The New Palgrave

A Dictionary of Economics

THE NEW
PALGRAVE
A DICTIONARY OF
ECONOMICS

EDITED BY

JOHN EATWELL

MURRAY MILGATE

PETER NEWMAN

Volume 1
A to D

THE MACMILLAN PRESS LIMITED, LONDON
THE STOCKTON PRESS, NEW YORK
MARUZEN COMPANY LIMITED, TOKYO

© The Macmillan Press Limited, 1987

The New Palgrave: A Dictionary of Economics
Edited by John Eatwell, Murray Milgate and Peter Newman
in four volumes, 1987

Published in the United Kingdom by
THE MACMILLAN PRESS LIMITED, 1987
London and Basingstoke
Associated companies in Auckland, Delhi, Dublin, Gaborone, Hamburg,
Harare, Hong Kong, Johannesburg, Kuala Lumpur, Lagos, Manzini,
Melbourne, Mexico City, Nairobi, New York, Singapore, Tokyo.

Published in the United States of America and Canada by
THE STOCKTON PRESS, 1987
15 East 26th Street, New York, NY10010, USA

Published in Japan by
MARUZEN COMPANY LIMITED, 1987
3–10, Nihonbashi 2-Chome, Chuo-Ku, Tokyo 103, Japan

Reprinted 1988 (twice)

The New Palgrave is a trademark of The Macmillan Press Limited

Library of Congress Cataloging-in-Publication Data
The New Palgrave: a dictionary of economics
  Sequel to: Dictionary of political economy/Robert
Harry Inglis Palgrave. 1910.
  Bibliography: p.
  Includes index.
  1. Economics—Dictionaries. I. Eatwell, John.
  II. Milgate, Murray. III. Newman, Peter K. 1928–.
  IV. Palgrave, Robert Harry Inglis, Sir, 1827–1919.
Dictionary of political economy.
HB61.N49   330′.03′21   87–1946
ISBN 0-935859-10-1 (set)

British Library Cataloguing in Publication Data
The New Palgrave: a dictionary of economics
  1. Economics—Dictionaries
  I. Eatwell, John. II. Milgate, Murray
  III. Newman, Peter.
330.03′21   HB61
ISBN 0-333-37235-2

Text keyboarded by Morton Word Processing Ltd, Scarborough, North Yorkshire.
Database management and text composition by Pergamon Orbit InfoLine Ltd, London.
Typeset by A. Wheaton & Co. Ltd, Exeter, Devon.
Printed and bound in Hong Kong.

Contents

First edition of *Dictionary of Political Economy*,
edited by Robert Harry Inglis Palgrave, in three volumes:

Volume I, printed 1894.
Reprinted pages 1–256 with Corrections, 1901, 1909.
Reprinted with Corrections, 1915, 1919.

Volume II, printed 1896.
Reprinted 1900.
Reprinted with Corrections, 1910, 1915.

Volume III, printed 1899.
Reprinted 1901.
Corrected with Appendix, 1908.
Reprinted with Corrections, 1910, 1913.
Reprinted, 1918.

New edition, retitled *Palgrave's Dictionary of Political Economy*,
edited by Henry Higgs, in three volumes:

Volume I, printed 1925.
Reprinted, 1926.

Volume II, printed 1923.
Reprinted, 1925, 1926.

Volume III, February 1926.
Reprinted, May 1926.

The New Palgrave: A Dictionary of Economics.
Edited by John Eatwell, Murray Milgate and Peter Newman.
Four volumes, 1987.

Reprinted 1988 (twice)

Publishers' Note

The New Palgrave: A Dictionary of Economics is a successor to the *Dictionary of Political Economy* edited by R.H. Inglis Palgrave and published in three volumes in 1894, 1896 and 1899. These were reprinted, with corrections and additions, during the first two decades of this century. A new edition, edited by Henry Higgs and incorporating all the corrections, was published in 1923–26 under the title *Palgrave's Dictionary of Political Economy*. (For an account of the genesis of the original and its subsequent development, see the entry PALGRAVE'S DICTIONARY OF POLITICAL ECONOMY in the present work.) To mark the publication of *The New Palgrave*, a reprint of the original Dictionary is being issued by the publishers.

The years since the original publication of Palgrave's *Dictionary* have seen a dramatic expansion in the content and influence of economics. When that work appeared, many topics now of great interest were either in their infancy or completely unknown: the serious study of urban economics, economic demography and mathematical economics was just beginning; fields such as econometrics, macroeconomics, game theory and the economics of uncertainty had hardly been explored. Those areas which were discussed in the original work have progressed dramatically since that time – money and finance, international trade and general equilibrium theory, to take only a few examples, have been transformed by the work of 20th-century economics. This is therefore an appropriate time for the production of a new Dictionary which, like its predecessor, attempts to define the state of the discipline by presenting a comprehensive and critical account of economic thought.

The preparation of the work began in 1983, when the editors – John Eatwell of Trinity College, Cambridge, Murray Milgate of Harvard University and Peter Newman of Johns Hopkins University, Baltimore – compiled the initial list of headwords and invited some 100 leading economists to participate in the creation of the work. After discussion and consultation, the editors refined the headword list and approached the many hundreds of writers who would represent the range of subjects and variety of viewpoints that comprise the discipline today.

The entries were commissioned by the editors from offices in Cambridge and Baltimore, and prepared for publication by the Macmillan Press in London. The resulting work contains nearly 2000 signed entries, written by more than 900 contributors; the four volumes are fully cross-referenced, and an explanation of the various aids to reference appears in the Introductory Notes.

Editors' Preface

In the preface to the first volume of his *Dictionary of Political Economy* (1894), R.H. Inglis Palgrave said that its 'primary object ... is to provide the student with such assistance as may enable him to understand the position of economic thought at the present time'. Although appearing almost a century later, when economics has changed and grown beyond anything imagined in his time, still much the same claim can be made for *The New Palgrave*.

In order to accommodate this growth, much that interested Inglis Palgrave has been jettisoned. Such topics as the administration of public exchequers, foreign coinage, land tenure systems, legal and business terms, social institutions, and many others, are all of interest but are, as Henry Higgs said in his preface to the second edition of the Dictionary, 'only remotely connected with economics'. Their place has been taken by whole disciplines unknown to the original editor (econometrics, game theory, Keynesian economics, optimization theory, risk and uncertainty and its application, social choice theory, urban economics), as well as by vast expansions of subjects which were in their infancy in his time (business cycle theory, general equilibrium theory, growth theory, industrial organization, labour economics, welfare economics).

There is so little remaining here of the original Dictionary that it would be disingenuous to call this its third edition. But just as the editor of *The New Grove* 'tried to ensure that something of the fine humane traditions of the earlier editions of Grove are to be seen in our pages', so we would like to believe that *The New Palgrave* has retained some of the liberal and scholarly spirit of Palgrave's enterprise. At least it is like its predecessor in dealing with economics mainly in its theoretical and applied aspects rather than in descriptive and institutional detail. The latter becomes outdated within a very few years, depreciating too rapidly for a publication meant for a longer shelf life than that.

Although it is not intended to contain a directory of economists, over 700 of the nearly 2000 entries in *The New Palgrave* are in fact biographical. We have aimed at reasonably complete coverage of the more important economists who have written primarily in English, especially in Britain itself, and a substantial treatment of major economists who have written in other languages. Palgrave, perhaps hoodwinked by his contributor C.P. Sanger, chose only Walras from economists living at that time, on the distinctly odd ground that 'he so closely carried on the work of his father Prof. Antoine Walras that it was not possible to mention the latter without also describing the works of his son'. We however have included a substantial number of living economists, arguing that economics has grown so much in this century that not to include many of its most eminent living practitioners would seriously limit the usefulness and scope of the work. To reduce obvious problems of evaluation we imposed a cut-off date: a necessary condition for inclusion is to have reached the age of seventy before 1 January 1986.

On many non-biographical subjects, large and small, we have tried to capture diversity and vivacity of view by having multiple entries, under similar but different titles. In this way we hoped to obtain essays that present the results and methods of research with fairness and accuracy, but not necessarily from a 'balanced' point of view. Such a view in these cases should be sought externally, as it were, using the system of cross-references to consult other relevant entries. This means more work for the reader but should yield correspondingly greater reward.

There is obviously a rough and ready correlation between size of entry and the importance which the editors attach to the person or subject concerned, but the correlation is very far from perfect. The actual realization of the project did not always turn out in accord with our original plans. And fortunately so, for we learned a great deal in the process of editing and as a consequence made continual revisions of those plans. Such adjustments have made for a better product, but not for one that displays perfect consistency. In this regard there can be no reader who will not wish that the Dictionary were different in some respects, a lot more here, rather less there, that tired or tiresome topic omitted, that important omission made good. While it is unrealistic to expect that all such errors of omission and commission can be avoided, our hope is that the reader will find that those which remain are unbiased, in almost every sense of the word.

There is, however, one major bias. We wanted not only to provide a thorough account of contemporary economic thought but also, like Palgrave himself, to have it set in historical perspective. So we asked authors to write accordingly, discussing for any particular subject its past and its prospects for the future, as well as its problems of the moment. Some topics are naturally more apt for this approach than others, and some contributors were of course more in sympathy with our aims than others. In the main, however, they responded very well indeed to our request, in some cases remarkably so.

Palgrave was the sole editor of his Dictionary, a labour of love for his subject over many years. Several of his authors did more than just write for him, however, by suggesting entries and contributors and by helping the work through the press. We have tried to preserve Palgrave's small editorial scale, but like him could not have done so without the generous and friendly help (far more than could be reasonably expected) of very many contributors, so many indeed that it would be invidious to acknowledge them all by name. We must however recognize the key part played by Margot Levy, the publishers' managing editor, whose enthusiasm and attention to detail contributed essentially to the timely completion of the work. It is also only simple justice to acknowledge, with gratitude, how much we have depended on the assistance of Ann Lesley in Cambridge and Donna Hall at Johns Hopkins, always cheerfully given and expertly rendered.

Editing this Dictionary has left us with a very strong sense, quite contrary to the layman's accepted view, of the solidarity of economics as a profession. This has been shown in many ways, not least by the extremely favourable response to our invitations to contribute, which were extended to economists of widely varying ideological and methodological persuasions. Over eighty per cent of those whom we asked agreed to write, and almost all of those who declined did so with words of regret and encouragement. Looking back, the hard work of editing subsides into the background, overwhelmed by the sheer enjoyment of putting it all together, by the continued pleasure of managing the flow of usually good and sometimes superlative copy from nearly a thousand authors. We hope that the reader will experience most of this enjoyment, and less of the work.

JOHN EATWELL, MURRAY MILGATE, PETER NEWMAN

January 1987

Introduction to the First Edition

The primary object of the *Dictionary of Political Economy* is to provide the student with such assistance as may enable him to understand the position of economic thought at the present time, and to pursue such branches of inquiry as may be necessary for that end.

The table of the contents of the work shows how large is the range of investigation which the student must follow at the present time.

During recent years the course of economic study has extended so widely that it was obviously impossible to restrict the work to the old and formerly well-recognized boundaries. The development of the historical school has opened out new and fertile fields, while the wants of those who follow the mathematical method of study have also to be considered. These two main lines of treatment are here but mentioned as examples. They are far from exhausting the countless ramifications of inquiry now rightly thought necessary for the complete investigation of a study bounded only by the requirements of human life in every social relation.

In making the selection necessitated by the limits of space, the requirements of different classes of students have throughout been borne in mind. On the one side purely business matters, such as banking, the foreign exchanges, and the operations of the mint come in; on the other, subjects of a philosophical character have been dealt with, such as questions of ethics and methods of definition, analysis, and reasoning; – and the ways in which diagrams and mathematical processes may lend assistance to economic inquiry have also been discussed. Again those interested in historical studies require an explanation of words found in early works, and those derived from classical and mediaeval times; also of legal phrases, now archaic, together with the modern correlative terms, for only thus can it be understood how ancient usage has influenced present habit. Life in the present day, even in the most modern settlements in the United States, in our British colonies, in the new countries coming into existence in different parts of the world, is influenced largely by the past. The stream of existence, if the simile may be permitted, reaches us deeply coloured by the soil of the fields through which it has flowed by the varied strata of the cliffs – some of them undermined by it – that have bounded its long and devious course.

Considerations of space have necessarily confined the scope of the work mainly to the developments of economic study in England, the United States, and our English-speaking colonies – and, in regard to these, an endeavour has been made to present under all the subjects treated an account of the best and most recent authorities; whilst the opinions held in other countries have also, as far as the required limits allowed, been considered and mentioned.

The biographies introduced have been selected with the same end. They show what has actually been written in former times, and hence will enable the reader to trace the progress of economic thought. Much attention has been given to the less-known writers. It is difficult for the student under ordinary circumstances to trace out when such authors lived, the surroundings which influenced their lives, and the opinions they held. While the oversights in science are sometimes as remarkable as the discoveries, these earlier labourers have not unfrequently been the precursors of other and better-known men, and have sometimes anticipated opinions that have held sway for long periods after them.

The different economic schools in the principal countries of the world are also described. Thus this volume contains notices of the American, Austrian, Dutch and English schools, and the French, German, Italian, and Spanish schools will follow in due course.

A work extending over so wide a range of subjects is, necessarily, the production of many minds, of writers whose pursuits, occupations, and studies are very diverse and varied. I desire to record my warm thanks to the contributors to the book, which is, I think, in itself an almost unique example of economic co-operation. Where all have assisted so heartily, it is less easy to select individual names; but I wish to be allowed to express my special thanks to Professor Dunbar, Dr. Keynes, Professor Marshall, Professor Montague, Professor Nicholson, Signor M. Pantaleoni, Mr. L.R. Phelps, Mr. L.L. Price, Mr. E. Schuster, Professor H. Sidgwick, and General Walker for valuable assistance in different directions, and particularly to Dr. Bonar, Professor Edgeworth, Mr. Henry Higgs, and Mr. H.R. Tedder, who have kindly helped in the more arduous labour of the preparation of the work for the press.

This is but an act of justice, that readers may know to whom they are specially indebted.

R.H. INGLIS PALGRAVE

Belton, near Great Yarmouth

Christmas 1893

Introductory Notes

The following notes contain an explanation of the style and method of this Dictionary, indicating the various aids to reference that appear throughout the work.

ABBREVIATIONS.   As is appropriate in an international work of reference, abbreviations have been kept to the minimum, thus avoiding the need for complex lists of abbreviated journal titles and the like. Abbreviations are used only for acronyms that have entered the ordinary vocabulary (thus IMF, GATT, R&D) or for common terms in economics where use of the full expression would be clumsy (e.g. MNC, LDC, DUP; in these cases, the term is explained in full on its first occurrence in each entry).

ALPHABETIZATION.   In entry headings, words are alphabetized as if continuous, ignoring spaces and hyphens, up to the first mark of punctuation, then again thereafter if that mark is a comma or a colon. These points may be illustrated by the following sequence of headings:

capital, credit and money markets
capital as a factor of production
capital as a social relation
capital budgeting
capital gains and losses
capitalism
.....
competition
competition: Austrian conceptions
competition: Classical conceptions
competition: Marxian conceptions
competition and efficiency
competition and selection
competition in international trade

ENTRY HEADINGS.   The dictionary headwords have been selected for ease of reference, avoiding the use of one main headword to cover a multiplicity of subjects. Thus, for example, we have preferred 'natural price' to 'price, natural' and 'equal rates of profit' to 'profit, equal rates of'; there are separate entries headed 'lump-sum taxes', 'indirect taxes', 'value-added tax' rather than many sub-entries under the heading 'taxes'. An exception has been made where entries involve direct comparison; thus in the example above, the entries on the Austrian, Classical and Marxian conceptions of competition are placed in alphabetical order under a generic heading.

As a general principle we have tried to place each entry where the majority of users of the Dictionary will expect to find it. The reader of the Dictionary who looks in the wrong place will be led to the right one by a cross-reference.

LIST OF ENTRIES.   As an additional aid to reference, the complete list of headwords and one-line cross-references is printed at the beginning of each volume, so that the reader can readily confirm whether a particular headword exists. If a term the reader has in mind does not appear under that title, a glance at the list will rapidly reveal entries on related topics.

AUTHORS.   The name of the author or authors appears at the foot of each entry, in the form approved by the authors themselves. Where the entry has been reprinted from Palgrave's *Dictionary of Political Economy* the author's name appears in square brackets, for example [F.Y. Edgeworth].

EDITORIAL STYLE.   In the editing of this dictionary, usage has followed the most natural style for the subject matter concerned. The orthography follows British practice in respect of spelling and punctuation, except that original sources are followed for titles and quoted matter. In keeping with modern stylistic practice, capitalization is restricted to proper names and to key terms in a specialized sense (thus 'Physiocrats' but 'neoclassical', 'post-Keynesian' but 'Institutional Economics'). Similarly, italics are used with discretion, either for emphasis or, in the case of foreign words that have entered English usage, to avoid ambiguity; thus *a priori* but 'ibid.', 'ex ante', etc.

Since *The New Palgrave* aims to allow each contributor to speak with an individual voice, no attempt has been made to impose a false stylistic uniformity. Those with an eye for minutiae will detect an inconsistency between entries in such matters as the capitalization of Marxist and Classical and the italicization of laissez-faire. Such inconsistencies are deliberate and represent an intention to reflect the subtle nuances of expression implied in these stylistic variations.

REPRINTS.   All entries in *The New Palgrave* are original contributions published in their present form for the first time, with two exceptions. The entry entitled Economic Theory and the Hypothesis of Rationality, and that on Mathematical Economics have appeared in learned journals. The source appears at the end of those entries in the same style used to designate articles reprinted from *Palgrave's Dictionary of Political Economy*.

FOREIGN LANGUAGES.   The use of foreign terms has been minimized. Where appropriate, an English translation is provided after the first appearance in an entry of a foreign term: for example 'Kathedersozialisten (socialists of the chair)'. In the bibliographies, no translation is provided for titles in French, German, Italian or Spanish; translations are however supplied for titles in Russian, Hungarian, Japanese and Polish. English is used for bibliographical details other than the title, thus 'Munich' not 'München', 'Rome' not 'Roma', 'January' not 'janvier', 'Vol. II' not 'Band II',etc. In German spellings the usage is ö (not oe), ss (not ß). French and German proper names are neither translated nor italicized (thus Ecole des Ponts et Chaussées, Privatdozent, Methodenstreit).

REFERENCES.   References appear in the text in author/date style, with page numbers where a particular passage is quoted. Thus (Samuelson, 1947, p. 73) is a reference to page 73 of Samuelson's work of 1947, which will appear in the bibliography of the article. References are always to the original date of publication, thus avoiding the solecism Mill (1965) where the author is referring to a modern edition of Mill's *Principles of Political Economy*; in this case, the citation will read Mill (1848), with details of the modern edition specified in the Bibliography. Where the page reference is to a modern collection, both dates may appear in the reference, with the original date of publication in square brackets.

Op. cit. and loc. cit., like other Latinisms, are avoided. An exception is made in the case of 'ibid.'; used to refer to the same work as the previous reference.

BIOGRAPHIES.   For reasons explained in the Editors' Preface, biographical entries on living economists are restricted to those who were born before 1 January 1916. All biographies include the subject's full names and dates with details of education, academic appointments and principal works. The emphasis is on an individual's contribution to economic thought – though of course other activities such as politics, business, government service and literary pursuits are briefly described – and each biography ends with a list of Selected Works, again with the emphasis on contributions to economics.

PROPER NAMES.   The prefix Mc or M' is alphabetized as 'Mac'. In the Romance languages names are alphabetized under the prefix when it includes the definite article (thus De Finetti, Le Trosne, Le Chatelier) unless common usage requires a departure from this rule; the name will then be cross-referenced (thus a cross-reference under De Tocqueville directs the reader to the entry heading Tocqueville). German names are alphabetized by the initial letter of the main surname, ignoring the prefix 'von' (thus Mises, Ludwig von; Böhm-Bawerk, Eugen von). An exception is made in the case of Von Neumann, whose name is alphabetized under 'V', following American usage and the style generally followed by economists. Where more than one spelling exists the form chosen for the entry heading (e.g. McCulloch, Tugan-Baranovsky, Bortkiewicz, Mao Zedong) will be immediately apparent from the List of Entries.

DATES.   Each biographical entry begins with the subject's full name followed by year of birth or a pair of dates showing years of birth and death. Where the date of birth is uncertain, the abbreviation *c* (*circa*) appears before the first date (e.g. *c*1610–1662); where the date of death is uncertain, a question mark appears before the second date (e.g. 1890–?1938); in the rare instances where neither date is known, the abbreviation *fl.* (*floruit*) is used.

ENTRIES FROM PALGRAVE'S DICTIONARY OF POLITICAL ECONOMY.   *The New Palgrave* includes some 50 entries reprinted from the original *Dictionary of Political Economy* edited by R.H. Inglis Palgrave and published between 1894 and 1899. These entries have been selected to reinforce the continuity between the 'old' Palgrave and the new. In some cases, for example, F.Y. Edgeworth's article on Agents of Production, they provide a classic statement of principle that could not be improved; in others, they also provide direct comparison with the modern interpretation – thus Henry Sidgwick's entry, Economic Science and Economics complements the modern treatment of Methodology while Edgeworth's essay on Mathematical Methods in Political Economy from the original Palgrave is a counterpart to Gerard Debreu's entry on Mathematical Economics. In other instances, such as Principal and Agent, and Experimental Methods in Economics, the old and new entries appear side by side. Another category includes biographical entries that can hold their own with modern scholarship, while a third comprises curiosities (James Asgill, for example) and some interpretations engagingly redolent of their time (here the interested reader may be referred to the entry on Babeuf).

BIBLIOGRAPHIES.   Most articles in the Dictionary are followed by bibliographies. These bibliographies serve a dual purpose: first, they give details for works referred to in the text of an article; and secondly, they provide additional information on studies on which the authors have drawn as well as recommended reading. In the case of biographical entries, the list is in two parts: a list of Selected Works in date order, and a Bibliography of secondary sources.

Bibliographies are arranged alphabetically by author/editor and chronologically under the author's/editor's name. Items written by the same author and published in the same year are given an alphabetical references (a, b, c, etc.) immediately following the year of publication; these same references appear in the text to refer the reader to the relevant publication. Where publications have been issued by an institution, the name of the institution is regarded as the author, and the item appears in the alphabetical sequence under that name. In the case of works by multiple authors, if an author has written works solely they are cited first, with joint authorship publications following in alphabetical and chronological order thereafter.

All bibliographies are intended to be complete and integral; that is, no other bibliography need be consulted to explain the references given in a particular entry. Where a citation is to another work – e.g. 'Reprinted in Robinson (1972)' – that citation will always refer to a work appearing in the same bibliography (in this case, Joan Robinson's *Collected Papers*, published in 1972).

The procedures of citation are broadly speaking self-evident, but it may nevertheless be helpful to outline here the main principles. For books that have appeared in several editions, information is given pertaining to the original date of publication and to the edition referred to in the text of the article. In some cases this may also include more detailed information about the first publication of the work. In the majority of cases a reference contains the title of the book, the date of publication, place of publication and publishers; where more than one edition or a reprint is cited, details of place and publisher are given. In the case of standard works such as *Capital* or the *Wealth of Nations* only one modern edition (of the author's choosing) is cited.

Details of English translations are normally noted; for items in less familiar languages where no English translation has been published, a translation of the title is given in parentheses. Minimum capitalization is used for titles in the Romance languages. Old orthography has been retained where necessary.

For references to multi-volume works, if the reference is to the work as a whole, the number of volumes is given. When a reference is to a specific volume, that volume is specified in the bibliography.

For articles in periodicals, the title of the article is cited, followed by the name of the periodical, volume (and fasicle number where appropriate), month of publication (where known) and page span. Readers calling up references through a photocopying or microfiche service will thus be able to locate the specific items they require. However, such information is not always available for foreign language publications, where only the journal title and month of publication may appear in the reference.

For chapters in books, the name of the chapter is cited, followed by the name of the author and the title of the book, publishing information (place and publisher) and in most cases either page references or a chapter reference. For edited works, the name of the editor (or editors) follows the title of the work, followed by publishing information (place and publisher) and in most cases either the page references or a chapter reference. Where a journal article has been subsequently reprinted, the details are included in the reference; for example, when an article is reprinted in the author's Collected Works or in a collection of essays.

For articles in encyclopedias or dictionaries, the name of the article is cited and the relevant volume number and page reference are given. For books published in series, the name of the series follows the title of the book, with its appropriate number therein (if necessary), and publication details.

Dissertations, working papers, lectures and other unpublished works are cited in roman type with the name of the place of the institution.

Where the author's name is given in square brackets this indicates that the article was unsigned in that publication, most often a periodical or newspaper. A date given in square brackets indicates the time of writing and the subsequent date, that of publication.

For biographical entries, a list of selected works has been appended to the article. The publications are cited in chronological order by date of publication, and the format of the citation is that of the bibliographies proper. The authors' names are not repeated in the lists of Selected Works and are to be inferred from the subject of the biography. In the case of joint authorship, the names of other authors are given in parentheses following the date.

Every effort has been made to check and cross-check all bibliographical references. However, in the case of more obscure references where data have not been accessible, or not supplied by an author, a short reference is cited, giving as much information as was available at the time of publication.

For publications which have not yet appeared in print, but for which some data are known, a short reference is cited. This usually pertains to articles forthcoming in periodicals.

AIDS TO REFERENCE.   *The New Palgrave* includes nearly 2000 entries, among them some 700 biographies. A variety of aids to reference is provided to guide the reader through the work. These include cross-references at the end of entries (and occasionally, within the entry) directing the reader to other articles in the Dictionary; one-line entries indicating the article where a particular topic is discussed; the list of fields of study, where Dictionary headwords are arranged in subject order (Appendix IV); and the analytical Index. Each of these complementary systems of reference is discussed below.

CROSS-REFERENCES.   Two kinds of cross-references appear in the work. One-line cross-references, which appear in bold type throughout the work, direct the reader to the entry where a particular topic is discussed, but under a different headword. Here we have tried to anticipate a term that the reader may have in mind and point the way to the relevant entry. Thus, for example,

> **distance function.** *See* GAUGE FUNCTIONS.
> **free rider.** *See* INCENTIVE COMPATIBILITY.

One-line cross-references are shown in the List of Entries, where they are printed in italics to distinguish them from headwords. While every effort has been made to make this list comprehensive, the publishers are aware that some terms will have eluded them; however, in this case readers should consult the analytical index.

Cross-references at the end of entries appear in SMALL CAPITALS and direct the reader to articles on related subjects for further elucidation of particular topics. Cross-references occasionally appear within the text, but this form of reference has been used very sparingly – our aim has been to avoid overloading the text with references, since each entry has been written as a discrete essay on the subject in question. The cross-references have been carefully selected to highlight particular entries elsewhere in the work, and are designed as a complement to the List of Entries and the Index.

APPENDICES. The four Appendices provide a further guide to the contents of *The New Palgrave* and its predecessor, *Palgrave's Dictionary of Political Economy*.

Appendix I is a list of entries in *The New Palgrave* arranged by author, showing those articles written by each contributor, whether alone or in collaboration with a colleague. The list shows the topics on which experts in any branch of the discipline have contributed entries to the Dictionary and is an indispensable guide to the current views of exponents of divergent viewpoints in every branch of the discipline.

Appendix II is a list of biographies included in the first edition of *Palgrave's Dictionary of Political Economy* (1894–99) and not reproduced in the present work. The list includes minor economists (whose entries in the original Dictionary may contain no more than a date and one or two publications) and a number of public and literary figures.

Appendix III amplifies the contrast between *The New Palgrave* and the old, and lists the contents of *Palgrave's Dictionary of Political Economy* with the full name of each author. This information was not provided in this form in the original Dictionary, where authors' signatures appeared only as initials. The list will enable the reader to compare the contents of the present work with its predecessor and to identify the contributors to the original Dictionary.

Appendix IV is an analysis of all the subject entries of *The New Palgrave* by 53 fields of study, together with a classification of all the biographies by country of the subject; each entry appears once and only once in these lists. Related subject fields appear together, both within ten general headings (denoted by a Roman numeral), and from one adjacent general heading to another. Ascription of author to country obviously poses serious problems, such as those caused by the mass exodus of scholars from Germany and Austria to the United States in the 1930s. Generally, the author is ascribed to that country in which he or she did his best-known work.

INDEX. The analytical index provides a detailed guide to key subjects discussed throughout the work. The index includes the complete List of Entries as well as many other essential items that do not have entries of their own but are central concepts in economic theory. In addition to providing concrete references to persons and topics, the index guides the reader to significant discussions of key subjects throughout the four volumes. The index can be thought of as revealing the detailed structure and contents which lie behind the list of entries: if the reader has a particular subject in mind, the index will show where the history, development and current status of that topic is amplified, with a page reference to the opening of the discussion. References are not given every time a particular word occurs; they appear only when tracing the reference will lead to a significant discussion on the topic in question. Index entries include analytical breakdowns in a form that will lead the reader directly to the relevant place.

In addition, the index includes the names of certain individuals and institutions referred to in the work. These include references to economists who do not have entries of their own, among them major living economists who do not qualify for biographical entries by virtue of their date of birth, and references to more minor figures of the past who are not the subject of separate entries. Bibliographical references are excluded from the index.

The compilation of a complex analytical index is of course subject to many difficulties but it is hoped that the present index, if imperfect in certain ways, will be a useful guide to the wealth of discussion in these volumes.

MARGOT LEVY

Acknowledgements

The editors and publishers wish to thank all those who assisted in the preparation of this work, and to acknowledge in particular the contribution of John Hodgson, in managing the project throughout its complex production cycle; Nigel Quinney, for bibliographical research; Keith Eady, for advice on the mathematical entries; Richard Max, for controlling the copy flow; and Ron Wood, for supervision of the final typesetting.

The following contributors (articles shown in parentheses) acknowledge support from public bodies or permission to reprint copyright material:

Andrew B. Abel (Ricardian equivalence theorem), financial support from the Amoco Foundation Term Professorship in Finance, the National Science Foundation and the Sloan Foundation. Kenneth J. Arrow (economic theory and the hypothesis of rationality), support from the Office of Naval Research, originally published as 'Rationality of Self and Others in an Economic System' in the *Journal of Business*, 1986, vol. 59, no. 4, pt.2, © University of Chicago Press. Hsaio Cheng (identification), financial support from the National Science Foundation. Gerard Debreu (existence of general equilibrium), support from the National Science Foundation; (mathematical economics), the article being a revised version of the Frisch Memorial Lecture delivered at the Fifth World Congress of the Econometric Society and published in *Econometrica*, November 1986. Giancarlo Gandolfo (stability), permission to quote from Hirsch and Smale (eds), *Differential Equations*, © Academic Press, Orlando, Florida. John C. Harsanyi (bargaining), financial support from The National Science Foundation through grant SES82-18938 administered by the Center for Research in Management, University of California, Berkeley. Werner Hildenbrand (cores), financial support by the Deutsche Forschungsgemeinschaft, Sonderforschungsbereich 303 and MSRI, University of California, Berkeley; (value judgements), financial support from the National Science Foundation through grant SES82-18938 administered by the Center for Research in Management, University of California, Berkeley. Gur Hubermann (arbitrage pricing theory), support from The National Science Foundation and the Center for Research in Security Prices. Mark Killingsworth (labour supply of women), for material published in *Handbook of Labor Economics*, Vol. I, ed. O. Ashenfelter and R. Layard, © Elsevier Science Publishers BV, 1986. R.G. King (business cycles), suppport from the National Science Foundation. Murray Milgate (Higgs, Henry), Cambridge University Press and the Royal Economic Society for permission to quote from the *Economic Journal*, 1940; (Palgrave's Dictionary of Political Economy), extracts from the Macmillan Archive held in the Library of the University of Reading. Marc Nerlove (time series analysis), financial support from the National Science Foundation. Marc Nerlove and Francis X. Diebold (autoregressive and moving-average time-series processes; estimation), financial support from the National Science Foundation. Don Patinkin (Keynes, John Maynard; neutrality of money), Central Research Fund of the Hebrew University of Jerusalem. Roy Radner (Marschak, Jacob), for material previously published in *Behavioral Science*, vol. 23, 1978; (uncertainty and general equilibrium), for material previously published in the *American Economic Review*, vol. LX, May 1970, in the *Journal of Economic Theory*, vol. 26, 1982, and in *Handbook of Mathematical Economics*, ed. K.J. Arrow and M. Intriligator, Vol. II, 1982, Amsterdam: North-Holland Publishing Company. Marcel K. Richter (revealed preference theory), support from the National Science Foundation. John Roberts (large economies), support from the National Science Foundation through grant SES83-08723. R. Wilson (exchange), support from Stanford University, Stanford; research support from the National Science Foundation (SES83-08723) and the Office of Naval Research (N00014-79C0685). J.E. Woods (invariable standard of value), provision of facilities by the Department of Economics, Queen Mary College, London.

LIST OF ENTRIES A – Z

One-line cross-references are shown in *italics*.

Abbott, Edith (1876–1957)
Abramovitz, Moses (born 1912)
absentee
absolute and exchangeable value
absolute income hypothesis
absolute rent
absorption approach to the balance of
    payments
absorptive capacity
abstinence
abstract and concrete labour
acapitalistic production
acceleration principle
accounting and economics
accumulation of capital
activity analysis
acyclicity
Adams, Henry Carter (1851–1921)
adaptive expectations
added worker effect
adding-up problem
additive preferences
additive utility function
adjustment costs
adjustment processes and stability
administered prices
advances
adverse selection
advertising
advisers
Aftalion, Albert (1874–1956)
ageing populations
agency costs
agent
agents of production
aggregate demand and supply analysis
aggregate demand theory
aggregate production function
aggregate supply function
aggregation of economic relations
aggregation problem
agrarianism
agricultural economics
agricultural growth and population
    change
agricultural supply
agriculture and economic development
aid
Akerman, Johan Gustav (1888–1959)
Akerman, Johan Henrik (1896–1982)
Alchian, Armen Albert (born 1914)
alienation
Allais, Maurice (born 1911)
Allais paradox

Allen, George Cyril (1900–1982)
Allen, Roy George Douglas (1906–1983)
allocation
allocation: strategy-proof mechanisms
allocation of time
Almon, Shirley Montag (1935–1975)
Almon lag
alternative technology
altruism
American Economic Association
Amoroso, Luigi (1886–1965)
amortization
analogy
analysis of variance
anarchism
Anderson, James (1739–1808)
Anderson, Oskar Nikolayevich
    (1887–1960)
Andreades, Andreas (1876–1935)
Andrews, Philip Walter Sawford
    (1914–1971)
Angell, James Waterhouse (1898–1986)
animal spirits
anomalies
anthropology, economic
antitrust policy
Antonelli, Giovanni Battista (1858–1944)
Aoyama, Hideo (born 1910)
appropriate technology
Aquinas, St Thomas (1225–1274)
arbitrage
arbitrage pricing theory
arbitration
ARIMA models
Aristotle (384–322 BC)
arms races
Armstrong, Wallace Edwin (1892–1980)
Arndt, Heinz Wolfgang (born 1915)
Arrow corner
Arrow–Debreu model of general
    equilibrium
Arrow's theorem
arts
Asgill, John (1659–1738)
Ashley, William James (1860–1927)
Ashton, Thomas Sutcliffe (1889–1968)
asset pricing
assets and liabilities
assignment problems
asymmetric information
atomistic competition
attributes
Attwood, Thomas (1783–1856)
auctioneer

auctions
Aupetit, Albert (1876–1943)
Auspitz, Rudolf (1837–1906)
Austrian conceptions of competition
Austrian School of Economics
autarky
autocorrelation
automatic stabilizers
autonomous expenditures
autoregressive and moving-average
    time-series processes
autoregressive-integrated-moving average
    models
average and normal conditions
average cost pricing
average industry
average period of production
Averch–Johnson effect
axiomatic theories
Ayres, Clarence Edwin (1891–1972)
Babbage, Charles (1791–1871)
Babeuf, François Noël (1764–1797)
Bachelier, Louis (1870–1946)
backwardation
backward bending supply curve
backward linkage
backwardness
Bagehot, Walter (1826–1877)
Bailey, Samuel (1791–1870)
Bain, Joe Staten (born 1912)
Bakunin, Mikhael Alexandrovitch
    (1814–1876)
balanced budget multiplier
balanced growth
balance of payments
balance of trade, history of the theory
balance of trade doctrine
balance sheet
Balogh, Thomas (1905–1985)
Banfield, Thomas Charles (1800–?1882)
Banking School, Currency School, Free
    Banking School
bank rate
banks
Baran, Paul Alexander (1910–1964)
Barbon, Nicholas (1637/40–?1698)
bargaining
Barone, Enrico (1859–1924)
barriers to entry
barter
barter and exchange
Barton, John (1789–1852)
basics and non-basics
basing point system

A

Abbott, Edith (1876–1957). Social reformer, economic historian and a pioneer in America of the study of the economic position of women, Edith Abbott was born on 26 September 1876 in Nebraska, and graduated from the University of Nebraska in 1901. She enrolled in a summer session at the University of Chicago in 1902, attracting the attention of James Lawrence Laughlin and Thorstein Veblen, and on their recommendation returned to Chicago in 1903 on a fellowship in political economy, taking her PhD in 1905 with a dissertation on the wages of unskilled labour in the USA between 1850 and 1900 (Abbott, 1905). It was during this period at Chicago that she met Sophonisba Breckinridge who became her mentor and lifelong friend. In 1906, on a Carnegie Fellowship, she went to the LSE to carry out research on women in industry. In London she was influenced by the social reformers of the day, including Charles Booth and Sydney and Beatrice Webb. She returned to the US in 1907 and taught political economy at Wellesley. In 1908 Breckinridge, now director of research at the newly established Chicago School of Civics and Philanthropy, invited her to become her assistant.

Abbott's work there involved her directly in action for the protection and education of juveniles and immigrants, for improvements in housing, and for the reform of correctional institutions. She also worked towards women's suffrage, the ten-hour law to protect women in employment, and the admission of women into trades unions. In the 1930s she was to become a staunch advocate of social insurance measures and the welfare state. Although sympathetic to the New Deal, she felt it to be entirely inadequate when it came to welfare policies.

Her publications ranged over a number of areas in social and public policy and, with Breckinridge, she was an influential proponent of the role of the state as the key element in any extensive programme of social welfare. The journal they jointly established in 1927, *Social Science Review*, was immediately recognized as a highly esteemed professional journal. Her main writings on economics were collected in her *Women in Industry* (1910), where a recurring theme was the distinction between the progress of 'professional' women (and the women's movements with which they were associated) and the relatively unchanged position of working-class women.

After 1920, although social work came increasingly to dominate her time, Abbott continued her role as an applied economist. She was a member of the advisory committee of the ILO on immigration, and succeeded Breckinridge as Dean of the School of Social Studies Administration at Chicago. She remained in the post until 1942, and continued editing the *Social Science Review* until 1953. She died at the age of 80 at her family home in Grand Island.

P. KERR

SELECTED WORKS

1905. Wages of unskilled labor in the United States, 1850–1900. *Journal of Political Economy* 13, 321–67.
1906. Industrial employment of women in the United States. *Journal of Political Economy* 14, 461–501.
1908. Study of early history of child labour in America. *American Journal of Sociology* 14, 15–37.
1910. *Women in Industry: A Study in American Economic History*. London: Appleton & Co; last reprinted in 1970.
1915. A forgotten minimum wage bill. *Life and Labour* 5, 13–16.

Abramovitz, Moses (born 1912). Born in Brooklyn, New York, Abramovitz was educated at Harvard (AB, 1932) and Columbia (PhD, 1939). He held faculty appointments at Columbia (1940–42, 1946–8) and Stanford University (1948–77) and was a member of the research staff of the National Bureau of Economic Research from 1938 to 1969. From 1942 to 1946 he worked as an economist for several organizations within the United States government. He was elected president of the American Economic Association in 1979–80.

Abramovitz's work, which was particularly influenced by Wesley C. Mitchell and Simon Kuznets, centres on the study of long-term economic growth and fluctuations in industrialized market economies. His first major contribution was an empirical study of business inventories that demonstrated the importance of inventory change in the shorter swings of the business cycle, and showed how the classification of inventories by stage of processing aided in the explanation of their behaviour (Abramovitz, 1950). From this, Abramovitz went on to the study of longer term fluctuations, Kuznets cycles of fifteen to twenty years duration, and formulated the most widely accepted interpretation of these cycles. Using Keynesian aggregate demand theory, Abramovitz developed a model linking Kuznets cycles to long swings in building cycles and demographic variables, and to shorter term business cycles (Abramovitz, 1959a, 1961, 1964, 1968).

Contemporaneously with his work on fluctuations, Abramovitz made important contributions to long term economic growth. He was one of the first to demonstrate that only a small share of long-term output growth in the United States was explained by factor inputs (Abramovitz, 1956). He documented and analysed the increasing role of government during long term economic growth (Abramovitz, 1957, 1981) and directed and coordinated a comparative study of the postwar economic growth of a number of industrialized market nations (Abramovitz, 1979b, 1986). Finally, he has challenged in characteristically perceptive fashion the facile linkage made by many economists between economic growth and improving human welfare (Abramovitz, 1959b, 1979a, 1982).

RICHARD A. EASTERLIN

SELECTED WORKS

1950. *Inventories and Business Cycles*. New York: National Bureau of Economic Research.
1956. Resource and output trends in the United States since 1870. *American Economic Review, Papers and Proceedings* 46, May, 5–23.

1957. (With Vera Eliasberg.) *The Growth of Public Employment in Great Britain*. Princeton: Princeton University Press.

1959a. Long swings in U.S. economic growth. Statement presented to Joint Economic Committee of the Congress. Hearings before Joint Economic Committee of the Congress of the U.S. on *Employment, Growth and Price Levels*, Part 2, 11–66, April 10.

1959b. The welfare interpretation of secular trends in national income and production. In M. Abramovitz et al., *The Allocation of Resources (Essays in Honor of Bernard F. Haley)*, Stanford: Stanford University Press.

1961. The nature and significance of Kuznets cycles. *Economic Development and Cultural Change* 9, April, 225–48.

1964. Evidence of long swings in aggregate construction since the Civil War. New York: National Bureau of Economic Research, *Occasional Paper No. 90*, Columbia University Press.

1968. The passing of the Kuznets cycle. *Economica*, November, 349–67.

1979a. Economic growth and its discontents. In *Economics and Human Welfare, Essays in Honor of Tibor Scitovsky*, ed. Michael Boskin, New York: Academic Press.

1979b. Rapid growth potential and its realization: the experience of capitalist economies in the postwar period. In *Economic Growth and Resources*, Proceedings of the Fifth World Congress of the International Economic Association, Vol. 1, London and New York: Macmillan Press.

1981. Welfare quandaries and productivity concerns. (Presidential Address to the American Economic Association.) *American Economic Review* 71(1), March, 1–17.

1982. The retreat from economic advance. In *Progress and its Discontents*, ed. G.A. Almond, M. Chodorow and R.H. Pearce, Berkeley: University of California Press.

1986. Catching up, forging ahead and falling behind. *Journal of Economic History* 46(2), June, 385–406.

absentee. An absentee may be variously defined (1) as a landed proprietor who resides away from his estate, or (2) from his country; or more generally (3) any unproductive consumer who lives out of the country from which he derives his income.

Examples of these species are (1) a seigneur under the *ancien régime* living in Paris at a distance from his estates; (2) an Irish landlord resident abroad; (3) an Anglo-Indian ex-official resident in England and drawing a pension from India. In writing briefly on the evils of absenteeism it is difficult to use general terms appropriate to all the definitions; but considerations primarily relating to some one definition may easily be adapted to another by the reader.

It is useful to consider separately the effects of the absentee proprietor's consumption upon the wealth of his countrymen; and the moral, as well as economical effects of other circumstances.

I. The more abstract question turns upon the fact that the income of an absentee is mostly remitted by means of exports. 'The tribute, subsidy, or remittance is always in goods ... unless the country possesses mines of the precious metals' (Mill). So far as the proprietor, if resident at home, would consume foreign produce, his absence, not increasing exports, does not affect local industry. So far as the proprietor's absence causes manufactures to be exported, his countrymen are not prejudiced. For they may have as profitable employment in manufacturing those exports as, if the proprietor had resided at home, they would have had in supplying manufactured commodities or services for his use. But if the proprietor by his absence causes raw materials to be exported, while if present he would have used native manufactures and services, his absence tends to deprive his countrymen of employment, to diminish their prosperity, and

perhaps their numbers. This reasoning is based on Senior's *Lectures on the Rate of Wages* (Lecture II), and *Political Economy* (pp. 155–61). Senior's position is in a just mean between two extremes – the popular fallacy and the paradox of McCulloch. On the one hand it is asserted that between the payment of a debt to an absentee and a resident there is the same difference as between the payment and non-payment of a tribute to a foreign country. On the other hand it is denied that there is any difference at all. The grosser form of the vulgar error, the conception that the income of the absentee is drawn from the tributary country in specie, is exemplified in Thomas Prior's *List of Absentees* (1727). McCulloch's arguments are stated in the essay on 'Absenteeism' in his *Treatises and Essays on Money*, etc., and in the evidence given by him before some of the parliamentary commissions which are referred to below. Asked 'Do you see any difference between raw produce and manufactured goods', McCulloch replies, 'I do not think it makes any difference' (compare *Treatises and Essays*, p. 232). He appeals to observation, and finds that the tenants of absentee landlords are 'subjected to less fleecing and extortion than those of residents'.

J.S. Mill attributes to absenteeism a tendency to lower the level of prices in the country from which the absentee draws an income; with the consequence that the inhabitants of that country obtain their imports at an increased cost of effort and sacrifice (*Unsettled Questions*, Essay i, p. 43). Mill's meaning may be made clearer by a study of the rest of the essay which has been cited, and of the parallel passage in his *Political Economy* (Book v, ch. iv, § 6), where he argues that an inequality between exports and imports results in an 'efflux of money' from one country to another.

Upon less distinct grounds Quesnay connects absenteeism with a development of trade and industry in an unhealthy direction (*Oeuvres*, ed. Oncken, p. 189). Among recondite considerations which may bear on the subject should be mentioned Cantillon's theory concerning the effect of the consumption of the rich on the growth of population (*Essai*, pt. i, ch. xv).

II. Other economical advantages lost by absenteeism are those which spring from the interest which a resident is apt to take in the things and persons about him. Thus he may be prompted to invest capital in local improvements, or to act as an employer of workmen. 'It is not the simple amount of the rental being remitted to another country', says Arthur Young, 'but the damp on all sorts of improvements'. D'Argenson in his *Considérations sur le gouvernement ancien et présent de la France* (1765, p. 183), attributes great importance to the master's eye.

The good feeling which is apt to grow up between a resident landlord and his tenantry has material as well as moral results, which are generally beneficial. The absentee is less likely to take account of circumstances (e.g. tenant's improvements), which render rack-renting unjust. He is less likely to make allowance for calamities which render punctual payment difficult. 'Miseries of which he can see nothing, and probably hear as little of, can make no impression' (A. Young). He is glad to get rid of responsibility by dealing with a 'middleman', or intermediate tenant – an additional wheel in the machinery of exaction, calculated to grind relentlessly those placed underneath it. Without the softening influence of personal communication between the owner and the cultivator of the soil, the 'cash nexus' is liable to be strained beyond the limit of human patience, and to burst violently. There can be little doubt but that absenteeism has been one potent cause of the misery and disturbances in Ireland. The same cause has produced like effects in cases widely different in other respects. The cruellest oppressors of the French peasantry before the Revolution were the *fermiers*, who purchased for an annual sum the right to collect the dues of absentee seigneurs. The violence of the Granger Railway legislation in the western states of America is attributed to the fact that the shareholders damnified were absentee proprietors (Seligman, *Journal of Political Science*, 1888).

There are also the moral advantages due to the influence and example of a cultivated upper class. The extent of this benefit will vary according to the character of the proprietors and the people. In some cases it may be, as Adam Smith says, that 'the inhabitants of a large village, after having made considerable progress in manufactures, have become idle in consequence of a great lord having taken up his residence in their neighbourhood'. The opposite view, presented by Miss Edgeworth in her *Absentee*, may be true in other states of civilization. Perhaps the safest generalization is that made by Senior that 'in general the presence of men of large fortune is morally detrimental, and that of men of moderate fortune morally beneficial, to their immediate neighbourhood'.

[F.Y. EDGEWORTH]
Reprinted from *Palgrave's Dictionary of Political Economy*.

BIBLIOGRAPHY
Brodrick, G.C. 1881. *English Land and English Landlords*. London.
Carey, H. 1835. *Essay on the Rate of Wages*. Philadelphia: Carey, Lea & Blanchard.
Lavergne, L. de. 1860. *Economie rurale de la France depuis 1789*. Paris: Guillamin.
Levasseur, E. 1889. *La population Française*. Paris.
Levasseur, E. 1885. A summary of the results of the recent Italian Commission. *Journal des Economistes*, November and December.
Montchrétien. 1615. *L'économie politique patronale. Traicté de l'oekonomie politique*. Ed. Th. Funck-Bretano, Paris, 1889.
Taine, H. 1876. *L'ancien régime*. Paris.
Tocqueville, A. de Clerel. 1856. *L'ancien régime et la révolution*. Paris, 3rd edn., 1857.
Smith, A. 1776. *An Inquiry into the Nature and Causes of the Wealth of Nations* London: W. Strahan & T. Cadell.
Wakefield, E. 1812. *An Account of Ireland, statistical and political*. London.
Young, A. 1780. *A Tour in Ireland*. London: T. Cannell & J. Dodsley.

absolute and exchangeable value.

No one can doubt that it would be a great desideratum in political economy to have such a measure of absolute value in order to enable us to know, when commodities altered in relative value, in which the alteration in value had taken place (David Ricardo, 1823, p. 399n).

The idea that changes in the relative or exchangeable value of a pair of commodities might usefully be attributed to alterations in the 'absolute value' of one or the other of them will appear rather odd to anyone accustomed to thinking of the basic problem of price theory as being the determination of sets of relative prices, with any consideration of 'absolute' value being confined to problems in monetary theory and the determination of the overall price level. Since in neoclassical theory it is the *relative* scarcity of commodities, or of the factor services which are used to produce them, which is the key to relative price formation, no conception of 'absolute' value, i.e. a price associated with the conditions of production of a single commodity, is either relevant or necessary.

Yet the notion of absolute value arose naturally within Ricardo's analysis of value and distribution. The central problem of classical theory is to relate the physical magnitude of surplus (defined as the social output *minus* the replacement of materials used in its production and the wage goods paid to the labourers employed) to the general rate of profit and the rents in terms of which the surplus is distributed. The key image is the distribution of a given magnitude of output between the classes of the society. 'After all', as Ricardo put it, 'the great questions of Rent, Wages and Profits must be explained by the proportions in which the whole produce is divided between landlords, capitalists, and labourers, and which are not essentially connected with the doctrine of value' (1820, p. 194). Ricardo was able to sustain this 'material' view of distribution only in the *Essay on Profits*, and only there by the implicit device of a sector in which all inputs and all output consist of the same commodity, corn, which is also used to pay wages in the other sectors of the economy. In the corn sector the division of the product may be expressed in physical terms, and the rate of profit expressed as a ratio of physical magnitudes.

This clear and direct analysis is no longer possible once the strong assumption of a self-reproducing sector is dropped.

The need to express heterogeneous surplus (net of rent) and heterogeneous capital as homogeneous magnitudes in order to determine the rate of profit created the need for a theory of value. Ricardo's materialist approach led him to the labour theory of value. The quantity of labour embodied directly and indirectly in the production of a commodity is determined by the conditions of production of that commodity, or as Ricardo put it, by the difficulty or facility of production, and will change only when the technique changes. Hence the aggregates of social surplus and capital advanced may be expressed as quantities of labour, these quantities being *invariant* to changes in the distribution of social product. So the rate of profit is determined as the ratio of surplus (on the land last brought into use) to the means of production, including wages.

Once, however, the impact of changes in distribution on exchangeable value is taken into account the picture is far less clear. The value of social output, and of the surplus, measured in any given standard, will typically now vary as distribution varies, even though the physical magnitude of social output remains unchanged. The direct deductive relationship between wages, surplus, and hence, the rate of profit, is no longer self-evident, or indeed, evident at all. It was Ricardo's desire to restore clarity to his analysis which led to his search for an invariable standard of value (a standard in terms of which the size of the aggregate would not vary as distribution was changed) and for what Sraffa describes as 'for Ricardo its necessary complement', absolute value (Sraffa, 1951, p. xlvi).

The term 'absolute value' was used by Ricardo but once in the first edition of the *Principles* and occasionally in letters. It was clarified in the papers on 'Absolute Value and Exchangeable Value', written in 1823 in the last few years of his life. These were discovered in a locked box at the home of F.E. Cairnes, the son of the economist John Elliot Cairnes, in 1943, and published for the first time in Sraffa's edition of Ricardo's *Works and Correspondence*.

There are two versions of the essay. One, a rough draft, is written on odd pieces of paper, some of them the covers of letters addressed to Ricardo. The other is a scarcely corrected draft, written on uniform sheets of paper. This clean draft breaks off, unfinished.

The importance of the essay derives from the reinforcement it provides to that interpretation of Ricardo's theory of value and distribution which suggests that the problem of the determination of the relative values of commodities stemmed from Ricardo's desire to relate his image of the division of social product as a physical magnitude to the wages, rents, and rate of profit of a market economy. Ricardo was not interested for its own sake in the problem of why two commodities produced by the same quantities of labour are not of the same exchangeable value. He was, rather, concerned by the fact that as distribution of social output *changes* exchangeable value *changes*, disrupting and obscuring an otherwise clear vision. It was this emphasis on the fact that *changes* in distribution lead to changes in exchangeable value, even though the quantity of social output and the method by which it is produced are unchanged, which led Ricardo into the intellectual cul-de-sac of the search for an invariable standard of value.

The absolute value of a commodity is the value of that commodity measured in terms of an invariable standard. An invariable standard of value may be found

> ... if precisely the same length of time and neither more nor less were necessary to the production of all commodities. Commodities would then have an absolute value directly in proportion to the quantity of labour embodied in them (Ricardo, 1823, p. 382).

Changes in the absolute values of commodities could then derive only from changes in the amount of labour embodied in them, and the value of social output would be invariate to its distribution.

Yet precisely because all commodities are not produced under the same circumstances, 'difficulty or facility of production is not absolutely the only cause of variation in value, there is one other, the rise or fall of wages' since commodities cannot 'be produced and brought to market in precisely the same time' (ibid., p. 368). Hence Ricardo must conclude, rather sadly, that 'there is no such thing in nature as a perfect measure of value' (ibid., p. 404) – there is no such thing as an invariable standard of value.

Marx (1883), who could not, of course, have seen the papers on Absolute and Exchangeable Value, was critical of Ricardo's absorption with the search for an invariable standard. The focus on changes in relative value obscured the fact that commodities do not exchange at rates proportional to their labour values (labour embodied). Yet Marx's attempt to restore clarity to the analysis of distribution by first determining the rate of profit as the ratio of quantities of labour, and then 'transforming' labour values into prices of production, encounters difficulties which derive from exactly the same source as those which bedevilled Ricardo – the difference in production conditions or 'organic composition of capital' of commodities.

The data of classical theory can be used to determine the rate of profit, as Sraffa (1960) has shown. But the determination cannot be 'sequential' – first specifying a theory of value and then evaluating the ratio of surplus to capital advanced by means of that predetermined theory of value. Rather the rate of profit and the rates at which commodities exchange must be determined simultaneously.

JOHN EATWELL

See also INVARIABLE STANDARD OF VALUE; RICARDO, DAVID.

BIBLIOGRAPHY

Marx, K. 1883. *Capital*, Vol. 3. London: Lawrence & Wishart, 1976.
Ricardo, D. 1820. Letter to J.R. McCullouch, 13 June 1820. In *Works and Correspondence of David Ricardo*, Vol. VIII, ed. P. Sraffa, Cambridge: Cambridge University Press, 1953.
Ricardo, D. 1823. Paper on 'Absolute and exchangeable value' (rough draft, and unfinished clean version). In *Works and Correspondence of David Ricardo*, Vol. IV, ed. P. Sraffa, Cambridge: Cambridge University Press, 1951.
Sraffa, P. 1951. Introduction to *Works and Correspondence of David Ricardo*, Vol. 1. Cambridge: Cambridge University Press.
Sraffa, P. 1960. *Production of Commodities by Means of Commodities*. Cambridge: Cambridge University Press.

absolute income hypothesis. *See* CONSUMPTION FUNCTION.

absolute rent. Marx's work on rent was based on his studies of the statistical reports published after the Russian Agrarian Reform of 1861. The importance of the Russian case on Marx's thinking is highlighted in Engels' 'Preface' to the third volume of Marx's *Capital*, which draws a parallel between the influence of Russia's diverse land tenure system on Marx's analysis of rent and the role of England on his analysis of industrial wage-labour.

Although the economic surplus normally takes the form of profits in the capitalist system, Marx gave considerable attention to rent. In chapter XLV of the third volume of *Capital* (1894), and in his critical comments on Ricardo's theory of rent, published in *Theories of Surplus-Value* (1905), Marx introduced the concept of absolute rent as the rent paid by capitalist tenant farmers to landowners, regardless of the fertility of the rented land.

Marx (1894, pp. 760, 771; 1905, pp. 244, 392) defined absolute rent as the difference between the value of the agricultural product of the least productive land and the *general* production price, $P(g)$. Absolute rent can absorb the entire $[value–P(g)]$ difference or a proportion of this difference. In contrast, differential rent is defined as the difference between the general production price and the *individual* production price, $P(i)$. These concepts are depicted in Figure 1. By definition, absolute rent is positive even on the worst cultivated land, A, whereas differential rent is zero on A, but then becomes positive and increases with improved land fertility, B, C, and D.

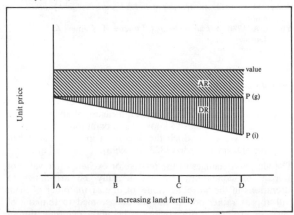

Figure 1 Marx's concept of absolute rent

Marx's concept of absolute rent is based on two assumptions: (1) the agricultural organic composition of capital is lower than the average of agriculture and industry; and (2) land is cultivated by capitalist tenant farmers. Assumption (1) implies that the value of an agricultural commodity will be *above* its production price; under assumption (2), landowners will lease land only to those capitalist tenants who can pay absolute rent even on the worst quality and most inconveniently located land.

In contrast to other commodities whose organic composition of capital is lower than the average of agriculture and industry, and thus have their values above their production prices, competition among capitalist producers does not reduce the values of the agricultural products to their production prices. The separation of landowners from tenant operators prevents the equalization of profit rates in agriculture with the single rate prevailing in industry. Landowners are therefore able to seize excess or above average agricultural profits and prevent them from entering the process by which the average profit rate is formed (see Marx, 1905, p. 37; Murray, 1977).

Under Marx's assumptions, the market price of an agricultural product will include the absolute rent above the general production price.

> If the worst soil cannot be cultivated – although its cultivation would yield the price of production – until it produces something in excess of the price of production, [absolute] rent, then landed property is the creative cause of *this* rise in price (Marx, 1894, p. 755).

There has been some confusion as to whether the upper limit of the market price of an agricultural product would be set by its individual value on the worst cultivated land. Marx (1905, p. 332) himself asked: 'If landed property gives the power to sell the product above its [production price], *at* its value, why does it not equally well give the power to sell the product *above* its value, at an arbitrary monopoly price?' Echoing Marx, Bortkiewicz (1911) and, much later, Emmanuel (1972) have also questioned why landlords limit absolute rent to the excess of value over the production price on the worst cultivated land. They suggest that since landowners have the power to withdraw land from cultivation until the market price covers both the absolute rent and the production price of the highest-cost producer, they could also charge a rent in excess of the corresponding value. In capitalist agriculture, absolute rent has a negative impact because it prevents agricultural prices from falling, and because it removes above average profits, a major source of capitalist technical innovation (see Lenin, 1901, pp. 119-29).

Despite some ambiguity in Marx's formulation of absolute rent, his argument is persuasive:

> Although landed property may drive the price of agricultural produce above its price of production, it does not depend on this, but rather on the general state of the market, to what degree market-price exceeds the price of production and approaches the value (Marx, 1894, p. 764, see also p. 762; Murray, 1977; Flichman, 1977).

According to Marx (1894, pp. 760, 765; 1905, pp. 244, 393), the lower composition of agricultural capital compared to that of industry 'is a *historical* difference and can therefore disappear', and so absolute rent would also tend to disappear as the productivity of agricultural labour approaches that of industry. In this case, the production price of an agricultural product would approach its value and any rent paid by the capitalist tenants would constitute a monopoly rent. The monopoly rent is paid above the value of the agricultural product, and it would thus be limited not by value, as in the case of absolute rent, but by foreign agricultural trade, competition among landowners, and the consumers budget (see Marx, 1894, pp. 758, 805, 810; 1905, p. 332).

Marx's theory of absolute rent has been by-passed by the controversy over the transformation of values into production prices, and has been little used as a conceptual device to analyse the effect of landownership on capitalist investment in agriculture or the effect of landownership on agricultural

prices. Unfortunately, absolute rent has been neglected by Marxist economists, while it seems to be a favourite *bête noire* among sympathetic critics of Marx, such as Bortkiewicz (1911) and Emmanuel (1972). As a result, absolute rent has an uncertain future as a useful theoretical device, despite the fact that in many countries capitalist agriculture still largely conforms to the two basic assumptions made by Marx more than a hundred years ago.

EDNALDO ARAQUEM DA SILVA

See also LAND RENT; MARX, KARL HEINRICH; RENT; UNEQUAL EXCHANGE.

BIBLIOGRAPHY
Bortkiewicz, L. 1911. La teoria della rendita fondiaria di Rodbertus e la dottrina di Marx sulla rendita fondiaria assoluta. In *La Teoria Economica di Marx e altri saggi su Böhm-Bawerk, Walras e Pareto*, Turin: Einaudi, 1971.
Emmanuel, A. 1972. *Unequal Exchange*. New York: Monthly Review Press.
Flichman, G. 1977. *La Renta del Suelo y el Desarrollo Agrario Argentino*. Buenos Aires: Siglo Veintiuno Editores.
Lenin, V.I. 1901. The agrarian question and the 'critics of Marx'. In V.I. Lenin, *Collected Works*, Vol. V, Moscow: Progress Publishers, 1973.
Marx, K. 1894. *Capital*, Vol. III. Moscow: Progress Publishers, 1971.
Marx, K. 1905. *Theories of Surplus Value*, Part II. Moscow: Progress Publishers, 1968.
Murray, R. 1977. Value and the theory of rent: I. *Capital & Class* 1(3), Autumn, 100-122.

absorption approach to the balance of payments. The absorption approach to the balance of payments states that a country's balance of trade will only improve if the country's output of goods and services increases by more than its absorption, where the term 'absorption' means expenditure by domestic residents on goods and services. This approach was first put forward by Alexander (1952, 1959).

The novelty of this approach may be appreciated by considering the particular question 'will a devaluation improve a country's balance of trade?' The elasticities approach, popular when Alexander was writing, answers this question by focusing on the price elasticities of supply and demand for exports and imports. It holds that the devaluation will be successful if the price elasticities of demand for exports and imports are large enough so that the increase in exports sold to foreigners and the reduction in imports bought by domestic residents together more than offset the terms of trade loss caused by the devaluation. (A special case of this result is formalized in the Marshall–Lerner conditions.) The absorption approach argues, by contrast, that the devaluation will only be successful if it causes the gap between domestic output and domestic absorption to widen. In effect Alexander criticizes the elasticities approach for focusing on the movement along given supply and demand curves in the particular markets for exports and imports (a microeconomic approach), instead of looking at the production and spending of the nation as a whole which shift these curves (a macroeconomic approach).

Alexander's criticism of the elasticities approach is valid. But without further elaboration the absorption approach is unhelpful in rectifying the inadequacy. This is because, taken at face value, the absorption approach merely states an identity. Let the symbols, Y, C, I, G, X and M stand for output, consumption, investment, government expenditure, exports and imports respectively. Then the Keynesian income-expenditure *identity* states that

$$Y = C + I + G + X - M \qquad (1)$$

which may be rewritten

$$X - M = Y - (C + I + G). \tag{2}$$

This *identity* states precisely that the trade balance will improve if output, Y, increases by more than absorption $(C + I + G)$.

What is needed, and what Alexander helped to provide, is an analysis of exactly how output and absorption change, in response to a devaluation, and indeed in response to other developments in the economy. Such a gap was also being filled at the time by Keynesian writers (Robinson, 1937; Harrod, 1939; Machlup, 1943; Meade, 1951; Harberger, 1950; Laursen and Metzler, 1950; see also Swan, 1956).

All of these authors grafted the Keynesian multiplier onto the elasticities approach. The resulting hybrid construct can be used to analyse the effects of a devaluation as follows. Suppose that the price elasticity effects do improve the balance of trade, $X - M$, by 'switching' expenditures towards domestic goods. Then these 'expenditure-switching' effects provide a positive stimulus to the Keynesian multiplier process, and drive up output Y and absorption $C + I + G$. Let x be the expenditure-switching effects on the trade balance of a devaluation of the currency by one unit, and let the overall effects of this devaluation on the trade balance be y. Let the propensity to consume be c, the tax rate be t and the propensity to import m, so that the Keynesian multiplier is $k = 1/[1 - c(1 - t) + m]$. The increase in output resulting from the devaluation is kx and the increase in absorption is $c(1 - t)kx$. And so

$$y = k[1 - c(1 - t)]x. \tag{3}$$

If the propensity to consume c is less than unity and the tax rate t is positive then absorption increases by less than output, and, as equation (3) shows the trade balance is improved by the devaluation. The above sketch shows how the combination of the elasticities approach and Keynesian theory is able to provide the needed analysis of how output and absorption change following a devaluation. And instead of describing the outcomes in terms of output and absorption, as Alexander did, it is possible to give a more conventional Keynesian description, which would proceed as follows. Since the multiplier $k = 1/[1 - c(1 - t) + m]$ times the propensity to import m is less than unity, the increase in imports induced by the multiplier, mkx, is less than the positive 'expenditure-switching effects', x, and so the trade balance improves.

We can also show how output and absorption change after an 'expenditure-changing' adjustment of policy. For example, a one unit increase in government spending will cause output to increase by k whereas absorption increases by the sum of the increase in government expenditure and the induced increase in consumption $(1 - t)ck$; the trade balance thus worsens by an amount z where

$$z = k - [1 + (1 - t)ck]$$
$$= k - [1 - c(1 - t) + m + c(1 - t)]k = -mk. \tag{4}$$

Again this outcome can be described in the more conventional Keynesian way: high government expenditure drives up output by the multiplier, k, and sucks in imports of an amount mk.

The combination of the elasticities approach and Keynesian multiplier theory was used to produce a theory of economic policy for an open economy, which involved the pursuit of full employment as well as a satisfactory balance of trade as policy objectives (Meade, 1951; see especially Swan 1956). This theory can be stated just as well in terms of Alexander's absorption approach. For example an improvement in the

balance of trade at full employment requires a reduction in absorption, without any change in output. It is obvious from the previous two paragraphs that this, in turn, requires both expenditure-switching policies and expenditure-changing policies, since both of these policies influence output as well as absorption. Johnson (1956) put this point masterfully, and I now express it algebraically. Let the desired increase in the trade balance be w, let the required devaluation of the currency be α units and let the required change in government expenditure be β. Then from equations (3) and (4)

$$w = [1 - c(1 - t)]kx\alpha - mk\beta \tag{5}$$

whereas, since output is not to be affected,

$$0 = kx\alpha + k\beta \tag{6}$$

Solving for β from equation (6) and substituting into equation (5), noting that $1 - c(1 - t) = 1/k - m$, gives

$$w = [1/k - m]kx\alpha + mkx\alpha = x\alpha.$$

Thus the required devaluation is simply $\alpha = w/x$ and substituting in equation (6) the required change in government expenditure is simply $\beta = -w$. This states what is obvious: government absorption must be reduced enough to release resources from domestic use—the expenditure-changing component of policy—and the devaluation must ensure that these resources are actually used to improve the trade balance, rather than leading to a fall in domestic output—the expenditure-switching component of policy.

Laursen and Metzler (1950) show that what is obvious must in fact be qualified. A more careful analysis would show that the positive expenditure switching effect of a devaluation on the trade balance is slightly smaller than the positive expenditure switching stimulus which devaluation imparts to the Keynesian multiplier process (whereas we have assumed both of these effects to be equal, and have denoted them by β). See also Harberger (1950) and Svensson and Razin (1983).

Modern balance of payments theory has carried criticisms much further than this. It has shown that the hybrid of the Keynesian multiplier and elasticities approaches is inadequate in providing a full analysis of how output and absorption change. First it does not deal with the inflationary effects of devaluation. But one way in which devaluation depresses absorption relative to output is through engendering rises in costs and prices which depress the real incomes (particularly real wages) of domestic consumers (Diaz Alexandro, 1966). Furthermore, devaluation may also engender a wage-price spiral so strong as to preserve the real incomes of domestic consumers, with the end result that prices rise by the full extent of the devaluation and there is no relative price change for the price elasticities effects to work on (Ball, Burns and Laury, 1977). In that case positive effects of devaluation on the trade balance can *only* emerge as a result of the effects of higher prices on absorption. (Higher prices lower the real wealth of consumers and perhaps also increase the tax burden if tax rates are progressive and not indexed with inflation.) Second, the multiplier-plus-elasticities analysis is not appropriate in analysing the effects of a devaluation not accompanied by any expenditure changing policy if the economy is at full employment, for in that case output cannot be expanded through the multiplier, and the effects of the devaluation must primarily work through the influence of inflation on absorption described above. Third, the multiplier-plus-elasticities analysis does not deal with monetary conditions. A devaluation, because it raises prices, may initially also cause higher interest rates which helps to curtail absorption. But if the improvement in the trade balance caused by the devaluation is allowed to lead to an expansion of the domestic money supply, then gradually interest rates will fall, absorption will rise, and the effects of the devaluation may turn out to be temporary. This issue has been analysed by the Monetary Approach to the Balance of Payments (Frenkel and Johnson, 1976; Kyle, 1976; McCallum and Vines, 1981). Alexander made many of these points in his articles whereas the authors cited at the end of the fourth paragraph tended to skate over them. For that reason his work prefigures much subsequent balance of payments theory.

In conclusion, the absorption approach provides a useful perspective from which to view the trade balance. But it must be supplemented by a theory both of what determines absorption and of what determines output. And of course, the absorption approach only deals with the trade balance; a full theory of the balance of payments requires a theory of capital account movements (and a discussion of how the exchange rate itself is determined).

DAVID VINES

See also ELASTICITIES APPROACH TO THE BALANCE OF PAYMENTS; MONETARY APPROACH TO THE BALANCE OF PAYMENTS.

BIBLIOGRAPHY

Alexander, S.S. 1952. Effects of devaluation on a trade balance. *International Monetary Fund Staff Papers*, Vol. 2, 263–78.

Alexander, S.S. 1959. A simplified synthesis of elasticities and absorption approaches. *American Economic Review* 49, 22–42.

Ball, J., Burns, T. and Laury, J.S.E. 1977. The role of exchange rate change in balance of payments adjustment – the United Kingdom case. *Economic Journal* 87, 1–29.

Caves, R.E. and Johnson, H.G. (eds) 1968. *Readings in International Economics*. London: George Allen & Unwin.

Diaz Alexandro, C. 1966. *Exchange Rate Devaluation in a Semi-Industrialized Country: The Experience of Argentina 1955–1961*. Boston: MIT Press.

Frenkel, J.A. and Johnson, H.G. (eds) 1976. *The Monetary Approach to the Balance of Payments*. London: George Allen & Unwin.

Harberger, A.C. 1950. Currency depreciation, income and the balance of trade. In Caves and Johnson (eds), (1968).

Harrod, R.F. 1939. *International Economics*. 2nd edn, Cambridge Economic Handbooks, VIII, London: Nisbet & Co.

Kyle, J.F. 1976. *The Balance of Payments in a Monetary Economy*. Princeton: Princeton University Press.

Laursen, S. and Metzler, L. 1950 Flexible exchange rates and the theory of employment. *Review of Economics and Statistics* 32, 281–99.

Machlup, F. 1943 *International Trade and the National Income Multiplier*. Philadelphia: Blakiston Co.

McCallum, J. and Vines, D. 1981. Cambridge and Chicago on the balance of payments. *Economic Journal* 91, 439–53.

Meade, J.E. 1951. *The Balance of Payments*. London: Oxford University Press.

Robinson, J.V. 1937. The Foreign Exchanges. In J. Robinson, *Essays in The Theory of Employment*, 2nd edn, 1947. Reprinted in *Readings in the Theory of International Trade*, ed. H.S. Ellis and L.A. Metzler, Philadelphia: Blakiston, 1949, 83–103.

Svensson, L. and Razin, A. 1983. The terms of trade and the current account: the Harberger–Laursen–Metzler Effect. *Journal of Political Economy* 91, 97–125.

Swan, T.W. 1956. Longer run problems of the balance of payments. In *The Australian Economy, a Volume of Readings*, ed. H. Arndt and W.M. Corden, Melbourne: Cheshire Press, 1963. Reprinted in Caves and Johnson (eds), (1968).

absorptive capacity. The idea that the productivity of new investment is a declining function of the rate of investment – the concept labelled 'absorptive capacity' – has attracted attention in development economics because of its implications as a constraint on growth.

The hypothesis began to emerge most clearly in the 1950s in the form of a limit on the total amount of investment which could be carried out and/or used in any period, as if the marginal productivity of resources devoted to investment would, at some level of total investment undertaken, fall to zero. This was the position taken by Horvath (1958), citing experience in Yugoslavia and Eastern Europe. An Economic Commission for Asia and the Far East (ECAFE) report claimed that 'capacity sets a limit to the amount of efficient investment physically possible', introducing the distinction between 'efficient' and, presumably, 'inefficient' investment (ECAFE, 1960). In the early discussions, the concept was used to represent all the constraints on development which economists could not easily put into the conventional production function, 'the supply of skilled labour, administrative capacity, entrepreneurship and social change' (Marris, 1970).

Rosenstein-Rodan (1961), Adler (1965) and others described the absorptive capacity concept as a relationship between the productivity and the rate of investment, rather than as an absolute ceiling on investment's productivity. The sources of the relationship were not discussed in depth nor investigated empirically and it remained a 'black box' whose inner workings were never fully explained. Nonetheless, by the mid-1960s the absorptive capacity idea had become a part of the standard toolbox of development economics and used readily to explain difficulties experienced in attempts to accelerate economic growth.

Research on growth and planning models led to both a refinement of the concept and new speculation about its sources. Kendrick and Taylor (1969), following a suggestion by Dorfman and Thoreson (1969), modelled the absorptive capacity constraint as a permanent reduction in the productivity of new investment related to the rate of investment, as if an increase in investment were accompanied by the use of progressively inferior engineering design and materials. Eckaus (1972) formulated the constraint by making the productivity of successive tranches of investment in any year decline relative to the original tranche with, however, the decline only being temporary. In subsequent periods after the new capital was completed, its productivity would grow to 'rated' levels. He offered the hypothesis that, as investment increases, less and less well qualified engineers and workers and less suitable equipment are employed in producing the new capital goods and bringing them into production.

The absorptive capacity concepts came to play a critical role in the economy-wide policy models which were formulated as linear programming problems. If the objective function in such models is linear, for example, the simple discounted sum of aggregate consumption over the plan period and, if all the constraints are linear and do not control the timing of consumption, the solutions of the models will exhibit 'flip-flop' or 'bang-bang' behaviour. Aggregate consumption will be concentrated either at the beginning or at the end of the planning period. This unrealistic and undesirable result can be controlled by constraints on the timing of consumption (Eckaus and Parikh, 1968). An aggregate utility function with declining marginal utility as a nonlinear objective function and/or absorptive capacity constraints, which are essentially nonlinear relations between investment and increments in output, are, however, theoretically more satisfactory means of avoiding 'bang-bang'.

The absorptive capacity concept is related closely to a generalization which emerged quite independently of the development literature from the study of factors constraining the growth of firms in advanced countries (Penrose, 1959). This was embodied in a theoretical growth model by Uzawa (1969). The concept is also a close relation, if not the twin, of an idea which appeared early in the macroeconomic analysis literature only to be lost and then revived once more. In chapter 11 of the *General Theory*, Keynes describes the marginal efficiency of capital, that is, the productivity of new investment, as declining with the rate of new investment because, 'pressure on the facilities for producing that type of capital will cause its supply price to increase' (Keynes, 1936). Under the title of 'adjustment costs', this characterization began to figure prominently in the macroeconomic literature in the late 1960s (Lucas, 1967).

'Adjustment costs' is a phrase which is as appealing as 'absorptive capacity'. The phenomenon is not explained by giving it a name, however. While the fact that economists continue to resort to the idea might be counted as evidence that it reflects a reality, the empirical research on its sources is still limited.

RICHARD S. ECKAUS

See also ADJUSTMENT COSTS; DEVELOPMENT ECONOMICS.

BIBLIOGRAPHY

Adler, J. 1965. *Absorptive Capacity and Its Determinants*. Washington, DC: Brookings Institution.

Dorfman, R. and Thoreson, R. 1969. Optimal patterns of growth and aid with diminishing returns to investment and consumption. *Economic Development Report* No. 142, Development Research Group, Harvard University, Cambridge, Mass.

Eckaus, R.S. 1972. Absorptive capacity as a constraint due to maturation processes. In *Development and Planning: Essays in Honour of Paul Rosenstein-Rodan*, ed. J. Bhagwati and R.S. Eckaus, Cambridge, Mass.: MIT Press.

Eckaus, R.S. and Parikh, K.S. 1968. *Planning for Growth*. Cambridge, Mass.: MIT Press.

Economic Commission for Asia and the Far East (ECAFE). 1960. *Programming Techniques for Economic Development*. Bangkok: United Nations.

Horvath, B. 1958. The optimum rate of investment. *Economic Journal* 68, 747–67.

Kendrick, D.A. and Taylor, L.J. 1969. A dynamic nonlinear planning model for Korea. In *Practical Approaches to Development Planning*, ed. I. Adelman, Baltimore: Johns Hopkins Press.

Keynes, J.M. 1936. *The General Theory of Employment, Interest and Money*. London: Macmillan.

Lucas, R. 1967. Adjustment costs and the theory of supply. *Journal of Political Economy* 75, August, 321–34.

Marris, R. 1970. Can we measure the need for development assistance? *Economic Journal* 80, 650–68.

Penrose, E. 1959. *The Theory of the Growth of the Firm*. Oxford: Blackwell.

Rosenstein-Rodan, P.N. 1961. International aid for underdeveloped countries. *Review of Economics and Statistics*. 43(2), 107–38.

Uzawa, H. 1969. Time preference and the Penrose effect in a two-class model of economic growth. *Journal of Political Economy* 77, 628–52.

abstinence. 'Abstinence' was Nassau Senior's term for that conduct for which profit is the reward (1836, p. 59). He meant it to convey two things: 'both the act of abstaining from the unproductive use of capital, and also the similar conduct of the man who devotes his labour to the production of remote rather than immediate results' (1836, p. 89). The term he knew was not ideal, but it was preferable to 'providence', which implies nothing of self-denial; and to 'frugality', which implies care and attention, that is, labour, which analytically Senior

wanted to keep distinct from the agent of production rewarded by profit. For the same reason he chose not to speak of profit in relation to 'capital'. Capital usually combines the services of natural agents, labour and abstinence, but it is desirable in an analysis to keep their several contributions distinct.

Despite the desirability of precision in analysis, Senior had to admit that in practice 'it is often difficult to distinguish profit from wages', or, for that matter, rent from profit (1848–9, pp. 149–50). Nor was he, nor any of the other classical writers who took over his terminology (e.g. J.S. Mill 1848, p. 34), able to quantify the reward of abstinence. Clearly it is the minimum return for there to be any accumulation, and, since profit is an uncertain expectation (1836, p. 187), must be at least equal to the rate of interest on a government bond; but beyond that exactly how the rate is settled was not paid much attention. It must not be thought, however, that profit is just the reward for the initial refraining from consuming one's capital. That would make any net return after the first period simply rent. The fact that Senior stressed abstinence also in relation to activity with remote results, suggests that he was fully aware that profit must be calculated as the present value of a stream of returns.

The notion of abstinence has been regarded by Marxian writers as a poor apology for a justification of the payment of interest. They have ridiculed it, using examples comparing the 'abstinence' of a Rothschild with the profligacy of a labourer who spends all his meagre income. Even John Stuart Mill, in his draft *Chapters on Socialism* wrote: 'The very idea of distributive justice, or proportionality between success and merit, or between success and exertion, is in the present state of society so manifestly chimerical as to be relegated to the regions of romance' (1879, p. 714).

These sentiments are misleading in relation to Senior's deployment of 'abstinence'. The idea derives from his Stoic perspective on supply. Production involves overcoming obstacles such as a natural preference for leisure and for present enjoyment; hence prudent behaviour to counter these impediments requires and merits recompense. Abstinence, for Senior, was on a par with the other agents of production – labour and natural agents – and is critical to one of his four fundamental propositions of economic science, the notion that the powers of labour 'may be indefinitely increased by using their Products as the means of further Production' (1836, pp. 26, 58). Senior's point is simply that abstinence is a necessary precondition for capital to emerge.

Marshall, with characteristic appositeness, insisted on a distinction between abstemiousness and waiting, and used the latter to replace abstinence (1890, pp. 232–3). He also saw the important point in Senior's discussion, namely, the need to encourage the 'faculty of realizing the future' or 'man's *prospectiveness*' (ibid., p. 233). Without encouragement to this faculty there will be no supply of capital. Others, such as Böhm-Bawerk and Fisher, argued against treating abstinence as a cost (Fisher, 1907, pp. 43–5). But this criticism scarcely touches Senior, and Fisher is basically at one with Marshall in stressing prospectiveness. Fisher's emphasis, however, is on time-preference and the fact that time-preference itself will depend on the size, distribution over time, composition and probability of the prospective income stream facing an individual (ibid., pp. 92–4). This is the natural link with recent models embodying inter-generational transfers and infinite time-horizons.

N. DE MARCHI

See also SENIOR, NASSAU WILLIAM; WAITING.

BIBLIOGRAPHY

Fisher, I. 1907. *The Rate of Interest*. New York: Macmillan.

Marshall, A. 1890. *Principles of Economics*. 9th (variorum) edn, 2 vols, London: Macmillan for the Royal Economic Society, 1961.

Mill, J.S. 1848. *Principles of Political Economy*. In *Collected Works of John Stuart Mill*, ed. J.M. Robson, Vols II, III, Toronto: University of Toronto Press, 1965.

Mill, J.S. 1879. *Chapters on Socialism*. In *Collected Works*, Vol. V, 1967.

Senior, N.W. 1836. *An Outline of the Science of Political Economy*. New York: Kelley Reprint, 1965.

Senior, N.W. 1848–9. Course of Lectures delivered in the University of Oxford. Unpublished; quoted in *Industrial Efficiency and Social Economy* by Nassau W. Senior, ed. S. Leon Levy, 2 vols, New York: Henry Holt & Co., 1928.

abstract and concrete labour. The reproduction of society requires the production and distribution of the mass of products which forms the material basis of its existence. This in turn means that each society must somehow ensure that its available social labour time is regularly directed, in particular quantities and proportions, towards the specific applications needed to ensure social reproduction. As Marx points out, 'every child knows that a nation which ceased to work ... even for a few weeks, would perish' (Marx, 1867a).

The above implies that all labour has two distinct aspects. As a part of the general pool of society's labour, it is merely one portion of the human energy available to the community. In this respect all labour is essentially the same, representing the expenditure of 'human labour-power in general' in its capacity as simply one part of the division of general social labour. This is labour as *social labour*. But at the same time, individual labour occurs in the form of a specific activity aimed at a specific result. Here it is the particular quality of the labour, its determination as labour of mining, metalworking, weaving, distribution, etc., which is relevant. This is labour as *concrete labour*, related to the concrete result of its activity.

Although the dialectic between concrete and social labour is a necessary part of social reproduction, their inter-connection is hard to discern within societies which produce things-for-exchange (commodities), because in this case individual activities are undertaken without any apparent consideration for the necessity of a social division of labour. All useful objects now appear to be naturally endowed with quantitative worth in exchange (*exchange value*), and this apparently natural property in turn seems to regulate the actual division of labour.

It is at this point that Marx introduces two crucial questions. What precisely is a commodity? And more importantly, why does it become socially necessary to attach an exchange value to it? He begins his answer by observing that as a useful good a commodity is simply a concrete bundle of different socially desirable properties. In this respect it is similar to particular, qualitatively distinct useful objects in all social forms of organization. But as an exchangeable good, its salient property is that it is treated socially as being qualitatively *identical* to every other commodity. This is manifested in the fact that when commodities are assigned differing quantities of exchange value, expressed in some common measure, they are thereby being socially regarded as qualitatively alike, all reducible to the same homogenous measure of quantitative worth. A commodity is therefore a doublet of opposite characteristics: a multiplicity of concrete useful properties (use value) on the one hand, and a single magnitude of homogenous quantitative worth (exchange value) on the other.

The double character of a commodity is strikingly reminiscent of the previously noted duality of labour as particular concrete labour and as general social labour. Indeed, in commodity producing society the various concrete labours 'only count as homogeneous labour when under *objectified husk*', that is, when they 'relate to one another as human labour by relating *their products to one another as values*'. The concrete labours are thus counted as social labour only when they are *valorized*, and the necessity of exchange value lies precisely in the fact that it is through this device that a society containing apparently independent private producers comes to grips with the social content of their individual labours. To answer Marx's second question, exchange value is the particular historical mode of expressing the general necessity of social labour.

The notion that exchange value is a historically specific way of accounting for social labour time does not imply that the terms of exchange of commodities always reflect the quantities of valorized social labour time that went into their respective production. Indeed, Marx distinguishes between the case in which particular useful objects are produced for direct use and only accidentally or occasionally find their way into the sphere of exchange, and the case in which goods are produced *in order* to be exchanged. In the first case, when for example otherwise self-sufficient tribes occasionally barter a few of their products, the relation between concrete labour and social labour is effectively determined within each social group, and exchange merely serves to create a temporary equivalence between the respective social labours involved. Because the objects in question are produced as useful objects and become commodities only when they enter exchange, the labours involved are valorized only in exchange itself. Moreover, since these activities do not depend fundamentally on exchange (and hence on the valorization of their labour), the precise conditions of exchange can in turn be decided by a variety of factors, ranging from broad structural influences to merely conjunctural or even accidental ones.

At the opposite extreme is the case of goods produced solely for exchange. Now, the particular labours involved are *aimed* at producing exchangeable goods, and the valorization of these labours is an intrinsic part of their reproduction. As producers of commodities, these labours create not only bundles of useful properties (use-values), but also amounts of abstract quantitative worth. In the former aspect, they are of course concrete labours; but in the latter, they are *value creating* activities whose content as social labour is manifest only in-and-through the abstract quantitative worth of their products. To emphasize this particular historical form of the duality of labour, Marx identifies that labour which is engaged in the production of commodities as being both concrete (use-value creating) labour, and *abstract* (value creating) labour.

Three further points must be briefly mentioned. First of all, Marx argues that abstract labour time not only stands behind the production of commodities, but that the magnitudes of these labour times actually regulate the exchange relations of these commodities. To this end, he defines the quantity of abstract labour 'socially necessary ... to produce an article under the normal conditions of production' as the (inner) *value* of the commodity, since it is the 'intrinsic measure' of the exchange value. Secondly, he distinguishes between the conditions under which the exchange relations of commodities are dependent on their (labour) values, and the conditions in which they are controlled by them. It is only in the latter instance, in which capitalism has effectively generalized commodity production, that the reproduction of society is regulated by the law of value. Lastly, he notes that once commodity production is indeed generalized, so that social labour appears only under objective husk, then the social relation among producers is actually regulated by the mysterious value-relation between their products. In this topsy-turvy world, a social relation among persons appears in their eyes to be in fact a relation among things. This is what Marx calls the Fetishism of Commodities which is characteristic of capitalism.

ANWAR SHAIKH

See also ADAPTIVE EXPECTATIONS; ADJUSTMENT COSTS; LABOUR POWER; MARXIST ECONOMICS; VALUE AND PRICE.

BIBLIOGRAPHY

Marx, K. 1867a. *Capital*, Vol. I. 1st edn, ch. 1 and Appendix to ch. 1. In *Value: Studies by Karl Marx*, trans. and ed. A. Dragstedt, London: New Park Publications, 1976.

Marx, K. 1867b. *Capital*, Vol. I. Introduced by E. Mandel, London: Penguin, 1976, ch. 1.

Marx, K. 1879. Marginal notes to A. Wagner's *Textbook on Political Economy*. In *Value: Studies by Karl Marx*, trans. and ed. A. Dragstedt, London: New Park Publications, 1976.

acapitalistic production. *See* CAPITALISTIC AND ACAPITALISTIC PRODUCTION.

acceleration principle. The acceleration principle has been proposed as a theory of investment *demand* as well as a theory determining the *supply* of capital goods. When combined with the multiplier, it has played a very important role in models of the business cycle as well as in growth models of the Harrod–Domar type. The acceleration principle has been used to explain investment in capital equipment, the production of durable consumer goods and investment in inventories (or stocks). In general, it has been used to explain aggregate investment, although it is sometimes used to explain investment by firms (micro-investment behaviour). The main idea underlying the acceleration principle is that the demand for capital goods is a derived demand and that changes in the demand for output lead to changes in the demand for capital stock and, hence, lead to investment. Its distinctive feature, then, is its emphasis on the role of (expected) demand and its de-emphasis on relative prices of inputs or interest rates.

The acceleration principle is a relatively new concept: it is possible to find its antecedents in Marx's *Theories of Surplus Value* Part II (1862–3, p. 531). Amongst the earliest exponents of the acceleration principle is Albert Aftalion in *Les Crises périodiques de surproduction* (1913). Later contributions by J. M. Clark (1917), A. C. Pigou (1927) and R. F. Harrod (1936) discussed the acceleration principle both as a determinant of investment and in its role in explaining business cycles. Haberler (1937) provides a fairly comprehensive account of the acceleration principle up to that date. Since then the contributions by Chenery (1952) and Koyck (1954) provide important extensions and developments of the theory. In recent years work by Eisner (1960) has employed the acceleration principle in econometric work. Almost all macro-economic models of the economy employ some variant of the acceleration principle to explain aggregate investment.

Underlying the acceleration principle is the notion that there is some optimal relationship between output and capital stock: if output is growing, an increase in capital stock is required. In the simplest version of the acceleration principle,

$$K_t^* = v Y_t$$

where K_t^* is planned capital stock, Y_t is output and v is a positive capital–output coefficient. Assuming that the capital stock is optimally adjusted in the initial period (that is $K_t = K_t^*$, where K_t is the actual capital stock) an increase in output (or planned output) leads to an increase in planned capital stock,

$$K_{t+1}^* = v Y_{t+1}$$

and again assuming optimal adjustment in the unit period

$$K_{t+1}^* - K_t^* = K_{t+1} - K_t = I_t = v(Y_{t+1} - Y_t) = v \Delta Y_t.$$

In other words, for net investment to be positive, output must be growing: v is called the accelerator.

The acceleration principle can be derived from a cost-minimizing model assuming either fixed (technical) coefficients and exogenous output, or variable coefficients with constant relative prices of inputs and exogenous output.

Some of the shortcomings of this simple model were well known; for example, the problem of being optimally adjusted: this was discussed in the context of whether or not the economy (or the firm) was working at full capacity. If the economy was operating with surplus capacity, an increase in aggregate demand would not lead to an increase in investment. Similarly, it was well known that the accelerator may work in an asymmetric fashion because of the limitations imposed on decreasing aggregate capital stock by the rate of depreciation: the economy as a whole could only decrease its capital stock by not replacing capital goods that were depreciating. Another important qualification to the simple accelerator model was than an increase in (expected) output would lead to an increase in investment only if it was believed that, in some way, the increase was 'permanent' or at least of long duration.

A generalization of the simple accelerator is provided by the flexible accelerator or the capital stock adjustment principle (also known as the distributed lag accelerator). It overcomes one of the major shortcomings of the simple accelerator, namely, the assumption that the capital stock is always optimally adjusted. The flexible accelerator also assumes that there is an optimal relationship between capital stock and output but allows for lags in the adjustment of the actual capital stock towards the optimal level. This is written as

$$I_t = b(K_t^* - K_{t-1})$$

where b is a positive constant between zero and one and K_t^* equals $v Y_t$. This equation implies that the adjustment path of actual capital stock towards the optimal level is asymptotic. In this version, the adjustment is not instantaneous either since, because of uncertainty, firms do not *plan* to make up the difference between K_t^* and K_{t-1} and/or because the *supply* of capital goods does not allow the adjustment to be instantaneous. A similar equation was derived by assuming increasing marginal costs of adjusting capital stock by Eisner and Strotz (1963).

In evaluating the acceleration principle it is worth stressing that, in some versions, it is used as an explanation of investment demand with the implicit assumption that the supply of capital goods will always satisfy that demand. In models where the acceleration principle is used to explain the *supply* of capital goods, it is assumed that they always satisfy the demand for them. The flexible accelerator is a hybrid version which includes both demand and supply elements.

Although there is no formal treatment of replacement investment, it is usually postulated to be determined in the same way as net investment. A major shortcoming of the acceleration principle is its simplistic treatment of *expectations* of future demand as well as its neglect of expectations of the time paths of output and input prices. Although most of the work in this field treats the acceleration principle as applying to the aggregate economy, it has also been used to explain investment by firms. It is especially important that the supply of capital goods is formally modelled along with the acceleration principle determining investment demand. Aggregation over firms is usually assumed to be a simple exercise of 'blowing up' an individual firm's investment demand. However, it should not be forgotten that in a modern capitalist economy an individual firm may invest by simply taking over an existing firm rather than by buying new capital goods. An important shortcoming of the acceleration principle is its neglect of technological change.

The acceleration principle is an important concept and has been used sucessfully in explaining investment behaviour as well as cyclical behaviour in a capitalist economy. It will continue to play an important role in macroeconometric models as well as in models of business cycles.

P.N. JUNANKAR

See also AFTALION, ALBERT; CLARK, JOHN MAURICE; INVESTMENT; MULTPLIER-ACCELERATOR INTERACTION.

BIBLIOGRAPHY

Aftalion, A. 1913. *Les crises périodiques de surproduction* . Paris: Rivière

Chenery, H. B. 1952. Overcapacity and the acceleration principle. *Econometrica* 20(1), January, 1–28.

Clark, J.M. 1917. Business acceleration and the law of demand: a technical factor in economic cycles. *Journal of Political Economy* 25(3), March, 217–35.

Eisner, R. 1960. A distributed lag investment function. *Econometrica* 28(1), January, 1–29.

Eisner, R. and Strotz, R. 1963. Determinants of business investment. In Commission on Money and Credit, *Impacts of Monetary Policy*, Englewood Cliffs, NJ: Prentice-Hall.

Haberler, G. 1937. *Prosperity and Depression*. Geneva: League of Nations.

Harrod, R.F. 1936. *The Trade Cycle*. Oxford: Oxford University Press.

Junankar, P.N. 1972. *Investment: Theories and Evidence*. London: Macmillan.

Knox, A.D. 1952. The acceleration principle and the theory of investment: a survey. *Economica* 19(75), August, 269–97.

Koyck, L.M. 1954. *Distributed Lags and Investment Analysis*. Amsterdam: North-Holland.

Pigou, A.C. 1927. *Industrial Fluctuations*. London: Macmillan. 2nd edn, 1929.

accounting and economics. Accounting and economics have been described by Boulding (1962) as 'the uncongenial twins'. They are both concerned with the same raw material, economic activity, but they approach it in very different ways. Each discipline has evolved over several centuries, developing its own concepts, language and culture with remarkably little help from the other. However, there has more recently been an increased interaction between the two disciplines, as the accountant's horizons have widened from recording to decision-making and the economist has become more concerned with the observation and measurement of economic phenomena in order to test his *a priori* theories.

The accountant's traditional concern has been with the accurate recording of economic events for the purposes of stewardship; that is, reporting to the owners of capital funds how those funds have been disbursed by their stewards or agents. The typical agent is the manager of a business, and the typical owner (or principal) is the shareholder or creditor, although tax authorities also typically have an interest, and many jurisdictions require corporate enterprises to be accountable to the wider public. Much of the effort of practising accountants is spent in auditing, which is a means of providing an independent validation of stewardship information. Thus accountants have traditionally sought to record past events in an objective manner. They have thus favoured recording transactions at their historical cost rather than attempting to revalue assets at current cost, which is more subjective. Thus the traditional posture of the accountant is backward-looking, recording past transactions, and giving great weight to objective description. Moreover, the accountant's methods have developed as pragmatic responses to practical difficulties, and early accounting theory was mainly an inductive *ex post* rationalization of accounting practice.

The economist, on the other hand, has traditionally had a broader perspective than the accountant. He has been concerned to analyse rather than merely to describe economic activity. He has therefore been concerned *inter alia* with normative issues, such as the optimal decisions a manager should make in order to maximize profit or the wealth of shareholders. Concern with decision-making naturally led to a concern with forward-looking information, reflecting the future consequences of the decision, in contrast with the accountant's concern with backward-looking information. Moreover, the analysis of the optimal decision required that the economist would develop deductive *a priori* theories, in contrast with the accountant's pragmatic inductive approach to theory.

Despite these traditional differences in orientation, the economist and the accountant have come much closer together during the 20th century, and this process is accelerating. From the accountant's standpoint, this is because of his widening responsibilities. Business enterprises have tended to be larger and more complex, and their accounting systems have tended to play an increasing role not only in stewardship and control but also in planning and decision-making. This has led the accountant into areas which are traditionally the province of the economist, and the accountant naturally turns to economic theory either for guidance or for justification of novel procedures. This has occurred most obviously in the development of management accounting (i.e. accounting for internal management purposes), which is clearly concerned with decision-making and which is not constrained by legal prescriptions. However, it has also occurred in the recent evolution of financial accounting; that is, financial reporting to providers of finance and other users of financial information who do not have access to the firm's internal management accounting system. In particular, there has been a concern, especially in the USA, with providing the capital market with information relevant to the valuation of stocks and shares.

From the economist's point of view, the closer relationship between economics and accounting can be attributed to two causes. Firstly, there has been an increased emphasis on testing economic theories and therefore increased concern with economic data, a rich source of which is accounts. Secondly, as microeconomic theory has developed in recent years, it has become increasingly concerned with uncertainty and the role of information in resolving uncertainty. Since the accountant is, in the real world, a major provider of information to economic agents, it is not surprising that these developments have brought accounting and economics closer together.

It is clear that, in terms of ideas, the contribution of economics to accounting has been much greater than that of accounting to economics. This is not surprising, in view of the different preoccupations of the two disciplines. The relationship might be likened to that between physics and engineering. The accountant, like the engineer, is concerned with essentially practical problems. In solving them, he draws upon the theoretical knowledge developed by the economist, just as the engineer draws upon the work of the physicist, but his contribution tends to be one of posing new problems for the theorist, or discovering inadequacies in his work, rather than developing new theory. This is a matter of emphasis rather than a rigid distinction, but it does explain the fact that the following brief account (a longer account is Whittington, 1977) of the exchanges between accounting and economics emphasizes the contribution of the latter to the former.

In the area of management accounting, the most obvious contribution of economists during the 20th century has been in the area of cost accounting. Accountants developed elaborate systems for recording and classifying costs and attributing them to different sources. These systems tended to be dominated by the accountant's obsession with clerical tidiness (e.g. a common view being that all overhead costs must be 'absorbed' by being attributed to a specific activity) and with the belief that a single 'objective' number, such as the historical cost of the ingredients of a product plus overhead costs allocated according to the accountant's rules, would serve for all purposes. The economist's view of costs, based upon the analysis of the optimal decision by a profit-maximizing management, was 'different costs for different purposes'; that is the nature and circumstances of the decision would determine the choice of cost measure (e.g. fixed overhead costs would not be relevant to a short-run decision for the purposes of which they could not be varied). Thus was the central message of *Studies in the Economics of Overhead Costs* (1923) by the distinguished economist J.M. Clark, which probably did more than any single book to interpret the economist's view of cost to the accountant. Other economists also set out to improve the accountant's understanding of the nature of the costs, notably in Britain at the London School of Economics. For example, R.H. Coase (1938) emphasized the importance of opportunity cost; that is, the cost of making a particular decision is not the historical cost of the resources committed but the net revenue foregone by not using the resources in the most profitable alternative. This literature is surveyed by Buchanan (1969).

More recently, the economist's contribution in this area has been extended by the application of opportunity cost to transfer pricing within the divisionalized firm, and by the recognition that linear programming can be applied to such problems. The shadow prices resulting from the dual solution of a programming problem can be used to identify opportunity costs (Samuels, 1965). This literature is surveyed by Arnold and Scapens (1981).

An even more recent contribution of economics to management accounting has been the application of agency theory, which was developed by economists in the 1970s as a result of the increased interest in information economics (Jensen and Meckling, 1976). This explores the problem of information asymmetry between principal and agent, and studies different forms of contract whereby the agent can be given incentives to act in the principal's interest, rather than exploiting his informational advantage at the principal's expense. This clearly has potential relevance to financial accounting, where the principal is the provider of capital and the agent is the manager. However, it also has relevance to the relationship between managers; for example, between central management and divisional management. Zimmerman (1979), for example, uses agency theory to justify the otherwise apparently irrational allocation of central overheads to divisions. Although such allocations may not seem to be rational from an opportunity cost perspective, they may be justified as a form of lump-sum tax on the perquisites of divisional managers which arise from their exploitation of their informational advantage.

Economists have also contributed notably to the area of financial management. Perhaps the most obvious of these contributions is in capital budgeting, where discounted cash-flow models of investment appraisal have become commonplace in textbooks and quite common in practice since the early 1960s. The discounted cash-flow approach is, of course, derived from neoclassical economics, and is found in the work of economists, such as Irving Fisher, early in the 20th century, although it also has earlier roots in actuarial science (see Parker, 1969, ch. 2). More recently, the capital budgeting decision has been elegantly integrated with the finance decision by Hirshleifer (1958), and there has been a considerable literature on the cost of capital and its relationship to the capital structure of the firm, arising from the classic paper by Modigliani and Miller (1958). Subsequently, the work of economists in the analysis of risk has influenced the accounting literature, notably the portfolio theory developed by Markowitz (1952) and the capital asset pricing model developed from it by Sharpe (1964). Of course, an influence on the accounting literature is not necessarily indicative of an influence on practice, but these contributions by economists to the analysis of the capital budgeting and financing decisions are now typically included in the examination syllabus of an accounting professional body, so they are likely to have an increasing influence on the practice of financial management in the future.

There are a number of other areas of management accounting to which economics and related disciplines have contributed; for example, the use of econometric techniques in estimating cost functions (Johnston, 1960) and in forecasting. However, the two areas described above, costing and financial management, have probably received the largest contribution. It is also important to note that economics is not the only discipline to contribute to management accounting; for example, the understanding of the budgeting process has been enhanced by the contributions of behavioural science, and some formal techniques have been borrowed direct from operational research.

Economics has made equally important contributions to the area of financial accounting during the 20th century. Most obviously, this has occurred in the debate on income measurement and asset valuation. One of the earliest critiques of accounting practice from the economist's point of view is J.B. Canning's *The Economics of Accountancy* (1929), which used as its ideal model Irving Fisher's concept of 'earnings' (as defined in Fisher, 1906). This concept is based upon the valuation of the net worth of the firm as the discounted present value of the future net cash receipts which it is expected to generate. This critique led Canning to dissatisfaction with the historical cost method of valuation and to advocate its substitution by current market values, which might provide better proxies for 'economic' values (i.e. net present values). This approach was reinforced by the influence of the Dutch and German schools of business economics, which also advocated the use of current market values (usually replacement costs) on the grounds of their relevance to the measurement of current economic performance.

The debate on various forms of current-cost or current-value accounting has persisted to the present time, and it has continued to draw on the work of economists. The economist who is the most frequently cited in this context is probably Hicks, whose definition of income, in *Value and Capital* (1946) is frequently quoted in the accounting literature. It is included in the collection of readings by Parker and Harcourt (1969), which has been very influential in introducing economists' writings to accountants.

Two specific techniques which owe their origins to economists and which have formed the basis of certain methods adopted to deal with inflation accounting are general price level adjustment and the value-to-the-owner approach to valuation. General price level adjustment owes its intellectual origins to Irving Fisher's *The Purchasing Power of Money* (1911), which was quoted in many of the earliest writings on inflation accounting. The value-to-the-owner method of valuation is commonly attributed to Bonbright (1937) but a similar concept is also found in the Dutch business economics literature and in Canning (1929). The central idea of this valuation method (which underlies current-cost accounting as at present implemented in the USA and the UK) is that the value of an asset has an upper limit imposed by the cost of replacement and, below this, a lower limit imposed by the net proceeds of sale or value in use. Thus value to the owner is the lower of replacement cost or recoverable amount, where recoverable amount is the higher of net selling value or value in use. This concept has clear antecedents in the economic theory of the late 19th century, particularly in the work of the Austrian school.

More recently, the accountants' debate on income measurement has shifted away from the idea of defining a unique 'true' income measure, because, under conditions of uncertainty and market imperfection, no such measure exists. The alternative approach is to regard an income statement as producing a set of information relevant to particular users or uses, rather than a single, all-purpose, 'bottom line' profit measure. The emergence of this approach owes a great deal to economists such as Alexander (1950), who produced an analysis of the effects of uncertainty and new information on ex ante and ex post income measures; Edwards and Bell (1961), who demonstrated how accounts could be designed in order to encompass a variety of measures of gain or profit, particularly under conditions of changing prices; and Beaver and Demski (1979) (the latter an economist), who demonstrated the formal result that were there is uncertainty and markets are incomplete, there can be no unique measure of income.

This informational view of financial reporting has had wider implications than its impact on income measurement. Beaver (1981) has aptly described information economics as causing 'an accounting revolution'. It has led, for example, to a large programme of empirical work to establish the value of particular pieces of information to particular users of accounts. This, in turn, has often focused on the capital market and has used models derived from economics (such as the capital asset pricing model and the assumption of market efficiency). There has also been a considerable debate about the accounting standard-setting process and its role in the market for financial information; for example, if that market were perfect there should be no need for accounting standards, and the nature of the imperfection which caused the need for standards should give some clue as to the type of standards which are required. Agency theory, which was discussed earlier in the context of management accounting, is another

application of information economics which has relevance to financial accounting. For example, the role of the auditor in monitoring accounts can be interpreted as being a technique for overcoming or limiting the information asymmetry between the agent (the manager) who prepares the accounts and the principal (the shareholder) who uses them.

Even this relatively brief and sketchy account of the contribution of economics to accounting during the 20th century should be sufficient to demonstrate that the contribution has been impressive. Economics has helped to transform accounting thought in a number of important areas, and it has had a significant impact on practice. We now turn, more briefly, to the less obvious, but nevertheless important, impact of accounting on economics.

It was suggested earlier that, because accounting is a practical art whereas economics is a theoretical discipline, we would expect the main flow of ideas to be from economics to accounting, and this has, in fact, been the case. The main contribution of accounting to economics has been in the provision of data about economic activity. Morgenstern has written, 'business accounts constitute the single most important source of information about the economic activity of a nation' (Morgenstern, 1963, p. 70). Accounts are the basis of much of the information about the corporate sector of the economy contained in the national income accounts. They also provide great deal of important information about microeconomic activity. Data banks of business accounts, such as the COMPUSTAT data bank in the USA, are widely used in applied economic research in such areas as finance and industrial economics.

However, the influence of accountants has not merely been confined to the provision of data. The concepts used by accountants have crept into the language and thought of economists, often surreptitiously but occasionally explicitly. An example of the latter type was Irving Fisher, whose early writings on income, capital and monetary theory are marked by meticulous attention to illustrating his theory in numerical examples, often explicitly in double-entry form. Fisher's appreciation of the nature of balance sheets, the distinct nature of flow statements and the double entry relationships between the two types of statement was fundamental to the way in which he thought about problems in monetary theory.

A more recent and perhaps more obvious importation of accounting concepts into economics has been in national income accounting. Although national income accounts were devised by economists, they are aggregations of data much of which have been prepared by accountants, and the aggregate accounts have therefore adopted many of the concepts and classifications used by accountants in preparing the basic data.

Accountants also have another function to which economists should perhaps pay greater attention in the future. They provide information for economic decision-makers, and any theory which hopes realistically to predict the outcome of a decision should take account of this information. An example of such work is the celebrated Hall and Hitch study (1939) of cost-plus pricing. This study led to a whole new field of empirical studies in the economics of pricing, but perhaps insufficient attention has been paid to the importance of the precise form of cost data which the accountant provides. However, there have been a number of studies of how the distortions inherent in historical cost accounting in periods of changing prices might lead to an exaggeration of the trade cycle (e.g. Baxter, 1955). It seems likely that, in the future, the further development of information economics will increase the economist's understanding of the role of accounting data in economic decisions.

G. WHITTINGTON

See also DOUBLE-ENTRY BOOKKEEPING; HISTORICAL COST ACCOUNTING; INFLATION ACCOUNTING; OVERHEAD COSTS.

BIBLIOGRAPHY

Alexander, S.S. 1950. Income measurement in a dynamic economy. In *Five Monographs on Business Income,* Study Group on Business Income, New York: American Institute of Accountants.

Arnold, J. and Scapens, R. 1981. The British contribution to opportunity cost theory. In *Essays in British Accounting Research,* ed. M. Bromwich and A. Hopwood, London: Pitman, ch. 7.

Baxter, W.T. 1955. The Accountant's contribution to the trade cycle. *Economica* 22(86), 99–112.

Beaver, W.H. 1981. *Financial Reporting: An Accounting Revolution,* Englewood Cliffs, NJ: Prentice-Hall.

Beaver, W.H. and Demski, J. 1979. The nature of income measurement. *Accounting Review* 54(1), January 1979, 38–46.

Bonbright, J.C. 1937. *Valuation of Property.* 2 vols. New York: McGraw-Hill.

Boulding, K.E. 1962. Economics and accounting: the uncongenial twins. In *Studies in Accounting Theory,* ed. W.T. Baxter and S. Davidson, London: Sweet and Maxwell.

Buchanan, J.M. 1969. *Cost and Choice: An Inquiry into Economic Theory.* Chicago: Markham.

Canning, J.B. 1929. *The Economics of Accountancy: A Critical Analysis of Accounting Theory.* New York: Ronald Press.

Clark, J.M. 1923. *Studies in the Economics of Overhead Costs.* Chicago: University of Chicago Press.

Coase, R.H. 1938. Business organisation and the accountant. *The Accountant,* 1 October–17 December.

Edwards, E.O. and Bell, P.W. 1961. *The Theory and Measurement of Business Income.* Berkeley: University of California Press.

Fisher, I. 1906. *The Nature of Capital and Income.* New York: Macmillan.

Fisher, I. 1911. *The Purchasing Power of Money.* New York: Macmillan.

Hall, R.L. and Hitch, C.J. 1939. Price theory and business behaviour. *Oxford Economic Papers* 2, May, 12–45.

Hicks, J.R. 1946. *Value and Capital.* 2nd edn, Oxford: Clarendon Press.

Hirshleifer, J. 1958. On the theory of optimal investment decision. *Journal of Political Economy* 66, August, 329–52.

Jensen, M. and Meckling, W. 1976. Theory of the firm: managerial behavior, agency costs and ownership structure. *Journal of Financial Economics* 3(4), October, 305–60.

Johnston, J. 1960. *Statistical Cost Analysis.* New York: McGraw-Hill.

Markowitz, H. 1952. Portfolio selection. *Journal of Finance* 7, March, 77–91.

Modigliani, F. and Miller, M.H. 1958. The cost of capital, corporation finance and the theory of investment. *American Economic Review* 48(3), June, 261–97.

Morgenstern, O. 1963. *On the Accuracy of Economic Observations.* Princeton: Princeton University Press.

Parker, R.H. 1969. *Management Accounting: An Historical Perspective.* London: Macmillan.

Parker, R.H. and Harcourt, G.C. (eds) 1969. *Readings in the Concept and Measurement of Income.* Cambridge: Cambridge University Press.

Samuels, J.M. 1965. Opportunity costing: an application of mathematical programming. *Journal of Accounting Research,* Autumn, 182–91.

Sharpe, W.F. 1964. Capital asset prices: a theory of market equilibrium under conditions of risk. *Journal of Finance* 19, September, 425–42.

Whittington, G. 1977. Accounting and economics. In *Current Issues in Accounting,* ed. A.B. Hope and B.V. Carsberg, Oxford: Philip Allan.

Zimmerman, J.L. 1979. The costs and benefits of cost allocations. *Accounting Review* 54(3), July, 504–21.

accumulation of capital. The accumulation of capital has been analysed by economists in two very different ways. The most common has been to see it as the expansion of the productive potential of an economy with a given technology, which may be improved in the process. But it has also been understood as the outright transformation of the technical and productive organization of the economy. The first approach leads to analyses based on the idea of steady growth, subsuming the concerns of the second under the heading of 'technical progress'. Such an approach rests on a conception of capital as productive goods or, in more sophisticated versions, as a fund providing command over productive goods. This is not wrong; it is merely inadequate. Capital must also be understood as a way of organizing production and economic activity, so that the accumulation of capital is the extension of this form of organization into areas in which production, exchange and distribution were governed by other rules. This conception of capital emphasizes the importance of organization; so understood, technology and engineering are not abstract science, they are ways of organizing production, and so have an institutional dimension. Accumulation then implies the transformation of institutions as well as production, and steady growth is not applicable (except perhaps as a benchmark).

Besides the distinction between steady state and transformational growth, there is another principal division in the way that economists have thought about accumulation. One side sees it as 'ploughing back' part of the surplus arising from production; the other as the process of adjusting a scarce resource to its optimal uses, as determined by the market. According to the classical 'surplus' approach, accumulation consists of the productive investment of part of society's net product – the surplus of output over necessary consumption and the requirements for maintaining capital intact – in order to expand productive capacity to take advantage of new or developing markets. The study of accumulation, therefore, needs to explain both the availability of the surplus and the motivation for ploughing it back, and this can be examined either as steady state expansion or as part of a process of transformation.

The originators of the classical tradition saw accumulation as a transformation of the economy. Smith stressed institutional changes, in particular the development of markets and the removal of state barriers, but his analytics were incomplete and partially incorrect. Ricardo offered only a rudimentary explanation of the surplus, in the 'iron law of wages'; accumulation, however, he saw as the natural activity of capitalists, although it would be limited by the rise of food prices caused by the extension of cultivation to marginal lands, shifting distribution in favour of rent. Marx located the origin of the surplus in the exploitation of labour and found the cause of the tendency of the rate of profit to fall in the interaction of competition and technological advance rather than in pressure on marginal land. Each offered a picture with a grand sweep, painted in large strokes. Modern 'surplus' theory is more circumspect and less interesting.

In most modern work accumulation is studied in the context of steady growth. Growth can be aimed at a specific target, or can continue indefinitely. The first is the subject of 'turnpike' studies (so called because to reach a target set of outputs most rapidly the economy first shifts to the balanced growth path – the 'turnpike' – and speeds along it, changing to the desired production mix when it reaches the right size), while the latter is analysed by models in which equilibrium paths of perpetual expansion are determined and their properties examined. So, given a system of production, we ask how that system can be set up so as to grow either over the indefinite future or over some finite stretch of time to reach some target set of outputs. In either case, however, accumulation, the central focus around which other economic questions are grouped, will result from the reinvestment of part of the surplus, and will be analysed either as a case of steady growth or as a deviation from steady growth.

The other approach sees accumulation or decumulation of capital simply as the adjustment of a particular factor of production to its equilibrium level, as determined by supply and demand. In this conception, factor equilibrium is defined in terms of the optimal allocation of scarce resources to competing tasks (in turn defined by the equilibrium final bill of goods, again determined by supply and demand.) The supply of capital may either be taken as given, along with that of land and labour, or it may be seen as governed by saving behaviour, and so responsive to the rate of interest. Demand for capital will be governed by its productivity at the margin, as with the other factors. Equilibrium in a particular sector comes when supply to that sector equals the demand for capital arising in it; equilibrium in general comes when the overall supply of capital equals the overall demand for it. So, according to this conception, accumulation occurs only when the economy is in disequilibrium – it is the movement along the path to equilibrium. The central economic problem is the optimal allocation of scarce resources, and accumulation of capital is a relatively minor matter.

Technical knowledge, however, is itself a scarce resource, and the incentives to produce it and allocate it optimally can be studied by neoclassical methods. Thus the allocation approach can give rise to an account of the long-term transformation of the economy.

But a reallocation process has a natural ending at the equilibrium point, whereas capital accumulation appears to be limitless. Locked into an allocation/disequilibrium framework, the supply and demand approach would be unable to tackle the main questions. It was saved from this fate by the development of the neoclassical growth model, based on the aggregate production function, and thus combining aspects of the traditional 'surplus' approach with supply and demand. This model provides an account of 'steady growth' over the long run; that is, uniform expansion of all outputs and all inputs, taking place together with regular technical progress. The working of this model, in turn, is based on the traditional theory of competitive factor markets with substitution between labour and capital in the process of production, where both factors are expressed in aggregate terms.

THE KEYNESIAN PROBLEMATIC. The question of substitution initially arose because a simple Keynesian growth model with a given capital–output ratio led to the disturbing conclusion that neither steady growth nor optimal allocation could be achieved. Aggregate demand equals Investment times the multiplier, or I/s, in the simplest case, where s is the average and marginal propensity to save. Aggregate supply, then, is the capital stock times its productivity, or K/v, where v is the capital–output ratio. So the growth rate, $G = I/K = s/v$. This is the rate which equates supply and demand; hence it is the one that business will find satisfactory. But nothing has been said about the labour force or employment; so the equilibrium growth rate need not be consistent with the growth of the labour force, a condition which cannot be optimal. Nor is that the only problem. When I is too low, so that $I/K <$ full employment s/v, $I/s < K/v$, and there will be excess capacity; so businesses will be inclined to reduce I still further. Similarly, when I is too large there will appear to be capacity shortage,

and businesses will be inclined to increase I still more. The system gives the wrong signals, and a deviation from steady growth will tend to worsen rather than correct itself.

THE NEOCLASSICAL RESPONSE. Substitution in response to price signals appears to correct this. The neoclassical model determines a path of steady and stable full-employment growth. For instance, when the rate of growth of labour, in efficiency units (the 'natural' rate of growth), persistently exceeds the rate, s/v, determined by the propensity to save and the capital–output ratio (the rate that will just balance aggregate demand and aggregate supply), the real wage will tend to fall, leading firms to substitute labour for capital. As a result, v, the capital–output ratio will decline, raising the rate of growth, s/v. So long as the production function is 'well behaved' (linear and homogeneous, positive first and negative second derivatives, marginal product of capital tends to infinity as K/L tends to zero, and tends to zero as K/L to infinity), there will exist a value of v that will equate s/v to any natural rate of growth. Technical progress which leaves the K/Y ratio unchanged (Harrod-neutral) will not affect the steady-growth path; technical progress which leaves the ratio of the marginal products of capital and labour unchanged (Hicks-neutral) will change the path, but the economy should adjust smoothly to the new equilibrium. In the Keynesian case, investment determined savings; here that causality is reversed (and so the instability disappears – by fiat): in the long run, all savings will be invested; persistent excess capacity (resulting from planned saving > planned investment at full employment) would drive down the rate of interest by lowering the return (or raising the risk) on existing securities; the lower rate of interest will then raise investment up to the full-employment level.

OPTIMALITY AND THE GOLDEN RULE. In neoclassical theory, equilibria tend also to be optimal, but in general the steady growth path will not be. An optimal path ought to be one along which per capita consumption is at a maximum. Consumption is output minus investment, and investment must grow at a fixed rate in order to fully employ the growing labour force. Now consider different capital–output ratios: if the marginal product of capital at a certain v adds more to output than is required to equip the labour force, consumption rises; if it adds less, consumption falls. Hence when the marginal product of capital just equals the additional investment required for the growing labour force, consumption will be at a maximum. But there is no reason to expect this level of the marginal product to be associated with the capital–output ratio that makes s/v just equal to the rate of growth of the labour force.

The proposition that consumption per head is maximized when the rate of profit equals the rate of growth is sometimes called the 'Golden Rule of Growth'. Under constant returns, it has another disconcerting implication for neoclassical theory. In the stationary state, a positive rate of profit implies that the choice of technique (of the capital–output ratio) is suboptimal. In the stationary state (the normal assumption underlying textbook price theory) only a zero rate of profit is consistent with optimal technique. But a zero rate of profit implies that the Labour Theory of Value governs long-run prices! Either long-run prices are determined by growth theory, or they reflect labour values, or the techniques in use are sub-optimal. (Non-constant returns make this more complicated, but the heart of the problem remains: allocation theory cannot determine long-run prices and optimal techniques independently of growth theory, and therefore of the 'surplus approach'.)

TECHNICAL PROGRESS. Treating technical progress as a shift of one kind or another in the production function limits the field of study to changes in method, overlooking the introduction of new products and, indeed, whole new sectors. Treating it as autonomous or as a function of time, even, as in 'learning-by-doing', time on the job, ignores the important influence of demand pressures. Neo-Keynesians, by contrast, treat technical progress as primarily occurring in manufacturing as a response to the growth of demand, so that the rate of technical progress depends on the relative size of manufacturing and on the rate of growth of demand, a relationship known as 'Verdoorn's Law', which has been widely confirmed.

CAPITAL THEORY. The standard version of neoclassical theory treats capital as a factor of production, on a par with labour and land, where factors are understood in broad terms and are supplied by households and demanded by firms. (The activity analysis version treats each capital good and each form of land or labour separately, determining its marginal product as a shadow price, thereby avoiding difficulties over capital-in-general, but for that very reason cannot easily analyse the forces that bear on capital as a whole; for instance, saving and investment and their relation to the rate of interest.) The 'surplus' approach of the classics, especially as developed by Marx, conceives capital as an institution: it is a way of organizing production by means of control over produced means of production, which permits processes of production to be valued so they can be bought and sold. These two approaches are obviously different, but are they necessarily incompatible? The capital theory controversy developed over the neoclassical attempt to show that the aggregate production function's implied ordering of techniques (according to an inverse relationship between profitability and capital-intensity) could be constructed in a disaggregated classical or 'surplus' model.

Each point on a neoclassical production function (whether aggregate or not) represents the adoption of a method of production: the firm or the economy as a whole has fully adjusted its plant and equipment. Moving from one point on a production function to another thus means scrapping old plant and replacing it with new, which implies a burst of exceptionally high activity in the capital-goods sector. This will normally be compatible with continuous full employment in the neoclassical framework only if the consumption goods sector is the more capital-intensive, a condition for which there is no economic rationale (Uzawa, 1961), or if certain other special conditions are met (Solow, 1962). But once we step outside the neoclassical framework the problem of 'traverse' (moving from one growth path to another), even with a *given* technique, can be shown to simply capacity surplus or shortages in one or more sectors, normally accompanied by temporary overall unemployment (Hicks, 1965; Lowe, 1975).

In marginal productivity theory a technique is thus uniquely designated by $(K/Y, K/L)$; moreover, each K/Y is uniquely paired to its corresponding K/L, and as a direct consequence, each K/L is uniquely associated with a marginal product of capital. But suppose a technique were most profitable at one rate of profit (marginal product of capital) and then also proved the most profitable at another level of the profit rate. If this could happen, the neoclassical production function would not uniquely determine the choice of method of production. Yet the general possibility of this phenomenon ('reswitching') is easily demonstrated. (Not only the neoclassical approach is at risk here; the Marxian doctrine of the falling rate of profit is likewise rendered suspect: Okishio, 1962).

Neoclassical production theory, whether aggregate or not, postulates diminishing marginal output as the amount used of a factor is varied in relation to other factors. If factors are paid the value of their marginal products, as the theory of competitive behaviour asserts, then factor reward (e.g. the rate of profit) should fall as the amount of the factor (capital) increases in relation to labour. (If reswitching occurs, it can be demonstrated that at least one of the switches will show a positive relation between capital per worker and the rate of profit.) Once we step outside the conventional approach, this inverse relationship is not intuitively plausible: increasing the amount of capital employed in a production process is a more complex matter than employing more labour. Capital consists of all the various means of production; it is a` *set* of inputs. In fact, it is more (and more complicated) than that: at the beginning of production the capital of an enterprise consists of its plant and equipment, its inventory of materials and its wage fund (minus various obligations). A little later it consists of somewhat depreciated plant and equipment, together with the worked-up inventory of marketable goods, while the materials and wage fund have disappeared. But (allowing for changes in indebtedness during production, etc.) although the actual goods in which its capital is embodied are different in the two situations, the business will sell for the same price – it has the same capital value. To vary the amount of capital is to change the size or the nature of the entire process, and it is not at all obvious what effect this will have on the rate of profit.

A second problem concerns influences running the other direction, from the rate of profit to the amount of capital. When the rate of profit changes, competition requires prices to change. (Suppose, *ceteris paribus*, that the real wage rose, requiring the general rate of profit to fall; to keep the rate uniform, so capital will not tend to migrate to the relatively high-profit industries, the prices of labour-intensive products will have to rise relative to capital-intensive ones.) But if the prices of produced means of production change, then the 'amount of capital' embodied in *unchanged* plant and equipment can vary, and this can come about because of variation in the rate of profit. Moreover, the amount of capital embodied in unchanged equipment can vary in either direction when the rate of profit changes, since the direction of relative price changes depends only on relative capital-intensity, about which no general rules can be given. The neoclassical ranking of techniques according to capital-intensity and the rate of return has to be considered an inadequate representation of the real complexities involved in choosing techniques and using capital in production. So the neoclassical answer to the Keynesian problem is not sufficient.

NEO-KEYNESIAN THEORY. An alternative to the neoclassical theory of steady growth, however, provides a similar answer by way of a different conception of price adjustments, while still remaining within the conception of accumulation as the expansion, rather than the transformation, of a given system. The overall saving ratio is considered the weighted average of saving out of wages and profits, the weights being the respective income shares. Here the propensity to save out of profits is assumed to be relatively high, and that out of wages to be low. Then, if the natural rate of growth $> s/v$, eventually the money wage rate would tend to fall, and this, *ceteris paribus*, would raise the profitability of investment. As a result the overall saving ratio would rise, bringing s/v up to the full-employment level. If s/v is greater than the natural rate, on the other hand, the resulting excess capacity would lower profitability and tend to bring s/v down. Thus it is not necessary to assume easy and unrealistic substitution; the capital/output ratio can remain fixed, and yet market adjustments will direct the system towards the full employment growth path.

Like the neoclassical, this scenario sees the natural rate of growth as the centre of gravitation towards which the system adjusts. But it has sometimes been given another, more Keynesian interpretation. If, at the level of normal capacity utilization, investment demand were to exceed savings, multiplier pressure would drive up prices – since output could not be (easily) increased. Money wages, on the other hand, would not be driven up, since employment could not be (easily) increased either, for when plant and equipment is operating at full capacity there are no more places on the assembly lines – the full complement of workers has already been hired. Thus the excess demand for goods will *not* translate into excess demand for labour, and prices will be driven up relative to money wages: a Profit Inflation. Thus the overall saving ratio will rise, until the pressure of excess demand is eased. So in the long run as well as in the short, savings adjusts to investment. Understood in this way, the second scenario contradicts the neoclassical one rather than complementing it.

INVESTMENT AND THE ACCELERATOR. But this is still not fully Keynesian, or at least not Harrodian, for the emergence of excess or shortage of capacity must be allowed to influence investment plans – the 'accelerator', or capital-stock adjustment principle. When $s/v >$ actual or current I/K, there will be a slump; when $s/v < I/K$ prices will be bid up relative to money wages. Money wages, in turn, will tend to rise or fall according to whether the actual rate of growth lies above or below the natural. If the actual rate lies above the natural, this will tend to raise the natural and lower the actual. There are thus three rates of growth: the actual, I/K, the warranted, s/v, and the natural, and six possible permutations of these. It can be shown that in only two cases is there an unambiguous tendency for all three rates to converge; in two others, plausible additional assumptions will bring a tendency to converge. But in two cases there seems to be no convergence at all; quite the opposite (Nell, 1982). So the Keynesian approach suggests that the full-employment (or, indeed, any) steady growth path should not be treated as a centre of gravitation; it may or may not be what the market tends to bring about.

CAPITAL VALUE AND PROFIT. Ironically, this neo-Keynesian approach runs afoul of the same problems that plague the neoclassical standard version. For once we leave the one-sector framework, the neo-Keynesian theory implies that excess aggregate demand will bid up, not the price level in general, but the relative price of capital goods – for the excess demand is entirely concentrated in the investment goods sector, and there is no discussion of how this could be transmitted to the consumer-goods sector. Moreover, if both prices did rise relative to money wages, consumer-goods demand would fall. But this would not indicate a possible equilibrium, for it leaves the profit rate unequal in the two sectors. Thus the neo-Keynesian claim must be that a bidding up of the relative price of capital goods will raise the rate of profit, leading to higher savings, etc., but in a two-sector model it is easily seen that this will only be the case when the capital-goods sector is the more capital-intensive. So the validity of the approach depends on an arbitrary condition (which becomes even more arbitrary as the number of sectors increases.)

Even worse, suppose that the capital-goods sector is the more capital-intensive, and consider a small rise in the growth rate to a new equilibrium level, requiring an increased production of capital goods (alternatively, a fall in the actual rate below the equilibrium). The corresponding new overall capital–labour ratio will be higher than the initial one; but to maintain full employment there will have to be a diversion of resources to the industry with the lower capital–labour ratio. To preserve full employment the capital-goods sector would have to be contracted; but to increase the growth rate it has to expand. (A similar argument holds for a decline in the equilibrium growth rate.) In the case where a rise in the price of capital goods would increase the rate of profit, permitting the neo-Keynesian mechanism to work, the system could not adjust to the new steady growth path, since the two conditions for adjustment contradict one another.

In fact, adjustment from one steady growth path to another turns out to be difficult in general, even without changes in technique. A change in the growth rate requires changes in the relative sizes of sectors, which means shifting labour and resources; but these are normally used in different proportions or in different combinations. And some can only be used in certain sectors and not in others. The 'traverse' from one steady path to another will normally involve both unemployment and shortages, and it may be difficult to actually reach a new path before the conditions determining it change. The 'steady growth' approach to accumulation may face insurmountable problems.

THE SIGNIFICANCE OF STEADY GROWTH. But, what then is the importance of the steady growth path? For the neoclassical approach it is an extension of the concept of equilibrium to the case of expansion over time; for some neo-Keynesians it represented a centre of gravitation, a point towards which the system would move, or around which it would oscillate. For others it may simply be a point of reference how the system would work *if* certain contrary-to-fact assumptions held. Real processes will normally be different and can be classified by their distance from such a point of reference.

Following Joan Robinson, steady growth with continuous full employment has been termed a 'golden age'; desired capital accumulation equals the natural rate of growth. But a low desired rate, well below the initial natural rate, might create a large reserve army of unemployed, forcing down real wages and lowering the birth rate, so that the natural rate would fall to the depressed desired rate a 'leaden age'. A desired rate above the natural rate may bid up real wages enough to lower the rate of profit until the desired rate falls to the natural – a 'restrained golden age'. A 'bastard golden age' occurs when the desired rate cannot be achieved because the real wage cannot be driven down sufficiently, the attempt resulting in inflation. Other possibilities can be envisioned, depending on the adjustment mechanisms postulated. For example, when the initial stock of capital is not appropriate to the desired rate of accumulation, it will have first to be adjusted, but the part of the capital-goods sector that produces capital goods for its own use may be too large or too small for easy adjustment to the desired rate, giving rise to 'platinum age' patterns of accumulation. The catalogue is endless, but its value is limited.

Steady growth, in fact, appears to be best analysed as a supply-side concept. Its most elaborate development, in fact, is strictly supply-side – as the von Neumann ray, or in Sraffa's terms, the Standard Commodity, where the industry sizes of the system have been so adjusted that the net product of the economy as a whole consists of the same commodities in the same ratios as its aggregate means of production. The warranted rate of growth, by contrast, balances supply and demand. But it is an imperfect growth concept, for it balances aggregate supply and aggregate demand *at a moment of time*; it does not balance the growth of supply with the growth of demand. The von Neumann ray is an analysis of the growth of supply – but so far there is no comparably detailed analysis of the growth of demand.

ACCUMULATION AND TECHNICAL CHANGE. This not only brings to light a defect in the theory of steady growth, it also raises the question of the relation of steady growth to the accumulation of capital. For the best-established empirical proposition in the study of consumer behaviour states that as income increases, consumer demand will increase non-proportionally – it will shift in a characteristic manner. Hence there is little point in trying to complete the theory of steady growth with an account of steady growth in demand; it doesn't happen.

In actual fact, steady growth has never taken place. The history of capitalism is a history of successive booms and slumps, but perhaps even more striking, of slow but persistent long-term shifts in crucial relationships. For two centuries labour shifted out of agriculture and migrated to the cities to work in manufacturing industry. For over half a century now labour has shifted into services, first from agriculture and then, later, from manufacturing as well. For almost a century the relative size of the government sector has been rising, whether measured by share of GNP or by share of employment.

These points lead to a major criticism of the treatment of technical progress in accumulation: whether it is presented as shifting the production function, as learning by doing, or in a 'technical progress' function, and whether conceived as embodied or disembodied, it has been treated as leading to the extraction of greater output from given resources, in the context of steady growth. But technical progress introduces new products as well as new processes, and together these change the forms of social life. This is reflected in the changing importance of the major sectors of the economy, in the changing class structure and in the changing patterns and nature of work. None of these points seems to be captured by the current analyses, in part because of the preoccupation with steady growth, based on an overly simplified concept of capital as productive goods. When capital is understood as also being a form of organization, then the link between accumulation and the transformation of institutions can be forged. Another reason, perhaps, may be that technical progress has been approached too timidly, and without understanding its dual relation to the growth of demand. For technical progress both stimulates the growth of demand and responds to it.

STEADY GROWTH VERSUS TRANSFORMATIONAL GROWTH. In practice, steady growth is an impossibility for at least three reasons. First, land and natural resources are limited, and high-grade ores and high-fertility lands are the first to be used. As they are used up over time, productivity falls unless and until technical progress offsets the decline – but such technical progress will have to involve new products. Second, as mentioned, Engel curves imply that consumption patterns will be changing. And finally, if propensities to save differ in the different social classes (and if workers receive interest on their savings, and capitalists salaries for managing capital), then the relative wealth of the classes will be changing over time, leading to changes in the composition of demand. The first point implies that costs will tend to rise; the second two, that demand for consumer goods will tend to rise more slowly as time passes. All three therefore point to long-term stagnation in the absence of major technological changes.

This does not simply mean increasing the productivity of currently employed processes; it means the development of new processes and new products – both for consumers and for industry. It means electrification, or the internal combustion engine, the aeroplane or, perhaps, the computer. The changes must be of sufficient importance to lead to an investment boom resulting from widespread scrapping of present plant and equipment, as well as the development, concurrently, of large-scale new markets, as consumers introduce the new products into their living patterns. And as new plants are built, economies of scale can be realized, making it possible to lower prices, so as to reach new markets in lower levels of the income distribution. Capital organizes markets and marketing as well as production.

New household products have emerged because a way has been found to perform some normal daily activity better or more cheaply by, in effect, shifting it from the household to industry, capitalizing it. New industrial processes, usually involving new products as well, have emerged as the result of mechanizing activities formerly performed by workers, enabling them to be done better, or more cheaply, or more reliably. Mass-production goods have replaced home crafts; the mechanization of agriculture, in conjunction with Engel's Law, has displaced farm labour; the rise of manufacturing, to build the factories and then to supply the new goods, has provided employment for the displaced labour – but at greatly reduced hours of work per week, providing more hours to spend on consuming.

The rise of mass production and the consequent urbanization have created new problems; among others, periodic mass unemployment, which in turn had to be dealt with by an expanded government. And today traditional mass production is being transformed by the computer and the chip, with consequences we cannot yet fully foresee.

The interlocking emergence of new products and new processes, creating new markets and new industries, can be termed 'transformational growth', in contrast to steady growth. It is here that the true story of the accumulation of capital, and the causes of the wealth of nations, will be found, but to date this study has been left the province of economic historians.

EDWARD J. NELL

See also CLASSICAL GROWTH MODELS; NEOCLASSICAL GROWTH MODELS.

BIBLIOGRAPHY

Domar, E.D. 1946. Capital expansion, rate of growth and employment. *Econometrica* 14, 137-47.

Harrod, R.F. 1939. An essay in dynamic theory. *Economic Journal* 49, 14-33.

Hicks, J. 1965. *Capital and Growth.* Oxford: Oxford University Press.

Kaldor, N. 1956. Alternative theories of distribution. *Review of Economic Studies* 23, 83-100.

Keynes, J.M. 1936. *The General Theory of Employment, Interest and Money.* London: Macmillan.

Laibman, D. and Nell, E.J. 1977. Reswitching, Wickell effects and the neo-classical production function. *American Economic Review* 67, 878-88.

Lowe, A. 1976. *The Path of Economic Growth.* New York: Cambridge University Press.

Marx, K. 1867-94. *Capital*, Vols. I, II, III. Moscow: Progress Publishers, n.d.

Nell, E.J. 1982. Growth, distribution and inflation. *Journal of Post-Keynesian Economics* 5, 104-13.

Nell, E.J. 1986. *Priority and Public Spending.* London: George Allen & Unwin.

Ricardo, D. 1817. *On the Principles of Political Economy and Taxation.* Vol. I of *The Works and Correspondence of David Ricardo,* ed. P. Sraffa, Cambridge: Cambridge University Press, 1951.

Robinson, J. 1956. *The Accumulation of Capital.* London: Macmillan.

Robinson, J. 1962. *Essays in the Theory of Economic Growth.* London: Macmillan.

Solow, R. 1956. A contribution to the theory of economic growth. *Quarterly Journal of Economics* 70, 65-94.

Solow, R. 1962 Substitution and fixed proportions in the theory of capital. *Review of Economic Studies* 29, 207-18.

Sraffa, P. 1960. *Production of Commodities by Means of Commodities*. Cambridge: Cambridge University Press.

Uzawa, H. 1961. On a two-sector model of economic growth. *Review of Economic Studies* 24, 40-47.

Von Neumann, J. 1937. A model of general economic equilibrium *Review of Economic Studies* 13, (1945-6), 1-9.

activity analysis. *See* LINEAR PROGRAMMING.

acyclicity. Acyclicity is a consistency property of preferences and other binary relations. It requires that the asymmetric part P of the relation (e.g. the subrelation of strict preference) contain no cycles; that is, for no sequence of alternatives x_1, $x_2, ..., x_n$ is it true that $x_1 P x_2, x_2 P x_3, ..., x_{n-1} P x_n$, and $x_n P x_1$. The study of cyclic preferences dates at least to Condorcet's (1785) treatment of the paradox of voting, in which transitive individual voters generate cyclic majority preferences.

Whenever a feasible set S contains more than two alternatives, some principle is needed to generate choices $C(S)$ from the pairwise comparisons summarized by the preference relation; one natural candidate is the set of undominated alternatives. Acyclicity is necessary and sufficient for the existence of a non-empty set of undominated elements in any finite feasible subset S of the universal set of alternatives In addition, defining the choice set as the undominated alternatives according to an acyclic relation guarantees that choices will exhibit a desirable consistency property: if S is a subset of T and if x belongs both to S and to $C(T)$, then x must belong to $C(S)$. In Sen's (1970) example, if the world champion is a Pakistani, then he must be champion of Pakistan as well. This property is attractive in piecemeal decision mechanisms in which choices are made from unions of choices over subsets. If an alternative fails to be chosen in some subset, it need not be reconsidered later, since the contrapositive of this property ensures that the alternative will not be among the final choices.

Acyclicity is a significantly weaker consistency property than transitivity; it permits intransitivities both of the strict preference relation P and the symmetric subrelation of indifference I. For example, the preferences xPy, yPz, and xIz are acyclic; so too are the preferences xIy, xIz, and xPz.

Acyclicity arises in several contexts in economics. Consumer theory's Strong Axiom of Revealed Preference (see Houthakker, 1950; Ville, 1951-2), for example, is an axiom asserting that a particular revealed preference relation is acyclic. It arose as well early in the development of game theory; the acyclicity of dominance relations is closely linked to the uniqueness of the von Neumann–Morgenstern (1947, ch. XII) solution.

Acyclicity has been studied most intensively, however, in connection with Arrow's (1951) Impossibility Theorem. This proposition concerns constitutions, which aggregate sets of individuals' preference orderings into social preferences. Arrow showed that the only constitutions satisfying two reasonable axioms and yielding transitive social preferences are dictatorial. Several writers have attempted to circumvent this conclusion by relaxing transitivity to the more defensible requirement of acyclicity. Non-dictatorial acyclic constitutions do exist, but they turn out to be hardly more attractive than dictatorships. Blair and Pollak (1982) review this literature and

show that such constitutions must endow at least one voter with extensive veto power over strict social preferences opposite his or her own. If egalitarian concerns force the vesting of such power in many such voters, the constitution will be highly indecisive, that is, frequently yield judgements of indifference between alternatives.

DOUGLAS BLAIR

See also ARROW'S THEOREM; ORDERINGS; PREFERENCES; PREORDERINGS, REVEALED PREFERENCE; SOCIAL CHOICE; TRANSITIVITY.

BIBLIOGRAPHY

Arrow, K. 1951. *Social Choice and Individual Values*. New York: Wiley.

Blair, D.H. and Pollak, R. 1982. Acyclic collective choice rules. *Econometrica* 50(4), July, 931–43.

Condorcet, Marquis de. 1785. *Essai sur l'application de l'analyse à la probabilité des decisions rendues à la pluralité des voix*. Paris.

Houthakker, H. 1950. Revealed preference and the utility function. *Economica* 17, May, 159–74.

Neumann, J. von and Morgenstern, O. 1947. *Theory of Games and Economic Behavior*. 2nd edn, Princeton: Princeton University Press.

Sen, A. 1970. *Collective Choice and Social Welfare*. San Francisco: Holden-Day.

Ville, J. 1952. The existence conditions of a total utility function. *Review of Economic Studies* 19(2), 123–8.

Adams, Henry Carter (1851–1921). Adams was born on 31 December 1851 in Davenport, Iowa, and died in Ann Arbor, Michigan, on 11 August 1921. In many respects typical of the new generation of late 19th-century American social scientists, Adams became a professional economist only after considering a career in the church or in reform political journalism. After graduating from Iowa (later Grinnell) College in 1874, he spent one year as a school teacher and another studying at Andover Theological Seminary before obtaining a fellowship at the newly founded Johns Hopkins University, where he received its first PhD, in 1878. At Hopkins, Francis Walker steered him towards public finance, a field to which Adams subsequently made major pioneering contributions. But he was no narrow specialist, and two years' further study in Europe, mainly at Berlin and Heidelberg, laid the foundations for the breadth of interest, historical perspective, and philosophical insight that characterized his later writings.

On returning to the USA Adams, like many of his contemporaries, found difficulty in obtaining a satisfactory permanent academic post and was obliged to spend several years in temporary or part-time employment before obtaining a permanent position at the University of Michigan in 1886, where he spent the remainder of his career. The frank and revealing correspondence between Adams and President Angell immediately prior to this appointment is a notable contribution to the chequered history of academic freedom in America (cf. Dorfman, 1954, editor's introduction; Coats, 1968), for Adams had only recently been dismissed from Cornell for having publicly expressed support for labour unions during the outcry over the Haymarket bomb incident. At Ann Arbor, Adams built up a distinguished department (Brazer, 1982) and achieved national recognition for his nearly two decades of service as Chief Statistician to the Interstate Commerce Commission, where by constructing and implementing a system of uniform railway accounts he made a lasting contribution to the development of public regulation.

A co-founder and staunch supporter of the American Economic Association, of which he was President in 1896–7, Adams endeavoured to bring the best elements in European economic, social, and political thought to bear on the study of contemporary problems. He made no significant contributions to economic theory, although he was one of the first American economists to incorporate Jevons's value theory into his teaching. A more temperate critic of laissez-faire individualism than Richard T. Ely, Adams preferred clear thinking to exhortation and was respected by his peers for his solid scholarship and balanced judgement, for example in his seminal essay on the 'Relation of the State to Industrial Action', the first systematic American examination of the respective spheres of private and public economic activity. While recognizing the force of competition as a principle he considered it inadequate as a curb to monopoly power, and liable to depress the ethical plane of economic activity as unscrupulous employers undercut their more reputable rivals. Arguing the need for increased government intervention as the economic system became more complex, Adams nevertheless opposed socialism and nationalization, initially preferring municipal and state to federal regulation. Later he viewed the regulatory commission as the ideal conservative instrument of reform. His analysis of the distinction between increasing, constant and diminishing returns underlay his concern at the growth of corporate power and at the end of his life he advocated cooperation as the most desirable basis for industrial reform. Like many later thinkers he emphasized the need for collaboration between the various organized groups in society, and his emphasis on the worker's proprietary rights in his employment became a significant theme in the writings of American labour economists. Another pioneering contribution was his appreciation of the interdependence of economics and jurisprudence, one of many elements drawn from the tradition of German historical economics. Although he displayed little interest in the monetary questions which troubled so many of his contemporaries, Adams was a versatile and fertile thinker, many of whose ideas became common currency among later generations of American social scientists.

A.W. Coats

SELECTED WORKS

1881. *Outline of Lectures upon Political Economy.* Amherst, Mass: C.A. Bangs Co. 2nd edn, Ann Arbor, 1886.

1884. *Taxation in the United States 1789–1816.* Baltimore: Johns Hopkins Press.

1887a. *Public Debts: an essay in the science of finance.* New York: D. Appleton Co. 2nd edn, 1898.

1887b. *Relation of the State to Industrial Action.* Baltimore: American Economic Association. New edn, ed. J. Dorfman, New York: Columbia University Press, 1954.

1897. *Economics and Jurisprudence.* London: Macmillan; New York: S. Sonnenschein & Co. New edn, ed. J. Dorfman, New York: Columbia University Press, 1954.

1898. *The Science of Finance: an investigation of public expenditures and public revenues.* New York: H. Holt Co. Revised edn, 1924.

1918. *American Railway Accounting: A commentary.* New York: H. Holt Co.

BIBLIOGRAPHY

Brazer, M.C. 1982. The Economics Department at the University of Michigan: a centennial perspective. In *Economics and the World Around It*, ed. S.H. Hymans, Ann Arbor, Michigan: University of Michigan Press.

Coats, A.W. 1968. Henry Carter Adams: a case study in the emergence of the social sciences in the United States, 1850–1900. *Journal of American Studies* 2, October, 177–97.

adaptive expectations. The adaptive expectations hypothesis may be stated most succinctly in the form of the equation:

$$E_t x_{t+1} = \sum_{i=0}^{\infty} \lambda (1-\lambda)^i x_{t-i}; \qquad 0 < \lambda < 1 \qquad (1)$$

where E denotes an expectation, x is the variable whose expectation is being calculated and t indexes time. What this says is that the expectation formed at the present time, E_t of some variable, x, at the next future date, $t + 1$, may be viewed as a weighted average of all previous values of the variable, x_{t-i}, where the weights, $\lambda(1-\lambda)^i$, decline geometrically. The weight attaching to the most recent, or current, observation is λ. The above equation can be manipulated readily to deliver:

$$E_t x_{t+1} = E_{t-1} x_t + \lambda (x_t - E_{t-1} x_t). \qquad (2)$$

What this equation says is that, viewed from time t, the expected value of the variable, x at $t + 1$, is equal to the value which, at time $t - 1$ was expected for t, plus an adjustment for the extent to which the variable turned out to be different at t from the value which, viewed from date $t - 1$, had been expected. The change in the expectation is simply the fraction λ multiplied by the most recently observed forecast error. In this formulation, the adaptive expectations hypothesis is sometimes called the error learning hypothesis (see Mincer, 1969, pp. 83–90).

The adaptive expectations hypothesis was first used, though not by name, in the work of Irving Fisher (1911). The hypothesis received its major impetus, however, as a result of Phillip Cagan's (1956) work on hyperinflations. The hypothesis was used extensively in the late 1950s and 1960s in a variety of applications. L. M. Koyck (1954) used the hypothesis, though not in name, to study investment behaviour. Milton Friedman (1957), used it as a way of generating permanent income in his study of the consumption function. Marc Nerlove (1958) used it in his analysis of the dynamics of supply in the agricultural sector. Work on inflation and macroeconomics in the 1960s was dominated by the use of this hypothesis. The most comprehensive survey of that work is provided by David Laidler and Michael Parkin (1975).

The adaptive expectations (or error learning) hypothesis became popular and was barely challenged from the middle-1950s through the late-1960s. It was not entirely unchallenged but it remained the only extensively-used proposition concerning the formation of expectations of inflation and a large number of other variables for something close to two decades. In the 1970s the hypothesis fell into disfavour and the rational expectations hypothesis became dominant.

The adaptive expectations hypothesis became and remained popular for so long for three reasons. First, in its error learning form it had the appearance of being an application of classical statistical inference. It looked like classical updating of an expectation based on new information.

Second, the adaptive expectations hypothesis was empirically easy to employ. Koyck (1954) showed how a simple transformation of an equation with an unobservable expectation variable in it could be rendered observable by performing what became a famous transformation bearing Koyck's name. If some variable, y, is determined by the expected future value of x, that is:

$$y_t = \alpha + \beta E_t x_{t+1} \qquad (3)$$

where α and β are constants, then we can obtain an estimate of α and β by using a regression model in which equation (1) [or equivalently (2)] is used to eliminate the unobservable expected future value of x. To do this, substitute (1) into (3). Then write down an equation identical to (3) but for one period earlier. Multiply that second equation by $1 - \lambda$ and subtract the result from (3) (Koyck, 1954, p. 22), to give:

$$y_t = \alpha\lambda + \beta\lambda x_t + (1-\lambda)y_{t-1} \qquad (4)$$

An equation like this may be used to estimate not only the desired values of α and β but also the value of λ, the coefficient of expectations adjustment. Thus, economists seemed to have a very powerful way of modelling situations in which unobservable expectational variables were important and of discovering speeds of response both of expectations to past events and of current events to expectations of future events.

Third, the adaptive expectations hypothesis seemed to work. That is, when equations like (4) were estimated in the wide variety of situations in which the hypothesis was applied (see above), 'sensible' parameter values for α, β, λ were obtained and, in general, a high degree of explanatory power resulted.

If the adaptive expectations hypothesis was so intuitively appealing, easy to employ, and successful, why was it eventually abandoned? There are three key reasons. First, the interpretation of the hypothesis as an application of classical inference came to be questioned, notably by John Muth (1960). Muth pointed out that the adaptive expectations hypothesis would only be optimal in the sense of delivering unbiased and minimum mean square error forecasts for a variable whose first difference was a first-order moving average process. Since this is likely to be a limited class of variables, the general validity of interpreting the adaptive expectations hypothesis as being consistent with classical inference came to be questioned. Second, in the area of macroeconomics, the adaptive expectations hypothesis was seen to be logically inconsistent with what came to be called the 'natural rate hypothesis' (Lucas, 1972). The latter hypothesis, that unemployment and other real variables are ultimately determined by real forces and not influenced by anticipations of inflation (at least not to a first-order) is so deeply entrenched in economics that the logical clash of the two hypotheses had to result in the modification of adaptive expectations (see Friedman, 1968, and Phelps, 1970). Third, and as almost always happens in scientific developments, a new, rational expectations alternative to adaptive expectations became available. The new theory had all the intuitive appeal of the old and, eventually, became equally tractable in empirical studies and began to show signs of success.

MICHAEL PARKIN

See also COBWEB THEOREM; EXPECTATIONS; HYPERINFLATION; KOYCK, LEENDERT MARINUS; PHILLIPS' CURVE; RATIONAL EXPECTATIONS.

BIBLIOGRAPHY

Cagan, P. 1956. The monetary dynamics of hyper-inflation. In *Studies in the Quantity Theory of Money*, ed. Milton Friedman. Chicago: University of Chicago Press.

Fisher, I. 1911. *The Purchasing Power of Money*. New York: Macmillan (latest edition, A.M. Kelley, New York, 1963).

Friedman, M. 1957. *A Theory of the Consumption Function*. Princeton: Princeton University Press.

Friedman, M. 1968. The role of monetary policy. *American Economic Review* 58, March, 1–17.

Koyck, L.M. 1954. *Distributed Lags and Investment Analysis*. Amsterdam: North-Holland.

Laidler, D. and Parkin, M. 1975. Inflation: a survey. *Economic Journal* 85, December, 741–809.

Lucas, R.E., Jr. 1972. Econometric testing of the natural rate hypothesis. In *The Econometrics of Price Determination*, ed. Otto Eckstein, Washington, DC: Board of Governors of the Federal Reserve System.

Mincer, J. 1969. *Economic Forecasts and Expectations*. New York: National Bureau of Economic Research.

Muth, J.F. 1960. Optimal properties of exponentially weighted forecasts. *Journal of the American Statistical Association* 55, 299–306.

Nerlove, M. 1958. *The Dynamics of Supply: Estimation of Farmers' Response to Price*. Baltimore: Johns Hopkins Press.

Phelps, E.S. (ed.) 1970. *Microeconomic Foundations of Employment and Inflation Theory*. New York: Norton.

added worker effect. *See* LABOUR SUPPLY OF WOMEN.

adding-up problem. In any theory of income distribution in which one type of return is determined residually, it will be tautologically true that the various different incomes, as determined by the theory, will add up so as to exhaust the total product. By contrast, *any* theory which provides a 'positive' explanation for every category or return, treating none as a residual, must show that the various returns so explained do indeed exhaust the product. In practice, it has been with reference to the marginal productivity theory that this consistency requirement has received considerable attention. By the early 1890s a number of authors had sought to extend the 'principle of rent' into a completely general theory of distribution but it was P.H. Wicksteed, in his *Co-ordination of the Laws of Distribution* (1894) who first clearly stated, and attempted to resolve, the resulting adding-up problem.

Consider first the simplest case, in which all markets are perfectly competitive, there is no uncertainty and 'entrepreneurs' are seen as mere hiring agents. If it is supposed also that all productive processes exhibit constant returns to scale, then the adding-up problem is shown by Euler's theorem on homogeneous functions to be a quite trivial problem, as Flux (1894) pointed out in his *Economic Journal* review of Wicksteed's book. When assuming constant returns one should, of course, be mindful of Samuelson's warning that 'Any function whatever in *n* variables may be regarded as a subset of a larger function in more than *n* variables which is homogeneous of the first order' (1983, p. 84, n. 13). Attention can also be drawn to the indeterminacy of the sizes of firms in the constant returns case, and thus to the question of how the perfect competition assumption can be underpinned, but these (perfectly proper) questions are not specific to the adding-up problem. It is, however, vital to appreciate that linear homogeneity of production relations does *not*, by itself, dispose of the adding-up problem; it is linear homogeneity in production, combined with perfectly competitive market conditions, which does that. This was forcefully demonstrated by Wicksteed himself in 1894. Whilst he upheld the assumption of constant returns to scale in production, he also held that a proportional increase of *all* inputs – both those used in production and those used in selling activities – would not result in an equal proportional increase in the quantity sold, at a given price. Thus there is not a 'constant returns' relationship between total outlays and total revenue. Wicksteed examined the consequences for 'adding-up', first in the case of monopoly and then with an ever-increasing number of firms in the industry, and was able to show that, as the number of firms became very large, marginal productivity pricing would approximately exhaust the product. Adding-up, or otherwise, is thus intimately related to market conditions.

Wicksteed's assumption of linear homogeneity in production, together with what was taken by Walras, at least, to be his implicit slighting of the work of others, resulted in his work receiving a hostile response from Pareto, Edgeworth and Walras. In the third edition of his *Eléments* Walras inserted an Appendix III, dated October 1895, which ended with the words 'Mr. Wicksteed . . . would have been better inspired if he had not made such efforts to appear ignorant of the work of his predecessors'. (This appendix was, however, dropped from subsequent editions; Stigler and Schumpeter have disagreed over the precise import of, and degree of justification for, Walras' displeasure.) More constructively, the second half of Walras' appendix outlined a proof of the adding-up theorem under competitive conditions (see below), a proof based on work by Barone. (It seems that Barone had submitted a review of Wicksteed's book to the *Economic Journal* and that Edgeworth had first accepted the review for publication but then subsequently withdrew his acceptance.) In his *Economic Journal* (1906) review of Pareto's *Manuale di Economia Politica* (1906), Wicksteed acknowledged the justice of the criticisms which Edgeworth and Pareto had made of his 1894 *Co-ordination* argument; and in the *Common Sense* (1910) he again referred to Edgeworth and Pareto and stated that paragraph 6 of the *Co-ordination* 'must be regarded as formally withdrawn' (p. 373, n. 1). (It is to be noted that Wicksteed does *not* refer to Walras in either of these acknowledgements of justified criticism.) In Volume I of his *Lectures on Political Economy* (1901), Wicksell expressed surprise that Wicksteed had 'declared – for reasons difficult to understand – that he desired to withdraw this work [the *Co-ordination*]' (1934, p. 101, n. 4). It must be noted clearly, first that Wicksteed did *not* withdraw the work as a whole, but only its paragraph 6, and secondly that Wicksteed's proof of the adding-up theorem under linear homogeneity and perfect competition is contained in paragraph 5. Paragraph 6, which he did declare to be withdrawn, concerns the extension of the result of paragraph 5 to the cases of imperfect product markets and of more than two inputs. This, together with Wicksteed's continued use of marginal productivity theory in his *Common Sense*, supports the view of Hutchison, Robbins and Stigler that Wicksteed's 'recantation' was 'merely verbal', and not a rejection of the substance of his earlier argument.

The solution to the adding-up problem which can be associated with the names of Barone, Walras and Wicksell dispenses with the linear homogeneity assumption but is still concerned with long run perfectly competitive equilibrium; it is centred not on the industry but on the individual firm. Any cost minimizing firm, which faces diminishing marginal products and given input prices, will so arrange its production that $w_i = (mc)(\partial q/\partial x_i)$, for each i, where w_i is the price of the ith variable input, $(\partial q/\partial x_i)$ its marginal product, and (mc) the marginal cost of the output in question. Multiplying both sides by x_i and then summing over i, one finds that $(avc)q = (mc) \Sigma x_i(\partial q/\partial x_i)$, where (avc) is average variable cost and q is output. For the cost minimizing firm, then, $\Sigma x_i(\partial q/x_i) \gtreqless q$ according as $(mc) \lesseqgtr (avc)$, that is according as average variable cost is falling, constant, or rising. If the average variable cost curve has a minimum point then, at that point, it will be *as if* there are constant returns to scale and 'adding-up' will obtain. Now introduce the assumption of profit maximization; the perfectly competitive firm will obey the rule $p = (mc) \geqslant (avc)$, where p is the product price. Hence $\Sigma x_i(\partial q/\partial x_i) \leqslant q$ for such a firm – and equality will hold in, and only in, the long-run equilibrium position (with $p = (mc) = (avc) =$ minimum average total cost.

Consider now the long-run equilibrium position under imperfect competition. The results given above for the cost minimizing firm will still hold, of course, but now (mc) is equal to marginal revenue rather than to product price. The consequence is that, in an 'imperfect' long run equilibrium, $\Sigma x_i(\partial q/\partial x_i) = (e/e - 1)q$, where '$e$' is the (absolute) elasticity of the demand curve at the equilibrium point. (This result

naturally tends to the corresponding perfectly competitive result as 'e' tends to infinity.) Analogous but inevitably more complex results can, of course, be obtained when both product and input markets are imperfect.

In the subsequently withdrawn paragraph 6 of his *Co-ordination*, Wicksteed noted that 'In practical cases there is usually a speculator who . . . buys the other factors, speculatively, at their *estimated* values' (p. 41, emphasis added) and that the speculator may make a gain or a loss, depending on how those anticipated values compare with the actual, realized values. He continued: 'But these gains and losses may be resolved into (1st) compensation for risk, and (2nd) the share that falls to this special speculating ability, regarded as a factor of production, and receiving its share of the production in accordance with the general formula [of marginal productivity]' (p. 42). Can entrepreneurship properly be regarded as simply 'another factor'? If not – and Edgeworth and Wicksell, for example, appear to have thought not – if entrepreneurship is related to true uncertainty (as opposed to risk) and if uncertainty leads to the existence of *residual* 'pure profits' then, as observed above, there is no 'adding-up problem' to be solved. For that problem arises, within the marginal productivity context, only when *every* form of income is related to the marginal product of some input.

IAN STEEDMAN

See also EULER'S THEOREM; MARGINAL PRODUCTIVITY THEORY; WICKSTEED, PHILLIP HENRY.

BIBLIOGRAPHY

Edgeworth, F.Y. 1904. The theory of distribution. *Quarterly Journal of Economics*, February. Reprinted in F.Y. Edgeworth, *Papers Relating to Political Economy*, Vol. I, London: Macmillan, 1925.

Flux, A.W. 1894. Review of Wicksell's Über Wert, Kapital und Rente and of Wicksteed's Co-ordination, etc. *Economic Journal* 4 June, 305–13.

Hicks, J.R. 1968. *The Theory of Wages.* 2nd edn, London: Macmillan.

Hutchison, T.W. 1953. *A Review of Economic Doctrines, 1870–1929.* Oxford: Clarendon Press, ch. 5.

Robbins, L. 1933. Editorial introduction to P.H. Wicksteed, *The Common Sense of Political Economy*. London: Routledge & Kegan Paul.

Robinson, J.V. 1934. Euler's theorem and the problem of distribution, *Economic Journal*, September. Reprinted in *Collected Economic Papers of Joan Robinson*, Vol. I, Oxford: Blackwell, 1966.

Samuelson, P.A. 1983. *Foundations of Economic Analysis* (enlarged edn). Cambridge, Mass.: Harvard University Press, ch. 4.

Stigler, G.J. 1968. *Production and Distribution Theories: The Formative Period.* New York: Agathon Press, ch. 12.

Walras, L. 1874–7. *Elements of Pure Economics.* London: Allen & Unwin, 1954 (Appendix III).

Wicksell, K. 1934. *Lectures on Political Economy,* Vol. I. London: Routledge & Kegan Paul (esp. pp. 101, 125–33).

Wicksteed, P.H. 1894. *An Essay on the Co-ordination of the Laws of Distribution.* London: Macmillan. Subsequent editions, ed. L. Robbins, LSE Reprints, 1932; ed. I. Steedman, London: Duckworth, 1987.

additive preferences. *See* SEPARABILITY.

additive utility function. *See* SEPARABILITY.

adjustment costs. Adjustment costs in general refer to the costs that economic agents incur when decision variables are changed. They appear in agents' optimization models to provide a basis for the derivation of the optimal rate of change, as distinct from the optimal level, of a decision variable and to establish a rationale for lags in the adjustment of choice variables to changes in exogenous variables.

The concept of adjustment costs was developed to provide a basis for a theory of investment in capital by the individual firm. As Haavelmo (1960) clearly pointed out, the static neoclassical theory of the firm yields a demand for capital as a stock but not a finite demand for investment. This implies in particular that the static theory is incapable of rationalizing the important prediction that changes in real interest rates cause inverse movements in investment in plant and equipment at the level of the individual firm.

In an effort to construct a dynamic framework capable of yielding a demand for investment, Eisner and Strotz (1963) first introduced adjustment costs into the neoclassical theory of the firm. Important early contributions to the development of the theory were made by Lucas (1967a, 1976b), Gould (1968), Treadway (1969, 1971), Uzawa (1969) and Mortensen (1973). See Brechling (1975) and Nickell (1978) for useful surveys of the literature. The early studies concentrated on the derivation of investment demand functions and the rationalization of flexible accelerator models of investment behaviour which are widely used in empirical work. Later work, for example Yoshikawa (1980), Hayashi (1982), used adjustment costs to establish a rigorous theoretical basis for Tobin's q-theory of investment.

THE NATURE OF ADJUSTMENT COSTS. If adjustment costs are to have economic content in a theory of investment, the nature of these costs needs to be illuminated. Several different types of adjustment costs have been identified in the literature. These can be usefully classified into costs that arise from activities internal to the firm and those that arise from market forces external to the firm.

Internal adjustment costs refer to the output the firm foregoes by diverting resources — capital and labour — from production to investment activities. They include mainly planning and installation costs. The formulation of investment plans absorbs resources in research and development and administrative activities. Similarly, the installation of new capital uses resources to 'bolt-down' the new capital, to reorganize production lines, to train workers to use the new equipment, etc. These activities result in lost output which constitutes the adjustment cost. Further, the larger is the rate of investment the larger are the relevant costs.

External adjustment costs arise when the firm is a monopsonist in the market for capital goods. Monopsony power is most likely to occur when capital is highly firm-specific in which case the individual firm's demand for capital may be a large fraction of the market demand for that type. In this case, the firm faces a rising supply price for capital goods. It must thus pay a premium in the form of higher prices the more capital goods it purchases per unit of time, that is, the larger is the rate of investment.

The two types of adjustment costs yield similar qualitative implications for investment behaviour. To avoid repetition, the subsequent discussion will focus on models with internal costs.

IMPLICATIONS FOR INVESTMENT. To identify the major implications of adjustment cost models for investment behaviour, it is helpful to focus on a basic model. Consider a firm that is a price-taker in product, factor and financial markets. It maximizes

$$V(t) = \int_t^\infty \pi(s) e^{-R(t,s)} \, ds \qquad (1)$$

subject to

$$\pi(s) = P(s)Q(s) - W(s)L(s) - G(s)\dot{K}(s) \qquad (2)$$

$$Q(s) = F[K(s), L(s)] - C[\dot{K}(s)] \qquad (3a)$$

$$F_K, F_L > 0, \quad F_{KK}, F_{LL} < 0, \quad F_{KK}F_{LL} - F_{LK}^2 \gtreqqless 0 \qquad (3b)$$

$$C(o) = 0, \quad \text{sgn}(C') = \text{sgn}(\dot{K}), \quad C'' > 0 \qquad (3c)$$

$$K(t) = K_t \qquad (4)$$

where V is the value of the firm, π is net revenue, Q is output, L is labour services, I is investment, K is capital stock, P is price, W is wage rate, G is price of capital goods, $R(t, s) = \int_t^s r(\tau) \, d\tau$, r is nominal interest rate, and the dot denotes time differentiation. All prices are expected prices. Further, $F(\cdot)$ is a standard concave, neoclassical production function, and $C(\cdot)$ is a strictly convex internal adjustment cost function. Depreciation is ignored for simplicity.

Define $\lambda(s)$ to be the imputed value or shadow price to the firm of an additional unit of capital, then the optimality conditions are:

$$P(s)F_L[K(s), L(s)] = W(s) \qquad (5)$$

$$\lambda(s) = G(s) + P(s)C'[\dot{K}(s)] \qquad (6)$$

$$\dot{\lambda}(s) = r(s)\lambda(s) - P(s)F_K[K(s), L(s)] \qquad (7)$$

$$\lim_{s \to \infty} \lambda(s)K(s) e^{-R(t,s)} = 0. \qquad (8)$$

These conditions yield interesting insights into the firm's decision process. Because labour can be changed without the firm incurring adjustment costs, it is a perfectly variable factor of production. Optimality therefore requires that the firm set the value of the marginal product of labour equal to the wage rate, a familiar condition from the static theory of the firm.

Capital, on the other hand, is a quasi-fixed factor; it can be changed but only if the firm is prepared to bear an adjustment cost. Condition (6) requires the firm to invest up to the point at which the shadow value of an additional unit of capital equals the marginal cost of investment, where the latter includes both the purchase price and the value of the marginal adjustment cost. To interpret (7), integrate it forward using the transversality condition, (8), to get that

$$\lambda(s) = \int_s^\infty P(\tau)F_K[K(\tau), L(\tau)] e^{-R(s,\tau)} \, d\tau. \qquad (9)$$

This states that the shadow price is the present value of the expected future marginal products of capital, which is essentially the marginal benefit to investment. Putting (6) and (9) together indicates that the investment decision is inherently a dynamic one in that optimality requires that the marginal cost of investment today be equated to the current and future values of the marginal gains to be derived from that investment. To highlight the role that adjustment costs play in the model, observe that if they are absent, i.e. $C(\dot{K}) \equiv 0$, then (6) and (7) reduce to

$$P(s)F_K[K(s), L(s)] = \left[r(s) - \frac{\dot{G}(s)}{G(s)} \right] G(s)$$

which requires the firm to equate the value of the marginal product of capital to its rental rate. This of course is the optimality condition for capital that emerges from static theory when capital is a perfectly variable factor. Hence, without adjustment costs the model reduces to the static neoclassical theory of the firm where all factors are variable.

This model yields several major implications for investment behaviour. These are quite general in the sense that they emerge from a wide variety of adjustment cost models. One is that the theory provides a rigorous basis for a finite demand for investment at the level of the individual firm. The latter is the optimal rate of capital accumulation that is the solution to the optimality conditions. Assume that the production function is strictly concave; i.e. it displays diminishing returns to scale to capital and labour due to some factor in the background, for example, managerial resources, land, etc., that is fixed in supply. Further, to obtain sharp results assume that expectations are static, i.e. $P(s) = P_t, W(s) = W_t, r(s) = r_t \, \forall s$. Then, the current investment demand function that emerges from the theory is

$$I(t) = \dot{K}(t) = I[K(t), r_t, g_t, w_t]$$
$$I_K < 0 \quad I_r < 0 \quad I_g < 0 \quad I_w \gtreqless 0$$

Most importantly, this relationship provides a theoretical underpinning for the proposition that current investment for the individual firm is inversely related to the (real) rate of interest.

Another implication is that the theory rationalizes flexible accelerator models of investment behaviour. Continue with the assumptions of decreasing returns to scale and static expectations, and consider the firm's long-run equilibrium position which is defined by setting $\dot{\lambda} = \dot{K} = 0$ in (5)–(7). Then

$$P_t F_L(K^*, L^*) = W_t$$
$$P_t F_K(K^*, L^*) = r_t G_t$$

where K^* and L^* are the optimal long-run or 'desired' values of capital and labour. Next, take a linear approximation of the optimality conditions about the firm's long-run equilibrium. Then investment can be expressed as a familiar flexible accelerator or stock adjustment model:

$$\dot{K}(t) = b[K^* - K(t)] \qquad 0 < b < \infty$$

where K^* is the 'desired' capital stock defined above and b is a 'reaction' coefficient. The theory thus provides a justification for models of investment behaviour that have been widely used in empirical work. The property that b is finite indicates that the adjustment costs cause the firm to close a discrepancy between the desired and actual stocks of capital only with a lag. The theory, however, implies that the reaction coefficient will not in general be a constant but rather will vary with economic variables, including the rate of interest and factor input prices; the latter has only rarely been recognized in empirical work.

The assumption that expectations are static can be relaxed without destroying the above implications of the theory, though to obtain results compromises on functional forms need to be made. Even with relatively general expected future price paths, the theory yields finite demand functions for investment. The derivation of the predictions of the theory for investment behaviour, however, becomes more complex, and the results depend on the precise assumptions that are imposed on expected future price paths (see, e.g., Gould, 1968). Still,

under plausible conditions, investment and current real interest rates are inversely related. Similarly, flexible accelerator formulations of investment behaviour can still be derived. Now, however, the 'desired' stock is a 'moving target' which depends on the discounted value of the paths of current and future expected prices (see, e.g., Sargent, 1979). Further, such a formulation implies that the effect of a change in a particular price will have a smaller effect on current investment the further in the future it is expected to occur.

Similarly, the theory can be modified to permit the production function to exhibit constant returns to scale. In this case, under static expectations the optimal level of investment is a constant depending only on expected prices and not on the capital stock (see, e.g. Brechling, 1975). Again, investment responds to expected prices in the usual fashion; in particular, investment is still inversely related to real interest rates. Under constant returns to scale, however, standard flexible accelerators cannot be derived because desired stocks of capital no longer exist.

A final implication of the theory is that it provides a rigorous justification for Tobin's q-theory of investment behaviour. On intuitive grounds, Tobin (1969) argued that investment should be positively related to the market value of an *additional* unit of capital relative to its replacement cost, or to what has been coined 'marginal q'. Two issues arise: Can the relationship between marginal q and investment be deduced from an optimization model of firm behaviour? Given that only 'average q', the market value of *existing* capital relative to its replacement cost, can be observed, can marginal q be related to average q so that the theory can be made operational for empirical work?

An adjustment cost model can be used to answer these questions. Assume now that expectations of future prices are unrestricted and that the production function displays constant returns to scale. Further, assume that the adjustment cost function is now

$$C(\dot{K}, K) = \hat{C}(\dot{K}/K)K \tag{10}$$

where $\hat{C}$ exhibits the same properties as $C(\cdot)$ above in (3c). Adjustment costs per unit of capital are thus inversely related to size of the firm as measured by the capital stock. Finally, assume that capital goods and consumer goods are perfect substitutes so that $G(s) = P(s)$. The optimality condition, (6), then becomes

$$q(s) = \frac{\lambda(s)}{P(s)} = 1 + \hat{C}[\dot{K}(s)/K(s)], \quad s \geqslant t.$$

Invert this relationship for $s = t$ to get

$$\frac{\dot{K}(t)}{K(t)} = f[q(t) - 1]$$
$$\dot{K} \gtreqless 0 \text{ as } q \gtreqless 1, \quad f' > 0$$

where $q(t) = \lambda(t)/P(t)$ is Tobin's q. This places a precise meaning on marginal q; from (9) above, it is the ratio of the shadow value to the firm of having an additional unit of capital in place to the price of acquiring new capital.

Marginal q, as defined here, is not easily observable. Consequently, many authors have used average q, the ratio of the market value of the firm's existing capital as measured in equity markets to the replacement cost of its capital stock, as a proxy for marginal q. Hayashi (1982) has shown that under the conditions assumed here marginal q and average q are equal. Specifically, the market value of the firm, $V(t)$, is

$$V(t) = \lambda(t)K(t)$$

or

$$\frac{\lambda(t)}{P(t)} = \frac{V(t)}{P(t)K(t)}$$

or

$$\text{marginal } q = \text{average } q.$$

Hence, empirically, under the assumed conditions investment may be written as

$$\frac{\dot{K}(t)}{K(t)} = f\left[\frac{V(t)}{P(t)K(t)} - 1\right].$$

Data are readily available to implement this relationship empirically. Further, since average q equals marginal q and the latter captures all the forces in the future, expected future prices, etc., that influence investment, the simplicity of the relationship for empirical work is clear.

SOME EXTENSIONS. Thus far, labour has been treated as a perfectly variable factor of production, that is, a factor not subject to adjustment costs. Labour, or more precisely the number of workers employed, however, may very well be subject to adjustment costs. These take the form of hiring and training costs, Salop (1973), Sargent (1979), or dynamic monopsony power, Mortensen (1970). In either case, such costs generate a finite flow demand for workers much like that for investment in capital. Further, when adjustment costs for labour are combined with those for capital, multivariate flexible accelerators in which the flow demand for one factor depends on the gaps between the desired and actual stocks of all factors can be derived.

In addition to the interaction of quasi-fixed factors of production with one another, quasi-fixed factors may interact with buffer stocks (see, e.g., Maccini, 1984). Firms hold buffer stocks, for example, finished goods inventories, to absorb random fluctuations in demand. Models of inventory holding behaviour yield investment demand functions for such stocks that may be expressed as flexible accelerators. When combined with a model of a quasi-fixed factor of production, the presence of excess stocks of finished goods, in the sense that the desired stock exceeds the actual stock, tends to reduce investment in capital because the firm can meet future demand needs at least for a time through excess inventories.

In a seminal paper, Hall and Jorgenson (1967) constructed measures of the cost of capital that take into account various aspects of the tax code, including the corporate income tax rate, investment tax credits, and various types of depreciation allowances. This analysis, however, was done in a model without adjustment costs. Several authors, for example Abel (1982), Summers (1981), have analysed the effects of changes in tax policies in models with adjustment costs. This permits a rigorous analysis of the effects of different tax policies on investment and a distinction between permanent and temporary tax changes.

Much of the theory of investment has been developed with essentially deterministic models where expectations of future prices are assumed to be held with probability one. Some work, for example Hartman (1972), Abel (1985), has extended the theory to accommodate stochastic future prices. This of course raises the complexity of the analysis, making it necessary to impose strong functional form assumptions to obtain results. The main result that emerges from this work

seems to be that increased uncertainty about future factor input prices tends to raise investment.

Although the concept of adjustment costs has been applied mainly to an analysis of investment in quasi-fixed factors of production, it is potentially quite general and has been used in other contexts. Rotemberg (1982) assumed that price-setting firms incur adjustment costs (costs to changing price lists, damage to the firm's reputation, etc.) when changing prices to rationalize 'sticky prices'. Bernanke (1985) incorporated adjustment costs into the utility function of a representative consumer to rationalize lagged adjustments in the demand for consumer durables. The adjustment costs take the form of foregone leisure that arises from the shopping for and learning how to use new durable goods. As these examples suggest, however, the underlying basis for adjustment costs, when applied to areas beyond quasi-fixed factors on production, is somewhat tenuous.

A CRITIQUE. To deduce the major implications of adjustment cost models for investment behaviour, what is crucial is not merely that the firm face adjustment costs, but that marginal adjustment costs rise with investment, i.e., $C'' > 0$ in (3c) or $\hat{C}'' > 0$ in (10). If alternatively adjustment costs are constant or diminish at the margin, the firm in general will immediately close any gap between desired and actual stocks of capital. This implies that investment is undefined at the point at which the gap is closed and that lagged adjustment disappears. Further, a positive relationship between investment and q will not in general exist.

As Rothschild (1971) pointed out, the difficulty with the assumption that marginal adjustment costs are increasing in investment is that it is a difficult assumption to justify in all, or even many, cases. Regarding internal adjustment costs, activities such as the reorganization of production lines or the training of workers may involve indivisibilities and the use of information as a factor input, which are standard sources of decreasing costs. Similarly, certain costs, for example the stopping of production lines, may be fixed in nature; that is, they are incurred as long as any investment is undertaken but do not vary much with the level of investment. These cases will give rise to internal adjustment cost functions that are not consistent with rising marginal costs. Further, while monopsony power may exist for certain types of highly specialized capital goods or workers, it is not clear that it applies to the bulk of investment activity. This raises questions about the importance of external adjustment costs in rationalizing investment behaviour.

While the incorporation of adjustment costs into the theory of the firm has generated much insight into investment behaviour, there is some disquieting uneasiness that the theoretical developments may rest on a weak foundation. But if adjustment costs cannot provide a basis for investment demand functions and lagged adjustment, the question of what else can remains open.

LOUIS J. MACCINI

See also ABSORPTIVE CAPACITY; FIXED FACTORS; INVESTMENT.

BIBLIOGRAPHY

Abel, A.B. 1982. Dynamic effects of permanent and temporary tax policies in a q model of investment. *Journal of Monetary Economics* 9, May, 353–74.

Abel, A.B. 1985. A stochastic model of investment, marginal q and the market value of the firm. *International Economic Review* 26, June, 305–23.

Bernanke, B. 1985. Adjustment costs, durables, and aggregate consumption. *Journal of Monetary Economics* 15, January, 41–68.

Brechling, F. 1975. *Investment and Employment Decisions*. Manchester: Manchester University Press.

Eisner, R. and Strotz, R.H. 1963. Determinants of business investment. In *Commission on Money and Credit: Impacts of Monetary Policy*, Englewood Cliffs, NJ: Prentice-Hall, 60–138.

Gould, J.P. 1968. Adjustment costs in the theory of investment of the firm. *Review of Economic Studies* 35, January, 47–55.

Haavelmo, T. 1960. *A Study in the Theory of Investment*. Chicago: University of Chicago Press.

Hall, R.E. and Jorgenson, D.W. 1967. Tax policy and investment behavior. *American Economic Review* 53, May, 247–59.

Hartman, R. 1972. The effects of price and cost uncertainty on investment. *Journal of Economic Theory* 5, October, 258–66.

Hayashi, F. 1982. Tobin's marginal q and average q: a neoclassical interpretation. *Econometrica* 50, January, 213–24.

Lucas, R.E. 1967a. Optimal investment policy and the flexible accelerator. *International Economic Review* 8, February, 78–85.

Lucas, R.E. 1967b. Adjustment costs and the theory of supply. *Journal of Political Economy* 75, August, 321–34.

Maccini, L.J. 1984. The interrelationship between price and output decisions and investment decisions. *Journal of Monetary Economics* 13, January, 41–65.

Mortensen, D.T. 1970. A theory of wage and employment dynamics. In *Microeconomic Foundations of Employment and Inflation Theory*, ed. E.S. Phelps, New York: Norton.

Mortensen, D.T. 1973. Generalized costs of adjustment and dynamic factor demand theory. *Econometrica* 41, July, 657–67.

Nickell, S.J. 1978. *The Investment Decisions of Firms*. Cambridge: Cambridge University Press.

Rotemberg, J. 1982. Sticky prices in the United States. *Journal of Political Economy* 90, December, 1187–211.

Rothschild, M. 1971. On the cost of adjustment. *Quarterly Journal of Economics* 85, November, 605–22.

Salop, S.C. 1973. Wage differentials in a dynamic theory of the firm. *Journal of Economic Theory* 6, August, 321–44.

Sargent, T.J. 1979. *Macroeconomic Theory*. New York: Academic Press.

Summers, L. 1981. Taxation and corporate investment: a q-theory approach. *Brookings Papers on Economic Activity* 1, 67–140.

Tobin, J. 1969. A general equilibrium approach to monetary theory. *Journal of Money, Credit and Banking* 1, 15–29.

Treadway, A.B. 1969. On rational entrepreneurial behaviour and the demand for investment. *Review of Economic Studies* 36, April, 227–39.

Treadway, A.B. 1971. On the multivariate flexible accelerator. *Econometrica* 39, September, 845–56.

Uzawa, H. 1969. Time preference and the Penrose effect in a two-class model of economic growth. *Journal of Political Economy* 77, July, 628–52.

Yoshikawa, H. 1980. On the 'q' theory of investment. *American Economic Review* 70, September, 739–43.

adjustment processes and stability. Economic theory is pre-eminently a matter of equilibrium analysis. In particular, the centrepiece of the subject – general equilibrium theory – deals with the existence and efficiency properties of competitive equilibrium. Nor is this only an abstract matter. The principal policy insight of economics – that a competitive price system produces desirable results and that government interference will generally lead to an inefficient allocation of resources – rests on the intimate connections between competitive equilibrium and Pareto efficiency.

Yet the very power and elegance of equilibrium analysis often obscures the fact that it rests on a very uncertain foundation. We have no similarly elegant theory of what happens *out* of equilibrium, of how agents behave when their plans are frustrated. As a result, we have no rigorous basis for believing that equilibria can be achieved or maintained if disturbed. Unless one robs words of their meaning and defines every state of the world as an 'equilibrium' in the sense that agents do what they do instead of doing something else, there is no disguising the fact that this is a major lacuna in economic analysis.

Nor is that lacuna only important in microeconomics. For example, the Keynesian question of whether an economy can become trapped in a situation of underemployment is not merely a question of whether underemployment equilibria exist. It is also a question of whether such equilibria are stable. As such, its answer depends on the properties of the general (dis)equilibrium system which macroeconomic analysis attempts to summarize. Not surprisingly, modern attempts to deal with such systems have been increasingly forced to treat such familiar macroeconomic issues as the role of money.

We do, of course, have some idea as to how disequilibrium adjustment takes place. From Adam Smith's discussion of the 'Invisible Hand' to the standard elementary textbook's treatment of the 'Law of Supply and Demand', economists have stressed how the perception of profit opportunities leads agents to act. What remains unclear is whether (as most economists believe) the pursuit of such profit opportunities in fact leads to equilibrium – more particularly, to a competitive equilibrium where such opportunities no longer exist. If one thinks of a competitive economy as a dynamic system driven by the self-seeking actions of individual agents, does that system have competitive equilibria as stable rest points? If so, are such equilibria attained so quickly that the system can be studied without attention to its disequilibrium behaviour? The answers to these crucial questions remain unclear.

A primary reason for that lack of clarity is the lack of a satisfactory theory about the disequilibrium behaviour of agents. A central example of the problem can be stated as follows. In perfect competition, all agents take prices as given. Then how can prices ever change? In a single market, for example, every firm believes that it will lose all its customers if it raises its price. Then who decides to go first when demand or cost increases? We are certain that such decisions are taken, but, at the level of satisfactory formal analysis, we do not know how.

While these issues arise in partial as well as general models, most of the literature on adjustment and stability has been at the general equilibrium level. (Search theory can be considered a partial modern-day exception.) Not surprisingly, that literature has largely begged the price-adjustment question, simply assuming that price somehow changes in the direction suggested by excess demand: $dp_i/dt = H^i(Z_i(p))$, where p is the vector of prices, $Z_i(p)$, the excess demand for the ith commodity, and $H^i(\cdot)$ a sign-preserving continuous function.

The question of who adjusts prices in this way is typically left unanswered or put aside with a reference to a fictitious Walrasian 'auctioneer'. That character does not appear in Walras (who did have prices adjusting to excess demands) but may have been invented by Schumpeter in lectures and introduced into the literature by Samuelson (who certainly did introduce the mathematical statement of price adjustment just given). Interestingly, however, the need for some such construct can reasonably be said to originate with Edgeworth, who wrote:

> You might suppose each dealer to write down his demand, how much of an article he would take at each price, without attempting to conceal his requirements; and these data having been furnished to a sort of market-machine, the price to be passionlessly evaluated (1881, p. 30).

There has been only moderate progress since Edgeworth's day in explaining just what one is to suppose in considering anonymous price adjustment in competitive markets.

General equilibrium theory has taken its most analytically satisfactory form in the Arrow–Debreu world where all markets for present and future commodities open and close before any other economic activity actually takes place. Despite the lack of realism, this made it natural to consider adjustment processes in which only prices move (in the way described above) and trade, production, and consumption only occur after equilibrium is reached. Such a dynamic process is called 'tâtonnement', and the study of tâtonnement models dominated the stability literature until 1960. In that year, the publication of Herbert Scarf's counterexample (Scarf, 1960) put an end to the hope that such models would turn out generally stable given only the ordinary assumptions of microeconomics. Tâtonnement stability requires extremely strong special assumptions.

This has extremely important implications. Indeed, it is not too strong to say that the entire theory of value is at stake. If stability requires trading (or production and consumption) to take place before equilibrium is reached, then the adjustment process itself changes the givens of the equilibrium problem (the endowments of agents, for example). This makes the set of equilibria also change in the course of adjustment, so that the equilibrium finally reached (assuming stability) differs from that computed by algorithms taking the initial situation as fixed. Moreover, comparative static analysis, that major tool of theory, will miscompute the effects of a displacement of equilibrium, for the equilibrium reached will depend on the adjustment process and not merely on the displacement itself. While such effects may be small, they are certainly not known to be small. The argument that they are likely to be negligible because prices adjust much faster than quantities is unconvincing. The limiting case of such relative speeds of adjustment is tâtonnement and is known to lack general convergence properties.

The failure of tâtonnement was by no means the end of the stability literature, however. The early 1960s were marked by two important insights. These were: first, that considerable gains might be achieved by restricting the adjustment process itself rather than the excess demand functions of agents (Hahn, 1961); second, that consideration of how trade takes place might lead to sensible restrictions. While logically separate, these two insights developed together in the study of 'non-tâtonnement processes', which are better called 'trading processes'.

In a pure-exchange trading process, prices continue to adjust as indicated by excess demands, but trade also takes place (consumption, however, still being postponed to equilibrium). The crucial question is how such trades should naturally be restricted, and here there are two leading candidates.

The first of these is the 'Edgeworth Process' (Uzawa, 1962; Hahn, 1962). Here the basic assumption is that trade takes place if and only if there is a group of agents, all of whom can gain in utility by trading among themselves at the current prices. With some complications due to the possibility that no such trades can be made at the initial configuration of prices, this assumption can be shown to generate a stable adjustment process. The crucial feature of the proof is that the sum of the utilities that would be achieved if trade ceases is increasing out of equilibrium, making that sum suitable for use as a Lyapunov function.

The basic assumption of the Edgeworth Process certainly seems attractive. Trade takes place because the agents participating make themselves better off thereby. Unfortunately, such attractiveness is somewhat superficial. First, the assumption places very large information requirements on the system. It is easy to construct examples where the only Pareto-improving trades require the participation of vast numbers of agents. While, as in the case of coalition formation in the theory of the core, the number of agents required cannot exceed the number of commodities, this is not a helpful limit when all future commodities are being traded. The assumption that trade readily takes place in such circumstances is not an easy one.

Second (and perhaps more important), the assumption that trade only takes place when participants each immediately gain in utility is only attractive when agents are supposed stupidly to expect prices constant and transactions to be completed. Once agents are allowed to become conscious of disequilibrium, transactions need not bring immediate utility gain; some transactions will be undertaken for speculative purposes, in the hopes that later transactions at profitable prices will materialize. While no rational agent ever trades without expecting to gain thereby, the basic assumption of the Edgeworth Process requires that every leg of a transaction bring a utility gain. It is crucial that the sum of the utilities agents would receive if trading ceased should always be increasing out of equilibrium. This is not true when arbitrage is involved – particularly when trade takes place for money. It is an open question whether the Edgeworth Process models can be adapted to allow more interesting behaviour.

The second major trading process model is the 'Hahn Process' (Hahn and Negishi, 1962). Its basic assumption (sometimes known as the 'Orderly Markets Assumption') is as follows. After trade, there may be unsatisfied demanders of a particular commodity, say apples, or there may be unsatisfied suppliers of that commodity, but if markets are sufficiently well organized there will not be both. The Hahn Process assumes that potential apple buyers and potential apple sellers can find each other. Indeed, it might be said that this is what we mean when we speak of such buyers and sellers as being in the same 'market'. As a result, we assume that – after trade – any agent with a non-zero excess demand for some commodity finds that his or her excess demand for that commodity is of the same sign as that commodity's aggregate excess demand.

This has a powerful consequence. Since prices move in the same direction as aggregate excess demand, any agent who cannot complete all planned transactions finds that the goods he or she would like to sell are falling in price, while the goods he or she would like to buy are becoming more expensive. The agent's target utility – the utility he or she would achieve if all transactions could be completed – is falling. As a result, out of equilibrium the sum of all target utilities falls and so can serve as a Lyapunov function. In effect, agents begin with unrealistically optimistic expectations and revise them downward until equilibrium is reached and expectations become mutually compatible. With some additional, relatively minor assumptions, the Hahn Process can be shown to be globally stable.

In fact, things are not so simple, for the assumption that buyers and sellers can find each other does not guarantee that unsatisfied excess demands for a given commodity will all have the same sign. This is because of the possibility that buyers will have nothing to offer that sellers are willing to accept. This problem cries out for the introduction of money as a medium of exchange (cf. Clower, 1965). That introduction was accomplished by Arrow and Hahn (1971) who assumed that offers to buy must be backed up with money in order to be active and that prices are affected only by active, rather than target excess demands. Applying the Hahn Process assumption to active excess demands, the same global stability results can be obtained – provided one assumes that agents never run out of money. This 'Positive Cash Assumption' is very difficult to justify from more primitive ones in the context of naïve expectations.

The introduction of money raises other problems. In particular, unless money is included in the utility function, it is hard to see why agents plan to hold it in equilibrium. Nevertheless, such introduction is essential, particularly if firms are to be included. Without a common medium of exchange in which profits are measured, firms producing an oversupply of some good, say toothpaste, will have no incentive to sell it, reckoning profits in toothpaste rather than in dollars.

With money, however, the inclusion of firms in the Hahn Process model is fairly easy (Fisher, 1974). Firms are assumed to sell promises to deliver outputs and acquire contracts to supply inputs, acting so as to maximize profits subject to ultimate production being feasible. Production itself is postponed until equilibrium (as is consumption in the pure exchange version). Again assuming that no household or firm ever runs out of cash, the target profits of firms decline if they cannot complete their planned transactions. Given that, the target utilities of the firms' owners – the households – also decline, and the stability result goes through much as before.

Despite its elegance, this is not a truly satisfactory result if one is interested in justifying the use of equilibrium economics. Apart from other difficulties, the equilibrium reached is one in which all trading opportunities have been exhausted. This is the consequence of working in an Arrow–Debreu framework, but it is not very satisfactory, and remains so even when some attempt is made to introduce production and consumption out of equilibrium (Fisher, 1976). One would rather expect equilibrium to involve the carrying out of planned trades at correctly foreseen prices.

Further, the agents in trading-process models are remarkably stupid, always expecting prices to remain constant and transactions to be completed, when their constant experience tells them that this is not so. A model that hopes to explain how arbitraging agents drive a competitive economy to equilibrium can hardly afford to assume that agents do not perceive the very arbitrage opportunities that characterize disequilibrium.

An ambitious, though not altogether successful attempt to deal with these problems was made in the disequilibrium model of Fisher (1983). Agents have point expectations and are allowed to expect price changes. They take advantage of arbitrage opportunities, limited only by rules as to short sales and credit availability. Households maximize utility and firms profits, planning and engaging in consumption and production, respectively, in real time. Trade in firms' shares takes place both because of differing price expectations and because households purchase expected dividend streams as a way of transferring liquidity across time periods.

Agents also realize that they are restricted as to the size of their transactions. They make price offers to get around such constraints. Thus each seller believes he or she faces a declining demand curve and has some monopoly power (similarly for buyers). The question of whether such perceptions disappear in equilibrium is the question of whether the equilibrium is Walrasian. In one form, it is also the question of whether there is equilibrium underemployment of resources. The answer turns out to be closely related to the extent to which the liquidity constraints are binding in equilibrium.

As this suggests, money plays a central role. The transactions demand for money does not disappear in equilibrium, which now involves the carrying out of previously planned transactions at the expected prices. On the other hand,

'money' in this model consists of very short-term bonds, bearing the same interest as all other assets in equilibrium. There is still no satisfactory theory in which agents hold non-interest-bearing bank notes in equilibrium.

Once one leaves equilibrium and leaves the theory of how the individual agent plans, matters become less satisfactory. This is largely because one has to deal with the behaviour of agents whose expectations are disappointed. The model handles this issue by making an extremely strong assumption called 'No Favourable Surprise'. This states that new, unexpected, favourable opportunities cease appearing. In effect, the kinds of shocks emphasized by Schumpeter (1911) – discovery of new products or processes, new ways of marketing, new sources of raw materials, and so forth – are ruled out if they are totally unforeseen. As in the Hahn Process, agents find that unexpected change makes them worse off as old opportunities disappear. With some technical complications, this ensures convergence to some equilibrium, although that equilibrium need not be Walrasian.

The problem is that 'No Favourable Surprise' is not a primitive assumption. One cannot hope to prove stability in a world constantly bombarded with exogenous Schumpeterian shocks. 'No Favourable Surprise', however, rules out the appearance of any unexpected opportunities, even those which arise in the course of adjustment to previous exogenous shocks. The Hahn Process model is a special case of this. So is the assumption of rational expectations. In a model with point expectations, however, rational expectations amounts to perfect foresight, and this begs the question of disequilibrium adjustment. It is unclear what happens under uncertainty and also unclear whether 'No Favourable Surprise' can be derived from other underlying premises.

Further, the very generality of the 'No Favourable Surprise' stability result has both satisfactory and unsatisfactory aspects. On the one hand, the price-adjustment mechanism left over from tâtonnement days can be dispensed with and individuals allowed to make price offers. On the other hand, just how those offers get made (or accepted) remains a mystery within the general confines of the 'No Favourable Surprise' assumption. We know that this depends on developing perceptions of demand and supply curves – of individual monopoly or monopsony power – but we do not know how those perceptions develop. As a consequence, the stability results give little insight into whether the system approaches a Walrasian or a non-Walrasian, quantity-constrained equilibrium. Similarly, we do not know the extent to which the adjustment process shifts the ultimate equilibrium or anything about adjustment speeds.

These remain questions of crucial importance for the under-pinnings of equilibrium analysis and, possibly, for the study of actual economies. They will remain unanswered without detailed analysis of how disequilibrium adjustment takes place when plans are frustrated. Equilibrium techniques will not succeed here, and new modes of analysis are needed if equilibrium economic theory is to have a satisfactory foundation.

FRANKLIN M. FISHER

See also AUCTIONEER; GENERAL EQUILIBRIUM; LYAPUNOV FUNCTIONS; STABILITY; SURPLUS AND THE EQUI-MARGINAL PRINCIPLE; TÂTONNEMENT AND RECONTRACTING.

BIBLIOGRAPHY

Arrow, K.J. and F.H. Hahn. 1971. *General Competitive Analysis.* San Francisco: Holden-Day; Edinburgh: Oliver & Boyd.

Clower, R.W. 1965. The Keynesian counterrevolution: a theoretical appraisal. In *The Theory of Interest Rates,* ed. F.H. Hahn and

F.P.R. Brechling, London: Macmillan; New York: St. Martin's Press.

Edgeworth, F.Y. 1881. *Mathematical Psychics*. Reprinted, New York: Augustus M. Kelley, 1967.

Fisher, F.M. 1974. The Hahn Process with firms but no production. *Econometrica* 42, May, 471–86.

Fisher, F.M. 1976. A non-tâtonnement model with production and consumption. *Econometrica* 44, September, 907–38.

Fisher, F.M. 1983. *Disequilibrium Foundations of Equilibrium Economics*. Cambridge: Cambridge University Press.

Hahn, F.H. 1961. A stable adjustment process for a competitive economy. *Review of Economic Studies* 29, October, 62–5.

Hahn, F.H. 1962. On the stability of pure exchange equilibrium. *International Economic Review* 3, May, 206–14.

Hahn, F.H. and Negishi, T. 1962. A theorem on non-tâtonnement stability. *Econometrica* 30, July, 463–9.

Scarf, H. 1960. Some examples of global instability of the competitive equilibrium. *International Economic Review* 1, September, 157–72.

Schumpeter, J. 1911. *The Theory of Economic Development*. 4th printing of English trans, Cambridge, Mass.: Harvard University Press, 1951.

Uzawa, H. 1962. On the stability of Edgeworth's barter process. *International Economic Review* 3, May, 218–32.

administered prices. Administered prices are prices set by enterprises, private or public, large or small, of their own volition in free markets for a period that they determine; so that prices do not fluctuate in the 'short run' with supply and demand. The market is cleared from moment to moment within this period by stock movements in the product and/or by queues of customers; and often by changes in production volume. The 'short run' includes periods long enough for it to *seem* bureaucratically possible to vary the price and thus to make more profit. Therefore *s.r.m.c./s.r.m.r.*, and administered prices constitute a failure to maximize profits. The administrator in this context is always the seller.

(A) We begin with the one great obvious exception: no prices in organized perfect markets, 'oriental' bazaars and auctions are administered. These markets do, of course, empirically exist: it is a myth that they are a myth. The principal examples are crops and metals (wholesale only); bonds, stocks and shares; foreign currency (wholesale only), houses; businesses (the latter two being disposed of in one-to-one higgling, as in an 'oriental bazaar'); most secondhand goods and antiques. Many homogeneous commodities, apt for organized perfect competition, are under state control; and many are dominated by oligopolies. But in perfect oligopoly, prices are not administered (the London Metal Exchange, in part).

Thus the textbook neoclassical description of the enterprise's price and output policy appears to be falsified by the very great majority of all turnover measured by value, and by the quite overwhelming majority of all individual prices. This has worried theorists far too little and they have not bothered to say much. But we must leave aside the reasons for that as belonging to methodological articles, and look at what might be said in favour of the text book. So here are the arguments that nevertheless long-run profits are being maximized despite, nay, because of, sticky prices (personal comments in brackets):

(B) (i) Very flexible prices annoy customers in an imperfectly competitive market; i.e. they lose good-will. So the firm that sets a not-too-high administered price gains customers and emerges with more total profit than it could gain from the average of the very short-run maximizing prices it could charge in an 'oriental' bazaar. (The writer knows of no research on this question, but finds the assertion plausible. It is alleged to be the foundation of many Quaker fortunes in the 17th century.)

(B) (ii) In most businesses there are very many products indeed, and it is junior employees that charge prices for them. They cannot be trusted to higgle on behalf of the firm, and senior employees are too busy. So the latter provide a list or other document, which their juniors apply. This document simply cannot be altered every moment, so the administered price is the best that can be done towards maximizing profits. (This is correct; note that single-or-few-product enterprises do tend to belong to perfect markets.)

And here (C) are the arguments that the phenomenon as defined does not exist:

(C) (i) Discounts from list price are extremely common. They are made *ad hoc* and *ad personam*, secretly. Therefore there are in fact no administered prices (the writer holds this to be a massive exaggeration of an admitted truth; but knows of no research that could tell us *how* massive, numerically speaking).

(C) (ii) Quality too can easily be manipulated in imperfect markets (but hardly – we must reply – in the short run, which is precisely how long an administered price is administered for).

Finally (D), here are the arguments for accepting that such prices are indeed a massive disproof of the doctrine that *m.c.* = *m.r.* even in the long run:

(D) (i) There is little empirical evidence that entrepreneurs or managers *ever* maximize even their long-run profits. The basic proposition of all neoclassical economics has never been properly researched; it has simply been elevated (or degraded?) into an axiom. We should reject its high philosophical claim and simply use our eyes. Our eyes may indeed confirm it, but only as an empirical generalization.

(D) (ii) Nevertheless it does seem probable, on mere inspection, that entrepreneurs and managers maximize their short- and simultaneously their long-run profits in perfect competition: what else could one be doing in a market where one is concerned with few products (see B (ii)), and there is no good-will (see B (i))? However that leaves wholly intact the possibility that entrepreneurs and managers behave differently in other types of market.

(D) (iii) In psychological terms homo economicus is a psychopath, though in situations (A) he has little choice. Now admittedly psychopathy is an arbitrary term, to be used with extreme care. But every psychologist would pale before calling almost all men psychopaths. There is nothing whatever in the other social sciences to indicate that profit-maximization is in fact a human norm.

(D) (iv) So far we have merely cleared the ground. The first positive argument is that it is obvious that when, in situations other than (A), we are making losses we do maximize our profits. But the fact that prices become more flexible in depression *confirms* that both long- and short-run profit-maximization are, in the majority of market situations, optional; for it entails that when there is no depression they become less flexible again. The often urged greater survival value of profit maximization refers to survival circumstances, not all circumstances.

(D) (v) Then there is the undoubted fact that FIFO accountancy influences prices. Ordinary observation tells us that in a period of prolonged but not very rapid price-rise the goods on sale in a shop are all priced by applying the customary gross profit margin (absolute or relative) to the historical cost of acquisition of the particular physical batch; so that on one shelf or in one drawer the identical object has different prices. It is very difficult indeed to attribute this to administrative difficulty – why not simply put a single general price label on the shelf or drawer, leaving individual items unmarked? And it certainly is not profit maximization. Again the business pages of the newspapers consistently refer to 'cost increases coming up through the pipe-line'; this banal, and generally accepted, phrase means the same thing.

(D) (vi) The happy hunting grounds of administered prices are manufacturing, retailing and the standard services of transportation. In construction 'cost-plus', where profit is an agreed percentage of whatever cost will turn out to be, is very notoriously the main method of price formation; still more so in pricing modifications to contracts. But cost-plus is the essence of practical price administration. R&D projects are also priced on 'cost-plus'; so indeed are all prototype machines and all non-standard repair jobs. 'Cost-plus' arises out of uncertainty as to costs; it induces profit-maximizers to raise their costs above the minimum for the contracted output. But to an ordinary customer like the writer it is evident that a high proportion of cost-plus chargers do not abuse their position.

In some situations $l.r.p.m.$ demands $s.r.p.m.$ These are the totally impersonal, or at least one-off, market situations listed above (A). In these, mere inspection, as we saw, tells us that $s.r.p.m.$ is practised; and it follows that $l.r.p.m.$ is too, since there is no good-will to be lost. But in situations (B) $l.r.p.m.$ forbids $s.r.p.m.$, since it loses good-will, and may also be too great an administrative burden. Now while again mere inspection tells us that $s.r.$ profit is not being maximized, we may not infer that $l.r.p.m.$ is being maximized. That is not evident, but can only be proved (or disproved) empirically.

Is satisficing a failure to maximize long-run profit? Certainly satisficing is implicit at every point above where administered prices are described. But if we accept it wholeheartedly it tells us nothing more. It means that we *pay attention to* the various costs of search: not that we minimize them (or indeed any other costs); not that we maximize profit net of search costs, nor again that we don't.

The trouble with satisficing is that it is all things to all men. Profit maximizing is an ex ante, or policy, concept; it requires, in the legal phrase, *mens rea* and cannot easily be proved or disproved from observation. This is truer the longer the run we consider and the more space we leave for human judgement. But satisficing is by itself simply a technique not a policy: a recognition that the setting of qualities, prices and outputs requires serious research and thought, but that a decision must come soon. Thus in terms of 'soonness' we have many courses open to us. If we decide very soon, we may be consciously following the full cost principle, and merely avoiding losses; or consciously maximizing profit but making a mistake about the time and resources required for optimization; or some third thing. If we decide at the 'right' moment, we may be consciously maximizing a concept of profit that includes decision-making costs and benefits; or consciously applying full cost but dithering too long; or again some third thing. There can also be systematic error as to how to maximize profits, despite a genuine wish to do it – notably ignorance of the marginal analysis at entrepreneurial level. But that undoubted fact is not quite what here concerns us. For those who do understand it still administer their prices. It should be remembered that a mere loss-avoider must also satisfice. He too faces an intellectual and information problem, though a simpler one: he too must eventually cut off his research and decide, though that point comes sooner. The sales-maximizer-subject-to-minimum-return (à la Baumol) is in the same boat too: with a problem of intermediate complexity. Satisficing, to repeat, is a universal tool.

Does *oligopoly* account for the whole phenomenon? Clearly not perfect oligopoly, but many have been tempted by the kinked demand curve of imperfect oligopoly, which gives such latitude to a price-setter. Hall and Hitch (1939), the pioneers,

certainly rested their work on this, and so does Sylos-Labini (1979 passim). But in reality the phenomenon is much more widespread, because the demand and marginal cost curves are *uncertain* also in monopolistic competition and monopoly, where kinks are unknown. Indeed the curves, though continuous, are thick bands and not narrow lines at all. This has the same effect as the kink, though for slightly different reasons. For the kink forms wherever the price happens to be, and the price may have been rationally set originally; but where the narrow lines become thick bands the situation is indeterminate a priori.

Nothing, then, except a methodologically false tradition forbids us to say that normal price-setting is merely cost-covering, or loss-avoidance plus a decent allowance for net profit; and that the quantification of the word 'decent' is a purely empirical task. It may, for all we know, differ more according to the ideology, nationality, religion or historical epoch of the entrepreneur/manager than according to the state (depressed or active) or the form (imperfect oligopoly, monopoly etc.) of the market. The work has not been done: we do not know.

Now the price that yields a 'decent' profit may be either lower or higher than the profit-maximizing price. It must however lie *below* the latter price much the most often. Why incur obloquy when for the same money you can be popular? The notion that prices administered in a long-run-non-profit-maximizing spirit are usually 'too' low is used by Baumol (1969, pp. 47–52, 63–6) to explain his observation that firms prefer sales volume to profit volume. In so doing he distances himself, to be sure, from the original Oxford full cost doctrine, but not importantly.

The 'lowness' of prices explains also cost inflation. In a climate of general price rises, where this is the general expectation for a long time ahead, the 'decent' price has a consequence quite incompatible with long-run profit maximization. The perpetual small cost increases, due to rises in import prices, wage-rates, variable and even fixed taxes, domestic fuel and raw material prices etc., can be accommodated without a damaging output shrinkage simply by raising the output price *towards* its profit-maximizing level. This is what cost inflation is. It never occurs in type A markets.

This is evidence indeed for a sceptical attitude towards neoclassical microeconomics. But better evidence would be more candid and straightforward empirical research, that simply treated homo economicus as a hypothesis like any other. The type A market reminds us that the hypothesis could easily be confirmed on many occasions.

The full-cost principle in particular, and administered prices in general, seem to be methodologically offensive to orthodox economic theory. No facts should be that. The immunity-system of the neoclassical body rejects every attempted transplant. Why? First, the whole theory, or generalization, is crude, indeterminate, superficial and unintellectual. The full-cost principle, or the cost-plus determination of all non-market-market prices from the fairly competitive parts of the private sector right through without distinction to the most protectedly monopolistic parts of the public sector, is the theory of value of the man in the street, and of most people in authority who set prices.

Yet, secondly, those four epithets above do not signify falsity. Many a good economist slips into such language *obiter*. The following passage from Okun, before he changed sides (1960, pp. 35–6), picked virtually at random from all the literature of economics, shows the same unthinking reflex:

The main element in the stubborn climb of prices and wages through most of 1969 was the enormous strength of demand for labour. After years of operating in a tight labour market, businessmen hired aggressively both to catch up and get ahead. They added far more workers to their payrolls than would have been dictated merely by short-run needs. Between mid–1968 and mid–1969, for example, wholesale and retail trade added 600,000 employees or a 4.5 per cent rise in their work force, while the volume of real goods flowing through trade barely increased. Such personnel policies get reflected in sagging productivity, a substantial addition to unit labour costs, and continued tightness in labour markets; the result is more inflationary pressure on both prices and wages.

The addition to demand through higher wages were certainly not upper-most in this author's mind. Yet the whole 53-page chapter (entitled Inflation: Problems and Prospects) is orthodoxly on the side of demand inflation, fiscal and monetary management, etc.

The idea has its place within the history of economic doctrine. It was dominant – unconsciously – in Smith, Ricardo and Marx. As pre-marginalist economists, they wrote always as if it were true, though they really had no systematic micro-economics. The idea certainly animated Marshall, an early and undogmatic marginalist who seems to have believed in loss minimization only. (For these 'forefathers', cf. Wiles, 1961.)

In the 1930s marginalism was completed by 'imperfect competition'; the marginalization of revenue rounded off that of cost. This both proved the necessity of a theory of value related to the theory of the firm, and ensured that it should be tidy and determinate – so non-empirical. Therefore, it has been hostile to these ideas. So much is evident all the way from William Stanley Jevons to Joan Robinson. The realistic pre-war reaction to marginalism came very shortly after Robinson, who may be said to have caused it. The reaction was called the full cost principle in UK, administered prices in USA. The former analysis was more complete since it had of course administered prices (Hall and Hitch, 1951 – originally 1938), but included a long analysis of costs. The latter was short in this latter respect, and so had too little regard for its own micro-foundations, being macro-economically biased, but made the contrast with perfect competition more clear (Means, 1935; cf. Sylos-Labini, 1969, p. 110). The erosion of both traditions after World War II is described in some detail by Lee, 1984. Yet they survive in business departments (e.g. Jackson, 1982), through not in 'industrial economics' courses within departments of economics. There, the view became widespread that all prices are somehow administered so as to maximize long-run profit, and full cost is an awkward and uneducated *language* only, for describing essentially marginalist decisions (Lee, op. cit.). The much praised text of Koutsoyiannis (1979) must be placed here in the last analysis – daring and unusual as she was to include such a subject in a textbook at all. Strong exceptions are Okun (1981, ch. 4 and p. 223) and Baumol (1967, pp. 48–52).

P.J.D. WILES

See also COST-PUSH INFLATION; KINKED DEMAND CURVE; MARK-UP PRICING; SATISFICING.

BIBLIOGRAPHY
Baumol, W. 1966. *Business Behavior, Value and Growth*. Revised edn, Princeton: Princeton University Press, 1967.
Hall, R.E. and Hitch, C.J. 1939. Price theory and business behaviour. In *Oxford Studies in the Price Mechanism*, ed. P.W.S. Andrews and T. Wilson, Oxford: Oxford University Press, 1951.
Jackson, D. 1982. *Introduction to Economics: Theory and Data*. London: Macmillan.
Koutsoyiannis, A. 1979. *Modern Micro-economics*. 2nd edn, London: Macmillan.
Lee, F. 1984. Whatever happened to the full-cost principle (USA). In *Economics in Disarray*, ed. P.J.D. Wiles and G. Routh, Oxford: Blackwell.
Means, G.C. 1935. Industrial prices and their relative inflexibility. *Senate Document No. 13*, 74th Congress, 1st Session, Washington, DC.
Okun, A.M. 1970. Inflation, problems and prospects. In *Inflation: the problems it creates and the policies it requires*, ed. A.M. Okun, H.M. Fowler and M. Gilbert, New York: New York University Press.
Okun, A.M. 1981. *Prices and Quantities*. Oxford: Blackwell.
Robinson, J. 1933. *The Economics of Imperfect Competition*. London: Macmillan.
Sylos-Labini, P. 1969. *Oligopoly and Technical Progress*. Cambridge, Mass.: Harvard University Press.
Wiles, P.J.D. 1961. *Price, Cost and Output*. 2nd edn, Oxford: Blackwell.

advances. The French Physiocrats used the term *avances* to indicate the outlays which had to be used in the process of production in order to yield a return in the future. In the *Essai sur la nature du commerce en général* (1755) Cantillon had already used the term advances, but it becomes prominent only in Physiocratic literature. The way in which Quesnay used this term clearly indicates that he was referring to what is now called either capital or means of production. The advances can be regarded as a sum of money, but more frequently the Physiocrats referred to the commodities which had to be 'advanced' in order to carry on the process of production. The different types of advances depend upon the methods of production adopted, which establish the relationships between the inputs and the output in each sector of the economy.

The Physiocrats dedicated particular attention to agriculture, where they distinguish three types of advances. The ground advances, *avances foncières*, include all the expenses which are necessary in order to prepare the soil for cultivation: drainage, cleaning of the soil, transportation and housing facilities (see Baudeau, 1767, pp. 154–6). This kind of advance had to be made once and for all; they were a sort of prerequisite for cultivation. Most of them were made by the landowners, whose rents were a compensation for this initial contribution to production (ibid.). The Physiocrats emphasize the importance of the advances of the agricultural entrepreneur, the farmer, which can be divided into two categories: the original advances, *avances primitives*, and the annual ones, *avances annuelles*. The former group includes all the instruments of cultivation like carts, ploughs etc., which can be used for many years and need annual repairs and maintenance. However, according to the Physiocrats the original advances also include the horses employed in cultivation and their fodder (see Quesnay, 1758, p. vi; Meek; 1962, p. 279). These original advances are like fixed capital, and they are assumed to wear out at a rate of 10 per cent a year. Thus, the farmers must use part of the annual output of cultivation to keep the stock of these advances at its initial level (see Quesnay, 1766, p. 152). The annual advances of agriculture are the raw materials, seeds etc. and the consumption goods necessary to allow the peasants and their families to work until the next harvest. These commodities are entirely consumed during the process of production and as such they must be regarded as circulating capital. In order to maintain the level of agricultural activity unchanged it is necessary to replace the entire annual advances. The whole annual advances plus the interest required to preserve the original ones from wear and tear make up the annual returns of cultivation, the *réprises* (see Quesnay, 1766, p. 154). The returns indicate which part of annual production must be set aside in order to be employed in the following production period. According to this way of examining the process of production, each year the annual output of agriculture must include all the types of commodities which have been used up during the previous productive process as advances. The Physiocratic concept of advances is then clearly linked to their view of the economy as a system which regularly reproduces itself. The part of the social product which is in excess of the returns is the surplus, or net product.

Quesnay used the concept of advances to establish some precise numerical relationships between the inputs and the output of the production process both in agriculture and in manufacturing. For instance, he believed that the best methods of cultivation required a ratio of one to five between the annual and original advances. A modern agricultural sector must have a large stock of original advances, which allows a net product equal to the amount of annual advances. Thus modern techniques of cultivation yield a revenue, or surplus, of 100 per cent (see Quesnay, 1766, p. 151). According to Quesnay the industrial sector employed only annual advances and its output is exactly equal to the value of these advances, thus there is no surplus. The notion of advances is an important element of the Physiocratic doctrine that only agriculture yields a net product.

Turgot, too, employed the concept of advances, but he did not clearly distinguish the analysis of the advances of agriculture from those of the other sectors of the economy (Turgot, 1766, pp. 147, 151). Turgot adopts Quesnay's definitions of annual and original advances as those commodities which must exist at the beginning of the process of production (ibid., pp. 153–4). For Turgot the term 'advances' also refers to the employment of money in one of the several types of investments; he also uses the terms 'moveable wealth' and 'capital' instead of that of 'advances' (see ibid., pp. 145, 152).

Adam Smith substitutes the term 'capital' for 'advances', even though he still uses Quesnay's notion of means of production, which must be advanced by the entrepreneur in order to carry on the process of production. Smith distinguishes fixed and circulating capital. The former notion refers to all the machines and the instruments which yield a profit to the entrepreneur without being sold. Circulating capital indicates all the commodities which yield a profit only when they are sold at the end of the productive process, but not when they still belong to the capitalist (see Smith [1776], 1976, vol. I, p. 279). However, contrary to Quesnay, in his theory of value Smith emphasizes the role of circulating capital. Thus the overall capital of society seems to be entirely made up by the wages advanced to the workers (ibid., pp. 66–7, pp. 110–11), because all machines are ultimately produced by labour.

Ricardo distinguishes fixed and circulating capital according to the durability of the input examined, but he admits that it is often difficult to draw a precise distinction between the two notions (Ricardo, 1821, pp. 31–2, 150–1). Ricardo accepts Smith's idea that from the point of view of society as a whole capital is made up of the value of the wages advanced to productive workers (ibid.). Malthus was the last classical economist to use the term 'advances', by which he meant all the commodities which had been accumulated in the past and whose value had to be subtracted from that of annual production in order to measure the profits of the entrepreneurs.

G. VAGGI

See also PHYSIOCRATS.

BIBLIOGRAPHY
Baudeau, N. 1767. Explication du Tableau économique à Madame de ***, par l'auteur des Ephémérides. In *Ephémérides du citoyen*, vols. XI and XII.
Malthus, T.R. 1820. *Principles of Political Economy*. In *The Works and Correspondence of David Ricardo*, ed. P. Sraffa, Cambridge: Cambridge University Press, 1951, vol. 2.
Meek, R.L. 1962. *The Economics of Physiocracy*. London: Allen & Unwin.
Quesnay, F. 1758. Explication du Tableau économique. In *Quesnay's Tableau Economique*, ed. M. Kuczynski and R. L. Meek, London: Macmillan, 1972.
Quesnay, F. 1766. Analyse de la formule arithmétique du Tableau économique. In Meek (1962).
Ricardo, D. 1821. *On the Principles of Political Economy and Taxation*, 3rd edn. *The Works and Correspondence of David Ricardo*, ed. P. Sraffa, Cambridge: Cambridge University Press, 1951, Vol. 1.
Smith, A. 1776. *An Inquiry into the Nature and Causes of the Wealth of Nations*. Oxford: Oxford University Press, 1976.
Turgot, A.R.J. 1766. *Réflexions sur la formation et la distribution des richesses*. In *Turgot on Progress, Sociology and Economics*, ed. R.L. Meek, Cambridge: Cambridge University Press, 1973.

adverse selection. Consider a market in which products of varying quality are exchanged. Both buyers and sellers rank products of different quality in the same way, but only the sellers can observe the quality of each unit of the good they sell. Buyers can observe at most the *distribution* of the quality of the goods previously sold. Without some device for the buyers to identify good products, bad products will always be sold with the good products. Such a market illustrates the problem of *adverse selection*.

Economists have long recognized that the problem of adverse selection can interfere with the effective operation of a market. However, the modern theoretical treatment of the problem began with a paper by George Akerlof, 'The Market for Lemons' (1970). As the title suggests, he considered a stylized market for used cars. The set of cars is indexed by a quality parameter q uniformly distributed between 0 and 1. For a car of quality q, he assumed that the reservation value of a buyer is $(3/2)q$ while the reservation value for a seller is just q. He then addressed the problem of determining the market price and the volume of trade in a situation where the number of potential buyers exceeds the number of sellers.

If both sides can observe the quality of cars in such a market, efficiency requires that all cars be exchanged and, if the market is competitive, cars of quality q are exchanged at a price of $(3/2)q$. Akerlof assumed, however, that buyers can observe the *average* quality of a car for sale at any price p. Since, in this case, any seller with a car of quality p or less offers the car for sale, the average quality of the cars for sale at any price p is equal to $q/2$. Given this relation between price and average quality, buyers value any car offered for sale at only $(3/4)p$. Consequently, the only market clearing price is 0 with no transactions occurring at all.

Akerlof's example presents the most extreme consequence of the problem of adverse selection. In general, not all trade is eliminated. Nevertheless, the market allocation is almost always inefficient. Briefly, the reason is as follows. Since sellers offer any good for exchange whose value is less than the price, the value to the sellers of the *average* product offered for sale is generally lower than the price. In contrast, the uninformed buyers purchase the product to the point where the value to them of the average product offered for sale is equal to the price. Consequently, in any Walrasian equilibrium, the value of the *marginal* car to the buyer exceeds its value to the seller. Furthermore, all buyers purchase from the same pool of products. To the extent that some buyers are willing to pay more for products of higher quality, a second source of inefficiency results.

Akerlof's analysis was generalized by Wilson (1980). He showed that when the buyers have heterogeneous preferences, there may be multiple Walrasian equilibria which can be ranked by the Pareto criterion. His argument is based on the following observation. If the average quality of the goods offered for sale increases sufficiently with the price, some buyers may actually prefer to buy at higher prices. Consequently, even in the absence of income effects, the demand curve may be upward sloping over some range of prices. If the demand and supply curves intersect more than once, multiple Walrasian equilibria result. Furthermore, since the supply curve must be upward sloping, demand must also be higher at higher equilibrium prices. It then follows by revealed preference that some buyers must also be better off at these prices. In fact, if the buyers have a constant marginal rate of substitution between the quality of the car and the consumption of other goods, Wilson showed that every buyer prefers a higher equilibrium price to a lower equilibrium price. Since sellers always prefer to sell at a higher price, it follows immediately that higher equilibrium prices are Pareto superior to lower equilibrium prices. It is also possible to construct examples where a price floor is Pareto superior to any equilibrium price even if the excess supply is rationed at random.

Based on these observations Wilson went on to argue that, in the presence of adverse selection, market forces may not lead to a single price. In fact, the nature of the equilibrium will generally depend on the nature of the institution or convention used to set the price. Akerlof's analysis implicitly assumed some kind of Walrasian mechanism. That is, in equilibrium all goods are exchanged at a single price which clears the market. Suppose instead, that each buyer must announce a price and then wait for offers. Then, if any buyer prefers a price which is higher than the Walrasian price, an equilibrium may result with excess supply which must be rationed. To increase the average quality of the product, sellers may prefer a price which is so high that supply exceeds demand, so that some suppliers are unable to sell their product.

This idea has been used by Stiglitz and Weiss (1978) to explain credit rationing. They considered a competitive banking system in which the supply of loanable funds is an increasing function of the deposit rate. Each borrower requires the same amount of funds and is indistinguishable to the banks from any other borrower. However, because of the possibility of default, borrowers differ in the expected return banks will earn at any given interest rate. In this model the banks assume the role of the uninformed buyers in Akerlof's used car example and the borrowers assume the role of the informed sellers. Stiglitz and Weiss then demonstrated that for a robust class of parameters, the market equilibrium implies an excess demand for loans.

I will illustrate their argument with a simple example. Suppose there are two types of borrowers. Both types use funds B to finance an investment project with the same expected return. Each of the n low risk borrowers earn a zero return with probability $1/2$ and a return $2B$ with probability $1/2$. Each of the n high risk borrowers earn a zero return with probability $3/4$ and a return $4B$ with probability $1/4$. In order to borrow the funds, banks require that firms put up collateral $C = B/2$. Then, at any (gross) interest rate r, a borrower repays the loan only if his return exceeds $[r - (1/2)B]$. Otherwise, he defaults and the bank collects whatever the firm earns plus the collateral.

Now consider the demand curve for loans. So long as this expected return exceeds the interest rate, a borrower will stay in the market. However, because of the differences in their distributions, the two types have different reservation values. Low risk borrowers earn non-negative profits only when $r \leqslant 3/2$, while high risk borrowers earn non-negative profits so long as $r \leqslant 5/2$. Consequently, the demand for loans is $2n$B for $0 < r \leqslant 3/2$, nB for $3/2 < r \leqslant 5/2$, and 0 for $r > 5/2$.

Finally, consider the supply of loanable funds. Since a bank is equally likely to lend to either a low or a high risk borrower when $r \leqslant 3/2$, for $0 < r \leqslant 3/2$, the expected (gross) rate of return to a bank is $[3r + (5/2)]/8$. For $3/2 \leqslant r \leqslant 5/2$, only the high risk borrowers are serviced, resulting in an expected rate of return $[2r + 3]/8$. Now suppose that the level of loans supplied by banks is $(16/13)n$B times the gross rate of return. Then we obtain a 'supply' curve of $n(16/13)B[3r + (5/2)]/8$ for $r \leqslant 3/2$ and $n(16/13)B[2r + 3]/8$ for $32 < r \leqslant 5.2$. Note that this supply curve is upward sloping everywhere except at $r = 3/2$ at which point it falls discontinuously from $n(14/13)B$ to $n(12/13)B$.Consequently, 'supply' is equal to demand at loan rate $r = 7/4$. At this loan rate, only high risk borrowers demand loans and the average rate of return to each bank is $13/16$.

Although an interest rate of $7/4$ clears the market, this is not the outcome we would expect if profit-maximizing banks could set their own interest rates, even in a competitive market. Since the interest rate is above $3/2$, the least risky borrowers have dropped out of the market. Consequently, by lowering the interest rate to $3/2$ and attracting the low risk borrowers, it is possible for a bank to raise its expected rate of return even though it earns a lower rate of return on each high risk borrower. In this example, any bank which lowers its interest rate to $3/2$ and attracts an equal number of both types of consumers will increase its expected rate of return to $7/8$. Since every borrower prefers the lower interest rate, the higher 'market clearing' rate is not sustainable. The result is an equilibrium rate of return with an excess demand for loans.

In his *Bell Journal* paper, Wilson suggested that a different equilibrium might emerge if the informed agents were the price setters. Refer back to the used car example. It is easy to show that the higher the reservation value of the seller, the smaller is the decrease in price he is willing to accept in order to increase his chances of finding a buyer. This observation suggests that it may be possible to sustain an equilibrium with a distribution of prices. Sellers of high-quality products announce high prices which attract only a few buyers. Sellers of low-quality products announce low prices which attract more buyers. Buyers are willing to purchase at both prices because the quality of the cars offered increases with the price. The quality of cars increases with the price because more buyers purchase at low prices than at high prices. This tradeoff between price and the probability of selling has also been exploited by Samuelson (1984) and others in the design of optimal mechanisms for allocating goods in environments with adverse selection.

Both of the non-Walrasian equilibria discussed above are the consequence of individual agents trying to exploit the relation between quality and price to avoid the problem of adverse selection. Indeed, the study of how agents try to compensate for the problems of adverse selection makes up a large part of the literature on markets with imperfect information. One of the most important ideas to come out of this line of research is the concept of market signalling first investigated by Michael Spence (1973). The idea is that sellers of higher-quality products will try to reveal themselves by undertaking some activity which is less costly to them than to sellers with lower-quality products.

In his example, more productive workers signal their productivity by purchasing education. In product markets, firms use guarantees to signal product reliability. In credit markets, lenders use collateral to signal credit worthiness (Bester, 1984).

CHARLES WILSON

See also ASYMMETRIC INFORMATION; CREDIT RATIONING; IMPLICIT CONTRACTS; INCENTIVE CONTRACTS; INCOMPLETE CONTRACTS; MORAL HAZARD; SELECTION BIAS AND SELF-SELECTION; SIGNALLING.

BIBLIOGRAPHY
Akerlof, G. 1970. The market for lemons. *Quarterly Journal of Economics* 84(3), August, 488–500.
Bester, H. 1984. Screening versus rationing in credit markets with imperfect information. University of Bonn Discussion Paper No. 136, May.
Samuelson, W. 1984. Bargaining under asymmetric information. *Econometrica* 52(4), July, 995–1005.
Spence, M. 1973. Job market signalling. *Quarterly Journal of Economics* 87(3), August, 355–74.
Stiglitz, J. and Weiss, A. 1981. Credit rationing in markets with imperfect information. *American Economic Review* 71, June, 393–410.
Wilson, C. 1980. The nature of equilibrium in markets with adverse selection. *Bell Journal of Economics* 11, Spring, 108–30.

advertising. Advertising has been controversial, probably more so than its economic importance would justify, at least since the emergence of the mass media in the last century. In the United States, advertising spending in recent years has been just above two per cent of GDP. This ratio has grown slowly over time; it is much lower in most other countries, especially in developing nations. In the US and elsewhere, the ratio of advertising to sales varies dramatically among industries, even if attention is limited to industries selling consumer goods and services.

Chamberlin's *Theory of Monopolistic Competition* (1933) was the first major work in economics to treat advertising formally, but its analysis led to few definite positive or normative conclusions. Perhaps reflecting the traditional distaste for advertising in the intellectual community, most early discussions of advertising by economists were generally critical, describing it as wasteful, manipulative, and anti-competitive. Its main redeeming feature was that it provided a source of revenue for the press. (Kaldor, 1950, is a leading example.) Most recent writers are less enthusiastic about the relation between advertising and the media, perhaps because of the rise of television.

CONSUMER DEMAND. We still know relatively little about how advertising affects consumer behaviour. Some writers distinguish between informative and persuasive advertising. Buyers are assumed to respond rationally to informative advertisements, while persuasive advertisements are somehow manipulative. But this distinction is of little value empirically: few if any advertisements present facts in a neutral fashion with no attempt to persuade, and even those with no obvious factual content signal consumers that the seller has invested money to get their attention.

Following Nelson (1974), a number of authors have explored the possibility that advertising affects behaviour through such signals. The core of the argument is that advertising is more profitable to high-quality than low-quality producers, all else equal, since the former are more likely to enjoy repeat sales. In sharp contrast, information processing models of human behaviour, explored in the marketing literature, suggest that advertising may affect behaviour mainly by enhancing a brand's chances of being on the short list ('evoked set') from which final choices are made.

It seems likely that the role of advertising varies considerably, depending on characteristics of products and distribution systems. In some markets advertised brands sell for substantially more than physically identical unadvertised brands; in others restrictions on advertising serve to increase prices (Benham, 1972). Porter (1976) has argued that advertising is less powerful when retailers are an important source of consumer information. The extent to which a buyer can judge quality prior to purchase (Nelson, 1974) should also affect the role of advertising. Similarly, buyers need more information to make decisions about new products than about established products, and advertising by retailers generally provides more price information than advertising by manufacturers.

Econometric analysis of the effects of advertising on consumer spending patterns is difficult because advertising is endogenous; it reflects sellers' decisions. This gives rise to simultaneous equations problems (Schmalensee, 1972). Survey evidence suggests that firms often follow percentage-of-sales decision rules in determining advertising budgets. If this were strictly true, the effect of advertising on sales would be impossible to identify. In fact, advertising/sales ratios are not constant over time, but it is difficult to find seller-related variables that explain the variations well. To the extent that advertising spending is based to some extent on actual or anticipated sales, but demand equations are estimated via least squares because the advertising spending decision cannot be modelled adequately, the importance of advertising as a determinant of consumer behaviour will be overstated.

Borden's (1942) massive study of the effects of advertising on demand concluded that advertising is not generally an important determinant of industry sales. Exceptions arise in new and growing sectors, where advertising can serve to accelerate growth that would occur in any case. Recent work seems generally to support these conclusions (see, for instance, Lambin, 1976). At the aggregate level, advertising tends to lag cyclical changes in total consumption slightly, not to lead those changes (Schmalensee, 1972, ch. 3). At the other extreme, while advertising is generally found to affect market shares, dollar advertising spending typically explains little of the variation in shares over time. This presumably reflects in part the fact that designing effective advertising themes and campaigns remains much more an art than a science.

Overall, advertising does not emerge from the empirical literature on consumer demand as an important determinant of consumer behaviour. Some have argued that advertising has fostered the long-run growth of materialism, but nobody has offered anything like a rigorous test of this proposition. Most practitioners contend that advertising follows rather than leads cultural trends, in part because most advertisers are reluctant to appear out of step with society.

SELLER BEHAVIOUR. All else equal, one would expect sellers to spend more on advertising in markets in which demand is more responsive to advertising, and one might expect demand to be more responsive when consumers need more information to make rational decisions (see Schmalensee, 1972, ch. 2). But we observe very intensive advertising, without much obvious factual content, of some products with which consumers are generally familiar, such as beer and soft drinks.

To the extent that advertising's effects persist over time, advertising outlays are an investment, and advertising budgets must be set using dynamic optimization methods (Sethi, 1977). The greater the profit on additional sales (i.e. the greater the gap between price and marginal cost), the more intensively it pays to advertise. Finally, advertising decisions by oligopolists must take into account the strategies of their rivals.

Consideration of these last two points indicates that the intensity of advertising may rise or fall with increases in market concentration (Schmalensee, 1972, ch. 2). On the one hand, reductions in the number of sellers would be expected to reduce the intensity of all forms of rivalry, and thus to reduce advertising spending. On the other hand, if sellers in concentrated markets manage to raise price far above marginal costs, they thereby enhance incentives to advertise.

Advertising competition can serve to erode excess profits. With a fixed number of sellers, it is likely to be more effective at doing so the more sensitive market shares are to differences in advertising outlays. Greater sensitivity encourages all sellers to advertise more without necessarily increasing the size of the market for which they are competing.

The evidence on scale economies in advertising is mixed. On the one hand, there is little or no evidence that doubling the number of advertisements seen by buyers will more than double the impact on demand. On the other hand, some media offer bulk discounts. And some media, particularly network television in the US, are such that the minimum required outlay is large in absolute terms. This may serve to disadvantage small sellers by effectively denying them the use of these media.

ECONOMIC WELFARE. One must distinguish between global and local welfare analysis in this context. Global analysis is concerned with questions like, 'Could one ban advertising (everywhere or in some particular market) and make society better off?' Local analysis deals with questions like, 'Would society be made better off by a reduction in the level of advertising spending (everywhere or in some particular market)?'

Global questions are difficult to treat formally and thus have not been answered rigorously. Since advertising does provide some information, one must specify how information would be provided if advertising were banned. In principle an omniscient bureaucrat can provide information to perfectly rational consumers optimally, so that a properly administered advertising ban can do no harm.

In practice, bureaucrats are far from omniscient, and the way in which information is presented to consumers affects the extent to which they retain and use it. Advertisers have every incentive to present information effectively, though they rarely have any incentive to present all information that might affect decisions. Advertising, like democracy, is terrible in principle but better than any known alternative in practice. Note also that advertising is practised, though not intensively by US standards, in socialist economies.

Local questions about the optimality of advertising are more susceptible of formal treatment. There are as many answers to these questions as there are papers that address them, however. The answers depend critically on exactly how advertising is assumed to affect behaviour. Butters (1977), for instance, assumes that advertising simply provides price information. He concludes that market-determined advertising levels are optimal if buyers cannot engage in search but are excessive if search is possible. Dixit and Norman (1978) assume that advertising simply changes tastes. If pre advertising tastes are assumed to be socially 'correct', a value-laden assumption, they show that advertising is generally socially excessive.

In general the literature offers no support for a presumption that market-determined advertising levels are socially optimal.

But it also fails to provide any workable scheme for regulating those levels in the public interest.

MARKET STRUCTURE. Discussions of the effects of advertising spending on the evolution of market structure have been dominated by two extreme views. Advertising's critics (e.g. Kaldor, 1950) stress its persuasive nature, argue that it builds loyalties and thus reduces price elasticities of demand within markets, and contend that it is a source of barriers to entry. Beginning with Telser (1964), advertising's defenders stress its role as a source of information, argue that it provides knowledge of alternatives and thus increases elasticities, and contend that it is a means of effecting, not deterring entry. Since the role of advertising seems to vary considerably among markets, neither of these extreme views is likely to be universally correct.

As a theoretical matter, the impact of advertising spending on price elasticities and barriers to entry depends, once again, on exactly how advertising is assumed to affect consumer behaviour. A good deal of empirical work has attempted to choose between the two extreme views outlined above, without producing any definitive results (see Comanor and Wilson, 1979, for a survey).

Many studies have examined the cross-section correlation between advertising and seller concentration; none has provided a satisfactory interpretation of this statistic. Telser (1964) found market shares to be less stable in markets with heavy advertising than in other markets, and Lambin (1976) found price elasticities to be lower in such markets. But neither study controlled for the product characteristics that affect share stability, price elasticity, and sellers' advertising spending decisions.

The clearest empirical regularity to emerge from this work is the strong, positive cross-section correlation between industry-level measures of advertising intensity (typically the advertising/sales ratio) and accounting measures of profitability. This stylized fact would seem to favour advertising's critics.

But profits are high when price/cost margins are large, and large margins encourage advertising (Schmalensee, 1972, ch. 7). Since it is difficult to model advertising spending decisions empirically, it is difficult to deal adequately with this simultaneous equations problem. Moreover, accounting measures of profit treat advertising as an expense, but it should be treated as a durable investment if its effects on demand persist over time. If those effects are assumed to be very long-lived, correcting the accounting profitability figures eliminates the correlation with advertising. Unfortunately, like so much in this area, the longevity of the impact of advertising on demand remains controversial.

RICHARD SCHMALENSEE

See also CHAMBERLIN, EDWARD HASTINGS; MARKET STRUCTURE; MONOPOLISTIC COMPETITION; SELLING COSTS.

BIBLIOGRAPHY
Benham, L. 1972. The effects of advertising on the price of eyeglasses. *Journal of Law and Economics* 15(2), October, 337–52.
Borden, N.H. 1942. *The Economic Effects of Advertising*. Chicago: Irwin.
Butters, G. 1977. Equilibrium distribution of sales and advertising prices. *Review of Economic Studies* 44(3), October, 465–91.
Chamberlin, E.H. 1933. *The Theory of Monopolistic Competition*. Cambridge, Mass.: Harvard University Press.
Comanor, W.S. and Wilson, T.A. 1979. The effect of advertising on competition: a survey. *Journal of Economic Literature* 17(2), June, 453–76.

Dixit, A. and Norman, V. 1978. Advertising and welfare. *Bell Journal of Economics* 9(1), Spring, 1–17.

Kaldor, N. 1950. The economic aspects of advertising. *Review of Economic Studies* 18(1), 1–27.

Lambin, J.J. 1976. *Advertising, Competition, and Market Conduct in Oligopoly over Time.* Amsterdam: North-Holland.

Nelson, P. 1974. Advertising as information. *Journal of Political Economy* 82(4), July/August, 729–54.

Porter, M. 1976. *Interbrand Choice, Strategy, and Bilateral Market Power.* Cambridge, Mass.: Harvard University Press.

Schmalensee, R. 1972. *The Economics of Advertising.* Amsterdam: North-Holland.

Sethi, S.P. 1977. Dynamic optimal control models of advertising. *SIAM Review* 19(4), October, 685–725.

Telser, L.G. 1964. Advertising and competition. *Journal of Political Economy* 72, December, 537–62.

advisers. Since olden times, princes, powers and potentates with widely differing economic backgrounds have availed themselves of advisers and advisory services of various kinds. Advisers sometimes assumed such positions of power and influence that, due either to their expertise or to their influence over the decisions of their employers, they became virtual rulers of a State. Father Joseph's influence over Cardinal Richelieu was such that he became known as the '*Eminence grise*', a term that became part of English usage. At the other end of the scale, monarchs would sometimes make use of court jesters and buffoons to advise them on public opinion judged from the reactions to the jesters' gibes and jokes.

Advisory opinions are frequently sought in English Common Law practice, as well as in the medical field. Advisory services are also frequently described as counselling services. In Embassies the title of Counsellor is generally used to indicate the most senior staff member after the Ambassador. The word in fact, derives from the French 'conseiller' or adviser. This is an indication of the importance attached to such functions in established diplomatic practice.

In more recent times, advisers have been better known in the economic field. A number of governments, including that of the United Kingdom have employed Economic Advisers. This practice has been extended, particularly in the postwar years, to the international scene, where various governments of the industrialized countries have sent economic or other technical advisers to dependent territories and to newly independent States at the latters' request. The various technical or Specialized Agencies of the United Nations system are predominantly purveyors of advisory services. These advisers, more often referred to as 'experts' are drawn from a wide range of member states of the UN and recruited on the basis of their specialized competence and may remain in overseas postings for extended periods. Consultative services are also provided by these agencies in the form of seminars, workshops and technical meetings, which could be described as collective advisory services. Shorter term consultant missions, generally under six months duration, are the usual vehicle for specific problems that can be resolved by such technical advice.

The effectiveness of advisers is, naturally, very much dependent on the status that their employers accord them and the level in a given hierarchy at which they have to work, and on their ability to make their views heard and respected. Much will also depend on the role that the adviser is implicitly expected to play. One employer may, for instance, be a genuine querrent in search of expertise in a field which may be unfamiliar to him, another may simply be using the adviser as a 'presence' by means of which he is able to lend greater credence to his own proposals or views. More frequently though, the adviser will be expected to provide outside opinions on a range of topics, not all of which may be within his specific range of competence or of his job description. The mere fact, however, of being able to express a reasonably unbiased opinion or of coming to conclusions by approaches different from those normally taken by his employer, is in itself an important contribution to the decision-making process of his employer.

Whatever role the adviser may play, it is important to stress the underlying principle behind the majority of such advisory positions, namely, that it provides a means of sharing or of diluting responsibility without any loss of authority on the part of the adviser's employer for decision-making.

Decision-makers, be they heads of state or junior managers, may be faced with a situation in which they realize that some possibly unpopular or risky decisions need to be taken, the results of which cannot be clearly predicted. In such cases an adviser would base his counsel on his own analyses of the problem. Should this agree in general terms with the employers' own views and inclinations, a decision would naturally be taken accordingly. Should the results of such advice, say for some unforeseen reason, turn out to be politically or economically disadvantageous, the employer can readily salvage his reputation by letting it be known that his decision was taken on the basis of the best available national or international advice. Should that not be sufficient to head off criticism, the adviser can be dismissed, carrying the blame for the erroneous decision. This would then enable the employer to take another course without undue damage to his own position or status. On the other hand, should the advice given to the employer be contrary to his views, he had the choice of either throwing it and the adviser out, or of allowing it to go forward into action with the responsibility for the consequences falling directly on the adviser. A successful outcome under such circumstances would then redound to the credit of both the employer and the adviser.

From this it can be seen that an important prerequisite for an adviser is an ability to use foresight to correctly forecast developments that are likely to flow from the advice given. Forecasting in a limited or specific isolated technical field is not particularly hazardous, but as soon as more complex issues relating, say, to economic policy, macroeconomic projections, or futures scenarios are considered, forecasting on the basis of often multiple variables, becomes, even with the aid of computer technology, much more prone to error. It should be borne in mind that under such circumstances the adviser represents and bases his advice on 'science', that is technical expertise, while his employer – generally a policy- or decision-maker – represents action. In practice the interface between these often becomes blurred. If the 'scientist' adviser limits his actions to factual data carrying no value judgements whatsoever, he may be failing in his assigned role of giving pertinent advice. Yet, if he draws too many conclusions from his data he may be usurping the prerogatives of his employer, a process that can lead to the adviser becoming an *éminence grise*.

The forecasting ability of an adviser is also conditioned by the level at which he is placed in a hierarchy. Complex issues of policy or of trend forecasting are nearly always contingent upon other related factors. If there are no clear guidelines from the level above that at which the adviser is working, he will not be able to provide much more than theoretical hypotheses. Again, if at a higher level he is unable to have access to other sectors of activity that may impinge on his own, his advice will be of limited value. Actively to seek out such information might be considered by the other sectors as an infringement or interference. This is particularly so in the case of governmental departments which tend to be rather rigidly hierarchized and jealous of their prerogatives. In order to provide an adviser with the freedom to range across such boundaries, they are often assigned to planning departments or Ministries. This practice is common in the case of internationally assigned economic or policy advisers. A disadvantage arising from this expedient is that the adviser becomes further removed from the action side of his role and more involved in theory and the elaboration of more utopian proposals that may not be realized.

An adviser can often be placed in a position where his advice has been overridden for, say, political or extraneous security reasons of which he may not have been cognizant, and yet retain the respect and support of his employer. He would then most likely be asked to assess the consequences of decisions he had not worked on, or perhaps not even envisaged. This situation occurs in Civil Services in respect of Ministerial decisions and requires both flexibility and a complete detachment on the part of the adviser from the implementation of his advice. This is a quality particularly valuable to decision-makers who are sometimes obliged for quite 'unscientific' reasons to embark on actions they have earlier condemned. The adviser could be relied upon to continue to provide unbiased technical advice based on new sets of parameters and probabilities.

Advisers can play important, and sometimes determinant roles in national and international affairs but remain as a general rule anonymous. It is consequently difficult for historians to assess their true role and contribution. When they have entered the pages of history it has often been for the wrong kind of notoriety. In the case of internationally assigned advisers this anonymity is subsumed into the collective efforts of the various organizations working in this field which in the case of intergovernmental organizations function as an international civil service.

JOHN WOOD

See also COURCELLE-SENEUIL, JEAN-GUSTAVE; FORECASTING.

BIBLIOGRAPHY
Jöhr, W.A. and Singer, H.W. 1955. *The Role of the Economist as Official Adviser*. London: George Allen & Unwin.

Aftalion, Albert (1874–1956). Aftalion was a Bulgarian-born French economist. He taught at the University of Lille and later at the University of Paris (Villey, 1968). His works include a study on Sismondi (1899), a treatise on crises of overproduction (1913), a critique of socialism (1923), two books on monetary issues (1927a, 1948) and several writings on issues related to international trade and the balance of payments (1937). His international reputation is mostly due to the 1913 work on overproduction, a summary of which exists in English (1927b).

Aftalion's approach to the problem of the trade cycle and overproduction is centred on the time lag between an expected increase in the demand for consumption goods and the production of equipment needed to generate the additional consumption goods. For this reason Aftalion has been considered as being among the inventors of the Accelerator Principle. However, his analysis differs significantly from the contemporary theories of the trade cycle based on such a principle. In those theories the Accelerator explains fluctuations in the investment component of effective demand without establishing any connection with the behaviour of prices. For

Aftalion, by contrast, the time required to obtain the extra amount of equipment necessary to produce the additional consumption goods is a basic ingredient to portray the link between fluctuation in output and changes in prices. His argument, based on purely intuitive grounds, runs as follows.

An expected expansion in consumption demand will lead to larger orders by wholesale traders. Since no unused capacity is assumed more machinery will be needed, the demand for which will be propogated to all stages of production. Capitalists are assumed to plan their output on the basis of current prices. Yet, the additional demand of capital goods and raw materials cannot be immediately satisfied. Hence prices will rise in these two sectors, and eventually in the consumption goods sector as well. When the new investment projects are finished and equipment is delivered, prices begin to fall. Entrepreneurs will cut current orders but deliveries due to past investment decisions will continue, thereby reducing price and orders further. This distinction between orders and deliveries influenced Kalecki's approach to the theory of economic fluctuations.

Aftalion did not produce a theory of output because he did not attempt any explanation of the adjustment of capacity to demand. Furthermore, it is not clear whether prices of consumption goods increase because of increases in the price of raw materials or because of the expansion of demand. Indeed, since no spare capacity exists, consumption goods prices should be sensitive to changes in demand. It follows, therefore, that Aftalion's assumption of a time lag between changes in raw material prices and those of consumption goods is theoretically confusing.

JOSEPH HALEVI

See also ACCELERATION PRINCIPLE.

SELECTED WORKS
1899. *L'oeuvre économique de Sismonde de Sismondi*. Paris: Pedone.
1913. *Les crises périodiques de surproduction*. 2 vols, Paris: Rivière.
1923. *Les fondements du socialisme: étude critique*. Paris: Rivière.
1927a. *La valeur de la monnaie dans l'économie contemporaine*, Vol. I. Paris: Sirey.
1927b. The theory of economic cycles based on the capitalistic technique of production. *Review of Economic Statistics* 9, October, 165–70.
1937. *L'équilibre dans les relations économiques internationales*. Paris: Domat-Montchrestien.
1948. *La valeur de la monnaie dans l'économie contemporaine*, Vol. 2. Paris: Sirey.

BIBLIOGRAPHY
Villey, D. 1968. Aftalion, A. In *International Encyclopedia of the Social Sciences*, New York: Macmillan.

ageing populations. Population ageing is represented by an increase in the relative number of older persons in a population and is associated with an increase in the median age of the population. The age structure of a population is determined by its mortality, fertility, and net migration experience. Although life tables and survivorship rates date from the 17th century, the development of mathematical demography is essentially a 20th-century innovation. The techniques of mathematical demography can be used to show how the age structure of a population changes with alternative transition rates.

The importance of these transition rates is shown by the observation that in the absence of migration two arbitrarily chosen populations that are subjected to identical fertility and mortality rates will ultimately generate the same age structure. Thus, as Coale (1972, p. 3) noted, populations gradually 'forget' the past in as far as their age compositions are concerned. Of course, the population age structure may echo past irregularities for several generations before these echo effects disappear (Easterlin, 1980).

Population projections illustrate that declining fertility produces population ageing, so do decreases in mortality rates; however, fertility changes dominate the age structure of a population. For example, even if man were to become immortal, high fertility rates would produce a relatively young population. Migration can modify the age composition of a population, but non-sustained migration will have only a transitory effect on the age distribution of a population unless the migration also alters the prevailing patterns of fertility and mortality (Keyfitz, 1968, p. 94).

Concern for the economic implications of ageing populations is essentially a 20th-century phenomenon. Populations with low life expectancies and high fertility rates will have only small fractions age 65 and older. For most of human history, these were typical population characteristics. Therefore, little attention was devoted to the macroeconomic implications of ageing. In summarizing economic thinking prior to the 20th century, Hutchinson (1967, p. 346) concludes that because the typical population age structure contained relatively few persons over age 65, not much attention was given to the ratio of workers to the total population. In most economic analysis, the population was simply assumed to be equivalent to labour supply.

Declining population growth occurred in Western Europe in the early part of the 20th century. The resulting ageing of populations began to attract attention. Economists focused their analyses on age structure ratios, such as the number of dependent persons (the young and the old) divided by the number of persons in the population or by the number of persons of working age. Much of the research examining the economic implications of ageing populations assesses the effects of changes in these dependency ratios or similar population ratios.

Dependency ratios are used to measure the relative productive potential of a population. The old-age dependency ratio generally measures the number of elderly persons at or above a certain age, say 65, divided by the number of persons of working age, say 16–64. This ratio has been widely used in economic analysis to measure the number of retired dependent persons per active member of the labour force. The old-age dependency ratio is used to illustrate the transfer of output from workers that is necessary to support retirees. This ratio rises with population ageing.

There are several problems concerning the economic interpretation of the old-age dependency ratio. First, if population ageing follows from reduced fertility, the total dependency ratio (youths plus elderly) may fall even as the old-age ratio is rising. The total cost to society of supporting the dependent populations will depend on the relative costs of maintaining the two dependent populations and the transfer mechanisms that are developed within the economic system (Sauvy, 1969, pp. 303–19). Second, the age-based dependency ratios are not perfect proxies for the ratio of inactive to active persons. Recently, some analysts have attempted to incorporate labour force participation into the dependency-ratio framework. Of course, over time, participation rates and the meaning of dependency may change. Third, significant compositional changes may occur within the elderly, youth, and working age populations. These changes have economic effects that may be as important as effects of changes in the dependency ratio itself (Clark and Spengler, 1980).

The cost of national pension systems rises with population ageing because a greater fraction of the population is receiving benefits and a smaller fraction is working and paying taxes to support the system (Munnell, 1977). This relationship has become one of the principal public policy issues associated with population ageing. The funding of pensions and the economic impact of alternative funding methods also has been subject to considerable examination. Feldstein (1974) argued that the pay-as-you-go financing of the US Social Security System substantially reduced the national savings rate. Subsequent research has produced a series of conflicting findings on this issue.

The growth of national pension systems has drawn attention to retirement ages. The impact of population ageing on pension funding requirements is exacerbated if the age of withdrawal from the labour force declines. During the past century, labour force participation rates of the elderly have fallen and the interaction of earlier retirement and population ageing has produced significant increases in income transfers to the elderly.

The changing age structure of a population may also alter the equilibrium unemployment rate and the average level of productivity in a society. Layoff and quit rates are a decreasing function of age. Since employment stability increases with age, national unemployment rates tend to decline with population ageing. Some attention has been given to the effect of ageing on productivity with emphasis on the ageing of the labour force and the ensuing slower rate of introduction of new human capital into the production process. The ability of older workers to maintain production standards has also been questioned. Data limitations preclude a definitive answer to the shape of the age-productivity profile. The macroeconomic significance of population ageing on national productivity depends on individual age-specific productivity, and any ensuing changes in investment, consumption, and savings behaviour. The net effect of these factors is unclear.

The effect of population ageing on national savings and therefore the rate of economic growth depends on age-specific savings rates and the age structure changes that occur as the population ages (Kelley, 1973). Although ageing of individuals tends to reduce their savings in old age, population ageing typically is associated with an increase in the fraction of the population in the high savings years and thus tends to stimulate increased saving and investment. The net effect of ageing on savings and growth will also depend on the cause of the population ageing. If population ageing results from slowing population growth, then the economic response to population size and rate of population growth will be observed simultaneously with the ageing effect. In general, the independent effect of population ageing will not be a major factor influencing future economic growth and development.

ROBERT L. CLARK

See also DECLINING POPULATION; DEMOGRAPHIC TRANSITION; SOCIAL SECURITY; STABLE POPULATION THEORY; STAGNATION.

BIBLIOGRAPHY

Clark, R. and Spengler, J. 1980. *Economics of Individual and Population Ageing.* Cambridge: Cambridge University Press.

Coale, A. 1972. *The Growth and Structure of Human Populations: A Mathematical Investigation.* Princeton: Princeton University Press.

Easterlin, R. 1980. *Birth and Fortune.* New York: Basic Books.

Feldstein, M. 1974. Social security, induced retirement, and aggregate capital accumulation. *Journal of Political Economy* 82(5), September, 905–26.

Hutchinson, E.P. 1967. *The Population Debate.* Boston: Houghton-Mifflin.

Kelley, A. 1973. Population growth, the dependency rate and the pace of economic development. *Population Studies* 27(3), November, 405–14.

Keyfitz, N. 1968. *Introduction to the Mathematics of Population.* Reading, Mass.: Addison-Wesley.

Munnell, A. 1977. *The Future of Social Security.* Washington, DC: The Brookings Institution.

Sauvy, A. 1969. *General Theory of Population.* New York: Basic Books.

agency costs. In the traditional analysis of the firm, profit maximization is assumed, subject to the constraints of a technological production function for transforming inputs into output. Optimum production solutions are characterized in terms of the equality between the ratio of marginal products of inputs and the ratio of input prices. While this analysis has provided valuable insights in understanding certain aspects of choices by firms, it completely ignores others having to do with the process through which the inputs are organized and coordinated. In essence, the traditional economic analysis treats the firm as a black box in this transformation of inputs into output. Rarely are questions raised such as: Why are some firms organized as individual proprietorships, some as partnerships, some as corporations, and others as cooperatives or mutuals? Why are some firms financed primarily by equity and others with debt? Why are some inputs owned and others leased? Why do some industries make extensive use of franchising while others do not? Why do some bonds contain call provisions, convertibility provisions, or sinking fund provisions while others do not? Why are some executives compensated with salary while others have extensive stock option or bonus plans? Why do some industries pay workers on a piece-rate basis while others pay at an hourly rate? Why do some firms employ one accounting procedure while others choose alternate procedures? To answer such questions requires the economic analysis of contractual relationships. Agency Theory provides a framework for such an analysis.

An agency relationship is defined through an explicit or implicit contract in which one or more persons (the principal(s)) engage another person (the agent) to take actions on behalf of the principal(s). The contract involves the delegation of some decision-making authority to the agent. Agency costs are the total costs of structuring, administering, and enforcing such contracts. Agency costs, therefore, encompass all contracting costs frequently referred to as transactions costs, moral hazard costs, and information costs. Jensen and Meckling (1976) break down agency costs into three components: (1) monitoring expenditures by principal, (2) bonding expenditures by the agent, and (3) the residual loss. Monitoring expenditures are paid by the principal to regulate the agent's conduct. Bonding expenditures are made by the agent to help assure that the agent will not take actions which damage the principal or will indemnify the principal if the prescribed actions are undertaken. Hence, monitoring and bonding costs are the out-of-pocket costs of structuring, administering, and enforcing contracts. The residual loss is the value of the loss by the principal from decisions by the agent which deviate from the decisions which would have been made by the principal if he had the same information and talents as the agent. Since it is profitable to invest in policing contracts only to the point where the reduction in the loss from non-compliance equals the incremental costs of enforcement, the residual loss is the opportunity loss when contracts are optimally, but incompletely enforced.

Jensen and Meckling (1976) point out that agency problems emanating from conflicts of interests are common to most cooperative endeavours whether or not they occur in the hierarchial manner implied in the principal–agent analogy. But, with the elimination of the difference between principal and agent, the distinction between monitoring and bonding costs is also lost; so, total agency costs are out-of-pocket costs plus the opportunity cost or residual loss.

It is crucial to recognize that the contracting parties bear the agency costs associated with their interaction and therefore have incentives to structure contracts to reduce agency costs wherever possible. Within the contracting process, incentives exist for individuals to negotiate contracts specifying monitoring and bonding activities so long as their marginal cost is less than the marginal gain from reducing the residual loss. Specifically, the contracting parties gain from forecasting accurately the actions to be undertaken and structuring the contracts to facilitate the expected actions. For example, with competitive and informationally efficient financial markets, unbiased estimates of agency costs should be included in the prices of securities when they are initially offered (as well as at any future date). This mechanism provides incentives to structure contracts and institutions to lower agency costs. Hence, in the absence of the usual externalities, the private contracting process produces an efficient allocation of resources.

Jensen (1983) describes two approaches to the development of a theory of agency which he labels the 'positive theory of agency' and the 'principal-agent' literatures. Both approaches examine contracting among self-interested individuals and both postulate that agency costs are minimized through the contracting process; thus, both address the design of Pareto-efficient contracts. However the approaches diverge at several junctures. The principal-agent literature generally has a mathematical and non-empirical orientation and concentrates on the effects of preferences and asymmetric information (for example, Harris and Raviv, 1978; Holmstrom, 1979; Ross, 1973; and Spence and Zeckhauser, 1971). The positive agency literature generally has a non-mathematical and empirical focus and concentrates on the effects of the contracting technology and specific human or physical capital (for example, Fama and Jensen, 1983a, 1983b; Jensen and Meckling, 1976; Myers, 1977; and Smith and Warner, 1979).

The investigation of agency costs has provided a deeper understanding of many dimensions of complex contractual arrangements, especially the modern corporate form. One can better understand the variation in contractual forms across organizations by studying the nature of the agency costs in alternative contractual arrangements. For example, Fama and Jensen (1983a) examine the nature of residual claims and the agency costs of separation of management and riskbearing to provide a theory of the determinants of alternative organizational forms. They argue that corporations, proprietorships, partnerships, mutuals and non-profits differ in the manner they trade off the benefits of risk-sharing with agency costs.

Agency cost analysis has been employed to examine the choice of organizational structure in the insurance (Mayers and Smith, 1981, 1986) and thrift industries (Smith, 1982; and Masulis, 1986). It has also been employed to examine the determinants of the firm's capital structure (Jensen and Meckling, 1976; Myers, 1977); the provisions in corporate bond contracts (Smith and Warner, 1979); the determinants of corporate leasing policy (Smith and Wakeman, 1985) and franchise policy (Brickley and Dark, 1987); the incentives for the development of a hierarchical structure within organizations (Zimmerman, 1979; Fama and Jensen, 1983b); and the determinants of corporate compensation policy (Smith and Watts, 1982). Finally, the analysis of agency costs has played a central role in the development of a positive theory of the choice of accounting techniques (Watts and Zimmerman, 1986).

Agency analysis has also afforded a different perspective in assessing the implications of observed contractual provisions. For example, typical discussions of mortgage loan provisions suggest that escrow accounts and limitations on renting the property are included in the loan contract for the benefit of the lender. However, if there is competition among lenders, these benefits must be reflected in compensating differentials in other loan terms, such as lower promised interest rates. If in addition, the rates on other securities are not affected by changes in the terms of this contract, then all of the benefits of these convenants must ultimately accrue to the borrower, not the lender.

CLIFFORD W. SMITH, JR.

See also INCENTIVE CONTRACTS; PRINCIPAL AND AGENT; TRANSACTION COSTS.

BIBLIOGRAPHY
Brickley, J.A. and Dark, F.H. 1987. The choice of organizational form: the case of franchising. *Journal of Financial Economics*.
Fama, E. and Jensen, M. 1983a. Agency problems and residual claims. *Journal of Law and Economics*, June, 327–49.
Fama, E. and Jensen, M. 1983b. Separation of ownership and control. *Journal of Law and Economics* 26, 301–25.
Harris, M. and Raviv, A. 1978. Some results on incentive contracts with applications to education and employment, health insurance and law enforcement. *American Economic Review* 68, 20–30.
Holmstrom, B. 1979. Moral hazard and observability. *Bell Journal of Economics* 10(1), 74–91.
Jensen, M. 1983. Organization theory and methodology. *Accounting Review* 58, 319–39.
Jensen, M. and Meckling, W. 1976. Theory of the firm: managerial behavior, agency costs and ownership structure. *Journal of Financial Economics* 3, 305–60.
Masulis, R. 1986. Changes in ownership structure: conversions of mutual savings and loans to stock charter. *Journal of Financial Economics*.
Mayers, D. and Smith, C. 1981. Contractual provisions, organizational structure, and conflict control in insurance markets. *Journal of Business* 54, 407–34.
Mayers, D. and Smith, C. 1986. Ownership structure and control: the mutualization of stock life insurance companies. *Journal of Financial Economics* 16.
Myers, S. 1977. Determinants of corporate borrowing. *Journal of Financial Economics* 5, 147–75.
Ross, S. 1973. The economic theory of agency: the principal's problem. *American Economic Review* 63, 134–9.
Smith, C. 1982. Pricing mortgage originations. *AREUEA Journal* 10, Fall, 313–30.
Smith, C. and Wakeman, L. 1985. Determinants of corporate leasing policy. *Journal of Finance*, July, 895–908.
Smith, C. and Warner, J. 1979. On financial contracting: an analysis of bond covenants. *Journal of Financial Economics*, June, 117–61.
Smith, C. and Watts, R. 1982. Incentive and tax effects of U.S. executive compensation plans. *Australian Journal of Management*, December, 139–57.
Spence, M. and Zeckhauser, R. 1971. Insurance, information, and individual action. *American Economic Review* 61, 119–32.
Watts, R. and Zimmerman, J. 1986. *Positive Accounting Theory*. Englewood Cliffs, NJ: Prentice-Hall.
Zimmerman, J. 1979. The costs and benefits of cost allocations. *The Accounting Review* 54, 504–21.

agent. *See* PRINCIPAL AND AGENT.

agents of production.   The causes or requisites of production, often called 'agents of production', may be divided into two classes: human action and external nature; commonly distinguished as 'labour', and 'natural agents'. The first category comprises mental as well as muscular exertion; the second, force as well as matter. To the second factor is sometimes applied the term *land*: in a technical sense, denoting not only the 'brute earth', but also all other physical elements with their properties. But this term is more frequently employed in another classification, according to which the agents of production are divided into three classes – land, labour, and capital. Of the two classifications which have been stated the former appears the more fundamental and philosophical. That 'all production is the result of two and only two elementary agents of production, nature and labour,' is particularly well argued by Böhm-Bawerk in his *Kapital und Kapitalzins*, pt. ii. p. 83. 'There is no room for a third elementary source,' he maintains. This view is countenanced by high authorities, of whom some are cited below. Even J.S. Mill, who is disposed to make capital nearly as important as the other members of the tripartite division, yet admits that 'labour and natural agents' are 'the primary and universal requisites of production' (*Political Economy*, bk. i, ch. iv, § 1). Prof. Marshall, dividing the subject more closely, thinks 'it is perhaps best to say that there are three factors of production, land, labour, and the sacrifice involved in waiting' (*Principles of Economics*, p. 614, note).

In the case where both labour and natural agents are required, the most frequent and important case, the question may be raised whether nature or man contributes more to the result. According to Quesnay (*Maximes*, p. 331), land is the sole source of riches. According to Adam Smith, in manufactures 'nature does nothing, man does all' (*Wealth of Nations*, bk. ii, ch. v). The better view appears to be that the division of industries into those in which labour does most and those in which nature does most is not significant. It is like attempting 'to decide which half of a pair of scissors has most to do in the act of cutting' (Mill, *Political Economy*, bk. i, ch. i, § 3).

Agents of production may be subdivided into those which are limited, and those which are practically unlimited. This distinction applies principally to natural agents. For labour may in general be regarded as an article of which the supply is limited. The ownership or use of those agents of production which are limited and capable of being appropriated acquires a value in exchange. Hence rent of land and wages of labour take their origin.

To account for the difference in the rents paid for different lands, it has been usual, after Ricardo, to arrange the lands in a sort of scale of fertility: No. 1, No. 2, and so on. Upon this classification it is to be remarked that productivity, the real basis of the differences in question, does not vary according to any one attribute, such as the indestructible powers of the soil, or proximity to the centres of industry; but upon a number of attributes (compare B. Price, *Practical Political Economics*, chapter on 'Rent'). Moreover, a scale in which lands, or other natural agents, were arranged according to their productive power, would hold good only so long as the other factor of production, human action, might remain constant. A light sandy soil may be more productive than a heavy clay, so long as the doses of labour applied to each are small. But the order of fertility may be reversed when the cultivation is higher. As Prof. Sidgwick remarks 'these material advantages' [afforded by natural agents] 'do not remain the same in all stages of industrial development: but vary with the varying amounts of labour applied, and the varying efficiency of instruments and processes' (*Political Economy*, bk. i, ch. iv, § 3). Compare Prof. Marshall, *Principles of Economics*, bk. iv, ch. iii, § 4.

A similar difficulty attends the attempt to arrange the other agent of production, human labour, in a scale of excellence; whereby to determine what has been called Rent of Ability. Prof. Macvane has noticed this difficulty in an article on 'Business Profits' in the *Quarterly Journal of Economics* (Harvard) for October 1887. Prof. Walker, in a reply to Prof. Macvane in the same journal, April 1888, admits and very happily illustrates the difficulty (p. 227).

[On this subject as many references might be given as there are treatises on political economy. The twofold classification above indicated is illustrated by the following: Hobbes, *Leviathan*, beginning of ch. xxiv ('The plenty of matter' consists of 'those commodities which from the two breasts of our common mother, land and sea, God usually either freely giveth, or for labour selleth to mankind'). Petty, *Treatises on Taxes* (3rd edn, 1685), ch. viii, p. 57 (labour the father, land the mother, of wealth). Berkeley, *Querist*, Query 4 ('Whether the four elements and man's labour therein be not the true source of wealth'). Cantillon, *Essay*, pt. i, ch. i (land the matter and labour the form of riches). Courcelle-Seneuil, *Traité théorique*, bk. i, ch. iii. Hearn, *Plutology*, ch. ii.]

[F.Y. EDGEWORTH]
Reprinted from *Palgrave's Dictionary of Political Economy*.

See also CAPITAL AS A FACTOR OF PRODUCTION.

BIBLIOGRAPHY
Berkeley, G. 1735–37. *The Querist*. Dublin.
Böhm-Bawerk, E. 1884. *Kapital und Kapitalzins*. Innsbruck.
Cantillon, R. 1752. *Essai sur la nature du commerce en général*. Paris.
Courcelle-Seneuil, J.G. 1858. *Traité theorique et practique d'économie politique*. Paris.
Hearn, W.E. 1864. *Plutology, or the theory of the efforts to satisfy human wants*. London.
Macvane, S.M. 1887. The theory of business profits. *Quarterly Journal of Economics* 2, 1–36.
Macvane, S.M. 1888. Business profits and wagers. *Quarterly Journal of Economics* 2, 453–68.
Marshall, A. 1890. *Principles of Economics*. London.
Mill, J.S. 1848. *Principles of Political Economy*. 2 vols, London.
Petty, W. 1685. *Treatise on Taxes and Contributions*. London.
Price, B. 1878. *Chapters on Practical Political Economics*. London.
Quesnay, F. 1846. *Maximes*. Ed. E. Daire, Paris.
Sidgwick, H. 1883. *Principles of Political Economy*. London.
Smith, A. 1776. *An Inquiry into the Nature and Causes of the Wealth of Nations*. London.

aggregate demand and supply analysis. 1 TEMPORARY EQUILIBRIUM; 2 PROCESS ANALYSIS; 3 PROCESSES WITH A CONSTANT LABOUR CAPITAL RATIO; 4 BUSINESS CYCLES WITH A CONSTANT LABOUR–CAPITAL RATIO; 5 KEYNESIAN INVESTMENT CYCLES; 6 NON-KEYNESIAN OVERINVESTMENT CYCLES.

1 TEMPORARY EQUILIBRIUM

Postulate an elementary period or instant, which may be arbitrarily short. There is a set of parameters given or determined at its outset. They change only from one instant to the next. Within an instant some markets are cleared. In this temporary equilibrium the economy moves from instant to instant in accordance with the laws governing the behaviour of the parameters.

Hicks (1939, p. 122) stated that there will nearly always be some goods whose production can be changed within the instant. Applying this principle to macroeconomics Hicks

(1937) treated labour as a perfectly variable factor for the individual entrepreneur, so that, in his interpretation, the Keynesian IS–LM equilibrium, or its full-employment counterpart, is the economy's temporary equilibrium, with employment, output and interest rates determined within the instant, given the parametric stock of capital etc. This is still the standard temporary-equilibrium concept in macroeconomics. A point not lying on the IS curve is usually regarded as indicating a net excess demand for goods.

But there are two serious difficulties. First there is the well-known crux concerning Walras' Law when there is involuntary unemployment in the IS–LM equilibrium. How can there be an excess supply of labour when there is no excess demand for anything else? The ingenious distinction made by Clower (1965, ch. 5) between 'notional' and 'effective' excess demands solves the problem formally, but prompts the question why it is required in macroeconomics when the rest of economics manages without it.

Secondly there is a strong case for assuming that labour, like capital, is a quasi-fixed factor for the individual entrepreneur, given or determined parametrically at the outset of each instant. For there are costs of hiring and firing people, and even of varying significantly hours worked, at short notice. But this suggests that macroeconomics should be based not on Hicks's principle but on the Marshallian concept of a temporary equilibrium relative to a given state of expectations, in which market prices equate demands in each instant to outputs predetermined at its outset.

Actually a macroeconomic temporary equilibrium of this kind was devised long ago. One of its inventors was Keynes himself. Keynes's economics was Marshallian in this respect from the *Treatise on Money* (1930, chs 9–11) to the *General Theory* (1936) and beyond. The contrary belief regarding the *General Theory* expressed, for example, by Hicks (1965, pp. 64–6) will be shown to be incompatible with the evidence.

Keynes's object in the *Treatise on Money* (1930, Preface, p. v) was to find a method of analysing dynamic processes towards and around a longer-run equilibrium. With the same end in view we shall present a model of temporary equilibrium under assumptions of constant returns to scale and labour-augmenting technical change, in order that a longer-run equilibrium may be one of steady growth. As in the Marshallian theory of relative prices, the dynamics will depend on revisions of short-term expected (or 'normal') prices when the prices of the temporary equilibrium turn out to be different from them. 'Hicksian' dynamics is somewhat pressed to find convincing substitutes for this lag, on which the Marshallian distinction between market and short-term normal prices is based. We shall show how it can be used in constructing a set of dynamic equations that accomplish Keynes's objective in the *Treatise on Money* and enable us to put into a unified framework a great variety of macrodynamic theories.

But it may be useful to begin by expressing our general approach to aggregative analysis. The subject-matter of macroeconomics is, we believe, the behaviour of index numbers, of final output, employment, the stock of capital, interest rates, the general price-level, etc. It is foolish to assume that their components are homogeneous, since index numbers are required just because they are not. We also dissent from the idea that there exists a fundamental non-aggregative system with which they should be consistent. The decision to be made is how far to disaggregate, not how to justify departures from this imaginary construct. Our purpose here will be served at the highest level of aggregation.

The index numbers are taken to reflect the average (or representative) behaviour and experience of economic agents.

The deviations from the average are not predicted by the model, and so could not be inferred from it even if everyone knew it in detail.

1.1 SUPPLY.

We assume a closed economy, so that total money income equals the value of final output. Real final output $Y = Kf(x)$, where K is the inherited stock of capital, $x = N/K$, and N is the demand for labour in efficiency units. For simplicity perfect competition is assumed. At the outset of an instant firms choose x by maximizing the profits expected to accrue in it. Thus optimum x depends on *short-term expectations*. If p is an index of prices expected for the instant and w an index of money wages per efficiency unit of labour, x maximizes $pf(x) - wx$. Necessary and sufficient conditions for an interior maximum are $f'(x) = w/p$ and $f''(x) < 0$. Given p, w, and K, then, both output, Y, and the sum of expected money incomes, pY, are parameters for the instant.

1.2 PRICES AND WINDFALL PROFITS.

Actual incomes may differ from pY. Let Q be the net sum of unexpected incomes deflated by pK. Thus money incomes deflated by K are $p[f(x) + Q]$. If π is the price level of final output, by definition $\pi f(x) = p([f(x) + Q]$, so that Q will turn out to be $\gtreqless 0$ according as the market determines π to be $\gtreqless p$ within the instant. Since output is completely inelastic within the instant, $pQ = (\pi - p)f(x) = [\pi f(x) - wx] - [pf(x) - wx]$ is the net sum of unexpected or *windfall* profits deflated by K. (In the *Treatise on Money* Keynes apparently defined windfall profits as the excess of entrepreneurs' actual over *long-term normal* renumeration (1930, pp. 124–5). The definition here follows from our having adopted his assumption in the *General Theory* (1936, ch. 5) that current employment of labour depends on *short-term* expectations, so that windfalls become the excess of actual over *short-term expected* profits.)

1.3 EXCESS DEMAND FOR FINAL OUTPUT.

We assume pK-deflated planned investment and saving to be functions $I(Q, r; x)$ and $S(Q, r; x)$. Planned saving is expected income minus planned consumption. r is an index of the general level of real interest rates. The pK-deflated excess demand for final output is

$$X_g = I(Q, r; x) - S(Q, r; x) - Q$$

The subscript g is for 'goods'. The semicolon preceding x indicates that it is a parameter for the instant. I_Q may be negative, since unexpectedly high prices may induce disinvestment in inventories. The sign of S_Q is ambiguous: a negative income effect may be outweighed by a positive substitution effect of unusually high or low π in relation to p. So is the sign of S_r. But we assume that $I_Q - S_Q - 1$ and $I_r - S_r$ are both negative. I_x is non-negative, but is positive if *long-term expectations* of profit move in the same direction as short-term expectations of it. Finally S_x, which has the sign of the marginal propensity to save, is assumed to be positive.

π will rise or fall (given p) according as X_g is positive or negative. So, therefore, will Q.

1.4 EXCESS FLOW DEMAND FOR MONEY.

There is a central-banking system. We abstract from the note issue. Commercial banks' reserves at the Central Bank, deflated by pK, are R. The public's pK-deflated demand for commercial banks' deposits is a function, $L(Q, r; x, \lambda)$, where λ is the parametric expected rate of inflation of p. L_r is negative and so is L_λ. L_Q may be zero. In any case its sign is ambiguous. There may be a positive income effect. But since a portion of loans is normally kept on deposit, when a rise in Q reduces the demand for inventories (and correspondingly the demand for bank loans) the borrow-

ers' demand for deposits may also be reduced. Finally L_x may be negative. For the rise in expected profits with x may increase confidence, reducing the demand for liquidity. (Transactions demand is already largely accounted for by expressing the demand as a ratio to pK.)

The public as a whole can make deposits whatever it wishes them to be by altering its borrowings from the banks. There can be no inevitable net creation of 'derivative' deposits by the banks themselves as they attempt to remove a net surplus of reserves, when the public commands the volume of bank loans at the banks' current loan rates. For a discussion of the genesis of deposits see Rose (1985, section 4).

It is convenient, but not essential, to assume that deposits are momently equal to the stock demand for them. The banks, however, have, at the outset of an instant, reserves that are not, in general, what they need. Let c be their desired ratio of reserves to deposits, assumed constant for simplicity. When cL differs from R they try to reduce the gap during the instant by *active net hoarding*. Its extent is assumed to be $\beta(cL - R)$, where β is a positive adjustment coefficient.

But there may also be *passive* net hoarding. The theory of the precautionary demand for money suggests that, since the terms for unexpected transactions between money and securities at short notice are apt to be worse than those for expected transactions between them, the optimum strategy should involve a temporarily passive response to unexpected net receipts, i.e., passive net hoarding of them. Now unexpected net receipts arise when Q is non-zero. We therefore assume that passive net hoarding is $\alpha Q (0 \leq \alpha \leq 1)$, with α constant.

The pK-deflated excess flow demand for money (reserves and deposits) is therefore

$$X_m = \beta[cL(Q, r; x, \lambda) - R] + \alpha Q - \dot{R}$$

the subscript m is for 'money'.

1.5 WALRAS' LAW.

Since final output is a parameter, the temporary equilibrium is an equilibrium of exchange. The sum of the values of the excess demands for goods, securities, and money must be zero. The excess demands for factors are irrelevant during the instant, owing to the assumption that factor employments are fixed at its outset. The problem encountered in the Hicksian theory simply does not arise here.

1.6 EXCESS FLOW DEMAND FOR LOANABLE FUNDS.

The excess supply of securities is the excess demand for lonable funds, whose pK-deflated value is X_f. Therefore by Walras' Law

$$X_f = I(Q, r; x) - S(Q, r; x)$$
$$- Q + \beta[cL(Q, r; x, \lambda) - R] + \alpha Q - \dot{R}$$

The subscript f is for 'funds'. r will rise or fall according as X_f is positive or negative.

1.7 THE TEMPORARY EQUILIBRIUM WITH PARAMETRIC R.

If the Central Bank sets R for the instant, $\dot{R} = 0$. The adjustment of r and π (or equivalently Q) puts X_f and X_g to zero, establishing a unique equilibrium if, in addition to the inequalities $I_Q - S_Q - 1 < 0$, $I_r - S_r < 0$, and $L_r < 0$, the condition $(I_Q - S_Q - 1)L_r - (I_r - S_r)L_Q > 0$ is satisfied. The equations are

$$I(Q^*, r^*; x) - S(Q^*, r^*; x) = Q^*$$
$$\alpha[I(Q^*, r^*; x) - S(Q^*, r^*; x)] = \beta[R - cL(Q^*, r^*; x, \lambda)]$$
$$\pi^* = p + p(I^* - S^*)/f(x).$$

(The asterisks indicate equilibrium values.) The first is Keynes's Fundamental Equation (viii) (1930, p. 138). The third is the form assumed by his Fundamental Equation (iv) (1930, p. 137) when windfalls are defined as in section 1.2 above. The second is more general than its counterpart in Keynes. For he assumed that there is no passive net hoarding, i.e., that $\alpha = 0$. The consequence is his 'liquidity preference' theory of interest, $L(Q^*, r^*; x, \lambda) = R/c$.

He held to this aspect of his temporary equilibrium not only in the *Treatise on Money* and immediately after it (Keynes, 1973a, pp. 224–5) but also in and after the *General Theory*. The net demand for funds represented by $I^* - S^*$ is matched by net loans from windfalls exactly equal to it. Thus in a letter to Hawtrey written soon after the publication of the *General Theory* he insisted that an increase in investment would not directly raise r^* because it would raise the demand for securities by precisely the same amount (Keynes, 1973b, p. 12).

But if α is positive $I^* - S^*$ is not fully matched by net loans from windfalls. Active net dishoarding must fill the gap, viz. $\alpha(I^* - S^*)$, and r^* must stand above or below the level corresponding to $L^* = R/c$ according as $I^* - S^*$ is positive or negative. This is essentially the 'loanable funds' theory of interest, for which see, e.g., Robertson (1940, pp. 1–20).

1.8 THE QUESTION OF SAY'S LAW. If rational conduct does imply that α is positive, there is a decisive answer to the question whether aggregate demand must be a determinant of the economy's behaviour, or equivalently whether the 'classical' theory of interest (Keynes, 1936, ch. 14) must be wrong. (For a fuller account of this subject see Rose (1985, pp. 1–17).) If for each pair of values of x and λ we can find a stock of reserves with which the temporary-equilibrium equations become

$$I(0, r^*; x) - S(0, r^*; x)$$
$$cL(0, r^*; x, \lambda) = R^*$$
$$\pi^* = p$$

with $r^* > 0$, the answer is no. The 'classical' theory of interest becomes valid, and, since $Q^* = 0$, aggregate money demand, $p[Y + K(I^* - S^*)]$, and money income, $\pi^* Y$, are equal to and determined by the given sum of expected incomes, pY. If such an R^* could always be found, inflation, fluctuations, unemployment there might be, but none of them due to movements of aggregate demand for output. Moreover the appropriate level of reserves can be found and sustained 'without the necessity for any special intervention or grandmotherly care on the part of the monetary authorities' (Keynes, 1936, p. 177). In effect Say's Law of Markets can be imposed whenever we wish; for the market mechanism itself will guarantee that supply, pY, creates its own demand. To impose it the Central Bank should stand passively ready to deal in securities with the member banks, at their current prices, in exchange for reserves. Both convenience and economic incentive will induce the banks to accomplish their active net hoarding via the Central Bank, the incentive being the tendency of security prices to move against them if they go to the market instead. Thus they will adjust their reserves to the demand for them in accordance with the equation $\dot{R} = \beta(cL - R)$. But then, since α is positive, the second equation in section 1.7 above implies $I^* - S^*$. The market cannot support a non-zero $I^* - S^*$ when the banks provide it with no active net dishoarding.

But if α were zero the second equation in section 1.7 would not imply $Q^* = 0$ when $R^* = cL^*$. Instead there would be many possible equilibria. Which of them would eventuate would depend on which value of R^* were fortuitously reached in the adjustment to cL^*. The Central Bank's policy could not succeed in imposing Say's Law. It would simply render indeterminate the equilibrium at which $I^* - S^*$ was matched by net loans from windfalls. No wonder Keynes was so insistent on his 'liquidity preference' theory of interest!

In a system with no Central Bank, all money consisting of the notes and deposits of *non-colluding* commercial banks holding each others' deposits as reserves, Say's Law would always rule if α were positive. For if $R = c = 0$ then $Q^* = 0$.

2 PROCESS ANALYSIS

2.1 COMPARATIVE STATICS OF TEMPORARY EQUILIBRIUM. Let m be the 'potential' supply of deposits, R/c. We shall refer to it as the supply of money deflated by pK.

The temporary equilibrium implies functions $Q^*(x, m, \lambda)$ and $r^*(x, m, \lambda)$. The signs of their partial derivatives are of the first importance in process analysis. What can be learnt about them from the formulae obtained by differentiating the equations of section 1.7 and applying Cramer's Rule, together with the inequalities assumed there?

Definite signs are attached to r_m^*, r_λ^*, Q_m^*, and Q_λ^*. The first two are negative, of course, and in consequence the last two are positive.

Sign $Q_x^* = \text{sign}[(I_r - S_r)L_x - (I_x - S_x)L_r]$. It may easily be positive; for the marginal inducement to invest, I_x, may exceed the marginal propensity to save, S_x, and L_x may be negative (see section 1.4).

Sign $r_x^* = \text{sign}[(\alpha + \beta c L_Q)(I_x - S_x) - (I_Q - S_Q - 1)\beta c L_x]$. If L_Q is zero and if, as one might expect, β is large, sign $r_x^* = $ sign L_x.

Since the banks' desired cash ratio will make no further explicit appearance, the letter c will be given a new definition in section 2.5 below.

2.2 CAPITAL ACCUMULATION. Since the goods markets are cleared, actual and planned investment are equal, Therefore $\dot{K}/K = I^*(x, m, \lambda)$. An essential requirement in some theories of growth and all 'overinvestment' theories of the business cycle (Haberler, 1937, ch. 3) is that I_x^* should be non-negative. Now $I_x^* = I_x + I_r r_x^* + I_Q Q_x^*$, so that all is well if I_r and L_x are negative and $|I_Q|$ is small. In a Say's-Law regime $I_x^* = (I_x S_r - I_r S_x)/(S_r - I_r)$, which is almost surely positive. The other two partials are positive if I_r is negative and $|I_Q|$ small.

2.3 THE DYNAMICS OF SHORT-TERM EXPECTATIONS. Three forces act on p from one instant to the next, namely expected inflation, the excess of windfall profits over windfall losses, and what we may call cost push. Their action is expressed by

$$\dot{p}/p = \lambda + H(Q^*) + \sigma(\dot{w}/w - \lambda), \qquad 0 \leqslant \sigma \leqslant 1,$$

with σ constant. H is an increasing function and $H(0) = 0$, because windfalls cause trial-and-error revision of short-term expectations. When $Q^* = 0$ and $\dot{w}/w = \lambda$ the inflation of expected prices equals the expected inflation of them, λ. The cost push term, $\sigma(\dot{w}/w - \lambda)$, allows for the possibility that when the index of efficiency wages rises or falls, firms expect prices to rise or fall in other affected industries, diverting demand to or from their own industry.

2.4 THE DYNAMICS OF EFFICIENCY WAGES. Similarly three forces act on w, namely expected inflation, the excess demand for labour, and the indexation of wages to expected prices. Their action is expressed by

$$\dot{w}/w = \lambda + F(x/v) + \tau(\dot{p}/p - \lambda), \qquad (0 \leqslant \tau \leqslant 1),$$

with τ constant. Let N^s be the supply of labour in efficiency units and v be N^s/K. Then $x/v = N/N^s$. When $x = v$ unemployment equals unfilled vacancies. The corresponding unemployment rate is the 'natural' rate, kept in being by the break-up of old jobs and imperfect information about the new jobs that replace them. (Firms with vacancies use their workers more intensively while seeking to fill them, so that the vacancies do not preclude the production of $Y = Kf(x)$.) The unemployment rate is a decreasing function of x/v. Unemployment is involuntary when x/v is <1. F is a non-decreasing function with $F(1) = 0$.

2.5 THE EQUATIONS OF MOTION. Logic requires $\sigma\tau < 1$; for $\dot{w}/w - \dot{p}/p$ cannot be both exclusively determined by x/v and exclusively determined by Q^*. Therefore the development of the economy is governed by the following equations:

$$\dot{x}/x = aH[Q^*(x, m, \lambda)] - bF(x/v)$$

$$\dot{p}/p - \lambda = cH[Q^*(x, m, \lambda)] - gF(x/v)$$

$$\dot{w}/w - \lambda = hH[Q^*(x, m, \lambda)] - cF(x/v)$$

$$\dot{v}/v = n - I^*(x, m, \lambda).$$

The first is from the derivative of $\log f'(x) = \log w/p$ with respect to time. The second and third combine the equations of sections 2.3 and 2.4. The fourth is from $\dot{v}/v = \dot{N}^s/N^s - \dot{K}/K$, with n defined as $\dot{N}^s/N^s$, the growth of the supply of labour in efficiency units. The coefficients are as follows:

$a = \phi(1 - \tau)/(1 - \sigma\tau) \geqslant 0$ with $\phi = -f'(x)/xf''(x) > 0$;

$b = \phi(1 - \sigma)/(1 - \sigma\tau) \geqslant 0$; $c = 1/(1 - \sigma\tau) > 0$;

$g = \sigma/(1 - \sigma\tau) \geqslant 0$; $h = \tau/(1 - \sigma\tau) \geqslant 0$.

In conjunction with particular assumptions about the behaviour of m, λ, and n, these equations enable us to capture the essential characteristics of many macrodynamic theories and to display their interrelationships.

3 PROCESSES WITH A CONSTANT LABOUR–CAPITAL RATIO

If $v = N^s/K$ is a constant, $\bar{v}$, the last equation in section 2.5 disappears. Two interpretations are possible: either the change in v over the relevant period is negligible, or labour-augmenting technical progress equals the growth of capital per worker. Processes with constant v can therefore be regarded as occurring in relation either to a short-period equilibrium without technical change or to a long-period equilibrium with endogenous growth. The formal structure is the same in both cases.

3.1 KEYNES'S GENERAL THEORY

3.1.1 *Expectations and short-period equilibrium.* In the *General Theory* the temporary equilibrium converges to a Marshallian short-period equilibrium with no technical change. Keynes imagines two ways by which it may be reached. In the *General Theory* for the most part he assumes as a short cut that short-term expectations are always fulfilled (Keynes, 1973a, pp. 602–3). At the outset of an instant, entrepreneurs, correctly anticipating the aggregate demand-price, choose the employment, x, that will maximize their actual profit, $\pi^*f(x) - wx$, since $p = \pi$. This is the case of the 'instantaneous multiplier'; Y^* is determined at the outset of each instant so as to make $Q^* = 0$, i.e., $I^* = S^*$, within it. However he does not insist on this. If short-term expectations are not always fulfilled, p is adjusted by trial and error from one instant to the next. This process, along with the assumption that during it the economy is in the temporary equilibrium, is actually contemplated at one point in the *General Theory* itself (Keynes, 1936, pp. 123–4), and indeed later he wished that he had made more of it there (Keynes, 1973b, pp. 180–1). We may also wish he had; for by not doing so he originated the myth that he was himself rejecting the *Treatise on Money*'s Marshallian conception of temporary equilibrium in favour of Hick's conception of it.

3.1.2 *Money wages and employment.* Keynes claims as a fundamental objection to the 'classical' theory the postulate that the real wages, w/p, on which employment, x, depends are *directly* affected by labour's bargaining about money wages (Keynes, 1936, p. 13). Keynesian unemployment is involuntary in a special way: it cannot be directly eliminated by flexibility of money wages. This dogma is first enunciated in the *Treatise on Money* (Keynes, 1930, p. 167), where changes in w have no direct tendency to bring about non-zero profits, Q^*, because, so long as they are not allowed to affect interest rates, they cause a proportionate change in the price level, $\pi^* = p + p(I^* - S^*)/f(x)$. But that is so only if they induce a proportionate change in expected prices, p, leaving w/p, and so x, unaffected. In fact he is assuming full cost push, $\sigma = 1$, so that, in section 2.5, $\dot{x}/x = aH(Q^*)$. Changes in employment are due solely to the effect of Q^* on *short-term expectations of prices in terms of wage units*, p/w, not at all to changes in the wage unit, w, itself, except in so far as they may affect the parameters determining Q^*.

Not a strong foundation for a *general* theory! Nevertheless there is a good reason for retaining this possibility in our process analysis. In the *Hicksian* temporary equilibrium the real wage is likewise determined independently of the money wage so long as m is given. When post-Keynesians who adopt the Hicksian viewpoint allow for some degree of money-wage flexibility, the qualitative behaviour of their models will be just as if there were full cost push.

3.1.3 *The trial-and-error process.* If, for simplicity, one treats as a parameter the supply of money 'in terms of wage units', so that $m = kf'(x)$ with k a positive constant, the process, with parametric λ, is $\dot{x}/x = aH[Q^*(x, kf'(x); \lambda)]$, $\dot{p}/p - \lambda = c[H(Q^*) + F(x/\bar{v})]$, $\dot{w}/w - \lambda = cF(x/\bar{v})$; for $g = c$ when $\sigma = 1$, and $h = 0$ because no wage-indexation is assumed. In the equilibrium [which is stable if $Q_x^* + Q_m^*kf''(x)$ is negative] $Q^* = 0$, $x^* < \bar{v}$, and $(\dot{p}/p)^* - \lambda = (\dot{w}/w)^* - \lambda = F(x^*/\bar{v})$. Thus Keynes really needs to assume wage inflexibility below full employment, $F(x/\bar{v}) = 0$ for $x < \bar{v}$, in addition to $\sigma = 1$. Otherwise the equilibrium would be upset by a systematic error about expected inflation. The underemployment equilibrium is then $I(0, r^*, x^*) = S(0, r^*, x^*)$, $L(0, r^*, x^*, \lambda) = m^* = kf'(x^*)$, $(\dot{p}/p)^* = (\dot{w}/w)^* = \lambda$, with $x^* < \bar{v}$.

3.2 SAY'S LAW. If m^* is such that $Q^* = 0$ for all x and λ, the process is $\dot{x}/x = -bF(x/\bar{v})$, $\dot{p}/p - \lambda = gF(x/\bar{v})$, $\dot{w}/w - \lambda = cF(x/\bar{v})$. When σ is less than unity and F is strictly increasing there is a convergence to equilibrium at the natural unemployment rate, with inflation of p and w at the rate λ, which is not determined by the system. The equilibrium equations are $I(0, r^*, x^*) = S(0, r^*, x^*)$, $x^* = \bar{v}$, $L(0, r^*, x^*; \lambda) = m^*$, $(\dot{p}/p)^* = (\dot{w}/w)^* = \lambda$.

Keynes (1936, p. 26) maintained that Say's Law would imply indeterminacy of x. Indeed it would under his assumption $\sigma = 1$, for then $b = 0$. However his allegation, that in these circumstances competition between entrepreneurs would lead to full employment, is a nonsequitur, as Hawtrey pointed out to him (Keynes, 1973b, pp. 31–2).

3.3 FULL WAGE-INDEXATION. If $\tau = 1$ then $a = 0$. The process is $\dot{x}/x = -bF(x/\bar{v})$, $\dot{p}/p - \lambda = cH[Q^*(x, m, \lambda)] + gF(x/\bar{v})$, $\dot{w}/w - \lambda = c[H(Q^*) + F(x/\bar{v})]$. As under Say's Law, there is convergence to the natural unemployment rate. But, whereas Say's Law leaves inflation indeterminate, full wage-indexation offers a painless means of manipulating it by changing the supply of money.

3.4 UNDEREMPLOYMENT EQUILIBRIUM IN A GROWING ECONOMY. The Keynesian equilibrium of section 3.1.3 can be interpreted as one of endogenous growth with involuntary unemployment.

This extension is due to Domar (1946, pp. 137–47). Actually he used the 'extreme Keynesian' assumptions that I is determined by entrepreneurs' animal spirits, with $I_x = I_r = 0$, and that $S = sf(x)$ with s a positive fraction, so that money has no effect on them. In his equilibrium (which is obviously stable, given I) $I = sf(x^*)$, and the ratio of actual output, $Y^* = Kf(x^*)$, to normal capacity output, $P = Kf(\bar{v})$, is less than unity unless I is large enough to imply $x^* - \bar{v}$.

4 BUSINESS CYCLES WITH A CONSTANT LABOUR–CAPITAL RATIO

4.1 A PURELY MONETARY THEORY OF CYCLES. The appellation is taken from Haberler (1937, ch. 2), where he expounds Hawtrey's theory, contrasting it with overinvestment theories, in which changes in v are an essential feature. The following version generalizes a model constructed by Phillips (1961, pp. 360–70) but conveying ideas much like those expressed by Hawtrey. For his first statement of them see Hawtrey (1928, ch. 5).

There are four assumptions: (i) F is strictly increasing; (ii) the ratio of the nominal money-supply to K grows at the constant rate μ; (iii) people expect inflation to be μ, i.e., $\lambda = \mu$; (iv) the equilibrium is stable.

Since m is the supply of money deflated by pK, $\dot{m}/m = \mu - \dot{p}/p$ by (ii). But from the second equation of motion in section 2.5 we have $\dot{p}/p = \lambda + cH + gF$, so that $\dot{m}/m = \mu - \lambda - cH - gF = -cH - gF$ by (iii). Hence the dynamic system in x and m is

$$\dot{x}/x = aH[Q^*(x, m; \mu)] - bF(x/\bar{v})$$

$$\dot{m}/m = -cH[Q^*(x, m; \mu)] - gF(x/\bar{v}),$$

with the equilibrium $x^* = \bar{v}$, $I(0, r^*, x^*) = S(0, r^*, x^*)$, $L(0, r^*, x^*; \mu) = m^*$. Notice that changes in μ have no real effect on it, merely altering m^*.

There is local stability if $\bar{v}[aH'(0)Q_x^* - bF_x] - m^*cH'(0)Q_m^*$ is negative. Thus even if the first term, representing the effect of x on $\dot{x}$, is positive, the second term, representing the effect of p on the course of real balances, and therefore on the course of interest rates, can (and we are assuming will) outweigh it. For Hawtrey the first term is positive. A shock induces a cumulative expansion (or contraction), which is eventually reversed because a growing shortage (or abundance) of money increases (or reduces) interest rates.

The discriminant of the linearized system is

$$D = \{\bar{v}[aH'(0)Q_x^* - bF_x] - m^*cH'(0)Q_m^*\}^2$$
$$- 4(ag + bc)\bar{v}m^*H'(0)F_xQ_m^*.$$

It implies that there will be oscillations if, *ceteris paribus*, Q_x^* is large. For $\partial D/\partial Q_x^*$ is negative when the stability condition is satisfied.

Examination of D reveals a very interesting point. With full cost push ($b = 0$) higher wage-flexibility (larger F_x) must, *ceteris paribus*, induce more rapid oscillations. Compare Keynes (1936, pp. 269–71). (Phillip's model, in which a coefficient β corresponds with our F_x, has this Keynesian characteristic.) For it increases the frequency of the turning points induced by the monetary factor without damping the cumulative process. But when b is positive high enough wage-flexibility eliminates the cumulative process entirely. No oscillations can occur.

4.2 STAGFLATION CYCLES. There have been periods during which inflation and the unemployment rate have risen or fallen simultaneously. Three assumptions are sufficient to explain this phenomenon: (i) expectations of inflation are adaptive: $\dot{\lambda} = \gamma(\dot{p}/p - \lambda)$ with γ positive and constant; (ii) monetary policy is to decrease (or increase) m when λ rises (or falls): $m = m(\lambda; \theta)$ with m_λ negative; θ is a shift parameter with m_θ positive; (iii) the equilibrium is stable.

We have then

$$\dot{x}/x = aH[Z(x, \lambda; \theta)] - bF(x/\bar{v})$$

$$\dot{\lambda} = \gamma\{cH[Z(x, \lambda; \theta)] + gF(x/\bar{v})\},$$

where $Z(x, \lambda; \theta)$ is $Q^*[x, m(\lambda; \theta), \lambda]$. The equilibrium equations are $x^* = \bar{v}$, $I(0, r^*, x^*) = S(0, r^*, x^*)$, and $L(0, r^*, x^*, \lambda^*) = m(\lambda^*; \theta)$. Observe that changes in θ affect only λ^*.

The equilibrium is locally stable if Z_λ and $\bar{v}[aH'(0)Z_x - bF_x] + \gamma cH'(0)Z_\lambda$ are both negative. The first condition is satisfied if and only if m_λ is more negative than L_λ. The authorities must ensure that real interest rates move in the same direction as λ. The second condition guarantees that the course of real interest rates eventually dissipates the cumulative expansions and contractions that may occur if $Z_x = Q_x^*$ is large.

If there are oscillations the turning points are due to the Central Bank's policy. As in the previous model higher wage-flexibility increases their frequency if b is zero, but weakens the cumulative forces if b is positive.

A shock due to a change in θ must initially cause x and λ to move in the same direction. But, whereas λ tends to a new equilibrium, x must tend back to the original $x^* = \bar{v}$. There must therefore be a period during which x and λ move in opposite directions, and since the inflation of both expected and actual prices tends to λ^*, there must also be a period during which inflation and the unemployment rate move in the same direction.

5 KEYNESIAN OVERINVESTMENT CYCLES

Henceforward we assume that $\dot{N}^s/N = n$ is a constant, thereby resuscitating the fourth equation in section 2.5.

Purely monetary theories fail to reproduce two observed features of business cycles: (1) The unemployment rate continues to fall (or rise) after entrepreneurs' expected profit-rates have begun to fall (or rise). (2) The real efficiency wage is not a monotonically increasing function of the unemployment rate. But overinvestment theories with a variable unemployment rate do reproduce them.

5.1 NATURAL AND WARRANTED RATES OF GROWTH. The natural rate is n, the sum of the growth rates of the supply of workers and efficiency per worker. The term 'warranted rate' was introduced by Harrod (1939, pp. 14–33) to designate a rate of growth of output which, if it occurs, will leave all parties satisfied that they have produced the right amount (ibid., p. 16). Several formulae are given for it there, and also in Harrod (1948, Lecture 3) and Harrod (1952, Essay 14), depending on alternative assumptions about the determinants of planned investment and planned saving. But the alternatives have one thing in common, namely that these plans are not significantly influenced by monetary policy; either the real rate of interest cannot easily be changed, or the plans are inelastic with respect to it (Harrod, 1952, pp. 95–100). Theories involving the warranted rate have an 'extreme Keynesian' bias.

In our equations of motion assume (i) $b = 0$; (ii) F is zero on a large interval around $x = v$; (iii) Q^* and I^* depend only on x; (iv) $\tau = 0$. Then $\dot{x}/x = aH[Q^*(x)]$, $\dot{p}/p - \lambda = cH[Q^*(x)]$, $\dot{w}/w = \lambda$, and $\dot{v}/v = n - I^*(x)$. The warranted rate is $\dot{Y}/Y = I^*$ with $Q^* = 0$, for it is justified by the realization, on the average, of short-term expectations.

Now as it stands this system is quite useless. The warranted rate is divorced from the natural rate, so that there is almost surely no equilibrium. But the defect can be remedied if either I or S can be assumed to depend on v.

5.2 AUTONOMOUS CONSUMPTION A rationale for making S depend on v was given by Matthews (1955, pp. 75–95), who suggested that planned consumption from a given income increases with the unemployment rate. Support for the unemployed is at the expense of planned saving. Such changes in consumption are 'autonomous' in that they are not in response to changes in income. Thus $S^* = S^*(x, v)$, with S_v^* negative. The system

$$\dot{x}/x = aH[Q^*(x, v)]$$
$$\dot{v}/v = n - I^*(x)$$

is assumed to have a unique equilibrium, $n = I^*(x^*) = S^*(x^*, v^*)$, with underemployment, i.e., $x^* < v^*$.

5.2.1 Shock-induced oscillations.
Assume that the equilibrium is stable. This is the case if $Q_x^* = I_x^* - S_x^*$ is negative and I_x^* is positive at the equilibrium point. It can be shown that there will be oscillations if $|Q_x^*|$ is sufficiently small. A shock induces overinvestment cycles, in that during the boom the growth of capital is excessive ($I^* > n$). The upper turning point is reached when the consequential fall in v pushes S^* above I^*. Similarly the lower turning point is reached when the rise in v, due to an excess of n over I^* during the slump, pushes S^* below I^*. For this kind of theory see Samuelson (1939, pp. 75–8). In his version n is zero and autonomous consumption spending is by the government.

5.2.2 Self-exciting oscillations.
Three conditions are sufficient for these: (i) The equilibrium is unstable but I_x^* is positive; (ii) nevertheless Q_x^* is negative for high and low values of x, say because short-term expected profit seems a less trustworthy guide to investment planning when it has moved far from its equilibrium; (iii) $H'(Q^*)$ is so large that the changes in x when Q^* is non-zero are much larger than the changes in v when I^* differs from n. By (i) the equilibrium is surrounded by centrifugal forces, and is almost surely not the initial state. By (ii) there are turning points for x, because when x and v are moving in opposite directions they combine to reduce windfalls, $|Q^*|$. By (iii) there are turning points for v, because of the rapidity with which net overinvestment, $|I^* - n|$, is reduced when x and v are moving in the same direction.

This essentially is Kaldor's theory (Kaldor, 1940, pp. 78–92). Only the first two conditions are given in his text, but the third is implicit there, and is explicitly stated in his appendix (Kaldor, p. 90).

5.3 AUTONOMOUS INVESTMENT.
Some investment may grow at the natural rate, n. Then $I^* = J(x) + Ae^{nt}/K$, where $KJ(x)$ is 'induced' investment, Ae^{nt} is 'autonomous' investment, and A is a positive constant. Since $e^{nt} = N^s/N_0^s$, $I^* = J(x) + (A/N_0^s)v$, or, more generally, $I^* = I^*(x, v)$ with I_v^* positive. The system

$$\dot{x}/x = aH[Q^*(x, v)]$$
$$\dot{v}/v = n - I^*(x, v)$$

is assumed to have a unique equilibrium, $n = S^*(x^*) = I^*(x^*, v^*)$, with $x^* < v^*$.

5.3.1 Shock-induced oscillations.
Assume that the equilibrium is stable. This is so if $x^* aH'(0)Q_x^* - v^* I_v^*$ is negative and $I_x^*(x^*, v^*)$ is positive. It can be shown that there must be oscillations if, ceteris paribus, Q_x^* is large. Overinvestment (underinvestment) leads to an upper (lower) turning point as changes in v push I^* below (above) S^*. For this alternative to the autonomous-consumption story see Kalecki (1939, Essay 6). He assumes that n is zero.

5.3.2 Self-exciting oscillations.
A persistent cycle follows from assumptions similar to those of Hicks (1950); cf. also Goodwin (1951, pp. 1–17): (i) The equilibrium is unstable. (ii) There is a full-employment ceiling, a rigid barrier, C, such that $x \leqslant Cv$. It is a constraint on x that is binding so long as its free motion would violate it. (iii) There is a value of x, viz. $\xi < x^*$,

such that $I_x^*(x, v)$ is positive for all $x > \xi$ but is zero for all $x \leqslant \xi$. For induced gross investment in fixed capital cannot be negative, and further induced disinvestment in inventories would disrupt the productive process (cf. Hicks, 1950, p. 104).

The cycle is attained in finite time from any non-equilibrium initial state. It has a *floor* implied by the fact that, if in its course the situation $I^*(x, v) = n$ occurs when $x \leqslant \xi$, v must remain constant until x has risen above ξ. The floor value of v is the solution to $I(\xi, v) = n$. The cycle must hit either the ceiling or the floor, but need not hit both.

6 NON-KEYNESIAN OVERINVESTMENT CYCLES

Henceforth we assume $\sigma < 1$ and some flexibility of money wages.

6.1 OSCILLATIONS WITH IMPERFECT WAGE-FLEXIBILITY.
F is strictly increasing, and there are positive constants q and l ($q > 1 > l$) such that F tends to $+\infty$ as x/v tends to q, and to $-\infty$ as x/v tends to l.

6.1.1 A 'non-monetary' theory.
Under a Say's-Law regime

$$\dot{x}/x = -bF(x/v)$$
$$\dot{v}/v = n - I^*(x),$$

where $I_x^* = (I_x S_r - I_r S_x)/(S_r - I_r) > 0$ (see section 2.2). The equilibrium, $n = I^*(v^*)$, is globally stable, but there will be shock-induced oscillations if F' is small and I_x^* is large in its neighbourhood. For the analysis and a comparison with Cassel's theory see Rose (1969, section III).

There will also be such oscillations if the elasticity of substitution between labour and capital (and therefore b) is small. The model then reproduces approximately Goodwin's growth cycle (Goodwin, 1967, pp. 54–8). (If, as he assumes, the elasticity is zero, and in addition all profits are saved and all wages consumed, every solution will be periodic in w/p and v).

If, however, wages were perfectly flexible the system would reduce to $\dot{x}/x = n - I^*(x)$, which is Solow's growth model (Solow, 1956, pp. 58–94).

6.1.2 A monetary theory.
Let monetary policy be to sustain a constant m. The system

$$\dot{x}/x = aH[Q^*(x; m, \lambda)] - bF(x/v)$$
$$\dot{v}/v = n - I^*(x; m, \lambda)$$
$$\dot{p}/p - \lambda = cH + gF$$

has only a 'quasi-equilibrium' if λ is arbitrarily given: for $\dot{x} = \dot{v} = 0$ does not imply $\dot{p}/p = \lambda$. To avoid this systematic error about long-run inflation we assume that the public foresees the value λ must take if $(\dot{p}/p)^*$ is to equal it. The equilibrium will then be $n = I(0, r^*, x^*) = S(0, r^*, x^*)$, $L(0, r^*, x^*, \lambda^*) = m$, $v^* = x^*$.

The interesting characteristic of this model is that, if the equilibrium is unstable and if I_x^* is everywhere positive, there must be self-exciting oscillations whose amplitude can be quite small. For the details see Rose (1967, pp. 153–73).

6.2 AN EQUILIBRIUM THEORY OF BUSINESS CYCLES.
Once upon a time cycles were thought to arise from unsustainable alterations in the structure of the production, brought about by inappropriate and unanticipated changes in the supply of money. Wage inflexibility was not an essential ingredient. This position, held by Hayek (1935, Lecture III) and a cohort of 'Austrian' economists, is surveyed in Haberler (1937, pp. 31–67). Recently, *Lucate duce*, there has been a remarkable attempt to recapture it (Lucas, 1975, pp. 1113–44).

The assumptions in our version of it are as follows: (i) there is continuous full employment; (ii) the growth rate of nominal money per unit of capital is a constant, μ. (iii) $\lambda = \mu$; (iv) there is no cost push ($\sigma = 0$). Therefore

$$\dot{x}/x = n - I^*(x, m; \mu)$$

$$\dot{m}/m = -H[Q^*(x, m; \mu)]$$

The equilibrium is almost certainly stable, but there can be oscillations if I_x^* and Q_m^* are small and Q_x^* is negative.

For simplicity we tell the story as if $n = \mu = \lambda = 0$. Equilibrium is disturbed by an unanticipated increase in nominal money. Interest rates fall, creating an investment boom and net windfall profits ('forced saving'). The investment boom increases capital, output, and capital intensity, $K/Y = 1/f(x)$, and is only weakly checked by the larger capital (lower x). But net windfalls raise p (reduce m) and so interest rates rise, eventually leading to an upper turning point for K and K/Y. Net windfalls are still positive, but, once K begins to fall, both higher interest rates and lower K (higher x) convert them into net losses. Now both K is falling and there are net windfall losses. But these reduce p and so interest rates fall, leading to a lower turning point for K and K/Y. Finally lower interest rates and higher K create net windfall profits once again, and a new boom of investment and windfalls begins.

This version may not please Lucas and his school. Persistent, recurrent, and unexploited profit opportunities are anathema to them. But for the inhabitants of their archipelago there persist also recurrent, unexploited profits to be made by discovering what is happening on other islands. Indeed the situations are not dissimilar. In our case what needs to be discovered is not only whether Q is positive or negative but also the whereabouts of its components, which are not predicted by the model.

HUGH ROSE

See also BUSINESS CYCLES; LOANABLE FUNDS; SAY'S LAW OF MARKETS; TEMPORARY EQUILIBRIUM; TRADE CYCLE.

BIBLIOGRAPHY

Clower, R.W. 1965. The Keynesian counterrevolution: a theoretical appraisal. In *The Theory of Interest Rates*, ed. F.H. Hahn and F.P. Brechling, London: Macmillan.

Domar, E.D. 1946. Capital expansion, rate of growth, and employment. *Econometrica* 14 April, 137–47. Reprinted in *Readings in the Modern Theory of Economic Growth*, ed. J.E. Stiglitz and H. Uzawa, Cambridge, Mass.: MIT Press, 1969.

Goodwin, R.M. 1951. The non-linear accelerator and the persistence of business cycles. *Econometrica* 19, January, 1–17.

Goodwin, R.M. 1967. A growth cycle. In *Socialism, Capitalism and Economic Growth*, ed. C.H. Feinstein, Cambridge: Cambridge University Press.

Haberler, G. 1937. *Prosperity and Depression*. Geneva: League of Nations.

Harrod, R.F. 1939. An essay in dynamic theory. *Economic Journal* 49, March, 14–33. (Errata, June, 377.) Reprinted in *Readings in the Modern Theory of Economic Growth*, ed. J.E. Stiglitz and H. Uzawa, Cambridge, Mass.: MIT Press, 1969.

Harrod, R.F. 1948. *Towards a Dynamic Economics*. London: Macmillan.

Harrod, R.F. 1952. *Economic Essays*. London: Macmillan.

Hawtrey, R.G. 1928. *Trade and Credit*. London: Longmans, Green. Reprinted in American Economic Association, *Readings in Business Cycle Theory*, Philadelphia: The Blakiston Company, 1944.

Hayek, F.A. 1935. *Prices and Production*, 2nd edn. London: George Routledge & Sons.

Hicks, J.R. 1937. Mr Keynes and the 'Classics'; a suggested interpretation. *Econometrica*. 5, April, 147–59. Republished in American Economic Association, *Readings in the Theory of Income Distribution*, Philadelphia: The Blakiston Company, 1946.

Hicks, J.R. 1939. *Value and Capital*. Oxford: Clarendon Press.

Hicks, J.R. 1950. *A Contribution to the Theory of the Trade Cycle*. Oxford: Clarendon Press.

Hicks, J.R. 1965. *Capital and Growth*. Oxford: Clarendon Press.

Kaldor, N. 1940. A model of the trade cycle. *Economic Journal* 50, March, 78–92. Republished in N. Kaldor, *Essays on Economic Stability and Growth*, London: Gerald Duckworth & Co., 1960.

Kalecki, M. 1939. *Essays in the Theory of Economic Fluctuations*. London: George Allen & Unwin.

Keynes, J.M. 1930. *A Treatise on Money*, Vol. I. London: Macmillan.

Keynes, J.M. 1936. *The General Theory of Employment, Interest and Money*. London: Macmillan.

Keynes, J.M. 1973a. *The General Theory and After*. Part I. *Preparation. The Collected Writings of John Maynard Keynes*, Vol. XIII, ed. D. Moggridge, London: Macmillan.

Keynes, J.M. 1973b. *The General Theory and After. Part II. Defence and Development. The Collected Writings of John Maynard Keynes*, Vol. XIV, ed. D. Moggridge, London: Macmillan.

Lucas, R.E. 1975. An equilibrium model of the business cycle. *Journal of Political Economy* 83(6), December, 1113–44.

Matthews, R.C.O. 1955. The saving function and the problem of trend and cycle. *Review of Economic Studies* 22, February, 75–95.

Phillips, A.W. 1961. A simple model of employment, money and prices in a growing economy. *Economica* 28, November, 360–70.

Robertson, D.H. 1940. Mr Keynes and the rate of interest. In D. H. Robertson, *Essays in Monetary Theory*, London: Staples Press. Republished in American Economic Association, *Readings in the Theory of Income Distribution*, Philadelphia: The Blakiston Company, 1946.

Rose, H. 1967. On the non-linear theory of the employment cycle. *Review of Economic Studies* 34, April, 153–73.

Rose, H. 1969. Real and monetary factors in the business cycle. *Journal of Money, Credit and Banking* 1(2), 138–53.

Rose, H. 1985. A policy rule for 'Say's Law' in a theory of temporary equilibrium. *Journal of Macroeconomics* 7(1), Winter, 1-17.

Samuelson, P.A. 1939. Interactions between the multiplier analysis and the principle of acceleration. In American Economic Association, *Review in Business Cycle Theory*, Philadelphia: The Blakiston Company, 1944.

Solow, R.M. 1956. A contribution to the theory of economic growth. *Quarterly Journal of Economics* 70, February, 65–94. Republished in *Readings in the Modern Theory of Economic Growth*, ed. J.E. Stiglitz and H. Uzawa, Cambridge, Mass.: MIT Press, 1969.

aggregate demand theory. Aggregate demand theory investigates the properties of market demand functions. These functions are obtained by summing the preference maximizing actions of individual agents. The study of aggregate demand theory is primarily motivated by the fact that market demand functions, rather than individual demand functions, are the data of economic analysis. In general, market demand functions do not inherit the structure which is imposed on individual demand functions by the utility hypothesis. Such structure, when present, enables us to obtain stronger predictions from available data.

Here we focus on three aspects of market demand functions. The first is that in certain special cases, market demand functions can be shown to satisfy the classical restrictions that characterize individual demand functions. The second is that aside from these very special cases, the economy cannot be expected to behave as an 'idealized' or 'representative' consumer. Finally, we verify that when the economy is modelled as a continuum of infinitesimally sized agents market demand functions may in some respects be better behaved than individual demand functions. For an elaboration of the material through Example 3 see Shafer and Sonnenschein (1982).

SECTION 1. This section presents the notation and briefly reviews the properties of individual demand functions. There are n consumers and l commodities. The consumption set of each consumer is R_+^l. The preferences of a consumer are described by a weak ordering $\succsim$ of R_+^l. If $x \succsim y$ we say 'x is at least as good as y'; if $x \succsim y$ and not $y \succsim x$, then we write $x \succ y$ and say 'x is preferred to y'; if $x \succsim y$ and $y \succsim x$, we write $x \sim y$ and say

'x is indifferent to y'. The preference relation $\succsim$ is continuous if $\{(x, y) : x \succsim y\}$ is closed; $\succsim$ is locally non-satiated if for each $x \in R_+^l$ and every $\eta > 0$ there exists a y such that $y \succ x$ and $\| x - y \| < \eta$; $\succsim$ is strictly convex if $x \succsim y$, $x \neq y$ and $0 < \alpha < 1$ implies that $\alpha x + (1 - \alpha) y \succ y$; $\succsim$ is representable if there exists a 'utility function' $U : R_+^l \to R$ such that $x \succsim y$ if and only if $u(x) \geq u(y)$; $\succsim$ is homothetic if it is representable by a utility function which is homogeneous of degree 1. It is assumed throughout that preference relations for all consumers are continuous, locally non-satiated and strictly convex. A continuous function $f : R_{++}^l \times R_+ \to R_+^l$ is a candidate consumer demand function if it satisfies (Budget balance) $p \cdot f(p, I) = I$ for all $(p, I) \in R_{++}^l \times R_+$ and (Homogeneity) $f(\lambda p, \lambda I) = f(p, I)$ for all $\lambda > 0$ and $(p, I) \in R_{++}^l \times R_+$. At prices p and income I, $f(p, I)$ denotes the commodity bundle purchased. If there exists a preference relation $\succsim$ such that for each $(p, I) \in R_{++}^l \times R_+$, $f(p, I)$ is the $\succsim$ maximal element in the set $\{x : p \cdot x \leq I\}$, then f is a consumer demand function.

Let f be a differentiable candidate consumer demand function. The Slutsky matrix associated with f is an $l \times l$ matrix denoted by $\Sigma(p, I)$ whose $(h, k)^{\text{th}}$ term is defined by

$$\sigma_{hk}(p, I) = \frac{\partial f_h}{\partial p_k}(p, I) + f_k(p, I) \cdot \frac{\partial f_h}{\partial I}(p, I).$$

The classical theorems of demand theory state that, if f is a consumer demand fucntion, then for all (p, I) $\Sigma(p, I)$ is symmetric and negative semi-definite. The integrability Theorem establishes the converse (see Hurwicz and Uzawa, 1971).

Let $\Delta^{n-1} = \{(x_1, x_2, \ldots, x_n) | x_i \geq 0 \text{ for all } i \text{ and } \Sigma x_i = 1\}$. Given prices p and income I, the distribution of income among consumers is defined by a mapping $\delta : R_{++}^l \times R_+ \to \Delta^{n-1}$. Thus $\delta^i(p, I) I$ is the ith individual's income when prices are p and income is I. A candidate demand function F is a market demand function relative to the distribution of income mapping δ if there exists n consumer demand functions $f^1, \ldots, f^n$ such that $F(p, I) = \Sigma_i f^i[p, \delta^i(p, I) I]$ holds for all $(p, I) \in R_{++}^l \times R_+$. If $(f^1, \ldots, f^n)$ are individual demand functions and if for all δ, $\bar{\delta} \in \Delta^{n-1}$, $\Sigma_i f^i(p, \delta^i I) = \Sigma_i f^i(p, \bar{\delta}^i I)$, then market demand is independent of the distribution of income.

SECTION 2. This section considers the conditions under which market demand functions belong to the class generated by a single consumer. The following classic result, due to Antonelli (1886) and later independently discovered by Gorman (1953) and Nataf (1953) gives necessary and sufficient conditions for a market demand function to be both independent of the distribution of income and generated by a preference relation.

Theorem 1 (Antonelli). Market demand is independent of the distribution of income and is preference generated if and only if there is a homothetic preference relation $\succsim$ such that each consumer demand function f^i is derived from $\succsim$. In this case, market demand is also generated by f^i.

Examples 1 and 2 demonstrate that if either the condition that preferences are homothetic or the condition that preferences of all consumers are identical is dropped, then market demand may depend on the distribution of income [for elaboration of, these examples, and of Example 3, see Shafer and Sonnenschein (1982)].

Example 1. Let two consumers have identical preferences on R_+^2 that are represented by $U(x, y) = xy + y$ and let prices be $(1, 1)$. If the distribution of income is $I_1 = 1$, $I_2 = 1$, then aggregate demand for x and y is 0 and 2 respectively. If the distribution of income is $I_1 = 2$, $I_2 = 0$, then aggregate demand for x and y is $\frac{1}{2}$ and $1\frac{1}{2}$ respectively.

Example 2. Let two consumers have homothetic preferences on R_+^2 represented by $U_1(x, y) = x$ and $U_2(x, y) = y$. Then market demand depends completely on the distribution of income.

If the income share of each consumer is fixed [i.e. $\delta(p, I)$ is a constant vector $(\delta^1, \ldots, \delta^n)$ for all (p, I)], then homotheticity of each individual preference relation is sufficient for market demand to be utility generated. This result is due to Eisenberg (1961).

Theorem 2 (Eisenberg). If the preferences of each agent can be represented by a homogeneous of degree one utility function U^i on R_+^l, and if income shares are fixed at $(\delta^1, \ldots, \delta^n) \in \Delta^{n-1}$, then market demand is generated by the homogeneous of degree one utility function U

$$U(x) = \max \prod_{i=1}^{n} [U^i(x^i)]^{\delta i} \text{ s.t. } \sum_i x^i = x.$$

Under the hypothesis of Theorem 2 market demand is determined by maximizing a social welfare function that gives each individual's preferences, a weight equal to his share of total income. The following example indicates that a fixed distribution of income, but no restrictions on agents' preferences is not sufficient to ensure that market demand is utility generated.

Example 3 (Hicks, 1957). There are two consumers who share market income equally. Market budgets for two different price ratios are indicated with dotted lines. The choices of the first individual are indicated by a cross and those of the second by a circle. Market demand at the steeper budget is denoted by D while demand at the flatter budget is denoted by D'. The choice of each individual is consistent with utility maximization; however, since D is chosen in the aggregate when D' is available and since D' is chosen when D is available, market demand is not utility generated.

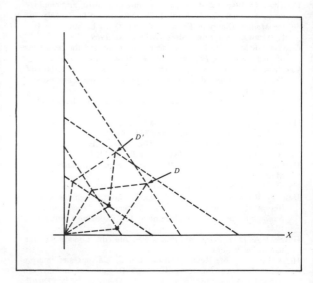

Theorems 1 and 2 referred to situations in which the distribution of income was determined exogenously. In a much

A final result, which illustrates a theorem due to Hildenbrand (1983), gives conditions under which market demand is neces-

referenced paper, Samuelson (1956) presented a theorem in which the distribution of income is determined as a solution to a maximization problem. Specifically, it is assumed that for every price-income combination, the government distributes income so as to maximize a Bergsonian social welfare function: let δ denote the distribution of income function determined by this process. Samuelson's theorem asserts that under these conditions, market demand relative to δ is utility generated. Proofs of the result may also be found in Chipman and Moore (1979), and Dow and Sonneschein (1983).

Theorem 3. Suppose that f^i is generated by U^i for $i = 1, \ldots, n$. If there exists a Bergsonian social welfare function $W(U^1, \ldots, U^n)$ that is increasing in all its arguments and such that for all $(p, I) \in R_{++}^l \times R_+$,

$$\delta(p, I) \in \operatorname*{arg\,max}_{(d^1, \ldots, d^n) \in \Delta^{n-1}} W\{U^1[f^1(p, d^1 I)], \ldots, U^n[f^n(p, d^n I)]\},$$

then aggregate demand $\Sigma_i f^i[p, \delta^i(p, I)I]$ is generated by the utility function

$$U(x) = \max W[U^1(x^1), \ldots, U^n(x^n)] \text{ s.t. } \sum_i x^i = x.$$

SECTION 3. Theorems 1–3 identify sets of assumptions under which market demand functions belong to the same class as consumer demand functions. Theorem 4 indicates that in the absence of these assumptions, none of the classical restrictions holds for market demand functions. In particular any values of demand and its derivatives that are consistent with Homogeneity and Budget Balance are possible.

Theorem 4 (Sonnenschein). Let F be an arbitrary C^1 candidate demand function for l commodities and let $n \geq l$. Then, for any $(p, I) \in R_{++}^l \times R_+$, there exists a market demand function generated by n consumers with demand functions $f^1, \ldots, f^n$ such that

$$F(p, I) = \sum_{i=1}^{n} f^i\left(p, \frac{I}{n}\right)$$

and

$$\frac{\partial F_k}{\partial P_j}(p, I) = \sum \frac{\partial f_k^i}{\partial p_j}\left(p, \frac{I}{n}\right), \quad \text{for each } k, j.$$

More general results of this nature exist for market excess demand functions; see Sonnenschein (1973a), Debreu (1974) and Shafer and Sonnenschein (1982) section 4.

SECTION 4. In this section an example of an economy with a continuum of infinitesimally sized agents is presented in which market demand is continuous despite the fact that individual demand functions are discontinuous: market demand is better behaved than individual demand. The point that is made here is quite general and is of importance in establishing the existence of competitive equilibrium without need for the assumption that preferences are convex; see Debreu (1982) section 4.

Example 4. There are two commodities x and y and the preferences of a consumer of type a are represented by the utility function $U(x, y, a) = x^2 + a^2 \cdot y^2$. The income of each consumer is fixed at unity and the consumption set of each consumer if R_+^2. The price of commodity y in terms of the numeraire commodity x is denoted by p. The distribution of

agent types is specified by defining the following density function g, over the domain of a:

$$g(a) = \begin{cases} 2 & \text{if } a \in [\frac{1}{4}, \frac{3}{4}] \\ 0 & \text{otherwise.} \end{cases}$$

Strict convexity of preferences is violated for each a, and consequently, the demand function of each consumer type is not single valued. The demand function for y as a function of p is given by

$$f^a(p) = \begin{cases} \dfrac{1}{p} & \text{if } p < a \\ 0 & \text{if } p > a \\ \left[\dfrac{1}{a}, 0\right] & \text{if } p = a. \end{cases}$$

The graph of f^a is drawn in Figure 2.

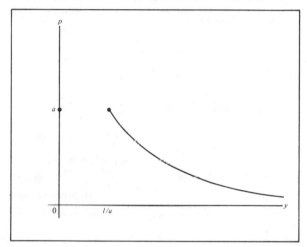

Figure 2

The multi valued function f^a is not well-behaved in the sense that it jumps at a. Let $F(p)$ denote market demand at price p. By definition

$$F(p) = 2\int_{a-1/4}^{a=3/4} f^a(p)\,da$$

$$= 2\int_{a=1/4}^{a=p} (0)\,da + 2\int_{a-p}^{a=3/4} \frac{1}{p}\,da$$

$$= \frac{3}{2p} - 2.$$

Thus, market demand is single-valued and differentiable in the entire domain of p, despite the fact that these properties do not hold for any given a. One way to understand the result is to observe that for each p, the relative mass of consumers whose demand is discontinuous at p is zero. This observation also illustrates the importance of the assumption that each agent is a 'small' part of the market and that preferences are dispersed. The result would not hold if the density function was assumed to be

$$h(a) = \begin{cases} 1 & \text{if } a \in [\frac{1}{4}, \frac{3}{4}] \\ \frac{1}{2} & \text{if } a = 1 \\ 0 & \text{otherwise} \end{cases}.$$

sarily downward sloping. Again, the point is that with the continuum of agents market demand may be better behaved than individual demand.

Theorem 5. Consider an economy in which all individuals have identical preferences but differ in their incomes. In particular, assume that income is uniformly distributed over the interval [0, 1] and let $f(p, I)$ denote the identical demands of the individuals with income I who face prices p. Under the above conditions, the mean demand for each commodity has a nonpositive slope.

A sketch of a proof of the theorem follows: It is well known from consumer demand theory that the sign of the term $\partial f_k(p, I)/\partial p_k$ can be either positive or negative. Since individual substitution effects are nonpositive, to prove the result it is sufficient to demonstrate that the mean income effect is nonpositive.

The income effect as a result of a change in the price of commodity k on the demand for k, for an individual with income I, is given by

$$-f_k(p, I)\frac{\partial}{\partial I}f_k(p, I).$$

Therefore, the mean income effect is given by

$$-\int_0^1 f_k(p, I)\frac{\partial}{\partial I}f_k(p, I)\, dI = -\frac{1}{2}\int_0^1 \frac{\partial}{\partial I}[f_k^2(p, I)]\, dI$$
$$= -\tfrac{1}{2}[f_k^2(p, 1) - f_k^2(p, 0)]$$
$$= -\tfrac{1}{2}f_k^2(p, 1) \leqslant 0,$$

which establishes the result.

H. SONNENSCHEIN

See also DEMAND THEORY; HOMOGENEOUS AND HOMOTHETIC RELATIONS; INTEGRABILITY OF DEMAND.

BIBLIOGRAPHY

Antonelli, G.B. 1886. *Sulla Teoria Matematica della Economia Politica*; Pisa: Nella Tipognafia del Folchetto. Translated by J.S. Chipman and A.P. Kirman in *Preferences, Utility and Demand*, ed. J.S. Chipman et al., New York: Harcourt Brace Jovanovich, 333–60.

Arrow, K.J. and Intriligator, M.D. (eds) 1981–6. *Handbook of Mathematical Economics*, Vols I, II and III. Amsterdam: North-Holland.

Chipman, J.S., Hurwicz, L. Richter, M.K. and Sonnenschein, H.F. (eds) 1971. *Preferences, Utility and Demand*. New York: Harcourt Brace Jovanovich.

Chipman, J.S. and Moore, J. 1979. On social welfare functions and the aggregation of preferences. *Journal of Economic Theory* 21, 111–39.

Debreu, G. 1974. Excess demand functions. *Journal of Mathematical Economics* 1, 15–23.

Debreu, G. 1982. Existence of competitive equilibrium. Chapter 15 in *Handbook of Mathematical Economics*, ed. K.J. Arrow and M.D. Intriligator, Amsterdam: North-Holland.

Dow, J. and Sonnenschein, H. 1983. Samuelson and Chipman – Moore on utility generated community demand. In *Prices, Competition and Equilibrium*, ed. M. Peston and R. Quandt, Oxford: Philip Allan Publishers.

Eisenberg, B. 1961. Aggregation of utility functions. *Management Science* 7, 337–50.

Gorman, W.M. 1953. Community preference fields. *Econometrica* 21, 63–80.

Hicks, J.R. 1957. *A Revision of Demand Theory*. Oxford: Clarendon Press.

Hildenbrand, W. 1983. On the 'law of demand'. *Econometrica* 51, 997–1020.

Hurwicz, L. and Uzawa, H. 1971. On the integrability of demand functions. In *Preferences, Utility and Demand*, ed. J.S. Chipman et al., New York: Harcourt Brace Jovanovich, 114-48.

Nataf, A. 1953. Sur des questions d'agrégation en économétrie. Publications de l'Institute de Statistique de l'Université de Paris 2, 5–61.

Samuelson, P. 1956. Social indifference curves. *Quarterly Journal of Economics* 70, 1–22.

Shafer, W. and Sonnenschein, H. 1982. Market demand and excess demand functions. Chapter 14 in *Handbook of Mathematical Economics*, ed. K.J. Arrow and M.D. Intriligator, Amsterdam: North-Holland.

Sonnenschein, H. 1973a. Do Walras' identity and continuity characterize the class of community excess demand functions? *Journal of Economic Theory* 6, 345–54.

Sonnenschein, H. 1973b. The utility hypothesis and market demand theory. *Western Economic Journal* 11, 404–10.

aggregate production function. *See* PRODUCTION FUNCTIONS.

aggregate supply function. John Maynard Keynes wrote *The General Theory* (1936) in order to show that Say's Law, where (aggregate) supply created its own (aggregate) demand, was not applicable to a monetary, production economy. In a Say's Law world, the aggregate demand function would be coincident with the aggregate supply function so that 'effective demand, instead of having a unique equilibrium value, is an infinite range of values all equally admissible; and the amount of employment is indeterminate except in so far as the marginal disutility of labour sets an upper limit' (Keynes, 1936, p. 26). In other words, Say's Law assumes there is no barrier to the economy obtaining, in the long run, a full employment output level.

Keynes claimed that Say's Law 'is not the true law relating the aggregate demand and supply functions' (1936, p. 26) and hence the 'true' relationship between the aggregate demand and the aggregate supply functions 'remains to be written and without which all discussions concerning the volume of aggregate employment are futile' (1936, p. 26). As Keynes pointed out in a letter to D. H. Robertson (Keynes, 1973), however, his aggregate supply function was 'simply the age-old supply function'. Keynes's revolutionary analysis stemmed from his belief that in a monetary economy, the aggregate demand function differed from, and was *not* coincident with, the aggregate supply function.

Keynes argued that the aggregate supply function could be readily derived from ordinary Marshallian micro-supply functions (1936, pp. 44–5) and that, therefore, the properties of the aggregate supply function 'involved few considerations which are not already familiar' (1936, p. 89). Keynes believed that 'it was the part played by the aggregate demand function which has been overlooked' (1936, p. 89). Hence, though Keynes briefly described the aggregate supply function (1936, pp. 25, 44–5) and its inverse, the employment function (1936, pp. 89, 280–1), the bulk of *The General Theory* was devoted to developing the characteristics of aggregate demand while the aggregate supply function was treated perfunctorily.

Consequently, the 'Keynesian Revolution' analytical structure (which Samuelson dubbed 'neoclassical synthesis Keynesianism') which was developed by Hicks (1937), Modigliani (1944), and Klein (1947) emphasized the novelty of the aggregate demand-side of Keynes's economic system. In losing sight of Keynes's well-known 'age-old' aggregate supply function, the Keynesian Revolution went off half-cocked and lost its foundation in Marshallian microeconomics.

In the 1954–7 period, there was a flurry of activity attempting to rediscover the basis of Keynes's aggregate supply function. This discussion culminated in Weintraub's 1957 article which Clower, in personal correspondence (dated 1 November 1957), characterized as 'a beautifully clear statement of what Keynes "should have meant" if we suppose that he was a rational being'.

The aggregate supply function as stated by Keynes and explicitly developed by Weintraub (1957), Davidson (1962), and Davidson and Smolensky (1964) relates the aggregate number of workers (N) that profit-maximizing entrepreneurs would want to hire for each possible level of expected sales proceeds (Z) – given the money wage rate, technology, the degree of competition (or monopoly), and the degree of integration of firms (cf. Keynes, 1936, p. 245). For any given degree of firm integration in the aggregate, GNP is directly related to total sales proceeds. If firms are fully integrated, aggregate sales proceeds equals GNP.

Following Keynes's argument (1936, p. 41) that money values and quantities of employment are the two 'fundamental units of quantity' to be used when dealing with aggregates, the aggregate supply proceeds are normally specified either in money terms (Z) or in Keynes's wage unit terms (Z_w) which is money sales proceeds divided by the money wage rate. Hence the aggregate supply function is specified as:

$$Z = f_1(N) \tag{1}$$

or

$$Z_w - f_2(N) \tag{2}$$

For purposes of simplicity and ease of comparability with the ordinary Marshallian micro-supply function, only the form of equation (1) will be developed in the following discussion. Equational form (2) of the aggregate supply function can then be derived merely by dividing all money sums expressed in equation (1) by the existing money wage rate.

The Marshallian supply curve for a single firm (s_f) indicates the profit-maximizing output possibilities for alternative market demand conditions. The supply schedule of profit-maximizing, alternative price–quantity combinations depend on the degree of competition (or monopoly) of the firm (k) and its marginal costs (MC).

The degree of monopoly of the firm depends on the market demand condition it faces. In the most simple case, as aggregate demand changes the demand curve facing the firm shifts without altering the degree of monopoly of the firm; for example, in the perfectly competitive case, shifts in the firm's demand curve do not alter the competitive market conditions. In more complex cases the degree of monopoly may vary as aggregate demand changes and the firm's demand curve shifts, i.e. $k = f(N)$.

Thus the firm's supply schedule can be specified in terms of its degree of monopoly power as given by a mark-up – whose magnitude depends on the price elasticity of demand facing the firm and its marginal costs:

$$s_f = f_3(k_f, MC_f) \tag{3}$$

where k_f is the firm's mark-up over its marginal costs (MC_f).

The profit-maximizing firm's mark-up is equal to Lerner's (1934) measure of the degree of monopoly power which is $[1/E_{df}]$ where E_{df} is the price elasticity of demand facing the firm for any given level of effective demand. Thus, for a perfectly competitive firm, $k = 0$ for all potential production flows and only marginal costs affect the position and shape

of its marginal cost curve. For conditions of less than perfect competition, $k > 0$, and hence both marginal costs and monopoly power at each potential output level affect the firm's market offerings as reflected in its supply curve offerings.

The firm's marginal cost (MC_f), assuming labour is the only variable input in the production process, equals the money wage (w) divided by marginal labour productivity (MP) where the latter is a function of employment (and the laws of returns involved in the technology of the firm). For any given 'law of returns' facing the firm, there will be a different marginal production cost structure. For example, with diminishing returns, the marginal production costs increase with increasing output; for constant returns, marginal production costs are constant, while for decreasing returns marginal costs decline with increases in output and employment. (Of course, the latter case is incompatible with perfect competition; it requires some degree of monopoly and hence some positive mark-up, $[k > 0]$ over marginal costs, so that market price covers average unit costs.) If marginal user costs (MUC) are not negligible, then $MC_f = [w/MP + MUC]$.

The Marshallian industry flow-supply schedule (s) is obtained simply by the usual lateral summation of the individual firm's supply curves; it is, therefore, related to the average industry mark-up or 'average' degree of monopoly and the industry's marginal cost schedule, i.e.,

$$s = f_4[k, MC] \tag{4}$$

where the symbols without subscripts are the industry's equivalent to the aforementioned firm's variables. Thus given (a) the production technology, (b) the money wage, and (c) the degree of monopoly based on specified market conditions for any given potential output and employment level, a unique industry supply function can be derived.

Although output across firms in the same industry may be homogeneous and therefore can be aggregated to obtain the industry supply schedule [equation (4)], this homogeneity of output assumption cannot be accepted as the basis for summing across industries to obtain the aggregate supply function (Keynes, 1936, ch. 4). Accordingly, the Marshallian industry supply function, s, which relates prices (p) and quantities (q) must be transformed into Keynes's industry supply function which relates total industry sales proceeds in money terms (z) with total industry employment hiring (n), i.e.,

$$z = f_5(n) \tag{5}$$

Since given returns, the money-wage, and the degree of monopoly, every point on the Marshallian industry supply function, s, is associated with a unique profit-maximizing price–quantity combination whose multiple equals total expected sales proceeds (i.e., $p \times q = z$) and since every industry output level (q) can be associated with a unique industry hiring level, i.e. $q = f(n)$, then every point of equation (4) of the s-curve in p–q space can be transformed to a point on a z-curve in pq–n space to obtain equation (5) supra.

Hence for each industry in which the traditional Marshallian supply function can be formulated in terms of equation (4), a Keynes industry supply function [equation (5)] can also be uniquely specified. All of Keynes's industry supply functions can then be aggregated together to obtain the aggregate supply function in terms of aggregate money proceeds (Z) and the aggregate quantity of employment units (N) as specified in equation (1), provided one reasonably assumes that corresponding to any given point of aggregate supply there is a unique distribution of proceeds and employment between the different industries in the economy (Keynes, 1936, p. 282).

PAUL DAVIDSON

See also KEYNES, JOHN MAYNARD; KEYNES'S GENERAL THEORY.

BIBLIOGRAPHY

Davidson, P. 1962. More on the aggregate supply function. *Economic Journal* 72, June, 452–7.

Davidson, P. and Smolensky, E. 1964. *Aggregate Supply and Demand Analysis.* New York: Harper & Row.

Hicks, J.R. 1937. Mr Keynes and the Classics; a suggested interpretation. *Econometrica* 5, April, 147–59.

Keynes, J.M. 1936. *The General Theory of Employment, Interest and Money.* New York: Harcourt, Brace.

Keynes, J.M. 1973. *The Collected Writings of John Maynard Keynes,* Vol.XIII, ed. D. Moggridge, London: Macmillan.

Klein, L.R. 1947. *The Keynesian Revolution.* New York: Macmillan.

Lerner, A.P. 1934. The concept of monopoly and the measurement of monopoly power. *Review of Economic Studies* 1, June, 157–75.

Modigliani, F. 1944. Liquidity preference and the theory of interest and money. *Econometrica* 12, January, 45–88.

Weintraub, S. 1957. The micro-foundations of aggregate demand and supply. *Economic Journal* 67, September, 455–70.

aggregation of economic relations. A simplification or aggregation problem is faced by a research worker whenever he finds that his data are too numerous or in too much detail to be manageable and feels the need to reduce or combine the detailed data in some manner. He will want to use aggregative measures for his new groups. But what will be the effect of this procedure on his results? How can he choose among alternative procedures? In grouping his data and/or relations he must also decide how many groups to use; a smaller number is more manageable but will cause more of the original information to be lost. The research worker seeks a solution of this problem that will best serve his objectives, or those of some decision-maker who will use his results.

For example, say that a true micro-model is

$$y = Px + v \tag{1}$$

where y is a vector of g endogenous variables and x is a vector of h predetermined variables. It is desired to work with a macro-model

$$\tilde{y} = \bar{P}\tilde{x} + \tilde{v} \tag{2}$$

where $\tilde{y}$ is a reduced *vector* of f aggregated endogenous variables, and $\tilde{x}$ is a reduced vector of j predetermined variables, where $f < g$, and $j < h$. The reduction is to be made in such a manner that when predictions are made with the macro-model, results will be as close as possible to those that could have been obtained with the micro-model.

General reviews of the aggregation problem in the various stages of its development may be found in Malinvaud (1956), Theil (1962), Fisher (1969) and Chipman (1976).

It is not surprising that the aggregation problem in economics began to attract attention with the development of econometrics since the task of inferring realistic models becomes particularly acute when only limited empirical data are available. It was only a dozen years or so after the founding of the Econometric Society that there occurred an early methodological discussion of the problem in Klein (1946), May (1946, 1947) and Shou Shan Pu (1946). This discussion related specifically to simultaneous equation macro-models.

The important and pioneering work of Theil (1954) treated the question of the consequences of aggregation in a stochastic model of simultaneous equations. Theil derived relationships between estimated parameters in detailed and aggregated models when the parameters are estimated by linear unbiased methods.

The approach of Theil, that of measuring the consequences of aggregation in terms of the discrepancies from a true micro-model, leads directly to the goal of optimal aggregation – that is, selecting a mode of aggregation resulting in a macro-model based on the data at hand and a given degree of detail, such that the expected discrepancies are minimized. To pursue this goal it is necessary to postulate a loss function in terms of the discrepancies and to have available a procedure for minimizing expected loss from a very large number of alternatives. Say that it is desired to predict y in (1) with small error, but that it is also desired to use a simplified model, $\tilde{P}$, of the same size as P, so the prediction will be

$$\tilde{y} = \tilde{P}x. \tag{3}$$

The simplified model $\tilde{P}$ is considered to be subject to certain a priori restrictions. For example, it may be assumed to be of a rank lower than that of P, or to be expressible in the form

$$\tilde{P} = T'\bar{P} \tag{4}$$

where $\bar{P}$ is an *aggregated matrix* of smaller order than P, and T' is given a priori.

Say that the cost of this procedure to the investigator is

$$c = E(\tilde{y} - y)'C(\tilde{y} - y), \tag{5}$$

where C is a known positive-definite matrix that weights the relative importance of forecast errors in the various endogenous variables and their interactions. It has been shown that

$$c = \operatorname{tr} C(\tilde{P} - P)M(\tilde{P} - P)' + \text{constant} \tag{6}$$

where $M = E(xx')$. The problem of choosing $\tilde{P}$ so as to minimize c may be called a *simplification problem*.

The lower the rank of $\bar{P}$, or the smaller the dimensions of $\bar{P}$, the more severe is the aggregation and simplification. To find the matrix $\bar{P}$, or $\tilde{P}$, that minimizes the cost c subject to a given level of severity of aggregation, is a well defined but not a trivial problem. It may be accomplished in two steps: first, finding the optimal $\bar{P}$ conditional on a partition and second, searching for the partition that gives a minimum minimorum c. For the second step a computer is necessary. First suggested by Hurwicz (1952) and ·Malinvaud (1956), the optimal aggregation approach has been extended and applied to a number of econometric problems by Fisher (1953, 1962, 1969) and Chipman (1975a, 1975b, 1976).

One of the most frequent applications and most strongly felt needs of aggregation is to Leontief inter-industry (input–output) models. We can make our equation (1) above into an input–output model by setting $g = h$, defining y as the set of outputs, x the set of final demands, and defining $P = (I - A)^{-1}$, where A is the matrix of technical coefficients. Here it is natural to require that the aggregation over both rows and columns of the matrix A involve the same partition, that is, that the combination of 'small industries' into 'large industries' implied by the row partition be the same as for the column partition. Some excellent preliminary discussion of the model is given by Leontief (1947). Conditions for obtaining perfect (without error) aggregation in this system were given by Hatanaka (1952).

Since the input–output model may be considered a special case of the simultaneous equations model, the same principles of optimal aggregation may be applied to find an aggregated or a simplified model. This approach is used in McCarthy (1956), Fisher (1958, 1969) and Neudecker (1970).

There is a well known correspondence between such concepts as distance, variance, and scatter, on the one hand, and entropy and information content on the other. If an m by n rectangular table contains a set X of numbers that sum to unity, the *entropy* of the table may be defined as

$$E(X) = - \sum_{i,j=1}^{n} x_{ij} \log x_{ij}. \qquad (7)$$

This may be considered a measure of the degree of sameness or homogeneity of the elements of the matrix X.

If X is aggregated by rows and by columns, an aggregated entropy may be found from the aggregated cells of the smaller matrix. This entropy will be larger than that of X. The difference may be regarded as a loss of information from the aggregation. The problem may be posed: to find the mode of aggregation (to a specified degree of detail) that minimizes this loss.

Skolka (1964) and Theil (1967) have applied this idea to input–output tables. Fisher (1969, ch. 6) has shown an exact correspondence between this problem and the minimization of his objective function (5). Recent insights into the aggregation problem in input–output analysis are found in Tintner and Sondermann (1977) and Laisney (1984).

Practically all of the work reviewed so far has proceeded on the assumption that the micro-model is true, or at least that the microdata with which the investigator works form an unbiased estimate of the truth. Thus, the expected loss from using an aggregated artefact can never be negative, and can be tolerated only if there is a compensating gain from aggregation, owing to increased manageability, understanding, etc., of a smaller model.

But in Grunfeld and Griliches (1960) an example was presented where the errors were *less* after aggregation. The monograph of Ringwald (1980) made the point that this situation is probably very frequent in economics, especially as so-called microdata have in reality undergone much processing and are a pre-aggregation of unobserved, yet more detailed data, probably subject to bias. Ringwald's critique has been followed up by Chipman (1985), who has developed formulae expressing the relationship between stage 1 and stage 2 models, where stage 1 is the result of some previous aggregation. The issue is obviously of considerable importance and it is evident that more work needs to be done.

WALTER D. FISHER

See also SEPARABILITY.

BIBLIOGRAPHY

Chipman, J.S. 1975a. The aggregation problem in econometrics. *Advances in Applied Probability*, September.

Chipman, J.S. 1975b. Optimal aggregation in large-scale economic models. *Sankhya* 37(4), 121–59.

Chipman, J.S. 1976. Estimation and aggregation in economics: an application of the theory of generalized inverses. In *Generalized Inverses and Applications*, ed. M.Z. Nashed, New York: Academic Press.

Chipman, J.S. 1985. Testing for reduction of mean-square error by aggregation in dynamic econometric models. In *Multivariate Analysis VI: Proceedings of the Sixth International Symposium on Multivariate Analysis*, Amsterdam: North-Holland.

Day, R.H. 1963. On aggregating linear programming models of production. *Journal of Farm Economics* 45, November, 797–813.

Fei, J.C.H. 1956. A fundamental theorem for the aggregation problem of input–output analysis. *Econometrica* 24(4), October, 400–412.

Fisher, W.D. 1953. On a pooling problem from the statistical decision viewpoint. *Econometrica* 21(4), October, 567–85.

Fisher, W.D. 1958. Criteria for aggregation in input–output analysis. *Review of Economics and Statistics* 40(3), August, 250–60.

Fisher, W.D. 1962. Optimal aggregation in multi-equation prediction models. *Econometrica* 30(4), October, 744–69.

Fisher, W.D. 1969. *Clustering and Aggregation in Economics*. Baltimore: The Johns Hopkins Press.

Fisher, W.D. 1979. A note on aggregation and disaggregation. *Econometrica* 47(3), May, 739–46.

Fisher, W.D. and Kelley, P.L. 1968. Selecting representative firms in linear programming. Ch. 13 in *Economic Analysis and Agricultural Policy*, ed. R.H. Day, Ames: Iowa State University Press, 1982.

Gorman, W.M. 1968. The structure of utility functions. *Review of Economic Studies* 35, October, 367–90.

Grunfeld, Y. and Griliches, Z. 1960. Is aggregation necessarily bad? *Review of Economics and Statistics* 42(1), February, 1–13.

Hatanaka, M. 1952. Note on consolidation within a Leontief system. *Econometrica* 20(2), April, 301–3.

Hurwicz, L. 1952. Aggregation in macroeconomic models [abstract]. *Econometrica* 20(3), July, 489–91.

Ijiri, Y. 1971. Fundamental queries in aggregation theory. *Journal of the American Statistical Association* 66, December, 766–82.

Klein, L.R. 1946. Remarks on the theory of aggregation. *Econometrica* 14(4), October, 303–12.

Laisney, F. 1984. Theory and practice in optimal aggregation of linear models. *Economic Letters*, 315–24.

Leontief, W. 1947. Introduction to a theory of the internal structure of functional relationships. *Econometrica* 15(4), October, 361–73.

Malinvaud, E. 1956. L'agrégation dans les modèles économiques. *Cahiers du Seminaire d'Économétrie* No. 4, Paris: Centre National de la Recherche Scientifique.

May, K. 1946. The aggregation problem for a one-industry model. *Econometrica* 14(4), October, 285–98.

May, K. 1947. Technological change and aggregation. *Econometrica* 15(1), January, 51–63.

McCarthy, J. 1956. Aggregation in the Leontief model. Joint Allied Social Science Association meeting in Cleveland, Ohio, 27 December.

Nataf, A. 1960. Résultats et directions de recherche dans la théorie de l'agrégation. *Logic, methodology and philosophy of science. Proceedings of the 1960 International Congress*, ed. E. Nagel, P. Suppes and A. Tarski, Stanford, California: Stanford University Press, 1962.

Neudecker, H. 1970. Aggregation in input–output analysis: an extension of Fisher's method. *Econometrica* 38(6), November, 921–26.

Ringwald, K. 1980. *A Critique of Models in Linear Aggregation Structures*. Boston: Oelgeschlager, Gunn & Hain.

Schneeweiss, H. 1965. Das Aggregationsproblem. *Statistische Hefte*.

Shou Shan Pu. 1946. A note on macroeconomics. *Econometrica* 14(4), October, 299-302.

Skolka, J. 1964. *The Aggregation Problem in Input–output Analysis*. Prague: Czechoslovakian Academy of Sciences.

Sondermann, D. 1973. Optimale Aggregation von grossen linearen Gleichungssystemen. *Zeitschrift für Nationalökonomie* 33(3–4), 235–50.

Theil, H. 1954. *Linear Aggregation of Economic Relations*. Amsterdam: North-Holland.

Theil, H. 1962. Alternative approaches to the aggregation problem. *Logic, methodology and philosophy of science. Proceedings of the 1960 International Congress*, ed. E. Nagel, P. Suppes and A. Tarski, Stanford, California: Stanford University Press.

Theil, H. 1967. *Economics and Information Theory*. Chicago: Rand McNally.

Tintner, G. and Sondermann, D. 1977. Statistical aspects of economic aggregation. In *Mathematical Economics and Game Theory*, ed. Henn and Moeschlin, Berlin: Springer.

aggregation problem. Microeconomic theory elegantly treats the behaviour of optimizing individual agents in a world with an arbitrarily long list of individual commodities and prices. However, the desire to analyse the great aggregates of macroeconomics–gross national product, inflation, unemployment, and so forth–leads to theories that treat such aggregates directly. What is the relation of such theory (or empirical work) to the underlying theory of the individual agent. When is it possible to speak of 'food' rather than of 'apples, bananas, carrots, etc?' When can one treat the investment decisions of all firms together as though there were a single good called 'capital' and all firms were a single firm?

LEONTIEF'S THEOREM.   Underlying many results on aggregation is a theorem of Leontief (1947a, 1947b). Let x and y be vectors of variables and $F(x, y)$ a twice-differentiable function. It is desired to aggregate over x, that is to replace x with a scalar aggregator function, $g(x)$, such that $F(x) \equiv H[g(x), y]$. This can be done if and only if, along any surface on which $F(x, y)$ is constant, the marginal rate of substitution between each pair of elements of x is independent of y.

HICKS–LEONTIEF AGGREGATION.   Since optimizing, price-taking agents equate marginal rates of substitution to price ratios, one restriction permitting aggregation over commodities is the assumption that the prices of all goods to be included in an aggregate always vary proportionally. This is called 'Hicks–Leontief aggregation' (Leontief, 1936; Hicks, 1939) and is a powerful expository tool. It requires no special assumptions as to the separability of utility or production functions, but is only applicable in relatively artificial situations. Under more general circumstances, and especially where aggregation over agents is involved, restrictions on utility or production functions become essential.

CONSUMPTION.   Consider a single household. Suppose that we wish to describe behaviour in terms of aggregate commodities such as 'food' or 'clothing'. By Leontief's Theorem, a food aggregate exists if and only if the marginal rate of substitution between any two kinds of food is independent of consumption of any non-food commodity. If a similar restrictive condition is satisfied for all the aggregates to be constructed, then the household's utility function can be written in aggregate terms.

Even such restrictive conditions will not always suffice. If we wish to represent the household as maximizing the aggregated utility function subject to an aggregated budget constraint, we must have aggregate prices as well as aggregate consumption goods. This requires that aggregates such as 'food' be homothetic in their component variables, again considerably restricting the household's utility function (Gorman, 1959; Blackorby et al., 1970).

Aggregation over agents presents a different set of questions. Suppose that we wish to treat the aggregate demands of a collection of households as the demands of a single, aggregate household. Then only aggregate income and not its distribution can influence demand. At given prices, this makes the income-derivative of every household's demand for a given commodity the same constant. Engel curves must be parallel straight lines. If zero income implies zero consumption, then all households must have the same homothetic utility function (Gorman, 1953).

In general, the only consumer-theoretic restrictions obeyed by aggregate demand functions are those of continuity, homogeneity of degree zero, and the various restrictions implied by the budget constraint. This corresponds to an important result (Sonnenschein, 1972, 1973) of general equilibrium theory on aggregate excess demand functions with Walras' Law replacing the budget constraint.

PRODUCTION.   Aggregation over inputs or outputs for a single firm also requires restrictive Leontief conditions on marginal rates of substitution. Aggregation over firms, however, leads to richer results.

Assume that every firm produces the same output from the same two inputs, capital and labour. Define Y, K, and L, as the totals over firms of output, capital and labour, respectively. We wish to represent the aggregate technology of the entire economy as $Y = F(K, L)$.

At first glance, this seems to lead to the same sort of result as in the case of households. Transfers of labour among firms must leave total output unchanged. Hence each firm's production function must be linear in labour with all firms having the same coefficient. If a similar condition applies to capital, every firm must have the same linear production function. Apparently, aggregation is not generally possible even if all firms are the same! (Nataf, 1948).

This formulation overlooks the fact that production functions involve efficiency conditions, giving *maximum* output for given inputs. If the total capital, K, and labour, L, available to the economy are assigned to firms to maximize total output, Y, then aggregate production can *always* be written as $Y = F(K, L)$. No further conditions are required.

This optimal-assignment is relatively natural for labour. It holds in competitive labour markets if all firms face the same wage (or in efficiently managed, centrally planned economies). It is not natural for capital, however, once we drop the assumption that all firms use the same type of physical capital. Suppose that technology is embodied in the capital stock and that capital cannot be shifted among firms. Then labour aggregation in this simple model remains easy, but capital aggregation is another matter.

Assume constant returns. If all firms had the same production function, differing amounts of capital would lead to differing amounts of labour with the labour–capital ratio the same in all firms. Then firms would differ only as to scale, and constant returns would make many small firms equivalent to one large one, permitting aggregation.

Unfortunately, capital augmentation is the *only* case permitting capital aggregation under constant returns in this model. Extensions to allow more types of capital in a given firm lead to similar results, as well as requiring that individual production functions permit capital aggregation. The requirements for the existence of partial capital aggregates such as 'plant' and 'equipment' are also very restrictive (Fisher, 1965, 1983; Gorman, 1968).

Now suppose that firms do not all have the same production function but that (for every v), the vth firm's production function can be written as $F(b_v K_v, L_v)$, where the function, $F(\cdot, \cdot)$ is common to all firms, but the parameter b_v can differ. This 'capital-augmenting' case is very restrictive, making one unit of one type of capital the exact duplicate of a fixed number of units of another. Having a different type of capital is equivalent to having more of the same type, and the argument given above shows that aggregation is permitted. The aggregate production function is $F(J, L)$, where J is the sum of the terms $b_v K_v$ (Solow, 1964).

Continue to assume capital to be firm-specific, but let there be several types of labour or of output. Output aggregation requires first that each firm's technology be separable in terms of output–the marginal rate of substitution between any pair of outputs must be independent of inputs. Further, under constant returns, the output-aggregator function must be the same for all firms (in contrast to the case of capital where production functions must be the same *after* capital aggregation). This means that firms cannot specialize; every firm must produce the same market-basket of outputs differing only as to scale. Similar conditions apply to labour (Fisher, 1968).

Perhaps surprisingly, the restrictive nature of such results does not really depend on the assumption that capital is firm-specific, once we leave the expository case of one output, one kind of capital, and one labour input for each firm. In general, aggregation over any set of inputs or outputs requires separability in each firm's production function. Further, under constant returns, even if capital is not firm-specific, aggregation over firms requires either that the aggregator functions applied to the firms all be the same (no specialization) or, if not, that the *only* difference in production functions be the nature of the aggregator function (generalized capital augmentation) (Fisher, 1982).

Abandoning constant returns does not provide practical help. Most non-constant returns cases do not permit aggregation even if all firms have the *same* production function. The cases that do are very restrictive (Fisher, 1965, 1968; Gorman, 1968; Blackorby and Schworm, 1984).

Such results show that the analytic use of such aggregates as 'capital', 'output', 'labour' or 'investment' as though the production side of the economy could be treated as a single firm is without sound foundation. This has not discouraged macroeconomists from continuing to work in such terms.

FRANKLIN M. FISHER

See also SEPARABILITY.

BIBLIOGRAPHY

Blackorby, C., Lady, G., Nissen, D. and Russell, R.R. 1970. Homothetic separability and consumer budgeting. *Econometrica* 38(3), May, 468–72.

Blackorby, C. and Schworm, W. 1984. The structure of economies with aggregate measures of capital: a complete characterization. *Review of Economic Studies* 51(4), October, 633–50.

Fisher, F.M. 1965. Embodied technical change and the existence of an aggregate capital stock. *Review of Economic Studies* 32(4), October, 263–88.

Fisher, F.M. 1968. Embodied technology and the existence of labour and output aggregates. *Review of Economic Studies* 35(4), October, 391–412.

Fisher, F.M. 1982. Aggregate production functions revisited: the mobility of capital and the rigidity of thought. *Review of Economic Studies* 49(4), October, 615–26.

Fisher, F.M. 1983. On the simultaneous existence of full and partial capital aggregates. *Review of Economic Studies* 50(1), January, 197–208.

Gorman, W.M. 1953. Community preference fields. *Econometrica* 21(1), January, 63–80.

Gorman, W.M. 1959. Separable utility and aggregation. *Econometrica* 27(3), July, 469–81.

Gorman, W.M. 1968. Measuring the quantities of fixed factors. In *Value, Capital, and Growth: Papers in Honour of Sir John Hicks*, ed. J.N. Wolfe, Edinburgh: University of Edinburgh Press.

Hicks, J.R. 1939. *Value and Capital*. Oxford: Clarendon Press.

Leontief, W.W. 1936. Composite commodities and the problem of index numbers. *Econometrica* 4(1), January, 39–59.

Leontief, W.W. 1947a. A note on the interrelation of subsets of independent variables of a continuous function with continuous first derivatives. *Bulletin of the American Mathematical Society* 53, 343–56.

Leontief, W.W. 1947b. Introduction to a theory of the internal structure of functional relationships. *Econometrica* 15(4), October, 361–73.

Nataf, A. 1948. Sur la possibilité de construction de certains macromodèles. *Econometrica* 16(3), July, 232–44.

Solow, R.M. 1964. Capital, labor, and income in manufacturing. In R.M. Solow, *The Behavior of Income Shares*, Studies in Income and Wealth, Princeton: Princeton University Press, 101–28.

Sonnenschein, H. 1972. Market excess demand functions. *Econometrica* 40(3), May, 549–63.

Sonnenschein, H. 1973. Do Walras' identity and continuity characterize the class of community excess demand functions? *Journal of Economic Theory* 6(4), August, 345–54.

agrarianism. *See* MANOÏLESCO, MIHAIL.

agricultural economics. Agricultural economics as described in this article is a distinctively American development. It was rooted in a unique set of institutions which grew up in a particular historical environment. Emerging as a separate discipline shortly after 1900, agricultural economics was firmly established by 1922. From that year until the early 1960s, agricultural economists set the pace for the parent discipline in empirical research, the cumulative development of data systems, and the joint application of economic theory and mathematical statistics to forecasting and policy analysis. Since 1965 the technical competence of agricultural economists has continued to increase but econometric methods are also being used by many other groups, and in newer fields such as economic development and environmental and natural resource studies, the skills of agricultural and other economists may be largely interchangeable.

For reasons of space and focus, we will concentrate on the relationship of agricultural economics to commercial agriculture. Many additional topics might reasonably be subsumed under the heading of 'agricultural economics': Chayanov's theory of peasant economy, agrarian reform, land and natural resource economics, rural poverty in developed countries, and so on. Moreover, we will give only cursory attention to developments since 1965, as these are discussed at length in the four-volume survey of agricultural economics literature edited by Martin (1977–86) on behalf of the American Agricultural Economics Association.

THE HISTORICAL SETTING, 1783–1900

Taylor and Taylor (1952, p. 79) say that 'the roots which seem to account for most of the early growth of agricultural economics in the United States' are found at six universities: Cornell, Illinois, Michigan State, Minnesota, Ohio State and Wisconsin. Their six states were linked by a common pattern of agricultural settlement, and the universities themselves were all members of the land-grant system; during the 1870s and 1890s farmers in these states (and others) shared common experiences of low prices and financial stress.

Agricultural settlement of the Midwest, 1783–1900. For a century after the formal conclusion of the War of Independence in 1783, settlers streamed westward across a vast continent previously occupied by a sparse aboriginal population. Before 1850 the great majority of settlers moving across the northern states came from New England, New York and Pennsylvania. They had never known peasantry (important in most of Europe) and had little experience with the separation of land ownership from actual farming (prevalent in England). They intended to own their land, clear it and improve it, and benefit from the increase in its value. They expected to farm it themselves and market the bulk of their produce.

After 1850 considerable numbers of German and Scandinavian immigrants joined the westward movement, though without changing its basic character. By 1900 the population of 11 Midwestern states in the path of this movement had grown to 23.2 million and substantially exceeded that of the New England and Middle Atlantic states.

Development of the land-grant system, 1860–1900. By 1890 the frontier was gone. Industry continued to grow and urban population to increase after 1890, accelerated by immigrants from Southern and Eastern Europe who congregated in the larger cities. Further increases in agricultural production from the nearly-fixed area would require more intensive cultivation, genetic improvements in crops and livestock, and better management.

Between 1860 and 1900 a unique set of institutions was developed to meet these objectives – a system of state agricultural colleges, experiment stations and extension services (Ross, 1942). Because grants of public lands had been used in the 1860s to help each state establish an agricultural college, the whole complex is often referred to as 'the land-grant system'. Initially, many supporters of the colleges expected them to accept students directly from the rural schools and teach them practical farming skills. By the 1880s that mission was being handled mainly in other ways, and the colleges were teaching principles of scientific agriculture; a common motto was 'science with practice'.

From the 1880s on, experiment stations were established in close association with the colleges to conduct research on soils, crops and livestock important to their states, and on the most relevant aspects of bacteriology and entomology. A little later, extension services were established to disseminate the results of this research to farmers, largely through demonstrations held in their local communities. By interacting with experiment station personnel, extension workers also encouraged them to focus much of their research on problems of direct concern to farmers.

Farm problems and protests, 1870–1900. The rapid expansion of agriculture in the United States has few parallels. As of 1783, the nation's land area was about 900,000 square miles, much of it still unsettled. The area was doubled shortly after 1800 by the Louisiana Purchase and other acquisitions, and more than tripled at mid-century (to a total of 3 million square miles) by the annexation of former Mexican territory. From 1850 on, settlement was facilitated by extension of the railroad network, and by 1900 millions of farmers were located more than a thousand miles from the Atlantic seaboard. Agricultural production outstripped domestic and foreign demand, and prices of farm products fell to punitively low levels during the 1870s and 1890s.

Many farmers felt that they were being victimized by the railroads, the meat packers, the international grain dealers, the New York City bankers, the monetary system, the tariffs which protected domestic manufacturers from foreign competition, and other forces far beyond their individual control. As farmers dominated several state legislatures and constituted two-fifths of the nation's population, they sought redress through political action. In concert with other groups, they succeeded in subjecting the railroads to federal regulation and in passing a not very effective antitrust law. They could not agree on specific proposals for government price supports and export subsidies on farm products, but these subjects were added to the political agenda for action in a later decade.

EMERGENCE OF AGRICULTURAL ECONOMICS AS A DISCIPLINE, 1900–1922

Taylor and Taylor (1952, pp. 53–79) note that courses labelled 'Agricultural Economy', 'Economics of Agriculture' and the like were taught sporadically at Cornell and a few other land-grant universities between 1868 and 1900. John M. Gregory influenced the content of several such courses through his teaching at the University of Illinois (1868–80) and through

his book, *A New Political Economy* (1882), which included a substantial chapter on 'Agricultural or Rural Economy'.

The farm management tradition. Meanwhile, some agricultural scientists were developing the field which came to be known as farm management. The more specialized agricultural scientists sought to 'help farmers' by advising them on specific techniques – soil analysis, seed selection, insect control, animal breeding, and so on. It was soon recognized that each farmer faced the very complicated task of integrating these bits and pieces of technology into a programme that would yield a satisfactory income from the farm as a whole.

George F. Warren (1913) of Cornell and a few others visualized 'farm management' as the vehicle for accomplishing this task in an orderly way. Their approach was empirical and holistic, featuring farm accounts, cost-of-production studies and the collection of input, output and financial information from large numbers of farmers. When such information was summarized for groups of farmers classified according to their degrees of financial success, it was expected that farmers generally would perceive ways of improving their own operations. This approach was given professional status through organization of the American Farm Management Association in 1910. Warren's view was that farm management deals 'with the internal organizations and management of specific farms' while 'rural economy deals with the public relations of farming' (quoted in Taylor and Taylor, 1952, p. 91).

The agricultural economics movement. Henry C. Taylor was the central figure in the emergence and establishment of agricultural economics. His interest was focused on rural economic problems by the farm crisis of the early 1890s. To pursue that interest, he transferred from Drake University to Iowa State, where he earned BS and MS degrees in Scientific Agriculture. In 1896 he began his doctoral studies at the University of Wisconsin under Richard T. Ely. His training also included a year of study in Germany and a year of research in England; his dissertation on *The Decline of Landowning Farmers in England* was published in 1904.

Taylor published his textbook, *Agricultural Economics*, in 1905. He discussed the factors of agricultural production and their economic properties; specified maximum net profit as the guiding principle in organizing and managing a farm; and cited works by Marshall, Ely, Smith, Mill, Carver, Böhm-Bawerk, Wieser and Clark. In an unpublished syllabus, he also dealt with economic principles applicable to 'public agricultural economics or an agrarian policy' (Taylor and Taylor, 1952, p. 87).

Taylor's view of agricultural economics could accommodate many of the interests of the farm management group. For a few years he and others of his persuasion maintained a separate Association of Agricultural Economists, but in 1919 the two groups merged amicably to form the American Farm Economic Association.

From 1863 on, the US Department of Agriculture (USDA) had developed a system of crop and livestock statistics. Decennial censuses of agriculture provided benchmark information. In response to congressional interests, the department took on an increasing variety of fact-gathering and reporting activities. In 1919 USDA's Office of Farm Management was reorganized to consolidate several of these along lines agreed upon by Warren and Taylor. Taylor left Wisconsin to head this organization. He was instrumental in consolidating all of USDA's statistical reporting and economic analysis activities in a single agency. The US Bureau of

Agricultural Economics, established in 1922 with Taylor as its Chief, became the central institution of the new discipline.

THE HISTORICAL AND INSTITUTIONAL CONTEXTS OF AGRICULTURAL ECONOMICS, 1922–1965

The next section after this one will emphasize the contributions of agricultural economists to economic theory and methodology. But before discussing the contributions themselves, we must comment on their historical and institutional contexts.

The historical context. Prices of farm products in the United States rose from 1900 to 1909 and remained quite stable during 1910–14 at a level representing moderate prosperity. World War I brought expanded production and also higher prices which peaked in mid-1920 at 235 per cent of the 1910–14 average. Land values rose sharply and many young farmers bought land on credit. Farm product prices plummeted 50 per cent between June 1920 and June 1921 and farm income remained at an unfavourable level throughout the 1920s while other sectors of the economy enjoyed high prosperity.

With the onset of the Great Depression, farm income declined by more than half from 1929 to 1932. Farm price support and acreage limitation programmes were introduced on a massive scale in 1933 and continued through 1940. Price and production programmes were extended throughout World War II, though with different objectives. With the removal of price controls in 1946, farm product prices shot up to new record levels. They receded somewhat in 1949 and rose again during 1950–52 as the hostilities in Korea seemed to threaten another round of shortages and inflation. With the end of these hostilities in mid-1953, US agriculture entered a period of 'burdensome surpluses', which continued unabated for nearly two decades.

The institutional context. Workers in the land-grant system and in USDA were strongly motivated to help farmers. From 1900 to 1940 their constituency included 30 million people living on 6 million farms. Geographically dispersed and with heterogeneous commodity interests, they could not (as a practical matter) organize for the purposes of maintaining economic data systems or programmes of production and marketing research. These services were provided by USDA and the land-grant universities.

By predilection and professional commitment, few agricultural economists were in a position to create new economic theory. Some who had the temperament and capacity to do so were co-opted by elite universities or research institutes (John D. Black from Minnesota by Harvard, E.G. Nourse from Iowa State by the Brookings Institution, T.W. Schultz from Iowa State by Chicago). J.K. Galbraith, with a PhD in Agricultural Economics from Berkeley, followed a somewhat erratic course to Harvard. These and other migrations helped to establish equivalencies between agricultural economists and members of the parent discipline: Black, Nourse, T.N. Carver (Harvard), and Joseph S. Davis (Stanford) served as presidents of both the American Farm Economic Association and the American Economic Association; Schultz and Galbraith served as presidents of the latter association but not the AFEA.

Prior to the 1950s, few general economists in the universities were in a position to do serious empirical research. In contrast, agricultural economists benefited from access to experiment station resources and from administrative recognition that they, like the agricultural scientists, needed supporting personnel, current-expense funds and substantial allocations of their own time to research. They studied (for the most part) tangible commodities, observable processes and measurable outcomes.

The Bureau of Agricultural Economics (BAE) provided an even richer environment. As of 1922, it included by far the largest group of research-oriented economists in the United States and could assign some of the most talented to full-time research.

SOME MAJOR CONTRIBUTIONS, 1922–1965

We first discuss some central figures and works of broad scope and then move successively to production economics, marketing and industrial organization, demand, supply and price analysis, and the analysis of government programmes.

Central figures and works of broad scope. As already observed, Henry C. Taylor (1873–1969) was without doubt the key figure in establishing agricultural economics. He adapted F.A. Walker's (1888) theory of profits to the explanation of differential returns to entrepreneurship in farming and gave convincing economic reasons for the decline of landowning farmers in England. Taylor's massive *Story of Agricultural Economics* (1952, co-authored with Anne Dewees Taylor) is indispensable for any future study of the origins and early literature of the discipline.

Edwin G. Nourse (1883–1974) published *Agricultural Economics* (1916), a selection of some 300 short readings in which economic principles are applied to agricultural topics. He became an authority on cooperative marketing and on international trade in farm products before moving to the Brookings Institution in 1923. In 1946 he became the first chairman of the President's Council of Economic Advisers.

John D. Black (1883–1960) was the most productive agricultural economist of his generation. He and his graduate students (at Minnesota during 1918–27 and then at Harvard) published in every subfield in the discipline. His *Agricultural Reform in the United States* (1929) reflects a comprehensive understanding of the agricultural sector and its role in the economy. A selection of his shorter writings is presented under 12 major headings in Black (1959) together with interpretive essays by a dozen of his most distinguished former students.

Joseph S. Davis (1885–1975) was particularly active in debates on agricultural policy during 1926–38; a selection of his papers in this area is contained in Davis (1939). His early training in economic history and his responsibilities as director of the Stanford Food Research Institute led him to emphasize the long-run effects and international repercussions of proposed policies.

T.W. Schultz (born 1902) rivalled Black in his comprehensive understanding of US agriculture. Schultz's *Agriculture in an Unstable Economy* (1945) incorporated new lessons from the 1930s and World War II. He trained and stimulated some of the most brilliant agricultural economists who began their careers in the 1940s and 1950s. His *Transforming Traditional Agriculture* (1964) was a major contribution to the theory of economic development, and he received the Nobel Prize for that and related works.

Howard R. Tolley (1889–1958) and Oris V. Wells (born 1903) were distinguished administrators of the US Bureau of Agricultural Economics. Like Henry C. Taylor, they inspired and challenged younger economists and maintained a high level of scientific freedom in the Bureau. Their intelligence was proverbial and their knowledge of the economic aspects of agriculture unsurpassed. Tolley (1917) was the first agricultural economist to use multiple- and partial-correlation measures; he also taught mathematical statistics in the USDA Graduate School to Mordecai Ezekiel and others in the early 1920s. Wells was a superb policy analyst who published very little under his own name; an example of his own research is Wells (1933). Wells completed his career as Deputy Director-General of the Food and Agriculture Organization of the United Nations.

Production economics. Farm management (Warren, 1913) was concerned with the profitable organization of production on individual farms. Taylor (1905) applied economic principles to the same subject matter and drew production functions (p. 98) showing stages of increasing, stationary and diminishing returns. Implicitly, he confined production economics within the farmer's fence-line.

John D. Black's *Introduction to Production Economics* (1926) far surpassed any earlier efforts. It is a remarkably modern book and deserves renewed attention.

The major divisions of Black's book are specialization and comparative advantage; the elements of production and their combination; the operating unit; the coordination of production; and the social organization of production (including chapters on social economy and the economies of cities and nations).

Tolley, Black and Ezekiel (1924), in a short bulletin of 44 pages, initiated a revolutionary way of utilizing data from farm-record surveys and cost-of-production studies which had been, and were being, collected in large quantities by farm management specialists. The three economists applied multiple regression analysis to such data, using a new technique originated by Ezekiel (1924) for handling curvilinear relationships among several variables. These equations, expressing the quantities of each output as a function of the quantities of the several inputs, were in fact *production surfaces* in several dimensions, showing diminishing physical returns to each input over most of its range. These surfaces, they pointed out, were logically analogous to those that might be derived by agricultural scientists from controlled experiments.

From the production surfaces, the authors derived *cost surfaces* and showed that the least-cost combinations of inputs would vary with changes in their relative prices. They also demonstrated that the highest-profit combination of inputs would almost always differ from the combination which yielded the lowest cost per unit of output. These differences were seldom recognized in the farm management tradition, and no previous empirical studies by agricultural scientists or economists had tried to deal with diminishing returns to more than one input at a time. The implications of this bulletin were so far-reaching that little more was done to realize them until Heady and his associates entered the field in the 1940s.

Earl O. Heady's classic *Economics of Agricultural Production and Resource Use* (1952) did more than any other book to revolutionize graduate training in agricultural economics during the 1950s and 1960s. Heady cites Arrow, Boulding, Carlson, Hicks, Hurwicz, Knight, Koopmans, Lerner, Morgenstern, Samuelson, Shackle, Tintner, von Neumann and others, along with an impressive range of empirical studies already completed under his direction. He uses the modern technical terminology of production functions (isoquants, isoclines, scale lines, etc.) throughout and employs many diagrams to illustrate these concepts. He employs mathematics as needed and reports regression surfaces from empirical studies. A later book, Heady and Dillon (1961), is devoted exclusively to agricultural production functions.

Marketing and industrial organization. Agricultural economists in the land-grant system and USDA gave substantial attention to the economics of cooperative marketing by farmers. Nourse clarified the conditions for successful operation of cooperative grain elevators in competition with private firms. Hibbard (1921) wrote an objective description of the marketing system for agricultural commodities and a realistic appraisal of the prospects for reforms (in the farmers' interests), through political action and through cooperative business organization.

Nicholls (1941) made a brilliant adaptation of Chamberlin's theory of monopolistic competition. While Chamberlin dealt with industries composed of a few *sellers*, Nicholls observed that farmers typically had to sell their products to industries composed of a few *buyers*. He stood Chamberlin's theory on its head, made the necessary mathematical derivations and illustrated the situations he perceived in the various agricultural processing industries – with empirical data where available, otherwise with hypothetical diagrams. On pages 358–63 he outlines the conditions for 'a complete and incontrovertible analysis' of 'the price and production policies of an agricultural industry'. They are extremely demanding; Holdren (1960), in his study of competition among food supermarkets, may be the only person who has met them successfully.

Hoffman's (1940) study of large-scale organization in the food industries also adapts Chamberlin's theory. Most of the references to imperfect competition in agricultural marketing textbooks during the 1950s and early 1960s were based on Nicholls and Hoffman.

Frederick V. Waugh (1898–1974) was the most sophisticated theorist to give major attention to agricultural marketing. A few of his marketing papers are reprinted in Waugh (1984), including 'Market Prorates and Social Welfare', originally published in the *Journal of Farm Economics*, May 1938, which provided the theoretical starting point for the first Food Stamp Plan. Waugh, Burtis and Wolf (1936) combined monopoly theory with statistical analysis in a study of the controlled distribution of a crop among independent markets. On behalf of the American Farm Economic Association, Waugh edited *Readings on Agricultural Marketing* (1954), containing several hundred short excerpts from writings of the more theoretically oriented contributors.

Demand, supply and price analysis. Henry L. Moore made the first serious, cumulative effort to estimate empirical demand functions. It was self-evident to him that 'the most ample and trustworthy data of economic science' then available were official statistics; also, that the best-developed official statistics were those of the USDA on prices and production of agricultural commodities. Moore turned his attention to these data, with the somewhat unexpected result that his empirical work had its first and greatest impact on agricultural economists. His books on *Economic Cycles* (1914) and *Forecasting the Yield and the Price of Cotton* (1917) furnished the inspiration for much of the work on statistical estimation of demand and supply functions that was carried on in the United States during the 1920s – most notably by Holbrook Working, F.V. Waugh, Mordecai Ezekiel, Louis H. Bean and E.J. Working.

One of the first to respond to Moore's influence was not an economist but the young associate editor of *Wallaces' Farmer* – Henry A. Wallace – later Secretary of Agriculture (1933–40) and Vice-President of the United States (1941–45). In *Agricultural Prices* (1920), Wallace estimated two alternative demand functions for hogs; his primary object was 'to promote a better understanding' among farmers, agricultural college students, extension workers and farm-organization leaders 'of the factors which influence prices of farm products and stimulate an intelligent interest in statistical economics' (p. 3). He had already sought Moore's advice in 1915 as to reference works on the method of least squares.

Wallace's father, Henry C. Wallace, became Secretary of Agriculture in 1921 in the midst of a precipitous drop in farm prices. By 1922 Henry C. Wallace had decided to provide farmers with the best possible forecasts of the demand and price outlook for their products, as a continuing aid to production adjustments on their individual farms. The newly organized BAE became the focus of quantitative economic research of unprecedented intensity; agricultural economists in the land-grant system were also involved. The leading contributors (already mentioned) entered the field in their early or mid-twenties.

Apart from Moore himself, these young agricultural economists were the first econometricians. They began their work in 1922, eight years before the founding of the Econometric Society and a full decade in advance of the first issue of *Econometrica*. Leontief (1971) cites their work as 'an exceptional example of a healthy balance between theoretical and empirical analysis... . They also were the first among economists to make use of the advanced methods of mathematical statistics.' In a private communication (1985) to the author, Tinbergen wrote that his 'early heroes' included 'several agricultural economists'. Tinbergen and Leontief were a few years younger than the most prominent of these, and were greatly impressed by them.

Looking back from 1985 it is difficult to realize how radical their activities were. J N Keynes (1917, p. 253) had observed that 'to some economists the very idea of a mathematical treatment of economic problems is not only repugnant, but seems even absurd'. This was a common view among general economists in the United States at that time. From 1920 on, Mitchell and his colleagues at the National Bureau of Economic Research were developing data bases of great ultimate promise, but they steadfastly avoided the explicit use of economic theory or of any but the very simplest descriptive statistical techniques. The leading English economists set great store by theoretical demand curves but doubted whether Jevons's hope of constructing empirical demand curves by statistics was capable of realization. Both groups were convinced that efforts to confront theory with data would be fruitless.

Moore experienced great difficulty in selling statistical demand analysis to *professors* of general economics; Wallace and others had little trouble in selling it to *students* of agricultural economics. In terms of Glenn L. Johnson's (1986a, 1986b) categories, Moore was engaged in 'disciplinary' research directed to his fellow professors; the agricultural economists were engaged in 'subject matter' and 'problem-solving' research of interest to farmers and policy-makers. The land-grant system set a premium on comprehensible and applicable results and could disseminate them very rapidly.

Tolley and Ezekiel (1923) presented an efficient and accurate method for fitting linear multiple regression equations, greatly increasing the accessibility of least-squares methods to economists and agricultural economists. Ezekiel (1924) published a partly-graphic method for fitting curvilinear regressions in any number of variables. Bean (1929a) created a short-cut version of Ezekiel's method which became very popular. H. Working (1925), Waugh (1984) and Ezekiel (1930) were very much aware of the presence and approximate magnitudes of errors (not necessarily random) in all variables and the biasing effects of random errors in the independent variables in multiple regression analyses.

The 'identification problem' in the simple case of demand and supply curves had been solved independently by three reviewers of Moore's 1914 book and was well understood by agricultural economists in the 1920s. The demand–supply–price structures for many farm products were recursive, and the bases for time-lags in the response of supply to price were well known. Apparent identification problems could usually be solved by temporal or spatial disaggregation and by the development of data for different market levels and different components of commodity supply and distribution. E.J. Working's 1927 article has received undue attention from general economists; Ezekiel (1928) dismissed it in a sentence or two so far as most agricultural commodities were concerned.

Had they needed to meet complicated identification problems head on, Ezekiel and his colleagues would most likely have called upon Sewall Wright, a young geneticist in USDA's Bureau of Animal Industry, with whom they were well acquainted. Wright's (1921) method of 'path coefficients' was capable of quantifying the implications of causal hypotheses for each separate path in very complicated systems. In his 1925 USDA bulletin, *Corn and Hog Correlations*, Wright reduced 510 observed correlations to a central system of 14 path coefficients connecting corn production, corn price, the summer price of hogs, the winter price of hogs, and the amount of hog breeding in successive years.

The pre-World War II literature of demand and supply analysis by agricultural economists remains widely scattered. Some 30 of the more important references are listed in Fox and Johnson (eds), (1969, pp. xxi–xxiii); several others are listed in Fox (1968). The techniques used in the late 1920s are reflected in Ezekiel's *Methods of Correlation Analysis* (1930), which remained the standard text on applied regression analysis for many years. Bean (1929b) summarizes a number of his own studies of supply response. Ezekiel (1938) presents a classic summary of theoretical and empirical work on 'cobweb' or recursive models. Waugh (1964, pp. 1–8) gives a concise and lucid history of demand and price analysis, with references overlapping those in Fox and Johnson but also citing Cournot, Dupuit, Marshall, Walras, Pareto, Hicks and others. The remaining 83 pages of Waugh's bulletin summarize a number of his own brilliant contributions to the field.

Fox (1953, 1958), like Waugh (1964), may be regarded as continuations of the tradition established by Ezekiel, Waugh and the two Workings but with full awareness of contributions made by Frisch, Koopmans, Wold, Henry Schultz and Tinbergen during 1934–39 and by Haavelmo and his associates during 1943–50.

During 1947–50 Fox, in association with James P. Cavin, designed a research programme which resulted in the most extensive and important body of statistical demand studies made in the United States during our period of interest (1922–65). Fox (1953) and the first part of Fox (1958), actually written during 1950–51, provided a prototype and the basic methodology for what came to be known as 'the demand and price structure series', the core of which was a set of USDA technical bulletins covering virtually all major farm commodities. Richard J. Foote gave direct supervision to this research from 1951 through 1957; several of the bulletins received awards for outstanding published research. Foote (1953) is an example of his own contributions to the series.

The spatial price equilibrium models in Fox (1958) are extensions of demand and supply analysis to a system of interconnected regions. Brandow (1961) extended the tradition to create a partly-synthetic model of the US food and agricultural sectors, consisting of consumer-demand functions for an exhaustive set of foods and food groups, a set of marketing margin equations and sets of demand and supply functions at the farm price level. Day's (1963) pathbreaking study, *Recursive Programming and Production Response*, may be regarded as an extension of the tradition of supply-response analysis.

J.B. Clark (1899, pp. 228–9) asserted that a commodity is 'a bundle of distinct utilities'. Waugh (1929) made the first effort to estimate the separate effects of the various attributes of farm products upon the prices paid for different lots. He found that a large percentage of the observed variation in prices could be explained by attributes which were generally lumped together as 'quality' but were in fact separately measurable. V.E. Smith (1964), working with consumer panel data collected by agricultural economists at his university, used linear programming techniques to estimate the implicit market values assigned by consumers to various food nutrients and food-habit restrictions. This also may be viewed as an extension of Waugh's 1929 work on 'quality' as a determinant of prices and Waugh's 1956 estimates of 'partial indifferences surfaces' for beef and pork (reprinted in Waugh, 1984).

Analysis of government programmes. Some farm leaders in the 1890s had advocated government price-support programmes for the major crops. With the collapse of farm prices in 1920–21, new versions of those proposals received political support. By 1924 it was clear that USDA's outlook work would not raise farm incomes sufficiently to satisfy widely-held perceptions of equity, and that political demands might well lead to large-scale programmes of price support and export subsidy. The depth and detail of BAE's studies during 1924–29 of factors affecting farm prices and farmers' responses to them were motivated in part by the need to explore and clarify the probable repercussions of such programmes. Haas and Ezekiel (1926) is one of many examples.

The Agricultural Marketing Act of 1929 provided $500 million for price-support operations on wheat, corn and cotton by the newly created Federal Farm Board. Joseph S. Davis and John D. Black served successively as the Board's chief economist; Ezekiel served as assistant economist under both. Coincidentally, a stock market crash (October 1929) marked the onset of the Great Depression. By 1932 some 25 per cent of the nation's labour force was unemployed. A new President, Franklin D. Roosevelt, took office in March 1933 and shortly named Henry A. Wallace as his Secretary of Agriculture; Ezekiel became Wallace's principal economic adviser.

As massive new programmes were initiated, Bean, Tolley, Wells and several other former BAE economists were recruited to programme-appraisal and programme-development roles in the action agencies. During 1933–41 they provided economic analysis of a quality unprecedented in the United States. The issues involved extended far beyond commercial agriculture and hence beyond the scope of this article. Kirkendall (1966) gives a masterly account of the roles played by Tolley and other agricultural economists in this larger arena.

The same expertise in programme analysis was applied to the rapidly changing problems of food production, distribution, price supports, price ceilings, rationing and subsidies during World War II. It was once again directed to the analysis of peacetime food and agricultural programmes after August 1945.

From 1946 on, Fox, Foote and others in BAE began to rebuild the research base in demand and supply analysis that had become somewhat depleted and scattered through personnel turnover during the war. The research base was needed both for the Bureau's continuing economic outlook reports and also for policy analysis. Fox's technical bulletin

(1953) and book (1958) were intended to serve both purposes. His contributions to Fox, Sengupta and Thorbecke (1966) were extensions of his earlier work on policy analysis in BAE.

NEW DEVELOPMENTS, 1945–1985

US farm population had remained quite stable from 1900 through 1940 at about 30 million. Its decline to 23 million in 1950 was generally regarded as a desirable response to wartime hyperemployment and postwar prosperity; as of 1940, there had been substantial underemployment in agriculture.

Technological change and emergence of the 'agribusiness' concept. But the decline continued. Production economists in the early 1950s recognized that the primary cause was substitution of purchased inputs (mechanical power and machinery, agricultural chemicals, and others) for labour on the farm. John H. Davis and Ray Goldberg (1957) surmised correctly that the true importance of agriculture in the national economy could be described by means of an input–output matrix containing a row for each industry that supplied some outputs *to* farming and a column for each industry that purchased some outputs *from* farming – in addition to farming as such. They subsumed this entire complex under the rubric of 'agribusiness'.

There were good reasons for expecting that farm-labour requirements would continue to decline rapidly during the 1950s and 1960s. The implications were that while relatively few farm boys and girls would find good opportunities in farming as such, their backgrounds would be very useful in other branches of agribusiness. As of 1952, one agricultural economics department had only 30 undergraduates majoring in Agricultural Economics; in 1953 it introduced an alternative programme, Agricultural Business, which enrolled 200 majors as of 1955 and eventually grew to 800!

Agricultural economists with graduate degrees also became diffused throughout the agribusiness complex. The American Farm Economic Association was renamed the American Agricultural Economics Association in 1968, recognizing that the interests and loyalties of its members were no longer confined to the farm population.

Expansion of agricultural economics into new fields. From 1950 on, many agricultural economists became involved in technical assistance programmes in the less-developed countries, and many students from those countries came to the United States for graduate training in the discipline. Some agricultural economists were attracted to the study of water-resource allocation, air and water pollution, or 'community', 'rural', or 'area' economic development programmes under USDA and land-grant university sponsorship. Fox (1962) and Fox and Kumar (1965) sought to provide conceptual frameworks for area economic development efforts.

As farm population dwindled and urban population grew, agricultural economics departments in some states changed their names to include references to food or natural resources; their clienteles changed correspondingly. At one university the general economics faculty expressed little interest in applications, so the agricultural economics department changed its name to Agricultural and Applied Economics.

The econometrics movement in general economics. Changes in the training of general economists after 1945 challenged the earlier leadership of agricultural economists in quantitative methods. It took time for the econometrics movement to spread, but by 1968 Strotz could write that it had become 'nearly coterminous with the parent discipline'. The skills of general economists in fields which lent themselves to quantification became largely interchangeable with those of agricultural economists working in the same or adjacent areas.

Continuing distinctions between agricultural and general economics as scientific communities. Despite considerable transferability of skills, agricultural and general economists continued, as late as 1985, to constitute two distinct scientific communities. Scholarly competition within each was so demanding that it was nearly impossible for anyone to be equally active, and to maintain high status and visibility, in both over any considerable period. Decisions to transfer from one community to the other in mid-career were not easily reversed.

CONCLUDING REMARKS

From its beginning, agricultural economics was devoted to problem-solving and to developing data systems and analyses which would enable farmers and others to understand their economic environments. Its practitioners observed production and marketing processes, measured inputs and outputs, and noted the attributes of commodities. They often worked closely with agricultural scientists and understood the logic of designing experiments and instruments to generate new data and make more accurate observations. The author believes that such continuing interaction between theory, observation, experiment (where feasible) and the development of new methods and data is still the most productive way to advance economic science.

KARL A. FOX

See also AGRICULTURAL SUPPLY; PEASANT ECONOMY.

BIBLIOGRAPHY

Bean, L.H. 1929a. A simplified method of graphic curvilinear correlation. *Journal of the American Statistical Association* 24, December, 386–97.

Bean, L.H. 1929b. The farmers' response to price. *Journal of Farm Economics* 11, July, 368–85.

Black, J.D. 1926. *Introduction to Production Economics.* New York: Henry Holt & Co.

Black, J.D. 1929. *Agricultural Reform in the United States.* New York: McGraw-Hill.

Black, J.D. 1959. *Economics for Agriculture: Selected Writings of John D. Black.* Ed. J. P. Cavin, with introductory essays, Cambridge, Mass.: Harvard University Press.

Brandow, G.E. 1961. *Interrelations among Demands for Farm Products and Implications for Control of Market Supply.* University Park, Pennsylvania: Pennsylvania Agricultural Experiment Station, Bulletin 680.

Clark, J.B. 1899. *The Distribution of Wealth: A Theory of Wages, Interest and Profits.* New York: Macmillan.

Davis, J.H. and Goldberg, R.A. 1957. *A Concept of Agribusiness.* Boston: Graduate School of Business Administration, Harvard University.

Davis, J.S. 1939. *On Agricultural Policy 1926–1938.* Stanford: Food Research Institute, Stanford University.

Day, R.H. 1963. *Recursive Programming and Production Response.* Amsterdam: North-Holland.

Ezekiel, M. 1924. A method of handling curvilinear correlation for any number of variables. *Journal of the American Statistical Association* 19, December, 431–53.

Ezekiel, M. 1928. Statistical analyses and the 'laws' of price. *Quarterly Journal of Economics* 42, February, 199–227.

Ezekiel, M. 1930. *Methods of Correlation Analysis.* New York: Wiley.

Ezekiel, M. 1938. The cobweb theorem. *Quarterly Journal of Economics* 52, February, 255–80.

Foote, R.J. 1953. *Statistical Analyses Relating to the Feed-Livestock Economy.* Washington, DC: US Department of Agriculture, Technical Bulletin 1070.

Fox, K.A. 1953. *The Analysis of Demand for Farm Products.* Washington, DC: US Department of Agriculture, Technical Bulletin 1081.

Fox, K.A. 1958. *Econometric Analysis for Public Policy.* Ames, Iowa: Iowa State University Press. Reprinted, 1977.

Fox, K.A. 1962. The study of interactions between agriculture and the nonfarm economy: local, regional, and national. *Journal of Farm Economics* 44, February, 1–34.

Fox, K.A. 1986. Agricultural economists as world leaders in applied econometrics 1917–1933. *American Journal of Agricultural Economics* 68, May, 381–6.

Fox, K.A. and Johnson, D.G. (eds) 1969. *Readings in the Economics of Agriculture.* Homewood, Ill.: Irwin. Published for the American Economic Association as Vol. 13 in its Series of Republished Articles on Economics.

Fox, K.A. and Kumar, T.K. 1965. The functional economic area: delineation and implications for economic analysis and policy. *Regional Science Association Papers* 15, 57–85.

Fox, K.A., Sengupta, J.K. and Thorbecke, E. 1966. *The Theory of Quantitative Economic Policy.* Amsterdam: North-Holland.

Gregory, J.M. 1882. *A New Political Economy.* New York: Van Antwerp, Bragg & Co.

Haas, G.C. and Ezekiel, M. 1926. *Factors Affecting the Price of Hogs.* Washington, DC: US Department of Agriculture, Bulletin 1440.

Heady, E.O. 1952. *Economics of Agricultural Production and Resource Use.* Englewood Cliffs, NJ: Prentice-Hall.

Heady, E.O. and Dillon, J.L. 1961. *Agricultural Production Functions.* Ames, Iowa: Iowa State University Press.

Hibbard, B.H. 1921. *Marketing Agricultural Products.* New York: D. Appleton & Co.

Hoffman, A.C. 1940. *Large-Scale Organization in the Food Industries.* Temporary National Economic Committee Monograph No. 35, Senate Committee Print, 76th Congress (2nd Session), Washington, DC: US Government Printing Office.

Holdren, B.R. 1960. *The Structure of a Retail Market and the Market Behavior of Retail Units.* Englewood Cliffs, NJ: Prentice-Hall. Reprinted, Ames: Iowa State University Press, 1968.

Johnson, G.L. 1986a. *Research Methodology for Economists.* New York: Macmillan.

Johnson, G.L. 1986b. Holistic modeling of multidisciplinary subject matter and problem domains. In *Systems Economics: Concepts, Models, and Multidisciplinary Perspectives,* ed. K.A. Fox and D.G. Miles, Ames, Iowa: Iowa State University Press.

Keynes, J.N. 1917. *The Scope and Method of Political Economy.* 4th edn, London: Macmillan & Co.

Kirkendall, R.S. 1966. *Social Scientists and Farm Politics in the Age of Roosevelt.* Columbia: University of Missouri Press. Reprinted by Iowa State University Press, 1982.

Leontief, W.W. 1971. Theoretical assumptions and non-observed facts. *American Economic Review* 61, March, 1–7.

Martin, L.R. (gen. ed.) 1977–87. *A Survey of Agricultural Economics Literature.* 4 vols, Minneapolis: University of Minnesota Press for the American Agricultural Economics Association. Vol. I. 1977. *Traditional Fields of Agricultural Economics, 1940s to 1970s,* ed. L.R. Martin. Vol. II. 1977. *Quantitative Methods in Agricultural Economics, 1940s to 1970s,* ed. G.G. Judge, R.H. Day, S.R. Johnson, G.C. Rausser and L.R. Martin. Vol. III. 1981. *Economics of Welfare, Rural Development, and Natural Resources in Agriculture, 1940s to 1970s,* ed. L.R. Martin. Vol. IV. 1987. *Agriculture in Economic Development,* ed. L.R. Martin.

Moore, H.L. 1914. *Economic Cycles: Their Law and Cause.* New York: Macmillan.

Moore, H.L. 1917. *Forecasting the Yield and the Price of Cotton.* New York: Macmillan.

Nicholls, W.H. 1941. *Imperfect Competition within Agricultural Industries.* Ames, Iowa: Iowa State University Press.

Nourse, E.G. 1916. *Agricultural Economics; a selection of materials in which economic principles are applied to the practice of agriculture.* Chicago: University of Chicago Press.

Ross, E.D. 1942. *Democracy's College: The Land-Grant Movement in the Formative State.* Ames, Iowa: Iowa State University Press.

Schultz, T.W. 1945. *Agriculture in an Unstable Economy.* New York: McGraw-Hill.

Schultz, T.W. 1964. *Transforming Traditional Agriculture*. New Haven: Yale University Press.

Smith, V.E. 1964. *Electronic Computation of Human Diets*. East Lansing: Bureau of Business and Economic Research, Graduate School of Business Administration, Michigan State University.

Taylor, H.C. 1904. *The Decline of Landowning Farmers in England*. Madison: University of Wisconsin, Bulletin 96, Economics and Political Science Series, Vol. I.

Taylor, H.C. 1905. *Agricultural Economics*. New York: Macmillan.

Taylor, H.C. and Taylor, A.D. 1952. *The Story of Agricultural Economics*. Ames, Iowa: Iowa State University Press.

Tolley, H.R. 1917. *The Theory of Correlation as Applied to Farm Survey Data on Fattening Baby Beef*. Washington, DC: US Department of Agriculture, Bulletin 504.

Tolley, H.R. and Ezekiel, M. 1923. A method of handling multiple correlation problems. *Journal of the American Statistical Association* 18, December, 993–1003.

Tolley, H.R., Black, J.D. and Ezekiel, M.J.B. 1924. *Input as Related to Output in Farm Organization and Cost of Production Studies*. Washington, DC: US Department of Agriculture, Bulletin 1277.

Walker, F.A. 1888. *Political Economy: Advanced Course*. 3rd edn, New York: Henry Holt.

Wallace, H.A. 1920. *Agricultural Prices*. Des Moines, Iowa: Wallace.

Warren, G.F. 1913. *Farm Management*. New York: Macmillan.

Waugh, F.V. 1929. *Quality as a Determinant of Vegetable Prices:* a *statistical study of quality factors influencing vegetable prices in the Boston wholesale market*. New York: Columbia University Press.

Waugh, F.V. (ed.) 1954. *Readings on Agricultural Marketing*. Ames, Iowa: Iowa State University Press.

Waugh, F.V. 1964. *Demand and Price Analysis: Some Examples from Agriculture*. US Department of Agriculture, Economic and Statistical Analysis Division, Economic Research Service, Technical Bulletin 1316.

Waugh, F.V. 1984. *Selected Writings on Agricultural Policy and Economic Analysis*. Ed. J.P. Houck and M.E. Abel, Minneapolis: University of Minnesota Press.

Waugh, F.V. Burtis, E.L. and Wolf, A.F. 1936. The controlled distribution of a crop among independent markets. *Quarterly Journal of Economics* 51, November, 1–41.

Wells, O.V. 1933. *Farmers' Response to Price in Hog Production and Marketing*. Washington, DC: US Department of Agriculture, Technical Bulletin 359.

Working, E.J. 1927. What do statistical 'demand curves' show? *Quarterly Journal of Economics* 41, February, 212–35.

Working, H. 1925. The statistical determination of demand curves. *Quarterly Journal of Economics* 39, August, 503–43.

Wright, S. 1921. Correlation and causation. *Journal of Agricultural Research* 20, January, 557–85.

Wright, S. 1925. *Corn and Hog Correlations*. Washington, DC: US Department of Agriculture, Bulletin 1300.

agricultural growth and population change. The macroeconomic theory of the relationship between demographic and agricultural change was developed by Malthus and Ricardo in the early stage of demographic transition in Europe, and interest in classical theory was revived in the middle of this century, when economists became aware of the unfolding demographic transition in other parts of the world. Ricardo (1817) distinguished between two types of agricultural expansion in response to population growth. One is the extensive margin, the expansion into new land which he supposed would yield diminishing returns to labour and capital because the new land was presumed to be more distant or of poorer quality than the land already in use. The other type, the intensive margin, is more intensive cultivation of the existing fields, raising crop yields by such means as better fertilization, weeding, draining, and other land preparation. This also was likely to yield diminishing returns to labour and capital. Therefore Ricardo assumed, with Malthus (1803), that population increase would sooner or later be arrested by a decline in real wages, increase of rents, and decline of per capita food consumption.

This theory takes no account of a third type of agricultural expansion in response to population growth: using the increasing labour force to crop the existing fields more frequently. This was in fact what was happening in England in Ricardo's time, when the European system of short fallow was being replaced by the system of annual cropping. Fallows are neither more distant nor of poorer quality than the cultivated fields, but if fallow periods are shortened or eliminated more labour and capital inputs are needed, both to prevent a decline of crop yields and to substitute for the decline in the amount of fodder for animals, which was previously obtained by the grazing of fallows. Therefore, this type of intensification is also likely to yield diminishing returns to labour and capital, but the additions to total output obtained by increasing the frequency of cropping are much larger than those obtainable by use of more labour and capital simply to raise crop yields. In fact, the Ricardian type of intensification is better viewed as a means not to raise crop yields, but more to prevent a decline of those yields as fallow is shortened or eliminated. When this third type of agricultural expansion by higher frequency of cropping is taken into account, elasticities of food supply in response to population growth are different from those assumed in classical theory.

The failure to take differences in frequency of cropping into account renders the classical theory unsuitable for the analysis of agricultural changes which accompany the demographic transition in developing countries in the second half of this century. Differences in population densities between developing countries are very large, and so are the related differences in frequency of cropping. The relevant classification for analysis of agricultural growth is not between new land and land which is sown and cropped each year, but the frequency at which a given piece of land is sown and cropped. Both in the past and today, we have a continuum of agricultural systems, ranging from the extreme case of land which is never used for crops, to the other extreme of land which is sown as soon as the previous crop is harvested. Increasing populations are provided with food and employment by gradual increase of the frequency of cropping.

In large, sparsely populated areas of Africa and Latin America, the local subsistence systems are pastoralism and long fallow systems of the same types as those used in most of Europe in the first millenium AD and earlier. In areas with extremely low population densities, twenty or more years of forest fallow alternate with one or two years of cropping, while four to six years of bush fallow alternate with several years of cropping in regions where population densities have become too high to permit the use of longer fallow periods. Methods of subsistence agriculture in developing countries with even higher population densities include short fallow systems (i.e. one or two crops followed by one or two years fallowing) or systems of annual cropping. In countries with very high population densities, including many Asian countries, some of the land is sown and cropped two or three times each year without any fallow periods.

If these differences in frequency of cropping are overlooked, or assumed to be adaptations to climatic or other permanent natural differences, the prospects for agricultural expansion in response to the growth of population and labour force look either more favourable, or more unfavourable, than they really are. In sparsely populated areas with long fallow systems, the areas which bear secondary forest or are used for grazing may be assumed incorrectly to be new land in the Ricardian sense, it being overlooked that they have the functions of recreating soil fertility or humidity, preventing erosion or suppressing troublesome weeds before the land is again used for crops. If neither the local cultivators nor their governments are aware of the risks of shortening fallow periods, and are not taking steps to avoid them, such shortening may damage the land and erosion, infertility or desertification may result. In such cases, the scope for accommodating increasing populations will prove to be less than expected, and later repair of the damage will become costly, if possible at all. On the other hand, if land presently used as fallow in long fallow systems is assumed to be of inferior quality, in accordance with Ricardian theory, the large possibilities for accommodation of increasing populations by shifting from long fallow to shorter or no fallow, will be overlooked or underestimated.

LABOUR SUPPLIES. When population growth accelerated in the developing countries in the middle of this century, economists applied Ricardo's distinction between expansion of cultivation to new land and attempts to raise crop yields by additional inputs of labour and capital. They therefore focused on the most densely populated countries in Asia, in which there was little new land. Since the possibilities for multicropping were not taken into account, it was assumed that the elasticity of food production in response to population growth would be very low in these countries, and that the acceleration of population growth would soon result in food shortages, high food prices, reduction of real wages, and steep increase of Ricardian rent.

Lewis (1954) suggested that in densely populated countries with little, if any uncultivated land, marginal returns to labour were likely to be zero or near to zero, and that a large part of the agricultural labour force was surplus labour, which could be transferred to non-agricultural employment without any diminution of agricultural output, even if there were no change in techniques. So Lewis recommended that rural-to-urban migration should be promoted, as a means of increasing marginal and average productivity in agriculture and of raising the share of the population employed in higher productivity occupations in urban areas. He confined his recommendation to densely populated countries, but many other economists made no distinction between densely and sparsely populated countries, assuming with Ricardo that uncultivated land must be of low quality so that a labour surplus would exist in all developing countries. The labour surplus theory contributed to create the bias in favour of industrial and urban development and the neglect of agriculture which has been a characteristic feature of government policy in many developing countries.

However, the labour surplus theory underestimates the demand for labour in agricultural systems with high frequency of cropping, based on labour intensive methods and use of primitive equipment. If population density in an area increases, fallow eliminated and multicropping introduced, then more and more labour-intensive methods must be used to preserve soil fertility, reduce weed growth and parasites, water the plants, grow fodder crops for animals, and protect the land. Some of the additional labour inputs are current operations, but others are labour investments. Before intensive cropping systems can be used, it may be necessary to terrace or level the land, build irrigation or drainage facilities, or fence the fields in order to control domestic animals. If these investments are made with human and animal muscle power, the necessary input of human labour is large. Even draught animals cannot reduce the work burden much, if fallows and other grazing land have been reduced so much that the cultivator must produce their fodder.

Part of the investments which are needed in order to increase the frequency of cropping are made by the cultivator with the same tools, animals and equipment that are used for current operations. Estimates of investments and savings in agricultural communities with increasing population are seriously low if they fail to include such labour investments. Due to the larger number of crops, the additional operations with each crop, and the labour investments, the demand for labour rises steeply when intensive land use is introduced. This contrasts with the assumptions of the labour surplus theory, which expects that the effect of population growth is always to add to the labour surplus.

When the theory of low supply elasticity and labour surplus in agriculture is combined with the theory of demographic transition, the prospects for densely populated countries with the majority of the population in agriculture look frightening. With the prospect of prolonged rapid growth of population (as forecast by the demographers) and with the poor prospects for expansion of food production and agricultural employment (implied by the labour surplus theory), it seemed obvious that sufficient capital could not be forthcoming for the enormous expansion of non-agricultural employment and output that was needed. So because the possibilities for adapting food production to population were underestimated, many economists suggested that the best, or even the only means to avoid catastrophe was the promotion of rapid fertility decline by family planning. This in turn overlooked the links between the level of economic development and the motivations for restriction of family size.

The motivation for adopting an additional work load in periods of increasing population, and the means to shoulder it, are different as between agricultural subsistence economies and communities of commercial farmers. In the former, the need to produce enough food to feed a larger family may be sufficient motivation for adopting a new agricultural system which, at least for a time, raises labour input more steeply than output. The way to shoulder a larger work load is to increase the labour input of all family members. In some regions most of the agricultural work is done by men, and in other regions, by women; but when the work load becomes heavier, women become more involved in agricultural work in the former regions, and men more involved in the latter; in both, children and old people have more work to do. For all members of agricultural families, average work days become longer and days of leisure fewer. The whole year may become one long busy season in areas with widespread multicropping, labour intensive irrigation, and transplanting from seed beds.

For commercial producers, the motivation for intensification of agriculture emerges when population growth or increasing urban incomes increase the demand for food, and push food prices up until more frequent cropping becomes profitable, in spite of increasing costs of production or need for more capital investment. By this change in sectoral terms of trade, a part of the burden of rural population increase is passed on to the urban population. The increase of agricultural prices is by no means all an increase of Ricardian rent, but is in good part a compensation for increasing costs of production. If the increase of food prices is prevented by government intervention or by imports of cheap food, the intensification will not take place.

Moreover, in regions with commercial agriculture, work seasons become longer when crop-frequency increases in response to population growth. Therefore the decline of real wages per work hour is at least partially compensated for by more employment in the off-seasons, and by more employment opportunities for women and children in the families of agricultural workers. The discussion of low or zero marginal productivity in agriculture suffers from a neglect of the seasonal differences in employment and wages. Many off-season operations are in fact required in order to obtain higher crop-frequency through labour intensive methods alone, and so may well appear to be of very low productivity if viewed in isolation from their real function. Wages for these operations, or indeed off-seasons wages generally, may be very low; but the seasonal differences in wages are usually larger. Therefore, accumulation of debt in the off-seasons with repayment in the peak seasons is a frequent pattern of expenditure in labouring families.

Low off-season wages are an important incentive for intensification of the cropping pattern in commercial farms, since much of the additional labour with multicropping, irrigation, labour intensive crops and feeding of animals falls in these seasons. But, when the same land is cropped more frequently in response to population growth, the demand for labour in the peak seasons also rises steeply, perhaps more than the supply of labour. In many cases, a large share of the agricultural population combines subsistence production on small plots of owned or rented land with wage labour for commercial producers in the agricultural peak seasons, and this contributes to considerable flexibility in the labour market. If real wages decline, because population increase pushes food prices up, full time agricultural workers have no other choice than to reduce their leisure and that of their spouse and children, and offer to work for very low wages in the off-season periods. But workers, who have some land to cultivate, may choose to limit their supply of wage labour, and instead cultivate their own land more intensively with family labour. Since they took wage labour mainly in the peak seasons, their limitation of the supply of wage labour may prevent a decline of, or cause an increase of, real wages in the peak seasons, and thus put a floor below the incomes of the full time workers.

The flexibility of the rural labour market is enhanced if not only labour but also land is hired in and out. A family that disposes of an increasing labour force may either do some work for other villagers, or rent some land from them, while a family that disposes of a reduced labour force may either hire some labour, or lease some land to others. With such a flexible system, prices for lease of land and wages will rapidly be adjusted to changes in labour supply. But the smooth adaptation of the system to population change will be hampered or prevented if, for political reasons, either hiring of labour or lease of land is made illegal, or changes in agricultural prices are prevented by government action.

TRANSPORT COST AND URBANIZATION. In Ricardian theory, marginal returns to labour and capital decline in response to population growth, partly because agricultural production is intensified, partly because it is expanded to inferior land, and partly because more distant land is taken into cultivation, thus increasing costs of transport. Thus, when population is increasing, producers have a choice between increasing costs of production, or increasing costs of transport between fields and consumers. However, there is a third possibility, which is to move the centre of consumption closer to land which is of similar quality to that which was used before the population became larger. Communities who use long fallow periods often move their habitations after long-term settlement in a forested area, and move to another area where the fertility of forest land has become high after a long period of non-use. Such movement of villages is likely to become more frequent, as population increases.

In other cases it is not the whole village which is moved, but an increasing number of villagers move their habitation to new lands, where they build isolated farmsteads or new hamlets. This may accommodate additional populations until all the space between the villages is filled up with habitations, and the choice in case of further population growth is between more frequent cropping, or use of inferior land, or long distance migration of part of the population.

The combination of shorter fallow periods and filling up of the space between the villages helps to create the conditions for emergence of small urban centres. Costs of transport are inversely related to the volume of transport, and roads, even primitive ones, are only economical, or feasible, with a relatively high volume of traffic. If fallow periods are very long, and distances between villages are large, there will be too few people in an area to handle both the production and transport which are necessary to supply a town with agricultural products. Urbanization and commercial agricultural production are only possible when population densities are relatively high, and fallow periods short. So when population in an area continues to increase a point may be reached when small market towns emerge, served by road and water transport, as happened in large parts of Europe in the beginning of this millenium.

With further growth of population it will again be necessary to choose between further intensification of agriculture at increasing costs, or moving the additional consumers (or some of them) to another location, where they can be supplied by less intensive agriculture, and with shorter distances of transport. So at this stage of development, new small market towns may emerge in between the old towns, or in peripheral areas together with agricultural settlement. In other words, instead of agricultural products moving over longer and longer distances, thus creating Ricardian rent in the neighbourhood of existing consumer centres, new centres of consumption may appear closer to the fields. In most of Europe, such a gradual spread of decentralized urbanization made it possible to delay the shift from short fallow agriculture to annual cropping to the late 18th or the 19th century. Areas with such a network of market towns have better conditions for development of small-scale and middle-sized industrialization than sparsely populated areas with a scattered population of subsistence farmers.

The long-distance migration from Europe to North America in the 19th century can be viewed as a further step in this movement of European agricultural producers and consuming centres to a region with lower population density, less intensive agriculture, and much lower agricultural costs. The urban centres in America were supplied by extensive systems of short fallow agriculture at a time when production in Western Europe had shifted to much more intensive agriculture with annual cropping and fodder production.

TECHNOLOGY. From ancient times, growth of population and increase of urbanization have provided incentives to technological improvements in agriculture, either by transfer of technology from one region to another, or by inventions in response to urgent demand for increase of output, either of land, or labour, or both. Until the 19th century, technological change in agriculture was a change from primitive technology, that is, human labour with primitive tools, to intermediate technology, that is, human labour aided by better hand tools, animal-drawn equipment, and water power for flow irrigation. In the classical theory of agricultural growth, such changes are means to promote population growth and urbanization, but they are assumed to be fortuitous inventions, and are not viewed as technological changes induced by population growth and increasing urbanization.

In the course of the 19th century, the continuing increase of the demand for agricultural products, and the increasing competition of urban centres for agricultural labour, induced further technological change in European and North American agriculture. The technological innovations of the industrial revolution were used to accomplish a gradual shift from intermediate to high-level technologies, that is, human labour aided by mechanized power and other industrial inputs. The chemical and engineering industries contributed to raise productivity of both land, labour and transport of agricultural products, and scientific methods were introduced in agriculture as a means of raising yields of crops and livestock.

The existence of such high-level technologies improves the possibilities for rapid expansion of agricultural production in developing countries as well, but because in North America and Europe these technologies were used to reduce direct labour input in agriculture, those economists who believed in the labour surplus theory feared that they would further increase labour surplus. However, the idea of a general labour surplus in agriculture in developing countries had never been unanimously agreed, and under the influence of empirical studies of intensive agriculture in densely populated regions, Schultz (1964) suggested that labour was likely to be fully occupied even in very small holdings, when primitive technology was used. Therefore output and income in such holdings could only be increased by introduction of industrial and scientific inputs, and human capital investment of the types used in industrialized countries.

Although the proponents and the opponents of the labour surplus theory had different views concerning the relationship between the demand for and supply of labour, they agreed in suggesting a low supply elasticity of output in response to labour inputs, because they overlooked, or underestimated, the large effects on output and employment which can be obtained by using high-level technologies to increase the frequency of cropping. The availability of new varieties of quickly maturing seeds, of chemical fertilizers, and of mechanized equipment for pumping water and land improvements, permits the use of multicropping on a much larger scale, and in much drier and colder climates than was possible before these new types of inputs existed. The new high-level technologies have changed the constraints on the size of the world population from the single one of land area to those of energy supply and costs, and of capital investment.

The new inputs permit a much more flexible adaptation of agriculture to changes in population and real wages. Intensive agriculture is no longer linked to low real wages, and it is possible, by changing the composition of inputs, to vary the rates of increase of employment and real wages for a given rate of increase of total output. By using a mixture of labour intensive and high-level techniques, adapted to the man-land ratio and the level of economic development, first Japan, and later many other densely populated countries, obtained rapid increases in both agricultural employment, output per worker, and total output. This 'Green Revolution' is an example of a technological change in agriculture induced by population change. The research which resulted in the development of these methods and inputs was undertaken and financed by national governments and international donors concerned about the effects of rapid population growth on the food situation in developing countries. Therefore, it focused mainly on improvement of agriculture in densely populated countries, where both governments and donors considered the problem to be most serious.

Agricultural producers who use high-level technologies are much more dependent upon the availability of good rural infrastructure than producers who use primitive or intermediate technologies. Transport and trade facilities are needed not only for the commercial surplus but also for the industrial inputs in agriculture; repair shops, electricity supply, technical schools, research stations, veterinary and extension services, are also needed. Therefore short-term supply elasticities differ between those regions which have and those which do not have the infrastructure needed for use of industrial and scientific inputs in agriculture. In the former, a rapid increase of output may be obtained by offering more attractive prices to the producers, while in the latter, increase of prices may have little effect on output, until the local infrastructure has been improved. Improvement of infrastructure may, on the other hand, be sufficient to obtain a change from subsistence production to commercial production, if it results in a major reduction in the difference between the prices paid to the local producers and those obtained in the consuming centres.

In densely populated regions with a network of small market towns, it is more feasible to introduce industrial and scientific inputs in agriculture, than in regions inhabited only by a scattered population of agricultural producers. Because per capita costs of infrastructure are lower in the first mentioned regions, they are more likely to have the necessary infrastructure, and if not, governments may be more willing to supply it. Thus sparsely populated regions are handicapped compared to densely populated ones, when high-level technologies are taken into use.

TENURE. Changes in output may also be prevented if the local tenure system is ill adapted to the new agricultural system. Land tenure is different in regions with different frequency of cropping. In regions with long fallow agriculture, individual producers have only usufruct rights in the land they use for cultivation, and the land, the pastures, and the forested land are all tribally owned. Before a plot is cleared for cultivation it is usually assigned by the local chief, and when large investments or other large works are needed the producers are organized by the chief as mutual work parties. If population increases and with it the demands for assignment of land, a stage may be reached when either the chief or the village community will demand a payment for such assignments, thereby changing the system of land tenure. Payments to the chief for assignment of land may turn him into a large scale landowner, and this payment may tip the balance and make more frequent cropping of land more economical than use of new plots, or settlement in new hamlets.

When frequency of cropping becomes sufficiently high that major permanent investments in land improvement are necessary, a change to private property in land may provide security of tenure to the cultivator, and make it possible for him to obtain credits. If at this stage no change of tenure is made by legal reform, a system of private property in land is likely to emerge by unlawful action and gradual change of custom; but in such cases the occupants, who have no legal rights to the land, may hesitate (or be unable) to make investments and land may remain unprotected against erosion and other damage.

In more densely populated areas, with more frequent cropping and need for large-scale irrigation and other land improvement, these investments may be organized by big landlords as labour service or by local authorities as wage labour, financed by local or general taxation. In order to change from a particular fallow system to another that is more intensive, it is likely that not only the ownership system in the cultivated plots but also that for uncultivated land must be changed, as must responsibility for infrastructure investment. Because of the links between the fallow system, the tenure system, and the responsibility for infrastructure investment, attempts to intensify the agricultural system by preservation (for political reasons) of the old tenure system and rural organization are likely to be unsuccessful, as are attempts to introduce new tenure systems that are unsuitable for the existing (or the desired, future) level of intensity and technology. Therefore, government policy is an important determinant of the agricultural response to population growth.

During fallow periods, the land is used for a variety of purposes: for gathering fuel and other wood, for hunting, for gathering of fertilizer, for grazing and browsing by domestic animals. Therefore, a change of the fallow system may create unintended damage to the environment unless substitutes are introduced for these commodities, or the pattern of consumption is changed. When hunting land becomes short, the right to hunt may be appropriated by the chiefs (or others), forcing the villagers to change their diet. When grazing land becomes short, enclosures may prevent the villagers (or some of them) from using it, or the village community may ration the right to pasture animals in the common grazing land and fallows, in order to prevent overgrazing and erosion, or desertification. These measures will impose a change of diet, and perhaps a change to fodder production in the fields.

NUTRITION. Both production and consumption change from land-using to less land-using products when population increases and agriculture is intensified. There may be a shift from beef and mutton to pork and poultry, from animal to vegetable products, from cereals to rootcrops for human consumption, and from grazing to production of fodder for animals. Under conditions of commercial farming, the changes in consumption and production are induced by increasing differentials between the prices of land-saving and land-using products. If the process of population growth is accompanied by decline of real wages, the changes in consumption patterns for the poorest families may be large. This may result in protein deficiencies and malnutrition with spread of the disease–malnutrition syndrome; this causes high child mortality because disease prevents the child from eating and digesting food, and malnutrition reduces the resistance to disease.

The classical economists had suggested that continuing population growth would result in malnutrition, famine and disease, which would re-establish the balance between population and resources by increasing mortality. But they also envisaged the possibility of an alternative model, in which population growth was prevented by voluntary restraint on fertility. Malthus (1803) talked of moral restraint and Ricardo (1817) of the possibility that the workers would develop a taste for comforts and enjoyment, which would prevent a superabundant population. However, it was not ethical or psychological changes but the economic and social changes resulting from increasing industrialization and urbanization which induced a deceleration of rates of population growth, first in Europe and North America, and later in other parts of the world.

GOVERNMENT POLICIES. The deceleration of rates of population growth in Europe and North America coincided with a decline in the income elasticity of demand for food due to the increase in per capita incomes. As a result the rate of increase in the demand for food slowed down, just as the rate of increase of production accelerated due to the spread of high-level technologies and scientific methods in agriculture. If it had not

been for government intervention in support of agriculture these changes would have led to abandonment of production in marginal land, and use of less industrial inputs in the land that was kept in cultivation. But this process of adjustment was prevented by attempts to preserve the existing system of family farming. Large farms could utilize high-level technologies (especially mechanized inputs) better than smaller ones, but governments wanted to prevent the replacement of small or middle sized farms by larger capitalist farms, or company farming. Therefore, both Western Europe and North America gradually developed comprehensive systems of agricultural protection and subsidization of agriculture, agricultural research, and other rural infrastructure. In spite of this support a large proportion of the small farms disappeared and much marginal land went out of cultivation, while the support actually encouraged large farms, and farms in the most favoured regions, to expand their production; they increased their use of fertilizer and other inputs, and invested in expansion of capacity for vegetable and animal production. So supply still continued to outrun demand, and protection against imports and subsidies to exports still continued to increase, while the industrialized countries turned from being net importers to net exporters of more and more agricultural products.

In the discussions about labour surplus and low elasticity of agricultural production in non-industrialized countries, Nurkse (1953) had suggested that an increase in agricultural production could be obtained if the surplus population was employed in rural work projects. In the period until such a programme, in conjunction with industrialization and a deceleration of population growth, could re-establish the balance between demand for and supply of food, he recommended that temporary food imports (preferably as food aid) should be used to prevent food shortage. Because of the increasing costs of financing and disposing of the food surplus, Nurkse's suggestion of food aid was well received by Western governments, and transfer of food, as aid or subsidized exports, reached large dimensions.

Some governments in developing countries did use food aid and commercial imports of the food surpluses of the industrialized countries as stop-gap measures, until their own promotion of rural infrastructure and other support to agriculture would make it possible for production to catch up with the rapidly increasing demand for food. But for many other governments the availability of cheap imports and gifts of food became a welcome help to avoid the use of their own resources to support agriculture and invest in rural infrastructure. Even in those developing countries with a large majority of the population occupied in agriculture, the share of government expenditure devoted to agriculture and related rural infrastructure is small, and within this small amount priority is usually given to development of non-food export crops, which often supply a large share of foreign exchange earnings. Exports of food crops are unattractive because of the surplus disposal of the industrialized countries, which exerts a downward pressure on world market prices. Therefore, both producers and governments in developing countries focus on the types of crops which do not compete with these subsidized exports. In regions in which the necessary infrastructure was available, employment and output of such export crops increased rapidly, not only in countries with abundant land resources but also in many densely populated countries, which shifted in part from food to non-food crops. This general shift from food to non-food crops contributed to a downward pressure on export prices of the latter crops in the world market.

Food imports can have important short-term advantages for the importing country. Rapidly increasing urban areas can be supplied at low prices and without the need to use government resources to obtain expansion of domestic production. Moreover, counterpart funds from food aid can be used to finance general government expenditure, and in countries with high levies on export crops, government revenue increases when production is shifted from food to export crops. However, although there might be short-term advantages of food imports and food aid, the long-term cost of neglecting agricultural and rural development can be very high. The lack of transport facilities and local stocks, and the lack of irrigation in dry and semi-dry areas, may transform years of drought to years of famine. When governments do not invest in rural infrastructure and fail to provide the public services which are necessary for the use of high technology inputs, the latter can be used only by large companies (who can themselves finance the necessary infrastructure) or in a few areas close to large cities.

Without cost reduction by improvement of the transport network and agricultural production, commercial food production may in many areas be unable to compete with imports. Commercial production will decline and subsistence producers will not become commercial producers. Instead, the most enterprising young villagers will emigrate in order to earn money incomes elsewhere. A larger and larger share of the rapidly increasing urban consumption must be imported, and food imports become a drug on which the importers become more and more dependent. The increasing dependency of many developing countries on food imports and food grants is often seen as a confirmation of the classical theory of inelastic food supply, and an argument for continuation of the policy of production subsidies and surplus disposal in America and Western Europe. Food imports are seen as gap fillers, bridging over increasing differences between food consumption and national food production in developing countries; but in many cases the gap is actually created by the food imports, because of their effect on local production and rural development.

FERTILITY. Contrary to the expectations prevalent in the middle of this century, government policy has proved to be a more important determinant of agricultural growth than the man–resource ratio, and the response to rapid population growth has often been better in densely populated countries than in sparsely populated ones with much better natural conditions for agricultural growth. The differences in agricultural growth rates and policies have in turn contributed to create differences in demographic trends, partly by their influence on industrial and urban development and partly by the effects on rural fertility, mortality and migration.

Because of their preoccupation with the man–land ratio, governments in densely populated countries not only devoted more attention and financial resources to agriculture than governments in sparsely populated countries, they also more often devoted attention and financial resources to policies aimed at reducing fertility. Moreover, tenure systems in densely populated countries usually provided less encouragement to large family size than tenure systems in sparsely populated countries.

In many densely populated countries with intensive agricultural systems, much of the rural population consists of small and middle-sized landowners, and such people are more likely to be motivated to a smaller family size than are landless labour and people with insecure tenure. They are less dependent upon help from adult children in emergencies and old age, because they can mortgage, lease, or sell land, or

cultivate with hired labour. They may also have an interest in avoiding division of family property among too many heirs. If they live in areas where child labour is of little use in agriculture, they may have considerable economic interest in not having large families, and be responsive to advice and help from family planning services.

In sparsely populated regions with large landholdings, the rural population seldom has access to modern means of fertility control, and motivations for family restrictions are weak. A large share of the rural population tends to be landless or nearly landless workers, and if not they may be without security in land. So they are much more dependent upon help from adult children in emergencies and old age than are landowners, or tenants with secure tenure. If, moreover, their children work for wages in ranches, farms and plantations, the period until a child contributes more to family income than it costs is too short to provide sufficient economic motivation for family restriction.

People who use long fallow systems in regions with tribal tenure have even more motivation for large family size than landless workers. The size of the area they can dispose of for cultivation is directly related to the size of their family, and most of the work, at least in food production, is done by women and children. So a man can become rich by having several wives and large numbers of children working for him. Moreover, unless he has acquired other property a man's security in old age depends on his adult children and younger wives, since he cannot mortgage or sell land in which he has only usufruct rights. Because of the differences in motivations for family size provided by individual and tribal tenure systems, the start of the fertility decline in regions with long fallow systems is likely to be linked to the time when population increase induces the replacement of the tribal tenure system by another system of tenure, and a decline is then more likely if it is replaced by small-scale land ownership than if it is replaced by large-scale farming.

In addition to the tenure system, changes in technological levels in agriculture and the availability of economic and social infrastructure may influence the timing of fertility decline in rural areas. The heavy reliance upon female and child labour in those densely populated areas in which agriculture is intensified by means of labour alone, may provide motivation for large families in spite of the shortage of land. Introduction of higher level technologies may then, in such cases, reduce a man's motivation to have a large family because it reduces the need for female and child labour. Use of intermediate and high-level technologies is nearly always reserved for adult men, while women and children do the operations for which primitive technologies are used. So when primitive technologies are replaced by higher level ones in more and more agricultural operations, men usually get more work to do and the economic contributions of their wives and children decline, thus reducing their economic interest in large family size. Moreover, in regions with little rural development high rates of child mortality may delay fertility decline, and the large-scale migration of youth from such areas may have a similar effect if parents can count on receiving remittances from emigrant offspring.

However, the relationship between rural development and fertility is complicated. Parents may want a large family for other than economic reasons, and increases in income due to rural development or to better prices for agricultural products make it easier for them to support a large family, thus preventing or delaying fertility decline. Other things being equal, fertility is positively related to income; but in developing societies most increases in income are caused and accompanied by technological, occupational and spatial changes that tend to encourage fertility decline, and the operation of these opposing effects may result in a relatively long time lag between rural modernization and fertility decline.

E. BOSERUP

See also DEMOGRAPHIC TRANSITION; HUNTING AND GATHERING ECONO-MIES; LABOUR SURPLUS ECONOMIES; MALTHUS'S THEORY OF POPULATION; NUTRITION; PEASANTS; THÜNEN, JOHAN VON.

BIBLIOGRAPHY

Boserup, E. 1965. *The Conditions of Agricultural Growth*. London: Allen & Unwin.
Boserup, E. 1981. *Population and Technological Change*. Chicago: Chicago University Press.
Lewis, W.A. 1954. Economic development with unlimited supplies of labour. *Manchester School of Economic and Social Studies* 22(2), May, 139-91.
Malthus, T.R. 1803. *An Essay on Population*. London: J.M. Dent, 1958.
Nurkse, R. 1953. *Problems of Capital Formation in Underdeveloped Countries*. Oxford: Oxford University Press.
Ricardo, D. 1817. *The Principles of Political Economy and Taxation*. Ed. P. Sraffa, Cambridge: Cambridge University Press, 1951.
Schultz, T.W. 1964. *Transforming Traditional Agriculture*. New Haven: Yale University Press.
Schuttjer, W. and Stokes, C. (eds) 1984. *Rural Development and Human Fertility*. New York and London: Macmillan.

agricultural supply. One of the earliest-investigated and most fruitful areas for econometric studies has been the estimation of agricultural supply functions. Studies date back at least to the work of Smith (1928) and Bean (1929) on US agriculture in the 1920s. Early studies adopted a fairly static view. Nerlove's (1958) work on *The Dynamics of Supply*, with adaptive price expectations and adjustment processes for United States agriculture, spawned renewed interest in specification and estimation issues on this topic. The roughly concurrent controversies about market responsiveness in developing-country agriculture (e.g., Schultz, 1964) led to a shift in emphasis towards this concern. In the last quarter century a veritable flood of such studies has appeared. More recently supply studies have incorporated more systematic emphasis on systemic characteristics, risk aversion, the household/farm model framework and alternative price expectations. This article reviews these basic developments in empirical studies of agricultural supply by starting with the most common framework for such analyses and then considering what questions arise when some of the traditional assumptions are weakened.

PERFECTLY-COMPETITIVE, EQUILIBRIUM SUPPLIES WITH NO RISK. Most empirical studies of agricultural supply have assumed perfect competition, equilibrium, no risk and separability be-tween the farm production decisions and the farm household consumption decisions. Under such conditions the supply func-tion for a specific product of an individual producer is the marginal cost function for product prices sufficiently high so that variable costs are covered (and zero otherwise). The market supply function is the sum of all individual supply functions. As such, the supply function depends on all relevant expected product and input prices, all fixed factors, and technology. There are two important elements of dynamics in the supply process: the adjustment of short-run fixed factors over longer time periods and the creation of expectations for product

harvest prices at the time that inputs, especially land, are commited.

Early studies basically posited a supply function as dependent on relevant expected prices (P^*):

$$S = f(P^*) \tag{1}$$

where S is a vector of supplies of different agricultural products and P^* is a vector of expected (or, at least after Nerlove's contributions, expected normal) prices.

Expected prices most commonly were represented by one-period lagged prices for products for which actual harvest prices would not be known until harvest time and by actual prices at the time of the input decision for inputs. Frequently, instead of using supplies as the dependent variable, areas devoted to individual crops were used since land is a critical input for which allocation among crops basically is under the control of the farmer.

The seminal contributions of Nerlove (1956, 1958) were: first to generalize the formation of price expectations with adaptive expectations and second, to incorporate a distributed-lag ad-justment process to reflect that adjustment is not costless. His basic model for an annual crop, thus, is:

$$A_t^* = a_0 + a_1 P_t^* + a_2 Z_t + u_t \tag{2}$$

$$A_t = A_{t-1} + \gamma(A_t^* - A_{t-1}) \tag{3}$$

$$P_t^* = P_{t-1}^* + \beta(P_{t-1} - P_{t-1}^*) \tag{4}$$

where

A_t is actual area under cultivation in period t,
A_t^* is 'desired' or equilibrium area under cultivation in t,
P_t is actual product price in t,
P_t^* is 'expected normal' price in t,
Z_t is other observed, exogenous factors, and
u_t is a disturbance term.

Relation (2) states that desired area is a function of expected normal prices, other exogenous factors, and a disturbance term; but neither the desired area nor the expected price typically is observed. Relation (3) states that there is a distributed-lag adjustment in actual area towards desired area, with γ the 'coefficient of adjustment'. Relation (4) states that the expected normal price in period t is the expected normal price in the previous period plus an adjustment for the discrepancy in the previous period between the expected normal and the actual price. Substitution of (3) and (4) into (2) gives an expression in terms of observable variables:

$$\begin{aligned} A_t = {} & [(1 - \beta) + (1 - \gamma)]A_{t-1} - (1 - \beta)(1 - \gamma)A_{t-2} \\ & + a_1\gamma\beta P_{t-1} + a_2\gamma Z_t - a_2\gamma(1 - \beta)Z_{t-1} \\ & + a_0 + \gamma u_t - \gamma(1 - \beta)u_{t-1}. \end{aligned} \tag{5}$$

Literally hundreds of estimates of some variant of this supply relation have been made. Initially they focused on developed-country agriculture. Due to the debate over the market-responsiveness of traditional developing agriculture, emphasis then shifted relatively to developing-country agriculture in studies by Krishna (1963, 1965), Behrman (1966, 1968b) and a host of others. Askari and Cummings (1976, 1977) noted over 600 such estimates by the mid 1970s. These studies vary substantially regarding the identification of relevant observed exogenous variables, the treatment of serial correlation in the disturbance term, what prices are included, and the role of yields. Despite such variations they point to a pattern of significant and often substantial price responses in agricultural supplies, with some indication of greater responses for higher-income and more-literate farmers, larger farms, own-operated farms, farms with access to irrigation, and crops with lower yield variability. This price responsiveness in developing-country agriculture suggests that measures to suppress particular agricultural prices significantly discourage domestic agricultural supplies of those products. An aggregate supply response study for a cross-section of developing countries by Peterson (1979) also reports substantial discouragement of aggregate agricultural production in these countries by price policies, though Binswanger, Mundlak, Yang and Bowers (1985) suggest that this result is an artifact of the price data used. The price responsiveness in developed countries suggests that price and income-support programmes induce expanded agricultural supplies for the products affected.

One subset of these studies merits particular mention: those that relate to perennials and livestock. Most of these studies have adapted the above model to incorporate long lags due to the long gestation between investment and production, with adjustment lags posited in respect to desired capital stock or desired investment. In a few cases (e.g. French and Matthews, 1971) there are extensive explicit empirical representations of the various critical variables in perennial and livestock production: production, investment, nonbearing new capital, and old capital removal. In many cases, however, the lack of basic data on capital stocks has left bearing stocks to be inferred from outputs or controlled for by differencing outputs for products such as cocoa in which there is a long period once trees have matured during which yields are approximately constant (e.g., Bateman, 1965, 1968; Behrman, 1968a, 1969). Despite the greater complexities of perennials and livestock production and the greater longevity of the related capital stock, there has been little effort to go beyond an essentially static formulation for the demand for the relevant capital stock. Conceptually this problem can be formulated as a dynamic programming model. But, as Nerlove (1979) notes, severe difficulties exist in the empirical implementation of such a strategy because of data inadequacies and because of the uncertainty of future technological developments.

Two additional modifications subsequent to the widespread use of the supply relation in (5) are worth noting. First, the more recent formulation of the supply relation is to start with a profit function and to note that the partial derivative with respect to a particular product price gives the supply function for that product and the partial derivative with respect to the price for a production input gives the input demand function. This approach has the advantage of focusing on the interrelations in a system of supply and demand relations within a multi-product and multi-input context and in indicating the nature of cross-equation systemic restrictions. The natural distinction between outputs and inputs within this context also sharpens the question about the frequent usage of area as the dependent variable in supply-response relations; such estimates presumably are characterized better as approximations to input demand relations though, as such, they provide information on the underlying parameters of the system that pertain to supply responses. Examples of profit-function-based agricultural supply studies include Lau and Yotopoulos (1971) and Bapna, Binswanger and Quizon (1984). In most applications of this approach, the concerns of Nerlove (1956, 1958) about the empirical dynamics of price expectation formulation and of adjustment have been ignored. Instead, assumptions of immediate adjustment and static product price expectations (i.e., the previous period's prices) prevail. There would seem to be further gains in understanding from the incorporation of such dynamic concerns into these

system estimates, though full incorporation of such dynamics leads to dynamic programming models with the problems mentioned above.

Second, representations of price expectations have changed. There has been growing emphasis throughout economics on 'rational expectations' (Muth, 1961), which are the minimum mean square forecasts based on the information available at the time of the forecast, including that about the structure of the system. There have been some efforts to incorporate rational price expectations into agricultural supply studies, though with reduced-form relations with the same variables as in relation (4) (e.g., Eckstein, 1984). The question remains open whether such rational expectations are preferable representations of expectations actually held by farmers and, if they are, about what information is available for farmers to utilize in their expectation formulation. Nerlove (1979) observes, for example, that the rejection of the proposition that farmers respond to the expectation of some average of prices in all future periods with adaptive expectations also implies the rejection of the notion that farmers are adjusting to a well-defined, longer-run equilibrium because such an equilibrium is well-defined only for stationary price expectations.

NON-SEPARABILITY BETWEEN FARM PRODUCTION AND CONSUMPTION. For the currently developed countries, the separability assumption probably is plausible. Most production is sold on markets, most consumption goods are purchased on markets, there probably are not consumption labour productivity links and markets are relatively complete (though risk may be a problem, see below).

For the developing countries, in contrast, the separability assumption may be misleading for millions of farm households. One respect in which these assumptions may be misleading is with regard to responses in total production versus the marketed surplus. Many of these households consume large shares of the basic staples that they produce. As a result, price responses in the marketed surplus may differ substantially from those in total production, depending on what is the household own consumption response. Krishna (1965) and Behrman (1966) presented early models of the price elasticity of the marketed surplus that incorporate the income elasticity of consumption within the household. Such models demonstrate that the price elasticity of the marketed surplus may differ greatly from those of total supply if own-consumption accounts for a substantial share of production and if either own-consumption price or income elasticities is large.

Two other reasons for which integrated household-farm models have been emphasized are incomplete markets (e.g., Lau, Lin and Yotopoulos, 1978; Barnum and Squire, 1979a, 1979b) and productivity–consumption links (e.g., Leibenstein, 1957; Bliss and Stern, 1978a, 1978b; Stiglitz, 1976; Pitt and Rosenzweig, 1986; Behrman and Deolalikar, 1987; Strauss, 1986). Both these phenomena are thought to be common in developing countries. If they are important, agricultural supply should be explored within the context of the household-farm model. This means that prices for consumption goods and services (e.g., for schools, clothing and health-care) and fixed household assets should enter into the determination of agricultural supplies, in addition to prices of agricultural products and inputs and fixed agricultural factors. For the examination of the determinants of some perennials and livestock, for instance, even the prices that determine births, infant and child mortality and migration in principle should be included since such prices simultaneously determine the long-run agricultural capital stocks (with the obvious link through the long-run availability of household labour). While there are a few studies of agricultural supply that have emphasized the conceptual importance of the farm-household model (e.g., Lau, Lin and Yotopoulos, 1978; Barnum and Squire, 1979a, 1979b), in empirical applications the full ramifications of such demand-production simultaneity are yet to be explored.

RISK AND RISK AVERSION. Farmers are subject to production risk and, for farmers who partake in markets, price and input-availability risks. Once it was established that developing-country farmers seem responsive to expected prices, considerable emphasis shifted to the role of risk and risk aversion in determining agricultural supplies. Many studies have attempted to test for the supply response to risk by including ad hoc empirical measures of risk (e.g., variances in prices or in yields as in Behrman, 1968b) and report some evidence of negative responses to risk. Several experiments have been undertaken to attempt to identify the nature and the magnitude of risk aversion among farms. The most satisfactory of these to date is by Binswanger (1980, 1981) in which the payoffs were real and substantial. He concludes that his results are consistent with expected utility maximizing behaviour (and not with security-based forms of behaviour in which farmers are concerned primarily with avoiding disaster) and that most individuals are risk averse, but not very risk averse.

How should supply responses be modelled given the possibility of risk and risk aversion? Newbery and Stiglitz (1981) provide a recent theoretical synthesis of the implications of risk and risk aversion for modelling supply in their discussion of the theory of commodity price stabilization. They demonstrate that risk may have an impact even on a risk-neutral farmer; such a farmer does not just maximize the product of expected prices and expected quantities minus costs if prices and quantities are correlated (as would be the case for a perfectly competitive farmer in an area which accounts for a large share of the market, as with West African cocoa production), but also must incorporate the price-quantity covariance in order to maximize expected profits. They also argue that rigorous specification of supply behaviour under risk aversion is difficult and should proceed from first principles of constrained utility maximization (which is likely to require a farm-household framework as well). Binswanger (1982) further elaborates on the difficulties of econometric estimation under risk preferences. I am unaware of empirical studies to date that are consistent with such a framework.

DISEQUILIBRIUM. The standard framework for empirical agricultural supply analysis assumes equilibrium, or adjustment towards equilibrium in which observed prices convey all the available information. As Schultz (1975) and Nerlove (1979) emphasize, however, for some important questions such as the nature of the historical transformation of developed-country agriculture and the current transformations of developing-country agriculture, disequilibria are likely to be common and visible prices are not likely to convey all of the relevant information available to farmers. For studies of agricultural supply responses in such contexts, a broader perspective is desirable to represent the impacts of differential capabilities of economic entities to deal with disequilibria, public investments, development of markets, technological and demographic changes, and governmental roles. Embedding

supply studies within this larger context in order to attain further understanding remains a major challenge.

JERE R. BEHRMAN

See also ADAPTIVE EXPECTATIONS; AGRICULTURAL ECONOMICS; COBWEB THEOREM; PRODUCTION AND COST FUNCTIONS.

BIBLIOGRAPHY

Askari, H. and Cummings, J.T. 1976. *Agricultural Supply Response: A Survey of the Econometric Evidence.* New York: Praeger Publishers.

Askari, H. and Cummings, J.T. 1977. Estimating agricultural supply response with the Nerlove model: a survey. *International Economic Review* 18, 257–92.

Bapna, S.L., Binswanger, H. and Quizon, J.B. 1984. Systems of output supply and factor demand equations for semi-arid tropical India. *Indian Journal of Agricultural Economics* 39(2), April–June, 179–202.

Barnum, H.N. and Squire, L. 1979a. An econometric application of the theory of farm-household. *Journal of Development Economics* 6(1), 79–102.

Barnum, H.N. and Squire, L. 1979b. *A Model of an Agriculture Household: Theory and Evidence.* Baltimore: Johns Hopkins for the World Bank, chs 3–6.

Bateman, M. 1965. Aggregate and regional supply functions for Ghanaian cocoa, 1946–62. *Journal of Farm Economics* 47, 384–401.

Bateman, M. 1968. *Cocoa in the Ghanaian Economy: An Econometric Model.* Amsterdam: North-Holland.

Bean, L.H. 1929. The farmers' response to price. *Journal of Farm Economics* 11, 368–85.

Behrman, J.R. 1966. Price elasticity of the marketed surplus of a subsistence crop. *Journal of Farm Economics* 48, 875–93.

Behrman, J.R. 1968a. Monopolistic cocoa pricing. *American Journal of Agricultural Economics* 50, 702–19.

Behrman, J.R. 1968b. *Supply Response in Underdeveloped Agriculture: A Case Study of Four Major Annual Crops in Thailand 1937–1963.* Amsterdam: North-Holland.

Behrman, J.R. 1969. Econometric model simulations of the world rubber market 1950–1980. In *Essays in Industrial Econometrics*, vol. 3, ed. L.R. Klein, Philadelphia: Economic Research Unit, Wharton School of Finance and Commerce, University of Pennsylvania.

Behrman, J.R. and Deolalikar, A.B. 1987. Health and nutrition. In *Handbook on Development Economics*, ed. H.B. Chenery and T.N. Srinivasan, Amsterdam: North-Holland.

Binswanger, H.P. 1980. Attitudes towards risk: experimental measurement evidence in rural India. *American Journal of Agricultural Economics* 62(3), 395–407.

Binswanger, H.P. 1981. Attitudes towards risk: theoretical implications of an experiment in rural India. *Economic Journal* 91, December, 867–90.

Binswanger, H.P. 1982. Empirical estimation and use of risk preferences: discussion. *American Journal of Agricultural Economics* 64(2), May, 391–3.

Binswanger, H., Mundlak, Y. Yang, M.C. and Bowers, A. 1985. Estimation of aggregate supply response. Washington: World Bank, Report No. ARU 48.

Bliss, C. and Stern, N. 1978a. Productivity, wages and nutrition, part I: the theory. *Journal of Development Economics* 5(4), 331–62.

Bliss, C. and Stern, N. 1978b. Productivity, wages and nutrition, part II: some observations. *Journal of Development Economics* 5(4), 363–98.

Eckstein, Z. 1984. A rational expectations model of agricultural supply. *Journal of Political Economy* 92(1), February, 1–19.

French, B.C. and Matthews, J.L. 1971. A supply response model for perennial crops. *American Journal of Agricultural Economics* 53, 478–90.

Jarvis, L. 1974. Cattle as capital goods and ranchers as portfolio managers: an application to the Argentine cattle sector. *Journal of Political Economy* 82, 489–520.

Krishna, R. 1963. Farm supply response in India–Pakistan: a case study of the Punjab region. *Economic Journal* 73, 477–87.

Krishna, R. 1965. The marketable surplus function for a subsistence crop: an analysis with Indian data. *Economic Weekly* 17, February.

Lau, L.J., Lin, W.-L. and Yotopoulos, P. 1978. The linear logarithmic expenditure system: an application to consumption-leisure choice. *Econometrica* 46(4), 843–68.

Lau, L.J. and Yotopoulos, P.A. 1971. A test for relative efficiency and application to Indian agriculture. *American Economic Review* 61, 94–109.

Leibenstein, H. 1957. *Economic Backwardness and Economic Growth.* New York: John Wiley.

Muth, J.F. 1961. Rational expectations and the theory of price movements. *Econometrica* 29, 315–35.

Nerlove, M. 1956. Estimates of supply of selected agricultural commodities. *Journal of Farm Economics* 38, 496–509.

Nerlove, M. 1958. *The Dynamics of Supply: Estimation of Farmers' Response to Price.* Baltimore: Johns Hopkins University Press.

Nerlove, M. 1967. Distributed lags and unobserved components in economic time series. In *Ten Economic Essays in the Tradition of Irving Fisher*, ed. W. Fellner et al., New York: Wiley, 126–69.

Nerlove, M. 1979. The dynamics of supply: retrospect and prospect. *American Journal of Agricultural Economics* 61(5), 867–88.

Newbery, D.M.G. and Stiglitz, J.E. 1981. *The Theory of Commodity Price Stabilization.* Oxford: Clarendon Press.

Nowshirvani, V. 1971. Land allocation under uncertainty in subsistence agriculture. *Oxford Economic Papers* 23, November, 445–55.

Peterson, W.L. 1979. International farm prices and the social cost of cheap food policies. *American Journal of Agricultural Economics* 61, 12–21.

Pitt, M.M. and Rosenzweig, M. 1986. Agricultural prices, food consumption and the health and productivity of farmers. In *Agricultural Household Models: Extensions, Applications and Policy*, ed. I.J. Singh, L. Squire and J. Strauss, Washington: World Bank.

Schultz, T.W. 1964. *Transforming Traditional Agriculture.* New Haven: Yale University Press.

Schultz, T.W. 1975. The value of the ability to deal with disequilibrium. *Journal of Economic Literature* 13, 827–46.

Smith, B.B. 1928. Factors affecting the price of cotton. US Department of Agriculture Technical Bulletin No. 50, Washington, DC.

Stiglitz, J. 1976. The efficiency wage hypothesis, surplus labour, and the distribution of income in LDC's. *Oxford Economic Papers, New Series* 28, 185–207.

Strauss, J. 1986. Does better nutrition raise farm productivity? *Journal of Political Economy* 94(2), April, 297–320.

agriculture and economic development. Most people in developing countries derive their livelihood from agriculture. Agricultural growth, and the conditions governing the distribution of its produce, are, therefore, of direct relevance to them. Agriculture is also important in that if it fails to develop at a suitable pace, it could prove to be a critical constraint on the growth of industrial and other sectors. It is the supplier of an essential wage good, viz. food; it also supplies raw materials to industry and, looked at from another angle, could provide the motive for industrial expansion by being a market for industrial goods.

Compared to just about one-fifteenth of the labour force engaged in agriculture in industrial countries, in developing countries the proportion is often in the range of half to four-fifths of the total. The proportion of output originating in agriculture, however, is much less – reflecting the lower output per man engaged in agriculture compared to other sectors. This disparity in productivity is greater in developing countries than in industrial countries.

The low productivity per worker implies that the proportion of output absorbed within agriculture itself, i.e. self consumption, is high, leaving little surplus for use outside agriculture. In a poor developing country, a farm family

produces enough food for itself and two other people; in contrast, in an industrial country like Britain, the proportion of labour force needed to provide food for the whole of its population is less than one-twentieth.

The importance of improved productivity in agriculture can also be viewed from another angle. The larger is the proportion of agricultural output not absorbed within agriculture itself, the greater is the market for non-agricultural goods. Agricultural growth, along with growth in exports and public investment, could constitute an important exogenous source of demand for industry.

The preceding argument can be illustrated with the help of Figure 1. In Figure 1, ON represents the level of employment in agriculture; and corresponding to it, there are OQ and OC, which trace the levels of total agricultural output and consumption within the agricultural sector respectively. At ON_1 level of employment, total output is $N_1 Q_1$, consumption is $N_1 C_1$, leaving a surplus of $C_1 Q_1$ for use outside agriculture. The surplus $C_1 Q_1$ sustains a level of employment in the non-agricultural (industrial) sectors, which results in an output level of $N_1 M_1$. The curve OQ has a declining slope reflecting diminishing returns in agriculture. This arises from the finiteness of land and other natural resources, yielding diminishing returns as the scale of other inputs is expanded. Technological progress, however, could result in outward shifts of the curve, so that for any given level of employment, output is higher. It would also result in larger surplus, enabling a larger level of employment to be sustained in the non-agricultural sector.

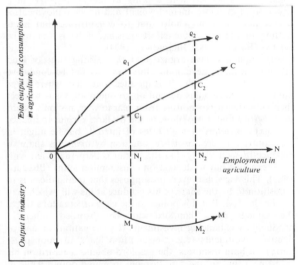

Figure 1

Productivity-enhancing investment in agriculture, however, depends not only on the state of knowledge, but also on conditions governing the adoption of technology: it depends on the land tenure system which determines how the agricultural produce is divided between owners of land and agricultural labour; on the terms of trade between agriculture and industry, which determine the relative cheapness of industrial inputs vis-à-vis agricultural produce; on the level of demand for agricultural produce; among other things. These issues are discussed below.

LAND REFORM. Land reforms were attempted in several countries not only with a view to improving the distribution of incomes, but also as a means of improving incentives to the farmer. In many countries, historically, land came to be concentrated in large holdings. In some cases, a portion of the landholding was cultivated directly by the landlord, the rest being leased out to tenants either in return for labour services or simply for rent, fixed or as a share of the produce. In some countries, large holdings of plantations developed, often owned and managed by expatriates; in some countries (e.g. the Caribbean, Mauritius, Fiji) labour to work on these plantations was brought over either as slaves or as indentured labour; the labourers were frequently given small plots of land to raise subsistence food and as a means of tying their services to the estate (Byres (ed.), 1983; Bagchi, 1982).

The conventional Marshallian argument for land reform was that in a situation where a tenant is obliged to pay a share of output as rent to the landlord, his incentive to maximize output is lost; instead of applying inputs to a point where the marginal output equals marginal cost, he would apply inputs only to the point where his share of marginal output is equal to the marginal cost. A tenant would also not undertake capital improvements if he did not enjoy security of tenure. It is suggested, therefore, that land reform which confers ownership rights on the tenant or improves the security of tenure would raise productivity. In practice, however, the situation is found to be far more complex than is implied in the above argument. It is found (e.g. South Asia) that land is leased-in and -out by all classes of farmers, big and small, largely because of reasons relating to operational efficiency. Moreover, crop-sharing is adopted to distribute risk, and is sometimes associated with sharing of inputs. Further, in a situation of endemic unemployment and underemployment, a tenant may have no choice but to demonstrate that he is putting in the maximum effort possible, if he is not to be evicted (Bagchi, 1982; Bharadwaj, 1974).

Some scholars have argued that the existing state of land relations in many developing countries may not be conducive to agricultural growth. It is pointed out that where large numbers of households depend on consumption loans to meet their subsistence expenditure from year to year, not only might the landlord find it profitable to use his farm surplus to finance consumption loans at high rates of interest, but he might in fact contrive to create such a situation by fixing his share of produce in such a way that the tenant is perpetually left with no alternative but to depend on consumption loans (Bhaduri, 1983). This view, however, presupposes that the landlord is in a position to fix the share of his produce at his will, which may not be the case. But this points to the class of situations where the savings of a landlord can be absorbed either in productivity-enhancing investments (e.g. irrigation) or unproductive investments (e.g. consumption loans to poor peasantry). In both instances, the landlord obtains a return on his investment, but in one case through increased output while in the other it would be through a change in the distribution of income. It could be argued that in a country such as India, the caste system effectively contrives to prevent a portion of the peasantry from gaining access to markets or resources in a free manner, creating conditions ripe for a strong demand for consumption loans. In such a situation, unless the rate of return on productive investment rises sharply through the availability of new technology (e.g. electrification, high yielding varieties of seeds), a large portion of rural savings might continue to be deployed in unproductive investment. Savings are in effect deployed to improve the share of produce rather than to improve output. In some instances this might even take the form of accumulating land which is not cultivated directly, but nevertheless acquired to prevent the

poorer peasantry from breaking out of the vicious circle of poverty.

A redistribution of land is expected to raise output in countries where there is widespread underemployment or unemployment, and labour effort is the main input in agriculture. In those situations, productivity of land is inversely related to size, as the small farmer who relies on family labour for cultivation puts in greater labour effort; the larger, capitalist, farmer who relies on wage labour, restricts labour input to the point where marginal output equals wage (Bharadwaj, 1974). In situations of endemic unemployment in rural areas, land is usually prized as a precious asset and many big farmers accumulate land since it gives them control over rural population, even if they do not put it to immediate use as an income yielding asset. For these reasons, a redistribution of landholdings could raise output. However, land reforms have rarely been successful. In countries where reforms were attempted as a once for all measure, they were widely evaded, and in the subsequent period land transfers were usually reversed through the market. Mexico, Egypt and India are good examples of this phenomenon (Bagchi, 1982).

Interesting exceptions to the above are South Korea and Taiwan, where the American military authorities in the post-World War II period implemented land reforms fairly rigorously in an attempt to ward off the threat of a communist revolution (Ghai et al., 1979). In South Korea, a ceiling of three hectares was imposed and the market in land was virtually abolished. This resulted in increased productivity as well as a reduction in poverty. The success of reform was facilitated by the fact that the industrial, urban population began to absorb a rising proportion of the labour force from about the early 1960s; this reduced the population pressure in the rural area, which usually heightens disequilibrating tendencies.

In general, the economies which inherited a large estate plantation economy, often under expatriate ownership, faced a difficult situation. If they were left as they were, the expatriate owners often did not plough back profit into capital formation, due to imagined or real political insecurity (e.g. Papua New Guinea, Guyana). In some countries, they were nationalized (e.g. Guyana) or schemes were developed to purchase a proportion of the estates and transfer them to the local communities, sometimes involving a degree of compulsion in the acquisition of land (e.g. Papua New Guinea, Kenya). While in some instances output improved as a result, the results were not uniformly positive. The failure by the erstwhile owners to replant properly had in some cases reduced profitability; in other cases, parcelling out of estates, lack of experience and poor management had reduced productivity (e.g. Papua New Guinea; Sawyerr (ed.), 1984, pp. 50–60).

In socialist countries, land reform occupied a central position in policy. An interesting case is that of China. Following the revolution of 1948, the Chinese agriculture was organized on a commune basis. There are various tiers, with the family as the basic unit. The family cultivates a private plot (which absorbs less than a tenth of total cultivated land), husbands small animals such as pigs, collects animal manure for private and collective use, and contributes labour to communal farming. Some 30 to 40 families constitute a production team, which is the basic production unit; it collectively owns the land it cultivates and the tools it uses. It makes the production decisions and distributes income. Superimposed over a production team are a production brigade, consisting of 7–8 production teams, and the peoples' commune, consisting of 13–15 brigades. The production brigade is responsible for services such as elementary schooling and health, and also organizes small-scale industries. The peoples' commune is responsible for services and small industries at a higher level, and also undertakes marketing and civil administration.

After deducting a proportion of net output (about a quarter) for collective use – taxes, cash and grain reserves, and a small welfare fund – the rest is distributed by the production team to its members, on the basis of work points accumulated by families at the team, brigade or commune level. But there is also distribution on the basis of an equality principle – on an adult equivalent basis – and to take care of families in persistently difficult circumstances (e.g. old people with no children) or to help maintain floor consumption levels among the poorest teams in the commune; such a distribution could absorb more than two-thirds of the output.

The state's control over the communes is exercised mainly through the supply and marketing system. The state collects produce through taxes, imposes quotas for delivery to the state at fixed prices, and additional deliveries at negotiated prices. It also allocates agricultural inputs and non-agricultural products for consumption. Agricultural plans are prepared at country and higher levels, and for aggregate commodity groups at the state level.

Through the commune system, China was able to improve income distribution. The provision of basic necessities, together with the maintenance of the food security system, has been a notable achievement of China. It was able to achieve this with little dependence on imports, and by absorbing not more than a fifth of the country's total investment resources. Collective labour at commune level was important in building rural infrastructure. China was at the same time able to maintain a rate of growth in total output comparable to that of, say, India (World Bank, 1983; Ghai et al., 1979).

It was clear, however, that for periods the Chinese farm output had suffered markedly as the output distributed on 'the equality principle' predominated and unrealistic physical targets were pursued. Poor management was another problem.

Since 1979, a form of *contractual collectivism* has been introduced in China under which individual or groups of peasant households can enter into a contract with the collective to undertake specialized work or crop production. Under some forms, the households are allocated work points, as before, on fulfilment of the contract; but under *da bao gan* or 'contracting in a big way' the households are allowed to keep the residual after paying the share of the collective's tax and grain sales quotas to the state and any additional sum agreed with the collective. Under the contractual collectivism, land continues to be owned by the collective, but the households can own implements and other working capital – and are sometimes allowed to hire labour. The market has also come to assume a greater role (Blecher, 1985). These changes have led to greater production, with luxury and cash crops expanding rapidly. Some observers see in this trend a resurgence of private property relations, even though, as land is still collectively owned and all households are members of collectives, it is difficult to describe it as such. These changes, while promoting growth, could result in increased rural inequalities, particularly as non-land inputs become important in agriculture. The conflict between working on one's own plot as against working for the collective, a conflict which was always present, could be heightened. The change is also likely to accentuate regional inequalities, as communes in areas endowed with poor natural resources find that the state cannot mediate a transfer of resources from the richer to the poorer communes.

TERMS OF TRADE. The availability of industrial inputs and consumer goods relatively cheaply in terms of agricultural produce enhances agricultural output by promoting productivity-raising investments, as well as by providing incentives to the agricultural sector. On the other hand, as the terms of trade faced by industry worsen, the surplus available within industry for reinvestment decreases; the market available for agricultural goods would also be reduced. For this reason, one could postulate 'equilibrium' terms of trade between agriculture and industry, deviations from which would have growth reducing effects (Thirlwall, 1986).

In market economies, the prices of agricultural products tend to be determined by the balance between supply and demand, whereas prices of industrial goods tend to be determined on the basis of a cost-plus principle. For this reason, improvements in productivity in agriculture are usually passed on through reduced prices to consumers, in contrast to industry where they may be absorbed within the sector itself. Historically, innovation and technological progress in agriculture has been sufficiently strong to outweigh the inherent tendency towards diminishing returns in agriculture, resulting in a favourable movement in terms of trade for industry. This had helped industrial growth.

In an attempt to maximize industrial growth, many governments adopted policies which tilted the terms of trade against agriculture. This was sometimes the result of an exchange rate policy which offered greater protection to industry than to agriculture. Where a country's exports consist of agricultural goods, while its inputs are sourced internally, a failure to adjust exchange rates for higher rates of inflation at home could result in an appreciation of exchange rates, tilting the terms of trade against agriculture. In some countries, overvalued exchange rates, pursued in an attempt to secure cheap food supplies for the urban population, seem to have had a negative effect on agricultural growth (e.g. Ghana, Nigeria, Tanzania and Papua New Guinea).

On the other hand, a movement that favours agriculture could depress industrial output by raising primary costs (i.e. costs of agricultural raw materials and money wage costs), and could also result in unacceptable rates of inflation. An end result could be a constraint on growth of aggregate demand in the economy, in an attempt to control inflationary pressures, which could prove to be a depressant of growth (Patnaik et al., 1976). Within rural areas, a favourable movement in terms of trade for agriculture could have the unforeseen consequence of worsening the distribution of income: in economies where land is cultivated by hired labour, money wage rates may fail to keep pace with prices of food; in economies where land is owned collectively (e.g. China), it could worsen the distribution of income between communes which are endowed with naturally rich land and those which are endowed with poor resources. There is some evidence that the favourable movement in terms of trade for agriculture such as that observed in India during the 1960s and 1970s has proved to be a constraint on industrial growth (Mitra, 1977); and in China, where in the late 1970s and early 1980s the terms of trade for agriculture were tilted favourably by supplying inputs at controlled prices and raising prices for output above quota, output seems to have responded favourably, even though the distribution of income between the poor and the rich communes may have worsened.

TECHNOLOGICAL CHANGE. The state played an important role in many developing countries in the provision of inputs for agriculture and in spreading new technology. The scale of this, and the access to it, varied greatly depending on the strength

73

of the farm lobbies and the character of the state. The absorption of these inputs, and their impact on output, also depended upon the land relations that characterized a country. The so-called 'Green Revolution', which consisted of cultivation of high yielding semi-dwarf varieties of wheat and rice, depended upon the availability of irrigation and more intensive application of fertilizer. The yields of these new varieties could be two to three times those of traditional varieties; by the late 1970s, over half the wheat acreage and one-third of paddy fields in developing countries were brought under these varieties. However, the success of the Green Revolution was confined to irrigated regions and somewhat affluent farmers, in countries where land was cultivated privately. It thus tended to increase inequalities across regions as well as classes (e.g. India, Mexico; see Bagchi, 1982). On the other hand, it boosted agricultural growth and enabled industrialization to proceed at a faster pace than might have been possible otherwise. The Green Revolution, by raising the prospect of higher yields, also tended to result in eviction of tenants, as landowners found it more profitable to cultivate land directly than to continue with output sharing arrangements with tenants. In some parts of the world, farmers responded by investing in tube-well irrigation to draw on underground water; where this was not accompanied by careful planning to ensure that adequate replenishment of underground water takes place (through, for example, construction of percolation tanks), it resulted in a gradual sinking of the water table, resulting in increased costs of irrigation all round. Another effect had been a reallocation of land use for the cultivation of high-yield crops, at the expense of others. Where the opportunities for foreign trade were not favourable, this resulted at times in stock accumulations of the favoured grains financed by the state – constituting a source of inflationary pressure.

The Green Revolution in general tended to increase intensity of cropping, and along with it the demand for labour input. In some countries, however, labour-saving mechanization began to displace labour use, partly motivated by the desire to reduce bottlenecks in the availability of labour in peak times, and partly to retain greater control of the labour process by the landowners. While mechanization thus helped in improving labour productivity – and to some extent land productivity – it also tended to result in a worsened distribution of income, even though absolute poverty may have declined. Mechanization facilitates the formation of large holdings and, therefore, can be expected to work in favour of concentration in landholdings.

INTERNATIONAL ENVIRONMENT. Agricultural exports are an important source of income for many developing countries, constituting nearly a quarter of their total export earnings (excluding oil exporting countries); in the case of many low income countries, they comprise virtually their total export earnings. Yet, the international trade environment has not moved propitiously for them in recent years. The terms of trade of agricultural exports deteriorated – by up to a quarter, for example, between 1974 and 1982. This was partly due to a change in the relationship between industrial country growth and the demand for commodities; and, partly, in recent years, due to attempts by developing countries to improve their export earnings simultaneously by substantial devaluations, which may have collectively worsened their terms of trade.

The environment for developing country agricultural exports was made worse by a high degree of protection in industrial countries. In general, farmers in Japan and Europe enjoy higher protection than farmers in those developing countries which depend on agricultural exports (World Bank, 1986). The problem is made worse by the attempts of industrial countries to off-load their farm surpluses at subsidized prices in the world market. By the early 1980s, the budgetary support expenditure in the USA, EEC and Japan has reached $35 billion, amounting to more than half of one per cent of their combined GDP.

While this is an advantage for those developing countries who could trade minerals or manufactures for food or other agricultural commodities, it has a negative impact on those countries which produced agricultural goods for export. Examples were sugar and beef, which were both heavily affected by industrial country protection; in these instances, the World Bank staff estimated that developing countries might have lost $12.5 billion in export revenues in 1983, as a result of industrial country protectionism; for comparison, the aid programmes of all industrial countries totalled $22·5 billion (both figures at 1980 prices; World Bank, 1985).

The policies of industrial countries also create substantial volatility in commodity prices, as the burden of balancing supply and demand is placed on a narrow market outside their own insulated domestic markets. This also increases the costs to the developing countries who depend more on agricultural exports.

An international trade regime which reduces protection for agriculture in industrial countries, and devises a scheme for reducing commodity price fluctuations, such as the Common Fund, will have a beneficial effect on agriculture in developing countries. However, in practice it has proved difficult to devise commodity agreements that can stabilize prices around a long-term trend level.

S.K. RAO

See also DEVELOPMENT ECONOMICS; LABOUR SURPLUS ECONOMIES; LAND REFORM; SHARECROPPING.

BIBLIOGRAPHY

Bagchi, A.K. 1982. *The Political Economy of Underdevelopment.* Cambridge: Cambridge University Press.

Bhaduri, A. 1983. *The Economic Structure of Backward Agriculture.* London: Academic Press.

Bharadwaj, K. 1974. *Production Conditions in Indian Agriculture.* Cambridge: Cambridge University Press.

Blecher, M. 1985. The struggle and contradictions of productive relations in socialist agrarian 'reform': a framework for analysis and the Chinese case. *Journal of Development Studies* 22(1), October, 104–26.

Byres, T.J. (ed.) 1983. Share cropping and share croppers. Special issue of *Journal of Peasant Studies*, January/April.

Ghai, D., Khan, A.R., Lee, E. and Radwan, S.R. 1979. *Agrarian Systems and Rural Development.* London: Macmillan.

Mitra, A. 1977. *Terms of Trade and Class Relations.* London: Frank Cass.

Patnaik, P., Rao, S.K. and Sanyal, A. 1976. The inflationary process: some theoretical comments. *Economic and Political Weekly*, 23 October.

Sawyerr, A. (ed.) 1984. *Economic Development and Trade in Papua New Guinea.* Port Moresby: University of Papua New Guinea Press.

Thirlwall, A.P. 1986. A general model of growth and development on Kaldorian lines. *Oxford Economic Papers* 38(2), July, 199-219.

World Bank. 1983. *China; Socialist Economic Development.* Washington, DC: World Bank.

World Bank. 1985. *World Development Report.* London: Oxford University Press.

World Bank. 1986. *World Development Report.* London: Oxford University Press.

aid. *See* FOREIGN AID.

Åkerman, Johan Gustav (1888–1959). Gustav Åkerman received perhaps the supreme accolade for any economist working in the theory of capital, Knut Wicksell's endorsement. Wicksell concluded his masterly review of the first part of Åkerman's doctoral dissertation with the following acknowledgement: 'I am convinced that on the whole the author has made a really significant contribution to the theory of capital' (Wicksell, 1934, Appendix 2(a), p. 273).

Born in 1888, Åkerman obtained his doctoral degree from the law faculty of the University of Lund in the days before economics, as a subject, had independent status, in 1923. He was appointed Docent (Associate Professor) in Lund the same year, on the strength of his brilliant doctoral dissertation: 'Realkapital und Kapitalzins'. He was subsequently appointed Professor of Political Economy and Sociology at what was later to become the University of Gothenburg in 1931, and remained there until his retirement. He died in 1959.

Wicksell's famous two-part review article (the second part being on 'Åkerman's Problem') of the first volume of his dissertation assured him international fame. The first volume of his dissertation dealt with the static problems of fixed-capital systems and the second volume with dynamic problems for analogous systems. His method of analysis, in the Austrian tradition, was very similar to Böhm-Bawerk's approach: copious numerical and special examples to illustrate subtle and deep general propositions. It is to his great credit that he seldom went wrong in deriving propositions by this primitive method; as a testimony to his insights we can cite concepts and issues at the frontiers of capital theoretic debates that owe much to the results of his dissertation of 1923–4: Wicksell effects, truncation of production flows, transverse flows, to name but a few.

He was, perhaps, also the first (after the early classical economists) to try to approach the problem of fixed capital as joint products – a method made famous by von Neumann and Sraffa in more recent times.

Even before his capital theoretic writings, he had engaged the grand old man of Swedish economics, Knut Wicksell, in a debate in the pages of the *Ekonomik Tidskrift* (1922) on the latter's proposals on norms for price stabilization.

His later work was mostly on practical problems of economic policy.

K. VELUPILLAI

SELECTED WORKS

1923. *Realkapital und Kapitalzins:Heft* I. Stockholm: Centraltryckeriet.
1924. *Realkapital und Kapitalzins:Heft II*. Stockholm: Centraltryckeriet.
1931. Om den Industriella Rationaliseringen och dess Verkningar · (bilaga 2 till Arbetslöshetsutredningens Betänkande). *SOU* 42, Stockholm.
1947. *Engelsk Arbetslöshet och Arbetslöshetspolitik*. Göteborg.
1956. Marginal productivity with different agricultural products. In *Twenty Five Economic Essays in Honour of Erik Lindahl*. Stockholm: Ekonomisk Tidskrift.

BIBLIOGRAPHY

Wicksell, K. 1934. Real capital and interest: Dr. Gustav Åkerman's *Realkapital und Kapitalzins*. Appendix 2(a) of K. Wicksell, *Lectures on Political Economy*, London: Routledge & Kegan Paul.

Åkerman, Johan Henrik (1896–1982). Somewhat lesser known internationally than his elder brother Gustaf, Johan Henrik Åkerman was, however, much better known inside Sweden. He was a prolific contributor to the theoretical, methodological, epistemological and policy debates in Sweden for almost fifty years. He challenged almost single-handedly (at least inside Sweden) the methodological position of the so-called Stockholm School and made valiant (but unsuccessful) attempts to provide an alternative vision which he described as the 'Lund School' method.

Johan Henrik Åkerman was born in Stockholm in 1896, graduated from the Stockholm Business School in 1918, and then spent two terms at Harvard University (1919–20) working with Warren M. Persons. On his return to Sweden, he continued his postgraduate studies in the Universities of Uppsala and Sweden. He obtained his PhD (Fil.Dr.) in 1929 from the University of Lund, where he was appointed Associate Professor in Political Economy and Economic Statistics in 1932. In 1943 he was appointed Professor in Political Economy in Lund and retained that position until his retirement in 1961. His scientific publications of more than 150 items included several books, some of which were translated into English and German. He was almost totally deaf from a very early stage in his life and totally deaf during his tenure as Professor in Lund. He died in 1982.

Johan Åkerman's outstanding doctoral dissertation had the title 'On the Rhythm of Economic Life' ('Om Det Ekonomiska Livets Rytmik'). It was an ambitious attempt to codify, theoretically and empirically, all aspects of the problem of fluctuations in economic life. It was based on the theoretical framework of Wicksell's *Geldzins und Guterpreise* (1898) and Cassel's 'Om kriser och dåliga tider' (On crises and bad times), *Ekonomisk Tidskrift*, 1904; and on the empirical methodology of the budding NBER work. Åkerman's dissertation was, perhaps, the earliest attempt to apply spectral analysis for studying time series phenomena in economics. His main examiner for the doctoral degree was Ragnar Frisch, whose more influential later work on 'Propagation Problems and Impulse Problems in Economic Dynamics' (1933) owes much to Åkerman's specific considerations of Wicksell's celebrated 'rocking-horse' example. This latter example, delineating one influential strand in business cycle methodology – the stochastic approach – stressed the important distinction between sources of propagation and impulse mechanisms. It is to Åkerman's great credit that he was able to revive and place in the centre of discussion on business-cycle methodology this important distinction, which was initially stressed by Wicksell in an obscure footnote to a review article in the *Ekonomisk Tidskrift*, 1918. It is both important and topical in view of recent developments in equilibrium business cycle theories, where these issues are central. Indeed, Åkerman's dissertation could claim to be an early manifesto of aspects of the New Classical Economics.

In the 1930s and 1940s Åkerman's research interests shifted towards methodological and epistemological problems – mainly under the influence and impact of the works of members of the Stockholm School (and, later, the Keynesians). He was severely critical of the rationality and individualistic assumptions underlying the then popular macroeconomic theories (and their microeconomic underpinnings). He developed a highly original alternative modelling strategy for macroeconomics based on a so-called dual principle of 'causal' and 'computing' ('Kalkyl') models where institutional details and socio-economic classes were explicit factors. His research and reflections on these matters, spread over a period of thirty years, were summarized and elegantly delivered as a lecture on the occasion of his retirement ('Avskedsföreläsning') from the Professorship in Lund on 9

May 1961 ('Fyra Methodologiska Moment', *Ekonomisk Tidskrift*, 1961). The depth of his understanding of recent developments in economic analysis and the scope of his comprehensive references to epistemological developments in theoretical physics and their relevance to economic theory, was displayed in that last, masterly, lecture.

His lifelong interest in the political economy of business cycles was also reflected in a highly original work on political business cycles, *Ekonomiskt Skeende och Politiska Förändringar*. He was continuing a Swedish tradition on this subject – and quite independently of Kalecki's important work on political business cycles – initiated by Herbert Tingsten's inter-war work on *Political Behaviour: Studies in Election Statistics* (1937).

Retrospectively, it is significant that Johan Åkerman's two pioneering studies on problems of fluctuations in mixed economies have their counterpart in research in the frontiers of the theory and empirical analysis of business, political and economic cycles even today.

K. VELUPILLAI

SELECTED WORKS
1928. *Om Det Ekonomiska Livets Rytmik*. Stockholm: Nordiska Bokhandeln.
1932. *Industriförbundets Produktionsindex: Motiv och Principer*. Stockholm: Sveriges Industriförbund.
1934. *Konjunkturteoretiska Problem*. Lund: C.W.K. Gleerup.
1936. *Ekonomisk Kausalitet*. Lund.
1939. *Ekonomisk Teori, I: De Ekonomiska Kalkylerna*. Lund and Leipzig.
1944. *Ekonomisk Teori, II: Kausalanalys av det Ekonomiska Skeendet*. Lund and Leipzig.
1945. *Banbrytare och Fullföljare inom Nationalekonomien*. Lund: C.W.K. Gleerup.
1946. *Ekonomiskt Skeende och Politiska Förändringar*. Lund: C.W.K. Gleerup.
1952. Innovationer och Kumulativa Förlopp. *Ekonomiskt Tidskrift*.
1960. Samhällsstruktur och Ekonomisk Teori. *Samhällsvetenskapliga studier* 18 (Lund).
1961. Fyra Methodologiska Moment. *Ekonomiskt Tidskrift*.

BIBLIOGRAPHY
Frisch, R 1933. Propagation problems and impulse problems in economic dynamics. *in Economic Essays in Honour of Gustav Cassel*, London: Allen & Unwin.
Tingsten, H. 1937. *Political Behaviour: Studies in Election Statistics*. Stockholm Economic Studies, No. 7, London: P.S. King & Son.

Alchian, Armen Albert (born 1914). Alchian was born in Fresno, California, in 1914. During his economic education at Stanford he inherited from his statistics teacher, Allen Wallis, an insatiable curiosity about real-world observations. Alchian invariably aims toward the derivation of testable implications. Whether his subject is charity, tenure, organization, money, inflation, or unemployment, he adheres firmly to the elementary principles of price theory.

His professional recognition began in 1950 with the publication of his paper on evolution and economic theory. This became an instant classic which launched a vigorous debate on economic methodology destined to enliven more than a decade. The work argues that the postulate of maximization may be false but that its use is justified by the tenets of 'survival of the fittest' under competition.

Justly famous, but not widely adopted because of its radical departure from traditional cost curves, is Alchian's seminal work on cost and output, published in 1959. Here he submits that in any productive activity the faster the production rate, the higher will be the unit cost because of diminishing returns, whereas the larger the production volume, the lower will be the unit cost because of greater choice in production methods. All costs, both average and marginal, are stated in discounted present values and expressed in terms of varying production programmes. Acceptance of this approach requires substantial modification of standard supply/demand analysis.

In all likelihood, Alchian will be best remembered for his works on property rights. To him, the economic system in any society is defined by its property rights, which constitute the 'rules' of competition. When these rights are altered, competitive behaviour will change, along with changes in income distribution and resource allocation. The use of price as a criterion for competition is inherent with private property rights and, in Alchian's view, it is less important to understand how price is determined than to understand what price does as a criterion for individuals competing for economic goods.

The Alchian approach to analyse property rights in terms of pricing and competition complements R.H. Coase's approach in terms of delimitation and enforcement of rights. Far from conflicting, the two merge in powerful accord. Together, they form a core in modern economic analysis, where the paradigm of property rights has now been firmly nailed in place.

STEVEN N.S. CHEUNG

SELECTED WORKS
1950. Uncertainty, evolution and economic theory. *Journal of Political Economy* 58, June, 211–21.
1953. The meaning of utility measurement. *American Economic Review* 43, March, 26–50.
1959. Costs and outputs. In *The Allocation of Economic Resources*, ed. M. Abramovitz, Stanford: Stanford University Press.
1962a. (With R.A. Kessel.) Competition, monopoly and the pursuit of money. *Aspects of Labor Economics*, pp. 157–75.
1962b. (With R.A. Kessel.) Effects of inflation. *Journal of Political Economy* 70, December, 521–37.
1965. Some economics of property rights. *Il Politico* 30, 816–29.
1968. Cost. In *International Encyclopedia of the Social Sciences*, New York: Macmillan, Vol. 3, 404–15.
1969. Information costs, pricing and resource unemployment. *Economic Inquiry* 7 June, 109–28.
1972. (With H. Demestz.) Production, information costs and economic organization. *American Economic Review* 62, December, 777–95.
1977. *Economic Forces at Work*. Indianapolis: Liberty Press.
1978. (With B. Klein and G.C. Crawford.) Vertical integration, appropriable rents and the competitive contracting process. *Journal of Law and Economics* 21, October, 297–326.
1983. (With W.R. Allen.) *Exchange and Production*. Belmont: Wadsworth.

alienation. This concept was introduced into economics from philosophy by Karl Marx, in his youthful *Economic and Philosophic Manuscripts*, written in 1844 but appearing in print only in 1932. Prior to the 1844 *Manuscripts*, alienation constituted a topic of purely philosophical speculation. Marx studied it in Hegel and Feuerbach, while present-day research claims to have observed anticipations of the idea in authors as old and as various as Jean-Jacques Rousseau, Calvin, Cicero and even Plato.

For a concept so widely used, no fully comprehensive definition seems possible. Its common element, in all authors, consists of the reference to a certain loss of self, accompanied by feelings of unhappiness or psychological *malaise*, arising from conditions of human bondage. This apart, Marx's immediate philosophical forerunners treated alienation in strikingly different manners. For Hegel, it represented a phase in the development of the Absolute Idea which, according to him, created nature by objectifying, materializing, itself and thereby losing its identity in the object of its own creation. The Idea would recover its original integrity by means of the conscious part of nature, the human being, when human history culminated, through suffering, to the point of the Absolute State (an ideal social regime defined by Hegel as totally free of alienation). In Feuerbach, on the other hand, it was not the Idea but man who became alienated, by submitting to the domination of – mainly religious – ideologies. These emanated from the human mind but were misunderstood by man to be autonomous, transcendental entities, superior to mankind. Man could get rid of alienation by simply rejecting such phantoms and exercising his faculties naturally, untrammelled by religious constraints.

Marx adopted Feuerbach's materialist, or rather anthropocentric, standpoint but shifted the ground of discussion decisively from psychology to economic reality, since '...the whole of human servitude is involved in the relation of the worker to production and every relation of servitude is but a modification of this relation' (Marx, 1844, p. 280). At the same time Marx also drew inspiration from Hegel's concept of the alienated Idea which suggested to him, by analogy, the concept of alienated labour: a creative force, producing not Nature, certainly, but the man-made human environment inside which, however, man lost his identity.

This transition, from the Idea to labour, apart from constituting the beginning of the introduction of historical materialism into modern thought by Marx, transformed the whole discussion of alienation by infusing economic concreteness into the prevailing, until then, philosophical generalities. Marx enriched the concept with real content, drawn from the classical economists (Smith, Say, Ricardo) as well as from some of their early socialist critics (Moses Hess, Proudhon) and on this basis built a dense but thorough critique of capitalist society. The economic morphology of alienation that he proposed can be summarized in the following four points:

(a) In the context of private property, the producer becomes alienated from his product through the mechanism of exchange, which makes the destination of his product a matter of indifference to him. This loss of interest in one's own product is pseudo-compensated by excessive though, from a human development point of view, pointless acquisitiveness towards the products of others. Passive consumerism of this kind is fanned into rapacious greediness by the intermediation in exchange of money.

(b) Trade in commodities leads, eventually, to trade in human labour as a commodity. This is alienated labour in a strict sense; its ownership actually passes from the worker to a person alien to him, the capitalist employer. The worker's product follows the fate of his labour. Both arrangements offend against man's natural sense of justice, which sanctions the inalienability of the human personality and awards ownership of products to the maker rather than the non-maker of them. Having to accept such violations degrades morally both worker and capitalist.

(c) Under alienation in the sense of (b), productive labour neither expresses nor satisfies any internal human need to create. It becomes a chore imposed by others and undertaken merely as a means of satisfying needs external to the labour activity itself. Work becomes boring, charmless, unsatisfying. The worker is treated as a mere tool, whom labour de-skills if not actually damages physically or mentally.

(d) From a broader point of view, man's specificity as a natural being (what Marx called man's 'species-being') resides in his capacity to adapt nature to his needs in a conscious manner rather than suffer natural selection to adapt his own characteristics to the dictates of the environment. In humanizing nature, labour produces results that reach beyond each individual's sphere to become beneficial for others. Production is inherently a mutually supportive activity, even when not undertaken jointly. It therefore provides a crucial basis for human solidarity. Economic antagonism based on private property, on the other hand, makes individuals act at cross-purposes, frustrating each other's aims and becoming subject to arbitrary domination by their products (a fact dramatized during economic crises). Hence alienation undermines both solidarity and the capacity for purposeful interaction with the environment. It affects the very substance of the 'species-being', giving rise to feelings of loneliness, powerlessness and aimlessness that afflict human lives.

For the overcoming of alienation Marx postulated the abolition of private property in Communism, which, with overtones from Hegel's Absolute State, he described as '...the genuine resolution of the conflict between man and nature and between man and man ... between objectification and self-confirmation, between freedom and necessity, between the individual and the species' (Marx, 1844, p. 296).

The success of Marx's morphology of alienation can be gauged by the fact that, during the modern revival of the idea, social science was unable to add to the concept any important new dimensions, limiting itself to assessing, sometimes empirically, the degree of presence, in various social groups, of the characteristics of alienation listed by Marx (Blauner, 1964). Marx in 1844 was less successful in the analysis of causal links between the moral, psychological and economic aspects of capitalist society. At times he argued as if causality ran from alienation to the economy; a clearly counter-marxian view if alienation were to be seen as a mainly psychological phenomenon. Even if one accepted this interpretation, as representative of a young, immature Marx, the question would still remain: what caused alienation?

In a sense Marx spent the rest of his life trying to answer this question. In the course of his research, however, he discovered that the explanation of the main aspects of social processes in capitalism, as well as the forecast of a future downfall of the capitalist system, could be founded on strictly economic grounds, without necessarily referring to concepts imported from ethics, psychology or philosophy. He, therefore, started losing interest in alienation as a *causal explanation* of capitalist institutions; in works published during his lifetime, the relevant term is little used. He did maintain a lively interest in the psychosomatic and moral degradation (i.e. the alienation) of people, particularly of workers, as an *effect* of capitalism. But he chose to place the emphasis on the 'hard science' rather than the ethical aspect of his teaching.

In this he was followed by most of the ideologists associated with the massive political movements which, inspired by his ideas, sprang up after his death in Europe by the end of the 19th and the beginning of the 20th century. They found it practically more expedient and more convincing to stress the economic rather than the ethical flaws of capitalism. In such climate, publication of the 1844 *Manuscripts* in 1932 (or the earlier independent rediscovery of the importance of certain aspects of alienation by Lukacs in his 1923 *History and Class Consciousness*) could not exert much influence on marxist thought.

The renaissance of interest in alienation – a most surprising intellectual event, for a concept that had lain hibernating for a whole century – came after World War II. The economic resilience of capitalism in industrially advanced countries; the desiccation of official marxist ideology, narrowly based on Marx's 'hard science'; the disillusionment caused by the persistence of hard and unequal conditions for labour in the Communist part of the world, despite abolition of private property there, all combined to lead socially critical thought to seek ethical and psychological, in addition to purely economic, underpinnings for its efforts.

In this reorientation, alienation played a central role, particularly among dissident intellectuals in Communist countries (Rudolph Barro, Agnes Heller, István Mészáros, Rudi Supek and others) to whom it offered a marxist platform for a humanistic criticism of the regime from the inside. At the same time non-marxists adopted the idea in their analysis of the present and future of capitalism, attributing certain symptoms of alienation (boredom, loneliness, purposelessness) to the achievement of affluence rather than the persistence of social antagonism (Kahn and Wiener, 1969). Thus alienation has, to some extent, transcended its original anticapitalist, strictly marxist, character to become a more widely accepted tool for the critical study of modern industrial society, irrespective of the ownership structure prevailing in each case.

GEORGE CATEPHORES

See also CAPITAL AS A SOCIAL RELATION; LABOUR POWER; MARXIST ECONOMICS.

BIBLIOGRAPHY
Main works
Feuerbach, L. 1841. *The Essence of Christianity*. New York: Harper, 1957.
Hegel, G.F.W. 1832. *The Phenomenology of Mind*. New York: Humanities Press, 1964.
Hegel, G.F.W. 1833–4. *The Science of Logic*. London: Allen & Unwin, 1929.
Marx, K. 1844. *Economic and Philosophic Manuscripts of 1844*. In Karl Marx and Frederick Engels, *Collected Works*, Vol. 3, London: Lawrence & Wishart, 1975.
Marx, K. 1857–8. *Grundrisse*. Ed. M. Nicolaus, London: Penguin Books, 1973.
Other works
Althusser, L. 1965, *For Marx*. New York: Pantheon, 1970.
Barro, R. 1978. *The Alternative in Eastern Europe*. London: New Left Books.
Blauner, R. 1964. *Alienation and Freedom: The Factory Worker and his Industry*. Chicago: University of Chicago Press.
Catephores, G. 1972. Marxian alienation – a clarification. *Oxford Economic Papers* 24(1), March, 124–36.
Elliot, J.E. 1979. Continuity and change in the evolution of Marx's theory of alienation: from the *Manuscripts* through the *Grundrisse* to *Capital*. History of Political Economy 11(3), Fall, 317–62.
Fromm, E. 1966. *Marx's Concept of Man*. New York: F. Ungar.
Godelier, M. 1966. *Rationalité et irrationalité en économie*. Paris: Maspero.
Heller, A. 1976. *The Theory of Need in Marx*. London: Alison & Busby.
Hook, S. 1950. *From Hegel to Marx*. New York: Humanities Press.
Hyppolite, J. 1969. *Studies on Marx and Hegel*. New York: Basic Books.
Kahn, H. and Wiener, A.J. 1969. *The Year 2000*. London: Macmillan.
Mandel, E. 1967. *The Formation of the Economic Thought of Karl Marx*. London: New Left Books, 1971.
Marcuse, H. 1954. *Reason and Revolution, Hegel and the Rise of Social Theory*. 2nd edn, New York: Humanities Press.
Mészáros, I. 1975. *Marx's Theory of Alienation*. 4th edn, London: Merlin Press.
Ollman, B. 1971. *Alienation: Marx's Conception of Man in Capitalist Society*. London: Cambridge University Press.
Supek, R. 1965. Dialectique de la pratique sociale. *Praxis*, No. 1.
Tucker, R.C. 1961. *Philosophy and Myth in Karl Marx*. Cambridge: Cambridge University Press.
Wood, A. 1981. *Karl Marx*. London: Routledge & Kegan Paul.

Allais, Maurice (born 1911).   Maurice Allais was born on 31 May 1911, in Paris. Originally a student at the Ecole Polytechnique he moved later to the Ecole Nationale des Mines (ENMP hereafter). He gained the doctorate of engineering of the University of Paris in 1949. He is currently director of Research at the Centre National de la Recherche Scientifique (CNRS) and Professor of Economic Analysis at the ENMP. The CNRS awarded him a gold medal in 1978, the first time this award was given to an economist.

His initial professional activity led him toward problems of applied economics and regulation. In France, the corps of mining engineers, one of the greatest branches of the civil service, is entrusted with the regulation of mining and energy and is very influential in the definition and control of public industrial policy. In some sense Allais' theoretical works are an attempt to find rational public economic public decisions. The title of his first book, *A la recherche d'une discipline économique. Première partie: l'économie pure* (1943) is very significant in this respect. One feels in Allais' thought a deep reluctance to accept any theory which cannot be made operative (Allais, 1978a). Thus a very important part of his activity, which will not be surveyed here, is devoted to applied economic studies, always directly supported by a theoretical analysis (cf. Allais, 1954, 1956a, 1977). In the brilliant tradition of Dupuit, Colson and Divisia this aspect of Allais' work has been essential for the development of the school of French economist engineers. As a professor Allais educated several generations of researchers and public managers; for example, M. Boiteux, G. Debreu and E. Malinvaud were his students.

In the line of descent from Walras, Fisher and Pareto, Allais' theoretical contributions are basic in four fields: general equilibrium and optimal allocation of resources ('*rendement social*' or '*efficacité maximale*' in Allais' terminology), capital and growth, money and business cycle, risky choices.

Allais is primarily a theorist of interdependence and optimum. It is impressive to observe that the research programme defined at the start in Allais (1943) has been almost wholly fulfilled, even though some of the initial basic assumptions have been drastically revised. When published in 1943, Allais' book was one of the most complete reports on general equilibrium and optimum theories, comparable to Hicks's *Value and Capital* and Samuelson's *Foundations of Economic Analysis*. Let us emphasize its differences. Allais gives the earliest formalization of an intertemporal general equilibrium and, in particular, all the arbitrage conditions between capital goods and land are made explicit. Then, the first results on global stability of Walrasian *tâtonnement* are proved by means of Lyapunov's second method under assumptions equivalent to gross substitutability (cf. Negishi, *Econometrica* (1962), for a report in English). The book also contains a complete account of optimum theory in terms of distributable surpluses and a precise and correct statement of the two welfare theorems. Finally, Allais outlined a theory of optimum population. Later, Allais' opinion on the relevance of the Walrasian model changed markedly (cf. Allais, 1967b, 1968, 1971, 1981). He would now define a state of general equilibrium as a position in which no distributable surplus can be obtained, and describes the whole motion of the system as governed by the search for such surpluses. In some way this new view is a true merging of general equilibrium and optimum theories (cf. Allais, 1981).

His main contributions to capital and growth theory are expressed in Allais (1947), (1960) and (1962). First, and sometimes with a lead of fifteen years, he found most of the results of so-called neoclassical theory of growth, including the famous golden rule of accumulation. Allais worked out a complete theory of capitalistic processes with a rigorous formalization of the concept of characteristic function first proposed by Jevons in 1871, by which is meant the sequence of past expenditures on primary inputs which have generated the present national income. The systematic use of this concept allowed Allais to build up a theory of economic growth. But its use has been even more fruitful in the analysis of capitalistic efficiency. Allais proved in 1947 that, in a stationary state, a zero rate of interest maximizes real income. This is the first version of the golden rule of accumulation obtained by Phelps some fourteen years later. In 1962 Allais widened this result and demonstrated that in steady states a capitalistic optimum is attained when the rate of interest is equal to the rate of growth (it is to be noted that Allais himself acknowledges that J. Desrousseaux had been the first to get this result in 1959, in a non-published paper). Thus Allais was completing his theory of optimal allocation of resources with a theory of capitalistic optimum.

To analyse intertemporal optimality, he assumes that each agent has preferences, on present and future consumption, possibly different in different periods. Hence it becomes possible to consider the psychological evolution of an individual over his lifetime, unlike the usual approach. In other respects Allais has been very careful to test the explicative power of his capitalistic optimum theory, by comparing the growth processes in different countries and trying to evaluate in every case the gap between the capitalistic optimum and the real state of accumulation.

Allais must be also considered as a major actor in the revival of the quantity theory of money (cf. Allais, 1956b, 1956c, 1965a, 1966, 1969, 1970, 1972, 1974). The reduced form of the model explaining the dynamics of national monetary expenditure is very similar to Cagan's contemporary formulation. But Allais claims that his model has very different foundations because it is supported by an alleged psychological law of the perception of time. The solutions of the integro-differential equation describing the evolution of income are shown to have three limit cycles, depending upon initial conditions. It is then possible to explain local stability of a steady state equilibrium, business cycles and hyperinflation state with the same basic model.

The last aspect of Allais' work concerns choice under risk (Allais, 1953b, 1953c, 1979). As usual, Allais' approach is both theoretical and empirical. He builds up his analysis on the basis of experimental psychological tests conducted in 1952 (cf. Allais, 1953c for a partial statement). For Allais the theory of choice under risk went, historically, through four steps. At first it was assumed that the mathematical expectation of the monetary gain was the natural evaluation of a lottery. Then the mathematical expectation of the gain in utility was used. The third step then considered subjective probabilities. The American school (Friedman, Marschak, Von Neumann, Morgenstern, Samuelson and Savage) takes into account only these three steps. So Allais claims that a fourth step must be reached: the value of a lottery is a functional depending upon the probability density parameterized by the gains. In effect the expected utility hypothesis implies a special such functional, so this last step seems very natural. Allais systematically criticizes the axioms on which the Bernoullian principle is based. According to him such axioms cannot help to define rationality in an uncertain environment. Through convincing examples he specially refutes Savage's independence and Samuelson's substitutability axioms. The major argument is in short that in the neighbourhood of certainty, a rational agent will prefer absolute safety. Then Allais proposes an alternative definition of rationality in risky situations: the set of choices must be ordered, an absolute preference axiom must be satisfied (i.e. if a lottery gives in every case larger gains than another, then any agent will prefer the first one) and only objective probabilities must be considered. The first two axioms seem quite reasonable and it is difficult, according to Allais, to disprove the last one. But it is clear that a decision rule following the Bernoullian principle cannot be deduced from these three axioms. They imply the use of a functional of more general form than the mathematical expectation of the psychological evaluation of gains. In fact Allais argues that the Bernoullian principle only takes into account the dispersion of the gains whereas the dispersion of their psychological values is pertinent.

Finally, Allais applies his theory of behaviour under uncertainty to a general equilibrium model (Allais, 1953a). He demonstrates this through an example where a competitive allocation of risks leads to an optimal allocation of resources, and where such an allocation can be obtained as a competitive equilibrium with an appropriate redistribution of initial endowments.

BERNARD BELLOC AND MICHEL MOREAUX

See also EXPECTED UTILITY HYPOTHESIS; UTILITY THEORY AND DECISION MAKING.

SELECTED WORKS
For a complete record of Allais' work on the period 1943–78 and an analysis by Allais himself, see Allais, 1978a, 1978b and 1978c.

1943. *A la recherche d'une discipline économique. Première partie: l'économie pure*. Paris. Ateliers Industria.
1947. *Economie et intérêt*. Paris: Imprimerie Nationale.
1953a. L'extension des théories de l'équilibre économique général et du rendement social au cas du risque. *Econometrica* 21, 269–90.
1953b. Le comportement de l'homme rationnel devant le risque: critique des postulats et axiomes de l'Ecole Américaine. *Econometrica* 21, October, 503 46. Trans. in *Expected Utility Hypotheses and the Allais Paradox*, ed. M. Allais and O. Hagen, Dordrecht: Reidel, 1979.
1953c. La psychologie de l'homme rationnel devant le risque. La théorie et l'expérience. *Journal de la Société de Statistique de Paris*, January, 47–72.
1954. Méthode d'évaluation des perspectives économiques de la recherche minière sur des grands espaces. Application au Sahara Algérien. Paris, mimeo. Trans. in *Management Science* 3(4), July 1957, 285–347.
1956a. *La gestion des houillères nationalisées et la théorie économique*. Paris: Imprimerie Nationale.
1956b. Explication des cycles économiques par un modèle non linéaire à régulation retardée. *Metroeconomica* 8, April, 4–83.
1956c. Explication des cycles économiques par un modèle non linéaire à régulation retardée. Mémoire complémentaire. In *Les modèles dynamiques en économétrie*, Collection des Colloques Internationaux du CNRS, Vol. 52:CNRS, Paris.
1960. L'influence du coefficient capitalistique sur le revenu réel par tête. *International Statistical Institute Bulletin* 38(2), 3–27.
1962. The influence of the capital-output ratio on real national income. *Econometrica* 30, October, 700–28.
1965a. Reformulation de la théorie quantitative de la monnaie. *Bulletin SEDEIS*, No. 928, Supplement.
1965b. The role of capital in economic development. In *The Economic Approach to Economic Development*, Amsterdam: North-Holland.
1966. A restatement of the quantity theory of money. *American Economic Review* 56, December, 1123–57.
1967a. Some analytical and practical aspects of the theory of capital. In *Activity Analysis in the Theory of Growth and Planning*, ed. E. Malinvaud and M. Bacharach, London: Macmillan.
1967b. *Les fondements du calcul économique*. Vol. I, Paris: Ecole Nationale Suprérieure des Mines (mimeo).
1968. *Les fondements du calcul économique*. Vols. II and III, Paris: Ecole Nationale Supérieure des Mines (mimeo).

1969. Growth and inflation. *Journal of Money, Credit and Banking* 1(3), August, 355–426.

1970. A reply to Michael R. Darby's comment on Allais' restatement of the quantity theory. *American Economic Review* 60(3), June, 447–56.

1971. Les théories de l'équilibre économique général et de l'efficacité économique. Impasses récentes et nouvelles perspectives. *Revue d'Economie Politique*, May. Trans. in *Equilibrium and Disequilibrium in Economic Theory*, ed. G. Schwödiauer, Dordrecht: Reidel.

1972. Forgetfulness and interest. *Journal of Money, Credit and Banking* 4(1), Part I, February, 40–73.

1974. The psychological rate of interest. *Journal of Money, Credit and Banking* 6(3), August, 285–331.

1975. The hereditary and relativistic formulation of the demand for money. Circular reasoning or a real structural relation? (A reply to Scadding's Note.) *American Economic Review* 65(3), June, 454–64.

1977. *L'impôt sur le capital et la réforme monétaire*. Paris: Hermann.

1978a. *Contributions à la science économique. Vue d'ensemble 1943–1978*. Paris: Centre d'Analyse Economique.

1978b. *Principaux ouvrages et mémoires 1943–1978*. Paris: Centre d'Analyse Economique.

1978c. *Titres et travaux scientifiques*. Paris: Centre d'Analyse Economique.

1979. The so-called Allais Paradox and rational decisions under uncertainty. In *Expected Utility Hypotheses and the Allais Paradox*, ed. M. Allais and T. Hagen, Dordrecht: Reidel.

1981. La théorie générale des surplus. Vol. I, Economie et sociétés. *Cahiers de l'ISMEA*, Series EM no. 8; Vol. II, Modèle illustratif, économie et sociétés. *Cahiers de l'ISMEA*, Series EM No. 9.

Allais paradox.

THE ST PETERSBURG PARADOX AND THE BERNOULLIAN FORMULATION. Let there be a random prospect $g_1, \ldots, g_i, \ldots, g_n, \ldots, p_1, \ldots p_i, \ldots, p_n$ ($\Sigma_i p_i = 1$) giving the probability p_i of positive or negative gains g_i. The early theorists of games of chance considered that a game was advantageous when the mathematical expectation

$$M = \sum_i p_i g_i \qquad (1 \leqslant i \leqslant n) \tag{1}$$

was positive (Allais, 1952b, pp. 68–9).

The principle of the mathematical expectation of monetary gains has proven to be open to question in the case of the *St Petersburg Paradox* outlined by Nicolas Bernoulli. For this game, we have: $g_i = 2^i$, $p_i = 1/2^i$, $n = \infty$ so that $M = \infty$. However, if the unit of value is the dollar, it can be seen that for most subjects, the psychological monetary value of the game (that is the price they are ready to pay for this random prospect) is generally lower than 20 dollars. This, at first sight, involves a paradox.

To explain this paradox, Daniel Bernoulli (1738) considered the mathematical expectation of cardinal utilities $u(C + g_i)$ instead of the mathematical expectation of monetary gains, C being the player's capital. Thus the formulation (1) is replaced by the Bernoullian formulation

$$u(C + V) = \sum_i p_i u(C + g_i) \tag{2}$$

in which V is the psychological monetary value of the random prospect. He proposed to take the logarithmic expression $u = \log(C + g)$ as cardinal utility (Bernoulli, 1738; Allais, 1952b, p. 68; 1977, pp. 498–506; 1983, p. 33). It can then be shown that we have approximately $V \sim a + [\log C/\log 2]$ with $a = 0.942$, which yields $V \sim 14$ or 18 US $ for C equal to 10,000 or 100,000 dollars respectively (Allais, 1977, p. 572).

THE NEO-BERNOULLIAN FORMULATION. In order to measure cardinal utility from random choice, von Neumann and Morgenstern demonstrated in the *Theory of Games* (1947), on the basis of a set of more or less appealing postulates, the existence of an index $B(C + g)$, such that

$$B(C + V) = \sum_i p_i B(C + g_i) \tag{3}$$

in which the index $B(C + g)$ is independent of the random prospect considered, but depends on the subject (von Neumann and Morgenstern, 1947, pp. 8–31 and 617–32; Allais, 1952b, p. 74; 1977, pp. 521–3, 591–603; 1983, p. 34).

Using other sets of postulates, Marschak, Friedman and Savage, Samuelson, Savage, etc. (Marschak, 1950 and 1951; Friedman and Savage, 1948; Samuelson, 1952; Savage, 1952 and 1954; Allais, 1952b, pp. 74–5, 88–92, and 99–103; 1977, pp. 464–5, 508–14; 1983, pp. 33–5) came to the same formulation (3), which may be referred to as the neo-Bernoullian formulation, but its interpretation differs depending on the postulates adopted. While von Neumann and Morgenstern believed, at least initially, that $B \equiv u$, the p_i being objective probabilities (Allais, 1952b, p. 74; 1977, pp. 591–2), Savage held that cardinal utility is a myth (Savage, 1954, p. 94), and that the neo-Bernoullian index B alone is real, the p_i being subjective probabilities, the existence of the function B and the p_i being proven on the basis of the axioms considered. Some authors (e.g. de Finetti, Krelle, Harsanyi) admit the existence of cardinal utility u, but they consider that $B \neq u$, and the index B is deemed to take account of the relative propensity for risk corresponding to the distribution of cardinal utility (de Finetti, 1977; Allais, 1952b, pp. 123–4; 1983, pp. 30–31).

Whereas von Neumann's and Morgenstern's opinion, accepted by most authors, is that the crucial axiom of their theory is axiom 3 Cb, I consider that their axioms 3 Ba and 3 Bb are the crucial ones (Allais, 1977, pp. 596–8). However, one way or another, irrespective of the nature of the axioms from which it is derived, the neo-Bernoullian formulation boils down to assuming the independence of the B_i for given values of the p_i. This is the principle of independence (Allais, 1952b, pp. 88–90 and 98–9; 1977, pp. 466–7).

THE ALLAIS PARADOX. When I read the *Theory of Games* in 1948, formulation (3) appeared to me to be totally incompatible with the conclusions I had reached in 1936 attempting to define a reasonable strategy for a repetitive game with a positive mathematical expectation (Allais, 1977, pp. 445–6). Consequently, I viewed the principle of independence as incompatible with the preference for security in the neighbourhood of certainty shown by every subject and which is reflected by the elimination of all strategies implying a non-negligible probability of ruin, and by a preference for security in the neighbourhood of certainty when dealing with sums that are large in relation to the subject's capital (Allais, 1952b, pp. 84–6, 88–90, 92–5; 1977, pp. 451, 466–7, 491–8).

This led me to devise some counter-examples. One of them, formulated in 1952, has become famous as the 'Allais Paradox'. Today, it is as widespread as its real meaning is generally misunderstood.

This counter-example consists of two questions, the gains considered being expressed in (1952) francs [one million (1952) francs is roughly equivalent to 10,000 (1985) dollars].

(1) *Do you prefer Situation A to Situation B?*
Situation A
   certainty of receiving 100 million.
Situation B
   a 10 per cent chance of winning 500 million,
   an 89 per cent chance of winning 100 million,
   a 1 per cent chance of winning nothing.

(2) *Do you prefer Situation C to Situation D?*

Situation C

    an 11 per cent chance of winning 100 million,

    an 89 per cent change of winning nothing.

Situation D

    a 10 per cent chance of winning 500 million,

    a 90 per cent chance of winning nothing.

It can be shown that, according to the neo-Bernoullian formulation, the preference $A > B$ should entail the preference $C > D$, and conversely (Allais, 1952b, pp. 88–90; 1977, pp. 533–41).

However, it is observed that for very careful persons, well aware of the probability calculus and considered as rational, and whose capital C is relatively low by comparison with the gains considered, the preference $A > B$ can be observed in parallel to the preference $C < D$. Since the neo-Bernoullians consider the axioms from which they deduce the neo-Bernoullian formulation as evident, they consider this result a paradox.

In 1952, Savage's answers to these two questions contradicted his own axioms. The explanation he gave is somewhat surprising. It boiled down to stating: 'Since my axioms are totally evident, my answers, which are indeed incompatible with my axioms, are explained by the fact that I did not give the matter enough thought' (Savage, 1954, pp. 101–103).

EMPIRICAL RESEARCH. After analysing the answers to the 1952 Questionnaire (Allais, 1952d). I found that the rate of violation of the neo-Bernoullian formulation coresponding to the Allais Paradox was approximately 53 per cent (Allais, 1977, p. 474).

This violation example is not an isolated one (Allais, 1977, pp. 636–6, n. 15). There is even one test for which the rate of violation is 100 per cent. It is based on the comparative analysis of, on the one hand, the monetary value x' attributed to a probability of $1/2$ of winning a sum between 0.0001 and 1000 million, with a probability of $1/2$ of winning nothing at all; and, on the other hand, of the monetary value x'' attributed to a probability p_i between 0.25 and 0.999 of winning 200 million, with a probability $1 - p_i$ of winning nothing at all. The two indexes $R_{1/2}$ and R_{200} deduced from these two series of questions, which according to the neo-Bernoullian formulation should be totally identical up to a linear transformation, in fact are completely different for all the subjects who answered the questions. Such was in particular the case of de Finetti (Allais, 1977, pp. 612–13, 620–31; 1983, pp. 61–2 and 110–11, n. 146).

Much empirical research has been carried out since 1952. It has shown that many subjects who can be viewed as rational may behave in contradiction with the neo-Bernoullian formulation (e.g. MacCrimmon and Larsson, 1975; Allais, 1977, pp. 507–8, pp. 611–54). Confronted with these results, the neo-Bernoullians always explain these violations as 'anomalies', 'errors', 'insufficient thought by the subjects', or 'ill constructed and inconclusive' experiments made by incompetent persons, 'inexperienced in experimental psychology' (e.g. Amihud, 1974 and 1977; Morgenstern, 1976). But these statements do not hold in the face of the very numerous violations observed by the many researchers, following different methods and operating in different countries at different times (Allais, 1977, pp. 541–2; 1983, p. 66).

THE ALLAIS PARADOX, A SIMPLE ILLUSTRATION OF ALLAIS' GENERAL THEORY OF RANDOM CHOICE. These violations can be explained very simply. Limiting consideration to the mathematical expectation of the B_i involves neglecting the basic element characterizing psychology vis-à-vis risk, namely the distribution of cardinal utility about its mathematical expectation (Allais, 1952b, pp. 51–5, 96–7; 1977, pp. 481–2,

520–23, 550–52; 1983, pp. 30–31), and in particular, when very large sums are involved in comparison with the psychological capital of the subject, the strong dependence between the different eventualities (g_i, p_i), and the very strong preference for security in the neighbourhood of certainty.

My 1952 inquiry (Allais, 1952d; 1977, pp. 447–9, 451–4, 604–54; 1983, pp. 28 and 41) showed that all the subjects questioned were able to answer questions on the intensity of their preferences for different possible gains, setting aside any consideration of random choices (only a few neo-Bernoullian authors refused to answer these questions) (Allais, 1943, pp. 156–77; 1952b, pp. 43–6; 1977, pp. 460–61, 475–80, 614–17, 632–3). The analysis of the answers made it possible to design a well defined cardinal utility curve, the structure of which is the same for all the subjects up to a linear transformation. It portrays their answers on average remarkably well (Allais, 1984a and 1984c).

This result is all the more significant in that this expression of cardinal utility shows a very striking similarity to the expression for psychophysiological sensation as a function of luminous stimulus, determined by Weber's and Fechner's successors (Allais, 1984c, § 4.3 and Charts III and XXV).

The existence of a cardinal utility $u(C + g)$ being proven and the neo-Bernoullian index $B(C + g)$, if it exists, being defined also up to a linear transformation, it can be shown that the two indexes are necessarily identical up to a linear transformation (Allais, 1952b, pp. 97–8, 103, 128–30; 1977, pp. 465, 483, 604–607; 1983, pp. 29–30; 1985).

As a consequence the neo-Bernoullian formulation reduces to considering the mathematical expectation of cardinal utility alone, neglecting its dispersion about the average. In so doing, it neglects what may be considered as the specific element of risk (Allais, 1952b, pp. 49–56; 1983, pp. 35–41).

In fact the cardinal utility corresponding to a monetary value V of a random prospect should be considered as a function

$$u(C + V) = F[u(C + g_1), \ldots, u(C + g_i), \ldots$$
$$\ldots, u(C + g_n), p_1, \ldots, p_i, \ldots, p_n] \quad (4)$$

of cardinal utilities u_i corresponding to the different gains g_i. Since utilities u_i are defined up to a linear transformation, it can be shown that (Allais, 1977, pp. 481–3, 550–52, 607–609; 1985, § 12 and 22)

$$u + \Delta = F(u_1 + \Delta, \ldots, u_i + \Delta, \ldots$$
$$\ldots, u_n + \Delta, p_1, \ldots, p_i, \ldots, p_n) \quad (5)$$

in which Δ is any constant (property of cardinal isovariation). Consequently it can be shown that relation (4) can be written

$$u(C + V) = \bar{u} + R(\mu_2, \ldots, \mu_l, \ldots, \mu_{2n-1}) \quad (6)$$

in which $\bar{u}$ represents the mathematical expectation of the u_i and the μ_l represent the moments of order l:

$$\mu_l = \sum_i p_i(u_i - \bar{u})^l. \quad (7)$$

The ratio $\rho = R/\bar{u}$ can be considered as an index of the propensity for risk. For $\rho = 0$, the behaviour is Bernoullian; for $\rho > 0$, there is a propensity for risk; for $\rho < 0$, there is a propensity for security. For a given subject, ρ can be nil, positive or negative, depending on the domain of the field of random choices considered (Allais, 1983, pp. 35–41; 1985).

The mistake made by the proponents of the neo-Bernoullian formulation is to want to impose restrictions on the preference index

$$I = f[g_1, \ldots, g_i, \ldots, g_n, p_1, \ldots, p_i, \ldots, p_n] \quad (8)$$

of any subject other than those corresponding to conditions of rationality, such as the existence of a field of ordered random choice or the axiom of absolute preference. According to this axiom, taking two random prospects g_i, p_i and g_i', p_i such that $g_i > g_i'$ for any p_i, the first is obviously preferable to the second (Allais, 1952b, pp. 38–41; 1977, pp. 457–8, 530–35; 1985, § 31.3).

Imposing other restrictions would, in the case of certain goods (A), (B), ..., (C) reduce to imposing special restrictions on the preference index $I(A, B, ..., C)$ which no author has ever envisaged. In fact, to have a marked preference for security in the neighbourhood of certainty together with a preference for risk far from certainty is not more irrational than preferring roast beef to chicken (Allais, 1952b, pp. 65–7; 1977, pp. 527–33; 1983, pp. 39–40; 1985, § 31.3).

FROM THE ST PETERSBURG PARADOX TO THE ALLAIS PARADOX. In sum, just as the St Petersburg Paradox led Daniel Bernoulli to replace the principle of maximization of the mathematical expectation of monetary values by the Bernoullian principle of maximization of cardinal utilities, the Allais Paradox leads to adding to the Bernoullian formulation a specific term characterizing the propensity to risk which takes account of the distribution as a whole of cardinal utility (Allais, 1978, pp. 4–7; 1977, pp. 548–52; 1983, pp. 35–42).

Neither the St Petersburg nor the Allais Paradox involves a paradox. Both correspond to basic psychological realities: the non-identity of monetary and psychological values and the importance of the distribution of cardinal utility about its average value.

For nearly forty years the supporters of the neo-Bernoullian formulation have exerted a dogmatic and intolerant, powerful and tyrannical domination over the academic world; only in very recent years has a growing reaction begun to appear. This is not the first example of the opposition of the 'establishments' of any kind to scientific progress, nor will it be the last (Allais, 1977, pp. 518–46; 1983, pp. 69–71, 112–14).

The Allais Paradox does not reduce to a mere counter-example of purely anectodal value based on errors of judgement as too many authors seem to think without referring to the general theory of random choice which underlies it. It is fundamentally an illustration of the need to take account not only of the mathematical expectation of cardinal utility, but also of its distribution as a whole about its average, basic elements characterizing the psychology of risk.

MAURICE ALLAIS

See also EXPECTED UTILITY HYPOTHESIS; MEAN VALUES.

BIBLIOGRAPHY

Allais, M. 1943. *A la recherche d'une discipline économique*, Première partie: l'économie pure. Ateliers Industria, 920 pp. Second edition under the title *Traité d'économie pure* Paris: Imprimerie Nationale, 1952, 5 vols. (The second edition is identical to the first, apart from the addition of a new introduction, 63 pp.)

Allais, M. 1952a. Fondements d'une théorie positive des choix comportant un risque et critique des postulats et axiomes de l'école Américaine. International Conference on Risk, Centre National de la Recherche Scientifique, May 1952. *Colloques Internationaux XL, Econométrie,* Paris, 1953, 257–332.

Allais, M. 1952b. The foundations of a positive theory of choice involving risk and a criticism of the postulates and axioms of the American school. English translation of 1952a. In Allais and Hagen (1979), 27–145.

Allais, M. 1952c. Le comportement de l'homme rationnel devant le risque: critique des postulats et axiomes de l'école Américaine. *Econometrica* 21(4), October 1953, 503–546. This paper corresponds to some parts of Allais, 1952a.

Allais, M. 1952d. La psychologie de l'homme rationnel devant le risque – la théorie et l'expérience. *Journal de la Société de Statistique de Paris,* January–March 1953, 47–73.

Allais, M. 1977. The so-called Allais' Paradox and rational decisions under uncertainty. In Allais and Hagen (1979), 437–699.

Allais, M. 1978. Editorial Introduction, Foreword. In Allais and Hagen (1979), 3–11.

Allais, M. 1983. The foundations of the theory of utility and risk. In *Progress in Decision Theory,* ed. O. Hagen and F. Wenstop, Dordrecht: Reidel, 1984, 3–131. ġ

Allais, M. 1984a. L'utilité cardinale et sa détermination – hypothèses, méthodes et résultats empiriques. Memoir presented to the Second International Conference on Foundations of Utility and Risk Theory, Venice, 5–9 June 1984.

Allais, M. 1984b. The cardinal utility and its determination – hypotheses, methods and empirical results. English version of 1984a, in *Theory and Decision,* 1987.

Allais, M. 1984c. Determination of cardinal utility according to an intrinsic invariant model. Abridged version of 1984a in *Recent Developments in the Foundations of Utility and Risk Theory,* ed. L. Daboni et al., Dordrecht: Reidel, 1985, 83–120.

Allais, M. 1985. Three theorems on the theory of cardinal utility and random choice. In *Essays in Honour of Werner Leinfellner,* ed. H. Berghel, Dordrecht: Reidel, 1986.

Allais, M. and Hagen, O. (eds) 1979. *Expected Utility Hypotheses and the Allais' Paradox; Contemporary Discussions and Rational Decisions under Uncertainty with Allais' Rejoinder.* Dordrecht: Reidel.

Amihud, Y. 1974. Critical examination of the new foundation of utility. In Allais and Hagen (1979), 149–60.

Amihud, Y. 1977. A reply to Allais. In Allais and Hagen (1979), 185–90.

Bernoulli, D. 1738. Specimen theoriae novae de mensura sortis. Trans. as 'Exposition of a new theory on the measurement of risk'. *Econometrica* 22, (1954), 23–36.

de Finetti, B. 1977. A short confirmation of my standpoint. In Allais and Hagen (1979), 161.

Friedman, M. and Savage, J.L. 1948. The utility analysis of choices involving risk. *Journal of Political Economy* 56, August, 279–304.

MacCrimmon, K. and Larsson, S. 1975. Utility theory: axioms versus paradoxes. In Allais and Hagen (1979), 333–409.

Marschak, J. 1950. Rational behavior, uncertain prospects and measurable utility. *Econometrica* 18(2) (April 1950), 111–41.

Marschak, J. 1951. Why 'should' statisticians and businessmen maximize moral expectation? In *Proceedings of the Second Berkeley Symposium on Mathematical Statistics and Probability,* Berkeley: University of California Press.

Marschak, J. 1977. Psychological values, and decision makers. In Allais and Hagen (1979), 163–75.

Morgenstern, O. 1976. Some reflections on utility. In Allais and Hagen (1979), 175–83.

Neumann J. von and Morgenstern, O. 1947. *Theory of Games and Economic Behavior.* 2nd edn, Princeton: Princeton University Press.

Samuelson, P. 1952. Utility, preference and probability. International Conference on Risk, Centre National de la Recherche Scientifique, Paris, May 1952. *Colloques Internationaux XL, Econométrie,* Paris, 1953, 141–50.

Savage, L. 1952. An axiomatization of reasonable behavior in the face of uncertainty. International Conference on Risk, Paris, May 1952. Centre National de la Recherche Scientifique, *Colloques Internationaux XL, Econométrie,* Paris, 1953, 29–33.

Savage, L. 1954. *The Foundations of Statistics.* New York: Wiley.

Allen, George Cyril (1900–1982). George Allen was born on 28 June 1900 at Kenilworth, Warwickshire, England and died at Oxford on 31 July 1982. His upbringing and education in Coventry and then in Birmingham, influenced the choice of topic – the industrial development of the Black Country – for his first book on what was to become one of his main professional interests, the history and organization of British industry. His second major interest, the economy of Japan, came from the three years he spent as a young man teaching at Nagoya, Japan. He returned to take up a post at Birmingham

University from which, while still in his twenties, he was appointed to a chair at Hull and later, at Liverpool. In World War II he worked at the Board of Trade and the Ministry of Economic Warfare. His wartime activities included playing a key part in the concentration of civilian industry and, with Hugh Gaitskell, writing the first paper on postwar policy on monopolies and restrictive practices. Later, he spent six months at the Foreign Office to advise on the economic reconstruction of Japan under the allied occupation. From 1947 to 1967 Allen headed the Department of Political Economy at University College, London, while continuing his participation in practical affairs as a member of the Monopolies (and Restrictive Practices) Commission and of other official bodies.

For Allen, economics was part of the study of man, not the application of specialized techniques. Therefore he favoured an historical approach, emphasizing the importance of institutional and social factors. At a time when government control and economic planning were widely considered as panaceas, Allen remained sceptical. Of his 17 books, perhaps the best known were *British Industries and their Organisation* (1933, revised edition 1970), *A Short Economic History of Japan* (1946, revised edition 1981) and *Monopoly and Restrictive Practices* (1968).

AUDREY DONNITHORNE

SELECTED WORKS
1933. *British Industries and their Organisation*. 5th edn, London: Longmans, 1970.
1946. *A Short Economic History of Modern Japan*. 4th edn, London: Macmillan, 1981.
1968. *Monopoly and Restrictive Practices*. London: Allen & Unwin.

Allen, Roy George Douglas (1906–1983). Allen was born on 3 June 1906 at Stoke-on-Trent, and died on 29 September 1983 at Southwold. He was knighted in 1966 and made a Fellow of the British Academy in 1952. He was educated at the Royal Grammar School, Worcester, and Sidney Sussex College, Cambridge (Wrangler, 1927). From 1928 he was assistant, then lecturer, then reader in economic statistics at the London School of Economics, becoming professor of statistics in 1944 and emeritus professor in 1973.

During the war, he was a statistician in HM Treasury from 1939 to 1941; from 1941 to 1942 he was Director of Records and Statistics for the British Supply Council in Washington, and from 1942 to 1945, he became British Director of Research and Statistics for the Combined Production and Resources Board in Washington. His other principal activities were as statistical adviser for HM Treasury (1947–8); member of the Air Transport Licensing Board (1960–72); and member of the Civil Aviation Authority (1972–3). He was President of the Econometric Society in 1951 and President of the Royal Statistical Society in 1969–70. He was also consultant to many international and professional organizations.

Allen was an economic statistician, mathematical economist and econometrician of exceptional competence and breadth of knowledge. His early and most original research, carried out in part with J.R. Hicks and A.L. Bowley, was on the theory of value, utility and consumers' behaviour: for example, Hicks and Allen (1934), Allen (1935), and Allen and Bowley (1935), the last an outstanding work on the econometrics of family budgets.

In the late 1930s he embarked on a series of successful textbooks based on his lectures. His *Mathematical Analysis for Economists* (1938) was intended to help students of economics whose training in mathematics was typically much less thorough than it is now. After the war, in addition to numerous papers on economic and statistical topics, including one reflecting his wartime work in Washington (Allen, 1946), and a compilation of papers on international trade statistics (Allen and Ely, eds, 1953), he continued the good work begun in 1938 with a succession of books on macroeconomics and the mathematical and statistical tools required in its study. Thus *Statistics for Economists* (1949) is an introduction to statistical methods in their application to economic material; *Mathematical Economics* (1956) is a text on economic theory, written in mathematical terms, which takes account of the growth of econometrics and the use of increasingly sophisticated mathematics by economists; *Basic Mathematics* (1962) provides a general introduction to mathematical ideas, applicable in both the natural and the social sciences; *Macro-Economic Theory* (1967) treats deterministic models from a positive rather than an optimizing or policy-oriented point of view; his 1975 work deals comprehensively with the design, construction and use of index-numbers, paying full attention to both the economic and the statistical aspects of the subject; his last book (Allen, 1980) is an introduction to national accounting, concentrating on the main aggregates at current and constant prices and illustrated by means of recent British official estimates.

Allen was an assiduous disseminator of ideas. His textbooks were translated into many languages and he continued to lecture until shortly before his death. As head of the Statistics Department of the LSE he was instrumental, with the help of M.G. Kendall, in expanding it from a staff of five in 1944 to one of 28, of whom seven were professors.

J.R.N. STONE

SELECTED WORKS
1934. (With J.R. Hicks.) A reconsideration of the theory of value: parts I and II. *Economica*, February, 52–76; May, 196–219.
1935. A note on the determinateness of the utility function. *Review of Economic Studies* 2, February, 155–8.
1935. (With A.L. Bowley.) *Family Expenditure*. London: P.S. King.
1938. *Mathematical Analysis for Economists*. London: Macmillan.
1946. Mutual aid between the US and the British Empire, 1941–45. *Journal of the Royal Statistical Society* 109(3), 243–71.
1949. *Statistics for Economists*. London: Hutchinson.
1953. (With J.E. Ely, eds.) *International Trade Statistics*. London: Chapman and Hall.
1956. *Mathematical Economics*. London: Macmillan.
1962. *Basic Mathematics*. London: Macmillan.
1967. *Macro-Economic Theory*. London: Macmillan.
1975. *Index Numbers in Theory and Practice*. London: Macmillan.
1980. *An Introduction to National Accounts Statistics*. London: Macmillan.

BIBLIOGRAPHY
Cairncross, A. 1985. Roy Allen, 1906–1983. In *Proceedings of the British Academy* 70, Oxford: Oxford University Press.
Grebenik, E. 1984. Roy George Douglas Allen, 1906–1983. *Journal of the Royal Statistical Society* 147(5), 706–7.

allocation. *See* EFFICIENT ALLOCATION OF RESOURCES.

allocation: strategy-proof mechanisms. *See* STRATEGY-PROOF ALLOCATION MECHANISMS.

allocation of time. *See* VALUE OF TIME.

Almon, Shirley Montag (1935–1975). Shirley Almon was born on 6 February 1935, in Saxonburg, Pennsylvania and died on 27 September 1975, in College Park, Maryland. She graduated from Goucher College in Baltimore, Maryland, in 1956, and received her PhD from Harvard University in 1964. The essence of her PhD dissertation was published in *Econometrica* (1965), a frequently cited article that introduced a new statistical technique for estimating distributed lags. This technique, now commonly known as the Almon lag, has been widely used in numerous econometric studies.

Almon worked at various times as an economist at the Women's Bureau in Washington, DC, at the National Bureau of Economic Research, at the Federal Reserve Bank of San Francisco, and at the Federal Reserve Board in Washington, DC. She taught elementary economics, industrial organization, and statistics at Wellesley College and Harvard University before joining the staff of the President's Council of Economic Advisers in 1966, where she continued until the onset of a brain tumour, discovered in 1967, ended her brief but significantly productive career.

Roger N. Waud

SELECTED WORKS

1965. The distributed lag between capital appropriations and expenditures. *Econometrica* 33, January, 178–96.
1968. Lags between investment decisions and their causes. *Review of Economics and Statistics* 50, May, 193–206.

Almon lag. The Almon distributed lag, due to Shirley Almon (1965), is a technique for estimating the weights of a distributed lag by means of a polynomial specification.

Consider the distributed lag model,

$$y_t = w_0 x_t + \cdots + w_n x_{t-n} + \epsilon_t \qquad (1)$$

where y_t is the value of the dependent variable at time t; x_t, $x_{t-1}, \ldots, x_{t-n}$ are the values of the regressor x at times, t, $t-1, \ldots, t-n$; and ϵ_t is the value of the disturbance ϵ at time t. The dependent variable y is influenced by the regressor x both contemporaneously and with a lag of up to n time periods. If the lag length, n, is finite and less than the number of observations, the regression coefficients w_i can be estimated by ordinary least squares (OLS).

It is often the case, however, that there is a high degree of multicollinearity among the regressors $x_t, \ldots, x_{t-n}$ so that most or all of the estimated regression coefficients are statistically insignificant, and powerful inferences about the true weights are impossible. This problem can be circumvented by introducing *a priori* information into the estimation procedure, typically by imposing restrictions on the true weights. If the restrictions are valid, the estimates of the weights will be unbiased, consistent, *and* more efficient than the OLS estimates. Similarly, the tests of hypotheses about the true weights will be valid *and* more powerful than the tests based on OLS estimation.

The Almon lag technique introduces *a priori* information by estimating the distributed lag model (1) subject to the restriction that the weights lie on a polynomial of degree p,

$$w_i = \lambda_0 + \lambda_1 i + \lambda_2 i^2 + \cdots + \lambda_p i^p, \qquad (2)$$

$i = 0, 1, \ldots, n$; $p \leqslant n$. This reduces the number of parameters from $n + 1$ $(w_0, w_1, \ldots, w_n)$ to $p + 1$ $(\lambda_0, \lambda_1, \ldots, \lambda_p)$. (A very readable description of the procedure for estimating the 'new' parameters $(\lambda_0, \lambda_1, \ldots, \lambda_p)$ and transforming these into estimates of the original weights $(w_1, w_2, \ldots, w_n)$ is provided by Kmenta (1971, pp. 492–3).) As with any *a priori* restriction, the restriction that the weights lie on a polynomial will lead to more efficient and more powerful tests if the restriction is valid, but will give biased and inconsistent and invalid tests if the restriction is false. Following are some important caveats to be borne in mind when using the Almon technique.

1. *The presence or absence of a lag is not a testable proposition when the Almon lag technique is used.* Suppose no lag is present so that x affects y only instantaneously; $w_0 \neq 0$ but $w_1 = w_2 = \cdots = w_n = 0$. Since a polynomial of degree p can equal zero in only p places (unless it is identically zero), any choice of $p < n$ involves a specification error; the n zeros $w_1, w_2, \ldots, w_n$ cannot lie on a polynomial of degree $p < n$. Therefore if the Almon lag technique is used in this case, the results will suggest the presence of a lag even though there is none.

2. *The use of end-point constraints.* It has been a rather common practice among users of the Almon technique to impose one or both end-point constraints

$$w_{-1} = 0; \quad w_{n+1} = 0 \qquad (3)$$

in estimation. In terms of (2) this involves the following restrictions on the λs:

$$\lambda_0 - \lambda_1 + \lambda_2 - \cdots \pm \lambda_p = 0 \qquad (4)$$
$$\lambda_0 + (n+1)\lambda_1 + (n+1)^2\lambda_2 + \cdots + (n+1)^p\lambda_p = 0. \qquad (5)$$

The imposition of (4) and (5) increases the efficiency of estimation if the restrictions are true, but gives biased and inconsistent estimates if they are false. In general, however, there are no convincing reasons for imposing these constraints. For example, it is tempting to argue that $w_{-1} = 0$ because it is the coefficient on x_{t+1} and x_{t+1} does not affect y_t. By the same logic one would conclude $0 = w_{-2} = w_{-3} = w_{-4} = \cdots$. However, this is not possible. If the weights w_i do in fact lie on a polynomial of degree p, no more than p of them can equal zero. This illustrates why one should be concerned only with the weights $w_0, w_1, \ldots, w_n$ – the behaviour of the polynomial outside this range is irrelevant.

3. *Choosing the lag length and polynomial degree.* Understating the length (choosing n less than the true lag length) is a specification error which results in biased and inconsistent estimates and invalid tests. A specification error is also committed by overstating the lag length. This occurs whenever the lag length is overstated by more than p minus the number of endpoint constraints because a p-degree polynomial can have only p zeros. Choosing a small value of p increases the possible efficiency gain from use of the Almon technique, but also makes specification error more likely. However, if p is not considerably less than n, using the technique may be pointless since the results will strongly resemble the OLS results; when $p = n$ the estimates are the same as OLS. A discussion of the procedures for testing for appropriate lag length and degree of polynomial, along with relevant literature citations, can be found in Judge et al. (1980, pp. 645–51).

Roger N. Waud

See also MULTIPLE TIME SERIES.

BIBLIOGRAPHY

Almon, S. 1965. The distributed lag between capital appropriations and expenditures. *Econometrica* 33(1), January, 178–96.
Judge, G., Griffiths, W., Hill, R. and Lee, T. 1980. *The Theory and Practice of Econometrics*. New York: Wiley.
Kmenta, J. 1971. *Elements of Econometrics*. New York: Macmillan.

alternative technology. *See* APPROPRIATE TECHNOLOGY; SCHUMACHER, E.F.

altruism. The French term 'altruisme' was introduced by Auguste Comte (1830–42) to signify devotion to the welfare of others, especially as a principle of action. It is closely related to concepts such as benevolence and unselfishness. It has long attracted the interest of moral philosophers (see e.g. Nagel, 1970; Milo, 1973; Roberts, 1973; Collard, 1978; Margolis, 1982). Rescher (1975, p. 11) categorizes it as one of the 'modalities' of unselfishness. Numerous social scientists in many fields, including sociobiology, have been interested in altruistic behaviour as helping to assure species and gene survival (Becker, 1976; Collard, 1978, ch. 5). While some economists have participated in such research, more have naturally concentrated upon the implications of altruism for economic outcomes–in particular, the allocation of resources and the distribution of income.

ALTRUISTIC PREFERENCES AND UTILITIES. Most of the problems presented by altruism are adequately captured in a simple model with n individuals who each consume a single transferable good – perhaps a Hicks composite commodity, because relative prices are fixed. So an economic allocation is described by an income distribution vector y in $\mathbb{R}^n$, whose typical non-negative component y_i denotes the income of person i. Even intergenerational altruism can be discussed in such a framework, with y_i denoting wealth, provided that capital markets are perfect and no transfers occur which affect real interest rates, and provided that we ignore the special problems that arise when both the time horizon and the number of individuals are infinite.

If individual i has selfish preferences, then income distribution y is preferred to y' if and only if $y_i > y_i'$ so that i has more income. But altruistic preferences allow y to be preferred to y' even if $y_i < y_i'$, provided enough other individuals j have gains $y_j - y_j'$ which are large enough to overcompensate. Thus altruistic preferences can be quite a general (complete and transitive) ordering $\gtrsim i$ on $\mathbb{R}^n_+$.

Some more care is needed here, however. Economists usually identify 'welfare' with 'preferences' and assume that it can be represented by a welfare function $w_i(y)$ on $\mathbb{R}^n_+$ which increases as y becomes more preferred. Recalling that altruism is regard for others' *welfare* then suggests that i must want to maximize a function of the form $w_i = \phi_i(y_i, \mathbf{w}_{-i})$, where $\mathbf{w}_{-i}$ denotes the vector of welfare levels w_j ($j \neq i$) with i excluded, and where ϕ_i is increasing in every other w_j. Given the income distribution y, finding the individual welfare levels $w_i(y)$ requires solving the n simultaneous equations:

$$w_i = \phi_i(y_i, \mathbf{w}_{-i}) \tag{1}$$

for every i. So each $w_i(y)$ is only well-defined provided that these equations have a unique solution. Becker (1974, pp. 1076–7) amongst others discusses this problem – for a special Cobb–Douglas case with two individuals. Assume that (1) does have a unique solution for every y in $\mathbb{R}^n_+$, though this is by no means innocuous. In particular, taking the total differential of (1) gives:

$$dw_i - \sum_{j \neq i} \phi_{ij}\, dw_j = \phi_{ii}\, dy_i \tag{2}$$

and the matrix formed by the coefficients of each dw_j on the left-hand side of each equation in (2) must be invertible (see Kolm, 1969, pp. 153–4).

PARETO INEFFICIENT REDISTRIBUTION. When everybody's altruistic utility function $w_i(y)$ depends upon the incomes of all, it seems obvious that there are externalities likely to cause Pareto inefficiency. Unlike standard externalities, however, individuals can translate their altruism into action by giving

income away to anyone they want to. Let $t_{ij}(\geqslant 0)$ denote the transfer made by i to j. Then, assuming that each w_i is differentiable, and recognizing the non-negativity constraints that prevent people taking income from others, transfers occur until the following first order conditions are satisfied for every i, j with $i \neq j$:

$$w_{ij} \leqslant w_{ii}, \quad t_{ij} \geqslant 0 \quad \text{and} \quad t_{ij}(w_{ii} - w_{ij}) = 0 \tag{3}$$

where w_{ii} denotes $\partial w_i / \partial y_j$. Thus $w_{ii} = w_{ij}$ unless the constraint $t_{ij} \geqslant 0$ binds, when one can have $w_{ij} < w_{ii}$, with i valuing his own income more than j's at the margin.

First order conditions for Pareto efficiency, on the other hand, require the existence of marginal welfare weights $\beta_i (i = 1 \ to \ n)$ such that, for every pair of individuals j, k:

$$\sum_i \beta_i(w_{ij} - w_{ik}) = 0 \tag{4}$$

so that the marginal social benefit of \$1 for j is equal to that of \$1 for k. This presumes an interior distribution in which all have income.

Now suppose that (3) is satisfied at a distribution y^* in which no individual wants to take income from anybody else. Then $w_{ii} = w_{ij}$ for all i, j and the efficiency conditions (4) are satisfied! But Winter (1969) notices how alleviating poverty can create externalities of the kind that occur when public goods have to be provided by private individuals. After all, a poor person is likely to benefit by receiving income from the rich, even if he is altruistic to the rich. Then $w_{ij} < w_{ii}$, where i is the poor person and j the rich. So (4) may well be violated. This is especially clear in Arrow (1981), where every individual's altruistic utility takes the form:

$$w_i(y) \equiv u_i(y_i) + \sum_{j \neq i} v(y_j) \tag{5}$$

and $y_i = y_j$ implies $u_i'(y_i) > v'(y_j)$. Arrow shows that, excluding trivial equilibria in which no voluntary redistribution at all takes place, redistribution is only Pareto efficient in a very special case when there is just one rich giver – e.g. the two person case by Hochman and Rodgers (1969). Obviously giving is then not a public good. But as soon as there are two or more givers, Pareto inefficiency is inevitable in Arrow's model at least (see also Bergstrom, 1970 and Nakayama, 1980).

POLICY RELEVANCE. If altruistic preferences make transfers to the poor a public good, this is a prima facie argument for public intervention to redistribute income. Yet this argument has been contested. It has even been claimed that redistributive policy is powerless because it merely substitutes for private charity. In Barro (1974), the issue is obscured by dynamic considerations and the fact that 'charity' takes the form of bequests to one's heirs. Public debt becomes irrelevant because its effects are totally offset by bequests. This presumes, however, that nobody wishes to make negative bequests, because otherwise the national debt is a way of reproducing the effects of negative bequests. Were Barro's arguments correct, Bernheim and Bagwell (1985) show that then many other policy instruments would also become ineffective; even distortionary income taxes could be offset by reducing bequests in order to pay them. Just as Barro's neutrality proposition fails when agents could gain from making negative bequests if they were allowed, so redistributive policies are effective *precisely* when the poor can gain by further transfers from the rich which the rich are unwilling to make because of the public good problem. This is true even when the poor feel altruistic toward the rich.

There are some special cases where neutrality does hold and policy is irrelevant. One is with just one giver, which is the Arrow (1981) sufficient condition for efficiency. Another is

Becker's (1974, p. 1080 and 1981) household with a head who is wealthy enough to want to control the intrafamily distribution of income. Then the 'rotten kid' theorem has the activities of selfish children completely offset by transfers from the head, provided that the household head is able to retain control even if he should die first (Hirshleifer, 1977). Becker never considers, however, a family with two heads, for which the rotten kid theorem would fail in general, with each head providing too little support for efficiency. Warr (1982, 1983) also argues that policy is irrelevant, but analyses only first order conditions like (3) without any inequalities, and so fails to consider the likely case in which charity is insufficient to make the poor want no more transfers from the rich. Bergstrom and Varian (1985) and Bergstrom, Blume and Varian (1986) provide further discussion.

IS CHARITY A PUBLIC GOOD? The flawed policy irrelevance argument is not the only way to contest treating redistribution as a public good when there is altruism. A better argument is due to Sugden (1982, 1983, 1985) who questions whether individuals' altruistic behaviour maximizes a utility function which can be expressed solely as a function of the income distribution. Suppose that A likes to give 10 per cent of his marginal income to charity C. Suppose too that B gives $10 less to charity C than before. Then this is like a $10 fall in A's total income, leading to a $1 drop in the amount A wants C to receive in total, so A increases his giving to C by $9 in order to bring this about. Conversely, if B gives $10 more to charity C, then A will reduce his giving by $9. This is a general feature of privately provided public goods: the more one person gives, the less others will want to. In the case of charity, however, such negative covariation between different people's giving seems implausible. It would imply (Sugden, 1983) that the main beneficiaries of a new gift to a charity are those other givers who respond by reducing their gifts to that charity! Sugden concludes that givers value charity *per se* as well as for the help it gives the recipients – a possibility discussed earlier by Arrow (1974), amongst others. Then each person's giving becomes a separate *private* good, and the public good argument for replacing charity by tax-financed transfer programmes becomes less convincing.

CHARITY: REAL OR APPARENT ALTRUISM? An obvious explanation of behaviour such as charitable giving is altruistic preferences. Yet it is not the only possible explanation. As just discussed, gifts may be made for their own sake as well as because of an altruistic regard for the recipient's welfare. They may also reflect egoistic cooperative behaviour, however, as discussed by Boulding (1973), Arrow (1974) and Hammond (1975), amongst economists, and by many sociobiologists – as has been pointed out by Becker (1976), Kurz (1977, 1978), etc. If persons A and B are in continual contact, both may gain from reciprocal cooperation as a form of mutual insurance. And if there is an infinite chain $A_1, A_2, A_3, \ldots$ with person A_n in contact with A_{n+1}, all can gain from maintaining cooperation into the indefinite future. Genes which promote such cooperation enhance their prospects of long-run survival. Maintaining such cooperation requires deviants to be punished suitably. But apparently altruistic behaviour emerges from entirely selfish preferences. The same is true when it is clear to all members of a group that *one* of their members must act for their mutual benefit, although there may be a costly or dangerous delay before the apparently altruistic behaviour emerges, as in Bliss and Nalebuff's (1984) model of brinkmanship. Finally, Sugden's (1984) theory of reciprocity is an interesting recent

explanation of apparently altruistic behaviour which is really selfish at bottom.

IS ALTRUISM RELEVANT? It has just been seen that altruistic preferences may be unnecessary to explain apparently altruistic behaviour. This limits the relevance of altruism for positive economics, though one cannot deny that some behaviour is indeed motivated by altruism in the sense of devotion to the welfare of others.

A more controversial claim is that altruism also has limited relevance for normative economics. This issue is addressed by Barry (1965, p. 65) because altruistic regard for others is an instance of a 'publicly oriented want', which 'carries a claim to satisfaction only as being a want for what ought to be done anyway', thus people's altruistic preferences are irrelevant in determining what should be the distribution of income, except in so far as they correspond to what is anyway ethically appropriate. In the language of welfare economics, each individual's welfare corresponds only to that person's 'privately-oriented' or selfish preferences. Altruism is therefore excluded, because it is regard for *others'* welfare. That is not to deny that welfare-relevant externalities may arise if, for instance, a rich person experiences revulsion on being confronted with extreme poverty. But avoiding such revulsion is *not* altruism so much as selfish behaviour.

A related reason for excluding altruistic preferences from welfare is to avoid undesirable double counting. Suppose that A is an altruist with utility $u(y^A) + (1/2)u(y^E)$ for the distribution of income between A and E, an egoist. Suppose that E, however, has a selfish utility function $u(y^E)$. Adding utilities then gives $u(y^A) + (3/2)u(y^E)$, with greater weight for the marginal utility of the undeserving egoist's income than for the deserving altruist's. A more appropriate welfare function is $u(y^A) + u(y^E)$ which disregards A's altruism and just adds selfish utilities. The main role of altruism in welfare economics is to help determine ethical views, not to determine individual welfare. Concepts of Pareto efficiency which include altruism in individual welfare have little normative significance, as do the alleged 'Pareto efficient' income redistributions. Altruistic behaviour often helps to promote social welfare, but it may not if the altruism happens to be directed toward those whose income should receive only small weight in the social welfare function.

PETER J. HAMMOND

See also ENVY; EQUITY; EXTERNALITY; FAMILY; GIFTS; PUBLIC GOODS; WICKSTEED, PHILIP HENRY.

BIBLIOGRAPHY

Arrow, K.J. 1974. Gifts and exchanges. *Philosophy and Public Affairs* 1, 343–62; reprinted as pp. 13–28 of Phelps (1975).

Arrow, K.J. 1981. Optimal and voluntary income distribution. In *Economic Welfare and the Economics of Soviet Socialism: Essays in Honour of Abram Bergson*, ed. S. Rosefield, Cambridge: Cambridge University Press, 267–88; reprinted as ch. 15 of *Collected Papers of Kenneth J. Arrow*, Vol. 1: *Social Choice and Justice*, Cambridge, Mass.: Belknap Press.

Barro, R. 1974. Are Government bonds net wealth? *Journal of Political Economy* 82, 1095–117.

Barry, B.M. 1965. *Political Argument*. London: Routledge & Kegan Paul.

Becker, G.S. 1974. A theory of social interactions. *Journal of Political Economy* 82, 1063–91.

Becker, G.S. 1976. Altruism, egoism and genetic fitness: economics and sociobiology. *Journal of Economic Literature* 14, 817–26.

Becker, G.S. 1981. Altruism in the family and selfishness in the market place. *Economica* 48, 1–16.

Bergstrom, T.C. 1970. A 'Scandinavian consensus' solution for efficient income distribution among nonmalevolent consumers. *Journal of Economic Theory* 2, 383–98.

Bergstrom, T.C., Blume, L. and Varian, H.R. 1986. On the private provision of public goods. *Journal of Public Economics* 29, 25–49.

Bergstrom, T.C. and Varian, H.R. 1985. When are Nash equilibria independent of the distribution of agents' characteristics? *Review of Economic Studies* 52, 715–18.

Bernheim, B.D. and Bagwell, K. 1985. Is everything neutral? Mimeo, Stanford University; forthcoming in the *Journal of Political Economy*.

Bliss, C.J. and Nalebuff, B. 1984. Dragon-slaying and ballroom dancing: the private supply of a public good. *Journal of Public Economics* 25, 1–12.

Boulding, K.E. 1973. *The Economy of Love and Fear: A Preface to Grants Economics*. Belmont: Wadsworth.

Collard, D.A. 1978. *Altruism and Economy: A Study in Non-Selfish Economics*. Oxford: Martin Robertson; New York: Oxford University Press.

Comte, A. 1830–42. *Cours de philosophie positive*. 6 vols, Paris: Bachelier.

Hammond, P.J. 1975. Charity: altruism or cooperative egoism? In Phelps (1975), 115–31.

Hirshleifer, J. 1977. Shakespeare vs. Becker on altruism: the importance of having the last word. *Journal of Economic Literature* 15, 500–2.

Hochman, H.M. and Rodgers, J.D. 1969. Pareto optimal redistribution. *American Economic Review* 59, 542–57.

Kolm, S.-C. 1969. The optimal production of social justice. In *Public Economics*, ed. J. Margolis and H. Guitton, London: Macmillan, 145–200.

Kurz, M. 1977. Altruistic equilibrium. In *Economic Progress, Private Values, and Public Policy: Essays in Honor of William Fellner*, ed. B. Balassa and R. Nelson, Amsterdam: North-Holland, ch. 8, 177–200.

Kurz, M. 1978. Altruism as an outcome of social interaction. *American Economic Review, Papers and Proceedings* 68, 216–28.

Margolis, H. 1982. *Selfishness, Altruism, and Rationality: A Theory of Social Choice*. Cambridge: Cambridge University Press.

Milo, R.D. (ed.) 1973. *Egoism and Altruism*. Belmont: Wadsworth.

Nagel, T. 1970. *The Possibility of Altruism*. Oxford: Clarendon Press.

Nakayama, M. 1980. Nash equilibria and Pareto optimal income redistribution. *Econometrica* 48, 1257–63.

Phelps, E.S. (ed.) 1975. *Altruism, Morality and Economic Theory*. New York: Russell Sage Foundation.

Rescher, N. 1975. *Unselfishness: The Role of the Vicarious Affects in Moral Philosophy and Social Theory*. Pittsburgh: University of Pittsburgh Press.

Roberts, T.A. 1973. *The Concept of Benevolence: Aspects of Eighteenth-Century Moral Philosophy*. London: Macmillan.

Sugden, R. 1982. On the economics of philanthropy. *Economic Journal* 92, 341–50.

Sugden, R. 1983. *Who Cares? An Economic and Ethical Analysis of Private Charity and the Welfare State*. London: Institute of Economic Affairs.

Sugden, R. 1984. Reciprocity: the supply of public goods through voluntary contribution. *Economic Journal* 94, 772–87.

Sugden, R. 1985. Consistent conjectures and voluntary contributions to public goods: why the conventional theory does not work. *Journal of Public Economics* 27, 117–24.

Warr, P. 1982. Pareto optimal redistribution and private charity. *Journal of Public Economics* 19, 131–8.

Warr, P. 1983. The private provision of a public good is independent of the distribution of income. *Economics Letters* 13, 207–11.

Winter, S.G. 1969. A simple remark on the second optimality theorem of welfare economics. *Journal of Economic Theory* 1, 99–103.

American Economic Association. The American Economic Association (AEA), the world's largest and most prestigious organization of professional economists, was inaugurated by a miscellaneous group of scholars, university administrators and public figures, in September 1885, in the early stages of a remarkable expansion in American academic life. Its original objectives of encouraging research, publications on economic subjects, and perfect freedom in economic discussions have been consistently maintained, sometimes not without difficulty given the disagreements among its members, and the persistent tension between the desire for scientific objectivity and non-partisanship and the urge to make an impact on public policy. This problem was especially acute during the AEA's early years, when economic questions were at the forefront of public discussion. A number of prominent American economists were then under attack, and some were dismissed from or forced out of their university posts because of their opinions. However under its first President, F.A. Walker, an internationally known figure who served for the first seven years, the AEA gradually lost some of its initial reformist tone and concentrated increasingly on more strictly scholarly issues. Unlike the British Royal Economic Society, which has frequently had a non-professional President, the AEA has invariably been dominated by academic economists, although in recent decades prominent government professional economists have occasionally held the office – for example, Alice Rivlin, the first woman President, in 1985.

While the AEA's contributions to economic knowledge through its periodicals – the *American Economic Review* (from 1911) and the *Journal of Economic Literature* (from 1963) and in various other ways, such as the publication of a superb multi-volume *Index of Economic Journals* – are undeniable, its services to the profession have perhaps been unnecessarily restricted because of the heterogeneity of its constituency, which has always included a substantial proportion of non-academic members, and its commitment to non-partisanship. Thus, for example, the AEA's reactions to the conflicts and tensions in American society during the later 1960s was distinctly less positive than those of some other learned societies, both within and outside the social sciences, with respect to academic freedom issues. However, in both World Wars the AEA played a notable and constructive part by organizing professional expertise for government service, and by conducting open debates and issuing publications on the economic problems of war and peace. The Association has also since 1945 occupied a leading role in the internationalization of the economic profession. It has always been an 'open' society, with no significant membership restrictions, partly because of the objections to control by a limited elite or coterie. Consequently it has not had, nor has it attempted to have, any direct influence on doctrinal developments in the field. Nevertheless, there have been periodic protests about the organization's unrepresentativeness and oligarchical management, a state of affairs reflecting the size, diversity, and geographical dispersion of its membership, which now stands at over 25,000 (including subscribers).

A.W. COATS

BIBLIOGRAPHY

American Economic Association, archives, Northwestern University Library, Evanston, Ill., and Secretary's Office, Vanderbilt University, Nashville, Tenn.

Coats, A.W. 1960. The first two decades of the American Economic Association. *American Economic Review* 50(4), September, 555–74.

Coats, A.W. 1964. The American Economic Association, 1904–1929. *American Economic Review* 54(3), June, 261–85.

Coats, A.W. 1969. The American Economic Association's publications: an historical perspective. *Journal of Economic Literature* 7(1), March, 57–68.

Coats, A.W. 1985. The American Economic Association and the economics profession. *Journal of Economic Literature* 23(4), December, 1697–728.

Dorfman, J. 1949, 1959. *The Economic Mind in American Civilization*, Vols III–V. New York: Viking Press.

Ely, R.T. 1936. The founding and early history of the American Economic Association. *American Economic Review* 26(1), 141–50.

Amoroso, Luigi (1886–1965).   A mathematician by training (at the Normale, Pisa), Amoroso was assistant professor of mathematics in Rome, then professor of financial mathematics in Bari, but soon turned to economics, which he taught from 1921 in Naples and then Rome; he was Fellow of the Econometric Society.

Leaving aside his contributions to pure mathematics (e.g. 1910), financial mathematics (e.g. 1921a), statistics (e.g. 1916), demography (e.g. 1929), four books (1921b, 1938, 1942, 1949) well summarize his contributions to economics, also contained in over 100 articles.

Inspired by Pareto, his mathematical background led him to develop the analogy between pure economics and classical mechanics: the principle of minimum (use of scarce) means is the equivalent of the principle of least action. He also saw analogies between Heisenberg's uncertainty principle and economic phenomena, but did not develop this idea. His existence and uniqueness proof (1928) of a meaningful solution to the system of equations defining consumer's equilibrium is the first modern treatment of existence and uniqueness problems in economics.

Amoroso stressed the need to analyse all optimum conditions in a dynamic context: for example, the consumer maximizes a functional under the balance constraint expressed as a differential equation; the problem is solved by applying the calculus of variations. He thus derived the extension of Pareto's static optimum conditions to a dynamic context. By considering the market determination of prices and introducing relationships between inventories and prices, he obtained systems of integro-differential equations capable of causing cycles around a trend, thus giving an explanation for crises and secular movements.

GIANCARLO GANDOLFO

SELECTED WORKS

A full bibliography of Amoroso's works up to 1959 and an evaluation of his scientific contributions by various authors is contained in: Onoranze al Prof. Luigi Amoroso, *Annali dell'Istituto di Statistica*, Vol. 30, Università di Bari, 1959.

1910. Sulla risolubilità della equazione lineare integrale di prima specie. *Rendiconti della Accademia dei Lincei*. Classe di Scienze fisiche, matematiche e naturali. Nota presentata dal socio Castelnuovo, nella seduta del 16.1.1910, Roma.

1916. Contributo al metodo delle minime differenze. *Giornale degli Economisti e Rivista di Statistica*, July, 50–86.

1921a. *Lezioni di matematica finanziaria*, Vol. 1 (1921), Vol. 2 (1923). Naples: Majo.

1921b. *Lezioni di economia matematica*. Bologna: Zanichelli.

1928. Discussione del sistema di equazioni che definiscono l'equilibrio del consumatore. *Annali di Economia*, March, 31–41.

1929. L'equazione differenziale del movimento della popolazione. *Rivista Italiana di Statistica*, April, 151–7.

1935. La dynamique de la circulation. *Econometrica* 3(4), October, 400–410.

1938. *Principi di economica corporativa*. Bologna: Zanichelli.

1942. *Meccanica economica*. Città di Castello: Macrì.

1949. *Economia di mercato*. Bologna: Zuffi.

amortization.   Amortization is an accounting term meaning to allocate a cost to several time periods. The term is derived from the Latin word for death and literally means to 'kill off' the liability. Debts which are paid off gradually are said to be amortized, and the term is also applied to the depreciation costs of the cost of certain assets which are used up in producing income.

Amortization in this second sense is illustrated by the following example (Table 1). A firm spends $10,000 to invent and patent a new product which is expected to yield revenue (net of operating expenses) of $5000 in the first year of production, $2000 in each of the next three years, and $1500 in the fifth year (see column (3) of Table 1). The product is assumed to become obsolete at the end of five years and to generate no additional revenue. The patent thus becomes valueless at that time.

Table 1 Amortization of Hypothetical Asset

(1) End of:	(2) Outlay	(3) Net Revenue	(4) Present Value*	(5) Amortization	(6) Profit
yr 0	$10000	0	$10000	0	0
yr 1	0	$5000	$ 6000	$4000	$1000
yr 2	0	$2000	$ 4599	$1401	$ 599
yr 3	0	$2000	$ 3058	$1541	$ 459
yr 4	0	$2000	$ 1364	$1694	$ 306
yr 5	0	$1500	0	$1364	$ 136

*Present value of remaining net revenue calculated using discount rate of 9.992%.

The present value of the net revenue stream associated with the invention is initially $10,000 at an approximate 10 per cent rate of discount. However, the present value of the remaining net revenue falls to $6000 at the end of the first year, to $4599 at the end of the second year, to $3058 and $1364 at the end of the third and fourth years, and to zero at the end of the product's useful life (see column (4)). This implies that the original $10,000 investment has been eroded by $4000 at the end of the first year, $1401 in the second year, and so on (see column (5)). In considering how much profit was earned in the first year, the loss in the value of the investment must be subtracted from revenue in order to keep the original value of the investment intact. Thus, profit in the first year is $1000, or 10 per cent of the original investment. Inspection of columns (4) and (6) reveals that the ratio of profit to remaining present value in the previous year is always 10 per cent.

If, on the other hand, the reduction in value is not recognized as a cost, one would erroneously conclude that the investment yielded $12,500 over the life of the asset (the sum of column (3)) rather than $2500 (the sum of column (6)). However, the value of the investment would have fallen from $10,000 to zero.

The year-to-year loss in asset value is termed 'amortization'. In this context, amortization is analogous to depreciation, although the former typically (but not always) refers to intangible assets while the latter typically (but not always) refers to tangible capital like plant and equipment. The concept of depreciation is, however, more intuitive since it is associated with physical deterioration and ultimate retirement from service. Intangible assets, on the other hand, are invisible and are difficult to measure or even value, so it is harder to believe that they are being used up in the production of income. For this reason, the term 'amortization' carries the connotation of an arbitrary and gradual killing off of asset value. This is unfortunate, since the true depreciation of tangible capital is hard to measure and arbitrary 'amortization' rules are typically used in tax and financial accounting.

The graduation write-off of a debt is another context in which the term 'amortization' is frequently used. The level-payment home mortgage is, for example, a common type of amortized loan. In the level-payment mortgage, the sum of the interest and principal payments is constant. During the early life of the loan, the bulk of this constant (or 'level') payment is for interest on the outstanding balance of the loan. The proportion of the level-payment allocated to the repayment of principal gradually increases as time goes by, since interest is paid on the outstanding balance of the loan. In the fully amortized loan, the sum of the period-by-period repayments of principal over the life of the loan is equal to the original value of the debt.

This type of arrangement may be contrasted with the case of the 'balloon' loan, in which the entire principal is repaid at the termination date of the loan. Loans may be a mixture of the two types: amortization of part of the principal with a balloon payment equal to the unamortized balance.

The amortization of a loan is conceptually related to the amortization of an intangible asset. The accompanying table could, for example, be reinterpreted as the payoff schedule for a $10,000 debt. Column (5) could be interpreted as annual return of principal (a non-level payment schedule), and column (6) as interest paid on the outstanding balance of the debt. However, the amortization of a loan involves the gradual write-off of a liability while the amortization of an intangible involves the gradual write-off of an asset. Both cases involve allocating a cost over several time periods.

CHARLES R. HULTEN

See also DEPRECIATION; MAINTAINING CAPITAL INTACT.

analogy. We say that something A is analogous to something B if, in some relevant respect, A is similar to but not identical with B. This is the basic relation upon which the use of analogy in various kinds of reasoning depends. We speak of reasoning by analogy when on the basis of some similarity which we discern between two things or processes or properties, or what you will, we infer some other similarity. Reasoning by analogy is a special case of inductive reasoning since we must be wary of the possibility that the further similarities which are presupposed in our inference may not actually obtain. Like all inductive inference reasoning by analogy is stepping from the known to the unknown. Clearly, then, analogical reasoning is not demonstrative or deductive.

A more refined analysis of the structure of the analogy can be made by distinguishing between those respects in which the analogues are similar, called the positive analogy, those respects in which they are different, called the negative analogy, and those respects in which we are unsure whether the property in question marks a similarity or a difference – the neutral analogy (Hesse, 1963). Once we have introduced the idea of neutral analogy the relation between the analogues is no longer symmetrical. If we think of analogy simply in terms of similarities and differences then if A is similar to B, B is similar to A, and if A is dissimilar to B, B is dissimilar to A. It does not matter which of A and B we say is analogous to which. But once we introduce the idea of neutral analogy we are obliged to decide which of the items under comparison is the one from which our reasoning will take a start and usually this decision is dependent on which of A or B we are confident we know. For example, if we argue that an illness is analogous to the invasion of a country by a hostile army, as van Helmont proposed in the 17th century, it seems reasonable to take the

invasion by the hostile army as the term about which we can in principle know a great deal and the cause of illness as the term about whose properties we are less certain. In reasoning by analogy, then, about the cause of disease, the idea of an invasion is the given term and the illness is the unknown. We can then take the known properties of invasions and armies and set out on an experimental programme to decide how many properties similar to them are to be found in the causes of disease. Thus: 'Soldiers are organisms', 'Are the causes of disease micro-organisms?' The logic of analogy then consists in picking out sets of properties and making comparisons between the members of the one set and of the other.

In judging the force of an analogy we must have some way of deciding which properties are important and which are not. If two things are similar only in unimportant or inessential ways and differ in other respects, then we generally take the analogy between them to be weak. Unlike deductive reasoning, analogy is, therefore, highly sensitive to context and to the interests of whoever is making use of it. It can hardly be said that there is anything intrinsic about a property which makes it important. Rather its importance depends upon the context and interests of the user. Furthermore, we need also to assume that we can make some sort of quantitative assessment of the degrees of similarities and differences between the analogues and this may be quite difficult to do in any principled way.

I have described the relation of analogy in terms of concrete relations of similarity and difference between the properties of analogous things. However, there are important linguistic phenomena which are in some ways like an analogy. The most obvious is simile. When we use that figure of speech we explicitly invite a comparison between the referents of the terms between which the simile is drawn by reference to likenesses. We tacitly assume that we draw a simile only where there are also differences. There are plenty of literary examples to illustrate this relationship.

The analogy relation seems to have another realization in language in metaphor. In a metaphorical use of a term an expression is employed in a novel context. Words which are customarily used for discussing one kind of subject matter, are used to describe some other. Some have said that in metaphor the sense of a word is displaced. In order for a metaphor to have any bite it must reflect some similarity. The metaphor 'life's journey' would hardly have had the currency that it enjoys in improving discourses, such as the speeches which accompany school prize-givings, had there been no way in which life could be seen as a journey. But unlike simile, metaphorical uses do not leave words unaffected. It has been pointed out by many students of metaphor that when a concept is displaced into a new domain it not only serves to highlight some hitherto unnoticed similarity between its old and new referents, but it changes its significance through coming to be used in a new domain. So the term 'current' was first used in the description of electricity, to highlight similarities between electricity and more easily observable fluids. The two centuries of use of this term in the electrical domain have certainly led to a change in its meaning (Martin and Harré, 1982).

ANALOGIES AND MODELS. The recent trend in philosophy of science to look more closely at actual examples of scientific reasoning has disclosed the quite central role that analogical reasoning plays in both the physical sciences and the social sciences. A special terminology has grown up in the sciences by which the term 'model' is appropriated for concrete analogues (Bunge, 1973).

Scientific models are of two main kinds. There are heuristic or homoeomorphic models and explanatory or paramorphic models. Each kind has a specific use.

Many phenomena are too complicated for ready examination. Salient features can be brought out by abstracting a simpler form from the original complexity and idealizing its properties. A homoeomorphic or heuristic model is a convenient representation of its subject. It may be a concrete thing, such as the scale models used in engineering. But it may be an abstract conceptual representation embodied in something like the 'rational actor' assumption in economics. Heuristic models are conservative. In a sense they merely represent what we already know but in some useful or convenient form.

Explanatory models (paramorphic analogues) are used creatively. They enable scientists to conceive of new kinds of beings and so far unobserved processes. Their main use is to complete theories by standing in for unobserved and so currently unknown causal processes. The kinetic theory depends on the idea of a swarm of molecules which are a model or analogue of the unknown constitution of real gases. The hypothetical behaviour of the molecular analogue must be like (analogous to) the behaviour of the real gas. Such models are of great interest to methodologists since they not only form the core of most scientific theories, but are also the vehicles for much creative scientific thinking. They are not devised at random. Their construction is always controlled by some implicit metaphysical assumptions (in the gas model case Newtonian atomism) which ensure their plausibility to the scientific community. This means that they are balanced between two analogy relations. They must behave analogously to the real thing they are a model for; and they are constructed by analogy with the real thing they are modelled on. For instance the popular rule-following models in social psychology should replicate the behaviour of the unknown cognitive systems they are models for while they must lie within the constraints imposed by the real cases of rule-following, say in ceremonial action, which they are modelled on. Both analogy relations are usually open, that is, though they exhibit positive and negative aspects, similarities and differences, there is usually a degree of unexplored neutral analogy. Theories develop by the conceptual exploration and, in favourable cases, the empirical testing of the neutral analogy.

Explanatory and heuristic models can be neatly distinguished by reference to their constitutive analogies. For a heuristic model source and subject are identical. A model plane is a model of a plane. But for an explanatory model source and subject are distinct. The idea of an implicit rule is modelled on that of an explicit rule, but the former is an analogue of some unknown regulative cognitive process.

ROM HARRÉ

BIBLIOGRAPHY

Bunge, M. 1973. *Method, Model and Matter*. Dordrecht: Reidel.

Hesse, M. 1963. *Models and Analogies in Science*. London: Sheed and Ward.

Martin, J. and Harré, R. 1982. Metaphor in science. In *Metaphor: Problems and Perspectives*, ed. D. Miall, Brighton, Sussex: Harvester Press.

analysis of variance. *See* HYPOTHESIS TESTING.

anarchism. A doctrine whose nature is suggested by its name, derived from the Greek *an archos*, meaning 'no government'.

The term *anarchist* appears to have been first used in a pejorative sense during the English Civil War, against the Levellers, one of whose enemies called them 'Switzerizing anarchists', and during the French Revolution by most parties in deriding those who stood to the left of them in the political spectrum. It was first used positively by the French writer Pierre-Joseph Proudhon in 1840 when, in his *Qu'est-ce-que la propriété? (What is Property?)*, a controversial essay on the economic bases of society, he defined his own political position by declaring, perhaps to shock his readers into attention, 'I am an anarchist.' Proudhon then explained his view that the real laws by which society operates have nothing to do with authority but are inherent in the very nature of society; he looked forward to the dissolution of authority and the liberation of the natural social order which it submerged. He went on, in his rather paradoxical manner, to declare: 'As man seeks justice in equality, so society seeks order in anarchy. Anarchy – the absence of a sovereign – such is the form of government to which we are every day approximating.'

Proudhon's attitude was typical of the anarchists in all periods. They have argued that man is a naturally social being, who through mutual aid evolves voluntary social institutions that can work effectively without the need for government, which in fact inhibits and distorts them. The important transformation of society, anarchists argue, will not be the political one of a change of rulers or a change of constitution, since political organization must be discarded; it must be replaced by the economic organization of the resources of a society without government. Thus, while they differ from socialists and communists in denying the state and any form of state control or initiative, anarchists agree with them in being opposed to capitalism, in seeking to abolish what one of their earliest thinkers, William Godwin, called 'accumulated property' and to replace it with some kind of common ownership of the means of production. Only a few extreme individualists have stood outside this pattern, as Max Stirner did.

The basic ideas of anarchism predate the use of the title *anarchist*. Some historians have found their origin in early religious movements that stood outside ordinary society, refused to obey its laws and attempted in some way to own their goods in common, like the Essenes, the Anabaptists and the Doukhobors. But in these cases the search seems to have been for spiritual salvation through a progressive retreat from involvement in the material world, and they have little in common with anarchism as a secular doctrine directed towards social transformation.

However, there are at least two social thinkers anterior to Proudhon who seem to fit the necessary criteria to be regarded as anarchists, since (a) they present a fundamental criticism of the existing governmental structure of society; (b) they present an alternative libertarian vision of a society based on cooperation rather than on coercion; and (c) they propose a method or methods of proceeding from one to the other.

The first is Gerrard Winstanley, the leader of the Diggers, a small communitarian group who emerged in England during the Commonwealth. In his 1649 pamphlet, *Truth Lifting Up its Head Above Scandals*, which departed entirely from religious orthodoxy by equating God with Reason, Winstanley laid down what afterwards became basic propositions among the anarchists: that power corrupts, that property and freedom are incompatible, and that authority and property between them are the main causes of crime; that only in a rulerless society where work and products are shared will men be both free and happy, because they will be acting according to their own judgements and not according to laws imposed from above.

Winstanley went beyond theory to direct action when he declared that only by their own action could the people change their lot, and he led his own followers in an occupation of English common lands, where they sought to set up an agrarian community in which all goods were shared. Despite the passive resistance they offered, the Diggers were finally forced off their land and Winstanley vanished into obscurity.

His ideas lingered in the dissenting sects of the 18th century, where they were picked up by William Godwin. In 1793 he published a massive treatise on the nature of government, *Political Justice*, which has often been described as the most thorough exposition of anarchist theory, though Godwin never called himself an anarchist. *Political Justice* does in fact admirably present the classic anarchist arguments that authority is against nature and that social evil exists because men are not free to act according to reason; 'accumulated property' is to be condemned because it is a source of power over other men.

Godwin anticipated the general anarchist emphasis on decentralization by sketching out a social organization in which the small autonomous community, or parish, would be the basic unit. He envisaged a loose economic system in which he anticipated Marx's slogan, 'From each according to his abilities, to each according to his needs', by proposing that – capital in the form of 'accumulated property' having been dissolved – men would freely transfer goods to each other according to need, and all would share in production. Though he seems to have imagined fairly accurately the labour-saving powers of machinery, since he prophesied a drastic reduction of the work day, he does not appear to have taken into account the more complex work relationships that the industrial revolution and factory production were already beginning to create. In the political organization of his parishes he anticipated later anarchists by rejecting such standard democratic procedures as voting, since he regarded the rule of the majority as a form of tyranny. He not only envisaged society moving to a practice of consensus after its liberation from government, but also hoped that such a liberation would come into being through education and peaceful discussion. His anarchism was evolutionary rather than revolutionary.

The distinction between evolution and revolution is important since, apart from variations in their proposals for the economic organization of society, the main differences between the anarchists who began to appear with Proudhon were in their views of the necessary strategies for achieving the aim they all held in common – the abolition of the state and all forms of government, and their replacement by voluntary and cooperative forms of administration.

Some, like Leo Tolstoy, Henry David Thoreau and the Dutch anarchist leader, Domela Nieuwenhuis, were pacifists, aiming to change society by the practice of civil disobedience. Mohandas K. Gandhi, who more than once termed himself an anarchist and who envisaged a decentralized society of village communes, was perhaps the most important of their company.

Proudhon was nearer to the pacifists in his view of the tactics of social change than he was to the later leaders of organized European anarchism. Though he often spoke of revolution, he hoped that peaceful change might come about through the creation of workers' economic organizations. Proudhon's mutualism, as he called it, was a mixture of peasant individualism and cooperativism aimed at the reorganization of society on an egalitarian basis. He set out to shock his readers by declaring that 'property is theft', but by this he really meant the use of property to exploit the labour of others. 'Possession' – the right of an individual worker or

group of workers to control the land or machines necessary for production – he regarded as necessary for liberty. In the book that may be his masterpiece, *The General Idea of the Revolution in the Nineteenth Century*, written in prison because of his criticisms of Napoleon III, he sketched out the picture of a society of independent peasants and artisans with their small farms and workshops, and of factories and utilities like railways run by associations of workers, linked together by a system of mutual credit based on productivity and administered by people's banks like that which he attempted to establish during the revolution of 1848. Instead of the centralized state, he suggested a federal system of autonomous local communities and industrial associations, bound by contract and mutual interest rather than by laws, with arbitration replacing courts of justice, workers' management replacing bureaucracy, and integrated education replacing academic education. Out of such a pattern, Proudhon believed, would emerge the natural social unity which he equated with anarchy and in comparison with which, he believed, the existing order would appear as 'nothing but chaos, serving as a basis for endless tyranny'.

Proudhon was the real founder of the organized anarchist movement. He laid down its theoretical foundations in a continental European context where Godwin was virtually unknown, so that Mikhail Bakunin, possibly the best-known and most influential of anarchists, once admitted: 'Proudhon is the master of us all.' Proudhon's followers, who called themselves mutualists, were active in the foundation of the International Working Men's Association, the so-called First International, which provided the first of many battlegrounds between the authoritarian socialism of the Marxists and the libertarian socialism of the anarchists.

In the early days of the International the struggle was between Marx and his followers and the disciples of Proudhon, who had died in 1864, the year the International was founded. Later the struggle took a new form, since Proudhon's disciples were replaced in opposing Marx by the followers of Bakunin, a Russian aristocrat turned conspirator, and the conflict between them eventually destroyed the organization. It was basically the conflict between Marx's idea of the workers seizing control of the state to carry out the revolution, and Bakunin's idea of the workers carrying out the revolution in order to destroy the state and all the other manifestations of political power.

Bakunin accepted Proudhon's federalism and the argument in favour of working-class direct action, which the latter had developed in his final posthumously published work, *De la capacité politique des classes ouvrières* (The political capability of the working classes). But he argued that the modified property rights (the rights of 'possession') which Proudhon contemplated for individual peasants and artisans were impractical, and instead he proposed that the means of production should be owned collectively (hence his followers were called 'collectivists'). However, he still held like Proudhon that each man should be remunerated only according to the amount of work he actually performed; in other words, though in a slightly different form, the wages system would continue.

The second important difference lay in views of revolutionary method. Proudhon believed that one could create within existing society the mutualist associations that would replace it, and for this reason he came to oppose violent revolutionary action which aimed at an abrupt transition. Bakunin did not believe that such a piecemeal method could work. As a romantic revolutionary, he argued that 'the passion for destruction is also a creative passion', and taught that a violent uprising was the necessary prelude to the construction of a free and peaceful society.

The individualism and non-violence implicit in Proudhon's vision were thrust into the side currents of anarchism; Tolstoy, who had known Proudhon, largely incorporated them in his teachings of a radical Christian anarchism. But down to the destruction of anarchism as a mass movement at the end of the Spanish Civil War in 1939, Bakunin's stress on violence and on a collectivized economic system remained dominant among anarchists in most countries.

The tactics of violent action varied, though they tended to be conditioned by the doctrine of propaganda by deed, which emerged during the 1870s among the Italian anarchists and was particularly propagated by Errico Malatesta. Individual assassinations, largely justified by this doctrine, became numerous around the turn of the century; a President of France and a President of the United States were among the victims. There were anarchist-inspired mass insurrections in Spain and Italy and, during the Russian Civil War, in the Ukraine, where for several years the anarchist leader Nestor Makhno established libertarian institutions over a wide area and protected them by a numerous Insurrectionary Army.

There were also variations in the concepts of collectivism which the anarchists pursued, exemplified particularly in anarchist communism and anarcho-syndicalism.

Anarchist communism was mainly developed by Peter Kropotkin, a Russian prince and a distinguished geographer who abandoned his privileges for the revolutionary cause, though the idea may have been developed first by the French geographer Elisée Reclus. Kropotkin wrote a number of the seminal works of anarchism, including *Mutual Aid: A Factor in Evolution*, in which he traced the development of cooperation among animals and men, and *Fields, Factories and Workshops*, in which he argued for the decentralization of industry that he considered an essential accompaniment to a non-governmental society.

The work in which Kropotkin most developed the idea of anarchist communism was *La Conquête du pain* (The conquest of bread), a kind of non-fictional utopia sketching out the vision of a revolutionary society organized as a federation of free communist groups. Kropotkin moved beyond Bakunin's collectivism, which envisaged common ownership of the means of production, to a complete communism in terms of distribution, which meant that need rather than merit would be the reason why a man should receive the means of life. Kropotkin argued that any payment according to the value of the work was a variant on the wages system, and that the wages system condemned man to economic slavery by regulating his patterns of work. Just as Kropotkin's anarchism was based on the idea (developed in *Mutual Aid*) that man was naturally social, so his idea of free communism was based on the notion that man was naturally responsible, and in a free society would neither shirk on his work nor take more than he needed from the common store.

Anarcho-syndicalism arose out of the involvement of anarchist activists in the French trade union movement, which revived during the 1880s after the proscriptions of working-class organizations that followed the Paris Commune of 1870. Industrial militancy seemed to offer a broad field for the direct action which the anarchists already advocated, and the anarcho-syndicalists tended to oppose to the gradualist tendencies of orthodox unionists, who sought the best possible deal with existing society, the intent to change that society by proceeding directly to the assumption of industrial control by the workers. Thus their unions, while not neglecting to fight for better conditions, were ultimately revolutionary in their intent, and a philosophy of incessant struggle developed among them. This concept was adapted by writers like Georges Sorel, who in *Réflexions sur la violence* suggested that the important aspect of revolutionary syndicalism was the myth of struggle and the cult of violence, which he believed had a regenerating effect on society. However, the working-class anarcho-syndicalist spokesmen, like Fernand Pelloutier, Emile Pouget and Paul Delesalle, rejected Sorel's theories, and believed that relentless industrial struggle, by violent and peaceful means, culminating in general strikes, could in fact destroy the capitalist system and the state at the same time. When that happened, the syndicates would be transformed from organs of struggle into the organizational bodies of the new society, taking over places of production and organizing transport and distribution. In this way they were developing Proudhon's concept of mutualist institutions evolving within the society they would eventually replace. Anarchist purists, notably Errico Malatesta, distrusted the anarcho-syndicalists, fearing that a trade union movement that controlled all industry might itself be corrupted by power.

For many years before World War I, the anarcho-syndicalists controlled the leading French trade union organization, the CGT (Confédération Générale du Travail); after the war it was taken over by the communists, who had gained added prestige among the workers through the success of the Russian Revolution.

Anarcho-syndicalism, however, spread from France to Spain, where it became a powerful working class movement. The anarchist federation of unions (Confederación Nacional del Trabajo) was the largest labour organization in Spain, at times reaching more than two million members. It was a model of anarchist decentralization, employing only one paid secretary in its federal office, the actual tasks of organization being carried out in their spare time by workers chosen by their fellows. The CNT was strong among the peasants of Andalusia as well as in the factories of Catalonia. The civil war in 1936–39 brought Spanish anarchism to its apogee, which was followed quickly by its downfall. The experience of decades of street fighting enabled anarchist workers in the eastern cities of Spain to defeat the generals in the early days of Franco's military uprising. Later they sent their militia columns to the various fronts. At the same time they tried to bring about their anarchist millenium behind the lines by expropriating the factories and the large estates. Reports suggest that many of the factories were well run by the workers and that the collectivization of the land induced the peasants to work with pride and devotion. But the experiments were too brief for valuable conclusions to be drawn from them, since the anarchists' hatred of authority made them as inefficient in creating armies as they seem to have been efficient in organizing collective work, and their experimental communes were suppressed at the time of Franco's victory.

The outcome of the Spanish civil war led to a general decline of anarchism during the 1940s and 1950s. However, in the generally radical atmosphere of the 1960s it underwent a revival; anarchist groups appeared once again in Europe and North America, the movement's history was written by scholars, and the works of the great anarchist theoreticians appeared again in print. Anarchism has not become again a mass movement of the kind that once flourished in Spain and to a lesser degree in France, Italy and briefly in the Ukraine. But it is a visible movement once more. Anarchist ideas of decentralization have spread widely and have merged with those of the environmental movement. It now survives more as an intellectual trend, encouraging a critical view of the institutions and practices of authority, than as a quasi-apocalyptic movement which envisaged the end of government as a possible and not distant goal.

GEORGE WOODCOCK

See also BAKUNIN, MIKHAIL; GODWIN, WILLIAM; PROUDHON, PIERRE JOSEPH.

BIBLIOGRAPHY
Joll, J. 1964. *The Anarchists*. London: Eyre & Spottiswoode.
Marshall, P.H. 1984. *William Godwin*. New Haven: Yale University Press.
Masters, A. 1974. *Bakunin, The Father of Anarchism*. New York: Saturday Review Press.
Read, H. 1954. *Anarchy and Order: Essays in Politics*. London: Faber & Faber.
Rocker, R. 1938. *Anarcho-Syndicalism*. London: Secker & Warburg.
Woodcock, G. 1956. *Pierre-Joseph Proudhon: A Biography*. London: Routledge & Kegan Paul.
Woodcock, G. 1962. *Anarchism: A History of Libertarian Ideas and Movements*. Cleveland: Meridian Books.
Woodcock, G. and Avakumovic, I. 1950. *The Anarchist Prince: A biographical study of Peter Kropotkin*. London: T.V. Boardman & Co.

Anderson, James (1739–1808).   Anderson farmed from the age of 15 first at Hermiston near Edinburgh, then at Monkshill, Aberdeenshire. Aberdeen honoured him with an LL D in 1780. He settled in Leith (near Edinburgh) in 1783, and founded *The Bee* (1790–94), a miscellany weekly magazine including literary, political and economic topics. He moved to London in 1797 and set up the magazine *Recreations ...* (1799–1802) along the same lines as *The Bee*. The most important primary and secondary sources are listed below.

A contemporary of Adam Smith and James Steuart, James Anderson was second to none as a development economist. His writings lay great stress on the deadening effects of outmoded (feudal) institutions, adverse political and historic legacies, poor communications allied with sparse population, and repressive English-inspired taxation – especially the duties on salt and coal – on Scottish development. His proposals for improvement emphasized the gradualist approach – abstract economic models and grandiose schemes attracted his scorn – where the latent desire of man to improve his lot was freed from constraint and encouraged by state action and private self-interested philanthropy. Thus, though Anderson in general supported laisser-faire as being an essential requisite of optimal development, the paternalistic encouragement of such development was frequently necessary, especially in the early stages. That he was no doctrinaire free-trader is seen in his espousal of the Corn Laws, on developmental grounds (see *An Inquiry into the Nature of the Corn Laws ...*). He took issue with Smith on this, and also on Smith's notion that corn regulates the price of all commodities (see especially his 'Postscript to Letter Thirteen' in his *Observations ...*). Smith never properly answered Anderson's criticisms (see Dow, 1984).

Anderson is regarded as an anticipator of Ricardo's rent theory (see, e.g., Schumpeter, 1954), but cannot in fact be cast in the narrowly abstract Ricardian mould. True, for Anderson an increase in corn price would have the differential effects on land rent as described by Ricardo; but such would be the first stage only of a development process. At the end of the process all land would have increased in fertility, and what was previously the least fertile cultivated land could well be now as fertile as the previously most fertile land (see *The Bee*, vol. 6, 28 December 1791).

Anderson was convinced of the harm caused by the Poor Laws, and was responsible for a successful appeal against the introduction of the poor rate in Leith.

In addition to his writings on agriculture and economic development and his literary magazine pieces, Anderson also wrote on slavery, archaeology and greenhouse and chimney design!

J.M.A. GEE

SELECTED WORKS
1777a. *Observations on the Means of exciting a spirit of National Industry....* Edinburgh.
1777b. *An Inquiry into the Nature of the Corn Laws....* Edinburgh.
1785. *An Account of the present State of the Hebrides, and Western Coasts of Scotland....* Edinburgh
1791–4. *The Bee*. Edinburgh.
1794. *A General View of the Agriculture and Rural Economy of the County of Aberdeen....* Edinburgh.
1799–1802. *Recreations....* London.

BIBLIOGRAPHY
Anderson, William. 1865. *The Scottish Nation*. Vol. 1, Edinburgh: A. Fullarton & Co., 126–9.
Dow, A. 1984. The hauteur of Adam Smith: an unpublished letter from James Anderson of Monkshill. *Scottish Journal of Political Economy* 31(3), November, 284–5.
Mullet, C.F. 1968. A village Aristotle and the harmony of interests: James Anderson of Monks Hill. *Journal of British Studies* 8(1), November, 94–118.
Schumpeter, J.A. 1954. *History of Economic Analysis*. London: George Allen & Unwin.

Anderson, Oskar Nikolayevich (1887–1960).   Anderson was born on 2 August 1887 in Minsk, Russia, and died on 12 February 1960 in Munich, Federal Republic of Germany. As a disciple of Aleksandr A. Tschuprow the younger in St Petersburg, Anderson was a pioneer in statistics and econometrics. After leaving Russia in 1920 he became professor of statistics at the Universities of Varna and Sofia in Bulgaria (until 1942), Kiel (until 1947) and Munich.

His oeuvre includes two textbooks and more than 150 articles in Russian, Bulgarian, English and German. Anderson participated during 1913–17 in the theoretical preparation and actual conduct of a sample on agricultural production in the Syr-Darja river area of Russia, one of the very earliest sample surveys. Later, he designed the sample plan for the processing of the Bulgarian Agricultural Census of 1926, with very good results which were decisive for further propagation and acceptance of sampling (1929, 1949).

Before and after World War I Anderson developed, independently of W.S. Gossett, the Variate Difference Method, a procedure to separate the smooth component (trend, business cycles) from the residual component, without making further assumptions about the underlying type of function (1929). Anderson wrote one of the first, much-noticed econometric papers, an effort to verify statistically the quantity theory of money, which was a very early analysis of causes by means of economic data (1931). Regarding index numbers, Anderson pointed particularly to the problem of chain index numbers, caused by error accumulation (1949, 1952).

Anderson was a charter member of the Econometric Society, a fellow or honorary member of numerous scientific associations, and held honorary doctorates from Vienna and Mannheim.

HEINRICH L. STRECKER

SELECTED WORKS

1929a. *Über die repräsentative Methode und deren Anwendung auf die Aufarbeitung der Ergebnisse der bulgarischen landwirtschaftlichen Betriebszählung vom 31. Dezember 1926.* Munich: Fachausschuss für Stichprobenverfahren der Deutschen Statistischen Gessel-schaft, 1949.

1929b. *Die Korrelationsrechnung in der Konjunkturfoschung. Ein Beitrag zur Analyse von Zeitreihen.* Bonn: Schroeder-Verlag.

1931. *Ist die Quantitätstheorie statistisch nachweisbar? Zeitschrift für Nationalökonomie* 2, Vienna.

1935. *Einführung in die Mathematische Statistik.* Vienna: Springer-Verlag.

1949. Mehr Vorsicht mit Indexzahlen! *Allgemeines Statistisches Archiv* 33, Munich.

1952. Wieder eine Indexverkettung? *Mitteilungsblatt für Mathematische Statistik* 4, Munich.

1954a. *Probleme der statistischen Methodenlehre.* 4th edn, Würzburg: Physica-Verlag, 1964.

1954b. *Über den Umgang mit systematischen statistischen Fehlern. Statistische Vierteljahresschrift* 7, Vienna.

BIBLIOGRAPHY

Fels, E.M. 1968. Anderson, Oskar N. In *International Encyclopedia of Statistics*, Vol. 1, London: Macmillan.

Strecker, H.L. 1965. Anderson, Oskar. In *Handwörterbuch der Sozialwissenschaften* (HDSW), Vol. 12, Stuttgart/Tübingen: Fischer-Verlag/Mohr-Verlag.

Strecker, H., Kellerer, H. et al. 1963. *Oskar Anderson Ausgewählte Schriften.* 2 vols, Tübingen: Mohr-Verlag, with a complete bibliography of Anderson's publications.

Andreades, Andreas (1876–1935).   Andreas (sometimes Andrew) Andreades was born in Corfu. His education (in France and England) and his academic affiliations were European, ranging from a doctorate in Law and Political Science from Paris University to the Bavarian Academy in Munich, the Romanian Academy in Bucharest and the Institut d'Egypte at Cairo. He became a lecturer at Athens University in 1902 and Professor of Economics in 1906.

The bulk of his writings were in Greek and French, effectively reducing his audience amongst English economists in the early 20th century. His interests were largely in the monetary and economic history of Greece. His financial history of ancient Greece was translated into English, but he was also concerned with contemporary Greek problems and Eastern Europe. In the late 1920s and early 1930s he lectured widely in Europe (UK, France, Belgium, Italy) and in Egypt.

In England Andreades was perhaps best known for his *History of the Bank of England,* translated into English from the French in 1909. This was the first complete history of the Bank and Foxwell's introduction to the translation describes it as

the best general survey of the subject which exists … . The author shows a remarkable familiarity with English methods and habits of thought, and his criticism is usually most just and temperate, and full of suggestion and stimulus (pp. xxiv–xxv).

Andreades attended the Paris and Danube Conferences in the interwar period and was a delegate to the assembly of the League of Nations in 1923, 1924 and 1929. He was chairman of the Greek League of Nations Union and president of the Athens branch of the Anglo-Hellenic League. He was honoured by the UK (CBE), Italy, Romania and Bulgaria, among other foreign countries.

R.J. BIGG

SELECTED WORKS

1909. *History of the Bank of England.* Trans. C. Meredith, with Introduction by H.S. Foxwell, London: P.S. King & Son.

Andrews, Philip Walter Sawford (1914–1971).   Andrews was born in Southampton and died in Lancaster. Most of his career was spent in Oxford and from 1946 until 1967, when he moved to his last post as Foundation Professor of Economics at the University of Lancaster, he was an Official Fellow of Nuffield College. He was founding editor of the *Journal of Industrial Economics*. In 1949, after conducting detailed case study investigations of business behaviour, Andrews published a potentially revolutionary analysis of firms in competitive oligopolistic markets. It included a non-marginalist, non-equilibrium theory of pricing and capacity choices. Firms were predicted to set prices by adding a mark-up to their 'normal' costs at their target levels of capacity utilization. The size of the mark-up would be limited by the difference between their own costs and their estimates of the opportunity costs of other firms with the knowledge to supply duplicates of their products and steal their markets. Only when their assessments of these cost conditions changed would they change their prices. Firms would also be expected to hold spare capacity in order to satisfy new customers without forcing established ones to turn their goodwill elsewhere.

After his death, Andrews's work was increasingly used as a building block in Post-Keynesian price theory. During his lifetime, however, his analysis failed to have a revolutionary impact, partly because most economists tried to make sense of it in orthodox terms; partly because Andrews generated confusion by writing in the language of business, not of textbook economics; and partly because it was not until 1964 that he published his incisive critique of the models he sought to displace.

PETER EARL

SELECTED WORKS

1949. *Manufacturing Business.* London: Macmillan.
1964. *On Competition in Economic Theory.* London: Macmillan.

Angell, James Waterhouse (1898–1986).   From 1924 until 1966 Angell was a member of the faculty at Columbia University, but most of his original work on monetary economics was undertaken in the decade between 1926 and 1936. This particular timing, together with the fact that Angell worked within the framework of the quantity theory of money, probably goes a long way towards explaining his comparative neglect in subsequent years – for this was the decade dominated by Keynes and his headlong assault on the quantity theory. Yet Angell was no mere expositor of that theory, and in his two most important books he contributed to its development in ways which were not to become fashionable until the influence of Keynesianism began to subside in the 1960s and 1970s.

Angell's first book, the *Theory of International Prices* (1926), was intended to provide a re-evaluation of classical theory in the light of the actual experience of the 18th and 19th centuries. Of the three main modifications he suggests – grounding the doctrine of comparative advantage on comparative money costs and prices rather than upon differential labour values; replacing the specie-flow adjustment mechanism with one based on adjustments via the domestic money supply and the price level; and the inclusion of the analysis of currency speculation in the determination of exchange rates – the last two are perhaps the most interesting. Angell's firm adherence to the quantity theory led him to appreciate that under the fixed exchange rate regime of the interwar gold standard, adjustment to international equilibrium had to be secured by movements in the domestic price level. On the opposite side of the Atlantic at about the same time, Keynes had made the same claim but had to waste much of his time in the famous debate over the return to gold in Britain simply trying to explain the point to his opponents. Of course, Keynes favoured abandoning fixed exchange rates in favour of managing the domestic money supply through Bank Rate policy, but in terms of his understanding of the international adjustment mechanism implied by the quantity theory his position was essentially the same as that of Angell.

Angell's other major contribution comes in his *Behavior of Money* published in 1936. This is an empirical study of the monetary history of the United States between 1890 and the 1930s. In it Angell analysed the relationship between the volume of bank deposits, the stock of notes and coins, the velocity of circulation, the general level of prices, and the volume of industrial production. He concluded that movements in nominal national income were highly correlated with changes in the stock of circulating medium. The velocity of circulation showed, he claimed, relative stability. With the customary 'real' forces determining real GNP, not only did this provide, to Angell's satisfaction, striking confirmation of the quantity theory, but it led him to a novel policy proposal: a quantitative rule for the restriction of the rate of change in the money supply. For Angell, 'the most effective ... procedure [for] induc[ing] a greater stability in national and individual money incomes ... is to stabilize the quantity of money itself' (1936, p. 163). It is relatively easy to see how closely both Angell's approach (an empirical analysis of actual monetary experience) and his specific policy prescription, anticipate the later work of Friedman and Schwartz. However, appearing as it did in the same year as Keynes's *General Theory*, it is not difficult to understand its lack of effect at the time.

It is not without interest to note that in his *Investment and Business Cycles* (1941), Angell directly criticized Keynes's theory of investment and that, in addition, Angell wrote a text on the interwar German recovery, *The Recovery of Germany* (1929). In 1945–6 he served as US representative on the Allied Commission on Reparations.

MURRAY MILGATE AND ALASTAIR LEVY

See also QUANTITY THEORY OF MONEY.

SELECTED WORKS

1926. *The Theory of International Prices: Criticism and Restatement.* Cambridge, Mass.: Harvard University Press.
1929. *The Recovery of Germany.* New Haven: Yale University Press.
1936. *The Behavior of Money: Exploratory Studies.* New York and London: McGraw-Hill.
1941. *Investment and Business Cycles.* New York and London: McGraw-Hill.

animal spirits. *See* INVESTMENT AND ACCUMULATION.

anomalies. *See* PARADOXES AND ANOMALIES.

anthropology, economic. *See* ECONOMIC ANTHROPOLOGY.

antitrust policy. Although many countries have adopted antitrust statutes and have an active antitrust enforcement programme, the United States was the first to enact national legislation on monopolies and monopolization. To be sure, English common law dealt with some of these matters long before the Sherman Act was passed in 1890. But the United States was and remains a leader in antitrust legislation, enforcement and research. The discussion herein focuses on the development of antitrust economics and related changes in antitrust enforcement within the United States.

Industrial Organization and, as a subfield therein, antitrust economics, is mainly a post-World War II development. The groundwork for this was laid by theoretical and empirical studies in the 1930s, of which Chamberlin's *Theory of Monopolistic Competition* (1933), Robinson's *The Economics of Imperfect Competition* (1933), Berle and Means's *The Modern Corporation and Private Property* (1932) and the series of studies by the Temporary National Economic Committee were especially important.

E.S. Mason was particularly influential in helping to give definition to the new field of Industrial Organization. Not only did he regard this as an important subject in its own right, but he perceived that informed antitrust enforcement was greatly in need of intellectual underpinnings. Interest in these matters mushroomed in the postwar period. Although the study of Industrial Organization was (and is) something of an art form, the leading texts – the one by Bain (1958), the other by Stigler (1968) – addressed the issues from the aforementioned standpoint of applied price theory. Not only was the firm regarded as a production function, but industry structure was thought to be virtually determinative of conduct and performance: 'an industry which does not have a competitive structure will not have competitive behavior' (Stigler, 1952, p. 167). The structure–conduct–performance paradigm rapidly gained ascendancy.

The size distribution of firms (usually measured as a four-firm concentration ratio) and the condition of entry (usually assessed with reference to Bain's [1956] pioneering treatment of 'barriers to entry') were the key structural features. Non-standard or unfamiliar business conduct was believed to be suspect if not outright antisocial. A monopoly presumption was thus applied to vertical integration of activities on the periphery. It was widely and readily accepted that such a presumption applied *a fortiori* to nonstandard or unfamiliar contracting practices.

The past twenty years have witnessed a vast reshaping of antitrust economics. Antitrust enforcement and policy have followed these changes with a lag. Although market power remains a centrepiece, barriers to entry are now treated in a more discriminating way. Also, there is much greater respect for the benefits of economies than there once was. Nonstandard or unfamiliar business practices are no longer regarded as presumptively unlawful. And the study of strategic behaviour has emerged as a central antitrust economics and public policy concern. Consider these seriatim.

BARRIERS TO ENTRY. Entry-barrier analysis made its appearance in the 1950s with the publication of books by Sylos-Labini (1956) and Bain (1956) and by Modigliani's formalization of the core argument (1958). It quickly made headway and was virtually determinative of antitrust enforcement in the 1960s. Enforcement uses were sweeping, and successes came easily. Dissent nevertheless appeared as entry-barrier arguments came to be used uncritically.

Objections of two kinds were registered. For one thing, the entry-barrier models purportedly dealt with oligopoly without ever addressing how the mechanics of collective action were realized (Stigler, 1968). Second, the existence of an 'entry barrier' was taken as a sufficient condition to warrant public-policy intervention. Comparative institutional analysis is not, however, concerned with defects judged with respect to a hypothetical ideal but with defects of a remediable kind.

Mistaken treatments of economies of scale are illustrative. To describe such a condition as a barrier to entry invites the conclusion that this is an antisocial outcome. Public policy hostility easily results. Thus the Federal Trade Commission declared that 'economic efficiency or any other social benefit [is] pertinent only insofar as it may tend to promote or retard the vigor of competition' (quoted in Bork, 1978, p. 254), where competition is defined in structural terms. The Supreme Court evidently concurred. It thus flatly held in Procter & Gamble that 'possible economies cannot be used as a defense to illegality' (386 US 568, 574 [1967]).

This preoccupation with entry barriers predictably gave rise to perverse responses. Rather than ask for affirmative if not mitigating consideration, Procter & Gamble responded to the government's claims of economies in the Clorox case by first denying them and thereafter insisting that the government was unable definitively to prove that such economies existed. Such inverted reasoning could not and did not survive.

ECONOMIES AS AN ANTITRUST DEFENCE. Although entry barrier analysis made rudimentary use of price theory, it made little appeal to applied welfare economics. This is regrettable, since application of the basic partial equilibrium welfare economics model to an assessment of the allocative efficiency trade-off between market power and economies disclosed that to sacrifice economies in favour of smaller price–cost margins often came at a high cost (Williamson, 1968b). Albeit subject to qualification, this view has made progressive headway (Liebeler, 1978; Bork, 1978; Muris, 1979; Fisher and Lande, 1983). Indeed, the 1984 Merger Guidelines of the Department of Justice now invite firms proposing a merger to present evidence of efficiencies. Although this is not without enforcement hazards, antitrust enforcement excesses of the 1960s – which led to the suppression, denial and perverse interpretation of efficiency – have been generally discredited.

Public policy towards vertical mergers has been similarly transformed. Thus, whereas the 1968 Vertical Merger Guidelines employed firm-as-production-function reasoning, whence vertical integration was proscribed if there was 'an appreciable degree of market control' at any stage in the system (Stigler, 1955, p. 183), the earlier limits have been relaxed under the firm-as-governance-structure approach to the study of economic organization (Coase, 1937; Williamson, 1985). Not only do the current Merger Guidelines make express provision for transaction cost economies, but they acknowledge that the characteristics of investments (especially the condition of asset specificity) are germane to an assessment of economic benefits. Vertical integration is now held to be problematic only where the market structure would support strategic behaviour.

VERTICAL MARKET RESTRICTIONS. The view that vertical market restrictions are presumptively anti-competitive has likewise been abandoned. The 'inhospitality tradition' maintained that nonstandard contracting practices (tie-ins, block booking, customer and territorial restrictions, and the like) had the purpose and effect of realizing leverage, facilitating price discrimination or erecting barriers to entry. More recent scholarship has taken a broader view of these matters. Two factors have been responsible for the new learning.

For one thing, the technological dichotomy between firm and market organization has been supplanted by a transactional view in which the existence and economic merits of a wide range of intermediate ownership and contracting modes are admitted. As a consequence, the earlier monopoly presumption has given way to an examination of transactions and the costs that attend alternative forms of contracting. Second, the focus on the *ex post* effects of contractual restraints has been supplanted by a more complete treatment of contract in which the *ex ante* bargain and the *ex post* terms are regarded simultaneously. The economic importance of intertemporal contractual integrity is emphasized by this latter perspective, whereas the focus of earlier piecemeal interpretations of contract had been on the momentary relationship between the parties. Different assessments of, for example, franchise terminations often result.

Thus, whereas the piecemeal approach to contract focuses on power disparities between the franchisor and the franchisee, the intertemporal approach examines *ex post* behaviour in relation to the *ex ante* bargain and asks whether efficiency considerations and reputation effects are operative. Successive studies of vertical restraints from an intertemporal perspective (Telser, 1960, 1981; Williamson, 1979, 1983; Klein and Leffler, 1981) urge that vertical market restrictions ought not to be regarded as presumptively unlawful but that their anti-competitive effects should be judged in strategic behaviour terms.

Inasmuch as conglomerate organization is at best an anomaly within the firm-as-production-function framework, conglomerate mergers in the pre-1970 period operated under a cloud. The monopoly presumption that was ascribed to nonstandard practices was thought to apply, whence vague monopoly purpose was imputed to conglomerate mergers. The 1968 Merger Guidelines of the Department of Justice, for example, held that 'Since reciprocal buying ... is an economically unjustified business practice which confers a competitive advantage on the favored firm unrelated to the merits', conglomerate mergers which create a prospect of reciprocity will ordinarily be challenged.

Subsequent study of nonstandard contracting, however, revealed that reciprocal trade can also serve efficiency purposes. In particular, reciprocity (of an appropriate kind) can help to create a mutual 'credible commitment'. To be sure, only the subset of contracts where trade is supported by investments in transaction specific assets will warrant such an efficiency rationale. Earlier claims that reciprocity is meritless, however, cannot be sustained.

Out of awareness, presumably, that the monopoly presumption had been overdone, the 1982 and 1984 Merger Guidelines are silent with respect to the special dangers of reciprocity. Instead, conglomerate acquisitions, which is the context where the reciprocity issue was originally expressed, are now held to pose antitrust problems only if the condition of potential entry is adversely effected. This is a much narrower conception and is one with which antitrust is legitimately concerned.

The upshot is that antitrust theory and policy were vastly transformed over the interval 1965 to 1985. Policy changes have followed theory, with lags of ten years and more as new theory was first subjected to the crucible of academic discourse. Although there is a real possibility that the antitrust pendulum could swing too far, the conceptual errors of the 1960s are unlikely to be repeated.

STRATEGIC BEHAVIOUR. Antitrust is in no position to settle for the quiet life. Issues of strategic business behaviour exploded onto the antitrust scene in the 1970s and have been prominently featured on the research and enforcement agenda since. A series of prominent antitrust suits and growing academic interest in business strategy were jointly responsible.

Major antitrust suits alleging predation were brought both by private firms and the Federal Trade Commission. Several private antitrust suits alleging predatory pricing by IBM against computer peripheral manufacturers illustrate the former. The Federal Trade Commission advanced novel theories of strategic anti-competitive behaviour in asserting predatory brand proliferation in the ready-to-eat cereals industry and pre-emptive investments in the titanium dioxide industry.

Academic interest in predation and, more generally, in strategic business behaviour was both responsive to and contributed to these antitrust developments. A consensus has yet to be reached, however, on such basic matters as the appropriate criteria for judging price predation.

Lack of such agreement encourages some to argue that predatory pricing is an antitrust fiction and ought to be disregarded. This derives, however, from a static assessment of predation. But the nub of the problem is intertemporal and features uncertainty. The study of these matters remains in flux.

A separate but nevertheless related academic literature has reformulated the earlier entry barrier work on more secure economic foundations. The study of pre-emptive investments (Spence, 1977) was successively elaborated by introducing the concept of credible threat (Dixit, 1979, 1980; Eaton and Lipsey, 1980, 1981). As it turned out, an investment took on credibility in the degree to which it was non-redeployable – which is precisely the issue with which the asset specificity literature is concerned. Subsequent work has extended the study of strategic behaviour to include an assessment of innovation (von Weizsäcker, 1980; Ordover and Willig, 1981) and to introduce probablistic gaming considerations into the calculus of predation (Milgrom and Roberts, 1982; Kreps and Wilson, 1982).

The study of strategic behaviour in the context of 'raising rivals costs' has also been progressing. The use of wage rates as a barrier to entry and of strategic forward integration (Williamson, 1968a, 1979) has since been generalized to encompass a wide class of cost-increasing strategies (Salop and Scheffman, 1983).

A third factor contributing to concern over and interest in the study of strategic behaviour has been posed by international competition. Allegations that strategic business behaviour – with respect both to foreign and domestic markets – is sometimes aided and abetted by government agencies are widespread. The joinder of the Industrial Organization literature and of the International Trade literature is needed to develop these issues in a more rigorous and systematic way. Work of this kind is in progress and is nicely summarized in Grossman and Richardson (1985). That there are very real and serious problems posed for which we do not presently have well-defined answers is plainly the case. Caution against protectionist use (or abuse) of antitrust to insulate markets against legitimate international competition is a matter of real concern. But the proposition that strategic behaviour is a myth in this and other contexts is simplistic and repeatedly refuted by the facts. Unpacking these issues poses a major intellectual challenge in the years ahead.

OLIVER E. WILLIAMSON

See also CARTELS; CONCENTRATION RATIOS; MONOPOLY; REGULATION AND DEREGULATION.

BIBLIOGRAPHY

Bain, J. 1956. *Barriers to New Competition*. Cambridge, Mass.: Harvard University Press.

Bain, J. 1959. *Industrial Organization*. New York: Wiley.

Berle, A.A. and Means, G.C. 1932. *The Modern Corporation and Private Property*. New York: Macmillan.

Bork, R.H. 1978. *The Antitrust Paradox*. New York: Basic Books.

Chamberlin, E. 1933. *Theory of Monopolistic Competition*. Cambridge, Mass.: Harvard University Press.

Coase, R.H. 1937. The nature of the firm. *Economica* 4, 386–405. Reprinted in *Readings in Price Theory*, ed. G.J. Stigler and K.E. Boulding, Homewood, Ill.: Richard D. Irwin, 1952.

Dixit, A. 1979. A model of duopoly suggesting a theory of entry barriers. *Bell Journal of Economics* 10, Spring, 20–32.

Dixit, A. 1980. The role of investment in entry deterrence. *Economic Journal* 90, March, 95–106.

Eaton, B.C. and Lipsey, R.G. 1980. Exit barriers are entry barriers: the durability of capital. *Bell Journal of Economics* 11, Autumn, 721–9.

Eaton, B.C. and Lipsey, R.G. 1981. Capital commitment and entry equilibrium. *Bell Journal of Economics* 12, Autumn, 593–604.

Fisher, A. and Lande, R. 1983. Efficiency considerations in merger enforcement. *California Law Review* 71, December, 1580–1696.

Grossman, G.M. and Richardson, J.D. 1985. Strategic trade policy: a survey of issues and early analysis. Special Papers in International Economics No. 15, Princeton University.

Klein, B. and Leffler, K.B. 1981. The role of market forces in assuring contractual performance. *Journal of Political Economy* 89, August, 615–41.

Kreps, D.M. and Wilson, R. 1982. Reputation and imperfect information. *Journal of Economic Theory* 27, August, 253–79.

Liebeler, W.C. 1978. Market power and competitive superiority in concentrated industries. *UCLA Law Review* 25, August, 1231–300.

Mason, E. 1957. *Economic Concentration and the Monopoly Problem*. Cambridge, Mass.: Harvard University Press.

Milgrom, P. and Roberts, J. 1982. Predation, reputation, and entry deterrence. *Journal of Economic Theory* 27, August, 280–312.

Modigliani, F. 1958. New developments on the oligopoly front. *Journal of Political Economy* 66, June, 215–32.

Muris, T.J. 1979. The efficiency defense under section 7 of the Clayton Act. *Case Western Reserve Law Review* 30, Fall, 381–432.

Ordover, J.A. and Willig, R.D. 1981. An economic definition of predatory product innovation. In *Strategic Views of Predation*, ed. S. Salop, Washington, DC: Federal Trade Commission, 301–96.

Robinson, J. 1933. *The Economics of Imperfect Competition*. London: Macmillan.

Salop, S. and Scheffman, D. 1983. Raising rivals' costs. *American Economic Review* 73, May, 267–71.

Spence, A.M. 1977. Entry, capacity investment and oligopolistic pricing. *Bell Journal of Economics* 8, Autumn, 534–44.

Stigler, G.J. 1952. The case against big business. *Fortune* 47, May, 123 et seq.

Stigler, G.J. 1955. Mergers and preventive antitrust policy. *University of Pennsylvania Law Review* 104, November, 176–84.

Stigler, G.J. 1968. *The Organization of Industry*. Homewood, Ill.: Richard D. Irwin.

Sylos-Labini, P. 1956. *Oligopoly and Technical Progress*. Trans. Elizabeth Henderson, Cambridge, Mass.: Harvard University Press, 1962.

Telser, L. 1960. Why should manufacturers want fair trade? *Journal of Law and Economics* 3, 86–104.

Telser, L. 1981. A theory of self-enforcing agreements. *Journal of Business* 53, February, 27–44.

Weizsäcker, C.C. von. 1980. *Barriers to Entry*. New York: Springer-Verlag.

Williamson, O.E. 1968a. Wage rates as a barrier to entry: the Pennington Case in perspective. *Quarterly Journal of Economics* 82, February, 85–116.

Williamson, O.E. 1968b. Economies as an antitrust defense: the welfare tradeoffs. *American Economic Review* 58, March, 18–35.

Williamson, O.E. 1979. Assessing vertical market restrictions. *University of Pennsylvania Law Review* 127, April, 953–93.

Williamson, O.E. 1983. Credible commitments: using hostages to support exchange. *American Economic Review* 73, September, 519–40.

Williamson, O.E. 1985. *The Economic Institutions of Capitalism*. New York: Free Press.

Antonelli, Giovanni Battista (1858–1944). Antonelli was born near Pisa in 1858. He studied mathematics and then went on to qualify as an engineer. Although his life was devoted to civil engineering, he made an important contribution to early mathematical economics. His *Sulla teoria matematica dell' economia politica*, intended to be the first part of a book, is remarkable, in particular for the conditions he gives for the 'integrability problem'.

This asks under what conditions are single valued demand functions generated by the maximization of a utility function. Antonelli studied the 'local' aspects of this problem. He started from what is now called the indirect demand function:

$$p = M[q]$$

where q is the vector of goods and p the vector of prices. He gave the symmetry of the matrix of the price substitution terms $\delta p_i / \delta q_j$ as a condition for the recoverability of the utility function but should have also required the negative semi definiteness of this matrix. The importance of this work has been recognized by Samuelson (1950) and later authors, but passed unappreciated if not unnoticed at the time.

In the same work Antonelli derives a condition for a market demand function to be derivable from a market utility function, that is, that individuals have linear parallel Engel curves. This condition was found much later by Gorman (1953) and Eisenberg (1961). Antonelli had an active and productive career in engineering and what would now be called 'operations research' but never came back to theoretical economics. He died in 1944.

A.P. Kirman

SELECTED WORKS

1886. *Sulla teoria matematica dell'economia politica*. Pisa. Reprinted, with an introduction by G. Demaria, Milan: Malfasi, 1952.

BIBLIOGRAPHY A detailed and careful account of Antonelli's contributions and a translation of his economic paper is given in:

Chipman, J.S., Hurwicz, L., Richter, M.K. and Sonnenschein, H.F. (eds) 1971. *Preferences, Utility and Demand*. New York: Harcourt Brace & Jovanovich. (See in particular Introduction to Part II by J.S Chipman, chapter 16: a translation of Antonelli and chapter 9 on the integrability problem by L. Hurwicz.)

Eisenberg, E. 1961. Aggregation of utility functions. *Management Science* 7, 337–50.

Gorman, W.M. 1953. Community preference fields. *Econometrica* 21, 63–80.

Samuelson, P.A. 1950. The problem of integrability in utility theory. *Economica* 17, 355–85.

Aoyama, Hideo (born 1910). Aoyama was born in Okayama, Japan. He obtained an MA (1932) and a doctorate (1951) in economics at Kyoto University, where he was Professor of Economics from 1946 to 1973.

In 1937 Aoyama wrote 'The Economic Theory of Monopoly', the first monograph on mathematical economics written in Japanese. He constructed a systematic classification of markets, providing a mathematical model of price determination for each type of market. His theory traces a path from isolated exchanges with numerous equilibrium points on a segment of the Edgeworth contract curve, towards perfect competition, where the equilibrium must be located on a particular point on the same curve. This view resembles the more recent theory of the core of an economy.

Between 1938 and 1943 Aoyama published a number of articles on the dynamics of economic fluctuation; these are included in the three volumes of his Collected Papers (1949, 1950 and 1953). He stressed the significance of distinguishing between the theory of the temporary state (in modern terminology, temporary general equilibrium) and the theory of process over time (macrodynamics). His general equilibrium model of production (1938) – influenced by the work of F.H. Knight, Gunnar Myrdal and Ragnar Frisch – expressed the supply and demand of all commodities as a function of their present prices, expected prices, and stocks. In the light of Hicks's *Value and Capital* (1939) he provided a rigorous mathematical treatment of the concept of the composite commodity grouping (1943). He was much influenced by the work of D.H. Robertson and attempted to reformulate his period analysis (1941a, 1941b).

Another of his interests was the theory of crisis, particularly Spiethoff's and Tugan-Baronovsky's interpretation of overinvestment. He demonstrated that Say's Law was an essential element in Spiethoff's theory and that the theory could not stand because errors in expectation were bound to cause general overproduction.

Like Yasuma Takata, his predecessor in the Kyoto chair of economics, Aoyama was a sociologist as well as an economist. In the 1940s he became particularly intersted in Max Weber and in his main works of this period (1948, 1949) he developed a typology of national economies based on Weber's theory of ideal types. He emphasized the common characteristics of rational systems of control such as the military, the bureaucracy and the corporation.

Aoyama was a pioneer of the scientific analysis of the economy and society during the dark age of Japanese social science. He introduced current Western theories to his students and influenced the new generation of Japanese mathematical economists in the postwar era.

Mitsuo Saito

SELECTED WORKS AVAILABLE IN ENGLISH OR GERMAN

1941a. A critical note on D.H. Robertson's theory of savings and investment (I). *Kyoto University Economic Review* 16(1), January, 49–73.

1941b. A critical note on D.H. Robertson's theory of savings and investment (II). *Kyoto University Economic Review* 16(2), April, 64–81.

1943. On the extension of the concept of a commodity: a note on Hicks's theory of the 'group of commodities'. *Kyoto University Economic Review* 18(2), April, 48–68.

1944. Die Rechnungsmässige Rationalität als Grundlegendes Merkmal der Modernen Volkswirtschaft, I. *Kyoto University Economic Review* 19(1), January, 44–60.

1959. (With Toru Nishikawa.) Business fluctuations in the Japanese economy in the inter-war period. *Kyoto University Economic Review* 28(1), April, 14–39.

appropriate technology. Depending on the decade, different criteria have provided the basis for judging the appropriateness of technology in developing countries. In the 1950s and 1960s, debate centred on whether the choice of technique ought to be guided by the objective of maximizing the growth rate, rather than the level, of output. In the 1970s, the maximand became employment. There was a surge in articles on employment creation through income redistribution and on the merits, more in theory than in practice, of alternative technology life-styles. Soon after, what was considered to be appropriate came once again to mean a competitive market outcome. So defined, the term 'appropriate technology' served no distinct purpose and dropped out of use.

Central to the economic literature in the 1950s and 1960s on how to accelerate development was lengthy discussion of choice of technique. A socialist like Dobb (1963) argued that insofar as the limiting factor consists in the available surplus of foodstuffs and other consumer goods, it will not be the best policy (from the growth standpoint) to invest in low productivity, 'labour-intensive' techniques (as advocated by the twin doctrines of Marginal Productivity and Comparative Cost). Techniques should be chosen that, by achieving a higher level of output per worker, make the surplus product larger. Dobb's point was also made by some adherents of the neoclassical production function who faulted the market model for being too preoccupied with static resource allocation (Sutcliffe, 1974, ch. 5).

Output grew very rapidly in developing countries in this period. Yet outside the socialist bloc, employment growth stagnated. The term 'appropriate technology' was popularized by economists seeking to understand this fact and what could be done about it.

The reasons proffered for slow employment growth amidst rapid rises in output were wide ranging. The majority blamed market distortions. The political clout of urban workers raised wages, subsidization of credit cheapened capital, and overvalued exchange rates invited machinery imports. Another group offered managerial explanations. A choice of technique was not a mere theoretical abstraction, as evidenced by different factor proportions among plants of the same firm ostensibly producing the same product in different countries. But 'engineering man' rather than *homo economicus* did the choosing, and in developing countries chose production processes to raise technical sophistication, reduce labour problems and enhance product quality (Stobaugh and Wells, 1984). A third set of reasons was elaborated by Frances Stewart (1972, 1985). First, she recognized a maximization conflict not merely between output and the growth of output, but also between output and employment. Two techniques of different factor proportions might incur the same total costs, but the technique with a higher ratio of capital to labour might produce higher output. In theory, this technique might generate more employment in the long run, but over time, new technologies would be devised, even more capital-using than those displaced, because innovation occurred in high wage countries. The assumption of a continuous spectrum of techniques to produce a given output, therefore, was belied by history (so lowering wages might succeed only in raising rents rather than employment). At the other extreme, 'technological determinists' were equally wrong in contending the absence of any choice. Yet by varying operating scale and discriminating among products to satisfy consumer wants, the technical menu could be widened.

By this line of reasoning, increasing employment was seen to depend upon choosing appropriate *products* and stimulating small-scale industry. The possibility of specializing through foreign trade in labour-intensive manufactures was under-played while it was assumed that the consumption bundle of the poor generally involved more labour-intensive production processes than that of the rich. Therefore, employment would rise with a redistribution of income from rich to poor to finance 'informal sector' markets.

The most radical articulation of this view, in the Proudhonian sense, was heard on the fringes of the economics profession. Adherents were sufficiently focused and active to be called a movement, the AT. The Appropriate Technology movement traced its intellectual heritage to Mahatma Gandhi and E.F. Schumacher (1973) and emphasized rural community development. Appropriate technology came to embody self-reliance, a rejection of the technico-economic values of industrialized nations, the use of locally available resources, especially solar energy, and not just a higher ratio of labour to capital (Jequier, 1976). Appropriate technology had to be developed by and for the people who lived by it.

Politically, even the most radical tendencies in the AT movement failed to mobilize mass support. In policy making, not even the moderates made much headway, except possibly in India. Political economy constraints had largely been ignored and demands for income redistribution proved fanciful. The difficulties of devising new technologies and developing local capabilities to assimilate and improve them were underestimated. And at best, all that might be expected was a small surplus and slow growth.

Into this void stepped enthusiasts of export-led growth. Through trade, developing countries could specialize in 'labour-intensive' products without having to redistribute income. With a reduction in market distortions, the choice by profit-maximizing firms of appropriate technology would be automatic. But the conflict between output growth and employment inherent in this reading of appropriate technology was never well understood. Governments in middle income countries with a long-term perspective, appreciative of the high risks of a trade reliant development strategy amidst rising wages, borrowed heavily abroad. Funds were used to establish new industries with long lead times and high capital requirements in order to stay ahead of competition from even lower wage countries in 'labour-intensive' goods. Debt servicing required access to the markets of advanced countries. Yet as advanced countries climbed up the ladder of comparative advantage, they became less capable of achieving full employment and less willing to relinquish their labour-using industries to imports. Neither the theoretical solution, lower wages, nor the politically popular one, protection, promised relief for indebted nations. Thus, the technologies that seemed appropriate to different groups of countries were out of synchronization. The fast growing, newly industrializing countries and the slower growing advanced economies collided in a widening range of markets for industrial products.

ALICE H. AMSDEN

See also BACKWARDNESS; CHOICE OF TECHNIQUE; SCHUMACHER, E.F.

BIBLIOGRAPHY
Dobb, M. 1963. *Economic Growth and Underdeveloped Countries*. London: Lawrence & Wishart.
Jequier, N. 1976. *Appropriate Technology*. Paris: Development Centre of the Organization for Economic Cooperation and Development.
Schumacher, E.F. 1973. *Small is Beautiful*. London: Blond & Briggs.
Stewart, F. 1972. Choice of technique in developing countries. *Journal of Development Studies* 9(1), October, 99–121.
Stewart, F. 1985. Macro policies for appropriate technology: an introductory classification. In *Technology, Institutions and Government Policies*, ed. J. James and S. Watanabe, London: Macmillan.
Stobaugh, R. and Wells, L.T., Jr. (eds) 1984. *Technology Crossing Borders*. Boston: Harvard Business School Press.
Sutcliffe, R.B. 1971. *Industry and Underdevelopment*. London: Addison-Wesley.

Aquinas, St Thomas (1225–1274). St Thomas Aquinas is generally acknowledged as the outstanding theologian of the high middle ages. A member of the Dominican order and a pupil of Albertus Magnus (1206–80), St Thomas taught at a number of centres including Paris, Anagni, Orvieto, Rome, Viterbo, and Naples. In his research he drew on an extensive range of sources, from the Christian tradition (based on the Scriptures, the Fathers, and the Roman writers) to Greek philosophy including the thought of the newly 'rediscovered' Aristotle. The writings of Aquinas are also wide-ranging, including commentaries on Aristotle's *Politics* and *Ethics*. Most celebrated among his major works is the *Summa Theologica*, which was set down between 1265 and 1273.

For St Thomas, economic reasoning is integrated with moral philosophy and the establishment of legal precepts. Analysis of economic activity is undertaken for the sake of determining appropriate standards in dealings between citizen and citizen, and so is an aspect of the inquiry into justice. The category of justice which Aquinas finds most relevant to economic life is commutative justice (from *commutatio*, i.e. transaction). Hence the focal points for his economic reasoning are value and price, money and interest.

On money, St Thomas stresses its roles as a medium for the exchange of commodities and as a unit of account, that is, a standard of value or measuring rod for comparing the relative worths of exchangeable things. In his treatments of compensation for delay in repayment of a money loan and of restitution of stolen money Aquinas also recognizes that money may have economic significance when held in balance (especially when held by businessmen). The stress on money as a medium of exchange and unit of account leads to a condemnation of most forms of interest-taking as usury, hence unjust. However, the analysis of restitution and compensation help pave the way for the later acceptance by theologians of *lucrum cessans* and *damnum emergens* as phenomena offering bases for a legitimate positive rate of interest.

The just price of any commodity for St Thomas is its current market price, established in the absence of fraud or monopolistic trading practices. It is a price established by *communiter venditur*, the price generally charged in the community concerned, rather than the price dictated by the preferences or needs of any one individual in that community. The value of a commodity will depend on subjective estimates of the utility of the good in question. It will also depend, in part, on cost of production, in that the latter influences supply conditions in any particular market. Aquinas does not achieve an effective synthesis of the utility and cost elements in his analysis of value, nor does he extend the analysis into a theory of distribution. These latter problems, however, were addressed by some of his Scholastic successors, often with reference to the analytical framework devised by St Thomas.

BARRY GORDON

See also SCHOLASTIC ECONOMIC THOUGHT.

SELECTED WORKS
An English translation of Aquinas' most celebrated work is: St Thomas Aquinas, *Summa Theologiae*, translated and edited by Marcus Lefebure (New York: Oxford University Press, 1975). There is also a translation of one of his commentaries on Aristotle, *Commentary on the Nicomachean Ethics* (Chicago: Library of Living Catholic Thought, 1964). Selected passages from the writings of St Thomas which are of interest for economists are included in A.E. Monroe, *Early Economic Thought* (Cambridge, Mass.: Harvard University Press, 1924), and in A.C. Pegis (ed.), *Basic Writings of St Thomas Aquinas*, 2 vols (New York: Random House, 1945). A Latin edition of Aquinas' works is: St Thomas Aquinas, *Opera Omnia*, 34 vols, ed. P. Mare and S.E. Frette (Paris: Vives, 1871–80).

BIBLIOGRAPHY
Baldwin, J.W. 1959. *The Medieval Theories of the Just Price.* Philadelphia: American Philosophical Society.

Gilchrist, J.T. 1969. *The Church and Economic Activity in the Middle Ages.* London: Macmillan.
Gordon, B. 1975. *Economic Analysis Before Adam Smith.* London: Macmillan.
Langholm, O. 1979. *Price and Value Theory in the Aristotelian Tradition.* Bergen: Universitetsforlaget.
Langholm, O. 1984. *The Aristotelian Analysis of Usury.* Bergen: Universitetsforlaget.
Noonan, J.T. 1957. *The Scholastic Analysis of Usury.* Cambridge, Mass.: Harvard University Press.
Stark, W. 1956. *The Contained Economy: an Interpretation of Medieval Economic Thought.* London: Blackfriars.
Viner, J. 1978. *Religious Thought and Economic Society.* Durham, NC: Duke University Press.
Weisheipl, J.A. 1974. *Friar Thomas D'Aquino: his Life, Thought and Work.* Garden City, New York: Doubleday.
Worland, S.T. 1967. *Scholasticism and Welfare Economics.* Notre Dame: University of Notre Dame Press.

arbitrage. An arbitrage opportunity is an investment strategy that guarantees a positive payoff in some contingency with no possibility of a negative payoff and with no net investment. By assumption, it is possible to run the arbitrage possibility at arbitrary scale; in other words, an arbitrage opportunity represents a money pump. A simple example of arbitrage is the opportunity to borrow and lend costlessly at two different fixed rates of interest. Such a disparity between the two rates cannot persist: arbitrageurs will drive the rate together.

The modern study of arbitrage is the study of the implications of assuming that no arbitrage opportunities are available. Assuming no arbitrage is compelling because the presence of arbitrage is inconsistent with equilibrium when preferences increase with quantity. More fundamentally, the presence of arbitrage is inconsistent with the existence of an optimal portfolio strategy for *any* competitive agent who prefers more to less, because there is no limit to the scale at which an individual would want to hold the arbitrage position. Therefore, in principle, absence of arbitrage follows from individual rationality of a single agent. One appeal of results based on the absence of arbitrage is the intuition that absence of arbitrage is more primitive than equilibrium, since only relatively few rational agents are needed to bid away arbitrage opportunities, even in the presence of a sea of agents driven by 'animal spirits'.

The absence of arbitrage is very similar to the zero economic profit condition for a firm with constant returns to scale (and no fixed factors). If such a firm had an activity which yielded positive profits, there would be no limit to the scale at which the firm would want to run the activity and no optimum would exist. The theoretical distinction between a zero profit condition and the absence of arbitrage is the distinction between commerce and simply trading under the price system, namely that commerce requires production. In practice, the distinction blurs. For example, if gold is sold at different prices in two markets, there is an arbitrage opportunity but it requires production (transportation of the gold) to take advantage of the opportunity. Furthermore, there are almost always costs to trading in markets (for example, brokerage fees), and therefore a form of costly production is required to convert cash into a security. For the purposes of this entry, we will tend to ignore production. In practical applications the necessity of production will weaken the implications of absence of arbitrage and may drive a wedge between what the pure absence of arbitrage would predict and what actually occurs.

The assertion that two *perfect* substitutes (e.g. two shares of stock in the same company) must trade at the same price is an implication of no arbitrage that goes under the name of the law of one price. While the law of one price is an immediate consequence of the absence of arbitrage, it is not equivalent to the absence of arbitrage. An early use of a no arbitrage condition employed the law of one price to help explain the pattern of prices in the foreign exchange and commodities markets.

Many economic arguments use the absence of arbitrage implicitly. In discussions of purchasing power parity in international trade, for example, presumably it is an arbitrage possibility that forces the spot exchange rate between currencies to equal the relative prices of common baskets of (traded) goods. Similarly, the statement that the possibility of repackaging implies linear prices in competitive product markets is essentially a no-arbitrage argument.

EARLY USES OF THE LAW OF ONE PRICE

The parity theory of forward exchange based on the law of one price was first formulated by Keynes (1923) and developed further by Einzig (1937). Let s denote the current spot price of, say, German marks, in terms of dollars, and let f denote the forward price of marks one year in the future. The forward price is the price at which agreements can be struck currently for the future delivery of marks with no money changing hands today. Also, let r_s and r_m denote the one year dollar and mark interest rates, respectively. To prevent an arbitrage possibility from developing, these four prices must stand in a particular relation.

To see this, consider the choices facing a holder of dollars. The holder can lend the dollars in the domestic market and realize a return of r_s one year from now. Alternatively, the investor can purchase marks on the spot market, lend for one year in the German market, and convert the marks back into dollars one year from now at the fixed forward rate. By undertaking the conversion back into dollars in the forward market, the investor locks in the prevailing forward rate, f. The results of this latter path are a return of

$$f(1 + r_m)/s$$

dollars one year from now. If this exceeds $1 + r_s$, then the foreign route offers a sure higher return than domestic lending. By borrowing dollars at the domestic rate r_s and lending them in the foreign market, a sure profit at the rate

$$f(1 + r_m)/s - (1 + r_s)$$

can be made with no net investment of funds. Alternatively, if the foreign route provides a lower return, then by running the arbitrage in reverse, i.e., by selling dollars forward, borrowing against them and converting the resulting marks into dollars on the spot market, the investor will collect an amount which, when lent in the domestic market at the dollar interest rate, r_s, will produce more dollars than were sold forward.

Thus, the prevention of arbitrage will enforce the forward parity result,

$$(1 + r_s)/(1 + r_m) = f/s.$$

This result takes on many different forms as we look across different markets. In a commodity market with costless storage, for example, an arbitrage opportunity will arise if the following relation does not hold:

$$f \leqslant s(1 + r).$$

In this equation, f is the currently quoted forward rate for the purchase of the commodity, e.g., silver, one year from now, s is the current spot price, and r is the interest rate. More generally, if c is the up-front proportional carrying cost, including such items as storage costs, spoilage and insurance, absence of arbitrage ensures that

$$f \leqslant s(1 + c)(1 + r).$$

(We normally would expect these relations to hold with equality in a market in which positive stocks are held at all points in time, and perhaps with inequality in a market which may not have positive stocks just before a harvest. However, proving equality is based on equilibrium arguments, not on the absence of arbitrage, since to short the physical commodity you must first own a positive amount.)

The above applications of the absence of arbitrage (via the law of one price) share the common characteristic of the absence of risk. The law of one price is less restrictive than the absence of arbitrage because it deals only with the case in which two assets are identical but have different prices. It does not cover cases in which one asset dominates another but may do so by different amounts in different states. The most interesting applications of the absence of arbitrage are to be found in uncertain situations, where this distinction may be important.

THE FUNDAMENTAL THEOREM OF ASSET PRICING

The absence of arbitrage is implied by the existence of an optimum for any agent who prefers more to less. The most important implication of the absence of arbitrage is the existence of a positive linear pricing rule, which in many spaces including finite state spaces is the same as the existence of positive state prices that correctly price all assets. Taken together with their converses, we refer collectively to these results as the *Fundamental Theorem of Asset Pricing*. (In the past, the emphasis has been on the linear pricing rule as an implication of the absence of arbitrage. Adding the other result emphasizes why we are concerned with the absence of arbitrage in the first place.) We state the theorem verbally here; the formal meanings of the words and the proof are given later in this section.

Theorem: (Fundamental Theorem of Asset Pricing) The following are equivalent:

(i) Absence of arbitrage
(ii) Existence of a positive linear pricing rule
(iii) Existence of an optimal demand for some agent who prefers more to less.

Beja (1971) was one of the first to emphasize explicitly the linearity of the asset pricing function, but he did not link it to the absence of arbitrage. Beja simply assumed that equilibrium prices existed and observed 'that equilibrium properties require that the functional q be linear', where q is a functional that assigns a price or value to a risky cash flow. The first statement and proof that the absence of arbitrage implied the existence of nonnegative state space prices and, more generally, of a positive linear operator that could be used to value risky assets appeared in Ross (1976a, 1978). Besides providing a formal analysis, Ross showed that there was a pricing rule that prices *all* assets and not just those actually marketed. (In other words, the linear pricing rule could be extended from the marketed assets to all hypothetical assets defined over the same set of states.) The advantage of this extension is that the domain of the pricing function does not depend on the set of marketed assets. We will largely follow Ross's analysis with some modern improvements.

Linearity for pricing means that the price functional or operator q satisfies the ordinary linear condition of algebra. If we let x and y be two random payoffs and we let q be the operator that assigns values to prospects, then we require that

$$q(ax + by) = aq(x) + bq(y),$$

where a and b are arbitrary constants. Of course, for many spaces (including a finite state space), any linear functional can be represented as a sum or integral across states of state prices times quantities.

To simplify proofs in this essay, we will make the assumption that there are finitely many states, each of which occurs with positive probability, and that all claims purchased today pay off at a single future date. Let Θ denote the state space,

$$\Theta = \{1, \ldots, m\},$$

where there are m states and the state of nature θ occurs with probability π_θ. Applying q to the 'indicator' asset e_θ whose payoff is 1 in state θ and 0 otherwise, we can define a price q_θ for each state θ as the value of e_θ;

$$q_\theta = q(e_\theta).$$

Now, if there were linearity, the value of any payoff, x, could be written as

$$q(x) = \Sigma_\theta q_\theta x_\theta.$$

Of course, this argument presupposes that $q(e_\theta)$ is well defined, which is a strong assumption if e_θ is not marketed.

We want to make a statement about the conditions under which all marketed assets can be priced by such a linear pricing rule q. We assume that there is a set of n marketed assets with a corresponding price vector, p. Asset i has a terminal payoff $X_{\theta i}$ (inclusive of dividends, etc.) in state of nature θ. The matrix $X \equiv [X_{\theta i}]$ denotes the state space tableau whose columns correspond to assets and whose rows correspond to states. Lower-case x represents the random vector of terminal payoffs to the various securities. An arbitrage opportunity is a portfolio (vector) η with two properties. It does not cost anything today or in any state in the future. And, it has a positive payoff either today or in some state in the future (or both). We can express the first property as a pair of vector inequalities. The initial cost is not greater than zero, which is to say that it uses no wealth and may actually generate some,

$$p\eta \leqslant 0, \tag{1}$$

and its random payoff later is never negative,

$$X\eta \geqslant 0. \tag{2}$$

(We use the notation that $\geqslant$ denotes greater or equal in each component, $>$ denotes $\geqslant$ and greater in some component, and $\gg$ denotes greater in all components. Note that writing the price of X_η as p_η for arbitrary η embodies an assumption that investment in marketed assets is divisible.) The second property says that the arbitrage portfolio η has a strict inequality, either in (1) or in some component of (2). We can express both properties together as

$$X_*\eta \equiv \begin{bmatrix} -p \\ X \end{bmatrix} \eta > 0. \tag{3}$$

Here, we have stacked the net payoff today on top of the vector of payoffs at the future date. This is in the spirit of the Arrow–Debreu model in which consumption in different states, commodities, points of time, and so forth, are all considered components of one large consumption vector.

The absence of arbitrage is simply the condition that no η satisfies (3). A consistent positive linear pricing rule is a vector of state prices $q \gg 0$ that correctly prices all marketed assets, i.e. such that

$$p = qX. \tag{4}$$

We have now collected enough definitions to prove the first half (that (i) $\Leftrightarrow$ (ii)) of the Fundamental Theorem of Asset Pricing.

Theorem: (First half of the Fundamental Theorem of Asset Pricing) There is no arbitrage if and only if there exists a consistent positive linear pricing rule.

Proof: The proof that having a consistent positive linear pricing rule precludes arbitrage is simple, since any arbitrage opportunity gives a direct violation of (4). Let η be an arbitrage opportunity. By (4),

$$p\eta = qX\eta,$$

or equivalently

$$0 = -p\eta + q(X\eta) = [1 \ q]X_*\eta.$$

By definition of an arbitrage opportunity (3) and positivity of q, we have a contradiction.

The proof that the absence of arbitrage implies the existence of a consistent positive linear pricing rule is more subtle and requires a separation theorem. The mathematical problem is equivalent to Farkas' Lemma of the alternative and to the basic duality theorem of linear programming. We will adopt an approach that is analogous to the proof of the second theorem of welfare economics that asserts the existence of a price vector which supports any efficient allocation, by separating the aggregate Pareto optimal allocation from all aggregate allocations corresponding to Pareto preferable allocations. Here we will find a price vector that 'supports' an arbitrage-free allocation by separating the net trades from the set of free lunches (the positive orthant).

The absence of arbitrage is equivalent to the requirement that the linear space of net trades defined by

$$s \equiv \{y \,|\, \text{for some } \eta, \; y = X_*\eta\}, \tag{5}$$

does not intersect the positive orthant $\mathscr{R}_+^{m+1} \equiv \{y \,|\, y \geqslant 0\}$ except at the origin, i.e., $S \cap \mathscr{R}_+^{m+1} = \{0\}$.

Since S is a subspace (and is therefore a convex closed cone), a simple separation theorem (Karlin, 1959, Theorem B3.5) implies that there exists of nonzero vector q_* such that for all $y \in S$ and all $z \in \mathscr{R}_+^{m+1}$, $z \neq 0$, we must have

$$q_* z > 0 \geqslant q_* y. \tag{6}$$

Letting z be each of the unit vectors in turn, the first inequality in (6) implies that q_* is a strictly positive vector.

Since S is a subspace, the second inequality in (6) must hold with equality for all $y \in S$. Define

$$q \equiv (q_{*2}, q_{*3}, \ldots, q_{*n})/q_{*1}.$$

Since $q_* \gg 0$, likewise $q \gg 0$. Dividing the second equality in (6) (which we now know to be an equality) by q_{*1} and expanding using the definition of X_* [from (3)], we have that

$$0 = -p + qX,$$

or

$$p = qX,$$

which shows that q is a consistent positive linear pricing rule. □

Before we can prove the second half of the pricing theorem, we need to define the maximization problem faced by a typical investor. In this problem, all we really need to assume is that more is preferred (strictly) to less, i.e. that increasing initial consumption or random consumption later in one or more states always leads to a preferred outcome. In fact, this is literally all we need: we do not need completeness or even transitivity of preferences, let alone a utility function representation or any restriction to a functional form. However, for concreteness, we will write down preferences using a state-dependent utility function of consumption now and in the future. The assumption that the investor prefers more to less is satisfied if the utility function in each state is increasing in comsumption at both dates.

The state-dependent restriction implies that the maximization problem faced by a particular agent is the maximization of the expectation of the state dependent utility function $u_\theta(\cdot,\cdot)$ of initial wealth and terminal wealth, given initial wealth w_0 and the possibility of trading in the security market. Then the maximization problem faced by a typical agent is the unconstrained choice of a vector α of portfolio weights to maximize

$$\Sigma_\theta \pi_\theta u_\theta[w_0 - p\alpha, (X\alpha)_\theta].$$

The quantity $p\alpha$ is the price of the portfolio, and therefore $w_0 - p\alpha$ is the residual amount of the initial wealth available for initial consumption. The preferences of the agent are said to be increasing if each $u_\theta(\cdot,\cdot)$ is (strictly) increasing in both arguments. Saying the agent prefers more to less is just another way of saying that preferences are increasing.

Here is the rest of the proof of the Fundamental Theorem of Asset Pricing.

Theorem: (Second half of the Fundamental Theorem of Asset Pricing) There is no arbitrage if and only if there exists some (at least hypothetical) agent with increasing preferences whose choice problem has a maximum.

Proof: If there is an arbitrage opportunity η, then clearly the choice problem for an agent with increasing preferences cannot have a maximum, since for every α,

$$\Sigma_\theta \pi_\theta u_\theta \{w_0 - p(\alpha + k\eta), [X(\alpha + k\eta)]_\theta\}$$

increases as k increases.

Conversely, if there is no arbitrage, by the first half of the Fundamental Theorem of Asset Pricing (proven earlier), there exists a consistent positive linear pricing rule q. Let $w_0 = 0$ and $\alpha = 0$. Consider the particular utility function

$$u_{*\theta}(c_0, c_1) \equiv -\exp[-(c_0 - w_0)] - (q_\theta/\pi_\theta)\exp(-c_1). \quad (7)$$

Each function $u_{*\theta}$ is strictly increasing and also happens to be strictly concave, infinitely differentiable, and additively separable over time. Using $p = qX$, it is easy to show that this utility function satisfies the first order conditions for a maximum, which are necessary and sufficient by concavity. (Note: by a more complicated argument, it can be shown that the von Neumann–Morgenstern 'state independent' utility function $-\exp(-c_0) - \exp(-c_1)$ has a maximum, but the maximum will not necessarily be achieved at $\alpha = 0$.) $\square$

As should be clear from the proof, it is not really important what class of preferences we use, so long as all agents having preferences in the class prefer more to less and the class includes the particular preferences used in the proof (which are additive over states and time, increasing, concave, and infinitely differentiable).

Recent research on arbitrage, starting with Ross (1978) and Harrison and Kreps (1979), has focused on extending these results to more general state spaces in which there are many time periods and, more importantly, infinitely many states. In these spaces, deriving a positive linear pricing rule for marketed claims is still straightforward (you can prove the algebraic linearity condition and positivity directly from the no arbitrage condition), but extending the pricing rule from the priced claims to all non-marketed claims requires some sort of extension theorem, such as a Hahn–Banach theorem. Obtaining a truly general result is complicated by the fact that the positive orthant is not typically an open set in these general spaces, and openness is a condition of the Hahn–Banach theorems. One part of the result that goes through in general is the implication that existence of an optimum implies existence of a linear pricing rule: so long as preferences are continuous in our topology, the preferred set will be open, and the linear pricing rule will be a hyperplane that separates the optimum from the preferred set.

ALTERNATIVE REPRESENTATIONS OF LINEAR PRICING RULES

There are many equivalent ways of representing a linear pricing rule. Which representation is simplest depends on the context. In one representation, the price is the expected value under artificial 'risk-neutral' probabilities discounted at the riskless rate. (The risk-neutral probability measure is also referred to as an equivalent martingale measure.) In another representation, the price is the expectation of the quantity times the state price density, which is the state price per unit probability. In yet another representation, the price is the expected value discounted at a risk-adjusted rate. The purpose of this section is to show the fundamental equivalence of these representations.

The motive for using a particular representation is usually found in the study of intertemporal models or models with a continuum of states. Nonetheless, we will continue our formal analysis of the single-period model with finitely many states, leaving the more general discussion of the merits of the various approaches until afterwards. Now, we have already seen the basic linear pricing rule representation. For any portfolio α,

$$\begin{aligned} p\alpha &= qX\alpha \\ &= \Sigma_\theta q_\theta (X\alpha)_\theta, \end{aligned} \quad (8)$$

i.e. the sum across states of state price times the payoff.

The risk-neutral or martingale representation asserts the existence of a vector Π of artificial probabilities and a shadow riskless rate r such that

$$\begin{aligned} p\alpha &= (1+r)^{-1}\Pi X\alpha \\ &= (1+r)^{-1}E_\Pi(x\alpha), \end{aligned} \quad (9)$$

i.e., the expectation E_Π of the payoff under the risk-neutral (martingale) probabilities Π, discounted at the riskless rate. It is easy to see the shadow riskless rate is equal to the riskless rate if one exists. The risk neutral approach is trivially equivalent to the positive linear pricing rule approach. Simply let

$$\Pi = q/\Sigma_\theta q_\theta \quad (10)$$

and

$$(1+r)^{-1} = \Sigma_\theta q_\theta. \quad (11)$$

For the converse, let

$$q = (1+r)^{-1}\Pi. \quad (12)$$

Therefore, the existence of a positive linear pricing rule is the same as the existence of positive risk-neutral probabilities. (The risk-neutral measure is equivalent to the original probability measure, i.e. Π has the same null sets as π. Here, that is simply the requirement that the list of states with positive probability is the same for both measures.)

A third approach emphasizes the role of the state price density, ρ_θ. In this case, the price is given by

$$\begin{aligned} p\alpha &= \Sigma_\theta \pi_\theta \rho_\theta (X\alpha)_\theta \\ &= E(\rho x\alpha). \end{aligned} \quad (13)$$

To see that this is equivalent to the linear pricing rule, simply let

$$\rho_\theta = q_\theta/\pi_\theta, \quad (14)$$

or, conversely, let

$$q_\theta = \rho_\theta \pi_\theta. \quad (15)$$

Clearly, ρ is positive in all states if and only if q is.

We have shown the equivalence of these three approaches. This equivalence is stated in the following theorem.

Theorem: (Pricing Rule Representation Theorem) The following are equivalent:

(i) Existence of a positive linear pricing rule
(ii) Existence of positive risk-neutral probabilities and an associated riskless rate (the martingale property)
(iii) Existence of a positive state price density.

The remaining representation is that the value is equal to the terminal value discounted at a risk-adjusted interest rate r_a.

$$p\alpha = (1 + r_a)^{-1} E(x\alpha) \qquad (16)$$

While this might at first appear to be inconsistent with the other representations, the risk-adjusted rate r_a is typically proportional to the covariance of return ($= x\alpha/p\alpha$) with some random variable, and consequently solving this equation for $p\alpha$ yields a linear rule. (See Beja, 1971, and Rubinstein, 1976, for general results concerning pricing rules using covariances.) For example, in the Capital Asset Pricing Model,

$$r_a = r + \lambda \, \text{cov}(x\alpha/p\alpha, r_m), \qquad (17)$$

where r_m is the random return on the market and λ is the market price of risk. Solving these two equations for $p\alpha$, we obtain

$$p\alpha = (1 + r)^{-1} E[x\alpha \{1 - \lambda [r_m - E(r_m)]\}], \qquad (18)$$

which is certainly linear in $x\alpha$. The subtle question is whether or not this is positive, and this hinges on whether the market return can get larger than $E(r_m) + 1/\lambda$ (Dybvig and Ingersoll, 1982). In any case, the important observation is that the basic form of the representation is linear even if verification of positivity depends on the exact form of the risk premium.

Now we return to the question of the comparative advantages of the various representations. The risk-neutral or martingale representation was first employed by Cox and Ross (1976a) for use in option pricing problems and was later developed more formally by Harrison and Kreps (1979) and a number of others. The risk-neutral representation is particularly useful for problems of valuation or optimization without reference to individual preferences, since under the martingale probabilities we can ignore risk altogether and maximize discounted expected value. In fact, for some problems, this approach tells us that risk-neutral results generalize immediately to worlds where risk is priced. However, this approach tends to be complicated when preferences are introduced, since von Neumann–Morgenstern (state independent) preferences under ordinary probabilities become state dependent under the martingale probabilities. As an aside, we note that in intertemporal contexts in which the interest rate is stochastic, the price is the risk-neutral expectation of the future value discounted by the rolled-over spot rate (which is stochastic).

The state price density representation (Cox and Leland, 1982, and Dybvig, 1980, 1985), is most useful when we want to look at choice problems. For von Neumann–Morgenstern preferences, the state price density is equal to the marginal utility of consumption, for some consistent positive state price density (Dybvig and Ross, 1982). (Note that if there is a non-atomic continuum of states, the state price density will typically be well-defined even though all primitive states have probability zero and state price zero.)

The representation of discounting expected returns using a risk-adjusted discount rate is most useful when we can get some independent assessment of the risk premium involved. Otherwise, it is needlessly complicated, since the price appears not only on the left-hand side of the equation but also in the denominator on the right-hand side. Discounting using a risk-adjusted rate is usually the method of choice for capital budgeting, since the risk adjustment is usually determined from comparables (e.g. from past returns on assets in similar firms). For capital budgeting, there may also be a pedagogical advantage that (so far) it has been easier to communicate to practitioners than the other methods. Furthermore, focusing on the risk adjusted discount rate sharpens the comparison of competing approaches (such as the Capital Asset Pricing Model and the dividend discount model).

It is useful to note how the various representations evolve over time. State prices are simply the product of state prices over subperiods. For example, for $t < s < T$, the state price of a state at T given the state at t is equal to the state price of the state at T given the state at s times the state price of the state at s given the state at t. (The state at s is determined by the state at T given the pervasive assumption of perfect recall, i.e. the assumption that the family of sigma-algebras is increasing. If we use some reduced specification of the state – as when looking at Markov processes – the state price is the product of the two, summed over all possible intermediate states.)

The martingale representation yields a price equal to the expected value under the martingale measure of the product of the terminal value times a discount factor that corresponds to rolling over shortest maturity default-free bonds. This representation makes particularly clear the interaction between term structure effects and other effects. If there is a significant term structure, the discount factor is random, and we cannot ignore the interplay between term structure risk and random terminal value unless the terminal value of the asset under consideration is independent of interest rates (under the martingale measure). If the terminal value is independent of interest rate movements, then the value of the asset today is the risk-neutral expected terminal value of the asset discounted at the riskless discount factor (which equals the risk-neutral expected discount factor from rolling over shorts).

The state price density has an evolution over time similar to that of the state price, namely the state price density over a long interval is the product of the state price density over short intervals. Since the state price density equals the state price divided by the probability, the ratio of the two evolutions gives us a relation involving only probabilities, which is Bayes' law.

Finally, the discounted expected value approach is more complicated than the others. The exact evolution over time depends on whether uncertainty is multiplicative, linear, a distributed lag, or whatever. This difficulty is usually overlooked in capital budgeting applications, which is probably not so bad in practice, given the imprecision of our estimates of risk premia and future cash flows.

MODERN RESULTS BASED ON THE ABSENCE OF ARBITRAGE

Most of modern finance is based on either the intuitive or the actual theory of the absence of arbitrage. In fact, it is possible to view absence of arbitrage as the one concept that unifies all of finance (Ross, 1978). In this section, we will try to provide a sample of how arbitrage arguments are used in diverse areas in finance. We will touch on applications in option pricing, corporate finance, asset pricing and efficient markets.

The efficient market hypothesis says that the price of an asset should fully reflect all available information. The intuition behind this hypothesis is that if the price does not fully reflect available information, then there is a profit opportunity available from buying the asset if the asset is underpriced or from selling it if it is overpriced. Clearly this is consistent with the intuition of the absence of arbitrage, even if what we have here is only an approximate arbitrage possibility, i.e. a large profit at little risk. Approximate arbitrage is always profitable to a risk-neutral investor. More generally, the issue is clouded somewhat by questions of risk tolerance and what is the appropriate risk premium. Happily, empirical violation of efficiency of the market (e.g. in event studies) is not significantly affected by the procedure for measuring the risk premium (Brown and Warner, 1980, 1985). Therefore, an empirical violation of efficiency is an approximate arbitrage opportunity that presumably would be attractive at large scale to many investors.

The Modigliani–Miller propositions tell us that in perfect capital markets, changing capital structure or dividend policy without changing investment is a matter of irrelevance to the shareholders. The original proofs of the Modigliani–Miller propositions used the law of one price and assumed the presence of a perfect substitute for the firm that was altering its capital structure. As an illustration of the Fundamental Theorem of Asset Pricing, Ross (1978) demonstrated that these propositions could be derived directly from the existence of a positive linear pricing rule.

To illustrate this argument, consider the proposition that the total value of the firm does not depend on the capital structure. The original argument assumed that there is another identical firm. If we change the financing of our firm, then the value of holding a portfolio of all the parts will give a final payoff equal to that of the identical firm, and must therefore have the same value under the law of one price. Alternatively, suppose that there exists a positive linear pricing rule q. Let x represent the total terminal value of a firm in a one period model and x_i the payoff to financial claim i on the assets of the firm. Then the sum of all the payoffs must add up to the total terminal value.

$$x = \Sigma_i x_i \qquad (19)$$

Using the positive linear operator, q, which values assets, we have that the value of the firm,

$$v = \Sigma_i q(x_i)$$
$$= q(\Sigma_i x_i)$$
$$= q(x_i), \qquad (20)$$

which is independent of the number or structure of the financial claims.

Note that both proofs make an implicit assumption that goes beyond what absence of arbitrage promises, namely that changing the capital structure of the firm does not change the way in which prices are formed in the economy. In the original proof this is the assumption that the other firm's price will not change when the firm changes its capital structure. In the linear pricing rule proof this is the assumption that the state price vector q does not change.

Another application of the absence of arbitrage is to asset pricing. The most obvious application is the derivation of the Arbitrage Pricing Theory (Ross, 1976a, 1976b). We will consider the special case without asset-specific noise. Assume that the mechanism generating the per dollar investment rates of return for a set of assets is given by

$$R_i = E_i + \beta_{i1} f_1 + \cdots + \beta_{ik} f_k, \quad i = 1, \dots, n, \qquad (21)$$

where E_i is the expected rate of return on asset i per dollar invested and f_i is an exogenous factor. This form is an exact

factor generating mechanism (as opposed to an approximate one with an additional asset specific mean zero term).

Applying the pricing operator, q, to equation (21) we have that

$$1 = q(1 + R_i)$$
$$= q(1 + E_i + \beta_{i1} f_1 + \cdots + \beta_{ik} f_k)$$
$$= q(1 + E_i) + \beta_{i1} q(f_1) + \cdots + \beta_{ik} q(f_k)$$
$$= (1 + E_i)/(1 + r) + \beta_{i1} q(f_1) + \cdots + \beta_{ik} q(f_k),$$

which implies that

$$E_i - r = \lambda_1 \beta_{i1} + \cdots + \lambda_k \beta_{ik}, \qquad (22)$$

where $\lambda_j \equiv -(1 + r)q(f_j)$ is the risk premium associated with factor j. Equation (22) is the basic equation of the Arbitrage Pricing Theory. We have derived it using absence of exact arbitrage in the absence of asset-specific noise. More general derivations account for asset-specific noise and use absence of approximate arbitrage.

The most important paper in option pricing, Black and Scholes (1973), is based on the absence of arbitrage, as is the whole literature it has generated. At any point in time, the option is priced by duplicating the value one period later using a portfolio of other assets, and assigning a value using the law of one price. We will illustrate this procedure using the binomial process studied by Cox, Ross and Rubenstein (1979). During each period, the stock price either goes up by 20 per cent or it goes down by 10 per cent and for simplicity we take the riskless rate to be zero. Assume that we are one period from the maturity of a call option with an exercise price of $100, and that the stock price is now $100 (the call is at the money).

How much is the option worth? To figure this out, we must find a portfolio of the stock and the bond that gives the same terminal value. This is the solution of two linear equations (one for each state) in two unknowns (the two portfolio weights). Explicitly, the terminal call value is the larger of 0 and the stock price less 100. In the good state, the stock value will be $120 and the option will be worth $20. In the bad state, the stock price will be $90 and the option will be worthless. If α_S is the amount of stock and α_B the amount of $100 face bond to hold in the duplicating portfolio, then we have that

$$20 = 120\alpha_S + 100\alpha_B$$

to duplicate the option value in the good state, and

$$0 = 90\alpha_S + 100\alpha_B$$

to duplicate the option value in the bad state. The solution to the two equations is given by

$$\alpha_S = 2/3$$
$$\alpha_B = -3/5$$

Therefore, each option is equivalent to holding 2/3 shares of stock and shorting (borrowing) 3/5 bonds. By the law of one price, the option value is the value of this portfolio, or $100\alpha_S + 100\alpha_B = 6\ 2/3$. In this context, we used arbitrage to value the option exactly. More generally, if less is known about the form of the stock price process, absence of arbitrage still places useful restrictions on the option price (Merton, 1973; Cox and Ross, 1976b).

An alternative to option pricing by arbitrage is to use a 'preference-based' model and price options using the first order conditions of an agent (Rubenstein, 1976). While using this alternative approach is very convenient in some contexts, the Fundamental Theorem of Asset Pricing tells us that we are not really doing anything different, and that the two approaches are simply two different ways of making the same assumption. The same point is true of the distinction some authors have made between the 'equilibrium' derivations of the Arbitrage Pricing Theory and the 'arbitrage' derivations: there is no substance in this distinction. One derivation may give a tighter approximation than another, but all derivations require similar assumptions in one form or another.

PHILIP H. DYBVIG AND STEPHEN A. ROSS

See also FINANCE; OPTION PRICING; OPTIONS; PRESENT VALUE; ZERO PROFIT CONDITION.

BIBLIOGRAPHY

Beja, A. 1971. The structure of the cost of capital under uncertainty. *Review of Economic Studies* 38, July, 359–68.

Black, F. and Scholes, M.S. 1973. The pricing of options and corporate liabilities. *Journal of Political Economy* 81(3), May–June, 637–54.

Brown, S. and Warner, J. 1980. Measuring security price performance. *Journal of Financial Economies* 8(3), September, 205–58.

Brown, S. and Warner, J. 1985. Using daily stock returns: the case of event studies. *Journal of Financial Economics* 14(1), March, 3–31.

Cox, J. and Leland, H. 1982. On dynamic investment strategies. *Proceedings, Seminar on the Analysis of Security Prices*, Center for Research in Security Prices, University of Chicago.

Cox, J. and Ross, S.A. 1976a. The valuation of options for alternative stochastic processes. *Journal of Financial Economics* 3(1/2), January/March, 145–66.

Cox, J. and Ross, S.A. 1976b. A survey of some new results in financial option pricing theory. *Journal of Finance* 31(2), May, 383–402.

Cox, J., Ross, S. and Rubinstein, M. 1979. Option pricing: a simplified approach. *Journal of Financial Economics* 7(3), September, 229–63.

Dybvig, P. 1980. Some new tools for testing market efficiency and measuring mutual fund performance. Unpublished manuscript.

Dybvig, P. 1985. Distributional analysis of portfolio choice. Yale School of Management, unpublished manuscript.

Dybvig, P. and Ingersoll, J., Jr. 1982. Mean-variance theory in complete markets. *Journal of Business* 55(2), April, 233–51.

Dybvig, P. and Ross, S. 1982. Portfolio efficient sets. *Econometrica* 50(6), November, 1525–46.

Einzig, P. 1937. *The Theory of Forward Exchange*. London: Macmillan.

Harrison, J.M. and Kreps, D. 1979. Martingales and arbitrage in multiperiod securities markets. *Journal of Economic Theory* 20(3), June, 381–408.

Karlin, S. 1959. *Mathematical Methods and Theory in Games, Programming, and Economics*. Reading, Mass.: Addison-Wesley.

Keynes, J.M. 1923. *A Tract on Monetary Reform*. London: Macmillan.

Merton, R. 1973. Theory of rational option pricing. *Bell Journal of Economics and Management Science* 4(1), Spring, 141–83.

Ross, S.A. 1976a. Return, risk and arbitrage. In *Risk and Return in Finance*, ed. I. Friend and J. Bicksler, Cambridge, Mass.: Ballinger.

Ross, S.A. 1976b. The arbitrage theory of capital asset pricing. *Journal of Economic Theory* 13(3), December, 341–60.

Ross, S.A. 1978. A simple approach to the valuation of risky streams. *Journal of Business* 51(3), July, 453–75.

Rubinstein, M. 1976. The valuation of uncertain income streams and the pricing of options. *Bell Journal of Economics and Management Science* 7(2), Autumn, 407–25.

arbitrage pricing theory. The Arbitrage Pricing Theory (APT) is due to Ross (1976a, 1976b). It is a one period model in which every investor believes that the stochastic properties of capital assets' returns are consistent with a factor structure. Ross argues that if equilibrium prices offer no arbitrage opportunities, then the expected returns on these capital assets are approximately linearly related to the factor loadings. (The factor loadings are proportional to the returns' covariances with the factors.)

In his introductory remarks, Ross (1976a) makes a heuristic argument based on the preclusion of arbitrage. That paper's formal proof shows that the theory's asserted pricing relation is a necessary condition for an equilibrium in a market where certain types of utility maximizing agents are present. The subsequent work, which is surveyed below, follows either the 'no arbitrage' or the equilibrium, utility based, route.

The APT is a substitute for the Capital Asset Pricing Model (CAPM) in that both assert a linear relation between assets' expected returns and their covariances with other random variables. (In the CAPM the covariances are with the market portfolio's return.) These covariances are interpreted as measures of risks which an investor cannot avoid by diversification. The slope coefficients of the linear relation between the expected returns and the covariances are interpreted as risk premia.

A FORMAL STATEMENT. The APT assumes that investors believe that the $N \times 1$ vector of the single period random returns on capital assets r satisfies the generating model

$$r = E + Bf + e, \tag{1.1}$$

where r and e are $N \times 1$ vectors of random variables, f is a $K \times 1$ vector of random variables (factors), E is an $N \times 1$ vector and B is an $N \times K$ matrix. With no loss of generality normalize (1.1) to make $E\{f\} = E\{e\} = 0$, where $E\{.\}$ denotes expectation. Thus, $E\{r\} = E$.

Restrictions on the diagonality of the covariance matrix $E\{ee'\}$ and on the relation between the eigenvalues of that covariance matrix and those of BB' are required for proofs of the APT. An additional customary assumption is that $E\{e|f\} = 0$, but this assumption is not necessary in some of the APT's developments (e.g. those of Ingersoll).

The number of assets N is assumed to be much larger than the number of factors K. In some models N approaches infinity and in some it is infinite. Thus, representation (1.1) applies to a sequence of capital markets; the first N assets in the $(N + 1)$st market are the same as the assets in the Nth market and the first N rows of the matrix B in the $(N + 1)$st market constitute the matrix B in the Nth market.

The APT asserts the existence of a $(K + 1) \times 1$ vector of risk premia u, an $N \times N$ positive definite matrix Z, and a constant a such that

$$(E - Cu)Z^{-1}(E - Cu) \leqslant a, \tag{1.2}$$

where the $N \times (K + 1)$ matrix $C = (i, B)$ and i is an $N \times 1$ column vector of 1's. The positive definite matrix Z is often the covariance matrix $E\{ee'\}$. If a risk-free asset is present in the investment universe under consideration then the first component of the vector of risk premia u is equal to the risk-free rate of return.

Exact arbitrage pricing obtains if (1.2) is replaced by

$$E = Cu. \tag{1.2'}$$

The interpretation of (1.2) is that each component of the vector E depends *approximately* linearly on the corresponding row of the matrix B. This linear relation is the same across assets. The approximation is better the smaller the constant a; if $a = 0$ the linear relation is exact and (1.2′) obtains.

A portfolio v is an $N \times 1$ vector. The cost of the portfolio v is $v'i$, the income from it is $v'r$, and its return is $v'r/v'i$ (if its cost is not zero).

INTUITION. The intuition behind the model draws from the intuition behind Arrow–Debreu securities pricing. K fundamental securities span all possible future states of nature in an Arrow–Debreu model. Each asset's payoff can be described as the payoff on a portfolio of the fundamental K assets. In other words, an asset's payoff is a weighted average of the fundamental assets' payoffs. If market clearing prices allow no arbitrage opportunities, then the current price of each asset must equal the weighted average of the current prices of the fundamental assets.

The Arrow–Debreu intuition can be couched in terms of returns and expected returns rather than payoffs and prices. If the unexpected part of each asset's return is a linear combination of the unexpected parts of the returns on the K fundamental securities, then the expected return of each asset is the same linear combination of the expected returns on the K fundamental assets.

To see how the Arrow–Debreu intuition leads from the factor structure (1.1) to exact arbitrage pricing (1.2′), set the idiosyncratic terms on the right-hand side of (1.1), e, equal to zero. Translate the K factors on the right-hand side of (1.1) into the K fundamental securities in the Arrow–Debreu model. Then (1.2′) follows immediately.

The presence of the idiosyncratic terms e in the factor structure (1.1) makes the model more general and realistic. It also makes the relation between (1.1) and (1.2′) more tenuous. Indeed, 'no arbitrage' arguments typically prove the weaker (1.2). Moreover, they require a weaker definition of arbitrage (and therefore a stronger definition of no arbitrage) in order to get from (1.1) to (1.2).

The proofs that lead from (1.1) to (1.2) augment the Arrow–Debreu intuition with a version of the law of large numbers. That law is used to argue that the average effect of the idiosyncratic terms is negligible. Here the independence of the e's is used. Indeed, the more one assumes about the (absence of) contemporaneous correlations among the e's, the tighter the bound on the deviation from (1.2′).

'NO ARBITRAGE' MODELS. Huberman (1982) formalizes the argument in the introduction of Ross (1976a). Huberman defines arbitrage as the existence of a subsequence of $N \times 1$ vectors w such that

$$w'i = 0, \qquad (1.3a)$$

$E\{w'r\}$ approaches infinity as N approaches infinity, (1.3b)

$\text{var}\{w'r\}$ approaches zero as N approaches infinity, (1.3c)

where $\text{var}\{\cdot\}$ denotes variance.

Requirement (1.3a) is that for each N, the portfolio w is costless. Requirement (1.3b) is that the expected income associated with w becomes large as the number of assets increases. Requirement (1.3c) is that the risk (as measured by the income's variance) vanishes as the number of assets increases.

A sequence of capital markets offers no arbitrage opportunities if there is no subsequence $\{w\}$ of portfolios which satisfies (1.3). Huberman shows that *if* (1.1) holds, the covariance matrix $E\{ee'\}$ is diagonal for all N and uniformly

bounded, and no arbitrage opportunities exist, *then* (1.2) holds with $Z = I$ and a finite bound a.

Ingersoll (1984) generalizes Huberman's result. He shows that (1.1), uniform boundedness of the elements of B and no arbitrage imply (1.2) with $Z = E\{ee'\}$, the covariance matrix of the idiosyncratic term e. A variant of Ingersoll's argument follows. Write the positive definite matrix Z as the product $Z = UU'$, where U is an $N \times N$ nonsingular matrix. Consider the orthogonal projection of the vector $U^{-1}E$ on the column space of $U^{-1}C$

$$U^{-1}E = U^{-1}Cu + g, \qquad (1.4)$$

where $g'U^{-1}C = 0$, the $(K+1)$-dimensional zero vector.

The position $w = U'^{-1}g$ (or kw, where k is a scalar) satisfies (1.3a) (because the first column of C is i). Compute $E\{kw'r\} = kg'g$ and $\text{var}\{kw'r\} = k^2g'g$. For $k = (g'g)^{-0.75}$, $E\{kw'r\} = (g'g)^{0.25}$ and $\text{var}\{kw'r\} = (g'g)^{-0.5}$. A violation of (1.2) implies that a subsequence of $\{g'g\}$ converges to infinity, which implies that (1.3) is satisfied by the costless positions $(g'g)^{-0.75}g$. A preclusion of (1.3) implies a bound on $g'g$. This last conclusion is equivalent to (1.2).

Stambaugh (1983) reconsiders the theory by assuming, in addition to the factor structure (1.1), that prices are set by investors who observe a vector of random variables y. The joint distribution of (r, y) is either multivariate normal or multivariate Student t. Thus, the factor structure (1.1) holds unconditionally but prices are set by investors who possess additional information. Stambaugh's distributional assumptions guarantee that the factor structure is maintained conditionally with the same matrix of factor loadings B as in the unconditional factor structure (1.1). This observation leads to an extension of the APT to a setting where investors have information about future returns (namely, they observe y) and it justifies tests of the APT which do not use that information.

Chamberlain and Rothschild (1983) employ Hilbert space techniques to study capital markets with (possibly infinitely) many assets. For two portfolios v and w they define the inner product $\langle v, w \rangle = E\{v'rw'r\}$. By the Riesz representation theorem both the expectation and the cost functional can be identified with inner products of unique members of the underlying Hilbert space. Chamberlain and Rothschild show that the minimum variance frontier (i.e., the set of portfolios whose return variance is minimal among all return variances of portfolios with the same expected return) in that space is generated by these two members of the space.

The preclusion of arbitrage implies the continuity of the cost functional in the Hilbert space. Letting $L(Z)$ equal the maximal eigenvalue of the limit covariance matrix $Z = E\{ee'\}$ and d equal the supremum of all ratios of expectation to standard deviation of the incomes on all costless portfolios with a non zero weight on at least one asset, Chamberlain and Rothschild argue that (1.2) holds with $a = L(Z)d^2$ and with the identity matrix replacing Z in the left-hand side of (1.2) if asset prices allow no arbitrage profits.

A portfolio w is *well diversified* if $\text{var}\{w'e\} = 0$, i.e., the portfolio's return contains only factor variance. Chamberlain (1983) assumes that K is the dimension of the subspace (in the Chamberlain–Rothschild Hilbert space) of all portfolio sequences $\{w\}$ such that $w'w$ converges to zero. He assumes also that if v is a portfolio sequence such that $v'v$ converges to zero and the covariance $\text{cov}(v'r, w'r) = 0$ for all w in that subspace and all v in the sequence, then the variance $\text{var}(v'r)$ converges to zero. The first assumption is that all the factors can be represented as limits (in the Hilbert space norm) of traded assets and the second is that the variances of the incomes on any sequence of portfolios which are well diversified in the limit, and which are uncorrelated with the factors, converge to zero. With

107

these additional assumptions Chamberlain provides explicit lower and upper bounds on the left-hand side of (1.2). He shows further that exact arbitrage pricing obtains if and only if there is a well diversified portfolio on the mean variance frontier.

UTILITY BASED ARGUMENTS. Connor (1984) shows that if the market portfolio is well diversified then every investor holds a well diversified portfolio (i.e. a $K + 1$ fund separation obtains; the funds are associated with the factors and with the risk-free asset which Connor assumes to exist). This and the first order conditions of any investor imply exact arbitrage pricing in a competitive equilibrium.

Connor and Korajczyk (1986) extend Connor's work to a model with investors with better information about returns than most other investors. The former class of investors is sufficiently small, so the pricing result remains intact and is used to derive a test of the superiority of information of the allegedly better informed investors.

Connor and Korajczyk (1985) extend the single period model of Connor to a multi-period model. They assume that the capital assets are the same in all periods, that each period's cash payoffs from these assets obey a factor structure, and that competitive equilibrium prices are set as if the economy had a representative investor who is an exponential utility maximizer. They show that exact arbitrage pricing obtains with time varying risk premia. (But, similar to Stambaugh (1982), with constant factor loadings.)

Chen and Ingersoll (1983) argue that if a well diversified portfolio exists and it is the optimal portfolio of some utility maximizing investor, then the first order conditions of that investor imply exact arbitrage pricing.

Dybvig (1983) and Grinblatt and Titman (1983) consider the finite asset case and provide explicit bounds on the deviations from exact arbitrage pricing. These bounds are functions of the per capita asset supplies, individual bounds on absolute risk aversion, variance of the idiosyncratic risk, and the interest rate. To derive his bound, Dybvig assumes that the support of the distribution of the idiosyncratic term e is bounded below, that each investor's coefficient of absolute risk aversion is non-increasing and that the competitive equilibrium allocation is unconstrained Pareto optimal. To derive their bound, Grinblatt and Titman require a bound on a quantity related to investors' coefficients of absolute risk aversion and the existence of K independent costless well diversified portfolios.

All the utility based developments of the model require that the vector of conditional means $E\{e|f\} = 0$.

ARBITRAGE PRICING AND MEAN VARIANCE EFFICIENCY. The APT was developed as a generalization of the CAPM, which asserts that the expectations of assets' returns are linearly related to their covariances (or betas, which are proportional to the covariances) with the market portfolio's return. Equivalently, the CAPM says that the market portfolio is mean variance efficient in the investment universe containing all possible assets. If the factors in (1.1) can be identified with traded assets then exact arbitrage pricing, (1.2′), says that a portfolio of these factors is mean variance efficient in the investment universe consisting of the assets r.

Huberman and Kandel (1985b), Jobson and Korkie (1982, 1985) and Jobson (1983) note the relation between the APT and mean variance efficiency to propose likelihood ratio tests of the joint hypothesis that a given set of random variables are factors in the statistical model (1.1) and that (1.2′) obtains.

Even when the factors are not traded assets, (1.2′) is a statement about mean variance efficiency: Grinblatt and Titman (1987) suppose that the factor structure (1.1) holds and a riskfree asset is available. They identify K traded assets such

that a portfolio of them is mean variance efficient if and only if (1.2′) holds. The work of Grinblatt and Titman is extended by Huberman, Kandel and Stambaugh (1986) who characterize the sets of K traded positions with that property and show that these assets can be described as portfolios if and only if the global minimum variance portfolio has nonzero systematic risk. To compute these sets of assets one must know the matrices BB' and $E\{ee'\}$. If the latter matrix is diagonal, factor analysis produces estimates of it and of BB'.

The interpretation of (1.2′) as a statement about mean variance efficiency contributes to the debate about the testability of the APT. (Shanken (1983, 1985) and Dybvig and Ross (1985) discuss the APT's testability without mentioning that (1.2′) is a statement about mean variance efficiency.) The theory's silence not only about the factors' identities but also about their number renders any test of the APT a joint test of the pricing relation and the correctness of the factors. As a mean variance efficient portfolio always exists, one can always find 'factors' with respect to which (1.2′) holds.

The factor structure (1.1) imposes restrictions which, combined with (1.2′), provide refutable hypotheses about assets' returns. The factor structure suggests looking for factors with two properties: (i) their time series movements explain a substantial fraction of the time series movements of the returns on the priced assets, and (ii) the unexplained parts of the time series movements of the returns on the priced assets are approximately uncorrelated across the priced assets.

EMPIRICAL WORK. The APT has generated a good deal of empirical work, not all of it as good as it claims to be. Much more empirical work is likely to be written, and by the time this section appears in print, it may seem obsolete; hence its brevity.

The APT is a one period model which makes an assertion about moments of a probability distribution function. That function is held in investors' minds and is not directly observable. The empirical implementation of the model assumes that the observed time series of asset returns are samples from the population which obeys the distribution function assumed in the model. Furthermore, a period of the model is interpreted to be any period with which the researcher feels comfortable (e.g. a day, a week or a month). Hence a licence to use the time series of asset returns to estimate the moments of the probability function which is assumed to be held by investors.

Empirical work inspired by the APT typically ignores (1.2) and studies instead exact arbitrage pricing, (1.2′). It consists of two steps: an estimation of factors (or at least of the matrix B in (1.1)) and then a check to see whether exact arbitrage pricing holds. Thus, these works can be interpreted as joint tests that the matrix B is correctly estimated and that exact arbitrage pricing holds. Estimation of the factor loading matrix B entails at least an implicit identification of the factors.

Three approaches have been used to estimate the matrix B. The first consists of algorithmic analysis of the estimated covariance matrix of asset returns. For instance, Roll and Ross (1980), Chen (1983) and Lehman and Modest (1985a) use factor analysis and Chamberlain and Rothschild (1983) and Connor and Korajczyk (1985, 1986) recommend using principal component analysis.

Factor analysis is a statistically more efficient method to estimate the matrix B in (1.1) than principal component analysis. It is also more expensive computationally. Indeed, it is so expensive that nobody has factor analysed the full covariance matrix $E\{rr'\}$ which has the estimated covariances of all the stocks on the NYSE (let alone the AMEX too). Factor analysis is typically applied to small subsets of asset returns. Lehman and Modest (1985b) compare different methods of factor loading estimation and conclude that the best is maximum likelihood factor analysis which uses as many securities as possible (they have as many as 750 securities in the factor analysis).

The second approach consists of the researcher's staring at the estimated covariance matrix of asset returns and using his judgement to choose factors and subsequently estimate the matrix B. Huberman and Kandel (1985a) note that the correlations of stock returns of firms of different sizes are increasing with the similarity in size. Therefore they choose an index of small firms, one of medium size firms and one of large firms to serve as factors.

The third approach is purely judgemental in that the researcher uses primarily his intuition to pick factors and then estimates the factor loadings and checks if they explain the cross sectional variations in estimated expected returns (i.e., he checks (1.2′)). Chan, Chen and Hsieh (1985) and Chen, Roll and Ross (1986) select financial and macroeconomic variables to serve as factors. They include the derivatives of the following variables: the return on an index of the New York Stock Exchange, the short and long term interest rates on US government debt, a measure of the private sector's default premium, the inflation rate, the growth rate of industrial production and the aggregate consumption rate.

The first two approaches are implemented to conform to the factor structure underlying the APT: the first approach by the algorithmic design and the second because Huberman and Kandel check that the factors they use indeed leave the unexplained parts of asset returns almost uncorrelated. The third approach is implemented without regard for the factor structure. Its attempt to relate assets' expected returns to the covariances of assets' returns with other variables is more in the spirit of Merton's (1973) intertemporal CAPM than in the spirit of the APT.

The empirical work cited above checks exact arbitrage pricing against a few alternatives: that the betas with the market are just as good in explaining the cross sectional variations of assets' mean returns (i.e. against the CAPM), and that other variables have marginal explanatory power above and beyond the factor loadings; these variables include firm size and the variance of the asset's return. Another test of the model, due to Brown and Weinstein (1983), checks the equality of the risk premia u across groups of assets.

By and large, the results support the APT except when it is tested against the alternative that small firms have higher mean returns than large firms even after differences in the factor loadings are accounted for. Results are mixed with respect to this alternative. Chen (1983), Chan, Chen and Hsieh (1985) and Chen, Roll and Ross (1986) and Huberman and Kandel (1985a) fail to reject the null hypothesis that factor loadings alone explain the cross sectional variations in assets' mean returns. Connor and Korajczyk (1985), Lehman and Modest (1985a), and Reinganum (1982) conclude the opposite. Before hastily interpreting this evidence as an overwhelming rejection of the APT, one must keep in mind that the competing model, the CAPM, fares even more poorly against the same alternative.

At the moment, then, the APT seems to describe the data better than competing models. It is wise to recall, however, that the purported empirical success of the APT may well be due to the weakness of the tests employed.

Which factors capture the data best? What are the relations among the factors which different researchers claim to have found? As any test of the APT is a joint test that the factors are correctly identified and that the linear pricing relation holds, we have within the APT's umbrella a host of competing theories. Each one accepts the APT but has its own factor identification procedure. The explosive number of factors and methods to construct them on the one hand, and the absence of a theory that interprets the factors and relates them to other aspects of economics on the other, leave us with a rich research agenda.

GUR HUBERMAN

See also ASSET PRICING MODEL; CAPITAL ASSET PRICING MODEL; FACTOR ANALYSIS; FINANCE.

BIBLIOGRAPHY

Admati, A.R. and Pfleiderer, P. 1985. Interpreting the factor risk premia in the arbitrage pricing theory. *Journal of Economic Theory* 35, 191–5.

Brown, S. and Weinstein, M. 1983. A new approach to testing asset pricing models: the bilinear paradigm. *Journal of Finance* 38, 711–43.

Chamberlain, G. 1983. Funds, factors and diversification in arbitrage pricing models. *Econometrica* 51, 1305–23.

Chamberlain, G. and Rothschild, M. 1983. Arbitrage, factor structure, and mean variance analysis on large asset markets. *Econometrica* 51, 1281–304.

Chan, K.C., Chen, N. and Hsieh, D. 1985. An exploratory investigation of the firm size effect. *Journal of Financial Economics* 14, 451–71.

Chen, N. 1983. Some empirical tests of the theory of arbitrage pricing. *Journal of Finance* 38, 1393–414.

Chen, N. and Ingersoll, J. 1983. Exact pricing in linear factor models with infinitely many assets: a note. *Journal of Finance* 38, 985–8.

Chen, N., Roll, R. and Ross, S.A. 1986. Economic forces and the stock markets. *Journal of Business* 59, 383–403.

Connor, G. 1984. A unified beta pricing theory. *Journal of Economic Theory* 34, 13–31.

Connor, G. and Korajczyk, R.A. 1985. Risk and return in an equilibrium APT: theory and tests. Banking Research Center Working Paper 129, Northwestern University.

Connor, G. and Korajczyk, R.A. 1986. Performance measurement with the arbitrage pricing theory: a framework for analysis. *Journal of Financial Economics* 15, 373–94.

Dhrymes, P., Friend, I. and Gultekin, B. 1984. A critical reexamination of the empirical evidence on the arbitrage pricing theory. *Journal of Finance* 39, 323–46.

Dybvig, P.H. 1983. An explicit bound on deviations from APT pricing in a finite economy. *Journal of Financial Economics* 12, 483–96.

Dybvig, P.H. and Ross, S.A. 1985. Yes, the APT is testable. *Journal of Finance* 40, 1173–88.

Gehr, A., Jr. 1978. Some tests of the arbitrage pricing theory. *Journal of the Midwest Finance Association* 7, 91–106.

Grinblatt, M. and Titman, S. 1983. Factor pricing in a finite economy. *Journal of Financial Economics* 12, 495–507.

Grinblatt, M. and Titman, S. 1987. The relation between mean-variance efficiency and arbitrage pricing. *Journal of Business*.

Huberman, G. 1982. A simple approach to arbitrage pricing. *Journal of Economic Theory* 28, 183–91.

Huberman, G. and Kandel, S. 1985a. A size based stock returns model. Center for Research in Security Prices Working Paper 148, University of Chicago.

Huberman, G. and Kandel S. 1985b. Likelihood ratio tests of asset pricing and mutual fund separation. Center for Research in Security Prices Working Paper 149, University of Chicago.

Huberman, G., Kandel, S. and Stambaugh, R. 1986. Mimicking portfolios and exact arbitrage pricing. Center for Research in Security Prices Working Paper 165, University of Chicago. *Journal of Finance*, 1987.

Ingersoll, J. 1984. Some results in the theory of arbitrage pricing. *Journal of Finance* 39(4), 1021–39.

Jobson, J.D. 1982. A multivariate linear regression test of the arbitrage pricing theory. *Journal of Finance* 37, 1037–42.

Jobson, J.D. and Korkie, B. 1982. Potential performance and tests of portfolio efficiency. *Journal of Financial Economics* 10, 433–66.

Jobson, J.D. and Korkie, B. 1985. Some tests of linear asset pricing with multivariate normality. *Canadian Journal of Administrative Sciences* 2, 114–38.

Lehman, B. and Modest, D. 1985a. The empirical foundations of the arbitrage pricing theory I: the empirical tests. Department of Economics Working Paper 291, Columbia University.

Lehman, B. and Modest, D. 1985b. The empirical foundations of the arbitrage pricing theory II: the optimal construction of basis portfolios. Department of Economics Working Paper 292, Columbia University.

Merton, R. 1973. An intertemporal capital asset pricing model. *Econometrica* 41, 867–87.

Reinganum, M. 1981. The arbitrage pricing theory: some simple tests. *Journal of Finance* 36, 313–22.

Roll, R. and Ross, S.A. 1980. An empirical investigation of the arbitrage pricing theory. *Journal of Finance* 35, 1073–103.

Roll, R. and Ross, S.A. 1984. A critical reexamination of the empirical evidence on the arbitrage pricing theory. *Journal of Finance* 39, 347–50.

Ross, S.A. 1976a. The arbitrage theory of capital asset pricing. *Journal of Economic Theory* 13, 341–60.

Ross, S.A. 1976b. Risk, return and arbitrage. In *Risk Return in Finance*, ed. I. Friend and J. Bicksler, Cambridge, Mass.: Ballinger.

Shanken, J. 1982. The arbitrage pricing theory: is it testable?. *Journal of Finance* 37(5), 1129–240.

Shanken, J. 1985. A multi-beta CAPM or equilibrium APT?: a reply. *Journal of Finance* 40, 1189–96.

Stambaugh, R. 1983. Arbitrage pricing with information. *Journal of Financial Economics* 12, 357–69.

arbitration.   Arbitration is the process of resolving disputes between two or more parties in which an individual or a board of arbitrators is authorized to appraise the facts and contending positions and to render a decision binding on the parties to the proceeding.

Arbitration is most extensively used in industrial relations, in disputes between labour organizations and managements. The process has been adapted to a widening variety of disputes such as in some landlord–tenant issues, divorce settlements, home or product warranties, in the interpretation of some commercial contracts and even in the settlement of some international questions, as in relative fishing rights between two countries.

Arbitration is said to be *voluntary* when the parties agree voluntarily to enter the process and to be bound by the decision. Arbitration is said to be *compulsory* when the parties are required by law to submit the dispute to a determination and to be bound by the decision. In voluntary arbitration the disputing parties are typically free to frame the question to be resolved, to select the arbitrator or the process of selection, to elect the form of arbitration and to shape the timing and the process. They also typically pay for the arbitration service. Under compulsory arbitration the parties may also have some role in selecting the arbitrator, or in the process of selection, or in influencing features of the process, but they have no choice but to submit to an arbitration procedure often specified in detail in statute.

Arbitration is to be distinguished from mediation, conciliation and fact-finding. While these processes are also widely used to facilitate the resolution of disputes, unlike arbitration there is no authorization to render a decision that is binding on the parties. Mediators typically seek to persuade contending parties to agree, and fact-finders typically make specific recommendations for a voluntary settlement, but they have no authority to issue a binding award.

The world of experience does not readily fit neatly into these definitional boxes; arbitration proceedings may involve mediation, and an arbitration award may in fact reflect full agreement of the parties, and the parties may prefer that the arbitrator(s) take responsibility for the 'award' before the public and their constituencies. The 'award' may in fact be an agreement of the parties or their representatives.

Arbitration is not a single invariant process, since at least in voluntary arbitration the parties have wide latitude to shape its form apart from the selection of the arbitrator(s). Arbitration may be of the last-best-offer variant in which the parties each present to the arbitrator(s) a final position, and the arbitrator(s) is required to select only one or the other proposal. By contrast in conventional arbitration the decision need not adopt either of the contending positions. The parties may also shape the arbitration process by defining the limits on the authority delegated to the arbitrator. The arbitrator may be restricted to the application or interpretation of an agreement or in the remedy the arbitrator may specify. Each of the parties may appoint an arbitrator, or a non-voting assessor to sit with an arbitrator, and they may in turn select the chair. The voting within the board of arbitration may be by majority vote or by the single vote of the chair, materially affecting the outcome in some cases. Thus the parties to the dispute may design the voluntary arbitration process in a wide variety of ways.

In the industrial relations system of the United States the distinction is drawn, as was not drawn historically in England, between issues of right (questions over the interpretation and application of a collective agreement) and issues of interest (questions concerning the terms of an agreement or issues outside an agreement). This distinction has been fundamental in the United States to the role of the grievance and arbitration procedure, the specified duration of collective agreements and the no-strike no-lockout provisions that limit industrial conflict in the United States .

Historically, in Great Britain, collective agreements had no fixed duration; an agreement could be reopened by either party on specified notice or with a specified change in some exterior event such as prices or trade. A dispute between a labour union and a management could equally be over an interpretation of an existing agreement or over a proposed change in the agreement itself. Such a distinction was not made. A strike or lockout could as readily be used as a tool to reach agreement in either case. Arbitration had no special role except as might be agreed upon in the particular dispute.

In the United States, in contrast, disputes over the interpretation or application of the agreement came voluntarily in many industries historically to be referred to standing arbitration tribunals or ad hoc arbitrators. The strike or lockout was precluded during the term of the agreement. Arbitration of issues of interpretation and application was the quid pro quo for both parties for giving up resort to economic force for a limited period. A no-strike, no-lockout clause was not possible in a labour agreement of any extended duration without arbitration to resolve grievances over the interpretation or application of that agreement.

This role for grievance arbitration in the United States long antedates the labour legislation of the 1930s or the 1960 decision of the Supreme Court in the *Steelworkers' Trilogy* that established a limited role for the courts to review arbitration awards. Thus the Anthracite Board of Conciliation, set up in 1903, and an early 'intermittent' umpire, Judge George A. Gray, established the rule that 'the Board could not write the law, but could only interpret it.' The clothing industries early used impartial umpires to settle disputes over piece rates and other terms of the agreement, but they also had a role in helping the parties by mediation and at times by arbitration to settle the terms of collective agreements. As industrial plants were organized on an industrial basis, the principle was carried over into these collective agreements with each collective bargaining relationship designing its own grievance arbitration procedures.

Beyond grievance arbitration in the United States, which encompasses the largest part of industrial relations arbitration, there are significant instances of arbitration over the terms of collective agreements, particularly in the public sector in some states.

There have been at least two contending views as to the nature of the arbitration process and the considerations that lead to the decision of the arbitrator. One view is that arbitrators act like judges are supposed to act: they weigh the facts and arguments against the standards and precedents urged by the parties to the conflict and render a decision with an articulated opinion. Another view is that arbitrators are primarily concerned to achieve a mutually acceptable solution, a position that the parties themselves would have achieved in their bargaining or administration had it not been frustrated and fallen short of full agreement. There are, no doubt, pairs of parties and arbitrators that follow each perspective; others fall in between. In their bargaining the parties seek to shape the process and the choice of arbitrators accordingly.

JOHN T. DUNLOP

See also BARGAINING; INDUSTRIAL RELATIONS; STRIKES AND LOCK-OUTS; TRADE UNIONS.

BIBLIOGRAPHY

Aaron, B. 1983. No labour courts, little arbitration: what's wrong with that? In *Comparative Industrial Relations: A Trans-Atlantic Dialogue*, Washington, DC: Bureau of National Affairs, 56–70.

Donovan, Lord. (Chairman.) 1968. *Royal Commission on Trade Unions and Employer Associations*. Cmd 3623. London: HMSO.

Dunlop, J.T. 1984. *Dispute Resolution, Negotiation and Consensus Building*. Dover, Mass.: Auburn House.

Elkouri, F. and Elkouri, E.A. 1985. *How Arbitration Works*. 4th edn, Washington, DC: BNA Books.

Kennedy, T. 1948. *Effective Labor Arbitration: The Impartial Chairmanship of the Full-Fashioned Hosiery Industry*. Philadelphia: University of Pennsylvania.

Lester, R.A. 1984. *Labor Arbitration in State and Local Government*. Princeton: Industrial Relations Section.

Lowell, J.S. 1893. *Industrial Arbitration and Conciliation*. New York: Putnam's Sons.

National Academy of Arbitrations. 1943 onwards. *Proceedings of the Annual Meetings*. Washington, DC: BNA.

Stevens, C.M. 1966. Is compulsory arbitration compatible with bargaining? *Industrial Relations Review* 5(2), February, 38–52.

Suffern, A.E. 1915. *Conciliation and Arbitration in the Coal Industry of America*. Boston: Houghton-Mifflin.

Walker, K.F. 1970. *Australian Industrial Relations Systems*. Cambridge, Mass.: Harvard University Press .

ARIMA models. Autoregressive-integrated-moving average (ARIMA) models are models which can be fitted to a single time series and used to make predictions of future observations. They owe their popularity primarily to the work of Box and Jenkins (1970), who defined the class of ARIMA and seasonal ARIMA models and provided a methodology for selecting a suitable model from that class.

The ARIMA class of models emerged as the result of a synthesis between the theory of stationary stochastic processes and certain *ad hoc* forecasting procedures based on the discounting of past observations. From the theoretical point of view the ability of an autoregressive-moving average (ARMA) process to approximate any linear stationary process was well known. On the other hand, it had been shown by Muth (1960) that the forecasts generated by the exponentially weighted moving average (EWMA) procedure, i.e.

$$\hat{y}_{t+1/t} = \lambda y_t + (1 - \lambda)\hat{y}_{t/t-1}, \tag{1}$$

where $\hat{y}_{t+1/t}$ is the prediction of y_{t+1} made at time t and λ is the smoothing constant, are identical to the optimal one step ahead forecasts which result when the differenced observations are modelled by a first order moving average process, i.e.

$$\Delta y_t = \xi_t + \theta\xi_{t-1}, \tag{2}$$

where ξ_t is a random disturbance term, Δ is the first difference operator and the MA parameter, θ, is equal to $\lambda - 1$. This result was extended to show that the forecasts produced by Holt's local linear trend procedure is the same as those given by a model in which second differences follow a second-order moving average process,

$$\Delta^2 y_t = \xi_t + \theta_1\xi_{t-1} + \theta_2\xi_{t-2}; \tag{3}$$

see Theil and Wage (1964), Nerlove and Wage (1964) and Harrison (1967). The nature of the synthesis effected by Box and Jenkins was to formulate a class of models in which the dth difference of the observations was taken to be stationary and hence capable of approximation by an ARMA process with p autoregressive parameters, $\phi_1, \ldots, \phi_p$ and q moving average parameters $\theta_1, \ldots, \theta_q$, i.e.

$$\Delta^d y_t = \phi_1\Delta^d y_{t-1} + \cdots + \phi_p\Delta^d y_{t-p}$$
$$+ \xi_t + \theta_1\xi_{t-1} + \cdots + \theta_q\xi_{t-q}. \tag{4}$$

The specification of (4) is denoted by writing it as ARIMA (p, d, q). Thus (2) is ARIMA $(0, 1, 1)$ while (3) is ARIMA $(0, 2, 2)$.

Given the ARIMA class of models, it was necessary to provide a methodology for choosing a suitable model from the class. Box and Jenkins (1970) proposed a model selection cycle based on three stages: identification, estimation and diagnostic checking. In the identification stage tentative choices are made for the values of p, d and q using statistical tools such as the correlogram and the sample partial autocorrelation function. Given a specification of these values, the parameters in the model are estimated by maximum likelihood (ML) or an approximation to maximum likelihood. The residuals from the model are then subject to diagnostic checking to determine if they appear to be approximately random. If the model fails these diagnostic checks the complete cycle is repeated, starting with an attempt to identify a new model. Once a suitable model has been fitted, it can be used to make predictions of future observations, together with estimates of the corresponding mean square errors.

ARIMA models of the form (4) are not, in general, appropriate for modelling monthly and quarterly observations as these typically contain a seasonal pattern. However, Box and Jenkins (1970, ch. 9) observed that taking an EWMA of the observations combined with an EWMA of the observations on the current month in previous years, not only produced a viable forecasting procedure but could also be rationalized by the stochastic process

$$\Delta\Delta_s y_t = (1 + \theta L)(1 + \Theta L^s)\xi_t \tag{5}$$

where Δ_s is the seasonal difference operator, and θ and Θ are parameters. Generalizing (5) gives the class of multiplicative seasonal ARIMA processes, in which a model of order $(p, d, q) \times (P, D, Q)_s$ is specified as

$$\phi(L)\Phi(L^s)\Delta^d\Delta_s^D y_t = \theta(L)\Theta(L^s)\xi_t, \tag{6}$$

where $\phi(L)$, $\Phi(L^s)$, $\theta(L)$ and $\Theta(L^s)$ are polynomials in the lag operator of order p, P, q and Q respectively. The methodology for selecting a model for the seasonal ARIMA class is essentially the same as that developed for the ARIMA class.

The application of the model selection methodology advocated by Box and Jenkins (1970) is not without its problems. Unless the sample size is very large, which it rarely is in economics, it is difficult to identify an ARIMA model of any degree of complexity using the correlogram and the sample partial autocorrelation function. These difficulties become even more acute when the observations have been differenced. One way of avoiding these problems is to select models by an automatic procedure, using a measure of goodness of fit such as the Akaike Information Criterion (AIC). This approach is now quite common, although it does move away from the spirit of the work of Box and Jenkins (1970), which emphasized the need for judgement on the part of the statistician.

A more radical criticism of Box–Jenkins methodology concerns the suitability of the ARIMA class itself. There is no overwhelming reason why an economic time series should, after an appropriate amount of differencing, be stationary. Furthermore, even if the stationarity assumption is a reasonable one for a differenced series, it does not follow that approximating the differenced series by an ARMA (p, q) process will necessarily lead to a model with desirable properties for forecasting. Some illustrations of this point can be found in Harvey and Todd (1983) and Harvey (1985). Thus while the ARIMA class may often be too restrictive because of its reliance on stationarity, it can also be argued that it is too general. Given the difficulties which arise in applying the Box–Jenkins methodology, it follows that there is ample scope for selecting an inappropriate model. As the examples cited by Jenkins (1982) show, the use of an automatic model selection procedure is only likely to make matters worse.

Recent work has suggested an alternative to ARIMA models, based on the idea that the components known to exist in economic time series, for example trends, seasonals and perhaps even cycles, are modelled explicitly. These components are unobserved but may be handled statistically by means of the state space form as in, say, Kitagawa (1981) or Harvey and Todd (1983). Thus more *a priori* information is put into the initial specification and the model selection methodology is closer to that of econometrics; see Harvey (1985). Following the terminology of simultaneous equation systems in econometrics, Engle (1978) has termed such models 'structural' models. If the model is linear, the 'reduced form' is an ARIMA process. Within this framework the reduced form provides a valid means of constructing forecasts, but it does not provide any direct information which can be used to describe the nature of the series in terms of components of interest.

A.C. HARVEY

See also AUTOEGRESSIVE TIME SERIES ANALYSIS; STATIONARY TIME SERIES; TIME SERIES ANALYSIS.

BIBLIOGRAPHY

Box, G.E.P. and Jenkins, G.M. 1970. *Time Series Analysis: Forecasting and Control.* San Francisco: Holden-Day.
Engle, R.F. 1978. Estimating structural models of seasonality. In *Seasonal Analysis of Economic Time Series,* ed. A. Zellner, Washington DC, Bureau of the Census, 281–308.
Harrison, P.J. 1967. Exponential smoothing and short-term sales forecasting. *Management Science* 13, 821–42.
Harvey, A.C. 1985. Trends and cycles in macroeconomic time series. *Journal of Business and Economic Statistics* 3, 216–27.
Harvey, A.C. and Todd, P.H.J. 1983. Forecasting economic time series with structural and Box–Jenkins models: a case study (with discussion). *Journal of Business and Economic Statistics* 1, 229–315.
Jenkins, G.M. 1982. Some practical aspects of forecasting in organisations. *Journal of Forecasting* 1, 3–21.
Kitagawa, G. 1981. A nonstationary time series model and its fitting by a recursive filter. *Journal of Time Series Analysis* 2, 103–16.
Muth, J.F. 1960. Optimal properties of exponentially weighted forecasts. *Journal of the American Statistical Association* 55, 299-306.
Nerlove, M. and Wage, S. 1964. On the optimality of adaptive forecasting. *Management Science* 10, 207–24.
Theil, H. and Wage, S. 1964. Some observations on adaptive forecasting. *Management Science* 10, 198–206.

Aristotle (384–322 BC). Aristotle (born Stagira, 384 BC, died Chalcis, 322), spent twenty years from the age of seventeen at Plato's Academy in Athens, to which city he returned in 335 to establish his own school, the Lyceum. He presided over the Lyceum until the death of Alexander the Great (whom he had once tutored) in 323. He then left Athens and died shortly thereafter.

Aristotle has been rightly called a 'universal genius': his works range over formal logic, epistemology and metaphysics; among the natural sciences, physics, meteorology and zoology; also ethics, politics, rhetoric and aesthetics. In each his contribution was a major one, as he defined and codified the subject-matter and indeed created much of the language required for scientific and philosophical discourse. He also established the first wide-ranging research organization, which collected masses of data that Aristotle and his associates employed for their systematic analyses.

The subject notably absent from this great corpus of research and publication is economics. The pseudo-Aristotelian work called *Oikonomikos* is no exception. Apart from the fact that it is a relatively late concoction, almost certainly not a single work in origin (whenever that was), the title and Book 3 (known only from a medieval Latin version) represent a type of literature on 'household management', now best represented from classical antiquity by the *Oikonomikos* of Xenophon, written in the first half of the 4th century BC, in which 'management' of the mistress and slaves of the household occupy a central role, but what we call 'economics' none at all. The other two books of the pseudo-Aristotelian compilation deal anecdotally with public revenue, but in large part only with the devices, based on force and fraud, employed by tyrants and other rulers in order to squeeze funds out of their subjects. In a rudimentary sense, therefore, there is an economic component in the work, but neither analysis nor any general conceptions.

For the latter there are only two relevant passages in the Aristotelian corpus, both of them digressions. One is in the *Politics* (1256a1–58b8) in the context of the 'natural' and 'unnatural' modes of acquiring wealth, the other in the *Nicomachean Ethics* (1132b20–34a24) in the context of the forms of justice. There has been a serious, though intermittent, modern discussion of these passages, chiefly among historians of economic thought, but there was no visible interest in antiquity. The period of paramount practical interest in Aristotle's economics was the later Middle Ages, from the early 13th century on, with Thomas Aquinas as the leading spirit. That was the time when Aristotle was both the great authority for the Church's assault on usury, for which the textual basis was firm and indeed obvious, and the authority for the doctrine of 'just price', which was in fact not Aristotelian but the consequence of a mistranslation (or at least a misinterpretation) by his Latin translators.

The digression in the *Politics* begins by establishing five means of 'natural' acquisition – pasturage, agriculture, hunting, fishing and, surprisingly to us, piracy; proceeds to indicate that as human groups became larger it became necessary to import necessaries lacking locally; argues that money was then invented to facilitate such acquisitions, then that money became converted into a good in itself and that its acquisition through profit, called *chrematistics*, was unnatural, with the taking of interest the worst of all. There is no concern here with how value in exchange is determined. For that one turns to the *Ethics*, where, after distinguishing distributive from corrective justice, Aristotle proceeds to digress about justice in exchange. His problem is the achievement of justice in the determination of exchange values, and the few pages are repetitive and unclear, as if the author were thinking aloud in a discussion or lecture. In consequence, virtually every translator and commentator since the Middle Ages has 'interpreted' Aristotle's thought to fit his own notions. The key sentences are these: 'There will therefore be genuine reciprocity when (the products) have been equalized, so that as farmer is to shoemaker, so is that of the shoemaker's product to that of the farmer's.' In that way, there will be no excess, which would be immoral, but 'each will have his own' (1133a33–b3).

This is repeated within a few lines and there can be no question that Aristotle meant 'as farmer is to shoemaker' to be taken literally. But to do so is intolerable under conventional economic thinking. Most commentators have therefore transmuted the thinking, and in the process they have reduced Aristotle's economic ideas to insignificance. No wonder that Schumpeter (1954, p. 57) dismissed Aristotle's analysis as 'decorous, pedestrian, slightly mediocre, and more than slightly pompous common sense'. However, on a straight reading of Aristotle's words, the conclusion seems clear to me that he never pretended to examine the price mechanism or any other aspect of market exchange *as it was practised*. He was offering a normative ethical analysis: much that went on in practice was unethical on his definition and therefore outside his discourse.

In sum, there is no economic analysis in Aristotle, not even in intention; judgements of his performance on that score or attempts to interpret his words so as to rescue them as economic analysis are doomed from the outset. In the more then fifteen years since I published this exposition at some length, I have seen no acceptable refutation of it in neoclassical economic terms, and I believe none to be possible. A more serious effort has been made by some Marxists, most powerfully in a sophisticated polemic by Meikle (1979), who argues that a Marxist view (and only a Marxist view) warrants a positive evaluation of Aristotle's efforts at economic analysis. I remain unpersuaded, firstly because the underlying proposition that Aristotle's age saw the rise for the first time of a genuine system of commodity production, which Aristotle appreciated and sought to grapple with, is one I hold to be historically false; secondly because Meikle fails to consider the critical phrase, 'as farmer is to shoemaker', which I believe undermines his interpretation. And there the debate stands.

M.I. FINLEY

See also CHREMATISTICS.

BIBLIOGRAPHY

Aristotle. *Nicomachean Ethics*. Trans. H. Rackham, London: Heinemann; Cambridge, Mass.: Harvard University Press (The Loeb Classical Library), revised edn, 1934.

Aristotle. *Politics*. Trans. E. Barker, Oxford: Clarendon, 1946.

Finley, M.I. 1970. Aristotle and economic analysis. *Past and Present* 47, May, 5–25.

Langholm, O. 1983. *Wealth and Money in the Aristotelian Tradition*. Oslo: Universitetsforlaget.

Langholm, O. 1984. *The Aristotelian Analysis of Usury*. Oslo: Universitetsforlaget.

Meikle, S. 1979. Aristotle and the political economy of the polis. *Journal of Hellenic Studies* 99, 57–73.

Schumpeter, J. 1954. *History of Economic Analysis*. New York: Oxford University Press.

arms races. Just as supply and demand curves have structured thinking about markets, most recent analytical work on arms races has been structured by two equations proposed by Lewis Fry Richardson (1881–1953), a Quaker and Fellow of the Royal Society, known also for his publications on meteorology and his quantification of war. His studies, begun during the First World War, only gained wider recognition with the posthumous publication of two books collecting his work, Richardson (1960a,b). His theories are reviewed in Rapoport (1957) and some biographical details are given in Richardson (1957).

The Richardson equations relate the evolution, over time (t), of the level of Arms, $A_i(t)$, for countries $i = 1, 2$; by an action–reaction process of the form:

$$dA_1(t)/dt = a_1 + b_1 A_2(t) - c_1 A_1(t)$$
$$dA_2(t)/dt = a_2 + b_2 A_1(t) - c_2 A_2(t)$$

The lower case letters denote parameters. The a's measure the exogenous increases in arms in each country; the b's the feedbacks as increases in the arms of one country stimulate the other to increase its arms; the c's the stabilizing fatigue effect by which larger stocks of arms reduce further increases. The model can also be given a familiar economic stock-adjustment interpretation, where

$$A_i(t)^* = d_i + e_i A_j(t);$$

and

$$dA_i(t)/dt = f_i[A_i(t)^* - A_i(t)]$$

with $A_i(t)^*$ being target levels of arms and f_i being adjustment coefficients.

This simple framework, with its analogies to mechanical and ecological models, has proved tremendously powerful in organizing thought about military interactions; raising research questions and allowing systematic discussion and comparison of the results. There are a great variety of results available, their precise form depending on the exact formulation of the model. However, the questions which naturally arise include the following.

1. What are the characteristics of the solution to this system and under what conditions will the interaction converge to a stable equilibrium? Richardson associated an explosive solution with the eventual outbreak of a war, but this interpretation has been widely challenged. The effect on the solution of more countries, alliances, different forms of equation for different types of country, non-linearities, and the like has also been investigated.

2. How should the A_i be measured: in physical stocks (number of missiles, warheads, battleships, etc.) or in monetary flows of military expenditure?

3. How should the parameters be interpreted and what are their likely values? Models of strategic calculation have been developed which give rise to reaction functions of this form and provide an interpretation of the parameters in terms of war-fighting considerations. The model can also be linked to game

theory and optimal control representations of the arms race to provide interpretations and likely values of the parameters.

4. How should the budget constraint be included in the model? The c_is are sometimes interpreted as measuring exhaustion effects, reflecting the economic burden of accumulating arms, or the A_i are measured by the shares of military expenditure in national income to proxy the economic constraints. But these adjustments are rather ad hoc. Once an explicit budget constraint is introduced, the arms race can be interpreted not just in terms of accumulating weapons for a potential war, but also in terms of imposing economic costs on the opponent; inducing them to spend so much on arms that they will bankrupt themselves.

5. What are the dynamics of the process? The model can be elaborated to allow for perception and decision lags, various types of expectation formation (rational or adaptive), and the possibility of deception.

6. How do you stop it? The Richardson type of framework has been used to consider what changes in institutional arrangements could damp the feedbacks or perhaps make the process run in reverse.

7. How can the model be estimated and tested? There are clearly problems of measurement, identification, and dynamic and stochastic specification that arise before the basic model is suitable for econometric application, and a variety of attempts have been made to solve these problems. There is also the difficulty that the parameters of the model, arising from game-theory or strategic calculations by the countries concerned, are unlikely to be stable over time.

Arms races appear to be pervasive phenomena, from the competitive accumulation of nuclear and conventional weapons by the super-powers to the regional competitions between countries like Greece and Turkey; Israel and the Arab States; and India and Pakistan. Arms races, thus, seem to be a characteristic form of international interaction. However, in general the quantitative evidence for the Richardson type action–reaction model has not been compelling, except perhaps for the relatively rare cases where there has been an explicit matching policy, such as the pre-1914 Anglo-German naval competition. Otherwise, the variety of complicating factors make econometric application and testing problematic.

There is also considerable criticism of the rather mechanical conception of an arms race embodied in the Richardson formulation. Instead, it is argued that the process is driven by autonomous forces in each country (objective evaluations of security needs or domestic political and economic pressures for military expenditure) rather than by some simple feedback process with an opponent. On this interpretation any observed correlations in arms are largely spurious.

The literature which addresses the questions raised above is vast and much of it is published in the *Journal of Conflict Resolution*. For economists who wish to get a taste of the issues, the theoretical paper by Intriligator (1975) and the discussion of econometric results by McGuire (1977 and 1981) and Desai and Blake (1981), provide a good entry. These papers are all concerned with the arms race in nuclear weapons between the US and USSR.

R. P. Smith

See also MILITARY EXPENDITURES; WAR ECONOMY.

BIBLIOGRAPHY

Desai, M. and Blake, N. 1981. Modelling the ultimate absurdity: a comment on 'A Quantitative Study of the Strategic Arms Race in the Missile Age'. *Review of Economics and Statistics* 63(4), November, 629–32.

Intriligator, M. 1975. Strategic considerations in the Richardson model of arms races. *Journal of Political Economy* 83, April, 339–54.

McGuire, M. 1977. A quantitative study of the strategic arms race in the missile age. *Review of Economics and Statistics* 59(3), August, 328–39.

McGuire, M. 1981. A quantitative study of the strategic arms race in the missile age: a reply. *Review of Economics and Statistics* 63(4), November, 632–3.

Rapoport, A. 1957. Lewis F. Richardson's mathematical theory of war. *Journal of Conflict Resolution* 1(3), 239–99.

Richardson, L.F. 1960a. *Arms and Insecurity: A Mathematical Study of the Causes and Origins of Wars*. Pittsburgh: Boxwood.

Richardson, L.F. 1960b. *Statistics of Deadly Quarrels*. Pittsburgh: Boxwood.

Richardson, S.A. 1957. Lewis Fry Richardson (1881–1953): a personal biography. *Journal of Conflict Resolution* 1(3), 300–304.

Armstrong, Wallace Edwin (1892–1980).   Born in England in 1892, W.E. Armstrong won an exhibition to Sidney Sussex College, Cambridge before World War I. At the outbreak of war he joined the Royal Medical Corps, but was wounded in action in 1915 and subsequently lost a leg. He returned to Cambridge and completed his degree in the Moral Sciences Tripos in 1918.

In his final year at Cambridge, Armstrong concentrated on psychology and was introduced to W.H.R. Rivers who interested him in anthropology. After completing his degree Armstrong studied anthropology under Haddon and from 1919 carried out field research in Papua New Guinea. Armstrong first worked in South-Eastern Papua, and early in 1921 was engaged by the Papuan government to collect further ethnographic material in this region (Armstrong 1922). He was later appointed Assistant Anthropologist to the government and spent two months on Rossel (Yela) Island in the far east of South-Eastern Papua.

Rossel Island was little known, but had acquired an infamous reputation after a French ship carrying over three hundred Chinese to Australia was wrecked on its coasts in 1858. Nearly all the survivors were killed and eaten by the islanders (Armstrong 1928a, Appendix 1). Anthropologically, the island is of considerable interest as its people speak a non-Austronesian language in contrast to the mostly Austronesian-speaking inhabitants of the Massim area to the west. Armstrong was probably attracted to the island on account of its ethnological significance, but his initial intention had been to study the islanders' kinship system. In the course of his research he discovered a unique 'monetary' system and concentrated on this aspect of the island's culture. The majority of Armstrong's ethnographic writings are concerned with the monetary system (Armstrong, 1923/24; 1924a; 1924b).

In 1922 Armstrong returned to Cambridge, where he was appointed to a temporary lectureship in social anthropology until 1925/26 when, because of changes in the teaching of anthropology, his post was not renewed, and his career in anthropology effectively ended. During the early 1920s Armstrong had become interested in economics and from 1926 to 1939 he acted as supervisor and occasional lecturer in economics at Cambridge. In 1939 he accepted a post as lecturer in economics at the University of Southampton. Eventually, after steady promotion, he became Professor of Economic Theory in the University and retired in 1961. He spent some of his retirement at the University of the West Indies (Armstrong et al., 1974). He died in 1980.

Armstrong's transformation from anthropologist to neoclassical economist did not involve a complete break with his intellectual past. The interest in psychology and *a priori* reasoning which he displayed in his anthropological writings (Urry, 1985) equipped him well for his career as a neoclassical theorist. What he did abandon, though, was an interest in empirical research. His contributions to economics were all in the area of pure theory and his arguments illustrated by use of counterfactual examples. For example his book, *Saving and Investment* (1936), explores the logical consequences of the assumption that human beings equate the marginal disutility of labour with the marginal utility of the product. A remarkable feature of this book is the extended use of the 'Robinson Crusoe' model of an imaginary island economy. Actual island economies bear no relation to this imaginary model and Armstrong's anthropological colleagues, such as Malinowski (1921; 1922) and Mauss (1925) were particularly critical of economists for this reason. Armstrong was well aware of these criticisms but never addressed them nor did he concern himself with empirical work or anthropology ever again.

Following the publication of his book (1936) Armstrong turned to the utility controversy. He developed a cardinal theory of utility (1939; 1948) and attempted to dismiss the ordinal theory on logical grounds (1950, p. 119). This involved him in a debate with Little (1950) and Georgescu-Roegen (1954) among others.

While Armstrong's book (1936) has passed largely unnoticed – his Pigovian-inspired theory was, after all, published in the same year as Keynes's *General Theory* – his writings on utility have attracted some attention. Ng (1975), for example, acknowledges his debt to Armstrong.

Armstrong's place in the history of anthropological thought is more secure. His ideas, while now outdated (Liep, 1983; Urry, 1985), are nevertheless of continued interest. His description of the Rossel Island 'monetary' system was until recently the only primary source on the subject and stimulated much secondary research.

C.A. GREGORY AND JAMES URRY

SELECTED WORKS

1922. Report on Suau Tawala. *Annual Report 1920–21* Melbourne: Government Printer.

1923/24. Rossel Island religion. *Anthropos* 18/19, 1-11.

1924a. Rossel Island money: a unique monetary system. *Economic Journal* 34, 423–9.

1924b. Shell money from Rossel Island, Papua. *Man* 24, 161–2.

1928a. *Rossel Island: An Ethnological Study*. Cambridge: Cambridge University Press.

1928b. Social Constructiveness III. *British Journal of Psychology* 18, 366–99.

1936. *Saving and Investment*. London: Routledge.

1939. The determinateness of the utility function. *Economic Journal* 49, 453–67.

1948. Uncertainty and the utility function. *Economic Journal* 58, 1–10.

1950. A note in the theory of consumer's behaviour. *Oxford Economic Papers* 2, 119–22.

1951. Utility and the theory of welfare. *Oxford Economic Papers* 3, 259–71.

1953. Marginal preference and the theory of welfare. *Oxford Economic Papers* 5, 249–63.

1955. Concerning marginal utility. *Oxford Economic Papers* 7, 170–76.

1958. Utility and the 'ordinalist fallacy'. *Review of Economic Studies* 25, 172–81.

BIBLIOGRAPHY

Armstrong, W.E., Daniel, S. and Francis, A.A. 1974. A structural analysis of the Barbados economy, 1968, with an application to the tourist industry. *Social and Economic Studies* 23, 493–520.

Georgescu-Roegen, N. 1954. Choice, expectations and measurability. *Quarterly Journal of Economics* 68, 503–34.

Liep, J. 1983. Ranked exchange in Yela (Rossel Island). In *The Kula*, ed. J.W. Leach and E.R. Leach, Cambridge: Cambridge University Press.

Little, I.M.D. 1950. The theory of consumer's behaviour: a comment.*Oxford Economic Papers* 2, 132–6.

Malinowski, B. 1921. The primitive economy of the Trobriand Islanders. *Economic Journal* 31, 1–16.

Malinowski, B. 1922. *Argonauts of the Western Pacific*. London: Routledge & Kegan Paul

Mauss, M. 1925. *The Gift*. London: Routledge & Kegan Paul.

Ng, Y-K. 1975. Bentham or Bergson? Finite sensibility, utility functions and social welfare functions. *Review of Economic Studies* 42, 545–69.

Urry, J. 1985. W.E. Armstrong and Social Anthropology at Cambridge. *Man* 20, 412–23.

Arndt, Heinz Wolfgang (born 1915).   Born February 1915 in Breslau, Germany (now Wroclaw, Poland), Arndt was educated at Oxford University (1933–38) and London School of Economics (1938–41). After two years as a research assistant at the Royal Institute of International Affairs, Arndt was Assistant Lecturer in Economics, University of Manchester (1943–46), Senior Lecturer, University of Sydney (1946–50) and then Professor of Economics in the School of General Studies and Research School of Pacific Studies. Australian National University (1951–80). He became Emeritus Professor of Economics, Australian National University in 1981. His many prestigious appointments include Member, Governing Council, United Nations Asian Institute for Economic Development and Planning (1969–75); Deputy Director, OECD (1972) and Chairman, Expert Group on Structural Change and Economic Growth Commonwealth Secretariat (1980).

Arndt first came to prominence in 1944 with his analytical economic analysis of the interwar period in which he argued the structuralist thesis that market forces could not correct the existing major disequilibria in the world economy. He recommended cooperative planning in the postwar period, involving controls on the volume and directions of international trade and investment and international cooperation if not supranational economic authorities.

His major contributions have been in policy-oriented economic research with particular reference to developing countries in the Pacific Basin. A leading authority on the Indonesian economy as well as other Asian economies, led Arndt to start the BIES in 1965 and the establishment in the Australian National University of a major research school on Asian economic development.

A prolific writer, Arndt was an important influence in Australian academic and policy circles in developing postwar understanding and acceptance of Keynesian macro-economic analysis.

R.D. FREEMAN

SELECTED WORKS

1944. *The Economic Lessons of the Nineteen-Thirties*. Oxford: Oxford University Press. Reprinted London: Frank Cass & Co., 1963; Italian trans., 1949, Japanese trans. 1978.

1954. A suggestion for simplifying the theory of international capital movements. *Economia Internazionale* 7, August, 469–81.

1955. External economies in economic growth. *Economic Record* 31, November, 192–214.

1957. *The Australian Trading Banks*. Melbourne: Cheshire. 2nd edn, 1960; 3rd edn (with C.P. Harris), 1965; 4th edn (with D.W. Stammer), 1973; 5th edn (with W.J. Blackert), Melbourne: Melbourne University Press, 1977.

1978. *The Rise and Fall of Economic Growth: A Study of Contemporary Thought*. Melbourne: Longman Cheshire.

1979. The modus operandi of protection. *Economic Record* 55, June, 149–55.
1981. Economic development: a semantic history. *Economic Development and Cultural Change* 29(3), April, 457–66.
1985. *A Course Through Life*. Canberra: Australian National University.

Arrow corner. *See* COST MINIMIZATION AND UTILITY MAXIMIZATION.

Arrow–Debreu model of general equilibrium. I INTRODUCTION; II THE MODEL; III EQUILIBRIUM; IV PARETO OPTIMALITY; V WHAT THE MODEL DOESN'T EXPLAIN.

I. INTRODUCTION

It is not easy to separate the significance and influence of the Arrow–Debreu model of general equilibrium from that of mathematical economics. In an extraordinary series of papers (Arrow, 1951; Debreu, 1951; Arrow–Debreu, 1954), two of the oldest and most important questions of neoclassical economics, the viability and efficiency of the market system, were shown to be susceptible to analysis in a model completely faithful to the neoclassical methodological premises of individual rationality, market clearing, and rational expectations, through arguments at least as elegant as any in economic theory, using the two techniques (convexity and fixed point theory) that are still, after thirty years, the most important mathematical devices in mathematical economics. Fifteen years after its birth (e.g. Arrow, 1969), the model was still being reinterpreted to yield fresh economic insights, and twenty years later the same model was still capable of yielding new and fundamental mathematical properties (e.g. Debreu, 1970, 1974). When we consider that the same two men who derived the most fundamental properties of the model (along with McKenzie, 1954) also provided the most significant economic interpretations, it is no wonder that its invention has helped earn for each of its creators, in different years, the Nobel Prize for economics.

In the next few pages I shall try to summarize the primitive mathematical concepts, and their economic interpretations, that define the model. I give a hint of the arguments used to establish the model's conclusions. Finally, on the theory that a model is equally well described by what it cannot explain, I list several phenomena that the model is not equipped to handle.

II. THE MODEL

Commodities and Arrow–Debreu Commodities (A.1) Let there be L commodities, $l=1,...,L$. The amount of a commodity is described by a real number. A list of quantities of all commodities is given by a vector in $\mathbb{R}^L$.

The notion of commodity is the fundamental primitive concept in economic theory. Each commodity is assumed to have an objective, quantifiable, and universally agreed upon (i.e. measurable) description. Of course, in reality this description is somewhat ambiguous (should two apples of different sizes be considered two units of the same commodity, or two different commodities?) but the essential quantitative aspect of commodity cannot be doubted. Production and consumption are defined in terms of transformations of commodities that they cause. Conversely, the set of commodities is the minimum collection of objects necessary to describe production and consumption. Other objects, such as financial assets, may be traded, but they are not commodities.

General equilibrium theory is concerned with the allocation of commodities (between nations, or individuals, across time, or under uncertainty etc.). The Arrow–Debreu model studies those allocations which can be achieved through the exchange of commodities at one moment in time.

It is easy to see that it is often important to the agents in an economy to have precise physical descriptions of commodities, as for example when placing an order for a particular grade of steel or oil. The less crude the categorization of commodities becomes, the more scope there is for agents to trade, and the greater is the set of imaginable allocations. Two agents may each have apples and oranges. There is no point in exchanging one man's fruit for the other man's fruit, but both might be made better off if one could exchange his apples for the other's oranges. Of course there need not be any end to the distinctions which in principle could be drawn between commodities, but presumably finer details become less and less important. When the descriptions are so precise that further refinements cannot yield imaginable allocations which increase the satisfaction of the agents in the economy, then the commodities are called Arrow–Debreu commodities.

A field is better allocated to one productive use than another depending upon how much rain has fallen on it; but it is also better allocated depending on how much rain has fallen on other fields. This illustrates the apparently paradoxical usefulness of including in the description of an Arrow–Debreu commodity characteristics of the world, for example the commodity's geographic location, its temporal location (Hicks, 1939), its state of nature (Arrow, 1953; Debreu, 1959; Radner, 1968), and perhaps even the name of its final consumer (Arrow, 1969), which at first glance do not seem intrinsically connected with the object itself (but which are in principle observable).

Hicks, perhaps anticipated by Fisher and Hayek, was the first to suggest an elaborate notion of commodity; this idea has been developed by others, especially Arrow in connection with uncertainty. Hicks was also the first to understand apparently complicated transactions, perhaps involving the exchange of paper assets or other noncommodities, over many time periods, in terms of commodity trade at one moment in time. Thus saving, or the lending of money, might be thought of as the purchase today of a particular future dated commodity. The second welfare theorem, which we shall shortly discuss, shows that an 'optimal' series of transactions can always be so regarded. By making the distinction between the same physical object depending, for example, on the state of nature, the general equilibrium theory of the supply and demand of commodities at one moment in time can incorporate the analysis of the optimal allocation of risk (a concept which appears far removed from the mundane qualities of fresh fruit) with exactly the same apparatus used to analyse the exchange of apples and oranges. Classifying physical objects according to their location likewise allows transportation costs to be handled in the same framework. Distinguishing commodities by who ultimately consumes them could allow general equilibrium analysis to systematically include externalities and public goods as special cases, though this has not been much pursued.

In reality, it is very rare to find a market for a pure Arrow–Debreu commodity. The more finely the commodities are described, the less likely are the commodity markets to have many buyers and sellers (i.e. to be competitive). More commonly, many groups of Arrow–Debreu commodities are traded together, in unbreakable bundles, at many moments in time, in 'second best' transactions. Nevertheless, this understanding of the limitations of real world markets, based on the concept of the Arrow–Debreu commodity, is one of the most powerful analytical tools of systematic accounting available to the general equilibrium theorist. Similarly, the model of Arrow–Debreu, with its idealization of a separate market for each Arrow–Debreu commodity, all simultaneously meeting, is the benchmark against which the real economy can be measured.

Consumers. (A.1) Let there be H consumers, $h = 1, \ldots, H$. □

Each consumer h can imagine consumption plans $x \in \mathbb{R}^L$ lying in some consumption set X^h. (A.2) X^h is a closed subset in $\mathbb{R}^L$ which is bounded from below. □

Each consumer h also has well defined preferences $\succcurlyeq h$ over every pair $(x, y) \in X^h \times X^h$, where $x \succcurlyeq y$ means x is at least as desirable as y. Typically it is assumed that (A.3) $\succcurlyeq$ is a complete, transitive, continuous ordering. □

Notice that in general equilibrium consumers make choices between entire consumption plans, not betweeen individual commodities. A single commodity has significance to the consumer only in relation to the other commodities he has consumed, or plans to consume. Together with transitivity and completeness, this hypothesis about consumer preferences embodies the neoclassical ideal of rational choice.

Rationality has not always been a primitive hypothesis in neoclassical economics. It was customary (e.g. for Bentham, Jevons, Menger, Walras) to regard satisfaction, or utility, as a measurable primitive; rational choice, when it was thought to occur at all, was the consequence of the maximization of utility. And since utility was often thought to be instantaneously produced, sequential consumer choice on the basis of sequential instantaneous utility maximization was sometimes explicitly discussed as irrational (see e.g. Böhm-Bawerk on saving and the reasons why the rate of interest is always positive).

Once utility is taken to be a function not of instantaneous consumption, but of the entire consumption plan, then rational choice is equivalent to utility maximization. Debreu (1951) proved that any preference ordering $\succcurlyeq_h$ defined on $X^h \times X^h$ satisfies (A.1)–(A.3) if and only if there is a utility function $u^h \colon X^h \to \mathbb{R}$ such that $x \succcurlyeq_h y$ exactly when $u^h(x) \geqslant u^h(y)$.

Under the influence of Pareto (1909), Hicks (1939) and Samuelson (1947), neoclassical economics has come to take rationality as primitive, and utility maximization as a logical consequence. This has had a profound effect on welfare economics, and perhaps on the scope of economic theory as well. In the first place, if utility is not directly measurable, then it can only be deduced from observable choices, as in the proof of Debreu. But at best this will give an 'ordinal' utility, since if $f \colon \mathbb{R} \to \mathbb{R}$ is any strictly increasing function, then u^h represents $\succcurlyeq_h$ if and only if $v^h \equiv f \circ u^h$ represents $\succcurlyeq_h$. Hence there can be no meaning to interpersonal utility comparisons; the Benthamite sum $\Sigma_{h=1}^{H} u^h$ is very different from the Benthamite sum $\Sigma_{h=1}^{H} f^h \circ u^h$. In the second place, the ideal of rational choice or preference, freed from the need for measurement, is much more easily extended to domains not directly connected to the market and commodities such as political candidates or platforms, or 'social states'. The elaboration of the nature of the primitive concepts of commodity and rational choice, developed as the basis of the theory of market equilibrium, prepared the way for the methodological principles of neoclassical economics (rational choice and equilibrium) to be applied to questions far beyond those of the market.

Although the rationality principle is in some respects a weakening of the hypothesis of measurable utility and instantaneous utility maximization, when coupled with the notion of consumption plan it is also a strengthening of this hypothesis, and a very strong assumption indeed. For example there is not

room in this theory for the Freudian split psyche (or self-deception), or for Odysseus-like changes of heart. Perhaps more importantly, a consumers's preferences (for example how thrifty he is) do not change according to the role he plays in the process of production (e.g. on whether he is a capitalist or landowner), nor do they change depending on other consumers' preferences, or the supply of commodities. As an instance of this last case, note that it follows from the rationality hypothesis that the surge in the microcomputer industry influenced consumer choice between typewriters and word processors only through availability (via the price), and not through any learning effect. (Consumers can 'learn' in the Arrow–Debreu model, e.g. their marginal rates of substitution can depend on the state of nature, but the rate at which they learn is independent of production or consumption – it depends on the exogenous realization of the state. We shall come back to this when we consider information.) If for no other reason, the burden of calculation and attention which rational choice over consumption plans imposes on the individual is so large that one expects rationality to give way to some kind of bounded rationality in some future general equilibrium models

Two more assumptions on preferences made in the model of Arrow–Debreu are nonsatiation and convexity:

(A.4) For each $x \in X^h$, there is a $y \in X^h$ with $y \succ_h x$, i.e. such that $y \succcurlyeq_h x$ and not $x \succcurlyeq_h y$. □

(A.5) X^h is a convex set, and $\succcurlyeq_h$ is convex, i.e., if $y \succ_h x$ and $0 < t \leqslant 1$, then $[ty + (1-t)x] \succ_h x$. □

The nonsatiation hypothesis seems entirely in accordance with human nature. The convexity hypothesis implies that commodities are infinitely divisible, and that mixtures are at least as good as extremes. When commodities are distinguished very finely according to dates, so that they must be thought of as flows, then the convexity hypothesis is untenable. In a standard example, a man may be indifferent between drinking a glass of gin or of scotch at a particular moment, but he would be much worse off if he had to drink a glass of half gin–half scotch. On the other hand, if the commodities were not so finely dated, then they would be more analogous to stocks, and a consumer might well be better off with a litre of gin and a litre of scotch, than two litres of either one. In any case, as we shall remark later, if every agent is small relative to the market (i.e. if there are many agents) then the nonconvexities in preferences are relatively unimportant.

Each agent h is also characterized by a vector of initial endowments

(A.6) $e^h \in X^h \subset \mathbb{R}^L$ for all $h = 1, \ldots, h$. □

The endowment vector e^h represents the claims that the consumer has on all commodities, not necessarily commodities in his physical possession. The fact that $e^h \in X^h$ means that the consumer can ensure his own survival even if he is deprived of all opportunity to trade. This is a somewhat strange hypothesis for the modern world, in which individuals often have labour but few other endowments, e.g. land. Doubtless the hypothesis could be relaxed; in any case, survival is not an issue that is addressed in the Arrow–Debreu model.

Each individual h is also endowed with an ownership share of each of the firms $j = 1, \ldots, J$

(A.7) For all $h = 1, \ldots, H$, $j = 1, \ldots, J$, $d_{hj} \geqslant 0$, and for all $j = 1, \ldots, J$, $\Sigma_{h=1}^{H} d_{hj} = 1$. □

Firms. (A.8) Let there be J firms, $j = 1, \ldots, J$. □

The firm in Arrow–Debreu is characterized by its initial distribution of owners, and by its technological capacity

$Y_j \subset \mathbb{R}^L$ to transform commodities. Any production plan $y \in \mathbb{R}^L$, where negative components of y refer to inputs and positive components denote outputs, is feasible for firm j if $y \in Y_j$. A customary assumption made in the Arrow–Debreu model is free disposal: if $l = 1, \ldots, L$ is any commodity, and v_l is the unit vector in $\mathbb{R}^L$, with one in the lth coordinate and zero elsewhere, then

(A.9) For all $l = 1, \ldots, L$ and $k > 0$, $-kv_l \in Y_j$, for some $j = 1, \ldots, J$. □

Although it is strange, when thinking of nuclear waste etc., to think that any commodity can be disposed without cost (i.e. without the use of any other inputs), as we shall remark later, this assumption can be relaxed, if negative prices are introduced (or if weak monotonicity is assumed).

The empirically most vulnerable assumption to the Arrow–Debreu model, and one crucial to its logic, is:

(A.10) For each j, Y_j is a closed, convex set containing 0. □

This convexity assumption rules out indivisibilities in production (e.g. half a tunnel), increasing returns to scale, gains from specialization, etc. As with consumption, if the indivisibilities of production are small relative to the size of the whole economy, then the conclusions we shall shortly present are not much affected. But when they are large, or when there are significant increasing returns to scale, the model of competitive equilibrium that we are about to examine is simply not applicable. Nevertheless, convexity is consistent with the traditionally important cases of decreasing and constant returns to scale in production.

We conclude by presenting three final assumptions used in the Arrow–Debreu model.

(A.11) Let $e = \Sigma_{h=1}^H e^h$,
let $F = \{y \in \mathbb{R}^L | y = \Sigma_{j=1}^J y_j, \; y_j \in Y^j, \; j = 1, \ldots, J\}$,
let $\bar{F} = \{y \in F | y + e \geqq 0\}$, and
let $K = \{(y_1, \ldots, y_J) \in Y_1 \times \cdots \times Y_J | \equiv y\Sigma_{j=1}^J y^j \in \bar{F}\}$.
Then $\bar{F} \cap \mathbb{R}_{++}^L \neq \phi$, and K is compact. □

Assumption (A.11) requires that the level of productive activity that is possible even if the productive sector appropriates all the resources of the consuming sector is bounded (as well as closed).

Notice that these assumptions are consistent with firms owning initial resources, as well as individuals. In the original Arrow–Debreu model (1954), the firms were prohibited from owning initial resources (they were assigned to the firm owners: with complete markets there is little difference, but with incomplete markets the earlier assumption is restrictive).

(A.12) The economy is irreducible. □

We shall not elaborate this assumption here. It means that for any two agents h and h', the endowment e^h of agent h is positive in some commodity l, which (taking into account the possibilities of production) agent h' could use to make himself strictly better off. It certainly seems reasonable that each agent's labour power could be used to make another agent better off.

Lastly, we assume that

(A.13) The commodities are not distinguished according to which firm produces them, or who consumes them. □

Assumption (A.13) is made simply for the purposes of interpretation. When put together with the definition of competitive equilibrium, it implies that there are no externalities to production or consumption, no public goods, etc. Mathematically, however, (A.13) has no content. In other words, if we dropped assumption (A.13), the Arrow–Debreu notion of competitive equilibrium would still make sense (even in the presence of externalities and public goods) and it would still have the optimality properties we shall elaborate in Section III, but it would require an entirely different interpretation. Consumers, for example, would be charged different prices for the same physical commodities (same, that is, according, to date, location and state of nature). In more technical language, a Lindahl equilibrium is a special case of an (A.1)–(A.12) Arrow–Debreu equilibrium, with the commodity space suitably expanded and interpreted. Thus each physical unit of a public good is replaced by H goods, one unit for the public good indexed by which agent consumes it. Also the physical technology set describing the production of the public good is replaced by a different set in the Arrow–Debreu model, lying in a higher dimensional space, where the output of the same amount of H goods. In an Arrow–Debreu equilibrium, consumers will likely pay different prices for these H goods, i.e. for what in reality represents the same physical public good. Hence the differential pay principle for the optimal provision of public goods elucidated by Samuelson, which appeared to point to a qualitative difference between the analytical apparatus needed to describe optimality in public goods and private goods economies, is thus shown to be explicable by exactly the same apparatus used for private goods economies, simply by multiplying the number of commodities. The same device can also be used for analysing the optimal provision of goods when there are externalities, provided that negative prices are allowed. Assumption (A.13) thus seriously limits the normative conclusions that can be drawn from the model. From a descriptive point of view, however, rationality and the price taking behaviour which equilibrium implies, make (A.13) necessary.

III. EQUILIBRIUM

Price is the final primitive concept in the Arrow–Debreu model. Like commodity it is quantifiable and directly measurable. As Debreu has remarked, the fundamental role which mathematics plays in economics is partly owing to the quantifiable nature of these two primitive concepts, and to the rich mathematical relationship of dual vector spaces, into which it is natural to classify the collections of price values and commodity quantities. Properly speaking, price is only sensible (and measurable) as a relationship between two commodities, i.e. as relative price. Hence there should be $L^2 - L$ relative prices in the Arrow–Debreu model. But the definition of Arrow–Debreu equilibrium immediately implies that it suffices to give $L - 1$ of these ratios, and all the rest are determined.

For mathematical convenience (namely to treat prices and quantities as dual vectors), one price is specified for each unit quantity of each commodity. The relative price of two commodities can be obtained by taking the ratio of the Arrow–Debreu prices of these commodities.

I shall proceed by specifying the definition of Arrow–Debreu equilibrium, and then I make a number of remarks emphasizing some of the salient characteristics of the definition. The longest remark concerns the differences between the historical development of general equilibrium, up until the time of Hicks and Samuelson and the particular Arrow–Debreu model of general equilibrium.

An Arrow–Debreu economy E is an array $E = \{L, H, J(X^h, e^h, \succcurlyeq_h), (Y^j), (d^{hj}), h = 1, \ldots, H, j = 1, \ldots, J\}$ satisfying assumptions (A.1)–(A.13). An Arrow–Debreu equilibrium is an array $[(\bar{p}_l), (\bar{x}_l^h), (\bar{y}_l^j), l = 1, \ldots, L, h = 1, \ldots, H, j = 1, \ldots, J]$ satisfying:

For all $j = 1, \ldots, J, \bar{y}_j \in$

$$\arg\max\left\{ \sum_{l=1}^L \bar{p}_l y_l | (y = y_1, \ldots, y_L) \in Y^j \right\} \quad (1)$$

For all $h = 1, \ldots, H$, $\bar{x}^h \in B^h(\bar{p})$, where $B^h(\bar{p})$

$$\equiv \left\{ x \in X^h \mid \sum_{l=1}^{L} \bar{p}_l x_l \leqslant \sum_{l=1}^{L} \bar{p}_l e_l^h + \sum_{j=1}^{J} d^{hj} \sum_{l=1}^{L} \bar{p}_l \bar{y}_l^j \right\} \quad (2)$$

and if $x \in B^h(\bar{p})$, then not $x \succ_h \bar{x}^h$,

For all $l = 1, \ldots, L$, $\sum_{h=1}^{H} \bar{x}_l^h = \sum_{h=1}^{H} e_l^h + \sum_{j=1}^{J} \bar{y}_l^j$. $\quad (3)$

The most striking feature of general equilibrium is the juxtaposition of the great diversity in goals and resources it allows, together with the supreme coordination it requires. Every desire of each consumer, no matter how whimsical, is met precisely by the voluntary supply of some producer. And this is true for all markets and consumers simultaneously.

There is a symmetry to the general equilibrium model, in the way that all agents enter the model individually motivated by self-interest (not as members of distinct classes motivated by class interests), and simultaneously, so that no agent acts prior to any other on a given market (e.g. by setting prices). If workers' subsistence were not assumed, for example, that would break the symmetry; workers income could have to be guaranteed first, otherwise demand would (discontinuously) collapse. As it is, at the aggregate level, supply and demand equally and simultaneously determine price; in equilibrium, both the consumers' marginal rates of substitution and the producers' marginal rates of transformation are equal to relative prices (assuming differentiability and interiority). There are gains to trade both through exchange and through production. This point of view represents a significant break with the classical tradition of Ricardo and Marx. We shall come to the main difference between the classical and neoclassical approaches shortly. Another difference is that there need not be fixed coefficients of production in the Arrow–Debreu model – the sets Y are much more general. Also in an Arrow–Debreu equilibrium, there is no reason for there to be a uniform rate of profit. There is none the less one aspect of the model which these authors would have greatly approved, namely the shares d^{hj} which allow the owners of firms to collect profits even though they have contributed nothing to production.

Notice that in general equilibrium each agent need only concern himself with his own goals (preferences or profits) and the prices. The implicit assumption that every agent 'knows' all the prices is highly non-trivial. It means that at each date each agent is capable of forecasting perfectly all future prices until the end of time. It is in this sense that the Arrow–Debreu model depends on 'rational expectations'. Each agent must also be informed of the 'price q_j of each firm j, where $q_j = \Sigma_{l=1}^{L} \bar{p}_l \bar{y}_l^j$. (Firms that produce under constant returns to scale must also discover the level of production, which cannot be deduced from the prices alone.) Assuming that the 'man on the spot' (Hayek's expression) knows much better than anyone else what he wants, or best how his changing environment is suited to producing his product, decentralized decision making would seem to be highly desirable, if it is not incompatible with coordination. Indeed, harmony through diversity is one of the sacred doctrines of the liberal tradition.

The greatest triumph of the Arrow–Debreu model was to lay out explicitly the conditions (roughly (A.1)–(A.13)) under which if is possible to claim that a properly chosen price system must always exist that, like the invisible hand, can guide diverse and independent agents to make mutually compatible choices. The idea of general equilibrium had gradually developed since the time of Adam Smith, mostly through the pioneering work of Walras (1874), Von Neumann (1937), Wald (1932), Hicks (1939) and Samuelson (1947). By the late 1940s the definition of equilibrium, including ownership shares in the firms, was well-established. But it was Arrow–Debreu (1954) that spelled out precise microeconomic assumptions at the level of the individual agents that could be used to show the model was consistent.

The axiomatic and rigorous approach that characterized the formulation of general equilibrium by Arrow–Debreu has been enormously influential. It is now taken for granted that a model is not properly defined unless it has been proved to be logically consistent. Much of the clamour for 'microeconomic foundations to macroeconomics', for example, is a desire to see an axiomatic clarity similar to that of the Arrow–Debreu model applied to other areas of economics. Of course, there were other earlier economic models that were similarly axiomatic and rigorous; one thinks especially of Von Neumann–Morgenstern's *Theory of Games* (1944). But game theory was, at the time, on the periphery of economics. Competitive equilibrium is at its heart.

The central mathematical techniques, convexity theory (separating hyperplane theorem) and Brouwer's (Kakutani's) fixed point theorem, used in Arrow-Debreu are, thirty years later, still the most important tools used in mathematical economics. Both elements had played a (hidden) role in Von Neumann's work. Convexity had been prominent in the work of Koopmans (1951) on activity analysis, in the work of Kuhn and Tucker (1951) on optimization, and in the papers of Arrow (1951) and Debreu (1951) on optimality. Fixed point theorems had been used by Von Neumann (1937), by Nash (1950) and especially by McKenzie (1954), who one month earlier than Arrow–Debreu had published a proof of general equilibrium using Kakutani's theorem, albeit in a model where the primitive assumptions were made on demand functions, rather than preferences. McKenzie (1959) also made an early contribution to the notion of an irreducible economy (assumption (A.9)).

The first fruit of the more precise formulation of equilibrium that began to emerge in the early 1950s was the transparent demonstration of the first and second welfare theorems that Arrow and Debreu simultaneously gave in 1951. Particularly noteworthy is the proof that every equilibrium is Pareto optimal. So simple and illuminating is this demonstration that it is no exaggeration to call it the most frequently imitated argument in all of neoclassical economic theory.

Among the confusions that were cleared away by the careful axiomatic treatment of equilibrium was the reliance of the discussions by Hicks and Samuelson on interior solutions and differentiability. When discussing the optimal allocation of housing, for example, it is evident that most agents will consume nothing of most houses, but this does not affect the Pareto optimality of a free (and complete) market allocation of housing. Similarly, it is not necessary to either the existence of Arrow–Debreu equilibrium, nor to the first and second welfare theorems, that preferences or production sets be either differentiable or strictly convex. In particular, it is possible to incorporate the 'neoclassical production function' with constant returns to scale with variable inputs, the classical fixed coefficients methods of production, and the strictly concave production functions of the Hicks–Samuelson vintage, all in the same framework.

This is not to say that differentiability has no role to play in the Arrow–Debreu model. In his seminal paper (1970), Debreu resurrected the role of differentiability by showing, via the methods of transversality theory (a branch of differential topology) that almost every differentiable economy is regular, in the sense that small perturbations to the economic data (e.g. the endowments) make small changes in all the equilibrium prices Before Debreu, comparative statics could be handled only under specialized hypotheses, for example, the invertibility of excess demand at all prices, etc. We shall give a fuller discussion of the three crucial mathematical results of the Arrow–Debreu model – existence, optimality and local uniqueness – in the next section.

Observe finally, that although the commodities may include physical goods dated over many time periods, there is only one budget constraint in an Arrow–Debreu equilibrium. The income that could be obtained from the sale of an endowed commodity, dated from the last period, is available already in the first period.

IV. PARETO OPTIMALITY

The first theorem of welfare economics states that any Arrow–Debreu equilibrium allocation $\bar{x} = (\bar{x}^h)$, $h = 1, \ldots, H$ is Pareto optimal in the sense that if $[(x^h), (y^j)]$ satisfies $y^j \in Y^j, \Sigma_{h=1}^H x^h = \Sigma_{j=1}^J y_n^j + e$, then it cannot be the case that $x^h >_h \bar{x}^h$ for all h. The second theorem of welfare analysis states the converse, namely that any Pareto optimal allocation for an Arrow–Debreu economy E is a competitive equilibrium allocation for an Arrow–Debreu economy $\hat{E}$ obtained from E by rearranging the initial endowments of commodities and ownership shares.

The first welfare theorem expresses the efficiency of the ideal market system, although it makes no claim as to the justice of the initial distribution of resources. The second welfare theorem implies that any income redistribution is best effected through a lump sum transfer, rather than through manipulating the market, e.g. through rent control, etc.

The connection between competitive equilibrium and Pareto optimality has been perceived for a long time, but until 1951 there was a general confusion between the necessity and sufficiency part of the arguments. The old proof of Pareto optimality (see Lange, 1942) assumed differentiable utilities of production sets, and a strictly positive allocation $\bar{x}$. It noted the first order conditions to the problem of maximizing the ith consumer's utility, subject to maintaining all the others at least as high as they got under $\bar{x}$, and feasibility, are satisfied at $\bar{x}$, if and only if $\bar{x}$ is a competitive equilibrium allocation for a 'rearranged' economy $\hat{E}$. This first order, or infinitesimal, proof of equivalence between competitive equilibrium and Pareto optimality could have been made global by postulating in addition that preferences and production sets are convex.

The Arrow and Debreu (1954) proofs of the equivalence between competitive equilibrium and Pareto optimality, under global changes, do not require differentiability, nor do they require that all agents consume a strictly positive amount of every good. In fact the proof of the first welfare theorem, that each competitive equilibrium is Pareto optimal, does not even use convexity.

The only requirement is local nonsatiation, so that every agent spends all his income in equilibrium. If (x, y) Pareto dominates the equilibrium allocation $(\bar{p}, \bar{x}, \bar{y})$, then for all $h, \bar{p} \cdot x^h < \bar{p} \cdot \bar{x}^h$. Since profit maximization implies that for all $j, \bar{p} \cdot \bar{y}^j \geqq \bar{p} \cdot y^j$, it follows that $\bar{p} \cdot (\Sigma_h x^h - \Sigma_j y^j) > \bar{p} \cdot (\Sigma_h \bar{x}^h - \Sigma_j \bar{y}^j)$, contradicting feasibility.

The proof of the second welfare theorem, on the other hand, does require convexity of the preferences and production sets (though not their differentiability, nor the interiority of the candidate allocation $\bar{x}$). Essentially it depends on Minkowski's theorem, which asserts that between any two disjoint convex sets in $\mathbb{R}^L$ there must be a separating hyperplane.

In this connection let us mention one more remarkable mathematical property of the Arrow–Debreu model. Let us suppose that all production takes place under constant returns to scale: if $y \in Y^j$, then so is λy, for $\lambda \geqslant 0$. We say that a feasible allocation $\bar{x}$ for the economy E is in the core if there is no coalition of consumers $S \subset \{1, \ldots, H\}$ such that using only their initial endowments of resources, as well as access to all the production technologies, they cannot achieve an allocation for themselves which they all prefer to $\bar{x}$. The core is meant to reflect those allocations which could be maintained when bargaining (the formation of coalitions) is costless. In a status quo core allocation, any labour union or cartel of owners that threatens to withhold its goods from the market knows that another coalition could form and by withholding its goods, prevent some members of the original coalition from being better off than they were under the status quo. It is easy to see that any competitive equilibrium is in the core. Debreu–Scarf (1963), building on earlier work of Scarf, showed by using the separating hyperplane theorem, that if agents are small relative to the market, in the sense they made precise through the notion of replication, then the core consists only of competitive allocations. Such a theorem can also be proved even if there are small nonconvexities in preferences (see Aumann (1964) for a different formulation of the small agent).

EXISTENCE OF EQUILIBRIUM. Suppose that agents' preferences and firms' production sets are strictly convex, and that agents strictly prefer more of any commodity to less (strict monotonicity) and that they all have strictly positive endowments. Let Δ be the set of L-price vectors, all non-negative, summing to one. Let $f^h(p)$ be the commodity bundle most preferred by agent h, given the strictly positive prices $p \in \Delta_{++}$. Similarly let $g^i(p)$ be the profit maximizing choice of firm j, given prices $p \in \Delta_{++}$. Finally, let $f(p) = \Sigma_{h=1}^H f^h(p) - \Sigma_{j=1}^J g^j(p) - e$. It is easy to show that f is a continuous function at all $p \in \Delta_{++}$. A price $\bar{p} \in \Delta_{++}$ is an Arrow–Debreu equilibrium price if and only if $f(\bar{p}) = 0$.

In general there is no reason to expect a continuous function to have a zero. Thus Wald could prove only with great difficulty in a special case that an equilibrium necessarily exists. Now observe that the function must satisfy Walras' Law, $p \cdot f(p) = 0$, for all p. So f is not arbitrary.

Consider the convex, compact set Δ_ϵ of prices $p \in \Delta$ with $p_l \geqq \epsilon > 0$, for all l. Consider also the continuous function $\phi: \Delta_\epsilon \to \Delta_\epsilon$ mapping p to the closest point $\hat{p}$ in Δ_ϵ to $f(p) + p$. By Brouwer's fixed point theorem, there must be some $\bar{p}$ with $\phi(\bar{p}) = \bar{p}$. From strict monotonicity, it follows that $\bar{p}$ cannot be on the boundary of Δ_ϵ, if ϵ is chosen sufficiently small. From Walras' Law it follows that if $\bar{p}$ is in the interior of Δ_ϵ, then $f(\bar{p}) = 0$. The demonstration of the existence of equilibrium by Arrow and Debreu, as modified later by Debreu (1959), followed a similar logic.

Note the essential role of convexity in two parts of the above proof. It was used with respect to agents' characteristics to guarantee that their optimizing behaviour is continuous. And it was also used to ensure that the space Δ_ϵ has the fixed point property. Smale (1976) has given a path-following proof (related to Scarf's (1973) algorithm) that on closer inspection does not require convexity of the price space. (Dierker (1974) and Balasko (1986) have given homotopy proofs.) This is not only of computational importance. It appears that there may be economic problems, dealing with general equilibrium with incomplete markets, in which the price space is intrinsically nonconvex, and in which the existence of equilibrium can only be proved using path-following methods (see Duffie-Shaffer, 1985).

To weaken the assumption of strict convexity, in the above proof, one can replace Brouwer's fixed point theorem with Kakutani's. An important conceptual point arises in connection with strict montonicity. If that is dropped, and the production sets do not have free disposal, then in order to guarantee the existence of equilibrium, the definition must be revised to require either $f_l(\bar{p}) = 0$, or $f_l(\bar{p}) < 0$ and $\bar{p}_l = 0$. There may be free goods, like air, in excess supply. One cannot drop monotonicity and free disposal without allowing for negative prices.

Finally, it can be shown that if there are small nonconvexities in either preference or production, and if all the agents are small relative to the market (either in the replication sense of Debreu-Scarf, or the measure zero sense of Aumann), then there will be prices at which the markets nearly clear. On the other hand, increasing returns to scale over a broad range is definitely incompatible with equilibrium.

LOCAL UNIQUENESS AND COMPARATIVE STATICS. Another property of the excess demand function $f(p)$ is that it is homogeneous of degree zero. So instead of taking $p \in \Delta$, let us fix $p_1 = 1$. Similarly, let $F(p)$ be the $L - 1$ vector of excess demands for goods $l = 2, \ldots, L$. If $F(p) = 0$, then by Walras' Law, $f(p) = 0$.

Suppose furthermore that agent characteristics are smooth. Then $F(P)$ is a differentiable function. If $D_p F(\bar{p})$ has full rank at an equilibrium $\bar{p}$, then $\bar{p}$ is locally unique. Moreover, the equilibrium p will move continuously, given continuous, small changes in the agents' characteristics, such as their endowments e. If $D_p F(\bar{p})$ has full rank at all equilibria $\bar{p}$, then there are only a finite number of equilibria. Debreu (1970) called an economy E regular if $D_p F(\bar{p})$ has full rank at all equilibrium $\bar{p}$ of E.

The problem of trying to give sufficient conditions on preferences etc. to guarantee that $D_p F$ has full rank in equilibrium has proved intractable (except for restrictive, special cases). But Debreu (1970) solved the problem in classic style, appealing to the transversality theorem of differential topology (or Sard's theorem), to show that if one were content with regularity for 'almost all' economies, then the problem is simple. He proved that for almost all economies, $D_p F$ has full rank at every equilibrium. Hence, in almost all economies comparative statics (the change in equilibrium, given exogenous changes to the economy) is well defined.

Observe that excess demand F depends on the agents' characteristics, including their endowments, so we could write $F(e, p)$. Now the transversality theorem says that (given some technical conditions) if $D_e F(e, \bar{p})$ has full rank at all equilibria $\bar{p}$ for the economy $E(e)$ with endowments e, for all e, then for 'almost all' e, $D_p F(e, \bar{p})$ has full rank at all equilibrium $\bar{p}$ of $E(e)$. But it is easy to show that $D_e F(e, p)$ always has full rank. Along similar lines, Debreu proved the 'generic regularity' of equilibrium.

There is one unfortunate side to this comparative statics story. One would like to show not only that comparative statics are well defined, but also that they have a definite form. In a concave programming problem, for example, a small increase in an input results in a decrease in that input's shadow price, and an increase in output approximately equal to the size of the input increase multiplied by its original shadow price. Given the strong rationality hypothesis of the Arrow–Debreu model, one would hope for some sort of analogous result. Following a conjecture of Sonnenschein, Debreu proved in 1974 that given any function $f(p)$ on Δ_c satisfying Walras' Law, he could find an Arrow–Debreu economy such that $f(p)$ is its aggregate

excess demand on Δ_c. Thus assumptions (A.1)–(A.13) do not permit any *a priori* predictions about the changes that must occur in equilibrium given exogenous changes to the economy. An increase in the aggregate endowment of a particular good, for example, might cause its equilibrium price to rise. The possibility of such pathologies is disappointing. It means that to make even qualitative predictions, the economist needs detailed data on the excess demands F.

V. WHAT THE MODEL DOESN'T EXPLAIN

We have already discussed the implications of the notion of Arrow–Debreu commodities and the second welfare theorem for insurance, namely that since every Pareto optimal allocation is supportable as an Arrow–Debreu equilibrium, every optimal allocation of risk bearing can be accomplished by the production and trade of Arrow–Debreu commodities, i.e. without recourse to additional kinds of insurance markets specializing in risks. Every Arrow–Debreu commodity is as much a diversifier in location, or time, or physical quality as it is for risk. This leads to a great simplification and economy of analysis. But it also means, that from the positive point of view, the Arrow–Debreu economy cannot directly provide an analysis of insurance markets (except as a benchmark case). In this section I shall try to point out a few of the other phenomena which recede into the background in the Arrow–Debreu model, but which would emerge if the assumption of a finite, but complete set of Arrow–Debreu commodities, and consumers was dropped.

There are four currently active lines of research which attempt to come to grips in a general equilibrium framework with some of these phenomena, while preserving the fundamental neoclassical Arrow–Debreu principles of agent optimization, market clearing, and rational expectations, that I think are particularly worthy of attention. They are the theory of general equilibrium with incomplete asset markets which can be traced back to Arrow's (1953) seminal paper on securities; overlapping generations economics, whose study was initiated by Samuelson (1958) in his classic consumption loan model; the Cournot theory of market exchange with few traders, first adapted to general equilibrium by Shapley-Shubik (1977), and the model of rational expectations equilibrium, pioneered by Lucas (1972).

Let us note first of all that in Arrow–Debreu equilibrium ther is no trade in shares of firms. A stock certificate is not an Arrow–Debreu commodity, for its possession entitles the owner to additional commodities which he need not obtain through exchange. Note also that in Arrow–Debreu equilibrium, the hypothesis that all prices will remain the same, no matter how an individual firm changes its production plan, guarantees that firm owners unanimously agree on the firm objective, to maximize profit. If there were a market for firm shares, there would not be any trade anyway, since ownership of the firm and the income necessary to purchase it would be perfect substitutes. In an incomplete markets equilibrium, different sources of revenue are not necessarily perfect substitutes. There could be active trade on the stock market. Of course, such a model would have to specify the firm objectives, since one would not expect unanimity. The theory of stock market equilibrium is still in its infancy, although some important work has already been done. (See Dreze, 1974, and Grossman-Hart, 1979.)

Bankruptcy is not allowed in an Arrow–Debreu equilibrium. That follows from the fact that all agents must meet their budget constraints. In a game theoretic formulation of equilibrium (such as I shall discuss shortly), it is achieved by imposing an infinite bankruptcy penalty. Since every Arrow–Debreu equilibrium is Pareto optimal, there would be no benefit in reducing the bankruptcy penalty to the point where someone might choose to go bankrupt. But with incomplete markets, such a policy might be Pareto improving, even allowing for the deadweight loss of imposing the penalties.

Money does not appear in the Arrow–Debreu model. Of course, all of the reasons for its real life existence: transactions demand, precautionary demand, store of value, unit of account, etc. are already taken care of in the Arrow–Debreu model. One could imagine money in the model: at data zero every agent could borrow money from the central bank. At every date afterwards he would be required to finance his purchases out of his stock of money, adding to that stock from his sales. At the last date he would be required to return to the bank exactly what he borrowed (or else face an infinite bankruptcy penalty). In such a model the Arrow–Debreu prices would appear as money prices. The absolute level of money prices and the aggregate amount of borrowing would not be determined, but the allocations of commodities would be the same as in Arrow–Debreu. There is no point in making the role of money explicit in the Arrow–Debreu model, since it has no effect on the real allocations. However, if one considers the same model with incomplete asset markets, the presence of explicitly financial securities can be of great significance to the real allocations.

In the Arrow–Debreu model, all trade takes place at the beginning of time. If markets were reopened at later dates for the same Arrow–Debreu commodities, then no additional trade would take place anyway. At the other extreme, one might consider a model in which at every date and state of nature only those Arrow–Debreu commodities could be traded which were indexed by the corresponding (date, state) pair. An intermediate case would also permit the trade of some (but not all) differently indexed Arrow–Debreu commodities. Now the Arrow–Debreu proofs of the existence and Pareto optimality of equilibrium do not apply to such an incomplete markets economy, as Hart (1975) first pointed out. We have already noted the existence problem. As for efficiency, the Pareto optimality of Arrow–Debreu equilibria might suggest the presumption that, though there might be a loss to eliminating markets, trade on the remaining markets would be as efficient as possible. In fact, it can be shown (generically) that equilibrium trades do not make efficient use of the existing markets.

The Arrow–Debreu model of general equilibrium is relentlessly neoclassical; in fact it has become the paradigm of the neoclassical approach. This stems in part from its individualistic hypothesis, and its celebrated conclusions about the potential efficacy of unencumbered markets. (Although Arrow, for example, has always maintained that a proper understanding of Arrow–Debreu commodities is also useful to showing how inefficient is the limited real world market system.) But still more telling is the fact that the assumption of a finite number of commodities (and hence of dates) forces upon the model the interpretation of the economic process as a one-way activity of converting given primary resources into final consumption goods. If there is universal agreement about when the world will end, there can be no question about the reproduction of the capital stock. In equilibrium it will be run down to zero. Similarly when the world has a definite beginning, so that the first market transaction takes place after the ownership of all resources and techniques of production,

and the preferences of all individuals have been determined, one cannot study the evolution of the social norms of consumption in terms of the historical development of the relations of production. One certainly cannot speak about the production of all commodities by commodities (Sraffa, 1960) (since at date zero there must be commodities which have not been produced by commodities, i.e. by physical objects which are traded).

It seems natural to suppose that as L becomes very large, so that the end of the world is put off until the distant future, that this event cannot be of much significance to behaviour now. But let us not forget the rationality imposed on the agents. Far off as the end of the world might be, it is perfectly taken into account. Thus, for example, social security (funded as it is in the US by taxes on the young) could not exist if rational agents agreed on a final stopping time to transactions.

Consider a model satisfying all the assumptions (A.1)–(A.13), except that L and H are allowed to be infinite, such as the overlapping generations model. It can be shown that there is a robust collection of economies which have a continuum of equilibria, most of which are Pareto sub-optimal, which differ enormously in time 0 behaviour. Thus in a model where time does not have a definite end, the optimality and comparative statics properties of equilibria are radically different. (For example, there may be a continuum of equilibria, indexed by the level of period 0 real wages (inversely related to the rate of profit) or the level of output or employment. The interested reader can consult the entry on OVERLAPPING GENERATIONS MODELS. A systematic study of economies where only L is allowed to be infinite was begun by Bewley (1972). Such economies tend to have properties similar to those of Arrow–Debreu.)

There is no place in the Arrow–Debreu model for asymmetric information. The second welfare theorem, for example, relies on lump sum redistributions, i.e. redistributions that occur in advance of the market interactions. But if agents cannot be distinguished except through their market behaviour, then the redistribution must be a function of market behaviour. Rational agents, anticipating this, will distort their behaviour and the optimality of the redistribution will be lost.

Similarly, in the definition of equilibrium no agent takes into account what other agents know, for example about the state of nature. Thus it is quite possible in an Arrow–Debreu equilibrium for some ignorant agents to exchange valuable commodities for commodities indexed by states that other agents know will not occur. This problem received enormous attention in the finance literature, and some claim (see Grossman 1981) that it has been solved by extending the Arrow–Debreu definition of equilibrium to a 'rational expectations equilibrium' (Lucas, 1972; see also Radner, 1979). But this definition is itself suspect; in particular, it may not be implementable.

Even if rational expectations equilibrium (REE) were accepted as a viable notion of equilibrium, it could not come to grips with the most fundamental problems of asymmetric information. For like Arrow–Debreu equilibrium, in REE all trade is conducted anonymously through the market at given prices. Implicit in this definition is the assumption of large numbers of traders on both sides of every market. But what has come to be called the incentive problem in economics revolves around individual or firm specific uncertainty, i.e. trade in commodities indexed by the names of the traders, which by definition involves few traders.

This brings us to another major riddle: how are agents supposed to get to equilibrium in the Arrow–Debreu model?

The pioneers of general equilibrium never imagined that the economy was necessarily in equilibrium; Walras, for example, proposed an explicit tâtonnement procedure which he conjectured converged to equilibrium. But that idea is flawed in two respects: in general, it can be shown not to converge, and more importantly, it is an imaginary process in which no exchange is permitted until equilibrium is reached. This illustrates a grave shortcoming of any equilibrium theory, namely that it cannot begin to specify outcomes out of equilibrium. The major crisis of labour market clearing in the 1930s, and again recently, argues strongly that there are limits to the applicability of equilibrium analysis.

One is led naturally to consider market games, in which the outcomes are well-specified even when agents do not make their equilibrium moves. The most famous market game is Cournot's duopoly model, which has been extended to general equilibrium by Shapley–Shubik (1977). When there are a large number of agents of each type, the Nash equilibria of the Shapley–Shubik game give nearly identical allocations to the competitive allocations of Arrow–Debreu. This justifies (to first approximation) the price taking behaviour of the Arrow–Debreu agents. But note that the informational requirements of Nash equilibrium are at least twice that of Arrow–Debreu competitive equilibrium (each agent must know the aggregates of bids and offers on each market). It is also extremely interesting that trade takes place in the Shapley–Shubik game even if there is only one trader on each side of the market. Hence many problems in asymmetric information which have no place in the Arrow–Debreu model, because they involve too fine a specification of the commodities to be consistent with price taking, might be sensible in a market game context. Finally, it can be shown that REE is not consistent with the Shapley–Shubik game, or indeed with any continuous game.

We have indicated some of the ways in which it is possible to extend general equilibrium analysis to phenomena outside the scope of the Arrow–Debreu model, while at the same time preserving the neoclassical methodological premises of agent optimization, rational expectations, and equilibrium. It is important to note that these variations have extended the definition of equilibrium as well; this is most obvious in the case of market games, where Nash equilibrium replaces competitive equilibrium. All of the models have retained, on the other hand, more or less the same notion of rationality, sometimes at the cost of increasing the demands on the rationality of expectations. A great challenge for future general equilibrium models is how to formulate a sensible notion of bounded rationality, without destroying the possibility of drawing normative conclusions.

JOHN GEANAKOPLOS

See also EXISTENCE OF GENERAL EQUILIBRIUM; GENERAL EQUILIBRIUM; INTERTEMPORAL EQUILIBRIUM AND EFFICIENCY; OVERLAPPING GENERATIONS MODEL; STABILITY; UNIQUENESS OF EQUILIBRIUM.

BIBLIOGRAPHY

Arrow, K.J. 1951. An extension of the basic theorems of classical welfare economics. *Proceedings of the Second Berkeley Symposium on Mathematical Statistics and Probability*, ed. J. Neyman, University of California Press, 507–532.

Arrow, K.J. 1953. Le rôle des valeurs boursières pour la répartition la meilleure des risques. *Économétrie*, Paris: Centre National de la Recherche Scientifique, 41–8.

Arrow, K.J. 1969. The organization of economic activity: issues pertinent to the choice of market vs nonmarket allocation, reprinted in *Collected Papers of Kenneth Arrow*, Cambridge, Mass.: Belknap Press, Vol. II, 133–55.

Arrow, K.J. and Debreu, G. 1954. Existence of an equilibrium for a competitive economy. *Econometrica* 22, 265–90.

Aumann, R.J. 1964. Markets with a continuum of traders. *Econometrica* 32, 39-50.

Balasko, Y. 1986. *Foundations of the Theory of General Equilibrium*. New York: Academic Press.

Bewley, T. 1972. Existence of equilibria in economies with infinitely many commodities. *Journal of Economic Theory* 4, 514–40.

Cournot, A. 1838. *Recherches sur les principes mathématiques de la théorie des richesses*. Paris: L. Hachette.

Debreu, G. 1951. The coefficient of resource utilization. *Econometrica* 19, 273–92.

Debreu, G. 1959. *Theory of Value, An Axiomatic Analysis of Economic Equilibrium*. New York: Wiley.

Debreu, G. 1970. Economies with a finite set of equilibria. *Econometrica* 38, 387–92.

Debreu, G. 1974. Excess demand functions. *Journal of Mathematical Economics* 1, 15–21.

Debreu, G. and Scarf, H. 1963. A limit theorem on the core of an economy. *International Economic Review* 4, 235–46.

Dierker, E. 1974. *Topological Methods in Walrasian Economics*. Berlin: Springer.

Drèze, J. 1974. Investment under private ownership: optimality, equilibrium, and stability. In *Allocation under Uncertainty*, ed. J. Drèze, New York: Macmillan.

Duffie, D. and Shafer, W. 1985. Equilibrium in incomplete markets: I–A basic model of generic existence. *Journal of Mathematical Economics* 14(3), 285–300.

Geanakoplos, J.D. and Polemarchakis, H.M. 1987. Existence, regularity, and constrained suboptimality of equilibrium with incomplete asset markets. In *Essays in Honor of Kennneth J. Arrow*, New York: Cambridge University Press.

Grossman, S. 1981. An introduction to the theory of rational expectations under asymmetric information. *Review of Economic Studies* 48, 541–60.

Grossman, S. and Hart, O. 1979. A theory of competitive equilibrium in stock market economies. *Econometrica* 47, 293–329.

Hart, O. 1975. On the optimality of equilibrium when the market structure is incomplete. *Journal of Economic Theory* 11(3), 418–33.

Hicks, J.R. 1939. *Value and Capital*. Oxford: Clarendon Press.

Koopmans, T.C. (ed.) 1951. *Activity Analysis of Production and Allocation*. New York: Wiley.

Kuhn, H.W. and Tucker, A.W. 1951. Nonlinear programming. *Proceedings of the Second Berkeley Symposium on Mathematical Statistics and Probability*, 481–92.

Lucas, R.E. 1972. Expectations and the neutrality of money. *Journal of Economic Theory* 4, 103–124.

McKenzie, L.W. 1954. On equilibrium in Graham's model of world trade and other competitive systems. *Econometrica* 22, 147–61.

McKenzie, L.W. 1959. On the existence of general equilibrium for a competitive market. *Econometrica* 27, 54–71.

Nash, J.F. 1950. Equilibrium points in n-person games. *Proceedings of the National Academy of Sciences of the USA* 36, 48–9.

Neumann, J. von. 1928. Zur theorie der Gesellschaftsspiele. *Mathematische Annalen* 100, 295–320.

Neumann, J. von. 1937. Uber ein ökonomisches Gleichungssystem und eine Verallgemeincrung des Brouwerschen Fixpunktsatzes. *Ergebnisse eines mathematischen Kolloquiums* 8, 73–83.

Neumann, J. von and Morgenstern, O. 1944. *Theory of Games and Economic Behavior*. Princeton: Princeton University Press.

Pareto, V. 1909. *Manuel d'économie politique*. Paris: Giard.

Radner, R. 1968. Competitive equilibrium under uncertainty. *Econometrica* 36(1), 31–58.

Radner, R. 1979. Rational expectations equilibrium: generic existence and the information revealed by prices. *Econometrica* 17, 655–78.

Samuelson, P.A. 1947. *Foundations of Economic Analysis*. Cambridge, Mass.: Harvard University Press.

Samuelson, P.A. 1958. An exact consumption-loan model of interest with or without the social contrivance of money. *Journal of Political Economy* 66, 467–82.

Scarf, H. (with the collaboration of T. Hansen.) 1973. *The Computation of Economic Equilibria*. New Haven: Yale University Press.

Shapley, L. and Shubik, M. 1977. Trade using one commodity as a means of payment. *Journal of Political Economy* 85, 937–68.

Smale, S. 1976. A convergent process of price adjustment and global Newton methods. *Journal of Mathematical Economics* 3, 107–120.

Sonnenschein, H. 1973. Do Walras' identity and continuity characterize the class of community excess demand functions? *Journal of Economic Theory* 6, 345–54.

Sraffa, P. 1960. *Production of Commodities by Means of Commodities.* Cambridge: Cambridge University Press.

Walras, L. 1874–7. *Eléments d'économie politique pure.* Lausanne: L. Corbaz.

Arrow's Theorem. Economic or any other social policy has consequences for the many and diverse individuals who make up the society or economy. It has been taken for granted in virtually all economic policy discussions since the time of Adam Smith, if not before, that alternative policies should be judged on the basis of their consequences for individuals; political discussions are less uniform in this respect, the welfare of an abstract entity, the state or nation, playing a role occasionally even in economic policy.

It follows that there are as many criteria for choosing social actions as there are individuals in the society. Furthermore, these individual criteria are almost bound to be different in some measure so that there will be pairs of policies such that some individuals prefer one and some the other. In the economic context, policies invariably imply distributions of goods, and in most policy choices, some individuals will receive more goods under one policy and others under the other. Individuals may also have different evaluations because of different concepts of justice or other social goals.

The individual criteria may be based on individual preferences over bundles of goods or individual preferences of a more social nature, with preferences over goods supplied to others. From the viewpoint of the formal theory of social choice, the criteria may even be judgements by others as to the welfare of individuals. The only assumption is that there is associated with each individual a criterion by which social actions are evaluated for that individual. Whatever their origin, these criteria differ from individual to individual.

Every society has a range of actions, more or less wide, which are necessarily made collectively. Much of the debate on the foundations of social decision theory began with criteria for evaluating alternative tariff structures, including as the most famous illustration moving from a tariff to free trade. The redistribution of income through governmental taxes and subsidies provides another important case of an inherently collective decision which would be judged differently by different individuals.

If every individual prefers one policy to another, it is reasonable to postulate, as is always done by economists, that the first policy should be preferred. The problem arises of making social choices (between alternative collective policies) when some individual criteria prefer one policy and some another.

The fundamental question of social choice theory, then, is the following: given a range of possible social decisions, one of which has to be chosen, and given the criteria associated with the individuals in the society, find a method of making the choice. Not all methods of decision would be regarded as satisfactory. The method should be in some measure representative of the individual criteria which enter into it. For example, we would want the Pareto condition to be satisfied, that an alternative not be chosen if there is another preferred by all individuals. The method should use all the data, that is,

both the range of possible actions and the individual criteria, and there are consistency conditions among the choices made for different data sets.

A pure case of social choice in action is voting, whether for the election to an office or a legislative decision. Here, the candidates or alternative legislative proposals are evaluated by each voter, and the evaluations lead to messages in the form of votes. The social decision, which candidate to elect or which bill to pass, is made by aggregating the votes according to the particular voting scheme used. The social decision then depends on both the range of alternatives (candidates or legislative proposals) available and the ranking each voter makes of the alternatives.

Voting procedures have one very important property which will play a key role in the conditions required of social choice mechanisms: only individual voters' preferences about the alternatives under consideration affect the choice, not preferences about unavailable alternatives.

Arrow's Theorem, or the Impossibility Theorem, states that there is no social choice mechanism which satisfies a number of reasonable conditions, stated or implied above, and which will be applicable to any arbitrary set of individual criteria.

Some terminology will be introduced in section 1 of this entry. In section 2, there will be a brief review of the relevant literature as it was known to me prior to the discovery of the theorem. In section 3, I state the theorem with some variants and discuss the meaning of the conditions on the social choice mechanisms.

1. THE LANGUAGE OF CHOICE. The formulation of choice and the criteria for it are those standard in economic theory since the 'marginalist revolution' of the 1870s as subsequently refined. There is a large set of conceivable *alternatives*; in any given decision situation, some given subset of these alternatives is actually available or feasible. This subset will be referred to as the *opportunity set*. Each individual can evaluate all alternatives. This is expressed by assuming that each individual has a *preference ordering* over the set of all alternatives. That is, for each pair of alternatives, the individual either prefers one to the other or else is indifferent between them (completeness), and these choices are consistent in the sense that if alternative x is preferred or indifferent to alternative y and y is preferred or indifferent to z, then x is preferred or indifferent to z (transitivity). This preference ordering is analogous to the preference ordering over commodity bundles in consumer demand theory. I have adopted the ordinalist viewpoint that only the ordering itself and not any particular numerical representation by a utility function is significant.

The *profile* of preference orderings is a description of the preference orderings of all individuals. For a given profile, the social choice mechanism will determine the choice of an alternative from any given opportunity set. In the case of an individual, it is assumed that the choice made from any given set of alternatives is that alternative which is highest on the individual's preference ordering. Analogously, it is assumed that social choices can be similarly rationalized. The social choice mechanism will have to be such that there exists a *social ordering* of alternatives such that the choice made from any opportunity set is the highest element according to the social ordering.

Therefore, a social choice mechanism or *constitution* is a function which assigns to each profile a social ordering.

2. THE RELEVANT LITERATURE. I will here review the literature on the justification of economic policy as I knew it in 1948–50.

There was some work in economics and more in the theory of elections of which I was unaware, which I will briefly note.

The best-known criterion for what is now known as social choice was Jeremy Bentham's proposal for using the sum of individuals' utilities. Curiously, despite its natural affinity with marginal economics, it received very little serious use, possibly because its distributional implications were unacceptably extreme. Edgeworth applied the criterion to taxation (1925: originally published in 1897): see also Sidgwick (1901, ch. 7).

The use of the sum-of-utilities criterion required interpersonally comparable cardinal utility. A reluctance to make interpersonal comparisons led to the proposal of the compensation principle by Kaldor (1939) and Hicks (1939). Consider a choice between a current alternative x and a proposed change to another alternative y. In general, some individuals will gain by the change and some will lose. The compensation principle asserts that the change should be made if the gainers *could* give up some of their goods in y to the losers so as to make the losers better off than under x without completely wiping out the gains to the winners. Notice that the compensation is potential, not actual. Since the only information used is the preference relation of each individual among three different alternatives, x, y, and a potential alternative derived from y by transfers of goods, no interpersonal comparisons are needed.

However, it turns out that the compensation principle does not define a social ordering. Indeed, Scitovsky (1941) showed that it was possible that the compensation principle would call for changing from x to y and then from y to x.

A different approach which sought to avoid not only interpersonal comparisons but also cardinal utility was the social welfare function concept of Bergson (1938). For each individual, first choose a utility function which represents his or her preference ordering. Then define social welfare as a prescribed function $W(U_1, \ldots, U_n)$ of the utilities of the n agents. For a given profile of preference orderings, if one of the utility functions is replaced by a monotone transformation (which represents therefore the same preference ordering), the function W has to be transformed correspondingly, so that social preferences defined by W are unchanged. In this formulation, a given social welfare function is associated with a given profile. There are no necessary relations among social welfare functions associated with different profiles.

It was also known to me, though I do not know how, that majority voting, which could be considered as a social decision procedure, might lead to an intransitivity. Consider three voters A, B and C and three alternatives, a, b and c. Suppose that A has preference ordering abc, B has ordering bca, and C the ordering cab. Then a majority prefer a to b, a majority prefer b to c, and a majority prefer c to a. Therefore, if we interpret a majority for one alternative to another as defining social preference, the relation is not an ordering. This paradox had in fact been discovered by Condorcet (1785), and there had been a small and sporadic literature in the intervening period (for an excellent survey, see Black, 1958, Part II; also, Arrow, 1973), but all of this literature was unknown to me when developing the Impossibility Theorem.

There was one further very important paper, which I did know, the remarkable paper of Black (1948) on voting under single-peaked preferences. Suppose the set of alternatives can be represented in one dimension, for example, a choice among levels of expenditure (this was the case studied by Bowen (1943) who anticipated part of Black's results). Suppose individuals have different preference orders over the alternatives, but these preferences have a common pattern; namely, there is a most preferred alternative from which preference drops steadily in both directions. Put another way, of any three alternatives, the one in the intermediate position is never inferior to both of the others. Under this *single-peakedness* condition, majority voting defined a transitive relation and therefore an ordering. Hence, if the preferences of individuals are restricted to satisfy the single-peakedness condition, there does exist a constitution as defined earlier.

3. STATEMENT OF THE IMPOSSIBILITY THEOREM. I now state formally the conditions to be imposed on constitutions and then state the Impossibility Theorem, which simply asserts the non-existence of constitutions satisfying all of the conditions. The theorem as stated in the original paper (Arrow, 1950) and in a subsequent book (Arrow, 1951) is not correct as written, as shown by Blau (1957). To avoid confusion, I give a corrected statement and then explain the error.

Condition U: The constitution is defined for all logically possible profiles of preference orderings over the set of alternatives.

Condition M (Monotonicity): Suppose that x is socially preferred to y for a given profile. Now suppose a new profile in which x is raised in preference in some individual orderings and lowered in none. Then x is preferred to y in the social ordering associated with the new profile.

Condition I (Independence of Irrelevant Alternatives): Let S be a set of alternatives. Two profiles which have the same ordering of the alternatives in S for every individual determine the same social choice from S.

To state the next condition, it is necessary to define an *imposed* constitution as one in which there is some pair of alternatives for which the social choice is the same for all profiles.

Condition N (Non-imposition): The constitution is not imposed.

A constitution is said to be *dictatorial* if there is some individual, any one of whose strict preferences is the social preference according to that constitution.

Condition D (Non-dictatorship): The constitution is not dictatorial.

Theorem 1: There is no constitution satisfying Condition U, M, I, N and C.

A sketch of the argument can be given. From Condition I, the preference between any two alternatives depends only on the preferences of individuals between them and not on preferences about any other alternatives. Define a set of individuals to be *decisive* for alternative x against alternative y if the social preference is for x against y whenever all the individuals in the set prefer x to y. First, it can be shown that a set which is decisive for one alternative against one other is decisive for any alternative against any other. Hence, we can speak of a set of individuals as being decisive or not without reference to the alternatives being considered. If a set is not decisive, its complement (the voters not in the given set) can guarantee a weak preference, that is, preference or indifference. The set of all voters can easily be shown to be decisive, so there are decisive sets. The second stage in the proof is to take a decisive set with as few members of possible. If there were only one member, then by definition there would be a dictator, contrary to Condition D. Therefore, split the smallest decisive set so chosen into two subsets, say V_1 and V_2, and let V_3 contain all other voters. We now use an argument similar to that which showed the intransitivity of majority voting. Take any three alternatives, x, y and z. Suppose the members of V_1 all have the preference ordering, xyz, the members of V_2 the ordering yzx, and the members of V_3 the ordering zxy.

Since V_1 and V_2 each have fewer members than the smallest decisive set, neither is decisive. Since all voters other than those in V_2 prefer x to y, x must be preferred or indifferent socially to y. Since V_1 and V_2 together constitute a decisive set and y is preferred to z in both sets, y must be preferred socially to z. By transitivity, then, x is socially preferred to z. But x is preferred to z only by the members of V_1, which would therefore be decisive for x against z and hence a decisive set. This, however, contradicts the construction that V_1 is a proper subset of the smallest decisive set and therefore is not a decisive set. The theorem is therefore proved.

Notice that Condition U, that the constitution be defined for all profiles, is essential to the argument. We consider the consequences of particular profiles.

In Arrow (1951, p. 59), the theorem is stated with a weaker version of Condition U (and a corresponding restatement of Condition M).

Condition U': The constitution is defined for a set of profiles such that, for some set of three alternatives, each individual can order the set in any way.

Since the contradiction requires only three alternatives, I supposed that the more general assumption would be sufficient. This is not so, as first pointed out by Blau (1957). The reason is that the non-dictatorship Condition D may hold for the set of all alternatives and not hold for a subset, such as the triple of alternatives just described. To illustrate, suppose there are four alternatives altogether. Let S be a set of three of them, and let w be the fourth. Suppose each individual may have any ordering such that w is either best or worst. There are two individuals in the society. The constitution provides that the social preference between any pair in S follows the preferences of individual 1, but w is best or worst according to individual 2's preference ordering. This constitution would satisfy all the conditions of the Arrow 1951 version and therefore provides a counter-example. What is true, of course, is that individual 1 is a dictator over the alternatives in S. If we still wish to retain the weaker Condition U', the theorem remains valid if a stronger non-dictatorship condition is imposed (see Murakami, 1961).

Condition D': No individual shall be a dictator over any three alternatives.

The conditions are fairly straightforward and need little comment. If it is reasonable to limit the range of possible individual orderings because of prior knowledge about the range of possible beliefs, then Condition U or U' could be replaced by a corresponding range condition. As has already been remarked, if preference orderings are restricted to the single-peaked type, then majority voting defines a constitution. There has been a considerable literature on range restrictions which imply that majority voting defines a constitution and some on more general voting methods. In a world of multi-dimensional issues, these restrictions are not particularly persuasive.

Conditions M and N embody different aspects of the value judgement that social decisions are made on behalf of the members of the society and should shift as values shift in a corresponding way. Condition D expresses a very minimal degree of democracy.

Condition I (independence of irrelevant alternatives) is central to the social choice approach whether in the Impossibility Theorem or in other, more positive, results. It is implicit in Rawls's difference principle of justice (Rawls, 1971), as well as in utilitarianism or methods based on voting.

The above conditions have not included the Pareto principle explicitly.

Condition P: If every individual prefers x to y, then x is socially preferred to y.

It is not hard to prove, however, that this condition is implied by some of the previous conditions, specifically Conditions M, I and N. Further, if the Pareto condition is imposed, then the Impossibility Theorem holds without assuming Monotonicity or Non-imposition. Of course, it is obvious that the Pareto principle implies Non-imposition, since any choice can be enforced by unanimous agreement.

Theorem 2: there is no constitution satisfying Conditions U, P, I, and D.

This entry has dealt with Arrow's Theorem itself and not with subsequent developments, which have been very abundant. The reader is referred to the entry on Social Choice in this work, and the surveys by Sen (1986) and Kelly (1978).

KENNETH J. ARROW

See also SOCIAL CHOICE; SOCIAL WELFARE FUNCTION; WELFARE ECONOMICS.

BIBLIOGRAPHY

Arrow, K.J. 1950. A difficulty in the concept of social welfare. *Journal of Political Economy* 58, 328–46.

Arrow, K.J. 1951. *Social Choice and Individual Values*. New York: Wiley. (2nd edn, New Haven: Yale University Press, 1963, identical except for an additional chapter.)

Arrow, K.J. 1973. Formal theories of social welfare. In *Dictionary of the History of Ideas*, ed. P.P. Wiener, New York: Scribner's, Vol. 4, 276–84.

Bergson (Burk), A. 1938. A reformulation of certain aspects of welfare economics. *Quarterly Journal of Economics* 52, 310–34.

Black, D. 1948. On the rationale of group decision-making. *Journal of Political Economy* 56, 23–34.

Black, D. 1958. *Theory of Committees and Elections*. Cambridge: Cambridge University Press.

Blau, J. 1957. The existence of social welfare functions. *Econometrica* 25, 302–13.

Bowen, H.R. 1943. The interpretation of voting in the allocation of economic resources. *Quarterly Journal of Economics* 58, 27–48.

Condorcet, M. de Caritat, Marquis de. 1785. *Essai sur l'application de l'analyse à la probabilité des decisions rendues à la pluralité des voix*. Paris: Imprimerie Royale.

Edgeworth, F.Y. 1897. The pure theory of taxation. In F.Y. Edgeworth, *Papers Relating to Political Economy*, London: Macmillan, 1925, Vol. II, 63–125.

Hicks, J.R. 1939. The foundations of welfare economics. *Economic Journal* 49, 696–700, 711–12.

Kaldor, N. 1939. Welfare propositions of economics and interpersonal comparisons of utility. *Economic Journal* 49, 549–52.

Kelly, J.S. 1978. *Arrow Impossibility Theorems*. New York: Academic Press.

Murakami, Y. 1961. A note on the general possibility theorem of social welfare function. *Econometrica* 29, 244–6.

Rawls, J. 1971. *A Theory of Justice*. Cambridge, Mass.: Harvard University Press.

Scitovsky, T. 1941. A reconsideration of the theory of tariffs. *Review of Economic Studies* 9, 92–5.

Sen, A.K. 1986. Social choice theory. In *Handbook of Mathematical Economics*, ed. K.J. Arrow and M. Intriligator, Amsterdam, North-Holland, Vol. III, 1073–81.

Sidgwick, H. 1901. *Principles of Political Economy*. 3rd edn, London: Macmillan.

arts. *See* PERFORMING ARTS.

Asgill, John (1659–1738). Asgill was born at Hanley Castle, Worcestershire, 1659, called to the English bar 1692, expelled from the Irish House of Commons 1703, and from the British Parliament 1707, for an eccentric pamphlet contending that man could be translated to heaven without dying. He left this world in the ordinary way, 1738. He wrote the following economic works:

Several Assertions proved in order to create another Species of Money than Gold and Silver, London, 1696 (based on the theory 'man deals in nothing but earth'; a contemporary pamphlet asserts that it is plagiarized from J. Briscoe's *Discourse on the Late Funds*, 1694).

Essay on a Registry for Titles of Land London, 1698 (4th edn. 1758). A *Collection of Tracts*, London, 1715, 8 parts, *Abstract of the Publick Funds Granted and Continued to the Crown since 1 W. & M.*, London, 1715, (reprinted in Somers's *Tracts*, 1815, xiii. p. 730–741).

[H.R. TEDDER]
Reprinted from *Palgrave's Dictionary of Political Economy*.

Ashley, William James (1860–1927). Sir William Ashley graduated from Oxford, remained there for several years as a tutor, and was elected fellow of Lincoln College in 1885. In 1888 he moved to the newly created professorship of political economy and constitutional history at the University of Toronto, and in 1892 was appointed to the world's first chair in economic history, at Harvard. In 1901 he became professor in Birmingham, where he helped to organize the first university school of commerce in Britain.

Ashley was drawn towards historical economics by Toynbee and Cliffe Leslie. From early on, his anti-theoretical, ethical and empirical bent drew him into conflict with Marshall, who feared that Ashley's teaching was detrimental to the success of his own analytical and theoretical programme. Later Ashley became closely associated with the German Historical School. As an evolutionist he accepted their research programme of searching for stages of development, but admitted later in his life that its results had not lived up to the early hopes.

He was an important and successful pioneer in economic history, both by his own contributions where he helped to lay the foundation of modern economic history, and by his efforts to establish it as an acknowledged discipline.

Ashley insisted that economic theories closely reflected economic reality, were only true relative to time and circumstances, and held that influential old doctrines, generally believed to be erroneous, had not been without truth and value in their time.

Ashley consistently attacked laissez-faire, advocating further social legislation and the extension of state ownership. He supported trade unions since they, together with trusts regulated by the state, would limit competition, which in his view was responsible for crises and unemployment. He was an important participant in the Tariff controversy in 1903 where he came down in favour of protection.

O. KURER

See also ENGLISH HISTORICAL SCHOOL.

SELECTED WORKS
1888–93. *An Introduction to English Economic History and Theory*. 2 vols, London and New York: Longmans.
1900. *Surveys, Historic and Economic*. London and New York: Longmans.
1903. *The Tariff Problem*. London: P.S. King.
1914. *The Economic Organisation of England: An Outline History*. London and New York: Longmans.

BIBLIOGRAPHY
Ashley, A. 1932. *William James Ashley: A Life*. London: King.
Clapham, J.H. 1927. Obituary: Sir William Ashley. *Economic Journal* 37, 678–83.
MacDonald, J.L. 1942. Sir William Ashley. In *Some Historians of Modern Europe: Essays in Historiography by Former Students of the University of Chicago*, ed. B.E. Schmitt, Chicago: University of Chicago Press.
Samuels, W.J. 1977. Ashley's and Taussig's Lectures on the History of Economic Thought at Harvard, 1896–1897. *History of Political Economy* 9, 384–411.
Semmel, B. 1957. Sir William Ashley as 'Socialist of the Chair'. *Economica* , NS 24, 343–53.
Wood, J.C. 1983. *British Economists and the Empire, 1860–1914*. Beckenham, Kent: Croom Helm.

Ashton, Thomas Sutcliffe (1889–1968). T.S. Ashton was born in Lancashire in 1889, graduated from Manchester University in 1909 and returned there in 1921 (after some years at the Universities of Sheffield and Birmingham) to teach political economy and economic history in the Faculty of Commerce. By the time he took up Eileen Power's chair of economic history at the London School of Economics in 1944, he had made a substantive and distinctive contribution to the history of the industrial revolution in three research monographs: *Iron and Steel and in the Industrial Revolution* (1924), *The Coal Industry of the Eighteenth Century* (1929, written with Joseph Sykes), and *An Eighteenth Century Industrialist: Peter Stubs of Warrington* (1939). Over the next decade this unassuming, humane, passionately non dogmatic scholar had become the leader of a new generation of economic historians, a generation whose members had been schooled in the theories and analytical techniques of economics rather than in the thinking habits of a history faculty.

The two industrial studies and the business history published while Ashton was in Manchester were exercises in applied economics, based on detailed investigation of primary sources (including a mass of business ledgers, letters and accounts) and of a wide range of 18th-century material reflecting economic and social events, transactions and opinions. These researches gave him a formidable armoury of qualitative and quantitative data from which he set out in the 1940s explicitly to 'find answers (partial and provisional though these may be) to the questions economists ask, or should ask, of the past'.

Ashton's last three books constituted a coherent and cumulative contribution to the economic history of the first country to make the transition to modern economic growth. His highly original essay *The Industrial Revolution* (1948) appeared just when the industrialization problems of developing countries were assuming major importance on the applied economists' research agenda and became a long-running bestseller. His *Economic History of England: The Eighteenth Century* (1955), the prime example of a new genre of economic history, contained the first systematic attempt to use standard economic theory to explain long-term changes in the general level of prices and economic activity over that century, and also injected a characteristic objectivity into the perennial controversy over the standard of living of workers in the industrial revolution. In his last book, *Economic Fluctuations in England 1700–1800* (1959), he shifted his analysis of 18th-century economic change to a short-run focus. But by then only the pure theorists and the econometricians were actively interested in cyclical analysis, and Ashton was effectively distanced from both groups by his persistent concern with taking account of social as well as economic factors in economic change and by his realistically discriminating approach to the use of either abstract concepts or statistical evidence.

PHYLLIS DEANE

SELECTED WORKS
1924. *Iron and Steel in the Industrial Revolution*. Manchester: Manchester University Press.
1929. (With Joseph Sykes.) *The Coal Industry of the Eighteenth Century*. Manchester: Manchester University Press.
1939. *An Eighteenth Century Industrialist: Peter Stubs of Warrington*. Manchester: Manchester University Press.
1948. *The Industrial Revolution*. London: Oxford University Press.
1949. The standard of life of the workers of England, 1790–1830. *Journal of Economic History*, Supplement 9, 19-38.
1955. *An Economic History of England: The Eighteenth Century*. London: Methuen.
1959. *Economic Fluctuations in England, 1700–1800*. Oxford: Clarendon Press.

asset pricing. In the early 1950s Harry Markowitz developed a theory of portfolio selection which has resulted in a revolution in the theory of finance leading to the development of modern capital market theory (1952, 1959). He formulated a theory of investor investment selection as a problem of utility maximization under conditions of uncertainty. Markowitz discusses mainly the special case in which investors' preferences are assumed to be defined over the mean and variance of the probability distribution of single-period portfolio returns, but he also treated most issues developed more fully in the subsequent literature.

J. Tobin (1958) utilized the foundations of portfolio theory to draw implications with regard to the demand for cash balances. He also demonstrated that given the possibility of an investment in a risk-free asset as well as in a risky asset (or portfolio), an investor can construct a combined portfolio of the two assets to achieve any desired combination of risk and return. Subsequently, W. F. Sharpe, using one of the efficient methods for constructing portfolios discussed in the appendices to the Markowitz book (1959), developed what he called the 'diagonal model' in his dissertation under the direction of Markowitz, the results of which were later summarized in an article (1963). This represented another step towards general equilibrium models of asset prices developed almost simultaneously by Treynor (1965), Sharpe (1964, 1970), Lintner (1965a, b), and Mossin (1966, 1969). Important contributions were made by Fama (1971, 1976) and by Fama and Miller (1972).

These works resulted in the development of the relationship between return and risk summarized in what has been called the Security Market Line of the Capital Asset Pricing Model (CAPM).

$$E(R_j) = R_F + \left[\frac{E(R_M) - R_F}{\sigma_M^2} \right] \text{COV}(R_j, R_M). \tag{1}$$

This equation says that the return required (*ex ante*) by investors on any asset is equal to the return, R_F, on a risk-free asset plus an adjustment for risk. Alternatively, the risk adjustment can be defined as the market risk premium weighted by the risk of the individual asset normalized by the variance of market returns. This latter measure has been referred to as the beta measure (β) of the risk of an individual asset or security. $[\beta = \text{COV}(R_j, R_M)/\sigma_M^2.]$ Leading synthesis papers on the CAPM are by Jensen (1972) and Rubinstein (1973).

The CAPM model assumes that the market functions in a reasonably perfect way in the sense that: all individuals act as if they are price-takers of all relevant prices; all securities are perfectly divisible and can be sold both long and short without margin and/or escrow requirements; there are no transaction costs or taxes; and, as in nearly all useful economic theory, arbitrage opportunities are absent so that an appropriate one price law obtains. Individuals are assumed to be risk averse, expected utility maximizers. In that differential assessment of probabilities generally explains too much, it is usual (although not necessary for all purposes) to require that probability beliefs are homogeneous (Krouse, 1986). Subsequent work established that the main principles of the CAPM held up with the successive relaxation of the above assumptions (Black 1972; Brennan 1971; Lintner 1969; Mayers 1972, 1973; Merton 1973).

Roll's critique (1977) has had a major impact. His major conclusions are: (1) The only legitimate test of the CAPM is whether or not the market portfolio (which includes *all* assets) is mean-variance efficient; (2) If performance is measured relative to an index which is *ex post* efficient, then from the mathematics of the efficient set, no security will have abnormal performance when measured as a departure from the Security Market Line; (3) If performance is measured relative to an *ex post* inefficient index, then any ranking of portfolio performance is possible depending on which inefficient index has been chosen. The Roll critique does not imply that the CAPM is invalid, but that tests of the CAPM are joint tests with market efficiency and that its uses must be implemented with due care.

Three basic types of models of asset pricing have been most frequently employed. The simplest, called the *market model*, is based on the fact that returns on security j can be linearly related to returns on a 'market' portfolio, namely:

$$R_{jt} = a_j + b_j R_{Mt} + \epsilon_{jt} \tag{2}$$

where ϵ_{jt} is the mean zero classical normally distributed error term. The market model assumes that the slope and intercept terms are constant over the time period during which the model is fit to the available data, a strong assumption.

The second model is the capital asset pricing theory. It requires the intercept term to be equal to the risk-free rate, or the rate of return on the minimum variance zero-beta portfolio, both of which may change over time. In its simplest form, the CAPM is written

$$R_{jt} - R_{Ft} = [R_{Mt} - R_{Ft}]\beta_{jt} + \epsilon_{jt}. \tag{3}$$

Systematic risk, β_{jt}, is generally assumed to remain constant over the interval of estimation.

The third model is the empirical counterpart to the CAPM, referred to as the *empirical market line*

$$R_{jt} = \hat{\gamma}_{0t} + \hat{\gamma}_{1t}\beta_{jt} + \epsilon_{jt}. \tag{4}$$

This formulation does not require that the intercept term equal the risk-free rate. No parameters are assumed to be constant over time. In contrast to the market model, which is a time series expression, both the intercept, $\hat{\gamma}_{0t}$, and the slope, $\hat{\gamma}_{1t} = (R_{Mt} - R_{Ft})$, are the estimates taken from cross-section data each time period (typically each month). The betas in (4) are (following Fama and MacBeth, 1973) calculated from the market model [equation (2)]. (See Copeland and Weston, 1983, chs 7 and 10.)

Empirical tests of the CAPM were conducted by Miller and Scholes (1972), Fama and MacBeth (1973), and Reinganum (1981), among others. Most of the studies use monthly total returns (dividends are reinvested) on listed common stocks.

Asset pricing models have been used to measure portfolio performance by mutual funds, pension fund advisers, etc., and in residual analysis of the impact of accounting reports, stock splits, mergers, etc. Some studies have used the market model to measure the error terms or residuals–positive or negative performance. However, the generally accepted procedure is first to calculate the β's from the market line [equation (2)]. Portfolios ranked by β's provide groupings to minimize errors in the measurement of variables problem. These portfolio betas are used to develop the parameters (intercept and slope terms) in equation (4) which is the empirical market line used to estimate the CAPM of equation (3). With estimates of the γ terms, the empirical market line can then be used to calculate 'abnormal' returns or residuals from predicted security returns.

The empirical tests of CAPM typically are conducted in excess return form. The equation in this form should have an intercept term not significantly different from zero, with a slope equal to the excess market portfolio return. The empirical tests have found an intercept term significantly above zero with a slope less than predicted. Thus the empirical securities market line is tilted clockwise implying that low beta securities earn more than the CAPM would predict and high beta securities earn less. But the main predictions of the CAPM of a positive market price for risk and a model linear in beta are supported.

The recognition that the market return alone might not explain all of the variation in the return on an asset or a portfolio gave rise to a multiple factor analysis of capital asset pricing. This more general approach formulated by Ross (1976b) was called the Arbitrage Pricing Theory (APT). Requiring only that individuals be risk averse, the APT has multiple factors and in equilibrium all assets must fall on the arbitrage pricing line. Thus the CAPM is viewed as a special case of the APT in which the return on the market portfolio is the single applicable factor.

Empirical work on the APT was performed by Gehr (1975), Roll and Ross (1980), Reinganum (1981), and Chen, Roll and Ross (1984). These studies use data on equity daily rates of return for the New York and American Stock Exchange listed stocks. The initial studies establish that other factors contribute to an explanation of required returns but did not identify them. Later studies suggest that economic influences such as unexpected changes in inflation rates, default premia (measured by the difference between high- and low-grade bond yields), and the term premium in interest rates (measured by the difference between yields on short- and long-term bonds) correlate highly with the identified explanatory factors.

The CAPM and APT have provided useful conceptual frameworks for business finance applications such as capital budgeting analysis and for measurement of the cost of capital. Although the CAPM has not been perfectly validated by empirical tests, its main implications are upheld: systematic risk (beta) is a valid measure of risk, the model is linear in beta, and the tradeoff between return and risk is positive. The earliest empirical tests of the APT have shown that asset returns are explained by three or possibly four factors and have ruled out the variance of an asset's own returns as one of the factors.

THOMAS E. COPELAND AND J. FRED WESTON

See also ARBITRAGE PRICING MODEL; CAPITAL ASSET PRICING MODEL; FINANCE; INTERTEMPORAL PORTFOLIO THEORY AND ASSET PRICING.

BIBLIOGRAPHY

Black, F. 1972. Capital market equilibrium with restricted borrowing. *Journal of Business* 45(3), July, 444–55.

Brennan, M.J. 1971. Capital market equilibrium with divergent borrowing and lending rates. *Journal of Financial and Quantitative Analysis* 6(5), December, 1197–205.

Chen, N.F., Roll, R. and Ross, S.A. 1986. Economic forces and the stock market. *Journal of Business* 59(3), July, 383–403.

Copeland, T.E. and Weston, J.F. 1983. *Financial Theory and Corporate Policy*. 2nd edn, Menlo Park, California: Addison-Wesley Publishing Company.

Fama, E.F. 1971. Risk, return, and equilibrium. *Journal of Political Economy* 79(1), January–February, 30–55.

Fama, E.F. 1976. *Foundations of Finance*. New York: Basic Books.

Fama, E.F. and MacBeth, J. 1973. Risk, return, and equilibrium: empirical tests. *Journal of Political Economy* 81(3), May–June, 607–36.

Fama, E.F. and Miller, M.H. 1972. *The Theory of Finance*. New York: Holt, Rinehart and Winston.

Gehr, A., Jr. 1975. Some tests of the arbitrage pricing theory. *Journal of the Midwest Finance Association* 7, 91–107.

Jensen, M.C. 1972. Capital markets: theory and evidence. *Bell Journal of Economics and Management Science* 3(2), Autumn, 357–98.

Krouse, C.G. 1986. *Capital Markets and Prices: Valuing Uncertain Income Streams*. New York: North-Holland Press.

Lintner, J. 1965a. Security prices, risk, and maximal gains from diversification. *Journal of Finance* 20, December, 587–616.

Lintner, J. 1965b. The valuation of risk assets and the selection of risky investments in stock portfolios and capital budgets. *Review of Economics and Statistics* 47, February, 13–37.

Lintner, J. 1969. The aggregation of investors' diverse judgments and preferences in purely competitive securities markets. *Journal of Financial and Quantitative Analysis* 4, December, 347–400.

Markowitz, H.M. 1952. Portfolio selection. *Journal of Finance* 7, March, 77–91.

Markowitz, H.M. 1959. *Portfolio Selection: Efficient Diversification of Investments*. New York: Wiley.

Mayers, D. 1972. Non-marketable assets and capital market equilibrium under uncertainty. In *Studies in the Theory of Capital Markets*, ed. M.C. Jensen, New York: Praeger.

Mayers, D. 1973. Non-marketable assets and the determination of capital asset prices in the absence of a riskless asset. *Journal of Business* 46(2), April, 258–67.

Merton, R. 1973. An intertemporal capital asset pricing model. *Econometrica* 41(5), September, 867–87.

Miller, M. and Scholes, M. 1972. Rates of return in relation to risk: a re-examination of some recent findings. In *Studies in the Theory of Capital Markets*, ed. M.C. Jensen, New York: Praeger, 47–78.

Mossin, J. 1966. Equilibrium in a capital asset market. *Econometrica* 34, October, 768–83.

Mossin, J. 1969. Security pricing and investment criteria in competitive markets. *American Economic Review* 59, December, 739–56.

Reinganum, M.R. 1981. The arbitrage pricing theory: some empirical results. *Journal of Finance* 36(2), May, 313–22.

Roll, R. 1977. A critique of the asset pricing theory's tests: Part I. *Journal of Financial Economics* 4(2), March, 129–76.

Roll, R. and Ross, S. 1980. An empirical investigation of the arbitrage pricing theory. *Journal of Finance* 35(5), December, 1073–103.

Ross, S.A. 1976a. Options and efficiency. *Quarterly Journal of Economics* 90(1), February, 75–89.

Ross, S.A. 1976b. The arbitrage theory of capital asset pricing. *Journal of Economic Theory* 13(3), December, 341–60.

Rubinstein, M.E. 1973. A mean-variance synthesis of corporate financial theory. *Journal of Finance* 28(1), March, 167–81.

Sharpe, W.F. 1963. A simplified model for portfolio analysis. *Management Science* 9, January, 277–93.

Sharpe, W.F. 1964. Capital asset prices: a theory of market equilibrium under conditions of risk. *Journal of Finance* 19, September, 425–42.

Sharpe, W.F. 1970. *Portfolio Theory and Capital Markets*. New York: McGraw-Hill.

Tobin, J. 1958. Liquidity preference as behavior toward risk. *Review of Economic Studies* 25, February, 65–86.

Treynor, J.L. 1965. How to rate management of investment funds. *Harvard Business Review* 43, January–February, 63–75.

assets and liabilities. The concepts of assets and liabilities are very closely related. Liabilities can be regarded as negative assets. The term 'assets' is related to the French 'assez', meaning 'enough'. It emerges as a legal concept, particularly in laws relating to bankruptcy, the question being whether in bankruptcy assets are enough to meet all the liabilities. Historically, there has been a tendency to distinguish between real, personal and equitable assets, but these distinctions are now of little importance.

In accounting, assets and liabilities come into prominence with the invention of double-entry book-keeping and the balance sheet, a concept which seems to have originated in Northern Italy at least by the 12th or 13th century. This concept was important as a prerequisite for the development of complex markets and profit-oriented economies as an improvement in the information system. Before the invention of the balance sheet it was hard for a merchant to know whether he had made any profit or not.

It is the convention of the balance sheet that assets are listed on one side and liabilities and equity on the other side, equity being defined fundamentally as net assets; that is, assets minus liabilities, which are negative assets. Accounting practice divides both assets and liabilities into a number of categories. Assets are commonly divided into current, deferred and fixed assets. Current assets consist of cash, bank deposits, short-term notes, accrued interest, inventories of goods in process or finished goods which are expected to be sold within the accounting period, usually six months or a year. Sometimes items like repair parts are included in this category, even though their life on the shelf may be longer. Another item may be deferred assets, such as insurance, advertising payments which are paid in advance where the services have not yet been performed. Finally, there are fixed assets of a lasting nature, such as buildings and machines. There is also a category of intangible assets, like goodwill, value of patents, and so on. These tend to have a rather dubious status in accounting practice.

Liabilities have a somewhat similar categorization. Current liabilities are those which are expected to be paid off in the accounting period – wage claims, short-term loans, accounts payable, and so on. Current assets minus current liabilities is sometimes called 'working capital'. Somewhat corresponding to fixed assets are long-term loan obligations. The sum of all assets minus the sum of all liabilities is the equity or net worth. This is usually divided into paid-up capital and undistributed profits.

Every time an event happens to an organization that has a balance sheet, the items in the balance sheet change. Thus, in production, when wheat is ground into flour the stock of wheat diminishes and of flour increases. Likewise, the stock of money may diminish as wages are paid, and the product of the work is added to assets. Assets diminish as machinery and buildings depreciate. Exchanges, purchases and sales are reflected in an increase in what is acquired and a decrease in what is given up for it. When money is borrowed, cash is increased on the asset side and the debt is increased on the liability side. It is a convention of cost accounting that both exchange and production represent transfers of equal values. When something is purchased, it is valued at the amount paid for it, so that the net worth does not change. Similarly, in production, the value of what is produced is equal to what has been consumed (i.e. destroyed) in the process, whether this is the money used to pay wages, raw materials used up or depreciation.

Profit is the growth of net worth, which happens when some asset is revalued, usually at the moment of sale. If it is sold for more than the accounting cost, the difference is an increase in net worth. Before sale, the asset is valued at cost. After the sale, if it is profitable, the asset disappears from the accounts but a larger sum of money than the value of the asset is entered, and this is why the net worth increases. When profits are distributed the liquid assets are diminished and the net worth diminishes by the same amount. Interest-bearing liabilities grow at the rate of interest, which accrues. This diminishes the net worth, this being the growth of a negative asset. Interest paid, cash or some liquid asset, diminishes by the same amount as accrued interest diminishes. There is no change in the net worth. Profit is made by constant manipulation of the assets through production and exchange to increase the total value of assests at a greater rate than interest on liabilities is accruing. Debt is presumably incurred because of a belief that it will increase the total volume of assets sufficiently so that some kind of economies of scale will permit a rate of growth of the increased assets more rapid than the rate of interest on the liabilities that are incurred in order to expand the assets.

An important problem in accounting, by no means satisfactorily solved, is how to deal with inflation and deflation. In order to get a net worth or 'bottom line', both assets and liabilities have to be expressed in terms of the monetary unit. In the case of physical assets, this means multiplying the quantity of the assets by some valuation coefficient which will turn it into a number of monetary units. Where the asset is constantly being bought and sold, the price, or ratio of exchange, is generally used as a valuation coefficient. In the case of fixed capital, the value is usually reckoned by taking an original purchase price and depreciating it over time by various methods, either at a constant percentage rate or at a constant amount per year. This figure is very arbitrary in any case and in periods of inflation and deflation becomes extremely misleading. Inflation tends to increase accounting profits because fixed capital tends to be undervalued.

Another element in the situation is that all profit-making involves buying something at a certain price or cost at one time and selling it at a later time. If in the time interval all prices have risen, there is a spurious profit, which is not really represented by purchasing power. Thus there is much to be said for having a profit figure indexed, although the technical difficulties in this have so far prevented very much application of this principle. Inflation, therefore, produces illusory high profits; deflation, likewise, produces illusory low profits. This happened in the Great Depression, when accounting profits in 1932 and 1933 were negative. Unfortunately, it is accounting profits rather than real profits which tend to govern business expectations and decisions.

Beyond accounting, assets and liabilities make a very important contribution to the understanding of both the description and the dynamics of the economic system. Every liability is or should be an asset in some other balance sheet, for every debt is an asset to the creditor and a liability to the debtor. When we sum all the balance sheets in society, therefore, we should come out with an overall balance sheet that consists merely of real assets on one side and the total net worth of the society on the other. There is some question as to whether we should include money of various kinds in real assets. Bank deposits, of course, are assets to the holder and liabilities to the bank, so if we sum all assets, including banks, deposits would disappear. Even paper money is in a certain sense a liability of the government, although it is not usually reckoned as such, for it has to be accepted by government in payment of taxes. An important proposition follows from the concept of the aggregate balance sheet, that an increase in net assets, that is, investment, will produce an increase in the total of net worth, which is profit. This may be offset by other events. This is an important clue, however, to the dynamics of a great depression, which exhibits positive feedback: a decline in investment produces a decline in profits, a decline in profits produces a further decline in investment, a further decline in profits, and so on. This is clearly what happened between 1929 and 1933 in the capitalist world.

The relation of assets and liabilities to income, production and consumption is very important. Real assets can be regarded as a kind of ecosystem of goods, with the stock of each good representing a population. Production is then equivalent to births, consumption to deaths. Production minus consumption is the increase in the total stock of a particular good. The net national product is equal to the total production of goods, which is equal to the total consumption, plus an increase in the total stock of goods, just as an increase in any population is equal to the number of births minus the number of deaths in a given period.

Production is a function of the size and structure of real assets themselves, which is particularly clear if we include the value of the human bodies and minds (i.e. human capital) in the total, as ideally we should. Economists have an unfortunate way of regarding households as a kind of black box outside the economy proper. Actually they are very much a part of it, and household capital – houses, furniture, automobiles, clothing, and so on – is very close to half of the total in a modern society. When we fly over a city we see far more houses than factories. If we compare the capital around us at our workplace with the capital around us in our home, for a considerable part of the population the home capital is much larger than the capital at work.

Another very important problem is the contribution of assets, particularly household assets to economic welfare. There is a long tradition in economics that regards consumption as the main method of measurement of riches. It is clear, however, that we get most of our satisfaction from the use and enjoyment of assets rather than from their consumption. I get no satisfaction out of the fact that my car, house and clothing are wearing out. What I get satisfaction out of is using them. An increase in durability, especially of household capital, therefore, is an addition to economic welfare. This is a point much neglected by economists. Consumption, then, can usually be seen as a bad thing, and production as what is necessary to offset it. There are exceptions to this rule. We like eating. We like the activity of producing in itself, even though it involves the using up of raw materials and so on. Thus the economic welfare function would include both assets of all kinds and certain forms of production and consumption, that is, income. Economists have often confused consumption with household expenditure or purchases, again because they regard the household as outside the economy. In modern society this can be very misleading, for household purchases are governed in no small degree by the depreciation of household capital to the point where it has to be replaced, so this depreciation is a very important aspect of consumption and income. Household purchases are exchange, not consumption. The production of assets inside households also tends to be neglected, and it is an important part of the total economy in terms of cooking, mending, painting and repairing. The household has a balance sheet of assets and liabilities just as much as a business does and cannot be understood without it.

Human capital, both in terms of assets and liabilities, is a concept which has achieved some recognition. Economic development is primarily a process in human learning and the increase in human capital. A natural catastrophe or a war which destroys physical capital is restored remarkably quickly if the human capital remains intact and the knowledge and the know-how are unimpaired. We often do not realize that an enormous destruction of capital takes place every year just by depreciation and consumption. Even spectacular disasters are often just a relatively small addition to this annual destruction. The fact that some human beings have a negative human capital, both for themselves and for society, cannot be overlooked, though our social accounting system is ill-equipped to deal with this problem. In political decisions, however, we do recognize it. The criminal justice system is at least intended to diminish negative human capital; the educational system, to increase positive human capital. The fact that there is very little capital accounting in government means that considerable parts of its activity, like unilateral national defence organizations, do not really have a 'bottom line', and their value is usually assessed in non-economic terms, which can easily lead into catastrophic mistakes of judgement.

KENNETH E. BOULDING

See also ACCOUNTING AND ECONOMICS; DOUBLE-ENTRY BOOKKEEPING.

assignment problems. Suppose each member i from one class of objects (persons, firms) $i = 1, \ldots, n$ is matched with one object j from another class of equal size (jobs, locations) $j = 1, \ldots, n$ and the economic outcome is measurable in money terms a_{ij}. Let $x_{ij} = 1$ when object i is assigned to object j and $x_{ij} = 0$ otherwise. The payoff of this matching is then $\Sigma_{ij} a_{ij} x_{ij}$. It represents gross profits (profits before wages or rents) in the assignment of persons to jobs and of firms to locations.

In the personnel or plant assignment problem this is to be maximized subject to the constraints that x_{ij} be integer and that

$$\sum_{j=1}^{n} x_{ij} = 1 \qquad (1)$$

and

$$\sum_{i=1}^{n} x_{ij} = 1. \qquad (2)$$

This *Linear Assignment Problem* (Thorndike, 1950; von Neumann, 1953; Koopmans and Beckmann, 1957) represents the simplest type of an allocation problem involving indivisible resources.

Since one of the constraints is redundant and a feasible linear programme can always be solved with no more positive variables than active constraints, an argument by induction shows that the integer constraints can be dropped so that the assignment problem becomes a special case of the transportation problem in linear programming (one unit to be removed from every point i and to be received at every point j). Even when partial assignments are meaningful (as in the case of assigning persons to jobs) an optimal assignment always exists that is a matching of persons with full-time jobs. This remains true when the constraints are relaxed ($\leqslant$ instead of $=$) and when the number m of objects i is unequal to the number n of objects j.

An important implication of the fact that the linear assignment problem is a linear programme is the existence of efficiency prices p_i, q_j that characterize and sustain the solution.

$$p_i + q_j \leqslant a_{ij}, \quad \text{and '=' when} \quad x_{ij} > 0. \qquad (3)$$

In the personnel assignment problem this means the following: the gross profits a_{ij} of an optimal assignment are split into wage p_i and job rent q_j, and this is the highest return that either labour or job owner can earn,

$$p_i = \max_j [a_{ij} - q_j]$$

$$q_j = \max_i [a_{ij} - p_i]. \tag{4}$$

In the locational assignment problem p_i is the firm's net profit or rent and q_j the location rent. An optimal assignment is thus sustained by competitive markets in which p_i and q_j are charged as competitive prices, for any non-optimal assignment would not earn these wages and rents and thus incur a loss. When the number of objects to be matched is equal, the efficiency prices p_i, q_j contain an arbitrary constant that may be added to all p_i and subtracted from all q_j. When all gross profits a_{ij} are positive, then a system of positive prices p_i, q_j exists. When there are more locations than firms, however, the efficiency prices of the non-occupied locations are zero and the arbitrariness disappears.

The dual problem requires one to find a minimal sum of wages and rents that covers all possible assignments

$$\min_{p_i, q_j} \sum_{i=1}^n p_i + q_i$$

such that $p_i + q_j \geqslant a_{ij}$ for all $i, j = 1, \ldots, n$.

Suppose we arrange persons in the order of decreasing wages p_i. Then the optimal assignment results when we let persons choose jobs among the remaining vacancies in this order. When all are allowed to bid, however, the payoffs of the more attractive jobs must then be handicapped by job rents until an equilibrium is found in which every job attracts one and only one interested bidder. This is the person for whom this job realizes his comparative advantage (the absolute advantage as measured by the payoff a_{ij} is achieved only by that person who secures the highest wage). A person who scores higher on every job than another person will receive a higher competitive wage than the other person.

These results for the linear assignment problem apply also when multiple copies of the same job (machine) or of the same (type of) person are present.

An interesting variant is the room-mate problem where the objects come from the same set and the set contains an even number. There is then a single constraint

$$\sum_{j=1}^n x_{ij} + x_{ji} \leqslant 2 \tag{5}$$

which has a feasible solution when n is even.

Notice that each assignment is counted twice. The efficiency condition is

$$p_i + p_j \geqslant a_{ij} \quad \text{and} \quad '=' \quad \text{when} \quad x_{ij} > 0. \tag{6}$$

Any fractional assignment would now generate a closed chain of positive x_{ij} which can always be broken by decreasing some x_{ij} while increasing some other x_{jk} until no chains are left, resulting in an integer assignment once more.

The dual problem $\min_{\mu_i} \sum_{i=1}^n \mu_i$ such that $p_i + p_j \geqslant a_{ij}$ all $i, j = 1, \ldots, n$ is clearly feasible, so that when (5) is also feasible an optimum solution exists.

The linear assignment problem ignores interdependencies among the pairs formed by the assignment. Such interdependencies exist, however, in the location example when 'linkages' occur between the different plants through the exchange of intermediate commodities. Let $b_{kl} \geqslant 0$ denote the commodity flow in weight units from plant k to plant l and assume these numbers to be technical constants independent of location. Let c_{ij} denote the distance from location i to location j, measured in transportation costs incurred in moving one weight unit from i to j, and assume transportation costs

for a commodity flow to be proportional to weight times distance. When plants k and l are assigned to locations i and j respectively, the total transportation cost incurred is

$$\sum_{i,j,k,l} x_{ik} b_{kl} x_{lj} c_{ij}. \tag{7}$$

An optimal assignment is now one that minimizes (7) subject to the constraints (1) and (2). The minimand is quadratic and not concave. Relaxing the integer constraints will always result in fractional solutions, and it is the fractional solutions that would be sustained by the efficiency prices that are market prices. It follows that in general

> no price system on plants, on locations, and on commodities in all locations that is regarded as given by plant owners and landlords will sustain any assignment. There will always be an incentive for someone to seek a location other than the one he holds. In the case of plants on the drawing board, competitive choices cannot be induced or sustained by such a price system. In the case of actual establishments already located the cost of moving is the only element of stability in the technological circumstances we have assumed. Without such a break on movement there would be a continual game of musical chairs. Whatever the assignment, prices of intermediate commodities and rents on locations cannot be so proportioned as to give no plant an incentive to seek a location other than the one it holds (Koopmans and Beckmann, 1957, p. 70).

Examples illustrating this have in fact been constructed. This is a disturbing case of market failure in the face of 'externalities', the externalities of the transportation costs incurred by others that result from the locational choice of any particular plant owner.

Mathematically the quadratic assignment problem turns out to be of the nonpolynomial type where the number of computations is not bounded by any polynomial function of the size of the problem (the number of plants), but workable algorithms have been developed (Graves and Whinston, 1970; Geoffrion and Graves, 1976; Reiter and Sherman, 1962).

Suppose now that there is no cardinal measure for the outcome of a matching but only a preference ordering on the sets of agents, for example, medical students and hospitals (Roth, 1984), or men and women (Gale and Shapley, 1962). When each agent of one set is assigned to at most one agent of the other set, this is known as the marriage problem; if to more than one as the college admissions problem.

The marriage problem is defined by two disjoint sets of men $M = \{m_1, \ldots, m_n\}$ and women $W = \{w_1, \ldots, w_n\}$; each man has a strict preference ordering over the set $W \cup \{u\}$ of women, where u represents the possibility of remaining unmarried; and each woman has a strict preference ordering over the set $M \cup \{u\}$.

Thus each agent can compare the desirability of marrying a potential assignment from the opposite sex or of staying unmarried.

Let $w_j P(m) w_k$ denote that man m prefers woman j to woman k and $m_j P(w) m_k$ that woman w prefers man j to man k. An outcome of the marriage problem is an assignment $w = x(m)$ of women to men and of men to women $m = y(w)$ such that $w = x(m)$ if and only if $m = y(w)$. An outcome thus matches a subset of the women with a subset of the men in monogamous marriage and leaves the rest of the men and the women unmarried. It is called *individually rational* if no woman prefers being unmarried to the assignment $y(w)$ and no man prefers being unmarried to the assignment $x(m)$. An outcome is called *unstable* if it is not individually rational or if there exists a woman w and a man m who prefer each other to their assignments $y(w)$ and $x(m)$, $mP(w) y(w)$ and $wP(m) x(m)$. An assignment that is not unstable is called *stable*.

The set of stable assignments is the core $C(P)$ of the game with the following rules: any woman and any man marry if and only if they both agree and may remain unmarried if they prefer. This core is not empty: there always exists a stable outcome. For instance, let men be arranged in a fixed but arbitrary sequence and let the first man propose in the order of his preference until a woman accepts him or he has exhausted the set W. The next man proposes in the order of his preferences to the women who have not yet married and so on. A man who precedes another man in this sequence would never prefer the other man's wife, or else the other man's wife would not prefer him.

For any man m the set of achievable assignments is the set $A_m(P) = \{x(m) | x \text{ is in } C(P)\}$ which represents the set of women to whom marriage is achievable with a stable outcome or if empty, the unmarried state. The set $A_w(P)$ of achievable assignments for women is defined analogously.

Proposition. The set $C(P)$ of stable outcomes of the marriage problem contains a M-optimal stable outcome x^* with the property that, for every man m in M, $x^*(m)$ is man m's most preferred achievable assignment; that is $x^*(m) R(m) x(m)$ for any other stable outcome x. Similarly, it contains a W-optimal stable outcome y^* such that $y^*(w) R(w) x(w)$ for every woman w and any stable outcome x. Thus all men are in agreement that x^* is the best stable outcome. By symmetry all women agree that y^* is the best stable outcome.

The M-optimal stable outcome has the following property reminiscent of Pareto-optimality: there is no outcome preferred by all men to the M-optimal stable outcome x^*. There is no outcome preferred by all women to the W-optimal stable outcome y^*. Thus even among unstable outcomes none is preferred by all men to the M-optimal stable outcome (similarly for women). An algorithm to discover x^* was proposed by Gale and Shapley (1962). In the first round each man proposes to the woman he ranks first. A woman rejects all proposals but one and accepts tentatively the man she prefers most among those who have proposed to her. In the second round the rejected suitors propose to their second choice. A woman may now jilt her first acceptance if she receives a proposal she prefers. This process continues until all men have been accepted or have exhausted their choice. This process represents a fair approximation to current practice in the US (i.e. 'sequential monogamy').

What interest does an agent have to reveal his true preferences which are only known to himself? Suppose some known procedure is applied by a planning board to produce a stable outcome with respect to the stated preferences of the agents, to be called a stable matching procedure. Any stable matching procedure gives rise to a game in which each agent's strategies are the preference orderings he/she might state.

There is no stable matching procedure which makes it a dominant strategy for all agents to state their true preferences. However,

> the matching procedure that yields the M-optimal stable outcome $x^*(P)$ for any stated preference P makes it a dominant strategy for every m in M to state his true preferences in the marriage problem. Similarly, a procedure that always yields $y^*(P)$ makes it a dominant strategy for every w in W to state her true preferences (Roth, 1985, p. 280).

Stable outcomes exist also for the college admissions problem,

but their properties are somewhat weaker (Roth, 1985). Also, every solution to the linear assignment problem is stable.

MARTIN BECKMANN

See also INDIVISIBILITIES; INTEGER PROGRAMMING.

BIBLIOGRAPHY
Dubins, L.E. and Freedman, D.A. 1981. Machiavelli and the Gale–Shapley algorithm. *American Mathematical Monthly* 88, 485–94.
Gale, D. and Shapley, L. 1962. College admissions and the stability of marriage. *American Mathematical Monthly* 69, 9–15.
Geoffrion, A.M. and Graves, G.W. 1976. Scheduling parallel production lines with changeover costs: practical application of a quadratic assignment–LP approach. *Operations Research* 24(4), 595–610.
Graves, G.W. and Whinston, A.B. 1970. An algorithm for the quadratic assignment problem. *Management Science* 17, 453–71.
Koopmans, T.C. and Beckmann, M. 1957. Assignment problems and the location of economic activities. *Econometrica* 25, (1) January, 53–76.
Reiter, S. and Sherman, G.R. 1962. Allocating indivisible resources affording external economies or diseconomies. *International Economic Review* 3, January, 108–35.
Roth, A.E. 1982. The economics of matching: stability and incentives. *Mathematical Operations Research* 7, 617–28.
Roth, A.E. 1984. The evolution of the labor market for medical interns and residents: a case study in game theory. *Journal of Political Economy* 92, 991–1016.
Roth, A.E. 1985. The college admissions problem is not equivalent to the marriage problem. *Journal of Economic Theory* 36, 277–88.
Thorndike, R.L. 1950. The problem of classification of personnel. *Psychometrika* 15, 215–35.
Von Neumann, J. 1953. A certain zero-sum two-person game equivalent to the optimal assignment problem. In *Contributions to the Theory of Games,* ed. H.W. Kuhn and A.W. Tucker, Vol. II, Princeton: Princeton University Press.

asymmetric information. The Arrow–Debreu model is the basic model in which the two classical welfare theorems of economics are expressed. Under quite general assumptions, it can be shown that, first, a competitive equilibrium allocation, or Walrasian allocation, is Pareto efficient (Pareto optimal); second, under somewhat different assumptions, any Pareto efficient allocation will be a competitive equilibrium allocation after some suitable redistribution of initial endowments. Implicitly or explicitly, the statement of the first welfare theorem assumes that all economic agents have the same information about all economic variables. This is not to say that uncertainty is ruled out; there may be uncertainty as long as all agents are identically uncertain. If this assumption of symmetric information is violated, the competitive outcome will no longer be guaranteed to be Pareto efficient. The introduction of asymmetric information into various economic problems has given us new insight into how market failures might arise and whether there may be governmental, or other non-market, corrections which can improve welfare. Several examples illustrating this are given below.

There may be a good which can vary in quality and whose quality will be known only by the owner. As an example, one can think of the objects being sold as used cars. Potential buyers will realize that there are good and bad quality cars and will rationally pay a price based on the average quality. This means that some cars will be underpriced (the highest quality cars), but which ones will be known only to the owner. Some underpriced cars may be so much underpriced that the owners will not be willing to sell them at the price based on the average quality. But the withdrawal of these quality cars causes the average quality of the cars in the market to decrease and consequently, potential buyers will rationally lower the price they are willing to pay for a car randomly drawn from those remaining. This in turn may lead to another round of withdrawal of some of the better remaining cars and a further lowering of the price buyers will pay. In the extreme, the equilibrium of this process may have no cars sold even in the case that all would have been sold had the quality of goods been symmetrically known, that is, when either everyone or no one could determine the quality. This problem is essentially that analysed by Akerlof (1970).

Asymmetric information has been introduced into a labour-management model to illustrate how it may distort the optimal labour contract. Assume that the demand function facing the firm is known to the firm but not to the workers. An optimal contract would generally be characterized by a constant labour force and a variable wage, lower wages being associated with lower levels of demand. This may not be feasible given the asymmetry, however. The firm would announce that the state of demand is low regardless of the truth since this lowers its wage bill without cost. The optimal contract with the asymmetry will typically involve a lower amount of labour employed when the firm announces that demand is low. Since this is more costly when demand is high (and the marginal revenue product of an additional hour is high), than when demand is low, optimal contracts in the presence of this sort of asymmetric information often take this form. Rosen (1985) surveys the literature on this problem.

A third area in which asymmetric information has been successfully introduced into traditional economic problems is that of industrial organization. As an example, it can be assumed that there are several firms within an industry and that each may know more about its own cost structure than about its competitor's (or potential competitor's). Equilibria in such models conform better to what is generally believed to be involved in predatory pricing and limit pricing than equilibria in models without asymmetric information. (Examples of such arguments can be found in Milgrom and Roberts, 1982a, 1982b.) It has also been shown that if small amounts of asymmetric information are introduced into the finitely played prisoners' dilemma game and into the chain store paradox, the paradoxes associated with these games disappear (see, e.g., Kreps et al., 1982).

In public economics, models have been investigated in which individuals know their own valuation for public goods but know nothing about other individuals' valuations. These models provide explanations of how and why governments may want to provide public goods. These explanations improve upon the explanations provided by models without asymmetric information; in addition, they provide a clearer understanding of the nature of the improvement in welfare that a government can effect. (Bliss and Nalebuff (1984) gives an insight into the problem of public goods with asymmetric information.)

The above examples focus on positive models which encompass asymmetric information. That is, they provide models which depend upon asymmetries in information to explain phenomena which are generally believed, but which are difficult to reconcile with optimizing behaviour in the absence of such asymmetries. There is extensive use of asymmetric information in normative models as well. We may want to devise governmental or non-governmental mechanisms to augment, alter, or replace markets; if so, we presumably want to do so in an 'optimal' manner, whatever notion of optimality we may want to rely on. To the extent that there is asymmetry among the agents in the economy in question, we must be able to predict the outcome after our

augmentation, alteration or replacement in the face of this asymmetry. This approach has been used extensively in optimal taxation. Suppose one feels that a given amount of tax revenue must be raised and that it is fairest to raise more revenue from those who are most able (most productive). If the ability of an agent is known to himself but not to anyone else, this asymmetry of information has to be taken into account. We must maximize social welfare subject to the constraint that it must be in the individuals' interest to reveal, indirectly or directly, these privately known abilities. In this manner, it is possible to derive characteristics of an optimal tax schedule under asymmetric information. In a similar manner we can determine the qualitative characteristics of other types of taxes to be levied in environments with asymmetric information. Atkinson and Stiglitz (1980) is an excellent reference to the literature in this area.

Similar normative models have been used to investigate the nature of optimal policy for many problems such as regulatory policy, anti-trust policy, monetary policy and other problems in which asymmetric information may play a role.

The common technique in analysing both normative and positive problems with asymmetric information is to model them as games with incomplete information and to use the Bayesian–Nash solution concept. This captures both the asymmetric information and the problems raised by economic agents sometimes having incentives to misrepresent the information they have. This modelling technique is not wholly satisfactory, however. Embedded in the technique is the assumption that the information structure is common knowledge. This is an assumption that while an agent may not know the exact information that another agent has, he knows the probability distribution of the information. Further, the second agent knows that the first knows this, the first knows that the second knows that he knows, and so on ad infinitum. The assumption that the information structure is common knowledge is extremely strong and the results of models using the assumption are correspondingly less convincing. Myerson (1979) is the standard reference here.

Much of the use of asymmetric information in economic models was motivated by a desire to understand seeming (Pareto) inefficiencies in particular market situations. The integration of asymmetric information into economic models accomplished this. In addition, the formalization of the asymmetry in the information among agents helped to clarify the notion of welfare in such circumstances as well. The question of whether or not a change from one allocation to another might make all agents better off is unambiguous in the case that there is no uncertainty. With uncertainty which is identical for all agents, it is also simple; each agent makes the comparison between the two allocations by taking the expected utility of the allocations using the commonly accepted probability distribution. When each agent has different information the problem becomes more complicated. Some agents may know that certain events cannot happen while others may not know this. What probabilities should be used to calculate an agent's expected utility – his own beliefs, those of the best informed agent, the totality of the information held by all agents or some entirely different probability? Holmstrom and Myerson (1983) provide a careful analysis of welfare judgements in the face of asymmetric information.

The introduction of asymmetric information into models in which agents behave strategically made it necessary to consider not only what agents knew, but what they thought other agents knew, what they thought other agents knew about what they knew and so forth. Addressing this directly resolved many of the dilemmas posed by welfare comparisons in an environment with asymmetric information.

A. POSTLEWAITE

See also ADVERSE SELECTION; IMPLICIT CONTRACTS; INCENTIVE CONTRACTS; INCOMPLETE CONTRACTS; MORAL HAZARD; PRINCIPAL AND AGENT.

BIBLIOGRAPHY

Akerlof, G. 1970. The market for lemons. *Quarterly Journal of Economics*, August, 488–500.

Atkinson, A. and Stiglitz, J. 1980. *Lectures on Public Economics*. New York: McGraw-Hill.

Bliss, C. and Nalebuff, B. 1984. Dragon-slaying and ballroom dancing: the private supply of a public good. *Journal of Public Economics* 25, August, 1–12.

Holmstrom, B. and Myerson, R. 1983. Efficient and durable decision rules with incomplete information. *Econometrica* 51, November, 1799–1820.

Kreps, D., Milgrom, P., Roberts, J. and Wilson, R. 1982. Rational cooperation in the finitely repeated prisoners' dilemma. *Journal of Economic Theory* 27, August, 245–52.

Milgrom, P. and Roberts, J. 1982a. Predation, reputation, and entry deterrence. *Journal of Economic Theory* 27, August, 280–312.

Milgrom, P. and Roberts, J. 1982b. Limit pricing and entry under incomplete information: an equilibrium analysis. *Econometrica* 50, 443–59.

Myerson, R. 1979. Incentive compatibility and the bargaining problem. *Econometrica* 47, 61–74.

Rosen, S. 1985. Implicit contracts: a survey. *Journal of Economic Literature* 23, September, 1144–75.

atomistic competition. This term was originally taken from the physical concept of matter as composed of atoms, the smallest irreducible elementary particles in a void. This idea, which originates with Democritus and Epicurus, was adopted in the 19th century by economists to convey two ideas. The first, which has persisted, is the notion that individuals are many and unimportant. This has led to an assimilation in the French literature of 'atomistic competition' to 'perfect competition'. However a second and more subtle idea was implied and received its clearest early expression in the work of Adam Smith. This is the concept of a society or economy as 'atomistic' rather than 'organic'. Thus it is the actions of many independent individuals which determine the evolution of the whole, rather than the collective organization of these individuals. This idea was contested in particular by Marx, whose position was the opposite of that of the utilitarians.

Paradoxically in modern terms the term atomistic competition is wholly inappropriate as a description of the perfectly competitive model. The mathematical idea which corresponds to perfect competition is that of an 'atomless measure space' of agents. This conveys accurately the idea that although no individual has any weight, collectively they can have positive weight or influence. An atom in this context is an individual who alone does have weight and thus can influence economic outcomes. This might correspond to a very wealthy agent, a firm or a monopolist (*see* MEASURE THEORY). Thus the appropriate modern term would be 'atomless competition'.

A.P. KIRMAN

See also LARGE ECONOMIES; MEASURE THEORY.

attributes. *See* CHARACTERISTICS.

Attwood, Thomas (1783–1856). In British social and political history the name of Thomas Attwood is usually connected with the Birmingham Political Union, of which he was a founder, and hence the part that movement played in the peaceful enactment of the great Reform Act of 1832. Later he was also associated with the Chartist movement. However, Attwood also has a place in the history of economic thought as an early exponent of anti-classical monetary and macroeconomic ideas and as the leading member of the so-called Birmingham School.

Thomas Attwood was born in 1783, the son of a banker and into whose profession he followed. From an early age he was also active in public affairs in the City of Birmingham. In 1811 he was elected high Bailiff of that town and the following year, with Richard Spooner (later to be another notable member of the Birmingham School) he represented Birmingham manufacturers' interests against the Orders in Council that had restricted UK trade with the USA and the Continent.

He was the first drawn into monetary controversy by the depression that followed the ending of the Napoleonic wars in 1815. Birmingham was then an important manufacturing town and had become the centre of small arms manufacture during the wars. Hence the abrupt reduction in government demand had a quick and sharp effect on the local economy. Attwood was particularly incensed by the cavalier attitude adopted by some orthodox classical economists towards the distress brought about by the postwar depression. Ricardo, for example, expressed little knowledge of it and doubted the claims of Birmingham industrialists. Attwood's first pamphlet – *The Remedy* – appeared anonymously in 1816 and this was followed in 1817, under his own name, by *A Letter to Nicholas Vansittart on the Creation of Money, and its Action upon National Prosperity*.

Those early pamphlets give us the theme that was to dominate all of Thomas Attwood's writings in the field of monetary economics. His prime object was the abolition of the metallic standard and its replacement with a flexible, managed, currency which, he believed was essential for a full employment policy. Throughout his many subsequent writings he never waivered from this position.

In 1830 Attwood was a founder of the Birmingham Political Union for the Protection of Public Rights: its aim was to secure middle and lower class representation in the House of Commons and the Union played a crucial role in supporting the Grey administration during the passage of the Reform Bill of 1832. In the same year together with Joshua Scholefield he was returned unopposed as a Member of Parliament for the new Parliamentary Borough of Birmingham. He continued to agitate for further Parliamentary reform and in 1839 was a presenter of the mammoth Chartist Petition to Parliament.

His place in the Chartist movement was uneasy and ambiguous. He never endorsed the use of physical force that was advocated by some of the more extreme leaders of the movement. More fundamentally the central tenet of Attwood's monetary proposals – the introduction of an inconvertible paper currency – was utterly rejected by the Chartists who attacked what they termed 'rag botheration' (paper currency) as enthusiastically as Cobbett.

Attwood felt, and rightly so, that his monetary ideas were never taken seriously by the establishment and he undoubtedly suffered from what may be termed a persecution complex. He was for example, caricatured by Disraeli in the *Runnymede Letters* and by J.S. Mill in the *Currency Juggle*.

Attwood died in 1856 a disappointed man. Birmingham honoured him with a statue in Stephenson's Place (1859).

His brother Matthias also wrote some important pamphlets in monetary matters but never took up the extreme position of his brother Thomas.

B.A. CORRY

See also BIRMINGHAM SCHOOL.

SELECTED WORKS
1964. *Selected Economic Writings.* Edited with an Introduction by F.W. Fetter, London: LSE Reprints of Scarce Works on Political Economy.

BIBLIOGRAPHY
Briggs, A. 1948. Thomas Attwood and the economic background of the Birmingham Political Union. *Cambridge Historical Journal* 9(2), 190–216.
Checkland, S.G. 1948. The Birmingham economists 1815–1850. *Economic History Review,* Second Series 1(1), 1–19.
Corry, B.A. 1962. *Money, Saving and Investment in English Economics.* London: Macmillan.
Wakefield, C.M. 1885. *Life of Thomas Attwood.* Printed privately.

auctioneer. Walras (1874) introduced the idea of a tâtonnement to provide a theoretical account of the formation of equilibrium prices. This account was not meant to be taken descriptively but rather as a 'Gedanken Experiment'. It was hoped that its study would provide insights into the actual *modus operandi* of the price mechanism.

Consider an economy of H households, F firms and n goods. Let $p \in \Delta \subset R^n_+$, where p is a price vector and Δ the simplex. Given the endowments of households ($e^h \in R^n_+$), $x^h - e^h$ is the net trade vector of household h where $x^h \in R^n_+$ is the vector of demand of household h. Assume that

$$x^h - e^h = \xi_h(p)$$

where $\xi_h(p)$ is a continuous function from Δ to R^n. Let $y^f \in R^n$ be an activity of firm f, where $y^f_i > 0$ is interpreted as 'the firm supplies good i' and $y^f_i < 0$ is interpreted as 'the firm demands good i as an input'. Let $y = \Sigma_f y^f$ and assume that

$$y = \eta(p)$$

is a continuous function from Δ to R^n. Then define

$$z = \sum (x^h - e^h) - y$$

which by our assumptions can be written as, say

$$z = \sum_h \xi_h(p) - \eta(p) = \theta(p).$$

It is known that addition of budget constraints implies

$$p \cdot z = 0 \qquad \text{all } p \in \Delta.$$

(Walras' Law). An equilibrium of the economy is $p^* \in \Delta$ such that

$$\theta(p^*) \leqslant 0.$$

It should be added that the net trades $\xi_h(p)$ are assumed to be utility maximizing for each household under the budget constraint:

$$p \cdot \xi_h(p) \leqslant \sum_f \lambda_{hf}(p \cdot y^f)$$

where $1 \geqslant \lambda_{hf} \geqslant 0$, $\Sigma_h \lambda_{hf} = 1$, is the share of h in the profits of firm f. Similarly $\eta^f(p) = y^f$ satisfies for all f:

$$p \cdot \eta^f(p) \geqslant p \cdot y^f \qquad \text{all } y \text{ which the firm can choose amongst.}$$

A tâtonnement is now described as follows. A fictitious agent called the *auctioneer* announces $p \in \Delta$. Households now report to this auctioneer their desired net trades $[\xi_h(p)]$ and firms report to him their desired activities $[\eta^f(p)]$. From these reports the auctioneer can deduce $\theta(p)$. In its light he calculates a new price vector p' as follows:

$$\frac{p'_i}{\sum p'_i} = \frac{p_i}{\sum p_i} \qquad \text{if } \theta_i(p) = 0 \text{ or if } \theta_i(p) < 0 \text{ and } p = 0$$

$$\frac{p'_i}{\sum p'_i} > \frac{p_i}{\sum p_i} \qquad \text{if } \theta_i(p) > 0$$

$$\frac{p'_i}{\sum p'_i} < \frac{p_i}{\sum p_i} \qquad \text{if } \theta_i(p) < 0.$$

He announces p' and agents send back messages which allow him to calculate $\theta(p')$. The process continues until and if the rule for calculating a new price vector yields the preceding price vector. *No actual trading occurs* during this process.

The rule which we have supposed the auctioneer follows in changing his price announcement is only one of a number of possible ones. Indeed, it is not the one proposed by Walras. He supposed the auctioneer to concentrate on one market at a time, specifically he changes only one price. Suppose he changes the ith price. Then he changes it until, given all other prices which are held constant, the ith market is in equilibrium. (He assumed that there always is such a price and that it is unique.) Thereafter he moves on to the next market. Of course, this process may never terminate in an equilibrium.

In all of this one ought to specify what it is that the auctioneer knows. So far we have assumed that he does not know the function $\theta(p)$. If, however, he does know this function we may think of the auctioneer as being concerned to find a solution to $\theta(p) \leqslant 0$ for $p \in \Delta$. He is then no more than a programmer. In this case, for instance, he may adopt Newton's method (Arrow and Hahn, 1971; Smale, 1976). That is he proceeds as follows: Let $J(p)$ be the $(n-1) \times (n-1)$ Jacobian of the first $(n-1)$ excess demand functions $[\hat{\theta} = \theta_1(p) \ldots \theta_{n-1}(p)]$. The price of the nth good is set identically equal to unity (it is the numeraire). Then define $\hat{p} = (p_1, \ldots, p_{n-1})$ and let $\hat{q} = (q_1, \ldots, q_{n-1})$ solve:

$$\hat{\theta}(\hat{p}) - J(\hat{p})(\hat{q} - \hat{p}) = 0$$

where it is assumed that a solution exists:

$$(\hat{q} - \hat{p}) = J(\hat{p})^{-1}\hat{\theta}(\hat{p}).$$

The auctioneer now follows the rule: raise p_i if $q_i - p_i > 0$, lower p_i if $q_i - p_i < 0$ and $p_i > 0$ and leave p_i unchanged if either $q_i = p_i$ or $q_i < p_i$ and $p_i = 0$. Under certain technical assumptions this way of calculating will lead the auctioneer to an equilibrium (see Arrow and Hahn, 1971).

This example demonstrates that it is possible to think of a tâtonnement as a kind of computer program. If one adopts this view, however, one will certainly not be mimicking the invisible hand. For instance, in the Newton method the price change in any one market depends on the excess demand functions in all markets and that is not what any version of 'the law of supply and demand' stipulates. Moreover the proposal violates the supposed economy in information of decentralized economies – that is much more is known to the auctioneer than can be known to any one agent. From the point of view of positive theory, therefore, this second interpretation of the auctioneer is not helpful, although it has found application in the theory of planning (e.g. Heal, 1973).

Assuming that the auctioneer only knows aggregate excess demands at the announced p, it has been customary ever since a famous paper by Samuelson (1941, 1942) on Hicksian stability to formulate the rule followed by the auctioneer dynamically. For instance:

$$\frac{dp_i}{dt} = 0 \qquad \text{if } \theta_i(p) < 0 \text{ and } p_i = 0$$

$$\frac{dp_i}{dt} = k_i \theta_i(p) \qquad \text{otherwise with } k_i > 0.$$

Even if this process leads to p^* it will do so only as $t \to \infty$. This is awkward since no one is allowed to trade while the process is still in motion. Some economists have by-passed this by saying that the time here involved is not calendar, but 'model-time'. On reflection it is not clear what that means unless it is 'computer time' which is meant and, if it is, one must again ask whether the construction will then have anything to do with any actual price mechanism.

Arrow (1959) has suggested an alternative interpretation which, however, much restricts the applicability of the tâtonnement. Suppose we think of time as divided into trading periods and let the auctioneer follow the rule:

$$p_i(t) = p_i(t-1) + k_i \theta_i [p(t-1)] \qquad k_i > 0$$

(with the usual boundary condition to avoid negative prices). Now suppose (a) that one is concerned with a pure exchange economy and (b) that all goods last for only one period so that agents in each period receive new endowments (identical for each period). Then we can allow the agents to trade during the process *without the trade in any one period* affecting the excess demand at any p in a subsequent period. So now (a) we think of the process in real time and (b) even if it converges to p^* only as $t \to \infty$ or does not converge at all, agents can trade.

This very restrictive case clarifies the reason why in general the tâtonnement prohibits trade out of equilibrium. Let $\hat{e} = (e^1, \dots, e^H)$, the endowment matrix of a pure exchange economy in which goods are durable. Let us now take explicit note of $\hat{e}$ in the excess demand function (since it was constant it was omitted hitherto) and write

$$\sum_h (x^h - e^h) = \hat{\theta}(p, \hat{e}).$$

Assuming that $\hat{\theta}(p, \hat{e}) = 0$ has a unique solution, the latter will depend on $\hat{e}$ and may be written as $p^*(\hat{e})$. If now trading takes place out of equilibrium, $\hat{e}$ will be changing and so therefore will $p^*(\hat{e})$. Thus when there is such out of equilibrium trading, the equilibrium which the tâtonnement is groping for will depend on the manner of the groping. To exclude this dependence was the purpose of excluding out of equilibrium trade. But there was another reason, namely the lack of any clear theory of how trade would proceed when either some prospective buyers or sellers could not carry out their trading intentions.

The fictitious auctioneer is also a consequence of theoretical lacunae and indeed of a certain logical difficulty. If prices are to be changed by the economic agents of the theory, that is either by households or firms or both then it is not easy to see how those same agents are also to treat prices as given exogenously as is required by the postulate of perfect competition. This difficulty was first noted by Arrow (1959) who argued that out of equilibrium price changes not brought about by an auctioneer require a departure from the perfect competition assumption if they are to be understood. Take for instance a situation for which $\hat{\theta}_i(p, \hat{e}) > 0$. Then at p there will be unsatisfied buyers. But that means that any firm raising its price for good i by a little will not, as in the usual perfect competition setting, lose all its customers. The reason is that buyers cannot be sure of obtaining the good from any of the other firms which have not yet raised their price. Hence the demand curve for good i facing a producer of that good is not perfectly elastic. (On the other hand, in equilibrium it well might be.) The postulate of the auctioneer sidesteps these problems at the cost of an understanding of how prices are

actually changed. It has enabled theorists to ignore the role of monopolistic competition in the process of price formation – a circumstance which until recently has left the whole matter without proper theoretical foundations.

But it must also be admitted that there are formidable theoretical difficulties to be faced in banishing the auctioneer. Whether we think of prices as formed by a bargaining process or by monopolistic competition or in some form of auction process, strategic considerations, that is to say, game theoretic tools, will be required. In addition, careful attention will have to be given to the information available to each of the agents involved in the process. Some progress has been made (e.g. Roth, 1979; Schmeidler, 1980; Rubinstein and Wolinsky, 1985) but there is a very long way to go. (Some economists have banished the auctioneer without considering these matters by the simple device of treating it as axiomatic that at all times the economy is in competitive equilibrium. There is nothing favourable to be said for this move.)

There is now also a somewhat subtler point to consider: the behaviour postulated for the auctioneer will implicitly define what we are to mean by an equilibrium: that state of affairs when the rules tell the auctioneer to leave prices where they are. But the auctioneer's pricing rules are not derived from any consideration of the rational actions of agents on which the theory is supposed to rest. Thus the equilibrium notion becomes arbitrary and unfounded. If, on the other hand, we had a theory of price formation based on the rational calculations of rational agents then the equilibrium notion would be a natural corollary of such a theory. For instance, one might then be led to describe a situation in which there is unemployment as one of equilibrium because neither firms nor workers, given their information and beliefs, find it advantageous to change the wage.

This line of reasoning leads one to a central objection to the auctioneer and indeed the tâtonnement: it sidesteps the important question of the co-ordinating power of the price mechanism. Here is an example. In an oligopolistic industry with excess supply it may not be advantageous for any one firm to reduce its price given its beliefs as to the strategies of its competitors. Yet it may be to all of the firms' advantage to have the price reduced: there is a co-operative solution which dominates the competitive one. Put another way, there are significant externalities in price-signalling. To leave these unstudied is to leave very important matters in darkness. The auctioneer is a co-ordinator *deus ex machina* and hides what is central.

These considerations are most striking in the context of Keynesian theory. As long as the auctioneer is in the picture no state of the economy in which there is involuntary unemployment can qualify as an equilibrium – the auctioneer would be reducing wages. But without the auctioneer the observation that a worker would prefer to work at the going real wage to being idle does not logically entail the proposition that the wage will be reduced. That proposition would require a great deal of further theoretical underpinning turning on the beliefs of workers, the strategies of other workers and the strategies of employers. It would also turn on the information available to agents. For instance, if lowering one's wage is regarded as a signal of lower quality of work then one may be reluctant to offer to work at a lower wage. The fictitious auctioneer makes sure that none of these matters is studied or understood. The use of this fiction encourages the view that all Pareto-improving moves will, in a competitive economy, be undertaken. This view, however, lacks any foundations other than the auctioneer himself.

One might just about convince oneself that notwithstanding all these objections, the tâtonnement and its auctioneer are worthwhile, if it were the case that it provided one story which showed how equilibrium was brought about. Unfortunately, however, it does not do this for there are only a few special cases for which the auctioneer process leads the economy to an equilibrium. In many others it will not do so. Indeed, in so far as one holds the view that an equilibrium is the normal state of an economy one should not be tempted to understand this circumstance by means of a tâtonnement.

F. HAHN

See also ADJUSTMENT PROCESSES; TÂTONNEMENT AND RECONTRACTING; WALRAS, MARIE-ESPRIT LÉON.

BIBLIOGRAPHY

Arrow, K.J. 1959. Towards a theory of price adjustment. In *The Allocation of Economic Resources,* ed. M. Abramovitz et al., Stanford: Stanford University Press, 41-51.

Arrow, K.J. and Hahn, F.H. 1971. *General Competitive Analysis.* San Francisco: Holden-Day; Edinburgh: Oliver & Boyd.

Heal, G.M. 1973. *The Theory of Economic Planning.* Amsterdam, London: North-Holland.

Roth, A.E. 1979. *Axiomatic Models of Bargaining.* Lecture Notes in Economics 170, Berlin: Springer-Verlag.

Rubinstein, A. and Wolinsky, A. 1985. Equilibrium in a market with sequential bargaining. *Econometrica* 53(4), 1133–50.

Samuelson, P.A. 1941, 1942. The stability of equilibrium. *Econometrica* 9, 97–120; 10, 1–25. Reprinted in Samuelson (1966), Vol. I, 539–62, 565–89.

Samuelson, P.A. 1966. *The Collected Scientific Papers of Paul A. Samuelson.* Ed. Joseph E. Stiglitz, Cambridge, Mass.: MIT Press.

Schmeidler, D. 1980. Walrasian analysis via strategic outcome functions. *Econometrica* 48, 1585-93.

Smale, S. 1976. A convergent process of price adjustment and global Newton methods. *Journal of Mathematical Economics* 3(2), 107–20.

Walras, L. 1874–7. *Eléments d'économie politique pure.* Definitive edn, Lausanne, 1926. Trans. by W. Jaffé as *Elements of Pure Economics,* London: George Allen & Unwin, 1954.

auctions. Herodotus reports the use of auctions as early as 500 BC in Babylon (see Cassady, 1967, pp. 26–40 for references to this and the following historical notes). The Romans made extensive use of auctions in commerce and the Roman emperors Caligula and Aurelius auctioned royal furniture and heirlooms to pay debts. Roman military expeditions were accompanied by traders who bid for the spoils of war auctioned *sub hasta* (under the spear) by soldiers. In AD 193 the Praetorian Guard seized the crown from the emperor Pertinax and auctioned it to the highest bidder, Didius, who, upon paying each guardsman the winning bid, 6250 drachmas, was declared emperor of Rome. It would appear that the Romans used the 'English' progressive method of auctioning, since the word auction is derived from the Latin root *auctus* (an increase).

TYPES OF AUCTION INSTITUTIONS

Auctions may be for a single object or unit, as in the unique object auctioning of paintings and antiques at Sotheby's and Christie's in London, or a lot or package of non-identical items, as in the family groups sold in the slave auctions of the antebellum South. Alternatively, auctions may be for multiple units where many units of a homogeneous standardized good are to be sold, such as gold bullion in the auctions conducted by the International Monetary Fund and the US Treasury in the 1970s, and in the weekly auctioning of 91-day and 182-day securities by the Treasury.

Auctions may also be classified according to the different institutional rules governing the exchange. Since the seminal work of Vickrey (1961), it has been recognized that these rules are important because they can affect bidding incentives, and therefore the terms and the efficiency of an exchange. The literature (Cassady, 1967; Arthur, 1976) has identified many different auction institutions throughout the world, but, following Vickrey (1961), it has become standard to distinguish four primary types of auctions which can be used either in single object or multiple (identical or non-identical) unit auctions.

English Auction. The auction customarily begins with the auctioneer soliciting a first bid for the object from the crowd of would-be buyers, or (where permitted by the auction house rules) announcing the seller's reservation price. Any bid, once recognized by the auctioneer, becomes the standing bid which cannot be withdrawn. Any new bid is admissible if and only if it is higher than the standing bid. The auction ends when the auctioneer is unable to call forth a new higher bid, and the item is 'knocked down' to the last (and highest) bidder at a price equal to the amount bid.

Where multiple units of identical, or nearly identical (close substitute), items are sold by one or more sellers at English auction, individual lots or units are put up for sale in some sequence with each lot or unit sold as a single object. Examples include livestock in the United States and wool in Australia. When there are Q strictly identical items to be sold in a progressive auction, the following alternative procedure has been suggested: '... the items are auctioned simultaneously, with up to (Q) bids permitted at any given level, the rule being that once (Q) bids have been made equal to the highest bid, any further bid must be higher than this' (Vickrey, 1976, p. 14).

Dutch Auctions. Under this procedure, originally called 'mineing', the price begins at some level thought to be somewhat higher than any buyer is willing to pay, and the auctioneer decreases the price in decrements until the first buyer accepts by shouting 'mine'. The item is then awarded to that buyer at the price accepted. Many years ago this procedure was automated by an electrical clock mechanism which is used widely in Holland for the sale of produce and cut flowers. The clock is normally located in a large amphitheatre (Cassady, 1967, p. 194) with buyers sitting at desks facing the clock. An indicator hand on the clock decreases counterclockwise through a series of descending prices. Any buyer can stop the indicator hand by pressing a button when the descending indicated price is acceptable.

The descending offer procedure is used in the sale of fish in England and Israel, in the sale of tobacco in Canada, and a variant of the procedure is used regularly to mark down clothing in Filene's department store in Boston. When the descending offer procedure is applied to multiple units, the first bidder exercises his option to take any part of the quantity offered. The offer price then continues its descent until the next bidder accepts and so on. Thus in fish markets in British ports, the auctioneer accepts 'book' bids for specified quantities. If the offer price reached this level before anyone accepts from the floor, the book bid is filled with any remaining quantity offered at descending prices to the crowd.

First Price Auction. This is the common form of 'sealed' or written bid auction, in which the highest bidder is awarded the item at a price equal to the amount bid. The multiple unit generalization of this procedure is called a *discriminative* auction. Thus if Q identical units are offered, the highest bids for the first Q units are all accepted at the prices and quantities stated in the bids tendered. The weekly primary auction of new short-term US. Treasury securities has used this institution for about fifty years.

Second Price Auction. This is a sealed bid auction in which the highest bidder is awarded the item at a price equal to the bid of the second highest bidder. The procedure is not common although it is used in stamp auctions. For example, the London stamp auction uses English oral bidding, but buyers not present may submit written 'book' bids. An award to a book bidder is made at one price interval or unit above the floor bid, or the second highest book bid, whichever is the largest. If the auctioneer has two book bids he starts the bidding at a unit interval above the second highest of the book bids. If the bid is not raised on the floor he declares it sold to the highest book bidder at this (approximately) second highest bid price.

The multiple unit extension of the second price sealed bid auction is called a *competitive* (or uniform price auction). Under this procedure if Q identical units of a good are offered, the highest bids for the first Q units are all accepted at one market clearing price equal to the bid for the $Q+1$st unit. The procedure was used experimentally by the US Treasury in the 1970s to sell long-term bonds, and in one gold bullion sale. Exxon corporation has sold bonds (usually to registered brokers and dealers) by this method on several occasions since the US Treasury experiments. Since 1978 Citicorp has been auctioning commercial paper weekly using the method, but the institution has not found general acceptance. These auctions are referred to as 'Dutch' auctions in the financial trade literature, but this is a misnomer because the long established 'mineing' procedure, known as the Dutch auction, follows a discriminative, not a uniform, multiple unit pricing procedure.

A summary of auction institutions should not omit some comment on the Walrasian *tâtonnement* hypothesis, which has long served the need of equilibrium price theory for a path independent process that precludes contracting at non-equilibrium prices. It appears that the only naturally occurring organized markets using a procedure similar to a Walrasian *tâtonnement* are the gold and silver bullion price 'fixing', or determining, markets (Jarecki, 1976). In the London Gold Market, representatives of the dealers in this market meet twice daily, and establish a price as follows: the chairman of the meeting begins with an initial starting price, and each representative indicates whether he is a seller, a buyer or neither at that price. Each dealer has orders from clients all over the world. To be a buyer means that at the trial price and volume of his client's buy orders exceed the volume of the sell orders. If at the starting price there are no sellers, the price is raised by varying amounts until one or more of the traders indicates that he is a seller at the standing price. Similarly, the price is moved down if there are no buyers at the starting price. At this juncture the chairman asks for 'figures'; i.e. for the net quantities each trader wishes to buy or sell. If the total indicated purchase quantity does not match the quantity offered by the traders the price is further adjusted until a match occurs. This Walrasian market also has a unanimity stopping rule. Each trader has a small Union Jack in front of him. When a trader is satisfied with the standing price, and has no further orders that require price adjustment, he puts the flag down. The chairman announces that the price is 'fixed' if and only if all flags are down.

THEORY OF AUCTIONS

The following analysis of auctions will adopt five principal assumptions: (1) Each bidder desires to purchase a single unit of the commodity. (2) Buyer i associates a cash value, v_i, with the item which represents i's maximum willingness to pay. In some auctions, notably the English institution, v_i can be interpreted as the cash equivalent of an uncertain item value. (3) The value v_i to i is independent of the value, v_j, to any j; i.e. v_i would not change if i had knowledge of v_j for all i and j. (4) Each i knows the value v_i, but has no certain knowledge of the values of others. (5) Transactions costs, including the cost of thinking, calculating, deciding and bidding, are negligible. Without loss of generality we can number the agents so that $v_1 > v_2 > \cdots > v_N$. An auction allocation is efficient (Pareto optimal) if it awards the offered unit(s) to the buyer(s) that value it most highly. When $Q = 1$ unit is offered, the allocation is efficient if it goes to buyer 1 with value v_1. If $Q = 7$ is offered, an efficient allocation requires buyers 1 to 7 each to receive one unit.

The English and Dutch systems are *continuous auctions* (in time) in which an agent may alter his/her bid in response to the bids of others, or the failure of a bid to be accepted; i.e. bid information is made available continuously by the process until the auction stopping rule is invoked. In *sealed bid* auctions each agent submits one bid message to a centre, which processes the messages according to the rules of the institution, then announces some form of aggregate or summary information describing the outcome. Either type of auction may be repeated over time, thereby generating a history of outcome information, but continuous auctions provide a message history between successive contracts, while sealed-bid auctions do not.

In auction theory it is convenient to define formal concepts of environment, institution, and agent behaviour (*see* EXPERIMENTAL METHODS IN ECONOMICS). The *environment*, $E = (E^1, \ldots, E^N)$, where each agent's characteristics, $E^i = (u^i, w^i, T^i)$, are defined by his preferences or utility (u^i), endowment (w^i), and state of knowledge (T^i). In the English or Second Price auction, $E^i = (v_i, N > 1)$ for agent i, indicating that i's preferences and endowment are defined by his/her value for one unit of the commodity, that i knows that there is at least one other bidder, and (by omission) that i knows nothing about any v_j, $j \neq i$.

The institution specifies (1) a language, $M = (M^1, \ldots, M^N)$, consisting of message elements $m = (m^1, \ldots, m^N)$, where M^i is the set of messages that can be sent by i, and m^i is the message sent by i; (2) a set of allocation rules $h = [h^1(m), \ldots, h^N(m)]$, and a set of cost imputation rules $c = [c^1(m), \ldots, c^N(m)]$, where $h^i(m)$ is the commodity allocation to agent i, and $c^i(m)$ is the payment required of i, given all the messages, m; (3) a set of adjustment process rules, $g(t_0, t, T)$, consisting of a starting rule, $g(t_0, \cdot, \cdot)$, a transition rule, $g(\cdot, t, \cdot)$, and a stopping rule, $g(\cdot, \cdot, T)$, after which the allocation and cost imputation rule become effective. Hence, an *institution* is defined by $I = (I^1, \ldots, I^N)$, where $I^i = [M^i, h^i(m), c^i(m), g(t_0, t, T)]$. In all auctions the messages are bids; i.e. $m^i \equiv b_i$, where b_i is a bid by agent i. Let the bids be numbered from highest to lowest $b_1 > b_2 > \cdots > b_N$ (the order and numbering of the bids need not be the same as for the values). In an English auction the process starts with some bid $b_j(t_0)$ by some agent j. This is the standing bid until, under the transition rule, some agent announces a higher bid which becomes the new standing bid, and so on in sequence. The process stops with a bid $b_1(T)$ when the auctioneer is unable to solicit a higher bid. Hence, $b_1(T)$ becomes the final message, and in the English auction institution, $I_e = (I_e^1, \ldots, I_e^N)$, the outcome rules are

139

$$I_e = [\cdot, h^1(m) = 1, c^1(m) = b_1;$$
$$h^i(m) = 0, c^i(m) = 0, \quad \text{for all} \quad i > 1, \cdot]$$

indicating that the last (and highest) bidder wins the item, pays the amount bid, and all others receive and pay nothing. In the Second Price sealed-bid auction the starting and stopping rules merely define the pre-auction time interval within which bids are to be tendered, and there is no transition rule. The bids are all examined at once, and the Second Price institution specifies $I_s = [h^1(m) = 1, c^1(m) = b_2; h^i(m) = 0, c^i(m) = 0, \text{ for all } i > 1]$, indicating that the high bidder is awarded the item at a price equal to the next highest bid, with all others receiving and paying nothing.

Within this framework we define *agent behaviour* as a function that carries each agent's characteristics, E^i, given the institution, I, into the (final) message m^i sent by i, $m^i = \beta(E^i | I)$. A *theory* of agent behaviour has the objective of specifying β as a *hypothesis* about the observed message responses of agents in alternative institutions such as the English and Second Price auctions.

English. Let $b_k(t)$ be the tth standing bid (in some sequence), announced by agent k. Then it is a dominant strategy for any $i \neq k$ to raise the bid if $v_i > b_k(t)$; i.e. this strategy is *best* for i whatever might be the response of any other agent. Note that since the winning bidder must pay the amount bid it is never optimal for any i to raise her own bid. If the auction has a standard bid increment, δ, assumed to be smaller than the distance between any two adjacent values, then i is motivated to bid $b_i(t+1) = b_k(t) + \delta$ if and only if $v_i \geqq b_i(t+1)$. Clearly, this process must stop with the Tth bid, when (eventually) agent 1 bids $b_1(T)$, where $v_2 - \delta < b_1(T) \leqq v_2 + \delta$, and agent 2 is unable to raise the bid without bidding in excess of v_2. Hence, in the English auction we have $m^i \equiv b_i = \beta(v_i, N > 1 | I_e) \equiv v_i$ for $i = 2, 3, \ldots, N$; i.e. each $i \neq 1$ is motivated to reveal demand by bidding up to his value v_i, with agent 1 *discovering* that she does not need to bid v_1, but at most $v_2 + \delta$ to obtain the award. It follows that the equilibrium price, p_e, must satisfy $v_2 - \delta < p_e \leqq v_2 + \delta$, and the award to agent 1 will be efficient.

Because individual units are sold sequentially in typical multiple unit English auctions ($N > Q > 1$), a theory of this case would require some hypothesized expansion of agent information sets which allows each i to weigh formally the prospect of underbidding v_i by some amount in earlier auctions in anticipation of possible lower prices in later auctions. But Vickrey's generalization (quoted above) of the English auction to multiple identical units, which preserves the information properties of the single unit case, does lead to determinate results: once the bidders with the Q highest values match bids at $b(T) \in (v_{Q+1} - \delta, v_{Q+1} + \delta)$, then no bidder will be motivated to raise this standing bid. Hence, the price for any Q units ($N > Q \geqq 1$) must satisfy $v_{Q+1} - \delta < p_e \leqq v_{Q+1} + \delta$, and the award to agents $1, 2, \ldots, Q$ will be efficient.

Second Price. In this auction the surplus obtained by the winning bidder depends upon the bid of the highest among the other $N - 1$ losing bidders; i.e. if i is the winner and j the highest losing bid, the surplus to i is $v_i - b_j$. Hence the optimal bid is the bid that maximizes the probability of winning a positive surplus. This occurs only if each i bids v_i. To bid less than v_i is to reduce the chance of being the high bidder, without affecting the surplus $v_i - b_j$. To bid more than v_i is to risk (without compensating benefit) winning at a price $b_j > v_i$, yielding a negative surplus. If each i *reasons* in this manner, then $m^i \equiv b_i = \beta(v_i, N > 1 | I_s) \equiv v_i$ for *all* i. It follows that the award will be to agent 1, which is efficient, and the price will be $p_s = b_2 = v_2$. This argument extends to the multiple unit case in

which N bidders each submit a bid for one of Q identical units ($N > Q > 1$). It is a dominant strategy for each i to bid v_i, the award will be to agents $1, 2, \ldots, Q$, and the competitive price paid by all Q winning bidders will be $p_c = b_{Q+1} = v_{Q+1}$.

In comparing the English and Second Price institutions it is seen that in the limit, as δ becomes small, the two institutions are isomorphic; that is, they lead to the same price and allocations. In the language of game theory these institutions are equivalent in the sense that they have the same normal form. They have quite different extensive (sequential process) forms. Analysis of the richer extensive form of the English auction leads to the conclusion that the high bidder wins with a bid of v_2 which makes the theoretical auction outcome identical to that of the Second Price auction, although the institutions have distinct cost imputation rules. It should be noted from our discussion in section I that the Second Price procedure appears to have arisen in practice in the British stamp (and some fish) markets which permitted 'book' bids at English auction. It is easy to see that in such circumstances auctioneers might soon 'discover' the equivalence of the English and Second Price procedure without having to resort to formal analysis.

The First Price and Dutch auctions use the same allocation and cost imputation rules that are used in the English auction; they are like the Second Price auction in that the auction is over before the bidders obtain informative data about their rivals from the auction itself. In these auctions it is of importance what each bidder assumes about the values and bidding behaviour of his rivals. In the analysis below we will follow Vickrey (1961) in supposing that the values are assumed by each agent to be independent occurrences from a constant density on the interval [0, 1]. Any bids and values can be mapped into this interval by expressing them as fractions of the largest possible value. Thus, if the maximum value is $\bar{v}$, a bid of b' and value v', can be represented by $b = (b'/\bar{v})$ and $v = (v'/\bar{v})$. With these assumptions about agent knowledge the environment is $E^i = [v_i; P(v) = v, N > 1]$ indicating that each i knows with certainty his/her own value $v_i \in [0, 1]$ for a single unit, that the other agent's values have the probability distribution, $\text{Prob}\{x < v\} \equiv P(v) = v$ and that there are N bidders.

First Price. Vickrey (1961) showed that if all agents are risk neutral the noncooperative (or Nash) equilibrium bid function in the First Price auction is

$$m^i \equiv b_i = \beta[v_i; P(v) = v, N | I_f] \equiv \left(\frac{N-1}{N}\right) v_i.$$

If all bidders have the same strictly concave utility function for surplus, say $u(v_i - b_i)$, the resulting bid function $b_A(v_i)$ will have the property

$$b_A(v_i) > \left(\frac{N-1}{N}\right) v_i$$

(Holt, 1980). In both of these cases, since the equilibrium bid function depends only on value, and not upon which agent has any particular value, any given ordering of the values induces the same ordering on the bids. Hence the highest value bidder will submit the highest bid, and the allocation is efficient. However, if each bidder i has constant relative risk averse (CRRA) utility, $(v_i - b_i)^{r_i}$, $r_i \in (0, 1)$, then it can be shown (Cox et al., 1982) that the Vickrey bid function generalizes to

$$b_i = \left(\frac{N-1}{N-1+r_i}\right) v_i, \quad \text{for} \quad b_i < \bar{b} = \frac{N-1}{N}.$$

Consequently, in this case (and in general when utility functions are distinct) the highest value bidder is not necessarily the highest bidder, since if he is less risk averse than the second, or third, highest bidder, his bid may be lower than theirs. All these results have been further generalized to the multiple unit discriminative auction ($N > Q > 1$) (see Vickrey, 1962; Harris and Raviv, 1981; Cox et al., 1984).

Dutch. The Dutch auction starting rule is to announce (or display on the clock) an initial asking price, $a(t_0)$. If the clock speed, measured in dollars, is s (\$ per second), then the transition rule states that at time t the asking price is $a(t) = a(t_0) - st$. If at T, agent i is the first to accept the standing offer (the stopping rule), then i's bid, and the price paid, is $b_i = a(t_0) - sT$. Each bidder must decide when to stop the descending offer price. Vickrey was the first to argue that the Dutch and First Price auctions are isomorphic; i.e. that a bidder i who would bid b_i in the First Price auction would stop the clock at T such that $b_i = a(t_0) - sT$ in the Dutch auction. This was demonstrated formally in Cox et al. (1982) by proving the equivalence of a pre-auction planning model of the Dutch (and First Price) auction with a Bayesian model of participation in the Dutch auction. The Bayesian model shows that the information at time t on the Dutch clock (no bidder by time t has stopped the clock) is non-informative; i.e. it provides no rational basis for modifying the optimal bid given any pre-auction postulated environment, such as $E^i = [v_i, P(v), N > 1]$. Hence, a Nash model of the Dutch auction (assuming CRRA utility) yields the behavioural hypothesis that

$$m^i \equiv b_i = \beta[v_i; r_i; P(v) = v, N > 1 | I_d] \equiv \left(\frac{N-1}{N-1+r_i}\right)v_i,$$

where each i is defined by the characteristics (v_i, r_i).

Because the Dutch auction has such a rich extensive form, containing parameters such as $a(t_0)$ and s that do not enter into the First Price auction, it would be surprising if these two auction procedures produced the same results in any particular parametric implementation. One can easily imagine an s so large that the standing price is not discernible on a Dutch clock, with a bidder having to guess at the bid price at which she is stopping the clock. Similarly, s might be so small that the waiting cost is significant leading to higher bids in the Dutch than in the First Price auction. The Dutch–First Price equivalence theorem abstracts from these extensive form parametric differences and analyses each institution as a mathematical game in normal form.

Theoretical behaviour in the standard single object auctions can be compared using the following compact representation:

$$b_i = \beta(E^i | I)$$

$$= \begin{cases} b_1 \in (v_2 - \delta, v_2 + \delta) \text{ for } i = 1, \text{ and } b_i \leqq v_i, \text{ for } i > 1, \\ \quad \text{if } E^i = (v_i), I = I_e \\ v_i, \text{ for all } i, \text{ if } E^i = (v_i; N > 1), I = I_s \\ \left(\frac{N-1}{N-1+r_i}\right)v_i, \text{ for all } i, \\ \quad \text{if } E^i = [v_i, r_i; \Phi(r), P(v) = v, N > 1], I = I_f \text{ or } I_d \end{cases} \quad (1)$$

These results generalize for multiple units, giving

$$b_i = \beta(E^i | I)$$

$$= \begin{cases} b_Q \in (v_{Q+1} - \delta, v_{Q+1} + \delta) \text{ for } i \leqq Q, \\ \quad \text{and } b_i \leqq v_i \text{ for } i > Q, \text{ if } E^i = (v_i), I = I_e \\ v_i, \text{ for all } i, \text{ if } E^i = (v_i; N > Q \geqq 1), \\ \quad I = I_{Q+1} \ (Q+1 \text{ price auction}) \\ b_a(v_i, r_i | E(r), N > Q \geqq 1), \\ \quad \text{if } E^i = [v_i, r_i; \Phi(r), P(v) = v, N > Q \geqq 1], \\ \quad I = I_D \text{ (discriminative auction)}, \end{cases} \quad (2)$$

where b_a is the CRRA bid function for multiple units [see Cox et al. (1984) and the references therein for the formula and its derivation], $\Phi(r)$ is the population distribution of the CRRA risk parameter and $E(r)$ is its expected value.

If we let $E[P(I)]$ be the (mathematical) expected selling price in a single object auction under institution I, using (1) it is easy to compare the four standard auctions in terms of this outcome measure (Vickrey, 1961) if we assume risk neutrality; i.e. $E^i = (v_i, r_i = 1; P(v) = v, N > 1)$:

$$E[P(I)] = \begin{cases} E(b_1) \in \left[\left(\frac{N-1}{N+1}\right) - \delta, \left(\frac{N-1}{N+1}\right) + \delta\right], \text{ if } I = I_e, \\ E(b_2) = \left(\frac{N-1}{N+1}\right), \text{ if } I = I_s, \\ E(b_1) = \left(\frac{N-1}{N+1}\right), \text{ if } I = I_f \text{ or } I_d, \end{cases} \quad (3)$$

since $E(v_2) = (N-1)/(N+1)$. It follows that for $\delta = 0$, all four auctions give the same expected selling price. It is also easy to show that if the bidders are risk averse, then $E[P(I_e)] = E[P(I_s)] < E[P(I_f)] = E[P(I_d)]$. Thus a testable outcome implication of the above models of bidding behaviour is that observed mean prices will be ordered

$$\bar{P}(I_e) = \bar{P}(I_s) = \left(\frac{N-1}{N+1}\right) \leqq \bar{P}(I_f) = \bar{P}(I_d).$$

Also, efficiency, measured by the percentage (probability) of awards to the highest value bidder will be 100 per cent in all the auctions if bidders are risk neutral or all have the same concave utility for surplus. But if bidders have CRRA utility with different parameters, r_i, then this measure of efficiency, ζ, will be ordered $100 = \zeta_e = \zeta_s > \zeta_f = \zeta_d$ in the English, Second, First and Dutch auctions respectively.

Experimental Tests of Auction Market Behaviour. Several studies (see Cox et al., 1984 and its citations) have tested the above models and various extensions of them using experimental methods. In all of the experiments summarized below, values are assigned from a uniform probability function whose parameters are common knowledge to all the participants. Each participant understands that he/she will be paid in cash the difference between the value assigned, and the price paid, conditional upon being a winning bidder in any particular auction.

From the numerous experimental studies reporting the results of perhaps 1500–2000 auctions, the following brief summary is offered.

1. The behaviour of prices in the four standard auctions is illustrated by the representative charts in Figures 1 and 2 comparing I_e and I_d prices using eight bidders, and I_f and I_s prices using five bidders. In these experiments, in each auction, a random sample of N values are assigned to the bidders from the uniform distribution on the interval $[\underline{v}, \bar{v}]$. From the distribution function (order statistic) for the Qth highest value in a sample of size N one can compute the expected Qth highest value, which is the expected (Marshallian) demand schedule, $E(v_Q | N) = [(\bar{v} - \underline{v})(N - Q + 1)/(N + 1)] + \underline{v}$. This schedule is graphed on the left of Figures 1 and 2 in normalized form by subtracting the expected second highest value; i.e. $E(v_Q | N) = (\bar{v} - \underline{v})(2 - Q)/(N + 1)$ is graphed. Similarly, on the right of Figures 1 and 2 are plotted the prices realized in each auction, normalized by subtracting the second highest value realized in each sample. Normalized in this way the risk neutral predicted average price is zero in all auctions. Figure 1 charts the prices in 36 sequential auctions in each of two experimental sessions with different groups of size $N = 8$. Session A con-

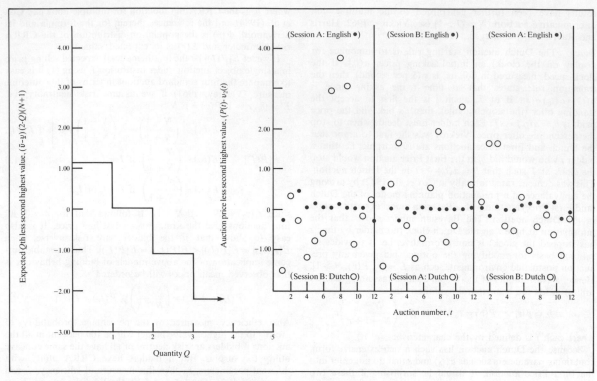

Figure 1 English–Dutch prices compared: eight bidders $[\bar{v}, \underline{v}] = [\$6.1, \$10]$

sisted of 12 English, followed by 12 Dutch, and ending with 12 English, auctions. Session B consisted of the opposite Dutch – English – Dutch sequence of 12 auctions each. A similar paired comparison of First and Second auctions using five bidders is shown in Figure 2. These charts should help to disabuse anyone of the notion that pricing institutions do not matter.

2. The mean observed prices in the four standard auctions (conducted under conditions which control for N, and other such parameters in the comparisons) for $N = 4$, 5, 6, 8 and 9 satisfy the ordering $\bar{P}(I_e) \cong E(v_2) \cong \bar{P}(I_s) < \bar{P}(I_d) < \bar{P}(I_f)$. Actually, mean prices in I_s tend to be below those in I_e because many subjects initially do not follow the dominant strategy rule $b_i = v_i$, but over time more and more subjects 'learn' to adopt this strategy. An example is shown in session C of Figure 2, in which six of the twelve prices in the First sequence of 12 auctions under I_s are below v_2, but in the second sequence (last panel) under I_s only two of the 12 prices are below v_2. Taking account of this convergence over time we can say that observed English and Second prices support the price implications of the theory as stated in (3).

3. Efficiences in the English and Second auctions are approximately the same (97 per cent and 94 per cent respectively) but are much lower in the First auction (88 per cent) and still lower in the Dutch (80 per cent).

4. These price and efficiency results support the following conclusions: (a) the English and Second auction are approximately equivalent; (b) the Dutch and First Price auctions are not isomorphic, behaviourally; (c) the First auction results are consistent with risk averse Nash equilibrium behaviour; and (d) both the efficiency data and observations on individual bidding support the CRRA model of Nash equilibrium bidding,

with different bidders exhibiting different degrees of risk aversion in their bidding behaviour; (e) the CRRA model of bidding in the First auction is also supported by the finding that increasing the payoff levels by a factor of three [paying the winning bidder $3(v_i - b_i)$ instead of $(v_i - b_i)$ dollars] has no effect on bidding behaviour – a theoretical result which follows if and only if utility is of CRRA form.

5. An extensive study of multiple unit discriminative auctions finds that the data are consistent with the CRRA Nash model of bidding behaviour over much but not all of the (N, Q) parameter space (Cox et al., 1984). Hence, anomalies remain, and in view of the highly replicable and non-artifactual character of the empirical results there is the strong implication that the resolution of these anomalies is an unfinished theoretical task.

6. The Second Price auction results do not extend to the multiple unit uniform price auction. Apparently, with multiple units, in those parameter cases that have been studied, the market is less effective in disciplining (with failure experiences) those strategies that depart from the dominant strategy.

ENRICHING THE ENVIRONMENT: DEPENDENCE, INFORMATION, COLLUSION AND COMBINATORIAL CONSIDERATIONS

Once replicable experimental results have been established and the strengths and weaknesses of a theory have been assessed, it is natural to extend both the theoretical and the empirical inquiry to richer environments. The required theoretical advances have been more difficult to achieve than the creation of richer environments in the laboratory (Kagel, et al., 1983).

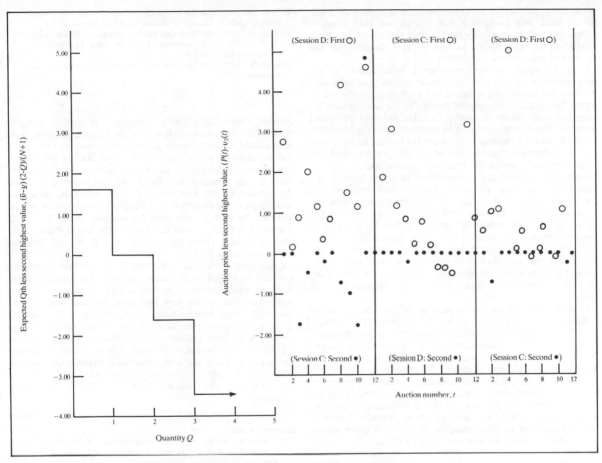

Figure 2 First-Second prices compared: 5 Bidders $[\bar{v}, \underline{v}] = [\$0.1, \$10]$

A limiting feature of the above theories is the assumption that agent values are independent. Consequently, each agent's willingness-to-pay as might be revealed in the open English auction has no information value to any other agent. Milgrom and Weber (1982) capture this important postulated property of some commodities by introducing the concept of positively dependent (affiliated) values. In this environment the English auction is no longer isomorphic to the Second Price auction; instead, prices in the former exceed those in the latter. Milgrom and Weber (1982) also argue that the Dutch–First isomorphism continues to hold when values are positively dependent, but this extension is of more limited scientific significance (than the extension of English–Second auction theory) since the experimental evidence is inconsistent with this implication in the independent values environment. Any theoretical implication found to be robust with respect to some generalization of the environment is a moot discovery if that implication is contrary to the evidence in the more special environment.

An important application of the case in which individual values are affiliated is to the sealed-bid auctions of oil exploration and development leases by the government. In this case we can think of each v_i as i's estimate of the value of the lease after obtaining seismic and other sample data providing information on the existence of possible oil bearing geological

structures. This application is often referred to as the common value of mineral rights model, since the analysis has assumed that all companies place the same value on any petroleum that might be discovered on the tract. This assumption is much too limiting since there is an active market for existing or proven petroleum reserves, and one cannot account for such exchanges if private values are indeed common. Hence petroleum exploration and development leases are best viewed as a case in which the commodity exhibits differing, but affiliated, private values. The first experimental study of 'common value' auctions (Kagel et al., 1983) reports bidding behaviour in which the bids are too high to be consistent with risk neutral utility functions and too diverse among individuals to be consistent with the implication of symmetrical bid functions. In effect these results, when values are affiliated, imply rejection of the common values model, and serve to establish the robustness of the experimental results when values are independent (Cox et al., 1984). These findings heavily underline the methodological point that evidence contrary to a postulate (e.g. symmetry) in any environment requires modification of the theory if one is to obtain empirically useful and observationally disciplined extensions of the theory to more complex environments.

The different standard auctions are not equivalent in terms of their collusive potential. The open-bid English auction is particularly vulnerable to collusion since a subset of $n < N$ buyers have only to agree not to bid against each other in order to reduce the expected price that will be paid. Furthermore, the English auction process assures that the agreement will be easy to monitor.

It is an open question whether a seller, such as the government in the sale of mineral leases, should publicize each bidder's bid every time a sealed-bid auction is conducted. It serves to reinforce the credibility of the auction process by allowing each bidder to verify that his bid was processed honestly. But if a buyers' ring is operating, such information makes it easy for the ring to monitor the bids of its members, and to determine the identity of outside bidders and the conditions under which the ring loses the auction.

Sealed bid auctions are vulnerable to collusion between the auctioneer and one or more buyers, and between the auctioneer and the seller. Thus, in the First Price auction, the terms of agreement between the auctioneer and a buyer might be that if the buyer enters the highest bid, then his bid is to be reentered slightly in excess of the second highest bid.

The Dutch auction is perhaps effective against all of the above examples of collusion. In this auction, since none of the losing bids is known to anyone, they cannot even be leaked, let alone announced, and these types of conspiracies are not feasible.

A new proposed auction institution which has yet to be implemented in practice, but has been subjected to limited testing in the laboratory is the combinatorial auction (Rassenti et al., 1982). This is a sealed-bid auction which allows bidders to submit bids for one or more combinations of non-identical items in a multiple unit auction. The problem was originally suggested in the context of designing a market for airport landing or takeoff slots. Airport slots are an extreme example of a resource whose productive value is enhanced in specified combinations. Thus a slot at New York's Kennedy International has no productive value except in combination with a flight compatible slot at Chicago's O'Hare Field.

VERNON L. SMITH

See also BIDDING; EXCHANGE; EXPERIMENTAL METHODS IN ECONOMICS.

BIBLIOGRAPHY

Amihud, Y. (ed.) 1976. *Bidding and Auctioning for Procurement and Allocation*. New York: New York University Press.
Arthur, H. 1976. The structure and use of auctions. In Amihud (1976).
Cassady, R. 1967. *Auctions and Auctioneering*. Berkeley: University of California Press.
Cox, J., Roberson, B. and Smith, V. 1982. Theory and behavior of single unit auctions. In *Research in Experimental Economics*, Vol. 2, Greenwich, Conn.: JAI Press.
Cox, J., Smith, V. and Walker, J. 1984. Theory and behavior of multiple unit discriminative auctions. *Journal of Finance* 39(4), September, 983–1010.
Harris, M. and Raviv, A. 1981. Allocation mechanisms and the design of auctions. *Econometrica* 49(6), November, 1477–99.
Holt, C. 1980. Competitive bidding for contracts under alternative auction procedures. *Journal of Political Economy* 88(3), June, 433–45.
Jarecki, H. 1976. Bullion dealing, commodity exchange trading and the London gold fixing. In Amihud (1976).
Kagel, J., Levin, J., Battalio, R. and Meyer, D. 1983. Common value auctions: some initial experimental results. University of Houston Working Paper, November.
Milgrom, P. and Weber, R. 1982. A theory of auctions and competitive bidding. *Econometrica* 50(5), September, 1089–122.
Rassenti, S., Smith, V. and Bulfin, R. 1982. A combinatorial auction mechanism for airport time slot allocation. *Bell Journal of Economics* 13(2), Autumn, 402–17.
Vickrey, W. 1961. Counterspeculation, auctions, and competitive sealed tenders. *Journal of Finance* 16(1), March, 8–37.
Vickrey, W. 1962. Auctions and bidding games. In *Recent Advances in Game Theory*, Proceedings of a Conference, Princeton: Princeton University Press.
Vickrey, W. 1976. Auctions, markets and optimal allocation. In Amihud (1976).

Aupetit, Albert

Aupetit, Albert (1876–1943). Aupetit was born in Sancerre (Cher). His two doctoral theses at the Faculté de Droit were respectively entitled *Théorie générale de la monnaie* (1901) and *Les accidents du travail dans l'agriculture*. Having twice failed the *concours d'agrégation*, the narrow gateway to a professorship at the Faculté de Droit, he entered the research department at the Banque de France, where he served as secretary-general from 1920 to 1926. He then entered private business. In 1936 he was elected a member of the Institut de France. His teaching was restricted to the Ecole Pratique des Hautes Etudes (1910–14) and to the Ecole des Sciences Politiques, from 1921 on.

Considered by Walras as his first disciple in France, Aupetit can best be judged by the master himself: 'He is in agreement with my social economics as well as with my pure and applied economics. He is the best and most brilliant disciple and successor I may wish to have' (Jaffé, 1965, p. 353). Aupetit's *Essai sur la théorie générale de la monnaie* is a faithful though simpler and more precise reformulation of Walras' general equilibrium and monetary theories. The postulates sustaining the quantity theory are made remarkably explicit. Questions of composite monetary standards, bimetallism, exchange rate determination and index numbers are also thoroughly discussed.

ROGER DEHEM

SELECTED WORKS

1901. *Essai sur la théorie générale de la monnaie*. Paris: Guillaumin. A truncated version of this book was published by Marcel Rivière, Paris, in 1957.
1905. L'oeuvre économique de Cournot. *Revue de métaphysique et de morale* 13, 377–93.

BIBLIOGRAPHY
Jaffé, W. 1965. *Correspondence of Léon Walras and Related Papers*. Amsterdam: North Holland, Vol. III.

Auspitz, Rudolf

Auspitz, Rudolf (1837–1906). Auspitz was born on 7 July 1837 in Vienna, where he died on 8 March 1906. He grew up in a well-educated Jewish family and studied mathematics and physics but without acquiring a degree. At the age of 26, apparently with some reluctance, he became a businessman and founded one of the first sugar refineries of the Austrian empire. As a lifelong opponent of cartels, he used to donate the extra profits he obtained from the sugar cartel to the employees' pension fund. Auspitz was also Richard Lieben's partner in the family bank, Auspitz, Lieben & Co.

A successful Liberal politician, Auspitz was a member of the Moravian Diet (1871–1900) and of the Austrian lower chamber (1873–90 and 1892–1905), where he acquired a reputation and influence as a financial expert. His first wife was Lieben's sister and a first cousin. They had two children, but the marriage was dissolved after 20 years because of the wife's insanity, whereupon Auspitz married his children's governess. He seems to have been a man of quiet energy and balanced judgement, untiring but of frail health. In some respects his life reminds one of Ricardo's.

All of Auspitz's significant scientific work was done jointly with Lieben; nothing seems to be known about their relative contributions. In 1889 appeared the *Researches on the Theory of Price*, the book that assured its authors of a place among the eminent mathematical economists. It is essentially an exhaustive partial-equilibrium analysis of price in terms of an ingenious geometrical apparatus.

The fundamental first chapter, preprinted in 1887 to fix priorities relative to Böhm-Bawerk, provides the basic tools. For every quantity of a given commodity, the 'curve of total satisfaction' indicates the maximum amount of money the buyer is willing to pay. The 'total cost curve', on the other hand, plots the minimum amount of money for which the seller (producer) is willing to supply each quantity. In modern terminology, these are indifference curves. The corresponding marginal curves, called respectively demand and supply curves, give the maximum (minimum) amount of money for which the buyer (seller) is willing to buy (sell) an additional unit.

On the assumption of a constant marginal utility of money, both parties choose the quantity in such a way that this marginal value is equal to the market place. The two marginal curves are thus equivalent to Marshall's reciprocal demand curves as applied to the exchange of one commodity against money. Auspitz and Lieben did not know Marshall's privately printed paper of 1879, however.

Competitive equilibrium is established where the demand curve intersects the supply curve. The vertical distances between the equilibrium point and the two indifference curves then measure the gains from trade, which leads to an analysis of consumer's and producer's surplus (but without these terms).

In subsequent chapters this apparatus is applied to a wide range of microeconomic problems and cases, including substitutes and complements, indivisibilities, disutility, technical progress, inventories, security markets, forward markets and options. Among many notable pieces of analysis one finds the argument that speculation is socially beneficial if it is profitable, and a derivation of long-run curves as envelopes of short-run curves which was not surpassed until Harrod and Viner. An important final chapter extends the analysis to monopoly, monopolistic competition, excise taxes and international trade, and includes a brilliant discussion of optimal tariffs (which disturbed free-trader Pareto; see *Giornale degli Economisti*, 1892).

Four appendices present the main argument in terms of univariate differential calculus, concluding with an extension to general equilibrium. In contrast to Launhardt, who, as an engineer, loved to compute numerical results for special functional forms, Auspitz and Lieben emphasize the logic of the problem.

Auspitz and Lieben, though highly regarded by men like Edgeworth, Pareto and Fisher, never received the credit they deserved. In their local environment, in view of the Austrian School's intolerance for mathematics, they were academic outcasts. This is illustrated by Menger's critical review (*Wiener Zeitung*, 8 March 1889, quoted in Weinberger, 1931) and by Auspitz's exchange with Böhm-Bawerk of 1894, which also shows Auspitz's analytical superiority. More importantly, Auspitz and Lieben, cut off from direct scholarly intercourse, were prisoners of their idiosyncrasy, never developing the knack for felicitous terminology and expository devices that in economics is so important for academic success. It also turned out that for partial analysis Cournot's price/quantity diagram is often more illuminating than the reciprocal demand curves.

Despite their gentle, scholarly personalities, Auspitz and Lieben also managed to stir up a controversy with Walras (see *Correspondence of Léon Walras and Related Papers*, ed. William Jaffé, 3 vols, Amsterdam, 1965). As early as 1887, Launhardt had warned Walras of the 'plagiarism' of those 'insolent Jewish pirates'. The preface to the *Researches*, while revealing Launhardt's diatribes as entirely unfounded, added a more substantive irritant by arguing that (1) Walras' simultaneous demand curves were not correctly constructed, in as much as the curve for one good presupposes a given price for the other, and (2) there cannot be multiple equilibria. This criticism stung Walras all the more since Edgeworth, in his presidential address of 1889, described Auspitz and Lieben as more accurate than Walras (an unwarranted observation, deleted in *Papers Relating to Political Economy*). Walras tried to mobilize Pareto and Bortkiewicz in his defence (without success) and began to polemicize against those who 'make bad theory in mathematical language'. His own reply, however (reprinted in the 4th edition of the '*Eléments*'), missed the essential point and only added to the confusion. Wicksell, as usual, got things right (*Wert, Kapital und Rente*, 1893). Auspitz and Lieben had overlooked the fact that Walras' curves, in effect, related to the demand and supply of one good in terms of the other, and the impossibility of multiple equilibria depended on the constancy of the marginal utility of money. After Auspitz's death Lieben graciously acknowledged their error (to which Walras, ungraciously, replied that the point was not important after all).

JÜRG NIEHANS

See also LIEBEN, RICHARD.

SELECTED WORKS

1885. *Meine parlamentarische Thätigkeit während der Reichsraths-Session 1879 85.* Vienna.
1887. (With Richard Lieben.) *Zur Theorie des Preises*. Leipzig: Duncker & Humblot.
1889. (With Richard Lieben.) *Untersuchungen über die Theorie des Preises*. Leipzig: Duncker & Humblot. French translation by Louis Suret, Paris: M. Giard & E. Brière, 1914.
1890a. (With Richard Lieben.) Reply. (To article by L. Walras in same publication.) *Revue d'économie politique* 4.
1890b. Die klassische Werttheorie und die Theorie von Grenznutzen. *Jahrbucher fur Nationalökonomie und Statistik* 55.
1894. Der letzte Maasstab des Güterwertes und die mathematische Methode. *Zeitschrift für Volkswirtschaft, Socialpolitik und Verwaltung* 3.

BIBLIOGRAPHY

Weinberger, O. 1931. Rudolf Auspitz und Richard Lieben. *Zeitschrift für die gesamte Staatswissenschaft* 91.
Weinberger, O. 1935. Rudolf Auspitz. *Neue Oesterreichische Biographie 1815–1918*, vol.VIII. Vienna.
Winter, J. 1927. *Fünfzig Jahre eines Wiener Hauses*. Vienna: F. Jasper.

Austrian conceptions of competition. *See* COMPETITION: AUSTRIAN CONCEPTIONS.

Austrian School of Economics. The birth of the Austrian School of Economics is usually recognized as having occurred with the 1871 publication of Carl Menger's *Grundsätze der Volkswirthschaftslehre*. On the basis of this work Menger (hitherto a civil servant) became a junior faculty member at the University of Vienna. Several years later, after a stint as tutor and travelling companion to Crown Prince Rudolph, he was appointed to a professorial chair at the University. Two younger economists, Eugen von Böhm-Bawerk and Friedrich von Wieser (neither of whom had been a student of Menger) became enthusiastic supporters of the new ideas put forward in Menger's book. During the 1880s a vigorous outpouring of literature from these two followers, from several of Menger's students, and in particular a methodological work by Menger himself, brought the ideas of Menger and his followers to the attention of the international community of economists. The Austrian School was now a recognized entity. Several works of Böhm-Bawerk and Wieser were translated into English; and by 1890 the editors of the US journal *Annals of the American Academy of Political and Social Science* were asking Böhm-Bawerk for an expository paper explaining the doctrines of the new school. What follows seeks to provide a concise survey of the history of the Austrian School with special emphasis on (a) the major representatives of the school; (b) the central ideas identified with the school; (c) the relationship between the school and its ideas, and other major schools of thought within economics; (d) the various meanings and perceptions associated today with the term Austrian Economics.

THE FOUNDING AUSTRIANS

Menger's 1871 book is recognized in the history of economic thought (alongside Jevons's 1871 *Theory of Political Economy*, and Walras's 1874 *Eléments d'économie politique pure*) as a central component of the 'Marginalist Revolution'. For the most part, historians of thought have emphasized the features in Menger's work that parallel those of Jevons and Walras. More recently, following especially the work of W. Jaffé (1976) attention has come to be paid to those aspects of Menger's ideas which set them apart from those of his contemporaries. A series of recent studies (Grassl and Smith, 1986) have related these unique aspects of Menger and the early Austrian economists to broader currents in the late 19th-century intellectual and philosophical scene in Austria.

The central thrust of Menger's book was unmistakable; it was an attempt to rebuild the foundations of economic science in a way which, while retaining the abstract, theoretical character of economics, offered an understanding of value and price which ran sharply counter to classical teachings. For the classical economists value was seen as governed by past resource costs; Menger saw value as expressing judgements concerning future usefulness in meeting consumer wants. Menger's book, offered to the German-speaking scholarly community of Germany and Austria, was thus altogether different, in approach, style and substance, from the work coming from the German universities. That latter work, while also sharply critical of classical economics, was attacking its theoretical character, and appealing for a predominantly historical approach. At the time Menger's book appeared, the 'older' German historical school (led by Roscher, Knies and Hildebrand) was beginning to be succeeded by the 'younger' historical school, whose leader was to be Gustav Schmoller. Menger, the 31-year-old Austrian civil servant, was careful not to present his work as antagonistic to that of German economic scholarship. In fact he dedicated his book – with 'respectful esteem' – to Roscher, and offered it to the community of German scholars 'as a friendly greeting from a collaborator in Austria and as a faint echo of the scientific suggestions so abundantly lavished on us Austrians by Germany ...' (Menger, 1871, Preface). Clearly Menger hoped that his theoretical innovations might be seen as reinforcing the conclusions derived from historical studies of the German scholars, contributing to a new economics to replace a discredited British classical orthodoxy.

Menger was to be bitterly disappointed. The German economists virtually ignored his book; where it was noticed in the German language journals it was grossly misunderstood or otherwise summarily dismissed. For the first decade after the publication of his book, Menger was virtually alone; there was certainly no Austrian 'school'. And when the enthusiastic work of Böhm-Bawerk and Wieser began to appear in the 1880s, the new literature acquired the appellation 'Austrian' more as a pejorative epithet bestowed by disdainful German economists than as an honorific label (Mises, 1969, p. 40). This rift between the Austrian and German scholarly camps deepened most considerably after the appearance of Menger's methodological challenge to the historical approach (Menger, 1883). Menger apparently wrote that work having been convinced by the unfriendly disinterest with which his 1871 book had been received in Germany, that German economics could be rescued only by a frontal attack on the Historical School. The bitter *methodenstreit* that followed is usually (but not invariably, see Bostaph, 1978) seen by historians of economics as constituting a tragic waste of scholarly energy. Certainly this venomous academic conflict helped bring the existence of an Austrian School to the attention of the international economics fraternity – as a group of dedicated economists offering a flood of exciting theoretical ideas reinforcing the new marginalist literature, sharply modifying the hitherto dominant classical theory of value. Works by Böhm-Bawerk (1886), Wieser (1884, 1889), Komorzynski (1889) and Zuckerkandl (1889) offered elaborations or discussions of Menger's central, subjectivist ideas on value, cost, and price. Works on the theory of pure profit, and on such applications as public finance theory, were contributed by writers such as Mataja (1884), Gross (1884), Sax (1887), and R. Meyer (1887). The widely used textbook by Philippovich (1893), who was a professor at the University of Vienna (but more sympathetic towards the contributions of the German school), is credited with an important role in spreading Austrian marginal utility theory among German-language students.

In these early Austrian contributions to the theory of value and price, emphasis was (as in the Jevonsian and Walrasian approaches) placed both on marginalism and on utility. But important differences set the Austrian theory apart from other early marginalist theories. The Austrians made no attempt to present their ideas in mathematical form, and as a consequence the Austrian concept of the margin differs somewhat from that of Jevons and Walras. For the latter, and for subsequent microeconomic theorists, the marginal value of a variable refers to the instantaneous rate of change of the 'total' variable. But the Austrians worked, deliberately, with discrete variables (see K. Menger, 1973). More importantly the concept of marginal utility, and the sense in which it decreases, referred for the Austrians not to psychological enjoyments themselves, but to (ordinal) marginal *valuations* of such enjoyments (McCulloch, 1977). In any event, as has been urged by Streissler (1972), what was important for the Austrians in marginal utility was not so much the adjective as the noun. Menger saw his theory as demonstrating the unique and exclusive role played, in the determination of economic value, by subjective, 'utility', considerations. Values are not seen (as they are in Marshallian economics) as *jointly* determined by subjective (utility) and objective (physical cost) considerations. Rather values are seen as determined *solely* by the actions of consumers (operating within a given framework of existing commodity and/or production possibilities). Cost is seen (by Menger, and especially by Wieser, whose name came to be associated closely with this insight) merely as prospective utility deliberately sacrificed (in order to command more highly preferred utility). Whereas in the development of the other marginalist theories, it took perhaps two decades for it to be seen that marginal utility value theory points directly to marginal productivity distribution theory, Menger at least glimpsed this insight immediately. His theory of 'higher-order' goods emphasizes how both the economic character and the value of factor services, are derived exclusively from the valuations placed by consumers upon the consumers products to whose emergence these higher order goods ultimately contribute. Böhm-Bawerk contributed not only to the exposition and dissemination of Menger's basic subjective value theory, but most prominently also to the theory of capital and interest. Early in his career he published a massive volume (Böhm-Bawerk, 1884) in the history of doctrine, offering an encyclopedic critique of all earlier theories of interest (or 'surplus value' or 'normal profit'). This he followed up several years later with a volume (Böhm-Bawerk, 1889) presenting his own theory. At least part of the renown of the Austrian School at the turn of the century derived from the fame of these contributions. As we shall note later on, a number of subsequent and modern writers (such as Hicks, 1973; Faber, 1979; and Hausman, 1981) have indeed seen these Böhm-Bawerkian ideas as constituting the enduring element of the Austrian contribution. Others, taking their cue from an oft-repeated critical remark attributed to Menger (Schumpeter, 1954, p. 847, fn. 8), have seen Böhm-Bawerk's theory of capital and interest as separate from, or even as somehow inconsistent with, the core of the Austrian tradition stemming from Menger (Lachmann, 1977, p. 27)). Certainly Böhm-Bawerk himself saw his theory of capital and interest as a seamless extension of basic subjectivist value theory. Once the dimension of time has been introduced into the analysis of both consumer and producer decisions, Böhm-Bawerk found it possible to explain the phenomenon of interest. Because production takes time, and because economizing men systematically choose earlier receipts over (physically similar) later receipts, capital-using production processes cannot fail to yield (even after the erosive forces of competition are taken into account) a portion of current output to those who in earlier periods invested inputs into time-consuming, 'roundabout' production processes.

Böhm-Bawerk became, indeed, so prominent a representative of the Austrian School prior to World War I that, largely due to his work, the Marxists came to view the Austrians as the quintessential bourgeois, intellectual enemy of Marxist economics (Bukharin, 1914). Not only did Böhm-Bawerk offer his own theory explaining the phenomenon of the interest 'surplus' in a manner depriving this capitalist income of any exploitative character, he had emphatically and mercilessly refuted Marxist theories of this surplus. In his 1884 work Böhm-Bawerk had systematically deployed the Austrian subjective theory of value to criticize witheringly the Marxist labour theory underlying the exploitation theory. A decade later (Böhm-Bawerk, 1896) he offered a patient, but relentless and uncompromising elaboration of that critique (in dissecting the claim that Marx's posthumously published Volume III of Capital could be reconciled with the simple labour theory forming the basis of Volume I). This tension between the Marxists and the Austrians was to find later echoes in the debate which Mises and Hayek (third- and fourth-generation Austrians) were to conduct, during the 1920–40 interwar period, with socialist economists concerning the possibility of economic calculation in a centrally planned economy.

Menger retired from his University of Vienna professorship in 1903. His chair was assumed by Wieser. Wieser has been justly described as

> the central figure of the Austrian School: central in time, central in the ideas he propounded, central in his intellectual abilities, that is to say neither the most outstanding genius nor one of those also to be mentioned ... He had the longest teaching record ... (Streissler, 1986).

Wieser had been an early and prolific expositor of Menger's theory of value. His general treatise on economics, summing up his life's contributions (Wieser, 1914), has been hailed by some (but certainly not all) commentators as a major achievement. (Hayek, 1968, sees the work as a personal achievement rather than as representative of the Austrian School.) In the decade prior to World War I, it was Böhm-Bawerk's seminar (begun when Böhm-Bawerk rejoined academic life after a number of years as Finance Minister of Austria) that became famous as the intellectual centre of the Austrian School. Among the subsequently famous economists who participated in the seminar were Josef A. Schumpeter and Ludwig von Mises, both of whom published books prior to the war (Schumpeter, 1908, 1912; Mises, 1912).

AFTER WORLD WAR I

The scene in Austrian economics after the war was rather different than it had been before. Böhm-Bawerk had died in 1914. Menger, who even in his long seclusion after retirement, used to receive visits from the young economists at the university, died in 1921. Although Wieser continued to teach until his death in 1926, the focus shifted to younger scholars. These included particularly Mises, the student of Böhm-Bawerk, and Hans Mayer, who succeeded his teacher Wieser, to his chair. Mises, although an 'extraordinary' (unsalaried) faculty member at the university, never did obtain a professorial chair. Much of his intellectual influence was exercised outside the university framework (Mises, 1978, ch. ix). Other notable (pre-war-trained) scholars during the Twenties included Richard Strigl, Ewald Schams, and Leo Schonfeld (later Illy). In the face of these changes the Austrian tradition thrived. New books were published, and a new crop of younger students came to the fore, many of whom were to become internationally famous economists in later decades. These included particularly Friedrich A. Hayek, Gottfried Haberler, Fritz Machlup, Oskar Morgenstern, and Paul N. Rosenstein-Rodan. Economic discussion among the Austrians was vigorously carried on, during the Twenties and early Thirties, within two partly overlapping groups. One, at the university, was led by Hans Mayer. The other centred around Mises, whose famed privatseminar met in his Chamber of Commerce office and drew not only the gifted younger economists, but also such philosophers, sociologists and political scientists as Felix Kaufmann, Alfred Schutz and Erik Voegelin. It was during this period that British economist Lionel Robbins came decisively under the influence of the intellectual ferment going on in Vienna. A distinctly important outcome of this contact was Robbins's highly influential book (Robbins, 1932). It was largely through this work that a number of key Austrian ideas came to be absorbed into the mainstream literature of 20th-century Anglo-American economics. In 1931 Robbins invited Hayek to lecture at the London School of Economics, and this led to Hayek's appointment to the Tooke chair at that institution.

Hayek's arrival on the British scene contributed especially to the development and widespread awareness of the 'Austrian' theory of the business cycle. Mises had sketched such a theory as early as 1912 (Mises, 1912, pp. 396–404). This theory attributed the boom phase of the cycle to intertemporal misallocation stimulated by 'too low' interest rates. This intertemporal misallocation consisted of producers initiating processes of production that implicitly anticipated a willingness on the part of the public to postpone consumption to a degree in fact inconsistent with the true pattern of time preferences. The subsequent abandonment of unsustainable projects constitutes the down phase of the cycle. Mises emphasised the roots of this theory in Wicksell, and in earlier insights of the British currency school. Indeed Mises was tempted to challenge the appropriateness of the 'Austrian' label widely attached to the theory (Mises, 1943). But, as he recognized, the Austrian label had become firmly attached to the doctrine. Hayek's vigorous exposition and extensive development of the theory (Hayek, 1931, 1933, 1939) and his introduction (through the theory) of Böhm-Bawerkian capital-theoretic insights to the British public, unmistakably left Hayek's imprint on the fully developed theory, and taught the profession to see it as a central contribution of the Austrian School. Given all these developments it is apparent that we must consider the early 1930s as constituting in many ways the period of greatest Austrian School influence upon the economics profession generally. Yet this triumph was to be short-lived indeed.

With the benefit of hindsight it is perhaps possible to understand why and how this same period of the early 1930s constituted, in fact, a decisive, almost fatal, turning point in the fortunes of the School. Within a few short years the idea of a distinct Austrian School – except as an important, but bygone, episode in the history of economics – virtually disappeared from the economics profession. While Hans Mayer continued to occupy his chair in Vienna until after World War II, the group of prominent younger economists who had surrounded Mises soon dispersed (for political or other reasons), many of them to various universities in the US. With Mises migrating in 1934 to Geneva and later to New York, with Hayek in London, Vienna ceased to be a centre for the vigorous continuation of the Austrian tradition. Moreover many of the group were convinced that the important ideas of the Austrian School had now been successfully absorbed into mainstream economics. The emerging ascendancy of theoretical economics, and thus the eclipse of historicist and anti-theoretical approaches to economics, no doubt permitted the Austrians to believe that they had finally prevailed, that there was no longer any particular need to cultivate a separate Austrian version of economic theory. A 1932 statement by Mises captures this spirit. Referring to the usual separation of economic theorists into three schools of thought, 'the Austrian and the Anglo-American Schools and the School of Lausanne', Mises (citing Morgenstern) emphasized that these groups 'differ only in their mode of expressing the same fundamental idea and that they are divided more by their terminology and by peculiarities of presentation than by the substance of their teachings' (Mises, 1933, p. 214). Yet the survival and development of an Austrian tradition during and subsequent to World War II, largely through the work of Mises himself and of Hayek, deserves and requires attention.

Fritz Machlup has, on several occasions (Machlup, 1981, 1982) listed six ideas as central to the Austrian School prior to World War II. There is every reason to agree that it was these six ideas that expressed the Austrian approach as understood, say, in 1932. These ideas were: (a) methodological individualism (not to be confused with political or ideological individualism, but referring to the claim that economic phenomena are to be explained by going back to the actions of individuals); (b) methodological subjectivism (recognizing that the actions of individuals are to be understood only by reference to the knowledge, beliefs, perception and expectations of these individuals); (c) marginalism (emphasizing the significance of prospective *changes* in relevant magnitudes confronting the decision maker); (d) the influence of utility (and diminishing marginal utility) on demand and thus on market prices; (e) opportunity costs (recognizing that the costs that affect decisions are those that express the most important of the alternative opportunities being sacrificed in employing productive services for one purpose rather than for the sacrificed alternatives); (f) time structure of consumption and production (expressing time preferences and the productivity of 'roundaboutness').

It seems appropriate, however, to comment further on this list. (1) With varying degrees of emphasis most modern microeconomics incorporates all of these ideas, so that (2) this list supports the cited Morgenstern–Mises statement emphasizing the common ground shared by *all* schools of economic theory. However (3) subsequent developments in the work of Mises and Hayek suggest that the list of six Austrian ideas was not *really* complete. While few Austrians at the time (of the early 1930s) were perhaps able to identify additional Austrian ideas, such additional insights were in fact implicit in the Austrian tradition and were to be articulated explicitly in later work. From this perspective, then, (4) important *differences* separate Austrian economic theory from the mainstream developments in microeconomics, particularly as these latter developments proceeded from the thirties onwards. It was left for Mises and Hayek to articulate these differences and thus preserve a unique Austrian 'presence' in the profession.

LATER DEVELOPMENTS IN AUSTRIAN ECONOMICS

One early expression of such differences between the Austrian understanding of economic theory and that of other schools, was Hans Mayer's paper criticizing 'functional price theories' and calling for the 'genetic-causal' method (Mayer, 1932). Here Mayer was criticizing equilibrium theories of price that neglected to explicate the *sequence* of actions leading to market prices. To understand this sequence one must understand the causal genesis of the component actions in the sequence. In the light of the later writings of Mises and Hayek, it seems reasonable to recognize Mayer as having placed his finger on an important and distinctive element embedded in the Austrian understanding. Yet the Austrians themselves during the 1920s (and such students of their works as Lionel Robbins) seemed to have missed this insight. What appears to have helped Hayek and Mises articulate this hitherto overlooked element, was the well-known interwar debate concerning the possibility of economic calculation under central planning. A careful reading of the contributions to that debate suggests that it was in reaction to the 'mainstream' equilibrium arguments of their opponents that Mises and Hayek made explicit the emphasis on process, learning and discovery to be found in the Austrian understanding of markets (Lavoie, 1985).

Mises had argued that economic calculation calls for the guidance supplied by prices; since the centrally planned economy has no market for productive factors, it cannot use factor prices as guides. Oskar Lange and others countered that prices need not be market prices; that guidance could be provided by non-market prices, announced by the central authorities, and treated by socialist managers 'parametrically' (just as prices are treated by producers in the theory of the firm, in perfectly competitive factor and product markets). It was in response to this argument that Hayek developed his interpretation of competitive market processes as processes of discovery during which dispersed information comes to be mobilized (Hayek, 1949, chapters 2, 4, 5, 7, 8, 9). An essentially similar characterization of the market process (without the Hayekian emphasis on the role of knowledge, but with an accent on entrepreneurial activity in a world of open-ended, radical uncertainty) was presented by Mises during the same period (Mises, 1940, 1949). In the light of these Mises–Hayek developments in the theory of market process (and recognizing that these developments constituted the articulation of insights taken for granted in the early Austrian tradition: Kirzner, 1985; Jaffé, 1976), it seems reasonable to add the following to Machlup's list of ideas central to the Austrian tradition: (g) markets (and competition) as processes of learning and discovery; (h) the individual decision as an act of choice in an essentially uncertain context (where the identification of the relevant alternatives is part of the decision itself). It is these latter ideas that have come to be developed in, and made central to the revived attention to the Austrian tradition that, stemming from the work of Mises and Hayek, has emerged in the US during the last decades.

AUSTRIAN ECONOMICS TODAY

As a result of these somewhat varied developments in the history of the Austrian School since 1930, the term Austrian Economics has come to evoke a number of different connotations in contemporary professional discussion. Some of these connotations are, at least partly, overlapping; others are, at least partly, mutually inconsistent. If seems useful, in disentangling these various perceptions, to identify a number of different meanings that have come to be attached to the term 'Austrian Economics' in the 1980s. The present status of the Austrian School of Economics is, for better or for worse, encapsulated in these current perceptions.

(a) For many economists the term 'Austrian Economics' is strictly a historical term. In this perception the existence of the Austrian School did not extend beyond the early Thirties: Austrian Economics was partly absorbed into mainstream microeconomics, and partly displaced by emerging Keynesian macroeconomics. To a considerable extent this view seems to be that held by economists in Austria today. Economists (and other intellectuals) in Austria today are thoroughly cognizant of – and proud of – the earlier Austrian School, as evidenced by several commemorative conferences held in Austria in recent years, and by several related volumes (Hicks and Weber, 1973; Leser, 1986), but see themselves today simply as a part of the general community of professional economists. Erich Streissler, present holder of the chair occupied by Menger, Wieser and Mayer, has written extensively, and with the insights and scholarship of one profoundly influenced by the Austrian tradition, concerning numerous aspects of the Austrian School and its principal representatives (Streissler, 1969, 1972, 1973, 1986).

(b) For a number of economists the adjective 'Austrian' has come to mark a revival of interest in Böhm-Bawerkian capital-and-interest theory. This revival has emphasized particularly the time dimension in production and the productivity of roundaboutness. Among the contributors to this literature should be mentioned Hicks (173), Bernholz (1971, 1973), Faber (1979) and Orosel (1981). In this literature, then, the term 'Austrian' has very little to do with the general subjectivist Mengerian tradition (which had, as noted earlier, certain reservations in regard to the Böhm-Bawerkian theory).

(c) For other economists (and non-economists) the term 'Austrian Economics' has come to be associated less with a unique methodology, or with specific economic doctrines, as with libertarian ideology in political and social discussion. For these observers, to be an Austrian economist in the 1980s is simply to be in favour of free markets. Machlup (1982) has noted (and partly endorsed) this perception of the term 'Austrian'. He has ascribed it, particularly, to the impact of the work of Mises. Mises' championship of the market cause was so prominent, and his identification as an Austrian was at the same time so unmistakable, that it is perhaps natural that his strong policy pronouncements in support of unhampered markets, came to be perceived as the core of Austrianism in modern times. This has been reinforced by the work of a leading US follower of Mises, Murray N. Rothbard, who has also been prominent in libertarian scholarship and advocacy. Other observers, however, would question this identification. While, as earlier noted, many of the early contributions of the Austrian School were seen as sharply antagonistic to Marxian thought, the school on the whole maintained an apolitical stance (Myrdal, 1929, p. 128). Among the founders of the school, Wieser was in fact explicit in endorsing the interventionist conclusions of the German Historical School (Wieser, 1914, pp. 490ff). While both Mises and Hayek provocatively challenged the possibility of efficiency under socialism, they too, emphasized the *wertfrei* character of their economics. Both writers would see their free market stance at the policy level as related to, but not as central to, their Austrianism.

(d) For many in the profession the term 'Austrian Economics' has come, since about 1970, to refer to a revival of interest in the ideas of Carl Menger and the earlier Austrian School, particularly as these ideas have been developed through the work of Mises and Hayek. This revival has occurred particularly in the US, where a sizeable literature has emerged from a number of economists. This literature includes, in particular, works by Murray N. Rothbard (1962), Israel Kirzner (1973), Gerald P. O'Driscoll (1977, 1985), Mario J. Rizzo (O'Driscoll and Rizzo, 1985), and Roger W. Garrison (1978, 1982, 1985). The thrust of this literature has been to emphasize the differences between the Austrian understanding of markets as processes, and that of the equilibrium theorists whose work has dominated much of modern economic theory. As a result of this emphasis, this sense of the term 'Austrian Economics' has often (and only partly accurately; see White, 1977, p. 9) come to be understood as a refusal to adopt modern mathematical and econometric techniques – which standard economics adopted largely as a result of its equilibrium orientation. The economists in this group of modern Austrians (sometimes called neo-Austrian) do see themselves as continuators of an earlier tradition, sharing with mainstream neoclassical economics an appreciation for the systematic outcomes of markets, but differing from it in its understanding of how these outcomes are in fact achieved. Largely as a result of the activity of this group, many classic works of the early Austrians have recently been republished in original or translated form, and have attracted a considerable readership both inside and outside the profession.

(e) Yet another current meaning loosely related to the preceding sense of the term, has come to be associated with the term 'Austrian Economics'. This meaning refers to an emphasis on the radical uncertainty that surrounds economic decision making, to an extent that implies virtual rejection of much of received microeconomics. Ludwig Lachmann (1976) has identified the work of G.L.S. Shackle as constituting in this regard the most consistent extension of Austrian (and especially of Misesian) subjectivism. Lachmann's own work

(1973, 1977, 1986) has, in the same vein, stressed the indeterminacy of both individual choices and market outcomes.

This line of thought has come to imply serious reservations concerning the possibility of systematic theoretical conclusions commanding significant degrees of generality. This connotation of the term 'Austrian Economics' thus associates it with a stance sympathetic, to a degree, towards historical and institutional approaches. Given the prominent opposition of earlier Austrians to these approaches, this association has, as might be expected, been seen as ironic or even paradoxical by many observers (including, especially, modern exponents of the broader tradition of the Austrian School of Economics).

[An earlier article on the Austrian School of Economics was begun and substantially drafted by Professor Friedrich A. Hayek – himself a Nobel laureate in economics whose celebrated contributions are deeply rooted in the Austrian tradition. The present author gratefully acknowledges his indebtness (in the writing of this essay) to the characteristic scholarship and treasure-trove of facts contained in Professor Hayek's unfinished article, as well as to Professor Hayek's other numerous studies that relate to the history of the Austrian School.]

ISRAEL M. KIRZNER

See also BÖHM-BAWERK, EUGEN VON; COMPETITION: AUSTRIAN CONCEPTIONS; HAYEK, FRIEDRICH VON; IMPUTATION; MENGER, CARL; MISES, LUDWIG EDLER VON; ROUNDABOUT METHODS OF PRODUCTION; WIESER, FRIEDRICH VON.

BIBLIOGRAPHY

Bernholz, P. 1971. Superiority of roundabout processes and positive rate of interest. A simple model of capital and growth. *Kyklos* 24(4) 687-721.

Bernholz, P. and Faber, M. 1973. Technical superiority of roundabout processes and positive rate of interest. A capital model with depreciation and n-period horizon. *Zeitschrift für die gesamte Staatswissenschaften* 129(1), February, 46-61.

Bostaph, S. 1978. The methodological debate between Carl Menger and the German Historicists. *Atlantic Economic Journal* 6(3), September, 3-16.

Böhm-Bawerk, E. von. 1884. *Geschichte und Kritik der Kapitalzins-Theorien.* English trans. as Vol. I of *Capital and Interest*, South Holland, Ill.: Libertarian Press, 1959.

Böhm-Bawerk, E. von. 1886. Grundzuge der Theorie des Wirtschaftlichen Guterwerths. *Conrad's Jahrbuch*, 1–88, 477–541.

Böhm-Bawerk, E. von. 1889. *Positive Theorie des Kapitales.* Innsbruck : Wagner.

Böhm-Bawerk, E. von. 1891. The Austrian economists. *Annals of the American Academy of Political and Social Science*, January, 361–84.

Böhm-Bawerk, E. von. 1896. *Zum Abschluss des Marxschen Systems.* Trans. (1898) as *Karl Marx and the Close of his System*, ed. P. Sweezy, New York: Kelley, 1949.

Bukharin, N. 1914. *The Economic Theory of the Leisure Class.* Translated from Russian (1927), London: M. Lawrence; reprinted, New York: Monthly Review Press, 1972.

Faber, M. 1979. *Introduction to Modern Austrian Capital Theory.* Berlin: Springer.

Garrison, R.W. 1978. Austrian macroeconomics: a diagrammatical exposition. In *New Directions in Austrian Economics*, ed. L.M. Spadaro, Kansas City: Sheed, Andrews & McMeel.

Garrison, R.W. 1982. Austrian economics as the middle ground: comment on Loasby. In *Method, Process, and Austrian Economics: Essays in Honor of Ludwig von Mises*, ed. I.M. Kirzner, Lexington, Mass.: Lexington Books.

Garrison, R.W. 1985. Time and money: the universals of macroeconomic theorizing. *Journal of Macroeconomics* 6(2), Spring, 197-213.

Grassl, W. and Smith, B. (eds) 1986. *Austrian Economics, Historical and Philosophical Background.* New York: New York University Press.

Gross, G. 1884. *Die Lehre von Unternehmergewinn.* Leipzig.

Hausman, D.M. 1981. *Capital, Profits, and Prices.* New York: Columbia University Press.

Hayek, F.A. 1931. *Prices and Production.* London: Routledge & Sons.

Hayek, F.A. 1933. *Monetary Theory and the Trade Cycle.* London: Jonathan Cape.

Hayek, F.A. 1939. *Profits, Interest and Investment: and Other Essays on the Theory of Industrial Fluctuations.* London: Routledge & Kegan Paul.

Hayek, F.A. 1949. *Individualism and Economic Order.* London: Routledge & Kegan Paul.

Hayek, F.A. 1968. Economic thought VI: the Austrian School. *International Encyclopedia of the Social Sciences*, ed. D.L. Sills, New York: Macmillan.

Hicks, J. 1973. *Capital and Time: A Neo-Austrian Theory.* Oxford: Clarendon Press.

Hicks, J.R. and Weber, W. 1973. *Carl Menger and the Austrian School of Economics.* Oxford: Clarendon Press.

Jaffé, W. 1976. Menger, Jevons and Walras de-homogenized. *Economic Inquiry* 14(4), December, 511-24.

Jevons, W.S. 1871. *The Theory of Political Economy.* London: Macmillan.

Kauder, E. 1965. *A History of Marginal Utility Theory.* Princeton: Princeton University Press.

Kirzner, I.M. 1973. *Competition and Entrepreneurship.* Chicago: University of Chicago Press.

Kirzner, I.M. 1981. Mises and the renaissance of Austrian Economics. *Homage to Mises, the First Hundred Years*, ed. J.K. Andrews, Jr., Hillsdale: Hillsdale College Press.

Kirzner, I.M. 1985. Comment on R.N. Langlois, 'From the knowledge of economics to the economics of knowledge: Fritz Machlup on methodology and on the "Knowledge Society" '. In *Research in the History of Economic Thought and Methodology*, ed. Warren J. Samuels, Greenwich, CT: JAI.

Komorzynski, J. von 1889. *Der Werth in der isolirten Wirthschaft.* Vienna: Manz.

Lachmann, L. 1973. *Macro-economic Thinking and the Market Economy.* London: Institute of Economic Affairs.

Lachmann, L. 1976. From Mises to Shackle: an essay on Austrian Economics and the Kaleidic Society. *Journal of Economic Literature* 14(10), March, 54-62.

Lachmann, L. 1977. Austrian Economics in the present crisis of economic thought. *Capital, Expectations, and the Market Process.* Kansas City: Sheed, Andrews & McMeel.

Lachmann, L. 1986a. Austrian Economics under fire: the Hayek–Sraffa duel in restrospect. In Grassl and Smith (1986).

Lachmann, L. 1986b. *The Market as a Process.* Oxford: Basic Blackwell.

Lavoie, D. 1985. *Rivalry and Central Planning: The Socialist Calculation Debate Reconsidered.* Cambridge: Cambridge University Press.

Leser, N. (ed.) 1986. *Die Wiener Schule der Nationalökonomie.* Vienna: Hermann Böhlau.

Machlup, F. 1981. Ludwig von Mises: the academic scholar who would not compromise. *Wirtschaftspolitischen Blätter*, No. 4.

Machlup, F. 1982. Austrian Economics. *Encyclopedia of Economics*, ed. Douglas Greenwald, New York: McGraw-Hill.

Mataja, V. 1884. *Der Unternehmergewinn.* Vienna.

Mayer, H. 1932. Der Erkenntniswert der Funktionellen Preistheorien. In *Die Wirtschaftstheorie der Gegenwart*, ed. H. Mayer, Vienna.

McCulloch, J.H. 1977. The Austrian theory of the marginal use and of ordinal marginal utility. *Zeitschrift für Nationalökonomie*, No. 3–4.

Menger, C. 1871. *Grundsätze der Volkswirtschaftslehre.* Translated (1950) as *Principles of Economics*, ed. J. Dingwall and B.F. Hoselitz; reprinted, New York: New York University Press, 1981.

Menger, K., Jr. 1973. Austrian marginalism and mathematical economics. In *Carl Menger and the Austrian School of Economics*, ed. J.R. Hicks and W. Weber, Oxford: Clarendon Press.

Meyer, R. 1887. *Das Wesen des Einkommens: Eine volkswirtschaftliche Untersuchung.* Berlin: Hertz.

Mises, L. von. 1912. *Theorie des Geldes und der Umlaufsmittel.* Translated as *Theory of Money and Credit* (1934), Indianapolis: Liberty Classics, 1980.

Mises, L. von. 1933. *Grundprobleme der Nationalökonomie.* Translated as *Epistemological Problems of Economics*, Princeton: Van Nostrand, 1960.

Mises, L. von. 1940. *Nationalökonomie, Theorie des Handelns und Wirtschaftens*, Geneva, Editions Union.

Mises, L. von. 1943. 'Elastic expectations' and the Austrian theory of the trade cycle. *Economica* 10, August, 251-2.

Mises, L. von. 1949 *Human Action, A Treatise on Economics.* New Haven: Yale University Press.

Mises, L. von. 1969. *The Historical Setting of the Austrian School of Economics.* New Rochelle: Arlington House.

Mises, L. von. 1978. *Notes and Recollections.* South Holland: Libertarian Press.

O'Driscoll, G.P., Jr. 1977. *Economics as a Coordination Problem: The Contributions of Friedrich A. Hayek.* Kansas City: Sheed, Andrews & McMeel.

O'Driscoll, G.P., Jr. and Rizzo, M.J. 1985. *The Economics of Time and Ignorance.* Oxford: Basil Blackwell.

Orosel, G.O. 1981. Faber's modern Austrian capital theory: a critical survey. *Zeitschrift für Nationalökonomie,* 141–55.

Philippovich, E. von Philippsberg. 1893. *Grundriss der Politischen Ökonomie.* Freiburg: Mohr.

Robbins, L. 1932. *The Nature and Significance of Economic Science.* London: Macmillan.

Rothbard, M.N. 1962. *Man, Economy, and State: A Treatise on Economic Principles.* Princeton: Van Nostrand.

Sax, E. 1887. *Grundlegung der Theoretischen Staatswirtschaft.* Vienna: Holder.

Schumpeter, J.A. 1908. *Das Wesen und der Hauptinhalt der Theoretischen Nationalökonomie.* Leipzig: Duncker & Humblot.

Schumpeter, J.A. 1912. *Theorie der wirtschaftlichen Entwicklung.* Leipzig: Duncker & Humblot. English translation (1934) *The Theory of Economic Development*, Cambridge, Mass.: Harvard University Press.

Schumpeter, J.A. 1954. *History of Economic Analysis.* New York: Oxford University Press.

Streissler, E. 1969. Structural economic thought: on the significance of the Austrian School today. *Zeitschrift für Nationalökonomie* 29(3-4), December, 237-66.

Streissler, E. 1972. To what extent was the Austrian School marginalist? *History of Political Economy* 4(2), Fall, 426-61.

Streissler, E. 1973. The Mengerian tradition. In *Carl Menger and the Austrian School of Economics*, ed. J.R. Hicks and W. Weber, Oxford: Clarendon Press.

Streissler, E. 1986. Arma virumque cano. Friedrich von Wieser, the bard as economist. In Leser (1986).

Walras, L. 1874. *Eléments d'économie politique pure.* Lausanne: Corbaz.

White, L.H. 1977. *The Methodology of the Austrian School Economists.* Revised edition, Auburn, AL: The Ludwig von Mises Institute of Auburn University, 1984.

Wieser, F. von 1884. *Ursprung des Wirtschaftlichen Wertes.* Vienna: Hölder.

Wieser, F. von 1889. *Der Naturliche Werth.* Vienna: Hölder. Trans. as *Natural Value*, ed. W. Smart, London: Macmillan, 1893; reprinted, New York: Kelley, 1956.

Wieser, F. von 1914. *Theorie der Gesellschaftlichen Wirtschaft.* Tübingen: Mohr. Translated (1927) as *Social Economics*, London: G. Allen & Unwin; reprinted, New York: Kelley, 1967.

Zuckerkandl, R. 1889. *Zur Theorie des Preises.* Leipzig: Stein.

autarky. Autarky means self-sufficiency, especially economic self-sufficiency. The term appears most frequently in economic literature, both as a theoretical construct deployed in the theory of comparative advantage, and as a policy of economic self-sufficiency.

In the theory of comparative advantage, the concept of autarky plays a central role. Originally developed by Torrens and Ricardo, the theory proceeds by considering at least two hypothetical commodity-producing economies. Each economy is supposed to be capable of existing in at least two states, one of which is autarky or no trade, and the other being free-trade. It is hypothesized that each economy can be compared under autarky independently of the other. For profitable trade between such hypothetical economies to take place, there must be some difference between the autarky or pre-trade prices. The various theories of comparative advantage proceed to postulate a variety of determinants of the autarky price differentials. There are at least three ways in which the autarky construct in the theory of comparative advantage is problematic.

First, when capital is treated as produced means of production in the economic model, either the conventional interpretation of the factor proportions theory of comparative advantage requires modification, or the autarky construct itself must be altered. The modern neo-Ricardian theory of comparative advantage takes the former route, arguing that when capital as produced means of production is included, independent determinants of income distribution must be added to the Ricardian theory of comparative advantage, which is based on technological differences between economies. (For an introduction to neo-Ricardian trade theory, see Steedman (ed.), 1979; see also Metcalfe and Steedman, 1981.) Neo-classical and some neo-Marxian interpretations of the theory of comparative advantage argue that the autarky construct itself must be modified to allow autarky comparisons at common prices between non-trading economies for the consistent valuation of produced means of production. The Heckscher–Ohlin–Samuelson factor proportions theory can then be applied in situations where there are produced means of production. The latter resolution of the difficulties created by produced means of production in the theory of comparative advantage is consistent with the empirical observation that no real economy is ever observed without trade or independently of other economies. In practical terms, the modified concept autarky really means 'less trade' rather than 'no-trade'. (See Ethier, 1981, and Smith, 1984, for a discussion of the neo-classical response to these issues.)

Second, the measurement of autarky price differentials when there are more than two commodities is not unambiguous. For a recent discussion of this problem and a generalization of the principle of comparative advantage, see Deardorff (1980).

A third problem with the use of the autarky construct in the theory of comparative advantage is that it is often defined in the context of an economic model which has no descriptive content. Whilst this is perfectly legitimate for some theoretical work, for empirical and policy purposes it is not appropriate to leave out a description of either the level of development of the forces of production, the relations of production which pertain to the economy or economics under consideration, or the superstructural arrangements in place. (For a modern re-statement of Marx's theory of history, see Cohen, 1978, 1983; see also Dobb, 1973.) This can lead to an over-emphasis on the role of the market and static efficiency criteria, and an understatement of dynamic and institutional factors, in the resultant theories of comparative advantage. (For a discussion of some of these issues, see Evans and Alizadeh, 1984.) The latter observation has an important bearing on the importance of autarky or self-sufficiency as a trading policy.

The main 19th-century exponents of economic self-sufficiency were Hamilton and List. They did not advocate autarky in the literal sense used in the theory of comparative advantage, but they did argue that new industrialized nations required protection of their infant industries before free trade could be embarked upon. There have been many 20th-century counterparts of List and Hamilton. In the 1920s, Preobrazhensky argued for import-substituting industrialization financed by the taxation of agriculture in a process called primitive socialist accumulation (for a formal statement of Preobrazhensky's problem, see Bardhan, 1970, ch. 9). In the early postwar period, Prebisch and Singer had a powerful influence on the Economic Commission for Latin America (ECLA), arguing for import-substituting industrialization to offset hypothesized adverse terms of trade movements and adverse monopoly conditions facing primary commodity producers. (By now, there is strong statistical evidence to support the Prebisch–Singer hypothesis on the declining trend of the net barter terms of trade between primary commodities and manufactures (excluding oil) for the whole of the 20th century; see Sapsford, 1985.) In Eastern Europe, in spite of considerable integration of their national economies, drives towards import substitution and self-sufficiency both nationally and as a trading bloc remain powerful tendencies in their economic mechanisms. Until recently, China followed a policy of near autarky, and only in the 1970s have there been moves in India to begin to dismantle powerful barriers to trade. An offshoot of the ECLA school, with strong neo-Marxian influences, has argued that by remaining open to the world economy, developing economies will not develop but will suffer a process of underdevelopment through mechanisms of dependency and unequal exchange. Amin, the leading advocate of a semi-autarkic development strategy, bases his argument on a model of unequal exchange which is not well founded theoretically or empirically. (For a statement and critique of Amin's theory of unequal exchange, see Amin, 1973, and Evans, 1981 and 1984.)

Some of the theoretical arguments for interfering with market mechanism, with direct and indirect consequences for the pattern and extent of trade, are agreed by all schools of thought. The presence of externalities and strong economies of learning combined with varying degrees of market distortion and market failure provide the basis for the modern theory of domestic market distortions. Within this context, protection through intervention in trade is likely to be worse than subsidies or other policies aimed directly towards policy objectives.

Increasingly, neoclassical economists and some of the main international agencies such as the World Bank and the International Monetary Fund, with a sharply enhanced policy role through the conditionality attached to debt re-negotiation agreements, argue that the development of dynamic comparative advantage is better served by imperfect markets than imperfect governments. This perspective is strongly disputed by many who stress the importance of state and parastatal institutions operating in conjunction with the market mechanism, often in the context of a rapidly growing national capitalist class and national capitalist firms (for an overview of some of these arguments, see Kaplinsky, 1984). Different views on the length of the learning period and the length of time for which it is appropriate for the state to be the driving force in a national development strategy lie behind the important policy debates on the role of freer trade and the world market in all economies, east, west and south. In the latter part of the 1980s, many debt-ridden developing countries are being asked to trade their way out of debt in the context of a sluggish and closing world economy, often with disastrous domestic consequences for the poorest and weakest citizens in their midst. The few countries which have a choice in the matter must find their sources of growth in their internal markets rather than through trade.

It is not easy to assess the degree of success of policies of economic self-sufficiency. Whilst a strong case can be made for greater economic self-sufficiency as a part of the process of developing a national economy, it is not clear how long such a policy should be carried on, or how selective government policies should be towards the protection of different industries. In practice, the remarkable growth performance of many developing countries in the postwar period has been achieved in very widely differing circumstances and with greater or less economic self-sufficiency. What is clear is that, excepting the special cases of some small city states, all late developers have gone through periods of development of their national economies with policies of greater economic self-sufficiency. Only in the very extreme cases of economic self-sufficiency, such as pursued in Cambodia under the Khmer Rouge in the 1970s, or of extreme protection, such as in Ghana, can it be said unequivocally that the drive for economic self-sufficiency, foregoing the static gains from trade, has contributed decisively to subsequent economic disaster.

DAVID EVANS

See also COMPARATIVE ADVANTAGE; FREE TRADE; HECKSCHER–OHLIN TRADE THEORY; NATIONAL SYSTEM; PROTECTION.

BIBLIOGRAPHY

Amin, S. 1973. L'échange inégal et la loi de la valeur: la fin d'un débat. Paris: Editions Anthropus – IDFP.

Bardhan, P.K. 1970. Economic Growth, Development and Foreign Trade: A Study in Pure Theory. New York: Wiley.

Cohen, G.A. 1978. Karl Marx's Theory of History: A Defence. Oxford: Oxford University Press.

Cohen, G.A. 1983. Forces and relations of production. In Marx: A Hundred Years On, ed. B. Mathews, London: Lawrence & Wishart.

Deardorff, A.V. 1980. The general validity of the law of comparative advantage. Journal of Political Economy 88, October, 941-57.

Dobb, M. 1973. Theories of Value and Distribution Since Adam Smith. Cambridge: Cambridge University Press.

Ethier, W. 1981. A reply to Professors Metcalfe and Steedman. Journal of International Economies 11, 273-7.

Evans, H.D. 1981. Trade, production and self-reliance. In Dependency Theory: A Critical Assessment, ed. D. Seers, London: Frances Pinter.

Evans, H.D. 1984. A critical assessment of some neo-marxian trade theories. Journal of Development Studies 20(2), 202-26.

Evans, H.D. and Alizadeh, P. 1984. Trade, industrialisation and the visible hand. In Kaplinsky (1984).

Kaplinsky, R. (ed.) 1984. Third World Industrialisation in the 1980's: Open Economics in a Closing World. Special Issue of The Journal of Development Studies, October.

Metcalfe, J.S. and Steedman, I. 1981. On transformation of theories. Journal of International Economics 11, 267-71.

Sapsford, D. 1985. The statistical debate on the net barter terms of trade between primary commodities and manufactures; a comment and some additional evidence. Economic Journal 95, 781-88.

Smith, A. 1984. Capital theory and trade theory. In Handbook of International Economics, ed. R.W. Jones and P.B. Kenen, Vol. 1, Amsterdam: North-Holland, 289-324.

Steedman, I. (ed.) 1979. Fundamental Issues in Trade Theory. London: Macmillan.

autocorrelation. See REGRESSION AND CORRELATION ANALYSIS.

automatic stabilizers. See BUILT-IN STABILIZERS.

autonomous expenditures. The idea of autonomous expenditures is usually associated with a simple Keynesian model of the economy and refers to those expenditures which are treated as exogenously given within the context of the model being used. The contrast is drawn between autonomous expenditures and induced expenditures. Autonomous expenditures are those which are unrelated to the other economic variables being considered, though it is income which is generally taken to be the key economic variable which does not influence autonomous expenditures. Induced expenditures are influenced by other economic variables, with the level of income being a major influence.

In the simplest formation of a Keynesian model, consumption expenditure is taken as $a + c.Y$ where Y is the level of income, and c the marginal propensity to consume out of income with a value of less than unity, and investment expenditure is taken as I (fixed). Then total expenditure equals $a + I + c.Y$. The component $a + I$ is the autonomous expenditure and $c.Y$ induced expenditure. In equilibrium, with income equal to expenditure, then $Y = a + I + c.Y$, so that $Y = (a + I)/(1 - c)$. This formula indicates the potential importance of autonomous expenditure in that it is autonomous expenditure which determines the level of income. Changes in autonomous expenditure are predicted to lead to changes in income.

Outside the simple model outlined above, the allocation of expenditure into categories of 'autonomous' and 'induced' is not straightforward. The difficulties which arise can be examined under two main headings. First, there will generally be some lags between the receipt of income and its effects on expenditure. A rise in income in the current period may have effects on expenditure in a number of future periods. Within the current period, there will be some expenditure induced by current income, some by previous income and some will be autonomous. Second, there are many categories of expenditure, besides consumption expenditure and investment, and these expenditures may be difficult to categorize as between induced and autonomous expenditures. Investment itself (and particularly investment in stocks and work-in-progress) may be related to income and hence partially induced expenditure. Government expenditure can vary automatically though inversely with the level of income (e.g. unemployment benefits), whilst taxation generally rises with income. But elements of government expenditure and taxation may be varied by the government in response to the level of income (particularly if the government was operating a Keynesian demand-management policy).

The simple Keynesian approach to macroeconomics paid particular attention to the importance of autonomous expenditures in the determination of the level of income. But in order to test that approach, different types of expenditure have to be classified as autonomous or induced. An attempt to do this, and to contrast the Keynesian approach with a monetarist approach, was made by Friedman and Meiselman (1963). The conclusion of that article was challenged by Ando and Modigliani (1965) and by de Prano and Mayer (1965). These articles did not reach any shared conclusions, but they did indicate the difficulties of making the concept of autonomous and induced expenditures operational (as well as raising a number of other methodological issues).

The actual definition of autonomous expenditure used by Friedman and Meiselman (1963) was the sum of net private domestic investment, government deficit on current account and the net foreign balance. These authors arrive at their definitions of autonomous expenditure by reference to the statistical relationship between various possible definitions of autonomous expenditure. Ando and Modigliani (1965) define autonomous expenditure as investment, exports, most government expenditure minus property taxes. Thus they regard most taxes as induced rather than autonomous. But they arrive at their definitions by their subjective views rather than the formal statistical tests applied by Friedman and Meiselman (which they reject).

The importance of the distinction drawn between autonomous and induced expenditures is threefold. First, it established a break with Say's Law that supply creates its own demand. In effect, under Say's Law, all expenditure is induced, so that an increase in the supply of goods and services would generate income for the suppliers, which in turn leads to a rise in demand. There could be some temporary disruption from such changes, but no prolonged effect from a discrepancy between supply and demand since the income generated for the suppliers is all spent. When the distinction between autonomous and induced expenditures is made, it is implicit that induced expenditures are less than total income and that the difference between the level of income which would be generated at full employment and the corresponding induced expenditures would not necessarily be filled by autonomous expenditures. Thus demand-deficient unemployment would then arise.

Second, there is usually an approximate identification of autonomous expenditures with investment, exports and government expenditures. It is a relatively short step to consider the different types of autonomous expenditures as substitutes for one another in the sense of contributing the same effect to the level of aggregate demand. In policy terms, this clearly would lead to suggestions that variations in government expenditure be used to offset fluctuations in private autonomous expenditure, particularly investment, in order to limit the extent of business fluctuations.

Third, autonomous expenditure is seen as the active ingredient in the level of aggregate demand, whilst induced expenditure is viewed as passive. Thus, induced expenditures are seen as adjusting passively to the level of income (as indicated above), whereas variations in autonomous expenditure are seen as leading to variations in the level of income (and in induced expenditure).

M. SAWYER

BIBLIOGRAPHY

Ando, A. and Modigliani, F. 1965. The relative stability of monetary velocity and the investment multiplier. *American Economic Review* 55(4), 693–728.

De Prano, M. and Mayer, T. 1965. Tests of the relative importance of autonomous expenditure and money. *American Economic Review* 55(4), 729–752.

Friedman, M. and Meiselman, D. 1963. The relative stability of monetary velocity and the investment multiplier in the United States, 1897–1958. In Commission on Money and Credit, *Stabilization Policies*, ed. E. Carey Brown et al., Englewood Cliffs, NJ: Prentice-Hall, 165–268.

autoregressive and moving-average time-series processes. Characterization of time series by means of autoregressive (AR) or moving-average (MA) processes or combined autoregressive moving-average (ARMA) processes was suggested, more or less simultaneously, by the Russian statistician and economist, E. Slutsky (1927), and the British statistician G. U. Yule (1921, 1926, 1927). Slutsky and Yule observed that if we begin with a series of purely random numbers and then take sums or differences, weighted or unweighted, of such numbers, the new series so produced has many of the apparent cyclic properties that are thought to characterize economic and other time series. Such sums or differences of purely random numbers are the basis for ARMA models of the processes by which many kinds of economic time series are assumed to be generated, and thus form the basis for recent suggestions for analysis, forecasting and control (e.g., Box and Jenkins, 1970).

Let L be the lag operator such that $L^k x_t = x_{t-k}$. Consider the familiar pth order linear, homogeneous, deterministic difference equation with constant coefficients common in discrete dynamic economic analysis (e.g. Chow, 1975):

$$\psi(L)y_t = 0$$

or

$$y_t - \psi_1 y_{t-1} - \cdots - \psi_p y_{t-p} = 0. \qquad (1)$$

Relationships are seldom exact, however, so we introduce a serially uncorrelated random shock ϵ_t with zero mean and constant variance:

$$E\epsilon_t = 0.$$
$$E\epsilon_t \epsilon_{t'} = \begin{cases} \sigma^2, & t = t' \\ 0, & \text{otherwise} \end{cases} \qquad (2)$$

Thus

$$\psi(L)y_t = \epsilon_t, \qquad (3)$$

which is the pth-order autoregressive process, AR(p), with constant coefficients studied by Yule (1927).

If the stochastic term in (3) as itself assumed to be a linear combination of past values of a variable such as ϵ_t, with properties (2), for example,

$$\psi(L)y_t = \mu_t, \qquad (4)$$

where $\mu_t = \phi(L)\epsilon_t$, and $\phi(\cdot)$ is a polynomial of order q, then the process is a mixed autoregressive moving-average process of order (p, q), ARMA (p, q). The process generating μ_t is simply a moving-average process of order q, MA(q).

Such dynamic processes, under appropriate conditions on the coefficients of ψ, ϕ, and the distribution of ϵ_t, have found wide application in both theoretical and empirical economics. The ability of such processes to describe the evolution of a series has made ARMA models a powerful tool for forecasting economic time series and other applications, such as seasonal adjustment. Moreover, because the models can capture a wide range of stochastic properties of economic time series, they have been widely used in models involving rational expectations (e.g. Whiteman, 1983).

UNIVARIATE ARMA MODELS. Conditions for weak stationarity and invertibility (i.e. capability of being expressed as a pure, but possibly infinite, AR) are most easily discussed in terms of the so-called z-transform or autocovariance-generating transform of the model. This is obtained for models (3) and (4) by replacing the lag operator by a complex variable z; thus, in general,

$$B(z) = \frac{\phi(z)}{\psi(z)}, \qquad (5)$$

where the expression on the right converges. If the roots of $\psi(z) = 0$ do not lie strictly outside the unit circle (i.e. some lie on or inside), the process described by (3) or (4) will not be stationary, nor will the expression on the right converge outside of a circle with radius less than one. (*See* TIME-SERIES ANALYSIS.) In order to find a purely AR representation of MA and ARMA models, we require that $1/\phi(z)$ converge in the same region, so that $\phi(z) = 0$ must also have roots outside the unit circle. In this case, $B(z)$ is well-defined everywhere outside of a circle inside the unit circle, and the model defined by (4) is both weakly

stationary and invertible; the representation

$$y_t = B(L)\epsilon_t \qquad (6)$$

is a one-sided, infinite-order MA, with $\Sigma_{j=-\infty}^{\infty} b_j^2 < \infty$.

In Wold (1938) it is shown that every discrete weakly stationary process may be decomposed into a purely linearly deterministic part (which can be predicted exactly from a sufficient past history) and a part which corresponds to (6) above. (See the discussions of stationarity and ergodicity in TIME-SERIES ANALYSIS.)

Let the autocovariances of a stationary, zero-mean time series, x_t, be given by

$$\gamma(\tau) = E x_t x_{t-\tau}. \qquad (7)$$

The function

$$g(z) = \sum_{\tau=-\infty}^{\infty} z^\tau \gamma(\tau) \qquad (8)$$

is called the autocovariance generating function. If the function $g(z)$ is known and analytic in a certain region, it is possible to read off the autocovariances of the time series as the coefficients in a Laurent series expansion of the function there. For a linearly nondeterministic time series with one-sided MA representation (6) the autocovariance generating transform is given by

$$g_{yy}(z) = \sigma^2 B(z)B(z^{-1}). \qquad (9)$$

This function is analytic everywhere in an annulus about the unit circle. If y_t is generated by a stationary ARMA model with invertible MA component then $g_{yy}(z)$ will have no zeros anywhere in this annulus. On the unit circle itself the *spectral density* of the series is proportional by a factor of $(2\pi)^{-1}$ to the autocovariance generating transform:

$$f_{yy}(\lambda) = (1/2\pi)g_{yy}(e^{i\lambda}), \qquad -\pi \leqslant \lambda < \pi. \qquad (10)$$

Stationary, invertible ARMA processes give rise to time series with spectral densities which are strictly positive in the interval $(-\pi, \pi)$.

Let $1/\beta_j, j = 1, \ldots, q$ be the roots, not necessarily distinct, of $\phi(z) = 0$, and let $1/\alpha_j, j = 1, \ldots, p$ be the roots of $\psi(z) = 0$. For a stationary, invertible ARMA model all these roots lie outside the unit circle. The autocovariances of the time series generated by this model are

$$\gamma(\tau) = (1/2\pi i) \oint_{|z|=1} z^{-\tau-1} g(z) \, dz$$

$$= (\sigma^2/2\pi i) \oint_{|z|=1} z^{p+|\tau|-q-1}$$
$$\times \left\{ \prod_{j=1}^{q} (1-\beta_j z)(z-\beta_j) \middle/ \prod_{k=1}^{P} (1-\alpha_k z)(z-\alpha_k) \right\} dz. \qquad (11)$$

By the residue theorem, the integral on the right-hand side of (11) is $2\pi i$ times the sum of the residues enclosed by the unit circle. This fact allows a particularly simple calculation of the autocovariances of a time series generated by an ARMA model (see Nerlove et al. 1979, pp. 78–85). For example, for the general pth-order autoregression, AR(p), with distinct roots, the result is

$$\gamma(\tau) = \sum_{k=1}^{p} \left[\alpha_k^{p+|\tau|-1} \middle/ \left\{ \prod_{j=1}^{p} (1-\alpha_j \alpha_k) \prod_{\substack{j=1 \\ j \neq k}}^{p} (\alpha_j - \alpha_k) \right\} \right], \qquad (12)$$

and for the ARMA(1, 1) model, it is

$$\gamma(\tau) = \alpha^{|\tau|}(1-\alpha\beta)(1-\beta/\alpha)/(1-\alpha^2), \qquad \tau = \pm 1, \pm 2, \ldots$$
$$= (1+\beta^2 - 2\alpha\beta)/(1-\alpha^2), \qquad \tau = 0. \qquad (13)$$

FORMULATION AND ESTIMATION OF UNIVARIATE ARMA MODELS. The problem of *formulating* an ARMA model refers to determination of the orders p and q of the AR and MA components, while the *estimation* problem is that of determining the values of the parameters of the model, for example, the roots $1/\alpha_j, j = 1, \ldots, p$, and $1/\beta_k, k = 1, \ldots, q$, and the variance σ^2 of ϵ_t.

Box and Jenkins (1970), among others, have suggested the use of the sample autocorrelation and partial autocorrelation functions as an approach to the problem of formulating an ARMA model. It is known, however, that the estimates of these functions are poorly behaved relative to their theoretical counterparts and, thus, provide a somewhat dubious basis for model formulation (Nerlove et al., 1979, pp. 57–68, 105–106; Hannan, 1960, p. 41).

More recently, information-theoretic approaches to model formulation, having a rigorous foundation in statistical information theory, have been proposed. These procedures are designated for order determination in general ARMA (p, q) models. The Akaike (1973) Information Criterion (AIC) leads to selection of the model for which the expression:

$$AIC(k) = \ln \hat{\sigma}^2_{ML} + 2k/T \qquad (14)$$

is minimized, where $\hat{\sigma}^2_{ML}$ is the maximum likelihood estimate of σ^2_ϵ, T is sample size, and $k = p + q$. It is well known that the AIC is not consistent, in the sense that it does not lead to selection of the correct model with probability one in large samples (Shibata, 1976; Hannan and Quinn, 1979; Hannan, 1980; Kashyap, 1980). The procedure does, however, have special benefits when selecting the order of an AR model, as shown by Shibata (1980). Specifically, he shows that if the true model can *not* be written as a finite AR, but an AR is fitted anyway, then use of the AIC minimizes asymptotic mean-squared prediction error within the class of AR models.

Schwarz (1978) and Rissanen (1978) develop a consistent modification of the AIC which has become known as the Schwarz Information Criterion (SIC). This criterion selects the model which minimizes:

$$SIC(k) = \ln \hat{\sigma}^2_{ML} + \frac{\ln T}{T}(k), \qquad (15)$$

and Hannan (1980) shows that this procedure identifies the true model with probability one in large samples, so long as the maximum possible orders of the AR and MA components are known.

Once the orders p and q are determined, the problem of *estimating* the parameters of the ARMA model remains. Various approaches in the time domain are available, such as least squares, approximate maximum likelihood (Box and Jenkins, 1970), or exact maximum likelihood (Newbold, 1974; Harvey and Phillips, 1979; Harvey, 1981). Approximate maximum likelihood in the frequency domain is also possible (Hannan, 1969b; Hannan and Nicholls, 1972; Nerlove et al., 1979, pp. 132–6). The latter is based upon the asymptotic distribution of the sample periodogram ordinates.

Estimation of pure AR models (no MA component) is particularly simple since ordinary least squares yield consistent parameter estimates. The basis of such estimation is the set of Yule–Walker equations (Yule, 1927; Walker, 1931). Consider the AR(p) process;

$$y_t = \sum_{i=1}^{p} \psi_i y_{t-i} + \epsilon_t. \qquad (16)$$

Multiplying (16) by $y_{t-\tau}$, $\tau \geq 0$, taking expectations, and recognizing that $\gamma(\tau) = \gamma(-\tau)$ gives

$$\gamma(\tau) = \sum_{i=1}^{p} \psi_i \gamma(\tau - i), \qquad \tau > 0. \qquad (17)$$

Dividing (17) by the variance $\gamma(0)$, we obtain the system of Yule–Walker equations:

$$\rho(\tau) = \sum_{i=1}^{p} \psi_i \rho(\tau - i), \qquad \tau > 0, \qquad (18)$$

which relate the autocorrelations of the process. This pth-order linear system is easily solved for the ψ_i, $i = 1, \ldots, p$, in terms of the first p autocorrelations. In practice, the theoretical autocorrelations are replaced by their sample counterparts, yielding estimates of the $\psi_i, i = 1, \ldots, p$. These parameter estimates may be conveniently used as start-up values for the more sophisticated, iterative estimation procedures discussed above.

Estimation of MA or mixed models by exact maximum likelihood methods is complicated further by a tendency to obtain a local maximum of the likelihood function at a unit root of the MA component, even when no roots are close to the unit circle (Sargan and Bhargava, 1983; Anderson and Takemura, 1984).

PREDICTION. Optimal linear least squares prediction of time series generated by ARMA processes may be obtained for known parameter values by the Wiener–Kolmogorov approach (Whittle, 1983). If y_t is generated by a stationary, invertible ARMA model with one-sided MA representation (6), a very simple expression may be given for the linear minimum mean-square error (MMSE) prediction of y_{t+v} at time t, y^*_{t+v}, in terms of its own (infinite) past

$$y^*_{t+v} - C(z)y_t, \qquad (19)$$

where

$$C(z) = \sum_{j=0}^{\infty} c_j z^j = \frac{1}{B(z)} \left[\frac{B(z)}{z^v} \right]_+.$$

The operator $\lfloor . \rfloor_+$ eliminates negative powers of z.

Suppose that y_t is AR(1):

$$y_t = \alpha y_{t-1} + \epsilon_t, \quad |\alpha| < 1,$$

then $y^*_{t+v} = \alpha^v y_t$. If y_t is AR(2):

$$y_t = (\alpha_1 + \alpha_2)y_{t-1} - \alpha_1 \alpha_2 y_{t-2} + \epsilon_t, \quad |\alpha_1|, |\alpha_2| < 1,$$

then $y^*_{t+1} = (\alpha_1 + \alpha_2)y_t - \alpha_1 \alpha_2 y_{t-1}$. In general, the result for AR(p) as in (1) is $y^*_{t+v} = \psi_1 y^*_{t+v-1} + \cdots + \psi_p y^*_{t+v-p}$, where $y^*_{t-j} = y_{t-j}$, for $j = 0, 1, \ldots$, at time t. Thus for pure autoregressions, the MMSE prediction is a linear combination of only the p most recently observed values.

Suppose that y_t is MA(1):

$$y_t = \epsilon_t - \beta \epsilon_{t-1}, \quad |\beta| < 1,$$

then $y^*_{t+1} = -\beta \sum_{j=0}^{\infty} \beta^j x_{t-j}$ and $y^*_{t+v} = 0$ for all $v > 1$. For moving-average processes, in general, predictions for a future period greater than the order of the process are zero and those for a period less distant cannot be expressed in terms of a finite number of past observed values.

Finally, suppose that y_t is ARMA(1, 1): $y_t - \alpha y_{t-1} = \epsilon_t - \beta \epsilon_{t-1}, |\alpha|, |\beta| < 1$, then $y^*_{t+v} = \alpha^{v-1}(\alpha - \beta)\sum_{j=0}^{\infty} \beta^j y_{t-j}$. For further examples, see Nerlove et al., 1979, pp. 89–102.

When an infinite past is not available and the parameter values of the process are not known, the problem of optimal prediction is more complicated. The most straightforward approach is via the state-space representation of the process and the Kalman filter (Kalman, 1960; Meinhold and Singpurwalla, 1983).

MULTIVARIATE ARMA PROCESSES. Let $\Psi(\cdot)$ and $\Phi(\cdot)$ be $K \times K$ matrix polynomials in the lag operator, y_t and ϵ_t be $K \times 1$ vectors. Then the K-variate ARMA(p, q) process is defined as

$$\Psi(L)y_t = \Phi(L)\epsilon_t, \quad \epsilon_t \overset{iid}{\sim} (0, \Sigma), \tag{20}$$

where $\Psi(L) = \Psi_0 - \Psi_1 L - \ldots - \Psi_p L^p$ and $\Phi(L) = \Phi_0 - \Phi_1 L - \ldots - \Phi_q L^q$, with each Ψ_j and Φ_j, $y = 0, 1, \ldots$, being a $K \times K$ matrix. The model is weakly stationary if all the zeros of $\det |\Psi(z)|$ lie outside the unit circle (Hannan, 1970), and invertible if all the zeros of $\det |\Phi(z)|$ also do.

In addition to the issues of formulation, estimation, and prediction, which arise in the univariate case as well, identification (in the usual econometric sense) becomes an important problem. Hannan (1969a) shows that a stationary vector AR process is identified if Φ_0 is an identity matrix (i.e. no instantaneous coupling), and Ψ_p is nonsingular. Hannan (1971) extends the analysis to recursive systems and systems with prescribed zero restrictions.

There are three approaches to the formulation of multivariate ARMA models. Nerlove et al. (1979) and Granger and Newbold (1977) develop an augmented single-equation procedure, and Wallis (1977) and Wallis and Chan (1978) develop another procedure which involves preliminary univariate analysis.

A second approach is due to Tiao and Box (1981), who use multivariate analogues of the autocorrelation and partial autocorrelation functions as a guide to model formulation. Their approach is computationally quite simple and usually leads to models with a tractable number of parameters. Identification is achieved by allowing no instantaneous coupling among variables.

Finally, the information-theoretic model formulation procedures which were discussed above generalize to the multivariate ARMA case. Quinn (1980) shows that Schwarz's criterion (SIC) again provides a consistent estimate of the vector AR order. In a large Monte Carlo comparison of criteria for estimating the order of a vector AR process (VAR), Lütkepohl (1985) shows the clear superiority of the SIC in medium-sized samples; the SIC chooses the correct model most often and leads to the best forecasting performance.

As in the case of univariate ARMA models, estimation in the multivariate case may be carried out in the frequency domain (Wilson, 1973; Dunsmuir and Hannan, 1976) or in the time domain (Hillmer and Tiao, 1979). An exact likelihood function in the time domain may also be derived by the Kalman filter by casting the multivariate ARMA model in state space form. Anderson (1980) provides a good survey of estimation in both time and frequency domains.

Prediction in the multivariate case with an infinite past is a straightforward generalization of the results for the univariate case (Judge et al., 1985, pp. 659–60). When only a finite past is available and the parameters of the process must be estimated, the most straightforward approach is again through the Kalman filter (see also Yamamoto, 1981).

APPLICATIONS. In addition to their obvious uses in forecasting, ARMA models, especially multivariate ARMA models, have a wide range of economic and econometric application.

The use of time-series methods in formulating distributed-lag models is discussed at length in Nerlove (1972) and Nerlove et al. (1979, pp. 291–353) and applied in the latter to an analysis of US cattle production. The notion of quasi-rational expectations introduced there is that the expectations on the basis of which economic agents react may, under certain conditions, be assumed to be the statistical expectations of the variables in question, conditional on observations of past history. If these variables are generated by time-series processes, such as those discussed in this entry, time-series methods may be used to derive expressions for the MMSE forecasts for any relevant future period; these MMSE forecasts are, by a well-known result, the aforementioned conditional expectations.

An econometric definition of causality based on time-series concepts has been developed by Granger (1969) and extended by Sims (1972). Let (x_t, y_t) be a pair of vectors of observations on some economic time series, and let Ω_{t-1} be the information available up to time t, which includes $\{(x_{t-1}, y_{t-1}), (x_{t-2}, y_{t-2}), \ldots\}$. Granger gives the following definitions in terms of the conditional variances:

Definition 1: x causes y if and only if

$$\sigma^2(y_t | \Omega_{t-1}) < \sigma^2(y_t | \Omega_{t-1} - \{x_{t-1}, x_{t-2}, \ldots\}),$$

where $\Omega_{t-1} - \{x_{t-1}, x_{t-2}, \ldots\}$ is the information set omitting the past of the series x_t.

Definition 2: x causes y instantaneously if and only if

$$\sigma^2(y_t | \Omega_{t-1}, x_t) < \sigma^2(y_t | \Omega_{t-1}).$$

It may happen that both x causes y, and y causes x; then x and y are related by a feedback system. In applications (x_t, y_t), is generally assumed to be generated by multivariate ARMA processes, and Ω_t is assumed to consist only of the past history of (x_t, y_t). Since ARMA models are applicable only to weakly stationary time series it must further be assumed that any transformation necessary to achieve stationarity is causality preserving. Granger's (1969) test for causal association is based on a multivariate AR representation, while Sims (1972) bases his on an equivalent MA representation. Sims also introduces a regression-based test related to the above which makes use of both future and past values of the series x_t in relation to the current value of y_t. Pierce and Haugh (1977) show that causality may also be tested in univariate representations of the series. Feige and Pierce (1979) and Lütkepohl (1982) show that the direction of causality so defined may be sensitive to the transformations used to achieve stationarity, and to the definition of the information set.

Time series methods have also been applied to the analysis of the efficiency of capital markets (Fama, 1970). The question is whether market prices fully reflect available information, for example, in a securities market. Efficiency requires that the relevant information set be that actually used by the market participants. Since the latter is inherently unobservable, tests of the efficiency of a market can be carried out only within the context of a particular theory of market equilibrium. Various alternatives lead to tests, based on AR or more general models, of the rates of return for different securities over time in the presence of shocks of various sorts which may or may not represent the introduction of new information (Ball and Brown, 1968; Fama et al., 1969; Scholes, 1972).

Finally, an important example of the use of time-series methods in econometrics has been put forth in the controversial revisionist views of Sargent and Sims (1977), and Sims (1980) on appropriate methods of econometric modelling. These views may be traced back to the work of T. C. Liu (1960) who argued that when only reliable *a priori* restrictions were imposed, most econometric models would turn out to be underidentified; furthermore, he argued that most of the exclusion restrictions generally employed, and the assumptions about serial correlation made to justify treating certain lagged values of endogenous variables as predetermined, were invalid; he concluded that only unrestricted reduced form estimation could be justified. The revisionist approach treats *all* variables as endogenous and, in general, places no restrictions on the parameters except the choice of variables to be included and lengths of lags. Attention in this approach is focused on the estimation of a general relationship among a relatively short list of variables rather than policy analysis and structural inference, which have been the emphasis of mainstream econometrics. As such, the approach has been mainly useful for data description and forecasting.

MARC NERLOVE AND FRANCIS X. DIEBOLD

See also ARIMA MODELS; ECONOMETRICS; ERGODIC THEORY; ESTIMATION; MULTIPLE TIME SERIES MODELS; SPECTRAL ANALYSIS; STATIONARY TIME SERIES; TIME SERIES ANALYSIS.

BIBLIOGRAPHY

Akaike, H. 1973. Information theory and an extension of the maximum likelihood principle. In *Second International Symposium on Information Theory*, ed. B.N. Petrov and F. Csaki, Budapest: Akademiai Kiado, Budapest, 267–87.

Anderson, T.W. 1980. Maximum likelihood estimation for vector autoregressive moving average models. In *Directions in Time Series*, ed. D.R. Brillinger and G.C. Tiao, Hayward, California: Institute of Mathematical Statistics. 49–59.

Anderson, T.W. and Takemura, A. 1984. Why do noninvertible moving averages occur? Technical Report No.13, Department of Statistics, Stanford University.

Ball, R. and Brown, P. 1968. An empirical evaluation of accounting income numbers. *Journal of Accounting Research* 6, 159–78.

Box, G.E.P. and Jenkins, G.M. 1970. *Time Series Analysis: Forecasting and Control*. San Francisco: Holden-Day.

Chow, G.C. 1975. *Analysis and Control of Dynamic Economic Systems*. New York: John Wiley.

Dunsmuir, W.T.M. and Hannan, E.J. 1976. Vector linear time series models. *Advances in Applied Probability* 8(2), June, 339–64.

Fama, E.F. 1970. Efficient capital markets: a review of theory and empirical work. *Journal of Finance* 25(2), May, 383–417.

Fama, E.F., Jensen, M., Fisher, L. and Roll, R. 1969. The adjustment of stock market prices to new information. *International Economic Review* 10(1), February, 1–21.

Feige, E.L. and Pierce, D.K. 1979. The casual causal relation between money and income: some caveats for time series analysis. *Review of Economics and Statistics* 61(4), November, 521–33.

Granger, C.W.J. 1969. Investigating causal relationships by econometric models and cross-spectral methods. *Econometrica* 37(3), July, 424–38.

Granger, C.W.J. and Newbold, P. 1977. *Forecasting Economic Time Series*. New York: Academic Press.

Hannan, E.J. 1969. The identification of vector mixed autoregressive-moving average systems. *Biometrika* 56(1), 223–5.

Hannan, E.J. 1969. The estimation of mixed moving average autoregressive systems. *Biometrika* 56(3), 579–93.

Hannan, E.J. 1970. *Multiple Time Series*. New York: John Wiley & Sons.

Hannan, E.J. 1971. The identification problem for multiple equation systems with moving average errors. *Econometrica* 39(5), September, 751–65.

Hannan, E.J. 1980. The estimation of the order of an ARMA process. *Annals of Statistics* 8(5), September 1071–81.

Hannan, E.J. and Nicholls, D.F. 1972. The estimation of mixed regression, autoregression, moving average and distributed lag models. *Econometrica* 40(3), May, 529–47.

Hannan, E.J. and Quinn, B.G. 1979. The determination of the order of an autoregression. *Journal of the Royal Statistical Society, Series B* 41(2), 190–95.

Harvey, A.C. 1981. *Time Series Models*. Oxford: Philip Allan.

Harvey, A.C. and Phillips, G.D.A. 1979. The estimation of regression models with ARMA disturbances. *Biometrika* 66(1), 49–58.

Hillmer, S.C. and Tiao, G.C. 1979. Likelihood function of stationary multiple autoregressive moving average models. *Journal of the American Statistical Association* 74(367), September, 652–60.

Judge, G.G., Griffiths, W.E., Hill, R.C., Lütkepohl, H. and Lee, T.C. 1985. *The Theory and Practice of Econometrics*. 2nd edn, New York: John Wiley.

Kalman, R.E. 1960. A new approach to linear filtering and prediction problems. *Journal of Basic Engineering, ASME Transactions* 82D, 35–45.

Kashyap, R.L. 1980. Inconsistency of the AIC rule for estimating the order of AR models. *Transactions on Automatic Control* 25(5), October, 996–8.

Liu, T.C. 1960. Underidentification, structural estimation, and forecasting. *Econometrica* 28(4), October, 855–65.

Lütkepohl, H. 1982. Non-causality due to omitted variables. *Journal of Econometrics* 19, 367–78.

Lütkepohl, H. 1985. Comparison of criteria for estimating the order of a vector autoregressive process. *Journal of Time Series Analysis* 6(1), 35–52.

Meinhold, R.J. and Singpurwalla, N.D. 1983. Understanding the Kalman filter. *American Statistician* 37, 123–7.

Nerlove, M. 1972. Lags in economic behaviour. *Econometrica* 40(2), March, 221–51.

Nerlove, M., Grether, D.M., and Carvalho, J.L. 1979. *Analysis of Economic Time Series: A synthesis*. New York: Academic Press.

Newbold, P. 1974. The exact likelihood function for a mixed autoregressive-moving average process. *Biometrika* 61(3), 423–6.

Pierce, D.A. and Haugh, L.D. 1977. Causality in temporal systems: characterizations and a survey. *Journal of Econometrics* 5(3), 265–93.

Quinn, B.G. 1980. Order determination for a multivariate autoregression. *Journal of the Royal Statistical Society, Series B* 42(2), 182–5.

Rissanen, H. 1978. Modelling by shortest data description. *Automatica* 14(5), September, 465–71.

Sargan, J.D. and Bhargava, A. 1983. Maximum likelihood estimation of regression models with moving average errors when the root lies on the unit circle. *Econometrica* 51(3), May, 799–820.

Sargent, T.J. and Sims, C.A. 1977. Business cycle modeling without pretending to have too much a priori economic theory. *In New Methods of Business Cycle Research*, ed. C.A. Sims, Minneapolis: Federal Reserve Bank of Minneapolis.

Scholes, M. 1972. The market for securities: substitution versus price pressure and the effects of information on share prices. *Journal of Business* 45(2), April, 179–211.

Schwarz, G. 1978. Estimating the dimension of a model. *Annals of Statistics* 6(2), March, 461–4.

Shibata, R. 1976. Selection of the order of an autoregressive model by the AIC. *Biometrika* 63(1), 117–26.

Shibata, R. 1980. Asymptotically efficient estimates of the order of a model for estimating parameters of a linear process. *Annals of Statistics* 8(5), September, 1147–64.

Sims, C. A. 1972. Money income and causality. *American Economic Review* 62(4), September, 540–52.

Sims, C. A. 1980. Macroeconomics and reality. *Econometrica* 48(1), January 1–47.

Slutsky, E. 1927. The summation of random causes as the source of cyclic processes. Trans. In *Econometrica* 5, 105–46.

Tiao, G.C. and Box, G.E.P. 1981. Modeling multiple time series with applications. *Journal of the American Statistical Society* 76, 802–816.

Walker, G. 1931. On periodicity in series of related terms. *Proceedings of the Royal Society London*, Series A 131, 518–32.

Wallis, K.F. 1977. Multiple time series analysis and the final form of econometric models. *Econometrica* 45(6), September, 1481–97.

Wallis, K.F. and Chan, W.T. 1978. Multiple time series modeling: another look at the mink–muskrat interaction. *Applied Statistics* 27(2), 168–75.

Whiteman, C.H. 1983. *Linear Rational Expectations Models*. Minneapolis: University of Minnesota Press.

Whittle, P. 1983. *Prediction and Regulation by Linear Least Squares Methods*. 2nd revised, Minneapolis: University of Minnesota Press.

Wilson, G.T. 1973. The estimation of parameters in multivariate time series models. *Journal of the Royal Statistical Society*, Series B 35(1), 76–85.

Wold, H. 1938. *A Study in the Analysis of Stationary Time Series*. Stockholm: Almqvist and Wiksell.

Yamamoto, T. 1981. Prediction of multivariate autoregressive-moving average models. *Biometrika* 68(2), 485–92.

Yule, G.U. 1921. On the time-correlation problem with special reference to the variate-difference correlation method. *Journal of the Royal Statistical Society* 84, July, 497–526.

Yule, G.U. 1926. Why do we sometimes get nonsense correlations between time series? A study in sampling and the nature of time series. *Journal of the Royal Statistical Society* 89, January, 1–64.

Yule, G.U. 1927. On a method for investigating periodicities in disturbed series with special reference to Wolfer's sunspot numbers. *Philosophical Transactions of the Royal Society of London,* Series A 226, 267–98.

autoregressive-integrated-moving average models. *See* ARIMA MODELS.

average and normal conditions. *See* NATURAL AND NORMAL CONDITIONS.

average cost pricing. Average cost pricing and its associated variations refer to the practice of firms' price decisions. With the exception of certain markets for primary commodities and financial transactions where either an auctioneer or jobbers make prices, the vast majority of goods and services are traded in markets where firms must set prices. Once set, firms' sales are limited by the size of the market and the competition of rivals.

Following developments in the theory of the firm (Chamberlin, 1933; Robinson, 1933), interest arose during the 1930s as to whether the pricing practices adopted by businesses provided supporting evidence for these theories. In their justly famous article of 1939, Hall and Hitch questioned 38 firms to discover what methods of price setting were actually applied and what motivated them to adjust prices. Their results revealed practices which appeared to be seriously at variance with the implications of received theory. Businesses typically set prices by calculating average costs of production and adding a mark up for profit. Firms did not habitually vary the mark up with variations in the strength of market demand. The findings were confirmed in other surveys after the War both in the UK (Andrews, 1949) and in the detailed studies carried out in the USA (Kaplan et al., 1958).

According to these studies the precise method of price setting varied widely with firms and industries. In some cases the cost reference was average prime or variable costs. (Kalecki's degree of monopoly theory used this concept (Kalecki, 1943).) In other cases fixed plus variable costs per unit of output or 'full cost' was common. Other variants reckoned unit costs at standard or normal levels of capacity utilization or of output. Depending therefore on the basis of unit cost adopted, the mark up might cover a target for gross profits alone, or would also include an allowance for fixed costs. While this type of price behaviour might be adopted by the industry leader, other firms might adopt a 'price minus' strategy of setting a target level of unit costs by deducting the firm's required mark up from the price set by the price leader or by foreign competition (Smyth, 1967). Business interviews suggested that mark ups were relatively stable so that price changes moved mainly with changes in unit costs.

The evidence apparently conflicted with the theory. While it was conceded that the equality of marginal cost and revenue was an impractical operational procedure for setting price, mark up pricing adjustments could be interpreted as a useful 'rule of thumb' by which profits might be maximized by trial and error (Machlup, 1946).

Econometric evidence has supplemented the original surveys. The literature is too large to summarize adequately here though Nordhaus (1971) provides a useful survey of US studies. An important aim of this literature was to use econometric methods to discover the extent to which the business cycle influenced the movement of prices. A disturbing feature of this work is the absence of uniform conclusions which can be made about price formation. There are no generally accepted measures of the relevant cost or demand variables and the results are often highly sensitive to the precise measures adopted. Some studies have generated a bewildering number of regressions correlating prices and indicators of costs and demand with little theoretical guidance or careful specification of hypotheses.

Although other economists (notably Kalecki, 1943 and Gardiner Means, 1935) have written about the concept of 'normal' or 'sticky' prices in the short run, Godley (1959) was the first to express the normal price hypothesis as a proposition about normal or standard unit costs. His hypothesis was that prices moved closely with normal unit costs and that the direct effect of demand on the mark up over normal unit costs was negligible. It assumed that firms operate with excess capacity and vary production principally by changing utilization rates. In forming price, firms are assumed to add a mark up to the average costs incurred when operating at a standard or normal rate of capacity utilization.

A series of empirical studies incorporated normal unit labour costs into price equations. Neild (1963) was the first to confirm support for this hypothesis using UK manufacturing data. Schultze and Tryon (1965), Fromm and Taubman (1968) and Eckstein and Fromm (1968) did similar studies for US data, though some of these found that capacity utilization measures of demand had an independent influence on price. Godley and Nordhaus (1972), in a study of the UK data, found that the effect of demand on prices was very small, once normal unit costs were measured appropriately in conformity with Godley's original hypothesis. Coutts, Godley and Nordhaus (1978) in a much larger study confirmed and extended the results to a number of sectors within manufacturing industry.

The empirical studies remain controversial, however, and have been subject to criticism. Rushdy and Lund (1967), using Neild's data, published alternative specifications of the price equation in which significant demand effects appeared. Laidler and Parkin (1975) were critical of the tests of demand used by Godley and Nordhaus. McCallum (1970) demonstrated that manufacturing price changes correlated well with an indicator of excess demand alone, i.e. no explicit cost variables were included at all.

It is essential, in understanding the debate on the cyclical behaviour of costs and prices, to distinguish clearly variations in actual unit costs which arise as a consequence of a firm's own variations in capacity utilization from those which arise caused by factors outside the firm's immediate control. The former occur because in the short run productivity changes are dominated by changes in capacity utilization which impart a counter-cyclical movement to actual unit costs. This is partially offset by the pro-cyclical movement of wage earnings arising from variations in hours worked, piece rate bonuses and overtime payments. The latter type of cost variations may arise because of changes in negotiated wage rates, in materials and technology. Some of these may have a pro-cyclical character to the extent that the prices of basic commodities are sensitive to the business cycle and that wage rates increase more rapidly when labour markets are tight. This implies that while firms' actual unit costs are likely to be counter-cyclical, normal unit costs are more likely to be mildly pro-cyclical. The normal price hypothesis asserts that prices will therefore be as pro-cyclical as are normal unit costs. A direct implication is that the actual mark up will vary pro-cyclically and hence generate highly pro-cyclical variations in profits.

Given these cyclical properties the data would be consistent with all of the following: price is a non-cyclical mark up on normal unit costs; price is a pro-cyclical mark up on actual unit costs; price changes are directly proportional to excess demand alone. The empirical tests of the normal price hypothesis can claim to establish only that relative to normal unit costs, prices do not rise or fall with the course of the business cycle. If this evidence is accepted it implies that the putative influence of demand on price over the cycle is almost completely offset by the decline in actual, relative to normal, unit costs and hence that demand effects are probably small compared with costs in determining industrial prices. How then can theory accommodate this conclusion about the relative importance of costs and demand?

Studies of industrial cost characteristics have indicated that, within the relevant range of output variation, marginal costs are typically falling or flat rather than rising as might be the case in agriculture or mining (Johnston, 1960). In the range where marginal costs are nearly constant they must also approximately equal average variable costs. By elementary manipulations of the profit maximizing conditions it follows that the optimal price may be expressed as a mark up on average variable cost – the mark up being a simple function of the firm's own elasticity of demand. This provides a common rationalization of the prevalence of mark up pricing practices in terms of the neoclassical theory of the firm. The interpretation apparently explains why costs have a major effect on prices while leaving a minor but significant role for demand (to alter the mark up) as theory predicts.

The difficulty in accepting this interpretation is that it does not explain the existence and persistence of underutilized capacity. It gives no convincing account why firms operate with a discretionary degree of spare capacity or why, in the absence of collusion, competition and profit maximizing behaviour does not force firms to operate at full capacity.

The requirement to set prices in industrial markets creates additional uncertainty for firms regarding expected market demand and the business strategies of current and potential rivals. Operating with a reserve capacity considerably increases the short-run flexibility of the firm to meet variations in demand, mainly by increasing hours of work and higher utilization of plant and machinery. Once prices are set, demand variations are first met by changing utilization rates.

By contrast prices perform a distinctive function in auction markets, conveying considerable information to buyers and sellers. Since the commodity can typically be classified into homogeneous trading grades, it is unnecessary for a customer to know which seller produced the commodity purchased by the customer. Each is an anonymous participant in an auction market. The markets for most industrial products require instead that firms cultivate relations with their customers to encourage repeat sales. Prices convey only limited information about the characteristics of the product offered. Okun (1981) classified the latter as 'customer markets'. He argued that customer markets encourage the development of pricing policies of mutual benefit to producers and customers in which prices are largely determined by costs. The needs of producers to promote good-will makes them forgo any short run temporary advantage in raising price when demand strengthens. Customers are offered a stable price at which orders are placed unless costs of production change. Customer markets encourage product differentiation and non-price competition as methods of establishing a distinctive reputation with customers.

This tendency to cost-determined pricing may occur in markets where competitive pressure, as measured by the number of rival firms, is high. It is reinforced in oligopolistic markets where price changes that are unrelated to costs risk conveying signals to competitors which produce retaliatory responses. This observation underlies the kinked demand curve rationalization of Hall and Hitch (1939) and Sweezy (1939).

Mark up pricing implies that firms do not behave as if they were aiming to maximize profits in the short run, although they may have this objective among others over a longer time horizon. The accumulated empirical work on average cost pricing demonstrates the inadequacy of current microeconomic theory to explain how most industrial markets operate. It provides challenging material for economists to develop a richer theory of industrial competition.

K.J. COUTTS

See also ADMINISTERED PRICES; MARGINAL AND AVERAGE COST PRICING; MARK-UP PRICING.

BIBLIOGRAPHY

Andrews, P.W.S. 1949. *Manufacturing Business*. London: Macmillan.
Chamberlin, E.H. 1933. *The Theory of Monopolistic Competition*. Cambridge, Mass.: Harvard University Press.
Coutts, K.J., Godley, W.A.H. and Nordhaus, W.D. 1978. *Industrial Pricing in the United Kingdom*. Cambridge: Cambridge University Press.
Eckstein, O. and Fromm, G. 1968. The price equation. *American Economic Review* 58, December, 1159-83.
Fromm, G. and Taubman, P. 1968. *Policy Simulations with an Econometric Model*. Washington, DC: Brookings.
Godley, W.A.H. 1959. Costs, prices and demand in the short run. In *Macroeconomic Themes*, ed. M.J.C. Surrey, Oxford: Oxford University Press, 1976.
Godley, W.A.H. and Nordhaus, W.D. 1972. Pricing in the trade cycle. *Economic Journal* 82, September, 853-82.
Hall, R.E. and Hitch, C. 1939. Price theory and business behaviour. *Oxford Economic Papers* 2, May, 12-45.
Johnston, J. 1960. *Statistical Cost Analysis*. New York: McGraw-Hill.
Kalecki, M. 1943. *Studies in Economic Dynamics*. London: Allen & Unwin.
Kaplan, A., Dirlam, J. and Lanzillotti, R. 1958. *Pricing in Big Business*. Washington, DC: Brookings.
Laidler, D. and Parkin, M. 1975. Inflation: a survey. *Economic Journal* 85, December, 741-809.
McCallum, B.T. 1970. The effect of demand on prices in British manufacturing: another view. *Review of Economic Studies* 37(1), January, 147-56.
Machlup, F. 1946. Marginal analysis and empirical research. *American Economic Review* 36, September, 519-54.
Means, G.C. 1935. Price inflexibility and the requirements of a stabilizing monetary policy. *Journal of the American Statistical Association* 30, June, 401-13.
Neild, R.R. 1963. *Pricing and Employment in the Trade Cycle*. Cambridge: Cambridge University Press.
Nordhaus, W.D. 1971. Recent developments in price dynamics. In *The Econometrics of Price Determination*, ed. O. Eckstein, Washington, DC: Federal Reserve.
Okun, A. 1981. *Prices and Quantities: a Macroeconomic Analysis* Washington, DC: Brookings.
Robinson, J. 1933. *The Economics of Imperfect Competition*. London: Macmillan.
Rushdy, F. and Lund, P.J. 1967. The effect of demand on prices in British manufacturing industry. *Review of Economic Studies* 34, October, 361-73.
Schultze, C.L. and Tryon, J.L. 1965. Prices and wages. *The Brookings Quarterly Econometric Model of the United States*, Chicago: Rand McNally.
Smyth, R. 1967. A price-minus theory of cost. *Scottish Journal of Political Economy*, June, 110-17.
Sweezy, P.M. 1939. Demand under conditions of oligopoly. *Journal of Political Economy* 47, August, 568-73.

average industry. *See* MARX, KARL HEINRICH; STANDARD COMMODITY.

average period of production. *See* AUSTRIAN SCHOOL OF ECONOMICS; PERIOD OF PRODUCTION; ROUNDABOUT METHODS OF PRODUCTION.

Averch–Johnson effect. The Averch–Johnson effect explores some unintended consequences of fair rate of return regulation (Averch and Johnson, 1962). Such regulation may cause the firm to select excessively capital-intensive technologies, and, thereby, not produce its output at minimum social cost. Specifically, the main Averch–Johnson result is that the capital–labour ratio selected by a profit-maximizing, regulated firm will be greater than that consistent with a cost-minimizing one for any output it chooses to produce. If the fair rate of return is greater than the cost of capital, a firm will have an incentive to invest as much as it can consistent with its production possibilities, because the difference between the allowed rate and its actual cost of capital is pure profit.

This brief overview discusses (1) the effects of rate of return regulation on a monopolist's inputs and outputs; (2) the effects on incentives to innovate; (3) the empirical evidence on the existence and strength of the Averch–Johnson effect; and (4) some of the main theoretical extensions. Since 1962, the Averch–Johnson literature has been extended to include objectives other than profit maximization, more subtle interactions between regulators and firms and more complex market conditions. By making the models more complex, the number of possible regulatory outcomes has been enlarged. But the basic Averch–Johnson result, as stated above, has proven remarkably robust. So the discussion here focuses on this result and some of the main corollary results.

CHOICE OF INPUTS IN THE BASIC AVERCH–JOHNSON MODEL

Suppose there exists a single-product, profit-maximizing monopolist subject to rate of return regulation. The firm's production function is

$$Q = F(K, L), \quad K, L > 0, \quad F(0, L) = F(K, 0) = 0,$$
$$F_1, F_2 > 0, \quad F_{11}, F_{22} < 0. \tag{1}$$

Suppose the firm's inverse demand function is

$$P = P(Q), \quad P'(Q) < 0. \tag{2}$$

Profit is

$$\Pi = PQ - rK - wL. \tag{3}$$

Assuming, as is standard, that there is no depreciation and that the acquisition cost of capital is adjusted to one, the rate of return constraint can be written

$$(PQ - wL)/K \leqslant s \quad \text{or} \quad PQ - wL - sK \leqslant 0, \tag{4}$$

or

$$\Pi \leqslant (s - r)K, \tag{5}$$

where s is the allowed rate of return. The fair rate of return is taken to be at least as great as the cost of capital ($s > r$) and less than the rate the firm could earn if it were unconstrained. Consequently, the constraint is effective, and the firm maximizes

$$\Pi = PQ - rK - wL \tag{6}$$

subject to (4) or (5). Letting R equal total revenue PQ, the

necessary first order conditions are

$$(1 - \lambda)R'F_1 - \lambda(s - r) = 0 \tag{7}$$
$$(1 - \lambda)R'F_2 - (1 - \lambda)w = 0 \tag{8}$$
$$R - wL - sK = 0. \tag{9}$$

λ is the standard Averch–Johnson Lagrange multiplier. Given that the constraint is effective, that $s > r$, and that the revenue function $R = PQ$ is concave, the multiplier λ is greater than zero and less than one. Consequently, the marginal rate of substitution of capital for labour for the regulated firm is

$$-dL/dK = [r - (\lambda/1 - \lambda)(s - r)]/w < r/w. \tag{10}$$

For any given output, the firm will not minimize cost, since this requires that the firm's marginal rate of technical substitution be equal to r/w.

This result can be shown graphically in several different ways (Baumol and Klevorick, 1970; Zajac, 1970). Zajac's formulation is shown here. Figure 1 shows the regulatory constraint (9) in relation to the firm's isoquants.

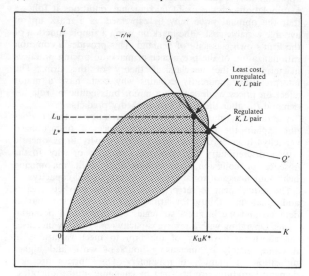

Figure 1   The Averch-Johnson (A-J) Effect

The shaded region inside the constraint curve shows input combinations resulting in rates of return greater than s. The firm wants to be as far up to the right on the constraint curve as possible, because, from (5), every increment of capital increases profit. Consequently, the firm will operate at the rightmost point of the constraint curve.

The output for this rightmost point can be obtained from the isoquant that intersects the constraint curve at its rightmost point. However, the least cost combination of capital and labour for producing this output, where $-dL/dK = r/w$, lies inside the proscribed shaded area, on the firm's efficient expansion path. For any given output, the firm cannot simultaneously be on the cost-minimizing price line with slope $-r/w$ and on the constraint curve.

THE OUTPUT OF THE REGULATED FIRM

One of the original rationales for regulation was that it would increase allocative efficiency by forcing monopolists to offer more output than ordinarily they would. If a larger output were always the result of rate of return regulation, then decreases in technical efficiency would be compensated by increases in allocational efficiency. In principle, regulatory agencies could seek an *s* that just balanced the marginal benefits of increased output against the marginal costs of decreased efficiency (Klevorick, 1971; Sheshinski, 1971; Bailey, 1973; Callen, Mathewson, and Mohring, 1976).

Increasing output, however, is not inevitable. The firm will use greater quantities of capital as *s* falls towards *r*, but the amount of labour the firm chooses to use will not necessarily be larger, and so output need not be larger. However, if labour is not an inferior input – the most likely case – then the optimal amount of labour for a regulated monopoly will also increase over the unregulated one, and, consequently, so will output (Baumol and Klevorick, 1970; Bailey, 1973). Firms with linear, homogeneous production functions will produce greater output. Given two firms with identical positive, homogeneous production functions – one regulated, one unregulated – the output of the unregulated one becomes a lower bound on regulated output, and the output such that 'regulated' average cost equals price becomes an upper bound (Murphy and Soyster, 1982).

Technological change and the regulated firm. Even if regulated firms are inefficient in static situations, technological change conceivably could induce more output through cost reductions. And rate of return regulation might conceivably induce regulated firms to be more innovative than unregulated firms. Regulation usually guarantees some profits, if not maximal ones, and these could be used for innovation.

If technological change is exogenous to the firm, but is factor-augmenting, then the optimal constrained K^* rises (Westfield, 1971; Magat, 1976). However, factor-augmenting technological advance will not necessarily result in increased output, since the firm may again use less labour to produce its output. Technological change, of course, is not usually entirely exogenous. Through their own research and development (R&D), firms gain knowledge of feasible innovation possibilities. Profit-maximizing firms subject to both a rate of return constraint and their own innovation possibilities constraint can, depending on production conditions, choose more labour-augmenting technologies than they would without regulation, reinforcing the bias the regulated firm has towards relatively capital-intensive technologies (Smith, 1974, 1975; Okuguchi, 1975).

In any case, regulation does not unambiguously increase innovation possibilities. The R&D expenditures of the regulated firm are not always larger than those that an unregulated firm would select under the same production and demand conditions (Magat, 1976). Furthermore, there is no systematic evidence that regulated firms select more high payoff R&D projects than unregulated ones and much anecdotal evidence to indicate that they are highly conservative.

Empirical tests. In the mid-1970s and early 1980s there were a number of attempts to determine whether Averch–Johnson effects actually existed and whether, if they existed, they imposed significant social costs. The empirical investigations used different tests for the effect and different data sets, most, however, relating to electric utilities. Unsurprisingly, the empirical evidence from these efforts was mixed. But overall the number of empirical investigations that find some evidence for the Averch–Johnson effect or its behavioural consequences outnumber those that find no evidence.

Using different methods but similar data, Courville (1974) and Spann (1974) concluded that Averch–Johnson effects existed. Petersen (1975), using a cost-minimizing version of the Averch–Johnson model, found that as the allowed rate of return approached the market cost of capital, capital costs

increased as did the share of those costs in total costs. Hayashi and Trapani (1976) confirmed that regulated firms have a capital–labour ratio greater than the cost-minimizing one and that tightening *s* decreases efficiency. However, Boyes (1976) concluded that there was no effect.

Smithson (1978) reported that there was static inefficiency among electric utilities, but he could not confirm that lowering the rate of return caused the optimal capital stock to increase. Tapon and Vander Weide (1979) found that only strictly regulated electric utility firms exhibit Averch–Johnson effects, but that less than half of the industry appears to be so regulated. Regulatory lag permits firms to avoid Averch–Johnson effects, but raises the question of the worth of public investments in regulatory institutions.

Gollop and Karlson (1980), using data on electric utilities and an intertemporal model, found no evidence of input distortions. But Filer and Hallas (1983), testing for the effects of regulation in the interruptable gas industry, found rate of return regulation induced investment in additional storage capacity. Giordano (1983), examining utilities during 1964–77, concluded that there was capital bias during the 1960s, but not in the 1970s, because increasing regulatory lag and rapidly rising factor prices wiped it out. Such a finding was consistent with Averch–Johnson predictions, but it made Averch–Johnson effects perhaps less relevant in the 1980s. However, Averch–Johnson effects continue to be reported. Mirucki (1984), for example, concludes that the Canadian Bell system overinvests in capital and does not minimize costs.

Some investigators have argued that even if Averch–Johnson effects exist, their impact may be small, for there may be deterrents to technical inefficiency such as open entry (Sharkey, 1982). Others have argued that even if Averch–Johnson effects existed in the 1960s and 1970s, the relevant problem for utilities in the 1980s has been one of avoiding actual rates of return that fall below the allowed rate *s*. The 1980s problem is underinvestment, because consumers are now able to prevent regulatory agencies from granting the price increases necessary to cover rising input costs (Navarro, 1983; Nelson, 1984; Rozek, 1984).

Theoretical extensions. The Averch–Johnson results have been extended and generalized in many ways. Three of the more significant extensions are discussed below.

Regulatory lag and stochastic review: The original Averch–Johnson result implicitly assumed regulatory agencies were always effective in enforcing the *s* they chose. In fact, regulators have great difficulty in keeping actual rates close to target rates. The regulatory process does its work episodically, through adjustments in price. Occasional adjustments, the regulator hopes, will bring the actual *s* to a tolerable level, if not back to the one originally set. Since regulation is a political, bureaucratic and legal process, there are almost always lags in enforcement. Consequently, firms may be able to escape the constraint for long periods of time (Bailey and Coleman, 1971; Klevorick, 1974).

Sufficient regulatory lag may allow the firm to be technically efficient at an unregulated monopolist's output, and it may induce more technological innovation than the case without enforcement lag. Continuous, effective regulation would prevent the firm from gaining the windfall profits that innovation may require, although Nelson argues that most technological change in the utilities industry is disembodied and has little relation to regulation (Nelson, 1984).

Demand uncertainty: Some authors argue that Averch–Johnson results hold only under some specifications of a stochastic demand function, but not others (Perrakis, 1976;

Peles and Stein, 1976). Most of this discussion goes to whether the optimal capital stock would be larger, if regulated firms faced stochastic demands. If, as in the original Averch–Johnson discussion, we assume that the firm selects K and L as part of a simultaneous, ex ante optimization process, then the basic Averch–Johnson result, the inefficient capital–labour ratio, still holds under stochastic demand (Das, 1980).

Dynamic analysis: Some authors have introduced time explicitly into the original static Averch–Johnson model. For example, El-Hodiri and Takayama (1981) interpret the 'Averch–Johnson effect' to be a larger optimal K^* for a regulated firm than an unregulated one, and they show that this is true even with the adjustment costs attributable to time. However, much of this dynamic literature has been devoted to showing that, given a firm that maximizes the present value of profits over any number of time periods, one or more Averch–Johnson results do not hold or hold only under special conditions (Niho and Musaccio, 1983; Dechert, 1984).

The significance of the Averch–Johnson effect. From the standpoint of microeconomic theory, the original Averch–Johnson results provided impetus for increasingly complex, analytical models of the regulatory process. The Averch–Johnson approach suggested that much of the conventional, qualitative wisdom about regulation could be modelled and tested and that it was necessary to do so. Without thinking through all the potential consequences, actions and rules could be quite flawed without anyone intending them to be so. But flaws generally become apparent only after actions and rules have become entrenched, difficult to change or reverse. So explicit modelling of regulatory rules became part of the economist's stock in trade.

From a public policy perspective, the Averch–Johnson results and the very large volume of follow-on research have made economists, legislators and administrators far more sensitive to the potential unintended consequences of regulatory alternatives in general and not just rate of return alternatives. The Averch–Johnson effect has also figured directly in rate cases with utilities sometimes forced to defend themselves against charges of inefficiency.

Future lines of development. By injecting changes into the Averch–Johnson formulation one at a time, theoretical work has sought to make the model more representative of the actual regulatory process. One set of writers has pursued the effects of stochastic demand. Another set has worked on regulatory lag and stochastic review processes, but without stochastic demand. Yet another set has had the firm making global optimizations over time without either stochastic demands or random review. Economists interested in welfare issues have tried to determine an optimal fair rate of return from a strict economics perspective, but neglected politics and bureaucratic behaviour in setting rates. No model builders to date have addressed firms and regulators as interacting organizations both suffering from bounded rationality and bounded information, although there is some recent work on what regulators might do when a firm's costs are unknown and it has incentives to lie (Baron and Meyerson, 1982).

Regulatory systems are so complex and interactive that the standard strategy of *a priori* modelling with a minimum number of plausible assumptions may no longer have sufficient pay off. In complex, interactive, relatively poorly understood situations, other analytical styles such as simulation or operational gaming can be useful. They have not been tried and probably should be. In fact, brute force, detailed descriptions of actual regulatory processes may be highly useful in suggesting guides for action. Regulation remains a problem in political economy.

Actual outcomes depend as much on political and bureaucratic necessity as they do on economic analysis and 'rational' benefit–cost estimates.

H.A. AVERCH

See also MARGINAL AND AVERAGE COST PRICING; PUBLIC UTILITIES; REGULATION AND DEREGULATION.

BIBLIOGRAPHY

Averch, H.A. and Johnson, L.L. 1962. Behavior of the firm under regulatory constraint. *American Economic Review* 52(5), December, 1052–69.

Bailey, E.E. 1973. *Economic Theory of Regulatory Constraint.* New York: D.C. Heath.

Bailey, E.E. and Coleman, R.D. 1971. The effect of lagged regulation in an Averch–Johnson model. *Bell Journal of Economics and Management Science* 2(1), Spring, 278–92.

Baron, D.P. and Meyerson, R.B. 1982. Regulating a monopolist with unknown costs. *Econometrica* 50(4), July, 911–30.

Baumol, W.J. and Klevorick, A.K. 1970. Input choices and rate-of-return regulation. *Bell Journal of Economics and Management Science* 1(2), Autumn, 162–90.

Boyes, W.J. 1976. An empirical examination of the Averch–Johnson effect. *Economic Inquiry* 14(1), March, 25–35.

Callen, J., Mathewson, G.F. and Mohring, H. 1976. The benefits and costs of rate of return regulation. *American Economic Review* 66(3), June, 290–97.

Courville, L. 1974. Regulation and efficiency in the electric utility industry. *Bell Journal of Economics and Management Science* 5(1), Spring, 53–74.

Das, S.P. 1980. On the effect of rate of return regulation under uncertainty. *American Economic Review* 70(3), June, 456–60.

Dechert, W. 1984. Has the Averch–Johnson effect been theoretically justified? *Journal of Economic Dynamics and Control* 8(1), October, 1–17.

El-Hodiri, M. and Takayama, A. 1981. Dynamic behavior of the firm with adjustment costs under regulatory constraint. *Journal of Economic Dynamics and Control* 3(1), 29–41.

Filer, J.E. and Hallas, D.R. 1983. Empirical tests for the effect of regulation on firms and interruptible gas service. *Southern Economic Journal* 50(1), July, 195–205.

Giordano, J.N. 1983. The changing impact of regulation on the U.S. electric utility industry, 1964–1977. *Eastern Economic Journal* 9(2), April–June, 91–101.

Gollop, F.M. and Karlson, S.H. 1980. The electric power industry: an econometric model of intertemporal behavior. *Land Economics* 56(3), August, 299–314.

Hayashi, P.M. and Trapani, J.M. 1976. Empirical evidence on the Averch–Johnson model. *Southern Economic Journal* 42(3), January, 384–98.

Klevorick, A.K. 1971. The 'optimal' fair rate of return. *Bell Journal of Economics and Management Science* 2(1), Spring, 122–53.

Klevorick, A.K. 1973. The behavior of a firm subject to stochastic regulatory review. *Bell Journal of Economics and Management Science* 4(1), Spring, 57–88.

Magat, W. 1976. Regulation and the rate of direction of induced technical change. *Bell Journal of Economics and Management Science* 7(2), Autumn, 478–96.

Mirucki, J. 1984. A study of the Averch–Johnson effect in the telecommunications industry. *Atlantic Economic Journal* 12(1), March, 121.

Murphy, F.H. and Soyster, A.L. 1982. Optimal output of the Averch–Johnson model. *Atlantic Economic Journal* 10(4), December, 77–81.

Navarro, P. 1983. Save now, freeze later: the real price of cheap electricity. *Regulation* 7, October, 31–6.

Nelson, R.A. 1984. Regulation, capital vintage, and technical change in the electric utility industry. *Review of Economics and Statistics* 66(1), February, 59–69.

Niho, Y. and Musaccio, R.A. 1983. Effects of regulation and capital market imperfection on the dynamic behavior of a firm. *Southern Economic Journal* 49(3), January, 625–36.

Okuguchi, K. 1975. The implications of regulation for induced technical change: comment. *Bell Journal of Economics and Management Science* 6(2), Autumn, 703–5.

Peles, Y.C. and Stein, J.L. 1976. The effect of rate of return regulation is highly sensitive to the nature of uncertainty. *American Economic Review* 66(3), June, 278–89.

Perrakis, S. 1976. On the regulated price-setting monopoly firm with a random demand curve. *American Economic Review* 66(3), June, 410–16.

Petersen, H.C. 1975. An empirical test of regulatory effects. *Bell Journal of Economics and Management Science* 6(1), Spring, 111–26.

Rozek, R.P. 1984. The over-capitalization effect with diversification and cross subsidization. *Economics Letters* 6(1–2), 159–63.

Sharkey, W.W. 1982. *The Theory of Natural Monopoly*. New York: Cambridge University Press.

Sheshinski, E. 1971. Welfare aspects of a regulatory constraint: note. *American Economic Review* 61(1), March, 175–8.

Smith, V.K. 1974. The implications of regulation for induced technical change. *Bell Journal of Economics and Management Science* 5(2), Autumn, 623–32.

Smith, V.K. 1975. The implications of regulation for induced technical change: reply. *Bell Journal of Economics and Management Science* 6(2), Autumn, 706–7.

Smithson, C.W. 1978. The degree of regulation and the monopoly firm: further empirical evidence. *Southern Economic Journal* 44(3), January 568–80.

Spann, R.M. 1974. Rate of return regulation and efficiency in production: an empirical test of Averch–Johnson thesis. *Bell Journal of Economics and Management Science* 5(1), Spring, 38–52.

Tapon, F. and Van der Weide, J. 1979. Effectiveness of regulation in the electric utility industry. *Journal of Economics and Business* 31(3), Spring–Summer, 180–89.

Westfield, F. 1971. Innovation and monopoly regulation. In *Technological Change in Regulated Industries*, ed. W.M. Capron, Washington, DC: Brookings Institution.

Zajac, E.E. 1970. A geometric treatment of Averch–Johnson's behavior of the firm model. *American Economic Review* 60(1), March, 117–25.

axiomatic theories. One of the first steps in axiomatizing a theory is to list the primitive notions. A familiar example is the classical case of Euclidean geometry. We can take as primitives the following three notions: the notion of point, the notion of betweenness – one point being between two others in a line – and the notion of equidistance – (the distance between given points being the same as the distance between two other given points). Other geometric notions can then be defined in terms of these three notions. For example, the line generated by two distinct points *a* and *b* is defined as the *set* of all points *c* which are between *a* and *b*, which are such that *b* is between *a* and *c*, or which are such that *a* is between *c* and *b*.

The primitive notions of a theory are seldom, if ever, uniquely determined by the intuitive content of the theory. Euclidean geometry has been developed in terms of a wide variety of primitive notions other than the three mentioned above. In Hilbert's well-known axiomatization (1899), for example, the five notions of point, line, plane, betweenness and congruence are taken as primitive. In contrast, in the same year, the Italian mathematician Pieri published an axiomatization of Euclidean geometry using only the primitive notions of point and motion.

An important preliminary step in fixing on the primitive notions of a theory is to make explicit what other theories are to be assumed in developing the axiomatization. For most axiomatic work in economics, a certain amount of standard mathematics is assumed, including of course logic and elementary set theory, as well as most of classical analysis. When such prior theories are not assumed, then a complete apparatus must be built from the ground up. This is quite uncommon in any of the empirical sciences, such as economics

or physics. For example, it would seem strange in a theoretical paper in economics to develop from scratch the concept of number or the concept of Riemann integral.

After making explicit what other theories are to be assumed and fixing on the primitive notions of the theory under study, the axioms of the theory can now be stated without ambiguity. The only concepts referred to in the axioms must be primitive notions, notions defined in terms of primitive notions, or notions belonging to the theories assumed *a priori*. It is also important to recognize that in deriving theorems of the theory in question, nothing may be assumed about the primitive notions except what is stated in the axioms or possibly follows from other theories assumed *a priori*.

Informally, there are other things that are often said about axioms which can be repeated here but which cannot always be satisfied. For instance, it is generally recognized that it is desirable to have as few axioms as feasible, and also to take as axioms statements which have a strong intuitive appeal. But minimization of number of axioms or the vague concept of intuitive appeal do not play explicitly a rigorous role in almost any critiques of actual axiom systems proposed. It is sometimes held that theories should always be formulated only in terms of their primitive notions; that is, without using any notions defined in terms of the primitives. The argument for this is that only in this fashion will the actual complexity of the theory be evident. Already in the case of axioms of geometry this can become an intolerable burden from the standpoint of perspicuity of formulation, and consequently it is again a recommendation that is to be followed when feasible but not taken as an inviolable injunction.

The rest of this article is organized in the following fashion. Section 1 provides a brief review of the history of the axiomatic method. Section 2 analyses the concept of the standard formalization of a theory in first-order logic, and points out why this approach does not work well in most scientific contexts. The positive approach of considering theories as being defined by set-theoretical predicates is developed in Section 3.

1. HISTORY

Euclid. As with many other things, the story of the axiomatic method begins with the ancient Greeks. It seems fairly certain that it developed in response to the early crisis in foundations; namely, the problem of incommensurable magnitudes as, for instance, of the side and diagonal of a square, which occurred in the 5th century BC. The axiomatic method as we think of it today was crystallized in Euclid's *Elements*. The important philosophical predecessor of Euclid is Aristotle, who discusses the first principles of any demonstrative science in the *Posterior Analytics*. According to Aristotle, a demonstrative science must start from indemonstrable principles. Of such principles Aristotle says in the *Posterior Analytics* that some are common to all sciences. These are what are termed *axioms* or *common notions*. Other principles are special to a particular science. A standard example of an axiom for Aristotle is the principle that if equals be subtracted from equals, the remainders are equal.

Euclid follows Aristotelian methodology by listing at the beginning of the *Elements* twenty-three definitions, five postulates (assumptions special to geometry) and five axioms or common notions. Euclid set the standard of rigour for nearly two thousand years of mathematics. Only in the 19th century did real flaws come to the surface in Euclid's axiomatic presentation. It should also be mentioned that in spite of the usefulness of the ancient distinction between postulates and axioms, it is not one that is explicitly made today. What Euclid called axioms are now taken up in what has been referred to above as the theories that are assumed *a priori*; for example, logic and classical mathematics. What are called axioms in the context of this article would be called postulates in ancient Greek terminology, but this ancient usage will not be followed here.

Although from a modern standpoint it is easy to pick out certain flaws in Euclid's *Elements* and to emphasize certain differences between his conception of the axiomatic method and modern ones, the essential point remains that the axiomatic method as reflected in his *Elements* is extremely close to modern views. Such important works of modern science as Newton's *Principia* (1687) were written in this geometrical tradition.

Modern geometry. The historical source of the modern viewpoint towards the axiomatic method was the intense scrutiny of the foundations of geometry in the 19th century. The most important driving force behind this effort was the discovery and development of non-Euclidean geometry at the beginning of the 19th century by Bolya, Lobachevski and Gauss.

It was above all the German geometer Pasch who formulated in the clearest and most explicit way the modern formal conception of geometry in his important book of 1882. Pasch emphasized that if geometry is to be a genuinely deductive science, then the deductions must everywhere be independent of the meaning of geometrical concepts. From a formal standpoint, the deductions should be valid without taking into account in any way the meaning of the terms. He emphasized the thoroughly modern point that if a theorem is rigorously derived from a set of axioms, and if we replace the primitive concepts by others of the same logical nature, then the theorem will remain valid. This has the effect of treating the primitive concepts as variables. The axiomatic approach in geometry continued to dominate conceptions of the axiomatic method well into the 20th century.

2. THEORIES WITH STANDARD FORMALIZATION

The most explicit and formally precise axiomatic versions of theories are ones that are formalized within first-order logic with identity. First-order logic can be easily characterized in an informal way. This is the logic that assumes (i) one kind of variable; (ii) logical constants, in particular the sentential connectives such as → for *if ... then ...*, and ∨ for *or*; (iii) the universal and existential quantifiers, (x), $(\exists x)$; and (iv) the identity symbol. A theory formulated within such a framework is called a theory with standard formalization. Three kinds of non-logical constants occur in axiomatizing the theory: the predicates or relation symbols, the operation symbols and the individual constants.

The expressions of the theory – i.e. finite sequences of symbols, of the language of the theory – are divided into terms and formulas. Recursive definitions of each are given. The simplest terms are variables or individual constants. New terms are built up by combining simpler terms with operation symbols in the appropriate fashion. Atomic formulas consist of a single predicate and the appropriate number of terms. Compound formulas are built up from atomic formulas by means of sentential connectives and quantifiers.

Theories with standard formalization are not often found in use in scientific context. They do have a role when particular questions are of interest. For example, a standard question about a theory with standard formalization is whether it is decidable. This means, is there a mechanical decision procedure for asserting whether or not a formula of the theory is a valid sentence of the theory, i.e. is a formula either an axiom or a theorem of the theory? In general, there is no decision procedure for theories with standard formalization. It was rigorously proved in 1936 by Alonzo Church that there is no mechanical test for the validity of arbitrary formulas in first-order logic. The most important positive decision result is probably that of Alfred Tarski's for the elementary algebra of real numbers, first published in 1948. A second important question is that of completeness. It is natural to ask of any scientific theory whether it is complete in the sense that it is possible to give a list of axioms of the theory from which all other true assertions of the theory may be derived. The most important result of modern logic is Kurt Gödel's result in 1931 that the elementary theory of positive integers is not complete in the sense just stated.

There are difficulties of casting ordinary scientific theories into first-order logic. The source of the difficulty has already been mentioned. Almost all systematic scientific theories assume a certain amount of mathematics *a priori*. There is no simple or elegant way to include such mathematical concepts in the standard formalization, which by definition assumes only the apparatus of elementary logic. For example, a theory that requires for its formulation an Archimedean-type axiom – for some n, n copies of a length however small are together longer than any given distance no matter how long – cannot be axiomatized in first-order logic. Because of these difficulties, standard axiomatic formulation of scientific theories follows the methodology outlined in the next section.

3. THEORIES DEFINED AS SET-THEORETICAL PREDICATES

From a formal standpoint, the essence of the approach that is close to the practice of modern mathematics and widely used in mathematical economics is to axiomatize scientific theories within a set-theoretical framework. From this standpoint, to axiomatize a theory is simply to define a certain set-theoretical predicate. The axioms as we ordinarily think of them are part of a definition, of course the most important part.

Here is the theory of weak orderings formulated as such a set-theoretical definition – for an elementary exposition of this approach, see Suppes (1957, ch. 12).

> *Definition.* Let A be a non-empty set and R a binary relation on A. A structure (A,R) is a *weak ordering* if and only if for every x, y, and z in A (i) if xRy and yRz then xRz, (ii) xRy or yRx.

Further formal work is then conducted in terms of the structures of a theory as thus defined. For many kinds of analysis a key definition is that of isomorphism of structures, here exemplified for the structures just considered.

> *Definition.* A structure (A,R) is isomorphic to a structure (A',R') if and only if there is a function f such that (i) the domain of f is A and the range of f is A', (ii) f is a one–one function, (iii) if x and y are in A, then xRy if and only if $f(x)R'f(y)$.

In terms of the definition of isomorphism, we then often seek for axiomatic theories a representation theorem which has the following meaning. A certain class of structures or models of a theory is distinguished for some intuitively clear reason and is shown to exemplify within isomorphism every structure of the theory. In the case of ordering relations, a typical representation theorem concerns representing any ordering by an isomorphic numerical ordering. Note that in the case of weak orderings, for example, we first form classes of objects that are equivalent in the ordering and then each equivalence class is assigned a number under the isomorphic representation.

Only the simplest kinds of structures have been discussed here, but the ideas developed apply without change to more complicated structures as exemplified in contemporary theories of pure mathematics, mathematical economics and other mathematically based disciplines. The development of axiomatic theories for such structures is now the widely accepted methodology for their investigation. The importance of identifying certain structures as basic is perhaps obvious, but a persuasive explicit argument is given in Bourbaki (1950) for the case of mathematics.

Finally, it should be emphasized that the commitment to a set-theoretical framework for the formulation of axiomatic theories is less essential than the general *formal* conception of the axiomatic method as it originated in modern geometry since Pasch and has been developed in detail in pure mathematics by Bourbaki.

PATRICK SUPPES

See also ORDERINGS; PHILOSOPHY AND ECONOMICS; PREFERENCES; PREORDERINGS.

BIBLIOGRAPHY
Bourbaki, N. 1950. The architecture of mathematics. *American Mathematical Monthly* 57, 231–2.
Euclid. *Elements*. Heath translation, 2nd edn, 1925; reprinted, New York: Dover, 1956.
Hilbert, D. 1899. *Gründlagen der Geometrie*. 9th edn, Stuttgart, 1962.
Pasch, M. 1882. *Vorlesungen über neuere Geometrie*. Leipzig: Springer.
Suppes, P. 1957, *Introduction to Logic*. New York: Van Nostrand.

Ayres, Clarence Edwin (1891–1972). Ayres was born on 6 May 1891 in Lowell, Massachusetts, and died on 25 July 1972 in Alamogordo, New Mexico. Trained as a philosopher, with degrees from Brown and Chicago (PhD, 1917), Ayres taught at Chicago, Amherst and Reed before moving to the University of Texas at Austin in 1930, from which he retired in 1968. For one year, 1924–5, he was an associate editor of *The New Republic*, associated with Herbert Croly, John Dewey, Alvin Johnson and R.H. Tawney. He had a lifelong correspondence with another philosophically oriented, but more traditional economist, Frank H. Knight.

He was profoundly influenced by Thorstein Veblen and Dewey and became a, if not the, leader of institutional economics after World War II. A truly charismatic lecturer, at Texas he had long-lasting influence on a coterie of students who continued his teachings in their own careers. As his ideas evolved, particularly with regard to the nature of and relations between institutions and technology, his students came away with coherent but varying substantive understandings.

Ayre's formulation of institutionalism stressed that science was a system of belief, that human values were only means to the continuation and enhancement of the life process, that technology, as he defined it, was a (largely) beneficent driving force in social change, and that considerations of rightness tended in practice to be matters of tradition and custom.

Technology, to Ayres, meant the use of tools, but he defined tools increasingly broadly to include intangible symbols and organizations. Technology was the surging force governing economic welfare, and constituted what he considered to be an objective industrial or developmental process. His conception of technologically instrumental value and truth emphasized the transcultural values of workability and efficiency which form a continuum. Opposed to technology was the binding force of established institutions which, through sanctioning ceremonial behaviour in favour of established or vested interests, were hostile to the conceptual and economic progress generated by technology. Economic progress was thus fundamentally a matter of industrialization; the logic of industrialization, or technological advancement in all respects, was continually at war with outworn, inhibitive institutions. Mankind's task was to develop new institutional forms and revise old ones in order to keep pace with evolving technology.

Ayres insisted that human behaviour was socially formed, and that for such behaviour to be explained and understood the economist had to study existing behaviour patterns (institutions) and general culture. In common with other institutionalists, Ayres insisted upon methodological collectivism and challenged what he considered to be the narrow focus on market equilibrium conditions maintained by mainstream economics.

Ayres influenced many development economists, who similarly perceived that modernization was inhibited by the continuance of traditional institutions or by the maintenance of positions of power antagonistic to modernization. More generally, Ayres, again like other institutionalists, argued that to understand the allocation of resources one had to go beyond the market to the institutions and cultural forces which, in part through adaptation to and incorporation of technology, constitute the real allocational mechanism. In a sense, the neoclassical juxtaposition between cost of production and utility became for Ayres something different, a juxtaposition between technology and the institutions which formed and weighted individual and collective choice.

WARREN J. SAMUELS

See also INSTITUTIONAL ECONOMICS.

SELECTED WORKS
1938. *The Problem of Economic Order*. New York: Farrar & Rinehart.
1944. *The Theory of Economic Progress*. Chapel Hill: University of North Carolina Press.
1946. *The Divine Right of Capital*. Boston: Houghton Mifflin.
1952. *The Industrial Economy*. Boston: Houghton Mifflin.
1961. *Toward a Reasonable Society*. Austin: University of Texas Press.

BIBLIOGRAPHY
Breit, W. 1973. The development of Clarence Ayres's theoretical institutionalism. *Social Science Quarterly* 54(2), September, 244–57.

B

Babbage, Charles (1791–1871). Charles Babbage is rarely regarded as a major contributor to economic thought. His name is synonymous with the early origins of the computer, and he was an important figure in early 19th-century scientific circles. He was educated at Trinity College and Peterhouse, Cambridge, and while still a student started the Analytical Society with Herschel and Peacock, for reforming mathematics in Britain. His interest in mathematics was the foundation for his later contributions to science, economics and statistics. After Cambridge, Babbage moved to London, where he began his lifelong work on his Analytical Engine and became a leading participant in scientific circles. He joined the Royal Society and was a founding member of the Cambridge Philosophical Society and the Royal Astronomical Society. Later he was to be one of Newton's illustrious successors in the Lucasian Chair of Mathematics at Cambridge. But he was also a radical if maverick intellectual and political critic. He wanted to see science reformed, to see British science play a leading part in theoretical advance, and to see this science related closely to applied technology. He also demanded a role for the state in providing support for science and university education, and for establishing a policy on technology. He wrote a controversial attack on the Royal Society, *Reflections on the Decline of Science and Some of its Causes* (1830), and was one of the founding trustees of the British Association for the Advancement of Science, with the purpose of bringing science and technology, from the provinces as well as the metropolis, into the forefront of culture and society.

Babbage was an early promoter of industrial exhibitions as a part of meetings of the British Association; he participated in the Mechanics Section of the Association and later wrote a book on the Great Exhibition of 1851. He took part in the great controversies over religion and science in the period, and wrote the *Ninth Bridgewater Treatise* in 1837 conveying his belief in a Newtonian universe, with a scientific Deity.

Politically, Babbage was a liberal Whig; he chaired an election committee and stood twice for Finsbury. He denounced election corruption and bribery, attacked church preferments and tithes, and was a firm supporter of the Reform Bill. His political pamphlet on the Income Tax showed a concept of moderate reform. He identified an electoral system based on one man, one vote with the 'advance of socialism', for where the poor were in the majority they would vote for low taxes for themselves and high taxes for the rich, 'thus destroying private enterprise'.

Babbage's social and academic context was clearly that of early 19th-century liberal–scientific circles, and he participated in the salon culture of the day. But there was another very important component to his intellectual make up: an abiding interest in practical mechanics and a fascination with contemporary industrial technology. He learned from manufacturers, large and small, mechanical engineers and above all from the skilled artisans he never ceased to praise. Developing the analytical engine was itself a task of scientific and mathematical reasoning combined with practical invention.

The continental tour he made in 1827–8, which was to be so formative to his later work, was not in the company of a scientific friend or even a servant, but with one of the artisans who had worked on the building of the analytical engine. Travelling through the Low Countries, Germany, Austria and Italy with a prolonged stay in Naples, Babbage lost no opportunity to visit local workshops and factories.

His transcendence of contemporary social and intellectual boundaries was the real basis for his brilliant and utterly original foray into political economy. *On the Economy of Machinery and Manufactures* (1832) was immensely popular: there were four editions in two and a half years, it was reprinted in the United States and translated into four continental languages. Babbage wanted to present his readers with the mechanical principles of arts and manufactures, and he hoped also to be read by the intelligent working man. To this extent the book fell within the contemporary genre of industrial–technological literature; indeed, part of it had been published in 1829 as a part of the *Encyclopedia Metropolitana*. Tracts on the steam engine, histories of the cotton industry and industrial manuals, dictionaries and encyclopedias were very popular at the time. Andrew Ure's later *Philosophy of Manufactures* (1835), an extraordinary panegyric on the factory system and steam-powered machinery, was very much a product of this genre, but it completely lacked the analysis of Babbage's contribution. For the latter was much more than popular industrial observation. It was an analysis based on economic principles, especially the Smithian account of the division of labour, of manufacturing technology and the organization of industrial work. Babbage's obvious first-hand knowledge of a wide variety of industrial and business processes, combined with general analysis of production systems, made the work a tour de force. At a time of anxiety and ambiguity over the reception of new technology, he also offered authoritative policy statements on a wide range of machinery issues including patent reform, export of machinery, crises of overproduction, and technological unemployment.

The book's intellectual situation in relation to political economy was not, however, easily apparent, and apart from Mill and Marx few appreciated its significance to their discipline. Before he wrote the book Babbage had intended to deliver a series of lectures in Cambridge on the Political Economy of Manufactures, but this never materialized. He himself conceded that his first edition did not profess to examine questions of political economy, and he attempted to correct this in the next edition by introducing three new chapters: 'The New System of Manufactures', 'The Effects of Machinery in Reducing the Demand for Labour', and 'On Money as a Medium of Exchange'. But most of the topics raised by Babbage were also foreign to contemporary classical political economy. Moving back to Smith, he analysed industrial organization and the microeconomics of the manufacturing firm, never losing sight of technological constraints and opportunities.

The book was initially criticized for failing to give due attention to the factory system and steam-powered textile technology. But this was precisely its strength. For it analysed the factory and the workshop as parts of the more general organization of work, and examined machinery in the context of a more general discussion of technology, including skill. Babbage's close observation of skills and hand processes as well as machinery, of the workshop as well as the factory was anyway a more accurate perception of contemporary industrial practice than a work concentrating on the outstanding and atypical phenomenon of the factory would have been.

Babbage analysed what he called 'the domestic economy of the factory'. He sought to specify what arrangement of production would succeed in selling articles at a minimum price, and he made a careful analysis of economies of scale in relation to the division of labour, distinguishing the dynamics of the factory from those of the workshop. He developed Smith's principle of the division of labour to a further refinement, introducing the significance of the division of skill, or the division of mental and manual labour. Vital, he believed, to the success of any organization of work was his 'Babbage Principle':

> that the master manufacturer by dividing the work to be executed into different processes, each requiring different degrees of skill or of force, can purchase exactly that precise quantity of both which is necessary for each process.

From this emphasis on the economy of skill, Babbage introduced novel discussions of the role of accounting, time and motion studies, communications innovations, and an analysis of machine functions. He was particularly concerned with the significance of precision and measurement in all processes, with the regularity of production, and with the planning of layout. He thus regarded as some of the greatest innovations not the celebrated power techniques themselves, but the processes which helped to make the new machines work properly, for example the steam engine governor and lubrication or grease. His interest in measurement led him to support all manner of instruments for counting machines and human actions; and he devised a detailed questionnaire as a basis for job studies and early time and motion studies. He also analysed as had no one before him the role of the speed of production and the intensity of labour in increasing output. Introducing machinery was only one incomplete route to increasing productivity; the productivity of labour could be rapidly improved through greater order, precision and labour discipline. Babbage noticed the convergence of technological and economic principles on topics such as velocity and copying; in a long discussion of the significance of copying techniques he pointed out the parallels between printing, casting and moulding, stamping and turning.

This core analysis of workshop organization was complemented by topical commentary on profit sharing, technological unemployment and trade unions. An important radical departure on wages and labour was provided in his 'New System of Manufactures' which argued for a piece-rate wage system and profit sharing, if not cooperation, as the key to overcoming the long–standing worker opposition to machinery. This was the problem which Babbage along with many of his contemporaries believed to be the major brake on Britain's industrial progress. The system was a far-reaching proposal for a worker's stake in increasing productivity, for collective decision-making on hiring, dismissal and the organization of the works. Where the system prevailed, modern methods would be chosen and an extensive division of labour introduced, not to control and subordinate labour, but as a cooperative decision by workers for the most efficient methods. The lengths to which his suggestions went were probably surpassed only by radical and Owenite cooperatives. When it came to practical implementation Babbage held out little hope of any appeal of the system to large established firms, but thought that groups of artisans and small firms would lead the way. Babbage's chapters on trade unions and machinery and employment were, however, the comments of a reformer not a radical. He attacked the truck system, but warned that trade unions could well lead to more rapid displacement of labour through machinery or industrial relocation. Dealing with technological underemployment, he used the case of hand-weaving and the power loom, arguing that the only solution lay in better workers' planning through such institutions as savings banks and Friendly Societies.

Babbage's use of practical observation and statistical data, and his critique of political economy's 'closest philosophers' induced him, with Richard Jones, J.E. Drinkwater, Malthus and Quetelet, to form a Statistics Section of the British Association in 1833, followed later by the Statistical Society of London. The Statistical Section, Section F, was confined to the presentation of statistical data, avoiding areas of political controversy. But the less restrictive London Society made its brief the connection of political economy to the statistical investigation of economic improvement. Babbage was the first President of Section F, and wrote several statistical papers. His earlier 'Letter to the Right Hon T.P. Courtenay on the Proportional Number of Births of the Two Sexes under Different Circumstances' (1829) compared the demographic structures of the Kingdom of Naples, France, Prussia and Westphalia. Much later he wrote 'On the Statistics of Light Houses' for the Brussels Congress of Statistics in 1853, and 'The Clearing House', read to the London Statistical Society and printed in its memoirs in 1856. Babbage also wrote a book on insurance, *A Comparative View of the Various Institutions for the Assurance of Lives* (1826), and is remembered for his revised actuarial tables and his popular presentation of a difficult subject.

Babbage certainly produced an original and farseeing economic analysis of industry in *On the Economy of Machinery and Manufactures*. He applied the principles of the division of labour he elaborated to his perception of the sciences. The ultimate result of the division of skills and especially the mental division of labour was the 'science of calculation'. He argued that the science of calculation, like any technology, would be developed to a degree where machinery would take over all numerical calculation. Arithmetical exercise would thus be separated from mathematical reasoning, and the 'science of calculation' harnessed to the Analytical Engine would become the science of all sciences. Babbage's ultimate vision for Britain's industrial progress was one of a computer-run technology.

MAXINE BERG

SELECTED WORKS

1830. *Reflections on the Decline of Science*. London: B. Fellowes.
1832. *On the Economy of Machinery and Manufactures*. London: Charles Knight. 4th edn, 1835.
1851. *The Exposition of 1851*. London: John Murray.
1864. *Passages from the Life of a Philosopher*. London: Longman & Co.

BIBLIOGRAPHY

Hyman, A. 1982. *Charles Babbage, Pioneer of the Computer*. Oxford: Oxford University Press.

Babeuf, François Noël (1764–1797).   François Noel Babeuf, called *Caius Gracchus*, was born in Saint Quentin in 1764 and died at Vendôme on 24 February 1797. Left to his own resources at the age of sixteen, his youth was stormy, and his whole life wild and irregular. From the commencement of the Revolution he wrote in the journal *Le correspondant Picard*, articles so violent in tone that he was brought to trial. His acquittal, 14th July 1790, did little to calm him. Appointed administrator of the Département of the Somme, he soon had to be dismissed from the office. This was the time at which he took the name of *Caius Gracchus*, posing as a *Tribun du peuple*. He gave the same name to a journal, which he had previously carried on under the sub-title of *Défenseur de la liberté de la presse*. All this took place shortly after the fall of Robespierre from power. This for a time had his approval; but he soon returned to his earlier views and appealed to those violent passions which, as a demagogue, he knew how to rouse. He gathered round him, under the name of the *Secte des Egaux*, all the old Montagnards who were dissatisfied with the régime of the Thermidorians. The object of this sect, which drew its inspiration from some of the sentimental ideas of J.J. Rousseau, was to destroy inequality of condition, with the object of attaining the general good. Sylvain Maréchal, author of a *Dictionnaire des Athées*, Buonarroti, who claimed to be descended from Michael Angelo, with Amand and Antonelle, who did not, it is true, remain associated long, and some others, formed the staff which recognised Babeuf as their chief. Working with feverish activity, they gathered round them a considerable number of adherents. The place where their club met was the Pantheon. At first orderly, their meetings became tumultuous and threatening and were prolonged far into the night. Attending armed, they prepared to resist by force the dissolution of the club which the authorities had determined on. General Bonaparte, acting with much tact, contrived to close the meetings of the club, but the members formed themselves forthwith into a secret society, and gradually, by winning over soldiers and police, became a formidable body, numbering nearly 17,000 able-bodied and armed men, without including the Faubourgs Saint-Antoine and Saint-Marceau, which were at their back. Addressing themselves to the masses, they published a manifesto written by Sylvain Maréchal in his most inflammatory style.

> We desire [said they] real equality or death. This is what we want. And we will have real equality, no matter what it costs. Woe to those who come between us and our wishes. Woe to him who resists a desire so resolutely insisted on... . If it is needful, let all civilization perish, provided that we obtain real equality... . The common good, or the community of goods. No further private property in land; the land belongs to no private person. We claim, we require the enjoyment of the fruits of the land for all; the fruits belong to the whole world [etc].

Instructions in great detail as to the methods of raising insurrectionary movements were added.

> Those who hinder us shall be exterminated; ... shall all alike be put to death: Those who oppose us or gather forces against us; strangers, of whatever nation they may be, who are found in the streets; all the presidents, secretaries, and officers of the royalist (*sic*) conspiracy of Vendémiaire, who may also dare to show themselves.

If the lives of men were to be treated thus, one may guess what fate was reserved for their property. But, after massacres and spoliations, what was to come of it all? The public authorities were to organise employment; there was to be only one source of employment, the state, with subdivisions devised to meet the wants, somewhat rudimentary, of the community. Every one was to have a right to lodging, clothes, washing, warming, and lighting, to food, *médiocre mais frugale*, to medical attendance. This is much what Louis Blanc, who appears to have sought his inspiration among the decrees of the *République des Egaux*, enunciated in more methodical and sober language. 'Every one is to work as he is able, and to consume according to his wants.'

The secret was well kept; it was only a few hours before the moment fixed for the explosion of the conspiracy (May 1796) that a captain, named Grisel, revealed it to the directory. Decisive steps were taken at once; a vigorous watch was kept, while the public authorities seized the leaders and their papers.

Babeuf and Darthé, condemned to death the 23rd of February 1797, stabbed themselves before the tribunal. Life still lingering on, they were guillotined the next day. Buonarroti and Sylvain Maréchal, condemned to exile (*déportation*), died, the first in 1837, the second in 1803.

It may be added that Babeuf seems to have had rather a disordered brain than an absolutely criminal disposition. He died with courage, leaving his wife a written paper declaring his conviction that he had always been a 'perfectly virtuous man'.

[A. COURTOIS]
Reprinted from *Palgrave's Dictionary of Political Economy*.

Bachelier, Louis (1870–1946).   Bachelier was born in Le Havre, France, on 11 March 1870 and died in Saint-Servan-sur-Mer, Ille-et-Villaine, on 28 April 1946. He taught at Besançon, Dijon and Rennes and was professor at Besançon from 1927 to 1937.

The unrecognized genius is one of the stock figures of popular history, and it is also a platitude that many examples dissolve upon careful examination. But the story of Louis Bachelier is in perfect conformity to all the clichés. He invented efficient markets in 1900, sixty years before the idea came into vogue. He described the random walk model of prices, ordinary diffusion of probability – also called Brownian motion – and martingales, which are the mathematical expression of efficient markets. He even attempted an empirical verification. But he remained a shadowy presence until 1960 or so, when his major work was revived in English translation.

This major work was his doctoral dissertation in the mathematical sciences, defended in Paris on 19 March 1900. Things went badly from the start: the committee failed to give it the 'mention très honorable', key to a University career. It was very late, after repeated failures, that Bachelier was appointed to the tiny University of Besançon. After he had retired, the University Archives were accidentally set on fire and no record survives, not even one photograph. Here are a few scraps I have managed to put together.

We begin with the proverbial episode of the grain of sand, or the lack of a nail. Bachelier made a mathematical error that is recounted in a letter the great probabilist Paul Levy wrote me on 25 January 1964:

> I first heard of him around 1928. He was a candidate for a professorship at the University of Dijon. Gevrey, who was teaching there, came to ask my opinion. In a work published in 1913, Bachelier had defined Wiener's function (prior to Wiener) as follows: In each interval $[n\tau, (n + 1)\tau]$, he considered a function $X(t\,|\,\tau)$ that has a constant derivative equal to either $+v$ or $-v$, the two values being equiprobable. He then proceeded to the limit $\tau \to 0$, keeping v constant, and claimed he was obtaining a proper function $X(t)$! Gevrey was scandalized by this error. I agreed with him and Bachelier was blackballed.

I had forgotten it when in 1931, reading Kolmogorov's fundamental paper, I came to 'der Bacheliers Fall.' I looked up Bachelier's works, and saw that this error, which is repeated everywhere, does not prevent him from obtaining results that would have been correct if only he had written $v = C\tau^{-1/2}$, and that, prior to Einstein [1905] and prior to Wiener [circa 1925], he has seen some important properties of the Wiener function, namely, the diffusion equation and the distribution of $\max_{0 < \tau < t} X(\tau)$.

We became reconciled. I had written to him that I regretted that an impression, produced by a single initial error, should have kept me from going on with my reading of a work in which there were so many interesting ideas. He replied with a long letter in which he expressed great enthusiasm for research.

That Levy should have played this role is tragic, for his own career also nearly foundered because his papers were not sufficiently rigorous for the mathematical extremists.

The second and deeper reason for Bachelier's career problems was the topic of his dissertation: 'Mathematical theory of speculation' – not of (philosophical) speculation on the nature of chance, rather of (money-grubbing) speculation on the ups and downs of the market for consolidated state bonds: '*la rente*'. The function $X(t)$ mentioned by Levy stood for the price of *la rente* at time t. Hence, the delicately understated comment by Henri Poincaré, who wrote the official report on this dissertation, that 'the topic is somewhat remote from those our candidates are in the habit of treating'. One may wonder why Bachelier asked for the judgement of unwilling mathematicians (assigning a thesis subject was totally foreign to French professors of that period), but he had no choice: his lower degree was in mathematics and probability was taught by Poincaré.

Bachelier's tragedy was to be a man of the past and of the future but not of his present. He was a man of the past because gambling is the historical root of probability theory; he introduced the continuous-time gambling on *La Bourse*. He was a man of the future, both in mathematics (witness the above letter by Levy) and in economics. Unfortunately, no organized scientific community of his time was in a position to understand and welcome him. To gain acceptance for himself would have required political skills that he did not possess, and one wonders where he could have gained acceptance for his thoughts.

Poincaré's report on the 1908 dissertation deserves further excerpting:

> The manner in which the candidate obtains the law of Gauss is most original, and all the more interesting as the same reasoning might, with a few changes, be extended to the theory of errors. He develops this in a chapter which might at first seem strange, for he titles it 'Radiation of Probability'. In effect, the author resorts to a comparison with the analytical theory of the propagation of heat. A little reflection shows that the analogy is real and the comparison legitimate. Fourier's reasoning is applicable almost without change to this problem, which is so different from that for which it had been created. It is regrettable that [the author] did not develop this part of his thesis further.

While Poincaré had seen that Bachelier had advanced to the threshold of a general theory of diffusion, he was notorious for lapses of memory. A few years later, he took an active part in discussions concerning Brownian diffusion, but had forgotten Bachelier.

Comments in a *Notice* Bachelier wrote in 1921 are worth summarizing:

> 1906: *Théorie des probabilités continues*. This theory has no

relation whatsoever with the theory of geometric probability, whose scope is very limited. This is a science of another level of difficulty and generality than the calculus of probability. Conception, analysis, method, everything in it is new. 1913: *Probabilités cinématiques et dynamiques*. These applications of probability to mechanics are the author's own, absolutely. He took the original idea from no one; no work of the same kind has ever been performed. Conception, method, results, everything is new.

The hapless authors of academic *Notices* are not called upon to be modest, but Louis Bachelier had no reason for being modest. Does anyone know more about him?

BENOIT B. MANDELBROT

See also CONTINUOUS TIME STOCHASTIC PROCESSES; WIENER PROCESSES.

SELECTED WORKS

1900. Théorie de la spéculation. *Annales de l'Ecole normale supérieure*, 3rd series, 17, 21–86. Trans. by A.J. Boness in *The Random Character of Stock Market Prices*, ed. P.H. Cootner, Cambridge, Mass.: MIT Press, 1967.
1901. Théorie mathématique des jeux. *Annales de l'Ecole normale supérieure*, 3rd series, 18, 143–210.
1906. Théorie des probabilités continues. *Journal des mathématiques pures et appliquées*, 6th series, 2(3), 259–327.
1910a. Les probabilités à plusieurs variables. *Annales de l'Ecole normale supérieure*, 3rd series, 27, 340–60.
1910b. Mouvement d'un point ou d'un système soumis à l'action des forces dépendant du hasard. *Comptes rendus de l'Académie des sciences* 151, 852–5.
1912. Calcul des probabilités. Paris: Gauthier-Villars.
1913. Les probabilités cinématiques et dynamiques. *Annales de l'Ecole normale supérieure*, 3rd series, 30, 77–119.
1924. Le jeu, la chance et le hasard. Paris: E. Flammarion.
1937. Les lois des grands nombres du calcul des probabilités. Paris: Gauthier-Villars.
1938. La spéculation et le calcul des probabilités. Paris: Gauthier-Villars.
1939. Les nouvelles méthodes du calcul des probabilités. Paris: Gauthier-Villars.

backwardation. Using the language of the London Stock Exchange, 'backwardation' is a fee paid by a seller of stocks (or securities) to the buyer for the privilege of deferring delivery of them. Hence it means that the futures price (i.e. the current price for the future delivery) falls short of the spot price (i.e. the current price of immediate delivery). 'Contango', the reverse of backwardation, is a fee paid by the buyer who wants to postpone delivery, and means that the futures price exceeds the spot price. These terms may be extended to any futures transaction.

Keynes (1923, pp. 255–66; 1930, ch. 29) and Hicks (1946 pp. 130–40) advanced the theory of 'normal' backwardation; namely, the situation where the futures price of commodities is a downwardly biased prediction of the spot price at delivery time. Since normal backwardation is tantamount to the presence of a positive risk premium, hedgers as a whole take a short futures position of the commodities, and speculators as a group a long position. The theory of normal backwardation attempts to explain why hedgers tend to go short in futures.

Keynes and Hicks explained the existence of normal backwardation on technological grounds. That is, technological conditions in production and consumption (including demand activities by manufacturers who use the commodities as inputs) are such that producers must look much further ahead than consumers, because the former may already have committed themselves to production while the latter have a freer hand about acquiring the commodities. Thus there exists a greater desire to cover planned production (supplies) than to cover planned consumption (demands), and hedgers as a whole have a tendency to go short in futures. In order to persuade speculators to assume a matching long position, a positive risk premium has to be offered, hence a 'normal' backwardation.

Although this technological explanation is valid for typical commodity markets, it does not apply to all markets. Consider the following equilibrium conditions in the spot and futures markets at time 0:

$$Q_{0,0} + Z_{-1} = C_{0,0} + K_0 \text{ (Spot Market Equilibrium)}$$

$$Q_{0,1} + K_0 - C_{0,1} = Z_0 \text{ (Futures Market Equilibrium)}.$$

The variables Q, C, K and Z denote output supply, consumption, storage and futures speculation, respectively. The subscripts signify time; $Q_{t,s}$ (or $C_{t,s}$) is output or consumption) planned at time t and actually supplied (or demanded) at time s, K_0 is the amount carried from time 0 to time 1, and Z_0 is the quantity of speculative futures contracts purchased (if $Z_0 > 0$, or sold if $Z_0 < 0$) at time 0 for time 1 delivery. In the case of typical commodities, Q, C, $K > 0$ and $Z \lessgtr 0$. (For more detailed discussions about the market equilibrium, see Kawai (1983).) The market clearing conditions yield:

$$Z_0 = Q_{0,1} + K_0 - C_{0,1} = C_{1,1} + K_1 - Q_{1,1}.$$

The arguments put forward by Keynes and Hicks assert that production is mostly planned and consumption is largely flexible so that $Q_{0,1} > C_{0,1}$ and $C_{1,1} > Q_{1,1}$. From this, $Z_0 > 0$ follows and there exists a 'normal backwardation' (or a positive risk premium). But when the adjustment cost of changing production is low and that of changing consumption high, such technological conditions may not be satisfied. Furthermore, in some markets (such as those for foreign exchange and financial instruments) the technological distinction between production (Q) and consumption (C) is unimportant and storage can be negative ($K < 0$); then, normal backwardation is not guaranteed. In essence, whether or not normal backwardation is generated depends on the nature of the commodities in question and is an empirical matter.

Considerable empirical effort has been devoted to detecting a positive or negative risk premium in various types of markets, with mixed result (see Peck, 1977). The 'efficient futures market hypothesis' (the hypothesis of no systematic risk premium combined with rational expectations) cannot be rejected for many markets, thus invalidating the theory of normal backwardation. In other markets, time-varying risk premia, positive or negative, have also been found.

MASAHIRO KAWAI

See also FUTURES TRADING; SPOT AND FORWARD MARKETS.

BIBLIOGRAPHY

Hicks, J.R. 1946. *Value and Capital*. 2nd edn, London: Oxford University Press.
Kawai, M. 1983. Price volatility of storable commodities under rational expectations in spot and futures markets. *International Economic Review* 24(2), June, 435–54.
Keynes, J.M. 1923. Some aspects of commodity markets. *The Manchester Guardian Commercial, Reconstruction Supplement*, 29 March. Reprinted in *The Collected Writings of John Maynard Keynes* Vol. 7, London: Macmillan.
Keynes, J.M. 1930. *A Treatise on Money*, Vol. 2. London: Macmillan.
Peck, A.E. (ed.) 1977. *Selected Writings on Futures Markets*, Vol. 2. Chicago: Chicago Board of Trade.

backward bending supply curve. *See* LABOUR SUPPLY OF WOMEN.

backward linkage. *See* LINKAGES.

backwardness. The term 'economic backwardness' is frequently used as a synonym for 'economic underdevelopment' and in this sense was first used by John Stuart Mill in the 1850s. Since 1950, however, the concept of 'relative economic backwardness', whereby characteristics of the development process are seen to be in the level or stage of development reached by a particular country, has come to be associated with the ideas put forward by Alexander Gerschenkron. It is Gerschenkron's concept which will be considered here.

The hypothesis that a nation's relative economic backwardness helps shape the contours of its subsequent development has a lengthy history. Versions of such a concept can be found in a number of 19th-century writings, most explicitly in relation to Russia. Thus both Herzen and Chernyshevskii, for example, specifically linked the expected path of Russia's industrialization with her level of backwardness. Although Gerschenkron himself made fullest use of his hypothesis in his writings on Tsarist Russia's industrial development, he never discussed the historical antecedents of his theories. Moreover it was Gerschenkron's contribution, not simply to link backwardness and economic change in one country, but to suggest a hypothesis of relative backwardness whereby the entire sequence of industrializing nations in 19th-century Europe fitted into a distinct pattern according to their level of development at the onset of their industrialization.

Gerschenkron first put forward his ideas in an influential essay published in 1952, 'Economic backwardness in historical perspective'. The concept was later refined and elaborated and was most clearly summarized in his 1962 paper 'The approach to European industrialization: a postscript'.

Gerschenkron's hypothesis relates specifically to the pattern of European industrialization in the 19th century. The concept of 'relative backwardness' depends first and foremost on the proposition that 'in practice, we *can* rank the countries according to their backwardness and even discuss groups of similar degree of backwardness' (Gerschenkron's italics). Once so ranked a number of further propositions appear. The more backward the country 'the more explosive was the great spurt of its industrialisation, if and when it came'. The pattern of industrialization exhibited by the late starter had a number of characteristics. These characteristics often showed 'the advantages of backwardness', a notion frequently stressed by Gerschenkron. Thus Gerschenkron suggested that the industrial upsurge of the backward late-developer was often associated with modern large-scale plant and enterprise and a tendency among the enterprises to form 'monopolistic compacts' such as trusts and cartels. Capital goods, rather than consumer goods, would dominate the industrial spurt of the late industrializer. The level of backwardness at the onset of industrialization tended to be associated with 'organized direction' of industrial development: the most backward were dominated by state activity, while the moderately backward had their industries largely controlled by investment banks. Also, the more backward the country the less likely was the agricultural sector to play a positive role in the industrialization spurt. Indeed, the industrial spurt would put increasing strains on consumption levels the lower the base from which industrialization started. Gerschenkron also suggested that as backward countries industrialized, and so became less backward, their patterns of further industrialization took on the character of the less backward: initial diversity gave way to subsequent convergence.

An influential notion inherent in Gerschenkron's hypothesis has been his concept of 'substitutes'; that is, the very backwardness of a country makes it necessary for that country to find substitutes for the internal demand, productive factors, or institutions which the backward country lacks. Thus in Russia the state was a 'substitute' for the entrepreneurial and financial facilities found in the less backward areas. Through the process of substitution, and by developing later, the less developed country could benefit from the 'advantages of backwardness', such as the adoption of the most advanced branches of industry with the latest technology.

Throughout Gerschenkron's writings Tsarist Russia stands as the prime example of the late industrializing backward country, while at the other extreme England was the relatively advanced early industrializer. Thus England's Industrial Revolution was characterized by a slow 'spurt', a concentration on small-scale competitive consumer goods industries, and with individual enterprises rather than banks or the state providing the bulk of industrial finance. Between the two extremes come the 'moderately backward' countries France and Germany, where the activities of investment banks play a crucial role in industrialization and where heavy industries played a larger role in the industrial spurt than they did in England.

The significance of Gerschenkron's scheme rests on several factors. Perhaps most fundamentally Gerschenkron opened up new avenues of historical enquiry by establishing a framework of analysis of differences rather than similarities in the process of modernization. In this way his concept of historical change differed both from Marxian and from other 'stage' theories such as Rostow's. By concentrating on sectoral industrial change rather than on aggregate national accounts Gerschenkron emphasized variables for which more data are available, and this has encouraged the application of statistical techniques to the study of economic history.

As mentioned already, Gerschenkron's major discussions and utilization of the concept of relative backwardness appear in his writings on Russia. He had also applied the concept to a number of individual case-studies which demonstrate how useful the hypothesis may be, even when historical reality does not conform to prior expectations. Of particular note are his studies of industrialization in Italy, Bulgaria, and Austria. For Italy Gerschenkron argued that the rate of industrial growth during the spurt after 1896 was less than might have been anticipated from the initial level of backwardness. The slower pace was due in part to inadequate support from investment banks and the state, and in part because the main burst of railway construction (which might have given impetus to the spurt) had occurred earlier. In Bulgaria, too, the state failed to provide an effective substitute for the lack of internal demand, entrepreneurship, and financial institutions. Austria, argued Gerschenkron, had indeed the potential for a successful industrial spurt in the early years of the 20th century. The problem here was that, in contrast to Witte's Russia, the state

was divided against itself: the Ministry of Finance obstructed the efforts of Prime Minister Koerber to introduce schemes for promoting large-scale industry, and, as in Italy, there had already been some measure of modern industrialization before the spurt.

These case studies are useful for the insights they provide into the process of industrialization even where the pattern suggested by Gerschenkron's scheme fails to materialize fully. Another brilliant application of the concept of relative backwardness was provided in Gerschenkron's 1970 study of European mercantilism, showing how the most backward countries around the beginning of the 18th century were those where mercantilist policies were most fully developed and applied.

Gerschenkron's hypothesis has come under critical scrutiny from several quarters. Some suggest that the concept of relative backwardness itself is too general and vague to be measured and tested in a meaningful way, although Sandberg has endeavoured to refine the concept by separating those countries backward through 'poverty' and those backward through 'ignorance' (a low level of educational attainment). Barsby has pointed out that several of Gerschenkron's key suggestions, such as the greater role of the state and of modern large-scale heavy industry in the industrial spurts of backward countries, are empirically difficult to determine; while Good has shown that the role of banking in European industrialization does not always conform to the Gerschenkronian pattern. Challenges, too, have come from historians of Russia. The roles played by the state, banks and agriculture in Russian industrialization suggested by Gerschenkron have been called into question (by Gregory and Crisp among others), while the suggested convergence of the Russian pattern towards that exhibited by less backward nations has also been denied. It has been noted, too, that Gerschenkron's hypothesis makes the nation-state rather than the region the unit of economic analysis, while other critics argue that Gerschenkron ignores such influences as military expenditure and the particular conjunction of railway and iron and steel development which influenced European growth rates at the close of the 19th century.

Literature specifically concerned with Gerschenkron's hypothesis, however, whether critical or otherwise, is an inadequate guide to the influence of the concept of relative backwardness on historiography. Gerschenkron's approach has proved both fruitful and enduring. Following Rosovsky's pioneering attempt to apply the concept to Japan, a number of studies have used the hypothesis of relative backwardness to analyse growth patterns in Africa, Asia, and elsewhere. Evidently, the approach will have widespread application far beyond the temporal and geographical limits set by Gerschenkron himself. Indeed, Gerschenkron's outstanding intellectual legacy may well lie not so much in his own studies of 19th-century European industrialization, which are increasingly subject to criticism and reinterpretation, but in the development of a major heuristic framework which will continue to provide insights into patterns of economic development across a wide spectrum of societies and time periods.

M. Falkus

See also catching-up; cumulative causation; development economics; gerschenkron, alexander; industrial revolution; periphery.

BIBLIOGRAPHY
Barsby, S.L. 1969. Economic backwardness and the characteristics of development. *Journal of Economic History* 29(3), September, 449–72.

Cameron, R. 1972. *Banking and Economic Development: Some Lessons of History*. New York: Oxford University Press.

Crisp, O. 1976. *Studies in the Russian Economy before 1914*. London: Macmillan.

Gerschenkron, A. 1952. Economic backwardness in historical perspective. In Gerschenkron (1962a).

Gerschenkron, A. 1955. Notes on the rate of industrial growth in Italy, 1881–1913. In Gerschenkron (1962a).

Gerschenkron, A. 1962a. *Economic Backwardness in Historical Perspective*. Cambridge, Mass.: Harvard University Press.

Gerschenkron, A. 1962b. Problems and patterns and Russian economic development. In Gerschenkron (1962a).

Gerschenkron, A. 1962c. Some aspects of industrialization in Bulgaria, 1878–1939. In Gerschenkron (1962a).

Gerschenkron, A. 1967. The discipline and I. *Journal of Economic History* 27(4), 443–59.

Gerschenkron, A. 1968. *Continuity in History and Other Essays*. Cambridge, Mass.: Harvard University Press.

Gerschenkron, A. 1970. *Europe in the Russian Mirror: Four Lectures in Economic History*. Cambridge: Cambridge University Press.

Gerschenkron, A. 1977. *An Economic Spurt that Failed: Four Lectures in Austrian History*. Princeton: Princeton University Press.

Good, D.F. 1973. Backwardness and the role of banking in nineteenth century European industrialisation. *Journal of Economic History* 33(4), December, 845–50.

Gregory, P. 1973–4. Some empirical comments on the theory of relative backwardness: the Russian case. *Economic Development and Cultural Change* 22(4), July, 654–65.

Rosovsky, H. 1961. *Capital Formation in Japan, 1868–1940*. New York: The Free Press.

Sandberg, L. 1982. Ignorance, poverty and economic backwardness in the early stages of European industrialisation: variations on Alexander Gerschenkron's grand theme. *Journal of European Economic History* 11(3), 675–98.

Bagehot, Walter (1826–1877).   Editor and literary critic as well as banker and economist, Bagehot was described in retrospect by Lord Bryce as 'the most original mind of his generation' (Buchan, 1959, p. 260). It is a difficult claim to sustain, certainly as far as his scattered economic writings are concerned. There was no doubt, however, about his intellectual versatility: there was an immediacy, a clarity and an irony – what he said of his friend Arthur Hugh Clough's poems, 'a sort of truthful scepticism' – about Bagehot's essays in different fields which make them still pre-eminently readable. Bagehot saw connections, too, between economics, politics, psychology, anthropology and the natural sciences – 'mind and character' – refusing to draw rigid boundaries between most of these subjects and 'literary studies', while recognizing in his later years that the frontiers of political economy needed to be more carefully marked. 'Most original' or not, he was, as the historian G.M. Young has observed, *Victoranum maxime*, if not *Victoranum maximus*: 'he was in and of his age, and could have been of no other.' He pre-dated academic specialization and professionalization, and he was never didactic in his approach.

His first writing on economics, a revealing if not a searching review of John Stuart Mill's *Principles of Political Economy*, appeared in 1848 before the sense of a Victorian age had taken shape. His last and most voluminous writing on the subject appeared posthumously in a volume of essays, the first on 'the postulates of English political economy', which his editor-friend Richard Holt Hutton entitled *Economic Studies* (1879). By then the economic confidence of the mid-Victorian years was over, and there were many signs both of economic and social strain, some of which Bagehot had predicted. It was in 1859, the *annus mirabilis* of mid-Victorian England, however, the year of Darwin's *Origin of Species*, Mill's *On Liberty* and

Smiles's *Self Help*, that Bagehot became editor of *The Economist*, a periodical founded by his father-in-law James Wilson, and it was through his lively editorship, which continued until his death, that he was in regular touch with an interesting and influential, if limited, section of his contemporaries. 'The politics of the paper', he wrote simply, 'must be viewed mainly with reference to the tastes of men of business.'

The mid-Victorian years constituted, in his own phrase, 'a period singularly remarkable for its material progress, and almost marvellous in its banking development'. It was the latter aspect of the period which provided him with the theme of his best-known and brilliantly written book *Lombard Street*, which was begun in 1870 and appeared in 1873. It dealt, however, as it was bound to do, not only with the 'marvellous development', but with the 'panics' of 1857 and 1866 to which the Bank of England, the central institution in the system, had to respond. Indeed, the germ of *Lombard Street* was an article written in *The Economist* in 1857, thirteen years after Peel's Bank Charter Act, and it was in 1866 that he took up the theme again.

Bagehot's conviction that the Bank of England neither fully understood nor fully lived up to its responsibilities was the product of years of experience which went back to his own early life between 1852 and 1859 as a country banker with Stuckey's at Langport, his birthplace, in the West of England, where his father also was a banker. The chapter on deposit banking reflects this. So, too, does his complaint that the Directors of the Bank of England were 'amateurs', and his insistence that the 'trained banking element' needed to be augmented.

Lombard Street is a book with a distinctive purpose rather than an essay in applied economics; and, as Schumpeter has observed, 'it does not contain anything that should have been new to any student of economics'. The main stress in it is on confidence as a necessary foundation of London's banking system. 'Credit – the disposition of one man to trust another – is singularly varying. In England after a great calamity, everybody is suspicious of everybody; as soon as that calamity is forgotten everybody again confides in everybody'. Bagehot underestimated the extent to which through joint stock banks' cheques trade was expanding without increases in note issue and the extent to which the Bank of England itself was beginning to develop techniques of influencing interest rates. He also overestimated the extent to which in 'rapidly growing districts' of the country 'almost any amount of money can be well employed'. In the last resort, too, his policy recommendations were deliberately restricted. He was disposed in principle to a 'natural system' in which each bank kept its own reserves of gold and legal tender, but in English circumstances he saw no more future in seeking to change the system fundamentally than in changing the political system. 'I propose to retain this system because I am quite sure that it is of no manner of use proposing to alter it'. With a characteristic glance across the Channel to France for a necessary comparison – things were done very differently there – he noted how the English system had 'slowly grown up' because it had 'suited itself to the course of business' and 'forced itself on the habits of men'. It would not be altered, therefore, 'because theorists disapprove of it, or because books are written against it'.

Bagehot had little use for 'theorists' and disdained the French for what he called their 'morbid appetite for exhaustive and original theories'. He described political economy 'as we have it in England' as 'the science of business' and did not object to the fact that it was 'insular'. Yet he talked of the 'laws of wealth' and believed that they had been arrived at in the same way as the 'laws of motion'. Free trade was such a law. It was impossible, he argued, to write the history of 'similar phenomena like those of Lombard Street' without 'a considerable accumulation of applicable doctrine': to do so would be like 'trying to explain the bursting of a boiler without knowing the theory of steam', a not very helpful analogy since the invention of the steam engine preceded the discovery of the laws of thermodynamics. Bagehot relied considerably on analogies. 'Panics', for example, were 'a species of neuralgia'. The 'unconscious "organization of capital" ' in the City of London, described by Bagehot as a 'continental phrase', depended on the entry into City business of a 'dirty crowd of little men'; and this 'rough and vulgar structure of English commerce' was 'the secret of its life' because it contained 'the propensity to variation' which was 'the principle of progress' in the 'social as in the animal kingdom'.

Such an approach to political economy was radically different from that of W.S. Jevons who, like Bagehot, had been educated at University College, London, or 'M. Walras, of Lausanne' who, according to Bagehot himself, had worked out 'a mathematical theory' of political economy 'without communication and almost simultaneously'. There were however three defects, Bagehot maintained, in the British tradition of political economy, which started with Adam Smith but was sharpened and 'mapped' by David Ricardo. First, it was too culture-bound; for example, it took for granted the free circulation of labour, unknown in India. Second, its expositors did not always make it clear that they were dealing not with real men but with 'imaginary' ones. Abstract political economy did not focus on 'the entire man as we know him in fact, but ... a man answering to pure definition from which all impairing and conflicting elements have been fined away'. It was not concerned with 'middle principles'. Third, considered as a body of knowledge, English political economy was 'not a questionable thing of unlimited extent but a most certain and useful thing of limited extent'. It was certainly not 'the highest study of the mind'. There were others 'which are much higher'.

Bagehot did not push such criticism far. He had much to say about primitive and pre-commercial economies, but he put forward no theory of economic development. Nor, despite an interest in methodology, did he draw out the full implications of his own behaviourist (and in places institutionalist) approach to economics. Finally, he offered no agenda for political economists in the future. He noted, as others noted, that during the 1870s political economy lay 'rather dead in the public mind. Not only does it not excite the same interest as it did formerly, but there is not exactly the same confidence in it.' His own precoccupations in that decade were more practical than theoretical despite the writing of such essays as 'The Postulates of English Political Economy', which first appeared in article form in the Fortnightly in 1876. He never completed a new essay on Mill, and an essay on Malthus, whom he took along with Smith, Ricardo and Mill to be the founders of British political economy, revealed more interest in the man than in his thought. In the year when the 'postulates' appeared, he successfully suggested to the Chancellor of the Exchequer the value to the Treasury of short-term securities resembling as much as possible commercial bills of exchange. The result was the Treasury Bill. The fact that the Chancellor was then a Conservative mattered little to the liberal-conservative Bagehot, who was described by his Liberal admirer W.E. Gladstone as a 'sort of supplementary Chancellor of the Exchequer'.

Bagehot was as out of sympathy with the liberal radicals of the 1870s as he was with the bimetallists, and he had never shown any sympathy for socialist political economy. He saw the capitalist as 'the motive power in modern production' in the 'great commerce', the man who settled 'what goods shall be made, and what not'. Nonetheless, he stated explicitly in several places that he had 'no objection whatever to the aspiration of the workmen for more wages', and he came to appreciate more willingly than Jevons the role of trade unions and collective bargaining. In his first review of Mill in 1848 he had stated that 'the great problem for European and especially for English statesmen in the nineteenth century is how shall the [wage] rate be raised and how shall the lower orders be improved'. Some of the views he expressed on this subject – and on expectations – were not dissimilar to those of the neoclassical Alfred Marshall. He did not use the term 'classical' himself in charting the evolution of British political economy.

Bagehot left no school of disciples. He was content to persuade his contemporaries. His sinuous prose style was supremely persuasive. So, too, was his skill in sifting and assessing inside economic intelligence. Yet while he devoted little attention to precise quantitative evidence in Lombard Street and, unlike Jevons, saw little point in developing economics in mathematical form, he was always interested in numbers as well as in words. One of his closest collaborators on the staff of The Economist, the statistician Robert Giffen, his first full-time assistant, paid tribute to 'his knowledge and feeling of the "how much" in dealing with the complex workings of economic tendencies'. 'He knew what tables could be made to say, and the value of simplicity in their construction.' Bagehot always maintained, however, that while 'theorists take a table of prices as facts settled by unalterable laws, a stockbroker will tell you such prices can be made'. Statistics were 'useful': they needed to be interpreted by 'men of business' who possessed the grasp of 'probabilities' and the 'solid judgement' which Bagehot most admired and which he sought to express. Indeed, business for him was 'really a profession often requiring for its practice quite as much knowledge, and quite as much skill, as law and medicine'. Businessmen did not go to political economy: political economy, as in the case of Ricardo, came to them.

ASA BRIGGS

SELECTED WORKS
All Bagehot's economic writings are collected in N. St. John Stevas (ed.), The Collected Works of Walter Bagehot, vols I–XV (1978–86), London: The Economist.

BIBLIOGRAPHY
Buchan, A. 1959. The Spare Chancellor. The Life of Walter Bagehot. London: Chatto & Windus.
Giffen, R. 1880. Bagehot as an economist. The Fortnightly, April.
Young, G.M. 1948. The greatest Victorian. In G.M. Young, Today and Yesterday, London: Rupert Hart-Davis.

Bailey, Samuel (1791–1870). Samuel Bailey was born in Sheffield, England, one of eleven children. His father was a cutler and merchant of substance. Samuel also became a merchant and banker. Throughout his life, he served on the Sheffield Town Trust (a quasi-governmental agency) and was twice a candidate for Parliament in the Reform elections of 1832 and 1835. Writing widely on banking, politics and philosophy, he lived his entire life in Sheffield, unmarried, and died there in 1870.

Bailey published his principal economic work, A Critical Dissertation..., in 1825, a time when Ricardian theory was nearing its peak of popularity and acceptance. The Westminster Review (1826) thought the Critical Dissertation inconsequential, and J.R. McCulloch (1845) later claimed that it had not shaken the foundations of Ricardo's labour theory of value. Robert Torrens, however, praised Bailey's book in 1831 at the London Political Economy Club, and John Stuart Mill brought it before his bi-weekly reading group. This attention, nevertheless, did not keep Bailey on front stage, and he had to be rediscovered later by E.R.A. Seligman (1905); the London School of Economics republished the *Critical Dissertation* in 1931. Schumpeter (1954) judged Bailey's tract to be a 'masterpiece of criticism' and to lie near the 'front rank in the history of scientific economics'. R.M. Rauner (1961) re-examined Bailey's work from a larger perspective.

The centrepiece of Bailey's argument was his definition of value as ultimately 'esteem' or a 'mental affection'. The 'specific feeling of value', however, arose only when items were subject to preference or exchange. This defined value as relative, not something intrinsic like labour in Ricardo's theory. Value is the amount of one commodity exchanged for another; it is measured in terms of a third commodity with which the two exchange if they are not directly bartered. From this position Bailey attacked Ricardo's postulate that labour effort defined value. He showed that despite Ricardo's claim to the contrary, constancy of labour used in production could not assure constancy in exchange value – unless value were defined differently. This, of course, is what Ricardo had done in shifting from exchange to 'real' or 'absolute' value.

Ricardo's conception of value as an absolute and his endless search for a standard of invariable value opened him to Bailey's stricture that constancy of value meant constancy in exchange ratios. Evidence and observation showed that exchange values rarely stayed constant. To the Ricardians, however, constancy of value meant constancy of labour cost of production; this, they believed, was necessary in the determination of whether individual economic welfare had changed over time. Bailey objected that exchange of commodities cannot take place between two different time periods. Exchanges occur at different times and these exchanges can be compared. But such comparisons are the only way economic welfare in different times or places can be assessed. In a later tract (1844), Bailey used this same argument, making the point that interperiod contracts could be fixed only in terms of quantities, not constancy of values. This enabled him to oppose the index number proposals (then called 'tabular standards') of Joseph Lowe and Poulett Scrope. Such standards could not assure constancy of quantities exchanged in different times, a criticism of index numbers that is still valid today.

Using relative value as his anchor, Bailey then demonstrated that Ricardo's theory of wages was faulty. He insisted that labour value – wages – was definitionally the same as all other value, namely, what a unit of labour exchanged for. Ricardo's theorem, that wages and profits varied inversely, was wrong since it implied that wages could be high (i.e. taking a large proportionate share of production) while labour value was low, wages exchanged for little and workers were near starvation.

The relative value concept applied to wages allowed Bailey an easy application of the principles of rent to labour. Just as with land, different values for labour were caused by the monopoly characteristics of labour supply, as well as by differential productivity due to varying labour skill or dexterity. This contrasted sharply with Ricardian–Malthusian subsistence wages. Unfortunately, Bailey did not use the same reasoning against capital and merely denoted profits as the gain over capital employed.

The *Critical Dissertation* prompted some serious attempts to

clear up the loose ends in Ricardo, most notably by McCulloch (1845); by the anonymous *Westminster Review* article (1826), probably written by James Mill (1826); and by Thomas DeQuincey (1844). But Ricardo's *system* held fast. Malthus (1827) devoted the largest part of his work on definitions to Bailey, mainly quarrelling over the purely relative value notion. He reaffirmed the importance of a constant, unvarying measure of value, defined as the quantity of labour commanded by commodities in exchange. Samuel Read (1829) drew on Bailey's destruction of the Mill–McCulloch theory that time used in production is congealed labour, but he did not follow Bailey on the relativity of value or the measure of value. C.F. Cotterill (1831) and H.D. Macleod (1863, 1866) both praised Bailey's work and used his treatment of the nature and measure of value in their own studies.

From a larger perspective, by stressing relative value exclusively, Bailey pulled economic analysis back from the Smith–Ricardo stream that sought a principal cause of value to explain the production and distribution of material wealth among the labouring, rentier and capitalist classes. In Bailey's argument relative values – prices – vary for all kinds of reasons affecting demand ('esteem') and supply (production under constant or increasing cost, supply-limiting) conditions. Hence, his view involves no notion of long-run growth, tendencies toward equilibrium, stationary states or other systemic visions. Everything is relative; individual economic welfare is expressed period-by-period solely in terms of relative values.

Bailey's is an incomplete treatment if one demands that value theory be integral with the determination of social, institutional and economic forces in an interdependent production system. On the other hand, Bailey's work freed analysis from the need to link production and distribution to socioeconomic class relationships. It pointed instead towards relationships between individual needs and perceptions, and the material goods that can satisfy them.

R.M. RAUNER

SELECTED WORKS

1821. *Essays on the Formation and Publication of Opinions and Other Subjects*. London.
1823. *Questions on Political Economy, Politics, Metaphysics, Polite Literature and Other Branches of Knowledge*. London.
1825. *A Critical Dissertation on the Nature, Measures and Causes of Value; chiefly in reference to the writings of Mr Ricardo and his followers*. London.
1826. *A Letter to a Political Economist; occasioned by an article in the Westminster Review on the subject of Value*. London.
1830. *A Discussion of Parliamentary Reform*. London.
1835. *The Rationale of Political Representation*. London.
1837. *Money and Its Vicissitudes in Value; as they affect National Industry and Pecuniary Contracts; with a Postscript on Joint-Stock Banks*. London.

BIBLIOGRAPHY

[Anon.] 1826. Letter to a Political Economist. *Westminister Review*, January.
Cotterill, C.F. 1826. *An Examination of the Doctrines of Value as set forth by Adam Smith, Ricardo, McCulloch, the Author of 'A Critical Dissertation', etc., Torrens, Malthus, Say, etc., being a reply to those distinguished authors*. London.
DeQuincey, T. 1844. *The Logic of Political Economy*. Edinburgh.
McCulloch, J.R. 1825. *Principles of Political Economy*. London.
McCulloch, J.R. 1845. *The Literature of Political Economy*. London.
Macleod, H.D. 1863. *A Dictionary of Political Economy*. London.
Macleod, H.D. 1866. *The Theory and Practice of Banking*. 2nd edn, London.
Malthus, T.R. 1827. *Definitions in Political Economy*. London.

Mill, J. 1826. *Elements of Political Economy*. 3rd edn, London.
Rauner, R.M. 1961. *Samuel Bailey and the Classical Theory of Value*. London: London School of Economics and Political Science, G. Bell & Sons.
Read, S. 1829. *An Inquiry into the Natural Grounds of Right to Vendible Property or Wealth*. Edinburgh.
Schumpeter, J.A. 1954. *History of Economic Analysis*. New York: Oxford University Press
Seligman, E.R.A. 1903. On some neglected British economists. *Economic Journal* 13, 335-63, 511-35.

Bain, Joe Staten (born 1912).   Joe S. Bain was born in Spokane, Washington, on 4 July 1912. After graduating from the University of California at Los Angeles in 1935 and gaining the doctorate from Harvard in 1940 (under Joseph Schumpeter), he spent his entire career at the University of California at Berkeley. He was appointed Distinguished Fellow of the American Economic Association in 1982.

A prolific and seminal writer, Bain helped to shape the field of industrial organization in its modern form, with special attention to market structure. Bain's analysis focused on the oligopoly group within an industry, and on barriers to new competition. He also worked on natural resource development by public enterprise, concentrating on the oil industry.

Bain's empirical work on economies of scale, entry barriers, and limit pricing broke new ground. He developed the field's intellectual format, in which technical factors may determine structure, and structure then influences behaviour and performance. Some of these concepts were already current as early as 1900. During 1925–40, as the field took shape, attention shifted to the industry and the oligopoly group within it.

In the 1930s, Bain entered a formative field which was rich in possibilities for giving new rigour to older concepts, for developing new ones, and for shaping the framework. That has been his main role and contribution. Though he did not create concepts, nor indeed the framework, he selected from among them and carried their scientific analysis further than anyone else.

The analysis grew after 1940 in a series of articles and chapters, culminating in *Barriers to New Competition* in 1956 and *Industrial Organization* in 1959. His analysis was verbal and graphical rather than mathematical. In Bain's analysis of the conditions of entry, the barriers have three possible economic sources; absolute cost advantages, product differentiation and size. Barriers then permit 'limit pricing' by a firm or firms which consciously apply their strategy toward entry.

Bain drew the main conclusions, and he noted the difficulties of empirical tests. The definition of barriers as a single, general phenomenon posed special problems, which are still unsolved. Since 1960, over seven new barriers 'sources' have been proposed, and the concept of barriers has tended to acquire just that *ad hoc* character which Bain frequently reproved in others' theories.

Measurement has also proven to be difficult. It requires a merging of disparate objective and subjective data about the barriers' causes. Whether these sources of barriers are additive, multiplicative or merely parallel was also left unclear by Bain (and all others).

Bain's measurement of scale economics was pioneering. Earlier studies had suffered from data problems and from a mingling of technical and pecuniary elements. Bain centred unerringly on technical economies. Thereby he gave the first solid normative basis for evaluating excess concentration.

By estimating 'best practice' conditions for scale for new capacity, Bain neatly avoided the normative–positive confusion which infects cross-section studies of past costs and survivor tests of emerging sizes. His 'engineering' estimates supply a normative basis for appraising how much concentration is socially 'necessary'.

Profitability was also analysed closely by Bain. He tried nearly every available method to factor out the concentration–profitability relationship. In a 1949 article (later extended in *Barriers*), Bain put the study of profitability on a firm scientific and normative basis. His findings of a step function, with a break at 70 per cent for eight-firm concentration, has tended to be replaced in recent research by a continuously sloping concentration–profitability relationship. Still, Bain set the basis for all good later research on the subject.

Bain's architectural choices in using and emphasizing individual elements were distinctive. Three features stand out – the triad, the industry basis, and the stress on the oligopoly group behind an entry barrier. (1) Bain developed the three-tier format of structure, behaviour and performance with what may be called a 'soft structuralist' emphasis. Bain used it as a broad set of concepts, by which the whole subject (theory, tests, policy lessons) is organized, not as just a format for individual cases. (2) Bain used the *industry* as the basic unit behaviour. It was a choice that shaped the images and methodology in distinctive ways. (3) The *oligopoly group*, setting limit price strategy behind an entry barrier, came to be the most distinctive part of Bain's analysis. As of 1949–50, Bain regarded concentration as the key determinant of market power and profitability.

By 1951 he appeared to regard barriers as the decisive element, which could be both necessary and sufficient to govern profitability. Yet Bain later suggested frequently that barriers would be highly correlated with the degree of concentration. In fact, all of the sources of barriers are also sources of high market shares and concentration. Do barriers shape the dominant firm's share, or do they operate jointly?

Any eventual resolution of barriers' role will probably assign barriers at least a significant role, thanks to Bain's stress on them. He put the concepts and relationships in testable form, and he began the testing of them. To a large extent he rescued the subject from a preoccupation with oligopoly interactions and games, and he gave it a strong framework.

Yet Bain's most durable contribution lies deeper, in the methods and research standards of the field. By 1960, he had helped to give it structure, precision, and high standards of research quality. He selected the main concepts and relationships, gave them extended analysis, tested them, and drew policy lessons. The individual parts were related within a framework of causation and performance.

His more specific methods and results have also continued to be valid because they met these standards. Beyond the individual concepts and tests is the fact that they fit together in a system, and that this system was carefully developed and tested. That is the way to scientific permanence.

WILLIAM G. SHEPHERD

See also COMPETITION AND EFFICIENCY; CONTESTABLE MARKETS; INDUSTRIAL ORGANIZATION; LIMIT PRICING; MARKET STRUCTURE.

SELECTED WORKS
1944, 1945, 1947. *The Economics of the Pacific Coast Petroleum Industry*. 3 vols, Berkeley: University of California Press.
1948. *Pricing, Distribution and Employment: Economics of an Enterprise System*. New York: Henry Holt; Italian and Spanish translations.

1956. *Barriers to New Competition: Their Character and Consequences in Manufacturing Industries*. Cambridge, Mass.: Harvard University Press.

1959. *Industrial Organization*. New York:Wiley; revised edn, 1968.

1966a. *International Differences in Industrial Structure: Eight Nations in the 1950s*. New Haven: Yale University Press.

1966b. (With R.E. Caves and J. Margolis.) *Northern California's Water Industry: The Comparative Efficiency of Public Enterprise in Developing a Scarce Natural Resource*. Baltimore: Johns Hopkins Press.

1972. *Essays on Price Theory and Industrial Organization*. Boston: Little, Brown & Co.

Bakunin, Mikhael Alexandrovitch (1814–1876). Mikhail Alexandrovitch Bakunin was unique amongst 19th-century revolutionaries. He combined a deep interest in political theory, philosophy and political economy with a love of political action. Not satisfied to merely outline the evils of existing society and draw blue-prints of superior ones, he propagandized, formed political secret societies and supported every political upheaval, large or small, hopeful or doomed to failure, of his era. Alexander Herzen said of him, 'Everything about this man is colossal, his energy, his appetite, yes, even the man himself.'

Bakunin was born in the Novotorschok district of Tver province. From his father he inherited an intellectual interest in the Encyclopédists and the ideas of Jean-Jacques Rousseau; from his pious sisters an interest in the cult of the inner life. At the age of 14 he was sent to the artillery school in St Petersburg but resiled against a military career and began studying Goethe, Schiller and Fichte – and later Hegel. Along with many other Russians of his generation, he was also deeply influenced by his fellow-Russian, Vissarion Belinsky, who preached a love of the poor.

After a period in Berlin, Dresden and various Swiss cities he moved to Paris in 1844, where he became acquainted with the French Socialists and various Russian exiles. At this time he was particularly influenced by Proudhon. As a result of Bakunin's calls for a revolution in his homeland and the establishment of a republican federation of all Slavic countries, Nicholas I issued a decree depriving him of all his civil, property and nobility rights and sentencing him to lifelong exile in Siberia should he ever return to Russia. Arrested in 1849 during the Dresden Revolution, he was sentenced to death, chained to a wall for a over a year, then returned to St Petersburg where he was kept in solitary confinement. Here he was pressured to write his famous *Confession*, on the insistence of the tsar. In 1857, when he was in bad health and close to suicide, his family succeeded in having him exiled to Siberia, from which he escaped by sailing down the Amur River. Over the next few years, he toured Europe and set up a secret *Fraternité Internationale* of like-minded revolutionaries. His last years were spent in destitution and ill health. Friends reported that his various imprisonments had taken a savage toll on his health. He died in Berne at the age of sixty-two.

Bakunin stood at the cross-roads of several intellectual currents. He was influenced by Slavophilism, Hegelianism, Marxism and Proudhonism. His impact on anarchism was two-tiered. He turned anarchism from a theory of political speculation into a theory of political action. Although he never joined any of the nihilist – 'propaganda by needs' – action groups in Russia or elsewhere, he provided great inspiration for those who did. His writings lacked the ponderous speculation of fellow anarchists such as Godwin, Proudhon or Stirner. They were appeals for action. Hence his most famous 1842 maxim: 'Let us have confidence in the eternal spirit which destroys and annihilates only because it is the unfathomable and eternally creative urge. The urge of destruction is at the same time a creative urge.'

Bakunin also turned anarchism from merely a philosophical position for radical sections of the petty bourgeoisie to a political philosophy which sought mass support from wage earners and the lumpenproletariat, even though its central cadres still tended to come from the intelligentsia. He was a vital influence behind the emergence of organized anarchist movements in Italy, France and Spain in particular in the three decades before World War I.

Bakunin's voluminous writings – Maximoff (1953) provides a good selection – have received little attention for three main reasons. The first is their fragmentary and issue- and incident-orientated style. The second is his identification with violence. To those unfamiliar with the richness of the anarchist intellectual tradition, Bakunin was far too easily equated with criminals and lunatics. The third reason is his conflict with Marx over the organization and aims of the First International. Marx won this battle but the battle of the giants destroyed the organization. Ever since, Marxist historians and others have done their best to either grossly distort Bakunin's role and position or banish him to historical oblivion, even though his writings deeply influenced both Marx and Lenin. (Bakunin also translated Marx's *Das Kapital* into Russian.)

E.H. Carr's bulky *Michael Bakunin* (1937) devotes litte attention to his ideas but does provide a detailed account of the First International battle. However, the work that is considered Bakunin's best and most mature, *Statism and Anarchism*, is not even mentioned. George H. Sabine's *History of Political Theory* gives him only a passing reference. The best short biography is that by Max Nettlau in Maximoff (1953). Many would consider Sir Isaiah Berlin's assessment of Bakunin – 'He has not bequeathed a single idea worth considering for its own sake; there is not a fresh thought, not even an authentic emotion, only amusing diatribes, high spirits, malicious vignettes, and a memorable epigram or two' (1978, p. 113) – too harsh.

In the history of political theory he remains an enigma. Despite his great emphasis on individual liberty, he believed he had founded a political philosophy to end all political philosophies and demanded unswerving allegiance from his followers. Bakunin will be long remembered for highlighting the greatest political dilemma of our age – how to achieve maximum individual liberty without resort to authoritarian methods and forms of social organization.

DAVID CLARK

See also ANARCHISM.

SELECTED WORKS

A complete edition of Bakunin's works has never been published, although a five-volume Russian edition was published by Golas Truda (Moscow and Petrograd, 1919–1922); a three-volume German edition by Verlag der Syndikalist, Berlin, 1921–240; and a six-volume French edition by P.V. Stock, 1895–1913). His *Statism and Anarchism* and *Confessions of a Revolutionary* have been published in many languages. See also A. Lehning (ed.), *Archives Bakounine*, Leiden, 1967.

BIBLIOGRAPHY

Berlin, I. 1978. *Russian Thinkers*. Ed. H. Hardy and A. Kelly, Harmondsworth: Penguin Books.

Carr, E.H. 1937. *Michael Bakunin*. London: Macmillan.

Maximoff, G.P. (ed.) 1953. *The Political Philosophy of Bakunin: Scientific Anarchism*. London: Collier Macmillan.

balanced budget multiplier. The balanced budget multiplier theorem is concerned with changes in aggregate demand consequent on simultaneous and equal changes in government expenditure and taxation. The essence of the theorem is that the expansionary effect of the former exceeds the contractionary effects of the latter. Thus the net effect is positive rather than zero which the commonsense of pre-Keynesian economics suggested. In other words, a tax-financed increase in public expenditure would be expansionary rather than neutral.

The theorem in its original form had a further remarkable characteristic. It was proved that the value of the balanced budget multiplier was not merely positive, but was precisely equal to unity. This appeared to be a rare example within economics of something rather less rare in natural science, namely the possibility of deriving a precise empirical magnitude from theoretical reasoning. Merely postulating, within the closed economy, a marginal propensity to consume and a marginal tax rate, both between zero and unity, led to a balanced budget multiplier of one.

The point may be seen most clearly by examining the multiplier in its form as an infinite series. The effect on aggregate demand of a unit increase in government expenditure on domestically produced goods and services is given by the series:

$$1 + c + c^2 + \cdots$$

The effect of a unit increase in income tax revenue is given by the series:

$$c + c^2 + \cdots$$

(where c in both cases is the marginal propensity to consume).

If the latter is deducted from the former, a value of unity follows for the net effect on aggregate demand.

It can be shown that if the increase in tax occurs because of an increase in the marginal tax rate, the same result follows. In addition, if imports are a function of consumption so that c is interpreted as the marginal propensity to consume domestically produced goods and services, once again the balanced budget multiplier is unity.

This, of course, immediately allows the examination of cases in which the balanced budget multiplier is positive but different from one, and even cases in which it is negative. Consider, for example, a unit increase in government expenditure, only a fraction b of which is spent on domestically produced goods and services, the remainder going on imports. The initial sequence above will then be multiplied by a number b lying between zero and one. In that sequence c will be the propensity to spend on domestic output (i.e., it is net of imports). Consider also an increase in taxation levied initially on households who spend on domestically produced goods and services a different fraction of the change in their income from the community at large. The second sequence above can then be rewritten as follows:

$$c' + c'c + c'c^2$$

where c' differs from c and is the initial decline in consumption.

The net effect on aggregate income will then be $(b - c')(1 + c + c^2 + \cdots)$. This equals $(b - c')/(1 - c)$. It is obvious that if c' is greater than b, the balanced budget multiplier is negative. If c' is sufficiently smaller than c, the balanced budget multiplier will be greater than unity.

Also, of course, the multiplier will change in value if the spending propensities relevant to the later stages of the government expenditure sequence are not the same as those in the tax sequence.

The matter may be complicated further by considering various forms of taxation. The impact effect of a unit increase

in income taxation is assumed to be c. The impact effect of a unit increase in indirect taxation is assumed to be unity – that is, a switch to indirect taxation leaving total tax revenue constant is contractionary. The impact effect of a unit increase in corporate taxation will, presumably, be on investment rather than consumption spending, unless it is passed on to households in higher prices.

All of this may be summarized by noting (i) that government expenditure may be on transfer payments or on goods and services; (ii) that the part devoted to goods and services may be further subdivided into that obtained from domestic production and that from abroad; (iii) that the tax effects depend on the nature of the taxes being levied; (iv) that the initial impact on aggregate demand of a tax increase depends on who it is levied on, relevant distinctions being between firms and households, and different types of households; and (v) that different categories of tax payers have different propensities to import. It follows that a tax-financed increase in government expenditure cannot be predicted without detailed consideration of the nature of the expenditure and the taxation. What is important, however, is that there is no presumption that a balanced budget is neutral with respect to aggregate demand. This itself is another way of putting the fundamental theorem of fiscal policy: fiscal stance is not measured correctly by the difference between public expenditure and tax revenue.

The history of the balanced budget multiplier is of some interest. The theorem was originally attributed to Haavelmo (1945). It is apparent that a prior claim to publication must go to Gelting (1941). An important early contribution was that of Wallich (1944). (Others have claimed to have known of the theorem and even to have written it down without publishing it, but that is not at all the same thing.) Important generalizations are attributable to Turvey (1953), and Peston and Baumol (1955).

M.H. PESTON

See also MULTIPLIER ANALYSIS.

BIBLIOGRAPHY

Gelting, J. 1941. Nogle Bemaerkninger om Finansieringen af offentlig Virksomhed. *Nationalökonomisk Tidsskrift* 79(5), 293–9.

Haavelmo, T. 1945. Multiplier effects of a balanced budget. *Econometrica* 13, October, 311–18.

Peston, M.H. and Baumol, W.J. 1955. More on the multiplier effects of a balanced budget. *American Economic Review* 45, March, 140–48.

Turvey, R. 1953. Some notes on multiplier theory. *American Economic Review* 43, June, 275–95.

Wallich, H.C. 1944. Income-generating effects of a balanced budget. *Quarterly Journal of Economics* 59, November, 78–91.

balanced growth. The idea of balanced growth can be traced back to John Stuart Mill's qualified restatement of Say's Law: 'Every increase in production, *if distributed without miscalculation among all kinds of produce in the proportions which private interest would dictate*, creates ... its own demand' (Mill, 1844). Say had the insight that all productive activity creates demand along with supply, and Mill added his no less important caveat that while production creates *specific* supplies, and investment creates *specific* productive capacities, the income they generate creates *general* demand, which then is distributed over many goods. Accordingly, for the structure of additional productive capacities to match the structure of additional demand, investment would have to proceed simultaneously in the economy's various sectors and industries in the same proportions in which the buying public apportions the expenditure of its additional income among the outputs of those sectors and industries. That implies a faster growth of sectors and industries for whose output the income elasticities of demand are high and a simultaneous but slower growth of those for whose products income elasticities of demand are low. Such is the meaning of balanced growth. A simplified version of balanced growth, *proportional* growth of all outputs, recurs in John von Neumann's celebrated growth model (Von Neumann, 1945).

On its customary nationalistic interpretation, the argument for balanced growth calls for inward-looking development policies: investment in productive capacities to match the expansion of *domestic* demand. It then conflicts with Ricardo's doctrine of comparative advantage, which says that rather than produce everything at home, each country does better if it specializes on the goods it is best at producing and trades its excess output of them for imports of those commodities in whose production it would have a comparative disadvantage. Moreover, the argument for nationally balanced growth also conflicts with the argument for exploiting economies of scale, whenever a country's domestic market for a particular good is too small to absorb the minimum output that is economical to produce. For in such cases, it is cheaper either to import that good from high-volume low-cost producers abroad, or to produce it at home on a large enough scale to render its cost competitive in world markets and export the surplus.

To resolve those conflicts, growth would have to be balanced, not on a national but on a world scale. Each country would then specialize in areas where its comparative advantage and economies of scale are the greatest, but they would have to keep their borders open to trade and let market forces assure the balanced growth of the world economy as a whole, in the sense of balancing each country's lopsided growth against the complementary lack of balance in the rest of world's growth. For example, the fast expansion of Great Britain's economy during her industrial revolution consisted in unbalanced growth in the direction of her comparative advantage to a degree that greatly increased her dependence on imports of food and primary products and her need of foreign markets for her exports with which to pay for those imports. To make that work, however, the developing world (which then was much larger) had to grow in an offsettingly unbalanced fashion by specializing on *its* comparative advantages in agricultural production, and also by growing at a much slower rate, given the much lower income elasticity of demand for food than for industrial products.

All this has long been known and more or less taken for granted by most economists; but the new problems and new thinking of the mid-20th century gave new prominence to the argument for nationally balanced growth. To begin with, the break-up of the colonial empires after World War II created many new, independent countries, all of them poor, undeveloped and anxious not only to grow but to catch up with the advanced industrial countries if possible. That brought the problem of accelerating economic development to centre stage and made the developing countries reluctant to acquiesce in their traditional role of primary producers, which, in a system of universal growth balanced on a worldwide scale, would have kept their growth rates well below those of the advanced countries (owing to the much lower demand elasticities for their exports), thereby further widening the gap between rich and poor countries.

Secondly, the Keynesian revolution stressed the importance of effective demand, and that, in the development context, was translated into a new emphasis on matching the structure of

supply to the structure of demand. Thirdly, the successful industrialization of Germany and the United States behind the shelter of protective tariffs led to the realization that a country's comparative disadvantage in some sectors is seldom unalterable but usually something that can be remedied through learning by doing; and that realization in turn greatly diminished the importance attached to the conflict between the doctrines of comparative advantage and nationally balanced growth. Finally, the dismal economic performance and protectionist stance of the industrial countries during the great depression of the 1930s led many economists, including some of the most distinguished and influential among them, to believe that, even apart from the argument of the previous paragraph, the developing countries would be well advised to limit their dependence on trade with the advanced countries and not make their own development contingent on the latter's parallel development.

All the above considerations contributed to making many, perhaps most, development economists advocate that the developing countries go their own separate ways, taking the route either of nationally balanced growth or of growth balanced for the developing world as a group, specializing among themselves in the framework of customs unions. Paul Rosenstein-Rodan was the first to advocate such a course in a celebrated article proposing a Danubian federation (Rosenstein-Rodan, 1943); but the foremost and most influential advocate of balanced growth was Ragnar Nurkse, who put the argument in the following way:

> The case for international specialization ... is as strong as ever, ... but if development through increased exports to the advanced industrial centers is ... retarded or blocked, there arises a possible need for promoting increases in output that are diversified in accordance with domestic income elasticities of demand so as to provide markets for each other locally (Nurkse, 1953).

Widespread agreement on the desirability of matching the structure of output to the structure of domestic demand contrasted with widespread disagreement as to the best way to achieve that goal. Nurkse and some others believed that, in poor countries, the market left to itself perpetuates poverty, because to emerge from it would require investment in increasing productivity, which is impeded not only by the low saving of the poor but even more by the lack of profit incentive to build high-productivity plants when the already existing local market for their output is too small. As a means of escaping that vicious circle of poverty, some favoured the central planning of investment to overcome the lack of private incentive; others (including Nurkse) believed that even indicative planning would provide enough additional incentive, especially when aided by tariff protection, tax concessions or cheap credit.

Albert Hirschman and his followers showed more faith in market forces but stressed the virtual impossibility of balanced growth in the narrow literal sense of the simultaneous establishment of many industries all at the same time. He pointed out (Hirschman, 1958) that most poor countries lack the resources for investing in more than one or very few modern projects at any given time, and therefore can aim at balanced growth only in the long run, through a sequential process of building first one then another plant, with each step correcting the worst imbalance in order to approach a more balanced structure gradually. He called that process 'unbalanced growth' and argued that market forces are likely to aid it, because imbalances create shortages, whose impact on prices render their relief or elimination more profitable. Note that Hirschman's unbalanced growth is the distribution over time of individual investment projects whose cumulative long-run aim and effect is still to balance and keep in balance the structure of domestic productive capacities and outputs.

Although the shortcomings of balanced growth were not forgotten (Scitovsky, 1959), it had become the fashionable doctrine of development economists in the period following World War II. The policy makers of developing countries were influenced by it to the extent of drawing up Three-, Four- or Five-Year Plans to coordinate investment; but they paid more lip service than serious attention to the doctrine of balanced growth. The fashionable policy was import-substituting industrialization, all too often centred on the most highly automated and therefore most prestigious industries. In consequence, the growth of many developing countries not only remained unbalanced but became unbalanced in the wrong direction, in favour of sectors with the country's greatest comparative *dis*advantage. Industry was favoured to the neglect of agriculture; automobiles, large kitchen appliances and petrochemicals were favoured to the neglect of the simpler manufactures and processed foods on which most of the newly generated income of the emerging urban working classes was spent. The unbalanced nature of such development manifested itself in the chronic underutilization of the new modern plants side by side with excess demand for food and its consequences, increasing imports and inflationary pressures. The disappointing record of import-substituting development in many countries led to a gradual shift towards export-led growth, which was equally unbalanced but in favour of industries with a comparative advantage.

Export-led growth therefore was much more successful, especially as long as it was favoured by expanding world trade. Nationally balanced growth continues to remain a theoretical doctrine more than a tried practical policy.

Mention should also be made in this connection of 'harmonic growth', a related but different concept, introduced by Janos Kornai and mainly applied, together with its opposite, 'rushed growth', to the growth policies of socialist countries (Kornai, 1972). Harmonic growth is a planner's value judgement of what list of things and in what proportions a country's growth policy ought to encompass. One of its elements, the balanced satisfaction of all the needs of the consuming public, corresponds to balanced growth; but most of its other elements go beyond a concern with market goods alone and call for such things as a parallel growth of public and private goods, an increase in leisure along with the increased availability of goods, an equitable distribution of income, a steady rate of growth over time, and the free unfolding of talents, which implies adequate and equal access to education, full employment and matching the training of specialists to the economy's demand for them. The opposite of harmonic growth, rushed growth, is the neglect or sacrifice of some of those or similar elements for the sake of the faster growth of the remainder. An obvious example is the policy of many socialist countries to ignore the housing shortage, neglect residential construction and use the resources so saved for a faster expansion of manufacturing capacity.

T. SCITOVSKY

See also LINKAGES; NURKSE, RAGNAR; UNEVEN DEVELOPMENT; VON NEUMANN MODEL.

BIBLIOGRAPHY
Hirschman, A. 1958. *The Strategy of Economic Development*. New Haven: Yale University Press.
Kornai, J. 1972. *Rush versus Harmonic Growth*. Amsterdam: North-Holland.
Mill, J.S. 1844. *Essays on Some Unsettled Questions of Political Economy*. London: London School of Economics, 1948.
Neumann, J. von. 1945-6. A model of general economic equilibrium. Trans. G. Morgenstern, *Review of Economic Studies* 13, 1–9.
Nurkse, R. 1953. *Problems of Capital Formation in Underdeveloped Countries*. Oxford: Basil Blackwell.
Rosenstein-Rodan, P.N. 1943. Problems of industrialisation of Eastern and South-Eastern Europe. *Economic Journal* 53, June–September, 202–11.
Scitovsky, T. 1959. Growth – balanced or unbalanced? In *The Allocation of Economic Resources*, ed. M. Abramovitz et al., Stanford: Stanford University Press.

balance of payments. *See* ABSORPTION APPROACH TO THE BALANCE OF PAYMENTS; ELASTICITIES APPROACH TO THE BALANCE OF PAYMENTS; MONETARY APPROACH TO THE BALANCE OF PAYMENTS.

balance of trade, history of the theory. The views of the earliest popular economists of England on the best manner of enriching the nation agree with the measures taken by the legislature and with the balance-of-bargain system, as enforced by the statutes of employment.

> The holl welthe of the reame is for all our riche commodities to gete owt of all other reamys therfore redy money; and after the money is brought in to the holl reame, so shall all peple in the reame be made riche therwith. (Clement Armstrong, *A treatise concerninge the Staple and the Commodities of this Realme*, 1530, pp. 32, 61.)

But when the English merchants had broken down the power of foreign companies and had formed companies of their own, they sought after a rule by which to ascertain what advantages the regulation of commerce afforded to the nation taken as a whole. Even during the prevalence of the balance-of-bargain system, a rough rule for the policy on which the coinage should be based had been given by an officer of the mint, Richard Aylesbury, who thought that

> provided the merchandise exported from England was properly regulated, that is, if no more of foreign commodities were allowed to be imported than the value of the native commodities which should be taken out, the money in England would remain, and great plenty would come from beyond the seas (*Rolls of Parliament*, vol. iii, p. 126; in Rudding, *Annals of the Coinage*, vol. i, p. 241).

These views, put forward in 1381 by Richard Aylesbury, contrary to the then prevalent opinion (Cunningham, *Growth of English Industry and Commerce, Early and Middle Ages*, 1890, p. 354), were formulated anew and with success by the anonymous author of 'A Discourse of the City of London'. He shows that the increase of prices, which followed the influx of the precious metals from the West Indies had induced the gentry to 'play the fermours, grasiars, brewers, or such like'. This mercantile spirit must be guided by the experience of the merchant's daily practice. England being in need of foreign commodities, and having no mines of its own,

> it followeth necessarily, that if we follow the councel of that good old Husband Marcus Cato, saying, 'oportet patrem familias vendacem esse, non emacem' and do carrie more commodities in value over the seas, then wee bring hether from thence: that then the Realme shall receive that Overplus in Money (*A Discourse of the Names and First*

Causes of the Institution of Cities, and peopled Towns; and of the Commodities that do grow by the same; and namely of the City of London, etc. (about 1578), in Stow's *Survey of London,* 1598, p. 450).

William Stafford accepted these principles, adding, that the imported commodities should be 'most apte to be either carried for or kepte in store', and he praised the bailiff of Carmarthen, who had forbidden a ship freighted with oranges to sell them (*A Compendious and Brief Examination,* 1581 edn, New Shakspere Society Edn, pp. 50, 54, 57). This rule of commercial politics has been accepted by John Wheeler (*A Treatise of Commerce,* 1601, pp. 7, 8) and by Gerrard de Malynes, who seems to have suggested the name of balance, saying that the prince should not suffer 'an overbalancing of forreine commodities with his home commodities or in buying more then he selleth' (*A Treatise of the Canker of England's Commonwealth,* 1601, p. 2). The underbalance of trade and the consequent scarcity of money he ascribed to the 'undervaluation of our Money in Exchange', effected by the practices of the bankers. His erroneous ideas and those of Thomas Milles concerning 'merchandising exchange' (*The Customer's Replie,* 1604) were attacked by Edward Misselden, who hoped to remedy this undervaluation of the coin by 'raising' it (*Free Trade or the meanes to make Trade florish,* 1622, pp. 103–5), similar views being expressed in the parliament (*Parliamentary History* vol. i, p. 1195); he calls, however, the balance of trade 'an excellent and politique invention, to shew us the difference of weight in the commerce of one kingdome with another in the scale of commerce' (*The Circle of Commerce, or the Balance of Trade, in defence of Free Trade,* by E.M., 1623, pp. 116, 117). He considers poverty and prodigality as the causes of the present underbalance, the Dutch at once growing rich by manufactures and restraining the home consumption (pp. 132–5). These opinions were generally accepted even by Francis Bacon (*Letter of Advice to George Villiers,* 1616; *Letters and Life,* ed. Spedding, vol. vi, pp. 22–49, and *History of Henry VII,* Works, vol. vi, p. 223), and King James I (*Parliamentary History,* vol. i, p. 1179).

As stress was laid upon the profit of exportation of manufactures, the uselessness of the prohibitions of the exportation of money and bullion became more and more evident. Commercial states like Tuscany and Holland, allowing its free exportation, grew rich, while those forbidding it, like Spain, became impoverished. This point was clearly elucidated by Lewes Roberts, *The Treasure of Traffike,* 1641, p. 77, and the whole doctrine, including the views of exchange as a symptom, not as an agent of trade, as Malynes had maintained, was most systematically explained by Thomas Mun in his posthumous treatise *England's Treasure by Forraigne Trade; or the Balance of our Forraigne Trade is the Rule of our Treasure,* 1664, who in his *Discourse of Trade* (new edn, 1621) had still advocated the statutes of employment. To him therefore the honour of its invention has often been ascribed. The obstacles to trade were for the most part caused by fiscal motives, and the Commonwealth sought to stimulate the exportation of English commodities by the Act of Navigation. The balance of trade was thought to be advantageous: by fetching the commodities from the immediate places of their production and by sending them to their best market, where they yield the greatest price, but above all by the cheapness of the exported manufactures and the reduction of the price of labour (*The Advocate: or a Narrative of the State and Condition of Things between the English and Dutch Nation,* 1651 edn). This programme was supported by the greatest economists of the end of the 17th century like Petty, Temple, Locke, having all the tendency to overwhelm

the Dutch power. Another body of practical men inquired into the advantage of some special trades, among which the French and east India trade was found ruinous, as absorbing money and bullion, and giving in its stead but wines or spices. To these at a later date acceded the fear of Irish competition in the matter of wool. This pessimistic series of writers begins with S. Fortrey's *England's Interest and Improvement,* 1663; the author of *Britannia Languens,* 1680, and J. Pollexfen, *England and East India Inconsistent in Their Manufactures,* 1697, were its foremost champions. The commercial treaty with France in 1713 was a new matter of complaint. In the *British Merchant,* all the arguments against the underbalance are restated by Sir Theodore Janssen in his *General Maxims in Trade,* 1713, and by Joshua Gee, who afterwards put forward his views in *The Trade and Navigation of Great Britain consider'd,* 1729. 'His writings', says Hume, 'struck the nation with an universal panic, when they saw it plainly demonstrated that the balance was against them for so considerable a sum as must leave them without a single shilling in five or six years.' Nevertheless, the creed of the balance of trade was shared not only by Cantillon and Sir J. Steuart (book ii, ch. xv), but even by freetraders like Thomas Gordon, *The Nature and Weight of the Taxes of the Nation,* 1722, Vanderlint, *Money answers All Things,* 1734, and the author of *An Essay on the Causes of the Decline of Foreign Trade,* 1743.

For some time, however, the belief in the doctrine had been shaken, partly by traders whose interest it was to refute its postulates, partly by the impossibility of giving the exact statistical statement of the balance, partly by the doubts raised by superior thinkers. One of the first, it seems, was the author of *Free Ports, the Nature and Necessitie of them Stated,* B. W., 1652:

> All consultations whatsoever about trade, if free ports bee not opened and this wholesale or general trade bee not incouraged, do still but terminate in som advice or other about regulating our consumption; and have no other good at farthest, but preventional, that our Ballance of Import exceed not our Export: which to confine ourselves to alone, is, on the other side a cours to short, as it will neither serv to rais the Strength of this Nation in shipping, or to Govern the Exchange abroad (p. 8).

But the first thorough refutation was given by Nicholas Barbon in 1690 and 1696, and his influence is to be traced in the writings of Sir Dudley North (*Discourses of Trade,* 1691 edn), who calls, evidently in reference to it, the balance of trade one of the current 'politick conceits in trade; most of which Time and better Judgment hath disbanded'. The increase of manufactures had in opposition to the former opinion that 'trade was the source of national riches' made way to the doctrine that the employment of population and labour was the primitive enriching power. 'Land and labour', says therefore John Bellers, 'are the foundations of riches, and the fewer Idle Hands we have the faster we increase in value; and spending less than we raise is a much greater certainty of growing Rich than any computations that can be made from our Exportation and Importation' (*Essays about the Poor,* 1699, p. 12). These views, though far more mingled with mercantilist beliefs, were upheld by the author of *The Advantages of the East India Trade to England consider'd* (1701 and 1720), who pointed out, that the only rule of foreign trade should be 'to get a greater for a less value', and by Defoe, who while refuting the authors of the *British Merchant,* declared himself to be 'a profess'd opposer of all fortuitous calculations, making estimates by guess work of the Quantities and Value of any Trade or Exportation' (*A Plan of the English commerce*, 1728; 2nd edn, 1737, p. 232). This confession and the doubts raised by Bishop Berkeley in his *Querist* (1735, Queries 555, 556), whether the rule of the balance of trade held always true, and whether it admitted not of exceptions, were indeed nothing new. For even Davenant, originally much devoted to these estimates (*Of the use of Political Arithmetic*, 1698, Works, vol. i, pp. 146 8), declared himself afterwards convinced that they were inaccurate for many important trades (*A Report to the Commissioners*, 1712, Works, vol. v, p. 382). Sir Josiah Child also stated, as Berkeley did, that by means of smuggling, and furthermore in the case of countries whose income was consumed by absentees, like Ireland, exports could exceed imports without enriching the people (*A new Discourse of Trade*, 1690, ch. ix). The doubts which all these expressions of opinion fostered, paved the way for the overthrow of the system. This was accelerated by the flourishing state of English trade, which continued to prosper through the 18th century notwithstanding all the predictions of evil expressed by the balance-of-trade theorists.

The successful onslaught on the system made by Hume in his Essays (1752) is now a matter of history. In these he restated Barbon's assertion that an equivalent must be paid in an export for every import received. Hume's refutation of the balance-of-trade theory had a considerable influence on the free trade doctrines of the physiocrats and also upon Adam Smith. The latter, like Barbon, controverted the theory on this subject which was laid down by Mun and by Locke. Adam Smith also, in the preference he gave to the home trade, and in his opposition to the mercantilist views, shows an inclination to incredulity in relation to the theory of foreign trade. The manner in which Adam Smith thus placed himself in opposition to the commonly-accepted opinions of his time explains the fact that his criticism of the theory of foreign trade obtained, when it first appeared, comparatively few adherents. Even Pitt, while proving the success of his policy by the growth of exports, said, when the authority of Adam Smith was quoted against him, that he considered 'that great author, though always ingenious, sometimes injudicious' (*Parliamentary History*, xxxiii, 562–3). The questioning, however, as to the complete applicability of the theory gradually extended as the 18th century waned. After the successful peace of Paris in 1763 the fear of a drain of specie began to spread in consequence of the growth of indebtedness to foreigners; and though the balance of trade seemed favourable, new doubts were expressed whether the values stated of the goods exported were accurate (*The Present State of the Nation*, 1769; by W. Knox, secretary to George Grenville, pp. 65–7). The observations of Burke on this occasion, though professedly designed to prove the balance to be favourable, are very acute. Though not allowing the statement as to the certificated goods for re-exportation to admit of error, he concedes the possibility for free goods, exported without drawback and bounty; he remembers that the costs of freight and the profits of the merchant are not taken into account, that in the balance of the Irish and West India trades import and export both refer to one nation, and he ridicules those who held that the foreign imports were a loss without even considering that part of it which enters into production (see Edmund Burke, *Observations on a late State of the Nation*, 1769, pp. 34–8. Also his *Letters on a Regicide Peace*, 1796, Works, vol. iv, p. 554). The refutation of the original theory of the balance of trade is justly ascribed to Adam Smith, and his predecessors in England, of whose principal works some notice has been given here. The work of Adam Smith was completed by Ricardo in his theory of international trade which has hitherto been the special domain of English economics.

[S. BAUER]
Reprinted from *Palgrave's Dictionary of Political Economy*.

balance of trade doctrine. *See* MERCANTILISM.

balance sheet. *See* ACCOUNTING AND ECONOMICS; DOUBLE-ENTRY BOOKKEEPING.

Balogh, Thomas (1905–1985). Balogh was one of that influential group of exiled Hungarian economists, for whose ambitions and talents Hungary was too small and poor. Experience of the power politics of the 1930s, as seen from a Hungary dominated by Germany, equipped him well to understand the adjustments of post-imperial Britain to a world in which power had ebbed away from her. Under the influence of the banker O.T. Falk, also the originator of many of Keynes's ideas, Balogh was converted from an anti-inflationary creed to his fierce hostility to dear money and deflationary policies. His *Studies in Financial Organization* (1947) combines a passion for reform with skilful command of intricate detail. After the war, Balogh turned his attention to the problems of the underdeveloped countries. As adviser to the Food and Agriculture Organization of the United Nations (1957–9) he transformed an afforestation project into a series of ambitious development plans of the countries round the Mediterranean.

After Harold Wilson resigned from the Cabinet in 1951 he came into close touch with Balogh. One of Balogh's lines of argument was that a Labour government should be committed to a policy of faster growth, sustained by a strong incomes policy and supported by more state intervention in industry and foreign exchange controls. After the Labour victory of 1964 Balogh was brought into the Cabinet Office as adviser on economic affairs, with special reference to external economic policy. After three-and-a-half years of service in Number 10 Downing Street he was made a life peer and returned to the University of Oxford.

Although often labelled an extreme left-wing economist, he challenged many cherished socialist clichés. Having moved gradually to the left (he had been a follower of Horthy, later a liberal, and did not become a socialist until the war), he believed in linking together like-minded nations, both rich and poor, which would build up their jointly planned economies behind protective barriers, on the basis of high investment, modernization and fair shares. He favoured central planning and controls because he believed that they alone could secure an efficient and fair allocation of resources.

He identified many problems before the bulk of the profession had turned its attention to them. Among these were the scale of German rearmament in the 1930s, the need for exchange control during the war, the dollar problem after the war, the importance of an incomes policy based on a social consensus, the need for international coordination of demand management, the role of rural education and agriculture in development, the content and style of higher education in Africa, and the need for professional expertise in the Civil Service.

Superficially, his views seem full of contradictions, such as his advocacy of administrative controls while denouncing administrators. Yet there is a unity of vision behind these paradoxes, often guided more by intuition than by formal analysis.

P. STREETEN

SELECTED WORKS

1947. *Studies in Financial Organization*. Cambridge: Cambridge University Press.
1949. *The Dollar Crisis*. Oxford: Basil Blackwell.
1963. *Unequal Partners*. Oxford: Basil Blackwell.
1964. *The Economic Impact of Monetary and Commercial Institutions of a European Origin in Africa*. Cairo: National Bank of Egypt.
1973. *Facts and Fancy in International Economic Relations*. Oxford: Pergamon.
1983. *The Irrelevance of Conventional Economics*. London: Weidenfeld & Nicolson.

Banfield, Thomas Charles (1800–?1882). Banfield resided for some years in Germany and was tutor to the sons of King Ludwig I of Bavaria. After his return to England he lectured on political economy at Cambridge from 1844 until 1855, but in 1846, through the patronage of Sir Robert Peel, he became Secretary to the Privy Council.

His residence in Germany enabled Banfield to act as an interpreter both of its economy and its economists to English audiences. His 1845 Cambridge lectures were expressly intended to direct attention to 'principles that foreign authors have laid down'; Banfield referred mainly to the works of Hermann, Storch and Rossi, and seems to have been the first English writer to mention von Thünen. His concept of organization of industry was based on a theory of consumption starting from the proposition: 'that the satisfaction of every lower want in the scale creates a desire of a higher character. If the higher desire existed previous to the satisfaction of the primary want it becomes more intense when the latter is removed' (Banfield, 1845, p. 11). Jevons quoted this approvingly in his *Theory of Political Economy*, but pointed out that satisfaction of lower wants does not create higher wants: 'it merely permits the higher want to manifest itself.'

The graduated scale of wants outlined by Banfield would then result in a corresponding graduated scale of industries. The organization of industry he thus related to the utility of the goods produced and pointed out the linkage between the demand for goods and the payments to factors of production. Banfield's theory of consumption led him to criticize the Ricardian theory of rent with its implications of a rising cost of satisfying primary wants, and to support free trade. His books on the *Industry of the Rhine* were purely factual, but remain useful as sources of historical information.

R.D. COLLISON BLACK

SELECTED WORKS

1843. *Six Letters to Sir Robert Peel on the Dangerous Tendency of the Theory of Rent advocated by Ricardo*, by a Political Economist. London.
1845. *Four Lectures on the Oganization of Industry, being part of a course delivered in the University of Cambridge in Easter Term, 1844*. London: Richard and John E. Taylor.
1846. *Industry of the Rhine, Series I, Agriculture*. London: Charles Knight & Co.
1848. *Industry of the Rhine, Series II, Manufactures*. London: C. Cox.
1852. *Free Production having Freed Trade! The Pressure of Taxation exposed in a Lecture delivered in the University of Cambridge*. London: W. Ridgway.
1855. *A Letter to William Brown Esq., MP, on the advantages of his proposed system of Decimal Coinage*. London: Robert Hardwicke.

Banking School, Currency School, Free Banking School. Historians of economic thought conventionally represent British monetary debates from the 1820s on as centred on the question of whether policy should be governed by rules (espoused by adherents of the Currency School), or whether authorities should be allowed discretion (espoused by adherents of the Banking School). In fact many other questions were in dispute, including those raised by neglected or misidentified participants in the debates – adherents of the Free Banking School.

Among the questions in dispute were the following: (1) Should the banking system follow the Currency School's principle that note issues should vary one-to-one with the Bank of England's gold holdings? (2) Were the doctrines of the Banking School – real bills, needs of trade and the law of reflux – valid? (3) Was a monopoly of note issue desirable or, as the Free Banking School contended, destabilizing? (4) Was overissue a problem and, if so, who was responsible? (5) How should money be defined? (6) Why do trade cycles occur? (7) Should there be a central bank? No, was the Free Banking School answer to the final question; yes, was the answer of the other two schools, with disparate views, as indicated, on the question of rules *vs.* authorities. What was not in dispute was the viability of the gold standard system with gold convertibility of Bank of England notes.

On what grounds did the schools oppose each other? Each of the first three questions identifies the central doctrines that the adherents of one of the schools shared; on the remaining questions, individual views within each school varied. Before establishing the positions of each school in the monetary debates, we introduce the institutional background and the principal participants.

INSTITUTIONAL BACKGROUND. The Bank of England, incorporated in 1694 as a private institution with special privileges, stood at the head of the British banking system at the time of the debates. Until 1826 the Bank's charter was interpreted to mean the prohibition of other joint stock banks in England. As a result banking establishments were either one-man firms or partnerships with not more than six members. Two types of banks predominated in England: the wealthy London private banks which had voluntarily surrendered their note-issuing privilege, and the country banks which depended almost exclusively on the business of note issues. Numerous failures among the country banks demonstrated that the effect of the Bank's charter was to foster the formation of banking units of uneconomical size.

Banking in Ireland was patterned on English lines. The Bank of Ireland, chartered in 1783 with the exclusive privilege of joint stock banking in Ireland, surrendered its monopoly in 1821 in places farther than fifty miles from Dublin. Joint-stock banking in the whole of Ireland was legalized in 1845.

The Bank of Scotland was founded in 1695 with privileges similar to those of the Bank of England, except that it was formed to promote trade, not to support the credit of the government. It lost its monopoly in 1716, and no further monopolistic banking legislation was enacted in Scotland. With free entry possible, many local private and joint stock banks, most of the latter well capitalized, where established, and a nationwide system of branch banking developed. Unlike the English system, overissue was not a problem in the Scottish system. The banks accepted each other's notes and evolved a system of note exchange. Shareholders of Scottish joint stock banks (except for three chartered banks) assumed unlimited liability. At the time of the debates banking in Scotland was at a far more advanced stage than in England.

PRINCIPALS IN THE DEBATES. The leading spokesmen for the Currency School side in the debates were McCulloch, Loyd (later Lord Overstone), Longfield, George Warde Norman, and Torrens. Norman, a director of the Bank of England for most of the years 1821–72, and of the Sun Insurance Company, 1830–64, was active in the timber trade with Norway. The principal Banking School representatives were Tooke, Fullarton, and John Stuart Mill, while James Wilson held views that straddled Banking and Free Banking School doctrines. The most prominent members of the Free Banking School were Parnell (later Baron Congleton), James William Gilbart, and Poulett Scrope. Gilbart, a banker, was general manager of the London and Westminster Bank, the first of the joint stock banks authorized by the Bank Charter Act of 1833.

CURRENCY SCHOOL PRINCIPLE. The objective of the Currency School was to achieve a price level that would be the same whether the money supply were fully metallic or a mixed currency including both paper notes and metallic currency. According to Loyd, gold inflows or outflows under a fully metallic currency had the immediate effect of increasing or decreasing the currency in circulation, whereas a mixed currency could operate properly only if inflows or outflows of gold were exactly matched by an increase or decrease of the paper component. He and others of the Currency School regarded a rise in the price level and a fall in the bullion reserve under a mixed currency as symptoms of excessive note issues. They advocated statutory regulation to ensure that paper money was neither excessive nor deficient because otherwise fluctuations in the currency would exacerbate cyclical tendencies in the economy. They saw no need, however, to regulate banking activities other than note issue.

The Banking School challenged these propositions. Fullarton denied that overissue was possible in the absence of demand, that variations in the note issue could cause changes in the domestic price level, or that such changes could cause a fall in the bullion reserve ([1844] 1969, pp. 57, 128–9). Under a fully metallic as well as under a mixed currency bank, deposits, bills of exchange, and all forms of credit might influence prices. Moreover, inflows and outflows of gold under a fully metallic currency might change bullion reserves but not prices. If convertibility were maintained, overissue was not feasible and no statutory control of note issues was required. An adverse balance of payments was a temporary phenomenon that was self-correcting when, for example, a good harvest followed a bad one. According to the Free Banking School, the possibility of overissue and inflation applied only to Bank of England notes but could not occur in a competitive banking system.

BANKING SCHOOL PRINCIPLES. The Banking School adopted three principles that for them reflected the way banks actually operated as opposed to the Currency School principle which they dismissed as an artificial construct of certain writers (White, 1984, pp. 119–28).

The first Banking School principle was the doctrine that liabilities of deposits and notes would never be excessive if banks restricted their earning assets to real bills. One charge levelled by modern economists against the doctrine is that it leaves the quantity of money and the price level indeterminate, since it links the money supply to the nominal magnitude of bills offered for discount. Some members of the school may be exculpated from this charge if they regarded England as a small open economy, its domestic money stock a dependent variable determined by external influences. However, because it ignored the role of the discount rate in determining the volume of bills generated in trade, the doctrine was vulnerable. In addition, the Banking School confused the flow demand for

loanable funds, represented by the volume of bills, with the stock demand for circulating notes, although the two magnitudes are non-commensurable.

Free Banking School members who also adopted the real bills doctrine erroneously attributed overissue by the Bank of England to its purchase of assets other than real bills, when overissue was possible with a portfolio limited to real bills, acquired at an interest rate that led to a stock of circulating medium inconsistent with the prevailing price level (Gilbart, 1841, pp. 103–5; 119–20). The Currency School regarded the real bills doctrine as misguided since it could promote a cumulative rise in the note issue and hence in prices.

A second Banking School principle was the 'needs of trade' doctrine, to the effect that the note circulation should be demand-determined – curtailed when business declined and expanded when business prospered, whether for seasonal or cyclical reasons. An implicit assumption of the doctrine was that banks could either vary their reserve ratios to accommodate lower or higher note liabilities, or else offset changes in note liabilities by opposite changes in deposit liabilities. For non-seasonal increases in demand for notes, the doctrine implied that expanding banks could obtain increased reserves from an interregional surplus of the trade balance. The Currency School regarded an increase in the needs of trade demand to hold notes accompanying increases in output and prices as unsound because it would ultimately produce an external drain. The Free Banking School countered that such an objection by the Currency School was paradoxical since the virtue of a metallic currency according to the latter was that it accommodated the commercial wants of the country, and therefore for a mixed currency to respond to the needs of trade could not be a vice. The modern objection to the needs of trade doctrine as procyclical is an echo of the Currency School view.

The third Banking School principle was the law of the reflux according to which overissue was possible only for limited periods because notes would immediately return to the issuer for repayment of loans. This was a modification of the real bills doctrine that Tooke and Fullarton advanced, since adherence to the doctrine supposedly made overissue impossible. They made no distinction between the speed of the reflux for the Bank of England and for competitive banks of issue – a distinction at the heart of the Free Banking position. For the latter, reflux of excess notes was speedy only if the notes were deposited in rival banks. These would then return the notes to the issuing banks and accordingly bring an end to relative overissue by individual banks. The Bank of England, on the contrary, could overissue for long periods because it had no rivals. Fullarton, however, made the unwarranted assumption that notes would be returned to the Bank to repay previous loans at a faster rate than the Bank was discounting new loans, hence correcting the overissue. Moreover, he believed that if the Bank overissued by open market purchases, the decline in interest rates would quickly activate capital outflows, reducing the Bank's bullion and forcing it to retreat. Tooke was sounder in arguing for the law of reflux on the ground that excess issues would not be held if they did not match the preferences of holders for notes rather than deposits.

The Banking School had no legislative programme for reform of the monetary system. Good bank management, in the view of the school, could not be legislated.

FREE BANKING SCHOOL PRINCIPLE. As the name suggests, the principle the Free Banking School advocated was free trade in the issue of currency convertible into specie. Members of the school favoured a system like the Scottish banking system, where banks competed in all banking services, including the issue of notes, and no central bank held a monopoly of note issue. They argued that in such a system banks did not issue without limit but indeed provided a stable quantity of money. Although the costs of printing and issuing were minimal, to keep notes in circulation required restraint in their issue. The profit-maximizing course for competitive banks was to maintain public confidence in their issues by maintaining convertibility into specie on demand, which required limiting their quantity.

Loyd's response to the argument for free trade in currency was that unlike ordinary trades, what was sought was not the greatest quantity at the cheapest price but a regulated quantity of currency. The Free Banking School denied that free banking would debase the currency, and contended that the separation of banking from note issue, the Banking School proposal, was impractical. Scrope (1833a. pp. 32–3) asked why the Currency School objected to unregulated issue of notes but not to that of deposits, questioning Loyd's assumption that an issuing bank's function was to produce money, when in fact its function was to substitute its bank notes for less well-known private bills of exchange that were the bank's assets. Scrope and other Free Banking adherents (Parnell, 1827, p. 143) neglected the distinction between a banknote immediately convertible into gold and a commercial bill whose present value varied with time to maturity and the discount rate. Contrary to Loyd, they reasoned that free trade and competition were applicable to currency creation because the business of banks was to produce the scarce good of reputation.

Loyd's second disagreement with the argument for free trade in banking was that miscalculations by the issuers were borne not by them but by the public. Moreover, individuals had no choice but to accept notes they received in ordinary transactions, and trade in general suffered as a result of overissue. The Free Banking School answer to this externalities argument turned on the ability of holders to refuse notes of issuers without reputation. Protection against loss could also be provided if joint stock banks were allowed to operate in place of country banks limited to six or fewer partners. In addition, if banks were required to deposit security of government bonds or other assets, noteholders would be further protected (Scrope, 1832, p. 455; 1833b, p. 424; Parnell, 1827, pp. 140–44). Free Banking School members who argued in this vein failed to recognize that they were thereby acknowledging a role for government intervention in currency matters.

In the 1820s the Free Banking School championed joint stock banking both in the country bank industry and in direct competition in note issue with the Bank of England in London. Although the six-partner rule for banks of issue at least 65 miles from London was repealed in 1826 after a spate of bank failures, the Bank retained its monopoly of note circulation in the London area. In addition, the Bank was permitted to establish branches anywhere in England. The Parliamentary inquiry in 1832 on renewal of the Bank's character was directed to the question of prolonging the monopoly. The Act of 1833 eased entry for joint stock banks within the 65-mile limit but denied them the right of issue and made the Bank's notes legal tender for redemption of country bank notes, in effect securing the Bank's monopoly. The doom of the Free Banking cause was finally pronounced by the Bank Charter Act of 1844. It restricted note issues of existing private and joint stock banks in England and Wales to their average circulation during a period in 1843. Note issue by banks established after the act was prohibited.

WAS OVERISSUE A PROBLEM? Participants in the debates understood overissue to mean a stock of notes, whether introduced by a single issuer or banks in aggregate, in excess of the quantity holders voluntarily chose to keep as assets, given the level of prices determined by the world gold standard. Was overissue of a convertible currency possible? According to the Free Banking School, interbank note clearing by competitive banks operated to eliminate excess issued by a single bank. The check to excess issues by the banking system as a whole was an external drain through the price-specie flow mechanism. In this respect the school acknowledged that the result of overissue by a competitive banking system as a whole was the same as for a monopoly issuer. However, they held that overissue was a phenomenon that the monopoly of the Bank of England encouraged but a competitive system would discourage.

The Currency School, on the other hand, regarded both the Bank of England and the Scottish and country banks as equally prone to overissue and did not grant that a check to overissue by a single bank or banks in the aggregate was possible through the interbank note clearing mechanism. For them, regulation of a monopoly issuer promised a stable money supply that was not attainable with a plural banking system.

The Free Banking School's explanation of the Bank of England's ability to overissue rested on the absence of rivals for the Bank's London circulation, so no interbank note clearing took place; the absence of competition in London from interest-bearing demand deposits; and the fact that London private banks held the Bank's notes as reserves. Hence the demand for its notes was elastic. The Free Banking and Currency Schools agreed that there was a substantial delay before an external drain checked overissue, so the Bank's actions inescapably inflicted damage on the economy. Scrope (1830, pp. 57–60), who attributed the Bank's willingness to overexpand its note issues to its monopoly position, advocated abrogating that legal status.

The Banking School dismissed the question of overissue as irrelevant, for noteholders could easily exchange unwanted notes by depositing them. What they failed to examine was the possibility that a broader monetary aggregate could be in excess supply resulting in an external drain.

HOW SHOULD MONEY BE DEFINED? Currency School members favoured defining money as the sum of metallic money, government paper money, and bank notes (Norman, 1833, pp. 23, 50; McCulloch, 1850, pp. 146–7). The Free Banking School, like the Currency School, focused on bank notes as the common medium of exchange, ignoring demand deposits that were not usually subject to transfer by check outside London. The Banking School definition of money is sometimes represented as broader than that of the other schools, but in fact was narrower – money was restricted to metallic and government paper money. Bank notes and deposits were excluded, since they were regarded as means of raising the velocity of bank vault cash but not as adding to the quantity of money (Tooke [1848], 1928, pp. 171–83; Fullarton [1844], 1969, pp. 29–36; Mill [1848], 1909, p. 523). In the short run, the school held that all forms of credit might influence prices, but only money as defined could do so in the long run, because the domestic price level could deviate only temporarily from the world level of prices determined by the gold standard.

WHY DO TRADE CYCLES OCCUR? The positions of the three schools on the impulses initiating trade cycles were not dogma for their members. In general the Currency and Banking Schools held that nonmonetary causes produced trade cycles, whereas the Free Banking School pointed to monetary causes, but individual members did not invariably hew to these analytical lines. McCulloch (1937, p. 63), Loyd (1857, p. 317), and Longfield (1840, pp. 222–3) essentially attributed cycles to waves of optimism and pessimism to which the banks then responded by expanding and contracting their issues. Banks accordingly never initiated the sequence of expansion and contraction. Hence the Currency School principle of regulating the currency to stabilize prices and business did not imply that cycles would thereby be eliminated. Cycles would, however, no longer be amplified by monetary expansion and contraction, if country banks were denied the right to issue and the Bank of England's circulation were governed by the 'currency principle'. Torrens (1840, pp. 31, 42–3), unlike other Currency School members, attributed trade cycles to actions of the Bank of England. That was also the position of the Free Banking School, although in an early work Parnell (1827, pp. 48–51) of that school held that cycles were caused by nonmonetary factors. For the Banking School, however, nonmonetary factors accounted for both the origin and spread of trade cycles. Tooke (1840, pp. 245, 277), for example, believed that overoptimism would prompt an expansion of trade credit for which the banks were in no way responsible. Collapse of optimism would then lead to shrinkage of trade credit. For Fullarton ([1844] 1969, p. 101) nonmonetary causes produced price fluctuations to which changes in note circulation were a passive response. Proponents of the nonmonetary theory of the onset of trade cycles provided no explanation of the waves of optimism and pessimism themselves. For the Free Banking School the waves were precipitated by the Bank of England's expansion and ultimate contraction of its liabilities. Initially, the Bank's actions depressed interest rates and ultimately forced them up, as loanable funds increased in supply and then decreased. The Bank's monopoly position enabled it to create such monetary disturbances, whereas competitive country banks had no such power.

SHOULD THERE BE A CENTRAL BANK? The Currency and Banking Schools were in agreement that a central bank with the sole right of issue was essential for the health of the economy. McCulloch (1831, p. 49) regarded a system of competitive note issuing institutions as one of inherent instability. Tooke (1840, pp. 202–7) favoured a monopoly issuer as promoting less risk of overissue and greater safety because it would hold sufficient reserves. The two schools differed on the need for a rule to regulate note issues, the Currency School pledged to a rulebound authority, the Banking School to an unbound authority. The Free Banking School disapproved of both a rule and a central bank authority, instead favouring a competitive note-issuing system that it held to be self-regulating. For that school proof that centralized power was inferior to a competitive system was revealed by cyclical fluctuations that had been caused by errors of the Bank of England.

A CONTINUING DEBATE. The Bank Charter Act of 1844 ended the right of note issue for new banks in England and Wales. Scottish banks, however, were treated differently from Irish banks by the Act of 1845 and from English provincial banks by the Act of 1844. Like the latter, authorized circulation for the Scottish banks was determined by the average of a base period, but they could exceed the authorized circulation provided they held 100 per cent specie reserves against the excess – a provision also imposed on the Bank of England.

The Free Banking School thus lost its case for an end of the note issue monopoly of the Bank of England. The death of Parnell in 1842, a leading Parliamentary spokesman, had hurt the cause. Others of the school were mainly country and joint stock bankers. The Acts conferred benefits on them by restricting entry into the note-issuing industry and by freezing market shares (White, 1984, pp. 78–9). Their voices were not raised in opposition. Only Wilson was critical of the privileges the Bank of England was accorded ([1847] 1849, pp. 34–66).

The Banking School objected not only to the Act but claimed vindication for its point of view by the necessity to suspend it in 1847, 1857 and 1866. The Currency School responded that the suspensions were of no great significance (Loyd, 1848, pp. 393–4). The recommendations of the Currency School prevailed to set a maximum for country bank note issues and the eventual transfer of their circulation to the Bank of England.

The monetary debates that were initiated in the 1820s were not conclusive. No point of view carried the day. Long after the original participants had passed from the scene, the doctrines of the schools found supporters. Even the Free Banking School position in opposition to monopoly issue of hand-to-hand currency that seemed to be buried has recently been revived by new adherents (White, 1984, pp. 137–50). The debate on all the questions in dispute in the 19th century continues to be live.

ANNA J. SCHWARTZ

See also BOYD, WALTER; BULLIONIST CONTROVERSY; CENTRAL BANKING; CLASSICAL THEORY OF MONEY; FULLARTON, JOHN; OVERSTONE, LORD; PENNINGTON, JAMES; REAL BILLS DOCTRINE; TOOKE, THOMAS.

BIBLIOGRAPHY

Fullarton, J. 1844. *On the Regulation of Currencies*. London: John Murray. Reprinted, New York: Augustus M. Kelley, 1969.

Gilbart, J.W. 1841. Testimony before the Select Committee of the House of Commons on Banks of Issue. British Sessional Papers, vol.5 (110).

Gregory, T.E. 1928. Introduction to *Tooke and Newmarch's A History of Prices*. London: P.S. King.

[Longfield, S.M.] 1840. Banking and currency. *Dublin University Magazine*.

Loyd, S.J. 1848. Testimony before the Secret Committee of the House of Commons on Commercial Distress. British Sessional Papers, 1847–8, vol. 8, part 1 (584).

Loyd, S.J. 1857. *Tracts and Other Publications on Metallic and Paper Money*. London.

[McCulloch, J.R.] 1831. *Historical Sketch of the Bank of England*. London: Longman.

[McCulloch, J.R.] 1837. The Bank of England and the country banks. *Edinburgh Review*, April.

[McCulloch, J.R.] 1850. *Essays on Interest, Exchange, Coins, Paper Money, and Banks*. London.

Mill, J.S. 1848. *Principles of Political Economy*, Ed. W.J. Ashley, London: Longmans & Co., 1909.

Norman, G.W. 1833. *Remarks upon Some Prevalent Errors, with Respect to Currency and Banking*. London: Hunter.

Parnell, H.B. 1827. *Observations on Paper Money, Banking and Overtrading*. London: James Ridgway.

Scrope, G.P. 1830. *On Credit-Currency, and its Superiority to Coin, in Support of a Petition for the Establishment of a Cheap, Safe, and Sufficient Circulating Medium*. London: John Murray.

[Scrope, G.P.] 1832. The rights of industry and the banking system. *Quarterly Review*, July, 407–55.

Scrope, G.P. 1833a. *An Examination of the Bank Charter Question*. London: John Murray.

Scrope, G.P. 1833b. *Principles of Political Economy*. London: Longman.

Tooke, T. 1840. *A History of Prices and of the State of the Circulation in 1838 and 1839*. London: Longman. Reprinted, London: P.S. King, 1928.

Tooke, T. 1848. *History of Prices and of the State of the Circulation, from 1839 to 1847 inclusive*. London: Longmans. Reprinted, London: P.S. King, 1928.

Torrens, R. 1840. *A Letter to Thomas Tooke, Esq. in Reply to His Objections against the Separation of the Business of the Bank into a Department of Issue and a Department of Discount: With a Plan of Bank Reform*. London: Longman.

White, L.H. 1984. *Free Banking in Britain: Theory, Experience, and Debate, 1800–1845*. Cambridge: Cambridge University Press.

Wilson, J. 1847. *Capital, Currency, and Banking; being a collection of a series of articles published in the Economist in 1845 ... and in 1847*. London: The office of the Economist. 2nd edn, London: D.M. Aird, 1859.

bank rate. This was the label applied to the rate at which the Bank of England would discount first-class bills of exchange in the London market: by extension, it has come to mean the rate at which any central bank makes short-term loans available to domestic commercial banks. The UK Bank Rate's practical significance dates from the Bank Charter Act of 1833, Section 7 of which exempted bills of a currency up to three months from the provisions of usury laws which had previously imposed a 5 per cent interest ceiling. This relaxation had been recommended in 1802 by Henry Thornton as a means of containing demand for discounts, which passed along a chain from country banks to London banks to the nascent last-resort central bank, and threatened to become excessive when market forces would have pushed rates above the ceiling. The urgency of such containment was increased as a result of (a) these 'internal' gold drains being reinforced by 'external' analogues related to the expansion of international trade and capital movements; (b) the imposition by the 1844 Bank Charter Act of a limit to the fiduciary issue, of Bank of England notes backed by holdings of securities, designed to ensure the maintenance of convertibility of notes into gold. The 1847 liquidity crisis forced the Government to promise a retrospective act of indemnity should this limit be breached, freeing the Bank to act as lender of last resort to whatever extent the exigencies of the crisis might require – but on condition that a Bank Rate of not less than 8 per cent be imposed.

Henceforward, and until the final abandonment of the gold standard in 1931, Bank Rate changes were the major technique by which the Bank of England protected its reserve. The technique was powerful at least until the First World War, after which its effectiveness was compromised by political and economic disorder, and by the rise of New York as an international financial centre alternative to London. Understanding of the causes of the pre-1914 power of Bank Rate increases (reductions tended to represent rather passive reactions to relaxation of pressures) is facilitated by distinguishing responses in the spheres of, respectively, the London money market; external trade and payments; and internal economic activity.

Within the London money market, matters hinged – in the manner adumbrated by Thornton – on bankers' response to the rise in Bank Rate to a 'penalty' level, above the market rate(s) at which the bankers had themselves acquired bills. Bank Rate thus operated, in Walter Bagehot's phrase, as a 'fine on unreasonable timidity' in regard to the liquidation of banks' assets with a view to strengthening reserve ratios, against the possibility of a run on banks by nervous depositors. Originally, it is to be noted, the initiative lay with the commercial banks rather than with the developing central bank; the shortage of cash (=deposits at the Bank of England) resulted from increased demand by the former, rather than from reduction of supply engineered by the latter; autonomous pressures were already raising (short-term) interest rates, and Bank Rate changes were an important – probably overriding – influence on the extent of the rise by virtue of the Bank of England's position as key supplier of an essential margin of funds. There was thus no real problem in 'making Bank Rate effective', that is to say ensuring that it exerted appropriate influence on market rates. Nor was there any call for assistance from the weapon, not in any case developed until after World War I, of open-market sales of securities at central bank initiative. These points warn modern theorists against the temptation to read back into the 19th century later-developed notions suggesting that the rise in *price* (short-term interest rates) either reflected, accompanied or caused a reduction in *quantity* (bank credit flows, or bank deposit totals). The relationship between Bank Rate changes and 'the quantity of money' was, as Keynes argued (see below) much more diffuse and complex than modern monetarist styles of theory can easily envisage; its character can hardly begin to emerge until repercussions outside the money market have been considered.

Of these repercussions, those relating to external flows, rather than to internal adaptations, were the main focus of attention in Bank Rate's classical period, and we first consider the external side. Ricardian thought, in the early part of the period, encouraged attention to the trade balance; but in practice, as the 19th century wore on, the action was increasingly seen to occur in the sphere of international payments and capital movements. This was mainly a reflection of structural changes which produced a consistently strong UK trade balance, massive long-term overseas lending, and a growing mass of internationally mobile bills of exchange (principally the 'bill on London'). It was also, by the turn of the century, a reflection of (probably fortuitously) helpful policy by the Bank of France, the focal point of London's only rival as a financial centre. The Bank of France kept more substantial gold reserves than the Bank of England; and it was willing to allow those reserves to vary in order to exert stabilizing influence on continental interest rates. As a result, a rise in London's Bank Rate tended to increase the differential between UK and foreign short-term rates, and to tilt the balance of short-term flows in London's favour. An increase in Bank Rate, opined the Cunliffe Committee in 1918, would 'draw gold from the moon'; in practice, the metal did not travel quite so far.

A highly significant implication of this (at the time, ill-understood) conjuncture, was that the Bank of England discovered a power to protect its reserve without significant damage to UK overseas trade. The validity of this judgement is witnessed by the decline in the volume of complaints from traders about the burden of high short-term interest rates. Such complaints were quite substantial in the early decades of intermittently high and rising Bank Rate levels. The present author has established (1962), however, that the grievances were much more closely related to the *availability* of short-term credit than to its *cost*. A rise in Bank Rate (from even quite low levels) was seen, with good reason, as heralding a potential liquidity shortage that might be transformed quickly into a liquidity crisis: alert bankers and traders at once began to exercise caution in undertaking new commitments. This is undoubtedly the historical origin of what would otherwise be a rather puzzling strand in the Bank Rate tradition, namely the idea that a rise in Bank Rate operated as an 'Index', a storm signal enjoining caution. This strand persisted in financiers' folk-memories long after its realistic institutional basis had declined, and resurfaced in the 1950s in a new form: sterling crises could be countered by a 'package deal' of measures, of which a Bank Rate rise constituted an essential element, as an *index* of the UK authorities' determination to inflict whatever pain might be necessary to rectify external imbalance.

In just what this pain might consist had been a matter of debate, intermittently vigorous, among academic economists – whose primary attention, in the 20th century, came to focus on the internal economy, and the effects thereon of what the 1918 Cunliffe Committee saw as a Bank Rate-induced (? accompanied) general rise of interest rates and restriction of credit. The emphasis on credit restriction was by then probably exaggerated, and traceable to the folk-memories just noted. The emphasis on generally rising interest rates undoubtedly exaggerated Bank Rate's *direct* influence on the structure of interest rates. It is true that, by 1900, commercial bank borrowing and lending rates were widely (not universally) linked to Bank Rate – an administrative link reflecting a market reality for, as indicated above and as Bagehot had argued, an institution (the Bank of England) that regularly supplied the market with the necessary residual margin of cash almost automatically exercised what we should call 'price leadership', its own price for short-term accommodation dominating other influences. Keynes was thus justified, in his *Treatise on Money* (1930), in treating Bank Rate as representative of the general level of *short* rates, on the assumption that Bank Rate changes were normally 'effective' in influencing market rates. The further link to *long* rates, however, was more problematic, and a source of disagreement between Keynes and R.G. Hawtrey (1938).

Hawtrey tended to downplay the link, on the argument that the direct influence on long rates of a rise in short rates depended on the period for which the rise was expected to last – which period, because of Bank Rate's external power described above, was typically brief. His view was doubtless influenced by his tenacious, and fairly isolated, adherence to the theory that Bank Rate's external power was mediated primarily by its influence on the cost of holding inventories. His theory was that individual merchants would have a strong inducement to respond to a Bank Rate increase by reducing purchases from manufacturers, designed to effect a temporary reduction of inventory levels during the limited period for which the higher Bank Rate was expected to last. But collectively these mercantile responses so reduced demand that manufacturers restricted their purchases of raw materials from merchants, and the 'vicious circle of deflation' was joined. Hawtrey claimed support for his theory from oral testimony, notably before House of Commons committees of inquiry into liquidity crises. But later investigation (Cramp, 1962) demonstrated that John Torr, Chairman of the Liverpool Chamber of Commerce during the 1857 crisis, was typical in arguing that what mattered to traders was 'not so much the rate of interest as the impossibility of getting the medium of exchange', that is, not so much the cost of credit as its availability, which gradually became more reliable as the techniques of commercial and central banking improved.

It was Keynes's view, in the *Treatise* and in the Report of the Macmillan Committee which he dominated, that exercised the more substantial and enduring influence on academic opinion. Unlike Hawtrey, he tended to emphasize the link through to long-term interest rates, perhaps implicitly assuming – by this juncture – the support of appropriate open-market operations, security sales by the central bank. He was by this stage urging

that such sales should include bonds as well as bills, facilitating direct influence on long rates. Such advocacy was not uncongenial to a central bank now ever-anxious to 'fund the floating debt', reflecting fears of repetition of the experience of feeling constrained by government borrowing needs during the inflationary boom of 1920–21.

Keynes was thus enabled to presume that a rise in Bank Rate would be accompanied by supporting measures appropriate to the exertion of a strong *indirect* influence on the structure of interest rates. In this way, he justified retrospectively the Cunliffe Committee's rejection of Alfred Marshall's dismissal of the effect of Bank Rate changes as 'a ripple on the surface', and also inaugurated the era of academic preoccupation with the link between 'the rate of interest' (essentially, the long-term rate) and the level of expenditures on fixed investment. He contended (*Treatise*, I, pp. 154–5) that 'a rise in Bank rate tends, in so far as it modifies the effective rates of interest, to depress price levels'.

The theoretical model deployed to explain this proposition is significant for the history of monetary theory as well as that of Bank Rate. Keynes appealed to Wicksell's celebrated (1898) concepts, to argue that a Bank Rate increase represented a rise in the market rate of interest, relative to the natural rate which would equate desired levels of investment and saving. The link to prices, however, would come principally, not through the monetary route of reduced bank-lending flows and bank-deposit stocks, but through the impact of higher market interest rates on the decision to invest. A higher rate of discount would be applied to the stream of future yields anticipated from an act of investment. Such acts would be postponed, the more readily when the higher Bank Rate was regarded as a temporary divergence from the normal level, the more ineluctably on account of the likely difficulty in such market conditions of floating new issues on the capital market. Aggregate demand and prices would thus tend to be depressed, by processes which would result in reduced demand for money balances. The money market tightness would be superficially eased from the domestic side, as it would also be relieved from the foreign side – quickly on account of reduced lending to overseas borrowers, more slowly and fundamentally as the domestic deflation improved the trade balance.

The *General Theory*, of course, was soon to initiate a prolonged phase of even greater scepticism about the strength of the linkage between money and prices. It appeared at a time when cheap money was also causing de-emphasis on the role of changes in Bank Rate. From 1932 to 1951, Bank Rate was held, apart from a hiccough when war began in 1939, at the level of 2 per cent. Academic discussion continued of the relationship between the level of interest rates and decisions to invest, but it was largely severed from consideration of money-market techniques and policies. When inflationary fears began to surface late in the cheap money era, as Professor R.S. Sayers (1979) notes, D.H. Robertson 'addressed the world not on the question "What has happened to Bank Rate?" but "What has happened to the Rate of Interest?"' '

The desire to restrain inflationary tendencies prompted the beginning in 1951 of a period of experimentation with the revival of monetary policy techniques, a trend which within a decade or so was to receive very substantial impetus from the anti-Keynesian monetarist counter-revolution originating principally in Chicago. In the earlier phases of this postwar period, Bank Rate changes were reintroduced to the authorities' armoury of measures, but somewhat tardily and half-heartedly, being subordinated to the then still quite fashionable preference for direct controls, e.g. on the volume of bank advances. As noted above, there was some disposition to regard a Bank Rate increase as an essential element in a restrictive 'package deal', but no-one seemed quite sure why, except that folk-memories even yet favoured it (*those* were the days, when even gold on the moon was magnetized!), and market enthusiasts instinctively welcomed a price element in a package consisting primarily of quantity controls. In the later, monetarist-influenced, phases of the postwar period, quantity controls were precisely what influential opinion desired, but because that opinion favoured achieving them by market rather than by administrative measures, interest-rate changes were acknowledged to have a significant, though subsidiary, role.

Thus was Keynes's sequence, which as we have seen began from Bank Rate, reversed. Bank Rate was renamed, under the 'Competition and Credit Control' regime operated in the UK in the 1970s. It became 'Minimum Lending Rate' (MLR). It was ostensibly linked to the Treasury Bill rate emerging from the weekly tender, and consequently moved much more frequently than of yore, although every so often the authorities uncoupled the link, when they desired an old-fashioned 'index effect' – on external fund flows – from a rise in short-term rates clearly engineered by themselves.

Under the new (and nameless) UK monetary control régime of the 1980s, the ghost of Bank Rate became yet more evanescent. The continuous posting of MLR was formally suspended, though the authorities reserved the right 'in some circumstances to announce in advance the minimum rate which, for a short period ahead, it would apply in lending to the market'. This right has on occasion been actified. Bank Rate lives, just. Treatises on money no longer contain, as did Keynes's, a chapter on its *modus operandi*. But as in so many directions in economics, it would be a bold observer who projected the existing trend indefinitely, and predicted Bank Rate's final demise. There are continuities in economics, albeit disguised by irregular cycles in opinion and practice; trends persist, even in a new high-technological age.

A.B. CRAMP

See also CHEAP MONEY; DEAR MONEY; MONETARY POLICY.

BIBLIOGRAPHY

Bank of England. 1971. Competition and credit control. *Quarterly Bulletin*, June.
Cramp, A.B. 1962. *Opinion on Bank Rate 1822–60*. London: G. Bell.
Cunliffe (Lord), et al. 1918. *Committee on Currency and Foreign Exchanges, First Interim Report*. London: HMSO.
Hawtrey, R.G. 1938. *A Century of Bank Rate*. London: Longman.
Keynes, J.M. 1930. *A Treatise on Money*. London: Macmillan.
Keynes, J.M. 1936. *General Theory of Employment, Interest and Money*. London: Macmillan.
Sayers, R.S. 1981. *Bank Rate in Keynes's Century*. London: The British Academy.
Wicksell, K. 1898. *Interest and Prices*. Trans. R.F. Kahn, London: Macmillan for the Royal Economic Society, 1936.

banks. *See* FINANCIAL INTERMEDIARIES.

Baran, Paul Alexander (1910–1964). Paul Baran, the eminent Marxist economist, was born on 8 December 1910 in Nikolaev, Russia, the son of a medical doctor who was a member of the Menshevik branch of the Russian revolutionary movement. After the October Revolution the family moved to Germany, where Baran's formal education began. In 1925 the father was offered a position in Moscow and returned to the USSR. Baran began his studies in economics at the University of Moscow the following year. Both his ideas and his politics were deeply and permanently influenced by the intense debates

and struggles within the Communist Party in the late 1920s. Offered a research assignment at the Agricultural Academy in Berlin in late 1928, he enrolled in the University of Berlin, and when his assignment at the Agricultural Academy ended he accepted an assistantship at the famous Institute for Social Research in Frankfurt. This experience too had a lasting influence on his intellectual development.

Leaving Germany shortly after Hitler's rise to power, Baran sought without success to find academic employment in France. He therefore moved to Warsaw, where his paternal uncles had a flourishing international lumber business. During the next few years he travelled widely as a representative of his uncles' business, ending up in London in 1938. With the approach of World War II, however, he decided to take what savings he had been able to accumulate, move to the United States, and resume his interrupted academic career.

Arriving in the United States in the fall of 1939, he was accepted as a graduate student in economics at Harvard. From there he went to wartime Washington, where he served in the Office of Price Administration, the Research and Development branch of the Office of Strategic Services, and the United States Strategic Bombing Survey, ending in 1945–6 as Deputy Chief of the Survey's mission to Japan. Back in the United States, he took a job at the Department of Commerce and gave lectures at George Washington University before being offered a position in the Research Department of the Federal Reserve Bank of New York. After three years in New York, he accepted an offer to join the economics faculty at Stanford University and was promoted to a full professorship in 1951, a position he retained until his death of a heart attack on 26 March 1964.

Baran was not a prolific writer, but his two main books, *The Political Economy of Growth* (1957) and (in collaboration with Paul M. Sweezy) *Monopoly Capital: An Essay on the American Economic and Social Order* (1966), are generally considered to be among the most important works in the Marxian tradition of the post-World War II period.

The Political Economy of Growth is concerned with the processes and condition of economic growth (or development, the terms are used interchangeably) in both industrialized and underdeveloped societies, with a special emphasis throughout on the ways the two relate to and interract with each other. It is at once an outstanding work of scholarship weaving an intricate pattern of theory and history, and at the same time a passionate polemic against mainstream economics. Its chief (innovative) analytical concept is that of 'potential surplus', defined as 'the difference between the output that *could* be produced in a given natural and technological environment with the help of employable productive resources, and what might be regarded as essential consumption.' (This concept presupposes Marx's 'surplus value', extending and modifying it for the particular purposes of the study in hand.) Two long chapters, totalling 90 pages, apply the concepts of surplus and potential surplus to the analysis of monopoly capitalism in ways that would later be refined and elaborated in *Monopoly Capital*. Three chapters (115 pages) follow on 'backwardness' (also called underdevelopment), and it is for these that the book has become famous, especially in the Third World.

Baran begins this analysis with a question which may be said to define the focus of the whole work: 'Why is it that in the backward capitalist countries there has been no advance along the lines of capitalist development that are familiar from the history of other capitalist countries, and why is it that forward movement there has been slow or altogether absent?' His answer, in briefest summary, is as follows: all present-day capitalist societies evolved from precapitalist conditions which

Baran for convenience labels 'feudal' (explicitly recognizing that a variety of social formations are subsumed under this heading). Viable capitalist societies could have emerged in various parts of the world; actually the decisive breakthrough occurred in Western Europe (Baran speculates on the reasons, but in any case they are not crucial to the subsequent history). Having achieved its headstart, Europe proceeded to conquer weaker precapitalist countries, plunder their accumulated stores of wealth, subject them to unequal trading relations, and reorganize their economic structures to serve the needs of the Europeans. This was the origin of the great divide in the world capitalist system between the developed and the underdeveloped parts. As the system spread into the four corners of the globe, new areas were added, mostly to the underdeveloped part but in a few cases to the developed (North America, Australia, Japan). One of the highlights of Baran's study is the brilliant historical sketch of the contrasting ways India and Japan were incorporated into the world capitalist system, the one as a hapless dependency, the other as a strong contender for a place at the top of the pyramid of power. Baran's message to the Third World was loud and clear: once trapped in the world capitalist system, there is no hope for genuine progress; only a revolutionary break can open the road to a better future. The message has been widely heard. Most of the revolutionary movements of the Third World have been deeply influenced, directly or indirectly, by Paul Baran's *Political Economy of Growth*.

The economic analysis of *Monopoly Capital* is a development and systematization of ideas already contained in *the Political Economy of Growth* and Paul Sweezy's *The Theory of Capitalist Development* (1942). The central theme is that in a mature capitalist economy dominated by a handful of giant corporations the potential for capital accumulation far exceeds the profitable investment opportunities provided by the normal *modus operandi* of the private enterprise system. This results in a deepening tendency to stagnation which, if the system is to survive, must be continuously and increasingly counteracted by internal and external factors (for an elaboration of this analysis, see MONOPOLY CAPITALISM). In the authors' estimation – not always shared, or even understood by critics – the new and original contributions of *Monopoly Capital* had to do mainly with these counteracting factors and their far-reaching consequences for the history, politics, and culture of American society during the period from roughly the 1890s to the 1950s when the book was written. They intended it, in other words, as much more than a work of economics in the usual meaning of the terms.

PAUL M. SWEEZY

See also MONOPOLY CAPITALISM.

SELECTED WORKS

There is a comprehensive bibliography of Baran's writings in English in a special issue of *Monthly Review*, 'In Memory of Paul Alexander Baran. Born at Nikolaev, the Ukraine, 8 December 1910. Died at San Francisco, California, 26 March 1964', 16(11), March 1965. This also includes statements on his life and work by more than three dozen contributors, most of whom had been his friends or colleagues.

1957. *The Political Economy of Growth*. New York: Monthly Review Press. 2nd edn, with a new preface, 1962.
1966. (With P.M. Sweezy.) *Monopoly Capital: An Essay on the American Economic and Social Order*. New York: Monthly Review Press.
1970. *The Longer View: Essays Toward a Critique of Political Economy*. Edited by J. O'Neill, preface by P.M. Sweezy, New York: Monthly Review Press. This volume, which follows an outline prepared before his death by the author, brings together his most important hitherto scattered essays and reviews.

Barbon, Nicholas (1637/40–?1698). Nicholas Barbon, son of Praisegod Barbon, a London leather merchant, was born in 1637 (or 1640), and after studying medicine at Leyden and Utrecht and taking the MD at Utrecht in 1661, was admitted an Honorary Fellow of the College of Physicians at London in 1664. He was elected a Member of Parliament in 1690 and 1695. His successful career in various mercantile activities is reported in the autobiography of Roger North, the brother, biographer, and co-author of Sir Dudley North. He was engaged in the building trade in London following the great fire of 1666, and in 1685 he published a pamphlet *Apology for the Builder: or a Discourse showing the Cause and Effects of the Increase of Building*. In 1681 he established the first fire insurance company, and in 1684 published an *Account of two insurance offices*. Barbon also established a large financial venture in banking. With John Asgill he operated a Land Bank in 1695 and in the same year published *An Account of the Land Bank, showing the design and manner of the settlement*, and prepared a scheme for a National Land Bank which did not, however, come into existence.

Barbon's place in the history of economics is due to his *Discourse of Trade* (1690) and his more important *Discourse concerning coining the new money lighter: An answer to Mr Locke's Considerations about raising the value of money*. Taking the same position as Josiah Child and arguing, against Locke, for a legal reduction of the maximum rate of interest, he published in 1694 *An Answer to ... reasons against reducing interest to four per cent*. His argument against trade restrictions and for international free trade principles places him in the front rank of anticipators of the doctrines that developed in the following century. He exhibited clearly the connection between the supply of money and the effective level of trade. Against the proposals to recoin the currency at the old standard he pointed out the potential deflationary effects of the reduction in the money supply that would result, 'the consequence whereof will be that trade will be at a stand'.

Barbon's concern with the 'disorder ... that attends a nation that want money to drive their trade and commerce' and the 'prejudice to the state by making money scarce' led him to argue, in contexts that elevated to priority the functional significance of money, that 'it is not absolutely necessary that money should be made of gold or silver'. 'Banks of credit ... are of great advantage to trade.' 'Money is the instrument and measure of commerce and not silver.' Barbon held a supply and demand theory of market price, based on a logically prior notion of use values, and what he called 'time and place' value. He argued that 'interest is the rent of stock and is the same as the rent of land', claiming that a lower interest rate would raise capital values, indirectly by remedying 'the decay of trade' and directly by increasing the capitalized value of income streams.

Consumption expenditures, Barbon argued, provided employment. In his argument that 'prodigality is a vice that is prejudicial to the man but not to trade ... covetousness is a vice prejudicial to both man and trade', he anticipated the prodigality and employment-creating expenditure argument of the following century.

DOUGLAS VICKERS

SELECTED WORKS

1690. *A Discourse of Trade*. London. Ed. Jacob H. Hollander, Baltimore: Johns Hopkins University Reprint, 1905.
1696. *A Discourse concerning coining the new money lighter*. London.

BIBLIOGRAPHY

Letwin, W. 1963. *The Origins of Scientific Economics: English Economic Thought 1660–1776.* London: Methuen.

Vickers, D. 1959. *Studies in the Theory of Money 1690–1776.* Philadelphia: Chilton.

bargaining. By bargaining we mean negotiations between two or more parties about the terms of possible cooperation, which may involve trade, employment (collective bargaining), a joint business venture, etc. For lack of space we will discuss only bargaining between two parties, and will restrict ourselves to the case of complete information. (For *n*-person bargaining, see Harsanyi, 1977, chs 10 to 13; for the case of incomplete information, see Harsanyi, 1982, and Harsanyi and Selten, 1987).

The outcome of bargaining is either an *agreement* about the terms of mutual cooperation, or it is a *conflict* in case no agreement can be reached.

For the purposes of economic analysis, any possible outcome can be identified with a vector $x = (x_1, x_2)$, where x_1 and x_2 are the commodity bundles (commodity vectors) that this outcome would yield to parties 1 and 2, respectively. (A simple special case of this is when x_1 and x_2 are not vectors but rather are scalars representing the two sides' money payoffs.) An alternative approach is to identify each outcome with a utility vector $u = (u_1, u_2)$, where $u_1 = U_1(x_1)$ and $u_2 = U_2(x_2)$ are the two sides' utility payoffs, i.e., the utilities they would derive from the commodity payoffs or the money payoffs x_1 and x_2 in accordance with their utility functions U_1 and U_2. For convenience, the vectors $x = (x_1, x_2)$ defined in terms of commodities or in terms of money will be called *physical outcomes* whereas the corresponding vectors $u = (u_1, u_2)$ will be called *utility outcomes*.

In terms of the physical outcomes, a bargaining situation can be characterized by its *physical feasible set F**, defined as the set of all its possible physical outcomes x, and by its *physical conflict point* $c^* = (c_1^*, c_2^*)$, whose two components are the commodity payoffs or the money payoffs c_1^* and c_2^* the two sides would receive if they were unable to reach an agreement. Of course always

$$c^* \in F^* \tag{1}$$

because c^* is one of the possible physical outcomes.

On the other hand, in terms of the utility outcomes, a bargaining situation can be characterized by its (utilistic) *feasible set F*, defined as the set of all its possible utility outcomes u, and by its (utilistic) *conflict point* $c = (c_1, c_2)$, specifying the two sides' utility payoffs c_1 and c_2 in the absence of an agreement, to be called the two sides' *conflict payoffs*. Obviously, we have

$$c_1 = U_1(c_1^*), \quad c_2 = U_2(c_2^*), \tag{2}$$

and

$$F = \{(u_1, u_2) | u_1 = U_1(x_1), \; u_2 = U_2(x_2) \text{ and } (x_1, x_2) \in F^*\}. \tag{3}$$

Moreover, in view of (1)

$$c \in F. \tag{4}$$

Most of the economic literature on bargaining is based on the assumption of:

Sufficiency of utility outcomes. No essential information is lost by basing the economic analysis of a bargaining situation solely on its possible utility outcomes as defined by its feasible set F and by its conflict point $c = (c_1, c_2)$.

This assumption is motivated by the fact that the two bargainers will be interested only in the *utility outcome* of their bargaining process, in the sense that they will be indifferent between two physical outcomes x and x' if both of them yield the same utility outcome u. (This follows from the very definition of the two sides' utility functions; cf. Roemer, 1985.)

BARGAINING IN CLASSICAL ECONOMIC THEORY

Prior to the advent of game theory, what economic theory had to say about two-person bargaining situations amounted to two rationality postulates:

1. Individual rationality. A rational bargainer will not agree to a utility payoff smaller than his conflict payoff so that

$$u_1 \geqslant c_1 \quad \text{and} \quad u_2 \geqslant c_2; \tag{5}$$

and:

2. Joint rationality. Two rational bargainers will not agree on a utility outcome $u = (u_1, u_2)$ if in the feasible set F there is another utility outcome $u' = (u_1', u_2')$ yielding higher payoffs $u_1' > u_1$ and $u_2' > u_2$ for both of them. (In other words, the outcome to be agreed upon will be a *Pareto optimal* – at least a weakly Pareto optimal – point of the feasible set F. See Figure 1.)

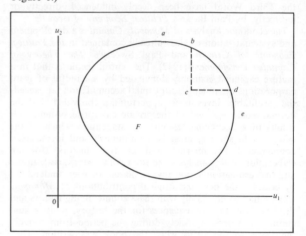

Figure 1

In Figure 1, the area F is the feasible set whereas the point c is the conflict point. The triangular area bcd is the set of all points satisfying the individual-rationality requirement. The upper-right boundary *abde* of F is the set of all Pareto optimal points, which satisfy the joint-rationality requirement. The intersection of the area bcd and of the boundary line *abde* is the arc bd: it is the set of all points satisfying *both* rationality requirements. Edgeworth (1881) called all points of bd possible *final settlements.* Pigou (1905) called bd itself the *range of practicable bargains.* Luce and Raiffa (1957) called it the *negotiation set.* We will follow this latter terminology. But we need also terms to describe the two end points of this set: We will call b party 1's *concession limit* because it is the least favourable outcome party 1 can rationally accept. By the same token, d will be called party 2's *concession limit.*

Neoclassical economics offers only what may be called a *weak* bargaining theory because it tells us no more than that the *agreement point* of two rational bargainers (i.e. the utility vector they will agree on) will lie somewhere within the negotiation set *bd*. But it does not tell us anything about *where* it will actually lie between the two sides' concession limits *b* and *d*, or about the economic forces that may move it closer to either limit.

THE NASH SOLUTION

It was the Danish economist Zeuthen (1930) who first realized the need for a *strong* bargaining theory predicting a *unique* agreement point, and who first understood that such a theory must be based on the two sides' attitudes toward *risk taking* and, more specifically, on the extent to which each side is willing to risk a conflict rather than accept unfavourable terms. But his path-breaking analysis of bargaining was seriously impaired by being done prior to von Neumann and Morgenstern's *Theory of Games and Economic Behavior* (1944), when neither the value of the axiomatic method in economic analysis nor the difference between expected-utility maximization and expected-money-income maximization was clearly understood.

Yet, even though von Neumann and Morgenstern's theory of games was an essential step toward a *strong* bargaining theory, their own analysis of two-person bargaining games did not go significantly beyond the *weak* bargaining theory of neoclassical economics. But they did provide the conceptual tools needed for a strong theory by introducing the concepts of moves, strategies, payoff functions, as well as games in extensive form, in normal form, and in characteristic-function form, etc. What is particularly important, they introduced the concept of von Neumann–Morgenstern utility functions, which offered a rigorous and convenient mathematical representation for the various players' attitudes toward risk taking – an essential prerequisite for a *strong* bargaining theory. Accordingly, the assumption of *sufficiency of utility outcomes* has to be restated as follows:

Necessity of von Neumann–Morgenstern utilities. A *strong* bargaining theory must be based on the feasible set *F* and on the conflict point $c = (c_1, c_2)$ defined in terms of the two sides' von Neumann–Morgenstern utilities. (But a *weak* bargaining theory can be based on defining *F* and *c* in terms of the two sides' *ordinal* utilities.)

The first author to use the analytical tools of game theory to propose a *strong* bargaining theory, was John Nash (1950, 1953), a brilliant student of von Neumann's. He assumed that the feasible set *F*, defined in terms of von Neumann–Morgenstern utilities, is a *compact* and *convex* set. (It will be convex because if *u* and *u'* are two feasible outcomes, then any probability mixture $pu + (1 - p)u'$ of the two will be likewise a feasible outcome.)

Nash postulates that the agreement point $\bar{u} = (\bar{u}_1, \bar{u}_2)$ of the game – commonly known as the *Nash solution* – will satisfy the following four axioms:

1. Efficiency. This is just the joint-rationality postulate of the last section.

A given game *G* is called *symmetrical* if interchanging the two players will not change the game. Geometrically this means that the feasible set *F* must be symmetrical with respect to the line λ defined by the equation $u_1 = u_2$, that is, with respect to the $+45°$ line going through the origin; and that the conflict point $c = (c_1, c_2)$ must lie on this line λ itself so that $c_1 = c_2$ (see Figure 2).

2. Symmetry. A symmetric game will have a symmetric agreement point $\bar{u} = (\bar{u}_1, \bar{u}_2)$ with $\bar{u}_1 = \bar{u}_2$. (In a symmetric game the two players have exactly the same strategic possibilities and have exactly the same bargaining power. Therefore, neither

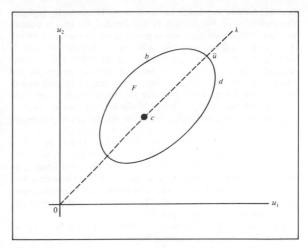

Figure 2

player will have any reason to accept an agreement yielding him a lower payoff than his opponent's.)

Axioms 1 and 2 already uniquely define the agreement point $\bar{u}$ of a symmetrical game: in such a game, $\bar{u}$ must be the intersection of line λ and of the upper-right boundary *bd* of the feasible set *F* (see Figure 2). The remaining two axioms are needed to extend the theory to nonsymmetrical games.

It is well known that two von Neumann–Morgenstern utility functions are behaviourally equivalent if one can be obtained from the other by an order-preserving linear transformation (i.e., by shifting the zero point of the utility scale and/or by changing the utility unit). This fact motivates axiom 3.

3. Linear invariance. Suppose that game *G'* can be obtained from game *G* by subjecting (say) player 1's utilities to an order-preserving linear transformation while keeping the other player's utilities unchanged so that, for any physical outcome $x = (x_1, x_2)$, the corresponding utility outcome $u = (u_1, u_2)$ is replaced by the transformed utility outcome $u' = (u_1', u_2')$ where

$$u_1' = au_1 + b \quad \text{with} \quad a > 0 \quad \text{and} \quad u_1' = u_2'. \qquad (6)$$

Suppose also that in the old game *G* the players would have agreed on the physical outcome $\bar{x} = (\bar{x}_1, \bar{x}_2)$ corresponding to the utility outcome $\bar{u} = (\bar{u}_1, \bar{u}_2)$. Then, in the new game *G'*, the players will agree on the *same* physical outcome $\bar{x}$, now corresponding to the utility outcome $\bar{u}' = (\bar{u}_1', \bar{u}_2')$ with

$$\bar{u}_1' = a\bar{u}_1 + b \quad \text{and} \quad \bar{u}_2' = \bar{u}_2. \qquad (7)$$

(In other words, the physical outcome $\bar{x}$ will not change if we choose to change the way we measure one player's von Neumann–Morgenstern utilities – even though, of course, the utility coordinates of $\bar{x}$ will change in accordance with the newly adopted method of measurement.)

Note that axiom 3 ensures that the outcome of bargaining will be independent of *interpersonal comparisons* of the two players' utilities. For by permitting transformation of one player's utilities without any transformation of the other player's it destroys the possibility that the outcome should depend on interpersonal utility comparisons.) Note also that in ethical contexts we cannot avoid making, or at least attempting, interpersonal utility comparisons. For instance, if I have to choose between giving my apple to Peter or to Paul, I may decide that Peter has a stronger moral claim to the apple because he would probably derive a *higher utility* from it (say, because he has not eaten for two days). In contrast, typically the outcome of bargaining is *not* decided by moral considerations. When one side makes a concession to the other he will do so out of *self-interest*, that is because he thinks it is unlikely that he can reach an agreement with the other side without making this concession. To be sure, sometimes people are guided by a mixture of pure bargaining considerations and of moral considerations. But in our theoretical analysis we must keep these two things apart. Unfortunately, many authors (including Luce and Raiffa, 1957) did not do so (see Harsanyi, 1977, pp. 13–15).

4. Independence of irrelevant alternatives. Let G be a bargaining game with conflict point c, with feasible set F, and with agreement point $\bar{u}$; and let G' be a game obtained from G by restricting the feasible set to a smaller set $F' \subset F$ in such a way that c and $\bar{u}$ remain within the new feasible set F', c remaining the conflict point also for G'. Then, $\bar{u}$ will be the agreement point also for this new game G'.

First, to explain the term 'irrelevant alternatives': by an 'alternative' we mean simply a feasible outcome. By an 'irrelevant' alternative we mean a feasible outcome *not* chosen by the players as their agreement point. Game G' is obtained from game G by excluding some of these irrelevant alternatives from the original feasible set F, without excluding the original agreement point $\bar{u}$ itself. What axiom 4 asserts is that by excluding such irrelevant alternatives from F we do not change the agreement point $\bar{u}$ of the game.

The upper-right boundary of the feasible set F will be called δF. The mathematical effect of axiom 4 is to make the agreement point $\bar{u}$ depend only on the shape of δF in the *neighbourhood* of $\bar{u}$, and to make the latter independent of the more distant parts of δF. The axiom is motivated by the way bargaining actually proceeds: It is a process of voluntary mutual concessions, which gradually *decreases* the set of possible outcomes under serious consideration from the entire boundary set δF to smaller and smaller subsets of δF around the eventual agreement point $\bar{u}$, and in the end to the one point $\bar{u}$ itself. What axiom 4 asserts is that this winnowing process does not change this agreement point $\bar{u}$ – which is a natural enough assumption since $\bar{u}$ is actually *chosen* by the winnowing process.

Yet even though axiom 4, it seems to me, has considerable intuitive appeal, it is no doubt the most controversial of Nash's axioms.

Nash has shown that these axioms imply the following theorem.

Theorem 1. The agreement point of the game is the unique utility vector $\bar{u} = (\bar{u}_1, \bar{u}_2)$ that maximizes the product

$$\pi = (u_1 - c_1)(u_2 - c_2), \tag{8}$$

called the *Nash product*, subject to

$$(u_1, u_2) \in F \tag{9}$$

and to

$$u_1 \geqslant c_1 \quad \text{and} \quad u_2 \geqslant c_2. \tag{10}$$

For a proof of this theorem, see Nash (1950, p. 59) or Harsanyi (1977, pp. 147–8).

Geometrically, the agreement point $\bar{u}$ can be characterized as follows: Let L_1 and L_2 be the horizontal and the vertical line going through the conflict point $c = (c_1, c_2)$. Then, $\bar{u}$ will be that particular point of the boundary set δF that lies on the highest rectangular hyperbola HH asymptotic to lines L_1 and L_2 and

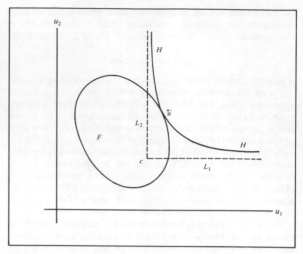

Figure 3

having a point in common with the feasible set F (see Figure 3).

ZEUTHEN'S BARGAINING MODEL

Even though Zeuthen's analysis is technically much inferior to Nash's it does usefully supplement tha latter because it makes the dependence of bargaining on the two sides' attitudes toward *risk taking* more explicit.

Suppose that, at a given stage of the bargaining process, player 1's last offer corresponded to the utility vector $v = (v_1, v_2)$ whereas player 2's last offer corresponded to the utility vector $w = (w_1, w_2)$ such that v and $w \in \delta F$, with $v_1 > w_1$ but $v_2 < w_2$. Which player will have to make the next concession? Zeuthen tries to answer this question as follows:

If player 1 accepts his oppenent's last offer w, then he will obtain the utility payoff w_1, with certainty. On the other hand, if he insists on his own last offer v, then he will obtain *either* payoff v_1 (if his opponent accepts this offer v) *or* will obtain the conflict payoff c_1 (if his opponent refuses to accept v). Suppose player 1 assigns the subjective probability p to the latter possibility and assigns the complementary probability $(1 - p)$ to the former possibility. Then, he must conclude that by insisting on his last offer u and by making no further concession he will obtain the expected payoff $(1 - p)v_1 + pc_1$, whereas by being conciliatory and accepting player 2's last offer w he will obtain payoff w_1.

Therefore, player 1 can rationally stick to his last offer only if

$$(1 - p)v_1 + pc_1 \geqslant w_1, \tag{11}$$

i.e., if

$$p \leqslant \frac{v_1 - w_1}{v_1 - c_1} = r_1. \tag{12}$$

By similar reasoning, if player 2 assigns probability q to the hypothesis that player 1 will stick to his last offer v, then he himself can rationally stick to his own last offer w only if

$$(1 - q)w_2 + qc_2 \geqslant v_2, \tag{13}$$

i.e., if

$$q \leqslant \frac{w_2 - v_2}{w_2 - c_2} = r_2. \tag{14}$$

Thus, the quantities r_1 and r_2 defined by (12) and by (14) can be interpreted as the *highest probability of a conflict* that player 1 and player 2, respectively, would face rather than accept the last offer of the other player. We will call r_1 and r_2 the two players' *risk limits*. Note that each player's risk limit is a ratio of two utility differences. The first one of these (such as the difference $v_1 - w_1$ in the case of player 1) measures the cost of *accepting the opponent's last offer* whereas the second (such as the difference $v_1 - c_1$ in the case of player 1) measures the cost of *provoking a conflict*.

Zeuthen suggests that the *next concession* must always come from the player with a *smaller* risk limit (except that if the two players' risk limits are equal then both of them must make concessions to avoid a conflict). We will call this suggestion *Zeuthen's principle*. This principle turns out to be closely related to the Nash solution.

Theorem 2. If the two players follow Zeuthen's principle then the next concession will always be made by the player whose last offer is associated with a higher Nash product (unless both are associated with equal Nash products, in which case both of them have to make concessions).

Proof. We have to show that $r_1 \geqslant r_2$ if and only if $(v_1 - c_1)(v_2 - c_2) \geqslant (w_1 - c_1)(w_2 - c_2)$, and then that if the first inequality is reversed then so is the second. But this follows from (12) and (14).

Corollary. If the two players act in accordance with Zeuthen's principle then they will tend to reach the Nash solution as their agreement point.

Proof. By Theorem 2, at each stage of the bargaining the offer point with the smaller Nash product will be replaced by a new offer point with a higher Nash product. The process will end at the utility vector with the highest possible Nash product, which is the Nash solution.

This statement, however, is subject to two qualifications.

1. If the two players make continually decreasing concessions to each other then the bargaining process may not converge to any agreement point at all. This can be prevented by requiring that all concessions should have a uniform lower bound (say, 1¢).
2. The process may 'overshoot' the Nash solution if either player makes unreasonably large concessions. But this can happen only if the players do not realize that they can always reach an agreement without accepting a payoff lower than the Nash solution would give them.

SELTEN'S AXIOMS FOR THE NASH SOLUTION

The Zeuthen–Nash theory in its original form postulates a feasible set F consisting of infinitely many feasible points. But it is worth considering a simpler bargaining situation where the players can choose only between *two* possible agreement points $v(v_1, v_2)$ and $w = (w_1, w_2)$. If they agree on which one to choose then this will be the outcome. But if they disagree then they will obtain only the conflict payoffs c_1 and c_2. Without loss of generality, we can choose the two players' utility functions in such a way that $c_1 = c_2 = 0$. The resulting 2×2 game can be represented by the payoff matrix shown in Game 1.

We will assume that outcome v is better for player 1 whereas outcome w is better for player 2 so that

$$v_1 > w_1 \quad \text{but} \quad v_2 < w_2. \tag{15}$$

Selten has shown that a game of this simple form can be fully analysed by using only two axioms (cf. Harsanyi and Selten, 1987, ch. 3).

One is the *linear-invariance* axiom (which is the same as Nash's axiom 3). The other is a *monotonicity* axiom (see below).

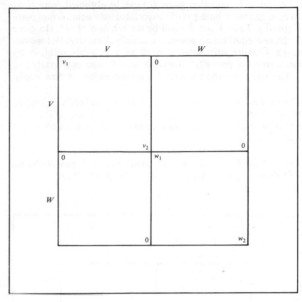

Game 1

Definition. A 2×2 game like Game 1 will be called *symmetrical* if $v_1 = w_2 = a$ and $v_2 = w_1 = b$. Thus, a symmetrical game will have the following form:

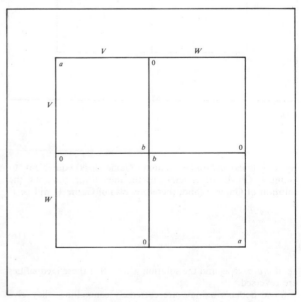

Game 2

Clearly, in a symmetrical game there can be no mathematical criterion which selects *either* one of the two equilibrium points $\bar{V}$ and $\bar{W}$ as the solution in preference to the other equilibrium point.

Monotonicity axiom. Suppose that game G is symmetrical (like Game 2), and that game G^* can be obtained from G by *increasing* one or both payoffs associated with equilibrium point $\bar{V}$ (or $\bar{W}$). Then $\bar{V}$ (or $\bar{W}$) will be the solution of G^*. (In game G the two equilibrium points are equally attractive. But we can make $\bar{V}$ more attractive than $\bar{W}$ as a possible solution by increasing the payoff(s) asociated with $\bar{V}$, and conversely.)

The linear-invariance and the monotonicity axioms imply:

Theorem 3. Game 1 will have $\bar{V}$ or $\bar{W}$ as its solution depending on whether $\pi(\bar{V}) > \pi(\bar{W})$ or $\pi(\bar{W}) > \pi(\bar{V})$, where $\pi(\bar{V}) = v_1 v_2$ and $\pi(\bar{W}) = w_1 w_2$ are the Nash products associated with $\bar{V}$ and with $\bar{W}$, respectively.

Proof. Suppose in game 1 we divide player 1's payoffs by w_1, and divide player 2's payoffs by v_2. Then we obtain:

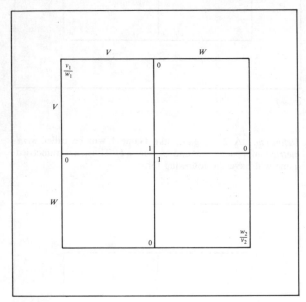

Game 3

By the linear-invariance axiom, Game 3 is equivalent to Game 1. On the other hand, by the monotonicity axiom, the solution of Game 3 (and, therefore, also of Game 1) will be $\bar{V}$ if

$$\frac{v_1}{w_1} > \frac{w_2}{v_2}, \tag{16}$$

i.e. if $v_1 v_2 > w_1 w_2$ and the solution will be $\bar{W}$ if these inequalities are reversed.

Since Selten's axioms are extremely compelling, they give strong intuitive support to the Nash solution.

THE CASE OF VARIABLE THREATS

Until now we have assumed that the two players' conflict payoffs c_1 and c_2 are simply *given*. But in many situations these payoffs will actually be determined by the retaliatory strategies t_1 and t_2 that players 1 and 2 would use against each other if they could not reach an agreement, so that we have to write

$$c_1 = H_1(t_1, t_2) \quad \text{and} \quad c_2 = H_2(t_1, t_2), \tag{17}$$

where H_1 and H_2 are the two players' payoff functions in the game.

To extend his theory to this kind of situation, Nash proposed the following model. The game is played in two stages. At stage 1, the two players announce their *threat strategies* t_1 and t_2, that is, the retaliatory strategies they would use in case of disagreement; and they will be *required* to implement these strategies if in fact no agreement is reached. (Implementation is assumed to be compulsory to exclude bluffing.) These threat strategies t_1 and t_2 then define the players' conflict payoffs c_1 and c_2 in accordance with (17).

Then, at stage 2 the two players will choose an agreement point $\bar{u} = (\bar{u}_1, \bar{u}_2)$ in accordance with Theorem 3 above, now regarding their conflict payoffs c_1 and c_2 as *given*.

In the bargaining model of Theorem 3 each player had only *one* possible threat, that of simple noncooperation. In contrast, in the model just described, each player may have a *choice* among various alternative threat strategies. The former is called the Nash model with *fixed threats*. The latter is called the Nash model with *variable threats*.

In this latter model, at stage 1 each player i must obviously choose his threat strategy t_i so as to maximize his final payoff $\bar{u}_i$. Maximization of his conflict payoff c_i would *not* be a rational objective because he expects $\bar{u}_i$ rather than c_i to be his actual payoff. (Prior to Nash, this was not properly understood. Even such distinguished economists as Hicks (1932) got it quite wrong (see Harsanyi, 1977, pp. 189–91).) The problem of how to choose an optimal threat strategy can be elucidated by the following theorem.

Theorem 4. Suppose that player 2's threat strategy t_2 is given. Then player 1 must choose his own threat strategy t_1 in such a way as to *maximize* the ratio

$$R = \frac{u_2 - c_2}{u_1 - c_1} = \frac{u_2 - H_2(t_1, t_2)}{u_1 - H_1(t_1, t_2)}. \tag{18}$$

On the other hand, given player 1's threat strategy t_1, player 2 must choose his own threat strategy t_2 so as to *minimize* this ratio R. (For a proof of the theorem, see Harsanyi, 1977, pp. 176–7.)

Note. When it comes to choosing threat strategies then the quantities $(u_2 - c_2)$ and $(u_1 - c_1)$ are to be interpreted as player 2's and player 1's *conflict costs* so that R itself becomes the *ratio* of these two costs.

CONCLUSION

Nash's theory of two-person bargaining is what we have called a *strong* theory: it defines a unique utility vector $\bar{u} = (\bar{u}_1, \bar{u}_2)$ as the agreement point to be chosen by two rational bargainers. For each player $i (i = 1, 2)$, this agreement point will yield a higher payoff $\bar{u}_i$:

(1) The greater his own willingness, and the less his opponent's willingness, to risk a conflict rather than accept unfavourable terms – as determined by his and his opponent's von Neumann–Morgenstern utility functions.

(2) The smaller the utility gain he could confer on his opponent at a given utility cost to himself if he made a further concession to him. (Thus, if the boundary curve δF were replaced by a *flatter* curve $\delta F'$ intersecting δF at agreement point $\bar{u}$ then this agreement point would move to the *right*, increasing player 1's payoff and decreasing player 2's.)

(3) The higher his own conflict payoff c_i and the lower his opponent's conflict payoff c_j would be if no agreement could be reached.

In case a player i has a choice among alternative threat strategies, he will maximize his final payoff u_i by maximizing the quantity $R = (u_i - c_i)/(u_j - c_j)$, that is, the ratio of his own conflict costs to his opponent's conflict costs, both measured in terms of von Neumann–Morgenstern utilities.

Finally, let me add the following qualification. Nash's theory is an attempt to predict how two rational bargainers will interact. But these predictions are based on the assumption that both sides' expectations about each other's behaviour are *endogenous*, that is are based on the intrinsic parameters of the bargaining situation (game situation) as such. But in many cases this may not be true. For example, the two parties may live in a society where it is customary for an older person to receive twice the payoff his younger opponent will receive. If each player *expects* the other player to follow this rule, it will become rational for him to follow it too. (For an experiment based on imparting exogenous expectations, see Roth and Schoumaker, 1983. For an excellent discussion of alternative axioms and of alternative solution concepts as well as for a very good bibliography, the reader is referred to Roth, 1979.)

JOHN C. HARSANYI

See also BILATERAL MONOPOLY; CONFLICT AND SETTLEMENT; CORES; EDGEWORTH, FRANCIS YSIDRO; EXCHANGE; GAME THEORY; SOCIAL WELFARE FUNCTION; ZEUTHEN, FREDERIK.

BIBLIOGRAPHY

Edgeworth, F.Y. 1881. *Mathematical Psychics*. London: C. Kegan Paul & Co.

Harsanyi, J.C. 1956. Approaches to the bargaining problem before and after the theory of games: a critical discussion of Zeuthen's, Hicks', and Nash's theories. *Econometrica* 24, 144–57.

Harsanyi, J.C. 1977. *Rational Behavior and Bargaining Equilibrium*. Cambridge: Cambridge University Press.

Harsanyi, J.C. 1982. Solutions for some bargaining games under the Harsanyi–Selten solution theory, I–II. *Mathematical Social Sciences* 3, 179–91 and 259–79.

Harsanyi, J.C. and Selten, R. 1987. *A General Theory of Equilibrium Selection in Games*. Cambridge, Mass.: MIT Press

Hicks, J.R. 1932. *The Theory of Wages*. London: Macmillan.

Luce, R.D. and Raiffa, H. 1957. *Games and Decisions*. New York: Wiley.

Nash, J.F. 1950. The bargaining problem. *Econometrica* 18, 155–62.

Nash, J.F. 1953. Two-person cooperative games. *Econometrica* 21, 128–40.

Neumann, J. von and Morgenstern, O. 1944. *Theory of Games and Economic Behavior*. Princeton: Princeton University Press.

Pigou, A.C. 1905. *Principles and Methods of Industrial Peace*. London: Macmillan.

Roemer, J.E. 1985. Axiomatic bargaining theory of economic environments. University of California, Davis, Working Papers Series No. 264.

Roth, A.E. 1979. *Axiomatic Models of Bargaining*. Berlin: Springer-Verlag.

Roth, A.E. and Schoumaker, F. 1983. Subjective probability and the theory of games: some further comments. *Management Science* 29, 1337–40.

Zeuthen, F. 1930. *Problems of Monopoly and Economic Warfare*. London: Routledge & Kegan Paul.

Barone, Enrico (1859–1924). Barone was born in Naples on 22 December 1859 and died in Rome on 14 May 1924. His education provided him with a solid grounding in the classics and in mathematics, with a view to embarking on a military career. He was appointed in 1894 to the Officers' Training School, where he was 'teacher in charge of military history'. He remained in this position until 1902, when be became the head of the historical office of the General Staff, and was given the rank of colonel.

He resigned in 1906, having already published an excellent series of biographical and historical military studies which altered the traditional concept of historical study in that field, by applying to it a method of successive approximation to which his growing interest in economics had introduced him.

His acquaintance with Maffeo Pantaleoni and Vilfredo Pareto provided him with the opportunity of collaborating with the *Giornale degli Economisti*. This association proved to be extremely valuable and productive and was to last from 1894 right up to the year of his death. It was in this periodical that in September/October 1908 he published the article 'Il Ministro della produzione nello stato collettivista'. This article was for a long time considered to be a mere 'curiosum'. However, after its publication in English in a volume edited by Hayek in 1935, it was destined to place its author, together with von Wieser and Pareto, alongside the founders of the pure theory of a socialist economy.

The whole discussion on collective economic planning, as it had developed since the 1920s, had ideological motivations and implications. These were totally excluded from Barone's article. The paper was, above all, a very ingenious illustration of one of Barone's deep beliefs: the usefulness of mathematical tools in clarifying questions which otherwise remain intricate and obscure. In fact it was Barone's use of equations which established the formal equivalence of the basic economic categories between a society based on private ownership in perfectly competitive conditions and a socialist society, in which the distinct need to establish the relative distribution of income was recognized. As Samuelson writes, the innovative meaning of Barone's contribution was that 'by avoiding all mention of utility and indeed without introducing even the notion of indifference curves, Barone was able to break new ground along lines which have in recent years become associated with the economic theory of index numbers'.

The importance of Barone's arguments in the 1930s debate on the economics of socialism in which he used the idea of a Pareto optimum and improved its application, was also not fully appreciated. It remained for Samuelson's *Foundations of Economic Analysis* to give a complete acknowledgement of Barone's development (adding different products after they have been weighted by their respective prices through a process of tâtonnement) of the Paretian optimum conditions as they relate to the planning of production under collectivism.

In addition to his connections with the economists already mentioned, Barone was acquainted with the famous academics of the time, both Italian and foreign (in particular, Walras) and they all in various ways underlined the enormous potential of Barone's intellect, his clever use of analytical tools, and the extreme clarity of his graphics. Walras, for example, wrote to him saying that

> Providence has singled you out to write the historical review of the various attempts made at mathematical economics over the last centuries, which promise to offer a doctrine which will become generally accepted in the next century. I strongly urge you to recognize this as your vocation and I hope that circumstances will allow you to undertake the task.

Alongside this appreciation, however, is the impression that Barone was overstretching his interests, a feeling which was stated in no uncertain terms by Luigi Einaudi: 'Because of the various vicissitudes of a life torn between activity, journalism, learning and the cinema ... Barone, who was not inclined to laborious and painstaking research, produced far fewer fruits than his supporters had anticipated.' The comment on the cinema refers to the fact that Barone, pressed by financial necessity and using his historical and military background, prepared treatments for the booming early Italian film industry.

This division of interests delayed until 1910 Barone's appointment to a chair in political economy at the Advanced Institute of Economics and Commerce in Rome, which later became the Faculty of Economics and Commerce. But with hindsight it cannot be said that Barone's admirers were justified in 'asking for more'. It is nearer the truth to say that he had not taken the trouble to put together his often very original and therefore extremely important papers on various subjects. As often happens, however, the very fact that his work on the pure theory of socialism received so much international acclaim was the cause for inadequate recognition of his other notable contributions. Of these, the much revised *Principi di Economia Politica* (1908) was an excellent text book, which, together with the booklet *Moneta e Risparmio* (1920), indicated that dynamic market forces constituted the main area of his intellectual interest. See also his works entitled *Economia coloniale* (1912), 'I costi connessi e l'economia dei trasporti' (1921), and 'Sindacati (cartelli e trust)' (1921). Of comparable importance are Barone's investigations in the field of financial studies, demonstrating an approach different from that of De Viti de Marco and Einaudi. Barone assumed an autonomous position inasmuch as he availed himself of Pareto's contributions on the stability of the distribution of incomes, using it as the basis of the distribution of taxes amongst the members of the community. There have been numerous criticisms of the statistical foundation of the Paretian income curve, and even Barone admitted that its shape could undergo change according to variations in social composition. Nevertheless, using its formulation, he provided an inductive basis for the study of a central issue in public finance. Barone's other research of recognized theoretical relevance was on the adverse welfare effects of indirect taxes on taxpayers as compared with direct taxes, for the same given tax returns. Barone was also a severe critic of the alternative versions of the financial theories of savings, in particular that of Edgeworth on minimum saving.

Although Barone was at the centre of the major theoretical debates of his time, he suffered from a conflicting loyalty to the two main formulators of general equilibrium theory, Walras and Pareto. Having been one of the first to grasp the logical aspects of general equilibrium theory, Barone was able to suggest ideas which Walras used to improve his formulation of the production function and the theory of distribution. When Pareto criticized the Walrasian formulation, Barone refrained from taking sides between the two exponents of

general equilibrium theory, and as a result Walras refused to recognize the suggestions Barone had given him. Barone himself confided to Wicksell that much of his work had aimed at 'bringing peace' between the two great antagonists. He considered their 'heated disputes' to be 'utterly and completely' deplorable. In spite of this show of fidelity, Barone should not be thought of merely as a follower of Walras and Pareto. As Gustavo del Vecchio, an excellent judge of both Italian and international economic thought, observed,

> Barone understood the deep systematic and critical significance of general equilibrium theory, but because he had been brought up on philosophy and history, he was able to fully appreciate how great were the writers who followed the partial approach, of whom Marshall was pre-eminent. For them, economic science existed only where it could be related to concrete and immediate reality by means of our instruments of observation.

F. CAFFÈ

See also ADDING-UP PROBLEM; ECONOMIC CALCULATION IN SOCIALIST ECONOMIES; PARETO, VILFREDO; SOCIAL WELFARE FUNCTION.

SELECTED WORKS

A complete bibliography of Barone's military studies is provided by a symposium on the fiftieth anniversary of his death, published in the periodical *L'Amministrazione della Difesa*, July/October 1974. The economic works of Enrico Barone have been reprinted in three volumes by Zanichelli (Bologna), 1937. The latest partial reprinting was carried out by Cedam (Padua), 1970. Of his works on economics, see:

1894a. Di alcuni problemi fondamentali per la teoria matematica dell'imposta. *Giornale degli Economisti*, March.
1894b. Sul trattamento di questioni dinamiche. *Giornale degli Economisti*, November.
1895. Studi sull distribuzione. *Giornale degli Economisti*, February/March.
1908a. *Principi di economia politica*. 7th edn, Rome: Sampaolesi, 1929.
1908b. Il Ministro della Produzione nello Stato Collettivista. *Giornale degli Economisti*, September/October. Reprinted as 'The Ministry of Production in the Collectivist State' in *Collectivist Economic Planning*, ed. F.A. Hayek, London: Routledge, 1935; translated into many other languages.
1912a. *Economia coloniale*. Rome: Sampaolese.
1912b. Studi de Economia e Finanza. *Giornale degli Economisti*, April/July.
1920. *Moneta e Risparmio*. Rome: Armani.
1921a. I costi connessi e l'economia dei trasporti. *Giornale degli Economisti*, February.
1921b. Sindacati (cartelli e trust). In *Nuova Collana di Economisti*, Vol. VII, Turin: Utet, 1956.

BIBLIOGRAPHY

Del Vecchio, G. 1925. L'opera scientifica di Enrico Barone. *Giornale degli Economisti*, November.
Einaudi, L. 1939. *Prefazione ai Principi di Economia finanziaria di A. De Viti de Marco*. Turin: Einaudi.
Jaffé, W. (ed.) 1965. *Correspondence of Léon Walras and related papers*. 3 vols, Amsterdam: North-Holland.
Samuelson, P.A. 1948. *Foundations of Economic Analysis*. Cambridge, Mass.: Harvard University Press.
Spinedi, F. 1924. Di un metodo nello studio della scienza sociale. *Rivista di scienze sociali e discipline ausiliarie*.

barriers to entry. *See* BAIN, JOE STATEN; CONTESTABLE MARKETS; ENTRY AND MARKET STRUCTURE.

barter. Barter is a simultaneous exchange of commodities, whether goods or labour services, with bargaining and without using money. It is thus a form of trade in which credit is absent or weak, where buyers and sellers compete and rates are not fixed, and which lacks an abstract measure of value in exchange or payment.

There is no economy known to ethnographers in which barter is the only means of exchange; but there are some in which it is dominant (e.g. Humphrey, 1985); and many marginal areas where barter plays a significant role alongside varieties of primitive trade and money transactions. Moreover barter is a major component of international trade, especially between east and west; it is an indispensable business tool of many modern corporations; and, with the rise of computerized exchange in the USA, it has begun to worry the Internal Revenue Service.

None of these contemporary examples, however, captures the interest of economists in barter. For it is as a central plank in the origin myth of classical and neoclassical economics that barter owes its prominence in modern thought. Adam Smith traced the 'wealth of nations' to division of labour:

> This division of labour, from which so many advantages are derived, is not originally the effect of any human wisdom ... It is the necessary, though very slow and gradual, consequence of a certain propensity in human nature which has in view no such extensive utility; the propensity to truck, barter and exchange one thing for another (Smith, 1776, I. ii, p. 13).

Linking this propensity to the faculties of reason and speech, Smith draws a line between ourselves and the animals: 'Nobody ever saw a dog make a fair and deliberate exchange of one bone for another with another dog' (ibid.). Given such a predisposition, mankind took advantage of differences in geography and skill to establish interdependence through primitive barter. Eventually the difficulties inherent in barter led to the emergence of certain commodities as normal means of exchange and eventually to money proper. Barter, as an expression of a natural human tendency, is thus the forerunner of modern markets based on money. It follows that these markets should be allowed to be self-regulating and spared the interventions of political agents claiming to possess superior 'wisdom'.

The founders of marginalist economics (Menger, Jevons) likewise traced the origins of money to the inefficiency of an earlier stage of barter. Most modern writers on money follow their example. In this they all echo a tradition first established by Plato and Aristotle. The Greek philosophers, however, imagined that, for money to come to express proportionate needs in a complementary division of labour, law rather than nature was required. To sum up the standard economists' myth, a natural propensity to exchange led human beings to establish a division of labour articulated by individualized barter in local markets; eventually long-distance trade evolved and with it more efficient markets based on money. The absence of a guiding political agency is an important feature of this story.

The most elegant refutation of such a construct is made by Polanyi in *The Great Transformation* (1944). He suggests that a more plausible historical sequence is the reverse of the above. Starting from a geographically based division of labour, highly placed political agents trade goods over long distances and routinize means of payment in a process leading to the establishment of money. Local markets are sometimes a spin-off of these channels of *grand commerce*, 'thus eventually, but no means necessarily, offering to some individuals an occasion to indulge in their alleged propensity for bargaining and haggling' (Polanyi, 1944, p. 58). Clearly, evolutionary parables should be treated with caution, especially when they fall under one pole or the other of an ideological struggle between liberalism and socialism. Barter is invariably found in an economic context marked by several institutions of exchange. What matters is to identify its structural features in juxtaposition with alternative mechanisms. In the following discussion the evidence for barter in primitive or backward economies will be reviewed, before turning briefly to its revival in capitalist economies. The principal conclusion is that an understanding of barter requires a synthetic approach combining politics and markets.

Grierson's classic article on the silent trade (1903) is a compilation of evidence for barter without face-to-face contact which captures the early fascination of armchair anthropology with the subject. The first modern fieldwork monograph in anthropology was also devoted to institutions of exchange. In *Argonauts of the Western Pacific* (1922) Malinowski set out to challenge what he took to be prevailing models of 'economic man'. His focus was the *kula*, a system of gift-exchange in the islands near New Guinea, involving armshells and necklaces. Under the cover of such an exchange between local leaders, the common people bartered for goods whose uneven distribution owed much to a geographically based division of labour. In addition maritime and inland villages exchanged fish for vegetables, sometimes through a formal rationing system organized by community leaders, sometimes through individual barter.

Malinowski emphasized the contrast of styles and status honour between ceremonial exchange and ordinary barter, although in the first case cited they were spatially united and in the second were institutional alternatives. The Melanesians were as anxious as the ethnographer to stress their absolute antipathy to confusion of the two extreme forms of exchange. Gift-giving was formal, characterized by generosity and delay of a return (implying credit and trust); barter was informal, characterized by conflict in bargaining and immediacy of return (implying no projection of the relationship into the future). One conferred high social standing, the other low status. In practice, ceremonial exchange is a means of establishing a fragile political order for trade through a transfer of tokens of alliance between leaders whose communities are on a footing akin to war; whereas individual barter and the appearance of hostility intrinsic to price negotiations can only be tolerated in a situation marked by peace and stable social order. Whatever the imputed social psychology, ceremonial exchange is a direct political intervention in the market, barter a manifestation of relatively free commodity exchange. Societies lacking states and money cannot rely exclusively on one form or the other. They must combine gift-exchange and barter pragmatically in response to variable degrees of 'peace for the trade'.

Recently, Humphrey (1985) has linked barter to economic disintegration in the periphery. Her case study of a people living near the Nepal–Tibet border accounts for the dominance of barter by the low supply of money. Being very poor, they cannot afford to keep much wealth in the form of money, preferring to satisfy demand immediately in the one-to-one transactions of barter. Under these circumstances money itself becomes an item of barter. Humphrey relates this temporary phenomenon to a collapse of the local political order which has left the population in a fragmented and individuated state. They have a high level of mutual tolerance but no hierarchy through which to organize inter-local trade as they once did. There is sometimes 'delayed barter' involving more valuable items and the extension of credit between trading partners. But his looks like a weak version of that more formalized trade based on trust which perhaps ought not to be confused with barter. Delay in making a return and associated relations of credit/debt are antithetical to barter; for bargaining is impossible if either party does not have the option of withdrawing from the negotiation.

Recent anthropological research has focused on the tendency of bartered goods to fall into distinct 'spheres of exchange'. In a classic article Bohannan (1955) argues that the Tiv of Nigeria prefer to exchange goods of the same broad category and look down on transactions across the boundaries between such spheres. Subsistence items are distinguished from prestige goods like cattle, slaves, metal bars and cloth. The highest level of exchange involves marriageable women only. In the colonial period money destroyed this compartmentalization of exchange by making conversion between spheres easier. Cultural disruption was the result.

This argument confuses several levels of analysis. First, as Marshall pointed out, utilities are never wholly commensurate: subsistence, luxury and prestige goods cannot be equalized simply by sharing a monetary medium of evaluation. It does not make any sense to ask how many sacks of potatoes an Eton education is worth, even though they both have a money price. Second, there are clearly problems of conversion in barter between low-bulk, high-value items and high-bulk, low-value items, typically between long-distance trade goods and small agricultural surpluses. Livestock and poultry offer one ready means of conversion, however. Again, nobody likes to sell a hi-fi set in order to pay the groceries bill, but such conversions are known to occur. Third – and most damaging – the main force restricting exchange to separate spheres is political and ideological, not economic in the technical sense. Tiv elders control commerce with the outside world and hold their junior kinsmen on the farm through a monopoly of marriageable women. Colonialism – not money as a fetishized abstraction – undermined that control by introducing markets for the young men's goods and labour.

The absence of money does not in itself present an insurmountable obstacle to efficient exchange. Much the most important precondition for barter lies in the forms of political order (or the lack of it); and it is this which is undermined by modern markets and by the states whose power is essential to their functioning. With this in mind we should consider briefly the survival of barter in the trading institutions of the advanced economies.

Much of the trade between the West and the Communist bloc takes the form of barter for the obvious reason that the East cannot accumulate hard currency reserves. Third World countries, such as some West African states, barter the products of an ecological division of labour (meat for grain) owing to a general lack of cash. Such activities are similar to the early trade between political agents emphasized by Polanyi. The multinational corporations have treasuries larger than those of many nations, yet they often choose to barter commodities they would normally be unable to sell in open markets – so many thousand gallons of paint for several months' lease of a Bahamas hotel chain. These activities are worrying to the tax authorities of nation states whose control over money supply has already been eroded by the rise of Eurodollar banking since early 1970s.

The *laisser-faire* economist's myth of barter as an expression of mankind's innate propensity to exchange ought to be replaced by a more complex historical appraisal of the institution's significance. Barter is an extremely widespread phenomenon, occurring in many times and places as a partial and often temporary solution to the problem of exchange. It is not abolished by money and indeed sometimes transforms money itself into an item of barter; and, if recent trends are a reliable indicator, it may now be undergoing a revival in the West. It was always a mistake to suppose that markets expanded without definite political conditions for their maintenance. Barter too rests on variable political conditions which are as much contemporary as they are primitive.

KEITH HART

See also ECONOMIC ANTHROPOLOGY; EXCHANGE; GIFTS.

BIBLIOGRAPHY
Bohannan, P. 1955. Some principles of exchange and investment among the Tiv. *American Anthropologist*. 57, 60–70.
Grierson, P. 1903. The silent trade. In *Research in Economic Anthropology*, Vol. 3, ed. G. Dalton, Greenwich, Conn.: JAI Press, 1980, 1–74.
Humphrey, C. 1985. Barter and economic disintegration. *Man* 20(1), 48–72.
Malinowski, B. 1922. *Argonauts of the Western Pacific*. London: Routledge.
Polanyi, K. 1944. *The Great Transformation*. Boston: Farrar.
Smith, A. 1776. *An Inquiry into the Nature and Causes of the Wealth of Nations*. Ed. E. Cannan, New York: The Modern Library, 1937.

barter and exchange. Barter, as distinct from exchange, is defined by the absence of money both as a medium of exchange and a measure of value. In the absence of a measure of value, complicated transactions between several dealers are hardly possible; and accordingly barter is generally characterized by the absence of competition. In the absence of competition bargains are not *determinate* in the same sense as in a perfect market. In the former, unlike the latter, case you might suppose the dispositions of the parties, their demand curves or 'schedules' (Marshall) known, and yet even theoretically be unable to predict what would be the terms of the bargain.

As Jevons says of such a case – with, in the context, unnecessary emphasis on the *indivisibility* of the commodity exchanged.

> The equations of exchange will fail ... I conceive that such a transaction must be settled upon other than strictly economical grounds. The result of the bargain will greatly depend upon the comparative amount of knowledge of each other's positions and needs which either bargainer may possess or manage to obtain in the course of the transaction (*Theory of Political Economy*, 2nd edn, pp. 130–34).

To which Mr Price adds, 'Nor indeed, did they possess the gift of clairvoyance, would the problem be necessarily solved' (*Industrial Peace*, p. 54). It is important to study this property of barter not so much on account of the rudimentary transactions to which the term is properly confined as for the sake of their analogy to the dealings of monopolists and combinations in advanced societies.

[The subject in question is discussed in the following passages: Auspitz and Lieben, *Theorie des Preises*, p. 381; Edgeworth, *Mathematical Psychics*, pp. 20–56; 'Observations on the Mathematical Theory of Economics', *Giornale degli Economist*, March 1891; Marshall, *Principles of Economics*, 'Note on Barter'; Menger, *Grundsätze*, ch. iv; Price, *Industrial Peace*, pp. 14 and 54; Sidgwick, *Political Economy*, book ii, ch. x.

The formation of appropriate conceptions on the subject is aided by those economists who, improving on the ordinary 'Robinsonnade', introduce a *second* primitive economic man.

Good examples occur in Courcelle Seneuil's *Traité théorique et pratique*, and Mr. Gonner's textbook of *Political Economy*.]

[F.Y. Edgeworth]

Reprinted from *Palgrave's Dictionary of Political Economy*.

BIBLIOGRAPHY
Auspitz, R. and Lieben, R. 1887. *Zur Theorie des Preises*. Leipzig.
Courcelle-Seneuil, J.G. 1858. *Traité théorique et pratique d'économie politique*. Paris: Amyot.
Edgeworth, F.Y. 1881. *Mathematical Psychics*. London: Kegan Paul.
Edgeworth, F.Y. 1891. Observations on the mathematical theory of economics. *Giornale degli Economisti*, March.
Gonner, E.C.K. 1888. *Political Economy*. London: R. Sutton & Co.
Marshall, A. 1890. Note on barter. In his *Principles of Economics*, London: Macmillan.
Menger, C. 1871. *Grundsätze der Volkwirtschaftslehre*. Vienna.
Sidgwick, H. 1883. *Principles of Political Economy*. London: Macmillan.

Barton, John (1789–1852). Barton is remembered in the history of economic thought for an early critical discussion of the impact of machinery on employment. A Sussex landowner, he combined an interest in statistical observation with a special concern for the impact of industrial and agrarian change on the condition of the labourer. He was the author of two important books, *Observations on the Circumstances which Influence the Condition of the Labouring Classes of Society* (1817) and *An Inquiry into the Causes of the Progressive Depreciation of Agricultural Labour in Modern Times* (1820). Later, in the 1830s, he wrote several tracts on the Corn Laws and on population and colonization. He was elected a fellow of the London Statistical Society in 1847 and read a paper in 1849, 'The Influence of the Subdivision of the Soil on the Moral and Physical Well-being of the People of England and Wales'. His early manuscript essays show a wide and careful grounding in political economy based on Hume, Smith and Ricardo. His first books were, however, written as interventions in the contemporary debates on the Poor Laws.

Barton's primary purpose in writing both the *Observations* and the *Inquiry* was to challenge Malthusian population theory, and the prevailing opinion that the cause of excess population and falling wages was the support offered by the Old Poor Law. Barton combined abstract reasoning with statistical data in a critique of Malthus and Ricardo that so impressed Schumpeter that he judged it 'a remarkable performance ... far above the rest of the literature that currently criticized the class leaders for their lack of realism, actual or supposed'.

Barton drew on population figures from the 16th to the 18th century to challenge Malthusian propositions of the dependence of population growth on levels of capital accumulation. Using data gathered from the agricultural districts, he also challenged assumptions of flexible supplies of labour in response to wage changes. His data provided no support for those who feared that population growth would follow on high wages. Custom and employment prospects, not changing wage rates, were the most important determinant of the age of marriage. Barton dissected the gap between population and labour supply, analysing age structure, apprenticeship, skills and labour immobility. His demographic work impressed Sismondi and induced McCulloch to give up Malthusianism.

The most influential analysis of the *Observations*, however, was Barton's critique of Ricardo's and Malthus' early optimistic assumptions of the impact of capital accumulation and machinery on the working classes. Another reason why high wages could not be blamed for inducing population growth, he argued, was that capital accumulation did not necessarily entail increases in employment. Capital had to be disaggregated into fixed (technological) and circulating (wage goods) capital before its impact on the labour market could be assessed. The demand for labour was dependent on circulating, not fixed, capital. And if wage rates rose relative to commodity prices, employers would substitute machinery for labour. The process of capital accumulation could, therefore, entail the release of rather than the demand for labour, and the amount of labour employed in the construction and repair of new machinery would provide only small compensation.

Barton's *Observations* was read by political economists and policy-makers – Huskisson and Malthus noted it, Sismondi praised it and McCulloch reviewed it. It was said to have induced Ricardo to make an about-turn in the third edition of his *Principles* and so to write his controversial chapter on machinery accepting the idea that the introduction of machinery could hurt the interests of manual labour. But Ricardo did not introduce this change until the third edition in 1821, and his analysis was rather different. Accepting Barton's point that the introduction of machinery might be induced by wage increases, he added his own novel analysis of autonomous technical change. It is likely that Ricardo changed his views on machinery not because he read Barton but because of contemporary political concern over the machinery issue combined with a timely reminder of Barton's work in a recent correspondence he had with McCulloch.

Barton's later pamphlets and newspaper articles of the 1830s and 1840s extended his early analysis into a general critique of industrialism. He defended the Corn Laws, arguing that labour thrown out of agriculture could not be transferred easily to manufacturing, and that the extension of manufacturing and machinery only concentrated wealth in fewer hands. He drew attention to an Adam Smith forgotten by his contemporaries – the Smith who conducted a radical critique of the monopoly spirit of merchants and manufacturers. John Barton's critique of industrialism and the introduction of machinery was a striking example of a special early 19th-century combination of traditional landed opinion with a radical concern for the condition of labour.

MAXINE BERG

SELECTED WORKS
1817. *Observations on the Circumstances which Influence the Condition of the Labouring Classes of Society*. London.
1820. *An Inquiry into the Causes of the Progressive Depreciation of Agricultural Labour in Modern Times*. London.
1962. *John Barton: Economic Writings*. Ed. G. Sotiroff, Regina, Saskatchewan.

basics and non-basics. The distinction between basic and non-basic commodities was introduced by Sraffa (1960). He first provided a definition valid for the single production case and then provided a general definition for the joint production case. In this entry single-output production is assumed except for a few remarks on the distinction between basics and non-basics in the joint production case.

Sraffa calls *basic* a commodity which enters directly or indirectly into the production of all commodities. He calls *non-basic* a commodity which does not have this property. The distinction is important since it is possible to prove that:

(a) basic commodities are indispensable; that is, they need to be produced whatever net output is produced (non-basic commodities are not indispensable and in particular are not produced if the net output consists only of basics);

(b) if the price of a non-basic is changed (i) because of a

specific tax on it or (ii) because its method of production is changed, then not all prices are affected, and, specifically, those of basics are not (if the price of a basic is changed, then any other price is changed);

(c) the Standard ratio is defined by the technology of basics only;

(d) relative prices of basics are defined and positive for all non-negative rates of profit lower that the Standard ratio (some non-basics may not have this property);

(e) if the *numéraire* includes only basic commodities, then the relationship between the wage rate and the rate of profit is determined by the technology of basics only;

(f) all basics and none of the non-basics enter into the Standard commodity.

All these statements can easily be shown after that some preliminaries are introduced.

Let us assume that there exist n commodities and n processes to produce them; each process produces *one* commodity. Let a_{ij} be the amount of commodity j used to produce one unit of commodity i; and let l_i be the amount of labour utilized to produce one unit of commodity i. Let $A = [a_{ij}]$ and $l = (l_1, l_2, \ldots, l_n)^T$.

Commodity j *enters directly* into the production of commodity i if and only if

$$a_{ij} > 0;$$

commodity j *enters directly or indirectly* into the production of commodity i if and only if there is a sequence $i_1, \ldots, i_z$ of indices such that

$$a_{i i_1} a_{i_1 i_2} \ldots a_{i_z j} > 0$$

that is, if and only if there is a natural number z such that $e_i^T A^z e_j > 0$, where e_i and e_j are the ith and the jth unit vectors respectively. Since z can be reduced to n at most, we can assert that commodity j enters directly or indirectly into the production of commodity i if and only if

$$e_i^T[A + A^2 + \cdots + A^n]e_j > 0.$$

Commodity j is *basic* if and only if

$$[A + A^2 + \cdots + A^n]e_j > 0. \tag{1}$$

Let c be the net output vector and x the operation intensity vector. Then

$$x^T = x^T A + c^T$$

i.e.

$$x^T = c^T[I - A]^{-1}$$

Statement (a) asserts that if j is basic then $x^T e_j > 0$ whatever the semipositive vector c is. This is so if and only if

$$[I - A]^{-1} e_j > 0$$

which is a direct consequence of inequality (1) since

$$[I - A]^{-1} = I + A + \cdots + A^m + \cdots \tag{2}$$

The reverse is also true since the vector $A^{n+h} e_j (h \geqslant 1)$ is a linear combination of vectors $A e_j, A^2 e_j, \ldots, A^n e_j$.

It is easily shown that if and only if all commodities are basic, i.e., if and only if

$$A + A^2 + \cdots + A^n > 0$$

matrix A is irreducible, that is, it is not possible to interchange the rows and the corresponding columns to reduce it to the form

$$A = \begin{bmatrix} A_{11} & 0 \\ A_{21} & A_{22} \end{bmatrix}$$

where A_{11} and A_{22} are square submatrices and 0 is a nul submatrix. If some non-basics exist, then matrix A is reducible and as a consequence can be transformed by the same permutation on rows and columns to the following 'canonical' form:

$$A = \begin{bmatrix} A_{11} & 0 & \ldots & 0 \\ A_{21} & A_{22} & \ldots & 0 \\ \vdots & \vdots & & \vdots \\ & & & 0 \\ A_{s1} & A_{s2} & \ldots & A_{ss} \end{bmatrix}$$

where A_{hh} $(h = 1, 2, \ldots, s)$ is a square irreducible matrix $[A_{hh} = 0$ only if $\dim(A_{hh}) = 1]$. That is, commodities are partitioned in s groups such that commodities in group h $(h = 2, 3, \ldots, s)$ do not enter either directly or indirectly into the production of commodities in groups $1, \ldots, h - 1$. Hence commodities in groups $2, \ldots, s$ are non-basic; commodities in group 1 may or may not be basic.

Sraffa assumes that at least one basic commodity exists. This is equivalent to assuming that

$$A_{21} \geqslant 0 \tag{3.1}$$
$$(A_{31}, A_{32}) \geqslant 0 \tag{3.2}$$
$$\ldots$$
$$(A_{s1}, A_{s2}, \ldots, A_{s,s-1}) \geqslant 0 \tag{3.s - 1}$$
$$\text{if} \quad \dim(A_{11}) = 1 \quad \text{then} \quad A_{11} > 0 \tag{4}$$

Inequality $(3.h - 1)$, $h = 2, 3, \ldots, s$, asserts that if commodities in group 1 enter directly or indirectly into the production of commodities in groups $1, \ldots, h - 1$, then they enter directly or indirectly into the production of commodities in group h (also since A_{hh} is irreducible). If $\dim(A_{11}) > 1$, then commodities in group 1 enter directly or indirectly into the production of themselves since A_{11} is irreducible; if $\dim(A_{11}) = 1$, then inequality (4) asserts that the commodity in group 1 enters directly into the production of itself.

If p is the price vector, w is the uniform *post factum* wage rate, and r is the uniform rate of profit, then the following equation holds

$$p = (1 + r)Ap + wl, \tag{5}$$

Let us partition vectors p and l in such a way that $p = (p_1^T, p_2^T, \ldots, p_s^T)^T$ and $l = (l_1^T, l_2^T, \ldots, l_s^T)^T$, where p_h and l_h are subvectors of the same dimension as A_{hh}. Then eq. (5) can be expanded as

$$p_1 = (1 + r)A_{11}p_1 + wl_1 \tag{6.1}$$
$$p_2 + (1 + r)[A_{21}p_1 + A_{22}p_2] + wl_2 \tag{6.2}$$
$$\ldots$$
$$p_s = (1 + r)[A_{s1}p_1 + A_{s2}p_2 + \cdots + A_{ss}p_s] + wl_s \tag{6.s}$$

Statement (b) is easily obtained from eq. (6) since inequalities (3) hold.

Let

$$R = \sup\{\rho \in \mathbb{R}/x \geqslant 0, x^T l = 1, x^T[I - (1 + \rho)A] \geqslant 0\}$$

It is easily recognized that there exists a vector q such that

$$q \geqslant 0, \quad q^T = (1 + R)q^T A, q^T l = 1. \tag{7}$$

R is called the Standard ratio (see Sraffa, 1960, pp. 21 and 26–7). Since the basic commodities are indispensable and non-basics are not [statement (a)], it is easily recognized that the entries of vector q corresponding to non-basics equal zero and the entries of q corresponding to basics are positive. That is, there exists a positive vector q_1 such that

$$q_1^T = (1 + R)q_1^T A_{11}$$

which proves statement (c).

Let

$$R^* = \sup\{ \rho \in \mathbb{R}/x \geq 0, x^T l = 1, x^T[I - (1 + \rho)A] > 0\}.$$

Obviously $R^* \leq R$. Assume that $0 \leq r \leq R^*$, then the theory of M-matrices ensures that matrix $I - (1 + r)A$ is invertible and

$$[I - (1 + r)A]^{-1} = I + (1 + r)A + \cdots + (1 + r)^m A^m + \cdots \geq 0.$$

Moreover,

$$[I - (1 + r)A_{11}]^{-1} > 0$$

because of inequality (1). Thus, if $0 \leq r < R^*$, all prices are non-negative (positive if labour enters directly or indirectly into the production of all commodities, i.e., directly into the production of at least one basic). Assume now that $R^* < R$ and that $R^* \leq r < R$. Then, it is still true that

$$[I - (1 + r)A_{11}]^{-1} > 0$$

but $I - (1 + r)A$ does not need to be invertible, and if it is so, its inverse has some negative entries. Thus, statement (d) is proven.

Let z be a semi-positive m-vector, where $m = \dim(A_{11})$. If the numeraire consists of z_1 units of commodity 1, z_2 units of commodity 2, . . . , z_m units of commodity m, i.e., if

$$(z^T, 0^T)p = z^T p_1 = 1$$

where 0 is a null vector of dimension $n - m$, then we obtain from eq. (6.1) that

$$w = \begin{cases} \dfrac{1}{z^T[I - (1 + r)A_{11}]^{-1}l_1} & \text{if } 0 \leq r \leq R \\ 0 & \text{if } r = R \end{cases}$$

which proves statement (e).

Sraffa (1960, ch 4) applies a special *numéraire* because of the useful properties it has. He normalizes prices by setting

$$q^T(I - A)p = 1$$

where q satisfies eq. (7). This *numéraire* is called the *Standard commodity*. Thus, statement (f) is also simply obtained.

The distinction between basics and non-basics is similar to, but different from, the distinction between 'necessary goods' and 'luxury goods'. Such a distinction is mentioned by Adam Smith, who asserted that a tax on one of the latter affects only the price of the taxed commodity; whereas a tax on one of the former affects all prices. Ricardo has remarked that if the real wage is given, a tax on a necessary good affects the profit rate, whereas a tax on a luxury good does not have this property. Dmitriev and Bortkiewicz have clarified that 'necessary goods' must include not only the commodities consumed by workers, but also the commodities which enter directly or indirectly into the production of those commodities (details can be found in Roncaglia, 1978).

The analysis by Ricardo, as elaborated by Dmitriev and Bortkiewicz, is definitely correct, if the real wage rate is given. Sraffa suggests that we consider as exogenously given the profit rate, rather than the real wage rate. In this case the distinction between basics and non-basics emerges as the fundamental one.

After the publication of *Production of Commodities*, the distinction between basics and non-basics was the central issue of an exchange of letters between Sraffa and Peter Newman, published as an appendix to an article by K. Bharadwaj (1970).

The main issue was the economic rationale of the assumption

$$R^* = R$$

which is necessary and sufficient for positivity of all prices for $0 \leq r \leq R$.

In Part 2 of *Production of Commodities by Means of Commodities*, Sraffa removes the assumption of single production and allows for joint products and here he provides a general definition of basic and non-basic commodities. Statements (b, i) and (f) are still valid. Statements (a), (b, ii), (c), (d) and (e) do not hold in general. Sraffa's distinction has been formalized by Manara, Steedman, and Pasinetti (see Pasinetti, 1980, chs 1, 3, 4).

NERI SALVADORI

See also ADVANCES; SRAFFA, PIERO; WAGES IN CLASSICAL ECONOMICS.

BIBLIOGRAPHY

Bharadwaj, K. 1970. On the maximum number of switches between two production systems. *Schweizerische Zeitschrift für Volkswirtschaft und Statistik* 106(4).

Flaschel, P. 1982. On two concepts of basic commodities for joint production systems. *Zeitschrift für Nationalömie* 42(3), 259-80.

Pasinetti, L.L. (ed.) 1980. *Essays on the Theory of Joint Production*. London: Macmillan.

Roncaglia, A. 1978. *Sraffa and the Theory of Prices*. New York: John Wiley.

Sraffa, P. 1960. *Production of Commodities by Means of Commodities*. Cambridge: Cambridge University Press.

basing point system. Americans generally consider apple pie, hot dogs, and baseball to be uniquely theirs in origin. Less pride of origin is assigned to the Basing Point System, originally known as Pittsburgh-Plus. However, this lack of pride in origin did not characterize American public opinion during the early years of Pittsburgh-Plus. In fact, at the turn of the century, the members of the Industrial Commission (the forerunner to the Federal Trade Commission), most members of the Congress of the United States, and later for many, many years the majority of those on the Supreme Court considered the system to be competitive and hence desirable. Before evaluating its pros and cons, a brief inquiry into its early history is in order.

According to testimony given by Henry P. Bope in November 1922 to the Federal Trade Commission, Pittsburgh-Plus was first used in 1880. He told the Commission that steel firms had previously priced their output f.o.b. mill. But beginning in 1880, beams (structural materials) were sold on the basis of the Pittsburgh price plus freight to a given buying point. He testified that this system originated with Carnegie Steel and three small firms, one of which was sited in eastern Pennsylvania, the other two in New Jersey. Having no competitors west of it, Carnegie Steel simply set the Pittsburgh price, and the others used that price plus freight *from Pittsburgh* to all destinations, regardless of the point of shipment. Carnegie Steel thus had access to all markets. The quid pro quo claimed for the small mills was on sales to locations proximate to their plant where they gained a phantom freight, as illustrated in the following hypothetical table 1. The justification for using Pittsburgh as base was that in those days *most* steel products were shipped from Pittsburgh. But inclusion in the system of tin plates and sheets shortly before the turn of the century is intriguing since there were no such mills in the Pittsburgh area (Fetter, 1931, p. 150).

Table 1 Sales from Chicago to Pittsburgh, Cleveland, Detroit, and Chicago

	Pittsburgh $	Cleveland $	Detroit $	Chicago $
Base Price	50	50	50	50
Plus Freight from Pittsburgh	0	4	6	8
Delivered Price	50	54	56	58
Minus Freight from Chicago	8	7	5	0
Mill Net Realization at Chicago	42	47	51	58
Freight Absorption	8	3	—	—
Phantom Freight	—	—	1	8

*Table taken from Wilcox, 1960, p. 269. Its perspective is that of a seller located in Chicago.

The arguments pro the system (TNEC paper, 1940) centred on the claim that the same price exists at a given time in each market with buyers having access to every seller: that is, pure competition. It was further argued that locations of steel plants were due to fundamental economic advantages. These arguments were patently extreme. For example, consider another industry in the United States which also practised base point pricing: the cement industry. Uniquely when Army Engineering opened eleven different bids for cement – each bid was for the same delivered price regardless of point of origin, $3.286854 a barrel (*The Aetna Co. Case*, 1946): pure competition? Consider the claim that it is desirable to have many seller alternatives. Under the base point system, each seller (and buyer) foregoes the competitive advantages of proximity. With respect to locational distribution, a small firm subject to basing point pricing can be shown to locate nearer the (base point) production centre than would the same size mill if pricing f.o.b. mill (Greenhut, 1970, chapter 7). When the system began to change toward multiple base points – due in part to increased freight rates and challenging litigations in cement, linseed oil, and hardwood flooring – steel industry locations did change considerably. Producers sprang up in the western portion of the United States where they were able to offer prices lower than the Pittsburgh mills by as much as $3 to $10 a ton (Fetter, 1931, p. 160).

What about another argument pro the system, namely that base point pricing prevents formation of local monopolies? This claim, too, is easily revealed to be invalid in theory (Greenhut and Greenhut, 1977; Greenhut, Norman and Hung, 1986). It also fails in practice since the prevalence of varying 'net mill' prices, that is, price discrimination, which typifies sales over geographic landscapes, signifies competitive impacts in place of local monopolies (Greenhut, Hwang and Li, 1980; Greenhut, 1981).

Phlips (1983, p. 6) defines a *non*-discriminatory price as that which occurs when two varieties of a product are sold by the same seller to two different buyers at the same *net* price, where by net price he means a price corrected for the cost associated with product differentiation. Phlips then claims that discrimination may be as common in the business world as 'it is rare in the economics textbooks' (p. 7). Indeed, it has been emphasized in spatial price theory that discriminatory pricing over geographic space is *the natural pricing* form because spatial markets are naturally separated. In turn, demand elasticities can be expected to differ in each submarket, and different demand elasticities generate different kinds of spatial price discrimination (Hoover, 1936–7; Greenhut, 1956, p. 157). Considering f.o.b. mill or base point pricing as competitive overlooks these conditions as well as the fact that invasion of markets becomes especially likely when firms discriminate over distances. Not surprisingly, delivered prices

of firms in West Germany and Japan were *often* found to be actually lower at greater freight cost distances than at proximate buying sites because of more intense competition at or near rival locations (Greenhut, 1981).

Present-day use of the base point system was recently spotlighted by Haddock (1982). By way of examples, Haddock (p. 290) cited the pricing of wheat based on Galveston, Texas, and the pricing of oil. On the intra-national level, cement in Great Britain has been sold under the system. Thus, between January 1982 and September 1983, Dunbar, Aberthaw, Padeswood, Aberdeen and Inverness were used as base points.

How, one may ask, is it possible in nations that consider conspiratorial restraints of trade to be illegal for widely dispersed sellers to quote identical delivered prices for a given product at each market point? The answer is that no specific communication is needed (Machlup, 1952, p. 90) *and* for a long time the judiciary in the United States was more concerned with *the means used* than the result itself. If the means did not involve communication, it was not considered a conspiracy (Averitt, 1980). However, consider in this regard the recent Southern Plywood Case in the United States.

Douglas Fir, with origins in the state of Washington, had customarily served as the production center for plywood shipments throughout the United States. As many as 100 firms operated 149 mills in the Northwest in 1963, the industry being described as loosely oligopolistic (Loescher, 1980, p. 11). In the early 1960s, suppliers of glue developed an adequate bond for manufacturing southern pine plywood; this led to dispersal of the industry.

Following the practice of West Coast producers, the new entrants in the South established a delivered pricing formula which assured the capture of the southern market. They accomplished this by quoting a Portland Base price at a slight differential 'below' the f.o.b. mill price on Douglas Fir plus *West Coast freight to southern destinations*. This signified high mill rates (phantom freight) on sales at southern delivery points close to a mill.

As suggested above, conscious parallelism of action had not typically been considered an unacceptable means. One might thus expect a favourable ruling for Southern Plywood. However, a change has taken place.

Obiter dictum in the *Triangle Conduit and Cable Co v FTC*, 1948, *suggested* that unilateral adoption of basing point systems could be prohibited if the firms were aware others were adopting similar practices. In the Brown Shoe Case (1966), the Federal Trade Commission was empowered to arrest trade restraints in their *incipiency* without proof of outright violation of the antitrust laws.

Now, the argument of the defendants in Southern Plywood was based on an econometric model for 1967–77 which suggested that Portland base prices varied with housing starts; hence, the defendants said no conspiracy prevails. But, as noted in the plaintiff's successful charge to the jury, individual self-interest would permit continuance of the system if and only if each expected the others '... to continue the common practice' (p. 330). Thus, Loescher (1980, p. 29), citing Turner (1962), Stigler (1949), Posner (1976) and himself (1959), notes that all of these writers are of the belief that *inferring a civil conspiracy* behind a basing point system is today intrinsic to American antitrust policy and practice. To assert next that the Basing Point system is therefore on its way out of use in the United States would, however, be a stronger inference than one can soberly make. This is especially so given the freight rate zones and basing lines of American railroads that sellers can avail themselves of in establishing difficult to evaluate variants of a *multiple* base point system. The prevalence of the system elsewhere in the world would also appear to depend on whether conspiracies and restraints of trade are strongly condemned *and* whether conscious parallelism of action can be identified and then inferred as a conspiracy.

M.L. GREENHUT

See also LOCATION OF ECONOMIC ACTIVITY; PRICE DISCRIMINATION.

BIBLIOGRAPHY

Aetna Portland Cement Co. v *FTC (1946)*. 157 F. 2nd 533 (1946), Respondents Brief p. 127.

Averitt, N.W. 1980. The meaning of 'unfair' methods of competition in Section 5 of the Federal Trade Commission Act. *Boston College Law Review* 21(2), 227–300.

Brown Shoe Co. (1966). 384 US 316.

Federal Trade Commission. 1922. Docket 760, Pittsburgh-Plus Complaint, Record pp. 10861–2.

Fetter, F.A. 1931. *The Masquerade of Monopoly*. New York: Harcourt, Brace & Co.

Greenhut, M.L. 1956. *Plant Location in Theory and Practice*. Chapel Hill: University of North Carolina Press; 4th printing, Westport, Conn.: The Greenwood Press, 1983.

Greenhut, M.L. 1970. *A Theory of the Firm in Economic Space*. New York: Appleton-Century-Crofts. 2nd printing, Austin, Texas: Lone Star Publishing Co., 1974.

Greenhut, M.L. 1981. Spatial pricing in the USA, West Germany, and Japan. *Economica* 48(189), 79–86.

Greenhut, M.L. and Greenhut, J. 1977. Nonlinearity of delivered price schedules and predatory pricing. *Econometrica* 45(8), 1871–5.

Greenhut, M.L., Greenhut, J. and Li, S. 1980. Spatial pricing patterns in the United States. *Quarterly Journal of Economics* 94, 329–50.

Greenhut, M.L., Norman, G. and Hung, G. 1986. *Imperfect Competition: A Spatial Approach*. Cambridge: Cambridge University Press.

Haddock, D.O. 1982. Basing-point pricing: competitive vs. collusive theories. *American Economic Review* 72(3), 289–306.

Hoover, E.M. 1936–7. Spatial price discrimination. *Review of Economic Studies* 4, 182–91.

In re *Plywood Antitrust Litigation (1978)*. MDL Docket Number 159, United States District Court, Eastern District of Louisiana.

Loescher, S.M. 1959. *Imperfect Collusion in the Cement Industry*. Cambridge, Mass.: Harvard University Press, 18–22, 232–40.

Loescher, S.M. 1980 Economic collusion, civil conspiracy, and treble damage deterrents: the Sherman Act breakthrough with Southern Plywood. *Quarterly Review of Economics and Business* 20(4), 6-35.

Machlup, F. 1952. *The Political Economy of Monopoly*. Baltimore: Johns Hopkins Press.

Phlips, L. 1983. *The Economics of Price Discrimination*. Cambridge: Cambridge University Press.

Posner, R.A. 1976. *Antitrust Law*. Chicago: University of Chicago Press.

Stigler, G.J. 1949. A theory of delivered prices. *American Economic Review* 39, December, 1143–59.

TNEC Papers. 1940. Vol. 3, *The Basing Point Method*. Published by The Corporation.

Triangle Conduit & Cable Co. v *FTC* (1948). 168 F 2nd 1975 (7th Cir. 1948).

Turner, D.F. 1962. The definition of agreement under the Sherman Act. *Harvard Law Review* 75, 655.

Wilcox, C. 1960. *Public Policies Toward Business*. Revised edn, Homewood: Richard D. Irwin.

Bastable, Charles Francis (1855–1945). Born in Co. Cork in 1855, Bastable graduated in history and political science from Trinity College, Dublin in 1878 and was called to the Irish Bar in 1881. The next year was to be the first of his fifty-year tenure of one of the oldest chairs of political economy in the British Isles – the Whately Chair at Trinity College. Throughout the whole of that period he also occupied a succession of chairs in legal subjects, including the Regius Chair of Laws at Trinity (1908–1932). He was a member of the first Council of the Royal Economic Society and among his scholastic honours were his presidency of Section F of the British Association in 1894 and his election as a Fellow of the British Academy in 1921. He died in Dublin in 1945.

Bastable's place in the history of economics is as an expositor of and commentator on classical doctrines, rather than as an original thinker. His main areas of interest were, first, trade and commercial policy and, second, public finance. His *The Commerce of Nations* is a spirited, semi-popular defence of free trade. Whilst written as a tract for the times, parts of this book have a continuing relevance and appeal, most notably in a chapter entitled 'Economic Arguments for Protection', which remained unchanged through successive editions over thirty years and which, while obviously tendentious, effectively rebuts some of the cruder fallacies which are still paraded today.

Bastable's concern for the pure and monetary theory of trade found expression in several journal papers (notably in the *Economic Journal*) and in his treatise, *The Theory of International Trade*. The latter is firmly in the English classical tradition, the discussion of comparative costs, for example, being essentially an exposition of Mill, defending him against such critics as Cournot.

Bastable's largest single work, *Public Finance*, was written explicitly as a textbook and, for its scope and clarity, deserves an honoured place in any history of that *genre*. The theory is, again, English classical, but the work as a whole is impressively eclectic, covering expenditure, taxation and debt with a wealth of institutional detail and juxtaposing arguments and examples from a large range of European and American sources.

In his writings at least, Bastable never appeared to recognize the significance of neoclassical innovations. He cites Marshall's *Principles* in various works, but not in a context which suggests that anything of analytical significance is contained therein. Indeed, he explicitly rejects as 'unsuitable' to the treatment of tax incidence the unity of value and distribution theory which he properly describes as 'the whole tendency of modern economic science' (*Public Finance*, 2nd edn, p. 331).

Perhaps the best indication of his doctrinal and methodological position is to be found in his 1894 presidential address to the British Association. He praises the German historical school, stresses the importance of sociology to the economist and urges the integration of economics with 'political science, jurisprudence and the scientific principles of administration'. This view that economics is part of the seamless garment of the social sciences informed all the work of this humane and scholarly man.

JOHN A. BRISTOW

SELECTED WORKS

1887. *The Theory of International Trade*. Dublin. 2nd–4th edns, London: Macmillan, 1897–1903.
1891. *The Commerce of Nations*. 9th edn, London: Methuen, 1923.
1892. *Public Finance*. 2nd edn, 1895; 3rd edn, London: Macmillan, 1903.

bastard Keynesianism. This is the name given by Joan Robinson to certain developments which occurred in Keynesian economics following the publication of the *General*

Theory, principally in the USA. They culminated in the system of thought which is more usually known as the neoclassical synthesis. The basic idea was that the notion of equilibrium of the economic system in traditional theory (traditional in the sense of Harrod, 1937), in which *all* markets (including the labour market) clear, was an accurate description of the outcome of tendencies in the economic system. However, the forces in the economy which allowed this position to be sought were weak, were often frustrated by rigidities and imperfections, and in any event took a long time to work themselves out. The economy would often be found for long periods of time experiencing sustained unemployment due to a deficiency of overall demand. Therefore there was a role for government intervention to reinforce and speed up the processes whereby the economy found its way to its full employment equilibrium position; once there, the traditional theory of resource allocation and income distribution would come into its own again. That is to say, an equilibrium position has been shown to exist within the bounds of traditional theory, so that Keynes has a place not so much as a theorist but as a sensible propagator and rationalizer of policies in the short period, over the cycle and perhaps permanently, as the average level of unemployment reflected a permanent tendency to a deficiency in aggregate demand.

The starting point of this analysis was the expression of what was argued to be the analytical core of the *General Theory* in terms of the IS/LM general-equilibrium framework, associated especially with Hicks (although both Harrod, 1937, and Meade, 1937, wrote down the same system in their interpretative papers of the *General Theory* in the same year – 1936 – as Hicks, 1937). The attempt to confine Keynes's contributions within a small general equilibrium model allowed the neoclassical synthesis to occur. For, following the contributions of Patinkin in the 1950s, recognition of the existence and role of the real balances or Pigou effect made it possible to define a full employment equilibrium: that is, to prove existence in the sense that, given the supply of money and that the key relationships of the system were stable and especially that their positions were independent of the processes and paths by which the equilibrium was found, there must always be a value of the general price level which implied a level of aggregate demand that was consistent with full employment. There was the additional proviso that as long as this position had *not* been attained, the general price level could not be constant because of competitive pressures on the money-wage rate in the labour market. This led to the interpretation of Keynes as the economics of dis-equilibrium, a situation which happened to be the usual state of the real world unless the government acted but which was not *theoretically* that interesting.

This interpretation of Keynes's contributions was regarded by Joan Robinson in particular (but also by Kahn, Kalecki and Shackle amongst others; for a contemporary view, see Chick, 1983) as illegitimate – hence the name, bastard Keynesianism. (Joan Robinson coined the phrase, 'the bastard Keynesians', in 1962 in her review of Harry Johnson's *Money, Trade and Economic Growth* (1962). She took particular exception to his assessment of the *General Theory* twenty-five years after its publication, arguing that what Johnson and other 'bastards' of his generation saw as weaknesses were in fact strengths – to wit, a sense of time, of the structure of society and of economic life as a process.) But for Joan Robinson and other kindred souls, Keynes *had* established, through his theories of investment behaviour and the consumption function, that there was no automatic tendency for the economy to gravitate towards a full-employment

equilibrium. Rather, there was an under-employment position (the interpretation of the characteristics of which varied according to whether it was Joan Robinson and her followers or Garegnani (1978, 1979), Eatwell (1979) and Milgate (1982) and their followers who described it). Keynes argued that, because of the uncertainty which of necessity must surround decisions about investment and holding money, and because producers in a monetary production economy of necessity must produce in anticipation of demand and of a money profit, and must make contracts in money terms, there are no necessary equilibrating forces which take the economy to full employment either at a point in time or over the cycle.

Moreover, Keynes himself stressed both the likely instability of his core functions, especially the investment and liquidity preference functions, *and* the dependence of this instability on movements in the economy itself, so that positions were not independent of paths. The IS/LM apparatus was therefore peculiarly unsuited to capture this vision of the operation of the economy, and the neoclassical synthesis itself was a denial of the revolution both in vision and in method which Keynes had provided. Furthermore, just because the neoclassical synthesis version dominated the profession when the monetarist counter-revolution came to prominence in the late 1960s and early 1970s, Keynesians were weakened in their fight back because they had already, unnecessarily and illegitimately, conceded the framework of the approach within which the battle was to be fought.

G.C. HARCOURT

See also ROBINSON, JOAN VIOLET.

BIBLIOGRAPHY
Chick, V. 1983. *Macroeconomics after Keynes, A Reconsideration of the General Theory*. Oxford: Phillip Allan.
Eatwell, J. 1979. *Theories of Value, Output and Employment. Thames Papers in Political Economy*. Summer, London: Thames Polytechnic.
Garegnani, P. 1978. Notes on consumption, investment and effective demand: I. *Cambridge Journal of Economics* 2, December, 335–54.
Garegnani, P. 1979. Notes on consumption, investment and effective demand: II. *Cambridge Journal of Economics* 3, March, 63–82.
Harrod, R.F. 1937. Mr Keynes and traditional theory. *Econometrica* 5, January, 74–86.
Hicks, J.R. 1937. Mr Keynes and the 'Classics'; a suggested interpretation. *Econometrica* 5, April, 147–59.
Johnson, H.G. 1962. *Money, Trade and Economic Growth*. London: Allen & Unwin.
Kalecki, M. 1936. Pare uwag o teorii Keynesa. *Economista* 3, reprinted in M. Kalecki, *Kapitalizm, Koniunktura i Zatrudmienie*, Warsaw: PWN, 1979. Trans. by F. Targetti and B. Kinda–Hass as 'Kalecki's review of Keynes' *General Theory*', *Australian Economic Papers* 21, December, 244–60.
Meade, J.E. 1937. A simplified model of Mr Keynes' system. *Review of Economic Studies* 4, 98–107.
Milgate, M. 1982. *Capital and Employment. A Study of Keynes's Economics*. London: Academic Press.
Robinson, J. 1962. Review of H.G. Johnson, *Money, Trade and Economic Growth*, 1962. *Economic Journal* 72, September, 690–92. Reprinted in J. Robinson, *Collected Economic Papers*, Vol. 3, Oxford: Basil Blackwell, 1965.

Bastiat, Claude Frédéric (1801–1850). French economist and publicist, born at Bayonne on 30 June 1801, the son of a merchant in the Spanish trade; died in Italy, at Rome, on 24 December 1850. Orphaned at the age of nine, Bastiat nevertheless received an encyclopedic education before entering his uncle's business firm in 1818. By 1824 he was expressing dissatisfaction with his employment. Upon inheriting his grandfather's estate in 1825, he left business and became a gentleman farmer at Mugron, but showed no more aptitude for agriculture than he had for commerce. So he became a provincial scholar, establishing a discussion group in his village and reading voraciously. His later writings show familiarity with the works of French, British, American and Italian authors, among them Say, Smith, Quesnay, Turgot, Ricardo, Mill, Bentham, Senior, Franklin, H.C. Carey, Custodi, Donato and Scialoja.

Bastiat left France in 1840 to study in Spain and in Portugal, where he tried unsuccessfully to establish an insurance company. Returning to Mugron, he learned (in the course of seeking information for his study club) of Cobden's Anti-Corn Law League and became an ardent free-trader (the 'French Cobden'). As a complete unknown in economics, he submitted a stirring article to the *Journal des économistes* in 1844, dealing with the influence of protectionism on France and England. It created an immediate sensation and raised a clamour for more from the editors. This response encouraged Bastiat's *Economic Sophisms*, which quickly sold out upon its publication in 1845, and was soon thereafter translated into English and Italian. In 1846 Bastiat moved to Paris, where he established the Association for Free Trade and quickened his literary activity, endangering his frail health in the process. A torrent of articles, pamphlets and books now flowed from his talented pen, undoubtedly made possible in such short order by the preceding twenty years of practically uninterrupted reflection. Some scholars say the frenzy produced more heat than light, yet on the whole, economics is better off for Bastiat's herculean efforts.

Bastiat was one of several writers (Quesnay, Smith, Say and Carey were the others) who formed the doctrine of Harmonism, or the optimistic idea that class interests naturally and inevitably coincide so as to promote economic development. The major challenge to this view came from Ricardo and Malthus, whose theories cast a sinister shadow over the prospect of economic progress. As against Ricardo's system, Bastiat erected a theory of value based on the idea of service. He distinguished between utility and service, identifying the former as insufficient, of itself, to establish value, because certain free goods (sun, air, water) have utility. Bastiat considered all commercial transactions as exchanges of service, with value measured in terms of the trouble a buyer saves by making the purchase.

J.E. Cairnes complained that this merely confounded what Ricardo had sought to delineate, namely those cases in which value is proportioned to effort and sacrifice from those in which it is not. A more fundamental criticism is that Bastiat's theory, notwithstanding denials to the contrary, is simply a labour theory in different guise. It is noteworthy, however, that Bastiat's idea bears a close resemblance to the notion of 'public utility' which Dupuit applied so successfully to the measure of gain from transport improvements, and in which reduction of costs effected by the improved service became the central issue. Yet any connection between the two, tenuous as it may be, must be considered to run from Dupuit to Bastiat rather than the reverse, since Dupuit published his famous article on public works and marginal utility before Bastiat abandoned his earlier polemics in favour of more 'constructive' attempts at theory. Bastiat's theory of rent, also clearly aimed against Ricardo, denied the notion of unearned income, again advancing the view that the value of land (always in the absence of government interference) derives entirely from the services it renders.

Generally, judgement on Bastiat has been that he made no original contributions to economic analysis. Cairnes, Sidgwick and Böhm-Bawerk discounted his pure economics completely. Marshall said that he understood economics hardly better than the socialists against whom he declaimed. And Schumpeter declared that Bastiat was not a *bad* theorist, he was simply no theorist at all.

Schumpeter also described Bastiat as 'the most brilliant economic journalist who ever lived', and so weighty a thinker as Edgeworth praised Bastiat's genius for popularizing, in the best sense of the term, the economic discoveries of his predecessors. Almost all commentators agree that Bastiat was unrivalled at exposing economic fallacies wherever he found them, and he found them everywhere. He was quite simply a genius of wit and satire, frequently described as a combination of Voltaire and Franklin. He had the habit of exposing even the most complex economic principles in amusing parables that both charmed and educated his readers. His writings retain their currency, even today. And as Hayek has reminded us in his introduction to Bastiat's *Selected Essays*, his central idea continues to command attention: the notion that if we judge economic policy solely by its immediate and superficial effects, we shall not only not achieve the good results intended, but certainly and progressively undermine liberty, thereby preventing more good than we can ever hope to achieve through conscious design. This principle is exceedingly difficult to elaborate in all of its profundity, but it is one which has galvanized the thought of contemporary economists, Hayek and Friedman.

Over the long haul, Bastiat's influence has waxed and waned. In his own day he received the ready support of Dunoyer, Blanqui, Chevalier and Garnier. Francis A. Walker introduced his doctrines into America at about the time of the Civil War. Pre-World War I French liberals such as Leroy-Beaulieu, Molinari and Guyot relied on his authority. Bastiat's ideas subsequently went into a long decline, only to become resurgent in the late 20th century among libertarian economists dissatisfied with Keynesian orthodoxy and Marxist alternatives. Ironically, Bastiat's originality is exhibited most in his contribution to political theory, which has drawn surprisingly little attention to this day.

R.F. HÉBERT

See also ECONOMIC HARMONY.

SELECTED WORKS
1844. De l'influence des tarifs français et anglais sur l'avenir des deux peuples. *Journal des économistes* 9, 244–71.
1964. *Economic Sophisms*. Trans. A. Goddard, Princeton: D. Van Nostrand.
1964. *Selected Essays on Political Economy*. Trans. S. Caine, Princeton: D. Van Nostrand.
1964. *Economic Harmonies*. Trans. W.H. Boyers, Princeton: D. Van Nostrand.

BIBLIOGRAPHY
Baudin, L. 1962. *Frédéric Bastiat*. Paris: Dalloz.
Hayek, F.A. 1964. Introduction to F. Bastiat, *Selected Essays on Political Economy*. Princeton: D. Van Nostrand.
Russell, D. 1963. *Frédéric Bastiat: Ideas and Influence*. Irvington-on-Hudson, New York: Foundation for Economic Education.

Baudeau, Nicolas (1730–c1792). Born at Amoise, Baudeau entered the church, becoming a Canon and Professor of Theology at the Chancelade Abbey. He was subsequently called to Paris in the service of Archbishop de Beaumont. In 1765, Baudeau founded the periodical *Éphémérides*, becoming its first editor till late 1768 and again during its two subsequent revivals. Converted to Physiocracy by Mirabeau in

1768, he became one of its most active propagandists through the many articles, pamphlets and books he produced. He died insane in Paris *circa* 1792 (Coquelin and Guillaumin, 1854, I, p. 148). Daire (1846, pp. 652–4) provides a bibliography of the economic writings and reprints his long introduction to economic philosophy (Baudeau, 1771) and his explanations of the *Tableau économique* (Baudeau, 1767–8), which Marx (1962, p. 324) found helpful for clarifying some of its more difficult points and which remains its most useful introduction to Physiocracy and the *Tableau's* intricacies. Baudeau (1771) is noteworthy for its concise definition of monopoly as 'everything which by force limits the numbers and competition of buyers and sellers' (p. 327) and its direct attribution to Gournay of the phrase, *laissez les faire* (p. 323).

Perhaps the most interesting of Baudeau's many writings is his systematic exposition and development of the Physiocratic theory of luxury (Baudeau, 1767), the most complete version of that doctrine and as such wrongly ignored (Dubois, 1912, pp. v–vi). Inspired by the Swedish sumptuary laws of 1767, and bearing in mind the Physiocratic division of output between necessary expenses and disposable net product, the essay clearly defines luxury as 'that subversion of the natural and essential order of national expenditure which increases the total of unproductive expenditure to the detriment of that which is used in production and at the same time to the detriment of production itself' (Baudeau, 1767, p. 14). In other words, disposal of the net product when in direct agricultural investment or in spending which directly or indirectly enhances the demand for agricultural produce, is productive: other uses of the surplus are wasteful, luxury spending. For example, hoarding which detracts from demand for agricultural produce, is luxury; importing commodities from abroad, if this increases overseas demand for domestic produce and thereby augments productive expenses, is not. Sumptuary laws are therefore not appropriate for curtailing luxury; free trade and a more simple pattern of consumption channelling more demand to the agricultural sector, are much more effective. In short, ostentation in consumption is to be preferred to ostentation in display and ornament, since the former creates a greater market for agricultural produce and hence for all production. As Meek (1962, p. 318) points out, this 'theory of luxury, with its distinction between productive and unproductive expenditure out of revenue, was much more useful to Smith and Ricardo than it was to the underconsumptionists', despite its emphasis on consumption spending as a factor in stimulating production.

PETER GROENEWEGEN

See also EPHÉMÉRIDES.

SELECTED WORKS

1767. Principes de la science morale et politique sur le luxe et les lois somptuaires. *Ephémérides* 1(1), January, and 1(3). Reprinted, ed. A. Dubois, Paris: Marcel Rivière, 1912.
1767–8. *Explication du Tableau économique à Madame de ****. Paris: Delalain, 1776.
1771. *Première introduction à la Philosophie économique ou analyse des états policés*. In *Physiocrates*, ed. E. Daire, Paris: Guillaumin, 1846.

BIBLIOGRAPHY

Coquelin, Ch. and Guillaumin, M. 1854. Baudeau. In *Dictionnaire de l'économie politique*, Paris: Guillaumin.
Daire, E. 1846. Notice sur la vie et les travaux de l'Abbé Baudeau. In E. Daire, *Physiocrates*, Paris: Guillaumin.
Dubois, A. (ed.) 1912. Nicolas Baudeau, *Principes de la science morale et politique*. Paris: Marcel Rivière.
Marx, K.H. 1962. *Theories of Surplus Value*, Part I. Moscow: Foreign Languages Publishing House.
Meek, R.L. 1962. *The Economics of Physiocracy*. London: Allen & Unwin.

Bauer, Otto (1881–1938). Born 5 September 1881, Vienna; died 4 July 1938, Paris. A member of a talented Jewish family and the only son of a textile manufacturer, Bauer became interested in Marxism and the 'revisionist' controversy while still in high school, and went on to study philosophy, law and political economy at the University of Vienna. He became the leader of the Austrian socialist party (SPÖ) and a prolific writer on economic and political questions. Bauer is best known for his study of nationalities and nationalism (1907), which remains the classic Marxist work on the subject, but he also wrote extensively on economics and his first major essay (1904), which brought him to the notice of Karl Kautsky, discussed the Marxist theory of economic crises. In his early writings he adopted a 'disproportionality' theory such as Hilferding expounded more fully in *Finance Capital* (1910); that is, a theory which sees the fundamental causes of crises in the 'anarchy of capitalist production', and particularly in the disproportion which regularly emerges between production in the two sectors of capital goods and consumer goods. However, in his last published book (1936) he propounded an underconsumption theory of crises which subsequently influenced the work of Sweezy. In the course of his analyses of economic crises Bauer introduced, or emphasized more strongly than other Marxist writers, such factors as the existing stock of capital, technical progress, and population growth.

Bauer also discussed economic questions in a broader context in his study of the development of capitalism and socialism after World War I, of which only the first volume was published (1931). In this work he examined the rationalization of capitalist production in three spheres: technical rationalization, the rationalization and intensification of work, and the rationalization of the enterprise (especially the growth of 'scientific management'). The final part of the book dealt with the limits to capitalist rationalization revealed by the economic crisis, its consequences for the working class, which he analysed in terms of a distinction between the 'labour process' (a concept which has become central in much recent Marxist political economy) and the 'life process', and the nature of rationalization in a socialist society.

Besides his major studies of nationalism and of the capitalist economy Bauer published many other important essays and books: on the Austrian revolution (where he strongly opposed the idea of a Bolshevik type revolution and began to elaborate his conception of the 'slow revolution'), on violence in politics and the doctrine of 'defensive violence', on fascism, on the philosophical foundations of Austro-Marxism, and on Marxism and ethics. His work as a whole represents one of the most important and interesting contributions to Marxist thought in the 20th century. The defeat of the SPÖ in the civil war of 1934, which drove Bauer into exile, was attributed by some critics to his excessively cautious and gradualist policies; on the other hand, the social, educational and cultural achievements of 'Red Vienna' in the 1920s and early 1930s showed the effectiveness of such policies when the socialists were in power, and they have had a major influence on Austria's development since 1945.

TOM BOTTOMORE

SELECTED WORKS

1904–5. Marx' Theorie der Wirtschaftskrisen. *Die Neue Zeit* 23.
1907. *Die Nationalitätenfrage und die Sozialdemokratie.* Vienna: Wiener Volksbuchhandlung. 2nd enlarged edition with new Preface, 1924.
1923. *Die Österreichische Revolution.* Abridged English version, New York: Burt Franklin, 1925; reprinted, 1970.
1931. *Kapitalismus und Sozialismus nach dem Weltkrieg.* Vol. I: *Rationalisierung oder Fehlrationalisierung?* Vienna: Wiener Volksbuchhandlung.
1936. *Zwischen zwei Weltkriegen?* Bratislava: Eugen Prager Verlag.

BIBLIOGRAPHY

Bottomore, T. and Goode, P. (eds) 1978. *Austro-Marxism.* Oxford: Clarendon Press.
Botz, G. 1974. Genesis und Inhalt der Faschismustheorien Otto Bauers. *International Review of Social History* 19, 28–53.
Braunthal, J. 1961. *Otto Bauer: Eine Auswahl aus seinem Lebenswerk.* Vienna: Wiener Volksbuchhandlung.

Bauer, Peter Tamas (born 1915).

Born in Hungary in 1915, Bauer became a fellow of Gonville and Caius College, Cambridge, from 1946 and Professor of Economics in the University of London at the London School of Economics from 1960 until he retired as Professor Emeritus in 1983. The earliest and most distinguished critic of development economics, he launched his research with a classic study of the rubber industry (1948), where he showed that the very rapid growth was a consequence of voluntary responses, usually of illiterate peasants, to expanded opportunities due largely to contacts with the West. In *West African Trade*, he showed that, contrary to the views of development economists and the evidence of official statistics, the extensive system of traders was efficient in providing production for the market and for expanding material welfare. State intervention in the form of marketing boards was shown to be a mechanism for exploiting monopsony power to the detriment of producers, particularly the small farmers, and to the benefit of the rulers. Stabilization of farm incomes did not require state marketing; it could be achieved by the farmers themselves.

Bauer's empirical studies and further reflection on the role of the state in development lead him to challenge the widespread belief, urged most eloquently by Myrdal, that comprehensive central planning, together with substantial aid from the governments of industrialized countries, was needed to overcome the vicious circle of poverty, low savings and low investment. Bauer pointed out that virtually all the rich countries had emerged from poverty without the supposed benefits of central planning or aid, and that even in very poor countries, provided there was security and suitable motivations, people saved and invested considerable sums efficiently. With central planning, on the other hand, investment was undertaken primarily for political motives and was much more likely to result in economic waste, such as premature industrialization behind high trade barriers. Bauer showed that aid was not a necessary condition of development and, since it reinforced government's grip on the economy, aid frequently inhibited material progress. He stressed the corrosive and corrupting politicization of economic life with its stultifying effects on development.

The meticulous scholarship and historical depth of Bauer's work was unusual if not unique in development studies. The veracity of Bauer's ideas and the poverty of development economics have become increasingly apparent in the 1970s and 1980s. In 1983 his elevation to the peerage as Baron Bauer of Market Ward in the City of Cambridge recognized his outstanding contributions to scholarship.

A.A. WALTERS

SELECTED WORKS

1948. *The Rubber Industry.* Cambridge, Mass.: Harvard University Press.
1954. *West African Trade.* Cambridge: Cambridge University Press.
1972. *Dissent on Development.* Cambridge, Mass.: Harvard University Press.
1984. *Reality and Rhetoric: Studies in the Economics of Development.* Cambridge, Mass.: Harvard University Press.

Bayes, Thomas (1702–1761).

The Rev. Thomas Bayes was the eldest son of Joshua Bayes, a minister in the Nonconformist church. He was probably educated at Coward's Academy. After assisting his father as pastor in Hatton Garden, London, he became, in 1731, Presbyterian minister at Mount Sion, Tunbridge Wells where he remained until his death on 17 April 1761. His fame today rests entirely on one paper, found by his friend Richard Price amongst Bayes' effects after his death and presented to the Royal Society: Bayes (1763). (A convenient recent reference is Bayes, 1958.) The paper appears to have aroused little interest at the time and a proper appreciation was left to Laplace. Even today there is much discussion over just what Bayes meant, but the fact that so much interest is taken in a paper over 200 years old testifies to the importance of the problem and the brilliance of Bayes' argument.

The problem was this (as stated at the beginning of the paper): 'Given the number of times in which an unknown event has happened and failed: *Required* the chance that the probability of its happening in a single trial lies somewhere between any two degrees of probability that can be named.'

Bayes' solution depended on two original ideas. The first, in the modern notation where $p(A \mid B)$ means the probability of A given B, says

$$p(B \mid A) = p(A \mid B)p(B)/p(A)$$

and is always known as Bayes' theorem. The second idea is more controversial and open to many interpretations. The question is what 'rule is the proper one to be used in the case of an event concerning the probability of which we absolutely know nothing antecedently to any trials made concerning it'?

To solve the problem Bayes took A to be the event of r happenings and s failures; B to be the unknown value θ of 'its happening in a single trial' so that $p(r, s \mid \theta) = \theta^r(1 - \theta)^s$; and supposed $p(r, s) = (r + s)^{-1}$ as a solution to the second question. This is equivalent to taking $p(\theta)$ constant.

The importance of Bayes' ideas goes beyond the initial problem. Let A be any *particular* event and B some *general* proposition. Then his theorem enables one to pass from the probability of the particular given the general, $p(A \mid B)$, which, as above, is often straightforward, to the difficult probability of the general given the particular, $p(B \mid A)$. As such it provides a solution to the central problem of induction or inference, enabling us to pass from a particular experience to a general statement. This Bayesian inference applies generally in science, economics and law. A special case with statistical problems is called Bayesian Statistics. It has been shown by Ramsey (1931), de Finetti (1974/5) and others that this is the only coherent form of inference. Despite this, eminent philosophers like Popper (1959) still misunderstand Bayes and deny probabilistic induction.

Bayes' solution to the second question has not been generally accepted and the probability to be assigned to the general proposition before the particular is observed, $p(B)$, has been the subject of much discussion. Solutions by Jeffreys (1985), and by Jaynes (1983) using entropy ideas, have all met with difficulties. The best solution currently available is to accept that *all* probabilities are subjective so that, in particular, $p(B)$ is the subject's probability for the general proposition. This view is primarily due to de Finetti. Enough data (in the form of particular events) enable subjects, despite differences in $p(B)$, to have close agreement on $p(B|A)$.

An interesting feature of Bayes' approach is that he defines probability in terms of expectation. The amount you would pay for the expectation of one unit of currency were B to occur is $p(B)$. Because of its confusion with utility concepts, this approach has not been much used.

It is hard to think of a single paper that contains such important, original ideas as does Bayes'. His theorem must stand with Einstein's $E = mc^2$ as one of the great, simple truths.

D. V. LINDLEY

BIBLIOGRAPHY
Bayes, T. 1763. An essay towards solving a problem in the doctrine of chances. *Philosophical Transactions of the Royal Society London* 53, 370–418.
Bayes, T. 1958. Reprint of the above with biographical note by G.A. Barnard. *Biometrika* 45, 293–315.
De Finetti, B. 1974/5. *Theory of Probability.* 2 vols, New York: Wiley.
Jaynes, E.T. 1983. *Papers on Probability, Statistics and Statistical Physics.* Ed. R.D. Rosenkrantz, Dordrecht: Reidel.
Jeffreys, H. 1985. *Theory of Probability.* Oxford: Clarendon Press.
Popper, K.R. 1959. *The Logic of Scientific Discovery.* London: Hutchinson.
Ramsey, F.P. 1931. *The Foundations of Mathematics and Other Logical Essays.* London: Kegan, Paul, Trench, Trubner.

Bayesian inference. Bayesian inference is a mode of inductive reasoning that has been used in many sciences, including economics. Bayesian inference procedures are available to evaluate economic hypotheses and models, to estimate values of economic parameters and to predict as yet unobserved values of variables. In addition, Bayesian inference procedures are useful in solving many decision problems including economic control and policy problems, firms' and consumers' stochastic optimization problems, portfolio problems, experimental design problems, etc. Many examples of these uses of Bayesian inference procedures are provided in Jeffreys (1967), De Groot (1970), Zellner (1971), Box and Tiao (1973), Leamer (1978), Boyer and Kihlstrom (1984), and Berger (1985).

A distinctive feature of Bayesian inference procedures is that they permit investigators to use both sample and prior information in a logically consistent manner in making inferences. This is important since prior information is widely used by Bayesian and non-Bayesian workers in making inferences. Bayes' Theorem, sometimes referred to as the Principle of Inverse Probability, serves as a fundamental learning model in the Bayesian approach. Initial or prior information is combined with current sample information by use of Bayes' Theorem to produce a 'post-data' or 'posterior distribution' that incorporates both prior and sample information. In this way prior or initial views are transformed by use of Bayes' Theorem to post-data views, a transformation that is a key, operational learning process.

Thomas Bayes, an 18th-century British Presbyterian minister, is usually given credit for solving the famous 'inverse proba-bility problem', stated by Bayes (1763) as follows: '*Given* the number of times in which an unknown event has happened and failed: *Required* the chance that the probability of its happening in a single trial lies somewhere between any two degrees of probability that can be named'. The solution, published two years after Bayes' death, was arrived at by an ingenious geometrical argument. (See Stigler (1983) for further consid-erations regarding the origins of the solution.) Note that Bayes' inverse problem is fundamentally different from those encoun-tered in games of chance, for example coin flipping, in which the probabilities of outcomes are known and the probabilities of various outcomes must be calculated. These are problems in *direct* probability; for example, calculate the probability of observing five heads in six flips of a fair coin. In Bayes' *inverse* probability problem, five heads in six flips of a coin are observed and what must be calculated or inferred is the chance that the probability of a head on a single flip lies in a given interval, say 0.4 to 0.7. Thus the probability of a head on a single toss is unknown and must be inferred from the outcomes. The modern solution, due to Laplace (see Molina, 1940) will be presented below. It is clear that the inverse problem is typical of scientific problems in which we observe data or outcomes and must infer the probabilistic mechanism or model that probably produced them. Cox (1961) and Jaynes (1984) provide fundamental analysis justifying Bayes' Theorem as a central tool in inductive reasoning.

Since Bayes' essay was published in 1763, Laplace (1820), Edgeworth (1928), Jeffreys (1967, 1973), de Finetti (1970), Wald (1950), Savage (1954), Good (1950, 1965), Lindley (1965, 1971), and many others have contributed to the development of Bayesian analysis and applications of it to many scientific estimation, prediction, testing, and other problems. In what follows, an overview of these developments will be presented and illustrated with analyses of selected problems.

I. ESTIMATION PROBLEMS

Bayes' Theorem plays a central role in estimation problems. Let $\mathbf{y}$ denote a vector of observations contained in a sample space $R_\mathbf{y}$ and θ a vector of parameters contained in a parameter space Θ. Given initial information I_0, let $p(\mathbf{y}, \theta | I_0)$ be the joint probability density function (pdf) for $\mathbf{y}$ and θ. Then

$$p(\mathbf{y}, \theta | I_0) = p(\theta | I_0)p(\mathbf{y} | \theta, I_0)$$

$$= p(\mathbf{y} | I_0)p(\theta | \mathbf{y}, I_0) \qquad (1.1)$$

where $p(\cdot | \cdot)$ is a generic symbol for a pdf labelled by its argument. Then from (1.1),

$$p(\theta | D) = p(\theta | I_0)p(\mathbf{y} | \theta, I_0)/p(\mathbf{y} | I_0)$$

$$\propto p(\theta | I_0)p(\mathbf{y} | \theta, I_0) \qquad (1.2a)$$

where $D \equiv (\mathbf{y}, I_0)$, the sample and prior information and '$\propto$' denotes 'is proportional to'. The result in (1.2a) is Bayes' Theorem where $p(\theta | D)$ is the posterior pdf for θ, $p(\theta | I_0)$ is the prior pdf for θ and $p(\mathbf{y} | \theta, I_0)$ is the pdf for $\mathbf{y}$ given θ and I_0, which when viewed as a function of θ is the likelihood function. Thus Bayes' Theorem can be stated as

Posterior pdf $\propto$ (Prior pdf) $\times$ (Likelihood function) (1.2b)

with the factor of proportionality being a normalizing constant.

In (1.2), $p(\theta | I_0)$, the prior pdf, represents information about possible values for θ *prior to observing* $\mathbf{y}$. The information in the observations $\mathbf{y}$ is incorporated in the likelihood function and (1.2) transforms the information in the prior pdf and the likelihood function into a posterior pdf for θ, $p(\theta | D)$, that is used to make inferences about the possible values of the elements of θ.

It is seen from (1.2) that the likelihood function plays an important role in Bayes' Theorem in summarizing the sample information. According to the likelihood principle, the likelihood function contains all the sample information and thus no sample information is disregarded when the likelihood function is employed. If there is uncertainty regarding the likelihood function's form, various forms can be considered as explained below and the sample and prior information can be employed in a Bayesian fashion to help resolve the uncertainty.

In the Bayesian approach to inference prior information about the possible values of θ is formally and explicitly introduced by use of a prior pdf, $p(\theta|I_0)$ in (1.2). If little prior information is available, a 'diffuse' or 'non-informative' prior pdf is employed, that is one that contains little information about the possible values of θ. On the other hand, if prior information about the possible values of θ is available, an 'informative' prior pdf would be employed. Prior information may be derived from past studies, economic theory, etc. For example, subject matter considerations and past studies may indicate that a parameter's value falls between zero and one and a prior pdf reflecting this restriction on the range of the parameter would be employed. This is but one type of prior information that may be available and can be incorporated in analyses by use of Bayes' Theorem.

To illustrate the use of Bayes' Theorem in estimation, several simple, important problems will be analysed.

Example 1: Normal mean with normal prior. Assume that the observations y_i, $i = 1, 2, \ldots, n$ have been independently drawn from a normal distribution with unknown mean θ, $-\infty < \theta < \infty$, and known variance, $\sigma^2 = \sigma_0^2$. The likelihood function is

$$p(\mathbf{y}|\theta, \sigma^2 = \sigma_0^2) = (2\pi\sigma_0^2)^{-n/2} \exp\left\{-\sum_{i=1}^{n}(y_i - \theta)^2\right\}$$
$$\propto \exp\{-n(\theta - \bar{y})^2/2\sigma_0^2\},$$

where

$$\bar{y} = \sum_{i=1}^{n} y_i/n$$

is the sample mean and

$$\sum_{i=1}^{n}(y_i - \theta)^2 = \sum_{i=1}^{n}(y_i - \bar{y})^2 + n(\theta - \bar{y})^2$$

has been employed. Further, assume that prior information regarding θ's possible values is well represented by a normal prior pdf with mean m and variance v, i.e. $p(\theta|m, v) = (2\pi v)^{-1/2} \exp\{-(\theta - m)^2/2v\}$. Then using Bayes' Theorem in (1.2), the posterior pdf for θ is

$p(\theta|D) \propto$ (prior pdf) × (likelihood function)
$$\propto \exp\{-[(\theta - m)^2/v + n(\theta - \bar{y})^2/\sigma_0^2]/2\}$$
$$\propto \exp\{-(\theta - \bar{\theta})^2/2\tau^2\} \qquad (1.3)$$

a normal pdf with mean $\bar{\theta}$ and variance τ^2 given by

$$\bar{\theta} = (h_0 m + h\bar{y})/(h_0 + h) \qquad (1.4)$$
$$\tau^2 = 1/(h_0 + h) \qquad (1.5)$$

where $h_0 = 1/v$, the prior precision and $h = n/\sigma_0^2$, the sample precision. It is seen that the posterior mean $\bar{\theta}$ is a weighted average of the prior mean m and the sample mean $\bar{y}$ with the prior precisions, $h_0 = 1/v$ and $h = n/\sigma_0^2$ as weights. As the prior

variance $v \to \infty$, that is the prior pdf is very spread out reflecting little information about θ's value, the posterior mean, $\bar{\theta} \to \bar{y}$, the sample mean and the posterior distribution approaches a normal pdf with mean $\bar{y}$ and variance σ_0^2/n. Also, as n grows large, the posterior pdf approaches a normal pdf with mean $\bar{y}$ and variance σ_0^2/n. For finite v and n, the normal distribution in (1.3) can be employed to make probability statements regarding θ's possible value. For example, the posterior probability that $a < \theta < b$ is given by

$$\Pr(a < \theta < b|D) = \int_a^b p(\theta|D)\,\mathrm{d}\theta$$
$$= F(b|D) - F(a|D) \qquad (1.6)$$

where $F(\cdot|D)$ is the cumulative posterior normal distribution associated with (1.3).

Example 2: Binomial Trials. Assume that θ, $0 \leqslant \theta \leqslant 1$, is the probability of 'success' on a given trial and that n independent trials yield r successes and $n - r$ failures. The likelihood function is given by

$$\binom{n}{r}\theta^r(1 - \theta)^{n-r}.$$

Further assume that prior information regarding θ's possible value is well represented by a beta pdf with parameters a and b, that is $p(\theta|a, b) = \theta^{a-1}(1 - \theta)^{b-1}/B(a, b)$ with $0 \leqslant \theta \leqslant 1$, a, $b > 0$ and where

$$B(a, b) = \int_0^1 \theta^{a-1}(1 - \theta)^{b-1}\,\mathrm{d}\theta,$$

the beta function. Then the posterior pdf for θ is

$$p(\theta|D) \propto \theta^{r+a-1}(1 - \theta)^{n-r+b-1} \qquad 0 \leqslant \theta \leqslant 1 \qquad (1.7)$$

which is in the beta form with parameters $a' = r + a$ and $b' = n - r + b$. Thus the normalized posterior pdf is $p(\theta|D) = \theta^{a'-1}(1 - \theta)^{b'-1}/B(a', b')$. With the posterior pdf in (1.7), it is possible to compute the posterior probability that $c_1 < \theta < c_2$, where c_1 and c_2 are any given numbers in the closed interval zero and one, as follows

$$\Pr(c_1 < \theta < c_2|D) = \int_{c_1}^{c_2} p(\theta|D)\,\mathrm{d}\theta. \qquad (1.8)$$

The integral in (1.8) can be evaluated using tables of the incomplete beta function or by numerical integration and is a solution to Bayes' inverse probability problem stated earlier. Note that if $a = b = 1$, the prior for θ is uniform over the interval zero to one, the Bayes–Laplace rule for representing little prior information about θ's value – see Jeffreys (1967, pp. 123–5) and Geisser (1984) for further discussion of this rule and other rules for representing knowing little about a binomial parameter.

In the two examples analysed above there were sufficient statistics, $\bar{y}$ for the normal mean problem and r for the binomial problem. It was the case that the posterior distributions were functions of these simple sufficient statistics. This is a general property of Bayesian analyses that is simply shown. Let $\mathbf{t}' = (t_1, t_2, \ldots, t_m)$ be a vector of sufficient statistics. Then $p(\mathbf{y}|\theta) = h(\mathbf{y})p(\mathbf{t}|\theta)$, where $h(\mathbf{y})$ is a function of just the data $\mathbf{y}$ and Bayes' Theorem in (1.2) yields

$$p(\theta|D) \propto p(\theta|I_0)p(\mathbf{y}|\theta, I_0)$$
$$\propto p(\theta|I_0)p(\mathbf{t}|\theta, I_0). \qquad (1.9)$$

Thus $p(\theta|D)$ depends on the data just through $\mathbf{t}$, the vector of sufficient statistics.

Further, in both examples analysed above, the prior distributions' forms were in the same form as the likelihood function. When this is the case, the prior distribution is said to have a 'natural conjugate' form – see, e.g. Raiffa and Schlaifer (1961) for further discussion of natural conjugate prior distributions.

Another property of Bayes' Theorem that is quite useful and appealing is that it can be applied sequentially to data sets with results that are identical to what is obtained by an application to an entire data set. To illustrate, consider two independent data vectors, $\mathbf{y}_1$, with pdf $p(\mathbf{y}_1|\boldsymbol{\theta})$ and $\mathbf{y}_2$ with pdf $p(\mathbf{y}_2|\boldsymbol{\theta}, I_0)$. If $p(\boldsymbol{\theta}|I_0)$ is the prior pdf, then the posterior pdf is

$$p(\boldsymbol{\theta}|D) \propto p(\boldsymbol{\theta}|I_0)p(\mathbf{y}_1|\boldsymbol{\theta}, I_0)p(\mathbf{y}_2|\boldsymbol{\theta}, I_0) \qquad (1.10)$$

where $D = (\mathbf{y}_1, \mathbf{y}_2, I_0)$. If we analyse the data sets sequentially, $p_1(\boldsymbol{\theta}|D_1) \propto p(\boldsymbol{\theta}|I_0)p(\mathbf{y}_1|\boldsymbol{\theta}, I_0)$ is the posterior pdf based on $D_1 = (\mathbf{y}_1, I_0)$. If $p_1(\boldsymbol{\theta}|D_1)$ is employed as a prior pdf for the analysis of the data set $\mathbf{y}_2$, the posterior pdf is $p(\boldsymbol{\theta}|D) \propto p_1(\boldsymbol{\theta}|D_1)p(\mathbf{y}_2|\boldsymbol{\theta}, I_0)$ which is just the same as (1.10). Thus the same posterior pdf is obtained by proceeding sequentially as by proceeding as shown in (1.10).

When a vector of parameters $\boldsymbol{\theta}$ is involved in Bayes' Theorem in (1.2), marginal and conditional posterior pdfs are of interest. Let $\boldsymbol{\theta}$ be partitioned as $\boldsymbol{\theta}' = (\boldsymbol{\theta}_1', \boldsymbol{\theta}_2')$ and suppose that interest centres on $\boldsymbol{\theta}_1$. For example $\boldsymbol{\theta}_2$ may be a vector of nuisance parameters that are of little interest to an investigator. The following integration can be performed analytically or numerically to obtain the marginal posterior pdf for $\boldsymbol{\theta}_1$, denoted by $p(\boldsymbol{\theta}_1|D)$,

$$p(\boldsymbol{\theta}_1|D) = \int_{\Theta_2} p(\boldsymbol{\theta}_1, \boldsymbol{\theta}_2|D)\, d\boldsymbol{\theta}_2 \qquad (1.11a)$$

where Θ_2 is the region containing $\boldsymbol{\theta}_2$. The capability of integrating out nuisance parameters is an extremely important property of the Bayesian approach. Further, writing $p(\boldsymbol{\theta}_1, \boldsymbol{\theta}_2|D) = p(\boldsymbol{\theta}_1|\boldsymbol{\theta}_2, D)p(\boldsymbol{\theta}_2|D)$ where $p(\boldsymbol{\theta}_1|\boldsymbol{\theta}_2, D)$ is the conditional posterior pdf for $\boldsymbol{\theta}_1$ given $\boldsymbol{\theta}_2$ and $p(\boldsymbol{\theta}_2|D)$ is the marginal posterior pdf for $\boldsymbol{\theta}_2$, the integral in (1.11a) can be expressed as

$$p(\boldsymbol{\theta}_1|D) = \int_{\Theta_2} p(\boldsymbol{\theta}_1|\boldsymbol{\theta}_2, D)p(\boldsymbol{\theta}_2|D)\, d\boldsymbol{\theta}_2. \qquad (1.11b)$$

Thus the marginal pdf, $p(\boldsymbol{\theta}_1|D)$ can be expressed as an average of conditional posterior pdfs, $p(\boldsymbol{\theta}_1|\boldsymbol{\theta}_2, D)$ with the marginal posterior pdf $p(\boldsymbol{\theta}_2|D)$ as the weight function.

The conditional posterior pdf, $p(\boldsymbol{\theta}_1|\boldsymbol{\theta}_2, D)$ is very important in performing sensitivity analyses. That is, $p(\boldsymbol{\theta}_1|\boldsymbol{\theta}_2, D)$ can be computed for various assigned values for $\boldsymbol{\theta}_2$ to determine how sensitive inferences about $\boldsymbol{\theta}_1$ are to what is assumed about $\boldsymbol{\theta}_2$. See Zellner (1971) and Box and Tiao (1973) for many examples of such sensitivity analyses. For example, $\boldsymbol{\theta}_2$ might be an autocorrelation parameter representing a possible departure from independence and $\boldsymbol{\theta}_1$ a vector of regression coefficients. How a departure from independence affects inferences about regression coefficients can be assessed using conditional posterior distributions.

The large sample properties of posterior distributions is also of interest. Under relatively mild conditions, it has been shown in the literature that as the sample size grows, posterior distributions assume a normal shape with mean approximately equal to the maximum likelihood (ML) estimate and covariance matrix equal to the inverse of the matrix of second derivatives of the log-likelihood function with respect to the parameters evaluated at the ML estimates. Jeffreys (1967, p. 193) views this result as a Bayesian justification for the ML estimate in large samples. For proofs of the asymptotic normality of posterior distributions, see Jeffreys (1967), Heyde and Johnstone (1979), and Hartigan (1983). Heyde and Johnstone (1979) show that when the observations are independently and identically distri-

buted, the conditions needed to prove the asymptotic normality of posterior distributions are identical to those needed to prove asymptotic normality of ML estimators. However, when observations are stochastically dependent, as in time series problems, they show that the conditions needed for asymptotic normality of posterior distributions are simpler and more robust than those needed for proving asymptotic normality of ML estimators.

In summary, Bayes' Theorem provides the complete, finite sample posterior pdf for parameters appearing in all kinds of econometric models. These posterior distributions can be employed to make probability statements about parameters' possible values – see e.g. (1.6) above for an example. If nuisance parameters are present, they can be integrated out of the joint posterior pdf to obtain a marginal posterior pdf for parameters of interest as shown in (1.11). Further, if the sample size is large, posterior pdfs assume a normal shape in general with a mean approximately equal to the ML estimate. However, if the sample size is not large, the ML estimate is often not a good approximation to the posterior mean and posterior pdfs' forms are usually non-normal – see Zellner and Rossi (1984) for illustrations of these points using logit models. While the complete posterior pdf is generally available in Bayesian analyses, often interest centres on obtaining an optimal point estimate for a parameter. The Bayesian solution to the problem of point estimation is presented below.

1.1. BAYESIAN POINT ESTIMATION. Given a posterior pdf for $\boldsymbol{\theta} \subset \Theta$, $p(\boldsymbol{\theta}|D)$ derived using Bayes' Theorem in (1.2), an estimate of $\boldsymbol{\theta}$, say $\hat{\boldsymbol{\theta}} = \hat{\boldsymbol{\theta}}(D)$, where $D = (\mathbf{y}, I_0)$, the sample and prior information, is desired. Some measure of central tendency relating to the posterior pdf, say the mean, modal value or median might be used as a point estimate. However, if the posterior pdf is asymmetric, these measures of central tendency will differ and the problem of choice among them remains. When a loss function, $L(\boldsymbol{\theta}, \hat{\boldsymbol{\theta}})$, is available, this problem can be solved by choosing the value of $\hat{\boldsymbol{\theta}}$ that minimizes expected loss and such a value is the Bayesian point estimate. Explicitly, the problem to be solved in Bayesian point estimation is $\min EL(\boldsymbol{\theta}, \hat{\boldsymbol{\theta}})$ with respect to $\hat{\boldsymbol{\theta}}$, or

$$\min_{\hat{\boldsymbol{\theta}}} \int_{\Theta} L(\boldsymbol{\theta}, \hat{\boldsymbol{\theta}})p(\boldsymbol{\theta}|D)\, d\boldsymbol{\theta} \qquad (1.12)$$

The solution to the minimization problem (1.12), denoted by $\hat{\boldsymbol{\theta}}^*$ is the Bayesian point estimate. Note that $-L(\boldsymbol{\theta}, \hat{\boldsymbol{\theta}})$ can be interpreted as a utility function and thus (1.12) is equivalent to choosing a value for $\hat{\boldsymbol{\theta}}$ that maximizes expected utility. Given the form of $L(\boldsymbol{\theta}, \hat{\boldsymbol{\theta}})$, the problem in (1.12) can be solved analytically or by numerical integration techniques. Below, solutions will be presented for some widely used loss functions.

a. *Quadratic loss functions.* Let $L(\theta, \hat{\theta}) = c_1(\hat{\theta} - \theta)^2$ where c_1 is a given positive constant. Then

$$EL = c_1 E(\theta - \hat{\theta})^2 = c_1 E[\theta - \bar{\theta} - (\hat{\theta} - \bar{\theta})]^2$$
$$= c_1[E(\theta - \bar{\theta})^2 + (\hat{\theta} - \bar{\theta})^2],$$

where $\bar{\theta} = E(\theta|D)$ is the posterior mean of θ. Then the value of $\hat{\theta}$ that minimizes expected loss is $\hat{\theta}^* = \bar{\theta}$, the posterior mean. This is a very general result applicable to all kinds of point estimation problems for which the above 'squared error' loss function is appropriate. For example, in the normal mean problem analysed above, the optimal point estimate relative to the above squared error loss function is the posterior mean given in (1.4). For the Binomial Trials problem with posterior pdf given in (1.7) the optimal point estimate relative to squared error loss is the mean of the posterior pdf, namely, $\hat\theta* = (r + a)/(n + a + b)$.

If θ is a vector of parameters and if the loss function is $L(\theta, \hat\theta) = (\hat\theta - \theta)'Q(\hat\theta - \theta)$, where Q is a given positive definite symmetric matrix, then

$$
\begin{aligned}
EL &= E(\hat\theta - \theta)'Q(\hat\theta - \theta) \\
&= E[\hat\theta - \bar\theta - (\theta - \bar\theta)]'Q[\hat\theta - \bar\theta - (\theta - \bar\theta)] \\
&= (\hat\theta - \bar\theta)'Q(\hat\theta - \bar\theta) + E(\theta - \bar\theta)'Q(\theta - \bar\theta) \quad (1.13)
\end{aligned}
$$

where $\bar\theta = E\theta \,|\, D$ is the posterior mean of θ. From the last line of (1.13), it is clear that the value of $\hat\theta$ that minimizes expected loss is $\hat\theta* = \bar\theta$, the posterior mean. Thus for multiparameter point estimation problems employing a quadratic loss function, the posterior mean is an optimal point estimate in terms of minimizing posterior expected loss.

b. *Absolute error loss functions*. If the loss function is $L(\theta, \hat\theta) = c_2|\hat\theta - \theta|$, where c_2 is a given positive constant, the value of $\hat\theta$ that minimizes expected loss is the median of the posterior pdf for θ, $p(\theta \,|\, D)$. With $a \leqslant \theta \leqslant b$, posterior expected loss is:

$$
\begin{aligned}
EL(\theta, \hat\theta) &= c_2 \int_a^b |\hat\theta - \theta| p(\theta \,|\, D) \, \mathrm{d}\theta \\
&= c_2 \left[\int_a^{\hat\theta} (\hat\theta - \theta) p(\theta \,|\, D) \, \mathrm{d}\theta + \int_{\hat\theta}^b (\theta - \hat\theta) p(\theta \,|\, D) \, \mathrm{d}\theta \right].
\end{aligned}
$$

Then

$$
\frac{\mathrm{d}EL(\theta, \hat\theta)}{\mathrm{d}\hat\theta} = c_2[F(\hat\theta \,|\, D) - 1 + F(\hat\theta \,|\, D)] \quad (1.14)
$$

where $F(\hat\theta \,|\, D) = \int_a^{\hat\theta} p(\theta \,|\, D) \, \mathrm{d}\theta$ is the cumulative posterior distribution function. The value of $\hat\theta$ that sets (1.14) equal to zero is $\hat\theta = $ median of the posterior pdf and this is the value that minimizes expected loss since $\mathrm{d}^2 EL/\mathrm{d}\hat\theta^2$, evaluated at the median is strictly positive. Thus for an absolute error loss function, the posterior median is an optimal point estimate. For the normal mean problem analysed above, the posterior pdf in (1.3) is normal and hence the median is equal to the mean, given in (1.4), since the normal posterior pdf is symmetric. For asymmetric posterior pdfs, such as that shown in (1.7), the median will not be equal to the mean.

c. *Zero-one loss functions*. If loss is equal to zero as $\hat\theta - \theta$ approaches zero and is equal to one for $|\hat\theta - \theta| \neq 0$, then the modal value of the posterior pdf is the value of $\hat\theta$ that minimizes expected loss – for a proof, see, e.g. Blackwell and Girshick (1954). Thus with a zero-one loss function, the modal value of (1.7), $\hat\theta* = (r + a - 1)/(n + a + b - 2)$ is optimal. Note that this value differs from the posterior mean $(r + a)/(n + a + b)$ that is optimal for a squared error loss function.

d. *Asymmetric LINEX loss function*. Let the loss function be given by

$$
L(\hat\theta - \theta) = b[e^{a(\hat\theta - \theta)} - a(\hat\theta - \theta) - 1], \qquad b > 0
$$
$$
a \neq 0 \quad (1.15)
$$

a class of asymmetric loss functions introduced and used by Varian (1975). For $\hat\theta - \theta = 0$, loss is zero and when $a > 0$, loss rises almost exponentially for $\hat\theta - \theta > 0$ and approximately linearly when $\hat\theta - \theta < 0$. The reverse is true when $a < 0$. Posterior expected loss is given by

$$
EL = b[e^{a\hat\theta} Ee^{-a\theta} - a(\hat\theta - E\theta) - 1]
$$

and the value of $\hat\theta$ that minimizes expected loss is

$$
\hat\theta* = -(1/a) \log Ee^{-a\theta} \quad (1.16)
$$

as shown in Zellner (1986). When (1.16) is evaluated using the normal posterior pdf in (1.3), the result is

$$
\hat\theta* = \bar\theta - a\tau^2/2 \quad (1.17)
$$

with $\bar\theta$ the posterior mean in (1.4) and τ^2 the posterior variance in (1.5). It is seen that the optimal point estimate in (1.17) is less than the posterior mean when $a > 0$ and greater than the posterior mean when $a < 0$ reflecting the asymmetry of the LINEX loss function in (1.15).

As the above examples indicate, the Bayesian point estimate is tailored to be optimal relative to the specific loss function that is deemed appropriate. For other loss functions, the problem of minimizing expected loss, shown in (1.12), can be solved, either analytically or by numerical integration to obtain an optimal Bayesian point estimate. This general procedure is applicable to all estimation problems in econometrics and statistics for which expected loss is finite, that is for which the integral in (1.12) converges to a finite value.

To appraise the general *sampling properties* of Bayesian estimates, $\hat\theta = \hat\theta(\mathbf{y}, I_0)$ is regarded as a random estimator. Relative to a specific loss function, $L(\theta, \hat\theta)$, the risk function is given by

$$
r(\theta) = \int_{R_y} L(\theta, \hat\theta) p(\mathbf{y} \,|\, \theta, I_0) \, \mathrm{d}\mathbf{y} \quad (1.18)
$$

and the Bayesian estimator is, by definition, the one that minimizes average or Bayes risk (BR),

$$
BR = \int_\Theta r(\theta) p(\theta \,|\, I_0) \, \mathrm{d}\theta, \quad (1.19)
$$

where $p(\theta \,|\, I_0)$ is a given prior pdf for θ that is assumed to be positive over the region Θ.

Upon substituting (1.18) in (1.19),

$$
BR = \int_\Theta \int_{R_y} L(\theta, \hat\theta) p(\mathbf{y} \,|\, \theta, I_0) p(\theta \,|\, I_0) \, \mathrm{d}\mathbf{y} \, \mathrm{d}\theta. \quad (1.20a)
$$

Using $p(\mathbf{y} \,|\, \theta, I_0) p(\theta \,|\, I_0) = p(\theta \,|\, D) p(\mathbf{y} \,|\, I_0)$, where $D = (\mathbf{y}, I_0)$, and interchanging the order of integration, (1.20a) can be expressed as

$$
BR = \int_{R_y} \left[\int_\Theta L(\theta, \hat\theta) p(\theta \,|\, D) \, \mathrm{d}\theta \right] p(\mathbf{y} \,|\, I_0) \, \mathrm{d}\mathbf{y}. \quad (1.20b)
$$

If the integral defining BR converges to a finite value and if $p(\mathbf{y} \,|\, I_0) > 0$ over the region R_y, then the value of $\hat\theta$ that minimizes the integral in square brackets in (1.20b) minimizes BR, i.e. it is the estimator that minimizes Bayes or average risk. Note that the integral in square brackets defines posterior expected loss. Thus the solution to the problem in (1.12), viewed as an estimator is the estimator that minimizes BR and is by definition the Bayesian estimator. This estimator is admissible since if there were another estimator that had lower risk, $r(\theta)$ given in (1.18), over Θ, it would have lower BR, a contradiction since the Bayesian estimator, by construction minimizes BR. These and other properties of Bayesian estimators are discussed in De Groot (1970), Berger (1985) and other works on decision theory. Thus Bayesian estimators relative to the loss function and prior pdf used to derive them have very good sampling properties under the condition that BR is finite, a sufficient condition for admissibility of the Bayesian estimator.

To illustrate some of the above concepts, consider estimation of a mean θ in the normal mean problem in Example 1 relative to a squared error loss function $L(\theta, \hat\theta) = (\theta - \hat\theta)^2$. As mentioned above, the posterior mean in (1.4) is the Bayesian estimator for this problem that we write as

$$\bar{\theta} = wm + (1-w)\bar{y} \qquad (1.21)$$

with $w = h_0/(h + h_0)$. Since $\bar{y}$ is normally distributed with mean θ and variance σ_0^2/n, the risk of $\bar{\theta}$ relative to a squared error loss function is

$$
\begin{aligned}
r(\theta) &= E_{\bar{y}}(\theta - \bar{\theta})^2 \\
&= \theta^2 - 2\theta E\bar{\theta} + E\bar{\theta}^2 \\
&= \theta^2 - 2\theta[wm + (1-w)E\bar{y}] + E[wm + (1-w)\bar{y}]^2 \\
r(\theta) &= w^2(\theta - m)^2 + (1-w)^2\sigma_0^2/n. \qquad (1.22)
\end{aligned}
$$

It is clear that $r(\theta)$ is smallest when $\theta = m$, the prior mean. To compute BR, we average $r(\theta)$ using the normal prior for θ with mean m and variance $v = 1/h_0$ to obtain

$$
\begin{aligned}
\text{BR} &= w^2 v + (1-w)^2 \sigma_0^2/n \\
&= 1/(h_0 + h) \qquad (1.23)
\end{aligned}
$$

where $\sigma_0^2/n = 1/h$. For comparison, the risk function for the sample mean, $\bar{y}$, is

$$
\begin{aligned}
r(\theta) &= E(\theta - \bar{y})^2 \\
&= \sigma_0^2/n. \qquad (1.24)
\end{aligned}
$$

On comparing (1.24) and (1.22), it is seen that when θ is close to the prior mean, (1.22) is smaller than (1.24). The BR of the sample mean is

$$\text{BR} = \sigma_0^2/n = 1/h \qquad (1.25)$$

which is larger than the BR of the posterior mean in (1.23). This is not surprising since the posterior mean is the estimator that minimizes BR.

Above, proper prior pdfs were employed to obtain Bayesian estimates and estimators. When *improper* prior pdfs are employed to represent vague or little prior information about parameters' values as in Jeffreys (1967) and others' works, posterior pdfs are usually proper and posterior probability statements can be made. Rényi (1970) – see also Hartigan (1983) – has provided an axiom system for probability theory that accommodates improper prior pdfs or unbounded measures and within the context of which Bayes' Theorem remains valid. When such prior pdfs are employed, the solution to the point estimation problem in (1.12) is termed a generalized Bayes estimate (GBE). Often BR is not finite for GB estimators and they need not in general be admissible. To illustrate, a normal mean problem and a regression problem will be analysed employing diffuse, improper prior pdfs.

Example 3: Normal mean with an improper prior. Assume that n observations have been independently drawn from a normal distribution with mean θ and variance σ^2, both of which have unknown values. The likelihood function is given by

$$
\begin{aligned}
p(\mathbf{y}|\theta, \sigma) &\propto \sigma^{-n} \exp\{-(\mathbf{y} - \iota\theta)'(\mathbf{y} - \iota\theta)/2\sigma^2\} \\
&\propto \sigma^{-n} \exp\{-[vs^2 + n(\theta - \bar{y})^2]/2\sigma^2\} \qquad (1.26)
\end{aligned}
$$

where $\mathbf{y}' = (y_1, y_2, \ldots, y_n)$, $\iota' = (1, 1, \ldots, 1)$, a $1 \times n$ vector with all elements equal to one,

$$\bar{y} = \sum_{i=1}^{n} y_i/n,$$

the sample mean and

$$vs^2 = \sum_{i=1}^{n} (y_i - \bar{y})^2 \quad \text{and} \quad v = n - 1.$$

Jeffreys's (1967) diffuse improper prior pdf for this problem is,

$$
\begin{aligned}
p(\theta, \sigma) &\propto 1/\sigma. \quad -\infty < \theta < \infty \\
&\qquad\qquad 0 < \sigma < \infty \qquad (1.27)
\end{aligned}
$$

That is θ and $\log \sigma$ are assumed independently and uniformly distributed. Since the integral of $p(\theta, \sigma)$ over the range $-\infty < \theta < \infty$ and $0 < \sigma < \infty$ does not converge to one, the prior pdf is termed 'improper'. See Zellner (1971, 1977) and Berger (1985) for further discussion of (1.27). On combining the likelihood function in (1.26) with the prior in (1.27) by Bayes' Theorem, the result is the joint posterior pdf for θ and σ, namely

$$p(\theta, \sigma|D) \propto \sigma^{-(n+1)} \exp\{-[vs^2 + n(\theta - \bar{y})^2]/2\sigma^2\}. \quad (1.28)$$

From (1.28), it is seen that the conditional posterior pdf for θ given σ is normal with mean $\bar{y}$ and variance σ^2/n. Also by integrating (1.28) with respect to σ, 0 to ∞, the marginal posterior pdf for θ is

$$p(\theta|D) \propto \{vs^2 + n(\theta - \bar{y})^2\}^{-(v+1)/2} \qquad (1.29)$$

which is a proper pdf, given $v > 0$, in the univariate Student-t form. That is $t = \sqrt{n}(\theta - \bar{y})/s$ has a standardised Student-t pdf with v degrees of freedom. Also, on integrating (1.28) with respect to θ, from $-\infty$ to ∞, the result is the marginal posterior for σ,

$$p(\sigma|D) \propto \sigma^{-(v+1)} \exp\{-vs^2/2\sigma^2\}, \qquad (1.30)$$

a proper pdf in the inverted-gamma form – see, e.g. Zellner (1971) for its properties. Thus even though the improper prior pdf in (1.27) was employed, the posterior pdfs in (1.29) and (1.30) are proper and can be employed to make posterior probability statements about the values of θ and σ.

To obtain an optimal point estimate for θ, assume that a squared error loss function is appropriate, that is $L(\theta, \hat{\theta}) = (\hat{\theta} - \theta)^2$. Relative to this loss function the value of $\hat{\theta}$ that minimizes posterior expected loss is the posterior mean of (1.29) which is $\bar{y}$ for $v > 1$. The risk of $\bar{y}$ relative to the squared error loss function is $E(\bar{y} - \theta)^2 = \sigma^2/n$ since $\bar{y}$ has a normal pdf with mean θ and variance σ^2/n. If we try to compute the BR of $\bar{y}$ relative to the improper prior in (1.27), it is clear that BR is unbounded, that is the integral defining

$$\text{BR} = \int_0^\infty \int_{-\infty}^\infty r(\theta) p(\theta, \sigma|I_0) \, d\theta \, d\sigma$$

diverges. Thus $\bar{y}$, the posterior mean does not minimize BR. A different argument must be used to establish the admissibility of $\bar{y}$ – see e.g. Blyth (1951) and Berger (1985) for proofs of the admissibility of $\bar{y}$.

As regards the posterior pdf for σ in (1.30), it can be transformed to a posterior pdf for σ^2 by a simple change of variable from σ to $\phi = \sigma^2$ to yield

$$p(\phi|D) \propto \phi^{-(n+2)/2} \exp\{-vs^2/2\phi\}. \qquad 0 < \phi < \infty \quad (1.31)$$

The posterior mean of ϕ is $\bar{\phi} = vs^2/(v - 2)$, for $v > 2$ which is optimal relative to a squared error loss function. Also, with respect to a relative squared error loss function, $L(\hat{\phi}, \phi) = (\hat{\phi} - \phi)^2/\phi^2$, the optimal value of $\hat{\phi}$ is $\hat{\phi}^* = vs^2/(v + 2)$ since $EL = \hat{\phi}^2 E1/\phi^2 - 2\hat{\phi} E1/\phi + 1$ and the minimizing value of $\hat{\phi}$ is $\hat{\phi}^* = E(1/\phi)/E(1/\phi^2) = vs^2/(v + 2)$. Finally the modal value of (1.30) that is optimal relative to a zero-one loss function is $\hat{\phi}_{m0} = vs^2/(v + 2)$. Thus point estimates that are optimal relative to various loss functions are readily obtained. Finally from (1.30), vs^2/ϕ has a χ_v^2 posterior pdf, a fact that is very useful in making posterior probability statements regarding ϕ's values.

Example 4: Normal regression model with a diffuse prior. Assume that the $n \times 1$ observation vector $\mathbf{y}$ is generated by $\mathbf{y} = X\boldsymbol{\beta} + \mathbf{u}$, where X is an $n \times k$ non-stochastic matrix with rank k, $\boldsymbol{\beta}$ is a $k \times 1$ vector of regression coefficients with unknown values and $\mathbf{u}$ is an $n \times 1$ vector of disturbance terms assumed independently drawn from a normal pdf with zero mean and finite variance σ^2 with unknown value. The likelihood function under these assumptions is

$$p(\mathbf{y}|X, \boldsymbol{\beta}, \sigma) \propto \sigma^{-n}\exp\{-(\mathbf{y} - X\boldsymbol{\beta})'(\mathbf{y} - X\boldsymbol{\beta})/2\sigma^2\}$$
$$\propto \sigma^{-n}\exp\{-[vs^2 + (\boldsymbol{\beta} - \hat{\boldsymbol{\beta}})'X'X(\boldsymbol{\beta} - \hat{\boldsymbol{\beta}})]/2\sigma^2\} \tag{1.32}$$

where $\hat{\boldsymbol{\beta}} = (X'X)^{-1}X'\mathbf{y}$, $vs^2 = (\mathbf{y} - X\hat{\boldsymbol{\beta}})'(\mathbf{y} - X\hat{\boldsymbol{\beta}})$ and $v = n - k$. The diffuse prior pdf that will be employed is

$$p(\boldsymbol{\beta}, \sigma|I_0) \propto 1/\sigma, \quad -\infty < \beta_i < \infty \quad i = 1, 2, \dots, k$$
$$0 < \sigma < \infty. \tag{1.33}$$

That is the elements of $\boldsymbol{\beta}$ and $\log \sigma$ are assumed to be uniformly and independently distributed. Since (1.33) does not integrate to a constant, it is an improper pdf. However on combining it with the likelihood function in (1.33) by means of Bayes' Theorem, the resulting joint posterior pdf is,

$$p(\boldsymbol{\beta}, \sigma|D) \propto \sigma^{-(n+1)}\exp\{-[vs^2 + (\boldsymbol{\beta} - \hat{\boldsymbol{\beta}})'X'X(\boldsymbol{\beta} - \hat{\boldsymbol{\beta}})]/2\sigma^2\}. \tag{1.34}$$

From (1.34), it is seen that the conditional posterior pdf for $\boldsymbol{\beta}$ given σ is normal with mean $\hat{\boldsymbol{\beta}}$ and covariance matrix $(X'X)^{-1}\sigma^2$. Since σ's value is unknown, this result is not very useful in practice. To get rid of the nuisance parameter σ, (1.34) is integrated with respect to σ to yield the marginal posterior pdf for $\boldsymbol{\beta}$,

$$p(\boldsymbol{\beta}|D) \propto \{vs^2 + (\boldsymbol{\beta} - \hat{\boldsymbol{\beta}})'X'X(\boldsymbol{\beta} - \hat{\boldsymbol{\beta}})\}^{-(v+k)/2} \tag{1.35}$$

a posterior pdf that is the multivariate Student-t form – see, e.g. Raiffa and Schlaifer (1961) and Zellner (1971) for its properties. For $v > 1$, the mean of (1.34) is $E(\boldsymbol{\beta}|D) = \hat{\boldsymbol{\beta}} = (X'X)^{-1}X'\mathbf{y}$, the least squares quantity and ML estimate. This then is another example wherein a non-Bayesian result has been produced by the Bayesian approach. Further, from (1.35), the marginal pdf for an element of $\boldsymbol{\beta}$, say β_i is in the univariate Student-t form; that is, $(\beta_i - \hat{\beta}_i)/s_{\beta_i}$ has a univariate Student-t pdf with v degrees of freedom where $\hat{\beta}_i$ is the ith element of $\hat{\boldsymbol{\beta}}$ and $s_{\beta_i}^2 = m^{ii}s^2$, where m^{ii} is the i-ith element of $(X'X)^{-1}$. Thus posterior probability statements about β_i's value, e.g. $\Pr(\beta_i > 0|D)$ can be made using properties of the univariate Student-t pdf.

Further, on integrating (1.34) with respect to the elements of $\boldsymbol{\beta}$, the following marginal posterior pdf for σ is obtained

$$p(\sigma|D) \propto \sigma^{-(v+1)} \exp\{-vs^2/2\sigma^2\} \tag{1.36}$$

a posterior pdf in the 'inverted gamma' form – see, e.g. Raiffa and Schlaifer (1961) and Zellner (1971) for its properties. By a change of variable in (1.36), the posterior pdf for $\phi = \sigma^2$, the variance is

$$p(\phi|D) \propto \phi^{-(v+2)/2} \exp\{-vs^2/2\phi\} \tag{1.37}$$

for which it is the case that vs^2/ϕ has a χ_v^2 pdf with $v = n - k$ degrees of freedom. The modal values and moments of (1.36) and (1.37) are readily available. Also, posterior probability statements regarding ϕ's possible values can be evaluated using tables of the χ_v^2 pdf; that is the posterior probability that ϕ lies between vs^2/a_2 and vs^2/a_1, given by $\Pr\{vs^2/a_2 < \phi < vs^2/a_1|D\}$, where $a_1, a_2 > 0$ are given constants, can be evaluated by use of χ_v^2 tables by noting that the required probability is equal to $\Pr\{a_1 < vs^2/\phi < a_2|D\}$, where vs^2/ϕ has a χ_v^2 posterior pdf.

As can be seen from what has been presented above, Bayesian point estimates can be readily computed from posterior pdfs that are optimal relative to loss functions that are deemed appropriate. They reflect both sample and prior information, as little or as much of the latter as is available. As regards sampling properties of point estimates, some properties of Bayesian estimators have been noted above. The relevance of sampling properties for making inferences from a *given* sample of data has been questioned by some – see e.g. Tiao and Box (1975). Indeed, it is difficult to state which sequence of future samples is most relevant for a given problem. Usually the sequence considered is *identical repetitions* of the process giving the sample data. This sequence is often not the most relevant sequence. However, before the sample data are drawn, it appears relevant to consider possible outcomes, particularly with respect to design of experiments, and it is here that sampling properties of procedures, including point estimation procedures, are most relevant. Once the data are drawn, the researcher's task is to make inferences based on the given sample and prior information.

With this said about point estimation, attention will now be given to interval estimation.

1.2 INTERVAL ESTIMATION. Given that a posterior pdf for a parameter θ, $p(\theta|D)$ is available that is unimodal, in interval estimation an interval is sought within which the parameter's value lies with a specified posterior probability, say 0.95. Since such intervals are not unique, it is necessary to impose a condition so that a unique interval is obtained. The condition is that of all intervals with posterior probability $1 - \alpha$, the one selected is the shortest. Formally, the length of the interval, say $b - a$ is minimized subject to the condition that $\Pr(a < \theta < b|D) = \int_a^b p(\theta|D) \, \mathrm{d}\theta = 1 - \alpha$, the given posterior probability. The solution for this constrained minimization problem is to take the values of a and b such that $p(a|D) = p(b|D)$ – see, e.g. Zellner (1971) for a proof. Given that $p(\theta|D)$ is unimodal, the posterior interval with probability content $1 - \alpha$ so computed has posterior densities associated with it that are greater than any other interval with posterior probability $1 - \alpha$ and thus has been called a posterior highest density (PHD) interval.

Example 5: PHD interval for a regression coefficient. In Example 4, it was indicated that the posterior pdf for a regression coefficient β_i is in the univariate Student-t form, that is $t_v = (\beta_i - \hat{\beta}_i)/s_{\beta_i}$ has a univariate Student-t posterior pdf with $v = n - k$ degrees of freedom. Then, with given probability $1 - \alpha$, say 0.95, $\Pr(-c < t_v < c|D) = 1 - \alpha$, where $c > 0$ is obtained from t-tables with v degrees of freedom. Note from the symmetry of the Student-t pdf, $p(-c|D) = p(c|D)$ as required for a PHD interval. Also the event $-c < t_v < c$ is equivalent to $\hat{\beta}_i - cs_{\beta_i} < \beta_i < \hat{\beta}_i + cs_{\beta_i}$ and thus the posterior probability that β_i is in the given interval $\hat{\beta}_i \pm cs_{\beta_i}$ is 0.95.

Further, a posterior region for the regression coefficient vector can be computed using the following result from (1.35), a property of the multivariate Student-t pdf, namely,

$$F_{k,v} = (\boldsymbol{\beta} - \hat{\boldsymbol{\beta}})'X'X(\boldsymbol{\beta} - \hat{\boldsymbol{\beta}})/ks^2 \tag{1.38}$$

has a posterior F distribution with k and v degrees of freedom. When $\boldsymbol{\beta}$ has two elements, (1.38) can be employed to compute a confidence region in the form of an ellipse with a given posterior probability, $1 - \alpha$ that β_1 and β_2 falls within it by choosing a value of $F_{k,v}$, say F_α such that $\Pr(F_{k,v} \leqslant F_\alpha) = 1 - \alpha$.

II. BAYESIAN PREDICTION PROCEDURES

Let $\mathbf{y}_f$ represent a vector of as yet unobserved variables and assume that the pdf for $\mathbf{y}_f$ is $f(\mathbf{y}_f|\theta)$, where θ is a vector of parameters with unknown values. The fact that θ has an unknown value makes it difficult to use $f(\mathbf{y}_f|\theta)$ to make probability statements about possible values of $\mathbf{y}_f$. However, if a posterior pdf for θ, $p(\theta|D)$ is available, provided by Bayes' Theorem in (1.2), then the joint pdf for $\mathbf{y}_f$ and θ is given by $f(\mathbf{y}_f|\theta)p(\theta|D)$, where D represents past data and prior information. Then the marginal or predictive pdf for $\mathbf{y}_f$, $p(\mathbf{y}_f|D)$, is given by,

$$p(\mathbf{y}_f|D) = \int_\Theta f(\mathbf{y}_f|\theta)p(\theta|D)\,d\theta. \qquad (2.1)$$

From (2.1) it is seen that the predictive pdf can be interpreted as an average of $f(\mathbf{y}_f|\theta)$ with $p(\theta|D)$ serving as the weight function. The result in (2.1) gives the complete predictive pdf for the vector of future values, $\mathbf{y}_f$ from which marginal pdfs for particular elements of $\mathbf{y}_f$ can be obtained by integration. Also, moments of the elements of $\mathbf{y}_f$ can be evaluated. As explained below, the mean of the predictive pdf (2.1) is an optimal point prediction relative to a quadratic loss function. Also, predictive intervals and regions for elements of $\mathbf{y}_f$ can be computed from (2.1).

As regards point prediction, given a predictive loss function, $L(\mathbf{y}_f, \hat{\mathbf{y}}_f)$, where $\hat{\mathbf{y}}_f = \hat{\mathbf{y}}_f(D)$ is some point prediction, an optimal value for $\hat{\mathbf{y}}_f$ is obtained by minimizing expected loss, that is by solving the following problem:

$$\min_{\hat{\mathbf{y}}_f} \int L(\mathbf{y}_f, \hat{\mathbf{y}}_f)p(\mathbf{y}_f|D)\,d\mathbf{y}_f. \qquad (2.2)$$

The solution, $\hat{\mathbf{y}}_f^*$ is the optimal point prediction. For example, for a quadratic loss function, $L(\mathbf{y}_f, \hat{\mathbf{y}}_f) = (\mathbf{y}_f - \hat{\mathbf{y}}_f)'Q(\mathbf{y}_f - \hat{\mathbf{y}}_f)$, where Q is a given positive definite symmetric matrix, expected loss is given by

$$\begin{aligned}
E(\mathbf{y}_f - \hat{\mathbf{y}}_f)'Q(\mathbf{y}_f - \hat{\mathbf{y}}_f) \\
= E[\mathbf{y}_f - \bar{\mathbf{y}}_f - (\hat{\mathbf{y}}_f - \bar{\mathbf{y}}_f)]'Q[\mathbf{y}_f - \bar{\mathbf{y}}_f - (\hat{\mathbf{y}}_f - \bar{\mathbf{y}}_f)] \\
= E(y_f - \bar{y}_f)'Q(y_f - \bar{y}_f) + (\hat{y}_f - \bar{y}_f)'Q(\hat{y} - \bar{y}_f) \qquad (2.3)
\end{aligned}$$

where $\bar{\mathbf{y}}_f$ is the mean of the predictive pdf. From (2.3), it is clear that taking $\hat{y}_f = \bar{y}_f$ minimizes expected loss. Thus, in general, the mean of a predictive pdf is an optimal point prediction relative to quadratic loss. As in the case of point estimation, if other loss functions are employed, point predictions that are optimal relative to them can be calculated by solving the problem in (2.2) analytically or numerically. This analysis for absolute error, zero-one and LINEX loss functions is similar to that presented above in connection with point estimation. Also, Bayesian point predictors based on proper prior distributions are admissible and minimize Bayes risk.

To illustrate the calculation of a predictive pdf for the multiple regression model with the posterior pdf for its parameters given in (1.34), let a future scalar observation, y_f be given by

$$y_f = \mathbf{x}_f'\boldsymbol{\beta} + u_f \qquad (2.4)$$

where $\mathbf{x}_f'$ is a $1 \times k$ given vector and u_f is a normal error term with zero mean and variance σ^2. Then noting from (1.34) that the posterior pdf of $\boldsymbol{\beta}$ given σ is $N[\hat{\boldsymbol{\beta}}, (X'X)^{-1}\sigma^2]$, the conditional distribution of y_f given σ is normal with mean $\mathbf{x}_f'\hat{\boldsymbol{\beta}}$ and covariance matrix, $[1 + \mathbf{x}_f'(X'X)^{-1}\mathbf{x}_f]\sigma^2$. On multiplying this conditional predictive pdf for y_f by the posterior pdf for σ, given in (1.36) and integrating over σ, the result is

$$p(y_f|D) \propto \{vs^2 + (y_f - \hat{y}_f)^2/a^2\}^{-(v+1)/2} \qquad (2.5)$$

where $\hat{y}_f = \mathbf{x}_f'\hat{\boldsymbol{\beta}}$, $a^2 = 1 + \mathbf{x}_f'(X'X)^{-1}\mathbf{x}_f$ and $v = n - k$, a pdf in the univariate Student-t form with v degrees of freedom with

mean $\hat{y}_f$. Thus

$$t_v = (y_f - \hat{y}_f)/as \qquad (2.6)$$

has a univariate Student-t pdf with v degrees of freedom. Using (2.6), a predictive interval for y_f can be computed that has a given probability, say $1 - \alpha$, of including y_f. Such an interval takes the form $\hat{y}_f \pm c_{\alpha/2} as$, where $c_{\alpha/2}$ is a constant obtained from tables of the t-distribution. The probability statement associated with this interval is:

$$\Pr\{\hat{y}_f - c_{\alpha/2} as < y_f < \hat{y}_f + c_{\alpha/2} as | D\} = 1 - \alpha. \qquad (2.7)$$

Note that y_f is random and the endpoints of the interval are non-random since they depend just on the given data D. A similar analysis can be performed to obtain the predictive pdf for a vector of future values $\mathbf{y}_f$, assumed generated by $\mathbf{y}_f = X_f\boldsymbol{\beta} + \mathbf{u}_f$ when the value of X_f is given.

Above in (2.4), $\mathbf{x}_f$ was assumed given. If $\mathbf{x}_f$'s value is unknown then the predictive pdf for y_f is given by

$$p(y_f|D) = \int p(y_f|x_f, D)p(\mathbf{x}_f|D_1)\,d\mathbf{x}_f \qquad (2.8)$$

where $p(x_f|D_1)$ is the predictive pdf for $\mathbf{x}_f$ given data D_1. The integration in (2.8) may be performed analytically or numerically. Further, predictive pdfs can be computed for linear combinations of future values, say $\mathbf{z} = A\mathbf{y}_f$ where A is a given matrix, for time series models – see Broemeling (1985), Monahan (1983) and Zellner (1971); for simultaneous equation models – see Richard (1973), and for many other models – see Aitchison and Dunsmore (1975).

III. BAYESIAN ANALYSIS OF HYPOTHESES

Bayesian methods are available for analysing hypotheses about parameters' values and for comparing and choosing between alternative hypotheses or models, be they nested or non-nested. Prior probabilities are assigned to hypotheses or models that reflect the degrees of confidence associated with them and Bayes' Theorem is employed to compute posterior probabilities for them that reflect the information in sample data. This approach differs radically from non-Bayesian testing procedures in which one hypothesis, e.g. the null hypothesis, or one of two models is assumed to be 'true' and a test statistics' distribution, derived under an assumed true null hypothesis or model is employed to 'accept' or 'reject' the assumed true hypothesis or model. For further consideration of these issues see Jeffreys (1967), Jaynes (1984), Kruskal (1978), Leamer (1978), and Zellner (1971, 1984).

To illustrate the Bayesian approach for analysing hypotheses, consider first a scalar parameter θ, say a population mean or a regression coefficient with possible values $-\infty < \theta < \infty$. Assume that the following two hypotheses are of interest, $H_1: \theta > 0$ and $H_2: \theta \leq 0$. Given a prior pdf for the parameter, $p(\theta|I_0)$, the prior probability that $\theta > 0$ is given by

$$\Pr(\theta > 0 | I_0) = \int_0^\infty p(\theta|I_0)\,d\theta \qquad (3.1)$$

and the prior probability that $\theta \leq 0$ is

$$\Pr(\theta \leq 0 | I_0) = \int_{-\infty}^0 p(\theta|I_0)\,d\theta = 1 - \Pr(\theta > 0 | I_0). \qquad (3.2)$$

Then the prior odds for H_1 versus H_2, denoted by K_{12}^0 is

$$K_{12}^0 = \Pr(\theta > 0 | I_0)/\Pr(\theta \leq 0 | I_0). \qquad (3.3)$$

These probabilities and K_{12} summarize initial views of the hypotheses H_1 and H_2. If data $\mathbf{y}' = (y_1, y_2, \ldots, y_n)$ are observed relating to θ's possible value, Bayes' Theorem in (1.2) can be employed to compute the posterior pdf for θ, $p(\theta|D)$, where $D = (\mathbf{y}, I_0)$ represents the sample and prior information. Then

$$\Pr(\theta > 0 | D) = \int_0^\infty p(\theta | D) \, d\theta \qquad (3.4)$$

and

$$\Pr(\theta \leqslant 0 | D) = \int_{-\infty}^0 p(\theta | D) \, d\theta \qquad (3.5)$$

are the posterior probabilities associated with H_1 and H_2, respectively and their ratio, K_{12}, is the posterior odds. The posterior probabilities in (3.4) and (3.5) differ from (3.1) and (3.2) because the former incorporate the information in the data. This approach can be extended to cases in which θ is a vector, say $\theta' = (\theta_1, \theta_2)$ and hypotheses such as H_1: $\theta_1 > 0$ and $\theta_2 > 0$; H_2: $\theta_1 \leqslant 0$ and $\theta_2 > 0$; H_3: $\theta_1 > 0$ and $\theta_2 \leqslant 0$ and H_4: $\theta_1 \leqslant 0$ and $\theta_2 \leqslant 0$. In analyses of these four hypotheses, bivariate prior and posterior pdfs for θ_1 and θ_2 can be employed to compute probabilities associated with each of the four hypotheses. These and other hypotheses, involving inequality constraints on parameters' values, are easily analysed. The integrals giving probabilities can be evaluated analytically or numerically – see Zellner (1971, pp. 194–200) for an example of this type of analysis relating to a second order autoregressive process.

Above, various probabilities associated with hypotheses have been computed. Given a loss structure, it is possible to choose a hypothesis so as to minimize expected loss. That is, in considering two hypotheses, a two-action-two-state loss structure is shown in Table 1, where L_{12} is the loss incurred when H_1 is selected and H_2 is appropriate, an error of type II, whereas loss L_{21} is incurred if H_2 is chosen when H_1 is appropriate, an error of type I. Given probabilities, $\Pr(H_1|D)$ and $\Pr(H_2|D)$, say computed from (3.4) and (3.5), respectively, they can be used to compute expected losses shown in the last column of the table. Then H_1 is chosen if $L_{12}\Pr(H_2|D) < L_{21}\Pr(H_1|D)$ and H_2 otherwise. The condition for choosing H_1 is:

$$1 < L_{21}\Pr(H_1|D)/L_{12}\Pr(H_2|D). \qquad (3.6)$$

In the special case of a symmetric loss structure, $L_{12} = L_{21}$, the decision rule in (3.6) reduces to choose H_1 if $\Pr(H_1|D) > \Pr(H_2|D)$. Note that the decision rule in (3.6) reflects prior and sample information as well as the loss structure.

Table 1

Acts	States of world		Expected loss
	H_1 is appropriate	H_2 is appropriate	
Choose H_1	0	L_{12}	$L_{12}\Pr(H_2|D)$
Choose H_2	L_{21}	0	$L_{21}\Pr(H_1|D)$
Probabilities:	$\Pr(H_1|D)$	$\Pr(H_2|D)$	

In the examples considered above, the hypotheses considered did not involve assigning a specific value to a parameter, e.g. $\theta = 0$ or $\theta = 1$. Since hypotheses such as these are frequently encountered in applied work, it is important to be able to appraise them. Jeffreys (1967, Chs V and VI), who is a pioneer in this area, has provided many Bayesian solutions for such testing problems. In this approach, a hypothesis H_1: $\theta = 0$ is considered relative to another hypothesis, H_2: $\theta = \theta_2$, where θ_2 is a given value different from 0. Prior probabilities, Π_1 and Π_2 are assigned to H_1 and H_2, respectively. Assume further that a

vector of observations $\mathbf{y}$ is available and that $p(\mathbf{y}|\theta = 0)$ is the likelihood function under hypothesis H_1 and $p(\mathbf{y}|\theta = \theta_2)$ is the likelihood function under hypothesis H_2. Then Bayes' Theorem is employed to obtain the following posterior odds, K_{12} relating to H_1 versus H_2:

$$K_{12} = (\Pi_1/\Pi_2) \times \{p(\mathbf{y}|\theta = 0)/p(\mathbf{y}|\theta = \theta_2)\}$$
$$= (\text{Prior Odds}) \times (\text{Bayes' Factor}). \qquad (3.7)$$

In (3.7) Π_1/Π_2 is the prior odds for H_1 versus H_2 while the Bayes' Factor (BF) is the ratio of likelihood functions, $p(\mathbf{y}|\theta = 0)/p(\mathbf{y}|\theta = \theta_2)$. The result in (3.7) can be regarded as a transformation of the prior odds into a posterior odds reflecting both prior and sample information. The following example illustrates use of (3.7).

Example 6: Posterior odds for two simple hypotheses. Let $y_i = \theta + \epsilon_i$, $i = 1, 2, \ldots, n$ where the ϵ_i's have been independently drawn from a normal distribution with zero mean and unit variance. Consider two hypotheses about the value of the mean, θ, H_1: $\theta = 0$ and H_2: $\theta = \theta_2 > 0$, with prior odds, $\Pi_1/\Pi_2 = 1$. Then the posterior odds are given by $K_{12} = (\Pi_1/\Pi_2) \cdot p(\mathbf{y}|\theta = 0)/p(\mathbf{y}|\theta = \theta_2)$, or with $\Pi_1/\Pi_2 = 1$,

$$K_{12} = \exp\left\{-\sum_1^n y_i^2/2\right\} \Big/ \exp\left\{-\sum_1^n (y_i - \theta_2)^2/2\right\}$$
$$= \exp\{n\theta_2(\theta_2/2 - \bar{y})\}. \qquad (3.8)$$

It is seen that if $\bar{y} = \theta_2/2$, $K_{12} = 1$ while if $\bar{y} < \theta_2/2$, $K_{12} > 1$, a result favouring H_1 and if $\bar{y} > \theta_2/2$, $K_{12} < 1$, evidence against H_1. If $\bar{y} = 0$, $K_{12} = \exp\{n\theta_2^2/2\} > 1$ with K_{12} larger the larger are n, the sample size and θ_2. Similarly, if $\bar{y} = \theta_2$, $K_{12} = \exp\{-n\theta_2^2/2\} < 1$ with K_{12} smaller the larger are n and θ_2. Note also that $\partial \log K_{12}/\partial \bar{y} = -n\theta_2 < 0$ indicating that K_{12} is a monotonically decreasing function of $\bar{y}$ with $\theta_2 > 0$.

Above two simple hypotheses have been analysed. Posterior odds can also be computed for composite hypotheses which do not involve assigning specific values for all parameters. For example in terms of Example 6, it is possible to compute posterior odds for the two hypotheses, H_1: $\theta = 0$ versus H_2: $\theta \neq 0$ or for pairs of the following three hypotheses, H_1: $\theta = 0$, H_2: $\theta > 0$ and H_3: $\theta < 0$. In these cases, there is a simple hypothesis, $\theta = 0$ and composite hypotheses, $\theta \neq 0$, $\theta > 0$ and $\theta < 0$. In the former case the posterior odds is given by $K_{12} = \Pi_1/\Pi_2 \times \text{BF}_{12}$ with the BF given as follows

$$\text{BF}_{12} = p(\mathbf{y}|\theta = 0) \Big/ \int_{-\infty}^\infty p(\mathbf{y}|\theta)\pi(\theta) \, d\theta \qquad (3.9)$$

where $\pi(\theta)$ is a prior pdf for θ under H_2: $\theta \neq 0$. Since in this case the two hypotheses are exhaustive, $K_{12} = P/(1 - P)$, where P is the posterior probability for H_1 and $1 - P$ is the posterior probability for H_2. For the three hypotheses, H_1: $\theta = 0$, H_2: $\theta > 0$ and H_3: $\theta < 0$, posterior odds, K_{12}, K_{13} and K_{23} can be computed given that prior probabilities Π_1, Π_2 and Π_3 for the hypotheses and prior pdfs for θ under H_2 and H_3, $\pi_2(\theta)$, $0 < \theta < \infty$, and $\pi_3(\theta)$, $-\infty < \theta < 0$ are available. For example, the posterior odds for H_1 versus H_3 and for H_2 and H_3 are:

$$K_{13} = (\Pi_1/\Pi_3)p(\mathbf{y}|\theta = 0) \Big/ \int_{-\infty}^0 p(\mathbf{y}|\theta)\pi_3(\theta) \, d\theta \qquad (3.10)$$

$$K_{23} = (\Pi_2/\Pi_3) \int_0^\infty p(\mathbf{y}|\theta)\pi_2(\theta) \, d\theta \int_{-\infty}^0 p(\mathbf{y}|\theta)\pi_3(\theta) \, d\theta. \qquad (3.11)$$

See Jeffreys (1967), Leamer (1978) and Zellner (1971, 1984) for further analysis of these testing problems. Also treated in these works are regression testing problems, for example computation of posterior odds for the hypotheses H_1: $\boldsymbol{\beta} = \mathbf{0}$ and H_2: $\boldsymbol{\beta} \neq \mathbf{0}$, where $\boldsymbol{\beta}$ is a vector of regression parameters in the usual linear regression model, $\mathbf{y} = X\boldsymbol{\beta} + \mathbf{u}$. Further, hypotheses referring to sub-vectors of $\boldsymbol{\beta}$ are considered in these works as well as non-nested regression models. For testing problems in multivariate regression, see Rossi (1980) and Smith and Spiegelhalter (1980). Also, asymptotic approximations to general posterior odds expressions have been considered by Jeffreys (1967), Lindley (1964), Schwarz (1978), Leamer (1978), and Zellner and Rossi (1984).

Finally, it is the case that posterior probabilities associated with alternative hypotheses can be used to obtain estimates and predictions that reflect uncertainties associated with alternative hypotheses. For example, consider the hypotheses for a regression coefficient vector $\boldsymbol{\beta}$, H_1: $\boldsymbol{\beta} = \boldsymbol{\beta}_1$, a given value, and H_2: $\boldsymbol{\beta} \neq \boldsymbol{\beta}_1$ with posterior probabilities P and $1 - P$, respectively, computed from the posterior odds $K_{12} = P/(1 - P)$. Using a quadratic loss function, $(\boldsymbol{\beta} - \bar{\boldsymbol{\beta}})'Q(\boldsymbol{\beta} - \bar{\boldsymbol{\beta}})$, where Q is a given pds matrix and $\bar{\boldsymbol{\beta}}$ is an estimate, Zellner and Vandaele (1975) show that the value of $\bar{\boldsymbol{\beta}}$ that minimizes expected loss is given by

$$\begin{aligned}\boldsymbol{\beta}^* &= P\boldsymbol{\beta}_1 + (1 - P)\bar{\boldsymbol{\beta}}_2 \\ &= \boldsymbol{\beta}_1 + 1/(1 + K_{12})\,(\bar{\boldsymbol{\beta}}_2 - \boldsymbol{\beta}_1)\end{aligned} \qquad (3.12)$$

where $\bar{\boldsymbol{\beta}}_2$ is the posterior mean of $\boldsymbol{\beta}$ under H_2. It is seen from (3.12) that the optimal estimate is a simple average of $\boldsymbol{\beta}_1$ and $\bar{\boldsymbol{\beta}}_2$ and that from the second line of (3.12) the estimate can be viewed as a 'shrinkage' estimate with shrinkage factor $1/(1 + K_{12})$. It is also possible to perform this analysis when more than two hypotheses are considered.

Bayesian posterior odds have also been derived and used for analysing non-nested models, say two different distributions for a set of observations or two completely different economic models, say a Keynesian model versus a monetarist model or a translog production model versus a Fourier series production model. For details, see Dyer (1973), Geisel (1975), Rossi (1980) and Zellner (1971).

In summary, Bayesian procedures for analysing many different kinds of hypotheses are available. They involve a statement of uncertainty about alternative hypotheses in the form of prior probabilities and prior distributions for parameters whose values are not specified by the hypotheses under consideration. Using these prior probabilities, likelihood functions, and Bayes' Theorem, posterior odds and probabilities can be computed, analytically or numerically. The posterior odds so obtained provide a representation of views regarding alternative hypotheses that reflects the information in the data.

The Bayesian approach to analysing hypotheses differs markedly from non-Bayesian approaches. In the latter, one hypothesis, the so-called null hypothesis is assumed to be true. A test statistic is chosen, say a t-statistic and its distribution under the null hypothesis, assumed to be true is derived. Then the value of the test statistic is computed from the data and compared with what is expected under the null hypothesis. If an unusually large value is obtained, the null hypothesis is rejected. The logic of this procedure seems to parallel that of deductive logic in which a proposition is assumed to be true and then a logical contradiction is deduced which implies that the proposition cannot be true. While this approach is valid in deductive logic, it is not valid in inductive logic wherein all propositions or hypotheses are uncertain and is the reason that Bayesians associate probabilities with hypotheses. Further, as Jaynes (1984) points out, if the null hypothesis is rejected in a

non-Bayesian analysis, then so too is the distribution of the test statistic that led to the decision rule for rejection. The fundamental difficulty with the non-Bayesian procedure is that it involves two contradictory assumptions, namely, the null hypothesis is true (with probability one) and the null hypothesis may not be true. In the Bayesian approach, the null hypothesis is not assumed to be true but rather it is assigned a probability between zero and one, a formal representation of an investigator's opinion about the inductive (not deductive) validity of the null hypothesis. As the following quotation from Lehmann (1959) indicates, non-Bayesians frequently have to use such subjective beliefs informally in order to get sensible results:

> Another consideration that frequently enters into the specification of a significance level is the attitude toward the hypothesis before the experiment is performed. If one firmly believes the hypothesis to be true, extremely convincing evidence will be required before one is willing to give up this belief, and the significance level will accordingly be set very low (p. 62).

Thus subjective beliefs are frequently employed in non-Bayesian tests but they are not formally incorporated in the theory of such tests in contrast to Bayesian theory in which they are. Further discussion of the comparative features of Bayesian and non-Bayesian testing procedures appears in Jeffreys (1967), Zellner (1971, 1984), Leamer (1978) and Berger (1985).

IV. ROBUSTNESS ISSUES IN BAYESIAN INFERENCE

It is desirable that Bayesian inferences and decisions not be overly sensitive to minor departures from assumptions about the forms of (a) prior distributions, (b) likelihood functions, and (c) loss functions. Various procedures have been suggested that attempt to deal with this issue which are called robust procedures. Robust procedures provide users of them some protection from the effects of various possible departures from assumptions but there is a price to be paid for such protection in terms of the precision of inferences. To illustrate, if there is some uncertainty about whether data follow a normal distribution, it is possible to consider a class of distributions containing the normal as a special case, say a Student-t distribution. Since the Student-t distribution contains more free parameters than a normal distribution, more parameters have to be estimated. If the data distribution is actually normal, there will be a loss of precision in using the Student-t distribution. However, if the normal distribution is inappropriate, use of the Student-t distribution may produce better results. Further, if there is little information regarding the form of a parametric data distribution, it is possible to use non-parametric methods; see, e.g. Jeffreys (1967, p. 211ff), Ferguson (1967) and Boos and Monahan (1983). In this last reference, 'boot-strapped' likelihood functions are employed in Bayesian analyses of data.

As regards prior distributions' forms, hierarchical prior distributions are often employed to guard against the possibility of assigning incorrect values to prior distributions' parameters. That is, if $p(\theta \,|\, \mathbf{a})$ is a prior pdf for θ and $\mathbf{a}$ is a vector of prior parameters and there is uncertainty about the value of $\mathbf{a}$, the prior pdf can be elaborated as follows, $p(\theta \,|\, \mathbf{a})f(\mathbf{a} \,|\, \mathbf{b})$ where $f(\mathbf{a} \,|\, \mathbf{b})$ is a prior pdf for $\mathbf{a}$ with parameter vector $\mathbf{b}$. Then the marginal prior pdf for θ is $p(\theta \,|\, \mathbf{b}) = \int p(\theta \,|\, \mathbf{a})f(\mathbf{a} \,|\, \mathbf{b})\,\mathrm{d}\mathbf{a}$, an average of $p(\theta \,|\, \mathbf{a})$ using $f(\mathbf{a} \,|\, \mathbf{b})$ as the weight function. Such hierarchical priors provide some protection against assigning an incorrect value for $\mathbf{a}$ in $p(\theta \,|\, \mathbf{a})$ but at a price of increased complexity of analysis. Also, if several prior pdfs are under consideration, say $p_1(\theta \,|\, \mathbf{a}_1)$, $p_2(\theta \,|\, \mathbf{a}_2)$, ..., $p_m(\theta \,|\, \mathbf{a}_m)$, it is possible to compute posterior odds given a likelihood function, $l(\theta \mid \mathbf{y})$ as follows

$$K_{ij} = (\Pi_i / \Pi_j) \frac{\int l(\theta \mid \mathbf{y}) p_i(\theta \mid \mathbf{a}_i) \, d\theta}{\int l(\theta \mid \mathbf{y}) p_j(\theta \mid \mathbf{a}_j) \, d\theta} \qquad (3.13)$$

where Π_i and Π_j are the prior probabilities associated with prior pdfs i and j, respectively. Assuming that $\Sigma_{i=1}^{m} \Pi_i = 1$, posterior probabilities, $P_1, P_2, \ldots, P_m$, with $\Sigma_{i=1}^{m} P_i = 1$, can be computed. These posterior probabilities can be employed to average results across different priors, as shown explicitly in (3.12), and thus to have some protection against using the 'wrong' prior. Also, Berger (1984) suggests using a particular class of prior distributions and checking to determine that inferences are not sensitive to the choice of prior pdf in the particular class. See Kadane (1984) for further discussion of these issues and for suggested measures of robustness.

Last, point estimates and other inference results are often sensitive to the form of the loss function employed. Thus it is important that the effects of possible errors in formulating loss functions be appraised; see Zellner and Geisel (1968), Varian (1975), and Zellner (1984, 1986) for some results relating to this problem area.

V. CONCLUDING REMARKS

An overview of Bayesian inference has indicated that Bayesian inference techniques are available for analysing many basic problems in science. These techniques are noteworthy for their conceptual simplicity and ability to combine prior and sample information in the solution of many scientific inference problems in a coherent manner. Perhaps the most commonly expressed criticism of the Bayesian approach is that it is 'subjective', the implication being that non-Bayesian procedures are 'objective'. In this connection, it is the case that non-Bayesians employ non-sample, subjective information informally in their analyses in choosing significance levels, functional forms for relations, appraising inference results, etc. The eminent non-Bayesian statistician Freedman (1986) has written:

When drawing inferences from data, even the most hard-bitten objectivist usually has to introduce assumptions and use prior information. The serious question is how to integrate that information into the inferential process and how to test the assumptions underlying the analysis (p. 127).

In a similar vein, the famous non-Bayesian statistician Tukey (1978) expressed the following views:

It is my impression that rather generally, not just in econometrics, it is considered decent to use judgment in choosing a functional form, but indecent to use judgment in choosing a coefficient. If judgment about important things is quite all right, why should it not be used for less important ones as well? Perhaps the real purpose of Bayesian techniques is to let us do the indecent thing while modestly concealed behind a formal apparatus. If so, this would not be a precedent. When Fisher introduced the formalities of the analysis of variance in the early 1920s, its most important function was to conceal the fact that the data was being adjusted for block means, an important step forward which if openly visible would have been considered by too many wiseacres of the time to be "cooking the data." If so, let us hope that day will soon come when the role of decent concealment can be freely admitted. . . .The coefficient may be better estimated from one source or another, or, even best, estimated by economic judgment . . .

It seems to me a breach of the statistician's trust not to use judgment when that appears to be better than using data (p. 52).

Thus, as is obvious, scientists use both sample and prior information in making inferences. Bayesian inference techniques provide a means of combining these two types of information. In many problems Bayesian inference techniques provide good solutions. Whether Bayesian inference techniques are superior to other inference techniques is an issue that is the subject of much past and current research.

ARNOLD ZELLNER

See also SPECIFICATION PROBLEMS IN ECONOMETRICS; STATISTICAL DECISION THEORY; STATISTICAL INFERENCE; SUBJECTIVE PROBABILITY.

BIBLIOGRAPHY

Aitchison, J. and Dunsmore, I.R. 1975. *Statistical Prediction Analysis*. Cambridge: Cambridge University Press.

Bayes, T. 1763. An essay toward solving a problem in the doctrine of chances. *Philosophical Transactions of the Royal Society* 53, 370–418.

Berger, J.O. 1984. The robust Bayesian viewpoint. In *Robustness of Bayesian Analysis*, ed. J. Kadane, Amsterdam: North-Holland, 64–144 (with discussion).

Berger, J.O. 1985. *Statistical Decision Theory and Bayesian Analysis*. 2nd edn. New York: Springer-Verlag.

Blackwell, D. and Girshick, M.A. 1954. *Theory of Games and Statistical Decisions*. New York: John Wiley & Sons.

Blyth, C.R. 1951. On minimax statistical decision procedures and their admissibility. *Annals of Mathematical Statistics* 22, 22–42.

Boos, D.D. and Monahan, J.F. 1983. Posterior distributions for boot-strapped likelihoods. Unpublished manuscript, North Carolina State University, December.

Box, G.E.P. and Tiao, G.C. 1973. *Bayesian Inference in Statistical Analysis*. Reading, Mass.: Addison-Wesley.

Boyer, M. and Kihlstrom, R.E. (eds) 1984. *Bayesian Models in Economic Theory*. Amsterdam: North-Holland.

Broemeling, L.D. 1985. *Bayesian Analysis of Linear Models*. New York: Marcel Dekker.

Cox, R.T. 1961. *The Algebra of Probable Inference*. Baltimore: Johns Hopkins University Press.

de Finetti, B. 1970. *The Theory of Probability*, Vol. 2. English trans., New York: John Wiley, 1974.

De Groot, M.H. 1970. *Optimal Statistical Decisions*. New York: McGraw-Hill.

Dyer, A.R. 1973. Discrimination procedures for separate families of hypotheses. *Journal of the American Statistical Association* 68, 970–74.

Edgeworth, F.Y. 1928. *Contributions to Mathematical Statistics*, ed. A.L. Bowley, London: Royal Statistical Society. Reprinted, Clifton, NJ: Augustus M. Kelley, 1972.

Ferguson, T.S. 1967. *Mathematical Statistics: A Decision Theoretic Approach*. New York: Academic Press.

Freedman, D.A. 1986. Reply. *Journal of Business and Economic Statistics*, January, 126–7.

Geisel, M.S. 1975. Bayesian comparisons of simple macroeconomic models, In *Studies in Bayesian Econometrics and Statistics in Honor of Leonard J. Savage*, ed. S.E. Fienberg and A. Zellner, Amsterdam: North-Holland, 227–56.

Geisser, S. 1984. On prior distributions for binary trials. *The American Statistician* 38, 244–7.

Good, I.J. 1950. *Probability and the Weighing of Evidence*. London: Griffin.

Good, I.J. 1965. *The Estimation of Probabilities*. Cambridge, Mass.: MIT Press.

Hartigan, J. 1983. *Bayes Theory*. New York: Springer-Verlag.

Heyde, C.C. and Johnstone, I.M. 1979. On asymptotic posterior normality for stochastic processes. *Journal of the Royal Statistical Society*, Series B 41, 184–89.

Jaynes, E.T. 1984. The intuitive inadequacy of classical statistics. *Epistemologia* 7, Special Issue on Probability, Statistics and Inductive Logic, 43–74.

Jeffreys, H. 1967. *Theory of Probability*. 3rd edn, Oxford: Clarendon Press (1st edn, 1939).

Jeffreys, H. 1973. *Scientific Inference*. 3rd edn, Cambridge: Cambridge University Press (1st edn, 1931).

Kadane, J.B. (ed.) 1984. *Robustness of Bayesian Analysis*. Amsterdam: North-Holland Publishing Co.

Kruskal, W.H. 1978. Tests of significance. In *International Encyclopedia of Statistics*, ed. W.H. Kruskal and J.M. Tanur, Vol. 2, New York: The Free Press, 944–58.

Laplace, P.S. 1820. *Essai philosophique sur les probabilités*. English translation as *A Philosophical Essay on Probabilities*, New York: Dover, 1951.

Leamer, E.E. 1978. *Specification Searches*. New York: John Wiley & Sons.

Lehmann, E. 1959. *Testing Statistical Hypotheses*. New York: John Wiley & Sons.

Lindley, D.V. 1964. The use of prior probability distributions in statistical inference and decisions. In *Proceedings of the Fourth Berkeley Symposium on Mathematical Statistics and Probability*, ed. J. Neyman, Berkeley: University of California Press, Vol. I, 453–68.

Lindley, D.V. 1965. *Introduction to Probability and Statistics from a Bayesian Viewpoint*. 2 vols. Cambridge: Cambridge University Press.

Lindley, D.V. 1971. *Bayesian Statistics: A Review*. Philadelphia: Society for Industrial and Applied Mathematics.

Molina, E.C. 1940. Some comments on Bayes' essay. In *Facsimiles of Two Papers by Bayes*, ed. W.E. Deming, Washington, DC: Graduate School, US Dept. of Agriculture, vii–xii.

Monahan, J. 1983. Fully Bayesian analysis of ARMA time series models. *Journal of Econometrics* 21, 307–31.

Raiffa, H. and Schlaifer, R. 1961. *Applied Statistical Decision Theory*. Boston: Graduate School of Business Administration, Harvard University.

Rényi, A. 1970. *Foundations of Probability*. San Francisco: Holden-Day.

Richard, J.F. 1973. *Posterior and Predictive Densities for Simultaneous Equation Models*. Berlin: Springer-Verlag.

Rossi, P.E. 1980. Testing hypotheses in multivariate regression: Bayes vs. non-Bayes procedures. H.G.B. Alexander Research Foundation, Graduate School of Business, University of Chicago. Paper presented at Econometric Society Meeting, September 1980, Denver.

Savage, L.J. 1954. *The Foundations of Statistics*. New York: John Wiley & Sons.

Schwarz, G. 1978. Estimating the dimension of a model. *Annals of Statistics* 6, 461–4.

Smith, A.F.M. and Spiegelhalter, D.J. 1980. Bayes factors and choice criteria for linear models. *Journal of the Royal Statistical Society*, Series B 42, 213–20.

Stigler, S.M. 1983. Who discovered Bayes's Theorem. *The American Statistician* 37, 290–96.

Tiao, G.C. and Box, G.E.P. 1975. Some comments on 'Bayes' estimators. In *Studies in Bayesian Econometrics and Statistics in Honor of Leonard J. Savage*, ed. S.E. Fienberg and A. Zellner, Amsterdam: North-Holland, 619–26.

Tukey, J.W. 1978. Discussion of Granger on seasonality. In *Seasonal Analysis of Economic Time Series*, ed. A. Zellner, Washington, DC: US Government Printing Office, 50–53.

Varian, H.R. 1975. A Bayesian approach to real estate assessment. In *Studies in Bayesian Econometrics and Statistics in Honor of Leonard J. Savage*, ed. S.E. Fienberg and A. Zellner, Amsterdam: North-Holland Publishing Co., 195–208.

Wald, A. 1950. *Statistical Decision Functions*. New York: John Wiley & Sons, Inc.

Zellner, A. 1971. *An Introduction to Bayesian Inference in Econometrics*. New York: John Wiley & Sons.

Zellner, A. 1977. Maximal data information prior distributions. In *New Developments in the Applications of Bayesian Methods*, ed. A. Aykac and C. Brumat, Amsterdam: North-Holland Publishing Co., 211–232.

Zellner, A. 1984. *Basic Issues in Econometrics*. Chicago: University of Chicago Press.

Zellner, A. 1986. Bayesian estimation and prediction using asymmetric loss functions. *Journal of the American Statistical Association* 81, 446–51.

Zellner, A. and Geisel, M.S. 1968. Sensitivity of control to uncertainty and form of the criterion function. In *The Future of Statistics*, ed. D.G. Watts. New York: Academic Press. 269–89.

Zellner, A. and Rossi, P.E. 1984. Bayesian analysis of dichotomous quantal response models. *Journal of Econometrics* 25, 365–93.

Zellner, A. and Vandaele, W. 1975. Bayes–Stein estimators for k-means, regression and simultaneous equation models. In *Studies in Bayesian Econometrics and Statistics in Honor of Leonard J. Savage*, ed. S.E. Fienberg and A. Zellner, Amsterdam: North-Holland, 317–43.

Beccaria, Cesare Bonsana, Marchese di (1738–1794). Italian economist, philosopher and statesman, Beccaria was born in Milan in 1738, educated at Parma and in law at Pavia, appointed Professor of Political (Public) Economy or Cameral Science in Milan (1768), resigned his chair to enter public service (1772), where he encouraged and implemented monetary, general economic and penal reforms and advocated a decimal system of weights, measures and coin. He died in Milan in 1794. Beccaria's greatest fame derives from his *Essay on Crimes and Punishment* (1764), which made his European reputation almost overnight and ensured his magnificent reception when he visited Paris in 1766. Among others, it exerted considerable influence on Bentham's utilitarian philosophy (Halévy, 1928) and popularized the phrase, 'the greatest happiness of the greatest number' (Beccaria, 1764, Introduction). He also enjoyed considerable reputation as an economist. This was based on his work on Milanese monetary problems of 1762 and the outline of his teaching programme and inaugural lecture of 1769 (translated into French and English). His most important economic work is an unfinished treatise, *Elementi di economia pubblica* (written in 1771 but not published till 1804) but his mathematical contribution to the economics of taxation and smuggling (1764b) is also of considerable interest (see Theocharis, 1961).

Beccaria (1764b) starts with a methodological point on the use of algebra in political and economic reasoning. He considered such use only legitimate when the analysis concerned quantities, hence not all subject matter of these sciences was amenable to mathematical reasoning. He then illustrates the use of algebra for solving an economic problem, namely how much of a given quantity of merchandise must merchants smuggle in order to break-even, even if the remainder of the goods is confiscated. The essay may have been inspired by Hume's 'Of the Balance of Trade' (1752, p. 76) with its comment on 'Swift's maxim' [that] 'in the arithmetic of the customs, two and two make not four, but often only one', because alterations in rates may alter revenue quite disproportionately.

Beccaria's plan for university instruction in economics and his inaugural lecture, develop a classification of the subject matter into five, interconnected parts: general principles and overview, agriculture, trade, manufactures and public finance. Further subdivisions into chapters are reminiscent of the table of contents of Cantillon (1755), a work he appears to have studied closely, though the historical part of his inaugural lecture only acknowledges Vauban, Melon, Montesquieu, Uztariz, Ulloa, Hume and Genovesi. The last is described as the father of Italian economics (Beccaria, 1769). Groenewegen (1983) demonstrates that Beccaria's economic sources also included Locke and Quesnay's articles published in the French *Encyclopédie*. The last gave parts of the *Elementi* a Physiocratic flavour; for example, in the analysis of large- and small-scale farming, productive and unproductive labour and, more generally, its emphasis on the importance of agriculture.

Beccaria sees political economy as a highly practical subject, because it is part of the science of legislation and politics. Its purpose is to 'increase the wealth of the state and its subjects, by giving instruction on the most appropriate and useful management of the national revenue and that of the sovereign' (Beccaria, 1769, p. 341). Although abstract treatment of the science is therefore largely rejected as inappropriate for such a practical subject, Beccaria maintains that serious discussion of its elements needs an introduction of general principles. A definition of wealth as 'things not only necessary but also convenient and elegant', starts these principles in Part I of the *Elementi*. Because wealth consists of goods designed to meet the needs of food, shelter and clothing, the science can be justifiably subdivided into parts derived from the sectors of production and exchange which supply the various wants of mankind. Raw materials are drawn from farming, pastoral activity, mineral exploitation and fishing, hence agriculture is the first part of political economy. Raw materials require work and preparation before they can be used, hence manufacturing is the second part. Efficient production of wealth creates a surplus available for exchange, hence commerce including value, money and credit constitutes the third part to be treated. Since protection of property is a prerequisite for efficient production and trade, public finance explaining how these expenses of government are met is the fourth element. Finally, Beccaria suggests a fifth topic to cover police and other government activity, but nothing of this nor the public finance part of his *Elementi* were ever completed. Having defined the scope of the subject in terms of wealth and the component parts helping its production, Beccaria elaborates on the principles in his theory of reproduction, or the combination of labour, time and capital which ensures the continuation of production activity. Here Beccaria demonstrates awareness of the links between division of labour and trade and recognizes that the prices which circulate commodities are regulated by necessary costs of production. A general analysis of the cost of labour or wages, of the advances and other means of production and of those incurred by the state in its essential protection of production activity, is therefore required. Beccaria further develops these general principles by examining the nature and interdependence of work and consumption introducing considerations of thrift, value, profit, useful work, variability of wants and difficulties in measuring the subsistence wage of workers. A discussion of the principle of population concludes the analysis of the 'simple truths' and 'self-evident axioms' from which the whole science of political economy can be deduced, as Beccaria intended to demonstrate in the other parts of his work. Of these, the completed chapters in Part IV on value, money and exchange are of the greatest interest.

PETER GROENEWEGEN

SELECTED WORKS
1764a. *An Essay on Crime and Punishment*. London: J. Almon, 1767.
1764b. An Attempt at an Analysis of Smuggling *Il Caffè*, Vol. I, Brescia, pp. 118–19. In *Precursors in Mathematical Economics: An Anthology*, ed. William Baumol and Stephan Goldfield, London: London School of Economics, 1968, 149–50.
1769. *A Discourse on Public Oeconomy and Commerce*. Translated from the Italian, London: J. Dodsley.
1771. *Elementi di economia pubblica*. In *Cesare Beccaria Opere*, ed. S. Romagnoli, Florence: Sansoni, 1958.

BIBLIOGRAPHY
Cantillon, R. 1755. *Essai sur la nature du commerce en général.* Reprint with English translation edited by H. Higgs for the Royal Economic Society, London: Macmillan, 1931.
Groenewegen, P.D. 1983. Turgot, Beccaria and Smith. In *Italian Economics Past and Present*, ed. P.D. Groenewegen and Joseph Halevi, Sydney: Frederick May Foundation for Italian Studies.
Halévy, E. 1928. *The Growth of Philosophic Radicalism*. Trans. Mary Morris, Boston: The Beacon Press, 1955.
Hume, D. 1752. Of the Balance of Trade. Reprinted in *David Hume, Writings on Economics*, ed. E. Rotwein, London: Nelson, 1955.
Theocharis, R.D. 1961. *Early Developments in Mathematical Economics*. London: Macmillan.

Beeke, Henry (1751–1837). The Rev. Henry Beeke has hitherto been known to historians of economics for his critique of the methods by which the value of Williams Pitt's income tax had been estimated, *Observations on the Produce of the Income Tax* (1800). This pamphlet is one of the better examples of the tradition of economics known as Political Arithmetic. It earned the praise of both J.R. McCulloch, who called it 'the best example of the successful application of statistical reasonings to finance that had then appeared', and Sir Robert Giffen, who examined the estimates with some care in *The Growth of Capital* and remarked that many of Beeke's calculations 'were fully justified by the results of the Income Tax' (p. 100).

Beeke was a good friend of such prominent Tories as Nicholas Vansittart, later Lord Addington, and J.C. Herries. It is probable that the publication of the *Observations* led to a meeting with the Younger Pitt at Addington's house in 1800. Thereafter Beeke regularly provided advice on a variety of economic topics to the Tory administration and Beeke became something of an unofficial economic adviser to the government. The topics on which he provided the most regular advice were funding and paper money. However, the most notable of Beeke's reports is one on the wheat harvest of 1800. Widespread rumours of a scarcity led Beeke to write a long report, now in the Devon Public Record Office, in which he detailed reasons why there was no real scarcity. In the process, he also provided the first clear statement of what is called a Giffen good:

> In all times of Dearness, there is an *Increase* in the consumption of whatever forms the *Basis* of the Food of the People, so long as by retrenching all other expense in Provisions they can possibly find Money to purchase it. They do not understand the Arts of Economical Cookery, they have not Utensils for it, their Stomachs are not used to novelties. With us the Consumption of Bread always increases when their Money, if divided, will not purchase an addition of Meat to the Diet which they cannot abandon. And this is true even when Bread is become in comparison far more costly.

It is not known whether this report was widely circulated, but if it was, then other early statements, such as that of the bureaucrat Simon Gray, may be indebted to Beeke.

In 1801 Beeke accepted the post of Professor of Modern History at Oxford and part of his duties involved delivering lectures on political economy, probably the earliest such lectures at Oxford. After about 1810 Beeke seems to have become less familiar with his Tory friends. In 1814 he became Dean of Bristol and for the rest of his long life appears to have eschewed all economic controversy.

S. RASHID

See also GIFFEN PARADOX; GRAY, SIMON; POLITICAL ARITHMETIC.

SELECTED WORKS
1799. *Observations on the Produce of the Income-Tax*. London.

BIBLIOGRAPHY
Giffen, R. 1890. *The Growth of Capital*. London.
McCulloch, J.R. 1845. *The Literature of Political Economy*. London.

Beer, Max (1864–1943).   Journalist and historian of socialism and economics. Born in the Polish district, Tarnobrzeg, of the then Austrian province of Western Galicia, he migrated to Germany in 1889 to work as journalist on the *Volksstimme*, a socialist newspaper. Subsequent political persecution, including a jail sentence, forced him to leave Germany for London in 1894. There he became one of the first students at the London School of Economics (1895–6) and until his return to Germany in 1915 he worked as London correspondent of *Vorwarts*. He made brief visits to Paris (1899) and New York (1900–1901). The triumph of National Socialism in 1933 caused his second period of political exile in London, where he died in 1943.

The importance of Beer's work for economics rests on his contributions to the history of economics, two of them written during the last years of his life. His *Early British Economics* (1938) combined a pioneering study in English of medieval economics together with the more usual discussion of mercantilism. Beer's remark (1938, p. 228) that William Petty 'was in economics what Francis Bacon was in philosophy – the emancipator from Aristotle', gives some of the flavour of the work. His *Inquiry into Physiocracy* (1939) deserves praise as the first English study on the subject since Higgs's work (1897) but is a 'somewhat bizarre interpretation' based on the argument that Quesnay wished to recreate medieval economic society (Meek, 1962, p. 368). Of greater interest is his still very readable and useful *History of British Socialism* (1912), particularly its detailed analysis of the sources of 'Ricardian socialism' and its consequent dichotomy between the cooperative socialism inspired by Owen and the 'economics of anti-capitalism' of Ravenstone and Hodgskin. He also wrote an excellent book on Marx (Beer, 1918).

PETER GROENEWEGEN

SELECTED WORKS
1912. *A History of British Socialism*. English edition in two volumes. London: G. Bell & Sons, 1921.
1918. *The Life and Teaching of Karl Marx*. Trans. from the German by T.C. Partington and H.J. Stenning, London, 1924.
1938. *Early British Economics from the XIIIth to the middle of the XVIIIth century*. London: George Allen & Unwin.
1939. *An Inquiry into Physiocracy*. London: George Allen & Unwin.

BIBLIOGRAPHY
Higgs, H. 1897. *The Physiocrats*. London: Macmillan.
Meek, R.L. 1962. *The Economics of Physiocracy*. London: George Allen & Unwin.

beggar-thy-neighbour.   The orthodox approach to international trade assumes full employment of a given amount of resources in the world economy. Within this framework, free trade (with certain exceptions such as the optimum tariff argument) is viewed to bring about the most efficient international division of labour, thereby maximizing world output as well as the output of individual trading economies.

A corollary to this argument is that, in general, interferences with the process of free trade leave both the intervening country and its trading partners as a whole worse off compared to the free trade situation.

Joan Robinson (1937) in what is now a classic article pointed out the problematic nature of this formulation. Elaborating on Keynes's notes on mercantilism in the *General Theory*, she argued that in times of worldwide unemployment, it is, indeed, possible for one country to increase its employment and total output by increasing its trade balance at the expense of other countries. She coined the phrase 'beggar-thy-neighbour' to describe such policies.

Robinson started her argument by pointing out that an increase in the trade balance, with a given level of home investment, is equivalent to the effect of an investment increase which would normally restore the level of employment in an economy with underemployment. The change in the trade balance and subsequently in home employment, can be brought about by policies which lead to the expansion of exports and/or of import-competing production. Robinson discussed four such policies: (1) exchange rate depreciation, (2) reductions in wages, (3) subsidies to exports and (4) restrictions by means of quotas and tariffs.

According to Robinson, a fall in the exchange rate or alternatively a fall in money wages stimulates output in exporting and import-competing industries and generally increases the trade balance. Although she had pointed out that an increase in the trade balance does not necessarily lead to higher employment, until recently, it was assumed that currency depreciation results in stimulating output and employment. It was argued that devaluation would have contractionary effects only when the Marshall–Lerner condition is violated. Since in the case of economies with underemployment this condition (that the sum of the absolute values of export and import elasticities must exceed unity) is assumed to be satisfied, currency depreciation was viewed as an output/employment stimulating device. More recently, Krugman and Taylor (1978) have discussed the contractionary effects of devaluation, pointing out that depreciation can lead to a reduction in national output if (1) imports initially exceed exports, (2) consumption propensities from wages and profits differ and (3) there are significant export taxes that cause an increase in government revenues as a result of devaluation.

There is another reason for exchange rate depreciation and/or reduction in money wages not to act as output stimulating policies. These two policies, if they succeed at all, stimulate exports and reduce imports if international competition takes place through prices. However, there are significant non-price factors in international competition which limit the role of devaluation and money wage reductions in increasing the trade balance or restoring full employment.

Historically, import controls and export subsidies have proved to be more effective devices. Import controls by means of tariffs and quotas are expected to increase the trade balance by protecting import competing sectors from external competition. Subsidies to exports are argued to increase the international competitiveness of such sectors.

For any of these expedients to succeed in terms of increasing employment in an economy, it is necessary that its trade partners do not retaliate. However, as Robinson pointed out, in times of general unemployment, a nation increasing its trade balance is faced with retaliation by others. What begins as a beggar-thy-neighbour remedy for unemployment in one country turns into an international beggar-thy-neighbour game with the total volume of international trade shrinking relative to world output and eventually leading to a decline in world economic output. Indeed, it was this kind of competitive behaviour that characterized the international trade policies of the thirties.

The postwar structuring of the world trade system through the establishment of institutions such as the IMF and GATT was based on efforts to avoid beggar-thy-neighbour policies. However, the new system failed to 'frame rules that would permit the right exceptions while ruling out the wrong ones'; it did not establish when the very same policies would be bad-neighbourly and when they would be good-neighbourly (Robinson, 1965). The rules that prohibit the use of devices that boost exports and check imports also prevent individual countries from employing them in times of necessity in constructive ways from the point of the world economy as a whole. For instance, in the case of a country that is attempting to stimulate its output by increasing its investment, initially imports may rise faster than exports. Such an economy would need to reduce its propensity to import while keeping its total level of imports constant so as not to develop a balance of payments problem.

The new system, instead of allowing the necessary exceptions, institutionalized a different type of bad-neighbourly conduct by advocating deflationary policies as the remedies for the balance of payments problems. In fact, institutions such as the IMF became the executioners of these deflationary policies which aim to bring about balanced trade starting from a deficit position by inducing a slump to cut down imports.

In recent times, these issues and problems have re-emerged under the present situation of the world economy in which there is widespread unemployment and the pressure for individual countries to respond with beggar-thy-neighbour policies has been building. The arguments developed by Joan Robinson have a great deal of freshness today in the light of these circumstances, making her contributions as relevant as when she first formulated them in the 1930s.

NILÜFER ÇAĞATAY

See also PROTECTION; ROBINSON, JOAN VIOLET.

BIBLIOGRAPHY

Krugman, P. and Taylor, L. 1978. Contractionary effects of devaluation. *Journal of International Economics* 8(3), August, 445-56.

Robinson, J. 1937. Beggar-my-neighbour remedies for unemployment. In J. Robinson, *Essays in the Theory of Unemployment*, London: Macmillan.

Robinson, J. 1965. The new mercantilism. An inaugural lecture delivered at the University of Cambridge, printed in *Collected Economic Papers of Joan Robinson*, Vol. 4, Oxford: Basil Blackwell, 1973.

behavioural economics. Since economics is certainly concerned with human behaviour – with, as Marshall put it, '[the] study of mankind in the ordinary business of life' – the phrase 'behavioural economics' appears to be a pleonasm. What non-behavioural economics can we contrast with it? The answer to this question is found in the specific assumptions about human behaviour that are made in neoclassical economic theory.

CONTRAST OF BEHAVIOURAL WITH NEOCLASSICAL THEORY

The neoclassical assumptions. How does human behaviour enter into classical and neoclassical economics? First, human goals and motivations are assumed to be given a priori in the form of a utility function, which allows an individual to make consistent choices among all possible bundles of goods and services. Second, economic actors are assumed always to choose, among the alternatives open to them, that one of the alternatives that yields the greatest utility (Savage, 1954).

These two assumptions – of a given utility function and of utility maximization (rationality) – are usually made explicitly. Other assumptions about human behaviour are often implicit in classical and neoclassical theory, and are not necessarily maintained through all variants of the theory. It is usually assumed that not only the utility function but also the set of available alternatives is given a priori. In search theory, this assumption is replaced by the assumption that new alternatives may be generated by a process of search, but at some cost, which is assumed to be known, as is the expected marginal return to the search.

With respect to the consequences of alternatives, it may be assumed that these are known completely and with certainty, or that what is known is a joint probability distribution of outcomes, although occasionally, forms of 'uncertainty' that are not reducible to probabilities are introduced into the theory. It is almost always assumed in neoclassical theory that, given their knowledge of utilities, alternatives, and outcomes, economic actors can compute which alternative will yield the greatest (expected) utility – although it is conceptually (if seldom practically) possible to incorporate a cost of computation into the theories that is analogous to the cost of generating alternatives in search theory.

Behavioural departures from neoclassical assumptions. With this characterization of classical and neoclassical economics, we can now, by a process of contrast, define rough boundaries for behavioural economics. Behavioural economics is concerned with the empirical validity of these neoclassical assumptions about human behaviour and, where they prove invalid, with discovering the empirical laws that describe behaviour correctly and as accurately as possible. As a second item on its agenda, behavioural economics is concerned with drawing out the implications, for the operation of the economic system and its institutions and for the public policy, of departures of actual behaviour from the neoclassical assumptions. A third item on its agenda is to supply empirical evidence about the shape and content of the utility function (or of whatever construct will replace it in a empirically valid behavioural theory) so as to strengthen the predictions that can be made about human economic behaviour.

Thus, behavioural economics is best characterized not as a single specific theory but as a commitment to empirical testing of the neoclassical assumptions of human behaviour and to modifying economic theory on the basis of what is found in the testing process. And not all of the economists who hold a behavioural point of view also hold a common theory, or are all preoccupied with examining the same parts of the economic mechanism.

Directions of behavioural research. Accordingly, we can distinguish a number of different foci and directions of inquiry in behavioural economics. Some investigations are concerned with the assumptions of utility and profit maximization, and with replacing these with alternative motivational assumptions that appear to describe human motivations in the marketplace more accurately (e.g. Baumol, 1959).

Another focus of behavioural research in economics is decision making under uncertainty – determining whether economic actors are able to and do maximize subjective expected utility, as called for by neoclassical theory. Here the interest is less in motivation than in the *ability* of human beings to carry out the calculations required to make the optimal decisions – the issues involved are largely cognitive.

The limitation in human ability to deal with uncertainty is just a special case of the numerous cognitive limitations that prevent economic actors from knowing and adopting the optimizing alternative of choice. The term 'bounded rationality' has been proposed to denote the whole range of limitations on human knowledge and human computation that prevent economic actors in the real world from behaving in ways that approximate the predictions of classical and neoclassical theory: including the absence of a complete and consistent utility function for ordering all possible choices, inability to generate more than a small fraction of the potentially relevant alternatives, and inability to foresee the consequences of choosing alternatives, including inability to assign consistent and realistic probabilities to uncertain future events (Simon, 1955).

CONVENTIONAL BEHAVIOUR

At the farthest remove from neoclassical economics are explanations of phenomena that do not rest at all on rationality assumptions. For example, it has been observed that the mean compensation of the top executive in corporations varies with the logarithm of the size of the corporation (Roberts, 1959). To explain this regularity in neoclassical terms one has to show that the marginal contribution of the top executive is proportional to the logarithm of company size; and this proposition implies, in turn, very specific conditions on the distribution of executive abilities (Lucas, 1978).

However, an explanation that requires no assumption about executive abilities can be derived from (a) the empirical observation that most companies are pyramidal, so that the number of organizational levels grows logarithmically with the number of employees; and (b) the empirical observation that most people regard it as 'legitimate' or 'appropriate' for a boss to be paid some multiple (about 1.5 times, say) of the salary of his or her immediate subordinates. The observed regularity in average salaries follows from these two observations (Simon, 1957). We may call this a 'sociological' explanation, since it postulates commonly held social beliefs or attitudes, but not rational calculation.

In the same way, the observed regularities in business firm size distributions (which usually fit closely to the Pareto distribution) follow from the assumption that expected growth is proportional to attained size (the Gibrat assumption). This assumption, in turn, can be derived from the postulate that access to internal and external investment funds is proportional to size, without postulating rational choice as part of the causal mechanism (Ijiri and Simon, 1977).

As a third example, the empirical observation that the labour share of total product has been nearly constant in the industrialized world during the past century may be explained from the premises: (a) that interest rates are nearly stable; (b) that at all levels of average per capita income, nearly the same fraction of total income is saved, hence the ratio of capital supply to total output is nearly constant (Simon, 1979). But premises (a) and (b) may be accepted as empirical (sociological) regularities that do not derive from assumptions of rationality or from assumptions that marginal costs are equal to marginal benefits.

If, in fact, important social phenomena, like salaries, access to capital for growth, or rates of saving, do not depend on rational calculations, but are conventionally determined, then the corresponding parts of economic theory need to be built

on empirical knowledge of socially accepted conventions rather than on derivations from the assumption of rationality. What phenomena are 'conventionally' rather than 'rationally' determined is itself an empirical question, and not one that can be settled by pure reasoning.

It is often possible to rationalize the kinds of behaviour that were described above as conventional, but the real work in such explanation is done by *ad hoc* auxiliary assumptions, which is quite different from inferring the behaviour uniquely from the assumptions of economic rationality alone. For example, almost any observed distribution of executive salaries would be compatible with Lucas's (1978) model provided that appropriate adjustments were made in the assumed (and unobservable) distribution of executive abilities. The proposed sociological explanation for the salary distribution is falsifiable, while Lucas's model is not.

In similar fashion, the historical stability of interest rates and of the saving to income ratio could be attributed in some measure to characteristics of individual utility functions. In this case, again, rationality assumptions play no important role. The argument rests on an unmotivated assumption about human preferences – an empirical assumption.

THE 'NEW INSTITUTIONAL ECONOMICS'

Less distant from neoclassical theory than the examples just cited are explanations that incorporate the rationality assumptions, but also invoke limits on the information available to actors or impose 'transaction costs' on their use of information in order to account for specific institutional phenomena. Much of the work of Williamson (1975) falls in this category.

For example, there is a fundamental difference between a sales contract and an employment contract. The former involves an exchange of specific commodities for money, while the latter involves the willingness of the employee to accept authority (i.e. to have his actions determined by the employer) in exchange for money. How can we predict which economic transactions will take the form of sales contracts, and which the form of employment contracts? It can be argued that if the employer has great uncertainty as to what specific duties he will want performed, and the employee is nearly indifferent among various ways of spending his time, then an employment contract will be the rational choice, otherwise a sales contract (Williamson, 1975, chs 4, 5; Simon, 1951).

Similar rational analyses have been proposed to explain the existence of various kinds of contractual instruments – for example, special forms of insurance and of forward contracting. 'Moral risk', that is, the practical unenforceability of some kind of contract clauses in the face of opportunistic behaviour of the parties, also commonly enters into explanations for the existence or non-existence of particular sorts of contracts. Williamson (1975) invokes the combination of bounded rationality and opportunism as the mechanism for explaining the relative roles of banks, conglomerates and divisionalized corporations in allocating investment capital.

The body of modern economic analysis that employs concepts like limited information, transaction costs, and opportunism to explain observed economic phenomena is often called the 'New Institutional Economics'. A common feature of these sorts of institutional analyses is that the real 'action' in the derivations comes not from the rationality assumptions, but from the assumptions of informational or other limits on rationality, or from what were in the previous section called sociological postulates. If employers had perfect foresight, or if they could costlessly renegotiate their contracts with employees for each new task to be performed, there would be no rationale for employment contracts. If householders made even roughly correct estimates of flood risk, purchases of flood insurance would rise sharply. Conglomerates can allocate investment funds more profitably than banks, because the former have inside information not available to the latter. And so on.

Moreover, since the institutional analyses usually involve the comparison of two, or a few, discrete alternatives rather than a continuum of choices, it is seldom necessary to evoke the assumption of maximization. Even a satisficing actor can be expected to select the better of two alternatives if the difference in expected outcomes is large. Conversely, if institutional arrangements are compatible with either maximizing or satisficing assumptions, evidence about them cannot be used to choose between these assumptions.

Explanations of institutional arrangements can often be reached by qualitative arguments about what is 'functional' rather than arguments about what is optimal. This reduction in dependence on rationality assumptions cuts two ways. By weakening the assumptions required for the arguments, it raises the prior probability of the explanation; by introducing into consideration a host of different potential auxiliary sociological assumptions, it increases the urgency of testing independently the empirical validity of these assumptions. Casual empiricism is especially inappropriate in these contexts.

It would be a valuable exercise to determine what part of neoclassical economics, and especially the new institutional economics, would survive the replacement of optimizing by satisficing or functional arguments. Presumably, theorems about Pareto optimality and market efficiency would be lost, but not necessarily theorems about stability of equilibrium. And as suggested above, many claims about the functionality of particular institutional arrangements would still be supported by the weaker assumptions.

THE 'UTILITY FUNCTION' OF THE FIRM

A good deal of neoclassical economic reasoning does not require any specific assumption about the shapes of the actors' utility functions. Much of the literature on the theory of the firm, however, requires the assumption that firms maximize profit or, in long-term analyses, the present value of stockholders' equity. There are many conceivable alternatives to the profit-maximization assumption, classifiable into three main categories: (a) that the firm seeks to maximize some other quantity than profit; (b) that individual executives strive to maximize their personal utilities, which are unlikely to coincide with the firm's utility; and (c) that executives and other participants identify with the subgoals of the organizational units to which they belong, and seek to maximize attainments of these subgoals (Marris, 1964).

An example of the first kind of alternative is Baumol's (1959) proposal that firms strive to maximize revenue rather than profits. Evolutionary arguments have been evoked against this sort of alternative to profit maximizing, but the objections rest on the assumption, much stronger than any in biological Darwinism, that only profit maximizers can survive. Again, it is clear that the issue has to be decided by empirical inquiry. In the biological world at least, many organisms survive that are not maximizers but that operate at far less than the highest achievable efficiency. Their survival is not threatened as long as no other organisms have evolved that can challenge the possession of their specific niches. Analogously, since there is no reason to suppose that every business firm is challenged by an optimally efficient competitor, survival only requires

meeting the competition. In a system in which there are innumerable rents, of long-term and short-term duration, even egregious sub-optimality may permit survival.

Nelson and Winter (1982) have examined evolutionary models of business firm growth that dispense with the assumption of profit maximization. Each firm, in their models, may have a different production function, and one that changes through imitation or, stochastically, from investment in R&D. With industry models of this sort, distributions of firm sizes may be obtained similar to those actually observed.

The second kind of deviation from the profit maximizing assumption – that which rests on considerations of executive behaviour – is perhaps the most frequently advanced. One form it takes is the 'organizational slack' hypothesis of Cyert and March (1963), which suggests that firms will ordinarily settle for 'satisfactory' profits, and that it is only when they fail to achieve these that they search for improved products or methods of operation. Leibenstein's (1976) concept of 'X-efficiency' has a similar flavour. One way to relate such behaviour to rationality assumptions is to postulate that 'comfort' is an important component in executive utility functions, and that there is a trade-off between the comfortable executive life and profits.

Another deviation from the neoclassical assumptions is to view the firm not as a system with a well-defined utility function, but as a coalition of partially cooperating and partially competing interests. The goal-defining process can then be viewed in terms of game theory. The notion of the corporation as a coalition has been developed by Cyert and March (1963) and by Williamson (1975).

Research on organizations has revealed the central importance of the mechanism of *identification* – the tendency of actors in an organization to internalize, and be guided by, the goals of the particular subparts of the organization with which they are most closely associated. In part, identification may be accounted for by systems of reward, but that is almost certainly an incomplete account. Cognitive mechanisms (especially focus of attention) and mechanisms of social motivation (including docility) appear to be at least as important as rewards in determining the criteria of choice that are applied to decisions. For example, departmental executives asked to identify the most important problem facing a company that has been described to them tend disproportionately to select problems in their own domain of expertise – the sales managers, sales problems; the production managers, production problems, and so on (Dearborn and Simon, 1958).

INDIVIDUAL UTILITY

In analysing the behaviour of consumers and employees, the outcomes often depend heavily on what is assumed about the structure and content of their utility functions. Changes in preferences between work and leisure, for example, will ordinarily produce corresponding changes in the labour supply function. Similarly, changes in social attitudes about women's roles may play a major part in determining the participation of women in the labour force, the number of children, and many other variables important to long-term social and economic development. As Becker (1981) has shown, this does not forestall economic analysis of these phenomena, but it does limit the power of the rationality principle to arrive at conclusions without numerous assumptions about the utility function.

The assumption of utility maximization is sometimes misunderstood to imply that only selfish motives play a role in human behaviour. However, except in the context of evolutionary theories that emphasize selection, the assumption of utility maximization, whether of business firms or of individuals, does not, of course, imply that human beings are selfish, only that they are consistent. Altruism can be accommodated in the utility function simply by including the well-being of other persons as one of its components. When utility maximization is not postulated directly, but is derived from Darwinian arguments of survival, then altruism, except for 'weak altruism' or 'enlightened self-interest', becomes more difficult to account for. Maximization of Darwinian fitness, as usually formulated, leaves little room for altruistic behaviour towards others who are not close relatives.

It is possible that this difficulty could be removed by closer attention to 'docility' (susceptibility to social instruction and influence) as a trait contributing strongly to fitness (Simon, 1983, ch. 2). Whether docility does, in fact, play a role in shaping preferences is an empirical question to be answered by behavioural research. And to what extent altruism (as distinguished from enlightened self interest) actually enters into human behaviour is also an issue that must be settled by empirical study.

DECISIONS UNDER UNCERTAINTY

Of all of the variables affecting, potentially or actually, the economic decision-making process, uncertainty has perhaps attracted the greatest amount of research attention, both theoretical and empirical. We now have substantial knowledge about the relation between actual human behaviour in the face of uncertainty and the behaviour predicted by the subjective expected utility model.

Data from the laboratory shows that, under different circumstances of choice, subjects depart from the predictions of the SEU model in diametrically opposite directions. At times when they view the world as stable or static, they place too much weight on past events in prediction; but when they perceive large structural changes taking place in the environment, they underestimate the significance of past experience for predicting the future.

Extensive studies of decisions to purchase or not to purchase flood insurance (Kunreuther, 1978) reveal behaviour that cannot be reconciled with any model of utility maximization. Specifically, it is found that people tend to ignore (hence, not to insure against) low-probability, high-consequence events, unless they have had rather direct past personal experience of them.

Assumptions about how people deal with uncertainty and predict future events have important consequences for macroeconomic theory. For example, rational expectations theories, adaptive expectations theories and cobweb theories make quite different predictions about the impact of government monetary and fiscal policies. But it can be shown that the bounds placed on rationality, and not the rationality assumptions, account for the main differences in prediction among, for example, leading business-cycle theories. A Keynesian theory of the cycle can be derived from a neoclassical model simply by assuming that labourers suffer from money illusion in their demands for wages; while a rational-expectations theory of the cycle can be derived from the same neoclassical model by assuming that businessmen mistake a general change in the price level for a relative change in the prices of the goods they purchase (another form of money illusion). As in institutional arguments, the real work in these theories is not being done by the rationality assumptions but by auxiliary assumptions about limits on rationality

(including limits on the accuracy of information) – assumptions often made on the basis of extremely casual evidence.

SEARCH AND CHOICE PROCESSES

Applications of the concept of bounded rationality to choice situations where uncertainty about outcomes is a dominant factor have been discussed above. Another line of research, mainly in the laboratory, seeks to examine the processes of search that people use, both in the exploration for alternatives and in their use of information about alternatives (Hogarth, 1980; Kahneman, Slovic and Tversky, 1982). A standard experimental paradigm confronts subjects with a number of alternatives, and allows them to obtain additional information about each until they make a choice or the available information is exhausted. Experiments in this paradigm show that decision makers usually satisfice, both in the sense of failing to examine all of the information that is available, and in the sense of choosing an alternative as soon as one has been found that is satisfactory along all the dimensions of concern.

A few studies have been made of situations where subjects must explore for new alternatives and must decide when to terminate the search. For example, a field study of the job search processes of business school students (Soelberg, 1966) showed students using a variety of rules of thumb to limit the list of firms they contacted and to choose among those who made offers to them.

In real-world situations, it is seldom realistic to talk about examining all alternatives or paying attention to all the potentially relevant information. Empirical evidence is still very scanty about the circumstances under which people will pay attention to particular variables in making their decisions (e.g. under what circumstances they will pay attention to the difference between real and nominal prices). Evidence is also very scanty (but see Cyert and March, 1963; Soelberg, 1966) about the circumstances under which people search for new alternatives.

The search for alternatives is, of course, a critical process in understanding entrepreneurial behaviour, decisions to invest in research and development activities, and generally in understanding the ways in which new economic activities and enterprises are spawned (Nelson and Winter, 1982; Winter, 1984). This Schumpeterian view toward economic development has recently been expanded and systematized by Nelson and Winter (1982), who model the growth of industries in which the development of new products and practices plays a major role in competition among firms. They show that in such models, evolutionary selection can replace or complement optimization as a driving force for change.

METHODS OF BEHAVIOURAL RESEARCH

Within the classical tradition, the principal evidence that has been used to test economic theories empirically has been public statistics, usually aggregated at least to the level of the industry (although limited use has been made, especially in investment theory, of financial data for individual firms). A powerful and sophisticated set of econometric tools has been developed for extracting from such data all the information that they contain. But it becomes increasingly clear that data of these kinds are simply too aggregated and noisy to reveal much about the decision-making processes of the economic actors. In neoclassical theory, those processes are simply postulated, in terms of the rationality assumptions, and never subjected to any really searching direct test.

What is even more troublesome, the typical inputs to econometric analysis provide little information that would be relevant to choosing the appropriate auxiliary assumptions (assumptions about the limits to rationality) that, we have seen, play a major role in drawing inferences from economic theories. In the absence of empirical evidence for choosing these assumptions, they are generally made in a casually empirical, armchair way.

The progress of economics, and especially the prospects for adequate empirical testing of economic theories, would seem to depend, therefore, on finding new kinds of data to supplement the sorts of aggregative evidence now typically employed. One important new kind of data comes from case studies, a second from survey research, and a third from laboratory experiments. Computer simulation models can provide a powerful tool for relating these kinds of data to theory. But successful use of such data will call for new methods for aggregating data that are gathered from individual firms or individual economic actors. Each of these points calls for a brief comment.

Case studies. A small, but growing, number of case studies have been made of the decision-making process in individual business firms (Cyert and March, 1963; Bromiley, 1981; etc.) and of individuals (Soelberg, 1966; Clarkson, 1962; Bouwman, 1982; etc.). That these studies have had little impact on economic theory must be attributed in considerable measure to the absence of a theory of aggregation that would indicate just how to use them. In general, economists, though willing to engage in casual introspective empiricism, have not been willing to treat the firms whose behaviour has been studied in depth as 'representative firms'.

Survey research. In the case of survey research, where appropriate sampling methods can be used, there is no such difficulty in relating the survey data to macromodels of industries or the economy. In fact, data on businessmen's expectations have been used, to a limited extent, as inputs into econometric models (Katona, 1975). The main limiting factors here appear to be the small number of economists who are trained to produce and interpret survey data, and the limited resources that have been applied to generating such data.

Experiments. The use of experiments to study economic behaviour is a relatively new, and rather rapidly spreading, development (see, e.g., Smith, 1976; Hong and Plott, 1982). A principal problem here is to produce in the laboratory motivational conditions that can be extrapolated to the real world. A principal limitation on the growth of laboratory experimentation is, again, the limited access of graduate students in economics to training in techniques of experimentation.

Computer modelling. Computers are widely used in economics, not only to run regressions, but also to model the economic system. Most of the models are aggregative, but there has been a certain amount of investigation of so-called 'micro-models', whose units are samples of individual actors and firms (e.g. Eliasson, 1984; Winter, 1984). In addition, one can point to a few models of decision-making within an individual firm (Bonini, 1963; Bromiley, 1981). Attention has been paid to the aggregation problem in constructing micro-models, but that problem remains a major barrier to acceptance of findings derived from models of these sorts as a part of the main stream of economic theory and knowledge.

HERBERT A. SIMON

See also BOUNDED RATIONALITY; SATISFICING.

BIBLIOGRAPHY

Baumol, W.J. 1959. *Business Behavior, Value and Growth.* New York: Macmillan.

Becker, G.S. 1981. *A Treatise on the Family.* Cambridge, Mass.: Harvard University Press.

Bonini, C.P. 1963. *Simulation of Information and Decision Systems in the Firm.* Englewood Cliffs, NJ: Prentice-Hall.

Bouwman, M.J. 1982. The use of accounting information: expert versus novice behavior. In *Decision Making*, ed. Ungson and Braunstein, Boston: Kent Publishing Co.

Clarkson, G.P.E. 1962. *Portfolio Selection: A Simulation of Trust Investment.* Englewood Cliffs, NJ: Prentice-Hall.

Cyert, R.M. and March, J.G. 1963. *A Behavioral Theory of the Firm.* Englewood Cliffs, NJ: Prentice-Hall.

Dearborn, D.C. and Simon, H.A. 1958. Selective perception. *Sociometry* 21, 140–44.

Eliasson, G. 1984. Micro heterogeneity of firms and the stability of industrial growth. *Journal of Economic Behaviour and Organization* 5, 249–74.

Hogarth, R.M. 1980. *Judgment and Choice: The Psychology of Decision.* New York: Wiley.

Hong, J.T. and Plott, C.R. 1982. Rate filing policies for inland water transportation: an experimental approach. *Bell Journal of Economics* 13, 1–19.

Ijiri, Y. and Simon, H.A. 1977. *Skew Distributions and the Sizes of Business Firms.* Amsterdam: North-Holland.

Kahneman, D., Slovic, P. and Tversky, A. (eds) 1982. *Judgment Under Uncertainty: Heuristics and Biases.* Cambridge: Cambridge University Press.

Katona, G. 1975. *Psychological Economics.* New York: Elsevier Publishing Co.

Kornai, J. 1971. *Anti-Equilibrium.* Amsterdam: North-Holland.

Kunreuther, H. et al. 1978. *Disaster Insurance Protection: Public Policy Lessons.* New York: Wiley.

Leibenstein, H. 1976. *Beyond Economic Man.* Cambridge, Mass.: Harvard University Press.

Lucas, R.E., Jr. 1978. On the size distribution of business firms. *Bell Journal of Economics* 9, 508–23.

Marris, R. 1964. *The Economic Theory of 'Managerial' Capitalism.* New York: Macmillan.

Nelson, R.R. and Winter, S.G. 1982. *An Evolutionary Theory of Economic Change.* Cambridge, Mass.: Harvard University Press.

Roberts, D.R. 1959. *Executive Compensation.* Glencoe, Ill.: The Free Press.

Savage, L.J. 1954. *The Foundations of Statistics.* New York: Wiley.

Simon, H.A. 1951. A formal theory of the employment relationship. *Econometrica* 19, 293–305. Reprinted as ch. 5.2 in Simon (1982).

Simon, H.A. 1955. A behavioral model of rational choice. *Quarterly Journal of Economics* 69, 99–118. Reprinted as ch. 7.2 in Simon (1982).

Simon, H.A. 1957. The compensation of executives. *Sociometry* 20, 32–5. Reprinted as ch. 5.6 in Simon (1982).

Simon, H.A. 1979. On parsimonious explanations of production relations. *Scandinavian Journal of Economics* 81, 459–74. Reprinted as ch. 4.4 in Simon (1982).

Simon, H.A. 1982. *Models of Bounded Rationality.* 2 vols, Cambridge, Mass.: MIT Press.

Simon, H.A. 1983. *Reason in Human Affairs.* Stanford: Stanford University Press.

Smith, V.L. 1976. Experimental economics: induced value theory. *American Economic Review* 66, 274–9.

Soelberg, P. 1966. *A Study of Decision Making: Job Choice.* Cambridge, Mass.: Alfred P. Sloan School of Management, MIT.

Williamson, O.E. 1975. *Markets and Hierarchies.* New York: Free Press.

Winter, S.G. 1984. Schumpeterian competition in alternative technological regimes. *Journal of Economic Behavior and Organization* 5, 287–320.

benefit principle. *See* LINDAHL ON PUBLIC FINANCE.

Bentham, Jeremy (1748–1832). Bentham was born in London on 15 February 1748, the son and grandson of a lawyer; he died in London on 6 June 1832. Destined by his father to be a lawyer, the law formed the centre of his long life. However, he turned at an early age from the idea of making money by the practice of law as it is and instead concentrated on the study of law as it ought to be. Bentham spent most of his life writing, accumulating piles of manuscript material on the theory of law and all associated subjects. At first these manuscripts were turned by him into books, but for most of his life he depended upon disciples to do the editing for him. Hence much of the important work which appeared in his lifetime appeared in French, edited by his Genevan disciple, Etienne Dumont, and other important material has only been published in this century. As well as the general theoretical work, Bentham wrote a mass of material designed to press particular schemes of improvement on the government, such as the design of prisons and poorhouses, new systems of taxation and a plan for interest-bearing currency. His economic work is contained in some of these occasional writings, largely unpublished in his lifetime, an early tract entitled *Defence of Usury* (1787), which was quite successful in its day, and some more theoretical treatises which also only existed in manuscript until edited by Werner Stark in 1952–4. Stark's edition, in three volumes, contains all the relevant material.

Whether engaged in writing, polemic or practical projects, Bentham spent most of his life in England, indeed in London. However, he travelled as far as Russia when relatively young, spending a couple of years on the new estates being opened up by Prince Potemkin. His *Defence of Usury*, just as his famous prison proposals, the *Panopticon*, (1791) was written as a series of letters from 'Crichoff, in White Russia'. Bentham also actively bombarded the new revolutionaries in France with proposals and was elected by them as an honorary citizen of the new French Republic. He developed a world-wide active discussion with promoters of reform and new legislation and became, appropriately enough for the inventor of the word 'international', an international figure.

Bentham's work in economics, as in most other particular areas of enquiry, is best seen as auxiliary to his central, overall project, the production of a complete, rational code of law. After asking himself at an early age how, by his own thought and invention, he might best aid humanity, Bentham, in typical 18th-century fashion, decided that this should be by the construction of legislation. The aim of such legislation was to be happiness; by making good laws, men would be made good; that is, seekers of their own and others' happiness. Right at the start of Bentham's first published work, the *Fragment on Government*, appears the famous formula, stating that the 'fundamental axiom' is that 'it is the greatest happiness of the greatest number that is the measure of right and wrong' ([1776] 1977, p. 393). This principle, variously called by him 'the greatest happiness principle' or 'the principle of utility' neither was, nor was claimed by Bentham to be, original. He took it as an obvious goal, and found not only its spirit but also the form of words in such predecessors as Helvetius and Beccaria (the famous formula occurs, for example, in the 1767 English translation of Beccaria, p. 2). The idea of attaining such an end by legislation is also something which he naturally took over from the same predecessors.

The central idea of Bentham's work, therefore, was to invent laws so that people would act so as to bring about the greatest happiness. Men, that is, acting naturally, would be placed in such a system of regulation and sanctions that, following these natural courses, they would not only satisfy themselves but

also produce the greatest happiness. The legislator, therefore, needs two principles to guide him in his work, one about what ought to happen, which sets his aim, and one about what naturally happens to human beings under various conditions, which tells him the nature of his raw material. The first is provided by the greatest happiness principle. The second is provided by a principle of psychological hedonism (also prevalent in Beccaria and Helvetius) declaring that people act so as to maximize their apparent interest. The legislator can hence plan reward and punishments designed to get such self-interested individuals to do as they ought. Acts contrary to the general happiness will be crimes, and crimes will be controlled because they will not pay: the certainty and amount of punishment will render them a bad bargain. Bentham's economics, like his psychology, is therefore an amplification of this natural principle of self-interest: it is shown what the effects of various legislative acts would be, and hence provides information of use to the legislator.

It is worth stressing that there are two principles at work in Bentham (or that, in more modern language, he is engaged in normative as well as descriptive welfare economics), because it is sometimes thought that there is just one principle at work, or that the normative one is meant to follow directly in some simple way from the descriptive one (persons making this mistake may be thinking of J.S. Mill's work *Utilitarianism* [1861], and its subsequent criticism, not of Bentham). Yet the famous declamatory start of Bentham's main theoretical work, the *Introduction to the Principles of Morals and Legislation*, which declares that 'Nature has placed mankind under the governance of two sovereign masters, *pain* and *pleasure*' ([1789] 1970, p. 11), goes on immediately to declare that these masters (which are for Bentham the elements of happiness) create both the standard of right and wrong and also the 'chain of causes and effects' (i.e. both what ought to happen and also what does happen). Similarly, to take the great work of the end of Bentham's life, the *Constitutional Code*, Bentham starts from two 'first principles': 'the greatest happiness principle and the self-preference principle' (1830b, vol. IX, p. 8). Analogously, it is a mistake to think that Bentham espouses the idea of a natural harmony of interests so that all men acting in a self-interested way will be kept by some hidden hand on course for universal happiness. On the contrary, Bentham is clear that legislative interference, that is, the threat of punishment to make some otherwise undesired conduct in someone's interest, is essential. Similarly, there is no conflict, as Elie Halévy supposed, between a Benthamite economics which supposes a natural identity of interests, and a legislative project which requires an artificial identification of interests (Halévy, 1928, pp. 17, 33). The economics merely provides natural facts about how men behave to be used by the legislator in his planning; knowing these facts, he knows when to interfere and when not; however, there can be no *a priori* supposition that the general happiness will come about anyway even if he does not interfere. As Bentham puts it in the *Manual of Political Economy*, 'the great object ... is to know what ought and what ought not to be done by government. It is in this view and in this view only that the knowledge of what is done and takes place without the interference of government can be of any practical use' (Bentham [1787], 1952, vol. I, p. 224).

Bentham spent much of his life constructing plans for institutions, whether they were very large institutions like nation states or much smaller ones like prisons, workhouses or banking systems. Following from the task set by his two leading principles, the leading idea of any such design could be set by the target enunciated in another specially named principle, the '*Duty and Interest* junction principle', which is 'to make it each man's *interest* to observe on every occasion that conduct which it is his *duty* to observe' (Bentham, 1798, vol. VIII, p. 380). In prisons and workhouses, this meant that he advocated contract management; with regard to state offices, their sale to the highest bidder; in general, an opposition to salaried officials. Here he is clearly influenced by Smith, who noted that in a University where a professor is salaried, 'his interest is ... set as directly in opposition to his duty as it is possible to set it' (Smith [1776], 1976, vol. II, p. 284); Bentham similarly talks of the salaries of professors in his *Rationale of Reward* (1825, p. 154). His concern for the management of institutions and his love of detailed planning is also shown by the work he did developing new systems of accounting for use in them (described in Goldberg, 1957).

The general principle of value from which such recommendations follow – namely that the greatest happiness of the greatest number should be promoted – may look as if it prescribes maximization in two different dimensions and hence has no solution. However, Bentham was quite clear that 'the greatest number' in the formula is just an auxiliary description; what the formula invokes is the greatest happiness, quite independently of how it is distributed. What is meant by 'happiness' is the occurrence of pleasure and the absence of pain, these two being supposed to be directly comparable with each other and it being supposed that all other elements of value or disvalue may be reduced to one or the other. Utility, the source of value for Bentham, is hence taken to be 'that property in any object, whereby it tends to produce benefit, advantage, pleasure, good, or happiness, (all this in the present case comes to the same thing) or (what comes again to the same thing) to prevent the happening of mischief, pain, evil, or unhappiness' ([1789] 1970, p. 12).

Such happiness, or such quantity of pleasure and pain, is supposed by Bentham to be calculable or measurable, and he takes it that empirical observation reveals that several factors have an influence on it. In chapter 4 of the *Introduction*, which is entitled 'Value of a lot of pleasure or pain: how to be measured' ([1789] 1970, p. 38), Bentham lists seven such factors: intensity, duration, certainty, propinquity, fecundity, purity and extent. Earlier manuscripts show a rough attempt to reduce these to numerical scales, and in this chapter he cites it as universally understood that the value of an article varies as its certainty of possession and the 'nearness or remoteness of the time at which, if at all, it is to come into possession' (p. 41). Bentham, that is, just takes it as an empirical fact that people exhibit time preference; and, taking this as a measure of the pleasure or pain which people find in things, hence discovers it to be a factor of their value. By 'fecundity' and 'purity' Bentham means the further pleasures or pains to which a particular one leads; given that he is summing up all the pleasures anyway, Bentham did not in fact need to list these as separate factors. Similarly, by the 'extent' of a pleasure he means the number of persons affected by it; again, since he can count all these separate pleasures separately, he did not need to list this as an additional factor of any one of them.

In accord with his view that utility was the single source of value, Bentham criticized Smith for distinguishing between value in use and value in exchange. He explains away the water and diamonds paradox (that useless diamonds are held to be more valuable than useful water), which Smith thought required this distinction by taking the value of an abundant commodity like water as its value at the margin. 'If the whole quantity required is available', as Bentham puts it, 'the surplus has no kind of value'; that is, it is of no use except, as he

notes, in cases of scarcity. Then water 'has a value in exchange superior to that of wine' (Bentham, 1954, vol. III, pp. 87, 88). The value of diamonds is also value in use for Bentham; giving pleasure, they possess utility.

Bentham's attempts at actual measurement were as sketchy as his conviction that measurement was possible was unshakeable. In early manuscripts he does talk of money as 'the instrument for measuring the quantity of pain or pleasure' and works with an example in which someone is indifferent between having a particular pleasure and having a particular sum of money. However, in the published work, money is not used as a measure; no doubt with good reason, because Bentham clearly held that equal increments of something which provided utility did not provide equal increments of utility. This follows from something which Bentham did produce and work out in a little detail: a set of psychological principles ('axioms of mental pathology', as he called them) which describe how happiness varies with variations of something which produces it. The key assumption, or axiom, here is that, although for unequal fortunes 'he who has the most wealth has the most happiness', 'the excess in happiness of the richer will not be so great as the excess of his wealth' (Bentham, 1802, vol. II, p. 20; 1864, p. 103). In other words, money (or any other producer of utility) has diminishing marginal utility, and Bentham clearly spells out the consequences of this, in particularly for equality. He frequently lists four subsidiary goals as means to the overall goal of general happiness: subsistence, security, abundance and equality. It follows from these axioms of mental pathology that, as long as the other subsidiary ends are not interfered with, greater happiness will be produced by promoting greater equality.

These subsidiary ends show that considerable interference by government is licensed by Bentham. Both security and subsistence demand action by the state; and the state should also do what it can to promote abundance and equality. Bentham indeed thinks that security, and the rights which make it up, such as rights to life or property, are produced by the state and do not exist antecedently to the state. Hence any tax proposals or measures of redistribution designed to produce poor relief or subsistence cannot be objected to because they are supposed to interfere with people's natural liberties or natural rights to property. For Bentham such things are complete chimeras, total fictions, nonsense. So, in a late pamphlet, the *Defence of a Maximum*, he can argue in favour of the state interference with the price of bread, saying that he will 'leave it to Adam Smith, and the champions of the rights of man ... to talk of invasions of natural liberty' (1954, vol. III, p. 258; he is presumably thinking of Smith [1776], 1976, vol. II, p. 208); for Bentham, there is no such thing to be interfered with. So as well as defence, justice and the public works permitted by Smith, Bentham also thought that the state should promote institutes for the propagation of knowledge, take control of health, insurance and possibly some communications – he notices that the benefits of a canal accrue 'in portions altogether unassignable, among individuals more clearly unassignable' in the *Institute of Political Economy* (1954, vol. III, p. 338); in other words, it is a public good. Bentham also produced a series of detailed proposals for state control of banking and the issue of paper currency.

Bentham was therefore not resistant to the idea of state activity, and he draws up several lists of 'agenda'; that is, areas where it is appropriate for the state to act. However, in spite of the specific criticisms, he does carry over the chief lines of Smithian economics so far as to hold that, in general, more happiness is produced if the state does not attempt to exercise control. The 'general rule' with respect to 'agenda' makes '*Be quiet* ... the motto, or watch word, of government' (1954, vol. III, p. 333). While considering any state intervention, it must be shown that it produces more good than the mischief of the most onerous current tax. It is assumed that, in general, once security and subsistence have been provided, more value (i.e. more pleasure) will be produced if people, who are supposed normally to know their own interests better than anyone else, are left free to pursue their own pleasures. Bentham's early pamphlet the *Defence of Usury* was indeed an attempt to out-Smith Smith by arguing that the rate of interest on money should be outside government control; and its last letter is a defence of 'projectors' against Smith. Indeed, Bentham not only defended projectors but was himself one to the extent that he hoped to make money out of his own project, the panopticon prison. He intended to be its first contract manager, having control of the criminals of England and setting them to work for profit.

Given Bentham's perspective as a legislator, political economy and the role of the state necessarily form a large part of any account of his work. However, having a theoretical mind, Bentham tended to become involved in issues for their own sake even if he had originally only considered them as means to an end. Hence his proposals for a new form of interest-bearing circulating currency led to a year's study of the effects of paper money and inflation, partly empirical and partly theoretical. The resulting work, the *Circulating Annuities* (1801), therefore not only consists of such typically Benthamite features as an engraving of the proposed new currency but also an analysis of the effects of the introduction of new paper money; and such analysis also occurs in the later occasional pamphlet *The True Alarm*. In his early work Bentham had thought that one reason why the scope for state interference was limited was that trade was always limited by capital; the government, not being able to increase capital, could hence do little for trade. Such is a predominant theme of the early *Manual of Political Economy*. However, when he reconsidered the matter, Bentham realized that, when there was unemployment, a monetary change might have a real effect by drawing new labour into the workforce. Hence money 'with regard to labour which as yet has not been brought into action, adds to the real quantity of wealth (according to the application made of the labour), and does not add to the nominal price of goods' (1952, vol. II, pp. 310–11). Discovering that monetary changes may lead to 'an increase of real wealth' (p. 313) leads Bentham into occasional criticism of Smith; leads him to say things like that, in one way, 'money, it would seem, is the cause, and the cause *sine qua non*, of labour and general wealth' (p. 324); means that he departs from his masters by extolling luxury expenditure and talking of forced saving; and by holding that new money may move wealth from the unproductive to the productive classes.

Although such remarks only form a passing part of an occasional work designed to encourage the government in a particular project, here, as elsewhere, Bentham throws out hints and insights which which have only properly been developed later by others. The general tenor of his *True Alarm* pamphlet, and in particular his account of these monetary effects, meant that he was sufficiently out of tune with orthodox opinion for his followers to think that it was not worth editing and publishing: Dumont consulted James Mill and Ricardo, and they advised against it (Ricardo's critical running commentary can be found in Ricardo, 1951). However, such Benthamite remarks are only occasional. The more persistent work is the account of how far the state should interfere in the running of the economy; which in turn is but part of the overall project of deciding the complete code of law for a state engaged in promoting the general happiness.

ROSS HARRISON

See also UTILITARIANISM.

SELECTED WORKS

1776. *A Fragment on Government.* London: T. Payne. Revised and edited by J.H. Burns and H.L.A. Hart, London: Athlone Press, 1977.
1787. *Defence of Usury.* London: T. Payne & Son. In Bentham (1952), vol. I.
1789. *An Introduction to the Principles of Morals and Legislation.* London: T. Payne & Son. Reissued, ed. J.H. Burns and H.L.A. Hart, London: Athlone Press, 1970.
1791. *Panopticon.* Dublin: Thomas Byrne. In Bentham (1843), vol. IV.
1793. *Escheat vice Taxation.* In Bentham (1952), vol. I.
1798. *Pauper Management Improved.* In Bentham (1843), vol. VIII.
1801. *Circulating Annuities.* London. In Bentham (1952), vol. II.
1802. *Traités de législation civile et pénale.* Ed. E. Dumont, 3 vols, Paris.
1808. *Scotch Reform.* London: J. Ridgway. In Bentham (1843), vol. V.
1811. *Théorie des peines et des récompenses.* Ed. E. Dumont. London.
1815. *A Table of the Springs of Action.* London: R. & A. Taylor. In Bentham (1843), vol. I.
1824. *The Book of Fallacies.* Ed. J.S. Mill, F. Place and P. Bingham, London: J. & H.L. Hunt.
1825. *The Rational of Reward.* Trans. and ed. R. Smith, London: J.L. & H.L. Hunt.
1827. *Rationale of Judicial Evidence.* Ed. J.S. Mill, London: Hunt and Clarke.
1830a. *The Rationale of Punishment.* Trans. and ed. R. Smith, London: Robert Heward.
1830b. *Constitutional Code.* In Bentham (1843), vol. IX.
1843. *The Works of Jeremy Bentham.* 11 vols. Ed. J. Bowring, Edinburgh: William Tait, 1838–43.
1864. *The Theory of Legislation.* Trans. Richard Hildreth from Bentham (1802), ed. C.K. Ogden, London: Kegan Paul & Co., 1931.
1952–4. *Jeremy Bentham's Economic Writings.* 3 vols, ed. W. Stark, London: George Allen & Unwin. Vol. I includes Bentham (1787), (1793) and the *Manual of Political Economy*; vol. II contains *Circulating Annuities*; vol. III contains *Defence of a Maximum, The True Alarm* and the *Institute of Political Economy*.
1970. *Of Laws in General.* Ed. H.L.A. Hart, London: Athlone Press.
1977. *A Comment on the Commentaries.* Ed. J.H. Burns and H.L.A. Hart, London: Athlone Press.
1983. *Deontology.* Ed. John Bowring, 2 vols, London: Longman & Co.; Edinburgh: William Tait, 1834; reissued, edited by Amnon Goldworth, Oxford: Clarendon Press.

BIBLIOGRAPHY

Goldberg, L. 1957. Jeremy Bentham: critic of accounting method. *Accounting Research* , July, 218-45.
Halévy, E. 1928. *The Growth of Philosophic Radicalism.* Trans. Mary Morris, London: Faber.
Harrison, R. 1983. *Bentham.* London: Routledge & Kegan Paul.
Hart, H.L.A. 1982. *Essays on Bentham.* Oxford: Oxford University Press.
Hume, L.J. 1981. *Bentham and Bureaucracy.* Cambridge: Cambridge University Press.
Hutchison, T.W. 1956. Bentham as an economist. *Economic Journal* 66, June, 288–306.
Mack, P. 1962. *Jeremy Bentham: An Odyssey of Ideas.* London: Heinemann.
Mill, J.S. 1832. Bentham. *London and Westminster Review.* In *Collected Works of John Stuart Mill*, ed. J.M. Robson, London and Toronto: Routledge & Kegan Paul and University of Toronto Press, 1969, vol. X.

Mill, J.S. 1861. *Utilitarianism*. In *Collected Works of John Stuart Mill* ed. J.M. Robson, London and Toronto: Routledge & Kegan Paul and University of Toronto Press, 1969, vol. X.

Petrella, F. 1977. Benthamism and the demise of classical economic Ordnungs Politik. *History of Political Economy* 92, Summer, 215–36.

Ricardo, D. 1951-73. *The Works and Correspondence of David Ricardo*. Ed. P. Sraffa, Cambridge: Cambridge University Press, Vol. III.

Robbins, L. 1952. *The Theory of Economic Policy in English Classical Political Economy*. London: Macmillan.

Robbins, L. 1970. *The Evolution of Modern Economic Theory*. London: Macmillan.

Smith, A. 1776. *An Inquiry into the Nature and Causes of the Wealth of Nations*. Ed. Edwin Cannan, Chicago: University of Chicago Press, 1976.

Stark, W. 1941. Liberty and equality, or Jeremy Bentham as an economist: I. Bentham's doctrine. *Economic Journal* 51, April, 56–79.

Stark, W. 1946. Liberty and equality, or Jeremy Bentham as an economist: II. Bentham's influence. *Economic Journal* 56, December, 583–608.

Taylor, W.L. 1955. Bentham as economist: a review article. *South African Journal of Economics* 23, March, 66–74.

Bergson, Abram (born 1914). Bergson was the intellectual father of US studies of the Soviet economy during World War II as chief of the Russian Economic subdivision of the Office of Strategic Services (OSS). After the war he played the major role in founding the US tradition of description and analysis of Soviet economic institutions, measurement of Soviet economic growth and evaluation of that growth. He had earlier made a major contribution to the development of welfare economics. His works on the Soviet economy are marked by a combination of encyclopaedic knowledge of Soviet statistics, theoretical analysis and immense industry. They had an enormous influence on the development of US economic Sovietology and established themselves as the dominant paradigm in that field.

Bergson's main contribution to economic Sovietology concerned the measurement of Soviet economic growth. The result of the combination of the 'propaganda of success' with Soviet economic institutions and the MPS method of calculating national income is that the data on economic growth published by the Soviet authorities are both incredible and clearly non-comparable with the data on economic growth of other countries. Bergson both developed a method which enabled internationally comparable national income statistics and growth rates to be calculated for the USSR and applied it to the USSR for 1928–55. The method was the 'adjusted factor cost' method. In essence it consists of adjusting actual Soviet transactions prices so as to bring them into line with the prices that would be observed if the USSR's prices were determined in accordance with neoclassical theory. These adjusted prices are then used as weights to aggregate the physical output series of branches and sectors of the economy as known from Soviet official data into a SNA type aggregate. This has the great advantage of producing data comparable to SNA data and hence suitable for international comparisons. At the same time, Bergson argued, this procedure enables a 'production potential' and possibly even a welfare interpretation to be given to the resulting national income data.

The development of this method and its application to the USSR for the period 1928–55 were enormous achievements. They clearly indicated that assessment of socialist economies did not have to remain at the level of ideological confrontation but was amenable to rational discourse and scientific inquiry.

Both the method and its results are controversial. The rationality of the adjusted factor cost prices, the representativeness of the physical products selected, the huge data requirements and skilled labour inputs necessary to apply the method, the relevance of neoclassical theory for interpreting Soviet economic data, and the accuracy of the picture of the Soviet economy resulting from application of the method, all came under fire. Other methods of generating internationally comparable data (e.g. the physical indicators method, or scaling up from NMP to GNP using data for the missing sectors) have also been used.

In welfare economics Bergson is famous for his 1938 paper which defined and discussed the concept of an individualistic social welfare function. The latter enables necessary conditions for an economic optimum to be calculated without the assumption of cardinal utility. This concept was subsequently utilized and developed by Samuelson and became an integral part of the welfare economics literature. Its usefulness remains a matter of controversy. According to Samuelson's contribution to the Bergson *festschrift* it was a major contribution, a 'flash of lightning' after which 'all was light' in the hitherto extraordinarily confused subject of welfare economics. A number of opinions of a less positive kind can be found on pp. 110–116 of M.H. Dobb, *Welfare Economics and the Economics of Socialism*. Bergson has also written on socialist economics and Arrow's Impossibility Theorem.

Besides his purely academic work on the Soviet economy, Bergson, with his OSS experience, played a major role in establishing and maintaining the close links between US academic studies of the Soviet economy and the intelligence community and other branches of the Federal Government. Besides being a professor of economics for many years, first at Columbia and then at Harvard, he was director of the Harvard Russian Research Center (1964–8, 1969–70), consultant to the Rand Corporation, member and subsequently Chairman of the Social Science Advisory Board of the US Arms Control and Disarmament Agency, consultant to various federal agencies, served as President of the Association for Comparative Economic Studies and has several times given testimony before the US Congress.

Bergson made a major contribution to 20th-century economics by establishing a school of economists who transformed the study of the Soviet economy, hitherto a reserve of partisan émigré and committed writers, into a field of sober academic inquiry.

MICHAEL ELLMAN

See also SOCIALIST ECONOMIES; SOCIAL WELFARE FUNCTION; WELFARE ECONOMICS.

SELECTED WORKS
Welfare economics
1938. A reformulation of certain aspects of welfare economics. *Quarterly Journal of Economics* 52(2), February, 310–34.
1966. *Essays in Normative Economics*. Cambridge, Mass.: Harvard University Press.
1982. *Welfare, Planning and Employment*. Cambridge, Mass.: MIT Press. *Soviet economic institutions*
1944. *The Structure of Soviet Wages*. Cambridge, Mass.: Harvard University Press.
1964. *The Economics of Soviet Planning*. New Haven: Yale University Press.
1984. Income inequality under Soviet socialism. *Journal of Economic Literature* 22(3), September, 1052–99.
Measurement of Soviet economic growth
1950. Ruble prices and the valuation problem. *Quarterly Journal of Economics* 64, August, 408–41.

1953. *Soviet National Income and Product in 1937*. New York: Columbia University Press.

1961. *The Real National Income of Soviet Russia since 1928*. Cambridge, Mass.: Harvard University Press. *Evaluation of Soviet economic growth*

1968. *Planning and Productivity under Soviet Socialism*. New York: Columbia University Press.

1978. *Productivity and the Social System – the USSR and the West*. Cambridge, Mass.: Harvard University Press.

Joint works

1954. (With H. Heymann, Jr.) *Soviet National Income and Product 1940–48*. New York: Columbia University Press.

BIBLIOGRAPHY

Birman, I. 1985. The Soviet economy: alternative views. *Survey* 29(2), Summer, 102–15.

Birman, I. 1986. The Soviet economy: alternative views. *Russia* 12, 60-74.

Dobb, M.H. 1969. *Welfare Economics and the Economics of Socialism*. Cambridge: Cambridge University Press.

Hanson, P. 1971. East–West comparisons and comparative economic systems. *Soviet Studies* 22(3), January, 327–43.

Holzman, F.D. 1957. The adjusted factor cost standard of measuring national income: comment. *Soviet Studies* 9(1), July, 32–6.

Marer, P. 1985. *Dollar GNPs of the USSR and Eastern Europe*. Baltimore: Johns Hopkins University Press.

Rosefielde, S. (ed.) 1981. *Economic Welfare and the Economics of Soviet Socialism*. Cambridge: Cambridge University Press. (The Bergson *Festschrift*; a full bibliography of Bergson's work in 1936–80 can be found on pp. 334–7 of this book.)

Seton, F. 1985. *Cost, Use and Value*. Oxford: Clarendon Press.

Wiles, P. 1955. Are adjusted roubles rational? *Soviet Studies* 7(2), October, 143–60.

Berkeley, George (1685–1753). George Berkeley was an Anglican clergymen of Anglo-Irish origins who rose to be Bishop of Cloyne. He is known today principally as the philosopher of immaterialism. It is possible to look upon the economic works of George Berkeley in two different ways. First, one may consider him solely as an economic thinker and evaluate the nature and content of the ideas espoused in Berkeley's principal economic pamphlet, *The Querist* (1735-7), some of whose ideas are foreshadowed in the *Essay towards preventing the Ruin of Great Britain* (1721) and in *Alciphron* (1732). Secondly, one may look upon the *Querist* as part of the programme of economic development espoused by a number of prominent Anglo-Irishmen, a substantial number of whom were Anglican clergymen and of whom Berkeley himself was one. Viewed primarily as an economist, the two most prominent features of Berkeley's thought are his emphasis upon industry as the true source of wealth and upon the stimulation of wants as the most effective way of eliciting increased industry (Queries 1, 4, 19–21 and *passim*). This balanced view, partially anticipated by John Law, synthesised both the typical Mercantilist emphasis upon work as well as the stress put upon demand by such economists as Bernard Mandeville. Berkeley goes on to emphasize that economic growth would be most stimulated if the Irish would develop a taste for Irish goods (144–6). However, since such a result could not be depended upon, Berkeley was prepared to have the state intervene in order to limit the influence of fashion upon consumer tastes (13–16). Berkeley was aware that everyone may not respond to his call for increased industry and he was even willing to force such people to work (380–87). In the first edition of the *Querist*, Berkeley emphasized the role of the monetary system as an important catalyst for economic growth and urged the need for a National Bank in Ireland. Due to a lack of popular interest, this section was largely omitted in subsequent editions. Most of the above ideas are very much a staple of British Mercantilist writing. Berkeley does however break new ground with his philosophical analysis of the sources of wealth and by his disdain for gold and silver *per se*; 'Whether there ever was, is, or will be, an industrious nation poor, or an idle rich?' (Query 1), 'Whether there be any virtue in gold or silver, other than as they set people at work, or create industry?' (Query 30), as well as by his emphasis upon the welfare of the common man as the true end of economic policy; 'Whether a people can be called poor, where the common sort are well fed, clothed and lodged' (Query 2).

In a wider sense, Berkeley is to be seen as a member of a group of public-spirited Irishmen, such as Thomas Prior and the Rev. Samuel Madden, who were moved by Ireland's poverty to form a group that would help ameliorate Ireland's misery – the Dublin Society. Instead of confronting hostile English colonial policy, this group took the view that one should do whatever was feasible within the constraints set by the English. With its emphasis upon simple, practicable measures, the philosophy of the Dublin Society was very congenial to Berkeley's general aim of returning philosophy from the elite to the common man. In terms of method, Berkeley followed an iconoclastic approach, believing that a clear statement of the problems would enable common sense to perceive proper solutions. In this sense, Berkeley may be considered an anti-deductive rather than an inductive economist.

The *Querist* was very influential. Ten editions were printed even in Berkeley's lifetime. Adam Smith owned a copy and may have learned from it. While the *Querist* continued to be read by many, such as Robert Southey and S.T. Coleridge, it was not written in a form which would endear itself to the systematizing tendencies of the classical economists. Isaac Butt tried hard to revive a Berkeleian approach in Ireland in the 1940s but failed. Nonetheless, Berkeley's genuine love for Ireland and for all the Irish people has endeared him to many, especially Irish patriots.

S. RASHID

SELECTED WORKS
The Works of George Berkeley. Ed. A.A. Luce and T.E. Jessop, London: Nelson, 1948–57.

BIBLIOGRAPHY
Ardley, G. 1968. *Berkeley's Renovation of Philosophy*. The Hague: M. Nijhoff.

Berle, Adolf Augustus, Jr. (1895–1971). A graduate at an early age of Harvard College and the Harvard Law School, Berle served in Army Intelligence in World War I and on the American delegation to the Paris Peace Conference, from which he emerged to denounce the terms of the Treaty, as did Keynes, though to a lesser audience. After practising law in New York, he joined the law faculty of Columbia University, where he became a member of the famous Brains Trust of Franklin D. Roosevelt. He was a close adviser of Roosevelt's, both before and after the latter's election to the Presidency.

In the later New Deal years, Berle served as an Assistant Secretary of State, then a senior position in the Department, and thereafter as Ambassador to Brazil. In the years following World War II, he was Chairman of the Liberal Party in New York and the long-time head of the Twentieth Century Fund, a foundation engaged in the active sponsorship of research in economic and social issues.

Berle's major contribution to economics, made in 1932 in conjunction with Gardiner C. Means in *The Modern Corporation and Private Property*, was in showing that authority in the modern large business enterprise moves ineluctably away from the owners of property to the managers and that by the time of research for the book the process was already far advanced. As a conclusion for conventional economics this, it is not too much to say, ranked in inconvenience with that of Keynes. Ownership no longer conveyed power in the great enterprise. Profit maximization was now by managers, not on behalf of themselves but for others largely unknown or, in pay and perquisites, for the managers themselves. Berle's conclusions also denied the independent, self-motivated, heroic role of the entrepreneur as offered in conventional economics, notably by Schumpeter.

Berle's contribution came from outside the conventional boundaries of the profession – from, of all things, a lawyer. Perhaps for this reason its importance was discounted, even denied, by many economists. In recent times, however, the truth of Berle's contentions has been recognized as personal profit maximization of managers – salaries, diverse perquisites, stock options, golden parachutes – has become one of the accepted scandals of the time. Nonetheless, Berle's role as one of the major innovating figures in economics has never been adequately recognized. In his textbook Paul Samuelson acknowledges *The Modern Corporation* as a classic; in Campbell R. McConnell's *Economics*, the most widely used text in the United States, Berle's name does not even appear.

In his later years Berle returned in a perceptive and informative way to the subject of power, though not with the innovative force of his earlier work.

J.K. GALBRAITH

SELECTED WORKS

1932. (With Gardiner C. Means.) *The Modern Corporation and Private Property*. New York: The Commerce Clearing House.
1959. *Power Without Property; A New Development in American Political Economy*. New York: Harcourt, Brace & World.
1963. *The American Economic Republic*. New York: Harcourt, Brace & World.
1969. *Power*. New York: Harcourt, Brace & World.

Bernoulli, Daniel (1700–1782). Swiss mathematician and theoretical physicist; born at Groningen, 8 February 1700; died at Basel, 17 March 1782.

Daniel Bernoulli was a member of a truly remarkable family which produced no fewer than eight mathematicians of ability within three generations, three of whom – James 1 (1654–1705), John 1 (1667–1748) and Daniel – were luminaries of the first magnitude.

Although initially trained in medicine, in 1725 Daniel Bernoulli accepted a position in mathematics at the newly founded Imperial Academy in St Petersburg, but returned to Basel in 1733, holding successively the chairs in anatomy and botany, physiology (1743), and physics (1750–77). He was elected to membership in all of the major European learned societies of his day, including those of London, Paris, Berlin and St Petersburg, and maintained an extensive scientific correspondence which included both Euler and Goldbach.

Original in thought and prolific in output, Bernoulli worked in many areas but his most important contributions were to the fields of mechanics, hydrodynamics and mathematics. He enjoys with Euler, his close friend from childhood, the distinction of having won or shared no fewer than ten times the annual prize of the Paris Academy. His masterpiece, the *Hydrodynamica* (1738), contains a derivation of the *Bernoulli equation* for the steady flow of a non–viscous, incompressible fluid, and the earliest mathematical treatment of the kinetic theory of gases, including a derivation of Boyle's Law.

Bernoulli also made important contributions to probability and statistics, including an early application of the method of maximum likelihood to the theory of errors and an investigation of the efficacy of smallpox inoculation (Todhunter, 1865, ch. 11). Nevertheless, his best-known contribution to this subject is unquestionably his 1738 paper 'Specimen theoriae novae de mensura sortis', which discusses utility, 'moral expectation' and the St Petersburg paradox.

The St Petersburg paradox (so called because Bernoulli's paper appeared in the *Commentarii* of the St Petersburg Academy) concerns a game, first suggested by Nicholas Bernoulli (Daniel's cousin) in correspondence with Montmort: a coin is tossed n times until the first head appears; 2^n ducats are then paid out. Paradoxically, the mathematical expectation of gain is infinite although common sense suggests that the fair price to play the game should be finite.

Bernoulli proposed that the paradox could be resolved by replacing the mathematical expectation by a moral expectation, in which probabilities are multiplied by personal utilities rather than monetary prices. Arguing that incremental utility is inversely proportional to current fortune (and directly proportional to the increment in fortune), Bernoulli concluded that utility is a linear function of the logarithm of monetary price, and showed that in this case the moral expectation of the game is finite.

Strictly speaking, Bernoulli's advocacy of logarithmic utility did not 'solve' the paradox: if utility is unbounded, then it is always possible to find an appropriate divergent series. Nor was he the first to adopt such a line of attack; the Swiss mathematician Gabriel Cramer had earlier written to Nicholas Bernoulli in 1728, noting that if utility were either bounded or proportional to the square root of monetary price, then the moral expectation would be finite. But it was via Bernoulli's paper that the utility solution entered the literature, and despite initial (and eccentric) criticism by D'Alembert, by the 19th century most treatises on probability would contain a section on moral expectation and the paradox.

An English translation of Bernoulli's 1738 paper on the St Petersburg paradox was published in *Econometrica* 22 (1954), 23–36, and is reprinted in *Precursors in Mathematical Economics: An Anthology*, ed. W.J. Baumol and S.M. Goldfeld, Series of Reprints of Scarce Works on Political Economy, No. 19, London: London School of Economics and Political Science, 1968, pp. 15–26. An English translation of Bernoulli's paper on maximum likelihood estimation appears in *Biometrika* 48 (1961), 1–18.

For further biographical information about Daniel Bernoulli and a detailed scientific assessment of his work, see the article by Hans Straub in *Dictionary of Scientific Biography*, Vol. 2 (1970). The DSB also contains excellent entries on several other members of the Bernoulli family. Eric Temple Bell's *Men of Mathematics*, (1937) contains a spirited, if not necessarily reliable, account of the Bernoullis.

Todhunter (1865, ch. 11) is still valuable as a summary of Bernoulli's work in probability; Todhunter's book is, as Keynes justly remarked, 'a work of true learning, beyond criticism'. For further information on Bernoulli's contributions to probability and statistics, see also Sheynin (1970 and 1972) and Maistrov (1974, pp. 106–7 and 110–18). The dispute with D'Alembert is discussed by Baker, (1975, pp. 172–5); see also Pearson (1978, pp. 543–55 and 560–65) and Daston (1979, pp. 259–79).

Useful discussions of Bernoulli's paper on the St Petersburg paradox include Leonard J. Savage (1954, pp. 91–5) and J.M. Keynes (1921, pp. 316–20). The mathematician Abel once wrote that one should read the masters and not the pupils; those who wish to follow Abel's advice will find challenging but rewarding Laplace's discussion of moral expectation in his *Théorie analytique des probabilités* (1812, ch. 10: 'De l'espérance morale').

The literature on the St Petersburg paradox up to 1934 is surveyed in Karl Menger (1934); an English translation of Menger's paper appears in M. Shubik (ed., 1967). For a discussion of the St Petersburg paradox in the context of an axiomatization of utility and probability other than that of Ramsey and Savage, see Jeffrey (1983, pp. 150–55). The paradox still continues to inspire interest and analysis; a recent example is Martin-Lof (1985).

S.L. ZABELL

BIBLIOGRAPHY
Baker, K.M. 1975. *Condorcet: From Natural Philosophy to Social Mathematics.* Chicago: University of Chicago Press.
Bell, E.T. 1937. *Men of Mathematics.* New York: Simon & Schuster; Harmondsworth: Pelican Books, 1953.
Daston, L.J. 1979. D'Alembert's critique of probability theory. *Historia Mathematica* 6, 259–79.
Jeffrey, R.C. 1983. *The Logic of Decision.* 2nd edn, Chicago: University of Chicago Press.
Keynes, J.M. 1921. *A Treatise on Probability.* London: Macmillan.
Laplace, P.S. 1812. *Théorie analytique des probabilités.* Paris. 2nd edn, 1814; 3rd edn, 1820.
Maistrov, L.E. 1974. *Probability Theory: A Historical Sketch.* New York: Academic Press.
Martin-Lof, A. 1985. A limit theorem which clarifies the 'Petersburg paradox'. *Journal of Applied Probability* 22, 634–43.
Menger, K. 1934. Die Unsicherheitsmoment in der Wehrtlehre. *Zeitschrift für Nationalökonomie* 5, 459–85. Trans. in *Essays in Mathematical Economics in Honor of Oskar Morgenstern,* ed. M. Shubik, Princeton: Princeton University Press, 1967.
Pearson, K. 1978. *The History of Statistics in the 17th and 18th Centuries.* New York: Macmillan.
Savage, L.J. 1954. *The Foundations of Statistics.* New York: Wiley.
Sheynin, O.B. 1970. Daniel Bernoulli on the Normal Law. *Biometrika* 57, 99–102.
Sheynin, O.B. 1972. D. Bernoulli's work on probability. *RETE Strukturgeschichte der Naturwissenschaften* 1, 273–300.
Straub, H. 1970. Bernoulli, Daniel. In *Dictionary of Scientific Biography,* ed. C.C. Gillispie, New York: Scribner's, Vol. 2, 136–46.
Todhunter, I. 1865. *A History of Mathematical Theory of Probability from the Time of Pascal to that of Laplace.* Cambridge: Cambridge University Press, repr. New York: Chelsea, 1961.

Bernoulli, James [Jakob, Jacques] (1654–1705). Bernoulli was born in Basel on 27 December 1654 and died there on 16 August 1705, a scion of a famous family of Swiss mathematicians. In 1687 he was appointed Professor of Mathematics in the University of Basel, and besides major contributions to probability theory he made advances in the calculus, the theory of series, and mechanics.

In the field of probability his *Ars conjectandi* was published posthumously in 1713. Part I is a commentary, with text, on Huygens's *De ratiociniis in aleae ludo* of 1657, in the course of which Bernoulli gave the expression for the binomial distribution for general chances. For this reason 'binomial trials' are sometimes called 'Bernoulli trials', although in fact De Moivre published the expression earlier. Part II is *The doctrine of permutations and combinations*, written in ignorance of Pascal's *Traité du triangle arithmétique* and therefore not as

novel as Bernoulli thought. Part III applies the theory of Part II to games of chance, while Part IV contains the celebrated limit theorem in probability in which Bernoulli derived an expression for the number of binomial trials required to ensure that the proportion of successes falls within stated limits with a certain specified probability. As the number of trials is increased, this probability tends to 1. He applied this theorem to the estimation of the binomial parameter, revealing a clear understanding of the problem of statistical estimation and thus inaugurating a continuing debate about the proper solution.

A.W.F. EDWARDS

Bernstein, Eduard (1850–1932). Born in Berlin, 6 January 1850; died in Berlin, 18 December 1932. The son of a Jewish railway engineer and the seventh child in a large family of fifteen children, Bernstein grew up in a lower middle-class district of Berlin in 'genteel poverty'. He did not complete his studies at the Gymnasium and in 1866 he began an apprenticeship in a Berlin bank. Three years later he became a bank clerk and remained in this post until 1878, but he continued to study independently and for a time aspired to work in the theatre. He became a socialist in 1871, largely through sympathy with the opposition of Bebel, Liebknecht and others to the Franco-Prussian war, and strongly influenced by reading Marx's study of the Paris Commune, *The Civil War in France* (1871). In 1872 Bernstein joined the Social Democratic Workers' Party, and in 1875 he was a delegate to the conference in Gotha which brought about the union of that party with Lassalle's General Union of German Workers to form a new Socialist Workers' party, later the Social Democratic Party (SPD). From that time Bernstein became a leading figure in the socialist movement, and in 1878, just before Bismarck's anti-Socialist law was passed, he moved to Switzerland as secretary to a wealthy young socialist, Karl Höchberg, who expounded a form of Utopian socialism in the journal *Die Zukunft* which he had founded. It was in 1878 that Bernstein read Engels's *Anti-Dühring* which, he said, 'converted me to Marxism', and he corresponded with Engels for the first time in June 1879. After some misunderstandings with Marx and Engels, who were suspicious of his relationship with Höchberg, Bernstein won their confidence during a visit to London and in January 1881, with their support, he became editor of *Der Sozialdemokrat* (the newspaper of the SPD, established in 1879). It was, as Gay (1952) notes, 'the beginning of a great career'.

In 1888 the Swiss government, under pressure from Germany, expelled Bernstein and three of his colleagues on the *Sozialdemokrat* and they moved to London to continue publication there. The period of exile in England, which lasted until 1901, was crucial in the formation of Bernstein's ideas. He became a close friend of Engels, who made him his literary executor (jointly with Bebel), and developed a stronger interest in historical and theoretical subjects, contributing regularly to Kautsky's *Die Neue Zeit* and publishing in 1895 his first major work, a study of socialism and democracy in the English revolution (entitled *Cromwell and Communism* in the English translation). Bernstein's major contributions in this study, which he later described as 'the only large scale attempt on my part to discuss historical events on the basis of Marx's and Engels's materialist conception of history', were to analyse the civil war as a class conflict between the rising bourgeoisie and both the feudal aristocracy and the workers, and to give prominence to the ideas of the radical movements in the revolution (the Levellers and Diggers), and in particular those of Gerrard Winstanley, who had been ignored by previous historians.

At the same time Bernstein established close relations with the socialists of the Fabian Society and came to be strongly influenced by their 'gradualist' doctrines and their rejection of Marxism. In a letter to Bebel (20 October 1898) he described how, after giving a lecture to the Fabian Society on 'What Marx really taught', he became extremely dissatisfied with his 'well-meaning rescue attempt' and decided that it was necessary 'to become clear just where Marx is right and where he is wrong'. Soon after Engels's death Bernstein began to publish in *Die Neue Zeit* (from 1896 to 1898) a series of articles on 'problems of socialism' which represented a systematic attempt to revise Marxist theory in the light of the recent development of capitalism and of the socialist movement. The articles set off a major controversy in the SPD, in which Kautsky defended Marxist orthodoxy and urged Bernstein to expound his views in a more comprehensive way, as he then proceeded to do in his book on 'the premisses of socialism and the tasks of social democracy' (1899; entitled *Evolutionary Socialism* in the English translation), which made him internationally famous as the leader of the 'revisionist movement'.

Bernstein's arguments in *Evolutionary Socialism* were directed primarily against an 'economic collapse' theory of the demise of capitalism and the advent of socialism, and against the idea of an increasing polarization of society between bourgeoisie and proletariat, accompanied by intensifying class conflict. On the first point he was attacking the Marxist orthodoxy of the SPD, expounded in particular by Kautsky, rather than Marx's own theory, in which the analysis of economic crises and their political consequences was not fully worked out, and indeed allowed for diverse interpretations (Bottomore, 1985). The central part of Bernstein's study, however, concerned the changes in class structure since Marx's time, and their implications. In this view, the polarization of classes anticipated by Marx was not occurring, because the concentration of capital in large enterprises was accompanied by a development of new small and medium-sized businesses, property ownership was becoming more widespread, the general level of living was rising, the middle class was increasing rather than diminishing in numbers, and the structure of capitalist society was not being simplified, but was becoming more complex and differentiated. Bernstein summarized his ideas in a note found among his papers after his death: 'Peasants do not sink; middle class does not disappear; crises do not grow ever larger; misery and serfdom do not increase. There *is* increase in insecurity, dependence, social distance, social character of production, functional superfluity of property owners' (cited by Gay, 1952, p.244).

On some points Bernstein was clearly mistaken. With the further development of capitalism, peasant production has declined rapidly and has been superseded to a great extent by 'agri-business'; economic crises did become larger, at least up to the depression of 1929–33. It was his analysis of the changing class structure which had the greatest influence, becoming a major issue in the social sciences, and above all in sociology, in part through the work of Max Weber, whose critical discussion of Marxism in his lecture on socialism (1918) largely restates Bernstein's arguments. There is a more general sense in which Bernstein's ideas have retained their significance; namely, in their assertion of the increasingly 'social character' of production and the likelihood of a gradual transition to socialism by the permeation of capitalist society with socialist institutions. In a different form the same notion is expressed by Schumpeter (1942) in his conception of a gradual 'socialization of the economy'; a conception which can also be traced back to Marx (Bottomore, 1985).

One other aspect of Bernstein's thought should be noted. Influenced by the neo-Kantian movement in German philosophy and by positivism (in an essay of 1924 he noted that 'my way of thinking would make me a member of the school of Positivist philosophy and sociology') Bernstein made a sharp distinction between science and ethics and went on to argue, in his lecture 'How is scientific socialism possible?' (1901), that the socialist movement necessarily embodies an ethical or 'ideal' element: 'It is something that *ought* to be, or a movement towards something that *ought* to be.' From this standpoint he criticized in a more general way a purely economic interpretation of history, and especially the kind of 'economic determinism' that was prevalent in the orthodox Marxism of the SPD; but in so doing he cannot be said to have diverged radically from the conceptions of Marx and Engels (and indeed he cited Engels's various qualifications of 'historical materialism' in support of his own views).

Bernstein's book met with a vigorous and effective response in Rosa Luxemburg's *Sozialreform oder Revolution* (1899), and the SPD became divided between 'radicals', 'revisionists', and the 'centre' (represented by Bebel and Kautsky); and although the latter retained control Bernstein remained a leading figure in the party until 1914. But his growing opposition to the war led him to form a separate organization in 1916 and then to join the left-wing Independent Social Democratic Party of Germany (USPD) in 1917. After the war Bernstein became increasingly disillusioned with the ineffectualness of the SPD in countering the reactionary nationalist attacks on the Weimar Republic, his influence waned, and his last years were spent in isolation.

TOM BOTTOMORE

See also SOCIAL DEMOCRACY.

SELECTED WORKS
1895. *Cromwell and Communism*. London: Allen & Unwin, 1930.
1899. *Evolutionary Socialism*. New York: Huebsch, 1909. Reprinted, New York: Schocken, 1961.
1901. Wie ist wissenschaftlicher Sozialismus möglich? *Sozialistische Monatshefte*.

BIBLIOGRAPHY
Bottomore, T. 1985. *Theories of Modern Capitalism*. London: Allen & Unwin.
Gay. P. 1952. *The Dilemma of Democratic Socialism*. New York: Columbia University Press.
Luxemburg, R. 1899. *Sozialreform oder Revolution*. Trans. as *Reform or Revolution*. New York: Three Arrows, 1937.
Schumpeter, J.A. 1942. *Capitalism, Socialism and Democracy*. London: Allen & Unwin. 5th edn, 1976.
Weber, M. 1918. Socialism. English trans. in *Max Weber: The Interpretation of Social Reality*, ed. J.E.T. Eldridge, London: Michael Joseph, 1970.

Berry, Arthur (1862–1929). A Cambridge mathematician who dabbled briefly in economics, Berry was born on 28 May 1862 in Croydon and died on 15 August 1929 in Cambridge. Entering King's College, Cambridge, in 1881, he was Senior Wrangler in the Mathematical Tripos of 1885 and became a Fellow of King's in 1886. After extension lecturing, he returned permanently to Cambridge in 1889. Thereafter, apart from administering Cambridge extension lecturing from 1891 to 1895, he devoted himself to King's and the teaching of mathematics, highly regarded but publishing little.

Berry's social and political interests were broad. As an undergraduate he had co-founded the Cambridge Economic Club, to which he delivered a paper on factory legislation (Berry, 1886). He must have attended Alfred Marshall's lectures and subsequently, at the latter's request, lectured on mathematical economics from 1891 to 1900, after which W.E. Johnson took over. Marshall also instigated Berry's only two publications on economic theory (Berry 1891a, 1891b). The first, which survives only as an abstract, was a significant contribution to the emerging marginal productivity theory of distribution on lines already sketched by Marshall. The second was a masterful resolution of a dispute between Marshall and F.Y. Edgeworth over the theory of barter, background letters on which are reproduced by Guillebaud (1961, Vol. II, pp. 791–8). After 1891 Berry drifted away from economics, partly because of heavy administrative work, and partly because of friction with Marshall over the question of women's status at Cambridge.

As an economist (and also more generally) Berry was talented but without a strong drive towards original work. His best-known publication was a history of astronomy for extension audiences (Berry, 1898). See *The Times* (1929) for further biographical information.

J.K. WHITAKER

SELECTED WORKS

1886. *Factory Legislation.* Text of a paper presented to the Cambridge Economic Club, Cambridge, privately printed.
1891a. The pure theory of distribution. *Report of the Sixtieth (1890) Meeting of the British Association for the Advancement of Science.* Reprinted in *Precursors in Mathematical Economics*, ed. W.J. Baumol. and S.M. Goldfeld, London: London School of Economics, 1968.
1891b. Alcune brevi parole sulla teoria del baratto. *Giornale degli Economisti*, June.
1898. *A Short History of Astronomy.* London: Murray.

BIBLIOGRAPHY

Guillebaud, C.W. (ed.) 1961. *Alfred Marshall: Principles of Economics.* 9th (Variorum) edn, London: Macmillan.
The Times. London. 1929. Obituary: Arthur Berry, 19 August.

Bertalanffy, Ludwig von (1901–1972). Primarily a biologist, Bertalanffy is recognized as the father of General Systems Theory and a founder of the Society for General Systems Research. Born near Vienna in 1901 he taught at the University of Vienna (1934–48), the University of Ottawa (1948–54), the University of Alberta (1961–9) and the State University of New York at Buffalo (1969–72). Like many pioneers, his work was recognized during his own lifetime by only a few, but his influence continues to grow. His work, especially on the theory of open systems, led the way to a more unified theory of organisms and organizations stretching from the biological to all the social sciences. He was an important contributor to what might be called the 'post-Newtonian' movement in the sciences, rejecting the reductionism of logical positivism, insisting that systems have hierarchies of complexity, each with its own patterns and methods, allowing for indeterminacy, recognizing that equilibrium is unknown in the real world except as an approximation, and stressing the generality of both ontogenetic and phylogenetic processes.

Main-line economics has remained solidly Newtonian, and the influence of Bertalanffy and of General Systems has been very small. Nevertheless the growing interest in evolutionary models and in more organic approaches to the growth and structure of firms suggest that the hope expressed by Alfred Marshall that economics could learn much from biology, and Veblen that economics might become an evolutionary science, may indicate a future somewhat different from the past. In such a case the importance of Bertalanffy's contribution will be more fully recognized.

KENNETH E. BOULDING

See also GENERAL SYSTEMS THEORY.

Bertrand, Joseph Louis François (1822–1900). Bertrand was born and died in Paris. He was an eminent but not great mathematician, graduate and professor of mathematics at the Ecole Polytechnique and from 1862 to 1900 a member of the Collège de France. His relevance to economic thought comes in his criticism of 'pseudo-mathematicians' in the *Journal des Savants* (1883) where he reviewed *Théorie mathématique de la richesse sociale* of Walras and *Recherches sur les principes mathématiques de la théorie des richesses* of Cournot. It is doubtful if Bertrand considered the problems of formal economic modelling more than casually, viewing the two works through the eyes of a mathematician with little substantive interest or understanding. His comments on Cournot were not only somewhat harsh, but as the subsequent developments in oligopoly theory and the theory of games have shown, both Cournot's model of duopoly and Bertrand's remodelling of duopoly with price rather than quantity as a strategic variable are worth investigation. Cournot's model has been (until recently) more generally treated than Bertrand's model. It remained for Edgeworth to point out the limitations of Bertrand's model (see Shubik, 1959). Bertrand also raised objections to the reference and realism of the process description of Walras of 'tâtonnement'.

It has been suggested (Blaug and Sturges, 1983) that Bertrand's critical review was used by opponents of mathematical economics as the basis for their position. Although explicit proof of this is hard to establish the tone and force of Bertrand's critique makes this highly probable.

MARTIN SHUBIK

SELECTED WORKS

1883. (Review of) *Théorie mathématique de la richesse sociale* par Léon Walras: *Recherches sur les principes mathématiques de la théorie des richesses* par Augustin Cournot. *Journal des Savants*, September, 499–508.

BIBLIOGRAPHY

Blaug, M. and Sturges, P. (eds) 1983. *Who's Who in Economics.* Brighton, England: Wheatsheaf Books.
Byron, G.H. 1899–1900. Joseph Bertrand. *Nature* 1591 (61), 614–16.
Shubik, M. 1959. *Strategy and Market Structure.* New York: Wiley.
Storick, D.L. 1970. Joseph Louis François Bertrand. *Dictionary of Scientific Biography*, Vol. 2, New York: Scribners.

best linear unbiased estimator (BLUE). *See* ESTIMATION.

Bettelheim, Charles (born 1913). Bettelheim has been a life-long Marxist for whom the theory and practice of the transition to socialism has been the central object of analysis. He has written influential theoretical works (e.g. *Economic Calculation and Forms of Property, The Transition to Socialist Economy, Studies in the Theory of Planning*), as well as studies of the political economy of different countries. The most important of these are on India (1968) – he was a consultant to the Indian government during the development of its planning system in the 1950s; on China (1974) he has visited China several times; and on the USSR (1946, 1976, 1978) – he reads Russian and has researched on the Soviet Union since the 1930s. He was influenced deeply by the Chinese cultural revolution, which shed new light on his view of the 'transition to socialism'. He considered that China had broken decisively (and correctly) from the Soviet Union's 'state capitalist' path. In the USSR, argued Bettelheim (following Mao), primacy was given to the 'development of the productive forces' at the expense of attempting to transform the system of unequal 'production relations', which formed the 'objective basis for the existence of classes'. His account of the Maoist attempt to break down workplace inequalities of power, income and status struck a powerful chord among many Western socialists at a time when Stalinism was being increasingly questioned, when confidence was high in the possibility of moving rapidly towards socialism, and before the mainstream of Western socialism had swung towards Euro-Communism.

PETER NOLAN

SELECTED WORKS
1946. *La planification sovietique*. Paris: Marcel Rivière.
1959. *Studies in the Theory of Planning*. Bombay.
1968. *India Independent*. London: Macgibbon & Kee.
1974. *Cultural Revolution and Industrial Organization in China*. New York: Monthly Review Press.
1975. *The Transition to Socialist Economy*. Hassocks: Harvester Press.
1976. *Class Struggles in the USSR, 1917–1923*. New York: Monthly Review Press.
1976. *Economic Calculation and Forms of Property*. London: Routledge.
1978. *Class Struggles in the USSR, 1923–1930*. New York. Monthly Review Press.

Beveridge, William Henry (1879–1963). Beveridge is chiefly remembered as a social and administrative reformer, whose *Social Insurance and Allied Services* (1942) set out the basic principles and structure of the postwar welfare state. Paradoxically, however, he thought of himself chiefly as an academic economist whose significance for posterity would lie in the fields of manpower policy and the theory of prices. Throughout his life his approach to economic problems were resolutely inductive and empirical, in contrast with the deductive and analytical method characteristic of most English economists. His early work, *Unemployment: a Problem of Industry* (1908), was based on detailed statistical analysis of the case-papers of applicants for unemployment relief. It drew attention to the structural, geographical and informational barriers that stood in the way of a perfect market for labour; and although its challenge to orthodox theory was practical rather than theoretical, it helped to erode belief in a natural economic equilibrium. Later editions of *Unemployment* (revised with the help of Lionel Robbins) were more strongly influenced by classical economic thought, but Beveridge never abandoned his belief that unemployment could only be cured by state intervention to organize and rationalize the market for labour. Beveridge in the 1930s was initially highly critical of the Keynesian analysis of unemployment; and although during the early 1940s he gradually absorbed many aspects of Keynesian thought, his *Full Employment in a Free Society* (1944) differed markedly from Keynes in its emphasis on the need for physical as well as fiscal controls over the economy and, in particular, on manpower planning.

Beveridge's early work on unemployment convinced him that there was a close and measurable connection between levels of economic activity and movements of prices. In the early 1920s he embarked upon what he came to see as his life's work; namely, the compilation of historical and statistical data relating to movements of prices since the 12th century. Beveridge's data convinced him that unemployment was caused, both nationally and internationally, by falls in the prices of primary products (though he failed to consider the possibility that the sequence of causation might lie in the other direction). Beveridge's resistance to the use of analytical models meant that his data was of limited value to (and indeed often mocked by) economic theorists. Since his death, however, his material has been a seam of gold to many economic historians. Only one volume of the proposed project was ever published, *Prices and Wages in England from the Twelfth to the Nineteenth Century*, vol. I (1939), but much unpublished material survives among Beveridge's papers in the British Library of Political Science and the Institute of Historical Research.

Although Beveridge is often seen as a leading protagonist of the 'mixed' economy, his writings on economic policy displayed a recurrent scepticism about how far it was possible to reconcile state intervention with consumer sovereignty. His study of *British Food Control* (1928) suggested that there were advantages and disadvantages in both a 'laissez-faire' and a 'command' economy, but that it was both logically and practically impossible to have the two in combination. Such doubts were partially allayed by the transformation of popular attitudes which Beveridge believed to have occurred during World War II, but were never fully resolved. In his writings on social welfare, Beveridge appears to have been little influenced by, and indeed largely unconscious of, the growing body of contemporary writings on welfare economics produced by theorists like Pigou. His approach to social insurance, and to transfer payments generally, was that of an early 19th-century utilitarian, modified by a sociological and humanitarian perspective. All his proposals on social security display a concern to maintain some of the central economic tenets of the Poor Law (maintenance of incentives, encouragement to private saving, strict avoidance of relief-in-aid-of-wages) together with more 'organic' goals such as national efficiency and the maintenance of civilized minimum standards. His arguments for or against various methods and degrees of 'redistribution' were nearly always rooted in pragmatism or rule-of-thumb propositions about human behaviour, rather than in rigorous marginal analysis. Even in the most collectivist and 'socialistic' period of his career, he was insistent that claims to welfare should be rooted as far as possible in 'contract' rather than 'status'. His general perception of social welfare should be seen as that of a popular political theorist rather than that of an academic economist; though clearly his ideas in this field were both influenced by, and had wider implications for, economic thought.

JOSE HARRIS

SELECTED WORKS
1909. *Unemployment: a Problem of Industry*. London: Longmans & Co. Another edn, *Unemployment: a Problem of Industry, 1909 and 1930*, London: Longmans & Co., 1930.
1928. *British Food Control*. London: Oxford University Press.
1931. *Tariffs: the Case Examined*. London: Longmans & Co. Popular edn, 1932.
1936. *Planning under Socialism, and Other Addresses*. London: Longmans & Co.
1939. *Prices and Wages in England, from the Twelfth to the Nineteenth Century*, Vol. 1. London: Longmans & Co.

1942. *Social Insurance and Allied Services. The Beveridge Report in brief.* London: HMSO.
1944. *Full Employment in a Free Society. A report.* Long: G. Allen & Unwin. 2nd edn, 1960. Also numerous articles in *Economic Journal, Economica, Sociological Review, Politica,* and elsewhere.

biased and unbiased technological change. Biased technical progress has commonly been classified as labour-saving or capital-saving. Relatively labour-saving and relatively capital-saving would be more accurate terms, since for example it is quite possible for a relatively labour-saving technological change to save some capital as well as labour. Unbiased technical change, commonly referred to as neutral technical change, lies at the watershed between these two categories.

There are rival definitions of neutrality in technical progress. Hicks (1932) proposed that an invention or innovation should be regarded as neutral if *with unchanged inputs of the two factors of production* the marginal product of labour is raised in the same proportion as the marginal product of capital. An innovation will then be relatively labour-saving if the marginal product of labour is raised in lesser proportion than the marginal product of capital, and relatively capital-saving if the former is raised in greater proportion than the latter.

The second definition of neutrality is due to Harrod (1948). Harrod proposed that technical progress should be regarded as neutral if, *with a constant rate of interest and rate of profit on capital,* the capital-output ratio is left unchanged.

The choice of definition should depend on the purpose in hand. Although in his discussion of the matter Harrod himself suggested otherwise, the Hicksian classification of technical progress would appear to be the more appropriate if one is concerned with the intrinsic character of a single invention or innovation. The Harrod definition of neutrality comes into its own if one is concerned with the effects of technical progress on the economy as a whole. Harrod-neutral technical progress has played an important part in the development of growth theory, and indeed it is for this purpose that Harrod introduced the concept. It is a well-established proposition that Harrod-neutrality of technical progress is a necessary condition for steady-state growth.

The main interest in the classification of technical progress lies in the light it can shed on the effects of technical progress on distributive shares and – more questionably – on levels of employment. If there is strict adherence to the assumption as to what is to be held constant in each case, both Hicks-neutral and Harrod-neutral technical progress will result in unchanged distributive shares. But the assumptions are very different and usually inconsistent with one another. Thus while Hicks holds the factor inputs unchanged, Harrod's assumption that the rate of profit remains unchanged normally implies an accumulation of capital relative to labour. The effect on distributive shares of an accumulation of capital relative to labour taken by itself is held to depend on the elasticity of substitution of capital for labour. Distributive shares will remain unchanged if and only if the elasticity of substitution is equal to unity. It follows from this that Hicks-neutrality and Harrod-neutrality will be mutually consistent if and only if the elasticity of substitution is equal to unity.

In the literature on growth economics, the concept of Harrod-neutral technical progress has often been rendered deceptively simple by the use of a hypothetical one-sector model of the economy, in which the single product can be used both as consumption good and as capital good. Harrod himself imposed no such limitation on his analysis. In such a one-sector model, there can be no change in the price of the capital good relative to the price of the consumption good, since they are one and the same good. It follows that if the capital-output ratio is to remain unchanged, capital must be accumulating in physical terms at the same rate of growth as output.

As soon as the one-sector model is abandoned, the analysis of the effects of a technical advance on distributive shares becomes a much more complex matter. They will depend not only on the character of the advance according to the Hicksian categories but also on the sector in which it takes place. By way of illustration, let it be supposed that the economy has two sectors, one producing a consumer good and one producing a capital good. The effects of a technical advance in the capital-good sector will be different from those of a technical advance in the consumer-good sector. A technical advance in the consumer-good sector will have no impact on the capital-good sector. Its effect on distributive shares in the consumer-good sector will depend solely on the Hicksian character of the advance. A technical advance in the capital-good sector, on the other hand, will impinge on both sectors. Whatever its Hicksian character, it will reduce the cost of the capital good relatively to the cost of labour in both sectors, so that there will be a tendency for capital to be substituted for labour. The effect on distributive shares will then depend on the elasticity of substitution.

Notwithstanding these complexities, which are further compounded when a two-sector model is replaced by a multi-sector model, Harrod's definition of neutrality of technical progress generalises satisfactorily so as to cover the various possibilities in a multi-sector economy, provided the capital-output ratio is understood to be measured in value terms. It has to be recognized, however, that the maintenance unchanged of the capital-output ratio in value terms can come about in more than one way, since not only are the quantities of the capital goods capable of variation but also their prices in terms of the consumption good.

From 1930 to 1960, economists were at pains to explain what was taken to be a broad historical constancy of distributive shares in advanced countries. Since 1960, there has been growing evidence, as for example that presented in Kendrick and Sato (1963), of a tendency for labour's share, broadly defined so as to include salaries as well as wages, to rise since World War I. Hicks had argued, plausibly enough, that there was likely to be a preponderance of relatively labour-saving inventions. If this is so, the question to be asked is why this did not lead to a falling share going to labour instead of to a maintained or even rising share. Part of the explanation is unconnected with the nature of technical progress. As people became wealthier, there was a shift in the consumption mix towards labour-intensive services. Although well established, this tendency is not held to provide a sufficient explanation of the facts. In so far as an explanation resting on the nature of technical progress is also required, the most plausible would seem to be that technical progress took place in the capital-good sector as well as in the consumer-good sector, reducing the cost of capital goods relatively to the cost of labour, but that the resulting substitution of capital for labour was insufficient to maintain capital's relative share.

The effect of technical progress on levels of employment must finally be considered. There is a recurring popular misconception during periods of rapid technical advance that technical progress, and especially labour-saving technical progress, will adversely affect the level of employment. Doubtless, any innovation that reduces the required input of labour per unit of product will reduce the level of employment if output does not rise. But the assumption of a constant level of output is here quite unwarranted. From the point of view of the economy as a whole, the benefit of technical progress is that it makes possible a greater output to be produced with a given endowment of resources.

This is not to deny that technical progress may put particular classes of workers out of work, giving rise to frictional or structural unemployment, the persistence of which will depend on the mobility or immobility of labour. It is also true that the individuals in a society may choose to enjoy some of the benefits of technical progress in the form of increased leisure. The notion often put forward, however, that labour-saving technical progress will somehow permanently reduce the opportunities for employment is not a proposition that has any basis in economic theory or that receives any corroboration from historical evidence.

A limitation of the whole analysis discussed above is that it is exclusively concerned with technical progress in the production process. The equally important contribution of technical progress in the provision of new consumer goods has perhaps been given less than its due share of attention from economists.

CHARLES KENNEDY

See also HARROD, ROY FORBES; INNOVATION; PROBLEMS IN MEASURING PRODUCTIVITY; SALTER, WILFRED EDWARD GRAHAM; TECHNICAL CHANGE.

BIBLIOGRAPHY
Harrod, R.F. 1948. *Towards a Dynamic Economics*. London: Macmillan.
Hicks, J.R. 1932. *The Theory of Wages*. London: Macmillan.
Kendrick, J.W. and Sato, R. 1963. Factor prices, productivity, and economic growth. *American Economic Review* 53(5), December, 974–1003.

Bickerdike, Charles Frederick (1876–1961). Bickerdike was born in England (whereabouts unknown) on 15 May 1876 and died in Wallington, Surrey, on 3 February 1961. He studied at Oxford from 1895 to 1899 where he received his BA degree in 1899 and MA in 1910. Upon winning the Cobden Prize for an essay summarized in Bickerdike (1902) he became a protégé of Edgeworth. After serving briefly as Lecturer on Economics and Commerce at the University of Manchester (1910–12) he entered the Civil Service with a position in the Board of Trade, where he remained until his retirement in 1941.

Bickerdike's published work consists of 15 articles and 38 book reviews, all (save two of the articles) in the *Economic Journal*. He is chiefly known as the originator of the theory of incipient and optimal tariffs (1906, 1907), according to which a country can always gain by imposing a sufficiently small tariff on its imports and can maximize its welfare by imposing a suitable tariff. To derive these results he developed a model (1907) in which nominal import and export prices were expressed as functions of the quantities of imports and exports respectively (with no cross-effects), each country being assumed to stabilize the value of its currency. The elasticities of demand for imports and supply of exports were defined as the reciprocals of the elasticities of these functions (with opposite sign). This has come to be known as the 'elasticity approach'. (For an interpretation of these demand and supply prices as prices relative to the price – assumed stabilized – of a non-tradable in a general-equilibrium model, see Chipman, 1978.) Bickerdike derived formulas for the effect on national 'advantage' of a small tariff (p. 100n) and for the optimal

tariff (p. 101n), and remarked – anticipating Lerner (1936) – that identical expressions would be obtained for an export tax. He noted that the optimal tariff depended only on the foreign elasticities (see also Kahn, 1947); this apparent paradox was explained by Graaff (1949, p. 56). The now-familiar, simpler and more general optimal-tariff formula expressed in terms of Marshallian elasticity was first introduced by Johnson (1950), who showed its relation to Bickerdike's formula.

Edgeworth (1908, p. 544) showed that the positive sign of the denominator of Bickerdike's expression for the advantage from an incipient tariff followed from dynamic stability. A related stability condition was later derived by Bickerdike (1920) for the analysis of a regime of fluctuating exchange rates, and was obtained as a condition for a transfer to lower the paying country's exchange rate. Equivalent formulas were subsequently adopted by Robinson (1937, p. 194n) and Metzler (1948), and – for the special case indicated by Bickerdike of infinite elasticities of supply of exports – by Lerner (1944, p 378).

Bickerdike's other contributions include two essays on local public finance (1902, 1912), a paper (1911) correcting a statement of Edgeworth's that price discrimination could improve upon competitive pricing, and papers on a number of other topics, the most noteworthy relating to business cycles and economic growth.

Although preceded by Carver (1903), Aftalion (1909, pp. 219–20) and Pigou (1912, pp. 144–5), Bickerdike (1914) may be considered one of the original developers of the acceleration principle (cf. Hansen, 1927, p. 112; Haberler, 1937, p. 87), providing a detailed numerical example and emphasizing (in contrast to Aftalion) the importance of durability of capital rather than the gestation period. Bickerdike regarded the phenomenon as an example of market failure. The paper was cited by Frisch (1931) – who erroneously attributed it to J.M. Clark – in the course of his criticism of Clark (1923) and reformulation according to which a deceleration of consumption will call forth a fall in gross investment only if it exceeds the rate of depreciation of capital. Bickerdike (1924, 1925) went on to develop an interesting mathematical model of economic growth according to which labour – the only factor – grows at a constant rate and produces only capital goods – of various durabilities and with various gestation periods – the services of which are consumed. On a path of balanced growth, the rate of interest is equal to the rate of growth, and interest is reinvested. The money supply grows at the same rate in order to maintain constant prices – or else it is constant and prices fall at a constant rate. Bickerdike's main object was to determine whether the process of saving benefited non-savers; in this he was not entirely successful, since his techniques limited him to balanced-growth paths. Nevertheless this work foreshadowed that of Lerner (1944, ch. 20) as well as many features of contemporary growth models, and attracted the attention of Hansen (1927, pp. 173ff).

Information on Bickerdike's life and work may found in Jha (1963) and in Larson (1983, 1987), where other relevant literature is also cited. According to Larson, after Bickerdike's death his papers, including some fifty letters from Edgeworth and twenty from Edwin Cannan, passed into the hands of one Godfrey Alan Dick who died in Oxford in 1981. They are presumed lost.

JOHN S. CHIPMAN

See also ELASTICITIES APPROACH TO THE BALANCE OF PAYMENTS; MARSHALL-LERNER CONDITIONS.

SELECTED WORKS

1902. Taxation of site values. *Economic Journal* 12, December, 472–484. Reprinted in Musgrave and Shoup (1959), 377–88.

1906. The theory of incipient taxes, *Economic Journal* 16, December, 529–35. Reprinted in Musgrave and Shoup (1959), 132–8.

1907. Review of *Protective and Preferential Import Duties* by A.C. Pigou. *Economic Journal* 17, March, 98–102.

1911. Monopoly and differential prices. *Economic Journal* 21, March, 139–48.

1912. The principle of land value taxation. *Economic Journal* 22, March, 1–15.

1914. A non-monetary cause of fluctuations in employment. *Economic Journal* 24, September, 357–70.

1920. The instability of foreign exchange. *Economic Journal* 30, March, 118–22.

1924. Individual and social interests in relation to saving. *Economic Journal* 34, September, 408–22.

1925. Saving and the monetary system, *Economic Journal* 35, September, 366–78.

BIBLIOGRAPHY

Aftalion, A. 1909. La réalité des surproductions générales, 3rd installment. *Revue d'économie politique* 23, March, 201–29.

Carver, T.N. 1903. A suggestion for a theory of industrial depressions. *Quarterly Journal of Economics* 17, *May*, 497–500.

Chipman, J.S. 1978. A reconsideration of the 'elasticity approach' to balance-of-payments adjustment problems. In *Breadth and Depth in Economics*, ed. J.S. Dreyer, Lexington, Mass.: Heath, 49–85.

Clark, J.M. 1923. *Studies in the Economics of Overhead Costs.* Chicago: University of Chicago Press.

Clark, J.M. 1931. Capital production and consumer-taking – a reply. *Journal of Political Economy* 39, December, 814–16. A further word, 40, October, 691–3.

Edgeworth, F.Y. 1908. Appreciations of mathematical theories, III. *Economic Journal* 18, September, 392–403; December, 541–556. Reprinted as: Mr. Bickerdike's theory of incipient taxes and customs duties, in F.Y. Edgeworth, *Papers Relating to Political Economy*, Vol. II, London: Macmillan, 1925, 340–66.

Frisch, R. 1931. The interrelation between capital production and consumer-taking. *Journal of Political Economy* 39, October, 646–54. A rejoinder, 40, April, 253–4. A final word, 40, October, 694.

Graaff, J. de V. 1949. On optimum tariff structures. *Review of Economic Studies* 17, 47–59.

Haberler, G. 1937. *Prosperity and Depression.* 3rd edn, Lake Success, NY: United Nations, 1946.

Hansen, A.H. 1927. *Business-Cycle Theory.* Boston: Ginn & Co.

Jha, N. 1963. *The Age of Marshall.* Patna: Novelty & Co.; 2nd edn, London: Frank Cass, 1973.

Johnson, H.G. 1950. Optimum welfare and maximum revenue tariffs. *Review of Economic Studies* 19, 28–35.

Kahn, R.F. 1947. Tariffs and the terms of trade. *Review of Economic Studies* 15, 14–19.

Larson, B.D. 1983. The analysis of interests in the economics of Charles Frederick Bickerdike. PhD dissertation, University of North Carolina, Chapel Hill, NC.

Larson, B. 1987. Bickerdike's life and work. *History of Political Economy* 19, Summer.

Lerner, A.P. 1936. The symmetry between import and export taxes. *Economica*, N.S. 3, August, 306–13.

Lerner, A.P. 1944. *The Economics of Control.* New York: Macmillan.

Metzler, L.A. 1948. The theory of international trade. In *A Survey of Contemporary Economics*, ed. H.S. Ellis, Philadelphia: Blakiston, 210–54.

Musgrave, R.A. and Shoup, C.S. (eds.) 1959. *Readings in the Economics of Taxation.* Homewood, Ill.: Irwin.

Pigou, A.C. 1912. *Wealth and Welfare.* London: Macmillan.

Robinson, J. 1937. The foreign exchanges. In Joan Robinson, *Essays in the Theory of Employment*, London : Macmillan, 183–209; 2nd edn, Oxford: Basil Blackwell, 1947, 134–55.

bidding. Auctions are studied because they are market institutions of practical importance. Their simple procedural rules to resolve multilateral bargaining over the terms of trade enjoy enduring popularity. They also present simply several basic issues of price determination: the role of private information, the consequences of strategic behaviour, and the effect of many traders. These issues have influenced the subject since the initial work of Vickrey (1961), the early contribution of Griesmer, Levitan, and Shubik (1967), and the influential dissertation by Ortega-Reichert (1968). Useful introductory surveys are by Engelbrecht-Wiggans (1980), Engelbrecht-Wiggans, Shubik and Stark (1983), Milgrom (1985), and MacAfee and McMillan (1986); bibliographies are in MacAfee and McMillan (1986) and Stark and Rothkopf (1979); and Cassady (1967) provides an historical perspective.

This note supplements the entry on Auctions by summarizing some additional theoretical contributions to these issues. This literature relies on the game-theoretic perspective that emphasizes the implications of complete optimizing behaviour. Omitted here are the experimental studies that offer alternative predictions of bidder behaviour. It remains to determine which better describes the behavior of experienced, savvy bidders in the major auction markets. Although general equilibrium models of closed economies have been studied (Schmeidler, 1980; Shapley and Shubik, 1977; Wilson, 1978), we focus on partial equilibrium models with bids and offers denominated in money terms. Also omitted are studies of markets with intermediaries such as brokers and specialists; models without private information (Dubey, 1982; Milgrom, 1986); and auctions in which losers also pay, as in price wars and wars of attrition.

In the traditional view, price determination is a consequence of market clearing: prices equate supply and demand. This clearing process is especially transparent in the case of auction markets. Essentially, auctions are markets with explicit trading rules that specify precisely how market clearing determines prices. For example, in a sealed-bid auction of one or more identical indivisible items, the (interval of) clearing prices is determined by intersecting the seller's supply schedule (reflecting the number of units available and announced reservation prices) with the demand schedule formed by arraying the buyers' bids in descending order. Non-discriminatory pricing sets the price at the highest rejected bid, discriminatory pricing charges each successful bidder the amount of his bid, and various intermediate cases are possible. Double auctions operate similarly except that the supply schedule is constructed by arraying the sellers' offers in ascending order. With divisible commodities, the aggregate schedules are obtained by constructing the sums of the traders' demand and supply schedules at each price. Oral auctions, such as the English auction, find a clearing price by calling for bids in ascending order. An oral double auction, or 'bid–ask' market, allows free outcry of bids and offers that can be accepted immediately and therefore depends on participants' judgments about the likely clearing price.

The variety of possible procedural rules is large, so theoretical studies emphasize the characterization of efficient trading rules, such as rules that are optimal for the buyers or the sellers. The design of trading rules is subject to the incentive compatibility constraints induced by the traders' private information and the option of any trader to forego participation or trade. Auctions are especially restrictive trading mechanisms because their rules are specified independently of information about the distribution of traders' attributes, even if this information is common knowledge. On the other hand, auctions have been important market institutions for millennia precisely because they are efficient or nearly so in a wide variety of environments.

Much of the theory of efficient trading rules studies 'direct revelation' games in which, in equilibrium, each trader's action consists of a direct report of his private information. This approach loses no generality in static models but the resulting optimal rules depend on the distribution of traders' attributes: only in special cases can they be implemented fully as auctions. (In the extreme case of highly correlated private information, an *optimal* trading rule can be designed by the seller to extract most or all of the potential revenue (Crémer and McLean, 1985; Myerson, 1981).) The theory therefore divides between the study of auctions, in which traders' strategies take account of the distribution of attributes, and the study of optimal direct revelation games, in which the trading rule incorporates this data. We concentrate on auctions here, but mention intersections with the general theory.

A trading rule specifies each trader's feasible actions and the prices and trades resulting from their joint actions. Models also specify each trader's information and preferences. Typically each trader i knows privately an observation s_i affecting his preferences, and the restrictive assumption is adopted that the joint probability distribution of these observations and any salient unobserved random variable v is common knowledge among the participants. (The observation s_i is often taken to be real valued for simplicity; it could be the bidder's posterior certainty-equivalent valuation of the item based on his private information.) A strategy therefore specifies a trader's actions depending on his observation and any further observations (such as others' bids) made in process. Trader i's expected utility u_i depends on the received quantity q_i, the price(s) p_i at which these units are traded, his observation s_i, the array $S_i = \{s_j | j \neq i\}$ of others' observations, and possibly on other variables v.

Interesting special cases of the probabilistic structure are: independent and identically distributed (iid) observations; conditionally iid observations given v; and more generally, affiliated observations (e.g., nonnegative correlation on any rectangle). In each case assume that the (conditional) distribution of an observation satisfies the monotone hazard rate or likelihood ratio property. Most of the familiar probability distributions satisfy these assumptions; e.g., lognormal distributions are often used in applications to oil-lease bidding.

Interesting special cases of the preference structure for a single item include: private values, $u_i = s_i - p_i$; a common value, $u_i = v - p_i$; mixed values, $u_i = u(s_i, v) - p_i$, where u is increasing; and private-value cases with common risk aversion, $u_i = U(s_i - p)$, where U is increasing and concave. Relevant features are summarized in the expected utility $\bar{u}(s_i, S_i) = \mathscr{E}\{u(s_i, v) | s_i, S_i\}$.

Other features are also addressed in some formulations: the seller's optimal reservation price, a trader's option to obtain costly further observations to improve his information, bids submitted jointly by syndicates of traders, and entry fees and auxilliary contingent payments such as royalties. (Bidding on the royalty rather than the price has been used in auctions of oil leases.) Uncertainty about the number of bidders is easily included if this number is independent of the bidders' observations; however, somewhat different comparative statics results ensue. If there are bid preparation costs, exposure constraints (total amount of bids submitted) or portfolio motives, then participation in an auction is itself a strategic action and may involve randomization if there are too many potential bidders for all to expect to recoup their costs. If information is costly and subject to choice then even with many bidders there is typically an upper bound on the bidders' total expenditures and each bidder may choose to collect relatively little information (Matthews, 1984). Repeated auctions introduce novel features, such as reputation effects, that severely

alter the results; e.g., one bidder with privileged information can win systematically (Bikhchandani, 1985).

Most theoretical studies assume that the traders' strategies form a Nash equilibrium, or in dynamic formulations, a sequential equilibrium: each strategy in each contingency is optimal for the remainder of the game. For many auction models the equilibrium strategies can be characterized elegantly in terms of the joint distribution of observations and bids (Milgrom and Weber, 1985). If the bidders (on the same side of the market) are positioned symmetrically *ex ante* then one focuses on the symmetric equilibrium in which all bidders use the same strategy, which is an increasing function of one's observation. A large class of symmetric discriminatory auctions have *only* symmetric equilibria (Maskin and Riley, 1986); they are usually characterized by differential equations, as illustrated for various cases in Milgrom and Weber (1982), Reece (1978), Wilson (1977, 1985). In non-discriminatory auctions a single equation specifies the optimal bid as the most one would be willing to pay conditional on one's observation being the most optimistic. Results about symmetric equilibria are fairly robust: examples indicate that under- or over-bidding by one participant engenders a similar but muted response by others, and the difference from the symmetric equilibrium varies smoothly. In sealed-bid discriminatory auctions with iid private values, one's bid is essentially the conditional expectation of the highest rejected valuation given that one's valuation is acceptable. An analogous property applies to mixed-value preferences. The important asymmetric cases occur when some bidders' information is superior to others' (e.g., direct information about v); in these cases any bidder with strictly inferior information obtains expected profits at most zero, and bidders may use randomized strategies. If all bidders have private information (with a positive density satisfying technical restrictions) then typically equilibrium strategies are not randomized and positive expected profits result.

We summarize results mainly for the special probabilistic and preference structures mentioned above, and for symmetric equilibria. Also, multiple-item auctions introduce few novelties when there is a single seller offering a fixed supply of identical items and each bidder wants at most one, so we focus on the single item case. An exception is a 'share auction', in which bidders offer demand schedules for shares of a divisible item in fixed supply: in this case there can be a continuum of symmetric equilibria, and the seller's expected revenue can be unaffected by more bidders (Wilson, 1979).

A main effect of risk aversion is to increase bids in symmetric discriminatory auctions with iid private values. The seller can enhance this effect by imposing an entry fee (preferably decreasing in the amount of the bid and ultimately negative for the highest bids) (Matthews, 1983; Maskin and Riley, 1984). Risk aversion induces bidders to bid higher under discriminatory pricing, and in fact this rule makes the winning bid a less risky random variable. The seller therefore prefers discriminatory pricing, and more so if he too is risk averse. However, if bidders have decreasing absolute risk aversion (ARA), they have the reverse preference (Matthews, 1987). With constant (or zero) ARA, a bidder's higher price with discriminatory pricing is exactly balanced by the riskier price associated with non-discriminatory pricing. With affiliated observations, the bidders prefer discriminatory pricing if they have constant ARA, and will be indifferent again at some degree of decreasing ARA. Affiliation biases the seller's preferences in the opposite direction, towards nondiscriminatory pricing.

Hereafter we assume no risk aversion. Then, in the iid private-values model of bidders' preferences, the seller's expected revenue is the same for discriminatory and non-discriminatory pricing (Harris and Raviv, 1981a, 1981b; Myerson, 1981; Riley and Samuelson, 1981). Moreover, subject to a technical restriction, either of these is optimal among all possible trading rules provided the seller adopts an optimal reservation price (Harris and Raviv, 1981a, 1981b; Myerson, 1981). With more general preferences, whenever $\bar{u}$ is increasing affiliation produces a distinct preference of the seller for (and the bidders against) non-discriminatory pricing $vs.$ discriminatory; indeed, the seller further prefers an oral auction (Milgrom and Weber, 1982). This illustrates the 'linkage principle': the seller wants to reduce the bidders' profits from their private information, and auction rules that reveal affiliated information publicly (inferences from bids in the case of oral auctions) or otherwise positively link one bidder's price to another's bid (non-discriminatory pricing) are advantageous when observations are affiliated and therefore positively correlated. Similarly, the seller prefers to reveal publicly any relevant affiliated information he has so as to reduce the bidders' informational advantages vis-$à$-vis each other. (However, revealing non-affiliated information may be disadvantageous, and in particular this applies to the number of bidders, even when it is independent of other data (Matthews, 1987).) The seller can gain further by conditioning payments ex $post$ on realized values, as in the case of a royalty (Riley, 1986).

The main results about bidders' strategies in single-item sealed-bid discriminatory auctions can be summarized for bidders with symmetric conditionally iid mixed-value preferences. Ex $ante$ each bidder has an equal chance of winning and the bidder with the most optimistic observation is predicted to win, namely i wins in the event $W(s_i) \equiv \{s_i > \max S_i | s_i\}$. (Failure to recognize that winning is an informative event, signalling that others' observations were less optimistic, is called the winner's curse (Capen, Clapp and Campbell, 1971); it is distressingly common in practice as well as in experiments. The implications of the fact that the maximum of several unbiased estimates is biased upward are apparently difficult to appreciate.) The most that i can profitably bid is therefore $\hat{u}(s_i) = \mathcal{E}\{\bar{u}(s_i, S_i)| W(s_i)\}$, whereas the optimal bid is less than this, by a percentage that is of the order of $1/n$ when there are n bidders, reflecting the bidder's monopoly rent both in terms of the limited number of bidders and the advantage of his private information, which are the two sources of bidders' expected profits. (In a nondiscriminatory auction, i bids $\hat{u}(s_i)$ computed from $\hat{W}(s_i) \equiv \{s_i = \max S_i | s_i\}$ but in equilibrium pays $\hat{u}(\max S_i)$ if he wins.) With many bidders these rents are dissipated and, remarkably, the winning bid conveys essentially all the information about v contained in $\max_i s_i$. In the common value model, the winning bid is a consistent estimator of the value whenever any consistent estimator exists that is a function of $\max_i s_i$: the winning bid is asymptotically as good an estimator as is possible from extrema of the bidders' observations. In particular, if the relative likelihood of a large observation is small for smaller values of v, then the maximum bid converges in probability to v as the number of bidders increases (Milgrom 1979a, 1979b; Palfrey, 1985; Wilson, 1977).

These features are reflected in the detailed calculations reported for models of oil-lease bidding (Reece, 1978). Other examples are shown in Table 1, which exhibits the equilibrium strategies for a model that roughly approximates firms' bidding for oil leases. Each bidder i observes $s_i = (s_{i1}, s_{i2})$ and $u(s_i, v) = s_{i1}v$, where s_{i1} represents a private factor (e.g., price or discount factor), and s_{i2} represents an estimate of the common factor v. Assume that, conditional on a location parameter $\bar{s}_1$, the private factors are conditionally independent and $\ln s_{i1}$ has mean $\ln \bar{s}_1$ and variance σ_1^2; and marginally $\ln \bar{s}_1$ has variance $\bar{\sigma}_1^2$. Similarly, conditional on v the estimates are conditionally independent and $\ln s_{i2}$ has mean $\ln v$ and variance σ_2^2; and marginally $\ln v$ has variance $\bar{\sigma}_2^2$. Consider the case adapted to the empirical fact that for Gulf of Mexico oil leases the logarithm of the bids typically has conditional variance about 1.0 whereas the estimating precision implies a variance of about 0.36 given that the prior variances ($\bar{\sigma}_1^2, \bar{\sigma}_2^2$) are comparatively so large that they can be considered infinite: assume that the conditional variance of the private factors accounts for the difference. In this case, the symmetric equilibrium bidding strategy specifies that each firm submits a bid that is a specified fraction (the bid factor) of the product of its private factor and its posterior expectation of the common factor given its estimate. The tabulation shows the percentage bid factor for four numbers n of bidders, assuming the seller's reservation price is zero, and it shows the winning bidder's expected percentage profit. The seemingly low bid factors are necessary to avoid the winner's curse; whereas the surprisingly large profit percentages reflect the role of the private valuation factors.

Table 1 Examples of Equilibrium Bidding Strategies Lognormal Distributions

$u_i = s_{i1}v, \sigma_1^2 + \sigma_2^2 = 1.0, \sigma_2^2 = 0.36$					
Number of Bidders	(n)	2	4	8	16
Bid Factor	(%)	30.9	39.0	40.5	39.6
Expected Profit	(%)	53.45	33.85	23.78	17.82

Analogous models in which a bidder can increase the precision of his information at increasing cost differ in that, even though bidders' total expenditures converge to a positive level as the number of bidders increases, each bidder's expenditure converges to zero. In this case the winning bid is not a consistent estimator of the common value v and the seller's expected revenue is reduced by the amount of the bidders' total expenditure on information, since in equilibrium this is necessarily recouped in expectation by the participating bidders (Matthews, 1984). An important policy conclusion is that bidders' expenditures on information are inefficiently large.

Single-item auctions with dynamic rules add a few new aspects. In a Dutch auction an exogenously specified price is lowered until a bidder accepts. This rule induces a game that for the bidders is strategically equivalent to a sealed-bid auction; it is also payoff equivalent unless they are impatient to trade, in which case a bidder is concerned about the sum of the interest rate and the hazard rate that trade will be unsurped by a competitor. For the seller it differs if he cannot commit to forego trading by stopping the price at a reservation price exceeding his valuation. In the iid private-values model of preferences, a generalized multi-item Dutch auction is an optimal selling strategy for a monopolist seller whenever potential demand exceeds supply (Harris and Raviv, 1981a, 1981b). Auctions with exogenously ascending prices, in which the items are awarded to the remaining bidders at the price at which the last of the others drops out, are a form of nondiscriminatory auction; but with affiliated observations, a bidder's strategy accounts for the learning enabled by seeing the prices at which others drop out – an instance of the linkage principle.

Double auctions have been studied only for the case of iid private values and non-discriminatory pricing. The price chosen is the midpoint of the interval of clearing prices derived from intersecting the schedules of bids (arrayed in descending order) and offers (arrayed in ascending order). Such an auction is actually an ex $ante$ efficient trading rule for the case of one buyer and one seller with values distributed uniformly on the same interval (Chatterjee and Samuelson, 1983; Myerson and

Satterthwaite, 1983); and by implication from the previous results for auctions, for one buyer *or* one seller. With several buyers and sellers and fairly general distributions, the *ex ante* efficient trading rule bears a strong resemblance to a double auction and has the remarkable property that the expected efficiency losses (compared to *ex post* efficiency) from strategic behaviour decline nearly quadratically to zero as the numbers of traders increase (Gresik and Satterthwaite, 1984). The weaker criterion of *interim* efficiency requires that no other trading rule is sure to improve every trader's expected gains from trade: a double auction satisfies this criterion if there are sufficiently many buyers and sellers (Wilson, 1985).

Oral multi-item discriminatory double auctions, allowing free outcry of bids and offers, are the most important practically (e.g. commodity markets) and the most challenging theoretically. Since trades are consummated in process at differing prices, 'market clearing' is dynamic and, for example, traders with extra-marginal valuations in the static sense can obtain gains from trade early on. Since traders are continually motivated to estimate the distribution of subsequent bids and offers, the learning process is a key feature. Theoretical studies have been attempted for both complete equilibrium models (Wilson, 1987) and others invoking some plausible behavioral assumptions (Easley and Ledyard, 1982; Friedman, 1984). These studies aim to explain the dramatic efficiency attained in experiments and the tendency for transaction prices to approximate or converge to the static Walrasian clearing prices (Smith, 1982; Plott and Sunder, 1982), especially with replication even when the subjects lack a base of common knowledge about distributional features. The efficiency realized in experimental settings is a major puzzle deserving better theoretical explanations.

In summary, auctions are important market institutions that ensure market clearing via explicit trading rules that are independent of the distribution of preferences and information among the participants. Over wide ranges of models of preferences and information, these trading rules are *ex ante* or *interim* efficient or nearly so, and both practically and experimentally they are evidently robust. The theory elaborates these properties and demonstrates the role of private information and strategic behaviour. The explicit construction of equilibrium strategies establishes the magnitudes of these effects and enables comparisons of trading rules, preference structures, informational conditions, and the number of participants; and additionally it explains phenomena such as the winner's curse that stem from adverse selection effects when there is dispersed information. Some models predict that the choice of pricing rule is inconsequential because bidders alter their strategies to compensate: the market clearing condition is the main determinant of welfare consequences.

In relation to the general economic theory of markets the theory of auctions addresses the special case of markets with explicit market-clearing trading rules and elaborates in fine detail the determination of prices and the efficiency and distributional consequences of particular assumptions about the attributes of participants. This endeavour is a useful step in the construction of a general theory of the micro-structure of markets that encompasses the full range from bilateral bargaining to 'perfectly competitive' markets.

ROBERT WILSON

See also AUCTIONS.

BIBLIOGRAPHY

Bikhchandani, S. 1985. Reputation in repeated second price auctions. Research Paper 815, Stanford Business School, July 1985; also in 'Market games with few traders', PhD dissertation, 1986.

Capen, E., Clapp, R. and Campbell, W. 1971. Competitive bidding in high-risk situations. *Journal of Petroleum Technology* 23, 641–53.

Cassady, R. Jr. 1967. *Auctions and Auctioneering.* Berkeley: University of California Press.

Chatterjee, K. and Samuelson, W. 1983. Bargaining under incomplete information. *Operations Research* 31, 835–51.

Crémer, J. and McLean, R. 1985. Optimal selling strategies under uncertainty for a discriminating monopolist when demands are interdependent. *Econometrica* 53, 345–63.

DeBrock, L. and Smith, J. 1983. Joint bidding, information pooling, and the performance of petroleum lease auctions. *Bell Journal of Economics* 14, 395–404.

Dubey, P. 1982. Price–quantity strategic market games. *Econometrica* 50, 111–26.

Easley, D. and Ledyard, J. 1982. A theory of price formation and exchange in oral auctions. Discussion Paper 461, Northwestern University, 1982.

Engelbrecht-Wiggans, R. 1980. Auctions and bidding models: a survey. *Management Science* 26, 119–42.

Engelbrecht-Wiggans, R., Milgrom, P.R. and Weber, R.J. 1983. Competitive bidding and proprietary information. *Journal of Mathematical Economics* 11, 161–9.

Engelbrecht-Wiggans, R., Shubik, M. and Stark, R. (eds) 1983. *Auctions, Bidding, and Contracting: Uses and Theory.* New York: New York University Press.

Friedman, D. 1984. On the efficiency of double auction markets. *American Economic Review* 74, 60–72.

Griesmer, J., Levitan, R. and Shubik, M. 1967. Towards a study of bidding processes, Part Four: Unknown competitive costs. *Naval Research Logistics Quarterly* 14, 415–33.

Gresik, T. and Satterthwaite, M. 1984. The rate at which a simple market becomes efficient as the number of traders increases: an asymptotic result for optimal trading mechanisms. Discussion Paper 641, Northwestern University, 1984.

Harris, M. and Raviv, A. 1981a. A theory of monopoly pricing schemes with demand uncertainty. *American Economic Review* 71, 347–65.

Harris, M. and Raviv, A. 1981b. Allocation mechanisms and the design of auctions. *Econometrica* 49, 1477–99.

Harris, M. and Townsend, R. 1981. Resource allocation under asymmetric information. *Econometrica* 49, 33–64.

Holt, C.A. Jr. 1979. Uncertainty and the bidding for incentive contracts. *American Economic Review* 69, 697–705.

Holt, C.A., Jr. 1980. Competitive bidding for contracts under alternative auction procedures. *Journal of Political Economy* 88, 433–45.

MacAfee, E.P. and McMillan, J. 1987. Auctions and bidding. *Journal of Economic Literature* 25.

Maskin, E. and Riley, J. 1984a. Monopoly with incomplete information. *Rand Journal of Economics* 15, 171–96.

Maskin, E. and Riley, J. 1984b. Optimal auctions with risk averse buyers. *Econometrica* 52, 1473–518.

Maskin, E. and Riley, J. 1986. Existence and uniqueness of equilibrium in sealed high bid auctions. Discussion Paper 407, University of California at Los Angeles, March 1986.

Matthews, S. 1983. Selling to risk averse buyers with unobservable tastes. *Journal of Economic Theory* 30, 370–400.

Matthews, S. 1984a. Information acquisition in discriminatory auctions. In *Bayesian Models in Economic Theory*, ed. M. Boyer and R. Kihlstrom, Amsterdam: North-Holland.

Matthews, S. 1984b. On the implementability of reduced form auctions. *Econometrica* 52, 1519–22.

Matthews, S. 1987. Comparing auctions for risk averse buyers: a buyer's point of view. *Econometrica* 55.

Milgrom, P.R. 1979a. *The Structure of Information in Competitive Bidding.* New York: Garland Publishing Co.

Milgrom, P.R. 1979b. A convergence theorem for competitive bidding with differential information. *Econometrica* 47, 679–88.

Milgrom, P.R. 1981. Rational expectations, information acquisition, and competitive bidding. *Econometrica* 49, 921–43.

Milgrom, P.R. 1985. The economics of competitive bidding: a selective survey. In *Social Goals and Social Organization*, ed. L. Hurwicz, D. Schmeidler and H. Sonnenschein, Cambridge: Cambridge University Press.

Milgrom, P.R. 1987. Auction theory. In *Advances in Economic Theory 1985*, ed. T. Bewley, Cambridge: Cambridge University Press.

Milgrom, P.R. and Weber, R.J. 1982a. A theory of auctions and competitive bidding. *Econometrica* 50, 1089–122.

Milgrom, P.R. and Weber, R.J. 1982b. The value of information in a sealed-bid auction. *Journal of Mathematical Economics* 10, 105–14.

Milgrom, P.R. and Weber, R.J. 1985. Distributional strategies for games with incomplete information. *Mathematics of Operations Research* 10, 619–32.

Moore, J. 1984. Global incentive constraints in auction design. *Econometrica* 52, 1523–5.

Myerson, R.B. 1981. Optimal auction design. *Mathematics of Operations Research* 6, 58–73.

Myerson, R.B. and Satterthwaite, M.A. 1983. Efficient mechanisms for bilateral trading. *Journal of Economic Theory* 29, 265–81.

Ortega-Reichert, A. 1968. *Models for Competitive Bidding Under Uncertainty*. Technical Report 8, Operations Research Department Stanford University

Palfrey, T.R. 1985. Uncertainty resolution, private information aggregation and the Cournot competitive limit. *Review of Economic Studies* 52, 69–83.

Plott, C.R. and Sunder, S. 1982. Efficiency of experimental security markets with insider information: an application of rational expectations models. *Journal of Political Economy* 90, 663–98.

Reece, D.K. 1978. Competitive bidding for offshore petroleum leases. *Bell Journal of Economics* 9, 369–84.

Reece, D.K. 1979. Alternative bidding mechanisms for offshore petroleum leases. *Bell Journal of Economics* 10, 659–69.

Riley, J. 1986. Ex post information in auctions. Discussion Paper 367, University of California at Los Angeles, March.

Riley, J. and Samuelson, W. 1981. Optimal auctions. *American Economic Review* 71, 381–92.

Schmeidler, 1980. Walrasian analysis via strategic outcome functions. *Econometrica* 48, 1585–93.

Shapley, L. and Shubik, M. 1977. Trade using one commodity as a means of payment. *Journal of Political Economy* 85, 937–68.

Smith, V. 1982. Microeconomic systems as experimental science. *American Economic Review* 72, 923–55.

Stark, R.M. and Rothkopf, M.H. 1979. Competitive bidding: a comprehensive bibliography. *Operations Research* 27, 364–90.

Vickrey, W. 1961. Counterspeculation, auctions and competitive sealed tenders. *Journal of Finance* 16, 8–37.

Vickrey, W. 1962. Auctions and bidding games. In *Recent Advances in Game Theory*, ed. O. Morgenstern and A. Tucker, Princeton: Princeton University Press.

Wilson, R. 1977. A bidding model of 'perfect' competition. *Review of Economic Studies* 44, 511–18.

Wilson, R. 1978. Competitive exchange. *Econometrica* 46, 557–85.

Wilson, R. 1979. Auctions of shares. *Quarterly Journal of Economics* 93, 675–89.

Wilson, R. 1985. Incentive efficiency of double auctions. *Econometrica* 53, 1101–16.

Wilson, R. 1987. Equilibria of bid–ask markets. In *Arrow and the Ascent of Economic Theory: Essays in Honour of Kenneth J. Arrow*, ed. G. Feiwel, London: Macmillan.

bid-rent function. *See* MONOCENTRIC MODELS.

bilateral monopoly. A bilateral monopoly is a market that is characterized by one firm or individual, a monopolist, on the supply side and one firm or individual, a monopsonist, on the demand side. The input markets of the monopolist and the output market of the monopsonist can be of any form. The essential ingredient is the single seller–single buyer situation. Because a buyer and a seller of a product, perforce, do business with each other, they are clearly able to make legally binding agreements. This contrasts with firms in the same industry, which do not sell to one another, and which are often precluded

by anti-collusion laws from making legally enforceable contracts. Of course, it is also possible to view bilateral monopoly noncooperatively.

The following coverage is chronological, starting first with the cooperative treatment due to Edgeworth (1881) and Marshall (1890). The noncooperative formulations, due to Wicksell (1925) and Bowley (1928) are considered next, along with Bowley's reformulation of the Marshallian cooperative contribution. Finally, bilateral monopoly is viewed in game-theoretic terms as a two-player cooperative game, principally in the manner of Nash (1950).

Bilateral monopoly is a special instance of two-person trade; therefore, the natural starting point is Edgeworth's (1881, pp. 20–30) well known analysis. Suppose the two agents, A and B, have utility functions $u^A(x, y)$ and $u^B(X - x, Y - y)$, where x and y are quantities of two goods consumed by A. The totals available to the pair are X and Y, respectively; hence, the consumption of B is $(X - x, Y - y)$. Edgeworth proposed that the two persons would trade to a Pareto optimal outcome that left each at least as well off as he would be in the absence of trade.

Marshall (1890, Appendix F and Mathematical Note XII) noted that, if both persons' marginal utilities are constant for one of the goods (say y), then any Pareto optimal trade will involve a fixed quantity of the other good (x). This is easily seen by recalling that a Pareto optimal (interior) trade requires equality of the two traders' marginal rates of substitution,

$$\frac{u_x^A(x, y)}{u_y^A(x, y)} = \frac{u_x^B(X - x, Y - y)}{u_y^B(X - x, Y - y)}$$

and then invoking Marshall's condition, which is

$$u^A(x, y) = v^A(x) + ay$$

and

$$u^B(X - x, Y - y) = v^B(X - x) + b(Y - y).$$

Note that Marshall's condition is actually that the two traders each have utility functions that are separable and linear with respect to one good. Equality of the marginal rates of substitution is given by

$$\frac{v_x^A(x)}{a} = \frac{v_x^B(X - x)}{b}$$

which is independent of y.

Bowley (1928) put Marshall's result in the following standard bilateral monopoly model: suppose the seller has the profit function $\pi^A = rx - C(x)$, where r is the firm's selling price, x is the amount sold, and $C(x)$ is the firm's total cost function; the buyer's profit function is $\pi^B = f(x) - rx$, where x is the buyer's only input, and $f(x)$ is its total revenue as a function of the sole input x. (That is, $f(x) = d[h(x)] \cdot h(x)$, where h is the production function and d is the inverse demand function for the firm.) The decision variables are x and r, and the Pareto optimality condition is

$$\frac{\partial \pi^A / \partial x}{\partial \pi^A / \partial r} = \frac{\partial \pi^B / \partial x}{\partial \pi^B / \partial r} \quad \text{or} \quad \frac{r - C'(x)}{x} = \frac{f'(x) - r}{-x}$$

The latter condition is independent of r and is equivalent to $f'(x) = C'(x)$, which states that the marginal revenue of the buying firm should equal the marginal cost of the selling firm – the condition for joint profit maximization. The way that the joint profit is split depends upon r, the transfer price between the two firms.

An equilibrium in a noncooperative vein was suggested by Wicksell (1925, pp. 223–5) and developed by Bowley (1928). Wicksell's equilibrium features a price announcement by the seller, followed by a quantity selection by the buyer. The seller is committed to deliver whatever amount the buyer wishes at the named price. Thus, the seller is a Stackelberg (1934) leader that knows the buyer will maximize $f(x) - rx$ with respect to x, and with r assumed constant. This allows the seller to solve $f'(x) = r$ for x as a function of r [denote this $x = \phi(r)$] and use this in its own profit function, $r\phi(r) - C[\phi(r)]$, which it then maximizes with respect to r to find the best price to announce.

In addition to working out the details of the foregoing model, Bowley suggested an alternative in which the roles of the two firms are exactly reversed: the buyer announces a price at which it will buy any quantity the seller cares to deliver, and the seller then chooses an amount to transact. The buyer can calculate the optimal choice of x for the seller as a function of r and then use this information to determine its most profitable price.

These noncooperative outcomes are not in general Pareto optimal; therefore, they are implausible in a setting such as this where there are only two agents who can discuss a transaction with one another and who are quite able to make binding agreements that do give them Pareto optimal outcomes.

Another way to visualize the possible outcomes in a bilateral monopoly is in the profit (or utility) space of the agents. In the Marshall–Bowley model the payoff possibility frontier is a straight line of slope $-b/a$. Were the two players a firm and a labour union, then, depending on the utility function assigned to the union, the payoff possibility frontier need not be a straight line. The union's utility function might well depend on the wage rate, the number of workers employed, and the average hours worked per employee. The representation of the model in profit, or utility, space is useful in approaching the model as a game-theoretic bargaining problem.

Perhaps the most famous two person cooperative game solution is that due to Nash (1950), in which there is a *threat outcome* that would prevail in the absence of agreement between the two players, with the bargained outcome being on the payoff possibility frontier at that point where the product of the players' gains from cooperation is maximized. Though this product maximization rule seems arbitrary on the surface, it is implied by several axioms that are plausible. For the bilateral monopoly model the threat of each firm is to refuse to trade with the other. This threat would force zero profit onto the buyer and $-C(0)$ onto the seller.

Nash's approach can be enriched in several ways. First, the threat of no trade need not leave the firms at profits of 0 and $-C(0)$. Perhaps the seller could enter the buyer's line of business. Similarly, the buyer may have other options open: there may be substitutes for the input supplied by the seller that are more expensive or less effective. If both possibilities hold at once, then 'no trade' does not completely specify the threat situation. The firms could become duopolists in a vertically integrated industry, and carry out threats in terms of the output levels that they decide to produce. This leads to a *variable threat* game, analysed by Nash (1953).

Neither of the Nash models appears to deal with the process of bargaining. Interestingly, the Nash outcome coincides with the outcome of a bargaining process proposed by Zeuthen (1930). On this, see Harsanyi (1956) who also shows the relationship between the Nash model and a suggestion of Hicks (1932).

Observation of labour–management bargaining indicates that agreements often are more costly than theory suggests. Strikes occur which impose costs on both sides even though both sides could have been better off by accepting the very same contract prior to a strike. Several directions are suggested in the literature in this regard. First, there are two-person cooperative game models in which offers and counter-offers are made until

a settlement is reached. During this process, real time is assumed to elapse, and the total size of the players' joint gain is supposed to shrink. Cross (1965) has such a model and, in an elegant paper, Rubinstein (1982) models the bargaining process in a way that turns the bargaining game into a noncooperative game having the Nash (1950) solution as its outcome. Second, it can be assumed, following Harsanyi and Selten (1972), that each player is ignorant of the payoff function of the other player. Each player makes a *demand*; however, if the two demands taken together lie beyond the payoff possibility frontier of the game, then no agreement is made. A third line of investigation, not formally applied to bilateral monopoly, is that of *repeated games* or *supergames*. Under this approach, one instance of bargaining between two players is seen as one episode in a larger game. For example, in labour–management negotiations, a contract is reached for a specific interval, say three years, and both firm and union are concerned with the effect that the current contract will have on later contract negotiations. This situation is easily seen as a game of many players, if it is added that the union may deal with more than one firm, and that the various contracts are interconnected. This latter consideration embeds a bilateral monopoly in a larger context; hence may be thought to go beyond the present topic. Additional discussion of bargaining models can be found in Roth (1979) and Friedman (1986).

JAMES W. FRIEDMAN

See also BARGAINING; COURNOT, ANTOINE AUGUSTIN; GAME THEORY; NASH EQUILIBRIUM; ZEUTHEN, FREDERIK.

BIBLIOGRAPHY

Bowley, A. 1928. Bilateral monopoly. *Economic Journal* 38, 651–9.
Cross, J. 1965. A theory of the bargaining process. *American Economic Review* 54, 67–94.
Edgeworth, F. 1881. *Mathematical Psychics*. London: Kegan Paul.
Fellner, W. 1949. *Competition Among the Few*. New York: Knopf.
Friedman, J. 1986. *Game Theory with Applications to Economics*. New York: Oxford University Press.
Harsanyi, J. 1956. Approaches to the bargaining problem before and after the theory of games. *Econometrica* 24, 144–56.
Harsanyi, J. and Selten, R. 1972. A generalized Nash solution for two-person bargaining games with incomplete information. *Management Science* 18, 80–106.
Hicks, J. 1932. *The Theory of Wages*. London: Macmillan.
Marshall, A. 1890. *Principles of Economics*. 9th (variorum) edn, with annotations by C.W. Guillebaud, London: Macmillan, 1961.
Nash, J. 1950. The bargaining problem. *Econometrica* 18, 155–62.
Nash, J. 1953. Two person cooperative games. *Econometrica* 21, 128–40.
Roth, A. 1979. *Axiomatic Models in Bargaining*. Berlin: Springer.
Rubinstein, A. 1982. Perfect equilibrium in a bargaining model. *Econometrica* 50, 97–109.
Stackelberg, H. von 1934. *Marktform und Gleichgewicht*. Vienna: Julius Springer.
Wicksell, K. 1925. Mathematical economics. In K. Wicksell, *Selected Papers on Economic Theory*, ed. E. Lindahl, Cambridge, Mass.: Harvard University Press, 1958.
Zeuthen, F. 1930. *Problems of Monopoly and Economic Warfare*. London: Routledge & Kegan Paul.

bimetallism. In a bimetallic monetary standard both gold and silver are given legal tender status and the ratio of their prices is fixed at the mint. Two conditions are required to fix the ratio of prices: standard coins in each of the two metals are given a fixed weight in terms of the unit of account (e.g., a US dollar from 1837 to 1873 was defined as 371.22 grains of fine silver and 23.22 grains of fine gold); and there must be free coinage of the two metals at the mint (allowing for brassage – the cost of certifying and minting of coins).

A bimetallic standard is a type of commodity standard, which is to be distinguished from a paper standard. Commodity standards may be based on metals, other commodities, or baskets of commodities including metals but in the past they have generally been based on silver, on gold or a bimetallic combination.

In a commodity standard the general price level is determined by the mutual interaction of the money market and the commodity market. Demand and supply conditions in the commodity market determine the real price of the commodity, and given the fixed (at the mint) nominal price of the commodity, the price level is determined by the demand and supply for the monetary stocks.

Via substitution between monetary and non-monetary uses of the commodity and an inverse relationship between the general price level and current production a metallic standard tends to be self regulating.

In a monometallic standard such as the gold standard the price level fluctuates with changing conditions of supply (such as gold discoveries or technological advances in mining) and changing conditions of demand (such as a growing preference for gold as real income rises). Bimetallism has long been viewed as providing a more stable price level than silver or gold monometallism.

This stabilizing mechanism operates via the substitution between monetary and non-monetary uses of each of the two metals. As long as the bimetallic ratio lies between the ratios that would yield monometallism for each metal taken in isolation – below the ratio of the price of gold to silver if silver alone were money and above the ratio if gold alone were money – then departures of the market ratio from the mint ratio would cause the undervalued (at the mint) metal to be transferred from monetary to non-monetary uses with the opposite occurring for the overvalued metal, thus tending to return the market ratio to the mint ratio. This substitution of cheaper for dearer metal is referred to as Gresham's Law, 'Bad money drives out good money' (originally discovered not by Sir Thomas Gresham in the 16th century but by Nicolas Oresme (Kindleberger, 1985) in 1360).

In addition production of the undervalued metal is encouraged, of the overvalued metal discouraged, tending also to return the market ratio to the mint ratio.

As long as the monetary gold stock is not completely displaced by the operation of Gresham's Law bimetallism will be successful. If the stock of silver increases sufficiently to displace the monetary gold stock, the bimetallic system breaks down and becomes a monometallic silver standard. Similarly, switching to a monometallic gold standard could occur in the case of a substantial increase in the stock of gold. In this event bimetallism degenerates into alternating monometallism.

A bimetallic standard would be more viable: the closer the proximity of the mint ratio to the long-run market ratio (the natural ratio); the larger the size of the currency area involved; the smaller the share of nonmonetary uses for each metal; the larger the relative sizes of the own and cross elasticities of nonmonetary demand for each metal, and the smaller and more similar the supply elasticities of production for each of the two metals (Walras, 1874–7; Fisher, 1922, Chen, 1972; Niehans, 1978).

Bimetallic standards can be traced in rudimentary form back to the middle ages. From Roman times the commercial world followed a silver standard but with the evolution of international trade gold coins, because of their higher value, gained in favour. By the mid-13th century Venice fixed the weights of both gold and silver coins, followed soon after by other Italian city states and in the 14th century by England, France and Burgundy (Cipolla, 1956; Munro, 1973).

The conversion to the gold standard and the ultimate demise of bimetallism began in England in 1717 when the Master of the Mint, Sir Isaac Newton, reduced the price of the silver guinea to 21s and raised the price of gold to £3 17s 10½d. This led to a cessation of the minting of silver guineas. Full demonetization of silver was achieved by 1798 (Yeager, 1976; Kindleberger, 1985).

While England was turning to the gold standard, France instituted 75 years of successful bimetallism in 1803 by fixing the ratio of silver to gold at $15\frac{1}{2}$:1. Until the late 1840s abundant supplies of silver threatened to displace gold but with the gold discoveries in California and Australia the process was reversed until the 1860s, when again major silver discoveries threatened the bimetallic standard. In 1865 France formed the Latin Monetary Union with Belgium, Switzerland and Italy (later joined by the Papal States, Greece and Romania). By agreeing to mint silver coins of the same fineness these countries expanded the size of the bimetallic currency area. The Latin Monetary Union continued the free coinage of silver until, swamped by massive supplies of new silver from discoveries in the Americas and the abandonment of the silver standard by several important countries, it limited silver coinage in 1874 and fully demonetized silver in 1878 (Kindleberger, 1985).

The United States adopted bimetallism in 1792 at a gold–silver price ratio of 15:1. Soon after its institution, the market ratio rose to the French ratio of $15\frac{1}{2}$:1 hence overvaluing silver at the mint and converting the currency to an effective silver standard. This was reversed when the ratio was raised to 16:1 in 1834 and the US followed an effective gold standard until the suspension of specie payments in 1861 (Laughlin, 1885; Martin, 1968). In 1873, silver was demonetized – a *de jure* recognition of its longstanding disuse – so that when the US resumed specie payments on 1 January 1879 it was on a gold standard. The succeeding two decades of deflation and falling silver prices produced a renewed interest in a return to bimetallism at 16:1 – the Free Silver movement – based on a coalition of silver mining interests, debtors, farmers and other groups adversely affected by deflation. The Free Silver movement achieved some of its aims in expanding the coinage of silver with the passage of the Bland Allison Act of 1878 and the Sherman Silver Purchase Act of 1890 but the resulting threat to the US adherence to the gold standard ultimately led to more deflation than would otherwise have occurred (Friedman and Schwartz, 1963).

Bimetallism was a great source of controversy in the 19th century. In England in the 1850s and 1860s concern over the inflationary effects of the Californian and Australian gold discoveries led to a renewed interest in the monetization of silver (Sayers, 1933). In this period there was considerable discussion over the 'parachute effect' of French bimetallism. Chevalier (1857) argued that the French bimetallic system, by absorbing the increased supplies of gold and releasing silver to be exported to the East, slowed down the rise in world prices. However, Jevons (1884) and Cairnes (1873) pointed out that the 'parachute effect' would not be as important as Chevalier maintained in preventing a rise in prices, since gold and silver can be considered as substitutes, so that as gold currency is substituted for silver, the price of silver will tend to fall along with the price of gold (Bordo, 1975).

The secular deflation of the last quarter of the 19th century led to considerable interest around the world in instituting a form of international bimetallism. This concern produced international conferences in 1878, 1881 and 1892, the important Gold and Silver Commission in England in 1886 and a Silver Commission in Germany in 1894. The conferences and commissions pitted the proponents and opponents of bimetallism against each other. Principal proponents of bimetallism were Nicholson (1888) and Walker (1896), principal opponents Jevons (1875 and 1884), Giffen (1898), and Laughlin (1885).

The key issues in the debate were whether bimetallism would produce greater price stability than gold monometallism and whether in the face of massive changes in the supply of silver, bimetallism was feasible.

None of the conferences succeeded in making any significant progress towards instituting an international bimetallic standard and once new gold supplies from South Africa and Alaska turned secular deflation into inflation interest in such schemes vanished.

The weight of the historical evidence on the operation of bimetallism suggests that it was a fragile standard. It was fragile in the sense that the bounds within which it could operate were on occasion broken by massive gold and silver discoveries and this fragility, ultimately, was the main cause for its demise. However, it did ensure greater price stability in the period when it was in force compared to the succeeding period of gold monometallism and, for the US at least, had it remained in effect from 1873 to 1920 it would have produced a more stable price level than was actually observed (Friedman and Schwartz, 1963; Timberlake, 1978; Drake, 1985).

MICHAEL D. BORDO

See also GOLD STANDARD.

BIBLIOGRAPHY
Bordo, M.D. 1975. John E. Cairnes on the effects of the Australian gold discoveries, 1851–73: an early application of the methodology of positive economics. *History of Political Economy* 7(3), 337–59.
Cairnes, J.E. 1873. *Essays in Political Economy: Theoretical and Applied.* Repr. New York: Augustus M. Kelley, 1965.
Chen, C.N. 1972. Bimetallism: theory and controversy in perspective. *History of Political Economy* 4(1), Spring, 89–112.
Chevalier, M. 1857. *On the Probable Fall in the Value of Gold.* London.
Cipolla, C. 1956. *Money, Prices and Civilization in the Mediterannean World, Fifth to Seventeenth Century.* Princeton: Princeton University Press.
Drake, L. 1985. Reconstruction of a bimetallic price level. *Explorations in Economic History* 22(2), April, 194–219.
Fisher, I. 1922. *The Purchasing Power of Money.* Reprinted, New York: Augustus M. Kelley, 1965.
Friedman, M. and Schwartz, A.J. 1963. *A Monetary History of the United States.* Princeton: Princeton University Press.
Giffen, R.G. 1898. *The Case Against Bimetallism.* London: George Bell & Sons.
Jevons, W.S. 1884. *Investigations in Currency and Finance.* Ed. H.S. Foxwell, London: Macmillan.
Kindleberger, C.P. 1985. *A Financial History of Western Europe.* London: Allen & Unwin.
Laughlin, L. 1885. *A History of Bimetallism in the United States.* New York: Appleton.
Martin, D.A. 1969. Bimetallism in the United States before 1850. *Journal of Political Economy* 76(3), May–June, 428–42.
Munro, J. 1973. *Wool, Cloth and Gold: The Struggle for Bullion in Anglo Burgundian Trade: 1340–1478.* Toronto: University of Toronto Press.
Nicholson, J.S. 1885. *Treatise on Money and Essays on Monetary Problems.* London.
Niehans, J. 1978. *The Theory of Money.* Baltimore: Johns Hopkins Press.
Sayers, R. 1933. The question of the standard in the eighteen fifties. *Economic History,* January.
Timberlake, R. 1978. Repeal of silver monetization in the late nineteenth century. *Journal of Money, Credit and Banking* 10(1), February, 27–45.
Walras, L. 1874–7. *Elements of Pure Economics.* Definitive edn of 1926, trans. by W. Jaffé, New York: R.D. Irwin, 1954.
Walker, F.A. 1896. *International Bimetallism.* London: Macmillan.
Yeager, L. 1976. *International Monetary Relations: Theory, History and Policy.* 2nd edn, New York: Harper & Row.

bioeconomics. The word *bioeconomics* (sometimes *bionomics*) has been used to describe two separate fields of investigation: (a) the economics of biological systems – that is the ways in which biological organisms and communities utilize scarce resources such as space, time, and sources of sustenance; and (b) biological resource economics – the ways in which the economic activities of human societies interact with the dynamics of biological systems. Bioeconomics is thus either a branch of biology (Wilson, 1975; May, 1981; Krebs and Davies, 1984), or of economics (Clark, 1976). For further discussion of the second interpretation, *see* RENEWABLE RESOURCES.

Two mathematical paradigms that play major, and complementary, roles in bioeconomics (both meanings) are optimization theory and the theory of competitive games. The philosophical basis for the use of optimization models in biology is the Darwinian theory of natural selection and evolution (Darwin, 1859): biological organisms are hypothesized to evolve so as to maximize their 'fitness', meaning (roughly) their ultimate contribution to the gene pool. Explicit models, however, usually employ more primitive objective functions, such as expected rate of food intake, probability of survival, or number of progeny produced per breeding cycle. Optimization models have been applied to the study of many aspects of animal behaviour, including foraging strategy, territoriality, reproductive strategy and life histories.

Game-theoretic models are also implied by the Darwinian paradigm, given that the strategies employed by an individual organism will interact with those of its competitors, predators, parasites and mutualist organisms.

Early models of the 'struggle for survival' were based largely on ordinary differential equation systems, following pioneering work of A.J. Lotka (1925) and V. Volterra (1931). These macroecological models did not attempt to describe the strategical behaviour of individual organisms, however. Game-theoretic models were introduced formally into biology by J. Maynard Smith (e.g. 1982) and other theoretical biologists. Maynard Smith's concept of an evolutionary stable strategy (ESS) is related to the notion of Nash competitive equilibrium in the theory of games. In biological terms, a strategy is said to be an ESS if, once established in a population, it cannot be invaded by a rare alternative strategy. The ESS concept has proved useful in modelling many strategic situations, such as aggression, foraging and anti-predation behaviour, mating systems, the evolution of sex, and so forth.

The phenomenon of altruistic behaviour was long considered a paradox for Darwinian theory. A related problem pertains to the natural regulation of animal population – how is it that populations do not regularly overrun their resource base in Malthusian fashion? Early theories of 'group selection' (Wynne-Edwards, 1962) have been rejected for the most part – animals do not adopt altruistic strategies 'for the good of the species'. The more recent theory of kin selection (see Dawkins, 1976), however, indicates that altruistic behaviour could evolve among closely related animals. An extreme case is found in insect societies, where all members of the group are essentially clones of the same queen. An alternative explanation of altruism is based on the concept of reciprocity in repeated games (Axelrod, 1984).

The overpopulation problem is resolved by many species through the institution of territoriality. Explanations for non-territorial species remain somewhat unsatisfactory. Many highly fecund species do respond rapidly to ephemeral resource supplies, and then experience high mortality rates when the resource base declines. Among these so-called r-selected species occur many of the major agricultural pests.

COLIN W. CLARK

See also LOTKA, ALFRED JAMES; PREDATOR-PREY MODELS; VOLTERRA, VITO.

BIBLIOGRAPHY

Axelrod, R.M. 1984. *The Evolution of Cooperation*. New York: Basic Books.

Clark, C.W. 1976. *Mathematical Bioeconomics: The Optimal Management of Renewable Resources*. New York: Wiley–Interscience.

Darwin, C. 1859. *On the Origin of Species by Means of Natural Selection, or, the Preservation of Favoured Races in the Struggle for Life*. London: John Murray.

Dawkins, R. 1976. *The Selfish Gene*. Oxford: Oxford University Press.

Krebs, J.R. and Davies, N.B. 1984. *Behavioural Ecology: An Evolutionary Approach*. 2nd edn, Oxford: Blackwell.

Lotka, A.J. 1925. *Elements of Physical Biology*. Baltimore: Williams and Wilkins.

May, R.M. (ed.) 1981. *Theoretical Ecology: Principles and Applications*. Oxford: Blackwell.

Maynard Smith, J. 1982. *Evolution and the Theory of Games*. Cambridge: Cambridge University Press.

Volterra, V. 1931. *Leçons sur la théorie mathématique de la lutte pour la vie*. Paris: Gauthier-Villars.

Wilson, E.O. 1975. *Sociobiology: The Modern Synthesis*. Cambridge, Mass.: Harvard University Press.

Wynne-Edwards, V.C. 1962. *Animal Dispersion in Relation to Social Behaviour*. Edinburgh: Oliver and Boyd.

biological applications of economics. Both Darwin and Wallace, the two independent discoverers of biological evolution, specifically said that the idea came to them while reading Malthus's work on population. Since Malthus was history's first professor of Economics, this was clearly the most important influence of economics on biology. It is particularly interesting because Malthus's book on population has turned out to have relatively little predictive value in dealing with the human race in the roughly 150 years since it was written, but does fit non-human specie rather well. In a way he was a better biologist than an economist.

Surprisingly, after this promising start, to a large extent, economics and biology developed independently. Herbert Spencer made some use of evolution in his economic work, and other economists – Armen Alchian is the name that comes immediately to mind – have also made use of evolutionary ideas in economics. But until very recently there was almost no evidence of any biological concern with economics. There would be occasional articles in each of these disciplines which would show some minor contact with the other, but the phenomena was of the second or third order of smalls.

This comparative lack of cross stimulation was quite surprising granted the fact that both disciplines involve essentially the same intellectual construct, maximization subject to constraint. If one looks at present-day articles, in the *American Naturalist* and the *American Economic Review*, their superficial resemblance is quite high and their basic structure is also rather similar. In both cases, the standard article consists of application of optimizing methods to predict phenomena in the real world, and then statistical testing. Interestingly, in both cases, these articles normally perform their statistical tests on data which has been collected by other people. In both cases of course, a certain amount of direct data collection either by observation or experiment is present, but basically the dependence is on data provided by others.

In fact, the structural similarity between biology and economics is extremely strong. The evolutionary hypothesis in biology implies quite strongly that individual plants and animals 'act' as if they were attempting to maximize the frequency of their genes in the future. Of course, there is no genuine 'acting'. The dandelion for example, doesn't do anything much. Nevertheless, the selection process together with random changes in the genes, makes the dandelion more and more efficiently adapted to its environment. Of course the other species are also changing so that the environment is continuously changing. It is equivalent to firing at a randomly moving target.

Biologists regularly use language which might imply to the careless reader that animals and plants do consciously make plans and attempt to maximize. This is of course not what the biologist means. The process of actual selection itself functions as a mapping of what in human beings would be a set of conscious if not (as Micheal Ghiselin emphasizes) terribly intelligent decisions.

But although there has been some recent biological interest in economics, the present rather economic appearance of the biological journals is I think an independent development. Once can find clear-cut examples of economic cross-stimulation. For a single example, a four-page note by the present author in the *American Naturalist* collected a grand total of 53 footnote citations in other parts of the biological literature (Tullock, 1971). This was a simple economic explanation for the observed feeding habits of an English bird. Nevertheless, although there are other examples of the same kind of thing, most of the development was independent.

Evidence of this independence was the simple fact that although the general structure of articles in the two journals is very similar, there is an important stylistic difference. Economic articles usually take the form of a theoretical exposition which is entirely deterministic. Statistical theory is then brought in when it is tested with real world data. The biologist usually begins with probabilistic equations. The biological method is clearly more elegant, but also much harder. It is not obvious which is the most efficient research tool, but it is obvious that the biologists have not copied the economists in this area.

That there was a long period in which the two disciplines were operating with rather similar theoretical structures but with almost no cross-stimulation, requires an explanation. The most likely explanation seems to be that from let us say, 1860 until quite recently, most biologists were engaged in cataloguing and understanding the immensely diverse body of species in the world. No one knows exactly how many species there are; the number certainly exceeds ten million and biologists have devoted most of their attention to simply trying to find out what is out there. Darwin's book on barnacles (1851–4) was more typical of 19th- and early 20th-century biological research than his book on evolution.

The diversity of the biological world is almost unbelievable to the non-biologist. Even after a specie has been studied and described and entered into his reference books, the total number of such species is so immense that some may remain totally unknown even to experts in that field. E.O. Wilson, for example, is a very prominent biologist and would be so even if he had never written *Sociobiology* (1975). His special field is non-human societies. The mole-rat, a mammal with a life pattern rather similar to that of social insects, and the social spiders have been catalogued in the formal literature for over fifty years now. In *Sociobiology*, Wilson showed no signs of knowing they even existed. This is not in any sense a criticism of Wilson, but an indication of the real problem posed by the extraordinary diversity of the biological world. Had he decided to go through the entire literature and look for all social species, it would have taken many hundreds of lifetimes.

Be that as it may, there was relatively little contact between the two disciplines until recently, and although there is now more intellectual contact, it tends to be in certain rather applied fields, particularly environmental concerns. Garrett Hardin for example, a prominent biologist concerned with certain environmental problems, reinvented the economics of overgrazing, which he called 'The Tragedy of the Commons'; when it was called to his attention that this was essentially economic, he began a serious study of that aspect of economics. Since then he has worked with economists to produce joint projects in this general area (see, for example, Hardin and Baden, 1977).

This is merely the most significant example of what is now quite a large body of cooperative research on such problems as pollution and environmental degradation. To a considerable extent the economic contribution to this joint research has amounted simply to pointing out that there are costs involved in preserving natural ecologies. Biologists tend to be extremely conservative in their approach to technology. The economist's role is frequently confined to pointing out that human welfare is also involved and suggesting trade-offs.

Another area where economists have for a long time been involved in biology is the specialized subdiscipline of agricultural economics. It should be said however, that in this case cross-fertilization has been rather minor. The basic objective of the professors of agricultural economics in our schools of agriculture has been to improve the returns of the farmers. For this purpose, they have engaged in applied economic research in a number of fields. In general, however, they do not seem to have had any particular influence on the biological research which goes on in the same schools of agriculture. It should also perhaps be said here, that a great many of the agriculture economists devote their time to rationalizing economic subsidy programmes which although they certainly benefit farmers, injure everyone else.

The only other area of application is of course in the field of sociobiology. This has attracted a great deal of attention from economists and other social scientists and hence it is perhaps wise to emphasize here that it is currently only a minor field within the biological disciplines themselves. Nevertheless, it seems an obvious area for application of economics and such applications have been made.

The first problem here is that of territoriality which is frequently confused with the property relations which we find in human society. In fact, the biological specie have no guarantee of ownership and must one way or another defend their territory. The situation thus, is rather similar not to property ownership, but to competing retail establishments in a geographical area. The work of Losch (1937, 1938) is obviously relevant here and biologists have made good use of it. Indeed, the author of this note has contributed a couple of minor communications to the development of this area (Tullock, 1979, 1983). The curious reader can find on page 272 of Wilson's *Sociobiology* a photograph of the Losch hexagons produced by a territorial species of fish.

As we move to more complex social structure it is more difficult to apply economics. Once again, Wilson used linear programming to study the distribution of Castes in the social insects. But an examination of the bibliography of his book will indicate that he was much more influenced by sociology than by economics in his general approach.

The dominance order, another important · organizational structure found in the animal kingdom does not seem to have any direct analogies in economic reasoning. It is of course possible to apply economic analysis to the dominance order, but so far little progress been made along these lines. There is no reason to believe that economics has any comparative advantage here.

The complex societies of the social insects, the mole rats, possibly the social spiders, and certainly the sponges clearly are subject to economic analysis. All of them engage in complex cooperative activity which should be readily amenable to economic analysis. So far the opportunity has appealed to only one economist, the author of this item. Since his manuscript was never published, the field is open to any ambitious pioneer.

Micheal Ghiselin has undertaken a serious project to create an organization which will bridge the gap. So far he has been able to stimulate little interest in either discipline. This is not because of conscious opposition, but because most scholars find themselves too involved in their own discipline to take on the extra work. It is a particularly clear case of the narrow specialization which, unfortunately, dogs the learned professions.

Altogether, the amount of cooperation between economists and biologists is surprisingly small. In spite of similar roots and similar methods, the two disciplines have gone their own ways. In a few areas practical problems have brought them together, and there are occasional cases of the use of tools from one field in the other. This item covers economic applications in biology, but there are examples of reverse influence, the evolutionarily stable strategy, for example. Basically these influences are minor. I would like to say that the situation is changing and that there are signs of greater inter-disciplinary cooperation developing. Unfortunately, this would be to mislead the reader. I hope such developments will occur but the present signs are unfavourable. Economic analysis probably has a greater future in dealing with the communities of the social insects, but so far, little has been done in this area.

GORDON TULLOCK

See also BIOECONOMICS; COMPETITION AND SELECTION; NATURAL SELECTION AND EVOLUTION.

BIBLIOGRAPHY

Darwin, C. 1851 and 1854. *A Monograph of the Sub-Class Cirripedia, with Figures of All the Species.* 2 vols, London: Ray Society.
Darwin, C. 1851 and 1854. *A Monograph of the Fossil Lepadidae; or Pedunculated Carripedes of Great Britain and A Monograph of the Fossil Balanidae and Verrucidae of Great Britain.* 2 vols, London: Palacontographical Society.
Ghiselin, M.T. 1974. *The Economy of Nature and the Evolution of Sex.* Berkeley: University of California Press.
Hardin, G. and Baden, J. 1977. *Managing the Commons.* San Francisco. W.H. Freeman and Company.
Losch, A. 1937. Population cycles as a cause of business cycles. *Quarterly Journal of Economics* 51, August, 649–62.
Losch, A. 1938. The nature of economic regions. *Southern Economic Journal* 5, July, 71–8.
Losch, A. 1964. *The Economics of Location.* Trans. by William H. Woglom, New Haven: Yale University Press.

Tullock, G. 1971. The coal-tit as a careful shopper. *The American Naturalist* 105, January/February, 77–80.

Tullock, G. 1979. On the adaptive significance of territoriality: comment. *The American Naturalist* 113(5), May, 772–5.

Tullock, G. 1983. Territorial boundaries: an economic view. *The American Naturalist* 121(3), March, 440–2.

Wilson, E.O. 1975. *Sociobiology*. Cambridge, Mass.: Belknap Press.

Birck, Laurits Vilhelm (1871–1933). Birck was born on 17 February 1871 in Copenhagen. He took his degree in economics at the University of Copenhagen in 1893, travelled in the United States in 1893 and in Britain and France in 1898–9. He served as a member of parliament and was active in wartime price control and postwar royal commissions on financial collapse and the great depression. He taught economics and public finance at his alma mater 1903–33 and died on 4 February 1933 in Copenhagen.

Birck received the foundations of his theory of value (1902, 1922) from his teacher Harald Westergaard, who in turn had received them from Jevons. Jevonian households were do-it-yourself households engaged in barter, and to Birck their positive and negative utilities remained cardinal to the end. To Jevons Birck added Marshall, whom he considered the greatest name in our discipline. Marshall separated industries from households. By keeping his firms and industries small, he could justify a *ceteris paribus* assumption and consider the supply and demand curves of a competitive industry to be independent of the rest of the economy, and hence of each other. The curves would intersect in two-dimensional, simple and tidy partial equilibria. Birck applied such equilibria to case studies in 1909 and 1915 of 12 important commodities: coffee, flour, grain, kerosene, matches, meat, potash, potatoes, powder, salt, sugar and tobacco. Applied to statistical and historical data, theory – however simple – came to life, and Birck was at his best.

Birck's theoretical method, the numerical example, was exemplified by his massive *Virksomhed* (1927–8) and, in English, by his variation (1927) on Wicksell's theme that the capitalist saver is the friend of labour, though the technical inventor is not infrequently its enemy.

HANS BREMS

SELECTED WORKS

1902. *Værditeori: En Analyse of Begrebet Eftersprøgsel og Tilbud* (Value theory: an analysis of the concept of demand and supply). Copenhagen: Søtofte.

1909. *Sukkerets Historie: En handels- og finanspolitisk Studie* (A history of sugar: a study in trade and public finance). Copenhagen: Gad.

1915. *Vigtige Varer: Deres Fremstilling, Forhandling og Beskatning* (Important commodities: their production, distribution and taxation). Copenhagen: Børsens Forlag.

1922. *The Theory of Marginal Value*. London: Routledge; New York: Dutton.

1927. Theories of over-production. *Economic Journal* 37, 19–32.

1927–8. *Den Økonomiske Virksomhed* (Economic activity). Copenhagen: Gad.

Birmingham School. Thomas Attwood is a signal example of good sense and general intelligence overborne by a futile monetary theory. He was the leader of the 'Birmingham School' who advocated high prices maintained by inflation of the currency. Attwood and his followers taught a lesson needed by some of their contemporaries when they insisted on the hardship inflicted on debtors by a fall in general prices, or rise in the value of the monetary standard. But the extent of the evil was greatly exaggerated when the resumption of specie payments in 1819 was made responsible for almost every trouble which subsequently befell the kingdom – the agricultural distress in England, the turbulence of O'Connell in Ireland, or the 'Rebecca' riots in Wales. The argument directed against the resumption deserves particular attention. It was held that the depreciation of paper with respect to gold just before the resumption was much less than the appreciation of gold with respect to things in general which followed the resumption. 'That measure (which it was said would only effect a charge to the extent of 3 per cent) had imposed an additional burthen of of 25, 30, or 40 per cent on every man in the community in all cases of deed, mortgage, settlement, or contact.' Prof. Walker appears inclined to ascribe some weight to this argument (*Money*, p. 388; *Money, Trade, and Industry*, p. 282).

Thomas Attwood's advocacy of monetary reform derived strength from his political influence. He was the founder of the 'Political Union' at Birmingham and took an active part in the agitation for parliamentary reform. It was believed that Attwood desired political reform principally as a means whereby to obtain a rectification of the currency. To that end he moved in the reformed parliament for a select committee to inquire into the causes of the general distress. This motion, like others which emanated from the Birmingham School, was lost.

Thomas Attwood was greatly assisted in this monetary crusade by his brother Mathias (born 1779, died 1851). Mathias's speech on the currency, 11th June 1822, is placed by Alison with Huskisson's speech on the other side, as 'containing all that ever has, or ever can be, said on the subject'. In 1830 Mathias proposed a double standard of silver and gold; at the rate of $15^{2859}/_{13640}$ lbs. of silver to 1 lb. of gold (Hansard, 1830, vol. xxv, pp. 102–145; Alison, *History of Europe*, 1815–52, vol. iv, ch. xxii. §32). Mathias, unlike his brother, was a Tory. He was a successful banker, co-founder of the National Provincial Bank of Ireland, the Imperial Continental Gas, and other companies. So little is business power alone a guarantee of sound economical theory.

There is an appreciative account of Thomas Attwood and the Birmingham School in a series of letters which were addressed to the *Midland Counties Herald* in 1843 by two Birmingham men (T.B. Wright and J. Harlow) signing themselves Gemini, and were republished in 1844 in the form of a book under that title. The title Gemini was appropriate according to Sir Robert Peel, for 'the efforts of no single writer are equal to the production of so much nonsense' (Speech on the Bank Charter, 1844). According to this par nobile 'the political economy of Mr. Attwood has this one great distinguishing feature, that it releases the nation from the thraldom of the heart-chilling doctrine of Malthus. The world is capable of multiplying its production to an almost unlimited extent; the governments of the world would have only to provide for the proper distribution of the productions, and the wants of all people will be supplied.' Such are the beneficent results of 'accommodating our coinage to man, and not man to our coinage' (Gemini, Letter 24). The cardinal tenets of the 'Birmingham economists' are compendiously stated at page 104, and again at page 285 of Gemini.

There is in the library of the British Museum a life of Thomas Attwood by his grandson, C.M. Wakefield, 'printed for private circulation'; which throws much light on the history of the Birmingham School. Mr. Wakefield does not profess to interpret his grandfather's views on currency.

J.S. Mill devotes a paragraph to the refutation of Attwood's theory of currency (*Political Economy*, book iii. ch. xiii. §4).

[F.Y. Edgeworth]

Reprinted from *Palgrave's Dictionary of Political Economy*.

See also ATTWOOD, THOMAS; PLACE, FRANCIS.

birth-and-death processes. Birth-and-death processes offer a helpful tool in analysing the growth process and the resulting size distribution of entities. The size of an entity is measured by the number of elements that belong to it. The birth-and-death process may comprise both the process by which elements are added to or deleted from the entity as well as to the process in which entities are added to or deleted from the population of entities. Examples of entities and their elements (stated in parentheses) are: cities (residents), firms (employees, customers, sales units, asset units), persons (income units), genera (species), authors (articles published), and words (appearances in a text).

Size distributions of entities have attracted attention because quite frequently empirical data show clear patterns that conform to the Pareto law, a linear relationship between the log of size of an entity and the log of rank of the entity, where rank is measured in such a way that the largest entity in the population has rank 1. Not only does the linearity hold well, especially for larger entities, but also the slope parameter changes little over time and over different regions from which data are taken. Birth-and-death processes help provide possible explanations for this observed regularity (Simon, 1955; Steindl, 1965; Singh and Whittington, 1968).

Birth-and-death processes are, in their basic form, stochastic processes in which the system moves within an ordered set of states, $E_0, E_1, E_2, \ldots$, through a series of transitions from a state E_n to its adjacent state E_{n+1} or E_{n-1} ($n \geqslant 0$ and $n > 0$, respectively), under a given set of transition probabilities that depend only upon the system's current state (Markov processes). If the system is in state E_n at time t, the probability that, between t and $t \pm \Delta t$, (a) the transition $E_n \to E_{n+1}$ occurs is $\lambda_n \Delta t + o(\Delta t)$, (b) the transition $E_n \to E_{n-1}$ ($n > 0$) occurs is $\mu_n \Delta t + o(\Delta t)$, (c) more than one transition occur is $o(\Delta t)$, and (d) no transitions occur is $1 - (\lambda_n + \mu_n)\Delta t + o(\Delta t)$.

The process is called a birth process if the probability of a transition $E_n \to E_{n-1}$ is zero for all $n > 0$. In particular, if λ_n in the birth process is a constant λ for all n, it becomes the Poisson process, which yields the Poisson distribution:

$$p_n(t) = e^{-\lambda t}(\lambda t)^n/n!, \qquad n = 0, 1, 2, \ldots, \tag{1}$$

where $p_n(t)$ is the probability that the system, starting from E_0 at $t = 0$, will be in state E_n at time t.

The above birth process assumes that the system has only a single birth mechanism operating independently of the state the system has attained. In many empirical systems such as those involving biological and economic populations, the expected number of births is often proportional to the size the system has attained. Hence an important special case of the birth process is when λ_n is set equal to λn, where λ is a constant. This leads to the negative binomial distribution:

$$p_n(t) = \binom{n-1}{a-1} e^{-a\lambda t}(1 - e^{-\lambda t})^{n-a}, \quad n \geqslant a, \tag{2}$$

where a (> 0) is the size of the population at $t = 0$. Similarly, the birth-and-death process in which $\lambda_n = \lambda n$ and $\mu_n = \mu n$ leads

to the following distribution:

$$\begin{cases} p_n(t) = \sum_{j=0}^{\min(a,n)} \binom{a}{j}\binom{a+n-j-1}{a-1}\alpha^{a-j}\beta^{n-j}(1-\alpha-\beta)^j, \\ \qquad \text{for } n > 0, \\ p_0(t) = \alpha^a, \end{cases} \tag{3}$$

where

$$\alpha = \{\mu[e^{(\lambda-\mu)t} - 1]\}/[\lambda\, e^{(\lambda-\mu)t} - \mu]$$

and

$$\beta = \{\lambda[e^{(\lambda-\mu)t} - 1]\}/[\lambda\, e^{(\lambda-\mu)t} - \mu]$$

(Bailey, 1964).

Each of the above systems involves only one entity whose distribution in size is at issue or multiple entities that all started at the same time and grow under the identical growth mechanism. But empirically interesting issues often relate to size distributions of entities that start at different times. Such analyses require not only a birth-and-death process of elements but also a birth-and-death process of entities to which elements belong.

If the birth process in which $\lambda_n = \lambda n$, leading to the probability distribution (2), is applied to the birth process of elements and also to the birth process of entities which are all born with size 1 ($a = 1$), the resulting size distribution as $t \to \infty$, is given by:

$$p_n = \rho B(n, \rho + 1). \tag{4}$$

Here, $B(n, \rho + 1)$ is the beta function of n and $\rho + 1$,

$$\begin{aligned} B(n, \rho + 1) &= \int_0^1 \tau^{n-1}(1 - \tau)^\rho \, d\tau \\ &= \Gamma(n)\Gamma(\rho + 1)/\Gamma(n + \rho + 1), \\ & \qquad 0 < n, \quad 0 < \rho < \infty \end{aligned} \tag{5}$$

where Γ is the gamma function and ρ is a parameter given by the ratio of the λ in the entity birth process to the λ in the element birth process. Since $\sum_{i=n}^{\infty} B(i, \rho + 1) = B(n, \rho)$, the distribution function, $F(n)$, cumulative from the right is:

$$F(n) = \sum_{j=n}^{\infty} f(n) = \rho B(n, \rho) = \rho\Gamma(n)\Gamma(\rho)/\Gamma(n + \rho). \tag{6}$$

Using a property of the gamma function, $\Gamma(n)/\Gamma(n + \rho) \to n^{-\rho}$ as $n \to \infty$. Thus, for a large n, $f(n) \to \rho\Gamma(\rho + 1)n^{-(\rho+1)}$ and $F(n) \to \rho\Gamma(\rho)n^{-\rho}$, hence:

$$\log F(n) \sim \log \rho\Gamma(\rho) - \rho \log n, \qquad \text{for large } n, \tag{7}$$

which shows a linear relation on the log–log scale between the size and rank ($F(n)$ times the number of entities in the population) of an entity.

The distribution given by (4) is called the Yule distribution (Yule, 1924). Yule constructed the probability model to explain the distribution of biological genera by numbers of species. However, its wide range of applicability to empirical size distributions in various fields has been recognized, and its properties and variations have been analysed extensively.

At the heart of many 'contagious' phenomena is the so-called Gibrat law of proportionate effect, which says that the expected percentage growth rate in size is independent of the size already attained. The assumption, $\lambda_n = \lambda n$, in (2)–(4) incorporates this law. While Gibrat's law without new entries leads to the log-normal distribution, the law plus a constant rate of entry of unit-size entities has been shown to generate the Yule distribution (Simon, 1955).

Simon and his colleagues have analysed many variations in the birth-and-death process that generate the Yule distribution and closely related distributions. In particular, the robustness of the Pareto law has been demonstrated under a variety of conditions. For example, (1) when all existing entities regardless of size have the same constant death rate, (2) when the entry rate of new entities is not a constant but a decreasing function of time, (3) when existing entities grow in proportion to their 'discounted size', the size whose components are discounted for the passage of time since birth so that entities with more recent growth have a better chance of growing than entities of comparable size but with an older growth history, and (4) when mergers and acquisitions are incorporated in the stochastic process (Ijiri and Simon, 1977), the system's steady state is approximately Pareto.

The birth process under Gibrat's law of proportionate effect is also related to Bose–Einstein statistics, developed to describe the behaviour of physical particles. This statistics is in contrast to Maxwell–Boltzmann statistics under which all m^r arrangements of r elements in m entities have equal probabilities of occurrence – an intuitively acceptable assumption. For example, each of the four arrangements of 2 elements, A and B, in 2 entities, (AB|), (A|B), (B|A), and (|AB), has a 1/4 chance of occurrence. However, modern theory in statistical mechanics has shown that this statistics does not apply to *any* known particles. This observation led to the construction of Bose–Einstein statistics, under which all elements are *in*distinguishable and all distinguishable arrangements of r elements in m entities have equal probabilities of occurrence. Thus, in the above example, each of (**|), (*|*), and (|**) has a 1/3 chance of occurrence as against 1/4, 1/2, and 1/4, respectively, under Maxwell–Boltzmann statistics.

It can be shown that the birth process under Gibrat's law of proportionate effect preserves Bose–Einstein statistics at every iteration of growth. To illustrate briefly, consider two entities (|) each with size 1, where size is defined as *one plus* the number of stars it contains (alternatively the number of spaces delimited by a bar, a star, and/or a parenthesis). A star is thrown in at each iteration, each entity having a probability of receiving the star in proportion to its size. Hence, if the first star lands on the first entity (*|), its chance of receiving the next star becomes twice as large as the second entity. Thus, the probability of obtaining (**|) or (|**) is $1/2 \times 2/3 = 1/3$, leaving (*|*) the remaining 1/3 probability. These are the probabilities under Bose–Einstein statistics.

The birth process may include the birth of entities (throwing in bars) as well as the birth of elements (throwing in stars). For example, at each iteration a bar instead of a star may be chosen with a constant probability. If the bar is thrown in a space giving each space an equal chance of receiving it, an existing entity may be split by the bar, making it more difficult for an entity to attain a large size. The resulting size distribution is a geometric distribution. If the bar is placed only in a space adjacent to an existing bar, thus always creating an entity of a unit size, the resulting size distribution is the Yule distribution as discussed earlier.

Birth-and-death processes offer not only a tool to gain insight into the growth of economic entities but also a basis for policy evaluation on such matters as industrial concentration and mergers and acquisitions.

YUJI IJIRI

See also DYNAMIC PROGRAMMING AND MARKOV PROCESSES; LIFE TABLES; PARETO DISTRIBUTION.

BIBLIOGRAPHY

Bailey, N.T.J. 1964. *The Elements of Stochastic Processes*. New York: Wiley.

Ijiri, Y. and Simon, H.A. 1977. *Skew Distributions and the Sizes of Business Firms*. Amsterdam and New York: North-Holland.

Simon, H.A. 1955. On a class of skew distribution functions. *Biometrika* 52(3/4), December, 425–40.

Singh, A. and Whittington, G. 1968. *Growth, Profitability and Valuation*. Cambridge: Cambridge University Press.

Steindl, J. 1965. *Random Process and the Growth of Firms: A Study of the Pareto Law*. New York: Hafner.

Yule, G.U. 1924. A mathematical theory of evolution, based on the conclusions of Dr. J.C. Willis, F.R.S.. *Philosophical Transactions* Series B, 213, 21-87.

birth rate. *See* FERTILITY.

Black, Duncan (born 1908).   Born on 23 May 1908 in Motherwell, Scotland, Black studied at the University of Glasgow, where he received an MA (Mathematics and Physics) in 1929, an MA (Economics and Politics) in 1932, and a PhD (Economics) in 1937. He also served there as Senior Lecturer in Social Economics, 1946–52. The bulk of his teaching career was at the University College of North Wales, Bangor: Lecturer in Economics, 1934–45; Professor of Economics, 1952–68; and Professor Emeritus 1968 onwards.

Black's very early research was in public finance, of which the major work is Black (1939). It is, however, his work in the 1940s and early 1950s (notably Black, 1948a, 1948b, 1948c, 1949, 1950 and Black and Newing, 1951), work which was integrated and expanded in Black (1958), which is the basis for his status as a father of the modern theory of public choice.

Roughly 200 years ago Condorcet (1785) demonstrated that majority rule need not yield a stable outcome when there are more than two alternatives to be considered. Although periodically rediscovered or reinvented by succeeding generations of scholars, the 'paradox of cyclical majorities' was, for all practical purposes, unknown to modern students of democratic theory until called to their attention by Duncan Black (see especially Black, 1948a, 1958). Black demonstrated that the 'paradox' was not just a mathematical curiosity but rather was connected to important political issues such as manipulability of voting schemes (1958, p. 44; see also 1948a, p. 29) and the absence of strong similarity of citizen preference structures (Black, 1958, pp. 10-14).

> Although Black was not the first to discover this phenomenon, his work is the foundation of all subsequent research on the problem. The investigations in this field of his principal predecessors, Condorcet and Lewis Carroll, had made no impact on the intellectual community of their day and had been completely forgotten. Their work is known today only because Black, after discovering the phenomenon himself, discovered his predecessors (Campbell and Tullock, 1965, p. 853).

Duncan Black's vision in the 1940s was a grand yet simple one: to develop a pure science of politics as a ramified theory of committees, so as to place political science on the same kind of theoretical footing as economics, with voters substituting for consumers. Because many of the basic ideas in his 1958 classic, *The Theory of Committees and Elections*, appear so 'obvious' in retrospect that it is hard to believe that they have not always been part of the stock of general human knowledge, and because this work understates by its silence the magnitude of Black's originality, the magnitude of Black's own contributions is often underappreciated. Black's great strength is that he has served both as synthesizer and pioneer. He rediscovered and reinterpreted for contemporary social science the strikingly modern probabilistic and game theoretic insights of long dead theorists such as Dodgson (Lewis Carroll), Borda and Condorcet (for example, the paradox of cyclical majorities, the Condorcet criterion, the Borda criterion, optimizing strategies under the limited vote, results on manipulability of voting schemes, the Condorcet jury theorem); while himself developing such seminal ideas as single-peakedness, the importance of the median voter given ordinal preferences, and the notion of equilibrium in a spatial voting game (Black and Newing, 1951; Black, 1958, 1967, 1969, 1976). Black's forthcoming biography of Lewis Carroll will emphasize Carroll's contributions to logic and the importance of his work on representation (under his real identity, that of the mathematician C.L. Dodgson) as a precursor to the modern theory of games and economic behaviour.

Underpinning virtually all of Black's work has been the deceptively simple insight of modelling political phenomena in terms of the preferences of a given set of individuals in relation to a given set of motions, the same motions appearing on the preference schedule of each individual, where motions can be represented as points on a real line or in an N-dimensional space. Black's work on what (after him) has come to be called 'the theory of committees and elections' has been 'one of the pillars on which rests the contemporary theory of public choice' (Grofman, 1981).

BERNARD GROFMAN

See also ARROW'S THEOREM; BORDA, JEAN-CHARLES DE; CARROLL, LEWIS; COMMITTEES; CONDORCET, MARQUIS DE; POLITICS AND ECONOMICS; PUBLIC CHOICE; SOCIAL CHOICE; VOTING.

SELECTED WORKS

1939. *The Incidence of Income Taxes*. London, Macmillan; reprinted, New York: A.M. Kelley, 1965.
1948a. On the rationale of group decision making. *Journal of Political Economy* 56(1), February, 23–34.
1948b. The decisions of a committee using a special majority. *Econometrica* 16(3), July, 245–61.
1948c. The elasticity of committee decision with an altering size of majority. *Econometrica* 16(3), July, 262–70.
1949. The theory of elections in single-member constituencies. *Canadian Journal of Economics and Political Science* 14(2), May, 158–75.
1950, 1964. The unity of political and economic science. *Economic Journal* 60, September, 506–14. Reprinted in *Game Theory and Related Approaches to Social Behavior*, ed. Martin Shubik, New York: John Wiley and Sons, 1964.
1951. (With R.A. Newing.) *Committee Decisions with Complementary Valuation*. Glasgow: William Hodge.
1958. *The Theory of Committees and Elections*. Cambridge: Cambridge University Press.
1966. A simple theory of non-cooperative games with ordinal utilities. *Papers on Non-Market Decision Making*, Fall.
1967. The central argument in Lewis Carroll's 'The Principles of Parliamentary Representation'. *Papers on Non-Market Decision Making*, Fall.
1969. Lewis Carroll and the theory of games. *American Economic Review* 59(2), May, 206–16.
1970. Lewis Carroll and the Cambridge Mathematical School of P.R.: Arthur Cohen and Edith Denman. *Public Choice* 8, Spring, 1–28.
1976. Partial justification of the Borda Count. *Public Choice* 28, Winter, 1–15.

BIBLIOGRAPHY

Campbell, C.D. and Tullock, G. 1965. A measure of the importance of cyclical majorities. *Economic Journal* 75, December, 853–7.

Condorcet, N.C. de. 1785. *Essai sur l'application de l'analyse à la probabilité des decisions rendues à la pluralité des voix*. Paris.
Grofman, B. 1981. The theory of committees and elections: the legacy of Duncan Black. In *Towards a Science of Politics: Essays in Honor of Duncan Black*, ed. G. Tullock, Blacksburg: Public Choice Center, Virginia Polytechnic Institute and State University.

black market. *See* SMUGGLING.

Blake, William (*c*1774–1852).   Blake was a member of the Political Economy Club from 1831 until his death, and in 1815–16 President of the London Geological Society (of which his friend Ricardo was also a member). His reputation as an economist was established by his 1810 tract, *Observations on the Principles Which Regulate the Course of Exchange; and on the Depreciated State of the Currency*, which came to be regarded as a standard work on the subject of foreign exchanges. He made the point that the actual (or *computed*) rate of exchange is determined by two different groups of causes. One, the demand and supply of foreign bills in the market, depending on the foreign payments the country has to make. The other, causes only affecting the value of the currency – i.e. the quantity and quality of metal in the coin, and the amount of currency compared with the commodities which have to be circulated by it. The rate of exchange as affected by the former causes he called the *real* exchange, the latter causes would instead affect what he called the *nominal* exchange. The combined effects of the two would determine the actual exchange (1810, p. 481). The distinction (which was then generally accepted: see e.g. Ricardo, *Works*, IV, p. 353) was not entirely well founded, however, because for instance changes in the price level caused by changes in the amount of money in circulation (Blake accepted the quantity theory) would affect the exports and imports of the country, and therefore could be seen as affecting the *real* exchange.

So far as currency questions are concerned, in this first work Blake adopted a straightforward bullionist position. He warned, however, on the dangers of deflation, and insisted that great caution be taken during the return to cash payments (1810, pp. 549 ff.).

In 1823, Blake published a book on the effects of government expenditure, which is more interesting for a modern reader than his 1810 work. He recanted his previous positions on depreciation, and maintained that during the inflation phase of the restriction of cash payments it was not paper to have depreciated, but gold to have risen. His argument was based on the importance of the foreign expenditure of the British government during the war years (a point largely neglected by the bullionists, and particularly by Ricardo). To this expenditure Blake attributed the fall in the exchange during the restriction, and saw the rise in the price of gold as a consequence of this fall (if the price of gold had not risen while the fall in the exchange continued, it would have been profitable to export it, but 'the holder of gold will not part with it, and transfer the power of making the profit to another person, unless at an advance in its price' :1823, p. 15).

He explained the rise in the prices of commodities (other than gold) during the restriction, with the increased *internal* expenditure of the government. In the course of this second argument, he made interesting remarks on government expenditure, and criticisms of the orthodox positions. He rejected the arguments of those who maintained that government expenditure is only a transfer of demand from one channel to another, and that it would be 'derived from a fund that would have been equally a source of demand if it had been left in the hands of the public' (1823, p. 44). He argued that the orthodox reasoning could not account for the great prosperity which during the war had accompanied the enormously increased government expenditure, and maintained that it was only '[i]f ... the productive powers of the country were exerted to the utmost, and there was no means of adding to the gross annual produce', that government expenditure would be made 'at the expense of that fund which has before supplied the capitalist' (pp. 48–9). '[T]he error [of the contrary position] lies in supposing, first, that the whole capital of the country is fully occupied; and, secondly, that there is immediate employment for successive accumulations of capital as it accrues from saving' (p. 54).

Blake's 1823 book caused quite a stir in the orthodox camp. Ricardo intended to write a review of it, but he could not complete it before his death (the unfinished draft and extensive notes on the book, together with Blake's replies, have reached us: see Ricardo, *Works*, IV, pp. 325 ff.). Unfavourable reviews were published by McCulloch in *The Scotsman*, and by the young J.S. Mill in the *Westminster Review*. Malthus, on the other hand, declared himself largely in favour of Blake (Malthus, 1823, p. 72).

A distinguished economist in his own times (he also published a work, in 1839, on the assessment of tithes), he was afterwards almost entirely forgotten. A very short entry (by F.Y. Edgeworth) was devoted to him in Palgrave's *Dictionary*. Viner dismissed him as 'hopelessly confused' (1937, p. 203n), and he is not even mentioned in Schumpeter's *History of Economic Analysis*. Some attention to him is given by Corry (1958, pp. 41–5; see also Tucker, 1960, p. 175).

G. DE VIVO

SELECTED WORKS

1810. *Observations on the Principles Which Regulate the Course of Exchange; and on the Present Depreciated State of the Currency.* As reprinted in *A Select Collection of Scarce and Valuable Tracts and Other Publications, on Paper Currency and Banking*, ed. J.R. McCulloch, privately printed, London, 1857.
1823. *Observations on the Effects Produced by the Expenditure of Government During the Restriction of Cash Payments.* London: Murray.

BIBLIOGRAPHY

Corry, B. 1958. The theory of economic effects of government expenditure in English classical political economy. *Economica* 25, February,34-48.
Malthus, T.R. 1823. *The Measure of Value, Stated and Illustrated, with an Application of It to the Alterations in the Value of the English Currency since 1790.* London: Murray.
Ricardo, D. 1951–73. *The Works and Correspondence of David Ricardo.* Ed. P. Sraffa with the collaboration of M.H. Dobb, 11 vols, Cambridge: Cambridge University Press.
Tucker, G.S.L. 1960. *Progress and Profits in British Economic Thought. 1650–1850.* Cambridge: Cambridge University Press.
Viner, J. 1937. *Studies in the Theory of International Trade.* Reprinted, Clifton: Kelley, 1975.

Blanc, Louis Joseph Charles (1811–1882). For Blanc, the problem of France is that of poverty; it is widespread:

> If there were only exceptional, isolated cases of suffering to alleviate, charity might perhaps be enough. But the causes of suffering are as general as they are profound, and it is by the thousand that one counts those amongst us who are deprived of clothing, food and shelter.

This suffering has its origins in competition which, through its tendency towards monopoly, has created poverty. Blanc

popularized the idea that competition is destructive: workers, competing against each other, lower their wages; manufacturers bankrupt themselves in their struggle against each other. Moreover, the machine, instead of helping workers, only forces large numbers of them into unemployment and further accentuates competition. In contemporary society the liberal thesis is straightforward: increasing the production of goods without taking account of their distribution leaves the fate of the weak at the mercy of chance. Work, which for the majority of people is the basis of their existence, is thrown into disarray and competition becomes systematic destruction rather than economic freedom. It is in no one's interest to maintain such a system because it deceives everyone. Social revolution is the only answer, and it must be undertaken because the existing social order will not last long and because revolution can be accomplished in a peaceful, orderly fashion.

What should be done? As the workers left to their own devices, cannot free themselves from their suffering, it is the duty of the government to help them. It must create workers' production associations, something Buchez had already advocated in 1834. But whereas Buchez thought above all of artisan and small businesses, Blanc had large industries in mind. By forming associations and cooperatives, workers would eventually win control of the means of production.

The State, which accordingly has to be strong, will initiate this movement for reform. It will be the 'poor man's banker'. After all, what can a free, talented man do if he has no capital? There is no liberty without real equality between citizens. The rights won by the Revolution of 1789 have no real force and no power to become effective. The State must distribute credit and so make it possible to create the tools of manufacture. It must set up a loan scheme to establish social workshops (*ateliers sociaux*) in all the main branches of industry.

All workers who so wished could work in these workshops, providing they showed some guarantee of dedication and morality. The hierarchy in these workshops would be established in their first year by the State, thereafter by election. In principal, all wages would be equal. Profits would be divided into three parts, the first to look after the old, the sick and the infirm, the second going towards easing crises in other industries, because all industries should help each other, and the third being set aside to help the workshops to expand by buying tools and instruments.

This socialization of the means of production will be achieved gradually. Private industries will progressively disappear, given the technical and social superiority of the social workshops; in effect, the social workshop constitutes a mode of organization where all workers, without exception, are encouraged to produce quickly and efficiently. The capitalists will not be expelled from the system, but will merely give up of their own accord. Although they may well be able to charge interest on the capital they invest in the workshops, Blanc refuses them any right to the profits, which will go first and foremost to the workers.

Moreover, this greatly increased feeling of cooperation and community would doubtlessly spread beyond the workplace. For Blanc, the 'obvious efficiency and incontestable richness of communal life' will give rise to the voluntary association of needs and pleasures.

Blanc was influenced by Necker and Sismondi but, like Turgot and Condorcet, he believed in progress. He wanted to build a new future without breaking with the past. He was the inventor of what came to be known as state socialism. He made specific that which Saint-Simon, Sismondi and Pierre Leroux had only sketched out. Later, interventionism came to enjoy a great deal of success in France and Germany, where it was propagated by Lassalle. But at the time Blanc was writing, public opinion, dominated by the liberals, thought the State incapable of effective intervention. An example of this is the rejection in 1838 of a bill proposing that the State complete the still largely unfinished railway network, and the decision to entrust this task to private companies. Blanc wanted the State to take this on, and he passionately defended his argument in the newspaper *Le bon sens*.

During the 1848 Revolution Blanc was a member of the Provisional Government and presided over the so-called Luxembourg Commission, which created the national workshops. But these were a mere caricature of his project for social workshops; they did not play their role of manufacture and instruction, and they foundered after disagreements between the members of the Provisional Government. After June 1848 Blanc left Paris and fled to London. He returned to Paris after the fall of the Second Empire in 1871, when he became a member of the National Assembly. He sat on the far Left and declared his opposition to the Commune.

J. WOLFF

SELECTED WORKS

1839. *L'organisation du travail*. Paris.
1841. *L'histoire de dix ans*. Paris.
1848. *Le droit au travail*. Paris.
1847–62. *L'histoire de la Révolution*. Paris.

BIBLIOGRAPHY

Leroy, M. 1946–54. *Histoire des idées sociales en France*. Paris: Gallimard.
Loubère, L.A. 1961. *L. Blanc. His life and his contribution to the rise of French Jacobin Socialism*. Evanston, Ill.: Northwestern University Press.

Blanqui, Jérôme-Adolphe (1798–1854). French labour economist, economic historian and first major historian of economic thought, Blanqui was born in Nice and educated both there and in Paris, subsequently teaching humanities at the Institution Massin. His teaching brought him into contact with J.B. Say, who 'wished him for a disciple' (Blanqui, 1880, p. ix) and to whose chair of political and industrial economy at the Conservatoire des Arts et des Métiers he succeeded in 1833. In addition, he was head of the Ecole Speciale du Commerce from 1830 to 1854, first editor of the *Journal des économistes* and from 1846 to 1848 served as member for Bordeaux in the Chamber of Deputies. In 1838 he was elected to the Académie des Sciences Morales et Politiques. He died in 1854 in Paris, more than a quarter of a century before his notorious younger brother, Louis Auguste, the revolutionary and member of the Paris Commune, with whom he is often confused.

Blanqui was a prolific writer but is now mainly remembered for his *Histoire de l'économie politique en Europe* (1837) which went through five editions. This is generally regarded as the first major history of political economy. In addition to doctrinal history it covered an enormous amount of economic history from the ancient world to the early 1840s. McCulloch (1845, p. 25) states that Blanqui's ancient economic history is 'brief and superficial; but his accounts of the political economy of the middle ages and modern times are more carefully elaborated, interesting and valuable.' Blanqui's treatment of history reflects his support of free trade and sympathy for the working class. Schumpeter (1954, p. 498, n.18) praises Blanqui's 1826 *Resumé de l'histoire du commerce et de l'industrie* as a valuable historical monograph, while his *Précis élémentaire d'économie politique* is also worthy of notice.

PETER GROENEWEGEN

SELECTED WORKS

Blanqui, J.A. 1837. *Histoire de l'économie politique en Europe depuis les anciens jusqu'à nos jours*. English trans. by E.J. Leonard as *History of Political Economy in Europe*, New York: G.P. Putnam's sons, 1880.

BIBLIOGRAPHY

McCulloch, J.R. 1845. *The Literature of Political Economy*. London: LSE Reprint, 1938.
Schumpeter, J.A. 1954. *History of Economic Analysis*. London: Allen & Unwin, 1959.

bliss. *See* OPTIMALITY AND EFFICIENCY; RAMSEY MODEL.

Bloch, Marc (1886–1944). In 1929 Lucien Febvre and Marc Bloch founded the *Annales d'histoire économique et sociale* (now called simply the *Annales*), a review that launched a new school of French historiography. Bloch and Febvre established this journal of sociological history as a '*une arme de combat*' against the traditional political and diplomatic history as taught by Langlois and Seignobos at the Sorbonne. Bloch and Febvre, colleagues at the University of Strasbourg since 1920, formed an ideal intellectual partnership. Febvre was arguably the more imaginative of the two superb scholars. A pioneer in what we now call the history of 'mentalities' and popular culture, Febvre drew upon cultural anthropology in his work a full generation before the 'Annales School' made this discipline one of its closest allies (*Le Problème de l'incroyance au XVIe siècle: la religion de Rabelais*, 1942). Bloch was, above all, a historian of Western agrarian regimes, meticulously explored over a millenium. His work reflects a thorough grounding in all of the historian's tools – archival, linguistic, geographic, archaeological and visual. Bloch was a medievalist by early training and his first work, *Les Rois thaumaturges* (1924) – a history of mentalities in its own right – gave little hint of his developing interest in economic history, a branch of history which had attracted little interest among French historians before Bloch was appointed to the Sorbonne in 1936. Bloch soon created an institute of economic and social history and planned a multiple-volume economic history of Europe, unfortunately never completed, except for his own *Esquisse d'une histoire monétaire de l'Europe* (1954).

Marc Bloch's most impressive achievement was his *Les Caractères originaux de l'histoire rurale Française* (1931), translated into English as *French Rural History*. In this now classic work on French rural society, Bloch traced a thousand years of history, demonstrating the slow evolution of field systems, farm technologies, the peasant household, the village community, communal usages, the incursion into the countryside of Church, State, noble and merchant, and the effects of long-run inflation on the various 'classes' in a complex rural hierarchy. One of Bloch's most original contributions was his linkage of a plough type (the heavy-wheeled plough drawn by heavy oxen or horses) to open elongated fields, which in turn necessitated communal farming and a whole package of collective rights of use. Bloch made a contrasting linkage between the light swing-plough, drawn by light oxen, to the closed irregular fields which necessitated fewer communal usages and led to a more absolute conception of private property. Yet in all of his hypotheses and interconnections, Bloch was extremely modest, always warning the reader of the limits beyond which the sources could not go.

Although his work pre-dates a more recent Annaliste awareness of ethnography and cultural anthropology, Bloch was a human geographer with a keen, even a visual grasp of *milieu* and locale. Appreciative of the work of folklorists such as Van Gennep, Bloch nevertheless preferred to identify the peculiar features of a locale by comparisons, among regions within France to be sure, but also with manors and fields on the other side of the Channel and the Rhine. His initial approach was rather to scrutinize a land survey (*cadastre*) or an aerial photograph of a field system than to 'decode' a village *fête*. At bottom, the 'original character' of French rural society was described by Bloch in structural rather than cognitive terms. Neither symbolic anthropologist nor econometrician, Marc Bloch was a positivist social historian who did not shy away from labels like 'agrarian individualism' when he thought them appropriate.

Marc Bloch's judiciousness, *bons sens*, and fair-mindedness, combined with his profound knowledge of every aspect of the agrarian structure from the 'gleaners of the stubble' to the precise curvature of the moldboard, has created great confidence in his work. This has been further reinforced by his personal testimony about history, especially in his *Métier d'historien* (1949), translated into English as *The Historian's Craft*. Like many of his compatriots, especially among those who have also mastered agrarian history like Georges Lefebvre, Georges Duby or Emmanuel LeRoy Ladurie, Marc Bloch was a model craftsman, not untouched by an underlying passion for the countryside.

R. FORSTER

SELECTED WORKS

1924. *Les rois thaumaturges*. Paris, Strasbourg: Faculté des lettres de l'Université de Strasbourg; London and New York: H. Milford, Oxford University Press. Trans. by J.E. Anderson as *The Royal Touch*, London: Routledge & Kegan Paul, 1973.

1931. *Les caractères originaux de l'histoire rurale française*. Paris; Cambridge, Mass.: Harvard University Press. Trans. by Janet Sondheimer as *French Rural History: An Essay on its Basic Characteristics*, Berkeley: University of California Press, 1966.

1939. *La société féodale*. Paris: A. Michel. Trans. by L.A. Manyon as *Feudal Society*, London: Routledge & Kegan Paul; Chicago: University of Chicago Press, 1961, 2 vols.

1941. *Testament*. Paris.

1946. *L'étrange défaite*. Paris: Société des Éditions Franc-tireur. Trans. by G. Hopkins as *A Strange Defeat: A Statement of Evidence Written in 1940*, London and New York: Oxford University Press, 1949.

1949. *Apologie pour l'histoire ou Métier d'historien*. Paris: Librairie Armand Colin. Trans. by Peter Putnam as *The Historian's Craft*, New York: Vintage Books, 1964.

1954. *Esquisse d'une histoire monétaire de l'Europe*. Paris: A. Colin.

1958. *La France sous les derniers Capétiens, 1223–1378*. Paris: A. Colin.

1960. *Seigneurie française et manoir anglais*. Paris: A. Colin.

1969. *Souvenirs de guerre, 1914–1915*. Paris: A. Colin.

For the principal articles of Marc Bloch, see his *Mélanges historiques* (Paris: SEVPEN, 1963), vols 1–2. See also: Hommages à Marc Bloch, *Annales d'histoire sociale* VII and VIII, 1945.

Bodin, Jean (1530–1596).   Bodin, who was a rival of Machiavelli and a precursor of Montesquieu, was born at Angers, 1530, and died of the plague, at Laon, 1596. His principal work, *De la République* (1577), published originally in French, then translated into Latin by the author himself, has not for its object, as its title might lead the reader to suppose, a panegyric on the republican form of government. While deriving everything from the sovereignty of the people, Bodin admits that the only practical method is the perpetual alienation of this sovereignty in favour of a monarch and his

heirs. He fixes no limits to this alienation, but he desires a 'Gouvernement tempéré sans être démocratique'. States-General like those at Blois (1576), in the deliberations of which he had shared, with more courage and ability than success, are, in his eyes, the proper remedy for an excess of absolute power. This was, in some respects, the representative monarchy of our days. He also supported the idea, developed later by Montesquieu, that climate has a dominant influence on the form of government; theocratic in the south and east, military in the north, free in the countries lying between these. Maintaining resolutely, through conviction, liberty of conscience, he was also a declared opponent of slavery. In political economy he supported principles universally admitted in our days against a *sieur de Malestroit*, who, had it not been for two pamphlets by Bodin, would be perfectly unknown at the present time (*Réponse aux paradoxes de M. de Malestroit touchant l'enchérissement de toutes les choses et des monnaies*, Paris, 1568, and *Discours sur le rehaussement et diminution des monnaies, pour réponse aux paradoxes du sieur de Malestroit*, Paris, 1578). He also published *La Démonomanie* (1587), and other similar works; for, strange as the fact is, this man, of such powerful intellect, was nevertheless a believer in sorcery and witchcraft.

[A.C. FIX]
REPRINTED FROM *Palgrave's Dictionary of Political Economy*.

Böhm-Bawerk, Eugen von (1851–1914).   As civil servant and economic theorist, Böhm-Bawerk was one of the most influential economists of his generation. A leading member of the Austrian School, he was one of the main propagators of neoclassical economic theory and did much to help it attain its dominance over classical economic theory. His name is primarily associated with the Austrian theory of capital and a particular theory of interest. But his prime achievement is the formulation of an intertemporal theory of value which, when applied to an exchange economy with production using durable capital goods, yields a theory of capital, a theory of interest, and indeed a theory of distribution in which the time element plays a crucial role. Both this construction and his equally famous critique of Marx's economics strongly influenced the development of economic theory from the 1880s until well into the 1930s.

Eugen Böhm Ritter von Bawerk was born in Brünn (now Brno) in Moravia on 12 February 1851, the youngest son of a distinguished civil servant who had been ennobled for his part in quelling unrest in Galicia in 1848, and who died in 1856 as deputy governor and head of the Imperial Austrian administration in Moravia. After reading law at the University of Vienna, Böhm-Bawerk entered the prestigious fiscal administration in 1872. In 1875, however, after taking his doctorate in law, Böhm-Bawerk obtained a government grant to do graduate work abroad and prepare himself for a teaching position in economics at an Austrian university, as did his class-mate and future brother-in-law Friedrich von Wieser. He worked for a year at Heidelberg with Karl Knies, and spent a term each at Leipzig, where Roscher taught, and at Jena, where Hildebrand taught. After working for another three years in the fiscal administration and the ministry of finance, he obtained his *Habilitation* (licence to teach) in 1880, and was immediately afterwards appointed to a professorship in economics at the University of Innsbruck which he held until 1889. From a scholarly point of view, Böhm-Bawerk's years in Innsbruck were the most fruitful of his life. A book on the theory of goods, based on his *Habilitation* thesis, appeared in 1881, the first volume of *Kapital und Kapitalzins* in 1884. In 1886 he published a monograph on the theory of value in the most influential German language journal in economics, and in 1889 the second volume of *Kapital und Kapitalzins*. These publications established him as one of the leading members of the group of economists around Carl Menger who came to be known as the 'Austrian School'. In 1889 Böhm-Bawerk preferred an appointment in the Austrian ministry of finance to a chair at the University of Vienna because it carried the assignment to work out a reform of the Austrian income tax. He distinguished himself in the execution of this task, and rapidly rose in rank, obtaining the position of a permanent secretary in 1891, and in 1892 also the vice-presidency of a commission to assess the proposal of a return to the gold standard. Having been appointed minister of finance in a caretaker government in 1893, Böhm-Bawerk was considered to have risen too high to return to his former position when it was replaced by a parliamentary post after a few months, and he was made president of one of the three senates of the Verwaltungsgerichtshof, the highest court of appeal in administrative matters. In 1896 he was again made minister of finance in a caretaker government, but returned once more to the Verwaltungsgerichtshof in 1897. He was yet again appointed minister of finance in 1900, this time in a civil servants' government which fell when he had resigned in 1904 after large increases in military expenditure had been voted which he deemed threatened financial stability. This time he was offered, among other positions, the post of governor of the central bank, the most lucrative position in the monarchy. Yet he turned it down in favour of a chair at the University of Vienna which was especially created for him. Alongside Friedrich von Wieser (who had succeeded Menger in 1902) and Eugen von Philippovich, Böhm-Bawerk lectured on economic theory and conducted a seminar that soon attracted many able students, among them Joseph Schumpeter, Rudolf Hilferding, Otto Bauer, Ludwig von Mises, Emil Lederer and Richard von Strigl. He did not, however, return to the quiet life of a scholar. Having been elected a member of the Austrian Academy of Sciences in 1902, he was elected its vice president in 1907, and its president in 1911. He had also been made a Geheimrat (privy councillor) in 1895, had been appointed to a seat in the upper house of the Austrian parliament in 1899, and was from time to time given various other official assignments. Böhm-Bawerk died on 27 August 1914 at Rattenberg-Kramsach in Tyrol where he had tried to restore his health after having fallen ill on his way to a congress of the Carnegie Foundation in Switzerland as the official Austrian representative.

Böhm-Bawerk was as much a civil servant as a scholar, and in his later years an elder statesman in academic affairs as much as in the public realm of what was still a Great Power. He was extremely successful as an administrator and economic policy maker. But it is for his contributions to economic theory that he is chiefly remembered today. *Kapital und Kapitalzins* has become an economic classic even though it is defective both in construction and exposition. The first edition was written in great haste, and although Böhm-Bawerk responded over-conscientiously and meticulously to almost every criticism in the two further editions which appeared in his lifetime, adding so much material that two slim volumes grew into three massive tomes, he never found the time to rethink the structure as a whole. This absorptive attention to criticism was due to temperament as well as to circumstances. Böhm-Bawerk had a lawyer's mind and found it difficult to think in terms other than disjunct categories or 'cases' which needed to be distinguished sharply and did not fit into a continuum in which things shade into one another. Moreover, writing in a thoroughly anti-theoretical environment dominated by the German Historical School, he felt obliged to take issue and to sharpen differences for the sake of discussion. As a result, Böhm-Bawerk acquired an undeserved reputation as a casuistic and ungenerous controversialist which did much to place his (admittedly in some respects imperfect) contributions in a more critical light than they merit.

The core of Böhm-Bawerk's theoretical endeavours is the development of an intertemporal theory of value, capital and interest. This attempt owes much to his teachers in economics. A.E.F. Schäffle, Menger's predecessor in Vienna, seems to have convinced him that it was necessary to respond on a theoretical plane to the social question, the most pressing economic policy problem of the day, by developing a satisfactory theory of distribution (see Schäffle, 1870). Karl Knies (1873–79) drew his attention to the problems of capital theory and the work of Marx. Carl Menger, finally, provided the starting point for his own theory.

In his *Grundsätze der Volkswirthschaftslehre* (1871), Menger had developed an atemporal theory of value, allocation and exchange. In his exposition and elaboration of that theory, Böhm-Bawerk (1886) strongly emphasized two of its aspects. Firstly, consumer behaviour is sharply distinguished from producer behaviour because only the former can evaluate goods directly; producers can do so only indirectly on the basis of their expectations of consumer's evaluations because production, being roundabout production, is necessarily time-consuming. Secondly, in both cases the evaluation of a commodity involves both the marginal utility of the commodity to the evaluating agent, and the marginal utility of the income available to him. In Böhm-Bawerk's usage, therefore, evaluations are shadow prices, or inverse demand schedules which imply an optimal allocation of commodities in the light of an agent's preferences as well as his income.

On the basis of such inverse demand schedules it was easy to show that the market price of a commodity could not be lower than the lowest price the 'last' buyer is prepared to offer, nor higher than the highest price the 'last' seller demands; here the 'last' seller is defined as the seller whose asking price is low enough to prevent any other seller from selling to the 'last' buyer: and the 'last' buyer as that buyer whose price offer is high enough to prevent any other buyer from buying from the 'last' seller. This definition, complicated as it is, is adapted to include the case of indivisible commodities which Böhm-Bawerk for one reason or another considered relevant.

Böhm-Bawerk also elaborated on Menger's seminal contribution by refining the analysis of distribution: he showed how inputs are evaluated by imputation, i.e. by imputing to them their proper share of the value of the output they help to produce. In essence this amounted to a marginal productivity theory along lines laid down by J.H. von Thünen, but again adapted to his peculiarly Austrian assumptions of limited substitutability and finite divisibility of inputs.

Böhm-Bawerk generalized (in 1889) this theory of price formation in atemporal exchange to include intertemporal exchange by assuming that agents evaluate and trade not only currently available commodities, but also subjectively certain prospects of commodities available in the future. In his theory of goods, Böhm-Bawerk (1881) had shown in a surprisingly modern manner that such prospects exist, and how they can be evaluated. Assuming further that a market exists on which currently available commodities can be exchanged for subjectively certain prospects of commodities available in the future, the same argument can be applied to intertemporal exchange as was applied to atemporal exchange. Böhm-

Bawerk did so in two stages, first considering a pure exchange economy without production, and then analysing an exchange economy with production.

In a pure exchange economy, all agents are consumers. Their inverse demand schedules, Böhm-Bawerk argued, involve for each agent a subjective rate of interest at which he is prepared, given his preferences over time and his (expected) income over time, to exchange subjectively certain prospects of commodities available in the future for the same amount of commodities available in the present. They also, Böhm-Bawerk maintained, typically exhibit positive time preference: commodities available in the present are typically evaluated at higher prices than subjectively certain prospects of the same commodities available in the future. This assertion is contained in the first two of Three Reasons he adduced for the positivity of the rate of interest. The first Reason postulates that the marginal utility of income will decline over the planning horizon because of higher expected incomes in the future. The second Reason postulates that for psychological reasons such as the finiteness of life, the marginal utility of a commodity declines as a rule with the length of time that elapses before it becomes available. As both these postulates have been much disputed it should be added immediately that Böhm-Bawerk regarded them as no more than testable assumptions which he deemed realistic but which admit exceptions. If these postulates are granted for all agents, their subjective rates of interest will always be positive, so that the market rate of interest will always be positive. The same will hold true if only the majority of agents behave according to these postulates. Böhm-Bawerk admitted that not all agents will always behave as postulated by him: but argued that as an empirical regularity they almost always did, and that his theory was applicable also when they did not. All that follows in the latter case is that the rate of interest is not positive. Note, therefore, that Böhm-Bawerk's argument establishes at one and the same time the existence of a (market) rate of interest in a pure intertemporal exchange economy, and identifies as the determinants of its height the relative intensities of the demand for, and supply of, commodities in the present and in the future, as expressed in agent's inverse demand schedules. Of course, these are commodity rates of interest which do not necessarily exhibit any particular term structure, nor uniformity across different types of commodities. Both these properties need the further assumption that intertemporal markets exist for all commodities, and that at least some agents are prepared to engage in arbitrage operations (see Nuti, 1974), Böhm-Bawerk did not explicitly make these assumptions, but he argued as if these properties were assured. Note also that Böhm-Bawerk conceived in this model of a pure exchange economy of the rate of interest as a property of an intertemporal price structure, and not as the specific price for something, be it abstinence, the productivity of money, waiting, or whatever.

In order to extend the model just considered to include production Böhm-Bawerk argued that producers can be shown to have intertemporal inverse demand schedules like consumers, and postulated in his third Reason that producers under-evaluate commodities available in the future on technical grounds. These assertions he derived from his analysis of the nature of production, and the role of capital in it. Production is assumed to be roundabout. It transforms non-produced or 'original' factors of production into consumable output with the help of capital goods which are internal to the production process. Because some capital goods are durable, production takes time. Böhm-Bawerk emphasized strongly the heterogeneity and specificity of capital goods. He

also denied that they can be aggregated into some physical measure for the capital stock; aggregation is in his view possible only by valuing capital goods. He employed a forward-looking measure of capital value in which durable capital goods are valued by the present value of their services, and indeed generalized this procedure to all durable goods by showing that their valuation involves a subjective rate of interest which is equalized when durable goods are traded on markets.

The view of production as roundabout led Böhm-Bawerk to postulate a correspondence between the amounts of different capital goods used in production and the time which elapses before a particular dose of non-produced inputs has matured in the form of consumable output. This correspondence he formalized in the concept of a period of production which is defined as the average period for which the various doses of non-produced inputs required for the production of a unit output remain 'locked up' in the production process. This definition was a mistake which got him into more than one difficulty, and provided material for heated debates. To get round all the difficulties raised in these debates, assume that it is possible to define a period of production as a technical property of a particular production system which does not depend on factor prices; and assume further (with Böhm-Bawerk) that it can be used to order different methods of production in such a way that methods with a longer period of production can be said to be more capital intensive. More specifically, assume a temporal production function which (for a unit output) has only the period of production as argument, and which exhibits diminishing returns but is not homogeneous.

On this basis Böhm-Bawerk formulated a theory of producer behaviour in which competition forces producers to choose production methods that generate just enough output to pay the costs of production. As Böhm-Bawerk showed, this implied a discounted marginal productivity doctrine of (original) factor pricing, and hence the existence of positive quasi-rents at the margin. He also showed that this construction involved inverse demand schedules for capital goods which for each period of production define a profit maximizing rate of interest for given factor prices. At this point in his analysis, Böhm-Bawerk assumed the capital stock of an economy as given, and argued that the profit maximizing rate of profit can be determined with the help of that assumption. While that is correct it was another mistake which was duly seized upon (see e.g. Garegnani, 1960) and which led to many debates. For the value of the capital stock associated with any method of production is an endogenous variable in his construction, as Böhm-Bawerk realized in other contexts. Nor was it necessary to make this assumption. It is sufficient to note that a single producer is forced by competition to pay neither less nor more than the discounted marginal value for the inputs he uses, if a time-consuming roundabout method of production is in operation. Translated into output prices this implies that he under-evaluates output available in the future. This is what Böhm-Bawerk asserted in the third Reason; the technical ground being the method of production in operation. Note that this is not so much a postulate or empirical regularity as it is an equilibrium condition.

Having thus established that producer behaviour can be characterized by derived inverse demand schedules for output which involve positive time preference, Böhm-Bawerk goes on to determine the market rate of interest in what is in effect a macroeconomic general equilibrium model. Attention is centred on the market for output available in the present, and the markets for claims to output available in the future. Supply on the market for output available in the present is fixed by decisions taken in the past; so is the supply available at all future dates whose production has already begun. Demand for output available in the present comes from consumers but will not exhaust supply if they save. Part of these savings will be taken up by other consumers in exchange for claims to output available in the future; transactions are consumption loans, and are likely, on Böhm-Bawerk's assumptions, to imply a positive rate of interest. Another part of savings will be taken up by producers, again in exchange for claims of future output, who use it to bid for more non-produced inputs in an attempt to expand the scale of production. As Böhm-Bawerk assumed that the amount of non-produced original factors is fixed, this results in higher factor prices and a change in the method of production (because higher factor prices can only be sustained if more output is produced). Net savings in the form of loans for productive purposes therefore imply a change in the method of production which, on Böhm-Bawerk's assumptions, implies capital deepening. Both kinds of transactions together determine the market rate of interest, which is thus seen to be determined by intertemporal consumer behaviour as summarized in the notion of positive time preference, and based on intertemporal preferences and the (expected) intertemporal distribution of incomes, on the one hand; and intertemporal producer behaviour as summarized in the period of production and the marginal product of extending it, and based on the intertemporal structure of roundabout methods of production on the other hand. Or, as Böhm-Bawerk put it, the rate of interest is determined by the relative evaluation of (output available in) the present and the future on the part of both, consumers and producers. On his assumptions, this rate of interest is positive.

In some passages Böhm-Bawerk suggested that the rate of interest determined in his model is equal to the marginal product of an extension of the period of production. That created the impression that he had done no more than to establish, in a more roundabout way, what Jevons (1871, ch. vii) had already demonstrated. In other passages, however, Böhm-Bawerk seems to be aware that a change in the method of production involves a change in the value of the capital goods it requires, and that these Wicksell (or revaluation) effects imply that the rate of interest is less than the marginal product of an extension of the period of production. Böhm-Bawerk also obscured his argument by introducing the concept of a subsistence fund, thereby suggesting that his theory was no more than a revamped wages fund theory. Neither these nor other infelicities in his exposition should obscure the fact, however, that the hard core of his argument is the determination of the rate of interest as the property of an intertemporal price structure which in turn is determined by an intertemporal theory of value and allocation in consumption and production.

Böhm-Bawerk's model consciously referred to a stationary state as he wished to show that the rate of interest has something to do with the efficient allocation of resources in stationary as well as in non-stationary states. This comes out most clearly when he considers a socialist economy and demonstrates that it would require a positive rate of interest as does a capitalist economy. He did, however, consider non-stationary states in an interesting comparative static analysis of the effects of an increase in savings, and of technical progress. That he obtained a positive rate of interest in a stationary state is of course due to his assumptions, and no contradiction to Schumpeter's argument (1912) which is based on a somewhat different model (see Böhm-Bawerk (1913) for a discussion of these differences).

The argument sketched on the preceding pages is expounded in Böhm-Bawerk's *Positive Theory* (1889) which he prefaced by a 'History and Critique of Interest Theories' (1884) in which he critically examined earlier (and in later editions also contemporary) attempts to explain the rate of interest. The purpose of this volume has often been misunderstood. It is not a history of the subject which generously corrects mistakes, nor an attempt to differentiate his own product. Rather it is a 'negative theory' (Edgeworth): an attempt to survey the building blocks for his own theory and to pinpoint the pitfalls a satisfactory theory should avoid. Yet it cannot be denied that it is often over-critical. Thus Böhm-Bawerk shows again and again that the rate of interest cannot be said to be *determined by* marginal productivity considerations, but does not add that these nevertheless have a role to play in a more complete explanation. A similar omission occurs when he discusses abstinence or more generally intertemporal preferences.

One of the conclusions Böhm-Bawerk drew from his demonstration is that the existence of the rate of interest is not due to exploitation. It is obvious that on his argument workers can get the whole product of labour only if production were instantaneous. As long as production is roundabout, the present value of the workers's share in the value of the output they have helped to produce is necessarily less than what it would be if production were instantaneous. This is due, of course, to the existence of capital; but Böhm-Bawerk argued that interest would have to be paid irrespective of who owns such capital goods. That was also the gist of his critique of Marx's economics (1896), in which he singled out the labour theory of value as the basis of all errors. Böhm-Bawerk was (apart from Schäffle and Knies) one of the first economists to discuss Marx's economics on a scholarly plane; but he remained curiously blind to Marx's critique of the social institutions of a capitalist society. Although his critique drew a long reply from one of his students (Hilferding, 1904) it was very influential and remained the best analytical performance of its kind until well into the 1950s (see Sweezy, 1949).

Böhm-Bawerk's single-minded concentration on economic phenomena is also evident in his discussion of the role of economic power on markets (1914): in the short run, he argued, economic power may cause deviations from the state of affairs as defined by economic forces; in the long run, however, the latter will prevail. Again he was blind to any changes economic power may cause to the environment in which economic forces operate.

The impact of Böhm-Bawerk's work was immense, but its reception was made difficult by its prolixity and its technical defects, which offered many openings to critics. In essence, Böhm-Bawerk combined elements of neoclassical economic theory with elements of classical economic theory. He was neoclassical in his concern with rational economic behaviour and its consequences for the demand and supply of commodities, their pricing on markets, the forces which bring about equilibrium on markets, and the interaction of different markets. By contrast, classical lines of thought predominate in Böhm-Bawerk's analysis of production. However much he denied any adherence to classical cost theories of value, his view of production and the role of capital and time in it bear the mark of the Ricardian tradition.

The neoclassical part of his argument, in particular his analysis of intertemporal consumer behaviour, was taken up by Irving Fisher (1907, 1930) and developed into a theory of interest which is based on the notion of time preference (which

Fisher transformed into a property of utility functions) and the concept of investment opportunities; these Fisher assumed rather than derived, thus cutting away Böhm-Bawerk's analysis of production and the role of capital in it. In this form, which admittedly offers insights into the problem of intertemporal allocation Böhm-Bawerk did not offer, Böhm-Bawerk's intertemporal theory of exchange became part of the heritage of orthodox neo-neoclassical economic theory.

The more classical part of Böhm-Bawerk's model was taken up and elaborated by Wicksell (1893, 1901). In an attempt to free it of its classical garb, Wicksell turned it into a marginal productivity theory of the rate of interest. He ran into difficulties, however, not only over the proper definition of the period of production, but also because his neglect of what Böhm-Bawerk had to say about intertemporal consumer behaviour forced him to assume a given capital stock in order to close his model. Wicksell used what had by then become the standard neoclassical concept of capital as a value sum, as proposed by J.B. Clark (1899), and (with good reason) combatted by Böhm-Bawerk (see Hennings 1986b). The shortcomings of such an argument, which was before long imputed to Böhm-Bawerk himself, were soon pointed out (see Cassel, 1903, and Garegnani, 1960). Nevertheless Wicksell's interpretation became the standard version of the 'Austrian' theory of capital and interest (see e.g. Lutz, 1956; Dorfman, 1959a, 1959b; Hirshleifer, 1967).

In the 1930s various attempts were made to reformulate Böhm-Bawerk's theory in such a way that it could be used as the basis of a theory of the short-run behaviour of an economy, particularly by Hayek (1931, 1939; and see Hicks, 1967), but also by Hicks (1939, parts iii and iv). This led to an intensive debate in which especially the capital theoretic foundations of his argument were examined, and found wanting (see Kaldor, 1947, and Reetz, 1971, for a survey). There were some attempts at reconstruction (Eucken, 1934; and Strigl, 1934), but the definition of the period of production provided a major stumbling block. At the same time, Hayek and Knight repeated the debate between Böhm-Bawerk and Clark about the concept of capital on a somewhat different level. Finally Hayek (1941) made a major attempt to get round the difficulties the debate had shown up, and achieved some advances: but in the end his contribution turned out to be the final word that did not persuade anybody. The major difficulty which he did not manage to overcome was the fact that Böhm-Bawerk's construction does not lend itself to dynamic analysis precisely because his classical, macroeconomic approach to production and the role of capital requires an equilibrium approach, and does not provide a suitable basis for a discussion of producer behaviour out of equilibrium, and its dynamics.

More recent restatements of Böhm-Bawerk's argument consequently emphasize its static nature (Weizäcker, 1971; Faber, 1979), but do not really go beyond an exact formulation, in terms of modern capital theory, of some aspects of his theory. By contrast, Hicks (1973) is an innovative attempt to salvage some of the salient features of Böhm-Bawerk's view of production and capital, especially his emphasis on the role of time in production processes, in a modern framework which once more attempts to formulate a dynamic analysis (see also Belloc, 1980; or Magnan de Bornier, 1980). It centres on the concept of a 'transition' from one steady state to another, i.e. a more long-term kind of economic dynamics than was considered in the 1930s; this is a promising approach which proves the vitality of Böhm-Bawerk's ideas.

Böhm-Bawerk posed a problem which had not been seen before in its full importance: the role of the rate of interest in the choice of an optimal method of production when production is roundabout, and its determination in a theory which takes seriously the impossibility to aggregate capital goods in physical terms. The solution he proposed is not without problems. But however much economic theory has progressed, some parts of his argument stand out as landmarks in the development of economic thought. Among them are his discussion of price formation on markets, especially those on which indivisible or finitely divisible commodities are traded, his analysis of time preferences, his analysis of intertemporal exchange, and his demonstration that the rate of interest is no more than a property of intertemporal price structures. His definition of the period of production turned out to be a cul-de-sac, but the possibilities his analysis of the role of time in production offers do not yet seem to have been exhausted.

Finally, the importance of his emphasis on the value aspect of the notion of aggregate capital and its implications has only recently been recognized as a seminal contribution. He can perhaps no longer be accorded the stature of a Ricardo or Marx. But the vitality of his ideas still ranks him among the great economists.

K.H. Hennings

See also AUSTRIAN SCHOOL OF ECONOMICS; PERIOD OF PRODUCTION; ROUNDABOUT METHODS OF PRODUCTION; VALUE AND PRICE.

SELECTED WORKS

1881. Rechte und Verhältnisse vom Standpunkte der volkswirtschaftlichen Güterlehre. Innsbruck: Wagner. Trans. as 'Whether legal rights and relationships are economic goods' in Böhm-Bawerk (1962).
1884. Kapital und Kapitalzins. Erste Abteilung: Geschichte und Kritik der Kapitalzins-Theorien. Innsbruck: Wagner. 2nd edn, 1900; 3rd edn, 1914; 4th edn, Jena: Fischer, 1921. Translation of 1st edn as Capital and Interest, London: Macmillan, 1890. Translation of 4th edn as Capital and Interest, vol. 1. South Holland, Ill.: Libertarian Press, 1959.
1886. Grundzüge der Theorie des wirthschaftlichen Güterwerthes. Jahrbücher für Nationalökonomie und Statistik 13, 1–82 and 477–541. Reprinted separately, London: London School of Economics, 1932.
1889. Kapital und Kapitalzins. Zweite Abteilung: Positive Theorie des Kapitales. Innsbruck: Wagner. 2nd edn, 1902; 3rd edn in two volumes 1909 and 1912; 4th edn in two volumes, 1921, Jena: Fischer. Translation of 1st edn as The Positive Theory of Capital, London: Macmillan 1891. Translation of 4th edn as Capital and Interest, vols. 2 and 3, South Holland, Ill.: Libertarian Press.
1896. Zum Abschluss des Marxschen Systems. In Staatswissenschaftliche Arbeiten, Festgaben für Karl Knies, ed. O. von Boenigk, Berlin: Haering. Trans. as Karl Marx and the Close of his System, London: Fisher Unwin, 1898. Reprinted in Sweezy (1949). Also trans. as 'Unresolved contradictions in the Marxian economic system' in Böhm-Bawerk (1962).
1913. Eine 'dynamische' Theorie des Kapitalzinses. Zeitschrift für Volkswirtschaft, Socialpolitik und Verwaltung 22, 520–85 and 640–57.
1914. Macht oder ökonomisches Gesetz? Zeitschrift für Volkswirtschaft, Socialpolitik und Verwaltung 23, 205–271.
1924. Gesammelte Schriften, ed. F.X. Weisz, Vienna and Leipzig: Hölder-Pichler-Tempsky.
1926. Kleinere Abhandlungen über Kaptial und Zins. Vienna and Leipzig: Hölder-Pichler-Tempsky.
1962. Shorter Classics. South Holland, Ill.: Libertarian Press.

BIBLIOGRAPHY

Belloc, B. 1980. Croissance économique et adaption du capital productif. Paris: Economica.
Cassel, G. 1903. The Nature and Necessity of Interest. London: Macmillan.
Clark, J.B. 1899. The Distribution of Wealth. New York: Macmillan.

Dorfman, R. 1959a. A graphical exposition of Böhm-Bawerk's interest theory. *Review of Economic Studies* 26, 153–8.

Dorfman, R. 1959b. Waiting and the period of production. *Quarterly Journal of Economics* 73, 351–72.

Eucken, W. 1934. *Kapitaltheoretische Untersuchungen.* 2nd edn, Tübingen: Mohr.

Faber, M. 1979. *Introduction to Modern Austrian Capital Theory.* Berlin: Springer.

Fisher, I. 1907. *The Rate of Interest.* New York: Macmillan.

Fisher, I. 1930. *The Theory of Interest.* New York: Macmillan.

Garegnani, P. 1960. *Il capitale nelle teorie della distribuzione.* Milan: Giuffrè.

Hayek, F.A. von. 1931. *Preise und Produktion.* Vienna: Springer. Trans. as *Prices and Production*, London: Routledge.

Hayek, F.A. von. 1939. *Profits, Interest and Investment.* London: Routledge.

Hayek, F.A. von. 1941. *The Pure Theory of Capital.* London: Routledge.

Hicks, J.R. 1939. *Value and Capital.* Oxford: Clarendon Press.

Hicks, J.R. 1967. The Hayek story. In J.R. Hicks, *Critical Essays in Monetary Theory*, Oxford: Clarendon Press.

Hicks, J.R. 1973. *Capital and Time.* Oxford: Clarendon Press.

Hilferding, R. 1904. Böhm-Bawerks Marx-Kritik. In *Marx Studien* 1, ed. M. Adler and R. Hilferding, 1–61. Trans. as 'Böhm-Bawerk's criticism of Marx' in Sweezy (1949).

Hirshleifer, J. 1967. A note on the Böhm-Bawerk/Wicksell theory of interest. *Review of Economic Studies* 34, 191–9.

Jevons, W.S. 1871. *The Theory of Political Economy.* London: Macmillan.

Kaldor, N. 1937. Annual survey of economic theory: the recent controversies on the theory of capital. *Econometrica* 5, 201–33.

Knies, K. 1873–9. *Geld und Credit.* 3 vols, Berlin: Weidemann'sche Buchhandlung.

Kuenne, R.E. 1971. *Eugen von Böhm-Bawerk.* New York and London: Columbia University Press.

Lutz, F.A. 1956. *Zinstheorie.* Tübingen: Mohr. Trans. as *The Theory of Interest*, Dordrecht: Reidel, 1967.

Magnan de Bornier, J. 1980. *Economie de la traverse.* Paris: Economica.

Menger, C. 1871. *Grundsätze der Volkswirthschaftslehre.* Vienna: Braumüller. Trans. as *Principles of Economics*, Glencoe, Ill.: Free Press, 1951.

Nuti, D.M. 1974. On the rates of return of investment. *Kyklos* 27, 345–69.

Reetz, N. 1971. *Produktionsfunktion und Produktionsperiode.* Göttingen: Schwartz.

Schäffle, A.E.F. 1870. *Kapitalismus und Sozialismus.* Tübingen: Laupp.

Schumpeter, J.A. 1912. *Theorie der wirtschaftlichen Entwicklung.* Leipzig: Duncker & Humblot. Trans. as *The Theory of Economic Development*, Cambridge, Mass.: Harvard University Press, 1934.

Schumpeter, J.A. 1914. Das wissenschaftliche Lebenswerk Eugen von Böhm-Bawerks. *Zeitschrift für Volkswirtschaft, Socialpolitik und Verwaltung* 23, 454–528. Trans. as ch. 6 in *Ten Great Economists*, ed. J.A. Schumpeter, London: Allen & Unwin, 1952.

Schumpeter, J.A. 1925. Eugen von Böhm-Bawerk. *Neue österreichische Biographie 1815–1918*, 2, 63–80.

Stigler, G.J. 1941. *Production and Distribution Theories.* New York: Macmillan.

Strigl, R. von. 1934. *Kapital und Produktion.* Vienna: Springer.

Sweezy, P.M. (ed.) 1949. *Karl Marx and the Close of his System by Eugen von Böhm-Bawerk and Böhm-Bawerk's Criticism of Marx.* New York: Kelley.

Weizsäcker, C.C. von. 1971. *Steady State Capital Theory.* Berlin: Springer.

Wicksell, K. 1893. *Über Wert Kapital und Rente nach neueren nationalökonomischen Theorien.* Jena: Fischer. Trans. as *Value, Capital and Rent*, London: Allen & Unwin, 1954.

Wicksell, K. 1901. *Föreläsningar i Nationalekonomi.* Vol. I: *Teoretisk Nationalekonomi.* Lund: Berlinska Boktryckeriet. Trans. as *Lectures on Political Economy*, Vol. 1, *General Theory*, London: Routledge, 1934.

Wicksell, K. 1911. Böhm-Bawerks kapitalteori och kritiken därav. *Ekonomisk Tidskrift* 13, 39–49. Trans. in K. Wicksell, *Selected Papers on Economic Theory*, London: Allen & Unwin, 1958.

Wicksell, K. 1914. Lexis och Böhm-Bawerk. *Ekonomisk Tidskrift* 16, 294–300, 322–34.

Boisguilbert, Pierre le Pesant, Sieur de (1645–1714). French economist and lawyer. Born at Rouen into a *noblesse de robe* family, Boisguilbert was educated at a Jesuit college in Rouen, the city where he spent most of his life and where he died in 1714. The famous Port Royal and the Paris law school trained him as an *avocat* but initially inspired a literary career. This produced translations from the Greek (Dion Cassius and Herodotus) and some historical novels, one of which, *Marie Stuart, Reyne d'Ecosse* (1675) went through three editions. Marriage to a rich heiress in 1677 allowed him to pursue profitable activities in trade and agriculture for several years and enter the magistrature of Normandy. Such experiences brought home to him the deteriorating French economic position and the need to reverse this through fiscal and economic reform. His first economic work, *Le détail de la France* (1695) reflects these concerns. For the remainder of his life he unsuccessfully pressed plans for fiscal reform on various finance ministers, ultimately republishing his ideas, including the new *Factum de la France*, in various collected editions from 1707 (a detailed biography and bibliography is in Boisguilbert, 1966).

Boisguilbert is largely remembered as a precursor of the Physiocrats and as the economist whom Marx (1859, p. 52) linked with Petty as marking the start of classical political economy. His influence was undoubtedly more extensive: much of Cantillon's (1755) circular flow analysis appears inspired by his work; while Roberts (1935, pp. 273–320) argues for considerable similarity between his fundamental economic ideas and some of Adam Smith's. A wealth of embryonic tools and concepts can be found in his work and include:

> division of labour, circular flow, velocity of money, hoarding, confidence, the multiplier, and variability of employment, supply and demand, diminishing utility, elasticity of demand, natural and market price, price variability, price flexibility, cobweb price-model, cost of production, diminishing returns, labour supply curve, bargaining range, impulse propagation, economic equilibrium, optimum and suboptimum price structures, and competition (Spengler, 1984, p. 77).

Tax criteria and class analysis need to be added to this list.

Boisguilbert's economic analysis ascribes France's economic distress to agricultural ruin from Colbert's edict prohibiting corn exports; excessive taxation worsened by tax farming; and financiers' power transforming money from a servant of trade into its tyrant. Underlying this diagnosis are models of equilibrium trade demonstrating the interdependence of the 200 occupations and professions exchanging their products at prices proportioned to necessary costs of production including a just profit. Hence buying, as the essential counterpart of selling and consumption, stimulates production. Disruptions to consumption prevent prices from covering costs, thereby initiating a downward spiral which ends in economic stagnation. Three causes for such disruptions are identified: low agricultural prices which lower rent and hence landlords' consumption demand; second, concentration of money among rich financiers leading to hoarding; third, lower consumption potential from excessive taxation. Since the livelihood of the poor depends on the consumption of the rich, unemployment and misery follow.

Boisguilbert's remedy follows from his identification of these causes of underconsumption. Free trade and encouragement of agriculture lead to a 'proper' corn price, conducive to high rents and consumption spending. Tax reform achieved by introducing a general proportional income tax removes the problem of excessive taxation and eliminates hoarding and leakages from the circular flow because the abolition of tax farming ends concentrated financier power. Subsequent encouragement of consumption allows prosperity to return and creates wealth for both the state and its citizens. Basic model, diagnosis and remedy are present with varying degrees of sophistication in Boisguilbert's major works, including *Traité de la nature, culture, commerce et intérêts des grains* (1704a) and *Dissertation de la nature des richesses, de l'argent et des tributs* (1704b), to name those not so far mentioned.

PETER GROENEWEGEN

SELECTED WORKS

1695. *Le détail de la France*. Reprinted in Boisguilbert (1966), 581–662.
1704a. *Traité de la nature, culture, commerce et intérêt des grains, tant par rapport au public, qu'à toutes les conditions d'un état*. Reprinted in Boisguilbert (1966), 827–78.
1704b. *Dissertation de la nature des richesses, de l'argent et des tributs, ou l'on découvre la fausse idée qui règne dans le monde à l'égard de ces trois articles*. Reprinted in Boisguilbert (1966), 973–1012.
1707. *Factum de la France*. Reprinted in Boisguilbert (1966) 879–956.
1966. *Pierre de Boisguilbert ou la Naissance de l'économie politique*. Paris: Institut National d'Etudes Demographiques.

BIBLIOGRAPHY

Cantillon, R. 1755. *Essai sur la nature du commerce en général*. London: Fletcher Gyles. Reprinted with an English translation and other material by Henry Higgs, London, for the Royal Economic Society, 1931.
Marx, K. 1859. *Contribution to the Critique of Political Economy*. With a new introduction by Maurice Dobb, London: Lawrence & Wishart, 1971.
Roberts, H. Van Dyke. 1935. *Boisguilbert, Economist of the Reign of Louis XIV*. New York: Columbia University Press.
Spengler, J.J. 1984. Boisguilbert's economic views vis-à-vis those of contemporary *réformateurs*. *History of Political Economy* (16)1, Spring, 69–88.

Bonar, James (1852–1941). Born at Collace in Perthshire (Scotland) on 27 September 1852, Bonar managed to combine a life-long career as a civil servant with the study of the history of economic thought, where his work focused on Smith, Ricardo, and especially Malthus. Somewhat ironically, given its rather poor reception at the time, his *Philosophy and Political Economy* (1893) is the book by which he is now principally remembered. Like Adam Smith, after graduating from Glasgow University, Bonar went as Snell Exhibitioner to Balliol College, Oxford, taking a first in 1877 and 'rounding-off' his studies at Leipzig and Tübingen (Shirras, 1941, p. 146). Afterwards he removed to the contrasting environment of the East End of London, lecturing there for three years as one of the pioneers of the University Extension Movement and founding an Adam Smith Club to promote the popular discussion of economic matters. In 1881 he joined the Civil Service, in which he remained until his retirement in 1919. From 1907 he was Deputy Master of the Royal Mint in Ottawa.

Bonar's early services to Ricardo scholarship were rendered in two compilations of correspondence: *Letters of David Ricardo to Thomas Robert Malthus: 1810–1823*, and *Letters of David Ricardo to Hutches Trower and Others: 1811–1823*, published in 1887 and 1899 respectively (the latter jointly with Jacob Hollander). In neither instance was Bonar able to recover the 'missing' Malthus and Trower letters which were not unearthed until the discovery of the so-called 'Ricardo Papers' in 1930. These are now published in Sraffa's edition of Ricardo's *Works and Correspondence*. In the Bonar edition of the letters to Malthus a number of errors of dating occurred, giving a rather misleading picture of the temporal development of Ricardo's work – most of these errors arose, it seems, from a mis-reading of Ricardo's handwriting, where the number '3' closely resembles a broken '0' (see Keynes, 1933, p. 112 n.2 and Sraffa, 1951–73, vol. VI, p. xxi n.1).

To Smithiana, Bonar bequeathed *A Catalogue of Adam Smith's Library* (1894), a handsomely printed volume even by the standards of the day, and *The Tables Turned* (1926), an imaginary discussion whose participants included (in addition to Smith), Ricardo, Malthus, Mill and Marx. It is difficult to believe that Bonar could have anticipated the quite extraordinary bout of antiquarianism that infected Smith studies as a consequence of the appearance of his catalogue. Around the substantive question of the extent of the direct indebtedness of Smith to Physiocracy (and, particularly, to Turgot) – where the content of the library is one quite minor piece of evidence – there sprang up an industry designed to track down, it would seem, every last item. The bug infected not only Scottish writers, but also American and Japanese economists, much to the detriment of obtaining a satisfactory answer to the original question.

Bonar's enthusiasm for Malthus (his 'services to general theory are at least equal to Ricardo's', 1885, p. vii) was rivalled only by that of Keynes. Aside from two books (1881 and 1885), his entry in Palgrave's *Dictionary*, and an *Economic Journal* article (1929), Bonar was engaged for much of his life on a full-scale intellectual biography of Malthus. How far this might have advanced the understanding of Malthus's contribution is impossible to say. However, since Bonar's published writings on Malthus appeared before both the discovery of Malthus's side of the Ricardo correspondence (in 1930) and Keynes's celebrated essay on Malthus (in 1933), the availability of additional material could hardly have failed to lead Bonar into new fields of interpretation.

While it was largely the above-mentioned works that secured Bonar's reputation during his lifetime – leading to honorary degrees from Glasgow and Cambridge, and election to the British Academy – much of it has now been superseded. His *Philosophy and Political Economy*, however, has proved more resistant to the passage of time. Its discussion of utilitarianism, for example, can still be read with profit. In places, Bonar's command of things 'German' – from Kant, Fichte and Hegel down to Richard Wagner – is impressive. Furthermore, with an early article (1888–9) and an entry for Palgrave's *Dictionary of Political Economy*, Bonar is credited in some circles with introducing the work of the Austrian School to an English-speaking audience.

At the age of sixty, Bonar climbed the Wetterhorn (3708 m) in a snowstorm – a feat which pales into insignificance when measured against the effort it must have required to complete upwards of seventy entries for the original edition of this Dictionary. He died on 18 January 1941 at the age of eighty-eight; his 'definitive' biography of Malthus (Keynes, 1933, p. 81n), the manuscript of which Shirras claimed to 'have with him' in 1941 ready for post-war publication, remains unpublished.

MURRAY MILGATE AND ALASTAIR LEVY

SELECTED WORKS

1881. *Parson Malthus*. Glasgow: James Maclehose.
1885. *Malthus and his Work*. London: Macmillan; 2nd edn, London: G. Allen & Unwin, 1924.

1887. *Letters of David Ricardo to Thomas Robert Malthus: 1810–1823*. Oxford: Clarendon Press.

1888–9. Austrian economists and their view of value. *Quarterly Journal of Economics* 3, October, 1–31.

1893. *Philosophy and Political Economy*. London: Swan Sonnenschein & Co; 4th edn, London: G. Allen & Unwin, 1927.

1894. *Catalogue of Adam Smith's Library*. London: Macmillan; 2nd edn, 1932.

1899. (With J.H. Hollander.) *Letters of David Ricardo to Hutches Trower and Others: 1811–1823*. Oxford: Clarendon Press.

1922. Knapp's theory of money. *Economic Journal* 32, March, 39–47.

1926a. Memories of F.Y. Edgeworth. *Economic Journal* 36, December, 647–53.

1926b. *The Tables Turned. A Lecture and Dialogue on Adam Smith and the Classical Economists*. London: P.S. King & Sons.

1929. Ricardo on Malthus. *Economic Journal* 39, June, 210–18.

1931. *Theories of Population from Raleigh to Arthur Young*. London: G. Allen & Unwin.

BIBLIOGRAPHY

Keynes, J.M. 1933. *Essays in Biography*. London: Macmillan. In the *Collected Works of John Maynard Keynes*, Vol. X, London: Macmillan, 1972.

Shirras, G.F. 1941. James Bonar. *Economic Journal* 51, April, 145–56.

Sraffa, P. (ed.) 1951–73. *The Works and Correspondence of David Ricardo*, 11 vols. Cambridge: Cambridge University Press.

bonds. A bond is a contract in which an issuer undertakes to make payments to an owner or beneficiary when certain events or dates specified in the contract occur. The term has medieval origins in a system where an individual was bound over to another or to land. Subsequently, goods were put in a bonded warehouse until certain conditions (e.g. payments of taxes or tariffs) were satisfied; individuals were released from jail when a bail bond guaranteeing their appearance in court was supplied; and individuals were allowed to perform certain tasks when a surety or performance bond guaranteeing satisfaction was provided. Governments and individuals have borrowed from others since earliest recorded history, as Sumerian documents attest. Perhaps public bonds first appeared in modern form with the establishment of the Monte in Florence in 1345. Monte shares were interest bearing, negotiable, and funded by the Commune.

In contemporary economic discourse, a bond is commonly understood to be a debt instrument in which a borrower, typically a government or corporation, receives an advance of funds and contracts to make future payments of interest and principal according to an explicit schedule. The remainder of this entry focuses exclusively on these debt instruments. Terms of bonds are designed to protect the rights of borrowers and creditors; they are heterogeneous and their interpretations and enforceability vary across legal jurisdictions.

The distinction between bonds and other evidences of debt such as loans or notes is inherently arbitrary and imprecise. Bonds tend to have rather long specified maturities when issued, or none at all in the case of consols. However, issuers may reserve the right to call them after they have been outstanding for a specified time interval. While bonds ordinarily convey no equity stake in an enterprise, some corporate bonds include a clause that allows bondholders to convert bonds to shares of the issuer's common stock at a specified conversion value. Formulas for determining the values of such options are discussed by Black and Scholes (1973).

Bonds tend to be negotiable and can usually be traded on an established secondary market. Once bonds are issued, bondholders are strategically vulnerable to actions of a firm's management, equity holders, and short-term lenders as has been argued by Bulow and Shoven (1978), especially if an issuer's financial condition deteriorates. Default occurs if a bond issuer fails to make scheduled payments of interest or principal or violates other covenants of a contract. A bondholder's rights in a default situation are circumscribed by terms of the contract and by judicial authority.

The yield on a bond is the flow of interest income to its holders. Apart from defaults, bonds traditionally pay interest in fixed amounts on specified dates that are indicated by coupons on the bond. Coupon bearing bonds may allow investors to choose portfolios that nearly match interest and amortization streams with their own nominal future requirements for funds. A portfolio is said to be perfectly *immunized* against interest rate fluctuations if such matching is achieved. Bonds that have no coupons are called discount bonds; they provide no interim cash flow and are retired at maturity with a payment equal to their face or par value, which is higher than the issue price. Default free bonds thus afford nominal *income certainty* to investors as was explained by Robinson (1951), but do not guarantee that an investor's spending goals can be achieved when inflation is unpredictable.

The nominal return from holding a bond is the sum of its interest payments and the change in its price over an arbitrary holding period. For example, if there are no transactions costs and taxes, the return from holding a multiyear bond for two years is:

$$\text{return} = y_1 + y_2 - P_p + P_s \tag{1}$$

where P_p and P_s are respectively the purchase and selling price and y_1 and y_2 are annual interest payments. If interest payments are assumed to be paid at year end, the nominal annual rate of return, r, from this two-year investment is obtained by solving the polynomial:

$$P_p = y_1/(1 + r) + (y_2 + P_s)/(1 + r)^2 \tag{2}$$

If the bond is actually bought at P_p and sold at P_s, a bond trader is said to *realize* a capital gain (loss) if P_p is less (more) than P_s.

A condition for equilibrium in a bond market is that expected rates of return from holding similar bonds are similar. If this condition were not satisfied, bond traders could improve portfolio earnings by selling the bond with the lower rate of return and buying the bond with the higher rate of return so long as the difference exceeds transactions costs. When transactions costs are zero, bonds are perfectly *reversible*. When expected rates of return rise, prices on outstanding bonds fall and rates of return *experienced* by existing bondholders fall; capital losses are experienced by holders of all but maturing bonds. Bond traders attempt to buy bonds immediately before market rates of return fall so that they may realize capital gains by buying at a low price and selling at a high price. Similarly, speculative traders of bonds seek to sell bonds immediately before market rates of return rise. A distinctive feature of bonds is that their future prices are unpredictable; rates of return and prices move inversely.

Bonds are issued by governments and corporations to finance deficits and acquire assets. While neither issuer can afford to ignore imminent movements in interest rates, their time schedules of outlays are somewhat inflexible. Deficits must be financed and it is shortsighted to delay purchasing high rate of return assets to take advantage of interest rate movements. Firms needing funds may choose to finance a long-term asset with short-term borrowings from banks, with a long-term bond whose interest rate varies or *floats* over time in a fixed relation to short-term rates, or with a long-term fixed coupon bond. Bank borrowing to finance long-term assets exposes firms to the risk that banks may unilaterally alter loan terms or refuse to renew maturing loans. Firms avoid non-renewal risk by borrowing with bonds. A firm's choice between issuing conventional fixed rate bonds or floating rate bonds to finance an asset depends in part on the correlation between returns from the asset being acquired and short-term interest rates for reasons that are developed by Cox, Ingersoll and Ross (1982). Other things being equal, a floating rate bond exposes a firm to less risk when short-term rates and the rate of return on the acquired asset are positively correlated.

Government deficits are financed by issuing fiat or *outside* money, short-term treasury bills and notes, and bonds. Central banks control the ratio of outside money to interest-bearing government debt when conducting monetary policy. Central bank sales (purchases) of bonds decrease (increase) bond prices and increase (decrease) bond interest rates in the market place. Other things being equal, an increase in bond interest rates increases the cost of financing new capital equipment and causes marginal investment projects to become unprofitable. Control of bond and other market interest rates by central banks is one handle through which monetary policy affects the level of macroeconomic activity. It has also been argued by Tobin (1963) that the composition of outstanding interest-bearing government debt can importantly influence the level of macroeconomic activity. If bonds are closer substitutes for physical capital in investors' portfolios than are treasury bills, a debt management policy of selling bonds and buying an equivalent amount of bills discourages private sector capital formation.

Since about 1970 bond markets have experienced a number of major institutional changes and innovations that promise to have enduring and uncertain consequences. The establishment of futures markets for bonds has modified the role of bonds in investor portfolios. Hedging and speculative positions are more inexpensively achieved in a futures market than they are by assuming long and/or short positions in a bond market. A market has also been established in *stripped* bonds where all a bond's coupons are separated from the body of a bond, and both parts are traded as separate entities. The body of the bond becomes a discount bond.

A large off-shore Eurobond market has developed where governments and corporations issue bonds denominated in currencies that may differ from the domestic currency unit of the issuer. This large and expanding market qualifies the effects of a monetary policy action in a country and complicates credit evaluation of potential bond issuers. In the United States and elsewhere, quasi-official agencies of governments have been issuing large amounts of bonds or collateralized securities that differ inconsequentially from government bonds; the effects of this development are similar to those of the expanding Eurobond market.

Finally, automation in bond markets has reduced costs of trading bonds and made them more convenient to hold. Most government bonds in the United States are no longer issued in certificate form; they are only computer entries. They are readily transferable in a computer and can be lent or sold at low cost whenever a borrower requires cash. By making bonds more reversible, automation has reduced the distinction between bonds and outside money, a distinction that is crucial for the success of central bank open market operations.

DONALD D. HESTER

See also CROWDING OUT; DEFICIT FINANCING; FINANCIAL INTERMEDIATES; NATIONAL DEBT; OPTION PRICING; PORTFOLIO ANALYSIS; PUBLIC DEBT.

BIBLIOGRAPHY
Black, F. and Scholes, M.S. 1973. The pricing of options and corporate liabilities. *Journal of Political Economy* 81(3), May/June, 637–54.
Bulow, J.I. and Shoven, J.B. 1978. The bankruptcy decision. *Bell Journal of Economics* 9(2), Autumn, 437–56.
Cox, J.C., Ingersoll, J.E., Jr. and Ross, S.A. 1981. The relation between forward prices and futures prices. *Journal of Financial Economics* 9(4), December, 321–46.
Robinson, J. 1951. The rate of interest. *Econometrica* 19, April, 92–111.
Tobin, J. 1963. An essay on the principles of debt management. In *Fiscal and Debt Management Policies*, prepared for the Commission on Money and Credit, Englewood Cliffs, NJ: Prentice-Hall.

booms and slumps. *See* BUSINESS CYCLES; CREDIT CYCLE; CRISES; CYCLES IN SOCIALIST ECONOMIES; FINANCIAL CRISIS; GROWTH AND CYCLES; TRADE CYCLE.

Borda, Jean-Charles de (1733–1799). The second half of the 18th century in France was one of the outstanding epochs of scientific thought and witnessed significant attempts to carry the methods of rigorous and mathematical thought beyond the physical and into the realms of the human sciences. A brilliant start was made in political science by three French academicians, namely Borda, Condorcet and Laplace, with contributions which now play a central role in the literature of public choice. It is a salutary warning to those who view science as endlessly progressive to note that the contributions of these outstanding academicians were lost for two centuries until they were rediscovered in 1958 by Duncan Black.

Borda was the first of the three to develop a mathematical theory of elections shortly after becoming a member of the Academy of Sciences. Born in 1733 in Dax, near Bordeaux, Borda was successively an officer of cavalry, a naval captain, and a scholar of mathematical physics as well as an innovator in the field of scientific instruments. Newly elected to the Academy of Sciences, Borda read a paper entitled 'Sur la forme des elections' on 16 June 1770. Four members were charged to report on it, but failed to do so.

The Academy was not to consider elections again during the succeeding fourteen years, until Borda again read a paper on elections in July 1784 following the favourable report by Bossut and Coulomb on Condorcet's manuscript, *Essai*. Borda's paper had been printed in the *Histoire de l'Academie Royale des Sciences* in 1781, three years prior to this reading. It was finally published in 1784. In essence, it reflected the content of his 1770 paper. Condorcet had become acquainted with Borda's contribution prior to writing his *Essai*, as a consequence of the strong oral tradition of the Academy. He acknowledged the powerful influence of Borda's ideas upon his own writings.

Borda was concerned that the single vote system of elections might select the wrong candidate. He illustrated by reference to a situation in which eight electors had candidate A as first preference, seven had candidate B, and six had candidate C. On the single vote, A would be elected, although the electors preferred B *or* C to A by a majority of 13 to 8. In essence, Borda was utilizing what later became known as the *Condorcet criterion*, though he failed to develop it himself. Instead, he attempted to remedy the defect of the single vote system by the method of marks, which he presented in two forms. Since one form is a special case of the other, only the more general form is here outlined.

The method of marks requires each elector to rank all the candidates by order of merit. The candidate is then allocated marks by reference to his ranking by each voter, for example, three marks for first place, two marks for second, and one mark for last in a three candidate election. The marks are then totalled across all elections. The candidate with the largest aggregate of marks is the winner.

To illustrate how the method of marks may provide a different result from that of the single vote, let us expand Borda's original example as outlined above into the form of Table 1.

Table 1 Rank Order of Candidates by Electors

A	A	B	B	C	C
B	C	A	C	A	B
C	B	C	A	B	A
1	7	1	6	1	5

In the Table 1 example, Candidate A would receive an aggregate of 39 marks, Candidate B receives an aggregate of 41 marks, and Candidate C receives an aggregate of 46 marks. Candidate C is the winner, reversing the single vote outcome.

The method of marks allows a role for preference intensities, albeit only on a strictly linear scale, within the electoral process. For this reason, it has been called a 'neo-utilitarian' approach (Sugden, 1981). The method is not strategy proof, since voters will tend to lower the ranking of the candidate most threatening to their preferred candidate to the lowest level, irrespective of their actual preferences. Borda himself clearly recognized this danger, but, in an age more honourable than our own, was merely moved to comment: 'My scheme is only intended for honest men.'

Borda's paper did not attempt to provide a comprehensive theory of elections. It failed to develop, though it implicitly embraced, the criterion of Condorcet. More important, it offered no real insight into the nature and/or the objectives of group decisions. It was, however, a significant first step in both directions. The method of marks is extremely effective if each elector genuinely desires to secure the election of 'that candidate who should be the most generally acceptable' (Black, 1958). In reality, most electors desire to secure the election of their most favoured candidate. Herein lies the weakness of the method of marks.

Shortly after hearing Borda's paper in 1784, the Academy adopted his method in elections to its membership. The method of marks remained in use until 1800, when it was attacked by a new member, and soon afterwards, was modified. The new member in question was Napoleon Bonaparte.

CHARLES K. ROWLEY

See also CONDORCET, MARQUIS DE; SOCIAL CHOICE; VOTING.

SELECTED WORKS

1781. Mémoire sur les élections au scrutin. *Histoire de l'Académie Royale des Sciences*, Paris.

BIBLIOGRAPHY

Black, D. 1958. *The Theory of Committees and Elections*. Cambridge: Cambridge University Press.

Condorcet, Marquis de. 1785. *Essai sur l'application de l'analyse à la probabilité des décisions rendues à la pluralité des voix*. Paris.

Lacroix, S.E. 1800. *Eloge historique de Jean-Charles Borda*. Paris.

Laplace, Marquis de. 1812. Leçons de mathématique données à l'Ecole Normale en 1885. *Journal de l'Ecole Polytechnique*.

Mascart, J. 1919. *La vie et les travaux du Chevalier Jean-Charles de Borda (1733–1799): épisodes de la vie scientifique au XVIIIe siècle*. Lyon.

Sugden, R. 1981. *The Political Economy of Public Choice: An Introduction to Welfare Economics*. Oxford: Martin Robertson.

Bortkiewicz, Ladislaus von (1868–1931). 'By far the most eminent German statistician since Lexis' (Schumpeter, 1932, p. 338), Bortkiewicz was born in St Petersburg into a family of Polish origin and educated in a Russian cultural environment (the University of St Petersburg included). Later, encouraged by W. Lexis and G.F. Knapp, he studied at the University of Strasbourg, where for two years he also taught, as *Privat-Dozent*, accident insurance and theoretical statistics. Back to St Petersburg, he worked from 1899 to 1901 at the Aleksandr Liceo – an elite secondary school of Russian *étatisme*. Then he was appointed 'extraordinary' (i.e. assistant) professor of economics and statistics at the University of Berlin, where he taught for 30 years, receiving his full professorship in 1920.

Bortkiewicz's work covers a wide range of subjects on statistics, economics, mathematics, even physics, and is scattered in a large number of publications. Bortkiewicz is considered one of the few great scholars of his time in the field of statistical methodology. His 'law of small numbers' or of 'rare events' (*Das Gesetz der Kleinen Zahlen*, 1898a) won great scientific attention – and unleashed an animated polemic in *Giornale degli Economisti* (1907–9) – particularly through the almost miraculous application of this law to the 280 Prussian soldiers killed by the kicks of their horses in the period 1875–94. An incomplete list of Bortkiewicz's writings published by Oskar Anderson in 1931 includes 54 entries – books, essays, notes – on 'theoretical statistics and calculus of probability'. Of these, Schumpeter pointed out to the economist a book (*Die Iterationen*, 1917) and papers on the measure of income inequality (1930), the quadrature of empirical curves (1926), homogeneity and stability in statistics (1918), variability under the Gaussian Law (1922), the property common to all laws of error (1923b) and the succession in time of chance events (1911).

As for economics, Bortkiewicz's writings – at least 24 papers – range from the theory of value of monetary theory and policy. (Contributions in the latter focus on the gold standard, banking credit, the velocity of circulation, and index numbers [1924].) As is known, some papers on the theory of value have particularly attracted an enduring attention. In 1949 Paul M. Sweezy published the English translation of an article on Marx (Bortkiewicz, 1907). In 1952, two sections of Bortkiewicz's 1906–7 long essay, 'Wertrechnung und Preisrechnung im Marxschen System', were translated in *International Economic Papers*. Finally, in 1971, a group of essays on the economic theories of Marx, Böhm-Bawerk, Walras and Pareto, was collected and published in Italian.

Bortkiewicz was essentially a critic. According to Oskar Anderson (1931) his analytic mind was extraordinarily acute, cold and merciless with mistakes and sloppy arguments, so that he was universally considered a stern and even quick-tempered judge, whose review articles nobody could overlook. To make his intellectual machine work he needed an external stimulus, often provided by scientific contributions of well-known authors. He entered into them, elaborated on them and sometimes confuted them.

These peculiarities are at work in his famous criticism of Böhm-Bawerk's theory of the origin of the interest on capital ('Der Kardinalfehler der Böhm-Bawerkschen Zinstheorie' 1906a). Bortkiewicz believed that the theses put forward by the 'theory of productivity' on this subject had been definitely confuted by Böhm-Bawerk, but that the alternative explanations suggested by him were also objectionable. According to Böhm-Bawerk's main argument, longer methods of production are technically more productive than shorter ones, so that present capital goods provide us with quantities of consumption goods greater than future capitals: this is the source of the interest of capital.

However, objects Bortkiewicz, a maximum level of production for each given capital invested always exists: because of physical reasons – if nothing else. Therefore, if we compare two investments, started at different times but equal in amount and composition, each of them will produce the same output, but at a temporal distance corresponding to the initial interval. Hence Böhm-Bawerk's superiority of present capital goods over future ones turns out to be a simple time span, which, in itself, is unable to explain the origin of interest.

At this point Bortkiewicz focuses his attention on a different explanation proposed by Böhm-Bawerk (and others): the scarcity of capital. The latter, Bortkiewicz maintains, can only be temporary and due to mistaken foresight. Since capital, according to Böhm-Bawerk, is nothing but an 'intermediate product', the working of the market mechanism will ease and eventually cancel out the shortages of the different capitals (vis-à-vis the workers) in the different lines of production.

On the other hand, this criticism of Böhm-Bawerk finds its *pendant* in Bortkiewicz's appreciation of Marx's theses on the origin of profit (and interest). 'Wertrechnung', Bortkiewicz's main article on Marx, was published shortly after 'Die Kardinalfehler ...' and is part of the same line of thinking. (Later, Bortkiewicz also came back to the problem in an essay significantly titled 'Böhm-Bawerk's main work in its relation to the socialist theory of the interest on capital' [1923a].)

'Wertrechnung' is divided into three parts. The first is dedicated to a long survey of opposers, followers and independent observers of Marx's conception of value and price. The author places himself among the 'mediators', in Lexis' footsteps (and recalls that Lexis' criticism [1885] had been favourably taken up by Engels in his preface to the third volume of *Das Kapital*).

The second part contains the well-known determination of prices and profit rate based on equations originally put forward by the Russian economist Dmitriev (1904) in his work on Ricardo. This solution that bears out many of Ricardo's propositions can be usefully compared with a second one published by the author at the same time (July 1907) in 'Zur Berichtigung'. Here, by taking into account Tugan-Baranovsky's contribution on the subject (1905), Bortkiewicz actually develops a suggestion made by Marx himself, according to which the values of inputs should be transformed into prices as well as the values of outputs.

The two solutions are shown to stem from different but connected ways of analysing (circulating) capital and therefore to be part of a single theoretical structure: they can be generalized, and eventually come to the same results (Garegnani, 1960; Meldolesi, 1971). Given the wage rate and the unit of account, they determine simultaneously prices and the profit rate, which in turn depend on the processes directly and indirectly used in the production of the wage commodities alone. However, from all this – and the connected results on the falling rate of profit, absolute rent (1910–11), and so on – an 'objectivist' stand should not be inferred. Bortkiewicz believed that both objective and subjective influences on prices should be recognized and that his cost equations could be inserted into the wider setting of general equilibrium analysis (1890, 1898b, 1906, 1907, 1921) – a hypothesis that, after the debate on Sraffa's 'reswitching of techniques' (1960, vol. III), is by now rather discredited.

The third part of 'Wertrechnung' discusses the theory of profit and culminates, as one might expect, on the *origin* of profit (and interest). In comparison to Ricardo, Bortkiewicz suggests, Marx had a fortunate inspiration in building a mode in which profit (as surplus-value) exists while commodities exchange according to values alone. For, in such a system, it is obvious that profit can neither come about through raising prices in the exchange, nor can it be the reward for 'capital productive services'. In other words, starting from values, Marx has defined in a clear and more significant way the theory of exploitation (or of deduction, as Bortkiewicz calls it with a neutral terminology) and has succeeded in making confusion on the matter impossible.

Luca Meldolesi

See also TRANSFORMATION PROBLEM; VALUE AND PRICE.

SELECTED WORKS

1890. *Eléments d'économie politique pure* de Léon Walras. *Revue d'économie politique.*
1898a. *Das Gesetz der kleinen Zahlen.* Leipzig.
1898b. Die Grenznutzentheorie als Grundlage einer ultraliberalen Wirtschaftspolitik. *Schmollers Jahrbuch* 22.
1906a. Der Kardinalfehler der Böhm-Bawerkschen Zinstheorie. *Schmollers Jahrbuch* 30.
1906b. Wertrechnung und Preisrechnung im Marxschen System. *Archiv für Sozialwissenschaft und Sozialpolitik* 23 and 25.
1907. Zur Berichtigung der grundlegenden theoretischen Konstruktion von Marx im dritten Band des 'Kapital'. *Jahrbücher für Nationalökonomie* 24.
1910–11. Die Rodbertus'sche Grundrententheorie und die Marx'sche Lehre von der absoluten Grundrente. *Archiv für Geschichte des Soziolismus und der Arbeiterbewegung* 1.
1911. Sterbeziffern und Frauenüberschuss. *Bulletin de l'Institut International de Statistique.*
1917. *Die Iterationen. Ein Beitrag zur Wahrscheinlichkeitstheorie.* Berlin.
1918. Homogeneitäl und Stabilität in der Statistik. *Skandinavisk Aktuarietidskrift.*
1921. Objektivismus und Subjektivismus in der Werttheorie. In *Nationalekonomiska Studier till Knut Wicksell*, Stockholm.
1922. Die Variabilitätsbreite beim Gausschen Fehlergesetz. *Nordisk Statistisk Tidskrift* 1.
1923a. Böhm-Bawerks Hauptwerk in seinem Verhältnis zur sozialstatistischen Theorie des Kapitalzinses. *Archiv für Geschichte des Sozialismus und der Arbeiterbewegung.*
1923b. Über eine verschiedenen Fehlergesetzen gemeinsame Eigenschaft. In *Sitzungsberichte der Berliner mathematischen Gesellschaft.* Berlin.
1924. Zweck und Struktur einer Preisindexzahl. *Nordisk Statistisk Tidskrift* 2 and 3.
1926. Über die Quadratur empirischer Kurven. *Skandinavisk Aktuarietidskrift.*
1930. Die Disparitätsmasse der Einkommensstatistik. In *XIX Session de l'Institut International de Statistique, Tokio 1930.* L'Aja.
1949. Appendix to E. von Böhm-Bawerk. *Karl Marx and the Close of His System*, ed. P.M. Sweezy, New York: A.M. Kelley.
1952. Value and Price in the Marxian System. *International Economic Papers* 2.
1971. *La teoria economica di Marx ed altri saggi su Böhm-Bawerk, Walras e Pareto.* Ed. L. Meldolesi, Turin: Einaudi.

BIBLIOGRAPHY

Anderson, O. 1931. Ladislaus v. Bortkiewicz [Obituary]. *Zeitschrift für Nationalökonomie* 3/2.
Dmitriev, V.K. 1904. *Economic Essays on Value, Competition and Utility.* Cambridge: Cambridge University Press, 1974.
Garegnani, P. 1960. *Il capitale nelle teorie della distribuzione.* Milan: Giuffrè.
Garegnani, P. et al. 1981. *Valori e prezzi nella teoria di Marx.* Ed. R. Panizza and S. Vicarelli, Turin: Einaudi.

Lexis, W. 1885. Die Marx'sche Kapitaltheorie. *Jarbücher für Nationalökonomie* 11.

Lexis, W. 1896. The concluding volume of Marx's Capital. *Quarterly Journal of Economics* 10.

Meldolesi, L. 1971. Il contributo di Bortkiewicz alla teoria del valore, della distribuzione e dell'origine del profitto. In *La teoria economica di Marx ed altri saggi su Böhm-Bawerk, Walras e Pareto*, ed. L. von Bortkiewicz, Turin: Einaudi.

Schumpeter, J.A. 1932. Obituary: Ladislaus von Bortkiewicz. *Economic Journal* 42, June, 338–40.

Sraffa, P. 1960. *Production of Commodities by Means of Commodities*. Cambridge: Cambridge University Press.

Sweezy, P.M. 1949. Editor's Introduction. In E. von Böhm-Bawerk, *Karl Marx and the Close of His System*, ed. P.M. Sweezy, New York: A.M. Kelley.

Tugan-Baranovsky, M. 1905. *Theoretische Grundlagen des Marxismus*. Leipzig: Duncker & Humblot.

Boulding, Kenneth Ewart (born 1910). Boulding was born on 18 January 1910 in Liverpool, England, and educated at Oxford and the University of Chicago. He has lived in the United States since 1937, teaching at Colgate, Fisk, Iowa State and McGill Universities, the University of Michigan and the University of Colorado. He was president of several learned societies including the American Economic Association and the American Association for the Advancement of Science.

The steadfast purpose that Boulding pursued in his work has been integration of knowledge. Instead of following the endlessly ramifying paths of specialized research in his chosen discipline, he sought to reach out from his 'home base' in economics to knowledge generated in other fields and, above all, to establish a leverage for deriving common vocabularies, conceptual frameworks, and methods.

This drive toward integration marks all of Boulding's contributions to economics. A typical example is the use of demographic models to describe macroeconomic aggregates. The sizes of biological populations are, of course, determined by birth rates and death rates. But these depend significantly on the age structure of the populations. Boulding conceives the aggregates of physical capital as a population of items, each characterized by an age. Production is analogous to births, consumption to deaths. Surely, the rates depend on the age structure of the 'population', as was vividly demonstrated in the post-war boom in the US automobile industry, when the population of automobiles was old (and hence had a high 'death rate') and by the eventual slump, which could have been predicted as a consequence of the same population becoming predominantly 'young'. The emphasis on 'structure' of aggregates marks also Boulding's treatment of income, the levels of prices and wages, price flexibility, etc.

To the extent that Boulding can be said to subscribe to any economic school of thought, he can be regarded as a Keynesian. His contribution in this direction has been in the macroeconomic theory of profits, which relates profits both to net investment and to distributions out of profits, what Keynes called the 'widow's cruse theory' (referring to the biblical legend of the cruse that never ran dry). While acknowledging an 'enormous debt to Keynes's brilliance of insight and imaginative sweep', Boulding points to a number of weaknesses in Keynesian macroeconomics, in particular failure to distinguish between exchanges, on the one hand, and the processes of production and consumption, on the other. In *A Reconstruction of Economics* Boulding developed separate theories of the two processes. In the same book he offered what he himself regards as, perhaps, the most original and controversial attempt to correct a weakness of Keynesian

theory. The central idea is based on a generalization from the context of microeconomics to macroeconomics of the gross growth in the value of net worth.

Grant economics, that is, the theory of one-way transfers (in contrast to exchanges) is a field that Boulding helped to found. Subsidies, philanthropy and welfare clearly fall within the scope of this field. But it may well be extended to taxation or generally to any transactions involving transfers difficult to define as exchanges, the prime concern of mainstream economics.

In 'evolutionary economics', as in 'demography of aggregates', Boulding again draws upon the conceptual repertoire of biological science. Economics is seen as an evolving ecosystem, following the general principles of mutation and selection. Mutation is interpreted as new ideas, new knowledge, modified, of course, by monopoly, government policy, etc. 'Know how' plays the role of the fundamental genetic factor, analogous to the seat of biological heredity, directing the development of the units of the ecosystem (analogues of organisms) whose interactions, in turn, shape the evolution of the system.

Recognition of Boulding's stature in the academic world has been lavish. Besides professorships in six universities and presidencies of several learned societies, he has held visiting research and teaching positions in about twenty institutions all over the world. He has been the recipient of at least ten honorary degrees and as many medals, awards, and prizes.

In contrast, Boulding's profession (as an 'establishment') has exhibited a marked coolness toward his work. In pursuing his commitment, Boulding abandoned the safety of established theoretical frameworks and conceptual schemes of his discipline. In particular, his major work, *A Reconstruction of Economics* (1950), which was, perhaps, meant to introduce new paradigms in the development of economic theory, met with a mixed response. There was no lack of appreciation of Boulding's originality and felicitous insights, the outstanding traits of his writings. The soundness of his specific contributions, however, was at times questioned. William Vickrey, in his review of *A Reconstruction of Economics* wrote:

> The most interesting and suggestive, but perhaps precarious section is the last, in which Boulding carries the analysis of macroeconomic identities to new and perhaps extravagant lengths. The new superstructure, though it leads to very interesting and even startling conclusions, depends, in many crucial spots, on precisely the kind of structural stability of relationship, and absence of unanalyzed side effects that Boulding has been at pains to warn us of in the preceding section (*American Economic Review*, 1951, pp. 671–6).

Not only the content but also the style of Boulding's rich output (about forty books and a thousand articles) must have contributed to widening the gulf between him and the economic 'establishment'. Integration is accomplished in consequence of seeing unity in diversity. Accordingly, analogy plays a prominent role in Boulding's thought, the sort of analogy that serves as the mortar of a general theory of systems, where structural similarities connecting situations of widely differing content are at the focus of attention. (Boulding was a co-founder of the Society for General Systems Research.)

Analogies occupy positions on a spectrum of rigour. At one end are mathematical isomorphisms, providing the most solid basis for unified theories of widely different phenomena. At the other end are the metaphors of poetry, triggering at times exhilarating insights but not guaranteeing any degree of objective validity or theoretical leverage. Boulding travels freely over that spectrum. In consequence, his style is wholly devoid of the dullness traditionally expected in works with a claim to scientific rigour or scholarly erudition. It seems that Boulding's attraction to what is interesting and paradoxical and his undisguised delight in iconoclasm, as well as the paucity of his references to the work of other economists ('It is easier to think it up than look it up'), contributed to the estrangement between him and his profession.

Boulding has no compunction against stating a profound principle as a quip, for example, 'Everything that exists is possible' (primacy of empirical evidence over doctrinaire conclusions), 'Things are the way they are, because they got that way' (commitment to the evolutionary point of view). There are gems to be found in Boulding's delightful jingles: 'That is reckoned wisdom which/Describes the scratch but not the itch' (a barb aimed at behaviourist dogma).

Boundaries between devotion to truth and devotion to values have no more meaning for Boulding than those between instruction and entertainment. He recognizes the stimulus that led many scientists to insist on a hermetic separation between 'what is' and 'what ought to be'. For instance, the superiority of 'price equilibrium' over a 'just price' as a fertile theoretical construct of economics is not disputed. But this emancipation from externally imposed morality has freed science in Boulding's estimation to develop its own system of values, apparent to anyone who, like Boulding, sees science not as an agglomeration of facts or techniques, not even as a system of theories but as an ongoing human enterprise, a passionate search for wisdom. Like Socrates, Boulding identifies wisdom with virtue. It is, perhaps, this insistence on the fundamental morality of science and of economics in particular that was the most important factor creating a distance between Boulding and the economic establishment.

Brought up as a Methodist and eventually becoming a Quaker, Boulding has remained a deeply religious person. For him Christianity is inseparable from pacifism. Rejection of war as an institution and of violence in all its manifestations is a cardinal principle in his political orientation. He has provided some outstanding leadership in the American peace movement, particularly during the turbulent years of the Vietnam war. He was a co-founder and director of the Center for Research in Conflict Resolution at the University of Michigan. This absorbing involvement in peace issues is reflected in several of his works, for example *The Economics of Peace* (1945), *Conflict and Defense* (1962), *Disarmament and the Economy* (1963).

In sum, Boulding is an economist who under pressure of intellectual curiosity and a devotion to freedom, justice, and progress (for which he has offered quite respectable operational definitions) has turned into a philosopher, be it noted, a scientifically literate one. The full flavour of his creative thought can be savoured in *The Meaning of the Twentieth Century* (1964), *Beyond Economics* (1968), and *The Image* (1956). The latter book, dictated in eleven days, was the 'product' of Boulding's sojourn at the Center for Advanced Study in the Behavioural Sciences in Palo Alto, California. There he met many of his contemporaries, who, he says, had a profound influence on his thinking.

ANATOL RAPOPORT

SELECTED WORKS

1941. *Economic Analysis*. New York: Harper. Rev. edn, Harper, 1948; 3rd edn, New York: Harper, 1955; 4th edn, New York: Harper & Row, 1966.

1945. *The Economics of Peace*. Englewood Cliffs, NJ: Prentice Hall; reissued, New York: Books for Libraries Press, 1972.

1950. *A Reconstruction of Economics*. New York: Wiley; reissued, Science Editions, 1962.

1953. *The Organizational Revolution: A Study in the Ethics of Economic Organizations*. New York: Harper, 1953; reissued, New York: Greenwood Press, 1984.

1956. *The Image; knowledge in life and society*. Ann Arbor: University of Michigan Press.

1958a. *The Skills of the Economist*. New York, Toronto: Clarke, Irwin.

1958b. *Principles of Economic Policy*. Englewood Cliffs, NJ: Prentice Hall.

1962. *Conflict and Defense: A General Theory*. New York: Harper.

1963. (With E. Benoit, ed.) *Disarmament and the Economy*. New York: Harper & Row; reissued, New York: Greenwood Press, 1978.

1964. *The Meaning of the Twentieth Century: The Great Transition*. New York: Harper & Row.

1968. *Beyond Economics: Essays on Society, Religion, and Ethics*. Ann Arbor: University of Michigan Press.

1970. *Economics as a Science*. New York: McGraw-Hill.

1973. *The Economy of Love and Fear: A Preface to Grants Economics*. Belmont, California: Wadsworth.

1978. (With T.F. Wilson, eds.) *Redistribution through the Financial System: The Grants Economics of Money and Credit*. New York: Praeger.

1981. *Evolutionary Economics*. London: Sage Publications.

1985. *Human Betterment*. London: Sage Publications.

bounded rationality. The term 'bounded rationality' is used to designate rational choice that takes into account the cognitive limitations of the decision-maker – limitations of both knowledge and computational capacity. Bounded rationality is a central theme in the behavioural approach to economics, which is deeply concerned with the ways in which the actual decision-making process influences the decisions that are reached.

The theory of subjective utility (SEU theory) underlying neo-classical economics postulates that choices are made: (1) among a given, fixed set of alternatives; (2) with (subjectively) known probability distributions of outcomes for each; and (3) in such a way as to maximize the expected value of a given utility function (Savage, 1954). These are convenient assumptions, providing the basis for a very rich and elegant body of theory, but they are assumptions that may not fit empirically the situations of economic choice in which we are interested.

Theories of bounded rationality can be generated by relaxing one or more of the assumptions of SEU theory. Instead of assuming a fixed set of alternatives among which the decision-maker chooses, we may postulate a process for generating alternatives. Instead of assuming known probability distributions of outcomes, we may introduce estimating procedures for them, or we may look for strategies for dealing with uncertainty that do not assume knowledge of probabilities. Instead of assuming the maximization of a utility function, we may postulate a satisficing strategy. The particular deviations from the SEU assumptions of global maximization introduced by behaviourally oriented economists are derived from what is known, empirically, about human thought and choice processes, and especially what is known about the limits of human cognitive capacity for discovering alternatives, computing their consequences under certainty or uncertainty, and making comparisons among them.

GENERATION OF ALTERNATIVES. Modern cognitive psychology has studied in considerable depth not only the processes that human subjects use to choose among given alternatives, but also the processes (problem-solving processes) they use to find possible course of action (i.e., actions that will solve a problem) (Newell and Simon, 1972). If we look at the time allocations of economic actors, say business executives, we find that perhaps the largest fraction of decision-making time is spent in searching for possible courses of action and evaluating them (i.e., estimating their consequences). Much less time and effort is spent in making final choices, once the alternatives have been generated and their consequences examined. The lengthy and crucial processes of generating alternatives, which include all the processes that we ordinarily designate by the word 'design', are left out of the SEU account of economic choice.

Study of the processes for generating alternatives quickly reveals that under most circumstances it is not reasonable to talk about finding 'all the alternatives'. The generation of alternatives is a lengthy and costly process, and one where, in real-world situations, even minimal completeness can seldom be guaranteed. Theories of optimal search can cast some light on such processes, but, because of limits on complexity, human alternative-generating behaviour observed in the laboratory is usually best described as heuristic search aimed at finding satisfactory alternatives, or alternatives that represent an improvement over those previously available (Hogarth, 1980).

EVALUATION OF CONSEQUENCES. Cognitive limits, in this case lack of knowledge and limits of ability to forecast the future, also play a central role in the evaluation of alternatives. These cognitive difficulties are seen clearly in decisions that are taken on a national scale: whether to go ahead with the construction of a supersonic transport; the measures to be taken to deal with acid rain; Federal Reserve policies on interest rates; and, of course, the supremely fateful decisions of war and peace.

The cognitive limits are not simply limits on specific information. They are almost always also limits on the adequacy of the scientific theories that can be used to predict the relevant phenomena. For example, available theories of atmospheric chemistry and meteorology leave very wide bands of uncertainty in estimating the environmental or health consequences of given quantities and distributions of air pollutants. Similarly, the accuracy of predictions of the economy by computer models is severely limited by lack of knowledge about fundamental economic mechanisms represented in the models' equations.

CRITERIA OF CHOICE. The assumption of a utility function postulates a consistency of human choice that is not always evidenced in reality. The assumption of maximization may also place a heavy (often unbearable) computational burden on the decision maker. A theory of bounded rationality seeks to identify, in theory and in actual behaviour, procedures for choosing that are computationally simpler, and that can account for observed inconsistencies in human choice patterns.

SUBSTANTIVE AND PROCEDURAL RATIONALITY. Theories of bounded rationality, then, are theories of decision making and choice that assume that the decision maker wishes to attain goals, and uses his or her mind as well as possible to that end; but theories that take into account in describing the decision process the actual capacities of the human mind.

The standard SEU theory is presumably not intended as an account of the process that human beings use to make a decision. Rather, it is an apparatus for predicting choice, assuming it to be an objectively optimal response to the situation presented. Its claim is that people choose as if they were maximizing subjective expected utility. And a strong *a priori* case can be made for the SEU theory when the decision

making takes place in situations so transparent that the optimum can be reasonably approximated by an ordinary human mind.

Theories of bounded rationality are more ambitious, in trying to capture the actual process of decision as well as the substance of the final decision itself. A veridical theory of this kind can only be erected on the basis of empirical knowledge of the capabilities and limitations of the human mind; that is to say, on the basis of psychological research.

The distinction between substantive theories of rationality (like the SEU theory) and behavioural theories is closely analogous to a distinction that has been made in linguistics between theories of linguistic competence and theories of linguistic performance. A theory of competence would characterize the grammar of a language in terms of a system of rules without claiming that persons who speak the language grammatically do so by applying these rules. Performance theories seek to capture the actual processes of speech production and understanding.

The question of the desirability and usefulness of a procedural theory of decision involves at least two separate issues. First, which kind of theory, substantive or procedural, can better predict and explain what decisions are actually reached. Does SEU theory predict, to the desired degree of accuracy, the market decisions of consumers and businessmen, or does such prediction require us to take into account the cognitive limits of the economic actors?

Second, are we interested only in the decisions that are reached, or is the human decision making process itself one of the objects of our scientific curiosity? In the latter case, a substantive theory of decision cannot meet our needs; only a veridical theory of a procedural kind can satisfy our curiosity.

BOUNDED RATIONALITY IN NEOCLASSICAL ECONOMICS. It should not be supposed that mainstream economic theory has been completely oblivious to human cognitive limits. In fact, some of the most important disputes in macroeconomic theory can be traced to disagreements as to just where the bounds of human rationality are located. For example, one of the two basic mechanisms that accounts for underemployment and business cycles in Keynesian theory is the money illusion suffered by the labour force – a clear case of bounded rationality. In Lucas's rational expectationist theory of the cycle, the corresponding cognitive limitation is the inability of businessmen to discriminate between movements of industry prices and movements of the general price level – another variant of the money illusion. Thus the fundamental differences between these theories do not derive from different inferences drawn from the assumptions of rationality, but from different views as to where and when these assumptions cease to hold – that is, upon differences in their theories of bounded rationality.

What distinguishes contemporary theories of bounded rationality from these ad hoc and casual departures from the SEU model is that the former insist that the model of human rationality must be derived from detailed and systematic empirical study of human decision making behaviour in laboratory and real-world situations.

HERBERT A. SIMON

See also BEHAVIOURAL ECONOMICS; RATIONAL BEHAVIOUR; SATISFICING.

BIBLIOGRAPHY
Cyert, R.M. and March, J.G. 1963. *A Behavioral Theory of the Firm.* Englewood Cliffs, NJ: Prentice-Hall; 2nd edn, 1975.

Hogarth, R.M. 1980. *Judgment and Choice: The Psychology of Decision.* New York: Wiley.

Nelson, R.R. and Winter, S.G. 1982. *An Evolutionary Theory of Economic Change.* Cambridge, Mass.: Harvard University Press.

Newell, A. and Simon, H.A. 1972. *Human Problem Solving.* Englewood Cliffs, NJ: Prentice-Hall.

Savage, L.J. 1954. *The Foundations of Statistics.* New York: Wiley.

Simon, H.A. 1982. *Models of Bounded Rationality.* 2 vols, Cambridge, Mass.: MIT Press (especially Sections VII and VIII).

Williamson, O. 1975. *Markets and Hierarchies.* New York: Free Press.

bounties. *See* TRADE SUBSIDIES.

bourgeoisie. The term *bourgeoisie* originally referred to the legal status of the town citizen in feudal France. In the *Encyclopédie* Diderot contrasted the political subordination of the *citoyen bourgeois* with the self-governing *citoyen magistrat* of ancient Greece. At the same time the French *bourgeoisie* (this term was first used in the 13th century) possessed certain economic and social rights, implicitly associated with the property required for trade, that distinguished it from the ordinary urban inhabitant or *domicilié* (Diderot, 1753, III, 486–9).

Something of the same concept can be found in Hegel's use of the term *bürgerliche Gesellschaft* ('civil society'). Civil society represented the legal and governmental framework required for the 'actual achievement of selfish ends', the independent sphere of activity for the economic individual. It was in contrast to what Hegel saw as the embodiment of 'absolute rationality', the State, representing the universal interest of the whole community (Hegel, 1820, p. 247).

Marx inherited, and initially used, *bourgeois* and *bürgerlich* in this restricted sense. Writing in 1842 on the opposition of the Rhineland urban estates to press freedom, he commented: 'we are faced here with the opposition of the bourgeois, not of the citoyen' (Marx, 1842, p. 168). The petty and philistine motivation of the bourgeois is contrasted with the revolutionary impulses of the wider *Tiers Etat* as defined, for instance, by Siéyes (1789). By 1843–4, however, Marx had adopted an analysis of social change in terms of economically defined class forces and consequently identified the bourgeoisie, rather than an undifferentiated *Tiers Etat*, as the revolutionary force which transformed feudal France. 'The negative general significance of the French nobility and the French clergy defined the positive general position of the immediately adjacent and opposed class of the *bourgeoisie*' (Marx, 1844, p. 185). Four years later Marx gave classic expression to this historically progressive role in the *Communist Manifesto*:

> The bourgeoisie, during its rule of scarce one hundred years, has created more massive and more colossal productive forces than all preceding generations together ... what earlier century had even a presentiment that such productive forces slumbered in the lap of social labour? (Marx, 1848, p. 489).

At the same time, Marx also made a historically specific redefinition of *bürgerlich* or civil society. Civil rights, far from being abstract freedoms which derived from the political character of the State, in fact expressed the material interests of a class, the private owners of capital, and it was these that ultimately determined the nature of the State. 'The political revolution against feudalism' regarded the sphere of civil society as 'the basis of its existence'. Man 'was not freed from

property, he received the freedom to own property' (Marx, 1844, p. 167).

The crux of Marx's innovation was, therefore, to reconceive the terms bourgeoisie and bourgeois society in forms which anchored them to a particular mode of production. In the *Manifesto* the bourgeoisie is used as a synonym for capital ('the bourgeoisie, i.e. capital') while the 'executive of the modern state' is described as 'but a committee for managing the common affairs of the bourgeoisie as a whole' (Marx, 1848, pp. 63 and 69).

Within this usage Marx invariably presents the bourgeoisie as historically contingent and subject to 'the immanent laws of capitalist production': to the 'centralisation of capital' and the contradictions bound up in its social relationship to labour. 'One capitalist kills many. Hand in hand with this centralisation, of the expropriation of many capitalists by few, develop on an ever extending scale, the co-operative form of the labour process ...' (Marx, 1867, p. 714–15). Accordingly, as Marx stressed in his *Eighteenth Brumaire of Louis Napoleon*, an analysis of the bourgeoisie, and of its internal 'factions' and 'interests', had to start with a concrete assessment of its particular forms of property and their changing place within capitalist production: 'upon the different forms of property, upon its social conditions of existence, rises an entire superstructure of distinct and differently formed sentiments ...' (Marx, 1852, p. 128).

The petty bourgeoisie, for instance, represented an unstable and transitional layer between the bourgeoisie and the proletariat:

> in countries where modern civilisation has become fully developed, a new class of petty bourgeoisie has been formed, fluctuating between proletariat and bourgeoisie and ever renewing itself as a supplementary part of bourgeois society ... as modern industry develops, they even see the moment approaching when they will completely disappear as an independent section of modern society and be replaced ... by overseers, bailiffs and shop assistants (Marx, 1848, p. 509).

They represented a 'transitional class in which the interests of two classes are simultaneously mutually blunted ...' (Marx, 1852, p. 133).

Conversely, within the bourgeoisie the centralization of capital ultimately reaches a point where management and ownership become divorced: 'the transformation of the actually functioning capitalist into a mere manager, an administrator of other people's capital and of the owner of capital into a mere owner, a mere money capitalist ....'

> Credit offers to the individual capitalist ... absolute control over the capital and property of others ... and thus to expropriation on the most enormous scale. Expropriation extends here from the direct producers to the smaller and medium-sized capitalists themselves ....

But 'instead of overcoming the antithesis between the character of wealth as social or a private wealth, the stock companies merely develop it in a new form' (Marx [1894], 1959, pp. 436–41).

Hence, in sum, Marx radically extended the significance of the concept to make the bourgeoisie that class which produced, but was itself continually modified by, the capitalist mode of production. Conversely, Marx gave a new and historically specific meaning to the term 'civil' (or *bürgerlich*) society, and argued that its endorsement of individual liberties extended only so far as they were compatible with capitalist property relations.

In the following generation a number of notable non-Marxist scholars adopted, at least in part, Marx's identification of the bourgeoisie as the class responsible for winning the social and political conditions necessary for capitalist production. But this process of wider adoption also saw a further reorientation of the concept. The new political and social institutions created by the bourgeoisie were now presented as the definitive basis for human freedom. The bourgeois character of civil society became the ultimate justification for the bourgeoisie.

Pirenne, writing in the 1890s, traced back the personal liberties of modern society to the medieval merchant bourgeoisie. It was the reliance of this class of merchant adventurers on individual enterprise and the unfettered application of knowledge that made the bourgeoisie the universal champion of 'the idea of liberty' (Pirenne, 1895 and 1925).

A little later Weber identified the origins of capitalist enterprise in the rational, resource-maximizing practices of medieval book-keeping. He then went one step further to claim that this 'capitalist spirit' was in turn derived from the doctrines of individual responsibility and conscientious trusteeship found in early protestant theology. Parallel to this within the political sphere, Weber argued that the same doctrines also underlay the creation of representative institutions and constitutional government (Weber, 1901–2 and 1920).

In the 1940s Schumpeter extended this derivation to democracy itself: 'modern democracy is a product of the capitalist process' (Schumpeter, 1943, p. 297). To do so he redefined the essence of democracy in individual, market terms as 'free competition for a free vote' (1943, p. 271), and warned that this was likely to be destroyed unless the advance of socialism could be halted. Schumpeter's thesis has since been generalized by Barrington Moore, who has sought to demonstrate that all forms of social modernization *not* led by the bourgeoisie have produced totalitarian forms of government (Moore, 1969).

This redefinition of Marx's original usage is also found in the continuing debate on the transition from feudalism to capitalism. Paul Sweezy, following Pirenne, argued that it was trade, and the role of the urban bourgeoisie as merchants, that destroyed feudalism as a mode of production. Towns and trade were alien elements that had corroded feudalism's non-market, non-exchange modes of appropriation (Sweezy, 1950). Maurice Dobb, following Marx's usage, had previously sought to show that the medieval bourgeoisie only became a revolutionary class in so far as it challenged feudalism as a mode of production (not distribution) and attempted to create a new type of exploitative relationship between capital and proletarianized labour (Dobb, 1946, p. 123; 1950). Dobb referred to Marx's own contention that the fully revolutionary overthrow of feudalism only took place when the struggle was under the leadership of the 'direct producers' rather than the merchant elite (Marx [1894], 1959, pp. 327–37).

Recently Anderson has revived this argument in a new form. Seeking the origins of the non-absolutist and democratic forms of government found in Western Europe, he argued that such institutions depended on a 'balanced fusion' between the feudalized rural remnants of Germanic society and the urban heritage of Roman *civiltas* and contract law. The role of the medieval merchant bourgeoisie within this fusion was to act as the bearer of the urban tradition (Anderson, 1974; see also Brenner, 1985).

The other major area of redefinition has been directed at the bourgeoisie in late or 'post' capitalist society. Its central feature is the claimed separation between the ownership and management of capital. If the bourgeoisie is defined by an ownership of capital that involves effective possession and control (Balibar, 1970), it is argued that in modern industrial society the actual owners of capital, the shareholders, have surrendered this to a 'new class' of corporate managers (Gouldner, 1979; Szelenyi, 1985). This concept of a managerial revolution was first popularized by Burnham (1942). It has since been developed to take account of the transnational concentration of capital. The resulting specialization of company functions has, it is argued, given executives the power to create autonomous spheres of decision-making with the result that corporate goals and strategies do not necessarily reflect the profit-maximizing interests of the nominal owners (Chandler, 1962; Pahl and Winkler, 1974).

In contrast, Marx has contended in his final writings that the growth of industrial monopoly and credit heightened the contradiction between private ownership and social labour, distorted exchange relationships and demanded systematic state intervention (Marx [1894], 1959, p. 438). Lenin later elaborated this perspective to argue that the growth of monopoly marked a new and final stage of capitalist development in which a fundamental split took place within the bourgeoisie. Utilizing an analysis first made by Hilferding (1910), Lenin argued that the fusion of banking and monopoly capital, producing 'finance capital', had created a new and parasitic relationship between state power and just one section of the bourgeoisie. The result was 'state monopoly capitalism' (Lenin, 1916 and 1917). A recent variant of this analysis has used the interlocking of company directorships to argue for the existence of a controlling elite of directors exercising a strategic dominance over all capital (Aaronovitch, 1961; Useem, 1984; Scott, 1984).

J. FOSTER

See also CAPITALISM; CLASS.

BIBLIOGRAPHY

Aaronovitch, S. 1961. *The Ruling Class.* London: Lawrence & Wishart.

Anderson, P. 1974. *Lineages of the Absolutist State.* London: New Left Books.

Balibar, E. 1970. Basic concepts of historical materialism. In L. Althusser and E. Balibar, *Reading Capital*, London: New Left Books.

Brenner, R. 1985. Agrarian class structure and economic development in pre-industrial Europe. In *The Brenner Debate*, ed. T. Aston, Cambridge: Cambridge University Press.

Burnham, J. 1942. *The Managerial Revolution.* London: Putnam.

Chandler, A. 1962. *Strategy and Structure.* Cambridge, Mass.: MIT Press.

Diderot, D. 1753. *Encyclopédie ou Dictionnaire raisonné des sciences.* Paris: Briasson.

Dobb, M. 1946. *Studies in the Development of Capitalism.* London: Routledge.

Dobb, M. 1950. A reply. *Science and Society*, Spring.

Gouldner, A. 1979. *The Future of Intellectuals and the Rise of the New Class.* New York: Seabury Press.

Hegel, G. 1820. *Naturrecht und Staatswischenschaft in Grundrisse.* In *Werke* VIII, ed. E. Gans, Berlin, 1833.

Hilferding, R. 1910. *Das Finanzkapital.* Vienna: I. Brand. Trans. M. Watnick and S. Gordon as *Finance Capital*, ed. T. Bottomore, London: Routledge & Kegan Paul, 1981.

Lenin, V.I. 1916. *Imperialism: The Highest Stage of Capitalism.* In *Collected Works* XXIII, Moscow, 1964.

Lenin, V.I. 1917. *The Impending Catastrophe and How to Combat it.* In *Collected Works* XXV, Moscow, 1964.

Marx, K. 1842. Debate on the law on thefts of wood. In *Collected Works* I, Moscow: Progress, 1975.

Marx, K. 1844. Contribution to the critique of Hegel's Philosophy of Law. In *Collected Works* III, Moscow: Progress, 1975.

Marx, K. 1848. *The Manifesto of the Communist Party*. In *Collected Works* VI, Moscow: Progress, 1976.

Marx, K. 1852. *The Eighteenth Brumaire of Louis Napoleon*. In *Collected Works* XI, Moscow: Progress, 1976.

Marx, K. 1867. *Capital*, Vol. I. Moscow: Progress, 1953.

Marx, K. 1894. *Capital*, Vol. III. Moscow: Progress, 1959.

Moore, B. 1969. *The Social Origins of Democracy and Dictatorship*. London: Penguin.

Pahl, R. and Winkler, J. 1974. The economic elite: theory and practice. In *Elites and Power in British Society*, ed. P. Stanworth and A. Giddens, Cambridge: Cambridge University Press.

Pirenne, H. 1895. L'origine des constitutions urbaines au moyen age. *Revue historique* 57.

Pirenne, H. 1925. *Medieval Cities: their origin and the renewal of trade*. Princeton: Princeton University Press.

Schumpeter, J. 1943. *Capitalism, Socialism and Democracy*. London: George Allen & Unwin.

Scott, J. 1984. *Directors of Industry: the British Corporate Network*. Cambridge: Polity Press.

Siéyes, E. 1789. *Qu'est-ce que le Tiers Etat?* Paris.

Sweezy, P. 1950. The transition from feudalism to capitalism. *Science and Society* 14(2), Spring, 134–57.

Szelenyi, I. 1985. Social policy and State Socialism. In *Stagnation and Renewal in Social Policy*, ed. G. Esping-Anderson, White Plains, NY: Sharpe.

Useem, M. 1984. *The Inner Circle*. New York: Oxford University Press.

Weber, M. 1901–2. Die protestantische Ethik und der Geist des Kapitalismus. *Archiv für Sozialwissenschaft und Sozialpolitik* 20.

Weber, M. 1920. *Gessämmelte Aufsätze zur Religionssoziologie*. Tübingen: Mohr.

Bowley, Arthur Lyon (1869–1957).   Bowley was born on 6 November 1869 in Bristol, and died on 21 January 1957 at Haslemere. In 1922 he was made a Fellow of the British Academy and knighted in 1950. He was educated at Christ's Hospital from 1879 to 1888, and Trinity College, Cambridge, from 1888 to 1891 (10th Wrangler, 1891). He stayed on another two terms studying physics, chemistry and, under the influence of Alfred Marshall, who remained a lifelong friend, economics. After a period as a schoolmaster, he became lecturer in mathematics, and then professor of mathematics and economics at University College, Reading, from 1900 to 1919. He concurrently taught at the London School of Economics from its inception in 1895, first as lecturer, then reader, then professor, and finally, from 1919, as the first holder of the newly established Chair of Statistics at the University of London, becoming Emeritus Professor on his retirement in 1936.

Among his other activities, he was Acting Director of the Oxford University Institute of Statistics from 1940 to 1944; foundation member in 1933, and then President from 1938 to 1939, of the Econometric Society; President of the Royal Statistical Societyfrom 1938 to 1940, and honorary President of the International Statistical Institute in 1949.

Bowley was an outstanding economic statistician who made substantial contributions to all areas in his field, from the theory of mathematical statistics to the methodology and practice of data collecting. His courses on statistics at the LSE formed the subject matter of two very successful textbooks (Bowley, 1901, 1910). He brought together and set out in a uniform way the developments of mathematical economics from Cournot to Pigou (Bowley, 1924). He wrote a detailed account of Edgeworth's contributions to mathematical statistics (Bowley, 1928). He collaborated with R.G.D. Allen on a masterly study of family budgets which deals with individual variation as well as average behaviour (Allen and Bowley, 1935).

One of his early interests was the course of wages, on which he wrote several books and over thirty articles, many jointly with G.H. Wood; his first paper on the subject was Bowley (1895) and his first book Bowley (1900). This led him to write extensively on index-numbers of prices and it is interesting that in 1899, on p. 641 of vol. III of *Palgrave's Dictionary of Political Economy*, he gave the index-number formula later to become famous as Irving Fisher's ideal index-number. He followed this work with studies of the national income in Bowley (1919, 1920, 1937) and jointly with J.C. Stamp in Bowley and Stamp (1927).

Bowley was a pioneer in the development of sampling methods and spoke strongly in their favour in his presidential address to the British Association in 1906. In 1912 he carried out a well-designed sample survey of Reading and soon followed this with similar enquiries in Northampton, Warrington, Stanley and Bolton (Bowley and Burnett-Hurst, 1915). A second survey of the same towns was made after the war (Bowley and Hogg, 1925). In the same period he prepared a substantial report on the precision attained in sampling (Bowley, 1926). He played an important role in the new survey of London life and labour (Llewellyn-Smith, 1930–35).

J.R.N. STONE

SELECTED WORKS

1895. Changes in average wages (nominal and real) in the United Kingdom between 1860 and 1891. *Journal of the Royal Statistical Society* 58, June, 223–78.

1900. *Wages in the United Kingdom in the Nineteenth Century*. Cambridge: Cambridge University Press.

1901. *Elements of Statistics*. London: P.S. King. 6th edn, 1937.

1910. *An Elementary Manual of Statistics*. London: P.S. King. 7th edn, London: Macdonald & Evans, 1951.

1915. (With A.R. Burnett-Hurst.) *Livelihood and Poverty: a study in the economic conditions of working-class households in Northampton, Warrington, Stanley and Reading*. London: G. Bell.

1919. *The Division of the Product of Industry: An Analysis of National Income before the War*. Oxford: Clarendon Press.

1920. *The Change in the Distribution of the National Income, 1880–1913*. Oxford: Clarendon Press.

1924. *The Mathematical Groundwork of Economics*. Oxford: Clarendon Press.

1925. (With M.H. Hogg.) *Has Poverty Diminished?* London: P.S. King.

1926. Measurement of the precision attained in sampling. *Bulletin de l'Institut International de Statistique* 22, pt I(3), 1–62.

1927. (With J.C. Stamp.) *The National Income 1924*. Oxford: Clarendon Press.

1928. *F.Y. Edgeworth's Contributions to Mathematical Statistics*. London: Royal Statistical Society.

1930–35. Contributions to H. Llewellyn-Smith, *New Survey of London Life and Labour*. 9 vols, London: P.S. King.

1935. (With R.G.D. Allen.) *Family Expenditure*. London: P.S. King.

1937. *Wages and Income in the United Kingdom since 1860*. Cambridge: Cambridge University Press.

BIBLIOGRAPHY

Allen, R.G.D. 1968. Bowley, Arthur Lyon. In *International Encyclopedia of the Social Sciences*, Vol. 2, New York: Macmillan and Free Press.

Allen, R.G.D. 1971. Bowley, Sir Arthur Lyon. *Dictionary of National Biography, 1951–1960*, Oxford: Oxford University Press.

Allen, R.G.D. and George, R.F. 1957. Professor Sir Arthur Lyon Bowley (with bibliography). *Journal of the Royal Statistical Society*, Series A (General) 120, pt 2, 236–41.

Bowley, Agatha H. 1972. *A Memoir of Professor Sir Arthur Bowley (1869–1957) and his Family*. Privately printed.

Darnell, A. 1981. A.L. Bowley, 1869–1957. In *Pioneers of Modern Economics in Britain*, ed. D.P. O'Brien and J.R. Presley, London: Macmillan.

Maunder, W.F. 1977. Sir Arthur Lyon Bowley. In *Studies in the History of Statistics and Probability*, Vol. II, ed. M.G. Kendall and R.L. Plackett, London: Griffin.

Bowley, Marian (born 1911). Marian Bowley was born in 1911, the daughter of the distinguished statistician A.L. Bowley. She was a student at the London School of Economics (1928–31), where she took her BSc (Econ) degree and later her PhD in 1936. She held a series of temporary teaching and research posts and was appointed to a lectureship at the Dundee School of Economics in 1938. After government service during World War II she was appointed to a lectureship at University College, London in 1947 and became successively reader and professor. She retired in 1975 and was made professor emeritus.

Marian Bowley's best-known contribution to economics is her work in the history of economic thought. Her major work in this field is undoubtedly her *Nassau Senior and Classical Economics* (1937) which still remains the standard work on that much misunderstood member of the classical school. Her book is more than just a study of Senior, it is really an overview of the whole classical system, both its economic theory and policy stance, woven into a study of Senior. One of her major points was to question the hegemony of classical value theory and argue rather that there were two distinct strands: the labour theory propagated by the Ricardians and a subjective approach espoused by people such as Lauderdale and Senior.

Bowley's other contributions to the history of economics are collected in her *Studies in the History of Economic Theory before 1870* (1973), where, incidently she somewhat repudiates her earlier views on classical value theory and sees more common features in the analysis.

Marian Bowley has also made important contributions to the understanding of the building industries in her *Innovations in Building Materials* (1960) and *The British Building Industry* (1966).

B.A. CORRY

SELECTED WORKS

1937. *Nassau Senior and Classical Economics*. London: George Allen & Unwin.
1960. *Innovations in Building Materials*. London: Duckworth.
1966. *The British Building Industry*. Cambridge: Cambridge University Press.
1973. *Studies in the History of Economic Theory before 1870*. London: Macmillan.

Bowman, Mary Jean (born 1908). Mary Jean Bowman, born in 1908 in New York City, obtained her PhD at Harvard (1938). Since 1958 she has taught at the University of Chicago. Her publications include ten books and monographs and over 100 articles, most of which relate to the economics of education.

Bowman's early writings are primarily expository: a clear description of measures of income inequality, and a stimulating textbook on economics written jointly with G.L. Bach. Much of her later writing deals with the effects of education on economic development and the personal distribution of income, using US, Japanese, Malaysian and Mexican data. These studies, which relate to schooling and on-the-job training, are well documented. Bowman also emphasizes the role of fertility and technological change, arguing that high rates of human capital formation and high rates of population growth are incompatible, unless sustained by technological change and the ability to learn rapidly in the post-school years.

Two characteristics typify her writings. First is her repeated attempts to bring expectations and uncertainty to bear on educational choices, using concepts inspired by G.L.S. Shackle. Secondly, Bowman often uses a multi-disciplinary approach. A contributor to the human capital and home economics literature, she draws on the education and sociological literature as well. An example of her tribute to sociological ideas is her insistence on the importance of 'information fields'. It remains to be seen whether these often disparate concepts, which Bowman has juggled so successfully, can be formalized in a synthetic fashion.

GILBERT R. GHEZ

SELECTED WORKS

1943. (With G.L. Bach.) *Economic Analysis and Public Policy*. New York: Prentice-Hall.
1945. A graphical analysis of personal income distribution in the United States. *American Economic Review* 35(3), September, 607–28.
1958. (ed.) *Expectations, Uncertainty and Business Behavior*. New York: Social Science Research Council.
1963. (With W.W. Haynes.) *Resources and People in East Kentucky: Problems and Prospects of a Lagging Economy*. Baltimore: Johns Hopkins Press for Resources for the Future.
1964. Schultz, Denison, and the contribution of 'Eds' to national income growth. *Journal of Political Economy*. 72(5), October, 450–64.
1965. (ed., with C.A. Anderson.) *Education and Economic Development*. Chicago: Aldine.
1966. The costing of human resource development. In *The Economics of Education*, ed. E.A.G. Robinson and J. Vaizey, London: Macmillan.
1967. (With R.G. Myers.) Schooling, experience, and gains and losses in human capital through migration. *Journal of the American Statistical Association* 62(3), September, 875–98.
1968. (ed.) *Readings in the Economics of Education*. Paris: UNESCO.
1972. (ed., with C.A. Anderson and V. Tinto.) *Where Colleges Are and Who Attends*. New York: McGraw Hill.
1972. Expectations, uncertainty and investments in human beings. In *Uncertainty and Expectations in Economics*, ed. C.F. Carter and J.L. Ford, Oxford: Basil Blackwell.
1973. (With D. Plunkett.) *Elites and Change in the Kentucky Mountains*. Lexington: University of Kentucky Press.
1978. (With A. Sohlman and B-C. Ysander.) *Learning and Earning*. Stockholm: National Board of Universities and Colleges.
1981. (With the collaboration of H. Ikeda and Y. Tomoda.) *Educational Choice and Labor Markets in Japan*. Chicago: University of Chicago Press.
1982. Choice in the spending of time. In *The Social Sciences, their Nature and Uses*, ed. W.H. Kruskal, Chicago: University of Chicago Press.
1984. An integrated framework for analysis of the spread of schooling in less developed countries. *Comparative Education Review*, 28(4), November, 563–83.
1986. (With B. Millot and E. Schiefelbein.) *Political Economy of Public Support of Higher Education: Studies in Chile, France and Malaysia*. Washington, DC: World Bank, Discussion Paper.

Boyd, Walter (1754–1837). Before the French Revolution, Walter Boyd was engaged as a banker in France but by the time his firm's property was confiscated by the French government in 1793, he was established in London as the leading member of the firm of Boyd Benfield & Co. At first this London venture was highly successful, and in 1797 Boyd entered Parliament as member for Shaftsbury, then a pocket borough owned by his partner. In this very year, however,

Boyd Benfield & Co began to encounter the difficulties which were to culminate in its liquidation in 1800. The basic cause of Boyd's ruin was his having entered into engagements in the expectation that his French property would be restored to him, an expectation that was finally disappointed in September 1797, but the events which precipitated the final collapse of his firm were the government's refusal to employ it as a contractor for the loan of 1799 and the Bank of England's final refusal to grant assistance in early 1800.

When, in 1801, Boyd published his 'Letter to William Pitt ...' attacking the Bank of England's policies since the suspension of specie convertibility of February 1797, he was hardly a disinterested observer. However, this pamphlet's appearance is widely regarded as marking the beginning of the 'Bullionist Controversy', and contains perhaps the first systematic, albeit crude statement of what came to be known as the Bullionist position. It argued that exchange depreciation and food price increases since 1797 were the result of an overissue of paper money by the Bank of England; that though foreign transfers could depreciate the exchanges this factor had not been important since 1797; and that the Country Bank note issue could not affect prices independently of Bank of England policies.

Boyd's pamphlet drew a number of replies, some, as Fetter (1965) notes, aimed more at Boyd than at his case, but one by Sir Francis Baring (1801) prefigured subsequent anti-bullionist positions. Baring argued (with some justice) that food price behaviour had had more to do with bad harvests than the exchange rate (which had moved much less), and that the exchange rate's fall had been the result of British remittances to Continental allies and not of overexpansionary policy on the part of the Bank of England.

Boyd made no further contributions to wartime debates. After the Peace of Amiens (1802) he visited France, only to be trapped there until 1814 by the renewal of hostilities. Upon his return to England he re-established his fortunes sufficiently to be able to re-enter Parliament in 1823, as member of Lymington, which he represented until 1830. He published two further pamphlets, on the Sinking Fund (1815 and 1828), but neither of these has the historical significance of his 1801 contribution.

DAVID LAIDLER

See also BULLIONIST CONTROVERSY.

SELECTED WORKS

1801. *Letter to the Right Honourable William Pitt on the Influence of the Stoppage of Issues in Specie at the Bank of England on the Prices of Provisions and Other Commodities.* London. 2nd edn, 1811.
1815. *Relections on the Financial System of Great Britain, and Particularly on the Sinking Fund.* London. 2nd edn, 1828.
1828. *Observations on Lord Grenville's Essay on the Sinking Fund.* London.

BIBLIOGRAPHY

Baring, Sir Francis. 1801. *Observations on the Publication of Walter Boyd.* London.
Fetter, F.W. 1965. *Development of British Monetary Orthodoxy: 1797–1875.* Cambridge, Mass.: Harvard University Press.

Brady, Dorothy Stahl (1903–1977). A mathematician and statistician, Dorothy S. Brady combined in her professional life extended periods in both universities and US federal agencies. Most of her empirical work entailed the design and interpretation of survey data on household income and expenditures and critiques of applications of such data.

This began with analysis of data collected in the large 1935–6 survey of incomes and expenditures of rural households which together with its urban counterpart provided the basis for new tests of the validity of Commerce Department estimates of the size and distribution of national income, consumption and savings. At the Bureau of Labor Statistics (1943–8, 1951–6) she assessed consumption and price data in connection with efforts to control inflation and she developed the statistical design for pricing the city workers' family budget which was used to estimate inter-area differences in the cost of living.

An active participant in the Conference on Income and Wealth of the National Bureau of Economic Research, Brady brought to its sessions a keen awareness of data limitations in the empirical identification of key elements in an analytical structure. Using statistical analysis to randomize effective unidentified factors, she found that the percentage of income saved by families tends to increase systematically with relative position in an income distribution, that the secular increase of income of a population tends to decrease the age at which children leave the family residence, often with financial help from parents, and that such leaving tends to increase the inequality of measured income distribution.

M. REID

See also SURVEY RESEARCH.

SELECTED WORKS

1940. (With others.) *Family Income and Expenditures, 5 Regions, Part 2.* US Department of Agriculture, Miscellaneous Publication No. 396.
1945. *Family Spending and Saving in Wartime.* US Bureau of Labour Statistics, Bulletin No. 872, Appraisal of survey data, p. 45.
1948. (With L.S. Kellog.) The city worker's family budget. *Monthly Labour Review* 66(25), 133–70.
1948. Family budgets, a historical survey. *Monthly Labour Review* 66(23), 171–5.
1949. The use of statistical procedures in the derivation of family budgets. *Social Service Review* 23(2), June, 141–57.
1952. Family savings in relation to changes in the level and distribution of income. *Studies in Income and Wealth,* New York: National Bureau of Economic Research, Vol. 15, 103–28.
1956. Family Savings, 1880 to 1950. Part II in *A Study of Savings in the United States,* Vol. III: *Special Studies,* ed. R.W. Goldsmith, D.S. Brady and H. Mendershausen, Princeton: Princeton University Press, 188–213.
1957. Measurement and interpretation of the income distribution in the United States. *Income and Wealth,* Series VI. London: International Association for Research in Income and Wealth.
1958. Individual incomes and the structure of consumer units. *American Economic Review, Papers and Proceedings* 48, 269–78.
1965. Age and the income distribution. *Research Report* No. 8, US Social Security Administration.
1966. Price deflators for final product estimates. *Studies in Income and Wealth,* Vol. 30: *Output, Employment, and Productivity in the United States After 1800.* Conference on Research in Income and Wealth. New York: National Bureau of Economic Research.
1971. The statistical approach: the input–output system. In *Approaches to American Economic History,* ed. G.R. Taylor and L.F. Ellsworth, Charlottesville: University Press of Virginia.

brain drain. *See* INTERNATIONAL MIGRATION.

Braudel, Fernand (1902–1985). One of the foremost social and economic historians of the 20th century, Fernand Braudel combined a perceptive grasp of historical interconnections, an exceptional skill of synthesis and an evocative, even 'poetic' style. Perception, scope and style were brought to successful fruition in Braudel's *La Méditerranée et le monde méditerranéen à l'époque de Phillipe II* (1949), which became a classic in historical literature and a model for a major school of French history known as the *Annales*. In this seminal volume and in many methodological articles that followed, Braudel proposed a triple notion of historical time – the long run (*longue durée*) over a millennium, trends (*conjonctures*) of a generation or more, and events (*événements*). According to Braudel, each of these notions or blocks of time involved unique historical problems, appropriate source materials, and even special approaches employing social-science disciplines neighbouring to history. Braudel's model emphasized the 'constraints' of human endeavour rather than the 'permissive' factors that had been so much a part of Whig history as practised by most early 20th-century historians. These constraints were imposed by geography, climate and soils, by demographic pressure and by a static social structure held together by the bonds of custom. Braudel likened this 'structure' to a glacier or to the sea depths, imparting both a physical metaphor and a sense of timelessness or immobility. His second temporal level, the *conjoncture*, made some room for change as new technologies, new forms of economic organization (especially capitalism), and subtle shifts in social relations and customs altered the 'structure'. Braudel likened these changes – he preferred the term 'mutations' – to the sea tides. Finally the 'event' was a kind of surface noise, an indication perhaps of deeper sea changes, but in itself of little significance for the historian. He likened these events to whitecaps on the vast ocean.

In addition to his emphasis on constraints and the obligation of historians to understand their deterministic effects on human behaviour, Braudel also stressed the cyclical nature of most of history – 'le temps, quasi immobile, fait de répétitions, de retours insistants, de cycles sans cesse recommencés.' There was about Braudel a strong sense of romantic conservatism that challenged Marxist and Whig historian alike. Braudel imparted to the Annales School a preference for metaphors taken from biology and anthropology (interconnection, *liens*, mutations, *glissements*) instead of the vocabulary, and indeed the goals of physics or economics (parsimonious cause, leanness of argument, elegance of formula or theory). It is also clear that for Braudel geography and demography were basic objects of study, that technology and economic and social organization were important, but that political history, biography and the history of formal ideas were secondary and even trivial historical pursuits. In a direct attack on the kind of history taught at the Sorbonne, Braudel insisted that 'events' tell us little about the deeper and interlocking structures and their subtle mutations. Indeed, such surface history may suggest a misguided 'voluntarism' in human history. With such a perspective, it is understandable that Braudel was most comfortable in the thousands of years of pre-industrial history. The more recent 19th century and its urban-industrial dynamism was unsettling to his outlook, his methodology and even to his aesthetic sense. But like a cultural anthropologist, Braudel never ceased to stress the fact that most of world history was pre-industrial.

Although Braudel was interested in quantification, he was never a model-builder, and in fact he used numbers illustratively rather than systematically. He had much to do with the Annales-style deployment of an array of graphic techniques – often very artfully designed – to demonstrate proportions and relationships, but as a descriptive technique in which the reader had to access the results by eye. Braudel did not use statistical measures, much less economic theory, perhaps because he considered them too abstract, a threat to

the living texture of social history that was his main concern. In the 1970s, like much of the Annales School, Braudel moved further toward cultural anthropology as reflected in his notion of 'day-to-dayness' (*la vie quotidienne*), in the cultural determinants of economic and social behaviour, in the values and attitudes (mentalities) of social groups, and in the *gestes* and *code* of an entire society or even a 'civilization'. These features were already present in the *Méditerranée*, but they became even more pronounced in his more recent *Civilisation matérielle et capitalisme (XV-XVIIIᵉ siècle)* (1967–79).

Fernand Braudel was also director of the Maison des Sciences de l'Homme in Paris, professor at the Ecole Pratique des Hautes Etudes and at the Collège de France, and co-editor of the *Annales: ESC*, one of the most prestigious journals of social and economic history in the western world today. Braudel's seminal writings, his provocative teaching, his administrative and editorial talents, and, not least, his powerful personality, made him an 'animateur' of the 'School of the Annales' for more than 30 years. Yet his work stands on its own as an appeal to approach history in its widest scope in time and place (*histoire totale*), in alliance with neighbouring disciplines, and presented with that special verve we call 'Braudelian'.

R. FORSTER

SELECTED WORKS

1949, 1966. *La Méditerranée et le monde méditerranéen à l'époque de Phillipe II*. Paris: Armand Colin. Trans. by Sian Reynolds as *The Mediterranean and the Mediterranean World in the Age of Philip II*, London: Collins; New York: Harper & Row, 1972–3.

1967, 1979. *Civilisation matérielle et capitalisme, XV-XVIIIᵉ siècle*. 1967 edn, 1 vol.; 1979 edn, 3 vols; Paris: Armand Colin. Trans. of 1st edn by Miriam Kochan as *Capitalism and Material Life, 1400–1800*, London: Weidenfeld & Nicolson, 1973. Trans. of 2nd edn by Miriam Kochan and Sian Reynolds as *Civilization and Capitalism, 15th–18th Century*, London: Collins; New York: Harper & Row, 3 vols, 1981, 1982, 1984.

1969. *Ecrits sur l'histoire*. Paris: Flammarion.

1973. *Mélanges en l'honneur de F. Braudel*. 2 vols, Toulouse: Edouard Privat.

Braverman, Harry (1920–1976). Harry Braverman was born in 1920 in New York City and died on 2 August 1976 in Honesdale, Pennsylvania.

Born into a working-class family, he was able to spend only one year in college before financial problems forced him out of Brooklyn College and into the Brooklyn Navy Yard. He worked there for eight years primarily as a coppersmith and then moved around the United States, working in the steel industry and in a variety of skilled trades. He became deeply involved in the trade union and socialist political movements. He helped found *The American Socialist* in 1954 and worked as its co-editor for five years. After the journal ceased publication for practical reasons, he moved into publishing, working first at Grove Press as an editor and eventually as vice-president and general business manager. In 1967 he became Managing Director of Monthly Review Press, where he worked until his death.

Braverman is best known for his classic study of the labour process under capitalism, *Labor and Monopoly Capital* (1974), awarded the 1974 C. Wright Mills Award. 'Until the appearance of Harry Braverman's remarkable book', Robert L. Heilbroner wrote in the *New York Review of Books*, 'there has been no broad view of the labour process as a whole ....' The book was all the more remarkable because of the void it filled in the Marxian analytic tradition – a literature ostensibly grounded in the analysis of the structural effects of class conflict but persistently reticent about the actual structure and experience of work in capitalist production.

Labour and Monopoly Capital advances three principal hypotheses about the labour process in capitalist societies.

First, Braverman helps formalize and extend Marx's resonant analysis, in Volume I of *Capital*, of the distinction between labour and labour power. Braverman highlights the essential importance and persistence of managerial efforts to gain increasing control over the labour process in order to rationalize – to render more predictable – the extraction of labour activity from productive employees.

Second, Braverman argues that such managerial efforts lead inevitably to the homogenization of work tasks and the reduction of skill required in productive jobs. He concludes (p. 83) that 'this might even be called the general law of the capitalist division of labor. It is not the sole force acting upon the organization of work, but it is certainly the most powerful and general.'

Third, as a corollary of the second hypothesis, Braverman argues both analytically and with rich empirical detail that this 'general law of the capitalist division of labour' applies just as clearly to later stages of capitalist development, with their proliferation of office jobs and white collars, as to the earlier stages of competitive capitalism and largely industrial work.

The first analytic strand of Braverman's work was both seminal and crucial in helping foster a renaissance of Marxian analyses of the labour process. The second and third hypotheses have proved more controversial. There are two grounds for concern. Braverman's analysis tends to reduce the character of the labour process to essentially one dimension – the level of skill required and control permitted by embodied skills – and therefore unnecessarily compresses the *many* essential dimensions of worker activity and effectiveness in production to a single monotonic index. At the same time, there is good reason for worrying about the simplicity of Braverman's argument of historically irreversible 'deskilling' for all segments of the productive working-class; it is quite plausible to hypothesize that for some labour segments in recent phases of capitalist development there has been a 'reskilling', as many have since called it, without in any way liberating these workers from capitalist exploitation or intensive managerial supervision.

DAVID M. GORDON

See also LABOUR PROCESS.

SELECTED WORKS

1974. *Labor and Monopoly Capital*. New York: Monthly Review Press.
1976. Two comments. Special issue on 'Technology, the Labor Process, and the Working Class', *Monthly Review*, July–August.

Bray, John (1809–1897). John Bray was born in the United States but spent his formative years (1822–42) in England. His attention was drawn to social and industrial questions during a period as an itinerant printer in the early 1830s and also through his work with the unstamped *Voice of the West Riding* (1833–4).

In 1837 Bray gave a series of lectures to the Leeds Working Men's Association – lectures which were to form the basis of his one major work *Labour's Wrongs and Labour's Remedy*, published in 1839. Shortly after (1842) he emigrated to the United States. However, his letters to the American papers show that he remained concerned with social and political

matters as they touched upon the interests of the labouring-classes; indeed, in the 1880s he became involved with the syndicalist Knights of Labor and was hailed in 1885, by the *Detroit News*, as the oldest living socialist born in America.

In *Labour's Wrongs* Bray traced the impoverishment of the labouring-classes to the skewed distribution of the ownership of the nation's productive capacity, which permitted the coercive exercise of economic power by the few against the interests of the many. This power was used to exploit those with only their labour to sell by means of unequal exchanges that reduced the value of labour to a bare subsistence level. Thus for Bray it was more by the infraction of the principle of equal exchanges 'by the capitalist, than by all other causes united that inequality of condition is produced and maintained and the working man offered up bound hand and foot, a sacrifice upon the altar of Mammon'. For Bray, therefore, exploitation occurred in the sphere of exchange with the crucial intermediation of money, which he saw as instrumental in ensuring that everything 'generated by the power of labour is perpetually carried off and absorbed by capital'. Further, the impoverishment of labour that resulted caused deficient demand and, in consequence, general economic depression.

Bray's solution to the iniquities and inequities of competitive capitalism was the creation of an economic system that would guarantee 'universal labour and equal exchanges'. Like other 19th-century socialist and anti-capitalist writers Bray sought to transmute the labour theory of value from a critical tool to an operational imperative. Thus goods should exchange at their labour values, for with labour exchanged against labour: 'That which is now called profit and interest cannot exist.' This was to be achieved by ensuring that the means of production were 'possessed and controlled by society at large' – something which was to be secured through purchase, the purchase price being met out of wealth created once the nation's productive capacity was under collective control.

Bray does no more than sketch the operational outlines of this socialist commonwealth, but it is clear that although influenced by Owenite thinking, his conception of socialism involved a move away from the idea of self-contained, self-sufficient, cooperative communities in the direction of central control over output, pricing, allocation and distribution. In this respect, while bearing many of the hallmarks of early 19th-century Owenite socialism, *Labour's Wrongs* points to the work of late 19th-century socialists where the market is supplanted by planning.

N.W. THOMPSON

SELECTED WORKS

1839. *Labour's Wrongs and Labour's Remedy or, the Age of Might and the Age of Right*. Leeds. Reprinted, New York: A.M. Kelley, 1968.

BIBLIOGRAPHY

Beales, H.L. 1933. *The Early English Socialists*. London: Hamish Hamilton.
Beer, M. 1953. *A History of British Socialism*. 2 vols, London: Allen & Unwin.
Carr, H.J. 1940. John Francis Bray. *Economica* 7, 397–415.
Cole, G.D.H. 1977. *A History of Socialist Thought*. Vol. 1: *Socialist Thought: the Forerunners, 1789–1850*. London: Macmillan.
Foxwell, H.S. 1899. Introduction to the English translation of A. Menger, *The Right to the Whole Produce of Labour*. London: Macmillan.
Gray, A. 1967. *The Socialist Tradition: Moses to Lenin*. London: Longman.
Henderson, J.P. 1985. An English communist, Mr Bray (and) his remarkable work. *History of Political Economy* 17, 73–95.
Hunt, E.K. 1980. The relation of the Ricardian socialists to Ricardo and Marx. *Science and Society* 44, 177–98.

King, J.E. 1981. Perish Commerce! Free trade and underconsumption in early British radical economics. *Australian Economic Papers* 20, 235–57.

King, J.E. 1983. Utopian or scientific? A reconsideration of the Ricardian socialists. *History of Political Economy* 15, 345–73.

Lloyd-Prichard, M.F. 1957. Introduction to J.F. Bray, *A Voyage from Utopia*. London: Lawrence & Wishart.

Lowenthal, E. 1911. *The Ricardian Socialists*. New York: Longman.

Thompson, N.W. 1984. *The People's Science: The Popular Political Economy of Exploitation and Crisis, 1816–34*. Cambridge: Cambridge University Press.

Breckinridge, Sophonisba Preston (1866–1948). Born on 1 April 1866 in Lexington, Kentucky; died on 30 July 1948 in Chicago, Illinois. Breckinridge (Wellesley '88), the first woman to pass the bar examination in Kentucky, abandoned legal work to take a PhD in political science at the University of Chicago, which she completed in 1901, followed by a law degree in 1904. Part of the circle of social reformers centred around Jane Addams at Hull House, Breckinridge pioneered in the professionalization of social work (as teacher, then as Dean and head of research of the Chicago School of Civics and Philanthropy, where social workers were trained). Her methodology was radically empirical; social problems were to be studied in their concrete context, by first-hand observation of the homes and communities of the poor. Working closely with Edith Abbott, she produced numerous monographs on tenement life and the effects of urban poverty on the breakdown of families. *New Homes for Old* (1921) detailed the dislocations and privations of the immigrant poor in big cities, while giving the social worker the leading role in helping these hapless victims construct a decent life. As early as the 1920s, Breckinridge was emphasizing the need for government responsibility for social welfare programmes, an idea not popular in America until the Depression of the 1930s. In 1927 she helped found the *Social Service Review* which she edited for the rest of her life.

B. BERCH

SELECTED WORKS

1912. (With E. Abbott.) *The Delinquent Child and the Home*. New York: Charities Publications Committee, Russell Sage Foundation.

1921. *New Homes for Old*. New York: Harper & Brothers.

1924. *Family Welfare Work in a Metropolitan Community*. Chicago: University of Chicago Press.

1927. *Public Welfare Administration in the United States*. Chicago: University of Chicago Press.

1931. *Marriage and the Civic Rights of Women*. Chicago: University of Chicago Press.

1933. *Women in the Twentieth Century*. New York: McGraw-Hill.

1934. *The Family and the State*. Chicago: University of Chicago Press.

Brentano, Lujo (Ludwig Josef) (1844–1931). Brentano was born in Aschaffenburg (Germany) into an old patrician family. Clemens Brentano, the poet, was his uncle; Bettina von Arnim, the writer, his aunt; and Franz Brentano, the philosopher, his brother. He was brought up in an atmosphere dominated by Catholicism (which he was later to abandon after the declaration of papal infallibility) and was particularly influenced by the anti-Prussian tradition of Southern Germany. He studied law and economics in Heidelberg and Göttingen. From 1871 he taught political economy as professor in Berlin, Breslau, Strassburg, Vienna, Leipzig and Munich.

A decisive point for his later career was his participation in the Statistical Seminar connected with the Prussian Statistical Office. Its director was Ernst Engel (originator of Engel's law), whose strong interest in the social conditions of the working classes was to have a lasting influence on Brentano. Engel advocated profit-sharing schemes as a means to the solution of the social question. In 1868 Brentano accompanied him on a visit to England, where they studied the effects of such measures. His experiences in England convinced Brentano of the inadequacy of profit-sharing for the reform of capitalism, but suggested another approach, which was to remain the main topic of Brentano's intellectual work: the improvement of the worker's position in the labour market through the establishment of trade unions.

While the individual worker was forced to sell his labour power under any conditions, this would not be the case for an organized coalition of workers. Such a coalition would enable them to become as free and independent as the sellers of other commodities and would allow for an effective control of the labour supply (1871–2, vol. 2; 1877, ch. 2). It was Brentano's deep conviction that trade unions were the only means to secure an adequate participation of the working classes in the general increase of wealth. He was especially interested in the history of the trade unions, which he traced back to the medieval guilds (1871–2, vol. 1). Especially interesting – particularly for the current debate – was his discussion of positive productivity effects of labour time reductions (1876).

He regarded the introduction of a general social security system as another important step for the reform of capitalism. He also favoured the cartelization of Germany industry. It was characteristic of him that he always intended to solve the social question within the framework of a capitalist economic system. He therefore rejected Marx and the Social Democrats of 19th-century Germany. Brentano emphasized that unequal conditions of material existence were absolutely necessary for the further cultural advancement of mankind (1877, pp. 303–4).

His concern for the social question shaped Brentano's attitude towards the classical economists: he opposed the classical notion of an abstract profit-maximizing individual as the central axiom of political economy, and found this particularly inadequate to describe working-class behaviour and the labour market (1923, ch. 1). It is in this context that his preoccupation with economic history (1916; 1927–9) must be seen. He intended to show that the relations between man and the economic system were changing through history, that the individual of classical economics was not the starting-point, but the result of economic development (1927–9, vol. 1, pp. iii–iv).

Further fields of interest were Malthus's theory of population development (1924), the theory of value (where he favoured the subjective theory of value; 1924), the German corn tariffs (which he opposed), and different forms of the law of estate.

Throughout his life Brentano remained an open-minded and enlightened liberal of whom an English trade union leader once said: 'He was our friend before it was fashionable to be our friend.' Brentano was a founding member of the Verein für Socialpolitik, which he left in 1929, when he thought that it had become reactionary. He opposed Bismarck in the Kaiserreich, the extreme German annexationists during World War I – although himself favouring limited territorial expansion – and the Socialist Revolutionaries in the postwar period. The republican government considered his appointment as first German postwar ambassador to Washington, but because of his advanced age he declined.

275

During the Weimar Republic Brentano was still concerned with social policy, mainly with the struggle for the eight-hour working day. He deplored the harsh austerity policy during the Great Depression. His memoirs, written in 1930, ended: 'I do not understand this policy. Do they want a social revolution?' (1931, p. 404).

B. SCHEFOLD

SELECTED WORKS

1870. *On the History and Development of Guilds, and the Origin of Trade Unions.* London: Trübner.

1871–2. *Die Arbeitergilden in der Gegenwart.* Vol. 1: *Zur Geschichte der englischen Gewerkvereine,* Leipzig: Duncker & Humblot, 1871; Vol. 2: *Zur Kritik der englischen Gewerkvereine,* Leipzig: Duncker & Humblot, 1872.

1876. *Über das Verhältnis von Arbeitslohn und Arbeitszeit zur Arbeitsleistung.* Leipzig: Duncker & Humblot. Trans. as *Hours and Wages in Relation to Production,* New York: Scribner; London: Sonnenschein, 1894.

1877. *Das Arbeitsverhältnis gemäss dem heutigen Recht.* Leipzig: Duncker & Humblot. Trans. as The *Relation of Labour to the Law of To-day,* New York: Putnam, 1898.

1889. *Über die Ursachen der heutigen socialen Noth.* Leipzig: Duncker & Humblot.

1916. *Die Anfänge des modernen Kapitalismus.* Munich: Königlich Bayerische Akademie der Wissenschaften.

1923. *Der wirtschaftende Mensch in der Geschichte.* Leipzig: Felix Meiner.

1924. *Konkrete Grundbedingungen der Volkswirtschaft.* Leipzig: Felix Meiner.

1927–9. *Eine Geschichte der wirtschaftlichen Entwicklung Englands.* 3 vols, Jena: Gustav Fischer.

1931. *Mein Leben im Kampf um die soziale Entwicklung Deutschlands.* Jena: Eugen Diederichs.

Bresciani-Turroni, Costantino (1882–1963). The last great exponent of old-time liberalism in Italian economics, Bresciani was an Italian counterpart of such distinguished libertarians as Robbins, Hayek or Friedman, a bit more moderate, perhaps, in his views and with a quantitative bent at least equal to Friedman's. Bresciani was born in Verona and his teachers in his homeland included Ricca-Salerno and Loria. After the completion of his studies at a number of universities in Italy he went to the University of Berlin, at that time at the height of its prestige, to study with historical economists such as Adolf Wagner and Gustav Schmoller, and with L. von Bortkiewicz, the mathematical statistician and pioneer in Marxian econometrics.

Amidst the push and pull of these intellectual influences Bresciani preserved an admirable independence of mind. Loria did not convert him to socialism and Schmoller did not turn him into an historical economist. More influenced by Pareto and Pantaleoni than by his great teachers, he became, first of all, an economic theorist, but again not a pure one but one looking for statistical verifications of theoretical propositions.

In his writings he would give a respectful hearing to the views of the classics and provide copious references to modern authorities, foreign languages and mathematical modes of expression constituting no barriers. As an Italian and libertarian, he was especially fond of citing Galiani. After the publication of Keynes's *General Theory* in 1936, Bresciani, like other contemporary economists, had to come to terms with the new economics. Again he showed his independence by continuing to adhere to such established doctrines as the quantity theory of money and the productivity theory of interest. This attitude, together with his insistence on the limitations rather than opportunities of public policies, gave

an old-fashioned flavour to his later writings, published, as they were, at a time when Keynes's influence reached its peak.

Bresciani's teaching career, which included chairs in statistics, led him eventually to the University of Milan (1926–57), but his work there was interrupted by various other activities. During the twenties he served as an adviser to the Berlin office of the Allied Reparations Commission, and from 1927 to 1940 he lectured at the newly established Egyptian University of Cairo. This multiplication of jobs again confirmed his penchant for independence and gave him the opportunity to absent himself from fascist Italy. After World War II he served the new Republic of Italy as president of an important bank and for a brief period also as minister of foreign trade. In this capacity he again demonstrated his independence, this time from ideological preferences, by sponsoring a government organization for export credit and insurance.

As a writer Bresciani started out, at age 22, with a critical review of Pareto's law of income distribution, a subject to which he returned later more than once. Much of his work was devoted to the theory of prices, domestic and international, present and future, as well as the relation between prices and interest. Among other topics that he investigated were the influence of speculation on prices, which he recognized as not always beneficial, economic forecasting, the inductive verification of the theory of international payments, and the relation between the harvest and the price of cotton in Egypt. Late in life he wrote a number of broad syntheses of economics, including a two-volume *Corso* that went into many editions.

Bresciani's masterpiece, and the work for which he is best known, is *The Economics of Inflation*, published originally in Italian in 1931 and in a revised English translation in 1937. The Italian title of the book – *Le vicende del marco tedesco*, or the vicissitudes of the German mark – conveys the substance of the book better than the title of the English translation, which claims a level of abstraction far higher than that embodied in the work, and, correspondingly, a much wider applicability of the content. The subtitle of the English translation is also carelessly worded. The subject of the work is the great German inflation after World War I, when prices had risen to astronomical heights and $1 in the end purchased 42 marks followed by eleven zeros. At that time this was considered a record, but the Hungarian inflation after World War II surpassed it, with the dollar then buying 145 pengö followed by 27 zeros.

Bresciani's book has been the standard work on the subject ever since. What was open to debate was never the completeness or reliability of the material that he presented but his interpretation. German students of the matter tended to adhere to the view that the rise in prices reflected the unfavourable rate of exchange, which in turn was ascribed, at least in part, to the burden of reparation payments that the Germans were eager to demonstrate as outrageously unreasonable. Bresciani opposed this interpretation. His principal argument was that foreign exchanges, by means of well-known mechanisms, will never fail to reach an equilibrium if only the external value of the currency falls deeply enough. Bresciani, instead of putting the blame on the foreign exchanges, placed it firmly on the German authorities which pursued policies of fiscal irresponsibility and unrestrained monetary expansion. Bresciani also discussed still other interpretations – conspiratorial or scandal theories – but found them unconvincing. One variant of these made the industrialists, who gained so much from the galloping inflation, responsible for it. Another one put the onus on the German authorites' desire to prove the impossibility of reparation payments. It may be of some interest that the second variant of the scandal theory would constitute a corollary of the policy of *deflation* which Chancellor Brüning adopted a few years later during the Great Depression, a policy instrumental in helping Germany to rid herself of reparation payments.

Critics of the work brought still other points of view before the reader. Joan Robinson, to give an example, stressed the role of ever-rising money wages that became indexed and subject to automatic increases. This would seem to lend support to the view blaming the foreign exchanges, because the rise in money wages offset the forces making for equilibrium of the foreign-exchange rates. But Robinson does not fully endorse Bresciani's or the German interpretation. In her view the eventual stabilization of the mark in November 1923 does not support the conclusion that monetary stringency is necessary and sufficient to put an end to inflation. In Robinson's view the stabilization succeeded because by that time the old German mark had shed almost all the standard functions that money is to serve.

HENRY W. SPIEGEL

SELECTED WORKS
1929. The movement of wages in Germany during the depreciation of the mark and after stabilization. *Journal of the Royal Statistical Society* 92, 374–414.
1931. *Le vicenda del marco tedesco*. Trans. by Millicent Sayers as *The Economics of Inflation: a study of currency depreciation in post-war Germany 1914–1923*, with a foreword by Lionel Robbins, London: Allen & Unwin; New York: Barnes & Noble, 1937.
1932. *Inductive Verification of the Theory of International Payments*. Cairo: Noury.
1934a. Egypt's balance of trade. *Journal of Political Economy* 42, June, 371–84.
1934b. The 'purchasing power parity' doctrine. *L'Egypte Contemporaine* 25, May, 433–64.
1936. The theory of saving. *Economica* 3, Part I, February, 1–23, Part II, May, 162–81.
1937. On Pareto's Law. *Journal of the Royal Statistical Society* 100, 421–32.
1938. The multiplier in practice: some results of recent German experience. *Review of Economics and Statistics* 20, May, 76–88.
1939. Annual survey of statistical data: Pareto's Law and the index of inequality of incomes. *Econometrica* 7, April, 107–33.
1942. *Economic Policy for the Thinking Man*. London: Hodge.
1964. Articles contributed by Costantino Bresciani-Turroni to the *Review of Economic Conditions in Italy* in the years from 1947 to 1962. Rome: Banco di Roma.

BIBLIOGRAPHY
Anon. 1964. Obituary of C. Bresciani-Turroni, with Bibliography. *Review of Economic Conditions in Italy* 3, Rome: Banco di Roma, 125–37.
Gambino, A. 1965. La politica monetaria e creditizia negli scritti di C. Bresciani-Turroni. *Studi economici* 20, 196–219.
Gambino, A. 1972. C. Bresciani-Turroni. *Dizionario biografico degli italiani*, Rome: Instituto della Enciclopedia Italiana, Vol. 14, 184–7.
Robinson, J. 1938. Review of *The Economics of Inflation*. *Economic Journal* 48, September, 507–13.
Tamagna, F.M. 1967. C. Bresciani-Turroni. *International Encyclopedia of the Social Sciences*, New York: Macmillan, Vol. 2, 149–50.

Bretton Woods. *See* INTERNATIONAL MONETARY INSTITUTIONS.

bribery. The economic analysis of political and bureaucratic institutions can productively begin with the study of bribery, not because it is necessarily pervasive but because it highlights the conflict between the public interest and the market.

Widespread bribery can transform a governmental procedure ostensibly based on democratic or meritocratic principles into one based on willingness-to-pay.

Most work on bribery is descriptive and taxonomic. While this makes for interesting reading and is an important source of background information on the range and diversity of corrupt deals, such research does not systematically examine the economic bases of bribery. When the latter are recognized, they are frequently treated in a cursory fashion so that either the underlying forces of supply and demand are seen as justifying payoffs or else the same forces are taken as reason to condemn the practice. Some of the best of this descriptive work appears in Clarke (1983), Gardiner and Olson (1974) and Heidenheimer (1970); other relevant books and articles are listed in the bibliography.

The theory of perfect competition emphasizes the impersonality of all market dealings. A manufacturer will sell to all customers irrespective of their race, gender, or inherent charm. Similarly, the ideal bureaucrat makes decisions on the basis of objective, meritocratic criteria and is not influenced by personal, ethnic or family ties. Bribes can replace an impersonal meritocratic procedure with an impersonal willingness-to-pay procedure, or can help to support a system of personalized favours based on close personal relations; conversely, payoffs may be a way for newcomers or members of pariah groups to obtain influence in the society. It follows that bribery can only be evaluated relative to a system without bribery. Then one's evaluation of the payoffs that occur will depend not only upon one's moral scruples concerning bribery as such, but also upon whether payoffs produce a more or a less impersonal, objective set of decisions and whether one values such a shift positively or negatively. The difficulties of analysis here are indicated, on the one hand, by those who see payoffs to officials in some underdeveloped countries as an extension of well-entrenched tribal customs, and on the other, those who see similar payoffs as a way of circumventing traditional attitudes and helping the country develop economically (see e.g. Clarke, 1983; Heidenheimer, 1970).

LEGISLATIVE CORRUPTION. Elected representatives care about being re-elected but they are also likely to care about their incomes. Consider a simple world in which voters are well-informed about the votes of legislators but cannot observe bribes directly. Assume that politicians run for re-election on their voting record and that no campaign spending is needed. Then a bribe designed to change a vote in the legislature will cost the politician some constituency support since otherwise no payoff would be necessary. Thus at a minimum, even if politicians have no moral qualms about accepting payoffs, the bribe must be sufficient to compensate the politician for the reduced chance of re-election. *Ceteris paribus* we would expect that the politicians with the lowest reservation bribes are those who are either quite certain of being elected or quite sure of defeat, for in each case a decline in electoral support can affect the ultimate outcome very little. It follows that, given the salience of the issue to the electorate, the closer the race, the higher will be the politician's reservation bribe.

In this simple model there is no need for campaign contributions, so bribes can be used only for personal gain, and there is a direct trade-off between bribes and the probability of re-election. But if payoffs *can* be spent either on a re-election campaign or used as personal income, then all types of politicians may be corruptible, depending on differences between legislators in moral scruples and in the salience to the voters of the issues of interest to the briber (see Rose-Ackerman, 1978, pp. 15–58).

PURCHASING AGENTS. In both public and private sectors and in both capitalist and socialist economies, purchasing agents are likely to have the opportunity either to pay or receive bribes. No bribes occur in a perfectly competitive market, where suppliers can sell and demanders can buy all they wish at the going price. Corruption requires market imperfections. For example, the government may be so large a purchaser that economies can be realized in filling its order; it may need products not available 'off-the-shelf' so that a negotiated contract is necessary. In short, if bribes are offered there must be some prospective excess profits out of which to pay them, and if bribes are accepted, it must be because the agent's superiors are either privy to the deal themselves or else cannot monitor the agent's behaviour adequately by such simple devices as comparing market prices with contract prices.

One might argue that in these situations corruption furthers efficiency, since the most efficient firm will have the highest prospective profits and so be willing to pay the highest bribe. This is simplistic. First, a firm may gain advantage by lowering quality in subtle ways not immediately obvious to government inspectors. Secondly, if managers of firms differ in respect for the law, the most unscrupulous have an advantage. Thirdly, keeping payoffs secret both wastes resources and causes the market to operate poorly because of the low level of available information. In short, the correspondence between efficiency and the size of the bribe is likely to be imperfect.

In other economic contexts purchasing agents may pay bribes to obtain supplies, instead of being paid to choose particular suppliers. This can happen when shortages of particular products develop and prices do not rise to reflect market conditions. This is especially important in planned economies. Indeed, discussions of corruption in the Soviet Union frequently point to this form as endemic (Grossman, 1977; Simis, 1979). Here again bribes can serve economic functions but have no advantage over prices, except the ideological one of hiding the pervasiveness of market-like processes from public view (see Montias and Rose-Ackerman, 1981).

The establishment of a legal and flexible price system is not always a realistic option. For example, the military purchases many complex and highly specialized weapons that cannot be effectively obtained through sealed bids. In such situations one must consider the role of detection and punishment. Here basic work on the economics of crime is relevant and, in fact, Becker and Stigler (1974) have themselves made the application to corrupt payments. They stress the importance of giving each employee a stake in his or her job by, for example, providing non-vesting pensions. This will make workers less likely to take risks that could lead to their dismissal. More generally, the expected punishment for bribery should be tied to the marginal gain from marginal increases in the payoff (Rose-Ackerman, 1978, pp. 109–35). Otherwise only some bribes will be deterred. Thus the marginal expected penalty for the bribe-taker, that is, the probability of apprehension and conviction times the penalty if convicted, must rise by at least one dollar for every dollar increase in expected payoff. If it does not, then even if a large lump-sum penalty is levied only relatively small bribes may be prevented. The bribe-payer's marginal penalty should be tied, not to the size of the bribe, but to the marginal increase in profit that a bribe makes possible. Penalties set at a multiple of the bribe paid may thus have little deterrent effect on bribe-payers, if the expected profits are many times larger.

DISPENSERS OF BENEFITS AND BURDENS. Low-level officials frequently have considerable discretion to decide who should receive a scarce benefit such as a unit of public housing, expedited access to an important person, a liquor licence, assignment to a particular judge. Others, such as health and safety inspectors and the police, have the power to impose costs and the discretion to refuse to exercise that power. While legal pricing systems can sometimes substitute for payoffs here, in many cases there is a strong public policy reason for opposing a market solution.

Given such programmes where market tests are undesirable, how can corruption be controlled? One option, explored in Rose-Ackerman (1978, pp. 137–66), is to introduce competitive pressures as a way of lowering the payoffs that people are willing to make and hence discouraging officials from accepting bribes which are low relative to the risk of detection and punishment. When a bureaucracy dispenses a scarce benefit, competition can be introduced by permitting an applicant to reapply if he has been turned down by one official. Then if the cost of reapplication is small, the first official cannot demand a large bribe in return for approving the application; in fact the offered bribe may be forced down so low that the official may turn it down and instead behave honestly. A few honest officials in this system may thus produce honesty in the others. Notice, however, that unqualified applicants will still wish to make payoffs and their willingness-to-pay increases if they expect that most other officials to whom they could apply are honest.

The case for competition among inspectors or police is somewhat different and depends upon the feasibility and cost of overlapping authority. Thus, the operator of a gambling parlour will not pay much to a corrupt policeman if a second independent policeman is expected to come along shortly. The whole precinct must be on the take, that is, monopolized, to make high bribes worthwhile.

In short, the role of competitive pressures in preventing corruption may be an important aspect of a strategy to deter the bribery of low-level officials, but requires a broad-based exploration of the impact of both organizational and market structure on the incentives for corruption facing both bureaucrats and their clients.

SUSAN ROSE-ACKERMAN

See also CRIME AND PUNISHMENT; DIRECTLY UNPRODUCTIVE PROFIT-SEEKING ACTIVITIES; RENT-SEEKING.

BIBLIOGRAPHY
Banfield, E. 1975. Corruption as a feature of governmental organization. *Journal of Law and Economics* 18(3), December, 587–605.
Becker, G.S. and Stigler, G.J. 1974. Law enforcement, malfeasance, and compensation of enforcers. *Journal of Legal Studies* 3(1), January, 1–18.
Benson, B.L. and Baden, J. 1985. The political economy of governmental corruption: the logic of underground government. *Journal of Legal Studies* 14(2), June, 391–410.
Clarke, M. (ed.) 1983. *Corruption: Causes, Consequences and Control.* New York: St Martin's Press.
Darby, M.R. and Karni, E. 1973. Free competition and the optimal amount of fraud. *Journal of Law and Economics* 16(1), April, 67–88.
Gardiner, J. 1970. *The Politics of Corruption: Organized Crime in an American City.* New York: Russell Sage Foundation.
Gardiner, J.A. and Lyman, T.R. 1978. *Decisions for Sale: Corruption in Local Land-Use Regulations.* New York: Praeger.
Gardiner, J.A. and Olson, D.J. (eds) 1974. *Theft of the City.* Bloomington: Indiana University Press.
Grossman, G. 1977. The 'second economy' of the USSR. *Problems of Communism* 26(5), September–October, 25–40.
Heidenheimer, A.J. (ed.) 1970. *Political Corruption: Readings in Comparative Analysis.* New York: Holt, Rinehart & Winston.

Jacoby, N., Nehemkis, P. and Eels, R. 1977. *Bribery and Extortion in World Business.* New York: Macmillan.

Johnson, O.E.G. 1975. An economic analysis of corrupt government with special application to less developed countries. *Kyklos* 28(1), 47–61.

Krueger, A.O. 1974. The political economy of the rent-seeking society. *American Economic Review* 64(3), June, 291–303.

LeVine, V.T. 1975. *Political Corruption: The Ghana Case.* Stanford: Hoover Institution Press.

Lui, F.T. 1985. An equilibrium queuing model of bribery. *Journal of Political Economics* 93(4), August, 760–81.

Montias, J.M. and Rose-Ackerman, S. 1981. Corruption in a Soviet-type economy: theoretical considerations. In *Economic Welfare and the Economics of Soviet Socialism: Essays in Honor of Abram Bergson,* ed. S. Rosefielde, Cambridge: Cambridge University Press.

Noonan, J. 1984. *Bribes.* New York: Macmillan.

Pashigan, B.P. 1975. On the control of crime and bribery. *Journal of Legal Studies* 4(2), June, 311–26.

Rashid, S. 1981. Public utilities in egalitarian LDC's: the role of bribery in achieving Pareto efficiency. *Kyklos* 34(3), 448–60.

Rose-Ackerman, S. 1975. The economics of corruption. *Journal of Public Economics* 4(2), February, 187–203.

Rose-Ackerman, S. 1978. *Corruption: A Study in Political Economy.* New York: Academic Press.

Rose-Ackerman, S. 1986. Reforming public bureaucracy through economic incentives. *Journal of Law, Economics and Organization* 2(1), 131–61.

Scott, J.C. 1972. *Comparative Political Corruption.* Englewood Cliffs, NJ: Prentice-Hall.

Sherman, L. (ed.) 1974. *Police Corruption.* Garden City, New York: Doubleday, Anchor Books.

Simis, L. 1978. The machinery of corruption in the Soviet Union. *Survey* 23(4), Autumn, 35–55.

Wraith, R. and Simkins, E. 1963. *Corruption in Developing Countries.* London: George Allen & Unwin.

Bright, John

Bright, John (1811–89). John Bright, a Lancashire mill-owner, became a national figure in the campaign that repealed the Corn Laws in 1846 and that came to be known as the Manchester School.

Elected to the House of Commons in 1843, he continued to represent industrial constituencies most of his life and worked tirelessly for radical reform which to him meant reducing the scope of government, making it more representative and keeping its foreign policy peaceful. He was a man of strong views but not doctrinaire or unwilling to change them.

Believing in the market, he opposed factory legislation but not as it applied to children. At one time he supported John Stuart Mill's effort to give women the vote but later opposed the idea. He was against a state church, yet proposed its funds be distributed to all denominations as a once-and-never-again subsidy which recalls Smith's artful scheme. Although a Quaker, he never condemned war in principle and said that violence, while rarely called for, was sometimes necessary.

In his day Bright was said to be the pacifist who could have been a pugilist if he had not been a Quaker. He does evoke truculence but what stands out a century later is his honesty and fierce independence. He combined them with an extraordinary speaking ability – in turns eloquent, persuasive, charming, brutally frank, cogent, and clever – all of which he could be because he had a first rate mind. Never quite the equal of his intimate friend and ally, Richard Cobden, he nevertheless was one of the great figures in the reform movements of the century.

WILLIAM D. GRAMPP

See also MANCHESTER SCHOOL.

SELECTED WORKS

1866. *Speeches on Political Reform.* London: Simpkin.
1878. *Speeches on Questions of Public Policy.* Ed. J.E. Thorold Rogers. London: Macmillan.
1879. *Public Addresses of John Bright.* Ed. J.E. Thorold Rogers. London: Macmillan.

Bronfenbrenner, Martin

Bronfenbrenner, Martin (born 1914). Bronfenbrenner received his AB from Washington University (St Louis) and his PhD from the University of Chicago in 1939. A student of Oskar Lange, Bronfenbrenner's professional career and writing reflect a catholicity of interests rare among modern economists. His books range from the careful and judicious treatise *Income Distribution Theory* (1971) to the playful collection of short stories on the American occupation of Japan, *Tomioka Stories* (1976). He is probably the only person to hold simultaneous memberships in the conservative Mt Pelerin Society and the Union of Radical Political Economists.

He has taught, and written on, macroeconomics, trade theory and policy, monetary economics, production theory, development economics, the history of economic thought, distribution theory, economic history, Marxian economics, and the Japanese economy. He is one of the most prolific of contemporary economists, his writings being characterized by elegance and felicitous phrasing and further adorned by verses from obscure poets and popular operettas.

As a 'neoclassical' economist, trained at Chicago, his contributions to economic analysis themselves blend a variety of themes and techniques. His major work on income distribution theory itself modifies neoclassical theory so that it can frame questions raised in both classical and neo-Marxian analysis. He has been a leader in the analysis of Japanese economic development and growth, an interest fostered during his military service as a Japanese language officer, and as an economist attached to the US occupation forces in Japan.

His regular academic appointments included positions at Wisconsin, Michigan State, Minnesota, Carnegie Tech, Aoyama Gakuin and Duke (where he was Kenan Professor of Economics). Many of his professional papers are held by the Manuscript Department of Perkins Library, Duke University.

E.R. WEINTRAUB

SELECTED WORKS

1945. Some fundamentals of liquidity theory. *Quarterly Journal of Economics* 59, May, 405–26.
1956. Potential monopsony in labour markets. *Industrial and Labour Relations Review* 9, July, 577–88.
1961. *Academic Encounter.* New York: Free Press.
1961. Some lessons of Japanese economic development, 1868 1938. *Pacific Affairs* 34(1), Spring, 7–27.
1963. (With F.D. Holzman.) Survey of inflation theory. *American Economic Review* 53, September, 593–661.
1959 (ed.) *Is the Business Cycle Obsolete?* New York: Wiley.
1971. *Income Distribution Theory.* Chicago: Aldine.
1976. *Tomioka Stories.* New York: Exposition Press.
1979. *Macroeconomic Alternatives.* Chicago: AHM Publishing Co.
1984. (With W. Sichel and W. Gardner.) *Economics.* Boston: Houghton Mifflin.

Brougham, Henry

Brougham, Henry (1773–1868). Baron Brougham and Vaux, Lord Chancellor, touched nearly all subjects and adorned some by his eloquence and dialectical skill. The contact seems least superficial, the ornament particularly solid, in the case of political economy. Brougham's first considerable work was *An Inquiry into the Colonial Policy of European Powers*, 1803.

Criticizing Adam Smith, he maintains that the monopoly of the colonial trade did not produce all the detrimental effects ascribed to it (Book I, §2, part ii). Referring to the slave colonies, Brougham not only denounces the slave trade as iniquitous – 'not a trade, but a crime' – but also argues that it is unprofitable. The argument is renewed in *A Concise Statement of the Question regarding the Abolition of Slave Trade* (1804). Slavery, as well as slave trade, was assailed by Brougham's oratory (*Speeches*, published in 1838, vol. ii.).

Free trade owes something to Brougham's advocacy. He exposed the folly of retaliation, as counsel (1808) for the merchants who petitioned parliament against the orders in council directed against Napoleon's continental system. After Brougham's masterly speech in 1812, the obvious orders were withdrawn (*Speeches*, vol. i). In the speech on manufacturing distress (1817) Brougham strikes at the complicated taxes which fettered trade (ibid.) But in the equally able speech on agricultural distress (1816) there is a good word for the corn law (ibid. p. 533).

Other economic topics handled by Brougham are: (1) depreciation of money, with reference to Sir E. Shuckburgh's standard (article on 'Currency and Commerce' [1803], *Contributions to Edinburgh Review*, published 1856, vol. iii, p. 22); (2) usury ([1816], *Contributions*, vol. iii p. 52); (3) over-population (speech on the Poor Laws, 1834, *Speeches*, vol. iii); (4) combinations (*Transactions of the Society for promoting Social Science* for 1860, p. 51). Brougham is also to be mentioned as a promoter of education and educational institutions – the London University, the Society for the Diffusion of Useful Knowledge, Mechanics' Institutes, and the Society for promoting Social Science.

In addition to the works which have been cited may be noticed: (1) *A Manual for Mechanics' Institutions*, 1839 (by B.F. Duppa, with outlines of lectures on political economy by Brougham); (2) *Political Philosophy*, 1842; (3) *Works*, 1st edn 1855–61, 2nd edn 1873. In the 11th volume of the 2nd edition there is a list of Brougham's publications, numbering 133.

[F.Y. EDGEWORTH]

Reprinted from *Palgrave's Dictionary of Political Economy*.

SELECTED WORKS

1803. *An Inquiry into the Colonial Policy of European Powers*. 2 vols, Edinburgh: E. Balfour.

1804. *A Concise Statement of the Question regarding the Abolition of Slave Trade*. London: J. Hatchard and T.N. Longman.

1838. *Speeches of Henry Lord Brougham*. 4 vols, Edinburgh: A. & C. Black.

1839. *Outlines of lectures on political economy*. In B.F. Duppa, *A Manual for Mechanic's Institutions,* London: Society for the Diffusion of Useful Knowledge.

1842. *Political Philosophy*. London: Society for the Diffusion of Useful Knowledge.

1855-61. *Works*. 11 vols, London, Glasgow: R. Griffin & Co.; 2nd edn, Edinburgh: A. & C. Black, 1873.

1856. *Contributions to the Edinburgh Review*. 3 vols, London, Glasgow: E. Griffin & Co.

Brown, (Ernest) Henry Phelps. See PHELPS BROWN, ERNEST HENRY.

Brown, Harry Gunnison (1880–1975). Harry G. Brown was born in Troy, New York, the son of an accountant. He was stricken from age four with tuberculosis of the hip. He graduated from Williams (1904) and took his PhD at Yale in 1909.

Brown instructed at Yale from 1909 to 1915, working closely with Irving Fisher. Herbert J. Davenport then hired him at the University of Missouri where he succeeded Davenport as Chair, remaining there through 1947. After retirement in 1950 he taught at The New School, The University of Mississippi, and Franklin and Marshall. During the Pennsylvania residence he campaigned vigorously, although in his eighties, for adoption of the graded tax in cities of that state, under its local-option law. He returned to Columbia, Missouri to retire, and continued publishing and speaking until his death at the age of 95.

Brown was the premier exponent among orthodox theorists of taxing land values and saw rail/utilities as generating taxable rents. There is producer surplus when rates exceed average cost. There is also consumer surplus when rates fall below average benefits. Both surpluses were locational and lodged in land rents. This led to a general interest in taxing land. He used conventional tools, careful craftsmanship, and a priori methods. Brown refuted J.B. Clark's idea that 'the lure of unearned increment' was a constructive incentive for pioneering; and Frank Knight's idea that land is like all other resources because it has an opportunity cost; and Ely's doctrine that 'ripening costs' of land speculators justify urban sprawl.

He criticized most non-land taxes, but opposed Federal deficits more than any tax, seeing deficits as competing directly for capital formation. He attributed macro problems to cost–push, pointing to overpricing of land and raw materials, which land taxation would abate; to high interest rates forced by inadequate bank reserves; to associationism in industry; and to the perverse behaviour of regulated rates under average-cost pricing, where reduced demand forces rates to rise and worsen a depression. He would increase investment opportunities by abating taxes on capital.

MASON GAFFNEY

SELECTED WORKS

1931. *Economic Science and the Common Welfare*. Columbia, Missouri: Lucas Bros.

1980. *The Selected Articles of Harry Gunnison Brown*. Ed. P. Junk, New York: The Robert Schalkenbach Foundation.

BIBLIOGRAPHY

Essays in Honor of Harry Gunnison Brown. *American Journal of Economics and Sociology* 11(3), April, 1952.

Brownian motion. *See* CONTINUOUS-TIME STOCHASTIC PROCESSES.

Brydges, Samuel Egerton, Bart. (1762–1837). To anyone disposed to make a psychological study of a defunct antiquary, topographer, essayist, bibliographer, poet, novelist, and critic, and who added to these occupations the study of political economy and occasional authorship in that science, Sir Egerton Brydges would afford an excellent subject. On the good side may be placed his industry and power of research, considerable originality, and a deep acquaintance with the ancient literature of England and of foreign countries. On the bad side should be ranged his excessively morbid temperament, a craze about an assumed right to an ancient barony, an intense suspicion of the motives of those who differed from him, and an unfounded notion that he was not sufficiently rewarded for his services in the cause of learning. Much material bearing on all this exists in his *Autobiography* and *Letters from the Continent*, as well as in his voluminous published and privately printed works, which in the course of his long life extended to no less than one hundred and forty volumes. We find in a quantity of his letters, which have never been printed, addressed, from 1818 to 1832, to Mr. James S. Brooks, member of a firm of solicitors who acted for him, and with whom, in a characteristic manner, he often fell out, many striking examples of Sir Egerton Brydges' talent as a political economist. It is a curious fact that in his most desponding and brooding moments he would fly to political economy as a relaxation of thought and as a favourite study, just as many of our first-class English statesmen have relieved tension of mind and the excitement of political conflict by Homeric studies or the composition of Greek and Latin verses.

Although Sir Egerton Brydges' works contain flashes of insight into correct deductions, practical as well as theoretical, they are a good deal disfigured by his want of study of the statistics and practice of commerce, and his ignorance of business generally.

[F. HENDRIKS]

Reprinted from *Palgrave's Dictionary of Political Economy*.

SELECTED WORKS

1799. *Tests of the National Wealth*. London.
1814. *Letters on the Poor Laws*. London.
1817. Reasons for a farther amendment to the Act of 54 George III cap. 156, being an act to amend the copyright act of 2 Anne. *Pamphleteer* 10, 493.
1818a. *A Vindication of the pending bill for the amendment of the copyright act from the misrepresentations and unjust comments of the syndics of the university library at Cambridge*. London.
1818b. *A Summary statement of the great grievance imposed on authors and publishers and the injury done to literature by the late copyright act*. London.
1818c. *Arguments for the Employment of the Poor*. London.
1818d. On the practicality of relieving the able-bodied poor. *Pamphleteer* 11, 133.
1819. *The Population and Riches of the Nation Considered*. Geneva: Lee Priory.
1820. *Answer to ... a Mode of Relieving ... the National Debt of Great Britain*. Florence.
1821. *What Are Riches?* Geneva. Reprinted, *Pamphleteer* 20, 479.
1822. *Letter on the Corn Question*. London.
1834. *Autobiography, Times and Opinions of Egerton Brydges*. 2 vols, London.

bubbles. A bubble may be defined loosely as a sharp rise in price of an asset or a range of assets in a continuous process, with the initial rise generating expectations of further rises and attracting new buyers – generally speculators interested in profits from trading in the asset rather than its use or earning capacity. The rise is usually followed by a reversal of expectations and a sharp decline in price often resulting in financial crisis. A boom is a more extended and gentler rise in prices, production and profits than a bubble, and may be followed by crisis, sometimes taking the form of a crash (or panic) or alternatively by a gentle subsidence of the boom without crisis.

Bubbles have existed historically, at least in the eyes of contemporary observers, as well as booms so intense and excited that they have been called 'manias'. The most notable bubbles were the Mississippi bubble in Paris in 1719–20, set in motion by John Law, founder of the *Banque Générale* and the *Banque Royale*, and the contemporaneous and related South Sea bubble in London. Most famous of the manias were the Tulip mania in Holland in 1636, and the Railway mania in England in 1846–7. It is sometimes debated whether a particular sharp rise and fall in prices, such as the German

hyperinflation from 1920 to 1923, or the rise and fall in commodity and share prices in London and New York in 1919–21, the rise of gold of $850 an ounce in 1982 and its subsequent fall to the $350 level, were or were not bubbles. Some theorists go further and question whether bubbles are possible with rational markets, which they assume exist (see e.g. Flood and Garber, 1980).

Rational expectations theory holds that prices are formed within the limits of available information by market participants using standard economic models appropriate to the circumstances. As such, it is claimed, market prices cannot diverge from fundamental values unless the information proves to have been widely wrong. The theoretical literature uses the assumption of the market having one mind and one purpose, whereas it is observed historically that market participants are often moved by different purposes, operate with different wealth and information and calculate within different time horizons. In early railway investment, for example, initial investors were persons doing business along the rights of way who sought benefits from the railroad for their other concerns. They were followed by a second group of investors interested in the profits the railroad would earn, and by a third group, made up of speculators who, seeing the rise in the railroad's shares, borrowed money or paid for the initial instalments with no intention of completing the purchase, to make a profit on resale.

The objects of speculation resulting in bubbles or booms and ending in numerous cases, but not all, in financial crisis, change from time to time and include commodities, domestic bonds, domestic shares, foreign bonds, foreign shares, urban and suburban real estate, rural land, leisure homes, shopping centres, Real Estate Investment Trusts, 747 aircraft, super-tankers, so-called 'collectibles' such as paintings, jewellery, stamps, coins, antiques etc. and, most recently, syndicated bank loans to developing countries. Within these relatively broad categories, speculation may fix on particular objects – insurance shares, South American mining stocks, cotton-growing land, Paris real estate, Post-Impressionist art, and the like.

At the time of writing, the theoretical literature has yet to converge on an agreed definition of bubbles, and on whether they are possible. Virtually the same authors who could not reject the no-bubbles hypothesis in the German inflation of 1923 one year, managed to do so a year later (Flood and Garber, 1980). Another pair of theorists has demonstrated mathematically that rational bubbles can exist after putting aside 'irrational bubbles' on the grounds not of their non-existence but of the difficulty of the mathematics involved (Blanchard and Watson, 1982).

Short of bubbles, manias and irrationality are periods of euphoria which produce positive feedback, price increases greater than justified by market fundamentals, and booms of such dimensions as to threaten financial crisis, with possibilities of a crash or panic. Minsky (1982a, 1982b) has discussed how after an exogenous change in economic circumstances has altered profit opportunities and expecta-tions, bank lending can become increasingly lax by rigorous standards. Critical exception has been taken to his taxonomy dividing bank lending into hedge finance, to be repaid out of anticipated cash flows; speculative finance, requiring later refinancing because the term of the loan is less than the project's payoff; and Ponzi finance, in which the borrower expects to pay off his loan with the proceeds of sale of an asset. It is objected especially that Carlo Ponzi was a swindler and that many loans of the third type, for example those to finance construction, are entirely legitimate (Flemming,

Goldsmith and Melitz, 1982). Nonetheless, the suggestion that lending standards grow more lax during a boom and that the banking system on that account becomes more fragile has strong historical support. It is attested, and the contrary rational-expectations view of financial markets is falsified, by the experience of such a money and capital market as London having successive booms, followed by crisis, the latter in 1810, 1819, 1825, 1836, 1847, 1857, 1866, 1890, 1900, 1921 – a powerful record of failing to learn from experience (Kindleberger, 1978).

CHARLES P. KINDLEBERGER

See also TULIPMANIA.

BIBLIOGRAPHY

Blanchard, O. and Watson, M.W. 1982. Bubbles, rational expectations and financial markets. In *Crises in the Economic and Financial Structure*, ed. P. Wachtel, Lexington, Mass.: Heath.

Flemming, J.S., Goldsmith, R.W. and Melitz, J. 1982. Comment. In *Financial Crises: Theory, History and Policy*, ed. C.P. Kindleberger and J.-P. Laffargue, Cambridge: Cambridge University Press.

Flood, R.P. and Garber, P.M. 1980. Market fundamentals versus price-level bubbles: the first tests. *Journal of Political Economy* 88(4), August, 745–70.

Kindleberger, C.P. 1978. *Manias, Panics and Crashes: A History of Financial Crises*. New York: Basic Books.

Minsky, H.P. 1982a. *Can 'It' Happen Again?: Essays on Instability and Finance*. Armonk: Sharpe.

Minsky, H.P. 1982b. The financial instability hypothesis. In *Financial Crises: Theory, History and Policy*, ed. C.P. Kindleberger and J.-P. Laffargue, Cambridge: Cambridge University Press.

Buchanan, David (1779–1848). Buchanan was born in Montrose, the eldest son of David Buchanan, the renowned printer, publisher, and amateur literary scholar. Unlike his father, David the younger did not attend university, but entered the family business. Primarily interested in economics, geography and statistics, Buchanan is generally regarded as a journalist and writer, but also as a 'Scottish economist' (*Encyclopedia of the Social Sciences*, 1935, iii. 27). Buchanan's career amply justifies all of these claims.

Invited by Francis Horner and Francis Jeffrey to act as editor for the short-lived *Weekly Register* in 1808, Buchanan moved to the *Caledonian Mercury* two years later and remained in this post until 1827. In the same year he became editor of the *Edinburgh Courant*, a position he held until his sudden death in 1848.

In 1835 Buchanan helped to compile the *Edinburgh Geographical Atlas*, and made a number of contributions to the *Edinburgh Gazetteer*. He also contributed pieces on geography and statistics to the seventh edition of the *Encyclopaedia Britannica* (1842), which were acknowledged in the preface. But the bulk of Buchanan's output was on economics, with numerous articles appearing in Cobbett's *Political Register* and in the *Edinburgh Review*. The latter in particular carried pieces on 'Lord Henry Petty's plan of Finance' (1807), 'Wheatley on Money and Finance' (1807), 'Spence on Agriculture and Commerce' (with Francis Jeffrey, 1809), the Corn Laws (1815), and 'Corn and Money' (1816).

This growing interest in economic subjects prepared Buchanan for his critical, annotated edition of the *Wealth of Nations* (1814), which in turn paved the way for his *Observations on the Subjects Treated of in Dr. Smith's Inquiry* published in the same year. In the Introduction to the latter work Buchanan set Smith's achievement in the context of the work done by Sir James Steuart and the physiocrats. While

expressing qualified admiration for both, Buchanan noted that the *Wealth of Nations* 'is a great display of reason on the business of the world; touching society in all its essential relations, containing lessons for government as well as for common life, and embracing subjects formerly placed without the limits of philosophy' (1814, p. viii).

Yet Dr Smith had 'not published a perfect work'. The critical 'dissertations' which follow supplement the notes with the intention of correcting 'what is amiss' (p. xv).

Less successful in his treatment of Ricardo, Buchanan elaborated on the determinants of price and criticized Smith's theory of rent. Other subjects covered include: metallic money and paper currency, wages, stock, productive and unproductive labour, the progress of opulence, the Corn Laws, commercial treaties, defence, public debt and the East India Company.

Buchanan included a section on taxation and went on to publish an *Inquiry into the Taxation and Commercial Policy of Great Britain* (1844) which subsequently attracted some critical acclaim.

In 1852 Buchanan was described as a man of 'unobtrusive habits, mild and gentle in his demeanour, and held in high respect by all who had an opportunity of forming an estimate of his character' (Anderson, 1863, p. 481).

ANDREW SKINNER

SELECTED WORKS

1814. (ed.) *Inquiry into the Nature and Causes of the Wealth of Nations*, in three volumes; to which is added *Observations on the Subjects Treated of in Dr. Smith's Inquiry* (1814), Edinburgh: Oliphant, Waugh & Innes; London: John Murray.

1844. *Inquiry into the Taxation and Commercial Policy of Great Britain, with Observations on the Principles of Currency and of Exchangeable Value*. Edinburgh: W. Tait.

BIBLIOGRAPHY

Anderson, W. 1863. *The Scottish Nation*. Edinburgh: A. Fullarton.

David Buchanan. In *Dictionary of National Biography*, Vol. VII. London: Smith, Elder & Co., 1886.

David Buchanan. In *Encyclopedia of the Social Sciences*, Vol. III. New York: Macmillan, 1935.

David Buchanan. In *Dictionary of Political Economy*, ed, R.H. Inglis Palgrave, Vol. I. London: Macmillan 1894.

Wellesley Index to Victorian Periodicals, 1824–1900. Ed. W.E. Houghton, Toronto: Toronto University Press 1966.

Bücher, Karl Wilhelm (1847–1930). Karl Bücher was born in Kirberg (Germany) into a poor family. He studied history and classical philology in Bonn and Göttingen. Bücher first worked as a journalist for the liberal *Frankfurter Zeitung*, and from 1881 taught political economy in Dorpat, Basle, Karlsruhe and Leipzig, where he retired in 1917.

Bücher is counted among the outstanding economists of the German 'younger' historical school. He remained, however, independent in his economic thinking. He did not adhere to the inductive method and in the Methodenstreit he sided with Menger against Schmoller. Although he advocated the adoption of social policy measures by the State, he confessed to being a liberal and did not follow the protectionist and state interventionist line of the 'Kathedersozialisten' (socialists of the chair). An important contribution to economics was Bücher's 'law of mass production', which described the relationship between production costs and output in industrial manufacturing. Moreover, Bücher carefully analysed the organization of the labour process and the division of labour (1893, pp. 261–334). His study on the importance of rhythm for the working process in pre-industrial societies is extremely interesting and may be regarded as his most original work (1896). He described how workers transformed monotonous physical labour through the adoption of rhythmic repetitions of their movements. By adjusting the work speed to this rhythm, the working process was both eased and intensified. Such a rhythm could be generated, for example, by singing. Bücher gave vivid examples of typical work songs and particularly described the role played by work songs in combining large masses of workers to carry out large-scale works. However, a precondition for all this was the worker controlling his individual work speed and dominating his working instruments. The fact that in modern industry this was no more the case led Bücher to interesting reflections on man and work in our industrial environment (1896, pp. 112–117).

Bücher's historical research focused on primitive people, antiquity and the Middle Ages. His analysis of primitive people (1893, pp. 1–82; 1918, pp. 1–26) was too generalized and did not grasp fully the extreme complexity of economic relations among these peoples. However, in his elaborate research on the distinction between exchange and gift he anticipated some of the problems which modern ethnology would later discuss. His studies on the economies of ancient Rome and Greece were important because they contributed to the refutation of authors who described these economies as simply capitalistic. Among his contributions on the Middle Ages were studies on the social situation of women and journeymen, and a demographic study on medieval Frankfurt, where Bücher applied statistical methods (1886; 1922).

Bücher developed a theory of stages of economic development (1893, esp. pp. 83–160), where he distinguished between the household economy (Hauswirtschaft) of classical antiquity (in accordance with I K Rodbertus' notion of the *oikos* economy), the town economy (Stadtwirtschaft) of the Middle Ages, and the national economy (Volkswirtschaft), i.e. the extensive exchange economy of modern times. The role of exchange served as the central distinctive criterion: exchange was supposed to be virtually absent in the household economy, which is the reason why the characterization of antiquity (where trade had been more important than Bücher thought) as a household economy was inaccurate. Exchange was confined to locally produced commodities and local markets in the medieval town economy, and dominating every sphere of economic life in the 'national economy'.

Bücher may also be regarded as one of the founders of journalism as an academic discipline. He especially focused on the role of the press for public opinion and the problems raised by the capitalist and profit-oriented structure of the press.

B. SCHEFOLD

SELECTED WORKS

1886. *Die Bevölkerung von Frankfurt am Main im XIV. und XV. Jahrhundert: Socialstatistische Studien*. Tübingen: Laupp.
1893. *Die Entstehung der Volkswirtschaft*. 1. Sammlung. 16th edn, Tübingen: Laupp, 1922. Trans. as *Industrial Evolution*, Toronto: University of Toronto Press, 1901.
1896. *Arbeit und Rhythmus*. Abhandlungen der Königlich Sächsischen Gesellschaft der Wissenschaft. Leipzig: Hirzel, 1897.
1918. *Die Entstehung der Volkswirtschaft*. 2. Sammlung. 8th edn, Tübingen: Laupp, 1925.
1922. *Beiträge zur Wirtschaftsgeschichte*. Tübingen: Laupp.

Buckle, Henry Thomas (1821–1862). Buckle led a student's recluse life, devoted to the great historic work which he left unfinished on his death in his forty-first year (1862). In the introduction to this work, the principle that human actions obey laws verifiable by statistics, was, as Mill says (*Logic*, bk. vi, ch. xi, § 1), 'most clearly and triumphantly brought out' by Buckle. Mill does not however agree in the opinion 'that the moral qualities of mankind are little capable of being improved,' and conduce little [to] the progress of society (ibid., § 2). Dr. Venn has protested more strongly against Buckle's fatalistic interpretation of statistics (*Logic of Chance*, 2nd edn, pp. 235–241). An erroneous impression of the futility of human effort is conveyed by such statements as 'suicide is merely a product of the general condition of society, and the individual felon only carries into effect what is a necessary consequence of preceding circumstances' (Venn, *Logic of Chance*, ch. xviii, § 14; Buckle, *History of Civilisation*, vol. i, ch. i). The same disposition to underrate the force of human will appears in Buckle's theories as to the influence of physical conditions on wages and population: 'There is a strong and constant tendency in hot countries for wages to be low, in cold countries for them to be high. The evil condition of Ireland was the natural result of cheap and abundant food' (*History of Civilisation*, ch. ii). He here maintains that 'potato philosophy of wages', which Walker stigmatized (*Political Economy*, bk. v, ch. iii). Buckle's economical reflections are indeed not always sound, but they bear the impress of originality, enhanced by copious learning and recondite references. His account of the discoveries made by political economists is masterly (ch. iv). The remarks on the leading economists, in particular Adam Smith and Hume, are instructive, even when disputable. The description of Adam Smith's method as *deductive*, is a half-truth characteristic of Buckle.

[F.Y. EDGEWORTH]
Reprinted from *Palgrave's Dictionary of Political Economy*.

SELECTED WORKS
1857–61. *History of Civilisation in England*. 2 vols. London.
1872. *Miscellaneous and Posthumous Works*. Ed. H. Taylor. London.

BIBLIOGRAPHY
Huth, A.H. 1880. *The Life and Writings of Henry Thomas Buckle*. London.
Mill, J.S. 1843. *A System of Logic*. London.
Stuart-Glennie, J.S. 1875. *Pilgrim Memories, or Travel and Discussion in the birth-countries of Christianity with the late Henry Thomas Buckle*. London.
Venn, J. 1866. *The Logic of Chance*. London.
Venn, J. 1881. *Symbolic Logic*. London.
Venn, J. 1889. *The Principles of Empirical or Inductive Logic*. London.
Walker, F.A. 1883. *Political Economy*. New York; London.

budgetary policy. The subject of budgetary policy in the period following the *General Theory* concerns the impact of public expenditure and taxation on aggregate demand. More recently some attention has also been paid to the relationship between the budget and aggregate supply. In both cases emphasis must be placed on the word 'aggregate'. The structure of government expenditure and taxation will also have an impact which can be studied at the microeconomic level in terms of effects on individual firms, households and markets, but that is not what is normally covered by the present heading.

Public expenditure may be classified into two main components; expenditure on goods and services, and transfer payments. The former may be divided into capital and current expenditure, and the latter into capital and current transfers. Theoretically, this division may correspond to the economic distinction between 'using up' and 'adding to stock'. In practice the division is more broad brush, and a great deal of what would be recognized as an addition to the public sector's stock of capital is treated as current expenditure.

What is regarded in practice as a transfer payment is also somewhat blurred, and sometimes depends on a distinction between someone being employed by the public sector as opposed to being supported by it. Within the transfer heading most systems of national accounts differentiate the costs of servicing the national debt from the remainder.

The issue of debt itself, both long term and short term, is connected with the financing of a budgetary deficit. Some systems of national accounts treat the purchase of private sector financial assets as public expenditure (and their sale by the government as negative public expenditure). Others more properly regard such activities as akin to the issue and redemption of debt, and, thus, falling within the orbit of financial policy.

Turning to the taxation side, the most straightforward classification is into direct and indirect taxes. The former, comprising income and capital taxes, may be divided into taxes levied on firms and taxes levied on households. Property taxes, i.e. the rates, will also be included in this category. Indirect taxes include sales taxes, purchase taxes and VAT. Even though these are sometimes nominally levied on firms, there is a tendency in macroeconomics to assume that their incidence is such that they are actually levied on households. A similar point applies to corporation taxes which may be passed forward and should be treated as indirect taxes on households.

Given all that as background, the central macroeconomic propositions are as follows. An increase in government spending raises aggregate demand. The extent to which it does so depends on the form of the spending as mentioned above, and on the value of the multiplier. A decrease in taxation also varies aggregate demand, and again the scale of the effect depends on the tax in question and the multiplier. In this case, however, the process depends on the tax cuts raising disposable income and private spending.

To the extent that taxes are a function of income and expenditure, they will influence the size of the multiplier. The larger the marginal tax rates, the more any income or expenditure will leak into the government's coffers, and the lower the value of the multiplier.

Transfer payments, although they are classified as government expenditure, work via their effect on disposable income and private expenditure. Some transfer payments may be endogenous, e.g. unemployment and other social security payments vary inversely with income. (In the longer run the *rate* at which these and similar payments are paid is likely to vary directly with income.)

Because aggregate demand is an increasing function of government expenditure and a decreasing function of taxation, these instruments in all their complexity may be used to manipulate it. If aggregate demand is forecast to be too low compared with aggregate supply, and is not expected to adjust automatically and quickly, a combination of public expenditure increases and tax cuts may be used to improve the position. A reversal of the instruments will deal with the case in which aggregate demand is excessive.

The government's budgetary position may be defined as the difference between tax revenues and expenditures. Because the various forms of expenditure and taxation have different effects on aggregate demand, the results of budgetary policy cannot be inferred simply from an examination of the budgetary position. It is necessary to look in detail at the budget to ascertain the net impact of fiscal action (*see* BALANCED BUDGET MULTIPLIER).

The totals of government expenditure and of taxation depend partly on the levels of national income and expenditure, i.e. they are endogenous. The multiplier is lower the more powerful these endogenous forces are. This means that exogenous shocks have smaller effects on the level of national income and employment. High marginal tax rates (and transfer payments) automatically cause expenditure to fall less as income falls. They are, therefore, called *automatic* or *built in stabilizers*. This automatic stability is not, of course, an unalloyed benefit. The economy may be stabilized well away from full employment, and endogenous leakages may make it very hard for increases in government or private expenditure to cause the economy to move in an appropriate direction.

The endogeneity of some government revenue and expenditure also complicates the interpretation of the budgetary position. Starting (say) from an initial position of budget balance, a surplus may result from an increase in private spending or a reduction in government spending. The former will cause national income and tax payments to rise. The latter will cause national income to fall. (It will also cause tax payments to fall but by less than the fall in government spending.) It follows that the emergence of a surplus does not mean that policy intervention has been actively contractionary. Indeed, if national income has risen as a result of greater monetary ease, policy will actually have been expansionary.

It may also be inferred that the budget surplus or deficit must be examined in relation to the level of national income. As a first approximation, the change in this surplus relative to income, and suitably weighted by the different aggregate demand effects of its expenditure and tax components, will indicate the extent to which fiscal policy has become more or less expansionary.

Another way of approaching this sort of issue is to ask what the budgetary position would be at a constant state of national income. The typical normalization is that corresponding to full employment. As has been noted, the budget may move into deficit if exogenous forces cause national income to fall below full employment. Tax revenues will be less and transfer payments more. Increases in rates of tax and cuts in rates of transfer payment may remove the deficit, but only by lowering aggregate demand further still. It may then be relevant to note that the exogenous restoration of full employment would also restore budget balance or even give rise to an excess of revenue over expenditure. It is suggested, therefore, that as well as the actual budgetary position, it is useful to calculate the full employment surplus (or deficit). This could indicate more accurately whether the net effect of policy is expansionary or not.

The question next arises of the relationship between fiscal policy and other forms of macroeconomic intervention, notably monetary policy and incomes policy. On the former, if the budgetary position is not one of balance, there will be consequences connected with the financing of the deficit or surplus. The government must borrow to finance its deficit, for example. It may do this in a way which increases the money supply. Alternatively, it may borrow long term from the non-bank private sector. It follows that there may be both flow wealth and liquidity effects causing private expenditure to change. To the extent that a deficit is financed in ways that make the private sector feel wealthier and more liquid, the direct expansionary fiscal effect will be accentuated. National income will rise further, and with tax revenue endogenous, eventually the deficit will disappear. It is also logically possible that the deficit is financed in ways which lower the private sector propensity to spend. Indeed, this may be strong enough to offset the original fiscal expansion. The deficit would then increase, and if this absolutely larger deficit continued to be financed in the same way, national income would go on contracting.

The connection between budgetary and financial policy is strengthened if the interest rate effects of the former are also taken into account. The interest on this year's national debt adds to required expenditure next year. An excessive deficit leading to a rise in the ratio of national debt to national income can in theory raise the ratio of interest payments to income, which *ceteris paribus* will increase indefinitely.

Turning to incomes policy, a larger fraction (usually more than half) of public expenditure consists of wages and salaries paid to public sector employees. Given the number of these workers, an increase in their pay adds to government expenditure and to aggregate demand. Whether control of the public sector pay bill is regarded as budgetary policy or incomes policy may seem more a matter of terminology than of fundamental economics. But it must also be borne in mind that government demand for labour is important in many sections of the labour market, and what the government is willing to pay may also be used to forecast its policy intentions especially in regard to inflation.

For some purposes of analysis it is important to place budgetary policy in an international context. The expansionary effect of an increase in public expenditure (especially if it is tax financed) will depend on the government's propensity to import compared with the private sector's, as will the change in the balance of payments or the exchange rate.

Possibly more important than that, the effectiveness of an increase in government expenditure depends on whether the exchange rate is fixed or variable, and the degree to which capital is mobile internationally.

On the former, starting from less than full employment, an increase in government expenditure will worsen the trade balance. If the nominal exchange rate is allowed to fall, and domestic prices do not rise, so that there is also a real devaluation of the currency, exports will rise relative to imports. In other words, in standard Keynesian terms, fiscal policy is more expansionary in the flexible exchange rate case than in the fixed.

Assume now that capital is mobile. With the money supply held constant, fiscal expansion causes the interest rate to rise and capital to flow in from abroad. This in turn causes the exchange rate to appreciate (or depreciate less). For sufficiently mobile capital the appreciation will offset the expansionary effects of the initial fiscal intervention, i.e. fiscal policy is rendered nugatory by perfectly mobile international capital. On the other hand, if the exchange rate is fixed, this same internationally mobile capital will finance a trade deficit. Thus, fiscal policy is most effective at least in the short term with a fixed exchange rate and highly sensitive international capital flows.

M.H. PESTON

See also DEFICIT FINANCING; DEFICIT SPENDING.

BIBLIOGRAPHY
The literature on budgetary policy is enormous. The following works contain useful bibliographies as well as being valuable in their own right.

Hansen, B. 1956. *The Economic Theory of Fiscal Policy*. London: Allen & Unwin.
Peacock, A.T. and Shaw, R. 1982. *The Economic Theory of Fiscal Policy*. 2nd edn, London: Allen & Unwin.

Peston, M. 1982. *Theory of Macroeconomic Policy*. 2nd edn, Oxford: Philip Allan.

budget constraint. *See* WEALTH CONSTRAINT.

budget deficit. *See* DEFICIT FINANCING; DEFICIT SPENDING.

buffer stocks. Sharp fluctuations in the prices of primary commodities seem to have been an integral part of the international economy for a long time. Keynes (1942) commented that 'One of the greatest evils in international trade before the war was the wide and rapid fluctuations in the world prices of primary products ...' and went on to argue that a stable post-war economic order would require a scheme to stabilize commodity prices. In this context he suggested the setting up of buffer stocks from which supply could be enhanced in periods of upward pressure on prices, and into which part of world supply could be withdrawn in periods of downward pressure on prices. As is documented in Volume XXVII of his collected works, Keynes lost the political battle to introduce such a buffer stock scheme. The post-war period saw attempts at price stabilization for individual commodities such as rubber, tin and sugar, but the major attempt at a comprehensive world wide scheme covering several commodities has been UNCTAD's 1976 proposal on an Integrated Program for Commodities. This proposal has also met with notable failure, and as things stand the case for buffer stocks on an international level seems to have lost its momentum. However, history teaches us that interest in buffer stocks is itself a cyclical phenomenon, and that concern for commodity price stabilization, particularly in the consuming nations of the North, is typically renewed in periods of commodity price booms.

To see the analytical arguments in favour of and against buffer stocks, consider the case where the demand curve for a commodity is fixed while the supply fluctuates for climatic or other reasons. Then the price of the commodity, determined by market forces, will also fluctuate. These fluctuations impose a cost on producers, but it is important to realize that (a) the root cause is supply uncertainty, and that (b) producers are interested not so much in price variability as in income variability. If the elasticity of demand is less than unity, then price fluctuations compensate for quantity fluctuations. In this situation, stabilizing price may actually increase income fluctuations. However, in the case where supply is certain but demand is variable, it is certain that price stabilization will also stabilize income. Newbery and Stiglitz (1981) carry out a comprehensive analysis of the benefits from price stabilization. Their conclusions are not supportive of buffer stock schemes: 'The major result of our analysis is to question seriously the desirability of price stabilization schemes, both from the point of view of the producer and of the consumer'.

So far as producers are concerned, the Newbery–Stiglitz conclusion follows from the observation that price changes typically compensate for supply fluctuations, and also because for observed values of the resultant income variability, and using experimental evidence on individual's risk aversion, the net 'risk premium' is not very large. The use of individual values for risk aversion, in evaluating the benefits to a nation of income stability, is questioned in Kanbur (1984). Also questioned is the direct identification of commodity earnings instability with instability of national income. Commodity earnings are foreign exchange, and in foreign exchange constrained regimes the cost of such instability may be much higher than viewing the instability in exactly analogous manner to an individual's insurance problem.

On the side of consumers, the Newbery–Stiglitz approach is again a microeconomic one, whereas the approach of Keynes (1942), Kaldor (1976) and Kanbur–Vines (1985) is macro-economic in nature. Newbery and Stiglitz view the costs of commodity price instability to the consuming nations just like the cost to an individual of price instability – which turns out to be small. But the Keynesian argument centres around the role of commodity price instability in fuelling the inflationary spiral in the consuming nations. Kanbur and Vines (1985) consider the benefits of stabilization in such a Keynesian setting, and find them to be larger than hitherto supposed.

The debate on buffer stocks will no doubt continue, but there are some lessons which have certainly been learned from the latest round of analysis. Firstly, supply responses are important. It is crucial to an understanding of the operation of buffer stocks to realize that a change in the degree of price instability will change supply conditions and hence the environment in which the scheme has to operate. This simultaneity must be taken into account. Secondly, the behaviour of agents other than producers has to be analysed – in particular, buffer stock schemes may be open to speculative attack rather in the manner of a central bank attempting to maintain a fixed exchange rate with limited reserves. Thirdly, the optimal behaviour of the buffer stock authority is a complicated matter. One approach to characterizing the solution, for a given economic environment, is to use stochastic dynamic programming; the analysis is further complicated by the fact that the solution will itself affect supply response and hence the economic environment. Also, the solution may be difficult to implement operationally. In actual operations, a 'band width rule' is often specified, which gives authority to the buffer stock managers to intervene above and below critical price levels.

Finally, there remains the question of why international negotiations on a comprehensive system of buffer stocks for major commodities have been singularly unsuccessful. Does this indicate that the benefits from commodity price stabilization are small? We have to be careful in separating out the intellectual pros and cons of stabilization from the political realities of international negotiations. For a start, in these negotiations the *stability* of prices gets confounded with the *level* of prices. The latter is a matter of the distribution of income between producers and consumers, while it is the former which has been the focus of most analysis. Also, while attempts to tie together a number of commodities in a single scheme can be justified from the point of view of being able to take advantage of the covariance between different prices, such tying together inevitably raises conflicts within the producing nations and within the consuming nations. Finally, discussions of and negotiations on UNCTAD's Integrated Program for Commodities inevitably became entangled with wider questions on the New International Economic Order. For these reasons it would be inappropriate to read the failures of such proposals to find acceptance as a sure sign of an intellectual weakness in the case for buffer stocks. The debate will continue, and the issue is still wide open.

RAVI KANBUR

See also COMMODITY RESERVE CURRENCY; INVENTORIES.

BIBLIOGRAPHY

Kaldor, N. 1976. Inflation and recession in the world economy. *Economic Journal* 86, December, 703–14.

Kanbur, S.M.R. 1984. How to analyse commodity price stabilization? A review article. *Oxford Economic Papers* 36(3), 336–58.

Kanbur, S.M.R. and Vines, D.A. 1987. North–South interaction and commod control. *Journal of Development Economics*.

Keynes, J.M. 1942. The international regulation of primary products. Reprinted in *Collected Writings of John Maynard Keynes*, Vol. XXVII, London: Macmillan, 1982.

Newbery, D.M.G. and Stiglitz, J.E. 1981. *The Theory of Commodity Price Stabilization – A Study in the Economics of Risk*. Oxford: Oxford University Press.

built-in stabilizers. Built-in stabilizers are automatic fiscal adjustments that reduce the national income multiplier and thus cushion the effect of changes in autonomous spending on the level of income. Suppose the multiplier is $1/(1 - c)$ in an economy with no tax or with a lump sum tax, where c is the marginal propensity to consume. With a proportional income tax, t, the multiplier is reduced to $1/_{c}[1 - c(1 - t)]$.

The two groups of stabilizers are taxes, in particular income taxes, and government transfer payments, such as unemployment compensation and welfare benefits. These stabilizers moderate the fall in income when private spending declines and restrain the increase in income when private spending rises. The properties of built-in stabilizers were discovered by many people soon after John Maynard Keynes's *General Theory of Employment, Interest and Money* (1936) was published, but the first person to use the term was Albert Gailord Hart (in De Chazeau et al., 1946); Hart (1945), Brown (1955), Richard A. Musgrave (1948) and Herbert Stein (De Chazeau et al., 1946) played a major role in the development and popularization of the theory of built-in stabilizers.

Two related statistical measures are used to describe fiscal responses to changes in economic activity. *Built-in flexibility* (b) is the change in tax revenues per unit of change in income dT/dY. *Elasticity* (e) is the ratio of the percentage change in tax revenues to the percentage change in income $[dT/T \div dY/Y] = (dT/dY)(Y/T)$. Denoting the effective rate T/Y as r, b can be expressed as a function of e: $b = e \times r$. Thus, the effectiveness of a tax (or expenditure) programme in cushioning changes in income is greater the higher its elasticity and the higher its effective rate. During periods of inflation, the increase in tax revenues or reduction in expenditures must be in *real* terms for the tax or expenditure programmes to qualify as automatic stabilizers.

Because of built-in stabilizers, the actual deficit or surplus reflects the prevailing levels of income and unemployment, as well as the government's fiscal policy. Thus, the effects of various fiscal programmes on demand may be compared only after removing the effects of the built-in stabilizers on the budget. By convention, the calculation is made at a high level of employment (say, 94 or 96 per cent of the labour force, depending on which rate is consistent with non-accelerating inflation) and the result is called the *high-employment deficit or surplus*. The stabilizing budget policy of the Committee for Economic Development, a non-profit organization of influential businessmen and educators, proposed that tax rates should be set to balance the budget or yield a small surplus at high employment.

The individual income tax is the most important stabilizer, both because of its size and progressive rate structure. When incomes fall, some people who were formerly taxable drop below the taxable level; others are pushed into lower tax brackets. When incomes rise, more people become taxable and others move into higher tax brackets. The result is that the yield of the individual income tax rises and falls more than in proportion to changes in income. Since consumption depends to a considerable extent on disposable personal income, automatic changes in individual income tax liabilities keep consumption more stable than it otherwise would be.

The cyclical elasticity of the corporation income tax is greater than that of the individual income tax because corporate profits fluctuate more widely than individual incomes. However, the corporate tax is less important as a stabilizer because it is much smaller. The policy of corporations to cut into saving rather than to reduce dividends when profits decline also stabilizes final demand. The reduction of retained corporate earnings prevents a corresponding decline in disposable personal income, thus helping to maintain spending of consumers.

Receipts from a general consumption tax (such as a general sales tax) or a proportional payroll tax respond about in proportion to changes in income. Excise taxes are even less effective automatic stabilizers than a general consumption tax because they are usually levied on the number of units (for example, cents per gallon) rather than as a percentage of the value of purchases and thus do not increase as prices increase.

The major built-in stabilizer on the expenditure side of the budget is unemployment compensation. These payments maintain consumption as output and employment fall. As incomes go up and employment increases, unemployment compensation declines. Other transfer payments (for example, social security and welfare benefits) also increase more rapidly during recessions as the number of beneficiaries increases, but their cyclical fluctuations are much smaller than the fluctuations of unemployment benefits.

Built-in flexibility is clearly desirable when inflation results from an overheated economy. But it may have perverse effects if prices are rising when employment and output are falling. In these circumstances, real tax receipts will rise if nominal income elasticity exceeds unity. Such a tax increase would aggravate the decline in economic activity.

Automatic increases in income taxes during periods of inflation raise real tax burdens without any action on the part of legislatures. To offset this 'bracket creep', many countries adjust income tax rates and exemptions automatically for inflation. In these indexed systems, the stabilizing effect of the income tax is limited to the change in tax liabilities from changes in real income, and not from the inflation component of income changes. Less attention has been paid in recent years to built-in flexibility, primarily because of the opposition to automatic increases in real tax burdens as a result of inflation.

JOSEPH A. PECHMAN

See also STABILIZATION POLICY.

BIBLIOGRAPHY
Brown, E.C. 1955. The static theory of automatic fiscal stabilization. *Journal of Political Economy* 63, October, 427–40.
Committee for Economic Development. 1947. *Taxes and the Budget. A Program for Prosperity in a Free Economy.* New York.
De Chazeau, M.G. et al. 1946. *Jobs and Markets.* A Committee for Economic Development Research Study, New York and London: McGraw-Hill.
Hart, A.G. 1945. Model building and fiscal policy. *American Economic Review* 35, September, 531–58.
Keynes, J.M. 1936. *The General Theory of Employment, Interest and Money.* London: Macmillan.
Musgrave, R.A. and Miller, M.H. 1948. Built-in flexibility. *American Economic Review* 38, March, 122–8.
Slitor, R.E. 1948. The measurement of progressivity and built-in flexibility. *Quarterly Journal of Economics* 62, February, 309–13.

Bukharin, Nikolai Ivanovitch (1888–1938). Nikolai Bukharin is commonly acknowledged to have been one of the most brilliant theoreticians in the Bolshevik movement and an outstanding figure in the history of Marxism. Born in Russia, he studied economics at Moscow University and (during four years of exile in Europe and America) at the Universities of Vienna and Lausanne (Switzerland), in Sweden and Norway and in the New York Public Library. While still a student, he joined the Bolshevik movement. Upon returning to Russia in April 1917, he worked closely with Lenin and participated in planning and carrying out the October Revolution. After the victory of the Bolsheviks he proceeded to assume many high offices in the Party (becoming a member of the Politbureau in 1919) and in other important organizations. In these various capacities he came to exercise great influence within both the Party and the Comintern. Under Stalin's regime, however, he lost most of his important positions. Eventually, he was among those who were arrested and brought to trial under charges of treason and was executed on 15 March 1938.

At the peak of his career Bukharin was regarded as the foremost authority on Marxism in the Party. He was a prolific writer: there are more than five hundred items of published work in his name, most of them written in the hectic twelve-year period 1916–1928 (for a comprehensive bibliography, see Heitman, 1969). Only a few of these works have been translated into English and these are the works for which he is now most widely known. A brief description of the major items gives an indication of the scope and range of his intellectual interests.

The Economic Theory of the Leisure Class (1917) is a detailed and comprehensive critique of the ideas of the Austrian school of economic theory, as represented by the work of its chief spokesman Eugen von Böhm-Bawerk, but situated in the broader context of marginal theory as it had appeared up to that time. In *Imperialism and World Economy* (1918) he formulated a revision of Marx's theory of capitalist development and set out his own theory of imperialism as an advanced stage of capitalism. This was written in 1914–15, a year before Lenin's *Imperialism*, and is credited with having been a major influence on Lenin's formulation. The theoretical structure of the argument is further elaborated in *Imperialism and the Accumulation of Capital* (1924) by way of a critique of the ideas of Rosa Luxemburg, another leading Marxist writer of that time. *The ABC of Communism* (1919), written jointly with Evgenii Preobrazhensky and used as a standard textbook in the Twenties, is a comprehensive restatement of the principles of Marxism as applied to analysis of the development of capitalism, the conditions for revolution, and the nature of the tasks of building socialism in the specific context of the Soviet experience. This book, taken with his *Economics of the Transition Period* (1920), constitutes a contribution to both the Marxist theory of capitalist breakdown and world revolution on the one hand and the theory of socialist construction on the other. *Historical Materialism: A System of Sociology* (1921), another popular textbook, combines a special interpretation of the philosophical basis of Marxism with what is perhaps the first systematic theoretical statement of Marxism as a system of sociological analysis. In style much of this work is highly polemical and geared to immediate political goals. But it reveals also a versatility of intellect, serious theoretical concern, and scholarly inclination. Arguably, his works represent in their entirety 'a comprehensive reformulation of the classical Marxian theory of proletarian revolution' (Heitman, 1962, p. 79). Viewed from the standpoint of their significance in terms of economic analysis, three major components stand out.

There is, first, the critique of 'bourgeois economic theory' in its Austrian version. Bukharin's approach follows that which Marx had adopted in *Theories of Surplus Value*, which is to give an 'exhaustive criticism' not only of the methodology and internal logic of the theory but also of the sociological and class basis which it reflects. He scores familiar points against particular elements of the theory, for instance, that utility is not measurable, that Böhm-Bawerk's concept of an 'average period of production' is 'nonsensical', that the theory is static. Such criticisms of the technical apparatus of the theory have since been developed in more refined and sophisticated form (see Harris, 1978, 1981; Dobb, 1969). Moreover, certain weaknesses in Bukharin's presentation, such as an apparent confusion between marginal and total utility and misconception of the meaning of interdependent markets, can now be readily recognized. But these are matters that were not well understood at the time, even by exponents of the theory. Bukharin views them as matters of lesser importance. What is crucial for him is 'the point of departure of the ... theory, its ignoring the social-historical character of economic phenomena' (1917, p. 73). This criticism is applied with particular force to the treatment of the problem of capital, the nature of consumer demand, and the process of economic evolution. As to the sociological criticism, his central thesis is that the theory is the ideological expression of the rentier class eliminated from the process of production and interested solely in disposing of their income through consumption. This thesis can be faulted for giving too mechanical and simplistic an interpretation of the relation between economic theory and ideology where a dialectical interpretation is called for (compare, for instance, Dobb, 1973, ch. 1, and Meek, 1967). But the issue of the social-ideological roots of the marginal revolution remains a problematic one, as yet unresolved, with direct relevance to current interest in the nature of scientific revolutions in the social sciences (see Kuhn, 1970; Latsis, 1976).

Secondly, Bukharin's work clearly articulates a conception of the development of capitalism as a world system to a more advanced stage than that of industrial capitalism which Marx had earlier analysed. This new stage is characterized by the rise of monopoly or 'state trusts' within advanced capitalist states, intensified international competition among different national monopolies leading to a quest for economic, political and military control over 'spheres of influence', and breaking out into destructive wars between states. These conditions are seen as inevitable results deriving from inherent tendencies in the capitalist accumulation process, at the heart of which is a supposed falling tendency in the overall average rate of profit. Altogether they are viewed as an expression of the anarchic and contradictory character of capitalism. The formation of monopolies is supposed to take place through reorganization of production by finance capitalists as a way of finding new sources of profitable investment and of exercising centralized regulation and control of the national economy. This transformation succeeds for a time at the national level but only to raise the contradictions to the level of the world economy where they can be resolved only through revolutions breaking out at different 'weak links' of the world-capitalist system. The idea of a necessary long-term decline in the rate of profit, and also the specific role assigned to financial

enterprises as such, can be disputed. A crucial ingredient of the argument is the idea of oligopolistic rivalry and international mobility of capital as essential factors governing international relations. In this respect the argument anticipates ideas that are only now being recognized and absorbed into the orthodox theory of international trade and which, in his own time, were conspicuously neglected within the entire corpus of existing economic theory. Much of the analysis as regards a necessary tendency to uneven development between an advanced *centre* and underdeveloped *periphery* of the world economy has also been absorbed into contemporary theories of underdevelopment. Underpinning the whole argument is a curious theory of 'social equilibrium' and of 'crisis' originating from a loss of equilibrium. 'To find the law of this equilibrium', he suggests (1979, p. 149), 'is the basic problem of theoretical economics and theoretical economics as a scientific system is the result of an examination of the entire capitalist system in its state of equilibrium'.

The third component is a comprehensive conception of the process of socialist construction in a backward country. These ideas came out of the practical concerns and rich intellectual ferment associated with the early period of Soviet development but have a generality and relevance extending down to current debates both in the development literature and on problems of socialist planning. The overall framework is one that conceives of socialist development as a long-drawn-out process 'embracing a whole enormous epoch' and going through four revolutionary phases: ideological, political, economic and technical. The process is seen as occurring in the context of a kind of war economy involving highly centralized state control, though there is an optimistic prediction of an ultimate 'dying off of the state power'. Room is allowed for preserving and maintaining small-scale private enterprise. The agricultural sector is seen as posing special problems, due to the assumed character of peasant production, which can only be overcome through transformation by stages to collectivized large-scale production. Even so, it is firmly held (in 1919) that 'for a long time to come small-scale peasant farming will be the predominant form of Russian agriculture', a view which Bukharin later abandoned in support of Stalin's collectivization drive. In industry, too, small-scale industry, handicraft, and home industry are to be supported, so that the all-round strategy is one that seems quite similar to that of 'walking-on two-legs' later propounded by Mao for China. An extensive discussion is presented of almost every detail of the economic programme, from technology to public health, but little or no attention is given to issues of incentives and organizational problems of centralization/decentralization which have emerged as crucial considerations in later work.

DONALD J. HARRIS

SELECTED WORKS

1917. *Economic Theory of the Leisure Class*. New York: Monthly Review Press, 1972.

1918. *Imperialism and World Economy*. New York: Monthly Review Press, 1973.

1919. (With E. Preobrazhensky.) *The ABC of Communism*. Harmondsworth: Penguin Books, 1969.

1920. The economics of the transition period. In *The Politics and Economics of the Transition Period*, ed. K.J. Tarbuck, London: Routledge & Kegan Paul, 1979.

1921. *Historical Materialism, A System of Sociology*. Ann Arbor: University of Michigan Press, 1969.

1924. *Imperialism and the Accumulation of Capital*. New York: Monthly Review Press, 1972.

BIBLIOGRAPHY

Dobb, M. 1969. *Welfare Economics and the Economics of Socialism*. Cambridge: Cambridge University Press.

Dobb, M. 1973. *Theories of Value and Distribution since Adam Smith*. Cambridge: Cambridge University Press.

Harris, D.J. 1978. *Capital Accumulation and Income Distribution*. Stanford: Stanford University Press.

Harris, D.J. 1981. Profits, productivity, and thrift: the neoclassical theory of capital and distribution revisited. *Journal of Post-Keynesian Economics* 3(3), Spring, 359–82.

Heitman, S. 1962. Between Lenin and Stalin: Nikolai Bukharin. In *Revisionism*, ed. Leopold Labedz, New York: Praeger.

Heitman, S. 1969. *Nikolai I. Bukharin: a Bibliography*. Stanford: Hoover Institution.

Kuhn, T. 1970. *The Structure of Scientific Revolutions*. 2nd edn, enlarged, Chicago: University of Chicago Press.

Latsis, S. (ed.) 1976. *Method and Appraisal in Economics*. Cambridge: Cambridge University Press.

Lenin, V.I. 1917. *Imperialism, the Highest Stage of Capitalism*. New York: International Publishers, 1939.

Meek, R.L. 1967. *Economics and Ideology and Other Essays*. London: Chapman & Hall.

Bullionist Controversy. 'Bullionist Controversy' is the label conventionally attached to the series of debates about monetary theory and policy which took place in Britain over the years 1797–1821, when the specie convertibility of Bank of England notes was suspended. The protagonists in this controversy are usually classified into two camps – 'bullionist' supporters of specie convertibility who were critics of the Bank of England, and 'anti-bullionist' adherents of an opposing viewpoint. Such labels are useful as organizing devices, but it is dangerous to apply them rigidly. The bullionist controversy was a series of debates about a variety of issues, and those debates involved a shifting cast of participants, whose views sometimes changed as controversy continued.

Although contemporary policy problems provided most of the immediate impetus for debate, the bullionist controversy was not a series of arguments about the application of well-known economic principles to a particular set of circumstances. On the contrary, much of the debate was about fundamental questions of economic theory; and though the literature of the controversy consists largely of pamphlets, reviews, letters to newspapers, parliamentary speeches and reports, it contains contributions of crucial and lasting importance to monetary theory.

1. The Bank of England, a privately owned joint stock company, was founded in 1694 with the aim of creating a market for, and an institution to manage, the government debt arising from William III's participation in the wars against the France of Louis XIV. By the end of the 18th century its monopoly of note issue in the London area, and its status as the only note-issuing joint stock bank in England, had given it a pivotal position in the British monetary system. It had in fact evolved into the central bank at least of England, though not of the United Kingdom; for Ireland at this time had its own largely independent monetary system, with commercial banks operating on a reserve base provided by the Bank of Ireland in Dublin, which held its reserves in specie rather than in claims upon London. Scottish Banks too belonged to a distinct system, albeit one which held its reserves in London. Though reforms of the coinage beginning in 1696 and culminating in that supervised by Sir Isaac Newton in 1717 had been intended to create a bimetallic system, their undervaluation of silver had instead placed Britain on a *de facto* gold standard that was firmly entrenched by the last decade of the century.

By the 1790s the 'circulating medium', to use a contemporary phrase, consisted of gold coin, Bank of England and Country (i.e., non-London) Bank notes, while bills of exchange and bank deposits were widely used means of payment in wholesale transactions. Country Banks mainly held reserves on deposit with private London banks, which did not emit notes, and which in turn held reserves in the form of Bank of England liabilities. Britain's specie reserves were mainly held by the Bank of England in the form of bullion. The degree of concentration here was not as absolute as it would become later in the 19th century, but, to put it in modern parlance, Bank of England liabilities were high-powered money, and any difficulties in the banking system at large quickly put pressure on the Bank's specie reserves.

The outbreak of hostilities between Britain and Revolutionary France in 1793 precipitated just such pressure. A drain of reserves from the banking system into domestic private sector portfolios, to which the Bank of England responded by contracting its note issue, created a liquidity crisis. The crisis was alleviated by a government issue of exchequer bills, and this very fact speaks eloquently of the lack of appreciation, on the part of the Bank and Government alike, of the role and responsibilities of a Central Bank in the monetary and financial system which characterized the state of knowledge at the beginning of the bullionist controversy. Not the least of that controversy's enduring contributions was to advance understanding of these matters.

As France recovered from the political chaos associated with the Terror, and the monetary chaos created by the Assignats, the war began to go badly for Britain and her allies. By the beginning of 1797 France was clearly in the ascendant. Indeed, the completion of Bonaparte's Italian campaign at the end of that year would see only Britain remaining in the field against her. During 1795–6 the Bank of England had again attempted to counter a continuing drain of specie from its reserves by a contraction of its liabilities, and had probably thereby accentuated its difficulties. This certainly was the opinion of commentators such as Walter Boyd (1800), while Henry Thornton's (1802) analysis of the general importance of a Central Bank's standing ready to lend freely in the face of a domestic run on its reserves in order to restore and maintain confidence may be read, in part, as a criticism of the Bank of England's behaviour during this episode.

Be that as it may, by February of 1797, pressure on the Bank was again strong, and rumours of an impending French invasion – a small force of French troops did land in Wales but was quickly captured – provoked a run on the banking system. This run began in Newcastle and quickly spread. To the Government and the Bank of England it seemed to put that institution in jeopardy, and an Order in Council of 26 February, confirmed in May by an Act of Parliament, suspended the specie convertibility of Bank of England notes. This 'temporary' suspension, initially supposed to end in June 1797, was to last until 1821. The management of an inconvertible currency – or rather partially convertible, for gold and some subsidiary silver coin continued to circulate, and during the suspension period of Bank did from time to time declare some of its small denomination notes convertible – would have been difficult enough in peacetime; but down to 1815 the Bank of England's task was frequently complicated by the need to make large transfers abroad to subsidise allies and support British forces fighting on the Continent, not to mention the disruptive effects of the Napoleonic 'Continental System' on British trade.

The body of economic analysis which a modern economist would deploy in dealing with these matters was not available in Regency Britain. The Cantillon (1734)–Hume (1752) version of the quantity theory of money, and its associated analysis of the price-specie flow mechanism was well enough known; but that dealt with a commodity money system, not with one dominated by banks, in which a large proportion of the 'circulating medium' consisted of bank notes and deposits (or cheques drawn upon them), not to mention various commercial bills. The *Wealth of Nations* (Smith, 1776) contained extensive discussions of banking, but those discussions, as Checkland (1975) has argued, were largely based on Scottish oral tradition; they therefore dealt with the competitive operations of commercial banks against the background of specie convertibility and had next to nothing to say about central banking.

Much available knowledge about the operation of inconvertible paper systems was of a practical nature. It drew on the French experience with John Law's scheme, and later the Assignats, on many North American experiments before, during and after the American War of Independence, and, to a lesser extent, the 18th-century experience of Russia and Sweden with paper money. Though the Swedish experience had generated controversy which in many respects anticipated the British bullionist debate, as Eagly (1968) has shown, there seems to be no evidence that the Swedish literature was known in Britain, even to those who, like Henry Thornton, were aware of the events that had generated it.

In short, by the 1790s, institutional developments in the British monetary system had run far ahead of systematic knowledge of what we would now call the theory of money and banking. The difficulties of the suspension period focused attention on this fact, and the analysis developed during the course of the bullionist controversy had to solve fundamental problems in monetary theory as well as cope with contemporary policy issues. It is because it dealt with the first of these tasks with such success that the controversy is of enduring importance to monetary economists, and not just to historians of economic thought and economic historians.

II. The 18th-century experiences with inconvertible paper referred to above were, with few exceptions, unhappy, and it is scarcely surprising that, at the very outset, opponents of restriction in Britain warned of dire inflationary consequences. However, it was not until 1800 that rising prices, a decline in the value of Bank of England paper in terms of bullion, and an associated depreciation of the sterling exchange rate on Hamburg gave warning that all was not well. (We need not concern ourselves here with the complications caused by the fact that Hamburg was on a silver and not a gold standard.) These events generated a flurry of pamphlets, and it is generally agreed that Walter Boyd's (1800) *Letter to ... William Pitt* was the most noteworthy of these. It stated a simple version of what was to become known as the bullionist position, namely that the suspension of convertibility had permitted the Bank of England unduly to expand its note issue and that overexpansion had in turn brought about the above-mentioned interrelated consequence.

The fact that agricultural prices had risen considerably more than the value of bullion made it possible for defenders of the Bank of England, such as Sir Francis Baring, to argue that the problem lay elsewhere than in the banking system *per se*. The Bank's defenders also raised at this early stage of the debate what was to become an important bone of contention in later monetary debates, namely the possibility that the Country Banks, by varying their note issue, could and indeed did exert an influence on the behaviour of the price level independently of the Bank of England. The preliminary 'skirmish' of 1800–1802 as Fetter (1965) called it was indecisive, but it produced Henry Thornton's *Paper Credit ...* (1802), an

extraordinary treatise which systematically expounds the intellectual basis of what Viner (1937) termed the 'moderate bullionist' position in subsequent discussions.

Von Hayek suggests in his introduction to *Paper Credit* that Thornton may have been working on it as early as 1796, but in its published form, this book was a defence, albeit a constructively critical defence, of the Bank of England's policy during the early years of restriction. It was published during a lull in the debate, and its *direct* influence on the course of the bullionist controversy was therefore minor. During the 19th century the work dropped from sight, and its true stature was not thereafter widely appreciated until the appearance of von Hayek's (1939) edition. Indirectly, however, *Paper Credit* was of the first order of importance. Its author was an influential member both of the Committee of the House of Commons that investigated Irish currency issues in 1804 – see Fetter (1955) on this episode – and of the so-called Bullion Committee itself, whose 1810 report marked the high point of the controversy. Moreover, the chairman of the latter committee, Francis Horner, who, with help from Thornton and William Huskisson, was the principal author of its Report, had devoted a long and favourable review article to *Paper Credit ...* in the first issue of the *Edinburgh Review*.

III. The immediate cause of the renewed controversy that led to the setting up by Parliament of the *Select Committee on The High Price of Gold Bullion* in February 1810 was a re-emergence of inflationary pressures in early 1890, whose most noticeable symptoms to observers not equipped with even the concept of a price index, let alone a serviceable example of such a device, were a declining exchange rate for sterling and marked rise in the price of specie in terms of Bank of England notes. Both of these symptoms were more marked than they had been in 1800–1802, but the positions taken up in the controversy that preceded the committee's formation and accompanied its deliberations were very much those established in the preliminary skirmish of those years.

What Viner (1937) terms the 'extreme bullionist' position had been stated by John Wheatley as early as 1803, and was subsequently maintained by him. David Ricardo, whose contributions to the *Morning Chronicle* in 1809 represent his first published work in economics also argued this position, though a little more flexibly than Wheatley, notably in his (1810–11) essay on *The High Price of Gold Bullion*. Simply put, the extreme bullionist position was that the decline in the exchanges, and the increase in the price of bullion, were solely due to an excessive issue of Bank of England notes, an excessive issue which could not have taken place under convertibility. Against such views, the anti-bullionist defenders of the Bank argued that the decline in the exchanges was due to pressures exerted by extraordinary wartime foreign remittances and had nothing to do with the Bank's domestic policy. Moreover, they argued, because the Bank confined itself to making loans on the security of high quality commercial bills, drawn to finance goods in the course of production and distribution, it was impossible that its note issue could be excessive and could cause prices to rise. The first of these arguments deals with what we would now call the 'transfer problem' and the second is a statement of the infamous *Real Bills Doctrine*.

At the outset of the bullionist controversy there existed little in the way of coherent analysis of the transfer problem under conditions of convertibility, let alone of inconvertibility. Adam Smith (1776) had stated that foreign remittances would in fact be effected by a transfer of goods rather than specie abroad, but had not explained how, while during the bullionist controversy the directors of the Bank of England consistently argued that any transfer must initially involve an outflow of specie equal in amount to the transfer itself. This position was not far removed from the naïve mercantilist analysis which Hume had so effectively attacked in 1752, and was, as Fetter (1965) has noted, quite inconsistent with the actual behaviour of the Bank's specie reserves during the French wars.

A key contributor to the analysis of the transfer problem was Thornton, and the influence of ideas first expounded in *Paper Credit* is quite evident in the Committee's *Bullion Report* of 1810 (Cannan, 1919). He had shown in *Paper Credit* how a transfer of goods would be brought about under a convertible currency as a result of monetary contraction in the country making the transfer and expansion in the recipient country, and had stressed income effects as well as price level changes as critical links in the mechanism. Though he did not distinguish clearly between a convertible and an inconvertible currency, he also argued that, under post-1797 arrangements (which because of the continued circulation of gold coin did not amount to a clear-cut inconvertible system), the mechanisms in question would lead to a temporary exchange rate depreciation, even if domestic policy was such as to promote what we would now term domestic price level stability. The limits to the possible depreciation here would be set by the costs of evading legal prohibitions on the melting and export of coin.

In 1802 this analysis had formed part of Thornton's defence of Bank of England policy against bullionist critics, and it was further refined in the course of the deliberations of the Parliamentary Committee of 1803 which investigated the depreciation of the Irish pound, and on which Thornton served. At least two authors, John Hill and J.C. Herries (both anti-bullionists) were later to supplement it with the observation that a temporary depreciation created scope for short-term capital movements to help in making a transfer effective.

By 1810–11, the view that transfers could temporarily depress the exchanges under conditions of inconvertibility, and a growing scarcity of gold coin had moved the system much closer to such conditions than it had been a decade earlier, set the analysis of moderate bullionists, including Thomas R. Malthus, and of course the Bullion Committee itself, apart from that of Ricardo and Wheatley, who denied that even a temporary exchange rate depreciation could take place in the absence of a simultaneous excessive issue of domestic paper. Either this latter argument involves an implicit definition of 'excessive' and is circular; or, as Viner has suggested, it is erroneous and provides an unfortunate example of the 'Ricardian vice' of giving answers relevant to the long run equilibrium outcome of particular situations to questions having to do with the intermediate stages whereby long run equilibrium is achieved.

Disagreement among the bullionists was about temporary effects, however. Moderate bullionists were in complete agreement with their more extreme colleagues that an apparently permanent exchange depreciation could not be put down to the effects of once and for all transfers. Their view, as expressed in the 1810 *Report*, was that sterling's initial depreciation had probably been the consequence of foreign remittances, and of the effects of the Continental System on trade, but that its subsequent failure to recover was caused by an overissue of paper money by the Bank of England. They thus rejected the Bank of England's claim that it was powerless to affect the purchasing power of paper money so long as it confined its issues to those called forth by the supply for discount of good quality bills of exchange.

The analysis of the Real Bills Doctrine set out in the *Bullion Report* is in all its essentials the same as that to be found in *Paper Credit*, and is marked by a careful discussion of the mechanisms whereby the policies espoused by the Bank could lead to overissue. In this respect it is superior to that of Ricardo, who in his essay of 1810–11, without going into any details about the processes whereby the economy might move from one long run equilibrium to another, concentrated on giving an exceptionally clear statement of the nature of the long run equilibrium relationship that rules between the quantity of paper money, the exchange rate and the price of specie (which, as Hollander (1979) persuasively argues, is to be understood in this context as standing as a proxy for what we would now term the general price level).

The Real Bills Doctrine is attributable to Adam Smith (1776) but in his work it appears mainly as a rule of behaviour for the individual commercial bank operating in a competitive system against a background of specie convertibility. To discount only good short-term bills is not perhaps bad practice for such an institution if it wishes to secure its long-term viability. To claim such a principle to be a sufficient guarantee of price level stability if adopted by a Central Bank managing something akin to an inconvertible paper currency is another thing altogether, but that is what the directors of the Bank of England did, giving to the Bullion Committee what Bagehot (1874) was later to term 'answers almost classical by their nonsense' when questioned on this matter. Adherence to the Real Bills Fallacy was by no means confined to the Bank of England. It had many defenders and even so able an economist as Robert Torrens espoused the doctrine during the bullionist controversy, though in later debates he was to be one of its most vigorous opponents. Moreover, despite its definitive refutation by Thornton and the Bullion Committee, this doctrine was to reassert itself with great regularity throughout the 19th century, and into the 20th, as Mints (1945) in particular has so carefully documented.

The critical flaw in the Real Bills Doctrine arises from its implicitly treating the nominal quantity of bills of exchange offered for discount as being determined, independently of the policies of the banking system, by the real volume of goods under production in the economy, rather than by the perceived profitability of engaging in production and trade. The latter, as Thornton, the Bullion Committee and all subsequent critics of the doctrine have pointed out, depends upon the relationship between the rate of interest at which the banking system stands ready to lend, and the rate of return that borrowers expect to earn. To put it in the language of Knut Wicksell (1898), whose analysis of these matters closely follows Thornton – even though he appears to have been unaware of *Paper Credit* – everything depends on the relationship between the 'money rate of interest' and the 'natural rate of interest'.

As the Bullion Committee argued, with the rate of interest at which banks would lend set below the anticipated rate of profit, the potential supply of bills for discount would be without limit. Under specie convertibility, a banking system that had fixed its lending rate too low would find the associated expansion of money causing a drain of reserves and the central bank would be forced to raise its lending rate. Without the crucial check of convertibility, prices and the money supply would begin to rise, as would the nominal value of new bills of exchange offered for discount in a self-justifying inflationary spiral. The Real Bills Doctrine, a relatively harmless precept under specie convertibility, thus becomes, under inconvertibility, a recipe for unlimited inflation and exchange depreciation. This conclusion is of enduring importance and is perhaps the most significant result that emerged from the bullionist controversy.

The Real Bills Doctrine was particularly dangerous in the circumstances of 1810. The then current usury laws set an upper limit of 5 per cent to the rate of interest at which loans could be made, and the ability of the public to convert paper money into gold coin, and then melt the latter for export, an illegal but seemingly widely practised check on overissue in the earlier days of the suspension, had become less effective by 1810 as gold coin had become scarce. Moreover, what we would now term inflationary expectations had begun to become established in the business community. Though the point was not raised explicitly in the *Bullion Report*, in a parliamentary speech of 1811 on the *Report*, Thornton showed himself well aware of the implications of this for the relationship between nominal and real interest rates and the inflationary process, thus anticipating the insights of Irving Fisher (1896) by 85 years.

In placing the blame for the persistence of sterling's depreciation on the Bank of England, the Bullion Committee also took the position that the Country Banks' note issue had not exerted a major independent influence on prices. Their *Report* contained nothing approaching a formal analysis of what we would nowadays term the 'bank credit multiplier'; such analysis did not appear until the early 1820s, when it was first developed by Thomas Joplin and James Pennington, and indeed it was not widely understood until well into the 20th century. The Committee nevertheless took the position that the Country Banks' note issue, not to mention the other privately emitted components of the circulating medium, tended to expand and contract in rough harmony with Bank of England liabilities. This is a point of some interest, since in the debates of the 1830s and 1840s, the Currency School, who in their opposition to the Real Bills Doctrine were the intellectual heirs to the bullionists, took a diametrically opposite view of the significance of the Country Bank note issue and were eventually successful in having it suppressed.

In matters of monetary theory and the diagnosis of contemporary problems it is hard to fault the Bullion Committee even today. No other discussion of economic policy issues prepared by working politicians has had so sound an intellectual basis and has stood the test of time so well. It is more difficult to praise the *Report*'s key policy proposal, however. So worried were its authors about sterling's depreciation, and about the capacity of the Bank of England to conduct policy competently, that in the midst of major war, and at a time when sterling had significantly depreciated, they recommended a return to specie convertibility at the prewar parity within two years. The *Bullion Report* was laid before the House of Commons in May 1811 where debate on its substance was organized around a series of resolutions and counter-resolutions. Though the Commons rejected the whole *Report* it is not without interest that the specific proposal to resume convertibility within two years failed by a significantly larger majority than did any other. It should be noted though, that in rejecting the Bullion Committee's recommendations, the House of Commons simultaneously supported resumption once peace was re-established.

IV. Subsequent experience was to prove the Bullion Committee's fears of future Bank of England profligacy unfounded. Whatever the Bank's directors may have said about their operating procedures, they clearly relied on more than a real bills rule, and, as commentators from Bagehot on have noted, their policy was, if judged by results, reasonably responsible, particularly after 1810, which saw the peak of

wartime inflationary pressures. Thus debate about monetary issues had died down by 1812, but that year saw the crucial defeat of Napoleon's army in Russia. The decline in his fortunes thereafter, leading to his final surrender in 1815, set the stage for the next phase of the bullionist controversy. This dealt mainly with the problems of implementing resumption, though the first decisive peacetime monetary measure, taken by Parliament in 1816, was to remove the legal ambiguity which had persisted since 1717 about the status of silver in Britain's monetary system by formally placing the country on a gold standard, albeit one in which convertibility was still suspended.

The end of a war that had lasted for more than two decades was inevitably an occasion for considerable economic dislocation. Agriculture and metalworking industries in particular suffered badly from the re-establishment of peacetime patterns of production and trade. A simultaneous general fall of prices in terms of gold, upon which was superimposed a contraction of Bank of England liabilities and therefore an approach of sterling to its prewar parity, was associated with widespread distress. In such circumstances, it is hardly surprising that there was much political opposition to early resumption. By and large, this opposition was not grounded in any coherent economic analysis, except in Birmingham. In this city, the centre of the metalworking industries, opposition to resumption was articulated by Thomas and Matthias Attwood and their associates, and the Birmingham School showed a keen appreciation of the effects of monetary contraction and deflation upon employment, and an understanding that an appropriately managed monetary system based on inconvertible paper might, in principle, be a viable method of avoiding such problems.

At their best the Birmingham School anticipated Keynesian insights of the 1930s, but their analysis often degenerated into crude inflationism, particularly in their later writings. In any event, they were always a small minority among those whom we would nowadays recognize as economists. The vast majority of these always supported the principle of resumption at the 1797 parity. The value of Bank of England paper in terms of gold was either regarded as a good measure of its purchasing power over goods in general, or stability in the good value of money was looked upon as 'natural' and desirable in its own right; and there was widespread agreement that wartime inflation had been unjust to creditors. The problems of those who had incurred debts during the war, after paper had depreciated, provided some of the impetus to popular opposition to resumption immediately after the war, particularly in agricultural areas, but it is nevertheless fair to argue that a curious moral one-sidedness about the redistributive effects of inflation emerged among the majority of economists during this stage of the bullionist controversy. This one-sidedness, which perhaps had its roots in Hume's view of credit markets in which the typical borrower is an improvident consumer and the typical lender a frugal producer, has played an important role in debates about inflation ever since.

If there was, then, wide agreement about the ultimate desirability of resuming convertibility at the 1797 parity, its advocacy was nevertheless tempered with caution after 1812. In contrast to the *Bullion Report*'s unconcern about such matters, later discussion did pay attention to the potentially disruptive effects on output and employment of the deflation needed to implement it. Two problems were recognized: first, deflation was needed to restore sterling to its old parity with gold; and, second, there was the possibility that the increased demand for gold implied by a resumption of convertibility might itself create more deflation by driving up the relative price of specie. The end of the war was, as we have already noted, the occasion for significant price level falls, both in terms of gold, but even more in terms of Bank of England paper, whose quantity in circulation contracted considerably. The latter contraction was not, according to Fetter (1965), the result of any conscious policy decision on the part of the Bank of England, but it did have the effect of weakening any practical case against resumption by reducing the amount of further deflation needed to implement it.

Ricardo dominated the later stages of the bullionist controversy, as Thornton had dominated its earlier stages, and he is often regarded as having been unconcerned about deflation. Such unconcern would be consistent with the Ricardian vice of underplaying the importance of the short run in economic life, but, as Hollander (1979) has shown, this view of his position is not sustainable. Ricardo's 1816 *Proposals for An Economical and Secure Currency* were motivated by a desire to mitigate further deflation as well as by a desire to put the British monetary system upon an intellectually sound basis. He argued that, with resumption, Britain adopt a paper currency rather than one with a high proportion of gold coin, and that the Bank of England should hold against it a reserve of gold ingots in terms of which notes could be redeemed. One practical advantage of this scheme was that by economizing on gold, it would put little upward pressure on its value when it was implemented, and Ricardo pointed out this advantage. He mainly justified his proposal in more general terms, though, stressing the desirability *per se* of economizing on scarce precious metals when paper would serve equally well as currency, an argument which harked back to Adam Smith's defence of paper money in the *Wealth of Nations*.

Ricardo's ingot plan was adopted in 1819 by Parliament, of which he was by then a member, as a basis for resumption; but second thoughts about it soon set it, for quite practical reasons. Counterfeiting of bank notes had been virtually unknown before 1797, but the increased circulation of low denomination Bank of England notes thereafter had offered considerable temptation to forgers. The years 1797–1817 saw over 300 capital convictions for the offence. These convictions and, as Fetter (1965) records, the fact that clemency seems to have been granted or refused on the recommendation of the Bank, brought much opprobrium upon that institution from a public among which opposition to the widespread use of capital punishment was becoming intense. A paper currency backed by gold ingots might have been economical and secure, but it did not remove the temptation to forgery. Hence Ricardo's ingot plan was dropped, and when resumption was finally implemented in 1821, gold coins replaced small denomination notes in circulation. Ricardo's ingot plan was not forgotten, however; it was to be the starting point of Alfred Marshall's symmetallic proposals of (1887), and something very like it was implemented in Britain in 1925 when the country once again resumed gold convertibility in the wake of a wartime suspension. The similarities here were no accident. The literature of the bullionist controversy, not least Ricardo's contributions to it, was much read and cited throughout the 19th century and into the 20th, not least by participants in the monetary debates of the 1920s.

V. The resumption of 1821 was not the unmitigated disaster that the 1925 return to gold was to be, not least because the amount of deflation needed after 1819 to make the 1797 parity effective was rather minor. Nevertheless, resumption did not put an end either to monetary problems or to debate. Even the rather small amount of deflation needed after 1819 was hard

for the economy to digest, and a fitful recovery thereafter ended, in 1825, in the first of a series of financial crises that were to recur at roughly decennial intervals for the next half century. Thus, if 1821 marked the end of the bullionist controversy, it also marked the beginning of a new period of debate about the monetary system, and in particular about the conduct of monetary policy and the design of monetary institutions under a gold standard. This debate would, in due course, culminate in a second famous controversy, that between the Currency School and the Banking School

There is considerable continuity between these later debates and the bullionist controversy, and this simple fact attests to the important contributions which were made during its course. In only a quarter century, 18th-century analysis of commodity money mechanisms had been adapted to the circumstances of a modern banking system, and the monetary economics of the open economy under fixed and flexible exchange rates had taken on a form that is recognizable even today. Moreover, the foundations of the theory of central banking under commodity and paper standards were also developed. It is hard to think of any other episode in the history of monetary economics when so much was accomplished in so short a period.

DAVID LAIDLER

See also BANKING SCHOOL, CURRENCY SCHOOL, FREE BANKING SCHOOL; CLASSICAL THEORY OF MONEY; HORNER, FRANCIS; QUANTITY THEORY OF MONEY; RICARDO, DAVID; THORNTON, HENRY.

BIBLIOGRAPHY

Bagehot, W. 1874. *Lombard Street, A Description of the Money Market.* Ed. Frank C. Genovese, Granston, Illinois: Richard Irwin, 1962.

Boyd, W. 1800. *Letter to the Right Honourable William Pitt on the Influence of the Stoppage of Issue in Specie at the Bank of England; on the Prices of Provisions, and other Commodities.* London.

Cannan, E. (ed.) 1919. *The Paper Pound of 1797–1821: The Bullion Report.* London: P.S. King & Son. Second (1921) edition, reprinted by Augustus M. Kelley, New York, 1969.

Cantillon, R. 1734. *Essai sur la nature du commerce en général.* Trans. and edited by Henry Higgs, London: re-issued for the Royal Economic Society by Frank Cass & Co., 1959.

Checkland, S. 1975. Adam Smith and the bankers. In *Essays on Adam Smith*, ed. A.S. Skinner and T. Wilson, Oxford: The Clarendon Press.

Eagly, R.V. 1968. The Swedish and English Bullionist Controversies. In *Events Ideology and Economic Theory*, ed. R.V. Eagly, Detroit, Mich.: Wayne State University Press.

Fetter, F.W. 1955. *The Irish Pound 1797–1826.* London: Allen & Unwin.

Fetter, F.W. 1965. *Development of British Monetary Orthodoxy 1797–1875.* Cambridge, Mass.: Harvard University Press.

Fisher, I. 1896. Appreciation and interest. *AEA Publications* 3(11), August, 331–442.

Hollander, S. 1979. *The Economics of David Ricardo.* Toronto: University of Toronto Press.

Hume, D. 1752. Of Money, Of the Balance of Trade and Of Interest. In *Political Discourses*, Edinburgh: Fleming. Subsequently incorporated in the 1758 edition of *Essays, Moral Political and Literary* London. Reprinted London: Oxford University Press, 1962.

Marshall, A. 1887. Remedies for fluctuations of general prices, *Contemporary Review*, March; reprinted as ch. 8 of *Memorials of Alfred Marshall*, ed. A.C. Pigou, London: Macmillan, 1925.

Mints, L. 1945. *A History of Banking Theory.* Chicago: University of Chicago Press.

Ricardo, D. 1809. Contributions to the *Morning Chronicle*. Reprinted in , *Works and Correspondence of David Ricardo*, ed. P. Sraffa, Vol. III, Cambridge: Cambridge University Press, 1951.

Ricardo, D. 1810–11. *The High Price of Gold Bullion, A Proof of the Depreciation of Bank Notes*. Reprinted in *Works* ..., ed. P. Sraffa, Vol. III, Cambridge: Cambridge University Press, 1951.

Ricardo, D. 1816 *Proposals for an Economical and Secure Currency*, Reprinted in *Works* ..., ed. P. Sraffa, Vol. IV, Cambridge: Cambridge University Press, 1951.

Smith, A. 1776. *An Inquiry into the Nature and Causes of the Wealth of Nations*. London. Reprinted in two vols, ed. R.H. Campbell, A.S. Skinner and W.B. Todd, Oxford: Clarendon Press, 1976.

Thornton, H. 1802. *An Enquiry into the Nature and Effects of the Paper Credit of Great Britain*. London. Edited with an Introduction by F.A. von Hayek, London: George Allen & Unwin, 1939; reprinted, New York: Augustus Kelley, 1962.

Viner, J. 1937. *Studies in the Theory of International Trade*. New York: Harper Bros.

Wheatley, J. 1803. *Remarks on Currency and Commerce*. London.

Wicksell, K. 1898. *Interest and Prices*. Trans. R.F. Kahn, London: Macmillan for the Royal Economic Society, 1936.

Bullock, Charles Jesse (1869–1941). Bullock was born in Boston on 21 May 1869. Trained partly by correspondence course directed by R.T. Ely, he graduated from Boston University in 1892 while employed as a high school principal, a combination not uncommon at the time. Following his Wisconsin PhD in 1895 he taught economics at Cornell, Williams (1899–1903) and Harvard (1903–34), where he directed the Committee on Economic Research from 1917 to 1929. While public finance was his principal field, he also made contributions to international economics, which was unusual before 1914, and the history of economics. The author of several successful textbooks, his major theoretical contribution was 'The Law of Variable Proportions' (1902). He served as adviser on taxation in Massachusetts and other states, and was president of the National Tax Association from 1917 to 1919.

A.W. COATS

SELECTED WORKS

1895. *The Finances of the United States, 1775–1789, with special reference to the budget*. Madison: University of Wisconsin Press.

1897. *Introduction to the Study of Economics*. Boston, New York etc: Silver Burdett & Co. 4th edn, revised and enlarged, 1913.

1900. *Essays on the Monetary History of the United States*. New York: Macmillan Co.

1902. The variation of productive forces. *Quarterly Journal of Economics* 16, August, 473–513.

1905. *Elements of Economics*. Boston, New York, etc.: Silver, Burdett & Co. Rev. enl. edn, 1923.

1936. *Economic Essays*. Cambridge, Mass.: Harvard University Press.

bunch maps. Bunch maps were developed by Ragnar Frisch (1934) to deal with the problems of confluence analysis. By 'confluence analysis' he meant the study of several variables in some sets of which a regression equation might have a meaning, while in others it might not because of the existence of more than one relation between the variables. Frisch's exposition of bunch maps was based on a situation where each variable in a set could be split into two components: one, the systematic component, was connected with the other variables; the other, the disturbance, was not so connected. The method was used to try to determine sets of variables in which one, and only one, exact linear relation held between the systematic components of the variables. Examples of the use of the method were given for constructed data where exact relations did exist. It is less clear whether they were assumed to exist in examples of applications to actual economic data. The other major applications of bunch maps were in Richard Stone's work on consumers' expenditure (Stone, 1945, 1954), but he did not consider an assumption of exact linear relations between systematic components as satisfactory.

In a full analysis of a number of variables, the bunch map was based on regressions calculated for every possible subset of two or more variables with minimization in the direction of every member of the subset. Each variable was normalized to give a unit sum of squares over observations of deviations from means. For any pair of variables, x_i and x_j (ij), in the subset, if the regression with minimization in the direction of x_k were written to express x_i in terms of the other variables, the coefficient of x_j would be minus the ratio of the cofactors of r_{jk} and r_{ik} in the correlation matrix of the variables in the subset. These cofactors were used as ordinate and abscissa respectively, but with one sign changed in such a way that the abscissa was positive, to obtain a point in a diagram. Similar points were plotted in the same diagram for all possible x_k in the subset and labelled with k. The points were joined to the origin to give the individual bunch with its beams. There was a separate bunch for every pair of variables in every subset. Together they formed the bunch map.

The bunch map was used mainly for comparing bunches of two subsets where the second contained the variables in the first plus an additional one. Attempts were made to classify the added variable as useful, superfluous or detrimental. Criteria which suggested that a variable was useful included the tightening of the bunch, a change in its general slope and the beam associated with the new variable being inside the bunch. The length of the beams and changes in length were also considered. An explosion of the bunch showed that the new variable was detrimental; that is, it introduced multiple relations.

The complexity of the procedure and the apparent subjectivity of combining different criteria in classifying variables may have contributed to the relatively small impact of bunch maps on applied econometrics, despite frequent references in textbooks and other works on econometric techniques. Frisch's analysis did, however, draw more attention to the dangers of errors of measurement in multicollinear situations than is common in more recent discussions of multicollinearity.

WILFRED CORLETT

See also ECONOMETRICS; FRISCH, RAGNAR ANTON KITTIL; MULTICOLLINEARITY; SIMULTANEOUS EQUATIONS MODELS.

BIBLIOGRAPHY

Frisch, R. 1934. *Statistical Confluence Analysis by Means of Complete Regression Systems*. Oslo: University Institute of Economics.

Stone, J.R.N. 1945. The analysis of market demand. *Journal of the Royal Statistical Society* 108, parts 3 and 4, 286–382.

Stone, J.R.N. 1954. *The Measurement of Consumers' Expenditure and Behaviour in the United Kingdom, 1920–1938*, Vol. 1. Cambridge: Cambridge University Press.

burden of the debt. Public debt constitutes private assets. The deficit of one sector of the economy is the surplus of another.

Thus, for a closed economy, internally held public debt is not the obvious burden it is to an individual. If the private sector pays taxes to service the debt, it is also the private sector which receives the proceeds of these taxes in payments of interest and principal. If taxes could be lump-sum, with no marginal effect upon economic behaviour, and were anticipated with certainty, and if public and private borrowing costs were the same, it could be argued that the public debt would be irrelevant, except for distributional effects.

This would imply that if would make no difference whether public expenditures were financed by current taxes or by borrowing (which would create a public debt that would be serviced by future taxes). This proposition, considered but dismissed by Ricardo, was labelled by Buchanan (1976; see also 1958) the Ricardo Equivalence Theorem after being refurbished by Barro (1974).

The public debt is not considered neutral, even with lump-sum taxation, if only because people are mortal. Those currently holding debt and receiving interest will escape some taxation by death. Barro's answer was to postulate agents with preference functions in which the assets and liabilities of their descendants were arguments. Hence the current generation's holdings of public debt in excess of the present value of their own consequent tax liabilities would be matched by their need to adjust their bequests to leave their heirs uninjured by future taxes necessary to service the debt.

To this there are many objections, including such obvious ones as the fact that some current agents have no heirs, that others do not care about their heirs, and that still others are at 'corner solutions', so that the amount that they give to (or receive from) their children will not be affected. There are further objections in terms of uncertainty as to life span, both for current agents and their children, and even with regard to the number of their heirs and of their heirs' heirs for whom provision should be made. These objections to the effective assumption of immortality, along with differences in public and private borrowing costs, and of course the fact that most taxation is not and cannot reasonably be expected to be of a lump-sum variety, had led to considerable rejection of the equivalence theorem (see Buiter and Tobin, 1979).

Whether (and if so, in what way) the public debt is a burden then becomes a highly conditional issue. While most theoretical discussions have apparently accepted the premise of full, market-clearing equilibrium, the more relevant circumstance is frequently one of underemployment related to insufficient aggregate demand. In this situation, public debt, far from being a burden, is likely to induce greater consumption, as is made particularly clear by Modigliani's life-cycle hypothesis (Modigliani and Brumberg, 1954; Ando and Modigliani, 1963). Those with greater wealth, in the form of public debt or other assets, will consume more now and plan to consume more in the future as well. Within a framework of rational expectations (without market-clearing), firms should then complement the increased consumption with increased investment to meet current and future consumption demand. Current output and employment would thus be higher, and a greater capital stock would be available for the future.

The existence of public debt, including non-interest-bearing debt in the form of government money, also facilitates inter-generational contracts. It permits the current working generation to save and exercise a claim for retirement support from the next generation in the absence of the ability to accumulate non-depreciating capital.

This possible benefit of widening available choices to saving and consumption leads some to view public debt as a burden. For if the public debt increases current consumption, it is argued that there must be less saving and hence a lesser accumulation of capital. Public debt proves a replacement for assets in the form of productive capital. The economy then suffers a lesser capital stock and hence less production, and, in equilibrium, less consumption as well. This argument has been extended by Feldstein (1974) to implicit government debt in the form of 'social security' or pension commitments.

While this argument, as indicated above, is clearly reversed in a situation of underemployment, where added consumption is likely to mean added investment as well, its macroeconomic applicability even in a condition of full-employment equilibrium, is questionable. For an increase in the public debt, in an economy already in full-employment equilibrium, would generate excess demand which would raise prices. If government non-interest-bearing debt in the form of money were increased in proportion to the increase in interest-bearing debt, the economy could then move to a new equilibrium in which prices would be higher but the *real* value of the public debt, the real value of the quantity of money, the rate of interest and all other real variables, including the rates of investment and consumption would be unchanged. If, again under conditions of full employment, the government imposes a permanent nominal deficit on a no-growth economy, it will generate a rate of inflation corresponding to the rate of increase of nominal debt. Hence real debt will not rise, and once more none of the presumed burden of increased debt will develop.

This suggests the existence of considerable confusion between real and nominal magnitudes. It is essentially the real public debt that matters. The nominal, par value of public debt has risen in many countries while rising interest rates and rising prices have caused substantial declines in its real, market values. It is hence important to correct measures of budget surpluses and deficits so that they correspond to *real* changes in the public debt. Suppose, for example, a nominal deficit of $100 billion and interest and price effects on the real value of an outstanding public debt of $2000 billion such that its real, market value, aside from the current deficit, declines to $1850 billion. In relevant, real terms the budget may then be viewed as in *surplus* by $50 billion, which is equal to the $150 billion 'capital gain' or 'inflation tax', minus the $100 billion nominal deficit (see Eisner and Pieper, 1984; Eisner, 1986).

Whether a burden or a blessing, public debt may, along these lines, be better evaluated in terms of its relation to the income or product of the economy. The debt may thus be viewed as rising, in a relative sense, only when it increases more rapidly than gross national product. In an economy with a debt-to-GNP ratio of 0.5, for example, this would mean that with a growth rate of, say, 8 per cent per annum (consisting, approximately, of 3 per cent real growth and 5 per cent inflation), the debt could grow at 8 per cent per year, implying a deficit equal to 4 per cent of GNP, with no change in the ratio of debt to GNP. A corollary of this is that, in a growing economy, there is always some equilibrium debt-to-GNP ratio consistent with any deficit-to-GNP ratio, that is

$$[\text{Debt/GNP} = (\text{DEF/GNP}) \div (\varDelta \text{GNP/GNP})].$$

If public debt is related to public assets, financial and tangible, the net public debt is likely to prove considerably less than the gross public debt, and the net worth or net assets of the public sector are likely to prove positive even in economies with large public debts. In a larger sense, public debt may well be related to total wealth of the economy, private as well as public, and human as well as non-human. A larger public debt may then be associated with greater public wealth. The public debt may properly be viewed as a burden on the economy, however, to the extent that it diminishes total real wealth. It may do so, if it does not increase public capital, by reducing the supply of private capital and/or the supply of labour.

That public debt would reduce the supply of private capital is, as already pointed out, questionable. With regard to the supply of labour, the force of the argument would depend upon agents finding their wealth in the form of public debt so

295

great that their supply of labour to secure additional income or wealth would be significantly curtailed. The real magnitudes of public debt, or ratios of public debt to gross national product, are nowhere sufficient to make this a serious concern. In the United States, for example, interest payments on the federal debt in 1986, despite half a decade of presumably huge deficits, represent no more than 3 per cent of gross national product. The real interest received by bondholders, after adjusting for the inflation loss in the principal of their bonds, is less than 2 per cent of gross national product. The public debt would have to be many times as large before private income from holding of the debt would be sufficient to have an appreciable effect in reducing the supply of labour (or other factors of production). Indeed, it may not be *possible* for the real debt to be sufficiently high to impinge significantly upon the supply of labour. For the necessary increases in nominal debt would generate such excess demand and consequent increases in the price level that an upper bound to the real debt would be reached before its effects upon supply could be significant.

All of this relates to internally or domestically held public debt. Public debt held by other countries or their nationals is another matter. If that debt is denominated in a country's own currency, it too can always be paid off by money creation and depreciated by inflation. If there is an external debt in foreign currencies, however, there is a real burden, which can, if the debt is sufficiently large, prove overwhelming. In the case of such external debt, this burden must be carefully balanced against any benefits in terms of income from the wealth or assets which the debt may have financed.

ROBERT EISNER

See also CROWDING OUT; NATIONAL DEBT; PUBLIC DEBT; RICARDIAN EQUIVALENCE THEOREM.

BIBLIOGRAPHY

Ando, A.K. and Modigliani, F. 1963. The 'life cycle' hypothesis of saving: aggregate implications and tests. *American Economic Review* 53, March, 55–84.
Barro, R.J. 1974. Are government bonds net wealth? *Journal of Political Economy* 82, November–December, 1095–117.
Buchanan, J.M. 1958. *Public Principles of Public Debt.* Homewood, Ill.: Irwin.
Buchanan, J.M. 1976. Barro on the Ricardian equivalence theorem. *Journal of Political Economy* 84, April, 337–42.
Buiter, W.H. and Tobin, J. 1979. Debt neutrality: a brief review of doctrine and evidence. In *Social Security versus Private Saving*, ed. George M. von Furstenburg, Cambridge, Mass.: Ballinger.
Eisner, R. 1986. *How Real Is the Federal Deficit?* New York: Free Press, Macmillan.
Eisner, R. and Pieper, P.J. 1984. A new view of the federal debt and budget deficits. *The American Economic Review* 74, March, 11–29.
Feldstein, M. 1974. Social security, induced retirement, and aggregate accumulation. *Journal of Political Economy* 82, September–October, 905–25.
Modigliani, F. and Brumberg, R. 1954. Utility analysis and the consumption function: an interpretation of cross-section data. In *Post-Keynesian Economics*, ed. K.K. Kurihara, New Brunswick: Rutgers University Press.
Ricardo, D. 1817. *On the Principles of Political Economy and Taxation.* In *The Works of David Ricardo*, ed. J.R. McCulloch, London: John Murray, 1846.
Ricardo, D. 1820. Funding system. In *The Works and Correspondence of David Ricardo*, ed. Piero Sraffa, Cambridge: Cambridge University Press, 1951, Vol. IV.

bureaucracy. The study of bureaucracy has to deal with an elemental paradox. The role of bureaucracy has obviously increased dramatically in modern times. This is true not only of government bureaucracies but business bureaucracies as well. Though there were a few bureaucracies of significant size in pre-industrial times, such as the hierarchy of the Roman Catholic Church and the civil services of various Chinese empires, they were clearly exceptional. By contrast, a very large proportion of the total resources in the developed nations are controlled by either governmental or private bureaucracies. The role of governmental bureaucracies, at least, has increased with some rapidity within the last few decades. The increase in the use of bureaucracies has occurred in so many countries that it could hardly be due entirely to chance, and thus must be due to what are, in some sense, social choices to use more bureaucracy.

Normally, when there are great increases in the demand for or use of some product or instrumentality, this is accompanied by independent evidence of enthusiasm for the product or instrumentality in question. When a society experiences a great increase in the demand for automobiles or for personal computers, there is at the same time a considerable amount of favourable commentary about whatever product is experiencing the boom in demand. There is pride in automobile ownership or awe at the power or compactness of personal computers. Nothing is more natural than that people's choices should be influenced by enthusiasms.

But where is the enthusiasm for bureaucracy that might have been expected to accompany the dramatic increase in the use of bureaucratic mechanisms? Any such enthusiasm is difficult to discern, and there are many conspicuous examples of dislike (or even contempt) of bureaucracy. Some of this negativism may be traced to particular ideological traditions, but this is not sufficient to explain the negativism; the problem is not only that the prevalence of the relevant ideology needs to be explained, but also that the lack of enthusiasm for bureaucracy prevails in a wide variety of ideological and cultural contexts and tends to apply (at least to some extent) to business as well as to governmental bureaucracies. There is no doubt that 'red tape' is viewed negatively by almost everyone, and that it is associated with bureaucracy, and especially governmental bureaucracy; the phrase is derived from the colour of the ribbons that were once used to tie folders of papers in the British government.

Some strands of the literature on bureaucracy are called into question by the paradox. Much of the admiring literature on bureaucracy is difficult to reconcile with the negative popular image of bureaucracy, whereas much of the negative literature suffers from the lack of any explanation of why virtually all societies, at least implicitly, keep choosing to use the instrumentality that is alleged to be so faulty.

Perhaps the most influential scholarly analysis of bureaucracy is not by an economist, but rather by the sociologist and historian, Max Weber. According to Weber:

> ... the fully developed bureaucratic mechanism compares with other organizations exactly as does the machine with the non-mechanical modes of production ...
>
> Precision, speed, unambiguity, knowledge of the files, continuity, discretion, unity, strict subordination, reduction of friction and of material and personal costs – these are raised to the optimum point in the strictly bureaucratic administration (1946, p. 214).

Although also critical of 'bureaucratic domination', Weber's more positive view of bureaucracy has been influential in sociology and political science. Yet it does not appear to have generated systematic or quantitative empirical studies that have tended to provide any confirmation for it, and it surely is not in accord with the popular image of bureaucracy. Weber himself fails to identify any strong incentives in bureaucracies that would lead to efficient allocations of resources or to high levels of innovation.

Similarly, the popular pejorative view of bureaucracy is inadequate to the extent that it offers no explanation why modern societies choose or accept an increasing degree of bureaucratization. There is, admittedly, a rapidly growing economic literature on the growth of government that attempts to identify incentives that lead to a supra-optimal size of government. Examining this large literature would take us a long way from bureaucracy, and it has not in any case yet advanced to the point of generating a professional consensus on any incentive that would systematically bring about the overuse of government and thus of governmental bureaucracy, though some contributions (e.g. Mueller and Murrell, 1985) are extremely promising. But even dramatic success in the literature on the growth of government would not be sufficient to solve the problem, as it would leave us with no explanation of the growth in modern times of business and other private bureaucracies.

Since an explanation of the growth of private bureaucracies is needed, and since an inquiry which begins with the growth of private bureaucracies may obtain some modest degree of detachment from the ideological controversies about the appropriate role of government, it may be best to consider private bureaucracies first. Here the basic question that must be answered is, 'Why do firms with hierarchies of employees exist?' Familiar economic theory explains that markets can under the appropriate conditions allocate resources efficiently, so we must ask why individuals in the business hierarchy, and owners of the buildings and equipment that a typical corporation uses, do not use the price signals of the market to coordinate their everyday interaction. As Ronald Coase pointed out in somewhat different language in his seminal article on 'The Nature of the Firm' (1937), the survival of firms with hierarchies of long-run employees and long-term ownership of complementary fixed capital can only be explained by a kind of market failure. The type of market failure that Coase, and Williamson (1964, 1975 and 1985) and the other economists that have developed the very important literature on private hierarchies have emphasized is 'transactions costs'. It would cost too much to contract out each day each of the very many separate tasks that are usually needed in any complex productive process, so in many cases it pays to forego the use of the market and to make long-term deals with employees who will perform such tasks each day as their superiors instruct them to do and receive in turn a regular salary. Though most of the literature in this tradition emphasizes only transactions costs, it is important to note that any market failure, such as that arising from an externality, could provide the incentive for the establishment of a firm that would internalize the externality, and all but the smallest firms have bureaucracies.

Though the foregoing argument also applies to small firms of the kind that predominated in pre-industrial times, there have been some changes since the industrial revolution that, within this Coasian–Williamson framework, can provide important insights into the growth of business bureaucracies. One factor that made for larger and more bureaucratic firms was the discovery of technologies subject to indivisibilities that only a large enterprise can profitably exploit.

But the extraordinary improvement in the technologies of transportation and communication was probably far more important. Reductions in transportation and communication costs make it economic for firms to draw factors of production

from farther away and also make it profitable for a firm to sell its output over a wider area. When transportation and communication technologies make it profitable for many firms to operate at a global rather than a village level, some very large firms can emerge. The improved transportation and communication also make it possible to coordinate the activities of a firm over a larger area. Superficial observers of the emergence of large firms have supposed that this growth of firm size entails a reduction in competition and a growth of monopoly. In fact, the dramatic reductions in transportation and communication costs have, of course, also increased the opportunities for market transactions over great distances, so the size of the market and the number of firms to which the typical consumer has access has (in the absence of extra trade barriers) also increased. At least in the Common Market or the United States, the average consumer, even if purchasing a product such as automobiles that is produced under greater-than-average economies of scale, has more firms competing for his business than did the average consumer in the typical rural village before the industrial revolution. Thus we see that the growth of business bureaucracy and the expansion of competitive markets are by no means necessarily obverse tendencies, but rather the kinds of things that often happen together.

The technologies that facilitated larger markets and larger firms also gradually led to the discovery of better methods of governing large-scale business organizations, as the historian Alfred D. Chandler has shown in some seminal historical studies of what he has called *The Visible Hand* (1977; see also 1962 and 1980). Several of these innovations occurred in the unprecedentedly large and geographically scattered railroads in the 19th-century United States, and many involved the creation of separate 'profit centres' and other devices that enabled larger firms to use market mechanisms to fulfill some functions within the firm (Williamson, 1985). This suggests that the costs and control losses in bureaucracies are still very considerable, so that business bureaucracy can only be explained in terms of rather substantial costs of using markets. The same conclusion emerges from the observation that activities that are highly space-intensive, such as most types of agricultural production, are quite resistant to bureaucratization, even after the development of modern technologies of transportation and administration; the firms that succeed in surviving in most types of farming are normally too small to have bureaucracies (Olson, 1985).

By contrast, in activities in which the transfer of new technologies and other information is especially important, market failure is likely to be fairly extensive, mainly because new information would only be rationally purchased by those who did not already have this information, and from this it follows that the market for new information is particularly handicapped by the asymmetrical information of the parties to any transaction. Thus, as J.C. McManus (1972), Buckley and Casson (1976) and, especially, Hennart (1982) have shown, the emergence of the multinational firms with bureaucracies that transcend national borders can be explained in this framework; capital can cross national borders through portfolio investment (almost all British and other foreign investment in the 19th century was portfolio investment), but the rise in the relative importance of firms with new technologies and methods that were often not well suited to market transfer via licensing of patents, gave rise to the multinational corporation.

The foregoing emphasis on the business bureaucracies that are generally neglected in discussions of bureaucracy makes possible a brief and unified explanation of governmental bureaucracy as well. Governmental bureaucracies are similarly necessary only because markets fail, at least to some degree; the theory of market failure is readily capable of being generalized to include all functions for which governmental are an efficient response (Olson, 1986). Since governmental as well as market mechanisms are obviously imperfect, it does not follow from the presence of market failure that government intervention is normatively appropriate, since the government might fail even worse than the market, but market failures are nonetheless often important and always a necessary condition for optimal governmental intervention. Of course, it would be absurd to suppose that actual government intervention is always optimal or that governments always intervene when it is Pareto-efficient for them to do so. It is nonetheless instructive to look at the existence of government bureaucracy, as of business bureaucracy, in terms of market failure.

Among other reasons, it is instructive because the very conditions that give rise to market failure inevitably generate, in governments, and to a considerable degree also in firms, exactly those inefficiencies and rigidities that are popularly and correctly attributed to bureaucracies. Some of these inefficiencies also occur when either governmental or business bureaucracy is used inappropriately, but the problem is most easily evident, and most serious, in precisely those cases where market failure makes bureaucratic mechanisms indispensable.

The reasons why the same conditions that make markets fail also generate difficulties and inefficiencies in bureaucracies unfortunately do not lend themselves to brief exposition. But perhaps a faint and intuitive sense of the matter will be evident from a moment's reflection about what could make a bureaucracy necessary. If, say, the fruits or vegetables grown on a farm are best picked by hand and the best way to pay each worker is by the number of bushels picked, there is no need to have any bureaucratic mechanism for getting the work done. When piece-rate or commission systems of reward work well, the market gives each worker a more or less optimal incentive to work and to be as efficient as the worker knows how to be. In essence, the reason is that the output is highly divisible into more or less homogeneous units or the revenue attributable to each worker is known, and so the output of different workers can be measured with reasonable accuracy.

Let us now shift to an opposite extreme. Consider a typical civil servant in the foreign ministry of a government. Even supposing that the only purpose of the foreign ministry in question was peacefully to maintain the country's independence, there would still be a stupendous difficulty in rewarding the civil servant on a piece-rate or commission basis, or in any way that is proportional to his productivity. The security of the country in question would normally depend in large part on what might loosely be described as the state of the international system – on world-wide indivisible or public good for which no one country could be entirely responsible. But even if the country in question were the only producer of this indivisible good, the foreign ministry would not be the only part of the government or the country that was relevant. Even in the foreign ministry, the typical civil servant is only one among thousands. How is his individual output to be measured, or even distinguished from that of his co-workers? The civil servant obviously cannot be paid in proportion to the revenue he generates, because if there really is market failure, the output cannot be sold in a market in the first place. Thus in practice, the remuneration of civil servants involved in producing public goods is not even a close approximation to each civil servant's true output; rewards in civil services will depend dramatically on proxy variables for performance such as seniority, education, and the fidelity of the employee to the

interests of his superior and to the 'culture' or ideology of that bureaucracy. The peculiarities of civil service personnel systems, competitive bidding rules, and red tape are mainly explained by this logic (Olson, 1973, 1974).

The knowledge of the 'social production function' of a government bureaucracy producing public goods will also be limited by the same indivisibility that has been described; there are fewer countries, or even airsheds for pollution abatement, than there are farms (or experimental plots at agricultural experiment stations), so in general less is known about how to run countries or control pollution than about agriculture or about production processes in other competitive industries (Olson, 1982). The same indivisibility that obscures the social production function and the productivity of individual civil servants and other public inputs also insures that there cannot be even an imperfectly competitive market, so there is also no direct information on what an alternative bureaucracy could have achieved in the same circumstances.

In large part, it is the lack of information due to the indivisibilities described above that allows some of the bureaucratic pathologies described in Niskanen (1971) and Tullock (1965) to occur. In Niskanen's widely cited formal model, it is assumed that only the government bureaucrats know how many resources are required to produce a given public output. These bureaucrats are assumed to gain from growth of the bureaucracy, because an official's power, opportunities for promotion and other perquisites are assumed to be an increasing function of the budget the bureaucrat administers. An agency faces the constraint, however, that the electorate will not sustain any government programme whose total costs exceed the total value of its output. The optimization of government bureaucrats therefore leads to a bureaucracy far larger than is Pareto-efficient; in essence the bureaucracy takes all of the surplus under the society's demand curve for the government output at issue. Critics of Niskanen's model have pointed out that it neglects the subordination of bureaucrats to politicians, and that politicians whose opportunities for re-election are positively correlated with the government's performance will endeavour to prevent bureaucracies from taking all of the surplus (see, for example, Breton and Wintrobe, 1975). These criticisms have substantial empirical support, but it is also true that there are many known cases where officials who fear a lower budget allocation than anticipated for their agency will eliminate or threaten to eliminate their politically most cherished activity rather than a marginal activity; this is precisely what Niskanen's model predicts. Though any final conclusion must await further research, the evidence available so far appears to suggest that the lack of information due to the indivisibilities described above does often allow bureaucracies to appropriate some of the surplus that consumers might otherwise be expected to receive, but that the incentives faced by politicians tends to keep bureaucracies from getting anything resembling the whole of this surplus.

Bureaucracies operating in a market environment share some of the information problems that confront government agencies providing public goods, but not others. The divisions of a large corporation that handle personnel, accounting, finance or public relations for the entire corporation provide collective goods to the corporation as a whole. They are in many ways in a situation analogous to the foreign ministry described above when deciding how much of the total profits of the firm to attribute to a given corporate employee; this accounts for the many similarities of large corporate and civil-service bureaucracies. But the corporation as a whole, and even the nationalized firm producing private goods in a market, does not, when it sells its output, have as great a difficulty as the government agency that produces a collective of public output that is indivisible and unmarketable. The firm produces a good or service that is divisible in that it may be provided to purchasers and denied to non-purchasers. This means that the output is directly measurable in some physical units or at least that the revenue obtained from this output is measurable. Since consumers, even in the absence of any high degree of competition, will have alternative uses for their money, the private corporation or nationalized firm in a market economy will get some feedback about how much value it is providing. If there is no legal barrier to the operation of a competitive enterprise and the market is contestable, the society will also have at least potential information about what value an alternative organization could provide. An enterprise in the market produces an output from which non-purchasers may be excluded, and this also means there is normally better knowledge of the production functions for private goods than of production functions for public goods. All this implies that the problems of bureaucracy are less severe in private business than in government agencies producing public goods. Interestingly, they are also less severe in government enterprises that unnecessarily produce private goods that private firms would readily provide than they are in agencies that produce public goods that would not have been provided by the market. The more flexible personnel policies in some nationalized firms than in classical civil service contexts thus provides support for the conception offered here.

The paradox of a vast growth of both public and private bureaucracy at the same time that there is almost a consensus that bureaucracies are not very efficient or flexible, thus appears to have a resolution. There are fundamental reasons, arising from the inherent conditions causing market failure that make both public and private bureaucracies inevitable. These same reasons also explain why bureaucracies lack the information needed for high levels of efficiency. But these same market failures show that (though the existing degree of bureaucracy may of course be far from optimal), it should not be surprising that societies choose to use more private and public bureaucracy even as they condemn such bureaucracy.

Mancur Olson

See also CONSTITUTIONAL ECONOMICS; HIERARCHY; PUBLIC CHOICE; RANK; SOCIALISM; WEBER, MAX.

BIBLIOGRAPHY

Breton, A. and Wintrobe, R. 1975. The equilibrium size of a budget maximizing bureau. Journal of Political Economy 83(1),February, 195–207.

Buckley, P. and Casson, M. 1976. The Future of the Multinational Enterprise. London: Macmillan.

Chandler, A.D. 1962. Strategy and Structure: Chapters in the History of American Industrial Enterprise. Cambridge, Mass.: MIT Press.

Chandler, A.D. 1977. The Visible Hand: The Managerial Revolution in American Business. Cambridge, Mass.: Harvard University Press.

Chandler, A.D. and Daems, H. (eds.) 1980. Managerial Hierarchies: Comparative Perspectives on the Rise of Modern Industrial Enterprise. Cambridge, Mass.: Harvard University Press.

Coase, R.H. 1937. The nature of the firm. Economica 4, November, N.S., 386–405.

Hennart, J.-F. 1982. A Theory of the Multinational Enterprise. Ann Arbor: University of Michigan Press.

McManus, J.C. 1972. The theory of the international firm. In The Multinational Firm and the Nation State, ed. Gilles Paquet, Donn Mills, Ontario: Collier Macmillan.

Mueller, D.C. and Murrell, P. 1985. Interest groups and the political economy of government size. In Public Expenditure and Government Growth, ed. F. Forte and A. Peacock, Oxford: Basil Blackwell.

Niskanen, W.A. 1971. Bureaucracy and Representative Government. Chicago: Aldine-Antherton.

Olson, M.L. 1973. Evaluating performance in the public sector. In The Measurement of Economic and Social Performance, ed. M. Moss, Studies in Income and Wealth, vol. 38, National Bureau of Economic Research, New York: Columbia University Press.

Olson, M.L. 1974. The priority of public problems. In The Corporate Society, ed. R. Marris, London: Macmillan.

Olson, M.L. 1982. Environmental indivisibilities and information costs: fanaticism, agnosticism, and intellectual progress. American Economic Review, Papers and Proceedings 72, May, 262–6.

Olson, M.L. 1985. Space, agriculture, and organization. American Journal of Agricultural Economics 67, December, 928–37.

Olson, M.L. 1986. Toward a more general theory of governmental structure. American Economic Review, Papers and Proceedings 76, May, 120–5.

Tullock, G. 1965. The Politics of Bureaucracy. Washington, DC: Public Affairs Press.

Weber, M. 1946. Bureaucracy. In From Max Weber: Essays in Sociology, ed. H. Gerth and C.W. Mills, New York: Oxford University Press.

Williamson, O.E. 1964. The Economics of Discretionary Behavior: Managerial Objectives in a Theory of the Firm. Englewood Cliffs, NJ: Prentice-Hall.

Williamson, O.E. 1975. Markets and Hierarchies: Analysis and Anti-trust Implications. New York: The Free Press.

Williamson, O.E. 1985. The Economic Institutions of Capitalism. New York: The Free Press.

Buridan, Jean (c1295–1356). French scientist and philosopher, Buridan studied philosophy with William of Ockham in Paris, where he became a professor and (in 1328 and 1340) rector. He made Ockham's nominalism the basis of an empirical physics, opposed to much in Aristotelian physics and paving the way for 17th-century mechanics. His *Consequentiae* addresses the theory of modal propositions in logic and attempts perhaps the first deductive derivation of the laws of deduction. But his name is best known from 'Buridan's Ass', the poor beast which is placed half-way between two identical bales of hay and starves to death for want of a reason for choosing one over the other. The example and name seem to have arisen later to refute his contention that will cannot operate without a sufficient reason, although Buridan himself mentions a dog in like state, in commenting on Aristotle's *De Coelo*. The topic is relevant to the theory of rational choice, where it could be awkward, if there were no way of resolving the problems of multiple equilibria. Presumably the ass must be allowed to have sufficient reason to pick at random, although that could still be awkward, if several asses had a coordination problem.

Martin Hollis

Burke, Edmund (1729–1797). Burke was born in Dublin and died at his estate at Beaconsfield. He is usually remembered as the champion of tradition, hierarchy, privilege and prejudice. His splendid defence of these in his *Reflections on the Revolution in France* has so overshadowed all his other writings that a different side of his thought – his unqualified embrace of the capitalist market economy – has pretty well dropped out of sight. Yet his market orientation was clear enough to his contemporaries. Adam Smith is reported to have said of Burke 'that he was the only man who, without communication, thought on these topics exactly as he did'. The topics were the naturalness and beneficence of the capitalist market economy. That Burke the traditionalist and believer in Divine and Natural Law could praise the self-regulating capitalist market economy, and urge on the government a policy of laissez-faire, is at first sight incredible, so incompatible do the two positions appear to be. In fact, as we shall see, they are not incompatible. And certainly Burke saw no inconsistency, for he regarded the market economy as part of the natural order of the universe, and even as divinely ordained. In spite of his gibe in the *Reflections*, lumping together 'oeconomists' and 'sophisters', Burke was himself a skilled economist. Indeed, he boasted in a later work how much he had done 'in the way of political oeconomy', which he had made 'an object of my humble studies, from my very early youth to near the end of my service in parliament...'. He was fully aware that the capitalist economy, driven by (in his words) monied men's avarice, their desire of accumulation, their love of lucre, could be appallingly hard on the wage-labourer. Nevertheless, as he wrote in his *Thoughts and Details on Scarcity*, it would be 'pernicious to disturb the natural course of things, and to impede, in any degree, the great wheel of circulation which is turned by the strangely directed labour of these unhappy people...'. For 'labour is a commodity like every other, and rises or falls according to the demand. This is in the nature of things.' Hence 'labour must be subject to all the laws and principles of trade, and not to regulation foreign to them...'. We should not try to escape calamity by 'breaking the laws of commerce, which are the laws of nature, and consequently the laws of God...'. Burke's grasp of *political* economy becomes evident in his recognition that the laws of commerce could not operate unless the mass of the people was kept subordinate and unless they accepted that position as natural. Referring to the nation's need for continuous capital accumulation, he wrote:

> To be enabled to acquire, the people, without being servile, must be tractable and obedient. The magistrate must have his reverence, the laws their authority. The body of the people must not find the principles of natural subordination by art rooted out of their minds. They must respect that property of which they cannot partake. They must labour to obtain what by labour can be obtained; and when they find, as they commonly do, the success disproportioned to the endeavour, they must be taught their consolation in the final proportions of eternal justice. Of this consolation whoever deprives them, deadens their industry, and strikes at the root of all acquisition as of all conservation. He that does this is the cruel oppressor... .

It was Burke's genius to see that the operation of the capitalist market economy *required* that the hard core of a hierarchical order should be maintained, and should be accepted even by those it oppressed. And the need for a hierarchical order could most easily be put as a need for the traditional order. So there is no inconsistency between his praise of tradition and his praise of the market economy.

C.B. MACPHERSON

BIBLIOGRAPHY

Of Burke's own works the most famous is the *Reflections on the Revolution in France* (1790); a modern reprint, in Pelican Classics, has an introduction by Conor Cruise O'Brien. Burke's equally important *Thoughts and Details on Scarcity* (1795) is only available in scarce editions of his Collected Works. Adam Smith's remark is reported in Robert Bisset, *Life of Edmund Burke,* 2nd edn, London 1800, vol. 2, p. 429.

Three recent studies of Burke's thought are:

Kramnick, I. 1977. *The Rage of Edmund Burke, Portrait of an Ambivalent Conservative.* New York: Basic Books.

Macpherson, C.B. 1980. *Burke.* Oxford: Oxford University Press.

O'Gorman, F. 1973. *Edmund Burke, his Political Philosophy.* London: Allen & Unwin.

Burns, Arthur Frank (1904–1987). Burns was born in Stanislau, Austria, on 27 April 1904. In 1914 his family emigrated to the United States, settling in Bayonne, New Jersey. Burns became a member of the economics faculty at Rutgers University in 1927, leaving in 1941 to accept an appointment at Columbia University, where he taught for many years and is presently John Bates Clark Professor of Economics Emeritus. He joined the staff of the National Bureau of Economic Research in New York in 1930, was director of research, 1945–53, and president 1957–67. In Washington Burns served as chairman of the Council of Economic Advisers, 1953–6; Counsellor to the President, 1969–70; chairman of the Federal Reserve System, 1970–78; and member of the President's Economic Policy Advisory Board since 1981. From 1981 to 1985 he was US Ambassador to the Federal Republic of Germany. In 1978–80 and again since 1985 he has been distinguished scholar in residence at the American Enterprise Institute.

Burns's economic studies have been primarily concerned with economic growth, business cycles, inflation, and economic policies bearing upon these phenomena. In *Production Trends in the United States since 1870*, published in 1934, he examined growth rates in individual industries, noting the nearly universal tendency towards retardation. An initial stage of rapid growth in a new industry is usually followed by slower growth as it loses part of its market or its resources to still newer industries. Despite the tendency toward slower growth and eventual decline of most industries, Burns noted that this did not imply that growth in total output would slow. The underlying cause, that is the rise of new industries, would itself help to maintain rapid growth in total output.

Burns's collaboration with Wesley Mitchell in the study of business cycles led to many innovations in measurement technique and to a vast accumulation of knowledge about the characteristics of cycles and the economic interactions that generated them. It also led to a more realistic view of what business cycle theory had to explain and what economic policy could be expected to accomplish. This in turn was useful to Burns in his later role as an economic policy-maker, that is as a Presidential adviser and as chairman of the Federal Reserve. Before taking on these responsibilities he wrote prophetically (1953): 'It is reasonable to expect that contracyclical policy will moderate the amplitude and abbreviate the duration of business contractions in the future ... But there are no adequate grounds, as yet, for believing that business cycles will soon disappear, or that the government will resist inflation with as much tenacity as depression ...' Burns's subsequent efforts were largely directed to improving the anti-recession, anti-inflation, and growth promoting policies of government.

G. MOORE

SELECTED WORKS

1930. *Stock Market Cycle Research.* New York: Twentieth Century Fund.

1934. *Production Trends in the United States since 1870.* New York: National Bureau of Economic Research.

1938. (With W.C. Mitchell.) *Statistical Indicators of Cyclical Revivals.* New York: National Bureau of Economic Research, Bulletin 69.

1946. (With W.C. Mitchell.) *Measuring Business Cycles.* New York: Columbia University Press.

1946. *Economic Research and the Keynesian Thinking of Our Times.* New York: National Bureau of Economic Research, 26th Annual Report.

1950. *New Facts on Business Cycles*. New York: National Bureau of Economic Research, 30th Annual Report. Reprinted in Burns, 1969.

1952. *The Instability of Consumer Spending*. New York: National Bureau of Economic Research. 32nd Annual Report.

1952. (et al.) *Wesley Clair Mitchell: The Economic Scientist*. New York: Columbia University Press.

1953. *Business Cycle Research and the Needs of Our Times*. New York: National Bureau of Economic Research, 33rd Annual Report.

1954. *The Frontiers of Economic Knowledge*. Princeton: Princeton University Press.

1957. *Prosperity without Inflation*. New York: Fordham University Press.

1960. Progress towards economic stability. *American Economic Review* 50, March, 1–19.

1966. *The Management of Prosperity*. New York: Columbia University Press.

1967.(With P.A. Samuelson.) *Full Employment, Guideposts, and Economic Stability*. Washington, DC: American Enterprise Institute for Public Policy Research.

1968. (With J.K. Javits and C.J. Hitch.) *The Defense Sector and the American Economy*. New York: New York University Press.

1968. Business cycles. *International Encyclopaedia of the Social Sciences*. New York: Macmillan and Free Press, pp. 226–44. Reprinted in Burns, 1969.

1969. *The Business Cycle in a Changing World*. New York: Columbia University Press.

1978. *Reflections of an Economic Policy Maker*. Washington: American Enterprise Institute.

1984. The American trade deficit in perspective. *Foreign Affairs*, Summer, 1058–69.

1985. Interview: an economist's perspective over 60 years. *Challenge*, Jan.–Feb., 17–25.

Burns, Arthur Robert (1895–1981). A native of London, Burns was educated at the London School of Economics, where he was a pupil of Edwin Cannan. His doctoral dissertation, *Money and Monetary Policy in Early Times*, appeared in a prestigious series in 1927 and is still a standard work on the subject. After the completion of his studies Burns moved to the United States and taught at Columbia University from 1928 to 1963. His service there overlapped with that of his wife Eveline M. Burns, with whom he published an introductory economics text in 1928, and with that of Arthur F. Burns, another noted economist.

In 1936 Burns, still an assistant professor, published *The Decline of Competition*, the bulk of which consisted of chapters on trade associations, price leadership, market sharing, price stabilization, price discrimination, non-price competition, and integration. The work formed part of a discussion that had been set in motion by the writings of Sraffa, Joan Robinson and Chamberlin and which explored the no-man's-land between competition and monopoly. It was to serve as a bridge that linked the abstractions of the theories of imperfect or monopolistic competition with the world of reality. Standing between abstraction and description, Burns's work was in the main an attempt at classification. It holds middle ground between the soaring abstractions of pure theory and the industry studies published by Walton Hamilton and Associates under the title *Price and Price Policies* in 1938. Hamilton was a follower of Veblen. Burns shared a friendly disposition toward institutional economics with other Columbia economists.

The Decline of Competition constitutes Burns's main claim to fame. In later years he directed a Twentieth-Century-Fund study of electric power and government policy, and in 1955 he published *Comparative Economic Organization*. The former

work was overtaken by the rise of atomic power as a source of electric energy, and the latter compared in isolation various factors affecting the national income.

HENRY W. SPIEGEL

SELECTED WORKS

1927. *Money and Monetary Policy in Early Times*. London: Kegan Paul; New York: Knopf.

1928. (With Eveline M. Burns.) *Economic World: A Survey*. London: Oxford University Press.

1936. *The Decline of Competition*. New York: McGraw-Hill.

1948. (Director of Research.) *Electric Power and Government Policy*. New York: Twentieth Century Fund.

1955. *Comparative Economic Organization*. New York: Prentice-Hall.

Burns, Emile (1889–1972). Burns was born in St Kitts, where his father was in the colonial administration. He was educated in London and Cambridge and earned his living in the shipping industry before working full-time for the Labour Research Department (1925–9) and later as an official of the Communist Party of Great Britain until he retired. He was a gifted expositor and popularizer of economic issues and problems and the books and pamphlets he wrote when at the Labour Research Department were much used in the trade union movement. They included a study of the textile industry (requested by the United Textile Workers Union), syllabuses on *Finance* and on *Imperialism* and a book on *Modern Finance* (1920) which set out the workings of the financial system.

He was active in the Independent Labour Party and then joined the Communist Party in 1921, an action which reinforced his interest in the contribution of Marxist economics to understanding contemporary economic problems. During the General Strike of 1926 he became propaganda organizer of the St Pancras Council of Action and published an invaluable survey of the work of Trades Councils and Councils of Action during the strike (1926).

He did not produce any substantial work of economic analysis but responded to or commented on key economic events and debates with a labour movement audience very much in his sights. *The Crisis: The Only Way Out* (1932) dealt forcibly with several of the favoured nostrums of the day such as 'managed credit', 'controlled and planned capitalism', the Fordist 'high wage' proposal etc., but in following the line of the CPGB at the time could only put forward as the solution a socialist revolution and fully planned economy on the Soviet model.

In 1940 he wrote a reply to Keynes's pamphlet *How to Pay for the War* (*Mr Keynes Answered*, 1940), which he saw as primarily a method of cutting workers' real wages in an imperialist war and as preparation for the slump which Emile Burns believed (and thought the capitalists also believed) would certainly and swiftly follow the end of the war. This was a widely held view among economists at the time. He treated the notion of 'equal sacrifice' in such an unequal society with the scorn it deserved.

Continuing his keen interest in financial and monetary issues his last book, published in 1968, was entitled *Money and Inflation*; he attacked both cost push and demand led theories of inflation, focusing rather on the *interests* of capital in using price increases as a way of cutting real wages, as offering a more plausible explanation.

His gift of clear exposition was shown in his *Introduction to Marxism* (1952), which went through many editions.

Whatever the direct impact of his writings on contemporary problems it is likely that his most lasting influence in the field of ideas came from his role as an editor and translator of the work of Marx and Engels. His compilation *Handbook of Marxism* published in the 1930s by the Left Book Club was widely circulated and contributed much to the spread of Marxist ideas in that period. Of special interest to economists was his translation of Part One of Marx's *Theories of Surplus Value* (sometimes described as Part IV of *Capital*), published in 1964 by the Foreign Languages Publishing House in Moscow and issued in Britain by Lawrence & Wishart.

His work as an economist was clearly limited by his continuous absorption in political and administrative activity (at one period he edited the busmen's rank and file journal) and his intense desire to serve all those struggling for improved conditions and deeper understanding of their problems.

SAM AARONOVITCH

SELECTED WORKS
1920. *Modern Finance*. London: Oxford University Press. 2nd edn, revised, 1922.
1922. *Finance: an introductory course for classes and study circles*. London: Labour Research Department.
1926. *The General Strike, May 1926: trades councils in action*. London: Labour Research Department.
1927. *Imperialism. An outline course*. London: Labour Research Department.
1932. *The Crisis: The Only Way Out*. London: Martin Lawrence.
1935. *A Handbook of Marxism: being a collection of extracts from the writings of Marx, Engels, and the greatest of their followers*. London: Victor Gollancz.
1939. *What is Marxism?* London: Victor Gollancz. Revised edn as *An Introduction to Marxism*, London: Lawrence & Wishart, 1952.
1940. *Mr Keynes Answered: an examination of the Keynes plan*. London: Lawrence & Wishart.
1964. Trans. of K. Marx, *Theories of Surplus Value: Volume IV of Capital*. Moscow: Foreign Languages Publishing House; London: Lawrence & Wishart.
1968. *Money and Inflation*. London: Lawrence & Wishart.

Burns, Eveline Mabel (1900–1985). Eveline M. Burns was Professor of Social Work at the School of Social Work of Columbia University (1946–67) and Lecturer in the Department of Economics (1928–42). She received her PhD in economics from the London School of Economics (1926) and was elected an Honorary Fellow of the School (1967). She was consultant to the Employment Opportunities Staff of the Committee on Economic Security (1934–5) and Chief of the Economic Security and Health Section of the National Resources Planning Board (1942).

Burns performed a significant role in translating the complexities of social security issues and programmes to both economists and the social welfare community and in influencing the development of income security policy in the United States. She was a member of several governmental advisory and research agencies and an adviser to numerous social welfare groups. She lectured on and published some of the early books and articles on social security and thus had an important impact on the administrators and future leaders during the initial period when the provisions of the Social Security Act were being implemented.

W. COHEN

SELECTED WORKS
1936. *Towards Social Security*. New York and London: McGraw-Hill Book Company.
1941. *British Unemployment Programs 1920–1938*. Washington, DC: Social Science Research Council.
1942. *Security, Work and Relief Problems*. A Report issued by the National Resources Planning Board, Washington, DC: US Government Printing Office.
1949. *The American Social Security Systems*. 2nd edn, Boston: Houghton-Mifflin, 1951.
1956. *Social Security and Public Policy*. New York: McGraw-Hill Book Company.
1973. *Health Services for Tomorrow: trends and issues*. New York: Dunellen.

business cycles. Development of rational expectations models of the business cycle has been the central issue on the macroeconomic research agenda since the influential analyses of Robert Lucas (1972a, 1972b). In this essay, we review these developments, focusing on the extent to which the rational expectations perspective has generated a new understanding of economic fluctuations.

Economists have long suspected that expectations play a central role in the business cycle, particularly in determining the relationship between money and economic activity. For example, Haberler's (1937) classic interwar survey of business cycle theory stresses the role of expectations, in a variety of theories that explain the business cycle as a Frischian (1937) interaction of external shocks and propagation mechanisms. Expectations also constitute an independent source of shocks in 'psychological' theories of the business cycle. However, as Haberler's survey makes clear, there has long been substantial disagreement among economists about the relative importance of various economic factors – sources of shocks and propagation mechanisms – in determining the observed character of business fluctuations. With the development of formal econometric analyses of business cycles – beginning with Tinbergen's work (1939) and proceeding through Sargent (1981) – it has become clear that unrestricted models of expectations preclude a systematic inquiry into business fluctuations.

The postulate that expectations are rational in the sense of Muth (1961), i.e. that economic agents accumulate information and utilize information efficiently, imposes considerable discipline on business cycle analysis. At present, no single rational expectations model has captured all of the central elements of the business cycle. One could take the view that an ultimate explanation of economic fluctuations will require a return to 'psychological influences'. We prefer to believe that existing individual models highlight specific features that are important and that the gradual accumulation of knowledge about shocks and propagation mechanisms will ultimately yield rational expectations models consistent with observed business cycles.

The organization of our discussion is as follows. First, we briefly consider a set of 'stylized facts' that any successful model must minimally produce. Then, we turn to four categories of rational expectations models of the business cycle, considering in turn how each has been developed to account for some specific set of stylized facts. We then review the empirical evidence regarding the overall performance of each class of models.

We begin by exploring the role of expectations in the basic real business cycle models of Kydland and Prescott (1982) and Long and Plosser (1983), in which dynamics of business cycles reflect the interaction of temporary real shocks and intertemporal (capitalistic) production. We then consider the monetary business cycle models of Lucas (1972, 1973) and Barro (1976, 1980) which utilize incomplete information as a rationale for temporary real effects of monetary disturbances.

Although agents have rational expectations in these models, lack of timely information on monetary shocks implies that agents erroneously perceive price level movements as representing changes in relative prices. After considering equilibrium models of the business cycle – in which prices are flexible – we turn to Keynesian models of business fluctuation constructed under the rational expectations postulate. Our discussion begins with the analyses of Fischer (1977) and Gray (1976), who model temporary wage stickiness arising from nominal wage contracts. Subsequently, we consider the emerging class of theories that focus on commodity price stickiness, beginning with a parable told by McCallum (1982) and then considering some alternative formal developments by Rotemberg (1982), Mankiw (1985) and Blanchard and Kiyotaki (1986).

Throughout our discussion, we follow the traditional macroeconomic practice of considering business cycles – defined as the stochastic components of macroeconomic time series – as stationary stochastic processes. This practice is followed in our description of stylized facts, but is also implicit in the theoretical economies that we consider, since the time series generated by these economies are stationary. If, in fact, economic time series exhibit nonstationarity, as argued by Nelson and Plosser (1982), then these classes of models are called into question. In a concluding section we briefly discuss the ongoing development of rational expectations business cycles that are capable of producing model economies that have nonstationary components.

STYLIZED FACTS

Much of our survey deals with the ability of various business cycle models to generate time series whose properties are consistent with commonly discussed summary statistics, i.e. the stylized facts of business cycles (see e.g. Lucas, 1977). Presentations of these stylized facts typically proceed as follows. First, certain smooth curves are removed from the data, frequently after a logarithmic transformation; these eliminate deterministic growth and seasonal components. Summary statistics are then calculated on the transformed data.

At a minimum the list of real quantity variables to be considered consists of the major national accounts aggregates – consumption, investment and output – along with measures of labour input (manhours, employment). In addition, real wages, real money balances and certain financial activity variables are frequently considered, as in the growth rate of some nominal variables such as the money stock, nominal interest rates and prices. All of the quantity series – including real balances – exhibit significant positive serial correlation at the annual or quarterly interval. They all also display positive covariation, both with output and with each other. They differ somewhat in relative volatilities, notably investment is more volatile than output, which in turn is more volatile than consumption. Evidence concerning the cyclical behaviour of the real wage is inconclusive; in part, this reflects a variety of constructs used. In general, however, there does not appear to be a pronounced cyclical relation. Measures of financial activity – such as deposit turnover and bank clearings – are strongly procyclical (Mitchell, 1957). As Lucas (1977) observes, there is little reason to qualify the observations by reference to specific time periods.

However, the relationship between nominal variables and the cycle exhibits less stability over time. In Mitchell's (1951) consideration of interwar data for the US, the price level and short-term nominal interest rate were strongly procyclical.

More recent investigations by Hodrick and Prescott (1980) into post-war US cycles, document a changing relation, price levels are countercyclical during the latter half of their sample and short-term rates are not systematically related to economic activity. However, most investigations do document a positive relation between income velocity and real activity that mirrors the financial transactions data.

When many sectors are included in this analysis, as in Mitchell (1951), there is a tendency for co-movement across sectors and considerable stability in lead–lag relations relative to aggregate output. There do appear to be different degrees of sectoral co-movement and amplitude. For example, agriculture does not covary closely with the rest of the economy. Producer and consumer durable goods manufacturing exhibits greater volatility than services.

EXPECTATIONS AND REAL BUSINESS CYCLES

In recent years, macroeconomists have begun the long postponed task of developing basic equilibrium models of economic fluctuations. That this is an essential first step was cogently argued by Hicks (1933) over fifty years ago, who stressed that one could not measure the extent of disequilibrium without first determining the content of equilibrium theory and that, in a dynamic stochastic system, there is rich content to equilibrium theory.

The analyses of Kydland and Prescott (1982) and Long and Plosser (1983) explain the dynamics of business cycles as reflecting the interaction of real shocks – to total factor productivity – and intertemporal (capitalistic) production possibilities. The Long and Plosser (1983) analysis develops some general economic principles – mentioned by Haberler (1937) – by studying the decisions of a representative consumer ('Robinson Crusoe') who directly operates the production technology of the economy. In this context the business cycles that arise are Pareto efficient. Thus, the mechanisms that generate cyclical activity are quite general and should carry over to richer macroeconomic models that possess incomplete information and nominal rigidities, including those that we consider below.

For example, the analysis of Long and Plosser shows that even if disturbances to production possibilities are temporally independent, real quantities – output, consumption and capital – display positive serial correlation. Shocks are propagated over time due to the preference of economic agents for smoothing consumption, and the fact that the intertemporal technology makes smoothing feasible. However, the persistence of shocks is limited by the existence of fixed factors (such as a fixed endowment of time); the ultimate effects of shocks are negligible. That is, in the periods after a productivity shock, there is negative net investment – relative to a trend value – as the economy adjusts back towards a steady-state. This residual role of investment implies that it displays great cyclical volatility (see King and Plosser, 1986). Thus, with temporally independent shocks, the basic equilibrium model predicts some of the central stylized facts – positive serial correlation in consumption and production, as well as the relative volatilities – but fails to capture the positive serial correlation of investment.

When there are many commodities, Crusoe's preference for diversity in his consumption bundle means that the effects of a temporary productivity shock in one sector are also transmitted across other sectors. Thus, as Long and Plosser (1983) stress, the basic equilibrium model also predicts that there will be comovement, with economic activity in diverse sectors tending to rise and fall together. Therefore, the basic equilibrium model also predicts another of the centralized stylized facts emphasized by Mitchell (1951).

Temporary shocks to factor productivity typically exert offsetting income and substitution effects on the effort decision, so that Crusoe's optimal cyclical variation in employment is ambiguous. In the parametric models of Long and Plosser, these two effects offset exactly, so that there is zero cyclical variation in labour input. Kydland and Prescott (1982) explore the implications of greater intertemporal substitution in preferences, using a non-time-separable but recursive preference specification. In this case, Crusoe finds it optimal to substitute effort toward periods in which its marginal reward is high, which leads effort to respond positively to temporary productivity shocks.

Even with temporary shocks to productivity, the intertemporal consequences of capital accumulation and effort decisions imply that Crusoe must form expectations about future production opportunities. In general, optimal decision rules will be different when Crusoe makes alternative assumptions about the nature of shocks and for alternative specifications of preferences and technology. Furthermore, the rational expectations assumption plays a pivotal role in the process of transforming optimal social decisions into a competitive theory of fluctuations, for there will be a coincidence between Crusoe's (or a social planner's) decisions and the decentralized actions of private agents only if expectations are rational.

Expectations have additional implications for Crusoe's decision rules when there is serial correlation in the exogenous factors, i.e. total factor productivity. For example, Crusoe's incentives for saving/investment to achieve consumption smoothing, are reduced if changes in (expected) future productivity accompany changes in current productivity because of larger wealth effects of such changes. Further, anticipated future variations in productivity also affect the marginal reward to current investment and the rewards to future effort, exerting additional substitution effects on current decisions.

EVIDENCE ON REAL BUSINESS CYCLES

Although real business cycle models produce some qualitative features of the business cycle it remains to determine whether they explain fluctuations *quantitatively*. The initial research effort addressing these questions has been undertaken by Kydland and Prescott in an influential series of papers (summarized in Prescott, 1985).

Following the methodological recommendations of Lucas (1980), Kydland and Prescott restrict the number of free parameters in their model economy by a number of steady-state conditions and also by the extensive use of behavioural parameter estimates taken from applied studies in other fields. For example, they use the observed constancy of labour's share to pin down the parameters in a Cobb–Douglas production function, and results from analyses of financial markets to restrict a preference curvature parameter governing the extent of intertemporal substitution/risk aversion. Following Solow (1957), they measure variations in total factor productivity as a residual from the aggregate production function and choose a simple Markovian stochastic process to capture the serial correlation in this series.

The results of the Kydland–Prescott studies have been surprising to most economists. The initial model economy produced summary statistics – second moments of consumption, investment, output, productivity, and effort – that accorded with the stylized facts described previously. (The specific presentation of the stylized facts to which the Kydland–Prescott model was compared is contained in Hodrick and Prescott, 1980). However, it is also clear that the basic neoclassical business cycle model as developed by Kydland and Prescott does not meet the stringent standards of rational expectations econometrics. Altug (1985) subjects the Kydland–Prescott model to rational expectations econometric procedures and finds that the model's restrictions are rejected by the data. Given the level of abstraction currently found in this model this is perhaps not surprising; it is encouraging that these types of models can loosely mimic some important aspects of cyclical activity.

The basic neoclassical model of Kydland and Prescott has been criticized on a number of other grounds that warrant further discussion. First, the model has no implications for any cyclical variation in employment or unemployment. That is, the model uses the representative agent paradigm and permits a smooth tradeoff between hours and output, so all adjustments in labour effort take place in terms of hours and not numbers of workers. Forcing a (more realistic) choice between working full time or not at all would generally introduce problematic nonconvexities in production possibilities. However, the important work of Rogerson (1985) provides a method for analyzing production nonconvexities in a representative agent model. Rogerson uses the fact that by introducing social arrangements that formally resemble lotteries – in that they specify probabilities of working full time or not at all – the representative agent problem can be made convex. This contrived randomness in the representative agent and corresponding social planner's problem improves welfare by smoothing the opportunities for effort by averaging across the population. It corresponds in a competitive, multi-agent framework to an economy in which some agents are employed and some are not, and in which their relative numbers can fluctuate over time. Further, the indivisibility of work effort results in a dramatic change in the corresponding social planner's problem that can be used to compute competitive outcomes. This optimum problem can be interpreted as that of a single agent with a greater degree of intertemporal substitution in labour supply than that of the identical agents that populate the economy. This is empirically important within the Kydland–Prescott model, since the greater degree of intertemporal substitution in aggregate labour supply is capable of producing quantitatively greater variations in employment (see Hansen, 1985).

The main potential theoretical alternative for smoothing production nonconvexities is to allow for heterogeneity of preferences. However, given the primitive state of methods for solution and estimation of dynamic macroeconomic models this alternative is not practical at the moment. It is, therefore, likely that Rogerson's insight will be widely employed. Overall, the focus of most business cycle models on hours and not on the number of employed workers represents a transient feature and is not an essential character of the real business cycle approach.

The social criticism of the Prescott model is that its internal mechanisms do not by themselves produce much serial correlation in economic time series. This is because, even though the model provides a mechanism for the propagation of shocks, the share of physical capital in output is small (about one-third). Therefore, consumption smoothing cannot be very important quantitatively in this framework (see King and Plosser, 1986). Rather, the cyclical character of the variation in total factor productivity – the Solow residual which is a Markov process that is close to a random walk – is used to generate persistence.

The stochastic nature of the shocks is therefore a key ingredient for generating the cyclical behaviour in the Kydland–Prescott model and there has also been some scepticism directed toward the nature of these shocks. For example, one questions whether this construct really captures an exogenous variable (technological change). If cyclical variations in the intensity of utilization of capital and labour inputs are significant, then important biases could arise, since endogenous decisions with respect to utilization will incorrectly be attributed to changes in technology. Further, in industries that are noncompetitive, there may be cyclical variations in the relationship between marginal cost and price (mark-ups) that would be counted as shocks to factor productivity by the Solow–Prescott procedure (see Bils, 1985). Also, Barro (1986) and others have expressed scepticism that there are real shocks of sufficient magnitude to generate observed cycles.

Finally, with the exception of King and Plosser (1984), these models cannot generate any of the observed correlations between money and economic activity, since financial sectors have been omitted from most real business cycle models.

King and Plosser (1984) extend the real business cycle model by incorporating accounting services as a factor in production of final goods. Consequently, when there are increases in total factor productivity in the final goods sector, there is an induced increase in the quantity of such services (an intermediate good), which rationalizes Mitchell's (1951) finding that measures of transactions activity in the banking sector are strongly procyclical. In considering extensions to incorporate demand deposits and outside currency, King and Plosser follow standard macroeconomic practice by assuming that service flows are proportional to asset stocks. Therefore, real quantities of currency and demand deposits covary positively with economic activity. Moreover, if price levels are not too countercyclical, then nominal demand deposits will move with the cycle, while movements in nominal currency may be unrelated to the evolution of the cycle, a hypothesis for which King and Plosser provide some supporting empirical evidence. However, as McCallum (1986) points out, if the central bank is targeting currency plus deposits, then these correlations can also arise in a monetary business cycle.

The main contribution of this literature is the detailed development of propagation mechanisms which may not be sensitive to the nature of the shock. Therefore, the real business cycle literature may serve as a useful complement to other equilibrium business cycle models, such as those involving monetary impulses. It is to this class of models that we now turn.

MONEY, EXPECTATIONS AND BUSINESS CYCLES

The pioneering work incorporating rational expectations into monetary models of the business cycle was undertaken by Lucas (1972a, 1972b, 1973). Macroeconomist's concern with linking the real and monetary sides of the economy probably stems from the influential work of Friedmand and Schwartz (1963), which appears to document an important causal role for nominal impulses including shifts in the money supply and the velocity of circulation.

The basic feature of imperfect information variants of equilibrium business cycle theory can be depicted in a simple log-linear business cycle model that essentially follows Lucas (1973). In this model, a non-storable commodity is produced at distinct locations indexed by z. Production in each location depends linearly on last period's output and on the perceived relative price, $p_t(z) - E_z p_t$, where $E_z p_t$ is the expected value of the log of the aggregate price level. Output demand at any location is positively related to factors influencing aggregate demand and a relative demand shock.

To close the model, one must specify a stochastic process governing the supply of money and the information set available to agents at each location. Agents are typically assumed to know the economy's structure, their current local price, $p_t(z)$, and past values of all variables and disturbances. They do not observe the contemporaneous values of aggregate data or of the disturbances.

This simple framework yields a number of key results that extend to other members of this class of equilibrium business cycle models. The primary result is that it is only *unperceived* monetary disturbances which produce real effects. Perceived changes in money affect both local and aggregate prices uniformly so that these are neutral toward relative prices and real activity. It is instructive to trace through the effects of a positive monetary shock. The demand for goods at location z rises, causing an increase in the price at location z. With incomplete information, suppliers in location z do not know whether any particular increase in $p_t(z)$ such as that arising from the monetary shock is due to aggregate or relative disturbances. Given the stochastic structure of the model, agents will generally attribute some of a money induced movement in $p_t(z)$ to an improvement in relative prices and therefore they will supply more. (The proportion of the price movement attributed to relative shifts in demand depends on the underlying variances of two shocks.) Therefore, an *unanticipated* increase in the money supply will cause output to rise precisely because it is mistakenly perceived as representing a change in relative prices. If, on the other hand, agents accurately perceived the shift in the money supply, they would neutralize the effects of this disturbance. Sargent and Wallace (1975) use this to develop the implication that anticipated movements in money supply have no real effects.

An initial criticism of Lucas's analysis involved the fact that this simple model could not generate the serial correlation evident in economic time series (Hall, 1975). But, as Lucas (1975) argues, linking the model of monetary shocks to capital accumulation and the other propagation mechanisms of real business cycle theory potentially overcomes this difficulty. For example, Sargent (1979) provides a nicely worked out linear business cycle model that utilizes adjustment costs to propagate temporarily misperceived nominal shocks.

The neutrality of perceived monetary disturbances represents a substantial problem for this class of equilibrium business cycle models. In reality, monetary data (although somewhat noisy) is produced in a very timely manner. If the relevant decision period is approximately one quarter, agents' information sets should plausibly be modelled as including the available contemporaneous monetary data. In this situation, King (1981) shows that fluctuations in output should be uncorrelated with the reported monetary statistics, essentially because expectation errors about relative prices should be uncorrelated with available information. Further, revisions in the monetary statistics should be correlated with real activity because the initial reporting errors induce misperceptions.

Thus, if monetary disturbances are accurately perceived, then they cannot be business cycle impulses for the reason suggested by Lucas (1972, 1973). It is important to stress that this does not rule out incomplete information as a rational for the non-neutrality of other nominal disturbances (such as money demand shocks) that may more plausibly be not directly observable over the relevant decision period.

Moreover, King's (1981) result is conditioned by the assumption that monetary disturbances are exogenous. If the central bank leans against changes in interest rates or if changes in inside money are correlated with real activity, then contemporaneous monetary statistics may be correlated with output even if they are accurately perceived. Moreover, King and Trehan (1984) show that monetary shocks can be non-neutral due to a signalling effect, if these statistics convey information about unobservable real economic conditions that influence agent's production and investment decisions.

It has also been suggested that King's result may be too strong, since although monetary data is available it may also be quite costly to process. Therefore, agents may in some sense ignore the data in making their labour/leisure decisions, which would imply that the initial specification of the information set was appropriate. (Edwards (1981) constructs a model in which there is a competitively determined fraction of agent that acquire costly information about the true monetary state, but it is unclear from his analysis whether business cycles can be a large social problem if the individual costs of information are small.) The preceeding argument reveals the arbitrary manner in which information structures are specified in this class of models and this is a problem that has not been dealt with satisfactorily in the macroeconomics literature to date.

There are numerous extensions and modifications of the simple model just considered. The most notable are those of Barro (1976, 1980), which are motivated by intertemporal substitution possibilities rather than by contemporaneous expected relative prices (as in Lucas, 1973, and Friedman, 1968). But these analyses preserve the central empirical implications of the simple model: (i) the irrelevance of predictable variations in monetary policy; and (ii) the causal link between unperceived monetary disturbances and real activity.

EMPIRICAL ANALYSES OF MONEY AND BUSINESS CYCLES

The empirical work on monetary impulses in equilibrium business cycle models is much too extensive to cover completely in this essay. Rather, we review three major lines of empirical investigation that bear on the relevance of the line of research. By and large, the evidence suggests that models of this class do not adequately represent links between money and business cycles.

Tests based on monetary decompositions. The first layer of tests examined the relationship between unanticipated movements in nominal variables and economic activity, with the key references being Sargent (1973, 1975) and Barro (1977, 1978). Following Barro's lead, subsequent investigations have focused on reduced form relations between money and economic activity, rather than estimation of systems incorporating a 'Lucas supply function' as in Sargent's early studies. The idea behind the Barro-type tests is to decompose the observed monetary time series into unanticipated and anticipated components by specifying a prediction rule. This two stage procedure involves estimation of a money supply process, with the residuals treated as unanticipated money and the fitted values treated as anticipated money. The empirical studies then investigate whether constructed unanticipated money influences various measures of economic activity and if the constructed anticipated components of money are neutral. Initial tests by Barro utilized a two-step procedure, with later investigations employing the econometrically more efficient method of estimating a simultaneous equation system and testing cross equation restrictions (Leiderman, 1980, and Abel and Mishkin, 1983).

These tests concern the joint hypothesis that expectations are rational, that the money supply process is correctly specified,

that the process governing the behaviour of the economy is correct, and that anticipated money is neutral. Thus, correct specification of all of these elements is necessary for successful execution of these tests. For example, if the Federal Reserve's reaction function is misspecified through the exclusion of relevant variables then measures of anticipated money will include the effects of these variables. If these excluded variables are correlated with explanatory variables in equations that depict the behaviour of the relevant economic magnitudes under consideration, which is likely to be the case, then coefficients will be biased and test statistics will be inappropriate.

The results of this type of tests are mixed. The analysis of Barro (1977) concerning the relationship between money and unemployment supports the implications of equilibrium business cycle theory. Working at the annual interval, Barro provides evidence that (i) anticipated monetary changes do not affect real activity in a statistically significant manner; and (ii) that unanticipated money growth affects output over three years, with the peak effect concentrated in the second year. A follow-up study of the price level at the annual interval, Barro (1978), provides evidence that price level movements accord less well with the predictions of theory. Although anticipated monetary changes have a one-for-one impact on the price level, the response of the price level to monetary shocks is more protracted than the response of real activity. Barro and Rush (1980) provide additional evidence using data on unemployment, output, and prices from the quarterly post-war time series, the interval that has subsequently been studied by most researchers. Generally this study confirms Barro's earlier results that unanticipated money influences real GNP (positively) and unemployment (negatively) but, as with the annual data, the results involving the price level are less persuasive. Although unanticipated money does affect the price level less than one for one, the lag structure for unanticipated money is inconsistent with lags found in output and unemployment equations.

Working at the quarterly interval, Mishkin (1982) and Merrick (1983) provide evidence against the neutrality hypothesis, where the hypothesized money supply process and lag lengths are altered from the Barro–Rush specification. Merrick essentially tries to replicate the Barro–Rush quarterly results on real GNP, after altering the money supply process by including lagged Treasury bill rates and stock market returns. He finds that unanticipated money no longer affects real GNP, but that anticipated money does. Mishkin also alters the money supply process by including past Treasury bill rates but finds that this does not affect the Barro-Rush results over a somewhat different sample period, where an eight quarter maximum lag is imposed. However, upon extending the lag lengths on unanticipated and anticipated money to twenty quarters, he is able to reject the joint hypothesis of rationality and neutrality. The Merrick and Mishkin results cast doubt on the robustness of the neutrality results obtained at the annual interval. However, in interpreting the above results, one must keep in mind that a composite hypothesis is being tested. For example, if anticipated money was neutral, but if the central bank engaged in interest-rate smoothing – as in Goodfriend (1986) – then variations in money growth would accompany changes in the real interest rate. If the factors that lead to these changes in the real interest rate are omitted in the output equation, anticipated money will spuriously appear to be non-neutral.

Leiderman (1983) investigates the cyclical pattern of real wage movements in response to money on both annual and quarterly data. According to neoclassical theory, the real wage should decline with application of an increased amount of effort to a fixed stock of capital. Thus, if misperceived monetary shocks fool labour suppliers into working more, then monetary shocks should lower real wages and increase output, so that a countercyclical relationship emerges between monetary shocks and real wages. Also, predictable shifts in money will leave real wages unaffected. Leiderman finds some support – at both the annual and quarterly intervals – for countercyclical variation in the real wage, which is strongest when the real wage is deflated by the wholesale price index and when overtime payments are excluded. However, in a recent study of a number of manufacturing industries, Kretzmer (1985) finds evidence that industry specific product wages (industry wage divided by the industry wpi component) are uniformly positively related to unanticipated monetary shocks.

Granger causality tests. Another type of neutrality test is based on the following observation: given the relevant state of the economy (capital, etc.), the history of monetary shocks should have no effects on real activity. Sargent (1976) and Sims (1980) utilized this perspective to construct neutrality tests along Granger causality lines. In a multivariate context nominal variables should not Granger-cause (predict) a vector of real variables if these contain the economy's state variables. (Conditions that assure that the state variable is reputable in this form are provided by Sargent (1979) – some may be unwilling to impose such lag length restrictions on error terms, which Sims (1980) argues incredible.) Sargent (1976), Sims (1980) and Eichenbaum and Singleton (1986) illustrate that the results of such tests are heavily dependent on variable selection and data processing, particularly treatment of non-stationarities.

A variant of this procedure is employed by Haraf (1983), who examines a four variable vector autoregression using real output, employment, inventories, and backorders. A constructed unanticipated money series does not Granger-cause the vector process governing the four real variables in the model, a result that is consistent with the simple equilibrium business cycle model. However, Haraf also finds that with the exception of real GNP, contemporaneous unanticipated movements in money have little explanatory power once lagged model variables are taken into account.

Tests based on contemporaneous monetary data. The previous tests concentrated on the distinction between unanticipated and anticipated changes in money. However, equilibrium business cycle theory typically predicts that the relevant distinction is between perceived and unperceived movements in money. Since monetary statistics are readily available, agents misperceive the true monetary state of the economy only to the extent that monetary statistics contain some reporting errors. Therefore, revisions in monetary statistics are indicators of misperceived money, and it is misperceived money that should be the relevant variable in explaining real economic fluctuations. Specific tests of the equilibrium business cycle theory using contemporaneous monetary data – historical statistical reports that were *potentially* available to private agents – are conducted by Barro and Hercowitz (1980) and Boschen and Grossman (1982).

Both of these papers contain evidence contradicting the implications of the simple equilibrium business cycle model outlined above. Barro and Hercowitz find that revisions in the monetary data do not help explain cyclical fluctuations of output or unemployment. Boschen and Grossman focus on King's (1981) observation that output should be uncorrelated with available monetary data. They begin by constructing a more elaborate procedure that yields valid tests of the real

effects of exogenous perceived money on output when misperceived money can affect output through a specific propogation mechanism. They find that contemporaneous monetary data is significantly (partially) correlated with real activity, which is inconsistent with the theory. Boschen and Grossman also test whether monetary reporting errors have real consequences and as in Barro–Hercowitz, there is no evidence of real effects. Thus, the Boschen and Grossman findings are inconsistent with the joint hypothesis of (i) a specific equilibrium business cycle model; (ii) that agents utilize contemporaneous information as money; and (iii) that measures of money (original and final reports) are exogenous.

Although properly specified tests are difficult to conduct, the mixed results of these three types of tests does not provide strong support for the equilibrium monetary business cycle view. Consequently, investigation of Keynesian alternatives seems warranted. We begin with the notion that multiperiod contracting imparts some stickiness to the nominal wage.

NOMINAL WAGE CONTRACTING MODELS

Much of the nominal wage contracting literature is based on two lines of work. One originates in Taylor (1979, 1980) and the other follows from Gray (1976) and Fischer (1977).

Taylor (1979, 1980) develops a model with multiperiod, overlapping nominal wage contracts and mark-up pricing. Simulations of the model under the assumption that wage contracts last for three or four quarters are used to investigate the dynamics of output or unemployment. Without any of the neoclassical propagation mechanisms, Taylor's models generate substantial serial correlation from the interactions of wage setting rules and expectations – shocks can last for more than the contract length because these are passed along via other, subsequent contracts. But Taylor's models have been criticized as departing too far from wage setting rules that could plausibly be rationalized by neoclassical methods – thus involving wage setting based on predetermined wage rates of others, which should be irrelevant – and for not containing the natural rate property (for further discussion of Taylor's models, see McCallum 1982).

The Gray (1976) Fischer (1977) perspective on wage contracts can be developed as follows. Production takes place at various locations or industries indexed by z, and depends negatively on the real wage $w_t(z) - p_t(z)$ in each location. (All variables are expressed in logarithms.) In the one period ahead contracting version of the model, the nominal wage $w_t(z)$ is set according to the rule $w_t(z) = E_{t-1} p_t + \gamma(z)(P_t - E_{t-1}P_t)$, $\gamma(z)$ indicates the extent of indexing in industry z. If $\gamma(z) = 1$, then wages in z are completely indexed to the aggregate price level. Given the nominal wage, firms determine employment along their marginal product curve, the efficiency condition being that the marginal product of labour equals $w_t(z) - p_t(z)$. Therefore a rise in the real wage reduces employment and output at location z.

Aggregate demand at any location is directly related to aggregate real balances and a relative demand shock, as in the equilibrium business cycle model. Also, the money supply is assumed to follow a random walk. In this setting, with incomplete indexing ($\gamma(z) < 1$), a positive money supply shock causes real wages to fall and output to rise. Also, with contracts set at one period in length, shifts in money that were anticipated at $t-1$ have no real effects. Therefore, tests that only consider the distinction between anticipated and unanticipated money cannot distinguish between equilibrium business cycle models with no contemporaneous information and models with nominal contracts extending for only one period.

However, as Fischer (1977) indicates, when contracts last for more than one period, shifts in money that are anticipated at $t-1$ will have real effects since some locations are locked into contracts conditioned on period $t-2$ information. However, Fischer (1979) reports some difficulties in implementing this strategy.

A direct test of the contracting model is performed by Ahmed (1986). Ahmed undertakes a careful study of the relationship between the Phillips curve slope and the degree of wage indexation in a particular industry. (The data set includes 19 Canadian industries.) The contracting model predicts that the responsiveness of industry specific output to unanticipated changes in money should be inversely related to the degree of indexing. That is, greater indexation by a particular industry reduces the responsiveness of real wages to unanticipated money and reduces the change in industry output to a monetary disturbance. Ahmed finds no evidence that there is any relationship between indexation and the magnitude of responsiveness of industry specific output to an aggregate monetary shock. These results are at variance with the implications of the contracting model.

Therefore, the strategy of producing monetary business cycles through nominal wage rigidities does not receive strong empirical support. This has lead Keynesians to refocus their attention on nominal rigidities that may occur in other areas of the economy, namely in the price of specific commodities.

STICKY PRICES AND BUSINESS CYCLES

After the Dunlop–Keynes–Tarshis controversy of the 1930s unveiled the lack of confirmation for countercyclical real wages, Keynesian macro theorists turned from models incorporating stickiness of wages to models featuring stickiness of product prices. This activity spanned the range from rationalizations of the pricing equations in large scale econometric models to the abstract dynamic pricing model of Phelps and Winter (1970) and the non-market clearing theory of Barro and Grossman (1976). Curiously, this prior path seems to have been ignored by the profession at large. Until recently, there has been substantial effort allocated to sticky wage models despite their reliance on a countercyclical path for the real wage. However, the past several years have seen increased attention to sticky price models. Although this line of research is still at an early stage and has, as yet, generated little empirical literature, we provide a brief review because of its likely importance in coming years.

Simultaneously with Fischer's wage contract model, Phelps and Taylor (1977) propounded a basic rational expectations model with price stickiness, in a paper that has received far less professional attention than Fischer (1977). However, research into sticky price models was continued by McCallum in an important series of papers. Initially, McCallum focused his investigations on the conditions under which sticky price models rationalized non-neutrality of monetary shocks while maintaining the neutrality of anticipated monetary policy (1978, 1979, 1980).

More recently, McCallum (1982, 1986) has provided a detailed outline of interactions between nominal shocks, price adjustment, and real activity, which presumably will be developed further in coming years. The key elements of this story are as follows. To economize on certain costs, firms find it optimal to maintain a set nominal price over some period, accommodating variations in relative and aggregate demand through alterations in production and inventories. Thus, monetary shocks have real effects. However, price adjustments incorporate firms' anticipations about monetary policy, so the real consequences of anticipated movements in money are much smaller than unanticipated movements and may be fully neutralized.

In McCallum's work the period over which stickiness prevails plays a crucial role. If price stickiness is to be assigned a major role in business cycles – even as an impulse mechanism – then the period over which firms elect to make prices sticky must be non-trivial. McCallum (1982, 1986) begins by reviewing theoretical explanations of why producers might temporarily stabilize relative prices against shocks, for example to attract a clientele of customers who prefer relative price stability. He then argues that the costs within period adjustment of nominal prices – or of indexation that would neutralize monetary shocks – cannot be the physical costs of adjusting prices, but rather are computational costs associated with the difficulties that agents face in understanding more complex contracts. He also argues that indexation provides only small reductions in risks to participants, although it is unclear how this is consistent with business cycles that are an important social problem.

Some other recent attempts to give theoretical content to the idea of price stickiness have proceeded along two different paths. One avenue emphasized by Mankiw (1985) and Blanchard and Kiyotaki (1985) involves models with monopolistically competitive firms that face fixed ('menu') costs of adjusting prices. So far, this line of research has concentrated on establishing that menu costs that are small can lead to large departures from socially efficient allocations when nominal shocks occur. These models are not yet dynamic, so that distinctions between anticipated and unanticipated movements in nominal variables have not yet been explored. But it stands to reason that there would be results that differed from McCallum's, since in his setup there are effectively zero costs of adjusting prices between periods and infinite costs of changing prices within the period. First, as in Mankiw(1985), large nominal shocks – even if unanticipated – would tend to be neutralized. Second, small anticipated changes in money would tend not to be neutralized, as the menu costs would be prohibitive. Irrespective of one's view on the plausibility of menu costs, these recent analyses provide a clue as to how individual agents might regard the gains to altering nominal contracts as small even though the social benefits would be large, due to the suboptimality of monopolistically competitive equilibria.

Another line of research has been pursued by Rotemberg (1981), who employs quadratic costs of price adjustment to induce gradual price adjustment. As in Phelps–Winter, these costs are viewed as arising from an erosion of the firm's clientele, with a specific interpretation involving an individual's dislike of price volatility. Using rational expectations methodology, Rotemberg provides evidence that prices adjust gradually, although the specific structural models which he employs are inconsistent with the cross equation constraints implied by the rational expectations postulate.

As the dynamic implications of sticky-price macro models are developed in more detail, it will become possible to discriminate between these models and the flexible price equilibrium theories considered earlier. In this process, since price level behaviour is a result of the interaction between private agents and the monetary authority, an adequate definition of price stickiness will be required. In particular most researchers have focused on the smoothing of price level variations that arises from private sector actions. However, smoothing can also arise from systematic actions by the monetary authority (see Goodfriend, 1986). Powerful tests will presumably require systematic examination of data generated prior to the creation of the Federal Reserve.

The microeconomic evidence developed by Carlton (1986) – working with the Stigler–Kindahl (1970) data – shows that some prices are fairly rigid. However, the rigidities do not seem to conform to those that have been postulated by macro-modellers. For instance, many price changes are extremely small, indicating that menu costs are not a pervasive factor. Carlton also does not find much evidence that buyers have strong preferences for products whose prices are relatively stable, implying that one rationalization of Rotemberg's costs of adjustment is apparently inoperative. As the particular mechanism that generates rigidities could be quite important for the dynamic implications of this class of models, identification of the empirically relevant sources of rigidities is necessary. At this stage, this class of models should be regarded as a potentially promising means of resurrecting long standing Keynesian notions. As of yet their value has not been proven.

CONCLUSION

In our overview of rational expectations models of business fluctuations, we have consciously emphasized the extent to which this class of models has generated cyclical interactions that are consistent with empirical evidence. Evidently, progress has not been rapid and there is currently no compelling evidence for any particular description of cycles, despite the fact that the models quite frequently have substantially distinct policy implications. We do not regard this assessment as a reason for departing from the discipline imposed by rational expectations, but feel that this is rather an indication of the amount of work that remains to be done.

In fact, some recent research has led us to become less sure that the conventional representation of business cycles – the stochastic components of economic time series – is appropriate. Nelson and Plosser (1982) have produced some provocative empirical work which cannot reject the hypothesis that the stochastic components of economic time series are nonstationary, possessing random walk components. Although their tests have low power against the alternative that the stochastic components are stationary but highly persistent (McCallum, 1986), these results represent a serious challenge to existing views. Further, there are now basic equilibrium models of fluctuations that imply non-stationarity if the intertemporal technologies are restricted so that the mean rate of economic growth is endogenously determined (King and Rebelo, 1986), basically because fixed factors are not too important. Further, these endogenous growth models have substantial implications for modelbuilding under the rational expectations postulate, for they imply that there are transformations of non-stationary economic variables that are stationary – that is, the macroeconomic data possess a cointegrated representation (King, Plosser, Stock and Watson, 1986).

Our forecast is that the construction of rational expectations model of the business cycle will be the centrepiece of the macroeconomic research agenda over the next fifteen years, as much as it has been over the fifteen that have passed since Lucas's influential contributions (1972a, 1972b). Recently, Lucas (1985a) has argued that economic fluctuations pale in welfare significance relative to the factors that determine the growth path of a particular country's economy; his research has recently turned to analyses of these factors (1985b). Most

macroeconomists presumably share McCallum's (1986) scepticism that economic fluctuations are second order problems relative to economic growth and, hence, would doubt that Lucas's current research direction will have the impact of his 1972 work. But we are not so sure, for if the analysis of King and Rebelo (1986) is sustained in richer models, then it is inappropriate to separate the study of economic fluctuations from that of economic growth. That is, the fact that economies grow tells us that temporary shocks to the economy's production possibilities will have permanent effects on the level of output.

MICHAEL DOTSEY AND ROBERT G. KING

See also CREDIT CYCLE; DEPRESSIONS; MULTIPLE TIME SERIES MODELS; RATIONAL EXPECTATIONS; TRADE CYCLE.

BIBLIOGRAPHY

Abel, A.B. and Mishkin, F.S. 1983. An integrated view of tests of rationality, market efficiency and the short-run neutrality of money. *Journal of Monetary Economics* 11, January, 3–24.

Ahmed, S. 1986. Wage indexation and the Phillip's curve slope: a cross-industry analysis. *Journal of Monetary Economics.*

Altug, S. 1985. Gestation lags and the business cycle: an empirical investigation. Unpublished working paper, University of Minnesota.

Barro, R.J. 1976. Rational expectations and the rôle of monetary policy. *Journal of Monetary Economics* 2, January, 1–32.

Barro, R.J. 1977. Unanticipated money growth and unemployment in the United States. *American Economic Review* 67, March, 101–15.

Barro, R.J. 1978. Unanticipated money, output and the price level in the United States. *Journal of Political Economy* 86, August, 549–80.

Barro, R.J. 1980. A capital market in an equilibrium business cycle model. *Econometrica* 48, September, 1393–417.

Barro, R.J. 1986. Comments of Eichenbaum and Singleton. Unpublished working paper, University of Rochester.

Barro, R.J. and Grossman, H.I. 1976. *Money, Employment and Inflation.* Cambridge: Cambridge University Press.

Barro, R.J. and Hercovitz, Z. 1980. Money stock revisions and unanticipated money growth. *Journal of Monetary Economics* 6, April, 257–67.

Barro, R.J. and Rush, M. 1980. Unanticipated money and economic activity. In *Rational Expectations and Economic Policy,* ed. S. Fischer, Chicago: University of Chicago Press for National Bureau of Economic Research.

Bils, M.J. 1985. Real wages over the business cycle: evidence from panel data. *Journal of Political Economy* 93, August, 666–89.

Bils, M. 1986. Cyclical behavior of marginal cost and price. Unpublished working paper, University of Rochester.

Blanchard, O.J. and Kiyotaki, N. 1985. Monopolistic competition, aggregate demand externalities and real effects of nominal money. National Bureau of Economic Research working paper No. 1770, December.

Boschen, J. and Grossman, H.I. 1982. Tests of equilibrium macroeconomics using contemporaneous monetary data. *Journal of Monetary Economics* 10, November, 309–34.

Carlton, D. 1986. The rigidity of prices. National Bureau of Economic Research working paper No. 1813, January.

Edwards, M. 1980. Informational equilibrium in a monetary theory of the business cycle. Unpublished working paper, University of Rochester.

Eichenbaum, M. and Singleton, K. 1986. Do equilibrium real business cycle theories explain post-war U.S. fluctuations? Unpublished working paper, Carnegie-Mellon University, April.

Fischer, S. 1977. Long term contracts, rational expectations and the optimal money supply rule. *Journal of Political Economy* 85, February, 191–205.

Fischer, S. 1980. On activist monetary policy with rational expectations. In *Rational Expectations and Economic Policy,* ed. S. Fischer, Chicago: University of Chicago Press for National Bureau of Economic Research.

Friedman, M. 1968. The role of monetary policy. *American Economic Review* 58, March, 1–17.

Friedman, M. and Schwartz, A.J. 1963. *A Monetary History of the United States, 1867–1960.* Princeton: Princeton University Press for National Bureau of Economic Research.

Frisch, R. 1933. Propagation problems and impulse problems in dynamic economics. In *Essays in Honour of Gustav Cassel*, London: George Allen & Unwin.

Goodfriend, M.S. 1986. Interest rate smoothing and price level trend-stationarity. Unpublished working paper, Federal Reserve Bank of Richmond, August.

Gray, J. 1976. Wage indexation: a macroeconomic approach. *Journal of Monetary Economics* 2, April, 221–35.

Haberler, G. 1937. *Prosperity and Depression.* Geneva: League of Nations.

Hall, R.E. 1975. Rigidity of wages and persistence of unemployment. *Brookings Papers on Economic Activity* No. 2, 301–49.

Hall, R.J. 1980. Comments on chapters 6 and 7. In *Rational Expectations and Economic Policy*, ed. S. Fischer, Chicago: University of Chicago Press for National Bureau of Economic Research.

Hansen, G. 1985. Indivisible labor and the business cycle. *Journal of Monetary Economics* 16, November, 309–28.

Haraf, W. 1983. Tests of a rational expectations–structural neutrality model with persistent effects of monetary disturbances. *Journal of Monetary Economics* 11, January, 103–16.

Hicks, J.R. 1933. Equilibrium and the cycle. Reprinted in J.R. Hicks, *Money, Interest and Wages: Collected Essays in Economic Theory*, Vol. 2, Cambridge, Mass.: Harvard University Press, 1982.

Hodrick, R.J. and Prescott, E.C. 1980. Post-war U.S. business cycles: an empirical investigation. Unpublished working paper, Carnegie-Mellon University.

King, R.G. 1981. Monetary information and monetary neutrality. *Journal of Monetary Economics* 7, March, 195–206.

King, R.G. and Plosser, C.I. 1984. Money, credit, and prices in a real business cycle. *American Economic Review* 24, May, 363–80.

King, R.G. and Plosser, C.I. 1986. Production, growth and business cycles. Unpublished working paper, University of Rochester, May.

King, R.G., Plosser, C.I., Stock, J. and Watson, M. 1986. Short run and long run relationships in macroeconomic time series. Unpublished working paper, University of Rochester.

King, R.G. and Rebelo, S. 1986. Business cycles with endogenous growth. Unpublished working paper, University of Rochester, March.

King, R.G. and Trehan, B. 1984. Money: endogeneity and neutrality. *Journal of Monetary Economics* 14, November, 385–94.

Kertzmer, P.E. 1985. Cross-industry tests of an equilibrium business cycle model with rational expectations. Unpublished working paper, Board of Governors of the Federal Reserve System, November.

Kydland, F. and Prescott, E.C. 1982. Time to build and aggregate fluctuations. *Econometrica* 50, November, 1345–70.

Leiderman, L. 1980. Macroeconomic testing of the rational expectations and structural neutrality hypotheses for the United States. *Journal of Monetary Economics* 6, January, 69–82.

Leiderman, L. 1983. The response of real wages to unanticipated money growth. *Journal of Monetary Economics* 1, January, 73–88.

Long, J.B. and Plosser, C.I. 1983. Real business cycles. *Journal of Political Economy* 91, February, 39–69.

Lucas, R.E., Jr. 1972a. Expectations and the neutrality of money. *Journal of Economic Theory* 4, April, 103–24.

Lucas, R.E., Jr. 1972b. Econometric testing of the natural rate hypothesis. In *The Econometrics of Price Determination*, ed. O. Eckstein, Washington: Board of Governors of the Federal Reserve System.

Lucas, R.E., Jr. 1973. Some international evidence on output–inflation tradeoffs. *American Economic Review* 63, June, 326–34.

Lucas, R.E., Jr. 1977. Understanding business cycles. In *Stabilization of the Domestic and International Economy*, ed. K. Brunner and A. Meltzer, Vol. 5 of the Carnegie-Rochester Series on Public Policy, Amsterdam: North Holland, 7–29.

Lucas, R.E., Jr. 1980. Methods and problems in business cycle theory. *Journal of Money, Credit and Banking* 2, November, 696–715.

Lucas, R.E., Jr. 1985a. Models of business fluctuations. Unpublished working paper, University of Chicago.

Lucas, R.E., Jr. 1985b. On the mechanics of economic development. Working paper, University of Chicago.

Mankiw, N.G. 1985. Small menu costs and large business cycles: a macroeconomic model of monopoly. *Quarterly Journal of Economics* 2, May, 529–38.

McCallum, B.T. 1978. Price level adjustments and the rational expectations approach to macroeconomic stabilization policy. *Journal of Money, Credit and Banking* 10, November, 418–36.

McCallum, B.T. 1979. A monetary policy ineffectiveness result in a model with a predetermined price level. *Economics Letters* 3, 1–4.

McCallum, B.T. 1980. Rational expectations and macroeconomic stabilization policy: an overview. *Journal of Money, Credit and Banking* 12, November (pt. 2), 716–46.

McCallum, B.T. 1986. On real and sticky price models of the business cycle. National Bureau of Economic Research working paper No. 1933, June.

McCallum, B.T. 1986. On real and sticky price of the business cycle. National Bureau of Economic Research working paper No. 1933, June.

Merrick, J.J., Jr. 1983. Financial market efficiency, the decomposition of anticipated versus unanticipated money growth, and further tests of the relation between money and real output. *Journal of Money, Credit and Banking* 40, May, 222–32.

Mishkin, F.S. 1982. Does anticipated money matter: an econometric investigation. *Journal of Political Economy* 90, February, 22–51.

Mitchell, W.C. 1951. *What Happens during Business Cycles.* New York: National Bureau of Economic Research.

Muth, J.F. 1961. Rational expectations and the theory of price movements. *Econometrica* 29, July, 315–35.

Nelson, C.R. and Plosser, C.I. 1982. Trends and random walks in macroeconomic time series: some evidence and implications. *Journal of Monetary Economics* 10, September, 139–62.

Phelps, E.S. 1967. Phillips curves, expectations of inflation and optimal unemployment over time. *Economica* 34, August, 254–81.

Phelps, E.S. and Winter, S.G. 1970. Optimal price policy under atomistic competition. In *Microeconomic Foundations of Employment and Inflation Theory*, ed. E.S. Phelps, New York: W.W. Norton and Company.

Phelps, E.S. and Taylor, J.B. 1977. Stabilizing powers of monetary policy under rational expectations. *Journal of Political Economy* 85, February, 163–90.

Prescott, E.C. 1986. Theory ahead of business cycle measurement. Federal Reserve Bank of Minneapolis Research Department Staff Report 102, February; also in *Carnegie-Rochester Conference Series on Public Policy*.

Rogerson, R. 1985. Indivisible labor, lotteries and equilibrium. Unpublished working paper, University of Rochester.

Rosen, S. 1985. Implicit contracts: a survey. *Journal of Economic Literature*, 23 September, 1144–75.

Rotemberg, J. 1982. Sticky prices in the United States. *Journal of Political Economy* 90, December, 1187–211.

Sargent, T.J. 1973. Rational expectations, the real rate of interest, and the natural rate of unemployment. *Brookings Papers on Economic Activity* No. 2, 429–72.

Sargent, T.J. 1976. A classical macroeconometric model for the United States. *Journal of Political Economy* 84, April, 207–37.

Sargent, T.J. 1979. Granger causality and the natural rate hypothesis. *Journal of Political Economy* 87, April, 213–48.

Sargent, T.J. 1981. Interpreting economic time series. *Journal of Political Economy* 89, April, 403–10.

Sargent, T.J. and Wallace, N. 1975. Rational expectations, the optimal monetary instrument and the optimal money supply rule. *Journal of Political Economy* 83(2), April, 241–54.

Solow, R.M. 1957. Technical change and the aggregate production function. *Review of Economics and Statistics* 39, August, 312–20.

Stigler, G. and Kindahl, J. 1970. *The Behavior of Industrial Prices.* New York: Columbia University Press for the National Bureau of Economic Research.

Tinbergen, J. 1932. *Business Cycles in the United States of America, 1919–1932.: Statistical testing of business cycle theories.* Geneva: League of Nations.

by-products. *See* JOINT PRODUCTION.

C

Cairnes, John Elliott (1823–1875).   Cairnes was born at Castlebellingham, County Louth, Ireland. At the height of his career he was probably the best-known political economist in England after John Stuart Mill, whose friend and associate he was from 1859 onwards; but his interest in economic questions developed relatively late, after periods spent working in his family's brewing business and in journalism. In 1856 he competed in the examination by which the Whately professorship of political economy at Trinity College, Dublin, was then filled, and was appointed for a five-year term. In 1859 he was also appointed Professor of Political Economy and Jurisprudence at Queen's College, Galway, a post which he held until 1870. However, he employed a deputy to perform his duties in Galway after he himself moved to London in 1865. In 1866 he became Professor of Political Economy at University College, London, but was forced to resign in 1872 by the progress of the rheumatic disease which left him almost completely paralysed before his death in 1875.

Cairnes has often been described as 'the last of the classical economists'. He always worked within the framework of the Ricardo–Mill tradition, devoting himself to refining and strengthening it and seeing no necessity for any radical reform or reconstruction. Within these self-imposed limits and in a career of less than twenty years as a professional economist he succeeded in making contributions to both theoretical and applied economics which earned him a high reputation among his contemporaries and a definite place in the history of economic thought.

Cairnes's first work in economics proved to be one of his most enduring contributions to the subject. This was *The Character and Logical Method of Political Economy* (1857; 2nd edition, 1875) which is still regarded as one of the best statements of the verificationist methodology of the English classical school. Following the lines laid down by Senior and Mill, Cairnes stressed the neutrality of economic science, emphasized the value of the deductive method and characterized the subject as a hypothetical science 'asserting, not what *will* take place, but what *would* or what tends to take place' ([1857] 1875, p. 55).

It was in the use of the deductive method to develop the central areas of economic theory that Cairnes's main interest came to lie. Yet it was through his work on applied economics and current issues of policy that he first came to be nationally and internationally known. In September 1859 Cairnes published the first of a series of 'Essays towards a solution of the Gold Question' in which he sought to 'apply the principles of economic science' in an attempt to 'forecast the directions in which the course [of trade and prices] would be modified by the increased supplies of gold'. This *a priori* approach was almost precisely the opposite of that used by Jevons to deal with the same problem, but their results coincided remarkably.

It was another application of this approach which first made Cairnes's work known to a much wider audience. In *The Slave Power* (1862) he sought to explain on economic grounds the appearance of slavery in the southern parts of the United States, tracing out both the conditions for and the consequences of the operation of a slave economy. As an indictment of the political economy of the Confederate States it strongly influenced public opinion in Britain towards support of the northern states in the American Civil War.

Between 1864 and 1870 Cairnes wrote a number of articles on the problems of land tenure in Ireland, in which he argued in favour of proposals to fix rent by law and contended that this was not inconsistent with classical rent theory. There is evidence that his views on this and other questions of the day, such as Irish university education, exerted considerable influence on (and through) Mill and Fawcett.

Cairnes's most important contribution to economic analysis, *Some Leading Principles of Political Economy newly expounded* (1874) was also to be his last work and that by which he came to be most widely known and judged. In it he re-stated, but with significant modifications, the essentials of classical doctrine on the central questions of value, distribution and international trade. His most important innovation was to show that the existence of 'non-competing groups' in labour markets implied that the cost of production theory must be supplemented by the analysis of reciprocal demand in the theory of domestic as well as international values.

Nevertheless his unsympathetic review of Jevons's *Theory of Political Economy* (*Fortnightly Review*, N.S., vol. 11, 1872) showed that he lacked interest in and understanding of the subjective approach to value theory which was then developing. Cairnes's treatment of distribution in the *Leading Principles* echoed Mill in showing sympathy for the position of the labourer combined with pessimism based on acceptance of Malthusian population theory; but it was chiefly notable for an elaborate but ultimately unsuccessful attempt to rehabilitate the wages-fund doctrine abandoned by Mill himself in 1869. The verdict of Schumpeter (1954, p. 533) still seems appropriate: Cairnes 'expounded the old analytical economics and explicitly distanced himself from the new'.

R.D. COLLISON BLACK

SELECTED WORKS

1857. *The Character and Logical Method of Political Economy*. London: Macmillan; 2nd edn 1875; repr. 1888.
1862. *The Slave Power; its Character, Career, and Probable Designs: Being an Attempt to explain the real issues involved in the American contest*. London: Macmillan; 2nd edn 1863.
1873a. *Political Essays*. London: Macmillan.
1873b. *Essays in Political Economy, theoretical and applied*. London: Macmillan.
1874. *Some Leading Principles of Political Economy newly expounded*. London: Macmillan.

BIBLIOGRAPHY

Black, R.D. Collison. 1960. Jevons and Cairnes. *Economica*, N.S. 27, 214–32.
Boylan, T.A. and Foley, T.P. 1984. John Elliott Cairnes, John Stuart Mill and Ireland: some problems for political economy. In *Economists and the Irish Economy*, ed. A.E. Murphy, Dublin: Irish Academic Press.

O'Brien, G. 1943. J.S. Mill and J.E. Cairnes. *Economica*, N.S. 10, 273–85.

Schumpeter, J.A. 1954. *History of Economic Analysis*. New York: Oxford University Press.

Weinberg, A. 1970. *John Elliott Cairnes and the American Civil War*. London: Kingswood Press.

calculus of variations. The development of the calculus of variations is attributed to Euler and Lagrange, although some of it can be traced back to the Bernoullis. A history of the calculus of variations is provided by Goldstine (1980). The calculus of variations deals with the problem of determining a function that optimizes some criterion that is usually expressed as an integral. This problem is analogous to the differential calculus problem of finding a point at which a function is optimized, except that the point in the calculus of variations is a function rather than a number. The function over which the optimum is sought is usually restricted to the class of continuous and at least piecewise differentiable functions.

A typical calculus of variations problem is of the form

$$\max_{x(t)} \int_{t_0}^{t_1} F[t, x(t), x'(t)] \, dt. \qquad \text{s.t. } x(t_0) = x_0, \qquad (1)$$

where $x'(t) = dx/dt$, and $t, x(t)$, and $x'(t)$ are regarded as independent arguments of the function F. The necessary conditions for $x^*(t)$ to maximize (1) are the Euler equation

$$F_x = dF_{x'}/dt, \qquad (2)$$

the Legendre condition

$$F_{x'x'} \leqslant 0 \qquad (3)$$

and the transversality conditions

$$\begin{cases} \text{a.} & F_{x'} = 0 \text{ at } t_1, \text{ if } x(t_1) \text{ is free,} \\ \text{b.} & F - x'F_{x'} = 0 \text{ at } t_1, \text{ if } t_1 \text{ is free,} \end{cases} \qquad (4)$$

where F_x and $F_{x'}$ refer to the partial derivatives of F with respect to x and x', respectively, and $F_{x'x'}$ is the second partial derivative of F with respect to x'. The Euler equation (2) is in general a nonlinear second order differential equation. The initial condition $x(t_0) = x_0$ and the transversality condition (4a) provide the means for determining the two constants of integration that arise in solving the Euler equation. The optimal value of the upper limit of integration, t_1, if it can be chosen, is determined by the transversality condition (4b). The problem posed in (1) can be extended to include additional arguments of the function F, to include a variety of additional constraints, and to involve double integrals (see Kamien and Schwartz, 1981). Concavity of F with respect to $x(t)$ and $x'(t)$ assures that the necessary conditions are also sufficient.

The earliest application of the calculus of variations to the analysis of an economic problem appears to have been attempted by Edgeworth (1881), who seems to have been greatly impressed by its successful employment in deriving some of the basic laws of physics. He sought to employ it to find a function for distributing income and assigning work among the members of society so as to maximize total social welfare. Many applications of the calculus of variations to economic problems have been conducted since then, a few of which will be described.

As the calculus of variations deals with the problem of finding a function or a path that maximizes some criterion, its major application in economics has been to problems involving optimal decision making through time where an entire course of actions is sought rather than a single action. One of the earliest and most influential applications along these lines is by Ramsey (1928). The question he addressed is how much should a nation save out of its national income through time so as to maximize its overall welfare over time. Ramsey argued that the discounting of future utilities was 'ethically indefensible' as it means that we give less weight to the utility of future generations than to our own. He posited, therefore, a maximum level of net utility, the utility of consumption minus the disutility of work, that he called bliss. This bliss level of utility is the asymptotic limit of the achievable level of net utility. Ramsey then sought the savings rate through time that would minimize the integral over the indefinite future of the difference between the bliss level of utility and the actual net utility level at each point in time, subject to the constraint that savings plus consumption equal total output at each instant of time. The rule he derived for the optimal savings rate, through the Euler equations, is that the 'rate of saving multiplied by the marginal utility of consumption should always equal bliss minus actual rate of utility enjoyed'. This is essentially a marginal sacrifice today equals marginal benefit tomorrow rule. The rationale for taking the upper limit of integration to be infinite in the objective function is that while individuals have finite lives, society as a whole goes on forever. Ramsey also took up the case where future utilities are discounted at a constant positive rate and derived what may be regarded as the fundamental equation of optimal consumption through time, namely that the proportionate rate of change of marginal utility of consumption should equal the difference between the marginal productivity of capital and the rate at which future utility is discounted. The Ramsey model became the basis for optimal growth theory that was intensely investigated in the late 1950s and 1960s.

Strotz (1956) addressed the question of the circumstances under which an individual would continue today to follow the optimal consumption plan through time that he had determined at an earlier date. In other words, he asked for the conditions under which an optimal consumption plan through time would be consistent. He found the necessary and sufficient conditions for consistency to be that 'the logarithmic rate of change in the discount function must be constant'. Exponential discounting at a constant rate satisfies this criterion.

Yaari (1965) addressed the question of an individual's optimal consumption plan through time when his lifetime is uncertain. He also allowed for the possibility that the individual derives utility form a bequest to his heirs. Yaari found that a major effect of the presence of uncertainty about one's lifetime is the same as an increase in the rate at which future utilities are discounted. Thus, the 'effective' rate at which future utilities are discounted has a risk premium term added to the discount rate in the absence of uncertainty about one's lifetime. The risk premium term is the instantaneous conditional probability of dying in the next instant given survival to the present. The presence of the risk premium means that the rate of consumption at any point in time is higher than it is in its absence. Uncertainty about one's lifetime increases one's rate of current spending, if there is no bequest motive.

While Ramsey applied the calculus of variations to the problem of optimal savings through time, Evans (1924) appears to have been the first to have employed it for determining the optimal rate of output through time. Evans used, as his vehicle for making the problem of choosing the level of output so as to maximize a monopolist's profit over an interval of time nontrivial, i.e. just simple maximization of profit at each instant of time, the assumption that the demand function for a good depended both on its current price and the rate of change of price. In particular, he assumed that the demand function was linear in price and its first derivative, and that the cost of production was a quadratic function of the level of output. Under these assumptions Evans sought the level of production that would maximize the integral of profits over a finite horizon. He was able to characterize this path and to show that a particular solution to the second order differential equation stemming from the Euler equation was the static monopoly profit maximizing level of output. Indeed, it is not difficult to show that when the problem is posed as one of maximizing the present value of an infinite horizon profit stream that the static monopoly profit maximizing level of output and the corresponding monopoly price constitute a steady-state towards which the output and price paths converge through time. This, of course, is intuitively plausible, as in the steady-state the rate of change of price with respect to time is zero, and so the demand function depends only on the current price level. Evans's work was extended by Roos (1925) to the case of duopolistic producers of a homogeneous product seeking to maximize their individual profits through time. The Roos paper may be regarded as the earliest analysis of what has come to be known as a differential game (see Freshtman and Kamien, 1987).

The last paper that deserves special mention because of its important application of the calculus of variations is Hotelling's (1931), dealing with the rate at which a mineral resource such as coal, copper or oil, should be extracted from a mine and sold so as to maximize the present value of its profits. Hotelling derived the fundamental equation for optimal extraction, under competitive production of the resource, namely that the extraction rate be such as to equate the percent change in price through time with the rate of interest at each instant in time. The intuitive reason for this is that if the percent change in the price of the resource exceeds the interest rate then it pays to extract and sell more today, because the alternative of extracting less and earning the interest on the revenue from that level of extraction yields less. The increase in the current rate of extraction, however, causes price to decline until the percent change in the price through time is equalized with the rate of interest. A similar analysis yields that current extraction will decline if the percent change in price is below the interest rate, which in turn will cause price to rise until equality is achieved. Along the optimal extraction path the mine owner is just indifferent between extracting an extra unit of resource today and extracting it tomorrow. A similar analysis can be carried out for a monopolistic mine owner, with the percent change in marginal revenue through time being equated with the interest rate.

There have been a very large number of applications of the calculus of variations since these early ones. Many have employed optimal control methods and dynamic programming methods, both of which constitute generalizations of the calculus of variations. As long as decision making though time is regarded as an important subject of economic analysis, the calculus of variations will continue to find use in economics.

MORTON I. KAMIEN

See also EDGEWORTH, FRANCIS YSIDRO; EVANS, GRIFFITH CONRAD; OPTIMAL CONTROL AND ECONOMIC DYNAMICS; RAMSEY MODEL; ROOS, CHARLES FREDERICK.

BIBLIOGRAPHY
Edgeworth, F.Y. 1881. *Mathematical Psychics*. Reprinted, New York: Augustus M. Kelley, 1967.
Evans, G.C. 1924. The dynamics of monopoly. *American Mathematical Monthly* 31, 75–83.
Fershtman, C. and Kamien, M. 1987. Dynamic duopolistic competition with sticky prices. *Econometrica*.
Goldstine, H.H. 1980. *A History of the Calculus of Variations*. New York: Springer-Verlag.
Hotelling, H. 1931. The economics of exhaustible resources. *Journal of Political Economy* 39, 137–75.
Kamien, M.I. and Schwartz, N.L. 1981. *Dynamic Optimization*. New York: North-Holland.
Ramsey, F.P. 1928. A mathematical theory of saving. *Economic Journal* 38, 543–59.
Roos, C.F. 1925. A mathematical theory of competition. *American Journal of Mathematics* 47, 163–75.
Strotz, R.H. 1956. Myopia and inconsistency in dynamic utility maximization. *Review of Economic Studies* 23, 165–80.
Yaari, M.E. 1965. Uncertain lifetime, life insurance and the theory of the consumer. *Review of Economic Studies* 32, 137–50.

cameralism. Cameralism is the specific version of mercantilism, taught and practised in the German principalities (*Kleinstaaten*) in the 17th and 18th centuries. Becher (1635-82), von Justi (1717–71) and von Sonnenfels (1732–1817) are the principal figures who contributed to a vast cameralist literature of about 14,000 titles (Humpert, 1935). The subject matter of *Kameralismus* reflected the political and economic phenomena and problems in the German territorial states. As a branch of 'science' it is a fiscal *Kunstlehre*, i.e. the practical art of how to govern an autonomous territory efficiently and justly via financial measures designed to fill the state's treasury. Its subject matter includes economic policy, legislation, administration and public finance. While there is no unifying analytical foundation of cameralism, it did develop in two distinct phases (a younger and an older branch) with varied emphasis on its different elements, and since the rising state was, in theory and reality, the focus and *ultima ratio* of political, economic and ethical (occasionally promotive) speculation, cameralism takes on a unitary form (*Gestalt*) only when viewed in retrospect.

The term 'cameralism' itself originates in the management of the state's or prince's treasure (*Kammer, caisse, camera principis*), seen as the principal instrument of economic and political power. In the age of enlightened absolutism, German-Austrian cameralism, based on a somewhat obscure natural-law philosophy, emphasized the paternalistic character of the governments' centralized fiscal policy (not, as is sometimes mistakenly thought, a Keynesian short-run instrument but rather a regulator for development which was to serve the general happiness of the subjects (*Untertanen*), i.e. an eudaemonistic utilitarianism). English and French mercantilism, on the other hand, stressed much more the wealth or 'riches' of the sovereign as an end.

The princely bureaucrats had been trained in their own universities (e.g. Halle, Frankfurt/Oder, Vienna) in 'fiscal jurisprudence' (von Stein) – a mixture of both formal budget and tax 'principles' – and a highly pedantic and descriptive systematization of facts and definitions. Analytical economics, insights into the laws of the market and the study of the interaction between market and state (or even of the bureaucratic and political mechanism) are relatively unknown in the simple textbooks of the cameralists, which show otherwise sound common sense. Statistics, important for census and grasping foreign trade, became a new discipline of the cameral curriculum.

The *practical* policy of cameralism concentrated on the development of a country which had been devastated and depopulated in the Thirty Years' War and impoverished by the discovery of the sea route to India and the fall of Constantinople. Under these abnormal circumstances a political and bureaucratic monopoly attempted to reconstruct the economic foundations of the country by an active population policy, the establishment of state manufactures and banks, the extension of infrastructure (canals, bridges, harbours and roads) and the promotion of modernization. It strictly regulated the still important agricultural sector, as well as trade and commerce.

The state protected the trades (*Gewerbe*) by means of high tariffs to restrict imports of unnecessary raw materials and it facilitated exports of manufactures and import substitution. On the other hand, the government removed internal trade barriers by abolishing the medieval guild organization and by unifying the law for municipalities. Mercantilist efforts to augment the state treasure via trade surplus and money policy were, of course, another main cameralisitc aim. Finally, it is notable that its monetary policy was inconsistent, insofar as the hoarding of precious metals as opposed to their circulating function were not clearly distinguished.

To set cameralism in secular perspective, the famous arguments of Smith and the physiocrats against the 'mercantile system' seem to be *mutatis mutandis* valid for neo-mercantilism, which also justifies both state intervention in the market and a greater GNP government share and often reverts to the regulatory rules and the principles of planning in this former epoch. However, neomercantilism fails to prove seriously both the state's competence to ensure efficiency and equity in the public sector and its ability to regulate the market reasonably. Some writers tend to overlook that in our times the basic conditions in the state and the economy are radically different from those of three centuries ago. For example, economic, political and administrative conditions in the German principalities differed strikingly from Ludwig Erhard's situation after World War II. And the wide gap between the Great Depression of the 1930s and the technologically influenced stagflation of today is obviously so fundamental that the regulatory Keynesian budget and employment theory, with its at present unrealistic assumptions, becomes rather obsolete. Thus any attempt to revive the strict regulating prescriptions of all-embracing cameralism, which lacks sufficient analysis and empirical testing, would apparently be a violation of both reason and experience. In this case we would use analytically poor (and old) tools to repair the wrong (and modern) machine.

H.C. RECKTENWALD

BIBLIOGRAPHY

Becher, J.J. 1668. *Politischer Diskurs*. Frankfurt/Main: Bielcke.
Humpert, M. 1935–7. *Bibliographie der Kameralwissenschaften*. Cologne: Schroeder. (Includes nearly 14,000 items.)
Justi, J.H.G. von. 1755. *Staatswirtschaft*. Leipzig: Breitkopf.
Mohl, R. von. 1855–8. *Geschichte und Literatur der Staatswissenschaften*, Vols 1–3. Erlangen: Enke.
Recktenwald, H.C. (ed.) 1973. *Political Economy: A Historical Perspective*. London: Collier-Macmillan.
Recktenwald, H.C. 1986. *Das Selbstinteresse – Zentrales Axiom der ökonomischen Wissenschaft*. Wiesbaden: Leibniz-Akademie der Wissenschaften.
Small, A.W. 1909. *The Cameralists*. New York: Franklin.
Sommer, L. 1920–25. *Die österreichischen Kameralisten in dogmengeschichtlicher Darstellung*. 2 vols, Vienna: Konegen.
Sonnenfels, J. von. 1765–76. *Grundsätze der Polizei, Handlungs- und Finanzwissenschaft*. Vienna: Camesina.

Canard, Nicolas-François (c1750–1833). French mathematician and economist, Canard was born in Moulins, near Vichy, around 1750, and died there in 1833. Little is known about his life other than the fact that he taught mathematics at the Ecole Centrale de Moulins. His other interests included economics, jurisprudence and meteorology.

Canard's reputation as an economist rests on his *Principes d'économie politique* (1801), a study of the incidence of taxes, which, however, has drawn more attention for its use of mathematics in economic analysis. Written in the year of Cournot's birth, the *Principes* was honoured by the French Institute, the same body that refused to recognize the later efforts of Cournot and Walras. Cournot (1877, p. i) reviled Canard's work as 'false', even as he admitted that it provided him an important starting point for his own researches. Other harsh critics were Francis Horner, J.B. Say, Joseph Bertrand, W.S. Jevons, and Léon Walras. Despite this rejection by French and English economists, Canard had considerable influence in Italy, where a group of writers, led most conspicuously by Francesco Fuoco, defended his method and adopted some of his ideas. In the present century, Seligman (1927, pp. 159–62) has credited Canard with the diffusion theory of taxation, Schumpeter (1954) has discounted his contribution completely, while Theocharis (1983) has defended him.

The *Principes* was influenced by Cantillon and to a lesser extent by the Physiocrats, whose doctrine Canard sought to refute. Cantillon's influence is obvious in two major areas. First, without using the terms, Canard advanced both an 'intrinsic' and a 'market' conception of price. He held that everything derives its value from the quantity of labour bestowed upon it. Different (unmeasurable) qualities of labour, however, render labour quantity an unsatisfactory measure. Therefore, one must look to the market to discover the determinants of price. Canard developed an equilibrium theory based on the relative bargaining power of buyer and seller, which he related to need and competition. (Clearly recognizing the forces of monopoly and monopsony, he nevertheless failed to develop a bilateral monopoly model.) Second, Canard revived Cantillon's 'three rents', and wove them into a general equilibrium conception of the economy, which he used to trace the effects of taxation (in the process, adumbrating the Ricardian theory of land rent).

Canard argued that the imposition of a new tax produces disequilibrium and sets in motion certain equilibrating adjustments which take time to work themselves through the economy. Each person who initially pays the new tax will attempt to pass it on to the purchaser of the good, but his success in doing so depends upon the 'forces' encountered; or as we would say today, the tax is shifted in proportion to the elasticities of demand and supply. Canard's maxim that 'every old tax is good, every new tax is bad', must be judged in this context.

R.F. HÉBERT

SELECTED WORKS

1801. *Principes d'économie politique*. Paris: F. Buisson.
1802. *Moyens de perfectionner le jury*. Moulins: P. Vidalin.
1808. *Traité élémentaire du calcul des inéquations*. Paris: Crapelet.
1824. *Eléments de météorologie*. Paris: P. Persan.
1826. *Mémoire sur les causes qui produisent la stagnation et le décroissement du commerce en France, et qui tendent à anéantir l'industrie commerciale*. Paris: Delaunay.

BIBLIOGRAPHY

Allix, E. 1920. Un précurseur de l'école mathématique: Nicholas-François Canard. *Revue d'histoire économique et sociale* 13, 38–67.
Baumol, W.J. and Goldfeld, S.M. 1968. *precursors in Mathematical Economics: An Anthology*. London: London School of Economics and Political Science.
Bousquet, G.H. 1957. N.F. Canard: Précurseur du marginalisme. *Revue d'économie politique* 50, 232–5.

Cournot, A.A. 1877. *Revue sommaire des doctrines économiques.* Paris: Hachette.

Seligman, E.R.A. 1927. *The Shifting and Incidence of Taxation.* 5th edn, New York: Columbia University Press.

Theocharis, R.D. 1983. *Early Developments in Mathematical Economics.* 2nd edn, London: Macmillan.

Cannan, Edwin (1861–1935). Cannan's name is linked inextricably with two great economic institutions: Adam Smith and the London School of Economics. His edition of the *Wealth of Nations* first appeared in 1904 and remains in print today (1986). Before the publication of the Glasgow edition of Smith's works in 1976, there was nothing that could even lay claim to being its rival. His association with the LSE began as a lecturer in 1895 (the year the School was founded), and continued (in the role of Professor from 1907) until his retirement in 1926.

Cannan was born on 2 February 1861 in Madeira, his mother having gone there on medical advice. Within three weeks of Edwin Cannan's birth his mother had died, and the family returned to Bournemouth where Cannan spent his boyhood. In 1880 he went to Balliol College, Oxford, and took his BA in 1884. He resided in Oxford for the remainder of his life although he was only once formally associated with that city's university when, in 1931, he held the Sidney Ball lectureship. Having a private income from a substantial family fortune, at no time in his life did Cannan have to rely upon securing paid employment for his living. Even after his appointment at the LSE, Cannan was in London on no more than two or three days a week. Cannan was twice President of Section F of the British Association (1902 and 1931), President of the Royal Economic Society (1932–4), and held honorary degrees from Glasgow (LL.D) and Manchester (Litt.D).

To Smith scholarship Cannan bequeathed not only his edition of the *Wealth of Nations* (1904) but also an edition of Smith's Glasgow lectures on jurisprudence (1896). Of the first of these, it is perhaps sufficient to note that subsequent scholarship has modified Cannan's editorial speculations as to its origins in only one major respect – concerning Smith's acquaintance with the work of Turgot – to demonstrate its value. The only other peculiarity of Cannan's commentary concerns his view of the theory of distribution, and it will be necessary to return to this point later. The publication of Smith's Glasgow lectures allowed scholars to observe for the first time just how many of Smith's subsequent views were to be found in his work on economics before his visits to France.

Cannan's original work in the history of economic thought is presented in a number of works, of which two call for separate attention: *A History of Theories of Production and Distribution in English Political Economy 1776–1848* (1893) and *A Review of Economic Theory* (1929). The former is the more carefully considered and better documented of the two, and although it would be difficult to agree with Hugh Dalton who in 1927 claimed that 'no one need ever do this particular piece of work again' (in Gregory and Dalton, 1927, p. 11), it is nevertheless the case that both books can be consulted with advantage even by modern students.

It seems that Cannan worked full-time on *Theories of Production and Distribution* from 1890 onwards. In the process of preparing the manuscript, he accumulated a personal library rich in materials form the 18th and 19th century (a library which was subsequently to contain, among other things, a collection of tracts by those Cannan called 'currency cranks' and all editions of Smith's *Wealth of Nations* down to 1900). Many of Cannan's original, if somewhat singular, views gain expression therein. There are two that warrant mention here: the claim that a theory of distribution properly understood requires an explanation of the *shares* of wages, profits and rent in total production (and not an explanation of their respective *rates*, which he calls pseudo-distribution), and the implied definition of 'classical economics' as the period between (and including) Smith's *Wealth of Nations* and the first edition of John Stuart Mill's *Principles* in 1848.

The former opinion is re-iterated in his introduction to the *Wealth of Nations* where it is argued that 'the theory of distribution ... is no essential part of the work and could easily be excised by deleting a few paragraphs in Book I, chapter vi, and a few lines elsewhere' (1904, p. xxxix). On Cannan's reading, Smith was sidetracked from what should have been his real target (a theory of distribution proper) into a discussion of distribution 'as a mere appendage or corollary of his doctrine of prices' (1893, p. 186), so that 'though Adam Smith had declared that the whole of annual produce is distributed into wages, profit, and rent, obviously meaning thereby total wages, profits, and rent, the last four chapters of Book I of the *Wealth of Nations* deal with wages per head, profits per cent, and rent per acre' (p. 231). Quite how Cannan felt that one might go about explaining his 'distribution properly understood' without a theory about the rates of wages, profits and rent, is impossible to determine from his extant writings. Indeed, his tenacious adherence to this peculiar conception introduces what is perhaps the only real blemish into his editorial introduction of the *Wealth of Nations*. As Higgs observed in his review of that edition in the *Economic Journal* for 1904, Cannan had not so ruthlessly abstained from introducing his own opinions about economic theory as might have been hoped.

Though Cannan does not use the epithet 'classical' to describe either the economics or the economists with which he deals in *Theories of Production and Distribution*, his implied definition of that school in terms of the work on economics in the years between 1776 and 1848 runs counter to the views of those historians of economic thought who prefer to construct a definition of classical economics in terms of some shared set of analytical precepts (a procedure which does not, of course, require that all classical economists reached the same conclusions). It should be noted, however, that Cannan did not subscribe to the view then beginning to emerge that there was a fundamental continuity in the history of economics from 1776 down to the present day. Indeed, like most historians of thought at the time, he was highly critical of Marshall's attempt to establish such continuity in Appendix I of his *Principles* which discusses Ricardo; such views were 'in defiance of all evidence' (1929, p. 177n) as far as Cannan was concerned. There will be cause to return to Cannan's reaction to Marshall later.

The *Review of Economic Theory* (1929) was based on Cannan's LSE lectures to second- and third-year undergraduates (see 1929, p. v). It is an interesting book perhaps more because of what is not said in it rather than what is. It contains no formal presentation of the formula for the elasticity of demand, the treatment of the theory of marginal utility is exceedingly brief, there is no discussion of equilibrium and no reference to the work of Cournot, Pareto, Edgeworth or Wicksell. These latter omissions are striking lacunae – the more so for a book written in the late 1920s. They take on even more significance when it is remembered that this book was an explicit attempt to supplement *Theories of Production and Distribution* with a consideration of work which followed it.

Indeed, it seems that Cannan was no great admirer of the mathematical school, and his opinion of Marshall was to say the least somewhat ambivalent (see, for example, Robbins, 1935, p. 396). On this latter point, one may take as an indication his article in *Economica* for 1924 which expresses no great admiration for the the quintessentially Marshallian concept of consumer's surplus: it is

a method which involves, not a single hypothesis, but an indefinite number of different hypotheses, each of which is inconsistent with all the others as well as with the actual facts ... inconsistent hypotheses which no one would ever have thought of it if it had not been suggested by the 'space' which happens to be included under the curve of a demand schedule (pp. 23–4).

Furthermore, in *An Economist's Protest* (1927) Cannan imagines Adam Smith to comment as follows on 'modern' economics:

The very ingenious speculations of Mr Jevons, Mr Marshall, Mr Edgeworth and others, ... have introduced a sort of algebra or geometry into the science ... . The followers of that system are very numerous; and as men are fond of appearing to understand what surpasses the comprehension of ordinary people, the cypher, as it may be called, in which they have concealed, rather than exposed, their doctrine, [they have] perhaps contributed not a little to increases the number of its admirers (p. 334).

It is doubtful whether the designers of the main doors of the new post-Cannan LSE building understood the irony of their decision to inscribe upon them the now familiar Marshallian demand-and-supply cross diagram.

No account of these two books should omit to mention the ample evidence they provide of Cannan's almost obsessive concern with the etymology of the terms used by economists. Sometimes this propensity led to interesting points, on other occasions it degenerated into farce.

Another of Cannan's contributions to the history of economic thought which may be singled out is his reprint of the Bullion Report (1810), which he published under the title *The Paper Pound* in 1919. The text of the Report runs to 72 pages, Cannan's introduction to it occupies 49 pages. It is of interest not only as an account of the debates which led up to the resumption of specie payments in England with the Act of the Elder Peel in 1819, but also as an indication of the position Cannan was to adopt in the monetary debates of the 1920s and 1930s. This position was to lead him into head-on collision with the views of Keynes on the question of the advisability of Britain's return to the gold standard after the First World War at the pre-war parity, and his adherence to it, in fact, helps to explain why *The Times* obituary for Cannan was headed 'An Orthodox Economist'. Moreover, the timing of its publication, as Cannan himself observes (1919b, p. xxxix), brings out very clearly the parallels between these two episodes in British monetary history.

Put bluntly, Cannan was probably one of the most strident advocates of the old-fashioned quantity theory around at the time, his solution to inflation being captured in his more than half-serious motto: 'Burn your paper money, and go on burning it till it will buy as much gold as it used to do' (1919b, p. xli). The experience of the policies adopted to deal with the inflation of the post-Napoleonic period were confirmation of the soundness of the return to gold after World War I. Cannan had no sympathy for the idea (still perfectly admissable under the quantity theory) of stabilizing the domestic price level through the management of the domestic supply of money, instead of fixing the exchange rate as the

return to gold required. Indeed, it is not always clear from his writings that he understood that the two possibilities were part and parcel of the theory he so vigorously defended.

Nor, it seems, was Cannan prepared to admit the seriousness of the short-run consequences of a policy of deflation on the domestic distribution of income, output and employment as a reason for being cautious about the return to gold – a factor which even someone like Pigou (the official adviser to the Cunliffe Committee and therefore no opponent of the return to gold) was more than prepared to take into account. According to Cannan the necessary adjustments 'must be regarded in the same light as those which a spendthrift or a drunkard is rightly exhorted by his friends to face like a man' (1919b, p. 105).

In addition to the works mentioned above (and those listed in the accompanying bibliography), Cannan contributed twenty-five entries to the original edition of this Dictionary, including those on 'capital' and 'profit'. The latter was cited by Friedman and Savage in their celebrated application of utility analysis to risk. Edwin Cannan was, it is said, a keen bicyclist; though in *Who's Who* he listed his recreation as work. He died on 8 April 1935.

MURRAY MILGATE

SELECTED WORKS
1888. *Elementary Political Economy*. London: Oxford University Press.
1893. *A History of Theories of Production and Distribution in English Classical Political Economy from 1776 to 1848*. London: P.S. King 2nd edn, 1903; 3rd edn, 1917.
1896a. *History of Local Rates in England*. London: Longmans, Green & Co. 2nd edn, London: P.S. King, 1912.
1896b. (ed.) A. Smith: *Lectures on Justice, Police, Revenue and Arms*. Oxford: Clarendon Press.
1904. (ed.) A. Smith: *An Inquiry into the Nature and Causes of the Wealth of Nations*. 2 vols, London: Methuen.
1912. *The Economic Outlook*. London: T. Fisher Unwin.
1914. *Wealth*. London: P.S. King & Son.
1918. *Money: its connexion with rising and falling prices*. London: P.S. King & Son, 7th edn, 1932.
1919a. *Coal Nationalisation*. London: P.S. King & Son.
1919b. *The Paper Pound: 1797–1821*. London: P.S. King; 2nd edn, 1925.
1924. 'Total utility' and 'consumer's surplus'. *Economica* 4, February, 21–6.
1927. *An Economist's Protest*. London: P.S. King & Son.
1929. *A Review of Economic Theory*. London: P.S. King & Son.
1931. *Modern Currency and the Regulation of Its Value*. London: P.S. King & Son.
1933. *Economic Scares*. London: P.S. King & Son.
BIBLIOGRAPHY
Bowley, A.L. 1935. Obituary: Edwin Cannan. *Economic Journal* 45, June, 385–92.
Robbins, L. 1935. A student's recollections of Edwin Cannan. *Economic Journal* 45, June, 393–8.
Gregory, T.E. and Dalton, H. (ed.) 1927. *London Essays in Economics*. London: George Routledge & Sons.

Cantillon, Philip (*fl.* 1725–1759). Author of '*The Analysis of Trade, Commerce, Coin, Bullion, Banks, and Foreign Exchanges*: ... Taken chiefly from a Manuscript of a very ingenious Gentleman deceas'd, and adapted to the present situation of our Trade and Commerce. By Philip Cantillon, late of the City of London, Merchant, London, 1759'. This Philip was the eldest son of James Cantillon of the city of Limerick, who was first cousin of Richard Cantillon, author of the *Essai sur la Nature du Commerce*. Philip carried on a banking business with David Cantillon at Warnford Court,

Throgmorton Street, London, at least as early as 1725. In 1738 he was a director of the Royal Exchange Assurance: in 1742 became bankrupt: in 1747 was trading alone as insurance agent and policy broker: in 1753 was partner with one Thomas Mannock in the same business: and in 1759 had retired. He married, 14 July 1733, Rebecca, daughter of William Newland of Gatton, Surrey, by whom he had two daughters. There is reason to think that he was engaged for a short time at Richard Cantillon's bank in Paris, but that his litigious character made him unamiable and brought about his speedy return. On the death of Richard, Philip intervened in the management of his estate, and thus obtained possession of several papers, including probably the English manuscript of the Essay, which professedly served as the groundwork of the Analysis of Trade. He must, however, have mutilated the manuscript almost beyond recognition. Much of the closely packed original is omitted, and much is replaced by vague and general summaries, most unskilfully made, with the result that little indeed of the Analysis fairly represents the views of Richard Cantillon. Philip added a preface on the history and importance of commerce, some strictures upon close corporations, new matter on inland and foreign trade, bankers and banks, and exchanges, interspersed with quotations from Hume's Essays, and from The Universal Merchant, etc., concluding with a criticism of the law relating to bills of exchange.

The book was reviewed in the Monthly Review or Literary Journal for April 1759, London, vol. xx. 309. Sir James Steuart (Works, 1805 edn, iii. 22) says, 'Mr. Cantillon, in his Analysis of Trade, which I suppose he understood by practice as well as by theory, has the following passage,' etc.

'A small treatise of Arithmetic,' explaining the foreign exchanges 'vulgarly and decimally' without 'unintelligible jargon,' was designed by the author of the Analysis (p. 85), but does not seem to have ever been published.

[HENRY HIGGS]
Reprinted from Palgrave's Dictionary of Political Economy.

SELECTED WORKS

1759. The Analysis of Trade, Commerce, Coin, Bullion, Banks, and Foreign Exchanges. London.

Cantillon, Richard (1697–1734). One Richard Cantillon, son of Philip Cantillon of Ballyheigue, County Kerry, was born in Ireland. Joseph Hone argued convincingly that this was the economist, on the ground that this Richard married Mary Ann Mahony, daughter of Lady Clare, and had with her a daughter Henrietta, who married Lord Farnham (after the death of her first husband, the Earl of Stafford). Earlier writers had estimated Cantillon's birth to have been as many as 17 years earlier, but subsequent scholars have tended to accept Hone's evidence; for example, Joseph J. Spengler (1954, p. 283) and Anita Page (1952, p. xxiv).

Richard Cantillon's close association with France has often been noted, but certain facts about his family go far to explaining this connection. An Anglo-Irish county family whose establishment in Ireland was Elizabethan or later would of course be Protestant, and the term 'Anglo-Irish Protestant ascendancy' would then apply strictly. But those families which came to Ireland in Norman times were Catholics, and some of these remained so for hundreds of years, in spite of dungeon, fire and sword (to use an old phrase). They often became Jacobites, and in that case Europe was for them a place of refuge and support. These were the 'Wild Geese', who joined foreign flags after one or other Irish rebellion failed.

Often educated in Europe, their ideas were cosmopolitan, their eyes on Paris and on Rome.

The Cantillons were established in Ireland in Norman times and remained Catholics, although not always very good ones. And in later centuries they became, and long remained, devoted to the Stuart cause. Roger Cantillon of Ballyheigue married Elizabeth Stuart in 1556, and his grandson Valentine fought for Charles I at Naseby, while his great-grandson Richard was wounded at the Boyne, went to France with James II and was made a chevalier for his pains. The chevalier, clearly more notable for gallantry than for worldliness, is said to have become banker to the Stuart Pretender in Paris (Spengler, 1954, p. 284) and died insolvent, a not unpredictable fate, in 1717. Our Richard appears to have come to the rescue of his uncle's honour, paying off most of the poor old Jacobite soldier's debts, many of which, indeed, were to him. This was not the end of the family's Stuart involvement; a James Cantillon, believed by Hone to be the young future economist's brother, followed King James to France and was decorated for valour, while a nephew, Thomas, mentioned in the economist's will, was with the Irish Brigade at Lauffelt. Migration to France and beyond was in the blood of these wild geese. It should cause no surprise that our Cantillon had houses in seven European cities, or that he lived much in Paris.

He was there, active in banking, between 1716 and 1720. Brilliantly anticipating the fate of John Law's scheme, he was also daring enough to profit immensely by it and, if the sources consulted by W. Stanley Jevons can be believed, 'made a fortune of several millions in a few days, but still, distrusting Law, prudently retired to Holland' (Jevons, 1881, p. 336) He appears again in Paris between 1729 and 1732, and seems to have had to engage in litigation with people who had lost through the collapse of Law's scheme, and blamed Cantillon for his part in this. Henry Higgs, after surveying the evidence, commented 'to have triumphed in the Courts over all his opponents' (Higgs, 1931, p. 373). One gets the feeling as one reads of rather ordinary people playing a game for stakes they could not afford with a master they could not match. Bankers fell like autumn leaves in Paris between 1717 and 1720, and as Higgs remarks, 'Their losses were probably very heavy in 1720 and much of them went into Cantillon's pocket' (ibid., p. 370).

Back in London in 1734, Cantillon's luck ran out. At the height of his success and his brilliance, he was robbed and murdered, left in the flames of his townhouse in Albermarle Street, Mayfair, during the early morning of 14 May. His precious manuscripts, the Marquis de Mirabeau tells us, perished with him (Higgs, 1931, p. 382). Lady Penelope Compton, who lived opposite, tells us that 'it burnt very feirce two houses intirely down before they could get any water' (ibid., p. 374). Given this furious blaze, the really remarkable thing to the modern reader is that even despite the primitive state of the forensic science of the day, evidence of foul play was nevertheless found. Higgs, who read the account of the subsequent trial at the Old Bailey, observes that

> it was soon evident that he had been murdered before the house was set on fire. His body was burned to ashes. The Journals for 6 June 1734 say 'Yesterday the refiners finished their search into the ashes of the late Mr Cantillon's house, when no plate, money, or jewels had been found; an undeniable circumstance of a robbery previous to the burning of the house' (ibid.).

Cantillon's servants were tried for murder, but quickly acquitted. Suspicion then fell on a Frenchman, Joseph Denier, alias Lebane, who, we are told by Higgs, had been Cantillon's cook for eleven years, but apparently had been dismissed a little more than a week before the murder. The French chef, whether in fact guilty or not, fled to Holland and thus evaded arrest.

So it came about that we possess only one work of Cantillon's, and that in what it has been claimed is a rough French translation. Even now its early publishing history is shrouded in mystery. The *Essay on the Nature of Trade in General* (1755) is thought to have been written between 1730 and Cantillon's death, but it was not published in a complete version until 1755, and then in the French translation, claiming on the title page to have been printed in London by Fletcher Gyles, a claim reasonably disputed by Jevons (1881, p. 341). The Marquis de Mirabeau, who revealed that the French translation was in his possession for 16 years, insisted that Cantillon 'never intended that the work should appear in French and only translated it for a friend' (Higgs, 1931, p. 383).

Yet, as we have seen, there would be nothing odd in someone of Cantillon's family background and personal habits *writing* a book in French and publishing it in Paris. It would appear, however, that an English original must have existed, and had been in the hands of Malachy Postlethwayt, since the latter incorporated large parts of Cantillon's *Essay* in publications beginning in 1749. The first complete English translation from the French text, which was printed alongside it, was that of Higgs in 1931. Higgs, incidentally, collated his English translation with parallel passages from Postlethwayt. In addition we now have the scholarly French edition, edited by Alfred Sauvy (1952) with a number of studies and commentaries.

Since the 'discovery' of Cantillon by the English-speaking world following Jevons's enthusiastic article (1881), no less than justice has been done to the merits of the *Essay* on those topics treated by Cantillon whose significance can be expressed satisfactorily in broadly neoclassical terms. Over these topics we may pass quickly. Jevons himself noted that Cantillon had presented a treatment of currency, foreign exchanges, banking and credit which, judged against the work of its period, he felt to be 'almost beyond praise' (Jevons, 1881, p. 342). This enthusiasm has proved infectious, and we find Joseph Spengler, 73 years later, writing that Hume, assuming he knew Cantillon's work, missed 'the import of Cantillon's brilliant analysis (which compares favourably with Keynes's) of the response of the price structure to changes in the quantity of money' (Spengler, 1954, p. 283). Spengler was not quite as impressed by Cantillon's treatment of the international specie flow mechanism, but Joseph A. Schumpeter found it a brilliant performance and insisted that 'the automatic mechanism that distributes the monetary metals internationally is ... almost faultlessly described' (1954, p. 223).

It was likewise recognized as early as Jevons that Cantillon had set out the leading ideas of Adam Smith's 'important doctrine concerning wages in different employments' (Jevons, 1881, p. 343), and that the *Essay* contained what Jevons (somewhat exaggeratedly) called 'an almost complete anticipation of the Malthusian theory of population' (p. 347). Jevons, with remarkable objectivity considering his own views on the formation of value, also singled out Cantillon's treatment of 'the whole doctrine of market value as contrasted to cost value' (ibid., p. 345). It was also customarily recognized by neoclassical scholars later than Jevons that Cantillon made important contributions to the founding of allocation theory.

To intellectual historians approaching the *Essay* in terms of the neo-Walrasian class of models for general equilibrium theory, it became natural to construe Cantillon's land and labour as given resources. In the *Essay*, however, while land is a given non-produced input, labour is a *produced commodity* available in return for subsistence. A reproduction structure thus exists, and surplus may be defined. Cantillon is largely concerned with the allocation of surplus output. This was understood by the first classical theorist to read Cantillon, Francois Quesnay. For all his one-sided preoccupation with *agricultural* surplus, Cantillon's French successor picked up the importance of the role of surplus, embodied it in a formal model and passed it on to later classical economists.

From a *modern* classical point of view Cantillon made several important contributions, which are not always stressed by traditional scholars. For one thing, he offered an early analysis of the respective roles of produced and nonproduced inputs in a more than minimally viable commodity reproduction structure. Developing Sir William Petty's concept of a 'par' between land and labour, Cantillon investigated the assumptions upon which a reduction of labour to land is legitimate. But, of course, Cantillon was reducing labour to the *produce* of land; that is, to corn. He noted that 'as those who labour must subsist on the produce of the Land it seems that some relation might be found between the value of labour and that *of the produce* of the Land' (Cantillon 1755b, p. 31; emphasis added). Cantillon had entered an area which even today bristles with problems, which would nowadays be described as concerning the aggregation of heterogeneous objects. Cantillon was well aware of some of them. He used a concept of subsistence, that of the 'meanest Peasant' (p. 39), as his unit of labour, but he was well aware that this differed all over Europe, and had apparently offered statistical material on this in the lost supplement. It is then necessary to be able to express units of more skilled labour in terms of common labour. He argues that 'it is easily seen that the difference of price paid for daily work is based upon natural and obvious reasons' (p. 23). Even today not much progress has been made on this problem, and highly sophisticated models blithely assume it out of existence by using a single homogeneous labour input. Land is also heterogeneous, as Cantillon was well aware; furthermore, any given kind of land can be used to grow different crops. But the analysis of heterogeneous land in the case of a single crop was not developed until Ricardo's period, and the formal analysis of the case where *different crops* are grown had to wait for Piero Sraffa (1960, pp. 74–8), and more recent work on the relations between produced and non-produced means of production, such as that of Alberto Quadrio Curzio (1980, pp. 218–40).

Leaving aside the difficulties of heterogeneous labour and heterogeneous land with multiple uses, the par is the quantity of corn needed for the subsistence of a labourer and his family during a given period. To get a consistent model, corn must be treated as the only commodity strictly necessary to the reproduction system (the only 'basic' in the Sraffian sense). Other outputs have to be treated as luxury goods (non-basics), so that one can accommodate the changing modes and fashions of Cantillon's prince and landowners. Cantillon in fact allowed even his meanest peasant a number of commodities: 'the married Labourer will content himself with Bread, Cheese, Vegetables, etc., will rarely eat meat, will drink little wine or beer' (Cantillon, 1755b, p. 37).

To accept this and retain the par, only two options seem open. The poor peasant's commodities other than bread (or other things made in the household from corn, labour, and any free ingredients) could be regarded as non-basic. Or one could construct a composite commodity, containing bread, cheese, vegetables, and so on, in fixed proportions, and use this as the unit of measurement for the par. Then, if one is to avoid the problems of different crops, one must assume that any parcel of the uniform land can produce these commodities in the standard proportions. Cantillon stressed how much even peasant consumption varied from country to country in Europe in his day. But it was not absurd to suppose, as he did, that consumption habits were fixed and traditional among the peasants of a *particular* area. None of this is meant to deny the justice of Marian Bowley's claim that 'the "par" between land and labour could only be found under special and unrealistic assumptions' (1973, p. 105).

In a model where corn is the only basic, or where a unit of composite commodity is always consumed in fixed proportions, one can express the surplus as corn output minus necessary corn input (seed, subsistence, feed for animals), or alternatively one can express surplus as net output of the composite commodity. Passages such as the following are then consistent with the measurement of the surplus in terms of corn (or units of the composite commodity) as required for the par:

> The Farmers have generally two thirds of the Produce of the Land, one for their costs and the support of their Assistants the other for the Profit of their Undertaking...The Proprietor has usually one third of the produce of his Land and on this third he maintains all the Mechanicks and others whom he employs in the City as well, frequently, as the Carriers who bring the Produce of the Country to the City (Cantillon, 1755b, pp. 43–45).

Cantillon's treatment of surplus strongly implies that it arises only in agriculture. All those in a state, we are told more than once, subsist at the expense of the proprietors of land. There are isolated passages where he seems to be recognizing that profits (in the sense in which these reflect the existence of surplus) can arise in manufacturing. Perhaps the classic case is the description of the master hatter, who, we are told, besides his upkeep, ought also to find 'a profit like that of the Farmer who has his third part for himself' (1755b, p. 203). Certainly Cantillon believed (unlike the physiocrats) that farmers kept two-thirds of the total produce, one-third representing their *profit*. But Cantillon used his term 'undertaker' (entrepreneur) to cover chimneysweeps and water-carriers, and Samuel Hollander is probably correct in saying that, in Cantillon, 'profits and wages were said to have a common source in, or to be dependent upon, the property of landowners' (1973, p. 40, n. 48). The concept of surplus throughout *industry*, and the dual concept of a rate of profit tending to equality across all sectors, including industrial sectors, would not be clearly and systematically expressed until the mature work of Adam Smith (see Walsh and Gram, 1980, pp. 40–77).

Cantillon, however, did pioneering work in developing the theory of the allocation of surplus. His model is remarkably sophisticated. It is an isolated economy – one might think of it as an island – ruled by a prince or landowner. Cantillon is perfectly clear that the prince's significant freedom of choice concerns only that part of output which constitutes the surplus he receives after providing for necessary inputs. He remarks that the prince, deciding on the use of the estate, 'will necessarily use part of it for corn to feed the Labourers, Mechanicks, and Overseers who work for him, another part to feed the Cattle, Sheep and other Animals' (Cantillon, 1755b, p. 59). The consumption pattern of workers is fixed, just like fodder for the animals: 'Labourers and Mechanicks who live from day to day change their mode of living only from necessity' (p. 63).

Cantillon is far from assuming, however, that the composition of *surplus* output is unchanging. Indeed, changes in the allocation of surplus, dictated by changes in the demands of the prince and any other landowners, are his explanation of deviations of current market prices from natural prices, or intrinsic values. In the original classics, and indeed as late as Alfred Marshall (as Pierangelo Garegnani has noted), natural prices are centres of gravitation to which market prices *tend* (Garegnani, 1976). This idea is clearly present in Cantillon. The prince or landlord, who is assumed to have a third of the produce of each of the farms he owns, and is mainly responsible for luxury consumption, is 'the principal Agent in the changes which may occur in demand' (Cantillon, 1755b, p. 63). If a few prosperous farmers engage in some luxury consumption, they will imitate the tastes of the prince. Thus changes in fashion were the leading cause of 'the variations of demand which cause the variations of Market prices' (p. 65). Cantillon is well aware that good or bad harvests, extraordinary consumption resulting from foreign troops, and so on, can disturb the gravitation of market prices towards natural prices, but he eliminates such accidents 'so as not to complicate my subject, considering only a State in its natural and uniform condition' (ibid.). This is precisely the concept of a long-period position common to all the great classical economists.

Even more surprisingly, Cantillon shows that he is quite aware that a planned economy directed by the prince, and a system of prices, can each achieve the identical allocation of surplus output – a result whose formal proof had to wait until the 20th century, and which lay fallow after Cantillon as classical political economy developed in other respects.

Cantillon, of course, was by no means the first to make *some* kind of distinction between market and natural prices. The Schoolmen had distinguished between the price ruling at a given moment on a market and the just price, sometimes relating the latter to costs. But in Cantillon the distinction between market and natural price is an integral part of a whole economic model. The natural price, or intrinsic value of a commodity 'is the measure of the quantity of Land and of Labour entering into its production' (ibid., p. 29). Labour is then reduced, through the par, to subsistence units, which, as we have seen, can either be measured in corn or in quantities of a composite commodity. These intrinsic values are assumed to be invariant (ibid., p. 31). Market prices may deviate from intrinsic values following a change in demand, as we have seen, but the actions of profit-maximizing capitalist farmers will then lead to supply changes, initiating the gravitation process. If the farmers 'have too much Wool and too little Corn for the demand, they will not fail to change from year to year the use of the land till they arrive at proportioning their production pretty well to the consumption of Inhabitants' (ibid., pp. 61–3).

Notice that since we are considering a change in *demand* for corn and wool, these goods are here being used for *luxury* consumption. Corn can be fed to servants and musicians, and wool makes fine garments. What is more, Cantillon can allow for the existence of a number of agricultural sectors producing *only* luxuries: fine wines, silks, blood horses, and so on. His model clearly implies that there is a tendency towards a long-period position in which capitalist farmers in each of these sectors would receive profits at the uniform rate of one-third of the intrinsic value of their total output. Thus the extraction of surplus, and its reflection in a uniform intersectoral rate of profit, is certainly understood by Cantillon for those sectors where capitalist production relations were firmly established in his period. It remained for Adam Smith to extend this analysis to the newly widespread phenomenon of his time, capitalist production throughout industry.

VIVIAN WALSH

SELECTED WORKS
1755a. *Essai sur la nature du commerce en général.* Traduit de l'Anglois, à Londres, chez Fletcher Gyles, dans Holborn.
1755b. *Essai sur la nature du commerce en général.* Ed. with English trans. and other material by Henry Higgs, London: Macmillan (for the Royal Economic Society), 1931.
1952. *Essai sur la nature du commerce en général.* Ed. Alfred Sauvy, Paris: Institut National d'Etudes Demographiques.

BIBLIOGRAPHY
Bowley, M. 1973. *Studies in the History of Economic Theory before 1870.* London: Macmillan.
Garegnani, P. 1976. On a change in the notion of equilibrium in recent work on value and distribution. In *Essays in Modern Capital Theory,* ed. M. Brown, K. Sato and P. Zarembka, Amsterdam: North-Holland.
Higgs, H. 1931. Life and work of Richard Cantillon. In *Essai,* ed. Henry Higgs (see Selected Works, 1755b).
Hollander, S. 1973. *The Economics of Adam Smith.* Toronto: University of Toronto Press.
Hone, J. 1944, Richard Cantillon, economist: biographical note. *Economic Journal* 54, April, 96–100.
Jevons, W.S. 1881. Richard Cantillon and the nationality of political economy. *Contemporary Review,* January. All citations from Higgs (1931).
Page, A. 1952. La vie et l'oeuvre de Richard Cantillon (1697–1734). In *Essai,* ed. Alfred Sauvy (see selected works, 1952).
Quadrio Curzio, A. 1980. Rent, income distribution, and orders of efficiency and rentability. In *Essays on the Theory of Joint Production,* ed. Luigi L. Pasinetti, New York: Columbia University Press.
Schumpeter, J.A. 1954. *History of Economic Analysis.* New York: Oxford University Press.
Spengler, J.J. 1954. Richard Cantillon: first of the moderns. *Journal of Political Economy* 62, Pt I, August, 281–95; Pt II, October, 406–24.
Sraffa, P. 1960. *Production of Commodities by Means of Commodities, Prelude to a Critique of Economic Theory.* Cambridge: Cambridge University Press.
Walsh, V. and Gram, H. 1980. *Classical and Neoclassical Theories of General Equilibrium, Historical Origins and Mathematical Structure.* New York: Oxford University Press.

capital, circulating. *See* CIRCULATING CAPITAL.

capital, constant. *See* CONSTANT AND VARIABLE CAPITAL.

capital, credit and money markets.   The markets for money, credit and capital represent a fundamental dimension of economic activity, in that the many and varied functions of the modern economy's financial markets both reflect and help shape the course of the economic system at large. Financial markets facilitate such central economic actions as producing and trading, earning and spending, saving and investing, accumulating and retiring, transferring and bequeathing. Development of the financial system is a recognized hallmark of economic development in the broadest sense.

Neither the important role played by the financial side of economic activity nor economists' awareness of it is a recent phenomenon. Economic analysis of the roles of money, credit and capital constitutes a tradition as old as the discipline itself. Nevertheless, in comparison with other equally central objects of economic analysis this tradition is as remarkable for its continuing diversity as for the richness of the insights it has generated. A century after Marshall and Wicksell and Bagehot, a half-century after Keynes and Robertson and Hicks, and a quarter-century after the initial path-breaking work of Tobin and Modigliani and Milton Friedman, there is still no firm consensus on many of the more compelling questions in the field: What are the most important determinants of an economy's overall level of capital intensity? How does risk affect the allocation of that capital? Do leverage and intermediation of debt matter for aggregate economic outcomes? Does money matter – and, if so, what is it?

The absence of universally accepted answers to these and other fundamental questions does not signify a failure to develop conceptual understanding of how the markets for money, credit and capital function, or of the basic elements of these markets' interactions with non-financial economic activity. The persistent diversity of thought on these unresolved questions has instead reflected the inability of empirical analysis, hindered by the continual and at times rapid evolution of actual financial systems, to provide persuasive evidence on issues characterized both by a multiplicity of plausibly relevant determining factors and by the inherent unobservability of some of the most important among them – for example, ex ante perceptions of risks as well as rewards.

THE MARKET FOR CAPITAL.   The essential reason for having a capital market in any economy stems from the nature of the productive process. In all economies anyone has ever observed, and the more so in the more developed among them, production of goods and services to satisfy human wants relies on capital as well as labour. If capital is to exist to use in production, someone must own it; and in economies in which this ownership function lies with individuals or other private entities, the primary initial role of the capital market is to establish the terms on which capital is held. In market-oriented economies the terms on which capital is (or may be) held provide incentives affecting the further accumulation of new capital, so that over time the capital market plays an additional, logically consequent role in determining the economy's existing amount of capital and hence its potential ability to produce goods and services.

In conceptualizing how the market mechanism sets the terms on which an economy's capital is held, economists have traditionally paired the role of capital as an input to the production process with the role of capital as a vehicle for conveying wealth – that is, ultimate command over goods and services – forward in time. The capital market is therefore the economic meeting place between the theory of production, often in the derivative form of the theory of investment, and the theory of consumption and saving. Different assumptions forming the underlying theory on either side in general lead to differing characterizations of how the capital market establishes the terms on which capital is held, and consequently differing characterizations of how the market affects the economy's accumulation of capital over time and hence its capital intensity at any point in time. Among the critical features of production theory and consumption-saving theory that have featured prominently in this analysis of their intersection are the substitutability of capital for other production inputs, the source and nature of technological progress, and the interest elasticity of saving. In most modern treatments, these specifics in turn depend on more basic assumptions like the respective specifications of the production function constraining producers and the intertemporal utility function maximized by wealth-holders.

Notwithstanding the central importance of this basic economic role of the capital market, as well as the insight and ingenuity with which economists over many years have elaborated their understanding of it, what gives the modern study of capital markets much of its particular richness is the focus on one particular factor that could, in principle, be entirely absent from this economic setting, but that is ever present in reality: uncertainty.

The essential feature of capital from this perspective is its durability. Because capital is durable – that is, its use in production does not instantly consume or destroy it – it provides those who hold it with not just the ability but the necessity to convey purchasing power forward in time in a specific form. Precisely because of this durability, capital necessarily exposes those who hold it to whatever uncertainties characterize both the production process and the demand for wealth-holding in the future.

Not just reward but risk too, therefore, are inherent features of capital that must accrue to some holders, somewhere in the economy, if the economy is to enjoy the advantages of production based in part on durable capital inputs. The introduction of risk has profound implications for consumption-saving behaviour. In addition, when the absence of perfect rental markets leads producers who use capital to be also among the holders of capital, the introduction of risk in this way affects production–investment behaviour too. Hence via at least one side of the capital market nexus, and via both sides under plausibly realistic assumptions, the risk consequent upon the durability of capital alters the determination of the terms on which capital is held, and thereby alters the determination of the economy's capital accumulation. Increasingly in recent years, the study of capital markets by economists has focused on the market pricing of this risk. The context in which this risk pricing of function matters, however, remains the consequences, for wealth-holding and for investment and production, of the terms on which capital is held.

The implications of the risk inherent in durable capital depend, of course, on many aspects of the capital market environment. Two prominent features of existing capital markets in particular have importantly shaped the explosive development of the capital markets risk-pricing literature during the past quarter-century. First, durable capital is not the only available form of wealth holding. Other assets may be risky too, but at least some assets exist which do not expose holders to the risks, involving unknown outcomes far in the future, that are consequent on the durability of typical capital assets. Second, even capital assets are not all identical. Heterogenous capital assets expose their holders to risks that not only are not identical but also, in general, are not independent.

Following Markowitz (1952) and Tobin (1958), the investigation of the allocation of wealth-holding between a single risk-free asset and a single risky asset readily establishes the terms on which (risky) capital is held, in the form of the excess of its expected return over the known return on the alternative (presumed risk-free) asset. In the simplest case of a single-period-at-a-time decision horizon, for example, the maximization of utility exhibiting constant relative risk aversion in the sense of Pratt (1964) and Arrow (1965), subject to the assumption that the uncertain return to capital is normally distributed, leads to the result that an investor's demand for capital, expressed in proportion to the inventor's total wealth, depends linearly on the expected excess return:

$$\frac{1}{W} \cdot A_K^D = \frac{1}{\rho \cdot \sigma_K^2} \cdot [E(r_K) - \bar{r}] \qquad (1)$$

where W is the investor's total wealth, A_K^D is the quantity demanded of the risky asset, ρ is the coefficient of relative risk aversion, $E(r_K)$ and σ_K^2 are respectively the mean and variance of the ex ante distribution describing assessments of the uncertain asset return, and $\bar{r}$ is the known return on the alternative asset. (This simple result is both convenient and standard, but it can be only an approximation because normally distributed asset returns are strictly incompatible with utility functions exhibiting constant relative risk aversion.) If it is possible to represent the economy's aggregate asset demands in a form corresponding to (1) for individual investors, then the requirement that the existing amount of each asset must equal to the amount demanded leads to the result that the expected excess return on capital depends linearly on the composition of the existing wealth:

$$E(r_K) = \bar{r} + \rho \sigma_K^2 \cdot \frac{A_K}{W} \qquad (2)$$

where A_K is the actual existing quantity of the risky asset. If the market equilibration process works via changes in the price of the risky asset, rather than its stated per-unit return, then both A_K and W are jointly determined with $E(r_K)$ and the resulting relationship is analogous though no longer linear:

$$E(r_K) = \bar{r} + \rho \sigma_K^2 \cdot \frac{P[E(r_K)] \cdot \bar{A}_K}{A_F + P[E(r_K)] \cdot \bar{A}_K} \qquad (3)$$

where A_F is the existing quantity of the risk-free asset (taken to have unit price), $\bar{A}_K$ is the quantity of the risky asset in physical units, and P is the price of the risky asset with $[dP/dE(r_K)] < 0$. (If capital is infinitely lived, $P = 1/E(r_K)$.) The addition of this element of the theory of risk pricing thus allows the capital market, in the context of a general economic equilibrium, to establish the terms on which durable capital is held – and hence the incentive to capital accumulation – when other, non-durable assets are also present.

The second major aspect of actual capital assets motivating the development of the economic analysis of capital markets is heterogeneity. Capital assets differ from one another not only because of actual physical differences but also because, with imperfect rental markets, the application of identical capital items to different uses in production has some permanence, so that ownership of a particular capital asset typically implies ongoing participation in a specific production activity. In general, each kind of capital asset, categorized not only by physical characteristics but also by production application, exposes those who hold it to a unique set of uncertainties. Moreover, in general the different risks associated in this way with different capital assets are not independent.

The elaboration of the single-risky-asset model in (1)–(3) due to Sharpe (1964) and Lintner (1965) readily represents the determination of relative returns in the capital market, in this context of heterogeneous capital assets with interdependent risks, and hence enables the outcomes determined in the capital market to affect not just the aggregate quantity but also the allocation of the company's capital accumulation. The multivariate analogues of (1) and (2) are simply

$$\frac{1}{W} \cdot \mathbf{A}_K^D = \frac{1}{\rho} \, \Omega^{-1}[E(\mathbf{r}_K) - \bar{r} \cdot \mathbf{l}] \qquad (4)$$

$$E(\mathbf{r}_K) = \bar{r} \cdot \mathbf{l} + \rho \Omega \cdot \frac{1}{W} \cdot \mathbf{A}_K \qquad (5)$$

where $\mathbf{A}_K^D$, $\mathbf{A}_K$ and $\mathbf{r}_K$ are vectors with individual elements respectively corresponding to A_K^D, A_K and r_K, Ω is the variance–covariance structure associated with expectations $E(\mathbf{r}_K)$, and $\mathbf{l}$ is a vector of units. In (4) the demand for each specific capital asset depends linearly on the expected excess return over the risk-free rate not only of that asset but of all other capital assets as well, with the substitutability between any two assets – that is, the response of the demand for one asset to the expected return on another – determined by the investor's risk aversion as well as by the interdependence among the respective returns on all of the risky assets. In (5) the equilibrium expected excess return on each capital asset at any time therefore depends (linearly) on the existing quantities of all assets expressed as shares of the economy's total wealth. Under conventional models of investment behaviour, the accumulation of each specific kind of capital over time depends in turn on the entire set of equilibrium returns determined in this way.

Moreover, this role of the capital market in guiding the allocation of capital does not depend in any fundamental way on the presence of an alternative asset with risk-free return. If all assets bear uncertain returns, either because capital assets are the only existing assets, or because even the returns on other assets are uncertain (because of uncertain price inflation, for example), the analogue of (4) is

$$\frac{1}{W} \cdot \mathbf{A}_K^D = \frac{1}{\rho} \, [\Omega^{-1} - (\mathbf{l}'\Omega^{-1}\mathbf{l})^{-1}\Omega^{-1} \, \mathbf{l}\mathbf{l}'\Omega^{-1}] \cdot E(\mathbf{r}_K)$$
$$+ (\mathbf{l}'\Omega^{-1}\mathbf{l})^{-1}\Omega^{-1}\mathbf{l}. \quad (6)$$

The second term in (6) represents the composition of the minimum-variance portfolio, which in the absence of a risk-free asset is a unique combination of risky assets, expressed as a vector of asset shares adding to unity. The first term in (6) expresses the investor's willingness to hold a portfolio different from this minimum-variance combination. The transformation of Ω contained in the first term maps what is in general a variance–covariance matrix of full rank into a matrix of rank reduced by one, as is implied by the balance sheet constraint emphasized by Brainard and Tobin (1968). Because the resulting matrix is of less than full rank, however, no exact analog of (5) then exists.

Combining the description of asset demands in (6) with the requirement of market clearing therefore determines the relative expected returns among all assets – in other words, determines the absolute expected returns on all assets but one, given the expected return on that one – but cannot determine absolute expected returns without at least some reference point fixed outside the risk pricing mechanism. This result is in fact analogous to the implication of (5) (or (3)), in that (5) determines the the expected return on each risky asset only in relation to the fixed benchmark of the known return on the alternative risk-free asset. In either case the analysis of risk pricing alone is insufficient to determine absolute returns without something else, presumably grounded in the fundamental interrelation between the respective roles of capital in production and in wealth-holding, to anchor the overall return structure.

Actual capital markets perform these functions of pricing risk and thereby guiding the accumulation and allocation of new capital, in essentially all advanced economies with well developed financial systems. In most such economies, the most immediately visible focus of the risk pricing mechanism is the trading on stock exchanges of existing claims to capital in the form of equity ownership shares in ongoing business enterprises. Equity shares are composite capital assets not only in the sense that each business firm typically owns a variety of different kinds of physical capital but also because the value of most firms consists in part of intangible capital in the form of existing knowledge, organization and reputation. In the context of what are often very large costs of establishing new enterprises, together with highly imperfect secondary markets for physical capital assets, even in principle the prices of equity securities need not correspond in any direct way to the liquidation value of a firm's separate items of plant and equipment. Given transactions costs and imperfect secondary markets, the existing enterprise itself is just as much an aspect of an advanced economy's long-lived production technology as is the sheer physical durability of capital.

Markets in which existing equity shares are traded also present the opportunity for the initial sale to investors of new equity shares issued by business enterprises in order to augment their available financial resources. In addition to guiding capital accumulation and allocation by establishing the relevant risk pricing, therefore, capital markets also play a direct role in facilitating capital accumulation by offering firms the opportunity to raise new equity funds directly. Even so, given firms' ability to increase their equity base by retaining their earnings rather than distributing them fully to shareholders – and also given the availability of debt financing (see the discussion of credit markets immediately below) – the extent to which firms actually rely on new issues of equity varies widely from one economy to another. In the United States, for example, well established firms typically do not issue new equity shares in significant volume, and the market for new issues is primarily a resource for new enterprises of a more speculative character. (The aggregate net addition to equity in the US market each year is typically negative, in that equity retirements and repurchases exceed gross new issues.) In most other economies, too, new issues of equity shares provide only small amounts of net funds for business.

Even when new equity additions via new shares issues are small, however, the risk pricing function of the capital market still guides an economy's capital accumulation and allocation process. Internal additions to equity from retained earnings are by far the major source of equity funds for the typical business in most economies, and – at least in theory – the retention or distribution of earnings by firms reflects in part considerations of expected return and associated risk as priced in the capital markets. Firms in lines of business in which new investment is less profitable (after allowance for risk) than the economy's norm not only cannot issue new equity shares on attractive terms but also must either distribute their earnings or face undervaluation of their outstanding shares by market investors. Conversely, firms with unusually profitable prospects at the margin of new investment can favourably issue new shares or can retain their earnings to fund their expansion.

Finally, two further features of actual modern capital markets bear explicit notice. Each, appropriately considered, is consistent with the notion of capital markets serving the basic function of pricing risk, and thereby guiding an economy's capital accumulation and allocation.

First, highly developed capital markets are characterized by enormous volumes of trading. In principle, the risk-pricing mechanism could function with little trading of existing securities, and under the right conditions it could function with none at all. If investors all agreed on the appropriate set of price relationships, there would be neither the incentive nor the need to effect actual transactions. The agreed-upon set of prices might fluctuate widely or narrowly, depending upon changes in assessments of risk and return, but as long as the assessments were universally shared there would be little if any trading.

The huge trading volumes typical of actual modern capital markets therefore suggest that, in fact, investors do not share identical risk and return assessments. Annual trading volume on the New York Stock Exchange, for example, is normally near one-half the total value of listed existing shares. Although the continually changing circumstances of both individual and institutional investors no doubt play some role, it is difficult to explain this phenomenon except in the context of substantial heterogeneity in the response of investors' risk and return assessments to the flow of new information.

The possibility that investors' opinions differ is only a minor complication for the theory of risk pricing as sketched above. Lintner (1969) showed that competitive capital markets with heterogeneous investors determine outcomes for the pricing of risky assets that just reflect an appropriately constructed aggregation over all individual investors' differing assessments (as well as their differing preferences), weighted by their respective wealth positions. The question remains, however, why investors' assessments differ. One line of analysis, initiated by Grossman (1976), has emphasized systematic differences in assessments due to underlying differences in information available to different investors. By contrast, Shiller (1984) suggested the importance of unsystematic differences not readily explainable within the conventional analytic framework based on rational maximization. The question remains unsettled but important nonetheless.

The second additional feature of actual modern capital markets that bears explicit attention is the proliferation of increasingly complex securities, including options, warrants, futures, and so forth. Given heterogeneity among investors, this development fits naturally in the context of the capital markets' basic economic role of establishing the terms on which the risks inherent in a capital-intensive production technology are to be borne. When investors differ among themselves in age, or wealth, or preferences, or risk and return assessments, in general the most efficient allocation of those risks does not consist of all investors' holding portfolios embodying identical risks and prospective returns. Instead, different investors will hold differing portfolios, and a further role of an economy's capital markets is to allocate the bearing of specific risks across different investors.

Heterogeneity among different kinds of physical assets would itself facilitate such specialization, and heterogeneity among the business enterprises whose equity shares constitute the asset units in actual capital markets typically does so to an even greater extent. Still, even this resulting degree of feasible specialization in risk bearing apparently falls well short of what would be fully consistent with the existing extent of investor heterogeneity.

Complex securities enable the capital markets to achieve a more efficient allocation of risk across heterogeneous investors by more finely dividing the risk inherent in an economy's production technology. Options, for example, permit an investor not merely to hold a (positive or negative) position in the equity of a specific firm but to hold positions corresponding only to designated parts of the distribution describing the possible outcomes for that firm's performance as reflected in the price of its equity shares. While the existing array of complex securities presumably does not approach the set of contingent claims necessary to span the space of possible outcomes in the sense of Arrow (1964) and Debreu (1959), developments along these lines in recent years have presumably rendered risk bearing more efficient. Moreover, following Merton (1973a) and Black and Scholes (1973), the analysis of the market pricing of risk has extended to explicitly contingent claims the central features of market equilibrium. The analysis is richer, therefore, and the outcome more efficient, but the end result of the economic process remains the pricing of the risk associated at any time with the existing stock of capital, with consequent effects on the total accumulation and allocation of capital over time.

THE MARKET FOR CREDIT. The presence of heterogeneity among different participants in a market economy also provides an economic rationale for credit markets. The primary initial role of the credit market is to facilitate borrowing and lending – that is, the transfer of purchasing power by the issuing and acquiring (and trading) of money-denominated debts. In establishing the terms on which such transfers take place, the credit market plays a role in guiding the allocation of the economy's resources that is parallel to that played by the capital market.

If all market participants were identical, such a market could establish terms on which the representative agents would be willing to borrow or lend, but no actual borrowing or lending would take place. Under those circumstances the credit market would be of little economic importance. By contrast, actual economies consist of an almost infinite variety of differently positioned participants. Individuals differ from business enterprises, and private-sector entities differ from governments. Even just among individuals, there are old and young, rich and poor, highly and weakly risk-averse, favourably and unfavourably taxed, home-owners and renters, and so on in ever more dimensions and ever greater detail. As a result, the credit market does not just establish a putative price for strictly hypothetical trades. It facilitates transfers that in turn make possible resource allocations which could not otherwise come about.

At the most basic level, economists since Fisher (1930) have emphasized the role of borrowing and lending in achieving a separation between production and consumption decisions. Here the function of the credit market is to enable individuals to shift purchasing power forward or backward in time, so as to free the timing pattern of consumption streams from the corresponding timing pattern of earnings from production (while still preserving, of course, the relevant constraint connecting the appropriately discounted totals). The overall result of this intertemporal separation is, in general, to achieve more efficient resource allocations in the sense both of greater production from given available inputs as well as higher utility from given available consumption. Without such a separation it would be impossible to construe the intertemporal theory of consumption and saving as in any way distinct from the theory of production and investment. Even the limited heterogeneity between firms and households is sufficient to give rise to borrowing and lending along these lines.

Nevertheless, the question of why money-dominated debts should serve this intertemporal transfer function – rather than having all obligations take the form of direct ownership claims to capital, for example – opens up a whole series of further important issues. Following the analysis of capital markets immediately above, the most readily apparent answer is that debt obligations isolate the specific risks associated with the purchasing power of the unit of denomination (in other words, inflation risk) and risks associated with the borrower's ability to meet the stated obligation (default risk), and that this conventional compartmentalization is evidently convenient for a variety of reasons. Inflation risk and default risk are in general not independent, however. In addition, it is just as easy to imagine alternative conventions that might be just as convenient, like the predominant use of debts denominated in purchasing-power units.

Given the conventional monetary denomination of debt obligations, the function of the credit market in most modern economies is to redistribute immediate claims to purchasing power, in exchange for future claims, along three major dimensions of heterogeneity: between individuals and firms, between the private sector and the government, and between domestic and foreign entities. In addition, redistributions among individuals (and, to a lesser extent, among firms) are often a further important credit market function.

Business firms typically apply to investment not only their equity additions from retained earnings and any new share issues but also funds raised by borrowing. Modigliani and Miller (1958) set forth conditions under which the firm's reliance on debt versus equity financing would be a matter of indifference, in that it would not affect the firm's total value, but conditions prevailing in actual economies and their capital and credit markets do not meet these conditions closely. Business reliance on debt financing is typically large, and it varies systematically across countries and across industries within a given country. Prominent aspects of the divergence of actual economies from the Modigliani–Miller irrelevance conditions which the ensuing voluminous literature has emphasized, include tax structures, risks and costs of bankruptcy by the firm, differential borrowing rates for firms and individuals (due to, for example, risks and costs of bankruptcy by individuals), monitoring costs required to minimize risks, and restrictive features of debt contracts intended to reduce risks due to moral-hazard effects of imperfectly compatible incentive structures.

The resulting substantial reliance on debt financing by business means that credit markets, like capital markets, play a major economic role in guiding an economy's accumulation and allocation of capital over time. When any or all of the factors cited above lead business enterprises to finance a new investment with some combination of additional equity (from retained earnings or new share issues) and additional debt, the appropriate calculation of investment incentives involves the cost to the firm in both the capital market and the credit market. In circumstances in which the financing margin corresponding to marginal new investment is a debt margin – as is often the case in the United States, for example, where firms' reliance on external funds is typically synonymous with issuance of debt – the relevant cost at the margin is the cost in the credit market.

Use of the credit market to finance government spending is among the oldest and most prevalent forms of financial transactions, and it has, understandably, generated an entire literature unto itself. In practical terms, government reliance on the credit markets in most modern economies is important not only in that governments often issue debt to finance large portions of their total spending but also because government borrowing often absorbs a large mount of the total funds advanced in the market by lenders. As is the case for private borrowers, government debt issues separate in time the ability to spend from the need to raise revenue. In addition, however, because under some circumstances governments need not repay debt obligations at all (they may refinance them forward indefinitely), and also because of uncertainty over the identity of the responsible taxpayers even in the case of future repayment, government debt is in part net wealth to the aggregate of private holders in a way that private debts are not.

The distinguishing feature of government debt in many economies is its essential freedom from default risk. In addition, in most economies the market for government debt is among the most efficiently functioning of all financial markets. Hence the existence of government debt enables the credit market to establish a base, with risk factors limited to inflation and real discounting values, from which it can then price privately issued debts subject to risks associated with default as well. The practice of giving government guarantees to the payment of interest and principal on selected private debts, which has greatly proliferated in recent years, has further increased the variety of forms of default-free debt securities. Yet another important implication of the default-free nature of government debt is that, to the extent that government borrowing takes the place of borrowing that individuals could do on their own account only at higher cost or not at all, government debt is in part net wealth to the private sector even if it is necessarily repaid and even if the identity of the responsible taxpayers is fully known.

International borrowing and lending has also greatly increased in recent years, as technological advances in communications have brought the world's financial markets closer together in the relevant physical sense, while individual countries' governments have progressively relaxed legal and regulatory barriers that impede international capital flows. From the perspective of any one country, the possibility of international borrowing and lending serves a separation function analogous to the fundamental Fisherian separation of production and consumption decisions in a closed economy. An economy that can borrow or lend abroad need not balance its imports and exports at each moment of time. Moreover, once an economy builds up a positive net international creditor position, it can indefinitely finance an excess of imports over exports from the associated interest income. (Conversely, once an economy builds up a net international debtor position, it must indefinitely export in excess of its imports so as to finance the debt service.) From the perspective of the world economy as a whole, international borrowing and lending is even more closely analogous to the closed economy model, in that it facilitates a more efficient allocation of resources across national boundaries.

Apart from these categorical heterogeneities, credit markets also reallocate immediate purchasing power among individuals and among business firms. The need for individuals in differing circumstances to make a complementary arrangements for divergences among their respective income and spending streams is basic to any life-cycle or overlapping-generations model of consumer behaviour. On the borrowing side, practical market limitations on individuals' issuance of equity-type claims contingent on their future earnings means that the only effective way for most individuals to shift command over purchasing power from the future to the present is through ordinary money-denominated debts. In fact, in most economies individuals' ability to borrow against no security other than future earnings is severely limited in any form, so that most borrowing by individuals occurs in conjunction with the purchase of homes, automobiles or other specific durable goods. On the lending side, individuals choosing to carry purchasing power into the future can hold wealth in any of its available forms, and in fact most individuals hold by far the greater part of their wealth in forms other than credit market instruments. Hence the great bulk of the borrowing done by individuals represents funds advanced by financial intermediary institutions rather than directly by other individuals.

Direct borrowing and lending among business firms is also a significant part of credit market activity especially in highly developed financial systems. On the borrowing side, firms' reliance on debt finance is readily understandable for reasons sketched above, irrespective of whether the funds raised come from individuals, from financial intermediaries or from other businesses. On the lending side, debt held by business firms usually takes the form of very short-term liquid instruments intended to provide maximum flexibility in the future disposition of the purchasing power thus deferred.

In sum, the credit markets pay the fundamental role of enabling an economy populated by heterogeneous agents to achieve superior resource allocations by redistributing immediate purchasing power in exchange for money-denominated claims on the future. Because of the intensive use of debt to finance both business and residential investment, in establishing the terms on which such transfers take place also play a consequent role in guiding the economy's capital accumulation and capital allocation over time that is analogous to – and, in some economies, as important as – the parallel incentives provided by the capital markets. In addition, in part because those elements of total spending that are typically debt-financed bulk large in aggregate demand, in many economies fluctuations of overall economic activity are as closely related to the movement of total credit as to the movements of any other financial aggregates (like any measure of money, for example).

Finally, as in the case for capital markets, several other features of actual credit markets that in principle need not be so, but in fact are so, have exerted a strong influence on the way in which economists have studied these markets over many years. One of the most important in this regard is the fact, noted above, that individuals directly hold relatively few credit market instruments. Instead, the great bulk of the borrowing and lending in any even moderately advanced economy takes place through specialized financial intermediaries, including commercial banks, non-bank thrift institutions, insurance companies, pension funds, mutual funds, and so on.

Standard rationales underlying financial intermediation include the minimization of information and transactions costs, and the diversification of risks, in a world in which assets are imperfectly divisible and both asset returns and wealth-holders' cash-flow positions are imperfectly correlated. In principle, these rationales apply to capital markets as well as credit markets, and in many countries institutions like mutual funds and pension funds do play an important role in holding equity shares. In practice, however, in many countries the bulk of the existing equity securities is still held directly by individuals rather than through financial intermediaries, while the opposite is true for debt instruments. As a result, the study of financial intermediation in general, and of specific kinds of intermediary institutions in particular, has been a major focus of the economic analysis of credit markets.

Another feature of actual credit markets that has likewise attracted a voluminous economic literature has been the simultaneous existence of a great variety of different debt instruments, especially including debts that differ according to their respective stated maturities. Although in principle only a single form of debt instrument, with a unique maturity, would enable the credit market to serve much of its economic functions, in fact almost all known credit markets are characterized by the simultaneous existence of many debt instruments with differing terms to maturity. The need for the market to price these debts – that is, to establish a term

structure of interest rates – not only raises issues of risk analogous to those discussed above in relation to capital markets but also makes explicit the need for a more general intertemporal framework of analysis.

At least since Hicks (1939), economists have been aware at some level that short-term and long-term debts are both risky assets, each from a particular time perspective. Apart from risks associated with default and inflation, short-term debt provides a certain return to holders over a short-time horizon, so that short-term government debt could plausibly constitute the risk-free asset in a no-inflation version of the standard capital asset pricing model represented by (1) and (2) above. Over a longer horizon, however, short-term debt preserves capital value only by exposing both borrowers and lenders to an income risk if interest rates fluctuate. Conversely, long-term debt maintains income streams only by exposing borrowers and lenders to the risk of fluctuating capital value over any time horizon shorter than the stated term to maturity. At an *a priori* level, there is no way to establish which form of risk is more important, and hence no way to establish even the sign of the expected return premium that risk-averse borrowers and lenders would establish in pricing short-term and long-term debts relative to one another.

Following both Hicks and Keynes (1936), most economists have assumed as an empirical matter that typically prevailing preferences are such that lenders require, and borrowers are willing to pay, a positive expected return premium for the capital risk inherent in long-term debt. Hence the subsequent development of the term structure literature has taken a form at least in principle compatible with the single-period capital asset pricing model. More recently, however, following Stiglitz's (1970) explicit demonstration of the connection between the risk pricing of receipt streams and preferences with respect to consumption streams, the economic literature of asset pricing has tended to return to the position that there is no general answer to the question of whether short-term or long-term debts are more risky. Instead, the preferred form of analysis has increasingly become an explicitly intertemporal model, like Merton's (1973b) intertemporal capital asset pricing model or, more recently, Ross's (1976) arbitrage pricing model as generalized by Cox et al. (1985).

MONEY MARKETS. The economic role played by the money market is more difficult to establish than that of the markets for capital and credit, in part because 'money' is not straightforward to define. The standard practice among non-economists, which often creates unexpected confusion for economists, is to refer to 'money' indistinguishably from short-term forms of credit, so that 'the money market' is just that segment of the credit market devoted to issuing and trading short-term debts, and 'money rates' are correspondingly the stated nominal interest rates on money market instruments thus defined. By contrast, economists have traditionally viewed money as distinct from credit, and have given money a central place in macroeconomic analysis which typically appeals to some form of aggregation argument to assume away the existence of credit altogether.

Two lines of thinking, neither necessarily easy to convert into an operational definition of 'money', have traditionally dominated economists' thinking on the subject. One has emphasized the role of money as a form of wealth (in traditional language, a store of value). The problem then is to define which forms of wealth constitute money and which do not. The emphasis in drawing such distinctions has typically rested on the safety and liquidity of the asset, in the sense of its relative freedom from default risk and its ease of conversion, at a predetermined rate of exchange, into whatever is the economy's means of payment. Although the general idea behind such thinking is clear enough, in actually existing economies it has proved impossible to draw the requisite line between money and non-money assets without imposing arbitrary distinctions. Typically, the more highly developed an economy's financial system, the greater is the need for such arbitrary judgements.

The alternative line of traditional thinking has been to emphasize the role of money in effecting transactions, and hence to define as money just those assets that are acceptable as means of payment. One problem here is that both legalities and common business practice sometimes make ambiguous what constitutes an acceptable means of payment. Indeed, in highly developed financial systems an increasing volume of transactions is effected without requiring the actual holding of any specific asset identifiable as money. Moreover, this approach leads to further difficulties, even apart from definitional problems. If money is used as one side of every transaction in the respective markets for all goods and services and all other assets, then the meaning of 'the money market' is unclear except in the sense that there exists a demand for money equal to the net supply of all other tradeables, and, correspondingly, a supply of money equal to the net demand for all other tradeables.

Under either the store-of-value approach or the means-of-payment approach, the central role conventionally attached to the money market in modern macroeconomic analysis primarily reflects the standard institutional structure within which monetary policy consists in the first instance of actions by the central bank that, either directly or through the financial intermediary system, affect the supply of money however it is defined. Market equilibrium then requires a corresponding change in the demand for money – that is, in the demand for highly liquid assets or for the means of payment, depending on the definitional approach assumed. In either case, the required shift in the public's aggregate portfolio demands presumably requires, in turn, a shift in the structure of expected asset returns, with consequent implications for non-financial economic activity under any of a variety of familiar theories of consumption, investment and production behaviour.

The specifics of this process, however, depend crucially on the definition of 'money'. Under the approach that identifies money with assets meeting sufficient criteria of safety and liquidity, the demand for money is merely a by-product of the theory of risk-averse portfolio selection under uncertainty. Under this approach, what is more difficult is to specify the process connecting the supply of money, so defined, to the central bank's actions. To the extent that the supply of assets defined as money consists largely of the liabilities of depository intermediaries, and to the extent that the relevant institutional arrangements require intermediaries to hold reserves against their liabilities, the connection between money supply and central bank actions that provide or withdraw intermediary reserves is apparent enough. When there is no reserve requirement, however – because either specific kinds of intermediary institutions or specific kinds of intermediary liabilities face no reserve requirement – the connection between monetary policy actions and money supply is more problematic.

The situation under the approach that identifies money with the means of payment is roughly the opposite. Because more economies' means of payment consist largely of the direct liabilities of the central bank and the reservable liabilities of specific intermediaries, connecting the supply of money to

central bank reserve actions is relatively straightforward. What is more difficult under this approach is establishing the link to the demand for money thus defined, and hence ultimately the effect on non-financial economic activity. When assets other than the means of payment also provide safety and liquidity, the standard theory of portfolio selection no longer suffices to determine the demand for the means of payment itself. Economic analysis of this problem has largely developed along the inventory-theoretic lines laid out initially by Baumol (1952) and Tobin (1956) and by Miller and Orr (1966). Especially in modern circumstances that readily permit transactions on a credit basis, however, the relevance of such 'cash in advance' models is unclear.

Regardless of the specific conceptual approach taken to define money, it is clear that the deposit liabilities of financial intermediaries bulk large in individuals' direct wealth holding in most actual economies, so that economists' study of money markets has heavily focused on the role of intermediaries and intermediation. The reasons for the prominent position of intermediary liabilities in individuals' direct wealth-holdings are not difficult to understand. The deposits of banks and similar intermediaries typically provide the most convenient means of settling most transactions, and the asset transformation provided by financial intermediations makes it attractive for most individuals to participate in the market for many kinds of assets via intermediaries rather than directly.

As a result, 'the money market' in most actual economies consists largely of financial intermediaries on one side and both individuals and business firms on the other. Here, as elsewhere in modern economies, the profusion of differentiated financial products is vast. Money market assets in this sense consist of checkable and non-checkable deposits, demand deposits and deposits for stated terms ranging from a few days to many months, deposits with fixed (nominal) returns and variable returns, and so on. Moreover, in the eyes of most market participants, short-term credit market claims that are close portfolio substitutes for intermediary deposits (commercial paper) are money market instruments too.

BENJAMIN M. FRIEDMAN

See also CREDIT; FINANCE; FINANCIAL INTERMEDIARIES; FINANCIAL MARKETS; MONETARY POLICY; MONEY SUPPLY.

BIBLIOGRAPHY

Arrow, K.J. 1964. The role of securities in the optimal allocation of risk-bearing. *Review of Economic Studies* 31, April, 91–6.

Arrow, K.J. 1965. *Aspects of the Theory of Risk-Bearing.* Helsinki: The Yrjo Jahnsson Foundation.

Baumol, W.J. 1952. The transactions demand for cash: an inventory theoretic approach. *Quarterly Journal of Economics* 66, November, 545–56.

Black, F. and Scholes, M. 1973. The pricing of options and corporate liabilities. *Journal of Political Economy* 81(3), May–June, 637–54.

Brainard, W.C. and Tobin, J. 1968. Pitfalls in financial model-building. *American Economic Review, Papers and Proceedings* 58, May, 99–122.

Cox, J.C., Ingersoll, J.E., Jr. and Ross, S.A. 1985. A theory of the term structure of interest rates. *Econometrica* 53(2), March, 385–407.

Debreu, G. 1959. *Theory of Value: An Axiomatic Analysis of Economic Equilibrium.* New Haven: Yale University Press.

Fisher, I. 1930. *The Theory of Interest.* New York: The Macmillan Company.

Grossman, S.J. 1976. On the efficiency of competitive stock markets when traders have diverse information. *Journal of Finance* 31(2), May, 573–85.

Hicks, J.R. 1939. *Value and Capital.* Oxford: Oxford University Press.

Keynes, J.M. 1936. *The General Theory of Employment, Interest and Money*. London: Macmillan; New York: Harcourt, Brace & World.

Lintner, J. 1965. The valuation of risk assets and the selection of risky investments in stock portfolios and capital budgets. *Review of Economics and Statistics* 47, February, 13–37.

Lintner, J. 1969. The aggregation of investors' diverse judgements and preferences in purely competitive securities markets. *Journal of Financial and Quantitative Analysis* 4(4), December, 347–400.

Markowitz, H. 1952. Portfolio selection. *Journal of Finance* 7, March, 77–91.

Merton, R.C. 1973a. Theory of rational option pricing. *Bell Journal of Economics and Management Science* 4(1), Spring, 141–83.

Merton, R.C. 1973b. An intertemporal capital asset pricing model. *Econometrica* 41(5), September, 867–87.

Miller, M.H. and Orr, D. 1966. A model of the demand for money by firms. *Quarterly Journal of Economics* 80, August, 413–35.

Modigliani, F. and Miller, M.H. 1958. The cost of capital, corporation finance, and the theory of investment. *American Economic Review* 48, June, 261–97.

Pratt, J.W. 1964. Risk aversion in the small and in the large. *Econometrica* 32, January–April, 122–36.

Ross, S.A. 1976. The arbitrage theory of capital asset pricing. *Journal of Economic Theory* 13(3), December, 341–60.

Sharpe, W.F. 1964. Capital asset prices: a theory of market equilibrium under conditions of risk. *Journal of Finance* 19, September, 425–42.

Shiller, R.J. 1984. Stock prices and social dynamics. *Brookings Papers on Economic Activity* No. 2, 457–510.

Stiglitz, J.E. 1970. A consumption-oriented theory of the demand for financial assets and the term structure of interest rates. *Review of Economic Studies* 37(3), July, 321–51.

Tobin, J. 1956. The interest-elasticity of transactions demand for cash. *Review of Economics and Statistics* 38, August, 241–7.

Tobin, J. 1958. Liquidity preference as behavior toward risk. *Review of Economic Studies* 25, February, 65–86.

capital, fictitious. *See* FICTITIOUS CAPITAL.

capital, fixed. *See* FIXED CAPITAL.

capital, measurement of. *See* CAPITAL THEORY: DEBATES; CAPITAL THEORY: PARADOXES; QUANTITY OF CAPITAL.

capital, quantity of. *See* QUANTITY OF CAPITAL.

capital accumulation. *See* ACCUMULATION OF CAPITAL.

capital as a factor of production. The role played by capital in production has frequently been in dispute: 'When economics reach agreement on the theory of capital they will shortly reach agreement on everything else' (Bliss, 1975, p. vii). Disagreements are due as much to divergent definitions, or uses, of the term 'capital' as to different views about what should be considered a factor of production. But above all there have been differing views about whether, and in what sense, capital can be said to be productive. In particular, there has been disagreement about whether it can be said that a more capital-intensive production method is more productive than a less capital intensive one. Preclassical, classical,

neoclassical and neo-neoclassical economic theory have given different answers to these questions. These will be considered below, but the discussion will be confined to the role of capital as a factor of production. It should be noted in particular that the problem why capital earns its owner an income depends as much on the social institution of ownership and the institutional organization of production as on the role capital plays in production. It is only the latter, in a sense technical, problem which will be addressed here.

TERMINOLOGY. Capital goods are produced commodities which are required for production no matter how much or how little they are subject to wear and tear. A stock (at a point of time; see Fisher, 1906) of different capital goods is a *capital*; this concept is to be taken in a vector sense. As long as they are required in production, all capital goods can be valued, even when they are not traded on markets, as many of them are. Because of their heterogeneity, different capital goods cannot be aggregated, but their values can. A *capital value* is therefore the sum of the capital values of those capital goods which constitute a capital. Note that this is a book-keeping term, which depends on the valuation of the capital goods involved; the capital value can change although there is no change in the stock of capital goods. The term *money capital* will be used in a similar sense, but with a somewhat different connotation: it denotes the sum of money necessary to buy a specified stock of capital goods. Real counterparts in a scalar sense to a given capital value or money capital can be constructed in principle (Hicks, 1974, p. 151), but not in an unambiguous manner.

PRODUCTION: BASIC NOTIONS. Production is the transformation of inputs into outputs. Inputs are those things which need to be increased in order to obtain more output by the same method of production, where the latter is defined as a blueprint which details what inputs are required when and in which proportions to produce a unit bundle of outputs. As there may be more than one method to produce the same unit bundle of outputs, a production process is defined as a particular method of production to produce a particular unit bundle of outputs. A production process always uses inputs in fixed proportions; variable proportions are represented by different production processes. If there exist various different production processes with which the same unit bundle of outputs can be produced, they will differ in the proportions in which they use various inputs; but in general it will not be possible to compare them from a purely technical point of view. Different production processes are comparable only if their costs are computed and related to the value of the outputs obtained. In general, however, any ordering obtained in this way need not be unique: two different production processes may have the same unit costs. Moreover, if the prices of inputs change a given ordering need not be preserved. Such difficulties affect the choice between different production processes; they do not, however, affect the role of capital in production, or its status as a factor of production.

Production typically is roundabout, i.e. proceeds in stages: what is produced as output in one production process is used as an input (alongside others) in another. If all these intermediate products (outputs which are used as inputs) are specific in the sense that they have only one possible use, all production processes required to produce a particular bundle of outputs can be strung together into a sequence of production processes. Consolidating all stages, one can view the sequence as transforming 'primary' inputs into 'final' outputs. Here primary inputs are these which are not produced within the sequence of production processes, if indeed they can be produced at all; final outputs are those which are not used, or used up, within the sequence.

Not all intermediate products are specific in the sense that they have only one possible use. In this case all interlocking sequences can be combined into a production system which again can be viewed as transforming primary inputs into final outputs. Without loss of generality one can assume that such a production system comprises all production processes in operation in an economy. Consolidating them amounts to adopting a 'black box' view of production. Disregarding the internal structure of the production system and of the production processes which constitute it, one links directly primary inputs to final outputs, and disregards all inputs produced and used, or used up, within the production system. The advantage of this procedure is that it reduces the number of inputs to be considered.

The definition of what is a primary input, or a final output, depends on the level of aggregation as well as the nature of the production processes involved. Production on a barren island will require many inputs as primary ones which are intermediate products in a production system comprising all production processes operating in a continent rich in resources. Similarly the final outputs produced by the island economy's production system may be confined to what are intermediate products in the production system of a continent.

By definition, an increase in output can only be obtained by an increase in inputs in fixed proportions. From this one can infer that all required inputs together are productive, and have a non-negative marginal production. This cannot, however, be inferred for any single input. This can only be done if either there are at least two different production processes for the production of the same unit bundle of outputs because then it is possible to calculate the marginal net value product of an input (Bliss, 1975, ch. 5); or if there are alternative uses for all inputs in production processes which produce other unit bundles of outputs (Uzawa, 1958). Only when there exists only one production process for a particular unit bundle of outputs and there are no alternative uses for some of the inputs it requires is it impossible to calculate their marginal contribution to the outputs obtained individually; it is of course still possible to calculate their contribution as a group of inputs.

FACTORS OF PRODUCTION. In modern usage, all primary inputs can be called 'factors of production'. Conventionally, however, primary inputs are considered, following Senior (1836), the services of agents or stocks, and the term 'factor of production' is reserved for the latter. If they are the services of natural agents or human beings, they are called 'original factors of production'; they are called simply 'factors of production' if they also include the services of stocks of durable commodities. Factors of production can therefore be defined as those agents or durable stocks the services of which are primary inputs in production processes.

Factors of production are productive and have a non-negative marginal product if their services are productive and have a non-negative marginal product.

The definition of factors of production just given is reasonably precise as far as natural agents and human beings are concerned. Land and labour have been considered factors of production at least since Petty (1662). Land was often understood, if tacitly, to include all beneficial powers of nature; the term 'natural agents' was introduced by Senior (1836). In preclassical theory durable stocks were called simply 'stocks' (see, e.g., Barbon, 1690), but usage of the term was often confined to trade and commerce. When production came to be seen as the dominant economic activity, produced means

of production, considered as a factor of production, came to be called 'capital'. This term had been in use for a long time (see Hohoff, 1918–19; Salin, 1930; Assel, 1953), but now acquired a new meaning, thus inviting confusion and controversy. It will be useful, therefore, to trace historically the use made of that term, and the notions attached to it.

PRECLASSICAL THEORIES OF CAPITAL AND PRODUCTION. There is very little about production and its relation to capital in economic writings before the mid-18th century. Barbon (1690) provides an early, but singular, instance of an analysis in which a surplus is seen to arise from the use of what he calls a 'stock' (of capital goods) in trade as well as in the production of commodities. In a similar vein, Hume used the term 'stock' somewhat indiscriminately to denote both a store of commodities and a sum of money. But he did distinguish, as had Barbon, between profits from 'stock' and interest on money (1752, p. 313), thus separating the investment of money from the productive use of 'stock', e.g. capital goods, although he is none too clear about the latter.

The Physiocrats were probably the first to develop a clear view of production and the role of capital in it. But they did not use the term 'capital'. Cantillon (1755) strongly emphasized the need for accumulated sums of money required to buy stocks of goods in which to trade, or with which to produce. But he called them 'funds' not 'capital'. Thus he speaks of the farmer who needs to have enough funds (*assed de fond*) to conduct his business. Quesnay used the term 'advances' (*avances*) in a similar way in the sense of money capital. Behind his usage is a clearly drawn picture of agricultural production which uses land and labour to produce output, and needs money capital to finance the lag between the expenditure on inputs and the sale of the output obtained. Probably deliberately, Quesnay eschewed the term 'capital'. Where he used it (1766b), he spoke explicitly of money capital (*capital d'argent*), but conceived it as invested in buildings, implements, stores of grain, cattle, and so on (1766a, pp. 172–3). These, however, he clearly conceived as productive. Moreover, his argument centres on the idea that larger advances would permit more productive production methods to be used (see Eltis, 1984, chs. 1 and 2).

Turgot (1770) was the first to develop a specific theory of capital as a factor in production when, possibly under the influence of Hume's ideas, he generalized Quesnay's theory. Quesnay had shown that advances were necessary for agricultural production. Turgot, in an attempt to develop Quesnay's theory of a society dominated by agriculture into a theory of a commercial society, places commerce and manufacture on an equal footing with agricultural production, and emphasized that advances are required in all branches of economic activity. Such advances are paid out of capital, which is defined as 'accumulated values' (1770, § LVIII). If account is taken of the various degrees of risks involved, the rates of return on all possible investments are equalized by competition between the owners of the various capitals (Turgot uses the plural, *capitaux*) such that the rate of interest can 'be regarded as a kind of thermometer of the abundance or scarcity of capitals in a Nation, and of the extent of the enterprises of all kinds in which it may engage' (1770, § LXXXIX). At the same time, Turgot argues emphatically that some return on all these kinds of investment is necessary in order to keep production on the same level; if the rate of return were lowered, capitals would be withdrawn, and production could not be kept on the same level as before (1770, § XCVI). Thus to Turgot 'capitals' are money capital. Money capital is required because production is roundabout and thus needs capital goods as well as original factors of production. Like Quesnay, Turgot assumed that larger amounts of money capital make possible higher levels of production. One might be inclined to argue that therefore money capital, i.e. advances, are productive; but although Turgot is not entirely clear on this point it seems that he considered not so much advances as the capital goods which represent them as productive.

THE CLASSICAL THEORY OF CAPITAL AND PRODUCTION. The classical view of the role of capital in production was worked out by Adam Smith. He began by emphasizing the division of labour, but then switched to a detailed consideration 'Of the Nature, Accumulation, and Employment of Stock' (1776, book II) in which he effectively adopted the theory put forward by Quesnay and Turgot. His attempts to integrate these two approaches were not entirely successful (Bowley, 1976); although the division of labour retained its status as a device which enhances the productivity of labour in classical economic theory, the emphasis was shifted to the accumulation of capital as the prime force making for growth. This was of course linked to the idea that production needs advances, and the proposition that labour was the more productive the larger these advances. Smith also changed the emphasis in another respect: he formally defined 'capital' as that part of a person's stock of commodities which is expected to yield an income. Smith described its function as assisting labour in production: fixed capital (machines, buildings, land improvements, and 'acquired and useful abilities') 'facilitates' labour by increasing its effectiveness; circulating capital (money, raw materials, goods in process and goods in stock) 'abridges' by providing (material) advances.

This distinction is ambiguous, but characteristic for Smith's position. Fixed capital, he argued, yields an income, i.e. is productive, by being used 'without changing masters': while circulating capital needs to be either given up (in trade) or be destroyed (in production) in order to be productive (1776, pp. 279–83). What is considered are capital goods; but only money capital can circulate in the way Smith described their circulation. The two approaches can be reconciled; but the way in which Smith expressed himself invited confusion between money capital on the one hand, and capital in the sense of capital goods on the other. In fact, Smith needed both concepts. James Mill (1821), Rae (1834) and other classical writers often used the term 'instrument' when emphasizing that they meant capital goods, and continued to speak of capital in the sense of money capital. Money capital played indeed an important role in classical economic thought for it permitted classical writers to argue, in a rather loose way, that production methods were the more productive, the more money capital they required. It is for this reason that Hicks (1974) called them 'Fundists'. At the same time, however, they also considered the role of capital goods in production processes (Sraffa, 1960), and thus maintained a 'real capital doctrine' (Corry, 1962, p. 18).

The view that capital assists labour was attacked by Lauderdale (1804), who pointed out that capital could, and frequently did, supplant labour when circulating capital was substituted for fixed capital. This initiated the debate on the 'machinery question', and confirmed the role of capital as a factor of production: what can supplant a factor of production surely must be considered as belonging to the same species.

Smith had separated a person's stock of commodities into durable consumer goods and capital by requiring that the latter be expected to earn an income. This led to many attempts to show that not only capital goods used in production are expected to yield an income (i.e. Hermann, 1832, or Menger, 1888). These discussions often confused the role of money capital in investment processes with the role of capital goods in production processes, and contributed to the survival of the concept of money capital as a factor of production referred to above.

The view that production requires advances in the form of capital goods was so dominant that the role of fixed capital was often pushed into the background. Thus Ricardo spoke of production as 'the united application of labour, machinery, and capital' (1817, p. 5), thus equating capital with circulating capital. As Smith had subsumed the consumer goods required for the maintenance of labour under circulating capital stocks, this particular part of the total stock of commodities in an economy acquired, under the name of the 'wages fund', a pivotal role in all discussions of the role of capital in production. Following a precedent set by Smith, the wage fund was seen to be derived from, and increased by, saving, i.e. non-consumption or 'abstinence', as Senior (1836) was to call it. Destined to supply the consumption goods required as advances while production processes continue, the concept was used as a theory of wage determination on the assumption that the wages fund was given at least in the short run and thus determines the wage level when workers compete freely for employment.

In spite of all the attention Smith gave to the accumulation of capital as a factor making for economic growth, he reserved a special role for human labour as the prime factor of production, expecially in those passages in which he set out his conjectural history. This emphasis, which is clearly based on the view that production requires advances, remained a feature of the classical theory of capital, and was a mainstay of the labour theory of value as developed by Ricardo and others. It is symptomatic that from this point of view the use of 'machinery and other fixed and durable capital' was considered no more than an (admittedly considerable) modification of the labour theory of value by Ricardo (1818, p. 30). More radical writers, such as Hodgskin (1827) emphasized the notion of capital goods as 'stored-up' labour (i.e. outputs produced by past labour) that had been worked out by James Mill (1821) and Ricardo (1817) and on its basis denied fixed capital the status as a factor of production.

The special role Smith has reserved for labour did not prevent him from juxtaposing labour, stock and land to parallel wages, profits and rent (1776, p. 69). This juxtaposition was elaborated into a strict parallelism between factors of production and their earnings by Say (1814) which became generally accepted by the middle of the 19th century. Thus when J.S. Mill (1848) summarized the classical theory of capital into his four propositions, he still adhered to the view that production required advances in the form of capital goods. But when he comes to discuss the laws of increase of factors of production, he treats them on an equal footing (though in exactly the order Smith had listed them: and not the land-labour-capital order which Say had made familiar). At the same time, however, Mill often gives the impression that he means money capital when he speaks of 'capital', especially in those passages in which he argues that competition will establish a uniform rate of return on capital because capital will be transferred from one industry to another.

In a similar way Marx (1867) used the term capital to mean both a stock of commodities, and a sum of values. In addition, Marx insisted that capital goods are capital only in a capitalistic society, and thus used the term also to describe a particular organization of production in society.

Finally, the view that production requires advances in the form of capital goods which Smith had expounded, and which most classical writers accepted, was developed by a few of them into a theory which strongly emphasized the time element in production. There are some traces of this in Ricardo (1817), especially in his recognition that all the difficulties he encountered in his theory of value are due to the temporal aspect of production processes. The view was worked out in detail by Rae (1834), by Longfield (1834), and also by Senior (1836). Their work foreshadows one aspect of the neoclassical theory of capital.

Classical economic theory considered three factors of production: land, labour, and capital. Each had its own dimension: land was a stock, labour a flow, and capital was money capital in the form of a stock of capital goods. In the original conception their standing was not equal: labour worked on land with the help of capital. Hence the capital intensity of production mattered: the more money capital was invested, the more productive was labour in its efforts to work up the bounty of nature into consumable output. These notions were not, however, made very precise: that was left for neoclassical theorists. Thünen's early discussion of the marginal productivity of capital (1850) remained an exception.

THE NEOCLASSICAL THEORY OF CAPITAL AND PRODUCTION. Neoclassical economic theory was not a coherent construct: up to the 1930s there were different versions of neoclassical theory as far as the treatment of capital as a factor of production is concerned (Stigler, 1941).

Perhaps the most contentious version was the Austrian one as worked out by Böhm-Bawerk (1889). To some extent it had been foreshadowed by Jevons (1871), even though Jevons had little to say about production. But there is a clear picture in Jevons of the necessity of money capital which is 'invested' in the form of advances in time-consuming production processes. What is more, Jevons formulated, very much *ad hoc*, a temporal production function which postulated that there are diminishing marginal returns to the length of investment of such advances: and used it to derive the marginal product of an extension of that length, which clearly is a measure for the capital intensity of production.

Böhm-Bawerk, by contrast, consciously and explicitly developed a theory of production. It very much follows classical lines: production requires time, and hence needs advances in the form of capital goods. Capital goods are seen as produced means of production, and at the same time as stored-up land-and-labour, even though they derive their value not, as the classics had maintained, from the fact that they represent land and labour services spent in the past: but from their prospective usefulness in the production of future output. Nevertheless Böhm-Bawerk emphatically denied that capital goods can be productive, and insisted that only the production processes which they make possible are productive. Although this could have meant that the notion of productiveness was transferred from factors of production to production processes, Böhm-Bawerk did not take this step. He seems to begin by saying that only land and labour should be called productive, and ends by postulating something very much like a productivity of the length of the period of production. As in Jevons (1871), this view is based on a temporal production function in which the degree of roundaboutness of production processes is explicitly taken as a measure for the capital intensity of the production processes in operation. Böhm-Bawerk attempted to overcome in this manner the difficulty of deriving any such measure from diverse sets of capital goods. The roundaboutness of production processes was turned into a variable which was chosen by profit-maximizing entrepreneurs subject to a given amount of money capital.

The relationship of this construction to classical economic thought is obvious. Nevertheless Böhm-Bawerk's attempt to provide a temporal theory of production based on the notion of capital as a derived factor of production, or intermediate good, turned out to be very contentious. The theory of interest which he had been built upon it was turned into what became the standard (neoclassical) theory of interest by Fisher (1907, 1930) – but only after it had been cut loose from its production-theoretic underpinnings: and after Fisher had substituted instead an analysis of investment opportunities based on the concept of money capital. Various attempts to reformulate Böhm-Bawerk's theory of the role of capital in production (Wicksell, 1893; Strigl, 1934; Hayek, 1940) generated much debate, but did not manage to rescue it.

The Austrian theory of capital is much more traditional than other versions of neoclassical theory which gave up the 'advances' view of capital. Thus Wicksteed (1894) placed all factors of production on an equal footing, including all kinds of capital goods, and postulated that 'The Product being a function of the factors of production we have $P = f(a, b, c, ...)$' (1894, p. 4) without even mentioning whether production takes time or not. Being considered akin to any other input in this respect, capital goods are of course productive; but nothing can be said about the capital intensity of production. Marshall (1890) argued in a similar way, although he kept to the classical tradition by reserving a place for money capital alongside the capital goods used in production. Taking up a distinction first made, it seems, by Menger (1888, p. 44), Marshall distinguished between capital goods which earn quasi-rents, and money capital which earns interest. In essence this is the distinction between production and investment: capital goods are used in production, and if used productively, earn quasi-rents; money capital is invested, and if invested successfully, earns interest. Clark (1899) equally rejected the advances view of production. In his view, production did not require advances once production processes were properly set up, or synchronized. As in Wicksteed, capital is a factor of production on an equal footing with land or labour. At the same time, Clark separated clearly between material capital goods or produced means of production, on the one hand, and capital as a 'quantum of productive wealth' (1899, p. 119), measured in money, which is invested in capital goods. Although Clark calls this 'a material entity' (1899, p. 119), his 'capital' is money capital, just as it was in Marshall (or Menger for that matter). Knight (1933) continued in this vein, but emphasized money capital, considered as a 'material entity', so much that capital goods were almost lost sight of. As a result, 'capital' came to be seen more and more as a homogeneous mass which was created by saving decisions, which could be invested in one industry and transferred to another, which was productive in the sense that is has a non-negative marginal product if used properly, and which guaranteed higher productivity if employed in larger amounts in relation to other factors of production. Not surprisingly, this conception was attacked by the heirs to the Austrian tradition in capital theory, especially Hayek (1936, 1940), as a 'mythology of capital'. But their own position was so much bound up with the deprecated notion of a period of production that Knight's conception (1933, 1934, 1935, 1936) became the dominant doctrine.

The notion of capital as a 'material entity' was formulated rigorously by Pigou, who provided a sophisticated definition of a capital stock, consisting of heterogeneous capital goods, which 'is capable of maintaining its quantity while altering its form' (1935, p. 239). This was possible only by making some rather strong assumptions on the way the capital stock was maintained. Thus Pigou assumed, among other things, that any item of a constant capital stock that needs to be replaced is replaced by another capital good yielding equal quasi-rents at the time of replacement. Later changes in quasi-rents are disregarded. While such assumptions may be objected to, they do allow in principle to give precise meaning to the notion of a capital stock as a chancing 'material entity' without aggregating heterogeneous capital goods, i.e. without negating its quality as a vector.

Walras (1874–7) and Pareto (1909) treated capital very much as Wicksteed had done: as yet another factor of production in a production system which was fully synchronized and which was not in need of advances. As they used production functions and thus assumed, as Wicksteed had done, that there always exist many production processes for the production of the same unit bundle of outputs, the productivity of capital goods was no problem for them. But because they espoused the black box view of production they somewhat lost sight of the internal structure of production, and hence of the character of capital goods as produced means of production: capital goods are in their conceptual scheme simply part of the endowment which economic agents use to maximize their satisfaction. Moreover they could not form a notion of the capital intensity of production as they had no way of aggregating capital goods in an unambiguous manner.

Wicksell, finally, in his later treatment of the matter (1901) attempted to provide a synthesis of neoclassical capital theory by combining the general equilibrium framework of Walras and Pareto with the Austrian view of production as a time-consuming process. This led him to emphasize capital goods and their productivity. But when he came to close his system he took refuge, as Böhm-Bawerk had done, to the idea of a given fund of money capital. The importance of a given fund of money capital which acted as a constraint on entrepreneurial choices between different degrees of roundaboutness of production processes was also emphasized by Schumpeter (1911) and Cassel (1918).

Neoclassical economists have in common that they attempted to formulate a theory of production; but they differed in their conceptions (Hennings 1985). Böhm-Bawerk and those who followed him made an attempt to formulate more precisely what they saw as the gist of the classical theory of the role of capital in production: but their efforts were not generally accepted. All other neoclassical writers except Wicksell jettisoned the advances view of capital, and were in consequence faced with the necessity of formulating a measure for the capital intensity of production if they wished to uphold the proposition that more capital intensive methods of production were more productive. Wicksteed as well as Walras and Pareto did not do so, and simply refrained from making such statements. Marshall, Clark, and Knight in one way or another attempted to solve the problem by taking refuge to a concept of capital which is in essence a notion of money capital, and which cannot unambiguously serve for that purpose. Only Pigou formulated an unambiguous concept of capital as a changeable 'material entity'.

THE NEO-NEOCLASSICAL THEORY OF CAPITAL IN PRODUCTION. The neo-neoclassical view of the role of capital in production is based on the work of Viner (1930), Stackelberg (1932), Schneider (1934) and others, who worked out the theory of production as well as a theory of production costs, and the syntheses later provided by Hicks (1939) and Samuelson (1947) of the various neoclassical theories on the basis of the

Walras–Pareto theory of general equilibrium (Arrow and Hahn, 1971). Originally strongly microeconomic in nature, capital goods held and stage. But as this theory was essentially static, little thought was given to dynamic considerations (Hicks (1939) was the exception), and hence to the problems that arise if concrete capital goods are shifted from one industry to another. Where such problems came up, refuge was taken in the Clark-Knight conception of capital as a fairly homogeneous and amorphous mass which could take on different forms. With the growth of macroeconomic one-sector thinking – Hicks (1932) is one of the earliest examples in this part of economic theory – this conception was more and more resorted to. It received the seal of approval in Samuelson's textbook (1948), and in numerous empirical studies based on the macroeconomic production function first proposed by Cobb and Douglas (1928). It was of course realized that capital consisted of capital goods: but their aggregation into a more or less homogeneous aggregate was considered an index number problem which could be solved in principle as well as in practice. It was against these notions that opposition arose in the 1950s and 1960s.

RECENT DEBATES. As Joan Robinson (1954, 1956) pointed out, the Clark–Knight concept of capital cannot serve in a macroeconomic production function à la Cobb–Douglas because it is essentially a monetary measure. Surprisingly, this contention engendered a major debate in capital theory. Essentially two answers were given to Robinson's objection. On the one hand it was argued that one should search for appropriate indices that can be used to aggregate heterogeneous capital goods into a scalar measure (Champernowne, 1954).

This created a specialist literature on aggregation problems which demonstrates that in general conditions for consistent aggregation are rather restrictive, although in many cases appropriate indices exist (Green, 1964). On the other hand, it was argued that macroeconomic analyses should be abandoned in favour of microeconomic ones if heterogeneity (which after all exists in land and labour as well as in capital goods) is the issue (Swan, 1962).

In the course of the debates referred to above it was demonstrated that the value paradoxes Joan Robinson had pointed out may invalidate the idea that different production processes can be brought into a continuous ordering which corresponds to their respective capital intensities. While this point was eventually accepted, its importance is still under dispute (see Harcourt (1972) and Blaug (1974) for summaries and evaluations from divergent points of view). To some, such demonstrations completely invalidate neoclassical and in particular neo-neoclassical economic theory, because both are considered to be founded on the idea that marginal products of factors of production need to be calculated on the basis of technical data alone. Others accept such demonstrations as exceptions to a general rule. What is sometimes lost sight of in these assessments is the fact that reswitching of production processes, capital revaluations, Wicksell effects, et hoc genus omne do not invalidate all propositions in capital theory (whether neoclassical or not). One can well do without capital in the sense of capital value (i.e. as a scalar magnitude) for some purposes (see, e.g. Nuti, 1970). Moreover, it should be appreciated that Robinson's objections do not apply to Pigou's notion of capital as a changeable 'material entity' even though it is not at all obvious that such a concept would serve well in a macro-economic production function.

Another attack on neoclassical capital theory was made by Garegnani (1960, 1970, and 1976). The gist of his argument seems to be that the Walrasian model of general equilibrium, if properly extended to include the production of capital goods, cannot generate equilibrium as well as a unique rate of return on all capital goods for all possible initial endowments. As Garegnani has not specified the dynamic adjustment processes he envisages, his claim is difficult to adjudicate. Nor is it clear in what respect, if any, it invalidates received notions of the role of capital in production processes. Recent debates (Hahn, 1982; Duménil and Lévy, 1985) have not thrown much light on these issues.

CONCLUSION. Capital always consists of heterogeneous capital goods; indeed it is useful precisely because goods are heterogeneous and specific in the sense that they cannot be used for all purposes. Attempts to represent them by some kind of aggregate are useful only if they preserve this aspect of capital goods. In classical economic theory the notion of advances was used as such an aggregate, although in a rather loose fashion, with an awareness of the heterogeneity of the capital goods that assisted labour in time-consuming production. Austrian neoclassical economic theory attempted unsuccessfully to make this notion more precise in the form of a temporal theory of production. Non-Austrian neoclassical and neo-neoclassical economic theory sacrificed the heterogeneity of capital goods together with the time element in production, and developed an atemporal theory of production on the basis of a concept of capital value, or money capital. Yet, as Wicksell pointed out (1901, p. 149), the valuation of capital goods in terms of prospective output is a 'theoretical anomaly'; it is nevertheless appropriate in view of their character as produced means of production. It is not surprising, therefore, that anomalies result when such concepts are used. The alternative is obviously to analyse the role of capital goods in a framework which admits their heterogeneity and permits them to be used for different purposes, i.e. in a general equilibrium framework. Such analyses have so far been mainly confined to stationary states. Some of the essential characteristics of capital goods, however, such as their specificity, are of importance only in non-stationary states. Much remains to be done, therefore, before the role of capital and of capital goods as factors of production can be said to be completely elucidated.

K.H. Hennings

See also QUANTITY OF CAPITAL; ROUNDABOUT METHODS OF PRODUCTION.

BIBLIOGRAPHY

Arrow, K.J. and Hahn, F.H. 1971. *General Competitive Analysis*. San Francisco: Holden Day; Edinburgh: Oliver & Boyd.

Assel, H.G. 1953. Der Kapitalbegriff und die Kapitallehre bis zum Beginn der Neuzeit. *Wirtschaft und Gesellung. Festschrift für Hans Proesler zu seinem 65. Geburtstag.* Erlangen.

[Barbon, N.] 1690. *A Discourse on Trade*. By N.B.M.D. London: Milbourn for the Author.

Blaug, M. 1974. *The Cambridge Revolution: Success or Failure?* London: Institute of Economic Affairs.

Bliss, C.J. 1975. *Capital Theory and the Distribution of Income.* Amsterdam and Oxford: North-Holland Publishing Company. Innsbruck: Wagner. Trans. as *The Positive Theory of Capital,* London: Macmillan, 1891.

Bowley, M. 1975. Some aspects of the treatment of capital in 'The Wealth of Nations'. In *Essays on Adam Smith*, ed. A.S. Skinner and T. Wilson, Oxford: Clarendon Press.

Cantillon, R. 1755. *Essai sur la nature du commerce en général.* Londres: Gyles. Edited with an English translation by Henry Higgs, London: Cass, 1959.

Cassel, G. 1918. *Theoretische Sozialökonomie.* Leipzig: Deichert. Trans. as *Theory of Social Economy*, London: Fischer Unwin, 1923.

Champernowne, D.G. 1954. The production function and the theory of capital: a comment. *Review of Economic Studies* 21, 112–35.

Clark, J.B. 1899. *The Distribution of Wealth.* New York: Macmillan.

Cobb, C.W. and Douglas, P.H. 1928. A theory of production. *American Economic Review* 18, March, 139–65.

Corry, B.A. 1962. *Money, Saving and Investment in English Economics 1800–1850.* London: Macmillan.

Duménil, G. and Lévy, D. 1985. The classicals and the neoclassicals: a rejoinder to Frank Hahn. *Cambridge Journal of Economics* 9, 327–45.

Eltis, W. 1984. *The Classical Theory of Economic Growth.* London: Macmillan.

Fisher, I. 1906. *The Nature of Capital and Income.* New York: Macmillan.

Fisher, I. 1907. *The Rate of Interest.* New York: Macmillan.

Fisher, I. 1930. *The Theory of Interest.* New York: Macmillan.

Garegnani, P. 1960. *Il capitale nelle teorie della distribuzione.* Milano: Guiffrè. Trans. as *Le capital dans les théories de la répartition,* Paris: Presses Universitaires de Grenoble et François Maspero, 1980.

Garegnani, P. 1970. Heterogeneous capital, the production function and the theory of distribution. *Review of Economic Studies* 37, 407–36.

Garegnani, P. 1976. On a change in the notion of equilibrium in recent work on value and distribution. In *Essays in Modern Capital Theory*, ed. M. Brown, K. Sato and P. Zarembka, Amsterdam, New York, Oxford: North-Holland.

Green, H.A.J. 1964. *Aggregation in Economic Analysis.* Princeton: Princeton University Press.

Hahn, F.H. 1982. The neo-Ricardians. *Cambridge Journal of Economics* 6, 353–74.

Harcourt, G.C. 1972. *Some Cambridge Controversies in the Theory of Capital.* Cambridge: Cambridge University Press.

Hayek, F.A. von. 1936. The mythology of capital. *Quarterly Journal of Economics* 50, February, 199–228.

Hayek, F.A. von. 1940. *The Pure Theory of Capital.* London: Routledge & Kegan Paul.

Hennings, K.H. 1985. The exchange paradigm and the theory of production and distribution. In *Foundations of Economics*, ed. M. Baranzini and R. Scazzieri, Oxford: Blackwell.

Hermann, F.B.W. 1832. *Staatswirthschaftliche Untersuchungen.* Munich: Weber.

Hicks, J.R. 1932. *The Theory of Wages.* London: Macmillan. 1963.

Hicks, J.R. 1939. *Value and Capital.* Oxford: Clarendon Press.

Hicks, J.R. 1974. Capital controversies, ancient and modern. *American Economic Review* 64, May, 307–16. Reprinted in J.R. Hicks, *Economic Perspectives*, Oxford: Clarendon Press, 1977.

[Hodgskin, T.] 1827. *Popular Political Economy.* London: Tait and Wait.

Hohoff, W. 1819–19. Zur Geschichte des Wortes und Begriffes 'Kapital'. *Vierteljahrshefte für Sozial- und Wirtschaftsgeschichte* 14, 554–74 and 15, 281–310.

Hume, D. 1752. Of Interest. *Political Discourses.* Edinburgh: Fleming. Reprinted in D. Hume, *Essays Moral, Political and Literary*, Oxford: Oxford University Press, 1963.

Jevons, W.S. 1871. *The Theory of Political Economy.* London: Macmillan.

Knight, F.H. 1933. Capitalistic production, time and the rate of return. In *Economic Essays in Honour of Gustav Cassel*, London: George Allen & Unwin.

Knight, F.H. 1934. Capital, time, and the interest rate. *Economica*, NS 1, August, 257–86.

Knight, F.H. 1935. Professor Hayek and the theory of investment. *Economic Journal* 45, March, 75–94.

Knight, F.H. 1936. The quantity of capital and the rate of interest. *Journal of Political Economy* 44, August, 433–63, and October, 612–42.

Lauderdale, J. Maitland, 8th Earl of. 1804. *An Inquiry into the Nature and Origin of Public Wealth.* Edinburgh: Constable.

Longfield, M. 1834. *Lectures on Political Economy.* Dublin: Milliken.

Marshall, A. 1890. *Principles of Economics.* London: Macmillan.

Marx, K. 1867–94. *Das Kapital.* 3 vols, Hamburg: Meisner. Trans. as *Capital*, 3 vols, Chicago: Kerr, 1906–9.

Menger, C. 1888. Zur Theorie des Kapitals. *Jahrbücher für Nationalökonomie und Statistik*, NF 17(51), 1–49.

Mill, J. 1821. *Elements of Political Economy*. London: Baldwin, Cradock and Joy.

Mill, J.S. 1848. *Principles of Political Economy*. London: Longmans, Green.

Nuti, D.M. 1970. Capitalism, socialism, and steady growth. *Economic Journal* 80, March, 32–57.

Pareto, V. 1909. *Manuel d'conomie politique* Paris: Giard & Brière. Trans. as *Manual of Political Economy*, London: Macmillan, 1972.

Petty, W. 1662. *A Treatise of Taxes and Contributions*. London: Brooke. Reprinted in *The Economic Writings of Sir William Petty*, ed. C.H. Hull, Cambridge: Cambridge University Press, 1899, Vol. 1.

Pigou, A.C. 1935. Net income and capital depletion. *Economic Journal* 45, June, 235–41.

[Quesnay, F.] 1766a. (Premier) Dialogue entre Mr. H. et Mr. N. *Journal d'Agriculture, du Commerce et des Finances*, June, 61–109. Reprinted in *Physiocrates*, ed. E. Daire, Paris: Guillaumin, 1846.

[Quesnay, F.] 1766b. Observations sur l'intérêt de l'argent (par M. Niasque). *Journal d'Agriculture, du Commerce et des Finances*, June, 151–71.

Rae, J. 1834. *Statement of Some New Principles of the Subject of Political Economy*. Boston: Hilliard Gray & Co.

Ricardo, D. 1817. *On the Principles of Political Economy and Taxation*. London: Murray. In *The Works and Correspondence of David Ricardo*, ed. P. Sraffa, Cambridge: Cambridge University Press 1951, vol. 1.

Robinson, J. 1954. The production function and the theory of capital. *Review of Economic Studies* 21, 81–106. Reprinted in *Collected Economic Papers of Joan Robinson*, Vol. II, Oxford: Blackwell.

Robinson, J. 1956. *The Accumulation of Capital*. London: Macmillan.

Salin, E. 1930. Kapitalbegriff und Kapitallehre von der Antike zu den Physiokraten *Vierteljahrsschrift für Sozial- und Wirtschaftsgeschichte* 23, 401–40.

Samuelson, P.A. 1947. *Foundations of Economic Analysis*. Harvard Economic Studies 80, Cambridge, Mass.: Harvard University Press.

Samuelson, P.A. 1948. *Economics: An Introductory Analysis*. New York: McGraw Hill.

Say, J.B. 1814. *Traité d'économie politique*. 2nd edn, Paris: Deterville.

Schneider, E. 1934. *Theorie der Produktion*. Vienna: Springer.

Schumpeter, J.A. 1911. *Theorie der wirtschaftlichen Entwicklung*. Leipzig: Duncker & Humblot.

Senior, N.W. 1836. *(An Outline of the Science of) Political Economy*. London: Griffin.

Smith, A. 1776. *An Inquiry into the Nature and Causes of the Wealth of Nations*. London: Strahan and Cadell. Ed. R.H. Campbell and A.S. Skinner with W.B. Todd, *The Glasgow Edition of the Works and Correspondence of Adam Smith*, Vol. II, Oxford: Clarendon Press, 1976.

Sraffa, P. 1960. *Production of Commodities by Means of Commodities*. Cambridge: Cambridge University Press.

Stackelberg, H. von. 1932. *Grundlagen einer reinen Kostentheorie*. Vienna: Springer.

Stigler, G.J. 1941. *Production and Distribution Theories*. New York: Macmillan.

Strigl, R. von 1934. *Kapital und Produktion*. Vienna: Springer.

Swan, T.W. 1956. Economic growth and capital accumulation. *Economic Record* 32, 334–61.

Thünen, J.H. von 1850. *Der isolierte Staat*. Theil II, 1. Abteilung: *Der naturgemässe Arbeitslohn und dessen Verhältnis zum Zinsfuss und zur Landrente*. Rostock: Leopold. Trans. by B.W. Dempsey as *The Frontier Wage*, Chicago: Loyola University Press, 1960.

Turgot, A.R.J. 1770. Réflexions sur la formation et la distribution des richesses *Ephémérides du Citoyen*, November and December 1769, January 1770. Trans. as 'Reflections on the Formation and Distribution of Wealth' in *Turgot on Progress, Sociology and Economics*, ed. R.L. Meek, Cambridge: Cambridge University Press, 1973.

Uzawa, H. 1958. A note on the Menger–Wieser theory of imputation. *Zeitschrift für Nationalökonomie* 18, 318–34.

Viner, J. 1930. Cost curves and supply curves. *Zeitschrift für Nationalökonomie* 3, 23–46.

Walras, L. 1874–7. *Eléments d'économie politique pure*. Lausanne: Corbaz. Trans. as *Elements of Pure Economics*, London: George Allen 1954.

Wicksell, K. 1893. *Über Wert, Kapital und Rente*. Jena: Fischer. Trans. as *Value, Capital and Rent*, London: George Allen & Unwin, 1954.

Wicksell, K. 1901. *Föreläsningar i Nationalekonomi*, Första Delen: *Teoretisk Nationalekonomi*. Lund: Berlingska Boktryckeriet. Trans. as *Lectures on Political Economy*, Vol. 1: General Theory, London: Routledge, 1934.

Wicksteed, P.H. 1894. *An Essay on the Co-ordination of the Laws of Distribution*. London: Macmillan.

capital as a social relation. Taken by itself, a sharp stone is simply a relic of some ancient and inexorable geologic process. But appropriated as a cutting instrument, it is a tool or, in a somewhat more murderous vein, a weapon. As a stone, it is a natural object. But as a tool or weapon, it is an eminently social object whose natural form is merely the carrier of the social relations which, so to speak, happen to have seized upon it.

Even any particular social object, such as a tool, can enter into many different sets of social relations. For instance, whenever a loom is used to weave cloth, it is a part of the *means of production* of a cloth-making labour process. However, because any such labour activity is itself part of the social division of labour, its true content can only be grasped by analysing it as part of a greater whole. For instance, the cloth-making process may be part of the collective labour of a family or community, in which the cloth is intended for direct consumption. Alternately, the very same people may end up using the same type of loom, in a capitalist factory in which the whole purpose of the labour process is to produce a profit for the owners. In the case of cloth produced for direct use, it is properties such as quality and durability which directly concern the producers. But in the case of cloth produced in a capitalist factory, the salient property of the cloth is the *profit* it can generate. All other properties are then reduced to mere vehicles for profit, and as we know only too well, the packaging of the product can easily displace its actual usefulness. This at any rate establishes that even two labour processes which are technically identical can nonetheless have substantially different dynamics, precisely because they exist within very different social frameworks.

The above result also applies to the tools of the labour process. For instance, in both communal and capitalist production, the loom serves as means of production in a labour process. But only in the latter case does it also function as *capital*. That is to say, for its capitalist owners, the significance of the loom lies not in its character as means of production, but rather in its role as means towards profit; while for the workers labouring alongside it, the loom functions not as their own instrument but rather as a proper capitalist tool. Indeed, if we look more closely at the capitalist factory, we will see that not only the loom, but also money, yarn, and even the capacity to labour all serve at various points as particular incarnations of the owners' capital. This is because *capital is not a thing, but rather a definite set of social relations* which belong to a definite historical period in human development, and which give the things enmeshed within these relations their specific content as social objects. To understand Capital, one must therefore decipher its character as a social relation (Marx, 1894, ch. 48; Marx, 1867, Appendix, II–III).

CAPITAL AND CLASS. Human society is structured by complex networks of social relations within which people exist and reproduce. The reproduction of any given society in turn requires not only the reproduction of its people, but also of the things they need for their existence, and of the social relations which surround both people and things.

The things which people need for their daily existence form the material base of society. Although the specific character of these things, and even of the needs they satisfy, may vary according to time and circumstance, no society can exist for long without them. Moreover, in all but the most primitive of societies, the vast bulk of the necessary social objects must be produced through human labour. Production, and the social allocation of labour upon which it rests, thus emerge as absolutely fundamental aspects of social reproduction. But social labour involves acting on nature while interacting with other people, in-and-through specific social relations. Thus, the labour process ends up as crucial not only in the production of new wealth, but also in the reproduction of the social relations surrounding this production, as well as of any other social relations directly contingent upon them.

The preceding point assumes particular significance in the case of class societies. In effect, a class society is structured in such a way as to enable one set of people to live off the labour of the others. For this to be possible, the subordinate classes must not only be able to produce more than they themselves appropriate, they must also somehow be regularly induced to do so. In other words, they must be made to work longer than that required by their own needs, so that their surplus labour and corresponding surplus product can be used to support their rulers. Thus, the very existence of a ruling class is predicated on the *exploitation of labour*, and on the reproduction of the social and material conditions of this exploitation. Moreover, since any such process is a fundamentally antagonistic one, all class societies are marked by a simmering hostility between rulers and ruled, punctuated by periods of riots, rebellions, and revolutions. This is why class societies always rely heavily on ideology to motivate and rationalize the fundamental social cleavage upon which they rest, and on force to provide the necessary discipline when all else fails.

Capitalism is no different in this respect. It is a class society, in which the capitalist class exists by virtue of its ownership and control of the vast bulk of the society's means of production. The working class is in turn comprised of those who have been 'freed' of this self-same burden of property in means of production, and who must therefore earn their livelihood by selling their capacity to labour (labour power) to the capitalist class. As Marx so elegantly demonstrates, the *general social condition* for the regular sale of labour power is that the working class as a whole be induced to perform surplus labour, for it is this surplus labour which forms the basis of capitalist profit, and it is this profit which in turn keeps the capitalist class willing and able to re-employ workers. And as capitalism itself makes abundantly clear, the struggle among the classes about the conditions, terms and future of these relations has always been an integral part of its history (Marx, 1867, Part II and Appendix).

CAPITAL AS INDIVIDUAL VERSUS DOMINANT SOCIAL RELATION. In the preceding section we spoke about already constituted capitalist society. But no social form springs full blown into being. Instead, its constituent elements must either already exist within other societies, albeit in disassociated form, or else

they must arise and be nurtured within the structure of its direct predecessor. This distinction between elements and the whole is important because it allows us to differentiate between capital as an individual social relation, and capitalism as a social formation in which capital is the *dominant* social relation.

Capital as an individual social relation is concerned most of all with the making of profit. In its most general form, this means advancing a sum of money M in order to recoup a larger sum of money M'. The general *circuit of capital* is therefore always attended by the two poles M and M', and their span is always the overall measure of its success. Note that money functions here as a means of making money (i.e. as money-capital), rather than merely as a means of purchasing commodities to be consumed (i.e. as money-revenue). Marx draws many significant and powerful implications from the above functional difference between money-capital and money-revenue.

Even within the circuit of capital, there are three distinct routes possible between its two poles. First, money capital M may be advanced as a loan, in return for a subsequent repayment M' which covers both the original advance and an additional sum over and above it. This is the circuit $M-M'$ of financial capital, in which an initial sum of money appears to directly beget a greater sum, through the apparently magical device of interest. Second, money capital M may be utilized to buy commodities C, and these very same commodities may then be resold for more money M'. This is the circuit $M-C-C-M'$ of commercial capital, in which the double appearance of C as an intermediate term signifies that it is the same set of commodities which first exists as the object of purchase of the capitalist, and then later as their object of (re)sale. Here, it is the acumen of the capitalist in 'buying cheap and selling dear' which appears to generate the circuit's profit. Finally, money capital M may be advanced to purchase commodities C comprising means of production (materials, plant and equipment) and labour power, these latter elements set into motion as a production process P, and the resultant product C' then sold for (expanded) money capital M'. This is circuit $M-C...P...C'-M'$ of industrial capital, in which the characteristic intermediate term is that of the production process P. Now, it is the capitalist's ability to keep the productivity of labour ahead of the real wage which appears as the fount of all profit.

The most prevalent early incarnations of capital are those of usurer's capital $M-M'$ and merchant capital $M-C-C'-M'$. Both of these are virtually as old as money itself, and have existed over the millennia within many different civilizations. However, they almost always appear as parasitic relations, either within a particular host society or between two or more cultures. Often despised and occasionally feared, these individual activities were nonetheless generally tolerated as long as they conformed to the overall structure of the social formation within which they existed. It is only in feudal Europe, particularly in England, that these antediluvian forms of capital fused together with industrial capital to form the entirely new social formation that we call the capitalist mode of production. Only then, on the foundation of surplus labour extracted directly by itself and for itself, do we find capital as the dominant social relation and its individual forms as mere particular moments of the same overall process (Marx, 1858, p. 266 and 1867, Appendix).

GENERAL LAWS OF CAPITAL. The social dominance of capital gives rise to certain patterns which are characteristic of the capitalist mode of production.

We have already encountered the first of these, which is that the class relation between capital and labour is a fundamentally antagonistic one, marked by an intrinsic struggle over the conditions and terms of the extraction of surplus labour. Though ever present, this antagonism can sometimes erupt with a force and ferocity which can shake the very foundations of the system itself.

Second, capitalism as a form of social organization pits each element against the other in a generalized climate of conflict: capitalist against worker in the labour process, worker against worker in the competition for jobs, capitalist against capitalist in the battle for market position and sales, and nation against nation in the world market. Like the class struggle, these other conflicts also periodically erupt into acute and open combat between the participants, whether it be the battles of strikers against scabs, or capitalists against their rivals, or even of world wars between one set of capitalist nations and another. It is precisely this real conflict which the bourgeois notion of 'perfect competition' is designed to conceal (Shaikh, 1982).

Thirdly, the relations among people are mediated by relations among things. This stems from the very nature of capitalist production itself, in which individual labours are undertaken solely with the aim of making a profit on their product. The various individual labours are thus articulated into a social division of labour only under the 'objectified husk' of their products. It is the products which therefore step to the fore, and the producers who follow behind. From this derives the famous Fetishism of Commodity Relations, i.e. exchangeability appears to be a natural property of all objects, rather than a historically specific way of evaluating the social content of the labour which produced them.

The fourth point follows directly from the third. As noted above, under capitalist relations of production individual labour processes are undertaken in the hope of private gain, with no prior consideration of a social division of labour. But any ensemble of such labours can survive only if they happen to collectively reproduce both the material and social basis of their existence: capitalist society, like all society, requires a particular pattern of labour in order to reproduce its general structure. Thus, under capitalist production, the various individual labours end up being *forcibly articulated into a moving social division of labour*, through a process of trial-through-error, of overshooting and undershooting, of discrepancy, disruption and even occasional ruptures in the process of reproduction. This pattern of apparent anarchy regulated by inner laws of motion is the characteristic form of capitalist reproduction. Notice how different this concept is from that of general equilibrium, where the whole process is reduced to one of immediate and perfect stasis.

The fifth point stems from the fact that capitalist production is driven by profit. Each capitalist is compelled to try and widen the gap between the initial advance M and the final return M'; those who are most successful prosper and grow, those who fall behind soon face the spectre of extinction. Within the labour process, this shows up in the tendency to stretch the length and intensity of the working day to its social limits, while at the same time constantly seeking to reshape the labour process along lines which are ever more 'rational' from the point of view of capital. This compulsion is directly responsible for capitalism's historically revolutionary role in raising the productivity of labour to new heights. And it is the associated capitalist rationality which is most perfectly expressed in the routinization of production, in the reduction of human activities to repetitive and automatic operations, and in the eventual replacement of the now machine-like human labour by actual machines. As Marx notes, the so-called Industrial Revolution is merely the signal, not the cause, of the advent of capitalist relations of production. And whereas earlier the tool was an instrument of labour, now it is the worker who is an instrument of the machine (Marx, 1867, Parts III–IV).

THE CONCEPTION OF CAPITAL WITHIN ORTHODOX ECONOMICS. Within orthodox economics, the term 'capital' generally refers to the means of production. Thus capital, along with labour, is said to exist in every society. From this point of view, social forms are to be distinguished from one another by the manner in which they 'bring together' the factors of production, the capital and labour, at their respective disposals. Capitalism is then defined as a system which utilizes the market to accomplish this task, in the context of the private ownership of the means of production (Alchian and Allen, 1983, chs 1 and 8).

By treating human labouring activity as a factor of production on a par with raw materials and tools, *hence as a thing*, orthodox economics succeeds in reducing the labour process to a technical relation between so-called inputs and outputs (e.g. a production function). All struggles over the terms and condition of labour thereby disappear from view.

Moreover, once labour is defined as a factor of production, every (able-bodied) individual is an owner of at least one factor. Of course, some may be fortunate enough to also own large quantities of capital. But that is a mere detail of the distribution of 'initial endowments', and on such things orthodox economics remains studiously neutral. What matters instead is that under capitalism the notion that everybody owns a factor of production bespeaks of an inherent equality among individuals. Any reference to the concept of class is therefore blocked from the start.

Next, because labour is merely one of the factors of production which individuals are free to utilize in any manner they choose, this labour-as-thing cannot be said to be exploited. The exploitation of labour thus drops out of sight, to be replaced by the notion of the cooperation of Capital and Labour, each of which contributes its component to the product and receives in turn its commensurate reward (as in marginal productivity theories of distribution). With this, the sanctification of capitalism is complete.

THE HISTORICAL LIMITS OF CAPITAL AS A SOCIAL RELATION. The last general point has to do with the historical specificity of capitalist production. On the one hand, capitalism is a powerful and highly flexible social structure. It has developed its forces of production to extraordinary heights, and has proved itself capable of dissolving or destroying all previous social forms. Its inherently expansive nature has led to the creation of vast quantities of wealth, and to a dominion which extends all over the globe. But on the other hand, this very same progressive aspect feeds off a dark and enormously destructive side whose nature becomes particularly clear when viewed on a world scale. The capital-labour relation is a profoundly unequal one, and the concentration and centralization of capital which attends capitalist development only deepens the inequality. The competitive struggle of all against all creates an alienated and selfish social character, imprisons each in an atmosphere of suspicion and stress, and heaps its miseries precisely on those who are in the weakest positions. Finally, as capitalism develops, so too does its level of mechanization, so that it is progressively less able to absorb labour. In the developed capitalist countries, this manifests itself as a growing mass of unemployed people at any given 'natural' rate of unemployment. In the Third World, as the incursion of capitalist relations lays waste to earlier social forms, the mechanized processes which replace them are able to pick up only a fraction of the huge numbers previously 'set free'. Thus the rising productivity of capitalist production is accompanied by a growing pool of redundant labour all across the globe. The presence of starving masses in the Third World, as well as of floating populations of unemployed in the developed capitalist world, are bitter reminders of these inherent tendencies.

The above perspective forcibly reminds us that capitalism is only one particular historical form of social organization, subject to deep contradictions which are inherent in the very structure of its being. Precisely because these contradictions are built-in, any successful struggle against their destructive effects must move beyond reform to the rejection of the structure itself. In the 20th century such efforts have taken a variety of forms, ranging from so-called parliamentary socialism to socialist revolution. Whatever we may think of the strengths and weaknesses of these various fledgling social movements, the general tendency is itself part of an age-old human process. History teaches us that no social form lasts forever, and capital as a social relation is no exception to this rule.

ANWAR SHAIKH

See also CLASS.

BIBLIOGRAPHY
Alchian, A.A. and Allen, W.A. 1983. *Exchange and Production: Competition, Coordination, and Control.* 3rd edn, Belmont, California: Wadsworth Publishing Co.
Mandel, E. 1976. Introduction to Vol. I of *Capital* by K. Marx (1867), London: Penguin.
Marx, K. 1858. *Grundrisse.* London: Penguin, 1973.
Marx, K. 1867. *Capital*, Vol I. London: Penguin, 1976.
Marx, K. 1894. *Capital*, Vol III. Introduced by Ernest Mandel, New York: Vintage, 1981.
Rosdolsky, R. 1977. *The Making of Marx's Capital.* London: Pluto Press.
Shaikh, A. 1982. Neo-Ricardian economics: a wealth of algebra, a poverty of theory. *Review of Radical Political Economics* 14(2), Summer, 67-83.

capital asset pricing model. Two general approaches to the problem of valuing assets under uncertainty may be distinguished. The first approach relies on arbitrage arguments of one kind or another, while under the second approach equilibrium asset prices are obtained by equating endogenously determined asset demands to asset supplies, which are typically taken as exogenous. Examples of the former range from the static arbitrage arguments which underlie the Modigliani–Miller theorem to the dynamic arbitrage strategies which are the basis for the Option Pricing Model: such arbitrage based models can only yield the price of one asset relative to the prices of other assets. The Capital Asset Pricing Model (CAPM) is an example of an equilibrium model in which asset prices are related to the exogenous data, the tastes and endowments of investors although, as we shall see below, the CAPM is often presented as a relative pricing model.

If they are to be of practical use, equilibrium asset pricing models must be parsimonious in their parameterization of asset demands. To date this parsimony has been achieved only by a choice of assumptions which leads to universal portfolio separation: this is the property that the asset demand vector of every agent can be expressed as a linear combination of a set of basis vectors which may be thought of as portfolios or mutual funds. The distinguishing feature of the set of models

which is collectively known as the CAPM is that each of these basis portfolios can be interpreted as the solution to a particular constrained portfolio variance minimization problem.

HISTORICAL PERSPECTIVE

The assumption that uncertainty about future asset returns can be described in terms of a probability distribution is at least as old as Irving Fisher (1906), although Hicks (1934b) appears to have been the first to suggest that preferences for investments could be represented as preferences for the moments of the probability distributions of their returns, and to propose that, as a first approximation, preferences could be represented by indifference curves in mean-variance space. Other writers such as J. Marschak (1938) adopted a similar view, but it remained for von Neumann and Morgenstern (1947) to place the theory of choice under uncertainty on a rigorous axiomatic basis, and their expected utility theory is now an essential element of the financial economics paradigm.

The story of modern portfolio theory really begins, however, with the classic contributions of Markowitz (1952, 1958) who assumed explicitly that investor preferences were defined over the mean and variance of the aggregate portfolio return, related these parameters to the portfolio composition and the parameters of the joint distribution of security returns, and for the first time applied the principles of marginal analysis to the choice of optimal portfolios.

Both Markowitz and Tobin (1958) showed that mean-variance preferences could be reconciled with the von Neumann/Morgenstern axioms if the utility function is quadratic in return or wealth. This assumption is objectionable since it implies negative marginal utility at high wealth levels. Tobin also showed, however, that mean-variance preferences could be derived by restricting the probability distributions over which choices are made to a two parameter family. After some initial confusion it was recognized that since portfolio returns are weighted sums of security returns, the two parameter family must be stable under addition, and the only member of the stable class with a finite variance is in the normal distribution. Subsequently Merton (1969) and Samuelson (1970) showed that mean-variance analysis is applicable for a broad class of continuous asset price processes if the trading interval is infinitesimal.

The major part of Tobin's analysis deals with the choice between a single risky asset and cash, but he demonstrated that nothing essential is changed if there are many risky assets, for they will always be held in the same proportions and can be treated as a single composite asset. This, the first separation theorem in portfolio theory, is illustrated in Figure 1 which plots mean returns, μ, against the standard deviation, σ. In this figure the curved locus $AMOVB$ corresponds to the set of portfolios offering the lowest standard deviation for each level of mean return: the positively sloped segment is referred to as the efficient frontier, for points along it offer the highest μ for a given σ. In the absence of any riskless investment opportunities, risk averse mean-variance investors will select portfolios corresponding to the points at which their indifference curves in (μ, σ) space are tangent to the efficient frontier (Tobin shows that the indifference curves of risk averters will have the requisite curvature). Point C represents cash which has zero risk and return. By combining cash with the portfolio of risky assets corresponding to the tangency portfolio O, investors are able to attain the (μ, σ) combinations along the line segment CO, and all investors who find it optimal to hold cash will find it optimal to combine their cash with the same risky portfolio O: their portfolio decisions can be *separated* into the choice of the

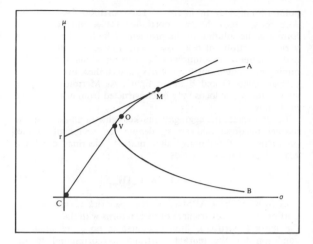

Figure 1 The efficient frontier and the CAPM.

optimal combination of risky asset (O) and the choice of the cash/risky asset ratio.

Six years elapsed before the equilibrium implications of the Tobin Separation Theorem were exploited by Sharpe (1964) and Lintner (1965). The reason for delay was undoubtedly the boldness of the assumption required for progress, namely that all investors hold the same beliefs about the joint distribution of security returns. Nevertheless, this assumption of homogeneous beliefs, combined with the further assumption that all investors can borrow as well as lend at the riskless rate, r, leads to the powerful conclusion that all investors hold the same portfolio of risky assets, denoted by M in the figure. Then the only risky assets that will be held by investors in equilibrium are those contained in portfolio M, and M must be the market portfolio of all risky assets in the economy. This identification of the tangency portfolio M with the aggregate market portfolio is the essence of the Sharpe–Lintner CAPM.

The interest of this result derives from the restriction that it imposes on expected asset returns: the excess of μ_j, the expected return on any security j, over the risk free rate r, must be proportional to the covariance of the security return with the return on the market portfolio, σ_{jM}:

$$\mu_j - r = \theta_M \sigma_{jM} \qquad \text{for all } j \tag{1}$$

where θ_M is a measure of aggregate risk aversion. The intuition behind this important result is that if investors are content to hold portfolio M, the marginal rate of transformation between risk and return obtained by borrowing to invest in a risky security must be the same for all risky securities. Frequently the unknown risk aversion parameter, θ_M, is eliminated and the relative pricing result is obtained:

$$\mu_j - r = \beta_j(\mu_M - r) \qquad \text{for all } j \tag{2}$$

where μ_M is the expected return on the market portfolio and $\beta_j \equiv \sigma_{jM}/\sigma_{MM}$ is the 'beta' coefficient, which corresponds to the slope of the regression line relating the return on the security to the return on the market portfolio.

During the first half of the 1970s extensive progress was made in relaxing the strong assumptions underlying the original

model, and new separation theorems and models were obtained. At the same time, extensive empirical investigations made possible by the development of new stock price data bases found results which were interpreted as favourable to the model. The model also has an influence on practical investment management and corporate finance.

A turning point was reached with the publication of a paper by Roll (1977); this argued that the market portfolio of the theory, which includes all assets, could never be empirically identified, and that therefore the CAPM, which simply asserts the efficiency properties of this portfolio, could never be empirically tested. This argument had substantial influence, and played a major role in shifting attention away from the CAPM to the newly emerging Arbitrage Pricing Theory of Ross (1976).

The CAPM is of great historical significance not only because it was the first equilibrium model of asset pricing under uncertainty, but also because it showed the importance of portfolio separation for tractable equilibrium models; and, being derivable from assumptions of either quadratic utility or normal distributions, it revealed that the requisite separation properties could be obtained by restrictions either on preferences or on distributions. Cass and Stiglitz (1970) clarified the rather restrictive assumptions necessary for preference based separation, and equilibrium models based on this have been constructed, for example, by Rubinstein (1976). Ross (1978) has identified the distributional assumptions required for separation in the absence of restrictions on preferences, and the Arbitrage Pricing Theory is based on a generalization of his 'Separating Distributions'. Thus both preference-based and distribution-based models of capital market equilibrium are lineal descendants of the CAPM.

An unfortunate consequence of the one period nature of the CAPM was a concentration of attention on equilibrium rates of return, rather than on prices, which are the fundamental variables of interest. However, Merton (1973) placed the CAPM in an intertemporal context, and his necessary condition for equilibrium rates of return forms one cornerstone (the other being an assumption of rational expectations) for the Cox, Ingersoll and Ross (1985) partial differential equation for asset prices.

FORMAL MODELS

While a complete asset pricing model endogenizes the riskless interest rate as well as the prices of risky securities, the CAPM adds nothing new to the theory of interest rate determination and we shall simplify by taking the interest rate and current consumption decisions as given, concentrating our attention on portfolio decisions and the pricing of risky securities.

In considering the various versions of the CAPM we shall pay particular attention to the implied demands of investors. It will be seen that in all cases in which risks are freely traded asset demands exhibit the separation property, and even when there are restrictions on trading as in the Mayers (1972) asset pricing model, an approximate separation property obtains.

The Sharpe–Lintner Model. Consider a setting in which each investor $i(i = 1, \ldots, m)$ is endowed with a fraction $\bar{z}_{ij}$ of security $j(j = 1, \ldots, n)$ and (a) investor utility is defined over the mean and variance of end of period wealth; (b) securities are traded in a competitive market with no taxes or transactions costs; (c) investors share homogeneous beliefs or assessments of the joint distribution of payoffs on the securities; there are no dividends; (d) there is an exogenously determined interest rate $r = R - 1$ at which investors may borrow or lend without default; (e) there are no restrictions on short sales.

Then define:

$\bar{P}_{j1}$ expected end of period value of security j;
$\bar{P}_{j0}$ initial value of security j;
ω_{jk} covariance between end of period value of j and k;
$\bar{W}_i, S_i^2$ expectation and variance of end of period wealth of investor i;
$V_i(\bar{W}_i, S_i^2)$ utility of investor i with $V_{i1} \equiv \partial V_i / \partial \bar{W}_i > 0$, $V_{i2} \equiv \partial V_i / \partial S_i^2 < 0$.

The investor's decision problem may be written as

$$\max_{z_{ij}} V_i(\bar{W}_i, S_i^2) \tag{3}$$

$$\text{s.t.} \quad \bar{W}_i = \sum_j z_{ij} \bar{P}_{j1} - R \sum_j (z_{ij} - \bar{z}_{ij}) P_{j0} \tag{4}$$

$$S_i^2 = \sum_j \sum_k z_{ij} z_{ik} \omega_{jk}. \tag{5}$$

The first order conditions for an optimum are

$$V_{i1}(\bar{P}_{j1} - RP_{j0}) + 2V_{i2} \sum_k z_{ik} \omega_{jk} = 0, \quad (j = 1, \ldots, n) \tag{6}$$

and the second conditions are satisfied by virtue of the assumption of risk aversion. Defining Ω^* as the variance covariance matrix $[\omega_{jk}]$ and using boldface type to denote vectors, the vector of fractional asset demands may be written

$$\mathbf{z}_i = \theta_i^{-1} \Omega^{*-1} (\bar{\mathbf{P}}_1 - R\mathbf{P}_0) \tag{7}$$

where $\theta_i^{-1} \equiv -V_{i1}/2V_{i2}$ is a measure of the investor's risk tolerance. Equation (7) is a statement of the Tobin Separation Theorem, that investor demands for risky assets differ only by a scalar multiple.

Market clearing requires that $\Sigma_i \mathbf{z}_i = \mathbf{1}$ where $\mathbf{1}$ is a vector of units. Then the equilibrium initial price vector is obtained by summing (7) over i and imposing the market clearing condition:

$$\mathbf{P}_0 = \frac{1}{R} \{\bar{\mathbf{P}}_1 - \theta_m \Omega^* \mathbf{1}\} \tag{8}$$

where $\theta_m \equiv (\Sigma_i \theta_i^{-1})^{-1}$. In this form the CAPM expresses equilibrium asset prices in terms of the exogenous variables, the distribution of end of period prices, investor risk aversion parameters and the interest rate, although it should be noted that in general the market risk aversion parameter θ_m will depend upon the endogenously determined distribution of wealth. This formulation corresponds to that of Lintner (1965) and emphasizes the one period nature of the model and the exogeneity of the end of period prices. However, the CAPM is most often written as a necessary condition for the equilibrium rates of return, although this obscures the distinction between endogenous and exogenous variables.

In what follows we shall work with the rate of return formulation; thus define $x_{ij} \equiv z_{ij} P_{j0}$, the amount invested in security j; $\mu_j \equiv \bar{P}_{j1}/P_{j0} - 1$, the expected rate of return and $\sigma_{jk} \equiv \omega_{jk}/P_{j0}P_{k0}$, the covariance of the rates of return between securities j and k. Making these substitutions in (4) and (5), the first order conditions (6) become

$$V_{i1}(\mu_j - r) + 2V_{i2} \sum_k x_{ik} \sigma_{jk} = 0, \quad (j = 1, \ldots, n). \tag{9}$$

Then, defining Ω as the variance covariance matrix of rates of return, the vector of asset demands $\mathbf{x}_i$ may be expressed as

$$\mathbf{x}_i = \theta_i^{-1} \Omega^{-1}(\boldsymbol{\mu} - r\mathbf{1}) \tag{10}$$

This is an alternative statement of the Tobin Separation Theorem and the portfolio $\Omega^{-1}(\boldsymbol{\mu} - r\mathbf{1}) \square$ corresponds to the

point of tangency in figure 1. This portfolio itself may be decomposed into the two portfolios $\Omega^{-1}\boldsymbol{\mu}$ and $\Omega^{-1}\mathbf{1}$. The former is the solution to the problem of finding the minimum variance portfolio of risky assets with a given expected payoff, and the latter is the solution to the problem of finding the global minimum variance portfolio of risky assets; these two portfolios plot at points O and V in the figure. As Merton (1972) has shown, the whole locus may be constructed from just these two portfolios.

Let V_m denote the aggregate market value of all assets in the market portfolio and let $\mathbf{v_m}$ denote the vector of market proportions. Combining the market clearing condition $\Sigma_i \mathbf{x}_i = V_m \mathbf{v_m}$ with (10) yields

$$\boldsymbol{\mu} - r\mathbf{1} = \theta_m V_m \Omega \mathbf{v_m} \tag{11}$$

This form of the CAPM expresses asset risk premia as proportional to the covariances of their returns with the returns on the market portfolio; this of course is no more than the condition for the market portfolio to correspond to the tangency point in figure 1. Equation (11) contains the market risk aversion parameter θ_m. This can be eliminated by premultiplying (11) by $\mathbf{v_m}$ and solving for $\theta_m = (\mu_m - r)/\sigma_m^2$, where μ_m and σ_m^2 are the expected return and variance of return on the market portfolio respectively. Then, substituting for θ_m in (11) we have the equation of the 'security market line':

$$\mu_j - r = \beta_j(\mu_m - r) \tag{12}$$

where $\beta_j \equiv \sigma_{jm}/\sigma_m^2$. In this form the CAPM is a relative pricing model which relates the risk premium on individual securities to the risk premium on the market portfolio. The proportionality factor, β_j, often referred to as the 'beta coefficient', is the coefficient from the regression of $\tilde{R}_j$, the return on security j, on $\tilde{R}_m$, the return on the market portfolio:

$$\tilde{R}_j = \alpha_j + \beta_j \tilde{R}_m + \tilde{e}_j \tag{13}$$

where $\tilde{e}_j$ is an orthogonal error term. Taking expectations in the market model equation (13), the asset pricing equation (12) is seen to imply the restriction $\alpha_j = (1 - \beta_j) r$. This restriction, and the existence of a positive risk premium on the market portfolio, are the major empirical predictions of the Sharpe–Lintner model. They have been the subject of extensive empirical tests.

Taxes and restrictions on riskless transactions. The absence of short sales restrictions is not critical to the Sharpe–Lintner model, since in equilibrium all investors hold the market portfolio, which does not involve short sales. The assumption is critical, however, for all the remaining models we shall consider which involve more than a single basis fund of risky securities.

Thus, following Black (1972) and Brennan (1970), assume that there are no opportunities for riskless borrowing or lending, and that each security pays pre-determined dividends which are taxed in the hands of the investor at the rate $t_i (i = 1, \ldots, m)$. Denoting the dividend yield by δ_j, and assuming that investor preferences are defined over the moments of after tax wealth, the first order conditions corresponding to (9) are:

$$V_{i1}(\mu_j - t_i \delta_j - \lambda_i) + 2V_{i2} \sum_k x_{ik} \sigma_{jk} = 0, \quad (j = 1, \ldots, n). \tag{14}$$

where λ_i is the Lagrange multiplier associated with the constraint that all wealth be invested in risky securities. The vector of asset demands may be written as:

$$\mathbf{x}_i = \theta_i^{-1}\mathbf{\Omega}^{-1}\boldsymbol{\mu} - (\theta_1^{-1}\lambda_1)\mathbf{\Omega}^{-1}\mathbf{1} - (\theta_1^{-1}\mathbf{t}_1)\mathbf{\Omega}^{-1}\delta \quad (15)$$

Note first that if $t_i = 0$ the optimal portfolio for any preferences can be constructed from the two mutual funds $\mathbf{\Omega}^{-1}\boldsymbol{\mu}$ and $\mathbf{\Omega}^{-1}\mathbf{1}$. Heterogeneous taxation of dividends introduces the third mutual fund, which can be interpreted as the solution to the problem of finding the minimum variance portfolio with a given total dividend. Aggregating the demand vectors, and imposing the market clearing conditions, yields an asset pricing equation which contains three utility dependent parameters, λ_m, θ_m, and t_m, corresponding to the three funds in (15):

$$\boldsymbol{\mu} - \lambda_m\mathbf{1} = \theta_m V_m\mathbf{\Omega}\mathbf{v_m} + \mathbf{t_m}\delta \quad (16)$$

t_m, the market tax rate, is a weighted average of the personal tax rates, and λ_m, the market shadow interest rate, is referred to for historical reasons as the zero beta return. When $t_m = 0$ (16) is just the condition for the market portfolio to be the tangency portfolio when the interest rate is λ_m. Thus the Black model, which does not include taxes, differs from the Sharpe–Lintner model only in leaving unspecified the relevant (shadow) riskless interest rate.

Non-marketable assets. Mayers (1972) has considered the effect of introducing an extreme form of market imperfection, namely an absolute prohibition on trading certain assets. This is important, for a substantial part of total wealth is not held as part of well diversified portfolios, on account either of prohibitions on trade (human capital), or of market imperfections such as transactions costs and information asymmetrics. Thus let $\bar{h}_i$ denote the expected payoff on the non-marketable wealth (human capital) or investor i, and let σ_{jh}^i denote the covariance between the return on marketable security j and the human capital of investor i. Then the expression for $\bar{W}_i$ must be increased by $\bar{h}_i$ and the variance of end of period wealth becomes $S_i^2 = \Sigma_j\Sigma_k x_{ij}x_{ik}\sigma_{jk} + 2\Sigma_j x_{ij}\sigma_{jh}^i + \sigma_{hh}^i$. The asset demand vector can then be written as

$$\mathbf{x}_1 = \theta_i^{-1}\mathbf{\Omega}^{-1}(\boldsymbol{\mu} - r\mathbf{1}) - \mathbf{b_i} \quad (17)$$

where $\mathbf{b_i} = \mathbf{\Omega}^{-1}\sigma_n^i$ is the vector of coefficients from the regression of the return on human wealth on the marketable security returns. Defining $\mathbf{x}_i^e \equiv \mathbf{x}_i + \mathbf{b_i}$ as the vector of effective asset demands, we see from (17) that effective asset demands exhibit the standard separation property. This reflects the fact that, while the returns on human capital are not directly marketable, the component of the return which is linearly related to the returns on the marketable securties is indirectly marketable by appropriate offsetting positions in the marketable securities. The asset holdings of the individual may be represented as the sum of effective asset holdings $\mathbf{x}_i^e$ and an investment in the component of human wealth whose return is orthogonal to the returns on marketable assets. We refer to this as approximate portfolio separation since the first component exhibits portfolio separation, and the second component has no effect on the relative demands for marketable assets.

The Mayers model leads to an asset pricing equation which is identical to that of the Sharpe–Lintner model if the market portfolio is defined as the sum of the effective investment vectors $\mathbf{x}_i^e$.

Inflation and international asset pricing. Stochastic inflation has no effect on the foregoing results, provided that a common inflation rate can be defined for all investors and returns are restated in real terms. However, the international asset pricing models of Solnik (1974) and Stulz (1981) distinguish between nationalities precisely on the basis of their price indices, which may differ on account of either a violation of commodity price parity or differences in tastes and consumption baskets (see Adler and Dumas, 1983).

Define $\tilde{\pi}_i$ as the inflation rate in the numeraire currency for investor i. Then, to a high order of approximation, which becomes exact as the time interval approaches zero, the mean and variance of real wealth can be written as

$$\bar{W}_i = \sum_j x_{ij}(\mu_j - r) + W_{0i}(1 + r - \tilde{\pi}_i + \sigma_{\pi\pi}^i) - \sum_j x_{ij}\sigma_{j\pi}^i \quad (18)$$

$$S_i^2 = \sum_j\sum_k x_{ij}x_{ik}\sigma_{jk} - 2W_{0i}\sum_j x_{ij}\sigma_{k\pi}^i + W_{0i}^2\sigma_{\pi\pi}^i \quad (19)$$

where W_{0i} is the investor's initial wealth.

The asset demand vector is then

$$x_i = \theta_i^{-1}\mathbf{\Omega}^{-1}(\boldsymbol{\mu} - r\mathbf{1}) + \mathbf{b}_i \quad (20)$$

where $\mathbf{b}_i \equiv W_{0i}\mathbf{\Omega}^{-1}\sigma_x^i$ is the vector of coefficients from the regression at the individual's aggregate inflation risk, $W_{0i}\tilde{\pi}_i$, on security returns. Comparing (20) with (17), it is apparent that this international asset pricing model is isomorphic to the Mayers' non-marketable wealth model with individual inflation risks playing the same role as human capital.

Black (1974) has modelled segmentation in international capital markets by introducing a tax on foreign security holdings for residents of one country. This model is isomorphic to Brennan's (1970) tax model, if the foreign securities are thought of as paying dividends on which only domestic residents are taxable. Stulz (1981) extends Black's model by prohibiting negative taxes on short sales: as one might expect, this causes some indeterminacy in the pricing relations since the marginal conditions of portfolio optimality are no longer always satisfied.

Intertemporal models. Merton (1973) has shown that the classical one period CAPM may be extended to intertemporal setting in which investors maximize the expected utility of lifetime consumption. With continuous trading and suitable restrictions on the stochastic process of asset prices, the essential mean-variance analysis is retained, the major innovation being that at each instant the individual may be represented as maximizing the expected utility of a derived utility function, defined over wealth and a set of S state variables describing the future investment and consumption opportunity sets. The state dependent derived utility function induces $(S + 1)$ fund separation in the risky asset portfolio, and the vector of risky asset demands may be written

$$\mathbf{x}_1 = \theta_1^{-1}\mathbf{\Omega}^{-1}(\boldsymbol{\mu} - r\mathbf{1}) - \sum_{s=1}^{s}\gamma_{is}\mathbf{\Omega}^{-1}\boldsymbol{\xi}_s \quad (21)$$

where ξ_s is the vector of covariances of asset returns with the change in state variable S and γ_{is} depends on the utility function. Aggregation of asset demands and the imposition of the market clearing condition leads to an asset pricing equation in which asset risk premia are a linear function of covariances with aggregate wealth *and* covariances with the state variables. In the absence of prior information about the relevant state variables this model is empirically indistinguishable from the Arbitrage Pricing Theory. Breeden (1979) has shown that this 'multi-beta' pricing model may be collapsed to a single beta measured with respect to changes in aggregate consumption if consumption preferences are time separable. Cornell (1981) has shown that unfortunately the relevant betas will be stochastic and Bergman (1985) has shown that the Breeden result does not generalize to non time-separable preferences.

Merton (1973) has employed the interest rate as a possible example of a relevant state variable. Since this obviously does vary stochastically over time it is of interest to enquire under what conditions the classic CAPM model will hold even with a stochastic interest rate. Constantinides (1980, 1982) has identified two sets of sufficient conditions. In his models the social investment opportunity set is stationary and consists only of risky investments: stochastic variation in the interest rate then does not affect the CAPM relation if either there is demand aggregation or full Pareto efficiency of asset markets. The intuition behind the result is that either condition is sufficient for prices to be determined as though there existed a single representative individual; for such an individual stochastic variation in the interest rate is irrelevant since the interest rate only represents a shadow price and not a real investment opportunity.

Finally, the single period nature of the CAPM is retained if individuals behave myopically, ignoring stochastic variation in the investment opportunity set in their portfolio choices: this occurs if and only if the utility function is logarithmic.

The foregoing models place restrictions on the joint distribution of security terms. As already mentioned, Cox, Ingersoll and Ross (1985) combine the Merton intertemporal model of returns with production and the assumption of rational expectations to yield a partial differential equation for asset prices. Stapleton and Subrahmanyam (1978) derive the only pure exchange discrete time intertemporal asset pricing model which is consistent with mean variance analysis. Their model assumes that investors have exponential utility functions and that asset cash flows follow a joint normal distribution; it is implicitly assumed that aggregate consumption follows a random walk.

Distributional assumptions. Comparatively little effort has been expended in relaxing the assumption of homogeneity of investor beliefs underlying the CAPM. However, progress has been made in generalizing the version of the model which is based on the normal distribution. As we have mentioned, Merton (1973) has shown that the model obtains as the decision making horizon shrinks to zero if asset returns belong to the family of *compact distributions*.

In a discrete time setting Ross (1978) has shown that the assumption of normality can be relaxed slightly to that of a two fund separating distribution. Dybvig and Ingersoll (1982) emphasize the critical nature of the distributional assumption since the CAPM result for all securities is vulnerable to the introduction of even a single security whose returns do not satisfy it. This would significantly reduce the usefulness of the model in capital markets which contain securities like options with truncated returns, except that if the market is fully Pareto efficient and return on the market portfolio is normally distributed, then those assets whose returns are jointly normal with the market portfolio will satisfy the CAPM. The reason for this is that Pareto efficiency permits the fiction of the representative investor who holds the market portfolio.

Sharpe (1977), in positing a factor model of returns, derived a multibeta version of the CAPM which is close in spirit to the equilibrium factor models developed more recently from antecedents in the Arbitrage Pricing Theory by Connor (1984) and others.

M. J. BRENNAN

See also FINANCE.

BIBLIOGRAPHY

Adler, M. and Dumas, B. 1983. International portfolio choice and corporation finance: a synthesis. *Journal of Finance* 38(3), June, 925–84.

Bergman, Y. 1985. Time preference and capital asset pricing models. *Journal of Financial Economics* 14(1), March, 145–59.

Black, F. 1972. Capital market equilibrium with restricted borrowing. *Journal of Business* 45(3), July, 444–55.

Black, F. 1974. International capital market equilibrium with investment barriers. *Journal of Financial Economics* 1(4), December, 337–52.

Breeden, D. 1979. An intertemporal asset pricing model with stochastic consumption and investment opportunities. *Journal of Financial Economics* 7(3), September, 265–96.

Brennan, M. 1970. Taxes, market valuation and corporate financial policy. *National Tax Journal* 23(4), December, 417–27.

Cass, D. and Stiglitz, J. 1970. The structure of investor preferences and asset returns, and separability in portfolio allocation: a contribution to the pure theory of mutual funds. *Journal of Economic Theory* 2(2), June, 122–60.

Connor, G. 1984. A unified beta pricing theory. *Journal of Economic Theory* 34(1), 13–31.

Constantinides, G. 1980. Admissible uncertainty in the intertemporal asset pricing model. *Journal of Financial Economics* 8(1), March, 71–86.

Constantinides, G. 1982. Intertemporal asset pricing with heterogeneous consumers and without demand aggregation. *Journal of Business* 55(2), April, 253–67.

Cornell, B. 1981. The consumption based asset pricing model: a note on potential tests and applications. *Journal of Financial Economics* 9(1), March, 103–8.

Cox, J., Ingersoll, J. and Ross, S. 1985. An intertemporal general equilibrium model of asset prices. *Econometrica* 53(2), March, 363–84.

Dybvig, P. and Ingersoll, J. 1982. Mean-variance theory in complete markets. *Journal of Business* 55(2), April, 233–51.

Fisher, I. 1906. *The Nature of Capital and Income.* New York: Macmillan.

Hicks, J.R. 1934a. A note on the elasticity of supply. *Review of Economic Studies* 2, October, 31–7.

Hicks, J.R. 1934b. Application of mathematical methods to the theory of risk. *Econometrica* 2, April, 194–5.

Lintner, J. 1965. The valuation of risk assets and the selection of risky investments in stock portfolios and capital budgets. *Review of Economics and Statistics* 47, February, 13–37.

Markowitz, H. 1952. Portfolio selection. *Journal of Finance* 7, March, 77–91.

Markowitz, H. 1958. *Portfolio Selection: Efficient Diversification of Investments.* New York: Wiley.

Marschak, J. 1938. Money and the theory of assets. *Econometrica* 6, October, 311–25.

Mayers, D. 1972. Non-marketable assets and capital market equilibrium under uncertainty. In *Studies in the Theory of Capital Markets,* ed. M. Jensen, New York: Praeger.

Merton, R. 1969. Lifetime portfolio selection under uncertainty: the continuous-time case. *Review of Economics and Statistics* 51(3), August, 247–57.

Merton, R. 1972. An analytic derivation of the efficient portfolio frontier. *Journal of Financial and Quantitative Analysis* 7(4), September, 1851–72.

Merton, R. 1973. An intertemporal capital asset pricing model. *Econometrica* 41, September, 867–87.

Roll, R. 1977. A critique of the asset pricing theory's test; Part I: On past and potential testability of the theory. *Journal of Financial Economics* 4(2), March, 129–76.

Ross, S. 1976. The arbitrage theory of capital asset pricing. *Journal of Economic Theory* 13(3), December, 341–60.

Ross, S. 1978. Mutual fund separation in financial theory: The separating distributions. *Journal of Economic Theory* 17(2), April, 254–86.

Rubinstein, M. 1976. The valuation of uncertain income streams and the pricing of options. *Bell Journal of Economics* 7(2), Autumn, 407–25.

Samuelson, P. 1970. The fundamental approximation theorem of portfolio analysis in terms of means, variances, and higher moments. *Review of Economic Studies* 37(4), October, 537–42.

Sharpe, W.F. 1964. Capital asset prices: a theory of market equilibrium under conditions of risk. *Journal of Finance* 19, September, 425–42.

Sharpe, W.F. 1977. The capital asset pricing model: a 'multi-beta' interpretation. In *Financial Decision Making under Uncertainty*, ed. H. Levy and M. Sarnat, New York: Harcourt Brace Jovanovich, Academic Press.

Solnik, B. 1974. An equilibrium model of international capital markets. *Journal of Economic Theory* 8(4), August, 500–24.

Stapleton, R. and Subrahmanyam, M. 1978. A multiperiod equilibrium asset pricing model. *Econometrica* 46(5), September, 1077–96.

Stulz, R. 1981. A model of international asset pricing. *Journal of Financial Economics* 9(4), December, 383–406.

Tobin, J. 1958. Liquidity preference as behavior towards risk. *Review of Economic Studies* 25, February, 65–86.

Von Neumann, J. and Morgenstern, O. 1947. *Theory of Games and Economic Behavior*. 2nd edn, Princeton: Princeton University Press.

capital budgeting. A sub-field within economics and finance, the principal concern of capital budgeting is the optimal deployment of funds into capital expenditures. The mainstream of the field, developed essentially in the 1950s and 1960s, consists of two threads of inquiry. (1) How should a company measure the investment worth of a capital expenditure proposal? (2) How should a company set the minimum required rate of return for a capital expenditure proposal?

HISTORICAL EVOLUTION. The concept of a *capital budget*, as opposed to an *operating budget*, originated in public finance. Many governments – the United States Federal government is a notable exception – have long maintained separate accounts for capital expenditures; that is, expenditures on capital assets that provide benefits over relatively long time periods.

In the private sector, separate budgeting for capital expenditure has an almost equally long history. The development, however, of the coherent body of thought now known as *capital budgeting* began only after World War II. Three forces drove that development:

(1) A dramatic postwar increase in private capital spending that led to increased interest in how such expenditures should be made.

(2) The postwar development of national income accounts which provided a vehicle for plausible economic projections, a necessary condition for rational choice.

(3) The publication in 1951 of two seminal books: *Capital Budgeting*, by Joel Dean, and *The Theory of Investment of the Firm*, by Friedrich and Vera Lutz.

Rational capital budgeting requires a correct basis for measuring the investment worth of each capital expenditure proposal.

Although capital expenditure decisions have long been regarded as one of the critical responsibilities of top-management (and, indeed, of Corporate Boards of Directors), before the 1950s the decisions themselves had been made on the basis either of intuitive judgements or poorly defined standards. Such inadequate approaches have been supplemented and, in some companies, supplanted by more robust and more quantitative criteria.

THE PAY-BACK PERIOD. One of the earliest quantitative yardsticks used for assaying the investment worth of a capital expenditure proposal (and one that is still in use) is the project's pay-back period – the number of years required to recoup the initial outlay. Because the measure ignores the size and duration of benefits beyond the pay-back period itself, it is a poor proxy for 'profitability'. Nonetheless, it provides a quick screening device for rejecting some proposals as well as for selecting among alternative investment proposals that involve purchases of equipment having approximately equal lives.

THE AVERAGE RATE OF PROFIT. The earliest measure used for a project's expected profitability is the ratio of the average annual flow of profit expected from the project to the average investment dedicated to the project – both measured in conventional accounting terms. The measure has been increasingly discarded because it is a poor proxy for true profitability on two counts: (1) it ignores the *timing* of expected benefits, and (2) it is subject, both with respect to the numerator and the denominator, to the vagaries of depreciation accounting.

THE DCF RATE OF RETURN. The discounted cash-flow rate-of-return measure (hence DCF), which relates the incremental cash inflows attributable to a project to the incremental cash outlays required by it, has gradually supplanted the average-rate accounting measure. In principle, the DCF rate of return (or internal rate of return) is identical to the long-used financial measure for the effective yield to maturity on a bond; that is, it is the rate at which the present value of all incremental cash or equivalent benefits expected from an investment is equal to the incremental outlays required by that investment.

NET PRESENT VALUE. If a company has a correct estimate for the rate of return that is required by the market on an investment with a given degree of riskiness, the DCF return offered by that investment proposal provides an infallible guide to whether or not it should be accepted. Exactly the same result can be achieved by an alternative process: if the present value of a project's net cash flows, discounted at its required rate of return, *exceeds* the present value of the outlays it entails, then the proposal should be accepted; that is, all proposals that have a positive *net* present value should be undertaken. Although both approaches yield the same correct result for accept–reject decisions, the net-present-value approach is a superior one in two special situations. (1) Some investment proposals (especially those designed to accelerate cash-inflows) have more than one DCF rate of return solution. In such cases (i.e. those with two or more positive solutions), none is a correct measure of the project's expected profitability. (2) When more than one proposal is acceptable by either standard, but only one can be executed because the two are mutually exclusive, the net-present-value approach invariably provides a better answer to the 'which is better?' question.

THE REQUIRED RATE OF RETURN. Both the DCF approach and the Net-Present-Value approach to investment decisions require a correct estimate of the required rate of return (or applicable discount rate) on the investment outlay that is being assayed. A number of increasingly sophisticated approaches to the estimation of that rate (also known as the appropriate

341

'cost of capital') have been developed. All such measures are now based on observable rates of return demanded in the marketplace by holders of the debt and equity securities that jointly finance the assets of the corporation. This rate, adjusted up or down for any differential riskiness of the particularly project that is being assayed, is now widely used as the 'hurdle' that any proposal must pass in order to be acceptable.

The rationale is a straightforward one. An investment that yields a *higher* rate of return than the market-determined cost of the funds it requires, has a positive net present value; that is, it creates wealth for the owners as well as for society as a whole. That is how Adam Smith's 'invisible hand' gets translated into practice.

E. SOLOMON

See also INVESTMENT DECISION CRITERIA; PRESENT VALUE.

BIBLIOGRAPHY

Bierman, H. and Smidt, S. 1960. *The Capital Budgeting Decision.* New York: Macmillan.

Dean, J. 1951. *Capital Budgeting.* New York: Columbia University Press.

Lutz, F. and Lutz, V. 1951. *Theory of Investment of the Firm.* Princeton: Princeton University Press.

Robichek, A. (ed.) 1967. *Financial Research and Management Decisions.* New York: John Wiley & Sons.

Solomon, E. (ed.) 1959. *The Management of Corporate Capital.* Glencoe, Ill.: Free Press. Contains an extensive bibliography of the literature up to 1959.

Solomon, E. 1962. *The Theory of Financial Management.* New York: Columbia University Press.

capital controversy. *See* CAPITAL THEORY: DEBATES; CAPITAL THEORY: PARADOXES.

capital flight. This term describes the phenomenon of funds fleeing across the national frontier in search of greater safety. The driving forces behind capital flight include actual or feared monetary instability, confiscatory taxation, war and revolution. Examples of the phenomenon can be found through several centuries. A low level of liquidity and high costs of international communication at first limited the potential scope of capital flight. The earliest 'modern' example was the large-scale movement of French funds to London during the Franco-Prussian war. Capital flight has reached in the 20th century a frequency and importance previously unseen.

The first major episode was the flight of capital during World War 1 out of France, Italy and the Central Powers, into the neutral countries – principally Switzerland, the Netherlands, and Sweden. The capital movements were 'accommodated' to a large extent by speculators in the neutrals buying the belligerent currencies at big discounts to their theoretical gold pars in the hope that large gains would be made once peace was restored.

Defeat brought a new outpouring of capital from Central Europe. Funds fled the Austro-Hungarian crown out of fear that the Successor States would 'nationalize' crowns on their own territory – blocking a substantial share of private holdings and insisting on tax-registration before converting the remainder into the new national money. At first, buyers of the Austro-Hungarian notes could be found in Italy's new territories (acquired from Austria–Hungary) in the expectation

(correct) that the Italian authorities would ultimately convert its new subjects' holdings into liras at a favourable rate. Then buyers appeared in the form of tourists attracted in swarms to Vienna during 1920–21 by the cheap crown.

The flight out of the mark was at first driven by fear that hurge taxes would be levied by the new Republic to meet the internal and external costs of defeat. After a brief respite in the last three-quarters of 1920, capital flight got new impetus from the gathering reparations crisis. The German government was suspected of deliberately inflating to demonstrate the 'impossibility' of paying reparations, whilst the danger of a French invasion of the Ruhr increased. Germany was again the source of huge capital flight in the years 1929–31, driven this time by the spectre of political instability (from mid-1929, the Nazi vote in elections rose strongly) and of national bankruptcy.

The next major episode of capital flight was from France. The fascist riots in February 1934, then the prospects of a 'Front Populaire' government coming to power (May 1935) and of a large devaluation of the franc to reflate the economy, unleashed a huge outflow of funds. The formation of a Centre–Centre Right government under Daladier in spring 1938 marked the turning point. In the next eighteen months, funds returned to France despite the growing menace of war. For Britain and the European neutrals (Holland, Belgium and Switzerland), by contrast, spring 1938 marked the start of a period of capital flight as funds sought refuge in the USA. There were three great waves and a final smaller wave between mid-1938 and the end of 1939: autumn 1938 (Munich crisis), spring 1939 (German occupation of Prague), August 1939 (Nazi–Soviet Pact and invasion of Poland) and November 1939 (feared invasion of the Low Countries). The Bank of England financed the outflows by undertaking massive dollar sales.

Capital flight changed direction dramatically as soon as France sued for an armistice (June 1940). Investors in Axis Europe and in the remaining European neutrals (particularly Switzerland) feared that the USA would freeze their funds and these were transferred into Swiss francs or to Latin America. For the next decade, Switzerland was the principal recipient of refuge funds – which in the early post-war years came largely from France. The USA was not regarded as a safe-haven – not just because of its wartime freeze of most foreign assets, but also because of the cooperation of the US authorities with European governments in securing the repatriation of flight capital.

In general, the postwar industrial world has not been struck by the huge waves of capital flight driven by political fears which marked the years 1914–40. The mid and late 1970s were a period of large movements of flight capital, but these were driven primarily by inflation. The inflows to Switzerland from France, Italy and Britain in 1976 reflected largely the high inflation in these countries and the non-indexation of their tax structures (particularly with respect to capital). During 1978, the spectre of high and rising inflation in the USA caused international funds to flee the dollar. Just when inflation fears began to moderate following the turn in US monetary policy of October 1979, a new fillip was given to capital outflows from the USA by the freezing of Iranian assets. Investors in much of the Third World, particularly OPEC, feared that if revolution brought to power a government unfriendly to Washington, their dollar assets might not be safe.

In almost all the episodes of capital flight mentioned, foreign investors and creditors have played a disproportionately large role. Foreign capital is less tied down by 'convenience factors'. Domestic residents in general have less to lose than foreigners from the introduction of exchange restrictions. Whereas foreigners might not be able to buy anything with frozen balances (except, perhaps, tourist services), residents would be able to use their funds freely on a normal range of goods – albeit possibly curtailed by import controls.

A general property of capital flight driven by fears of future disaster is that it occurs in waves, not continuously. The wave-like motion reflects discontinuous changes in the probability of the possible 'bad state of the world' becoming reality. News – a frequent cause of shifts in probability assessments – is by its nature sudden. Alarming new information causes investors to revise upwards the share of hedge-assets (usually foreign) in their portfolio. During the period of portfolio-adjustment a wave of capital flight becomes apparent. Once adjustment is complete, the wave subsides. Under a floating exchange rate system, the waves are sublimated into abrupt fluctuations in currency values. The exchange rate falls to a point where investors see sufficient return on holding the 'troubled' money at the margin to delay re-arranging their portfolio. As trade flows respond to the exchange rate change, the portfolio adjustment begins to take place.

Capital flight can reach such a force as to cause national bankruptcy (meaning that foreign credits are frozen and exchange restrictions introduced). For example, the official foreign exchange reserves may have become exhausted; foreign loans be impossible to obtain; interest rate rises (which in principle might stem capital outflows) be infeasible because they would intensify deflation, increasing the risk of domestic political tumult or bank failures; a downward float of the currency be ineffective in strengthening the capital account because it gives rise to a wage–price spiral or invites retaliation by other nations concerned with 'unfair' competition in trade. Governments sometimes pre-empt a forced bankruptcy by coming to a 'voluntary' re-scheduling arrangement with foreign creditors and imposing a range of controls on domestic capital exports. Such measures are costly. The country's credit-rating would be adversely affected for decades to come. A tradition of economic and political liberalism might well be damaged irreparably. In some respects, a liberal government which prevents its citizens from protecting their wealth against the coming to power of a dictatorship or against a foreign invader is already in league with the enemy.

The fear of forced bankruptcy is not the only motive for government to seek to limit capital flight. Measures may be introduced as a 'sop' to labour when economic policy is being tightened. Alternatively, the authorities may hope that the measures will raise the level of domestic investment and employment of real wages. A reduced degree of capital flight should mean that interest rates can settle at a lower level. In general, though, measures against capital flight are largely ineffective, unless policed by methods inconsistent with a liberal society. Traffic in banknotes is one obvious loophole, especially where the given country has land frontiers and is a tourist centre. Other loopholes include false invoicing in trade and compensation payments.

Such transactions often lie behind the large negative 'errors and omissions' items in balance of payments statistics for countries susceptible to capital flight. They may also be responsible for the positive 'errors and omissions' for the countries receiving flight capital. The positive errors could reflect foreign hoarding demand for the domestic currency (for example, Swiss franc notes accumulated outside Switzerland) or inflows of flight capital being hidden behind domestic names for fear of freezing (for example, much of the inflows to the USA in 1939-40 were disguised behind US names and gave

rise to a large positive errors item in the US balance of payments at that time).

Measures against capital flight might indeed increase its extent. Domestic investors would realize that they could not quickly raise the proportion of foreign currency in their portfolio. Hence, if the political and economic climate at home worsened, they could be 'underprotected' for a long time. To hedge this possibility, they might painstakingly via available loopholes accumulate foreign holdings to a level higher than justified simply by present risks.

BRENDAN BROWN

See also EXCHANGE CONTROLS; HOT MONEY; INTERNATIONAL CAPITAL FLOWS.

BIBLIOGRAPHY
Blankart, C. 1919. *Die Devisenpolitik während des Weltkrieges.* Zurich: Orell Fussli.
Gutmann, I. 1913. *Das Französische Geldwesen im Kriege 1870–78.* Strassborg: Trubner.
Koeppel, W. 1931. *Kapitalflucht.* Berlin: Wilhelm Christians.

capital gains and losses. National accounting has made the definition of capital gains and losses rather precise in practice, but fundamentally their distinction from income raises quite subtle issues, about which great economists have long been wavering. Whenever it becomes important, inflation gives to some of these issues a fresh relevance. Much remains to be learned, moreover, on how capital gains affect economic behaviour and how the allocation of resources ought to deal with the capital losses resulting from current activity.

DEFINITION. Although the reference books such as United Nations (1969) are not explicit enough about this basic notion, national accounting systematically applies the following

$$\Delta W = Y + CT + CG - C \qquad (1)$$

where ΔW is the variation of wealth between the beginning and end of the period under consideration, Y is income, CT the net capital transfer received (gifts, bequests, capital taxes and subsidies), CG the net capital gain and C consumption. The identity applies to any agent or group of agents. This identity may be taken as the *de facto* definition of net capital gains (i.e. gains *minus* losses), to the extent that well-defined rules are used for the flows Y, C and CT, which appear in the current accounts, and to the extent that wealth is assumed to be unambiguously determined.

Looking carefully at the existing rules, one, however, realizes that the distinction between income and net capital gain is conventional to a large extent. It is precisely on the choice of this convention that some important questions about the definition of incomes lie.

Chapter 7 of Fisher (1906) shows that defining the concept of income was not an easy task for economists. Fisher's own preferred definition, 'the services of capital', may not seem quite clear, but it can be identified with consumption. This would make the whole of investment belong to capital gains, a solution that was seriously discussed by Samuelson (1961) but has hardly any advocate today. At the other extreme, the 'comprehensive definition of income', also called the Haig–Simons definition, was proposed by economists studying income taxes (Haig, 1921; Simons, 1938); income would be equal to the sum of consumption and wealth increase, thus leaving neither capital gains, nor capital transfers in equation

(1). One now most commonly refers to the definition introduced by Hicks (1939), 'A man's income is the maximum value which he can consume during a week, and still expect to be as well off at the end of the week as he was at the beginning' (p. 172).

National accountants, however, measure income as the sum of the value of production and net current transfers. Production is essentially computed from physical outputs and inputs, valued at current prices and aggregated. This means that stock revaluations that explain part of the change of wealth are not incomes but capital gains or losses. Hicks's definition, on the contrary, implies that expected stock revaluations belong to income. In equation (1) only windfalls would be true capital gains. But whether the change of value of an asset should be classified as expected or not is most often not clear. (How long in advance should it have been expected? Should an outside observer be able to make sure that the asset holder had expected the change?) The distinction between expected and unexpected capital gains or losses, however, remains essential in economic analysis.

INFLATION. The most sizeable asset revaluations result from changes of the price level. When inflation is important, a good proportion of these revaluations are, moreover, expected by all agents. Their occurrence then plays a role in the determination of the equilibrium of all exchanges and economic operations, inducing in particular high interest rates. On the other hand, the change of nominal wealth becomes of little interest in comparison with the change of real wealth; 'real capital gains' should then be distinguished from nominal ones. Hence, inflation perturbs the significance of normal accounting rules; new measurements are required for correct assessments of income flows (Jump, 1980).

This applies first to business accounting, in which reference to historical costs underestimates physical assets and depreciation of fixed capital, while it overestimates net returns from financial assets. This explains the search for new or alternative accounting rules that would be better suited in cases of fast inflation and would more correctly draw the line between income and capital gains or losses. This search went as far as the stage of implementation in the United Kingdom (see Walton, 1978).

At the level of the whole economy, when the rules of national accounting are applied, real capital gains and losses resulting from variations of the general level of prices are important. Typically they benefit enterprises and government, which are net debtors, whereas they mean large losses for households. When all these capital gains and losses are imputed to incomes, on the ground that they must have been expected, the current accounts of firms and government appear substantially more favourable, whereas sizeable redistribution is also found as between groups of households (see Bach and Stephenson, 1974; Babeau, 1978; Wolff, 1979).

The question has been considered whether national account practices should not be revised so as to better record true incomes in times of inflation (see Hibbert, 1982). A prerequisite is the regular production of national balance sheets. When this is done, important capital gains and losses, due for instance to booms in real estate or share prices, also appear beyond those due to changes of the general price level.

CAPITAL GAINS IN ECONOMIC BEHAVIOUR. Most econometric studies tend to neglect capital gains as flows, although wealth and indebtness are often taken into account. The role of capital gains on the consumption behaviour of households has, however, been studied. Up to now the results have been rather inconclusive (Bhatia, 1972; Peek, 1983; Pesaran and Evans, 1984).

In all likelihood the difficulty comes from the fact that some capital gains are purely transitory, whereas most of them have some degree of permanence, but this degree varies widely from one to the other. A pure windfall is comparable to an exceptional gift; accidental losses or war damages occur once for all, whereas capital losses due to an inflation that is expected to last may appear to be as permanent as interest incomes, even sometimes as wage incomes. But to classify capital gains according to their supposed permanence is far from being an obvious operation.

Gains on the value of corporate shares have a permanent component following from the firms' policy of retaining part of their profits. This is why increases of retained earnings have been considered as likely to increase household consumption, but not as much as an increase of permanent income would, since the size of undistributed profits varies a good deal with business conditions (Feldstein and Fane, 1973; Malinvaud, 1986).

The problem becomes still more complex when capital gains are correlated with cost changes for items of household wealth. An extreme case occurs when prices of residential real estate increase: owners of houses make a capital gain, but simultaneously the cost of housing increases by the corresponding amount; whether houses are let or used by their owners, a stimulating effect on real consumption is doubtful.

CAPITAL LOSSES, CONSERVATION AND WELFARE. The existence of capital gains and losses raises a number of issues for the theory of allocation of resources, for instance what should be the taxation of capital gains (David, 1968; Green and Sheshinski, 1978), or how best to organize insurance against capital losses. But particular attention nowadays concerns the damages that economic activity causes to the environment and to reserves of exhaustible resources (Fisher, 1981).

Not all environmental effects mean capital losses; many of them are just externalities in the normal course of economic activity. But irreversible damages to the forests, the soil or even the climate must also be recognized and are usually not recorded as consumption or as inputs to production. Depletion of non-renewable reserves are similarly often treated as capital losses.

The detrimental effects of many of these losses will appear mainly in a rather distant future. Whether or not losses should be accepted – what for instance should be the optimal speed of depletion of natural resources – raises difficult questions of intergenerational equity, on which economists have uncomfortably to enter the field of social philosophy.

The problem cannot be discarded here on the ground that proper discounting makes the distant future negligible. Indeed, in the purest case, the shadow discounted price of an exhaustible resource is as high in the future as it is now, for as long as the resource will remain used (Hotelling, 1931). The remote future must then be taken into account for present decisions.

It is moreover notorious that enormous uncertainties affect the purely physical estimation of the consequences involved. Neither the effects of carbon dioxide emission on the climate, nor the existing reserves of fossil fuels, nor the future emergence of appropriate technologies for the wider use of renewable energy can be securely assessed. Under such circumstances, the emergence of an objective methodology for economic decisions is particularly difficult.

E. MALINVAUD

See also SOCIAL ACCOUNTING

BIBLIOGRAPHY

Babeau, A. 1978. The application of the constant price method for evaluating the transfer related to inflation: the case of French households. *Review of Income and Wealth* 24(4), December, 391–414.

Bach, G. and Stephenson, J. 1974. Inflation and the redistribution of wealth. *Review of Economics and Statistics* 56(1), February, 1–13.

Bhatia, K. 1972. Capital gains and the aggregate consumption function. *American Economic Review* 62(5), December, 866–79.

David, M. 1968. *Alternative Approaches to Capital Gains Taxation.* Washington, DC: Brookings Institution.

Feldstein, M. and Fane, G. 1973. Taxes, corporate dividend policy and personal savings: the British experience. *Review of Economics and Statistics* 55(4), November, 399–411.

Fisher, A. 1981. *Resource and environmental economics.* Cambridge: Cambridge University Press.

Fisher, I. 1906. *The Nature of Capital and Income.* New York: Macmillan.

Green, J. and Sheshinski, E. 1978. Optimal capital-gains taxation under limited information. *Journal of Political Economy* 86(6), 1143–58.

Haig, R. 1921. The concept of income: economic and legal aspects. In *The Federal Income Tax*, ed. R. Haig, New York: Columbia University Press.

Hibbert, J. 1982. *Measuring the effects of inflation on income, saving and wealth.* Paris: OECD.

Hicks, J. 1939. *Value and Capital.* 2nd edn, Oxford: Oxford University Press, 1946.

Hotelling, H. 1931. The economics of exhaustible resources. *Journal of Political Economy* 39, 137–75.

Jump, G. 1980. Interest rates, inflation expectations, and spurious elements in measured real income and saving. *American Economic Review* 70(5), December, 990–1004.

Malinvaud, E. 1986. Pure profits as forced saving. *Scandinavian Journal of Economics* 88(1), 109–30.

Peek, J. 1983. Capital gains and personal saving behaviour. *Journal of Money, Credit and Banking* 15(1), February, 1–23.

Pesaran, M. and Evans, R. 1984. Inflation, capital gains and UK personal savings: 1953–81. *Economic Journal* 94, June, 237–57.

Samuelson, P. 1961. The evaluation of 'social income': capital formation and wealth. In *The Theory of Capital*, ed. F. Lutz and D. Hague, London: Macmillan.

Simons, H. 1938. *Personal Income Taxation.* Chicago: University of Chicago Press.

United Nations. 1969. *A System of National Accounts.* New York: United Nations.

Walton, J. 1978. Current cost accounting: implications for the definition and measurement of corporate income. *Review of Income and Wealth* 24(4), December, 357–90.

Wolff, E. 1979. The distributional effects of the 1969–75 inflation on holdings of household wealth in the United States. *Review of Income and Wealth* 25(2), June, 195–208.

capital goods. Capital goods are a series of heterogeneous commodities, each having specific technical characteristics. Outside the hypothetical case where real capital consists of a single commodity, it is impossible to express the stock of capital goods as a homogeneous physical entity. As a consequence of capital's heterogeneous nature its measurement has become the source of many controversies in the history of economic thought.

The function of capital goods is production. Unlike labour ('in the raw') and (non-cultivated) land, capital goods are not given, they are themselves produced. Being an output as well as an input, the size and variation of the capital stock are intra-economic phenomena. Because real capital is not an 'original' factor of production but is the result of economic processes in which it participates as one of the determinants, the formation of real capital or investment is the central channel through which all other determinants, be they technical progress, changes in labour supply or the exploitation of natural resources, influence the long-run development of an industrial system.

A distinction is normally made between durable or fixed capital, including not only plant and machinery but also buildings and other essential parts of the industrial infrastructure which are used up only partially during the year, and circulating capital, consisting of stocks of raw materials, semi-finished goods, etc., capital which is fully used up during the production period and must therefore be replaced in full.

Capital has at least two different aspects: capital as goods and capital as value. From a technological point of view, produced means of production are a condition for the operation of any social and economic system, once Smith's early and rude state of society is overcome. It was Marx who emphasized that these necessary physical instruments of production become 'capital' only under the capitalistic rules of the game when the means of production are separated from the labourers and owned by the capitalists. Thus the means of production possess a double aspect in capitalistic societies: on the one hand 'capital' is understood to mean the total of heterogeneous goods and equipment designed for specific uses (productive concept), on the other hand it is regarded as a homogeneous fund of value and source of 'unearned' income in the form of profits (portfolio concept).

The value of the capital goods corresponding to each system of production, even with a constant technique, will change with income distribution whichever the unit in which they are measured. Current relative prices change when the rate of profits or the real wage rate changes, so that the same physical capital represents a different value whereas different stocks of capital goods can have the same value. Furthermore, only in long-run equilibrium will a given stock of capital goods have the same value whether it be determined as the accumulated sum of past investment expenditures or as the expected future net returns discounted back to the present at the ruling rate of profits.

Another way of measuring capital goods is in terms of labour time directly and indirectly required to produce them, the appropriately dated quantities of labour compounded at the various given rates of profits. As the analyses of Joan Robinson (1956), who called it 'real capital', and Sraffa (1960) show, it is impossible to get any notion of capital as a measurable quantity independent of distribution and prices.

Whereas the individual is concerned with the extent to which he owns capital goods as a store of wealth and a source of income, society as a whole is never faced with problems of buying or selling capital goods against money or credit. Greater output unambiguously requires a greater amount of capital goods, given the degree of capacity utilization and technology. These additional capital goods can be provided only by a process of accumulation or net investment.

Emphasis on the strategic role of the capacity to produce capital goods in the domestic economy plays a decisive role in the analyses of Fel'dman (1928) and Lowe (1955, 1976). Both authors take as their starting point Marx's famous two-departmental scheme of expanded reproduction, modifying it in an adequate way to include all activities that increase the capacity of an economy to produce output in one sector. During the Soviet industrialization debate in the late twenties, Fel'dman formalized the notion that investment-priority for the capital-goods sector was a precondition for attaining a higher growth rate. Structural incapacity to supply enough capital goods will prevent a rise in the saving ratio from being fully transformed into the desired level of investment. But it has to be taken into account that a one-sided preoccupation with this 'Fel'dman constraint' on the investment capacity side may bring the 'Preobrazhenski constraint' on the consumption side into action. If the initial capacity of the capital goods industry is just sufficient to replace the worn-out machines, growth can only take place as a result of a temporary reduction in the output of consumer goods which may be impossible for subsistence reasons. In this case a *circulus vitiosus* will emerge.

The strategic role of the machine tools sector and the compulsion to enlarge first the equipment in capital goods industries were also dealt with by economists discussing the growth and planning problems of underdeveloped countries in the Fifties and Sixties (see, for example, Dobb, 1960 and Mathur, 1965). Countries like India which lack a self-sufficient machine tools sector can speed up their transformation process by foreign trade. The Fel'dman constraint would be binding only if the domestic output of machine tools could not be supplemented with imports.

The perception that there is a group of fixed capital goods which hold the strategic position in any industrial system like seed corn for agricultural production, led Lowe to the conclusion that it is useful to split up the capital goods sector in the Marxian scheme of reproduction into two subsectors. In his 'tripartite' scheme of three vertically integrated sectors, the first produces primary equipment goods or 'machine tools' which are directly used for production in sectors I and II. Sector II produces the secondary equipment goods which are used as inputs only in sector III producing consumer goods, which means that the capital stock in the latter is not transferable. Thus sector I is the only one capable not only of producing machines for other sectors but also for itself; it is therefore a *self-reproducible sector*. In Sraffa's terminology, sector I represents the 'basic system'.

The sub-division of the capital goods group is relevant for investigating the structural conditions for steady growth and, even more, in addressing questions of 'traverse analysis', when the problem of structural change is moved to the centre of the stage. The decisive problem that the economy faces upon departing from a steady growth path is the inadequacy of the old capital stock. The dynamic traverse from one steady growth path to another necessarily involves a change in the whole quantity structure, especially the rebuilding of the capital stock. The economy cannot change output unless it first changes inputs, i.e. the capital goods group must provide the commodities demanded for changing the inputs to produce the new output pattern. The production of machine tools is the bottle-neck which any process of rapid expansion must overcome. The key to a higher growth rate lies in increasing the shares of sector I. The same logic requiring that the system as a whole first has to change inputs before it can change output makes such an increase dependent on the prior expansion of the capital stock of this sector. Whereas in the two-sectoral Fel'dman model this is only possible by a policy of putting a larger proportion of new machine tools into the production of more machine tools, in the Lowe model an additional *ex post* transfer of machines from sector II to sector I is possible, thereby shortening the time of adjustment. Both models come to the same result, namely that in order to increase the growth rates of total output and consumption output in the long run, at first a temporary fall in the growth rate of consumption output is necessary.

The neo-Austrian theory developed by Hicks is characterized by a completely different treatment of the durable means of production. In his neo-Austrian model, a stream of labour inputs is converted into a stream of final outputs (consumption goods). 'Capital goods are simply stages in the process of production' (Hicks, 1973, p. 5), i.e. they are regarded as intermediate products which don't appear explicitly but are implied and produced within each process of 'maturing' of original inputs into the final product. Thus the intertemporal aspect of production and consumption is placed into the forefront of the analysis; time is the essence of capital in the Austrian view. By treating fixed capital as if it were working capital, Hicks does not recognize the need for a special machine-tools sector. There is no basic product in this model. Hence, the production process is not 'circular'; the neo-Austrian approach turns out to be a further variant of the production theoretic paradigm of marginalist analysis, which conceives of the production process as a 'one-way avenue that leads from "Factors of production" to "Consumption goods"' (Sraffa, 1960, p. 93).

It is precisely the focus on the adjustment problems caused by the impact of technical innovations that has led Hicks to his vertical representation of the productive structure. In contrast to Leontief–Sraffa–Lowe systems, in Hicks neither intersectoral transactions, nor therefore the effects of innovation upon industrial structure, are shown. Hicks sees the decisive advantage of the Austrian method in its ability to cope with the important fact that process innovations nearly always involve the introduction of new capital goods. This would lead to insurmountable difficulties in the traverse analysis if capital goods were physically specified because 'there is no way of establishing a physical relation between the capital goods that are required in the one technique and those that are required in the other' (Hicks, 1977, p. 193). A similar explanation is given by Pasinetti who develops his theory of structural change in terms of vertically integrated sectors. While conceding that the input-output model gives more information on the structure of an economic system at any point in time, he points out that because of the change of input-output coefficients and the 'breaking down' of the inter-industry system over time, the vertically integrated model is superior for dynamic analysis (see Pasinetti, 1981, pp. 109–17). Measuring capital goods in units of vertically integrated productive capacity of the final commodity 'has an unambiguous meaning through time, no matter which type of technical change, and how much of it, may occur' (p. 178).

Whilst it is true that a sectorally disaggregated approach encounters difficulties when the effects of innovations connected with the introduction of new capital goods are studied, the price that Austrian-type models have to pay for their linear 'imperialism' is rather high. Technical change takes place at the industry level, a characteristic which is completely washed out in vertically integrated models. The industry-specific nature of technical change also implies that, contrary to Pasinetti's assumption, rates of productivity growth in the different vertically integrated sectors cannot be thought of as being independent of each other. How could the new capital goods be produced without the old ones existing at the beginning of the traverse? Thus the existence of a basic system remains relevant, even when the basic product(s) is(are) changing its(their) quality. Innovations introducing new consumption goods cannot be dealt with in a satisfactory way. All this does not imply that the concept of vertically integrated sectors is meaningless, on the contrary, it can be very helpful as a complementary perspective. But it illustrates that input-output models emphasizing intersectoral interdependencies retain conceptual priority.

Fixed capital has two other important dimensions: its degree of capacity utilization, and its durability. Thus the choice of cost-minimizing technique involves the choice of the 'planned' degree of capital utilization and the choice of the economic lifetime of a fixed capital good. The latter can best be dealt with on the basis of a von Neumann–Sraffa treatment of fixed capital goods (which contains Hicks's neo-Austrian model as a special case) as a joint part of the gross output, thus identifying machines of different ages as different commodities. To every technically possible lifetime corresponds a specific w-r relation which may slope upwards over some range for a given truncation (in which case the prices of partly worn-out machines become negative and premature truncation is advantageous), whereas the w–r frontier is always downwards sloping. The analysis of the choice of the optimal lifetime or truncation period shows that with constant or increasing efficiency the maximum technical lifetime will always be chosen, independently of income distribution. With decreasing or changing efficiency, however, premature truncation may become profitable (see Hagemann and Kurz, 1976). A change in the wage rate (rate of profits) will generally lead to changes in the optimal economic lifetimes of fixed capital goods. With more complex patterns of the time profile of efficiency, the return of the same truncation period at different intervals of the rate of profits is possible, a phenomenon closely linked to reswitching of techniques (see also Schefold, 1974).

HARALD HAGEMANN

See also CAPITAL AS A FACTOR OF PRODUCTION; QUANTITY OF CAPITAL.

BIBLIOGRAPHY

Dobb, M. 1960. *An Essay on Economic Growth and Planning*. London: Routledge.

Fel'dman, G.A. 1928. On the theory of growth rates of national income, I and II. In ed. N. Spulber, *Foundations of Soviet Strategy for Economic Growth*, Bloomington: Indiana University Press, 1964.

Hagemann, H. and Kurz, H.D. 1976. The return of the same truncation period and reswitching of techniques in neo-Austrian and more general models. *Kyklos* 29(4), 678–708.

Harcourt, G.C. 1972. *Some Cambridge Controversies in the Theory of Capital*. Cambridge: Cambridge University Press.

Hicks, J. 1973. *Capital and Time. A Neo-Austrian Theory*. Oxford: Clarendon Press.

Hicks, J. 1977. *Economic Perspectives. Further Essays on Money and Growth*. Oxford: Clarendon Press.

Lowe, A. 1955. Structural analysis of real capital formation. In ed. M. Abramovitz, *Capital Formation and Economic Growth*, Princeton: Princeton University Press.

Lowe, A. 1976. *The Path of Economic Growth*. Cambridge: Cambridge University Press.

Mathur, G. 1965. *Planning for Steady Growth*. Oxford: Blackwell.

Pasinetti, L.L. 1981. *Structural Change and Economic Growth. A theoretical essay on the dynamics of the wealth of nations*. Cambridge: Cambridge University Press.

Robinson, J. 1956. *The Accumulation of Capital*. London: Macmillan.

Schefold, B. 1974. Fixed capital as a joint product and the analysis of accumulation with different forms of technical progress. In *Essays on the Theory of Joint Production*, ed. L.L. Pasinetti, London: Macmillan.

Sraffa, P. 1960. *Production of Commodities by Means of Commodities. Prelude to a critique of economic theory*. Cambridge: Cambridge University Press.

capitalism. Capitalism is often called *market society* by economists, and the *free enterprise system* by business and government spokesmen. But these terms, which emphasize certain economic or political characteristics, do not suffice to describe either the complexity or the crucial identificatory elements of the system. Capitalism is better viewed as a historical 'formation', distinguishable from formations that have preceded it, or that today parallel it, both by a core of central institutions and by the motion these institutions impart to the whole. Although capitalism assumes a wide variety of appearances from period to period and place to place – one need only compare Dickensian England and 20th-century Sweden or Japan – these core institutions and distinctive movements are discoverable in all of them, and allow us to speak of capitalism as a historical entity, comparable to ancient imperial kingdoms or to the feudal system.

The most widely acknowledged achievement of capitalist societies is their capacity to amass wealth on an unprecedented scale, a capacity to which Marx and Engels paid unstinting tribute in *The Communist Manifesto*. It is important to understand, however, that the wealth amassed by capitalism differs in quality as well as quantity from that accumulated in precapitalist societies. Many ancient kingdoms, such as Egypt, displayed remarkable capacities to gather a surplus of production above that needed for the maintenance of the existing level of material life, applying the surplus to the creation of massive religious or public monuments, military works or luxury consumption. What is characteristic of these forms of wealth is that their desirable attributes lay in the specific use values – war, worship, adornment – to which their physical embodiments directly gave rise. By way of decisive contrast, the wealth amassed under capitalism is valued not for its specific use-values but for its generalized exchange-value. Wealth under capitalism is therefore typically accumulated as *commodities* – objects produced for sale rather than for direct use or enjoyment by their owners; and the extraordinary success of capitalism in amassing wealth means that the production of commodities makes possible a far greater expansion of wealth than its accumulation as use-values for the rulers of earlier historical formations.

Both Smith and Marx stressed the importance of the expansion of the commodity form of wealth. For example, Smith considered labour to be 'productive' only if it created goods whose sale could replenish and enlarge the national fund of capital, not when its product was instrinsically useful or meritorious. In the same fashion, Marx described the accumulation of wealth under capitalism as a circuit in which money capital (M) was exchanged for commodities (C), to be sold for a larger money sum (M′), in a never-ending metamorphosis of M–C–M′.

Although the dynamics of the M–C–M′ process vary greatly depending on whether the commodities are trading goods or labour power and fixed capital equipment, the presence of this imperious internal circuit of capital constitutes a prime identificatory element for capitalism as a historical genus. As such, it focuses attention on two important aspects of capitalism. One of these concerns the motives that impel capitalists on their insatiable pursuit. For modern economists the answer to this question lies in 'utility maximization', an answer that generally refers to the same presumed attribute of human nature as that which Smith called the 'desire of bettering our condition'. The unappeasable character of the expansive drive for capital suggests, however, that its roots lie not so much in these conscious motivations as in the gratification of unconscious drives, specifically the universal infantile need for affect and experience of frustrated aggression. Such needs and drives surface in all societies as the desires for prestige and for personal domination. From this point of view, capitalism appears not merely as an 'economic system' knit by the appeals of mutually advantageous exchange, but as a larger cultural setting in which the pursuit of wealth fulfils the same unconscious purposes as did the pursuit of military glory or the celebration of personal majesty in earlier epochs. Such a description conveys the force of the 'animal spirits' (as Keynes referred to them) that both set into motion, and are appeased by, the M–C–M' circuit. (Heilbroner, 1985, ch. 2; Sagan, 1985, chs 5, 6).

A second general question raised by the centrality of the M–C–M' circuit concerns the manner in which the process of capital accumulation organizes and disciplines the social activity that surrounds it. Here analysis focuses on the institutions necessary for the circuit to be maintained. The crucial capitalist institution is generally agreed to be private property in the means of production (not in personal chattels, which is found in all societies). The ability of private property to organize and discipline social activity does not however lie, as is often supposed, in the right of its owners to do with their property whatever they want. Such a dangerous social licence has never existed. It inheres, rather, in the right accorded its owners to *withhold* their property from the use of society if they so wish.

This negative form of power contrasts sharply with that of the privileged elites in precapitalist social formations. In these imperial kingdoms or feudal holdings, disciplinary power is exercised by the direct use or display of coercive force, so that the bailiff or the seneschal are the agencies through which economic order is directly obtained. The social power of capital is of a different kind – a power of refusal, not of assertion. The capitalist may deny others access to his resources, but he may not force them to work with them. Clearly, such power requires circumstances that make the withholding of access an act of critical consequence. These circumstances can only arise if the general populace is unable to secure a living unless it can gain access to privately owned resources or wealth. Capital thus becomes an instrument of power because its owners can establish claims on output as their *quid pro quo* for permitting access to their property.

Access to property is normally attained by the relationship of 'employment' under which a labourer enters into a contract with an owner of capital, usually selling a fixed number of working hours in exchange for a fixed wage payment. At the conclusion of this 'wage-labour' contract both parties are quit of further obligation to one another, *and the product of the contractual labour becomes the property of the employer.* From this product the employer will pay out his wage obligations and compensate his other suppliers, retaining as a profit any residual that remains.

In detail, forms of profit vary widely, and not all forms are specific to capitalism – trading gains, for example, long predate its rise. Explanations of profit vary as a consequence, but as a general case it can be said that all profits depend ultimately on inequality of economic position. When the inequality arises from wide disparities of knowledge or access to alternative supplies, profits typically emerge as the mercantile gains that were so important in the eyes of medieval commentators, or as the depredations of monopolistic companies against which Adam Smith inveighed. When the inequality stems from differentials in the productivity of resources or productive capability we have the quasi-rents to which such otherwise different observers as Marshall and Schumpeter attribute the source of capitalist gain. And when the inequality is located in the market relationship between employer and worker it appears as the surplus value central to Marxian and, under a different vocabulary, to classical political economy. As Smith put it, 'Many a workman could not subsist a week, few could subsist a month, and scarce any a year without employment. In the long-run the workman may be as necessary to his master as his master is to him; but the need is not so immediate' (Smith [1776], 1976, p. 84).

This is not the place to enter into a discussion of these forms of profit, all which can be discerned in modern capitalist society. What is of the essence under capitalism is that gains from whatever origin are assigned to the owners of capital, not to workers, managers or government officials. This is a clear indication both of the difference of capitalism from, and its resemblance to earlier social formations. The difference is that product itself now flows to owners of property who have already remunerated its producers, not to its producers – usually peasants in precapitalist societies – who must then 'remunerate' their lords. The resemblance is that both arrangements channel a social surplus into the hands of a superior class, a fact that again reveals the nature of capitalism as a system of social domination, not merely of rational exchange.

Thus we can see that the successful completion of the circuit of accumulation represents a political as well as an economic challenge. The attainment of profit is necessary for the continuance of capitalism not alone because it replenishes the wherewithal of each individual capitalist (or firm) but because it also demonstrates the continuing validity and vitality of the principle of M–C–M' as the basis on which the formation can be structured. Profit is for capitalism what victory is for a regime organized on military principles, or an increase in the number of adherents for one built on a proselytizing religion.

THE EVOLUTION OF CAPITALISM. Capitalism as a 'regime' whose organizing principle is the ceaseless accumulation of capital cannot be understood without some appreciation of the historic changes that bring about its appearance. In this complicated narrative it is useful to distinguish three major themes. The first concerns the transfer of the organization and control of production from the imperial and aristocratic strata of precapitalist states into the hands of mercantile elements. This momentous change originates in the political rubble that followed the fall of the Roman empire. There merchant traders established trading niches that gradually became loci of strategic influence, so that a merchantdom very much at the mercy of feudal lords in the 9th and 10th centuries became by the 12th and 13th centuries an estate with a considerable measure of political influence and social status. The feudal lord continued to oversee the production of the peasantry on his manorial estate, but the merchant, and his descendant the guild master, were organizers of production in the towns, of trade between the towns and of finance for the feudal aristocracy itself.

The transformation of a merchant estate into a capitalist class capable of imagining itself as a political and not just an economic force required centuries to complete and was not, in fact legitimated until the English revolution of the 17th and the French revolution of the 18th centuries. The elements making for this revolutionary transformation can only be alluded to here in passing. A central factor was the gradual remonetization of medieval European life that accompanied its political reconstitution. The replacement of feudal social relationships, mediated through custom and tradition, by market relationships knit by exchange worked steadily to improve the wealth and social importance of the merchant against the aristocrat. This enhancement was accelerated by many related developments – the inflationary consequence of the importation of Spanish gold in the 16th century, which further undermined the rentier position of feudal lords; the steady stream of runaway serfs who left the land for the precarious freedom of the towns and cities, placing further economic pressure on their former masters; the growth of national power that encouraged alliances between monarchs and merchants for their mutual advantage; and yet other social changes (see Pirenne, 1936; Hilton, 1978).

The overall transfer of power from aristocratic to bourgeois auspices is often subsumed under the theme of the rise of market society; that is, as the increasingly *economic* organization of production and distribution through purchase and sale rather than by command or tradition. This economic revolution, from which emerge the 'factors of production' that characterize market society, must however be understood as the end product of a *political* convulsion in which one social order is destroyed to make way for a new one. Thus the creation of a propertyless waged labour force – the prerequisite for the appearance of labour-power as a commodity that would become enmeshed in the M–C–M' circuit – is a disruptive social change that begins in England in the late 16th century with the dispossession of peasant occupants from communal land and does not run its course until well into the 19th century. In similar fashion, the transformation of feudal manors from centres of social and juridical life into real estate, or the destruction of the protected guilds before the unconstrained expansion of nascent capitalist enterprises, embody wrenching socio-political dislocations, not merely the smooth diffusion of pre-existing economic relations throughout society. It is such painful rearrangements of power and status that underlay the 'great transformation' out of which capitalist market relationships finally arise (Polanyi, 1957, Part II).

A second theme in the historical evolution of capital emphasizes a related but distinct aspect of political change. Here the main emphasis lies not so much in the functional organization of production as in the separation of a traditionally seamless web of rulership, extending over all activities within the historical formation, into two realms, each concerned with a differentiated part of the whole. One of these realms involved the exercise of the traditional political tasks of rulership – mainly the formation and enforcement of law and the declaration and conduct of war. These undertakings continued to be entrusted to the existing state apparatus which retained (or regained) the monopoly of legal violence and remained the centre of authority and ceremony. The other realm was limited to the production and distribution of goods and services; that is, to the direction of the material affairs of society, from the marshalling of the workforce to the amassing and use of the social surplus. In the fulfilment of this task, the second realm also extended its reach beyond the boundaries of the territorial state, insofar as commodities were sold to and procured from outlying regions and countries that became enmeshed in the circuit of capital.

The formation of these two realms was of epoch-making importance for the constitution of capitalism. The creation of a broad sphere of social activity from which the exercise of traditional command was excluded bestowed on capitalism another unmistakable badge of historic specificity; namely, the creation of an 'economy', a semi-independent state within a state and also extending beyond its borders.

This in turn brought two remarkable consequences. One of these was the establishment of a political agenda unique to capitalism, in which the relationship of the two realms became a central question around which political discussion revolved, and indeed continues to revolve. In this discussion the overarching unity and mutual dependency of the two realms tends to be overlooked. The organization of production is generally regarded as a wholly 'economic' activity, ignoring the political function performed by the wage–labour relationship in disciplining the workforce in lieu of bailiffs and seneschals. In like fashion, the discharge of political authority is regarded as essentially separable from the operation of the economic realm, ignoring the provision of the legal, military and material contributions without which the private sphere could not function properly or even exist. In this way, the presence of two realms, each responsible for part of the activities necessary for the maintenance of the social formation, not only gives to capitalism a structure entirely different from that of any precapitalist society but also establishes the basis for a problem that uniquely preoccupies capitalism; namely, the appropriate role of the state vis-à-vis the sphere of production and distribution.

More widely recognized is the second major effect of the division of realms in encouraging economic and political freedom. Here the capitalist institution of private property again takes centre stage, this time not as a means of arranging production or allocating surplus, but as the shield behind which designated personal rights can be protected. Originally conceived as a means for securing the accumulations of merchants from the seizures of kings, the rights of property were generalized through the market into a general protection accorded to all property, including not least the right of the worker to the ownership of his or her own labour-power.

Now the wage–labour relationship appears not as means for the subordination of labour but for its emancipation, for the crucial advance of wage-labour over enslaved or enserfed labour lies in the right of the working person to deny the capitalist access to labour-power on exactly the same legal basis as that which enables the capitalist to deny the worker access to property. There is, therefore, an institutional basis for the claim that the two realms of capitalism are conducive to certain important kinds of freedom, and that a sphere of market ties may be necessary for the prevention of excessive state power. This is surely an important part of Smith's celebration of the society of 'natural liberty', and has been the basis of the general conservative endorsement of capitalism. Unquestionably, the greatest achievements of human liberty thus far attained in organized society have been achieved in certain advanced capitalist societies. One cannot, however, make the wider claim that capitalism is a sufficient condition for freedom, as the most cursory survey of modern history will confirm.

A third theme in the evolution of capitalism calls attention to the cultural changes that have accompanied and shaped its institutional framework. Much emphasis has been given to this theme in the work of Weber and Schumpeter, both of whom stress the historic distinctions between the essentially rational that is, means – ends calculating – culture of capitalist civilization compared with the 'irrational' cultures of previous social formations. Here it is important to recognize that rationality does not refer to the *principle* of capitalism, for we have seen that the impetus to amass wealth is only a sublimation of deeper-lying non-rational drives and needs, but to the behavioural paths followed in the pursuit of that principle. The drive to amass capital can be analysed in terms of a calculus that is less readily apparent, if indeed present at all, in the search for other forms of prestige and power. This pervasive calculating mind-set is itself the outcome both of the abstract nature of exchange-value, which makes possible commensurations that cannot be carried out in terms of glory or sheer display, and of the pressures exerted by the marketplace, which penalize economic actors who fail to follow the arrow of economic advantage. Capitalism is therefore distinguishable in history by the predominance of a prudent, accountant-like comparison of costs and benefits, a perspective discoverable in the mercantile pockets of earlier formations but highly uncharacteristic of the tempers of their ruling elites (see Weber, 1930; Schumpeter, 1947, ch. XI).

The cultural change associated with capitalism goes further, however, than the rationalization of its general outlook. Indeed, when we examine the general culture of capitalist life we are most forcibly struck by an aspect that precedes and underlies that highlighted above. This is the presence of an ideological framework that contrasts sharply with that of precapitalist formations. I do not use the word *ideology* in a pejorative sense, as denoting a set of ideas foisted on the populace by a ruling order in order to manipulate it, but rather as a set of belief systems to which the ruling elements of the society themselves turn for self-clarification and explanation. In this sense, ideology expresses what the dominant class in a society sincerely believes to be the true explanations of the questions it faces.

That which is characteristic of the ideologies of earlier formations is their unified and monolithic character. In the ancient civilizations of which we know, an all-embracing world view, usually religious in nature, explicates every aspect of life, from the workings of the physical universe, through the justification of rulership, down to the smallest details of social routines and attitudes. By way of contrast, the ideology that emerges within capitalism is made up of diverse strands, more of them secular than religious and many of them in some degree of conflict with other strands. By the end of the 18th century, and to some degree before, the explanation system to which capitalist societies turn with respect to the workings of the universe is science, not religious cosmology. In the same manner, rulership is no longer regarded as the natural prerogative of a divinely chosen elite but perceived as 'government'; that is, as the manner in which 'individuals' create an organization for their mutual protection and advancement. Not least, the panorama of work and the patterns of material life are perceived not as the natural order of things but as a complex web of interactions that can be made comprehensible through the teachings of political economy, later economics. The individual threads of these separate scientific, political-individualist and economic belief systems originate in many cases before the unmistakable emergence of capitalism in the 18th century, but their incorporation into a skein of culture provides yet another identifying theme of the history of capitalist development.

Within this skein, the ideology of economics is obviously of central interest for economists. A crucial element of this belief system involves changes in the attitude towards acquisitiveness itself, above all the disappearance of the ancient concern with good and evil as the most immediate and inescapable consequence of wealth-gathering. As Hirschman has shown, this change was accomplished in part by the gradual reinterpretation of the dangerous 'passion' of avarice as a benign 'interest', capable of steadying and domesticating social intercourse rather than disrupting and demoralizing it (Hirschman, 1977). Other crucial elements of understanding were provided by Locke's brilliant demonstration in *The Second Treatise on Government* (1690) that unlimited acquisition did not contravene the dictates of reason or Scripture, and by the full pardon granted to wealth-seeking by Bentham, who demonstrated that the happiness of all was the natural outcome of the self-regarding pursuit of the happiness of each.

The problem of good and evil was thus removed from the concerns of political economy and relegated to those of morality; and economics as an inquiry into the workings of daily life was thereby differentiated from earlier inquiries, such as the reflections of Aristotle or Aquinas, by its explicit disregard of their central search for moral understanding. Perhaps more accurately, the constitution of a 'science' of economics as the most important form of social self-scrutiny of capitalist societies could not be attempted until moral issues, which defied the calculus of the market, were effectively excluded from the field of its investigations.

THE LOGIC OF THE SYSTEM. This conception of capitalism as a historical formation with distinctive political and cultural as well as economic properties derives from the work of those relatively few economists interested in capitalism as a 'stage' of social evolution. In addition to the seminal work of Marx and the literature that his work has inspired, the conception draws on the writings of Smith, Mill, Veblen, Schumpeter and a number of sociologists and historians, notable among them Weber and Braudel. The majority of present-day economists do not use so broad a canvas, concentrating on capitalism as a market system, with the consequence of emphasizing its functional rather than its institutional or constitutive aspects.

In addition to the characteristic features of its institutional 'nature', capitalism can also be identified by its changing configurations and profiles as it moves through time. Insofar as these movements are rooted in the behaviour-shaping properties of its nature, we can speak of them as expressing the logic of the system, much as conquest or dynastic alliance express the logic of systems built on the principle of imperial rule, or the relatively changeless self-reproduction of primitive societies expresses the logic of societies ordered on the basis on kinship, reciprocity and adaptation to the givens of the physical environment.

The logic of capitalism ultimately derives from the pressure exerted by the expansive M–C–M' process, but it is useful to divide this overall force into two categories. The first of these concerns the 'internal' changes impressed upon the formation by virtue of its necessity to accumulate capital – its metabolic processes, so to speak. The second deals with its larger 'external' motions – changes in its institutional structure or in important indicia of performance as the system evolves through history.

The internal dynamics of capitalism spring from the continuous exposure of individual capitals to capture by other capitalists. This is the consequence of the disbursement of capital-as-money into the hands of the public in the form of wages and other costs. Each capitalist must then seek to win back his expended capital by selling commodities to the public, against the efforts of other capitalists to do the same. This process of the enforced dissolution and uncertain recapture of money capital in the circuit of accumulation is, of course, the pressure of competition that is the social outcome of generalized profit-seeking. We can see, however, that competition cannot be adequately described merely as the vying of suppliers in the marketplace. As both Marx and Schumpeter recognized, competition is at bottom a consequence of the mutual encroachments bred by the capitalist drive for expansion, not of the numbers of firms contending in a given market.

The process of the inescapable dissolution and problematical recapture of individual capitals now gives rise to the activities designed to protect these capitals from seizure. The most readily available means of self-defence is the search for new processes or products that will yield a competitive advantage – the same search that also serves to facilitate the expansion of capital through the development of new markets. Competition thus reinforces the introduction of technological and organizational change into the heart of the accumulation process, usually in two forms: attempts to cheapen the cost of production by displacements of labour by machinery (or of one form of fixed capital by another); or attempts to gain the public's purchasing power by the design of wholly new forms of commodities. As a consequence, one of the most recognizable attributes of capitalist 'internal' dynamics has been its constant revolutionizing of the techniques of production and its continuous commodification of material life, the sources of its vaunted capacity to change and elevate living standards.

A further internal change also arises from the expansive pressures of the core process of capital accumulation. This is a threat to the capacity of capital as a whole to extract a profit from the production of commodities. This tendency arises from the long-run effect of rising living standards in strengthening the bargaining power of labour versus capital. There is no way in which individual enterprises can ward off this threat by cutting wages, for in a competitive market system they would thereupon lose their ability to marshall a workforce. Their only protection against a rising tendency of the wage level is to substitute capital for labour where that is possible. For the system as a whole, the need to hold down the bargaining power of labour must therefore hinge on a generalization of individual cost-reducing efforts, through the system-wide displacement of labour by machinery, or by the direct use of government policies to maintain a profit-yielding balance between labour and capital, or by systemic failures – 'crises' – that create generalized unemployment. Whether attempted by deliberate policy or brought about by the outcome of spontaneous market forces, the pressure to secure a profit-compatible level of wages thus becomes a key aspect in the internal dynamics of the system.

A final attribute of the internal logic of capitalism must also be traced to its core process of accumulation. This is the achievement of a highly adaptive method of matching supplies against demands without the necessity of political intervention. This cybernetic capacity is surely one of the historical hallmarks of capitalism, and is regularly emphasized in the 'comparative systems approach' in which the responsive capacities of the market mechanism are compared with the inertias and rigidities of systems in which tradition or command (planning) must fulfil the allocational task. A critique of the successes and failures of the market system cannot be attempted here. Let us only emphasize that the workings of the system itself derive from institutional attributes whose genesis we have already observed – namely, the establishment of free contractual relations as the means for social coordination; the establishment of a social realm of production and distribution from which government intervention is largely excluded; the legitimation of acquisitive behaviour as the social norm; and activating the whole, the imperious search for the enlargement of exchange-value as the active principle of the historical formation itself.

LARGE-SCALE TENDENCIES. From the metabolism of capitalism also emerges its larger 'external' motions – the overall trajectory often described as its macroeconomic movement, and the configurational changes that are the main concern of institutional economics. It may be possible to convey some

sense of these general movements if we note three general aspects characteristic of them.

We have already paid heed to the first of these, the tendency of the capitalist system to accumulate wealth on an unparalleled scale. Some indication of the magnitude of this process emerges in the contrast between the increase in per capital GNP of developed (capitalist) and less-developed (noncapitalist) countries:

Table 1 GNP per capita (1960 dollars and prices)

	Presently developed countries	Presently less-developed countries
Around 1750	$180	$180–90
Around 1930	780	190
Around 1980	3,000	410

Source: Paul Bairoch in Faaland (1982), p. 162.

After our lengthy discussion of the central role of accumulation within capitalism it does not seem necessary to relate this historic trend to its institutional base. Two somewhat neglected aspects of the overall increase in wealth seem worth mentioning, however. The first is that the increase in per capita GNP includes both augmentations in the volume of output and an extension of the M–C–M' process itself within the social world. This is manifested in a continuous implosion of the accumulation process within capitalist societies – the process of the commodification of material life to which we earlier referred – and its explosion into neighbouring noncapitalist societies.

This explosive thrust calls attention to the second attribute of the overall expansion of wealth. It is that capital, as such, knows no national limits. From its earliest historic appearance, capital has been driven to link its 'domestic' base with foreign regions or countries, using the latter as suppliers of cheap labour-power or cheap raw materials or as markets for the output of the domestic economy. The consequence has been the emergence of self-reinforcing and cumulative tendencies towards strength at the centre, to which surplus is siphoned, and weakness in the periphery, from which it is extracted. The economic dimensions of this global drift are immediately visible in the previous table. This is the basis for what has been called the 'development of underdevelopment' as the manner in which ancient patterns of international hegemony are expressed in the context of capitalist relationships (Myrdal, 1957, Part I: Baran, 1957, chs V–VII).

We turn next to a different overall manifestation of the larger logic of capitalist development – its changes in institutional texture. There have been, of course, many such changes in the long span of Western capitalist experience – indeed, it is the very diversity of the faces of capitalism that prompted our search for its deep-lying identifying elements. Nonetheless, two changes deserve to be singled out, not only because of their sweeping magnitude and transnational occurrence, but because they have deeply altered the evolutionary logic of the system itself. These have been the emergence within all modern capitalisms of highly skewed size distributions of enterprise, and of very large and powerful public sectors.

The general extent of these transformations is sufficiently well known not to require detailed exposition here. Suffice it to illustrate the trend by contrasting the largely atomistic composition of manufacturing enterprise in the United States at the middle of the 19th century with the situation in the 1980s, when seven-eighths of all industrial sales were produced by 0.1 per cent of the population of industrial firms. The enlargement of the public sector is not so dramatic but is equally unmistakable. During the present century in the United States, its size (measured by all government purchases of output plus transfer payments) has increased from perhaps 7.5 per cent of GNP to over 35 per cent, a trend that is considerably outpaced by a number of European capitalisms.

The first of these two large-scale shifts in the configuration can be directly traced to the pressures generated by the M–C–M′ circuit. The change from a relatively homogeneous texture of enterprise to one of extreme disparities of size is the consequence not only of differential rates of growth of different units of capital, but of defensive business strategies of trustification and merger, and the winnowing effect of economic disruptions on smaller and weaker units of capital. There is little disagreement as to the endemic source of this transformation in the dynamics of the marketplace and the imperative of business expansion.

The growth of large public sectors is not so immediately attributable to the accumulation process proper but rather results from changes in the logic of capitalist movements after the concentration of industry has taken place. Here the crucial change lies in the increasing instability of the market mechanism, as its constituent parts cease to resemble a honeycomb of small units, individually weak but collectively resilient, and take on the character of a structure of beams and girders, each very strong but collectively rigid and interlocked. It seems plausible that this rigidification was the underlying cause of the increasingly disruptive nature of the crises that appeared first in the late 19th century and climaxed in the great depression of the 1930s; and it is widely accepted that the growth of the public sector mainly owes its origins to efforts to mitigate the effects of that instability or to prevent its recurrence.

This brings us to the last general aspect of capitalist development; namely, the tendency for interruptions and failures to break the general momentum of capital accumulation. Perhaps no aspect of the logic of capitalism has been more intensively studied than these recurrent failures in the accumulation process. In the name of stagnation, gluts, panics, cycles, crises and long waves a vast literature has emerged to explain the causes and effects of intermittent systematic difficulties in successfully negotiating the passage from M to M′. The variables chosen to play strategic roles in the explanation of the phenomenon are also widely diverse: the saturation of markets; the undertow of insufficient consumption; the technological displacement of labour; the pressure of wages against profit margins; various monetary disorders; the general 'anarchy' of production; the effect of ill-considered government policy, and still others.

Despite the variety of elements to which various theorists have turned, a common thread unites most of their investigations. This is the premise that the instabilities of capitalist growth originate in the process of accumulation itself. Even theorists who have the greatest confidence in the inherent tendency of the system to seek a steady growth path, or who look to government intervention (in modern capitalism) as the main instability-generating force, recognize that economic expansion tends to generate fluctuations in the rate of growth, whether from the 'lumpy' character of investment, volatile expectations, or other causes. In similar fashion, economists who stress instability rather than stability as the intrinsic tendency of the system do not deny the possibility of renewed accumulation once the decline has performed its surgical work; indeed, Marx, the most powerful proponent of the inherently unstable character of the M–C–M′ process, was the first to assert that the function of crisis was to prepare the way for a renewal of accumulation.

In a sense, then, the point at issue is not whether economic growth is inherently unstable, but the speed and efficacy of the unaided market mechanism in correcting its instability. This ongoing debate mainly takes the form of sharp disagreements with respect to the effects of government policy in supplementing or undermining the corrective powers of the market. The failure to reach accord on this issue reflects more than differences of informed opinion with regard to the consequences of sticky wages or prices, or ill-timed government interventions, and the like. It should not be forgotten that, from the viewpoint of capitalism as a regime, interruptions pose the same threats as did hiatuses in dynastic succession or breakdowns of imperial hegemony in earlier formations. It is not surprising, then, that the philosophic predilections of theorists play a significant role in their diagnoses of the problem, inclining economists to one side or the other of the debate on the basis of their general political sympathies with the regime, rather than on the basis of purely analytic considerations.

PERIODIZATION AND PROSPECTS. All the foregoing aspects of the system can be traced to its inner metabolism, the money–commodity–money circuit. This is much less the case when we now consider the overarching pattern of change described by the configuration of the social formation as a whole as it moves from one historic 'period' to another.

Traditionally these periods have been identified as early and late mercantilism; pre-industrial, and early and late industrial capitalism; and modern (or late, or state) capitalism. These designations can be made more specific by adumbrating the kinds of institutional change that separate one period from another. These include the size and character of firms (trading companies, putting-out establishments, manufactories, industrial enterprises of increasing complexity); methods of engaging and supervising labour (cottage industry through mass production); the appearance and consolidation of labour unions within various sectors of the economy; technological progress (tools, machines, concatenations of equipment, scientific apparatus); organizational evolution (proprietorships, family corporations, managerial bureaucracies, state participation). David Gordon has coined the term 'social structure of accumulation' to call attention to the changing framework of technical, organizational and ideological conditions within which the accumulation process must take place. Gordon's concept, applied to the general problem of periodization, emphasizes the manner in which the accumulation process first exploits the possibilities of a 'stage' of capitalism, only to confront in time the limitations of that stage which must be transcended by more or less radical institutional alterations (Gordon, 1980).

The idea of an accumulation process alternately stimulated and blocked by its institutional constraints provides an illumining heuristic on the intraperiod dynamics of the system, but not a theory of its long-run evolutionary path. This is because not all national capitalisms make the transitions with equal ease or speed from one social structure to another, and because it is not apparent that the pressures of the M–C–M′ process push the overall structure in any clearly defined direction. Thus Holland at the end of the 17th century failed to make the leap beyond mercantilism, and England in turn in the second half of the 19th century failed to create a successful late industrial capitalism. In this regard it is interesting that the explanatory narratives of the great economists apply with far greater cogency to the evolutionary trends within periods than across them – Smith's scenario of growth in *The Wealth of Nations*, for instance, containing no suggestion that the system would move into an industrial phase with quite different dynamics, or Marx's depiction of the laws of motion of the industrialized system containing no hint of its worldwide evolution towards a state-underwritten structure. Although the inner characteristics of the M–C–M′ process enable us to apply the same generic designation of capitalism to its successive species-forms, it does not seem to be possible to demonstrate, even after the fact, that the transition from one stage to another had to be made, or to predict before the fact what the direction of institutional adjustment will be.

These cautions apply to the prospects confronting capitalism in our day. Its long post World War II boom seems to have been based on three attributes of the social structure of accumulation of that time. One of these was the increasing interconnection between the political and the economic realms, not merely to provide a public base for mass consumption but to utilize the state's power of finance and international leadership to promote foreign private trade and production. Japanese capitalism has been the much cited case in point for the latter development. A second characteristic of the boom was the extraordinary development of technology, based on the close integration of scientific research and technical application. A third was the pronounced bourgeoisification of working-class life, especially in Europe and Japan, greatly reducing the spectre of class conflict in capitalist politics.

On the basis of these developments capitalism enjoyed the longest uninterrupted period of accumulation in its history, from the early 1950s to the mid-1970s. Not only was the boom uninterrupted save for minor and shortlived recessions, but on the wings of its new technological breakthroughs, and under the auspices of its active state cooperation, capitalism made extraordinary advances in introducing its core institutions into many areas of the underdeveloped world.

This halcyon period came to a sharp end in 1980 when growth rates in the United States and Europe fell precipitously. Some, although not all of the causes of this depression can be ascribed to an exhaustion of the expansionary possibilities within the postwar social structure of accumulation. The effect of enlarged and sustained public expenditure gradually shifted from the encouragement of production to the inducement of inflation, thus setting the stage for the adoption of the tight money policies that finally broke the back of the boom. As markets became saturated, the advances in technology lost their capacity to stimulate capital expansion and attention was increasingly directed to their system threatening aspects – ecologically dangerous products, employment-eroding processes and sovereignty-defying enhancements of the international mobility of money capital and commodities. The international character of capital acquired extraordinary importance, as multinational corporations transplanted fixed capital into underdeveloped regions, from which it launched artillery barrages of commodities back on its domestic territory. And not least, the bourgeoisification of labour may have removed a traditional source of adaptational pressure from capitalism.

It is not possible to foretell how these challenges will be met, or what institutional changes will be forced upon the capitalist world as their consequence, or which capitalist nations will find the institutional and organizational means best suited to continue the accumulation process in this newly emerging milieu. Thus there is no basis for predicting the longevity of the social formation, either in its national instantiations or as a formational whole.

But while history forces on us a salutary agnosticism with regard to the long-term prospects for capitalism, it is interesting to note that all the great economists have envisaged an eventual end to the capitalist period of history. Smith describes the accumulation process as ultimately reaching a plateau when the attainment of riches will be 'complete', followed by a lengthy and deep decline. Ricardo and Mill anticipate the arrival of a 'stationary state', which Mill foresees as the staging ground for a kind of associationist socialism. Marx anticipates a series of worsening crisis, each crises serving a temporary rejuvenating function but bringing closer the day when the system will no longer be able to manage its internal contradictions. Keynes foresees 'a somewhat comprehensive socialization of investment'; Schumpeter, an evolution into a kind of bureaucratic socialism. By way of contrast, contemporary mainstream economists are largely uninterested in questions of historic projection, regarding capitalism as a system whose formal properties can be modelled, whether along general equilibrium or more dynamic lines, without any need to attribute to these models the properties that would enable them to be perceived as historic regimes and without pronouncements as to the likely structural or political destinations towards which they incline. At a time when the need for institutional adaptation seems pressing, such an historical indifference to the fate of capitalism, on the part of those who are professionally charged with its self-clarification, does not augur well for the future.

ROBERT L. HEILBRONER

See also ECONOMIC INTERPRETATION OF HISTORY; SOCIALISM.

BIBLIOGRAPHY

Baran, P. 1957. *The Political Economy of Growth.* New York: Monthly Review Press.

Faaland, J. 1982. *Population and the World Economy in the 21st Century.* Oxford: Blackwell.

Gordon, D. 1980. Stages of accumulation and long economic cycles. In *Processes of the World System,* ed. T. Hopkins and I. Wallerstein, Beverly Hills: Sage.

Heilbroner, R.L. 1985. *The Nature and Logic of Capitalism.* New York: W.W. Norton.

Hilton, R. (ed.) 1978. *The Transition from Feudalism to Capitalism.* London: Verso.

Hirschman, A. 1977. *The Passions and the Interests.* Princeton: Princeton University Press.

Myrdal, G. 1957. *Rich Lands and Poor.* New York: Harper & Bros.

Pirenne, H. 1936. *Economic and Social History of Medieval Europe.* London: K. Paul, Trench, Trubner & Co.

Polanyi, K. 1957. *The Great Transformation.* Boston: Beacon Press.

Sagan, E. 1985. *At the Dawn of Tyranny: The Origins of Individualism, Political Oppression, and the State.* New York: Knopf.

Schumpeter, J. 1942. *Capitalism, Socialism and Democracy.* New York: Harper & Bros.

Smith, A. 1776. *The Wealth of Nations.* Oxford: Clarendon Press. 1976.

Weber, M. 1930. *The Protestant Ethic and the Spirit of Capitalism.* London: Allen & Unwin.

capitalism, contradictions of. *See* CONTRADICTIONS OF CAPITALISM.

capitalistic and acapitalistic production. If 'capital' is the set of produced means of production, (almost) all production is capitalistic. Thus, the presence of capital in this sense can at most be (and in the history of economic doctrines was taken to represent) a necessary condition for defining capitalistic production. Differences arose as to the relative emphasis put on the social or techno-economic aspects of such transformation processes.

In Marx's analysis, capitalistic production is the organization of social production specific to a society characterized by private ownership of the means of production and by its separation from 'labour'. This historically given Mode of Production is contrasted with pre- and post-capitalistic forms, where power relationships are regulated according to different principles. By contrast, the distinction between production with and without capital focuses upon the relationship between means and objectives (consumption goods) of production activity. It played a role in the era of the full articulation of neoclassical thought. Its analytical use obviously depended upon the specific conception (and representation) of capital.

According to perhaps the most common theory, Capital is a factor of production, a member of a triad with Labour and Land. This view emphasizes the aspect of capital as a stock of man-produced goods which are at any point of time available in fixed quantities. (A)capitalistic production entails the application of (un)aided labour to natural resources. On the other hand, according to the Austrian (Böhm-Bawerk) definition, capital is the set of intermediate goods (or 'maturing consumption goods') emerging in the transformation of labour services into final goods when indirect methods of production are employed. This conception emphasizes the functional relationship whereby capital is the mode of realization of advanced production activity. Accordingly, acapitalistic production is direct production of consumption goods through application of bare labour to natural resources. Finally, in Wicksell's theoretical compromise, capital is a stock of used-up services of both labour and land. Production without capital is carried on by means of labour and natural resources in a state where capital goods either do not exist or are free goods relative to the available technology. (See Part II of the first volume of Wicksell's Lectures, 1934.) This definition obviously overlooks the fact that capital goods are themselves a byproduct of the advancement of technological knowledge, an idea implicit in Böhm-Bawerk and hinted at by Schumpeter.

At any rate, in all its various interpretations, acapitalistic production was a logical abstraction meant to illustrate, in a simpler analytical context, some basic principles holding for capitalistic production. In Böhm-Bawerk, this is the principle of the higher productivity of indirect (i.e. capitalistic) methods of production. In Wicksell, the distinction is meant to illustrate the marginalistic approach to the distribution of income and to show how it can be extended from the simpler production with labour and land only to production involving capital goods. In the former case, wage rate and rent are regulated by the marginal productivities of the two factors, in a state of full employment of labour and zero entrepreneurial profits. However, the extension of the marginal productivity principle to the theory of interest meets a crucial conceptual difficulty due to the fact that capital, being an aggregate of produced goods, has to be measured in value and the latter depends itself on income distribution. It is to avoid a circular argument that Wicksell proposes to regard capital as 'a single coherent mass of saved up resources'. Hence, interest would be (equal to) the difference between the marginal productivity of saved up labour and land and the marginal productivity of current labour and land. According to Wicksell, 'experience' shows that capital has a higher productivity and this is the reason why its share in the national product is normally positive.

It has been proved, in the debate on capital theory in the 1960s, that Wicksell's attempt at finding a way out of the difficulties of the marginalistic approach to income distribution is unsatisfactory. However, the recurrence of the theme of the distinction between acapitalistic and capitalistic production is interesting for it indicates the neoclassical authors' awareness of the theoretical difficulties they met in the treatment of capital and distribution.

LIONELLO F. PUNZO

See also CAPITAL PERVERSITY; WICKSELL, JOHAN GUSTAF KNUT.

BIBLIOGRAPHY

Böhm-Bawerk, E. von. 1889. *Positive Theorie des Kapitals*. Trans. by G.D. Huncke as Vol. 2 of *Capital and Interest*, South Holland, Ill.: Libertarian Press, 1959.

Schumpeter, J.A. 1954. *History of Economic Analysis*. London: Allen & Unwin.

Wicksell, K. 1934. *Lectures on Political Economy*. 1st English edn, ed. L. Robbins, London: George Routledge & Sons.

capitalization. *See* PRESENT VALUE; RENT; TIEBOUT HYPOTHESIS.

capital markets. *See* CAPITAL, CREDIT AND MONEY MARKETS.

capital perversity. Neoclassical capital theory regards the interest rate as the market price of the composite factor 'capital'. In this theory the interest rate is equal to the marginal product of capital, since the demand curve for capital is its marginal productivity schedule. Moreover, the theory assumes that capital obeys the law of diminishing returns just like any other factor, so that its demand curve is downward-sloping. In an economy where labour is the only primary factor and constant returns to scale prevail, this implies the following postulate: *as the interest rate falls, the capital–labour ratio increases*, which plays an important role in neoclassical growth theory and in comparative static analyses of interest rate determination.

Neoclassical capital theory also makes another closely related postulate: *as the interest rate falls, the output–labour ratio increases*. This postulate does not explicitly use the concept of aggregate capital. However, it too implies that 'capital' obeys the law of diminishing returns. For the output–labour ratio can be raised only when some input other than labour is increased behind the scenes, and in this economy capital is the only such input available.

Both postulates necessarily hold if output is produced by labour and a *single* capital input in a linear homogeneous production function, as in the Clark–Ramsey production function. Cambridge economists, led by Robinson (1953–4, 1956), Champernowne (1953–4) and Sraffa (1960), criticized these postulates, however, for economies with heterogeneous capital goods, thus kindling the so-called Cambridge controversies in capital theory as surveyed by von Weizsäcker (1971), Harcourt (1972), Blaug (1974), and Burmeister (1980). Eventually, counter-examples that appeared in Pasinetti et al. (1966) showed irrefutably that both postulates can fail to hold in such economies. These paradoxical phenomena are called *capital perversities*. They showed very clearly that 'capital' is different from other factors in that diminishing returns do not hold for it even in contexts quite free of aggregation problems.

In order to examine the first postulate for economies with heterogeneous capital goods, one has to aggregate heterogeneous capital goods into a single dollar value of capital. Such a measure could well be specious, however, due to the index number problem involved in the aggregation, the interest rate affecting the prices of capital goods with different gestation periods differently. Since the second postulate does not depend on a particular aggregate measure of capital, it may appear a more robust characterization of diminishing returns from roundabout processes than the first. In fact, the following proposition due to Burmeister and Dobell (1970, Corollary 7.2) implies that the two postulates are equivalent once a proper price index is chosen for evaluating capital.

Suppose than an exogenous increase in interest rate shifts one stationary-state production equilibrium to another. Then, as long as the interest rate is positive, the ratio of output to labour moves in the same direction as the ratio of 'constant-price capital' to labour, where the 'constant-price capital' is the dollar value of the new capital input vector measured at the initial input price vector.

For this reason we will examine only the failure of the second postulate to hold.

RESWITCHING. Capital perversity was demonstrated via examples of the so-called reswitching phenomenon; the simplest and most illuminating is Samuelson's (1966). He assumes that output this year is produced by applying labour inputs in three preceding years according to the following production function:

$$Y = y(x_1, x_2, x_3), \qquad (1)$$

where Y is this year's output level and x_1, x_2, and x_3 are labour inputs one, two, and three years ago, respectively. Let p_t be the present value of the wage rate t periods prior to the production year. Producers chose the cost-minimizing input vector (x_1, x_2, x_3) for the given output level under the input price vector (p_1, p_2, p_3). Samuelson also assumes free entry, so that maximized profit is zero.

Now consider a steady-state economy where Y is produced every year and prices are constant. Then we have

$$p_t = w \cdot r^t, \qquad (2)$$

where w is the (constant) wage rate and r is 1 plus the interest rate. Input and output variables for each year may be shown as in Table 1. Each column shows the total amount of labour L applied in the entire production process that year as

$$L = x_1 + x_2 + x_3. \qquad (3)$$

As the macroeconomist sees it, this economy as a whole produces Y every year by applying capital inputs in the form of goods-in-process and an amount L of labour.

Samuelson considered the case where the technology (1) consists of only two techniques α and β: α's input vector (x_1, x_2, x_3) for producing a unit output is $(0, 7, 0)$ and β's $(6, 0, 2)$. He showed that β minimizes cost when the interest rate lies between 50 and 100 per cent per year, while α does so otherwise. As the interest rate increases from zero, therefore, the cost-minimizing technique switches first from α to β, and then back to α. This phenomenon, that as the interest rate increases, a once-abandoned technique becomes re-employed, is called *the reswitching of techniques*. It is obvious that when it happens capital perversity necessarily occurs. In Samuelson's case, for example, when the interest rate is increased past 100 per cent, technique β with $Y/L = 1/8$ is switched to α with $1/7$, falsifying the second postulate. It can readily be shown that at this switching interest rate the first postulate also fails, even after the index number problem is removed.

WHAT CAUSES PERVERSITY? Examples of reswitching had to be given for economies with discrete technologies, since it occurs with probability zero in a smoothly substitutable production function. But neither reswitching nor a discrete technology is necessary for perversity itself. Indeed, Hatta (1976) constructed an example of a smoothly substitutable and linear homogeneous function of type (1) that behaves perversely.

To see how this might work, consider a generalized version of (1):

$$Y = y(x_1, x_2, \ldots, x_n), \qquad (4)$$

where y is quasi-concave, linear homogeneous, and differentiable. Then we have the following proposition due to Hatta (1976), which was independently hinted at by Solow (1975, p. 52):

For capital perversity to occur in (4) it must have at least one complementary input pair. (A)

Equivalently, if all input pairs in (4) are (Hicksian) substitutes, perversity cannot occur.

According to a standard Hicksian demand rule (1946, ch. 3), (net) complementarity among inputs can occur in (4) only if n is greater than 2. Thus Proposition (A) implies that for perversity to occur in (4), n must be greater than 2. When $n = 2$, on the other hand, the economy has only one capital good, i.e., the one produced by the labour input applied in the previous year. Proposition (A) therefore implies that:

Heterogeneity of capital is necessary for perversity in (4). (B)

We now prove (A) for the case $n = 3$. The cost-minimizing input vector for output level Y under the input price vector (p_1, p_2, p_3) is given by the following set of input demand functions:

$$x_s = a_s(p_1, p_2, p_3, Y) \qquad s = 1, 2, 3.$$

We assume that the interest rate is positive, i.e.,

$$r > 1. \qquad (5)$$

Noting (2) and the zero-degree homogeneity of a_s in the prices, the following must hold when cost is minimized:

$$x_s = a_s(1, r, r^2, Y) \qquad s = 1, 2, 3.$$

In view of equation (3), therefore, the total labour movement requirement in this stationary economy is

$$L = a_1(1, r, r^2, Y) + a_2(1, r, r^2, Y) + a_3(1, r, r^2, Y)$$

By definition perversity occurs if the L necessary to produce a constant Y every year is lowered when the interest rate is raised, i.e., if

$$\partial L / \partial r < 0. \qquad (6)$$

Carrying out this differentiation, we obtain

$$\frac{\partial L}{\partial r} = (r-1) \cdot a_{12} + 2(r^2-1) \cdot a_{13} + (r^2-r) \cdot a_{23}. \qquad (7)$$

Table 1

1986	1985	1984	1983	1982	1981	1980
			Y	x_1	x_2	x_3
		Y	x_1	x_2	x_3	
	Y	x_1	x_2	x_3		
Y	x_1	x_2	x_3			

355

where

$$a_{st} \equiv \partial a_s / \partial p_t.$$

This and (5) imply that $\partial L / \partial r$ is positive if all a_{st}'s (i.e. Hicksian cross-substitution terms) are positive. This in turn implies that for perversity to occur, there must be at least one complementary input pair. Q.E.D.

For general n, Proposition (6) is proved similarly, since (7) generalizes to

$$r \cdot \frac{\partial L}{\partial r} = \sum_{s=1}^{n-1} \sum_{t=s+1}^{n} (t-s)(p_t - p_s) \cdot a_{st}.$$

Now look at Samuelson's example in the light of (A). Assume that for given Y and given prices, β is cost-minimizing. Now let p_1 increase, keeping p_2 and p_3 constant. Eventually this will make β more costly than α, so α will be employed. But α uses less x_3 than β in order to produce the same output, so the rise in p_1 has caused a reduction in x_3, i.e. pair $(1, 3)$ is complementary. Thus Samuelson's discrete model is consistent with our Proposition (A), obtained for the neoclassical production function.

Hence perversity is simply one of the many paradoxes caused by complementarity. The reason why the Clark–Ramsey production function always behaves well is now clear: it has only two inputs, which must be substitutes.

WHY COMPLEMENTARITY? Why does complementarity cause perversity? Note first that when $n = 3$ perversity cannot occur if either the input pair $(1, 2)$ or the pair $(2, 3)$ is complementary. Indeed, when $n = 3$ the following stronger version of (A) holds: For perversity to occur in (1), a_{13} must be negative, i.e., the specific input pair $(1, 3)$ must be complementary.   (C)

Just as a complementary pair of consumption goods can be regarded as a composite good, a complementary pair of inputs (e.g. truck and garage) may be treated as a composite input. When a neighbouring input pair is complementary in the production function (1), therefore, that function can be regarded as containing just two inputs: one (composite) labour and a (composite) capital. For example, when $(1, 2)$ is complementary, the pair $(1, 2)$ can be regarded as composite labour. In such cases the production function is essentially of Clark–Ramsey form and so behaves well.

When $(1, 3)$ is complementary, on the other hand, the technology's two (composite) inputs $(1, 3)$ and 2 cannot be ranked in terms of their gestation periods. The two inputs can interchange the roles of capital and labour for different levels of interest rate, which explains why perversity can occur in this situation. Observe that $(1, 3)$ is also complementary in Samuelson's model with a discrete technology, and the above explanation is applicable to his model.

Proposition (C) can be extended in various ways to the case where $n > 3$. For example, perversity never occurs if the structure of complementarity is such that the n inputs can be classified into one composite labour and one composite capital. Thus perversity occurs only if complementarity creates a composite input that cannot be unequivocally ranked with another (composite) input vis-à-vis their gestation periods. As Hatta (1976) argues, Bruno, Burmeister and Sheshinski's (1966) non-reswitching condition can be interpreted in this spirit.

The proof of (C) is straightforward. Noting that $a_{11} + r a_{12} + r^2 a_{13} = 0$ and $a_{31} + r a_{32} + r^2 a_{33} = 0$, from the homogeneity property of the input demand functions in prices, we can rewrite (7) as:

$$\frac{r}{w} \cdot \frac{\partial L}{\partial r} = (1 - r) \cdot a_{11} + (r^3 - r) \cdot a_{13} + (r^3 - r^4) \cdot a_{33}.$$

This implies that a_{13} must be negative if perversity occurs, since r is greater than 1 and a_{11} and a_{33} are negative from the Hicksian demand rule. Thus (C) is proved.

CONCLUSION To construct models of growth and the interest rate in an economy with heterogeneous capital–good inputs, the concept of 'capital' is not at all necessary: microeconomic production functions can be specified directly in terms of the physical units of those inputs. The main focus of the Cambridge controversies in capital theory was rather on the question of how well the simple Clark–Ramsey production function can approximate the qualitative properties of a production economy with heterogeneous capital–good inputs.

It was established through these controversies that the monotonic relationship between output–labour ratio and interest rate, a basic property of the Clark–Ramsey production function, fails to hold in a world of heterogeneous capital inputs. Since this relation has nothing to do with the index number problem, the fact that it breaks down in a general model clearly contradicted that part of neoclassical capital theory which was based upon the Clark–Ramsey production function. This was a genuinely new finding that came out of the capital controversies. As we have seen, however, it is fully explicable within neoclassical theory, being no more (and no less) than one of the many intractable problems caused by the presence of complementarity.

TATSUO HATTA

See also CAPITAL THEORY: PARADOXES; REVERSE CAPITAL DEEPENING.

BIBLIOGRAPHY
Blaug, M. 1974. *The Cambridge Revolution: Success or Failure?* London: The Institute of Economic Affairs.
Bruno, M., Burmeister, E. and Sheshinski, E. 1966. The nature and implications of the reswitching of techniques. *Quarterly Journal of Economics* 80, 526–53.
Burmeister, E. 1980. *Capital Theory and Dynamics.* Cambridge: Cambridge University Press.
Burmeister, E. and Dobell, R. 1970. *Mathematical Theories of Economic Growth.* New York: Macmillan Co.
Champernowne, D.G. 1953–4. The production function and the theory of capital: a comment. *Review of Economic Studies* 21, 112–35.
Harcourt, G.C. 1972. *Some Cambridge Controversies in the Theory of Capital.* London: Cambridge University Press.
Hatta, T. 1976. The paradox in capital theory and complementarity of inputs. *Review of Economic Studies* 43, 127–42.
Hicks, J. 1946. *Value and Capital.* 2nd edn, London: Oxford University Press.
Pasinetti, L.L. et al. 1966. Paradoxes in capital theory: a symposium. *Quarterly Journal of Economics* 80, 503–83.
Robinson, J. 1953–4. The production function and the theory of capital. *Review of Economic Studies* 21, 81–106.
Robinson, J. 1956. *The Accumulation of Capital.* London: Macmillan.
Samuelson, P.A. 1966. A summing up. *Quarterly Journal of Economics* 80, 568–83.
Solow, R. 1975. Brief comments. *Quarterly Journal of Economics* 89, 48–52.
Sraffa, P. 1960. *Production of Commodities by Means of Commodities Prelude to a Critique of Economic Theory.* Cambridge: Cambridge University Press.
von Weizsäcker, C.C. 1971. *Steady State Capital Theory.* Berlin: Springer-Verlag.

capital structure. See DIVIDEND POLICY.

capital taxation. *See* TAXATION OF CAPITAL.

capital theory: debates. Capital theory is notorious for being perhaps the most controversial area in economics. This has been so ever since the very inception of systematic economic analysis. Much of the interest in the theory of capital lies in the fact that it holds the key to the explanation of profits. Since the notion of 'capital' is at the centre of an inquiry into the laws of production and distribution in a capitalist economy, controversies in the theory of capital are reflected in virtually all other parts of economic analysis.

We can distinguish between debates *within* different traditions of economic analysis and debates *between* them. In what follows our concern will be mainly with the latter. At the cost of severe simplification, the various traditions in the theory of capital and distribution may be divided into two principal groups, one rooted in the surplus approach of the classical economists from Adam Smith to Ricardo and the other in the demand and supply approach of the early marginalist economists. The so-called 'Cambridge controversies' (cf. Harcourt, 1969), triggered off by a seminal paper by Joan Robinson (1953), consisted essentially in a confrontation of these two radically different traditions. The debate is still continuing. Currently, the discussion focuses on some of the neoclassical authors' claim that the classical theory, as it was reformulated by Sraffa (1960), is a 'special case' of modern general equilibrium theory. We shall come back to this questionable proposition towards the end of the entry.

THE SURPLUS APPROACH. The general method underlying the classical economists' approach to the theory of capital and distribution was that of 'normal' or 'long-period' positions. These were conceived as centres around which the economy is assumed to gravitate, given the competitive tendency towards a uniform rate of profit. Because of the assumed gravitation of 'market values' to the 'normal' levels of the distributive and price variables, the former were given little attention only, being governed by temporary and accidental causes, a proper scientific analysis of which was considered neither necessary nor possible. Emphasis was on the persistent or non-temporary causes shaping the economy. Accordingly, the investigation of the permanent effects of changes in the dominant causes was carried out by means of comparisons between 'normal' positions of the economic system.

The development of a satisfactory theory to determine the general rate of profit was thus the main concern of the classical economists. As regards the content of this theory, profits were explained in terms of the *surplus product* left after making allowance for the requirements of reproduction, which were conceived inclusive of the wages of labour (Ricardo, 1817, vol. 1, p. 95). As Sraffa (1951, 1960) emphasized, the determination of the social surplus implied taking as data (i) the system of production in use, characterized, as it is, by the dominant technical conditions of production of the various commodities and the size and composition of the social product; and (ii) the ruling real wage rate(s). In accordance with the underlying 'normal' position the capital stock was assumed to be so adjusted to 'effectual demand' (Adam Smith) that a normal rate of utilization of its component parts would be realized and a uniform rate of return on its supply price obtained. Thus the classical authors separated the determination of profits and prices from that of quantities. The latter were considered as determined in another part of the theory i.e. the analysis of accumulation and economic and social development.

The rate of profit was defined by the ratio between social surplus and social capital, i.e. two aggregates of heterogeneous commodities. Thus the classical theory had to face the problem of value. Ricardo's ingenious device to solve this problem consisted in relating the exchange values of the commodities to the quantities of labour directly and indirectly necessary to produce them. This led to the first formulation of one of the key concepts in the theory of capital ever since – the inverse relationship between the real wage and the rate of profit (Ricardo, vol. 8, p. 194).

It was not until Marx that additional important steps in the development of the surplus approach were taken. In particular, in Marx the analytical role of the 'labour theory of value' in the determination of the general rate of profit was brought into sharp relief. According to him the explanation of profits in terms of the surplus approach would have been trapped in circular reasoning if the value expression of either aggregate (surplus and capital) were to depend on the rate of profit. The measurement of both aggregates in terms of labour values, which themselves were seen to be independent of distribution, was considered a device to circumvent this danger and provide a non-circular determination of the rate of profit, $r = s/(c + v)$, where r is the general rate of profit, s the 'surplus value', c the value of the means of production or 'constant capital', and v the wages advanced or 'variable capital'. A central meassage of Marx's *Capital* reads that the rate of profit is positive if and only if there is 'exploitation of workers', i.e. there is a positive 'surplus value'.

In Marx's opinion it was only after the rate of profit had been determined that the problem of normal prices, or 'prices of production' as he called them, could be tackled. Marx dealt with it in terms of a multisectoral analysis of the production of commodities by means of commodities; the deviations of relative prices from labour values are systematically traced back to sectoral differences in the 'organic composition of capital', i.e. the proportion of 'constant' to 'variable' capital (cf. the so-called 'transformation' of values into prices of production; Marx, 1959, Part II).

Yet Marx did not fully succeed in overcoming the analytical difficulties encountered by the classical economists in the theory of capital and distribution. He was particularly wrong in assuming that the determination of the rate of profit is logically prior to that of normal prices. Given the system of production and the real wage the rate of profit and prices can be determined only simultaneously. This was first demonstrated by Bortkiewicz (1907). For a rigorous and comprehensive formulation of the classical surplus approach see Sraffa (1960), whose contribution will be dealt with in more detail below.

THE NEOCLASSICAL APPROACH. The abandonment of the classical approach and the development of a radically different theory, which came to predominance in the wake of the so-called 'marginalist revolution' in the latter part of the 19th century, was motivated (apart from ideological reasons ever present in debates in capital theory) by the deficiencies of the received (labour) theory of value. Since the new theory was to be an alternative to the classical theory, it had to be an alternative theory about the same thing, in particular the normal rate of profit. Consequently, the early neoclassical economists, including, for example, Jevons (1871), Walras (1874), Böhm-Bawerk (1889), Wicksell (1893, 1901) and J. B. Clark (1899), adopted fundamentally the same method of analysis: the concept of 'long-period equilibrium' is the neoclassical adaptation of the classical concept of normal positions.

The basic novelty of the new theory consisted in the following. While the surplus approach conceived the real wage as determined *prior* to profits (and rent), in the neoclassical approach all kinds of incomes were explained simultaneously and *symmetrically* in terms of the 'opposing forces' of supply and demand in regard to the services of the respective 'factors of production', labour and 'capital' (and land). It was the seemingly coherent foundation of these notions in terms of *functional* relationships between the price of a service (or good) and the quantity supplied or demanded elaborated by the neoclassical theory that greatly contributed to the latter's success.

As regards the supply side of the neoclassical treatment of capital, careful scrutiny shows that its advocates, with the notable exception of Walras (at least until the fourth edition of the *Eléments*), were well aware of the fact that in order to be consistent with the concept of a long-period equilibrium the capital equipment of the economy could not be conceived as a set of given physical amounts of produced means of production. The 'quantity of capital' in given supply rather had to be expressed in *value* terms, allowing it to assume the physical 'form' best suited to the other data of the theory, i.e. the technical conditions of production and the preferences of agents. For, if the capital endowment is given in kind only a short-period equilibrium, characterized by differential rates of return on the supply prices of the various capital goods, could be established by the forces constituting demand and supply. However, under conditions of free competition, which would enforce a tendency towards a uniform rate of profit, such an equilibrium could not be considered a 'full equilibrium' (Hicks, 1932, p. 20).

Thus the formidable problem for the neoclassical approach in attempting the determination of the general rate of profit consisted in the necessity of establishing the notion of a market for 'capital', the quantity of which could be expressed *independently* of the 'price of its service', i.e. the rate of profit. If such a market could be shown to exist, profits could be explained analogously to wages (and other distributive variables) and a theoretical edifice erected on the universal applicability of the principle of demand and supply.

Now, the plausibility of the supply and demand approach to the problem of distribution was felt to hinge upon the demonstration of the existence of a unique and stable equilibrium in the market for 'capital'. (On the importance of uniqueness and stability see, for example, Marshall, 8th edn, 1920, p. 665n.) With the 'quantity of capital' in given supply, this, in turn,

implied that a monotonically *decreasing* demand function for capital in terms of the rate of profit had to be established (see Figure 1). This inverse relationship was arrived at by the neoclassical theorists through the introduction of two kinds of substitutability between 'capital' and labour: substitutability in consumption and in production. According to the former concept a rise in the rate of profit relatively to the wage rate would increase the price of those commodities, whose production is relatively 'capital intensive', compared to those in which relatively little 'capital' per worker is employed. This would generally prompt consumers to shift their demand in favour of a higher proportion of the cheapened commodities, i.e. the 'labour intensive' ones. According to the latter concept a rise in the rate of interest (and thus profits) relatively to wages would make cost-minimizing entrepreneurs in the different industries of the economy employ more of the relatively cheapened factor of production, i.e. labour. Hence, through both routes 'capital' would become substitutable for labour and for any given quantity of labour employed a decreasing demand schedule for capital would obtain. In Figure 1 the demand schedule DD' corresponding to the *full employment* level of labour L^* (determined simultaneously in the labour market) together with the supply schedule SS' would then ensure a unique and stable equilibrium E with an equilibrium rate of profit r^*. Accordingly, the division of the product between wages and profits is expressed in terms of the 'scarcity of factors of production', including 'capital' conceived as a value magnitude that is considered independent of the rate of profit.

Let us now briefly look more closely at some of the characteristic features of neoclassical capital theory and point out differences between the main versions in which it was presented.

To define 'capital' as an amount of value requires the specification of the standard of value in which it was to be measured. A rather common procedure was to express capital in terms of consumption goods or, more precisely, to conceive of it as a 'subsistence fund' in support of the 'original' factors of production, labour and land, during the period of production extending from the initial expenditure of the services of these factors to the completion of consumption goods. This notion corresponded to the view that capital resulted from the investment of past savings, which, in turn, implied 'abstention' from consumption. Thus it appeared to be natural to measure 'capital' in terms of some composite unit of consumption goods. However, there was a second dimension of capital contemplated by these authors: the *time* for which capital is invested in a process of production. The idea was that capital can be increased either by using more of it or by lengthening the period of time for which it is invested.

The first author to use time as a single measure of capital was Jevons (1871). The gist of his argument consisted in the concept of a 'production function' $y = f(T)$, where output per unit of labour, y, is 'some continuous function of the time elapsing between the expenditure of labour and the enjoyment of results, T; this function is assumed to exhibit diminishing returns (1871, pp. 240–41). Jevons showed that in equilibrium $r = f'(T)/f(T)$.

Jevons's contribution was the starting point of the Austrian theory of capital and interest with Böhm-Bawerk and Wicksell as its main representatives. Böhm-Bawerk's concern was with establishing a temporal version of the demand and supply approach. This involved the appropriate reformulation of the data of the theory. The central elements of his analysis were the concepts of 'time preference' and the 'average period of production', used in describing consumer preferences and technical alternatives, respectively. As in Jevons social capital was conceived as a subsistence fund and was seen to permit the adoption of more productive but also more 'roundabout', i.e.

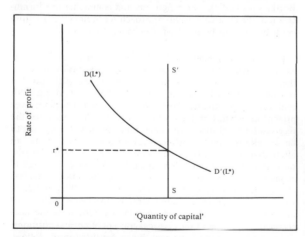

Figure 1

time-consuming, methods of production. It was to the concept of the 'average period of production' that the marginal productivity condition was applied in the determination of the rate of interest.

Among the older neoclassical economists it was perhaps Wicksell who understood best the difficulties related to the problem of a unified treatment of capital in terms of the demand and supply approach. In particular, Wicksell was critical of attempts to work with the value of capital as a factor of production alongside the physically specified factors of labour and land in the production function of single commodities. This implied 'arguing in a circle' ([1901] 1934, p. 149), since capital and the rate of interest enter as a cost in the production of capital goods themselves. Hence the value of the capital goods inserted in the production function depends on the rate of interest and will change with it. Moreover, Wicksell expressed doubts as to the possibility of providing a sufficiently general definition of the 'average period of production' that could be used to represent capital in a way that is not threatened by this kind of circularity. In the *Lectures* he tried to overcome these difficulties by introducing production functions in terms of *dated* services of the 'original' factors labour and land.

While Wicksell shared Böhm-Bawerk's procedure of conceiving the 'capital endowment' of the economy as a value magnitude, he become increasingly sceptical whether it was admissible to identify it with some unspecified stock of subsistence goods, which, in turn, was seen to provide some measure of 'real' capital. With capital as a value magnitude Wicksell showed that the rate of interest is generally not equal to the marginal productivity of 'capital'. This discrepancy is due to the revaluation of the capital stock entailed by a change in distribution. The phenomenon is known as the 'Wicksell effect' and was regarded by Joan Robinson as the key to a criticism of the marginal productivity theory of income distribution.

Authors like J.B. Clark and Marshall appear to have been less aware of the fact that the conditions of production of single commodities cannot be defined in terms of production functions that include 'capital' among the factors of production. Obviously, the criticism levelled against these versions applies also to the concept of the 'aggregate production function', which boomed in the late 1950s and throughout the 1960s in conjunction with neoclassical growth theory.

Alternative views of the fundamentals of capital theory were expressed in a controversy between Böhm-Bawerk and J.B. Clark around the turn of this century (cf. in particular Böhm-Bawerk, 1907, and Clark, 1907). Böhm-Bawerk criticized Clark's attempt to differentiate between 'true capital', a permanent abiding fund of productive wealth, and 'concrete capital goods', each of which is destructible and has to be destroyed in order to serve its productive purpose; in Böhm-Bawerk's view this is 'dark, mystical rhetoric'. Furthermore, Böhm-Bawerk refuted Clark's claim that no concept of 'waiting' or 'abstinence' is needed to explain interest in stationary equilibrium. Without some concept of time preference, and thus a theory of saving, the determination of the rate of interest is left hanging in the air.

Irving Fisher (1930) extended general equilibrium theory to intertemporal choices. However, he proceeded as if there were a single composite commodity to be produced and consumed at different dates. In his discussion of the theory of interest all prices, wages and rents are assumed to be fixed. Hence the interrelationship between the rate of interest, prices and the remaining distribution variables is set aside. The 'investment opportunities' available to an individual and to society as a whole are summarized in intertemporal production possibility frontiers. Due to the assumption of diminishing returns Fisher arrived at a decreasing demand function for saving with respect to the rate of interest. As Keynes noted, this is equivalent to his 'marginal efficiency of capital' schedule (Keynes, 1936, p. 140). Because of 'impatience' the supply of saving is considered to be positively related to the rate of interest. The market equilibrium between the supply of, and the demand for, saving gives the rate of interest, which is equal to the marginal rate of return over the cost of the marginal increase in the capital stock. (For an attempt to generalize Fisher's rate of return approach see Solow, 1967. For a critique of Fisher and Solow see Pasinetti, 1969, and Eatwell, 1976.)

The 1930s brought a further controversy on the theory of capital (cf. Kaldor, 1937). This was triggered off by a series of articles by F.H. Knight (e.g. Knight, 1934), in which he launched an attack on the concept of the 'period of production' revived a few years earlier by Hayek, among others. In particular, Knight argued that there is no need to refer to a 'quantity of capital' and that therefore the 'vicious circle' disappears. The rate of interest could be ascertained with reference to the instantaneous rate of investment and the present value of the additional stream of future income generated by it, However, Knight's proposed solution to the problem of circularity in terms of a 'theory of capital without capital' is illusory, since if the accusation of circularity applies at all (because the value of capital goods cannot be ascertained independently of the rate of interest), it applies both to the stock variable 'capital' and the corresponding flow variable 'investment'.

Finally, some recent attempts to revive and reformulate basic elements of the doctrines of the older neoclassical and Austrian authors should be noted, in particular: Weizsäcker (1971), Hicks (1973) and Faber (1979) on the Austrian theory, Morishima (1977) on Walras, and Hirshleifer (1970) and Dougherty (1980) on Fisher. (For a critical assessment of the older theories see especially Garegnani, 1960.)

THE RECENT CRITIQUE OF NEOCLASSICAL THEORY. Sraffa (1960) deserves the credit for having elaborated a consistent formulation of the classical surplus approach to the problem of capital and distribution. His analysis provided the fundamental basis for a critique of the prevalent neoclassical theory during the so-called 'Cambridge controversies in the theory of capital' (see Harcourt, 1969; Kurz, 1985).

Sraffa starts from a given system of production in use in which commodities are produced by means of commodities. If wages are assumed to be paid at the end of the uniform production period, then, in the case of single-product industries (i.e. circulating capital only) and with gross outputs of the different products all measured in physical terms and made equal to unity by choice of units, we have the price system

$$p = (1 + r)Ap + wl,$$

where p is the column vector of normal prices, A is the square matrix of material inputs, l is the vector of direct labour inputs and w is the wage rate. Under certain economically meaningful conditions, for any given feasible wage rate in terms of a given standard the above equation yields a unique and strictly positive price vector in terms of the standard and a unique and non-negative value of the rate of profit. The investigation of the 'effects' of variations in one of the distribution variables on the other one and on the prices of commodities, assuming that the methods of production remain unchanged, yields the following results. First, the system possesses a finite maximum rate of profits $R > 0$ corresponding to a zero wage rate. Second, the vector of prices in terms of the wage rate p/w (prices in terms of quantities of *labour commanded*) is positive and rises monotonically for $0 \leqslant r < R$, tending to infinity as r approaches R.

Third, at the maximum level of wages corresponding to $r = 0$ relative prices are in proportion to their labour costs, while at $r > 0$ relative prices generally deviate from relative labour costs and vary with changes in r (or w); it is only in the special case of uniform 'proportions' of labour to means of production in all industries that prices are proportional to 'labour values' for all levels of r (w). (For a discussion of joint production, fixed capital and land, see Pasinetti, 1980.)

While earlier authors were of the opinion that the capital–labour or capital–output ratios of the different industries could be brought into a ranking that is independent of distribution, this is generally not possible: 'the price of a product . . . may rise or it may fall, or it may even alternate in rising and falling, relative to its means of production' (Sraffa, 1960, p. 15). This result destroys the foundation of those versions of the traditional theory that attempted to define the conditions of production in terms of production functions with 'capital' as a factor. Moreover, as regards the concept of the 'capital endowment' of the economy conceived as a value magnitude, the same 'real' capital may assume different values depending on the level of r. Sraffa concludes that these findings 'cannot be reconciled with *any* notion of capital as a measurable quantity independent of distribution and prices' (1960, p. 38).

Samuelson (1962), in an attempt to counter Joan Robinson's (1953) attack on the aggregate production function, claimed that even in cases with heterogeneous capital goods some rationalization can be provided for the validity of simple neoclassical 'parables' which assume there is a single homogeneous factor called 'capital', the marginal product of which equals the rate of interest. But, alas, Samuelson based his defence of traditional theory in terms of the construction of a 'surrogate production function' on the assumption of equal input proportions (cf. 1962, pp. 196–7). By this token the 'real' economy with heterogeneous goods was turned into the 'imaginary' economy with a homogeneous output, i.e. the 'surrogate production function' was nothing more than the infamous aggregate production function. (For a critique of Samuelson's approach see particularly Garegnani, 1970.)

Implicit in the above system of price equations is the inverse relationship between the wage and the rate of profit, or *wage curve*, of the given system of production, $w = w(r)$. We may now turn to the hypothesis that for one or several industries alternative technical methods are available for the production of the corresponding commodity. The technology of the economic system as a whole will then be represented by a series of alternative techniques obtained from all the possible combinations of methods of production for the various commodities. Expressing w and p in terms of a commodity produced in all the alternative systems, we obtain as many different wage curves as there are alternative techniques. In Figure 2 it is assumed that only two techniques, α and β exist. Clearly, at any level of the wage rate (or rate of profit), entrepreneurs will choose the *cost-minimizing* system of production. It can be shown that, whichever the system initially in use, the tendency of producers to switch to the cheaper system will bring them to the one giving the highest rate of profit (wage rate), whereas systems giving the same r for the same w will be indifferent and can coexist. Thus, in the example of Figure 2, in the two intervals $0 < w < w_1$ and $w_2 < w \leqslant W_\alpha$ technique α will be chosen, while in the interval $w_1 < w < w_2$ technique β turns out to be superior; at the two switch points P and Q both techniques are equiprofitable. It follows that with a choice of technique the relationship between w and r, or *wage frontier*, will be represented by the outermost segments or envelope of the intersecting wage curves.

Figure 2 shows that the same technique (α) may be the most profitable of a number of techniques at more than one level of the wage rate even though other techniques (here β) are more profitable at wage rates in between. The implication of this possibility of the *reswitching* of techniques is that the direction of change of the input proportions cannot be related unambiguously to changes of the so-called 'factor prices'. The central element of the neoclassical explanation of distribution in terms of supply and demand is thus revealed as defective. This element consisted in the proposition that a rise of r must decrease the 'quantity of capital' relative to labour in the production of a commodity because of the assumed substitutability in production and consumption. The demonstration that a rise in r may lead to the adoption of the more 'capital intensive' of two techniques clearly destroys the neoclassical concept of substitution in production. Moreover, since a rise in r may cheapen some of the commodities, the production of which at a lower level of r was characterized by a relatively high 'capital intensity', the substitution among consumption goods contemplated by the traditional theory of consumer demand may result in a higher, as well as in a lower, 'capital intensity'. It follows that the principle of substitution in consumption cannot offset the breakdown of the principle of substitution in production. Finally, it is worth mentioning that reswitching is not necessary for *capital-reversing* cf. Symposium, 1966, p. 516).

The negative implication of reverse capital deepening for traditional theory can be illustrated by means of the example of Figure 3, in which the value of capital corresponding to the full employment level of labour is plotted against the rate of profit. Obviously, if with traditional analysis we conceived the curve KK' as the 'demand curve' for captial, which, together with the corresponding 'supply curve' SS', is taken to determine the 'equilibrium' level of r, we would have to conclude that this equilibrium, although unique, is unstable. With free competition and perfectly flexible distributive variables a deviation of r from r^* would lead to the complete extinction of one of the two income categories. According to the critics of traditional theory, the finding that the quantity of a factor demanded need not be related to the price of the factor service in the conventional, inverse manner demonstrates the failure of the supply and demand approach to the explanation of normal distribution, prices and quantities.

NEOCLASSICAL RESPONSES. Neoclassical economists tried to counter the attack in various ways. At first it was claimed that reswitching is impossible. When this claim was shown conclusively to be false (cf. Symposium, 1966), doubts were raised as to its empirical importance (see, for example, Ferguson, 1969),

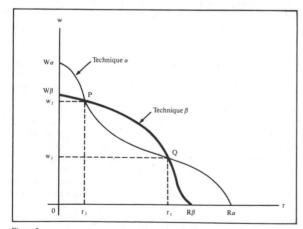

Figure 2

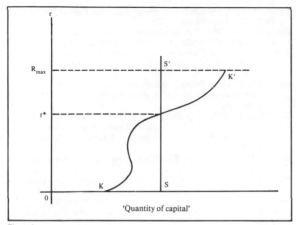

Figure 3

threatened by the difficulties concerning the notion of capital a drastic methodological reorientation was advocated (cf. Garegnani, 1976; Milgate, 1979). Most influential in this move away from the traditional method was apparently Hicks's *Value and Capital* (1939; second edition 1946). Interestingly enough, Hicks himself appears to have become increasingly sceptical as to the usefulness of the 'temporary equilibrium method' then suggested by him (see, for example, Hicks, 1965, pp. 73–4).

The second observation concerns Hahn's attempt to interpret Sraffa's analysis as a special case of general equilibrium theory. Since the latter takes as data (i) the preferences of consumers, (ii) the technical conditions of production, and (iii) the physical endowments, Hahn's view necessarily leads to the question of which constellation of these data is compatible with a uniform rate of profit. Clearly, to superimpose the latter specification on an ordinary general equilibrium system would render it over-determined, as some of the older neoclassical authors were well aware of. Hence, following the interpretation under consideration, (i), (ii) or (iii) cannot be taken as independent variables. Now it is Hahn's contention that at the basis of Sraffa's price equations there must be a special proportion between the initial endowments; i.e. (iii) is tacitly assumed to be specified accordingly. However, as we have seen there is no evidence in support of this presupposition. The surplus approach does not require given endowments of produced means of production in order to determine distribution and normal prices. In fact, looking at classical analysis as a whole the quantities of the capital goods available may be considered as dependent rather than indepen-dent variables. In analysing the problem of value, capital and distribution the classical economists took the capital stocks installed in the different industries as exactly adjusted to *given outputs*, such that the latter could be produced at minimum costs. The tendency towards normal capital utilization and a uniform rate of profit was seen to be the outcome of the working of the persistent forces of the system reflected in the competitive decisions of producers.

Since the opinion entertained by Hahn that Sraffa's analysis can be subsumed as a 'special case' under modern neoclassical theory has to be rejected, the question remains, which of the two is the more powerful instrument of analysis. There does not seem to exist a ready-made answer at present. The following remarks on the dominant neoclassical theory must suffice.

Obviously, to take the capital endowment as given in kind implies that only 'short-period' equilibria can be determined. Because firms 'prefer more profit to less' (Hahn, 1982, p. 354) the size and composition of the capital stock will rapidly change. Thus, major factors which general equilibrium theory envisages as determining prices and quantities are themselves subject to quick changes. This, in turn, makes it difficult to distinguish them from those accidental and temporary factors, which, at any given moment of time, prevent the economy from settling in the position of equilibrium. More important, the fast variation in relative prices necessitates the consideration of the influence of future states of the world on the present situation.

This can be approached in two different ways. First, if there were complete futures markets the analysis could be carried out in terms of the concept of *intertemporal equilibrium*. However, the assumption that all intertemporal and all contingent mar-kets exist, which has the effect of collapsing the future into the present, can be rejected on grounds of realism and economic reasoning (see, for example, Bliss, 1975, pp. 48 and 61). Moreover, there is the following conceptual problem (see Schefold, 1985). If in equilibrium some of the capital stocks turn out to be in excess supply these stocks assume zero prices. This possibility appears to indicate that the expectations entre-preneurs held in the past when deciding to build up the present

thereby insinuating that neoclassical theory was a simplified picture of reality, the basic correctness of which would not be endangered by 'exceptions' of the kind analysed in the capital debate. Other advocates of the neoclassical approach were conscious of how defective the attempt was to play down the importance of reswitching and capital-reversing using the 'empirical' route. Since the phenomenon was irrefutable it had to be absorbed and shown to be compatible with the more sophisticated versions of the dominant theory.

Perhaps the first move in this direction was made by Bruno, Burmeister and Sheshinski (1966), who drew an analogy be-tween reswitching and the long-known possibility of the exist-ence of multiple internal rates of return. However, whereas the latter phenomenon is a discovery within the partial, 'fixed-price' framework of microeconomic theory of investment, reswitching presupposes a total, general framework. Moreover, we are not told how traditional theory was both able to cope with re-switching and yet preserve its basic structure.

A more interesting challenge came from authors such as Bliss (1975) and Hahn (1982). They contended that because of its concern with a uniform rate of profit Sraffa's analysis can be considered a 'special case' of general equilibrium theory. Ac-cording to these authors the criticism of traditional neoclassical capital theory implicit in Sraffa is correct but has no bearing upon modern general equilibrium theory. Since in the latter the distribution of income is explained in terms of given *physical* endowments of agents, there is no need to find a scalar representation of the capital stock. The uniformity of profit rates is taken to be 'a very special state of the economy' (Hahn, 1982, p. 363) which, for given preferences and production sets, presupposes a particular composition of initial endowments. In general, there will be as many own rates of return as there are different assets in the endowment set.

The first thing to be noticed is that the preservation of the basic supply and demand approach to the explanation of prices, distribution and quantities in modern general equilibrium theory is effectuated at the cost of the abandonment of the traditional long-period method. As we have seen, this method was shared by all 'forerunners' of this theory, including, most notably, Walras and von Neumann (1936). Indeed, the change in the notion of equilibrium involved expresses a fundamental break with the analytical method used by all economic theory up to the 1930s, when partly because of a growing perception among neoclassical economists that the whole approach was

capital stocks are not realized. Hence, strictly speaking we are faced with a disequilibrium situation because otherwise the wrong stocks could not have accumulated. Therefore, the problem arises how the past or, more exactly, possible discrepancies between expectations and facts influence the future.

Since the notion of intertemporal equilibrium cannot be sustained the theory is ultimately referred back to the introduction of individual price expectations concerning future deliveries of commodities for which no present markets exist. This leads to the *temporary equilibrium* version of modern neoclassical theory. The basic weakness of the theories of temporary equilibrium concerns the necessarily arbitrary choice of hypotheses about individual price expectations. Indeed, as Burmeister stresses, 'all too often "nearly anything can happen" is the only possible unqualified conclusion' (Burmeister, 1980, p. 215). Moreover, the stability properties of this kind of equilibrium are unclear, since small perturbations caused by accidental factors may entail changes in expectations, which define that very equilibrium.

The danger of lapsing into empty formalism and of depriving the theory of clear-cut results was of course recognized by several supply and demand theorists and considered a fundamental weakness. In view of it some of them were prepared to dispence with the alleged generality of general equilibrium theory and return to some version of traditional neoclassical analysis. After the recent debate in capital theory this involved ruling out reswitching and other 'perverse', i.e. non-conventional, phenomena in terms of sufficiently bold assumptions about available techniques. It comes as no surprise that given these assumptions the central neoclassical postulate of the inverse relation between the capital-labour ratio and the rate of profit should re-emerge as 'one of the most powerful theorems in economic theory' (Sato, 1974, p. 355). However, in order to be clear about this move it deserves to be stressed that it was motivated, as one author expressly admits, by the fact that 'regular economies' have 'desirable properties' (Burmeister, 1980, p. 124).

HEINZ D. KURZ

See also MARGINAL PRODUCTIVITY THEORY; QUANTITY OF CAPITAL; REVERSE CAPITAL DEEPENING.

BIBLIOGRAPHY

Bliss, C.J. 1975. *Capital Theory and the Distribution of Income*. Amsterdam: North-Holland.
Böhm-Bawerk, E. von. 1889. *Positive Theorie des Kapitales*. Jena: Gustav Fischer. Trans. as *Positive Theory of Capital*, London: Smart, 1891.
Böhm-Bawerk, E. von. 1906–7. Capital and interest once more. *Quarterly Journal of Economics* 21, Pt. I, November 1906, 1–21; Pt. II, April 1907, 247–82.
Bortkiewicz, L. von. 1907. Zur Berichtigung der grundlegenden theoretischen Konstruktion von Marx im dritten Bande des 'Kapital'. *Jahrbücher für Nationalökonomie und Statistik*, July. English trans. in Appendix to E. von. Böhm-Bawerk, *Karl Marx and the Close of his System*, ed. P. Sweezy, New York, 1949.
Bruno, M., Burmeister, E. and Sheshinski, E. 1966. The nature and implications of the reswitching of techniques. *Quarterly Journal of Economics* 80, November, 526–53.
Burmeister, E. 1980. *Capital Theory and Dynamics*. Cambridge: Cambridge University Press.
Clark, J.B. 1899. *The Distribution of Wealth*. London: Macmillan.
Clark, J.B. 1907. Concerning the nature of capital: a reply. *Quarterly Journal of Economics* 21, May, 351–70.
Dougherty, C. 1980. *Interest and Profit*. London: Methuen.
Eatwell, J. 1976. Irving Fisher's 'Rate of return over cost' and the rate of profit in a capitalistic economy. In *Essays in Modern Capital Theory*, ed. M. Brown, K. Sato and P. Zarembka, Amsterdam: North-Holland.

Faber, M. 1979. *Introduction to Modern Austrian Capital Theory*. Berlin: Springer-Verlag.
Ferguson, C.E. 1969. *The Neoclassical Theory of Production and Distribution*. Cambridge: Cambridge University Press.
Fisher, I. 1930. *The Theory of Interest*. London: Macmillan.
Garegnani, P. 1960. *Il capitale nelle teorie della distribuzione*. Milan: Giuffrè.
Garegnani, P. 1970. Heterogeneous capital, the production function and the theory of distribution. *Review of Economic Studies* 37(3), July, 407–36.
Garegnani, P. 1976. On a change in the notion of equilibrium in recent work on value. In *Essays in Modern Capital Theory*, ed. M. Brown, K. Sato and P. Zarembka, Amsterdam: North-Holland.
Hahn, F.H. 1982. The neo-Ricardians. *Cambridge Journal of Economics* 6(4), December, 353–74.
Harcourt, G.C. 1969. Some Cambridge controversies in the theory of capital. *Journal of Economic Literature* 7(2), June, 369–405.
Hicks, J.R. 1932. *The Theory of Wages*. London: Macmillan.
Hicks, J.R. 1939. *Value and Capital*. 2nd edn, Oxford: Clarendon Press, 1946.
Hicks, J.R. 1965. *Capital and Growth*. Oxford: Oxford University Press.
Hicks, J.R. 1973. *Capital and Time – a Neo-Austrian Theory*. Oxford: Oxford University Press.
Hirshleifer, J. 1970. *Investment, Interest and Capital*. Englewood Cliffs: Prentice-Hall.
Jevons, W.S. 1871. *The Theory of Political Economy*. Reprint, New York: Kelley, 1970.
Kaldor, N. 1937. The recent controversy on the theory of capital. *Econometrica* 5, July, 201–33.
Keynes, J.M. 1936. *The General Theory of Employment, Interest and Money*. London: Macmillan.
Knight, F.H. 1921. *Risk, Uncertainty and Profit*. Chicago: University of Chicago Press.
Knight, F.H. 1934. Capital, time and the interest rate. *Economica* 1, August, 257–86.
Kurz, H.D. 1985. Sraffa's contribution to the debate in capital theory. *Contributions to Political Economy* 4, 3–24.
Marshall, A. 1890. *Principles of Economics*. 8th edn (1920). Reprint, reset, London: Macmillan, 1977.
Marx, K. 1894. *Capital*. Vol. III. Moscow: Progress Publishers; Harmondsworth: Penguin, 1959.
Milgate, M. 1979. On the origin of the notion of 'intertemporal equilibrium'. *Economica* 46, February, 1–10.
Morishima, M. 1977. *Walras' Economics: a Pure Theory of Capital and Money*. Cambridge: Cambridge University Press.
Neumann, J. von. 1936. Über ein ökonomisches Gleichungssystem und eine Verallgemeinerung des Browerschen Fixpunktsatzes. In *Ergebnisse eines Mathematischen Kolloquiums*, ed. K. Menger, Vienna: F. Deuticke. Trans. as 'A Model of General Economic equilibrium', *Review of Economic Studies* 13(1), (1945–6), Winter, 1–9.
Pasinetti, L.L. 1969. Switches of technique and the 'rate of return' in capital theory. *Economic Journal* 79, September, 508–31.
Pasinetti, L.L. (ed.) 1980. *Essays on the Theory of Joint Production*. London: Macmillan.
Ricardo, D. 1951–73. *The Works and Correspondence of David Ricardo*. 11 vols, ed. P. Sraffa in collaboration with M.H. Dobb, Cambridge: Cambridge University Press.
Robinson, J. 1953. The production function and the theory of capital. *Review of Economic Studies* 21(2), Winter, 81–106.
Samuelson, P.A. 1962. Parable and realism in capital theory: the surrogate production function. *Review of Economic Studies* 29, June, 193–206.
Sato, K. 1974. The neoclassical postulate and the technology frontier in capital theory. *Quarterly Journal of Economics* 88(3), August, 353–84.
Schefold, B. 1985. Cambridge price theory: special model or general theory of value? *American Economic Review, Papers and Proceedings* 75(2), May, 140–45.
Smith, A. 1776. *An Inquiry into the Nature and Causes of the Wealth of Nations*. Ed. E. Cannan, introduced by G.J. Stigler, Chicago: Chicago University Press, 1976.

Solow, R.M. 1967. The interest rate and the transition between techniques. In *Socialism, Capitalism and Economic Growth, Essays presented to Maurice Dobb*, ed. C.H. Feinstein, Cambridge: Cambridge University Press.

Sraffa, P. 1951. Introduction. In D. Ricardo, *The Works and Correspondence of David Ricardo*, Vol. 1.

Sraffa, P. 1960. *Production of Commodities by Means of Commodities*. Cambridge: Cambridge University Press.

Symposium. 1966. On paradoxes in capital theory: a symposium. *Quarterly Journal of Economics* 80(4), November, 526–83.

Walras, L. 1874–7. *Eléments d'économie politique pure*. Lausanne: Corbaz. 4th edn 1900. Trans. by W. Jaffé of definitive edn (1926) as *Elements of Pure Economics*, London: Allen & Unwin, 1954.

Weizsäcker, C.Ch. von. 1971. *Steady State Capital Theory*. Berlin, Heidelberg, New York: Springer-Verlang.

Wicksell, K. 1893. *Über Wert, Kapital und Rente*. Jena: Gustav Fischer. Trans. as *Value, Capital and Rent*, New York: Kelley, 1954.

Wicksell, K. 1901. *Föreläsingar i Nationalekonomi*, Vol. 1. Lund: Berlingska Boktryckeriet. Trans. as *Lectures on Political Economy*, Vol. 1, London: Routledge & Kegan Paul, 1934.

capital theory: paradoxes.

PROLOGUE. The idea that capital theory might lead economists to discover forms of 'paradoxical' behaviour has emerged in the economic literature of the 1960s largely as an outcome of developments in the field of production theory (theory of linear production models). What happened in capital theory is in fact a special instance of a more general phenomenon. Economists sometimes tend to examine a large domain of economic phenomena by adapting theoretical concepts that had originally been devised for a much narrower range of special issues. The discoveries of 'paradoxical' relations derive from the fact that their process of generalization often turns out to be ill-conceived and misleading, if not entirely unwarranted.

For a long time, in capital theory, it had been taken for granted that there is a unique, unambiguous profitability ranking of production techniques in terms of capital intensity, along the scale of variation of the rate of interest. The discovery that this is not necessarily true has induced many economists to speak of 'paradoxes' in the theory of capital. But the roots of apparently paradoxical behaviour are to be found, not in the economic phenomena themselves, but in the economists' tendency to rely on too simple 'parables' of economic behaviour.

Traditional beliefs about capital are deeply rooted in the history of economic analysis, and may be traced back to pre-classical literature. As will be shown in the next section, a long post-classical tradition was then developed on that basis. The length of ancestry might explain the survival of conventional beliefs.

THE EMERGENCE OF THE CONVENTIONAL VIEW. The notion of 'capital' was associated for a long time with investible wealth and its income generating power, and was largely independent of detailed consideration of the function of invested wealth in the production process. The earliest development of capital theory took place within the analytical framework of a pure exchange economy (Petty, Locke). Within this perspective, capital was often associated with purely financial transactions (lending and borrowing) and the relationship between capital and rate of interest came quite naturally to be conceived as the relationship between loanable funds and their price. The origin of the belief in the inverse monotonic relation between the demand for capital and the rate of interest may be traced back to this phase of the literature on capital.

The association of capital with the process of production did not come to the fore until quite late, in spite of certain isolated anticipations. (Hicks (1973, p. 12) even quotes Boccaccio's *Decameron* on the issue.) The description of capital as a stock of means of production became common with the Physiocrats and the Classical Economists. In this period, Cesare Beccaria (1804, ms 1771–72) presented what J.B. Say considered to be the first analysis of 'the true functions of productive capitals' (Say, 1817, p. xliii). Soon after him, Adam Smith (1776) built upon the distinction between 'productive' capital and 'unproductive' consumption his theory of structural dynamics and economic growth. Finally, David Ricardo gave a definite shape to classical capital theory by examining the relationship between capital accumulation and diminishing returns and by considering in which way different proportions of capital in different industries might influence the relative exchange values of the corresponding commodities (Ricardo, 1817, ch. I, sections IV and V). Classical capital theory is characterized by lack of interest in the purely financial dimension of investment. As a result, the relation between capital accumulation and the rate of interest recedes into the background and is substituted by the relation between real capital accumulation and the rate of profit. (In Ricardo, the rate of profit is determined by equality with the rate of net output on the least fertile land.)

In this way, the foundations of capital theory shifted from the exchange to the production sphere, and the demand-and-supply mechanism was confined to the process by which the rate of interest is maintained equal to the rate of profit in the long run. However, certain aspects of the pre-classical approach maintained a foothold in economic analysis. In particular, a number of economists (starting with Thünen, Longfield and Senior) continued to be interested in the income-generating function of capital at the level of the individual investor, and tried to combine this approach with the emphasis on the productive function of capital that had emerged in the classical literature. The marginal productivity theory of capital and interest was developed as an answer to this conceptual problem. The essential features of that theory may be clearly seen in Thünen:

> The return, which the total amount of capital provides since the moment in which it is lent, is determined by the utility of that portion of capital which is last employed (Thünen [1850], 1857, p. 131).

> It must then be known at which point the agriculturist should stop along the ranking of improvements which he might either introduce or give up. The answer is as follows: he would find an advantage in introducing all those improvements that bring him a return which, when compared to the capital employed, is greater than the rate of interest that could be obtained by lending the same amount of capital (Thünen [1850], 1857, p. 186).

Thünen's theory suggests a relationship between the rate of interest (i) and the rate of profit (r) quite different from the one found in Ricardo. The reason for this is that Ricardo had taken r to be fixed for the individual entrepreneur, so that equality between i and r was brought about by adjustment between the supply and demand for loans in the financial markets. Thünen suggested a different adjustment mechanism by taking r to be variable for the individual entrepreneur, so that the attainment of the long run equality between the rate of profit and the rate of interest came to depend on the change in the physical productivity of capital as much as on adjustment in the financial markets.

This view is founded upon a thorough transformation of the Ricardian theory of diminishing returns and provided the logical starting point for the later marginalist theory of diminishing returns from aggregate capital. The analytical and historical process leading to this outcome is a rather complex one, and it is best understood by distinguishing two separate stages. In the first stage, the law of diminishing returns, which Ricardo considered to hold for the economy as a whole in the long-run, was applied to the short-run behaviour of the individual entrepreneur. As a result, the change in input proportions within any given productive unit is associated with the change in the physical productivity of capital. Here the variation of the capital stock is unlikely to influence the system of prices, so that the decrease (or increase) in the return from the last 'increment of capital' could be unambiguously associated with an increase (or decrease) in the physical capital stock. The second stage consisted in extending the above result to the variations in the aggregate quantity of capital available in the economic system as a whole (quantity of 'social capital').

The process which we have described permitted to transform the classical conception of diminishing returns from a macro-social law into a microeconomic relation derived from the law of variable proportions. This new type of diminishing returns was then extended to the 'macro-social' sphere once again. As a result, it became possible to think that the rate of interest and the rate of profit (tending to be equal to each other) are associated with the physical marginal productivity of social or aggregate capital: an increase in the relative quantity of capital with respect to the other inputs would be associated with lower marginal productivity of capital and thus with a lower equilibrium rate of interest and rate of profit. This inverse monotonic relation between the rate of interest (or the rate of profit) and the quantity of capital per man eventually became an established proposition of capital theory. Its relevance can be seen from the attempts by Jevons (1871), Böhm-Bawerk (1889) and Clark (1899) to found on the theory of the marginal productivity of factors the explanation of the distribution of the social product among factors of production under competitive conditions.

Further light on the conceptual roots of the marginalist view of capital is shed by the contributions of Jevons and Böhm-Bawerk. In their theories, profit is considered as the remuneration due to the capitalist as a result of the higher productiveness of 'indirect' or 'roundabout' processes of production when compared with processes carried out by 'direct' labour only. The generalization of the marginal principles which they carried out is thus associated with the description of the production process as an essentially 'financial' phenomenon in which final output, like interest in financial transactions, could be considered as 'some continuous function of the time elapsing between the expenditure of the labour and the enjoyment of the result' (Jevons [1871], 1879, p. 266). The subsequent discovery of 'anomalies' in the field of capital accumulation was possible when economists started to question this extension of capital theory from the financial to the productive sphere, and when the technical structure of production was examined on its own grounds independently of the 'financial' aspect which might be considered to be characteristic of 'the typical business man's viewpoint' (Hicks, 1973, p. 12).

ANTICIPATIONS OF DEBATE. It has just been shown that microeconomic diminishing returns provided the foundations for a theory of the diminishing marginal productivity of social

capital, which was extended from the microeconomic sphere by way of logical analogy.

The pitfalls of this approach did not take long to emerge, as economic analysis came to grips with the full complexity of the production process. Knut Wicksell, discovered that, in the case of an economic system using heterogeneous capital goods, it might be impossible to describe diminishing returns from aggregate capital. The reason for this is that a variation in the capital stock might be associated with a change in the price system that would make it impossible to compare the quantities of capital before and after the change (see Wicksell [1901–6], 1934, pp. 147 and ff., and p. 180). Wicksell also recognized that this difficulty is characteristic of capital because 'labour and land are measured each in terms of its own *technical* unit ... capital, on the other hand, ... is reckoned, in common parlance, as a sum of *exchange value*' (Wicksell [1901–6], 1934, p. 149).

The special difficulty associated with heterogeneous capital goods is in fact an outcome of a particular procedure by which the fundamental theorems concerning capital and interest had been formulated with reference to the idealized setting of an isolated producer, and then extended by analogy to the case of the 'social economy'. The drawbacks of this methodology were perspicaciously noted by Nicholas Kaldor in the late Thirties:

> it is rather unfortunate that, following Böhm-Bawerk and his school, we have been generally accustomed to start with a more specialised set-up, with the picture of Robinson-Crusoe engaged in net-making. This Crusoe-approach makes it unnecessarily difficult to single out features which are merely the property of a special case from the demonstration of general principles. Had the analysis started with the 'general case' – by imagining a society where *all* resources are produced and the services of all resources co-operate in producing further resources – a great deal of the controversies concerning the theory of capital might not have arisen (Kaldor, 1937, p. 228.)

It is remarkable that so many 'paradoxical' results of modern capital theory were subsequently discovered precisely as an outcome of the procedure here described by Kaldor.

The stage of modern controversy was set by the consideration of two distinct problems: (i) the measurement of 'social capital' in models with heterogeneous capital goods; (ii) the discovery that production techniques that had been excluded at lower levels of the rate of profit might 'come back' as the rate of profit is increased (this phenomenon is known as *reswitching of technique*).

Joan Robinson started the discussion by calling attention to the difficulties inherent in any physical measure of social capital (Robinson, 1953–4). She also pointed out the 'curiosum' that the degree of mechanization associated with a higher wage rate and a lower rate of profit might be lower than the degree of mechanization associated with a lower wage rate and a higher rate of profit. (She attributed this 'curiosum' to Miss Ruth Cohen, but later on she attributed it to the reading of Sraffa's Introduction to Ricardo's *Principles*.)

Immediately afterwards, David Champernowne discovered that, in general, we must admit 'the possibility of two stationary states each using the same items of equipment and labour force yet being shown as using different quantities of capital, merely on account of having different rates of interest and of food-wages' (Champernowne, 1953–4, p. 119). Champernowne also admitted that the inverse monotonic relation between the rate of profit and the quantity of capital per man (as well as the inverse monotonic relation between the rate of profit and capital per unit of output) might not be generally true: 'it is logically possible that over certain ranges of the rate of interest, a fall in interest rates and rise in food-wages will be accompanied by a *fall* in output per head and a *fall* in the quantity of capital per head' (Champernowne, 1953–4, p. 118). Champernowne's explanation of what appeared to be perverse behaviour from the point of view of traditional theory was that changes in the interest rate can be associated with changes in the cost of capital equipment even if the capital stock is unchanged. As a result, perverse behaviour was attributed to pure 'financial' variations and a physical measure of capital was still thought to be possible. This Champernowne tried to obtain by introducing a chain index method for measuring capital (Champernowne, 1953–4, p. 125). A few years later, Joan Robinson again took up the same issue in her *Accumulation of Capital* (1956, pp. 109–10). The reason she gave for the 'Ruth Cohen curiosum' is quite different from the one proposed by Champernowne. She explicitly recognized that 'financial' factors such as a higher wage rate and a lower rate of interest would have 'real' consequences by influencing the actual choice of technique. (In the 'perverse' case a lower rate of interest would be associated with the choice of the less mechanized technique.)

When a few years later Michio Morishima attempted a multi-sectoral generalization of Joan Robinson's Simple Model he confirmed the possibility of a positive relationship between the rate of interest and the degree of mechanization of a technique: (Morishima, 1964, p. 126.) Finally John Hicks came up with the same problem when examining 'the response of technique to price changes' in the framework of a simple economy consisting of a consumption good 'industry' and a net investment good 'industry', and in which the same capital good is used in both industries (see Hicks, 1965, pp. 148–56).

But in spite of all these anticipations, it must be admitted that the issue of technical reswitching was not given an important place in economic theory before the publication of Piero Sraffa's *Production of Commodities by Means of Commodities* (1960). It is with Sraffa's work that the phenomenon took a prominent place. Sraffa's result is in fact remarkable not only for the discovery that the choice of the production technique is not in general a monotonic function of the rate of profit but also for the special route that he followed to obtain that result. Sraffa was able to show that heterogeneity of capital goods and of 'capital structures' (different proportions between labour and intermediate inputs in the various processes of production) would normally give rise, with the variation of the rate of profit and of the unit wage, 'to complicated patterns of price-movement with several ups and down' (Sraffa, 1960, p. 37). This phenomenon would in turn bring about changes in the 'quantity of capital' that are not generally related to the rate of profit in a monotonic way. Reswitching of technique and reverse capital deepening are thus derived from a general property of production models with heterogeneous capital goods. (See RESWITCHING OF TECHNIQUE and REVERSE CAPITAL DEEPENING.)

NEOCLASSICAL PARABLES AND THE CAPITAL CONTROVERSY. Following the publication of Sraffa's book, a lively debate on capital theory suddenly flared up in the 1960s, and the way it did is itself an interesting event.

It is known that when propositions derived from individual behaviour are applied to the more complex case of the 'social economy', the extension is admittedly possible on condition that the social economy has a number of special features making it identical, from the analytical point of view, to the case of the isolated individual. To test these features, the social economy is often described in terms of a 'parable' in which those particular conditions are satisfied. This 'parable', though unrealistic, is taken to be useful, from the heuristic or a persuasive point of view.

In this vein Paul Samuelson attempted to construct a 'surrogate production function' by analogy with microeconomic behaviour (Samuelson, 1962). His work can be considered as the first explicit attempt to get rid of the complexities of an economic system with heterogeneous capital goods by constructing a model in which that system is described in terms of an 'aggregate parable' with physically homogeneous capital. After introducing the assumption that 'the same proportion of inputs is used in the consumption-goods and [capital-] goods industries' (Samuelson, 1962, pp. 196–7), Samuelson was able to prove that 'the Surrogate (Homogeneous) Capital ... gives exactly the same result as does the shifting collection of diverse capital goods in our more realistic model' (Samuelson, 1962, p. 201). In particular, 'the relations among w, r, and Q/L that prevail for [the] quasi-realistic complete system of heterogeneous capital goods' could 'be shown to have the same formal properties as does the parable system' (Samuelson, 1962, p. 203). This result was taken to be a justification for using the surrogate production function 'as a useful summarizing device' (ibid.). In fact, Pierangelo Garegnani, who was present at a discussion of a draft of Samuelson's paper, did point out that Samuelson's result is crucially dependent on the assumption of equal proportions of inputs (see Garegnani, 1970). Samuelson acknowledged Garegnani's criticism in a footnote to his paper and admitted that it would be a 'false conjecture' to think that the 'extreme assumption of equi-proportional inputs in the consumption and machine trades could be lightened and still leave one with many of the surrogate propositions' (Samuelson, 1962, p. 202n). But Samuelson and various other economists continued to look for conditions that would ensure a monotonic relation between the rate of profit and the choice of technique even in presence of a non-linear relation between w and r.

The outcome appeared a few years later. David Levhari, a PhD student of Samuelson's, in his dissertation and then in a paper for the *Quarterly Journal of Economics*, claimed he had proved that reswitching of the whole technology matrix would be impossible if this matrix is of the 'irreducible' or 'indecomposable' type (Levhari, 1965). This property – Levhari claimed – would exclude reswitching and thus make it possible to extend the use of a 'surrogate production function' to the non-linear case with production technologies for basic commodities.

However, Levhari's theorem was disproved by Luigi Pasinetti in a paper at the Rome 1st World Congress of the Econometric Society in 1965. Pasinetti's final draft of his paper was published in the November 1966 issue of the *Quarterly Journal of Economics* (Pasinetti, 1966) together with papers written in the meantime by Levhari and Samuelson (1966), Morishima (1966), Bruno, Burmeister and Sheshinski (1966) and Garegnani (1966). This set of papers was called by the journal editor 'Paradoxes in capital theory: a symposium', thereby originating the term. Paul Samuelson concluded the discussion with a 'Summing up' in which he admitted that 'the simple tale told by Jevons, Böhm-Bawerk, Wicksell, and other neoclassical writers', according to which a falling rate of interest is unambiguously associated with the choice of more capital-intensive techniques, 'cannot be universally valid' (Samuelson, 1966, p. 568).

The various contributions to this discussion showed that reswitching might occur both with 'decomposable' and 'indecomposable' technologies. This result was proved in different ways by Pasinetti (1965 and 1966), Morishima (1966), Bruno, Burmeister and Sheshinski (1966) and Garegnani (1966). Samuelson stated in his summing up that 'reswitching is a logical possibility in any technology, indecomposable or decomposable' (Samuelson, 1966, p. 582). He then called attention to the associated phenomenon of reverse capital deepening and concluded that 'there often turns out to be no unambiguous way of characterizing different processes as more "capital-intensive", more "mechanized", more "roundabout" ' (Samuelson, 1966, p. 582).

Although the logical possibility of reswitching was admitted by all participants in the discussion, Bruno, Burmeister and Sheshinski raised doubts as to its empirical relevance: 'there is an open empirical question as to whether or not reswitching is likely to be observed in an actual economy for reasonable changes in the interest rate' (Bruno, Burmeister and Sheshinski, 1966, p. 545n). The same doubt was expressed in Samuelson's summing up (Samuelson, 1966, p. 582). Bruno, Burmeister and Sheshinski also mentioned a theorem, which they attributed to Martin Weitzman and Robert Solow, according to which reswitching of technique may be excluded, in a model with heterogeneous capital goods, provided at least one capital good is produced by 'a smooth neoclassical production function', if 'labour and each good are inputs in one or more of the goods produced neoclassically' (Bruno, Burmeister and Sheshinski, 1966, p. 546). This theorem is based on the idea that 'setting the various marginal productivity conditions and supposing that at two different rates of interest the *same* set of input-output coefficients holds, the proof follows by contradiction' (Bruno, Burmeister and Sheshinski, 1966, p. 546).

It is worth noting that Weitzman–Solow's theorem is simply a consequence of the idea that, in the case of a commodity produced by a neoclassical production function, each set of input–output coefficients ought to be associated in equilibrium with a one-to-one correspondence between marginal productivity ratios and input price ratios. No ratio between marginal productivities would be associated with more than one set of input prices, and this is taken to exclude the possibility that the same technique be chosen at alternative rates of interest, and thus at different price systems. The Weitzman–Solow theorem is at the origin of a line of arguments that has been followed up by a number of other authors, such as Starrett (1969) and Stiglitz (1973). These authors have pursued the idea that 'enough' substitutability, by ensuring the smoothness of the production function, is sufficient to exclude reswitching of technique. However, non-reswitching theorems of this type involve that, for each technique of production, the capital stock may be measured either in physical terms or at given prices. For in a model with heterogeneous capital goods, if we allow prices to vary when the rate of interest of the unit wage are changed, there is no reason why the same physical set of input–output coefficients might not be associated with different price systems: even in the case of a continuously differentiable production function, the marginal product of 'social' capital cannot be a purely real magnitude independent of prices. Once it is admitted that 'in general marginal products are in terms of net value at constant prices, and hence may well depend upon what those prices happen to be' (Bliss, 1975, p. 195), it is natural to allow for different marginal productivities of the same capital stock at different price systems. It would thus appear that reswitching of technique does not carry with it any logical contradiction even in the case of a smoothly differentiable production function.

Pasinetti also pointed out that the concept of *neoclassical* substitutability is itself a very restrictive concept indeed, as it requires the possibility of infinitesimal variations of each input at a time. In fact, Pasinetti pointed out that it is possible to have a *continuous* variation of techniques (i.e. continuous substitutability) along the *w-r* relation and yet wide discontinuities in the variation of many inputs between one technique and another, thus making reswitching a quite normal phenomenon (see Pasinetti, 1969). Moreover, a non-monotonic relation between the rate of profit and capital per man may also be obtained in the absence of reswitching (Pasinetti, 1966; Bruno, Burmeister and Sheshinski, 1966). This last possibility calls attention to the phenomenon that lies at the root of the various 'paradoxes' in the theory of capital: the fact that, unless special assumptions are made, a change in the rate of profit and in the unit wage at given technical coefficients is associated with a change of relative prices.

This debate continued for a few years in the late 1960s and early 1970s, with a series of journal articles (see for example Robinson and Naqvi, 1967) and books (see for example Harcourt, 1972). In particular, Hicks presented a 'Neo-Austrian' model in *Capital and Time* (1973), concluding that reswitching of technique can be excluded only in the special case in which all the techniques have the same 'duration parameters', which means the same 'construction period' and 'utilization period' (pp. 41–4).

In the end, therefore, numerous details were added. Yet the essential results remained those that had emerged from Sraffa's book and from the symposium on 'Paradoxes in capital theory'.

SYNTHESIS. The source of most of the difficulties that have emerged in capital theory may be traced back to the fact that 'capital' may be conceived in two fundamentally different ways: (i) capital may be conceived of as a 'free' fund of resources, which can be switched from one use to another without any significant difficulty: this is what may be called the 'financial' conception of capital; (ii) capital may be conceived of as a set of productive factors that are embodied in the production process as it is carried out in a particular productive establishment: this is what may be called the 'technical' conception of capital.

The idea that there exists an inverse monotonic relation between the rate of interest and the demand for capital was born in the financial sphere. The parallel idea of an inverse monotonic relation between the rate of profit and the 'quantity of capital' employed in the production process is the outcome of a long intellectual process of extensions and generalizations. But the recent debate on capital theory has conclusively proved that such extensions and generalizations are devoid of any foundation.

It is logically impossible to make the 'financial' and the 'technical' conceptions of capital coincide, except under very restrictive conditions indeed. There is no unambiguous way in which a decreasing rate of profit may be related to the choice of alternative techniques, in terms of a monotonically increasing capital intensity, or for that matter in terms of monotonically increasing profiles of net production flows over time.

These analytical results are hardly in dispute by now. But their ultimate significance and relevance for economic theory remain highly controversial.

A group of economists now maintain that the new discoveries in capital theory concerning the relations between the rate of profit, capital per man and technical choice call for a reconstruction of economic theory from its foundations. It is stressed that the traditional beliefs are due to mistaken generalizations from the theory of short-run microeconomic behaviour, and it is argued that the economic theory (marginal economic theory) that led to the inconsistencies should be abandoned. It is pointed out that the obvious alternative is a resumption and development of the more comprehensive approach of the classical economists. A characteristic feature of this view is the attention accorded to the 'fully settled' and long-run positions of the economic system, which are made to emerge independently of the forces, such as demand and supply, that determine the level of the economic magnitudes in the short-run (see Garegnani, 1970, and in a different context, Pasinetti, 1981).

A second line of interpretation maintains that economic theorists should be prepared to give up the analytical tools of equilibrium analysis but should concentrate on the actual historical dynamics of the economic system. A characteristic argument associated with this view is that the analysis of the 'capital paradoxes' was carried out through comparison of the virtual positions of the economic system at different levels of the rate of profit and of the unit wage, and that it would be impossible in this way 'to describe an actual process of moving from one equilibrium point to another' (Robinson, 1975, p. 87). A similar argument has been put forward by Hicks (1979, p. 57), according to whom 'nothing can be shown about the *accumulation* of capital' by means of comparison among virtual positions of the economic system. As a result, reswitching of technique is acknowledged as a logical possibility but doubts are expressed on its importance in actual economic history.

A third line of interpretation is taken by more traditionally minded economists. It is argued that the discovery of 'anomalies' in the field of capital theory does point to an important deficiency in traditional economic theory, which leads to the inevitable abandonment of the concept of 'aggregate capital' in neoclassical theory. However it is also argued that there is a way of overcoming this deficiency without giving up the basic premises of traditional theory, and in particular without rejecting the application of the demand-and-supply framework to the study of production. This way leads to concentrating the analysis either on the study of 'short-run' ('temporary') equilibria, in which the physical stocks of technical capital are given, or on the equilibrium of an intertemporal economy, in which goods are described by taking their date of delivery into account. In either case, the logical possibility (or 'existence') of an equilibrium price vector is studied without explicitly considering the movement of 'free' capital from one use to another, and the importance of 'capital paradoxes' is explicitly recognized but the associated difficulties are transferred to the field of stability analysis. In fact the issue of 'stability' of equilibrium is often left open and simply stated in a problematic way (see Hahn, 1982). The traditional 'parables' are thus abandoned in pure economic theory, even if they are still retained to play a role in the fields of applied economics.

Whatever the view that is taken, the major victim of the debate has been the Böhm-Bawerk–Clark–Wicksell theory of capital that was patiently constructed towards the end of the 19th century. This theory relied on a conception of 'aggregate capital' that was taken as measurable independently of the rate of profit and of income distribution. Such a conception of 'capital' has had to be jettisoned. This has on the one hand led to a return to the Walrasian formulation of general equilibrium theory, and on the other hand to the revival of classical political economy. In any case the debate has induced theoretical economists to be much more rigorous about the nature and limits of their assumptions. In many important cases, it has also brought about a change in the main focus of their analyses. Yet it is unlikely that the next generations of economists will leave the issue of capital theory at rest.

LUIGI L. PASINETTI AND ROBERTO SCAZZIERI

See also QUANTITY OF CAPITAL; RESWITCHING OF TECHNIQUE; REVERSE CAPITAL DEEPENING; ROBINSON, JOAN VIOLET; SRAFFA, PIERO; WICKSELL'S THEORY OF CAPITAL.

BIBLIOGRAPHY

Beccaria, C. 1804. *Elementi di economia pubblica* (ms 1771–72). In *Scrittori Classici Italiani di Economia Politica*, ed. Pietro Custodi, Vol. XVIII, 17–356 and Vol. XIX, 5–166, Milan: Destefanis.

Bliss, C.J. 1975. *Capital Theory and the Distribution of Income.* Amsterdam and Oxford: North–Holland; New York: American Elsevier.

Böhm-Bawerk, E. von. 1889. *Positive Theorie des Kapitales (Kapital und Kapitalzins, Zweite Ableitung).* Translated as *The Positive Theory of Capital,* London: Macmillan.

Bruno, M., Burmeister, E., and Sheshinski, E. 1966. The nature and implications of the reswitching of techniques. *Quarterly Journal of Economics* 80(4), November, 526–53.

Burmeister, E. 1980. *Capital Theory and Dynamics.* Cambridge: Cambridge University Press.

Champernowne, D. 1953–4. The production function and the theory of capital: a comment. *Review of Economic Studies* 21(2), 112–35.

Clark, J.B. 1899. *The Distribution of Wealth.* New York: Macmillan.

Garegnani, P. 1966. Switching of techniques. *Quarterly Journal of Economics* 80(4), November, 554–67.

Garegnani, P. 1970. Heterogeneous capital, the production function and the theory of distribution. *Review of Economic Studies* 37(3), July, 407–36.

Hahn, F. 1982. The neo-Ricardians. *Cambridge Journal of Economics* 6(4), December, 353–74.

Harcourt, G.C. 1972. *Some Cambridge Controversies in the Theory of Capital.* Cambridge: Cambridge University Press.

Hicks, J. 1965. *Capital and Growth.* Oxford: Clarendon Press.

Hicks, J. 1973. *Capital and Time. A Neo-Austrian Theory.* Oxford: Clarendon Press.

Hicks, J. 1979. *Causality in Economics.* Oxford: Basil Blackwell.

Jevons, W.S. 1871. *The Theory of Political Economy.* London: Macmillan and Co; 2nd edn, 1879.

Kaldor, N. 1937. Annual survey of economic theory: the recent controversy on the theory of capital. *Econometrica* 5(3), July, 201–33.

Levhari, D. 1966. A nonsubstitution theorem and switching of techniques. *Quarterly Journal of Economics* 79(1), February, 98–105.

Morishima, M. 1964. *Equilibrium, Stability and Growth. A Multi-Sectoral Analysis.* Oxford: Clarendon Press.

Morishima, M. 1966. Refutation of the nonswitching theorem. *Quarterly Journal of Economics* 80(4), November, 520–25.

Pasinetti, L.L. 1965. Changes in the rate of profit and degree of mechanization: a controversial issue in capital theory. (Unpublished) paper presented at the First World Congress of the Econometric Society, Rome, 1965.

Pasinetti, L.L. 1966. Changes in the rate of profit and switches of techniques. *Quarterly Journal of Economics* 80(4), November, 503–17.

Pasinetti, L.L. 1969. Switches of technique and the 'rate of return' in capital theory. *Economic Journal* 79(3), September, 508–31.

Pasinetti, L.L. 1981. *Structural Change and Economic Growth: A theoretical essay on the dynamics of the wealth of nations.* Cambridge: Cambridge University Press.

Ricardo, D. 1817. *On the Principles of Political Economy and Taxation.* Vol. I of the *The Works and Correspondence of David Ricardo,* ed. Piero Sraffa with the collaboration of M.H. Dobb, Cambridge: Cambridge University Press, 1951.

Robinson, J. 1953–4. The production function and the theory of capital. *Review of Economic Studies* 21(2), 81–106.

Robinson, J. 1956. *The Accumulation of Capital.* London: Macmillan.

Robinson, J. 1975. The unimportance of reswitching. In Joan Robinson, *Collected Economic Papers,* Vol. V, Oxford: Basil Blackwell, 1979, 76–83.

Robinson, J. and Naqvi, K.A. 1967. The badly behaved production function. *Quarterly Journal of Economics* 81(4), November, 579–91.

Samuelson, P. 1962. Parable and realism in capital theory: the surrogate production function. *Review of Economic Studies* 29(3), June, 193–206.

Samuelson, P. 1966. A summing up. *Quarterly Journal of Economics* 80(4), November, 568–83.

Say, J.B. 1817. *Traité d'économie politique*. Paris: Déterville.

Smith, A. 1776. *An Inquiry into the Causes of the Wealth of Nations*. General editors R.H. Campbell and A.S. Skinner; textual editor W.B. Todd, Oxford: Clarendon Press, 1976.

Sraffa, P. 1960. *Production of Commodities by Means of Commodities*. Cambridge: Cambridge University Press.

Starrett, D. 1969. Switching and reswitching in a general production model. *Quarterly Journal of Economics* 83(4), November, 673–87.

Stiglitz, J. 1973. The badly behaved economy with the well-behaved production function. In *Models of Economic Growth*, ed. J.A. Mirrlees and N.H. Stern, London: Macmillan.

Thünen, J.-H. 1857. *Le salaire naturel et son rapport au taux de l'intérêt*. Translated by Mathieu Wolkoff, Paris: Guillaumin et Cie (German original published in 1850).

Wicksell, K. 1901–6. *Lectures on Political Economy*. Vol. I, *General Theory*. London: Routledge, 1934.

capital utilization. Capital utilization is given different interpretations in the economic literature. If a machine is available for use during, say, a day then various levels of utilization can be obtained by varying the duration of operations within the day. For any fixed duration within the day, however, it is also possible to vary the machine's rate of utilization by varying its speed. In each case there is variation in capital utilization, but both physical and economic characteristics differ widely in the two cases. Moreover, even with duration and speed constant within the day, some writers define variations in capacity utilization via variations in the variable inputs employed with a given machine per day relative to some maximum or optimum daily output. Unfortunately, these as well as other writers frequently use the terms 'capital utilization' and 'capacity utilization' interchangeably.

The discussion here will focus on the analysis of variations in the duration of operations. A brief historical perspective sets the stage for a presentation of current theorizing on this topic. Finally, the links to the issues of speed and capacity are set forth in detail.

HISTORICAL PERSPECTIVE. Concern with the duration of operations dates to the late 18th century and the spread of the factory system in England. Early writing emphasized the appropriate length of the working day relative to its social consequence for workers and its economic consequence for capitalists. Positions on these issues were developed in the context of debates over the various Factory Acts in England. These discussions usually assumed the length of the working day to be the same for capital and labour.

Marx provides a most interesting example of the development of economic thinking on duration up to his time. The length of the working day is given substantial attention in his work (1867, ch. 10); indeed, it provides the cornerstone for his theory of exploitation (see, e.g. Morishima, 1973, ch. 5); yet Marx pays only minor attention to the separation of capital's work-day from labour's work-day which is at the centre of modern analysis.

Marshall, like his predecessors, was interested in duration because of its implications for the well-being of workers and the viability of the economic system. But he saw the separation of the work-day of labour from the work-day of capital inherent in shift-work systems as an opportunity for resolving the conflicting interests of workers and capitalists with respect to the length of the work-day. Thus he becomes an advocate of the adoption of multiple shifts early in his professional career (1874) and maintained his interest in the topic throughout his career (e.g. see his work on Industry and Trade [1923, p. 650] and the *Principles* [1920, p. 578]).

Marshall's emphasis became the basis for the work of Robin Marris (1964), who treats capital utilization as a synonym for shift-work. Interestingly enough, the other modern pioneer, Georgescu-Roegen (1969, 1970, 1972), stresses the choice of the daily duration of operations, acknowledges Marx's emphasis on the topic but overlooks Marshall as well as Marris. Both view the choice of duration at the plant level, either directly or through the selection of a shift-work system, as a long-run or ex-ante decision; that is, before the plant is built. Moreover, both assume the ex-post elasticity of substitution to be zero; that is, within the day no variations in choice of technique are allowed once the factory is built. However, while Marris uses discrete techniques of production and discrete systems of utilization to describe the structure of the firm's optimization problem, Georgescu-Roegen uses a continuous production function and a continuous index of the daily duration of operations; these differences of method do not generate substantial differences in results.

Both economists use their analyses to argue against anachronistic social legislation and draw implications from their work for an important contemporary economic problem, namely for the improvement of economic conditions in developing countries.

Before presenting the modern theory it is useful to note a few salient facts. Thanks to Foss's efforts (1981) there are reliable estimates of the average work-week of capital (plant hours) in US manufacturing for 1929 and 1976, 67 and 82 hours, respectively. These estimates can be compared to an average work-week for labour of 50 hours in 1929 and 40 hours in 1976. Furthermore, Foss views the rise in capital's work-week between 1929 and 1976 as an underestimate of the increase in shift-work, because of the decrease in the number of days worked per week during this same period. These facts underlie recent interest in the topic and the frequent identification of capital utilization with shift-work.

CURRENT STATE OF THE THEORY: DURATION. A substantial number of recent contributions, based on the work of Marris and Georgescu-Roegen, have incorporated the choice of duration into the neoclassical theory of the firm. This work is most concisely exposited using a model which relies on duality theory to generate the main results available in this literature (cf. Betancourt, 1986).

The firm's optimization problem is viewed as a two-stage procedure. In the first stage the decision-maker generates a cost function for each given level of duration; in the second stage the decision-maker selects from these cost functions that one which leads to least total cost. The end result in the two-input case is:

$$C^* = dC(w^*, r^*, x^*). \qquad (1)$$

For a given reference unit of duration, w^* represents the average wage rate, r^* the price of capital services, x^* the level of output, while d represents an index of duration of operations, C is a classical cost function, and C^* represents the total cost of operations at the optimal level of duration.

For example, if an eight-hour shift starting during normal hours is the reference unit of duration, as duration increases beyond this reference period: the average wage rate (w^*) increases because of shift differentials due to workers' preferences for normal hours or social legislation; and the price of capital services per eight-hour shift decreases, although there will be two opposite tendencies in this case. The daily price of a unit of capital increases due to the additional wear and tear created by the longer duration, but this price is now spread over a greater number of hours, and the price of capital services per eight-hour shift (r^*) decreases. Betancourt and Clague (1981, ch. 2, sect. 2) provide a detailed discussion of why the second effect predominates. Finally, as duration increases, the same daily output is spread over a greater number of hours, and the level of output per eight-hour shift (x^*) decreases.

The formulation in (1) yields all but one of the main insights about capital utilization or shift-work offered by, for example, Winston and McCoy (1974), Baily (1976) and Betancourt and Clague (1975). A brief listing of these results is as follows: (i) high shift differentials or overtime rates discourage capital utilization by increasing w^*, (ii) technologies with high degrees of returns to scale discourage utilization by raising the costs of operating at low levels of output (x^*); (iii) technologies with high degrees of capital intensity encourage capital utilization because the consequent fall in the relevant cost of capital (r^*) affects a higher percentage of costs; (iv) technologies with abundant ex-ante substitution possibilities encourage utilization because they lower the costs of taking advantage of the consequent fall in the cost of capital (r^*) through the building of a more capital intensive factory.

These four factors are the main long-run determinants of optimal duration on the cost side. In addition, two other characteristics of the utilization decision are worth stating. First, factories built to operate at high levels of utilization will be designed to use capital-intensive techniques. Second, how exogenous changes in input costs affect duration depends critically on the ex-ante elasticity of substitution. For instance, if this elasticity is greater than unity, under constant returns to scale, an exogenous fall in the price of capital lowers the costs of building the plant to operate longer hours.

A logical extension of (1) allows for an endogenous choice of daily output under the assumption of profit maximization. While the main results discussed earlier continue to hold, an additional result is obtained: when the degree of returns to scale depends on the level of output (x^*), as in the standard U-shaped cost curve, the higher the level of daily output, dx^*, permitted by demand conditions, the more likely that the high utilization systems are the most profitable.

One application of the model is as the theoretical basis for empirical studies of the choice of duration (cf. Betancourt and Clague, 1981, chs 4–8). It is worth noting that the model's implications emphasized above were not rejected by several different bodies of data. Furthermore, the duality formulation provides a convenient point of departure for empirical analyses that are directed at more familiar topics in the economics of production but make duration endogenous. Another application has been to include choice of duration in standard general equilibrium models of international trade. For example, using the specific-factors model with variable utilization, Betancourt, Clague and Panagariya (1985) reconcile the dual scarcity explanation of Anglo-American trade in the 19th century with the empirical evidence on observed utilization levels. Since the same general equilibrium models underlie the analysis of many topics in the public-finance literature, one would expect applications to this field in the near future.

A short-run perspective has played an important role in dramatizing the implications of high levels of utilization for employment and output, since in this perspective a doubling of utilization implies a doubling of employment and output. For a forceful and optimistic discussion of the feasibility of this outcome through policy manipulation, see Schydlowsky (1979); for a less optimistic, long-run appraisal, see Betancourt and Clague (1981, chs 9–11). From a theoretical standpoint the heterogeneous capital-goods model of Solow, as developed in Mann (1984), provides the most drastic departure from the previous model. To analyse utilization at aggregate levels, Mann's model has a very attractive property: one can predict the effect on utilization of exogenous changes in the prices of capital and labour without knowing the elasticity of substitution. This same characteristic, however, limits its usefulness for understanding the duration decision at the plant or process level.

RELATED ISSUES: SPEED AND CAPACITY. The relations between duration, speed and capacity are difficult to analyse and are neglected in the literature. To start, consider a dual representation of the cost function in (1). Namely;

$$x = dF(K, L) \qquad (2)$$

where x is the level of daily output, i.e. $x = dx^* = dF$; F is a neoclassical production function defined over the reference period of duration; K represents both the level of the capital stock employed and the rate of capital services, which implies that the speed of operations (v) is constant and set at unity; and L represents labour services per reference period of duration. Alternatively, those who analyse variations in utilization through choice of speed represent the productive process as follows:

$$x = F(vK, L) \qquad (3)$$

where all variables have been previously defined. In (3) duration is set at unity.

Writers who employ (3) assume that the price of the capital stock is an increasing function of speed or utilization (e.g. Smith, 1970). Since costs are defined as $C = r(v)K + wL$, where $r'(v) > 0$, the cost of a unit of capital services obtained by increasing speed is an increasing function of v. While in the duration model the price of the capital stock $r(d)$ is an increasing function of duration ($r'(d) > 0$), the cost of a unit of capital services obtained by increasing duration is a decreasing function of duration, i.e. $r^* = r(d)/d$ and $r^{*\prime}(d) < 0$. This difference implies that models with one utilization variable to describe the productive process can generate nonsensical economic results if this variable is interpreted as representing either duration or speed, because the behaviour of costs can only represent one of the two interpretations.

Another interesting feature of the 'speed' model stems from the first-order conditions for cost minimization, which can be used to show that, if v, K and L are treated as choice variables, at the optimum, $r(v) = r'(v)v$. When duration and speed are endogenous this characteristic generalizes to $r(v, d) = r_v(v, d)v$ and optimal speed is determined by optimal duration (cf. Madan, 1985).

Consider now the representation of the productive process underlying the typical definitions of capacity utilization. Namely:

$$x = F(K, L) \qquad (4)$$

where all variables are defined as before and speed and duration set at unity. Using (4), Panzar's (1976) definition of capacity becomes:

$$h(K) = \max_L F(K, L) \qquad (5)$$

where $h(K)$ is an increasing function of K. This definition leads to an output-based definition of short-run capacity utilization; that is:

$$CU = x/x \max \qquad (6)$$

where x max is given by (5).

When capital equipment is capacity rated in terms of output

369

units, as in electricity generation, one can measure directly the denominator of (6) and short-run capital and capacity utilization coincide (cf. Winston, 1982, ch. 5). In general, however, the denominator in (6) is not well defined. An alternative procedure is to define the denominator in (6) as the optimal level of output, x^0. For instance, in the literature on dynamic factor demand models (e.g. Morrison, 1985) x^0 is defined as the optimal level of output when the capital stock is endogenous. Since this literature implicitly assumes constant duration in both the short-run and the long-run, there is no relation between this measure of capacity utilization and capital utilization. Moreover, 'optimal' output varies with the specification of the optimization problem, and one can generate a variety of reasonable definitions of capacity utilization which measure different concepts. Not surprisingly, the corresponding empirical definitions fail to move together (de Leeuw, 1979). To conclude, many theoretically plausible alternatives for integrating capital and capacity utilization exist.

ROGER BETANCOURT

See also FIXED FACTORS; HOURS OF WORK.

BIBLIOGRAPHY

Baily, M. 1976. The effect of differential shift costs on capital utilization. *Journal of Development Economics* 3(1), 27–47.

Betancourt, R. 1986. A generalization of modern production theory. *Applied Economics* 18, 915–28.

Betancourt, R. and Clague, C. 1975. An economic analysis of capital utilization. *Southern Economic Journal* 42(1), 69–78.

Betancourt, R. and Clague, C. 1981. *Capital Utilization: A Theoretical and Empirical Analysis.* New York: Cambridge University Press.

Betancourt, R., Clague, C. and Panagariya, A. 1985. Capital utilization and factor specificity. *Review of Economic Studies* 52, 311–29.

de Leeuw, F. 1979. Why capacity utilization rates differ. In *Measures of Capacity Utilization: problems and tasks,* ed. Frank de Leeuw et al., Board of Governors of the Federal Reserve System Staff Studies, no. 105.

Foss, M. 1981. Long-run changes in the workweek of fixed capital. *American Economic Review, Papers and Proceedings* 71, 58–63.

Georgescu-Roegen, N. 1969. Process in farming versus process in manufacturing: a problem of balanced development. In *Economic Problems of Agriculture in Industrial Societies,* ed. Ugo Papi and Charles Nunn, New York: Macmillan.

Georgescu-Roegen, N. 1970. The economics of production. *American Economic Review* 60(2), 1–9.

Georgescu-Roegen, N. 1972. Process analysis and the neoclassical theory of the firm. *American Journal of Agricultural Economics* 54, 279–94.

Madan, D. 1985. Optimal duration and speed in the long run. Mimeo, University of Sydney.

Mann, B. 1984. Capital heterogeneity, capital utilization, and the demand of shiftworkers. *Canadian Journal of Economics* 17(3), 450–70.

Marris, R. 1964. *The Economics of Capital Utilization.* Cambridge: Cambridge University Press.

Marshall, A. 1873. The future of the working classes. In *Memorials of Alfred Marshall,* ed. A.C. Pigou, London: Macmillan, 1925.

Marshall, A. 1920. *Principles of Economics.* 8th edn, London: Macmillan.

Marshall, A. 1923. *Industry and Trade.* 4th edn. Reprints of Economic Classics, New York: Augustus M. Kelley, 1970.

Marx, K. 1867. *Capital.* Vol. I. Vintage Books edn, New York: Random House, 1979.

Morishima, M. 1973. *Marx's Economics.* Cambridge: Cambridge University Press.

Morrison, C. 1985. On the economic interpretation and measurement of optimal capacity utilization with anticipatory expectations. *Review of Economic Studies* 52, 295–310.

Panzar, J. 1976. A neoclassical approach to peak load pricing. *The Bell Journal of Economics* 7(2), 521–30.

Schydlowsky, D. 1979. Capital utilization, growth, employment, balance of payments, and price stabilization. In *Planning and Short-Term Macro-Economic Policy in Latin America,* ed. J. Behrman and J. Hanson, Boston: Ballinger.

Smith, K. 1970. Risk and the optimal utilization of capital. *Review of Economic Studies* 37, 253–9.

Winston, G. and McCoy, T. 1974. Investment and the optimal idleness of capital. *Review of Economic Studies* 41, 419–28.

Winston, G. 1982. *The Timing of Economic Activity.* Cambridge: Cambridge University Press.

Carey, Henry Charles (1793–1879). American social scientist. Born in Philadelphia, the son of Mathew Carey, he was a prolific author, and his influence, though shortlived, spread from Pennsylvania throughout the nation and to Europe.

Carey's economic views were sharply at variance with those of Ricardo and Malthus, and reflect the optimism characteristic of American conditions favourable to economic expansion, conditions from which Carey himself benefited as a successful entrepreneur and promoter. The two leading themes of his writings were protectionism and harmony of interests. In his first book, *Essay on the Rate of Wages* (1835), he opposed trade restrictions as running counter to the providential order. But in *The Past, the Present and the Future* (1848) and in later writings, he vigorously appealed for tariff protection as fulfilling his law of association, a law that called for diversified and balanced regional development. Narrow specialization and foreign trade would violate this law. In *The Slave Trade* (1853) Carey suggested protectionism for the South, where it would foster industrial development.

The scope of Carey's optimistic belief in a harmonious order gradually widened. In his first book he postulated harmony between capitalists and workers, the former benefiting from rising profits and the latter from wages that rose as a result of the accumulation of capital. In his *Principles of Political Economy* (1837–40) the landowner becomes part of the harmonious order, with his earnings depicted as a return on his capital rather than a gift of nature. Population growth does not disturb the harmony as it is restrained by social conditioning. There are further attacks against the Ricardian rent theory in *The Past, the Present and the Future,* where cultivation is said to move from inferior to superior land, not vice versa as Ricardo had taught, and with returns increasing rather than decreasing. In the *Principles of Social Science* (1858–9) Carey expands his vision of a harmonious order to apply to the universe, and in *The Unity of Law* (1872) he maintains that cosmic and social laws are identical. Carey has been characterized as 'easily the most perverse and the most original American political economist before Veblen' (Conkin, 1980, p. 261).

HENRY W. SPIEGEL

SELECTED WORKS

1835. *Essay on the Rate of Wages.* Philadelphia; Carey, Lea & Blanchard.

1837–40. *Principles of Political Economy.* 3 vols, Pennsylvania: Carey, Lea & Blanchard.

1838. *The Credit Systems in France, Great Britain and the United States.* Philadelphia: Carey, Lea & Blanchard.

1848. *The Past, the Present, and the Future.* Philadelphia: Carey & Hart; London: Longman, Brown, Green, and Longmans.

1851. *The Harmony of Interests, Agricultural, Manufacturing and Commercial.* Philadelphia: J.S. Skinner; 2nd edn, New York: M. Finch, 1852.

1853. *The Slave Trade, Domestic and Foreign; why it exists, and how it may be extinguished.* Philadelphia: A. Hart.

1858–59. *Principles of Social Science*. 3 vols, Philadelphia: J.B. Lippincott & Co.; London: Trübner & Co.

1863. *Financial Crises: their causes and effects*. Philadelphia: Baird.

1867. *Reconstruction: industrial, financial & political*. Philadelphia: Collins.

1872. *The Unity of Law; as exhibited in the relations of physical, social, mental and moral science*. Philadelphia: H.C. Baird.

BIBLIOGRAPHY

Conkin, P.K. 1980. *Prophets of Prosperity: America's first political economists*. Bloomington: Indiana University Press.

Dorfman, J. 1946. *The Economic Mind in American Civilization 1606–1865*. New York: Viking, Vol. 2.

Green, A.W. 1951. *Henry Charles Carey: nineteenth-century sociologist*. Philadelphia: University of Philadelphia Press.

Kaplan, A.D.H. 1931. *Henry Charles Carey: a study in American economic thought*. Baltimore: Johns Hopkins Press.

Carey, Mathew (1760–1839). American publicist. Carey came to America as a poor immigrant from Ireland. He settled in Philadelphia, where in 1785 he founded a publishing, printing and bookselling business that eventually became the largest of its kind in the United States; a successor firm is still in the publishing business. Carey became a leading citizen of Philadelphia, got involved in politics, and participated in many local and regional controversies. When, after the end of the War of 1812, the Pennsylvania manufacturers were threatened by a flood of imports, Carey became a leader of the protectionist movement. A prolific writer, he supported its cause by a flood of publications that reached a wide public and helped to establish Hamilton's 'American system'.

In his *Olive Branch* (1814), Carey attempted to reconcile the Federalists and Democrats. A statement promoting protectionism was inserted in later editions of the work, which embodied Carey's message in over 10,000 copies – according to Carey himself, a record for a book not religious in nature.

Among the many pamphlets that Carey wrote in support of various causes, some thirty contain philanthropic appeals aiming to improve the wages and working conditions of the poor. An example of these is his *Address to the Wealthy of the Land* (1831). The free-trade economists with whom he had battled for so long he now takes to task for allegedly discouraging aid to the poor. People, he argues, may be unemployed or casually employed against their wishes, and some work in employments where their supply is large relative to the demand for their labour. He proposes to arouse public opinion against employers who fail to pay a living wage, and points to education and increased mobility of labour as means to improve the position of the poor. Ideas such as these are now commonplaces, but when Carey wrote about them, his was a lonely voice.

HENRY W. SPIEGEL

BIBLIOGRAPHY

Nuesse, C.J. 1945. *The Social Thought of American Catholics*. Washington, DC: The Catholic University of America Press.

Rowe, K.W. 1933. *Mathew Carey: A Study in American Economic Development*. Baltimore: Johns Hopkins Press.

Spiegel, H.W. 1960. *The Rise of American Economic Thought*. Philadelphia: Chilton, ch. 5.

Carlyle, Thomas (1795–1881). The eldest of nine children of Margaret Aitkin and James Carlyle, Thomas Carlyle was born at Ecclefechan in Scotland on 4 December 1795. While Carlyle's contributions ranged over many fields (including history, literary and social criticism, biography, translation and political commentary), in economics he is remembered chiefly as the originator of the epithet 'the dismal science' ('The Nigger Question', 1849; in *Miscellaneous Essays*, vol. 7 p. 84). Among 'the professors of the dismal science', one M'Croudy (J.R. McCulloch) is a principal target of Carlyle's criticism. Yet Carlyle's writings on economics are more extensive than this small measure of recognition might suggest, and his key criticisms of the economic and political tendencies of the 'present times' (as he called them) are contained essentially in three works: *Chartism* (1840), *Past and Present* (1843) and *Latter-Day Pamphlets* (1850). Almost inevitably, Carlyle's characteristically romantic reaction to the decline of authority and the rise of utilitarian individualism led him into head-on collision with the prevailing economic doctrines of the day. Since, for Carlyle, the challenge of democracy to the *ancien régime* had been carried forward under the mistaken banner 'Abolish it, let there henceforth be no relation at all' (1850, p. 21), it was natural for him to hold that *laissez-faire*, free competition, the law of supply and demand, and the 'cash nexus' were no more than 'superficial speculations ... to persuade ourselves ... to dispense with governing' (1850, p. 20). Although Carlyle's account of the 'cash-nexus' was adopted verbatim by Marx and Engels in the opening pages of *The Communist Manifesto*, in the latter sections of that document his overall position is roundly attacked (see there the reference to the 'Young England' movement, of which Carlyle was a prominent member).

There is also a thinly veiled attack on Carlyle's 'dissatisfaction with the Present ... and affection and regret towards the Past' in John Stuart Mill's *Political Economy* (pp. 753–4). However, at Carlyle's hands the utilitarian calculus of pleasure and pain fared little better. It was charged with ignoring all those sentiments, aspirations and interests which distinguished the human from other animals and was dubbed by Carlyle 'the Pig Philosophy' (1850, p. 268). Though Carlyle had few if any followers among economists, he exerted a profound impact upon the thinking of John Ruskin, and he may correctly be regarded as a principal exemplar in England of that reactionary or feudal brand of 'socialism' criticized by Marx and Engels in the *Communist Manifesto*. Carlyle died in Chelsea on 5 February 1881 and was buried in Ecclefechan.

MURRAY MILGATE

SELECTED WORKS

1888–9. *Works*. 37 vols. London: Chapman & Hall. (Page references above are from this edition.)

1896–9. *Works*. The centenary edition in 30 vols. London: Chapman & Hall.

BIBLIOGRAPHY

Mill, J.S. 1848. *Principles of Political Economy*. Ed. W.J. Ashley from the 7th edn (1871), London: Longmans, 1909.

Carroll, Lewis (Charles Lutwidge Dodgson) (1832–1898). Born on 27 January 1832, he was Student at Christ Church, Oxford, 1852–98, and Lecturer in Mathematics 1856–81. He died on 14 January 1898.

Lewis Carroll was the author of *Alice's Adventures in Wonderland* (1865), *Through the Looking Glass and What Alice Found There* (1872), and a large number of humorous poems of which 'The Hunting of the Snark' (1876) is the best known. In his real identity, that of Charles L. Dodgson, he was a mathematician of modest repute in the areas of geometry, recreational mathematics, and logic: author of *Euclid and his Modern Rivals* (1879), *Curiosa Mathematica* (1888, 1893), and *Symbolic Logic, Vol. I* (1896). Under either identity, however, he may appear to be a rather unlikely candidate for inclusion in an encyclopedia of economics. Yet his work on mechanisms for political representation anticipates important ideas in game theory and that branch of public choice theory having to do with committees and elections. The earliest work appeared in three privately printed pamphlets on *The Theory of the Committee* (1873, 1874, 1876) and dealt with a number of topics in majority rule procedures including a discussion of what is known today as the Borda count. Only recently has it been rediscovered and the significance of its contributions realized – almost entirely because of the historical scholarship of Duncan Black (1958, 1967, 1969, 1970).

The Principles of Parliamentary Representation (1st edn, Nov. 1884, 2nd edn, Jan. 1885), applies techniques which we now associate with two-person zero-sum games to solve the problem of the optimal strategy for a two-party competition in a class of voting games in which each party must decide how many candidates it wishes to nominate in a constituency in which each voter may cast v votes (no more than one to each candidate) and there are m seats to be filled. If $v < m - 1$ we have what is called the limited vote. If $v = m$ we have plurality or the bloc vote. To make the problem tractable, Dodgson supposes that each of the parties knows the number of its own supporters and those of the opposing party and that each party is able to direct the voting of each of its supporters exactly as it chooses. While not, of course, referring to it as such, he makes use of the idea of a maximin strategy in which each party chooses under the assumption that the opposing party will be optimally distributing its voting strength among an optimal number of candidates.

In this same work, Dodgson considers the question of what voting rule of the type specified above will be optimal in the sense of minimizing the expected proportion of voters whose votes are 'wasted'. By a 'wasted' vote Dodgson here means that the voter's ballot played no part in effecting the outcome; e.g. if a party with s per cent of the electorate elects h candidates but would have elected that same number of candidates even if it had received support from only s' per cent of the electorate ($s' < s$), then $(s - s')$ per cent of the electorate has had its votes wasted. In Dodgson's view, the existence of wasted votes implies that some voters are not having their preferences fully represented. He finds $v = 1$, a special form of the limited vote, commonly called the single non-transferable vote (used in post-World War II Japan) to be optimal under this standard. Under the assumption of a rectangular distribution of party voting support, he finds that the reduction in the magnitude of the expected wasted vote drops off rapidly with increasing m, for $m > 4$.

In related work, Dodgson uses a game-theoretic style of argument to consider optimal party candidate strategies under a cumulative voting system (a semi-proportional system in which each voter may cumulate up to v votes on a single candidate) and under the Hare system (the single transferable vote, a proportional system in which voters indicate their relative orderings of the candidate). For the latter election system, Dodgson looks at the problem of rational coalition forming and provides some examples to show that the results of the Hare system need not be consistent with the expected outcome of a coalitional bargaining game between political parties. However, Dodgson's results are at best suggestive. Indeed the problem he posed has only just been solved (Sugden, 1983).

Dodgson's work on proportional representation was guided by his familiarity with research done by a number of Cambridge mathematicians (most involved to some degree with the Proportional Representation Society), a group whom

Black (1970) identifies as the Cambridge School of Mathematical Politics. While Dodgson's treatment of proportional representation takes some essential ingredients from these earlier writers, his systematic treatment of the limited vote is a new creation. 'Where there had been only scattered fragments, he leaves a completed edifice' (Black, 1970). In making use of the maximin strategy to obtain an equilibrium solution to a particular two-person zero sum game and in examining optimal coalitional strategies in the context of election politics, Dodgson's long-neglected work deserves recognition as a step on the road toward the development of the modern theory of political economy.

BERNARD GROFMAN

See also BLACK, DUNCAN; BORDA, JEAN-CHARLES DE; VOTING.

SELECTED WORKS

1865, 1872. Carroll, Lewis. *The Annotated Alice: Alice's Adventures in Wonderland* and *Through the Looking Glass*. Ed. Martin Gardner, New York: New American Library, 1960.
1873, 1874, 1876. Dodgson, Charles L. *The Theory of the Committee*. Privately printed.
1879. Dodgson, C.L. *Euclid and his Modern Rivals*. London: Macmillan.
1884, 1885. Dodgson, C.L. *The Principles of Parliamentary Representation*. London: Harrison.
1888, 1893. Dodgson, C.L. *Curiosa Mathematica*. London: Macmillan.
1896. Dodgson, C.L. *Symbolic Logic, Vol. I*. Reprinted, along with *Symbolic Logic, Vol. II*, ed. William W. Bartley, III., London: Macmillan.

BIBLIOGRAPHY

Black, D. 1958. *The Theory of Committees and Elections*. Cambridge: Cambridge University Press.
Black, D. 1967. The central argument in Lewis Carroll's 'The Principles of Parliamentary Representation'. *Papers on Non-Market Decision Making*, Fall.
Black, D. 1969. Lewis Carroll and the theory of games. *American Economic Review Proceedings* 59(2), May, 206–16.
Black, D. 1970. Lewis Carroll and the Cambridge Mathematical School of P.R.: Arthur Cohen and Edith Denman. *Public Choice* 8, Spring, 1–28.
Black, D. (forthcoming) *Lewis Carroll*.
Lennon, F.B. 1962. *The Life of Lewis Carroll*. New York: Macmillan.
Phillips, R. (ed.) 1971. *Aspects of Alice*. New York: Vanguard; London: Gollancz; reprinted, New York: Vintage, 1977.
Sugden, R. 1983. Free association and the theory of proportional representation. *American Political Science Review* 78(1), 31-43.

cartel. A cartel, according to Webster, can be either 'a written agreement between belligerent nations' such as a prisoner exchange arrangement, or 'a voluntary, often international combination of independent private enterprises supplying like commodities or services' (Webster's, 1967). The second concept is our concern here. The majority of cartels have dealt with national or smaller markets, but many of the best known have been international in coverage. Economists often distinguish private cartels and public cartels. In the latter, the government theoretically makes the rules, typically under strong influence from the affected industry and enforces them. Private cartels involve private agreements. They may or may not be publicly enforced depending on the nation, the period and the agreement. Some international cartels are private, but the best known have resulted from agreements among national governments.

Cartels may involve price fixing, output controls, bid-rigging, allocation of customers, allocation of sales by product or territory, establishment of trade practices, common sales agencies or combinations of these. Many medieval cities and mercantilist nations were tightly bound by such restraints of trade, but the cartel movement is usually pictured as arising with the large private firm in the late 19th century. Cartels were carried farthest in Germany in the half-century ending with World War II, but they were also important in Austria, Switzerland, Italy, France, Scandinavia and Japan in the same period. They reached their peak during the great depression of the 1930s. Cartelization was slower to develop in Britain and other nations with a common law tradition such as the United States. A prohibition of contracts in restraint of trade (largely a refusal of the courts to enforce) goes back at least to the early 15th century in English common law. The prohibition was written into the American Sherman Anti-Trust Act when it was passed in 1890. Even in the United States, however, the National Industrial Recovery Act, passed at the bottom of the great depression in 1933, permitted industries to formulate enforceable 'codes of fair competition'. The Act was ruled unconstitutional by the Supreme Court in 1935, but the United States continued public cartels in such fields as coal-mining, oil production, interstate transportation, and agriculture for many years.

In the years since World War II most private and public industrial cartels have weakened. America's prohibition of private cartels was strengthened and many of its public cartels ended. The Western occupation forces in Japan and Germany imposed cartel prohibitions there. The subsequent national governments revised these rules to permit certain cartels, but they are far removed from the prewar, pro-cartel policies of the same countries. Most other industrial non-communist countries have adopted anti-cartel laws since the war, but few have gone as far as the United States. On the other hand, some international commodity agreements established extremely high prices in the 1970s. In a number of cases such as bauxite and copper the agreements failed within a few years. But the Organization of Petroleum Exporting Countries (OPEC) was able to keep world oil prices far above their costs for more than a decade. This was possible because Saudi Arabia, with more than a quarter of world capacity, was willing to reduce output greatly as smaller producers inside and outside OPEC expanded.

A 'perfect cartel' is one that maximizes the sum of the profits of its members. This requires that output be allocated among participants so that cost is minimized. That, in turn, implies that different producers operate their capacities at different rates. In the long run, some participants' plants would be closed. The traditional solution for private cartels is side payments from the expanding to the contracting producers. In fact, although such payments have been made, perfect cartels have generally been beyond the reach of private cartels short of merger. A perfect cartel would be difficult to distinguish from a well-run firm. The classic example was the prewar German chemical firm, I.G. Farben (Interessen Gemeinschaft Farbenindustrie meaning 'Community of Interests in the Dye Industry'). It did begin as an eight-firm cartel, but by 1925 they had all merged (Michels, 1928).

Enforcement is a crucial aspect of cartels. This requires (a) detection of violations and (b) sanctions on violators. Detection is easy in oral auctions. Violations are immediately obvious when they occur. In the more common cases where firms must bid for customers in sealed-bid auctions or through salesmen, detection is much more difficult, unless winning bids are publicly announced. Cumulative changes in market shares seem to be the most credible evidence of whether 'cheating' is going on or not, but the usefulness of such evidence rapidly declines as the numbers of competing firms increase (Stigler, 1964). The implication is that purely private cartels with many members are weak. If they have serious social cost it is most likely to work via changes in institutions such as the establishment of a basing point system or political pressure for oral auctions. Public enforcement seems essential for cartels to raise price for any length of time on unconcentrated markets.

Private enforcement also requires privately imposed sanctions. Oral auctions help here also. Only one conspirator per bid need incur any risk in punishing a violator, and even he need not always 'win'. Punishment in these cases is not severe. Since the violator is usually free to withdraw from the bidding, he need not pay a price that involves a loss. He can be deprived of the gain from collusion and, perhaps, access to the objects being bid for. With sealed bids or where the rivals solicit customers through salesmen, punishment is apt to mean general price wars – the temporary suspension of the cartel. As the numbers in a cartel grow, the gain from violating it generally increases faster than the loss from such punishment when detected (Lambson, 1984). Here is another reason to expect purely private cartels to be weak unless the market is concentrated.

In private cartels prices are unlikely to be set at joint maximizing levels. The bargaining power of major participants is apt to reflect their potential profitability without the cartel. Usually the low-cost firms have the best prospects without the cartel. If they determine cartel price, it is likely to be lower than that of a monopolist with the same plants. Small firms may also have a special influence on cartel price. A firm that is too small to be worth disciplining will probably sell at a discount from cartel price. Such a small firm as a cartel member is apt to favour high cartel prices from which it then discounts. If the numbers of such small firms become large, the majors may try to discipline the fringe as a whole to limit their discounts. In fact, however, the growth of a large fringe commonly leads to the collapse of the cartel.

Public cartels are also unlikely to be perfect cartels, but they often differ from private cartels. Many American public cartels (such as those in agriculture, oil prorationing, import quotas for oil refiners, and airlines under the Civil Aeronautics Board) allocated output, access to cheap imports of oil or to profitable markets in favour of small and high-cost firms, just the opposite of what would have occurred under successful private cartels.

Effective cartels are likely to result in excess capacity for several reasons. High-profit prospects attract entrants – as in American oil prorationing in the 1940s, 1950s and early 1960s or the famous oil glut that grew up in the 1980s after the huge price increases imposed by OPEC in the 1970s. High prices permit continued excess capacity that would be driven from the field in a competitive market – as in much of American agriculture. Existing firms will often build excess capacity if it increases sales because with prices far above marginal cost, additional sales are worth the additional cost to the firm (Posner, 1975) – as occurred on competitive airline routes in 1945–77 even though entry was prohibited (Douglas and Miller, 1974). An equilibrium at high cartel prices is reached when excess capacity has forced cost up to the point where profits are reduced to normal levels and entry and expansion is no longer attractive. Excess capacity can be avoided if members' output does not depend on current capacity. For instance, American flue-cured tobacco production depends on acreage allotments set in the late 1930s. As a result, the government was able over many years to prevent the development of excess capacity which presented such problems in other crop programmes.

Excess capacity may arise in private cartels also. In addition to entry and expansion attracted by high prices, excess capacity may be intentionally built or maintained so that the threat of retaliation against violators of the cartel can be credible (Brock and Scheinkman, 1985).

Many nations have permitted and enforced cartels of certain sorts which were seen to be in the public interest. Most of the industrial non-communist countries of the world including the United States permit export cartels. From a narrow national point of view this makes some sense at least for large countries. Their national incomes are enhanced by exploitation of any powerful positions they occupy abroad. With all major countries following such strategies, however, the overall effect must be some net loss for most of them. Another reason for export cartels arises when a major importing country negotiates a restriction on exports from foreign sources. The Americans negotiated many such quotas with major foreign exporters to the United States in the 1960s and 1970s.

Import quotas almost always involve public cartels in form. Import licences are distributed among importers by the government and are kept valuable by the trade restriction itself. In the 1930s Germany used import restrictions along with complex foreign-exchange policies to exploit its special position with respect to many of its trading partners. The main purposes of import quotas today are protectionism and/or the allocation of scarce foreign exchange. Exploitative import cartels seem to be few. The large countries employ import quotas very little today, and small nations have little monopsony power. Because of international specialization, small countries can often be large in their main export markets, but specialization in consumption and imports is rare.

A number of countries use cartels to aid temporarily depressed industries. The Japanese 'depression cartels' are an example (Hadley, 1970). Depressed industries can form cartels for one year or less if approved by a specified government agency. The state of the industry need not derive from a general depression, but the case for such cartels seems strongest in such a setting. No long-term adjustment by the industry is called for, and a temporary cartel may be one of the less costly ways of assisting industries seriously hurt by general economic decline. In normal times occasional bankruptcies may serve to weed out badly managed firms, and economic pressure on a declining industry serves to transfer resources to more productive uses, but widespread financial disasters during a depression seem of little social value. The crucial thing is that the depression cartel be truly temporary and that the problems that made the industry 'depressed' do not call for long-term adjustments.

Japanese cartel law also provides for 'rationalization cartels' (Hadley, 1970), which are not so limited in duration as the depression cartels. They require the approval of the appropriate public agency, once more. A number of European nations also provide for rationalization cartels. Rationalization refers to long-term adjustments by an industry such as the replacement of suboptimal or obsolete capacity or the elimination of excess capacity. It is conceivable that joint action by the firms in an industry could offer a better solution to excess capacity than a fight to the finish on the open market might yield. At least the transition would be less painful if a joint decision were made about which plants should be closed and the survivors bought out the firms which were to go out of business. In practice, rationalization cartels have done little of this. Rather, they set price and/or output that reduced the pressure on their members to adjust. They accomplished little or no rationalization as a result.

Where rationalization means replacing suboptimal or obsolete capacity, the cartel approach seems even less promising. It would call upon efficient producers to help their high-cost rivals to become more competitive. A theoretically appealing exception is the specialization cartel. The firms in such a cartel agree to assign products to particular members, thus permitting optimal-scale capacity for each subproduct. Governments that permit such cartels often try to reduce their competitive effects by limiting the combined shares of the market of the cartel. For instance, in the European Coal and Steel Community such cartels may not have more than 15 per cent of industry sales. However, four such groups permitted in Germany, each with a common sales agency, accounted for most of German steel and half of ECSC steel in the 1960s. Most of the specialization involved output quotas which permitted economies of long production runs. Little specialization of plant and equipment was accomplished, so few economies of scale were realized (Stegemann, 1979).

In general, most rationalization cartels have turned out in fact to be oriented primarily toward short-term restraint of trade.

LEONARD W. WEISS

See also ANTI-TRUST POLICY; COLLUSION; COOPERATIVE EQUILIBRIUM; INDUSTRIAL ORGANIZATION; MARKET STRUCTURE; MONOPOLY; OLIGOPOLY; RATIONALIZATION OF INDUSTRY.

BIBLIOGRAPHY

Brock, W.A. and Scheinkman, J. 1985. Price setting supergames with capacity constraints. *Review of Economic Studies* 52(3), July, 371–82.

Douglas, G.W. and Miller, J.C., III. 1974. *Economic Regulation of Domestic Air Transport,* Washington, DC: Brookings.

Fuller, J.G. 1962. *The Gentlemen Conspirators.* New York: Grove. (About the American electrical equipment cartel of the 1940s and 1950s.)

Hadley, E. M. 1970. *Anti-Trust in Japan.* Princeton: Princeton University Press, ch. 15.

Lambson, V. 1984. Self-enforcing collusion in large dynamic markets. *Journal of Economic Theory,* 34(2), December, 282–91.

MacAvoy, P.W. 1965. *The Economic Effects of Regulation.* Cambridge, Mass.: MIT Press.

Michels, R.K. 1928. *Cartels, Combines, and Trusts in Post-War Germany.* New York: Columbia University Press; London: P.S. King & Co.

Osborn, D.K. 1976. Cartel problems. *American Economic Review* 66, September, 835–44.

Posner, R.A. 1975. The social cost of monopoly and regulation. *Journal of Political Economy* 83(3), August, 807–27.

Pribram, K. 1935. *Cartel Problems.* Washington, DC: Brookings.

Stegemann, K. 1979. The European experience with exempting specialization agreements and recent proposals to amend the Combines Investigation Act. In *Canadian Competition Policy,* ed. J.R.S. Prichard, W.T. Stanbury and T.A. Wilson, Toronto: Butterworths, 449–86.

Stigler, G. 1964. A theory of oligopoly. *Journal of Political Economy* 72(1), February, 44–61.

Stocking, G.W. and Watkins, M.W. 1946. *Cartels in Action.* New York: The Twentieth Century Fund.

Webster's Unabridged International Dictionary. 1967. 3rd edn, Springfield, Mass.: Meriam–Webster.

Carver, Thomas Nixon (1865–1961). Carver's career exemplifies the blend of scientific economics and popular social science so characteristic of his period. He was born on 25 March 1865 in Kirkville, Iowa. After a disrupted undergraduate education at Iowa Wesleyan and the University of Southern California (AB, 1891), he studied at Johns Hopkins under Richard T. Ely and John Bates Clark, eventually obtaining his PhD at Cornell in 1894. A joint appointment in economics and sociology at Oberlin led to a professorship in political economy at Harvard (1900–32), where for a time he taught the only course in sociology. His principal theoretical work in economics was an extension of Clark's marginalism to a synthesis of abstinence and productivity theories of interest. He also made pioneering contributions to the economics of agriculture and rural sociology, and published several textbooks and numerous magazine articles. Carver's attacks on radicalism and socialism, his forthright advocacy of individualism, thrift and free enterprise, and his insistence on the crucial value of natural resources conservation and social balance, made him a cult figure among Harvard students. Acceptance of Malthusian population theory and recognition of the dangers of corporation power did not quench his optimism, although he favoured public works and credit expansion as a corrective to the 1930s depression. Carver served as adviser to the Department of Agriculture and Director of its rural organization service in 1913–14. An energetic and successful Secretary-Treasurer of the American Economic Association from 1909 to 1913, he was elected President in 1916. He died in Santa Monica, California, on 8 March 1961.

A.W. COATS

SELECTED WORKS

1893. The place of abstinence in the theory of interest. *Quarterly Journal of Economics* 8, October, 40–61.

1904. *The Distribution of Wealth.* New York, London: Macmillan; reprinted, 1932.

1911. *Principles of Rural Economics.* Boston, New York: Ginn & Co; reprinted, 1932.

1912. *The Religion Worth Having.* Boston and New York: Houghton Mifflin; revised edn, Los Angeles: Ward Ritchie Press, 1940.

1915. *Essays in Social Justice.* Cambridge, Mass.: Harvard University Press; repr. 1940.

1919. *Principles of Political Economy.* Boston, New York: Ginn & Co.

1921. *Principles of National Economy.* Boston, New York etc: Ginn & Co.

1925. *The Present Economic Revolution in the United States.* Boston: Little, Brown & Co.

1935. *The Essential Factors of Social Evolution.* Cambridge, Mass.: Harvard University Press.

1949. *Recollections of an Unplanned Life.* Los Angeles: Ward Ritchie Press.

cash balances. *See* MONEY SUPPLY.

Cassel, Gustav (1866–1944). Along with Knut Wicksell and David Davidson, Gustaf Cassel was the founder of modern economics in Sweden. He started as a mathematician and began his career as an economist by treating problems of railway rates and progressive taxation from a mathematical point of view. In order to deepen his understanding of economics he went to Germany, where he attended the seminars of Schönberg, Cohn and other traditional representatives of the economic profession. After visits to England, where he made the acquaintance of Marshall and of Sidney and Beatrice Webb, and a short period of lecturing at the university of Copenhagen, in 1902 Cassel took up a position as associate professor in economics at the university of Stockholm. In 1904 he was appointed a professor in economics and public finance. As holder of the chair he acquired a series of gifted pupils, Gunnar Myrdal and Bertil Ohlin among others, who, although they developed the theoretical heritage

of Wicksell rather than that of Cassel, became the founders of the Stockholm School of economics. Before World War I Cassel frequently served as a government expert on problems of railway rates, taxation, state budgets and banking and his involvement in problems of economic policy increased with the post-War economic problems. During the 1920s he became an adviser to the League of Nations on monetary problems and was commonly regarded as a leading international authority in this field, lecturing and publishing widely. All his life he worked also as a columnist for the Swedish daily paper *Svenska Dagbladet*. Although Cassel was originally liberal, he progressively turned more and more conservative denouncing the labour movement, the welfare state and Keynesianism in the name of 'Modern Scientific Principles'.

It is no easy task to evaluate the contributions of Gustav Cassel to economics. He never cared much about paying homage to his predecessors, from whom he sometimes took over fruitful ideas, while at the same time being unjustifiably critical towards other theorists. His expositions are not seldom marred by contradictions and a vagueness in expression, only scantily veiled by his mastery in round and polished sentences. At the same time Cassel took a keen interest in very many fields of economic theory and practice, he had a firm grip on empirical economics and his gifts in tracking down the relevant and essential aspects of economic problems were unusual. These qualities, in combination with a forceful and pedagogical exposition and, on the top of this, an imperturbable conviction of being the chosen spokesman for progress and the principles of science, made him influential not only among men of practical matters but also among fellow economists.

Cassel's main work is his *Theoretische Sozialökonomie* (1918) but his most important theoretical ideas were in fact conceived already around the turn of the century. In his essay *Grundsätze für die Bildung der Personentarife auf den Eisenbahnen* (1900), he criticized the idea of calculating railway rates on the basis of average costs and instead advocated marginal cost-pricing. For a railway enterprise as a monopolistic business unit, rates which equalized marginal costs and marginal revenues were the optimal ones, though this might imply that some rates were lower than average costs. Even if the principle had been advocated already in 1885 by the American railway economist A.T. Hadley, it was succinctly formulated by Cassel.

Venturing into general economic theory, Cassel in these years also criticized Ricardo's labour theory of value in the essay *Die Produktionskostentheorie Ricardos und die ersten Aufgaben der theoretischen Volkswirtschaftslehre* (1901), presented an outline of his own theory of price, *Grundriss einer elementaren Preislehre* (1899) and developed a theory of interest in *The Nature and Necessity of Interest* (1903). The Ricardian labour theory of value was, according to Cassel, untenable because it assumed that the labour-capital ratio was equal in different enterprises and industries, that labour was homogeneous and that the marginal land did not pay any rent. He did not care to take issue with the Marxian development of the labour theory of value. The labour theory of value belonged to the so-called one-sided value theories. But so did the marginal utility theory of value, which was deficient primarily because it lacked a clearly conceptualized unit of measurement for utility but also because goods, according to Cassel, are not generally divisible and the valuations of goods are not continuous functions of the supply. Therefore, Cassel suggested that one should do away with all conceptions of value and rest content with money prices and not bother with what might lie behind money prices. Thus Cassel did not consider the fact that money itself may vary in value, nor that the marginal utility of money certainly varies between individuals. Following Marshall, Cassel explained prices by reference to supply and demand and, following Walras, he devised a general equilibrium model for market prices in the form of a system of simultaneous equations. In fact, Cassel's price theory is a simplified version of the theory of Walras, who was characterized as 'in a sense one of my precursors'. However, by popularizing Walras, Cassel contributed much towards the understanding of the mutual interdependencies in a market economy. It was quite logical that the theory of interest that Cassel devised also should be based upon supply and demand, viz. supply of waiting and demand for the use of capital, as a special case of the general theory of price, and he boldly asserted that waiting and use denoted the same thing. Although his theory of interest, showing a close resemblance to that of Senior, was not original, it still merits our attention because of its vivid illustrations and some striking applications. This is particularly the case for Cassel's argument against the idea of a continually falling rate of interest. Given that most saving is made in order to safeguard a permanent future level of income, the shortness of life puts a ceiling under the rate of interest. This was the necessary and sufficient condition for the necessity of interest.

The year after the publication of *The Nature and Necessity of Interest*, Cassel also published his theory of the business cycle and his theory of the secular development of the general level of prices in two articles in the Swedish journal *Ekonomisk tidskrift*, 'Om kriser och dåliga tider' (1904) and 'Om förändringar i den allmänna prisnivän' (1904). Both these theories were later incorporated and somewhat elaborated in his *Theoretische Sozialökonomie* (1918). In his theory of the business cycle Cassel was evidently influenced by Spiethoff and Tugan-Baranowsky, who recently had made public their theories explaining the business cycle with reference to the variations in investment of fixed capital and of loanable funds. What is really new in Cassel's treatment is his precise formulation of the accelerator principle, which he expounds with reference to the relationship between the demand for freights and the output of ships. The treatment of growth theory had to await the publication of his *Theoretische Sozialökonomie* and also on this point Cassel was wholly original, in fact foreshadowing the Harrod growth formula by his own formula for 'the uniformly progressing economy', the only difference being that Cassel worked with an average instead of a marginal capital coefficient.

Cassel's theory of the secular development of the general level of prices also demands our attention as a piece of brilliant imagination and was as late as 1930, after Kitchin's refinements, accepted as the theoretical basis for the first interim report of the gold delegation of the League of Nations. Cassel's theory was a straight-forward quantity theory of money. By calculating the relative variations of gold output in relationship to a calculated normal need of gold for preserving a constant general level of prices Cassel showed that there was a very good correlation between the relative variations of gold output and the corresponding variations in the general level of prices. Cassel's theory met with all the objections the quantity theory of money usually meets and in addition a series of more specific criticism: that it presupposes a constant ratio between velocity (V) and transactions (T), which is difficult to believe; that it overlooks the important role of silver in the 19th century as well as the varying proportions of the more relevant variable monetary gold; and that a case as good as Cassel's could be made, and in fact was made by Warren and Pearson, by making the gold price rather than gold output the effective cause of price changes. But since Kitchin's (and Woytinski's)

calculations, taking only monetary gold in regard, showed a still better fit between the variations of gold output and prices, Cassel's theory is still a serious candidate.

After this first period of theoretical activity around the turn of the century, Cassel mainly devoted his energy to synthesizing and propagating his ideas on the national and the international scene. The only really new element in his theoretical set-up was the famous purchasing power parity theory of the exchange rates, according to which the international rates of exchanges are determined by the purchasing power of the national currencies. It is easy to show that this is a rather poor general theory for the explanation of the exchange rates. But it contained a pragmatic truth during and after World War I, when trade balances and, hence, the supply and demand of currencies, to a great extent, were determined by the course of rapid inflation in different countries. It is precisely this instinct for pragmatic truths that explains Cassel's success and influence in the international community of bankers and politicians during the 1920s. In his memoranda to the international conferences of the League of Nations Cassel first and foremost advocated stability of monetary affairs by means of control of the quantity of money, increased interest rates and cut-downs of state expenditures. But he was also critical towards the subsequent ruthless policy of deflation creating widespread unemployment and new disequilibria in world trade as well as intolerable debt burdens. Together with Keynes he criticized the unwillingness of the claimants to the German war debt to receive German goods as payment. When confronted by the permanent unemployment of the 1920s, Cassel concentrated his attacks on trade unions and the level of wages and untiringly explained the gospel contained in Say's Law. During the course of the 1930s it became all too clear that Gustav Cassel had been left behind by the march of events and of economic theory. It was his tragedy that he himself, who once waved his magic wand over international economic affairs, could not bear the truth. After some years of protracted rearguard skirmishes he devoted himself to more philosophical problems and wrote up a voluminous autobiography characteristically entitled 'In the Service of Reason' (*I förnuftets tjänst*, 1940–41). His last words on his death-bed were 'A world currency!'

BO GUSTAFSSON

See also PURCHASING POWER PARITY; WICKSELL, JOHAN GUSTAF KNUT.

SELECTED WORKS

1899. Grundriss einer elementaren Preislehre. *Zeitschrift für die gesamte Staatswissenschaften* 55, 395–458.

1900a. *Das Recht auf den vollen Arbeitsertrag*. Göttingen: Vandenhoeck & Ruprecht.

1900b. Grundsätze für die Bildung der Personentarife auf den Eisenbahnen. *Archiv für Eisenbahnwesen*. Trans. as 'The principles of railway rates for passengers', *International Economic Papers* 6, (1956), 126–47.

1901. Die Produktionskostentheorie Ricardos und die ersten Aufgaben der theoretischen Volkswirtschaftslehre. *Zeitschrift für die gesamte Staatswissenschaft* 57, 68–100.

1902a. Der Ausgangspunkt der theoretischen Ökonomie. *Zeitschrift für die gesamte Staatswissenschaft* 58, 668–98.

1902b. *Sozialpolitik*. Stockholm: H. Geber.

1903. *The Nature and Necessity of Interest*. London, New York: Macmillan.

1904a. Om kriser och dåliga tider. *Ekonomisk Tidskrift* 6, 21–35 and 51–81.

1904b. Om förändringar i den allmänna prisnivån. *Ekonomisk Tidskrift* 6, 311–31.

1917. *Dyrtid och sedelöverflöd*. Stockholm: P.A. Norstedt & Söner.

1918. *Theoretische Sozialökonomie*. Leipzig: C.F. Winter. (In manuscript in 1914. There are five German editions.) Trans. into English as *Theory of Social Economy*, London: T.F. Unwin, 1923; new revised edn., London: E. Benn, 1932. French, Japanese and Swedish editions also available.

1921. *The World's Monetary Problems. Two memoranda presented to the International Financial Conference of the League of Nations in Brussels in 1920 and to the Financial Committee of the League of Nations in September 1921*. London: Constable & Co.

1922. *Penningväsendet efter 1914*. Stockholm: P.A. Norstedt. Trans. into English as *Money and Foreign Exchange after 1914*, London: Constable & Co., 1922. German, French, Spanish and American editions also available.

1925. *Fundamental Thoughts in Economics*. London: T.F. Unwin.

1927. *Memorandum till den Internationella ekonomiska Konferensen i Genève 1927*. Stockholm: P.A. Norstedt.

1928. *Socialism eller framåtskridande*. Stockholm: P.A. Norstedt & Söners.

1935. *On Quantitative Thinking in Economics*. Oxford: Clarendon Press.

1936. *The Downfall of the Gold Standard*. Oxford: Clarendon Press.

1940–41. *I förnuftets tjänst, en ekonomisk självbiografi*. 2 vols, Stockholm: Bokfölaget Natur och Kultur.

1942. *Vår bildnings fåfänglighet*. Stockhom: Bonniers.

1944. *Den odelbara människan*. Stockholm: Natur och Kultur.

BIBLIOGRAPHY

A good biography of Cassel has yet to appear. The biography by his secretary, Ingrid Giobel-Lilja (1948), may be consulted for biographical details, especially as regards his family life. Böhm-Bawerk (1914) made a critical examination of Cassel's theory of interest, and Wicksell (1919) published a very critical review of *Theoretische Sozialökonomie*. A more descriptive account of Cassel's main work is to be found in Mitchell (1969); Gunnar Myrdal (1945) wrote an obituary; and Gustafsson (1964) offers another overall evaluation with emphasis on Cassel's theory of long-run prices.

Böhm-Bawerk, E. von. 1914. Exkurs XIII, Kritische Glossen zur Zinstheorie Cassels, Exkurse zur 'Positiven Theorie des Kapitals'.

Giobel-Lilja, I. 1948. *Gustav Cassel, En livsskildring*. Stockholm: Natur och Kultur.

Gustafsson, B. 1964. Gustav Cassel (1866–1944). *Vär Tid* no. 3.

Mitchell, W.C. 1969. *Types of Economic Theory*, Vol. 2. New York: A.M. Kelley, chapter XVI.

Myrdal, G. 1945. Gustav Cassel in memoriam. *Ekonomisk Revy*. Republished (in Swedish) in J. Schumpeter, *Stora national-ekonomer*, Stockholm: Natur och Kultur, 1953.

Wicksell, K. 1919. Professor Cassels nationalekonomiska system. *Ekonomisk Tidskrift* 21, 195 226. Republished in *Schmollers Jahrbuch* 52(5), 1928, and in K. Wicksell, *Lectures on Political Economy*, Vol. I, London: G. Routledge & Sons, 1934, Appendix I

catallactics. The term, meaning 'the science of exchanges', was proposed as a replacement for the name 'political economy' by the Rev. Richard Whately in his 1831 Drummond Lectures at Oxford on political economy (Whately, 1831). As the leader of the group of embattled religious and economic liberals at Oriel College, Oxford, during the 1820s, Whately, a distinguished logician, had become tutor and lifelong friend of the economist Nassau W. Senior. In his Drummond Lectures, Whately was concerned to refute the dominant Oxford view that political economy, being concerned with wealth, was materialistic and opposed to Christianity. In focusing on exchanges, Whately denounced Adam Smith's definition of the scope of political economy as the science of wealth.

Whately defined man as 'an animal that makes exchanges', pointing out that even the animals nearest to rationality have not 'to all appearance, the least notion of bartering, or in any way exchanging one thing for another' (Whately, 1831, p. 7).

Focusing on human acts of exchange rather than on the *things* being exchanged, Whately was led almost immediately to a subjective theory of value, since he saw that 'the same thing is different to different persons' (p. 8) and that differences in subjective value are the foundation of all exchanges.

In 1831 Whately was named Archbishop of Dublin, where he promptly used his influence to create and financially support a permanent five-year Whately Chair of Political Economy at Trinity College. For the rest of his life Whately personally selected the holders of the chair; as a result, the Whately professors carried on their mentor's tradition of catallactics and subjective utility theory. In contrast to John Stuart Mill's development of economics as a science of the abstraction 'economic man', man engaged only in avaricious pursuit of wealth, the third holder of the Whately Chair, James Anthony Lawson (1817–87), developed the idea of economics as catallactics, as studying exchanging man. Lawson, holder of the chair in his twenties (1841–6), and later to become an MP and Attorney-General for Ireland, stated in his first lecture that economics views man 'in connection with his fellow-man, having reference solely to those relations which are the consequences of a particular act, to which his nature leads him, namely, the act of making exchange' (Lawson, 1844, pp. 12–13). Yet, Lawson himself fell back on discussions of wealth in his second lecture, demonstrating that, in their specific exposition, the catallacticians had not yet fully emancipated themselves from the older definitions of the scope and nature of political economy (Kirzner, 1960).

One pseudonymous English writer who adopted catallactics in this period was Patrick Plough, who included and explained the term in the title of his tract, *Letters on the Rudiments of a Science, called, formerly, improperly, Political Economy, recently more pertinently, Catallactics* (London, 1842).

Catallactics reached the status of a self-conscious school of thought in the writings of the zealous and indefatigable Scottish lawyer and economist Henry Dunning Macleod. Stressing value as the result of a subjective desire of the mind, Macleod furthered the emancipation of economics from material wealth by showing that immaterial goods or services are also subjects of exchange. Macleod insisted that catallactics was the only correct school of economic thought and traced back the origins of the school beyond Whately to the late 18th-century French philosopher Etienne Bonnot de Condillac. While Condillac, in his *Le commerce et le gouvernement* (1776), did not actually use the term catallactics, he defined economics as the philosophy of commerce, or the science of exchanges. Condillac also noted that value stems only from mental desires, and hence demand, for exchangeable goods, and proclaimed that men engage in exchange precisely because each man values what he gains in exchange more than what he gives up. Hence both parties to an exchange gain in value (Macleod, 1863, pp. 530–35).

The catallactic school found its culmination in the United States, in Arthur Latham Perry (1830–1905), for half a century a highly influential professor of political economy at Williams College. Perry endorsed the Macleod view of the history of economic thought, the sound catallactic school descending from Condillac through Whately and Macleod. He went beyond the inconsistencies of his forerunners, however, by purging the word 'wealth' from economics altogether, and proposing that 'property' – that which can be bought and sold – be used as a term denoting valuable things not yet sold and therefore in need of an estimate of their value (Perry, 1865).

While interest in the catallactic approach faded after the work of Perry, a variant appeared in the early work of Schumpeter (1908). In this manifesto for the reconstruction of economic theory, Schumpeter wished to purge economics of all concern about purposeful human motives or actions and replace it with exclusive concentration on mechanistic alterations of economic quantities. Exchanges then become 'purely formal' variations in economic quantities of goods (Schumpeter, 1908, pp. 49–55, 86, 582; Machlup, 1951; Kirzner, 1960).

Schumpeter did, however, manage to contribute positively to the catallactic approach. Whately and his followers had strongly rejected any element of Crusoe economics, since for them economic analysis had to be confined to interpersonal exchange. In Schumpeter's formalistic approach, actions of Crusoe could alter the placement of quantities of economic goods and therefore could be considered 'exchanges'.

It remained for Ludwig von Mises (1949) to bring back the term catallactics in his treatise on economics, and to broaden it by embedding its analysis of the market, or the science of exchanges, in the wider discipline of 'praxeology', the science of human action. Crusoe economics then becomes vindicated in the broader sense of analysing Crusoe's actions and his use of resources to achieve his values and goals, as well as in the sense of exchanging his present state for a more satisfying one.

MURRAY N. ROTHBARD

See also MACLEOD, HENRY DUNNING; WHATELY, RICHARD.

BIBLIOGRAPHY

Condillac, E.B. de 1776. *Le commerce et le gouvernement considérés relativement l'un à l'autre.* In *Oeuvres philosophiques de Condillac*, ed. George LeRoy, Paris: Presses Universitaires de France, 1947–51, vol. 2.

Kirzner, I.M. 1960. *The Economic Point of View: an Essay in the History of Economic Thought.* Princeton: Van Nostrand.

Lawson, J.A. 1844. *Five Lectures on Political Economy*, delivered before the University of Dublin, 1843. London and Dublin.

Machlup, F. 1951. Schumpeter's economic methodology. *Review of Economics and Statistics* 33, May, 145–51.

Macleod, H.D. 1863. *A Dictionary of Political Economy.* Vol. I, London.

Mises, L. von. 1949. *Human Action: a Treatise on Economics.* New Haven: Yale University Press.

Perry, A.L. 1865. *Political Economy.* 21st edn, New York: Scribners, 1892.

Plough, P. 1842. *Letters on the Rudiments of a Science, called, formerly, improperly, Political Economy, recently more pertinently, Catallactics.* London.

Schumpeter, J.A. 1908. *Das Wesen und der Hauptinhalt der theoretischen Nationalökonomie.* Leipzig: Duncker & Humblot.

Whately, R. 1831. *Introductory Lectures on Political Economy.* 2nd edn, London, 1832.

catastrophe theory. The theory of general equilibrium defines equilibrium prices p as the solutions in the commodity space of the vector equation defined by equality of supply and demand, namely $z(p) = 0$, where z denotes aggregate excess demand. This formulation leads to a purely mathematical problem, namely the study of the properties of the solutions of the equation $z(p) = 0$. The first problem to come into the picture is that of existence. Its positive solution leads to new issues such as the determinateness of the solutions or their number. The fact that these problems cannot be solved uniformly with exactly the same answer for every economy necessitates the introduction of suitable parameters in terms of which the properties of the solutions of the equilibrium equation can be properly described. Let ω denote this parameter chosen in some suitable vector space Ω. This means that the aggregate demand function z can be viewed as depending on $\omega \in \Omega$ which we now denote by $z(\cdot, \omega)$ and the goal of equilibrium theory becomes one of relating the properties of the solutions to $z(p, \omega) = 0$ with the parameter ω. In practice, one chooses for ω the initial endowments of every consumer, the equilibrium model simply describing a pure exchange economy.

This way of handling problems by parameterizing them had been introduced by Poincaré, who called it the continuation method. It has also been extensively used by engineers dealing with applied issues involving solving equations dependent on parameters. The topic popularized by Thom under the name catastrophe theory consists simply in combining Poincaré's continuity method with the tools of singularity theory. As a first approximation, a singularity is just another word for a multiple root of the equation $z(p, \omega) = 0$ where the unknown is the vector p. One easily sees, at least intuitively, that multiple roots, and especially double roots, correspond to borderline cases associated with changes in the number of solutions, the standard picture being that solutions appear or disappear in pairs at these double roots. Clearly enough, this may entail discontinuous behaviour of the equilibrium solution despite the fact every other feature of the model is continuous or even smooth. Catastrophe theory has often been unduly identified to this discontinuity property.

In a pure exchange economy consisting of l commodities and m consumers, the parameter space Ω, namely the set of initial endowments, can be identified to $(\mathbb{R}^l)^m$. Prices can conveniently be normalized, for example, with the help of the numeraire convention, so that the price space can be identified to $S = \mathbb{R}^{l-1}_{++}$. Then, the problem is to describe the set E of solutions (p, ω) to $z(p, \omega) = 0$, i.e., $E = \{(p, \omega) \in S \times \Omega / z(p, \omega) = 0\}$ (global approach), and the solutions $(p, \omega) \in E$ when ω varies (local approach). The main results are the following ones:

(1) Under smoothness assumptions for preferences, E is a smooth submanifold of $S \times \Omega$ diffeomorphic to Ω. Furthermore, the natural projection $\pi : E \to \Omega$ defined by the formula $(p, \omega) \to \omega$ is proper (and smooth).

(2) The set Σ consisting of $\omega \in \Omega$ for which the equilibrium equation possesses a multiple root is closed with Lebesgue measure zero.

(3) Let P be the set of Pareto optima. This subset does not intersect Σ. Furthermore, there is uniqueness of equilibrium when ω describes the connected component containing the set of Pareto optima P in the complement of the set Σ in Ω.

This latter result implies that, for an economy where the trade vector remains small to some extent, equilibrium is unique and depends smoothly on the parameters defining the economy. On the other hand, when this trade vector is large, the economy is likely to have multiple equilibria so that, when the parameter vector ω varies, 'catastrophic' changes of the equilibrium prices and allocations are susceptible of being observed.

These relationships between the properties of equilibria and their number are special cases of a far more general property of the general equilibrium model. We state it as follows. Let $N(\omega)$ denotes the number of solutions of the equilibrium equation $z(p, \omega) = 0$, with $p \in S$. Then, assume that N is given (i.e., the number of solutions of the equilibrium equation is known for every $\omega \in \Omega$). Furthermore, assume there exists an economy ω with at least two equilibria, i.e., $N(\omega) \geqslant 2$. Then, there is enough information to determine all the equilibrium prices associated with every economy $\omega \in \Omega$. In other words, the economic model possesses the quite remarkable property that knowing the number of solutions suffices to determine the precise value of these solutions (provided there is an economy with multiple equilibria). If there is uniqueness of equilibrium, the above statement does not hold true any more. In that case, one finds that this unique equilibrium price vector is constant, i.e., does not depend on the economy $\omega \in \Omega$.

Y. BALASKO

See also GLOBAL ANALYSIS; REGULAR ECONOMIES.

catching-up. The search for a pattern in the observed wide variation in the cross-country growth rate of output per man hour has led to the observation that the latecomers in industrialization should, and in fact do, tend to innovate faster than does the world's 'technology frontier area' (TFA), the latter defined as the regions in which the world's best technology is employed. The reason behind this observation is the commonsense notion that in technology or organization, as well as in science, learning and imitating is typically cheaper and faster than is the original discovery and testing. The distance between the level of development of the TFA and that of a less developed country (LDC) may be taken as a measure of the backlog of technological opportunities to exploit. The larger the backlog, the greater may be expected to be the economic incentive to take advantage of some of these opportunities and, other things being equal, the greater the rate of international technology transfer. The idea that there might be 'advantages of backwardness' in this sense is usually associated with the names of Thorstein Veblen and Alexander Gerschenkron. Veblen (1915) applied it to Germany vis-à-vis England; Gerschenkron (1962) updated and extended the work to include Russia, France and Italy. A formalization of this idea by Nelson and Phelps (1966) assumed that an increase in the level of technology of an LDC is proportional to the technology gap between it and the TFA. This assumption implies that the relationship between the rate of innovation and the relative technology gap is, for any LDC and in the course of time, positive and linear. Moreover, the LDCs' innovation rate would always exceed that of the TFA but fall toward it asymptotically, the relative gap falling as a result toward a country-specific positive constant, called the 'equilibrium technology gap'. This falling of the relative technology gap between an LDC and the TFA is what is meant by (international and/or technological) catching-up.

Studies of the world pattern of productivity growth rates in the period 1950–85 have led to the important qualification of the original Veblen–Gerschenkron hypothesis, namely that for the group of highly backward LDCs, the rate of innovation tends to be lower the greater the relative technology gap. The relationship across all countries is thus of the 'hat-shaped type' (Gomulka, 1971; Horvat, 1974). The usual interpretation of the negative part of the Hat-shape Relationship rests on the notion of 'absorptive capacity' being the severely limiting factor in the initial phase of the catching-up. As educational standards and physical infrastructure are improved and export capabilities developed, a larger amount of foreign technology becomes profitable. Technology imports themselves also help upgrade skills and increase exports, attracting still larger technology imports, and so forth. It is this causality sequence which gives rise to the relationship's negative part. However, before absorptive capacity is developed to reach a level at which an LDC's rate of innovation is the same as that of the TFA, an LDC's relative backwardness would be increasing.

The Hat-shape Relationship may be interpreted as an international, macroeconomic equivalent of logistic or S-shaped diffusion curves observed often for individual inventions. Theoretical research has been centred on modelling the dynamics of catching-up under different channels of technology transfer, such as direct foreign investment (Findlay, 1976), a cost-free diffusion (Gomulka, 1971), or trading conventional goods for embodied technology (Gomulka, 1970). The most recent development of the theory also takes into account economic dualism and technology transfer costs. This particular theory combines international technology transfer with internal diffusion from the modern to the traditional sector, and interprets 'appropriate technology' in a dynamic context. Empirical studies indicate that embodied technology transfer is an important, perhaps the main, channel for most LDCs (Gomulka and Sylvestrowicz, 1976). However, in the postwar catching-up of the US by countries with large R and D sectors, such as Japan, West Germany and the USSR, the import of capital goods from the US has apparently played a small role, indicating that disembodied diffusion, both (virtually) cost-free and commercial, have probably played the main role. The post-1975 labour productivity slowdown in countries of the latter character may be interpreted as evidence of these highly developed countries approaching their specific equilibrium technology gaps. These equilibrium gaps, as well as innovation rates in the course of the catching-up itself, appear to be strongly influenced by cultural and systemic factors. Consequently, the process of catching-up is bringing about a state of international growth equilibrium in which the innovation rate would be common to all countries, but in which productivity and technology levels would continue to vary significantly among the world's countries.

STANISLAW GOMULKA

See also BACKWARDNESS; CUMULATIVE CAUSATION; DIFFUSION OF TECHNOLOGY; PERIPHERY.

BIBLIOGRAPHY

Ames, E. and Rosenberg, N. 1963. Changing leadership and industrial growth. *Economic Journal* 73, March, 13–31.
Findlay, R. 1976. Relative backwardness, direct foreign investment, and the transfer of technology: a simple dynamic model. *Quarterly Journal of Economics* 92(1), February, 1–16.
Gerschenkron, A. 1962. *Economic Backwardness in Historical Perspective.* Cambridge, Mass.: Harvard University Press.
Gomulka, S. 1970. Extensions of the 'Golden Rule of Research' of Phelps. *Review of Economic Studies* 37, January, 73–93.
Gomulka, S. 1971. *Inventive Activity, Diffusion, and the Stages of Economic Growth.* Aarhus: Institute of Economics.
Gomulka, S. and Sylvestrowicz, J.D. 1976. Import-led growth: theory and estimation. In *On the Measurement of Factor Productivities: Theoretical Problems and Empirical Results,* ed. Altman et al, Göttingen: Vendenhoeck and Ruprecht.
Horvat, B. 1974. Welfare and the common man in various countries. *World Development* 2(7), 29–39.
Nelson, R.R. and Phelps, E.S. 1966. Investment in humans, technological diffusion, and economic growth. *American Economic Review* 56(2), May, 69–75.
Veblen, T. 1915. *Imperial Germany and the Industrial Revolution.* London: Macmillan.

Cattaneo, Carlo (1801–1861). Cattaneo was a leading spokesman for social and political reform in his native Lombardy. A polymath, he made important contributions to history, geography, linguistics and philosophy and took a prominent role in politics, as well as writing on economics and engaging in various business ventures. However, he preferred the title of economist to all others, and a concern with economic reform runs through his work. An admirer of Charles Bonet, a follower of Condillac, he developed his own theory of human progress from barbarism to civility. At the heart of his thesis was a sensationalist epistemology adapted from Vico, which he called the psychology of associated minds. He argued that if individuals were allowed to experience sufficient contrasting ideas and situations then humankind would gradually improve and both our needs and the means of satisfying them infinitely multiply. He was therefore a staunch advocate of both political liberty and free trade, which he regarded as linked. He criticized the feudal privileges and economic nationalism of the period, calling for the abolition of the decrees against the Jews and opposing the protectionist doctrines of Friedrich List, but defended private property as an inalienable right essential to individual liberty and vehemently attacked socialist proposals for public ownership, especially Proudhon's.

He regarded the contrast between the highly developed Lombard agriculture, based on irrigation schemes devised by small proprietors, and the backward cultivation of the vast feudal estates in the south as illustrating the links between liberalism and economic development. He believed the collective enterprises of Lombard farmers, based on mutual self-interest, provided a model for republican self-government, but were only feasible within small territories where a relative homogeneity of interest and culture obtained. He therefore attacked the projects of both Cavour and Mazzini for Italian unification under a single government, devising an alternative proposal for a federal republic. He felt federalism provided the best antidote to the centralizing tendencies of the age, and ultimately hoped for a United States of Europe on the North American model.

His ideas, largely disseminated through reviews such as *Politecnico* (which he founded in 1839 and ran from 1839 to 1844 and from 1860 to 1863), were very influential at the time, and he was even asked by Gladstone to devise a scheme for agricultural reform in Ireland. He took a major part in the development of the Italian railway network, arguing that the lines should be constructed according to economic rather than political considerations. Participation in the revolution of 1848 against Austrian rule led to his exile in Switzerland. Although Garibaldi and Cavour separately sought his advice and aid in 1860, his federal republicanism led him to fall out with both of them and he was excluded from academic and political posts in the new Italian kingdom.

R.P. Bellamy

SELECTED WORKS

1958. *Scritti Economici*. 3 vols, ed. A. Levi, Florence: Le Monnier.
1960. *Scritti Storici e Geografici*. 4 vols, ed. G. Salvemini and E. Sestan, Florence: Le Monnier.
1964. *Scritti Politici*. 4 vols, ed. M. Boneschi, Florence: Le Monnier.

BIBLIOGRAPHY

Ambrosoli, L. 1960. *La Formazione di Carlo Cattaneo*. Milan and Naples: Ricciardi.
Greenfield, K.R. 1965. *Economics and Liberalism in the Risorgimento: a study of nationalism in Lombardy 1814–48*. Revised. edn, Baltimore: Johns Hopkins Press.
Lovett, C.M. 1972. *Carlo Cattaneo and the Politics of the Risorgimento*. The Hague: Nijhoff.

causal inference. When a particular event is observed, such as an economic variable taking a value in some region of the set of all possible values, it is natural to ask why that event occurred rather than some other. If, just earlier, some other event was observed to occur, it is also natural to ask if the joint observation of the two events indicates a relationship and possibly one that could be called an influence of one event by another, or even a causation. For a unique, or very rare event, such as the start of a world war, it will be very difficult to present more than sensible and suggestive statistical evidence about causation. However, in economics, values for many variables are observed with great regularity, such as daily stock market prices or monthly production figures and so a generating mechanism can be postulated that produces these values and the investigation and understanding of this mechanism is obviously one of the main tasks for the economist. In such studies, ideas such as theories, laws and causation arise very naturally, and economists in their workings use such words very frequently. It is unfortunately true that not all writers give the same meanings to these words. The understanding of causality is not the same for all economists, but this is hardly surprising as statisticians and philosophers are also not in agreement among themselves.

Economists who have attempted to discuss the meaning of causation in economics include Herbert Simon (1953), Herman Wold (1954), Julian Simon (1970), Sir John Hicks (1979), and Arnold Zellner (1979). Most of the writers emphasize the difference between a mere association and the deeper sub-class of associations that might be called causal relationships. To distinguish these, some statisticians have emphasized the use of experimental studies, but these are rarely available in economics and so this aspect of causation will not be further considered.

One can either discuss causation in very general, abstract terms or the discussion can be focused on the specific question of whether it is possible to test for causation using the data available. The latter requires an operational procedure and definition. There are basically two types of causal testing situations. In the first, a population of economic agents is observed and some variables measured for each, for example, the amount of electricity used by a household. The totality of these measurements gives a distribution. A question can then be asked – why does this household use more electricity than that one? This is a cross-sectional causality question. It is also possible to measure parameters of the distribution, such as the mean or the variance, and to ask why these parameters are changing through time. Thus, the question is asked, why is electricity demand higher this year than last? This could be called a temporal causality question. The definitions of causality and their interpretations may differ between these two cases.

It is convenient to assume the existence of a quantity called the 'degree of belief' held by an individual about the correctness of some causal theory or proposition and to assume further that this quantity can be represented as a probability. The objective of any causal analysis, such as a statistical test, might be to try to influence the degree of belief of oneself or of others. For this purpose, the analysis need not be complete or perfect, but merely to have enough value to make one reconsider one's beliefs.

A mere association between a pair of economic variables, such as a correlation or a non-independent joint distribution, is insufficient to determine a causation, partly because such associations are symmetric between the variables, the extent to which X is correlated to Y, or can be explained by Y, is exactly the same as Y is correlated, or explained, by X. It is generally thought that causation is a non-symmetric relationship, and there are various ways in which asymmetry can be introduced, the most important of which are controllability, a relevant theory, outside knowledge, and temporal priority. Amongst the economic writers, each has its advocates and detractors.

Concerning controllability, Strotz and Wold (1960) write:

z is a cause of y if, by hypothesis, it is or 'would be possible' by controlling z indirectly to control y, at least stochastically. But it may or may not be possible by controlling y indirectly to control z this way.

Essentially this idea is from their experimental background and uses hypothetical experiments. By utilizing enough knowledge about lack of controllability in a system, so that some possible causal links are put to zero, tests can be constructed on the remaining links. This would obviously be the case if a system of variables, all measured at the same time, could be displayed recursively, so that the jth equation involved only the first j variables. However, by redefining variables as linear combinations of the original set, such a recursive system can always be achieved and not uniquely, unless there are sufficient identifying qualifications on the system. J. Simon suggests that controllability is required to make causal analysis useful for policy-makers. The equivalence of causation and controllability is not generally accepted, the latter being perhaps a deeper relationship. If a causal link were found and was not previously used for control, the action of attempting to control with it may destroy the causal link.

Hicks, Zellner and J. Simon, in discussing causal links, all emphasize the relevance of a sound economic theory. Hicks (1979) accepts static or equilibrium theory as sufficient for use, while J. Simon (1970) suggests that a statement that is 'logically connected to the general framework of systematic economics is much more likely to be considered causal than one that stands alone'. Thus, the theory is used to increase the degree of belief, and these writers suggest that a strong degree of belief cannot be achieved without a convincing theory. Zellner (1979) takes a much stronger view, leaning heavily on the work of the philosopher H. Feigl who says that 'the clarified (or purified) concept of causation is defined in terms of *predictability according to a law* (or more adequately, according to a set of laws)'. In his work, Zellner appears to be saying that for him a degree of belief cannot be anything but very small unless the causal analysis is based on some generally acceptable economic theory. He gives no examples of such economic laws and it is interesting to note that Hicks (1979, p. 2) says the 'there are few economic laws that are at all firmly based'.

Concerning temporal priority, it is generally, although not universally, accepted that the cause cannot occur after the effect. It is also frequently assumed that the cause will occur before the effect, providing a convenient asymmetry, but this view is certainly more controversial. Both Zellner and Hicks firmly reject it and Hicks maintains that instantaneous and contemporaneous causality is the 'characteristic form of the causal relation in modern economics'. It is certainly true that much economic theory is written as though causation is instantaneous. However, as Hicks also points out, all economic variables are accumulations of the outcomes of economic decisions and it is difficult to present a sensible decision mechanism in which there is an instantaneous relationship between the observed inputs to the decision (the causes) and the observed outputs (the effects). Thus, for statistical testing purposes, which has to use just observed variables, the temporal priority assumption appears to be more reasonable. It is also clear that if any part of the cause cannot occur later than any part of the variable being effected, instantaneous causation cannot occur between some pairs of stock and flow variables. For example, production of steel in a month could not instantaneously cause production of automobiles in the month, as part of one variable occurs after part of the other. There is always the possibility of apparent instantaneous causation occurring because of temporal aggregation or missing common causes.

Occasionally other outside information is used to break the symmetry of association. One variable may be thought to be generated outside the economic system, such as a weather variable, so that causation can only flow from it to part of the economy. This idea is the classical one of exogeneity. For a discussion of this topic with generalizations concerned with estimation problems, see Engle et al. (1983). A particular case is when a variable is thought to be completely controlled, such as tax rates or possibly money supply, so that controlled money could cause price changes but not vice versa. In all these cases, the outside information may be useful, if it is correct.

Although many important economic questions can be phrased in the cross-sectional causal situation, they have received little causal testing in that context, except under the 'outside information' assumption. However, many tests have been conducted for economic questions that can be stated as temporal causation. These tests have been conducted using the concepts known in the literature as 'Granger-causation'. This approach is based on two axioms – that the cause will occur before the effect (strict temporal priority) and that the cause contains unique information about the effect. The second can be stated more formally as follows. Let A_t represent all the observable information available at time t and $A_t - Y_t$ represent all this information except that contained in the series $Y_{t-j}, j \geq 0$. Then Y_t will be said to cause X_{t+1} if

$$\text{Prob}(X_{t+1} \text{ in } C | A_t) \neq \text{Prob}(X_{t+1} \text{ in } C | A_t - Y_t)$$

for any region C. The two axioms have the simple consequence that any well-behaved function $f(X_{t+1})$ will be generally better forecast using any cost function as a criterion. Thus, tests of this type of causation potentially can be based on forecastability but to be operational some simplifications are required. If one has a belief about a temporal causation then it could be called a prima facie causality. If a test is based on the above definition, but with the unusual universal information-set replaced by a restricted but practical information set I_t, and if the test finds evidence for causation, then the relationship remains a prima facie cause. The set I_t will consist of a group of time series and the larger and more relevant it is, the more stringent will be the test; it is then more likely that degrees of belief will change. The choice of the causation to investigate and the choice of I_t will probably depend on some theory, but this could be a low-level theory and, if the tests so suggest, may be worth further development. In practice, tests are rarely based on distributions but on parameters of the distributions such as means. This could be stated as 'Y_t is a prima facie cause in mean of X_{t+1} with respect to I_t' if

$$E[X_{t+1} | I_t] \neq E[X_{t+1} | I_t - Y_t].$$

It will follow that X_{t+1} is better forecast, using a least squares criterion, if Y_t is used than if it is not used. Standard time-series modelling techniques will provide models of X_{t+1} based on I_t and on $I_t - Y_t$ and the post-sample forecasting ability of the two models can then be used to test this particular form of causation. Some of these tests are described in Pierce and Haugh (1977) and evaluated in Nelson and Schwert (1982). They are generally linear in data, although do not have to be, and, if misapplied, can of course lead to incorrect results. To correspond strictly to the definition, tests should be based on the post-sample forecasting abilities of the alternative models.

The definition has both some advantages and some problems, and these are discussed in Granger (1980). In theory, the tests are not altered if backward filters are applied to the data, but some kinds of seasonal adjustments or measurement errors can give problems. If Y_t causes X_{t+1} the X_t may, but need not cause

381

Y_{t+1}, so that feedback can occur but need not. Similarly, if Y_t causes X_{t+1} and X_t causes Z_{t+1} then Y_t may, but need not cause, Z_{t+2}. It has to be remembered when interpreting results based on tests that missing common causal variables can always alter the interpretation, that causation may be lost if one variable is controlled so as to reduce the strength of the causal link, and that temporal aggregation or using data measured over intervals much wider than actual causal lags can also destroy causal interpretation.

C. W. J. GRANGER

See also AUTOREGRESSIVE TIME SERIES ANALYSIS; CAUSALITY IN ECONOMIC MODELS; ENDOGENEITY AND EXOGENEITY; SPECTRAL ANALYSIS; STATIONARY TIME SERIES; TIME SERIES ANALYSIS.

BIBLIOGRAPHY

Engle, R.F., Hendry, D.F. and Richard, J.F. 1983. Exogeneity. *Econometrica* 51, 277–304.

Granger, C.W.J. 1980. Tests for causation – a personal viewpoint. *Journal of Economic Dynamics and Control* 2, 329–52.

Hicks, Sir J. 1979. *Causality in Economics*. New York: Basic Books.

Nelson, C.R. and Schwert, G.W. 1982. Tests for predictive relationships between time series variables. *Journal of the American Statistical Association* 77, 11–18.

Pierce, D.A. and Haugh, L.D. 1977. Causality in temporal systems. *Journal of Econometrics* 5, 265–93.

Simon, H. 1953. Causal ordering and identifiability. *Studies in Econometric Method*, Cowles Commission Monograph No. 14, ed. W.C. Hood and T.C. Koopmans. New York: John Wiley.

Simon, J.L. 1970. The concept of causality in economics. *Kyklos* 23, 226–52.

Strotz, R.H. and Wold, H. 1960. Recursive versus nonrecursive systems: an attempt at synthesis. *Econometrica* 28, April, 417–27.

Wold, H. 1954. Causality and econometrics. *Econometrica* 22, 162–77.

Zellner, A. 1979. Causality and econometrics, policy and policy making. *Carnegie-Rochester Conference Series on Public Policy* 10, 9–54.

causality in economic models. Causal notions arise when we seek to understand the workings of a complex system by analysing it into component subsystems and mechanisms. Thus, if we wish to understand the quantities of strawberries that are produced and consumed and the prices at which they are exchanged, we may consider a number of mechanisms that affect quantity and price. What mechanisms we will include depends on how widely we draw the boundaries of the system to be examined.

For example, we may include (1) a weather mechanism that determines the amount of rainfall; (2) a productivity mechanism that determines the yield of strawberries per acre; (3) a supply mechanism that determines the acreage sowed in strawberries; and (4) a demand mechanism that determines the quantity of strawberries purchased. In this formulation, each mechanism, which might be represented by an equation, determines the value of a particular variable as a function of some other variables (not specified in the account above). The variable whose value is so determined (dependent variable) may be called the *effect* of the working of that particular mechanism, while the values of other variables entering into the mechanism (independent variables) are the *causes* of that effect.

In the example before us, we might write:

$$R = r \tag{1}$$

$$Y = f_1(R, F, T) \tag{2}$$

$$A = f_2(p) \tag{3}$$

$$Q = YA \tag{D}$$

$$p = f_3(Q) \tag{4}$$

Here R is rainfall, and r a positive constant; Y is the yield per acre, F the amount of fertilization, and T the amount of tillage; A is the acreage sowed, and p the market price; and Q is the total yield. Equation (D) represents a definition, not a separate mechanism. In equation (4), p is taken as the dependent variable, since Q is assumed already to be determined by (2) and (3) (cobweb assumption).

CAUSAL ORDERING. The system of equations defines a *causal ordering* among the variables. The value of R is determined exogenously, as are the values of F and T. That is to say, they are determined in some larger system of which the mechanisms described in the equations are only a subset. The value of Y follows from those of R, F, and T. The values of A, Q, and p are determined simultaneously. Thus, the equations determine a partial ordering:

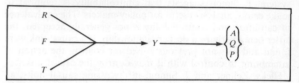

Figure 1

Notice that the asymmetry that underlies this ordering cannot be interpreted as the asymmetry of logical implication, for from 'A implies B' we can infer that 'not-B implies not-A', while from, 'Heavy rainfall causes the yield to be large' we cannot conclude that 'A small yield causes a scanty rainfall.' The most accurate mode of expression is: 'The amount of rainfall determines (causes) the amount of yield' – large or small in both cases. The asymmetry reflects a distinction between exogeneity and endogeneity of variables, based, in turn, upon controllability (in the case of variables that can be manipulated directly), or time precedence. Thus R is exogenous to mechanism (2) on the assumption that the weather is unaffected by changes in the yield of strawberries. (That this is an empirical assumption is clear from the fact that widespread cultivation *can* cause changes in climate).

If we wish to remove the ambiguity from the causal relations among A, Q, and p, we may assume (as in the classical cobweb theory) a time lag, replacing p in equation (3) by the exogenous and predetermined variable, p_{-1}. Then the causal ordering becomes:

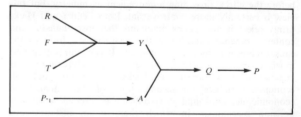

Figure 2

Now it is clear why we took p as the dependent variable in equation (4). Introducing the time lag requires making an empirical assumption – specifically an assumption about how farmers form expectations about future prices. In a rational expectations model, for example, this lag would not be admissible.

FORMALIZATION. To formalize these ideas, consider a system of n simultaneous linear equations in n variables (*linear structure*). We assume that each equation represents a mechanism. In some linear structures, certain subsets of equations can be solved independently of the remaining equations (*self-contained sub-*

sets). Consider the *minimal self-contained subsets* of a system (those that do not themselves contain smaller self-contained subsets). With each such subset, associate the variables that can be evaluated from the subset alone (endogenous variables), and call them *variables of order zero*. Next, substitute the values of these variables in the remaining equations of the system, and repeat the whole process, obtaining the variables of order one, two, and so on, and the corresponding minimal self-contained subsets of equations. If a variable of some order occurs with non-zero coefficient in an equation belonging to a subsystem of higher order, then that variable is one of the causes of the values of the endogenous variables of the latter set.

Thus, in our original example, equation (1) is the minimal self-contained subset of zero order, and R is its variable; (2) is the minimal subset of first order, and Y its variable; while (3), (D), and (4) constitute the minimal self-contained subset of second order, and A, Q, and p are their variables. The exogenous variables, F and T, can be regarded as parameters of the system, or equations parallel to (1) can be added for them, so that each belongs to a separate minimal self-contained subset of order zero.

IDENTIFIABILITY OF CAUSAL ORDERING. The causal ordering among variables in a linear self-contained structure depends on which variables appear with non-zero coefficients in which equations. Consider a set of observations of the variables satisfying the equations of such a structure. Clearly these observations will also satisfy a new structure made up of equations that are arbitrary linear combinations of equations drawn from the original set. But different combinations of variables will generally appear in the equations of the new structure than appeared in the equations of the original structure. Taking these linear combinations 'blends' the separate mechanisms represented by the original equations. Hence, the causal ordering is not preserved under such a transformation, although the same empirical observations are compatible with both sets of equations.

From this consideration it follows that causal ordering cannot be inferred from simultaneous observations, no matter how numerous, of the variables of a structure. Additional assumptions must be made to identify a unique structure from the observations. The *identification problem* of econometrics is the problem of finding a sufficient number of prior assumptions to determine a unique set of equations, each corresponding to a mechanism, that fits the observations. The equations thus determined are usually called *structural equations*, while algebraically equivalent equations derived from them by linear combination are called *reduced form* equations.

The assumptions needed to identify structural equations may be derived from prior knowledge about mechanisms (e.g., our knowledge that the weather affects crops, but crops do not usually affect the weather). Where experimentation is possible, holding particular variables constant while varying others, experimental findings are a powerful source of empirically valid identifying assumptions. Sometimes, there is prior knowledge, also, that particular mechanisms are independent of each other (that farmers make their decisions independently of consumers, and vice versa). Whatever their source, the identifying assumptions are genuine empirical assertions, and cannot be made arbitrarily or for reasons of statistical convenience if the correct causal inferences are to be drawn. So-called 'spurious' correlation is best interpreted as a relation between variables that does not have causal force because it was estimated from equations that did not correspond to independent mechanisms.

HERBERT A. SIMON

See also SIMULTANEOUS EQUATION MODELS.

BIBLIOGRAPHY
Goldberger, A.S. and Duncan, O.D. 1973. *Structural Equation Models in the Social Sciences.* New York: Academic Press.
Hood, W.C. and Koopmans, T.C. 1953. *Studies in Econometric Method.* New York: Wiley.
Simon, H.A. 1977. Causes and possible worlds. Section 2, in H.A. Simon, *Models of Discovery,* Dordrecht: D. Reidel.

Cazenove, John (1788–1879). Cazenove wrote nine books and pamphlets on political economy, dealing with a wide variety of theoretical concepts and practical issues. In addition, he made a valuable contribution to political economy as an editor of Richard Jones's *Literary Remains* (1859, p. xl), and T.R. Malthus's *Definitions in Political Economy* (1853). There is also strong evidence to suggest that he was the anonymous editor of the second edition of Malthus's *Principles of Political Economy* (Pullen, 1978). He contributed a review to the *British Critic* ('Chalmers – On Political Economy', October 1832, a vigorous criticism of James Mill and Ricardo), and could possibly have contributed others (Gordon, 1985, pp. 17–19).

Malthus had a high regard for Cazenove. He recommended to his publisher that the first edition of his *Principles* should be reviewed by Cazenove in the *Quarterly Review* (letter of 26 January 1821, in the archives of John Murray), and he nominated Cazenove for membership of the Political Economy Club, at its second meeting in 1821. J.L. Mallet recorded in his diary that, in the Club debates, 'on most occasions Ricardo and Mill led on one side, and Malthus and Cazenove on the other'. In a letter to Thomas Chalmers of 6 February 1833, Malthus described Cazenove as 'a particular friend' and as 'a very clever man, and good political economist'. When Malthus died in 1834, Cazenove applied (unsuccessfully) for his position as professor of history and political economy at the East India College (James, 1969, pp. 355–6). But Cazenove's friendship with Malthus, and his agreement with some of Malthus's main doctrines, did not prevent him from criticizing Malthus on occasions and adopting an independent line (Pullen, 1978, pp. 293–4).

Cazenove's omission from the first two editions of *Palgrave's Dictionary* and the absence of any entry under 'Cazenove' in the *Index of Economic Articles* up to 1979, indicate that his writings have so far attracted very little attention. But Gordon (1985) has shown that Cazenove does not deserve this neglect. His writings are a worthwhile contribution to political economy in their own right, and an important part of the anti-Ricardian tradition. In particular, Cazenove opposed Say's Law and recognized the possibility of a general glut. Like Malthus he emphasized the role played by effective demand, and denied that continued economic growth can be achieved merely through saving and capital accumulation. He stressed the idea – also put forward by Malthus, under the name of 'the doctrine of proportions' – that economic progress requires a balance between saving and consumption.

Cazenove's grandfather, David de Cazenove, and his father, James de Cazenove, were merchants of French Huguenot origin who migrated to London from Geneva in 1777 (*Burke's Landed Gentry*). Cazenove was born and died in London. He appears to have worked in his father's firm, Jas. Cazenove & Co., which he described (1861, pp. 42–3) as 'a large commercial firm' with 'some sixty or seventy foreign correspondents'. He retired from the business early – in 1832, at the age of 44, he described himself as 'late a continental merchant' – but his literary output continued until 1861. His father's brother, Phillip Cazenove, founded the present London firm of stockbrokers, Cazenove & Co. His brother, Philip Cazenove, was for many years the senior partner of Cazenove & Co., but there is no evidence that John Cazenove ever worked in that firm (information from Mr H. de L. Cazenove, of Cazenove & Co.) John Cazenove's son, John Gibson Cazenove, MA, DD (1822–96) of Brasenose College, Oxford, was Chancellor of Edinburgh Cathedral and author of theological works.

J.M. PULLEN

SELECTED WORKS

1820. *A Reply to Mr Say's Letter to Mr Malthus on the Subject of the Stagnation of Trade*. London: J.M. Richardson. (The copy annotated by Ricardo is in Edinburgh University Library. See Ricardo, *Works and Correspondence*, ed. P. Sraffa, Cambridge, Cambridge University Press, Vol. X, 405–10.)

1822. *Considerations on the Accumulation of Capital and its Effects on Profits and on Exchangeable Value*. London: J.M. Richardson.

1829. *Questions Respecting the National Debt and Taxation Stated and Answered*. London: J.M. Richardson. (The British Library copy contains MS alterations, presumably intended for a 2nd edition.)

1832a. *Outlines of Political Economy ...* . London: Pelham Richardson.

1832b. *The Evidence that WOULD have been given by Mr ——, late a continental merchant, before the Committee of Secrecy appointed to inquire into the expediency of renewing the Bank Charter*. London: Pelham Richardson. (The British Library copy contains a MS note by Cazenove correcting an error on p. 15.)

1840. *An Elementary Treatise on Political Economy ...* . London: A.H. Baily.

1847. *The Money Crisis*. London.

1859. *Thoughts on a Few Subjects of Political Economy*. London: Simpkin Marshall.

1861. *Supplement to Thoughts on a Few Subjects of Political Economy*. London: Simpkin Marshall.

BIBLIOGRAPHY

Gordon, B. 1985. John Cazenove (1788–1879): critic of Ricardo, friend and editor of Malthus. Paper presented at the Third Conference of the History of Economic Thought Society of Australia held at La Trobe University.

James, P. 1979. *Population Malthus: His Life and Times*. London: Routledge & Kegan Paul.

Jones, R. 1859. *Literary Remains, Consisting of Lectures and Tracts on Political Economy, of the Late Rev. Richard Jones*. Edited, with a Prefatory Notice, by the Rev. William Whewell, D.D., London: John Murray.

Malthus, T.R. 1853. *Definitions in Political Economy ...* . A New Edition, with a Preface, Notes, and Supplementary Remarks by John Cazenove, London: Simpkin & Marshall.

Pullen, J.M. 1978. The editor of the second edition of T.R. Malthus' *Principles of Political Economy*. History of Political Economy 10(2), 286–97.

censored data models. The *censored* normal regression model considered by Tobin (1958), also commonly known as the 'tobit' model, is the following:

$$y_i^* = \beta x_i + u_i \qquad u_i \sim \mathrm{IN}(0, \sigma^2)$$

The observed y_i are related to y_i^* according to the relationship

$$\begin{aligned} y_i &= y_i^* \qquad \text{if } y_i^* > y_0 \\ &= y_0 \qquad \text{otherwise} \end{aligned} \tag{1}$$

where y_0 is a prespecified constant (usually zero). The y_i^* could take values $< y_0$. The only thing is that they are not observed. Thus, y_i is set equal to y_0 because of *non-observability*. The values x_i are observed for all the observations. If *both* y_i and x_i

are unobserved for $y_i \leqslant y_0$ then we have what is known as a *truncated* regression model.

The problem is essentially one of missing data. Data on y are missing for some observations. Hence, we have to ask why data are missing. In some cases this is owing to the design of the experiment, as in the case of the data from the negative income tax experiment. These data have been analysed by Hausman and Wise (1977), who consider a truncated regression model. In almost all other cases y_0 is the outcome of choices of individuals. In this case the model is incomplete unless the determinants of y_0 are studied.

SOME EARLY DEVELOPMENTS. The first application of the censored regression model (1) is that of Tobin (1958) who studied the expenditures on durable goods by 735 non-farm households. y_i^* is the ratio of total durable expenditures to disposable income and $y_0 = 0$. However, y_i is not equal to zero here because of non-observability, but because of individuals' choices. Thus, the censored regression model (1) is inappropriate for this problem. In fact, the tobit model is inappropriate for almost all the applications in which it has been used (including that by Tobin).

The model by Cragg (1971) considers this as a sequential decision problem. For the case of demand for automobiles, the decisions are whether or not to buy a car and how much to spend if the decision to buy a car is made. In this model we have the latent variable:

$$I_i = x_i \delta_1 + \eta_{1i} \qquad \eta_{1i} \sim \mathrm{IN}(0, 1) \tag{2}$$

The subscript i denotes the ith individual. We observe the dummy variable D_i which is defined as

$$\begin{aligned} D_i &= 1 \text{ if } I_i > 0 \qquad \text{(buyers)} \\ &= 0 \text{ otherwise} \qquad \text{(non-buyers)} \end{aligned} \tag{3}$$

For those who purchased a car, Cragg specifies a log normal model. Thus, denoting expenditures by y_i, we have

$$\log y_i = x_i \delta_2 + \eta_{2i} \qquad \eta_{2i} \sim \mathrm{IN}(0, \sigma^2) \tag{4}$$

The equation is defined only for the individuals for which $D_i = 1$.

In practice, however, it is questionable whether individuals make their decisions this way. The decision of whether or not to buy a car and how much to spend if a car is bought are often joint decisions. One can formulate this model in terms of two latent variables. Though there are several variants of this that one can think of, one formulation is the following.

y_1 = the cost of the car the individual wants to buy.
y_2 = the maximum expenditure the individual can afford.

The actual expenditure y is given by

$$\begin{aligned} y &= y_1 \qquad \text{if } y_1 \leqslant y_2 \\ &= 0 \qquad \text{if } y_1 > y_2 \end{aligned} \tag{5}$$

We can, in fact, consider y_1 and y_2 both to be log normal. This model is discussed in Nelson (1977), though not with reference to the example of automobile expenditures.

It is tempting to use the simple tobit model (1) every time that one has a bunch of zero (or other limit) observations on y. However, this is inappropriate. For instance, if hours worked for a number of individuals in a sample are zero, it does not mean that one can apply the tobit model to explain hours worked. One has to construct a model where hours worked are zero because of some decisions about labour force participation, in terms of reservation and market wages, as done by Heckman (1974). Estimation of this model from censored as well as truncated samples is discussed in Wales and Woodland (1980).

SELECTION MODELS. In the estimation of censored regression models we often have to formulate the censoring function that incorporates individual decisions. This function is also called a *selection criterion*. Usually the selection criterion involves the choice variables and other explanatory variables. Thus, the model is formulated as:

$$y_1 = \beta_1 x_1 + u_1 \qquad \text{Choice 1} \qquad (6)$$

$$y_2 = \beta_2 x_2 + u_2 \qquad \text{Choice 2} \qquad (7)$$

and

$$I^* = \gamma_1 y_1 + \gamma_2 y_2 + \beta_3 x_3 + u \qquad \text{Selection criterion} \qquad (8)$$

The observed y is defined as

$$y = y_1 \qquad \text{if } I^* > 0$$
$$= y_2 \qquad \text{if } I^* \leqslant 0.$$

Interest centres on the determinants of γ_1 and γ_2 (see Lee, 1978; Willis and Rosen, 1979). One can substitute y_1 and y_2 in (8) and get a reduced form for the selection criterion. In this approach interest mainly centres on the so-called 'selectivity bias' in the estimation of (6) and (7) by OLS. Since both y_1 and y_2 are censored, we have to estimate the parameters in (6) and (7) by the use of ML methods. Heckman (1979) suggests a simple correction to the OLS, which involves the addition of an extra explanatory variable to each of (6) and (7) obtained from the estimation of the criterion function (8) in its reduced form. This criterion is based on the assumption of normality. Goldberger (1983) made some calculations with alternative error distributions and showed that this adjustment for selection bias is quite sensitive to departures from normality.

There have been two solutions to this problem. One is the extension of the analysis of selectivity to general error distributions. This is the approach considered in Lee (1982, 1983), a summary of which is also given in Maddala (1983, pp. 272–5) along with earlier suggestions by Olsen. The other alternative approach is to consider distribution-free estimates (see Cosslett, 1984), though this methodology is in early stages of development. Thus, there are computationally feasible alternatives available to explore the selectivity problem without assuming normality and there are procedures available to test the assumption of normality as well (see Lee and Maddala, 1985).

The 'Heckman correction' for selectivity bias is very popular, mainly because it is easy to apply. But for this same reason it has also been applied in cases where it is not applicable; such cases are cited in Maddala (1985).

SOME OTHER PROBLEMS. Many of the problems connected with the estimation of the censored regression model, assuming parametric distributions, are discussed in Maddala (1983, chs 6 and 9) and Amemiya (1984). For distribution-free methods one can refer to Miller and Halpern (1982), Cosslett (1984) and Powell (1984). It is now well known that the properties of the estimators change with the violation of some basic assumptions. For instance, heteroskedasticity and errors in the dependent variable do not affect the consistency property of OLS estimators in the normal regression model. With the censored regression model, the ML estimators are no longer consistent under these assumptions. Stapleton and Young (1984) suggest that with errors in the dependent variable, the 'correct' ML estimation appears computationally difficult but find some alternative estimators promising.

There has been some progress made in the development of distribution free estimation and estimation when the standard assumptions are violated. For tests of some of the standard assumptions, see Lee and Maddala (1985).

G.S. MADDALA

See also LATENT VARIABLES; LIMITED DEPENDENT VARIABLES; LOGITS, PROBITS AND TOBITS; SELECTION BIAS AND SELF-SELECTION.

BIBLIOGRAPHY

Amemiya, T. 1984. Tobit models: a survey. *Journal of Econometrics* 24, 3–61.

Cosslett, S.R. 1984. Distribution-free estimator of a regression model with sample selectivity. Discussion Paper, CEDS, University of Florida.

Cragg, J.G. 1971. Some statistical models for limited dependent variables with application to the demand for durable goods. *Econometrica* 39, 829–44.

Goldberger, A.S. 1983. Abnormal selection bias. In *Studies in Econometrics, Time-Series and Multivariate Analysis*, ed. S. Karlin, T. Amemiya and L.A. Goodman, New York: Academic Press.

Hausman, J.A. and Wise, D.A. 1977. Social experimentation, truncated distributions, and efficient estimation. *Econometrica* 45, 919–38.

Heckman, J.J. 1974. Shadow prices, market wages, and labor supply. *Econometrica* 42, 679–93.

Heckman, J.J. 1979. Sample selection bias as a specification error. *Econometrica* 47, 153–61.

Lee, L.F. 1978. Unionism and wage rates: a simultaneous equations mode with qualitative and limited dependent variables. *International Economic Review* 19, 415–33.

Lee, L.F. 1982. Some approaches to the correction of selectivity bias. *Review of Economic Studies* 49, 355–72.

Lee, L.F. 1983. Generalized econometric models with selectivity *Econometrica* 51, 507–12.

Lee, L.F. and Maddala, G.S. 1985. The common structure of tests for selectivity bias, serial correlation, heteroscedasticity, and non-normality in the tobit model. *International Economic Review* 26, 1–20.

Maddala, G.S. 1983. *Limited Dependent and Qualitative Variables in Econometrics*. New York: Cambridge University Press.

Maddala, G.S. 1985. A survey of the literature on selectivity bias as it pertains to health-care markets, In *Advances in Health Economics*, ed. R.M. Scheffler and L.F. Rossiter, Greenwich, Conn.: JAI Press.

Miller, R. and Halpern, J. 1982. Regression with censored data. *Biometrika* 69, 521–31.

Nelson, F.D. 1977. Censored regression models with unobserved stochastic censoring thresholds. *Journal of Econometrics* 6, 309–27.

Powell, J.L. 1984. Least absolute deviations estimation for censored regression models. *Journal of Econometrics* 25, 303–26.

Stapleton, D.C. and Young, D.J. 1984. Censored normal regression with measurement error on the dependent variable. *Econometrica* 52, 737–60.

Tobin, J. 1958. Estimation of relationships for limited dependent variables. *Econometrica* 26, 24–36.

Wales, T.J. and Woodland, A.D. 1980. Sample selectivity and the estimation of labor supply functions. *International Economic Review* 21, 437–68.

Willis, R.J. and Rosen, S. 1979. Education and self-selection. *Journal of Political Economy* 87, S5–S36.

central banking. When the first government-sponsored banks were founded in Europe, for example the Swedish Riksbank (1668) and the Bank of England (1694), there was no intention that these should undertake the functions of a modern central bank, that is, discretionary monetary management and the regulation and support, for example through the 'lender of last resort' function, of the banking system. Instead, the initial impetus was much more basic, generally relating to the financial advantages a government felt that it could obtain from the support of such a bank, whether a State bank, as in the case of the Prussian State Bank, or a private bank, like the Bank of England. This naturally involved some favouritism, often supported by legislation, by the government for this particular bank in return for its financial assistance. The favoured bank was often granted a monopoly advantage, for example over the note issue in certain areas, or as the sole chartered joint stock bank in the country; and this may have had the effect in some countries, such as England and France, of weakening the early development of other commercial banks, so that, at the outset, the foundation of a government-sponsored bank was a mixed blessing for the development of banking in such countries.

Other government-sponsored central banks, for example the Austrian National Bank founded in 1816 at the end of the Napoleonic wars, were established to restore the value of the national currency, notably after its value had been wrecked by government over-issue in the course of war finance. Others were founded partly in order to unify what had become in some cases (e.g. in Germany, Switzerland and Italy) a somewhat chaotic system of note issue; to centralize, manage and protect the metallic reserve of the country, and to facilitate and improve the payments system. While these latter functions were seen as having beneficial economic consequences, the ability to share in the profits of seignorage and greater centralized control over the metallic (gold) reserve had obvious political attractions as well. In any case, prior to 1900, most economic analysis of the role of Central Banks concentrated on the question of whether the note issue, and the gold reserves of the country, should be centralized, and, if and when centralized, how controlled by the Central Bank.

Once such government-sponsored banks had been established, however, their central position within the system, their 'political' power as the government's bank, their command (usually) over the bulk of the nation's specie reserve, and, most important, their ability to provide extra cash, notes, by rediscounting commercial bills made them become the bankers' bank: commercial banks would not only hold a large proportion of their own (cash) reserves as balances with the Central Bank, but also rely on it to provide extra liquidity when in difficulties. In several early cases, such as the Bank of England's, this latter role had not been initially intended; in most cases of Central Banks founded in the 19th century the full ramifications of their role as bankers' bank were only dimly perceived at the time of their founding; these functions developed naturally from the context of relationships within the system.

Initially, indeed, the role of Central Banks in maintaining the convertibility of their notes, into gold or silver, was not different, nor seen as different, from that of any other bank. Their privileged legal position, as banker to the government and in note issue, then led naturally to a degree of centralization of reserves within the banking system in the hands of the Central Bank, so it became a banker's bank. It was the responsibility that this position was found to entail, in the process of historical experience, that led Central Banks to develop their particular art of discretionary monetary management and overall support and responsibility for the health of the banking system at large.

This management has had two (interrelated) aspects: a macro function and responsibility relating to overall monetary conditions in the economy, and a micro function relating to the health and wellbeing of the (individual) members of the banking system. Until 1914 such management largely consisted of seeking to reconcile the need to maintain the chosen metallic standard, usually the gold standard, on the one hand

with concern for the stability and health of the financial system, and beyond that of the economy more widely, on the other. Thereafter, as the various pressures of the 20th century disrupted first the gold standard and thereafter the Bretton Woods' system of pegged exchange rates, the macroeconomic objectives of monetary management have altered and evolved. Yet at all times concern for the health of the banking system has remained a paramount concern for the Central Bank.

This concern for the wellbeing of the banking system as a whole was, at least for those Central Banks founded in the 19th century or before, largely an evolutionary development and not one that they had been programmed to undertake from the start. Indeed in England the legislative framework of the 1844 Bank Charter Act was to prove something of a barrier to the development of the micro-supervisory functions of the Bank: for this Act divided the Bank into two Departments – the Issue Department, whose note issuing function was to be closely constrained by strict rules (to maintain the Gold Standard); and the Banking Department, which was intended to behave simply as an ordinary competitive, profit-maximizing, commercial bank.

Nevertheless the micro-functions of a Central Bank in providing a central (and therefore economical) source of reserves and liquidity to other banks, and hence both a degree of insurance and supervision, cannot be undertaken effectively by a commercial competitor, basically because of competitive conflicts of interest. The advantages of having some institutions providing such micro-Central Banking functions are such that even in those various countries initially without Central Banks there was some natural tendency towards their being provided, after a fashion, from within the private sector – for example by clearing houses in the United States, or by a large commercial bank providing quasi-Central Bank functions. Nevertheless, because of conflicts of interest, such functions were not, and cannot be, adequately provided by competing commercial institutions.

Some Central Banks, mainly those that began their existence under private ownership (e.g. the Bank of England, the Banca d'Italia, but also some that were subject to political oversight, e.g. the Banque de France, the Commonwealth Bank of Australia), retained for a considerable time a large role in ordinary commercial banking. It was, however, the metamorphosis from their involvement in commercial banking, as a competitive, profit-maximizing bank among many, to a non-competitive, non-profit-maximizing role that marked the true emergence in those countries of proper Central Banking. This metamorphosis occurred naturally, but with considerable difficulty in England, the difficulty arising in part from the existence of property rights in the profits of the Bank, and in part from concern about the moral hazards of the Bank consciously adopting a supervisory role, (as evidenced in the arguments between Bagehot and Hankey, reported in Bagehot's *Lombard Street*).

Indeed, with the Central Bank coming to represent the ultimate source of liquidity and support to the individual commercial banks, this micro-function does bring with it naturally a degree of 'insurance'. Such insurance, in turn, does involve some risk of moral hazard: commercial banks, believing that they will be protected by their Central Bank from the consequences of their own follies, may adopt too risky and careless strategies. That concern has led Central Banks to become involved – to varying extents – in the regulation and supervision of their banking systems. In all countries the Central Bank plays *some* role in the support of its commercial banks, because it alone can provide 'lender of last resort' assistance; but the extent to which it shares the insurance, supervisory, and regulatory function, both for the banking system more narrowly and for the wider financial system, with government and private bodies set up specifically for such purposes, varies from country to country. With structural changes apparently breaking down the barriers between the banking system on the one hand and other financial intermediaries on the other in the course of the 1970s and 1980s, the question of the division of responsibility of the Central Bank on the one hand, and other supervisory government bodies and insurance agencies on the other, has become topical.

The Central Bank's more glamorous function is the conduct of macro-monetary policy. The main objective of this function in normal times has been to maintain the (internal and external) value, and reputation, of the national currency. At times of national crisis, notably during wars, however, the financial needs of the State have generally overridden the desire for financial stability, with the conduct of monetary policy then being mainly determined by questions of how the necessary finance can most effectively be mobilized to support the urgent needs of the State. Apart from such national emergencies, the desire to achieve financial stability became synonymous, during the 19th and early 20th centuries, with adherence to the Gold Standard.

The break-down of the Gold Standard in the interwar period left many countries with high unemployment, a falling price level, and international trade and capital flows increasingly constrained by direct controls. In this context it became widely felt that monetary policy was relatively powerless: once interest rates were brought down to low levels, there was little more, it was argued, that monetary policy could do. The management of aggregate demand would, therefore, have to be left to fiscal policy, with direct controls of various kinds used to constrain subsequent inflationary pressures (e.g. in World War II) and international disequilibria.

The erosion of direct controls in the late 1940s and 1950s, and the establishment of the Bretton Woods system of pegged, but adjustable, exchange rates, meant that Central Banks generally were able, during the 1950s and 1960s, to return to their accustomed policy of maintaining the value of their national currencies by seeking to hold these pegged to the US dollar and thence, until the late 1960s, to gold. With the US dollar at the centre of the world financial system, the Federal Reserve System had a different and special responsibility, to maintain the internal stability of the $. After many successful years, US monetary policy and the Bretton Woods system were overwhelmed by pressures arising from the Vietnam War, political strains within the Western Alliance, and, finally, the 1973 Oil Shock.

Up till then, most Western governments had sought to maximize employment and growth, along broadly Keynesian lines, subject to trying to maintain the exchange rate peg. With that peg no longer in place after 1972, governments then placed various emphases on supporting full employment on the one hand and monetary constraint on the other. In the event, however, there seemed no evidence that countries with more expansionary monetary policies, and thence more inflation, did achieve notably higher rates of growth or employment. This experience led directly to the adoption of 'pragmatic' monetarist policies by the Central Banks of the main industrialized countries, whereby they sought to achieve publicly announced, steadily declining rates of growth for certain domestic monetary intermediate target aggregates.

This policy shift has, in turn, had a chequered history. Monetarists claim that the commitment to, and technical execution of, monetary targetting has been unsatisfactory.

Keynesians claim that it has involved no more than simple deflation, with the policy's success in reducing inflation in the early 1980s tarnished by a dramatic growth in unemployment and a poor rate of growth of real output. Moreover, the conduct of policy has been complicated by a generally growing instability, partly induced by structural change, in the relationship between money and nominal incomes, an unstable velocity of money, and also by serious and persistent volatility in exchange rates and interest rates, often leaving these seemingly way out-of-line with economic fundamentals.

As of 1985, it seems difficult to see how a fully international system of pegged exchange rates could be re-established, though this would provide the traditional, and simplest, milieu for Central Bank policy. (This, though, would still allow regional groupings of countries to seek to maintain a stable exchange rate system between themselves, such as the European Monetary System, generally based on a central key currency within the group.) On the other hand, previous enthusiasm for rules, and for fixed targets for monetary growth, is dissipating, partly as the evolving structure of the financial system once again brings into question the appropriate definition, role, and essential properties, of money and banks. So for the moment, there seems no valid alternative to a discretionary conduct of monetary policy, with an eye not only both to monetary and exchange rate developments, but also to the broader evolution of the economy.

CHARLES GOODHART

See also BANK RATE, CHEAP MONEY; DEAR MONEY; FINANCIAL INTERMEDIARIES; MONETARY POLICY.

BIBLIOGRAPHY
Classical
Bagehot, W. 1873. *Lombard Street*. London: Henry S. King.
Fetter, F. 1965. *Development of British Monetary Orthodoxy, 1797–1875*. Cambridge, Mass.: Harvard University Press.
Thornton, H. 1802. *An Inquiry into the Nature and Effects of the Paper Credit of Great Britain*. London: Hatchard.
Evolution
Goodhart, C.A.E. 1985. *The Evolution of Central Banks*. ICERD Monograph, London School of Economics.
Hawtrey, R.G. 1932. *The Art of Central Banking*. London: Longmans.
Sayers, R. 1957. *Central Banking after Bagehot*. Oxford: Clarendon Press.
Smith, V. 1936. *The Rationale of Central Banking*. London: P.S. King & Son.
Timberlake, R., Jr. 1978. *The Origins of Central Banking in the United States*. Cambridge, Mass.: Harvard University Press.
US National Monetary Commission. 1910–11. (Twenty volumes of papers and original material on banking and Central Banking in all major industrialized countries.) Washington, DC: Government Printing Office.
Veit, O. 1969. *Grundriss der Wahrungspolitik*. 3rd edn, Frankfurt: Fritz Knapp Verlag.
Contemporary
Bank of England. 1984. *The Development and Operation of Monetary Policy, 1960–1983*. Oxford: Clarendon Press.
Board of Governors of the Federal Reserve System. *The Federal Reserve System: Purposes and Functions*. Washington, DC: Federal Reserve Board.
Duwendag, D. et al. 1985. *Geldtheorie und Geldpolitik*. 3rd edn, Cologne: Bund-Verlag.
Federal Reserve Bank of New York. 1983. *Central Bank Views on Monetary Targeting*. New York: Federal Reserve Bank of New York.
Meek, P. 1982. *US Monetary Policy and Financial Markets*. New York: Federal Reserve Bank of New York.
Woolley, J. 1984. *Monetary Politics*. Cambridge: Cambridge University Press.

centralization. *See* DECENTRALIZATION.

central place theory. First formulated by the German economic geographer Walter Christaller in 1933, central place theory is recognized as one valid though partial explanation of why cities and towns exist, what determines their growth and how their ordering within regions and nations comes about. Christaller developed his deductive theory by building upon the work of three previous analysts of the relationship between space and the economy. The work of von Thünen on the Isolated State (1826) had pointed to the principles determining the distribution in space of different types of agricultural production. Alfred Weber's theory of the Location of Industries (1922) had delineated how transport costs for inputs and to markets shaped the location of production and Oskar Engländer pinpointed how selling prices are shaped by consumer preferences, travel to shop behaviour and spatially variable production costs.

The critical focus of Christaller's theory is that urban areas, or 'central places' exist to provide goods and services for the territory surrounding them. Thus producers of such services as retailing, wholesaling, banking, insurance and leisure, all locate their facilities so as to capture the expenditure of local consumers. Christaller delineated two principles at the centre of these locational decisions. Starting from assumptions of a featureless plain devoted to agriculture (his region of study was Southern Germany) a uniform density of population, no variation in consumer tastes, invariant transport costs per kilometre and a uniform spread of natural resources, he showed that producers must locate so as to obtain a minimum level of demand – the *demand threshold* – below which normal profits would not be earned and the business could not survive. This threshold can be expressed in terms of the minimum local population times their expenditure needed to match minimum demand. The *market range*, the second key concept, is that distance which consumers are willing to travel to obtain the good or service. It represents the outer geographical limit beyond which consumers will give their custom to other nearer outlets in other centres. Now for each good or service consumers will have a different willingness to incur the physical and monetary costs of travel. For some goods, perhaps bought every day, such as bread or newspapers, they will only be prepared to travel short distances. For other much less frequent and usually more expensive purchases, such as furniture or a motor car, they will be willing to travel much farther since the cost of travel relative to the value of the good purchased is regarded as insignificant.

It follows from these two principles that goods and services bought frequently and with consumers only willing to travel short distances will have many small trading areas with each supplier locating at the centre of one such trading area. By contrast, goods bought infrequently will require much larger trading areas so as to achieve the minimum demand threshold with consumers being willing to travel to the much more limited number of central places up to the limit of their market range.

From these two principles and the ensuing spatial extent of the market for each good, Christaller delineated a *hierarchy* of market areas and of their central places serving them. Christaller argued that these market areas would be hexagonal in shape (an efficient form for covering territory) and that the increase in market sizes would be governed by geometrical rules. Moreover he argued that the centre of each market area

of a given size would supply goods and services not only characteristic of its size class but also the goods and services provided in lower order centres as well. This would come about because consumers, in economizing upon travel costs, would attempt to obtain as many goods as possible in their trips to higher-order centres and because consumers located around such centres would require small central places to supply their frequent purchases. Thus numerous small central places would 'nest' within the trading areas of larger central places, but the trading areas of these larger places would not overlap.

In delineating seven types of central places from the hamlet to the metropolitan city, Christaller argued that as this hierarchy was ascended the number of places decreased but the distance between the places, the local population of these places, the geographical extent and the population of their hinterlands, all would increase by constant factors. The actual determinants of these constants would be shaped by whether *marketing, transporting* or *administration* factors were at work. In the first case each central place would control all the trade in its own area and one third of the trade in all contiguous hexagonal areas. Under the transporting principle the distance between lower-order centres and a main centre is minimized so that the latter dominates the trade of its own area and half of the trade of the sub-centre. And finally on the administrative arrangement each main centre controls the trading allegiance of all the sub-centres.

August Lösch was the first to attempt a re-formulation of Christaller's rigid geometrical portrayal of market sizes. He argued that the hierarchy of sizes could increase in any number of possible ways. Lösch's realism was not matched by a simple expression of his own theory and it has been left to others, particularly Parr, to delineate a theory of market sizes taking account of the advantages to consumers and producers of clustering and of the development of business and public services.

Since its inception central place theory has been subjected to constant criticism. The assumptions of uniform distribution of population and of linear transportation costs have been thought to be unrealistic. But complicating these assumptions to accord with different realities does not affect the validity of the case that consumers will attempt to minimize travel distance, that they are willing to travel longer distances to obtain some goods, that demand thresholds for each good will vary and that wherever possible multiple goods buying will be preferred to single goods buying. Consequently a more realistic set of assumptions may change the number and shape of the trading areas and the precise form of the hierarchical pattern but not their essential characteristics.

The assumptions of uniform tastes and a uniform spread of natural resources are much more problematic. Consumers with the same income in cities and in rural areas have spending patterns which differ and this will shape the nature of trading areas. And the exploitation of natural resources in particular regions will result in the creation of employment, population growth and inward migration, all of which will affect local trading areas and the central place hierarchy in ways which may be related to, but are not caused, by the buying habits of the existing hinterland population.

Similar criticisms can be made of the theory's unrealistic assumptions about manufacturing location. Much manufacturing locates in particular areas because of natural and/or man made endowments. Frequently the growth of this activity is determined not by the expenditure of local population but by buyers within the nation or even internationally. And increasingly modern producer services such as banking, insurance and consultancy may serve international markets from 'world central places' with demand being determined less by the physical access of buyers within the international trading area but by price, quality, reliability and the ingenuity of the producers in developing services. The theory is also weak in explaining the dynamics of change within the hierarchy. This is not only because it assumes perfect competition and unrestricted freedom of entry but also because it was developed at a time when land use planning restraints were much less significant.

In sum, central place theory is incomplete in terms of its explanatory power, but nonetheless is a crucial ingredient in any proper understanding of why cities and towns exist and what shapes their hierarchical distribution over national space.

GORDON C. CAMERON

See also CHRISTALLER, WALTER; GRAVITY MODELS; LOCATION OF ECONOMIC ACTIVITY; SPATIAL COMPETITION; SPATIAL ECONOMICS; URBAN ECONOMICS.

BIBLIOGRAPHY
Beavon, K.S.O. 1977. *Central Place Theory: a re-interpretation.* London: Longman.
Berry, B.T.L. and Garrison, W.L. 1958. Recent developments of central place theory. *Papers and Proceedings of the Regional Science Association* 4, 107–20.
Lösch, A. 1954. *The Economics of Location.* Trans. W.H. Woglom and W.F. Stolper, New Haven: Yale University Press.
Parr, J. 1978. Models of the central place system: a more general approach. *Urban Studies* 15(1), 35–50.
Richardson, H.W. 1972. *Regional Economics.* London: Weidenfeld & Nicolson.

central planning. Central planning denotes the total body of government actions to determine and coordinate directions of national economic development. The process of central planning is composed of pre-plan studies and forecasts, formulation of aims for given periods of time, establishment of their priorities (order of importance), listing ways and means, and, eventually, the plan's implementation. Central planning is a term usually associated with Centrally Planned Economies (CPE) as opposed to Private Enterprise (or Market) and Mixed Economies (UN official classification), but it is often used in a broader sense to denote any systematic macroeconomic control by the government. For Tinbergen (1964), central planning means planning by governments, or national planning (in the Netherlands as well as in some other countries there are Central Planning Bureaux, even though these economies cannot be classed with the group of CPEs).

In this broader meaning, central planning takes several different names, specifically: 'direct', 'hierarchical' (Bauer, 1978) or 'centralistic' as practised in most centrally planned economies; 'financial' as in Hungary; 'indicative' as in France.

The term 'planning' often stirs emotions. For some people, especially for many Communist economists, central planning is good by definition. Others use it to denounce socialism and indeed any kind of government intervention as 'planned chaos' (Mises, 1947). The scope and meaning of central planning varies along with changing fashion. When Arthur Lewis confessed 'we are all planners now' (Lewis [1949] 1956, p. 74), it was fashionable to described any kind of state interventionism as 'planning'. Robbins (1947, p. 68) termed his proposal for a modest anti-inflationary or anti-deflationary fiscal policy as 'overall financial planning'. Since the 1970s, though, general opinion seems to have been increasingly wary of planning, indeed sceptical about its effectiveness. Accordingly, even some

planners in the state administration who staunchly stood by that idea preferred to cover their activity under less emotionally charged terms (such as 'steering').

Initially, central planning used to be generally regarded as an inalienable feature of socialist economy and hence as the exact opposite of market and commodity production typical of capitalism. It was interpreted as planning in physical units, by central command, based upon a hierarchical structure of national economy which had at its disposal ways and means to enforce decisions by administrative order. Precisely this kind of planning system developed in the Soviet Union, less as a product of any definite concept or vision of socialist economy than as an outcome of many different interacting factors – doctrine and ideology, the specific situation of Russia at that time, and the political ends to which the victorious revolutionary authorities subordinated the economy.

ORIGINS. After the Bolshevik victory in Russia Lenin's writings, apart from the above-mentioned view of planning as the exact opposite of market (which was shared by many other Marxists), provided two other theoretical contributions to the formidable task of organization of the economy. Following Rudolf Hilferding, Lenin (like Bukharin) described imperialism as an ante-chamber of socialism on account of the steadily accelerating process of production concentration (trusts) and the centralization of banks which were rapidly expanding their control of domestic industries. The German wartime economy with its large-scale combination of latest technology, planning and efficient organization, was viewed by Lenin as something like an archetype for a future socialist economy.

In the period of 'War Communism' (1918–20) the need for planning was repeatedly proclaimed but no national plan could actually be drawn up. It was only towards the end of the period that Gosplan, a planning commission, was created, although its job was modest and only vaguely defined for years thereafter. No firm way could be found to reconcile planning with the New Economic Policy (NEP) introduced in 1921.

The most important accomplishment of the early 1920s was the plan for electrifying all Russia, which was drawn up at Lenin's personal initiative in 1920 and which came to be referred to as GOELRO. That plan provided for the building, within the following 10–15 years, of power stations and related infrastructure in major industrial regions. At that stage, planning was viewed as primarily an engineering rather than economic activity (as can be seen if only from the composition of the commission, which included mostly engineers and agriculture specialists).

From 1925 onwards, Gosplan began to publish each year what were called economy-wide 'control figures' initially for a year only but later for five-year periods. Those figures were regarded as a non-binding set of estimations and forecasts. Their main contribution to the development of planning was that they eventually led up to the design of what is called the balancing method, which juxtaposes demand for goods with their output. First five-year plans also began to be drafted outside Gosplan.

The Soviet economy became a 'centrally planned' economy only at the time of the First Five-Year Plan (1928/9–1932/3). That was a time of tough internal struggle in the party and one of escalating heroic development programmes. Each new draft version of the five-year plan, beginning with the first one after the Party Congress in December 1927 through to its final approval, set up increasingly ambitious tasks. But the balancing of tasks with resources in the plan was based mainly on overly optimistic (and largely unfeasible) forecasts of labour productivity growth. The party and the state authorities soon began to mobilize the population to over-fulfil the plan, or, more precisely, those targets in the plan which were arbitrarily recognized as the most important ones (priority tasks). Thenceforward, plans became tools for mobilization rather than for balanced allocation of resources. Annual plans often shook up the current five-year plan to accommodate it to these new priorities (or super-priorities).

The First Five-Year Plan (which was officially declared fulfilled in four-and-a-quarter years) generated many bottle-necks and disproportions; this suggested that the pace should perhaps be slowed down – and priorities rearranged, as to some extent was attempted in the final version of the next five-year plan (for 1933–37). At the same time the new plan was even more detailed and its scope expanded significantly (the number of branches comprised by the plan increased to 120 from the original 50). The authors of the first five-year plans apparently did not realize the full institutional and political implications of over-ambitious tasks, the scale of which were in some cases downright unfeasible. In order to rescue those regarded as top priorities (especially those concerning heavy industries and manufacturing), others had to be sacrificed (those relating to standards of living were the first victims). This could only be accomplished by methods typical of wartime economy, that is, highly centralized organization, rigid subordination and discipline, all-embracing rationing, various kinds of coercion, and political mobilization. That was exactly what was attempted during the first two five-year plan periods.

To a considerable extent this amounted to a revival of the methods tried in the period of 'War Communism', including compulsory labour and rationing, however not as formal and lasting institutions like, for example, labour mobilization during the civil war, but either as side-effects of other campaigns (mass deportations during the collectivization drive, purges of the 1930s, etc), or as emergency responses to situations of extreme penury (rationing) which eventually should make room for allocation of labour and consumer goods through some kind of market (for ideological reasons the term was never used in relation to labour). This was combined with abandonment of the original egalitarianism in incomes policy; increased reliance on material incentives geared to plan and fulfilment and piece rates became a distinctive mark of the Stalinist period.

MAIN FEATURES (FORMAL ASPECTS). The first two five-year plans set the general shape for a model of Soviet central planning, transplanted after World War II to communist Eastern Europe. That model survived unchanged through to the mid-1950s (except in Yugoslavia), and in most communist countries it functions to this day in its general outline.

In both its design and implementation stages, central planning is based on a hierarchical pattern of national economy, which in turn presupposes obedience and discipline. Freedom of choice (which is lifted only temporarily or partly) applies to purchases of consumer goods within the existing commodity supply and the state-determined purchasing power, as well as to choice of occupation and workplace within the statutory obligation to be in employment.

Using information on the economy's shape and tendencies at any given moment, the central authority formulates a set of general guidelines of the plan, possibly based on prior special studies and forecasts. The plan's guidelines include such aggregates as the distribution of the national income between accumulation and consumption, the shares and main directions of investment by sectors, the desired rate of overall economic growth etc. These guidelines as a rule are pre-defined by the leading bodies of the ruling party, and are then disaggregated by the government into guidelines for particular industrial ministries and local authorities to produce their own draft plans, which are further disaggregated and communicated to industrial associations and individual enterprises. Government guidelines include two kinds of indices; directives, which are mandatory for local planners in drafting their blueprints (whatever alteration may prove necessary can only be made by a superior agency) and information indices. The enterprise draft plans are then aggregated by industrial associations and branch ministries, and their draft plans are in turn aggregated into a national (or central) economic plan for one or five years which is usually approved by parliament. Only after that are final corrections and adaptations introduced into lower-level plans. This particular procedure of plan construction has been called the 'spindle technique' in reference to textile machines, for guidelines and draft versions first travel from the top downwards, then up, and then again down the hierarchy.

One pivotal point in this procedure is the plan's internal consistency. The idea is to match demand for each particular resource with the level of its supply during the plan period. A whole system of balance sheets (indeed thousands of them) is used for that purpose. Balance sheets set – in physical or equivalent units – available amounts of materials, capacities, energy, labour, as well as financial means (personal income and spending, foreign trade balance, the budget) against anticipated demand in each case.

Plan fulfilment is a fundamental obligation of each economic organization. Managers and, to some extent the workforce as well, are evaluated for their plan performance and rewarded or penalized accordingly. Tasks named in an enterprise plan are both commands by a superior authority and obligations to supply enough resources to safeguard smooth cooperation. Although enterprises are given not only quantitative targets but also qualitative ones (e.g. technological input/output coefficients for materials, power etc, the importance of output–quantity performance is overriding.

ADVANTAGES AND FAILURES. This particular model of planning was conceived in a country with abundant resources of labour (open or disguised unemployment) and primary products; it was applied also in several other countries with large unused capacities. Proving able to mobilize idle resources initially produced very high growth rates, although one cannot take official statistical records at their face value. Determination of obligatory priorities on a national scale enabled countries to concentrate resources and efforts on several selected spectacular tasks. The successful bid to transform the Soviet Union into a superpower in a relatively brief time is perhaps the least debatable success of this planning model.

However, from the mid-1950s onwards centrally planned economies have been coming under growing criticism both from professional economists and from the general public. The criticism became particularly sharp as growth indicators declined and started to affect the (slow anyway) improvement of living standards; the system's weakness in generating and absorbing technological innovations became increasingly evident. However, critical voices – even when acknowledged by political authorities – did not lead, as a rule, to consistent and effective changes in the economic system.

The main lines of criticism of deficiencies of the existing system of central planning can be summarized as follows:

The procedure for building plans outlined above cannot guarantee efficient allocation of resources. The tasks and resources for their implementation are not decided by the central planning agency in a truly 'sovereign' way because such an agency is bound to rely on the supply of information from lower-rank agencies. But that information, apart from some natural delays or mistakes made in its transmission upwards, is often deliberately distorted by enterprises, which use it as a weapon in plan bargaining. Enterprises usually want to wrench as large means and as small tasks as possible from the central economic authority for themselves. Industrial association, indeed even branch ministries, often helps them achieve this purpose. At that stage, too, the main battle for investment funds begins. Enterprises and local authorities try to get 'put on' the plan by deliberately underrating estimated costs of their undertakings. Eventually, the plan is apparently brought into balance, but it has built-in significant disproportions right from its start, which leads to a waste of resources.

Even greater waste results from the centralistic bureaucratic method of controlling the execution of plan tasks, which eventually leads to equating planning with management. The over-taut plan, based as it is on unrealistic assumptions, especially regarding labour productivity growth, can later be 'fulfilled' only by setting up a whole system of ad hoc priorities and superpriorities which makes a reduction of nonpriorities unavoidable. As a rule, the victimized sectors are those related to the sphere of personal incomes or social or municipal services (public transport), the health service, housing, education – treated as residuum.

Once they have been assigned the required resources by the central economic authority, enterprises no longer feel compelled to seek ways of saving materials or energy. Because deliveries of materials and energy are as a rule irregular, enterprises try to provide against such risks by hoarding excessive inventories of materials and reducing employment only reluctantly. Moreover, enterprises are given no effective inducements to seek new technology, indeed even to emulate existing new techniques.

Prices set by the central authority are as a rule rigid and random, reflecting neither costs nor relative scarcities of individual goods. As a consequence, both at the central level and at enterprise level clear criteria of choice are largely absent.

Viewed from the consumer's vantage point, centrally planned economies provide poor-quality goods and a meagre product mix. Their incapability of meeting greater diversification of needs, which inevitably progresses along with increase in income levels, is one of the major reasons for the growth of a 'second economy' (moonlighting, corruption etc).

Over-taut plans, implemented through commands, unavoidably generate an inflated control system and subject the economy to political goals. Subordination of economies to politics is often presented as expression of general (social) interest; in reality this subordination often conceals vested interests of small informal groups. In the process of plan negotiations and rearrangement of priorities in the course of implementation, centralistic administrative planning engenders informal lobbies which exert growing pressure on the central authority. A product of quasi-missionary zeal to develop the production of means of production, the heavy industry lobbies are the strongest of all. Gradually, the central authority is losing its 'sovereignty' to them. Even when the authority begins to appreciate 'harmony' more than 'rush' (Kornai, 1972) it is unable to shed that pressure.

This very role of lobbies goes against the widely held belief that in the centrally planned economies the superior position belongs to the preferences of the central planners. Increasingly concrete decisions are made under growing pressures of various informal vested interest groups. In this situation,

criteria of choice cannot be clear or unequivocal, which makes public control of the central planning agency's operations even more difficult. For the same reason, and even more because of the secretive style of work of state agencies, as well as absence or limitation of consumer organizations, environmental groups, independent trade unions, and with restricted press freedom, the central authorities cannot play the part of an umpire reconciling different social interests. Protection of public interest becomes fictitious under these conditions. Thus, when official doctrines proclaim unity of interests, this may simply conceal a growing tendency towards a peculiar kind of 're-privatization' of centrally planned economics.

EVOLUTION AND PROSPECTS. Since the mid-1950s, in the system of central planning as practised in countries of the so-called 'real socialism' two categories of change have taken place.

The growth and mathematization of economics, in particular the expansion of linear programming, operations research, input–output analysis, cybernetics and systems analysis, the wide extension of computer applications etc., have supplied planners with subtler tools for their work. The development of these tools fuelled hopes, already in the 1960s, that planning would proceed 'from balancing the plan towards the choice of optimal plan' (Lange, 1965). 'Planometrics' came into use then, indeed even something like a 'computopia' began to develop.

The second kind of change was more institutional in character. It came along with de-Stalinization, of which economic reform was and still remains a part. Unlike in Yugoslavia, where the economic system was to correspond to an entirely different model of socialist society compared with the Soviet-type one, in the countries belonging to CMEA institutional changes amounted, generally speaking, to a transfer of some economic decision-making to lower-level units, an expansion of material incentives for managers and workers alike, and an extension of market mechanisms.

As a result of the new techniques and of the partial decentralization, central planning has probably become a slightly more efficient tool of economy-wide control. However, all those improvements were ultimately too negligible and inconsistent to stand up to the growing complexity of economy, in particular to offset the depleting reserves of extensive-type growth factors (excess labour, cheap raw materials) by more intensive methods of growth stimulation. The technology gap between CMEA and advanced Western countries, which became clear in the 1960s and has kept widening since then, has not been bridged; if anything, it has continued to widen. Hence, repeated calls for more or less radical economic reform are still the order of the day.

PLANNING AND FREEDOM. Ever since its inception, the question of economic planning has set off disputes about democracy and individual freedom. In its original purely ideological concept, planning used either to be equated with democracy or presented as democracy's exact opposite: suffice it to mention the New Leftist utopia of a social system based on the belief that production and distribution can somehow be planned by the people with a total absence of market and state. The eternal Kingdom of Freedom was to come simply as soon as market and state alike have been abolished.

More elegant, albeit no less utopian, is the free-marketeers' blueprint for rejecting any governmental planning as a threat to efficiency and freedom. Although quite fashionable (and not only in the West), this mode of thinking is nonetheless outside the mainstream of disputes over planning versus freedom.

In fact, most major currents of social thinking have undergone a process of radical re-thinking in the course of recent decades. This holds for liberalism (Mannheim, 1940; Galbraith, 1973; Lindblom, 1977) and for non-Communist socialism (Crosland, 1956; Crossman, 1965; Nove, 1983) as well as for Marxism (Brus, 1975; Horvat, 1982; Kornai, 1985). Whatever differences may divide all these currents of thought, as indeed individual thinkers within each current, all of them are aware of two kinds of threat to freedom – one that comes from all-embracing, hierarchical and bureaucratic planning, and another that comes from the failure to plan anything at all. The market mechanism is regarded as something like a barrier to bureaucratic arbitrariness. But its failures in turn may put at hazard not only economic but even political stability, thereby destroying the foundations of the desired social order. Planning, within given limits, thus turns out to be an indispensable condition of freedom. While making a plea for a polycentric model of economy – both in the sense of providing for different forms of ownership and of decision-making – all these currents of thinking believe that society as a whole should have an authentic say (via its representatives) on the main lines of investment and on general rules for national income distribution.

Of course, there is nothing inevitable in the long-run direction this movement will take either in the West or in the East. The chance to create a social order which would be based upon the three main tiers of plan, the market and freedom would be much greater if it were clear that each of these is a necessary condition for high socio-economic efficiency, and that freedom too can be viewed not only as a value in itself but also as a specific kind of production factor. Some authors have questioned this dependence of economic efficiency on political democracy (Gomulka, 1977). However, neither studies of this relationship in many Third World countries (Adelman and Taft, 1967) nor the record of previous reforms in the Communist world supply any definite answer to this question. On the other hand, the analysis of pressures on, and prospects of, the evolution of Communist systems in Eastern Europe has led to a rather persuasive argument (Brus, 1980) that without democratizing internal political relations these systems will be unable to remove (or at least to reduce substantially) central planning's chronic deficiencies, such as insufficient and distorted information flows, negative selection of managerial personnel, chronic investment failures, labour alienation etc. The stagnation threatening the Communist countries presses the ruling groups to more radical reforms which would combine plan, market and freedom. At the same time, repeated setbacks of neoliberal economic policies in the West may well generate fresh and strong public pressure for changes in a similar direction.

TADEUSZ KOWALIK

See also COMMAND ECONOMY; DECENTRALIZATION; MARKET SOCIALISM; MATERIAL BALANCES; SOCIALISM.

BIBLIOGRAPHY

Adelman, I. and Taft, C.M. 1967. *Society, Politics and Economic Development: A Quantitative Approach.* Baltimore: Johns Hopkins Press.

Bauer, T. 1978. Investment cycles in planned economies. *Acta Oeconomica* 21(3), 243–60.

Brus, W. 1975. *Socialist Ownership and Political Systems.* London: Routledge & Kegan Paul.

Brus, W. 1980. Political system and economic efficiency: the East European context. *Journal of Comparative Economics* 4(1), March, 40–55.

Cave, M. and Hare, P. 1981. *Alternative Approaches to Economic Planning.* New York: St Martin's Press.

Crosland, C.A.R. 1956. *The Future of Socialism.* London: Jonathan Cape.

Crossman, R.H.S. 1965. Planning and freedom. In R.H.S. Crossman, *Essays in Socialism,* London: Hamish Hamilton.

Davies, R.W. and Carr, E.H. 1974. *Foundations of a Planned Economy 1926–1929.* Harmondsworth: Penguin.

Ellman, M. 1983. Changing views on central economic planning: 1958–1983. *The ACES Bulletin, A Publication of the Association for Comparative Economic Studies* (Tempo, Arizona) 25(1), Spring.

Galbraith, J.K. 1973. *Economics and the Public Purpose.* Boston: Houghton Mifflin.

Gomulka, S. 1977. Economic factors in the democratization of socialism and the socialization of capitalism. *Journal of Comparative Economics* 1(4), December, 389–406.

Horvat, B. 1982. *The Political Economy of Socialism. A Marxist Social Theory.* Armonk, NY: M.E. Sharpe.

Kornai, J. 1972. *Rush versus Harmonic Growth.* Amsterdam: North-Holland.

Kornai, J. 1985. *Contradictions and Dilemmas, Studies on the Socialist Economy and Society.* Corvina: Kner Printing House.

Lange, O. 1965. Od bilansowania do wyboru optymalnego planu (From balancing the plan to the choice of optimal plan). *Nowe Drogi* (Warsaw), No.2.

Lewis, W.A. 1949. *The Principles of Economic Planning.* London: George Allen & Unwin Ltd, 1956.

Lindblom, C. 1977. *Politics and Markets. The World's Political-Economic Systems.* New York: Basic Books.

Mannheim, K. 1940. *Man and Society in an Age of Reconstruction. Studies in Modern Social Structure.* London: Routledge & Kegan Paul, 1974.

Mises, L. von. 1947. *Planned Chaos.* Irvington-on-Hudson, NY: The Foundation for Economic Education.

Nove, A. 1983. *The Economics of Feasible Socialism.* London: Allen & Unwin.

Robbins, L. 1947. *The Economic Problem in Peace and War.* London: Macmillan.

Tinbergen, J. 1964. *Central Planning.* New Haven and London: Yale University Press.

centre of gravitation. In the Classical theory concerning the price of commodities there are two notions of price: the *market price*, which is the price actually prevailing, and the *natural price*, which is equal to 'what is sufficient to pay the rent of the land, the wages of the labour, and the profits of the stock . . . according to their natural rates' (Smith, 1976, p. 72); and the natural price is a *centre of gravitation* for the actual price, i.e. the latter is continually tending to the former.

In the description of this tendency given by the Classics, one can distinguish two main propositions. According to the first one, the market price depends on the difference between current supply and 'effectual demand' – which is 'the demand of those who are willing to pay the natural price of the commodity' (Smith, 1776, p. 73) – the market price being higher, lower than, or equal to the natural price, if such a difference is, respectively, negative, positive or zero. According to the second proposition, the difference between market price and natural price gives rise to movements of capitals and changes in the structure of production, so that the output of a commodity increases (decreases) if such a difference is positive (negative).

The position of the economy in which market price equals natural price and output equals effectual demand is a 'centre of repose and continuance' (Smith, 1776, p. 75), a position which is bound to repeat itself unaltered, until an exogenous change (e.g. in the available techniques of production) takes place.

On the basis of current definitions and methods of dynamical analysis (see, e.g. Lasalle, 1976), one can recognize in the above theory the description of a dynamical system, in which the state variables are prices and output (or capital) quantities and for which the vector formed by natural prices and the corresponding output (or capital) quantities is an equilibrium.

The notion of a uniform rate of profit price vector, towards which actual prices tend to move, having been accepted – after Ricardo – by generations of economists, including Marshall and Walras, was then abandoned in the works on general equilibrium of recent decades.

The uniform-rate-of-profit price vector – let us call it *production price vector* – had a central place in Sraffa's book *Production of Commodities by Means of Commodities, Prelude to a Critique of Economic Theory* (1960), but nothing was said in it about the relation between such price vector and actual prices.

As a 'prelude to a critique of economic theory' Sraffa's analysis does not require such a relation; but it does, if it is to be used as a building block for a 'reconstruction' of economic theory. For this reason the Classical theory, according to which 'long period positions' are 'centres of gravitation' for actual prices, has been recently reintroduced (Garegnani, 1976).

This reintroduction, however, also requires a critical re-examination today in the light of the contemporary methodology of dynamics. In order to illustrate this point, we shall try to formalize the gravitation theory of the Classics in a simple way.

Let us consider an economy in which there are n sectors, each producing a different commodity. The production of every commodity requires capital advances, which must cover the purchases of material inputs as well as the payment of a subsistence wage rate to each employed worker.

To simplify the discussion further, we also *assume* that for our economy a unique semi-positive price vector exists, such that in each sector the following two conditions hold together:

(a) a uniform rate of profit prevails;
(b) demand and supply are equal.

We call this vector 'the production price vector' of our economy and denote it by $p^* = (p_i^*)$, $i = 1, 2, 3, \ldots, n$. The existence of such a vector can be *proved* in various kinds of models (see, e.g. Boggio, 1985).

Let us now reconsider the two propositions in which we have summarized the description of the gravitation process given by the Classics and call d_{it}, p_{it} and q_{it}, respectively, the effectual demand for, the actual price and the current output of the i-th commodity at time t, $t \in R_+$.

Then a simple way to model the first proposition is the following

$$p_{it} - p_i^* = g_i(d_{it} - q_{it}), \qquad i = 1, 2, \ldots, n \qquad (1)$$

where g_i is a continuous sign-preserving function.

As for the second proposition, that is, the relation between output changes (as determined by capital movements across sectors) and profitability (as expressed by the difference between market and natural price), it can be modelled as

$$\dot{q}_i = s_i(p_{it} - p_i^*), \qquad i = 1, 2, \ldots, n \qquad (2)$$

where $\dot{q}_i = dq_{it}/dt$ and s_i is a continuous sign-preserving function.

These two equations, however, are not sufficient to prove the gravitation thesis. They must be supplemented by some specific assumption about the time-pattern of d_t, the vector of effectual demands. Let us assume that d_t is constant

$$d_t = d^* \qquad (3)$$

where d^* is a fixed semi-positive vector. Then from (1), (2) and (3) we get

$$\dot{q}_i = s_i[g_i(d_i^* - q_{it})] \qquad (4)$$

Since $d(q_{it} - d_i^*)/dt$ is always equal to $\dot{q}_i$, one can see that, by equation (4), its sign is always opposite to that of $(q_{it} - d_i^*)$. Therefore as t grows $|q_{it} - d_i^*|$ decreases monotonically, i.e. q_{it}

tends to d_i^*. This implies that as t tends to $+\infty$, p_{it} must also, by equation (1), tend to p_i^*.

Hence the couple (p^*, d^*) is a globally asymptotically stable equilibrium for system (1)–(2)–(3). Notice that the same conclusion could be reached if we assumed that d_{it}, instead of being constant, were growing at a constant proportional rate.

This result means that, according to our model, although exogenous changes may shift the actual price vector and/or the production price vector, the gravitation mechanism will always tend to close the gap between them.

However, our model and the gravitation theory of the Classics are rather crude and, in several points, unsatisfactory. A clear example of this is the assumed equivalence between a positive (negative) value of $(p_{it} - p_i^*)$ and a capital-attracting (-repelling) sectoral rate of profit. If the higher than average rates of profit are capital-attracting and the lower than average rates are capital-repelling, one can show that such an equivalence does not hold in general (see Steedman, 1984). The ratio between a given sectoral profit rate and the average rate depends also on the prices of the commodities required as input in that sector. The Classical description neglects these interindustry links and any attempt to incorporate them in the analysis requires the simultaneous consideration of all prices, output levels, etc. thereby disrupting the beautiful simplicity of the Classical theory of gravitation.

The study of the stability of production prices by means of the methods of contemporary dynamic analysis has recently begun (for references and more comments, see Boggio, 1985). Two main approaches have been followed. In the first approach the process of price formation is based on some kind of mark-up or full-cost rule. Very strong stability results are obtained. But the assumption of exogenous mark-ups or target profit rates is not entirely satisfactory. In the second approach the original description of the Classics is followed more closely: actual price changes depend upon supply and demand and output changes depend upon profit differentials.

We notice that in the latter approach the equilibrium vector is formed by both production (relative) price vector and steady state output proportions. Since no economy grows in a balanced way, the reference to balanced growth is often considered such a weakness as to deprive a theory of any usefulness. Actually, the meaning of balanced growth, as of every equilibrium concept, is not necessarily to offer in itself a description of reality. If the equilibrium is stable, the effects of changes in the data of the system can be approximately studied by means of the displacements of equilibrium positions: in the case under discussion, the effects on prices by the displacements of production prices, the effects on output proportions by the displacements of balanced growth proportions. A condition for the correct use of this method, an outstanding example of which in the field of economics, is the above described theory of the Classics, is that the changes in the data should be slower than the movements of the state variables of the (dynamical) system. These remarks suggest the great advantage of studying change by means of comparisons or sequences of equilibria: the more fundamental aspects of change are selected out of the variety of accidental and transitory ones.

As for the results obtained in the latter approach to the study of the stability of production prices, they are mainly against stability, except for the case when strong price substitution effects in consumption are introduced. A more promising approach, in terms both of realism and of stability results, consists, probably, in assuming that price changes depend *mainly* on cost changes, but some role in determining the former is also played by excess demand.

Much more work in this field, however, seems necessary. Its

importance derives not only from the question of 'gravitation' itself, but also from more general issues of economic theory.

By specifying in a rigorous and formal way a dynamical process for which Sraffa prices are (part of) an equilibrium and by showing that such a process is not reducible to a neo-Walrasian disequilibrium process – in which prices react to excess demands, supply *instantaneously* adjusts to prices and expected future prices are replaced by current prices of 'futures' – such a work can establish in the clearest way that Sraffa prices are not simply reducible to a special case of neo-Walrasian general equilibrium theory.

Secondly, if it can show that, to give a stylized description of price-quantity dynamical interrelationships, there are more plausible ways than the neo-Walrasian one, such a work can give a contribution in the direction of replacing the neo-Walrasian paradigm.

LUCIANO BOGGIO

See also COMPETITION; EQUILIBRIUM, DEVELOPMENT OF THE CONCEPT OF; LONG RUN AND SHORT RUN; MARKET PRICE; NATURAL AND NORMAL CONDITIONS.

BIBLIOGRAPHY
Boggio, L. 1985. On the stability of production prices. *Metroeconomica* 37(3), October, 241–67.
Garegnani, P. 1976. On a change in the notion of equilibrium in recent work on value and distribution; a comment on Samuelson. In *Essays in Modern Capital Theory*, ed. M. Brown, K. Sato and P. Zarembka, Amsterdam: North-Holland.
Lasalle, J.P. 1976. *The Stability of Dynamical Systems*. Philadelphia: SIAM.
Ricardo, D. 1817. *On the Principles of Political Economy and Taxation*. Ed. P. Sraffa, Cambridge: Cambridge University Press, 1951.
Smith, A. 1776. *An Inquiry into the Nature and Causes of the Wealth of Nations*. Ed. R.H. Campbell and A.S. Skinner, Oxford: Oxford University Press, 1976.
Sraffa, P. 1960. *Production of Commodities by Means of Commodities: Prelude to a Critique of Economic Theory*. Cambridge: Cambridge University Press.
Steedman, I. 1984. Natural prices, differential profit rates and the Classical competitive process. *The Manchester School of Economic and Social Studies* 52(2), 123–40.

certainty equivalent. In order to take a decision in an uncertainty context, it is necessary, from a theoretical point of view, to build a model and specify all the consequences in every possible state of the world. In applied work this method is much too involved. Consequently, for applied purposes, it would be interesting to have a model where uncertainty is treated in such a way that the decision problems are as simple as the equivalent ones in a certainty framework. The identification of the conditions under which such an isomorphism between the optimal decisions under uncertainty and the optimal decisions in an equivalent certainty context holds is called the certainty equivalent problem.

Theil (1954) has been the first to point out the problem and to suggest a specific model in which the certainty equivalent property holds.

Theil imposes the following two assumptions: (i) the vector x of instruments and the vectory y of result variables are related by a simple equation

$$y = g(x) + S \qquad (1)$$

where S is a vector of random variables, that we can take to have a zero expected value without loss of generality. (ii) The decision-maker's objective function is quadratic and can be written as

$$u(x, y) = A(x) + \sum_{i=1}^{m} A_i(x) y_i + \frac{1}{2} \sum_{i=1}^{m} \sum_{y=1}^{m} A_{ij} y_i y_j \qquad (2)$$

Using such a model it is straightforward to show that whenever the optimal solution to the problem of maximizing the expected utility under the constraint (1) exists, it is the same as the optimal solution to the equivalent certain problem:

$$\begin{cases} \text{Max } u(x, y) \\ y = g(x) \end{cases}$$

This result is extended not only to the multiperiod problem but also to the case where the decision-maker receives more and more information as time elapses. The resulting stochastic problem is then more involved, but it is simply solved by use of dynamic programming, the optimal strategy in period t being a function of the previously observed signals η_{t-k}

$$X_t^* = x_t^*(\eta_1, \eta_2, \ldots, \eta_{t-1})$$

Again, the conditions for the first period solution to this problem to be the solution of the equivalent certain problem are very strong. As before, it has to be the case that the objective function is quadratic, but in addition the constraint relating instruments to results is restricted to be of the following type:

$$y = RX + S$$

where R is a matrix with some required specifications (namely, the value of the instrument variables of one period have no effect on the result variables of the preceding periods).

The conditions that guarantee the equivalence between the uncertainty problem and the certainty problem are so restrictive, that an alternative view of the problem has been suggested. Instead of setting restrictions on the parameters of the model, the uncertainty itself is restricted to be 'small'. Formally, this is equivalent to consider an entire class of problems that can be ranked in their uncertainty as measured by a parameter ϵ and whose limit is the certain problem. The question is then to know under what conditions the solution to the limit of the random problems, that is equal to the one of the certain problem, is independent of ϵ to the first order, so that

$$\frac{dE\,[x_t^*(\eta_1, \ldots, \eta_t)\epsilon]}{d\epsilon} = 0 \qquad \text{for} \quad \epsilon = 0.$$

This slightly different point of view is called the 'first order certainty equivalence' problem and has been dealt with by Theil (1957) and Malinvaud (1969).

The very general conditions obtained by Malinvaud for the first order certainty equivalent to hold are (i) that the objective function is twice differentiable and (ii) that the optimal strategy is continuous with respect to the degree of uncertainty. If this condition holds, the optimal values of the instruments at time 1 are, to the first order approximation, independent of the degree of uncertainty.

It is clear that this condition cannot be met if there are constraints on the future instrument variables, since this will bring in a kink. A particular and natural example of a framework where the first order certainty equivalence does not hold is when decisions are irreversible. As pointed out in Henry (1974), it is then the case that the value of the decision in the first period will affect the decision set in the following periods, and consequently, the use of the certainty equivalent would generate a systematic error.

XAVIER FREIXAS

See also RISK.

BIBLIOGRAPHY
Henry, C. 1974. Investment decisions under uncertainty: the irreversible effect. *American Economic Review* 64, 1996–2012.
Malinvaud, E. 1969. First order certainty equivalence. *Econometrica* 37, 706–18.

Simon, H. 1956. Dynamic programming under uncertainty with a quadratic criterion function. *Econometrica* 24, 74–81.

Theil, H. 1954. Econometric models and welfare maximization. *Weltwirtschaftsiges Archiv* 72, 60–83.

Theil, H. 1957. A note on certainty equivalence in dynamic planning. *Econometrica* 25, 346–9.

CES production function. The CES (Constant Elasticity of Substitution) production function, including its special case the Cobb–Douglas form, is perhaps the most frequently employed function in modern economic analysis. Not only is the CES function used for the formal depiction of production technology, it is used as a convenient tool for empirical analysis as well. In addition to production theory, the CES function, more commonly known as the Bergson family of utility functions, is employed in utility theory.

ORDINARY CES PRODUCTION FUNCTIONS. The simplest form of CES function utilized in production theory is the constant returns to scale type (Arrow et al., 1961):

$$Y = T[\alpha K^{-\rho} + (1-\alpha)L^{-\rho}]^{-(1/\rho)} \qquad (1)$$

where Y = output, K = capital, L = labour, and the parameters T, α, and ρ satisfy the conditions: $T \geqslant 0$, $0 \leqslant \alpha \leqslant 1$ and $\rho \leqslant -1$. As is implied by its name, the elasticity of factor substitution between capital and labour for production function (1) is expressed as some constant value.

For any neoclassical production function $Y = f(K, L)$, the elasticity of factor substitution between capital and labour is defined as the proportionate change in the K/L ratio (k) relative to the proportionate change in the marginal rate of factor substitution $r = f_L/f_K$ along a given isoquant curve, where $f_L = \partial Y/\partial L$ and $f_K = \partial Y/\partial K$ are the respective marginal products. That is,

$$\sigma = \frac{\mathrm{d}\log k}{\mathrm{d}\log r} = \frac{f_K f_L(f_K K + f_L L)}{KL(2f_{KL}f_K f_L - f_K^2 f_{LL} - f_L^2 f_{KK})}, \qquad (2)$$

where σ represents the elasticity of substitution and f_{KL}, f_{KK} and f_{LL} represent the cross and own derivatives of the respective marginal products.

Applying definition (2) to production function (1) we obtain:

$$\sigma = \frac{1}{1+\rho} \quad \text{or} \quad \rho = \frac{1-\sigma}{\sigma}. \qquad (3)$$

Consequently, it is easy to see why ρ is often referred to as the 'substitution' parameter. The α parameter in production function (1) is the 'distribution' parameter that permits the relative importance of capital and labour to vary in production. In the extreme case where $\rho \to 0$ or $\sigma = 1$, the CES function (1) converges to the Cobb–Douglas form:

$$Y = TK^\alpha L^{1-\alpha}. \qquad (4)$$

In this form, it is evident that α and $1 - \alpha$ are the production elasticities of capital and labour respectively. Under conditions of perfect competition, α and $1 - \alpha$ will also equal the respective relative income shares (or income distribution). The T parameter in both production functions (1) and (4) is the 'efficiency' (or technical progress) parameter.

With the exception of its special case the Cobb–Douglas form, the ordinary CES production function is cumbersome and difficult to manipulate. However, the underlying expression for the marginal rate of factor (technical) substitution has a simple form and this is the primary reason for the popularity and wide use of this production function.

HOMOTHETIC AND NON-HOMOTHETIC CES PRODUCTION FUNCTIONS. Any monotonic transformation of the ordinary CES production functions (1) belongs to a class of CES production functions called the homothetic class, i.e.

$$Y = F(f), \qquad F' > 0,$$

where

$$f = T[\beta K^{-\rho} + (1-\beta)L^{-\rho}]^{-(1/\rho)}. \qquad (5)$$

In addition to the class of homothetic CES production functions, there is a more general, and perhaps more meaningful, class of non-homothetic CES production functions. One can refer to the class of non-homothetic CES functions as the 'general class' of CES production functions as it contains the homothetic class as a special case.

The class of non-homothetic CES production functions is derived as a solution to the differential equation that defines a constant elasticity of factor substitution. However, unlike the case of the homothetic CES production functions where the marginal rate of factor substitution is (implicitly) assumed to be independent of either the output level or the process of technical change, the family of non-homothetic CES production functions explicitly assumes that output level and technical change will have some kind of impact on the factor input ratio.

The class of non-homothetic CES production functions can be expressed as follows (Sato, 1975):

$$C_1(Y)K^{-\rho} + C_2(Y)L^{-\rho} = 1, \quad \rho = \frac{1-\sigma}{\sigma}, \quad \sigma \neq 1, \quad (6a)$$

$$C_1(Y)\log K + C_2(Y)\log L = 1, \quad \sigma = 1, \qquad (6b)$$

where C_1 and C_2 are functions of the output level Y. When $C_1 = aC_2$, where a is a constant, we can express (6a) as

$$K^{-\rho} + aL^{-\rho} = \frac{1}{C_1(Y)} = B(Y)$$

or

$$Y = B^{-1}(K^{-\rho} + aL^{-\rho}).$$

Note that with the appropriate choice of B and a, we can always express the above in the form of the ordinary CES production function. In general, the non-homothetic CES production functions are in an implicit form and can never be expressed in an explicit form.

CLASSIFICATION OF NON-HOMOTHETIC CES PRODUCTION FUNCTIONS. The general class of non-homothetic CES production functions can be classified in a number of ways, depending on the specific purpose in mind. For example, it is well known that the ordinary CES production function belongs to the explicit and separable class of homothetic CES functions. In a similar fashion, we can derive an explicit and separable class of non-homothetic CES functions (Sato, 1974). Another way of classifying non-homothetic CES production functions is to consider the form of the underlying marginal rate of factor substitution function. However, the most precise way of classifying the family of non-homothetic CES production functions is to utilize Lie group theory.

A HISTORICAL NOTE. It was Arrow et al. (1961) who first utilized the ordinary CES production function expressed in (1) for the estimation of constant returns to scale aggregate production functions using cross-country data. Since then, the ordinary CES function and its variants have been widely applied in both theoretical and empirical work involving production behaviour.

Prior to its application to production analysis, the ordinary CES function, was utilized in the study of demand as the Bergson family of utility functions (Samuelson, 1965). Earlier writers in growth economics, such as Dickinson (1955) and

Solow (1956), used special cases of the CES function, such as $\sigma = 2$. In the field of mathematics, Courant (1959, vol. 1, pp. 557, 601) has used the explicit form of the ordinary CES function in conjunction with the so-called Jensen inequalities.

A published note by McElroy (1967) contains the first reference to the non-homothetic CES production family. However, it was not until later that Sato (1974) derived an explicit form of the non-homothetic CES production function. The application of Lie group theory to CES production functions was first presented in 1975. This work demonstrated that the 'projective' type of technical change with eight essential parameters can be used most effectively to classify the general non-homothetic CES family of production functions. This work is summarized in Sato (1981, ch. 5).

RYUZO SATO

See also COBB-DOUGLAS FUNCTIONS; ELASTICITY OF SUBSTITUTION; HUMBUG PRODUCTION FUNCTION; PRODUCTION AND COST FUNCTIONS; QUANTITY OF CAPITAL.

BIBLIOGRAPHY

Arrow, K., Chenery, H., Minhas, B. and Solow, R. 1961. Capital–labor substitution and economic efficiency. *Review of Economics and Statistics* 43(3), August, 225–50.

Courant, R. 1959. *Differential and Integral Calculus*. 2 vols, New York: Wiley.

Dickinson, H. 1955. A note on dynamic economics. *Review of Economic Studies* 22(3), 169–79.

McElroy, F. 1967. Note on the CES production function. *Econometrica* 35(1), January, 154–6.

Samuelson, P. 1965. Using full duality to show that simultaneously additive direct and indirect utilities implies unitary price elasticity of demand. *Econometrica* 33(4), October, 781–96.

Sato, R. 1974. On the class of separable non-homothetic CES production functions. *Economic Studies Quarterly* 25(1), April, 42–55.

Sato, R. 1975. The most general class of CES functions. *Econometrica* 43(5–6), September-November, 999–1003.

Sato, R. 1981. *Theory of Technical Change and Economic Invariance*. New York: Academic Press.

Solow, R. 1956. A contribution to the theory of economic growth. *Quarterly Journal of Economics* 70(1), February, 65–94.

ceteris paribus. The Latin phrase 'ceteris paribus', which translates as 'other things the same', is much invoked by economists. Its popularity stems from its prominent use by Alfred Marshall ([1890] 1920, pp. xiv-xv, 366–70), who invented the metaphor of 'the pound called Coeteris Paribus' – pound being used here in the same sense as in impoundment – in which are imprisoned 'those disturbing causes, whose wanderings happen to be inconvenient' (1920, p. 366).

The term ceteris paribus has no clearly settled technical meaning among economists, so that an attempt to chronicle its usage would be both difficult and unrewarding. Instead, it seems preferable to distinguish the most important alternative ways in which the phrase might be employed, alluding only briefly to the pertinent literature. It is important to distinguish at the outset three broad ways in which the phrase might be used. These are:

(i) As a reminder that any practicable theory must take for granted the stability and continuance of certain background circumstances.

(ii) As a warning, when using a theory predictively, that certain variations in circumstances admitted by the theory have been assumed not to occur.

(iii) An an instruction to hold hypothetically constant some members of a set of *necessarily* covarying variables while changes in the others are contemplated.

For example, an analysis of the movement of a group of adjacent cooling towers during gales might (i) abstract from earthquakes, or (ii) hold constant ambient temperature while considering the effects of varying wind speed, or (iii) analyse the swaying of one tower in a high wind on the assumption that the other towers are perfectly rigid, even though they too must actually sway in a way that subtly alters the wind currents buffeting the first tower. In the language of econometric models, these three usages of 'ceteris paribus' can be characterized as (i) a reminder that the model's structure is assumed not to change, or (ii) a warning that certain *exogenous* variables are presumed to remain constant when others change, or (iii) an instruction to hold constant certain *endogenous* variables while varying others, even though this is not justified by any separability properties of the model's structure.

The first two usages pose no difficulties. In each, the invocation of ceteris paribus merely serves as a reminder that a more comprehensive or elaborate analysis might have been attempted. The risk of earthquakes could have been incorporated into the analysis of cooling-tower stability at the price of added complexity. But a failure to do so is without methodological significance. The incidence of earthquakes is unlikely to be affected by any movement of the towers, so that the exclusion merely singles out a convenient stopping place on the inevitable trade-off between comprehensiveness and complexity. Analogously, in predicting with an econometric model it would be possible to make careful predictions of the changes in all exogenous variables that accompany a tax cut. But a failure to do so involves no logical inconsistency, and the resulting ceteris-paribus prediction of the tax-cut's effects will still have substantive interest.

It is the third usage alone, with its implied logical inconsistency, which poses distinct difficulties of interpretation and methodological justification. To start with, the assertion that certain variables are mutually interdependent presumes knowledge, at least in principle, of a correct comprehensive theory in which these variables are endogenous. For economists, the requisite background theory has usually been that of Walrasian competitive general equilibrium. In such a context, the invocation of ceteris paribus in its third sense to freeze hypothetically certain endogenous variables (or, more generally, to treat them as if exogenous) can itself be given at least three alternative rationalizations.

I. PARTIAL EQUILIBRIUM ANALYSIS AS AN APPROXIMATION. The focus here is on the demand-supply interactions in one market or a few closely interrelated markets as exogenous shifts occur, prices in all other markets being treated as hypothetically constant (or perhaps in some cases varied exogenously). Such a procedure is inconsistent with the supposed background general-equilibrium theory which implies that all prices vary interdependently. But it may give an adequate *approximate* representation of the particular markets being examined (see Viner [1931] 1953, p. 199). This is more likely the weaker and more diffuse are connections to, and feedbacks from, markets outside the examined set. Smallness relative to the entire economy is usually helpful in this regard, but such questions have received surprisingly little detailed analysis.

II. APPROACH BY SUCCESSIVE APPROXIMATION. Here the use of ceteris paribus restrictions is viewed as a necessary transitional step towards the evolution or understanding of a fully-comprehensive general-equilibrium theory. The limitations of human comprehension, its need to understand and test only one link of a complete chain at a time, calls for a piecemeal step-by-step progression from the crude but simple to the sophisticated but more complex, even though such a proceeding would appear illogical to an all-comprehending Cartesian intelligence. It should, however, be observed that this progression could well take place by starting with a highly aggregated general equilibrium model and successively reducing the degree of aggregation, instead of by starting with a simple partial-equilibrium model and gradually expanding its coverage until general equilibrium is reached – as is Marshall's clearly stated strategy (1920, pp. xiv–xv).

III. ILLUMINATING THOUGHT EXPERIMENT. Conceptual experiments which hold constant certain endogenous variables, or vary them arbitrarily, may perform a valuable heuristic role in aiding comprehension of the attainment and character of general equilibrium, even though they are not part of the theory's logical structure. Thus, the construction of Walrasian market excess demand functions, by the mental experiment of facing each individual with the same arbitrary price vector and then aggregating, is heuristically valuable despite the fact that all market excess demands must be zero in equilibrium. In part this heuristic value comes from pertinence to the disequilibrium meta theory in which any equilibrium theory must be embedded, a meta theory which might be visualized only vaguely and informally. Mental experiments of this type have been termed 'individual' or 'ceteris paribus' experiments by Patinkin, who contrasts them with 'market' or 'mutatis mutandis' experiments in which endogenous variables are always constrained to satisfy the requirements of the underlying general equilibrium structure (1965, pp. 11–12).

These three different ways of invoking ceteris paribus to freeze or 'exogenize' some endogenous variables may be contrasted briefly by saying that the first views partial-equilibrium theory as sometimes preferable to general-equilibrium theory, the second regards partial equilibrium theory as an interim step towards general equilibrium theory, and the third interprets ceteris-paribus experiments as heuristic aids sustaining general equilibrium theory.

The partial-equilibrium approach is closely associated with Marshall, who popularized its use, although Cournot (1838) among others had employed it previously. But Marshall's *methodological* discussion of the use of ceteris paribus restrictions arose in the narrower context of his time-period analysis, which is conducted within a framework already partial-equilibrium in character (1920, pp. 366–80). Considering a single industry (his example is fishing), he imprisons in the pound of ceteris paribus those variables, exogenous or endogenous, whose movement is very rapid or very slow compared to those whose equilibrium and comparative-static properties he wishes to explore. The aim is to gain rough insight into likely time paths, given that explicit dynamic analysis is not feasible (see Viner [1931] 1953, p. 206).

The use, other than for frank approximations, of ceteris paribus assumptions which conflict with underlying general-equilibrium requirements (i.e., the use of individual rather than market experiments) has been attacked as illogical or misleading by Friedman (1949) and Bailey (1954) in the context of demand functions, and by Buchanan (1958) more generally. A judicious assessment and summing up is provided by Yeager (1960).

Applications of ceteris paribus ideas to growth paths rather than stationary equilibria have been pioneered by Fisher and Ando (1962).

In closing, mention might be made of the classical notion of 'disturbing causes' as set out by J.S. Mill (1844, Essay V). Any deductive theorist who regards his assumptions as true, rather than mere means for generating refutable statements, must view his (valid) deductions as also true in the absence of disturbing causes not allowed for in his assumptions (see Keynes, 1891, pp. 204–13). Are such disturbing causes to be viewed as ruled out by a ceteris paribus assumption? According to Mill, they are in the statement of general economic theory (when e.g. other motives than the pursuit of wealth are excluded) but not in its specific applications, when due allowance must be made *ex ante* for all likely disturbing causes. Thus, the ruling out of disturbing causes is meant as nothing but a device to permit statement and development of a common theoretical skeleton which must be fleshed out whenever specific use is made of it.

J.K. WHITAKER

See also MARSHALL, ALFRED.

BIBLIOGRAPHY
Bailey, M.J. 1954. The Marshallian demand curve. *Journal of Political Economy* 62, June, 255–61.
Buchanan, J.M. 1958. Ceteris paribus: some notes on methodology. *Southern Economic Journal* 24, January, 259–70.
Cournot, A.A. 1838. *Mathematical Principles of the Theory of Wealth.* Trans., New York: Macmillan, 1897.
Fisher, F.M. and Ando, A.K. 1962. Two theorems on ceteris paribus in the analysis of dynamic systems. *American Political Science Review* 56, March, 108–13.
Friedman, M. 1949. The Marshallian demand curve. *Journal of Political Economy* 57, December, 463–95. Reprinted in M. Friedman, *Essays in Positive Economics*, Chicago: University of Chicago Press, 1953.
Keynes, J.N. 1891. *The Scope and Method of Political Economy.* London: Macmillan.
Marshall, A. 1890. *Principles of Economics*, Vol. 1. 8th edn, London: Macmillan, 1920.
Mill, J.S. 1844. *Essays on Some Unsettled Questions of Political Economy.* London: Parker.
Patinkin, D. 1965. *Money, Interest and Prices.* 2nd edn, New York: Harper & Row.
Viner, J. 1931. Cost curves and supply curves. *Zeitschrift für Nationalökonomie* 3, September, 23–46. Reprinted in American Economic Association, *Readings in Price Theory*, Homewood: Irwin, 1953.
Yeager, L.B. 1960. Methodenstreit over demand curves. *Journal of Political Economy* 68, February, 53–64.

Ceva, Giovanni (1647/48–1734). Mathematician, hydraulic engineer and mathematical economist, Ceva was born in Milan in 1647 or 1648 and died in Mantua in 1734. He studied at the University of Pisa; later he obtained a post at Gonzaga's court in Mantua, where he became the chief technician and applied his mathematical skill to technical and administrative problems.

As a mathematician he is known for the theorem (1678) concerning the concurrency of the transverse lines from the vertices of a triangle, which is named after him; his work on fluvial hydraulics is summed up in *Opus hydrostaticum* (1728). His studies in economics are contained in a work of 1711, where he studied monetary problems. Here we find a statement of the quantity theory of money: *ceteris paribus*, the value of money varies inversely with its quantity and directly with the number of people. The latter assertion may seem odd, but it is not if we interpret 'number of people' as a proxy for the transaction variable in the quantity theory equation (as is implicit in Ceva's Postulate II). We also find an independent statement of Gresham's Law and a study of the problems of a plurimetallic standard.

The interest of this work, however, does not lie in its economics, where no objectively new contributions are made, but in its methodological content and message. Ceva was the first to conceive, to state lucidly and to apply unhesitatingly the idea of *systematically* employing the mathematical method in economics as an indispensable tool with which to reason rigorously, to understand difficult and otherwise obscure phenomena and to put them in order. His analytico-deductive treatment, which proceeds by definitions, postulates, remarks, propositions, theorems and corollaries, is indeed the first example of mathematical economics as we now understand it.

GIANCARLO GANDOLFO

SELECTED WORKS

1678. *De lineis rectis se invicem secantibus statica constructio.* Mediolani. (A static construction concerning straight lines which intersect one another. Milan.)
1711. *De re numaria quoad fieri potuit geometrice tractata.* Mantuae. (On money, treated mathematically as far as has been possible. Mantua.) Reprinted, with editor's Preface by E. Masè-Dari, as *Un precursore della econometria. Il saggio di Giovanni Ceva 'De re numaria' edito in Mantova nel 1711,* Modena: Pubblicazioni della Facoltà di Giurisprudenza, 1935. French translation, with translators' Introduction and notes by G.-H. Bousquet and J. Roussier, in *Revue d'histoire économique et sociale,* 1958, No. 2, 129–69.
1728. *Opus hydrostaticum.* (A work on hydrostatics.) Mantua.

BIBLIOGRAPHY

Dictionary of Scientific Biography. 1971. New York: Scribner's Sons, Vol. 3, 181–3. (On Ceva's contribution to mathematics.)
Dizionario biografico degli italiani. 1980. Rome: Istituto dell'Enciclopedia Italiana, Vol. 24, 316–19. (On Ceva's life and works.)
Nicolini, F. 1878. Un antico economista matematico. *Giornale degli Economisti,* October 11–23. (On Ceva's contribution to mathematical economics; see also *De re numaria* [1711], Preface to 1935 reprint and Introduction to 1958 French translation.)

Chadwick, Edwin (1800–1890). Public administrator and social reformer, Sir Edwin Chadwick was born at Longsight, near Manchester, on 24 January 1800 and died at East Sheen, Surrey, on 6 July 1890. He was trained as a lawyer and qualified for the bar in 1830. His early radicalism led him into contact with the utilitarians and the reforming political economists who drew their inspiration from Ricardo. He acted as Bentham's secretary and assistant for the last two years of his life. He was also a friend of the economist Nassau Senior, and he and Senior were largely responsible for the Report which led to the complete restructuring of the Poor Law in 1834, along lines which the economists had been urging for years. For the next 20 years Chadwick was employed in a variety of public administrative positions, becoming best known for his *Report on the Sanitary Condition of the Labouring Population* (1842) which laid the foundations for modern urbanized sewerage and public health measures throughout the country, and even the world. But he was a difficult man to deal with and was eventually pensioned off by the government in 1854. He wrote a large number of pamphlets, as well as being responsible wholly or partly for many important government reports (Finer, 1952).

Chadwick's principal claim to fame lies in the way in which he applied his knowledge of, and passionate commitment to, utilitarian and economic analysis to many social problems of the first half of the 19th century, but only after a minute empirical investigation of the nature of the problems. Much of his work (such as the Poor Law Report) shows the influence of the orthodox economic analysis of the times, but in some respects Chadwick was years ahead of his time. In particular, there are signs of some grasp of the problem of externalities in connection with industrial accidents costs. Chadwick wanted to throw the costs of industrial accidents incurred in the construction of the railways onto the railway companies themselves. He was struck by the heavy social costs imposed by these accidents which were not borne by the railway companies, nor by the actual construction companies, and he argued that the solution to this problem was to internalize these costs to the railway companies themselves (Lewis, 1950). But it was fifty years before workers' compensation legislation was introduced in Britain, and over a hundred before some theoretical justification was offered in economic terms for this legislation.

P.S. ATIYAH

BIBLIOGRAPHY

Finer, S.E. 1952. *The Life and Times of Sir Edwin Chadwick.* London: Methuen.
Lewis, R.A. 1950. Edwin Chadwick and the railway labourers. *Economic History Review,* 2nd Series, 3(1), 107.

Chalmers, Thomas (1780–1847). Chalmers was born in Anstruther, Fife, and died in Edinburgh. Though he was strongly attracted to mathematics and physics in his youth, he is famous as a theologian and economist and as an active worker in the field of poor relief. Appointed to a parish in 1803, he later moved to Glasgow, where he began a famous and influential experiment in the administration of poor relief through dividing up the large parish of St John into small units and relying on a large number of voluntary helpers. He left Glasgow to become Professor of Moral Philosophy at St Andrews in 1823; in 1828 he became Professor of Divinity at Edinburgh and in 1843 he was centrally involved in the famous ecclesiastical divisions which produced the Free Church.

Endorsing Malthus's theory of population, he argued fervently (and repetitively) that the answer to the problem lay in moral education which would, in turn, lead to moral restraint. He opposed the poor law: it stimulated population, and interfered with private charity, which, his Glasgow experience had convinced him, was more effective. His work on aggregate demand and gluts – he argued that there could be both overproduction and oversaving since aggregate demand could be diminished not increased in proportion to both production and saving – is generally regarded as following the work of Malthus; but the essence of the argument, in terms of his aggregate demand and employment-creating analysis of trade, is present in his 1808 pamphlet, and thus precedes Malthus's own concern with aggregate demand.

D.P. O'BRIEN

SELECTED WORKS

1808. *An Inquiry into the Extent and Stability of National Resources.* Edinburgh: Oliphant & Brown.
1821–6. *The Christian and Civic Economy of Large Towns.* 3 vols, Glasgow: Chalmers & Collins, Collins.
1832. *On Political Economy, in connexion with the Moral State and Moral Prospects of Society.* Glasgow: Collins.

BIBLIOGRAPHY

Blaikie, W.G. 1887. Chalmers, Thomas. In *Dictionary of National Biography,* Oxford: Oxford University Press, 1973, Vol. 3.
Bonar, J. 1894. Chalmers, Thomas. In *Palgrave's Dictionary of Political Economy,* ed. H. Higgs, London: Macmillan, 1925.

Chamberlin, Edward Hastings (1899–1967). A major innovator in modern microeconomic theory, Chamberlin was born in

La Conner, Washington, on 18 May 1899, and died in Cambridge, Massachusetts, on 16 July 1967. He received his PhD from Harvard in 1927, became a full professor there in 1937, and occupied the David A. Wells chair from 1951 until his retirement in 1966. He edited the *Quarterly Journal of Economics* from 1948 to 1958.

Chamberlin's career exhibits a unity of professional purpose and thematic dedication over its more than forty-year length that is rare for modern theorists. Beginning with the start of his thesis research in 1925, its publication in 1933 as the seminal *Theory of Monopolistic Competition*, and continuing through eight editions, Chamberlin devoted his life to his vision of realistic market structures as mixtures of monopoly and competition.

He opposed the alternative polar frameworks of pure competition and monopoly of the 1920s as unrealistic; proselytized for his merger of them at the level of the firm in both broad and narrow contexts; strove tirelessly (and rather stridently) to distinguished his concepts from Joan Robinson's similar constructs; and manned the academic ramparts in full echelon against all who sought either to criticize the concepts or, alternatively, take credit for their genesis.

In so doing, Chamberlin's broad contributions to microeconomic analysis were of fundamental and insufficiently acknowledged importance. His 'large group case' and revival of interest in oligopoly theory created the notion of market structure as a continuum between pure competition and monopoly with location dictated by numbers of firms and product differentiation. With his work he fathered modern industrial organization analysis by giving a theoretical core to what was previously institutional and anecdotal. He reoriented the interest of microeconomics from the industry to the firm, revealing the latter's target variables to include selling cost and product variation as well as price. And his frameworks led economists to comprehend the importance of differentiated oligopoly in developed economies through his emphasis upon product differentiation, his formalization of monopoly power as control over price, and his perception of the core feature of oligopolistic market structure as perceived mutual interdependence of decision making.

MONOPOLISTIC COMPETITION THEORY. In its generic sense, which Chamberlin stressed increasingly in his later career, monopolistically competitive market structures are those in which the firm feels the external compulsions of competitive forces tempered in varying degrees by a monopolistic power to price its product. Central to monopolistic competition in this wider sense is *product differentiation*, or the ability of the firm to distinguish its product in the preferences of consumers, where product is defined to include a complex of qualities in addition to those inherent in the physical good (e.g. location, repair services, ambience etc.). The existence of differentiation (1) implies the possibility of *selling costs*, or costs aimed at adapting demand to the product (advertising, catalogues, discounts etc.) as distinguished from *production costs*, or expenditures that adapt the product to demand, and (2) *product variation*, or the variability of the complex of qualities and attributes that characterize the firm's output in the mind of the consumer.

In his original presentation of monopolistic competition and into the 1940s, Chamberlin tended to identify it more narrowly with a specific market structure that isolated product differentiation as its distinctive component. This was the *large-group case* with the 'tangency solution' as the firm's long-run equilibrium position, as shown in Figure 1. Each firm produces a slightly differentiated product which may be closely

approximated by competing firms. Hence, a large number of close substitutes ensure that the firm's demand curve is only slightly tilted from the pure competitor's horizontal position. If, for simplicity, all firms are assumed to have identical cost functions and to share sales equally (the *symmetry* assumption) then competition will reduce profit to zero by equating average cost and price at a tangency of the demand curve *dd'* and the average cost function *AC*. Where the tangency occurs marginal revenue *MR* will equal marginal cost *MC*. Hence, at price p° and sales x° each firm will be maximizing its profits at zero and neither entry into nor exit from the industry will occur: no internal or external force will exist to upset the long-run status quo.

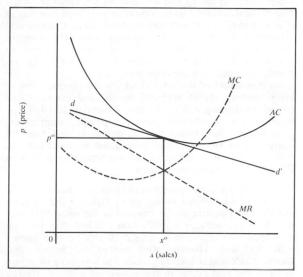

Figure 1   The firm's optimal solution in the large-group case.

Despite Chamberlin's later disclaimers, there is little doubt that the large group case was featured as the novel contribution of his theory, and it became identified with monopolistic competition theory. But from the beginning, Chamberlin did identify a second species in the generic theory: monopolistic competition caused by fewness of sellers of a homogeneous product. In the preface to the first edition of the *Theory* he includes oligopoly in the concept of monopolistic competition. Oligopoly – he coined the word independently but later recognized its prior usage in 1914 by Karl Schlesinger – in the pure (i.e. undifferentiated product) case formed the mirror image of the large-group case, with small rather than large numbers of sellers and undifferentiated rather than differentiated products. Surprisingly, given the centrality of product differentiation in his thought, he had little to say about differentiated oligopoly as a composite of the two purer cases of monopolistic competition – as late as 1948 the sixth edition of the *Theory* devoted only five pages to informal discussion of it – although he realized increasingly in his later work the prominent position it held in realistic market structures.

Chamberlin's contributions to the theory of pure oligopoly were noted above in listing his broader impacts on the field. More narrowly, they were not great advances. He ignored formal treatment of collusion and tended to urge that tacit collusion would lead to joint profit maximization for pure oligopoly and to a price solution intermediate between joint profit maximization and the large-group case for differentiated oligopoly. In his later, more informal, treatment of oligopoly, however, he asserted a general tendency toward 'live-and-let-live' limitations on oligopolistic rivalry.

But from the 1950s on, Chamberlin moved away from the large-group case as the featured form of monopolistic competition theory and shifted emphasis to oligopoly in its differentiated form. In part this was an aspect of his continuing desire to distance his theory from Joan Robinson's imperfect competition, in which she had independently developed the large-group case complete with tangency solution in the symmetry case. But more importantly, the evolution of his thought reflected his increasing awareness that few market structures contained the uniform product competition implied by that solution. Rather, closer investigation of most realistic market structures with large numbers of sellers of slightly differentiated products revealed hierarchical clusters of oligopolistically competing firms. His book of essays (Chamberlin, 1957) reveals clearly his attempt to prevent monopolistic competition theory from being too closely identified with the large-group case.

Another aspect of this later effort was the playing down of his pioneering use of marginal revenue and marginal cost curves. In denying P.W.S. Andrews's assertion that full cost pricing was antithetical to monopolistic competition, Chamberlin asserted that it was integral to that body of analysis from the beginning, since profit maximization was never an exclusive motivation of the firm – as it was in Robinson's imperfect competition.

OTHER MICROECONOMIC CONTRIBUTIONS. An implication of the large-group equilibrium illustrated in Figure 1 is that firms would have long-run *excess capacity* in the sense that they would be operating at a production rate less than the rate associated with minimum average cost. This led to a dispute with Sir Roy Harrod, who seemed to believe that Chamberlin's results occurred because he was using short-run demand and cost curves in the large-group analysis. Harrod argued that businessmen would follow their long-run revenue and cost prospects and that excess capacity would not result. Chamberlin properly pointed out that his functions were long-run functions and that the long-run demand in Harrod's case did not attain the horizontality needed to eliminate excess capacity (Harrod, 1952, Essays, 7,8; Chamberlin, 1957, pp. 280–95; Kuenne, 1967, pp. 67–70). Later, Chamberlin argued that excess capacity also occurred in an industry when entrants flooded in irrationally even when profits disappeared (whose counter-argument was probably what Harrod had in mind) (Chamberlin, 1957, p. 290).

Chamberlin devoted a large portion of his writing to rationalizing the U-shaped average cost curve that was so fundamental to his market structures. Building upon the notion of the long-run average cost curve as the envelope of short-run average cost curves with fixed plants, he distinguished between using a fixed plant curve optimally in the short-run at its minimum-cost rate and producing a given rate of output optimally in the long-run by building an over-sized plant and using it at less than minimum cost capacity. Also, he denied that the rising portion of the long-run average cost curve was caused solely by management complexity or lumpy factors at higher output rates. In so doing, Chamberlin challenged the assertions of Knight (1921, pp. 98–9), Lerner (1944, pp. 165–7, 174–5), Stigler (1952, pp. 133, 202n.), and Kaldor (1934, p. 65n; 1935, p.42) that if all factors could be reduced to finely divisible units with (explicitly or implicitly assumed) constant efficiency, the average total cost would be constant as all product would be produced with optimal factor

proportions. He argued that such factors would experience economies of scale as a function of factor-complex size owing to the ability to exploit specialization possibilities. These possibilities – \$100 in capital might be concretized in 10 shovels but \$10,000 in capital might materialize as one back-hoe – permitted resource aggregates to become qualitatively different complexes with increased scale, rendering the notion of factor units with unchanged efficiency meaningless. The argument turns upon the semantics of constant efficiency units and the usefulness of the assumption, however, and was seen by most theorists to be non-illuminating and, as Chamberlin emphasized, tautological.

Two other contributions by Chamberlin are worthy of brief note. One was his destruction of Joan Robinson's notion of worker 'exploitation', because in non-purely competitive industries workers received marginal revenue product rather than marginal value product. Chamberlin demonstrated conclusively that the difference between the two was not received by any other factor, including the entrepreneur, but was experienced as an external revenue constraint by the firm. The second, quite different, contribution was Chamberlin's role as a founder of modern experimental market research by his publication of the results of mock market operations with his students.

THE DEBATE WITH ROBINSON. Chamberlin, like most microeconomic theorists of his generation, was thoroughly Marshallian in vision and methodology, and his innovations integrated neatly into the concerns of the post-Marshallian school. It was somewhat ironic, therefore, that Chamberlin found his major (and reluctant) opponent in Joan Robinson, as thoroughly Marshallian as himself. Chamberlin spent much of his professional life urging the fundamental divisions between his theory of monopolistic competition and Robinson's theory of imperfect competition.

The basis of the distinction changed fundamentally over his career. In the earlier objections, Chamberlin perceived correctly that Robinson's aim was to implement Sraffa's suggestion that microeconomic theory be rewritten in terms of a general theory of monopoly (Robinson, 1933, p.v). In so doing, he urged, Robinson failed to achieve the true blending of monopoly and competition that his theory achieved. Robinson evolved the large-group case in every detail, but passed quickly over it in pressing on to her larger goal of creating a general theory of 'monopoly' in industries with more than one firm. To Chamberlin, who in this early period stressed the large-group case, her emphasis upon near-homogeneous commodities with some differentiation of sellers in the consumers' minds slighted the competition among differentiated products and resulted in an analysis of industry 'monopoly', very close to the one-firm monopoly of standard theory.

There was some truth in this, although Chamberlin was ungenerous to Robinson in interpreting her achievements, for in addition to her large-group case development she paralleled him in isolating selling costs and in defining two types of imperfect markets: (1) firms which were not alike in customers' preferences, and (2) oligopoly. But she saw the threat to the existence of the 'industry' that nonhomogeneous products posed, and her overall goal needed that solid Marshallian construct. Chamberlin from the beginning was willing to abandon the concept and speak of 'product groups'.

However, as the large-group case came under criticism as incorporating too much of the purely competitive and as oligopolistic structures received more attention in the literature, Chamberlin, as we have seen, shifted his ground and began to criticize Robinson for the opposite fault. The problem was, he now said, that imperfect competition failed to achieve the union of the competitive and the monopolistic because there was not enough monopoly content at the level of the firm. Implicitly, Robinson's large-group case was now focused upon for this fault, in comparison with his increasingly emphasized generic concepts that stressed oligopolistic elements.

The profession has ignored Chamberlin's strictures as distinctions without meaningful differences, and quite properly rewarded both theorists for their innovations. But the goals of the theorists were different, and, in most instances, Chamberlin's greater stress upon product differentiation and variation, selling cost and oligopoloy proved to be more seminal in their professional impact.

ROBERT E. KUENNE

See also FIRM, THEORIES OF THE; MONOPOLISTIC COMPETITION.

SELECTED WORKS

1933. *The Theory of Monopolistic Competition.* 6th edn, Cambridge, Mass.: Harvard University Press, 1948.
1954. (ed.) *Monopoly and Competition and Their Regulation.* London: Macmillan.
1957. *Towards a More General Theory of Value.* New York: Oxford University Press.

BIBLIOGRAPHY

Harrod, R.F. 1952. *Economic Essays.* London: Macmillan.
Kaldor, N. 1934. The equilibrium of the firm. *Economic Journal* 44, March, 60–76.
Kaldor, N. 1935. Market imperfection and excess capacity. *Economica* 2, February, 33–50.
Knight, F.H. 1921. *Risk, Uncertainty, and Profit.* Boston: Houghton Mifflin.
Kuenne, R.E. (ed.) 1967. *Monopolistic Competition Theory: Studies in Impact.* New York: Wiley.
Lerner, A.P. 1944. *The Economics of Control.* New York: Macmillan.
Robinson, J. 1933. *The Economics of Imperfect Competition.* London: Macmillan.
Stigler, G.J. 1952. *The Theory of Price.* New York: Macmillan.

Champernowne, David Gawen (born 1912). It was fortunate for the economics profession that the schoolboy Champernowne, a keen and able mathematician, was advised to read something in the school library to broaden his horizons: he chose Marshall's *Principles*.

David Champernowne was born on 9 July 1912 into an Oxford academic family. He was sent to school at Winchester and went from there as a scholar to King's College, Cambridge. Whilst still an undergraduate he published his first paper (on 'normal numbers'). Early contact with Dennis Robertson confirmed his previous interest in economics, and he was advised by J.M. Keynes to abandon his thoughts of becoming an actuary and switch to the Economics Tripos by taking his Part II Mathematics in one year rather the normal two. He obtained firsts throughout in both subjects.

His academic career spanned the London School of Economics (1936–8) Oxford (1945–59), and Cambridge (1938–40 and 1959–78). During the war period he served with Lindemann as Assistant in the Prime Minister's Statistical Section (1940–41) and worked with Jewkes at the Ministry of Aircraft Production's Department of Statistics and Programming.

He proved to be a genuine pioneer both in economic theory and statistics. His King's fellowship dissertation (submitted in 1936, but published thirty-seven years later) laid the foundations for the application of stochastic process models to the analysis of income distributions. His prewar interest in Frank Ramsey's theory of probability led on to work at Oxford on the application of Bayesian analysis to autoregressive series (at a time when the Bayesian approach was decidedly unfashionable), and culminated in his major trilogy on *Uncertainty and Estimation*. However although he is thought of today primarily as a theoretician, his flashes of technical insight have always been tempered with healthy doses of practical scepticism. This is evident in his early work with Beveridge on the regional and industrial distribution of employment and unemployment.

Champernowne has acted as midwife to a number of major theoretical contributions over and above his own work. He provided an invaluable 'translation' to von Neumann's seminal paper on multisector growth. His role as behind-the-scenes expert at Cambridge over many theoretical issues is legendary: Joan Robinson acknowledged the assistance of his 'heavy artillery' in underpinning, and extending, her major work on capital and growth: A.C. Pigou's later writings on output and employment, Nicholas Kaldor's work on savings and economic growth models, and Dennis Robertson's *Principles* were all indebted to his intellectual influence.

He has held Chairs at both Oxford and Cambridge, was director of the Oxford Institute of Statistics and has been editor of the *Economic Journal*. He was elected Fellow of the British Association in 1970.

F.A. COWELL

SELECTED WORKS

1935. A mathematical note on substitution. *Economic Journal* 15, 246–58.
1936. Unemployment, basic and monetary: the classical analysis and the Keynesian. *Review of Economic Studies* 3, 201–216.
1938. The uneven distribution of unemployment in the United Kingdom. 1929–36, I. *Review of Economic Studies* 5, February, 93–106.
1939. The uneven distribution of unemployment in the United Kingdom. 1929–36, II. *Review of Economic Studies* 6, February, 111–24.
1945. A note on J.von Neumann's article on 'A model of general economic equilibrium'. *Review of Economic Studies* 13, 10–18.
1948. Sampling theory applied to autoregressive sequences. *Journal of the Royal Statistical Society, Series*B, 204–42.
1952. The graduation of income distributions. *Econometrica* 20, 591–615.
1953. A model of income distribution. *Economic Journal* 63, 318–51.
1954. The production function and the theory of capital: a comment. *Review of Economic Studies* 21(2), 112–35.
1958. Capital accumulation and the maintenance of full employment. *Economic Journal* 68, June, 211–44.
1969. *Uncertainty and Estimation in Economics.* 3 vols, Edinburgh: Oliver and Boyd.
1971. The stability of Kaldor's 1957 model. *Review of Economic Studies* 38, 47–62.
1973. *The Distribution of Income Between Persons.* Cambridge: Cambridge University Press.
1974. A comparison of measures of income distribution. *Economic Journal* 84, 787–816.

chance. *See* PROBABILITY; RANDOM VARIABLES.

changes in tastes. It is often analytically convenient to abstract from the phenomenon of changing tastes in explaining or evaluating economic phenomena. Alfred Marshall for example defended the assumption of given wants as a useful, if crude, starting point in developing utility theory.

Since the 1930s, however, the assumption of given wants has hardened increasingly into dogma. A notable step in that direction was taken in 1932, when Lionel Robbins gave wide currency to the definition of economics as the study of the relations between ends and means, the ends taken as given (Robbins, 1932, ch. 2).

Nobody, of course, supposes that tastes for goods and services are literally biological givens. (Stigler and Becker (1977) do deploy this claim, perhaps for its shock value, but it is natural to read them as saying that certain deep-lying wants, as for nourishment and self-esteem, are given and these deep-lying preferences interact with prices and incomes to explain changes in tastes for particular goods and services.)

The more common view is that it is efficient to divide the intellectual labour between economists who study the consequences of given tastes and sociologists, psychologists and others who explain formation of and changes in tastes. Yet on the whole, economists (with a few notable exceptions like Scitovsky (1976)) have shown little interest in what psychologists and others have had to say about preference formation and change. At a minimum, there would seem to be a need for interdisciplinary collaboration on problems, such as long run economic development or cross-national comparisons in consumption patterns, where both causes and consequences of tastes are likely to be important (see, e.g. Felix, 1979). If the causes of the taste changes are non-economic, the economists on such teams might usefully concentrate on analysing their consequences.

Sometimes, however, the division of labour will not be so neat. First, tastes may change because of changes in economic variables, making tastes *endogenous* to the economic system. The alleged influence of advertising on tastes is a standard example; another is the claim that the extension of market production into traditional societies affects tastes for material consumption relative to communal 'leisure' activities (Galbraith, 1958; Hefner, 1983). When such interactions are empirically important, adequate economic models need to include them.

Second, when a consumer's tastes differ at different points in time, problems of temporal inconsistency in preferences and of intrapersonal preference conflict arise. A consumer who expects to have different preferences in the future faces a planning problem between his present and future self somewhat analogous to that involved in allocating resources between two consumers with different tastes. The challenge of extending the theory of rational intertemporal choice to cover such cases – with the consumer making plans he or she will actually carry out and will not regret – is considerable (Hammond, 1976). Further problems arise when preferences change rhythmically or recurrently (Winston, 1980). A consumer who is periodically assailed by an impulse to spend or to overeat may take steps in advance to control the consequences of those impulses, burning credit cards or locking the refrigerator. Thomas Schelling has given the label *egonomics* to the study of such strategic attempts to reconcile intrapersonal preference conflicts (Schelling, 1978, 1980; Elster, 1979, 1985).

The taste changes discussed so far may simply 'happen' to consumers, without their active participation or indeed sometimes without their knowledge. A further degree of complexity is introduced when it is recognized that consumers may have preferences regarding what their tastes should be. A consumer may, for example, prefer that she lose the taste for smoking, say, or acquire a taste for jogging. An adequate economic theory of consumer choice should include such second-order preferences or *meta-preferences* (Frankfurt, 1971;

Sen, 1977). Such an extension is necessary, most simply, in order to explain the non-trivial expenditures that consumers in advanced societies make on deliberately changing their own tastes – for example, through music-appreciation classes, weight-control clinics, and SmokEnders. More broadly, tension between consumers' everyday expenditure patterns and their larger views about how they should live – what one might call their *values* rather than mere preferences (Hirschman, 1985) – plays a role in explaining various features of human experience, including ambivalence, ideological commitment and the capacity for self-discipline and self-criticism. These features of behaviour will not always matter for economics, but sometimes they will. Savings behaviour and workplace relations (where willingness to identify with the organization's goals is an important variable) are obvious applications; Albert Hirschman (1982) has argued that the explanation of fluctuations in the 'taste' for political involvement relies heavily on the formation and revision of ideological metapreferences towards politics.

The fact that preferences can change raises issues for the normative as well as the explanatory dimensions of economics. One set of questions involves the role social policy should play in resolving questions of intrapersonal conflict among preferences. Society can provide support for self-control devices, for example by allowing people to enter contracts that bind their future behaviour (such as agreeing to be confined to an alcohol treatment facility). This would then involve overruling the person's future demands to be released. It is difficult to know from what standpoint to judge the effects of a decision either way on the person's welfare or liberty (Schelling, 1984). Social policy can also undermine self-control, as state-run lotteries show.

Severe difficulties also arise if economic institutions or policies can change preferences. To evaluate such policies or institutions in terms of either the preferences *ex ante* or *ex post* (unless the two happen to agree) seems arbitrary. But to decide which set of preferences is itself 'objectively' better seems to most contemporary economists just as arbitrary, as well as threatening to liberty. (Many earlier economists, including notably Marshall and J.S. Mill, were much more willing to make and defend value judgements about desirable preferences). An appeal to meta-preferences may help – basing judgment on what preferences people themselves prefer. But of course meta-preferences may themselves depend on economic institutions and policies, so this solution doesn't go very deep.

From a normative standpoint, both kinds of problems – those of preference conflict and of endogenous preferences – suggest the need to move away from the strictly 'want-regarding' moral systems that underlie most neoclassical welfare economics. Such moral systems, labelled 'welfarist' by A.K. Sen (1979), exclude as morally irrelevant all information about a society except the degree to which individuals' preferences are satisfied. Other information enters the analysis only insofar as it affects the amount of preference satisfaction achieved. (Utilitarianism and Paretian welfare economics are the most important examples of welfarist moral systems.)

Relaxing the welfarist constraint admits several kinds of information that may help with 'preference change' problems. First, procedural issues about how preferences are formed may be recognized as morally important. Processes of preference formation or change that rely on misrepresentation or distortion of facts, or on emotional manipulation, may be morally downgraded irrespective of any judgement about the worth of the preferences that result (McPherson, 1982, 1983). Second, measures of individual well-being may be constructed that depend on the *resources* available to an individual or on the *capabilities* he or she can exercise, rather than (only) on the amount of preference satisfaction attained (Sen, 1982; Rawls, 1982). This may partly free evaluations of states of affairs from dependence on existing preferences. Finally, a society can use its public deliberative processes to come to agreement on the objective value of promoting (say, through education) certain preferences or common values (Scanlon, 1975). Such agreement need not presuppose that those same preferences would be valuable in other societies or times, and procedural protections could be applied to the means by which these values are promoted.

All the problems discussed in this essay – the dependence of preferences on institutions and policies, the presence of conflicting desires within the person, and the human capacity to evaluate one's own preferences – were well known to Plato and Aristotle, and were recognized by them as central issues for social theory. That the problems have remained central and largely unresolved for twenty-five hundred years no doubt makes some economists think it wise to define them out of the discipline, at whatever cost in realism and relevance. Others, however, welcome the resurgence of interest in problems of changing tastes as an opportunity to re-establish links with the other social sciences and with political philosophy.

M.S. McPHERSON

See also ADVERTISING; PREFERENCES; WANTS.

BIBLIOGRAPHY

Elster, J. 1979. *Ulysses and the Sirens: Studies in Rationality and Irrationality.* Cambridge: Cambridge University Press.

Elster, J. 1985. Weakness of will and the free-rider problem. *Economics and Philosophy* 1(2), Fall, 231–66.

Felix, D. 1979. De gustibus disputandum est: changing consumer preferences in economic growth. *Explorations in Economic History* 16, 260–96.

Frankfurt, H. 1971. Freedom of the will and the concept of a person. *Journal of Philosophy* 68, 14 January, 5–20.

Galbraith, J.K. 1958. *The Affluent Society.* Boston: Houghton-Mifflin.

Hammond, P. 1976. Changing tastes and coherent dynamic choice. *Review of Economic Studies* 43, February, 159–73.

Hefner, R.W. 1983. The problem of preference: economics and ritual change in Highland Java. *Man* 17, November–September, 323–41.

Hirschman, A.O. 1982. *Shifting Involvements: Private Interest and Public Action.* Princeton: Princeton University Press.

Hirschman, A.O. 1985. Against parsimony: three easy ways of complicating economic discourse. *Economics and Philosophy* 1, April, 7–21.

McPherson, M.S. 1982. Mill's moral theory and the problem of preference change. *Ethics* 92, January, 252–73.

McPherson, M.S. 1983. Want formation, morality, and some 'interpretive' aspects of economic inquiry. In M.S. McPherson, *Social Science as Moral Inquiry,* New York: Columbia University Press.

Rawls, 1982. Social unity and primary goods. In *Utilitarianism and Beyond,* ed. A. Sen and B. Williams, Cambridge: Cambridge University Press, pp. 159–86.

Robbins, L. 1932. *An Essay on The Nature and Significance of Economic Science.* London: Macmillan; New York: St. Martin's Press, 1969.

Scanlon, T.M. 1975. Preference and urgency. *Journal of Philosophy* 72, 655–69.

Schelling, T.C. 1978. Egonomics, or the art of self-management. *American Economic Review* 68, May, 290–94.

Schelling, T.C. 1980. The intimate contest for self-command. *The Public Interest* 60, Summer, 94–118.

Schelling, T.C. 1984. Ethics, law and the exercise of self-command. In T.C. Schelling, *Choice and Consequence,* Cambridge: Harvard University Press.

Scitovsky, T. 1976. *The Joyless Economy.* New York: Oxford University Press.

Sen, A.K. 1977. Rational fools: a critique of the behavioral foundations of economic theory. *Philosophy and Public Affairs* 6, Summer, 317–44.

Sen, A.K. 1979. Utilitarianism and welfarism. *Journal of Philosophy* 76, 463–89.

Sen, A.K. 1982. On weights and measures: informational constraints in social welfare analysis. In A.K. Sen , *Choice, Welfare, and Measurement,* Cambridge, Mass.: MIT Press, 226–63.

Stigler, G.J. and Becker, G.S. 1977. De gustibus non est disputandum. *American Economic Review* 67, March, 76–90.

Winston, G. 1980. Addiction and backsliding: a theory of compulsive consumption. *Journal of Economic Behavior and Organization* 1(4), 295–324.

characteristics. If Eve had not insisted that 'an apple is an apple is an apple', Adam would probably have brought down the wrath of Jehovah himself by characterizing things, unsurprisingly, by their characteristics, thus bringing man-made order into chaos. There remains the problem: what characteristics? Here a little mathematics is useful. Suppose goods Y are sold only in bundles X, and that there are a_{ij} units of Y_j in X_i. The total quantity of it will be

$$y_j = \sum_i a_{ij} x_i, \tag{1}$$

and the total value of a bundle X_i

$$p_i = \sum_j a_{ij} q_j, \tag{2}$$

in an obvious notation, so that expenditure

$$\sum_i p_i x_i = \sum_{ij} a_{ij} q_i x_i = \sum_j q_j y_j, \tag{3}$$

for all q, x, and expenditure, m, is invariant, a fact brought to the attention of young economists at large by Samuelson when he published his *Foundations* just after the war. That immediately suggested that we might instead consider the X as goods, thought of as bundles of characteristics Y. Were we to try $y_j = f^j(x)$, $p_i = g^i(q)$ instead of (1)–(2), the notion that total expenditure should be invariant would yield $m = \sum g^i(q)x_i \equiv \sum q_j f^j(x)$, so that $\partial^2 m/\partial x_i \partial q_j = f^j_i(x) = g^i_j(q) = a_{ij}$, say, the subscripts denoting differentiation, and hence back to the linear characteristics model (1)–(2), which had already been used extensively, if implicitly, by Rowntree when studying working-class budgets in York before and after World War I, by Miss Schulz in her monthly 'human needs' budgets during World War II, by numerous nutritionists, and finally by Stigler, in a paper cited in Koopmans' Cowles Commission monograph on activity analysis in 1951 as a precursor of linear programming, a topic very fashionable among young economists at the time.

Why did demand analysts not immediately take up a model which was at once so obvious, so often used, and so in keeping with the spirit of the early Fifties? They realized, of course, that people do not eat what is good for them, so that $a_i = (a_{ij})$ each j would have to be estimated, not taken from manuals of nutrition. Hotelling's Method of Principal Components, which had been introduced to econometricians at large by Stone in 1947, immediately suggested itself as a way of estimating them, or more precisely and relevantly, the space they span. The real problem was that the model, to be useful, would have to work with many fewer characteristics than goods to be characterized; that this seemed certain, *in practice*, to yield infinite price elasticities; and that at a time when econometric research was consistently turning up what then seemed dramatically low ones.

To see why, return to (2). What are these mysterious q's? Nobody buys and sells raw characteristics. In fact the q's are the values which particular households put on the characteristics, and there is no reason why they should be the same for households with notably different tastes or incomes. What happens when there are two characteristics is illustrated in Figure 1. $P_1, \ldots, P_9$ display the amounts of them available for a dollar spent on $X_1, \ldots, X_9$. One hundred times as much would be available for \$100, so that we can rescale the diagram to match the amounts particular households decide to spend on these goods as a group. Clearly nobody would buy X_2, X_5 or X_6 at these prices, so that p_5 will presumably fall to $p_5' = (0P_5/0P_5')p_5$, for instance, at which price X_5 would be at least potentially competitive. Now consider a household whose indifference curve, appropriately scaled, is II. Its chosen bundle, y, of characteristics can be bought equally cheaply in many different ways, so that x_3, x_4, x_5, x_6 and x_7 are indeterminate. In particular it may or may not buy X_5. Should p_5 fall any further, however, it would buy a definite amount $x_5' > 0$, say, of it, while X_4 and X_6 would become uncompetitive from everybody's point of view. Hence the infinite elasticities, as we pass through *equilibrium points*.

Suppose Y_2 is a luxury. Then sufficiently rich households, like that represented by JJ, may value it sufficiently highly to *buy* X_1 and X_2, in the technical sense that it would actually buy either if its price were to fall at all. If there are too few of them to make these goods viable, their prices will have to fall for them to stay in production possibly until P_1'', P_2'' lie on P_7–P_3 extended, but possibly not. Equally, poor households may buy X_8 and X_9.

People who have never heard of a linear characteristics model often talk of the mass market, X_3–X_7, an up-market sector, X_1–X_3; and a down-market one, X_7–X_9. Even the idea of goods at the top and bottom end of the mass market, like X_3 and X_7, is quite common. That is mildly reassuring. They tend to speak of specialist markets, too, such as that for sports cars; these can easily be handled when there are more than two characteristics.

If we know the goods which fall into any one of these sectors we can fit a stochastic version of (2) to them using, for instance, some variant of principal components analysis, given enough data. The key phrase here is 'given enough data'. Demand analysts have to deal with short inter- and autocorrelated series, subject to error, generated by the interactions between many agents, and have to be sure that the goods in question remain in the same sector throughout the period under analysis, or over the regions, for example. In practice, therefore, there have to be far fewer characteristics than goods in each sector they examine, and they commonly deal with goods bought by virtually everyone.

It is, we think, fairly generally accepted that such models are most appropriate for groups of closely related goods, to which the obvious alternative, additive separability, seems particularly badly adapted, though it has often been used by theorists interested in monopolistic competition. This is because they seem likely to differ in several ways, or, if you like, interact through several channels, which is impossible under additive separability; while the fact that they are often somewhat similar to each other suggests that linear approximations such as (1)–(2) may work quite well. It is consistent with the evidence from market research that households buying breakfast cereals, for instance, commonly buy many types in quite a short period, and has been borne out by studies in the demand for related foods – although these are perhaps particularly favourable cases since we can imagine each mouthful being churned up in the stomach, the relevant components being extracted and possibly processed further to yield the characteristics in question. Labour economists quite soon began to make valiant efforts to estimate the characteristics of individual workers, or groups of workers, and to fit them to those of the functions they perform, though segmentation of the market seems more likely here, while the existence of specialization suggests that two workers with the endowment (y_1^*, y_2^*) appropriate to the job in hand may be more productive than one with $(y_1^* + \delta, y_2^* - \epsilon)$ and another with $(y_1^* - \delta, y_2^* + \epsilon)$.

There remains the problem of infinite elasticities.

There are two obvious routes around it: to drop linearity and hence the strong invariance property (4), or to recognize that we are oversimplifying, so that the characteristics in question do not represent the goods perfectly. In the latter case, the natural requirement would be that the characteristics catch what these goods have in common, allowing each to have a specific value of its own, in addition, largely to be explained by the amount of it consumed. This model has been tried out with some limited success: for instance it would require at least six common characteristics Y to fit data on sources of meat protein taken from the British National Food Survey (NFS), as one plus the specific just mentioned, and either does much better than the specific alone, which is rather like an old-fashioned demand equation; the estimates were reasonably consistent in different regions; while the own price elasticities, the shadow prices of the characteristics being held constant, almost always lay between 0 and -2. Stephen Pudney estimated it by more sophisticated methods in 1980 and submitted it to formal statistical tests. It failed the tests, but did better than the alternatives he had considered – *in the particularly favourable case of food*.

If one drops linearity, the same statistical methods can be

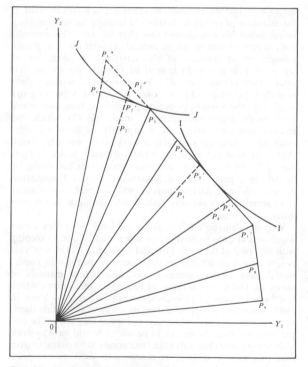

Figure 1

used to estimate models with

$$y_j^\epsilon = \sum_i a_{ij} x_i^\epsilon, \quad \text{each } j, \tag{4}$$

for instance. When $\epsilon < 1$ these are strictly concave, so that we can no longer match any particular good perfectly by baskets of others. In this case, each unit of X_i contributes towards each Y_j for which $a_{ij} \neq 0$. An alternative model

$$y_j^\epsilon = \sum_i a_{ij} x_{ij}^\epsilon, \quad \sum_j x_{ij} = x_i, \tag{5}$$

implies that some electricity, for instance, is used for cooking, some for lighting, some for heating, etc. Since the consumer has to get the same value at the margin in each use, these are best characterized in the dual. In that case, they become a special, additive, example of the composite commodities described in the entry SEPARABILITY, which were not included among the alternatives examined by Pudney. As it happens, much modern demand analysis runs in terms of composites like (5), though these are commonly interpreted as modes of behaviour appropriate to *households with particular characteristics* – of which income is the most important – rather than as *characteristics of goods*. The ϵ, too, are usually taken to vary from one composite commodity Y_j to another in such analyses, because poor families are commonly thought to have less flexibility in their budgets. As against this, they cannot deal with utility functions which are general in terms of the components in question, while the linear characteristics model can and does.

In practice characteristics models have commonly been applied to survey data. In the case of the NFS, for instance, each household keeps detailed records for a week. Even if this had no effect on their behaviour, they clearly buy quite different goods in different weeks quite independently of any variations in prices, and the like. The smallest units to which research workers had access contained about one hundred households: even at this level of aggregation, variability between households buying fresh beef and veal, for instance, commonly contributed less to the variance in their consumption per household than did the decision to buy it, rather than fresh mutton and lamb, and so on. This would not matter were it not for the fact that different foods may commonly be bought together: pork and apples, for instance, or strawberries and cream. Principal components analysis is based on the covariances; those between 'temporary' components may therefore contaminate the estimates of the 'permanent' characteristics, which commonly interest us most, though this should be mitigated by the use of instrumental variables as in Pudney's later work.

An alternative route would be to model the decision to buy explicitly on its own. Here the most obvious analogue is that of modal choice in transport economics, though that is considerably simplified by the fact that just one mode is chosen on any single occasion, while many different and overlapping collections of goods might be. Here the leading work was done by McFadden in 1974, building on foundations laid by Quandt and the psychologist Luce, employing an additively separable stochastic utility function to obtain choice probabilities based on the characteristics of each mode. In a manner similar to hedonic analysis these characteristics and their values for each model are assumed known, both to the consumer and to the econometrician, in contrast to the models discussed above whose aim was to identify the relevant components.

The early applications of the theory estimated, on the grounds of computational ease, multinomial logit models but this specification suffers from the 'Independence of Irrelevant Alternatives', introducing a new transport mode changes the probabilities of choosing existing modes so as to keep their ratios constant. However, alternatives are now available: Hausman and Wise discuss and estimate a conditional probit model and McFadden has introduced generalized extreme value models. At this stage, application has not yet caught up with theory.

Domenich and McFadden visualized utility being separable into seven components, one encompassing non-travel decisions and the other six travel-related decisions. These six would be made sequentially, first residential location, then vehicle ownership, trip no-trip, destination, times of day and finally mode of travel, each based on optimal decisions at lower stages. Furthermore, each choice would be made on the basis of the characteristics of the alternatives.

Despite this rich framework, studies reported in the economic journals have concentrated on either a single level or, at most, two levels of this process taking other decisions as given. This is no doubt due to the formidable data requirement of a broader analysis, detailed disaggregated data are required both on those who choose a particular mode and those who do not.

Given these difficulties, the studies that have been completed should be considered illustrative of possibilities rather than definitive. The results obtained are certainly promising, with a typical model predicting in excess of 85 per cent of actual choice correctly. However, there is as yet no basis for evaluating the forecasting ability of the model. Winston has recently used this approach to forecast the demand for a newly established West Coast shipping line but does not provide data on the actual impact; he notes, however, that the response of incumbents to the additional competitor may invalidate his forecast.

The other main use of characteristics in empirical work is in the hedonic analysis of the prices paid for goods like houses, of which families commonly own one, so that linearity and additivity are beside the point, while the characteristics at risk are normally taken to be known. The obvious tool here is the compensating variation – that is the money $h(p, y, u) = g(p, y, u) - g(p, \bar{y}, u)$, say, required to compensate a family for living in a house with characteristics y rather than a standard house $\bar{y}$, in the obvious definition, on the demand side, and the extra cost $k(p, y) = \phi(p, \bar{y}) - \phi(p, y)$, say, of providing y rather than $\bar{y}$, on the supply. Clearly the distribution of household characteristics is important in any equilibrium analysis, as is the structure we put on these functions. The temptation to assume separability, $h(p, y, u) = H(p, \psi(y), u)$, should probably be rejected.

How much more people are willing to pay to live in one environment rather than another is obviously important evidence in the planning of land use: how much more for a better gearbox, for directing research. Yet hedonic analysis has not provided much hard evidence so far, for lack of a secure theoretical foundation until Sherwin Rosen entered the field in the Seventies; because the potential characteristics tend to be numerous, and highly intercorrelated, while principal component analysis has often been inappropriately used; and finally because, in comparing different results, people have tended to forget what was held constant when the characteristic which interested them was varied to determine its shadow price.

A great deal of theoretical work, both in industrial and fiscal economics, has run in terms of the characteristics of the goods produced or potentially produced. Such studies are at once highly important, and difficult. Lacking hard information about the differences between goods, protagonists have tended to go for analytical convenience, or comparability with earlier work. In particular, the analogy with geographical position is often used, as has symmetry in the analysis of monopolistic competition, though there seems to be no obvious justification for them other than custom and convenience, not that either is to be despised. The results have been illustrative, therefore, of what might happen, rather than statements of what would, and in what circumstances.

There are two bridges between the empirical and theoretical schools.

Houthakker (1952) is itself purely theoretical, but clearly springs from the need to make sense of the budget data which he and Prais had been studying. He distinguishes n goods, each available in a range of qualities $v_i^- \leqslant v_i \leqslant v_i^+$, for instance at prices $p_i = a_i + b_i v_i$, where a_i and b_i are parametrically variable. He shows that a reduction in the price b_i of 'quality' accompanied by an increase in the base price a_i which leaves a family just as well off as before, leads to it buying less of i, but of a higher quality, for instance, and envisages future applications in industrial economics, in which v_i might be a vector.

Building on earlier work with Cowling, Cubbin (1975) looked at the car market in Britain in the Sixties, combining a well-chosen characteristics model, with explicit consideration about pricing, changes in quality, and advertising; concluding from the profit margins that the industry acted oligopolistically, effective monopoly being ruled out by competition in quality.

Return to Adam. Had he known how long the first five days had lasted in the other foundation myth, and that the species around him had evolved slowly, prospering when they fitted appropriate niches, dying when they did not, he would probably have used a dynamic model, in which the characteristic space itself expanded, as new species defined new niches and new possibilities as Nalebuff and Caplin have recently argued. The economies of scale, and the political power associated with them, probably make a direct analogy with economic production inappropriate; but something like it seems to be needed when technology is changing as fast as now.

One last point. We have talked throughout as if everybody was hungry for all the characteristics. That is by no means necessarily the case. Some may be universally hated, some positively liked by some, disliked by others, though that would lead to a segmented market in the linear case.

W.M. GORMAN and G.D. MYLES

See also DEMAND THEORY; GOODS AND COMMODITIES; HEDONIC FUNCTIONS AND HEDONIC INDICES; SEPARABILITY.

A FEW REFERENCES:

Caplin, P. and Nalebuff, B. 1986. Multidimensional product differentiation and price competition. *Oxford Economic Papers* 38, November.

Cubbin, J. 1975. Quality change and pricing behaviour in the United Kingdom car industry 1956–68. *Economica* 42, 43–58.

Domencich, T.A. and McFadden, D. 1975. *Urban Travel Demand.* Amsterdam: North Holland.

Gorman, W.M. 1956. A possible procedure for analysing quality differentials in the egg market. Journal paper No. 3129, Iowa Agricultural Experiment Station, and *Review of Economic Studies* (1980) 47, 843–56.

Hausman, J. and Wise, D. 1978. A conditional probit model for qualitative choice: discrete decisions recognising interdependence and heterogeneous preferences. *Econometrica* 46, 403–26.

Hotelling, H. 1933. Analysis of a complex of statistical variables into principal components. *Journal of Educational Psychology* 24, 417–44 and 498–520.

Houthakker, H.S. 1952. Compensated changes in quantities and qualities consumed. *Review of Economic Studies* 19, 154–84.

Ironmonger, D.S. 1972. *New Commodities and Consumer Behaviour.* Cambridge: Cambridge University Press.

Koopmans, T.C. (ed.) 1951. *Activity Analysis of Production and Allocation.* New York: John Wiley & Son.

Lancaster, K.J. 1966. A new approach to consumer theory. *Journal of Political Economy* 74, 132–57.

Luce, R.D. 1959. *Individual Choice Behaviour.* New York: John Wiley & Sons.

McFadden, D. 1981. Econometric models of probabilistic choice. In *Structural Analysis of Discrete Data with Econometric Applications,* ed. C.F. Manski and D. McFadden, Cambridge, Mass.: MIT Press.

Quandt, R. 1956. Probabilistic theory of consumer behaviour. *Quarterly Journal of Economics* 70, 507–36.

Rowntree, P.S. 1918. *The Human Needs of Labour.* London: Thomas Nelson & Sons.

Samuelson, P.A. 1947. *Foundations of Economic Analysis.* Cambridge, Mass.: Harvard University Press.

Schultz, T. 1943–59. *Bulletin of the Oxford University Institute of Statistics,* various issues.

Stigler, G.J. 1945. The cost of subsistence. *Journal of Farm Economics* 27, 303–314.

Stone, J.R.N. 1947. On the interdependence of blocks of transactions. *Journal of the Royal Statistical Society* (Supplement), 1–45.

Winston, C. 1981. A multinational probit prediction of the demand for domestic ocean container services. *Journal of Transport Economics and Policy* 15, 23–42.

charity. *See* ALTRUISM; GIFTS.

chartism. The chartist movement was in its origin and its aim economic. It arose out of the economic necessities of the time, and its leaders had before them, as their ultimate object, social and industrial amelioration. To understand fully this aspect of chartism we must study the movement in its two phases: (1) from 1836 to 1839; (2) from 1840 to 1848.

(1) 1836 TO 1839. Three circumstances may be regarded as bringing about the chartist movement: the commercial and industrial distress immediately preceding it in time; the introduction of machinery with its effects; and the new poor law of 1834. Various men were of course variously affected by these causes; but their common action was secured by the predominant influence of one man, and the action of another, supported as he was by his colleagues. The influence referred to was that of Robert Owen, who had preached the gospel of optimism and social regeneration when all around seemed overshadowed with a gloomy present and a threatening future, and, further, urged on his followers and all with whom he came in contact, the need of education and moral elevation. It was, however, the action of Lord John Russell that brought into united action bodies so diverse in aim and constitution as the working men's association of London, the Birmingham political union, and the unions of the north, these latter being under the guidance of Feargus O'Connor. Briefly described, the first was educational and moderate, the second unstable, partly desirous of bringing about the adoption of Mr Attwood's currency scheme, and partly anxious for general industrial amelioration, while the latter formed centres for violent denunciation of the rise of machinery, and of the application of the new poor laws. All, however, hoped to attain their ends by bringing pressure to bear on parliament, itself to be rendered more amenable by a further extension of the franchise; and hence Lord John Russell's declaration against all further reform united them together and led to the formation of the national convention. The task to which this body devoted itself was mainly political, and to attain its object recourse was had first to menaces and then to open revolt. The former were disregarded and the latter was suppressed. Meantime, however, in the northern unions an almost socialistic attitude had been taken by some of the

leaders. Throughout the entire movement, indeed, there had been symptoms that many were thinking of and aiming at an entire social reconstruction.

(2) 1840 TO 1848. The second phase of chartism differed essentially from the first. It was of smaller account in every way but one. Its strength was less, its adherents fewer, its organization less stable; but the views of its leaders were much more advanced. In theory, Bronterre O'Brien stood far ahead of any other. He was socialistic in his aims, but, unlike some of his associates, he did not confuse socialism and industrial retrogression. His schemes were, it is true, somewhat immature, but he may be described as feeling about for a new social organization. Feargus O'Connor, on the other hand, was neither so consistent nor so advanced in his aims. Thus at one time he was advocating the claims of the 'National Charter Association', for so the organization of the chartists was called, while at another, in defiance of the advice of his associates, he advocated a new scheme for bringing the people into connection with the land. In opposing the Anti-Corn Law League, it should be noticed, however, that he based his antagonism on the need which he alleged to exist of general social reconstruction (see especially speech, 5 August 1844). But the direct effect of the agitation at this period was small. Discussions among the leaders and mutual accusations 'of interested motives' diminished their following, and it was to little or no purpose that O'Connor sought to win them back by his apparent advocacy of their interests in a periodical called *Labour*, or by his national land scheme. The latter, as a matter of fact, was financially unsound. The movement failed. That the leaders were really in earnest in their agitation is probable from the circumstances which have been alluded to, as also from their decided refusal to form any alliance with the middle class, or capitalist, reformers of Birmingham.

In its two phases, then, chartism was of economic importance. During the earlier period it aimed at economic regeneration; during the second, it not only aimed at this, but assumed a socialistic character.

[E.C.K. GONNER]
Reprinted from *Palgrave's Dictionary of Political Economy*.

BIBLIOGRAPHY
Gammage, R.G. 1894. *History of the Chartist Movement, 1837–54*. Newcastle-on-Tyne.

chartism: the points of the Charter. The Charter itself was a document in the form of an act of parliament, drafted by Francis Place from materials supplied by William Lovett. Its proposals were always summed up under six heads or 'points' viz. Universal, i.e. adult male, Suffrage, the Ballot, Annual Parliaments, Payment of Members, Equal Electoral Districts, and Abolition of Property Qualification. No one of these proposals was in any sense new, and the great majority of them had been continuously agitated for more than fifty years. The Duke of Richmond introduced a proposal for adult suffrage and equal electoral districts into the House of Lords in 1780. All or nearly all the charter 'points' were adopted by the Society of the Friends of the People, and the Corresponding Society in the earlier years of the French Revolution, and by that Edinburgh Convention for taking part in which Muir and Palmer were sentenced in 1793. The 'points' were generally spoken of as the Duke of Richmond's, or Sir Francis Burdett's, or Major Cartwright's 'plan of radical reform', and were undisguisedly intended by all their working class supporters to be used for bringing about economic as well as political equality. During the ten years following the French war every period of high prices and low wages produced a fierce agitation for 'radical reform' in the manufacturing districts and sometimes also in London. In 1830–32 the 'plan' was for a time given up in favour of the Reform Bill, but in London amendments in favour of universal suffrage were carried at the public meetings held in support of Lord Grey's bill. These were generally moved by members of the 'Rotunda Gang', or national Union of the Working Classes, many of whom had been personal disciples of Robert Owen. The reformers of 1790–1820 had advocated Tom Paine's proposal of a graduated income tax, or had been followers of 'Spence's plan' of land municipalization. These men went further, and were strongly though vaguely socialistic in tone. Place describes them as

filled with bitter notions of animosity against everybody who did not concur in the absurd notions they entertained, that everything which was produced belonged to those who by their labour produced it, and ought to be shared among them; that there ought to be no accumulation of capital in the hands of any one to enable him to employ others as labourers, and thus by becoming a *master* make slaves of others under the name of workmen, to take from them the produce of their labour, to maintain themselves in idleness and luxury while their slaves were ground down to the earth or left to starve. They denounced every one who dissented from these notions as a *political economist* under which appellation was included the notion of a bitter foe to the working classes – enemies who deserved no mercy at their hands.

Place also gives a good specimen of their teaching in a song published about this time:

'Wages should form the price of goods,
　Yes, wages should be all;
Then we who work to make the goods
　Should justly have them all.
But, if the price be made of rent,
　Tithes, taxes, profits all,
Then we who work to make the goods
　Shall have – just none at all.'

From among these men came Lovett, Cleave, Hetherington, and others who were afterwards leaders of the chartist movement. It is significant that their organization was called successively the 'British Association for Co-operative Knowledge' (i.e. of Robert Owen's principles) in 1829; 'The Metropolitan Trades Union' in 1830, when one of their declared objects was to 'enhance the value of labour by diminishing the hours of employment', and 'The National Union of the Working Classes', for nominally political purposes, in 1831.

After the complete failure of the chartist movement in 1848, working-class reformers generally returned to the work of co-operation and trade-unionism, so that the economic side of the agitation which carred the Reform Bills of 1867 and 1884 was not so apparent as the political side. But the bill of 1867 was opposed on economic grounds by Robert Lowe (afterwards Lord Sherbrooke), Lord Shaftesbury, and others. Lord Shaftesbury on that occasion said:

I am sure that a large proportion of the working classes have a deep and solemn conviction – and I have found it among working people of religious views – that property is not distributed as property ought to be; that some checks ought to be kept on the accumulation of property in single hands; that to take away, by a legislative enactment, that which is in excess, with a view to bestow it on those who have insufficient means, is not a breach of any law, human or divine.

[G. WALLACE]

Reprinted from *Palgrave's Dictionary of Political Economy*.

Chayanov, Alexander Vasil'evich (1888–?1939). Chayanov is the best-known exponent of the theory of peasant economy developed by the Organization and Production School of Russian agricultural economists. The latter were active from around 1905 down to the period of the New Economic Policy adopted by the Soviet regime.

Little is known of Chayanov's early life except that he probably came of genteel stock in European Russia. He came into early prominence and in 1913 was appointed assistant professor at the Agricultural Institute of Petrovskoe Razumovskoe (later renamed the Timiriyazev Agricultural Academy), near Moscow. In 1919, he was put in charge of the seminar on agricultural economics of the Timiriyazev Academy, later to be renamed once again as the Institute of Agricultural Economy. He directed the Institute until 1930 when, at the height of the collectivization campaign, he was dismissed. He is alleged to have died on 30 March 1939 at Alma-Ata (Smith, 1976).

Chayanov was a tireless investigator into the conditions of agriculture in Russia in the era succeeding the Stolypin reforms and in the first ten years or more of the Soviet regime. He published numerous studies on cooperation, credit, peasant farming etc. in other European countries such as Italy, Belgium and Switzerland. But his main area of research centred on problems of Russian peasant production, including the question of cooperation among the peasant producers. He also took part in the organization of cooperation among the peasantry. In 1914 Chayanov proposed the organization of a central cooperative for the export of flax. Russia was then the leading exporter of flax in the world. In 1916–17 the Central Cooperative Association of Flax Growers, of which Chayanov was a director, obtained a monopoly of flax exports, after signing an agreement with a private firm interested in the same field.

During and after the period of the Bolshevik Revolution, Chayanov became concerned with the appropriate form of agrarian reforms. He emphasized the diversity of production conditions in the different regions of Russia and of the needs of different types of products such as grain or flax. He also stressed the need to give the peasant adequate incentive to produce and market the crops needed by other sectors of the economy. By and large, he was against forcible collectivization and nationalization of land, and for voluntary cooperation among peasants who would retain control over their land. But in the period when the creation of state farms came on the political agenda, he worked out a locational plan for such farms and tried to figure out their optimum size.

The most complete bibliography of Chayanov's works available so far lists one hundred items of economic or agro-economic studies under his own name, spanning the years 1909 to 1930, sixteen items edited or with a preface by him (published over the years 1915–28), and twelve other works by him in the field of literature, history and arts, published over the period 1912–28 (Thorner, Kerblay and Smith, 1966, pp. 279–96). Chayanov was a cultured Russian intellectual, typical of his generation, and he wrote many of his 'non-professional pieces' under a variety of pseudonyms such as 'Botanik X', 'Moskovskii Botanik X', and 'Ivan Kremnev'.

The utopia published by him under the last guise has been translated into English as *The Journey of my Brother Alexei to the Land of Peasant Utopia* (Kremnev, 1920). However, it is the translation of two of his major theoretical studies into English in 1966 that kindled interest in his work among English-language readers (Thorner, Kerblay and Smith, 1966).

The centrepiece of Chayanov's theory is the concept of the family labour farm. Such a farm is supposed to employ only family labour on the family farm and on other activities such as crafts and services; on the other side, no part of this labour is hired out. Chayanov largely ignored the non-farm activities of the family labour farm. Then the equilibrium output of the farm was taken to be determined by the equation of the consumption needs of the family and the drudgery of effort (Kerblay, 1966, p. xxxii).

Chayanov claimed that 90 per cent of the farms in Russia before the October Revolution were family labour farms. He used the area sown per family as the primary criterion for stratifying peasant households and claimed, on the basis of the data analysed by himself and by other researchers such as B.N. Knipovich, N.P. Makarov and S.N. Prokopovich, that it was the size of the family that determined the size of the area sown rather than the other way round. The direction of causality was established by means of a life cycle theory: a young family would have a high proportion of consumers to producers, and as the children grow up, the size of the family farm would increase at first to accommodate the growing needs of the family. The farm would in turn grow as more working hands are added to the family units. Then some of the young adults would move away, and settle down either on a portion of the partitioned family farm or on a new farm (Chayanov, 1966, pp. 53–69).

Chayanov considered the family farm or the 'family economy' to be not only typical of pre-revolutionary or early post-revolution Russia, but to underlie a wide variety of economic systems (Chayanov, 1924; this has been translated as 'On the theory of non-capitalist economic systems' in Thorner, Kerblay and Smith, 1966, pp. 1–28). In Chayanov's view, this family economy underlies not only the natural economy and 'the commodity economy' but is really at the basis of what he calls the feudal system, where the peasant household and the landlord's demesne form a symbiotic unity.

Chayanov's views on the structure of Russian rural society as well as his general view of the peasant economy as more or less a universal category have been challenged by his critics, who include the Russian Agrarian Marxists led by L.N. Kritsman (1926) and later researchers (Harrison, 1975, 1977a, 1977b, 1979; Littlejohn, 1977; Ennew, Hirst and Tribe, 1977; Chandra, 1985). It has been claimed that once a multi-dimensional matrix of stratification is used, Russian rural society is found to have been highly stratified along class lines as Lenin had argued in his *Development of Capitalism in Russia* (1899) and later works. Chayanov's critics point out that changes in social structure cannot be explained by demographic factors alone so that the life cycle theory advanced by him does not have much of an empirical basis. Chayanov failed to take into account the fact that small peasants, rich peasants, and 'family labour farms' are held together in a web of market relationships, and that family labour farms are vulnerable to vagaries of the market as well as to natural or biological factors (see Bagchi, 1982, ch. 6). Once capital is assumed to be mobile as between different farms and other sectors of the economy, the theoretical basis of an enduring family labour farm is thoroughly undermined. A peasant mode of production cannot have a theoretical validity either, because it ignores the relations of production that hold the peasantry together but also differentiate them in particular ways.

Although Chayanov's life cycle model would hold ideally only in a land-abundant economy, attempts have been made to adapt the model of the self-exploiting family farm to densely populated underdeveloped countries with widespread underemployment of labour (Georgescu-Roegen, 1960) and to Polish feudalism (Kula, 1962). The utopianism underlying some of the theories favouring small peasant farming under capitalist countries and explicitly spelled out by Chayanov (Kremnev, 1920), has been assailed for its lack of realism and its reactionary overtones (Patnaik, 1979). But there is no doubt that Chayanov raised a number of questions which, in combination with the work of Kautsky, Lenin, Mao and other Marxists, will provide a rich crop of research programmes on rural social structures wherever the peasantry formed or continue to form a large fraction of the population (Harrison, 1979; Chandra, 1985).

AMIYA K. BAGCHI

See also PEASANT ECONOMY; PEASANTS.

SELECTED WORKS

1924. 'Zur Frage einer Theorie der nichtcapitalistischen Wirtschaftssysteme', von A. Tschayanoff. *Archiv für Sozialwissenschaft und Sozialpolitik* 51. Trans. as 'On the theory of non-capitalist economic systems', in Thorner, Kerblay and Smith (1966).

1925. *Organizatsiia krest'ianskogo khoziaistva. Iz rabot Nauchno-Issledovatel'skogo Instituta s.-kh. ekonomii.* Moskva Tsentral'noe tovarichestvo kooperativnogo izd. Trans. as 'Peasant farm organization', in Thorner, Kerblay and Smith (1966).

1966. *A.V. Chayanov on the Theory of the Peasant Economy.* Ed. D. Thorner, B. Kerblay and R.E.F. Smith, Homewood, Ill.: Richard D. Irwin.

BIBLIOGRAPHY

Bagchi, A.K. 1982. *The Political Economy of Underdevelopment.* Cambridge: Cambridge University Press.

Chandra, N.K. 1985. Peasantry as a single class. In *Truth Unites: Essays in Honour of Samar Sen*, ed. A. Mitra, Calcutta: Subarnarekha.

Ennew, J., Hirst, P. and Tribe, K. 1977. 'Peasantry' as an economic category. *Journal of Peasant Studies* 4(4), July, 295–322.

Georgescu-Roegen, N. 1960. Economic theory and agrarian economics. *Oxford Economic Papers*, Vol. 12. Reprinted in N. Georgescu-Roegen, *Analytical Economics: Issues and Problems*, Cambridge, Mass.: Harvard University Press, 1966.

Harrison, M. 1975. Chayanov and the economics of the Russian peasantry. *Journal of Peasant Studies* 2(4), July, 389–417.

Harrison, M. 1977a. The problems of social mobility among Russian peasant households, 1880–1930. *Journal of Peasant Studies* 4(2), January, 127–61.

Harrison, M. 1977b. The peasant mode of production in the work of A.V. Chayanov. *Journal of Peasant Studies* 4(4), July, 323–36.

Harrison, M. 1979. Chayanov and the Marxists. *Journal of Peasant Studies* 7(1), October, 86–100.

Kerblay, B. 1966. A.V. Chayanov: life, career, works. In Thorner, Kerblay and Smith (1966).

Kremnev, I. 1920. *Puteshestvie moego brata Alekseya v stranu krest'ianskoi utopii*, Moscow. Trans. as 'The journey of my brother Alexei to the land of peasant utopia' (introduced by R.E.F. Smith), *Journal of Peasant Studies* 4(1), October 1976, 63–108.

Kritsman, L.N. 1926. *Klassovoe rassloenie sovetskoi derevni (po dannym volostnykh obsledovanii).* Translated, condensed and edited by G. Littlejohn as 'Class stratification of the Soviet countryside', *Journal of Peasant Studies* 11(2), January 1984, 85–143.

Kula, W. 1962. *Teoria ekonomiczna ustroju feudalnego.* Warsaw: Państwowe Wydawnictwo Naukowe. Translated into English from the Italian edition by L. Garner as *An Economic Theory of the Feudal System*, London: New Left Books, 1976.

Littlejohn, G. 1977. Chayanov and the theory of peasant economy. In *Sociological Theories of the Economy*, ed. B. Hindess, London: Macmillan.

Patnaik, U. 1979. Neo-populism and Marxism: the Chayanovian view of the agrarian question and its fundamental fallacy. *Journal of Peasant Studies* 6(4), July, 375–420.

Smith, R.E.F. 1976. Introduction. *Journal of Peasant Studies* 4(1), October, 1–8.

cheap money. 'By a long-established convention the rate of discount or the short-term rate of interest is called the "price" of money, so that "dear money" means a high rate, "cheap money" a low rate' (Hawtrey, 1938, p. 28n). By the time Hawtrey was writing, however, the meaning of cheap money was changing, as a result of changes in both economic theory and monetary policy, to include low *long*-term interest rates. In the late 20th century money has not often been cheap in either sense, so that cheap or cheaper money now usually refers simply to a fall in (real) interest rates.

In the late 19th century and early 20th century, 'cheap money' meant low money market rates of interest, the rate at which commercial bills could be discounted. Since in England these rates were strongly influenced by the Bank of England's rediscount rate (Bank Rate), which was generally higher than the market rate, a 3% Bank Rate could be regarded as the upper limit of cheap money (Hawtrey, 1938, p. 133). On this criterion there was cheap money for varying periods of time in all but nine years from 1844 to 1914 (Palgrave, 1903, p. 98; Hawtrey, 1938, Appendix I). The Bank of England, committed to maintaining the pound sterling on the gold standard with the aid of a relatively small gold reserve, varied its rate very frequently, so that these periods were of short duration, except for the spells of cheap money that followed upon the dear money of financial crises. In 1844–5, 1848–53, 1858–60, 1867–8, 1876–7, 1893–6, and 1908–9 Bank Rate was usually *below* 3% for a year of more. The most prolonged of these spells, occurring in the last years of the 'Great Depression', was permitted by a large inflow of American gold into Britain, at a time of increasing gold production, falling prices, and high unemployment (Hawtrey, 1938, pp. 110–12; Sayers, 1936, ch. 1; Sayers, 1976, p. 51). Bank Rate stood at 2% for $2\frac{1}{2}$ years, the longest period at its historical minimum before the 1930s. In the previous decade, though Bank Rate was more variable, interest rates had also been generally low. As they were to do again in the 1930s, the British government took advantage of falling long-term rates to reduce the interest paid on a large proportion of outstanding national debt: the famous 'Goschen conversion' of 1888 reduced the interest rate on 3% Consols to $2\frac{3}{4}$% until 1903 and $2\frac{1}{2}$% thereafter (Clapham, 1944, Vol. 2, pp. 318–21; Spinner, 1973, pp. 139–503; G.J. Goschen was Chancellor of the Exchequer).

After World War I Bank Rate changes were less frequent than before 1914, partly because a high Bank Rate was now associated with high unemployment (Committee on Currency and Foreign Exchanges after the War, 1918; Moggridge, 1972; Sayers, 1976, chs 6, 7 and 9; Howson, 1975, chs 2 and 3). At the same time Bank Rate was generally higher than before the war, having been raised and kept high to curb the postwar boom in 1919–20, and again as part of the attempts to return to and stay on the gold standard at prewar parity. It was 3% only twice in 1919–31, in 1922–3 and 1930–31, and $2\frac{1}{2}$% once, for 10 weeks in mid-1931. By the time Britain left the gold standard there was a widespread desire for 'cheap money', for the sake of both the economy and the budget. Developments in monetary theory in these years (for example, Robertson,

409

1926; Keynes, 1930) implied that low *long-term* interest rates would be needed to increase investment in fixed capital and hence income and employment, rather than just low short-term rates to boost investment in working capital (inventories) as in the older views of, say, Hawtrey (1913, 1919, 1938). In 1932 the British government embarked upon a 'cheap money policy' to provide a spell of low long-term rates as well as to enable the conversion of high interest bearing government debt contracted during World War I. This also involved the establishment of an Exchange Equalization Account (EEA) to manage the exchange rate and provide sterilization of the effects of reserve changes on the monetary base. The announcement of the conversion of £2000 million 5% War Loan 1929–47 to 3½% War Loan 1952 or after was made on 30 June 1932, when Bank Rate was reduced to 2%. Apart from a short-lived rise at the outbreak of World War II, Bank Rate remained at 2% until 7 November 1951 (Nevin, 1953 and 1955, ch. 3; Howson, 1975, ch. 4, and 1980; Sayers, 1976, ch. 18).

Similar, although more complex, developments in monetary theory and policy had been taking place in the USA in the interwar years (Friedman and Schwartz, 1963, chs 6–9; Chandler, 1971, chs 8). On both sides of the Atlantic the persistence of low interest rates and high unemployment in the 1930s induced considerable scepticism as to the efficacy of cheap money (however defined) as well as increased confidence in the monetary authorities' power to bring it about (Sayers, 1951 and 1957, chs 3 and 6; Keynes, 1936; Wallich, 1946; Morgan, 1944). The decisions to maintain cheap money during and immediately after World War II reflected the scepticism, the confidence, and the desire to avoid the high borrowing costs of World War I. Monetary policy became a matter of issuing sufficient quantities of suitable debt instruments to satisfy the public's asset preferences and allowing the money supply to expand to whatever extent was necessary to maintain the fixed pattern of interest rates (Sayers, 1956, chs 5 and 7; Friedman and Schwartz, 1963, ch. 10; Chandler, 1971, pp. 346–8). Interest rates ranged from $\frac{3}{8}$% on Treasury bills to $2\frac{1}{2}$% for long-term government bonds in the USA, and from 1% on Treasury bills to 3% for long-term government bonds in the UK. In Britain after the war, Hugh Dalton, Chancellor of the Exchequer 1945–7, also tried to go further and pursue a 'cheaper money policy', specifically to lower interest rates for government debt by $\frac{1}{2}$% all the way along the yield curve. There was soon a reaction against the monetization of debt implied in these policies, and in 1947 official support of the markets for government securities was weakened in both countries, although the cheap money policies were not finally abandoned until 1951 (Paish, 1947; Sayers, 1957, ch. 2; Friedman and Schwartz, 1963, ch. 11; Dow, 1964, ch 2 and 9; Howson, 1985).

Monetary theory and practice have changed the concept of 'cheap money' again since 1951. In a more inflationary world the importance of controlling the money supply has been recognized – in the 1970s if not before – as have the inadequacies of interest rates (short or long) as an indicator of monetary conditions. When prices are rising rapidly, money can be 'cheap' even if nominal interest rates are at historically high levels. The stance of a central bank's monetary policy is now more often represented by the rate of the growth of the money supply, rather than by interest rates.

SUSAN HOWSON

See also CREDIT CYCLE; DEAR MONEY; MONETARY POLICY.

BIBLIOGRAPHY

Chandler, L.V. 1971. *American Monetary Policy 1928–1941*. New York: Harper & Row.

Clapham, J.H. 1944. *The Bank of England*. Cambridge: Cambridge University Press.

Committee on Currency and Foreign Exchanges after the War 1918. *First Interim Report*, Cd. 9182, London: HMSO.

Dow, J.C.R. 1964. *The Management of the British Economy 1945–60*. Cambridge: Cambridge University Press.

Friedman, M. and Schwartz, A.J. 1963. *A Monetary History of the United States 1867–1960*. Princeton: Princeton University Press.

Hawtrey, R.G. 1913. *Good and Bad Trade*. London: Constable & Co.

Hawtrey, R.G. 1919. *Currency and Credit*. London: Longmans, Green & Co.

Hawtrey, R.G. 1938. *A Century of Bank Rate*. London: Longmans, Green & Co.

Howson, S. 1975. *Domestic Monetary Management in Britain 1919–38*. Cambridge: Cambridge University Press.

Howson, S. 1980. *Sterling's Managed Float: The Operations of the Exchange Equalisation Account, 1932–39*. Princeton Studies in International Finance No. 46, November.

Howson, S. 1985. The origins of cheaper money, 1945–47. Economic History Workshop, University of Toronto.

Keynes, J.M. 1930. *A Treatise on Money*. London: Macmillan for the Royal Economic Society, 1971.

Keynes, J.M. 1936. *The General Theory of Employment, Interest and Money*. London: Macmillan for the Royal Economic Society, 1973.

Moggridge, D.E. 1972. *British Monetary Policy 1924–1931*. Cambridge: Cambridge University Press.

Morgan, E.V. 1944. The future of interest rates. *Economic Journal* 54, December, 340–51.

Nevin, E. 1953. The origins of cheap money, 1931–32. *Economica* 20, February, 24–37.

Nevin, E. 1955. *The Mechanism of Cheap Money*. Cardiff: University of Wales Press.

Paish, F.W. 1947. Cheap money policy. *Economica* 14, August, 167–79.

Palgrave, R.H.I. 1903. *Bank Rate and the Money Market*. London: John Murray.

Robertson, D.H. 1926. *Banking Policy and the Price Level*. London: P.S. King & Son.

Sayers, R.S. 1936. *Bank of England Operations 1890–1914*. London: P.S. King & Son.

Sayers, R.S. 1951. The rate of interest as a weapon of economic policy. In *Oxford Studies in the Price Mechanism*, ed. T. Wilson and P.W.S. Andrews, Oxford: Clarendon Press.

Sayers, R.S. 1956. *Financial Policy 1939–45*. London: HMSO.

Sayers, R.S. 1957. *Central Banking after Bagehot*. Oxford: Clarendon Press.

Sayers, R.S. 1976. *The Bank of England 1891–1966*. Cambridge: Cambridge University Press.

Spinner, T.J., Jr. 1973. *George Joachim Goschen*. Cambridge: Cambridge University Press.

Wallich, H.C. 1946. The changing significance of the interest rate. *American Economic Review* 36, December, 761–87.

Cherbuliez, Antoine Elisée (1797–1869). Swiss lawyer and economist, Cherbuliez was born in Geneva into a family of French Protestants who were uprooted by the Edict of Nantes. Trained in law, Cherbuliez held a judgeship until 1835, at which time he succeeded Pellegrino Rossi at the University of Geneva as professor of public law and political economy. He also served in the Swiss Constituent Assembly and the Grand Council, but after the fall of the Conservative Republican Party in 1848 he moved to Paris and became a naturalized French citizen. A short time later, however, he returned to his homeland as professor of political economy at the University of Lausanne, preceding Léon Walras in the position.

Concurrently, he held the chair of political economy at the University of Zurich from 1855 until his death in 1869.

As an economist, Cherbuliez produced nothing original, but he excelled in exposition. His writings represent a kind of mature classicism. The diadem in a collection of sparkling gems is his *Précis de la science économique et ses practicales applications*, a masterpiece of erudition, described by Schumpeter (1954, p. 501) as 'one of the best textbooks of "classic" economics'. Luigi Cossa (1880) put it on a par with Mill's *Principles*, judging it 'possibly superior'. J.E. Cairnes, in quiet affirmation of Cossa's judgement, followed Cherbuliez in his reformulation of the classical theory of value.

Cherbuliez wrote for the *Dictionnaire d'économie politique* and for the *Journal d'économie politique*, on such topics as socialism (which he opposed), charity, transportation, money and banking, taxation (he accepted Canard's theory), entrepreneurship, economic history and the history of economic thought. If he was an apostle at all, he followed Say and Bastiat. Like the former, he partitioned economics systematically into 'theory' and 'practice'. Like the latter, he wrote pamphlets in support of liberalism and the deductive method. Despite the clarity of his style and exposition, however, Cherbuliez was not widely read. He left no distinctive imprint on French economics, nor is he remembered by most textbooks in the history of economic thought.

R.F. HÉBERT

SELECTED WORKS
1840. *Riche ou pauvre*. Paris: A. Cherbuliez.
1848. *Le Socialisme c'est la barbarie*. Paris: Guillaumin.
1862. *Précis de la science économique et de ses principales applications*.
   2 vols. Paris: Guillaumin.

BIBLIOGRAPHY
Cossa, L. 1880. *Guide to the Study of Political Economy*. Trans. from the 2nd Italian edn. London: Macmillan.
Gide, C. and Rist, C. 1949. *A History of Economic Doctrines*. Trans. R. Richards, Boston: D. C. Heath.
Schumpeter, J. A. 1954. *History of Economic Analysis*. Ed. E.B. Schumpeter, New York: Oxford University Press.

Chernyshevskii, Nikolai Garilovich (1828–1889). Nikolai Chernyshevskii was born in Saratov in 1828 and died there in 1889. He was one of a group of 'revolutionary democrats' which included Herzen and Belinskii among its number, and Chernyshevskii became the group's outstanding intellectual leader during the critical decade following the accession of Tsar Alexander II in 1855. His greatest period of activity thus came in the aftermath of the European revolutionary upheavals in 1848–9, and coincided with Russia's defeat in the Crimean War (1853–6), the debate leading up the Emancipation of the Serfs (1861), and the subsequent post-emancipation reaction and gathering of revolutionary sentiment.

Chernyshevskii's influence both on his contemporaries and on later generations of Russian revolutionaries was profound. He undoubtedly influenced both Marx and Lenin, and Lenin admired Chernyshevskii more than any other non-Marxist revolutionary writer. Chernyshevskii therefore holds an honoured place in Soviet literature on the development of socialist thought, and he is viewed as the main precursor of Marxism in Russia. His ideas also helped prepare the way for the development of Russian Populism (the Narodnik movement) in the 1870s.

Several major threads run through Chernyshevskii's voluminous and wide-ranging writings. He was an admirer of Western achievements and believed that Russia must modernize in order to catch up with the more civilized West.

Thus although he was opposed to capitalism, he was by no means opposed to industrialization and urbanization. In this he was at odds both with the Slavophils and with the later *Narodniki*. He was a strong believer in individualism and in the benefits of enlightened self-interest. He believed that societies, shorn of such oppressive institutions as autocracy and serfdom, or of exploitative capitalism, could grow towards socialism in a rational manner. His ideas were rooted also in a belief in the Laws of History, and in the 'necessary' transition from one stage of development to another. But he also believed that societies, like individuals, could progress by revolutionary means at an accelerated pace. In particular, he argued that Russia could progress to a socialist state without having to undergo a period of capitalism (a viewpoint unacceptable to Leninists, who argued that Russia already was a capitalist country). Chernyshevskii was thus the first Russian writer to put forward a theory of accelerated social change.

In so far as Chernyshevskii perceived that Russia might 'skip' a stage of historical development by virtue of her backwardness, he may be considered a precursor of the 'concept of relative backwardness' later elaborated by Alexander Gerschenkron. In particular, Russia could take advantage of her backwardness by borrowing both institutional forms and technology from the more developed West without incurring the costs of the pioneer. But Chernyshevskii failed to develop the concept, and, as Gerschenkron has pointed out, added little to the ideas already advanced by Herzen. Indeed, in Gerschenkron's opinion 'it is not clear at all that Chernyshevskii made any independent contribution to economic analysis' (Gerschenkron, 1962, p. 171).

Chernyshevskii came from a humble background. He was the son of a poor village priest and at first trained for the priesthood himself, attending the theological seminary at Saratov between 1842 and 1845. His literary and linguistic skills took him to St Petersburg, where he graduated from the department of history and philology in 1850. It was during these years that he became a radical and a revolutionary, influenced profoundly by the revolutions of 1848–9 and the debate over serfdom in Russia. His ideas were influenced by Herzen and Belinskii and also by the German philosophers (especially Feuerbach and Hegel), by French utopian socialists and by English political economists (especially Ricardo and Mill).

Following two years teaching in his native Saratov, Chernyshevskii returned to St Petersburg in 1853 and in the following year joined the staff of the literary journal *Sovreminnik* (The Contemporary). Between 1854 and 1857 he wrote most of his literary criticism, using this as a vehicle to expound his social views. He rejected any concept of 'art for art's sake', arguing the essentially political nature of aesthetics. From 1857 Chernyshevskii devoted himself almost entirely to political and social issues and wrote a series of major articles. These included *Capital and Labour* (1859), *A Critique of Philosophical Prejudices Against the Communal Ownership of Land* (1858) and *The Anthropological Principle of Philosophy* (1860). He also translated John Stuart Mill's *Principles of Political Economy* in (1860) and wrote a lengthy critique of Mill's theories.

In these and other works Chernyshevskii criticized the workings of liberal capitalism, which he condemned for its exploitation of the masses and for periodic economic crises. From Mill's wage-fund theory Chernyshevskii drew a theoretical demonstration of the inevitability of mass poverty under capitalism. He thought that under capitalism the division of labour would inevitably decrease wages, as each operation would require less skill and training and therefore would be rewarded less. And he drew the conclusion that industry, while not to be avoided, must have a different form of social organization. Social evils sprang ultimately from poverty, and 'whoever says "poverty of the people" also says "the government is bad" '.

Chernyshevskii was a strong defender of the peasant village commune (*mir*) both on social and economic grounds. He viewed the village commune as a possible bridge which would enable Russia to avoid the capitalist stage of development, and he argued that the commune should be modernized along rational lines and become similar to workers' associations in western Europe. He attacked vehemently the terms of the Emancipation, arguing that the peasants should be given their land without having the obligation to pay redemption taxes.

Long under suspicion for propagating revolutionary views (though their message was always subtly disguised in order to escape censorship), Chernyshevskii was arrested on a pretext in July 1862 and imprisoned in the Fortress of St Peter and Paul. He was charged with 'plotting the overthrow of the existing order', and after a trial lasting two years, was ultimately sentenced to seven years' hard labour and exile for life in Siberia.

During his imprisonment Chernyshevskii continued to write a number of important works, including his most famous and influential novel *Chto Delat'* (*What is to be Done?*) (1862–3). The heroes of the novel were the 'new radicals', guided by rational self-interest ('egoism') rather than irrational beliefs. The message of the book was an optimistic one – much could be achieved by individuals who were guided by sound principles even though living in a corrupt society. The novel was serialized in *The Contemporary* (due to an oversight by the censor) and it had an immediate and profound impact on the Russian intelligentsia.

After his exile in 1864 Chernyshevskii's productive life was virtually over. He remained in Siberia – despite vain attempts by radical groups to free him – until 1883, when he was allowed to live in Astrakhan under police supervision. But only in 1889, shortly before his death, was he allowed to return to his native Saratov.

There is no doubt that Chernyshevskii's honoured place in Soviet histories of revolutionary thought owes much to the approval given his writings by Marx, Engels and Lenin. This in turn may be explained in part by Chernyshevskii's championship of the masses, his emphasis on historical forces and his materialism, as well as his own humble origins and his suffering at the hands of the Tsarist authorities. If his writings seem turgid and sometimes coarse, he was nonetheless a powerful and original thinker who did much to adapt the various strands of Western European political economy and philosophy to Russian conditions. He influenced a generation of Russian revolutionaries and did much to prepare the ground in Russia for the *Narodnik* movement of the 1870s and, later, for the spread of Marxism. There is no evidence that Chernyshevskii himself was influenced by Marx, or even that he had read Marx's works. It is probable, though, that he had read the *Communist Manifesto*, and the first volume of *Das Kapital* was sent to him in Siberia in 1872.

M. FALKUS

SELECTED WORKS

1862–3. *A Vital Question: or What is to be Done?* Trans. by N.H. Dale and S.S. Skidelsky, New York: T.Y. Crowell & Co., 1886.
1853. *Selected Philosophical Essays*. Moscow: Foreign Languages Publishing House.

BIBLIOGRAPHY

Gerschenkron, A. 1962. *Economic Backwardness in Historical Perspective*. Cambridge, Mass.: Havard University press.

Pereira, N.G. 1975. *The Thought and Teachings of N.G.Chernyshevskii*. The Hague: Mouton.
Randall, F.B. 1967. *N.G. Chernyshevskii*. New York: Twayne Publishers.

Chevalier, Michel (1806–1879). Born in Limoges, 13 January 1806; died in Paris, November 1879. Undoubtedly one of the most eminent 19th-century French economists, Chevalier belongs to that most typical brand of engineer-economists. First in his class (*major*) at the Ecole Polytechnique in 1830 and member of the Corps des Mines as an economist, Chevalier came very early under the spell of Saint-Simon's utopian doctrine. From his early editorship of the Saint-Simonian newspaper *Le Globe* (1830–32) and his subsequent sentence to a year in jail (for 'outrage to morals' for publishing advanced ideas on the liberation of women, sexual liberty and the need for communal life) to a made-to-measure niche as economic adviser to Napoleon III and 'éminence grise' to the Second Empire business and banking establishment, Chevalier applied his brilliant mind to various current problems and policy issues without managing however to escape completely from the Saint-Simonian mystique. His main claim to fame, the Anglo-French Treaty of 1860 (the Cobden–Chevalier Treaty), an important if short-lived interruption in the general protectionist policy of France, is one of the best illustrations of these twin components of Chevalier's approach to economics and economic policy: weak on the analytics and very strong on the factual analysis with a touch of Saint-Simonian idealism.

Together with public works, cheap bank credit and education, free trade is one of the articles of faith he took over from the Saint-Simonian doctrine. Chevalier returned to these issues throughout his life (notably in his penetrating analysis of the American economy and banking system in the early 1830s which earned him later the nickname of 'Economic Tocqueville'). Binding these various elements with a quasi-philosophical concept of association (as the cornerstone of social order), Chevalier suggests a broad theory of economic growth which he considered flexible enough to be applied to different times and countries.

His Saint-Simonian antecedents and his extensive travelling (to England, Egypt and foremost to the United States) rendered Chevalier suspicious of all 'absolutist' economic theory. In fact, in his most technical chapters (particularly on money) Chevalier never digs beneath the surface of things and contributes very little, if anything, to analytic economics. His only systematic work, his *Cours* (1843, 1844, 1850) delivered at the Collège de France offers little more in the field of theory than a lengthy (and flat) apology for Say's brand of 'vulgar' liberalism. With Rossi, his predecessor, and Leroy-Beaulieu, his successor at the Collège de France, Chevalier was in fact largely responsible for introducing and perpetuating in academic circles the liberal orthodoxy that was to bar Walras from getting an appointment in the 1860s and that dominated French economics for so long that as late as in 1939 Keynes could still quip about its lack of 'deep roots in systematic thought' (1939, p. xxxii).

P. BRIDEL

SELECTED WORKS

1843, 1844, 1850. *Cours d'économie politique*. 3 vols. Paris: Capelle.

BIBLIOGRAPHY

Keynes, J.M. 1939. French Preface to *The General Theory of Employment, Interest and Money*. In *Collected Writings*, Vol. VII, London: Macmillan, 1973, 31–5.
Walch, J. 1975. *Michel Chevalier, économiste, saint-simonien. 1806–1879*. Paris: Vrin (with extensive bibliography).

Cheysson, Jean-Jacques Emile (1836–1910). French engineer, economist and statistician, Cheysson was born in Nîmes and died in the Swiss Alps. Schooled at the Ecole Polytechnique and the Ecole des Ponts et Chaussées, he served with distinction in the Corps of Civil Engineers, demonstrating his ingenuity during the German siege of Paris (1870) by converting train stations to flour mills (using locomotive engines as the power source), thereby increasing bread production. Only when wheat supplies were eventually exhausted did the city finally capitulate. After the armistice, Cheysson became factory director at Creusot, the huge industrial complex that was bombed during World War II, where he immersed himself in the microeconomics of the firm and began to develop an analytical programme which anticipated the main lines of what we now call econometrics.

Calling his method 'geometric statistics', Cheysson presented its outline to the Paris Statistical Society in 1885 as a scientific approach to 'the practical solution of business problems'. His technique rested on the twin pillars of theory and observation. It combined the spirit of Cournot's economics with attention to recorded data, using geometry to display concrete facts and to interpolate gaps in available statistics. In spirit and scope, but considerably ahead of its time, it mirrored the objectives of the Econometric Society, established at Lausanne in 1931.

A potential alliance between Cheysson and Léon Walras eventually soured, thus cutting off what might have been a productive channel of communication for Cheysson's new method. Cheysson taught geometric statistics to his students at the Ecole des Mines and the Ecole des Sciences Politiques (he held the first chair of economics at each institution), but inspired no group of followers the way Walras or Marshall did, and the powerful originality of his contribution gradually faded, only to be rediscovered in the present century by Staehle (1942, p. 322) and Schumpeter (1954, p. 842), and reconstructed piecemeal by Hébert (1972, 1973, 1974).

Within the narrow compass of 35 pages Cheysson enriched the theories of statistical demand; revenue and cost curves; profit maximization; spatial market boundaries for raw materials and finished products; wages; product and quality variation; investment; and taxation. His deft handling of these difficult subjects while the titans of economic theory were debating the psychological premises of value theory, constitutes a remarkable performance, even by modern standards.

After 1890 Cheysson turned his energies increasingly towards that branch of ideas that the French call 'social economy'. A follower of LePlay since their first meeting in 1864, Cheysson shared his colleague's interest in social and economic reform. LePlay's school emphasized moral and religious considerations in the economic order, especially the primacy of the family, the rights of workers and the duties of employers. Under Cheysson's leadership, the Société d'Economie Sociale (founded by LePlay in 1856) wedged itself between the socialists on the left and the liberals on the right. Unwilling to accept the evils of poverty and the misfortunes of the workers, yet rejecting socialist remedies, LePlay's school sought amelioration through the encouragement of private initiative. They considered social reform as much a matter of economics as morality. Cheysson was thrice president of the Société d'Economie Sociale, and was elected to the Académie des Sciences Morales et Politiques in 1901. He left behind a literary legacy that numbered over 500 publications, embracing such diverse topics as economics, statistics, geography, agriculture and social hygiene.

R.F. HÉBERT

SELECTED WORKS

1911. *Oeuvres choisies.* 2 vols, Paris: A. Rousseau.

BIBLIOGRAPHY

Colson, L.C. 1913. Notice sur la vie et les travaux de M. Emile Cheysson. Académie des Sciences Morales et Politiques. *Séances et travaux* 179, 153–87.
Hébert, R.F. 1972. A note on the historical development of the economic law of market areas. *Quarterly Journal of Economics* 86, November, 563–71.
Hébert, R.F. 1973. Wage cobwebs and cobweb-type phenomena: an early French formulation. *Western Economic Journal* 11, December, 394–403.
Hébert, R.F. 1974. The theory of input selection and supply areas in 1887: Emile Cheysson. *History of Political Economy* 6, 109–13.
Schumpeter, J.A. 1954. *History of Economic Analysis.* Ed. E.B. Schumpeter, New York: Oxford University Press.
Staehle, H. 1942. Statistical cost functions: appraisal of recent contributions. *American Economic Review* 32, June, 321–33.

Chicago School. To identify a Chicago School of economics requires some demarcations, both of ideas and persons, that may not be universally accepted. Justification for these decisions must be heuristic; that is, they facilitate the story to be told. But it is not denied that there may be alternative accounts that would entail different demarcations. In this account, the 'Chicago School' is and has been centred in the University of Chicago's Economics Department from about 1930 to the present (1985). However, it is convenient to define the School so as to include many members of the large contingent of economists in the Graduate School of Business and the group of economists and lawyer-economists in the Law School. Largely because of the intellectual loyalty of former students, the influence of the Chicago School extends far beyond the University of Chicago to the faculties of other universities, the civil service, the judiciary and private business. Moreover, this influence is not confined to the United States.

To restrict the retrospective horizon of the School to 1930 implies exclusion of a number of famous economists who had been on the University of Chicago faculty before that time; for example, Thorstein Veblen, Wesley C. Mitchell, J.M. Clark, J. Laurence Laughlin, C.O. Hardy. However, none of these shared the intellectual characteristics that have typified members of the Chicago School as defined here.

In a nutshell, the two main characteristics of Chicago School adherents are: (1) belief in the power of neoclassical price theory to explain observed economic behaviour; and (2) belief in the efficacy of free markets to allocate resources and distribute income. Correlative with (2) is a tropism for minimizing the role of the state in economic activity.

Before discussing these characteristics in detail, let me give a brief historical account in which it is convenient to divide the history of the School into three periods: (1) a founding period, in the 1930s; (2) an interregnum, from the early 1940s to the early 1950s; and (3) a modern period, from the 1950s to the present.

During the founding period, the Chicago Economics Department contained a wide diversity of views both on methodology and public policy. Institutionalist views were well represented among the senior faculty, and institutionally oriented students constituted a large part of the graduate student population. Among the prominent Institutionalists were the labour economists H.A. Millis and (one side of) Paul H. Douglas; the economic historians John U. Nef and C.W. Wright, and Simeon E. Leland, a Public Finance specialist and long-time department chairman.

Like other social science departments at Chicago, economics was actively engaged in developing the (then) embryonic 'quantitative techniques'. The leading figures in quantitative methods were Henry Schultz, a pioneer student of statistical demand curves, who taught the graduate courses in mathematical economics and mathematical statistics, and Paul Douglas who was (during the 1920s and 1930s) a leader in the estimation of production functions and the measurement of real wages and living costs.

However, it is generally agreed that the progenitors of the Chicago School were Frank H. Knight and Jacob Viner. These two scholars shared an intense interest in the history of economic thought and both were, broadly speaking, devotees of neoclassical price theory. However, their intellectual styles and temperaments were quite different, and their personal relations were not close. Apart from his interest in the history of thought, Viner was primarily an applied theorist working on problems in international trade and related issues in monetary theory. Knight's work was focused on the conceptual underpinnings of neoclassical price theory, and his main concerns were to clarify and improve its logical structure.

Temperament and intellectual focus combined to make Knight a formidable critic, both of ideas and their protagonists. This led to a good deal of friction between him and both Douglas and Schultz. Personalities aside, Knight was strongly averse to the quantification of economics and was very outspoken on this, as on most other matters. (For further details, see Reder, 1982, pp. 362–5.)

By contrast, Viner was rather sympathetic to the aspirations of 'quantifiers', though sceptical of their prospects for success, at least in the near future. Viner's sympathy for quantitative work was prompted by the strong empirical bent of his own research, although friendship for Douglas and Schultz may also have been involved. On the other hand, Knight's purely theoretical studies of capital theory, risk, uncertainty, social costs, and so on, generated neither need for empirical verification nor exposure to research that might have offered it. As a result, Knight's relations with Douglas and Schultz were ridden with conflict, and theoretical disagreements with Viner spilled over into barbed comments to graduate students and kept personal relations (between Knight and Viner) from becoming more than merely correct (Reder, 1982, p. 365).

What Knight and Viner had in common was a continuing adherence to the main tenets of neoclassical price theory and resistance to the theoretical innovations of the 1930s, Monopolistic Competition and Keynes's *General Theory*. This theoretical posture paralleled an antipathy to the interventionist aspects of the New Deal and the full employment Keynesianism of its later years. Viner, who was actively consulting the government throughout the period, was much less averse to New Deal reforms than Knight and his protégés. However, there was a sharp contrast between the views of Knight and Viner, on the one hand, and those of avowed New Deal supporters such as Douglas, Schultz and some of the Institutionalists.

As a result of the division of faculty views, on both economic methodology and public policy, the graduate student body was exposed to a diversity of thought patterns and did not exhibit a great degree of conformity to any particular one. But despite their many disagreements, an effective majority of the Chicago faculty concurred in a set of degree requirements (for the PhD) that stressed competence in the application of price theory. These requirements were quite unusual in the 1930s and the process of satisfying them exercised a great influence in forming a (common) view of the subject among the students, in which price theory was of major importance.

The most important of the requirements was that all PhD candidates, without exception, pass preliminary examinations in both price theory and monetary theory. These examinations were difficult and attended with an appreciable failure rate. Even on second and third trials, there was a non-negligible probability of failure, with the result that some students were (and are) unable to qualify for the doctorate. For most students, the key to successful performance on the examinations was mastery of the material presented in relevant courses, especially the basic price theory course (301) and study of previous examinations.

For over half a century, the need to prepare for course and preliminary examinations, especially in price theory, has provided a disciplinary–cultural matrix for Chicago students. Examination questions serve as paradigmatic examples of research problems and 'A' answers exemplify successful scientific performance. The message implicit in the process is that successful research involves identifying elements of a problem with prices, quantities, and functional relations among them as these occur in price theory, and obtaining a solution as an application of the theory.

Although the specific content of examination questions has evolved with the development of the science, the basic paradigm remains substantially unchanged: economic phenomena are to be explained primarily as the outcome of decisions about quantities made by optimizing individuals who take market prices as data with the (quantity) decisions being coordinated through markets in which prices are determined so as to make aggregate quantities demanded equal to aggregate quantities supplied.

Of course, students vary in the degree to which they assimilate price theoretic ideas to their thought processes, and resistance to these ideas was probably greater in the 1930s than later. Nevertheless, regardless of their special field of interest, all students were compelled to absorb and learn to use a considerable body of economic theory. In the 1980s these skills are very widespread, but in the 1930s they were rarely found and served to distinguish Chicago-trained PhD's – especially in applied fields – from other economists.

Despite the common elements of their training, as in other institutions, doctoral students tended to identify themselves with one or another particular faculty member, usually their dissertation supervisor. Thus each of the major figures in the department was associated with a cluster of advanced students. One such cluster, associated with Knight in the mid-1930s, became of very great importance in the history of the Chicago School. Key members of this cluster were Milton Friedman, George Stigler and W. Allen Wallis. The group established close personal relations with two junior faculty members, Henry Simons and Aaron Director, who were also protégés of Knight. Another member of the group was Director's sister, Rose, who later married Milton Friedman.

It was this group that provided the multigenerational linkage in intellectual tradition that is suggested by the term 'Chicago School'. Although they admired Knight, and were devoted to him, the intellectual style of Friedman, Stigler, et al. was very different from Knight's. They were thoroughgoing empiricists with a distinct bias toward application of quantitative techniques to the testing of theoretical propositions. In their empirical bent and concern with 'real world' problems, they were much closer to Viner than to Knight, but, whatever the reason, they identified with the latter.

Partly because of his important role in the teaching of theory to undergraduates and (less well-prepared) beginning graduates, in the 1930s and until his untimely death in 1946, Henry Simons exercised an important influence on Chicago students.

But he is remembered mainly for his essays on economic policy (collected in Simons, 1948) which constituted the principal statement of Chicago laissez-faire views during this period.

Simons's view had a distinctly populist flavour that is absent from those more recently associated with Chicago economics. For example, he favoured use of government power to reduce the size of large firms and labour unions. Where such policies would lead to unacceptable losses of efficiency (e.g. 'natural monopolies'), Simons favoured outright public ownership. In sharp contrast to more recent Chicago statements on the matter, Simons emphatically supported progressive income taxation to promote a more egalitarian distribution of income (Simons, 1938).

Finally, Simons proposed a requirement of 100 per cent reserves against demand deposits and restriction of Federal Reserve discretion in monetary policy in favour of fixed rules designed to stabilize the price level (Simons, 1948). In this he was the direct forbear of Chicago monetarism, as later developed by Friedman and Friedman's students.

Historically, Friedman, Stigler and Wallis were both the intellectual and the institutional heirs of Knight and Viner. The story of Chicago economics would be less convoluted if the succession had been a matter of the older generation appointing their best students to succeed them. But it was not that simple. On the eve of World War II there was great concern, within the Economics Department and (probably) in the central administration as well, that Chicago had none of the leading figures in the new theoretical developments of the period; that is, in nonperfect competition and Keynesian macroeconomics.

To rectify this, in 1938, they appointed Oscar Lange as assistant professor. In addition to his credentials as a contributor to the literature of Keynes's *General Theory*, especially its relation to general equilibrium theory, Lange was a leading participant in the current debate on the possibility of market socialism and its (alleged) advantages relative to laissez-faire capitalism in terms of efficiency. Further, he had made a number of contributions to mathematical economics and was able to provide backup support for Henry Schultz in that subject area, and in mathematical statistics as well.

As an outspoken and politically active socialist, Lange's views were diametrically opposed to laissez faire. That he managed to stay on friendly terms with virtually all of his colleagues was a testimonial both to his own tact and to their tolerance of dissent. Of course, it was no accident that the principal socialist in the Chicago tradition should have been a *market* socialist.

Within a few months of Lange's appointment, Henry Schultz was killed in an automobile accident and Lange became the sole mathematical economist in the Chicago department. Within a year the loss of Schultz was compounded by the partial withdrawal of Douglas from academic life to pursue a political career. Still further, with the outbreak of World War II, Viner became increasingly involved in Washington and, ultimately, in 1945, he resigned to accept an appointment at Princeton.

As a result of these losses, the Department had to be rebuilt. The process of reconstruction began during the war years, with Lange taking a leading role. He was very anxious to recruit colleagues who were leaders in current theoretical developments, especially in mathematical economics. Failing to obtain his first choice, Abba Lerner, he readily accepted Jacob Marschak and, for a short period, collaborated with the latter in making further appointments both to the Department and to the Cowles Commission, which had located at the University of Chicago in 1938. The collaboration ended abruptly in 1945 when Lange resumed Polish citizenship to become ambassador to the United States and, subsequently, to fill many other high positions in the socialist government of Poland.

During the war years, T.W. Schultz was attracted from Iowa State. A leading figure in agricultural economics, Schultz soon became chairman, a position from which he exercised much influence for over two decades. In addition to Schultz, in 1946 the Department acquired Lloyd Metzler to teach international trade and a number of younger theorists and econometricians associated mainly with the Cowles Commission. Whatever was the intention, these appointments served as a counterweight to the more or less contemporaneous appointments of Friedman (to the Economics Department) and Wallis (to the Business School).

There then ensued a struggle for intellectual pre-eminence and institutional control between Friedman, Wallis and their adherents on one side, and the Cowles Commission and its supporters on the other. The struggle persisted into the early 1950s, ending only with the partial retirement of Lloyd Metzler (due to ill health) and the departure of the Cowles Commission (for Yale) in 1953. While not monolithic, the Chicago economics department that emerged from this conflict had a distinctive intellectual style that set it apart from most others.

In positive economics, this style involves de-emphasizing the role of aggregate effective demand as an explanatory variable and stressing the importance of relative prices and 'distortions' thereof. In economic policy, it involves stressing the beneficial effects of allowing prices to be set by market forces rather than by government regulation. In an important sense, 'Chicago economics' in the 1950s and 1960s was simply an extension of the ideas of the Knight coterie of the 1930s. Indeed, some of the key figures – notably Friedman, Stigler and Wallis – of that group were leading Chicago economists in the later period as well. Moreover, they were consciously concerned with explicating the continuity of the tradition and preserving it (see below).

The close personal relations of the members of the Knight coterie, maintained for over a half century, has reinforced the strong common elements in their idea-systems and made it easy to ignore the (important) points of disagreement, both among themselves and with others. As already mentioned, Friedman, Stigler and Wallis, like most Chicago economists of their own and subsequent cohorts, believe strongly in use of statistical data and techniques for testing economic theories. In this they differ from Knight, Simons, James Buchanan, Ronald Coase (1981) and a significant minority of other economists associated with Chicago, either as graduate students or faculty, who believe (on various grounds) that the validity of an economic theory lies in its intuitive appeal and/or its compatibility with a set of axioms, rather than in the conformity of its implications with empirical observation.

A second disagreement concerns the consistency of policy advocacy in any form, with the methodology applied in positive economics. (The most influential general description of this methodology is chapter 1 of Friedman, 1953.) This methodology recommends that explanations of economic behaviour be based on a model of (individual) decisions of resource allocation (among alternative uses) designed to maximize utility subject to the constraints of market prices and endowments of wealth. Market prices are presumed to be set so as to equate quantities supplied with those demanded, for all entities traded.

As traditionally applied by neoclassical economists with a

predilection for laissez faire, this methodology coexists with advocacy of government policies designed to promote that objective. But in the late 1960s one group of Chicago economists led by Stigler (who had returned to Chicago in 1958 as Walgreen Professor in both the Economics Department and the Business School) began to apply the tools of economic analysis to the investigation of the determinants of political activity, especially government intervention in resource allocation. Thus study of the regulatory and taxing activities of the state became directed not simply at demonstrating their adverse effects upon economic efficiency, but primarily to explaining their occurrence as an outcome of the operation of 'political markets' for such activities.

So analysed, interventions traditionally viewed as efficiency impairing, such as tariffs, require reinterpretation. An individual's resources include not only his command over goods and services acquired through conventional markets, but also his political influence (however measured). Government interventions are considered to be endogenous outcomes of a political-economic process, reflecting the political as well as the economic wealth of decision making units, and not as aberrations of an exogenous state (e.g. see Stigler, 1982). So viewed, criticism of political outcomes is no more warranted than criticism of the expenditure behaviour of sovereign consumers; both are outcomes of the free choice of resource owners.

This is not to suggest that the 'political economy' wing among Chicago economists has become indifferent to laissez faire. On the contrary, opposition to government intervention (e.g. regulation) among Stigler and his allies is quite as strong as it ever has been. During the past decade many economists and lawyers at some time affiliated with the Law and Economics group at Chicago have been prominent advocates of deregulation. However, tension between advocacy of reform, and positive analysis of the political process through which reform must be achieved, presents a continuing existential problem to the heirs of the Chicago tradition. Although they are well aware of the problem, thus far they have refrained from divisive dispute and treat exercises in political advocacy as a consumption activity by those engaged.

Political science is only one of the fields into which Chicago economics has expanded during the past quarter century. Beginning in the early 1940s and accelerating in the last two decades under Richard Posner's leadership, the economic analysis of legal institutions has become an important area of research both for economists and for legal scholars. Further, using the theory of labour supply as a point of departure, the economic analysis of the family has become an important part of the study of population, marriage, divorce and family structure. This development has challenged sociological and psychological modes of explanation in fields that had long been considered provinces of these other disciplines. Still further, the theory of human capital has had a major impact on the study of education.

It is convenient to date the 'disciplinary imperialist' phase of the Chicago School as beginning in the early 1960s and continuing to the present. However, its roots go back into the 1930s; since that time there has been, at least in the oral tradition, a tropism for application of the tools and concepts of price theory to (seemingly) alien situations, and for taking delight in confronting conventional wisdom with the results. Correlatively, there has been a strong tendency to resist explanations of behaviour that do not run in terms of utility maximization by individual decision-makers coordinated by market clearing prices.

However, until well into the 1950s, the disciplinary imperialist aspect of the Chicago paradigm was overshadowed by the struggle to defend the integrity of neoclassical price theory from the attacks of Keynesians at the macro level and the attempts of various theorists of nonperfect competition to provide alternatives at the micro level. The counterattack on the *General Theory* produced a revival of neoclassical monetary theory in a refined and empirically implemented form; this revival is associated with the work of Milton Friedman (1956).

The struggle to re-establish the competitive industry as the dominant model for explaining relative prices was led by Stigler (1968, 1970), and generated much of the theoretical and empirical literature of the field of Industrial Organization. Both in Industrial Organization and Money-Macro, the earlier debates continue, with Chicago-based participants being identifiable as partisans of the standpoints of Friedman and Stigler a quarter of a century ago. However, in the 1970s and 1980s the topics related to these debates have been forced to share centre stage with newer subjects.

The expansion of Chicago economics beyond the traditional boundaries of the discipline began in the middle and late 1950s; two early examples were H.G. Lewis's application of price theory to the 'demand and supply of unionism' (Lewis, 1959) and Gary Becker's dissertation on racial discrimination (Becker, 1957). These were followed in the 1960s and 1970s by a number of others, as already mentioned. Many of these are more or less straightforward applications of conventional price theory to new problems. However, the analysis of time as an economic resource (Becker, 1965) has led to important improvements in the theory of household behaviour.

The analysis of time is also related to a methodological tendency to reject differences in tastes (including attitudes, opinions and beliefs in 'tastes') as a source for explanations of cross-individual differences in behaviour (Stigler and Becker, 1977; Becker, 1976). The rejection is based on the contention that (1) seeming differences of taste are usually reducible to differences of cost and (2) statements about cost differences are much more amenable to empirical test. While this methodological principle has met with resistance, at Chicago as elsewhere, it is reflected in a great deal of ongoing research, especially where cost of time is an important variable.

A separate path of disciplinary expansion has arisen in the field of Finance. Whether, prior to the 1960s, this field was a province of Economics, is a point that it is convenient to bypass. But unquestionably, prior to the theoretical developments initiated by Modigliani and Miller's famous paper (1958) on the (non) relation of stock prices and dividends, the theory of corporate finance, asset prices, risk-bearing and related topics had at best only a tenuous relationship with the theory of price. Subsequent developments have completely reversed that situation, so that in the mid-1980s, the 'capital asset pricing model' has become an integrating matrix for the theories of security prices, asset structure of the firm, and, via the study of executive compensation, wages.

The dominant idea underlying these developments is that, save for transaction costs, *on average* no opportunity for arbitrage gains goes unexploited. One implication of this is the proposition that there is 'no free lunch'; another implication is that no specifiable algorithm can be found that will enable a resource owner to utilize publicly available information to predict movements of asset prices well enough to gain by trading. The latter implication is tantamount to the 'hypothesis of efficient markets'.

While not formally identical with rational expectations, efficient markets will support any behaviour conforming to rational expectations, but will be compatible with other models of expectations only where one or another set of correlated forecast errors (across individuals) is assumed. Moreover, so long as expectations are rational, and regardless of how they are generated, there is no way in which variables operating through expectations can improve upon the neoclassical explanation of relative prices and quantities. This obviates any need for augmenting economic theory by variables reflecting psychological or sociological factors that operate upon individual decision-making via expectations. Obviously, such a theory of expectations is strongly supportive of the claims of economic theory in interdisciplinary competition.

The interrelated ideas of rational expectations and efficient markets originated at Carnegie-Mellon in the work of Muth (1961) and Modigliani and Miller (1958) rather than at Chicago. However, their consonance with the Chicago paradigm is such that they have found a home in the Chicago Business School under the leadership of Miller and his students, and (since the mid-1970s) in the Economics Department under Robert Lucas, rather than in their place of origin. While the claim of Chicago to be the primary locus for research in these fields is a strong one, it is a claim more subject to challenge than analogous claims in some other fields.

Yet a third Chicago innovation of the late 1950s is the 'Coase Theorem' (Coase, 1960). In essence this theorem states that, ignoring transaction costs, if there is any reallocation of goods, claims, rights (especially property) or alteration of institutions that – after making compensating side payments to losers – increases the utility of everyone, said reallocation will occur. If rationality is a maintained hypothesis and transaction costs are negligible, the theorem becomes a tautology. Thus the empirical content of the theorem will vary inversely with the importance attributed to transaction costs, which serve as a conceptual receptacle for all forces bearing upon decision-making other than those explicitly incorporated in the theory of price. To consider the Coase Theorem empirically important is to believe that transaction costs and departures from rationality are unimportant.

Put differently, the Coase Theorem suggests that the real world tends towards a position of Pareto optimality. Of course, for given tastes and technology, there may be a different Pareto optimum for each distribution of wealth. Therefore, to the extent that the distribution of wealth is exogenous and has important behavioural consequences, the predictive implications of both Pareto optimality and the Coase Theorem are less salient. Thus the rise in influence of the Coase Theorem at Chicago has more or less paralleled a decline in the marked concern with income distribution that existed in the 1930s and 1940s, especially in the work of Henry Simons (Reder, 1982, p. 389).

When objects of exchange are taken to include legislation and other political variables, the Coase Theorem strongly suggests that the forces of decentralized decision-making that govern production and exchange also control changes in laws and institutions. Thus belief in the Coase Theorem is – or should be – conducive to political passivity. Nevertheless, not all Chicago economists are politically quiescent. But with few exceptions, they are generally conservative, though with considerable differences of shading and intensity of belief, and in taste for political controversy. Probably these differences parallel differences in the degree to which they accept economic explanations of political behaviour. Perhaps the most common characteristic of Chicago economists is distrust of the state. This distrust, together with the belief that, given time, voluntary exchange will usually generate truly desirable reforms, acts as a powerful brake on wayward impulses to improve society through political action.

The saga of the Chicago School is at once the story of the evolution of a set of ideas – a paradigm – and of a particular institution with which its leading protagonists have been associated. In this essay I have emphasized certain central theoretical ideas and historical events to the exclusion of detailed coverage of applied work and mention of the individuals responsible for it. However, it is the association of these central ideas with an identifiable, multigenerational group of individuals located at a particular institution that justifies the title of this article. Many of the key individuals in this history – Director, Friedman, Stigler, Wallis – are still alive, intellectually active and in close touch with their successors on the Chicago faculty. This continuity, both of personalities and ideas, is a distinctive feature of the intellectual tradition called the Chicago School.

In the mid-1980s the vitality of this tradition is threatened more by the growing acceptance of many of its key ideas than by resistance to them. A quarter century ago, Chicago economics was distinguished by its emphasis on the importance of competition and money supply. Arguably, in 1985, these views and their extensions have become mainstream economics, leaving the story of the Chicago School as a nearly closed episode in the history of economic thought. While such an argument may prove valid, it is too soon to tell.

M.W. REDER

See also COASE, RONALD HARRY; DOUGLAS, PAUL HOWARD; FRIEDMAN, MILTON; KNIGHT, FRANK HYNEMAN; LANGE, OSKAR; LAUGHLIN, JAMES LAURENCE; METZLER, LLOYD APPLETON; SCHULTZ, HENRY; SCHULTZ, THEODORE WILHAIN; SIMONS, HENRY CALVERT; STIGLER, GEORGE JOSEPH; VINER, JACOB.

BIBLIOGRAPHY

Becker, G.S. 1957. *The Economics of Discrimination*. Chicago: University of Chicago Press.

Becker, G.S. 1965. A theory of the allocation of time. *Economic Journal* 75, September, 493–517.

Becker, G.S. 1976. *The Economic Approach to Human Behavior*. Chicago: University of Chicago Press.

Coase, R.H. 1960. The problem of social cost. *Journal of Law and Economics* 3(1), October, 1–44.

Coase, R.H. 1981. How should economists choose? Washington, DC: American Enterprise Institute for Public Policy Research.

Friedman, M. 1953. *Essays in Positive Economics*. Chicago: University of Chicago Press.

Friedman, M. 1956. *Studies in the Quantity Theory of Money*. Chicago: University of Chicago Press.

Lewis, H. Gregg. 1959. Competitive and monopoly unionism. In *The Public Stake in Union Power*, ed. P.D. Bradley, Charlottesville: University of Virginia Press.

Modigliani, F. and Miller, M.H. 1958. The cost of capital, corporation finance and the theory of investment. *American Economic Review* 48, June, 261–97.

Muth, J.F. 1961. Rational expectations and the theory of price movements. *Econometrica* 29, July, 315–35.

Reder, M.W. 1982. Chicago economics: permanence and change. *Journal of Economic Literature* 20(1), March, 1–38.

Simons, H.C. 1938. *Personal Income Taxation*. Chicago: University of Chicago Press.

Simons, H.C. 1948. *Economic Policy for a Free Society*. Chicago: University of Chicago Press.

Stigler, G.J. 1968. *The Organization of Industry*: Homewood, Ill.: Richard D. Irwin.

Stigler, G.J. 1982. Economists and public policy. Washington, DC: American Enterprise Institute for Public Policy Research.

Stigler, G.J. and Becker, G.S. 1977. De gustibus non est disputandum. *American Economic Review* 67(2) March, 76–90.

Stigler, G.J. and Kindahl, J.K. 1970. *The Behavior of Industrial Prices*. New York: Columbia University Press for the National Bureau of Economic Research.

Child, Josiah (1630–1699).

Child, Josiah (1630–1699). The second son of Richard Child, a London merchant, Sir Josiah Child was born in 1630 and enjoyed a highly successful merchant career during which he amassed a considerable fortune. His business ventures, which included the provisioning of Navy ships, led to his appointment as Deputy to the Navy's Treasurer at Portsmouth in 1655 and he became Mayor of that city in 1658. He was appointed a Director of the East India Company in 1674, and with the exception of 1676 he was re-elected to a Directorship in every subsequent year until his death. In 1681 he was elected Governor of the Company and established a close relationship with the Crown. Following the Revolution of 1688, and in response to mounting attacks on his conduct of Company affairs, he relinquished some of his active management responsibilities.

Child's claim to recognition as an economist rests on his *Brief Observations concerning Trade and Interest of Money*, first published in 1668 and reissued (anonymously) in expanded form as *A Discourse about Trade* in 1690 and again as *A New Discourse of Trade* (with Child's name on the title page) in 1693. The work summarizes the views he presented to the Council of Trade appointed by the King in 1668 (following the appointment of a Select Committee on the State of Trade by the House of Commons in the preceding year) and to a similar House of Lords Committee in 1669.

Among the reasons for the mercantile supremacy of the Dutch, he cites the establishment of banks and the widespread use of transferable bills of exchange, which he strongly argued should be adopted in England. He argued for a reduction of the legal maximum rate of interest from six to four per cent (referring to this as 'my old theme'), claiming that the lower rate of interest in the Netherlands was 'the *causa causans* of all the other causes of the riches of that people'. He saw the beneficial effects on trade of a lower cost of money capital, but he did not discuss, as did John Locke at the same time, the relation between a legally established rate of interest and the rate established by natural market forces.

Child's argument that the beneficial effect of lower interest rates would cause 'all sorts of labouring people that depend on trade (to be) more constantly and fully employed' took up the then widespread concern with the employment problem and he concluded: 'it is our duty to God and nature so to provide for and employ the poor'. A significant discussion of the question of the poor and a scheme for their relief and employment is included in Chapter II of the *Discourse of Trade*.

Notwithstanding his scattered observations that appear to support free trade principles and his assertion of the principles of competitive markets, Child was an exponent of monopoly when it suited his and the East India Company's advantage. He recognized the need to export bullion if that gave rise to further export trade opportunities. But his work abounds in arguments for trade restrictions in specific cases, such as those requiring the transportation of traded commodities in English vessels and requiring that colonial trade should be conducted only with England, thereby emphasizing the domestic employment-creating effects of the colonies. He stands as a latter-day mercantilist rather than an analytical anticipator of the *laissez faire* doctrines of genuine and generalized freedom of trade.

DOUGLAS VICKERS

SELECTED WORKS

1668. *Brief Observations concerning Trade and Interest of Money*. London.
1693. *A New Discourse of Trade*. London.

BIBLIOGRAPHY

Letwin, W. 1959. *Sir Josiah Child, Merchant Economist*. Boston: Harvard Graduate School of Business.
Macauley, Thomas (Lord). 1848, 1855, 1861. *The History of England from the Accession to James the Second*. New York: AMS Press, 1968.
Schumpeter, J.A. 1954. *History of Economic Analysis*. New York: Oxford University Press.

choice of technique and the rate of profit.

CAPITALISTIC CRITERION. In a capitalistic economy the main production decisions are made by private capitalists. The choice of technique is one of the decisions in their hands, and the criterion for that choice is to maximize the expected profit rate. In order to calculate that rate they must have expectations of the prices of various commodities, and of the wage rate.

Assuming a linear technology, in the ith sector capitalists have T_i alternative techniques:

$$a_{i1}(k_i), a_{i2}(k_i), \ldots, a_{in}(k_i), \tau_i(k_i) \qquad k_i = 1, 2, \ldots, T_i$$

where $a_{ij}(k_i)$ is the amount of the jth commodity used as input to produce one unit of the ith commodity by the k_ith technique and $\tau_i(k_i)$ is the amount of labour necessary to produce one unit of the ith commodity by the k_ith technique.

Capitalists have expected prices and the wage rate:

$$p_1^e, p_2^e, \ldots, p_n^e, w^e$$

where p_i^e is the expected price of the ith commodity and w^e is the expected wage rate.

The expected profit rate from the k_i technique, which is denoted as $r_i^e(k_i)$, is calculated as

$$p_i^e = [1 + r_i^e(k_i)]\left[\sum a_{ij}(k_i)p_j^e + \tau_i(k_i)w^e\right].$$

Capitalists choose the technique which yields the highest expected profit rate. If

$$r_i^e(k_i^*) \geqq r_i^e(k_i) \qquad k_i = 1, 2, \ldots, T_i \qquad (1)$$

then they choose the k_i^*th technique among T_i alternatives. As is easily seen, (1) can be rewritten as

$$\sum a_{ij}(k_i^*)p_j^e + \tau_i(k_i^*)w^e \leqq \sum a_{ij}(k_i)p_j^e + \tau_i(k_i)w^e$$
$$k_i = 1, 2, \ldots, T_i \qquad (2)$$

The means that the expected unit cost is smallest in the k_i^*th technique. So in this case *the maximum profit rate criterion* is equivalent to *the minimum unit cost criterion*. However, this equivalence does not hold in general. If we introduce durable equipment the two criteria are not equivalent. But for simplicity here we will ignore durable equipment.

PROFIT RATE AND TECHNIQUES. In the ith sector by the minimum unit cost criterion capitalists adopt the technique

$$a_{i1}, a_{i2}, \ldots, a_{in}, \tau_i$$

and labourers receive the commodity basket

$$b_1, b_2, \ldots, b_n$$

per unit of labour. Then an equal rate of profit r between n

sectors is determined by the following equations:

$$p_i = (1 + r)\left(\sum_{j=1}^{n} a_{ij} p_j + \tau_i w \right) \qquad i = 1, 2, \ldots, n$$

$$w = \sum_{i=1}^{n} b_i p_i \tag{3}$$

From these equations it is clear that the profit rate r depends on techniques (a_{ij}, τ_i) and the real wage basket (b_i).

In order to examine the relationship between the profit rate and techniques in various sectors, we must introduce a new concept: *basic sectors*. P. Sraffa has used this terminology, defining basic sectors as those whose outputs are directly or indirectly necessary in the production of every commodity (see ch. 2 in Sraffa, 1960).

However, it is not guaranteed a priori that such basic sectors exist; and even if they do exist, the concept is not useful for our purpose here.

Now we redefine basic sectors as those whose products are wage goods, or whose products are directly or indirectly necessary to produce wage goods. 'Wage goods' means commodities which are included in the real wage basket $(b_1, \ldots, b_n)$. If $b_i > 0$ then the ith commodity is a wage good. Basic sectors in this sense necessarily exist, for there must be at least one commodity which is a wage good.

Suppose there are m basic sectors, with $m \leqslant n$; after renumbering, let the 1st, 2nd, $\ldots$, mth sectors be basic sectors. Then the equations

$$p_i = (1 + r)\left(\sum_{i=1}^{m} a_{ij} p_j + \tau_i w \right) \qquad i = 1, 2, \ldots, m$$

$$w = \sum_{i=1}^{m} b_i p_i \tag{4}$$

are sufficient to determine the profit rate r, where prices $(p_1, \ldots, p_m)$ and the wage rate w are both positive. Therefore we can say that the profit rate does not depend on techniques in the non-basic sectors. For example, pure luxury goods are non-basic commodities. Whatever great improvement may occur in the techniques in those sectors, the (equalled) rate of profit is not influenced at all. This conclusion was first found by Ricardo, but Marx did not accept it (Ricardo, 1821, p. 132; Marx, 1867–94, Vol. III, ch. 5, pp. 83–4).

Hereafter in this essay we confine ourselves to techniques in the basic sectors only, and we assume that the classification into basics and non-basics remains unaffected by the technical changes considered here.

TECHNICAL PROGRESS. Let us suppose the profit rate r to be determined by (4), and that in the kth sector $(1 \leqslant k \leqslant m)$ a *new* alternative technique

$$a'_{k_1}, a'_{k_2}, \ldots, a'_{k_m}, \tau'_k$$

becomes feasible. Capitalists must then calculate the expected profit rate of this new technique and compare it with those of alternative techniques to decide whether or not to adopt it, so we now need an assumption about how capitalists form their expectations. For simplicity we assume

$$p_i^e = p_i, \quad w^e = w \qquad i = 1, 2, \ldots, m$$

i.e. capitalists expect that current prices and the wage rate, as given by (4), will remain the same (static expectations).

If the following inequality holds, capitalists adopt the new technique:

$$\sum_{j=1}^{m} a'_{kj} p_j + \tau'_k w < \sum_{j=1}^{m} a_{kj} p_j + \tau_k w \tag{5}$$

Supposing this to be so, the previous technique in the kth sector $(a_{k_1}, a_{k_2}, \ldots, a_{k_m}, \tau_k)$ is replaced by the new technique $(a'_{k_1}, a'_{k_2}, \ldots, a'_{k_m}, \tau'_k)$. How does the profit rate r as given by equation (4) then change, under the requirement that the real wage basket remain unchanged? We can prove that the profit rate r necessarily rises, as follows:

Putting

$$\beta = 1/(1 + r), \quad q_i = p_i/w,$$

equations (4) are rewritten as

$$\beta q_i = \sum a_{ij} q_j + \tau_i, \qquad i = 1, 2, \ldots, m \tag{6}$$

$$1 = \sum b_i q_i \tag{7}$$

Let the solution of (6) and (7) be

$$(\beta, q_1, \ldots, q_m).$$

When $(a_{k_1}, a_{k_2}, \ldots, a_{k_m}, \tau_k)$ is replaced by $(a'_{k_1}, a'_{k_2}, \ldots, a'_{k_m}, \tau'_k)$, the profit rate is determined by

$$\beta q_i = \sum a_{ij} q_j + \tau_i, \qquad i = 1, \ldots, k - 1, k + 1, \ldots, m \tag{8}$$

$$\beta q_k = \sum a'_{kj} q_j + \tau'_k \tag{9}$$

and (7). Let the solution of (8), (9) and (7) be

$$(\beta', q'_1, \ldots, q'_m).$$

As $q'_i > 0$ for all i, the coefficients matrix of q_i $(i = 1, 2, \ldots, m)$ satisfies the Hawkins–Simon conditions (see Simon and Hawkins, 1949).

From (6)–(9), we get

$$\beta' \Delta q_i = \sum a_{ij} \Delta q_j - q_j \Delta \beta,$$
$$i = 1, \ldots, k - 1, k + 1, \ldots, m \tag{10}$$

$$\beta' \Delta q_k = \sum a'_{kj} \Delta q_j - q_k \Delta \beta + \left\{ \sum q_j \Delta a_{kj} + \Delta \tau_k \right\} \tag{11}$$

$$0 = \sum b_i \Delta q_i \tag{12}$$

where

$$\Delta q_i = q'_i - q_i, \qquad \Delta \beta = \beta' - \beta$$
$$\Delta a_{kj} = a'_{kj} - a_{kj}, \qquad \Delta \tau_k = \tau'_k - \tau_k.$$

The third term on the right side of (11) is negative, by (5). If $\Delta \beta \geqslant 0$, then in (10) and (11) $\Delta q_k < 0$ and $\Delta q_i > 0$ for all $i \neq k$, because as shown above the coefficient matrix of Δq_i in (10) and (11) satisfies the Hawkins–Simon conditions. If the kth commodity is a wage good, $\Delta q_k < 0$ contradicts (12). If the kth commodity is a means of production (that is it belongs to the basic sectors), there must be at least one kind of wage good whose $\Delta q_i < 0$; again this contradicts (12). So $\Delta \beta > 0$, or in other words the profit rate r rises.

The proposition that any new technique which satisfies the profit rate criterion (5) and so is introduced into the basic industries necessarily increases the general rate of profit, cannot be compatible with the Marxian law of the tendency for the profit rate to fall. However large the organic composition of production may become, the general rate of profit must increase without exception, provided that the newly introduced technique satisfies the profit rate criterion and the rate of real wage remains constant (see Okishio, 1961, for further discussion).

JOINT PRODUCTION. So far we have disregarded joint production as well as durable equipment. Even if we introduce durable equipment, the conclusion obtained in the former section still holds (see Nakatani, 1984). However, when we consider the joint production it is possible (though not necessary) to find a case in which the proposition does not hold, a perverse conclusion that was originally presented by Salvadori (1981).

	Input			Output	
Technique	1	2	Labour	1	2
1	0.5	0.5	1	1	2
2		0.5	1	1	
3		0.5	1	2	

In order to show such a case we examine the following numerical example. In this economy, shown in table 1, there are two kinds of commodity. The second commodity is a wage good and it is produced jointly with the first commodity. Let the real wage rate be 0.7 unit of the second commodity. At the first stage we assume that techniques 1 and 2 only are feasible.

The profit rates of techniques 1 and 2 are determined by

$$p_1 + 2p_2 = (1 + r_1)(0.5p_1 + 0.5p_2 + w)$$
$$p_1 = (1 + r_2)(0.5p_2 + w)$$
$$w = 0.7p_2$$

where r_1, r_2 are the profit rates of techniques 1 and 2, respectively. Putting $p = p_1/p_2$ these equations are rewritten as

$$p + 2 = (1 + r_1)(0.5p + 1.2)$$
$$p = 1.2(1 + r_2)$$

The profit rates of both technique are drawn on Figure 1.

Now we examine the condition in which both techniques 1 and 2 are used. If technique 1 only is used at activity level x, then the surplus products consist of $(1 - 0.5)x$ units of commodity 1 and $(2 - 0.5 \simeq 0.5)x$ units of commodity 2. Therefore if the capitalists' demand for the surplus products (for their consumption or investment) are 100 units of commodity 1 and 50 units of commodity 2, then there must be excess demand for commodity 1 or excess supply for commodity 2 and the relative price p_1/p_2 increases.

When p rises above p^* the expected profit rate r_2 becomes greater than r_1, so technique 2 is introduced. However, technique 2 cannot replace technique 1 completely because technique 2 cannot produce commodity 2. Therefore both techniques must be used, which requires that the equal rate of profit be determined at r^*.

At the next stage we assume that technique 3 becomes feasible. Technique 3 is apparently superior to technique 2, because in the new technique capitalists get more output from

the same input, so it replaces technique 2. The profit rate of technique 3 is calculated from

$$2p_1 = (1 + r_3)(0.5p_2 + w)$$
$$w = 0.7p_2$$

which can be rewritten as

$$2p = 1.2(1 + r_3)$$

This equation is also plotted on figure 1, from which it can be seen that the equalized rate of profit falls to r'.

SUBSTITUTIONAL TECHNICAL CHANGE. In the previous sections we treated the relationship between the profit rate and technical change under the condition that the real wage basket remain unchanged. The change in the technique adopted was not induced by a change in the real wage rate, but was caused by the introduction of a new process.

The question now is the relationship between the profit rate and technical change that is induced by a change in the real wage rate. We define the level of the real wage rate λ as follows. Assume that each labourer spends his wage income on various wage goods in fixed proportions. Then we have

$$w = \lambda \sum b_i p_i,$$

where the b_i are all constant and λ is the level of the real wage rate.

At the first stage $\lambda = 1$, and the profit rate is determined by equations (6) and (7). At the next stage $\lambda > 1$, which means a rise in the real wage rate. Then the profit rate is determined by the following equations

$$\beta q_i = \sum a'_{ij} q_j + \tau'_i \qquad i = 1, 2, \ldots, m \qquad (13)$$
$$1 = \lambda \sum b_i q_i \qquad \lambda > 1. \qquad (14)$$

As shown in (13) the techniques used in every sector may differ from the techniques used at the first stage, because of the rise of the real wage rate and the change of prices which accompanies it. What can we say about the relationship between the newly adopted technique (a'_{ij}, τ'_i) and the old technique (a_{ij}, τ_i)? (Of course we assume that no technique becomes newly feasible for capitalists between the first stage and the next stage.)

Let the solution of (6) and (7) be

$$(\beta, q_i, \ldots, q_m).$$

Then

$$\sum a_{ij} q_j + \tau_i \lessgtr \sum a'_{ij} q_j + \tau'_i \qquad (15)$$

because technique (a_{ij}, τ_i) would not have been adopted at the first stage if inequality (15) had not held; rather they would have adopted (a'_{ij}, τ'_i).

Let the solution of (13) and (14) be

$$(\bar{\beta}, \bar{q}_1, \ldots, \bar{q}_m).$$

Then, arguing as for (15),

$$\sum a_{ij} \bar{q}_j + \tau_i \gtrless \sum a'_{ij} \bar{q}_j + \tau'_i. \qquad (16)$$

Using inequalities (15) and (16) we can prove that in going from the first stage to the second the profit rate necessarily falls, as follows:

From (6), (7), (13) and (14) we get

$$\bar{\beta} \delta q_i = \sum a'_{ij} \delta q_j + q_i \delta \beta + \left\{ \sum (a'_{ij} - a_{ij}) q_j + (\tau'_i - \tau_i) \right\}$$
$$i = 1, 2, \ldots, m \qquad (17)$$
$$0 = \sum b_i \delta q_i + (\lambda - 1) \sum b_i \bar{q}_i \qquad (18)$$

where

$$\delta q_i = \bar{q}_i - q_i, \quad \delta \beta = \bar{\beta} - \beta.$$

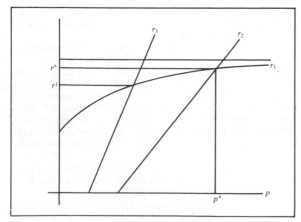

Figure 1

From (15) we know that the third term on the r.h.s. of (17) is non-negative. If we assume $\delta\beta \leqslant 0$ then all the δq_i become non-negative because the coefficient matrix of δq_i satisfies the Hawkins–Simon conditions. But since $\lambda > 1$ that contradicts (18). So $\delta\beta$ must be positive, or in other words the profit rate must fall.

When the real wage rate rises capitalists cannot avoid a fall in the profit rate, even if they substitute techniques to avoid it; only the introduction of new and superior feasible techniques can prevent the fall. However, we cannot say that the capitalists' efforts to substitute with exciting techniques are of no use to them. Though they cannot avoid a fall in the profit rate, they can mitigate it. We can prove this as follows.

If in spite of the rise in the real wage rate capitalists adhere to the techniques adopted at the first stage, the profit rate is determined by

$$\beta q_i = \sum a_{ij} q_j + \tau_i \qquad i = 1, 2, \ldots, m \tag{19}$$

$$1 = \lambda \sum b_i q_i \qquad \lambda > 1 \tag{20}$$

Let the solution of (19) and (20) be

$$(\beta^*, q_1^*, \ldots, q_m^*).$$

From (13), (14), (19) and (20) we get

$$\beta^* \, dq_i = \sum a_{ij} \, dq_j - q_i^* \, d\beta + \left\{ \sum (a_{ij}' - a_{ij}))\bar{q}_j + (\tau_i' - \tau_i) \right\}$$
$$i = 1, 2, \ldots, m \tag{21}$$

$$0 = \lambda \sum b_i \, dq_i \tag{22}$$

where

$$dq_i = \bar{q}_i - q_i^*, \quad d\beta = \bar{\beta} - \beta^*.$$

From (16) the third term of the r.h.s. of (21) is non-positive. However, if we now consider the case in which substitution actually occurs, then for some i the third term on the r.h.s. of (21) is negative. If we assume $d\beta \geqslant 0$, then all the dq_i become non-positive and some actually negative, because the coefficient matrix of dq_i satisfies the Hawkins–Simon conditions. This contradicts (22) so $d\beta < 0$. In other words, when the substitution is carried out the profit rate is greater than it would have been if capitalists had adhered to the old optimal technique, which corresponded with the former level of the real wage rate.

N. OKISHIO

See also INVESTMENT DECISION CRITERIA; INVESTMENT PLANNING; NON-SUBSTITUTION THEORIES.

BIBLIOGRAPHY

Marx, K. 1867–94. *Capital*. Translated from the third German edition by Samuel Moore and Edward Aveling, ed. Frederick Engels. Reprinted, New York: International Publishers, 1967.

Nakatani, T. 1984. Technical change and the rate of profit: considering fixed capital. *Kobe University Economic Review* 30, 65–78.

Okishio, N. 1961. Technical changes and the rate of profit. *Kobe University Economic Review* 7, 85–99.

Ricardo, D. 1821. *On the Principles of Political Economy and Taxation*. Vol. 1 of *The Works and Correspondence of David Ricardo*, ed. P. Sraffa, Cambridge: Cambridge University Press, 1951.

Salvadori, N. 1981. Falling rate of profit with a constant real wage: an example. *Cambridge Journal of Economics* 5(1), March, 59–66.

Simon, H.A. and Hawkins, D. 1949. Some conditions of macroeconomic stability. *Econometrica* 17, July–October, 245–48.

Sraffa, P. 1960. *Production of Commodities by Means of Commodities: Prelude to a Critique of Economic Theory*. Cambridge: Cambridge University Press.

choice theory. *See* UTILITY THEORY AND DECISION-MAKING.

chrematistics. A Greek word occasionally taken over into English (and some other western European languages) to mean 'money-getting', often but not always with pejorative overtones. After a great flurry in the 5th and 4th centuries BC in the original Greek, the word became uncommon and would not be worth noticing here were it not that the major debates among Greek thinkers, chiefly ethical, were revived in the 13th century by the scholastic philosophers though without actually using the term 'chrematistic'. The earliest English example given by the *Oxford English Dictionary* dates from the mid-18th century, in Henry Fielding's last novel, *Amelia* (1752): 'I am not the least versed in the chrematistic art ... . I know not how to get a shilling, or how to keep it in my pocket if I had it' (Book IX, ch. 5). This pedantry implied no familiarity by readers, for Fielding promptly gave them the sense of it. Nor is there much to be drawn from the unimportant 19th-century terminological disagreement over the propriety of the term 'political economy', for which Gladstone and a few others preferred 'chrematistics'.

The word had a long and complex history in early Greek, which we cannot trace properly because of insufficient evidence. The ultimate root was the verb *chrao*, to 'need' or 'use', hence *chrema* (more common in the plural form, *chremata*), 'goods', 'property', 'wealth', and the verbal forms meaning 'to seek wealth'. (Other extensions, such as 'to engage in discussion or negotiations' or 'to consult an oracle' need not concern us.) Alongside these *chrao* words there were others with the same sense of goods, property, wealth, but all attempts to codify distinctions in usage, for instance between real property and moveable wealth, have proved not to reflect the actual practice of Greek speakers and writers.

Concomitant with this linguistic history there was a related development in commercial practice and attitudes. One thread that persisted in attitudes, however, was a distrust, even outright condemnation, of trading for profit, of making a profit out of the sheer act of exchange without any additions to, or transformation of, the goods being traded. This motif was already apparent in the *Odyssey*: when Odysseus declined the invitation to join in the games arranged following a feast at the court of King Alcinous of the Phaeacians, he was taunted by one of the courtiers with an unbearable insult:

> No indeed, stranger, I do not think you are like a man of games, ... but like one who travels with a many-benched ship, a master of sailors who traffic, one who remembers the cargo and is in charge of merchandise and coveted gains (*Odyssey*, 8, 145–64).

This distrust of trade can be amply exemplified right through pagan antiquity and then among the Church Fathers (on whom see Baldwin, 1959, pp. 12–16), with differences in nuance from culture to culture and from author to author that are sometimes interesting and at times paradoxical in their practical implications. Cicero provides a neat illustration. In the *De officiis* (1, 150–1) he dismisses those 'who buy from merchants in order to re-sell immediately, for they would make no profit without much outright lying', whereas commerce that is 'large-scale and extensive, importing much from all over the distributing to many without misrepresentation (*vanitas*), is not to be greatly censured'. In that nuance there was an exception because of the social usefulness of the large-scale merchant in his role as importer, with the consequent suggestion that he, unlike the petty trader in the market, was able to avoid outright lying. Not all moralists allowed such an exception, and Cicero gives no hint why one was in practice possible in this particular instance.

What I have been calling a paradox revealed itself when the moral judgements of a given culture or society conflicted with its legal system and rules of practice. Obviously large numbers of Greeks and Romans behaved contrary to the norms of commercial exchange laid down by Aristotle or Cicero, and on the whole both Greek and Roman law accepted the validity of private agreements provided only that they did not require actions specifically prohibited by the law. However, there were also major differences between the two, most obviously with respect to usury. Barring unimportant exceptions, especially in emergency situations, it was the rule among Greek states that no attempt was made to restrict or otherwise regulate rates of interest, whereas from earliest times the Roman law kept a tight reign on moneylending. Hence in Rome the professional moneylender, the *fenerator*, was a figure of distrust and contempt while men of means ranked moneylending at legal rates second only to land ownership as a source of income, and did not often blanch at charging exorbitant rates for loans to communities outside the sphere of the Roman law. There we see several paradoxes at work simultaneously.

This apparent detour has brought us back to the heart of the discussion of money-getting, of chrematistics. We can examine the formulations of moralists and we can match them against the legal precepts, but the critical question of practice in actual exchanges largely escapes us. Not only are we driven to outright guesses about pricing procedures (as about the actual practice with respect to interest charges), but there is no useful ancient testimony about the mechanism of price determination. Much of what is written about the meaning or the reality behind Aristotle's ambiguous formulation, or about Aquinas' concept of just price, is nothing but a backward projection of a modern author's own notions, for which there is no warrant (and often contrary evidence) in the ancient texts themselves (Finley, 1970).

In the end, we have only one surviving analysis from antiquity of the complex of issues raised by the notion of chrematistics (and no reason to think that other systematic accounts once existed and were eventually lost). That is the account by Aristotle and it is not only unsatisfactory but there can be no doubt that Aristotle himself thought it merely tentative and incomplete. It is enough to indicate that the term 'chrematistics' is used in three incompatible senses, with the pejorative one predominant (see in detail Newman, 1887–1902, II, 165–208). Nevertheless, Aristotle had made a serious start in grappling with a major social and moral problem, and one could have expected further discussion and development. Instead, the whole discussion promptly died for some 1,500 years until it was apparently revived with Albertus Magnus and Thomas Aquinas in the 13th century following the translation into Latin of the *Ethics* and the *Politics*. This is a curious puzzle in the history of ideas, and it must be said that modern accounts are dominated by illusions.

One is that not only was Aristotle one of the greatest figures in the history of philosophy, but that this was acknowledged in the generations after his death by the way in which philosophical questions were treated. Perhaps this was not often stated explicitly (since there was no textual foundation for such a view), but the implication was never far beneath the surface. Yet it is a fact that in the field of social thought the *Politics* was effectively lost sight of and unknown for some three centuries after the death of Aristotle's successor Theophrastus (see Sandbach, 1985), and that it continued to be neglected for a millennium. Between Cicero and the 13th century no more than a dozen references in Greek are known,

half of them in Byzantine lexica and scholia (Susemihl and Hicks, 1894, p. 18 n.7). Stoicism had quickly become the dominant school and the concept of natural law was its pivotal one. From the Greeks it passed to the Romans, and under the influence notably of Cicero and Seneca, it became one of the three foundation-stones of European ethics until the beginning of the modern era (and even beyond). How 'pure' this Stoic ethics remains is irrelevant. What is essential is its dominance and the fact that it by-passed the Aristotelian concern with chrematistics, justice in exchange, and the like.

The second foundation-stone was the Roman law, a confusing and ambiguous one. The Roman jurists were in practice firm supporters of the principle that any agreements made in good faith and not specifically prohibited by the law were acceptable. There was no place in that sphere for Aristotelian doctrines about chrematistics. Nor was there in the third foundation, the Church Fathers, despite their 'misgivings about the merchant' (Baldwin, 1959, pp. 12–16). The attitude of the New Testament to economic matters, unlike the Old, was a subject of controversy from the beginning, but what matters in our context is first that there was a hardening of attitudes on some matters, especially usury and the morals of commerce, over the final centuries of antiquity and the early Middle Ages, and that secondly, chrematistics hardly entered the discussion. From the 6th century on, church councils and later, in the Carolingian period, imperial enactments produced a stream of warnings about the 'morally dangerous character of buying and selling' (Baldwin, 1959, p. 34). The fullest account of this material remains Schaub (1905), with its revealing subtitle, 'eine moralhistorische Untersuchung'. By the 12th century, an impressive body of doctrine had been developed regarding usury, business practices and trade. The contrast is striking with the almost total emptiness on these subjects in the vast corpus of the writings of St Augustine (Cranz, 1954).

It is remarkable how the conventional histories of economic thought tend to skip over some seven centuries of 'moral history' as they leap from antiquity to the rediscovery of Aristotle and the apogee of scholasticism in the 13th century. In an important and neglected article published by the Pontifical Medieval Institute in Toronto, Eschmann (1943, p. 134) rightly concluded that in that century, dominated by Albertus Magnus and Thomas Aquinas, the rediscovery of Aristotle merely 'reinforces the Roman–patristic ideas and plays a decorative rather than a constructive role'. By then the fundamental principles had already been laid down in the solution of concrete problems arising from usury, buying and selling, and the conduct of trade. Aquinas may have codified such doctrines as just price, but he neither invented them nor found them in Aristotle. Because of the way he worked, in particular because he never produced a synthesis of social philosophy, there are puzzles that continue to plague commentators.

How, in particular, was the just price determined? That was Aristotle's problem (though in different language) with chrematistics, and, as we have seen, he never resolved it satisfactorily. But at least he made a serious effort: we know of none made by Aquinas. The common view today is that for the latter the just price was the prevailing one in normal practice, and I cannot avoid the suspicion that this is merely a projection into scholasticism of the thinking of neoclassical economists (e.g. Viner, 1978). As one historian who accepts the common view has conceded, nowhere did Aquinas 'state in practical terms what exactly comprised the just price' and the only textual support for the notion that the just price is the prevailing price comes from writers in the next generation or two (Baldwin, 1959, pp. 75–6). There is an alternative interpretation that at least merits more consideration than it has hitherto received: Aquinas, writes a neo-Thomist economist (Stark, 1956, p. 5), 'does not stop to consider the question how the just price is arrived at' because 'it is taken for granted ... like all the other rules and regulations of an orderly social existence'; 'the price is part and parcel of the system of custom on which all social life is built'.

Ironically, at the moment when the Aristotelian questions in their latter-day versions reached their intellectually most sophisticated formulation they were already moribund in practice, and they soon effectively dropped from sight, despite the lingering canon law and theological interest, in usury in particular. The slogan 'treasure by foreign trade' can be thought to have been the death-knell.

M.I. FINLEY

See also ARISTOTLE.

BIBLIOGRAPHY
Baldwin, J.W. 1959. The medieval theories of the just price. *Transactions of the American Philosophical Society* 49(4), 1–92.
Cranz, F.E. 1954. The development of August ideas on society. *Harvard Theological Review* 47(4), October, 255–316.
Eschmann, I.T. 1943. A Thomistic glossary on the principle of the preeminence of the common good. *Mediaeval Studies* 5, 123–65.
Finley, M.I. 1970. Aristotle and economic analysis. *Past and Present* 47, May, 5–25.
Newman, W.L. 1887–1902. *The Politics of Aristotle*. 4 vols, Oxford: Oxford University Press.
Sandbach, F.H. 1985. Aristotle and the Stoics. *Cambridge Philological Society, Supplement*, 10.
Schaub, F. 1905. *Der Kampf gegen den Zinswucher, ungerechten Preis und unlautern Handel im Mittelalter*. Freiburg: Herder.
Stark, W. 1956. The contained economy. Paper no. 26 of the Aquinas Society of London.
Susemihl, F. and Hicks, R.D. (eds) 1894. *The Politics of Aristotle, Books I–V*. London: Macmillan & Co.
Viner, J. 1978. Religious thought and economic society. *History of Political Economy* 10(1), Spring, 9–189.

Christaller, Walter (1894–1975). Christaller, who never held an academic post but worked throughout his life in association with the University of Erlangen, is known for one seminal book *Die zentralen Orte in Süddeutschland* (Central places in Southern Germany). Published in Germany in 1933 it remained largely unnoticed by English-speaking scholars until a translation of August Lösch's *Economics of Location* (1954) brought it widespread attention. Later an accurate translation of Christaller's book by C.W. Baskin (in 1966) confirmed the elegance of his deductive theorizing.

Christaller sought to clarify and explain the laws which determine the number, sizes and distribution of towns Drawing upon the work of von Thünen, Alfred Weber and Engländer, Christaller developed a general theory of why a *hierarchy* of villages and towns providing different services should appear and why this hierarchy should differ region by region. Making use of key concepts of market threshold, and normal travelling distance, he showed how the geographical extent of the trading areas for different goods and services vary and how low order centres provide limited ranges of goods to small trading areas whereas larger centres service much wider areas and contain all the goods of the lower centres as well as goods unique to their size.

Christaller's work has been criticized as ignoring the role of manufacturing in shaping the growth of towns and cities, of underplaying the effects of an unequal distribution of natural resources and of an all too rigid expression of the laws of market size and of the hierarchy of central places. Of the last point Christaller was fully aware and by 1950 he had modified his stance allowing for greater variability in the determinants of the hierarchy. And though his general theory of spatial relations is incomplete, all subsequent analysts of retail trade, of the location of services and of urban growth, recognize the rigour of his approach and the elegance of his attempt to provide the 'economic theoretical foundations of town geography'.

GORDON C. CAMERON

See also CENTRAL PLACE THEORY.

SELECTED WORKS
1933. *Die zentralen Orte in Süddeutschland: eine ökonomisch-geographische Untersuchung uber die Gesetzmässigkeit der Verbreitung und Entwicklung der Siedlungen mit stadtischen Funktionen*. Jena: G. Fischer. Trans. by C.W. Baskin as *Central Places in Southern Germany*, Englewood Cliffs, NJ: Prentice-Hall, 1966.
BIBLIOGRAPHY
Beavon, K.S.O. 1977. *Central Place Theory – a Re-interpretation*. London: Longman.
Berry, B.J.L. and Harris, C.D. 1970. Walter Christaller: an appreciation. *The Geographical Review* 60, 116–19.
Lösch, A. 1954. *The Economics of Location*. Trans. from the 2nd (1944) edn. by William H. Woglom with the assistance of Wolfgang F. Stolper, New Haven: Yale University Press. (1st German edn, 1940.)

Christian Socialism. Christian Socialism is a name which properly belongs to the propagation of cooperative production or working men's associations by F.D. Maurice and his disciples in the years 1849 to 1853. Its origin is to be found in a letter from J.M. Ludlow to Maurice (March 1848) saying that the socialism of Paris workmen was a real power which would shake Christianity if it were not Christianized. After the publication of Henry Mayhew's letters on the London poor in the *Morning Chronicle*, in 1849, Maurice and his followers at Lincoln's Inn, who had already been trying to persuade the Chartists, in *Politics for the People* (6 May to 29 July 1848), and in discussions at the Cranbourne Tavern, that moral and sanitary reform were of much more importance than extension of the suffrage, turned their attention to economic questions. They were led to deny any beneficence to the operation of self-interest. 'Free competition', said Ludlow, 'mars everywhere, instead of making, the wisest distribution of labour' (*Christian Socialism*, p. 35). 'We have protested', Maurice wrote to Dr Jelf, 12 November 1851, 'against the spirit of competition and rivalry precisely because we believe it is leading to anarchy, and must destroy at last the property of the rich as well as the existence of the poor' (*Life*, ch. ii, p. 83). As a remedy they proposed 'Christian socialism', or friendly association for productive purposes. They sometimes went so far as to imagine a state of things in which all producers might 'combine regularly into one body which should, after mutual explanations and by mutual concert, fix the terms upon which each member should dispose of his wares to the others' (Ludlow, *Christian Socialism*, p. 35); but they suggested no principle of distribution on which this agreement should be based. They founded an association of tailors (February 1850) of which Walter Cooper, formerly a Chartist, was manager, and organized a society for promoting working men's associations under a council of promoters among whom were Maurice, Charles Kingsley, T. Hughes, E.V. Neale, and F.J. Furnivall. *Alton Locke*, which represents the ethical side of the Christian Socialist doctrine, was published early in 1850, and was followed by *Tracts on Christian Socialism*, *Tracts by Christian Socialists*, and the *Christian Socialist*, a weekly penny paper which lasted from 20 November 1850 to the end of 1851. Its place was then taken by the *Journal of Association*, which endured till 28 June 1852. The evidence of the 'Promoters' before Slaney's Committee of the House of Commons on 'Investments for the savings of the middle and working classes' in 1850, aided in bringing about the legislation of cooperative societies by the 'Industrial and Provident Partnerships Act' of 1852. After the passing of that Act the society for promoting associations was remodelled and the term 'Christian Socialism', as employed in this connection, was abandoned. It was offensive alike to theologians, economists, and socialists. The hostility displayed towards the Christian Socialists in many quarters was more due to the name they assumed, and to the vehemence with which Kingsley denounced competition, than to dislike of their Associations, though these were doubtless looked on with some suspicion as copies from French models.

[E. CANNAN]
Reprinted from *Palgrave's Dictionary of Political Economy.*

BIBLIOGRAPHY
Brentano, L. 1883. *Die christlichsoziale Bewegung in England.* 2nd edn, Leipzig, 1883.
Hughes, T. 1884. Prefatory Memoir in the Eversley edn of *Alton Locke*, 2 vols, London: John Murray, 1881.
Ludlow, J.M. 1851. *Christian Socialism and its Opponents.* London.
Maurice, F. 1884. *Life of Frederick Denison Maurice, chiefly told in his own letters.* London.

circular flow. The analysis of the social process of production and consumption must start from some notion of commodity circulation. Consideration of the simple cycle of agricultural production suggests that production is an essentially circular process, in the sense that the same goods appear both among the products and among the means of production. From this viewpoint, commodity (as well as money) circulation is a triviality, whose discovery cannot really be attributed to any particular economist.

It has been suggested that the notion was originally developed by François Quesnay, a surgeon, by analogy with the circulation of the blood. However the popular analogy between money and blood is much older (see for instance 'Money is for the state what blood is for the human body', *Etats généraux*, 1484); and the process of money and commodity circulation among different classes (landlords, labourers, merchants) and areas (town and country) was clearly described by Boisguillebert and Cantillon several decades before the physiocrats.

What is truly novel with Quesnay is the idea that the essential task of economic science is the investigation of the technical and social conditions which allow the repetition of the circular process of production. This approach (at least in the extreme form given it by the physiocrats), and the peculiar model building activity that sprang from it, was later abandoned by economists. More than a century had to pass before the theme could be resumed, following the publication of Marx's own *tableaux* in the second volume of *Capital* (1885), but merely within the rather limited and isolated group of the German and Russian theoretical economists.

Tugan-Baranowsky considered circularity as the essential feature of capitalist economy, in which production was the end of consumption rather than the other way round; in his view,

the economists were unable to understand this 'paradox' because (with the remarkable exception of Marx) they had strayed from the way opened up by Quesnay. The young Schumpeter, in a justly celebrated essay, dated the birth of economics as a science from the physiocratic analysis of the circular flow. And Leontief (1928) wrote in a similar vein, arguing in favour of the substitution of the principle of circular flow (the 'reproducibility viewpoint') for that of *homo oeconomicus* (the 'scarcity viewpoint') as the cornerstone of economic theory.

The reproducibility viewpoint is shared by the whole classical tradition of political economy. However, within this broad theoretical tradition, we can single out a radical strand which considers the economic behaviour of every individual as completely determined by the reproduction requirements of the system. This peculiar approach characterizes the pure theorists of the circular flow, with whom we will now briefly deal. Not surprisingly, this theoretical approach is often associated with a practical attitude in favour of some sort of central planning (as a consequence of the distrust for the 'anarchy' of the market).

The *Tableau Economique* depicts all the transactions taking place during the year among the three basic classes of society: the class of landowners (L), the 'productive' class of farmers (P_a), and the 'sterile' class of manufacturers (P_m). These transactions can be summarized by a graph, where three points – one for each class – are connected by lines, representing the transactions; the lines are oriented according to the direction of the money flows, whose value is shown by numbers (thousand millions of *livres*). Figure 1 is drawn on the data of Quesnay (1766); since the sum of the money flows leaving each point equals that of those coming in, the system is reproducible.

Marx's (simple) reproduction scheme can also be easily adapted to the same type of three-point graph, once capitalists are substituted for landowners, and the two industries producing intermediate goods ('constant' capital) and consumption goods ('variable' capital and luxuries) are substituted for the two classes of manufacturers and farmers respectively. It should be noted that, while Quesnay's *tableaux* are inherently static, Marx does also consider expanded reproduction: in his own words, the picture shifts from a circle to a spiral. A modern

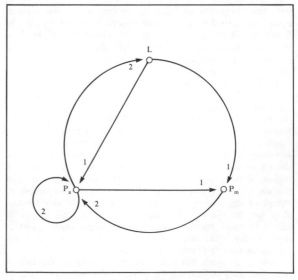

Figure 1

example of a circular representation of an expanding economy is the well-known von Neumann model, which, from this point of view, can be considered as the most sophisticated heir to the Marxian schemes.

Quesnay's and Marx's *tableaux* were offered in value terms; but there is no conceptual difficulty in imagining analogous schemes in physical terms. Now, if all the physical transactions taking place among all the agents of the economy are known, there is a unique set of relative prices which makes it possible for the process to be repeated.

Let us consider an economy in which n producers produce n goods. If we know all the physical amounts x_{ij} of the various goods consumed by the different producers, and if the economy is closed (i.e. production equals consumption for each good), relative prices p_i are determined by the following linear homogeneous equations:

$$\sum_i x_{ij} p_i = p_j \sum_h x_{jh}. \tag{1}$$

This theory or prices has now come to be associated with the closed Leontief model (1941), but it was originally formulated in the late 18th century by Achille Isnard. He considered a simple example with three producers and consistently computed the corresponding prices.

His example is illustrated by the graph of Figure 2: three points, one for each producer, are connected by lines, corresponding to the amounts exchanged; the lines are now oriented according to the physical commodity flows. Relative prices have to be such as to equalize the value of the flows leaving each point with that of the flows coming in; the loops at the vertices (self-consumption) are not relevant to our problem.

When Leontief, a century and a half later, rediscovered the theory, he recognized in it the 'objective' theory of value. One year later, the German mathematician Robert Remak interpreted system (1) as determining the rational prices for an economy in which the individual standards of living are fixed by a central authority. He showed that the system has in general meaningful solutions; and maintained that these prices could be practically computed and implemented.

Until now, we have considered only closed systems, in which all transactions are assumed as known irrespective of their

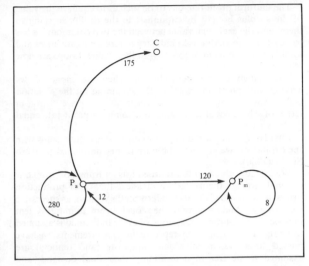

Figure 3

nature (technical inputs or human 'final' uses). We can now open the model, by considering as given only those transactions which are dictated by the technology in use (including workers' subsistence) and leaving undetermined the final utilization of the surplus thus appearing.

There is now room for an additional relation, stating the way in which the surplus is distributed. If we assume that it is entirely appropriated by profit-earners in proportion to the capital advanced, we land on the familiar ground of the classical theory of production prices.

The case can be illustrated by a simple numerical example supplied by Sraffa: there are only two industries, producing wheat (P_a) and iron (P_m) respectively; the class of capitalists (C) gets the entire surplus, consisting only of wheat. In Figure 3 the numbers on the oriented graph refer to the physical quantities (quarters and tons) in the example.

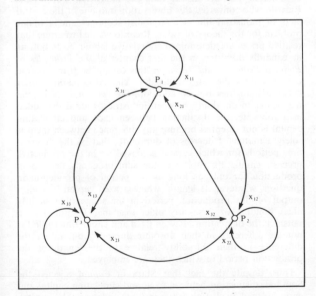

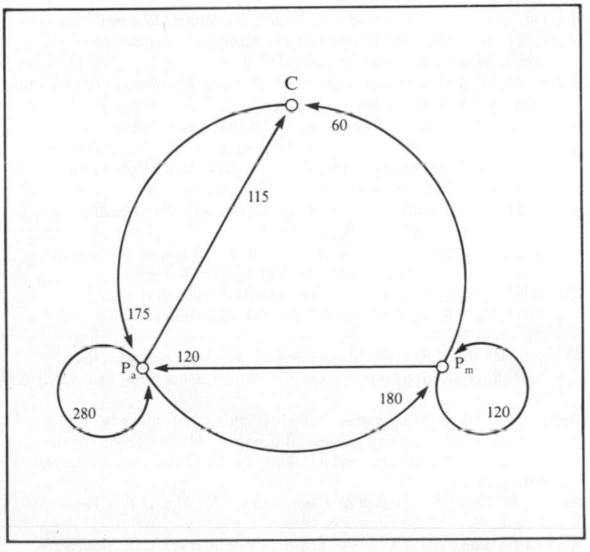

Figure 2

Figure 4

The uniform profit rate has to be such as to equalize the value of the surplus bought by capitalists to the profits accruing to them; and the exchange value between the two commodities has to be such as to enable each industry to replace its advances and to distribute profits in proportion to their value. Loops are now relevant.

The system is then reproducible when the money flows leaving each point are equal to those coming in; the situation is illustrated in Figure 4, and corresponds to a price of iron in terms of wheat equal to 15 and to a common profit rate equal to 25 per cent.

Finally, if we allow the wage earners to share the surplus with the capitalists, we generate the pure theory developed by Piero Sraffa (1960).

We are now able to interpret the abstract transition from our original circular theory to the classical theory of production prices, and eventually to its modern Sraffa version, as successive steps in a gradual opening of the model. From an initial system in which the economic behaviour of every individual is assumed to be rigidly determined by reproduction requirements, we have passed to a system in which capitalists (and rentiers) are assumed to be free in determining their final demand; and finally we have also granted some degree of freedom to the workers.

The term 'free' means here only that the composition of final demand is an issue which lies outside the domain of the pure theory of prices; of course, it can be the object of a distinct section of economic theory. In this perspective, we could say that the neoclassical theory of prices corresponds to a vision of the economy in which the individuals are supposed to be undifferentiated (i.e. there are no classes) and all equally free (the reproduction requirements do not play any essential role in determining prices).

GIORGIO GILIBERT

See also PHYSIOCRATS; QUESNAY, FRANÇOIS.

BIBLIOGRAPHY

Boisguillebert, P. de. 1707. *Dissertation de la nature des richesses*. In *Oeuvres manuscrites et imprimées*, Paris: INED, 1966.

Cantillon, R. 1755. *Essai sur la nature du commerce en général*. Paris: INED, 1952.

Isnard, A.N. 1781. *Traité des richesses*. Lausanne: Grasset.

Leontief, W. 1928. Die Wirtschaft als Kreislauf. *Archiv für Sozialwissenschaft und Sozialpolitik* 3.

Leontief, W. 1941. *The Structure of American Economy*. Oxford and New York: Oxford University Press.

Marx, K. 1885. *Das Kapital*, Vol. II. Hamburg: Meissner.

Neumann, J. von. 1937. Über ein ökonomisches Gleichungssystem und eine Verallgemeinerung des Brouwerschen Fixpunktsatzes. *Ergebnisse eines mathematischen Kolloquiums* VIII.

Peter, H. 1954. *Mathematische Strukturlehre des Wirtschaftskreislaufes*. Göttingen: Schwartz.

Quesnay, F. 1766. *Analyse de la formule arithmétique du Tableau économique*. In *Textes annotés*, Paris: INED, 1958.

Remak, R. 1929. Kann die Volkswirtschaftslehre eine exakte Wissenschaft werden? *Jahrbücher für Nationalökonomie und Statistik* 76.

Remak, R. 1933. Können superponierte Preissysteme praktisch berechnet werden? *Jahrbücher für Nationalökonomie und Statistik* 80.

Schumpeter, J. 1914. *Epochen der Dogmen und Methodengeschichte*. In *Grundriss der Sozialökonomik*, Tübingen: Mohr. Trans. by R. Aris as *Economic Doctrine and Method: an historical sketch*, Oxford: Philip Allen, 1954.

Sraffa, P. 1960. *Production of Commodities by Means of Commodities*. Cambridge: Cambridge University Press.

Tugan-Baranowsky, M. 1894. *Les crises industrielles en Angleterre*. French trans., Paris: Giard, 1913.

circulating capital. The explicit distinction between fixed and circulating capital first makes its appearance in Book II, chapter 1 of Adam Smith's *Wealth of Nations*, who derived it from ample hints in Quesnay and Turgot. Circulating capital goods, according to Smith, consist of those intermediate goods that embody a quantity of purchasing power that perpetually returns to the capitalist as he disposes of the final goods into the making of which they entered, in contrast to fixed capital goods, whose value is never fully recovered in one production cycle. The simplest example of circulating capital is raw materials, just as the simplest example of fixed capital is buildings and machines. However, all the classical economists, including Smith, included in circulating capital not just raw materials but also the consumer goods that support labour during the process of production; that is, wage goods.

This is the origin of the notorious 'wages fund doctrine', according to which wages are said to be 'advanced' to workers at the outset of a production period as a result of which they are determined by the ratio between the volume of capital advanced and the size of the labour force. The notion arose out of a pronounced tendency in 18th-century economics to regard agriculture as an industry typical of production as a whole and to view wheat as both a representative output of agriculture and the staple article of consumption of workers. The fact that wheat only becomes available in the form of annual harvests, which must be willy-nilly stored as a 'fund' for future consumption if its actual use is to be more or less continuous throughout the year, made it possible to define capital simply as 'advances' to workers to support them from seedtime to harvest. Despite the fact that this agrarian model was gradually abandoned in the century after Smith, the wages fund doctrine lived on until J.S. Mill's recantation of the doctrine in 1867, and with it the definition of circulating capital as including all consumer goods that enter into the wage basket (Blaug, 1985, pp. 185–8). Surprisingly enough, this conception of capital as consisting largely if not solely of wage goods survived even beyond the 'marginal revolution': it lies at the heart of the theoretical schema adopted by Böhm-Bawerk in his *Positive Theory of Capital* (1887).

Adam Smith noted that fixed and circulating capital combine in different proportions in different industries, but it was Ricardo who converted this observation into one of the central facts of industrial life in a capitalist economy and a major problem for the theory of value. Ricardo wanted to argue that relative prices are determined by relative labour costs but, as he candidly admitted in the first chapter of the *Principles of Political Economy and Taxation*, this cannot be true, because not only does the ratio of fixed to circulating capital differ between industries but, in addition, the two kinds of capital may differ in durability between industries. Indeed, he added in a footnote, the distinction between fixed and circulating capital is not essential because any difference between them is solely a matter of degrees of durability; that is, the different time periods for which capital is locked up in the productive process: circulating capital is the sum of goods tied up in production for only as long as the period of production in question, whatever its length, whereas fixed capital is a joint output of this production period in the shape of a slightly older building or a slightly older machine. To put it in a nutshell: the distinction between fixed and circulating capital is not the difference in their absolute durability but rather the difference in their durability relative to the length of the production period in which they are employed.

Thus, despite the fact that Marx in *Capital* rejected the Smithian distinction between fixed and circulating capital and chose instead to distinguish 'constant' and 'variable' capital, confining the former to the wage bill and the latter to everything else on the grounds that wages might vary for a given production system even if all the technical input coefficients remained the same, he operated throughout the first volume of the book with a circulating capital model by virtue of the assumption that the capital stock of every industry in the economy turns over once a year: despite all the references to machinery in this first volume, all the analytical problems created by the use of fixed capital are eliminated by assuming that every industry operates with an annual production period. It is only in Volume 2 of *Capital*, and particularly chapters 8–14, that Marx takes account of differences in the durability or turnover rates of capital invested in different industries, and it is here that he begins to confront the problems created by the fact that fixed capital, unlike circulating capital, only transfers part of its value to the final product during each turnover of capital. This is the now famous problem of joint production, which, it has been argued (Steedman, 1977, ch. 10), may produce such anomalies as negative labour-costs for some products.

In the same way, all of the work of Böhm-Bawerk and most of that of Wicksell on the theory of capital is confined to the question of the optimum investment period of continuously applied circulating capital; that is, to what Ragnar Frisch has called the 'flow input–point output' case. It is only when we take up the 'point input–flow output' or the even more typical case of 'flow input–flow output' that we confront the question of fixed capital, an issue that Böhm-Bawerk consistently avoided and that Wicksell only took up in one essay in later life (Blaug, 1985, pp. 563–4). The difficulty created by the use of fixed capital is simply that there is no obvious way of linking particular units of input embodied in fixed capital with particular units of finished output: all the inputs embodied in fixed equipment are jointly responsible for the whole stream of future outputs. Thus, by limiting itself to circulating capital, Austrian capital theory avoided such vexing questions as the optimum rate of depreciation and replacement of old equipment that are always linked with the decision to invest in new equipment, questions which perhaps are not completely resolved even to this day.

The increasing use of fixed capital is said to be one of the distinguishing characteristics of a capitalist system. If so, we might well expect capital theory to have been largely devoted to an analysis of fixed capital. It is one of the ironies of the history of economic thought, however, that capital theory from Turgot to the late Wicksell always treated circulating and not fixed capital as 'capital' *par excellence*.

MARK BLAUG

See also ADVANCES.

BIBLIOGRAPHY
Blaug, M. 1985. *Economic Theory in Retrospect*. 4th edn, Cambridge: Cambridge University Press.
Steedman, I. 1977. *Marx After Sraffa*. London: New Left Books.

circulating media. *See* CURRENCIES.

city planning. *See* URBAN ECONOMICS.

Clapham, John Harold (1873–1946). Sir John Clapham, who became in 1928 the first professor of economic history in the University of Cambridge, was born in Lancashire, the son of a prosperous jeweller. From the Cambridge boarding school (Leys) to which he was sent at the age of 14, he went up to King's College in 1892 to read history at a time when Acton, Maitland and Cunningham dominated the history school. It was as a graduate student at King's researching into the French Revolution, that he attracted the attention of Alfred Marshall, who characteristically set about pressuring the promising young historian to devote his research efforts to filling the gaps in modern English economic history. There is an oft-quoted letter which Marshall wrote in 1897 to Acton saying:

> I feel that the absence of any tolerable account of the economic development of England during the last century and a half is a ... grievous hindrance to the right understanding of the problems of our time ... but till recently the man for the work had not yet appeared. But now I think the man is in sight. Clapham has more analytic faculty than any thorough historian whom I have ever taught: his future work is I think still uncertain: a little force would I think turn him this way or that. If you could turn him towards XVIII or XIX century economic history, economists would ever be grateful to you.

Unfortunately Marshall did not live to read Clapham's massive, three-volume *Economic History of Modern Britain*, the first volume of which appeared in 1926 (dedicated to Marshall and his old enemy William Cunningham), and the last in 1938. No doubt he approved of the scholarly monograph on *The Woollen and Worsted Industries* (1907), written when young Clapham was professor of economics at the University of Leeds – an appointment in which it is hard not to suspect that Marshall's influence was decisive. Nevertheless, when Clapham returned to a King's fellowship in 1908, he resumed his researches in French political history and joined his fellow historians in criticizing the new Economics Tripos for being far too theoretical. It was not until after World War I (during which he served in the Board of Trade and gained first-hand experience of the process of economic decision-making as a member of the Cabinet Committee on Priorities) that he in effect rejoined the path that Marshall had pointed out to him. His *Economic Development of France and Germany* (1921) was the first modern study in comparative economic development, but typically it involved juxtaposing his detailed analyses of two differing experiences of development, rather than relating them to a general theory of economic development, or even generalizing from these case histories.

The truth is that Clapham had no interest in theoretical economics except in so far as it supplied concepts and categories that would permit him to classify and analyse the empirical detail of economic history. He was repelled by the blatant unrealism of orthodox theorizing. His famous article 'Of empty economic boxes', published in the September 1922 *Economic Journal*, accused the theorists of operating with concepts which were empty and irrelevant. 'I think a great deal of harm has been done', he complained, 'through omission to make clear that the Laws of Return have never been attached to specific industries: that we do not, for instance, this moment *know* under what conditions of returns coals or boots are being produced.' But his complaints fell on deaf ears. The interwar theorists saw no point in relating the strategic concepts of their models to real-world constructs and were agreed that, as Keynes put it, Clapham was 'barking up the wrong tree'.

What Clapham had learned from Marshall was that

economics is the study of mutually interacting quantities and that it was the function of an economic historian to put the key quantitative questions to the historical record – for example, how large? how long? how often? how representative? – when spelling out the chains of cause and effect linking economic events. He made it his business to demolish, or qualify, facile generalizations that did not stand up to the available statistical evidence; for example, the Malthusian law of population, or the Marxian predictions of the pauperization of the masses. Though alive to the defects of historical statistics, he was bold enough to make the best of them, 'to offer dimensions, in place of blurred masses of unspecified size' and to analyse the bare aggregates into their strategic components. His training as a historian, however, kept a balance between quantitative and qualitative data, and his large-scale study of the economic development of modern Britain was diversified and illuminated by a continuous stream of vivid factual detail. His last book, *The Bank of England: A History, 1694–1914* (1944), commissioned by the Bank to commemorate its 250th anniversary, gave him access to the voluminous manuscript records of the first Central Bank. Writing its history and setting its operations and policies within their political and economic context was a task which by training and interests he was peculiarly well-equipped to perform. His intellectual energy seemed enhanced rather than diminished by his retirement from the Cambridge chair, and his sudden death in 1946 cut short a research programme which was still in full swing.

PHYLLIS DEANE

SELECTED WORKS
1907. *The Woollen and Worsted Industries*. London: Methuen.
1921. *The Economic Development of France and Germany, 1815–1914*. Cambridge: Cambridge University Press.
1922. Of empty economic boxes. *Economic Journal* 32, September, 305–14.
1926–38. *An Economic History of Modern Britain*. 3 vols. Cambridge: Cambridge University Press. Vol. 1, *The Early Railway Age 1820–1850*, (1926); Vol. 2, *Free Trade and Steel*, (1932); Vol. 3, *Machines and National Rivalries (1887–1914) with an Epilogue (1914–1929)*, (1938).
1944. *The Bank of England: A History, 1694–1944*. 2 vols, Cambridge: Cambridge University Press.

Clark, Colin Grant (born 1905).   Colin Clark, one of the most fertile minds in 20th-century applied economics, was born in London. After graduating in chemistry at Oxford University in 1924, he worked as assistant to W.H. Beveridge, Allyn Young and A.M. Carr-Saunders, stood unsuccessfully as a Labour candidate in the May 1929 General Election, then joined the staff of the Economic Advisory Council, recently set up by Ramsay MacDonald, of which Keynes was a member. In 1931, rather than agree to write a protectionist manifesto for MacDonald, he accepted an appointment as lecturer in statistics at Cambridge, where he remained until, in 1937, he went to Melbourne University, initially as visiting lecturer. In Australia he occupied government posts, chiefly as economic adviser to the state government of Queensland, until 1952. After spells as visiting professor at the University of Chicago and as Director of the Oxford Institute of Agricultural Economics, he returned to Australia in 1968. He remains active as a research consultant at the University of Queensland.

In the first decade of an astonishingly prolific half-century of research and writing, Colin Clark established himself as one of the pioneers of national income estimates. He greatly improved existing estimates for the United Kingdom, and later for Australia and the Soviet Union, and in so doing made methodological contributions so fundamental that he has justly been described as co-author, with Simon Kuznets, of the 'statistical revolution' that accompanied the revolution in macroeconomics of the 1930s. He was the first to use the gross national product (GNP) and to present estimates in the framework of the main components of aggregate demand $(C+I+G)$; he made some of the earliest estimates of Keynes's multiplier and, in an article published in 1937, one of the first international comparisons of the purchasing power of national currencies and thus of real national product. These were carried further in his monumental *Conditions of Economic Progress* (1940), which was important chiefly because it signalled the revival of interest among the profession in secular economic growth and development but which also supplied the first substantial statistical evidence of the gulf in living standards between rich and poor countries (the 'Gap') and developed the thesis that, in the course of economic growth, the occupational structure shifts from primary to secondary and tertiary industries. During World War II, in *The Economics of 1960*, Clark made one of the first ambitious attempts at a macroeconomic model of the world economy.

Recognized also as one of the 'Pioneers in Development', Colin Clark has in the past thirty years made significant contributions to empirical study of the relations between food supply and population growth, the economics of irrigation and subsistence agriculture, of determinants of economic growth and of productivity in agriculture in developing countries. At the same time, he has been a gadfly in the political economy of developed countries, arguing against growthmanship, against high taxation and against welfarism long before it became fashionable to do so.

H.W. ARNDT

See also SOCIAL ACCOUNTING; STONE, JOHN RICHARD NICHOLAS.

SELECTED WORKS
1932. *The National Income, 1924–31*. London: Macmillan.
1937. *National Income and Outlay*. London: Macmillan.
1939. *A Critique of Russian Statistics*. London: Macmillan.
1940. *Conditions of Economic Progress*. London: Macmillan. Revised edn, 1957.
1942. *The Economics of 1960*. London: Macmillan.
1961. *Growthmanship*. London: Institute of Economic Affairs.
1964. (With M.R. Haswell.) *Economics of Subsistence Agriculture*. London: Macmillan.
1967. *Population Growth and Land Use*. London: Macmillan. Revised. edn, 1977.
1982. *Regional and Urban Location*. St Lucia: University of Queensland.
1984. Development economics: the early years. In *Pioneers in Development*, ed. G.M. Meier and D. Seers, New York: Oxford University Press.
BIBLIOGRAPHY
Clark, Colin. In *International Encyclopedia of the Social Sciences Biographical Supplement*, New York: The Free Press, 1979.

Clark, John Bates (1847–1938).   John Bates Clark, the first American economist to deserve and gain an international reputation, was born at Providence, Rhode Island, on 26 January 1847 into a modestly prosperous merchant family. His father's struggle with tuberculosis prompted a move to Minneapolis in search of a better climate and later required Clark to discontinue his studies at Amherst (he had transferred from Brown after two years) in order to run the family business. The business involved selling a line of ploughs to receptive but credit-needy country storekeepers throughout Minnesota. Following his father's death, the business was sold at a profit and Clark returned to Amherst, graduating with highest honours in 1872.

Clark's New England forebears had included many Congregational ministers and he seriously considered entering the Yale Divinity School. (He remained a communicant throughout his life and saw one son enter the ministry.) But encouraged by President Julius Seelye of Amherst, who had taught him political economy out of Amasa Walker's textbook, he chose instead the high-risk course of an academic career in a country still without universities. After Amherst, he went abroad, enrolling for two years at Heidelberg and six months at Zurich.

While Clark has left no detailed account of his European studies, his early work indicates that he was much influenced by the German historical school, and especially by the lectures of Karl Knies. Whether the influence was for good or ill is not clear. It probably slowed his development as a theorist. (His formulation of the marginal utility principle was worked out before he had heard of Jevons.) But it also taught him that an economist needed a far more professional training than that provided by the thin textbook gruel offered in the American colleges of the day. Clark was one of three young 'Germans' (the other two being Richard Ely and Henry Carter Adams) who, at a meeting of the American Historical Society at Saratoga in 1885, issued the call that led to the formation of the American Economic Association. Their plainly avowed purpose was to encourage German-style empirical research and give a sympathetic hearing to the critics of laissez faire. The dogmatic social Darwinism of William Graham Sumner epitomized all that they disliked in American economics. Clark became the third president of the new group and his diplomacy and moderation are credited with making it more acceptable to the country's older economists, most of whom eventually joined (but not Sumner).

Shortly after going to his first professorship at Carleton College in Northfield, Minnesota, in 1876, Clark was incapacitated for two years by an illness that, according to his son, John Maurice, permanently lowered his energy level. Whatever its nature – the family memorial to Clark provides no details – the illness seems only to have strengthened his determination and powers of organization. Following his recovery, Clark worked steadily and with a notable economy of effort until shortly before his death at the age of ninety-one. Most of his contributions to economic theory, however, were worked out in the first fifteen years of his career though the most polished formulations did not come until *The Distribution of Wealth* (1899). Clark's need to choose his projects carefully may explain why, despite his admiration for the work of historians and institutionalists, he never tried to emulate them. All of his life Clark remained a theorist who often wrote on issues of the day.

Clark first gained recognition with a series of articles in *The New Englander* that, with revisions, were published in 1886 as *The Philosophy of Wealth*. Clark's admirers have found this first book something of an embarrassment and not without reason. It is a young Victorian's book, full of grand historical generalizations and the elevated expressions of sentiment that have long been out of fashion. Still, on close reading, it reveals the qualities that were to make him a major figure in the history of economics – a superb command of language (Böhm-Bawerk, who debated capital theory with Clark, claimed that his literary elegance gave him an unfair advantage), a willingness to take a position on controversial issues, and, above all, a remarkable talent for economic theory.

The collection contains a totally original and quite sophisticated statement of the principle of marginal utility ('effective utility' in Clark's vocabulary), a reasoned rejection of Malthusian pessimism, and many perceptive comments on the rise of labour unions, cartels, and corporations. Even the main outlines of Clark's treatment of capital and interest are discernible in the *Philosophy*.

Clark's intellectual distinction was fully revealed two years later with the publication of his monograph, *Capital and its Earnings* (1888a) which has a good claim to stand as the foundation stone of modern capital theory. While the distinction between labour and capital is still accepted (though even here Clark wavers), all other things including land that directly or indirectly enter into the production of consumer goods are treated as capital. The existence of interest is firmly placed in the productivity of capital. The creation of income as a concomitant of the destruction of individual capital goods is emphasized. The irrelevance of the 'period of production' of individual capital goods to anything of importance is shown and the fallacy underlying the wages fund doctrine is exposed.

Clark has been criticized for introducing the 'neoclassical fairy tale' into capital theory – the notion that capital is some strange substance that, 'transmutes itself from one machine form into another like a restless reincarnating soul' (Samuelson, 1962). While the neo-classical fairy tale has its limitations as a construct for understanding capital accumulation in the real world, Samuelson's jibe is off target. Clark's view of the production process is perfectly correct. Machines do 'transmute' themselves into other machines in the course of wearing out.

A more serious challenge to capital theory in the Clark tradition goes back to Böhm-Bawerk. If there is such a thing as a quantity of capital 'embodied' at any given moment in a set of heterogeneous specialized capital goods, what is its unit of measure? Unlike Irving Fisher, Clark faced the question squarely and attempted an answer. Unfortunately, the effort led him to bring forth his 'universal measure of value' – the product of a strange and nearly unintelligible fusion of utility analysis and the labour theory of value. While Clark was inordinately proud of his measure (and credited its inspiration to some lectures of Knies) it quickly found a merciful oblivion.

Later writers in the Clark tradition – or, at any rate, those who have felt the need for an impeccably consistent set of assumptions – have curbed their ambitions and been content to solve (or evade) the measurement problem by positing a surrogate production function where all capital goods are moulded from some homogeneous putty-like substance. The limit case in the Clark tradition is the 'Crusonia plant' named by Frank Knight but first suggested by W.S. Jevons's 'whole produce'. It supplies all human wants and, in the absence of consumption, grows at a constant geometric rate. Here the quantity of capital can be found either by measuring Crusonia directly or by dividing the plant's yield (income) in perpetuity by its natural growth rate, that is, the marginal (and average) productivity of investment.

Whether one prefers capital theory in Clark's tradition to its principal rival – capital theory in the Sraffa tradition – is ultimately a matter of personal taste. Both employ simplifications that take one far from reality. However, notwithstanding the measurement conundrum, to date capital theory in the Clark tradition has provided the basis for virtually all empirical work on wealth and income. This is not surprising. To statisticians, measuring changes in the quantity of capital (which they rename the real value of the stock of capital assets) is just another index number problem.

Very early in his career Clark began to work on the problem of factor shares (possibly because of his interest in Henry George) and concluded that the treatment of land rent as a surplus whose size is not determined by marginal productivity was gross error. The most complete statement of his views on distribution is in *The Distribution of Wealth* (1899) which drew heavily on his earlier articles and monographs. Despite its flaws (which include the universal measure of value) the *Distribution* is a remarkable book and, by any reasonable test, a landmark treatise in the development of economics.

The *Distribution* represents an advance on the prior art in two important respects. It offers a discussion of the relation of statics to dynamics – the terms were introduced into economics by Clark – superior to that of previous treatments. And it offers, for the first time, a complete and lucid exposition of the neo-classical theory of distribution. The *Distribution* also brought Clark's views on capital to a much wider audience.

Clark was as conscious of the rapid pace of economic change as any German or American institutionalist of his day, but he stressed that, at any given moment, there are 'natural' values in the marketplace and permanent pressures pushing actual values toward them.

Reduce society to a stationary state, let industry go on with entire freedom, make labor and capital absolutely mobile – as free to move from employment to employment as they are supposed to be in the theoretical world that figures in Ricardo's studies – and you will have a regime of natural values. These are the values about which rates are forever fluctuating in the shops of commercial cities. You will also have a regime of natural wages and interest; and these are the standards about which the rates of pay for labor and capital are always hovering in actual mills, fields, mines, etc.

Only by a careful separation and delineation of static and dynamic forces, Clark believed, can the process of price formation in real-world markets be understood. His methodology is not as formal and austere as F.H. Knight's in *Risk, Uncertainty, and Profit* (1921), but it is essentially the same. (In the version of Knight's doctoral dissertation accepted at Cornell in 1916 his intellectual debts to Clark are gratefully and fully acknowledged; for reasons unknown, almost all of the favourable references to Clark are omitted in the rewritten version published five years later.)

To demonstrate that, in the static state, payments to the factors exhaust the product when each receives its marginal product, Clark devised a set of diagrams to show that, in a two-factor model, what is viewed as rent and what is viewed as a factor payment is a matter of perspective. One becomes the other by interchanging the fixed and variable factors in the diagrams. Clark's treatment of rent has been followed by an admiring Paul Samuelson in all of the many editions of his *Economics*.

Clark's approach to distribution is set forth in 'words and pictures' (his mathematical training did not include calculus) and so lacks the precision of the versions of Wicksell and Wicksteed. But being more accessible to student readers, it was Clark's treatment that first gained widespread attention for the neo-classical theory of distribution.

Clark has often been reproved for implying both that factor payments ought to be according to marginal productivity and that in a real-world market economy most factor payments do closely approximate marginal productivity (see, for example,

Stigler, 1941). A reading of the *Distribution* without reference to Clark's other writings would indicate that he did hold these views. Certainly his advocacy of compulsory arbitration to end long labour disputes assumed that economic justice consisted in giving striking workers the wages prevailing in comparable employments elsewhere. However, a brilliant essay, 'The Theory of Economic Progress' (1896) leaves no doubt that he placed a far higher value on economic growth than on short-run justice or efficiency.

Well before Schumpeter, Clark wrote:

The picture of a stationary state presented by John Stuart Mill as the goal of competitive industry is the one thing needed to complete the impression of dismalness made by the political economy of the early period. A state could not be so good that that lack of progress would not blight it; nor could it be so bad that the fact of progress would not redeem it. ... The decisive test of an economic system is the rate and direction of movement.

Clark was a leading participant in the trust controversy that occupied American politics in the thirty years before World War I. His moral seriousness and literary ability (and, one suspects, his ability to meet deadlines) made him a favourite of magazine editors – he once described himself as 'writing my trust article again'. Like all economists of that era he had to think through his attitude toward the many large firms with large market shares that had so suddenly appeared.

As recorded in the *Philosophy of Wealth*, Clark's first reaction to the American business scene on returning from Germany was one of fascinated revulsion joined to an expression of hope that businessmen could be led to behave in more acceptable ways by pressures from labour unions, Church, and State. As the years passed, his views of commerce became much more favourable and his policy recommendations more worldly and specific. He early pointed out that the conduct of most so-called trusts was influenced by the fear of entry and he never depreciated the efficiency gains made possible by large-scale production. At first he urged only a modest amount of government intervention as in, *The Control of Trusts: An Argument in Favor of Curbing the Power of Monopoly by a Natural Method* (1901). Clark's 'natural method' was little more than the competition of the marketplace purged of its 'destructive' ingredients plus government regulation of railroad rates to prevent unjustified differentials. A much expanded version of *The Control of Trusts*, with John Maurice Clark, his son, as co-author and the subtitle omitted, appeared in 1912. The revisions were mostly the work of the son and contain a virtual blueprint for an antitrust policy. The Clayton and Federal Trade Commission Acts of 1914 which followed shortly received their enthusiastic approval.

By his writing Clark did more than any other economist to confer intellectual respectability on an antitrust policy that had had its origins in the populist discontent that produced the Sherman Act. In retrospect, this may seem to have been a dubious achievement. But in Clark's favour it can be said that he was dealing with new and difficult issues and approached them with more objectivity than most of his contemporaries, for example, W.Z. Ripley and F.A. Fetter.

Clark's life as a teacher was at Carleton, Smith, Amherst, and from 1895 to 1923 at Columbia. At Carleton his kindness helped Thorstein Veblen (a thoroughly unpopular undergraduate in that church college) to find his way. At Columbia it helped Alvin Johnson to gain the income needed to complete his doctoral programme. His encouragement led F.H. Giddings to leave provincial journalism for a seminal career in sociology. He was, of course, the omnipresent influence in the life of John Maurice Clark, who succeeded to his chair at Columbia. Still, Clark's direct influence through the classroom seems to have been surprisingly limited. His quiet and self-sufficient personality did not require disciples and his probing but loosely organized lectures appealed only to very able students. Then too, Clark was a theorist in an era when, in the United States, institutional economics, not theory, was the height of academic fashion.

From 1911 onward Clark's great concern became the contribution that social scientists could make to ending war. When the Carnegie Endowment for International Peace was formed in 1910, he became the first director of its economics and history section serving until 1923. There he took the initiative in obtaining support for the studies that became the *Social and Economic History of the World War*. The general editor was his friend and Columbia colleague in history, James T. Shotwell. The Carnegie *History* ultimately ran to over a hundred volumes and still stands as the most ambitious research project in the social sciences ever undertaken by a private foundation. Unfortunately, its initial promise was never realized. Shotwell sought to organize the Carnegie *History* on the strange principle that an accounting of the great war was too important to be left to historians. As a result, while the series contains a few memorable studies, for example, J.M. Clark, *The Costs of the World War to the American People* (1931), it served mainly to preserve the recollections of wartime ministers and civil servants that would otherwise have been lost. J.M. Keynes disdainfully withdrew from the *History* in the planning stage.

Clark's work for peace continued to the end of his life. His last small book was a moving plea for collective action to deter aggression, *A Tender of Peace: The Terms on Which Civilized Nations Can, if They Will, Avoid Warfare* (1935). Clark died in New York City on 21 March 1938.

An abundance of honours came to him in his lifetime both in the United States and abroad. They were all deserved.

DONALD DEWEY

See also CAPITAL PERVERSITY; CLARK, JOHN MAURICE; DISTRIBUTION THEORIES: NEOCLASSICAL; FISHER, IRVING; MARGINAL PRODUCTIVITY THEORY.

SELECTED WORKS

1886. *The Philosophy of Wealth: Economic Principles Newly Formulated*. Boston: Ginn & Co.
1888a *Capital and Its Earnings*. Baltimore: American Economic Association.
1888b. (With F.H. Giddings.) *The Modern Distributive Process*. Boston: Ginn & Co.
1893. The ultimate standard of value. *The Yale Review* 1, February–May, 252–74.
1896. The theory of economic progress. *American Economic Association: Economic Studies* 1, April, 1–22.
1899. *The Distribution of Wealth: A Theory of Wages, Interest and Profits*. New York: The Macmillan Co.
1901. *The Control of Trusts: An Argument in Favor of Curbing the Power of Monopoly by a Natural Method*. New York: The Macmillan Co.
1904. *The Problem of Monopoly: A Study of a Grave Danger and of the Natural Mode of Averting It*. New York: Columbia University Press.
1907. *The Essentials of Economic Theory: As Applied to Modern Problems of Industry and Public Policy*. New York: The Macmillan Co.
1912. (With J.M. Clark.) *The Control of Trusts*. New York: The Macmillan Co.
1914. *Social Justice without Socialism*. Boston: Houghton Mifflin.

1935. *A Tender of Peace: The Terms on which Civilized Nations Can, If They Will, Avoid Warfare*. New York: Columbia University Press.

A nearly complete listing of Clark's publications is in *A Bibliography of the Faculty of Political Science, Columbia University, 1880–1930*, New York: Columbia University Press, 1931; also in *Economic Essays Contributed in Honor of John Bates Clark*, ed. J.H. Hollander, New York: The Macmillan Co., 1927.

BIBLIOGRAPHY
Böhm-Bawerk, E. 1906. Capital and interest once more. *Quarterly Journal of Economics* 21, 1–21, 247–82.
John Bates Clark. A memorial volume prepared by his children. New York, privately printed, 1938.
Samuelson, P. 1962. Parable and realism in capital theory: the surrogate production function. *Review of Economic Studies* 29, 193–206.
Stigler, G. 1941. *Production and Distribution Theories: The Formative Period*. New York: The Macmillan Co.

Clark, John Maurice (1884–1963).   Clark was born on 30 November 1884 in Northampton, Massachusetts, and died on 27 June 1963 in Westport, Connecticut. Educated at Amherst College and Columbia University (PhD, 1910), he taught at Colorado College (1908–10), Amherst (1910–15), University of Chicago (1915–26) and Columbia University (1926–52), where he succeeded his father, John Bates Clark. He was president of the American Economic Association in 1935 and received its Francis A. Walker Medal in 1952. His dissertation, 'Standards of Reasonableness in Local Freight Discrimination', was written under the supervision of his father. He was associated with the National Bureau of Economic Research, the National Resources Planning Board, the Twentieth Century Fund, the Attorney General's National Committee to Study the Anti-Trust Laws, and other organizations.

Clark worked within both orthodox and heterodox economics, making important contributions to microeconomics, macroeconomics and institutional, or social, economics. Eclectic and open-minded, he was critical of the apologetic uses of economic theory, particularly of the drawing of narrow and misleading welfare implications. He emphasized the limits of economics as a science.

Clark's contributions within conventional theory dealt principally with economic dynamics. He developed and stressed the implications of overhead, fixed costs in capital intensive industry for competitive structure, business pricing policy, and economic stability. He was the principal of several discoverers of the acceleration principle, with its important implications for instability. His career-long concern with competitive structure and behaviour led to his formulation of the concept of 'workable competition', with a stress on potential competition and intercommodity substitution. The major result of his equally long work in macroeconomics was an exploration of the strategic factors in business cycles which effectively summarized, in a general theoretical context, the state of empirical knowledge at the time. He also wrote extensively on railroad and public utility rates, basing-point pricing, economic planning, the economics of war and of peacetime conversion, wage-price (cost-push inflation) theory and policy, and related topics.

Clark departed from the conventional mainstream in his social economics, which was akin to the Institutional Economics of John R. Commons and Wesley C. Mitchell and which reflected the influence of Thorstein Veblen and John Dewey. Clark's work on the social control of business and the theory of regulation explored the fundamental legal-economic nexus of society in a non-ideological manner stressing the

substance and inexorable presence of formal (legal) and
informal controls in an economic system, even in a pluralistic
and voluntaristic economy, controls typically obscured in
conventional analysis of markets. Law was important to the
structure of freedom, not something solely antagonistic to
freedom. His work in welfare economics emphasized the role
of institutions, the necessity of psychological realism, and the
inexorable role of moral or ethical values. His concern with
the costs of labour that are registered in neither the market
nor by industry presaged later Institutional work on
externalities and social costs.

WARREN J. SAMUELS

SELECTED WORKS
1912. (With J.B. Clark.) *The Control of Trusts*. New York:
    Macmillan.
1923. *Studies in the Economics of Overhead Costs*. Chicago: University
    of Chicago Press.
1926. *Social Control of Business*. New York: McGraw-Hill.
1934. *Strategic Factors in Business Cycles*. New York: H. Wolff for
    the National Bureau of Economic Research.
1936. *Preface to Social Economics*. New York: Farrar and Rinehart.
1948. *Alternative to Serfdom*. New York: Knopf.
1949. *Guideposts in Time of Change*. New York: Harper.
1957. *Economic Institutions and Human Welfare*. New York: Knopf.
1961. *Competition as a Dynamic Process*. Washington, DC: Brookings
    Institution.

class. The word originates from the Latin 'classis', which
included among its uses the subdivision of the population by
wealth (most notably in the constitution of Servius Tullius). In
modern usage it was adopted by Defoe (1728) to define 'classes
of people' in terms of occupation and income. It was widely
used by the Physiocratic School (Cantillon, 1755, and Steuart,
1767) and most centrally by Quesnay (1758) to define
socio-economic functions. Quesnay's *Tableau Oeconomique*
made farmers the *classe productive*, landlords the *classe
distributive* and merchants the *classe sterile*.

Adam Smith, while referring to this usage by Quesnay, did
not himself adopt it. His categorization of economic
relationships was by direct reference to landlords, capitalists
and labourers, and his analysis of social relationships was
posed separately in terms of 'ranks' and 'orders'. The first use
of the term in a way that specifically linked economic function
to social activity was, most probably, by the Scottish lawyer
and historian, John Millar (1787). He described the Dark Ages
as marked by the 'separation of a whole people into two great
classes', and argued that in a commercial nation the division of
labour and the unequal distribution of wealth held the danger
of 'the class of mechanics and labourers' being 'debarred from
extensive information' and 'becoming the dupes of their
superiors'.

By the beginning of the 19th century the term was in wide
popular use: 'lower', 'middle' and 'upper' classes being the
most frequent but with increasing reference to the 'working
classes' (as in Robert Owen's *A New View of Society* in 1816).

The connotation of 'class' as a social collectivity was clearly
present in 1817 when Ricardo (1817, p. 5) established the term
as a central concept of political economy. The *Principles* begin:

> the produce of the earth – all that is derived from its
> surface by the united application of labour, machinery and
> capital, is divided among these classes of the commu-
> nity... . In different stages of society, the proportions of
> the whole produce of the earth which will be allotted to
> each of these, under the name of rent, profit and wages,
> will be essentially different ... . To determine the laws

which regulate this distribution is the principal problem in
political economy.

Subsequently Ravenstone (1821) and Hodgskin (1825) argued
from Ricardo's work that there existed an inherent conflict of
interest between the 'classes' of labour and capital. Hodgkin
additionally claimed that this could only be resolved by the
collective action of labour.

It was this usage that Marx and Engels inherited and then
extended radically. The individual elements within their
analysis were not new. The concept of social progress, of
transformation through the unfolding contradictions of
thought and consciousness, was common to all young
Hegelians. The idea of economically defined stages was present
in Smith, Millar and Adam Ferguson. The explanation of
political action in terms of economically defined classes was
also widespread.

What was new in the work of Marx and Engels was the way
in which they combined these elements and then embodied
them in the one central concept of 'class'. Class struggle
became, for them, the motive force of human history. The
progressive advance of productive capacity demanded, they
argued, the existence of labour surpluses. Historically, these
had been achieved exploitatively within a series of social
systems, each marked by different forms of property relations
and distinguished by the precise way in which its 'ruling class'
was able to extract the surplus from the direct producers.

> At a certain stage of their development, the material
> productive forces of society come into conflict with the
> existing relations of production... . From forms of
> development of the productive forces these relations turn
> into fetters. Then begins the epoch of social revolution... .
> In broad outlines Asiatic, ancient, feudal and modern
> bourgeois modes of production can be designated as
> progressive epochs in the economic formation of society
> (Marx, 1859, pp. 20–22).

Hence, in the words of the *Communist Manifesto*, 'the history
of all hitherto existing society is the history of class struggles'
(Marx and Engels [1848] 1976, p. 478). The Manifesto argued,
on the basis of its analysis of previous stages of human
history, that the social injustices of capitalist society could
only be overcome through the collective exercise of power by a
new revolutionary class. Under capitalism this revolutionary
class was the working class, and its historical objective,
springing from its experience of the material conditions of
capitalist production, was to be the establishment of an
ultimately classless society in which the surplus would be
controlled collectively. Initially, this would require the working
class to destroy the capitalist state and constitute its own state
power.

Marx gave this working class, as a class 'in itself', a very
comprehensive definition. He included within it all those who
had to sell their labour power in order to subsist. Marx
argued, in contrast to Adam Smith, that productive labour
was not to be conceived narrowly in terms of the manual
character of the task, a definition which broke what he saw as
the central linkage between hand and head, consciousness and
physical action. On the contrary, productive labour within
capitalism was to be defined by its social relationship to
capital. Moreover, as capitalism's means of production
became progressively more social in character, and the division
of labour more marked 'so, as a necessary consequence, does
our notion of productive labour, and of its agent the
productive labourer, become extended. In order to labour
productively it is no longer necessary for you to do manual
work yourself; enough if you are an organ of the collective

labourer, and perform one of its subordinate functions' (Marx, 1867, pp. 476–7). In *Theories of Surplus Value* Marx pointed out that productive labour included artists and writers as long as they were employees whose labour assisted in the creation of surplus value (Marx, 1905, p. 157).

However, at the same time as insisting on this broad definition of productive labour, Marx also argued that the 'class consciousness' necessary for the working class to constitute itself as a class 'for itself' developed unevenly and did so first and foremost among workers within large-scale industry. The *Communist Manifesto* presents this as a historical process, with 'various stages of development' in which workers are cumulatively exposed to the material contradictions of capitalist production (Marx and Engels, 1848, p. 492). Marx first systematically enumerated these stages in *The Poverty of Philosophy* (Marx, 1847). They were the need of all workers to combine in face of competition, the erosion of craft through the division of labour, the loss of control over labour through 'real subordination' to the machine, the exposure to capitalist crisis which brought an understanding of the system's contradictions and finally the industrial concentration which provided an awareness of collective strength. The end result was the unification of local struggles into national struggles and 'consequently into a political party'.

This classic usage of the term 'class' may, in sum, be said to possess the following characteristics. First, it defines class in terms of collective position within a series of historically definite production relations:

> It is always the direct relationship of the owners of the conditions of production to the direct producers – a relation always naturally corresponding to a definite stage in the development of the methods of labour and thereby its social productivity – which reveals the innermost secret, the hidden basis of the entire social structure, and with it the political form of the relation of sovereignty and dependence, in short, the corresponding form of the state (Marx, 1894, p. 791).

Second, it understands these relations to be exploitative and hence to be sustained coercively through the exercise of state power. Third, it conceives social progress, the process by which human beings made their own history, as dialectical, driven by its own contradictions. Each successive stage is achieved through collective, conscious class struggle in which the new revolutionary class destroys the state power of the old and creates its own. The state, therefore, is entirely the product of, and based within, existing class relations – *not* 'an independent entity that possesses its own intellectual, ethical and libertarian basis' (Marx, 1891, p. 25).

Marx gave this perspective precise definition in 1852 when he described his essential discovery not as the existence of classes or class struggle but 'that the *existence of classes* is only bound up with *particular, historic phases in the development of production*; that the class struggle necessarily leads to the *dictatorship of the proletariat*; that this dictatorship itself only constitutes the transition to the *abolition of all classes* and to a *classless* society' (Marx, 1983, pp. 64–5).

Since Marx's death most re-definitions of class have attempted to untie this tight knot of argument and claim that its dialectical linkage of production relations, state power and class struggle is empirically or theoretically illegitimate.

Max Weber, while never making an explicit critique of Marx's usage of 'class', left a number of comments which have provided the basis for most counter-hypotheses.

Weber proposed three conceptually distinct dimensions for the analysis of social position. These were: 'class situation' which referred to a person's material 'life chance' (or economic advantages) within any market situation, be it as consumer, employee or landlord; 'status situation' which was determined by the social 'honour' accorded to particular social groupings and any objective 'life chance' advantages which flow from this; and 'power' which defined a group's differential access to the legitimate use of force (Weber, 1922).

These categories reasserted the separateness of economic, social and political spheres. In this way, it was claimed, it was possible to test empirically for any correspondence of position between the three dimensions rather than simply asserting it. It also made it possible to categorize societies by the degree to which status stratification or class formation (conceived as conflict within a market) was dominant.

None of these categories, however, directly corresponds to Marx's concept of class. All three refer to different forms of *distribution* – with Weber's concept of class referring to the distribution of resources which occurs 'economically' within a market situation. To this extent, it is quite distinct from the classical usage which refers to position with the social relations of *production* and categorizes social systems by the particular way in which the surplus is extracted.

Recent elaborations of the Weberian approach maintain this distinction. Parkin argues that the principal class division within modern society is that deriving from the different market opportunities of manual and non-manual occupations. This is because those in non-manual occupations are able to exploit the mechanism of 'social closure': a 'process by which collectivities seek to maximise rewards by restricting access to a limited number of eligibles'. For Parkin, therefore, the class division between the 'bourgeoisie and the proletariat' is not defined by the ownership or non-ownership of capital but occurs *within* the occupational labour market and results from the way in which 'social closure' gives non-manual occupations a significantly greater control over resources (Parkin, 1971 and 1974).

Giddens also bases his analysis on market strength but sees modern society as divided into three 'social classes': 'groupings whose class – or market – situation are sufficiently similar to justify the aggregate being termed a social class.' These are defined by the particular character of their power within the market (or 'mediate structuration'), and consist of an 'upper class' (having ownership and control of property), a 'middle class' (possessing technical and educational skills) and a 'lower class' (having only labour to sell) (Giddens, 1973).

A somewhat similar re-definition of class was provided by Poulantzas. He also argues that modern capitalist society contains three 'social classes'. These are the bourgeoisie defined by its possession and real economic control of capital, the working class whose labour is employed manually in material production of use values and the 'new petty bourgeoisie' which includes all other wage workers. Unlike Marx, therefore, Poulantzas uses a narrow definition of productive labour. Additionally, and following Althusser, he sees the 'structural determination of class' as taking place at a 'political' and 'ideological' as well as 'economic' level. Accordingly, he places non-manual wage workers in the petty bourgeoisie on the grounds that politically they supervise manual workers and that ideologically, as mental workers, they participate in 'secret knowledge' (Poulantzas, 1973).

Olin Wright, taking a position somewhat closer to that of classical Marxism, contests the validity of Poulantzas's 'new petty bourgeoisie'. He argues that Poulantzas's rationale for excluding non-manual employees from the working class elevates the 'political' and 'ideological' spheres above the economic, and reduces the economic to a market opposition similar to that used by Weber. Instead Olin Wright argues that there exists between the working class and the bourgeoisie a number of 'contradictory class locations' (Wright, 1978).

The most succinct 20th-century restatement of Marx's original linkage of class to state coercion and systems of production remains Lenin's *State and Revolution* (1917) and *A Great Beginning* (1919).

J. FOSTER

See also BOURGEOISIE; CAPITAL AS A SOCIAL RELATION; MARXIST ECONOMICS.

BIBLIOGRAPHY

Cantillon, R. 1755. *Essai sur la nature du commerce en générale*, Ed. H. Higgs, London: Macmillan, 1931.

Defoe, D. 1728. *Extracts from the Plan of the English Commerce*. In *A Select Collection of Scarce and Valuable Tracts on Commerce*, ed. J. McCulloch, London, 1859.

Giddens, A. 1973. *The Class Structure of the Advanced Societies*. London: Hutchinson.

Hodgskin, T. 1825. *Labour Defended against the Claims of Capital*. London.

Lenin, V.I. 1917. State and Revolution. *Collected Works*, XXV, Moscow, 1964.

Lenin, V.I. 1919. A Great Beginning. *Collected Works*, XXIX, Moscow, 1965.

Marx, K. 1847. Poverty of Philosophy. *Collected Works*, VI, Moscow, 1976.

Marx, K. 1859. *A Contribution to the Critique of Political Economy*. Moscow, 1970.

Marx, K. 1867. *Capital*, Vol. I. Moscow, 1953.

Marx, K. 1891. *Critique of the Gotha Programme*. Moscow, 1966.

Marx, K. 1894. *Capital*, Vol. III. Moscow, 1959.

Marx, K. 1905. *Theories of Surplus Value*, Part I. Moscow, 1971.

Marx, K. 1983. *Collected Works*, XXXIX. Moscow.

Marx, K. and Engels, F. 1848. The Manifesto of the Communist Party. *Collected Works*, VI. Moscow, 1976.

Millar, J. 1787. *An Historical View of English Government*, Vol. IV. London, 1803.

Owen, R. 1816. *A New View of Society*. London.

Parkin, F. 1971. *Class Inequality and Political Order*. London: MacGibbon.

Parkin, F. 1974. Strategies of social closure in class formation. In *The Social Analysis of Class Structure*, ed. F. Parkin, London: Tavistock.

Poulantzas, N. 1973. *Political Power and Social Classes*. London: New Left Books.

Quesnay, F. 1758. *Tableau Oeconomique*. Paris.

Ravenstone, P. 1821. *The Source and Remedy of the National Difficulties*. London.

Ricardo, D. 1817. *The Principles of Political Economy*. In *Works and Correspondence of David Ricardo*, ed. P. Sraffa, Vol. I, Cambridge: Cambridge University Press, 1951.

Steuart, J. 1767. *Inquiry into the Principles of Political Economy*. Ed. A. Skinner, Edinburgh: Oliver & Boyd, 1966.

Weber, M. 1922. *Wirtschaft und Gesellschaft: grundriss der verstehenden Soziologie*, Parts II and III. Tübingen, 1922.

Wright, E. 1978. *Class, Crisis and the State*. London: New Left Books.

classical conception of competition. *See* COMPETITION: CLASSICAL CONCEPTIONS.

classical economics. The label 'classical economics' is sometimes employed to refer quite simply to an era in the history of economic thought from, say, 1750 to 1870, in which a group of predominantly British economists used Adam Smith's *Wealth of Nations* as a springboard for analysing the production, distribution and exchange of goods and services in a capitalist economy. So broad a definition of classical economics must include such contemporary Continental writers as Cournot, Dupuit, Thünen and Gossen, not to mention such British writers as Bailey, Lloyd and Longfield, who at first glance seem to stand outside the tradition founded by Adam Smith. It is difficult to resist the implication, therefore, that classical economics is more than a period in the history of economic thought: it seems to involve a definite approach to economic problems. The difficulty, however, is how to characterize this approach.

Shrugging aside such tendentious definitions of classical economics as those of Marx and Keynes – for Marx (1867, pp. 174–5n) classical political economy begins with Petty in the 17th century and ends with Ricardo, and for Keynes (1936, p. 3n) the classical school begins with Ricardo and ends with Pigou – the first question is whether it was Adam Smith or David Ricardo who established the 'essence' or 'core' or classical economics. Of course, Adam Smith laid down the main issues that economists debated for a century after him, but there is also little doubt that the Smithian tradition was in some sense transformed with the appearance of Ricardo's *Principles of Political Economy and Taxation* in 1817. Some writers have nevertheless insisted that Smith and not Ricardo was the lasting influence on the character of classical economics, contending that the leading features of Ricardo's theoretical system were soon rejected even by his avowed followers in the decade after his death in 1823. Others, however, have insisted that, despite all the criticisms of Ricardo that no doubt appeared in the late 1820s and early 1830s, later writers like John Stuart Mill and John Elliott Cairnes continued to operate right up to the 1870s with the central Ricardian theorem that the rate of profit and hence the accumulation of capital depends critically on the marginal cost of production in agriculture; in that sense, they remained trapped in the Ricardian system. But even this assertion presupposes the notion that the Ricardian system is essentially characterized as a theory about the determination of the rate of profit, a proposition which is by no means accepted by all historians of economic thought.

It is only after clearing up this problem of the relative significance of Smith's and Ricardo's ideas in shaping the central current of classical economics that we can take up the question of where to place the utility theories of value put forward by such writers as Lloyd, Longfield, Senior, Dupuit and Gossen, the abstinence theories of interest of Bailey, Senior, Rae and John Stuart Mill, the use of both supply and demand forces in the determination of international prices by Mill, the theory of general gluts and the denial of Say's Law of Markets by Malthus, and the exploitation theory of profits by Marx – in short, all the elements of economic theorizing in the period 1770 to 1870 that so clearly do not belong to the corpus of doctrines bequeathed by Adam Smith and David Ricardo. Likewise, it is only then that we can start talking about the end of classical economics in the 1870s and the nature of the 'marginal revolution' that may or may not have marked a decisive break in the continuity of orthodox economics.

The endless debate on what was classical economics is neatly illustrated by the simultaneous appearance of three books on classical economics: *Classical Economics Reconsidered* by Thomas Sowell (1974), *The Structure of Classical Economic Theory* by Robert Eagly (1974) and *The Classical Economists* by Denis O'Brien (1975). Of the three, Eagly takes the widest view of the length of time over which something called 'classical economic theory' ruled the roost, beginning with the physiocrats in the 1750s and ending with the Walrasian theory of general equilibrium in the 1870s. His view is not only that the whole of classical economics can be defined in terms of a single conceptual framework but that this framework revolves essentially around a particular concept of capital as a stock of intermediate goods invested in staggered production periods, the question of the pricing of final goods always relegated to the next period after output has already been determined by the size of the labour force and the technology of the previous period; in short, the key to classical economics is to be found in the so-called 'wages fund doctrine'. Whether this thesis is convincing or not, Eagly's book represents an extreme example of the tendency to define classical economics as one coherent body of ideas organised around a central unifying principle. The secondary literature is, of course, replete with other attempts to pin down once and for all the classical theory of economic growth (e.g. Lowe, 1954; Samuelson), 1980, but few allege, as Eagly does, that their modelling of classical economics captures all the essentials of the writings of Quesnay, Smith, Ricardo, Mill and Marx, as well as McCulloch, Torrens, Bailey, Jones, Senior, Longfield, Babbage, Tooke, Wakefield, etc.

Sowell, on the other hand, adopts the traditional definition of classical economics as in effect the School of Adam Smith, and he therefore excludes Marx and, more surprisingly, Malthus, Torrens and Senior at least in some respects from the mainstream of the tradition stemming from *The Wealth of Nations*. That tradition consisted, according to Sowell, of a common set of philosophical presuppositions, common methods of analysis and common conclusions regarding matters of substantive economic analysis: it comprised such major propositions as the labour theory of value, the Malthusian theory of population, Say's Law and the quantity theory of money and was predominantly oriented towards the issue of economic growth (although not in the modern sense of the term as a theory of the steady-state equilibrium growth path of an economy). However, Sowell admits that this picture has to be qualified after 1817 by such phrases as 'classical economics in its Ricardian form' because Ricardo worked a major change in Smith's eclectic mode of economic reasoning by adopting static equilibrium analysis as the only valid method of conducting an economic argument. At any rate, Sowell's treatment of classical economics leaves little doubt of the extensive and varied character of economics in the classical period, posing problems for anyone who seeks to define classical economics in one or two sentences.

Both Eagly's and Sowell's books are dwarfed by O'Brien's wide-ranging and comprehensive review of classical economics, which alone among the three begins with an incisive discussion of the extent to which the classical writers formed a 'scientific community'. (O'Brien's book also contains excellent annotated bibliographical notes on classical economics; indeed, O'Brien, Blaug (1985) and Spiegel (1983) between them review the whole of the secondary literature.) O'Brien follows Schumpeter in arguing that the Ricardian system represented an analytical detour from the main line of advance running from Adam Smith to John Stuart Mill; it was not a fatal detour, however, because the full Ricardian apparatus attracted hardly any followers and in any case was more or less abandoned by the 1830s. As we noted earlier, this Schumpeter–O'Brien thesis has been questioned by some (e.g. Blaug, 1958; Hollander, 1977). The point is, however, that O'Brien's book perfectly illustrates our contention that any stand taken on the nature of classical economics as a whole

depends critically on the attitude adopted towards the Ricardian metamorphosis of Smithian economics.

THE SRAFFA INTERPRETATION OF RICARDO. Still more recently a new note has been struck in the old argument about the essential meaning of classical economics. Inspired by the publication of Sraffa's *Production of Commodities by Means of Commodities* (1960), a number of commentators have argued that classical economics is in effect a Sraffa-system, that is, an analysis of the manner in which a capitalist economy invests its surplus of net output over consumption, which is to say an output in excess of that required to reproduce that level of output, subject to the condition that goods and services are so priced as to maintain a uniform rate of wages and a uniform rate of profit on capital in all lines of investment. This approach, they contend, was buried in the 1870s when the central object of economic analysis became that of investigating the optimum allocation of resources whose quantities are given at the outset of the analysis; in reviving classical surplus analysis, Sraffa not only provides a promising new way of studying economic problems but also illuminates precisely what it was that united Smith, Ricardo and Marx, thus licensing the use of a single label such as 'classical economics' to cover them all (see Meek, 1973, 1977, the originator of the argument; and Dobb, 1973; Roncaglia, 1978; Walsh and Gram, 1980; Bradley and Howard, 1982; Eatwell, 1982; Garegnani, 1984; Howard and King, 1985).

As is well known, a Sraffa-system consists of a set of linear production equations, one for each commodity in the economy, and is intended to demonstrate that these equations are sufficient to determine all relative prices in long run equilibrium irrespective of the pattern of demand, provided that (1) the output of each commodity is given; (2) rate of profit on capital is uniform throughout the economy and (3) the real wage or (alternatively the rate of profit on capital) is somehow determined exogenously. On the face of it, such a theory does indeed appear to be very much like 'classical economics'. For example, after distinguishing between 'natural' and 'market' prices of commodities – or, as we would nowadays say, the long-run and short-run prices of commodities – Adam Smith focused much of his analysis on the determination of 'natural' prices, a tendency which became even stronger in the writings of Ricardo. Moreover, Smith and certainly Ricardo, not to mention Marx, always wrote as if demand played no role whatever in the determination of 'natural' price. We have all known ever since the work of Marshall that this neglect of demand can be justified if one assumes that commodities are produced under conditions of constant unit costs or constant returns to scale, the long-run supply curves of all industries being perfectly horizontal over the relevant range of output. Sraffa's production equations imply fixed coefficients of production and, again, we have known ever since the work of Leontief that fixed coefficients of production are sufficient (but not necessary) to produce constant costs. In short, Sraffa's demonstration that prices in his model are determined independently of demand is eminently 'classical'.

Likewise, there is no doubt that the concept of a uniform rate of return on capital, or rather defining 'natural' prices to be those generated by a stationary equilibrium in which the rate of profit has become equalized by interindustry mobility of capital, is typical of all economic writing in the century between 1770 and 1870. Finally, the real wage rate in classical economics is determined by so-called 'subsistence' requirements and these were defined by Ricardo, Mill and Marx in historical rather than physiological terms; in other words, it was assumed that the current 'natural' price of labour reflected the past history of the 'market' price of labour. The 'natural' price of labour was in effect determined by workers' attitudes to the size of their families but since the classical economists did little to analyse these attitudes, it is not too much to say that the so-called 'subsistence *theory* of wages' actually amounts to taking 'subsistence' as a datum (Schumpeter, 1954, p. 665). Once again, it can be argued that the Sraffian assumption of an exogenous real wage is 'classical' in spirit.

There is no doubt that Sraffa's system captures many of the elements of 'classical economics'. It provides a further bonus, however, in illuminating classical economics. Generations of critics have tried to make sense of Ricardo's lifelong quest for an 'invariable measure of value' and have given it up as a hopeless task. Ricardo was troubled by the fact that any change in money wages will alter the structure of relative prices owing to the fact that capital and labour are combined in different proportions in different industries. Thus, a rise in wages or a fall in the rate of profit raises the prices of labour-intensive goods relative to the price of capital-intensive goods. This violates the labour theory of value according to which relative prices are determined by the physical quantities of labour expended on production independently of the rate at which labour is rewarded. To remedy this difficulty, Ricardo struck upon the notion of expressing all prices in terms of a commodity produced by a ratio of capital to labour that is a weighted average of the entire spectrum of capital–labour ratios in the economy; such a commodity, he believed, constitutes an 'invariable measure of value' in the sense of providing a standard of measurement that is invariant to changes in the ratio of wages to profits. In the same way, Sraffa measures all prices in terms of a 'standard composite commodity' that consists only of outputs combined in the same proportions as the non-labour inputs that enter into all the successive layers of its manufacture. Moreover, in one of the many elegant demonstrations in his book, Sraffa succeeds in showing that such a 'standard commodity' is in fact embedded in any actual economic system and that the proportion of net output going to wages in that reduced-scale system determines the rate of profit in the economy as a whole.

The explanation of this result depends on Sraffa's distinction between 'basic' commodities which enter directly or indirectly into the production of every commodity in the economy, including themselves, and 'non-basic' commodities which enter only into final consumption. If we treat labour itself as a produced 'means of production' then wage goods constitute examples of 'basic' commodities, that is, they are technically required to cause households to produce the flow of labour services. Ricardo clearly believed that wheaten bread was 'basic' in this sense but Sraffa parts company with Ricardo in rejecting any and all versions of the subsistence theory of wages; workers in Sraffa are primary, non–reproducible inputs. Nevertheless, there are plenty of other basics besides wage goods in an actual economy and the upshot of Sraffa's distinction between basics and non-basics is that the 'standard composite commodity' consists only of basics and indeed of all the basics in the economy; this collection of basics enters into the production of the invariant yardstick in a 'standard ratio', that is, in the same proportion as they enter into their own production. It turns out that relative prices and either the rate of profit or the rate of wages (depending on which one is given exogenously) depend only on the technical condition of producing the 'standard commodity' and are in no way affected by what happens to nonbasic commodities. In a way this is obvious: a change in the cost of producing a nonbasic no doubts alters its own price but, by the definition of a nonbasic commodity, the effect stops there since the product in question never becomes an input into any other technical process. It is also obvious, at least intuitively, that an exogenous change in wages unconnected with a change in productive techniques alters the rate of profit but has no effect on relative prices measured in terms of the standard commodity for the simple reason that the change alters the measuring rod in the same way as it alters the pattern of prices being measured. The 'standard commodity' therefore provides an 'invariable measure of value', and Ricardo's old problem is at long last solved.

In developing his own ideas, Sraffa also advanced an entirely new interpretation of how Ricardo came to connect his theory of the determination of the rate of profit with the question of finding an invariable yardstick for measuring relative prices. In his early pamphlet *Essays on the Influence of a Low Price of Corn on the Profits of Stock* (1815), Ricardo wanted to show that the extension of cultivation to inferior soils depresses the rate of profit on capital throughout the economy by raising the marginal cost of producing 'corn', that is, wheat, the principal wage good consumed by workers. This is easy to demonstrate in a one-sector economy where the only output is wheat. However, from the beginning Ricardo operated with a two-sector economy in which an agricultural industry produces 'corn' and a manufacturing industry produces 'cloth'. Of course, if wage goods consist entirely of corn and if cloth is always purchased out of profits and rents, it is still easy to show that the rate of profit on capital depends decisively on the action of diminishing returns in agriculture. In agriculture, wheat is the only output and it is also the input both in the form of wages 'advanced' to workers to tide them over the annual production cycle and seeds to plough back into the next agricultural cycle; hence, the 'money' rate of profit in agriculture cannot possibly diverge from the 'wheat' rate of profit because any change in the price of wheat affects inputs and output in the same degree. Manufacturing, however, only uses wheat as one of its inputs (namely, in the form of wage goods), and since the rate of profit earned on capital must be equal in between the two industries in equilibrium, the price of wheat determines a definite price for cloth. If, for example, the rate of profit in agriculture falls due to the operation of diminishing returns, the price of cloth in terms of wheat must likewise fall to prevent cloth from being more profitable to produce than wheat. To reiterate: measuring all prices in terms of wheat, the 'money' rate of profit in industry is governed by the 'wheat' rate of profit in agriculture, which, in turn, depends entirely on the technology of producing wheat, the unique wage good; in one of Ricardo's famous catch phrases: 'it is the profits of the farmer which regulate the profits of all other trades'.

This ingenious argument, which appears to explain the determination of the rate of profit in purely physical terms without the use of a theory of value, is known in the literature as the 'corn model'. In the preface to his edition of *The Works of David Ricardo* (1951), Sraffa argued that the corn model is implicit in Ricardo's 1815 *Essay*. To be sure, Ricardo never wrote it down in so many words because even in the *Essay* he could not swallow the assumption that wages are entirely spent on wheat, that all agricultural products are wage goods and that all manufactured products are luxuries which are never consumed by workers. Nevertheless, he did use wheat in the *Essay* as a measure for aggregating the heterogeneous inputs of agriculture on the assumption that all prices rise and fall with wheat prices, and he also employed arithmetical examples in which all inputs and outputs of both agriculture and manufacturing are expressed in terms of wheat. In the

Principles he analysed an economy with many sectors in which a change in the terms of trade between wheat and cloth will alter real wages and hence the rate of profit on capital. Nevertheless, his preoccupation in this mature work with the 'invariable measure of value' may be read as an attempt to secure the same results obtained earlier with the aid of the corn model, that is, to tie the determination of the rate of profit directly to the production function of agriculture. Of course, if Ricardo could have ignored the varying proportions of labour and capital in different industries, he could have reached all his conclusions without the aid of an invariable yardstick of value. He had placed so much emphasis, however, on what Marx was to call the unequal 'organic composition of capital' that this route was closed to him. Hence, the quest for an 'invariable measure' with which to recapture the simple truth of the corn model. Here then is a rational reconstruction of Ricardo's arguments that accounts neatly for both the form and the drift of his reasoning.

A GENERAL EQUILIBRIUM INTERPRETATION OF RICARDO. Sraffa's interpretation of Ricardo has won wide assent even among those who otherwise remain sceptical about Sraffa's system in its own right. However, Samuel Hollander's recent re-examination of the whole of Ricardo's writings has taken sharp exception to Sraffa's reading (Hollander, 1979, pp. 123–90, 684–9). Ricardo, according to Hollander, never entertained the corn model even implicitly, never assumed that corn alone enters the wage basket, never argued that the rate of profit in agriculture determines the general profit rate and, above all, never assumed that real wages remain constant either because they are determined by the subsistence requirements of workers or because they are determined exogenously. What Hollander really objects to is the notion that 'distribution', that is, the rate of wages and the rate of profit, are determined in Ricardo as in Sraffa's own model independently of and indeed prior to the value of commodities, so that the former causally determines the latter. This is to be contrasted with the approach of Walrasian general equilibrium theory in which the pricing of factor services is determined simultaneously with the pricing of final consumption goods. It is simply not true, argues Hollander, that the history of economic thought can be neatly divided into two great branches, a general equilibrium branch leading down from Walras and Marshall to Samuelson, Arrow and Debreu today, in which all relevant economic variables are mutually and simultaneously determined, and a completely different branch leading down from Ricardo and Marx to Sraffa in which distribution takes priority over pricing because economic variables are causally determined in a sequential chain starting from a predetermined real wage (Pasinetti, 1974, pp. 42–4, even enlists Keynes into the ranks of the Ricardo–Marx–Sraffa school). Ricardo, Hollander insists, was essentially a general equilibrium theorist – and so were Adam Smith, John Stuart Mill and even Karl Marx (Hollander, 1973, 1981, 1982).

Before passing judgement on this dispute, it is worth noting that what has been called the 'neo-Ricardian' or 'Cambridge' interpretation of the history of economic thought claims superior merit for Ricardo because Ricardo divorced the question of distribution from the question of pricing. But this is precisely the grounds on which many pre-war historians of economic thought attacked Ricardo! Thus, Frank Knight in a famous essay on 'The Ricardian Theory of Production and Distribution' (1956) poured scorn on classical writers like Ricardo because they utterly failed to approach the problem of distribution as a problem of valuation and this despite the fact that the effective demand for any factor of production depends on the distribution of income, which in turn depends at least to some extent on the pricing of factor services; in short, 'distribution theory has little meaning apart from a theory of general equilibrium' (Knight, 1956, pp. 41, 63). Similarly, Schumpeter (1954, pp. 473, 568–9, 1171) spoke scathingly of the 'Ricardian Vice' whereby an already oversimplified economic model is further reduced by freezing one endogeneous variable after another by special *ad hoc* assumptions. First, rent in Ricardo is determined as an intra-marginal return to land treated as a factor in fixed supply; the location of the margin depends of course on the demand for agricultural produce, but this is in turn explained by the size of the population via the assumption of a perfectly inelastic demand for corn. Second, having 'gotten rid of rent' on the margins of cultivation, Ricardo then employed a subsistence theory of wages to determine the share of total-output-minus-rent that accrues to labour. Third, total profits in Ricardo are treated as a pure residual after the deduction of wages and rents, the rate of profit being determined as the quotient of total profits and the inherited stock of capital. In other words, the problem of distribution is explained by three totally different types of theories, which in turn are quite different from the principles employed to explain the pricing of goods and services, namely, the labour theory of value. How amazed Knight and Schumpeter would have been to see their critique stood on its head, so that what they regarded as vices are now viewed in certain quarters as virtues.

RICARDO VERSUS SMITH. Having expounded various interpretations of classical economics, it is time to attempt some sort of general assessment. To collect our thoughts, consider the number of problematic issues we have outlined above. Is the economics of Adam Smith something different from the economics of David Ricardo? Obviously there is no total break in the continuity of thinking, but nevertheless, is there a sufficient break to warrant the use of such dramatic language as the 'Ricardian Revolution'? Was this 'Ricardian Revolution' the implicit resort to something like the 'corn model' to produce a clear-cut explanation of the determination of the rate of profit, or was it simply a change in the style of economic reasoning? Was Ricardo soon repudiated, so that the Smithian tradition survived right down to John Stuart Mill and beyond, or are the later phases of classical economics dominated by the ideas of Ricardo rather than those of Adam Smith? Is there sufficient coherence around a definite core of ideas to permit us to talk at all of 'classical economics'? Is this core the notion of the origin and disposition of the 'economic' surplus and the proposition that distribution is independent of valuation? And, finally, is all of classical economics a primitive but prescient version of general equilibrium analysis?

We can deal quickly with the first question, the so-called 'Ricardian Revolution'. With the exception of Hollander (1979, ch. 1), all modern commentators on classical economics agree that Ricardo altered both the scope, method and focus of economics. Even if we take only *The Wealth of Nations* among Smith's books and essays, the scope of economics for Adam Smith is enormous and perhaps wider than that for any economist before or after him. The first two books of *The Wealth of Nations* consists largely of what later came to be regarded as the very hallmark of orthodox economics: the theory of value and the theory of production and distribution, employing in the main the method of comparative statics. But even the 'Digression' on the value of silver in chapter 11 of Book I takes up an unorthodox topic, namely, changes in the structure of prices over centuries with the aid of a method of analysis that might be called 'inductive' or 'historical'. Moreover, here as elsewhere in *The Wealth of Nations* there is a remarkable emphasis on the notion of 'increasing returns' so widely defined as to include the effects of both increases in the scale of production and changes in the method of production or technical progress. Despite the flowering of a considerable literature in recent years purporting to model Smith's 'theory of economic growth', few have succeeded in capturing this vital element in Smith's thinking, which Kaldor (1972) has consistently emphasized (but see Eltis, 1984, ch. 3). Moreover, this notion of increasing returns soon dropped out of classical economics, coming back only ninety years later with the writings of Karl Marx.

Similarly, there is the famous distinction in Book III of *The Wealth of Nations* between productive and unproductive labour with Ricardo and Mill accepted, which McCulloch and Senior denied, which Marx reinterpreted in a different way, but which nevertheless was never followed up and developed in any fruitful way. A simple explanation for this failure to elaborate Smith's distinction was that Smith made a mess of it, defining productive labour alternatively as labour which produces something tangible, produces a profit for its employer, and generates productive capacity that then creates a demand for additional employment. But another explanation is that the distinction between the employment of 'manufacturers' and 'menial servants', between wealth-creating and wealth-consuming activities, is only relevant in the context of long-run economic development, being partly a 'positive' account of different patterns of economic change in different nations and partly a 'normative' proposal for legislators seeking to maximize the rate of net investment in an economy. Although Mill was profoundly concerned with questions of economic development (see O'Brien, 1975, ch. 8), Ricardo had no real interest in the forces that govern the historical patterns of economic change, and for that reason alone the Smithian distinction between productive and unproductive labour, and the associated discussion of an optimum investment pattern between industries in chapter 5 of Book II of *The Wealth of Nations*, was effectively laid to rest all through the heyday of classical economics.

Smith's interest in 'the different progress of opulence in different ages of nations' totally dominates Book III of *The Wealth of Nations* and is at work even in Book IV on mercantilist theory and policy and Book V on public finance. In this latter half of *The Wealth of Nations* there is little appeal to the comparisons of steady-state equilibria, which was to figure so heavily in practically everything that Ricardo wrote. But there are two other elements in these pages that are totally missing in Ricardo and even in Mill, namely, a concern with the incentive effects of different institutional devices for rewarding self-employed professionals and individuals employed in the public sector (Rosenberg, 1960) and a keen sense of the role of pressure groups in the formulation of economic policies (Peacock, 1975; West, 1976; Winch, 1983). Thus, the modern theory of property rights as well as the economic theory of politics may properly claim Smith as a forerunner. At any rate, neither of these two aspects of *The Wealth of Nations* has any echoes in the writings of those that came immediately after Smith.

Consider next the theory of international trade. There is a static equilibrium theory of the gains of foreign trade in Smith based on the principle of absolute rather than comparative advantage, and here no doubt, Ricardo saw further than Smith. But there is also a dynamic theory of the gains of trade in Smith, the so-called 'vent-for-surplus' doctrine, according to which foreign trade widens the extent of the market and generates new wants; this view of foreign trade disappears in Ricardo and only comes back to classical economics with Mill (Bloomfield, 1975, 1978, 1981).

Smith's theory of money is also profoundly different from that of Ricardo, typically invoking the quantity theory of money in its dynamic 18th-century version in which the emphasis falls on the disequilibrium 'transition period' between an increase in the quantity of money and the rise in prices and not on the final equilibrium adjustment between money and prices (Laidler, 1981). In addition, Smith was an advocate of private, unregulated banking (qualified only by the prohibition of the issue of banknotes for small sums), reflecting the operation of Scottish banking, which was unregulated for over a century between 1716 and 1844. It was Henry Thornton who first rejected the Smithian tradition in his *Paper Credit of Great Britain* (1802), explicitly denying that the note issue in a free banking system would be self-regulating as Smith had argued. By the time of Ricardo it was orthodox to argue that the issue of banknotes was an obvious exception to the doctrine of laissez faire (White, 1984, ch. 3). Here too, the gulf between Smith and Ricardo is almost total.

There is no need to underline Ricardo's differences with Adam Smith over the labour theory of value, since Ricardo set out explicitly to criticize Smith's failure to apply the labour theory of value to a modern economy rather than a purely conjectural 'early and rude state of society'. But what is not so obvious is the fact that even in respect of labour as a measure of the 'real price' of commodities – Smith's tortured language in Book I, chapter 5, for the problem of specifying an index number of economic welfare – Smith's view of labour is profoundly subjective, whereas Ricardo in his comparable chapter 20 of the *Principles of Political Economy and Taxation* on 'value and riches' consistently treats labour as an objective, physical expenditure of energy. In the masterly tenth chapter of Book I of *The Wealth of Nations* on 'relative wages', Smith demonstrated that competition in labour markets equalize the net advantages of different occupations, that is, the monetary returns to units of disutility of labour. In other words, to the extent that labour is a 'measure of value' in Smith, it is labour conceived as 'toil and trouble' and reflects the preferences of workers as much as those of their employers. Although Ricardo, and for that matter Marx, never disputed this analysis of Smith, they ignored its implications and blithely treated labour as fundamentally homogeneous in quality, its role in the production of commodities being conceived as a brute reflection of purely technological data; in short, they took as given something like Sraffa's production equations. It is this and not the famous debate over whether the value of commodities in Smith is determined by the labour 'commanded' by goods or the labour 'embodied' in their production that represents the real watershed in the history of the labour theory of value (Robertson and Taylor, 1957; Gordon, 1959; Blaug, 1985, pp. 49–53).

But the most profound departure in Ricardo from the Smithian tradition is the notion that rent is in a class by itself as a source of income: it is 'unearned income', being an intramarginal return to purely natural differences in the quality of land which have nothing whatever to do with the activity of landlords. Despite Smith's references to landlords who 'love to reap where they have never sowed' and the 'conspiracy' of merchants, the Smithian world is one in which all economic interests are essentially harmonious or, at any rate, capable of being made harmonious by wise legislators. The Ricardian world, however, is one which conflicting class interests are unavoidable. It is this unique element in the

Ricardian system, which gave classical economics its sharp political edge, an edge that clearly worries so many of the minor classical economists, such as Jones, Senior and Longfield.

Finally, the central and indeed sole focus of the Ricardian system is the question: what determines the rate of profit on capital, or rather, what governs its changes over time? This is a question which never really troubled Adam Smith. He made it clear that profit is equalized among industries in the long run, but he had no explanation of how the level of the rate of profit is determined. To be sure, Smith believed that the rate of profit was eventually doomed to fall because of the exhaustion of profitable investment outlets. But he never emphasized this proposition and on balance he took an extremely optimistic view of the future prospects for economic growth. Ricardo too was essentially an optimist about the long-run growth potential of the British economy but only if the Corn Laws were repealed; he was thus motivated to argue the strongest possible connection between the rate of profit on capital and the real cost of producing wheat exclusively with domestic resources. In consequence, Ricardo viewed absolutely every aspect of economic activity, including monetary forces, currency arrangements, taxation, the financing of the public debt, and of course foreign trade, through the lenses of his theory of profits. Many readers of Ricardo have been deceived by the preface to his *Principles* – 'To determine the laws which regulate this distribution (of rent, profit, and wages), is the principal problem in Political Economy' – into believing that the Ricardian system is largely devoted to an analysis of the determination of the relative shares of land, capital and labour. But while Ricardo certainly had much to say about the issue of relative shares, and indeed was responsible for introducing this theme into economics, his analysis is in fact concentrated on rents per acre, the rate of the profit per unit of capital and the rate of wages per man. It is, in a word, a book about the pricing of factor services and that is (surely?) much less than the subject-matter of *The Wealth of Nations*.

There is little doubt, therefore, that the scope of the science of political economy as conceived in *The Wealth of Nations* was sharply contracted in Ricardo's *Principles of Political Economy*. But, in addition, Adam Smith wrote much besides *The Wealth of Nations*. Quite apart from *The Theory of Moral Sentiments* and the remarkable essay on the *History of Astronomy*, the publication of the new University of Glasgow edition of the complete *Works and Correspondence of Adam Smith* (1976–83) strongly suggests that he intended to round off his contributions by a major work on the theory of jurisprudence which he never lived to write; nevertheless, even in *The Wealth of Nations* he never lost sight of the fact that political economy may be considered as 'a branch of the science of a statesman or legislator', the latter being therefore something more comprehensive than the former. A number of recent commentators (Cropsey, 1957; Lindgren, 1973; Winch, 1978; Skinner, 1979) have indeed insisted that all of Adam Smith's writings are held together by a unified vision of an all-embracing social science, which he unfortunately never succeeded in realizing to the full. Whether this thesis is persuasive or not, it certainly strengthens the contention that the economics of Adam Smith is conceived on grander lines than the economics of David Ricardo.

THE CORN MODEL AGAIN. So there was what might be described in highly coloured language as a 'Ricardian Revolution': what began as a criticism of some of 'Professor Smith's opinions' ended up as a wholesale revision of the legacy of Adam Smith.

What was the cornerstone of this 'Revolution'? Was it the 'corn model'? It certainly was a denial of the Smithian cost-of-production theory according to which a rise in money wages would raise all prices, thus leaving the rate of profits unaffected. But that is not to say that Ricardo's fundamental theorem that 'profits vary inversely as wages' was based on an implicitly held corn model. It is true that the corn-model interpretation neatly rationalizes Ricardo's arguments in the early *Essay on Profits* in which the economy is conceived as consisting of two sectors but the rate of profit is determined exactly as it would be in a one-sector economy. In other words, Ricardo should have held the corn model for without it the *Essay* is simply logically inconsistent. Nevertheless, the corn-model version simply attributes far more rigour and consistency to Ricardo's analysis than is warranted (Peach, 1984). What Ricardo later put in place of the missing corn model was the 'invariable measure of value' which was designed to surmount two of his unresolved difficulties at one and the same time: (1) that workers consume both manufactured and agricultural goods, so that one can never be sure that the rising cost of producing wheat is directly transmitted to the rate of profit; and (2) that capital and labour combine in different proportions in different industries, so that a change in real wages for any reason whatsoever alters the structure of prices and, thus, affects the rate of profit even if nothing has happened to the technology of agriculture.

We noted earlier that Sraffa's *Production of Commodities by Means of Commodities* may be said to have vindicated Ricardo's belief in the existence of an 'invariable measure of value', capable of separating and measuring the effects of changes in technology from those due to changes in the rate of wage and profits. But doubts remain about the validity of this claim. In Ricardo, the divining rod of the invariable measure is supposed to be invariant (as Ricardo kept saying) not just to changes in wages in profits but also to changes in its own methods of production. Sraffa's 'standard commodity' fills the bill on the first score but fails on the second score: it is not invariant to changes in its own techniques of production and therefore falls short of solving Ricardo's problem of linking the determination of the rate of profit directly and unambiguously to the action of diminishing returns in agriculture. The truth is that there is no such thing as an 'invariable' yardstick that will satisfy all the requirements that Ricardo placed upon it (Ong, 1983). All of which is to say that, despite the fact that Ricardo was the first truly rigorous analytical economist, it is impossible to exonerate him from all analytical errors: he was at times inclined to square a circle using only a ruler and a compass!

CLASSICAL ECONOMICS AS SURPLUS THEORY. We turn next to the thesis that classical economics is the economics of the creation and disposition of surplus output over consumption – a theory of the reproducibility of economic systems in the making – in sharp contrast to the later neoclassical theme of the allocation of *given* resources between competing ends, subject to the constraints of technology and existing property rights. Now, there can be little doubt that this is precisely the nature of the economics of physiocracy (Eltis, 1984, ch. 2), and it is little wonder that those who argue the surplus interpretation include the physiocrats in classical economics (Walsh and Gram, 1980, ch. 2). There is also little doubt that it captures much of the drift of *The Wealth of Nations* and turns up again in Mill's *Principles* and in Marx's *Capital*. On the other hand, it does not begin to do justice to dominant features of the Ricardian system and leaves out almost as much as it manages to include in the writings of the classical economists.

What does it tell us, for example, about the jewel in the crown of classical economics: Ricardo's law of comparative advantage as the foundation of the belief in free trade, which served throughout the whole of the 19th century as the litmus-paper test of an economic liberal? Ricardo treated foreign trade as a matter of moving along a static world production-transformation curve, constructed on the basis of *given* resources and the *given* techniques of production of the trading countries; the gains of foreign trade in his celebrated cloth–wine example show up in a global increase in physical output from given labour resources in Portugal and England. There is no hint here of 'surplus theory' and perhaps that is why the surplus interpretation of classical economics studiously avoids discussion of the theory of international trade.

It might be argued, however, that the subject of foreign trade lies outside the mainstream of classical economics because it violates the assumption of a uniform rate of profit on capital – if capital were mobile between countries, international trade would be based like intranational trade on absolute cost advantages. As a matter of fact, Thweatt (1976) has argued that Ricardo's view of foreign trade never went beyond the conception of absolute advantage and this despite the three-paragraph illustration of comparative advantage in his *Principles*, which may well have been written by James Mill rather than Ricardo. After all, free trade for Ricardo meant a policy appropriate to an advanced manufacturing nation in its relation with agrarian nations supplying it with food; the point of the chapter on foreign trade in the *Principles* is not to explain the gains of trade but to demonstrate that foreign trade only affects the rate of profit insofar as it leads to the importation of cheaper wage goods.

Be that as it may, less than a decade after the death of Ricardo, the young Mill (1844, but written in 1829) completed Ricardo's argument by showing that the division of the overall gains from foreign trade in the two countries depends on 'reciprocal demand', thus putting another nail in the coffin of the labour theory of value: even when goods are produced by labour alone within countries, the barter terms of trade between countries depend on both demand and supply. Cairnes subsequently extended the reciprocal demand approach even to domestic trade at least in respect of exchange between 'non-competing groups'. None of this has anything to do with the creation, accumulation and allocation of an economic surplus, and so the surplus interpretation must leave to one side the classical theory of international prices, the classical theory of balance of payment adjustments and with it the classical theory of monetary management.

But the shortcomings of the surplus interpretation extend even to classical theorizing about the operations of a closed economy. It can throw no light on the care with which Adam Smith spelt out the effects of a public mourning on the price of black cloth in Book I, chapter 7, of *The Wealth of Nations*, so as to demonstrate that 'market' prices cannot permanently diverge from 'natural' prices because they imply profit opportunities for producers that will sooner or later be exploited; all this is to say that the surplus interpretation has little time for those short-run adjustments that formed the staple of much of the practical wisdom of classical economists grappling with day-to-day economic problems. Similarly, the surplus interpretation must pass over the doctrine of opportunity costs that was part and parcel of the legacy of Adam Smith, namely, that effective costs to producers are not expenditures incurred in the past but present opportunities foregone. As Buchanan (1929) showed many years ago, Ricardo's characteristic doctrine of 'getting rid of rent' by

concentrating attention on the rentless margin of production implies that land has no uses alternative to the growing of wheat; while this may at a pinch be justified at a macroeconomic level, Smith's theory of rent, which recognizes the fact that land employed in cultivation must compete with land for grazing or urban use, is thus more truly in the tradition of analysing allocation with given resources than is Ricardo's. This Smithian emphasis on the competing uses for land, so that ground rent does enter into the price of agricultural goods, was never lost sight of by classical writers between Ricardo and Mill and comes back into its own in Mill's *Principles*, notably in Book II, chapter 16, on rent theory.

The surplus interpretation is thus a limited view of classical economics, but it is not a misrepresentation. In one sense it is only fancy language for the old view that classical economics is essentially the economics of development, which starts from a fundamental contrast between augmentable labour and non-augmentable land given in quantity and asks how, under these circumstances, growth in the sense of per capita income can be maximized (Myint, 1948). Indeed, the notion that growth of population and the accumulation of capital are the great themes of classical economics in contrast to the question of efficient allocation of given supplies of the factors of production in neoclassical economics after 1870 is endorsed in many, if not in all, textbooks on the history of economic thought (e.g. Blaug, 1985, pp. 295–6). So why all the fuss? Why all this insistence on the surplus interpretation in recent years?

A close reading of those who have advocated a reading of classical economics in terms of surplus analysis suggests two rather different motivations for the 'new' interpretation: one is to provide Marx with a respectable pedigree, or at least to display Marx as the true heir of bourgeois economics in its days of glory, solving the riddles that baffled Quesnay, Smith and Ricardo; the other is to reveal Sraffa as the true heir of the classical tradition, demonstrating that there is an old and venerable tradition of explaining the determination of prices without resorting to the preferences and satisfactions of consumers and without relying on a market mechanism to price both capital and labour. Each of these two strands of the surplus interpretation produces its own special distortions of classical economics.

It is certainly true that Marx was in many ways a direct descendant of Smith and Ricardo, and particularly of Ricardo. He took over from Smith the distinction between use value and exchange value (as well as the denial that the former had anything to do with the determination of the latter), the distinction between market and natural prices, together with the notion that the business of the economist is to explain natural prices as terminal states of long-run equilibrium outcomes, the distinction between productive and unproductive labour, the conception of historically increasing returns as a major force in the process of development, the tripartite division of national revenue into wages, profits and rents as the incomes of three distinct social classes – and much else. But he learned even more from Ricardo and particularly Ricardo's discovery that all the problems of the labour theory of value are reducible to the undeniable fact that capital and labour combine in different proportions in different industries, difficulties which may be resolved however by measuring all prices in terms of the price of a commodity produced by the 'average' industry. This was the key to Marx's 'transformation problem', which demonstrated that 'prices of production' must systematically diverge from labour 'values' if the rate of profit is to be uniform between industries, an insight which, Marx thought, had always eluded Ricardo. Marx hardly noticed that in correcting Ricardo's answer, he also corrected his question. Ricardo's problem had been: what determines the rate of profit? Marx's problem, however, was: what determines the rate of profit if profit is in the nature of unpaid labour, a mark-up on the outlays of wages disguised as a mark-up on all cost-outlays? But the nature of profit as 'earned' or 'unearned' income did not interest Ricardo: he devoted one sentence to this subject in the *Principles* and even this sentence was a throw-away remark.

Marx also learned from Ricardo how to reduce skilled labour to common labour by simply taking the structure of relatives wages as given, thus missing the thrust of Smith's theory of relative wages, namely, that wages are not determined solely by the demand side in labour markets. Marx discarded the Malthusian theory of population but retained the subsistence theory of wages relying on the 'reserve army' of the unemployed to keep wages fluctuating around subsistence levels. He failed to notice, however, that this made wages a function of the play of demand and supply in labour markets and not the labour-costs of producing wage goods; in short, the pricing of wage goods in Marx does not conform to the labour theory of value. Like Ricardo, Marx conceded that the level of 'subsistence' is itself historically conditioned: it is a standard of living that workers have become accustomed to expect by past experience. Thus, even the 'natural' price of labour in Marx is not entirely cost-determined but depends on the preferences of workers. Once again, the 'value of labour-power' in Marx does not conform to the labour theory of value.

Marx never paid much attention to Ricardo's doctrine of comparative advantage and apparently failed to notice that it too violates the labour theory of value. It is also doubtful whether he ever truly grasped the import of Ricardo's theory of differential rent and particularly its central implication that prices everywhere, and not just in agriculture, are determined by marginal rather than average costs of production.

Nevertheless, despite all the obvious differences between Smith and Ricardo on the one hand and Ricardo and Marx on the other in both analytical constructs and social vision, there are so many striking similarities between them that Marxian economics is simply unimaginable without Smith, Ricardo and (although Marx did not like to admit it) John Stuart Mill. Marx went further than any of them in his grasp of business cycles, his treatment of technical change and the so-called 'reproduction schema' – the true starting point of the modern theory of steady-state growth – but he never emancipated himself from his starting point in classical economics with all its strengths and all its weaknesses.

There can be little quarrel, therefore, with a surplus interpretation of classical economics that treats Marx squarely as one of the last classical economists. However, it is when this Marxian strand in the surplus interpretation is combined with the Sraffian strand that we begin to encounter a mythical classical economics that never existed. We are told that the data for the analysis of prices in classical economics are the same as those for Sraffa, namely, (1) the size and composition of output, (2) the techniques of production in use, and (3) the real wage rate; these are contrasted with the data of neoclassical economics, namely, the preferences of individuals, the initial endowment of the factors of production among individuals and the existing techniques of production (e.g. Eatwell, 1977, p. 62). We are even told that long-run prices in classical theory are *not* the outcome of the opposing forces of demand and supply and that classical 'natural' prices are *not* what (ever since Marshall) are called long-run 'normal' prices

(Harcourt, 1982, p. 265) or that, although classical 'natural' prices are indeed the same as neoclassical long-run 'normal' prices, the theories advanced by classical and neoclassical economists for the determination of these long-run equilibrium prices are quite different (Garegnani, 1976, pp. 28–9). But there is actually no warrant for any of these assertions.

The size and composition of output is certainly not treated as given in Smith and to say so is to make nonsense of Smith's emphasis on secular economic development and the optimum balance of manufacturing and agriculture in the course of secular growth. Ricardo, on the other hand, frequently but not invariably treats the output of agricultural produce to be determined by the size of population via a perfectly inelastic demand for wheat (Barkai, 1965; Stigler, 1965). Thus, he does not assume the output of wheat (or any other product) to be a datum but to be an endogenously determined variable, a function of population growth, which in turn is treated as an endogenous variable. He never squarely faced up to all the difficulties created for his argument by commodity-substitution as the price of 'corn' rises relative to 'cloth', but he certainly recognized the problem. There is no support, therefore, for the contention that he took the composition of output to be a datum, except provisionally at certain points in his argument for the sake of producing what he called 'strong results'. What we have said about Smith and Ricardo follows with double force for both Mill and Marx. So much then for this part of the attempt to bring the classical economists fully into the Sraffian fold.

We can agree that the classical economists took for granted an existing state of techniques – has there ever been an economist, apart possibly from Marx, who has not? – but the real question is whether they conceived of this state of techniques *à la* Sraffa as ruling out factor substitution. On balance, as we noted earlier, the answer to this question must be yes. Ricardo of course recognized the problem the moment he introduced the chapter on machinery in the third edition of the *Principles* (1821), but by then he was thoroughly committed to his invariable standard of value, which necessarily rules out factor substitution. On the other hand, a special kind of factor substitution was built into his theory of differential rent in which variable doses of capital-and-labour combined in fixed proportions are applied in increasing amounts to a fixed quantity of heterogeneous land; it is this idea which of course led John Bates Clark and Philip Wicksteed in later years to hail Ricardo as the 'father' of marginal productivity theory. When we consider that the theory of differential rent was the very cornerstone of the Ricardian system, we can only gasp at Sraffa's bold declaration in the preface to his *Production of Commodities by Means of Commodities* (1960) that his own system, concerned as it is 'exclusively with such properties of an economic system as do not depend on changes in the scale of production or in the proportions of "factors" ' is identical to the 'standpoint ... of the old classical economists from Adam Smith to Ricardo'.

Next, can it be argued that the classical economists took the real wage rate as a datum for their analysis of value and distribution? It is perfectly true that the much-maligned theory of subsistence wages in factor amounts to saying that the subsistence wage is whatever has been the real wage for a long time. How long is long? About a generation, Malthus said, and Ricardo agreed. But such assertions did not help much in specifying the subsistence wage, since annual population growth had been positive for as long as anyone could remember, and a positive rate of population growth implied that market wages exceed the natural subsistence wage rate. So, in effect, the classical economists regarded real wages as data but that is not what they thought they were doing; after all, the only reason that the Malthusian theory of population was so quickly incorporated into the mainstream of classical economics was that it appeared to provide a truly endogeneous explanation of the determination of real wages. The long-run equilibrium wage rate, Malthus had taught, was that wage rate, which, given the historically conditioned habits and customs of the working class, encouraged them to reproduce a family of given size. Some classical economists, like Senior and McCulloch, came to doubt the validity of the Malthusian theory but never managed to put any other theory of the determination of long-run wages in its place. John Stuart Mill, on the other hand, found the Malthusian theory so suitable for his purpose of alleviating poverty through the self-help of the poor – birth control, education and the formation of consumer and producer cooperatives – that he espoused it more vehemently than even Malthus himself. All in all, there is simply no warrant for arguing that any classical economist (including Marx) *intended* to explain real wages by forces outside the purview of economic analysis.

Lastly, we come to the most grotesque distortion of all: the idea that any appeal to the forces of demand *and* supply in determining prices is necessarily alien to classical economics and that classical 'natural' prices have nothing whatsoever in common with Marshall's long-run 'normal' prices. Now, it is true that Ricardo (and Marx after him) propagated the misleading idea that demand-and-supply explanations only pertain to 'market' prices, whereas 'natural' prices are to be explained solely in terms of costs of production, as if costs can influence prices without acting through supply. Ricardo lacked the analytical apparatus to appreciate the fact that supply-side explanations of prices hold only if goods are produced under conditions of constant costs; this might well justify the neglect of demand in the case of the pricing of 'cloth' but certainly not on his own grounds in the case of the pricing of 'corn'. This marvellous confusion of language, encouraged by Ricardo's tendency to think of demand and supply as quantities actually bought and sold and not as schedules of demand and supply prices, was almost entirely cleared up by Mill in his masterful treatment of value in Book III of his *Principles* in which he noted that an equilibrium price is one which equates demand and supply in the sense of a mathematical equation and concluded that 'the law of demand and supply ... is controlled but not set aside by the law of cost of production, since cost of production would have no effect on value if it could have none on supply'. In fact, this is not very different from what Ricardo (1952, Vol. IX, p. 172) once said in private to Jean Baptiste Say: 'You say demand and supply regulates the price of bread; that is true, but what regulates supply? the cost of production.'

Marshall's schema of market-period, short-period and long-period prices, of constant-cost, increasing-cost and decreasing-cost industries, and their accompanying diagrams of demand and supply, are indispensable aids to clear thinking about the determination of prices and imply nothing whatsoever about the truth or falsity of any particular theory of prices. To treat demand and supply as dirty words that classical economists would never have employed in the explanation of natural prices is to take their outmoded language at its face value and, indeed, to deny any analytical progress in the history of economics.

To reject Sraffian interpretations of classical economics is not to reject Sraffa's system on its own grounds. Whether or not it is faithful to both the spirit and the letter of classical economics, it is undeniably true that, like all advances in economic theory, it casts a new light on the ideas of the past.

It has certainly made us think again about Ricardo's invariable measure of value and its intimate connection with Marx's transformation problem; it has illuminated the problem of joint production and the difficulties which this creates for the labour theory of value, however formulated; and it has highlighted the fact that any theory of prices necessarily involves some proposition about how total output is divided between wages and profits. Its impact on the ongoing debate about the great ideas of the past is perhaps best illustrated by the furore which it has created among Marxian economists, suggesting for example, that the labour theory of value in Marx is both unnecessary and incapable of producing Marx's results (Steedman, 1977, 1981). But to endorse Sraffa's system as a tool for historical exegesis is not to say that it successfully models the essence of classical economics. Smith, Ricardo, Mill and Marx are simply richer than anything captured in *Production of Commodities by Means of Commodities*.

CLASSICAL ECONOMICS AS GENERAL EQUILIBRIUM THEORY. Every extreme reaction produces a counter-reaction. The surplus interpretation of classical economics is a reaction against Marshallian interpretation of classical economics in which Ricardo and Mill are viewed as neoclassical theorists in embryo; for Marshall there was one and only one thread of continuous thought from Adam Smith to his own times (e.g. Marshall, 1890, App. I). In reaction to the surplus interpretation, Hollander has argued that from Ricardo onwards, classical economics was, for all practical purposes, general equilibrium theory; there never was any 'marginal revolution'. Since this assertion is, to say the least, surprising, let us quote his own words:

> Ricardian economics – the economics of Ricardo and J.S. Mill – in fact comprises in its essentials an exchange system fully consistent with the marginalist elaborations. In particular, their cost–price analysis is pre-eminently an analysis of the allocation of scarce resources, proceeding in terms of general equilibrium, with allowance for final demand, and the interdependence of factor and commodity markets (Hollander, 1982, p. 590).

It is evident that by 'general equilibrium theory', Hollander means a number of interconnected propositions, such as efficient allocation of given resources among alternative uses subject to the principle of diminishing marginal returns, the simultaneous determination of both quantities and relative prices with the aid of the principle of equality between demand and supply, and the consequent interdependence between equilibrium in product and factor markets. Perhaps we have already said enough to suggest that if this what is meant by general equilibrium theory, there is no sense in which we can subscribe to Hollander's interpretation of classical economics.

Hollander has spelled out his meaning in great detail in a major work on *The Economics of David Ricardo* (1979). In interpreting Ricardo as a general equilibrium theorist, Hollander found himself revising more or less the entire body of Ricardian scholarship, implying that absolutely everybody else before him had radically misinterpreted Ricardo. To convey the flavour of his iconoclasm, consider the following small sample of the extraordinary conclusions of this book (for a complete list, see O'Brien, 1981, pp. 354–5): (1) Ricardo's method of analysis was identical to that of Adam Smith; (2) Ricardo's theory of money was not very different from that of Smith; (3) Ricardo treated the pricing or products and the pricing of factors as fully interdependent; (4) Ricardo's profit theory did not originate in a concern over the Corn Laws, and Ricardo never believed, even in his early writings, that profits in agriculture determine the general rate of profit in the economy; (5) Ricardo's value theory was essentially the same as that of Marshall in that it paid as much attention to demand as to supply, and Ricardo never regarded the invariable measure of value as an important element in his theory; (6) Ricardo could have established his fundamental theorem of the inverse wage–profit relationship without his invariable yardstick and he frequently took the short-cut of assuming identical capital–labour ratios in all industries to give the answers he looked for; (7) wages in Ricardo are never conceived at any time as constant or fixed at subsistence levels; (8) Ricardo never assumed a zero price-elasticity of demand for corn, making the demand for agricultural produce a simple function of the size of population; (9) Ricardo did not predict a falling rate of profit or a rising rental share and never committed himself to any clear-cut predictions about any economic variable; and (10) Ricardo was never seriously concerned about the possibility of class conflict between landowners and everybody else or between workers and capitalists.

There must be something wrong with an interpretation of Ricardo that produces so many conclusions diametrically opposed to what every commentator has found in Ricardo, not only since his death but even while he was still alive. The distortions produced by the surplus interpretation of classical economics are therefore as nothing compared to those generated by Hollander's general equilibrium interpretation.

Walsh and Gram (1980) provide a more reasonable version of the general equilibrium characterization of classical economics: they take the view that general equilibrium analysis encompasses more or less the whole of the history of economic thought, but they distinguish between pre-Walrasian general equilibrium analysis of the allocation of the economic surplus over successive time periods and post-Walrasian general equilibrium analysis of the allocation of given resources within the same time period. One difficulty with their argument is that they never inform the reader what precisely is meant by 'general equilibrium analysis'. If we mean a discussion of the determination of both product and factor prices which proceeds in terms of an explicit or implicit set of simultaneous equations in order to ensure that the number of unknowns to be determined are equal to the number of equations written down, then obviously classical economics is not general equilibrium analysis: factor pricing in classical economics is invariably explained on different principles from those governing the pricing of products. If we go further and demand that such a discussion must include not just a demonstration of the existence of a unique equilibrium solution for the vector of factor and product prices but also an analysis of the stability and determinacy of the set of equilibrium prices, such as Walras himself struggled to provide, then even more obviously classical economics is not general equilibrium analysis. But what Walsh and Gram seem to mean by general equilibrium analysis is simply any analysis that involves the simultaneous determination of prices and one distributional variable on the assumption that other factor prices are given; in short, they define general equilibrium analysis to be nothing more nor less than Sraffian economics. Their book therefore collapses the general equilibrium interpretation of classical economics into the surplus interpretation, sharing the deficiencies of both in equal proportions.

Finally, Arrow and Hahn (1971, pp. 1–3) join the fray in the introduction to their textbook on general equilibrium theory. In contrast to Walsh and Gram, they are perfectly explicit about what is meant by general equilibrium theory: if it means anything it implies some notion of both determinateness and

stability, that is, the relations describing the economic system are sufficient to determine the equilibrium values of its variables, and a violation of any one of these relations sets in motion forces to restore it. They go on to introduce a new note into the argument: general equilibrium theory is typically associated with the doctrine of unintended consequences – equilibrium outcomes may be and usually are different from those intended by individual actors – and the doctrine that competition is a social mechanism that is capable of achieving a determinate and stable set of equilibrium prices. In all these senses of the term, they count Adam Smith as a 'creator' of general equilibrium theory and Ricardo, Mill and Marx as early expositors. They add, however, that there is another sense in which none of the classical economists had a 'true general equilibrium theory': no classical economist gave explicit attention to demand as a coordinate element with supply in determining prices, and hence classical economics determined the prices but not the quantities of commodities, the only exception to this statement being their treatment of agricultural output; on the other hand, Mill's theory of foreign trade was 'a genuine general equilibrium theory'.

To this brief but incisive discussion of the sense in which classical economics is or is not general equilibrium theory, one must add one word of caution: it is the subtle but nevertheless unmistakable difference in the conception of 'competition' before and after the 'marginal revolution'. The modern concept of perfect competition, conceived as a market structure in which all producers are price-takers and face perfectly elastic sales curves for their outputs, was born with Cournot in 1838 and is foreign to the classical conception of competition as a process of rivalry in the search for unrealized profit opportunities, whose outcome is uniformity in both the rate of return on capital invested and the prices of identical goods and services but not because producers are incapable of making prices. In other words, despite a steady tendency throughout the history of economic thought to place the accent on the end-state of competitive equilibrium rather than the process of disequilibrium adjustments leading up to it, this emphasis became remorseless after 1870 or thereabouts, whereas the much looser conception of 'free competition' with free but not instantaneous entry to industries is in evidence in the work of Smith, Ricardo, Mill, Marx and of course Marshall and modern Austrians (Stigler, 1957; McNulty, 1967; Littlechild, 1982). For that reason, if for no other, it can be misleading to label classical economics as a species of general equilibrium theory except in the innocuous sense of an awareness that 'everything depends on everything else'.

SUMMING UP. We have reviewed the recent upswell of new and startling interpretations of classical economics in the light of developments in modern economics, such as the economics of development, growth theory, general equilibrium theory, and Sraffian analysis. In itself there is nothing surprising about this, nor is it a new phenomenon: every turn and twist in the history of economic thought has always been attended by a fresh look at the past. Marx in propounding his own treatment of the 'laws of motion' of capitalism felt impelled to re-examine the ideas of his predecessors over more than a thousand pages. Jevons, Menger and Walras, the triumvirate that is said to have launched the 'marginal revolution', accompanied the exposition of their 'new' economics by scathing denunciations of the fallacies of classical political economy. Marshall, in seeking unsuccessfully to reconcile a static with a dynamic treatment of economic problems, naturally looked with sympathy at the work of his classical forebears and struggled to depict them as slightly exaggerating one side of the truth in contrast to Jevons, who exaggerated the other. Perhaps therefore the recent proliferation of definitely new but conflicting interpretations of the essential meaning of classical economics is simply an expression of the fact that modern economists are divided in their views and hence quite naturally seek comfort by finding (or pretending that they can find) these same views embodied in the writings of the past.

MARK BLAUG

See also CLASSICAL GROWTH MODELS; MARX, KARL HEINRICH; MILL, JOHN STUART; RICARDO, DAVID; SMITH, ADAM.

BIBLIOGRAPHY

Arrow, K.J. and Hahn, F.H. 1971. *General Competitive Analysis*. San Francisco: Holden-Day.

Barkai, H. 1965. Ricardo's static equilibrium. *Economica* 32, February, 15–31.

Blaug, M. 1958. *Ricardian Economics: An Historical Study*. New Haven, Conn.: Yale University Press.

Blaug, M. 1985. *Economic Theory in Retrospect*. 4th edn, Cambridge: Cambridge University Press.

Bloomfield, A.I. 1975. Adam Smith and the theory of international trade. In Skinner and Wilson (1975).

Bloomfield, A. I. 1978. The impact of growth and technology of trade in nineteenth-century economic thought. *History of Political Economy* 10(4), Winter, 608–35.

Bloomfield, A.I. 1981. British thought on the influence of foreign trade and investment of growth, 1800–1880. *History of Political Economy* 13(1), Spring, 95–120.

Bradley, I. and Howard, M.C. 1982. *Classical and Marxian Political Economy*. London: Macmillan.

Buchanan, D. 1929. The historical approach to rent and price theory. *Economica* 9(26), June, 123–55.

Cropsey, J. 1957. *Polity and Economy: An Interpretation of the Principles of Adam Smith*. The Hague: Nijhoff.

Dobb, M. 1973. *Theories of Value and Distribution since Adam Smith*. London: Cambridge University Press.

Eagly, R.V. 1974. *The Structure of Classical Economic Theory*. New York: Oxford University Press.

Eatwell, J. 1977. The irrelevance of returns to scale in Sraffa's analysis. *Journal of Economic Literature* 15(1), March, 61–8.

Eatwell, J. 1982. Competition. In Bradley and Howard (1982).

Eltis, W. 1984. *The Classical Theory of Economic Growth*. London: Macmillan.

Garegnani, P. 1976. On a change in the notion of equilibrium in recent work on value and distribution. In *Essays in Modern Capital Theory*, ed. M. Brown, K. Sato and P. Zarembka, Amsterdam: North-Holland.

Garegnani, P. 1984. Value and distribution in the classical economists and Marx. *Oxford Economic Papers* 36(2), June, 291–325.

Gordon, D.F. 1959. What was the labour theory of value? *American Economic Review* 49(2), May, 462–72.

Harcourt, G.C. 1982. The Sraffian contribution: an evaluation. In Bradley and Howard (1982).

Hollander, S. 1973. *The Economics of Adam Smith*. Toronto: University of Toronto Press; London: Heinemann Educational Books.

Hollander, S. 1977. The reception of Ricardian economics. *Oxford Economic Papers* 29(2), July, 221–57.

Hollander, S. 1979. *The Economics of David Ricardo*. Toronto: University of Toronto Press; London: Heinemann Educational Books.

Hollander, S. 1981. Marxian economics as 'general equilibrium' theory. *History of Political Economy* 13(1), Spring, 121–55.

Hollander, S. 1982. On the substantive identity of the Ricardian and neoclassical conception of economic organization: the French connection in British classicism. *Canadian Journal of Economics* 15(4), November, 586–612.

Howard, M.C. and King, J.E. 1985. *The Political Economy of Marx*. 2nd edn, London: Longman.

Kaldor, N. 1972. The irrelevance of equilibrium economics. *Economic Journal* 82, December, 1237–55.

Keynes, J.M. 1936. *The General Theory of Employment, Interest and Money*. In *The Collected Writings of John Maynard Keynes*, Vol. VII, London: Macmillan, 1973.

Knight, F.H. 1956. *On the History and Method of Economics*. Chicago: University of Chicago Press.

Laidler, D.E.W. 1981. Adam Smith as a monetary economist. *Canadian Journal of Economics* 14(2), May, 187–200.

Lindgren, J.R. 1973. *The Social Philosophy of Adam Smith*. The Hague: Martinus Nijhoff.

Littlechild, S.C. 1982. Equilibrium and the market process. In *Method, Process, and Austrian Economics*, ed. I.M. Kirzner, Lexington, Mass.: D.C. Heath.

Lowe, A. 1954. The classical theory of economic growth. *Social Research* 21, Summer, 127–58.

Marshall, A. 1890. *Principles of Economics*. London: Macmillan.

Marx, K. 1867. *Capital: A Critique of Political Economy*. Trans. B. Fowkes, Harmondsworth: Penguin Books, 1976.

McNulty, P.J. 1967. A note on the history of perfect competition. *Journal of Political Economy* 75(4), August, 395–9.

Meek, R.L. 1967. *Economics and Ideology and Other Essays*. London: Chapman & Hall.

Meek, R.L. 1973. *Studies in the Labour Theory of Value*. 2nd edn, London: Lawrence & Wishart.

Meek, R.L. 1977. *Smith, Marx and After*. London: Chapman & Hall.

Mill, J.S. 1844. *Essays on Some Unsettled Questions Political Economy*. London: London School of Economics, 1948.

Myint, H. 1948. *Theories of Welfare Economics*. Cambridge, Mass.: Harvard University Press.

Myint, H. 1958. The 'classical theory' of international trade and underdeveloped countries. *Economic Journal* 68, June, 317–37.

O'Brien, D.P. 1975. *The Classical Economists*. London: Oxford University Press.

O'Brien, D.P. 1981. Ricardian economics and the economics of David Ricardo. *Oxford Economic Papers* 33(3), November, 352–86.

Ong, N-P. 1983. Ricardo's invariable measure of value and Sraffa's 'standard commodity'. *History of Political Economy* 15(2), Summer, 207–27.

Pasinetti, L.L. 1974. *Growth and Income Distribution: Essays in Economic Theory*. Cambridge: Cambridge University Press.

Peach, T. 1984. David Ricardo's early treatment of profitability: a new interpretation. *Economic Journal* 94, December, 733–51.

Peacock, A. 1975. The treatment of the principles of public finance in *The Wealth of Nations*. In Skinner and Wilson (1975).

Ricardo, D. 1951–73. *The Works and Correspondence of David Ricardo*. Ed. P. Sraffa, Cambridge: Cambridge University Press.

Robertson, H.M. and Taylor, W.L. 1957. Adam Smith's approach to the theory of value. *Economic Journal* 67, June, 181–98.

Roncaglia, A. 1978. *Sraffa and the Theory of Prices*. New York: Wiley.

Rosenberg, N. 1960. Some institutional aspects of the *Wealth of Nations*. *Journal of Political Economy* 68(6), December, 557–70.

Samuelson, P. 1978. The canonical classical model of political economy. *Journal of Economic Literature* 16(4), 1415–34.

Schumpeter, J.A. 1954. *History of Economic Analysis*. New York: Oxford University Press.

Skinner, A.S. and Wilson, T. 1975. *Essays on Adam Smith*. Oxford: Clarendon Press.

Skinner, A.S. 1979. *A System of Social Science: Papers Relating to Adam Smith*. Oxford: Clarendon Press.

Sowell, T. 1974. *Classical Economics Reconsidered*. Princeton: Princeton University Press.

Spiegel, H.W. 1983. *The Growth of Economic Thought*. Durham, North Carolina: Duke University Press.

Sraffa, P. 1960. *Production of Commodities by Means of Commodities*. Cambridge: Cambridge University Press.

Steedman, I. 1977. *Marx after Sraffa*. London: New Left Books.

Steedman, I. (ed.) 1981. *The Value Controversy*. London: Verso Editions and New Left Books.

Stigler, G.J. 1957. Perfect competition, historically contemplated. *Journal of Political Economy* 65(1), February, 1–17.

Stigler, G.J. 1965. Textual exegesis as a scientific problem. *Economica* 33, November, 447–50.

Thweatt, W.O. 1976. James Mill and the early development of comparative advantage. *History of Political Economy* 8(2), Summer, 207–34.

Walsh, V. and Gram, H. 1980. *Classical and Neoclassical Theories of General Equilibrium*. Oxford: Oxford University Press.

West, E.G. 1976. Adam Smith's economics of politics. *History of Political Economy* 8(4), Winter, 515–39.

White, L.H. 1984. *Free Banking in Britain: Theory, Experience and Debate, 1800–1845*. Cambridge: Cambridge University Press.

Winch, D. 1978. *Adam Smith's Politics: An Essay in Historiographic Revision*. Cambridge: Cambridge University Press.

Winch, D. 1983. Science and the legislator: Adam Smith and after. *Economic Journal* 93, Winter, 501–20.

classical growth models. Analysis of the process of economic growth was a central feature of the work of the English classical economists, as represented chiefly by Adam Smith, Thomas Malthus and David Ricardo. Despite the speculations of others before them, they must be regarded as the main precursors of modern growth theory. The ideas of this school reached their highest level of development in the works of Ricardo.

The interest of these economists in problems of economic growth was rooted in the concrete conditions of their time. Specifically, they were confronted with the facts of economic and social changes taking place in contemporary English society as well as in previous historical periods. Living in the 18th and 19th centuries, on the eve or in the full throes of the industrial revolution, they could hardly help but be impressed by such changes. They undertook their investigations against the background of the emergence of what was to be regarded as a new economic system – the system of industrial capitalism. Political economy represented a conscious effort on their part to develop a scientific explanation of the forces governing the operation of the economic system, of the actual processes involved in the observed changes that were going on, and of the long-run tendencies and outcomes to which they were leading.

The interest of the classical economists in economic growth derived also from a philosophical concern with the possibilities of 'progress', an essential condition of which was seen to be the development of the material basis of society. Accordingly, it was felt that the purpose of analysis was to identify the forces in society that promoted or hindered this development, and hence progress, and consequently to provide a basis for policy and action to influence those forces. Ricardo's campaign against the Corn Laws must obviously be seen in this light, as also Malthus's concern with the problem of population growth and Smith's attacks against the monopoly privileges associated with mercantilism.

Of course, for these economists, Smith especially, progress was seen from the point of view of the growth of national wealth. Hence, the principle of national advantage was regarded as an essential criterion of economic policy. Progress was conceived also within the framework of a need to preserve private property and hence the interests of the property-owning class. From this perspective, they endeavoured to show that the exercise of individual initiative under freely competitive conditions to promote individual ends would produce results beneficial to society as a whole. Conflicting economic interests of different groups could be reconciled by the operation of competitive market forces and by the limited activity of 'responsible' government.

As a result of their work in economic analysis the classical economists were able to provide an account of the broad forces that influence economic growth and of the mechanisms underlying the growth process. An important achievement was their recognition that the accumulation and productive investment of a part of the social product is the main driving force behind economic growth and that, under capitalism, this takes the form mainly of the reinvestment of profits. Armed with this recognition, their critique of feudal society was based on the observation among others, that a large part of the social product was not so invested but was consumed unproductively.

The explanation of the forces underlying the accumulation process was seen as the heart of the problem of economic growth. Associated with accumulation is technical change as expressed in the division of labour and changes in methods of production. Smith, in particular, placed heavy emphasis on the process of extension of division of labour, but there is, in general, no systematic treatment of the relation between capital accumulation and technical change in the work of the classical economists. It later becomes a pivotal theme in the work of Marx and is subjected there to detailed analysis (see, for instance, *Capital*, I, part 4). To these basic forces in economic growth they added the increase in the supply of labour available for production through growth of population. Their analysis of the operation of these forces led them to the common view, though they quite clearly differed about the particular causes, that the process of economic growth under the conditions they identified raises obstacles in its own path and is ultimately retarded, ending in a state of stagnation – the 'stationary state'.

The conception of the stationary state as the ultimate end of the process of economic growth is often interpreted as a 'prediction' of the actual course of economic development in 19th-century England. There is no doubt that it was for a time so regarded by some, if not all, of the economists and their contemporaries, though the weight that was assigned to this particular aspect of the conception by Ricardo himself is a matter of some dispute. What is more significant, however, is that this conception served to point to a particular social group, the landlord class, who benefited from the social product without contributing either to its formation or to 'progress' and who, by their support of the corn laws and associated restrictions on foreign trade, acted as an obstacle to the only effective escape from the path to a stationary state, that is, through foreign trade.

In examining the work of the classical economists we find also that problems of economic growth were analysed through the application of general economic principles, viewing the economic system as a whole, rather than in terms of a separate theory of economic growth as such. These principles were such as to recognize basic patterns of interdependence in the economic system and interrelatedness of the phenomena of production, exchange, distribution, and accumulation. In sum, what we find in classical economic analysis is a necessary interconnection between the analysis of value, distribution, and growth. Because of these interconnections it was by no means possible to draw a sharp dividing line between the inquiry into economic growth and that into other areas of political economy. As Meek (1967, p. 187) notes:

> To Smith and Ricardo, the macroeconomic problem of the 'laws of motion' of capitalism appeared as the primary problem on the agenda, and it seemed necessary that the whole of economic analysis – including the basic theories of value and distribution – should be deliberately oriented towards its solution.

Distribution of the social product was seen to be connected in a definite way with the performance of labour in production and with the pattern of ownership of the means of production. In this regard, Labour, Land, and Capital were distinguished as social categories corresponding to the prevailing class relationships among individuals in contemporary society: the class of labourers consisted of those who performed labour services, landlords were those who owned titles or property in land, and capitalists were those who owned property in capital consisting of the sum of exchangeable value tied up in means of production and in the 'advances' which go to maintain the labourers during the production period. Each class received income or a share in the product according to specified rules: for the owners, the rule was based on the total amount of property which they owned – so much rent per unit of land, so much profit per unit of capital (and, for the class of finance capitalists or 'rentiers' who lent money at interest, so much interest per unit of money lent). For labourers it was based on the quantity of labour services performed: so much wages per hour.

Accumulation and distribution were seen to be interconnected through the use that was made by different social classes of their share in the product. Basic to this view was a conception, taken over from the Physiocrats, of the social surplus as that part of the social product which remained after deducting the 'necessary costs' of production consisting of the means of production used up and the wage goods required to sustain the labourers employed in producing the social product. This surplus was distributed as profits, interest, and rent to the corresponding classes of property owners. For the classical economists, the possibility of accumulation was governed by the size and mode of utilization of this surplus. Accordingly, their analysis placed emphasis upon those aspects of distribution and of the associated class behaviour which had a direct connection with the disposal of the surplus and therefore with growth. In particular, it was assumed that, typically, workers consumed their wages for subsistence, capitalists reinvested their profits and landlords spent their rents on 'riotous living'. On the other side, accumulation would also influence the distribution of income as the economy expanded over time.

It was this absolutely strategic role of the size and use of the surplus, viewed from the perspective of the economy as a whole and of its process of expansion, which dictated the significance of the distribution of income for classical economic analysis. Thus, for Ricardo especially, investigation of the laws governing distribution became the focus of analysis. In a letter to Malthus, Ricardo wrote (*Works*, VIII, pp. 278–9): 'Political Economy you think is an inquiry into the nature and causes of wealth; I think it should rather be called an inquiry into the laws which determine the division of the produce of industry among the classes which occur in its formation.' What was of crucial significance in this connection was the rate of profits because of its connection with accumulation, both as the source of investment funds and as the stimulus to further investment.

Having 'got rid of rent' as the difference between the product on marginal land and that on intra-marginal units, the Ricardian analysis focused on profits as the residual component of the surplus. Under the simplifying conditions on which the analysis was constructed, there emerged a very clear and simple relationship between the wage rate and the overall rate of profits, determined within a single sector of the economy – the corn-producing sector. The special feature of corn as a commodity was that it could serve both as capital good (seed corn) in its own production and as wage good to be advanced to the workers. With the wage rate fixed in terms of corn, the rate of profit in corn production is uniquely determined as the ratio of net output of corn per man minus the wage to the sum of capital per man consisting of seed corn and the fund of corn as wage good. Competition ensures that the same rate of profit enters into the price of all other commodities that are produced with indirect labour. The overall rate of profits, determined in this way, varies inversely with the corn wage. But, as soon as it is recognized that the wage and/or the capital goods employed in corn production consist of other commodities besides corn, the rate of profits can no longer be determined in this way. For the magnitude of the wage and of the total capital then depends on the prices of those commodities, and these prices incorporate the rate of profit. Attention then has to be directed to explaining the rate of profit by taking account of the whole system of prices. For this purpose the theory of value is called upon to provide a solution and Ricardo struggled with this problem until the end of his life. An elegant solution has now been worked out by Sraffa (1960) which shows that, in a system of many produced commodities, with the real wage rate given at a specified level, the rate of profit is determined by the given wage and the conditions of production of the commodities that are 'basics'. It so happens that Ricardo's case of corn is just such a 'basic' commodity in the strict sense that it enters directly and indirectly into the production of every commodity including itself.

Given the perceived centrality of the rate of profit in a capitalist economy, for classical political economy it becomes a crucial problem in the theory of economic growth to account for movements in the rate of profit associated with the process of capital accumulation and development of the economy. Such movements are a decisive reference point for understanding the long-term evolution of the economy. The classical answer to this problem, as worked out most coherently by Ricardo, is that in a closed economy there is an inevitable tendency for the rate of profit to fall in the course of the accumulation process and, hence, that the accumulation process itself is brought to a halt by its own logic.

Marx was later to propose this falling tendency of the rate of profit (FTRP) as a *law*. He considered it to be 'the most important law of modern political economy' (*Grundrisse*, p. 748; *Capital*, III, part 3). He was, of course, following in the tradition of the classical economists in which the same idea had been firmly entrenched, though supported on different grounds. But, interestingly enough, it is also the case that there exists a distinct conception of a FTRP within neoclassical theory (see Harris, 1978, ch. 9; 1981). In Keynes, as well, the idea is embodied in his projection of the long-term prospects for capitalism resulting in the 'euthanasia of the rentier' (1936, pp. 375–6). In Schumpeter (1934), it occurs in the form of the idea that the profitability of innovations tends inevitably to be eroded so that the economy settles back to the conditions of the 'circular flow' in the absence of new innovations. Though it is based in each case on quite different foundations, this conception is one of the most striking and persistent uniformities across different schools of economic thought. (For a discussion of the long history of the idea of a falling rate of profit, see Tucker, 1960.)

A MODEL OF ACCUMULATION. The essential features of the classical argument regarding the accumulation process can be exhibited with a simple model adapted from Kaldor (1956) and Pasinetti (1960). This model formalizes the Ricardian conception of an agricultural economy producing a single product, 'corn', under capitalist conditions. Land is of differing fertility and labour is applied in fixed proportion to less and less fertile land. Accordingly, the average and marginal product of labour falls as the margin of cultivation is extended through capital accumulation and increase of employment on the land. The system may indifferently be assumed to expand on the extensive or intensive margins of available land. Also, it does not matter for this analysis that there exists any production outside agriculture. It would turn out, in any case, that the overall average rate of profit for the economy as a whole is determined by the agricultural rate of profit or, in the general case, by the conditions of production of 'basics' (cf. Sraffa, 1960; Pasinetti, 1977). Of course, in a system with many produced commodities, it is not possible to define 'less fertile land' independently of the rate of profit (Sraffa, 1960). However, this problem does not arise in this simplified model of a corn-producing economy. We deliberately abstract from complications associated with the Malthusian population dynamics. This is perhaps the most problematic feature of the classical conception and we return to it below. Meanwhile, it is simply assumed, as in Lewis (1954), that a labour force is in perfectly elastic supply at some conventionally fixed real wage rate equal to 'subsistence'.

Let the production function relating output Y to labour input L be

$$Y = F(L) \qquad F(0) \gtreqless 0$$
$$F' > w^* > 0$$
$$F'' < 0 \qquad\qquad (1)$$

which satisfies the law of diminishing returns and allows for the existence of a surplus product above the 'subsistence' wage-rate w^*. Total capital K consists entirely of wages W (the 'wage fund') advanced at the beginning of the production period to hire labour. Thus

$$K = W = wL \qquad\qquad (2)$$

We are here, for simplicity, neglecting capital as seed-corn and inputs of fixed capital are ignored. Total output is distributed between payment of rent R to landlords, profits P to capitalists, and replacement of the wage fund:

$$Y = R + P + W \qquad\qquad (3)$$

Given the margin of cultivation reached at any time, the level of land rent is determined as the difference between the average and marginal product of labour at the prevailing level of employment:

$$R = \left(\frac{F(L)}{L} - F'\right)L \qquad\qquad (4)$$

Profit emerges as the residual

$$P = (F' - w^*)L \qquad\qquad (5)$$

It follows that the rate of profit r is determined from

$$r = \frac{P}{W} = \frac{F'}{w^*} - 1 \qquad\qquad (6)$$

It is the dynamics of the wage fund which represents the process of accumulation in this model. Accumulation of capital consists of the growth of the wage fund with a corresponding increase of employment. Additions to the wage fund come entirely from investment of capitalists' profits since the spendthrift landlords consume their share of the surplus. If the capitalists invest a proportion of profits equal to α, then

$$\Delta W = \alpha P \qquad 0 < \alpha < 1 \qquad\qquad (7)$$

The proportion α need not be a constant. It could vary in a manner dependent on the rate of profit as suggested by Ricardo's idea that

[the capitalists'] motive for accumulation will diminish with

every diminution of profit, and will cease altogether when their profits are so low as not to afford them an adequate compensation for their trouble and the risk which they must necessarily encounter in employing their capital productively (*Works*, I, p. 122).

In that case we have

$$\alpha = \alpha(r) \qquad \alpha' > 0$$
$$\alpha(r^*) = 0 \qquad\qquad (8)$$

where r^* is the capitalists' minimum acceptable rate of profit. By definition the rate of capital accumulation is $g = \Delta W / W$, and from (6), (7), and (8) it follows that

$$g = \alpha(r) \cdot r \qquad\qquad (9)$$

Thus, the rate of accumulation is uniquely dependent on the profit rate.

The movement in the profit rate as accumulation proceeds can be derived from (6). Evidently, as employment increases the marginal product of labour falls. The rate of profit must therefore fall. It continues to fall as long as there is any increment to the wage fund so as to employ extra labour on the available land. The process comes to a half when the profit rate is so low that accumulation ceases. The economy is then at the stationary state.

In this model, the capitalists are caught between, on the one hand, the diminishing productivity of labour as the margin of cultivation is extended and, on the other, the need to pay the ongoing wage rate in order to secure labour for employment. As the productivity of labour falls on the marginal land the pressure of land rent increases for the existing intra marginal units. The capitalists must therefore pay out an increasing share of the surplus to the landlords. In this way they gradually lose command over the investible surplus of the economy to the landlord class. This distributional conflict between the landlord class and the capitalists constitutes a central feature of the process that drives the economy towards its ultimate stationarity. The impenetrable barrier in the process is the diminishing fertility of the soil. More generally, it is the limitation of natural resources, in this case land, which brings the process to a halt. In this respect the classical model is a particular case of resource-limited growth. Any other limited resource would have the same effect, through increasing 'rents' for that resource. At the same time, this consequence is also the product of the capitalists' own actions in relentlessly seeking to expand the size of their capital.

The underlying dynamic process which expresses this conflictive evolution of capitalist accumulation has usually been assumed in the literature to converge towards the stationary state (cf. Pasinetti, 1960; Samuelson, 1978). Some reservation on this question of convergence was originally expressed by Hicks and Hollander (1977) and followed up by Gordon (1983). Subsequent discussion by Casarosa (1978), Caravale and Tosato (1980) and Caravale (1985) further emphasized the problematic nature of the convergence process. Much of the complexity of this process arises from the intertwined dynamics of distributional change and population growth typical of the Ricardian system. Day (1983) has shown that characterization of the population dynamics by itself may be sufficient to generate extremely erratic or 'chaotic' motions. In a recent paper, Bhaduri and Harris (1986) analyse the essential dynamics of the Ricardian system as it is governed solely by the interplay of distribution and accumulation in a model similar to the present one. They find that the model can generate very complex 'chaotic' movements instead of any smooth and gradual convergence to the stationary state. The possibility of such behaviour is shown to depend uniquely on the initial configuration of parameters. This result should lead one to question the presumption that the Ricardian system necessarily converges to a stationary state.

THE MALTHUSIAN POPULATION DYNAMICS. A crucial role is played in the classical analysis by the population dynamics deriving from the Malthusian Law of Population Growth. In particular this law requires that population grows in response to a rise of wages above subsistence. This response mechanism is supposed to provide the labour requirements for expansion and thereby hold wages in check. But this is evidently a highly implausible principle on which to base an account of the process of capitalist expansion. If capitalism had to depend for its labour supply entirely upon such a demographic-biological response, it seems doubtful that sustained high rates of accumulation could continue for long or even that accumulation could ever get started. This is because, first, there must exist a biological upper limit to population expansion. Accumulation at rates above this limit would drive up the wage to such a level as to reduce or perhaps choke off the possibility of continued accumulation. For the classical labour supply principle to work it must be presumed arbitrarily that this limit is sufficiently far out or, equivalently, that the supply curve is sufficiently elastic over a wide range.

Even if it is granted that population growth is significantly responsive to the level of wages, it is still the case that the adjustment of population is inherently a long drawn-out process having only a negligible effect on the actual labour supply in any short period of time. In the interim, any sizeable spurt of accumulation must then cause wages to be bid up, eat into profits, and bring accumulation itself, to a halt. From the start, therefore, accumulation could never get going in such a system. Even if it did, its continuation would always be in jeopardy because the mechanism of adjustment of labour supply is an inherently unreliable one, fraught with the possibility that at any time wages may rise to eat up the profits that are the well-spring of accumulation.

This feature of classical analysis was soundly criticized and rejected by Marx (*Capital*, I, pp. 637–9). In its place, he sought to introduce a principle that was internal to the accumulation process, that would account for the continuing generation of a supply of labour to meet the needs of accumulation from within the accumulation process itself. This was the principle of the reserve army of labour or the 'law of relative surplus population' (*Capital*, I, ch. 25, sections 3 and 4). The reserve army results from a process of 'recycling' of labour through its displacement from existing employment due to mechanization and structural changes in production. In addition to this pool of labour there are other possible sources of increased labour supply to feed the accumulation process. These originate, for instance, in increased labour force participation rates among existing workers, in labour migration, and in the erosion of household work and other forms of non-capitalist production. Capital export to other regions can play the same role. These sources have been observed historically to be more or less significant at various times and places. It appears, therefore, that there is considerable flexibility of labour supply, and hence of accumulation, even without taking account of population growth. The existence of population growth certainly adds to the pool of available labour, as is now widely recognized. But the singular and unique role attributed to it by the Malthusian theory has by now been discredited and abandoned.

CONCLUSION. The Classical economists are often regarded as 'pessimistic' in their prognosis for economic growth. It is said

that they constituted economics as the 'dismal science'. Still, there is much to be learned, that is of contemporary relevance, from a close examination of their analytical system. What emerges from such an examination is a complex structure of ideas expressing a deep understanding of the nature of capitalism as an economic system, the sources of its expansionary drive, and the barriers or limits to its expansion. Their ideas were essentially limited, however, to the conditions of a predominantly agrarian economy, without significant change in methods of production, in which, because of the limited quantity and diminishing fertility of the soil, growth is arrested by increasing costs of production of agricultural commodities. Their analysis underestimated the far-reaching character of technological change as a powerful and continuing force in transforming the conditions of productivity both in agriculture and in industry. While they clearly perceived the possibilities opened up by international trade and foreign investment, they failed to incorporate these elements as integral components of a systematic theory of the growth process. It remained for Marx to pinpoint some of the major limitations and deficiencies of the classical analysis and to develop an analysis of the capitalist accumulation process that went beyond that of the classical economists in many respects while also leaving many unresolved questions. Subsequent work has continued to address the issues with limited success. Until today, the theory of growth of capitalist economies continues to be one of the most fascinating and still unresolved areas of economic theory.

DONALD J. HARRIS

See also CLASSICAL ECONOMICS; DISTRIBUTION THEORIES: CLASSICAL; SMITH, ADAM.

BIBLIOGRAPHY

Bhaduri, A. and Harris, D.J. 1986. The complex dynamics of the simple Ricardian system. *Quarterly Journal of Economics.*

Caravale, G.A. (ed.) 1985. *The Legacy of Ricardo.* Oxford: Blackwell.

Caravale, G.A. and Tosato, D.A. 1980. *Ricardo and the Theory of Value, Distribution and Growth.* London: Routledge & Kegan Paul.

Casarosa, C. 1978. A new formulation of the Ricardian system. *Oxford Economic Papers* 30(1), March, 38–63.

Day, R.H. 1983. The emergence of chaos from classical economic growth. *Quarterly Journal of Economics* 98(2), May, 201–13.

Gordon, K. 1983. Hicks and Hollander on Ricardo: a mathematical note. *Quarterly Journal of Economics* 98(4), November, 721–6.

Harris, D.J. 1978. *Capital Accumulation and Income Distribution.* Stanford: Stanford University Press.

Harris, D.J. 1981. Profits, productivity, and thrift: the neoclassical theory of capital and distribution revisited. *Journal of Post Keynesian Economics* 3(3), Spring, 359–82.

Hicks, J.R. and Hollander, S. 1977. Mr. Ricardo and the moderns. *Quarterly Journal of Economics* 91(3), August, 351–69.

Kaldor, N. 1956. Alternative theories of distribution. *Review of Economic Studies* 23, 83–100.

Keynes, J.M. 1936. *The General Theory of Employment, Interest, and Money.* New York: Harcourt, Brace.

Lewis, W.A. 1954. Economic development with unlimited supplies of labour. *The Manchester School* 22, May, 139–91.

Malthus, T.R. 1798. *Essay on the Principle of Population,* 1st edn. London: Macmillan, 1926.

Malthus, T.R. 1820. *Principles of Political Economy.* Reprinted in *The Works and Correspondence of David Ricardo,* ed. P. Sraffa and M. Dobb, Vol. II, Cambridge: Cambridge University Press, 1951.

Marx, K. 1867. *Capital,* Vol. I. New York: International Publishers, 1967.

Marx, K. 1973. *Grundrisse.* Harmondsworth: Penguin Books.

Meek, R.L. 1967. *Economics and Ideology and Other Essays.* London: Chapman & Hall.

Pasinetti, L. 1960. A mathematical formulation of the Ricardian system. *Review of Economic Studies* 27(2), February, 78–98.

Pasinetti, L. 1977. *Lectures on the Theory of Production.* New York: Columbia University Press.

Ricardo, D. 1951–73. *The Works and Correspondence of David Ricardo.* Ed. P. Sraffa with the collaboration of M. H. Dobb, Cambridge: Cambridge University Press.

Samuelson, P. 1978. The canonical classical model of political economy. *Journal of Economic Literature* 16, 1415–34.

Schumpeter, J. 1934. *The Theory of Economic Development.* New York: Oxford University Press.

Smith, A. 1776. *An Inquiry into the Nature and Causes of the Wealth of Nations.* New York: Modern Library, 1937.

Sraffa, P. 1960. *Production of Commodities by Means of Commodities.* Cambridge: Cambridge University Press.

Tucker, G. 1960. *Progress and Profits in British Economic Thought 1650–1850.* Cambridge: Cambridge University Press.

classical theory of distribution. *See* DISTRIBUTION THEORIES: CLASSICAL.

classical theory of money. The classical theory of money is an integral part of the classical theory of value and distribution; and its conceptual categories have real counterparts in historical experience. These categories begin with metallic money and progress to the more complex forms of fiduciary money and credit.

CLASSICAL FRAMEWORK. The equation of exchange forms a common point of reference for all approaches to monetary theory, since the relationships it expresses simply constitute a truism and do not in themselves imply causality: $MV = PT$, where M denotes the money supply, V the velocity of circulation, P an index of prices and T the number of commodity transactions. This equation may also be written: $MV = PY$, where Y denotes total output, the index P is correspondingly adjusted and V no longer reflects the circulation of a stock of commodities but the rate of expenditure of a flow of income (corresponding to the flow of output). We shall use this alternative formulation to specify the classical approach to monetary theory. The only difference of substance is the replacement of the sum of commodity transactions with a measure of net output over a given period, hence excluding non-produced assets (such as land) from the exchange process.

The classical theory of money was developed largely as a response to the practical issue of the relationship between changes in the money supply and the price level. This issue was central to three historical episodes which form the background to our discussion: the Price Revolution of the 16th and 17th centuries, the Napoleonic war inflation and the industrial crises of the mid-19th century. It was not the existence of an empirical correlation that was in dispute, but the direction of causation. A solution would therefore require a *theoretical* approach as well as knowledge of the facts.

The basic structure of the solution arose from discussion of the Price Revolution. Instead of augmenting wealth in the manner suggested by mercantilist doctrine, the influx of gold and silver from the newly discovered American mines seemed only to devalue the unit of account. An immediate interpretation was offered by the quantity theory of money, which attributed the increase in the price level throughout Europe entirely to monetary expansion. According to David Hume, money had no intrinsic value and was simply a means of circulation, in which capacity it served simultaneously as money of account (1752, p. 33). This approach 'essentially amounted to treating money not as a commodity but as a

voucher for buying goods' (Schumpeter, 1954, p. 313). Once in circulation, money acquired merely a 'fictitious value', whose magnitude was established by demand and supply (Hume, 1752, p. 48 also Montesquieu, 1748, pp. 50–51; Vanderlint, 1734, pp. 2–3; Locke, 1691, p. 233).

Classical economists, by contrast, treated money as a *real commodity*, whose value was determined like other commodities by the labour time socially necessary for its production (Petty, 1963, I, pp. 43–4; Smith, 1776, p. 24; Ricardo, 1821, pp. 85–6). They traced the cause of the Price Revolution not to monetary phenomena but to lowered production costs at the mines (Nef, 1941; Onthwaite, 1969, esp. p. 29; Vilar, 1976, esp. p. 343). It followed that, in the long run, when economic activity is regulated by permanent forces, the magnitude of P in the equation of exchange is determined on the basis of value theory and both Y and V are fixed due to Say's Law and institutional factors respectively. Hence P is the independent variable in the equation and M the dependent variable. Any movement in P as a result of changes in the production costs of commodities (or money) has a commensurate effect on M. This determination of aggregate monetary requirements in the 'real' sector of the economy became known as the 'classical dichotomy' and constitutes the basic classical law of circulation (Petty, 1963, I, p. 36; Smith, 1776, pp. 332–3; Ricardo, 1923, p. 158; Marx, 1867, pp. 123–4). In other words, causation runs from prices to money in classical economics and not the reverse as we find in both traditional quantity theory and neoclassical monetarism (Eatwell, 1983; Green, 1982). All things being equal, 'The quantity of money that can be employed in a country must depend on its value' (Ricardo, 1821, p. 352). The type of money employed in the circulation process has no bearing on this conclusion, since V will be determinate whatever *its* numerical value.

Had the scope of classical economics extended no further than the study of permanent economic forces, the question of whether it possessed a 'quantity theory of money' would not have arisen. But the limitations of a long run approach in explaining concrete developments and formulating relevant policies convinced most classical writers to take into account the role of temporary factors. In particular, the effect of exogenous changes in the money supply needed to be explained. Now the problem became complicated by the definition of money and the nature of financial organization. If Say's Law kept Y constant, only two possibilities remained open: a price adjustment, i.e. a change in P, or a quantity adjustment, i.e. a change in V (by hoarding or dishoarding). This was the essence of the division among the classical economists. One group was led by Ricardo and included the bullionists (i.e. supporters of the 1810 Bullion Report), and later, the currency school. The other group comprised the anti-bullionists and the banking school and was given qualified approval by Marx.

The dominant Ricardian group held consistently that both Y and V were always fixed. The quantity 'theory' of money was therefore no theory at all in this view, but simply a logical outcome of assuming Say's Law. The inflationary process was seen as the transitional mechanism by which monetary deviations were corrected: 'That commodities would rise or fall in price, in proportion to the increase or diminution of money, *I assume as a fact which is incontrovertible*' (Ricardo, 1923, p. 93 fn., emphasis added).

The opponents of quantity theory, on the other hand, were prepared to sacrifice logical consistency in an attempt to interpret the real events with which they were confronted. Their often pioneering expositions generally placed the weight of adjustment on V, although the extent was seen as contingent upon the composition of M – whether the money supply was metallic, fiduciary or credit. The flaw in their approach was their failure to overthrow Say's Law and develop an analysis of the saving–investment process, i.e. a theory of output. Had they done so, their challenge to the incorporation of quantity theory into classical economics may have been more successful.

CURRENCY AND CREDIT. By the time the Bank of England suspended cash payments in 1797, a body of principles on the role and behaviour of paper money had already been formed. The collapse of Law's system led to considerable discussion which culminated in Smith's authoritative exposition of banking in the *Wealth of Nations*. There Cantillon's view was accepted – as against Law and Steuart – that banking could not increase the quantity of capital but only its turnover (Smith, 1776, p. 246). This accorded with the given output assumption of Say's Law. It was also established that paper money would not depreciate provided its total amount did not exceed the value of gold and silver that would otherwise have circulated at any given level of economic activity (ibid., p. 227).

More contentiously, Smith argued that the economic convertibility of paper and metallic money could be maintained not only by enforcing legal convertibility but also by having banks adopt the practice of discounting 'real bills', i.e. securities backed by real assets (ibid., p. 239 and *passim*). This became known as the 'real bills doctrine'. It was repudiated first by Thornton and then by Ricardo and the currency school, but rehabilitated as the 'law of reflux' by the banking school.

The Bank Restriction period was marked by high inflation accompanied by a rise in the market price of bullion over its mint price. This indicated a depreciation of paper currency in terms of the monetary standard, a phenomenon which could not have existed when convertibility was enforced by law. The central problem was to explain the appearance of this premium on bullion, and to find a principle whose practical implementation would restore and maintain economic convertibility, thus ensuring that the bank notes conformed to the behaviour of metallic currency. The explanation which gained widest acceptance was based upon the quantity theory of money. It was presented officially in the Bullion Report and then developed by Ricardo. The remedy for inflation implied by this approach was control over the money supply by the authorities.

Ricardo began his analysis by recognizing the need to replace gold and silver in the sphere of circulation by paper – provided only that it was issued in the same amount, i.e. the amount prescribed by the value of the metal which served as the monetary standard: 'A currency is in its most perfect state when it consists wholly of paper money, but of paper money with an equal value with the gold which it professes to represent' (Ricardo, 1821, p. 355). Ricardo's discussion of legally convertible bank notes followed Smith, with some of Thornton's modifications. Since their equivalence with gold was guaranteed, they could not be issued in a greater quantity than the value of the coin which would otherwise have circulated. Any attempt to exceed this sum would precipitate a return of notes for specie, a depreciation of both paper and metallic currency, and the subsequent export of superfluous bullion (Ricardo, 1923, pp. 7–13). Overextension of inconvertible notes in a 'mixed currency' of notes and coins had the same effect so long as the degree of excess was no greater than the amount of coin in circulation (ibid., p. 13, n., pp. 108–12).

In 1809, however, when Ricardo entered the bullion controversy, the currency was composed almost entirely of inconvertible paper. He therefore ascribed the rise in commodity prices, insofar as it corresponded with the premium on bullion, wholly to monetary overissue. Such an overissue would have no other effect than to 'raise the *money* price of bullion without lowering its *value*, in the same manner, and in the same proportion, as it will raise the prices of other commodities' (ibid., p. 13 n. and p. 109). In other words, although paper money was depreciated, the 'bullion price' of commodities was unaltered. Hence the deterioration of the foreign exchanges 'will only be a *nominal*, not a *real* fall, and will not occasion the exportation of bullion' (ibid).

Ricardo was criticized for ignoring the real reasons for the inflation, which had more to do with harvest failures, war subsidies and the Napoleonic blockade (Morgan, 1965, pp. 46–7). Moreover, he left himself open to the charge of superimposing a theory of *fiduciary* money on a *credit* system. Had bank notes been issued at will by the state, Ricardo would have been correct in his characterization of their relationship to the price level. Fiduciary money only *represents* gold in the circulation process, and is depreciated to the extent of its overissue. The depreciation persists until the quantity is reduced, for there are no self-correcting tendencies as in the case of convertible paper. However, the fact that the notes of the Bank Restriction period were not forced currency but credit responding to the demand of the non-bank public was excluded from Ricado's consideration by Say's Law. He treated the notes as though they were fiduciary because output and velocity were independently given. The possibility of disintermediation when the authorities tried to contract the note issue was also excluded. The fixed velocity assumption implied that the rest of the spectrum of credit would shrink commensurately with the notes. In fact, as the banking school was to demonstrate, credit instruments simply expanded in their place.

The resumption of specie payments in 1819 on the advice of Ricardo and the bullionist spokesmen did nothing to eliminate price instability from Britain's developing industrial economy. In 1825 and 1836, phases of vigorous expansion ended with an adverse balance of payments, a gold drain from the Bank of England and an inflationary collapse into recession. The currency school – a new orthodoxy which Morgan describes as the 'heirs of the Bullion Report' – attributed the recurrent dislocation to excessive monetary growth. The convertibility of bank notes was no longer seen as a sufficient safeguard against overissue and consequent depreciation. The currency school argued that rules would have to be devised to make the paper currency fluctuate as though it were metallic, in other words to replicate the 'automatic' operation of Ricardo's international specie-flow mechanism. This implied regulation of the note issue by the monetary authorities in strict conformity with the foreign exchanges; the export and import of bullion was treated as an index of monetary excess or deficiency, and thus of the value of the notes.

The currency principle was given practical effect by the Bank Charter Act of 1844, which set the pattern of the UK financial system for almost a century. It was challenged by the banking school, which Morgan calls 'the heirs to the opposition to the Bullion Report, but the opposition as it might have been rather than as it was'.

The long-run determination of aggregate monetary requirements by nominal output – the 'supply side' of the equation of exchange – was common ground in the debate. The real point at issue was again the *short-run* behaviour of the variables. Whereas the currency school adopted Ricardian quantity theory and applied it to a credit system made up of convertible bank notes, the banking school took the alternative view of metallic circulation and tried to develop a theory specific to credit. Both sides recognized the importance of theorizing the laws of metallic circulation as a precondition for the analysis of paper currency. The entire currency school case for monetary control rested upon the assertion that the note issue would not by itself emulate the behaviour of a metallic system. Despite legal convertibility, it might depart at least temporarily from the amount and value of the metallic money which would otherwise have circulated. In practice, therefore, economic convertibility could only be ensured by quantitative intervention on the part of the authorities (Torrens to Lord Melbourne, *cit*. Tooke, 1844, p. 7).

Banking school criticism took three main lines. First, starting from the assumption that legal convertibility necessarily implied economic convertibility, they pointed out that any discrepancy between the note issue and a purely metallic system arose from the currency school's erroneous theory of metallic circulation rather than from the supposed autonomy of the notes. Second, any effect of prices attributed to bank notes could not be denied to a range of financial assets excluded by the currency school from their definition of money. Third, bank notes were in any case not money but credit, and therefore never could be overissued, through the credit structure as a whole might be extended beyond the limits of real accumulation by 'speculation and overtrading'.

The banking school emphasized that the volume of notes in circulation could not be increased at will by the authorities, but only in response to the demand of the non-bank public. This crucial difference between fiduciary money and bank notes was explained by Tooke as consisting, 'not only in the limit prescribed by their convertibility to the amount of them, but in the *mode of issue*' (Tooke, 1844, pp. 70–71, emphasis added; see also Fullarton, 1845, ch. 3 and Wilson, 1859, pp. 48, 51–2, 57–8). The currency principle, by contrast, 'completely identifies *monetary turnover* with *credit*, which is economically wrong' (Marx, 1973, p. 123). An advance of bank notes did not *add* to the money supply, but merely changed its *composition*, allowing the substitution of one financial asset for another in the hands of the public. Excess notes returned automatically to the bank 'in the shape of deposits or of a demand for bullion' (Tooke, 1844, p. 60; see also Wilson, 1859, p. 58; Marx, 1867, III, pt. 5). This was the basis of the law of reflux, which Fullarton called 'the great regulating principle of the internal currency'. It held that economic convertibility could be ensured not only by a legal right to exchange notes for specie but also by maintaining a balance between the notes advanced on loan and those returned to the bank at maturity. Provided lending took place on commercial paper which represented a real or (within a given timescale) potential sum of values, 'the reflux and the issue will, in the long run, always balance each other' (1845, pp. 64–7; also p. 207; Marx, 1973, p. 131).

The banking school did not imagine that the economic cycle could be eliminated by monetary measures. Instead, they evolved a new set of criteria by which the authorities could operate on the 'state of credit' through interest rate and reserve management (Tooke, 1844, p. 124; Fullarton, 1845, p. 164; Marx, 1867, III, p. 447). In practice, all that lay between the currency and banking schools was ultimately a matter of timing, but this reflected profound theoretical differences. Within the framework of classical analysis, it was the banking school which came closer to constructing a modern philosophy of monetary regulation.

ROY GREEN

See also BANKING SCHOOL, CURRENCY SCHOOL, FREE BANKING SCHOOL; BULLIONIST CONTROVERSY; HUME, DAVID; QUANTITY THEORY OF MONEY; RICARDO, DAVID; THORNTON, HENRY.

BIBLIOGRAPHY
Cantillon, R. 1755. *Essai sur la nature du commerce en général.* London: Macmillan, 1931.
Eatwell, J. 1983. The analytical foundations of monetarism. In *Keynes's Economics and the Theory of Value and Distribution*, ed. J. Eatwell and M. Milgate, London: Duckworth.
Fullarton, J. 1845. *On the Regulation of the Currency.* London: John Murray.
Green, R. 1982. Money, output and inflation in classical economics. *Contributions to Political Economy* 1, 59–85.
Hume, D. 1752. *Writings on Economics.* Oxford: Oxford University Press, 1955.
Law, J. 1705. *Money and Trade Considered.* Edinburgh: Anderson.
Locke, J. 1691. Consequences of the lowering of interest and raising the value of money. In J.R. McCulloch, *Principles of Political Economy*, London: Ward, Lock & Co., 1825.
Marx, K. 1867. *Capital.* Moscow: Progress Publishers, 1971.
Marx, K. 1973. *Grundrisse.* Harmondsworth: Penguin.
Montesquieu, C. 1748. *The Spirit of Laws.* London: George Bell & Sons, 1900.
Morgan, E.V. 1965. *The Theory and Practice of Central Banking, 1797–1913.* London: Frank Cass.
Nef, J.U. 1941. Silver production in central Europe: 1450–1618. *Journal of Political Economy* 49, June, 575–91.
Outhwaite, R.B. 1969. *Inflation in Tudor and Early Stuart England.* London: Macmillan.
Petty, W. 1963. *Economic Writings.* New York: Kelley.
Ricardo, D. 1821. *Principles of Political Economy and Taxation.* Ed. P. Sraffa, Cambridge: Cambridge University Press, 1951.
Ricardo, D. 1923. *Economic Essays.* London: Frank Cass.
Schumpeter, J. 1954. *A History of Economic Analysis.* London: Allen & Unwin.
Smith, A. 1776. *An Inquiry into the Nature and Causes of the Wealth of Nations.* London: Routledge, 1890.
Steuart, J. 1767. *An Inquiry into the Principles of Political Economy.* Edinburgh: Oliver and Boyd, 1966.
Thornton, H. 1802. *An Enquiry into the Nature and Effects of the Paper Credit of Great Britain.* London: LSE reprint series, 1939.
Tooke, T. 1844. *An Inquiry into the Currency Principle.* London: LSE reprint series, 1959.
Vilar, P. 1976. *A History of Gold and Money: 1450–1920.* London: New Left Books.
Viner, J. 1937. *Studies in the Theory of International Trade.* London: Allen & Unwin.
Wilson, J. 1859. *Capital, Currency and Banking.* 2nd edn, London. The Economist.

classical theory of production. *See* PRODUCTION: CLASSICAL THEORIES.

classical theory of wages. *See* WAGES IN CLASSICAL ECONOMICS.

classification. *See* MEASUREMENT, THEORY OF.

Cliffe Leslie, Thomas Edward (1827–1882). T.E. Cliffe Leslie was both the pioneer (with J.K. Ingram) and the most radical member of the English Historical School. Born in Co. Wexford, he was educated at King William's College, Isle of Man, and at Trinity College, Dublin. In 1853 he became professor of jurisprudence and political economy at Queen's College, Belfast. His inaugural lecture 'The Military Systems of Europe Economically Considered' was published in 1856 and set the empirical, comparative tone that informed all his work. It was, however, Leslie's Irish context that did most to sharpen his onslaught on orthodox economics. To the Irish tenant-farmers, lacking either security of tenure or the right to be compensated for improvements they had made, liberal economists offered only free trade and the assurance that no good could come from specific legislation for Ireland. Thus Robert Lowe (shortly to become Gladstone's Chancellor) in 1868 urged Parliament to oppose land reform 'with the principles of political economy'. That Mill dissented, supporting what eventually became the Irish Land Act of 1870, was perhaps the crucial episode in Leslie's becoming a self-proclaimed disciple of Mill.

In 1870 Leslie published a volume of essays entitled *Land Systems and the Industrial Economy of Ireland, England and Continental Countries*. Highly praised by Mill in the *Fortnightly Review*, it was the last and most important of his works directly on the Irish question. In the same year he fired his opening salvo in the English *Methodenstreit* with 'The Political Economy of Adam Smith' (1888). Here Leslie lauded Smith as an inductive, historically minded economist whose brand of economics should never have been supplanted by the grotesque abstractions and unbalanced methodology of Ricardo. In 'On the Philosophical Method of Political Economy' (1888), Leslie reiterated that man was not, as the classical economists had assumed, a being whose 'great variety of different and heterogeneous motives' could be compounded into a homogenous desire for wealth when deductive analysis was required. He went on to attack orthodox political economy for its failure – inability, indeed, as it stood constituted – to go behind the individual economic agent and weigh up the social and historical forces moulding his actions and preferences. But perhaps his most radical paper, and certainly the one which strikes the strongest chord today, is 'The Known and the Unknown in Economics' (1888), in which the limits of the economist's information – and the blithe unconcern of many economists about the fact that these limits exist – are laid sharply bare. Here, again, historical relativism is the mainspring, Leslie arguing that only in a primitive village economy, with predictable 'reproduction' of economic activities and prices set by custom, can the economist have something approaching complete knowledge. When prices are set in a competitive market, when credit and default weaken certainty and trust, when technical change accelerates to the point where products rapidly become obsolete, then universalist economic 'laws' represent little more than an (unwitting) confession of ignorance as to the really important features of any particular episode until it can be written up from a historian's perspective.

Leslie's intended *magnum opus*, a work on the economic and legal history of England, had only reached manuscript stage when he lost it in France in 1872. For the remaining ten years of his life, his contribution was more critical than constructive. However, in the 1870s, radical criticism of deductive economics was badly needed, as both Marshall and John Neville Keynes were later to admit.

J. MALONEY

SELECTED WORKS
1888. *Essays in Political Economy*. Dublin: Hodges, Figgis & Co.
BIBLIOGRAPHY
Hutchison, T.W. 1978. *On Revolutions and Progress in Economic Knowledge*. Cambridge: Cambridge University Press.
Koot, G. 1975. T.E. Cliffe Leslie, Irish social reform, and the origins of the English historical school of economics. *History of Political Economy* 7(3), Fall, 312–36.

cliometrics. Clio, the muse of history, has inspired many ways of studying the past. The narrative of Herodotus or Thucydides, the medieval chronicle, the prosopography of Namier and Neale, the *'histoire totale'* of the *Annales* school, all represent different solutions to the problem of understanding and describing what happened in past time. Each has suited its age, each gained its adherents and its detractors, and each has ultimately been displaced by a new method.

Cliometrics, the most influential but never predominant mode of historical enquiry in the 1960s and 1970s, is like its predecessors, an amalgam of methods. Even its name is in dispute; some of its adherents prefer 'econometric history', some 'quantitative history', some 'the new economic history', some even 'the new history', while the most recent and all-inclusive term is 'social science history'. Whatever the exact name, each denotes a set of methods 'born of the marriage contracted between historical problems and advanced statistical analysis, with economic theory as bridesmaid and the computer as best man' (Fogel and Elton, 1983, p. 2).

The marriage was first conducted in the United States by priests drawn from a generation of young economists trained in theory and econometrics, who were interested in history and anxious to apply their skills to historical problems. Two of its earliest offspring were attempts to solve a central problem in American history, that of the role of the railroad in the economic development of the nation in the 19th century (Fogel, 1964; Fishlow, 1965). Both were careful to specify the subject of enquiry in the language of economic theory and both used a technique which came to be regarded as typical of early cliometrics, that of the counterfactual. They imagined what might have happened within the American economy if the railroad had not been brought into use and measured its impact as the reduction in the real cost of transport, the difference between the actual rail costs and the hypothetical non-rail costs. Finding that this difference was small, they argued, threw doubt on old-established views that the railroad caused the economic development of the United States.

The counterfactual, familiar to economists used to the assessment of opportunity cost and the methods of comparative statics, was either unknown or alien to most historians in the United States and Britain, to whom 'hypothetical history' was a pejorative term. Taught to eschew speculation about what might have happened in history, they reacted with horror to the building of imaginary networks of canals across the mid-West. More fundamentally, many historians rejected the concepts of causation which they judged to be implied in the closed and deterministic models of the economists; they argued, instead, that historical statements of causation were much weaker, multi-factorial, and unsuitable to be tested by the economist's method of removing one possible cause and assessing the outcome, *ceteris paribus* (McClelland, 1975).

The theory and practice of the counterfactual occupied a great deal of the time and attention of cliometricians and their intellectual opponents during the 1960s and early 1970s. Research on the United States railroads stimulated similar enquiries into the economic impact of the British, German, Russian and other railways, using essentially the same methods as Fogel and Fishlow, although with modifications to suit each country, and with essentially the same results; the railways made a significant difference to the speed of economic growth but that growth could have been achieved with other forms of transport (O'Brien, 1977). Similar results came from the only major counterfactual study of innovation outside the railway, that by Von Tunzelmann (1978) of the steam engine in Britain.

These findings were successful in demolishing myths of the revolutionary effects of a single new technology but, once this was done, the counterfactual itself dropped out of favour both as an explicit technique and a subject of controversy. Historians admitted that they should be more careful in the phrasing of statements about causation, economists that counterfactual models were of limited use in studies of long-term societal change.

The debate over counterfactuals was symptomatic, however, of a gulf not only between two methods of studying history but, more fundamentally, between two modes of thought and two forms of scholarly training. As Sir John Habakkuk has put it, 'one man cannot think in two ways'; the economist's search for carefully specified models of collective behaviour, susceptible to test by quantitative methods, leads him to approach history in a way which differs fundamentally from the search for the sources of individual behaviour which is characteristic of the work of many historians. Moreover, even when economists are drawn to discuss the behaviour of individuals, or historians to discuss collectivities, the tendency to reason from generalization or to emphasize specificity still remains.

The conflict has been muted, however, by closer contact between the two modes of thought. Early studies in cliometrics in the United States were written by economists and principally for economists; its frame of reference was neoclassical economics and its protagonists were seeking to establish themselves within the economics profession. Contacts with historians were limited. In Britain, by contrast, cliometrics developed more slowly than in the United States but always remained in contact with historians; it was often carried out in university departments of history or economic history, only rarely by economists. Its style and theoretical origin were more eclectic, its topics for research closer to the interests of historians.

The methodological conflicts aroused by cliometric studies of the railroad were thus largely absent from the primary topic of British cliometrics in the 1970s, even though much of the research was the work of economists from the United States. The topic was the performance of the British economy between 1850 and 1914 and, specifically, the extent to which British entrepreneurs could be blamed for slowing British growth. Here, cliometrics demonstrated much of its power in sharpening the questions under debate and in devising tools and identifying data to test the hypotheses which were formulated.

Complementing the development of historical national accounts by Deane and Cole (1976) and Feinstein (1972), a number of studies were completed of individual British industries and their responsiveness to profit opportunities and to technical change. A secondary focus of debate was created by continuing discussion of differences between the British and American economies, stimulated by the work of Habakkuk (1962), a debate marked by considerable theoretical complexity and the inadequacies of conventional theories of technical change. Although debate continues, it is now generally accepted that British entrepreneurs can be absolved from wilder charges of incompetence (McCloskey and Sandberg, 1974) even if other features of the British economy and society militated against faster growth.

Even in the case of the third major controversy stimulated by cliometrics, that following the publication of *Time on the Cross: The Economics of American Negro Slavery* by R.W. Fogel and S.L. Engerman (1974), methodological argument was secondary to discussion of the substantive issues and findings. Although the book received withering criticism,

both from historians and from economists, the debate which ensued has demonstrated an acceptance of the validity of cliometrics in general, if not of specific descriptions, analyses or conclusions (Gutman, 1975; David et al., 1976). Indeed, much of the vigour of the debate sprang from the ability of critics to re-analyse data gathered by Fogel and Engerman but made available for general use.

Despite the criticisms, the major finding of *Time on the Cross* in the field of economic history, that Southern slave agriculture before the Civil War was profitable and efficient relative to Northern free agriculture, is now generally accepted, although Fogel and Engerman's conclusions in the field of social history, concerned with the behaviour and attitudes of the slaves, remain controversial.

The methods and topics of cliometric research have spread far beyond the economic history of the United States and Britain. The work of Kovalchenko and Kahk in the Soviet Union has demonstrated the potential of the methods within the framework of Marxist analysis (1977), while German-speaking historians have been active in the development of quantitative political history. A particularly productive area of research has been demographic history, where the quantitative skills of the demographer have been allied to intensive archival research and to sophisticated economic models (Wrigley and Schofield, 1981). Quantitative methods increasingly form part of the training of historians, so that they may understand, if not undertake, cliometric research.

Cliometrics in the 1980s is not, however, uncontroversial. Attacks on its methods, and on the cost of the large-scale data collection which has accompanied much cliometric research, continue to be made by historians calling for a revival of narrative history. More seriously, a general attack on the use of quantitative methods in history has come from historians who espouse 'people's history' or '*alltagsgeschichte*'; to such historians, who seek to study and recreate the experience of working people in the past, cliometrics is seriously flawed. Not only are quantitative data seen as the product of the exercise of state power in the past, thus reflecting the concerns of the ruling classes rather than the life of the working classes, but (despite the growth of cliometrics in the Soviet Union) cliometric analysis is seen as irredeemably tainted by its early and continued association with neoclassical economics. It imposes, it is alleged, a capitalist, individualist and rationalist world-view, failing to recognize many important features of the life of individuals in the past (Floud, 1984).

Criticism of the restrictive models used by cliometricians is also made, from a different ideological stance, from within the economics profession. In particular, it is argued that the use of comparative statics is unlikely to be adequate for the analysis of large systems, such as national economies, which are changing over time; by contrast, it is believed, the methods of general equilibrium analysis offer more chance of capturing the main features of economic development in the past (James, 1984). While many cliometricians assent to this argument in principle, few have been brave enough to try to develop such analyses; a notable exception is Williamson (1974, 1985).

Cliometrics is, however, now able to play an increasingly important role within the study of economics. Its methods, often borrowed from contemporary applied economics and econometrics, are increasingly sophisticated. Allied with a greater interest on the part of economists in the parallels that can be drawn with, or the lessons that can be learned from, the past this ensures that cliometricians play an important part in such controversies as that about the existence of the Phillips curve or the causes of high unemployment between 1919 and 1939. Indeed, what is time series analysis but cliometrics?

Cliometrics has not, it is true, been able to satisfy either its protagonists or its critics. It has not become, as some predicted, the dominant mode of historical analysis in the 1980s; nor has it proved to be a passing fad. Within economics, it has a secure if minor place as an aid to the understanding of the present. Within history, cliometrics has achieved the place which all but its most fanatic acolytes wished it to fill, that of one among the many methods by which we can hope to understand the past.

RODERICK FLOUD

See also COUNTERFACTUALS; ECONOMIC HISTORY.

BIBLIOGRAPHY

David, P.A., Gutman, H.G., Sutch, R., Temin, P. and Wright, G. 1976. *Reckoning with Slavery*. New York: Oxford University Press.

Deane, P. and Cole, W.A. 1976. *British Economic Growth 1688–1959*. Cambridge: Cambridge University Press.

Feinstein, C.H. 1972. *National Income. Expenditure and Output of the United Kingdom, 1855–1965*. Cambridge: Cambridge University Press.

Fishlow, A. 1965. *American Railroads and the Transformation of the Ante-Bellum Economy*. Cambridge, Mass: Harvard University Press.

Floud, R.C. 1984. Quantitative history and people's history: two methods in conflict? *Social Science History* 8(2), 151–68, reprinted in *History Workshop Journal* 17, 113–24.

Fogel, R.W. 1964. *Railroads and American Economic Growth*. Baltimore: Johns Hopkins Press.

Fogel, R.W. and Elton, G.R. 1983. *Which Road to the Past? Two Views of History*. New Haven and London: Yale University Press.

Fogel, R.W. and Engerman, S.L. 1974. *Time on the Cross: The Economics of American Negro Slavery*. Boston: Little, Brown.

Gutman, H.G., 1975. *Slavery and the Numbers Game*. Urbana, Ill.: University of Illinois Press.

Habakkuk, H.J. 1962. *American and British Technology in the Nineteenth Century*. Cambridge: Cambridge University Press.

James, J.A. 1984. The use of general equilibrium analysis in economic history. *Explorations in Economic History* 21(3), 231–53.

Kovalchenko, I.D. et al. 1977. *Mathematical Methods in Historical-Economic and Historical-Cultural Studies*. Moscow: Nauka.

McClelland, P.D. 1975. *Causal Explanation and Model Building in History, Economics and the New Economic History*. Ithaca, New York and London: Cornell University Press.

McCloskey, D.N. and Sandberg, L. 1974. From damnation to redemption: judgments on the late Victorian entrepreneur. *Explorations in Economic History* 9, 89–108.

O'Brien, P. 1977. *The New Economic History of the Railways*. London: Croom Helm.

Von Tunzelmann, G.N. 1978. *Steam Power and British Industrialisation to 1860*. Oxford: Clarendon Press.

Williamson, J.G. 1974. *Late Nineteenth-Century American Development: A General Equilibrium History*. Cambridge: Cambridge University Press.

Williamson, J.G. 1985. *Did British Capitalism Breed Inequality?* London: Allen and Unwin.

Wrigley, E.A. and Schofield, R.S. 1981. *The Population History of England, 1541–1871: A Reconstruction*. Cambridge, Mass.: Harvard University Press.

clubs. The economic theory of clubs has its roots independently in two seminal articles, one by James Buchanan (1965) and the other by Charles Tiebout (1956). Buchanan's motivation was to define a broad spectrum of economic goods on a continuum between pure public goods and pure private goods and to understand the relations between characteristics of the good, its cost and the group which consumes it. Tiebout's concern, on the other hand, was with whether individual preference revelations might be inferred from the mobile consumer/voter's choices among location-specific public goods. If this were possible, it might resolve the dilemma whereby efficiency in the provision of a collective good is so difficult to reach because consumers conceal their preferences. Each of these papers has stimulated a large intertwining literature on all aspects of the provision of goods to groups.

A club is an organization which offers a shared collective good exclusively to its members, defraying the cost of the good from member's payments (typically dues payments or user fees in the form of head taxes) according to some more or less equal or in some cases discriminatory tax rule. The quality (or quantity) of the good available to each member may or may not depend on the size of the membership or on its composition. In the former case, congestion or impurity is said to exist in the provision of the club's good; otherwise none. In either case, the greater the level of resources applied to the provision of the club's good, the greater the quantity or quality available to any fixed membership.

Abstracting from the fact that sometimes the provision of a club's good occurs simultaneously with land utilization, congestion–consumption relationships can be written as:

$$C = f(X, N); \quad \text{or} \quad X = \Phi(C, N)$$

where C indicates total cost, X the amount of the good, and N the size of the club. Here we assume all N individuals consume identical quantity or qualities of the good. For a fixed value of C, X declines if N increases, while, for fixed N, X increases with gains in C.

Drawing on such a simple representation of the club's technology, the economic theory of clubs studies a menu of normative and positive issues related to demand and supply for the club's good. What is the optimal club membership size and the optimal provision of the good? Is there a best assignment of individuals to clubs? In particular, should clubs consist of similar individuals so that the membership is homogeneous? Can optimality be achieved on a decentralized basis, through population mobility and independent club management? In this event, what is the nature of the equilibrium among clubs?

The answer to these questions is known to depend strongly on a number of factors: (1) overall size of population to be distributed relative to the number of optimal-sized clubs; (2) whether entry in the creation of clubs is free or restricted; (3) pricing rules and other objectives followed by club management (e.g. whether all members pay the same price, whether the club management prices at marginal or average cost, and whether profit, or rent maximization is a management objective); (4) diversity or variation among individuals as to their demands/tastes for the club's good.

Intensive analysis of these problems has produced several prominent and robust results:

(1) In general it is Pareto-efficient to have a size of club such that per-person cost is minimized – provided such a minimum exists, each club provides only one good and enough people exist.

(2) Club memberships are Pareto-efficient if similar (as close to identical as the overall population permits) individuals are assigned to each club. That is, narrow economic efficiency indicates that populations should be segregated by demand for quality or quantity of the club's good.

(3) Provided clubs serve solely as consumption locations, and therefore all the income of each member is given exogenously, equal head taxes (dues) should be employed to finance the provision of the good. Any attempt by clubs to discriminate in the taxes-dues charged to different members will drive out the rich and thereby generate unstable equilibria.

(4) If 'clubs' in addition to providing for collective

consumption also provide a location for production, and if club sites thereby yield diminishing returns to input application, *and* if free entry obtains so that new clubs are created costlessly, then all club goods should be financed from the location-specific surplus (rent) attributable to each club. Club membership should be increased and marginal private productivity of members thereby driven down, until the corresponding site rent will pay for that club's good.

(5) If the optimum number of clubs does not divide total population into an integer, so that too few or too many people exist to occupy just evenly the clubs at the optimal level, then no equilibrium assignment of individuals to clubs exists (the core is empty).

(6) Under conditions of freely mobile populations a system of club managements each of which sets dues and services so as to maximize the economic asset value of the club is efficient.

(7) In most situations, a club can be efficiently run by its members, the government or private firms. In the case of private firms, the optimal charges are identical to the optimal tolls or user fees for member-owned and operated clubs.

The theory of clubs finds its strongest application in the analysis of and rationale for government decentralization, of hierarchical government and ultimately of fiscal federalism. Thus the formal structure of the theory has been fruitfully applied to questions such as the viability of discriminatory taxation at the local level, the implications of alternative maximizing objectives for local policy-makers and the inter-dependencies between urban land/housing markets and local government service provision when people can freely move about.

The results of such analysis frequently shed light on the structure of population grouping by segregated or desegregated patterns, on the forces behind the dynamics of community change, especially in so far as such change is caused by local tax and service provision policies, on proper division of tax/expenditure decision-making among levels of government and on the conditions under which intervention by the central government in the fiscal affairs of lower levels is justified in the name of equity or efficiency.

MARTIN C. MCGUIRE

See also CONSTITUTIONAL ECONOMICS; PUBLIC CHOICE; TIEBOUT HYPOTHESIS.

BIBLIOGRAPHY

Berglas, E. 1976. Distribution of tastes and skills and the provision of local public goods. *Journal of Public Economics*, November, 409–23.

Bewley, T.F. 1981. A critique of Tiebout's theory of local public expenditures. *Econometrica* 49, 713–40.

Buchanan, J.A. 1965. An economic theory of clubs. *Economica* 32, 1–14.

McGuire, M. 1974. Group segregation and optimal jurisdictions. *Journal of Political Economy* 82, 112–32.

Pauly, M. 1970. Cores and clubs. *Public Choice* 9, 53–65.

Samuelson, P. 1954. The pure theory of public expenditure. *Review of Economics and Statistics* 36, 387–9.

Sandler, T. and Tschirhart, J.T. 1980. The economic theory of clubs: an evaluative survey. *Journal of Economic Literature* 18(4), 1481–521.

Stiglitz, J. 1977. Theory of local public goods. In *The Economics of Public Services*, ed. M. Feldstein and R. Inman, London: Macmillan.

Tiebout, C. 1956. A pure theory of local expenditures. *Journal of Political Economy* 64, 416–24.

Westhoff, F. 1977. Existence of equilibria in economies with a local public good. *Journal of Economic Theory* 14, 84–112.

Wheaton, W. 1975. Consumer mobility and community tax bases. *Journal of Public Economics* 4, 377–84.

Williams, A. 1966. The optimal provision of public goods in a system of local governments. *Journal of Political Economy* 74, 18–33.

Wooders, M. 1978. Equilibria, the core, and jurisdiction structures in economies with a local public good. *Journal of Economic Theory* 18, 328–48.

coalitions. *See* CORES; SHAPLEY VALUE.

Coase, Ronald Harry (born 1910). R.H. Coase was born in Middlesex, England, in 1910. After graduating from the London School of Economics in 1932, he taught at the Dundee School of Economics (1932–34), the University of Liverpool (1934–5), the London School of Economics (1935–51), the University of Buffalo (1951–8), the University of Virginia (1958–64), and the University of Chicago, where he also assumed editorship of the *Journal of Law and Economics* (1964–82). Influenced by his mentor, Arnold Plant, Coase developed a deep conviction that one cannot understand the behaviour of something unless he sees and touches its reality. Throughout his academic career he has persistently turned from what he calls 'blackboard economics' to economics relevant to the real world.

As a student, Coase was captivated by two books introduced to him by Lionel Robbins. To Frank Knight's *Risk, Uncertainty, and Profit*, Coase owes his enduring interest in economic organizations and institutions. Philip Wicksteed's *Commonsense of Political Economy* initiated Coase's uncanny ability to analyse constrained choices without recourse to higher mathematics. A seminal mind, fed with what we today would regard as a bare minimum of knowledge, was sufficient to see the world in its own way and to exert profound influence on the profession. We owe to Coase much of our present understanding of how economic systems operate.

At age 21, even before receiving his bachelor's degree, Coase visited the United States on a travelling scholarship. During this tour he conceived and drafted 'The Nature of the Firm', destined to be published later (in 1937). Considering how the work began, as the equivalent of an undergraduate term paper, one stands in awe of the insights it offers. The impact of that precocious piece is sharply rising even today. A check with indices reveals 17 citations of the 'firm' paper during 1966–70, 47 during 1971–5, and 105 during 1976–80.

In that paper Coase addresses the question: Why, in a free-enterprise economy, would a worker voluntarily submit to direction by an entrepreneur or an agent instead of selling his own output or service directly to customers in the market? For an answer, Coase looked at the costs of operating the market, notably the costs of 'discovering prices'. He decided that a central agent who employs and directs workers avoids the costs of the numerous negotiations and measurements which would otherwise be required in determining prices for multiple transactions. The organization called a 'firm' emerges for that reason to supersede the market, or a factor market emerges to supersede a product market. As the process expands, however, the costs of monitoring workers and of making erroneous decisions increase. The firm size is found when, at the margin and as a group, these costs equal the costs implicit in operating in the market.

In a nutshell, the thesis rests on the choice of contracts. However, with this view it is not quite correct to say that a firm supersedes a market or that a factor market supersedes a product market; rather, one type of contract (e.g. wage and rental contracts) supersedes another type (i.e. product market contracts). An input owner will choose the arrangement with lower transaction costs. Because contracts may take a great variety of forms and the chain of contractual relationships may spread to the entire economy, both the firm and its size are often ambiguous. In any event, Coase's original work launched the transaction cost approach to analysing economic organization.

Although the term 'transaction costs' was not coined until the 1960s, Coase has always been preoccupied by costs not directly incurred in the physical process of production. His next major paper, for example, dealt with the marginal cost controversy. It was published in 1946, a period when economists were beginning to understand the Pareto condition involving marginal cost yet were puzzling that for a producer facing decreasing cost, the case of so-called 'natural monopoly', the practice of marginal cost pricing would necessarily incur a loss. The standard argument implicated governmental subsidy along with regulations or the involvement of government itself in production. To this view Coase introduced the costs of administering marginal cost pricing, including the cost of bureaucracy and the cost of determining the value of output to consumers. The real costs of marginal cost pricing would then presumably exceed its gain. Indeed, Coase has never believed in the existence of a natural monopoly; to him, in a situation of decreasing cost competition merely takes a different form.

For a full twenty years after the paper on the firm, only the marginal cost controversy had attracted much attention to Coase. During this period his works were almost invariably associated with monopoly and, oddly enough, with monopoly in broadcasting. And it was from his interest in broadcasting that Coase would shape economic thinking later. When he did so, however, it was not with monopoly, but with the chaotic competition of broadcasting rights.

Meantime, at Chicago, Aaron Director had quietly brought out the first issue of a new journal, the *Journal of Law and Economics*, in 1958. This was Chicago at its best, and excitement mounted as economists examined what may now be called the 'new institutional economics'. From his post in Virginia, Coase took a look at this issue and submitted a paper on broadcasting entitled 'The Federal Communications Commission'. Director promptly responded by setting it at the forefront of his second issue, which was to appear in 1959.

However, Director himself and his colleagues, especially Reuben Kessel, felt that amendments to the article were needed. Coase has taken issue with Pigou's classic view that in a case of conflicting uses (such as a piece of land being used simultaneously for growing wheat and parking cars) the party inflicting damage should be restrained. If that were done, said Coase, the restrained party would be harmed. The goal – to reduce damage – could be reached more efficiently through the market itself simply by a clear delineation of property rights.

That thesis was wrong, said the Chicago group, and they urged that Coase delete the attendant arguments. The author stood firm, but he agreed to come to Chicago later to defend his position, and that offer led to one of the most legendary debates in the history of economics. Participants in that after-dinner performance at the home of Director in 1960 called it 'the most exciting debate in their experience' and unanimously mourned that it had not been recorded.

For the occasion, Director assembled a stellar cast: Martin Bailey, Milton Friedman, Arnold Harberger, Reuben Kessel, Gregg Lewis, John McGee, Lloyd Mints, George Stigler, and of course Coase and Director themselves. The debate began with everyone siding with Pigou against Coase. It is recalled that Coase stood stoutly on his views. According to Stigler, in the midst of the debate Friedman opened fire and the bullets hit everyone except Coase. Coase himself remembers that

when he found himself still standing after Friedman's slaughter, he knew he was home free. (Did he fail to realize he was already safely home with the FCC paper?)

According to McGee, as the debaters left Director's home in a state of shock they mumbled to one another that they had witnessed intellectual history. Kessel, who began as the strongest opponent of Coase's views, confessed to this writer years later his view that one would have to go back to Adam Smith to find another economist with insights on the working of economic systems comparable to those of Coase.

In many ways the FCC paper is Coase's outstanding work. Not only is its scholarship unsurpassed, it first spelled out what came to be known as the Coase Theorem. However, what captured the imagination of economists then was its total novelty. Why, of all the valuable assets on earth, would an economist select radio frequencies as a subject for the economic analysis of property rights? These wavelengths are not even physically observable! And the idea of delineating property rights in frequencies so as to allow the market to resolve the chaotic interference when people compete to broadcast was most disturbing. For if this could be applied to radio frequencies – and it obviously could – the same approach would surely be applicable for any other resource!

A direct outcome of the debate was publication of 'The Problem of Social Cost' (1960). This may well be the most cited economic work of our time: 99 citations in 1966–70; 186 citations in 1971–5; and 331 citations in 1976–80. The term Coase Theorem, coined perhaps by Stigler and popularly associated with the social-cost paper (actually it first appeared in the FCC piece), will go down in history as certainly as Say's Law. A term cannot be suppressed when around it a paradigm is in the making. Coase himself did not endorse the term, feeling that it was somewhat misleading. In this he is correct, for what he did was to specify the conditions under which the traditional theorem of exchange becomes operative. In the FCC paper he succinctly states that 'the delineation of rights is an essential prelude to market transactions'. In the social cost piece he simply clarifies further the role of transaction cost.

Coase's analysis of social cost is a natural extension of his early work on the firm in that it urges specification of constraints inherent in the real world. Its thrust has stimulated economic inquiry on three fronts. First, it spotlights those constraints on property rights and transaction costs that decisively affect behaviour and in this way discloses possible explanations of a whole spectrum of observations commonly avoided by economists. Second, it interprets economic efficiency, or Pareto optimality, in the light of constraints ignored by neoclassical economists, and in the process it deals a telling blow to welfare economics. Third, Coase offers a fresh approach to theories of regulation and of the state.

After Coase became editor of the *Journal of Law and Economics* he held that position for nineteen years and brought the publication to towering heights. Some of us feel that a genius at his prime should not have burdened himself with so time-consuming a task. Although he continued to write, with emphasis on transaction costs and institutional arrangements (notably his works on the lighthouse and on the payola system), the editorial responsibilities must have curtailed to some extent his eager research on such charming diversities as buffaloes, contracts, Alfred Marshall and the host of other subjects he has examined with fresh eyes through almost half a century.

Coase admires Marshall for his total dedication to economics. Coase has surely been equally dedicated. He delves with intense concentration into problems. He thrives on hunches and possesses an inspired sense of generalization, but declines to jump to any conclusion without meticulous fact-finding and thorough reasoning. He has no interest in theory for its own sake – the world he sees is always the real world. He holds no standardized arguments sacred. He dislikes the concepts of equilibrium, of utility and of long and short runs. That he has gone so far without bowing to conventional wisdom is one measure of a creative mind.

Historians seem uncertain about whether events make heroes or heroes make events. In this case, both causal directions are clear. Events made a hero: Coase was fortunate that his innovative work on social cost (and transaction costs) appeared just as a tide was turning. The call for policy recommendations which had dominated earlier economic thinking was being replaced by a desire for economic explanations. And a hero made events: what Coase had to say turned the rising tide into a ground swell.

Many economists now are confident that the place which marginalism held in neoclassical economics will one day be rivalled by the position of transaction costs and the choice of contracts as the fount of fruitful analysis in the economics of the real world.

STEVEN N.S. CHEUNG

SELECTED WORKS

1937. The nature of the firm. *Economica* 4, November, 386–405.

1938. Business organization and the accountant. A series of 12 articles in *The Accountant*, October–December.

1946. The marginal cost controversy. *Economica* 13, August, 169–82.

1959. The Federal Communications Commission. *Journal of Law and Economics* 2, October, 1–40.

1960. The problem of social cost. *Journal of Law and Economics* 3, October, 1–44.

1961. The British Post Office and the messenger companies. *Journal of Law and Economics* 4, October, 12–65.

1970. The theory of public utility pricing and its applications. *Bell Journal of Economics* 1(1), 113–28.

1974. The lighthouse in economics. *Journal of Law and Economics* 17(2), October, 357–76.

1979. Payola in radio and television broadcasting. *Journal of Law and Economics* 22(2), October, 269–328

BIBLIOGRAPHY

Cheung, S.N.S. 1983. The contractual nature of the firm. *Journal of Law and Economics* 26(1), April, 1–21.

Kitch, E. (ed.) 1983. The fire of truth: a remembrance of Law and Economics at Chicago, 1932–1970. *Journal of Law and Economics* 26(1), April, 163–233.

Coase Theorem. Anyone who has taught the Coase Theorem to fresh minds has experienced first hand the wonder and admiration which it inspires, yet Coase never wrote it down, and, when others try, it probably turns out to be false or a tautology. The proposition, or propositions, called the Coase Theorem was originally developed through a series of examples (Coase, 1960). Like a judge, Coase steadfastly refused to articulate broad generalizations in his original paper. Like a judge's opinion, for every interpretation of his paper there is a plausible alternative. Instead of trying to arrive at the ultimate answer, I will offer several conventional interpretations of the Coase Theorem and illustrate them with one of his examples. After more than twenty years of debate the conventional interpretations appear to have exhausted its meanings.

A central insight in microeconomics is that free exchange tends to move resources to their highest valued use, in which case the allocation of resources is said to be Pareto efficient. Besides ownership of resources, the law creates many other entitlements, such as the right to use one's land in a certain way, the right to be free from a nuisance, the right to compensation for tortuous accidents, or the right to performance on a contract. Coase can be regarded as having generalized propositions about the exchange of resources to cover propositions about the exchange of legal entitlements. Under this interpretation, the Coase Theorem states that *the initial allocation of legal entitlements does not matter from an efficiency perspective so long as they can be freely exchanged.* In other words, misallocation of legal entitlements by law will be cured in the market by free exchange.

This interpretation suggests that insuring the efficiency of law is a matter of removing impediments to the free exchange of legal entitlements. Legal entitlements often suffer from vagueness, which makes their value difficult to assess. Furthermore, the courts are not always willing to enforce contracts for the sale of legal entitlements. Consequently, under the 'free exchange interpretation', the efficiency of law is to be secured by defining entitlements clearly and enforcing private contracts for their exchange.

Besides freedom of exchange, there are other conditions which economists usually regard as necessary for markets to allocate resources efficiently. One such condition concerns the elusive, but unavoidable, concept of transaction costs. Narrowly conceived, transaction costs refer to the time and effort required to carry out a transaction. In some circumstances these costs can be very high, as when a deal involves several parties at different locations. High transaction costs can block the workings of markets which would otherwise be efficient. Broadly conceived, transaction costs refer to any use of resources required to negotiate and enforce agreements, including the cost of information needed to formulate a bargaining strategy, the time spent higgling, and the cost of preventing cheating by the parties to the bargain. Stressing the 'transaction cost interpretation', the Coase Theorem can be regarded as stating that *the initial allocation of legal entitlements does not matter from an efficiency perspective so long as the transaction costs of exchange are nil.*

Like a frictionless plane in physics, a costless transaction is a logical construction, rather than something encountered in life. Keeping this fact in mind, the policy prescription following from the transaction cost interpretation of the Coase Theorem is to use law to minimize transaction costs, not eliminate them. According to this line of reasoning, rather than allocating legal entitlement efficiently in the first place, lawmakers are more likely to achieve efficiency by lubricating their exchange. Legal procedure is rife with devices whose purpose is to avoid litigation by encouraging private agreements involving an exchange of legal entitlement.

The 'transaction costs' interpretation focuses attention on some obstacles to exchanging legal entitlement, specifically the cost of negotiating and enforcing private agreements. When 'transaction costs' are given a reasonably circumspect definition, there are additional obstacles to private exchange besides transaction costs. The theory of regulation has developed a finer, richer classification based upon deviations from perfect competition (Schultze, 1977). To illustrate, a monopolist can increase his profits by supplying less than the competitive amount of the good and forcing the price up. Thus monopoly is a form of market failure which is usually distinguished from transaction costs. Stressing this 'market failures interpretation', the Coase Theorem can be regarded as stating that *the initial allocation of legal entitlements does not matter from an efficiency perspective so long as they can be exchanged in a perfectly competitive market.*

This interpretation suggests that ensuring the efficiency of law is a matter of ensuring the existence of perfectly competitive markets for legal entitlements. The conditions of perfect competition include the existence of many buyers and sellers, the absence of external effects, full information about price and quality by the participants in the market, and no transaction costs.

The three interpretations can be illustrated by an historical example which Coase made famous. Wood and coal-burning locomotives emit sparks that set fire to farmers' fields from time to time. Each of the parties can take precautions to reduce the damage caused by fires. To illustrate, the farmers can avoid planting and storing crops along the margins of the railroad tracks, and the railroad can instal spark arresters or run fewer trains.

Upon first inspection, it seems that the law controls the incentives for precaution by the parties, and, consequently, determines the amount of damage from fires. To illustrate, injunction is the conventional remedy in property law for a nuisance. If the farmers have a right to enjoin the railroad and shut it down until it stops emitting sparks, it seems that there will be little or no damage from sparks. Conversely, if the railroad has the right to operate trains with impunity, it seems that there will be a lot of damage. According to the Coase Theorem, these appearances are misleading, because while the law creates the initial allocation of entitlements, the market determines the final allocation. To illustrate, if farmers have a right to enjoin the railroad, they can sell this right. Specifically, the railroad could pay a sum of money to the farmers in exchange for a legally binding promise not to enjoin the railroad. Conversely, if the railroad has the right to emit sparks with impunity, it can sell this right. Specifically, farmers could pay a sum of money to the railroad in exchange for a legally binding promise to reduce spark emissions.

Whatever the initial allocation of rights, the farmers and the railroad have an incentive to continue trading entitlements so long as there are potential gains from trade. As with ordinary goods, the gains from trading legal entitlements are not exhausted until each entitlement is held by the party who values it the most. To illustrate, if, say, farmers have a right to be free from sparks, and if the entitlement to emit sparks is worth more to the railroad than the right to be free from sparks is worth to farmers, both parties will benefit from the farmers selling their rights to the railroad. The potential gains from trade are exhausted when entitlements are allocated efficiently. Thus, when the market works, the equilibrium allocation of legal entitlements will be efficient.

The three interpretations of the Coase Theorem give different accounts of the conditions that must be satisfied in order for this market to work. According to the 'free exchange' interpretation, the equilibrium allocation of entitlements will be efficient if entitlements are clearly defined and contracts for their exchange are enforceable. In the example, the conditions of the 'free exchange' interpretation are apparently met when the farmers have the right to enjoin the nuisance, or when the railroad has the right to emit sparks with impunity. Thus, according to the free exchange interpretation of the Coase Theorem, it does not matter from an efficiency perspective whether farmers have the right to enjoin the railroad or the railroad has the right to pollute with impunity.

The conclusion about efficiency is different under the 'transaction cost' interpretation. If there are many farmers, the cost of negotiating and enforcing an agreement among them would be high, especially since individual farmers might hold out for a larger share of the surplus, so inefficiencies in the initial allocation of entitlements would probably persist in spite of opportunities for private agreements. On the other hand, if there are just a few farmers, the cost of negotiating and enforcing an agreement between them and the railroad would be low, so the theorem predicts that the equilibrium allocation of entitlements would be efficient.

Turning to the third version, according to the 'perfect competition' interpretation, the equilibrium allocation of entitlements will be efficient if the conditions of perfect competition are satisfied in the market for legal entitlements. In the example of the railroad and the farmers, there is only one railroad, so the market is characterized by monopoly rather than perfect competition. Furthermore, there may be other types of failure in the conditions of perfect competition. For example, farmers may have more information than the railroad about the harm caused by sparks, whereas the railroad may have more information than the farmers about the technology for reducing spark emissions. In view of these facts, the exchange of legal entitlements between the farmers and the railroad would depart far from the conditions of perfect competition, so the market might fail to cure inefficiencies in the initial allocation of legal entitlements.

Of course, the initial allocation of rights always matters from the perspective of income distribution. To illustrate, if efficiency requires the railroad to be free from injunction, granting the farmers the right to injunctive relief will motivate the railroad to try to buy this right. The purchase is a cost to the railroad and income to the farmers. Conversely, granting impunity to the railroad will save it the cost of purchasing the right and deprive farmers of the income from selling it. Like scarce resources, scarce legal rights are valuable.

IS THE COASE THEOREM TRUE OR FALSE? In economics, a 'proof' is a derivation from generally accepted behavioural assumptions. As I will show, attempts to formulate the Coase Theorem in any of its three interpretations encounter obstacles which suggests that it is probably false or a mere tautology.

The weakest form of the theorem asserts that legal entitlements will be allocated efficiently under perfect competition. When Arrow (1969) examined externalities similar to those discussed by Coase, he showed that the efficiency conditions can be interpreted as the equilibrium conditions in a competitive market for the exchange of externality rights. But, as indicated by Arrow and others (Starrett, 1972), this formal demonstration has little practical value because externalities by their nature have characteristics which prevent the formation of competitive markets.

To illustrate, suppose that pollution is forbidden except by holders of resaleable pollution coupons issued by the government. Each pollutee who holds a coupon thereby prevents pollution from occurring, whereas each polluter who acquires a coupon uses it to increase the amount of pollution. Obviously, the social benefits of an individual pollutee retaining a coupon exceed his private benefits, so pollutees will sell too many of them. Equivalently, the social cost of a polluter acquiring a coupon exceeds his private cost, so pollutees will acquire too many of them. This divergence between private and social costs is itself an externality. So the attempt to eliminate externalities by setting up a market for pollution coupons just gives rise to a new type of externality (for details, see Cooter, 1982.) In reality, there are no perfectly competitive markets for externalities of the type discussed by Coase, and it seems impossible for them to arise spontaneously by private agreement. There might be some way for the government to create a pseudo-market (e.g. Groves, 1976), but none has been implemented.

Turning from the perfectly competitive market interpretation to the transaction cost interpretation of the Coase Theorem, observe that a private solution is likely to be efficient in cases affecting only a few parties, as, say, when contiguous land owners negotiate concerning a nuisance caused by one of them. If only a few parties are involved, the prices of entitlements will be negotiated instead of the parties acting as price-takers, which violates an assumption of perfect competition, but such negotiations often succeed anyway. According to the transaction cost interpretation of the Coase Theorem, externality problems affecting small numbers of people should have efficient solutions.

Although accurate as a rule of thumb, the transaction cost interpretation is not strictly true. It rests upon the proposition that bargaining reaches an efficient conclusion when the costs of negotiating and enforcing agreements is nil (Regan, 1972). In reality, bargaining among small numbers of people sometimes breaks down – unions strike, hijackers kill hostages, realtors lose sales because of disagreements over the price, disputes go to trial, and so forth. The essential obstacle, which has nothing to do with the cost of communicating or enforcing agreements, is the strategic character of bargaining. By definition, a bargaining situation has the characteristic that a surplus can be achieved by agreement, but there is no settled way for dividing it up among the beneficiaries. A self-interested negotiator will press his claim to a share of the surplus as far as he dares without destroying the basis for cooperation. In economic jargon, the rational negotiator demands an additional dollar so long as the resulting increase in the probability of noncooperation creates an expected loss of less than a dollar. When negotiators underestimate an opponent's resolve, they press too hard and the negotiations fail to reach an agreement. Thus bargaining situations are inherently unstable.

Seen in this light, the transaction cost interpretation of the Coase Theorem errs in the direction of optimism by assuming that cooperation will always occur when bargaining is costless. The polar opposite viewpoint, which has been called the 'Hobbes Theorem' (Cooter, 1982), errs in the direction of pessimism by assuming that the problem of dividing the surplus can only be solved by coercive force, not by cooperation. Reality lies in between the poles of optimism and pessimism, because strategic behaviour causes bargaining to fail in some cases, but not in every case.

The challenge to theory and empirical research raised by this interpretation of the Coase Theorem is to predict when legal entitlements will be allocated efficiently by private agreements. To advance this debate, broad labels such as 'transaction costs' and 'free exchange' must yield to substantive, detailed descriptions of the conditions under which private bargaining about legal entitlements succeeds. Fortunately, a more satisfactory bargaining theory has begun to emerge in recent years which adheres more closely to reality. According to this account, bargaining will break down for strategic reasons in a percentage of cases, but in equilibrium no one is surprised by the frequency with which breakdowns occur. (The key concept is the Bayesian Nash equilibrium; see Harsanyi, 1968, and Cooter and Marks, 1982.)

In economics, an 'empirical test' is a comparison between a prediction and facts. Recently, attempts have been made to test the Coase Theorem, for example, by determining the conditions under which bargaining in small groups reaches an efficient conclusion (Spitzer, 1982). The new developments in game theory, combined with the associated empirical research, hold the promise of finally establishing a scientific account of the conditions under which inefficient allocations of legal entitlements will be cured by private agreements.

WHAT IS THE SIGNIFICANCE OF THE COASE THEOREM? Pigou used economics to defend the common law principle that a party who causes a nuisance should be enjoined or required to pay damages. According to Pigou, the common law rules tend to promote economic efficiency by internalizing social costs. In some cases, he found gaps in the common law which require supplementary legislation, such as imposing a tax upon polluters equal to the social cost of pollution.

Coase's paper was framed as an attack upon Pigou's analysis of the law of nuisance. Coase disagreed with the conclusion that government action, through nuisance law or taxation, is typically required to achieve efficiency. The Coase Theorem suggests that the externalities represented by nuisances will sometimes, or perhaps usually, be self-correcting. I have argued that the forms of market failure are too diverse to be subsumed under a reasonably circumspect concept of transaction costs, and, consequently, the transaction cost interpretation of the Coase Theorem should be regarded as false or as a tautology whose truth is achieved by inflating the definition of transaction costs. Although the obstacles to spontaneous, private solutions of externalities are broader than suggested by the Coase Theorem, the role of government in lubricating private agreements, rather than issuing commands, is much favoured in the contemporary economic understanding of regulation.

In the event that government action is required to correct a nuisance, Coase denied Pigou's claim that the common law concept of causality is a useful guide to assigning responsibility. In Coase's view, the fact that someone 'causes' a nuisance, as judged by common law principles, does not imply that holding him liable or enjoining him is efficient. For Coase, the question of efficiency is to be decided by a balancing of cost and benefits in which the role of causality is not decisive. Coase's suggestion that causality should have little bearing upon legal responsibility contradicts countless court decisions and appears to have had little impact upon the practice or theory of law.

Whatever the merits of his arguments, Coase offered a challenge to widely accepted views in public finance. Before his article appeared, not much attention was paid to the possibility that externalities could be cured by private bargains. Thus Coase's claim went to the heart of a major debate in economics. Furthermore, the publication of Coase's article can be regarded as a breakthrough for the subject which has acquired the name of 'law and economics'. Before publication of Coase's article, economic *analysis* (as opposed to economic thought) had received little application to the common law, which is at the core of legal theory and method as taught in law schools. By analysing cases from property law in a lawyerly style, yet drawing upon microeconomics to guide the analysis, Coase demonstrated the fruitfulness of the economic analysis of the common law. He inspired a generation of scholars who pioneered the economic analysis of law, although he did not use the mathematical tools which have come to characterize the subject twenty years later.

ROBERT D. COOTER

See also COMMON PROPERTY RIGHTS; ECONOMIC ORGANIZATION AND TRANSACTION COSTS; EXTERNALITY; LAW AND ECONOMICS.

BIBLIOGRAPHY
Arrow, K. 1969. The organization of economic activity: issues pertinent to the choice of market versus non-market allocation. In *The Analysis and Evaluation of Public Expenditure: the PPB System*. US Congress, Joint Economic Committee, Washington, DC: GPO. Reprinted in *Public Expenditure and Policy Analysis*, ed. R. Haveman and J. Margolis, Chicago: Rand McNally, 1977.

Coase, R. 1960. The problem of social cost. *Journal of Law and Economics* 3(1), October, 1–44.

Cooter, R. 1980. How the law circumvents Starrett's nonconvexity. *Journal of Economic Theory* 22(3), June, 145–9.

Cooter, R. 1982. The cost of Coase. *Journal of Legal Studies* 11(1), January, 1–34.

Cooter, R. and Marks, S. 1982. Bargaining in the shadow of the law; a testable model of strategic behavior. *Journal of Legal Studies* 11(2), 225–52.

Groves, T. 1976. Information, incentives, and the internalization of production externalities. In *Theory and Measurement of Economic Externalities*, ed. A.Y. Steven, London: Academic Press.

Harsanyi, J.C. 1967–8. Games with incomplete information played by 'Bayesian' players, I–III. *Management Science*, Part I, 14(3), November 1967, 159–82; Part II, 14(5), January 1968, 320–34; Part III, 14(7), March 1968, 486–502.

Pigou, A.C. 1920. *The Economics of Welfare*. London: Macmillan. 4th edn, 1932.

Regan, D. 1972. The problem of social cost revisited. *Journal of Law and Economics* 15(2), October, 427–37.

Schultze, C. 1977. *The Public Use of Private Interest*. Washington, DC: Brookings.

Spitzer, M. 1982. The Coase Theorem: some experimental tests. *Journal of Law and Economics* 25(1), 73–98.

Starrett, D. 1972. Fundamental non-convexities in the theory of externalities. *Journal of Economic Theory* 4(2), April, 180–99.

Cobb–Douglas functions. The Cobb–Douglas function is perhaps the most ubiquitous form in economics, owing its popularity to the exceptional ease with which it can be manipulated and to the fact that it possesses the minimal properties that economists consider desirable. It appeared early (at least by 1916, see Wicksell, 1958, p. 133), notably in the theory of distribution where it was used to prove the adding-up theorem of factor shares when the production elasticities sum to unity. It is the first form that many embryonic mathematical economists squeeze and buffet to obtain nice expressions for marginal products and utilities. It has been applied econometrically countless times, still surprising people that it can explain the data so well (Mairesse, 1974). It forces itself into relatively new areas such as frontier production functions (see Førsund et al., 1980). And it has been used both as a utility and production function in analyses of growth, development, macroeconomics, public finance, labour and just about any other applied area in economics. Yet, it possesses restrictive properties and perhaps for that reason it has become for some an object of disdain, often regarded as a child's toy in the world of real economics. But for others, the Cobb–Douglas is at least a venerable form and, effectively, it and its putative inventor are regarded fondly.

In its unrestricted form, the Cobb–Douglas can be written as $f(\mathbf{x}) = A \prod_{i=1}^{n} x^{a_i}$, where A is an efficiency parameter, a_i is the elasticity of $f(x)$ with respect to x_i, and $\mathbf{x}$ is confined to R_{++}^n. Defining the x_i as goods consumed, it has been used as a utility function; defining them as inputs in the production process, it is a production function; as normalized prices, it is an indirect utility function; and so on. We focus here on its use as a production function for a single output.

A large part of the appeal of the form stems basically from the fact that if $0 < a_i < 1$, $f(\mathbf{x})$ is strongly pseudo-concave on its domain. That entails that if the firm is a profit maximizer and factor supply and product demand functions are continuously differentiable on their domains, then the input demand and supply of output functions have the immensely useful property of continuous differentiability everywhere on their respective domains. Also, if $\Sigma_i a_i \le 1$ and if factor supply and product demand functions are well-behaved, the input demand functions are downward sloping with respect to own price and the output supply function does not slope downward with regard

to product price. What could be better and, moreover, it is all so simple to demonstrate.

Another attractive property of the form is that it has a function coefficient that is identical to its degree of homogeneity, calculated by summing the factor production elasticities. Thus, $\Sigma_i a_i \lessgtr 1$ for all i easily and succinctly characterizes decreasing, ·constant and increasing returns to scale, respectively. This characteristic also has important implications for the cost, profit and revenue duals of the production function. For example, the cost function of a price-taking firm which has a Cobb–Douglas technology decomposes into two parts, one a linear homogeneous function of factor prices and the other a function of output q, that is $C(q, \mathbf{w}) = B \prod_{i=1} w_i^{c_i} q^{c_0}$, where B is a positive constant, $\mathbf{w}$ is a (positive) price vector of the inputs, $c_i = a_i/\Sigma_i a_i$ and $c_0 = 1/\Sigma_i a_i$.

The list of attractive properties extends to the aggregation problem since the Cobb–Douglas is homogeneous and weakly separable. First consider the question of aggregation across inputs. Suppose one can write a generalized Cobb–Douglas function as follows:

$$q = \prod_{s=1}^{S} \left(\prod_{j=1}^{J_s} x_{sj}^{b_{sj}} \right)^{Y_s},$$

where $b_{sj} = a_{sj}/\Sigma_j a_{sj}$, $Y_s = \Sigma_j a_{sj}$, J_s is the number of factors in the sth group, S is the number of groups, $s = 1, 2, \ldots, S$ and $j = 1, 2, \ldots, J_s$. Notice that $\Sigma_j b_{sj} = 1$. Since each expression in the parentheses is homogeneous of degree one for each s, the profit maximization procedure can be decomposed into two stages and there exist quantity and price indexes (call them x_s and W_s, respectively) such that the expenditure on the sth group is $W_s x_s$ for $s = 1, 2, \ldots, S$.

With respect to aggregation across firms, suppose the rth firm's production function were

$$q_r = A_r x_{1r}^{c_{1r}} x_{2r}^{c_{2r}}, \ldots, x_{nr}^{c_{nr}},$$

where $\Sigma_i c_{ir} = 1$ and $i = 1, 2, \ldots, R$. It is evident that the expansion paths for all firms are straight lines through their respective origins. Then under the extremely restrictive conditions that the expansion paths for each firm are parallel (i.e. if $c_{ir} = c_{it} = c_i$ for each i and for all r and t), and that the first order conditions are satisfied, the R functions consistently aggregate to

$$q = x_1^{c_1} x_2^{c_2}, \ldots, x_n^{c_n},$$

a nicely behaved aggregate production function.

There is another way to look at the aggregation-across-firms problem that involves the Cobb–Douglas function. Suppose that factors in each firm are used in fixed proportions with the Leontief coefficients being distributed across all firms according to a Pareto distribution. Then a surprising result by Houthakker (see Sato, 1975) is that the aggregate production function of the industry is a Cobb–Douglas form.

Of course, there is a price for these desirable implications and most of it is owing to the fact that the Cobb–Douglas technology entails that the elasticity of substitution takes on the knife-edge value of unity. If there is no technological change, a unit substitution elasticity implies that the income shares of all factors of production remain constant in the face of changes in things that are deemed germane such as saving, the rate of growth of the economy and relative factor supplies. Only the state of the technology matters in this instance, a highly disputable outcome. When technological change is allowed to proceed in a Cobb–Douglas world, it is a fact that Hicks-, Solow- and Harrod-neutral technological change are equivalent, thus blurring these distinctions. Another implication of the unit substitution elasticity of the (linear homogeneous) Cobb–Douglas form is that, used in growth models, it guarantees the existence and stability of equilibrium growth, again obscuring an important problem in economics.

Furthermore, it is a fact that the Cobb–Douglas form requires that each factor of production be essential in the sense that no factor may be completely substituted for another. Hence the domain of the function must be confined to the set of strictly positive real numbers. This is not particularly disturbing for situations in which the factors can be taken to be large aggregates but it does limit the analysis in other contexts.

Technological change is represented in the Cobb–Douglas by changes in the efficiency parameter A which are Hicks neutral, by changes in the scale of the factor inputs which are factor augmenting and also Hicks neutral, and by changes in the elasticities of production which may be Hicks non-neutral. However, the unit elasticity of substitution is restrictive in still another way: it cannot represent a technological advance that results in a change in the ease of substitution among factors of production.

What is the form's provenance? It is generally attributed to Paul Douglas and although he gracefully acknowledged (Douglas, 1967) that Wicksteed and Walras were cognizant of it, he neglected to add Wicksell's name to the list. Be that as it may, Douglas relates in his gentle comments that in 1927 he asked a professor of mathematics, Charles Cobb, to devise a formula that could be used to measure the comparative effect of each of two factors of production upon the total product to satisfy a linear log–log relationship in his input and output data. His work encountered a host of theoretical concerns (see Brown, 1966 for a discussion) aside from the capital, output and labour measures for which he was faulted. But the production form remained in spite (or perhaps because) of its restrictive properties.

Subsequent work has demonstrated that the Cobb–Douglas is a special case of a variety of forms and approaches. The constant elasticity of substitution (CES) production function is perhaps the most well known of the forms that yield the Cobb–Douglas as a special case, either by using L'Hôpital's rule when the elasticity of substitution goes to unity or it can be derived from certain expressions used in deriving the CES function (see Brown and De Cani, 1963). Parenthetically, the CES, itself, is known to mathematicians as a mean of order t [i.e. $(\Sigma_{i=1} a_i x_i^t)^{1/t}$ for $t \neq 0$] so that if one takes the limit as $t \to 0$, of course, the Cobb–Douglas emerges. Also, it can be derived from the translog production form (Christensen *et al.*, 1973) and many others, besides, by judiciously restricting certain parameters. A different approach to the derivation of the Cobb–Douglas form has been taken by P. Zarembka (see the entry on transformation of variables in econometrics) who specifies each variable as $z(\lambda) = (z^\lambda - 1)/\lambda$ for $\lambda \neq 0$ and $z(\lambda) = \ln z$ for $\lambda = 0$. Then, applying this transformation to the production function, we would have $z_0 = q$ and $z_i = x_i$ for all i. Thus, if the z_k $(k = 0, 1, \ldots, n)$ are related linearly, the transformation turns out to be a useful procedure in econometrics to treat the general problem of functional form, an important special case of which is the Cobb–Douglas.

In sum, though it is restrictive and sometimes regarded as an economic toy, the Cobb–Douglas form is remarkably robust in a vast variety of applications and that it will endure is hardly in question.

MURRAY BROWN

See also CAPITAL THEORY: PARADOXES; CES PRODUCTION FUNCTION; DOUGLAS, PAUL HOWARD; HUMBUG PRODUCTION FUNCTION; PRODUCTION AND COST FUNCTIONS.

BIBLIOGRAPHY

Brown, M. 1966. *On the Theory and Measurement of Technological Change*. Cambridge: Cambridge University Press.

Brown, M. and DeCani, J. 1963. Technological change and the distribution of income. *International Economic Review* 4, September, 289–309.

Christensen, L.R., Jorgenson, D.W. and Lau, L.J. 1973. Transcendental logarithmic production frontiers. *Review of Economics and Statistics* 55(1), February, 28–45.

Douglas, P.H. 1948. Are there laws of production? *American Economic Review* 38, March, 1–41.

Douglas, P.H. 1967. Comments on the Cobb–Douglas production function. In *The Theory and Empirical Analysis of Production*, ed. M. Brown, National Bureau of Economic Research, Studies in Income and Wealth, No. 31, New York: Columbia University Press.

Førsund, F.R., Lovell, C.A.K. and Schmidt, P. 1980. A survey of frontier production functions and of their relationship to efficiency measurement. *Journal of Econometrics* 13(1), May, 5–25.

Mairesse, J. 1974. *Comparison of Production Function Estimates*. Paris: Institut National de la Statistique et des Etudes Economiques.

Sato, K. 1975. *Production Functions and Aggregation*. Amsterdam: North – Holland.

Wicksell, K. 1958. *Selected Papers on Economic Theory*. Ed. Erik Lindahl, Cambridge Mass.: Harvard.

Cobbett, William (1763–1835). William Cobbett was born, appropriately, at the 'Jolly Farmer' in Farnham, Surrey, in 1763. He was by turns soldier, clerk, teacher, journalist and political agitator but whether in his early literary career as an anti-Jacobin pamphleteer or later in his role as combative radical his voice was that of the small farmer threatened by the forces of economic and social change which characterized the early phases of Britain's industrial revolution.

Cobbett's acerbic castigation of its major theorists shows he had little time for political economy and he would certainly have greeted with a wry guffaw his inclusion in a dictionary of economic thought. Nevertheless it was the case that much of his writing in the *Twopenny Register* (1816–20) and works such as *Paper against Gold* (1815) was given over to a discussion of economic questions and in particular the economic difficulties that confronted Britain in the post-Napoleonic war period, and even in his *Rural Rides* (1830) few opportunities were lost of discoursing on matters economic.

For Cobbett material impoverishment was a consequence of the political decisions affecting taxation, the Debt, the convertibility of the currency etc., which emanated from a Parliament corrupted by the influence of tax-gatherers, 'Change Alley men, sinecurists, placemen, Jews and Borough-tyrants. Crucial here was the passage of the Bank Restriction Act of 1797, which in suspending cash payments by the Bank of England had created a 'Paper money system' that robbed the 'industrious' of their 'earnings' producing 'that monster in civil society, starvation in the midst of abundance'. This paper money system was seen in itself as a means of appropriating the product of labour but most importantly, with the return to cash payments in 1819, it created a situation where the nation was compelled to pay in an appreciated medium of exchange debts contracted in a depreciated paper currency. The industrious were therefore forced to pay in gold what had been contracted in paper. Thus both the inflation of the Revolutionary and Napoleonic wars and the deflation that followed were seen by Cobbett as redistributing wealth in favour of the idle generally and the fundholders and bankers in particular. Justice demanded, therefore, that there should be an equitable adjustment in the level of taxation to take account of the appreciation in the value of money. For this, parliamentary reform and an end to political corruption were necessary prerequisites.

Under the undifferentiated heading of 'The Thing', Cobbett sought to attack all those who jeopardized his vision of a stable, hierarchically structured, rural economy and society, dominated by the independent yeoman farmer and free from 'the all-devouring Jew and tax-eater'. Specifically, he condemned 'the Funding and Manufacturing and Commercial and Taxing System' for their tendency to draw 'wealth into great masses ... [and] man also into great masses', like 'the Great Wen' [London], which both corrupted its inhabitants and impoverished the country as a whole.

Cobbett's was an anti-industrial, anti-commercial, anti-urban and anti-City political economy with its ideological roots in the political radicalism of the 18th century and with Paine's *Decline and Fall of the English System of Finance* (1797) as its basic text. Yet if, with the growth of industrial capitalism, this 'old corruption' critique became increasingly irrelevant and inadequate; if by the 1830s it was being supplanted in the working-class press by an anti-capitalist and socialist analysis of contemporary ills which deployed to critical effect the tools and concepts of political economy, this should not obscure the remarkable longevity of Cobbettian ideas. Thus even a superficial survey of Chartist literature will show just how indelible was the mark left by the *Twopenny Register* upon a generation of political radicals. In a sense too Cobbett's vision of a pastoral England peopled by free-born, hearty, independent cultivators will remain indestructible, drawing sustenance as it does from an ineradicable human craving for the permanence, the certainty, the order and the stability which rural self-sufficiency seems to offer.

N.W. THOMPSON

SELECTED WORKS

1802–36. *Cobbett's Political Register*. The paper was published throughout this period but the cheap, popular post-Napoleonic war edition of the paper referred to as *Cobbett's Twopenny Register* ran from 12 October 1816 until 29 July 1820.
1815. *Paper against Gold and Glory against Prosperity*. London.
1830. *Rural Rides in the Counties of Surrey, Kent, Sussex....* London.

BIBLIOGRAPHY

Beer, M. 1953. *A History of British Socialism*. 2 vols, London: Allen & Unwin.
Cole, G.D.H. 1947. *The Life of William Cobbett*. 3rd edn, London: Home & van Thal.
Cole, G.D.H. 1977. *A History of Socialist Thought*. 5 vols. Vol. 1, *Socialist Thought: The Forerunners, 1789–1850*. London: Macmillan.
Green, D. 1983. *Great Cobbett: The Noblest Agitator*. Oxford: Oxford University Press.
Sambrook, J. 1973. *William Cobbett*. London: Routledge & Kegan Paul.
Spater, G. 1982. *William Cobbett: The Poor Man's Friend*. 2 vols, Cambridge: Cambridge University Press.
Thompson, N.W. 1984. *The People's Science: The Popular Political Economy of Exploitation and Crisis*. Cambridge: Cambridge University Press.

Cobden, Richard (1804–1865).   Cobden led the campaign that repealed the Corn Laws in 1846, after which there was free trade in grain. The son of a Middlesex farmer, he sought his fortune in Manchester, became an owner of a mill that employed 2000 workers and was noted for excellence of its calicoes. At 35, he was a rich man.

His calling, however, was politics. After taking part in the successful effort to incorporate Manchester, he entered the movement against the Corn Laws in 1838. Until then it had been conducted by middle class radicals and various business interests, among them the Manchester Chamber of Commerce. Cobden, John Bright, and others like them wanted to enlarge the movement, make it bold and uncompromising. They were exasperated by the businessmen who so wanted to look respectable that they could not see where their interest lay. Thomas Tooke had said the same about the London merchants, when on their behalf he drafted the celebrated petition of 1820 for free trade and they were reluctant to sign it.

The militants of Manchester formed the National Anti-Corn Law League and agitated for free trade up and down the country. They become known as the Manchester School of Economics and were celebrated as arch advocates of laissez-faire. Actually they were a coalition of diverse interests that agreed on only one issue – repeal of the Corn Laws – and each did so for its particular reasons.

Cobden's reason was peace. He believed free trade would break down national barriers and give everyone a material interest in avoiding war. This was not an argument gotten up for the occasion but the expression of a view he had long held. When young he wrote two long tracts on foreign policy which denounced alliances among nations and political engagements of all kinds, decried the idea of a balance of power, was especially disapproving of colonies, then went on to extol free trade as the way to peace and its guarantor. Years later, after he and Bright had brought down the Corn Laws, he told him, 'I have always had an instinctive monomania against the system of foreign interference, protocolling, diplomatising, etc.'

That scarcely expressed the horror he had of violent action, even the suggestion of it. When the southern states of America seceded, he thought Lincoln was wrong in bringing the issue to battle although he had no sympathy with them (except their fondness for free trade). He was shocked by the massacres in India and was opposed to wars of independence and to revolution. He thought duelling was barbarous, was against capital punishment, objected to boxing, couldn't stand brass bands, and asked the Pope to prohibit bull fighting in Spain. He favoured free trade so long as its effect was peaceful, as he believed it usually was, but when he believed it was not he quickly put it aside. He opposed the sale of foreign bonds in the London market if the proceeds were to be used to buy arms. 'No free trade in cutting throats,' he said.

Pacifism, not laissez-faire, was Cobden's guiding principle; and he applied laissez-faire less to domestic than to foreign markets. He did not care for the Factory Acts but only spoke, never voted, against them. He approved of increasing the monopoly powers of the Bank of England and of regulating aspects of railway construction. He had no use for the New Poor Law, of which most economists of the day approved, and spoke derisively of McCulloch's 'usual dogmatism'. But he carefully read the latter's edition of the *Wealth of Nations* and wrote in the margins of the chapters that moved him. His notes are especially lively where Smith condemns the colonial policy of Great Britain. However, where he describes the operation of the invisible hand, the margins are quite untouched.

WILLIAM D. GRAMPP

See also CORN LAWS; MANCHESTER SCHOOL.

SELECTED WORKS

1835. *England, Ireland and America, by a Manchester manufacturer*. London.
1836. *Russia, by a Manchester manufacturer*. Edinburgh.
1849. *Speeches on peace, financial reform and other subjects*. London.

1867. *Political Writings*. London: Ridgeway.
1868. *Speeches on questions of public policy*. 2 vols, ed. J. Bright and J.E. Thorold Rogers, Oxford: Oxford University Press.

BIBLIOGRAPHY

Ritchie, J.E. 1865. *The Life of Richard Cobden*. London: Ward and Lock.
Ashworth, H. 1877. *Recollections of Richard Cobden, M.P., and the Anti-Corn Law League*. London: Cassell.
Morley, J. 1881. *The Life of Richard Cobden*. London: Fisher Unwin.

cobweb theorem. The persistent fluctuations of prices in selected agricultural markets have attracted the attention of economists from time to time, and the theory of the cobweb was developed to explain them. The theory is applicable to those markets where production takes time, where the quantity produced depends on the price anticipated at the time of sale and where supply at time of sale determines the actual market price.

One strand of the cobweb literature (the term was coined by Kaldor, 1934) concentrates on how expectations are formed and the effect of the price expectations mechanism on the stability of equilibrium. Cobweb theory was first developed under static price expectations where the predicted price equalled actual price in the last period. The cobweb theorem proved that the market price would (not) converge to (long run) equilibrium price if the absolute value of the price elasticity of demand was greater (smaller) than the price elasticity of supply. This stability condition was modified later as more sophisticated expectations models were adopted. Early articles by Tinbergen (1930), Ricci (1930) and Schultz (1930) appeared in German (see Waugh, 1964, for a review of this literature). Ezekiel's important article (1938) spells out in greater detail the conditions for convergence, divergence or perpetual oscillation and shows how cycles of different lengths could be generated under static expectations.

Why the theory was developed in the 1930s and not earlier is a bit of mystery, for recurring price cycles for some agricultural products had been reported by agricultural economists for some time. Economists may have been attracted to the cobweb theory in the 1930s because of the events of the Depression. A theory that explained both oscillation and long departures from stationary equilibrium was more attractive after the events of the Depression. The fact that Ezekiel's paper was reprinted in the 1944 American Economic Association volume on business cycles lends credence to this view.

The impression left by Ezekiel and subsequent contributors is that the cobweb theory is a valuable tool for explaining price cycles. Ezekiel was aware of the simplicity of static expectations and not unmindful of the importance of shocks on the demand and the supply sides of the market in causing aberrant price fluctuations (e.g. weather and the randomness of yields). Even so, agriculture economists, who were presumably more familiar with price fluctuations in agricultural markets, have been more prone to accept the theory, while theorists have given the theory more of a mixed reception.

The price expectations mechanism has undergone many refinements over the years. In 1958 Nerlove proposed the use of adaptive expectations. This suggestion is motivated by the findings of econometric studies which showed the price elasticity of demand to be less than the price elasticity of supply for many agricultural goods. Under these conditions the static expectations version of the cobweb model predicts a price cycle of increasing amplitude. However, the observed price cycles in agricultural markets showed no sign of being explosive. Nerlove attempted to reconcile theory with evidence and to show that convergence is possible under a broader set of conditions provided expectations are adaptive. During the 1930s the attractiveness of the cobweb model seemed to be in its ability to explain persistent or even explosive price cycles. By the late 1950s these were no longer attractive features, and Nerlove felt compelled to offer an explanation of why price cycles of increasing amplitude are not observed even when demand elasticities are smaller than supply elasticities. Waugh (1964) took a different tack and attempted to reconcile the theory with the evidence of stable price cycles by suggesting that the price elasticity of supply becomes smaller (larger) than the price elasticity of demand at prices well above (below) the long-run equilibrium price. Under this assumption, a stable price cycle will eventually be reached.

The length of the cobweb price cycle is determined by the length of the production process. If it takes one year to bring a fattened hog to the market, then the complete price cycle should take two years. At first, little attention and superficial explanations were given to explain why the predicted length is often shorter than the actual length of the price cycle. It was left to the critics to point out these discrepancies.

The critics are responsible for the other strand of the literature. They appeared early but were not very influential at first although their criticisms were ultimately given more weight. The critics questioned the rationality of using an arbitrary expectations mechanism by otherwise profit-maximizing agents, and pointed out that the theory implies that producers would expect to lose wealth if they entered and remained in an industry with a cobweb price cycle. In a perceptive article on the pig cycle in England, Coase and Fowler (1935) questioned the realism of static expectations. They showed that the price of a bacon (mature) pig less the cost of feeding for the next five months and less the cost of a feeder (young) pig, which would be stable in a competitive market if farmers had static expectations, fluctuated over time. Hence the empirical evidence contradicted the assumption of static expectations. They presented evidence that pig breeders reacted quickly to a change in expected profits, and this implied that the pig price cycle should be only two years instead of the observed four-year period. The fluctuation in the profits per pig were attributed to the difficulty of predicting both demand and foreign imports. The Coase–Fowler paper advanced, if only in faint outline, the essence of the rational expectations hypothesis which was to blossom some 35 years later. They hinted that anticipated prices would not be formed in a mechanistic way because profits would be higher the more accurate are the forecasts. Prediction errors were due to the difficulty of predicting shifts in demand and in foreign supply.

Buchanan's paper (1939) criticized the cobweb model because it implied that producers suffer aggregate losses over the price cycle when output is determined by the long-run supply curve. He pointed out that the theory was based on the dubious assumption of a continued supply of entrepreneurs standing ready to dissipate their capital. The critics were also disturbed by the ambiguity of whether the supply curve is of the short- or long-run variety, and the failure to clarify how the adjustment from the short-run to the long-run supply curve is made. These early criticisms and ambiguities aside, references to the cobweb theory continued to appear in textbooks.

Nerlove's paper (1958) briefly rekindled the controversy. His purpose was to resurrect the theory and show that it could explain price behaviour if adaptive expectations were employed. Mills (1961) criticized the use of adaptive and other autoregressive expectations mechanisms in the deterministic model because they implied a simple pattern of forecast errors that producers could detect, incorporate into their forecasts and thereby improve the accuracy of their price forecasts. While Nerlove's suggestion did rectify one limitation of the cobweb theory, it did not address the critical issue of why producers relied on any particular forecasting mechanism. Muth (1961) developed the implications of rational expectations for cobweb theory in his now famous paper. Muth postulated that expectations were the predictions of the economic structure of the market and incorporated all available information. Under certain conditions the predicted price equals the conditional expectation of price, given currently available information. Adaptive expectations can be rational only under special conditions, and the coefficient of adaptation is determined by the values of the slopes of the demand and supply curves.

The rational expectations formulation has powerful implications for cobweb theory. If the price forecasts incorporate all available information and are on average correct, then forecast errors will not be serially correlated and the pattern of past forecast errors cannot be used to improve the accuracy of the forecasts. Moreover, what is then left of the supposed ability of the cobweb theory to explain the cyclical behaviour of prices? Price fluctuations would have to be explained either by the cyclical pattern of exogenous variables or by the summation of random shocks (Slutsky, 1937). Muth's paper represents a frontal attack on the traditional cobweb model. He notes that the traditional model tends to predict a shorter price cycle than is observed and indicates that the rational expectations version predicts a longer price cycle.

Interest in the cobweb model has ebbed in recent years and few articles on it have appeared in the major journals. Economists have found it more rewarding to apply the rational expectations hypothesis to areas like monetary or business-cycle theory than to the study of particular markets, even though the analysis of markets with inventories raises issues that are just as difficult and subtle. The question of whether the cobweb does or does not explain price cycles has not really been resolved. Freeman (1971) has suggested that the traditional cobweb model explains cycles in the markets for lawyers, physicists and engineers. Tests of the rational expectations hypothesis have been suggested by Pashigian (1970) when expectations data are available and by Hoffman and Schmidt (1981) when expectations data are unavailable. So the methodology exists for distinguishing between the competing hypotheses. Few econometric tests have been made of the rational expectations hypothesis in markets where the assumptions of the cobweb model apply. The fundamental question of whether observed price cycles are better explained by systematic errors in price forecasts or by the cumulative impact of unpredictable shocks, has not as yet been definitively addressed.

B. PETER PASHIGIAN

See also ADAPTIVE EXPECTATIONS; RATIONAL EXPECTATIONS; STABILITY.

BIBLIOGRAPHY

Buchanan, N. 1939. A reconsideration of the cobweb theorem. *Journal of Political Economy* 47, February, 67–81.

Coase, R.H. and Fowler, R.F. 1935. Bacon production and the pig-cycle in Great Britain. *Economica* 2, May, 142–67.

Ezekiel, M. 1938. The cobweb theorem. *Quarterly Journal of Economics* 52, February, 255–80.

Freeman, R.B. 1971. *The Market for College-Trained Manpower*. Cambridge, Mass.: Harvard University Press.

Hoffman, D.L. and Schmidt, P. 1981. Testing the restrictions implied by the rational expectations hypothesis. *Journal of Econometrics* 15(2), February, 265–87.

Kaldor, N. 1934. A classificatory note on the determinateness of equilibrium. *Review of Economic Studies* 1, February, 122–36.

Mills, E.S. 1961. The use of adaptive expectations in stability analysis: comment. *Quarterly Journal of Economics* 75, May, 330–35.

Muth, J.F. 1961. Rational expectations and the theory of price movements. *Econometrica* 29, July, 315–35.

Nerlove, M. 1958. Adaptive expectations and cobweb phenomena. *Quarterly Journal of Economics* 72, May, 227–40.

Pashigian, B.P. 1970. Rational expectations and the cobweb theory. *Journal of Political Economy* 78(2), March–April, 338–52.

Slutsky, E.S. 1937. The summation of random causes as the source of cyclical processes. *Econometrica* 5, April, 105–46.

Waugh, F.V. 1964. Cobweb models. *Journal of Farm Economics* 46, November, 732–50.

Coddington, Alan (1941–1982). Born in Doncaster, Yorkshire, Coddington began his academic career with a degree in physics at Leeds University. After a year teaching mathematics in a school in York, he returned to university in that city for his D.Phil. in Economics. On taking his degree in 1966 he was appointed Assistant Lecturer in Economics at Queen Mary College, London, where he rose steadily to become Professor in 1980.

His theoretical work has three main strands: an early interest in the theory of bargaining, resulting in several articles and a much-respected book (1968); various aspects of environmental economics; and, continuing throughout his career, methodology and the history of 20th-century economic thought.

It is this last area which one immediately associates with Coddington's name. From his work on interpretations of Keynes, his characterizations of the 'neoclassical synthesis' of the textbooks as 'hydraulic Keynesianism' and of the 'fundamentalists' as 'Chapter 12 Keynesians' (referring to the chapter of the *General Theory* which discusses the precariousness of long-term expectations) have entered economists' everyday language.

His coverage of modern economic thought included not only Keynes, but also Hicks, Shackle, Friedman, Hahn, Malinvaud, Clower and Leijonhufvud. His article on Hicks (1979) and much of his work on Keynes, with an invaluable new chapter ('The Keynesian Dichotomy') were reworked into his posthumously published book, *Keynesian Economics: The Search for First Principles*, to which every reviewer responded first with enthusiasm, then with regret that they had been deprived by Coddington's suicide of the intellectual stimulus of debating with him.

VICTORIA CHICK

SELECTED WORKS

1968. *Theories of the Bargaining Process*. London: George Allen & Unwin.

1973. Bargaining as a decision process. *Swedish Journal of Economics* 75(4), December, 397–405.

1974a. The economics of conservation. In *Conservation in Practice*, ed. A. Warren and F.B. Goldsmith, New York: Wiley.

1974b. Creaking semaphore and beyond: a consideration of Shackle's *Epistemics and Economics. British Journal for the Philosophy of Science* 26(2), 151–63.

1975. The rationale of general equilibrium theory. *Economic Inquiry* 13(4), December, 539–58.

1978. Review of *The Theory of Unemployment Reconsidered* (Malinvaud). *Journal of Economic Literature* 16(3), September, 1012–18.

1979. Hicks' contribution to Keynesian economics. *Journal of Economic Literature* 17(3), September, 970–88.

1983. *Keynesian Economics: The Search for First Principles*. London: George Allen & Unwin.

codetermination and profit-sharing. The contract regulating labour employment by capitalist firms usually embodies three basic elements: a fixed money wage rate per unit of time, the subjection of workers to the employer's authority in the workplace and the short-term nature of the hiring commitment. Explicit or implicit departures from this standard can be observed; they are the result of individual or collective negotiations in the labour market, which balance out their advantages and disadvantages for each party, either directly or through accompanying changes in other parameters of the labour contract. Government legislation and economic policy set limits or fix actual values for some of these parameters and stipulations; within these bounds the market determines the rest.

Long tenure, i.e. the employee's option on continued employment, like all options has a value (for the employee) and a cost (for the employer), which is matched by correspondingly lower pay than that associated with shorter-term contracts. The partial and delayed indexation of money wages to a consumer price index for the period between successive rounds of wage negotiations favours employees when inflation decelerates and employers when it accelerates. Piece-rates, i.e. wages related to *individual* performance, give employees a short term reward (penalty) for effort supply higher (lower) than that which otherwise could be contractually fixed, as well as automatic participation in productivity gains due to learning by doing, subject to a ratchet effect on the determination of subsequent rates; employers save on the costs of recruitment, supervision, and contractual enforcement, lose short term productivity gains but can use more fully their contractual power in exacting effort and speeding up progress when rates are reviewed. Government policy influences directly or indirectly market choice, in the pursuit of policy targets such as distributive fairness, employment, price stability, efficiency and growth.

The same combination of private interest and government policy determines the degree of workers' participation in decision-making processes (codetermination) and in the performance (profit-sharing) of enterprises (for a bibliographical survey, see Bartlett and Uvalic, 1985).

CODETERMINATION. Employee participation in enterprise decision-making in cooperatives amounts to full entrepreneurship through participation in assemblies, the election of representative organs and involvement in the appointment of managers. In other enterprises it takes the form of access to information and right to consultation, participation in decisions on conditions and organization of work and on internal social questions, through a workers' council or similar organ; right up to the minority (or even parity) participation and vote in the board of directors of a joint-stock company (as in German *Mitbestimmung*; see Nutzinger, 1983) with a possibility of influencing decisions about employment, the level and structure of investment and other crucial factors were the other board members to be sufficiently divided.

The effects of codetermination are three-fold:

(i) The reduction in labour disutility obtainable when workers have a say in the division of labour and work organization, since enterprises may neglect workers' preferences about the specific uses to which their labour is put or at any rate respond to the needs of a hypothetical average worker: if the number of enterprises is not large enough, workers' control is necessary to reduce disutility and alienation. The effect of workers' control on productivity has an indeterminate sign (Pagano, 1984).

(ii) The reduction of the number and intensity of conflicts in the workplace in general and, in particular, the more likely acceptance by workers of unpopular decisions by management, when workers receive detailed and credible information and participate in decision making, identifying themselves partly with the enterprise and above all lengthening their time horizon in view of continued participation in decision-making (Aoki, 1984; Cable, 1984; Fitzroy and Mueller, 1984). Of course conflicts within the firm are made more tractable by the *introduction* of codetermination but *afterwards* are bound to reappear over time (Furobotn, 1985); also there remains a basic conflict between employed and unemployed' workers which may even be exacerbated by the employment protection policies conceivably encouraged by those already employed in their exercise of codetermination.

(iii) The greater correspondence between workers' powers and responsibilities, codetermination being the counterpart of workers' exposure to enterprise risks. The very fact that workers, unlike capitalists, cannot diversify between different enterprises when selling their services exposes them to an employment and income risk which induces them to make a claim to control; a claim which up to a point the employer may prefer to accept instead of granting higher wages or longer tenure.

PROFIT-SHARING. In pre-capitalist systems workers' participation in the results of their enterprise took the forms – now little used – of sharecropping in agriculture and of sliding scales (indexing wage rates to the price of the product), for instance, in English coalmines. In modern capitalism such participation – for which 'profit-sharing' is a shorthand label – takes the form of cooperatives' net revenue sharing, production prizes based on group or overall performance, participation in gross/net revenue/profit, share options, participation in investment funds and pay increases graded according to productivity growth.

The effects of an element of profit-sharing in labour earnings are three-fold:

(i) An expected increase in labour productivity. This is not due to workers gaining from the product of *individual* extra-effort (as in the case of piece-rates) since each of n workers employed will only get at most $1/n$ of the product of his own extra-effort (Samuelson, 1977) and on the contrary may *reduce* effort if he can, being exposed to at most only $1/n$ of the output loss from his own lower effort. The productivity gain can be expected from workers, costlessly to themselves, gaining from intelligent and effective use of any given individual level of effort, from cooperating with other workers and management and from monitoring and supervising each other's effort, efficiency and cooperation (Reich and Devine, 1981; Fitzroy and Kraft, 1985).

(ii) Cyclical flexibility of labour earnings and therefore greater stability of profit levels and rates. Employment will not be stabilized during the cycle by labour earnings flexibility obtained through profit-sharing because the marginal cost of labour to firms – i.e. the fixed component of pay – does not vary automatically. Workers, who are normally risk-averse, will prefer a fixed sum of money to a profit-sharing formula of equivalent amount while employers, who are normally risk-lovers, may or may not prefer greater stability of profit rates (according to their actual attitude to risk and the alternative cost of reducing risk through diversification) to the point of granting higher average earnings on a profit-sharing formula than a fixed wage to mutual advantage. Therefore profit-sharing is favoured primarily in risky ventures; otherwise on this ground alone profit-sharing would be favoured by firms only in a recession (when workers would only accept it as an alternative to a permanent wage cut) and by workers only during a boom (when firms would only accept it as an alternative to a permanent wage increase).

(iii) Higher level of labour employment, for a given level of labour earnings with respect to a fixed wage regime, due to the lower marginal cost of labour to profit-sharing firms. Vanek finds that higher employment will be associated with higher aggregate income, lower prices (because of higher output), higher export volume and domestic import substitution (with undetermined effects on the balance of payments depending on price and income elasticities), lower after-tax and after-labour-share profits and higher labour-share in national income (Vanek, 1965).

Rediscovering Vanek's macroeconomic benefits from profit-sharing (though not its impact on net profits and relative income shares), Weitzman claims that these benefits are neglected by individual firms, as in other instances of 'public goods', 'externalities' and 'market failures', therefore necessitating public policy measures (Weitzman, 1983, 1984). However, there is no reason why a firm should object to granting a given increase in earnings under the guise of a profit-share instead of an equivalent fixed amount unless that represents forced insurance against profit variability; and why workers – at least at the level of nation-wide collective bargaining – should not take into account the potential employment and price stability benefits of this formula and offset them against the greater variability of their earnings in between negotiations, due to both cyclical factors and random factors affecting their firm's performance.

Contrary to Weitzman's belief, in fact, profit-sharing is not absolutely superior to wage contracts. For workers, profit-sharing transforms the probability distribution of uncertain employment at a fixed and certain income into a probability distribution of employment with a higher mean (because of lower marginal cost of labour) but no less variable over the cycle, at a more variable income (both over the cycle and for other factors affecting dispersion of enterprise performance) and at a higher (real) mean. For firms it transforms a more into a less variable probability distribution of money profit rates around the same mean (or a lower mean if workers are protected from actual losses; the effect on real profit rates depending on accounting conventions and choice of *numéraire*). In the pursuit of greater employment and price stability of course a government may grant tax relief to shared profits, just as effectively and with just as much reason as it may subsidize the marginal cost of labour to firms under a wage regime. Otherwise there is no reason why profit-sharing should be forced upon unwilling workers and firms by well-meaning reformers, beyond the extent they are prepared to consider in their market transactions. These propositions are developed further below (see also Nuti, 1985 and 1986).

INTERDEPENDENCE BETWEEN CODETERMINATION AND PROFIT-SHARING. The respective effects of codetermination and of profit-sharing are not independent. The productivity increase expected from profit-sharing can be raised by workers having collective discretion over the organization of labour; or the productivity fall which might derive from workers' control over labour organization might be tempered by profit-sharing. Greater variability of earnings – during the cycle and across firms – strengthens under profit-sharing the case for codetermination already present in workers' exposure to employment risk in the wage régime. The income premium required by risk-averse workers to replace some of their fixed wage with a variable profit-share can be reduced by their involvement in the decisions which expose them to income variability in the first place. The reduction in conflict frequency and intensity expected from codetermination is enhanced by profit-sharing because for each worker it partly internalizes the conflict between 'us' and 'them' otherwise manifested and enacted externally; in any case it is a requirement of any effective incentive system that power and responsibility should not be separated.

The quantification of degrees of 'codetermination' and to a lesser extent of 'profit-sharing' raises conceptual and practical difficulties (though see Cable, 1985). By and large we can observe a certain correlation between the two: both codetermination and profit-sharing are zero in the pure capitalist enterprises and unity in cooperatives and other forms of partnerships of capital and labour; minor forms of codetermination (or conversely of profit-sharing) tend to go hand in hand with minor forms of profit-sharing (or of codetermination); a high degree of one without the other is virtually unknown.

The combination of 100 per cent codetermination (= self-determination) and 100 per cent profit-sharing (= net revenue sharing) obtained in cooperative firms, according to conventional literature, is subject to economic stimuli of a somewhat 'perverse' kind. These are primarily: restrictive employment (= membership) policies; destabilizing and Pareto-inefficient reactions (or at best inelasticities) to price changes and technical progress; a low propensity towards self-financed investment (Ward, 1958; Vanek, 1970). In empirical studies of cooperative firms there is no incontrovertible evidence of these phenomena, which are probably partly offset by other economic (job security, growth-mindedness, etc.) and non-economic stimuli; but there is a presumption that – albeit in a weak form – the same tendencies and, in particular, employment restrictive policies might be associated with codetermination. We can also presume that workers' eagerness to press and ability to assert demands for codetermination, as in the case of other demands, increase as unemployment diminishes. Hence the employment-generating benefits of profit-sharing can be at least partly offset by the restrictive employment policies possibly associated with codetermination brought about by profit-sharing and by greater proximity to full employment. Recent empirical studies suggest modest but sizeable improvements in economic performance from codetermination and profit-sharing (Cable and Fitzroy, 1980; Estrin et al., 1984) when and where they occur but there may have been costs that remained unobserved and, in any case, the improvements cannot be generalized.

MARKETS AND POLICY. Degrees of codetermination and profit-sharing may well be regarded as desirable on 'political' (as opposed to 'purely technical') grounds such as equity and social peace. They may also be the best policy instruments in the pursuit of public objectives such as stability, employment and growth, in the sense of having the least cost in terms of public funds or offering the most attractive trade-offs between alternative targets. Otherwise, as Jensen and Meckling argue for codetermination and one can also argue for profit-sharing, if it is truly beneficial to both stockholders and labour no laws would be needed to force firms to undertake reorganization (1979, p. 474). Yet renewed and insistent calls for public intervention in favour of *profit-sharing without codetermination* have been put forward by M.L. Weitzman in recent writings (1983, 1984, 1985a, 1985b, 1986). The proposal has been enthusiastically received in certain academic and political circles and hailed as a breakthrough in the specialist press.

Weitzman's novelty, the foundation for this renewed fascination with profit-sharing, is the rash assertion of two propositions. First, that long-run full employment equilibrium under profit-sharing is associated with permanent but non-inflationary excess demand for labour, which cushions off the economy from contractionary shocks and gives new dignity and status to labour. In adman's language we are told, for instance:

> A share system has the hard-boiled property of excess demand for labour, which turns into a tenacious natural enemy of stagnation and inflation. The share economy possesses a built-in, three-pronged assault on unemployment, stagnant output, and the tendency of prices to rise. This is a hard combination to beat (Weitzman, 1984, p. 144).

Second, that even in the short run the share economy can achieve and maintain full employment. For instance:

> The share system, ..., has a strong built-in mechanism that automatically stabilizes the economy at full employment, even before the long-run tendencies have had the chance to assert their dominance. ... a share economy has the direct 'strong force' of positive excess demand for labor ... pulling it towards full employment. ... the strong force of the share system will maintain full employment (Weitzman, 1984, p. 97).

Were these claims well founded an enlightened government possessing these truths would be justified in forcing profit-sharing on to a yet unconverted and disbelieving public, thus achieving full employment, price stability and growth at a stroke. Unfortunately miracles exist only for the uninformed and the faithful, but do not bear the weight of sober scrutiny. First, excess demand for labour at full employment cannot be sustained and can only be a temporary disequilibrium. Second, permanent excess demand for labour is inconsistent with lack of codetermination, and when this is introduced restrictive employment policies will alter the picture. Third, and most important, there is no guarantee that full employment can necessarily be achieved. Without these benefits the alleged 'public good' merits of the sharing contract disappear.

EXCESS DEMAND FOR LABOUR AT FULL EMPLOYMENT. Suppose that the share economy reaches a state of full employment. Weitzman maintains the presence and persistence of excess demand for labour in long-run equilibrium on the basis of the following argument:

$$\text{labour total pay} = \text{marginal revenue value of labour productivity at full employment} \quad (1)$$

because long-run equilibrium must be full-employment equilibrium and because of the underlying homomorphism of profit-sharing and wage contracts in long-run equilibrium (Weitzman, 1983). By definition of profit-sharing

$$\text{labour total pay} = \text{fixed pay} + \text{share of net profits} \quad (2)$$

where fixed pay is greater than or equal to zero, and the share of net profits is greater than zero. It follows from (1) and (2) that:

$$\text{marginal revenue value of labour productivity at full employment} > \text{fixed pay} = \text{marginal cost of labour to firms} \quad (3)$$

i.e. firms will wish to employ more workers than are available. A permanent state of excess demand for labour will exist, which will protect full employment from contractionary shocks, as long as shocks do not reduce the marginal revenue

value of labour productivity at full employment below the fixed element of pay, in which case the maintenance of over-full employment requires a reduction of the fixed element without cutting earnings as much as necessary in the wage regime.

There are three grounds for refuting this syllogism. First, firms should be well aware that, whatever their pay formula, they can only attract workers by offering the going rate for labour total pay and should regard this, and not the fixed element of pay, as marginal cost of labour. If firms behave as they should, excess demand for labour disappears.

Second, if firms regard the fixed element of pay as the marginal cost of labour they should find its being lower than the marginal revenue value of labour productivity disquieting enough to experiment with alternative combinations of pay parameters without raising total pay above labour productivity. Risk-averse workers preferring fixed pay to potentially variable earnings of identical mean, risk-neutral or risk-loving employers will reduce their labour cost by raising the fixed element of pay at the expense of workers' profit share; even without taking into account attitude to risk it is plausible to expect managers to experiment with alternative pay parameters and not to rest until they have equalized their marginal cost and marginal value of labour, i.e.

$$\text{marginal revenue value of labour productivity at full employment} = \text{fixed pay} \quad (3')$$

which can only be reconciled with the definition (2) of a profit sharing contract if the workers' share of net profit is zero: with the sharing component of earnings the 'share economy' also vanishes and reverts to the fixed wage economy without any excess demand for labour.

Third, workers perceiving excess demand for labour are likely to reduce their supply of effort and/or increase turnover – as they do in the only known instances of permanent excess demand for labour, i.e. Soviet-type economies (see Lane, 1985) – if not right down to the point where their marginal product equals fixed pay at least as close to that level as they are allowed to get by monitoring and supervising arrangements. This is another mechanism which can reduce and eliminate excess demand for labour if it occurred.

CODETERMINATION AND EMPLOYMENT. The lack of codetermination is an explicit precondition of Weitzman's claims (though not of Vanek's, who does not claim full and over-full employment of labour and does not need this restriction). (In the earlier version of his analysis Weitzman takes a sanguine view of the possibility of keeping codetermination in check: '... the bargaining power of labor unions is not a natural right ...' (1984a, p. 109); '... the decisions on output, employment and pricing are essentially made by capitalists' in his model (p. 132); 'I can see no *compelling* reason why a capitalist firm should be more prone to allow increased worker participation in company decision making under one contract form than under another' (p. 133, emphasis added). His latest version is more open-minded: workers' participation in decision-making becomes not only possible but desirable as 'a question of justice and practical politics' as long as it excludes *employment* decisions (1986). It is extremely hard to imagine *any* major decision, in which workers might have a voice, that would *not* directly or indirectly also affect employment. Either this limitation or workers' participation would have to give way.) We know that it is possible to exclude workers from codetermination in the presence of persistent unemployment; such exclusion might be difficult at full employment, and it would certainly be very difficult with excess demand for labour, but the *persistent* state of excess demand for labour postulated by Weitzman should make the exclusion of codetermination, whether or not employment questions are directly involved, impossible without an authoritarian or military regime. This is not a moral, or legal, or legalistic proposition; it is a question of 'practical politics'.

Once workers have a say on output, employment and pricing and related questions (investment, innovation, etc.) they will try and resist the very possibility of dilution of their own shares just as shareholders usually resist the dilution of share capital; for better or worse they are likely to adopt, or are tempted to adopt, other things being equal, restrictive employment policies in the possibly misguided and self-defeating purpose of raising or maintaining individual earnings. This is not a case *against* profit-sharing, but an argument for not expecting that over-full employment, if achievable, can be sustained necessarily, i.e. an argument against the plausibility of Weitzman's model (see Nuti, 1985).

PROFIT-SHARING AND FULL EMPLOYMENT. The foundation of Weitzman's claims on behalf of profit-sharing is the assertion that, even in the short run, the share economy 'delivers' full employment of labour. ('Resources are always fully utilised in a share system' (Weitzman, 1985b, p. 949); real world frictions, inertias and imperfections are mentioned only to be exorcised, and to reassert the full employment claim at least as a 'natural tendency' (p. 949, p. 952) of the share economy which, we are told, 'delivers full employment' (1986); see also Weitzman, 1984, p. 97.)

For a share economy to 'deliver' full employment three necessary conditions must be satisfied simultaneously:

(i) the physical marginal productivity of labour at full employment must be positive;

(ii) the marginal revenue obtained by firms from that physical marginal product of labour must also be positive;

(iii) the fixed element of pay in share contracts must be flexible enough to fall down to the level of the marginal revenue product of labour at full employment, positive as it may be.

The first condition rules out the possibility of *classical* unemployment, i.e. due to lack of equipment, land or other resources in the quantities necessary to employ all workers efficiently. Yet, after over a decade of deep and protracted recession, deindustrialization and decapitalization, even advanced industrialized countries such as Britain or France today cannot be expected to be able to satisfy this condition as a matter of course, not to speak of Italy or, say, Spain, or of less developed countries. In his formal model Weitzman (1985b) postulates constant physical productivity of labour; this is a plausible assumption *up to near-full capacity* but Weitzman gives no reason why the capacity should be constrained by labour instead of other resources.

The second condition rules out the possibility of *Keynesian* unemployment, i.e. aggregate demand constraints making the marginal product of labour valueless before full employment is reached. Even if the first condition was satisfied, imperfect competition – which in all of Weitzman's work provides the environment in which the share contract is to operate – provides an excellent reason why firms might not give to additional physical products a positive value. Weitzman can assert that '... a "pure" sharing system not having any base wage would possess an infinite demand for labor' (1985b, p. 944), which implies positive marginal revenue for any level of output, because of the very special assumption that the elasticity of demand is *greater than unity* (p. 938), which

makes demand curves absurdly and indefinitely elastic even for imperfectly competitive firms. The proposition cannot have any claim to general validity.

Even if demand for labour *were* to be infinite in the pure share economy, i.e. with a zero fixed element of pay, it would not necessarily be infinite, or even large enough to reach full employment, for a positive fixed element of pay. Weitzman neglects the determination of the relative weight of the fixed and variable components of the share contract but recognizes the impossibility of total dependence of pay on profit; yet he takes for granted, for no good reason, that the fixed element of pay can be compressed down to whatever is the full employment marginal revenue product of labour, which we do not even know for sure is positive.

It is a non-controversial feature of the sharing contract, known from Vanek (1965), that the replacement of part of the wage by a profit-share of identical average cost to firms will lead to greater employment, higher output and lower prices – in the absence of large enough adverse feedback on investment (which Weitzman recognizes as a possible short run effect of the introduction of sharing) and in the absence of large enough feedbacks of accompanying codetermination on firms' employment policy. But there is a world of difference between higher employment and full employment and another world of difference between full employment and persistent over-full employment; no serious work can afford to switch indifferently and cavalierly from one to the other.

SHARE CONTRACTS AND PUBLIC GOOD. If the share economy could really guarantee, as general and necessary consequences of its establishment, the achievement and stability of full employment without adverse drawbacks there would be a case for public policy treating the share contract as 'public good' to be pressed on an unenlightened public still largely unaware of potential benefits, as in the case of safe vaccination against infectious disease. The case for the share economy would not be much greater than that for enforced wage flexibility, which would also guarantee full employment and stability under the same circumstances. A downward flexible wage would not deliver excess demand for labour but this is a questionable achievement and would not be necessary to absorb contractionary shocks if wages were flexible; downward flexible wages would also require a greater fall of money earnings to achieve full employment in the short run and may be more likely to bring about adverse effects on aggregate demand; otherwise there is little to choose between the two, except for the lower degree of public resistance that can be expected for share contracts with respect to wage cuts.

In fact if the share contract could really deliver and maintain full employment, while a wage economy could not, the greater variability of workers' earnings associated with profit-sharing over the cycle would disappear and, between firms, could be eliminated by labour freely redeploying itself at will across labour-hungry firms; the variability of employment would also disappear; workers would have *de facto* free access to a job in any firm of their choice, as in forgotten utopias (Hertzka, 1890; Chilosi, 1986). Thus it could be said that '... a move towards profit sharing represents an unambiguous improvement for the working class' (Weitzman, 1985b, p. 954). But we have seen that profit-sharing cannot guarantee full (let alone over-full) employment. Without full employment, the higher variability of earnings associated with profit-sharing remains and it may or may not be compensated by the higher mean value of employment probability and perhaps real earnings. Outside over-full employment, in fact, the share economy is just as vulnerable to contractionary shocks as the wage economy because, in spite of flexibility of labour earnings in the share regime, the marginal cost of labour to firms (which is the fixed component of workers' pay) remains constant just as does the wage. Thus the higher stability of employment to be found in Japan simply cannot be the result of profit-sharing, as Weitzman firmly believes, seeing that Japan has never known a state of over-full employment; higher employment stability would require workers' shares in GNP instead of their enterprise's profits.

The fact that the adoption of a share contract, without the guarantee of stable full employment, has a cost for workers, eliminates the necessity, but not the possibility, of the share contract having 'public good' features. A vaccine may be somewhat unsafe, its degree of unsafety acceptable to all if vaccination is universal and all benefit from reduced exposure to infection, yet individuals benefit from free-riding strategies and the enforcement of universal vaccination as 'public good' can still be beneficial to all. If labour contracts were negotiated exclusively at the level of individuals or firms the external beneficial effects of the share contract might be lost from sight; but these external benefits – unlike the case of genuine 'public goods' – are completely internalized in nationwide negotiations between associations of employers and employees. Admittedly the benefits, such as they are, of profit-sharing may be still unknown to the public at large and deserve wider publicity. But it is counterproductive to foist a good medicine on a sceptical public by claiming that it can guarantee longevity or immortality. At the first signs that such excessive claims are unfounded it may be thrown away despite its real lesser benefits.

D.M. NUTI

BIBLIOGRAPHY

Aoki, M. 1984. *The Co-operative Game Theory of the Firm*. Oxford: Oxford University Press.
Bartlett, W. and Uvalic, M. 1985. Bibliography on labour-managed firms and employee participation. European University Institute Working Paper, No. 85/198, Florence.
Cable, J.R. 1984. Employee participation and firm performance: a prisoners' dilemma framework. European University Institute Working Paper, No. 84/126, Florence.
Cable, J.R. and Fitzroy, F.R. 1980. Productive efficiency, incentives and employee participation: some preliminary results for West Germany. *Kyklos* 33(2), 100–121.
Chilosi, A. 1986. The right to employment principle and self-managed market socialism: a historical account and an analytical appraisal of some old ideas. European University Institute Working Paper, No. 86/214, Florence.
Estrin, S., Jones, D.C. and Svejnar, J. 1984. The varying nature, importance and productivity effects of worker participation: evidence for contemporary producer cooperatives in industrialised Western societies. CIRIEC Working Paper, No. 84/04, University of Liège.
Fitzroy, F.R. and Kraft, K. 1985. Profitability and profit-sharing. *Discussion Papers of the International Institute of Management*, WZB, Berlin, IIM/IP 85–41, December.
Fitzroy, F.R. and Mueller, D.C. 1984. Cooperation and conflict in contractual organisations. *Quarterly Review of Economics and Business* 24(4), Winter, 24–49.
Furobotn, E.G. 1985. Codetermination, productivity gains and the economics of the firm. *Oxford Economic Papers* 37, 22–39.
Hertzka, T. 1980. *Freiland. Ein soziales Zukunftsbild*. Dresden: Pierson. English translation, London: Chatto & Windus, 1891.
Jensen, M.C. and Meckling, W.H. 1979. Rights and production functions: an application to labor-managed firms and codetermination. *Journal of Business* 52, October, 469–506.
Lane, D. (ed.) 1985. *Employment and Labour in the USSR*. London: Harvester Press.
Nuti, D.M. 1985. The share economy: plausibility and viability of Weitzman's model. European University Institute Working Paper,

No. 85/194, Florence; Italian translation in *Politica ed Economia* 1, January 1986.
Nuti, D.M. 1986. A rejoinder to Weitzman. (In Italian.) *Politica ed Economia* 4, April.
Nutzinger, H.G. 1983. Empirical research into German codetermination: problems and perspectives. *Economic Analysis and workers' Management* 17(4), 361–82.
Pagano, U. 1984. Welfare, productivity and self-management. European University Institute Working Paper, No. 84/128, Florence.
Reich, M. and Devine, J. 1981. The microeconomics of conflict and hierarchy in capitalist production. *Review of Radical Political Economics* 12(4), Winter, 27–45.
Samuelson, P.A. 1977. Thoughts on profit-sharing. *Zeitschrift für die Gesamte Staatswissenschaft* (special issue on profit-sharing).
Vanek, J. 1965. Workers' profit participation, unemployment and the Keynesian equilibrium. *Weltwirtschaftliches Archiv* 94(2), 206–14.
Vanek, J. 1970. *The General Theory of Labor-Managed Market Economies*. Ithaca: Cornell University Press.
Ward, B.M. 1958. The firm in Illyria: market syndicalism. *American Economic Review* 48(4), 566–89.
Weitzman, M.L. 1983. Some macroeconomic implications of alternative compensation systems. *Economic Journal* 93(4), 763–83.
Weitzman, M.L. 1984. *The Share Economy*. Cambridge, Mass.: Harvard University Press.
Weitzman, M.L. 1985a. Profit sharing as macroeconomic policy. *American Economic Review, Papers and Proceedings 75(2), May, 41–5.*
Weitzman, M.L. 1985b. The simple macroeconomics of profit sharing. *American Economic Review* 75(5), December, 937–53.
Weitzman, M.L. 1986. Reply to Nuti. (In Italian.) *Politica ed Economia* 4, April.

Coghlan, Timothy (1855–1926). Coghlan was the son of a poor family in Sydney, and obtained his education through scholarships. Like several other distinguished economists, his original career was in engineering, in this case civil engineering, which led to his taking an interest in statistics. New South Wales had been established as a penal colony under military rule, and therefore right from the colony's beginning people and governments were accustomed to statistical enumeration much more thorough than in the rest of the world. Coghlan was appointed statistician by the colonial government, and produced over a long period of years a large output of excellent statistical papers.

Before Federation in 1901, there were six separate colonial governments in Australia, often pursuing different objectives. This was particularly the case in the highly controversial matter of free trade or protection. The two most populous colonies were Victoria and New South Wales. Victoria had attracted a large population through the abundance of alluvial gold in its riverbeds. This was soon exhausted; and deep mining fell far short of taking its place. The Victorian Government considered that the only way to provide employment to make up for the decline in mining was to establish manufacturing industries under high tariff protection. New South Wales (which admittedly had not had such a destabilizing gold rush) was determined to adhere to free trade, with the object of promoting agricultural and pastoral production. Some of Coghlan's writings were polemic, strongly stating the free trade case. In the *Wealth and Progress of New South Wales*, in succeeding editions, the available statistics of the colony were assembled, pointing to a superior rate of growth to that of Victoria.

Coghlan was fifty years ahead of his time in making national product estimations for New South Wales. Without any experience in any other country to guide him, he devised methods which would pass muster today. His work however was not followed up. There was no further estimate of Australian national product until the study by Benham in the 1920s, using less precise methods, and then another gap until Sir John Crawford and I prepared a study in 1937.

Coghlan prepared a series of publications on a more extensive basis, *The Seven Colonies of Australasia* (i.e. including New Zealand; it was thought at the time New Zealand might enter the Australian federation).

The free trade case was lost in 1908, when Victoria, with its allies in some other states, persuaded the new federal government to impose highly protective tariffs.

Coghlan was posted to London, where he performed most of the duties (but without the title, which went to the political head) of Agent General for New South Wales. The duties were varied and responsible, including the raising of large sums in loans.

In partial retirement, Coghlan embarked upon a *magnum opus, Labour and Industry in Australia*, which was published in England in 1918, giving a most full and detailed account of its subject, but illuminated by stories and anecdotes which make it readable.

COLIN G. CLARK

SELECTED WORKS
1893. *Sheep and Wool in New South Wales, with History and Growth of the Pastoral Industry of the Colony as Regards Both These Items of Production*. Sydney: Potter.
1898a. *Notes on the Financial Aspect of Australian Federation*, n.t.p. Sydney: W.A. Gullick.
1898b. *Notes on the Financial Aspect of Australian Federation. The Position of Tasmania and Western Australia*. Sydney: W.A. Gullick.
1898c. *Notes on the Financial Aspect of Australian Federation. The Incidence of the Federal Tariff*. Sydney: W.A. Gullick.
1898d. *Tables to Accompany Notes on Financial Aspects of Federation*. Sydney: W.A. Gullick.
1898e. *A Statistical Account of the Seven Colonies of Australasia 1861–1897*. Sydney: W.A. Gullick.
1902. *The Progress of Australasia in the Nineteenth Century*. London, Philadelphia: The Linscott Publishing Company.
1903a. (With T.T. Ewing.) *The Progress of Australia in the Century*. London, Edinburgh: W. & R. Chambers Ltd.; Philadelphia, Detroit: The Bradley-Garretson Co., Ltd.
1903b. *The Decline in the Birth-Rate of New South Wales and Other Phenomena of Childbirth: an essay in statistics*. Sydney: W.A. Gullick.
1918. *Labour and Industry in Australia, from the First Settlement in 1788 to the establishment of the Commonwealth in 1901*. London, New York: Oxford University Press.

write for the Cambridge Economic Handbooks, of which he was then editor.

In common with most of the leading British economists of her generation she became a temporary civil servant soon after the outbreak of World War II, serving first at the Ministry of Food and later at the Board of Trade when questions of postwar reconstruction were rising to the top of the economic policy agenda of government. In 1945 she returned to Cambridge as lecturer in the Faculty of Economics and Politics and as Director of Studies in Economics at Newnham College, to which she had been elected a Fellow in 1939 and of which she was to become an active Principal in 1954. Soon after retiring from her university post in 1972 she was elected to the Cambridge City Council, where for a decade and a half she has devoted her formidable energy and talent as an applied economist to local government problems.

Ruth Cohen's reputation among contemporary economists has rested largely on her capacity to offer forceful, direct and perceptive oral comments on issues of current economic debate – theoretical as well as applied. This is the kind of salutary influence on the discipline that is rarely acknowledged in print, except in the occasional footnote. In the event, however, her typically terse intervention in the torrid capital theory debates that raged in the learned journals of the 1950s and 1960s has been duly credited with having triggered off a spate of articles in the capital-switching and capital-reversing phase of the debate – a phase which eventually ended in general agreement that her observation had revealed what some would describe as a fatal flaw, and others an awkward anomaly, in the orthodox neo-classical theory of the production function. To have stimulated this degree of consensus in a theoretical controversy which has carried unusually heavy methodological and ideological undertones is no mean achievement.

PHYLLIS DEANE

SELECTED WORKS
1936. *A History of Milk Prices*. Oxford: Agricultural Economics Research Institute.
1940. *The Economics of Agriculture*. Cambridge: Cambridge University Press.
BIBLIOGRAPHY
Harcourt, G.C. 1972. *Some Cambridge Controversies in the Theory of Capital*. Cambridge: Cambridge University Press.
Johnson, H.G. 1978. Ruth Cohen: a neglected contributor to contemporary capital theory. In E.S. Johnson, *The Shadow of Keynes*, Oxford: Blackwell.

Cohen, Ruth Louisa (born 1906).   Ruth Cohen is one of the select band of leading professional economists whose importance is measured more by her emphatically common-sense influence on colleagues and pupils than by the length of her publications list. Born in 1906, she entered Newnham College, Cambridge, in 1926 to read for the Economics Tripos within a Faculty that contained a galaxy of outstanding individuals and included such stars as Keynes, Pigou, Robertson, Maurice Dobb and Piero Sraffa. She had already developed a research interest in agricultural economics when, after spending a couple of years as Commonwealth Fund Fellow at Stanford and Cornell, she joined the Oxford University Agricultural Economics Research Institute in 1933. For the next six years she pursued that specialization and completed two well-received books – one an analytical and statistical history of milk prices and the other a text on the economics of agriculture which J.M. Keynes invited her to

Cohen Stuart, Arnold Jacob (1855–1921).   Born in The Hague, Cohen Stuart was an engineer who took up the challenge put forward by the famous Dutch economist and politician N.G. Pierson to study the mathematical foundations of what we would call nowadays an optimal tax structure. His thesis (Cohen Stuart, 1889) has been reprinted in part (Musgrave and Peacock, 1958).

The international attention to Cohen Stuart's exposition is due to the thorough discussion by F.Y. Edgeworth in his article on the pure theory of taxation (Edgeworth, 1897). Following a lead by Pierson, Cohen Stuart studied the impact of the principle that each taxpayer should sacrifice an equal proportion of the total utility which he derives from material resources. He proved that it depends on the decrease of marginal utility of income, whether the income taxed above a certain minimum will be progressive, regressive or proportional in relation to the level of income. Cohen Stuart argues that in most practical cases a modest progressive tax rate will emerge.

Although based on old-fashioned concepts of measurable utility, Cohen Stuart's contribution to the analysis of the optimal income tax is part of the modern theory of optimal taxation (Mirrlees, 1971) and therefore comparable to Cournot's role in the development of the theory of oligopoly.

ARNOLD HEERTJE

SELECTED WORKS

1889. *Bijdrage tot de theorie der progressieve inkomstenbelasting*. The Hague: Nijhoff.

BIBLIOGRAPHY

Edgeworth, F.Y. 1897. *Papers Relating to Political Economy*, Vol. II. London: Macmillan, 1925.
Mirrlees, J.A. 1971. An exploration in the theory of optimum income Taxation. *Review of Economic Studies* 38, 175–208.
Musgrave, R.A. and Peacock, A.T. (eds) 1958. *Classics in the Theory of Public Finance*. London: Macmillan.

Cohn, Gustav (1840–1919). Lecturer (*Privatdozent*) at the University of Heidelberg in 1869, Cohn was appointed professor of economics at the Riga Polytechnic Institute (1869–72). After spending some years in England he was appointed to a chair of economics at the Zürich Polytechnic Institute in 1875 and then in Göttingen in 1884. There he lived up to his death in 1919.

Cohn is noted for his pioneering contributions to the theory and policy of transportation and public finance. In his *Untersuchungen* (1874–5), *Eisenbahnpolitik* (1883) and *System* (1898, vol. 3), utilizing biased materials produced by parliamentary commissions, he strongly recommended railway centralization and government ownership while opposing canal construction; yet he failed to test the efficiency of these policy recommendations. In the field of public finance he is (like Rau, Roscher, von Stein and Wagner) the typical German exponent of Smith's liberal principles (not his moral theory) coupled with his own historical and ethical ideas, which were based on relatively poor analysis and synthesis. Cohn attributed to the state an economic and moral competence which he unquestioningly assumed. Advocating the legitimacy of value judgements (*Werturteile*) and ethical norms in economic science, he dealt with equity in taxation, particularly the controversial subsistence level and progressive taxation. Seligman rightly classes Cohn among the founders of the science of public finance.

His writings on general economics (1885–98, 1886) are distinguished by a philosophical foundation and a brilliant essayistic style which earned him a great reputation among his contemporaries.

H.C. RECKTENWALD

SELECTED WORKS

1874–5. *Untersuchungen über die englische Eisenbahnpolitik*. Leipzig: Duncker & Humblot.
1883. *Die englische Eisenbahnpolitik der letzten zehn Jahre (1873–1883)*. Leipzig: Duncker & Humblot.
1885–98. *System der Nationalökonomie*. 3 vols, Stuttgart: Enke.
1886. *Nationalökonomische Studien*. Stuttgart: Enke.

BIBLIOGRAPHY

Recktenwald, H.C. (ed.) 1973. *Political Economy: A Historical Perspective*. London: Collier-Macmillan.

Colbert, Jean-Baptiste (1619–1683). Colbert was born at Reims on 29 August 1619 and died on 6 September 1683. In no way at all could he be called an economist. He was,

however, one of the most powerful administrators, known to history, of measures affecting the economic life of a nation, to such an extent and with such lasting influence that his name is preserved in the notion of Colbertism.

He came of a mercantile family which had acquired some public offices. He learned his job as economic administrator by entering the service, in 1651, of a man he was effectively to succeed, Cardinal Mazarin. Once successfully installed in the service of Louis XIV, after Mazarin's death in 1661, his climb to power was rapid. He soon came to hold numerous offices of state: finance, commerce, buildings, the navy, and more besides. His achievements rested in part upon his exercising virtually undisputed power for twenty-two years as the dominant minister of the grandest of absolute monarchs; and in part upon his own qualities of character which he brought to bear upon the economic problems of France as he perceived them. Those qualities included energy, tenacity, shrewdness, honesty, a notable ability to deploy the techniques of the courtier, and a wholly remarkable capacity for hard work. His hand was felt in every aspect of French economic life; and everywhere he exercised that passion for order which is so often the hallmark of the bureaucrat. Adam Smith sniffed at him as a 'laborious and plodding man of business ... accustomed to regulate the different departments of public offices' (Smith, 1776, p. 627). But he was a lot more than that. Cold, humourless, and devoted, he was the super-servant of a super-king.

Those qualities did not, on the other hand, include any original economic ideas whatever. He had absorbed, with characteristic thoroughness, all the assumptions, maxims, dogmas, and assorted notions about economic matters which circulated in 16th- and 17th-century Europe, and to which the label of mercantilism has become attached. Consequently, by dint of his position and activities, and because a very large volume of his papers have survived for the historian, he has come down to posterity as the embodiment of conventional mercantilism in practice. Non-existent as a theoretical entity, mercantilism has acquired the appearance of a coherent economic policy probably more from Colbert's activities than from any other single historical source. And because it appeared, and was continued after his death, in the grandeur which was France, it was copied or adapted in other aspiring monarchies. French mercantilism or Colbertism thus became a recognizable reality in a way that the English 'mercantile system' did not.

The nature of his economic ideas can often be gathered from the explanatory memoranda which he addressed to Louis XIV (who was not always as interested in such matters as Colbert thought he should be). They have a familiar ring. He wanted money circulating in the kingdom, not because he identified money with wealth, but because it facilitated the payment of taxes and helped to stimulate economic activity; those branches of overseas trade which brought in precious metals were therefore to be especially favoured. Manufacturing industry deserved encouragement because it lessened French dependence on imports, because it was the basis of an export trade which brought in wealth, and because it employed the idle (the Catholic Colbert had the zeal for work and the disapproval of idleness normally thought of as peculiar to Puritanism). In the interest of the economic unification of France, internal trade and transport needed improvement by the removal of tolls and the repair of roads and bridges. Royal support was needed, and was secured, for the construction of canals – of which the most spectacular achievement was the opening in 1681 of the Canal des Deux Mers, providing a waterway between the Atlantic and the Mediterranean.

Colbert shared the pervasive belief in a fixed cake of trade, so that, as he patiently explained to Louis in March 1669, the whole trade of Europe was carried in a fixed number of vessels and therefore 'le commerce cause un combat perpétuel en paix et en guerre entre les nations de l'Europe, à qui on emportera la meilleure partie'. The Dutch, the English and the French were the 'acteurs de ce combat' (*Lettres* VI, p. 266). France's gain was to be secured by Holland's and/or England's loss. It followed that shipbuilding should be encouraged and the French navy and mercantile marine greatly enlarged. France should move in on trades hitherto dominated by her rivals. Hence his setting up in the 1660s of privileged trading companies: a French East India Company, a French West India Company to improve and exploit French colonies, and the Company of the North to tap the Baltic trade. Such views also provided an economic justification for the war which Louis launched against Holland in 1672. Colbert had to find the revenue for these and others of his master's military activities. Consequently, he devoted much time to trying to reform the royal finances. Many of his measures – for example, to improve the collection of taxes or to unify the customs system – were thus again part of a policy designed to improve the performance of the economy so that it could in turn yield more wealth to the greater glory of *le roi soleil*.

How much success attended Colbert's policies has been a matter of debate. *Laissez-faire* economists and economic historians of similar views have inevitably disparaged them and stressed the rigidities which were built into the French economy in the 18th century. His efforts to unify the chaotic diversity of French fiscal and customs administration were only very partially successful; his overseas trading companies were inadequately financed and generally unprofitable; his comparative neglect of agriculture left the basis of the economy in a poor state. But his work did greatly improve the size and efficiency of the French navy and mercantile marine; stimulate – albeit at a high cost – certain areas of French manufacturing industry; and encourage French merchant enterprise in branches of trade hitherto the preserve of others. Not all of this was evident in his own lifetime. But one thing was: Colbert died a very rich man, ennobled as Marquis de Seignelay, his brothers and sisters and cousins amply provided with lucrative sinecures, his sons as ministers or army officers, and his three daughters married off to dukes. Such were the 17th-century rewards of administering an economy.

D.C. COLEMAN

BIBLIOGRAPHY

Clément, P. (ed.) 1861–2. *Lettres, Instructions et Mémoires de Colbert.* 8 vols. Paris.

Cole, C.W. 1939. *Colbert and a Century of French Mercantilism.* 2 vols, New York: Columbia University Press.

Smith, A. 1776. *An Inquiry into the Nature and Causes of the Wealth of Nations.* Ed. E. Cannan, New York: Modern Library edn, 1937.

Colbertism. Colbertism is a term used to describe the economic policies associated with the French statesman, Jean-Baptiste Colbert; and sometimes, confusingly, as a synonym for mercantilist policies in general.

In the course of his account, and denunciation, of the mercantile system, Adam Smith presented it as something foisted upon governments by conspiring businessmen. Extending this view from England to France, he said of Colbert that he had been 'imposed upon by the sophistry of merchants and

manufacturers' (Smith, 1776, p. 434). Whatever degree of truth there may be in his account so far as it related to England – and there is some – it wholly misrepresents the mind of Colbert and the nature of Colbertism. Distrusting the self-interest of businessmen as a power for the greater good of society, Colbert believed profoundly that, although their pursuit of profits should be encouraged, the way to ensure that such activities redounded to the greater wealth, and hence power and glory, of France was by regulation and order. So Colbertism was essentially a systematic treatment of economic activities imposed from above by the King through his servant. It could be described as a version of the mercantile system appropriate to an absolutist state. It owed little or nothing to mercantile or manufacturing pressures brought to bear on governments. Although there were some similarities between Colbertism and English mercantilism, both in the ideas which lay behind it and in its outward forms as it affected overseas trade, the creation of Colbertian policies did not in the least resemble the process of bargaining and compromise between Crown and Parliament by which English mercantilism was muddled into existence. For this reason alone the term 'Parliamentary Colbertism', coined by Cunningham and used by him to describe English economic policy, 1689–1776 (Cunningham, 1907, II, pp. 403–68), was singularly inappropriate. It was also inapt for the different reason that Colbertism was distinguished by a concern for the direct control of production which was wholly absent from the English version of mercantilist policies.

The quintessence of Colbertism is strikingly illustrated in Colbert's approach to manufactures. Observing that France had great industrial potential, with many and scattered crafts and substantial manpower, he set about the country's industrial rehabilitation. He used a variety of weapons: subsidies, special tax reductions or exemptions, protection against foreign imports, the encouragement of early marriage and large families, grants of special privileges, and the establishment of *manufactures royales*. Disapproving, for example, of the way in which his countrymen imported and wore the woollen cloth or serges of Holland and England, he set up *manufactures royales* to stimulate their production in France; and in 1667 very sharply increased import duties against the offending English and Dutch imports. Similar techniques were used to promote the making of lace, silk stockings, tapestries, carpets, glassware, tinplate, soap, naval supplies, and cannon. Luxury items and textiles received particular attention. It has been said that 'the greatest industry in France was supplying the wants of the King and his court' (Cole, 1939, II, p. 303). In quantitative terms this was probably untrue but its significance was very real; and such a statement could not possibly be made about English industry. Stimulation demanded regulation. So Colbert established a Code of Commerce, promulgated for textiles elaborate controls covering precise lengths, widths and other details of all types of textiles; established an apparatus of industrial inspection; and insisted upon all labour being organized within the guild structure.

Three points need to be stressed about these measures. First, Colbertism was here a continuation and codification, a new ordering of old practices; it was part of an *étatisme* with medieval roots. Second, at the time that Colbert was imposing these measures on the French economy, their English counterparts were withering away; the last legislative attempt at general regulation of the English cloth industry failed in 1678. Third, Colbert's regulative achievements were continued after his death: Colbertism brought many more detailed regulations in the seventy years after 1683.

Colbert's founding of privileged monopolistic trading companies shows a certain resemblance to the prior establishment of their counterparts in Holland and England. Again, however, the special nature of Colbertian mercantilism is evident both in the preponderance of royal and government finance in the early years of these companies because of inadequate mercantile enthusiasm for them; and in the degree of personal control which Colbert himself exercised, especially over the French East India Company. So far from being a product of mercantile pressures Colbertism ran foul of merchants on more than one occasion. Colbert made himself very unpopular with those of Marseilles, for example, when, obsessed by the need to keep money circulating so that taxes could be paid, he tried to prevent them from exporting coin in order to conduct their trade with the Levant. And the highly protective anti-Dutch tariff of 1667 attracted internal opposition because it so obviously invited retaliation.

The vast regulative apparatus built up by Colbert and his successors showed more contempt than understanding of the role of businessmen. French commercial and industrial advance during the 18th century, though owing something to Colbert's initiating stimuli, continued despite, rather than because of, the perpetuation of Colbertism. Indeed, one of the reasons for the final reaction against it was the extent to which the bureaucratic machine had become both corrupt in its operation and irrelevant to the needs of the French economy. It helped the proliferation in 18th-century France of a congerie of fiscal office-holders and a concomitant trade in offices and privileges functioning in and around an overblown court. Such practices certainly existed before Colbert's day; but just as Colbert brought a new administrative zeal to old economic ideas, so Colbertism came to provide a still more fertile soil for the growth of ancient corruptions. Meanwhile, however, it appealed to other states – Prussia and the German principalities, Russia, Austria, Spain – intent on building up or repairing economic bases for the support of absolutist courts, territorial ambitions, or the urge for military glory. The sorts of mercantilism which they adopted all varied a good deal, despite the common name and some common economic ideas. But those of central, eastern and southern Europe were often much nearer in spirit to Colbertism than to the mercantile system which Smith discerned in England or to the particular variety which the Dutch had erected in Holland. Colbertism was in this sense *sui generis*.

D.C. COLEMAN

See also MERCANTILISM.

BIBLIOGRAPHY
Cole, C.W. 1939. *Colbert and a Century of French Mercantilism.* 2 vols, New York: Columbia University Press.
Cole, C.W. 1943. *French Mercantilism, 1683–1700.* New York: Columbia University Press.
Cunningham, W. 1907. *The Growth of English Industry and Commerce.* 3 vols. Cambridge: Cambridge University Press.
Smith, A. 1776. *An Inquiry into the Nature and Causes of the Wealth of Nations.* Ed. E. Cannan, New York: Modern Library edn, 1937.

Cole, George Douglas Howard (1889–1959). A British socialist intellectual, G.D.H. Cole was born in Cambridge in 1889. He grew up in London and was educated at Balliol College, Oxford. As a young Oxford don, Cole came to prominence during the second decade of the century as a leading advocate of guild socialism (a doctrine of workers' control in industry) and adviser to the labour and trade union movements. After the collapse of guild socialism, Cole continued to be the outstanding socialist theorist and Labour Party intellectual in Britain during the interwar and immediate postwar periods, always combining academic work with political commitment. An encyclopaedist and polymath, Cole's published output was prodigious in both volume and range. He produced over a hundred books, and at different periods held academic posts in three disciplines (philosophy, economics, political theory) and could easily have held posts in at least two others.

Cole's central and lifelong preoccupation was with the advocacy of a decentralized, self-managing and participatory form of socialism. It is against this background that his work in economics has to be seen. Although he immersed himself in economic matters during the interwar period (when he was Reader in Economics at Oxford), he regarded this as a labour of necessity. In a basic sense, he did not *like* economics, and railed against the 'algebraic sterilities' of those economic theorists who divorced the subject both from social values and from the solution of pressing problems in the real world. He was, anyway, not equipped to enter the higher reaches of theoretical economics, and his own economic theory therefore remained essentially derivative. His early guild socialism had been remarkably innocent of any serious economic theory at all.

Yet, instead of confirming Cole as of only minor importance, what this really serves to emphasize is the remarkable nature of his contribution to practical economics between the wars. If his economic theory was derivative, he derived it from sources that enabled him to construct radical policy proposals to combat slump and unemployment. Drawing particularly upon the 'underconsumption' (or 'over-saving') analysis of capitalism developed by J.A. Hobson, Cole mounted a sustained critique of economic orthodoxy in relation to unemployment throughout the 1920s and argued the need for demand stimulation and a bold programme of public works and investment. The great merit of Hobsonian economic theory for a socialist like Cole was that it provided the materials from which capitalism could be both indicted and reformed.

Cole's recovery programme remained substantially the same in the 1930s, but from the early years of that decade he displayed a clearer understanding of how such a programme was to be financed. His policy proposals were already proto-Keynesian, but from the early 1930s (when he worked with Keynes on the Economic Advisory Council) he analysed the economic situation from a recognizably Keynesian perspective. Reviewing Keynes's *General Theory* in the *New Statesman* (the house magazine of the British Left), Cole described it as 'the most important theoretical economic writing since Marx's *Capital*, or, if only classical economics is to considered as comparable, since Ricardo's *Principles*'. Above all, it provided the theoretical credentials for his own dissenting economics.

However, if Keynes had to be absorbed by the Left, and mobilized for a recovery programme, Cole also took the view that it was necessary to look beyond the conditions of short-term stabilization and towards the development of a 'new' economics of socialism. He therefore emerged as a leading advocate of socialist economic planning in the 1930s, but for the rest of his life (and after the war from the vantage point of the Chichele Chair of Social and Political Theory at Oxford) he continued to search for a form of socialist economy consistent with his prior commitment to a form of non-bureaucratic socialist democracy.

ANTHONY WRIGHT

SELECTED WORKS
1929. *The Next Ten Years in British Social and Economic Policy*.
    London: Macmillan.
1932. *Economic Tracts for the Times*. London: Macmillan.
1935. *Principles of Economic Planning*. London: Macmillan.
1950. *Socialist Economics*. London: Gollancz.

BIBLIOGRAPHY
Cole, M. 1971. *The Life of G.D.H. Cole*. London: Macmillan.
Wright, A.W. 1979. *G.D.H. Cole and Socialist Democracy*. Oxford:
    Clarendon Press.

collective action.   For a long while, economists, like specialists
in other fields, often took it for granted that groups of
individuals with common interests tended to act to further
those common interests, much as individuals might be
expected to further their own interests. If a group of rational
and self-interested individuals realized that they would gain
from political action of a particular kind, they could be
expected to engage in such action; if a group of workers would
gain from collective bargaining, they could be expected to
organize a trade union; if a group of firms in an industry
would profit by colluding to achieve a monopoly price, they
would tend to do so; if the middle class or any other class in a
country had the power to dominate, that class would strive to
control the government and run the country in its own
interest. The idea that there was some tendency for groups to
act in their common-interests was often merely taken for
granted, but in some cases it played a central conceptual role,
as in some early American theories of labour unions, in the
'group theory' of the 'pluralists' in political science, in
J.K. Galbraith's concept of 'countervailing power', and in the
Marxian theory of class conflict.

More recently, the explicit analysis of the logic of individual
optimization in groups with common interests has led to a
dramatically different view of collective action. If the
individuals in some group really do share a common interest,
the furtherance of that common interest will automatically
benefit each individual in the group, whether or not he has
borne any of the costs of collective action to further the
common interest. Thus the existence of a common interest
need not provide any incentive for individual action in the
group interest. If the farmers who grow a given crop have a
common interest in a tariff that limits the imports and raises
the price of that commodity, it does not follow that it is
rational for an individual farmer to pay dues to a farm
organization working for such a tariff, for the farmer would
get the benefit of such a tariff whether he had paid dues to the
farm organization or not, and his dues alone would be most
unlikely to determine whether or not the tariff passed. The
higher price or wage that results from collective action to
restrict the supply in a market is similarly available to any firm
or worker that remains in that market, whether or not that
firm or worker participated in the output restriction or other
sacrifices that obtained the higher price or wage. Similarly, any
gains to the capitalist class or to the working class from a
government that runs a country in the interests of that class,
will accrue to an individual in the class in question whether or
not that individual has borne the costs of any collective action.
This, in combination with the extreme improbability that a
given individual's actions will determine whether his group or
class wins or loses, entails that a typical individual, if rational
and self-interested, would not engage in collective action in the
interest of any large group or class.

Analytically speaking, the benefits of collective action in the
interest of a group with a common interest are a public or
collective good to that group; they are like the public goods of
law and order, defence, and pollution abatement in that
voluntary and spontaneous market mechanisms will not
provide them. The fundamental reality that unifies the theory
of public goods with the more general logic of collective action
is that ordinary market or voluntary action fails to obtain the
objective in question. It fails because the benefits of collective
or public goods, whether provided by governments or
non-governmental associations, are not subject to exclusion; if
they are received by one individual in some group, they
automatically also go the others in that group (Olson, 1965).

Since many groups with common interests obviously do not
have the power to tax or any comparable resource, the
foregoing logic leads to the prediction that many groups that
would gain from collective action will not in fact be organized
to act in their common interests. This prediction is widely
supported. Consumers have a common interest in opposing
the legislation that gives various producer groups supra-
competitive prices, and they would sometimes also have a
common interest in buyers' coalitions that would countervail
producer monopolies, but there is no major country where
most consumers are members of any organization that works
predominantly in the interest of consumers. The unemployed
similarly share a common interest, but they are nowhere
organized for collective action. Neither do most taxpayers, nor
most of the poor, belong to organizations that act in their
common interest (Austen-Smith, 1981; Brock and Magee,
1978; Chubb, 1983; Hardin, 1982; Moe, 1980; Olson, 1965).

Though some groups can never act collectively in their
common interest, certain other groups can, if they have
ingenious leadership, overcome the difficulties of collective
action, though this usually takes quite some time. There are
two conditions either of which is ultimately sufficient to make
collective action possible. One condition is that the number of
individuals or firms that would need to act collectively to
further the common interest is sufficiently small; the other is
that the groups should have access to 'selective incentives'.

The way that small numbers can make collective action
possible at times is most easily evident on the assumption that
the individuals in a group with a common interest are
identical. Suppose there are only two large firms in an industry
and that each of these firms will gain equally from any
government subsidy or tax loophole for the industry, or from
any supra-competitive price for its output. Clearly each firm
will tend to get half of the benefit of any lobbying it does on
behalf of the industry, and this can provide an incentive for
some unilateral action on behalf of the industry. Since each
firm's action will have an obvious impact on the profits of the
other, the firms will have an incentive to interact strategically
with and bargain with one another. There would be an
incentive to continue this strategic interaction or bargaining
until a joint maximization or 'group optimal' outcome had
been achieved. This same logic obviously also applies to
collective action in the form of collusion to obtain a
supra-competitive price, and thus we obtain the well-known
incentive for oligopolistic collusion in concentrated industries
whenever there are significant obstacles to or costs of entry. As
the number in a group increases, however, the incentive to act
collectively diminishes; if there are ten identical members of a
group with a common interest, each gets a tenth of the benefit
of unilateral action in the common interest of the group, and if
there are a million, each gets one millionth. In this last case,
even if there were some incentive to act in the common
interest, that incentive would cease long before a group-
optimal amount of collective action had taken place. Strategic
interaction or voluntary bargaining will not occur since no two

individuals have an incentive to interact strategically or to bargain with one another. This is because the failure of one individual to support collective action will not then have any perceptible effect on the incentive any other individual faces so there is no incentive for strategic interaction or rational bargaining. Thus we obtain the result that, in time, sufficiently small groups can act collectively, but that this incentive for collective action decreases monotonically as the group gets larger and disappears entirely in sufficiently large or 'latent' groups.

When the parties that would profit from collective action have very different demand curves, the party with the highest absolute demand for collective action will have an incentive to engage in some amount of collective action when no other member of the group has such an interest. This leads to a paradoxical 'exploitation of the great by the small'. This is true to a greater degree and is evident much more simply if income effects are ignored, as in the demand curves for a collective good depicted in the figure below. When the party with the highest demand curve for the collective good, D_h, has obtained the amount of the collective good, Q_1, that is in its interest unilaterally to provide, any and all parties with a lower demand curve, such as D_s, will automatically receive this same amount, and thus have no incentive to provide any amount at all! (Olson, 1965). When income effects and certain 'private good' aspects of some collective goods are taken into account the results are less extreme, but a distribution of burdens disproportionality unfavourable to the parties with the absolutely larger demands tends to remain. This disproportion has been evident, for example, in various military alliances and international organizations, in cartels, and in metropolitan areas in which metropolis-wide collective goods are provided by independent municipalities of greatly different size (Olson and Zeckhauser, 1966; Sandler, 1980).

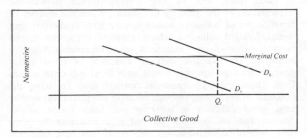

Figure 1

The other condition, besides small numbers, that can make collective action possible, is 'selective incentives'. Those large groups that have been organized for collective action for any substantial period of time are regularly found to have worked out special devices, or selective incentives, that are functionally equivalent to the taxes that enable governments to provide public goods (Olson, 1965; Hardin, 1982). These selective incentives either punish or reward individuals depending on whether or not they have borne a share of the costs of collective action, and thus give the individual an incentive to contribute to collective action that no good that is or would be available to all could provide. The most obvious devices of this kind are the 'closed shop' and picket line arrangements of labour unions, which often make union membership a condition of employment and control the supply of labour during strikes (see, for example, McDonald, 1969; Gamson, 1975). Upon investigation it becomes clear that labour unions are not in this respect fundamentally different from other large

organizations for collective action, which regularly have selective incentives that, though usually less conspicuous than the closed shop or the picket line, serve the same function.

Farm organizations in several countries, and quite notably in the United States, obtain most of their membership by deducting the dues in farm organizations from the 'patronage dividends' or rebates of farm cooperatives and insurance companies that are associated with the farm organizations. The professional associations representing such groups as physicians and lawyers characteristically have either relatively discreet forms of compulsion (such as the 'closed bar') or subtle individual rewards to association members, such as access to professional publications, certification, referrals, and insurance. In small groups, and sometimes in large 'federal' groups that are composed of many small groups, social pressure and social rewards are also important sources of selective incentives.

The selective incentives that are needed if large groups are to organize for collective action are less often available to potential entrants or those at the lower levels of the social order than to established and well-placed groups. The unemployed, for example, obviously do not have the option of making membership of an organization working in their interest a condition of employment, nor do they naturally congregate as the employed do at workplaces where picket lines may be established. Those who would profit from entering a cartelized industry or profession are similarly almost always without selective incentives. Experience in a variety of countries also confirms that those with higher levels of education and skill have better access to selective incentives than lower income workers; highly trained professionals such as physicians and attorneys usually come to be well organized before labour unions emerge, and the unions of skilled workers normally emerge before unions representing less skilled workers. The correlation between income and established status and access to selective incentives works in the same direction as the lesser difficulty of collective action of small groups of large firms in relatively concentrated industries explained above. Together these two factors generate a tendency for collective action to have, in the aggregate though not in all cases, a strong anti-egalitarian and pro-establishment impact (Olson, 1984).

The study of collective action goes back to the beginnings of economics, but then came to be strangely neglected during most of the rest of the history of the subject. Though this is not generally realized, the study of collective action, admittedly only in an inductive and intuitive way, was a crucial part of Adam Smith's analysis of the inefficiencies and inequities in the economies he observed (Smith, 1776). Smith even noted that the main beneficiaries of collective action in his time were by no means the poor or those of average means. He also emphasized the tendency for urban interests to profit from collective action at the expense of rural people, because the geographical dispersion of agricultural interests areas made it more difficult for them to combine to exert political influence or to fix prices; this emphasis presumably owed something to the poor transportation and communication systems in his day, which presumably obstructed the organization of rural interests more in his time than it does in developed countries now.

The label that Adam Smith gave to the set of public policies, monopolistic combinations, and ideas that he attacked was, after all, 'mercantilism', because the single most important source of the evils was the collective action of merchants, or merchants and 'masters', especially those organized into guilds or 'corporations'. In his discussions of the 'Inequalities

Occasioned by the Policy of Europe' and of 'The Rent of Land' (Bk. I, ch. 10, pt. ii and ch. 11), Smith emphasized that 'whenever the legislature attempts to regulate the differences between masters and their workmen, its counsellors are always the Masters'. Similarly,

> it is everywhere much easier for a rich merchant to obtain the privilege of trading in a town corporate, than for a poor artificer to obtain that of working in it ... . Though the interest of the labourer is strictly connected with that of the society ... his voice is little heard and less regarded.

The rural interests are similarly at a disadvantage, according to Smith, especially as compared with those in 'trade and manufactures':

> The inhabitants of a town, being collected into one place, can easily combine together. The most insignificant trades carried on in towns have accordingly, in some place or another, been incorporated, and even where they have never been incorporated ... voluntary associations and agreements prevent that free competition which they cannot prohibit .... The trades which employ but a small number of hands run most easily into such combinations .... People of the same trade seldom meet together, even for merriment and diversion, but the conversation ends in a conspiracy against the public, or in some contrivance to raise prices.

By contrast, 'the inhabitants of the country, dispersed in distant places, cannot easily combine together'.

These passages, though not in the order they appear in Smith, nonetheless correctly convey his alertness to collective action. Though the handicap that rural interests face in organizing for collective action is far less in developed countries today than it was in Smith's time, even this part of his argument still generally holds true in the developing countries, where transportation and communication in the rural areas are poor, peasants are generally unrepresented, and agricultural commodities normally underpriced (Anderson and Hayami, 1986; Schultz, 1978; Olson, 1985).

Adam Smith's insights into collective action and its consequences were ignored until recent times. Presumably one reason is that most economists in the 19th and early 20th centuries were mainly interested in the logic of the case for competitive markets. The logic of collective action, by contrast, is really a general statement of the logic of market failure; it embodies the central insight of the theories of public goods and externalities, that markets and voluntary market-type arrangements do not generally work in those cases where the beneficiaries of any collective good or benefit cannot be excluded because they have not paid any purchase price or dues (Baumol, 1952). It was not until Knut Wicksell's 'New Principle of Just Taxation' was published in German in 1896 (Musgrave and Peacock, 1967) that any economist revealed a clear understanding of the nature of public goods, and only with the publication of Samuelson's articles in the 1950s (Samuelson, 1955) that this idea came to be generally understood in the English-speaking world.

A second obstacle to the development of the logic of collective action was that collective action by governments was normally taken for granted. Notwithstanding the difficulties of collective action, anarchy is relatively rare because a government that provides some sort of law and order quickly takes over. This in turn is due to conquerors and the gains they obtain in increased tax revenues from establishing some system of law and order and property rights. In the absence of the provision of these most elemental collective goods, there is not much for a conqueror to take, so the historic first movement of the invisible hand is evident in the incentive conquerors have to establish law and order. Those who lead the governments that succeed conquerors obviously must maintain a system of law and order if they are to continue collecting significant tax revenues. Since governments providing basic collective goods have been ubiquitous, the classic writers on public goods like Wicksell and Samuelson did not even ask how collective goods emerged in the first place. They focused instead on how to determine what was an appropriate sharing of the tax burdens and on the difficulty of determining what level of provision of public goods was Pareto-optimal. This in turn naturally led to Wicksell's recommendation that only those public expenditures that could, with an appropriate allocation of the tax burdens, command approximate unanimity, should normally be permitted, and to Samuelson's and Musgrave's (1959) concern for the non-revelation of preferences for public goods. The difficulties of collective action and public good provision on a voluntary basis therefore naturally did not gain any theoretical attention.

When, as in the new political economy or public choice, the focus is also on the efforts of extra-governmental groups to obtain the gains from lobbying, cartelization, and collusion, and on private action to obtain collective benefits of other kinds, a more general conception becomes natural (Barry and Hardin, 1982; Olson, 1965; Taylor, 1976). It then becomes clear that the likelihood of voluntary collective action depends dramatically on the size of the group that would gain from collective action. When a group is sufficiently small and there is time for the needed bargaining, the desired collective goods will normally be obtained through voluntary cooperation (Frohlich, Oppenheimer, and Young, 1971). If there are substantial differences in the demands for the collective good at issue, there will be the aforementioned paradoxical 'exploitation of the great by the small'. When the number of beneficiaries of collective action is very large, voluntary and straightforward collective action is out of the question, and taxes or other selective incentives are indispensable. Selective incentives are available only to a subset of those extra-governmental groups that would gain from collective action. Even those extra-governmental groups that do have the potential of organizing through selective incentives will usually have great difficulty in working out these (often subtle) devices, and will normally succeed in overcoming the great difficulties of collective action only when they have relatively ingenious leadership and favourable circumstances.

If follows that it is only in long-stable societies that many extra-governmental organizations for collective action will exist. In societies where totalitarian repression, revolutionary upheavals, or unconditional defeat have lately destroyed organizations for collective action, few groups will have been able in the time available to have overcome the formidable difficulties of collective action. It has been shown elsewhere (Mueller, 1983; Olson, 1982), that (unless they are very 'encompassing') organizations for collective action have extraordinarily anti-social incentives; they engage in distributional struggles, even when the excess burden of such struggles is very great, rather than in production. They also will tend to make decisions slowly and thereby retard technological advance and adaptations to macroeconomic and monetary shocks. It follows that societies that have been through catastrophes that have destroyed organizations for collective action, such as Germany, Japan, and Italy, can be expected to enjoy 'economic miracles.' An understanding of collective action also makes it possible to understand how Great Britain, the country that with the industrial revolution discovered modern economic growth and had for nearly a century the world's fastest rate of economic growth, could by now have fallen victim to the 'British disease'. The logic of collective action, in combination with other theories, also makes it possible to understand many of the other most notable examples of economic growth and stagnation since the Middle Ages, and also certain features of macroeconomic experience that contradict Keynesian, monetarist, and new classical macroeconomic theories (Balassa and Giersch, 1986).

MANCUR OLSON

See also BARGAINING; PUBLIC CHOICE; SOCIAL CHOICE.

BIBLIOGRAPHY
Anderson, K. and Hayami, Y. 1986. *The Political Economy of Protection*. Sydney: George Allen & Unwin.
Austen-Smith, D. 1981. Voluntary pressure groups. *Economica* 48, May, 143–53.
Balassa, B. and Giersch, H. (eds) 1986. *Economic Incentives*. Proceedings of the International Economic Association, London: Macmillan.
Barry, B. and Hardin, R. (eds) 1982. *Rational Man and Irrational Society*. Beverly Hills: Sage.
Baumol, W.J. 1952. *Welfare Economics and the Theory of the State*. Cambridge, Mass.: Harvard University Press.
Brock, W. and Magee, S. 1978. The economics of special interest groups: the case of the tariff. *American Economic Review* 68(2), May, 246–50.
Chubb, J. 1983. *Interest Groups and Bureaucracy*. Stanford: Stanford University Press.
Frohlich, N., Oppenheimer, J. and Young, O. 1971. *Political Leadership and Collective Boards*. Princeton: Princeton University Press.
Gamson, W.A. 1975. *The Strategy of Social Protest*. Homewood, Ill: Dorsey.
Hardin, R. 1982. *Collective Action*. Baltimore: Johns Hopkins University Press for Resources for the Future.
McDonald, D.J. 1969. *Union Man*. New York: Dutton
Moe, T.M. 1980. *The Organization of Interests*. Chicago: University of Chicago Press.
Mueller, D.C. (ed.) 1983. *The Political Economy of Growth*. New Haven: Yale University Press.
Musgrave, R.A. 1959. *The Theory of Public Finance*. New York: McGraw-Hill.
Musgrave, R.A. and Peacock, A.T. (eds) 1967. *Classics in the Theory of Public Finance*. 2nd edn, New York: McGraw-Hill.
Olson, M.L. 1965. *The Logic of Collective Action*. Cambridge, Mass.: Harvard University Press.
Olson, M.L. and Zeckhauser, R. 1966. An economic theory of alliances. *Review of Economics and Statistics* 48, August, 266–79.
Olson, M.L. 1982. *The Rise and Decline of Nations*. New Haven: Yale University Press.
Olson, M.L. 1984. Ideology and growth. In *The Legacy of Reaganomics*, ed. C.R. Hulten and I.V. Sawhill, Washington: Urban Insitute Press, DC.
Olson, M.L. 1985. Space, organization, and agriculture. *American Journal of Agricultural Economics* 67, December, 928–37.
Samuelson, P.A. 1955. Diagrammatic exposition of a theory of public expenditure. *Review of Economics and Statistics* 37, November, 350–56.
Sandler, T. (ed.) 1980. *The Theory and Structure of International Political Economy*. Boulder, Colorado. Westview.
Schultz, T.W. 1978. *Distortion of Agricultural Incentives*. Bloomington: Indiana University Press.
Smith, A. 1776. *An Inquiry into the Nature and Causes of the Wealth of Nations*. London: J.M. Dent, 1910.
Taylor, M. 1976. *Anarchy and Cooperation*. London: John Wiley.
Wicksell, K. 1896. A new principle of just taxation. Trans. from the German by J.A. Buchanan, in Musgrave and Peacock (1967).

collective agriculture. The socialist countries have generally modelled their rural institutions on those of the USSR in the 1930s. For the most part, means of production were owned by the so-called collective, farmwork was 'collectively' organized, and personal income 'collectively' distributed. At their peak, over one-third of the world's farmers worked under this system.

'Socialist' countries have favoured collectives for the following principal reasons.

Firstly, the leadership in most 'socialist' countries initially was afraid of an economically independent peasantry with ideas shaped by individualistic 'petty commodity production'. As Stalin put it: 'a great deal of work has to be done to remould the collective-farm peasant, to correct his individualistic mentality and to transform him into a real working member of a socialist society' (Stalin, 1929, p. 469). Collectives were not intended as independent co-operatives: collectivization was party-led and collectives were subject to considerable external control (see e.g. Davies, 1980; Volin, 1970; Selden, 1982; Unger, 1984). Such a rationale is deeply undemocratic, especially given the peasants' numerical dominance in those countries (see, in particular, Cohen, 1974, ch. 6).

Second, it was believed that state intervention through party-led collectives would improve rural economic performance (see e.g. Stalin, 1929; General Office, 1956). Collectives could raise savings and investment rates through reinvesting income and mobilizing 'surplus' labour for capital construction. Unfortunately, success in these respects can damage labour motivation by reducing current returns to collective labour. Collectives also could provide a vehicle for rapidly introducing new technology. However, this applies to bad as well as good technology – examples of the former are legion in 'socialist' agriculture, including the various programmes in the Soviet Union associated with Lysenko (discussed in Volin, 1970) and the ill-fated introduction of the double-wheeled, double-share plough, in China (Kuo, 1972, ch. 12).

Third, party-led collectives were viewed as a means to attain high farm marketing rates and an outflow of farm sector savings to finance non-farm investment:

> By transferring the disposal of agricultural output from individual peasants to government-supervised collective farm managements, collectivization destroys the basis for the peasants' resistance to the 'siphoning-off' of the economic surplus (Baran, 1957, p. 268).

However, without, for example, adequate supplies of appropriately priced industrial commodities, forcibly raising the rate of farm sector marketings can reduce the growth rate of farm output and the future volume of farm marketings. Moreover, it has proved difficult to achieve a net farm savings outflow due, for example, to agriculture's need for industrial incentive goods and farm inputs (increased, insofar as inputs are inefficiently used and collectivization adversely affects livestock holdings, motive power and fertilizer supplies), and the state's inability to control private market prices (Ellman, 1975; Ishikawa, 1967).

Fourth, it was considered that collectives would prevent 'capitalist' polarization alongside farm modernization, with the majority of peasants becoming wage labourers (Stalin, 1929; Mao, 1955). Evidence from other developing countries contradicts Stalin and Mao's crude vision of rural class polarization (see, especially, Hayami and Kikuchi, 1981). It indicates too that appropriate state policies (e.g. land reform, provision of education and credit, infrastructure construction, progressive taxation) can mitigate rural class inequalities.

Class polarization is not the inevitable accompaniment of rural modernization, nor is collectivization the only way to resolve problems of rural class inequality (e.g. Hayami and Kichuchi, 1981).

Fifth, Lenin, Stalin and Mao all believed that agriculture was characterized by lumpiness and economies of scale (Lenin, 1899; Stalin, 1929; Mao, 1955). In many farm tasks, large scale is indeed an advantage, for example in research, processing, building and maintaining irrigation facilities. However, many modern farm inputs are divisible. Provided they are appropriately priced, credit is available and they have access to lumpy complementary inputs, all farm strata in modernizing areas tend to acquire them (Hayami and Kikuchi, 1981). Moreover, in large agricultural units labour supervision is a major problem (Bradley and Clark, 1971). If a collective's members trust each other and are motivated to work hard for the group irrespective of relative income then labour supervision is not an issue. However, this is rarely the case (Morawetz, 1983) and collective farm managers have had to devise payment systems to motivate farm workers. In certain farm tasks (notably harvesting) it is easy to pay labour according to its product, but for most farm tasks it is more difficult than in industry to devise payment systems that strongly motivate wage labour: farm work often requires a flexible response from the worker which is difficult to anticipate in the payment system; the final produce takes a long time to produce, with different workers' contributions difficult to isolate; work is physically dispersed and production conditions vary greatly from one part of the production unit to another; the main task specializations are seasonal, and permanent minute sub-division of work into easily measurable segments is not generally possible. These problems have meant that under private agriculture, if labour is relatively abundant and capital relatively expensive, the normal outcome is for land to be rented out beyond a certain farm size, so that a relatively high output per acre can be attained through self-operating, self-motivated, rent-paying farmers, rather than cultivated with large numbers of hired workers. In collective farms, the attempt to supervise large numbers of farm workers has resulted in powerful managerial diseconomies of scale and reduced farm efficiency.

Collective agriculture has not performed well. Collective farms in the USSR in 1929–31 and in China in 1959–61 experienced massive institutionally caused declines in farm output, accompanied by demographic disasters (on the Soviet Union, see Volin 1970, ch. 10; on China, see Ashton, 1984). It is, indeed, a terrible indictment of collective farming, that the worst famines of the 20th century have occurred under that system. The USSRs long-term growth of farm output has required colossal capital outlays so that by the 1970s, the agricultural sector was absorbing over one quarter of Soviet new fixed investment (Carey, 1976). From the mid-1950s to the later 1970s Chinese farm output per caput was stagnant: 'de-collectivization' of agriculture in the early 1980s was accompanied by a huge rise in farm output (Nolan and Paine, 1986).

The 'socialist' countries' poor agricultural performance is in part attributable to shortcomings in the supply of industrial goods (Smith, 1981). Part is also due to extensive state intervention in collective farms. However, there are fundamental problems in principle even with relatively independent collective farms. Large units (whether state, collective or private) are necessary to undertake activities exhibiting lumpiness or economies of scale. However, for many farm tasks powerful managerial diseconomies of scale exist, and even given favourable policies in other respects, in most

circumstances this would prove a barrier to good performance of collective farms.

PETER NOLAN

See also AGRICULTURAL GROWTH AND POPULATION CHANGE; PEASANTS.

BIBLIOGRAPHY

Ashton, B. et al. 1984. Famine in China, 1958–61. *Population and Development Review* 10(4), December, 613–45.
Baran, P. 1957. *The Political Economy of Growth.* New York: Monthly Review Press.
Bradley, M.E. and Clark, M.G. 1972. Supervision and efficiency in socialized agriculture. *Soviet Studies* 23(3), January, 465–73.
Carey, D.W. 1976. Soviet agriculture: recent performance and future plans. In USCJEC, 1976.
Cohen, S.F. 1974. *Bukharin and the Bolshevik Revolution.* London: Wildwood House.
Davies, R.W. 1980. *The Socialist Offensive: the collective action of Soviet agriculture, 1929–1930.* London: Macmillan.
Ellman, M. 1975. Did the agricultural surplus provide the resources for the increase in investment in the USSR during the First Five Year Plan? *Economic Journal* 85(4), December, 844–63.
General Office of the Central Committee of the Chinese Communist Party. 1956. *Socialist high tide in China's villages (Zhongguo nongcun de shehuizhuyi gaochao).* 3 vols, Peking: People's Publishing House.
Hayami, Y. and Kikuchi, M. 1981. *Asian Village Economy at the Crossroads.* Tokyo: University of Tokyo Press.
Ishikawa, S. 1967. Resource flow between agriculture and industry. *The Developing Economies* 5(1), March, 3–49.
Kuo, L.T.C. 1972. *The Technical Transformation of Agriculture in Communist China.* London: Praeger.
Lenin, V.I. 1899. *The Development of Capitalism in Russia.* Moscow: Progress Publishers, 1964.
Mao Tsetung. 1955. On the co-operative transformation of agriculture. In Mao (1977).
Mao Tsetung. 1977. *Selected Works of Mao Tsetung*, Vol. V. Peking: Foreign Languages Press.
Morawetz, D. 1983. The kibbutz as a model for developing countries. In Stewart (1983).
Nolan, P. and Paine, S. 1986. Towards an appraisal of the impact of rural reform in China, 1978–85. *Cambridge Journal of Economics* 10(1), March, 83–99.
Selden, M. 1982. Co-operation and conflict: co-operative and collective formation in China's countryside. In Selden and Lippit (1982).
Selden, M. and Lippit, V. (eds) 1982. *The Transition to Socialism in China.* New York: M.E. Sharpe.
Smith, G.A.E. 1981. The industrial problems of Soviet agriculture. *Critique*, No. 14, 41–65.
Stalin, J. 1929. Concerning questions of agrarian policy. In J. Stalin, *Problems of Leninism*, Peking: Foreign Languages Press, n.d.
Stewart, F. (ed.) 1983. *Work, Income and Inequality.* London: Macmillan.
Unger, J. 1984. *Chen Village.* Berkeley: University of California Press.
US Congress, Joint Economic Committee (USCJEC). 1976. *Soviet Economy in a New Perspective.* Washington, DC: US Government Printing Office.
Volin, L. 1970. *A Century of Russian Agriculture.* Cambridge, Mass.: Harvard University Press.

collective bargaining. Collective bargaining is a term applied to a variety of methods of regulating relationships between employers and their employees. Its distinctive feature is that it clearly acknowledges a role for trade unions. In contrast with, for example, autocratic paternalism or producer co-operatives, the employer who engages in collective bargaining accepts the right of independent representatives of employees, acting as a collectivity, to argue their point of view on matters that affect their interests. Pay and working conditions are the most common subjects of collective bargaining, but it can encompass any aspect of management.

The impact of collective bargaining upon management, and its effectiveness from the point of trade union members, vary enormously between different employment circumstances. They depend ultimately upon the collective strength that can be mobilized by employees within the legislative constraints laid down by the state. Collective bargaining is thus best seen as a political institution. It provides a means of bringing at least temporary reconciliation of divergent interests between employers and employees in circumstances in which each side can, to a greater or lesser extent, inflict damage on the other. It is, however, a political institution that is intimately linked with economic processes. The relative power of the bargaining partners owes much to their respective labour and product markets. At the same time the outcome of their bargaining has a major impact upon both the wages and the productivity of labour.

THEORETICAL APPROACHES. This view of collective bargaining as primarily a political rather than an economic institution is relatively recent. Beatrice Webb claimed, according to Marsh (1979), to have originated the expression in 1891 in her study *The Co-operative Movement of Great Britain*. She analysed it further with her husband Sidney Webb in *Industrial Democracy* (1897). Although they did not define it, they saw it as an alternative to individual bargaining, so that the employer, instead of making separate deals with isolated individuals, 'meets with a collective will and settles, in a single agreement, the principles on which, for the time being, all workmen of a particular group, or class, or grade, will be engaged'. They identified it as one of three methods used by trade unions to meet their objectives, the other two being to establish mutual assurance arrangements for their members and to press governments to enact favourable laws. For all the richness of the Webbs' analysis, collective bargaining remained for them essentially an economic institution, imposed upon the employer by a labour cartel whereby workers secured better terms of employment by controlling competition among themselves. A naive version of this view can be seen to underlie much formal analysis of collective bargaining by present day labour economists.

For the next half century Marsh reports no substantial development of the concept apart from in Leiserson's *Constitutional Government in American Industries* (1922). Then in 1951 Chamberlain, in his book *Collective Bargaining*, argued that there were, in essence, three distinct theories. 'They are that collective bargaining is (1) a means of contracting for the sale of labour, (2) a form of industrial government, and (3) a method of management.' The first, 'marketing' theory was much the same as that of the Webbs. The second, 'governmental' aspect was concerned with the procedural needs of dispute resolution. The third 'managerial' theory referred to the way in which management and unions in practice combined 'in reaching decisions on matters in which both have vital interests'; unions through collective bargaining become not the usurpers of management functions but 'actually *de facto* managers'. At much the same time Harbison (1951) was stressing the very constructive social role that collective bargaining played in resolving industrial conflict and in pushing for the enhancement of the 'dignity, worth and freedom of individuals in their capacity as workers'.

This more complex view of collective bargaining has been refined by Dunlop (1967) and Kochan (1980) in the United States, but probably the most influential discussion has been Flanders' attempt of 1968 to create a comprehensive theoretical analysis. He argued that the economic associations of the term 'collective bargaining' are misleading. The collective agreement commits no one to either buy or sell labour, but rather ensures that, when labour is bought or sold, the terms of the transaction will accord with the provisions of the agreement. Above all else collective bargaining is a rule-making process covering many aspects of the employment relationship besides pay and conditions of work. The second characteristic feature of collective bargaining that Flanders stressed is that of the power relationship between the protagonists whose negotiations ('the diplomatic use of power') create the rules. Thus, while there are also technical rules and legal rules regulating work, what distinguishes the legitimacy of those that result from collective bargaining is their authorship. They are jointly determined by the accepted representatives of both employers and employees who consequently share responsibility for both the rules' contents and their observance.

Flanders' analysis has proved fertile in several respects. It has drawn attention to the extent to which collective bargaining is a positive management technique rather than just an impediment to effective management imposed by trade unions. As a result of this shift in emphasis, a major part of academic research into collective bargaining in the 1980s has explored managerial, as opposed to trade union, strategies, and has exposed the extent to which union behaviour is shaped by these management strategies. In addition, what could be seen as the Weberian under-current in Flanders' analysis has focused policy-makers' attention upon the importance of procedural clarity in conflict resolution, and thereby upon the dangers of ambiguity in the legitimation of agreements. The most obvious example is provided by the influential central recommendation of the British Royal Commission on Trade Unions and Employers' Associations of 1968. The emphasis it placed upon employer initiated procedural reform, rather than legislative constraints on trade unions, owed much to the evidence that Flanders had submitted. Finally, by conceptualizing wages as part of a broader package of regulations and as embodying strongly normative principles, the theory opened the way to a more fruitful understanding of wage determination than is offered simply by the market models of orthodox theory.

Two crucial features of the employment relationship ensure that the process of collective bargaining is fundamentally unlike that of non-labour commercial bargains. They are its open-endedness and its continuity. The labour contract is open-ended because the recruitment of an employee does not ensure the performance of work; the employee has to be motivated, by whatever means, to perform to the required standard. In all but highly oppressive societies such motivational techniques tend to be varied and complex, differing not least in the extent to which they place emphasis upon levels of pay and upon employee participation. Since social comparisons (and especially very local ones) play an important part in the motivation and demotivation of labour, the bureaucratic standardization of terms of employment, which is generally a characteristic of collective agreements, often fits in well with management's preferred personnel techniques. In this way, properly conducted collective bargaining can provide a socially stable working environment which facilitates the employer's prime aim of eliciting labour productivity. In short, the conduct of the bargain affects the quality of the labour bargained over.

The second distinctive feature of the employment relationship is its continuity. Employer and employees are bound together, for better or worse, for an indeterminate duration.

Additions to and departures from the workforce generally occur in a piecemeal way. A host of potentially contentious issues feature in the relationship, only a small minority in contention at any one time, and many affecting only a minority of the workforce. Thus a bargain over a particular issue, such as a pay grievance, cannot be evaluated in isolation, but as one fibre in a thick rope of regulations, with many largely implicit trade-offs with respect to other issues, past, present and future.

CHARACTERISTICS. The definition of collective bargaining as the joint regulation of the employment relationship by employer and employee representatives is one that covers a broad range of processes. It is helpful to analyse these further. An initial distinction has to be made between negotiation and consultation. In a negotiation the discussions are characterized, first, by the awareness of each side of the possibility of one inflicting costs on the other in the absence of an acceptable outcome. Second, a negotiation has to result in some sort of agreement, however informal, to which the two sides are, at least for the time being, committed. Consultation, by contrast, is unaccompanied by either the threat of sanctions or the need to reach binding agreement. Actions taken by management in the light of consultation result from a reappraisal of the facts of the case; those taken after negotiation reflect a compromise which has taken into account the threat (or experience) of sanctions inflicted by either or both sides. Under most collective bargaining arrangements it is felt advisable by both sides to distinguish as far as is possible between negotiations and consultations, at any rate in formal procedures. It is, for example, now normal in large unionised workplaces in Britain to deal with them in specifically different committees, even though the membership of those committees may be much the same.

In practice the distinction is far from clear-cut. The blend of approaches adopted in a particular collective bargaining episode depends very much upon the issue in question and the relationship between the parties involved. In their study *A Behavioral Theory of Labor Negotiations* (1965), Walton and McKersie distinguished four classes of negotiation. First, there were 'distributive' bargains: zero-sum negotiations typified by annual wage bargains and characterized by very formal proceedings. Second were 'integrative' bargains: problem-solving discussions aiming at non-zero-sum gains for both sides and generally much more informal in procedure. Third, was 'attitudinal structuring', an almost didactic form of bargaining dialogue in which one side tries to alter the way in which their opponents perceive the problem and its context. Finally, 'intra-organizational' bargains were aimed at altering positions and attitudes, not on the other side, but within the negotiator's own side.

An important influence upon the way in which bargaining is conducted is the personal 'bargaining relationship' between the two individuals who have to take the lead in representing the two sides. This is a term given to the level of trust and facility of communication that exists between them. However acrimonious the collective dispute over which they are bargaining, the better the bargaining relationship between the individual negotiators, the more efficiently they will be able to assess each other's relative power position and the better the chance of the dispute being settled without recourse to expensive sanctions. In a mature bargaining relationship it is common for the negotiators to protect each other from their own sides by, for example, avoiding the humiliation of a bargaining opponent by helping him to gloss over the magnitude of a defeat and by manipulating public statements from one's own side so as to help in his intra-organizational bargaining with his own.

It is normal to draw a clear distinction between the substantive and procedural aspects of collective bargaining. A substantive agreement sets out the actual pay levels, working conditions, or whatever that have been agreed and will be worked to. A procedural agreement defines the way in which such substantive terms might be altered, added to, or interpreted. An effective procedure for negotiation or grievance settlement will state which agents on each side are entitled to be involved in negotiations, in what sequence different sets of negotiators are entitled to consider the matter, what their precedence is, and possibly also matters such as rights of appeal, time constraints, ratification methods and the form of the substantive outcome.

This distinction is particularly obvious in countries whose labour laws cause collective agreements to be tested in the courts; the substantive agreements tend to be written, detailed, formal, and established for specified duration. There are other countries where employer preference, or legal opportunity, makes it unusual for the bargaining opponents to use legal sanctions against each other. In these circumstances the great bulk of substantive regulation may be unwritten and in the form of verbal agreements, custom, and tacit understandings. Because of this a greater emphasis is placed upon the rectitude of the procedural agreements (which may still be very informal) whereby this amorphous body of substantive rules is interpreted and altered, not through comprehensive periodic negotiations, but by a constant incremental process of piecemeal adjustment. Although the United States might be described as exemplifying the legalistic extreme, and Great Britain the 'voluntaristic', most bargaining arrangements have elements of each, with the degree of legalism and formality varying by issue and industry, as well as by country.

BARGAINING STRUCTURE. The structure of bargaining in a country, industry, or enterprise, refers to several different characteristics of collective bargaining. The two most important are the 'bargaining units' and 'bargaining levels' employed. A bargaining unit is a group of employees covered by a particular agreement. Within this basic territory of industrial government there is a coherence of terms of employment, procedures, and trade union representation that is not necessarily to be found between different bargaining units. The level of bargaining refers to the role played by the principal negotiators within their organizations; whether, for example, the employer representative responsible is a factory manager, a company director, or an employers' association representative.

These two characteristics are involved in the single most important decision in the shaping of any bargaining structure which is whether the employers confront the unions singly or in alliance. Single-employer bargaining, resulting in agreements at company-level or lower, is the majority practice in the United States and Japan and now in Britain. Multi-employer bargaining, in which associations of employers conclude industrywide agreements, remains the most important form in most of continental Europe. In practice there is often some employer collusion in industries where single-employer bargaining dominates, and there is usually room for individual employer discretion in industries with strong employers' associations, but the distinction remains one of fundamental economic, political, and managerial significance.

Two other defining characteristics of bargaining structure are its 'form' and 'scope'. The first refers to the extent to which proceedings and agreements are formalized and codified. As already mentioned, this depends in part upon the labour legislation of the country. The second matter, scope, refers to the range of issues covered by collective bargaining. At its narrowest it may include no more than pay and hours, while elsewhere it may take in issues as diverse as training policy, investment decisions and child-care facilities.

The most comprehensive theory seeking to explain industrial and national differences in bargaining structure is to be found in Clegg's *Trade Unionism under Collective Bargaining* (1976). This sees the strategy adopted by employers as the main determinant of bargaining structure, although changes in strategy may be slow to take effect. The legislative framework of a country is also of crucial importance. It defines the limits of rights to strike, the status of the employment contract, any guarantees of security for trade unions, and the legally responsible agents on each side.

Most countries acquired their principal labour legislation at some historic period of crisis – war, defeat, depression, or extreme industrial unrest – and the institutional arrangements that developed from that have become consolidated in subsequent, more peaceful times. This helps to account for the very great variations in collective bargaining practice to be found in different countries; they often owe their origin to a distant panic measure based upon a fashionable idea (such as, for example, compulsory arbitration in Australia or compulsory conciliation in Canada) to which employers and unions have adjusted so firmly that radical reformation is all but impossible. A recurring experience around the world is of legislatures finding extreme difficulty in reforming collective bargaining, other than in times of extremes crisis, because of the essential privacy of the bargaining relationship between employers and union.

Most industrialized countries publicly assert a commitment to collective bargaining as a necessary part of a democratic society, and for most it is the normal means of conducting industrial relations in the public sector. Convention 84 (1947) of the International Labour Organization asserts that 'all practical measures shall be taken to assure to trade unions which are representative of the workers concerned the right to conclude collective agreements with employers and employers' associations'. In practice the freedom of collective bargaining in both public and private sectors varies substantially between countries and over time.

No discussion of collective bargaining would be complete without a mention of the debate concerning its relationship with industrial democracy.

One view is that, because collective bargaining is essentially concerned with compromise, trade unions are sucked into collaborating with capitalism and thereby denied the opportunity of uniting the working class in overthrowing existing employers and then instituting true industrial democracy through workers' control. Opposing this is a view that deplores the fact that collective bargaining institutionalizes the opposition of capital and labour: them and us. It considers that the best form of industrial democracy is to be found where workers are brought to perceive an ultimate identity of interest with employers. Between these positions is that most clearly expressed by Clegg in *A New Approach to Industrial Democracy* (1960). This argues that there can never be complete identity of interest between employer and employee, and also that if employee representatives are given managerial responsibilities they will be forced to behave very similarly to the employers they have replaced. Consequently the role of the trade union is best seen as one of constant opposition, acting to modify management actions in the light of members' interests insofar as their organized power permits.

Far from undermining the common interests of capital and labour, collective bargaining permits the joint regulation of aspects of employment which would otherwise generate greater disharmony and division.

WILLIAM BROWN

See also ARBITRATION; INDUSTRIAL RELATIONS; TRADE UNIONS; WAGE POLICY; WAGES, REAL AND MONEY.

BIBLIOGRAPHY

Chamberlain, N.W. 1951. *Collective Bargaining*. New York: McGraw-Hill.

Clegg, H.A. 1960. *A New Approach to Industrial Democracy*. Oxford: Blackwell.

Clegg, H.A. 1976. *Trade Unionism under Collective Bargaining*. Oxford: Blackwell.

Dunlop, J.T. 1967. The social utility of collective bargaining. In *Challenges to Collective Bargaining*, ed. L. Ulman, New York: Prentice-Hall.

Flanders, A. 1968. Collective bargaining: a theoretical analysis. *British Journal of Industrial Relations*, March; reprinted in A. Flanders, *Management and Unions*, London: Faber & Faber, 1975.

Harbison, F.H. 1951. *Goals and Strategies in Collective Bargaining*. New York: Harper.

Kochan, T.A. 1980. *Collective Bargaining and Industrial Relations*. Homewood: Irwin.

Leiserson, W.M. 1922. Constitutional government in American industries. *American Economic Review*, Supplement.

Marsh, A. 1979. *Concise Encyclopedia of Industrial Relations*. Farnborough: Gower.

Walton, R.E. and McKersie, R.B. 1965. *A Behavioral Theory of Labor Negotiations*, New York: McGraw-Hill.

Webb, S. and B. 1897. *Industrial Democracy*. London: Longmans Green.

collective goods. *See* PUBLIC GOODS.

collegium. *See* SOCIAL CHOICE.

Collet, Clara Elizabeth (1860–1948). After a period as a schoolteacher in Leicester, Clara Collet became one of Charles Booth's assistants on his Survey of London Life and Labour in 1886. In 1893 she entered the civil service as Labour Correspondent and later Senior Investigator for Women's Industries in the newly established Labour Department of the Board of Trade. The earnings and employment of women became and remained Clara Collet's main concern; her contemporaries recognized her as the principal authority on the subject in Britain. Articles on female labour and earnings were among her contributions to the first edition of Palgrave's *Dictionary of Political Economy* in 1894 and the thorough and lucid reports which she produced on women's industrial employment figured in Parliamentary Papers, contributing to the passing of the original Trade Boards Act of 1906. After her retirement in 1920 from what had by then become the Ministry of Labour, Collet herself served on a number of Trade Boards, and wrote the section on Domestic Service for the *New Survey of London Life and Labour* directed by her former chief, Sir H. Llewellyn Smith.

The first woman Fellow of University College, London, where she took her MA degree in 1885, Clara Collet was one of the founders in 1890, along with Henry Higgs and

H.R. Beeton, of the Economic Club which met there monthly, and acted as its secretary from 1905 until 1922.

She was also a founder member of the British Economic Association, which later became the Royal Economic Society; she served on its Council from 1920 to 1941, and on that of the Royal Statistical Society from 1919 until 1935.

R.D. COLLISON BLACK

SELECTED WORKS

1893–4. Royal Commission on Labour. Employment of Women. Miss C.E. Collet. Report. *Parliamentary Papers* 1893–4 [C.6894, *XXIII*] xxxvii, pt. I.

1894. Statistics of employment of women and girls. Miss Collet. Report. *Parliamentary Papers* 1894 [C.7564], lxxxi, Pt. II.

1894. (With Dora M. Barton.) Female labour. In Palgrave's *Dictionary of Political Economy,* London: Macmillan & Co., Vol. II.

1894. Females and children, earnings of. In Palgrave's *Dictionary of Political Economy,* London: Macmillan & Co., Vol. II.

1898. The collection and utilization of official statistics bearing on the extent and effects of the industrial employment of women. *Journal of the Royal Statistical Society* 61, 219–60.

1899. Money wages of in-door domestic servants. Miss Collet. Report. *Parliamentary Papers* 1899 [C.9346] xcii.

1931. Domestic service. Chapter VIII in *New Survey of London Life and Labour,* ed. H. Llewellyn Smith, London: P.S. King, Vol. II.

1933. Appendix to *The Private Letter Books of Joseph Collet, sometime Governor of Fort St. George Madras.* Ed. H.H. Dodwell, London: Longmans.

collusion. Although collusive practices are not restricted to the economic relationships of a well-defined sub-group in society, it is common to use the term collusion in the context of cooperative activity between different firms. With regard to the study of collusion, research has centred on the conditions most conducive to collusion and, in both theoretical and empirical work on the operation of collusive arrangements (see Scherer, 1980, chs 6 and 7).

If economic agents are self-interested maximizers then, given that cooperation between a group of firms will almost certainly make possible higher profits for each member of the group than is possible without cooperation, there is a presumption that collusive arrangements will be widespread. Thus it is important to understand why collusion should fail to be universal. In fact, a more general issue is also raised by this. Taking the argument one stage further, direct cooperation between a group of firms and its consumers is likely to make possible benefits to everybody as compared with a situation where firms and consumers are separated by an anonymous market. This cannot be the case for the economy as a whole if it is Pareto efficient (e.g. the standard perfectly competitive economy without externalities) but it will still be the case that cooperative action by a group of agents within the economy will allow that group to gain at the expense of the rest of the economy. The study of the problems faced by colluding firms should hope to throw light on these more general issues.

1. Consider a well defined group of firms producing identical or similar products, the implication being that demand for the products is interrelated. As a first step, assume that cost and demand functions faced by each firm are common knowledge (every other firm in the group knows these functions, every firm knows this, and so on). If the firms meet together to collude then some joint action will emerge. Cooperative game theory concerns itself with this solution but, for the present exercise, it is sufficient to note two of the main determinants of the eventual solution. First, there are the outcomes made possible by cooperative action. Assume profits can be redistributed within the group – side-payments can be made. Then if cooperative action fails to maximize joint profits all firms can be made better off. Given the common knowledge assumption so that there is no argument for inefficiency based upon the misperceptions of firms, joint profit maximization, with the group of firms acting like a multi-product monopolist, should emerge.

Side-payments may not always be possible. For instance, collusive behaviour is outlawed in many countries and, though it may be difficult to detect whether actions by firms are part of some collusive arrangement, the transfer of money between firms is much more likely to be capable of detection. But without side-payments, actions which influence the size of joint profits also influence the distribution of those profits; the consequence of this being that distributional considerations will influence the actions chosen by firms. For instance, the cooperative Nash bargaining solution (Nash, 1950) leads to actions which maximize the *product* of individual gains above some status quo position – compared with joint-profit maximization, there is movement towards the equalization of gains above the status quo. This may be viewed as a compromise between ignoring distributional considerations and the other extreme where only distributional considerations count.

The second major determinant of the solution reached will be what each firm can expect to achieve if it refuses to accept a particular proposed collusive action for the group. The status quo of the Nash bargaining solution may be interpreted in this way. This is the most obvious component of 'bargaining power' for an agent. The requirement that firms must prefer the collusive action to what can be achieved by reneging, places restrictions on the collusive solution. Under the assumption that firms are interrelated only through the demand structure and that this interrelationship implies that the goods produced by the collusive firms are substitutes, then the worst that can happen to a firm if it refuses to accept a collusive arrangement is that all other firms maximize their production and the reneging firm chooses production to maximize profits in this hostile environment. Given this scenario, there will usually be a large range of collusive actions which offer more to firms than can be achieved by reneging. However, it is not enough for firms to say that they will 'punish' a reneging firm in this way, there must be grounds on the part of the reneging firm for believing that punishments will be carried out – it must be a credible threat in the sense that if the firm reneges, other firms have an incentive to punish the firm. The credibility restriction in this environment is captured by the so-called 'perfect folk theorem' of repeated games (see Rubinstein, 1979, for a published version of the theorem) – firms called upon to punish will have the strongest incentive to punish if all other firms punish that firm for not punishing in the first place. This argument leads to the conclusion that any collusive outcome can be maintained as long as all firms are better-off than the best they could achieve under maximum retaliation from other firms. Here it should be noted that as, by definition, a firm will be happy to choose its Nash strategy if all other firms do the same, the Nash equilibrium is a feasible punishment solution. Thus there will always be an effective deterrent if all firms are better-off under collusion than in the Nash equilibrium (Friedman, 1971).

2. Thus far, the story has assumed that there are no information problems for the (potentially collusive) group of firms. Exogenous uncertainty faced by all firms is not a particular problem but when there are informational asymmetries between firms, the study of collusion is much richer. In fact, almost all the theoretical literature on collusion takes some informational asymmetry as a starting point and it is useful to survey some

of this literature from the viewpoint of the informational asymmetry which is being postulated.

It is convenient to distinguish between two forms of asymmetry – adverse selection where, for instance, some firms do not know the cost and demand conditions of other firms, and moral hazard where it is the behaviour of other firms which cannot be observed. In the former case, it is preferences that cannot be observed, in the latter case it is actions. Both forms of asymmetry can have important effects upon the structure of collusive arrangements that could be expected to emerge.

3. Taking the adverse selection case first, it is fairly reasonable to assume that a firm will have a better knowledge of the demand and cost conditions that it faces than other firms. Although firms may be attracted by the simplicity of adopting a collusive arrangement based upon solely common information, this solution ignores the efficiency gains that may be achieved from making the collusive outcome sensitive to the privately held information of firms. Clearly, the main problem that arises is that each individual firm must have the incentive to reveal this private information. Consider a simple model with just two firms, 1 and 2. Assume that the revenues they receive when they produce outputs q_1 and q_2 are given by $R_1(q_1, q_2)$ and $R_2(q_1, q_2)$. Each firm has a constant marginal cost of production β_1 and β_2 and assume that this is private information, firm 1 knowing the true value of β_1, firm 2 knowing the true value of β_2. Assume, for simplicity, that β can take on only two values, $\underline{\beta}$ and $\bar{\beta}$, $\underline{\beta} < \bar{\beta}$. Collusion will result in the adoption of output levels for each firm and the levels may be sensitive to the private information β_1 and $\beta_2 - q_1(\beta_1, \beta_2)$ and $q_2(\beta_1, \beta_2)$. However, this can only be implemented if a firm does not pretend to be a high cost firm ($\bar{\beta}$) when it is low cost ($\underline{\beta}$) and vice versa; for firm 1, profit maximization implies

$$R_1[q_1(\underline{\beta}, \beta_2), q_2(\underline{\beta}, \beta_2)] - \underline{\beta} q_1(\underline{\beta}, \beta_2)$$
$$\geqslant R_1[q_1(\bar{\beta}, \beta_2), q_2(\bar{\beta}, \beta_2)] - \underline{\beta} q_1(\bar{\beta}, \beta_2)$$

and

$$R_1[q_1(\bar{\beta}, \beta_2), q_2(\bar{\beta}, \beta_2)] - \bar{\beta} q_1(\bar{\beta}, \beta_2)$$
$$\geqslant R_1[q_1(\underline{\beta}, \beta_2), q_2(\underline{\beta}, \beta_2)] - \bar{\beta} q_1(\underline{\beta}, \beta_2)$$

This places restrictions on the class of solutions that can be implemented. Combining the inequalities gives

$$(\bar{\beta} - \underline{\beta})[q_1(\underline{\beta}, \beta_2) - q_1(\bar{\beta}, \beta_2)] \geqslant 0$$

which implies that the lower the marginal cost, the more a firm is allowed to produce. Given that the collusive solution will usually entail a restriction in output as compared with what a firm would like to choose (the other firm's output remaining constant), the firm must be provided with a disincentive from pretending to be a low-cost firm when it is high-cost and this will come from variations in q_2 – to provide the right incentives to firm 1, the output of firm 2 should be negatively correlated with the marginal cost of firm 1.

The foregoing demonstrates that the implementability requirement gives some structure to the collusive solution. But the exact outcome chosen will be the result of bargaining between the firms concerned. This bargaining process may involve the transfer of information prior to collusive agreements being reached (Roberts, 1985).

Recognition of the adverse selection problem gives theoretical insight into the form of collusive practices that are discussed in the more applied literature. In general discussions a distinction is drawn between implicit and explicit collusion. However, in models without information problems, each firm is aware of the agreement that would be decided upon if it met

with other firms and is aware how reneging firms would be dealt with. In this case, there is no need for firms to collude explicitly and the distinction between implicit and explicit collusion is not useful. But when adverse selection exists, it is clear that a rule which makes other firms' behaviour depend upon the private information of some firm will require information transmission between firms. The idea of implicit collusion can be rationalized as a situation where either no information is transmitted or, to take a less extreme case, where information is transmitted through aggregate market-wide indices, e.g. the equilibrium price in the industry.

The existence of adverse selection can also provide a theoretical rationale for mark-up pricing as a collusive outcome (Roberts, 1983). When firms are selling in the same market, cost conditions facing firms are more likely to be the source of private information than demand conditions. While it may be impossible for other firms to observe the cost *function* of a firm, it may be possible to observe the level of costs at the output being produced. As this observation can be used as a proxy for the private information of the individual firm, a collusive agreement will involve the output and price levels of firms being dependent upon cost levels – this provides a rationale for why the firms' behaviour may be sensitive to average, rather than the conventional marginal, costs.

4. Over the last twenty years, most of the theoretical literature on collusion has considered situations where the actions of firms fail to be perfectly observed by other firms – a situation of moral hazard. If the preferences of firms are common knowledge then the problem is not one of deciding upon the collusive solution but, instead, of policing that solution.

The simplest example of imperfect monitoring arises when there is a delay before the action of a firm is observed by others. If time units are set equal to the delay time then a firm will gain from reneging on a collusive agreement if

$$(1 - \beta)\Pi^R + \beta \Pi^P > \Pi^C$$

where Π^C is the profit per unit time under the collusive agreement, Π^R is the maximum profit that the firm can achieve by reneging given that other firms keep to the collusive agreement Π^P is the profit the firm can achieve when it is being punished by the other firms and β is the discount factor for the firm. Obviously, $\Pi^R \geqslant \Pi^C$ so that the longer the delay before other firms perceive reneging (the smaller the β), the more incentive a firm has to renege. As the degree of punishment that can be inflicted is restricted by the requirement that other firms have to punish, and this incentive itself is diminished when there is a delay in observing behaviour, the smallest possible Π^P will rise as the delay time increases so reinforcing the incentive to renege. For a detailed analysis of this problem, see Abreu (1986).

The other main form of imperfect monitoring that has been considered deals with the case where individual firm behaviour is never observable but market-wide aggregates can be observed by all firms. This was the situation which was studied by Stigler (1964) in his seminal paper on collusion and by many authors since (a recent analysis is to be found in the work of Porter, 1983, and Green and Porter, 1984). In the case studied by Stigler, firms observe the demand conditions for their own output and this gives an indication of the prices that other firms are charging. Green and Porter take the simple case of a homogeneous product being produced by similar firms. There is some uncertainty in demand so that a 'low' market price may be a result of this uncertainty or of 'cheating' on the collusive agreement by some firms. Green and Porter consider 'trigger-price' punishment strategies which take the form of the group moving to the Cournot equilibrium for a fixed time T if the market price drops below some level $\bar{p}$. A feature of this informational set-up is that all firms suffer from this punishment. The trigger-price strategies are set so that cheating does not occur though, because of the uncertainty, a proportion of time is spent in the punishment regime. There is a direct trade-off between the gains from a collusive agreement that severely restricts output and the costs of punishment that will be suffered in the maintenance of this agreement. Notice that as there is no adverse selection, there are no requirements for the firms to meet together to decide upon collusive behaviour – it may be far-fetched but there is nothing to rule out a system of implicit collusion with trigger-price strategies. For this reason, these moral hazard models are often described as non-cooperative models of collusion.

5. The theory and practice of collusion are much discussed in texts on industrial organization. The foregoing has tried to make clear that the structure of information asymmetry in the market is crucial for understanding the operation of collusive agreements. With a particular informational set-up, the structure of the set of collusive agreements which will not entail reneging is now quite well understood. Despite much work, there is rather less understanding of the exact agreement that will be settled upon.

KEVIN ROBERTS

See also CARTELS; COOPERATIVE EQUILIBRIA; COOPERATIVE GAMES.

BIBLIOGRAPHY

Abreu, D. 1986. Extremal equilibria of oligopolistic supergames. *Journal of Economic Theory* 39(1), June, 191-225.

Friedman, J. 1971. A non-cooperative equilibrium for supergames. *Review of Economic Studies* 38(1), January, 1-12.

Green, E. and Porter, R. 1984. Noncooperative collusion under imperfect price information. *Econometrica* 52(1), January, 87-100.

Nash, J. 1950. The bargaining problem. *Econometrica* 18(2), April, 155-62.

Porter, R. 1983. Optimal cartel trigger price strategies. *Journal of Economic Theory* 29(2), April, 313-38.

Roberts, K. 1983. Self-agreed cartel rules. IMSSS Discussion Paper No. 427, Stanford.

Roberts, K. 1985. Cartel behaviour and adverse selection. *Journal of Industrial Economics* 33(4), 401-13.

Rubinstein, A. 1979. Equilibrium in supergames with the overtaking criterion. *Journal of Economic Theory* 21(1), August, 1-9.

Scherer, F. 1980. *Industrial Market Structure and Economic Performance.* 2nd edn, Chicago: Rand McNally.

Stigler, G.J. 1964. A theory of oligopoly. *Journal of Political Economy* 72(1), February, 44-61.

colonialism.

> Everywhere do I perceive a certain conspiracy of rich men seeking their own advantage under the name and pretext of the commonwealth (Sir Thomas More).

Modern colonialism, as a historical phenomenon of territorial expansion, is intimately entwined with the rise and expansion of the modern capitalist world system. So colonialism is entwined with the history, economics, politics and ruling ideas of the modern capitalist society. On the other hand, and to avoid any terminological confusions, the term *imperialism* should be reserved to designate the new nexus of financial and technological dependency relations and arrangements marking the new distinct stage of mature capitalism (Magdoff, 1970).

During the modern colonial period (1870–1945) colonialism has emerged as a general description of the state of subjection – political, economic and intellectual – of a non-European society as a result of the process of colonial organization (Fieldhouse, 1981).

THE AGE OF COLONIALISM: HISTORICAL BACKGROUND. The age of colonialism began about 1500, following the European discoveries of a sea route around Africa's southern coast (1488) and of America (1492). Colonialism thus expanded by conquest and settlement after a period of extensive exploration. The improvement in navigational instruments helped a great deal to make substantial progress in the discovery of new geographical territories.

Portugal emerged as the leading nation in such process of overseas expansion. 'The search for wealth in the form of gold, ivory, spices and slaves spurred the Portuguese and may have been the strongest motivating force behind the colonization drive of the Portuguese during the 16th century' (*Encyclopaedia Britannica*, 1768, Vol. 4, p. 881).

The old colonial period, which lasted nearly three centuries, following the major Portuguese and Spanish conquests, may be viewed largely as a commercial venture. The Spaniards and the Portuguese resorted to their warships, gunnery and seamanship to keep the main trade routes open. The Spanish sovereigns created in 1504 the House of Trade (Casa de Contracion) to regulate commerce between Spain and the New World. Their purpose was to establish state monopoly over overseas trade, and thus pour the maximum amount of bullion into the royal treasury (*Britannica*, 1768, Vol. 5, pp. 882–3).

The old colonial system was disrupted in the 18th century as new contradictions developed due to the rapid advance of the Industrial Revolution in England, and by the progressive control England was able to exercise over world shipping. Such new developments led to a policy of opening the American ports to international trade, a policy at variance with the type of colonial relations prevailing between Spain, Portugal and their colonies. These relations were organized exclusively around the exploitation of precious metals (Furtado, 1970, p. 20).

The century between the 1820s and the outbreak of the World War I saw the establishment of the modern colonial order. For during that period European countries had achieved complete dominance over world trade, finance and shipping. On the other hand, the political and military authority of the European conquerors was backed by superiority in technology, applied science, organization and information systems (Bagchi, 1982).

Between the late 1870s and World War I (1914–18), the colonial powers added to their possessions an average of about 240,000 square miles (620,000 sq. km.) a year, while during the first 75 years of the 19th century the rate of increase in new territories acquired by colonial powers averaged about 83,000 square miles (215,000 sq. km.) a year. By the year 1914, the colonies extended over approximately 85 per cent of the surface of the globe.

Against this historical background, John Hicks establishes a useful distinction between two types of colony: colonies of settlement and trading-post colonies (Hicks, 1969, p. 51). A third type of colony was identified as 'the plantation colonies'. In such case, the colony which started as a colony of settlement was gradually transformed into a trading colony (ibid., p. 53).

THE COLONIZATION DEBATE. While there is a strong connection between mercantile expansion and colonization, it would be a mistake to emphasize the crude economic interpretation of colonialism by narrowing down colonialism to the process of control of supplies of raw materials, mineral resources and markets in underdeveloped and precapitalist regions. In fact, such a narrow economistic approach eliminates a vital aspect of colonialism relating to political activity and the drive for dominance over the daily lives of the people of the colonized regions (e.g. French colonialism).

Nonetheless, colonialism must be viewed, dialectically, as a complex phenomenon of capitalist expansion, operating in terms of time and space. To illustrate this point, S.H. Frankel described such a process as a *disintegrating* but also a *formative* process, a unique process in the history of mankind (Frankel, 1953). Some other writers justified colonial rule on the ground that 'Colonialism was a necessary instrument of "modernization" which would help other peoples to do what they could not have done, or have done as well, by themselves' (Fieldhouse, 1981, p. 43). At the other end of the spectrum, radical theorists, notable among them Walter Rodney, claim that under colonialism 'the only things that developed were dependency and underdevelopment' (Rodney, 1972, p. 256).

One of the most articulate arguments put forward in defence of the colonial rule in underdeveloped areas is that of Lord Bauer, who contends that:

> The colonial governments established law and order, safeguarded private property and contractual relations, organized basic transport and health services, and introduced some modern financial and legal institutions. This environment also promoted the establishment or extension of external contacts, which in turn encouraged the inflow of external resources, notably administrative, commercial and technical skills as well as capital.
>
> These contacts also acquainted the population with new wants, crops, commodities and methods of cultivation and opened new sources of supply of a wide range of commodities. These changes engendered a new outlook on material advance and on the means of securing it: for good or for evil these contacts promoted the erosion of the traditional values, objectives, attitudes and customs obstructing material advance (Bauer, 1976, p. 149).

This argument only confirms the deep-seated Western biased view, claiming that material progress and advance can only be achieved by eroding the traditional values, customs and production structures of pre-capitalist and primitive societies. Rosa Luxemburg (1913) would see in Lord Bauer's view an eloquent proof of her radical contentions about colonialism and territorial expansion, by the emerging capitalist nations.

But what is at issue is not the possibility or not of achieving material progress or advancement, but the terms on which these transformations in the material and socioeconomic structures were operated. From our viewpoint, what needs to be stressed is the loss of sovereignty which the process of European colonization entailed for practically all colonized peoples. In Africa, for instance, European colonizers often crushed, suppressed or amalgamated states at will. In most instances, the direct colonial rule was designed to direct and reorder the day-to-day lives of the African peoples (Ajayi, 1969).

Seen in a radically different light, thinkers such as Albert Memmi, Jean-Paul Sartre and Franz Fanon placed greater emphasis on the ideological implications and the sociopsychological consequences of the process of colonization. According to Fanon, colonialism tended not only to deprive a society of its freedom and its wealth, but of its very character, leaving its people intellectually and morally disoriented (Fanon, English edition, 1966).

PATTERNS OF COLONIAL TRADE. Historians tend to agree that the conquest of colonies was designed to the economic advantage of the European conquerors. Some historians (e.g. E.J. Hobsbawm) would go as far as to claim that the Industrial Revolution in England would not have been accomplished without the conquest and penetration of 'underdeveloped' markets overseas (Hobsbawm, 1968, p. 54).

In fact, the primary aim of all European states was to use commercial regulations to maximize their share of colonial trade in both directions and the profits they made from it. The English Navigation Acts, dating from the 1650s, may be taken as typical in this respect. According to these Acts, all colonial trade must be carried in British-owned and registered ships. All goods imported to the colonies must either be the product of Britain or be transhipped and pay duty there. Any colonial exports so 'enumerated' must be carried direct to a British port in the first instance (Deane, 1965, p. 204). The aim of such rules and regulations was to give British shipowners, merchants and manufacturers an assured benefit from colonial commerce and to enable the government to tax colonial trade. This clearly indicates the close association between the process of colonization and the rise of various foreign-trade monopolies held by the charted colonial companies.

Hence, against all claims of the 'Free-Trade' school, the British cotton industry did not rely on its competitive superiority, but relied heavily on the monopolistic practices embodied in colonial trade-regulations, and enforced by the British commercial and naval supremacy (Hobsbawm, 1968, p. 58). On the other hand, the terms of trade between the colonized areas and the metropolitan countries had a tendency to deteriorate steadily over time, so that the primary producers in colonized areas tended to obtain proportionally less with their labour than they could have done had they concentrated on producing food or other subsistence crops for their own use or for the home market (Fieldhouse, 1981, p. 78). This may be characterized, in modern terminology, as 'unequal exchange', which emphasizes once again the exploitative nature of colonial trade.

THE INTERNAL CONTROL OF THE COLONIAL ECONOMY. The key to understanding colonialism as a historical phenomenon lies in analysing the mechanism of the internal control of the colonial economy. In this connection, one has to answer two fundamental questions. Why did the Western countries spend so much energy, blood and money in seeking to procure colonial possessions? What are the direct and indirect economic benefits of colonialism?

In the colonial economy, top priority was given to infrastructure investment: railways, harbours, telegraphs, rivers and roads, since it was believed that these constitute the prerequisites of a modern economy, making it possible to link internal areas of production to the world commodity markets. In the agricultural sector, it is still an open question whether plantations, owned and run by foreigners, made any significant contribution to the development of the colonial economy. On the positive side, they served as the main vehicle of introducing new crops, attracting foreign capital, expanding the base of the cash economy and the wage-labour force, and increasing agricultural productivity. On the negative side, the crops of such plantations were subject to severe fluctuations on the international commodity markets, thus subjecting the colonial economy to severe cyclical fluctuations.

In matters of industrialization, many observers tend to agree that the colonial powers did not positively encourage industrialization in their dependencies, and in many instances their basic policies led to some sort of de-industrialization (Bagchi, 1982). In this respect, many writers invoke the record of colonization in India from the days of the East Indian Company. For the balance of historical evidence points to the fact that up to the 18th century the economic conditions of India were relatively advanced, and Indian methods of industrial production were comparable with those prevailing in any other advanced part of the world (Baran, 1957, p. 144).

On the other hand, Bill Warren has offered a neo-Marxist view, opposed to the 'Dependency School', regarding the effects of colonialism on the development of productive forces in Third World countries. His main argument runs as follows: 'Direct Colonialism, far from having retarded or distorted indigenous capitalist development that might otherwise have occurred, acted as a powerful engine of progressive social change' (Warren, 1980).

Nonetheless, Warren's positive account of the effects of colonialism on the process of capitalist development in Third World countries tends to be rather unitary in spirit. For the pattern of resource allocation in colonial territories had been shaped and administered largely by forein investors, bankers and merchants. According to Paul Baran, the principal impact of foreign enterprise on the development of the underdeveloped and precapitalist regions 'lies in hardening and strengthening the sway of merchant capitalism, in slowing down and indeed preventing its transformation into industrial capitalism' (Baran, 1957, p. 205).

This very nature of the process of capitalist development under colonialism led some authors, such as H. Alavi, to offer the highly controversial concept of the 'colonial mode of production'. This concept was offered as a theoretical construction designed to allow for a variety of relations other than those which characterize the 'capitalist mode of production', as experienced in the advanced capitalist economies of the 'centre' (Alavi, 1975). In this respect, Alavi and company established the distinctive features of the 'colonial mode of production' on the basis of empirical investigation of the circuits of capital and forms of labour recruitment of what comes to be called by other authors (i.e. Samir Amin and Gunder Frank) 'colonial capitalism' or 'peripheral capitalism' (Booth, 1985, p. 169). Yet the difficulties and confusions surrounding the concept of a 'colonial mode of production', as a distinct mode of production, remain formidable.

DECOLONIZATION AND NEOCOLONIALISM: TWO SIDES OF THE SAME COIN. The drive towards decolonization in the post-World War II period was a response to the economic crisis of an ageing colonial system. This colonial system was found to involve considerable, and sometimes unacceptable, financial costs to the metropolis. Moreover, colonialism had become increasingly discredited among the people of the colonizing nations themselves, just as the emotional strains of suppressing nationalistic movements in colonized regions had become largely intolerable for public opinion (Fieldhouse, 1981, p. 24).

Nonetheless, the process of decolonization proved to be a nominal process in the sense that the formal end of colonial rule did not necessarily result in genuine economic independence for the former colonies. There is now a community of view among left-wing economists and writers that decolonization took place when and because foreign monopoly capital felt confident that the colonial society and economy had been so restructured that their interests could be preserved without direct political control. In other words, colonialism had been merely transmitted into perpetual neocolonialism (Baran, 1957).

The term 'neocolonialism', which has gained wide acceptance since the mid-1950s, is meant to designate a state of affairs characterized by a structure of dependency relationships whereby the former colonial territories are kept in their subordinate place within the imperialist system. This is maintained and sustained by means of chronic and structural balance of payments difficulties, arising from the trade, aid and investment relationships with their former or new metropolitan countries (Warren, 1973, p. 35).

In sum colonialism may be seen in a historical perspective as one decisive and dramatic stage in the evolution of international economic relationships. The establishment of colonial rule constituted an arbitrary break in the normal course of history, splitting up regions and creating new artificial entities, transplanting new alien values and institutions into colonized societies. One may finally wonder whether it would not have been better for the people of the colonized regions to remain autonomous until certain indigenous forces could gain momentum and generate new conditions for socioeconomic development and material progress.

M. ABDEL-FADIL

See also IMPERIALISM.

BIBLIOGRAPHY

Ajayi, J.F. 1969. Colonialism: an episode in African history. In *Colonialism in Africa 1870–1960,* ed. L.H. Gann and P. Duignan, vol. 1, London: Cambridge University Press.

Alavi, H. 1975. India and the colonial mode of production. In *The Socialist Register, 1975,* ed. R. Miliband and J. Saville, London: Merlin Press.

Bagchi, A.K. 1982. *The Political Economy of Underdevelopment.* London: Cambridge University Press.

Baran, P. 1957. *The Political Economy of Growth.* New York: Monthly Review Press.

Bauer, P.T. 1976. *Dissent on Development.* London: Weidenfeld & Nicolson.

Booth, D. 1985. Marxism and development sociology: interpreting the impasse. *World Development* 13(7), 761-87.

Deane, P. 1965. *The First Industrial Revolution.* London: Cambridge University Press.

Encyclopaedia Britannica. 1768. 5th edn, 1977, Vol. 4.

Fanon, F. 1966. *The Wretched of the Earth.* New York.

Fieldhouse, D.K. 1981. *Colonialism, 1870–1945: An Introduction.* London: Weidenfeld & Nicolson.

Frankel, S.H. 1953. *The Economic Impact of Colonialism on Under-Developed Societies.* Oxford: Basil Blackwell.

Furtado, C. 1970. *Economic Development of Latin America.* London: Cambridge University Press.

Hicks, J. 1969. *A Theory of Economic History.* Oxford: Clarendon Press.

Hobsbawm, E. 1968. *Industry and Empire.* London: Weidenfeld & Nicolson.

Luxemburg, R. 1913. *The Accumulation of Capital.* London: Routledge & Kegan Paul, 1951.

Magdoff, H. 1970. Is imperialism really necessary? *Monthly Review,* Part I, 22(5), October, 1–14; Part II, 22(6), November, 1–11.

Rodney, W. 1972. *How Europe Underdeveloped Africa.* London: Bogle.

Warren, B. 1973. Imperialism and capitalist industrialization. *New Left Review* No. 81, September–October, 3-44.

Warren, B. 1980. *Imperialism: Pioneer of Capitalism.* London: New Left Books.

colonies. The economic advantages and disadvantages of colonies, the best means of establishing them and ensuring their development, and the principles that should govern trade and other relations with the mother country, have persistently served as fertile topics for policy and theoretical debate in the history of political economy. The treatment given here will be confined to the British debate on colonies from the late 18th to the first decades of the 20th century.

The British empire was composed of colonies and ex-colonies which had differing histories of acquisition and varying political and economic relationships with the mother country. It follows that the problems which they posed were equally diverse, as illustrated by the differences between the economies of the British West Indies before and after slavery was abolished, the question of public land disposal and emigration to Canada, Australia and New Zealand, and the tasks of administering an Indian sub-continent with a largely peasant population living close to minimum subsistence levels. To this list can be added the problems of integrating Scotland and Ireland into the English economy and polity after the respective Acts of Union in 1707 and 1808, where 'colonial' issues – in a technical rather than emotive sense – were often at stake, even if the term was not used to describe them. Indeed, Ireland and India as subsistence farming economies posed similar problems to British administrators, despite major differences in their cultural backgrounds and political status within the empire. For that matter, even the United States after independence could for some purposes be treated as having a 'colonial' relationship with Britain, largely because it remained a major outlet for British capital and labour.

The sheer magnitude of the problems of empire and their changing nature over more than two centuries would guarantee that they bulked large in the minds of British economists. A few strategic examples will show that there has always been a fairly intimate relationship between economics, economists, and empire. Adam Smith may well have advised the imposition of the Townshend duties on North America in 1763, and he was certainly involved in advising the British government on the consequences of American break-away when these earlier attempts to exert fiscal control led to successful revolt. Malthus held the first Chair of political economy in Britain at an educational institution at Haileybury established to train the servants of the East Indian Company; and James and John Stuart Mill together devoted nearly 40 years to the service of the Company. The younger Mill was also a consistent supporter of schemes involving the 'systematic colonization' of Australia and New Zealand, as well as taking a major interest, along with most of his classical predecessors and successors, in the problems of the Irish economy. The controversy over imperial preference at the turn of the 20th century underlined the gulf that existed between historical or institutionalist economists and their more orthodox opponents, led by Alfred Marshall, who believed that the increasing challenge to Britain's industrial hegemony did not justify abandonment of deductive methods of economic reasoning or those cosmopolitan free trade principles which had spurred British prosperity earlier. Finally, of course, there is Keynes, whose first employment as a civil servant was within the India Office, and whose first major economic work was a treatise on *Indian Currency and Finance* (1913) – a work which attempted to do for its day what Sir James Steuart had done when he wrote *The Principles of Money Applied to the Present State of the Coin of Bengal* in 1772.

A treatment based on chronology and recurring themes seems the best way of dealing with the diversity of Colonies as a topic of economic interest, though it should be remembered that colonies and empire was never treated solely as *economic* problems, even after the inauguration, largely under Marshall's auspices, of a measure of professional distance in these matters.

The initial and longest period in the history of colonial policy began in England during Elizabethan times and effectively ended with the dismantling of what had become known as the 'old colonial system' in the 1820s. This system was loosely based on the amorphous doctrines which Adam Smith subjected to attack in the *Wealth of Nations* as a central part of his condemnation of the 'mercantile system' (later known as Mercantilism). During this mercantile period colonies generated a large body of literature which reflected the overwhelming concern with national power and economic self-sufficiency as the prime objectives of state intervention. Thus colonies not only served direct strategic purposes as naval or military bases, they were also treated as sources of precious metals, and of strategic and other raw materials necessary to Britain's early manufacturing industries – of particular value when carried in British ships and bought through monopolistic arrangements at prices lower than could be obtained on the world market. Colonies were variously regarded as protected export markets, outlets for surplus population, and sources of tribute, in addition to serving occasionally as prison settlements. Although the development of free trade doctrines, together with associated monetary ideas on specie-flow mechanisms, eventually succeeded in undermining many of the arguments in favour of colonial possessions and regulations, economic nationalism and neo-mercantilistic ideas and policies have always exerted a powerful attraction, especially in countries that were industrial later-comers or anxious to overcome the problems of underdevelopment by means of import-substitution and/or export promotion.

During the 18th century, the established wisdom on the subject of colonies came under question largely because the supposed benefits of trade controls to the mother country were connected with the growing cost to Britain of defending and governing her North American colonies. Among the earliest critics of the colonial system from this point of view was Josiah Tucker, who argued that existing benefits in the form of export markets and imported goods would accrue to Britain under free trade, and without the attendant military and economic burdens of empire. Provoked by David Hume's essays on commerce and money, Tucker also engaged in an important dispute with Hume on the question of whether trade relations between rich and poor countries could be considered as equalizing or not, and if so, by what process – perhaps through rising labour costs and prices in the richer trading partner, or through some other mechanisms of stimulus and emulation in the poorer country. The dispute was of relevance to free-trade relations between England and Scotland after Union, and of potential relevance to Britain's relations with Ireland and other 'colonies', whether acknowledged as such or not. Indeed the Hume–Tucker debate was an early example of recognition of the essential similarities between international and interregional trade in a world in which currencies were linked through the gold standard. It also concerned relative rates of growth and the respective merits of agriculture and manufacturing as the basis for a nation's wealth and prospects for economic development. Would those who had the advantages of an early start acquire world dominion and monopoly; and hence would poorer and later starters in the race be forced to employ protective measures to establish and maintain their infant industries? If noticed, the debate would have foreshadowed later issues raised by Friedrich List and Henry Carey with Germany and the United States in mind, as well as other questions such as 'free trade imperialism', the 'permanence' of the dollar problem after World War II, and the debate on 'dependency' and the development of post-colonial underdevelopment in the 1960s and 1970s.

Smith's extensive treatment of colonies in the *Wealth of Nations* (especially Book IV, chapter 7) became the *locus classicus* of the anti-mercantile position, where much of his discussion was interwoven with an account of the founding of the European colonies which brought matters up to the present, namely to the issues underlying Britain's dispute with its American colonies. Whereas Edmund Burke had advocated the relaxation of trade controls and taxation as a means of preserving the political status quo, Smith maintained that Britain's pretensions to empire would remain those of a shortsighted shopkeeper unless some system could be found whereby the debts and current burdens of empire could be shared by the colonies themselves; and he emphasized the point by closing the *Wealth of Nations* with a warning about the potential long-term effects on British growth prospects of existing arrangements. Hence the elaborate scheme he advanced for an imperial (Anglo-American) free trade zone, with provision for complete fiscal harmonization and legislative union. However, since he regarded this proposal as utopian, its purpose was chiefly to underline the precise conditions under which the burdens of empire could be made acceptable. Much the same result could be achieved through free trade and a treaty of friendship, without provision for imperial government.

Smith's close dissection of the various gains and losses involved in maintaining the monopoly of colonial trade employed a quasi-mercantilist idea of 'vent for surplus', as well as other arguments about the effects on profits of colonial markets which could not be squared with later Ricardian orthodoxy on the doctrine of comparative costs, capital accumulation, Say's Law, and the permanent causes of declining profits. Ricardo also pointed out circumstances in which it was possible for the mother country to so regulate the trade of a colony as to make it less beneficial to the colony, and more advantageous to the mother country than free trade – an early version of the terms-of-trade argument for tariffs (not meant for use) which in the hands of Robert Torrens was to blossom into a case for an imperial *Zollverein* a few years later.

With the support of most political economists, however, the system of colonial preferences was gradually and unilaterally dismantled, beginning with the efforts of Huskisson and Robinson in the 1820s. The views of special interest groups, especially those connected with shipping and the West Indies, which Smith had expected to prevail, were outflanked by an uncertain combination of intellectual argument, political opportunism, and a general realization that Britain's industrial dominance meant that mutual restrictions merely restricted the dominant partner without conferring equivalent benefit. A similar combination involving humanitarian arguments prevailed on the related matter of West Indian slavery and the slave trade. The keystone of Britain's rather isolated status as a free-trading nation was installed with the abolition of the Corn Laws in 1846, a policy that had considerable long-term significance for British agriculture and Britain's relationship to colonial suppliers of food and raw materials, including the United States as well as colonies of recent settlement.

During the 1830s and 1840s public debate on colonies and colonization was dominated by the activities of Edward Gibbon Wakefield and the colonial reformers, a group of radicals dedicated to the revival of 'the lost art of colonization'. Their programme entailed the creation of self-governing colonies as outlets for Britain's surplus capital and labour, avoiding the evils of simply 'shovelling out paupers', abolishing penal settlements, and creating 'civilized' communities enjoying the benefits of free trade and high rates of growth. Wakefield's diagnosis of the simultaneous existence in Britain of surplus capital and labour, and the consequent need for new fields of employment abroad, was developed in opposition to Ricardian orthodoxy on the wage fund and Say's Law. His ideas on the optimal economic development of colonies also conflicted with Smith's view that countries of European settlement enjoying an abundance of land were likely to make rapid economic progress. The key to high rates of growth lay in achieving the correct balance between capital, labour, and their 'field of employment' by restricting access to land. This could be achieved by setting a price on land sufficient to delay dispersal of the wage-labour force, and by using the proceeds of land sale for the purpose of bringing in new immigrants. This policy meant that public land disposal and immigration had to remain an imperial rather than purely local concern, thereby creating scope for conflict when colonies achieved self-government. The Wakefield policy came to be seen as a symbol of imperial oppression, an attempt to place colonial development within a straitjacket designed with European conditions in mind. It also entailed loss of freedom in disposing of one of the main sources of revenue available to self-governing colonies. The colonial reformers' hopes of establishing an empire in which free trade ruled were another casualty of self-government when it led to tariffs being raised by Canada and Australia against British and other goods.

What now seems remarkable is the rapidity and extent of influence exerted over British colonial policy by Wakefield's untried theories, though modern development economics may yield comparable examples. He was also highly successful in convincing a number of leading political economists, not least John Stuart Mill, that his ideas deserved to form the basis for future policy. Mill gave prominence to Wakefield's ideas in his *Principles of Political Economy* and other writings by consistently championing 'systematic colonization' as a solution to Britain's population difficulties; and by treating its application to new countries as a valid exception to the general principle of *laissez faire*, namely as a case where the self-interest principle acting under competitive conditions would lead to a sub-optimal result as far as the community was concerned. As part of his general modification of Ricardo's assumptions concerning capital scarcity and the distant prospect of the stationary state, Mill also endorsed the conclusions of Wakefield's heterodox diagnosis of Britain's economic condition, while denying that it was in conflict with Say's Law and other received Ricardian doctrines. By acknowledging the importance to Britain of the export of capital and labour to colonies, Mill not only removed an obstacle to support for colonization, and hence to the extension of empire, he opened up a major exception to the comparative cost doctrine as an interpretation of Britain's trading pattern: the trade with colonies now became akin to interregional trade. It should also be noted that Mill, confirming the tradition that the only new economic arguments for protection have been advanced by those who favour free trade as a general rule, gave a cautious endorsement to the infant industry case for tariffs.

India was never a colony in the same sense that North America, Australia and New Zealand were British colonies. Attempts were often made to prevent or discourage European colonization before 1830, and until 1858 India was governed by the East India Company acting on a renewable Charter granted by Parliament. The Company had been subjected to closer government control in the late 18th century, deprived of its commercial monopoly in 1813, and finally ceased trading altogether in 1833 when it lost its exclusive privileges over the China trade. These developments represented another victory for the forces of free trade, and they blunted the force of Smith's criticisms both of monopolies and government by trading companies. As we have seen in the case of Tucker, free trade ideas could be associated with a case for complete 'emancipation' (Bentham's term) of all colonies. (It was an association of free trade with anti-imperialism which was an invitation for revisionist historians to counter with a neat, perhaps over-neat, inversion by drawing attention to 'free-trade imperialism'.) But there were fewer spokesman for such ideas in relation to India, where other notions of European superiority and responsibility held sway, along with more mundane considerations connected with the retention of investment, employment, and trading opportunities.

India had provided Smith with a prime example of a stationary or declining state, something that could either be attributed to the deficiencies of its system of government and taxation, or to those of a backward people whose culture constituted a barrier to economic progress, though usually to a combination of both. In addition, criticism from divergent quarters was made of the flow of tribute leaving India for Britain, much of it financed by exports of textiles that competed with domestic industry: Indian commerce came in conflict with British manufacturing interests, which were placated by the imposition of duties on Indian imports. But with the reorganization of the Company, especially after 1813, came new priorities and opportunities for those with ambitions to bring the light of post-Smithian, and more especially, Ricardian political economy to bear on the problems of Indian administration. Such a task proved highly congenial to James Mill, a critic of the Company's monopoly powers who was appointed by the Company in 1819 and rose to the rank of Chief Examiner in charge of political, judicial, and fiscal correspondence with India. It was largely through Mill's efforts, later endorsed by his son, John Stuart Mill, that the Ricardian rent doctrine came to play such a large part in the conduct of Indian affairs. It provided the basis for the *ryotwari* system of land tenure, whereby the state became the sole landlord and met its revenue needs by levying *ryots* or peasant-farmers according to Ricardian principles of pure rent. By confining the state's exactions to rent it was thought that the peasant farmer would enjoy normal profits and wages, and the state would eliminate an intermediary or landowning class of *zemindars* or rent-receivers. The system embodied action according to a clear analytical proposition, antagonism to rent as a form of private income, and a view of the prospects for Indian economic development that treated the peasant proprietor as a capitalistic entrepreneur, freed from the arbitrary exactions of landowners and responding to market incentives – which is not to say that the application of these Western economic ideas to Indian conditions was any more successful than the *zemindari* alternative.

In Ireland, where similar economic conditions of a growing population dependent on a backward agriculture obtained, it proved more difficult to bypass the Irish landowner in order to grant the kind of security of tenure to the peasant proprietor that either existed or was the aim of administrators in India. Indeed, the initial view of economists during the early classical period was unsympathetic to the preservation of peasant proprietorship in Ireland. The favoured solution was consolidation of tenant-holdings as a preliminary to the

creation of a capitalistic form of farming employing agricultural wage-labour along English lines, together with emigration or absorption of the displaced population into alternative employment. Before, but especially after the Great Famine of 1846, emigration, largely unplanned, was the only part of this programme that operated. Under the leadership of John Stuart Mill, J.E. Cairnes, W.T. Thornton and Henry Fawcett, the earlier diagnoses and remedies were entirely recast; a more positive evaluation of the possibilities of transforming cottier tenants into peasant proprietors enjoying security of tenure was registered and advocated as the basis for a solution to Irish problems. It was a position that ran directly counter to English property ideas and involved recognition of the role of custom as opposed to contract in designing policies and institutions for societies that did not conform to the English model.

Mill's deployment of a more relativist approach in policy matters was later to be seen as a welcome, though incomplete concession to a succeeding generation of more full-blooded historical and institutionalist critics of deductive economic theory, with its built-in bias in favour of rational economic man – a creature originally invoked by Mill to underline the contrast with societies where custom prevailed. Such critics were more numerous and vocal after 1870, and the resulting split within the economists' ranks coincided with a campaign for 'fair trade' in the 1880s which blossomed into Joseph Chamberlain's scheme of tariff reform along imperial preference lines – an unwitting return to Torrens's imperial *Zollverein*. The historical economists, led by William Cunningham and W.J. Ashley, had already followed Schmoller and other German exemplars in according a more positive valuation to Mercantilism, and this presaged their endorsement of tariff reform as an imperial remedy for Britain's declining competitiveness. At the price of forsaking free trade, Britain could offer preferential treatment to imperial food and raw materials in return for similar preferences in the markets of her ex-colonies. There had already been a revival of interest in imperial federation, which could be portrayed, as it was by John Shield Nicholson, as a return to Adam Smith's project of empire. While much of this belongs to the larger subject of imperialism, a term which has always carried more nationalistic and ideological oxygen, the episode is chiefly of interest here because it was the occasion for a major challenge to economic orthodoxy. Chamberlain's use of arguments supplied by such economists as W.A.S. Hewins brought Marshall into the professional and political fray with his *Memorandum on Fiscal Policy of International Trade* (1908), a work which is still perhaps the best brief restatement of the free trade position based on a combination of neoclassical trade theory and an empirical analysis of contemporary conditions in the colonies as well as in Britain.

Marshall's pupil, John Maynard Keynes, was not as impressed by his master's memorandum when he looked back on it from the vantage point of 1930. At this time Keynes had decided that a revenue tariff was an acceptable policy for Britain to follow, though not for reasons connected with imperial solidarity. Thus when Neville Chamberlain achieved his father's goal with the passage of the Import Duties Act in 1932, followed by the Ottawa Agreements which began the period of imperial preference, Keynes withdrew his support for tariffs. Nevertheless, any account of the revolution associated with Keynes's name is likely to be incomplete without some reference to the ending of free trade in Britain, coupled as it was with the inauguration of an era in which external monetary constraints on British domestic policy were weakened. Of more long-term significance to imperial policy in the interwar period, however, was the revival of interest in state-assisted settlement in the white dominions and the new emphasis on colonial development, with Africa as well as India now assuming a larger role in official, if not professional, economic thinking. At this point colonies and colonial policy become something else, the beginnings of modern development economics.

DONALD WINCH

See also MERIVALE, HERMAN; MILL, JAMES; TRADE UNIONS; WAKEFIELD, EDWARD GIBBON.

BIBLIOGRAPHY
Ambirajan, S. 1978. *Classical Political Economy and British Policy in India*. Cambridge: Cambridge University Press.
Barber, W.J. 1975. *British Economic Thought and India, 1600–1858*. Oxford: Clarendon Press.
Black, R.D.C. 1960. *Economic Thought and the Irish Question, 1817–1870*. Cambridge: Cambridge University Press.
Black, R.D.C. 1968. Economic policy in Ireland and India in the time of J.S. Mill. *Economic History Review* 21, 321–36.
Drummond, I.M. 1974. *Imperial Economic Policy, 1917–1938*. London: Allen & Unwin.
Knorr, K. 1944. *British Colonial Theories, 1570–1850*. Toronto: Toronto University Press.
Semmel, B. 1970. *The Rise of Free Trade Imperialism*. Cambridge: Cambridge University Press.
Stokes, E. 1959. *The English Utilitarians and India*. Oxford: Clarendon Press.
Winch, D. 1965. *Classical Political Economy and Colonies*. London: Bell & Sons.
Wood, J.C. 1983. *British Economists and the Empire*. London: Croom Helm.

Colquhoun, Patrick

Colquhoun, Patrick (1745–1820). Colquhoun was born in Dundee. A successful early career in business led to the position of Lord Provost of Glasgow in 1782 and 1783. In 1789 Colquhoun moved to London and became active as a magistrate. He worked on the provision of poor relief and put forward plans for the reform of London's police. He died in London in 1820.

Colquhoun's interest in poor relief led to his *New and Appropriate System of Education for the Labouring People* (1806), a pamphlet based on his own experience of running a school in Westminster. Like Thomas Chalmers later, he argued for the necessity of education to raise the standards and aspirations of the poor, though primarily in order to curb vice rather than population. This, he believed, was the most cost-effective way of tackling poverty. His *Wealth, Power and Resources of the British Empire* (1814), his last important work, is the one for which he is best known. This contained detailed figures on incomes and occupations and the relative importance of agriculture and manufacturing in Great Britain and Ireland. He also included a history of the public revenue, and descriptive material on the colonies. The work was not very securely based; McCulloch, who had first-hand experience of trying to construct large-scale statistical data for his *Commercial Dictionary*, was severely critical of it in the *Edinburgh Review* and in *Brande's Dictionary*. But it was followed by later writers and Colquhoun's estimate that unproductive labour, one fifth of the total, received one third of output was widely quoted.

D.P. O'BRIEN

SELECTED WORKS
1806. *A New and Appropriate System of Education for the Labouring People*. London: J. Hatchard.

1814. *A Treatise on the Wealth, Power and Resources, of the British Empire, in every quarter of the world, including the East Indies; the rise and progress of the funding system explained; with observations on the national resources for the beneficial employment of a redundant population*. London: J. Mawman.

BIBLIOGRAPHY
Blaug, M. 1958. *Ricardian Economics*. New Haven: Yale University Press.
Deane, P. 1956. Contemporary estimates of national income in the first half of the nineteenth century. *Economic History Review* 8, 339–54.
Espinasse, F. 1887. Colquhoun, Patrick. In *Dictionary of National Biography*; reprinted, Oxford: Oxford University Press, 1973.
[McCulloch, J.R.] 1835. State and defects of British statistics. *Edinburgh Review* 61, 154–181.
McCulloch, J.R. 1837. *A Statistical Account of the British Empire; exhibiting its extent, physical capacities, population, industry, and civil and religious institutions*. London: C. Knight.

Colson, Léon Clément

Colson, Léon Clément (1853–1939). French engineer, economist and statistician, Colson was born at Versailles on 13 November 1853, and died at Paris on 24 March 1939. Trained in mathematics as an engineer at the Ecole Polytechnique and the Ecole des Ponts et Chaussées, Colson extended his interests to statistics and economics, eventually teaching the latter at both his alma maters and at the Ecole des Hautes Etudes Commerciales and the Ecole des Sciences Politiques. Despite a lifelong career in the French Ministry of Public Works, he found time to produce several notable works, including his monumental *Cours d'économie politique*.

Colson received high marks for the technical competence of his theoretical exposition. According to Antonelli, his *Cours* rendered the doctrines of the French Liberal School 'scientific'. Divisia hailed it as the best work on pure theory since Walras. Colson particularly demonstrated his competence in the field of production by erecting a theory of full employment on the idea of capital–labour substitution and the equalization of factor returns at the margin. He followed the Austrian theory of value, but at the same time showed more sympathy to Walras than his contemporaries did. His work also had a certain affinity with Marshall's in that it integrated mathematics and geometry into the exposition of economic theory. As with Cheysson, Colson's economic views were affected by his statistical studies as much as the latter were affected by the former. Despite exceptional difficulties, he was one of the first to attempt an estimate of French national income in the early years after World War I.

Colson was elected to the Institut International de Statistique in 1906, to the Academie des Sciences Morales et Politiques in 1910 (replacing Cheysson), and to the Conseil Supérieure de Statistique in 1912. He belonged to the French Legion of Honour and the Société d'Economie Politique, of which he was president from 1929 to 1933. He became an honorary fellow of the Royal Statistical Society (London) and was elected an original fellow of the Econometric Society, founded in 1931. His most imposing legacy, however, was the generation of 20th-century French economists and engineers he trained at the *grandes écoles* during the interwar period.

R.F. HÉBERT

SELECTED WORKS
1901–7. *Cours d'économie politique*. 3 vols, Paris: Gauthiers-Villars.
1912. *Organisme économique et désordre social*. Paris: E. Flammarion.
1914. *Railway Rates and Traffic*. Trans. L.R. Christie, G. Leedham and C. Travis. London: George Bell & Sons.

BIBLIOGRAPHY

Divisia, F. 1950. *Exposés économiques. L'Apport des ingénieurs français aux sciences économiques*. Paris: Dunod.

Flux, A.W. 1939. Clément-Léon Colson. *Royal Statistical Society Journal* 102(4), 624.

Marshall, A. 1933. Alfred Marshall, the mathematician, as seen by himself. *Econometrica* 1, 221–2.

Colwell, Stephen (1800–1871). Stephen Colwell, American protectionist, was born in Virginia (now West Virginia). After practising law, he eventually became a successful industrialist and entrepreneur in Philadelphia, where he was a leading citizen and philanthropist. He was a friend of Henry Carey's and shared many of Carey's views, especially his ardent protectionism. Colwell's appeal for high tariffs on iron manufactures and other goods resounded in many publications. Some of these were addressed to the Presbyterian clergy and he drew on religion to fortify his economic views. Colwell buttressed his appeal by making it part of a wider view of the world that may be characterized as elitist and supportive of high wages but also of inequalities of wealth and status. These were to be offset by a stewardship of wealth, that called for private charity rather than public relief for the poor, which Colwell opposed. High wages and private charity thus became complements of high tariffs.

Colwell's arguments ran counter to the teachings of the classical economists, whom he criticized on grounds that were similar to the criticisms made by the exponents of German historical economics and economic romanticism. Colwell was impressed by the protectionist views of Frederick List and found a translator for the original German of the latter's *National System of Political Economy*, to which he himself wrote an introduction.

Colwell is also remembered as the author of *The Ways and Means of Payment: A Full Analysis of the Credit System with its Various Modes of Adjustment* (1859), a massive volume that treats of the financial controversies of the time. In this work Colwell supported a private national bank, inconvertible paper money, the real-bills doctrine, the demonetization of gold, and a national clearing system, all amidst an economy of high prices. He denied the validity of the quantity theory of money and advised against a 100 per cent reserve plan. He wrote the book from a point of view that considered money the handmaiden of commerce.

HENRY W. SPIEGEL

SELECTED WORKS

1851. *New Themes for the Protestant Clergy*. Philadelphia: Lippincott, Grambo & Co.

1856. Preliminary essay to List, F. *National System of Political Economy*. Trans. by G.A. Mantile, Philadelphia: J.B. Lippincott & Co.

1859. *The Ways and Means of Payment: A Full Analysis of the Credit System with its Various Modes of Adjustment*. Philadelphia: J.B. Lippincott & Co.

BIBLIOGRAPHY

Dorfman, J. 1946. *The Economic Mind in American Civilization 1606–1865*. Vol. 2, New York: Viking.

Mints, L.W. 1945. *A History of Banking Theory in Great Britain and the United States*. Chicago: University of Chicago Press.

combination. 'Combination' is a term used for a variety of forms of organization. An obsolescent usage relates to business firms which have come together in some kind of merger and today are usually referred to as monopoly, cartel, industrial combination or multinational. In Britain during the 18th century and for most of the 19th century combination was understood to mean associations of working men whose purposes were the raising of wages or the alteration of working conditions. The term 'trade union' did not come into common use until after 1830 and only in the second half of the century did it supplant 'combination'.

Combined labour action in the 18th century was widespread although by no means was it all directed by or channelled through formal organizations. The Webbs (1894, ch. 1) were in error in insisting that only those associations that were formally constituted and in continuous existence should properly be counted among the early trade unions. In the 18th century, especially, it was the collective presence of workers that was the crucial determinant of industrial response. Formal organization was not a necessary condition of industrial militancy, and 'collective bargaining by riot' is a well-documented phenomenon (Hobsbawm, 1964, ch. 2). In 1718 and 1724 West of England clothiers complained to Parliament that weavers had 'threatened to pull down their houses and burn their work unless they would agree to their terms'. A study of Lancashire textile workers (Turner, 1962) emphasized that the essence of 18th-century unionism was the persistence of collective pressures which in given circumstances encouraged collective action. Associations among the Lancashire textile workers developed informally out of the occupational life-style within the community. A settled group would encourage habits of association and common action, and skill was always a consolidating factor, but there was also much activity among the unskilled and migrant groups.

An incomplete listing of recorded industrial disputes gives a total of 383 for the whole of Britain between 1717 and 1800 (Dobson, 1980, ch. 1). Most of these were in England, and of the English figure of 333 disputes just over a third (120) occurred in London, the main centre of the artisan trades in the 18th century. The occupational breakdown for the whole country shows 64 incidents from among the textile workers, mostly in the wool industry; only seamen and ships-carpenters (each with 37) and tailors (with 22) exceed a total of twenty. Those between ten and twenty include coalminers, workers in the shipbuilding industries, textile workers other than those in wool or silk, shoemakers, and most trades in building. The range of additional trades for which some disputes were listed is considerable, and hardly any occupation except the service industries was free from industrial conflict (Rule, 1981, ch. 6).

The London journeymen tailors were the most effective combination in Britain during the 18th century. Their organization seems to have been established around 1700 as the result of the coming together of five 'box' clubs: box clubs being a version of the friendly society. In order to function effectively the clubs were associations in continuous existence, and their rules and regulations later provided the basis for the discipline of a trade union. The meeting places of the box clubs were public houses recognized by the trade and known as the 'house of call'. The box club and the house of call were the type of organization common to all the trades that succeeded in establishing more or less continuous associations. The tailors' combination first came into prominence as the result of a petition presented to the House of Commons in 1721, which asserted that 15,000 London journeymen had entered into a combination and engaged upon a strike. The report of a House of Commons committee was followed by an Act (7 Geo 1, c. 13) which fixed wages by the day for summer and winter, and which also prohibited combinations. While the Act was going through Parliament the journeymen briefed counsel, at a reported cost of £700.

Legislation against combinations in specified trades was common during the next hundred years; examples affect the wool trade, (12 Geo I, c. 34), hatters (22 Geo II, c. 27), silk weavers (17 Geo III, c. 55), and the paper trade (36 Geo III, c. 111). At the end of the century, in 1799, there was passed a general Act (to be repealed and replaced the next year by 40 Geo III, c. 60) which made illegal all combinations whose purpose was obtaining an advance in wages or the lessening in the number of hours worked; and for the next quarter of a century the Combination Laws were in force, although in respect of certain trades they were not always rigorously applied (Webb, 1894, ch. 2). In 1824 all previous statutes in respect of combinations were repealed but this Act was in turn repealed and replaced the following year by 6 Geo IV, c. 129, which permitted combinations on strictly defined terms and listed punishments for the use or the threatened use of intimidation, molestation or violence in the pursuit of the declared objects of the industrial action.

The ending of the complete legal prohibition of combinations was largely due to a growing appreciation of the requirements of a labour market in the period of early industrialization. It was also in part the result of adroit political pressure by Francis Place and, inside Westminster, Joseph Hume. The most weighty supporter of those who accepted the demand that workingmen's combinations should be free of legal restraint was J.R. McCulloch, who spoke in the name of orthodox political economy. McCulloch argued that the Combination Laws were unjust in that employers and their workmen were not put on the same level; they were dangerous because they engendered contempt for the law and encouraged class hatred; and they were futile because no action could permanently drive up the level of wages above the natural rate. McCulloch believed in peaceful combination: 'There is no good reason why workmen should not, like the possessors of every other valuable and desirable article, be allowed to set whatever price they please upon the labour they have to dispose of' – but he was clear above all that no artificial levels of wages could possibly maintain themselves in a competitive market. He saw the usefulness of combinations in a strictly narrow context. He warned against strikes, as normally benefitting those employers outside the strike action, and underlined the danger of industry-wide strikes in reducing the competitiveness of home industry compared with foreign production (O'Brien, 1970, pp. 366–70). He was notably adamant against any use of force or intimidation in the day-to-day activities of the combinations and was particularly opposed to attempts to compel workmen to join combinations or participate in strikes or other action; and he commended the clauses in the 1825 Act which imposed prison sentences for those convicted of such intimidation. McCulloch elaborated his ideas in the *Essay on Wages* of 1826, which he published in a revised version in the *Treatise on Wages* of the early 1850s, and he summarized his views in an article on 'Combination' in the 8th edition of the *Encyclopaedia Britannica* of 1854.

The character of trade unionism changed in certain respects during the second quarter of the 19th century as a result of the influence of Owenism and the ideas of the anti-capitalist theorists such as Hodgskin, Gray and Thompson (wrongly designated as the 'Ricardian socialists'). It is important not to exaggerate the nature of the change since unions remained what they had always been: defensive-offensive bodies concerned with the betterment of their members. But in the decade after the legalization of combinations for peaceful agitation there was a notable growth of cooperative organizations and some support for Owen's communitarian ideas. Radical political economy worked in the same direction.

The distortion of exchange values, so it was argued, meant that labour exchanged below and commodities above their natural values, and under-consumption and the usual accompaniments of economic crisis were the result. Hence a concern with equitable exchange relations with an emphasis upon the Labour Exchanges of the early 1830s and a longer term preoccupation with money and the banking system (N.W. Thompson, 1984). Owenism, with its ideas of cooperation was a central strand in the organization of the Grand National Consolidated Trades' Union in 1834–5 from which, it should be noted, a number of skilled societies held aloof; and Owenism, which was critical of policies such as mutual support funds for unemployment, sickness and death, and remained only a partial influence upon union attitudes. After the failure of the Grand National in the mid-1830s the combinations which survived – almost entirely made up of skilled workers and craftsmen – continued with their traditional sectional approaches to industrial problems. There remained a residue of Owenite ideas – in cooperative production for example which the Christian Socialists of 1848–1854 were able to draw upon (Raven, 1920; Saville, 1954) – but these were attitudes which became progressively weaker in the decades after the half century.

Combinations of working men for industrial purposes generated a continuous opposition, amounting to hatred, among the employing classes, whose distrust and dislike goes back to the early beginnings of modern industrial society. This hostility, as well as fear, has been a component part of the English liberal tradition and has influenced politicians, administrators and the judiciary. The last group is especially important in that while politicians have slowly modified their views and gradually legislated in more sympathetic ways in respect of trade union rights and status – at least until the last quarter of 20th century – the judiciary have been more wayward in their judgements and have followed quite closely the vagaries of middle class opinion. This opinion has moved between reluctant acquiescence and straight hostility, and the history of the law relating to combinations and trade unions has exhibited batches of legal decisions which have negated the intentions of Parliament. This was true of the late 1860s and during the 1890s, the latter period culminating in the Taff Vale decision. The hostility of educated opinion towards these industrial associations of working men was well illustrated in a letter written by Richard Cobden, the quintessential middle-class liberal of the 19th century, addressed to his brother in 1844: 'Depend upon it, nothing can be got by fraternising with the trade unions. They are founded upon principles of brutal tyranny and monopoly. I would rather live under a Dey of Algiers than a Trade Committee' (Morley, 1882, p. 299). These have been enduring sentiments.

JOHN SAVILLE

See also INDUSTRIAL RELATIONS.

BIBLIOGRAPHY
Dobson, C.R. 1980. *Masters and Journeymen. A Prehistory of Industrial Relations 1717–1800*. London: Croom Helm.
Hobsbawm, E.J. 1964. *Labouring Men*. London: Weidenfeld & Nicolson.
Morley, J. 1881. *The Life of Richard Cobden*. Abridged edn, London: Nelson's Shilling Library, 1910.
Musson, A.E. 1972. *British Trade Unions, 1800–1875*. London: Macmillan.
O'Brien, D.P. 1970. *J.R. McCulloch: A Study in Classical Economics*. London: Allen & Unwin.
Raven, C.E. 1920. *Christian Socialism 1848–54*. London: Macmillan.
Rule, J. 1981. *The Experience of Labour in Eighteenth-Century Industry*. London: Croom Helm.

Saville, J. 1954. The Christian Socialists of 1848. In *Democracy and the Labour Movement*, ed. J. Saville, London: Lawrence & Wishart.

Thompson, E.P. 1963. *The Making of the English Working Class*. London: Victor Gollancz.

Thompson, N.W. 1984. *The People's Science. The popular political economy of exploitation and crisis, 1816–34*. Cambridge: Cambridge University Press.

Turner, H.A. 1962. *Trade Union Growth, Structure and Policy. A Comparative Study of the Cotton Unions*. London: Allen & Unwin.

Webb, S. and Webb, B. 1894. *The History of Trade Unionism*. London: Longmans & Co.

combinatorics. Combinatorics, or combinatorial mathematics, is a difficult field to define. It cuts across many branches of mathematics yet a mathematician will clearly sense which problems are of a combinatorial nature. Perhaps the simplest definition is that it is concerned with configurations or arrangements of elements, usually finite in number, into sets. Three basic types of problem are posed. Firstly the existence of certain configurations; secondly, once their existence is proved, the classification or enumeration of the configurations meeting the requirements imposed; and thirdly the construction of algorithms for finding the configurations in question.

Why has combinatorics been the poor relation of the mathematical tools used in economics? The first and most obvious explanation is that the evolution of theoretical or mathematical economics has led us in the opposite direction to that in which combinatorics is useful. Ever since the 'marginal revolution' there has been clear emphasis on the use of differential methods and an implicit acceptance of the perfect divisibility of goods. Indeed if we consider the most elaborate extension of the basic Arrow–Debreu model it is to one in which there is a continuum of agents and a continuum of goods. This is just the sort of context in which the combinatoric approach is of little use.

Yet the economist may well feel that discrete problems are of importance and that indeed the world is best represented as one where goods are not infinitely divisible and where the number of agents is finite. Now given the standard assumptions of convexity, at least in production, the perfectly competitive model may indeed be regarded as a satisfactory ideal or limiting case and the finiteness of a real economy is just an inconvenience. In this case it would seem that combinatorics has little role to play.

However although we may consider taking divisibility as a reasonable idealization in a large economy (even this may be questioned – *see* INDIVISIBILITIES) as soon as convexity is dropped as an assumption for production the problem of finiteness cannot be avoided. If there are increasing returns to scale there will be a minimum profitable plant size and there will be a fundamental indivisibility. At this point combinatoric analysis comes back into its own, and no argument can be made for using infinitely divisible goods as a reasonable approximation. Thus the existence of non-convexities will lead us back into a situation which may, for example, be game-like and in which we will be looking for a solution with a finite number of large plants.

This is to suggest that realism may lead us away from the smooth differential world to which economists are accustomed towards a discrete one in which combinatorics plays an important role.

Nevertheless, till now, finiteness and the combinatoric approach have not occupied a significant place in economics.

However, some examples will show that certain branches, although not central, have made extensive use of such an approach.

The development of mathematical programming, in particular of linear programming, has relied particularly on combinatorics. The algorithms developed to solve such problems are essentially combinatoric. Many economic models have been built on the basis of the 'activity analysis' or fixed coefficient production approach.

Game theory has made extensive use of combinatorics and provides an interesting example of how the combinatoric approach can be confronted with one using continuous functions or compact sets.

Combinatoric arguments are used to show that the core of a balanced game is non-empty. A simple argument shows that a market game is balanced and further it can be shown that the only allocations remaining if we replicate a given economy are competitive. This leads us to the conclusion that a competitive or Walrasian allocation exists. Now the latter statement is known to be equivalent to the existence of a fixed point for a continuous mapping. Thus we arrive by combinatorical methods at the same result as that obtained by an apparently very different tool.

This argument is reinforced by the fact that the algorithms developed for finding approximate competitive equilibria are essentially combinatoric in nature. They consist in systematically examining points in the price space, of evaluating the total excess demand of an economy at these points and finding a path which leads to a reduction in the excess demand until it is close to zero. Again, the approximation of fixed points of continuous functions is obtained by a combinatoric approach.

There are many other examples of ways in which combinatoric analysis has proved useful. Arrow's theorem on the impossibility of a social welfare function is typically proved in the case of a finite number of individuals faced with a finite number of social alternatives. The problem is to find a way of aggregating individual preference orders on these alternatives into a social order in a way which satisfies certain simple axioms. The usual line of proof consists of finding certain configurations of individual preferences which lead via the axioms to a contradiction with the existence of a social order. The reasoning here too is combinatoric. The introduction of graph theory to describe communication patterns in economics has brought into economic theory a field which has long been regarded as fundamentally combinatoric. The use of 'matching' models to analyse job search and unemployment is yet another example.

Whilst these few rather arbitrary examples show that combinatorial analysis has not been absent from economic theory it is also clear that it has not been central.

However, it seems likely that economics is to evolve towards the sort of models now widely studied in computer science, away from global optimization towards more simple forms of 'rationality' as embodied in simple automata. Furthermore the computation of equilibrium even for underlying continuous models is becoming increasingly important. All this together with a recognition of certain fundamental indivisibilities in economics is likely to move combinatorics to a much more central position on the stage of economic theory.

A.P. KIRMAN

See also CORES; FIXED-POINT THEOREMS; GAME THEORY; GRAPH THEORY; RAMSEY, FRANK PLUMPTON.

BIBLIOGRAPHY
Three elegant and elementary introductions to combinatorics are Berge (1971), Polya, Tarjan and Woods (1983) and Ryser (1963). A more advanced text is Aigner (1979).

Aigner, M. 1979. *Combinatorial Theory*. Berlin: Springer.
Berge, C. 1971. *Principles of Combinatorics*. New York; Academic Press.
Polya, G., Tarjan, R.E. and Woods, D.R. 1983. *Notes on Introductory Combinatorics*. Boston: Birkhauser.
Ryser, H.J. 1963. *Combinatorial Mathematics*. Mathematical Association of America, New York: John Wiley.

command economy. A command economy is one in which the life-cycle and activity of firms, their adjustment to disturbance, and coordination between them, are typically and in the main governed by administrative means – commands, directives, and regulations – rather than by a market mechanism. Perhaps the most distinctive feature of such an economy is the setting of the firm's production targets by higher directive, often in fine detail. The administrative means rely on planning, budgets, material balances, quotas, rationing, technical coefficients, price and wage controls, and other techniques. While the command principle is likely to clash with the operation of market forces, a command economy may nonetheless contain and rely on the market mechanism in some of its sectors and areas: for example labour allocation or small-scale private production.

The phrase 'command economy' comes from the German '*Befehlswirtschaft*', and was originally applied to the Nazi economy, which shared many formal similarities with that of Soviet Russia. Synonymous or near-synonymous terms are: 'centrally planned economy', 'centrally administered economy', 'Soviet-type economy', 'bureaucratic economy' and 'hierarchy'.

The command economy's conceptual origins go back to the Viennese economist Otto Neurath, who in the years before and after World War I developed an extreme version (to the point of moneylessness) based chiefly on prior experience with wartime economies (Raupach, 1966). Apart from the relatively short-lived Nazi case and even briefer ones under emergency conditions in some other countries, especially in wartime, actual instances of command economies are virtually limited to communist-ruled countries, with the USSR as the prototype and prime exemplar. Thus, what follows is mainly inspired by the Soviet example, at the time of writing (1986) still systemically little altered since its appearance in the early 1930s. The means of production are taken to be predominantly state-owned.

A command economy is a creature of state authority, whose marks it bears and by whose hand it evolves, exists, and survives. Except in cases of external duress or mere imitation, it is established for specific purposes or reasons, such as: (1) maximum resource mobilization towards urgent and over-riding national objectives, e.g. rapid industrialization or the prosecution of war; (2) radical transformation of the socio-economic system in the collectivist direction based on ideological tenets and power-political imperatives; (3) not the least, as an answer to the disorganization of a market economy through price control, possibly occasioned by inflationary pressure arising from (1) and/or (2).

It requires a formal, centralized, administrative hierarchy staffed by a bureaucracy; it also needs to be embedded in (at least) an authoritarian, highly centralized polity if it is not to dissolve or degenerate into something else. At the same time, each office or firm and every economic actor within the command structure holds interests which, if only in part, do not coincide with those of superiors or of the overall leadership. This generates important problems of vested interests, principal–agent interaction, incentives, and general enforcement of the leadership's will, and calls for a variety of monitoring organizations (party, police, banks, etc.). The term 'command' must not be taken to preclude self-serving behaviour, bureaucratic politics, bargaining between superiors and subordinates, corruption, peculation and (dis)simulation. On the contrary, such behaviour tends to be widespread in a command economy; yet, the concept of a 'command economy' remains valid so long as, in the main, authority relations and not a market mechanism govern the allocation of resources.

Rational application of the command principle calls for planning, which is basically of two types. Longer-term, developmental planning expresses the leadership's politico-economic strategy (e.g. five-year plans); shorter-term, coordinative planning ideally translates the strategy into resource allocation while aiming to match resource requirements and availabilities for individual inputs, goods, etc., in a disaggregated way for given time periods and locations. Coordinative planning serves, thus, as the basis for specific operational directives to producers and users. A major problem is that detailed planning and the corresponding directives may lack the requisite information, often cannot be effectively coordinated, and owing to their rigidity are peculiarly vulnerable to uncertainty (cf. Ericson, 1983). Information in the command sector tends to flow vertically, up and down, rather than horizontally, between buyer and seller, adding to difficulties of demand-supply coordination. In addition, problems of motivation, accountability (down as well as up), inappropriate decision-making parameters, and divergent interests complicate the procedure. Even at best, this manner of resource allocation can hope to attain only internal consistency (in the sense of effectively matching disaggregated requirements and availabilities) but not a high order of economic efficiency. Economic calculus in quest of efficiency tends to enter more at the project-planning stage than in short-term resource allocation and use.

Though money is used in the command sector (as well as in the household sector), its role as a bearer of options and as the means of pecuniary calculation for decision-making tends to be limited and deliberately subordinated to the planners' will and the administrators' power. Banks and the treasury accommodate the money needs of production, ensuring a soft budget constraint for the individual firm. At the same time, the 'moneyness' of money at the firm level is low, hemmed in as it is by administrative constraints and impediments, including the rationing of nearly all producer goods, and by the widespread 'seller's market' (shortages of goods). This monetary ease plus the seller's market play an important role in ensuring individual worker's job security at the firm level and full employment in the large, while keeping the firm relatively insensitive to money cost.

Producer prices (and most retail prices), wages, prices of foreign currencies, etc., are generally centrally set and controlled, often remaining fixed for long periods of time. Micro-disequilibria abound. The widely perceived dubious meaningfulness of such prices and the administrative allocation of most producer goods in physical terms combine to sustain the traditional system of detailed production plans and directives in terms of physical indicators – yet another bar to more efficient planning and management.

While administrative orders are the rule in a command economy, backed up by greater or lesser degree of state coercion (depending on country and period), Soviet-type economies rely heavily on monetary ('material') incentives to elicit desired individual compliance and performance. A difficulty is that the physical and other indicators to which the material incentives are linked may often be poor measures of social benefit (as seen by the leadership). In any case, liberal resort to such rewards widens the distribution of official earnings and raises questions of permissible limits of income inequality. Yet there may be little choice in that the state must in effect compete with the much higher incomes from the second economy (*infra*). (The Soviet Union during War Communism, Cuba in the 1960s, and the People's Republic of China during some periods before Mao's death in 1976, tended to downgrade material incentives in favour of normative controls, but never did quite abolish them.)

The behaviour of the Soviet-type firm has been much studied. Because its directives ('plan') and the corresponding managerial incentives stress physical output, produced or shipped, and thanks to its low sensitivity to cost and the ambient seller's market, the firm often sacrifices product cost, quality, variety, innovation and ancillary services to its customers, for sheer product quantity. It should be noted that firms in such an economy are largely protected from any product competition, both from the outside world and from other domestic firms, thanks to the climate of administrative controls and the prevalent excess demand for their output. Difficulties with supply, frequent revision of its plans, interference by party and other authorities, and other systemic problems also stand in the way of its more efficient and effective operation. To function at all the firm's management is frequently forced to break rules and even resort to criminally punishable acts.

Such acts, together with ubiquitous and protean illegal activity on private account, add up to a large underground economy characteristic of every command economy. Together with legal private activity (allowed in varying degree in different countries), the underground economy comprises an important 'second economy', which at once supports and supplements the 'first economy' and is inimical to it. While the second economy significantly adds to the supply of goods and services, especially for consumption, it also redistributes private income and wealth, contributes to the widespread official corruption, and generally criminalizes the population (cf. Grossman, 1977).

Command economies have been instrumental in radically transforming societies more or less according to their drafters' intents, in mobilizing resources for rapid industrialization and modernization, at times on a vast scale, and in rapidly amassing industrial power and military strength. Economic growth has been especially marked (though not unparalleled by market economies) where large amounts of un- and underemployed labour and rich natural resources could be mobilized and combined with existing (Western) technology, and where the public's material improvement could be restrained, or even seriously depressed, under strong political control. As these possibilities waned, and as the economies grew in size and complexity, and thus became less amenable to centralized administrative management, rates of growth have tended to decline sharply. At the same time, their shortcomings in adapting production to demand and its changes – providing consumer welfare, effecting innovation, serving export markets – became more apparent and less tolerable. This has led to much discussion and occasional measures of institutional reform.

Some actual reforms have gone so far as to introduce or extend the market mechanism to such a degree that one can no longer regard the economy as a Soviet-type command economy, even if one cannot speak of it as a full-fledged market economy either. Yugoslavia since the early 1950s, Hungary since 1968 and especially since the early 1980s, and post-Mao China, are the most important cases in point; their analysis cannot be undertaken here. Other actual reforms have been of the minor or 'within-system' nature, aiming to decentralize certain types of decision while eschewing the market mechanism and retaining the hierarchical form of organization and the command principle. (Usually the decentralizing measures have been accompanied by a number of other measures relating to organizational structure, prices (still controlled), incentives, indicators, etc.) The Soviet reform of 1965 was of that kind; many similar ones have taken place in other communist countries since the mid-1950s. On the whole, such reforms have had little success in addressing the problems of the command economy. Bureaucratic and political obstacles apart, the attempt to decentralize economic decisions without bringing in a market mechanism almost inevitably leads to economic difficulties. The beneficiaries of devolution of decision-making often lack the necessary information to produce just what the economy requires or to invest to meet prospective needs. Moreover, they may apply the additional power at their disposal to advance particularist causes or to divert resources into illegal channels. Micro-disequilibria mount. Before long, superior authorities step in to recentralize on a case-by-case basis and the reform withers away. The command economy contains a strong immanent – perhaps even congenital – centralizing force (cf. Grossman, 1963; Wiles, 1962, ch. 7).

GREGORY GROSSMAN

See also CENTRAL PLANNING.

BIBLIOGRAPHY
Ericson, R.E. 1983. A difficulty with the 'command' allocation mechanism. *Journal of Economic Theory* 31(1), October, 1–26.
Grossman, G. 1963. Notes for a theory of the command economy. *Soviet Studies* 15, October, 101–23.
Grossman, G. 1977. The 'second economy' of the USSR. *Problems of Communism* 26(5), September, 25–40.
Raupach, H. 1966. Zur Entstehung des Begriffes Zentralverwaltungs-wirtschaft. *Jahrbuch für Sozialwissenschaft* 17(1), 86–101.
Wiles, P.J.D. 1962. *The Political Economy of Communism.* Cambridge, Mass.: Harvard University Press.

commerce. *See* INTERNATIONAL TRADE.

commodities. *See* GOODS AND COMMODITIES.

commodities, contingent. *See* CONTINGENT COMMODITIES.

commodity fetishism. This term used by Marx to characterize the perception of social relations under the sway of commodity exchange. It is under capitalism that fetishism of commodities assumes its most comprehensive form. In *Capital*, the notion is developed initially with reference to commodity exchange between atomistic self-employed producers. The principal characteristic of such an economy is that each economic agent produces goods which he himself does not consume, and, in turn, consumes goods which he has not produced. For Marx, the important feature is that the mutual interdependence of economic agents is established *ex post* when they come to exchange their products rather than *ex ante* when they embark on production. Marx draws attention to the contrast between the coordination of production decisions through the 'invisible hand' of the market, and that through a production plan.

The notion of fetishism of commodities is premissed on the contention that the coordination mechanism is not neutral but has an effect on the way in which economic agents perceive their mutual interdependence and the terms in which they are characterized. Under commodity production in general, and capitalism in particular, economic agents are characterized first and foremost as potential buyers and sellers of commodities, and commodity exchange serves as a paradigm of relations between them. It may be argued that the 'rational economic man' of economic theory is not a fiction but an effect of coordination through the invisible hand of the market. The fact which singles out capitalism is that under it labour-time (labour power, in Marx's terminology) too becomes a commodity appearing on a par with other commodities. This appearance masks the special character of the labour market. For the participants in the labour market are on the one hand the labourers who have nothing to sell but their labour-time, and on the other, the capitalists who own means of production. On the surface, the relations between capitalists and labourers appear as no more than those of sellers and purchasers masking the fact that the value-added by the employed labourers exceeds their wages, thus giving rise to profit or 'surplus value'.

What has been the effect of the notion of fetishism of commodities on Marxist analyses? First of all, it has furnished the foundation for the analyses of ideology under capitalism, an exemplar of which is Althusser's essay on ideology. Further, Pashukanis, a Soviet jurisprudential theorist of the 1920s, used the notion of fetishism of commodities to sketch a Marxist theory of law. In economic analyses it has led to a denigration of exchange relations and the emphasis on production relations as the vantage point for the analysis of economic systems. As a result, the formation of prices and the systems of market exchange have remained a neglected area in Marxist economic analyses. Furthermore, it has instituted an unquestioned distinction between ideological and scientific categories. The former is to be avoided in favour of the latter. It has led Marxist economists to spurn marginal calculus, including linear programming, as ideological. In all, the notion of fetishism of commodities, while fecund in the formation of theories of ideology and law, has been an obstacle in the development of Marxist economic analyses.

A. HUSSAIN

See also MARX, KARL HEINRICH.

BIBLIOGRAPHY

Althusser, L. 1971. Ideology and ideological state apparatus. In L. Althusser, *Lenin and Philosophy and Other Essays,* London: New Left Books.

Marx, K. 1867. *Capital,* Vol. I. Moscow: Progress Publishers, 1965.

Pašukanis, E.B. 1970. *La théorie générale du droit et le Marxisme.* Paris: EDI.

commodity money. Although money in the shape of goods has its origin at the earliest stages of civilization in the social division of labour, money as a commodity appeared only with the development of a market economy. We may define 'commodity money' as a special commodity which has been set aside from the mass of commodities to perform the role of a 'universal equivalent'; in this capacity, it serves as a measure of value, medium of exchange and means of payment. We shall examine these distinct attributes of money in turn.

The main difficulty for monetary analysis 'lies not in comprehending that money is a commodity, but in discovering how, why, and by what means a commodity becomes money' (Marx 1867, p. 95). The classical economists showed that goods were transformed into commodities by the process of exchange, thus acquiring an 'exchange value' as well as 'use value'. Moreover, the exchange of commodities began not within primitive communities, but at their point of contact with other communities. As a result of barter, certain goods were more quickly established as commodities, and became the first money (Morgan, 1965). In some communities, shells or cattle served this purpose; in most, however, the precious metals were selected for reasons of their durability, uniformity and divisibility.

Much has been written about the nature and origins of metallic money from the viewpoint of anthropology and even psychoanalysis (e.g. Freud, 1959, vols. II and III). Among economists, it became generally accepted that money was simply a technical device to overcome the limitations of barter: 'The inconveniences of barter are so great, that without some more commodious means of effecting exchanges, the division of employments could hardly have been carried to any considerable extent' (Mill, 1848, p. 299; see also Smith, 1776, pp. 17–22); yet it is important to recognize that these limitations or 'inconveniences' themselves stemmed from the evolution of exchange value as an economic category, and hence from the conversion of individual labour into social labour (Marx [1859] 1970, pp. 50–51). In practical terms, only one commodity can function adequately as money, the universal commodity; after attempts to operate a 'bimetallic' system proved unworkable, *gold* became the dominant monetary commodity (Feaveryear, 1931).

MEASURE OF VALUE. During the period when commodity production was localized and restricted in character, exchange value in the form of money was treated as the sole embodiment of a nation's wealth; this approach became known as 'mercantilism'. It was challenged by the 'founder of political economy', Sir William Petty, who expanded the conception of wealth to reflect the growth of the division of labour and the emergence of *generalized* commodity production. He reduced the exchange value of heterogeneous commodities to a common denominator in social labour, hence determining the value of money like other commodities by the labour time necessary for its production (Petty, 1963, I, pp. 43–4). For the classical economists, money was first and foremost a 'produced commodity': 'The same general rule which regulates the value of raw produce and manufactured commodities, is applicable also to the metals; their value depending ... on the total quantity of labour necessary to obtain the metal, and to bring it to market' (Ricardo, 1951/52, I, pp. 85–6; also Marx, 1867, p. 97). This approach clearly identified the function of money as 'the uniform Measure and Rule for the Value of all Commodities' (Petty, 1963, I, p. 183), and as the standard in which their prices are expressed.

Later economists showed that, as a measure of value, money transforms the values of commodities into prices, into imaginary quantities of gold whose value is potentially variable; and, as a standard of price, it measures those quantities of gold in terms of invariable units of weight: 'The excellence of any thing as a measure of value, is altogether independent of its own variableness in value' (Bailey, 1837, p. 10). It was the inevitable discrepancy between the face value of coin and its intrinsic value due to wear and tear and debasement which led to the regulation of this standard by law, and ultimately to the creation of token or 'fiduciary' money (Feaveryear, 1931).

MEDIUM OF EXCHANGE. Since money enters circulation with a given value and commodities with a given price, the quantity of money required as a medium of exchange will be determined by the magnitude of its value, all other things being equal. This is the 'classical law of circulation' which was a central feature of classical monetary thought (Petty, 1963, I, p. 36; Smith, 1776, pp. 332–3; Ricardo, 1951/52, I, p. 352, 1966, p. 158; Marx, 1867, pp 123–4). It suggests the possibility of replacing all the precious metals in circulation with tokens, provided only that such tokens are issued in the same amount as the metals they purport to represent: 'A currency is in its most perfect state when it consists wholly of paper money, but of paper money of an equal value with the gold which it professes to represent' (Ricardo, 1951/52, I, p. 361; see also Smith, 1776, p. 227; Marx, 1867, p. 128).

Supporters of a long-run quantity theory of money, however, took the opposite approach. The fact that commodity money could be replaced by symbols indicated to them that money was itself a mere symbol. This impression was confirmed by the experience of the Price Revolution of the 16th and 17th centuries. The increased quantity of precious metals from the American mines did not augment wealth, but seemed only to devalue the unit of account. Money was thus treated as having no intrinsic value; it *represented commodities* in the exchange process, serving only as *numéraire* (Hume, 1752, p. 33); yet the evidence tends to support the classical view that the Price Revolution was due to the lowered production costs of gold and silver (Nef, 1941; Outhwaite, 1969; Vilar, 1976).

The quantity theory, as Schumpeter points out, 'essentially amounted to treating money not as a commodity but as a voucher for buying goods' (1954, p. 313). Although gold and silver had no value and hence were not real commodities when they entered circulation, once in circulation they acquired a 'fictitious value' whose magnitude was determined by supply and demand (ibid., p. 48; Vanderlint, 1734, pp. 2–3). Consequently, instead of the quantity of money depending on its value, the value of money and prices of commodities were established by their relative quantities.

MEANS OF PAYMENT. The separation of purchase and sale in the exchange process gave rise to credit, and the further role of money as a means of payment (Cantillon, 1755 p. 141; Thornton, 1802, pp. 76 and 92). Whereas tokens simply represent commodity money, credit instruments are *claims* which must eventually be met. The development of special institutions for setting off claims, such as the *virements* of medieval Lyons, economized the means of payment, leaving only a single balance to be paid (Cantillon [1755] 1931, pp. 311–13; Postan, 1928); and the modern credit system, by confining bullion to a centralized reserve fund, allows transactions to be conducted and claims met with fiduciary money issued by the state (Feaveryear, 1931).

The growing network of payments promoted by credit on the one hand increases the velocity of money to such an extent that its presence is no longer required in the majority of transactions and, on the other, creates a propensity for industrial crises to assume a more explosive monetary form:

> The faith of each man in the continuance not only of his own prosperity, but of that of his neighbour, becomes so strong, that the most boundless credit is frequently lavished in the support of the most worthless schemes. Everything

in the nature of value puts on an aspect of bloated magnitude; till at last the exchange becomes affected by the unnatural rise of prices, the bullion is sent abroad, a panic ensues, and the bubble bursts, with a destruction of capital which relieves the money-market for a season of the load which had oppressed it, abates competition, and restores the market-rate of interest to the level from which it had declined (Fullarton, 1844, pp. 163–4).

On the eve of the crisis, as Marx later observed, money was declared to be a 'vain imagination': commodities alone are money. Then, as the ensuing panic swept through the markets, 'the cry is everywhere: money alone is a commodity' (1867, p. 138). This became the familiar pattern of crises under the gold standard.

Although legal convertibility has long been abolished, *economic* convertibility remained an implicit target of post-war monetary policy, at least until the formal repudiation of the Bretton Woods agreement. Even now, a demonetized gold is a significant component of national bank reserves, a broad indicator of currency values and an international means of payment. Society still clings tenaciously to its 'barbarous relic'.

ROY GREEN

See also CURRENCIES; FIAT MONEY; FIDUCIARY ISSUE; MONEY SUPPLY.

BIBLIOGRAPHY
Bailey, S. 1837. *Money and its Vicissitudes in Value: as they affect National Industry and Pecuniary Contracts.* London.
Cantillon, R. 1755. *Essai sur la nature du commerce en général.* London: Macmillan, 1931.
Feaveryear, A.E. 1931. *The Pound Sterling: A History of English Money.* Oxford: Clarendon Press.
Freud, S. 1959. *Collected Papers.* Ed. E. Jones, New York: Basic Books.
Fullarton, J. 1844. *On the Regulation of Currencies.* London: John Murray.
Hume, D. 1752. *Essays, Literary, Moral and Political.* London: Ward, Lock, n.d.
Marx, K. 1859. *A Contribution to the Critique of Political Economy.* Moscow: Progress Publishers, 1970.
Marx, K. 1867. *Capital,* Vol. I. Moscow: Progress Publishers.
Mill, J.S. 1848. *Principles of Political Economy.* London: Longmans, Green, Reader and Dyer, 1873.
Morgan, E.V. 1965. *A History of Money.* Harmondsworth: Penguin.
Nef, J.U. 1941. Silver production in Central Europe: 1450–1618. *Journal of Political Economy* 49, June, 575–91.
Outhwaite, R.B. 1969. *Inflation in Tudor and Early Stuart England.* London: Macmillan.
Petty, W. 1963. *Economic Writings.* Ed. C. Hull, New York: Kelley reprint.
Postan, M. 1928. Credit in medieval trade. In *Essays in Economic History,* ed. E.M. Carus-Wilson, London: Edward Arnold, 1954.
Ricardo, D. 1951-73. *Works.* Ed. P. Sraffa, Cambridge: Cambridge University Press.
Ricardo, D. 1966. *Economic Essays.* Ed. E.C.K. Gonner, London: Frank Cass & Co.
Schumpeter, J.A. 1954. *History of Economic Analysis.* London: Allen & Unwin.
Smith, A. 1776. *An Inquiry into the Nature and Causes of the Wealth of Nations.* London: Routledge, 1890.
Thornton, H. 1802. *An Enquiry into the Nature and Effects of the Paper Credit of Great Britain.* London: LSE Reprint Series, 1939.
Vanderlint, J. 1734. *Money answers all Things.* New York: Johnson reprint, n.d.
Vilar, P. 1976. *A History of Gold and Money: 1450–1920.* London: New Left Books.

commodity price stabilization. *See* BUFFER STOCKS.

commodity reserve currency. Commodity Reserve Currency (CRC for short) is a proposal for re-establishing an international monetary 'standard' – basing it upon a 'basket' of widely used commodities. Recent experience shows the inconvenience of lacking a standard. While restoration of a gold standard has many supporters, gold has become so remote from the goods-and-services economy that for decades now governments have had scope to play tricks with its price; and since the early 1970s, the value of gold has been highly unstable. Can there be a commodity standard other than gold, less abstract and linked to articles of everyday use? A good way to study this question is to examine the feasibility and desirability of CRC.

Pioneers of the CRC proposal were Jan Goudriaan and Benjamin Graham. Variant proposals have come from a number of economists, including Lord Keynes and Friedrich Hayek. The nearest approach to a standard version is probably still the submission of 1964 to the United Nations Conference of Trade and Development by Albert Hart, Nicholas Kaldor and Jan Tinbergen. No governments or major multilateral bodies have sponsored CRC, though there has been official and private use of 'baskets' of currency units (ECU, etc.), and of 'baskets' of securities (traded on various private commodity exchanges).

Advocates of CRC propose that it be administered by a multinational agency, which we may call IMA – presumably to be a branch of the International Monetary Fund. A currency unit (which following Lord Kaldor we may call the Bancor) is to be defined as the value of a basket of primary commodities, with fixed physical composition.

Like the administrator of a traditional gold standard, IMA must buy or sell at a stated price (plus or minus a margin to avoid a hair-trigger effect) as much of the monetary commodity (i.e. the commodity baskets) as may be offered or demanded. As to the margin, some CRC proponents suggest 5 per cent on each side of par; but a wider range would have great advantages. Prices of the individual component commodities could fluctuate more than the basket. Any one commodity price could rise; but if its rise would bring the basket above the posted selling price, sales of baskets by IMA would bring a compensating fall of other prices.

The price of a basket with fixed physical composition is an index number of commodity prices, weighted by the quanta of the various items included. Hence CRC may be viewed as a scheme to stabilize an index of primary-commodity prices. CRC thus would have a counter-cyclical effect – holding within bounds the fluctuation of income for the world's exporters and producers of primary commodities, and by the same token the fluctuation of major elements in the world's cost of living.

An effective CRC would require that national currencies be tied to the Bancor by fixed exchange rates, or at least by not-too-movable pegs. The general stabilization effect of the proposal would vanish if major currencies were allowed to float against the Bancor.

Many primary commodities have been proposed for a CRC basket. Major criteria for inclusion are:

(1) *Standardization*, of the sort necessary to run futures markets on a commodity exchange – with rules for dealing with quality differences.

(2) *Storability* for at least a year or two without excessive cost or loss of quality. Security against fire, looting, requisition by local governments, etc., is implied.

(3) *Improbability of major price manipulations* by governments or by combinations of producing enterprises. Long

before OPEC rose to power in 1973, this criterion led advocates of CRC to omit petroleum from the proposed basket.

(4) *Reliability of commodity contracts*, enabling the IMA to replace physical holdings with contracts for future or spot delivery if this will reduce costs. Use of futures could be of humanitarian importance in case of shortages of foodstuffs such as rice.

These criteria would admit most of the world's important grains, fibres, fats and oils, beverage crops, primary metals – and probably a number of basic chemicals and forest products. Amounts of the various commodities in the basket would reflect their weight in world production and/or trade.

The CRC basket must be large (worth several million US dollars), because for efficient trading each element must be a multiple of a wholesale lot. This large basket-size would be appropriate, since CRC is designed as a vehicle for holding national monetary reserves rather than for retail or even wholesale trade.

IMA holdings of the various commodities must be parcelled out to points of delivery and storage along the normal trade routes of the commodities. Correspondingly, IMA purchases and sales must be handled by agents at the various trading points. To tell whether at any moment baskets must be bought or sold, IMA must sum up bids or offers reported by these agents. IMA must take the initiative – instructing all agents to sell or buy – whenever the sum of bid prices for the elements of the basket adds up to the posted selling price for the basket, or the sum of asked prices to the buying price.

Objections to CRC have hinged primarily on costs and/or on the difficulties of getting a CRC system under way. There has been continuing debate about the size of the reserve needed to validate IMA selling offers, about the cost of holding stocks of various suggested commodities, etc. Such costs must be compared with benefits from reducing cyclical fluctuations in primary producers' incomes, etc. – and of doing so without engaging in commodity-by-commodity operations. Benjamin Graham used to stress that the success of such operations hinges on restriction of commodity production, whereas success of CRC would stimulate production. For this and other reasons, the cost/benefit problem is complex.

During episodes of worldwide commodity stringency, accumulation of a commodity reserve has seemed impossible. When there has been a great piling up of stocks (as at this writing in early 1986), it has seemed as if mobilization of stocks held by the European Economic Community, the United States, various other governments such as Brazil, cartels such as that for tin, and private concerns such as copper companies, might permit a very rapid start.

Starting a CRC during a period of widespread shortages could be highly inflationary; starting it during a general economic downswing could mitigate a recession. There is debate as to whether accumulation of a reserve must stick to previously agreed proportions of the different commodities, or whether (as proposed by Keynes and more recently by Kaldor) the IMA should buy individual commodities at such dates and prices as seem wise. On this route, the composition of the CRC basket and the selling-price offer would grow out of the process of accumulation. This variant, plainly, would increase the similarity of IMA's operations to those of commodity 'stabilization' groups and remove the impersonality held to be the central virtue of the Goudriaan/Graham scheme.

ALBERT GAILORD HART

See also CURRENCIES; GOLD STANDARD; INTERNATIONAL MONETARY POLICY.

BIBLIOGRAPHY

Bennett, M.K. et al. 1949. *International Commodity Stockpiling as an Economic Stabilizer*. Stanford: Stanford University Press.

Goudriaan, J. 1932 *How to Stop Deflation*. London: The Search Publishing Company.

Grubel, H.G. 1965. The case against international commodity reserve currency. *Oxford Economic Papers* 17(1), March, 130–35.

Hallwood, P. 1986. External economy arguments for commodity stockpiling: a review. *Bulletin of Economic Research* 38(1), January, 25–41.

Harmon, E. 1959. *Commodity Reserve Currency*. New York: Columbia University Press.

Hart, A.G., Kaldor, N. and Tinbergen, J. 1964. The case for an international Commodity Reserve Currency. Geneva, United Nations Conference on Trade and Development, 17 February 1964. E/CONF.46/p/7. Conveniently accessible in N. Kaldor, *Essays on Economic Policy–II*, London: Gerald Duckworth & Co., 1964.

Hayek, F.A. 1984. The future monetary unit of value. In *Money in Crisis*, ed. Barry N. Siegel, San Francisco: Pacific Institute for Policy Research.

Newbery, D.M.G. and Stiglitz, J.E. 1981. *The Theory of Commodity Price Stabilization*. Oxford: Clarendon.

common land. The legal status of common land is a source of considerable popular confusion. With the notable exception of some village greens, commons do not represent areas which are owned by nobody, nor areas which are owned by everybody, nor even by everybody within a given locality. Since the early medieval period, commons have been owned by specific individuals, usually the lord of the manor within which they lie. The term 'common' refers not to ownership, but to rights held in common by certain people to use the product of the soil of the area in question. In turn, this means that the owner cannot enclose the land; hence the unfenced open space which is still the most characteristic feature of a common (Campbell and Clayden, 1980).

These rights are not now, nor have they been in the historic past, generally shared by everyone living within a given locality. Instead they are usually attached to specific dwellings, or to their sites. Except, therefore, where the owner has so decreed, the use of commons as recreational open spaces by a wide public is not in the strict sense defensible in law.

Commons, of course, were not in origin primarily places for recreation. They formed a vital element in the pre-industrial rural economy. Commons represent the attenuated remnants of the medieval wastes: areas which were not used to produce arable crops, but to provide a range of other resources. The principle rights exercised by commoners were, and are: *common of pasture*, or the right to pasture animals; *pannage*, or the right to allow pigs to eat acorns or beech mast; *common in the soil*, or the right to take minerals, gravel, stone, sand etc. for use on the commoner's holding; *estovers*, or the right to take small branches, bracken etc. for fuel, fencing or animal litter; *turbary*, or the right to dig peat or turf for use as fuel; and *piscary*, the right to take fish from streams or ponds on the common. Of these rights, that of common of pasture has normally been by far the most important.

The early history of common land is obscure. It appears that in the early Saxon period, areas of open waste were much more extensive than they were to become in the medieval period, and the rights to their use were more loosely defined and often exercised by much wider groups. The name of Sherwood Forest, for example – the Shire Wood – indicates that it was once the common woodland of the entire shire of Nottingham. Limitation and closer definition of rights to common waste occurred during the population increase of the early medieval period (Hoskins and Stamp, 1967). As arable expanded, common grazing dwindled, and areas of waste which had formerly been shared by communities were now divided between them, often after violent disputes. But there were also disputes within communities, as manorial lords, in association with their more prosperous tenants, attempted to take areas of the common waste into private ownership. The medieval struggle for the commons culminated in the Statute of Merton (The Commons Act of 1235), which decreed that freeholders had to be left with sufficient pasture to maintain the mixed farming of their holdings. However, the rights of the customary tenants were not protected by statute law, and the passing of the law for the first time clearly enshrined in national law the concept that the manorial lord rather than the community itself was the *owner* of the common waste of a manor.

The continual expansion of arable at the expense of the common wastes during the period before 1300 had other effects. There was an increasing tendency for commons to be *stinted*, that is, for the number of beasts put out by each commoner to be more carefully regulated. There were a number of ways in which this could be organised, the most usual being by the rules of levancy and couchancy, that is, where the right to turn out was measured by the capacity of the commonable tenement in such a way that only as many animals could be turned out as the tenement was able to support (with the aid of hay etc.) through the winter.

The extent to which the commons survived during the medieval period varied considerably from region to region, as the result of the interplay of a number of factors. Essentially, commons survived best where population densities were low and where much land was unsuitable for arable agriculture. Thus large areas survived in the uplands of the north and west. But there may have been more complex social and economic factors which were also important in the preservation of common grazing, especially in lowland areas, for the distribution of commons in medieval England does not appear to be a direct and simple reflection of demographic pressure or environmental factors. In certain parts of the south and east of England – areas of dispersed settlement and irregular field systems, poorly developed communal controls and individualistic agriculture – some communities seem to have lacked the management structures necessary to act corporately to plough up areas of common grazing, even in areas of high population and moderately fertile soils, such as Norfolk. In addition, poor controls on the alienation of land and the practice of partible inheritance led to an early proliferation of smallholders for whom the resources provided by the commons were of vital importance. In such areas the conversion of waste to arable agriculture ground to a halt rather earlier than in the classic open-field areas of the Midlands.

In the latter areas, communities were more cohesive and communal controls on agriculture and land-use better developed. There were often stronger manorial controls on the alienation of land, holdings did not fragment to the same extent and there was less economic polarisation within the farming community. It may be this that explains why in many of these areas so much of the wastes were ploughed up in the 12th and 13th centuries, as arable prices, and the need for food for consumption, increased. Whatever the explanation, it appears that in many parts of the central Midlands, areas of common grazing were almost entirely destroyed by the end of the 13th century. The arable strips of many villages ran right up to the parish boundary, meeting with those of neighbouring villages.

This was not true of all areas in the Midlands, however. Conversion of grazing to arable was more retarded in the Forest areas. Such areas were not necessarily densely wooded; the term *forest* was a legal rather than a descriptive or environmental term, referring to areas to which forest law applied. This was a body of rules and restrictions originally intended to preserve deer for the royal chase and which *inter alia* attempted to limit the destruction of suitable habitats through the expansion of arable cultivation. In reality, forest law functioned more as a source of revenue, for encroachments on the wastes were tolerated if a fine was paid. Nevertheless, in areas like Rockingham Forest in Northamptonshire, these institutional factors combined with the relatively marginal nature of local soils to preserve extensive areas of open waste.

As arable expanded at the expense of grazing, in the areas of irregular field systems and dispersed settlement surviving commons often became foci for settlement. The poorly developed nature of communal controls in such areas was probably the stimulus for this development; farmers and smallholders moved to the edge of areas of common grazing not only for the convenience provided by such a location, but also, as it were, to stake a visible claim to their use. The freedom to alienate land and the irregular nature of field systems in these areas made such settlement migration possible, for they allowed the acquisition of blocks of land adjacent to the common upon which farmsteads could be established. This development seldom occurred in areas of regular open-field systems, nucleated settlement, and strong community controls.

Thus it was mainly in the south–east and the north–west of England that the medieval period saw the development of straggling settlements around the perimeter of commons. This process went furthest in parts of East Anglia, where complex manorial organisation and the presence of substantial numbers of free tenants practising partible inheritance led to a proliferation of smallholdings and wholesale migration away from earlier village sites. Farmsteads clustered around areas of common which thus became large village greens, leaving the parish church – marking the original Saxon site of settlement – isolated in the fields some distance away (Wade Martins, 1975).

Lowland commons have a distinctive form. They have straggling, concave outlines, formed by a series of rough arcs; roads funnel into the common where these arcs join. This characteristic shape probably derives from the fact that commons are the remnants of more extensive areas of waste which had been continuously encroached upon for centuries before their outline became fossilised, usually in the early medieval period. The perimeters of commons are often defined by particularly massive and ancient banks and ditches.

Today, many commons are wooded, but this is normally a relatively recent feature, resulting from a relatively recent decline in the intensity of grazing. By the end of their medieval period, commons had usually lost whatever woodland they had formerly carried; it had been destroyed by felling and over-grazing, and only names like 'Wood Green' sporadically reflect their former nature. Medieval woodland, in contrast, was not usually common land, but land which had been enclosed from the waste and over which the use and access of others had been limited (Rackham, 1976).

By the end of the Middle Ages, there were considerable regional variations in the extent of common land. Commons survived better in the upland areas of the north and east than in the more fertile lowland zone. Within the lowland areas, they tended to survive better in the south and east of England, and in the west country, than in the classic open-field areas of the Midlands, with the exception of the forest areas, where they usually also survived well.

These variations were a factor in the local and regional development of rural society in the post-medieval period. In particular, areas in which extensive commons survived tended also to be the areas in which the decline of the small freehold farmer, which continued at varying rates throughout the post-medieval period, was retarded. In areas like the Fens, small farmers used their rights to extensive commons to adopt forms of livestock farming as specialized agricultural regions emerged in the 15th century. Survival of commons also allowed small cottagers to maintain a measure of economic independence, and the more extensive commons attracted large numbers of squatters, often part-time craftsmen. As a result, areas in which large commons survived tended to have a reputation for lawlessness. The opportunities which such areas offered to the poor also ensured that they often experienced particularly rapid population growth in the early modern period. In Northamptonshire, for example, forest villages in the 17th century were on average around half as populous again as non-forest villages (Hoskins and Stamp, 1967, p. 52).

Much enclosure of common land occurred during the 16th and 17th centuries. Nevertheless, in 1688 Gregory King estimated that there were still 10 million acres of heaths, moors, mountains and barren land in England and Wales, and a further 3 million acres of forests, parks, and commons, the majority of which was common land. Today, the total area of common land in England and Wales is around 1.5 million acres. Even allowing for a high degree of inaccuracy in King's estimates, there has clearly been a dramatic reduction in the area of common land as a result of Parliamentary enclosures, mainly in the late 18th and early decades of the 19th centuries. Enclosure was principally inspired by a desire on the part of the larger landowners to profit from the conversion of the remaining commons to arable, or their improvement as pasture, both of which were difficult or impossible where the land was subject to the use and access of a large number of local inhabitants. The high prices of arable during the Napoleonic Wars were a particular stimulus to enclosure of open heaths and wastes, especially on the light soils of eastern England (Turner, 1980, pp. 63–93).

The enclosure of commons was, like the enclosure of open fields, closely connected with the decline of the small owner-occupier which had continued almost uninterrupted throughout the early modern period. As land fell into the hands of relatively few people, so it became easier to obtain the agreement necessary to enclose, especially as with the advent of Parliamentary Enclosure a majority in favour of enclosure was judged on the basis of the area of land which the agreeing landowners held, rather than on their number.

Yet as well as being in part a consequence of the decline of the small proprietor, enclosure of commons also served to accelerate this process. The allotments received by those small farmers or cottagers who were able to prove the legality of their claim to common rights were seldom sufficient compensation for the advantages lost through enclosure, especially when legal and fencing costs were taken into account. For many small farmers, enclosure was the final misfortune which led to their departure from farming; for the small cottager, enclosure often led to increased, if seasonal, reliance on poor relief (Snell, 1985).

Today, the distribution of surviving common land in

England and Wales continues to be very uneven, with more in the highland zone than in the lowlands. Within the lowlands, there are still fewer commons in the Midland counties than in the south and east, or in the west country. In lowland areas, most commons are now principally valued for their amenity value, or for their role as nature reserves or Sites of Special Scientific Interest. Common land now survives as such only where it has been registered under the terms of the Commons Registration Act of 1965. All existing common land is listed in the final register, which was closed on 1 August 1972.

T. WILLIAMSON

See also COMMON PROPERTY RIGHTS; OPEN FIELD SYSTEM.

BIBLIOGRAPHY

Campbell, I. and Clayden, P. 1980. *The Law of Commons and Village Greens*. Henley-on-Thames, Oxon: Open Spaces Society.
Hoskins, W.G. and Dudley Stamp, L. 1967. *The Common Lands of England and Wales*. London: Collins.
Rackham, O. 1976. *Trees and Woodland in the British Landscape*. London: Dent.
Snell, K. 1985. *Annals of the Labouring Poor: social change and agrarian England 1660–1900*. Cambridge: Cambridge University Press.
Turner, M.E. 1980. *English Parliamentary Enclosure*. Folkestone, Kent: William Dawson.
Wade Martins, P. 1975. The origins of rural settlement in East Anglia. In *Recent Work in Rural Archaeology*, ed. P.J. Fowler, Bradford on Avon: Moonraker Press.

common law. Common law is a system of law and legal processes which originated in England shortly after the Norman Conquest and after several centuries of continuous development was exported to the English colonies, and so came to be the basis of the law of the greater part of United States, as well as of Australia, New Zealand, most of Canada and (to a lesser degree) also of India, Pakistan, Bangla Desh and many parts of Africa. The chief characteristic of the common law has always been that its development has lain largely in the hands of the judges, and that it has therefore grown and changed incrementally, case by case, in the course of actual litigation.

In modern times the term 'common law' is used in a variety of senses. In the broadest sense, it continues to be used to refer to the entire system of law originating in England which now forms the basis of the law in the greater part of the former British Empire, often nowadays called the 'common law world'. In this sense the common law is often contrasted with the 'civil law' which derives from the law of ancient Rome, and today operates in most of Western Europe, as well as in a number of other countries (such as Japan and Egypt) which have borrowed their law from European countries. One of the chief characteristics of the modern civil law is that it derives its authority from one or more basic Codes of law; and it remains a principal distinction between common law and civil law countries that the former have not generally codified their law. And even in common law jurisdictions (such as California, for example) where there does today exist a kind of common law Code, it differs fundamentally in nature from the civil law Codes; in particular the system of precedent, and the authority of the judges to interpret and develop such common law Codes are quite different from those recognised in civil law countries.

The term 'common law' is also often used in various narrower senses. In the most important of these narrower senses, the common law is often contrasted with legislation, so that the lawyer in a common-law country still thinks of legislation as a type of law different from the 'common law', which is basically judge-made law. The term 'common law' is sometimes used in yet a third relevant sense in which it is distinguished from a body of law, known technically as 'Equity' which was originally supplementary to the common law, and was developed in the separate Court of Chancery. Today common law (in this narrow sense) and 'Equity' are almost everywhere merged and administered by a single set of courts.

The common law (in the first two senses identified above) has traditionally been associated with the economics of the free market in at least two different ways. First, there is a strain of thought, represented in particular by Hayek (1973), which seems to suggest that a system of law, like the common law, which is largely judge-made, is inherently more likely to favour and protect individual freedoms, and among them (or especially) economic freedoms. But this is an implausible and indeed eccentric claim, which seems to involve confusion of the first two senses of the term of 'common law' referred to above. Because most redistribution is accomplished in modern democracies by legislative measures, it is easy to assume that a legal system which owes little to legislation will be more likely to recognize and protect the freedom of the market, but the amount of redistribution which occurs in a legal system does not necessarily depend upon whether that society is part of the common law world. There is no *a priori* reason to suppose that judges left to themselves by a legislature will necessarily favour the economics of the market. In the last analysis, the policies favoured by judges will depend upon their own preferences, their culture and traditions.

But there is a second way in which the common law has traditionally been associated with the freedom of the market, and this association rests upon the historical facts of the last three centuries. The concept of the Rule of Law which came to be recognized and defended in England after the revolution of 1688 has been seen by many as having favoured the development of a free market economy in England prior to and during the early years of the industrial revolution. Because of this historical fact it was for a long time almost an article of faith among English writers that the common law and the freedom of the market were closely associated. This view is today less strongly held in England, as a result no doubt of the fact that, while Englishmen still like to believe in the Rule of Law (despite grave doubts in some quarters as to whether this concept has much meaning), they are by no means so wedded to the free market as they were. In America, where the Constitution of 1788 substantially embodied the English traditions as to the Rule of Law, as well as the then accepted ideology of the free market, the association between the two has survived rather more strongly.

The reasons for the traditional belief in the close association between the common law and the freedom of the market must therefore be sought in history, and in particular in English history during the period from approximately 1770 to 1870, when the free market economy was largely in process of being established. And of all parts of the common law, none was more important for this purpose than the law of contract, because this was the part of the law most intimately related to the economic system. Indeed, the story of English law between 1770 and 1870 was to a large degree the story of how the law of contract was converted into the law of the free market, and of how the ideology of freedom of contract became one of the great intellectual movements of history (Atiyah, 1979).

The first three-quarters of the 18th century was a period of transition in England, during which many older ideas about contract and the market were being displaced by the newer ideas which gradually became dominant towards the end of the century. Among the older ideas at least three can be identified as particularly hostile to the laws needed to serve the emerging free market economy. First, there was a regulatory element in the law and the economy dating back to Tudor times, represented for instance by statutory controls of wages and prices of many commodities, and by the apprenticeship laws which controlled entry to many trades with outdated and largely unnecessary restrictions. Secondly, there was a paternalistic element in much contract law at this time, with the courts being still willing to relieve various classes of persons from the consequences of bad bargains which they had made. This paternalism was particularly pronounced under various doctrines of Equity, such as rules for the relief of mortgagors, rules against the enforcement of contractual penalties and forfeitures, rules for the protection of seamen and 'expectant heirs', and so forth. Thus, in the third sense of the term the 'common law' identified above, it can be said that the common law was always more market-oriented than Equity. Thirdly, there was a traditional moralistic element in the contract law of the 18th century, and this also took different forms, such as the general hostility to usury (as to which see Simpson, 1975, pp. 510–18), and the attempts to regulate the way in which essential foods and drinks were sold by use of the traditional marketing offences. The 'moral' roots of older law were also related to ideas about 'just prices' which, though rarely openly recognized in the common law, seem to have been influential at least in some of the cases in Equity, where there are signs that the Chancellors did have some vague sense of unease if they were asked to enforce contracts at prices which seemed to them very unfair, or on terms which were (in the language of the law) 'unconscionable'.

In addition to these specific instances of interference with the binding force of private contracts, there were important respects in which the whole concept of a general contract law remained relatively undeveloped at this time. Thus, while the law recognized and enforced specific types of contracts, such as contracts for the sale of land, contracts of insurance and so forth, there was, as yet, little sign of a general law of contract, governing all types of transaction. Then also, it remains unclear how far the contract law of this period actually recognized and enforced wholly executory contracts, in the sense of awarding damages for breach of a contract prior to any acts of performance or detrimental reliance by any of the parties. And finally, it is clear that, from the standpoint of today, the law of contract in the 18th century had not yet freed itself from dependence on the law of property. Of course, in one sense contract law can never be free from a dependence on property entitlements, because contract law is the mechanism by which entitlements are exchanged; but there are clear signs in the 18th century that contract law was still closely tied to property law in another sense, in the sense (for instance) that the proprietary aspects of many transactions were still regarded as more important than the promissory or contractual aspects. So, for instance, the right of a mortgagor to redeem the mortgaged property was protected by the courts even when by the terms of the mortgage documents he had forfeited that right by delay in repaying the loan. It was assumed that if the mortgagee received back his money, with interest and costs, he was adequately protected by the law, even though the contract itself would have given him more extensive rights.

During the century beginning around 1770 these older ideas and traditions gradually gave way before the ideology of freedom of contract; but it would be wrong to think that this ideology did not have long roots and antecedents in still earlier periods. There are, even in the 16th and 17th centuries, many signs of incipient economic liberalism among the lawyers such as Coke, who bequeathed to the common law a hatred of monopolies as well as a passion for individual liberties (Wagner, 1935). And Thomas Hobbes, in a well-known passage in *Leviathan*, had swept away all the medieval learning about 'just prices' and declared that '[t]he value of all things contracted for, is measured by the Appetite of the Contractors; and therefore the just value, is that which they be contended to give' (Hobbes [1651] 1968, p. 208). So the ideology of freedom of contract certainly had origins going back well beyond the 18th century. Nevertheless, it does seem (though the matter remains controversial) that major changes in the law began during the course of that century which gathered pace as the century progressed.

Certainly, a great deal occurred to change the character of contract law from the last quarter of the 18th century until well into the 19th century, and there is much evidence that many of these changes in the law were profoundly influenced by classical economic theory, and perhaps still more by popular versions of classical economic theory. First, the relics of the Tudor regulatory economy gradually disappeared. Wage regulation had become increasingly obsolete in practice during the 18th century, and a major challenge to the older laws in the name of freedom of contract had taken place in the celebrated case of the Gloucestershire Weavers (1756–7), (Atiyah, 1979, pp. 73–4). By the early 19th century most of the legislation authorizing the fixing of wages had been repealed. So too was the Statute of Apprentices, after many years during which its operation had been gradually whittled down by the judges. Secondly, the signs of paternalism which are still found in 18th-century Equity seem to have disappeared gradually as the judges hardened their hearts and toughened their minds. For example, signs of an attempt to introduce implied warranties on the sale of good for the protection of buyers, which can be detected in the 18th century, were largely scotched, and the principle of *caveat emptor* reasserted with full vigour. The equitable doctrines allowing the courts to relieve various unfortunates from the effects of hard bargains were gradually whittled down, although they never disappeared altogether. Third, the moralistic elements in the law were also gradually whittled down. The law of contract came increasingly to be seen to be neutrally enforcing agreements which must be presumed to be beneficial to both parties. The only moral component left in the law of contract during the 19th century seemed to derive from the binding nature of promises.

The subjective theory of value also seems to have been largely accepted by the judges even before it had been wholly accepted by economists. Although the common law had always insisted that a promise be supported by some 'consideration', some reason, before it would be enforced (and to that extent at least contained a paternalist element), the growing acceptance of the subjective theory of value meant that the doctrine of consideration became much less important during the 19th century. So for instance, in *Haigh* v. *Brooks* (1840, 113 English Reports 124) the judges enforced a promise to pay £9000 in return for the giving up of a guarantee previously given by the promisor, even though it now appeared that the guarantee might be unenforceable and legally worthless. The promisor had valued it at £9000, said the judges; it was not for them to say that the document was worthless. For similar reasons, the prejudice against usury had gradually been overcome, and the usury laws were totally repealed in England in 1854.

In these ways, then, the principle that contracts are binding and must be strictly enforced had been greatly strengthened, and exceptional cases had been whittled down by the middle of the 19th century. In addition, other changes had occurred in the general nature of contract law, which were closely related to the growing trend to see contract law as the law of the free market. First, it was during this period that a general law of contract came into existence for the first time in the common law world. And the process of generalization was important to the ideology of the law in a number of respects. In particular, the generalizing of contractual ideas meant that the law had to become more abstract, more broadly principled. Principles had to be developed which could be applied equally to (say) commercial contracts for the sale of wheat, to contracts of employment, and (for instance) to personal contracts such as the contract to marry. This abstraction may have helped the law become more neutral, less inclined to pursue any redistributive tendencies, such as may exist where (say) there is a separate body of legal doctrine dealing with contracts of employment, or with residential leases, or with loan transactions.

Next, it seems clear that another major development during this period was the gradual shift in emphasis in contract law away from treating contracts as present, or partly performed exchanges, and towards treating them as private planning devices, made in advance to allocate risks. The wholly executory contract became clearly recognised by the law, so that it now became possible for a person to sue for damages for breach of a pure promise, even where no performance or detrimental reliance had taken place. The justification for requiring damages to be paid in such circumstances was never clearly enunciated, and indeed, specific justification was rarely seen to be necessary. It was widely assumed that the broad principle of freedom of contract required, not only that parties be left free to make their own exchanges, but that the law should be available in aid of a party to enforce his claim to damages where the other failed to perform. John Stuart Mill was the first economist to point out that a policy of *laissez-faire* could not be used to justify the enforcement of executory contracts (Mill, 1848, vol. 2, p. 386), but even modern economists do not generally pursue this line of thought, though some libertarians have done so.

And finally, 19th-century contract law increasingly freed itself from its dependence on property law. Although obviously entitlements still remain the subject matter of all contracts, contract law has become much less concerned with specific items of property, and is more concerned with wealth as a kind of fungible property. The reason for this was basically that 19th-century contract law was dominated by the needs of merchants and traders, to whom all property is in principle replaceable with money. A merchant can be assumed to be indifferent between a piece of property, and the value of that property. Similarly, as contracts came to be increasingly seen as fundamentally risk-allocation devices, the particular entitlements or property to which the risks attached became less important.

By the last quarter of the 19th century, the process of developing a mature body of general contract law had largely been completed in England, and although a similar process took place in America (Horwitz, 1977), there is ground for believing that that was not completed for another fifty years or so. Freedom of contract had, apparently, reached its highest point. But although this was true of the ideology of freedom of contract among lawyers and judges, it was not really true of the views of economists or of the politicians, or of the public. By the late 19th century, neoclassical economists were already beginning to write sceptically about the sweeping effects of freedom of contract which had been attributed to the classical economists, and were pointing out the many possible causes of market failure such as information difficulties, externalities and monopoly. And although most of the older regulatory legislation had been repealed in the first half of the 19th century, Parliament had at the same time been gradually building up a completely new body of regulatory enactments dealing with new industrial problems – factories, coal mines, safety at sea for seamen and emigrant passengers, public health, the adulteration of food and drink, regulation of the weights and measures used for sales, and so on. Much of this new legislation had been a pragmatic response to perceived evils, and though some of it could have been justified economically by arguments concerning misinformation or externalities, much of it would have been difficult to justify except on the assumption of paternalistic or redistributive motives. Some of it may have been inspired by sheer impatience, an unwillingness to give the market time to work, or a belief that the short-term costs of market failures were so severe that legislative correction was necessary without regard to the long term distortions this might produce.

What is quite clear is that by the time the English common law and common lawyers had accepted the teachings (as they were thought to be) of the classical economists on freedom of contract, these teachings were already somewhat out of date. The result was that the mature common law of contract was seriously deficient in a number of respects. It was first of all deficient in its almost total neglect of the problem of externalities. Contracting parties were entitled to pursue their own interests, regardless of the effect of their contract on third parties, or the public. Only in the most extreme cases of actual illegality would the courts generally refuse to uphold a contract. Secondly (although this certainly could not be laid at the door of the classical economists), there had been, during the 19th century, a serious neglect by common lawyers of the problem of monopoly. This may well have been largely due to the fact that for the greater part of this period the British economy was itself highly competitive, and in little danger from monopolies. But the complacent assumption that cartels were unstable and were always vulnerable to internal or external competition was in England (though not in America) carried over by lawyers and courts into new conditions towards the end of the 19th century, and well into the present century, when it was utterly out of date. A second result of this failure of the common law to keep pace with economic theory and political reality, was the growing gulf between the common law and legislation. Once again, extensive legislative intervention with freedom of contract began to become commonplace, and much of it was increasingly redistributive in character.

During the course of the present century this process continued at an increasing pace until 1980 or thereabouts, since when there are signs that history has virtually reversed itself. Disillusion with the free market, particularly in England, increased during the great depression in the 1930s until, by the end of World War II, a Labour Government was elected to power with a massive majority and with a mandate to lay the foundations for a socialist state and a socialist economic system. Since then England has increasingly learned to live with a 'mixed economy', to a large part of which the traditional law of contract seems irrelevant because the public sector is often controlled by public laws rather than by contract law. But even in areas where private law continues to operate, the common law of contract has become increasingly affected by legislative intervention. Virtually all types of consumer transactions are today controlled or affected to some degree by legislation, including consumer credit contracts, contracts of employment, residential leases, and insurance contracts. Unconscionable, or unfair contracts are increasingly subjected to judicial control. Many areas of law which were formerly controlled largely by contract, such as family law, are now subject to extensive judicial discretionary control. Even business and commercial contracts are subject to vast bodies of legislative and regulatory laws, some, such as the modern monopoly or anti-trust laws, being designed to preserve the operation of a competitive market, but much of it still being designed to restrict competition or the operation of the free market.

America has not gone so far down this road as Britain and other common-law countries, and indeed, for a long time, in the late 19th and early 20th centuries, constitutional decisions of the United States Supreme Court in the name of freedom of contract, actually prevented similar developments. Much legislative intervention with freedom of contract was, during this period, declared unconstitutional, frequently over the dissent of Justice Holmes. By the late 1930s, however, the majority of the court had largely accepted Holmes's view, and since then, legislative intervention with freedom of contract has not been regarded as per se unconstitutional. This shift in the court opened the door to the same kind of regulation and intervention which had already been taking place in Britain, and although America has not, like Britain, brought large-scale industries within the public sector and therefore partially outside the control of contract law, most of the other legislative developments of the British type certainly have their parallel in America. No doubt some contracts are more regulated in Britain, but conversely there are plenty of examples of legislative interference with freedom of contract in America which are not to be found in Britain.

These vast changes in the operation of the common law have accompanied or brought with them a change in ideology once again. Paternalism and redistribution were, at least until around 1980, increasingly favoured by many writers and teachers of contract law, as well as large sectors of the electorate. Even the judges became much more sympathetic to arguments based on concepts like unconscionability and inequality of bargaining power. In America, unconscionability was given express legitimacy as a device for overturning unfair contracts by the Uniform Commercial Code, and was increasingly used by the judges as a matter of common law as well. Many relationships of a contractual character (for instance, that of physician and patient) and others of a virtually contractual character (for instance, that between manufacturers of products and ultimate purchasers and consumers) are, both in American and Britain, increasingly regulated by tort law rather than contract law, at least where things go badly wrong and legal actions for damages are brought based on negligent conduct, or on defects in the goods. In such malpractice or products liability actions the appropriate standards of care or quality are set by judges and juries and not by the contracting parties, and contractual exculpatory clauses are often denied legal validity.

Since about 1980 there have been increasing signs that the tide has turned yet again, both in Britain and America. Obviously, and visibly, British and American governments have since then been trying to reassert the virtues of the free market and roll back the frontiers of regulation, and in this they are being vigorously supported by some lawyers and law teachers in America, though not to any real extent in Britain. It is not yet clear what the impact of this is going to be on the future of the common law of contract. One possible scenario is

that, as in the late 19th century, the courts will be behind the times, but that on this occasion they will be hostile to the reasserted belief in the free market and will continue to defend paternalist and redistributive intervention in free contracts, particularly where one of the parties to the contract is a consumer or 'small man' thought to be weak in bargaining power. But another possible scenario is that the new enthusiasm for the free market will prove but a short-lived hiccup in the long-term trend towards paternalist and redistributive policies. In either event it seems unlikely that for many years to come British or American courts will be enforcing contracts according to the full rigour of the common law.

P.S. ATIYAH

See also LAW AND ECONOMICS.

BIBLIOGRAPHY

Atiyah, P.S. 1979. *The Rise and Fall of Freedom of Contract*. Oxford: Oxford University Press.

Hayek, F.A. 1973. *Law, Legislation and Liberty*, vol. 1, *Rules and Orders*. London: Routledge & Kegan Paul.

Hobbes, T. 1651. *Leviathan*. Ed. C.B. Macpherson, Harmondsworth: Penguin Books, 1968.

Horwitz, M.J. 1977. *The transformation of American Law 1780–1860*. Cambridge, Mass. and London: Harvard University Press.

Mill, J.S. 1848. *Principles of Political Economy*. From the fifth London edition, New York: D. Appleton & Co., 1908.

Simpson, A.W.B. 1975. *A History of the Common Law of Contract*. Oxford: Clarendon Press.

Wagner, D.O. 1935. Coke and the rise of economic liberalism. *Economic History Review* 6(1), October, 30.

common markets. *See* CUSTOMS UNIONS; ECONOMIC INTEGRATION.

common property rights. In a society where individuals compete for the use of scarce resources, some rules or criteria of competition must exist to resolve the conflict. These rules, known as property rights, may be established in law, in regulation, in custom or in hierarchy ranking. The structures of rights may take a variety of forms, ranging from private property rights at one extreme to common property rights at the other. Most fall somewhere in between: either set of rights would be rare in its purest form.

In a private property, the delimitation of the right to its use is expressed in dimensions or characteristics inherent in the property itself. These rights are exclusive to some private party, are freely transferable, and the income derived from them is not attenuated, restrained or infringed by laws or regulations. Hence price control, taxation, and social restriction of transferability may be regarded as violations of private property rights. In a common property, there is no delimitation or delineation of its use rights to any private party. No one has the right to exclude others from using it, and all are free to compete for its use. Hence there are no exclusive use rights, no rights to be transferred, and in the limiting case, no net income can be derived from using the common property.

This last condition rests on an economic proposition known as the dissipation of rent. It argues that because of the lack of exclusive use rights, individuals competing for the use of a common property will reduce its rental value or net worth to zero. The reason is that if no one has an exclusive claim to the value (i.e. rent) of that property, its use will invite competition to the point that each and every competing user can earn no more than the alternative earning of his own resources required in the exploitation of that common property. In other words, under competition and with no one having a special advantage, a 'prize' that has no exclusive claimant will be dissipated or absorbed by the costs of other resources which must be dedicated to its winning. Hence the net value of the prize won is zero.

The usual examples of common property rights cite a public beach and marine fisheries, and the dissipation of rent typically implies excessive use or over-exploitation. However, the dissipation may take the form of under-exploitation. For example, a piece of fertile land under common ownership may be used for herd grazing, or left idle, instead of being planted as an orchard.

In the real world, the complete dissipation of rent is rare indeed. This is because the supply curve of labour or of other inputs may be rising (some intramarginal rent may be captured), the competing users may have different opportunity costs (the non-marginal users may be enjoying rent), or entry may be restricted by regulations, by customs or by information costs. Still, with common property rights some dissipation of rent is inevitable, and no society can afford to surrender a large portion of its valuable resources to this structure of property rights.

A property may be held in common because its capturable rent is lower than the cost of enforcing exclusivity. In this case, the dissipation of rent is no waste. However, to the extent that rent dissipation is viewed as a waste, its occurrence must be attributable to the omission of some constraints in the analysis. Attempts to reduce rent dissipation go far to explain why common property in its 'pure' form is seldom observed. In marine fisheries, for example, numerous regulations govern the fishing season, the size of fish caught, the boat size and the mesh size, and various licensing arrangements restrict the number of boats and fishermen. The market value of a fishing licence, sometimes enormous, is one measure of the ocean rent captured. Even for public beaches, regulations of some type will often be found to govern the use of those most in demand.

Whereas regulations and restrictions on entry in the use of a common property often serve to reduce dissipation, the rent that can be captured is usually less than if the property were privately owned. To reconcile this observation with constrained maximization, we must infer that, enforcement costs aside, other transaction costs associated with the changing of institutional arrangements must restrain the formation of private property rights.

No economy can survive if the majority of its scarce resources are commonly owned. Regulations may, indeed, reduce rent dissipation; but in the process they not only distort the use of the resources but also invite corruption and the emergence of special interests. An unrestrained common property, strictly speaking, is propertyless in ownership; if its structure is extended to all resources, starvation for all must result. If one rules out private property rights, then to avoid the imposition of an infinite array of regulations the remaining alternative is the communal system or the communist state.

In a communist state there is no private owner of productive resources: each constituent is propertyless, in the literal sense of the word. Since the dissipation of rents associated with common properties will guarantee starvation, in a communist state the rights to use resources, and to derive income therefrom, are defined in terms of rank. That is, stripped of all ownership rights over valuable and productive resources, the citizens of a communist state hold differing rights to use resources and to obtain income according to their status. In

the people's communes in China under the Great Leap Forward, for example, no one owns the productive resources (i.e. everyone is propertyless), but comrades of different ranks enjoy different rights and privileges. 'Rank' as such has value and is subject to competition, therefore a system of 'property' rights is implicit. However, the valuable rights are now defined in terms other than the inherent properties of the productive resources.

This is, in fact, the key distinction between a private property system and a communist state: the former delineates rights in terms of certain dimensions of the productive resources themselves; the latter delineates rights in terms of a characteristic (rank) of people deprived of productive human capital. In the communist state, the competition for and protection of rank will draw on the use of valuable and productive resources (another form of rent dissipation). Moreover, the lack of market prices increases the cost of information, and the lack of contractual choices increases the cost of enforcing performance. What is saved in return are the costs of delineating and enforcing rights in properties.

It is among these varied costs – broadly defined as transaction costs – that we find the key divergence in economic performance between the communist and the private property systems. If one ignores transaction costs, the delineation of rights in terms of rank will produce the same use of resources as would the delineation of rights in properties. However, it can be convincingly argued that the broadly defined transaction costs are generally higher with communal than with private rights. Communism fails, not because it does not work in theory, but precisely because in practice its costs of transaction are higher than those in a system of private property rights. Still, the delineation of rights in ranks is a way to reduce rent dissipation in a propertyless state.

Strictly speaking, the dissipation of rent associated with common property is no 'theory' at all, because dissipating rent merely to produce an equilibrium does not explain behaviour. Worse, to stand aside and simply permit rent to dissipate is inconsistent with the postulate of constrained maximization.

What is useful and important from the standpoint of economic explanation is to view whatever rent dissipation does occur as necessarily a constrained minimum because, under the maximization postulate, each and every individual has an incentive to reduce that dissipation. Behaviour associated with the dissipation of rent must therefore be regarded as attempts to reduce that loss, and this altered view explains many observations. That some dissipation remains must then be attributable to the constraints of transaction costs. The challenge to the economist is to specify and identify what these costs are and how they will vary under differing circumstances.

STEVEN N.S. CHEUNG

See also COASE THEOREM; FISHERIES.

BIBLIOGRAPHY
Alchian, A.A. 1965. Some economics of property rights. *Il Politico* 30(4), 816-29.
Bottomley, A. 1963. The effect of the common ownership of land upon resource allocation in Tripolitania. *Land Economics* 39, February, 91-5.
Cheung, S.N.S. 1970. The structure of a contract and the theory of a non-exclusive resource. *Journal of Law and Economics* 13, April, 49-70.
Cheung, S.N.S. 1974. A theory of price control. *Journal of Law and Economics* 17, April, 53-71.
Cheung, S.N.S. 1982. *Will China Go 'Capitalist'?* Hobart Paper 94, London: IEA.
Coase, R.H. 1960. The problem of social cost. *Journal of Law and Economics* 3, October, 1-44.

Demsetz, H. 1964. The exchange and enforcement of property rights. *Journal of Law and Economics* 7, October, 11–26.

Gordon, H.S. 1954. The economic theory of a common property resource: the fishery. *Journal of Political Economy* 62, April, 124–42.

Knight, F.H. 1924. Some fallacies in the interpretation of social cost. *Quarterly Journal of Economics* 38, August, 582–606.

Commons, John Rogers (1862–1945). Commons was born on 13 October 1862 in Hollandsburg, Ohio, and died on 11 May 1945 in Raleigh, North Carolina. He studied at Oberlin College (BA, 1888) and Johns Hopkins University (1888–90). He taught at Wesleyan, Oberlin, Indiana, Syracuse, and Wisconsin (1904–32).

The founder of the distinctive Wisconsin tradition of institutional economics, Commons derived his theoretical insights (generalized in his *Legal Foundations of Capitalism* and *Institutional Economics*) from his practical, historical and empirical studies, particularly in the field of labour relations and in various areas of social reform. He drew insight not only from economics but also from the fields of political science, law, sociology and history. A principal adviser and architect of the Wisconsin progressive movement under Robert M. La Follette, Commons was active as an advisor to both state and federal governments. He was instrumental in drafting landmark legislation in the fields of industrial relations, civil service, public utility regulation, workmen's compensation and unemployment insurance. He served on federal and state industrial commissions, was a founder of the American Association for Labor Legislation, was active in the National Civic Federation, National Consumers' League (president, 1923–35), National Bureau of Economic Research (associate director, 1920–28), and the American Economic Association (president, 1917). He participated in antitrust litigation (especially the Pittsburgh Plus case) and in movements for reform of the monetary and banking system (often associated with Irving Fisher, who considered Commons one of the leading monetary economists of the period).

The critical thread uniting Commons's diverse writings was the development of institutions, especially within capitalism. He developed theories of the evolution of capitalism and of institutional change as a modifying force alleviating the major defects of capitalism. Commons came to recognize and stress that individual economic behaviour took place within institutions, which he defined as collective action in control, liberation, and expansion of individual action. The traditional methodologically individualist focus on individual buying and selling was not capable, in his view, of penetrating the forces, working rules and institutions governing the structural features of the economic system within which individuals operated. Crucial to the evolution and operation of the economic system was government, which was a principal means through which collective action and change were undertaken.

Commons rejected both classical harmonism and radical revolutionism in favour of a conflict and negotiational view of economic process. He accepted the reality of conflicting interests and sought realistic, evolutionary modes of their attenuation and resolution. These modes focused on a negotiational psychology in the context of a pluralist structure of power. He sought to enlist the open-minded and progressive leaders of business, labour and government in arrangements through which they could identify problems and design solutions acceptable to all parties.

In other contexts, he sought to use government as an agency for working out new arrangements to solve problems, such as worker insecurity and hardship, rather than promote systemic restructuring, although to many conservatives his ventures were radical enough. To these ends Commons and small armies of associates engaged in fact finding – his look-and-see methodology – in a spirit of bringing all scientific knowledge to bear on problem solving. From these experiences, indeed already manifest in the underlying strategy, Commons developed: a theory of government as alternately a mediator of conflicting interests and an arena in which conflicting interests bargained over their differences; a theory of the complex organization – in terms of freedom, power and coercion – and evolution of the legal foundations of capitalism, which centred in part on the composing of major structural conflicts through the mutual accommodation of interests; and a theory of institutions with an affirmative view of their roles in organizing individual activity and resolving conflict.

The institutions Commons studied most closely were trade unions and government, particularly the judiciary. He developed his theory of the economic role of government in part on the basis of his study of the efforts of workers to improve their market position and in part on the use of government by both enemies and friends of labour. Commons's was an interpretation of trade unions as a non-revolutionary development, as collective action seeking to do for workers what the organizations of business attempted to do for their owners and managers. His study of the reception given unions and reform legislation led him to recognize the critical role of the United States Supreme Court (and the courts generally), and its conception of what was reasonable in the development and application of the working rules which governed the acquisition and use of power in the market. Accordingly, Commons developed a theory of property which stressed its evolution and role in governing the structure of participation and relative withholding capacity in the market.

Commons also developed a theory of institutions which focused on their respective different mixtures of bargaining, rationing and managerial transactions, all taking place within a legal framework which was itself subject to change.

Although Commons's institutionalism had different emphases from that of Thorstein Veblen, for example, in that Commons stressed reform of the capitalist framework, they shared a view of economics as political economy and of the economy as comprising more than the market. Unlike Veblen, Commons was not antagonistic toward businessmen, and indeed accepted capitalism, though not necessarily on the terms given or preferred by the established power structure.

Commons was one of the few American economists to found a 'school', a tradition that was carried forward by a corps of students, especially Selig Perlman, Edwin E. Witte, Martin Glaeser and Kenneth Parsons. Much mid-20th-century American social reform, the New Deal for example, drew on or reflected the work of Commons and his fellow workers and students.

WARREN J. SAMUELS

SELECTED WORKS

1893. *The Distribution of Wealth*. New York: Macmillan.
1905. *Trade Unionism and Labor Problems*. Boston: Ginn.
1910–11. (With others.) *Documentary History of American Industrial Society*. 10 vols. Cleveland: A.H. Clark.
1916. (With J.B. Andrews.) *Principles of Labor Legislation*. New York: Harper.
1919. *Industrial Goodwill*. New York: McGraw-Hill.
1919–1935. (With others.) *History of Labor in the United States*. 4 vols. New York: Macmillan.
1921. *Industrial Government*. New York: Macmillan.

1924. *The Legal Foundations of Capitalism*. New York: Macmillan.
1934. *Institutional Economics*. New York: Macmillan.
1934. *Myself*. New York: Macmillan.
1950. *The Economics of Collective Action*. Madison: University of Wisconsin Press.

communications. The economics of communications is a loose, somewhat vaguely defined amalgam of topics in applied microeconomics. Although having close ties to the microeconomic theory of the economics of information, it is probably best characterized as a subfield of industrial organization, regulation and public enterprise that deals with the communications sector: telecommunications, broadcasting, the print media, the performing arts and the postal system. Of course, the activities that constitute this list are somewhat arbitrary, but they reflect what is both taught and studied by people in the subfield as well as some important economic realities that make specialized studies of the communications sector a valid category among distinct intellectual pursuits. First among these realities is that the industries in the communications sector are closely linked. Broadcasting competes with the performing arts for both audience and inputs, and telecommunications competes with the postal service. Moreover, telecommunications networks are capable of delivering broadcast services, and vice versa. Among the products over which the postal system, telecommunications and cable television compete is the delivery of the output of the print media.

Another unifying theme across communications industries is the connection of the study of the sector to the economics of public goods and externalities. Communications is the production and dissemination of information. Some aspects of the production of information are public goods, and the dissemination and use of information can have important external effects. Moreover, most of these external effects are non-economic phenomena such as political participation, the cultural values held by members of a society or the level of violence. Because of the unique character of these externalities, the motives for public policy in communications are closely linked with a society's fundamental political and social values. Thus, freedom of speech and the extent of the right to privacy, as well as the use of control of communications to manipulate the political process, are at the heart of debates over communications policy.

RATIONALES FOR GOVERNMENT INTERVENTION. Not surprisingly, the role of the public sector is very large in the communications sector in nearly every nation. Subsidization, nationalization and extremely detailed regulation of prices and attributes of the product are common. In market-oriented societies, telecommunications and mail are nationalized or subject to economic regulation for much the same reasons that underpin the same policies in other infrastructural industries: that these industries are natural monopolies and that their performance and pattern of development profoundly affect the development of much of the rest of the economy. But even here, unique externality arguments are brought forth as additional factors to be taken into account by policy-makers. First, subscription to the telecommunications network or access to mail delivery creates the capability to receive communication from others. A person who decides to mail a letter or place a telephone call presumably considers only his or her net benefits from the communication; the willingness to pay of the recipient (positive or negative) is not taken into account. Thus, for example, the extent of phone service and

the pattern of calling can be expected to be inefficient if each person bears the full cost of, first, subscribing to the network, and then placing telephone calls. In particular, if some potential customers have too low a willingness to pay to become subscribers, but are also desired objects of communications by others, the number of subscribers will be too low if subscribers must bear the full cost of connecting them to the network. This argument constitutes the foundation for the 'universal service' objective; that is, a policy of maximizing the number of subscribers to the telephone network, and the policy practised nearly everywhere of adopting a price structure for telephone services that subsidizes installation charges, pay-telephone prices and/or monthly access charges to the local network, especially for customers in high-cost areas such as rural communities.

A second externality of the telecommunications system is said to be its contribution to national security. A joint product of a private telecommunications network is a ready resource that can be commandeered and used by government in times of national emergency, such as foreign attack, natural disasters or accidents. The use of communications to coordinate a response to such an event, then, should play a role in affecting the capacity and design of the telecommunications system, and often is the basis of an argument for building into the system more redundancy and interconnectability than might otherwise be optimal and than independent private concerns would undertake on their own. These contingent needs by government have been said to constitute a separate natural-monopoly argument, an example of 'economies of scope' between private and public uses that can only be captured if the private system is a single, integrated whole. In the United States, for example, the Department of Defense was a consistent critic of proposals to relax regulation and increase competition in the telecommunications industry during the 1960s and 1970s.

The externalities associated with the mass media have to do with the social, political and psychological consequences of the content of information, and for the most part are dealt with by scholars from disciplines other than economics. (The main exception is research on the effects of advertising, where an inconclusive debate has raged for decades as to whether the informational value of advertising exceeds the sum of its direct costs and possible resource misallocation owing to manipulation and misperceptions of consumers.) The analytical foundation for the belief in the importance of informational externalities is the proposition that people's behaviour as citizens, parents, consumers, workers, friends, and so on, can be significantly affected, at least in the short run, by the informational content of the mass media. Once one accepts this proposition, the next logical step is to entertain the idea that censorship by the state, at least in principle, can prevent some of the external diseconomies of destructive content, while proactive state interventions to channel the content of the media towards greater educational and otherwise uplifting content can provide additional social benefits.

The most obvious manifestations of these ideas are in broadcasting. The British Broadcasting Corporation was founded on openly paternalistic principles about the potential of radio broadcasts for educational and other uplifting purposes. Until the recent move towards decentralization through cable television and towards private, commercial television, a core principle of French broadcasting policy was to preserve French culture and values by limiting and censoring programmes from other nations. In Germany, decentralized, regional quasi-public broadcast monopolies were created after World War II to protect simultaneously against capture by the national government or by the national print media barons, either of which, it was feared, might use broadcasting to arouse nationally destructive political passions. And in the United States, broadcast licensing has, until recently, enforced a long set of standards for evaluating competitors for a given license, including personal characteristics and other business holdings of the licensee and both performance and promise about the extent of 'public service' programming offered by commercial as well as non-commercial (educational) outlets.

Of course, other mass media are not free of similar policy constraints, although the print media and the arts are usually accorded greater freedom in the content of their messages than are broadcasters. The areas of policy controversy are the definition of the liability for slanderous attacks and the concomitant definition of privacy rights, the boundaries between pornography and legitimate expression, and the principles separating sedition from reasonable political discourse.

The core economic issue in this debate is whether the 'marketplace for ideas' works well without intervention, or at least better than is the case with active political intervention by the very government authorities whose security and power can be affected by the content of communications. The argument for non-intervention is twofold. Positively, it is that in the end people's tastes in ideas should be accorded the same status as their tastes in other goods as long as the consumption of communications produces no external diseconomies. If communications cause bad behaviours, then if people are informed about this fact – and about the punishments exacted if those behaviours are manifest – they will efficiently anticipate this in making decisions about which communications to receive and how to treat those that are received. And, as with goods, ideas about how the world works that prove correct will be perceived, at least eventually, as superior to less correct ideas. Negatively, the argument for an unregulated marketplace for ideas is a pessimistic forecast of how political intervention is likely to work: a combination of orientation towards propaganda to serve the interests of preserving the status quo and an extreme sensitivity to either vocal, organized single-issue groups seeking to impose their values on others or a tyranny of the majority that persecutes those who stray too far from current norms.

The other side of the dispute, usually advocated more by non-economists, is rooted in observed relationships between communications and behaviour, perhaps best documented in the study of the effects of television on violence (especially by children) and on the manipulation of the news for short-term political objectives. This position regards the efficiency of the marketplace for ideas as demonstrably poor, at least in the short run; implicitly, it accords less credence to the proposition that individuals are as rational – indeed, are even proactive – in selecting among competing communications as economic theory assumes. Proponents of intervention especially emphasize the unformed and manipulable attitudes of children.

The final pervasive feature in the communications sector that deserves further elaboration is the partially non-rivalous nature of the consumption of information. All information is a public good in the sense that once a new information product has been created for a first user, it does not have to be created again for subsequent users: in principle, at least, the first use of information does not preclude its use by others. In practice, this characteristic may be unimportant. Information must be disseminated in some way to subsequent users, and the cost of dissemination may exceed the cost of secondary creation – as for example can be the case for a simple computer program.

Or, information may be very cheaply privatized so that the public goods characteristic introduces no significant inefficiency to a private market system of distribution. Nevertheless, the publicness of information is a serious issue in an assessment of the performance of allocational institutions in the communications sector, and in the design of private market processes for allocating resources the problems of publicness must be addressed. Whether the product is a written news report, a novel, a theatrical production, a television broadcast, or 'Dial-A-Joke' on the telephone, the problem is fundamentally the same: producers will not supply a product unless they can recover the opportunity cost for creating it, yet the marginal cost of providing the product to one more consumer does not include any of the production costs of the information. Hence, efficient provision of information requires one of the following: subsidies of the production of information, or price discrimination with protection against arbitrage so that consumers with relatively low willingness to pay for information will not be inefficiently excluded. In practice, both are common. Governments subsidize broadcasting and performing arts by direct payments, and certain users of the postal and telecommunications system either directly or by engaging in price discrimination (e.g. the differences in basic monthly service rates of telephones between residences and businesses, and the lower postal rates for circulating the print media). Of course, neither direct subsidies nor discriminatory prices are explicitly designed in a quantitative sense to offset the inefficiencies of private provision of public goods, so that the issue of optimal pricing of communications services is an active and still-developing field of research. The focus here is on the two fields in which most of the work has been done: telecommunications and broadcasting. Moreover, the discussion includes research on market structure issues because of their close connection to the implications of alternative pricing policies.

PRICING AND MARKET STRUCTURE IN TELECOMMUNICATIONS. The telecommunications industry in the United States offers an array of services that until very recently were provided as joint products by a legally protected monopoly. When the monopoly was secure and unquestioned, the pricing problem was to devise a price structure that recovered joint and fixed costs with minimal loss of efficiency. As the natural monopoly presumption came to be called into question, the pricing problem began to incorporate another dimension, to provide appropriate signals to potential competitors so that the market structure would evolve efficiently.

To understand the rudiments of the telephone pricing problem requires some basic knowledge about the technical characteristics of the telecommunications network. The traditional telephone system is best conceptualized as having four components: customer terminal equipment (a telephone, a computer terminal, a switchboard); a pair of copper wires connecting each terminal device to a central switch; the central switch that serves the local community; and a hierarchy of transmission conduits and additional switches that serve to connect the local switches. Typically the telephone price structure has three elements: an installation charge for activating a customer's copper wire pairs; a basic monthly service charge for renting terminal equipment and the copper wire pairs; and a message toll for placing telephone calls. The common practice is for the installation charge to cover only a fraction of installation costs as a means of encouraging universal service, and for the basic monthly charge to entitle the subscriber to unlimited local calling – sometimes not confined to other telephones connected to the same local switch, but also including calls through adjacent local switches. Usually the basic monthly charge is much higher (by a factor of two or three) for business than for residences, but within each of these categories it tends to be approximately the same over wide geographic areas regardless of differences in cost of service.

Until about 1960, the revenues from installation charges and the basic monthly rate approximately covered the cost of local service (including local switches). But as long-distance toll calls became more important, telephone companies increasingly used toll revenues to cover part of the cost of the local system. This required no increase in toll prices; indeed, long-distance prices generally were falling because technological change was extraordinarily rapid in this segment of the system. By simply letting prices fall a little more slowly than costs, a large and growing fraction of local network costs could be paid for by toll. These revenues could be used to construct systems in high-cost rural areas without causing increased prices for basic service elsewhere, again to encourage universal service.

Since toll calls pass through local switches they impose a cost on the local network, because local switches must be designed to be large enough and complex enough to accommodate them. Consequently, toll prices would bear some local system costs in an efficient pricing structure. In addition, however, toll calls also contributed to 'non-traffic sensitive' (NTS) costs – the terminals and copper wire – even though, by definition, the magnitude of investment required for this equipment was unrelated to the amount of calling.

Obviously, this pricing structure not only encouraged universal service but encouraged local calling (with a zero price at the margin) while discouraging long-distance calling compared to an efficiency standard. Encouraging subscriptions to the system may be warranted on efficiency grounds, although the magnitude of the subscription externality has not been quantified, and so it is not possible to tell whether the amount of the subsidy is justified. Likewise, a subsidy of local calls may be desirable, but the method of subsidization is of doubtful validity. The external benefit (or cost) of a call falls on the person being called, not on society generally.

Hence, the optimal pricing structure involves a sharing of the costs of calling between the parties to a conversation, where the costs involve the operating costs of the system and the effect of calls on the required capacity of the switching system. Only if metering costs were large in comparison with the costs of calling would it make sense not to charge for calls, but with modern electronic switching metering costs are not significant, so that one cannot justify a subsidy for local calls. Moreover, even if one could, there is no justification for taxing long-distance calls to pay the subsidy unless one believes that the externality of a local call is substantially more important than the externality of a long-distance call.

The general structure of an optimal price structure for the telephone network, given important externalities and natural monopoly, can be derived as follows. Begin with a basic monthly charge that would pay the marginal cost of terminals and copper wire connections to the local switch, and toll charges on all calls that pay the marginal cost of the switching and transmission facilities that are traffic sensitive. These prices need further adjustment, for they may collect too much or too little total revenue. But prior to this adjustment they must also be uniformly adjusted downwards to account for the externality of subscribing and calling (assuming that people like to receive phone calls). The adjustment for the toll rate can simply be passed on to the recipient of the call; however, the basic monthly rate must come down for everyone. At this

point the likely case is that the basic monthly rate does not cover the NTS costs, so that further adjustments must be made. One possibility is a subsidy paid from an economy-wide tax, but more likely the additional revenues will come from the rate structure of the telephone company. The first-best solution is to raise infra-marginal prices, such as the cost of the first few calls made per month, producing what amounts to quantity discounts for all types of calls. Alternatively, one could adopt Ramsey pricing, raising the price the most for services with relatively inelastic demand.

The resulting price structure would have a number of very interesting features. Call recipients would pay a share of the price of a call. To implement this so as only to charge for calls with a positive benefit, the shared cost would start a decent interval after the call is answered, and subscribers who desired it could be permitted to designate in advance that they would bear the full cost of their calls. All prices would be built on marginal costs, which means peak-load pricing of calling and prices for both basic access and calling that were higher in high-cost areas. To the extent that Ramsey prices were invoked, they would most certainly rely primarily on basic monthly charges, for this has by far the lowest demand elasticity: estimates range between -0.02 and -0.10. Thus, even if there is a significant externality associated with subscribing to the network, the Ramsey pricing method for paying for it involves raising the price of basic access. Or, putting the matter another way, ignoring this externality in setting prices will have very little effect on subscriptions to the system, and hence very little effect on efficiency. Finally, differences between residential and business basic monthly charges would exist only if their externality value differed, they imposed different costs on the system or they had different price elasticities.

Obviously, the pricing structure of telephone service has never reflected these principles. Until the 1970s, government officials perceived the extent of inefficiency of the pricing structure as something of an academic issue and largely ignored it. But technological change and the false signals to entrants from the price structure have led to strong pressures for competitive entry into the formerly secure telephone monopoly. Computer technology has vastly diversified the demand for telecommunications, as well as vastly increased its magnitude, and computers and other advances in micro-electronics have altered the technology of supply. Examples of the broad range of new computer-based services include on-line connections to mainframes and data bases for technical and business use, automatic teller machines, remote sensing for protection against fires and burglars, and reservation services. Each of these uses has somewhat different technical requirements, so that the optimal market structure for the industry may well be to have a product-differentiated oligopoly, even if each has unexploited economies of scale. Moreover, the greater demand created by these technical advances allows considerable exploitation of scale economies even in a segmented system.

On the supply side, advances in electronics have changed the basic character of the local network. No longer are high-density networks built of dedicated copper wire pairs for each terminal. Instead, micro-electronic technology allows multiple signals on the same wires, and small-scale switches distributed throughout the local network that serve to concentrate lines from many terminals into a smaller number of active circuits, taking advantage of the fact that not all terminals are in use simultaneously. This reduces the unit cost of capacity and hence the significance of scale economies in the local network. Moreover, it undermines a cornerstone of the optimal-pricing structure that was developed above by eliminating most of the NTS costs. If, as is becoming the case, customers own their terminal equipment, and if line concentration begins when a small number of terminals are aggregated into a single pathway to the first switch, then nearly all of the system that is owned by the local telephone company consists of traffic-sensitive investment. Hence, the trend should be away from reliance on the basic monthly charge and towards greater reliance on message tolls for calling.

The failure to adjust the pricing system to the realities of costs and technology adds to the pressure for competitive entry in the parts of the system where prices are higher than the costs of service. Specifically, the attempt to tax long-distance service in order to subsidize local calling makes relatively intense users of long-distance service ripe candidates for a competitive long-distance supplier. Large companies with many telephone lines who can provide their own concentrated connections between their facilities have a strong incentive to bypass subscriptions to the local network. And other electronic pathways for communications, such as cable television and point-to-point uses of the radio spectrum, can be exploited to bypass the telecommunications network.

Thus far, government officials responsible for telecommunications policy whether as operators of public enterprises or regulators of private utilities, have focused more on the structural aspects of the problem than on pricing issues. Even in the United States, which has perhaps the greatest commitment to competition, government policy regarding entrants has been the binding constraint on the growth of competition, and the price structure is still replete with inefficiencies. The likely explanation for this phenomenon is the belief by political actors that the cost of local service to residences is the price that is most visible politically and that rationalized pricing will cause residential service to become more expensive, either from raising basic monthly charges or from message toll for local calls. To avoid raising residential prices, political actors therefore believe that they have to keep some other prices above the cost of service, and to maintain these prices in the face of diminished or perhaps even non-existent natural monopoly they must erect barriers to competitive entry aimed at the overcharged customers.

PRICES AND MARKET STRUCTURE IN BROADCASTING. The most common way to pay for broadcasting is to provide signals to the audience at no charge, and to rely on either advertising or government subsidies as to the source of revenues. In one sense such an arrangement seems to fit the fact that broadcasts are a classic public good; the marginal cost to the broadcaster of one more person receiving a broadcast is zero, and consumption among members of the audience is completely non-rivalrous. Hence, any attempt to charge a viewer for a programme can introduce inefficiency to the extent that anyone is thereby excluded from participation who also has a positive willingness to pay to join the audience.

The difficulty with free broadcasting, however, is that it does not necessarily result in programmes that maximize the net willingness to pay of the audience. Ignoring for a moment the frictions in the political process and the incentives of political actors to manipulate programme content to their private benefit, both subsidized and advertiser-supported television lead broadcasters to measure their success primarily on the basis of the size of audience. In a subsidized system, the objective would be to make certain that political support is as high as possible, and in an advertising system, in which the broadcaster is selling the attention of viewers, revenues are

more or less proportional to audience size. The issue in both cases is not whether audience satisfaction is maximized but whether it is kept high enough for a large enough number of people to maximize revenues from a payment system that is not based on the intensity of preferences but on the number of satisfied customers. In particular, small groups with intense willingness to pay for an unusual type of programming material will generally not have their preferences satisfied even if their aggregate willingness to pay exceeds that of a large audience for the traditional mass-audience programme.

Three means are available for coping with this state of affairs. One is to expand the number of broadcast options until all groups are satisfied. Suppose that there is a large mass audience and a series of small, specialized ones. As the number of stations expands, the audience for mass programmes each can expect will be the total mass audience divided by the number of stations. Eventually, there will be enough stations so that the largest specialized taste will constitute a larger audience than the share of the mass audience the next station could expect to capture, so that a strategy to maximize audience will lead to specialization. In the United States, this is more or less the policy with respect to radio broadcasting. In the early years of radio, the Federal Communications Commission tried to assure diversity in commercial broadcasting by specifying the format (e.g. type of programmes) that a station could broadcast. Recently, station formats have been deregulated, yet the multiplicity of categories remain, in much the same fashion that there is a broad spectrum of magazines and books by type of material.

In television, the strategy of increasing the number of stations is more difficult to follow. Television stations consume far more radio frequency space than radio stations, and no nation has thus far been willing to allocate enough high-quality radio spectrum to television to provide much of a test as to whether specialization might take place in a more extensive industry. An unplanned test, however, is under way in Italy, where in the 1970s the courts declared that the government had no constitutional right to limit the number of television stations, and largely unregulated entry has taken place on a massive scale. It is too soon to tell what the ultimate outcome of this system will be.

The second mechanism to produce more diversity in television is to allow the audience to express a willingness to pay, commonly by installing cable television with much higher capacity than off-air television and charging customers on the basis of the number and type of channels that they elect to receive. The inefficiency inherent in this system is the cost of privatizing broadcasts so that on either a per programme or per channel basis they can be sold. Prior to the extensive development of cable television in the United States, the common speculation was that privatization of broadcasts would cause a diversion from traditional mass audience programming, with more activity in cultural programmes, educational broadcasting and public affairs. The expectation was based upon the belief that higher-income groups were more interested in diversity and would have more influence in determining the content of for-pay systems. In practice, this expectation has not been realized. The new cable-oriented networks for the most part offer programming that is like that provided by off-air broadcasters, such as movies, sports events and regular series. The principal exception is in public affairs, where national cable news and public events networks have succeeded. Educational and cultural programming, however, has been largely unsuccessful. The inference to be drawn is that scarcity in television stations caused an excess demand for television, but primarily for programmes that were much like those featured by off-air stations, largely oriented towards the mass audience.

The third means for increasing diversity is to create a single, multi-outlet monopoly broadcasting entity. If such an entity seeks to maximize total audience, it will not have as much incentive to duplicate mass programming, because audience substitution from one channel to the next will have no value. A second or third mass-audience station will increase the size of the total audience, but the evidence indicates that the effect is small compared to audience diversion. For example, in the United States the first television station captures a little less than half of the potential audience available in prime evening viewing time. No matter how many additional stations are added, the maximum viewing share appears to be about 80 per cent, and this is almost totally achieved after three or four stations are operating. This suggests that a multi-channel monopolist would either diversify programming on the second or third channel, or simply elect not to broadcast on more than one or two channels, depending on the relationship between the value of a net increment to the audience and the costs of adding another channel.

American public television provides an example of a novel method of support, for it is one of the few attempts to implement a decentralized decision process for acquiring a public good (here programmes). The first component of the system is the method of public financing, which involves multiple year, advance funding to erect some barrier to political manipulation of programmes. The public funds are then divided into three components: a budget for experimental programming that is spent by an independent, quasi-public entity (the Corporation for Public Broadcasting); a budget for the technical operation of the national network (Public Broadcasting Service); and a direct subsidy of local stations. This subsidy is based in part on the success of the station in obtaining private contributions from its audience. Thus the station subsidy amounts to an attempt to overcome the free-rider problem faced by viewers by providing matching funds for their contributions.

The second component of the system is the mechanism by which stations decide which programmes will appear on the network. This is accomplished by a combination voting and price system. The price of a programme for each station is determined by the size of the community it serves, and stations then vote on each programme proposal. If some stations vote against the proposal, the prices faced by the supporters are increased by an amount necessary to allow the programme to cover its costs, and voting proceeds again. The process continues until programmes are either purchased or discarded; usually fewer than a dozen iterations are required to reach a decision. Stations voting against a programme are excluded from broadcasting it; however, stations may later join the group paying for it by paying a premium price.

The programme acquisition process decentralizes network programming to the stations, thereby serving two ends. First, because the station budgets depend on contributions, or the voluntary willingness to pay of the audience, there exists a feedback mechanism from the audience to the network that is similar to a pay-TV system. Second, the network schedule becomes less vulnerable to political attack, for centralized government officials who might seek to control it face a collective of over 150 station licensees, who, in turn, are actively using contributions patterns to make decisions about which programmes to acquire.

The American system of financing public television does not, of course, have pristine efficiency properties; neither the voluntary audience contributions nor the mechanism whereby stations select programmes is an incentive-compatible mechanism. Nevertheless, in the inherently imperfect world of public goods acquisition, they appear to perform remarkably well, and experimental investigations in a laboratory setting suggest that the method of acquiring programmes can be productively employed in a variety of settings for collective decisions.

REMAINING ISSUES. Two aspects of the communications sector make it a ripe area for continuing study. First is the rapidly evolving technology of supply and demand, and the second is the pervasive and changing influence of political processes on the structure and performance of the sector.

With changing technology has come a significant change in the pattern of demand for services. This suggests that historical patterns of use and estimates of service-specific demand are unreliable predictors of the future. Yet relatively little research has investigated how changing technology – lower costs, greater possibilities of use, more technical capabilities – have affected key aspects of demand: the rate of growth by service and customer category and the own- and cross-elasticities of demand.

Changing technical possibilities and demand should also feed back into the political forces that guide the development of the sector. Most advanced industrialized nations are in the midst of transition in at least some policies regarding communications, such as the privatization and introduction of competition in telecommunications in Japan and Great Britain, and the elimination of the state broadcasting monopolies in France and Italy. These changes deserve study on two counts: how these dramatic policy changes affect performance, and what political forces they may be creating that will shape policy and industry structure in the future.

A period of rapid change is one in which important new knowledge is likely to be forthcoming. One can anticipate that a summary of the economics of communications a decade or two hence will contain significant and surprising new insights.

ROGER G. NOLL

See also PUBLIC UTILITY PRICING.

BIBLIOGRAPHY

Bloch, H. and Wirth, M. 1984. The demand for pay services on cable television. *Information Economics and Policy* 1(4), 311–32.

Brock, G. 1981. *The Telecommunications Industry: The Dynamics of Market Structure*. Cambridge, Mass.: Harvard University Press.

Coase, R. 1959. The Federal Communications Commission. *Journal of Law and Economics* 2(1), 1–40.

Courville, L., de Fontenay, A. Dobell, R. 1983. *Economic Analysis of Telecommunications*. Amsterdam: North-Holland.

Evans, D. (ed.) 1971. *Breaking Up Bell*. Amsterdam: North-Holland.

Levin, H. 1971. *The Invisible Resource*. Baltimore: Johns Hopkins Press.

Machlup, F. 1980. *The Production and Distribution of Knowledge in the United States*. Princeton: Princeton University Press.

Mitchell, B. 1978. Optimal pricing and local telephone services. *American Economic Review* 68(4), September, 517–37.

Network Inquiry Special Staff. 1980. *New Television Networks: Entry, Jurisdiction, Ownership and Regulation*. Washington, DC: Federal Communications Commission.

Noll, R. 1985. 'Let them make toll calls': A state regulator's lament. *American Economic Review* 75(2), May, 52–6.

Noll, R., Peck, M.J. and McGowan, J.J. 1973. *Economic Aspects of Television Regulation*. Washington, DC: Brookings.

Owen, B. 1975. *Economics and Freedom of Expression*. Cambridge, Mass.: Ballinger.

Owen, B., Beebe, J. and Manning, W. 1974. *Television Economics*. Lexington, Mass.: D.C. Heath.

Park, R.E. 1972. Prospects for cable in the 100 largest television markets. *Bell Journal of Economics* 3(1), Spring, 130–50.

Park, R.E. 1975. New television networks. *Bell Journal of Economics* 6(2), Autumn, 607–20.

Rosse, J. 1967. Daily newspapers, monopolistic competition, and economies of scale. *American Economic Review* 52(2), May, 522–33.

Rosse, J., Dertouzos, J., Robinson, M. and Wildman, S. 1979. Economic issues in mass communications industries. *Proceedings of the Symposium of Media Concentration.* Washington, DC: Federal Trade Commission. Vol. I, 40–192.

Snow, M. 1986. *Marketplace for Telecommunications: Regulation and Deregulation in Industrialized Democracies.* White Plains, NY: Longman.

Spence, A.M. and Owen, B. 1977. Television programming, monopolistic competition and welfare. *Quarterly Journal of Economics* 91(1), February, 103–21.

Steiner, P. 1952. Program patterns and preferences, and the workability of competition in radio broadcasting. *Quarterly Journal of Economics* 66(2), May, 194–223.

Spitzer, M. 1985. Controlling the content of print and broadcast. *Southern California Law Review* 58(6), September, 1349–405.

Taylor, L. 1980. *Telecommunications Demand: A Survey and Critique.* Cambridge, Mass.: Ballinger.

von Weiszacker, C. 1984. Free entry into telecommunications? *Information Economics and Policy* 1(3), 197–216.

communism. The term 'communism' was first used in modern times to designate a specific economic doctrine (or regime), and a political creed intending to introduce such a regime, by the French lawyer Etiénne Cabet in the late 1830s; his works, especially the utopia *L'Icarie*, were influential among the Paris working class before the revolution of 1848. In 1840, the first 'communist banquet' was held in Paris – banquets and banquet speeches were a common form of political protest under the July monarchy. The term spread rapidly, so that Karl Marx could entitle one of his first political articles of 16 October 1842 'Der Kommunismus und die Augsburger *Allgemeine Zeitung*'. He noted that 'communism' was already an international movement, manifesting itself in Britain and Germany besides France, and traced its origin to Plato. He could have mentioned ancient Jewish sects and early Christian monasteries too.

In fact, some of the so-called 'Utopian socialists', in the first place the German Weitling, called themselves communists and spread the influence of the new doctrine among German itinerant handicraftsmen all over Europe, as well as among the more settled industrial workers of the Rhineland. Under the influence of Marx and Engels, the League of the Just (Bund dez Gerechten) they had created, changed its name to Communist League in 1846. The League requested the two young German authors to draft a declaration of principle for their organization. This declaration would appear in February 1848 under the title *Communist Manifesto*, which would make the words 'communism' and 'communists' famous the world over.

Communism, from then on, would designate both a classless society without property, without ownership – either private or nationalized – of the means of production, without commodity production, money or a state apparatus separate and apart from the members of the community, and the social-political movement to arrive at that society. After the victory of the Russian October revolution in 1917, that movement would tend to be identified by and large with Communist parties and a Communist International (or at least an 'international communist movement'), though there exists a tiny minority of communists, inspired by the Dutch astronomer Pannekoek, who are hostile to a party organization of any kind (the so-called 'council communists', *Rätekommunisten*).

The first attempts to arrive at a communist society (leaving aside early, medieval and more modern christian communities) were made in the United States in the 19th century, through the establishment of small agrarian settlements based upon collective property, communally organized labour and the total absence of money inside their boundaries. From that point of view, they differed radically from the production cooperatives promoted for example by the English industrialist and philanthropist Robert Owen. Weitling himself created such a community, significantly called Communia. Although they were generally established by a selected group of followers who shared common convictions and interests, these agrarian communities did not survive long in a hostile environment. The nearest contemporary extension of these early communist settlements are the *kibbutzim* in Israel.

Rather rapidly, and certainly after the appearance of the *Communist Manifesto*, communism came to be associated less with small communities set up by morally or intellectually selected elites, but with the general movement of emancipation of the modern working class, if not in its totality at least in its majority, encompassing furthermore the main countries (wealth-wise and population-wise) of the world. In the major theoretical treatise of their younger years, *The German Ideology*, Marx and Engels stated emphatically:

> Empirically, communism is only possible as the act of dominant peoples 'all at once' and similtaneously, which presupposes the universal development of productive forces and the world intercourse bound up with them. ...The proletariat can thus only exist world-historically, just as communism, its activity, can only have a 'world-historical' existence.

And, earlier in the same passage,

> ... This development of productive forces (which at the same time implies the actual empirical existence of men in their *world-historical*, instead of local, being) is an absolutely necessary practical premise, because without it privation, is merely made general, and with *want* the struggle for necessities would begin again, and all the old filthy business would necessarily be restored ... ([1845-6] 1976, p.49).

That line of argument is to-day repeated by most orthodox marxists (communists), who find in it an explanation of what 'went wrong' in Soviet Russia, once it was isolated in a capitalist environment as a result of the defeat of revolution in other European countries in the 1918–1923 period. But many 'official' Communist Parties still stick to Stalin's particular version of communism, according to which it is possible to successfully complete the building of socialism and communism in a single country, or in a small number of countries.

The radical and international definition of a communist society given by Marx and Engels inevitably leads to the perspective of a *transition* (transition period) between capitalism and communism. Marx and Engels first, notably in their writings about the Paris Commune – *The Civil War in France* – and in their *Critique of the Gotha Programme* [of the German social-democratic party], Lenin later – especially in his book *State and Revolution* – tried to give at least a general sketch of what that transition would be like. It centres around the following ideas:

The proletariat, as the only social class radically opposed to private ownership of the means of production, and likewise as the only class which has potentially the power to paralyse and overthrow bourgeois society, as well as the inclination to collective cooperation and solidarity which are the motive forces of the building of communism, conquers political (state) power. It uses that power ('the dictatorship of the proletariat') to make more and more 'despotic inroads' into the realm of private property and private production, substituting for them collectively and consciously (planned) organized output, increasingly turned towards direct satisfaction of needs. This implies a gradual withering away of market economy.

The dictatorship of the proletariat, however, being the instrument of the majority to hold down a minority, does not need a heavy apparatus of full-time functionaries, and certainly no heavy apparatus of repression. It is a state *sui generis*, a state which starts to wither away from its inception, i.e. it starts to devolve more and more of the traditional state functions to self-administrating bodies of citizens, to society in its totality. This withering away of the state goes hand in hand with the indicated withering away of commodity production and of money, accompanying a general withering away of social classes and social stratification, i.e. of the division of society between administrators and administrated, between 'bosses' and 'bossed over' people.

That vision of transition towards communism as an essentially evolutionary process obviously has preconditions: that the countries engaged on that road already enjoy a relatively high level of development (industrialization, modernization, material wealth, stock of infrastructure, level of skill and culture of the people, etc.), created by capitalism itself; that the building of the new society is supported by the majority of the population (i.e. that the wage-earners already represent the great majority of the producers and that they have passed the threshhold of a necessary level of socialist political class consciousness); that the process encompasses the major countries of the world.

Marx, Engels, Lenin and their main disciples and co-thinkers like Rosa Luxemburg, Trotsky, Gramsci, Otto Bauer, Rudolf Hilferding, Bukharin et al. – incidentally also Stalin until 1928 – distinguished successive stages of the communist society: the lower stage, generally called 'socialism', in which there would be neither commodity production nor classes, but in which the individual's access to the consumption fund would still be strictly measured by his quantitative labour input, evaluated in hours of labour; and a higher stage, generally called 'communism', in which the principle of *satisfaction of needs* for everyone would apply, independently of any exact measurement of work performed. Marx established that basic difference between the two stages of communism in his *Critique of the Gotha Programme*, together with so much else. It was elaborated at length in Lenin's *State and Revolution*.

In the light of these principles, it is clear that no socialist or communist society exists anywhere in the world today. It is only possible to speak about 'really existing socialism' at present, if one introduces a new, 'reductionist' definition of a socialist society, as being only identical with predominantly nationalized property of the means of production and central economic planning. This is obviously different from the definition of socialism in the classical marxist scriptures. Whether such a new definition is legitimate or not in the light of historical experience is a matter of political and philosophical judgement. It is in any case another matter altogether than ascertaining whether the radical emancipatory goals projected by the founders of contemporary communism have been realized in these really existing societies or not. This is obviously not the case.

ERNEST MANDEL

See also CENTRAL PLANNING; COLLECTIVE AGRICULTURE; FULL COMMUNISM; MARX, KARL HEINRICH; PEASANTS; PLANNED ECONOMY; SOCIALIST ECONOMICS.

BIBLIOGRAPHY
Marx, K. and Engels, F. 1845-6. *The German Ideology*. As in Karl Marx and Frederick Engels, *Collected Works*, Vol. 5, London: Lawrence & Wishart, 1976.

community indifference curves. The idea of a community indifference curve, as the term is commonly used, is due to Scitovsky (1942). The genesis of the idea is the fact that comparative statics and welfare analysis in economic models is simplified considerably if there is a social preference ordering over aggregate commodity bundles which reflects the collective individual preferences of agents. Scitovksy's notion of a 'community indifference curve' essentially allows the analytical convenience of social indifference curves, in certain circumstances, without having to assume a specific Bergson–Samuelson social welfare function or having to assume the restrictive assumptions on agents' preferences needed to guarantee that agents act collectively as a single individual.

The definition of a community indifference curve is basically simple. Suppose there are m commodities and n agents. Let x denote a commodity vector (as m-vector with non-negative coordinates) and u_i a utility function representing agent i's preferences. We will assume that u_i is monotone increasing and quasi-concave. Given a vector $u' = (u'_1, \ldots, u'_n)$ of utility numbers, the community indifference curve at u', $CIC(u')$, is defined to be the set of all commodity vectors x such that there is a distribution $(x_1, \ldots, x_n)$ of commodity vectors satisfying $\Sigma_i x_i = x$ and $u_i(x_i) = u'_i$, $i = 1, \ldots, n$, and there is no $x' \leqslant x$, $x' \neq x$ which also has this property. Thus one can obtain any vector $x \in CIC(u')$ by fixing the quantities of all but one good and minimize the amount of the remaining good subject to achieving u'. As pointed out by Samuelson (1956), the community indifference curve can be interpreted as a 'dual' to the utility possibility frontier. The utility possibility frontier, for a given x, is the set of all vectors u' of utility numbers achievable by a Pareto efficient distribution of x to the agents. Let $U(x)$ denote the utility possibility frontier for the commodity vector x. Then it is easy to see that $CIC(u') = \{x . u' \in U(x)\}$ and that $U(x) = \{u' : x \in CIC(u')\}$.

We will now describe the most important properties of community indifference curves. First, each $CIC(u')$ looks like the indifference curve of a monotone quasi-concave utility function. That is, the set of vectors x such that $x \geqslant x^1$ for some $x^1 \in CIC(u')$ is a convex set. For example, when $m = 2$, $CIC(u')$ is a curve with a diminishing marginal rate of substitution. Second, unlike the utility possibility frontier, the community indifference curve is essentially an ordinal concept, that is it does not depend on the choice of utility functions representing agents' preferences, in the following sense. Suppose, for each i, u_i and v_i are two utility functions representing agent i's preferences, and let $(x_1, \ldots, x_n)$ be a Pareto efficient allocation to the agents. Define $u' = [u_1(x_1), \ldots, u_n(x_n)]$ and $v' = [v_1(x_1), \ldots, v_n(x_n)]$. Then $CIC(u') = CIC(v')$. Clearly, community indifference curves can be parameterized by a given Pareto efficient allocation of goods rather than a given vector of utilities. Third, assuming smooth utility functions, the marginal rate of substitution for any two commodities on a community indifference curve is equal to the common marginal rate of substitution of each agent. Specifically, pick an $x \in CIC(u')$, and let $(x_1, \ldots, x_n)$ be the Pareto efficient allocation of x such that $u_i(x_i) = u'_i$, $i = 1, \ldots, n$. Then for any two commodities h and h', the marginal rate of substitution of h and h' evaluated at $x \in CIC(u')$ is equal to the marginal rate of substitution of h for h' at x_i on agent i's indifference curve through x_i. Fourth, and very important, community indifference curves are not, in general, 'indifference' curves in the sense of being level curves of some function. Pick any x, and u', $u'' \in U(x)$ such that $u' \neq u''$. Then by definition, $x \in CIC(u') \cap CIC(u'')$. Thus $CIC(u')$ must either coincide with $CIC(u'')$ or intersect properly. The condition for two community indifference curves never to intersect properly is then that $CIC(u') = CIC(u'')$ for all u', $u'' \in U(x)$, for all x. It turns out that this is true if and only if the agents have identical homothetic preferences, in which case the family of all community indifference curves will coincide with the family of indifference curves for the common preferences of the agents.

From the above definition and properties, the following observation constitutes the basic use of community indifference curves: if the economy is currently at a vector of utility numbers u', then x' is a commodity vector which lies above $CIC(u')$ if and only if there is some distribution of x' to the agents which will achieve a vector of utilities u'' such that $u'' > u'$. In this sense, x' is 'better' than any $x \in CIC(u')$. However, since from above community indifference curves can intersect properly, it may also be that there is a u''' such that $x' \in CIC(u''')$ and an $x \in CIC(u')$ such that x lies above $CIC(u''')$, in which case x is also 'better' than x'. Thus it is important to realize that community indifference curves cannot be used to define a social ordering of aggregate output vectors. Nevertheless, community indifference curves can still be a useful analytical device. For example, consider a market economy with two produced goods. Consider an equilibrium in which all consumers face the same prices, in terms of the aggregate output vector x' and the vector of utilities u' obtained by the agents. Graphically this equilibrium can be represented by drawing the production posssibility frontier and $CIC(u')$, noting they meet at x'. The slope of the production possibility frontier at x' represents the price ratio faced by firms, and the slope of the $CIC(u')$ at x' the common price ratio faced by consumers. If firms and consumers face the same price ratio, then the $CIC(u')$ must be tangent to the production possibility frontier at x. Thus no feasible x can be produced which can make all agents better off, so the situation is Pareto optimal. If however, firms face different prices than the agents because of, for example, taxes or tariffs, then the slope of the $CIC(u')$ will be different from the slope of the production possibility frontier, and thus the two curves will intersect properly. In this case there must exist an x' on the production possibility frontier which lies above $CIC(u')$, so the original situation is Pareto inefficient.

WAYNE SHAFER

See also ARROW'S THEOREM; OPTIMALITY AND EFFICIENCY; SOCIAL WELFARE FUNCTION; WELFARE ECONOMICS.

BIBLIOGRAPHY

Samuelson, P.A. 1956. Social indifference curves. *Quarterly Journal of Economics* 70(1), February, 1–22.
Scitovsky, T. 1942. A reconsideration of the theory of tariffs. *Review of Economic Studies* 9(2), Summer, 89–110.

comparative advantage. The modern economy, and the very world as we know it today, obviously depends fundamentally on specialization and the division of labour, between individuals, firms and nations. The principle of comparative advantage, first clearly stated and proved by David Ricardo in 1817, is the fundamental analytical explanation of the source of these enormous 'gains from trade'. Though an awareness of the benefits of specialization must go back to the dim mists of

antiquity in all civilizations, it was not until Ricardo that this deepest and most beautiful result in all of economics was obtained. Though the logic applies equally to inter*personal*, inter*firm*, and inter*regional* trade, it was in the context of inter*national* trade that the principle of comparative advantage was discovered and has been investigated ever since.

What constituted a 'nation' for Ricardo were two things – a 'factor endowment', of a specified number of units of labour in the simplest model, and a 'technology', the productivity of this labour in terms of different goods, such as Cloth and Wine in his example. Thus labour can move freely between the production of cloth and wine in England and in Portugal, but each labour force is trapped within its own borders. Suppose that a unit of labour in Portugal can produce 1 unit of cloth or 1 unit of wine while in England a unit of labour can produce 4 units of cloth or 2 units of wine. Thus the opportunity cost of a unit of wine is 1 unit of cloth in Portugal while it is 2 units of cloth in England. Assuming competitive markets and free trade, it follows that *both* goods will never be produced in *both* countries since wine in England and cloth in Portugal could always be undermined by a simple arbitrage operation involving export of cloth from England and import of wine from Portugal. Thus wine in England or cloth in Portugal must contract until at least one of these industries produces zero output. If both goods are consumed in positive amounts, the 'terms of trade' in equilibrium must lie in the closed interval between 1 and 2 units of cloth per unit of wine. Which of the two countries specializes completely will depend upon the relative size of each country (as measured by the labour force *and* its productivity in each industry) and upon the extent to which each of the two goods is favoured by the pattern of world demand. Thus Portugal is more likely to specialize the smaller she is compared to England in the sense defined above and the more world demand is skewed towards the consumption of Wine relative to the consumption of Cloth.

Viewed as a 'positive' theory, the principle of comparative advantage yields *predictions* about (a) the *direction* of trade, that each country exports the good in which it has the lower comparative opportunity cost ratio as defined by the technology in each country, and about (b) the *terms* of trade, that it is bounded by these comparative cost ratios. From a 'normative' standpoint the principle implies that the citizens of each country become 'better off' as a result of trade, with the extent of the gains from trade depending upon the degree to which the terms of trade exceed the domestic comparative cost ratio. It is the 'normative' part of the doctrine that has always been the more controversial, and it is therefore necessary to evaluate it with the greatest care.

In Ricardo's example the labour force is presumably supplied by different households, each of which has the same *relative* productivity in the two sectors as the national average. Thus *all* households in *each* country must become better off as a result of trade if the terms of trade lie strictly in between the domestic comparative cost ratios. The import-competing sector in each country simply switches over instantaneously and costlessly to producing the export good (moving to the opposite corner of its linear production-possibilities frontier, in terms of the familiar geometry), obtaining the desired level of the other good by imports, raising utility in the process. When one country is incompletely specialized, then all households in that country remain at unchanged utility levels, all of the gain from trade going to the individuals in the 'small' country. Thus we have a situation in which *everybody gains*, in at least one country, while *nobody loses* in either country, as a result of trade.

This very strong result depends upon Ricardo's assumption of perfect occupational mobility in each country. Suppose we take the opposite extreme of completely *specific* labour in each sector, so that each country produces a fixed combination of cloth and wine, with no possibility of transformation. In this case labour in the import-competing sector in each country must necessarily *lose*, as a result of trade, while labour in each country's export sector must gain. It can be shown, however, that trade will improve *potential* welfare in each country in the Samuelson (1950) sense that the utility-possibility frontier with trade will dominate the corresponding frontier without trade, so that no one need be worse off, and at least some one better off, if lump-sum taxes and transfers are possible (Samuelson, 1962).

Another very important normative issue is the question of the relationship between the free-trade equilibrium and *world* efficiency and welfare. In the Ricardian model world welfare in general will *not* be maximized by free trade. In the numerical example considered here Ricardo stresses the fact that England can still gain from trade even though she has an *absolute* advantage in the production of *both* goods, her productivity being greater in both cloth and wine, though comparatively greater in cloth. Suppose that labour in Portugal could produce at English levels, *if it moved to England*; i.e. the English superiority is based on climatic or other 'environmental' factors and not on differences in aptitude or skill. Then, if labour were free to move, and in the absence of 'national' sentiment, all production would be located in England, and Portugal would cease to exist. The former Portuguese labour would be better off than under free trade, since their real wage in terms of wine will now be 2 units instead of 1. English labour would be worse off, if the terms of trade were originally better than 0.5 wine per 1 cloth, but it is easy to show that they could be sufficiently compensated since the utility-possibility frontier for the world economy as a whole is moved out by the integration of the labour forces.

The case when each country has an absolute advantage in one good is more interesting. As is easy to see (see Findlay, 1982) this case will involve a movement of labour to the country with the higher real wage under free trade, increasing the production of this country's exportable and reducing that of the lower-wage country under free trade. The terms of trade turn against the higher-wage country until eventually the real wage is equalized. The terms of trade that achieve this equality of real wages will be equal to the ratio of labour productivities in each country's export sector; i.e. the 'double factoral' terms of trade will be unity. This solution of free trade *combined* with perfect labour mobility will achieve not only efficiency for the world economy but equity as well. 'Unequal exchange' would not exist, while liberal, Utilitarian and Rawlsian criteria of distributive justice would be satisfied as well, as pointed out in Findlay (1982). Despite all this, it still seems utopian to expect a policy of 'open borders', in *either* direction, for the contemporary world of nation-states.

The two-country, two-good Ricardian model was extended to many goods and countries by a number of subsequent writers, whose efforts are described in detail by Haberler (1933) and Viner (1937). In the case of two countries and *n* goods the concept of a 'chain of comparative advantage' has been put forward, with the goods listed in descending order in terms of the *relative* efficiency of the two countries in producing them. It is readily shown that with a uniform wage in each country all goods from 1 to some number *j* must be exported, while all goods from (*j*+1) to n must be imported. The number *j* itself will depend upon the relative sizes of the two countries and the composition of world demand. An analogous chain concept applies to the case of two goods and countries, this time ranking the countries in terms of the ratio of their productivities in the two goods, with country 1 having the greatest *relative* efficiency in cloth and country n in wine. World demand and the sizes of the labour forces will determine the 'marginal' country *j*, with countries 1 to *j* exporting cloth and (*j*+1) to n exporting wine.

The simultaneous consideration of comparative advantage with many goods and many countries presents severe analytical difficulties. Graham (1948) considered several elaborate numerical examples, his work inspiring the Rochester theorists McKenzie (1954) and Jones (1961) to apply the powerful tools of activity analysis to this particular case of a linear general equilibrium model. It is interesting to note in connection with mathematical programming and activity analysis that Kantorovich (1965) in his celebrated book on planning for the Soviet economy worked out an example of optimal specialization patterns for factories that corresponds *exactly* to the Ricardian model of trade between countries.

While most of the literature on the Ricardian trade model has concentrated on the model of chapter 7 of the *Principles*, in which it appears that labour is the sole scarce factor, his more extended model in the *Essay on Profits* has been curiously neglected, though the connections between trade, income distribution and growth which that analysis explores are quite fascinating. The formal structure of the model was laid out very thoroughly in Pasinetti (1960). The economy produces two goods, corn and manufactures, each of which has a one-period lag between the input of labour and the emergence of output. Labour thus has to be supported by a 'wage fund', an initially given stock that is accumulated over time by saving out of profits. Corn also requires land as an input, which is in fixed supply and yields diminishing returns to successive increments of labour. The wage-rate is given exogenously in terms of corn, and manufactures are a luxury good consumed only by the land-owning class, who obtain rents determined by the marginal product of land. Profits are the difference between the marginal product of labour and the given real wage, which is equal to the marginal product 'discounted' by the rate of interest, in this model equal to the rate of profit, defined as the ratio of profits to the real wage that has to be advanced a period before. Momentary equilibrium determines the relative price of corn and manufactures, the rent per acre and the rate of profit, as well as the output levels and allocation of the labour force between sectors. The growth of the system is at a rate equal to the product of the rate of profit and the propensity to save of the capitalist class. It is shown that the system approaches a stationary state, with a monotonically falling rate of profit and rising rents per acre.

The opportunity to import corn more cheaply from abroad will have significant distributional and growth consequences. Just as Ricardo argued in his case for the repeal of the Corn Laws, cheaper foreign corn will reduce domestic rents and raise the domestic rate of profit, and thus the rate of growth. The approach to the stationary state is postponed, though of course it cannot be ultimately averted. The growth consequences for the corn exporter, however, are adverse (Findlay, 1974).

The main doctrinal significance of this wider Ricardian model, however, is to reveal the extent to which the subsequent 'general equilibrium' or 'neoclassical' approach to international trade is already present within the Ricardian framework. For one thing, the pattern of comparative advantage itself depends upon the complex interaction of technology, factor proportions and tastes. In the chapter 7 analysis the pattern of comparative advantage is *exogenous*, simply given by the four fixed technical coefficients indicating the productivity of labour in cloth and wine in England and Portugal. The production-possibility frontiers for each country are linear, and comparative advantage is simply determined by the magnitude of the slopes. As demonstrated in Findlay (1974), however, the *Essay on Profits* model implies a concave production-possibilities frontier at any moment, since there are diminishing returns to labour in corn even though the marginal productivity of labour in Manufactures is constant. With two countries the pattern of comparative advantage will depend upon the slopes of these curves at their autarky equilibria, which are *endogenous* variables depending upon the sizes of 'wage fund' in relation to the supply of land and the consumption pattern of landowners, as well as the technology for the two goods.

As Burgstaller (1986) points out, however, the steady-state solution of the model restores the linear structure of the pattern of comparative advantage. The zero profit rate in the steady state requires the marginal product of labour to be equal to the given real wage, and this implies a fixed land–labour ratio and hence output per unit of labour in corn. We thus once again have two fixed technical coefficients, so that the slope of the linear production-possibilities frontier is once again an exogenous indicator of comparative advantage.

The 'neo-Ricardian' approach of Steedman (1979a, 1979b) considers more general time-phased structures of production. Technology alone determines negatively sloped wage-profit or factor-price frontiers, any point on which generates a set of relative product prices and hence a pattern of comparative advantage relative to another such economy.

While J.S. Mill, Marshall and Edgeworth all made major contributions to trade theory, the concept of comparative advantage did not undergo any evolution in their work beyond the stage at which Ricardo had left it. They essentially concentrated on the determination of the terms of trade and on various comparative static exercises. The interwar years, however, brought fundamental advances, stemming in particular from the work of the Swedes Heckscher (1919) and Ohlin (1933). The development of a diagrammatic apparatus to handle general equilibrium interactions of tastes, technology and factor endowments by Haberler (1933), Leontief (1933), Lerner (1932) and others culminated in the rigorous establishment of trade theory and comparative advantage as a branch of neoclassical general equilibrium theory.

The essentials of this approach can be expounded in terms of the familiar two-country, two-good, two-factor model (see Jones (1965) for an algebraic and Findlay (1970) for a diagrammatic exposition). The given factor supplies and constant returns to scale technology define concave production-possibility frontiers, assuming that the goods differ in factor-intensity. This determines the 'supply side' of the model, which is closed by the specification of consumer preferences. Economies that have identical technology, factor endowments and tastes will have the same autarky equilibrium price-ratio and so will have no incentive to engage in trade. Countries must therefore differ with respect to at least one of these characteristics for differences in comparative advantage to emerge. With identical technology and factor endowments, a country will have a comparative advantage in the good its citizens prefer *less* in comparison to the foreign country, since then this good will be cheaper at home. Similarly, if factor endowments and tastes are identical, differences in comparative advantage will be governed by relative technological efficiency; i.e. a country will have a comparative advantage in

the good in which its relative technological efficiency is greater, just as in the Ricardian model. These differences in technological efficiency could be represented, for example, by the magnitude of multiplicative constants in the production functions; i.e. 'Hicks-neutral' differences.

In keeping with the ideas of Heckscher and Ohlin, however, it is differences in factor proportions that have dominated the explanation of comparative advantage in the neoclassical literature. The Heckscher–Ohlin Theorem, that each country will export the commodity that uses its relatively abundant factor most intensively, has been rigorously established and the necessary qualifications carefully specified. Among the more important of these is the requirement that factor-intensity 'reversals' do not take place; i.e. that one good is always more capital-intensive than the other at all wage-rental ratios or at least within the relevant range defined by the factor proportions of the trading countries.

Associated with the Heckscher–Ohlin Theorem is the Stolper–Samuelson Theorem (1941), that trade benefits the scarce factor, and the celebrated Factor Price Equalization Theorem of Lerner (1952, though written in 1932) and Samuelson (1948, 1949, 1953), which states that under certain conditions free trade will lead to complete equalization of factor rewards even though factors are not mobile internationally. The normative significance of this theorem is that free trade alone can achieve world efficiency in production and resource allocation, unlike the case of the Ricardian model. The requirements for the theorem to hold, however, are very stringent. In particular it requires factor proportions to be sufficiently close to each other in the trading partners so that the production patterns are fairly similar. Thus it would be far-fetched to expect the price of unskilled labour to be equalized between Bangladesh and the United States, for example.

One limitation of the Heckscher–Ohlin model was that the stock of 'capital', however conceived, should be an endogenous variable determined by the propensity to save or time preference of each trading community. The model has been extended by Oniki and Uzawa (1965) to a situation where the labour force is growing in each country at an exogenous rate and capital is accumulated in response to given propensities to save in each country. One of the goods is taken to be the 'capital' good, conceived of as a malleable 'putty-putty' instrument. They demonstrate that the system will converge in the long run to a particular capital–labour ratio for each country, which will be higher for the country with the larger saving propensity. As the capital–labour ratios evolve, the pattern of comparative advantage for a given 'small' country in an open trading world will also shift over time towards more capital-intensive goods in the process of economic development. Thus comparative advantage should not be conceived as given and immutable, but evolving with capital accumulation and technological change. Much of the loose talk about 'dynamic' comparative advantage in the development literature, however, is misconceived since it attempts to change the pattern of production by protection *before* the necessary changes in the capacity to produce efficiently have taken place. Other models which endogenize the capital stocks of the trading countries are Stiglitz (1970) and Findlay (1978), which utilizes a variable rate of time preference and an 'Austrian' point-input/point-output technology, which implies a continuum of capital goods as represented by the 'trees' of different ages.

Empirical testing of the positive side of the theory of comparative advantage only begins in a systematic way with the work of MacDougall (1951) on the Ricardian theory and the celebrated article of Leontief (1954) which uncovered the apparent paradox that US exports were more labour-intensive than her imports. Leontief's dramatic finding spurred considerable further empirical research motivated by the desire to find a satisfactory explanation. The role of natural resources, the increasing scarcity of which in the US caused capital to be substituted for it in import-competing production, was stressed by Vanek (1963). The role of 'human' capital was stressed by Kenen (1965) and a number of empirical investigators, who found that US exports were considerably more skill-intensive than her imports, even though physical capital-intensity was only weakly correlated with exports and imports. This pointed to the need to reinterpret the simple Heckscher–Ohlin model in terms of skilled and unskilled labour as the two factors, rather than labour of uniform quality and physical capital. Since the formation of skill through education is an endogenous variable, a function of a wage differential that is itself a function of trade, we need a general equilibrium model that can simultaneously handle both these aspects, a task that was attempted in Findlay and Kierzkowski (1983).

Many other extensions of the Heckscher–Ohlin theory are surveyed in Jones and Neary (1984), while Deardorf (1984) gives a very incisive account of the attempts at empirical testing of the theory of comparative advantage in its different

RONALD FINDLAY

See also HECKSCHER–OHLIN TRADE THEORY; INTERNATIONAL TRADE; RICARDO, DAVID.

BIBLIOGRAPHY

Burgstaller, A. 1986. Unifying Ricardo's theories of growth and comparative advantage. *Economica*.
Deardorf, A. 1984. Testing trade theories. In *Handbook of International Economics*, ed. R.W. Jones and P.B. Kenen, Vol. 1, Amsterdam: North-Holland.
Ethier, W. 1984. Higher dimensional issues in trade theory. In *Handbook of International Economics*, ed. R.W. Jones and P.B. Kenen, Vol. 1, Amsterdam: North Holland.
Findlay, R. 1970. *Trade and Specialization*. Harmondsworth: Penguin.
Findlay, R. 1974. Relative prices, growth and trade in a simple Ricardian system. *Economica* 41, February, 1–13.
Findlay, R. 1978. An 'Austrian' model of international trade and interest equalization. *Journal of Political Economy* 86(6), December, 989–1007.
Findlay, R. 1982. International distributive justice. *Journal of International Economics* 13, 1–14.
Findlay, R. and Kierzkowski, H. 1983. International trade and human capital: a simple general equilibrium model. *Journal of Political Economy* 91(6), December, 957–78.
Graham, F. 1948. *The Theory of International Values*. Princeton: Princeton University Press.
Haberler, G. 1933. *The Theory of International Trade*. Trans. by A. Stonier and F. Benham, London: W. Hodge, 1936; revised edn 1937.
Heckscher, E. 1919. The effects of foreign trade on the distribution of income. *Ekonomisk Tidskrift*. English translation in H.S. Ellis and L.A. Metzler (eds), *Readings in the Theory of International Trade*, Philadelphia: Blakiston, 1949.
Helpman, E. and Krugman, P. 1985. *Market Structure and Foreign Trade*. Cambridge, Mass.: MIT Press.
Jones, R.W. 1961. Comparative advantage and the theory of tariffs. *Review of Economic Studies* 28, 161–75.
Jones, R.W. 1965. The structure of simple general equilibrium models. *Journal of Political Economy* 73, December, 557–72.
Jones, R.W. and Neary, J. 1984. Positive trade theory. In *Handbook of International Economics*, ed. R.W. Jones and P.B. Kenen, Vol. 1, Amsterdam: North-Holland.
Kantorovich, L. 1965. *The Best Use of Economic Resources*. Cambridge, Mass.: Harvard University Press.
Kenen, P.B. 1965. Nature, capital and trade. *Journal of Political Economy* 73, October, 437–60; Erratum, December, 658.
Leontief, W.W. 1933. The use of indifference curves in the analysis of foreign trade. *Quarterly Journal of Economics* 47, May, 493–503.
Leontief, W.W. 1954. Domestic production and foreign trade: the American capital position re-examined. *Economia Internazionale* 7, February, 9–38.
Lerner, A.P. 1932. The diagrammatic representation of cost conditions in international trade. *Economica* 12, August, 345–56.
Lerner, A.P. 1952. Factor prices and international trade. *Economica* 19, February, 1–15.
MacDougall, G.D.A. 1951. British and American exports. *Economic Journal* 61, December, 697–724.
McKenzie, L.W. 1954. Specialisation and efficiency in world production. *Review of Economic Studies* 21(3), 165–80.
Ohlin, B. 1933. *Inter-regional and International Trade*. Cambridge, Mass.: Harvard University Press.
Oniki, H. and Uzawa, H. 1965. Patterns of trade and investment in a dynamic model of international trade. *Review of Economic Studies* 32, 15–38.
Pasinetti, L. 1960. A mathematical formulation of the Ricardian system. *Review of Economic Studies* 27, 78–98.
Ricardo, D. 1951. *The Works and Correspondence of David Ricardo*. Ed. P. Sraffa, Cambridge: Cambridge University Press, Vols I and IV.
Samuelson, P.A. 1948. International trade and the equalization of factor prices. *Economic Journal* 58, June, 163–84.
Samuelson, P.A. 1949. International factor price equalization once again. *Economic Journal* 59, June, 181–97.
Samuelson, P.A. 1953. Prices of factors and goods in general equilibrium. *Review of Economic Studies* 21, 1–20.
Samuelson, P.A. 1962. The gains from international trade once again. *Economic Journal* 72, December, 820–29.
Steedman, I. 1979a. *Trade Amongst Growing Economies*. Cambridge: Cambridge University Press.
Steedman, I. (ed.) 1979b. *Fundamental Issues in Trade Theory*. London: Macmillan.
Stiglitz, J. 1970. Factor–price equalization in a dynamic economy. *Journal of Political Economy* 78(3), May June, 456–88.
Stolper, W. and Samuelson, P.A. 1941. Protection and real wages. *Review of Economic Studies* 9, 58–73.
Vanek, J. 1963. *The Natural Resource Content of U.S. Foreign Trade 1870–1955*. Cambridge, Mass.: MIT Press.
Viner, J. 1937. *Studies in the Theory of International Trade*. New York: Harper.

comparative dynamics. *See* MODELS OF GROWTH; NEOCLASSICAL GROWTH MODELS.

comparative statics. Comparative statics is the method of analysing the impact of a change in the parameters of a model by comparing the equilibrium that results from the change with the original equilibrium. The term 'statics' is not usually meant to have descriptive content: although terms like 'comparative dynamics' and 'comparative steady states' are sometimes used, comparative statics analysis can be performed on dynamic economic models. The restrictive aspects of this analysis are that there is no analysis of the historical forces that have brought about the original equilibrium position and no analysis of the transitional process involved in the adjustment from one equilibrium position to another. The use of comparative statics, of comparing one equilibrium position with another, is as old as economics itself. It was, for example, the method used by Hume (1752) in his analysis of an increase in the stock of gold on prices in an economy.

The neoclassical method of comparative statics analysis was formalized by Hicks (1939) and, most clearly, by Samuelson (1947). This method makes heavy use of differential calculus to analyse the impact of small (infinitesimal) changes in the parameters of model on its equilibrium. Samuelson considered a system of equations involving endogenous variables and exogenous variables, or parameters, of the form:

$$f_1(p_1, \ldots, p_n, \alpha_1, \ldots, \alpha_m) = 0$$
$$\vdots$$
$$f_n(p_1, \ldots, p_n, \alpha_1, \ldots, \alpha_m) = 0.$$

Here $(\alpha_1, \ldots, \alpha_m)$ is a vector of parameters that specifies the economic environment. It may include the government policy parameters such as tax rates; it may also include completely exogenous factors such as variables describing the state of the weather or consumers' tastes and preferences. The vector $(p_1, \ldots, p_n)$ is a vector of endogenous variables that specifies the state of the economic system. It may include production levels and allocation levels for different goods. For the neo-classical economist, however, the typical endogenous variable is the price of a good. The equations themselves are the equilibrium conditions. A solution to them is taken to specify completely the state of the economic system.

Samuelson's type of model can be written out compactly in vector notation as

$$f(p, \alpha) = 0$$

where $f: P \times A \to R^n$, $P \subset R^n$, and $A \subset R^m$. The important thing to notice is that the number of endogenous variables and the number of equilibrium conditions are equal. Assume that (p^0, α^0) is a solution to this system of equations, that the function f is continuously differentiable, and that the $n \times n$ matrix of partial derivatives

$$\begin{bmatrix} \dfrac{\partial f_1}{\partial p_1}(p^0, \alpha^0) \ldots \dfrac{\partial f_1}{\partial p_n}(p^0, \alpha^0) \\ \vdots \qquad \qquad \vdots \\ \dfrac{\partial f_n}{\partial p_1}(p^0, \alpha^0) \ldots \dfrac{\partial f_n}{\partial p_n}(p^0, \alpha^0) \end{bmatrix}$$

is invertible. Then the inverse function theorem of differential calculus says that, in a small neighbourhood of p^0 in P, this implies that $p^0 = f^{-1}(0, \alpha^0)$ is the locally unique solution to the equilibrium conditions. Furthermore, under the same assumptions, the implicit function theorem says that the locally unique vector p that satisfies $f(p, \alpha) = 0$ varies continuously with α near α^0. In other words, there exists a continuous function $p(\alpha)$ such that

$$f[p(\alpha), \alpha] \equiv 0.$$

To calculate the impact of small changes in α on p we differentiate with respect to α using the chain rule:

$$Df_p[p(\alpha), \alpha]Dp(\alpha) + Df_\alpha[p(\alpha), \alpha] \equiv 0$$
$$Df_p(p^0, \alpha^0)Dp(\alpha^0) + Df_\alpha(p^0, \alpha^0) = 0$$
$$Dp(\alpha^0) = -Df_p(p^0, \alpha^0)^{-1}Df_\alpha(p^0, \alpha^0).$$

The elements of the $n \times m$ matrix

$$Dp(\alpha^0) = \begin{bmatrix} \dfrac{\partial p_1}{\partial \alpha_1}(\alpha^0) \ldots \dfrac{\partial p_1}{\partial \alpha_m}(\alpha^0) \\ \vdots \qquad \qquad \vdots \\ \dfrac{\partial p_n}{\partial \alpha_1}(\alpha^0) \ldots \dfrac{\partial p_n}{\partial \alpha_m}(\alpha^0) \end{bmatrix}$$

are called the comparative statics multipliers: for example, when the first parameter changes from α_1^0 to α_1, the equilibrium value of the second endogenous variable changes from p_2^0 to

approximately

$$p_2^0 + \frac{\partial p_2}{\partial \alpha_1}(\alpha^0)(\alpha_1 - \alpha_1^0),$$

at least if $\alpha_1 - \alpha_1^0$ is small enough.

The prototypical model to which Samuelson applied such comparative statics analysis was Walras's (1874) model of economic equilibrium. Here the endogenous variables are the prices of the n goods in the economy and the equilibrium conditions are requirements that excess demands (demand minus supply) for these goods be equal to zero. Since the number of endogenous variables and the number of equilibrium conditions are both equal to n, it would seem that the method of analysis described above is immediately applicable. Walras realized, however, that there were two offsetting complications. First, multiplying all prices by any positive constant leaves excess demands unchanged, that is, excess demands are homogeneous of degree zero, since this is merely a change in accounting units. Second, the total value of all demands equals the value of all supplies since all income is spent on goods. This second requirement, known as Walras's Law, can be written out as

$$\sum_{i=1}^n p_i f_i(p, \alpha) \equiv 0.$$

Walras considered an economy in which all prices were strictly positive. He used the homogeneity condition to reduce the numbers of endogenous variables by one, setting $p_1 = 1$ as numeraire. He used Walras's Law to reduce the number of equilibrium conditions by one, ignoring the first one since

$$f_1(p, \alpha) \equiv -\sum_{i=2}^n p_i f_i(p, \alpha).$$

Walras gave two arguments for the existence of equilibrium. The first involved the counting of equations and unknowns given above. The second involved a transitional process for adjusting prices when not in equilibrium, which he called

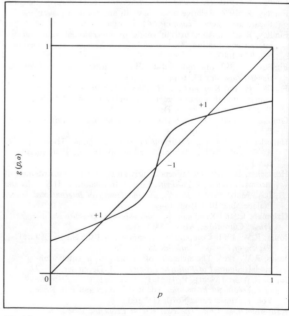

Figure 1

tâtonnement. Samuelson formalized this process in a system of differential equations:

$$\frac{\mathrm{d}p_i}{\mathrm{d}t} = f_i(p, \alpha), \qquad i = 1, \ldots, n.$$

Near an equilibrium p^0 this system can be linearized as

$$Dp(t) = Df_p(p^0, \alpha)[p(t) - p^0].$$

The requirement that the equilibrium p^0 be locally stable involves restrictions on the eigenvalues of the matrix $Df_p(p^0, \alpha)$. This is the same matrix whose inverse plays the crucial role in determining the comparative statics multipliers. Samuelson's view was that, by making assumptions on the sign pattern of the elements of $Df_\alpha(p^0, \alpha)$, the responses of excess demands to changes in the parameters, and by imposing the requirement of local stability on $Df_p(p^0, \alpha)$, 'meaningful theorems' about the signs of the comparative statics multipliers $Dp(\alpha)$ could be derived. He called this methodology 'The Correspondence Principle'. Unfortunately, however, except for very low dimensional cases ($n = 2, 3$) very few such theorems seem available.

The *tâtonnement* process itself is unattractive because it offers no real time interpretation: an auctioneer calls out prices and agents announce their excess demands. The auctioneer then adjusts prices until excess demands equal zero. Until this point is reached no production or consumption takes place; once it is reached all production and consumption take place, and the economy shuts down.

In the 1950s attention turned away from derivation of the comparative statics properties of a model to proofs of the existence of equilibrium. Wald (1936) had pointed out the inadequacy of Walras' existence arguments and had provided existence proofs. The role of differential calculus in providing the mathematical tools was assumed by topology and convexity theory. Using these tools, Arrow and Debreu (1954) and others were able to provide proofs of the existence of equilibrium for very general models. The principal mathematical tool employed was Brouwer's fixed point theorem, which says that any continuous mapping g of a non-empty, compact, convex set into itself has a point that stays fixed under the mapping, that is, where $p^* = g(p^*)$. This theorem is illustrated in Figure 1, where

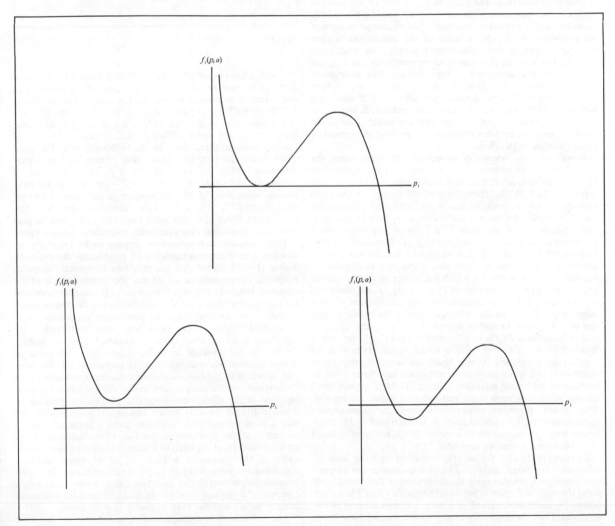

Figure 2

519

the non-empty, compact convex set is the interval (0, 1). Notice that there are three fixed points.

To use Brouwer's fixed point theorem it is necessary to convert equilibrium conditions of the form $f(p, \alpha) = 0$ into the form $p - g(p, \alpha) = 0$, where the mapping g has the right properties. The price domain is often taken to be the simplex

$$S = \left\{ p \in R^n | \sum_{i=1}^{n} p_i = 1, p_i \geqslant 0 \right\},$$

which is a non-empty, compact, convex set. The mapping g is constructed by manipulating $p + f(p, \alpha)$ until it only takes on values in S.

Scarf (1973) developed a computational algorithm for finding the fixed points of mappings that satisfy the conditions of Brouwer's fixed point theorem. As our discussion above indicates, this algorithm can be used to compute equilibria of economic models. Following this development, a number of economists have employed large-scale numerical general equilibrium models to analyse the impact of policy changes such as changes in tax systems and tariff rates on individual countries or groups of countries. The methodology is that of comparative statics: The parameters of the model are calibrated or econometrically estimated to match a historically given state of the economy. A change in some of the parameters is then introduced and a new equilibrium position is calculated. Finally, the new equilibrium is compared with the original equilibrium. Such models have been developed to incorporate such phenomena as fixed prices, rationing, government intervention, and simple dynamic considerations. Shoven and Whalley (1984) offer a survey. An earlier tradition in large-scale use of comparative statics started with the work of Johansen (1960), who used calculus techniques to analyse the impact of small changes in parameters.

Proofs of the existence of an equilibrium leave many important questions unanswered: for example, is the equilibrium price vector unique? If not, is it locally unique? Does it vary continuously with the parameters of the model? Answers to such questions are essential in any application of comparative statics analysis. To answer such questions, economists have made heavy use of the tools of differential topology, which combines those of calculus and topology (see Mas-Colell, 1985). Debreu (1970) developed the concept of a regular economy to answer the questions of local uniqueness and continuity. A regular economy is one for which the matrix of partial derivatives of $p - g(p, \alpha)$ with respect to p, $I - Dg_p(p, \alpha)$, where I is $n \times n$ identity matrix, is invertible at every equilibrium p^*. Not surprisingly, this turns out to be equivalent to the condition that the $(n - 1) \times (n - 1)$ matrix formed by deleting the first row and column from $Df_p(p, \alpha)$ is invertible. That this latter matrix is invertible is, of course, what is meant by the claim that the equilibrium conditons involve equal numbers of independent equations and unknowns once one price has been fixed as numeraire and one equation deleted. Debreu proved that almost all models, in a strict mathematical sense, are regular. This result provides some justification for Samuelson's comparative statics methodology. It is illustrated in Figure 2, where small perturbations to a model that is not regular result in it becoming a regular economy.

Dierker (1972) and Varian (1975) realized that the tools of differential topology could also be used to answer the uniqueness question. Consider again the illustration of Brouwer's fixed point theorem in Figure 1. Suppose that neither 0 or 1 is a fixed point of g and that the graph of g never becomes tangent to the diagonal. Then the graph of g must cross the diagonal one more time from above than it does from below. Associate an index

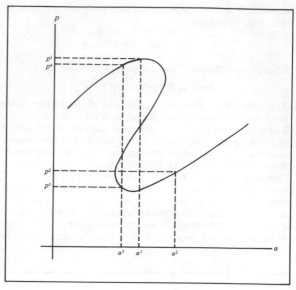

Figure 3

+1 with a fixed point p^* if the graph of g crosses the diagonal from above and an index -1 if it crosses from below. This index can be computed by finding the sign of the expression $1 - (\partial g / \partial p)(p^*, \alpha)$. The sum of the indices of all fixed points is +1. Consequently, if index $(p^*) = +1$ at every equilibrium, then there is only one equilibrium, but, if index $(p^*) = -1$ at any equilibrium, there must be multiple equilibria. The fixed point index theorem says that these results hold in higher dimensions when the index of a fixed point is computed by finding the sign of the expression $\det[I - Dg_p(p^*, \alpha)]$. We have already seen that, if this expression is non-zero, then the equilibrium p^* is unique and varies continuously with α. The fixed point index theorem says that this expression is also crucial for conditions that guarantee uniqueness of equilibrium.

Unfortunately such conditions appear to be extremely restrictive. For Walrasian models with production, for example, Kehoe (1985b) argued that the only two such conditions with economic interpretations are (i) that the consumer side of the economy behaves as though there were only one consumer, and (ii) that the conditions of the non-substitution theorem are met, so that prices are determined by production conditions alone. In applied models where taxes and other distortions play significant roles not even these conditions suffice (see Kehoe, 1985a). In the presence of multiple equilibria, the value of comparative statics analysis becomes problematical. We must pay attention to the historical forces that have brought about the original equilibrium position and to the transitional process involved in the adjustment from one equilibrium position to another. Even if we start with a historically given equilibrium that is locally stable with respect to some adjustment process, we can run into problems in the face of mathematical catastrophes of the sort depicted in Figure 3. Here the change in the value of the parameter α from α^1 to α^2 brings about a discontinuous jump from p^1 to p^2. Another danger that non-uniqueness presents is the possibility that a researcher might compute p^4 as the new equilibrium after changing the parameter from α^1 to α^3, without even knowing that p^4 exists.

The problem of non-uniqueness of equilibrium is even more acute in dynamic models (such as Samuelson's, 1958 overlapping generations model) that involve an infinite number of consumers and goods. Such models need not have even locally unique equilibria, and no current version of comparative statics analysis seems to be applicable (see Kehoe and Levine, 1985).

TIMOTHY J. KEHOE

See also ENVELOPE THEOREM; LE CHATELIER PRINCIPLE.

BIBLIOGRAPHY

Arrow, K.J. and Debreu, G. 1954. Existence of an equilibrium for a competitive economy. *Econometrica* 22, 265–90.

Debreu, G. 1970. Economics with a finite set equilibria. *Econometrica* 38, 387–93.

Dierker, E. 1972. Two remarks on the number of equilibria of an economy. *Econometrica* 40, 951–3.

Hicks, J.R. 1939. *Value and Capital*. Oxford: Clarendon Press.

Hume, D. 1752. Of the balance of trade. In *Essays, Moral, Political and Literary*, London: Longmans Green, 1898.

Johansen, L. 1960. *A Multi-Sectoral Study of Economic Growth*. Amsterdam: North-Holland.

Kehoe, T.J. 1985a. The comparative statics properties of tax models. *Canadian Journal of Economics* 18, 314–34.

Kehoe, T.J. 1985b. Multiplicity of equilibria and comparative statics. *Quarterly Journal of Economics* 100, 119–47.

Kehoe, T.J. and Levine, D.K. 1985. Comparative statics and perfect foresight in infinite horizon economics. *Econometrica* 53, 433–53.

Mas-Colell, A. 1985. *The Theory of General Economic Equilibrium: A Differentiable Approach*. Cambridge: Cambridge University Press.

Samuelson, P.A. 1947. *Foundations of Economic Analysis*. Cambridge, Massachusetts: Harvard University Press.

Samuelson, P.A. 1958. An exact consumption-loan model of interest with or without the social contrivance of money. *Journal of Political Economy* 66, 467–82.

Scarf, H.E. 1973. *The Computation of Economic Equilibria*. New Haven: Yale University Press.

Shoven, J.B. and Whalley, J. 1984. Applied general equilibrium models of taxation and international trade. *Journal of Economic Literature* 22, 1007–51.

Varian, H.R. 1975. A third remark on the number of equilibria of an economy. *Econometrica* 43, 985–6.

Wald, A. 1936. Über einige Gleichungssysteme der mathematischen Ökonomie. *Zeitschrift für Nationalökonomie* 7, 637–70. Translated as 'On some systems of equations in mathematical economics', *Econometrica* 19, (1951), 368–403.

Walras, L. 1874–7. *Eléments d'économie politique pure*. Lausanne: Corbaz. Translated by W. Jaffé as *Elements of Pure Economics*, London: Allen & Unwin, 1954.

compensated demand. I. HICKS COMPENSATION – DEFINITION; II. BASIC PROPERTIES; III. UNCOMPENSATED DEMAND; IV. SLUTSKY COMPENSATION; V. HISTORICAL NOTES.

I. HICKS COMPENSATION – DEFINITION

When a consumer faces a price change under a given nominal income, his utility (or real income) level as well as his demand vector changes. Suppose, however, that his income level is simultaneously changed as the price is changed so as to keep his utility at the initial level. This operation may be regarded as a compensation for the price change, and we call the resulting demand vector the *compensated demand* for the new price.

Thus the compensated demand is a function of the price vector and the utility level, and we may write it as

$$x = h(p, \mu), \qquad (1)$$

where x and p are the consumption and price vectors, while μ is the utility level. We call h the *compensated (or Hicks) demand*

function. Formally, it may be defined as the solution function of the following minimization problem:

$$\min_x p'x \text{ subject to } u(x) = \mu, \qquad (2)$$

where u is the utility function.

II. BASIC PROPERTIES

(*a*) *Hicksian Demand Rules.* The Jacobian matrix of h with respect to p, denoted as h_p, is nothing but the Hicks substitution matrix. It has well-known properties:

$$p'h_p(p, \mu) = 0. \qquad (3)$$

$$yh_p(p, \mu)y \leqslant 0 \quad \text{for all } y. \qquad (4)$$

$$h_p(p, \mu) = h'_p(p, \mu). \qquad (5)$$

Condition (3) is called the homogeneity condition, since it shows that the function h is homogeneous of degree zero with respect to p. Conditions (4) and (5) are called the negative semi-definiteness and the symmetry conditions, respectively. We will call these three conditions the *Hicksian Demand Rules*.

(*b*) *Shephard–Samuelson Lemma.* The minimized expenditure value of problem (2) is a function of p and μ. This is called the *expenditure function*. Formally, we define it by

$$e(p, \mu) \equiv \min_x \{p'x \,|\, u(x) = \mu\}.$$

By definition, we obviously have

$$e(p, \mu) \equiv p'h(p, \mu). \qquad (6)$$

There is a less obvious, but extremely useful, relationship between the compensated demand and the expenditure functions:

$$e_p(p, \mu) = h(p, \mu). \qquad (7)$$

This identity usually referred to as the *Shephard–Samuelson Lemma* was obtained by Hicks (1946, p. 331), Samuelson (1947, p. 68; 1953–54, pp. 15–16), Shephard (1953).

To prove the Shephard–Samuelson Lemma, let x^* be an expenditure-minimizing vector that yields μ at the price p^*, i.e.,

$$x^* \equiv h(p^*, \mu). \qquad (8)$$

Define the *gain function* g by

$$g(p) \equiv e(p, \mu) - p'x^*. \qquad (9)$$

This and the definition of e imply that $g(p) \leqslant 0$. Also from (6) and (8), we have $g(p^*) = 0$. Hence the function g takes its minimum value of 0 when $p = p^*$. Therefore, the first and the second order minimization conditions yield

$$g_p(p^*) = 0 \qquad (10)$$

and

$$y'g_{pp}(p^*)y \geqslant 0 \quad \text{for all } y \neq 0. \qquad (11)$$

Equation (10) immediately proves (7).

To demonstrate the usefulness of the Shephard–Samuelson Lemma, let us prove the Hicksian Demand Rules from this Lemma. From (7) we have

$$e_{pp}(p, \mu) \equiv h_p(p, \mu).$$

This immediately yields (5). In view of (9) and (11), this also proves (4). On the other hand, (6), (9) and (10) yield

$$h(p^*, \mu) + p^{*\prime}h_p(p^*, \mu) - x^* = 0.$$

From (8), therefore, we obtain (3).

III. UNCOMPENSATED DEMAND

(a) *Reflection*. The concept of the compensated demand is essential in analysing properties of the ordinary demand function. To see this, consider a maximization problem:

$$\max u(x) \quad \text{subject to } y = p'x, \tag{12}$$

where y is the income level. Its solution function $m(p, y)$ is called the *ordinary* (or *Marshallian*) *demand function*. Define the *indirect utility function* by

$$v(p, y) \equiv u[m(p, y)]. \tag{13}$$

Problem (2) may be regarded as the expenditure minimization problem associated with (12). Newman (1982) calls it the *reflection* or the *mirror image* of maximization problem (12). If we let $\mu = v(p, y)$ in problem (2), the resulting minimum expenditure must equal y and the compensated demand must be equal to $m(p, y)$ in Problem (12). Thus we have

$$y \equiv e[p, v(p, y)] \tag{14}$$

and

$$m(p, y) \equiv h[p, v(p, y)]. \tag{15}$$

(b) *Roy's Identity*. These identities yield *Roy's identity*,

$$v_p(p, y) \equiv -v_y(p, y)m(p, y). \tag{16}$$

To see this, differentiate (14) with respect to p and y to get

$$e_\mu[p, v(p, y)]v_p(p, y) \equiv -e_p[p, v(p, y)] \tag{17}$$

and

$$1 \equiv e_\mu[p, v(p, y)]v_y(p, y), \tag{18}$$

respectively. Multiplying by $v_y(p, y)$ on both sides of (17), and then applying (18), (7) and (15), we obtain (16).

(c) *Slutsky–Hicks Decomposition*. Identities (14) and (15) also yield the *Slutsky–Hicks decomposition*,

$$m_p(p, y) \equiv h_p[p, v(p, y)] - m_y(p, y)m(p, y). \tag{19}$$

Thus the slope of the ordinary demand function equals the slope of the compensated demand function adjusted to the income effect.

To prove (19), differentiate (15) with respect to p and y to get

$$m_p(p, y) \equiv h_p[p, v(p, y)] + h_\mu[p, v(p, y)]v_p(p, y) \tag{20}$$

and

$$m_y(p, y) \equiv h_\mu[p, v(p, y)]v_y(p, y), \tag{21}$$

respectively. The only difference between (19) and (20) is their income terms. Applying (16) and (21) to the last term of (20), we get (19).

IV. SLUTSKY COMPENSATION

After a price change takes place, the Hicks compensation keeps the consumer on the same utility level as before the price change. As Mosak [1942] pointed out, however, Slutsky had a different concept of compensating the loss of real income. Slutsky considered a compensation that 'makes possible the purchase of the same quantities of all the goods that had formerly been bought', When a price change takes place, the Hicks-compensated and the Slutsky-compensated demand effects are generally different. When the price change is infinitesimal, however, they become equal, and this equality is called Mosak's Equality.

Mosak's equality has played an important role in index number theory. The Laspeyres index, which is widely adopted

in practice, is based on the Slutsky compensation, since it indicates the change in income that would be needed in the current year in order to buy the commodity bundle bought in the base year. Under the Slutsky substitution effect, the individual can be no worse off and is likely to be better off since he is able to purchase at least the bundle he had before the price change. Thus he is 'overcompensated' for the price change (see Samuelson, 1953, pp. 4–5). The price index that truly reflects the utility change should be based on the Hicks compensation. Such an index is difficult to compute because utility levels are not observable. Mosak's equality reveals, however, that for small price changes the Laspeyres index is a good approximation to the 'ideal' index.

Let us now formally state Mosak's equality. Define the function s by

$$s(p, x) \equiv m(p, p'x). \tag{22}$$

The function s is the demand function with the fixed endowment bundle x. We call $s_p[p, m(p, y)]$ the *Slutsky substitution matrix*. It represents the variation in demand when the price change is accompanied by an income compensation that keeps the original consumption bundle $m(p, y)$ on the budget plane. Mosak's Equality may now be expressed as

$$s_p[p, m(p, y)] \equiv h_p[p, v(p, y)]. \tag{23}$$

To prove this, first define the function w by

$$w(p, x) \equiv v(p, p'x). \tag{24}$$

The value of $w(p, x)$ represents the maximized utility level when the endowment bundle x is given. Differentiating this and applying Roy's identity, we get

$$w_p[p, m(p, y)] = 0. \tag{25}$$

Thus, if the utility maximizing bundle under a certain price vector happens to be equal to the endowment bundle, the utility level is hardly changed by a slight change of the price vector away from the initial one. Equations (15), (22) and (24) yield

$$s(p, x) = h[p, w(p, x)].$$

Differentiating this with respect to p and noting (24), we immediately have (23).

V. HISTORICAL NOTES

Slutsky (1915) first established the homogeneity and symmetry conditions on the substitution matrix. Since he did not have the concept of utility-maintaining compensation or the compensated demand function, he derived these properties for the Slutsky compensated substitution matrix $s_p[p, m(p, y)]$ rather than for the Hicksian matrix $h_p[p, v(p, y)]$. During the 1930s, Hicks and Allen (1934) and Hicks (1939, 1946) gave verbal interpretations to the substitution matrix in terms of the Hicksian compensation. But in their formal derivation of its properties, they defined the substitution matrix to be the Slutsky substitution matrix, as is clear from the following passage from the Mathematical Appendix of Hicks (1946, p. 309):

> ... it follows from the equation that the substitution term represents the effect on the demand for x_s of a change in the price of x_r, combined with such a change in income as would enable the consumer, if he chose, to buy the same quantities of all goods as before, in spite of the change in P_r.

Thus they too did not explicitly state the function h, much less gave a name to it.

To the writer's knowledge, Samuelson (1947) is the first author who explicitly stated (1) and derived Hicksian rules directly from it, though he did not give a name to it (see Samuelson, 1947, (43) on p. 103 and (99) on p. 114). Subsequently, Samuelson (1953, p. 8, n1) gave a heuristic proof of the symmetry and the negative-semidefiniteness condition of the Slutsky-compensated substitution matrix as envelope properties, i.e. in a spirit very much similar to the one given above. In this path-breaking proof, however, he relied upon the indirect utility function rather than the expenditure function, thus without using the mirror image minimization problem or the compensated demand function.

McKenzie (1956) and Karlin (1959) explicitly defined the function h, and derived its properties by taking full advantage of the Shephard–Samuelson Lemma. However, they had to use a *global* property of the expenditure function in deriving the negative semidefiniteness condition, which is a *local* property. The proof of this condition employed above is solely based on a *local* minimization condition, and serves as the mirror image counterpart of Samuelson's (1953) proof for the Slutsky substitution matrix. Diamond and McFadden (1973) attribute this proof method to Gorman (see Gorman, 1976). The above proof of Mosak's equality is due to Hatta and Willke (1982).

Silberberg (1974) considered the general maximization problem with possibly many constraint functions where both target and constraint functions may be non-linear. Extending Samuelson's (1965) proof method, he showed that the compensated solution function of that problem satisfies generalized forms of the symmetry and non-negative definite conditions, as long as the constraint functions do not contain shift parameters. Silberberg's proof boils down to Gorman's in the standard expenditure minimization problem. Hatta (1980) extended the concept of the compensated demand function to the case where the same shift parameters may appear simultaneously in both target and constraint functions in the general problem. He showed that the properly compensated solution function in that problem satisfies generalized forms of symmetry and non-negative definite conditions. He also established an envelope theorem that contains both the Shephard–Samuelson Lemma and Roy's Identity as special cases. His proof integrates Samuelson's (1953) and Gorman's into one. The global characterization of the compensated demand function by McKenzie and Karlin was extended into *duality theory*, as surveyed by Diewert (1982).

In many branches of economics outside the demand theory, the concept of the compensated demand function was implicitly used without being explicitly stated. Examples are Hotelling's (1938) and Harberger's (1974) analysis of the *excess burden of taxation*, Hicks's (1956) *compensating* and *equivalent variation* that illuminate the concept of consumers' surplus, and Alonso's (1964) *rent bid function*, which keeps a consumer's utility constant regardless of the location he chooses. A number of economists of the Chicago School, including Friedman (1949), Bailey (1954) and Becker (1971), used the concept of the Hicks compensation in various welfare analyses. Each of these authors gave a different name to the concept. Friedman called its graph the *Marshallian demand curve* contrary to the current usage of this term; Bailey, the *constant-real-income demand curve*, and Becker, the *pure demand curve*.

The explicit use of the compensated demand function gave rise to dramatically clearer restatements and proofs of many existing theorems. Its usefulness has reached far beyond that, however. Since the early 1970s, this function has been used for the analyses of the welfare impacts of parametric shifts in various general equilibrium models, as stated by Ohyama (1974), Takayama (1974), Diamond and MacFadden (1974),

Dixit (1975) and Hatta (1977, 1980), and comprehensively studied by Dixit and Norman (1980) and Woodland (1982).

The history of the compensated demand function is curious. The properties of its derivatives were known and the concept of Hicks compensation used in many fields of economics before the function itself was stated or named. Perhaps this is because economists had an unconscious reluctance in putting the elusive concept of the utility level as a variable of a function. Once explicitly stated and well understood, however, the compensated demand function has found a powerful use in welfare economics, precisely because it has the utility level, rather than income, as an explicit variable.

TATSUO HATTA

See also DEMAND THEORY; DUALITY; INDEX NUMBERS.

BIBLIOGRAPHY

Alonso, W. 1964. *Location and Land Use*. Cambridge, Mass.: Harvard University Press.

Bailey, M.J. 1954. The Marshallian demand curve. *Journal of Political Economy* 62, 255–61.

Becker, G.S. 1971. *Economic Theory*. New York: Alfred A. Knopf.

Diamond, P.A. and McFadden, D.L. 1974. Some uses of expenditure function in public finance. *Journal of Public Economics* 3, 3–21.

Diewert, W.E. 1982. Duality approaches to microeconomic theory. In *Handbook of Mathematical Economics*, Vol. 2, ed. K.J. Arrow and M.D. Intriligator, Amsterdam: North-Holland, 535–99.

Dixit, A.K. 1975. Welfare effects of tax and price changes. *Journal of Public Economics* 4, 103–23.

Dixit, A.K. and Norman, V. 1980. *Theory of International Trade*. Cambridge: Cambridge University Press.

Friedman, M. 1949. The Marshallian demand curve. *Journal of Political Economy* 57, 463–95.

Gorman, W.M. 1976. Tricks with utility functions. In *Essays in Economic Analysis*, ed. M. Artis and R. Nobay, Cambridge: Cambridge University Press.

Harberger, A.C. 1974. *Taxation and Welfare*. Boston: Little, Brown.

Hatta, T. 1977. A recommendation for a better tariff structure. *Econometrica* 45, 1859–69.

Hatta, T. 1980. Structure of the correspondence principle at an extremum point. *Review of Economic Studies* 47, 987–97.

Hatta, T. and Willke, R.J. 1982. Mosak's equality and the theory of duality. *International Economic Review* 22, 361–4.

Hicks, J.R. and Allen, R.D.G. 1934. A reconsideration of the theory of value, I, II. *Econometrica*, N. S. 1, 52–75, 196–219.

Hicks, J.R. 1939. *Value and Capital*. London: Oxford University Press.

Hicks, J.R. 1956. *A Revision of Demand Theory*. London: Oxford University Press.

Hotelling, H.S. 1938. The general welfare in relation to the problems of taxation and of railway and utility rates. *Econometrica* 6, 242–69.

Karlin, S. 1959. *Mathematical Methods and Theory in Games Programming and Economics*, Vol. 1. Reading, Mass.: Addison-Wesley Publishing Company.

McKenzie, L. 1956. Demand theory without a utility index. *Review of Economic Studies* 24, 185–9.

Mosak, J. 1942. On the interpretation of the fundamental equation of value theory. In *Studies in Mathematical Economics and Econometrics*, ed. O. Lange, Chicago: University of Chicago Press, 69–74.

Newman, P.K. 1982. Mirrored pairs of optimization problems. *Economica* 49, 109–19.

Ohyama, M. 1974. Tariffs and the transfer problem. *Keio Economic Studies* 11(1).

Samuelson, P.A. 1947. *Foundations of Economic Analysis*. Cambridge, Mass.: Harvard University Press.

Samuelson, P.A. 1953. Consumption theorems in terms of overcompensation rather than indifference comparison. *Economica* 20, February, 1–9.

Samuelson, P.A. 1965. Using full duality to show that simultaneously additive direct and indirect utilities implies unitary price elasticity of demand. *Econometrica* 33, 781–96.

Shephard, R. 1953, 1970. *Cost and Production Functions*. Princeton: Princeton University Press.

Silberberg, E. 1974. A revision of comparative statics methodology in economics, or, how to do comparative statics on the back of an envelope. *Journal of Economic Theory* 7, 159–72.

Slutsky, E. 1915. Sulla teoria del bilancio del consumatore. *Giornale degli Economisti* 51, 1–26. English trans. in *Readings in Price Theory*, ed. G.J. Stigler and K.E. Boulding, Chicago: Chicago University Press, 1953.

Takayama, A. 1974. On the analytical framework of tariffs and trade policy In *Trade Stability and Macroeconomics, Essays in Honor of Lloyd A. Metzler*, ed. G. Horwich and P.A. Samuelson, New York: Academic Press, 153–78.

Woodland, A.D. 1982. *International Trade and Resource Allocation*. Amsterdam: North-Holland.

compensation. *See* INCENTIVE CONTRACTS.

compensation principle. The term 'compensation principle' refers to the principle that in comparing two alternative states in which a given community of persons might find itself, one of the states constitutes an improvement over the other (in the weak sense including equivalence) if it is possible for the gainers to compensate the losers for their losses and still be at least as well off as in the original state.

If the hypothetical compensation is actually carried out, the principle reduces to the Pareto criterion: all are at least as well off, in one state compared to the other. There is no need to invoke the compensation principle in such a case. On the other hand, if the principle is used to compare two unique alternative states in which a community might find itself, neither of which is Pareto-superior to the other, the principle seems quite arbitrary unless interpreted in a broader context. There is a sense in which one person might be said to be basically healthier than another even though, at the particular moment, such a person might have a cold and the other one not. The compensation principle is usually used to make comparisons in this sense; one state of the economy is sounder, healthier, more robust, or has greater productive potential, than another. What this implies is that states under comparison are usually not unique, singleton states but composite ones, or sets of states. Formally, the objects being compared are usually sets of commodity bundles that could be made available to the aggregate of consumers, described in the literature as 'situations' in contrast to single 'points' in such sets (cf. Baldwin, 1954).

Examples of comparisons in which the compensation principle is typically used are those between (a) a perfectly competitive system of industrial organization and an imperfectly competitive one; (b) free trade and no trade (or restricted trade); (c) the state of an economy before and after a war, or depression, or change in productive techniques. Most but not all of these types of comparisons are relevant to policy decisions; and the policy decisions are usually not of an *ad hoc* type (for which the compensation principle would hardly be appropriate) but of a fundamental nature concerning the underlying system of industrial organization and trade.

Inasmuch as the principle can be applied without the need to make interpersonal comparisons, some of its more ardent proponents have maintained that it is 'value-free'. However, there can be no doubt that it does require acceptance of some value judgements, since the Pareto criterion itself constitutes one – albeit a widely accepted one. Another value judgement implicit in the principle as it has usually been applied is that each individual is the best judge of his or her own well-being; while also quite widely accepted, this one is obviously controversial, and in fact government policy measures are often called for precisely in those instances where it is clearly an untenable assumption. But the most important and controversial way in which value judgements enter into the compensation principle is in the conflict between potentiality and actuality: one situation is judged better than another if everybody *could* be made better off in the new situation even though some in fact become worse off. This lacuna in the principle has led Little (1950) and Mishan (1959) to formulations in which compensation tests are combined with explicit distributional value judgements, and Samuelson (1947, 1956) into a full-fledged ethical system in which compensation is carried out to the extent that the ethical norms dictate.

In many applications the compensation principle is difficult to formulate in a precise manner unless one assumes absence of externalities in consumption, so it is usually formulated (but with some notable exceptions, e.g. Coase, 1960) under the assumption that each person's welfare depends only on his or her own consumption of goods and services. In most applications, the data available for making comparisons are, almost inevitably, limited to aggregative information on the actual state of the economy in each situation; much of the work in applying the principle therefore consists in using economic theory to make inferences from the actual observations concerning underlying conditions in the economy. By its nature, the compensation principle is limited in its application to comparing alternative states (or sets of states) of a given community of individuals; thus, it cannot be applied (at least not literally) to historical comparisons of a country's condition over time (since the population has changed) or to comparisons of the living conditions of different countries (since the populations are different). However, extensions of the principle to cover such comparisons are possible provided suitable additional empirical assumptions and value judgements are accepted; for example, if all individuals are assumed to have identical preferences, one could ask whether there exists a redistribution of income in each period (or country) such that each individual in the one situation would be better off than each individual in the other. This would obviously entail additional value judgements along with the additional empirical assumptions.

1. HISTORICAL DEVELOPMENT: FROM DUPUIT TO HOTELLING. The compensation principle may be traced back to Dupuit (1844, pp. 359–60; 1969, p. 272) and Marshall (1890, p. 447; 1920, p. 467) who used the concept of consumers' surplus to compare the losses of consumers (say from a bridge toll or an excise tax) with the gains to the government. The demonstration that the former exceed the latter, so that consumers cannot be compensated for their losses out of the government revenues, provided a convincing case for the superiority of an income tax to an excise tax (or for the superiority of government subsidization of bridge construction to its financing of it by tolls), and at the same time provided scientific prestige and great intuitive appeal to a method that was able to reach such a definitive conclusion and furnish a measure of the 'deadweight loss'.

While Dupuit and Marshall used partial-equilibrium analysis, Pareto (1894, p. 58) was the first to introduce the concept into general-equilibrium theory, in the course of an article devoted to proving the optimality of competitive equilibrium. In the first part of this article (summarized by Sanger, 1895),

Pareto used as his criterion of optimality the sum of individual utilities; in the second part, however – acknowledging the criticisms and suggestions of Pantaleoni and Barone (both admirers of Marshall, which Pareto was not) – he reformulated the problem so as to sum not the utilities of different consumers but the quantities they consume. His criterion of optimality (1894, p. 60) was that it should be impossible for one person to gain without another losing – 'Pareto optimality' – a criterion that had also been introduced by Marshall (1890, pp. 449–50; 1920, pp. 470–71). A more refined version of Pareto's argument later appeared in the *Cours* (Pareto, 1896–7, I, pp. 256–62; II, pp. 88–94).

The proposition formulated by Pareto (1894) anticipated what has now come to be known as the 'fundamental theorem of welfare economics', namely that every competitive equilibrium is Pareto optimal and, conversely, every Pareto optimum can be sustained by a competitive equilibrium. Pareto considered the problem faced by a socialist state striving to attain an outcome in which it was impossible for one person to gain without another losing. The Ministry of Justice would concern itself with problems of income distribution, and the Ministry of Production with resource allocation and choice of production coefficients. A weakness of Pareto's argument was that he assumed a price system already to be established – perhaps our socialist state needs the prices of its capitalist neighbours to guide it. Pareto further assumed that each individual's budget constraint was adjusted by the addition of a parameter (a lump-sum subsidy or tax) controlled by the government. The government's objective was to maximize the sum of these parameters, which he showed was equal to aggregate profit – the value of commodities consumed less the value of factor services supplied, equal to the value of firms' output less the outlay on their factor inputs. If it were possible to increase all the parameters, the existing situation would not be Pareto optimal; if their sum were a maximum, it would not be possible to increase one of them without decreasing another, and the outcome would be Pareto optimal. Pareto showed that maximization of aggregate profit at the given prices, subject to the resource allocation and production-function constraints, would lead to cost-minimization and zero profits. (For mathematical details of Pareto's argument see Chipman, 1976, pp. 88–92.) Pareto summarized this result by stating (1896–7, II, p. 94):

> Free competition of entrepreneurs yields the same values for the production coefficients as would be obtained by determining them by the condition that commodity outputs should be chosen in such a way that, for some appropriate distribution, maximum ophelimity would be achieved for each individual in society.

The last clause was Pareto's unfortunately awkward way of stating the criterion of Pareto optimality.

Barone (1908), who had originally spurred Pareto on to this line of argument, developed it further himself. He noted that a competitive equilibrium has the property that aggregate profit is at a maximum at the equilibrium prices, hence for any feasible departure from this equilibrium, valuing consumption and factor services at the equilibrium prices, some individuals may gain and others will lose, the losses outweighing the gains so that even if the gainers part with all their gains, the rest will still be worse off than originally. (Barone used what is now known as the criterion of revealed preference to make inferences concerning preferences from data on prices and incomes.) Such a state was described by Pareto and Barone as 'destruction of wealth', and its measure by aggregate income loss at the competitive-equilibrium prices provided an

alternative to the deadweight loss considered by Dupuit and Marshall. Barone (1908) also related his arguments to those of Marshallian consumers'-surplus analysis.

Lerner (1934) invoked the compensation principle in his proposed method for measuring monopoly power, describing it as 'a loss to the consumer which is not balanced by any gain reaped by the monopolist'. In this paper Lerner also formulated, apparently independently, the concept of Pareto optimality.

Hotelling (1938) made a noteworthy contribution by providing an alternative demonstration of the inferiority of excise taxes to income taxes, using the compensation principle directly. He considered a single individual consuming n commodities in amounts q_j and facing market prices p_j. Prior to the imposition of the excise taxes (or tolls), the individual consumes a bundle q^0 at prices p^0 and income (or fixed component of income) m^0, which maximizes a utility function $U(q)$ subject to the budget constraint $p^0 \cdot q = m^0$. Subsequent to the introduction of taxes, market (tax-inclusive) prices and after-tax income are p^1 and m^1 respectively, and a bundle q^1 is chosen which maximizes $U(q)$ subject to $p^1 \cdot q = m^1$. The government collects $r = (p^1 - p^0) \cdot q^1 - (m^1 - m^0)$ in revenues. Since the government is assumed to collect $(p_j^1 - p_j^0) \cdot q_j^1$ in taxes on commodity j, p_j^0 must be identified with the production cost after the tax (as well as with the market price = production cost before the tax); this is a fairly restrictive assumption, since it implies that the tax does not affect production costs. (In this respect Hotelling's treatment is less general than Dupuit's and Marshall's, involving infinite elasticities of supply.) We may denote the ad valorem excise-tax rate on commodity j by $t_j = p_j^1/p_j^0 - 1$, and a proportional income-tax rate by $t_0 = 1 - m^1/m^0$ (negative taxes are interpreted as subsidies). The government's revenues are

$$r = \sum_{j=1}^{n} t_j p_j^0 q_j^1 + t_0 m^0 - 0,$$

assumed zero since the government distributes the total proceeds of these excise taxes back to the consumer (or taxes the consumer if these are negative). The consumer's budget constraint after the imposition of the taxes is

$$\sum_{j=1}^{n} (1 + t_j) p_j^0 q_j^1 = (1 - t_0) m^0.$$

These two equations together imply that q^1 satisfies the budget constraint $p^0 \cdot q^1 = m^0$, hence q^1 was in the consumer's original budget set. Therefore, setting aside the 'infinitely improbable . . . contingency' that q^0 and q^1 lie on the same indifference surface, Hotelling concluded (p. 252) that 'if a person must pay a certain sum of money in taxes, his satisfaction will be greater if the levy is made directly on him as a fixed amount than if it is made through a system of excise taxes which he can to some extent avoid by rearranging his production and consumption.'

Unfortunately Hotelling overlooked the fact that if $t_j = t$ for all j then the government's budget constraint implies $p^0 \cdot q^1 = -m^0 t_0/t$, whence $t_0 = -t$ and $q^1 = q^0$. That is, a system of uniform ad valorem excise taxes is equivalent to a proportional income tax. This was pointed out by Frisch (1939) and accepted by Hotelling (1939). As Frisch made clear, what Hotelling really proved was the nonoptimality of a system of nonproportional excise taxes or subsidies when selling prices are given. If these selling prices are equal to marginal costs, Hotelling's theorem shows that market prices should be proportional to marginal costs. Since incomes are fixed in Hotelling's formulation, income taxes may be regarded as lump-sum taxes. If institutional considerations make excise taxes impossible for one commodity (say leisure), then they

525

must be zero for all commodities and optimality requires that prices be equal to marginal costs. (For a less charitable interpretation of Hotelling's contribution see Silberberg, 1980.)

Hotelling went on to assert that his proposition could be extended to many consumers (though no details or proof were provided), and he proceeded to examine the consumers'-surplus measure of loss $\frac{1}{2}(p^1 - p^0) \cdot (q^1 - q^0) = \frac{1}{2} T p^0 \cdot (q^1 - q^0)$ (where T is a diagonal matrix of excise-tax rates t_j). He also made some general observations (p. 267) that, to this day, constitute what is probably the best statement to be found of the philosophy underlying the compensation principle.

2. THE YEARS OF THE NEW WELFARE ECONOMICS. In the cases to which the compensation principle was applied by Dupuit, Marshall, Lerner and Hotelling, compensation was made between the class of consumers on the one hand and a government or a monopolist on the other. While Pareto and Barone had discussed compensation between different classes of consumers (as had Hotelling in his general remarks) their work was unknown to English-speaking economists until the publication in 1935 of the English translation of Barone's 1908 work. Even this seems not to have struck home, however, since Kaldor (1939) cited passages from Harrod (1938) and Robbins (1938) to the effect that since movement towards free trade would affect different classes differently, no scientific statement could be made concerning the beneficial effect of free trade without making interpersonal comparisons of utility.

Kaldor (1939) proceeded to sketch an argument to the effect that removal of an import duty (using the classical example of repeal of the Corn Laws) would result in a situation in which the losses incurred by the landlords could be compensated by the gains (through lower import prices) obtained by the other consumers. Such an argument cannot be correct, however, since as Kaldor (1940) pointed out only a year later, it follows from Bickerdike's theory of optimal tariffs that a country can gain from the imposition of a sufficiently small duty, and as Graaff (1949) and others later demonstrated, the compensation principle can be used to show that, with suitable compensation, all persons can gain. Unless the rate of corn duty was above the optimal tariff rate, the opposite conclusion would follow to that indicated by Kaldor (1939).

A previous attempt by Pareto (1895) to show by means of the compensation principle that a tariff would lead to 'destruction of wealth' was defective, since he assumed trade to be balanced in domestic prices and thus he failed to take account of the improvement in the terms of trade and the beneficial effect of the tariff revenues.

Other attempts prior to 1939 to make the case for free trade suffered from vagueness both in specifying the criterion of gain and in specifying the alternative with which free trade was being compared. Ricardo (1815, p. 25) stated: 'There are two ways in which a country may be benefited by trade – one by increase of the general rate of profits ... the other by the abundance of commodities, and by a fall in their exchangeable value, in which the whole community participate.' According to Cairnes (1874, p. 418), 'the true criterion of the gain on foreign trade [is] the degree in which it cheapens commodities, and renders them more abundant.' A hint of a compensation principle is found in Viner (1937, pp. 533–4):

> free trade ... necessarily makes *available* to the community *as a whole* a greater physical real income in the form of more of *all* commodities, and ... the state ... can, by appropriate supplementary legislation, make certain that removal of duties shall result in more of *every* commodity for *every* class of the community.

Like Kaldor's statement, this is formally incorrect; but it was sufficiently suggestive to stimulate Samuelson (1939) into providing a formal proof of a gains-from-trade theorem, albeit under very restrictive assumptions.

Samuelson (1939) assumed that an open economy had a locus $\phi(y, l) = 0$ of efficient combinations of outputs y and (variable) factor services l, and asserted that vectors of prices p and factor rentals w in competitive equilibrium would be such that aggregate profit $p \cdot y - w \cdot l$ is a maximum. This is the same as the proposition of Pareto (1894) and Barone (1908) referred to above. Letting x denote the bundle of commodities consumed, under both (balanced) free trade and autarky the budget equation $p \cdot x = p \cdot y$ holds. Letting superscripts 0 and 1 denote equilibrium values under autarky and free trade respectively, it follows that

$$p^1 \cdot x^1 - w^1 \cdot l^1 \geqslant p^1 \cdot x^0 - w^1 \cdot l^0.$$

Assuming all N individuals to be identical in their preferences and ownership of factors, and dividing this inequality through by the number of individuals, it states that each person chooses $(x^1/N, l^1/N)$ under free trade when $(x^0/N, l^0/N)$ is available, hence (if $p^1 \neq p^0$) each person prefers $(x^1/N, l^1/N)$ to $(x^0/N, l^0/N)$. Therefore free trade is Pareto-superior to autarky.

Samuelson went on to assert (p. 204) that if the assumption of identical individuals is dropped, then although it could no longer be said that each individual was better off under free trade, 'it would always be possible for those who desired trade to buy off those opposed to trade, with the result that all could be made better off.' This argument went unchallenged until Olsen (1958) pointed out that if compensation were paid from gainers to losers, a new equilibrium price constellation p^1 would result, and the argument no longer follows. For this reason Samuelson's 1939 results has come to be known as the gains-from-trade theorem for the 'small-country case', though this interpretation was not suggested by Samuelson at the time. But this description of Samuelson's result is inaccurate. Generalizing his argument we can say that if (x_i^t, l_i^t) are the allocations of (x^t, l^t) to individual i, where $\Sigma_{i=1}^N x_i^t = x^t$ and $\Sigma_{i=1}^N l_i^t = l^t$, then given the allocations (x_i^1, l_i^1) of (x^1, l^1) under free trade one can find Pareto-optimal allocations (x_i^0, l_i^0) of (y^0, l^0) under autarky such that

$$p^1 \cdot x_i^1 - w^1 \cdot l_i^1 \geqslant p^1 \cdot x_i^0 - w^1 \cdot l_i^0 \quad \text{for} \quad i = 1, 2, \ldots, N.$$

This proves that for *any* free-trade equilibrium it is possible to find a weakly Pareto-inferior Pareto-optimal autarky equilibrium. It does not prove the obverse proposition that for any autarky equilibrium it is possible to find a weakly Pareto-superior free-trade equilibrium. A general gains-from-trade theorem was therefore yet to be established, but Samuelson had provided an important first step.

Hicks (1939) ushered in the 'new welfare economics' with a synthesis building on Hotelling (1938) and Kaldor (1939) and based on the compensation principle, making it possible, according to him, to make policy proposals in favour of economic efficiency which were free of value judgements. Hicks's most original contribution (Hicks, 1940) was his attempt to apply the compensation principle to data on a country's real national income. This was a natural thing to try to do, since Pigou's (1920) main work was devoted to evaluating a country's welfare by national-income comparisons, and it was largely Pigou's resort to interpersonal comparisons in order to justify this that was the object of Robbins's (1938) criticism.

Hicks's (1940) basic tool was the 'revealed-preference' comparison which had been employed by Barone (1908) and

Hotelling (1938). If observations are available at times 0 and 1 of a country's national income in period-1 prices, and it is recorded that $p^1 \cdot y^1 \geqslant p^1 \cdot y^0$ (where p^t, y^t are vectors of prices and outputs at time t), what can be inferred? In the first place, to make any headway one must assume that the observed situations are competitive equilibria. Let us define an allocation of a commodity bundle x as an $N \times n$ matrix X whose ith row, x_i, is the bundle of n commodities allocated to individual i, and whose row sum $\sigma(X) = \Sigma_{i=1}^N x_i$ is equal to x. As between two bundles x_i^0, x_i^1 consumed by individual i, let us define $x_i^1 R_i x_i^0$ to mean that x_i^1 is preferred or indifferent to x_i^0 by individual i, where R_i is a continuous, convex, monotonic total order, with P_i denoting strict preference and I_i indifference. (This relation assumes the absence of externalities in consumption.) Finally, let $X^1 R X^0$ (resp. $X^1 P X^0$) mean that X^1 is weakly (resp. strictly) Pareto-superior to X^0 (i.e., $x_i^1 R_i x_i^0$ for all i, resp. $x_i^1 R_i x_i^0$ for all i and $x_i^1 P_i x_i^0$ for some i). Then from the real-income comparison $p^1 \cdot y^1 \geqslant p^1 \cdot y^0$, Hicks noted that there does not exist an allocation X of y^0 that is weakly Pareto-superior to the actual allocation X^1 of y^1. This follows from the same argument that establishes the Pareto optimality of the assumed competitive equilibrium in period 1. The non-existence of an allocation X of y^0 such that $X R X^1$, where $\sigma(X^1) = y^1$, constituted for Hicks the definition of an 'increase in real social income'.

Kuznets (1948) pointed out by an example that in the case considered by Hicks, it could also be true that there is no allocation X of y^1 which is weakly Pareto superior to the actual allocation X^0 of y^0. Accordingly he suggested that Hicks's criterion be supplemented by the condition that there should exist an allocation $\bar{X}$ of y^1 that is weakly Pareto superior to the actual allocation X^0 of y^0. But while the latter criterion implies $p^0 \cdot y^1 \geqslant p^0 \cdot y^0$, it is not implied by it, so a national-income comparison using current and base prices would still not yield Kuznets's criterion.

Kuznets's criticism of Hicks was similar to the objection raised by Scitovsky (1941) to the criterion proposed by Kaldor (1939). According to Scitovsky's interpretation of Kaldor an allocation X^1 of y^1 is better than an allocation X^0 of y^0, if there exists a reallocation $\bar{X}^1$ of y^1 which is Pareto superior to X^0. Scitovsky objected that this gave preference to the *status quo ante*, and besides, he pointed out that the criterion was internally inconsistent in the sense that it allowed two such pairs (X^t, y^t) to be superior to each other. He therefore proposed that Kaldor's test be supplemented by the criterion that there exist a reallocation $\bar{X}^0$ of y^0 that is Pareto inferior to X^1.

The literature on 'compensation tests' suffered from ambiguity as to the domain of definition of the relations and internal inconsistency of the relations. It was pointed out by Gorman (1955) that the relations were intransitive. It was shown in Chipman and Moore (1978) that the Hicks–Kuznets and Scitovsky double criteria, as well as the national-income comparisons in terms of base- and current-year prices, could lead to cycles of three competitive equilibria each superior to its successor.

The definitive contribution to the subject of national-income comparisons was that of Samuelson (1950) who introduced what Chipman and Moore (1971) described as the 'Kaldor–Hicks–Samuelson (KHS) ordering'. The objects under comparison in this approach are sets Y of commodity bundles y, e.g. production-possibility sets. Letting $A(Y)$ denote the set of allocation matrices X such that $\sigma(X) \in Y$, this ordering is defined by

$$Y^1 >_R Y^0 \Leftrightarrow [\forall X^0 \in A(Y^0)][\exists X^1 \in A(Y^1)]\, X^1 R X^0.$$

In words, Y^1 is potentially superior to Y^0 if, for all allocations of commodity bundles in Y^0, there exists a (weakly) Pareto

superior allocation of a commodity bundle in Y^1. This is a reflexive and transitive relation; it also satisfies the condition that $Y^0 \subseteq Y^1$ implies $Y^1 >_R Y^0$. Samuelson also introduced the important concept of a utility-possibility frontier, which is the relative boundary of a utility-possibility set $U(Y, R; f)$; this in turn is a set of N-tuples of individual utilities, $u = f(X)$, for some $X \in A(Y)$, where f is an N-tuple of positive-valued utility functions representing R. If the sets Y are 'disposable' (i.e., containing for every $y \in Y$ the bundles y' with $0 \leqslant y' \leqslant y$), and the R_i continuous and monotonic, then the utility-possibility sets are also disposable. If Y is non-empty, compact disposable, and convex, and the R_i are continuous, monotonic, and convex, then provided the f_i are continuous and concave, $U(Y, R: f)$ is non-empty, compact, and convex (cf. Chipman and Moore, 1971, p. 24). If the f_i are only quasi-concave and not concave, $U(Y, R; f)$ need not be convex (cf. Kannai and Mantel, 1978). The KHS ordering among consumption-possibility sets translates into set-inclusion of the corresponding utility-possibility sets. Samuelson (1959, p. 10) gave an example of a case of crossing utility-possibility frontiers in which $X^2 \in A(Y^2)$ was Pareto superior to $X^1 \in A(Y^1)$ yet Y^1 would be ranked higher than Y^2 in terms of some value judgement. This established that the 'compensation tests' were not 'relatively *wertfrei*'.

Another approach was followed by Chipman and Moore (1973, 1976a) who asked the following question: if competitive equilibria (X^t, y^t, p^t) are observed satisfying $p^1 \cdot y^1 \geqslant p^1 \cdot y^0$ and $p^0 \cdot y^1 \geqslant p^0 \cdot y^0$, where $y^t \in Y_t$ for $t = 0, 1$, under what conditions on preferences must this imply that $Y^1 >_R Y^0$? For the case $Y^t = \{y^t\}$ they showed that the preference relations R_i must be identical and homothetic. This is a global result; with positive consumptions of all commodities the condition could no doubt be weakened to the aggregation criterion of Antonelli (1886), Gorman (1953), and Nataf (1953), namely that consumer i's demand for commodity j have the form

$$x_{ij} = a_{ij}(p) + b_j(p) m_i$$

where m_i is consumer i's income.

Samuelson (1956) applied the compensation principle in a striking way in his proposed alternative to the New Welfare Economics. He discovered that if a social-welfare function has the separable form $W[f(X)]$, then a social utility function $f_w(x) = \max\{W[f(X)]: X \in A(x)\}$ has the property that it can be achieved in a decentralized manner by means of an income-distribution policy assigning individual shares of aggregate income as functions of prices and aggregate income. The first complete proof of this result was presented in Chipman and Moore (1972) (see also Chipman and Moore, 1979; Chipman, 1982). The main tool of analysis used was the concept of a Scitovsky indifference surface (Scitovsky, 1942) which is defined as the boundary of the set $\Sigma_{i=1}^N R_i x_i$, where $R_i x_i$ is the set of all commodity bundles preferred or indifferent to x_i by individual i. This set is necessarily a subset of the set $R_w x$ of aggregate bundles preferred or indifferent to x by the Samuelson social ordering. In a competitive equilibrium the aggregate consumption bundle minimizes aggregate expenditure at the equilibrium prices over both sets, hence the bundle x_i minimizes each individual's expenditure over $R_i x_i$ (cf. Koopmans, 1957, pp. 12–13).

3. GAINS FROM TRADE AND OPTIMAL TARIFFS. The new tools developed by Scitovsky (1942) and Samuelson (1950, 1956) made possible a rigorous proof of a gains-from-trade theorem, as well as of the proposition that a country could gain by a tariff.

Kemp (1962) noted that Samuelson's 1939 theorem implied that for any point on the free-trade utility-possibility frontier, the autarky utility-possibility frontier must pass below it; he reasoned that, as a result, for any point on the autarky utility-possibility frontier, the free-trade utility-possibility frontier must pass above it. If this argument can be accepted, it follows that for every allocation $X^0 \in A(Y^0)$, where Y^0 is the autarkic production-possibility set, there exists a (weakly) Pareto-superior allocation $X^1 \in A(Y^1)$, where Y^1 is the free-trade consumption-possibility set. Then free trade is superior to autarky by Samuelson's 1950 criterion.

The trouble with this argument, however, is that it requires that one can define a free-trade utility-possibility frontier (or consumption-possibility frontier) with the strong topological property of homeomorphism to the $(N-1)$-dimensional unit simplex (intuitively, absence of 'holes'). That this need not always be possible, was shown by Otani (1972, p. 149), and indeed admitted by Kemp and Wan (1972, p. 513). It is always possible if world prices are fixed, beyond our country's control. In that case the free-trade consumption-possibility set Y^1 is the budget set enclosing the production-possibility set Y^0 (cf. Samuelson, 1962, p. 821), and the gains-from-trade theorem follows immediately from the property $Y^1 \supseteq Y^0 \Rightarrow Y^1 >_R Y^0$. In similar fashion the famous 'Baldwin envelope' (Baldwin, 1948) defines a well-behaved consumption-possibility set containing the production-possibility set, from which one can prove the superiority of restricted trade (with an optimal tariff) to autarky (cf. Samuelson, 1962).

For the general case in which a country can influence world prices, a method was shown by Kenen (1957). If all but 1 of the N individuals are constrained to have the same level of satisfaction under trade as achieved under autarky, a net production-possibility set can be constructed which indicates the amount available for the Nth person. It remains only to show that the Nth person will gain from a movement from autarky to free trade. A similar approach was indicated by Vanek (1964).

Grandmont and McFadden (1972) and Chipman and Moore (1972) both used the concept of an income-distribution policy to establish the gains-from-trade theorem. In Chipman and Moore this policy was chosen to be one that maximizes a separable Bergson-Samuelson social-welfare function. A standard argument is used to show that social utility is at least as high under free trade as under autarky. It remains to show that a function $W(u)$ can be chosen so that the corresponding distribution policy ensures that an increase in social utility implies an increase in each individual's utility. This is achieved by choice of $W(u) = \min_i (u_i - u_i^0)/c_i$ where $c_i > 0$ and u_i^0 is the level of utility achieved by individual i under autarky.

4. GENERAL-EQUILIBRIUM THEORY. The compensation principle is used in the proof of the theorem that every competitive equilibrium is Pareto-optimal (Arrow, 1952, pp. 516, 519; Koopmans, 1957, p. 49; Debreu, 1959, pp. 94–5), in the sense that arbitrary allocations of feasible output bundles among consumers are assumed possible, regardless of resource-ownership constraints. A pair (X^0, p^0) is a competitive equilibrium for the production-possibility set Y if $X^0 R X$ for all $X \in A(Y)$ satisfying $Xp^0 \leqslant X^0 p^0$, and $y^0 p^0 \geqslant y p^0$ for all $y \in Y$, where $y^0 = \sigma(X^0) \in Y$. Pareto-optimality means that one cannot find an $X \in A(Y)$ such that XPX^0. The proof is by contradiction: XPX^0 implies $Xp^0 \geqslant X^0 p^0$ (the vector inequality being weak in all components and strict in at least one) hence taking column sums, $yp^0 > y^0 p^0$.

The converse theorem, that every Pareto optimum can be sustained by a competitive equilibrium, requires stronger assumptions which are awkward to state (cf. Arrow, 1952, p. 518; Koopmans, 1957, p. 50; Debreu, 1959, p. 95). The basic idea of the proof (Koopmans, 1957, pp. 50–52; Debreu, 1959, p. 96) can be sketched in terms of the concept of a Scitovsky (1942) indifference surface. If X^0 is a Pareto-optimal allocation for a closed, convex production-possibility set Y, then the interior of the Scitovsky set of X^0 can be written $P_k x_k^0 + \Sigma_{i \neq k} R_i x_i^0$ for some k. Defining the allocation X^1 by $x_k^1 P_k x_k^0$ and $x_i^1 R_i x_i^0$ for $i \neq k$, we have $X^1 P X^0$ hence $X^1 \notin A(Y)$. Therefore the interior of the Scitovsky set does not intersect Y, and these convex sets can be separated by a hyperplane defining the equilibrium prices. It is then verified that at these prices the properties of a competitive equilibrium are satisfied.

Debreu (1954, p. 590) introduced an alternative equilibrium concept according to which the condition that consumer preferences be maximized subject to their budget constraints was replaced by the condition that consumer expenditures be minimized subject to the constraints that the bundles considered be at least as desirable as the equilibrium bundles. (The second of the above theorems follows more easily under this alternative definition.) For a given set of positive-valued utility functions representing consumer preferences, Arrow and Hahn (1971, p. 108) called this a 'compensated equilibrium'. As a means of proving existence of the latter they studied the utility-possibility frontier or 'Pareto frontier' (p. 96), and obtained a new proof of the result of Chipman and Moore (1971) that the set of Pareto-optimal allocations X of Y (the 'contract curve') and the utility-possibility frontier are topologically homeomorphic to the unit simplex of dimension one less than the number of individuals. These results were further developed by Moore (1975).

5. COST-BENEFIT ANALYSIS. Hicks (1941, p. 112) made an interesting distinction between two tasks of welfare economics: (1) the study of (Pareto)-optimal organizations of the economy and (2) the study of deviations from such optima. More precisely, the first was concerned with when there was a deviation and the second with the size of the deviation. He also identified these two tasks with general- and partial-equilibrium analysis respectively, although there appears to be no justification for this other than the historical accident that consumers' surplus developed as a partial-equilibrium tool. He remarked that consumers' surplus is not needed for the first task, since lack of fulfilment of the proportionality between marginal utilities and marginal costs provides the needed information immediately. For the second task, he was not content with a ranking of the non-optimal states, but with measuring the size of their deviations from optimality, which of course would provide such a ranking. Thus, the staunch ordinalist in consumer theory became an equally ardent cardinalist in welfare theory.

Hicks's concepts of compensating and equivalent variation (Hicks, 1942) may most conveniently be defined in terms of the minimum-income or income-compensation functions of McKenzie (1957) and Hurwicz and Uzawa (1971). Denoting the ith consumer's demand function by $x_i = h_i(p, m_i)$ (where x_i and p are n-vectors), and defining the indirect preference relation R_i^* by $(p^0, m_i^0) R_i^* (p^1, m_i^1)$ if and only if $h_i(p^0, m_i^0) R_i h_i(p^1, m_i^1)$, the income-compensation function is defined by

$$\mu_i(p; p^0, m_i^0) = \inf \{ m_i : (p, m_i) R_i^* (p^0, m_i^0) \}.$$

Following Chipman and Moore (1980), the generalized compensating variation in going from (p^0, m_i^0) to (p, m_i) is defined as

$$C_i(p, m_i; p^0, m_i^0) = m_i - \mu_i(p; p^0, m_i^0)$$

and the generalized equivalent variation by

$$E_i(p, m_i; p^0, m_i^0) = \mu_i(p^0; p, m_i) - m_i^0.$$

These reduce to Hicks's concepts when $m_i = m_i^0$.

The compensating variation expresses for each consumer the amount of money income he or she would be willing to give up (or the negative of the amount by which he or she would have to be compensated), at the new prices, to make up for the change in prices and income. One of the reasons for the great appeal of the concept is that these are amounts that can be added up over the set of consumers. In Hicks's words (1942, p. 127):

> the general test for a particular reform being an *improvement* is that the gainers should gain sufficiently for them to be able to compensate the losers and still remain gainers on balance. This test would be carried out by striking the balance of the Compensating Variations.

Denoting by m^t the vector of N incomes in state t, and by M^t their sum, we can define a dual potential-improvement ordering between pairs of price-income pairs (p^t, M^t) as follows. Let $A^*(p, M)$ be the set of $(n + N)$-tuples (p, m) such that $\Sigma_{i=1}^N m_i = M$, and let R^* be the relation such that $(p^0, m^0) R^*(p^1, m^1)$ if and only if $(p^0, m_i^0) R_i^*(p^1, m_i^1)$ for $i = 1, 2, \ldots, N$. Then we define the dual KHS relation $>_{R^*}$ by

$$(p^0, M^0) >_{R^*} (p^1, M^1) \Leftrightarrow [\forall (p', m') \in A^*(p^1, M^1)$$

$$(\exists (p, m) \in A^*(p^0, M^0)] : (p, m) R^*(p', m').$$

Choosing price-income pairs (p^0, m^0) and (p^1, m^1) satisfying this definition, since $\mu_i(p'; p, m_i)$ is an indirect utility function representing R_i^* for $t = 0$ or 1, we have $\mu_i(p'; p^0, m_i^0) \geqslant \mu_i(p'; p^1, m_i^1)$ for all individuals i, hence

$$M^0 = \sum_{i=1}^N m_i^0 = \sum_{i=1}^N \mu_i(p^0; p^0, m_i^0) \geqslant \sum_{i=1}^N \mu_i(p^0; p^1, m_i^1).$$

so one obtains a multi-consumer analogue to the compensating variation from the formula

$$M^0 - \sum_{i=1}^N \mu_i(p^0, p^1, m_i^1) \geqslant M^1 - \sum_{i=1}^N \mu_i(p^1, p^1, m_i^1) = 0.$$

Likewise for the equivalent variation,

$$0 = \sum_{i=1}^N \mu_i(p^0; p^0, m_i^0) - M^0 \geqslant \sum_{i=1}^N \mu_i(p^0; p^1, m_i^1) - M^0.$$

In the latter case the same indirect utility functions are summed on both sides of the inequality sign; it is a case where Benthamites and compensationists can find common ground.

Boadway (1974) considered the relationship between the condition of positive summed compensating variations and the fulfillment of compensation tests and came to the negative conclusion that the former was neither necessary nor sufficient for satisfaction of the latter in general, but was sufficient in the case of identical and homothetic preferences. Foster (1976) showed that if there are no price distortions (but not otherwise), satisfaction of the compensation tests implies satisfaction of the 'cost–benefit criterion' (positive summed compensating variations). This conclusion is in accord with the above inequalities.

What about the Hicksian tenet that the size of the compensating variation is important so that one can compare two suboptimal states? This would require one to be able to conclude that if the compensating variation from state 0 to state 2 is positive and greater than the compensating variation from state 0 to state 1, then state 2 should be superior to state 1 in terms of the dual KHS ordering. But this is not true even in the case of the single consumer. It was shown in Chipman and Moore (1980) that the function $C_i(p, m_i; p^0, m_i^0)$ cannot be an indirect utility function for unrestricted domain $(p, m_i) > 0$, and can be if m_i is held constant if and only if preferences are homothetic, and if p_1 is held constant if and only if preferences are 'parallel' with respect to commodity 1. If preferences are identical and homothetic, since $\mu_i = \mu$ is homogeneous of degree 1 in m_i, $\Sigma_{i=1}^N \mu_i(p^0; p, m_i) = \mu(p^0; p, M)$, so exact aggregative analogues are obtained to both the compensating and equivalent variations. If the equivalent variation, which is an indirect utility function, is used, restrictions on consumer preferences are not needed, and the problem of finding an adequate indicator of the size of the deviation from a given Pareto optimum is satisfactorily resolved.

6. GAME THEORY. One of the striking aspects of von Neumann and Morgenstern's theory of games (1947) was not only its postulate of measurability of utility but also that of its transferability between players. Since this was introduced as a positive rather than a normative assumption, it has met with even greater resistance of the part of economists than the hedonist calculus. Indeed, it was not until Debreu and Scarf (1963) showed how game theory could be liberated from this restriction with their development of the concept of the core of an economy that game theory began to be taken really seriously by economists. The replacement of transferability of utilities by transferability of commodities bears a striking resemblance to the replacement in welfare economics of the calculus of utilities by the principle of compensation.

In some branches of game theory the assumption of transferable utility is still retained, but it has been made somewhat more plausible, or at least interpretable, by means of the postulate that the utility functions of all individuals are linear in one distinguished commodity used for making side payments (cf. Owen, 1982, p. 122). These utility functions have the form

$$U_i(x_{i1}, x_{i2}, \ldots, x_{in}) = c_i x_{i1} + V_i(x_{i2}, \ldots, x_{in}).$$

This form of the utility function goes back to Edgeworth (1891, p. 237n) and even earlier (though in garbled form) to Auspitz and Lieben (1889, p. 471). In Edgeworth it was used to illustrate the phenomenon of exchange when the marginal utility of one commodity serving as money was held constant, in accordance with one possible interpretation of Marshall's theory of consumers' surplus. (In the case $n = 2$ he showed that the exchange in commodity 2 would be constant, but in commodity 1 'indeterminate'; see the reply by Berry (1891) on behalf of Marshall, and Marshall (1891, p. 756; 1920, p. 845).) The above form for the utility function has been rediscovered many times, by Wilson (1939), Samuelson (1942), and others; cf. Chipman and Moore (1976b, p. 115). Barone (1894, p. 213n) gave the name 'ideal money (numéraire)' to a good with a constant marginal utility (commodity 1 in the above). For the case $c_i = c$ for all i, these 'parallel' preferences (cf. Boulding, 1945) yield a special case of the family of aggregable Antonelli–Gorman–Nataf demand functions referred to above.

7. CONCLUDING OBSERVATIONS. As Scitovsky (1941) pointed out, the compensation principle has been used in two quite different ways. Prior to Hicks (1940), it was used only to compare efficient with inefficient states of a given economy with a given technology or trading system. Starting with Hicks (1940), its use was extended to comparison of efficient states of an economy under different technologies. It has turned out that in order for national-income comparisons to provide a correct indicator of potential-welfare improvement, very strong conditions are required concerning similarity of individual preferences: locally, the Antonelli–Gorman–Nataf conditions, and globally, identical homothetic preferences. It is not even enough to assume that aggregate demand can be generated by an aggregate preference relation, e.g., that

preferences are homothetic and relative income-distribution constant (cf. Chipman and Moore, 1980a). Even in such cases, strong value judgements (such as acceptance of a particular Bergson–Samuelson social-welfare function) are required in order to draw welfare conclusions from national-income comparisons.

When attention is restricted to the efficient operation of an economy with a given technology, it turns out that in most cases of interest, the ranking of consumption-possibility sets according to the Kaldor–Hicks–Samuelson criterion follows from their ranking by set-inclusion. This does not mean, however, that the set-inclusion is always obvious or easy to prove.

The KHS ordering of consumption-possibility sets could be given simply a factual interpretation as indicating the 'productive potential' of an economy. But if it is given a normative interpretation then it obviously involves a value judgement, since a more efficient outcome, if it is not Pareto-superior, can obviously be judged worse in terms of some social-welfare function.

Samuelson's (1956) model of the 'good society', elegant though it is, is too sweeping for most economists to accept, and it begs the question of how the social-welfare function will be chosen. Little's (1950) and Mishan's (1969) attempts to link plausible distributional value judgements with compensation criteria have encountered unresolvable logical difficulties (cf. Chipman and Moore, 1978). The hope that the compensation principle would allow policy decisions to be made free of value judgements has not been fulfilled. Nevertheless, much has been learned about the interrelationships among values, facts, and policies, and it can certainly be said that the development of the compensation principle has led to clearer thinking about economic policy issues.

JOHN S. CHIPMAN

See also SOCIAL WELFARE FUNCTION; WELFARE ECONOMICS.

BIBLIOGRAPHY

Antonelli, G.B. 1886. *Sulla teoria matematica della economia politica.* Pisa: Folchetto. English translation: On the mathematical theory of political economy, in *Preferences, Utility, and Demand*, ed. J.S. Chipman, L. Hurwicz, M.K. Richter and H.F. Sonnenschein, New York: Harcourt Brace Jovanovich, 1971, 332–64.

Arrow, K.J. 1951. An extension of the basic theorems of classical welfare economics. In *Proceedings of the Second Berkeley Symposium on Mathematical Statistics and Probability*, ed. J. Neyman, Berkeley and Los Angeles: University of California Press, 507–532.

Arrow, K.J. and Hahn, F.H. 1971. *General Competitive Analysis.* San Francisco: Holden-Day.

Arrow, K.J. and Scitovsky, T. (eds) 1969. *Readings in Welfare Economics.* Homewood, Ill.: Irwin.

Auspitz, R. and Lieben, R. 1889. *Untersuchungen über die Theorie des Preises.* Leipzig, Duncker & Humblot.

Baldwin, R.E. 1948. Equilibrium in international trade: a diagrammatic analysis. *Quarterly Journal of Economics* 62, November, 748–62.

Baldwin, R.E. 1954. A comparison of welfare criteria. *Review of Economic Studies* 21, 154–61.

Barone, E. 1894. Sulla 'consumers' rent'. *Giornale degli Economisti* Series 2, 9, September, 211–24.

Barone, E. 1908. Il Ministerio della produzione nello stato colletivista. *Giornale degli Economisti* Series 2, 37, August, 267–93; October, 391–414. English translation: The Ministry of Production in the Collectivist State, in *Collectivist Economic Planning*, ed. F.A. Hayek, London: Routledge & Kegan Paul, 1935, 245–90.

Berry, A. 1891. Alcune brevi parole sulla teoria del baratto di A. Marshall. *Giornale degli Economisti* Series 2, 2, June, 549–53.

Boadway, R.W. 1974. The welfare foundations of cost-benefit analysis. *Economic Journal* 84, December, 926–39. A reply, *ibid.*, 86, June 1976, 358–61.

Boulding, K.E. 1945. The concept of economic surplus. *American Economic Review* 35, December, 851–69.

Cairnes, J.E. 1874. *Some Leading Principles of Political Economy Newly Expounded.* New York: Harper & Brothers.

Chipman, J.S. 1976. The Paretian heritage. *Revue européenne des sciences sociales et Cahiers Vilfredo Pareto* 14(37), 65–171.

Chipman, J.S. 1982. Samuelson and welfare economics. In *Samuelson and Neoclassical Economics*, ed. G.R. Feiwel, Boston: Kluwer-Nijhoff Publishing, 152–84.

Chipman, J.S. and Moore, J.C. 1971. The compensation principle in welfare economics. In *Papers in Quantitative Economics*, Vol. 2, ed. A.M. Zarley, Lawrence: University Press of Kansas, 1–77.

Chipman, J.S. and Moore, J.C. 1972. Social utility and the gains from trade. *Journal of International Economics* 2, May, 157–72.

Chipman, J.S. and Moore, J.C. 1973. Aggregate demand, real national income, and the compensation principle. *International Economic Review* 14, February, 152–81.

Chipman, J.S. and Moore, J.C. 1976a. Why an increase in GNP need not imply an improvement in potential welfare. *Kyklos* 29(3), 391–418.

Chipman, J.S. and Moore, J.C. 1976b. The scope of consumer's surplus arguments. In *Evolution, Welfare, and Time in Economics*, ed. A. Tang, F.M. Westfield and J.S. Worley, Lexington, Mass.: Heath, 69–123.

Chipman, J.S. and Moore, J.C. 1978. The New Welfare Economics, 1939–1974. *International Economic Review* 19, October, 547–84.

Chipman, J.S. and Moore, J.C. 1979. On social welfare functions and the aggregation of preferences. *Journal of Economic Theory* 21, August, 111–39.

Chipman, J.S. and Moore, J.C. 1980a. Real national income with homothetic preferences and a fixed distribution of income. *Econometrica* 48, March, 401–422.

Chipman, J.S. and Moore, J.C. 1980b. Compensating variation, consumer's surplus, and welfare. *American Economic Review* 70, December, 933–49.

Coase, R.H. 1960. The problem of social cost. *Journal of Law and Economics* 3, October, 1–44.

Debreu, G. 1951. The coefficient of resource utilization. *Econometrica* 19, July, 273–92.

Debreu, G. 1954. Valuation equilibrium and Pareto optimum. *Proceedings of the National Academy of Sciences* 40, July, 588–92.

Debreu, G. 1959. *Theory of Value.* New York: Wiley.

Debreu, G. and Scarf, H. 1963. A limit theorem on the core of an economy. *International Economic Review* 4, September, 235–46.

Dupuit, J. 1844. De la mesure de l'utilité des travaux publics. *Annales des Ponts et Chaussées, Mémoires et documents relatifs à l'art des constructions et au service de l'ingénieur* Series 2, 2, 2e semestre, 332–75, Pl. 75. English translation: On the measurement of the utility of public works, in Arrow and Scitovsky (1969), 255–83.

Edgeworth, F.Y. 1891. Osservazioni sulla teoria matematica dell'economia politica con riguardo speciale ai principi di economia di Alfredo Marshall. *Giornale degli Economisti* Series 2, 2, March, 233–45. Ancora a proposito della teoria del baratto, *ibid.*, October, 316–18. Abridged English translation: On the determinateness of economic equilibrium, in F.Y. Edgeworth, *Papers Relating to Political Economy*, Vol. II, London: Macmillan, 1925, 313–19.

Foster, E. 1976. The welfare foundations of cost-benefit analysis – a comment. *Economic Journal* 86, June, 353–8.

Frisch, R. 1939. The Dupuit taxation theorem. *Econometrica* 7, April, 145–50. A further note on the Dupuit taxation theorem, ibid., 156–7.

Gorman, W.M. 1953. Community preference fields. *Econometrica* 21, January, 63–80.

Gorman, W.M. 1955. The intransitivity of certain criteria used in welfare economics. *Oxford Economic Papers*, N.S. 7, February, 25–35.

Graaff, J. de V. 1949. On optimum tariff structures. *Review of Economic Studies* 17, 47–59. Reprinted in Arrow and Scitovsky (1969), 523–40.

Graaff, J. de V. 1957. *Theoretical Welfare Economics*. Cambridge: Cambridge University Press.

Grandmont, J.M. and McFadden, D. 1972. A technical note on classical gains from trade. *Journal of International Economics* 2, May, 109–125.

Harrod, R.F. 1938. Scope and method of economics. *Economic Journal* 48, September, 383–412.

Hicks, J.R. 1939. The foundations of welfare economics. *Economic Journal* 49, December, 696–712.

Hicks, J.R. 1940. The valuation of social income. *Economica*, N.S. 7, May, 105–24.

Hicks, J.R. 1941. The rehabilitation of consumers' surplus. *Review of Economic Studies* 8, February, 108–116. Reprinted in Arrow and Scitovsky (1969), 325–35.

Hicks, J.R. 1942. Consumers' surplus and index-numbers. *Review of Economic Studies* 9, Summer, 126–37.

Hicks, J.R. 1957. *A Revision of Demand Theory*. Oxford: Clarendon Press.

Hotelling, H. 1938. The general welfare in relation to problems of taxation and of railway and utility rates. *Econometrica* 6, July, 242–69. Reprinted in Arrow and Scitovsky (1969), 248–308.

Hotelling, H. 1939. The relation of prices to marginal costs in an optimum system. *Econometrica* 7, April, 151–5. A final note, ibid., 158–9.

Hurwicz, L. and Uzawa, H. 1971. On the integrability of demand functions. In *Preferences, Utility, and Demand*, ed. J.S. Chipman, L. Hurwicz, M.K. Richter and H.F. Sonnenschein, New York: Harcourt Brace Jovanovich, 332–64.

Kaldor, N. 1939. Welfare propositions in economics and interpersonal comparisons of utility. *Economic Journal* 49, September, 549–52. Reprinted in Arrow and Scitovsky (1969), 387–9.

Kaldor, N. 1940. A note on tariffs and the terms of trade. *Economica*, N.S. 7, November, 377–80.

Kannai, Y. and Mantel, R. 1978. Non-convexifiable Pareto sets. *Econometrica* 46, May, 571–5.

Kemp, M.C. 1962. The gains from international trade. *Economic Journal* 72, December, 803–19.

Kemp, M.C. and Wan, H.Y., Jr. 1972. The gains from free trade. *International Economic Review* 13, October, 509–22.

Kenen, P.B. 1957. On the geometry of welfare economics. *Quarterly Journal of Economics* 71, August, 426–47.

Koopmans, T.C. 1957. *Three Essays on the State of Economic Science*. New York: McGraw-Hill.

Kuznets, S. 1948. On the valuation of social income – reflections on Professor Hicks' article. *Economica*, N.S. 15, February, 1–16, May, 116–31.

Lerner, A.P. 1934. The concept of monopoly and the measurement of monopoly power. *Review of Economic Studies* 1, June, 157–75.

Little, I.M.D. 1950. *A Critique of Welfare Economics*. 2nd edn, London: Oxford University Press, 1957.

McKenzie, L.W. 1957. Demand theory without a utility index. *Review of Economic Studies* 24, June, 185–9.

Marshall, A. 1890. *Principles of Economics*. London: Macmillan. 2nd edn, 1891; 8th edn, 1920.

Mishan, E.J. 1969. *Welfare Economics: an Assessment*. Amsterdam: North-Holland.

Moore, J.C. 1975. The existence of 'compensated equilibrium' and the structure of the Pareto efficiency frontier. *International Economic Review* 16, June, 267–300.

Nataf, A. 1953. Sur des questions d'agrégation en économétrie. *Publications de l'Institut de Statistique de l'Université de Paris* 2(4), 5–61.

von Neumann, J. and Morgenstern, O. 1947. *Theory of Games and Economic Behavior*. 2nd edn, Princeton: Princeton University Press.

Olsen, E. 1958. Udenrigshandelens gevinst (The gains of international trade). *Nationaløkonomisk Tiddskrift* 98(1–2), 76–9.

Otani, Y. 1972. Gains from trade revisited. *Journal of International Economics* 2, May, 127–56.

Owen, G. 1982. *Game Theory*. 2nd edn, Orlando, Florida: Academic Press.

Pareto, V. 1894. Il massimo di utilità dato dalla libera concorrenza. *Giornale degli Economisti* Series 2, 9, July, 48–66.

Pareto, V. 1895. Teoria matematica del commercio internazionale. *Giornale degli Economisti* Series 2, 10, April, 476–98.

Pareto, V. 1896, 1897. *Cours d'économie politique*. 2 vols, Lausanne: F. Rouge.

Pigou, A.C. 1920. *The Economics of Welfare*. London: Macmillan. 4th edn, 1932.

Ricardo, D. 1815. *An Essay on the Influence of a low price of corn on the profits of stock*. London: John Murray. In *The Works and Correspondence of David Ricardo*, Vol. IV, ed. Piero Sraffa, Cambridge: Cambridge University Press, 1951, 9–41.

Robbins, L. 1938. Interpersonal comparisons of utility: a comment. *Economic Journal* 48, December, 635–41.

Samuelson, P.A. 1939. The gains from international trade. *Canadian Journal of Economics and Political Science* 5, May, 195–205.

Samuelson, P.A. 1942. Constancy of the marginal utility of income. In *Studies in Mathematical Economics and Econometrics in Memory of Henry Schultz*, ed. O. Lange, F. McIntyre and T.O. Yntema, Chicago: University of Chicago Press, 75–91.

Samuelson, P.A. 1947. *Foundations of Economic Analysis*. Cambridge, Mass.: Harvard University Press.

Samuelson, P.A. 1950. Evaluation of real national income. *Oxford Economic Papers*, N.S. 1, January, 1–29. Reprinted in Arrow and Scitovsky (1969), 402–33.

Samuelson, P.A. 1956. Social indifference curves. *Quarterly Journal of Economics* 70, February, 1–22.

Samuelson, P.A. 1962. The gains from international trade once again. *Economic Journal* 72, December, 820–29.

Sanger, C.P. 1895. Recent contributions to mathematical economics. *Economic Journal* 5, March, 113–28.

Scitovsky, T. 1941. A note on welfare propositions in economics. *Review of Economic Studies* 9, November, 77–88. Reprinted in Arrow and Scitovsky (1969), 390–401.

Scitovsky, T. 1942. A reconsideration of the theory of tariffs. *Review of Economic Studies* 9, Summer, 89–110.

Silberberg, E. 1980. Harold Hotelling and marginal cost pricing. *American Economic Review* 70, December, 1054–7.

Vanek, J. 1964. A rehabilitation of 'well-behaved' social indifference curves. *Review of Economic Studies* 31, 87–9.

Viner, J. 1937. *Studies in the Theory of International Trade*. New York: Harper & Brothers.

Wilson, E.B. 1939. Pareto versus Marshall. *Quarterly Journal of Economics* 53, August, 645–50.

competition. Competition is a rivalry between individuals (or groups or nations), and it arises whenever two or more parties strive for something that all cannot obtain. Competition is therefore at least as old as man's history, and Darwin (who borrowed the concept from economist Malthus) applied it to species as economists had applied it to human behaviour.

A concept that is applicable to two cobblers or a thousand shipowners or to tribes and nations is necessarily loosely drawn. When Adam Smith launched economics as a comprehensive science in 1776, he followed this usage. He explained why a reduced supply of a good led to a higher price: the 'competition [which] will immediately begin' among buyers would bid up the price. Similarly if the supply become larger, the price would sink more, the greater 'the competition of the sellers' (Smith, [1776], 1976, pp. 73–4). Here competition was very much like a race: a race to obtain part of reduced supplies or to dispose of a part of increased supplies. Almost nothing except a number of buyers and sellers was necessary for competition to operate. And the greater the number of each, the greater the vigour of competition:

> If this capital [sufficient to trade in a town] is divided between two different grocers, their competition will tend to make both of them sell cheaper, than if it were in the hands of one only; and if it were divided among twenty, their competition would be just so much the greater, and the chance of their combining together, in order to raise the price, just so much the less (ibid., pp. 361–2).

With such a loose concept, there was little occasion to speak of one market as being more or less competitive than another, although this very passage presented the commonsense idea that larger numbers of rivals increased the intensity of competition.

The competition of grocers in a town pertained to competition *within* a market or an industry. Smith made much of the competition of different markets or industries for resources, and he developed what has always remained the main theorem on the allocation of resources in an economy composed of private, competing individuals or enterprises. The argument may be stated: Each owner of a productive resource will seek to employ it where it will yield the largest return. As a result, under competition each resource will be so distributed that it yields the same rate of return in every use. For if a resource were earning more in one use than another, it would be possible for its return in the lower-yielding use to be increased by reallocating it to the higher-yielding use. And this theorem led to what John Stuart Mill called the most frequently encountered proposition in economics: 'There cannot be two prices in the same market' (Mill, 1848, Book II, ch. IV, s. 3).

The competition of different markets or industries for the use of the same resources called attention to some problems which are less important within a single market such as the grocery trade in a town. One must possess knowledge of the investment opportunities in these different employments, and that knowledge is less commonly possessed than knowledge within one market. It often requires a good deal of time to disengage resources from one field and instal them elsewhere. Both of these conditions were recognized by Smith, who spoke of the difficulty of keeping secret the existence of extraordinary profits, and of the long run sometimes required for the attainment of equality of rates of return.

For the next three-quarters of a century the prevailing treatment of competition followed the practice of Smith. One can find occasional hints of a more precise definition of competition, well illustrated by Nassau W. Senior:

> But though, under free competition, cost of production is the regulator of price, its influence is subject to much occasional interruption. Its operation can be supposed to be perfect only if we suppose that there are no disturbing causes, that capital and labour can be at once transferred, and without loss, from one employment to another, and that every producer has full information of the profit to be derived from every mode of production. But it is obvious that these suppositions have no resemblance to the truth. A large portion of the capital essential to production consists of buildings, machinery, and other implements, the results of much time and labour, and of little service for any except their existing purposes ... few capitalists can estimate, except upon an average of some years, the amount of their own profits, and still fewer can estimate those of their neighbours (1836, p. 102).

Senior is hinting at a concept of perfect competition, but the hint is not pursued.

The classical economists felt no need for a precise definition because they viewed monopoly as highly exceptional: Harold Demsetz has counted only one page in 90 devoted to monopoly in *The Wealth of Nations* and only one in 500 in Mill's *Principles of Political Economy*. Indeed the word 'monopoly' was usually restricted to grants by the sovereign of exclusive rights to manufacture, import or sell a commodity; witness the entry in the *Penny Cyclopedia* (1839):

> It seems then that the word monopoly was never used in English Law, except when there was a royal grant authorizing some one or more persons only to deal in or sell a certain commodity or article.

> If a number of individuals were to unite for the purpose of producing any particular article or commodity, and if they should succeed in selling such article very extensively, and almost solely, such individuals in popular language would be said to have a monopoly. Now, as these individuals have no advantages given them by the law over other persons, it is clear they can only sell more of their commodity than other persons by producing the commodity cheaper and better (XV, p. 341).

The ability of rivals to seek out and compete away supernormal profits, unless prevented by legal obstacles, was believed to be the basic reason for the pervasiveness of competition.

In the last third of the 19th century the concept of competition became the subject of intense study. The most popular reason given for this attention is that the growth of large-scale enterprises, including railroads, public utilities, and finally great manufacturing enterprises, made obvious the fact that a simple concept of competition no longer fit the economy of an industrial nation such as England.

A second source of misgiving with the broad definition of competition is that it might not lead to the uniformity of returns to a resource predicted by the theory. The Irish economist Cliffe Leslie repeatedly made this charge:

> Economists have been accustomed to assume that wages on the one hand and profits on the other are, allowing for differences in skill and so forth, equalized by competition, and that neither wages nor profits can anywhere rise above 'the average rate', without a consequent influx of labour or of capital bringing things to a level. Had economists, however, in place of reasoning from an assumption, examined the facts connected with the rate of wages, they would have found, from authentic statistics, the actual differences so great, even in the same occupation, that they are double in one place what they are in another. Statistics of profits are not, indeed, obtainable like statistics of wages; and the fact that they are not so, that the actual profits are kept a profound secret in some of the most prominent trades, is itself enough to deprive the theory of equal profits of its base (1888, pp. 158–9).

The easiest way to combat such criticisms was not to confront them with data – that path was not chosen for many years – but to define competition in such a way as to ensure the desired results such as uniformity of price.

The complications possible with competition were raised also on the theoretical side. William T. Thornton, in his book *On Labour* (1869), denied the fact that prices were determined by the 'law of supply and demand', particularly within labour markets. He employed bizarre examples, such as supply and demand curves which coincided over a vertical range, to show that price could be indeterminate or unresponsive to changes in supply or demand. These objections naturally called forth responses, from both J.S. Mill (*Collected Works*, V) and Fleeming Jenkin, a famous engineer.

The most persuasive reason for the increasing attention to the concepts of economics was the gradual move of economic studies to the universities, which proceeded rapidly in the last decades of the century. The expanding use of mathematics was one major symptom of the development of the formal and abstract theory of economics by Walras, Pareto, Irving Fisher and others. That formalization would scarcely be possible without a more precise specification of the nature of competition, and the replies to Thornton's criticisms were a precursor to this literature.

The groundwork for the development of the concept of perfect competition was laid by Augustin Cournot in 1838 in his *Mathematical Principles of the Theory of Wealth*. He made the first systematic use of the differential calculus to study the implications of profit-maximixing behaviour. Starting with the definition, Profits = Revenue − Costs, Cournot sought to maximize profits under various market conditions. He faced the question: How does revenue (say, pq) vary with output (q)? The natural answer is to *define* competition as that situation in which p does not vary with q – in which the demand curve facing the firm is horizontal. This is precisely what Cournot did:

> The effects of competition have reached their limit, when each of the partial productions D_k [the output of producer k] is *inappreciable*, not only with reference to the total production $D = F(p)$, but also with reference to the derivative $F'(p)$, so that the partial production D_k could be subtracted from D without any appreciable variation resulting in the price of the commodity (Cournot [1838] 1927, p. 90).

This definition of competition was especially appropriate in Cournot's system because, according to his theory of oligopoly, the excess of price over marginal cost approached zero as the number of like producers became large. The argument is as follows:

> Let the revenue of the firm be $q_i p$, and let n identical firms have the same marginal costs, MC. Then the equation for maximum profits for one firm would be

$$p + q_i(\mathrm{d}p/\mathrm{d}q) = MC.$$

> The sum of n such equations would be

$$np + q(\mathrm{d}p/\mathrm{d}q) = nMC,$$

> for $nq_i = q$. This last equation may be written,

$$p = MC - p/nE,$$

> where E is the elasticity of market demand (Cournot, 1838, p. 84).

Cournot believed that this condition of competition was fulfilled 'for a multitude of products, and, among them, for the most important products'.

Cournot's definition was enormously more precise and elegant than Smith's so far as the treatment of numbers was concerned. A market departed from unlimited competition to the extent that price exceeded the marginal cost of the firm, and the difference approached zero as the number of rivals approached infinity. This definition, however, illuminated only the effect of number of rivals on the power of individual firms to influence the market price, on Cournot's special assumption that each rival believed that his output decisions did not affect the output decisions of his rivals. It therefore bore only on what we term market competition.

Cournot did not face the question of the role of information possessed by traders, and this question was taken up by William Stanley Jevons in 1871 in his *Theory of Political Economy*. He characterized a perfect *market* by two conditions:

> (1.) A market, then, is theoretically perfect only when all traders have perfect knowledge of the conditions of supply and demand, and the consequent ratio of exchange; ... (2.) ... there must be perfectly free competition, so that any one

will exchange with any one else upon the slightest advantage appearing. There must be no conspiracies for absorbing and holding supplies to produce unnatural ratios of exchange (Jevons, 1871, pp. 86, 87).

By perfect knowledge Jevons meant only that each trader in a market knew the price bids of every other trader. The second condition ruled out any joint actions by two or more traders, without his noticing that with knowledge so perfect as to know the behaviour of rivals, there might appear the very conspiracies he ruled out. The two conditions dictated that 'there cannot be two prices for the same kind of article' in a perfect market, which he called the 'law of indifference'.

The merging of the concepts of competition and the market was unfortunate, for each deserved a full and separate treatment. A market is an institution for the consummation of transactions. It performs this function efficiently when every buyer who will pay more than the minimum realized price for any class of commodities succeeds in buying the commodity, and every seller who will sell for less than the maximum realized price succeeds in selling the commodity. A market performs these tasks more efficiently if the commodities are well specified and if buyers and sellers are fully informed of their properties and prices. Also a complete, perfect market allows buyers and seller to act on differing expectations of future prices. A market may be perfect and monopolistic or imperfect and competitive. Jevons's mixture of the two has been widely imitated by successors, of course, so that even today a market is commonly treated as a concept subsidiary to competition.

Edgeworth was the first economist to attempt a systematic and rigorous definition of perfect competition. His exposition deserves the closest scrutiny in spite of the fact that few economists of his time or ours have attempted to disentangle and uncover the theorems and conjectures of the *Mathematical Psychics* (1881), probably the most elusively written book of importance in the history of economics. His exposition was the most influential in the entire literature.

The conditions of perfect competition are stated as follows:

> The *field of competition* with reference to a contract, or contracts, under consideration consists of all individuals who are willing and able to recontract about the articles under consideration ...
>
> There is free communication throughout a *normal* competitive field. You might suppose the constituent individuals collected at a point, or connected by telephones – an ideal supposition [1881], but sufficiently approximate to existence or tendency for the purposes of abstract science.
>
> A *perfect* field of competition professes in addition certain properties peculiarly favourable to mathematical calculation; ... The conditions of a *perfect* field are four; the first pair referable to the heading *multiplicity* or continuity, the second to *dividedness* or fluidity.
>
> I. An individual is free to *recontract* with any out of an indefinite number, ...
>
> II. Any individual is free to *contract* (at the same time) with an indefinite number; ... This condition combined with the first appears to involve the indefinite divisibility of each *article* of contract (if any X deal with an indefinite number of Ys he must give each an indefinitely small portion of x); which might be erected into a separate condition.
>
> III. Any individual is free to *recontract* with another independently of, *without the consent* being required of, any third party, ...

IV. Any individual is free to *contract* with another independently of a third party; ...

The failure of the first [condition] involves the failure of the second, but not *vice versa*; and the third and fourth are similarly related (Edgeworth, 1881, pp. 17–19).

The essential elements of this formidable list of conditions are two:

(1) There are an indefinitely large number of independent traders on each side of a market (the Cournot condition).

(2) Each trader can costlessly make tentative contracts with everyone (hence the divisibility of commodities) and alter these contracts (recontract) so long as a more favourable contract can be made. The result is perfect knowledge (the Jevonian condition).

Edgeworth gave an intuitive argument for the need for an indefinitely large number of traders on both sides of a market. It proceeds as follows. Let there be one seller and two buyers, and let the seller gain all the benefits of the sale: each buyer is charged the maximum price he would pay rather than withdraw from the market. If now a second seller appears, he will find it advantageous to offer better terms to the two buyers: 'It will in general be possible for *one* of the [sellers] (without the consent of the other), to *recontract* with the two [buyers], so that for all those three parties the recontract is more advantageous than the previously existing contract' (ibid., p. 35). As the numbers of traders on each side increase, the price approaches the competitive equilibrium level where no individual trader can influence it.

A defect in this argument is that it ignores the fact that if the traders on one or both sides of the market, be they 2, or 2000 or 2,000,000, join together they can do better *individually* than by competing. If traders on each side join, however, there will be bilateral monopoly, not competition. Edgeworth gives no reason why the combination of traders fails to take place. Only in modern times has the reason for independent behaviour by rivals been established: the costs of reaching and enforcing agreements on joint action increase with both the number of rivals and the complexity of the transactions. At a certain level – quite possibly with only two traders under some conditions – the costs of joint action exceed the gain to at least some of the traders, and independent behaviour emerges.

Edgeworth's 'conjecture', as it is now often called, that a unique, competitive price would emerge when the number of traders became large, has given rise to a modern literature vast in scope and often highly advanced in its mathematical techniques (for references, see Hildenbrand, 1974). One result in this literature is that in the case of a large (infinite) number of traders, no coalition of a portion of the traders can exclude traders outside the coalition from trading at the price-taking equilibrium.

Edgeworth's introduction of the requirement that the commodity or service that is traded by highly divisible is a response to the following problem:

Suppose a market, consisting of an equal number of masters and servants, offering respectively wages and service; subject to the condition that no man can serve two masters, no master employ more than one man; or suppose equilibrium already established between such parties to be disturbed by any sudden influx of wealth into the hands of the masters. Then there is no *determinate*, and very generally *unique*, arrangement towards which the system tends under the operation of, may we say, a law of Nature, and which would be predictable if we knew beforehand the real requirements of each, or of the average, dealer; ... (Edgeworth, 1881, p. 46).

Consider the simple example: a thousand masters will each employ a man at any wage below 100; a thousand labourers will each work for any wage above 50. There will be a single wage rate: knowledge and numbers are sufficient to lead a worker to seek a master paying more than the going rate or a master to seek out a worker receiving less than the market rate. But any rate between 50 and 100 is a possible equilibrium. But if a single worker leaves the market, the wage will rise to 100, and if a single employer withdraws, the wage will fall to 50. This ability of a single trader to affect the price arises because of the lumpiness of the article traded (here a worker's labour for a given period). Once a worker can work for two masters, the withdrawal of one worker in a thousand will reduce the available hours of work per day to each employer by only 8/1000 hours or 4.8 minutes per day, with only a negligible influence upon the wage rate. Alternatively, a distribution of wage offers and demands would also eliminate the indeterminacy and market power.

Edgeworth's analysis was limited to competition within a market, and it was left to John Bates Clark to emphasize the need for mobility of resources if the return on each resource was to be equalized in every use.

... there is an ideal arrangement of the elements of society, to which the force of competition, acting on individual men, would make the society conform. The producing organism actually shapes itself about his model, and at no time does it vary greatly from it ... We must use assumptions boldly and advisedly, make labour and capital absolutely mobile, and letting competition work in ideal perfection (Clark, 1899, pp. 68, 71).

Perfect and free mobility of resources is of course an even more extreme assumption than the other conditions required for perfect competition because there is less reason to believe that free movement of resources is even approached in the real economy. Nor is the assumption of perfect mobility necessary to eliminate monopoly power in a market: in the Victorian age, the price of wheat of Iowa was set in Liverpool even though transportation costs were substantial. The assumption is usually necessary to attain strict equality in the price of a good at every point (the law of one price), although even this is not strictly true (as in the factor price equalization theorem). Clark also demanded that the economy be stationary for perfect competition, a condition we shall return to later.

All the elements of a concept of perfect competition were in place by 1900, and this concept increasingly became the standard model of economic theory thereafter. The most influential statement of the conditions for perfect competition was made by Frank H. Knight in his doctoral dissertation, *Risk, Uncertainty and Profit* (1921). The conditions were stated in extreme form; for example, 'There must be perfect, continuous, costless intercommunication between all individual members of the society' (Knight, 1921, p. 78) – so Jones in Seattle would know the price of potatoes and be able costlessly to ship to Smith in Miami a bushel of potatoes at every moment of time.

Of course these conditions are not *necessary*, but only sufficient, to achieve the competitive equilibrium. For example, if even a considerable fraction of buyers knows that seller A is charging more than B for a given commodity, their patronage may be quite enough to force A to reduce his price to that of B. Nor are the various conditions independent of one another: for example, if it is very cheap for either a commodity or its buyers or sellers to move between two places, that will insure that the prices in the two places will be widely known.

Along with the development of the concept of competition as a standard component of the theory of prices and the allocation of resources, it acquired a growing role as the criterion by which to judge the efficiency of actual markets. Adam Smith had already advanced the proposition that output was maximized in a private enterprise economy with competition. If each owner of a resource maximized the return from his resources, then (in the absence of 'external' effects of one person's actions on others) aggregate output would be maximized. This theorem (labelled 'on maximum satisfaction') was developed and qualified by Léon Walras (1874), Alfred Marshall (1890), Pareto (1895–6, 1907), Pigou (1912) and a host of modern economists.

Competition is much too central a concept in economics to remain unaffected when economists change their interests or analytical methods. We may illustrate this fact by the problem of economic change.

In a regime of change, of growing population and capital or innovations or new consumer demands, the problem of defining competition is much more difficult than it is for the stationary economy. Unless the change is predictable with precision, knowledge must necessarily be incomplete and errors and lags in adaptation to new conditions can be large. For this reason, indeed, J.B. Clark believed that perfect competition was achievable only in the stationary economy.

Even short-run changes in market price raise the question: is the change in price initiated by a particular seller or buyer, and if so, is this trader not facing a negatively sloping demand curve or a positively sloping supply curve? The infinitely elastic supply and demand curves of perfectly competitive equilibrium seem inapplicable to periods of changing market conditions. Some economists nevertheless retain the condition that individual traders cannot influence price by introducing a hypothetical auctioneer who announces price changes.

A partial adaptation of the competitive concept to change is made by making it a long-run equilibrium concept. Even if resources are not costlessly mobile and even if entrepreneurs do not have perfect foresight, one can analyse the rate of approach of returns on resources to equality. If an industry experiences a once-for-all large change, it could be in competitive equilibrium before and after the change, and the equilibria could be studied by competitive theory (comparative statics).

This adaptation did not satisfy Joseph Schumpeter, who believed that incessant change in products and production methods was the very essence of competitive capitalism. He argued that the displacing of one product or method by another, a process which he called creative destruction, made the concept of perfect competition irrelevant to either positive analysis or welfare judgements. If the monopoly that reduced output, compared to competition, by 10 per cent in one year, increased output by 100 per cent over the next two decades, then monopoly might be preferred to stagnant competition.

It is crucial to this argument that monopoly provides large, though temporary, rewards to successful innovators but competition does not:

But perfectly free entry into a *new* field may make it impossible to enter it at all. The introduction of new methods of production and new commodities is hardly conceivable with perfect – and perfectly prompt – competition from the start. And this means that the bulk of what we call economic progress is incompatible with it. As a matter of fact, perfect competition is and always has been temporarily suspended whenever anything new is being introduced – automatically or by measures devised

for that purpose – even in otherwise perfectly competitive conditions (Schumpeter, 1942, pp. 104–5).

Schumpeter relies on instantaneous rivalry to eliminate the incentives to innovation under competition, and the conclusion would not hold if competition is defined in terms of long-run equilibrium.

Nevertheless the issue is not disposed of so easily. If change is continuous rather than sporadic, long-run equilibria will never be fully achieved. Several economists have emphasized that alterations in the concept of competition are called for in periods of historical change. Kirzner has emphasized the role of entrepreneurial rivalry in competition, whereas such rivalry is nonexistent in a perfectly competitive equilibrium. Demsetz has proposed a concept of laissez-faire competition, in which freedom of resources to move into any use is the central element. Such realistic reversions to the competitive concept of the classical economists have not been systematically formalized into theoretical models.

The concept of perfect competition, or indeed any theoretically precise concept of competition, will not be met by the actual condition of competition in any industry. John Maurice Clark made the most influential effort to create a concept of 'workable competition' which would serve as a working rule for public policies which seek to preserve or increase competition.

Clark emphasized the fact that if one requisite of perfect competition is absent, it may be desirable that a second requisite also be unfulfilled. For example, with instantaneous mobility but imperfect knowledge, members of an occupation would keep shifting back and forth between two cities, always overshooting the amount of migration which would equalize wage rates. This propensity to overshoot equilibrium would be corrected with less mobility of labour. This problem was later formalized as the theory of the 'second best'.

The essence of the concept of workable competition was the belief that 'long-run curves, both of cost and of demand, are much flatter than short-run curves, and much flatter than the curves which are commonly used in the diagrams of theorists' (J.M. Clark, 1940, p. 460). This correct and sensible view led to a proliferation of studies, usually in doctoral dissertations, of individual industries, in which the workableness of competition in each industry was appraised. Unfortunately there were no objective criteria to guide these judgements, and there was no evidence that the studies were accepted by the governmental agencies which administered competitive policies.

The popularity of the concept of perfect competition in theoretical economics is as great today as it has ever been. The concept is equally popular as first approximation in the more concrete studies of markets and industries that comprise the field of 'industrial organization' (applied microeconomics). The limitations of the concept in dealing with conditions of persistent and imperfectly predicted change will not be removed until economics possesses a developed theory of change. Even within a stationary economic setting the concept is being deepened by mathematical economists (see Mas-Colell, 1982). Meanwhile the central elements of competition – the freedom of traders to use their resources where they will, and exchange them at any price they wish – will continue to play a major role in the economics of an enterprise economy.

See also EXCHANGE; LARGE ECONOMIES; PERFECT COMPETITION; PERFECTLY AND IMPERFECTLY COMPETITIVE MARKETS.

GEORGE J. STIGLER

BIBLIOGRAPHY

Clark, J.B. 1899. *The Distribution of Wealth.* London: Macmillan.

Clark, J.M. 1940. Toward a concept of workable competition. *American Economic Review*, June; reprinted in *Readings in the Social Control of Industry*, Philadelphia: Blakiston, 1942.

Cournot, A. 1838. *Researches into the Mathematical Principles of the Theory of Wealth*. Reprinted New York: Macmillan, 1927.

Demsetz, H. 1982. *Economic, Legal and Political Dimensions of Competition*. Amsterdam: North-Holland Publishing Company.

Edgeworth, F.Y. 1881. *Mathematical Psychics*. London: Kegan Paul, 1932.

Hildenbrand, W. 1974. *Core and Equilibria of a Large Economy*. Princeton: Princeton University Press.

Jevons, W.S. 1871. *The Theory of Political Economy*. London: Macmillan.

Kirzner, I.M. 1973. *Competition and Entrepreneurship*. Chicago: University of Chicago Press.

Knight, F.H. 1921. *Risk, Uncertainty and Profit*, Part 2. Boston: Houghton Mifflin Co.

Leslie, T.E. Cliffe. 1888. *Essays in Political Economy and Moral Philosophy*. London: Longmans Green.

McNulty, P.J. 1967. A note on the history of perfect competition. *Journal of Political Economy* 75(4), August, 395–9.

Marshall, A. 1890. *Principles of Economics*. London: Macmillan.

Mas-Colell, A. (ed.) 1982. *Noncooperative Approaches to the Theory of Perfect Competition*. New York: Academic Press.

Mill, J.S. 1848. *Principles of Political Economy*. In *Collected Works*, ed. J.M. Robson, Toronto: University of Toronto Press, 1965.

Nutter, G.W. 1951. *The Extent of Enterprise Monopoly in the United States, 1899–1939*. Chicago: University of Chicago Press.

Penny Cyclopedia. 1839.

Schumpeter, J.A. 1942. *Capitalism, Socialism and Democracy*. New York: Harper & Bros.

Senior, N.W. 1836. *Political Economy*. London: W. Clowes.

Shepherd, W.G. 1982. Causes of increased competition in the US economy, 1939–1980. *Review of Economics and Statistics* 64(4), November, 613–26.

Smith, A. 1776. *The Wealth of Nations*. Glasgow edn, Oxford University Press, 1976.

Stigler, G.J. 1957. Perfect competition, historically contemplated. *Journal of Political Economy* 65, February, 1–17.

Stigler, G.J. and Sherwin, R. 1985. The extent of the market. *Journal of Law and Economics* 28(3), 555–85.

Thornton, W.T. 1869. *On Labour*. London: Macmillan.

competition: Austrian conceptions. The essence of Austrian economics is its emphasis on the ongoing economic process as opposed to the equilibrium analysis of neoclassical theory. Austrian concepts of competition reflect this emphasis. Indeed, one of the central challenges by Austrians to the neoclassical model, and a common denominator of virtually all Austrian economics, is the rejection of the concept of perfect competition. In this respect, a number of economists who cannot be considered Austrian in all aspects of their work, share, nonetheless, the Austrian emphasis on actual market activities and processes – for example, Joseph Schumpeter (1942), J.M. Clark (1961), Fritz Machlup (1942) and others.

When the concept of competition entered economics at the hands of Adam Smith and his predecessors, it was not clearly defined, but it generally meant entry by firms into profitable industries (or exit from unprofitable ones) and the raising or lowering of price by existing firms according to market conditions. There was little recognition, and virtually no analysis, of entrepreneurship as it might be reflected in these and other forms of competition, but there was a recognition that business firms do in most situations have some control over market prices, with the degree of control varying inversely with the number of firms in the industry. These basic ideas, expanded and supplemented, are generally compatible with most modern Austrian analysis.

What is objectionable to Austrian economists is the neoclassical concept of perfect competition, developed during the 19th and early 20th centuries. The development began with Cournot (1838), whose concern it was to specify as rigorously as possible the *effects* of competition, after the *process* of competition had reached its limits. His conceptualization of this situation was a market structure in which the output of any one firm could be subtracted from total industry output with no discernible effect on price. Later contributions by Jevons, Edgeworth, J.B. Clark and Frank Knight led to the model of perfect competition as we know it today (Stigler, 1957; McNulty, 1967).

The trouble with the concept from the Austrian point of view, as Hayek has emphasized, is that it describes an equilibrium situation but says nothing about the competitive process which led to that equilibrium. Indeed, it robs the firm of all business activities which might reasonably be associated with the verb 'to compete' (Hayek, 1948). Thus, firms in the perfectly competitive model do not raise or lower prices, differentiate their products, advertise, try to change their cost structures relative to their competitors, or do any of the other things done by business firms in a dynamic economic system. This was precisely the reason why Schumpeter insisted on the irrelevance of the concept of perfect competition to an understanding of the capitalist process.

For Schumpeter, any realistic analysis of competition would require a shift in analytical focus from the question of how the economy allocates resources efficiently to that of how it creates and destroys them. The entrepreneur, a neglected figure in classical and neoclassical economics, is the central figure in the Schumpeterian analytical framework. The entrepreneur plays a disequilibrating role in the market process by interrupting the 'circular flow' of economic life, that is, the ongoing production of existing goods and services under existing technologies and methods of production and organization. He does this by innovating – i.e. by introducing the new product, the new market, the new technology, the new source of raw materials and other factor inputs, the new type of industrial organization, etc. The result is a concept of competition grounded in cost and quality advantages which Schumpeter felt is much more important than the price competition of traditional theory and is the basis of the 'creative destruction' of the capitalist economic process. It produces an internal efficiency within the business firm, the importance of which for economic welfare is far greater, Schumpeter argued, than the allocative efficiency of traditional economic theory (Schumpeter, 1942).

His emphasis on the advantages of the firm's internal efficiency led Schumpeter to a greater tolerance for large-scale business organizations, even for those enjoying some degree of monopoly power, than was typical of many more traditional theorists of his time. This is a not uncommon characteristic of Austrian economics. Hayek, for example, makes the distinction between entrenched monopoly, with its probable higher-than-necessary costs, and a monopoly based on superior efficiency which does relatively little harm since in all probability it will disappear, or be forced to adjust to market conditions, as soon as another firm becomes more efficient in providing the same or a similar good or service (Hayek, 1948). And that is precisely Schumpeter's point. The ground under even large-scale enterprise is constantly shaking as a result of the competitive threat from the new firm, the new management, or the new idea. Schumpeter's competitive analysis was less a defence of monopoly power than of certain business activities which were judged to be monopolistic only from the comparative standpoint of the model of perfect competition. He insisted that the quality of a firm's entrepreneurship was of far greater significance than its mere size.

The leading contemporary Austrian theorist of competition is Israel Kirzner (1973). Kirzner's approach draws on the analysis of market processes and the concept of 'human action' developed earlier by Ludwig von Mises. For von Mises, entrepreneurship is human action in the market which successfully directs the flow of resources toward the fulfilment of consumer wants (von Mises, 1949). Kirzner's more fully developed theory of competition is based on the idea that the means–end nexus of economic life is not given but is itself subject to creative human action. This creative role Kirzner defines as entrepreneurship, and it is essentially the ability to detect new but desired human wants, as well as new resources, techniques, or other ways through which to satisfy them. Whether he discovers new wants or new means of satisfying old ones, the Kirznerian entrepreneur is the one who sees and exploits what others fail to notice – the profit opportunities inherent in any situation in which the prices of factor inputs fall short of the price of the final product.

There is a difference between Kirzner's theory of entrepreneurship and that of Schumpeter. Schumpeter's entrepreneur is a disequilibrating force in the economic system; he initiates economic change. Kirzner's entrepreneur plays an equilibrating role; the changes he brings about are responses to the mistaken decisions and missed opportunities he detects in the market. Unlike Schumpeter's entrepreneur, he is not so much the creator of his own opportunities as a responder to the hitherto unnoticed opportunities that already exist in the market. Thus, in the competitive market process, the Schumpeterian and Kirznerian entrepreneurs may complement each other – the one creating change, the other responding to it.

Austrian dissatisfaction with the perfectly competitive model extends to the theories of imperfect and monopolistic competition. Hayek's and Kirzner's criticisms are the same as of perfect competition, i.e., that the analysis is limited to an equilibrium situation in which the underlying data are assumed to be adjusted to each other, whereas the relevant problem is the process through which adjustment occurs. Schumpeter criticized monopolistic competition for its continued acceptance of an invarying economic structure and forms of industrial organization. Nonetheless, the incorporation into economic theory of quality competition and sales efforts, complementing the traditional and limited focus on price competition, as well as the efforts on the part of some industrial organization specialists and institutional economists to analyse and explain actual market processes, are developments that are generally within the Austrian tradition.

PAUL J. MCNULTY

See also AUSTRIAN SCHOOL OF ECONOMICS; CREATIVE DESTRUCTION.

BIBLIOGRAPHY

Clark, J.M. 1961. *Competition as a Dynamic Process*. Washington, DC: Brookings.

Cournot, A.A. 1838. *Recherches sur les principes mathématiques de la théorie des richesses*. Paris: Hachette.

Hayek, F.A. von. 1948. The meaning of competition. In F.A. Hayek, *Individualism and Economic Order*, London: George Routledge & Sons.

Kirzner, I. 1973. *Competition and Entrepreneurship*. Chicago: University of Chicago Press.

Machlup, F. 1942. Competition, pliopoly, and profit. Pts I–II. *Economica*, N.S. 9, Pt. I, February, 1–23, Pt. II, May, 153–73.

McNulty, P. 1967. A note on the history of perfect competition. *Journal of Political Economy* 75(4), Part 1, August, 395–9.

Mises, L. von. 1949. *Human Action*. New Haven: Yale University Press.

Schumpeter J. 1942. *Capitalism, Socialism, and Democracy*. New York: Harper & Row, 1962.

Stigler, G. 1957. Perfect competition, historically contemplated. *Journal of Political Economy* 65, February, 1–17.

competition: classical conceptions.

Only through the principle of competition has political economy any pretension to the character of a science. So far as rents, profits, wages, prices, are determined by competition, laws may be assigned for them. Assume competition to be their exclusive regulator, and principles of broad generality and scientific precision may be laid down, according to which they will be regulated (John Stuart Mill, *Principles of Political Economy*, p. 242).

In all versions of economic theory 'competition', variously defined, is a central organizing concept. Yet the relationship between different definitions of competition and differences in the theory of value has not been fully appreciated. In particular, the characteristics of 'perfect' competition (notably the conditions which ensure price-taking) are often read back, illegitimately, into classical discussions of competition.

The mechanisms which determine the economic behaviour of industrial capitalism are not self-evident. As a form of economy in which production and distribution proceed by means of a generalized process of exchange (in particular by the sale and purchase of labour) it possesses no obvious direct mechanisms of economic and social coordination. Yet, in so far as these operations constitute a system, they must be endowed with some degree of regularity, the causal foundations of which may be revealed by analysis. The first steps in economic investigation which accompanied the beginnings of industrial capitalism consisted of a variety of attempts to identify such regularities, often by means of detailed description and enumeration, as in the works of Sir William Petty, and hence to establish the dominant causes underlying the behaviour of markets. But what was required was not simply the description and classification which precedes analysis, but abstraction, the transcendence of political arithmetic (Smith, 1776, p. 501).

The culmination of the search for a coherent abstract characterization of markets, and hence the foundation of modern economic analysis, is to be found in chapter 7 of Book I of Adam Smith's *Wealth of Nations* – 'Of the natural and market price of commodities'. In this chapter Smith presented the first satisfactory formulation of the regularity inherent in price formation. The idea, partially developed earlier by Cantillon, and by Turgot in his discussion of the circulation of money, was that

There is in every society ... an ordinary or average rate of both wages and profits ... When the price of any commodity is neither more nor less than what is sufficient to pay the rent of land, the wages of labour, and the profits of stock employed ... according to their natural rates, the commodity is then sold for what may be called its natural price.

and that

The natural price ... is, as it were, the central price, to which the prices of all commodities are continually gravitating. Different accidents may sometimes keep them suspended a good deal above it, and sometimes force them down somewhat below it. But whatever may be the obstacles which hinder them from settling in this center of repose and continuance, they are continually tending towards it (Smith, 1776, p. 65).

Thus the natural price encapsulates the persistent element in economic behaviour. And that persistence derives from the ubiquitous force of competition: or, as Smith put it, the condition of 'perfect liberty' in which 'the whole of the advantages and disadvantages of the different employments of labour and stock must ... be either perfectly equal or continually tending to equality' (p. 111), for the natural price is 'the price of free competition' (p. 68).

The relationship between competition and the establishment of what Petty called 'intrinsic value' had been discussed in the works of Petty, Boisguillebert, Cantillon and Harris as the outcome of rival bargaining in price formation, competition being the greater when the number of bargainers was such that none has a direct influence on price. Quesnay expressed the formation of competitive prices as being 'independent of mens' will ... far from being an arbitrary value or a value which is established by agreement between the contracting parties' (in Meek, 1962, p. 90), but he did not relate the *organization of production* to the formation of prices in competitive markets. Consideration of that relationship required the development of a general conception of the role of capital, and with it the notion of a general rate of profit formed by the competitive disposition of capital between alternative investments (Vaggi, 1987).

A significant step in this direction was made by Turgot, who both conceived of the process of production as part of the circulation of money:

> We see ... how the cultivation of land, manufactures of all kinds, and all branches of commerce depend upon a mass of capitals, or movable accumulated wealth, which, having been first advanced by the Entrepreneurs in each of these different classes of work, must return to them every year with a regular profit ... It is this continual advance and return of capitals which constitutes *what ought to be called the circulation of money* (Turgot, 1973, p. 148)

and saw that the structure of investments would tend to be that which yielded a uniform rate of profit:

> It is obvious that the annual products which can be derived from capitals invested in these different employments are mutually limited by one another, and that all are relative to the existing rate of interest on money (Turgot, 1973, p. 70).

However, Turgot neither related the determination of the rate of profit to production in general – he accepted the Physiocratic idea that the incomes of the industrial and commercial classes were 'paid' by agriculture – nor developed the conceptual framework which linked the formation of prices and of the rate of profit to the overall organization of the economy. These were to be Smith's achievements:

> If ... the quantity brought to market should at any time fall short of the effectual demand, some of the component parts of its price must rise above their natural rate. If it is rent, the interest of all other landlords will naturally prompt them to prepare more land for the raising of this commodity; if it is wages or profit, the interest of all other labourers and dealers will soon prompt them to employ more labour and stock in preparing and bringing it to market. The quantity brought thither will soon be sufficient to supply the effectual demand. All the different parts of its price will soon sink to their natural rate, and the whole price to its natural price (Smith, 1776, p. 65).

So in a competitive market there will be a tendency for the actual prices (or 'market prices' as Smith called them) to be relatively high when the quantity brought to market is less than the effectual demand (the quantity that would be bought at the natural price) and relatively low when the quantity brought to market exceeds the effectual demand. This working of competition was known as the 'Law of Supply and Demand'. The working of competition which constitutes the 'Law' do not identify the phenomena which *determine* natural prices. The 'Law' of supply and demand should not be confused with supply and demand *theory*, i.e. the neoclassical theory of price determination which was to be developed one hundred years later. Nor should Smith's discussion of the tendencies of concrete market prices be confused with supply and demand functions, which are loci of equilibrium prices.

Adam Smith's conception of 'perfect liberty' consists of the mobility of labour and stock between different uses – the mobility that is necessary for the establishment of 'an ordinary or average rate both of wages and profits' and hence for the gravitation of market prices toward natural prices. Smith identifies four reasons why market prices may deviate 'for a long time together' above natural price, creating differentials in the rate of profit, all of which involve restriction of mobility:

(a) extra demand can be 'concealed', though 'secrets of this kind ... can seldom be long kept';

(b) secret technical advantages;

(c) 'a monopoly granted either to an individual or a trading company';

(d) 'exclusive privileges of corporations, statutes of apprenticeship, and all those laws which restrain, in particular employments, the competition to a smaller number than might otherwise go into them.'

For Smith there is some similarity in the forces acting on wages and profits which derives from his conceiving of the capitalist as personally involved in the prosecution of a particular trade or business. So the rate of profit, like the rate of wages, may be differentiated between sectors by 'the agreeableness or disagreeableness of the business', even though 'the average and ordinary rates of profit in the different employments of stock should be more nearly upon a level than the pecuniary wages of the different sorts of labour' (1776, p. 124). Landlords, capitalists and workers are all active agents of mobility. In Ricardo's discussion the emphasis shifted towards the distinctive role of capital:

> It is, then, the desire, which every capitalist has, of diverting his funds from a less to a more profitable employment, that prevents the market price of commodities from continuing for any length of time either much above, or much below their natural price (Ricardo, 1817, p. 91).

Ricardo used the term 'monopoly price' to refer to commodities 'the value of which is determined by their scarcity alone', such as paintings, rare books and rare wines (pp. 249–51) which have 'acquired a fanciful value', and he argued that for 'Commodities which are monopolised, either by an individual, or by a company ... their price has no necessary connexion with their natural value' (p. 385). His analysis of value and distribution is accordingly confined to 'By far the greatest part of those goods which are the object of desire ... such commodities only as can be increased in quantity by the exertion of human labour, and on the production of which competition operates without restraint' (p. 12).

For Marx competition is synonymous with the generalization of capitalist relations of production. Competition is thus related to the rise to dominance of the capitalist mode of production:

> While free competition has dissolved the barriers of earlier relations and modes of production, it is necessary to observe first of all that the things which were a barrier to it were the inherent limits of earlier modes of production, within which they spontaneously developed and moved. These limits became barriers only after the forces of production and the relations of intercourse had developed sufficiently to enable capital as such to emerge as the dominant principle of production. The limits which it tore down were barriers to its motion, its development and realization. It is by no means the case that it thereby suspended all limits, nor all barriers, but rather only the limits not corresponding to it ... Free competition is the real development of capital (Marx, 1973, pp. 649–50).

And as capitalism itself develops so does competition:

> On the one hand ... [capital] creates means by which to overcome obstacles that spring from the nature of production itself, and on the other hand, with the development of the mode of production peculiar to itself, it eliminates all the legal and extra-economic impediments to its freedom of movement in the different spheres of production. Above all it overturns all the legal or traditional barriers that would prevent it from buying this or that kind of labour-power as it sees fit, or from appropriating this or that kind of labour (Marx, 1867, p. 1013).

The concentration of capital (increasing unit size of firms) and, in particular, the centralization of capital (cohesion of existing capitals) destroys and *recreates* competition. Competition is one of the most powerful 'levers of centralization', and

> The centralization of capitals, or the process of their attraction, becomes more intense in proportion as the specifically capitalist mode of production develops along with accumulation. In its turn centralization becomes one of the greatest levers of its development (Marx, 1867, p. 778n).

Like Smith and Ricardo, Marx, relates the development of competition to the establishment of the general rate of profit:

> What competition, first in a single sphere, achieves is a single market value and market price derived from the individual values of commodities. And it is competition of capitals in various spheres, which first brings out the price of production equalising the rates of profit in the different spheres. The latter process requires a higher stage of capitalist production than the previous one (Marx, 1894, p. 180).

It is in his conception of the circuit of capital that Marx best portrays capitalist competition. The image is one of capital as a homogeneous mass of value (money) seeking its maximum return. Profits are created by embodying capital in the process of production, the commodity outputs of which must be realized, i.e. returned to the homogeneous money form to be reinvested. Competition is thus characteristic of the capitalist mode of accumulation; mobility and restructuring are two aspects of the same phenomenon.

Marx's general conception of capital as a system corroborates Quesnay's notion of an economy operating 'independent of men's will'. This does not mean that there may not be circumstances in which individual capitals exercise some control in particular markets – indeed such limitations may be necessary for the accumulation process to proceed in certain lines. Capital removes only those barriers which *limit* its accumulation. The market control exercised in some lines of modern industry is not necessarily a limitation but may be a prerequisite of production on an extended scale. Aggregate capital flows discipline the actions of individual capitals, and hence endow the system with the regularity manifest in the perpetual tendency, successfully contradicted and recreated, towards a general rate of profit and associated prices.

Competition not only establishes the object of analysis, natural prices and the general rate of profit, but makes meaningful analysis possible, since it allows the operations of the capitalist economy to be characterized in a manner which permits theoretical statements of general validity to be made about them.

Theory proceeds by the extraction from reality of those forces which are believed to be dominant and persistent, and the formation of those elements into a formal system, the solution of which is to determine the magnitude or state of the variables under consideration. It is obvious that the solution will not, except by a fluke, correspond to the actual magnitudes of the variables ruling at any one time, for these will be the outcome not solely of the elements grouped under the heading 'dominant and persistent', but also of the myriad of other forces excluded from the analysis as transitory, peculiar or specific (lacking general significance) which may, at any moment, exert a more or less powerful effect. Nonetheless, the practice of analysis embodies the assumption that the forces comprising the theory *are* dominant, and that the determined magnitudes will, on average, tend to be established. In any satisfactory analytical scheme these magnitudes must be centres of gravitation, capturing the essential character of the phenomena under consideration.

The importance of Smith's use of competition is now apparent. Theory cannot exist in a vacuum. Simply labelling forces dominant is not enough. These forces must operate through a process which establishes their dominance and through which the 'law-governed' nature of the system is manifest. That process is competition, which both enforces and expresses the attempt of individual capitals to maximize profits. Thus important aspects of the behaviour of a capitalist market economy may be captured at a sufficient level of generality to permit the formulation of general causal statements, i.e. to permit analysis. Without this step, which constitutes the establishment of what was called above the *method* of analysis, it would have been impossible to develop any general form of economic *theory*.

The classical theory of value and distribution may be shown to provide a logically coherent explanation of the determination of the general rate of profit and hence of natural prices (prices of production) taking as data (see Sraffa, 1960):

(a) the size and composition of social output;

(b) the technique in use; and

(c) the real wage.

The classical achievement is thus composed of two independent elements: (a) the characterization of the object of the theory of value; and (b) the provision of a theory for the determination of that object. Underlying the former is the concept of gravitation imposed by competition, and underlying the latter the concept of gravitation inherent in theoretical abstraction. Any alternative system must not simply provide a different theory but also achieve a similar congruence with the traditional method.

The development in the final quarter of the 19th century of what was to become known as the neoclassical theory of value and distribution was an attempt to provide an alternative to a classical theory embroiled in the logical difficulties inherent in the labour theory of value and sullied by unsavoury associations with radicalism and Marxism. But despite the dramatic change in theory that was to be heralded by the works of Jevons, Menger and Walras, the method of analysis which characterized the object the theory was to explain stayed fundamentally the same; the new theory was an alternative explanation of the same phenomena. Marshall labelled natural prices 'long-run normal prices', and declared that, as far as his discussion of value was concerned 'the present volume is chiefly concerned ... with the normal relations of wages, profits, prices etc., for rather long periods' (1920, p. 315). The same continuity of method may be found in the work of Walras (1874–7, pp. 224, 380), Jevons (1871, pp. 86, 135–6), Böhm-Bawerk (1899, p. 380) and Wicksell (1934, p. 97).

Nonetheless, the structure of neoclassical theory is such that a different notion of competition is required. The classical emphasis on mobility must be supplemented by a precise definition of the relationships presumed to exist between individual agents. The fundamental concept of 'perfect' competition, for example, encompasses the idea that the influence of each individual participant in the economy is 'negligible', which in turn leads to the idea of an economy with infinitely many participants (Aumann, 1964). Such formulations are entirely absent from the classical conception of competition, since the classical theory is not constructed around individual constrained utility maximization.

JOHN EATWELL

See also CENTRE OF GRAVITATION; NATURAL AND NORMAL CONDITIONS; SURPLUS APPROACH TO VALUE AND DISTRIBUTION.

BIBLIOGRAPHY

Aumann, R.J. 1964. Markets with a continuum of traders. *Econometrica* 32, 39–50.

Böhm-Bawerk, E. von. 1899. *Capital and Interest*, Vol. II. South Holland, Illinois: Libertarian Press, 1959.

Jevons, W.S. 1871. *Theory of Political Economy*. Harmondsworth: Penguin, 1970.

Marshall, A. 1920. *Principles of Economics*. 8th edn, London: Macmillan.

Marx, K. 1867. *Capital*, Vol. I. Harmondsworth: Penguin, 1976.

Marx, K. 1894. *Capital*, Vol. III. New York: International Publishers, 1967.

Marx, K. 1973. *Grundrisse*. Harmondsworth: Penguin.

Meek, R.L. 1956. *Studies in the Labour Theory of Value*. London: Lawrence & Wishart.

Meek, R.L. 1962. *The Economics of Physiocracy*. London: Allen & Unwin.

Meek, R.L. 1973. Introduction to Turgot (1973).

Mill, J.S. 1848. *Principles of Political Economy*. London: Parker.

Ricardo, D. 1817. *Principles of Political Economy and Taxation*. Ed. P. Sraffa, Cambridge: Cambridge University Press, 1951.

Smith, A. 1776. *An Inquiry into the Nature and Causes of the Wealth of Nations*. London: Methuen, 1961.

Sraffa, P. 1960. *Production of Commodities by Means of Commodities*. Cambridge: Cambridge University Press.

Turgot, A.J.R. 1973. *Turgot on Progress, Sociology and Economics*, ed. R.L. Meek, Cambridge: Cambridge University Press.

Vaggi, G. 1987. *The Economics of François Quesnay*. London: Macmillan.

Walras, M.E.L. 1874–7. *Elements of Pure Economics*. Homewood, Ill.: Irwin, 1954.

Wicksell, K. 1934. *Lectures on Political Economy*, Vol. I. London: Routledge & Kegan Paul.

competition: marxian conceptions. In the works of the classical economists such as Smith (1776) and Ricardo (1817), competition was identified as a central concept in economic theory. Free competition was regarded as the organizing and equilibrating force in an exchange society, bringing about natural prices as centres of gravity for market prices through capital flows from areas with low rates of returns to areas with high rates. Yet compared with the theory of perfect competition, classical free competition was defined more in terms of economic behaviour than of market structure (Stigler, 1957; McNulty, 1968; Eatwell, 1982). Marx's concept of competition, rooted in the classical theory of free competition, also refers to the behavioural activities of the capitalist firm. Marx, however, more than the classics, cast serious doubts on the stability properties of the competitive process, and he conceptualized competition as inter-firm dynamics carried out through reorganization of the firm and technical change. In this it somewhat resembles the modern theory of oligopolistic rivalry (Friedman, 1982) and Schumpeter's notion of competition as a process of 'creative destruction' (1943).

THE DYNAMICS OF COMPETITION IN MARX. The marxian concept of competition though already adumbrated in his early writings (1847, 1857/8) is systematically developed in his later work (1861/3, 1867, 1893, 1894). It is derived from his theory of the behaviour of the capitalist firm (Kuruma, 1973). The driving force for economic change and growth is the goal of the capitalist firm to grow and to expand ('the self-expansion of capital'). From the inter-firm dynamics results economic evolution, accumulation and growth, but also the downfall of old firms and the centralization of capital (Marx, 1867, ch. 25) by which the competition and rivalry become fiercer. Firms are not conceived as powerless economic agents adjusting passively toward parametrically given techniques, prices and quantities but as actively seeking the reorganization of production and market activities in the context of rivals' possible reactions. Firms also are not seen as price takers but rather as price-setting firms with their market shares adjusting through the reaction of the rivals or as quantity-setting firms (Marx, 1894, ch. 10) with prices and profits determined through market interactions. Price differentiation even for homogeneous products is assumed to exist under disequilibrium conditions (Marx, 1894, ch. 10). Monopoly firms are considered exceptional cases as 'temporary monopolies' (Marx, 1894, p. 178) when the demand exceeds supply for a considerable period or as 'natural monopolies' (Marx, 1894, p. 861) when there is ownership of land or natural resources (Marx, 1894, pp. 178, 861).

In production activities, the reorganization of the firm and technical change are seen as the main weapons of competition (Marx, 1867, pp. 623). The goal of the firm is to capture a transient surplus profit and to transform it into long-run growth potentials, leading to disequilibria and imbalances through irreversible technical change and innovation, taking place not in time-continuous form but in discrete steps. Moreover, competition through technical change results not in the existence of one optimal technique but in the coexistence of multiple techniques, and the weighted average technique is – excluding some exceptional cases such as decreasing returns to scale and rent – considered the regulating technique determining the long-run normal price (Marx, 1894, ch. 10).

Contrary to those forces generating disequilibria and imbalances through inter-firm dynamics competition is also conceived as a balancing force. Capital as a homogeneous fund (money capital) seeks its maximum return by flowing between sectors ('competition between industries', Marx 1894, ch. 10). Free mobility of labour and capital, no artificial or natural barriers for its entry or exit and sufficiently widespread knowledge of fields of investment are considered preconditions for the free flow of funds. In Marx (1894, ch. 10) as in Smith (1776, ch. 7) and Ricardo (1817, ch. 4) a dynamical process is conceived in which capital funds flow into industries with high rates of return away from industries with low rates of return. Thus the relative output proportions in industries will change, creating imbalances of supply and demand. These, in turn, cause relative market prices and profit rates to change, tending to establish for the economic system long-run prices of production as centres of gravity for market prices. Yet the stability properties of such a dynamic . process were not demonstrated rigorously. The arguments were put forward intuitively by analogy with Newton's theory of the planetary system that profit rates fluctuate or oscillate within a bounded interval and actual prices gravitate around their long-run production prices. Differentials of profit rates between industries and firms were expected to exist for a shorter or longer period due to disequilibrium dynamics and due to speed and ease of adjustment varying from one industry to another (Marx, 1894, p. 208). Though Marx anticipated possible institutional and structural changes, due to 'concentration and centralization of capital', he did not, however, assume that inter-firm and inter-industry competition would become less severe with the evolution of capitalism.

POST-MARXIAN THEORY. In the post-marxian theory since Hilferding (1910) the elimination of competition and the delay and disruption of the formation of a general profit rate through monopolization became the main theoretical concern. Three causes are posited as reasons for monopolization: industrial concentration, increasing constraints for the mobility of capital (in particular due to high proportion of fixed capital in total capital outlay), and collusion (cooperative behaviour and cartels). In this view these three causes result in monopoly prices and the persistence of differential profit rates between industries and size classes of firms (Sweezy, 1942). For those theories, the large firms are conceived as economic units endowed with discretionary price setting power determining their own environment (Kalecki, 1938, 1943; Sweezy, 1939, 1942; Baran and Sweezy, 1966; and Eichner, 1976). Here the ideas of mark up pricing, target rate of return pricing and entry-preventing pricing have replaced the classical and marxian theory of production prices (natural prices, prices of production).

Given this general trend in post-marxian theory there are, however, many differences among theorists regarding (i) the causes of the monopolization; (ii) the determination of the mark-ups and the rates of return; (iii) the different role of inverse demand function and quantity reactions in their theory of price setting firms; (iv) the impact of the rise of oligopolies and firms size on technical change; and (v) the impact of large oligopoly firms on the stability of the economic system (increasing stability or instability with stagnation tendencies). Yet in spite of these differences, post-marxian theory is influenced by the theory of imperfect competition arising in the 1930s, and competition is thus identified more with market structure than with rival behaviour. Moreover, the theory of mark-up pricing was built more on a partial equilibrium view and thus not well-founded in an interdependent economic system. Though in the writings of some of the post-Marxian scholars the existence of large oligopoly firms does not preclude rivalry and competition (in particular concerning technical change, see Baran and Sweezy, 1966, ch. 3), post-marxian writers seemed to have considered the theory of imperfect competition a more adequate framework for their analysis of advanced capitalism.

RECENT DISCUSSIONS. In recent discussions there is a certain revival of the concepts of competition of the classics and Marx,

in particular concerning the role of competition for (1) industrial and corporate price and profit determination; (2) technical change and innovation; and (3) the formation of a general rate of profit.

(1) In new contributions attempts have been made to elaborate a theory of mark-up pricing for large corporations in the context of a dynamic theory of competition and long-run prices of production. In this context the economic behaviour of large corporations is explained more in terms of change of the production processes and the organization of the firm and less in terms of a change of market structures (Clifton, 1977, 1983; Semmler, 1984a) as was attempted by post-marxian theory. According to this new view, mark-up and target rate of return pricing have their origin not in new market structures but in the rise of a new type of firm: the multi-plant and multi-product corporations and their new financial management techniques. Though there is, as the theory of mark-up pricing predicts, sufficient empirical evidence of differential profit rates among industries and size classes of firms – depending, however, also on the time-period and the measure chosen for the rate of profit – it has not been sufficiently demonstrated that these differentials stem from imperfect market structures or from a disequilibrium dynamics. In addition, the empirically observed mark-up, target rate of return, and entry-preventing pricing, originally developed by large corporations in the 1920s, can be made consistent with a concept of long period prices of production. Since, however, large corporations are no longer single product firms, it is more appropriate to apply the theory of joint production to the economic behaviour of large corporations (Semmler, 1984a). On this basis fruitful attempts have been made to analyse the dynamics of competition, mark-ups, and rates of return on the basis of an interdependent system of prices and outputs.

(2) The theory of technical change in marxian economics has recently been given a firmer foundation in the theory of competition (Okishio, 1961; Shaikh, 1978; Roemer, 1979). In this discussion, the marxian statement (Marx, 1867, ch. 12; 1894, ch. 15) that under competitive pressure individual firms will implement technical change and innovations and capture a transient surplus profit, but that the diffusion of techniques will entail a falling general profit rate, was debated anew with the tools of mathematical economics. The Okishio theorem seemed to invalidate this statement, since it implies that the capitalist firm in competition will always choose a cost minimizing technique that raises the individual as well as the general profit rate (Okishio, 1961). This Okishio result was disputed by Shaikh (1978) and extended by Roemer (1979). The latter extended the Okishio result to a production price model including fixed capital. In the debate, however, it became clear that the Okishio result holds only under the conditions of perfect competition with perfect information about the current and future cash flow and capital cost of an innovation where rivals' reactions either do not occur or can be foreseen (Semmler, 1984b). In the context of the dynamics of competition as conceived by Marx – and also in the Schumpeterian tradition – due to unforeseen rivals' reactions certainty concerning future technology and markets cannot be expected when firms choose or are forced to choose a technique through competition. Thus the theory of perfect competition does not seem to be applicable as a framework in this context. But choice of techniques with market and technological uncertainties due to unforeseen rivals' reactions is by its nature difficult to model appropriately and thus more precise results are not yet available.

(3) In post-marxian theories the competitive formation of a

general profit rate was either taken for granted or completely disputed (as in the tradition since Hilferding). Recently, however, it became clear that if it cannot be established theoretically how profit rate differentials are dynamically equalized through the forces of competition then the concept of prices of production would become empirically irrelevant. In order to solve this problem, many scholars have begun to formalize Marx's conceptualization of competition by means of dynamical systems with price and quantity changes over time. Nikaido (1983) presented results on the dynamic equalization of profit rates and the stability properties of prices of production showing that in general they are not even locally stable. In subsequent discussion, however, it was shown by Duménil and Lévy (1984), Steedman (1984), and Flaschel and Semmler (1987) that better results may be obtained if the dynamics of competition are formalized as indicated above. For an n-sector model, a dynamics which includes changes not only in prices but also in production levels can be formulated as follows:

$$\dot{x}_i = d_i[r(p, x)_i - \bar{r}(p, x)] \tag{1}$$

and

$$\dot{p}_i = k_i[\bar{D}(p, x)_i - S(p, x)_i] \tag{2}$$

where $\bar{D}(p, x)_i$ is the average or expected demand for an industry i for a growing economic system, $S(p, x)_i$ the industry's supply, $r(p, x)_i$ the industry's profit rate, $\bar{r}(p, x)$ the average profit rate and $\dot{p}_i$, $\dot{x}_i$ the time rate of change of prices and outputs. This dynamical process of competition refers to capital flows across industries according to differential profit rates (and changes in respective production levels) as well as to changes in prices due to imbalances in supply and demand. The results obtained in recently published articles on this process range from the demonstration of complete instability of the dynamic equalization of profit rates (Nikaido, 1983) to the demonstration that prices of production are at least locally stable (Duménil and Lévy, 1984). It can also be demonstrated (by utilizing a proper Lyapunov function) that prices, outputs, and profit rates are fluctuating or oscillating within boundaries (Flaschel and Semmler, 1987). Most of these attempts, however, refer only to a circulating capital model when the inter-industry competitive process is analysed, and the demonstrated results depend on the type of formalization, the reaction coefficients as well as on additional stabilizing forces (such as substitution in capitalist consumption, rate of change of inventories or rate of change of profit rate differentials). Models of inter-industry competition including fixed capital, returns to scale, or multiple techniques are still rare.

WILLI SEMMLER

See also MONOPOLY CAPITALISM; SURPLUS APPROACH TO VALUE AND DISTRIBUTION.

BIBLIOGRAPHY

Baran, P. and Sweezy, P. 1966. *Monopoly Capital.* New York: Monthly Review Press.
Clifton, J.A. 1977. Competition and the evolution of the capitalist mode of production. *Cambridge Journal of Economics* 1(2), June, 137–51.
Clifton, J.A. 1983. Administered prices in the context of capitalist development. *Contributions to Political Economy* 2, 23–38.
Duménil, G. and Lévy, D. 1984. *The Dynamics of Competition: a restoration of the Classical analysis.* CEPREMAP, No. 8416, Paris.
Eatwell, J. 1982. Competition. In *Classical and Marxian Political Economy: Essays in Memory of R. Meek*, ed. I. Bradley and M. Howard, London: Macmillan.

Eichner, A.S. 1976. *The Megacorp and Oligopoly: Microfoundations of Macrodynamics.* Cambridge: Cambridge University Press.
Flaschel, P. and Semmler, W. 1987. Classical and neoclassical competitive adjustment processes. *The Manchester School of Economic and Social Studies.*
Friedman, J. 1982. Oligopoly theory. In *Handbook of Mathematical Economics*, ed. K.J. Arrow and M.D. Intriligator, Amsterdam: North-Holland, Vol. II.
Hilferding, R. 1910. *Das Finanzkapital.* Trans. as *Finance Capital*, London: Routledge & Kegan Paul, 1981.
Kalecki, M. 1938. Distribution of national income. Reprinted in M. Kalecki, *Selected Essays on the Dynamics of the Capitalist Economy*, Cambridge: Cambridge University Press, 1971.
Kalecki, M. 1943. Cost and prices. Reprinted in M. Kalecki, *Selected Essays* (1971).
Kuruma, S. 1973. *Marx Lexikon zur Politischen Oekonomie*, Vol. 1: Konkurrenz. Berlin: Oberbaum.
Marx, K. 1847. *Lohnarbeit und Kapital.* Trans. as *Wage Labor and Capital*, New York: International Publishers, 1933.
Marx, K. 1857/8. *Grundrisse der Kritik der Politischen Ökonomie.* Trans. as *Grundrisse*, New York: Random House, 1973.
Marx, K. 1861/3. *Theorien über den Mehrwert.* Trans. as *Theories of Surplus Value*, 3 vols, Moscow: Progress Publishers, 1963.
Marx, K. 1867, 1893, 1894. *Das Kapital, Kritik der Politischen Ökonomie.* 3 vols. Trans. as *Capital, A Critique of Political Economy*, New York: International Publishers, 1967.
McNulty, P.J. 1968. Economic theory and the meaning of competition. *Quarterly Journal of Economics* 82, November, 639–56.
Nikaido, H. 1983. Marx on competition. *Zeitschrift für Nationalökonomie* 43(4), 337–62.
Okishio, N. 1961. Technical changes and the rate of profit. *Kobe University Economic Review* 7, 85–99.
Ricardo, D. 1817. *Principles of Political Economy and Taxation.* In *Works and Correspondence*, ed. P. Sraffa, Vol. 1, Cambridge: Cambridge University Press, 1951.
Roemer, J.E. 1979. Continuing controversy on the falling rate of profit: fixed capital and other issues. *Cambridge Journal of Economics* 3(4), December, 379–98.
Schumpeter, J. 1943. *Capitalism, Socialism and Democracy.* London: George Allen & Unwin.
Semmler, W. 1984a. *Competition, Monopoly and Differential Profit Rates.* New York: Columbia University Press.
Semmler, W. 1984b. Marx and Schumpeter on competition, transient surplus profit and technical change. *Economie Appliquée* 37(3–4), 419–55.
Shaikh, A. 1978. Political economy and capitalism: notes on Dobb's theory of crisis. *Cambridge Journal of Economics* 2(2), June, 233–51.
Smith, A. 1776. *An Inquiry into the Nature and Causes of the Wealth of Nations.* Ed. E. Cannan, London: Methuen, 1961.
Steedman, I. 1984. Natural prices, differential profit rates, and the classical competitive process. *The Manchester School of Economic and Social Studies* 52(2), June, 123–40.
Stigler, G.J. 1957. Perfect competition, historically contemplated. *Journal of Political Economy* 65(1), February, 1–17.
Sweezy, P.M. 1939. Demand under conditions of oligopoly. *Journal of Political Economy* 47, August, 568–73.
Sweezy, P.M. 1942. *The Theory of Capitalist Development.* New York: Monthly Review Press, 1968.

competition, imperfect. *See* IMPERFECT COMPETITION.

competition, monopolistic. *See* MONOPOLISTIC COMPETITION.

competition, perfect. *See* PERFECT COMPETITION.

competition and efficiency. The association between economic efficiency and competition goes back at least as far as Adam Smith's 'invisible hand' metaphor. Indeed, a goodly portion of the vast body of subsequent work in value theory has dealt with the normative issues arising from the workings of the competitive economy. Thus any short essay on the topic must be somewhat idiosyncratic, focusing upon the points which are of greatest interest to the author. Therefore, I shall limit my attention to the properties of the (static, partial equilibrium) *economic model* of perfect competition and how its use has recently been extended to add to our understanding of a larger range of real world markets. I must leave to others the tasks of sorting out the importance of competition in, for example, the Schumpeterian process of 'creative destruction', the aggregation and transmission of society's stock of information, or the evolutionary progress of technological advance.

Fortunately for my purposes, the historical development of the competitive model has been thoroughly analysed by Stigler (1957). The formulation of the model, as we know it today, was completed in the work of Knight (1921). It is interesting to note that the last refinement to be added was the free mobility of resources across industries: i.e. the entry and exist of firms. In his insightful concluding section, Stigler points out that competition can flourish *within* a market without this last ingredient. (Consider an agricultural market with Ricardian rents.) He suggested that the term 'market competition' be used to describe such situations, and that the term 'industrial competition' be applied when mobility across industries is present. The work that I shall discuss deals with the converse possibility: perfectly contestable markets, situations in which competition may not necessarily exist within a particular market, but firms (and resources) are assumed to be perfectly mobile across industries.

The role of entry and exit in assuring the equalization of returns across markets is not logically limited to those cases in which it is technologically feasible for the market to be populated by a large number of firms, each capable of achieving an efficient scale of operation. It may be expected that the lure of profits might serve to make relevant certain aspects of competitive theory even under conditions of 'natural monopoly'. The most striking practical illustration of this point was the recent deregulation of airlines in the United States. This took place, in part, because the free mobility of resources (aircraft) across markets led policy makers to believe that satisfactory economic performance could be achieved without the stultifying effects of economic regulation. This, despite the fact that most city-pair airline markets are natural monopolies and none can be expected to support the large numbers of firms required by the perfectly competitive model. Thus the need to extend at least part of the competitive paradigm to incorporate such cases had become apparent.

In a classic article, Demsetz (1968) set forth one way to break the commonly perceived link between monopoly provision of certain increasing returns services and monopoly conduct on the part of the firm providing the service at any point in time. By pointing out that the impossibility of competition within the market need not preclude effective competition *for the market*, Demsetz raised a fundamental challenge to the conventional wisdom that the only effective ways to deal with a technological natural monopoly were through economic regulation or public enterprise.

Demsetz chose to elaborate this idea in the context of a franchise bidding scheme, in which the franchise was to be awarded, not to the firm offering the greatest lump sum payment to the municipal coffers, but to the firm offering to serve the market at the lowest price. Subsequent authors have criticized this as a policy proposal, focusing on the problems raised by considerations of sunk costs and incomplete contracts, from which Demsetz explicitly sought to abstract. However, there is another sense in which the franchise bidding example may have been an unfortunate expository choice. Because it introduced a new institution between the firm and the market the franchise auctioneer – this illustration may have obscured the link between the analysis of competition for the market and the earlier notion of the role of free entry and exit in ensuring effective industrial competition. Furthermore, Demsetz's simple bidding scheme cannot handle the realistic cases in which the monopolist produces two or more technologically related services.

The theory of contestable markets developed by Baumol, Panzar and Willig (1982) is most usefully viewed as an attempt to extend the neoclassical (partial equilibrium) theory of long-run competitive equilibrium to the case of increasing returns to scale. In so doing, they developed a model which achieved the Demsetz solution to the monopoly problem as the result of a market equilibrium process. This extension was accomplished by emphasizing the role played by potential entry in characterizing the defining properties of long-run competitive equilibrium.

To see this reinterpretation most clearly, the following definitions are necessary:

Definition 1: A Feasible Industry Configuration (FIC) is a collection of firms, $i = 1, \ldots, m$; output vectors for each, $y^1, \ldots, y^m$; and a market price vector p such that each firm earns non-negative profits and the total quantity supplied equals the quantity demanded: i.e. $py^i - C(y^i) \geq 0$, for all $i = 1, \ldots, m$ and $\Sigma y^i = D(p)$, where C is the (multiproduct) minimum cost function and D the market demand function.

Feasibility surely reflects the minimal conditions one would expect to prevail in long-run industry equilibrium in a private enterprise economy: All firms must earn non-negative profits and the total quantity supplied by firms equals the amount demanded by consumers at the market price. While feasibility requires financial viability, it does not preclude the positive profits which may attract entry. Therefore, the neoclassical notion of long-run competitive equilibrium must encompass some additional restrictions. More specifically,

Definition 2: A long-run competitive equilibrium is any FIC which also has the property that $py - C(y) \leq 0$ for all y.

While this characterization of long-run competitive equilibrium may be unfamiliar, it is equivalent to the standard notion of price taking firms earning zero economic profits by equating marginal cost to price. (To see this, note that since profits are nonpositive for all output levels, the fact that $py^i - C(y^i) \geq 0$ means that output level y^i maximizes the ith firm's profits. This, in turn, implies that $MC(y^i) = p$ if firm i is producing.)

Characterizing competitive equilibrium via Definitions 1 and 2 has the advantage of focusing attention on the role played by potential entry. The strictures of Definition 2 can be interpreted to mean that the firms in an industry in long-run competitive equilibrium act as if they were policed by potential entrants prepared to enter the market in pursuit of any profit opportunity calculated at current market prices. While this lack of attention to the possibility of retaliatory price responses by rivals reflects the noncooperative spirit of the competitive paradigm, it ignores the response of consumers to a change in the market price. Therefore it is useful to consider making potential entrants 'less optimistic' in the following sense:

Definition 3: A Sustainable Industry Configuration (SIC) is any FIC which also satisfies the condition that $p^e y^e - C(y^e) \leqslant 0$ for all $p^e \leqslant p$ and $y^e \leqslant D(p^e)$.

Thus firms in a SIC behave as if the market were policed by potential entrants that calculate the profitability of entry under the assumption that incumbent firms' prices remained unchanged, but that do take account of the reality that consumers can be induced to purchase a larger quantity only at a lower price. Put another way, an FIC is also an SIC when no potential entrant can anticipate earning a positive profit by quoting a price at or below that prevailing in the market and serving all or a part of the resulting demand. The following semantic clarification completes the characterization of a contestable market:

Definition 4: A perfectly contestable market is one in which perfectly free entry and exit ensure that the only possible long-run equilibria are SICs.

An immediate implication of Definitions 1–4 is:

Proposition 1: Any long-run competitive equilibrium is an SIC, but not conversely. Thus all perfectly competitive markets are perfectly contestable, but not all perfectly contestable markets are perfectly competitive.

The proof follows from the fact that the conditions which an FIC must satisfy in order to be a long-run competitive equilibrium are stronger than those required of an SIC. Thus a long-run competitive equilibrium is, by construction, an SIC. To see that the converse is not true, consider the case in which the average costs of production fall throughout the relevant range; i.e. at least as far as the intersection of the average cost curve and the market demand curve. The point of intersection, the Demsetz outcome, characterizes a sustainable industry configuration, since profits are non-positive and no point on or below the demand curve can yield non-negative profits at a lower price. However this outcome is clearly not a long-run competitive equilibrium because price is equal to average cost which, by hypothesis, is strictly greater than marginal cost.

The above demonstration points out the fact that the concept of contestable markets can be applied beyond the large-numbers case of perfect competition. However it also raises questions about the efficiency properties of such markets. The fact that equilibrium may involve a price greater than marginal cost means that the First Best optimality properties of the competitive model need no longer apply. What efficiency properties, then, *can* be associated with equilibria in contestable markets? In the case of single product markets it is intuitively clear (and straightforward to prove) that, when they exist, sustainable industry configurations are solutions to the Second Best optimization problem: maximize welfare (as measured, for example, by the sum of producers' and consumers' surpluses) subject to the constraint that firms earn non-negative profits. Clearly, when increasing returns to scale render marginal cost pricing unprofitable, the best that can be done, in the absence of lump sum transfers and discriminatory or non-linear pricing, is to set price equal to average cost.

However, even this level of performance can no longer be guaranteeed once one moves to the realistic realm of multiple products. For example, a monopolist producing two or more products can, in general, find an infinite number of price combinations which will yield it exactly zero economic profits. Some of these prices and resulting market demand quantities may represent SICs. Call this set P. If the underlying cost and demand functions are sufficiently well-behaved, there will exist a unique constrained welfare maximizing price vector p^*. The most desirable efficiency result would be for the set P to consist of the single element p^*. Unfortunately, it is easy to construct examples in which P does not contain p^*, as well as cases in which P is empty.

What efficiency properties does this generalized process of industrial competition possess when extended beyond the realm of perfect competition? The results that pertain generally lie entirely on the cost side.

Proposition 2: In any SIC, the industry's output is divided among the firms in a way that minimizes total industry costs.

The proof is by contradiction. Consider an initial SIC composed of m firms producing output vectors, $y^1, \ldots, y^m$, at market prices p. Suppose, contrary to hypothesis, that there exists an alternative group of k firms with output vectors, $z^1, \ldots, z^k$, that could produce the current industry output at a lower total cost. That is $\Sigma_j z^j = D(p) = \Sigma_i y^i$, but $\Sigma_j C(z^j) < \Sigma_i C(y^i)$. Then the new group, in total, would earn positive economic profits at the initial price p. This is true because, by hypothesis, total revenues would be equal, but total costs would be lower for the alternative group, while the initial group of firms must have been earning non-negative profits. Therefore at least one firm, say firm j, in the alternative group would anticipate earning strictly positive profits at the price vector p. But then there exists an entry plan $p^e = p \leqslant p$ and $y^e = z^j \leqslant D(p^e)$ such that $p^e y^e - C(y^e) > 0$, which contradicts the hypothesis that the initial group of firms constituted a SIC.

Additional efficiency results for contestable markets are presented in chapter 11 of Baumol, Panzar and Willig. Here, I shall mention specifically a class of results which are relevant only in the multiproduct context. One implication of the fact that equilibrium in a contestable market presents no profit opportunities for potential entrants is that no subset of services of a multiproduct enterprise can generate revenues in excess of the cost of providing them alone. Thus, equilibrium in perfectly contestable markets cannot involve one gorup of services subsidizing another. Whether or not this property is a desirable efficiency result is unclear. Consider, for example, a situation in which a monopoly firm uses common facilities to produce two services, one of which has a very elastic demand curve while that of the other is very inelastic. Maximizing total surplus subject to a break-even constraint leads to the well-known inverse elasticity rule: the markup of price over marginal cost is greater for services whose demand is least elastic. However, this pricing policy may easily lead to revenues from the inelastic service in excess of the cost of providing it alone. Such an outcome would not be an SIC and could not persist in a perfectly contestable market. Thus while the mobility of firms and resources can, even without the presence of market competition, ensure productive efficiency, it cannot in general guarantee that an optimal relationship of output prices in a multiproduct industry will prevail outside the perfectly competitive realm.

JOHN C. PANZAR

See also CONTESTABLE MARKETS; INCREASING RETURNS; MONOPOLY; NATURAL MONOPOLY.

BIBLIOGRAPHY

Baumol, W., Panzar, J. and Willig, R. 1982. *Contestable Markets and the Theory of Industry Structure*. New York: Harcourt Brace Jovanovich.
Demsetz, H. 1968. Why regulate utilities? *Journal of Law and Economics* 11, April, 55–65.
Knight, F. 1921. *Risk, Uncertainty, and Profit*. Chicago: University of Chicago Press.
Stigler, G. 1957. Perfect competition, historically contemplated. *Journal of Political Economy* 65, February, 1–17.

competition and selection. Under competitive conditions, a business firm must maximize profit if it is to survive – or so it is often claimed. This purported analogue of biological natural selection has had substantial influence in economic thinking, and the proposition remains influential today. In general, its role has been to serve as an informal auxiliary defence, or crutch, for standard theoretical approaches based on optimization and equilibrium. It appeared explicitly in this role in a provocative passage in Milton Friedman's famous essay on methodology (Friedman, 1953, ch. 1), and it seems that many economists are familiar with it in this context only.

There is, however, an alternative role that the proposition can and does play. It serves as an informal statement of the common conclusion of a class of theorems characterizing explicit models of economic selection processes. A model in this class posits, first, a range of possible behaviours for the firm. This range must obviously extend beyond the realm of profit maximization if the conclusion of the argument is to be non-trivial, and it must include behaviour that is appropriately termed 'profit maximizing' if the conclusion is to be logically attainable at all. The model must also characterize a particular dynamic process that in some way captures the general idea that profitable firms tend to survive and grow, while unprofitable ones tend to decline and fail. A stationary position of such a process is a 'selection equilibrium'.

Models of this type occupy an important but non-central position in evolutionary economic theory (Nelson and Winter, 1982). They establish that the equilibria of standard competitive theory can indeed be 'mimicked' (in several different senses) by the equilibria of selection models. More importantly, by making explicit the strong assumptions that apparently are required to generate this sort of result, they are the basis for a critique of its generality and an appraisal of the strength of the crutch on which standard theory leans. They also provide a helpful entry-way to the much broader class of evolutionary models in which mimicry results fail to hold. This entry-way has the convenient feature that the return path to standard theory is well marked; the sense in which evolutionary theory subsumes portions of standard theory becomes clear.

The concept of competition need not, of course, be considered only in the context of perfectly competitive equilibrium. In a broader sense of the term, any non-trivial selection model in which the 'fit' prosper and the 'unfit' do not is a model of a 'competitive' process. The process need not have a static equilibrium, or any equilibrium, and it may easily lead to results that are clearly non-competitive by the standards of industrial organization economics.

The remainder of this essay first considers in more detail the theoretical links between selection processes and competitive equilibrium outcomes. It then examines a more interesting and less well-explored area that involves selection and, in a broad sense, competition; Schumpeterian competition.

COMPETITIVE EQUILIBRIUM AS A SELECTION OUTCOME. The intention here is to describe the heuristic basis of existing examples of this type of theorem, or, alternatively, to describe the basic recipe from which an obviously large class of broadly similar results could be produced. There may be other basic recipes, as yet unknown. There certainly are ways to ignore individual instructions of the recipe and yet preserve the result, though at the cost of delicately contrived adjustments in other assumptions.

(To avoid confusion, it should be noted at the outset that the word 'equilibrium' is used in two different senses in this discussion, the 'no incentives to change behaviour' sense

employed in economic theory and the 'stationary position of a dynamic process' sense that is common outside of economics. The point of the discussion is, in fact, to relate these two equilibrium ideas in a particular way.)

(1) Constant returns to scale must prevail in the specific sense that the supply and demand functions of an individual firm at any particular time are expressible as the scale (or 'capacity') of that firm at that time multiplied by functions depending on prices, but not directly on scale or time. Increasing returns to scale must be excluded for familiar reasons. Decreasing returns must be excluded because they will in general give rise to equilibrium 'entrepreneurial rents' which could be partially dissipated by departures from maximization without threatening the survival of the firm. Thus, for example, the U-shaped long run average cost curve of textbook competitive theory does not provide a context in which selection necessarily mimics standard theory if competitive equilibrium would require some firms to be on the upward sloping portion of the curve.

(2) Firms must increase scale when profitable and decrease scale (or go out of business entirely) when unprofitable. Alternatively, profitability of a particular firm must lead to entry by perfect imitators of that firm's actions. In the absence of such assumptions, it is plain that there will in general be equilibria with non-zero profit levels, which under assumption (1) cannot mimic the competitive result. While the 'decline or fail' assumption is a plausible reflection of long-run breakeven constraints characteristic of actual capitalist institutions, no such realistic force attaches to the requirement that profitability lead to expansion. If firms do not pursue profits in the long-run sense of expanding in response to positive profitability, stationary positions may involve positive profits. Such stationary positions fail to mimic competitive equilibria for that reason alone (given constant returns), but they also introduce once again the possibility that the short-run behavioural responses of surviving firms may dissipate some of the positive profit that is potentially achievable at selection equilibrium scale.

In standard theory, expansion in response to profitability may be seen as an aspect of the firm's profit-seeking on the assumption that it regards prices as unaffected by its capacity decisions. In turn, this ordinarily requires that the firm in question be but one of an indeterminately large number of firms that all have access to the same technological and organizational possibilities.

While the assumption that firms have identical production sets and behavioural rules is common and appears inoffensive in orthodox theorizing, it is very much at odds with evolutionary theory. The orthodox view comes down to the assertion that all productive knowledge is freely available to one and all – perhaps it is all in the public library. By contrast, evolutionary theory emphasizes the role of firms as highly individualized repositories of productive knowledge, not all of which is articulable. From the evolutionary perspective, the fact that mimicry theorems rely on assumptions of unimpaired access to a public knowledge pool is by itself sufficient to make it clear that the selection argument can provide only a weak and shaky crutch for standard competitive theory.

(3) A firm that is breaking even with a positive output at prevailing prices must not alter its behaviour; a potential entrant that would only break even at prevailing prices must not enter. This assumption is needed to assure that the competitive equilibrium position is in fact a stationary position of the selection process.

Models of natural selection in biology do not typically involve this sort of assumption, but neither do they conclude that only the fittest genotypes survive – the biological analogue of the proposition discussed here. Rather, they show how constant gene frequencies come to prevail as the selection forces that tend to eliminate diversity come into balance with mutation forces that constantly renew it. A strictly analogous treatment of economic selection would be much more appealing than the sort of result discussed here. It would admit that occasional disruptions may arise from random behavioural change, or from over-optimistic entrants. Thus, potentially at least, it could better serve the purpose of establishing the point that the results of standard competitive theory are in some sense robust with respect to its behavioural assumptions. Unfortunately, standard theory offers no clue as to what this sense might be. It is plain that the adjustment processes of the system are centrally involved, and there is no behaviourally plausible theory of adjustment that is the dynamic counterpart in the disciplinary paradigm of static competitive equilibrium theory.

Within the limits defined by the requirement for a strictly static competitive outcome, the most plausible approach combines the idea of characterizing the firms in the selection process by their 'rules of behaviour' – an idea advanced in a seminal paper by Armen Alchian (1950) – with Herbert Simon's idea of satisficing (1955). In the simplest version, each firm simply adheres unswervingly to its own deterministic behavioural rule (or 'routine', in the language of Nelson and Winter, 1982). Such a rule subsumes or implies the firm's supply and demand functions, and given the conditions set forth in (1) and (2) above, a constant environment evokes a constant response. Satisficing may be introduced as a complication of this picture by an assumption that a firm that sustains losses over a period of time will search for a better behavioural rule; this adds behavioural plausibility to the adjustment process but does not introduce the possibility that random rule change might disrupt an otherwise stationary competitive equilibrium position.

(4) The final requirement can be succinctly but inadequately stated as 'some firms must actually be profit maximizers'. Although this formulation does adequately cover some simple cases, it does not suggest the depth and subtlety of the issues involved.

Two points deserve particular emphasis here. The first is the distinction between profit maximizing *rules of behaviour* (functions) and profit maximizing *actions*. In general, a selection equilibrium that mimics a particular competitive equilibrium must clearly be one in which some firms take actions that are profit maximizing in that competitive equilibrium, and in this sense are profit maximizers. But this observation does not imply that the survivors in the selection equilibrium possess maximizing *rules*, and in general it is not necessary that survivors be maximizers in this stronger sense. (Proof: Consider a competitive equilibrium with constant returns to scale. Restrict the firms' supply and demand functions to be constant up to a scale factor at the values taken in the given equilibrium. Embed this static equilibrium in a dynamic adjustment system in which firms' scales of output respond to profitability in accordance with assumption (2). Then the given competitive equilibrium becomes a selection equilibrium – since the only techniques in use make zero profit – but the firms are not profit maximizers in the stronger sense.)

The second point extends the first. The notion of profit maximizing behavioural rules itself rests on the conceptual foundation of a production set or function that is regarded as a given. In evolutionary theory, however, it is the rules themselves that are regarded as data and as logically antecedent to the values (actions) they yield in particular environments. Thus, in this context, a problem arises in interpreting the basic idea of a selection equilibrium mimicking a standard competitive one: there is no obvious set of 'possibilities' to which one should have reference.

The most helpful approach here emphasizes internal consistency. Assumptions about the structure of what is 'possible' can be invoked without the additional assumption that there is a given set of possibilities – for example, additivity and divisibility may be assumed without implying that the set of techniques to which these axioms apply is a given datum of the system. Such an approach provides a basis for discussing whether a particular selection equilibrium is legitimately *interpretable* as a competitive equilibrium given the other assumptions in force. Along this path one can explore a rich variety of selection equilibrium situations that may be thought of as competitive equilibria. Precisely because the variety is so rich, to know only that an outcome is interpretable in this fashion is to know very little about it.

In the light of formal analysis of selection models of the sort described above, how strong is the crutch that selection provides to standard theory? For many analytical purposes, it is a crucial weakness that the crutch relates only to equilibrium actions and not to behavioural rules; it is from the knowledge that the rules are maximizing that the results of comparative statics derive. A selection system disturbed by a parameter change from a 'mimicking' equilibrium does not necessarily go to a new 'mimicking' equilibrium, let alone to one that is consistent, in standard theoretical terms, with the information revealed in the original equilibrium. More fundamentally, selection considerations cannot compensate for the inadequacies of standard theory that arise from the basic assumption that production possibilities are given data of the system.

SCHUMPETERIAN COMPETITION. In two great works and in many other writings, Joseph Schumpeter proclaimed the central importance of innovative activity in the development of capitalism. His early book, *The Theory of Economic Development*, focused on the role and contribution of the individual entrepreneur. From today's perspective the work remains enormously insightful and provocative but may seem dated; the image of the late 19th-century captains of industry lurks implicitly in the abstract account of the entrepreneur. The late work, *Capitalism, Socialism and Democracy*, is likewise insightful, provocative and a bit anachronistic. In this case, the anachronism derives from the predictions of a future in which the innovative process is bureaucratized, the role of the individual entrepreneur is fully usurped by large organizations, and the sociopolitical foundations of capitalism are thereby undercut. Present reality does not correspond closely to Schumpeter's predictions, and it seems increasingly clear that he greatly underestimated the seriousness of the incentive problems that arise within large organizations, whether capitalist corporations or socialist states.

Substantial literatures have accumulated around a number of specific issues, hypotheses and predictions put forward in Schumpeter's various writings. Regardless of the verdicts ultimately rendered on particular points, everyday observation repeatedly confirms the appropriateness of his emphasis on the centrality of innovation in contemporary capitalism. It confirms, likewise, the *in*appropriateness of the continuing tendency of the economics discipline to sequester topics related to technological change in sub-sectors of various specialized fields, remote from the theoretical core.

The purpose of the present discussion is to assess the relationships of selection and competition from a

Schumpeterian viewpoint, that is, to extend the discussion above by considering what difference it makes if firms are engaged in inventing, discovering and exploring new ways of doing things. Plainly, one difference it makes is that 'competition' must now be understood in the broad sense that admits a number of additional dimensions to the competitive process, along with price-guided output determination. In particular, costly efforts to innovate, to imitate the innovations of others, and to appropriate the gains from innovation are added to the firm's competitive repertoire.

Selection now operates at two related levels. The organizational routines governing the use made of existing products and processes in every firm interact through the market place, and the market distributes rewards and punishments to the contenders. These same rewards and punishments are also entries on the market's scorecard for the higher level routines from which new products and processes derive – routines involving, for example, expenditure levels on innovative and imitative R&D efforts. Over the longer term, selection forces favour the firms that achieve a favourable balance between the rents captured from successive rounds of innovation and the costs of the R&D efforts that yield these innovations.

In formal models constructed along these lines, it is easy to see how various extreme cases turn out. One class of cases formalizes the cautionary tale told by Schumpeter (1950, p. 105), in which competition that is 'perfect – and perfectly prompt' makes the innovative role non-viable. Sufficiently high costs of innovation and low costs of imitation (including costs of surmounting any institutional barriers such as patents) will lead to the eventual suppression of all firms that continue to attempt innovation, and the system will settle into a static equilibrium. (The character of this equilibrium may, however, depend on initial conditions and on random events along the evolutionary path; the production set ultimately arrived at is an endogenous feature of the process.) One can also construct model examples to illustrate the cautionary message 'innovate or die', the principal requirement being simply a reversal of the cost conditions stated above.

With the exception of some extreme or highly simplified cases, models of Schumpeterian competition describe complex stochastic processes that are not easily explored with analytical methods. Of course, the activity of writing down a specific formal model is often informative by itself in the sense that it illuminates basic conceptual issues and poses key questions about how complex features of economic reality can usefully be approximated by a model. Some additional insight can then be obtained using simulation methods to explore specific cases (Nelson and Winter, 1982, Part V; Winter, 1984). One of the most significant benefits from simulation is the occasional discovery of mechanisms at work that are retrospectively 'obvious' and general features of the model.

The discussion that follows pulls together a number of these different sorts of insights, emphasizing in particular some issues that do not arise in the related theoretical literature that explores various Schumpeterian themes using neoclassical techniques. (For the most part these neoclassical studies explore stylized situations involving a single possible innovation, and thus do not address issues relating to the cumulative consequences of dynamic Schumpeterian competition. See Kamien and Schwartz (1981) and Dasgupta (1985) for references and perspectives on this literature.)

A fundamental constituent of any dynamic model of Schumpeterian competition is a model of technological opportunity. Such a model establishes the linkage between the resources that model firms apply to innovative effort and their innovative achievements. The long run behaviour of the model

as a whole depends critically on the answers provided for a set of key questions relating to technological opportunity. Does the individual firm face diminishing returns in innovative achievement as it applies additional resources over a short period of time? If so, from what 'fixed factors' does the diminishing returns effect arise, and to what extent are these factors subject to change over time either by the firm's own efforts or by other mechanisms? Are selection forces to be studied in a context in which technological opportunity presents more or less the 'same problem' for R&D policy over an extended period, or is the evolutionary sorting out of different policies for the firm a process that proceeds concurrently with historical change in the criteria that govern the sorting?

Technological opportunity is said to be *constant* if R&D activity amounts to a search of an unchanging set of possibilities – in effect, there is a meta-production set or meta-production function that describes what is ultimately possible. *Increasing* technological opportunity means that possibilities are being expanded over time by causal factors exogenous to the R&D efforts in question – implying that, given a level of technological achievement and a level of R&D effort, the effort will be more productive of innovative results if applied later. With constant technological opportunity, returns to R&D effort must eventually be decreasing, approaching zero near the boundary of the fixed set of possibilities.

It is all too obvious that it may be very difficult to develop an empirical basis for modelling technological opportunity in an applied analysis of a particular firm, industry or national economy. There is no easy escape from the conundrum that observed innovative performance reflects both opportunity and endogenously determined effort, not to mention the fact that neither performance nor effort is itself easily measured or the even more basic question of whether analysis of the past can illuminate the future. These difficulties in operationalizing the concept of technological opportunity do not, unfortunately, in any way diminish its critical role in Schumpeterian competition.

The evolutionary analysis of Schumpeterian competition has not, thus far, produced any counterpart for the sorts of mimicry theorems that can be proved for static equilibria. That is, there is no model in which it can be shown that selection forces, alone or in conjunction with adaptive behavioural rules, drive the system asymptotically to a path on which surviving firms might be said to have solved the remaining portion of the dynamic optimization problem with which the model situation confronts them – except in the cases where the asymptotic situation is a static equilibrium with zero R&D. The list of identified obstacles to a non-trivial positive result is sufficiently long, and the obstacles are sufficiently formidable, so as to constitute something akin to an impossibility theorem. It seems extremely unlikely that a positive result can be established within the confines of an evolutionary approach – that is, without endowing the model firms with a great deal of correct information about the structure of the total system in which they are embedded.

The most formidable obstacle of all derives from the direct clash between the future-oriented character of a dynamic optimization and the fact that selection and adaptation processes reflect the experience of the past. If firms cannot 'see' the path that technological opportunity will follow in the future, if their decisions can only reflect past experience and inferences drawn therefrom, then in general they cannot position themselves optimally for the future. They might conceivably do so if the development of technological opportunity were simple enough to validate simple inference schemes. Such simplicity does not seem descriptively plausible; who is to say that it is implausible that in a particular case technological opportunity might be constant, or exponentially increasing, or following a logistic, or some stochastic variant of any of these? And absent some restriction on the structural possibilities, how are model firms to make inferences to guide their R&D policies?

This obstacle is not featured prominently in the simulations reported by Nelson and Winter, which are largely confined to very tame and stylized technological regimes in which opportunity is summarized by a single exponentially increasing variable, called 'latent productivity'. Such an environment, reminiscent in some ways of neoclassical growth theory, seems at first glance to be a promising one for the derivation of a balanced growth outcome in which actual and latent productivity are rising at the same rate, the problem facing the firms is in a sense constant, and selection and adaptation might bring surviving firm R&D policies to optimal values.

In fact, such a result remains remote even under the very strong assumption just described. Demand conditions for the product of the industry (or the economy) affect the long run dynamics, and in this area also assumptions must be delicately contrived to avoid excluding a balanced growth outcome. For example, consider an industry model with constant demand in which demand is (plausibly) less than unit elastic at low prices. Then, cost reduction continued indefinitely would drive sales revenue to zero. Zero sales revenue will not cover the cost of continuing advance. What is involved here is a reflection of the basic economics of information; costs of discovery are independent of the size of the realm of application, and on the assumption stated the economic significance of that realm is dwindling to nothing. The implication is that demand conditions may check progress even if technological opportunity is continually expanding. Indeed, this may well be the pattern that is typically realistic for any narrowly defined sector.

This difficulty too can be dispatched by an appropriately chosen assumption. Beyond it lie some further problems. A model that acknowledges the partially stochastic nature of innovative success will display gradually increasing concentration (Phillips, 1971), unless some opposing tendency is present. A good candidate for an opposing tendency is the actual exercise of market power that has been acquired by chance (Nelson and Winter, 1982, ch. 13). But this market power can, presumably, also shelter various departures from present value maximization, including departures from dynamically optimal R&D policy.

To reiterate, the quest for mimicry theorems in the context of Schumpeterian competition seems foredoomed to failure. Since models of Schumpeterian competition plainly provide a much better description of the world we live in than do models of static equilibrium, the overall conclusion with regard to the strength of the selection crutch is distinctly more negative than the conclusion for static models alone. Assumptions that firms maximize profit or present value will have to stand on their own, at least until somebody invents a better crutch for them. In the meantime, it will continue to be the case that predictions based on these assumptions are sometimes sound and sometimes silly, and standard theory does not offer a means of discriminating between the cases. More direct attention should be paid to the mechanisms of selection, adaptation and learning, which among them probably account for as much sense as economists have actually observed in economic reality, and also leave room for a lot of readily observable nonsense.

SIDNEY G. WINTER

See also NATURAL SELECTION AND EVOLUTION.

BIBLIOGRAPHY
Alchian, A. A. 1950. Uncertainty, evolution and economic theory. *Journal of Political Economy* 58, June, 211–21.
Dasgupta, P. 1985. The theory of technological competition. In *New Developments in the Analysis of Market Structure*, ed. J. Stiglitz and G.F. Mathewson, Cambridge, Mass.: MIT Press.
Friedman, M. 1953. *Essays in Positive Economics*. Chicago: University of Chicago Press.
Kamien, M. and Schwartz, N. 1981. *Market Structure and Innovation*. Cambridge: Cambridge University Press.
Nelson, R. and Winter, S. 1981. *An Evolutionary Theory of Economic Change*. Cambridge, Mass.: Belknap Press of The Harvard University Press.
Phillips, A. 1971. *Technology and Market Structure: a study of the aircraft industry*. Lexington, Mass.: D.C. Heath.
Schumpeter, J.A. 1912. *The Theory of Economic Development*. Trans. Redvers Opie, Cambridge, Mass.: Harvard University Press, 1934.
Schumpeter. J. A. 1950. *Capitalism, Socialism and Democracy*. 3rd edn, New York: Harper.
Simon, H. 1955. A behavioral model of rational choice, *Quarterly Journal of Economics* 69, February, 99–118.
Winter, S. G. 1964. Economic 'natural selection' and the theory of the firm. *Yale Economic Essays* 4(1), Spring, 225–72.
Winter, S. G. 1971. Satisficing, selection and the innovating remnant. *Quarterly Journal of Economics* 85(2), May, 237–61.
Winter, S. G. 1984. Schumpeterian competition in alternative technological regimes. *Journal of Economic Behavior and Organization* 5(3–4), September–December, 287–320.

competition and stability. *See* ADJUSTMENT PROCESSES AND STABILITY; STABILITY.

competition in international trade. In international markets the equivalent of the owned assets and the skills of individuals and firms in internal markets is the difference in relative national resource endowments. In elementary theory, the effects of international competition are defined by comparison with an initial state of no trade. The typical question addressed is 'What will happen if trade is opened up?' On this view, international competition 'causes' trade because of the differences there would be, in the absence of trade, in the relative costs of production of pairs of goods in two countries. And the effect of international competition, and the ensuing trade, is to have ironed out some of these differences and to have increased in the process the aggregate equilibrium output of each good.

In each country, initially, the cheaper good is the one whose production technology calls for a lot of the input that is relatively plentiful there. When trade is opened up, the producers of the dearer commodity in each country face competition from the country better suited to produce it. Through international competition, differences in the relative scarcity (and cost) of labour, land and capital and consequent differences in the ratio of the price of, say, food to the price of, say, machinery are lessened. With the growth of multinational companies (MNCs), choices are made between competing by offering products (i.e. by exporting) and by licensing domestic producers overseas or setting up subsidiary companies to produce and market on the spot. These choices depend upon the importance of economies of scale in production; transport costs; the costs of transferring capital, technology and management; and upon the restrictions imposed by governments upon the free movement of goods: that is, tariffs, import quotas and other barriers.

If all industries were subject to diminishing returns and perfect competition ruled, with homogeneous products, differences in the factor endowments of two countries starting to compete would lead to specialization up to the point where, at the margin, the relative costs of each pair of goods were the same in each country. In fact, with increasing returns to scale, equal relative marginal costs are no guarantee of equilibrium. Competitive advantage may accrue to an industry in the country where home demand expands and is protected for a time, so that relative costs fall as output increases. This so-called 'infant industry' case is still the most striking illustration of the inadequacy of simple static theorems about the effects of international competition upon trade flows.

The account of trade flows due to Heckscher and Ohlin (namely that it depends on differing input requirements for different goods and differing input endowments in different countries) remains the most important observation about international competitive advantage.

This model of specialization through trade can be modified to cope quite well with such market imperfections as transport and other transaction costs, limited information, a degree of imperfect competition in factor markets and limited trade barriers. It becomes seriously strained however when one tries to use it to explain the results of international competition in the world of many traders and many commodities. The number of separate 'factors of production' has to be increased to equal the number of traded commodities and defined to suit the observed trade flows. Competitive advantage became something 'revealed', rather than predictable by taking a census of resources. Cheap US skilled labour might be redefined as capital, but since physical capital was also cheap in the US the paradox which Leontief observed – that the US tended to import capital-intensive goods and export labour-intensive – could not be resolved this way.

On another view, out of which grew an alternative and more robust model of international competition, high technology was regarded as complementary to (skilled) labour explaining the bias of US trade. But a theory which relied first on separating factors of production but then required them to be lumped together is not a good theory. Furthermore, competitive advantages were found to be continuously changing in ways that could not be predicted by counting heads or hectares.

In the 1950s and 1960s, when industrial international competition became much more open and many countries were newly industrializing, trade both ways in different variants of the same products grew prodigiously. It has become clear that international competition drives intra-industry trade in imperfectly competitive differentiated markets; that in very many markets today's net exporter is tomorrow's importer; and that international competition involves the international transfer of capital and knowhow as well as of goods.

Something is needed then to supplement the explanation of broad directions of trade advantage in terms of fixed differences in factor endowments and given technology. There has arisen a less determinate, more detailed account of disequilibrium change in trade flows under conditions of imperfect competition. This account makes it clear how international competition leads to two-way flows of trade within the same industry. Where there are economies of scale in each of eight plants, four in each country, producing four variants of one product, a likely outcome is that four of the eight will survive, perhaps two in each country, and in each country the loyal customers of each type will import or buy at home accordingly. *Net* trade flows might be zero but gross

trade might be half of total consumption. Or two countries, one rich and one poor, might have developed at home (through domestic competition) lower relative costs in the 'superior' variant in the richer country and in the 'down-market' variant in the poorer country. As trade becomes easier, with cheaper transport and communications or lower tariff barriers, the poor country exports its variant to the poorer consumers in the richer country and vice versa. As incomes grow in both countries, demand in both will shift more and more towards the rich country's variant, and the poorer country loses overall market share.

Where the pressures of competition are leading to successive shifts in state-of-the-art technology in a discontinuous way, competitive advantage may move from the technological leader nation to the fast followers as they acquire this technology; and back to the leader again with the next major breakthrough, as has been observed in industries as different as radio receivers and textiles.

These models of changing comparative advantage owe much to Joseph Schumpeter. They focus upon the temporary monopoly advantages that accrue to the innovator, extended sometimes by patent protection and economies of scale.

As the technology gap is closed by imitators competing away the monopoly profits, the technological leader nation, like Schumpeter's individual innovator, jumps to new dry stepping-stones in today's 'sunrise' industries. The technology gap is moved but kept open.

Whenever this evolution involves new products, it becomes closely linked to a now well-established view of the development of product markets: namely, that products move through a life cycle of youthful growth as comparative luxuries; into explosive growth as they are mass-produced and become available to poorer consumers; into maturity, stagnation and sometimes death as they are superseded by a more efficient or desirable way of satisfying the same underlying needs. As products move through their life cycles, international competitive advantage will tend to shift from developed technological leader economies to newer or poorer industrializing economies, particularly those with large domestic markets allowing home-grown scale economies.

Technology gap and product life-cycle theories do not explain why some economies lead and others follow. The underlying point is that industrial leadership creates a kind of human and physical capital infrastructure, usually reflected in vigorous R&D. This intellectual property is partly external to the individual competitors in the leader economics and acts as a catalyst for new processes and products. There is a virtuous circle at work so long as resources can move freely from yesterday's staples to tomorrow's winners. When structural adaptation is slow, international competition can remove a historical leadership position from an economy whose high relative wages then prevent it from competing later in the cycle with newly-industrializing fast-followers. The UK is an economy, open to fierce international competition, which has lost its place in this way and is rapidly de-industrializing.

The typical market in international trade nowadays is one in which there is a small number of firms each with a strong home base but competing in each other's markets and in third markets. Price cuts are typically quickly matched, so oligopolists compete (and try to secure their segment of the market) by differentiating their products. Cars, clothes and computers are therefore both imported and exported as international competition drives individual producers to specialize.

Much of the most recent work on international competition examines how trade develops under conditions of imperfect competition. Intra-industry trade flows are affected by increasing returns to scale in individual product lines, by product differentiation, by competition in *non-price* terms (design, reliability, durability, variety, packaging, servicing, distribution, delivery speed, advertising) and by the scope for vertically integrated corporations to choose the separate locations of the different stages of production of the final product.

With intra-industry trade specialization, the threat of re-entry into each other's specialisms, as well as the possibilities of new entry, limit monopoly power. Other things being equal, entry is easier where world demand is growing fast and when the background technology is changing fast. Trade under conditions of imperfect competition tends to lead to increasing 'narrow market' specialization but decreasing 'wide market' monopoly power, together with lower costs and equal or greater breadth of consumer choice.

Two final international competition issues are important: the occasionally perverse effects of increased price competitiveness through currency depreciation; and the effect upon trade flows of the competitive options open to MNCs.

Suppose, through successive devaluations, one country's relative unit labour costs fall. (Relative unit labour costs are a better measure of price competitiveness than relative export prices because the latter catch only actual transactions, not lost orders.) The benefit to its trade in manufactures may be short-lived. Orders will come in at the most price-sensitive end of each of its industrial markets. Since this is usually the less sophisticated end, the nation's industries tend to become less competitive in *non-price* terms: to be impelled to specialize in those product versions whose demand grows least fast as incomes grow. In the longer run, scale economies (and overall market share) may be lost. Paradoxically, devaluation may have its best chance of increasing trade competitiveness when *domestic* competition is limited, so that home currency prices can be raised in price-inelastic markets, and the higher margins be used to overcome *non-price* disadvantages in world markets.

Large firms can move technology, capital and management skills, as well as goods, and change domestic factor supplies by training. International competition drives firms to look for the lowest cost way of creating value-added. It is often cheaper for a MNC to transfer key inputs than to ship final products. Exporting, licensing, local assembly or packaging, joint ventures with local producers, and complete local production and marketing are alternative modes of international competition. Each mode has private benefits and costs. The choice between them is affected by the expected reactions of competitors and by the policies of the consumer governments. Protection, and its threat, and dramatic improvements in communications in recent years have led to a large increase in international competition between local subsidiaries of MNCs and an increase in the proportion of trade in intermediate goods within vertically integrated firms. The overall volume of trade is nowadays a poor measure of the importance or strength of international competition.

D.K. STOUT

See also INTERNATIONAL TRADE.

BIBLIOGRAPHY

Caves, R.E. 1971. International corporations: the industrial economics of foreign investment. *Economica* 38, February, 1–27.

Caves, R.E. and Jones, R.W. 1981. *World Trade and Payments: An Introduction*. 3rd edn, Boston: Little Brown.

Cornwall, J. 1977. *Modern Capitalism, Its Growth and Transformation.* London: Martin Robertson, ch. 10.

Grubel, H. and Lloyd, P. 1975. *Intra-Industry Trade: The Theory and Measurement of International Trade in Differentiated Products.* New York: Wiley.

Houthakker, H.S. and Magee, S.P. 1969. Income and price elasticities in world trade. *Review of Economics and Statistics* 51(2), May, 111–25.

Kanamori, H. 1968. Economic growth and exports. In *Economic Growth: the Japanese Experience Since the Meiji Era*, ed. L. Klein and K. Onkawa, Homewood, Ill.: Richard Irwin.

Leontief, W.W. 1934. Domestic production and foreign trade. *Economica Internazionale* 7, February, 3–32. Reprinted in American Economic Association, *Readings in International Economics*, Homewood, Ill.: Richard Irwin, 1968.

Linder, S. 1961. *An Essay on Trade and Transformation.* Stockholm: Almqvist & Wiksell.

Schumpeter, J.A. 1942. *Capitalism, Socialism and Democracy.* New York: Harper.

Stout, D.K. 1977. *International Price Competitiveness, Non-Price Factors and Export Performance.* London: National Economic Development Office.

Thirlwall, A.P. 1980. *Balance of Payments Theory and the UK Experience.* London: Macmillan.

Venables, A.J. 1985. *International Trade, Trade and Industrial Policy and Imperfect Competition: A Survey.* Centre for Economic Policy Research Discussion Paper No. 74, October.

Vernon, R. (ed.) 1970. *The Technology Factor in International Trade.* National Bureau of Economic Research Conference Series No. 22, New York.

Wells, L. 1972. International trade: the product life cycle approach. In *The Product Life Cycle and International Trade*, ed. L. Wells, Cambridge, Mass.: Harvard University Press.

competition policy. The content and direction of competition policy is inevitably conditioned by the domestic structure and international relations of the economy in which the policy is applied. Since my discussion, although theoretical, is essentially concrete, I will direct my analysis to the case of competition policy in the UK. However, the argument may readily be generalized to other economies.

ECONOMIC EFFICIENCY. In the postwar period there have been considerable changes in the industrial structure and performance of the UK economy. In general, these changes have been associated with a decline in international competitiveness across broad areas of manufacturing industry, and a more concentrated structure of output in the hands of fewer, major, domestic producers in many manufacturing and non-manufacturing sectors. The increased exposure of the UK to international competition following entry to the EEC, and the more general progressive liberalization of international trade in the world economy, have been associated, in this country, with the development of substantial structural unemployment, surplus capacity, and an inability to match, by exports, the increased penetration of domestic markets by foreign producers.

The policy response to these changes has involved a constant interplay between macroeconomic demand management on the one hand, and interventionist, cooperative and competitive supply side strategies on the other. As one industrial policy weapon, on the supply side, the regulation of competition has evolved gradually in the postwar years in response to the accumulation of evidence about the effects of particular types of market behaviour upon the amount, quality and price of output supplied, and upon the responsiveness of supply to changing domestic and international demand patterns. This evolution has occurred against a background of other supply side industrial policies, in particular planning and cooperative initiatives, and policies towards price and profit margin controls. Any discussion of the appropriate current, and future, stance of competition policy must therefore be carried out in the context of specific assumptions about the objectives and form of industrial policy; and about the form of overall economic strategy, in particular about policies towards the balance of payments and international trade.

In an open economy we may define the role of industrial policy to be the maintenance of efficient production of output. By efficiency in this sense we mean that the economy must be able to meet the demands for goods and services of consumers at home, as well as sell enough of its products abroad to pay for the nation's import requirements subject to the constraint that this objective is fulfilled at socially acceptable levels of output, employment and the exchange rate (Singh, 1977).

It will be assumed that the role of competition policy within this framework must be to regulate economic behaviour to assist in the achievement of the efficiency objective. In more operational terms we shall interpret this to mean that competitive behaviour should be so regulated as to ensure the production, currently and in the future, of internationally tradeable output of a sufficiently high quality and at a sufficiently low cost and price to compete effectively with international suppliers at home and abroad, along with least-cost production of those non-tradeable elements of domestic consumption. This means that the competitive process must so far as is possible allocate sufficient inputs, including investment, to those uses necessary to achieve those objectives, and ensure operation at lowest possible cost. To the extent that certain forms of competitive behaviour are not compatible with the achievement of the appropriate levels and allocations of investment, employment and output, and hinder the achievement of the overall efficiency objective, then competition policy must be sufficiently flexible to accommodate non-competitive behaviour shown to be necessary for this.

I am therefore abstracting throughout from arguments in favour of a competition policy based on the notion of competitive behaviour as a 'good thing' *in itself*, irrespective of its implications in terms of an overall economic efficiency objective. Such arguments may be considered by some to be of overriding importance. It must, however, be recognized that they are based on political, philosophical or moral grounds, and are not in themselves susceptible to positive economic analysis.

COMPETITIVE AND COMPETITION POLICY. In order to distinguish competitive and non-competitive behaviour, and to consider the link between market behaviour and some notion of economic efficiency we obviously need to define a concept of competition. The best-developed notion of competition in formal economic analysis is that inherent in the state of affairs known as perfect competition. It is easy to show that, under certain very restrictive conditions, perfect competition will lead to economic efficiency in the traditional Pareto sense in which resources are so allocated that no one can be made better off without someone else being made worse off. Unfortunately, both the notion of perfect competition and the related Pareto efficiency criterion are too restrictive to serve as useful foundations for the analysis of competition policy. The state of affairs embodied in perfect competition assumes away nearly all those aspects of business behaviour with which competition policy is concerned (such as rivalry in terms of price setting, innovation in products and processes, and advertising) and ignores the static welfare gains to be had by improving the internal organization of enterprises, in favour of an analysis concentrating exclusively on the gains to be had by

reallocating resources between perfectly internally efficient producers. Moreover, even within its own restricted ambit, it yields few helpful decision rules for an imperfect world to adopt since it is unfortunately the case that if the conditions necessary for perfect competition are unavoidably absent in any single market then nothing can be said in general about the correct behaviour to be followed in the rest of the economy. In particular, it does not follow, for example, that the perfectly competitive partial equilibrium solution of setting prices equal to marginal cost, so that normal profits are earned in all sectors but the affected one, is the next best solution to setting prices equal to marginal cost everywhere. This 'problem of the second best' means that appropriate pricing rules can only be derived after a piecemeal approach to individual cases in which the input–output links with the distorted sectors are examined in order to gauge in which direction, and to what extent, price should diverge from marginal cost. The Pareto efficiency criterion is, of course, limited because of its inability to deal with those economic changes which involve alterations in the distribution of income. It is inevitable that the achievement of the kind of efficiency we have described above as the objective of UK economic policy will involve changes in the distribution of income, not least between different industrial nations, and between sectors of the domestic economy. For all these reasons we have preferred to adopt another approach to competition to use in relation to our efficiency criterion set out earlier.

This approach analyses competition, not as a state of affairs, but as a dynamic process linking structural change with market behaviour. Competition is taken to mean that range of activities aimed at meeting the objectives of one producer at the expense of others, and is thus defined in the business sense of the word, as a process involving rivalry between producers. Competitive rivalry takes both the form of contests within existing markets, and the form of potential entry into new areas when prospective returns appear relatively attractive. It includes rivalry in terms of price, but also in terms of altered or improved techniques of production or products, and in terms of the provision of information to consumers about products. All these forms of rivalry have consequences for the level and rate of growth of the technical efficiency of production and standards of consumption, for the allocation of resources between industries, and for the evolution of the structures of markets themselves.

There are a number of theories from which we may choose, which involve notions of competition as a dynamic process. The best known are those of Marx (1867–94), Schumpeter (1942), Downie (1958) and Clark (1961). This entry is based on the characterization of the competitive process by Downie. This is because he provides in a relatively simple manner, an analysis which is both more precise for our purposes than Clark, and avoids the complications imposed by the richer, more cosmic, implications of the Marxian and Schumpeterian analyses of capitalism. Moreover, the Downie model includes the main beneficial effects usually claimed to follow from competitive rivalry, in terms of cost efficiency, resource allocation, and technical progress, whilst emphasizing the possible structural changes flowing from competition which may change its nature and effects. We can then, following Downie, sketch an outline of a simple competitive process in a given market and consider its efficiency implications.

In any market we may expect that firms with the lowest cost structure (inherited from the past) will for any given market price have the highest profits to finance expansion. In their own pricing policy, firms are expected to set a price which promises to attract customers and provide sufficient retained profits to finance the capacity necessary to serve them in a balanced manner. In this way, within markets, relatively low costs will be associated with relatively fast growth, and a competitive transfer of market shares from the less to the more efficient will occur. Moreover, this transfer mechanism may have a feedback effect on efficiency in the sense that the previously less efficient will be threatened with an ever-diminishing share of the market unless they can improve their cost position, for instance by introducing more recent innovations in production technique.

The transfer and innovation mechanisms within markets thus have beneficial effects, both upon allocative efficiency, by transferring output and resources to the currently most efficient producers, and upon technical progressiveness, by encouraging the introduction of the least-cost techniques available. The outcome of this competitive process, however, in terms of the changing allocation of output between different firms over time, and the impact of this upon competitive behaviour itself, will depend ultimately on the answer to a number of empirical questions about the relationship between past and future efficiency, and company size and performance. If past success is repeated, and resulting gains in relative size offer efficiency advantages in themselves, through economies of scale or enhanced innovative ability, then particular markets may come to be dominated by ever fewer, ever larger, firms as a result of the transfer mechanism, whilst the innovative mechanism, acting as a spur for past losers to improve performance, may not be powerful enough to offset this tendency. Past failure may raise the desire, but inhibit the ability, to recover. Innovation in process or product may be expensive, and low profits, or relatively small scale, may limit the power of losers to respond actively enough to prevent the transfer mechanism from leading to the concentration of ever more output in fewer hands. Thus, in the absence of revival the end product of the competitive process may be domination of the market by the single producer whose efficiency in the past has outstripped all rivals.

However, before this stage is reached, the private gains from collusion between remaining producers may become apparent, since it can offer both lower costs of competition and a higher market price. The costs of adding to the stock of goodwill accumulated by past advertising can be reduced, and the necessity to indulge in competitive process and product innovation is modified. Moreover, collusion can offer the leading firms higher margins by concerted pricing policies, at least in the short run, and possibly in the long run too, if the scales of production and advertising created by the competitive process itself form effective barriers to entry. Thus the competitive process seems to end inevitably in dominant-firm monopolistic or oligopolistic structures, and in the suppression of the process itself. This reduces the pressure to increase the level of efficiency through time and, in the case of collusion, to reduce the dispersion of efficiency. Market price is higher, and to some extent output is lower than it might otherwise be. High-cost plants and firms can remain in production at the higher market price and the incentive to improve products and production methods falls. Thus, both levels and rates of growth of efficiency in any market may be worsened by the cessation of the competitive process in structural conditions which may themselves limit the chances of substantial new entry.

In terms of this analysis the objective of competition policy would appear to be the identification and regulation of those structures, restrictions on entry and kinds of behaviour which arrest the competitive process, and produce the efficiency

losses described above. This clearly poses problems of establishing links between structure and behaviour, of specifying behaviour inimical to the competitive process and of establishing the existence of markets where the competitive process has atrophied, and where it appears that efficiency gains are possible. In the case of an open economy such as the United Kingdom the relevant markets, and standards of comparison for efficiency, are international in character, and we must recognize that in many industries the degree of concentration of purely domestic producers will be of little use in assessing the fierceness of the transfer mechanism, because of the importance of foreign competition.

However, more fundamental problems have also to be recognized. It may be that a competitive process of the kind outlined above may not be the only, or the most efficient, means of achieving the same ends, either before or after the stage is reached at which the possibilities of market dominance or collusion arise. Thus, we must consider planned or cooperative solutions to the problem of raising efficiency. Moreover, there is no guarantee that the end result of the competitive process itself, in terms of the levels and rates of change of operating efficiency of producers, and their distribution between activities, will, for any individual country, necessarily meet the overall efficiency objective outlined earlier, in terms of output, inflation, employment and international trade performance targets. There is then, for both the above reasons, the possibility of conflict, in industrial policy *methods*, between the promotion of arm's-length competitive behaviour through competition policy, and the possible reduction in such behaviour encouraged by other aspects of government policy in pursuit, for instance, of industrial strategy. The possibility of conflict is most obvious in relation to restrictive trade practices, but is also present in the creation or encouragement of domestic dominant-firm positions through government-sponsored mergers or rationalization schemes (NEDO, 1978).

These conclusions run in some cases contrary to the majority of recent academic argument in this area, where increasing emphasis has been paid to the claimed welfare losses due to merger, increased monopoly power, and restrictive trade practices. However, in the context of current UK industrial performance and within the current overall economic policy framework a detailed scrutiny of the current evidence for the UK yields no foundation for a generally more aggressive approach towards large-firm dominance than the current legislation already adopts. This is not to deny that competition policy is necessary, but to assert that an *appropriate* competition policy must be designed in the light of existing economic conditions; of the evidence of the effects of various forms of market structure and behaviour; and of the overall objectives of economic policy.

ALAN HUGHES

See also ANTI-TRUST POLICY; MARKET STRUCTURE.

BIBLIOGRAPHY

Clark, J.M. 1961. *Competition as a Dynamic Process*. Washington, DC: Brookings Institution.
Downie, J. 1958. *The Competitive Process*. London: Duckworth.
Marx, K. 1867–94. *Capital*. London: Lawrence & Wishart, 1970–72.
NEDO. 1978. *Competition Policy*. National Economic Development Office; London: HMSO.
Schumpeter, J.A. 1942. *Capitalism, Socialism and Democracy*. London: George Allen & Unwin, 1968.
Singh, A. 1977. The UK industry and the world economy: a case of de-industrialisation? *Cambridge Journal of Economics* 1(2), June, 113-36.

competitive market processes. 1. Do fully competitive price signals from intense rivalry in the market justify the moral sentiment of laissez-faire? On grounds of distributive justice among risk-takers, the answer has generally been 'yes' throughout the history of economic analysis.

In considerations of optimum economic efficiency, however, the answer seems to have become more difficult over the course of development. The cheapening of commodities witnessed by the classical economists is the most virtuous example of efficient competitive market processes in which the distribution of returns tends to be equalized. Against the theoretical standard of perfect competition, non-price forms of competition came to be viewed in the 1930s as second-class virtues - imperfectly or monopolistically competitive practices.

Questions of intervention on grounds of allocative inefficiency have continued to hinge on the existence of classical monopoly profits. By the 1970s, the weight of empirical evidence and the acknowledged fact of intensified global competition served to eliminate the credibility of the market concentration doctrine derived from perfect and imperfect competition (see Demsetz, 1973, 1982).

At a more fundamental level, Joan Robinson was persuaded to abandon imperfect competition in favour of trying to more fully develop a classical line of analysis only partially worked out by the classical economists and largely ignored ever since (see Clifton, 1977).

Yet, after a decade of deregulation and the strongest sentimentality to let the free market reign, evidence of static and dynamic inefficiencies in industry is accumulating (*Business Week*, 1986). Has the sheer intensity of competition in the rate of economic change and the pace of economic life become so severe as to hinder economic efficiency even under the strongest possible tendencies to equalized returns in the market? Competition, however complex and full of discontinuities, is still evident as a systematic and general force in the empirically observed fact that accounting rates of return across firms and industries tend toward uniformity over time.

This dynamic tendency is stronger among larger than smaller firms and is stronger today than a century ago (see Singh and Whittington, 1968 chapter 6; Brozen, 1970, 1971, 1982, pp. 239–40). But it is not explained by the neoclassical theory of perfect competition, which requires atomism of independent agents under static premises of maximization. It is not explained by imperfect or monopolistic competition for stable positions of some degree of monopoly power are less and less in evidence all the time. Yet this dynamic tendency is not associated with any optimum or unique state of industrial efficiency, as under perfect competition. Finally, the intensity of competitive rivalry that leads to this tendency cannot be measured by neoclassical standards – the number of firms in a market. It exists primarily under market conditions of concentrated oligopoly.

It seems pointless to try to reconstitute the general theory of competitive value by still more *a priori* game theorizing which only adds to the false perception of indeterminacy and lack of systematic generality in 'price behaviour' under contemporary market conditions. A recent alternative has been to apply game theory to perfect competition (see Mas-Colell, 1980). What used to be a static state of affairs distinguished by the absence of any and all rivalry is now a non-cooperative equilibrium, independent of the number of agents, that may entail dynamic strategies of M periods contingent on past histories.

This re-introduces the long forgotten classical principle that interdependent, dynamic rivalries are what lead to the tendency toward uniformity in returns across the price system.

A possible virtue of the approach is that not all games need have positive sum outcomes, so the question of competitive rivalry and economic efficiency is left open, not closed as in the pure neoclassical doctrine of perfect competition.

With all the intellectual baggage imposed by perfect and imperfect competition, however, is it not preferable to start fresh by examining and explaining in classical price–theoretic terms that systematic empirical tendency toward uniformity in returns? The first point is that the institutional conditions for free capital mobility in the industrial context of fixed capital have developed gradually and progressively over the course of economic development during the past two hundred years. They are to be found in the first instance not in the atomistic enterprise but in the evolution of the organizational structure and competitive strategies of today's representative firm, the industrially and geographically diversified, publicly held corporation. Top management in industry has increasingly assumed the role once reserved for bankers in day-to-day affairs, moving capital from areas of lower to areas of higher returns.

When finance is committed to industry as fixed capital, it is at once immobilized for its economic life. It does not have the character of putty which enables it to be moulded for any use promising today's highest return in the market. The greatest barriers to capital mobility existed for the single factory enterprise which typified organizational structures in the United States in the 1840s. Railroad firms created the first degree of capital mobility directly within the enterprise by pioneering the coordinated, multi-unit organization. From the 1890s on, a degree of capital mobility across industries was added by integrated manufacturing companies and by mass retailers. Truly diversified industrial corporations began appearing in the 1920s and by the 1930s, mass retailers were national in scope (see Chandler, 1977, for a definitive history).

Beyond these structural elements in the development of capital mobility in the firm, the number of competitive strategies available to it from economies of large-scale organization and the intensity of the search for competitive advantage available from large budgets and staffs have also increased. Product innovations from a permanent R&D staff, advertising campaigns, takeovers and divestitures, together with price and credit competition give the firm added flexibility in responding to changes in market conditions and in initiating them.

Free capital mobility is not synonomous with the ability of atomistic firms or individual agents to move freely throughout the economy, whatever utopian analogies with a system of perfect liberty and individual freedom that may conjure up. What matters is the freedom of capital, however organized, so to move. As theoretical constructs, perfect and imperfect competition left a vision of capitalist development that is at complete odds with the actual historical development of conditions of free capital mobility. In this view, which is also espoused by many non-neoclassical economists, barriers to free capital mobility have grown with the evolution of large corporations, and the system has become less competitive, not more competitive.

Even beyond considerations of corporate organization and strategy, free capital mobility is nowhere more fully developed in history than in the institutions of today's capital markets. Ever more integrated on a world scale, ever more innovative in the range of 'products' and services offered, the large firms which dominate these markets have such powerful and all-encompassing information networks as to approximate the economic assumption of perfect information in the short run, if not rational expectations in the long run.

The acceptance of market processes in ever more spheres of human existence beyond basic needs is a third sense in which free capital mobility is more highly developed today. Scale economies in automobile production are not barriers to entry into new fields of endeavour like the child care industry. Finally, with the growth of labour-intensive services as a proportion of the economy, more businesses take on the characteristics of merchant capital once again in history since even learned human capital is more malleable than fixed stock.

2. Beyond considerations of free capital mobility in explaining the uniformity in returns are other key issues that fall outside the scope of perfect and imperfect competition, whether or not amalgamated with game theory.

If today's oligopolistic firms are the slaves of the market as never before in history, in what sense are they 'pure price takers'? Such corporations are entirely unable to dictate their ex post rate of return in the market, whatever their ex ante pricing behaviour. It is with the ex post rate of return that the theory of competitive price is concerned, and that will be determined by many forms and intensities of competitive behaviour in the market, of which a suggested mark-up ex ante is only one. Partial equilibrium mark-up theories have never comprehended the difference between ex ante and ex post and err in believing ex ante pricing discretion implies some degree of ex-post monopoly power.

The very interdependence in decision-making between oligopolistic firms is what causes that ebb and flow of business and profits across firms, industries and markets so as to render the ex post rate of return fully competitive and beyond the control of the individual firm. Unfortunately, game theory was used for decades to deny the generality of contemporary competitive behaviour rather than to explain its most systematic feature in the convergence of accounting rates of return over the long run.

A virtue of the neoclassical theory of perfect competition was to provide a readily quantifiable means of measuring the intensity of competition – by the number of firms in a market. In consideration of non-price forms of competition, this precision in economic theory became lost, appearing in lieu of theory as an industrial organization 'paradigm' of market structure *and* conduct *and* performance. Can quantitative precision be resurrected in a general theory of competitive value for the modern age?

Observation tells us that the intensity of rivalry in contemporary markets can be measured by the *frequency* and *voracity* of changes in market conditions – the sum total of strategic moves and countermoves made by firms in that market per unit of time. The common denominator among all types of competition is to what measured degree does the action move business and profits from one sphere to another or one firm to another.

There is a clear analogy to perfect competition that can be made here. Were oligopolists in a market limited to the type of action an atomistic firm entering that market could take, pure price taking behaviour would emerge as the frequency of such strategic moves and countermoves increased without limit. Price for a homogeneous good would be bid down to its normal competitive minimum not by unlimited entry by one small firm after another, but by an unlimited number of atomistic-like strategic moves by the competing oligopolists.

Game theory to date appears to have overlooked the primacy of numbers of actions in the marketplace over numbers of actors in resurrecting the general theory of competitive value, on measuring the intensity of competition as the frequency of strategic moves and countermoves in the first instance.

Of course, large firms are not restricted to atomistic competition. Cut-rate 'two percent' financing by General Motors Corporation in August 1986 was a competitive move that had the potential to draw a great amount of business and profits away from other firms. For that reason, this voracious move was imitated quickly by Ford and Chrysler.

Competition in the personal computer market has been intense not only because of voracious price breaks from time to time, but because the frequency of changes in market conditions has been enormous from real and cosmetic innovations in hardware and software. The frequency of competition among the commercial television networks in changing the time slots of programmes has at times approached the irrational from the consumer's standpoint.

3. When market processes are intensely competitive in the frequency, voracity or complexity of strategic moves and countermoves applied, what will be the nature of decision-making by the individual firm? Does active rivalry in the market necessarily mean 'maximizing behaviour', optimally efficient performance from decision-making at the margin?

One strong clue to the answer is the rejection of the marginal method *and* the assumption of constant returns to scale in recent classical general equilibrium models of competitive price determination (see Sraffa, 1960). If maximizing behaviour underlies the classical approach, it certainly is not of pure neoclassical vintage, for decision-making at the margin requires marginal units which, according to Sraffa, are 'nowhere to be found' in the pure classical theory of competitive value.

Nor is any notion of maximization or optimal efficiency to be found in the statement of technology or 'production function' of the pure classical system. The technology is not specified by input–output coefficients, which imply minimum input per unit of output. Only viability conditions for each industry at a given scale of output are listed. Viability is not the same thing as optimum efficiency in the use of a technique of production, whether under conditions of simple reproduction or the production of a surplus.

The entirely unsophisticated requirements for specifying technology in the classical determination of competitive value is an advantage, because it formally leaves open the question of whether fully competitive price behaviour in ongoing market processes is always efficient.

The empirically observed tendency of accounting rates of return to converge in the long run seems more assuredly decision-making by oligopolists where the intensity of competitive behaviour is asymmetric around a normal or average rate of profit. Whether from creditor or stockholder admonition, team pride or the threat of takeover, firms whose performance is below the normal rate of return are under stronger pressure to improve profitability than those whose performance is above the norm (see Cyert and March, 1956).

Further, the attributes of intensely competitive market processes cause decision-making by the firm facing such discontinuities and complexities in its external environment to be the kind of 'bounded rationality' highlighted in the administrative theories of decision-making for different reasons related to the internal characteristics of large organizations (see Simon, 1947).

The paradox of how 'maximum' effort or greater and greater rivalry directed through market processes can result in sub-optimal outcomes is precisely the question the business world, especially in America, seems to be asking itself today (see President's Commission, 1985). While associated with even stronger and faster movements to capture new markets or eliminate excess profitability than less intensely competitive behaviour in bygone eras, classifying it as 'maximizing behaviour' or 'satisficing' can only lead to confusion. The former implies efficiency where no such implication is warranted *a priori*, while the latter implies an absence of highly energetic behaviour from constantly striving, an implication at complete odds with the facts. A more neutral term like 'competitive behaviour' seems preferable.

4. If fully competitive price signals can exist under different degrees of industrial efficiency, then the moral sentiment of laissez-faire is not so readily justified in a competitive free enterprise system. Welfare economics must focus on competition as both virtue and vice, rather than competition as virtue and monopoly as vice, as in the past fifty years. Consider Figure 1, which relates the intensity of competition to the degree of economic efficiency. In modern economic doctrine there are three unambiguous situations: pure monopoly (point γ), perfect competition (point π) and the long run shutdown point beyond which a firm cannot cover its total costs (point ϕ).

In the context of a single industry, ruinous competition is rightly viewed as self-correcting by market forces. Therefore, the entire scope of economic investigation is believed to have been between θ and β. The curve $\sigma\,\pi$ expresses the sentiment that the more competition the better for efficiency as measured by the rate of return. The curve $\gamma\,\pi$ expresses the proposition that the more competition, the lower the degree of monopoly, and the stronger the tendency toward uniformity in returns around a normal rate of profit ρ. All inefficiency is due to the absence of competition in sufficient degree, and may be measured as social welfare losses like the area $\gamma\,\sigma\,\pi$.

The principle justification for laissez-faire through history has been that 'competition without limit' must always enhance the general welfare by improving static or dynamic efficiencies, as expressed in the positive slope of $\sigma\pi$. Competition in effect can never become so intense, or of a character or complexity, that it pushes a market or an economic system beyond point π in the long run. In neoclassical theory, this is expressed as an increase in the number of firms without limit tending to produce a state of perfect competition.

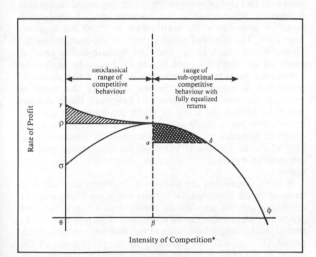

Figure 1 Efficiency and Inefficiency in Competitive Resource Allocation

*For neoclassical theory, this axis measures the number of competitors, where the limit, represented by the vertical dashed line, is the familiar large numbers case of atomistic or perfect competition. For classical theory, the axis measures the frequency and magnitude of changes in market conditions. There is no limit to the intensity of such competitive behaviour.

Yet once we admit that ruinous competition has existed in history, is there no range of sub-optimal competitive behaviour between π and ϕ? Competition that is sufficiently intense to bid away all excess profits, but too intense to maximize efficiency and the general welfare? Fully competitive market processes that lead to sub-optimal outcomes – zero sum or even negative sum games?

If and only if such business practices are isolated in one or a few markets will they be self-correcting by the market. If they are, or have become, systemic throughout the economy, there is no reason to believe they will be self-regulating in the market in a way which leads to movement from a position like δ to the unique point of optimum efficiency associated with equality of returns, π.

I submit that today's general competitive equilibrium in resource allocation lies at a point like δ and that the free enterprise system in an atmosphere of laissez-faire is experiencing social welfare losses of the form $\pi\,\alpha\,\delta$, not of the form $\pi\,\rho\,\gamma$ from monopolistic distortions.

There is no distortion in price signals associated with contemporary social welfare losses. They exist in a climate of intensely competitive market processes where the tendency toward equality of returns is stronger, not weaker. The real issue is becoming whether all this incessant change still represents a Schumpeterian process of creative destruction or an inefficient process of 'destructive creations'.

Free capital mobility has become so highly developed in financial markets and top management behaviour in corporations that it has led to the virtual collapse of the long period in setting aspiration levels for the rate of return on real capital formation in industry. This increase in the intensity of competition is generating an ongoing bias against efficiency-enhancing forms of strategic corporate behaviour in favour of stop-gap or crisis management forms of competition such as 'asset juggling', which does not affect the quality of products or the efficiency with which they are produced, distributed and sold.

The rate of change in and complexity of market conditions to which the firm must respond strategically has accelerated, not only in product and input markets, but also in economic policy variables here and abroad. The intensity of these competitive pressures is leading to the creation of corporate cultures that are very risk averse, and to decision-making of strictly bounded rationality that, however energetic, can hardly be called 'maximizing behaviour'.

The growing inability to protect positions of differential rent or supra-normal profits for a period necessary to sustain some of the most productive forms of risk-taking entrepreneurial behaviour is caused by the very intensity of competition in contemporary market processes. The crowding out of these Schumpeterian forms of dynamically efficient market processes is a third social welfare loss that exists in today's laissez-faire atmosphere.

The capitalization of finance on pure finance rather than real asset creation has become almost an epidemic of market processes that are of dubious value to the general welfare and that, moreover, increase the cost of capital for productive uses. For example, the increase in takeover divestiture type activities is associated with the creation of a distinct market for corporate control which simply changes the distribution of ownership and/or control of existing productive assets.

5. All seem to be agreed that competition has become more intense in recent decades and especially in recent years. I continue to maintain, as well, that there has been a secular increase in the intensity and complexity of competition over

the course of capitalist development and that the free enterprise system continues to develop fundamentally along the lines of ever greater capital mobility.

But it is also my contention that over the course of capitalist development and especially evident in recent years in America, the intensity of competition has become so great as to hinder industrial efficiency. Change for the sake of change rather than for economic and social progress. Competition, that engine of prosperity that has propelled us forward for two centuries, now seems to be of a character that it is holding us back.

This suggests a very different role for economic doctrine and public policy than either laissez-faire or the regulation of monopolistically competitive practices. It implies that intervention in the market which reduces the intensity or scope of certain fully competitive practices will not inexorably lead to protected positions of monopoly or associated inefficiencies. Intervention may in all probability enhance economic growth or improve statical resource allocation while fully maintaining that attribute of distributive justice among risk-takers, insofar as the equality of returns is concerned, that is the hallmark of capitalism and freedom.

J.A. CLIFTON

See also COMPETITION; COMPETITION: AUSTRIAN CONCEPTIONS; COMPETITION: CLASSICAL CONCEPTIONS; COMPETITION: MARXIAN CONCEPTIONS.

BIBLIOGRAPHY

Brozen, Y. 1970. The antitrust Task Force deconcentration recommendations. *Journal of Law and Economics* 13(2), October, 279-92.

Brozen, Y. 1971. The persistence of 'high rates of return' in high stable concentration industries. *Journal of Law and Economics* 14(2), October, 501-12.

Brozen, Y. 1982. *Concentration, Mergers and Public Policy*. New York: Macmillan.

Business Week. 1986. The hollow corporation. 3 March.

Chandler, A.D., Jr. 1977. *The Visible Hand*. Cambridge, Mass.: Harvard University Press.

Clifton, J.A. 1977. Competition and the evolution of the capitalist mode of production. *Cambridge Journal of Economics* 1(2), June, 137-51.

Cyert, R. and March, J. 1956. Organizational factors and the theory of oligopoly. *Quarterly Journal of Economics* 70, February, 44-64.

Demsetz, H. 1973. The market concentration doctrine. American Enterprise Institute for Public Policy Research, Hoover Institution on War, Revolution and Peace.

Demsetz, H. 1982. *Economic, Legal, and Political Dimensions of Competition*. New York: North-Holland.

Mas-Colell, A. 1980. Noncooperative approaches to the theory of perfect competition: presentation. *Journal of Economic Theory* 22(2), 121-35.

President's Commission on Industrial Competitiveness. 1985. *Global Competition: The New Reality*, Vol. 1, Washington, DC.

Simon, H. 1945. *Administrative Behavior*. New York: Macmillan and Free Press.

Singh, A. and Whittington, G. 1968. *Growth, Profitability and Valuation*. Cambridge: Cambridge University Press.

Sraffa, P. 1960. *Production of Commodities by Means of Commodities*. Cambridge: Cambridge University Press.

complementarity. *See* SUBSTITUTES AND COMPLEMENTS.

computation of general equilibria. The general equilibrium model, as elaborated by Walras and his successors, is one of the most comprehensive and ambitious formulations in the current body of economic theory. The basic ingredients with which the Walrasian model is constructed are remarkably spare: a specification of the asset ownership and preferences for goods and services of the consuming units in the economy, and a description of the current state of productive knowledge possessed by each of the firms engaged in manufacturing or in the provision of services. The model then yields a complete determination of the course of prices and interest rates over time, levels of output and the choice of techniques by each firm, and the distribution of income and patterns of saving for each consumer.

The Walrasian model is essentially a generalization, to the entire economy and to all markets simultaneously, of the ancient and elementary notion that prices move to levels which equilibrate supply and demand. No intellectual construction of this scope, designed to address basic questions in a subject as complex and elusive as economics, can be described as simply true or false – in the sense in which these terms are used in mathematics or perhaps in the physical sciences. The assertions of economic theory are not susceptible to crisp and immediate experimental verification. Moreover, the Walrasian model disregards obvious aspects of human motivation which are of the greatest economic significance and which cannot be addressed in the language of our subject: economic theory is mute about our affective lives, about our opposing needs for community and individual assertion, and about the non-pecuniary determinants of entrepreneurial energy.

There are, in addition, aspects of economic reality which are capable of being described in the framework of the Walrasian model but which must be assumed away in order for the model to yield a determinate outcome. Uncertainty about the future is an ever-present fact of economic life, and yet the complete set of markets for contingent commodities required by the Arrow–Debreu treatment of uncertainty is not available in practice. Economies of scale in production are a central feature in the rise of the large manufacturing entities which dominate modern economic activity; their incorporation into the Walrasian model requires the introduction of non-convex production possibility sets for which the competitive equilibrium will typically fail to exist.

In spite of its many shortcomings, the Walrasian model – if used with tact and circumspection – is an important conceptual framework for evaluating the consequences of changes in economic policy or in the environment in which the economy finds itself. The effects of a major shock to the economy of the United States – such as the four-fold increase in the price of imported oil which occurred in late 1973 – can be studied by contrasting equilibrium prices, real wages and the choice of productive techniques both before and after the event in question. Generations of economists have used the Walrasian model to analyse the terms of trade, the impact of customs unions, changes in tariffs and a variety of other issues in the theory of International Trade. And much of the literature in the field of Public Finance is based on the assumption that the competitive model is an adequate description of economic reality.

In these discussions the analysis is frequently conducted in terms of simple geometrical diagrams whose use places a severe restriction on the number of consumers, commodities and productive sectors that can be considered. This is in contrast to formal mathematical treatments of the Walrasian model, which permit an extraordinary generality in the elaboration of the model at the expense of immediate geometrical visualization. Unfortunately, however, it is only under the most severe assumptions that mathematical analysis will be capable of providing unambiguous answers concerning the direction and magnitude of the changes in significant economic variables, when the system is perturbed in a substantial fashion. In order for a comparative analysis to be carried out in a multi-sector framework it is necessary to employ computational techniques for the explicit numerical solution of the highly non-linear system of equations and inequalities which represent the general Walrasian model.

THE USE OF FIXED-POINT THEOREMS IN EQUILIBRIUM ANALYSIS

One of the triumphs of mathematical reasoning in economic theory has been the demonstration of the existence of a solution for the general equilibrium model of an economy, under relatively mild assumptions on the preferences of consumers and the nature of production possibility sets (see Debreu, 1982). The arguments for the existence of equilibrium prices inevitably make use of Brouwer's Fixed-Point Theorem, or one of its many variants, and any effective numerical procedure for the computation of equilibrium prices must therefore be capable of computing the fixed points whose existence is asserted by this mathematical statement.

Brouwer's Fixed-Point Theorem, enunciated by the distinguished Dutch mathematician L. E. J. Brouwer in 1912, is the generalization to higher dimensions of the elementary observation that a continuous function of a single variable which has two distinct signs at the two endpoints of the unit interval, must vanish at some intermediary point. In Brouwer's theorem the unit interval is replaced by an arbitrary closed, bounded convex set S in R^n, and the continuous function is replaced by a continuous mapping of the set S into itself: $x \rightarrow g(x)$. Brouwer's Theorem then asserts the existence of at least one point x which is mapped into itself under the mapping; that is, a point x for which $x = g(x)$. To see how this conclusion is used in solving the existence problem let us begin by specifying, in mathematical form, the basic ingredients of the Walrasian model.

The typical consumer is assumed to have a preference order for, say, the non-negative commodity bundles $x = (x_1, x_2, \ldots, x_n)$ in R^n; the preference ordering is described either by a specific utility function $u(x_1, x_2, \ldots, x_n)$ or by means of an abstract representation of preferences. The consumer will also possess, prior to production and trade, a vector of initial assets $w = (w_1, w_2, \ldots, w_n)$. When a non-negative price vector $p = (p_1, p_2, \ldots, p_n)$ is announced the consumer's income will be $I = p \cdot w$ and his demands will be obtained by maximizing preferences subject to the budget constraint

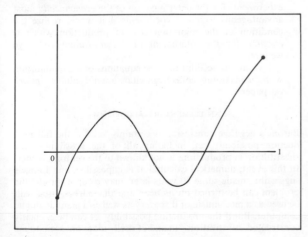

Figure 1

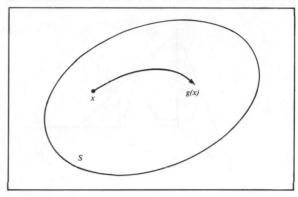

Figure 2

$p \cdot x \leqslant p \cdot w$. If the preferences satisfy sufficient regularity assumptions, the consumer's demand functions $x(p)$ will be single-valued functions of p, continuous (except possibly when some of the individual prices are zero), homogeneous of degree zero and will satisfy the budget constraint $p \cdot x(p) = p \cdot w$.

The market demands are obtained by aggregating over individual demand functions and, as such, will inherit the properties described above. The market *excess* demand functions, which I shall denote by $f(p)$, arise by subtracting the supply of assets owned by all consumers from the demand functions themselves. It is these functions which are required for a complete specification of the consumer side of the economy in the general equilibrium model: they may be obtained either by the aggregation of individual demand functions – as we have just described – or they may be directly estimated from econometric data. The following properties will hold, either as a logical conclusion or by assumption:

1. $f(p)$ is homogeneous of degree zero.
2. $f(p)$ is continuous in the interior of the positive orthant
3. $f(p)$ satisfies the Walras Law $p \cdot f(p) = 0$.

The first of these properties permits us to normalize prices in any one of several ways; for example, $\Sigma p_j = 1$ or $\Sigma p_j^2 = 1$. Given either of these normalizations, I personally do not find it offensive to extend the property of continuity to the boundary, even though there are elementary examples of utility functions, such as the Cobb–Douglas function, for which this would not be correct.

The production side of the economy requires for its description a complete specification of the current state of technical knowledge about the methods of transforming inputs into outputs – with commodities differentiated according to their location and the time of their availability. This can be done by means of production functions, an input/output table with substitution possibilities and several scarce factors rather than labour alone, or by a general activity analysis model:

$$A = \begin{bmatrix} -1 & 0 & \ldots & 0 & a_{1,n+1} & \ldots & a_{1,k} \\ 0 & -1 & & 0 & a_{2,n+1} & & a_{2,k} \\ \vdots & \vdots & & \vdots & \vdots & & \vdots \\ 0 & 0 & & -1 & a_{n,n+1} & & a_{n,k} \end{bmatrix}$$

Each column of A describes a particular productive process, with inputs represented by non-negative entries and outputs by positive entries. The activities are assumed capable of being used simultaneously and at arbitrary non-negative levels $x = (x_1, x_2, \ldots, x_k)$; the net production plan is then $y = Ax$.

557

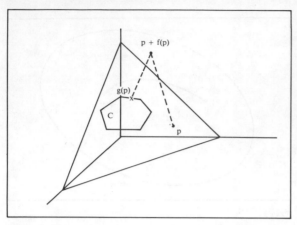

Figure 3

sions obtained by constructive procedures. In spite of the many simplifications in the proof of Brouwer's Theorem offered during the subsequent half-century, it was not until the mid-1960s that constructive methods for approximating fixed points of a continuous mapping finally made their appearance on the scene (Scarf, 1967) – aided by the development of the modern electronic computer and by the rapid methodological advances in the discipline of operations research.

In the early decades of this century, the question of the explicit numerical solution of the general equilibrium model was an active topic of discussion – not by numerical analysts – but rather by economists concerned with the techniques of economic planning in a socialist economy. The issue was raised in the remarkable paper published by Enrico Barone in 1908, entitled 'The Ministry of Production in a Socialist Economy'. Barone, and subsequently Oskar Lange (1936), accepted the Walrasian model – with suitable transfers of income – as an adequate description of ideal economic activity in an economy in which the means of production were collectively owned. In the absence of markets, prices, levels of output and the choice of productive techniques were to be obtained by an explicit numerical solution of the Walrasian system. A key feature of Barone's analysis was the concept of the 'technical coefficients of production' – the input/output coefficients associated with those activities in use at equilibrium. Barone's contention was that the equilibrium could be found – by an extremely laborious calculation which might indeed claim a significant share of the national product – only if the correct activities were known in advance. For Barone, rational economic calculation in a socialist economy was defeated by the many opportunities for substitution in production: the particular activities in use at equilibrium would be impossible to determine by a prior computation. It is instructive to quote Barone on this point.

With this formulation, a competitive equilibrium is defined by a non-negative vector of prices $p = (p_1, p_2, \ldots, p_n)$ and a non-negative vector of activity levels $x = (x_1, x_2, \ldots, x_k)$ satisfying the following conditions:

1. $f(p) = Ax$,
2. $pA \leqslant 0$.

The first condition states that supply and demand are equal in all markets, and the second that there are not opportunities for positive profits when the profitability of each activity is evaluated at the equilibrium prices. Taken in conjunction with the Walras's Law, these conditions imply that those activities which are used at a positive level in the equilibrium solution make a profit of zero.

Given the assumption of continuous and single-valued excess demand functions and the description of the production possibility set by means of an activity analysis model, the following rather direct application of Brouwer's Theorem is sufficient to demonstrate the existence of a equilibrium solution. Under weaker assumptions on the model, variants such as Kakutani's Fixed-Point Theorem may be required.

Let prices be normalized so as to lie on the unit simplex $S = \{p = (p_1, p_2, \ldots, p_n) | p_i \geqslant 0, \Sigma p_i = 1\}$. The set of prices p for which $pA \leqslant 0$ is termed the *dual* cone of the production possibility set generated by the activity analysis matrix A. Its intersection with the unit simplex is a convex polyhedron C consisting of those normalized prices which yield a profit less than or equal to zero for all activities.

We construct a continuous mapping of S into itself as follows: for each p in S consider the point $p + f(p)$; a point which is generally not on the unit simplex itself. We then define $g(p)$ – the image of p under the mapping – to be that point in C which is closest, in the sense of Euclidean distance, to $p + f(p)$. It is then an elementary application of the Kuhn–Tucker Theorem to show that a fixed point of this mapping is, indeed, an equilibrium price vector.

THE EQUILIBRIUM MODEL AS A TOOL FOR POLICY EVALUATION

Brouwer's original proof of his theorem was not only difficult mathematically, but it was decidedly non-constructive; it offered no method for effectively computing a fixed point of the mapping. Brouwer did, in fact, reject his own argument during the later 'intuitionist' phase of his career, in which he proclaimed the acceptability of only those mathematical conclu-

> The determination of the coefficients economically most advantageous can only be done in an *experimental* way: and not on a *small scale*, as could be done in a laboratory; but with experiments on a *very large scale*, because often the advantage of the variation has its origin precisely in a new and greater dimension of the undertaking. Experiments may be successful in the sense that they may lead to a lower cost combination of factors; or they may be unsuccessful, in which case the particular organization may not be copied and repeated and others will be preferred, which *experimentally* have given a better result.
>
> The Ministry of Production could not do without these experiments for the determination of the *economically* most advantageous technical coefficients if it would realize the condition of the minimum cost of production which is *essential* for the attainment of the maximum collective welfare.
>
> It is on this account that the equations of the equilibrium with the maximum collective welfare are not soluble *à priori*, on paper.

AN ELEMENTARY ALGORITHM

Barone's negative conclusion is certainly valid if the full production possibility set, including all of the possibilities for substitution in production, is not known to the central planner. In this event, numerical calculation is impossible, and Lange's suggestion, made some 20 years later, may be appropriate: the problem can be turned on its head and the market, itself, can be used as a mechanism of discovery as well as a giant analogue computer. But if the production possibility set can be explicitly constructed, substitution – in and of itself – does not seem to me to be a severe impediment to numerical computation.

At the present moment, some 20 years after the introduction and continued refinement of fixed-point computational techniques, I have in my possession a small floppy disk with a computer program which will routinely solve – on a personal computer – for equilibrium prices and activity levels in a Walrasian model in which the number of variables is on the order of 100. (The authors of the program suggests that examples with 300 variables can be accommodated on a mainframe computer.) Substantial possibilities of substitution, if known in advance, offer no difficulty to the successful functioning of this algorithm. In my opinion, the modern restatement of Barone's problem is rather that even 300 variables are extremely small in number in contrast to the millions of prices and activity levels implicit in his account. The computer, while expanding our capabilities immeasurably, has taught us a severe lesson about the role of mathematical reasoning in economic practice and forced us to shift our point of view dramatically from that held by our predecessors. We realize that our preoccupations are not with universal laws which describe economic phenomena with full and complete generality, but rather with intellectual formulations which are an imperfect representation of a complex and elusive reality. The application of general equilibrium theory to economic planning, and more generally to the evaluation of the consequences of changes in economic policy, must be based on highly aggregated models whose conclusions are at best tentative guides to action.

An exercise in comparative statics is begun by constructing a general equilibrium model whose solution reflects the economic situation existing prior to the proposed policy change. The number of parameters required to describe demand functions, initial endowments and the production possibility set is considerable, and in practice the constraint of reproducing the current equilibrium must be augmented by a variety of additional statistical estimates in order to specify the model. The limitations of data in the form required by the Walrasian model inevitably make this estimation procedure less than fully satisfactory.

The second step in the exercise is to calculate the solution after the proposed policy changes are explicitly introduced into the model. In some cases the policy variables being studied can be directly incorporated as parameters in the equations whose solution yields the equilibrium values; if the changes are small, their effects on the solution may be obtained by differentiating these equations and solving the resulting linear system for the corresponding changes in the equilibrium values themselves. This approach was adopted by Leif Johansen (1960) and by Arnold Harberger (1962) in his study of the incidence of a tax on corporate profits. The use of this method in policy analysis continues in Norway, and it forms the basis of the amibitious programme carried out by Peter Dixon and his collaborators in Australia (1982). If, on the other hand, the policy changes are large, the equilibrium position may be shifted substantially, and its determination may require the use of more sophisticated computational methods.

Fixed-point algorithms can be divided into two major classes: those based on the elements of differential topology, surveyed by Smale (1981), and those which are combinatorial in nature. The most elementary of the combinatorial algorithms for approximating a fixed point of a continuous mapping of the unit simplex $S = \{x = (x_1, x_2, \ldots, x_n) | x_i \geqslant 0, \Sigma x_i = 1\}$ begins by dividing the simplex into a large number of small subsimplices as illustrated in Figure 4. In our notation the simplex is of dimension $n - 1$ and has faces of dimension $n - 2, \ldots, 1$. It is a requirement of the subdivision that the intersection of any two of the subsimplices is either empty or a full lower dimensional face of both of them.

Each vertex of the subdivision will have associated with it an integer label selected from the set $(1, 2, \ldots, n)$. When the method is applied to the determination of a fixed point of a particular mapping, the labels associated with a vertex will depend on the mapping evaluated at that point. For the moment, however, the association will be arbitrary aside from the requirement that a vertex on the boundary of the simplex will have a label i only if the ith coordinate of that vertex is positive.

The remarkable combinatorial lemma demonstrated by Emanuel Sperner (1928) in his doctoral thesis is that at least one subsimplex must have all of its vertices differently labelled. Assuming this result to be correct, let us consider a mapping of the simplex in which the image of the vector $x = (x_1, \ldots, x_n)$ is $f(x) = [f_1(x), \ldots, f_n(x)]$. The requirement that the image be on the simplex implies that $f_i(x) \geqslant 0$ and that $\Sigma f_i(x) = 1$. It follows that for every vertex of the subdivision v, unless v is a fixed point of the mapping, there will be a least one index i for which $f_i(v) - v_i < 0$. If we select such an index to be the label associated with the vertex v, then the assumptions of Sperner's Lemma are clearly satisfied, and the conclusion asserts the existence of a simplex whose vertices are distinctly labelled.

If the simplicial subdivision is very fine, the vertices of this subsimplex are all close together; at each vertex a different coordinate is decreasing under the mapping, and by continuity every point in the small subsimplex will have the property that each coordinate is not increasing very much under the mapping. Since the sum of the coordinate changes is by definition zero, the image of any point in the completely labelled subsimplex will be close to itself, and such a point will therefore serve as an approximate fixed point of the mapping. A formal proof of Brouwer's Theorem requires us to construct a sequence of finer and finer subdivisions, to find, for each subdivision, a completely labelled simplex, and to select a convergent sequence of these simplices tending to a fixed point of the mapping.

Sperner's Lemma may be applied to the equilibrium problem directly. For simplicity, consider the model of exchange in which the market excess demand functions are given by $g(p)$, with p on the unit price simplex. As before, we subdivide the simplex and associate an integer label from the set $(1, \ldots, n)$ with each vertex v of the subdivision, according to the following rule: the label i is to be selected from the set of those indices of which $g_i(p) \leqslant 0$. It is an elementary consequence of Walras' Law that a selection can be made which is consistent with the assumptions of Sperner's Lemma, and there will therefore be a subsimplex all of whose vertices bear distinct labels. By virtue

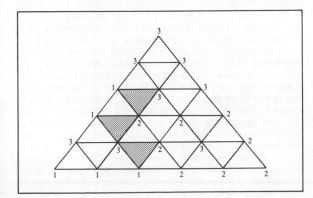

Figure 4

of the particular labelling rule, any point in such a completely labelled simplex will be an approximate equilibrium price vector in the sense that all excess demands, at this price, will be either negative or, if positive, very small.

Sperner's original proof of his combinatorial lemma was not constructive; it was based on an inductive argument which required a complete enumeration of all completely labelled simplices for a series of lower dimensional problems. In order to develop an effective numerical algorithm for the determination of such a simplex let us begin by embedding the unit simplex, and its subsimplices, in a larger simplex T, as in Figure 5. The larger simplex is subdivided by joining its n new vertices to those vertices of the original subdivision lying on the boundary of the unit simplex. The assumptions of Sperner's Lemma permit the new vertices to be given distinct labels from the set $(1, \ldots, n)$, in such a way that no additional completely labelled simplices are generated. For concreteness, let the new vertex receiving the label i be denoted by v^i.

We begin our search for a completely labelled simplex by considering the simplex with vertices $v^2, \ldots, v^n$ and one additional vertex, say v^*. If v^* has the label 1, this simplex is completely labelled and our search terminates; otherwise we move to an adjacent simplex by removing the vertex whose label agrees with that of v^* and replacing it with that unique other vertex yielding a simplex in the subdivision. As the process continues, we are, at each step, at a simplex whose vertices bear the labels $2, \ldots, n$, with a single one of these labels appearing on a pair of vertices. Precisely two $n - 2$ dimensional faces have a complete set of labels $2, \ldots, n$. The simplex has been entered through one of these faces; the algorithm proceeds by exiting through the other such face.

The argument first introduced by Lemke (1965) in his study of two person non-zero sum games was carried over by Scarf (1967) to show that the above algorithm never returns to a simplex previously visited and never requires a move outside of T. Since the number of simplices is finite, the algorithm must terminate, and termination can only occur when a completely labelled simplex is reached.

IMPROVEMENTS IN THE ALGORITHM

The algorithm can easily be programmed for a computer, and it provides the most elementary numerical procedure for

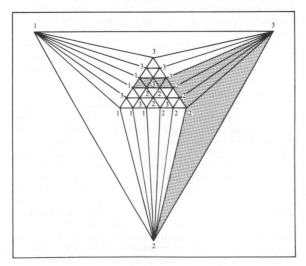

Figure 5

approximating fixed points of a continuous mapping and equilibrium prices for the Walrasian model. Since its introduction in 1967, the algorithm, in this particular form, has been applied to a great number of examples of moderate size, and it performs sufficiently well in practice to conclude that the numerical determination of equilibrium prices is a feasible undertaking. The algorithm does, however, have some obvious drawbacks which must be overcome to make it available for problems of significant size. For example, the information which yields the labelling of the vertices, and therefore the path taken by the algorithm, is simply the index of a coordinate which happens to be decreasing when the mapping is evaluated at the vertex. More recent algorithms make use of the full set of coordinates of the image of the vertex instead of a single summary statistic.

Second, this primitive algorithm is always initiated at the boundary of the simplex. If the approximation is not sufficiently good, the grid size must be refined, and a recalculation, which makes no use of previous information, must be performed. It is of the greatest importance to be able to initiate the algorithm at an arbitrary interior point of the simplex selected as our best *a priori* estimate of the answer.

The following geometrical setting (Eaves and Scarf, 1976) for the elementary algorithm suggests the form these improvements can take. Let us construct a piecewise linear mapping, $h(x)$, of T into itself as follows: for each vertex v in the subdivision let $h(v) = v^i$, where i is the label associated with v. We then complete the mapping by requiring h to be linear in each simplex of the subdivision. The mapping is clearly continuous on T and maps every boundary point of T into itself. Moreover, every subsimplex in the subdivision whose vertices are not completely labelled is mapped, by h, into the boundary of T. If none of the simplices were completely labelled, this construction would yield a most improbable conclusion: a continuous mapping of T into itself which is the identity on the boundary and which maps the entire simplex into the boundary. That such a mapping cannot exist is known as the Non-Retraction Theorem, an assertion which is, in fact, equivalent to Brouwer's Theorem. The impossibility of such a mapping reinforces our conclusion that a completely labelled simplex does exist.

Select a point c interior to one of the boundary faces of T and consider the set of points which map into c; that is, the set of x for which $h(x) = c$. As Figure 6 indicates, this set contains a piecewise linear path beginning at the point c, and transversing precisely those simplices encountered in our elementary algorithm. There are however, other parts of the set $\{x \mid h(x) = c\}$: closed loops which do not touch the boundary of T and other piecewise linear paths connecting a pair of completely labelled simplices. Stated somewhat informally, the general conclusion, of which this is an example, is that the inverse image of a particular point, under a piecewise linear mapping from an n dimensional set to an $n - 1$ dimensional set, consists of a finite union of interior loops, and paths which join two boundary points, (see Milnor, 1965, for the differentiable version).

To see how this observation can be used, consider the product of the unit simplex S and the closed unit interval [0, 1]; that is, the set of points (x, t) with x in S and $0 \leqslant t \leqslant 1$, as in Figure 7. Extend the mapping from the unit simplex to this large set by defining $F(x, t) = (1 - t)f(x) + tx^*$, with x^* a preselected point on the simplex, taken to be an estimate of the true fixed point. The set of points for which $F(x, t) - x = 0$ is, by our general conclusion, a finite union of paths and loops. Precisely one of these paths intersects the upper boundary of the enlarged set. If the path is followed, its other endpoint must lie in the face $t = 0$ and yield a fixed point of the original mapping. The path leading to the fixed point can be followed on the

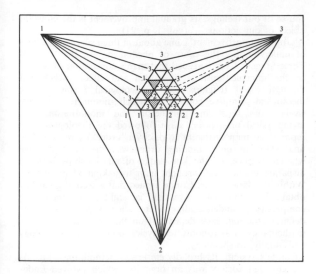

Figure 6

computer in several ways. We can, for example, introduce a simplicial decomposition of the set $S \times [0, 1]$ and approximate F by a piecewise linear mapping agreeing with F on the vertices of the subdivision. Following the path involves the same type of calculation we have become accustomed to in carrying out linear programming pivot steps. There are a great many variations in the mode of simplicial subdivision leading to substantial improvements in the efficiency of our original fixed-point algorithm (Eaves, 1972; Merrill, 1971; van der Laan and Talman, 1979).

An alternative procedure, adopted by Kellogg, Li and Yorke (1976) and Smale (1976), is to impose sufficient regularity conditions on the underlying mapping so that differentiation of $F(x, t) - x = 0$ yields a set of differential equations for the path joining x^* to the fixed point on $t = 0$. This leads to a variant of Newton's method which is global in the sense that it need not be initiated in the vicinity of the correct answer. But whichever of these alternatives we select, the numerical difficulties in computing equilibrium prices can be overcome for all problems of reasonable size.

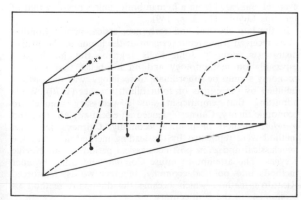

Figure 7

APPLIED GENERAL EQUILIBRIUM ANALYSIS

During the last 15 years, the field of Applied General Equilibrium Analysis has grown considerably; instead of the few tentative examples illustrating our ability to solve general equilibrium problems, we have seen the construction of a large number of models of substantial size designed to illuminate specific policy issues. The number of books and papers which have appeared in the field is far too large for a complete enumeration in this essay, and I shall mention only a few publications which may be consulted to obtain an indication of the diversity of this activity. The paper by Shoven and Whalley (1984) in the *Journal of Economic Literature* is a survey of applied general equilibrium models in the fields of taxation and international trade constructed by these authors and their colleagues. The volume by Adelman and Robinson (1978) is concerned with the application of general equilibrium analysis to problems of economic development. Whalley (1985) has written on trade liberalization, and Ballard, Fullerton, Shoven and Whalley (1985) on the evaluation of tax policy. Jorgenson (Hudson and Jorgenson, 1974) and Manne (1976) have made extensive applications of this methodology to energy policy, and Ginsburg and Waelbroeck (1981) provide a refreshing discussion of alternative computational procedures applied to a model of international trade involving over 200 commodities. The volume edited by Scarf and Shoven (1985) contains a collection of papers presented at one of an annual series of workshops in which both applied and theoretical topics of interest to researchers in the field of Applied General Equilibrium Analysis are discussed.

HERBERT E. SCARF

See also GENERAL EQUILIBRIUM.

BIBLIOGRAPHY

Adelman, I. and Robinson, S. 1978. *Income Distribution Policy in Developing Countries: A Case Study of Korea.* Stanford: Stanford University Press.

Ballard, C.L., Fullerton, D., Shoven, J.B. and Whalley, J. 1985. *A General Equilibrium Model for Tax Policy Evaluation.* Chicago: University of Chicago Press.

Barone, E. 1908. Il Ministero della Produzione nello stato colletivista. *Giornale degli Economisti e Revista di Statistica.* Trans. as 'The Ministry of Production in the Collectivist State', in *Collectivist Economic Planning*, ed. F.A. Hayek, London: G. Routledge & Sons, 1935.

Brouwer, L.E.J. 1912. Über Abbildungen von Mannigfaltigkeiten. *Mathematische Annalen* 71, 97–115.

Debreu, G. 1982. Existence of competitive equilibrium. In *Handbook of Mathematical Economics*, ed. K.J. Arrow and M. Intriligator, Amsterdam: North-Holland.

Dixon, P.B., Parmenter, B.R., Sutton, J. and Vincent, D.P. 1982. *ORANI: A Multisectoral Model of the Australian Economy.* Amsterdam: North-Holland.

Eaves, B.C. 1972. Homotopies for the computation of fixed points. *Mathematical Programming* 3, 1–22.

Eaves, B.C. and Scarf, H. 1976. The solution of systems of piecewise linear equations. *Mathematics of Operations Research* 1, 1–27.

Ginsburg, V.A. and Waelbroeck, J.L. 1981. *Activity Analysis and General Equilibrium Modelling.* Amsterdam: North-Holland.

Harberger, A. 1962. The incidence of the corporation income tax. *Journal of Political Economics* 70, 215–40.

Hudson, E.A. and Jorgenson, D.W. 1974. U.S. Energy policy and economic growth. *Bell Journal of Economics and Management Science* 5, 461–514.

Johansen, L. 1960. *A Multi-Sectoral Study of Economic Growth.* Amsterdam: North-Holland.

Kellogg, R. B., Li, T.Y. and Yorke, J. 1976. A constructive proof of the Brouwer Fixed Point Theorem and computational results. *SIAM Journal of Numerical Analysis* 13, 473–83.

Kuhn, H.W. 1968. Simplicial approximation of fixed points. *Proceedings of the National Academy of Sciences* 61, 1238–42.

Lange, O. 1936. On the economic theory of socialism. *Review of Economic Studies* 4, 53–71, 123–42.

Lemke, C.E. 1965. Bimatrix equilibrium points and mathematical programming. *Management Science* 11, 681–9.

Manne, A.S. 1976. ETA: a model of energy technology assessment. *Bell Journal of Economics and Management Science* 7, 379–406.

Merrill, O.H. 1971. Applications and extensions of an algorithm that computes fixed points of certain non-empty convex upper semicontinuous point to set mappings. Technical Report 71–7, University of Michigan.

Milnor, J. 1965. *Topology from the Differentiable Viewpoint*. Charlottesville: University of Virginia Press.

Scarf, H.E. 1967. The approximation of fixed points of a continuous mapping. *SIAM Journal of Applied Mathematics* 15, 1328–43.

Scarf, H.E., with the collaboration of T. Hansen. 1973. *The Computation of Economic Equilibria*. London, New Haven: Yale University Press.

Scarf, H. and Shoven, J.B. (eds) 1984. *Applied General Equilibrium Analysis*. Cambridge: Cambridge University Press.

Shoven, J.B. and Whalley, J. 1972. A general equilibrium calculation of the effects of differential taxation of income from capital in the U.S. *Journal of Public Economy* 1, 281–321.

Shoven, J.B. and Whalley, J. 1984. Applied general-equilibrium models of taxation and international trade. *Journal of Economic Literature* 22, 1007–51.

Smale, S. 1976. A convergent process of price adjustment and global Newton methods. *Journal of Mathematical Economics* 3, 107–20.

Smale, S. 1981. Global analysis and economics. In *Handbook of Mathematical Economics*, ed. K.J. Arrow and M. Intriligator, Amsterdam: North-Holland, Vol. I.

Sperner, E. 1928. Neur Beweis für die Invarianz der Dimensionszahl und des Gebietes. *Abhandlungen an den mathematischen Seminar der Universität Hamburg* 6, 265–72.

van der Laan, G. and Talman, A.J.J. 1979. A restart algorithm for computing fixed points without an extra dimension. *Mathematical Programming* 17, 74–84.

Whalley, J. 1985. *Trade Liberalization among Major World Trading Areas*. Cambridge, Mass.: MIT Press.

Comte, Isidore Auguste Marie François Xavier

Comte, Isidore Auguste Marie François Xavier (1798–1857). Auguste Comte, co-founder of sociology and positivist philosopher, was born at Montpellier in 1798 and died in Paris in 1857. A student at the Ecole Polytechnique until he was dismissed for disobedience and incorrigible behaviour, Comte became the secretary to Henri de Saint-Simon in 1818, a position he held until 1824. Over this period Comte developed the kernel of positivist philosophy and, along with Saint-Simon, modern sociology. The irascible Comte spent the rest of his life – often in the face of frequent poverty and desperate personal circumstances including mental breakdowns and a failed marriage – establishing, altering and working out positivism as a philosophical system of knowledge and as the foundation for the 'science of society'. Comte's *chefs d'oeuvre* included the encyclopedic *Cours de philosophie positive* (1830–42) and his *System of Positive Polity* (1851–4).

Comte's social philosophy encompassed all aspects of life, which he believed to be the harmonious working together of two inseparable elements – an organism and its environment. The 'true' methods of science were empirical (or inductive), and Comte, as did his mentor Saint-Simon, believed that they could be applied, *mutatis mutandis*, to all branches of thought including the social sciences, of which economics was a part. He succinctly described this basis in the *System of Positive Polity*: 'It [the positivist synthesis of all knowledge] rests at every point upon the unchangeable Order of the World. The right understanding of this order is the principal subject of our thoughts; its preponderating influence determines the general course of our feelings; its gradual improvement is the constant object of our actions ...' (vol. 1, p. 21).

'Gradual improvement' came about in three successive stages of understanding the cause of phenomena. In the 'Law of Three Stages', Comte argued that man's conception of 'order' or the interrelationships of causes and effects, went first through a religious or theological stage, the theological–primitive content of which diminished progressively from fetishism, polytheism and monotheism. The metaphysical or *a priori* stage followed the theological and represented man's attempt to discover 'order' by reason. The final stage in understanding order was the positive stage wherein science, or the knowledge of relationships between disparate phenomena, brought man to a kind of perfection. Within this latter stage, Comte argued that a second great law obtained – that of decreasing generality and increasing complexity of understanding. Here, sciences progressed in a definite ordering,. each dependent on the previous one, from mathematics to astronomy to physics to chemistry to biology and, finally, to sociology.

Comte's system, its broadly empirical methodology, and its precept that society was an organism which evolved under constraints that were themselves ultimately altered by social activities and behaviour, had a measurable impact upon classical economics and upon the *form* that economic analysis would take in the neoclassical period and beyond. J.S. Mill introduced Comte's ideas to England and, for a time at least, was deeply influenced by the French philosopher. Mill's *Logic* (1843) contains copious and favourable references to Comte's inverse-deductive (empirical-historical) method for use in the broader and more important investigation of integrated social studies. In the end, however, Mill reaffirmed the *a priori* 'Ricardian' method for the narrower concerns of political economy. Again, Comte's influence surfaced in Mill's *Principles of Political Economy* (1848) in the form of the famous 'statics and dynamics' distinction and in Mill's admissions that the ultimate aim of social science was a broader conception of the process than political economy had to offer. In his *Principles*, however, Mill reaffirmed the (admittedly provisional) *a priori* deductive method as the essential and proper one for studying political economy. Ultimately, Mill and a number of Comte's followers totally rejected the 'religion of humanity' that Comte later made of his positivist principles (1851–77). Mill was especially aghast at the infringements on individual liberty that Comte's quasi-medieval 'Catholicism without Christianity' envisioned. In his *Autobiography* Mill attacked Comte's planned society as 'the completest system of spiritual and temporal despotism which ever yet emanated from a human brain, unless possibly that of Ignatius Loyola' (1873, p. 149).

In the late classical and early neoclassical period Comte's ideas received some reinforcement at the hands of the British historicists, notably John Kells Ingram. But his impact, especially on methodology and on his belief that political economy should be subordinate to sociology, was successfully nullified by the efforts of John Elliott Cairnes (1870). While admitting that empiricism was a necessary adjunct to economic theory, Cairnes defended an essentially abstract and *a priori* method in political economy. Cairnes's ideas on method were replicated by the leading methodologist of the neoclassical and even post-neoclassical periods, John Neville Keynes. The attempt to infuse Comtian and other broader methods into political economy, in other words, reinforced Ricardo's method which became the dominant method of economists in the 20th century.

ROBERT B. EKELUND, JR.

See also POSITIVISM; SPENCER, HERBERT.

SELECTED WORKS

1830–42. *Cours de philosophie positive*. 5th edn, 2 vols, translated by H. Martineau; 3rd edn, London, 1893.

1851–4. *Système de politique positive, ou Traité de sociologie instituant la religion de l'humanite*. Trans by J.H. Bridge et al. as *System of Positive Polity*, London, 1875–7; New York: Burt Franklin Reprint, 4 vols, 1968.

1899. *Lettres inédites de John Stuart Mill à Auguste Comte*, publiées avec les réponses de Comte et un introduction par Lucien Lévy-Bruhl. Paris: Felix Alcan.

BIBLIOGRAPHY

Abrams, P. 1968. *The Origins of British Sociology 1834–1914*. Chicago: University of Chicago Press.

Adelman, P. 1971. Frederic Harrison and the 'Positivist' attack on orthodox political economy. *History of Political Economy* 3(1), Spring, 170–89.

Cairnes, J.E. 1870. M. Comte and political economy. *Fortnightly Review* 13, 579–602.

Ekelund, R.B., Jr. and Olsen, E. 1973. Comte, Mill and Cairnes: the positivist-empiricist interlude in late classical economics. *Journal of Economic Issues* 7(3), September, 383–416.

Hayek, F.A. 1955. *The Counter-Revolution of Science, Studies in the Abuse of Reason*. New York: The Free Press.

Ingram, J.K. 1899. *A History of Political Economy*. London: A. and C. Black, 1915.

Mill, J.S. 1865. *Auguste Comte and Positivism*. London: N. Trübner.

Mill, J.S. 1873. *Autobiography*. New York: Columbia University Press, 1924.

Seligman, B.B. 1969. The impact of positivism on economic thought. *History of Political Economy* 1(2), Fall, 256–78.

concavity. *See* CONVEXITY.

concentration ratios. These standard indicators of the degree of oligopoly in markets are used in studying market conditions. The ratio is the combined market shares of the 'oligopoly group' of firms which, being few, are closely interdependent. The ratio is usually based on three, four or five firms.

In theory the ratio indicates the market power held by the interdependent group. When the ratio is high, a few firms dominate the market and, with some degree of collusion, can raise prices and perform other conventional monopoly actions. Higher concentration makes effective collusion more probable. If the oligopolists achieve perfect joint maximization of profits, then the market power they exert is as great as if the firms were unified into one dominant firm. Concentration is therefore an indicator of diluted monopoly power.

How diluted it is depends on the degree of firms' cohesion. The fewer the firms, the more impact a departure from collusion will have on the joint outcome. Also, such departures will tend to be discovered more quickly, and therefore be open to more effective punishment by the other oligopolists. Therefore, higher concentration tilts the oligopolists' choices away from maverick price-cutting and toward collusion. Accordingly, high concentration should avoid the disintegration that often afflicts efforts to fix prices.

The distinction between tight oligopoly (a four-firm ratio above 60 per cent) and loose oligopoly (a ratio below 40 per cent) has come to be regarded as particularly important. In tight oligopoly, collusion is likely to crystallize effectively into strong cooperation, as the oligopolists' common interests overwhelm the rewards from cheating. Loose oligopoly, by contrast, is seen as a setting for disintegration, where the many oligopolists with low market shares are jointly unable to avert the endemic price cutting. This reasoning, which is broadly confirmed by the common run of experience in actual markets, suggests that a threshold value of concentration in the 50–60 per cent range should present a clear divide between the effective competition seen in loose oligopoly and the high market power that tight oligopoly may create.

Concentration is usually second in importance to individual market shares, as an element of market structure. Thus, for example, a General Motors may have a market share of 50 per cent, while it and the other three leading firms have a combined concentration ratio of 90 per cent. GM's own price–profit, innovation and other results are likely to be influenced more closely by its own 50 per cent share – giving it a dominant-firm position – than by the fact that it is in a market with high concentration in four firms.

Concentration's effects, such as they are, may be modified by entry conditions. Free and vigorous entry can limit the tight oligopolists' ability to exert market power. This is a controversial area, for there may be few active entrants actually ready to take advantage of free-entry conditions. Also, entry may be slow or marginal, so that it does not strongly affect the core of the market positions held by the leading firms.

Starting in the 1930s, the ratios soon gained pre-eminence in studying the degrees of market power. One was the then-new focus on oligopoly. The other was the new availability of the actual ratios for hundreds of US manufacturing industries for the year 1935. (US and UK ratios appear about every four or five years, as part of the industrial census. Only manufacturing industries are covered, although ratios on urban US banking markets are prepared by other sources.)

Econometric analysis has made extensive use of these ratios, with scores of papers reporting regressions relating concentration to price–cost patterns, growth rates, efficiency, rates of innovation, etc. In fact, concentration ratios reigned as the research focus for analysis of market power and its effects. Indeed, from 1939 to about 1970 the abundant availability of the ratios reinforced the tendency to regard (perhaps over-regard) oligopoly as a central issue. With the growing focus on individual market shares, the role of concentration ratios became less important in the 1970s. Even so, the ratios continue to be an indispensable descriptive statistic, used widely in research into the several elements of structure and their effects.

Before summarizing some of the results, one needs to note that the ratios are subject to a serious technical fault. A correct definition of the market is important, if true concentration within the market is to be measured. The US Bureau of the Census has a detailed system of standard industrial classification (SIC). All sectors are grouped by numbers, ranging from SIC 1 to 100. The manufacturing sector covers 'industry groups' 20 through 39, and so forth. Differing degrees of fineness are given. The five-digit product level is, on balance, about correct in fitting the average scope of true markets. Yet most research has focused on the much broader four-digit 'industries', which now number about 450 in the US.

About half of these four-digit census 'industries' depart seriously from correct market boundaries. The use of raw census ratios has undermined a good deal of the past research on structure and its effects. Commonly, the ratios are too broad, lumping together distinct products and geographic markets (for example, the national four-firm US ratio is 14 per cent for newspapers, but concentration ratios in true local newspaper markets probably average close to 100 per cent). Some cases go the other way, with the official ratios too high (for example, imports are not included in the ratios, and this is important for steel, television sets, shoes, cameras, automobiles and many others).

Adjusting the ratios to fit true market conditions requires care and judgement. Thus the weighted average degree of four-firm concentration in US manufacturing industries has been actually about 60 per cent, rather than the 40 per cent indicated by the raw census ratios.

Properly adjusted to eliminate these biases, a concentration ratio is an excellent descriptive statistic. It conveys the degree of oligopoly 'tightness'. It can show changes in structure pretty accurately. Thus the market power indicated by a ratio of 53 or 63 may be a matter of debate, but a rise in ratio from 53 to 63 for a given industry strongly suggests that there has been a rise in market power.

By 1975, the ratios have provided enormously valuable lessons, in several directions. They were the workhorse statistic in describing the structure of hundreds of industries, in case studies of industries, in antitrust investigations and in other straightforward treatments. They had become a pivotal basis for antitrust policy choices, such as in merger cases, where the degree of concentration was one basis for deciding whether to oppose the merger. During 1960–75 they gave rise to many scores of regression analyses, which tried to relate concentration to the possible effects of market power.

The correlation of concentration with price behaviour drew the largest volume of testing. These estimations were commonly plagued by the use of uncorrected, raw census ratios, which introduced substantial errors. Even so, a broad and significant correlation did emerge, enough to establish a presumption that the theoretical effects of oligopoly market power on pricing activity do occur in practice. The most successful testing involved multivariate models of five to eight independent variables, including filter variables such as capital intensity and growth, and other structure-related variables such as market shares, advertising intensity and capital-requirements barriers to entry.

Another important line of research attempted to explain concentration as the dependent variable. Growth rates were one possible causative variable, while economies of scale were another. Growth emerged as a very weak influence, and scale economies turned out to explain only a limited amount of actual concentration in important national markets. The weakness of these results may, in part, have reflected errors in the concentration ratios themselves.

Finally, concentration's possible effects on innovation, stability and wealth distribution have been explored. These studies often were forced to adopt quite creative approaches, in light to the data problems. Again, the general patterns have confirmed the main predictions of theory, that high concentration tends to affect results much as high monopoly power does. High concentration was associated, on the whole, with slowed innovation, greater instability of production and the disequalizing of the distribution of wealth.

Yet testing continues on all of these points, and the concentration ratios have tended only to suggest patterns, not resolve them. Studies since 1970 have focused more on individual market shares, showing them to have stronger effects than concentration, just as theory predicts. Though the use of concentration ratios in regression analysis may have peaked, the ratios (adjusted as appropriate) will undoubtedly continue as a main basis for describing the degree of market power in a wide array of markets in the US, UK, Canada, Japan and certain other countries.

WILLIAM G. SHEPHERD

See also DEGREE OF MONOPOLY; MARKET SHARE; MARKET STRUCTURE.

BIBLIOGRAPHY

Bain, J.S. 1956. *Barriers to New Competition.* Cambridge, Mass.: Harvard University Press.

Bain, J.S. 1968. *Industrial Organization.* Revised edn, New York: Wiley.

Blair, J.M. 1972. *Economic Concentration.* New York: Harcourt, Brace, Jovanovich.

Chamberlin, E.H. 1933. *The Theory of Monopolistic Competition.* 8th edn, Cambridge, Mass.: Harvard University Press, 1962.

Collins, N. and Preston, L.E. 1968. *Concentration and Price–Cost Margins in Manufacturing Industries.* Berkeley: University of California Press.

Comanor, W.S. and Smiley, R.H. 1975. Monopoly and the distribution of wealth. *Quarterly Journal of Economics* 89, May, 177–94.

Comanor, W.S. and Wilson, T. 1975. *Advertising and Market Power.* Cambridge, Mass.: Harvard University Press.

Goldschmid, H.J., Mann, H.M. and Weston, J.F. (eds) 1974. *Industrial Concentration: The New Learning.* Boston: Little, Brown.

Mann, H.M. 1966. Seller concentration, barriers to entry, and rates of return in thirty industries, 1950–1960. *Review of Economics and Statistics* 48, August, 296–307.

Mansfield, E. 1964. Industrial research and development expenditures. *Journal of Political Economy* 72, August, 319–40.

Scherer, F.M. 1980. *Industrial Market Structure and Economic Performance.* 2nd edn, Boston: Houghton Mifflin.

Shepherd, W.G. 1969. Market power and racial discrimination in white-collar employment. *Antitrust Bulletin* 14, Spring, 141–61.

Shepherd, W.G. 1970. *Market Power and Economic Welfare.* New York: Random House.

Shepherd, W.G. 1979. *The Economics of Industrial Organization.* Englewood Cliffs, NJ: Prentice-Hall.

Shepherd, W.G. 1982. Causes of increased competition in the US economy, 1939–1980. *Review of Economics and Statistics* 64, November, 613–26.

Stigler, G.J. (ed.) 1955. *Business Concentration and Price Policy.* Princeton: Princeton University Press.

Stigler, G.J. and Kindahl, J.K. 1970. *The Behavior of Industrial Prices.* New York: Columbia University Press for the National Bureau of Economic Research.

US Bureau of the Census. 1980. *Concentration Ratios in Manufacturing, 1977.* MC77 (SR) 2. Washington, DC: Government Printing Office.

Condillac, Etienne Bonnot de, l'Abbé de Mureau (1714–1780). Philosopher and economist. Born at Grenoble, the third son of a well-to-do aristocratic family, Condillac took his name from an estate purchased by his father in 1720. As a sickly child with poor eyesight he had little early education and was apparently still unable to read by the age of 12. After his father's death in 1727 he moved to Lyon to live with his oldest brother, continuing his education at its Jesuit college. Through this brother he may have first met Jean Jacques Rousseau, who was tutor to his nephews in 1740 and became a life-long friend. His second brother, l'Abbé de Mably, took Condillac to Paris in c1733 to study theology at Saint Sulpice and the Sorbonne. He was ordained in 1740 and for the rest of his life 'ever faithful to the Christian church, would always wear his cassock, always remain l'Abbé' (Lefèvre, 1966, p. 11).

For the next fifteen years he lived the life of a Paris intellectual, studying the philosophy of Descartes, Malebranche, Leibniz and Spinoza, 'to whose speculative systems he formed a life-long aversion, preferring the English philosophers Locke (who particularly influenced his thinking), Berkeley, Newton and rather belatedly, Bacon (Knight, 1968, pp. 8–9). In this period he published the works which made his philosophical reputation: the *Essay on the Origin of Human Knowledge* (1746), the *Traité des Systèmes* (1749), his most famous philosophical work *Treatise on the Sensations* (1754) described as the 'most rigorous demonstration of the

[18th-century] sensationalist psychology' (Knight, 1968, p. 12) and his *Traité des Animaux* (1755).

Apart from giving him entry to the Paris salons, where at Mlle de Lespinasse's salon he is reputed to have first met Turgot, another life-long friend (Le Roy, 1947, p. ix), his intellectual reputation gained him the position of tutor to Louis XV's grandson, the Duke of Parma. From 1758 to 1767 he resided in Parma. Because of its prime minister's economic development policies, inspired by a mixture of 'mercantilism, physiocracy and the ideas of Gournay', Condillac developed an interest in economic matters, an interest 'indirectly confirmed by his known contacts with the Italian political economists, Beccaria and Gherardo' (Knight, 1968, pp. 231–2). In 1768 he returned to Paris, but by 1773 had retired to his estate of Flux near Beaugency, where he died in 1780. During the last decade of his life he published his *Cours d'Etudes* (1775), his work on economics (1776), a text on logic (1780) for use in Polish Palatinate schools and commenced the unfinished *La Langue des Calculs* (1798). In 1752, he became a member of the Royal Prussian Academy; in 1768 after his return from Parma he was elected to the French Academy. His works have been frequently collected, most recently by Le Roy (1947–51).

The impetus for Condillac's writing *Le Commerce et le Gouvernement* has been ascribed to a desire to assist his friend Turgot in the difficulties he faced in 1775 as finance minister over the grain riots induced by his restoration of the free trade in grain (Le Roy, 1947, p. xxv; Knight, 1968, p. 232). This fits with the work's unqualified support for free trade in general and the grain trade in particular (1776, esp. pp. 344–5, which seems directly inspired by the Paris events of 1775). Writing the book may also be explained as a return favour for Turgot's assistance in getting Condillac (1775) published (cf. Knight, 1968, pp. 13, 232). Despite Condillac's strong support for this major part of Physiocratic policy and his close adherence to other aspects of Physiocracy, his argument that manufacturing was productive brought critical replies from Baudeau and Le Trosne (1777). In this context it may be noted that his work bears little direct Physiocratic influence, the major influence being Cantillon (1755), the only work directly cited apart from Plumard de Dangeul (1754). It is, however, possible to detect some influence from the economics of Turgot, Galiani and Verri on the theory of value, price and competition (cf. Spengler, 1968, p. 212).

As published, the work is divided into two parts. The first provides the elements of the science. Its starting point is the foundation of value, which Condillac finds in the usefulness of an object relative to subjective needs making relative scarcity the key variable determining value. Value is distinguished from price because price can only originate in exchange. It is determined by the competition between buyers and sellers guided by their subjective estimation of value. Gains from exchange arise from differences in value; for Condillac, value cannot exchange for equal value. Although Condillac did discuss the costs of acquiring commodities, his emphasis is on exchange, trade and price. Exchange presumes surplus production and a need for consumption. Hence trade inspires and animates production and is essential to increasing wealth. Only simple pictures of production are presented: farm labourers producing prime necessities of food and materials; artisans transforming raw materials into essentials and luxuries; traders who circulate these products at home and abroad. By this circulation trade distributes the annual product and under competitive conditions settles its true prices. Condillac is more concerned with developing the institutions associated with trade; growth of towns and

villages, money, banking, credit, interest and the foreign exchanges, the defence of property by government and hence the need for taxation, the effects of restraints on trade, including the grain trade. The second part is almost completely devoted to examining effects of specific obstacles to trade ranging from war, tariffs, taxes, excessive government borrowing to luxury spending in the capital city and exclusive trading privileges. Moderate wants combined with complete freedom constitute his recipe for the best form of economic development.

Condillac's economic work received a mixed reception from later economists. J.B. Say (1805, p. xxxv) described it as an attempt 'to found a system of ... a subject which [the author] did not understand'. Jevons (1871, p. xviii) praised Condillac's 'charming philosophic work [because] in the first few chapters ... we meet perhaps the earliest distinct statement of the true connections between value and utility ...'. Macleod (1896, p. 73) described it as a 'remarkable work ... utterly neglected but in scientific spirit ... infinitely superior to Smith'. Since then, it has remained neglected even though as 'a good if somewhat sketchy treatise on economic theory and policy [it was] much above the common run of its contemporaries' (Schumpeter, 1954, pp. 175–6).

PETER GROENEWEGEN

SELECTED WORKS

1746. *An Essay on the Origin of Human Knowledge*. Trans. by Thomas Nugent, London: Nourse, 1756.
1749. *Traité des Systèmes, où l'on en démêle les inconvénients et les avantages*. Paris and Amsterdam.
1754. *Treatise on the Sensations*. Trans. by Geraldine Carr, London: Favill Press, 1930.
1755. *Traité des Animaux, où après avoir fait des observations critiques sur le sentiment de Descartes et sur celui de M. Buffon on entreprend d'expliquer leurs principales facultés ...* . Amsterdam.
1775. *Cours d'Etude pour l'instruction du Prince de Parma, Aujourd'hui Ferdinand, Duc de Parma*. Parma (and Paris).
1776. *Le Commerce et le gouvernement considerés relativement l'un à l'autre*. In *Oeuvres complètes de Condillac*, Vol. 4, Paris: Brière, 1821.
1780. *The Logic*. Trans. by Joseph Neef, Philadelphia, 1809.
1798. *Le langue des Calculs, Ouvrage Posthume et élémentaire*. Paris.

BIBLIOGRAPHY

Cantillon, R. 1755. *Essay on the Nature of Commerce in General*. Trans. by H. Higgs, London: Macmillan, 1931.
Jevons, W.S. 1871. *Theory of Political Economy*. 4th edn, London: Macmillan, 1911.
Knight, I.F. 1968. *The Geometric Spirit. The Abbé de Condillac and the French Enlightenment*. New Haven and London: Yale University Press.
Lefèvre, R. 1966. *Condillac ou la joie de vivre*. Paris: Editions Seghers.
Le Roy, G. (ed.) 1947–51. *Oeuvres philosophiques de Condillac*. Paris: Presses Universitaires de France.
Le Trosne, G.F. 1777. *De L'intérêt Social, par rapport à la Valeur, à la circulation, à l'Industrie, & au commerce intérieur & extérieur: Ouvrage élémentaire dans lequel on discoute quelques Principes de M. l'Abbé de Condillac*. Paris.
MacLeod, H.D. 1896. *The History of Economics*. London: Bliss, Sands & Co.
Plumard de Danguel. 1754. *Remarques sur les avantages et les désavantages de la France et de la Gr. Bretagne par rapport au commerce et aux autres sources de la puissance des états*. Leyden (and Paris).
Say, J.B. 1805. *A Treatise on Political Economy of the Production, Distribution and Consumption of Wealth*. Trans. C.R. Prinsep, new American edition, Philadelphia, 1880; reissued New York: Kelley, 1963.
Schumpeter, J.A. 1954. *History of Economic Analysis*. London: Allen & Unwin, 1959.
Spengler, J.J. 1968. Condillac, Etienne Bonnot de. In *Encyclopedia of the Social Sciences*, 2nd edn, Chicago: Chicago University Press, Vol. 3.

Condorcet, Marie Jean Antoine Nicolas Caritat, Marquis de (1743–1794). Condorcet was a French mathematician and philosopher. With many of his fellow *encyclopédistes* he shared the conviction that social sciences are amenable to mathematical rigour. His pioneer work on elections, the *Essai sur l'application de l'analyse a la probabilité des decisions rendues a la pluralité des voix* (1785) is a major step in that direction.

The aim of the *Essai* is to 'inquire by mere reasoning, what degree of confidence the judgment of assemblies deserves, whether large or small, subject to a high or low plurality, split into several different bodies or gathered in one only, composed by men more or less wise' (*Discours préliminaire* to the *Essai*, p. iv).

In modern words, this is the jury problem: to decide whether the accused is guilty or not requires converting the opinions of several experts, with varying competence, into a single judgement. Systematic probabilistic computations for this problem occupy most of the *Essai*, often camouflaging the essential contributions. The opaqueness and technicality of the argument meant that a full recognition of its importance did not occur until more than 150 years later (Black, 1958). Since then Condorcet's findings have strongly influenced modern social choice theorists (e.g. Arrow, Guilbaud and Black), and still play a central role in many of its recent developments.

The starting point is that majority voting is the unambiguously best voting rule when only two candidates are on stage. This fact, whose modern formulation is known as May's theorem (May, 1952) was clear enough to the encyclopedists, too. How, then, can we extend this rule to three candidates or more? The naive, yet widely used, answer is plurality voting (each voter casts a vote for one candidate; the candidate with most votes is elected). Both Condorcet and Borda (his colleague in the Academy of Sciences) raise the same objection against the plurality rule. Suppose, says Condorcet (*Discours préliminaire*, p. lviii) that 60 voters have the opinions shown in Table 1 about three candidates A, B, C.

Table 1

	23	19	16	2
top	A	B	C	C
	C	C	B	A
bottom	B	A	A	B

In the illustration, candidate A wins by plurality. Yet if we oppose A against B only, A loses (25 to 35) and in A against C, A loses again (23 to 37). Thus the plurality rule does not convey accurately the opinion of the majority. From these identical premises, Borda proposes his well-known scoring method (each candidate receives 2 points from a voter who ranks him first, 1 point from one who ranks him second, and none from one who ranks him last; hence C is elected with score 78), whereas Condorcet opens a quite different route.

Condorcet posits a simple binomial model of voter error: in every binary comparison, each voter has a probability $1/2 < P < 1$ of ordering the candidates correctly. All voters are assumed to be equally able, and there is no correlation between judgements on different pairs. Thus for Condorcet the relevant data is contained in the 'majority tournament' that results from taking all pairwise votes:

B beats A, 35 to 25; C beats A, 37 to 23;

C beats B, 41 to 19.

Condorcet proposes that the candidates be ranked according to 'the most probable combination of opinions' (*Essai*, p. 125). In modern statistical terminology this is a maximum likelihood criterion (see Young, 1986).

In the above example the most probable combination is given by the ranking: CBA since the three statements C over B, C over A, B over A agree with the greatest total number of votes. Condorcet's ranking criterion implies that an alternative (such as C) that obtains a majority over every other alternative must be ranked first. Such an alternative, if one exists, is known as a 'Condorcet winner'.

As Condorcet points out, some configurations of opinions may not possess such a winner, because the majority tournament contains a cycle (a situation known as 'Condorcet's paradox'). He exhibits the example shown in Table 2:

Table 2

23	17	2	10	8
A	B	B	C	C
B	C	A	A	B
C	A	C	B	A

Here A beats B, 33 to 27; B beats C, 42 to 18; C beats A, 35 to 25. According to Condorcet's maximum likelihood criterion, this cycle should be broken at its weakest link (A over B), which yields the ranking B over C over A. Therefore in this case B is declared the winner.

Somewhat later in the *Essai* (pp. 125–6), Condorcet suggests that one may compute the maximum likelihood ranking of n candidates by, first, choosing the $n(n-1)/2$ binary propositions that have the majority in their favour; then, if there are cycles, *successively deleting* those with smallest majorities until a complete ordering of the candidates is obtained. Unfortunately, for $n > 3$ this heuristic algorithm does not necessarily yield the ranking that accords with the greatest number of votes. An axiomatic characterization of Condorcet's rule is given in Young and Levenglick (1978).

Condorcet's idea of reducing individual opinions to all pairwise comparisons between alternatives proved essential to the aggregation of preferences approach initiated by Arrow (1953). The key axiom Independence of Irrelevant Alternatives (IIA) requires that voting on a pair of candidates be enough to determine the collective opinion on this pair: this generalizes majority tournaments by dropping the symmetry across voters and across candidates. In this sense Arrow's impossibility theorem means that the Condorcet paradox is inevitable in any nondictatiorial voting method satisfying IIA.

Many more useful insights can be discovered in the *Essai*. For instance the issue of strategic manipulations, which has played a central role in the theory of elections since the late 1960s, is suggested in places, although it is never systematically analysed. For example, on page clxxix of the *Discours Preliminaire*, Condorcet criticizes Borda's method as more vulnerable to a '*cabale*'. His argument is supported by the modern game theoretical approach: whenever the configurations of individual opinions guarantee existence of a Condorcet winner, it defines a strategyproof voting rule. This is one of the principal arguments in favour of Condorcet consistent voting rules, namely rules electing the Condorcet winner whenever it exists (see e.g. Moulin, 1983, ch. 4).

H. MOULIN AND H.P. YOUNG

See also BORDA, JEAN-CHARLES DE; SOCIAL CHOICE; VOTING.

SELECTED WORKS
1785. *Essai sur l'application de l'analyse à la probabilité des décisions rendues à la pluralité des voix.* Paris.

BIBLIOGRAPHY
Arrow, K. 1951. *Social Choice and Individual Values.* New York: Wiley.
Black, D. 1958. *The Theory of Committees and Elections.* Cambridge: Cambridge University Press.
May, K. 1952. A set of independent necessary and sufficient conditions for simple majority decision. *Econometrica* 20(4), 680–84.
Moulin, H. 1983. *The Strategy of Social Choice.* Amsterdam: North-Holland.
Young, H.P. 1986. Optimal ranking and choice from pairwise comparisons. In *Information Pooling and Group Decisionmaking* ed. B. Grofman and G. Owen, Greenwich, Conn.: JAI Press.
Young, H.P. and Levenglick, A. 1978. A consistent extension of Condorcet's election principle. *SIAM Journal of Mathematics* 35(2), 285–300.

conflict and settlement. All living beings are competitors for the means of existence. Competition takes the more intense form we call *conflict* when contenders seek to disable or destroy opponents, or even convert them into a supply of resources. Conflict need not always be violent; we speak, for example, of industrial conflicts (strikes and lockouts) and legal conflicts (law suits). But physical struggle is a relevant metaphor for these ordinarily non-violent contests.

THE STATICS OF CONFLICT

Involved in a rational decision to engage in conflict, economic reasoning suggests, will be the decision-maker's *preferences*, *opportunities* and *perceptions*. These three elements correspond to traditional issues debated by historians and political scientists about the 'causes of war': Is war mainly due to hatred and ingrained pugnacity (hostile preferences)? Or to the opportunities for material gain at the expense of weaker victims? Or is war mainly due to mistaken perceptions, on one or both sides, of the other's motives or capacities?

Of course it is quite a leap from the choices of individuals to the war-making decisions of collectivities like tribes or states. Group choice-making processes notoriously fail to satisfy the canons of rationality, most fundamentally owing to disparities among the interests of the individual members. Thus the internal decision-making structures of the interacting groups may also be implicated among the causes of war.

Setting aside this last complication, Figures 1 and 2 are alternative illustrations of how preferences, opportunities, and perceptions might come together in a simple dyadic interaction. In each diagram the curve QQ bounds the 'settlement opportunity set' – what the parties can jointly attain by peaceful agreement or compromise – drawn on axes representing Blue's income I_B and Red's income I_R. The points P_B and P_R, in contrast, indicate the parties' separate *perceptions* of the income distribution resulting from conflict. The families of curves labelled U_B and U_R are the familiar utility indifference contours of the two agents.

Figure 1 shows a relatively benign situation: settlement opportunities are complementary, so there is a considerable mutual gain from avoiding conflict; the respective preferences display benevolence on each side; and the perceptions of returns from conflict are conservative and agreed (P_B and P_R coincide). The 'Potential Settlement Region' PSR (shaded area in the diagram), that is, the set of income distributions such that *both* parties regard themselves as doing better than by fighting, is therefore large – which plausibly implies a high probability of

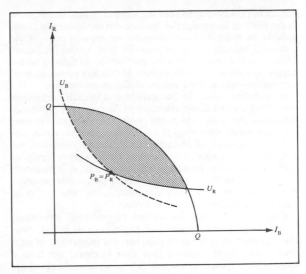

Figure 1 Statics of conflict – large potential settlement region.

coming to an agreement. Figure 2 shows a less pleasant situation: antithetical opportunities, mutually malevolent preferences, and divergently optimistic estimates of the returns from conflict. The PSR is therefore small, and the prospects for settlement much poorer.

What might be called the *materialistic theory* attributes conflict, ultimately, to competition for resources. Primitive tribes attack one another for land, for hoards of consumables, or for slaves. Similar aims evidently motivated barbarian invasions of civilized cities and empires in ancient times, and European colonial imperialism in the modern era. Yet, between contending parties there will almost always be some element of complementary interests, an opportunity for mutual gain represented by the potential settlement region PSR. Orthodox eco-

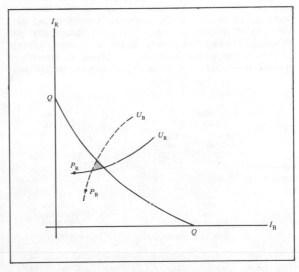

Figure 2 Statics of conflict - small potential settlement region.

nomics has always emphasized the scope of mutual benefit, even to the point of losing sight of conflict; certain dissident schools, notably the Marxists, have commited the opposite error. While a detailed analysis cannot be provided here, among the factors underlying the relative material profitability of fighting versus negotiating are wealth differentials, Malthusian pressures, military technology, and the enforceability of agreements.

In contrast with the materialistic approach, *attitudinal theories* of conflict direct attention to the respective preference functions. An issue which has excited considerable interest concerns the relative weights assignable to genetic versus cultural determinants of attitudes. One extreme viewpoint, for example, regards xenophobic wars of family against family, of tribe against tribe, or nation against nation, as biologically 'normal' in the human species. An opposite interpretation pictures man as an innately compliant being, who has to be culturally indoctrinated into bellicosity.

Finally, what might be termed *informational theories* of conflict emphasize differences of perceptions or beliefs. Neo-classical economics tends to minimize the importance of such divergences – partly because they tend to cancel out from a large-numbers point of view, partly because incorrect beliefs are adjusted by experience in the process of establishing an economic equilibrium. But conflict and war are pre-eminently small-numbers, disequilibrium problems. Indeed, conflict may be regarded as in a sense an *educational process*. The school of actual struggle teaches the parties to readjust their perceptions to more realistic levels. Wars end by mutual consent when the potential settlement opportunities are seen as more attractive than continued fighting.

THE DYNAMICS OF CONFLICT

Static and dynamic elements are both importantly involved in conflict or settlement processes. In game theory terms, the *payoff environment*, represented by the familiar normal-form matrix, is the static element. The dynamic element may be called the *protocol of play*; as pictured in the game tree, the protocol specifies the allowable step-by-step moves in the light of the players' information at each stage.

A few very simple payoff environments are shown in Matrices 1 to 4. The numbers in each cell indicate ordinally ranked payoffs for each player, 1 being the poorest outcome in each case. In Matrix 1, 'Land or Sea', the environment is characterized by completely antithetical (constant-sum) payoffs. The other three matrices – 'Chicken', 'Reciprocity' and 'Prisoners' Dilemma' – represent several of the many different possible mixed-motive situations combining an element of opposition of interests with an opportunity for mutual gain.

The simplest protocol to analyse is *one-round sequential play*: first Row selects one of his options, then Column makes his move in the light of Row's choice, and the game ends. In a sequential-play protocol it is always possible to find a 'rational' solution. If Column can be relied to choose his best final move then Row, knowing this, can calculate his best first move accordingly. (This process results in what is called a 'perfect equilibrium'.) In contrast, where the protocol dictates that players in a single-round game choose *simultaneously* – or, equivalently, where each chooses in ignorance of the other's move – solution concepts are harder to justify. The most commonly employed is called the 'Nash equilibrium' (or 'equilibrium point'), a pair of strategies from which neither player would want to diverge unilaterally.

In the 'Land or Sea' payoff environment, under the one-round *sequential-move* protocol, it is the second-mover or defender who has the advantage. If Row moves first, for example, Column can always successfully counter; e.g. if Row attacks by land, Column will defend by land. Hence the (1, 2) payoff-pair is the outcome regardless of Row's initial move. In military terms the defence has an intrinsic advantage whenever the attacker must visibly commit his forces to one or another line of attack. And, of course, where the defence has such an advantage neither party is motivated to initiate warfare through aggression. But if 'Land or Sea' is played under the *simultaneous-move* protocol, both parties are groping in the dark and little can be said with confidence. (Here the Nash equilibrium would have each side choosing its move at random, in effect tossing a coin.)

In the payoff environment of 'Chicken' (Matrix 2), while the opportunities remain highly antithetical there is now a mutual interest in avoiding the disastrous (1, 1) outcome that comes about when both play Tough. In contrast with 'Land or Sea', in the 'Chicken' payoff environment the advantage lies with the *first-mover*. Specifically, Row should rationally play Tough, knowing that Column then has to respond with Soft. For, Column must accept the bad (payoff of 2) to avoid the worst (payoff of 1). If the protocol dictates simultaneous moves, however, once again the players are groping in the dark. Under the Nash equilibrium concept they choose probabilistically, which implies that the disastrous (1, 1) outcome will indeed occur a percentage of the time. There is a suggestive application of this model to industrial conflict. If union (or management) becomes committed to play Soft, it will be at a disadvantage in negotiations – the other side will then surely play Tough. But if both play Tough, there is no hope for peaceful settlement. Hence each side should rationally adopt a 'mixed' strategy, with the consequence that strikes and lockouts will occur in a certain fraction of the dealings.

The 'Reciprocity' payoff environment (Matrix 3) is more rewarding to cooperative behaviour. The idea is that each player would answer Soft with Soft – leading to the mutually preferred (4, 4) payoffs – but failing this, would respond to Tough with Tough. If the *sequential-move* protocol applies, the first-mover would then always rationally choose Soft, and so the ideal (4, 4) payoff-pair should be achieved. But under the *simultaneous-move* protocol, with each party in the dark about the other's move, again the outcome is quite unclear. In fact there are three Nash equilibria: pure-strategy solutions at (4, 4) and (2, 2), and a mixed-strategy solution as well.

Finally, in the famous 'Prisoners' Dilemma' payoff environment (Matrix 4) the parties are likely to find themselves in the Defect–Defect 'trap' with (2, 2) payoffs, even though (3, 3) could be achieved were each to play Cooperate. Here the 'trap' takes hold under both sequential-move and simultaneous-move protocols.

Matrix 1
LAND OR SEA

	Defend by land	Defend by sea
Attack by land	1,2	2,1
Attack by sea	2,1	1,2

Matrix 2
CHICKEN

	Soft	Tough
Soft	3,3	2,4
Tough	4,2	1,1

Matrix 3
RECIPROCITY

	Soft	Tough
Soft	4,4	1,3
Tough	3,1	2,2

Matrix 4
PRISONERS' DILEMMA

	Co-operate	Defect
Co-operate	3,3	1,4
Defect	4,1	2,2

The preceding discussion could only be suggestive, limited as it was to 2-player single-round games, within that category to only a few 2-strategy symmetrical payoff environments, and finally to the very simplest protocols – excluding, for example, all negotiations and communications between the parties. Space limitations permit comment upon only a few additional points:

Perceptions. Standard game models assume that players know not only their own payoffs but also their opponents'. Unintentional error on this score, or else deliberate deception, may play a crucial role. Suppose two parties in the 'Reciprocity' payoff environment of Matrix 3 find themselves initially playing Tough–Tough with outcome (2, 2). Imagine now they are given a chance to shift strategies under a *sequential-move* protocol. As first-mover, Row would be happy to change from Tough to Soft if only he could rely upon Column to respond in kind. But Row may, mistakenly, believe that Column's payoffs are as in 'Chicken', from which he infers that Column would stand pat with Tough. Row would therefore not shift from Tough, hence Column in his turn would not change either. (Some authors have gone so far as to attribute all or almost all of human conflict to such mistaken 'self-fulfilling beliefs' about the hostility of opponents, but of course this pattern is only one of many possibilities.)

Commitment and deterrence. In some circumstances the second-mover in point of time (Column) may be able to *commit* himself to a given response strategy before Row makes his first move. While Column thereby surrenders freedom of choice, doing so may be advantageous. Consider threats and promises. A *threat* is a commitment to undertake a second-move punishment strategy even where execution thereof is costly. A *promise* similarly involves commitment to a costly reward strategy. Matrices 5 and 6 illustrate how a threat works. Row's choices are Attack or Refrain, while Column's only options are to Retaliate or Fold if Row attacks. Column's problem, of course, is to deter Row's attack. In Matrix 5 Column prefers to Retaliate if attacked, a fact that – given Row's preferences – suffices for deterrence. Commitment is not required. (Since Column prefers to Retaliate, there is no need to *commit* himself to do so.) In Matrix 6 the Column player prefers to turn the other cheek; if attacked, he would rather Fold than Retaliate. Unfortunately, this guarantees he will be attacked! (Note that here it is not excessive hostility, but the reverse, that brings on conflict.) But if Column could *commit* himself to Retaliate, for example by computerizing the associated machinery beyond the possibility of his later reneging, then deterrence succeeds. In short, if a pacific player can reliably *threaten* to do what he does not really want to do, he won't have to do it! (Needless to say, so dangerous an arrangement is not to be casually recommended.)

	Matrix 5 DETERRENCE WITHOUT COMMITMENT			Matrix 6 DETERRENCE REQUIRING COMMITMENT	
	Fold	Retaliate		Fold	Retaliate
Refrain	2,3	2,3	Refrain	2,3	2,3
Attack	3,1	1,2	Attack	3,2	1,1

THE TECHNOLOGY OF STRUGGLE

Conflict is a kind of 'industry' in which different 'firms' compete by attempting to disable opponents. Just as the economist without being a manager or engineer can apply certain broad principles to the processes of industrial production, so, without

claiming to replace the military commander, he can say something about the principles governing how desired results are 'produced' through violence.

Battles typically proceed to a definitive outcome – victory or defeat. *Wars* on the whole tend to be less conclusive, often ending in a compromise settlement. These historical generalizations reflect the working of increasing versus decreasing returns applied to the production of violence:

(1) Within a sufficiently small geographical region such as a battlefield, there is a critical range of increasing returns to military strength – a small increment of force can make the difference between victory and defeat.

(2) But there are decreasing returns in projecting military power away from one's base area, so that it is difficult to achieve superiority over an enemy's entire national territory. The increasing-returns aspect explains why there is a 'natural monopoly' of military force *within* the nation-state. The diminishing-returns aspect explains why a multiplicity of nation-states have remained militarily viable to this date. (However, there is some reason to believe, the technology of attack through long-range weapons has now so come to prevail over the defence that a single world-state is indeed impending.)

Going into the basis for increasing returns, at any moment the stronger in battle can inflict a more-than-proportionate loss upon his opponent, thus becoming progressively stronger still. Important special cases of this process are modelled via Lanchester's equations. In combat, in the ideal case where all the military units distribute their fire equally over the enemy's line, the process equations are:

$$dB/dt = -k_R R$$

$$dR/dt = -k_B B$$

Here B and R are the given force sizes for Blue and Red, and the per-unit military efficiencies are given by the k_B and k_R coefficients. It follows that military strengths are equal when:

$$k_B B^2 = k_R R^2$$

But even where military strength varies less sensitively than as the square of force size, it remains quite generally the case that in the combat process the strong become stronger and the weak weaker, leading to ultimate annihilation unless flight or surrender intervene. (Of course, a skilful commander finding himself with an adverse force balance will attempt to change the tactical situation – by timely withdrawal, deception, or other manoeuvre.)

One implication of increasing returns may be called the 'last-push principle'. In the course of a conflict each side will typically not be fully aware of the force size and strength that the opponent is ultimately able and willing to put in the field. Hence the incentive to stand fast, even at high cost, lest a potentially won battle be lost. (Foch: 'A battle won is a battle in which one will not confess oneself beaten.') This valid point unfortunately tends to lead to battlefield carnage beyond all reasonable prior calculations, as experienced for example at Verdun.

On the other hand, an effective substitute for force size is superior *organization*. An integrated military unit is far more powerful than an equally numerous conglomeration of individual fighters, however brave. Organizational superiority, far more than superiority in weapons, explains why small European expeditionary contingents in early modern times were able to defeat even vast indigenous forces in America, Africa and Asia. Battles are thus often a contest of organizational forms; the army whose command structure first cracks under pressure is the loser.

As for diminishing returns, in the simplest case an equilibrium is achieved at a geographical boundary such that:

$$M_B - s_B x_B = M_R - s_R x_R$$

Here M_B and M_R are military strengths at the respective home bases, s_B and s_R are decay gradients, and x_B and x_R are the respective distances from base. The condition of equality determines the allocation of territory.

The 'social physics' of struggle is of course far more complex than these simplistic initial models suggest. There are more or less distinct offence and defence technologies, first-strike capability is not the same as retaliatory strength, countering insurgency is a different problem from central land battle, etc.

CONFLICT, SOCIETY AND ECONOMY

Conflict theory can help explain not only the size and shape of nations, but the outcomes of competition in all aspects of life: contests among social classes, among political factions and ideologies, between management and labour, among contenders for licences and privileges ('rent-seeking'), between plaintiffs and defendants in law suits, among members of cartels like OPEC, between husband and wife and sibling and sibling within the family, and so on. Whenever resources can be seized by aggression, invasion attempts can be expected to occur. Invasive and counter-invasive effort absorb a very substantial fraction of society's resources in every possible social structure, whether egalitarian or hierarchical, liberal or totalitarian, centralized or decentralized. Furthermore, every form of human social organization, whatever else can be said for or against it, must ultimately meet the survival test of internal and external conflict.

Notes on the literature of conflict (of special relevance for economists). Classical military thought from Machiavelli to Clausewitz to Liddell Hart, though rarely analytical in the economist's sense, remains well worth study. An excellent survey is Edward Mead Earle (1941). Modern work in this classical genre understandably concentrates upon the overwhelming fact of nuclear weaponry and the problem of deterrence; the contributions of Herman Kahn (1960, 1962) are notable. There is of course a huge historical literature on conflict and war. An interesting economics-oriented interpretive history of modern warfare is Geoffrey Blainey (1973). William H. McNeil (1982) examines the course of military organization and technology from antiquity to the present, emphasizing the social and economic context. On a smaller scale John Keegan (1976) provides a valuable picture of how men, weapons, and tactics compete with and complement one another on the battlefield. There is also a substantial body of statistical work attempting in a variety of ways to summarize and classify the sources and outcomes of wars; the best known is Lewis F. Richardson (1960b). Mathematical analysis of military activity, that is, quantifiable modelling of the clash of contending forces, is surprisingly sparse. The classic work is Frederick William Lanchester (1916 [1956]).

The modern analysis of conflict, typically combining the theory of games with the rational-decision economics of choice, is represented by three important books by economists: Thomas C. Schelling (1960), Kenneth E. Boulding (1962) and Gordon Tullock (1974). Works by non-economists that are similar in spirit include Glenn H. Snyder and Paul Diesing (1977) and Bruce Bueno de Mesquita (1981). A tangentially related literature, making use of the rather mechanical psychologistic approach of Richardson (1960a), includes a very readable book by Anatol Rapoport (1960).

JACK HIRSHLEIFER

See also BARGAINING; GAME THEORY.

BIBLIOGRAPHY
Blainey, G. 1973. *The Causes of War.* New York: The Free Press.
Boulding, K.E. 1962. *Conflict and Defense: A General Theory.* New York: Harper & Brothers.
Bueno de Mesquita, B. 1981. *The War Trap.* New Haven and London: Yale University Press.
Earle, E.M. (ed.) 1941. *Makers of Modern Strategy: Military Thought from Machiavelli to Hitler.* Princeton, NJ: Princeton University Press.
Kahn, H. 1960. *On Thermonuclear War.* Princeton, NJ: Princeton University Press.
Kahn, H. 1962. *Thinking About the Unthinkable.* New York: Avon Books.
Keegan, J. 1976. *The Face of Battle.* New York: Viking Press.
Lanchester, F.W. 1916. *Aircraft in Warfare: The Dawn of the Fourth Arm.* London: Constable. Extract reprinted in *The World of Mathematics,* ed. James R. Newman, vol. 4, New York: Simon & Schuster, 1956, 2138–57.
McNeill, W.H. 1982. *The Pursuit of Power: Technology, Armed Force, and Society since AD 1000.* Chicago: University of Chicago Press.
Rapoport, A. 1960. *Fights, Games, and Debates.* Ann Arbor: University of Michigan Press.
Richardson, L.F. 1960a. *Arms and Insecurity: A Mathematical Study of the Causes and Origins of War.* Pittsburgh: Boxwood; Chicago: Quadrangle.
Richardson, L.F. 1960b. *Statistics of Deadly Quarrels.* Pittsburgh: Boxwood; Chicago: Quadrangle.
Schelling, T.C. 1960. *The Strategy of Conflict.* Cambridge, Mass.: Harvard University Press.
Snyder, G.H. and Diesing, P. 1977. *Conflict Among Nations: Bargaining, Decision Making, and System Structure in International Crises.* Princeton, NJ: Princeton University Press.
Tullock, G. 1974. *The Social Dilemma: The Economics of War and Revolution.* Blacksburg, Virginia: University Publications.

congestion. With ambient conditions of scarcity, congestion (like 'shortages'), appears either when the property rights are not well defined or when mutual trading and contracting is excluded. Thus, consider an elevator with a capacity of 10 persons when 15 people appear to demand a ride, so that at least 5 people must incur the costs of a wait for the next available space. In most modern societies there is no inherent investiture of the right to a place in the first elevator. However, social behaviour sometimes recognizes a rule of convenience or status – such as that of the elderly, the handicapped, the chief executive officer and women to take priority. But to avoid all possibility of conflict, such rules would have to be enormously complex. In practice, most societies recognize a simple rule of the queue, first come first served. It is remarkable that queuing rules are to be found ubiquitously, and that very different societies appear to find that rule fair, although rather wasteful; seemingly, equity is worth the cost.

Even with the rule, however, there is considerable scope for making mutually advantageous trades. The eleventh man in the queue might offer to buy the place of one of the first ten, and someone with an assured place may be willing to trade his place and wait for the next elevator in exchange for the offer of the eleventh man. Deals may be struck so that those who value a speedy lift highly may buy the places of those who do not. Since all contracts are freely negotiated, people must be at least as well off and so there is Pareto improvement. However, the queue is still an inefficient rationing device; clearly, it would have been better if no more than ten people had arrived for the lift, and that those ten had been the people who valued most highly the service at that time. The queue involves waste in waiting. Yet, in principle, it is easy to devise alternative schemes for the allocation of property rights which do not involve the waste of time and resources in queuing. For example, a lottery might allocate the ten places in the elevator, and indeed such a system was used at the London School of Economics to allocate parking places; but, of course, only to the faculty.

Suppose the ownership of the right to designate the qualifications for travel in the elevator to be vested in its owner. Then, assuming that the owner wants to maximize his profits, he will find it profitable – transactions costs and stochastic variations aside – to *sell* the right to travel on the elevator directly to the travelling public. There will be no queue and no evidence of congestion. Well-specified property rights, zero transactions costs, profit maximization and freedom to contract are sufficient, but clearly not necessary, to banish congestion. The private provision of elevators, often by the users themselves, ensures that there is in fact no persistent or structural congestion.

Persistent or structural congestion, as distinct from accidental or transitory stochastic congestion, is normally to be found in the lack of specification of a property right, usually involving the public sector. For example, it is widely believed that there is considerable congestion in many fishing grounds – too many fishermen chasing too few fish. The number of fish is limited and so for a particular boat the marginal cost of fishing should reflect the fact that additional fish netted will increase the costs of other vessels catching fish; there are fewer fish and less spawn, etc. The point is that the fish are not *owned* by a profit-maximizing entity which extracts a royalty for each fish caught. They are nominally in the ownership of the state, if in national waters, but the state charges no royalty per fish caught. Scarce fish are not priced but treated as free. Thus the fishing grounds are congested and over-fished.

HIGHWAY CONGESTION. The most important form of congestion is on the highways, particularly on city streets, normally owned and operated by the state. If the state authorities were profit-seeking entities then they would charge prices for the use of the city streets that reflect the intensity of demand relative to the scarce capacity available. They would levy tolls in order to maximize their net revenue from the street system. But traditionally the state has not charged for the use of city streets prices or tolls that reflect their scarcity. The urban roads are 'free' for all users; provided they have paid their licence duty and acquired the right to use any of the roads in the national network as intensively as they wish. Thus people try to make too much use of the road network in areas where road capacity is scarce relative to demand. The urban streets become overcrowded, vehicle speeds slow as they get in one another's way, and the costs of a journey rise. Congestion is rather different from queuing; one cannot buy a place up front of a traffic jam as one can with negotiable positions in the disciplined queue. But in other respects – for example the waste of resources involved – queuing and congestion have the same characteristics.

The formal economic modelling of congestion can proceed either by analysing the phenomenon in terms of demand, or in the form of supply and cost conditions. Following the historical precedent of Dupuit (1844) and Pigou (1912) the approach is usually from the cost and supply side. The first assumption is that traffic consists of homogeneous vehicles with identical technical characteristics and cost functions. Each vehicle is operated by people with the same utility functions and the same levels of income, and so the same valuation of time. In order to avoid problems at the end or beginning of the road, we might conveniently assume that the road is a circle, with traffic going round and round. Let $c(x)$ be the cost incurred for travelling one kilometre, where x is the number of kilometres travelled by all the vehicles on the circular route of k kilometres in circumference. The density of vehicles is then x/k. Thus the total cost of the x vehicle-trips of 1 kilometre each is then $C(x) = x \cdot c(x)$.

As the number of trips on the road increases, the density of vehicles on the road rises, and so the speed of the traffic flow falls, and $c(x)$ rises. These are the familiar conditions of increasing congestion on the road. An individual deciding whether to make another trip will reckon the cost involved as $c(x)$ per kilometre, and will make that trip if his valuation of the worth of the trip is at least as great as $c(x)$ per kilometre. But the addition of another vehicle on the road will slow down all existing vehicles and so increase the costs of all other road users. Consequently the marginal costs of the additional trip consist not merely of the private costs of the particular motorist but the additional costs he inflicts on others by adding to the congestion of the highway. With C defined as the total cost of x trips, the marginal costs of the trip are $dC/dx = c + x \cdot dc/dx$, where c measures the private marginal cost of the individual and $x \cdot dc/dx$ measures the increase in cost to each user (dc/dx), multiplied by the number of user-trips (x). Clearly, if (as we have assumed) no price is levied for the use of the highway, then private marginal costs are less than the true marginal costs. Private decisions will then result in too much traffic on the road.

This state may be conveniently defined as the condition of *congestion*. In common usage, congestion may be used to denote circumstances where there is *some* interaction and slowing of vehicles below their traffic-free speed. With this wider definition, some congestion is virtually always efficient and actually there may be too little congestion on some highways. In this essay the common usage definition will be eschewed and throughout the technical definition, denoting *too much* traffic and too dense a traffic flow, will be employed.

The underlying reason for congestion is that the authorities do not charge an appropriate rent for the use of the highway. Were the highway to be owned by a profit-seeking agent, a toll would be levied for the use of the road at least as high as the cost which the marginal motorist imposes on other ($x \cdot dc/dx$). (If the road owner were to enjoy some monopoly power, rather than be a member of a large number of agents competing to supply the services of roads, then he would exact a monopoly rent in excess of ($x \cdot dc/dx$). But we shall continue with the fiction of a large number of privately owned competitive road suppliers so that the analogue with private business is clear.) In his classic work, Pigou (1912) used the priceless road illustration as a paradigm for competitive industry and thereby concluded that the competitive industry would always over-expand and degenerate into conditions of congestion. As Knight (1924) pointed out, under conditions of private ownership of resources, including roads, there would be no such overuse (congestion), since the road-owners would charge a competitive price for their services. Pigou was correct in the particular illustration of the 'free' road, but it was a distortion introduced by the public sector which would have not appeared under conditions of private ownership.

The normative conclusion is that it would be best, or at least better, if the authorities adopted a pattern of road pricing that simulated the behaviour of a competitive, privately-owned road system. For a specified level of traffic, say $x = x_i$, the authorities should charge a toll for the use of the road of $x \cdot (dc/dx)$ evaluated at $x = x_i$. This can be interpreted as the product of the private cost of a trip (c) multiplied by the elasticity of that cost with respect to the number of trips $[(x/c) \cdot (\mathrm{d}c/\mathrm{d}x)]$, evaluated at $x = x_i$.

This calculation gives the optimum supply price of road space when the traffic is at the level x_i. If, however, the level x_i represents the traffic equilibrium when there is a zero charge for the road service, as shown in Figure 1, then one must take into account the fact that raising the price of the total trip from $c(x_i)$ to $[c(x_i) + x \cdot (\mathrm{d}c/\mathrm{d}x)]$ will give rise to a reduction of traffic along the demand curve. As traffic falls, both cost and the optimum toll also decline. The new equilibrium toll will be $x_0 \cdot (\mathrm{d}c/\mathrm{d}x)$ for the optimum level of traffic x_0 and private cost $c(x_0)$. The optimum toll will always be below that calculated for the existing level of toll-free equilibrium traffic flow.

A rising value for the $c(x)$ function is intuitively plausible and fits in well with corresponding notions of the theory of the firm and industry. In Figure 1, however, the $c(x)$ function becomes vertical at a level of trips shown as *max*, but instead of the cost curve staying vertical for all values exceeding c(max), it is shown as backward-bending, eventually becoming asymptotic to the vertical cost axis. The rationalization for the backward-bending segment is best considered in terms of the flow/density/speed relationship by which trips are produced. Clearly the flow of vehicles past any given point of our circular road represents the number of trips completed. But the flow per hour is equal to the product of the density of vehicles (number per kilometre) and the speed of those vehicles (kilometres per hour). As vehicles join the road, density increases and speed is reduced. At low densities the reduction in speed is small, so that additional vehicles and increases of density will increase flow. However, as more vehicles jam into the existing road-space the effects of the additional density on speed will be so important that the slower speeds reduce the flow of trips. Ultimately one can imagine the bumper to bumper conditions of the complete jam. Then flow is zero and costs approach very high values indeed.

In this description of traffic flow, there is an obvious analogue with the theory of fluid dynamics (Walters, 1961). In the simplest form of the steady state flow theory:

$$s = b[\log D (s = 0) - \log D(s)]$$

where s is the speed and D is the density at which that specified speed is attained, and $x = sD$. This gives a very simple form to the elasticity of speed with respect to traffic flow, namely $\mathrm{d}\log s / \mathrm{d}\log x = b/(b - s)$. The parameter b measures the critical speed at which flow is maximized. In statistical studies of traffic flow one finds values of b ranging from about 12 kph for city streets to 26 to 30 kph for urban freeways and motorways. There is thus some evidence that the fluid-dynamic model is useful for interpreting conditions of very dense traffic.

There is obviously considerable difficulty in dealing with such backward bending curves. For any given level of trips there are two conceivable levels of cost – one high level associated with a high density, and one low level corresponding to the light density. In any rational arrangement of affairs one would expect that the backward-bending high-density conditions would be avoided by some system of exclusion, by pricing or other means. But it would be foolhardy to assume that such rational arrangements would be the norm; clearly the observed frequent traffic jams are not consistent with economic rationality. The possibility of a high-density, high-cost equilibrium being stable, a point such as A in Figure 1, cannot be dismissed. There is however also another locally stable equilibrium at point C, on the rising part of $c(x)$. There may be many such locally stable equilibria and some unstable ones, such as that represented by point B in Figure 1. The chaotic nature of traffic flow in many

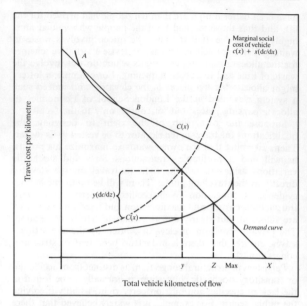

Fig. 1. Demand and supply on a congested highway.

cities suggests that it would not be entirely wise to ignore such phenomena – although one might argue that such conditions are likely to be transitory and of limited interest. Very little analytical or empirical attention has been paid to such problems of multiple equilibria and stability.

Various other models derived from the theory of thermodynamics and the statistical theory of queues have been used to model the congested aspects of road traffic. Although useful for simulating the interaction of congestion and flows in networks, the thermodynamic analogue has not been of much use in understanding the economics of congestion (Haight, 1963). The theory of queues and the stochastic processes derived to model lightly congested traffic have not been notably successful in producing theoretical simulations of observed processes, so again little has been done to interpret them in economic terms.

The empirical study of congestion has, however, found that the studies by traffic engineers of the relationship between speed, flow and density have been an invaluable basis for the economic assessment of the costs of congestion and the levels of the appropriate road tolls. Regression analysis of speed on flow has been the staple of analysis, sometimes using a rather unsatisfactory linear approximation for the rising section of the cost curve (and the falling section of the speed curve), and occasionally using the logarithmic form of the fluid dynamics analogue. The job of the economist was to translate a speed-flow relationship into a cost-flow form. The simplest approximation for very congested traffic is that cost is inversely proportional to speed. For less congested traffic, however, the approximation usually adopted is: $c = m + n/s$, where m and n are constants which depend on the currency of measurement, and c is cost per kilometre (Smeed, 1968).

Since the speed-flow relationships conform to theoretical expectation (with the exception of those with light flow and low density), the cost-flow version of the relationship is also consistent with the form displayed in Figure 1. Taking observed levels of flow, density, speed and cost on urban highways, one may calculate the gap between marginal social cost and private cost (i.e. a measure of $x \cdot (\mathrm{d}c/\mathrm{d}x)$). For cost inversely proportional to speed and with the fluid dynamic model, the optimum toll $t(s)$ at speed s is then $(cb)/(s-b)$. For some urban highways, however, the situation is clearly on the backward-bending part of the cost curve. Formally, the optimum toll at that point is infinite. But such a conclusion takes no account of the reaction of demand; one may merely take it as a reminder that it is patently wasteful to have so highly congested a road. Even if the demand curve lies to the right of the whole of the rising section of the cost curve, the optimum arrangement will always be to bring traffic down so that the equilibrium flow is on the rising section of the cost curve. This makes it important to know the shape of the demand curve and the values of the elasticities of demand over the relevant ranges of flow.

Unfortunately we know much less about the elasticity of demand for trips than we do about the cost functions. Substitution of elasticities between one road and another can be adduced from minimum cost (usually minimum time) routings by programming models, but substitutions between modes and the long run development of urban areas and movement are more intractable. Nevertheless some work by John Tanner, reported in Smeed (1968), showed that the level of optimum tolls was not very sensitive to different assumptions about elasticities of demand; but this result has not been fully explored and explained.

The empirical studies suggest that the optimum toll for town and city traffic during peak periods is probably at least 50 per cent – and in many cases as much as 100 per cent – of the private cost of the journey. Off-peak, the appropriate tolls are perhaps nearer to 10 to 40 per cent of the private cost. Note that in many cities, particularly those in the Third World such as Bangkok, Lagos and Sao Paulo, the peak can last for more than eight hours. The main implication for policy is that the wastes of congestion are very high and that there is a good prima facie case for reducing the demand for trips, probably by some sort of pricing mechanism.

The best policy to deal with urban road congestion is likely to be some form of road pricing. However, road pricing is the exception rather than the rule. Most governments have simply stood idly by as the wastes of congestion mount. When the traffic jams become quite unacceptable, the normal procedure is to impose regulations to ration the use of the streets. In Lagos, for example, odd-numbered licence plates were allowed on odd days and even numbers on even days. The most ubiquitous policy is to discourage the private motorist, with a particularly low occupancy to road space ratio, and to promote mass transit by rail or bus. Various priority systems with special bus lanes and impediments for cars have been the usual policy. A proper application of road pricing has been practised in only one case – Singapore. There the private motorist pays a daily or a monthly fee to enter the restricted area of downtown Singapore during the morning rush hours. The scheme was instituted in 1975 and has been judged by both the government and independent observers as a considerable success on economic and political criteria (World Bank, 1985). Rather similar schemes have been considered for London, Washington DC, and many other cities, but political considerations have prevented their implementation. The development of information technology has made feasible many sophisticated systems of computer controlled pricing. One such system has been introduced on an experimental basis in Hongkong (World Bank, 1985). The technical objections to road pricing have been largely overcome, but the distributional, vested interests and political hurdles have yet to be surmounted.

CONGESTION IN AIRPORTS AND PORTS. After highways, perhaps the most important examples of congestion are to be found in airports and ports. Both differ from the urban road congestion in so far as it is the normal practice to charge fees for landing aircraft and for harbouring ships. The problem of congestion arises when such fees do not reflect the scarcity of the facilities. (For some examples in ports, see Bennathan and Walters, 1979, and in airports, Park, 1971.) Landing fees or port dues may be subject to legal limitations or political pressure. Yet in practice it has been much easier to adjust airport and port fees to reflect scarcity, including seasonal or diurnal peaks, than to introduce congestion tolls on the highways.

CONCLUSION. The economic analysis of congestion has made some useful progress and the ideas and the policy measures that flow from those notions have a firm place in the economics of public policy. However, the policy of congestion tolls has been resisted by most governments, presumably because it is believed that there is not sufficient electoral support for such measures. In that sense, the political economy of congestion pricing has been largely a failure. It is difficult to see what changes would ensure its success.

A.A. WALTERS

See also MARGINAL AND AVERAGE COST PRICING; TRANSPORT.

BIBLIOGRAPHY

Bennathan, E. and Walters, A.A. 1979. *Port Pricing and Investment Policy for Developing Countries*. New York: Oxford University Press.

Dupuit, J. 1844. On the measurement of the utility of public works. Reprinted in *Transport*, ed. Dennis Munby, London: Penguin, 1968, 19–57.

Demsetz, H. 1982. *Economic, Legal, and Political Dimensions of Competition*. Amsterdam: North-Holland.

Haight, F. 1963. *Mathematical Theories of Traffic Flow*. New York: Academic Press.

Knight, F. 1924. Some fallacies in the interpretation of social cost. *Quarterly Journal of Economics* 38, August, 582–606.

Park, R. 1971. Congestion tolls for commercial airports. *Econometrica* 39, September, 683–94.

Pigou, A.C. 1912. *Wealth and Welfare*. London: Macmillan.

Smeed, R. 1968. Traffic studies and urban congestion. *Journal of Transport Economics and Policy* 2, January, 33–70.

Vickrey, W. 1969. Congestion theory and transport investment. *American Economic Review* 59, May, 251–60.

Walters, A.A. 1961. The theory of measurement of private and social costs of highway congestion. *Econometrica* 29, October, 676–99.

World Bank. 1985. *Urban Transport*. Washington, DC: World Bank.

conglomerates. The overall output of a firm may be composed of activity in more than one product market. The growth of individual firms will be composed of changes in the scale of their activities in each of the markets in which they operate and in the numbers of those markets. In any period these changes will consist of horizontal expansion in the market(s) in which they operated at the beginning of the period and entry into new markets; where there is a supplier or buyer relationship with the original market then this expansion will be vertical integration. Expansion which fits neither of these categories is termed diversifying or conglomerate expansion. Growth in any of these directions may be by the purchase of new assets (internal growth), or by the purchase of existing assets through takeover or merger (external growth). Although it is common to refer to non-horizontal and non-vertical expansion as diversified, or conglomerate, the latter term also has a more specific connotation emphasizing particularly diverse external expansion. It has in particular been used to mean a company which has by a deliberate strategy of external growth, often away from declining sectors, developed a highly diversified product range which cannot easily be characterized in terms of a single, or well defined, group of production technologies, a single set of major competitors, or a stable place in a well defined industry group (Steiner, 1975; Weston, 1980). (And in the US context to have financed that expansion with issues of paper rather than cash, accompanied by accounting techniques for consolidating acquired companies designed to boost earnings per share and make future paper issues even more profitable (Blair, 1972; Steiner, 1975).)

Although diversified businesses predate World War II (often in the form of financial holding companies in Europe and Japan) conglomerate companies in the above sense are essentially a postwar phenomenon, and have been associated with the widespread adoption of decentralized divisionalized management structures. In particular, in the United States the growth of merger activity in the 1960s was dominated by diversified acquisitions, the most spectacular of which were associated with the emergence of a group of particularly aggressive conglomerates. For instance, between 1961 and 1969 ITT, already a very large multinational telecommunications company, acquired amongst other concerns, the largest US bakery, the largest US hotel chain, and the largest US house builder, the second largest US car rental service and a number of large insurance and finance companies. Gulf and Western over a similar period acquired companies in sugar, tobacco, steel, paper, banking, insurance and motion pictures (Blair, 1972).

These are extreme examples of a general longer run tendency for diversification to increase in the post-war period in all the major industrial economies (Berry, 1975; Jacquemin and De Jong, 1977; Utton, 1979). Case studies of corporate growth strategies, and estimates of levels of, and changes in, diversification in the 1960s and 1970s reveal that rapid unrelated product expansion is outweighed by expansion based on a related product, or 'narrow spectrum' diversification strategy (e.g. outside a fairly finely defined (say 3 or 4 digit) primary product group but within a broader (say 2 digit) industry, of which the primary group is a part (Wood, 1971; Channon, 1973; Rumelt, 1974; Berry, 1975; Biggadike, 1979; Utton, 1979; Caves et al., 1980; Spruill, 1981). Nevertheless, these studies also suggest an increase in the importance of unrelated product expansion and a situation has now been reached where the largest companies in the major industrial countries have, by the long-term pursuit of such strategies, come to occupy leading positions in many different industries (Shepherd, 1970; Blair, 1972; Utton, 1979) and where the market in corporate takeovers, and divisionalized management structures, permit the easy pursuit of further conglomerate growth by external means (Mueller, 1969). This has inevitably raised questions about the relationship between market competition and conglomerate growth, and about the effects of conglomerate merger upon corporate performance.

Estimating the impact of conglomerate activity in an industry upon levels of, and trends in, its concentration are surrounded by empirical problems. These arise from lack of precise data on the market shares of individual firms in different industries, and on the evolution over time of those shares. Similar problems limit attempts to measure the impact of conglomerate entry, either by merger, or new investment. The evidence suggests that conglomerate mergers have had little impact on levels of, or trends in market concentration in the US (Goldberg, 1973, 1974) whilst in the UK and the US neither the presence of diversified firms, nor new entry by diversification, seems to lead to increased levels of concentra-

tion. If anything the reverse seems to be the case (Berry, 1975; Utton, 1979). Effects on competitive behaviour rather than market structure are a little better documented. Here the argument is that operating over many markets enhances power in each of them individually (Edwards, 1955). Thus it is argued that conglomerate firms may impose reciprocal buying pressures upon suppliers to encourage them to use, as inputs, the products of other divisions of the parent conglomerate; may employ predatory pricing in newly entered markets, cross-subsidized by activities elsewhere; and practice mutual forebearance with accepted spheres of influence agreed with other conglomerates. More difficult to detect may be other effects claimed to arise from reductions in potential competition, where it is argued, for instance, that entry by a large conglomerate may deter other likely entrants, or lead to subsequent anti-competitive behaviour, which could not, or otherwise would not, occur. Where entry is by merger it may also be argued that this is at the expense of new investment in the market, either by incumbents, or the new entrant itself (Markham, 1973; Steiner, 1976; Scherer, 1979). Examples can be found in the US, and in the UK and Europe, of most these practices. There is little to suggest however that these are persistent, typical, or pervasive features of conglomerate behaviour. Where they have been most prominent they appear to have been due at least as much to individual market power as to overall conglomerate strength (Markham, 1973; Scherer, 1979; Utton, 1979).

Corresponding to claims of the anti-competitive losses which may follow from the spread of conglomeration are claims of likely benefits. Here it is claimed that such firms may allocate more resources per unit of sales to research and development, since the chances of utilizing spin-offs and unexpected findings within the organization are higher (Nelson, 1959); may experience economies of scope (Panzar and Willig, 1981) and may enjoy lower costs of raising capital on the stock market in response to more stable earnings streams, and the reduced risk of bankruptcy that conglomerate spread may bring. There is no consistent evidence to suggest that these effects lead to any superiority in profit performance, either for the individual firm, or for industries in which conglomerate firms play an important role, some studies finding positive, and others negative, effects on profit levels or stability (Rhoades, 1973, 1974; Utton, 1979; Caves et al., 1980; Kelly, 1980). There is, however, some evidence to support the view that diversified firms have higher R&D inputs and patent outputs than specialized firms, although there is an obvious problem of causation involved (Wood, 1971; Kennedy and Thirlwall, 1972; Scherer, 1979). The effects of conglomerate merger have been much more extensively investigated than the impact of conglomerate firms as such. Those studies for the US which examine periods beyond the stock market conglomerate boom years of the late 1960s show such merging conglomerate companies either doing less well, or at best as well, as other companies (or portfolios of shares) in terms of profitability, profit stability and shareholder returns. This is especially so when profitability measures are used which allow for the loan financing techniques used to build up the most spectacular conglomerate empires in the 1960s merger boom (Mueller, 1977). Evidence for other countries is more fragmentary but that for the UK, for instance, suggests that conglomerate mergers perform relatively well in terms of profitability compared to mergers in general, though neither outperform companies relying on internal growth (Meeks, 1977; Cosh, Hughes and Singh, 1980).

Most of this work may be set in the context of a static neoclassical perspective to trade off monopoly welfare losses against efficiency gains. On this basis it would be hard to mount a significant case for or against conglomerates. To look at the problem in this way is however, to distract attention from what may be regarded as more fundamental questions about the working of the economic system as a whole. There are three interrelated issues here. What are the comparative advantages of organizing economic activity on the basis of interfirm market processes as opposed to intra-firm administrative and organizational processes, what is the impact of the spread of conglomeracy upon the flow of economic resources between alternative prospective uses, and how does diversification and the spread of conglomeracy affect the flow of information upon which a market economy is based.

On one view of the world the growth of divisionalized conglomerate companies may be regarded, in many instances, as a superior resource allocation mechanism to interfirm market transactions. Internal administrative allocative decisions to move resources between the company's individual markets and divisions, it is argued, are based upon more and better information than that available to outsiders in the stock market (Williamson, 1975, 1985; Chandler, 1962, 1977). From this point of view appropriately organized conglomerates are efficient mini-capital markets, and represent that potent source of new entry by mobile capital, and adjustment away from declining sectors which lies at the heart of the competitive adjustment process (Clifton, 1977, and, from a different perspective, Weston, 1980). Moreover, the wider the spread of industries covered by any firm, and the wider the threat of takeover of the inefficient, or sleepy, or of entry by new investment, the more forceful this argument becomes. On the other hand conglomerate firms are not all embracing in their industrial coverage, their acquisitions may not be especially driven by industrial logic or production efficiency, and it may be argued that in addition they reduce the efficiency of operation of the capital market itself, given that financial reporting by large firms is notoriously aggregative.

In this sense the defining characteristics of conglomerates are to be found in their internal financial and administrative arrangements, which have in principle freed them from the particular constraints of individual product markets and production technologies. They represent the latest boundary between organization and the market (Coase, 1937) and as such fit uneasily into any generally accepted model of the workings of the macro or micro economy as a whole.

ALAN HUGHES

See also ANTI-TRUST POLICY; MARKET STRUCTURE.

BIBLIOGRAPHY

Berry, C.H. 1975. *Corporate Growth and Diversification*. Princeton: Princeton University Press.

Biggadike, E.R. 1979. *Corporate Diversification Entry Strategy and Performance*. Boston: Harvard University, Graduate School of Business.

Blair, J.M. 1972. *Economic Concentration*. New York: Harcourt Brace Jovanovich.

Caves, R.E. 1980. Industrial organisation, strategy and structure. *Journal of Economic Literature* 18(1), March, 64-92.

Caves, R.E. et al. 1980. *Competition in the Open Economy*. Cambridge, Mass.: Harvard University Press.

Chandler, A. 1962. *Strategy and Structure: Chapters in the History of the Industrial Enterprise*. New York: Anchor Books.

Chandler, A. 1977. *The Visible Hand: The Managerial Revolution in American Business*. Cambridge, Mass.: Harvard University Press.

Channon, D.F. 1973. *The Strategy and Structure of British Enterprise*. London: Macmillan.

Clifton, J.A. 1977. Competition and the evolution of the Capitalist mode of production. *Cambridge Journal of Economics* 2, June, 137–51.

Coase, R.H. 1937. The nature of the firm. *Economica* 4, November, 386–405.

Cosh, A., Hughes, A. and Singh, A. 1980. The causes and effects of takeovers in the United Kingdom. In *The Determinants and Effects of Mergers*, ed. D.C. Mueller, Cambridge, Mass.: O.G.H. Publishers.

Edwards, C.D. 1955. Conglomerate bigness as a source of power. In *Business Concentration and Price Policy*, ed. G. Stigler, New York: National Bureau for Economic Research.

Goldberg, L.G. 1973. The effect of conglomerate mergers on competition. *Journal of Law and Economics* 16(1), April, 137-58.

Goldberg, L.G. 1974. Conglomerate mergers and concentration ratios. *Review of Economics and Statistics* 56(2), August, 303-9.

Hughes, A. and Singh, A. 1980. Mergers concentration and competition in advanced capitalist economies: an international perspective. In *Determinants and Effects of Mergers*, ed. D.C. Mueller, Cambridge, Mass.: O.G.H. Publishers.

Jacquemin, A.P. and De Jong, H.W. 1977. *European Industrial Organisation*. London: Macmillan.

Kelly, M. 1980. The effects of diversification on market structure and monopoly power. In K. Cowling et al., *Mergers and Economic Performance*, Cambridge: Cambridge University Press.

Kennedy, C. and Thirlwall, A.P. 1972. Technical progress: a survey. *Economic Journal* 82, March, 11-72.

Markham, J.W. 1973. *Conglomerate Enterprise and Public Policy*. Boston: Harvard Graduate School of Business.

Meeks, G. 1977. *Disappointing Marriage*. Cambridge: Cambridge University Press.

Mueller, D.C. 1969. A theory of conglomerate mergers. *Quarterly Journal of Economics* 83(4), November, 643-59.

Mueller, D.C. 1977. The effects of conglomerate mergers. A survey of the empirical evidence. *Journal of Banking and Finance* 1(4), December, 315-47.

Mueller, D.C. (ed.) 1980. *The Determinants and Effects of Mergers: An International Comparison*, New York: O.G.H. Publishers.

Nelson, R. 1959. The simple economics of basic scientific research. *Journal of Political Economy* 67, June, 297-306.

Panzar, J.C. and Willig, R.D. 1981. Economies of scope. *American Economic Review, Papers and Proceedings* 71(2), May, 268-72.

Rhoades, S.A. 1973. The effect of diversification on industry profit performance in 241 manufacturing industries in 1963. *Review of Economics and Statistics* 55(2), May, 146-55.

Rhoades, S.A. 1974. A further evaluation of the effect of diversification on industry profit performance. *Review of Economics and Statistics* 56(4), November, 557-9.

Rumelt, R.P. 1974. *Strategy, Structure and Economic Performance*. Boston: Harvard Graduate School of Business.

Scherer, F.M. 1979. *Industrial Market Structure and Economic Performance*. 2nd edn, Chicago: Rand McNally, 1980.

Shepherd, W.G. 1970. *Market Power and Economic Welfare*. New York: Random House.

Spruill, C.R. 1981. *Conglomerates and the Evolution of Capitalism*. Carbondale: Southern Illinois University Press.

Steiner, P.O. 1976. *Mergers: Motives, Effects, Policies*. Ann Arbor: University of Michigan Press.

Utton, M.A. 1979. *Diversification and Competition*. Cambridge: Cambridge University Press.

Weston, J.F. 1980. Industrial concentration, mergers and growth. In *Mergers and Economic Efficiency*, Vol. I, Washington, DC: U.S. Government Printing Office.

Williamson, O.E. 1975. *Markets and Hierarchies: Analysis and Anti-Trust Implications*. New York: Free Press.

Williamson, O.E. 1985. *The Economic Institutions of Capitalism*. New York: Free Press.

Wood, A.J.B. 1971. Diversification, merger and research expenditure: a review of empirical studies. In *The Corporate Economy*, ed. R. Harris and A.J.B. Wood, London: Macmillan.

conjectural equilibria. In an economy with very many agents the market environment of any one of these is independent of the market actions he decides upon. More generally one can characterize an economy as *perfectly competitive* if the removal of any one agent from the economy would leave the remaining agents just as well off as they were before his removal. (The economy is said to satisfy a 'no surplus' condition; see Makowski, 1980; and Ostroy, 1980.) When an economy is not perfectly competitive, an agent in making a decision must take note of its effect on his market environment, for example, the price at which he can sell. This effect may not be known (or known with certainty) and will therefore be the subject of *conjecture*. A conjecture differs from expectations concerning future market environments which may, say, be generated by some stochastic process. It is concerned with responses to the actions of the agent.

In the first instance then the topic of Conjectural Equilibria is that of an economy which is not perfectly competitive by virtue of satisfying a no surplus condition. But, as we shall see, an economy could fail to satisfy this condition and yet have a perfectly competitive equilibrium.

By an equilibrium in economics we usually mean an economic state which is a rest (critical) point of an (implicit) dynamic system. For instance, it is postulated in the textbooks that when at going prices the amount agents wish to buy does not equal the amount they wish to sell, prices will change. Strictly this should mean that there would, in such a situation, be an incentive for some agent(s) to change prices. This causes difficulties when the economy is perfectly competitive (Arrow, 1959) since it implies that the agent can influence his market environment by his own actions. That is one reason why a fictitious auctioneer has been introduced to account for price changes.

When the economy is not perfectly competitive these difficulties are avoided. A price will be changed if some agent conjectures that such a change would be to his advantage. As a corollary then a conjectural equilibrium must be a state from which it is conjectured by each agent that it would be disadvantageous to depart by actions which are under the individual agent's control. (For a formal definition see below.)

But there are other difficulties. In particular, there is the question of the source of conjectures. If these are taken as given exogenously then there are many states which could be conjectural equilibria for *some* conjectures. It should be noted that a similar objection can be raised in conventional equilibrium analysis. There it is the preferences of agents which are taken as exogenous and there too there are many equilibria which are compatible with some (admissible) preferences. However, while conjectures may turn out to be false and this may occasion a change in conjectures it is less easy to point to equally simple and convincing endogenous mechanisms of preference change. For that reason one may feel that conjectural equilibrium requires that conjectures are in some sense correct ('rational'). For if they are not they will change in the light of experience. This argument is considered below.

The reason why the idea of conjectural equilibria is of interest is that economies which are not intrinsically perfectly competitive (e.g. because of the large number of agents) are of interest and because it allows one to study price formation without an auctioneer.

AN ILLUSTRATION. Consider two agents each of whom can chose an action a_i from a set of action A_i. Let $A = A_1 \times A_2$ with elements $a = (a_1, a_2)$. Then a conjecture c_i is a map from $A \times A_i$ to A_j written as

$$C_i = \theta_i(a, a_i').$$

Its interpretation is this: given the actions of the two agents (a), C_i is the action of j conjectured by i to be result from his choice of a_i'. (In a more general formulation the conjecture can be a probability distribution but that is not considered here.) We require conjectures to be *consistent*:

$$\theta_i(a, a_i) = a_j \qquad (1)$$

This says that if agent i continues in his action a_i then he conjectures that j will do likewise. [This use of the word 'consistent' is *not* that of Bresnahan (1981) and others who use it to mean 'correct'.]

Suppose now that there is a function v from A to R^2, written as $v(a) = [v_1(a), v_2(a)]$, which gives the payoffs to the agents as a function of their joint action a. Consider a^* to be one such joint action. One says that a^* is a *conjectural equilibrium* for the two agents if

$$v_i[a_i, \theta_i(a^*, a_i)] \leqslant V_i[a_i^*, \theta_i(a^*)] \qquad \text{all } a_i \in A_i, \quad i = 1, 2 \;\; (2)$$

That is, the joint action a^* is a conjectural equilibrium if no agent, given his conjecture, believes that he can improve his position by deviating to a different action.

It is not the case that conjectural equilibrium, as defined, always exists. For instance in the case of a duopoly in a homogeneous product where the action is 'setting the price', v may not be concave and a sensible conjecture may have discontinuities. One thus needs special assumptions to ensure existence or one must face the possibility that agents do not chose actions but probability distributions over actions (mixed strategies); e.g. Kreps and Wilson (1982) in their work on sequential equilibrium employ conjectures which are probability distributions.

Supposing that a conjectural equilibrium exists, one may reasonably argue that until conjectures are less arbitrarily imposed on the theory not much has been gained – almost any pair of actions could be a conjectural equilibrium. A first attempt to remedy this is to ask that conjectures be correct (rational). If that is to succeed in any simple fashion it will be necessary to suppose that each agent has a unique best action under this conjecture. This is very limiting and it means that some of the classical duopoly problems cannot be resolved in this way.

Let the status quo again be a^*. Then if θ_1^* and θ_2^* are correct conjectures it must be that

$$v_2\{\theta_1^*(a^*, a_2), \theta_1^*[(a_1, a_1^*), \theta_2^*(a^*, a_2)]\}$$
$$> v_1\{a_1', \theta_1^*[(a_1^*, a_2), a_1']\} \qquad \text{all } a_1' = A_2 \quad (3)$$
$$v_1\{\theta_2^*(a^*, a_2), \theta_1^*[(a_1^*, a_2), \theta_2^*(a^*, a_2)]\}$$
$$> v_1\{a_s', \theta_1^*[(a_1^*, a_2), a_1']\} \qquad \text{all } a_1' = A_1 \quad (4)$$

A *Rational Conjectural Equilibrium* is then a conjectural equilibrium a^* [with conjectures $\theta_1^*(\cdot)$, $\theta_2^*(\cdot)$ which satisfy (3) and (4)]. It must be re-emphasized that such an equilibrium may not exist for some A and v (see Gale, 1978; Hahn, 1978).

However the idea is simple and where applicable, coherent. It has however been criticized (in a somewhat intemperate and muddled paper) by Makowski (1983). This criticism appears to have had some appeal to some game theorists who like to think of games in extensive form (which they sometimes like to call dynamic). The criticism is this: when agent one deviates from a^* he is interested in the payoffs which he will get given this deviation and agent two's response. This payoff Makowski thinks of as accruing in the 'period' after agent one's deviation. But when agent two responds in that period he is interested in this payoff in the period following this response. So the agents expect 'the game to end' in different periods (Makowski, 1983, p. 8). Moreover, after agent two has responded, agent one, in his turn will again want to respond, i.e. deviate from the deviation he started with. This criticism is then illustrated with an example in which one agent expects the other to return to the status quo *after* he has deviated from it.

All of this however is wrong. Firstly, if one wants to give a time interpretation to conjectures etc. then actions must be thought of as strategies. That is, the deviating agent deviates in one or more elements of his plan over the whole length of the game (perhaps infinite). Under correct conjectures responses and counter responses are taken into account in evaluating the benefits of deviation. Hence, and secondly, a deviating agent is in this situation never surprised by the response of the other, which therefore does not lead him to further revise his deviation. On the definition, agent 1 expects the response to his deviation to be $\theta_1(a^*, a_1)$. Suppose this gives a_2 which is correct. Then that agent knows that the new status quo will be $(a_1, a_2) = a$ and if he has calculated benefits correctly he will not wish to deviate again.

However, there is the following to be said in favour of Makowski's criticism. Deviations in strategies may not be observable by the other agent. Therefore in traditional duopoly models with a sequential structure the re-interpretation of actions as strategies may be inappropriate. There is some evidence that in the duopoly literature with conjectures the consequent difficulties have not always been appreciated. It is also the case that too little attention has been paid to the assumption of a unique best response on which the above formulation depends.

An alternative to rational conjectures are *reasonable conjectures* (Hahn, 1978). A conjecture is reasonable if acting on any other conjecture would lower profits given the conjectures of other firms. Suppose that $\bar{\theta}$ is the set of all possible consistent conjectures. For any $\theta_i \in \bar{\theta}$, assume that there is a unique optimizing choice of output by firm i of $y_i(\theta_i)$. Then i's conjecture $\theta_i^0 \in \theta$ is reasonable if given jth conjecture θ_j:

$$v_i[y_i(\theta_i^0), y_j(\theta_j)] \geqslant \hat{v}_i[y_i(\theta_i'), y_j(\theta_j)] \quad \text{all } \theta_i' \in \theta. \quad (5)$$

But then a *reasonable conjectural equilibrium* is a pair (θ_1^0, θ_2^0) each in θ such that

$$v_i[y_i(\theta_i^0), y_j(\theta_j^0)] \geqslant \hat{v}[y_i(\theta_i'), y_j(\theta_j^0)], \quad i, j-1, 2, \quad \theta_i' \in \bar{\theta} \quad (6)$$

This is just a Nash-equilibrium where conjectures are interpreted as strategies (Hart, 1982).

While this is still quite demanding it is significantly weaker than (3). If equilibria exist they may be 'bootstrap equilibria', that is they will depend on beliefs about the actions of others, which beliefs may be incorrect. There is certainly no ground for believing that they will be efficient.

One can go one step further in the direction of plausibility by requiring that conjectures be reasonable only for small, or infinitesimal, deviations from the status quo. After all, large experiments are likely to be costlier than small ones. This will allow a larger class of reasonable conjectures and equilibria.

GENERAL CONJECTURAL EQUILIBRIUM. It is fair to say that at present General Equilibrium Theory is in some way complete only for a perfectly competitive economy, that is one where the returns to an individual agent are just equal to the contribution which he makes (Makowski, 1980; Ostroy, 1980). In general (although there are exceptions) such an economy exists when it is large (e.g. it consists of a non-atomic continuum of agents). But there is now another possibility: an economy can be perfectly competitive if agents conjecture that their market actions will have no effect on the prices at which they can trade.

The following assertion will be clear from what has already been discussed. Let us say that an economy is *intrinsically* perfectly competitive if it satisfies the *no-surplus condition*. Then perfectly competitive conjectures are rational if an economy is intrinsically perfectly competitive. But perfectly competitive conjectures can be reasonable even when the economy is not intrinsically perfectly competitive. That is conjectures may be such that if an agent acts on any conjecture other than the perfectly competitive one, his profits will be lower. For instance, this may even be the case for two duopolists with constant marginal costs whose conjectures refer to the price charged by the rival firm. It will also be clear that if we do not require conjectures to be either reasonable or rational then, in general, conjectures can be found to support a competitive equilibrium in an economy which is not intrinsically perfectly competitive.

In a general equilibrium context it is not clear what it is that firms are supposed to conjecture. In some sense the conjecture must refer to the reaction of the whole economy to the action of the conjecturing agent. In other words, it is not obvious how to define a game which adequately represents the economy. But in what sense?

Consider an economy with n produced goods and m non-produced goods. For simplicity suppose that all firms are single product firms and that all firms producing the same good are alike, including their conjectures. There are very many households whose reasonable conjectures are always the competitive one. Households receive the profits of firms. Since the action of any one firm can affect the prices at which households can trade it is not at all clear what it is in the households' interest that the firms should maximise (Gabszewicz and Vial 1972). If all households are alike it could be their common utility function, but that seems far removed from the world. I shall arbitrarily assume that firms maximize their profits in terms of one of the non-produced goods, say the first. This is arbitrary but it seems to me equally dubious to suppose that firms always choose in the 'best interests of shareholders', especially when that interest is often difficult and sometimes impossible to define.

Let $p \in R^n$, $w \in R^{m-1}_+$ be the price vectors in terms of good m of produced and non-produced goods respectively (so $w_m \equiv 1$). Let $y_j \in Y_j \subset R^{n+m}$ be the production of firm j where $y_{ij} > 0$ is its output of good j, $y_{ii} < 0$ is an input of good i, produced or non-produced. Let $y = \Sigma y_j$, where $y_j \in Y_j$ all j. Let $z \in R^m_+$ be the endowment of non produced goods and

$$F = \{y \mid y \geqslant (0, -z)\}$$

so that F is the set of feasible net production vectors Y. Let θ_{hj} be the share of household h in firm j.

Given any $y \in F$ we think of each household as endowed with a certain strictly positive stock of non-produced goods and $\theta_{hj} Y_j$ of the production of firm j. To avoid unnecessary complications assume θ_{hj} $(j = 1, \ldots, n)$ to be such that if z_h is the stock of non-produced goods owned by household h:

$$\text{For all } y \in F: z_h + \sum_j \theta_{hj} y_j \geqslant 0 \quad \text{all } h. \quad (7)$$

Households consume both types of goods. Hence for any $y \in F$ there is now an associated pure exchange economy where each household's endowment is given by (7). Making the usual assumptions there will exist at least one equilibrium $[p(y), w(y)]$. Suppose for the moment that there is only one for each $y \in F$.

Now firm j in this equilibrium observes $[p(y), w(y)]$ and will deviate from y_j (if it deviates at all) if it can thereby increase its conjectured profits. Let

$$\hat{\pi}_j[p(y), w(y), y_j']$$

be the conjectural profit function of firm j. Then y^0, $p(y^0)$, $w(y^0)$ is a conjectural equilibrium if for all $j = 1, \ldots, n$:

$$\hat{\pi}_j[p(y^0), w(y^0), y_j^0] \geqslant \hat{\pi}_j[p(y^0), w(y^0), y_j'] \quad \text{all } y_j' \in Y. \quad (8)$$

Such a conjectural equilibrium will exist if all $\hat{\pi}_j(\cdot)$ are quasi-concave, an assumption for which there is scant justification (Hahn, 1978).

If we demand that conjectures be rational then conjectured and actual profit must coincide for all y_k' (the two coincide for $y_k' = y_k^0$ by the requirement that conjectures be consistent). One proceeds as follows. Let $y_k' = y_k^0$. Given the conjectures of the remaining firms find the conjectural equilibrium of the economy $p\{y^*(k), w[y^*(k), y^*(k)]\}$, where $y(k)$ is the vector y with y_k' in the kth place and condition (8) is not imposed for firm k. One then requires that for all $y_k' > 0$

$$\hat{\pi}_k[p(y^0), w(y^0), y_k'] = \pi_k\{p[y^*(k)], w[y^*(k)], y_k'\}$$

where $\pi_k(\cdot)$ is actual profit. For rational conjectures this should be true for all k.

It will be seen that rational conjectural equilibrium is very demanding. For a certain class of conjectures it will not even exist (Gale, 1978; Hahn, 1978). More importantly, the whole procedure breaks down if given a deviation by k, the conjectural equilibrium, is not unique. Lastly, even if by sufficient assumptions one overcomes these difficulties, it is not agreeable to commonsense to suppose that firms can correctly calculate general equilibrium responses to their actions, nor is it obvious that they should always be only concerned with equilibrium states.

Reasonable conjectures do not fare much better, although a notable contribution to their study has recently been made by Hart (1982). Hart notices that conjectures of firms induce a supply correspondence (not generally convex) on their part. Here let us suppose that we can in fact speak of supply functions. These can be thought of as strategies in a manner already discussed. A reasonable conjectural equilibrium then satisfies the condition that, given the supply functions of other firms, no deviation by firm k to another supply response can increase its profits. In (8) one then substitutes on the right-hand side for y_j', $\eta_j'[p(y^0), w(y^0)]$, an admissible supply function (see Hart, 1982) of j and requires the inequality to hold for all such functions. Of course, one has

$$y_j^0 = \eta_j^0[p(y^0), w(y^0)]$$

for a reasonable conjectural equilibrium.

To show existence of such an equilibrium will require strong assumptions. The technicalities will be found in Hart (1982). However one of the assumptions which he makes is not only technically useful but economically sensible since it leads firms to face a simpler task in forming conjectures. Hart supposes the economy to consist of a number of islands each of which has many consumers and one firm of each type ($j = 1, \ldots, n$). The islands are small replicas of the whole economy. But households have shares in firms on all islands so that if there are enough islands their share in any firm on their own island is very small. That means that any firm can disregard the effect of a change in its own profits on the demand for the good it produces. To make this work one supposes that produced goods are totally immobile between islands while non-produced goods are totally mobile. By an appropriate assumption on consumers on each island one ensures that they all have the same demand. Lastly, since shares in a firm are held on many different islands the firm, in acting in the shareholder's interest is justified in neglecting the effect of its actions on relative prices on its own island and so is justified in maximizing profits.

From the point of view of conjectural equilibrium the island assumption allows firms (both reasonably and rationally) to ignore effects of their own actions on w – the price vector of non-produced goods. These will be determined by demand and supply over all islands and in this determination any one firm can be regarded as playing a negligible role. This is some gain in realism. But after all allowances have been made it is still true that (a) the assumptions required for the existence of reasonable conjectural equilibrium are uncomfortably strong and (b) even when that is neglected such an equilibrium seems to have small descriptive power.

SIMPLER APPROACHES. Negishi (1960) made the first, justifiably celebrated, attempt to incorporate imperfect competition in general equilibrium analysis. He did this by letting single product firms have consistent inverse demand conjectures (the case he studies most thoroughly makes these linear). Consistency is all he asked for of conjectures but he also needed the uncomfortable postulate that the resulting conjectural profit functions be quasi-concave. Later Hahn (1978), Silvestre (1982) and others added the requirement that besides being consistent, the conjectured demand functions have, if differentiable, the correct slope at equilibrium (i.e. that the conjecture be *infinitesimally* or 'first order' *rational*). It turns out that this extra requirement does not much restrict conjectures, nor thus the set of equilibria which can be generated by some conjectures. The reason roughly is this: in conjectural equilibrium, when conjectured profit functions are twice differentiable, the partial derivative of the conjectured profit function of firm j with respect to its own output must vanish. Suppose the economy to be in such an equilibrium and consider an infinitesimal output deviation by firm k. To find the equilibrium which ensues, differentiate all equilibrium relations, other than that for firm k, with respect to the output of firm k. Amongst these will be the condition that the marginal profit conjectured of every firm (other than k), be zero. Hence differentiation of that condition will yield second order terms. But we can choose these arbitrarily since we are only requiring first order rationality. One can show in fact that these second order terms can be chosen so as to make the first order conjectured change in profit of any firm k correspond to the actual change. (Details in Hahn, 1977.) Hence first order rationality imposes few restrictions.

Both Hahn (1978) and Negishi (1979) have also considered kinked conjectures. The idea is this. If an agent can transact at the going price as much as he desires his conjectures are competitive. If he is quantity constrained (e.g. if a firm cannot sell an amount determined by equality between marginal cost and price) his conjectures are non-competitive. That is he considers that a price change is required to relax the quantity constraint. The fix-price methods of Drèze (1975) and others can be interpreted as an extreme form of such conjectures – for instance to relax a constraint on sales, price, it is conjectured, must be reduced to zero.

To such conjectures there have been two objections. Firstly, they assume that an agent's conjectures are not influenced by constraints on others. For instance, a firm which can hire as much labour as it wants at the going wage while workers cannot sell as much as they like does not conjecture that it could have the same amount of labour at a lower wage. To this one can answer that it is not easy for an agent to observe the quantity constraints on others. For instance, unemployment statistics do not tell us whether workers have chosen not to work or whether they are constrained in their sale of labour. None the less this objection has some force and needs further study with proper attention to the information of agents.

The other objection is that these kinked conjectures are not explained. That is true if explanation turns on what an agent knows or can learn. None the less the hypothesis seems to be to have psychological verisimilitude. If I can always sell my labour at the going wage there is little occasion for the difficult conjecturing of what would happen if I raised my wage. This is not so if I find that I cannot find employment at the going wage.

In any event these simpler approaches allow one to incorporate traditional monopolistic competition in a general equilibrium framework. Of course, some of the assumptions such as concave conjectured profit functions are strong. On the other hand, one can now allow for a certain amount of increasing returns (Silvestre, 1982).

SOME CONCLUSIONS. The conjectural approach has this merit: it takes proper and explicit note of the perceptions by individuals of their market environment. Economic theory perhaps too often neglects the possibility that what is the case may depend on what agents believe to be the case. Historians and others have long since studied the intimate mutual connection between beliefs and events but economists have not made much headway here. The conjectural approach is perhaps a small beginning. For it deals with the theories agents hold and this must plainly enter into our theory of agents.

In particular one should not pay too much attention to the objection that conjectures may not be derivable from some first principles of rationality. It seems to me quite proper to find their description in history. Nor, as has been argued, will an appeal to learning render conjectures in some sense objectively justifiable. This is clear from the discussion of reasonable conjectures and from the costs of experimentation. For hundreds of years witches were burned in the light of a reasonable theory which few would now regard as having proper objective correlatives. There is no reason to suppose that it is possible for businesses or governments now to do better than some of the best minds of the past.

From a more immediately relevant standpoint, conjectural theories are of interest because they attempt a general equilibrium analysis of non-perfect competition. It is good to know that in a proper sense perfectly competitive economies can be viewed as Limiting Cournot Conjectural Equilibrium economies (Novshek and Sonnenschein, 1978). But this knowledge does not contribute to the study of properly imperfectly competitive economies. Again the study of fix-price equilibria has borne some fruits, but not those which were first sought by Triffin (1940) when he proposed a framework for general equilibrium with monopolistic competition. If it is the case that actual economies are not perfectly competitive nor that they behave 'as if' they were, then the task set by Triffin requires serious attention and it is likely that conjectural theories will have a role to play.

Recent developments in game theory (e.g. Kreps and Wilson, 1982) suggest that these two conjectures will have to play a part. Indeed quite generally in that theory, players conjecture that their opponent is 'rational' in an appropriate sense. It is not the case that the conjectural equilibrium approach is an alternative to the game theoretic one.

F. HAHN

See also AUCTIONEER; MONOPOLISTIC COMPETITION IN GENERAL EQUILIBRIUM THEORY; NASH EQUILIBRIUM.

BIBLIOGRAPHY

Arrow, K.J. 1959. Toward a theory of price adjustment. In M. Abramovitz et al., *The Allocation of Economic Resources*, Stanford: Stanford University Press, 41–51.

Bresnahan, T.F. 1981. Duopoly models with consistent conjectures. *American Economic Review* 71(5), 934–45.

Dreze, J. 1975. Existence of equilibrium under price rigidity and quantity rationing. *International Economical Review* 16, 301–20.

Gabszewicz, J.J. and Vial, J.D. 1972. Oligopoly 'à la Cournot' in general equilibrium analysis. *Journal of Economy Theory* 4, 381–400.

Gale, D. 1978. A note on conjectural equilibria. *Review of Economic Studies* 45(1), 33–8.

Hahn, F.H. 1977. Exercise in conjectural equilibria. *Scandinavian Journal of Economics* 79, 210–26.

Hahn, F.H. 1978. On non-Walrasian equilibria. *Review of Economic Studies* 45, 1–17.

Hart, O. 1982. Reasonable conjectures. Suntory Toyota Centre for Economics and Related Disciplines. London School of Economics.

Kreps, D.M. and Wilson, R.B. 1982. Sequential equilibria. *Econometrica* 50, 863–94.

Makowski, L. 1980. A characterisation of perfectly competitive economies with production. *Journal of Economic Theory* 22(2), 208–21.

Makowski, L. 1983. 'Rational conjectures' aren't rational and 'reasonable conjectures' aren't reasonable. SSRC Project on Risk, Information and Quantity Signals. Cambridge University Discussion Paper 60.

Negishi, T. 1960. Monopolistic competition and general equilibrium. *Review of Economic Studies* 28, 196–202.

Negishi, T. 1979. *Micro-Economic Foundations of Keynesian Macro-Economics*. Amsterdam: North-Holland.

Novshek, W. and Sonnenschein, H. 1978. Cournot and Walras equilibrium. *Journal of Economic Theory* 19, 223–66.

Ostroy, J. 1980. The no-surplus condition as a characterisation of perfectly competitive equilibrium. *Journal of Economic Theory* 22(2), 183–207.

Silvestre, J. 1977. A model of a general equilibrium with monopolistic behaviour. *Journal of Economic Theory* 16(2), 425–42.

Triffin, R. 1940. *Monopolistic Competition and General Equilibrium Theory*. Cambridge: Mass.: Harvard University Press.

Ulph, D. 1983. Rational conjectures in the theory of oligopoly. *International Journal of Industrial Organization* 1(2), 131–54.

conjectural variation. *See* DUOPOLY; OLIGOPOLY.

consols (Consolidated Fund). *See* BONDS.

conspicuous consumption. Conspicuous consumption means the use of consumer goods in such a way as to create a display for the purpose of impressing others rather than for the satisfaction of normal consumer demand. It is consumption intended chiefly as an ostentatious display of wealth. The concept of conspicuous consumption was introduced into economic theory by Thorstein Veblen (1899) in the context of his analysis of the latent functions of 'conspicuous consumption' and 'conspicuous waste' as symbols of upper class status and as competitive methods of enhancing personal prestige.

Veblen argued that the leisure class is chiefly interested in this type of consumption, but that, to a certain degree, it exists in all classes. The leisure class undoubtedly has much more opportunity for this kind of consumption. The criterion as to whether a particular outlay fell under the heading of conspicuous consumption was whether, aside from acquired tastes and from the canons of usage and conventional decency, its result is a net gain in comfort or in fullness of life.

It is widely thought that Veblen introduced the concept of conspicious consumption into economic literature, but it was known much earlier. Adam Smith (1776, Book I, ch.11) wrote about people who like to possess those distinguishing marks of opulence that nobody but themselves can possess. In the eyes of such people the merit of an object that is in any degree either useful or beautiful is greatly enhanced by its scarcity, or by the great amount of labour required to accumulate any considerable quantity of it. This is the labour for which nobody but themselves can afford to pay. Smith concludes that this domain is ruled by fashion. J.B. Say and McCulloch wrote about this issue in a similar way. But the author who first used the term 'conspicuous consumption' was the Canadian economist John Rae (1796–1872). His explanation of the nature and effects of luxury was based on the meaning of vanity in human life. He understood vanity to be the mere desire for superiority over others without any reference to merit. The aim is to have what others cannot have, whereas the stimulus to productivity in economic life is the passion for effective accumulation: 'Articles of which consumption is conspicuous, are incapable of gratifying this passion' (Rae, 1834).

However, it was Veblen who introduced the concept of conspicuous consumption as a phenomenon important for the understanding of consumption as a whole. He gave Rae no reference at all.

Veblen's historical and socio-economic explanation of this institution gave as a result the so-called 'Veblen effect'. This is the phenomenon whereby as the price of an article falls some consumers construe this as a reduction in the quality of the good or loss of its 'exclusiveness' and cease to buy it.

F. STANKOVIĆ

See also RAE, JOHN; VEBLEN, THORSTEIN.

BIBLIOGRAPHY
Mason, R.S. 1981. *Conspicuous Consumption: A Study of Exceptional Consumption Behaviour*. New York: St Martin's Press.
Rae, J. 1834. *The Sociological Theory of Capital*. Ed. C. Mixter, New York: Macmillan.
Smith, A. 1776. *An Inquiry into the Nature and Causes of the Wealth of Nations*. Ed. E. Cannan, London: Methuen, 1981.
Sweezy, P. 1952. *Veblen and Marx–History of American Socialism, Socialism in American Values*. Ed. E. Donald and Person, Princeton: Princeton University Press.
Veblen, T. 1899. *The Theory of the Leisure Class*. London: George Allen & Unwin.

constant and variable capital. 1 DEFINITION; 2 VARIABLE CAPITAL AND SOURCE OF PROFIT; 3 ORGANIC COMPOSITION AND PRODUCTION PRICE; 4 ORGANIC COMPOSITION AND THE RATE OF PROFIT; 5 ORGANIC COMPOSITION AND UNEMPLOYMENT.

1 DEFINITION

In *Das Kapital* Marx defined Constant Capital as that part of capital advanced in the means of production; he defined Variable Capital as the part of capital advanced in wages (Marx, 1867, Vol. I, ch. 6). These definitions come from his concept of Value: he defined the value of commodities as the amount of labour directly and indirectly necessary to produce commodities (Vol. I, ch. 1). In other words, the value of commodities is the sum of C and N, where C is the value of the means of production necessary to produce them and N is the amount of labour used that is directly necessary to produce them. The value of the capital advanced in the means of production is given to C.

However, the value of the capital advanced in wages is obviously not equal to N, because it is the value of the commodities which labourers can buy with their wages, and has no direct relationship with the amount of labour which they actually expend. Therefore, while the value of the part of capital

that is advanced in the means of production is transferred to the value of the products without quantitative change, the value of the capital advanced in wages undergoes quantitative change in the process of transfer to the value of the products. This is the reason why Marx proposed the definitions of constant capital C and variable capital V.

The definition of constant capital and variable capital must not be confused with the definition of fixed capital and liquid capital. Fixed capital is a part of constant capital which is totally used in production process but transfers its value to produces only partially. Liquid capital is a part of constant capital which is totally used up and transfers its whole value within one production process. So constant capital is composed of both fixed capital and liquid capital, and on the other hand liquid capital belongs partly to constant capital and partly to variable capital.

Marx introduced the concept 'value-composition of capital', μ, which is defined as the ratio of constant capital C to variable capital V.

$$\mu \equiv \frac{C}{V} \qquad (1.1)$$

Marx knew well that the value composition of capital reflects not only material characteristics of the process of production but also the social relationship between capitalists and labourers. In fact definition (1.1) can be rewritten as

$$\mu = \frac{C}{N} \cdot \frac{N}{V} \qquad (1.2)$$

C/N reflects the character of the process of production and N/V reflects the class relationship between capitalists and labourers. C/N is the ratio of the amount of labour necessary to produce the means of production to the amount of labour directly bestowed, which is completely determined by the material condition in the process of production, while N/V is the ratio of the amount of labour which labourers actually expend to the amount of labour that is necessary in order to produce commodities which labourers can purchase with their wages. If labourers are forced to work longer with less wages, this ratio must rise.

Marx proposed to call the value-composition of capital, insofar as it is determined by the material condition of the process of production, 'the organic composition of capital'. More explicitly, 'The value-composition of capital, inasmuch as it is determined by, and reflects, its technical composition, is called the *organic* composition of capital' (*Capital*, Vol. III, ch. 8). However, as shown above, the value composition of capital is not determined by the material condition of the process of production alone. So it is better to introduce the ratio C/N in the place of the organic composition of capital, which is determined only by the material condition in the process of production. In order to avoid confusion, I call this ratio the 'organic composition of production'. This is the ratio of dead labour to living labour, which Marx himself frequently used in *Das Kapital*.

2 VARIABLE CAPITAL AND SOURCE OF PROFIT

In contrast to Smith, Ricardo and others, Marx attached great importance to analysis to find the source of profit. He found that source in surplus labour, which is the excess of labour expended by labourers over the value of commodities which labourers can obtain with their wages (*Capital*, vol. I, ch. 5). Using the notation introduced above, $N > V$ is the necessary condition for profit to exist. In order to illuminate this fact, he called capital advanced in wages *Variable Capital*. So the validity of this name depends on his analysis of the source of profit. How is it justified?

For simplicity we set up the simplest model which can reflect the fundamental characteristics of a capitalistic economy; these characteristics are the prevalence of commodity production, and the existence of class relationships between labourers and capitalists. There are only two kinds of commodities: the means of production (commodity 1) and consumption goods (commodity 2). In order to produce one unit of the ith commodity an amount of a_i unit of means of production and an amount of labour τ_i are necessary as input. Labourers are forced to work for T hours per day and earn the money wage rate w.

In order for profit to exist in both industries the following inequalities are necessary

$$p_1 > a_1 p_1 + \tau_1 w \qquad (2.1)$$

$$p_2 > a_2 p_1 + \tau_2 w \qquad (2.2)$$

where p_1 and p_2 denote the price of the means of production and consumption goods respectively. As labourers work for T hours a day at money wage w per hour, they can purchase an amount B of consumption goods.

$$B = \frac{wT}{p_2}, \qquad B/T = R \qquad (2.3)$$

where R is the real wage rate.

In the first volume of *Das Kapital*, Marx assumed that all commodities are exchanged at prices exactly proportionate to their unit value (equivalent exchange). Unit values of commodities are determined by the following equations

$$t_1 = a_1 t_1 + \tau_1 \qquad (2.4)$$

$$t_2 = a_2 t_1 + \tau_2 \qquad (2.5)$$

which assure unique and positive values, provided $a_1 < 1$ (Dmitriev, 1898; May, 1949–50; Okishio, 1955a, 1955b).

Under the assumption of equivalent exchange, we have

$$p_i = \lambda t_i \qquad (2.6)$$

where λ is a constant which converts the dimension from hours to, say, dollars. Substituting (2.3) and (2.6) into (2.1) and (2.2) we get

$$t_1 > a_1 t_1 + \tau_1 \frac{B}{T} t_2 \qquad (2.7)$$

$$t_2 > a_2 t_1 + \tau_2 \frac{B}{T} t_2. \qquad (2.8)$$

By equations (2.4) and (2.5) and the above inequalities, we have

$$\tau_1 \left(1 - \frac{B}{T} t_2\right) > 0 \qquad (2.9)$$

$$\tau_2 \left(1 - \frac{B}{T} t_2\right) > 0. \qquad (2.10)$$

Consequently we arrive at the conclusion

$$T > Bt_2. \qquad (2.11)$$

This inequality implies the existence of surplus value, because surplus value is the excess of working hours T over the amount of labour necessary to produce commodities which labourers can receive with wages B. If the number of workers employed is n, then total expended labour is nT and variable capital measured in terms of value is $Bt_2 n$. So the inequality (2.11) can be rewritten as

$$N > V \qquad (2.12)$$

This is the reason Marx called capital advanced in wages variable capital.

As shown above, Marx proved the theorem of the source of profit under the assumption of equivalent exchange. Though this is a clear-cut way to show the results, it has induced various critiques. Many critics have said that Marx's theorem would be right if all exchanges were equivalent exchange, but that in reality exchanges are seldom equivalent so his theorem cannot be valid. In order to refute such a criticism we must prove the theorem without the assumption of equivalent exchange (see Okishio 1955a, 1955b, 1963, 1972, 1978; Morishima, 1973). Mathematically, our task is to find necessary and sufficient conditions for inequalities (2.1), (2.2) and (2.3) to have non-negative solutions for p_1, p_2. From (2.1) we know easily that the condition

$$1 - a_1 > 0 \qquad (2.13)$$

is necessary for p_1 to be positive. This condition ensures that the society will obtain net output.

Next, substituting (2.3) into (2.1), and from (2.13) we have

$$\frac{p_1}{p_2} > \frac{\tau_1 B}{T(1 - a_1)}. \qquad (2.14)$$

On the other hand, from (2.2) and (2.3) we get

$$\frac{p_1}{p_2} > \frac{T - \tau_2 B}{T a_2}. \qquad (2.15)$$

We can easily get from (2.14) and (2.15)

$$\frac{a_2 \tau_1 B}{(1 - a_1)} < T - \tau_2 B. \qquad (2.16)$$

Inequality (2.16) is rewritten as

$$T > B \left(\frac{a_2 \tau_1}{1 - a_1} + \tau_2\right). \qquad (2.17)$$

By (2.17), (2.4) and (2.5) the above becomes

$$T > Bt_2. \qquad (2.18)$$

Thus we can arrive at Marx's result.

For later convenience we show another expression for the existence of surplus value.

Dividing (2.1) and (2.2) by w, we get

$$\frac{p_1}{w} > a_1 \frac{p_1}{w} + \tau_1 \qquad (2.19)$$

$$\frac{p_2}{w} > a_2 \frac{p_1}{w} + \tau_2 \qquad (2.20)$$

By comparing (2.19) and (2.20), and (2.4) and (2.5), we get

$$\frac{p_i}{w} > t_i, \qquad (i = 1, 2) \qquad (2.21)$$

Equation (2.21) implies that if positive profit exists, then the price–wage ratio (the amount of commanded labour) is greater than the amount of value (necessary labour). In the famous controversy with Ricardo, Malthus pointed out this difference between labour commanded and labour embodied. Though he wrongly thought that this difference injured the validity of the labour theory of value, he had come near to the Marxian theory of the source of profit (see Malthus, 1820, pp. 61–3, 120).

Condition (2.21) is rewritten as

$$1/t_i > w/p_i$$

This condition shows that if positive profit exists, then the productivity of labour $(1/t_i)$ must be greater than the rate of real wages (w/p_i).

581

3 ORGANIC COMPOSITION AND PRODUCTION PRICE

The concept of organic composition of capital plays an important role in Marx's analysis of prices.

The price of production (Ricardo's 'natural price') that gives every industry the equal rate of profit is determined by the following equations:

$$p_1 = (1 + r)(a_1 p_1 + \tau_1 w) \tag{3.1}$$

$$p_2 = (1 + r)(a_2 p_1 + \tau_2 w) \tag{3.2}$$

$$w = R p_2 \tag{3.3}$$

where r is the general (equal) rate of profit.

The first problem is to examine the relationship between

$$\frac{t_1}{t_2} \sim \frac{p_1}{p_2}.$$

If they are equal then we have equivalent exchange, if not we have non-equivalent exchange from the point of view of the labour theory of value. The values of the commodities are determined by (2.4) and (2.5). The ratio of the value of production-goods to consumption-goods t_1/t_2 is given as

$$\frac{t_1}{t_2} = \frac{\tau_1 \left(\dfrac{a_1 t_1}{\tau_1} + 1 \right)}{\tau_2 \left(\dfrac{a_2 t_1}{\tau_2} + 1 \right)}. \tag{3.4}$$

The relative price of production-goods to consumption-goods determined by (3.1) and (3.2) is given as

$$\frac{p_1}{p_2} = \frac{\tau_1 \left(\dfrac{a_1 p_1}{\tau_1} + w \right)}{\tau_2 \left(\dfrac{a_2 p_1}{\tau_2} + w \right)}. \tag{3.5}$$

Comparing (3.4) with (3.5), we obtain

$$\frac{t_1}{t_2} - \frac{p_1}{p_2} = \frac{\tau_1}{\tau_2} \left[\frac{\dfrac{a_1 t_1}{\tau_1} + 1}{\dfrac{a_2 t_1}{\tau_2} + 1} - \frac{\dfrac{a_1 p_1}{\tau_1} + w}{\dfrac{a_2 p_1}{\tau_2} + w} \right]. \tag{3.6}$$

The expression in brackets on the RHS of (3.6) is given by

$$[\;] = (t_1 w - p_1) \left(\frac{a_1}{\tau_1} - \frac{a_2}{\tau_2} \right) A, \qquad A > 0. \tag{3.7}$$

If profit is positive, from (2.21) $t_1 w - p_1$ is negative. So we can conclude

$$\frac{t_1}{t_2} \gtreqless \frac{p_1}{p_2} \Leftrightarrow \frac{a_1}{\tau_1} \lesseqgtr \frac{a_2}{\tau_2}. \tag{3.8}$$

The RHS of the above means the comparison of the organic composition of production and also the organic composition of capital, because as shown above the organic composition of production is $a_i t_1 / \tau_i$ and the organic composition of capital is $a_i t_1 / \tau_i R t_2$.

The second problem is to examine the influence of the change in real wage rate on the relative prices determined by (3.1), (3.2) and (3.3):

$$d \left(\frac{p_1}{p_2} \right) \Big/ dR.$$

Denoting the relative price of production-goods to consumption-goods as p, from (3.1), (3.2) and (3.3) we obtain

$$f(p) \equiv a_2 p^2 + (\tau_2 R - a_1) p - \tau_1 R = 0. \tag{3.9}$$

Differentiating (3.9) with respect to R, we have

$$\frac{dp}{dR} = \frac{\tau_1 - \tau_2 p}{2 a_2 p + \tau_2 R - a_1}. \tag{3.10}$$

The denominator above is positive, because from (3.9)

$$\text{denominator} \times p = a_2 p^2 + \tau_1 R > 0.$$

We shall show that the sign of the numerator depends on the comparison between the organic composition of capital in both sectors.

The function $f(p)$ in (3.9) is drawn in Figure 1. The meaningful solution of the equation (3.9) is given at p^*. Substituting τ_1/τ_2 into $f(p)$, we get

$$f \left(\frac{\tau_1}{\tau_2} \right) = \tau_1 (a_2 \tau_1 - a_1 \tau_2).$$

Therefore if $a_2 \tau_1 - a_1 \tau_2 > 0$ then $f(\tau_1/\tau_2) > 0$, so considering the graph of $f(p)$ we know that $\tau_1/\tau_2 > p^*$. In the same way we can conclude that if $a_2 \tau_1 - a_1 \tau_2 \gtreqless 0$, then $\tau_1/\tau_2 \gtreqless p$. Consequently, from (3.10) we can conclude

$$d \left(\frac{p_1}{p_2} \right) \Big/ dR \gtreqless 0 \Leftrightarrow \frac{a_1}{\tau_1} \lesseqgtr \frac{a_2}{\tau_2}.$$

This proposition is first established in Ricardo's *Principles* (1821, p. 43).

4 ORGANIC COMPOSITION AND THE RATE OF PROFIT

The concept of organic composition of capital plays an important role in Marx's analysis of the movement of the rate of profit.

Marx defined the rate of profit as

$$r = \frac{S}{C + V}. \tag{4.1}$$

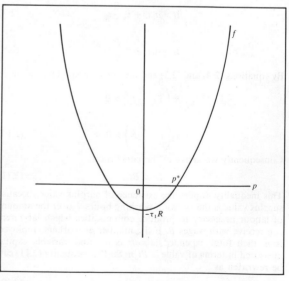

Figure 1

By (1.1), equation (4.1) is rewritten as

$$r = \frac{e}{\mu + 1}, \qquad e = S/V \qquad (4.2)$$

where e is the rate of exploitation.

He asserted that if the organic composition of capital μ increases sufficiently then the rate of profit r must inevitably decrease. This is the famous 'law of the tendency for the rate of profit to fall' (*Capital*, vol. III, ch. 13).

Many people have criticized this theorem. They have said that if the rate of exploitation e increases sufficiently, r may increase in spite of the increase of μ. So r does not necessarily decrease, even if μ increases sufficiently (Robinson, 1942; Sweezy, 1942). Such a critique overlooks the logic of Marx's argument.

Marx stated:

> Since the mass of the employed living labour is continually on the decline as compared to the mass of materialized labour set in motion by it, i.e., to the productively consumed means of production, it follows that the portion of living labour, unpaid and congealed in surplus-value, must also be continually on the decrease compared to the amount of value represented by the invested total capital. Since the ratio of the mass of surplus-value to the value of the invested total capital forms the rate of profit, this rate must constantly fall (*Capital*, vol. III, ch. 13, p. 213).

Therefore Marx's true intention is to insist that if the organic composition of production $v = C/N$ (the ratio of the mass of materialized labour to the mass of living labour) increases sufficiently, the rate of profit must fall.

This can be proved as follows (Okishio, 1972). From (4.1) and (4.2), and

$$v = C/N \qquad (4.3)$$

we have

$$
\begin{aligned}
r_{t+1} - r_t &= \frac{S_{t+1}}{C_{t+1} + V_{t+1}} - r_t \\
&= \frac{e_{t+1}}{v_{t+1}(1 + e_{t+1}) + 1} - r_t \\
&= \frac{1}{v_{t+1}(1/e_{t+1} + 1) + 1/e_{t+1}} - r_t
\end{aligned} \qquad (4.4)
$$

where suffixes t, $t + 1$ denote periods.

The RHS of (4.4) is an increasing function of e. If we take the limiting value as e tends to infinity, we have

$$r_{t+1} - r_t < \frac{1}{v_{t+1}} - r_t.$$

Therefore we conclude, if $v_{t+1} > 1/r_t$, then $r_{t+1} - r_t < 0$.

The above reasoning can be restated. The reciprocal of the organic composition of production sets an upper limit to the rate of profit, because

$$r = \frac{S}{C + V} < \frac{S + V}{C} = \frac{N}{C} \qquad (4.5)$$

If this upper limit decreases sufficiently, the rate of profit must eventually decrease, as shown in Figure 2.

In response to criticisms of this view we must say that as far as we accept Marx's assumption that the inverse of the organic composition (N/C) tends toward zero, Marx's conclusion inevitably follows.

So far we have defined the rate of profit as (4.1) and C, V,

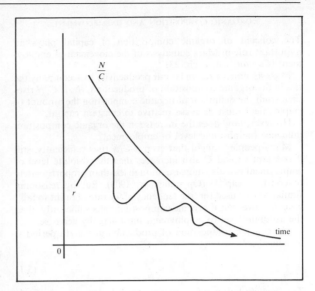

Figure 2

S are all measured in terms of labour value. However, the general rate of profit r must be determined by (3.1), (3.2) and (3.3). Can we derive the same conclusions for such a redefined r ?

Eliminating p_1, p_2, w from (3.1), (3.2) and (3.3) we have

$$f(r, R) \equiv (1 + r)^2 R(a_1 \tau_2 - a_2 \tau_1)$$
$$- (1 + r)(a_1 + \tau_2 R) + 1 = 0 \qquad (4.6)$$

Differentiating $f(r, R)$ we have

$$f_r \, dr + f_R \, dR = 0 \qquad (4.7)$$

where

$$f_r = 2(1 + r) R(a_1 \tau_2 - a_2 \tau_1) - (a_1 + \tau_2 R)$$
$$f_R = (1 + r)^2 (a_1 \tau_2 - a_2 \tau_1) - (1 + r) \tau_2$$

Considering (4.6)

$$(1 + r) f_r = (a_1 + \tau_2 R)(1 + r) - 2 \qquad (4.8)$$

From (3.1), (3.2), (3.3), we know

$$1 - (1 + r) a_1 > 0 \qquad 1 - (1 + r) \tau_2 R > 0 \qquad (4.9)$$

From (4.8) $f_r < 0$. f_R is rewritten as

$$f_R = (1 + r)\{[(1 + r) a_1 - 1] \tau_2 - (1 + r) a_2 \tau_1\}$$

So by (4.9) $f_R < 0$, from which $dr/dR < 0$. As R goes to zero r tends to its upper limit, which is obtained from (4.6)

$$r_{max} = \frac{1 - a_1}{a_1}. \qquad (4.10)$$

Since the value of the means of production is determined by (2.4), we have

$$\frac{1 - a_1}{a_1} = \frac{(1 - a_1) t_1}{a_1 t_1} = \frac{\tau_1}{a_1 t_1} = \frac{N_1}{C_1} \qquad (4.11)$$

Thus the upper limit of the general rate of profit is given by the reciprocal of the organic composition of production in the means of production sector. Therefore if the organic composition in that sector rises sufficiently, the general rate of profit must fall.

5 ORGANIC COMPOSITION AND UNEMPLOYMENT

The concept of organic composition of capital plays an important role in Marx's analysis of the movement of employment (*Capital*, vol. I, ch. 23).

Marx assumed a rise in labour productivity to accompany the rise in the organic composition of production C/N. If C/N rises then from the definition of organic composition the amount of employment must decrease relative to constant capital.

However, how does the increase in the organic composition influence the absolute level of employment?

Many people thought that even if C/N rises sufficiently, still if constant capital C also increases then the absolute level of employment can also increase, though less than proportionately to constant capital (Oppenheimer, 1903). But by reasoning similar to that used for 'the tendency of the rate of profit to fall', we can prove that if organic composition rises sufficiently, then the absolute level of employment must actually decrease.

The organic composition of production in the tth period v_t is defined as

$$v_t = \frac{C_t}{N_t}. \tag{5.1}$$

The accumulation of constant capital $\Delta C = C_{t+1} - C_t$ is financed from surplus value S.

$$C_{t+1} - C_t < S_t. \tag{5.2}$$

The surplus value S is a part of the amount of living labour which labourers expend

$$S_t < N_t. \tag{5.3}$$

By (5.1), we obtain,

$$N_{t+1} - N_t = \frac{1}{v_{t+1}} C_{t+1} - \frac{1}{v_t} C_t$$

$$= \frac{1}{v_{t+1}} (C_{t+1} - C_t) + C_t \left(\frac{1}{v_{t+1}} - \frac{1}{v_t} \right).$$

From (5.2) and (5.3) we get

$$N_{t+1} - N_t < \frac{1}{v_{t+1}} S_t + C_t \left(\frac{1}{v_{t+1}} - \frac{1}{v_t} \right) < \frac{N_t}{v_{t+1}} + C_t \left(\frac{1}{v_{t+1}} - \frac{1}{v_t} \right)$$

$$= \frac{C_t}{v_{t+1} v_t} (1 + v_t - v_{t+1}).$$

We can say, if $(1 + v_t - v_{t+1}) < 0$, then $N_{t+1} - N_t < 0$. Therefore, if the organic composition of production in the $t + 1$th period, v_{t+1}, increases sufficiently so as to exceed $1 + v_t$, then the amount of employed labourer, N_{t+1} must inevitably become less than N_t, however high the rate of accumulation of capital may be (Okishio, 1972). The rate of accumulation of capital $\Delta C/C$ itself is bounded by the reciprocal of the organic composition. From (5.2) and (5.3)

$$\frac{\Delta C}{C} < \frac{N}{C} = \frac{1}{v}$$

so that, because it is reasonable to assume that the growth rate of labour supply is non-negative, we can say that if the organic composition rises sufficiently the rate of unemployment inevitably rises. Though Marx did not state this explicitly, we think that this is what he wanted to say.

In analysing Marx's theorem on the movement of the rate of profit and employment, we have accepted his central assumption that the organic composition of production rises sufficiently over time. However, there arises the problem: under what conditions do capitalists choose techniques that have sufficiently high organic compositions of production?

Marx seemed to think that the rise in labour productivity and the rise in the organic composition are two aspects of the same thing. But these two do not always go together. Marx himself knew that if labour productivity in the means of production sector rises very high then even if technical composition rises, still the value composition may remain constant or decrease.

As to the capitalists' introduction of new techniques we have the following propositions:

(1) if the real wage rate remains constant and capitalists introduce new techniques which raise the rate of profit (calculated at the current prevailing prices and wage) then the new general rate of profit does not decrease, whatever the organic composition may be.

(2) if the real wage rate rises and capitalists adapt to this situation with the introduction of new techniques, then the new general rate of profit is higher than the one which would be expected if such a new technique were not introduced.

For the proofs of these propositions, see CHOICE OF TECHNIQUE AND THE RATE OF PROFIT.

N. OKISHIO

See also MARXIAN VALUE ANALYSIS; ORGANIC COMPOSITION OF CAPITAL; SURPLUS VALUE.

BIBLIOGRAPHY

Dmitriev, V.K. 1898. The theory of value of David Ricardo. In V.K. Dmitriev, *Economic Essays on Value, Competition and Utility*, ed. D.M. Nuti, Cambridge: Cambridge University Press, 1974.

Malthus, R. 1820. *Principles of Political Economy considered with a View to their Practical Application*. 1st edn, London.

Marx, K. 1867–94. *Capital*. Translated from the third German edition by Samuel Moore and Edward Aveling, ed. Frederick Engels. New York: International Publishers, 1967.

May, K. 1949. The structure of classical theories. *Review of Economic Studies* 17(1), 60–69.

Morishima, M. 1973. *Marx's Economics: A Dual Theory of Value and Growth*. Cambridge: Cambridge University Press.

Okishio, N. 1955a. Kachi to Kakaku (Value and production price). *Keizaigaku Kenkyu Nempo* (The Annals of Economic Studies), Kobe University, No. 19.

Okishio, N. 1955b. Monopoly and the rates of profit. *Kobe University Economic Review* 1, 71–88.

Okishio, N. 1963. A mathematical note on Marxian theorems. *Weltwirtschaftliches Archiv* 91, pt. 2, 287–98.

Okishio, N. 1972. A formal proof of Marx's two theorems. *Kobe University Economic Review* 18, 1–6.

Okishio, N, et al. 1978. Three topics on Marxian fundamental theorems. *Kobe University Economic Review* 24, 1–18.

Oppenheimer, T. 1903. *Das Grundgesetz der Marxschen Gesellschaftslehre*. Book II, ch. 25. Berlin: Reimer.

Ricardo, D. 1821. *On the Principles of Political Economy and Taxation*. Vol. 1 in *Works and Correspondence of David Ricardo*, ed. P. Sraffa, Cambridge: Cambridge University Press, 1951–73.

Robinson, J. 1942. *An Essay on Marxian Economics*. London: Macmillan.

Sweezy, P.M. 1942. *The Theory of Capitalist Development: Principles of Marxian Political Economy*. New York: Oxford University Press.

constant elasticity of substitution production function. *See* CES PRODUCTION FUNCTION.

constant returns. *See* EULER'S THEOREM; RETURNS TO SCALE.

constitutional economics. The term *Constitutional Economics* (Constitutional Political Economy) was introduced to define and to classify a distinct strand of research inquiry and related policy discourse in the 1970s and beyond. The subject matter is not new or novel, and it may be argued that 'constitutional economics' is more closely related to the work of Adam Smith and the classical economists than its modern 'non-constitutional' counterpart. Both areas of inquiry involve positive analysis that is ultimately aimed at contributing to the discussion of policy questions. The difference lies in the level of or setting for analysis which, in turn, implies communication with different audiences.

Orthodox economic analysis, whether this be interpreted in Marshallian or Walrasian terms, attempts to explain the choices of economic agents, their interactions one with another, and the results of these interactions, within the existing legal–institutional–constitutional structure of the polity. Normative considerations enter through the efficiency criteria of theoretical welfare economics, and policy options are evaluated in terms of these criteria. The policy analyst, building on the analysis, presents his results, whether explicitly or implicitly, to the political decision-makers, who then make some ultimate determination from among the available set. In this role the policy analyst directly, and the theorist indirectly, are necessarily advising governmental decision-makers, whoever these may be.

By both contrast and comparison, constitutional economic analysis attempts to explain the working properties of alternative sets of legal–institutional–constitutional rules that constrain the choices and activities of economic and political agents, the rules that define the framework within which the ordinary choices of economic and political agents are made. In this sense, constitutional economics involves a 'higher' level of inquiry than orthodox economics; it must incorporate the results of the latter along with many less sophisticated subdisciplines. Normative considerations enter the analysis in a much more complex manner than through the artificially straightforward efficiency criteria. Alternative sets of rules must be evaluated in some sense analogously to ranking of policy options within a specified institutional structure, but the epistemological content of the 'efficiency' criteria becomes more exposed.

The constitutional economist, precisely because the subject matter is the analysis of alternate sets of rules, has nothing to offer by way of policy advice to political agents who act within defined rules. In this sense, constitutional economics is not appropriately included within 'policy science' at all. At another level, however, the whole exercise is aimed at offering guidance to those who participate in the discussion of constitutional change. In other words, constitutional economics offers a potential for normative advice to the member of the continuing constitutional convention, whereas orthodox economics offers a potential for advice to the practising politician. In a real sense, constitutional economics examines the *choice of constraints* as opposed to the *choice within constraints*, and as this terminology suggests, the disciplinary attention of economists has almost exclusively been placed on the second of these two problems.

A preliminary illustration of the distinction may be drawn from the economics of monetary policy. The constitutional economist is not directly concerned with determining whether monetary ease or monetary restrictiveness is required for furthering stabilization objectives in a particular setting. On the other hand, he is directly concerned with evaluating the properties of alternative monetary regime (e.g. rule-directed versus discretionary, fiat versus commodity standards). The ultimate objective of analysis is the choice among the institutions within which political agents act. The predicted behaviour of these agents is incorporated in the analysis of alternative sets of constraints.

I CONSTITUTIONAL ECONOMICS AND CLASSICAL POLITICAL ECONOMY. As suggested, Constitutional Economics is related to classical political economy and it may be considered to be an important component of a more general revival of the classical emphasis, and particularly as represented in the works of Adam Smith. (The closely related complementary components are discussed briefly in section III.) One obvious aim of the classical political economists was to offer an explanation and an understanding of how markets operate without detailed political direction. In this respect, orthodox neoclassical economics follows directly in the classical tradition. But the basic classical analysis of the working of markets was only a necessary step toward the more comprehensive purpose of the whole exercise, which was that of demonstrating that, precisely because markets function with tolerable efficiency independently of political direction, a powerful normative argument for constitutional structure exists. That is to say, Adam Smith was engaged directly in comparing alternative institutional structures, alternative sets of constraints within which economic agents make choices. In this comparative analysis, he found it essential to model the working properties of a non-politicized economy, which did not exist in reality, as well as the working properties of a highly politicized mercantilist economy, which could be directly observed.

There is no need here to enter the lists on either side of the 'ideas have consequences' debate. We know that the economy of Great Britain was effectively de-politicized in the late 18th and early 19th centuries, and from the analysis of Smith and his classical fellow travellers there emerged both positive understanding of economic process and philosophical argument for a particular regime. The normative argument for laissez faire was, perhaps inevitably, intermingled with the positive analysis of interaction within a particular structure of constraints, essentially those that describe the minimal, protective, or night-watchman state. Economics, as a social science, emerged, but in the process attention was diverted from the institutional structure. Even the predicted normative reaction against the overly zealous extension of the laissez faire argument was couched in 'market failure' terms, rather than in the Smithian context of institutional comparison. The early socialist critique of market order, both in its Marxist and non-Marxist variants, was almost exclusively negative in that it elaborated putative failures of markets within an unexamined set of legal-political rules while it neglected analysis of the alternative rules that any correction of the alleged failures might require. Only with the debates on socialist calculation in the decades prior to World War II did the issues of comparative structure come to be examined.

It was only in the half-century after these debates that political economy, inclusively defined, returned, in fits and starts, to its classical tradition. Given the legal order of the protective state (the protection of property and the enforcement of contracts), we now know that under some conditions 'markets fail' when evaluated against idealized criteria, whether these be 'efficiency', 'justice', or other abstract norms. We also know that 'politics fails' when evaluated by the same criteria. Any positive analysis that purports to be of use in an ultimate normative judgment must reflect an informed comparison of the working properties of alternative sets of rules or constraints. This analysis is the domain of Constitutional Economics.

II CONSTITUTIONAL ECONOMICS AND SOCIAL PHILOSOPHY. Classical political economy emerged from moral philosophy, and its propounders considered their efforts to fall naturally within the limits of philosophical discourse. As a modern embodiment, Constitutional Economics is similarly located, regardless of disciplinary fragmentation. How can persons live together in liberty, peace and prosperity? This central question of social philosophy requires continuing contributions from many specialists in inquiry, surely including those of the constitutional economists. By their focus directly on the ultimate selection of a set of constraining rules within which ordinary social interaction takes place, constitutional economists remove themselves at least one stage further from the false position of 'social engineer' than their counterparts in orthodox economics. Precisely because there is no apparently simple evaluative criterion analogous to 'allocative efficiency' at hand, the constitutional economist is less tempted to array alternatives as if an unexamined criterion commands universal assent. The artificial abstraction of 'social utility' is likely to be less appealing to those who concentrate on choices among constraints than to those who examine choices within constraints.

If, however, there is no maximand, how can ultimate normative consequence emerge? In this respect, one contribution lies at the level of positive analysis rather than in a too-hasty leap into normative evaluation. Classical political economy contains the important principle of spontaneous coordination, the great discovery of the 18th century. This principle states that, within the legal umbrella of the minimal state and given certain conditions, the market 'works'. Even if in the principle's modern embellishment we must add 'warts and all', we still have come a long way toward a more comprehensive understanding of the alternatives for social order. To the extent that his efforts expand the public understanding of this principle, in application to all institutional settings, the constitutional economist remains under less apparent compulsion to advance his own privately preferred 'solutions' to the ultimate choice among regimes.

III THE NEW POLITICAL ECONOMY. Care should be taken not to claim too much for Constitutional Economics, especially if a narrow definition is used. As noted earlier, this research programme, by designation, emerged in the 1970s to describe efforts at analysing the effects of alternative sets of rules, as opposed to analyses of choices made within existing and unexamined structures. In a more comprehensive overview of developments after World War II, Constitutional Economics takes its place among an intersecting set of several research programmes, all of which have roots in classical political economy. Critical emphases differ as among the separate programmes, but each reflects efforts to move beyond the relatively narrow confines of orthodox neoclassical economics.

In continental Europe, the whole set of subdisciplines is included under the rubric 'The New Political Economy'. Within this set we can place (1) Public Choice, from which Constitutional Economics emerged; (2) Economics of Property Rights; (3) Law and Economics or Economic Analysis of Law; (4) Political Economy of Regulation; (5) the New Institutional Economics, and (6) the new Economic History. Defined imperialistically, Constitutional Economics would parallel the inclusive term and embrace all of these programmes, since some attention is drawn in each case to the legal–political constraints within which economic and political agents choose. Differences can be identified, however, and it may be useful to summarize some of these here, even if detailed discussion of the other research programmes cannot be attempted.

Public Choice, in its non-constitutional aspects of inquiry, concentrates attention on analyses of alternative political choice structures and on behaviour within those structures. Its focus is on predictive models of political interactions, and is a preliminary but necessary stage in the more general constitutional inquiry. The economics of property rights, law and economics, and the political economy of regulation remain somewhat closer to orthodox economic theory than Constitutional Economics or Public Choice. The standard efficiency norm remains central to these subdisciplines, both as an explanatory benchmark and as a normative ideal. The new institutional economics is directed more toward the interactions within particular institutional forms rather than toward the comprehensive structure of political rules (Furubotn and Richter, 1980; Frey, 1984). Some elements of the new economic history closely parallel Constitutional Economics, with, of course, an historical rather than a comparative emphasis (North and Thomas, 1973).

IV PRESUPPOSITIONS. Constitutional Economics, along with the related research programmes mentioned above, shares a central methodological presupposition with both its precursor, classical political economy, and its counterpart in modern neoclassical microeconomics. Only individuals choose and act. Collectivities, as such, neither choose nor act and analysis that proceeds as if they do is not within the accepted scientific canon. Social aggregates are considered only as the results of choices made and actions taken by individuals. The emphasis on explaining non-intended aggregative results of interaction has carried through since the early insights of the Scottish moral philosophers. An aggregative result that is observed but which cannot, somehow, be factored down and explained by the choices of individuals stands as a challenge to the scholar rather than as some demonstration of non-individualistic organic unity.

Methodological individualism, as summarized above, is almost universally accepted by economists who work within mainstream, or non-Marxian, traditions. A philosophical complement of this position that assumes a central role in Constitutional Economics is much less widely accepted and is often explicitly rejected. A distinction must be drawn between the methodological individualism that builds on individual choice as the basic unit of analysis and a second presupposition that locates the ultimate sources of value exclusively in individuals.

The first of these presuppositions without the second leaves relatively little scope for the derivation of constitutional structures from individual preferences. There is no conceptual normative bridge between those interests and values that individuals might want to promote and those non-individualistic values that are presumed to serve as ultimate normative criteria. The whole constitutional exercise loses most if not all of its *raison d'être* in such a setting. If the ultimate values which are to be called upon to inform the choices among institutions are non-individualistic, then there is, at best, only an instrumental argument for using individually expressed preferences in the process of discovering those values.

On the other hand, if the second presupposition concerning the location of the ultimate sources of value is accepted, there is no *other* means of deriving a 'logic of rules' than that of utilizing individually expressed interests. At base, the second presupposition implies democracy in governance, along with the accompanying precept that this structure of decision-making only takes on normative legitimacy with the prefix 'constitutional' appended to it.

V WICKSELL AS PRECURSOR. The single most important precursor to Constitutional Economics in its modern variant is Knut Wicksell, who was individualist in both of the senses discussed above. In his basic work on fiscal theory (*Finanztheoretische Untersuchungen*, 1896), Wicksell called attention to the significance of the rules within which choices are made by political agents, and he recognized that efforts at reform must be directed toward changes in the rules for making decisions rather than toward modifying expected results through influence on the behaviour of the actors.

In order to take these steps, Wicksell needed some criterion by which the possible efficacy of a proposed change in rules could be judged. He introduced the now-familiar unanimity or consensus test, which is carried over into Constitutional Economics and also allows the whole research programme to be related closely to the contractarian tradition in political philosophy. The relationship between the Wicksellian and the Paretian criteria is also worthy of note. If only individual evaluations are to count, and if the only source of information about such evaluations is the revealed choice behaviour of individuals themselves, then no change could be assessed to be 'efficient' until and unless some means could be worked out so as to bring all persons (and groups) into agreement. If no such scheme can be arranged, the observing political economist remains silent. The Wicksellian contribution allowed the modern economist to bring the comparative analysis of rules or institutions within a methodological framework that utilizes and builds on the efficiency criterion, which, when interpreted as indicated, does not require departure from either of the individualistic presuppositions previously discussed.

VI *Homo Economicus* IN CONSTITUTIONAL CHOICE. Constitutional Economics, as distinct from the complementary research programme on political constitutions that are within the boundaries of law, political science, sociology and other disciplines, goes beyond the logical presuppositions of individualism to incorporate non-tautological models of individual utility maximization. *Homo economicus* takes a central role in comparative institutional inquiry. Individuals are assumed to seek their own interests, which are defined so as to retain operational content.

Two quite different arguments can be made in support of this postulate in Constitutional Economics. The first is based simply on methodological consistency. To the extent that individuals are modelled as utility maximizers as they participate in market relationships, there would seem to be no basis for postulating a shift in motivation as they behave within non-market constraints. There is at least a strong presumption that individuals do not undergo character transformation when they shift from roles as buyers or sellers in the market-place to roles as voters, taxpayers, beneficiaries, politicians, or bureaucrats in the political process. A more sophisticated reason for postulating consistency in behaviour lies in the usefulness of the model for the whole exercise of institutional comparison. If the purpose is to compare the effects of alternative sets of constraints, some presumption of behavioural consistency over the alternatives is necessary in order to identify those differences in results that are attributable to the differences in constraints.

A second argument for introducing *homo economicus* in Constitutional Economics is both more complex and more important. It is also the source of confusion because it is necessary to distinguish carefully between the use of *homo economicus* in predictive social science, specifically in positive Public Choice and in neoclassical economics, and in Constitutional Economics. There is an argument for using the construction in the latter, even if there are demonstrated empirical limits on the explanatory power of the model in the former.

The argument is implicit in the work of the classical economists. It was stated as a methodological principle by both David Hume and J.S. Mill:

> In constraining any system of government, and fixing the several checks and controls of the constitution, each man ought to be supposed a knave, and to have no other end, in all his actions, than private interest (Hume [1741], 1963, pp. 117–18).

> The very principle of constitutional government requires it to be assumed that political power will be abused to promote the particular purposes of the holder; not because it is always so, but because such is the natural tendency of things, to guard against which is the special use of free institutions (Mill [1861], 1977, p. 505).

The ultimate purpose of analysing alternative sets of rules is to inform the choice among these sets. The predicted operating properties of each alternative must be examined, and these properties will reflect the embodied models of individual behaviour within the defined constraints. Behavioural departures from the presumptive models used in deriving the operating properties will, of course, be expected. But the costs of errors may not be symmetrically distributed around the single best predictive model. The predicted differential loss from behavioural departures from a model that involves 'optimistic' motivational assumptions may be much larger than the predicted differential gain if the model is shown to be an accurate predictor. Hence, comparative evaluation of an institution based on an altruistic model of behaviour should take into account the possible non-linearity in the loss function that describes departures from the best estimates. (In legal practice, formal contracts include protections against worst-case behaviour patterns.) In constitutional choice, therefore, there is an argument for incorporating models of individual behaviour that presume more narrowly defined self-interest than any empirical record may warrant (Brennan and Buchanan, 1985).

VII APPLICATIONS. Applications of Constitutional Economics, as a research programme, have emerged in several settings. First, consider taxation. Post-Marshallian economic theory, either in its partial or general equilibrium model, was often applied to tax incidence. Analysis was directed toward predicting the effects of an exogenously imposed tax on the private economizing behaviour of persons in their varying capacities as demanders and suppliers of goods and services in the market-place. Building on this base of positive analysis, normative welfare economics allows a ranking among alternative equi-revenue tax instruments in terms of the Paretian standard. In both the positive and normative aspects, neoclassical tax theory embodies the presumption that taxes, as such, are exogenous to the choice process.

The major contribution of modern Public Choice, as a subdiscipline in its own right, has been that of endogenizing political decision-making. In its direct emphasis, public choice theory examines the political decision rules that exist with a view toward making some predictions about just what sort of tax institutions or tax instruments will emerge. Constitutional Economics, as an extended research programme that emerges from Public Choice, goes a step further and uses the inputs from both neoclassical economics and public choice theory to analyse how alternative political rules might generate differing tax rules.

The relevant constitutional choice may be that of granting government authority to levy taxes on Tax Base A or Tax Base B. Suppose that under the neoclassical equi-revenue assumption, analysis demonstrates that the taxing of A generates a lower excess burden than the taxing of B. Analysis of the political choice process may demonstrate, however, that government, if given the authority to tax A, will tend to levy a tax that will generate *more* revenue than would be forthcoming under an authority to tax B. The equi-revenue alternatives may not be effective political alternatives under any plausibly acceptable modelling of the behaviour of political agents. Once this simple point is recognized, the normative significance of the neoclassical ranking of tax instruments is reduced. Discussion shifts necessarily to the level of interaction between political decision structures and fiscal institutions.

A second application of Constitutional Economics is found in the post-Keynesian discussion of budgetary policy. The Keynesian advocacy of the use of governmental budgets to accomplish macroeconomic objectives was based on a neglect of the political decision structure. The proclivity of democratic governments to prefer spending over taxing, and hence to bias budgets toward deficit, is readily explained in elementary public choice theory (Buchanan and Wagner, 1977). This essential step in public choice reasoning leads naturally to inquiry into the relationships between the constraints that may be placed on political choice and predicted patterns of budgetary outcomes. Out of this intensely practical, and important, application of Constitutional Economics emerged the intellectual bases for the normative argument that, in the post-Keynesian era when moral constraints on political agents have lost much of their previous effectiveness, formal rules limiting deficit financing may be required to insure responsible fiscal decisions. In the modern setting, such rules would limit spending rates. But it is perhaps worth noting that, in the political environment of Sweden in the 1890s, Wicksell advanced analytically similar proposals for reform in the expectation that, if the suggested reforms should be implemented, public sector outlay would increase.

The analysis of alternative rules for 'the transfer constitution' represents a third application of constitutional economics. With the 1971 publication of John Rawls's *A Theory of Justice*, renewed attention came to be placed on principles of distributive justice. Although explicitly pre-constitutional, Rawls's work has a close relationship with the efforts to derive criteria for political and economic rules of social interaction. Economists, as well as other social scientists and social philosophers, have come increasingly to recognize that the untrammelled interplay of interest-group politics is unlikely to further objectives for distributive justice. Analysis of how this politics operates in the making of fiscal transfers suggests that principled adjustments in the post-tax, post-transfer distribution of values is only likely to be achieved if the institutional rules severely restrict the profitability of investment in attempts to subvert the transfer process.

Further applications include the regulatory constitutions, along with the organization of public enterprises. In its inclusive definition, Constitutional Economics becomes the analytical route through which institutional relevance is reintroduced into a sometimes sterile social science. In its less inclusive definition, Constitutional Economics, along with its related and complementary research programmes, restores 'political' to 'economy', thereby bringing a coherence that was absent during the long hiatus during which 'economics' made putative claims to independent status.

JAMES M. BUCHANAN

See also BLACK, DUNCAN; LAW AND ECONOMICS; PUBLIC CHOICE; SOCIAL CHOICE; VOTING.

BIBLIOGRAPHY

Brennan, G. and Buchanan, J. M. 1980. *The Power to Tax: Analytical Foundations of the Fiscal Constitution.* Cambridge: Cambridge University Press.

Brennan, G. and Buchanan, J.M. 1985. *The Reason of Rules: Constitutional Political Economy.* Cambridge: Cambridge University Press.

Buchanan, J.M. 1974. *The Limits of Liberty: Between Anarchy and Leviathan.* Chicago: University of Chicago Press.

Buchanan, J.M. and Tullock, G. 1962. *The Calculus of Consent: Logical Foundations of Constitutional Democracy.* Ann Arbor: University of Michigan Press.

Buchanan, J.M. and Wagner, R.E. 1977. *Democracy in Deficit: The Political Legacy of Lord Keynes.* New York: Academic Press.

Frey, B. 1984. A new view of economics: comparative analysis of institutions. *Scelte Pubbliche* 1, 17–28.

Furubotn, E.G. and Richter, R. (eds) 1980. The New Institutional Economics – a symposium. *Zeitschrift für die gesamte Staatswissenschaft,* 140.

Hayek, F.A. 1973–9. *Law, Legislation, and Liberty.* 3 vols, Chicago: University of Chicago Press.

Hume, David. 1741. On the interdependencey of Parliament. In *Essays, Moral, Political and Literary,* London: Oxford University Press, 1963.

McKenzie, R. 1982. *Bound to Be Free.* Palo Alto: Hoover Press.

McKenzie, R. (ed.) 1984. *Constitutional Economics.* Lexington, Mass.: Lexington Books.

Mill, J.S. 1861. Considerations on representative government. In *Essays on Politics and Society,* Vol. XIX of *Collected Works of J.S. Mill,* Toronto: University of Toronto Press, 1977.

North, D.C. and Thomas, R.P. 1973. *The Rise of the Western World: A New Economic History.* Cambridge: Cambridge University Press.

Rawls, J. 1971. *A Theory of Justice.* Cambridge, Mass.: Harvard University Press.

Wicksell, K. 1896. *Finanztheoretische Untersuchungen.* Jena: Gustav Fischer. Central portions of this work were published in English translation as 'A new principle of just taxation' in *Classics in the Theory of Public Finance,* ed. R.A. Musgrave and A.T. Peacock, London: Macmillan, 1959.

constraint qualification. *See* CONVEX PROGRAMMING.

consumer durables. Applied work on the demand for durable goods has usually analysed two kinds of data. The first is time-series data on purchases, aggregated over consumers and typically with different kinds of durables aggregated into one or two groups. The second is cross-section data on the ownership of different kinds of durables. There has been a corresponding specialization in economic theory with that appropriate to the first type of data neglecting the issues of discreteness of ownership emphasized in the second and instead focusing on the dynamics of investment, expectations and adjustment costs, these being neglected in the theory of discrete choice at the level of individual households. The discussion below is in this tradition. In the first part, the focus is on the dynamics of purchases and in the second on the microeconomics of discrete choice.

A good which is durable yields a flow of services into the future. Whatever other issues arise, the analysis of the demand for durables must take into account the distinction between stocks of goods and flows of services and the intertemporal character of the decision to purchase or own a durable good. The simplest coherent model which captures these two essential features was first exposited by Cramer (1957) though somewhat analogous analyses of the demand for investment goods had been in the literature for some time (Fisher, 1930).

The assumptions made in this model are the following. Consumers maximize utility through time. They can lend and borrow at the same interest rate. They can instantly buy or sell a durable good at the same price. There are no psychic adjustment costs or habits associated with purchasing or owning a durable good. The service flow from owning a durable is proportional to the stock. Deterioration of the service flow through time is geometric. New vintages of durables are exactly the same as the old, when converted into efficiency units. Durable goods are perfectly divisible and no discreteness issues arise: thus they need not be owned in integer amounts and the question of scrapping never arises though durables can be traded on the second-hand market. Stating the assumptions this baldly when it is plain how counter-factual many of them are serves to anticipate some of the discussion below.

On these 'neoclassical' assumptions, the consumer maximizes

$$u_t = V(q_t, S_t, q_{t+1}, S_{t+1}, \ldots, q_T, S_T, A_T) \quad (1)$$

subject to a sequence of period to period budget constraints of the form, for example, at t,

$$A_t = A_{t-1}(1+r_t) + y_t - q_t - (p_t^D/p_t)(S_t - (1-\delta)S_{t-1}) \quad (2)$$

where q is the flow of non-durable consumption, S is the stock of durables and A is the stock of real financial assets defined as the nominal stock deflated by the price index for non-durable goods. Its presence in (1) reflects the bequest motive. The budget constraint (2) which looks slightly formidable just expresses the fact that the change in financial assets equals financial saving, i.e. income minus expenditure. The change in real financial assets is $A_t - A_{t-1}$ and income is $r_t A_{t-1} + y_t$, where r is the real rate of return and y is real non-property income. Note that the real rate of return includes any capital gains or losses so that property income $r_t A_{t-1}$ is an economist's rather than a national income accountant's measure. Expenditure in real terms, i.e. in terms of the flow of non-durable consumption, consists of q_t and money expenditure on durables deflated by the price index for non-durables p_t. Money expenditure on durables is $p_t^D[S_t - (1-\delta)S_{t-1}]$, where p^D is the price index for durables and where the stock of durables $S_t = q_t^D + (1-\delta)S_{t-1}$, where q_t^D is the flow of purchases and δ is the rate of deterioration of durables so that $(1-\delta)S_{t-1}$ is the amount of durables owned at $t-1$ that survives into period t. The generalization of (1) and (2) when q and S are vectors is easy.

It is conventional in intertemporal consumer theory under point expectations to convert the period to period budget constraints into the present value form by eliminating financial assets from the sequence of constraints (2) for t, $t+1$, $t+2, \ldots$. Life-cycle wealth is defined as the value of initial durables plus financial assets plus human wealth (the present value of current and expected non-property income):

$$W_t \equiv p_t^D/p_t(1-\delta)S_{t-1} + A_{t-1}(1+r_t) + \sum_{j=t}^{T} \rho_j y_j \quad (3)$$

where the real discount factor ρ_j is defined by

$$\rho_j = \prod_{i=t+1}^{j} (1+r_i)^{-1}, \quad t+1 \leqslant j \leqslant T$$
$$\rho_t = 1. \quad (4)$$

The budget constraint for the decision variables q_t, S_t, q_{t+1}, S_{t+1} etc. correspondingly is:

$$W_t = \sum_{j=t}^{T} \rho_j q_j + (p_t^D/p_t)S_t$$
$$+ \sum_{j=t+1}^{T} \rho_j(p_j^D/p_j)[S_j - (1-\delta)S_{j-1}]. \quad (5)$$

The effective relative price associated with S_t can then be written in the 'user cost' form

$$\Pi_t = (p_t^D/p_t)\left\{1 - (1-\delta)\left[1 + \frac{\Delta(p_{t+1}^D/p_{t+1})}{p_{t+1}^D/p_{t+1}}\right]\Big/(1+r_{t+1})\right\}$$
$$\approx p_t^D/p_t[\delta - \Delta \ln(p_{t+1}^D/p_{t+1}) + r_{t+1}] \quad (6)$$

which is the approximation familiar from Jorgenson's (1963) neoclassical theory of investment. Thus (5) becomes

$$W_t = \sum_{j=t}^{T} \rho_j q_j + \sum_{j=t}^{T} \rho_j \Pi_j S_j. \quad (7)$$

Maximizing (1) subject to (7) gives demand functions

$$q_t = g(\rho, \rho\Pi, W_t)$$
$$S_t = g^D(\rho, \rho\Pi, W_t) \quad (8)$$

where ρ, $p\Pi$ are the vectors (ρ_j), $(\rho_j\Pi_j)$ which appear in (7). In the above, ρ_j, Π_j, y_j for $j > t$ are, of course, forecasts made at t of the respective real interest rates, relative user costs of durables and real non-property incomes prevailing in the future. In empirical work, as well as choosing tractable restrictions on preferences and so for (8), some assumptions need to be made about how consumers make these forecasts.

Considering the forecasts necessary to construct the relative user cost of durables Π_t immediately raises a potential problem. In recent experience, the variability in ex post Π_t has been tremendous. In the 1970s in most Western economies, the ex post real rate of interest r_{t+1} was frequently negative and, particularly when accompanied by relative price declines in durable goods, it is quite likely that ex post the user cost Π_t was sometimes negative. It is true that there are expectations mechanisms such as the adaptive one which, combined with a low adjustment parameter, might have made the ex ante user cost less variable than the ex post and perhaps prevented it from becoming negative. However, in practice, even fairly crude extrapolations of past experience would have led to a highly variable series for the relative user cost Π_t, much more so than is plausibly consistent with the relative smooth behaviour of purchases of durables if (8) were the true model. In Muellbauer (1981), I tested a model based on (8) for British quarterly data. The evidence strongly rejects such a model both because of the failure of cross-equation restrictions and because of the obvious statistical mis-specification of the durables equation.

It seems that one needs a theory which gives rise to much more sluggishness or 'persistence' in purchases of durables. The standard way of building in such persistence is to posit adjustment costs for durables. There has been much work over the years (see Stone and Rowe, 1957; Chow, 1957; and Nerlove, 1957), on the stock adjustment model which is an ad hoc way of building in sluggish adjustment. Weissenberger (1984) has estimated a model for quarterly British data on non-durable and durable demands based on a quadratic utility function with quadratic adjustment costs and rational expectations. Apart from the coefficients on financial assets he finds a reasonable degree of coherence between the two equations and the durables equation fits well and its residuals are well behaved. Muellbauer and Pashardes (1982, revised 1987) build persistence effects into preferences in a rather more general way though, in the context of a quadratic utility function, the effect is similar to Weissenberger's. Since their empirical results on annual British data for a system of nine demand functions, one of which is for durables, are rather satisfactory, it is worth examining the approach.

They assume that the utility function is intertemporally separable in *transformed* quantities z_{ij}:

$$u_t = V[v_t(z_{1t}, \ldots, z_{nt}), \ldots, v_T(z_{1T}, \ldots, z_{nT}), A_T] \qquad (9)$$

where

$$z_{ij} = (S_{ij} - a_i S_{ij-1})(\delta_i / 1 - a_i)$$
$$= [q_{ij} + (1 - \delta_i - a_i) S_{ij-1}](\delta_i / 1 - a_i) \qquad (10)$$

and where the stock $S_{ij} = q_{ij} + (1 - \delta_i)q_{ij-1} + (1 - \delta_i)^2 q_{ij-2} + \cdots$. In a steady state $S_i = q_i/\delta_i$ and so $z_i = q_i$. In the case of a non-durable good (for which $\delta_i = 1$),

$$z_{ij} = \frac{q_{ij} - a_i q_{ij-1}}{1 - a_i}.$$

The parameter a_i can be thought of as a 'habit' or 'persistence' parameter when $0 < a_i < 1$. With diminishing marginal utility, the more the consumer consumed of good i last period the greater is his or her marginality utility and so 'need' for the good this period. When $a_i < 0$, it can be interpreted as a shortlived durability parameter since, with $\delta_i = 1$, a purchase last period but not earlier gives utility this period.

It was Spinnewyn (1979, 1981) who first extended the user cost concept of price of a durable good to more general transformed quantities of the type defined in (10) above. As long as these are linear functions of $(q_{ij}, q_{ij-1}, q_{ij-2}, \ldots)$, a user cost price p_{ij}^v can be defined. Then, since the intertemporally separable form of the utility function permits two-stage budgeting (see Gorman, on SEPARABILITY below), there exist demand functions

$$z_{it} = g_i(p_t^v, x_t^v) \qquad (11)$$

where

$$x_t^v \equiv \sum_{i=1}^{a} p_{it}^v z_{it}.$$

From (10), purchases of good i

$$q_{it} = [a_i - (1 - \delta_i)]S_{it-1} + \frac{1 - a_i}{\delta_i} z_{it}. \qquad (12)$$

This can also be written in the form

$$\Delta q_{it} = \frac{1 - a_i}{\delta_i} \Delta z_{it} + (1 - a_i)(z_{it-1} - q_{it-1}). \qquad (13)$$

This elegantly expresses an extended kind of partial adjustment model termed an 'error correction model' by Hendry. Changes in q respond to changes in z but with a stabilizing feedback to last period's deviation between q and z. The lower is durability, i.e. the higher is δ_i and the higher is a_i, the slower is the speed of adjustment. This makes it clear that in the absence of persistence effects, one should expect greater volatility of purchases for durables than for non-durables. In the empirical results reported for annual British data by Muellbauer and Pashardes, there are strong persistence effects both for durables and for non-durables though generally a little larger for durables. Thus the volatility of purchases for durables is higher than for non-durables but much lower than it would be for a zero persistence parameter a_i.

Equation (13) can be estimated in two ways. The one adopted by Muellbauer and Pashardes uses the identity

$$x_t^v \equiv \sum_{i=1}^{n} p_{it} z_{it}.$$

Potentially it suffers from the possible correlation between a disturbance term added to (13) and the z_{it}'s embodied in the budget x_t^v. The alternative is to solve the intertemporal optimization problem to give a solution for x_t^v as a function of life-cycle wealth and price and rate of return expectations. Under this alternative some assumptions, as in the study of the life-cycle consumption function, need to be made to model expectations empirically and the results are likely to be sensitive to which assumptions are made.

Models of this type give good results for aggregate time series data, at least relative to formulations that ignore persistence or durability. But one may well wonder about the source of persistence to which the above analysis gives simple expression. In many ways the most plausible explanation is the gap between buying and selling prices of durables due to installation costs, transactions costs or to information asymmetries. According to Akerlof's (1970) 'lemon effect' the potential buyer of a used durable fears that the reason the owner wishes to sell is that the durable is a lemon. Since there may be no way that the seller can convince the buyer that it is not, a car that is only a few weeks old and has suffered no physical deterioration is likely to be saleable only at a price substantially below the showroom price. Thus even if a consumer expects substantial capital gains on a durable, there is little incentive to buy in order to sell at a profit. The most that can then be expected is some advancement of purchases that are likely to have been made soon anyway.

At the individual level, such a gap between buying and selling prices makes corner solutions likely (see Deaton and Muellbauer (1980), pp. 360–64 for a discussion). It is then very difficult to derive tractable econometric models that reflect the theory at all precisely. One might take something like (13) as a starting point and try to build in additional elements such as the asymmetric response that larger restrictions on selling than on buying suggest. For specific durables such as automobiles where most buyers of new cars trade in a used one, the differential of new and used car prices could be added to (13) as an extra, somewhat *ad hoc* explanatory variable.

There are alternative ways of modelling the effects of prices of complementary goods such as the gasoline needed to run a car. One way is just to include this price in the vector of prices p_t^v as long as the form of preferences embodied in $g_i(\ )$ is quite general, e.g. a flexible functional form (Diewert, 1971). But imposing rather more structure often yields rewards. If it is car services that appear in the utility function and the cost of these consists both of a user cost or rental equivalent and a running cost that depends on the fuel efficiency of the car, price effects are likely to be modelled more accurately. This kind of approach also suggests vintage effects that could be observable even on aggregate data. In response to the fuel price increases in the 1970s manufacturers eventually brought models to the market which were much more fuel efficient than previous vintages. The effective price differential between new models and the existing stock is likely to be an important element in the replacement decision. As the fuel efficiency gap between the existing stock and new models narrows, *ceteris paribus*, one would expect replacement demand to fall off. Similar vintage effects can arise through other quality improvements in new durables. The only way quality improvements could show up in the simple model leading to (13) is through falls in the quality adjusted price p^D.

Among the advantages of the assumption that new and used durables, when converted into efficiency units, are perfect substitutes is that it simplifies the analysis of the interaction of supply and demand. Total market supply of stock is the sum of the surviving stock $(1 - \delta_i)S_{it-1}$, which is given, plus new supply, which if firms are competitive is a function of current and expected values of p_t^D and costs of production. Aggregate demand for stock given (11) can be written in the form

$$S_{it} = a_i S_{it-1} + \frac{1-a_i}{\delta_i} g_i(p_t^v, x_t^v).$$

If prices clear the market, equating supply and demand determines p_{it}^D which is thus endogenous and ought to be treated as such in econometric work. In practice, however, new and used durables may not be perfect substitutes, new prices may be set by oligopolistic producers and the second-hand market, despite its imperfections, may be more demand responsive in its prices. Nevertheless, the above model is a bench-mark that raises issues which applied economists working on the demand for durables need to face.

The other source of data on the demand for the durables is household surveys. In such cross-sections, the discreteness of ownership must be explicitly recognized. The classic paper by Farrell (1954) was one of the first to analyse the threshold effects which govern ownership. The modern economic treatment in its simplest form can be explained as follows. Let p^D be the rental price of a durable good and the budget constraint be

$$pq + p^D S = x \tag{14}$$

Suppose $S = 1$ if the durable is owned and $S = 0$ if not. Let the single period utility function be

$$u = v(q, S, b, \epsilon) \tag{15}$$

where b is a vector of observable household characteristics and ϵ summarizes unobservable ones in a scalar. If $S = 0$, we can solve for $q = x/p$ from the budget constraint and if $S = 1$, $q = (x - p^D)/p$. Thus the durable is owned if the utility from owning $v[(x - p^D)/p, 1, b, \epsilon]$ exceeds that from not owning $v[x/p, 0, b, \epsilon]$. These solved out utility functions are termed 'indirect utility functions'. This ownership criterion is still valid if, in fact, durables of this type vary in size, performance, luxuriousness or other characteristics that can be summarized in a quality index. $S = 1$ then refers to the minimum quality available while $S > 1$ for higher qualities. Maximizing (15) subject to (14) then gives conventional demand functions, given $S \geq 1$, $q = g(x, p, p^D; b, \epsilon)$, $S = g^D(x, p, p^D; b, \epsilon)$ and the durable is owned if

$$g^D(x, p, p^D; b, \epsilon) \geq 1. \tag{16}$$

Here p^D is a quality corrected price index, which in a single cross-section, like p, is usually assumed to be the same for all consumers. Equation (16) suggests the use of Probit or Logit analysis to examine ownership variations on micro-data (see McFadden, 1973, 1981). Given information on rental expenditure defined as $p^D S = p^D g^D(x, p, p^D; b, \epsilon)$ if $g^D(\ ) \geq 1$, Tobit analysis is the appropriate technique (see Tobin, 1958).

Equation (16) also has implications for 'quasi'-Engel curves which link ownership in an income bracket to the income level. Suppose that (16) holds if $\epsilon < \theta(x, p, p^D, b)$. Then the proportion of households with budget x and characteristics b owning the durable is

$$\int_{-\infty}^{\theta} f(x, b, \epsilon)\, d\epsilon \bigg/ \int_{-\infty}^{\infty} f(x, b, \epsilon)\, d\epsilon \tag{17}$$

where $f(\ )$ is the joint probability density of x, b and ϵ. Provided the budget x can be plausibly linked to observable income, this provides a justification for the 'quasi'-Engel curves estimated, for example, by Aitchison and Brown (1957), Cramer (1962), Pyatt (1964), and Bonüs (1973). These studies have not always, however, given as much attention to the household character-

istics b as they might have done. If b and ϵ were independently distributed of x and θ monotonic in x, then there must be a sigmoid relationship between the level of x and the proportion owning the durable given the sigmoid shape of the cumulative distribution function for x. In practice, though there is quite a high correlation between such household characteristics as size and income, empirical 'quasi'-Engel curves are usually sigmoid in shape. In aggregate, as average income rises over time there is also a sigmoid relationship between the average income level and the aggregate proportion owning a durable. As Deaton and Muellbauer (1980, pp. 370–1) note, this sigmoid shape could be partly due to the sigmoid shape of the cumulative distribution function of income and partly due to other causes of diffusion such as epidemic models of the spread of a disease which may be appropriate when new goods such as television are introduced.

For simplicity the discussion above has taken the case of a single type of durable. But as McFadden (1981) and Dubin and McFadden (1984) demonstrate, the generalization to a portfolio of different kinds of durables still results in tractable models which can be estimated by maximum likelihood techniques. All these models of ownership, however, need to be given a long-run interpretation which abstracts from transactions costs and imperfections in second-hand markets. The latter may cause specific households to have ownership patterns that differ from those they would have in a steady state. In cross-sections, information on past decisions and past income is usually missing, so that the kind of dynamic elements discussed in the earlier part of this entry cannot be analysed empirically.

JOHN MUELLBAUER

See also HOUSEHOLD BUDGETS; HOUSING; SEPARABILITY.

BIBLIOGRAPHY

Aitchison, J. and Brown, J.A.C. 1957. *The Lognormal Distribution.* Cambridge: Cambridge University Press.

Akerlof, G. 1970. The market for 'lemons'. *Quarterly Journal of Economics* 84(3), August, 488–500.

Bonüs, H. 1973. Quasi-Engel curves, diffusion, and the ownership of major consumer durables. *Journal of Political Economy* 81(3), May–June, 655–77.

Chow, G. 1957. *Demand for Automobiles in the US: a study in consumer durables.* Amsterdam: North-Holland.

Cramer, J.S. 1957. A dynamic approach to the theory of consumer demand. *Review of Economic Studies* 24, February 73–86.

Cramer, J.S. 1962. *A Statistical Model of the Ownership of Major Consumer Durables.* Cambridge: Cambridge University Press.

Deaton, A. and Muellbauer, J. 1980. *Economics and Consumer Behaviour.* Cambridge: Cambridge University Press.

Diewert, W.E. 1971. An application of the Shephard duality theorem: a generalized Leontief production function. *Journal of Political Economy* 79(3), May–June, 481–507.

Dubin, J.A. and McFadden, D. 1984. An econometric analysis of residential electric appliance holdings and consumption. *Econometrica* 52(2), March, 345–62.

Farrell, M.J. 1954. The demand for motor cars in the United States. *Journal of the Royal Statistical Society,* Series A 117(2), 171–201.

Fisher, I. 1930. *The Theory of Interest.* New York: The Macmillan Company.

Jorgenson, D.W. 1963. Capital theory and investment behaviour. *American Economic Review, Papers and Proceedings* 53, May, 247–59.

McFadden, D. 1974. Conditional logit analysis of qualitative choice behavior. In *Frontiers in Econometrics,* ed. P. Zarembka, New York: Academic Press.

McFadden, D. 1981. Econometric models of probabilistic choice. In *Structural Analysis of Discrete Data,* ed. C. Manski and D. McFadden, Cambridge, Mass.: MIT Press.

Muellbauer, J. 1981. Testing neoclassical models of the demand for durables. In *Essays in the Theory and Measurement of Consumer*

Behaviour, ed. A.S. Deaton, Cambridge: Cambridge University Press.

Muellbauer, J. and P. Pashardes 1982, 1987. Tests of dynamic specification and homogeneity in a demand system. Discussion paper 125, Birkbeck College, 1982; revised as Institute of Fiscal Studies discussion paper, 1987.

Nerlove, M. 1957. A note on long-run automobile demand. *Journal of Marketing* 21, July, 57–64.

Pyatt, G. 1964. *Priority Patterns and the Demand for Household Durable Goods.* Cambridge: Cambridge University Press.

Spinnewyn, F. 1979. The cost of consumption and wealth in models with habit formation. *Economics Letters* 2(2), 145–8.

Spinnewyn, F. 1981. Rational habit formation. *European Economic Review* 15(1), January, 91–109.

Stone, R. and Rowe, D.A. 1957. The market demand for durable goods. *Econometrica* 25, July, 423–43.

Tobin, J. 1958. Estimation of relationships for limited dependent variables. *Econometrica* 26, January, 24–36.

Weissenberger, E. 1984. An intertemporal system of dynamic consumer demand functions. Centre for Labour Economics, London School of Economics, Discussion Paper No. 186.

consumers' expenditure. The study of consumers' expenditure, both in total and in composition, has always been of major concern to economists. Neoclassical economics sees the delivery of individual consumption as the main object of the economic system, so that the efficiency with which the economy achieves this goal is the criterion by which alternative systems, institutions and policies are to be judged. Within a capitalist economy, such considerations lead to an examination of the relationship between *prices* and consumption behaviour, and theoretical development and empirical analysis have been a major continuous activity since the middle of the last century. Even older is the tradition of using individual household budgets to dramatize poverty, and the relationship between household incomes and household expenditure patterns has occupied social reformers, statisticians and econometricians since at least the 18th century. In more modern times, it has been recognized that the study of public finance and of taxation depends on a knowledge of how price changes affect the welfare and behaviour of individuals, and the recent development of optimal tax theory and of tax reform analysis has placed additional demands on our understanding of the links between prices, expenditures and welfare.

In the last fifty years, aggregate consumption has become as much as an object of attention as has its composition, and in spite of a common theoretical structure, there has been a considerable division of labour between macro economists, interested in aggregate consumption and saving, and micro economists whose main concern has been with composition, and with the study of the effects of relative prices on demand. The interest of macroeconomics reflects both long-term and short-term interests. What is not consumed is saved, saving is thrift and the basis for capital formation, so that the determinants of saving are the determinants of future growth and prosperity. More immediately, aggregate consumption accounts for a large share of national income, typically more than three-quarters, so that fluctuations in behaviour or 'consumption shocks' have important consequences for output, employment, and the business cycle. Since Keynes's *General Theory*, the consumption function, the relationship between consumption and income, has played a central role in the study of the macroeconomy. Since the 1930s, there has been a continuous flow of theoretical and empirical developments in consumption function research, and some of

the outstanding scientific achievements in economics have been in this field.

In this essay, the major themes will be the interplay between theory and evidence in the study of consumers' expenditure and its composition. If economists have any serious claim to being scientists, it should be clearly visible here. The best minds in the profession have worked on the theory of consumption and on its empirical implementation, and there have always been more data available than could possibly be examined. I hope to show that there have been some stunning successes, where elegant models have yielded far from obvious predictions that have been well vindicated by the evidence. But there is much that remains to be done, and much that needs to be put right. Many of the standard presumptions of economics remain just that, assumptions unsupported by evidence, and while modern price theory is logically consistent and theoretically well developed, it is far from having that solid body of empirical support and proven usefulness that characterizes similar central theories in the natural sciences.

1. A SIMPLE THEORETICAL FRAMEWORK. Almost all discussions of consumer behaviour begin with a theory of *individual* behaviour. I follow neoclassical tradition by supposing that such behaviour can be described by the maximization of a utility function subject to suitable constraints. The axioms that justify utility maximization are mild, see any microeconomic text such as Varian (1984) or Deaton and Muellbauer (1980b), so that utility maximization should be seen as no more than a convenient framework that rules out the grossest kind of behavioural inconsistencies. The assumptions that have real force are those that detail the constraints facing individuals or else put specific structure on utility functions. Perhaps the most general specification of preferences that could be considered is one that is written

$$u_t = E_t\{f(q_1, q_2, \ldots, q_t, \ldots, q_T)\} \qquad (1)$$

where u_t is utility at time t, E_t is the expectation operator for expectations formed at time t, q_1 to q_T are vectors of consumption in periods 1 to T, and $f(\ )$ is a quasi-concave function that is non-decreasing in each of its arguments. Several things about this formulation are worth brief discussion. The function $f(\ )$ yields the utility that would be obtained from the consumption vectors under certainty, and it represents the utility from a *life-time* of consumption; the indices 1 to T therefore represent *age* with 1 the date of birth and T that of death. The expectation operator is required because choice is made subject to uncertainty, not about the choices themselves, which are under the consumer's control, but about the consequences of current choices for future opportunities. It is not possible to travel backward through time, so that choices once made cannot be undone, and yet the cost of current consumption in terms of future consumption foregone is uncertain, as is the amount of resources that may become available at future dates. The consumer must therefore travel through life, filling in the slots in (1) from left to right as best as he or she can, and at time (or age) t, everything to the left will be fixed and unchangeable, whether now seen to be optimal or not, while everything ahead of t is subject to the random buffeting of unexpected changes in interest rates, prices, and incomes. The solution to this sort of maximization problem has been elegantly characterized by Epstein (1975); here I shall work with something that is more restrictive but more useful and note in Section 3 below some phenomena that are better handled by the more general model.

Intertemporal utility functions are frequently assumed to be *intertemporally additive*, so that the preference rankings between consumption bundles in any two periods or ages are taken to be independent of consumption levels in any third period. If so, the utility function (1) takes the more mathematically convenient form

$$u_t = E_t \sum_{r=0}^{T} v_r(q_r). \tag{2}$$

Note that by writing utility in the form (2), since the expectation operator is additive over states of the world preferences are in effect assumed to be *simultaneously* additive over both states and periods, an assumption that can be formally defended, see Gorman (1982) and Browning, Deaton and Irish (1985). It has the consequence that risk aversion and intertemporal substitutability become two aspects of the same phenomenon. Individuals that dislike risk, and will pay to avoid it, will also attempt to smooth their consumption over time and will require large incentives to alter their preferred consumption and saving profiles. Note also that the additive structure of (2) means that, unlike the case of (1), previous decisions are irrelevant for current ones. For decision-making at time t, bygones are bygones, and conditional on asset and income positions, future choices are unaffected by what has happened in the past. There can therefore be no attempt to make up for lost opportunities, nor can such phenomena as habit formation be easily modelled.

Because utility in (2) is intertemporally separable, maximization of life-time utility implies that, within each period, the period subutility function $v_t(\ )$ must be maximized subject to whatever total it is optimal to spend in that period. The period by period allocation of consumption expenditure to individual commodities need not, therefore, be planned in advance, but can be left to be determined when that period or age is reached, and period t allocation will follow according to the rule

$$\text{maximize } v_t(q_t) \quad \text{subject to } p_t \cdot q_t = x_t, \tag{3}$$

where p_t is the price vector corresponding to q_t, and x_t is the total amount to be spent in t. Problem (3) is one of standard (static) utility maximization, though note that x_t is not given to the consumer, but is determined by the wider intertemporal choice problem. Nevertheless, not the least advantage of the intertemporally additive formulation is its implication that the composition of expenditure follows the standard utility maximization rule. It allows separate attention to be given to demand analysis on the one hand, i.e. to the problem (3), and to the consumption function on the other hand, this being understood to be the intertemporal allocation of resources, i.e. the determination of x_t.

Write the maximized value of utility from the period t problem as $\psi_t(x_t, p_t)$, where $\psi(\ )$ is a standard indirect utility function. The original intertemporal utility function then takes the form

$$u_t = E_t \sum_{r=0}^{T-t} \psi_r(x_{t+r}, p_{t+r}). \tag{4}$$

The constraints under which this function is maximized are most conveniently analysed through the conditions governing the evolution of wealth from period to period. If A_t is the (ex-dividend) value of assets at the start of period t, N_{it} is the nominal holdings of asset i with price P_{it}, d_{it} is the dividend on i paid immediately before the beginning of t, and y_t is income in period t, then

$$A_{t+1} = \sum_i N_{it}(P_{it+1} + d_{it+1}) \tag{5}$$

$$\sum_i N_{it} P_{it} = A_t + y_t - x_t. \tag{6}$$

Conditions (5) and (6) determine how wealth evolves from period to period, and the picture is completed by requiring that the consumer's terminal assets be positive, i.e.

$$A_{T+1} \geqslant 0 \tag{7}$$

To solve this problem, the technique of backward recursion is used. This rests on the observation that it is impossible to know what to do in period t without taking into account the problem in period $(t + 1)$, nor that in $(t + 1)$ without thinking about $(t + 2)$, and so on. However, in period T there is no future, so that looking ahead from date t, we can write subutility in period T in terms of that period's price and inherited assets, and we write this as v_T, i.e.

$$v_T = v_T(A_T) = \psi_T(A_T + y_T, p_T). \tag{8}$$

Given this, the consumer can look ahead from period t to period $(T - 1)$ and foresee that the problem then will be to choose the composition of assets N so as to maximize v_{T-1}, where

$$v_{T-1}(A_{T-1}) = \max_N \left[\psi_{T-1}(A_{T-1} + y_{T-1} - N \cdot P_{T-1}, p_{T-1}) \right.$$
$$\left. + E_{T-1}\{v_T[N \cdot (P_T + d_T)]\} \right]. \tag{9}$$

At the next stage, assets in $(T - 2)$ will be allocated so as to trade off the benefits of consumption in $(T - 2)$ versus the benefits of A_{T-1} in v_{T-1} in (9) above and again yielding a maximized value v_{T-2}. As we follow this back through time, the consumer finally reaches the current period t, where he or she faces an only slightly complicated version of the usual 'today tomorrow' trade-off; the asset vector N must be chosen to solve the problem,

$$u_t = \max_N \left[\psi_t(A_t + y_t - N \cdot P_t, p_t) \right.$$
$$\left. + E_t\{v_{t+1}[N \cdot (P_{t+1} + d_{t+1})]\} \right]. \tag{10}$$

From this sequence of problems, several important results readily follow. Firstly, consider the derivatives of each of the functions $v_r(A_r)$ which represent the marginal value of an extra unit of currency for the remaining segment of life time utility from r through to T. By the envelope theorem (see for example Dixit (1976) for a good exposition), it is legitimate to differentiate through the maximization problem, from which

$$v_r'(A_r) = \partial \psi_r / \partial x_r = \lambda_r, \text{ say,} \tag{11}$$

so that λ_r is the marginal utility of money in period r. Secondly, the maximization of (10) with respect to portfolio choice gives the relationship, for each asset i,

$$P_{it} \partial \psi_t / \partial x_t = E_t\{(P_{it+1} + d_{it+1}) \partial \psi_{t+1} / \partial x_{t+1}\} \tag{12}$$

which, defining the asset *return* R_{it+1} as $(P_{it+1} + d_{it+1})/P_{it}$, and using (11) can be rewritten in the simple form

$$\lambda_t = E_t(\lambda_{t+1} R_{it+1}). \tag{13}$$

This equation, in current parlance often referred to as the 'Euler equation', can be used to derive many of the implications of the theory of consumption. Note first that it is little more than the standard result that the marginal rate of substitution between today's and tomorrow's consumption should be equal to the relative price. However, the equation is set in a multiperiod framework, not a two-period one, and it explicitly recognizes the uncertainty in both asset returns and in the value of money in subsequent periods. The equation also holds for all i, i.e. for all assets, so that the result also has implications for asset pricing as well as for consumption and saving, and for this reason the model is often referred to as the consumption-asset pricing model. I shall return to these implications below.

The theory as presented above is the modern equivalent of the life-cycle theory of consumption that dates back to Irving Fisher (1930) and Frank Ramsey (1928), and that had its modern genesis in the papers by Modigliani and Brumberg (1954) and (1954, published 1979). Modigliani and Brumberg's treatment differs from the above only in not explicitly modelling uncertainty, and by including only a single asset. The modern version appears first in Breeden (1979) and in Hall (1978), see also Grossman and Shiller (1981).

2. PREDICTIONS AND EVIDENCE. One of the most important implications of the theory above, and of equation (13) in particular, is that the evolution of consumption over the life-cycle is independent of the pattern of income over the life-cycle. The asset evolution equations (5) and (6) allow consumers to borrow and lend at will, so that the only ultimate constraint on their consumption is one of life-time solvency. In consequence, consumption patterns are free to follow tastes, the evolution of family structure, or the different needs that come with ageing, provided that in the end, total life-time expenditure lies within (total) life-time resources, whether from inherited wealth, or from labour income. It is often assumed that tastes are such that consumers prefer to have a relatively smooth consumption stream, and this can be illustrated from a special case of equation (13). Assume that the within period utility function is homothetic so that $\psi(x, p)$ is $\phi[x/a(p)]$ for some linearly homogeneous function $a(\ )$, and that $\phi(\ )$ has the isoelastic form with elasticity $(1 - \sigma)$. Life-time utility takes the form

$$u_t = \sum_{r=0}^{T} (1 + \delta)^{-r} [x_{t+r}/a(p_{t+r})]^{1-\sigma} \qquad (14)$$

where δ is the rate of pure time preference, and $\sigma \geqslant 0$ is the coefficient of relative risk aversion and the reciprocal of the intertemporal elasticity of substitution. Equation (14) can be used to evaluate (13), and gives immediately

$$E[\{(1 + r_{t+1})/(1 + \delta)\} \{c_t/c_{t+1}\}^{\sigma}] = 1 \qquad (15)$$

where r_{t+1} is the real after tax rate of interest from t to $t + 1$ on any asset, and c_t is real consumption, $x_t/a(p_t)$. Equation (15) shows that, if expectations are fulfilled, consumption will grow over the life cycle if the real rate of interest is greater than the rate of pure time preference, and vice versa, while with $r_t = \delta$, consumption is constant with age. These results are of course an artefact of the specific assumptions about utility, and for any real household, consumption can be expected to vary predictably with age according to patterns of family formation, growth, and ageing; Modigliani and Ando (1957) have suggested that consumption per 'equivalent adult' might be constant over the life-cycle. But whatever the shape of preferences, there need be no relationship between the profiles of consumption and of income; income can be saved until it is needed, or borrowed against if it is not yet available.

Independent of the life-time *pattern* of consumption is its level, which under the life-cycle model is determined by the level of total life-time resources, so that individuals with the same tastes but with higher incomes or higher inherited assets will have higher levels of consumption throughout their lives. If the future were entirely predictable, the consumption plan at any point in time could be decided with reference to the level of total wealth, this being the value of financial assets and the discounted present value of current and future incomes. In this sense, the life-cycle model is a permanent income theory of consumption, where permanent income is the annuity value of

life-time wealth, though the life-time interpretation is only one of the many that are offered in Friedman's (1957) original statement. Whether life-cycle or not, linking consumption to *future* incomes has important consequences. First, consumption will respond only to 'surprises' or 'shocks' in income; changes in income that have been foreseen are already discounted in previous behaviour and should not induce any changes in plans. Of course, this does *not* mean that consumption will not change along with changes in income; a change may have been planned in any case, and some proportion of any actual change may well have been unforeseen. However, if a substantial fraction of the regular changes in income over the business cycle are foreseen by consumers, or if unanticipated fluctuations in income are regarded as only temporary with limited consequences for total life-time resources, then consumption will not respond very much to cyclical fluctuations in income. Aggregate consumption is indeed much smoother than is aggregate income, and this has been traditionally accepted as an important piece of confirmatory evidence. I shall take up the matter again below when I deal with the recent econometric evidence.

The distinction between measured income and permanent income is also important for the interpretation of cross-sectional evidence. Since measured income can be regarded as an error-ridden proxy for permanent income, the regression of consumption on measured income will be biased downward (rotated clockwise) compared with the true regression of consumption on permanent income. Cross-sectional regressions, or time-series regressions of simple Keynesian consumption functions will therefore tend to understate the long-run marginal propensity to consume. Well before the work on life-cycle models, Kuznets (1946) showed that the long-run saving ratio in the United States had been roughly constant in spite of repeated cross-sectional analyses showing that the saving ratio rose with income, and the life-cycle theory could also readily account for these findings. It is interesting to note that the constancy of the saving ratio is far from being well established as an empirical fact; the evidence for other countries with long-run data is very mixed, and even the United States saving ratio is clearly influenced in the long-run by technical change, migration patterns, and demographic shifts, see Kuznets (1962) and Deaton (1975). Life-cycle and permanent income theories also predict that households with atypically high income will tend to save a great deal of it, a prediction which explained the apparently anomalous finding that black households tend to save more than white households at the same level of measured income; since blacks typically have lower household income than whites, those with the same measured income can be expected to have a higher transitory component.

The Modigliani and Brumberg life-cycle story was also important because it offered a story of capital accumulation in society as a whole that relied on the way in which people made preparation for their own futures, particularly for their future retirement. In a stationary life-cycle economy, in which there is neither economic nor population growth, aggregate saving is zero, and the old, as they dissave, pass on the ownership of the capital stock to the next generation who are, in turn, saving for their own retirement. With either population or income growth, the aggregate scale of saving by the young would be greater than that of dissaving by the old, so that, to a first approximation, the aggregate saving ratio, while in the long-run independent of the *level* of national income, would depend on the sum of its population and per capita real income growth rates. Modigliani (1986), in his Nobel address, has given an account of how very simple stylized models of saving and refinement yield quite accurate predictions of the saving ratio and of the ratio of wealth to national income, and the predictions about the growth effects have been repeatedly borne out in international comparisons of saving rates, see Modigliani (1970), Houthakker (1961, 1965), Leff (1969) and Surrey (1974). Perhaps the only problem with these interpretations is that there is little evidence that the old actually dissave, except by running down state social security or pension schemes, see for example Mirer (1979). Partly, this may be a rational response to uncertainty about the date of death and about possible medical expenses near the end of life (Davies, 1980), partly there may be statistical problems of measurement, (Shorrocks, 1975), and partly consumers may wish to leave bequests. However, most countries' tax systems penalize donors who do not pass on assets prior to death, so the reason for the size of actual bequests remains something of a mystery. Bernheim, Schleiffer and Summers (1985) have gone so far as to suggest that parents retain their wealth until death in order to control their heirs and to solicit attention from them. They claim empirical support for a positive relationship between visits by children to their parents and parents' bequeathable assets; visits are apparently especially frequent to rich sick parents, but not at all frequent to poor sick parents. Related to the dispute about the reason for bequests is a parallel dispute on their importance in the transmission of the capital stock, see the original contribution by Kotlikoff and Summers (1981) and Modigliani's reply, summarized in his (1986) Nobel lecture.

The life-cycle and permanent income models also provided the econometric specifications for a generation of macroeconometric models. Ando and Modigliani (1963) suggested a simple form for the aggregate consumption function in which real aggregate consumption was a linear function of expected real labour income, YL, and of the real value of financial assets, i.e.

$$c_t = \alpha E_t(YL) + \delta W_t. \qquad (16)$$

In practical econometric work, the expectation was typically replaced by a linear function of current and past values of labour income, a procedure that can be formally justified by modelling labour income as a linear ARIMA process, a topic to which I shall return below. Wealth or a subset of wealth was included as data allowed, although sometimes the return to wealth was included with labour income which could then be replaced by total income, so that, with smoothing, (16) becomes a permanent (total) income model of consumption. A favourite variant, suggested in Friedman (1957), was to model permanent income as an infinite moving average of current income with geometrically declining weights,

$$y_t^p = (1 - \lambda) \sum \lambda^r y_{t-r}, \qquad (17)$$

so that if current consumption is proportional to permanent income, substitution yields

$$c_t = kc_{t-1} + k(1 - \lambda)y_t, \qquad (18)$$

a formulation that is also easy to defend if consumers 'partially adjust' to changes in current income. Models like (18), possibly with additional lags, and with the occasional appearance of more or less 'exotic' regressors, such as wealth, interest rates, inflation rates, money supply, as well as various dummy variables for 'problem' observations, were the standard fare of macroeconometric models in their heyday, from the early sixties for about a decade and a half. They fit the data well, they accounted for the smoothness of consumption relative to income, and they accorded at least

roughly with the general features of the life-cycle and permanent income formulations which provided them with pedigree and general theoretical legitimacy. Dozens of papers could be cited within this tradition; those by Stone (1964), (1966), Evans (1967), Davidson, Hendry, Srba and Yeo (1978) will perhaps stand as good examples.

3. RECENT ECONOMETRIC EXPERIENCE. In the mid-1970s, the general state of complacency of macroeconomic modelling was rapidly eroded, largely by the apparent inability of the standard models to explain, let alone to predict, the co-existence of unemployment and inflation. The relationship between consumption and income did not escape some of the blame, although the main focus of attack was elsewhere. Standard consumption functions, that had worked well into the early seventies, seriously under-predicted aggregate saving during the period of (at least relatively) rapid inflation that characterized most Western economies in the middle of the decade. The implementation of the theory of the consumption function was also singled out for discussion in Lucas's famous (1976) essay that became known as the Lucas 'critique'. As Lucas forcefully argued, if consumption is determined by the discounted present value of *expected* future incomes, the response of consumption to a change in income is not well-defined until we know how expectations of income are formed. Each observed realization will cause a re-evaluation of future prospects in accordance with formulae that depend on the nature of the stochastic process governing income. If the nature of the stochastic process is changed, for example by a fundamental change in the tax code, then the way in which information is processed will change, and new information about incomes will have different implications for future expectations and for future consumption. This insight is of great importance, although its implications for econometric modelling were initially taken much too negatively; if the rules keep changing, econometric models will be inherently unstable (as evidenced by their performance in the mid-seventies) and we should give up trying to find stable relationships. Instead, as events have shown, the introduction of rational expectations has given a whole new lease of life to the study of consumption, with developments as positive as anything that has happened since the life-cycle and permanent income models were the 'new' theories in the mid-fifties. Lucas's critique suggested at least two lines for research. First, could the failure of consumption functions, or indeed of macroeconometric models in general, really be traced to a change in the way expectations were formed? If so, it ought to be possible to detect changes in the stochastic process generating real income. Second, and more generally, if expectations are important, there ought to be high returns to the simultaneous modelling of consumption and income, so that knowledge of the structure of the latter can be used either to estimate the consumption function, or to test for the validity of the expectations mechanism. My own reading of the evidence is that the Lucas critique is *not* capable of explaining the failure of the empirical consumption function, but that the under-prediction of saving resulted from ignorance of the fact that saving appears to respond positively to inflation, or at least to unanticipated inflation. There is overwhelming evidence from a large number of countries, see in particular Koskela and Viren (1982a, 1982b), that saving increased with inflation in the 1970s, even when we allow for real income and its various lags. Such a finding is also consistent with the life-cycle theory since unanticipated inflation imparts a negative shock to real assets, so that risk-averse, low intertemporal elasticity consumers will save to replace the lost

assets so as to avoid the chance of low consumption later. It is also possible to explain the relationship through the confusion between relative and absolute price changes that is engendered by unanticipated inflation in an environment in which goods are bought sequentially, see Deaton (1977), but it would be hard to devise a test that would separate this from the life-cycle explanation. But if inflation was indeed the cause of the failure of the empirical consumption functions, then it is a standard enough story. An important variable was omitted from the analysis, it had not been very variable in the past so that its omission was hard to detect, and economists had not been imaginative enough to perceive its importance in advance. The Lucas critique is only one of the many problems that can beset an econometric equation, and it does not seem to have been the fatal one in this case.

The second research direction, the joint examination of income and consumption, has proved more productive. The first important step was taken by Hall (1978), who pointed out that equation (15) implies that, as an approximation consumption should follow a random walk with drift. To see why, assume that the real interest rate r is constant and known, and write (15) in the form

$$c_{t+1}^{-\sigma} = \{(1+\delta)/(1+r)\}c_t^{-\sigma} + \epsilon_{t+1} \qquad (19)$$

where the expectation at t of ϵ_{t+1} is zero. Equation (19) is exact, but a convenient expression can be reached by factoring c_t out of the right hand side, taking logarithms, and approximating. This gives

$$\ln c_{t+1} = \ln c_t + g + v_{t+1} \qquad (20)$$

where g is positive or negative as r is greater than or less than δ, and the 'innovation' v_{t+1}, like ϵ_{t+1}, has expectation zero at time t. Equation (20) shows that, in the absence of 'news', consumption will grow or decline at a steady rate g, so that nothing that is known by the consumer at time t or earlier should have any value for predicting the deviation of the rate of change of consumption from its constant mean. The result is often referred to as the 'random walk' property of consumption, though the theory does not predict that v_{t+1} has constant variance, so that, strictly speaking, the stochastic process is not a random walk.

For someone used to thinking about the consumption function as the relationship between consumption and income, Equation (2) is notable for the apparent absence of any reference to income. But of course income can appear through the stochastic term v_{t+1} if current income contains new information about its own value or about future values of income, and this will generally be the case. The random walk model does not predict that consumption should not respond to current income. It does however predict that, conditional on lagged consumption, past income or changes in income should not be correlated with the current change in consumption, and a considerable amount of effort has recently gone into testing this proposition. In Hall's (1978) original paper, to the surprise of the author and of much of the profession, the model worked well for an aggregate of United States consumption of non-durables and services. The level of consumption certainly depends on its own lagged value, but the addition of one or more lagged values of income or of further lagged values of consumption did not significantly add to the explanatory power of the model. Hall examined the role of the number of other lagged variables and discovered that lagged stockmarket prices had predictive power for the change in consumption, so that he concluded by formally rejecting the model. However, the overwhelming impression was favourable, at least relative to expectations.

Hall's test procedures are attractive because they do not depend on the properties of the income process, and focus only on consumption and its lags. But robustness comes at the price of power, and later work has devoted considerable attention to the joint properties of consumption and real income. Perhaps the natural route to modelling is to find a representation of real income as a stochastic process, typically as some sort of ARIMA. Once this is known, changes in income can be decomposed into anticipated and unanticipated components using the standard forecasting formulae from statistical time series analysis, so that it becomes possible to test whether consumption responds to one but not to the other. The random walk model seemed not to survive these tests so well. Papers by Flavin (1981) and by Hayashi (1982) showed that, for United States data, consumption is sensitive to *anticipated* changes in income, something that should not be the case in a thoroughgoing life-cycle model in which consumers are efficiently looking into the future. The phenomenon became known as the 'excess sensitivity' result, and was typically ascribed to the existence of a substantial number of consumers who wish to borrow against future income but are unable to do so. Such liquidity constrained consumers can be expected to consume all their available income, so that their consumption will increase one for one with all income changes, whether anticipated or not. However, it is not clear that the excess sensitivity finding is itself robust. First, it is becoming increasingly recognized that the problems of econometric testing in the time-series models are more severe than had been generally supposed. The time series of both consumption and income are non-stationary, and it sometimes seems as if hypothesis testing in models involving non-stationary variables is like building on shifting sands; see Mankiw and Shapiro (1985, 1986) and Durlauf and Phillips (1986) for some of the problems. Second, there are a large number of variables other than income which can affect consumption, so that, according to (20), surprises in wealth and in inflation should affect consumption, as should the level of real interest rates. Adding even a few of these variables reduces degrees of freedom and diminishes the probability of being able to reject the basic model. Both Bean (1985) and Blinder and Deaton (1985) find that time-series models of consumption with several variables are more easily reconciled with the theory than are the simple two variable models. Not all of this should be ascribed to lack of degrees of freedom; for example Blinder and Deaton consistently find that unanticipated changes in wealth affect consumption and that anticipated changes do not. Third, even in a bivariate income-consumption model, Campbell (1985) has found that the model is largely consistent with the time series evidence. Campbell recognizes the possibility of time-series feedback from lagged consumption to income, and models saving and the change in income as a bivariate vector-autoregressive system in which each series is regressed on lagged values of both. The structure of this representation then turns out to be very close to what it would have to be if the life-cycle rational expectations model were correct. The conflict between Campbell's results and the excess sensitivity findings are presumably accounted for by the feedback from saving to changes in labour income, since his model is otherwise compatible with the earlier ones.

Similarly mixed findings are also being uncovered from longitudinal panels that follow individual households over time. In contrast to the situation with labour supply, there are few panel data in the United States that cover household consumption, and most work has used the data on expenditure on food that is contained in the Michigan Panel Study of

Income Dynamics (PSID). In an elegant paper, Hall and Mishkin (1982) found results that were in accord with the excess sensitivity results; there is a strong negative correlation in their data between changes in consumption and changes in lagged income that is inconsistent with the view that only surprises in income should matter. However, since in their data changes in income are negatively correlated over time, a negative correlation between the lagged income change and the change in consumption can be interpreted as a positive correlation between consumption changes and changes in actual income, as predicted by the model of liquidity constraints. Hall and Mishkin conclude that these results would be consistent with a model in which about one fifth of consumers were unable to borrow as much as they wished. Once again, these results were supported by other similar evidence, see in particular Zeldes (1985) and Bernanke (1984), also using the PSID, Runkle (1983), using data from the Denver Income Maintenance Experiment, and Hayashi (1985a) using panel data from Japan. However, one potential problem with the use of panels is the importance of errors of measurement in such data. There is a considerable body of evidence that PSID income changes are subject to very substantial reporting errors, see in particular Altonji (1986), Duncan and Hill (1985), and Abowd and Card (1985). Altonji and Siow (1985) have recently estimated a model similar to Hall and Mishkin's using the PSID but with allowance for measurement error, and they find little conflict with the view that consumption responds only to news. However, it is unclear, at least to this reader, whether the acceptance of the model represents low power once errors of measurement are allowed for, or whether such errors really offer a plausible explanation for Hall and Mishkin's findings.

A more formal line of research has attempted to estimate the Euler condition (15) directly, thus avoiding the approximations made by Hall and by others. Rewrite (15) once more, this time as

$$(1 + r_{t+1})(c_{t+1})^{-\sigma} - (1 + \delta)(c_t)^{-\sigma} = \epsilon_{t+1} \qquad (21)$$

where, as before ϵ_{t+1} is orthogonal to any variable known in period t or earlier. Hansen and Singleton (1982) proposed that the parameters in (21) be estimated by a generalized methods of moments scheme. Suppose that we have two variables or instruments z_{1t} and z_{2t}, each known at time t, so that we have $E_t(z_{it}\epsilon_{t+1}) = 0$ for $i = 1, 2$. We can then estimate the two unknown parameters, σ and Δ, by equating sample and theoretical moments, and solving the two equations, $i = 1, 2$

$$T^{-1}\sum [z_{it}\{(1 + r_{t+1})(c_{t+1})^{-\sigma} - (1 + \delta)(c_t)^{-\sigma}\}] = 0. \qquad (22)$$

If, as is typically the case, we have more than two z-variables, then it will not generally be possible to choose the two parameters so that (22) is exactly zero. Instead, the vector can be made as small as possible, or more specifically, the parameters can be estimated by minimizing a quadratic form that can be thought of as a weighted sum of squares of the left-hand side of (22); see Hansen and Singleton for details. If the model were true, this minimized value ought to be small, so that with more instruments than parameters, the generalized method of moments procedure yields a test-statistic that is diagnostic for model adequacy.

Test procedures based directly on the Euler conditions have several notable advantages. As was the case for Hall's procedures, few assumptions have to be made about the structure of the income process, and the model satisfies the best professional standards of seeking a direct confrontation between theory and data with as few approximations and supplementary assumptions as possible. The model can also be readily extended to test the implications of the consumption asset pricing model by repeating the tests using the returns on a range of alternative assets, see (13) above. Hansen and Singleton's study, as well as several others, find that the test statistics are much too large to be consistent with the theory and so reject the intertemporal model implied by the Euler conditions. Given the apparent superiority of the tests, these results have been accorded a great deal of weight in the literature. However, while I believe that Hansen and Singleton's work represents a very important methodological advance, I think that there are good reasons for not treating their results as a definitive rejection of life-cycle theory. The high level of technique that is embodied in deriving the Euler equation, not to mention the complexity of generalized methods of moments estimation, should not blind us to the very simple, even simple-minded, economic story that underlies these models. Fundamentally, the Euler equation says that the marginal rate of substitution between today's and tomorrow's consumption should be equal to the rate of return on assets between today and tomorrow, so that estimation of the Euler equation, unlike the Hall or excess-sensitivity tests, focuses very directly on the relationship between real interest rates and changes in real consumption, and the model will not fit the data if there is no close association between the two. And it only takes a very cursory inspection of United States time-series data to see that there is no such association. Real consumption grew in all but one year between 1954 and 1984, while real after-tax interest rates were as often negative as positive, so that consistency with the theory would require that the pure rate of time preference be negative. Nor is there any association between the rate of growth of consumption and the level of real after-tax interest rates, see Deaton (1986b) for some data. But this in no way reflects badly on the life-cycle theory. As was made perfectly clear in the original Modigliani and Brumberg papers, and it is the *essence* of the life-cycle model, aggregate consumption cannot be expected to behave like individual consumption. Imagine a stationary economy with neither population nor real income growth, in which there is an excess of real interest rates over the rate of pure time preference, and in which all consumers have identical additive life-time preferences with isoelastic subutility functions. In such an economy, each individual has a consumption path that is growing over time, but aggregate consumption is constant, a result that is achieved by old people dying and being replaced by young people who have much lower consumption levels relative to their incomes. Unless we believe that there is some automatic and immediate relationship between real interest rates, time preference and growth, as would obtain for example along a 'golden age' growth path, or unless we believe that consumers have infinite lives, then there is no reason at all to suppose that aggregate consumption should look at all like the life-cycle path of a representative consumer. Representative agent models are frequently useful, and it is not very constructive to dismiss macroeconomics because it requires implausible aggregation assumptions. However, the life-cycle model provides a well-worked out account of individual and aggregate saving, an account that is consistent with a good deal of other evidence and theory, and it *does not* predict that aggregate consumption should be consistent with the intertemporal optimization conditions for a single individual. The general question of the effects of interest rates on consumption is something that has remained in dispute for a long time, and in spite of repeated attempts to isolate the effect, careful studies have tended to be unable to do so, or at least to find effects that are at all robust, or that can be replicated on even slightly different data sets or data periods. Economic theories or policy prescriptions that rely on intertemporal substitution of consumption in response to changes in real interest rates are not well-buttressed by any solid body of empirical evidence.

Another useful approach to testing the life-cycle model is to consider the stylized facts of the income and consumption processes, and to see whether consumption behaves in the way that is to be expected given the stochastic process of income. Most people who have studied the time series for quarterly real disposable income in the United States agree that, like GDP, the series can be parsimoniously described by a model that is linear in its first two lags, i.e. an autoregression of the form

$$y_t = \alpha_1 + \alpha_2 y_{t-1} + \alpha_3 y_{t-2} + u_t \tag{23}$$

where u_t is the income innovation, that part of current income that cannot be anticipated from previous observation of the series. Of course, real income is not a stationary series, but has a strong upward trend, and there is considerable disagreement about the nature of this trend, what is the economic story behind it, and how it should be modelled. One possibility is that real income contains a *deterministic* time trend, so that there is some sort of equilibrium growth path that cannot be altered by shocks to the economy. Shocks certainly exist, but they cause only short term temporary deviations from the path and have little or no long-term temporary deviations from the path and have little or no long-term significance. In this view, equation (23) applies to the *deviations* of income from trend, not to income itself; equivalently, (23) can be modified by including a linear or quadratic time trend. The alternative view is that there is no deterministic trend, but that the rate of change of income is a stationary stochastic series with constant mean. In practice, this can look very like the previous model, but there is the vital conceptual difference that in the second, non-deterministic model, there is nothing that will ever bring income back to any deterministic path. In consequence, shocks to current income have permanent and long-lasting effects. The version of (23) that corresponds to this view can be written.

$$\{(y_t - y_{t-1}) - \gamma\} = \rho\{(y_{t-1} - y_{t-2}) - \gamma\} + u_t \tag{24}$$

which can readily be seen to be a special case of (23), though note that it is the case where the time series possesses a unit root, or is stationary in first differences. For (24) to be a valid specialization of (23), the quadratic equation with the α's of (23) as coefficients must have a unit root, hence the term. Equation (24) appears to fit the data well and the parameter ρ turns out to be around 0.4, so that (24) says that if the increase in real income in one quarter is greater than its long term mean, then the next quarter's increase is also likely to be above the mean, though by less. While the long-term mean of the rate of change of income is constant and equal to γ, good fortune (positive u's) and bad fortune (negative u's) never have to be paid for (or made up), since shocks are immediately consolidated into the income level, and growth goes on in the same way as before, but from the new base. As Campbell and Mankiw (1986) have emphasized, the unit root model exhibits shock *persistence*, while the deterministic trend model does not; they suggest that shock persistence is what we should expect if supply shocks predominate over demand shocks, with the reverse in standard Keynesian models where shocks are typically attributed to fluctuations in aggregate demand.

It turns out that it is almost impossible to tell these two processes apart on United States time series data. Processes with unit roots are inherently difficult to tell apart from processes that are stationary around deterministic trends, and the tests that are available, Dickey and Fuller (1981), Phillips

and Perron (1986), certainly cannot reject the hypothesis that (24) is a valid specialization of (23). Nor would the tests convince a believer in the deterministic model that income does not have a deterministic trend, even though it will readily be recognized that the deviations from trend are themselves close to non-stationarity. Since both processes are special cases of (23) with the inclusion of a time trend, and since each assumes parameter values that are very close to one another, one might think (and hope)' that the two models would have very similar implications. But it is easy to see this is not true. If permanent income is taken as the annuity value of discounted future incomes, then (24) implies that any innovation u_t to current income, because it will persist forever, and because it can be expected to be followed by another infinitely persistent innovation of the same sign, will change permanent income by more than the amount of the innovation, equation (25) below gives the formula for the change in permanent income, if the real interest rate is r, and if real income follows (24), see Flavin (1981) or Deaton (1986b),

$$\Delta y_t^p = \frac{(1+r)^2}{r+1-\rho} u_t \tag{25}$$

so that the change in permanent income is between one and a half and twice as large as the innovation in current income. By contrast, fitting the deterministic model yields a much smaller effect, with the change in permanent income about one fifth of the shock in measured income. Since consumption should change by about the same amount as does permanent income, the life-cycle model, together with the unit root formulation, yields the uncomfortable prediction that consumption should be *more* variable than income over the business-cycle, not less. If the unit root model is correct, then the life-cycle and permanent income models can be rejected because they predict what they were designed to predict, that consumption is smooth relative to real income! The deterministic model gives no such problems, but as yet we have no way of being sure that it is correct, unless, of course we assume from the start that the life cycle story is true.

There is insufficient space in this essay to follow these issues further, or to discuss in detail the evidence for and against the two formulations of the stochastic process governing real income; the interested reader can refer to Deaton (1986b) and to the evidence on persistence in GDP presented by Campbell and Mankiw (1986) and by Cochrane (1986). There are a number of possible solutions to these puzzles, and a great deal of empirical work remains to be done, though I suspect that the time-series data on income are insufficiently long to allow the isolation of the very long-run properties on which the permanent income theory rests, see in particular the interesting paper by Watson (1986).

4. VARIATIONS ON THE BASIC THEME. There exist many interesting developments of the basic life-cycle model, and I have space to discuss only a few. I have already mentioned the role of liquidity constraints, and many people would take it as transparent that many consumers do not have access to unlimited credit, or else face borrowing rates that are higher than the rates at which they can lend. Of course, many consumers may be able to smooth their consumption without recourse to borrowing, and the borrowing needs of many others may be met by the typically rather good markets in home mortgages. For consumers who nevertheless wish to borrow but cannot, their spending will be closely tied to their actual income. For some of the theoretical and empirical literature on this point see Flemming (1973), Dolde and Tobin (1971), and Hayashi (1985b). The theoretical consequences of uncertainty about the

date of death have been worked out by Yaari (1965), and as argued above, play a possibly important part in the explanation of the saving behavior of the elderly.

Another line of research is the possible relaxation of the assumption that preferences are intertemporally additive. Allowing all periods (or ages) to interact with all other periods in an unrestricted way, as in equation (1), would be much too general to be useful, and the search has been for simple models that break the restriction in a natural and straightforward way. One useful analogy is with the theory of durable good purchases, where utility depends on the *stock* of assets possessed, the stock in turn being the integral of past purchases less depreciation. Purchases in one period therefore have consequences for utility in subsequent periods, something that will be taken into account by a forward looking consumer. In the case of durable goods, the assumption of perfect capital markets effectively converts durable into non-durable goods, with the price of a unit of stock for one period being the implicit rental or user cost, the latter being defined as the sum of interest cost, depreciation, and expected capital loss, see for example Diewert (1974) or Deaton and Muellbauer (1980, ch. 13).

However, various authors, Houthakker and Taylor (1970) perhaps being the first, have extended the durable model to encompass 'psychic' stocks which, like physical stocks, are augmented by purchases and diminished by depreciation, but unlike physical stocks, can either increase or decrease utility. The latter case covers habit formation; consumption of an addictive good generates pleasure now, but engenders a hungry habit that is pleasureless but costly in the future. The model has been given an elegant formulation in two papers by Spinnewyn (1979a, 1979b). As an example, see also Muellbauer (1985), take the utility function

$$u = \sum (1 + \delta^{-1} v(c - \alpha c_{t-1}), \quad \alpha > 0. \tag{26}$$

where α is a measure of habit formation. Spinnewyn maximizes this function with respect not to c_t, but with respect to the 'net' quantities $z_t = c_t - \alpha c_{t-1}$, and shows how to rewrite the budget constraint so as to define corresponding prices of the z's that reflect not only market prices of the goods, but also the costs of consumption now in terms of pleasure foregone later. Under certainty, and looking ahead from time t, the full shadow price of an additional unit of consumption now is

$$p_z = \sum_{k=0}^{T-t} [\alpha/(1+r)]^k p_{t+k} \tag{27}$$

because the habits that are built up now have to be paid for later. Note that this sort of formulation also predicts that it is $c_t - \alpha c_{t-1}$, not c_t, that is proportional to permanent income, so that consumption itself will adjust only sluggishly to changes in permanent income with habits causing a drag. Other formulations of non-separable preferences can be found in the papers by Kydland and Prescott (1982), and by Eichenbaum, Hansen, and Singleton (1984), both of which are concerned to reconcile fluctuations in the aggregate economy with the behaviour of a single representative agent.

Many of the models discussed so far assume that the consumption function actually exists, hence taking for granted the essentially keynesian assumption that income is given to the consumer, and is not chosen together with consumption. A considerable body of work has grown up in the last ten years that is concerned with the simultaneous choice of labour supply and consumption in a life-cycle setting. Heckman (1971) and Ghez and Becker (1975) are among the pioneers of this approach. Unlike the price of goods, the price of leisure tends to show a systematic pattern over the life-cycle, so that, if consumers are free to choose their hours, and if they can freely borrow and lend so as to transfer resources between periods, it will pay them to work hardest during those periods in their life-cycles when the rewards for doing so are highest, and to take their life-time leisure when wage rates are low and leisure is cheap. There is superficial evidence in favour of this story, and Ghez and Becker, followed by Smith (1977) and Browning, Deaton and Irish (1985), all find that workers tend to work longest hours in middle age when wage rates are high and the lowest number of hours at the beginning and end of the economically active life, when wage rates are relatively low. Consumption also tends to peak in middle age, and this can be brought into the story by assuming that consumption and leisure are complements, so that the lack of leisure in middle age is partially compensated by high levels of expenditure. This elegant fable has also been made much of in equilibrium theories of the business cycle, which accounts 'unemployment' as a voluntary vacation taken when the real wage is low and leisure is on sale, see in particular Lucas and Rapping (1969) and Lucas (1981).

There now exists a growing volume of literature that shows just how much violence to the facts is done by this story. All the evidence quoted above looks across different individuals at different points in their life-cycles, while the theory says that the same individual will change his or her hours of work along with changes in the real wage over the life-cycle. Time-series and panel data from the United States and time-series of cross-sections from the united Kingdom suggest that this is simply not the case, see for example Mankiw, Rotemberg and Summers (1985), Ashenfelter and Ham (1979, Ashenfelter (1984), and Browning, Deaton and Irish (1985), and even MaCurdy's (1981) more postive study provides only very weak evidence, see in particular Altonji (1986). The joint consumption and labour supply story fares even less well than the labour supply model alone, and there is clear evidence that the way in which consumption and hours fluctuate over the cycle (sometimes together and sometimes in opposite directions) is not consistent with the way in which they move together over the life-cycle. The attempt to provide a unified theory of business and life-cycles has been an interesting and important one, but it cannot be said to have been successful.

I have been somewhat cavalier in my treatment of aggregation issues, choosing to emphasize them when I believe them to be important, for example in the fitting of Euler conditions, and ignoring them when it has been convenient to do so. Attempts to do better than this have not been notably successful. Formal conditions that allow aggregation in consumption function models are typically too restrictive to be useful, so that, in theory, changes in the distribution of income should have detectable effects on aggregate consumption. However, attempts such as that by Blinder (1975) to link the distribution of income to consumption have not been notably successful, perhaps because the income distribution is not variable, or because it changes smoothly enough over time to preserve a stable relationship between average income and average consumption. There is also an issue of aggregation over goods in order to define real consumption at all, even at the level of the individual agent. In the derivation in section 1 above, I made the convenient assumption that within-period preferences were homothetic, so that an index number of real consumption could be formed. But homotheticity, although very convenient for studying the consumption function, is very inconvenient for studying the allocation of expenditure among goods since it implies that the within-period total expenditure elasticities of each good are all equal to unity. Fortunately, there are aggregation results of Gorman's (1959), see also Deaton and Muellbauer (1980b, ch. 5) for an exposition that allows us to have the best of both worlds, at least if we remain with intertemporally additive preferences. If the single-period indirect utility function $\psi(x, p)$ takes the form known as the 'generalized Gorman polar form'

$$\psi(x, p) = F[x/a(p)] + b(p) \qquad (28)$$

where $a(p)$ and $b(p)$ are linearly homogeneous functions of prices and $F(\ )$ is monotone increasing, then the real expenditure index $x/a(p)$ can serve as an indicator of real consumption just as in the homothetic case. This happens because when the consumer chooses the allocation of life-time expenditure over periods so as to maximize the intertemporal sum of terms like (28), the $b(p)$ terms are irrelevant. However, the intra-period demand functions that correspond to (28) do not display unitary elasticities unless the $b(p)$ is identically equal to zero, and quite general functional forms are permitted. There is therefore no real conflict between the analysis of the consumption function on the one hand, and the analysis of demand on the other. It is to the latter that I now turn.

5. THEORETICAL AND EMPIRICAL DEMAND FUNCTIONS. Demand functions are the relationships between the purchase of individual goods, income or total expenditure, prices, and a variety of other factors depending on the context. Economists have attempted to make empirical links between demand and price since Gregory King's famous demand curve for wheat, see Davenant (1699), and since the middle of the 19th century, there has been a great development in the theory of consumer behaviour. Much practical work continues in the tradition of King, paying little attention to formal theory, concerning itself instead with finding empirical regularities. For a firm studying the demand for its product, or for anyone interested in establishing a single price elasticity, this probably remains the best approach; the major developments in econometric technique and empirical formulation have not been much concerned with, or relevant to, these very practical questions. The pragmatic approach (the term comes from Goldberger's famous but unpublished (1967) study), probably reached its peak with the publication of Richard Stone's great monograph, Stone (1954a), and much is still to be learned by a careful study of Stone's procedures for measuring income and price elasticities. However, in this essay, I shall follow the literature, and follow its more methodological approach.

The theory outlined in Section 1 above suggests that the demand functions of an individual consumer can be derived by maximizing a utility function $v(q)$ subject to a budget constraint $p \cdot q = x$, where x is total expenditure. In the analysis here, x is chosen at some previous level of decision making, but traditionally it is treated as if it were a datum by the consumer, the utility maximization yields a vector q that is some function $g(x, p)$, say, of total expenditure and prices. These demand functions cannot simply be any functions, but must have certain properties as a result of their origins in utility maximization. Obviously, the total value of the demands should be equal to total outlay x, the 'adding-up' property, and it must be true that proportional changes in x and in p do not have any effect on quantities demanded, the 'homogeneity' or 'absence of money illusion' property. Somewhat less obvious are the famous symmetry and negativity properties. These apply to the Slutsky (1915) matrix, S, the typical element of which is defined as

$$s_{ij} = \partial q_i / \partial p_j + q_j \partial q_i / \partial x.$$

As any intermediate text shows, see for example Deaton and Muellbauer (1980b, ch. 2), the Slutsky matrix must be symmetric and negative semi-definite. The symmetry property is not readily turned into simple intuition; negativity implies that the diagonal elements of the matrix are non-positive, a proposition often referred to as 'the law of demand'. The four properties, adding-up, homogeneity, symmetry and negativity, essentially exhaust the implications of utility maximization, so that any empirical demand functions that satisfy them can be regarded as having been generated by utility maximization, or by rational choice, with 'rational' defined, following Gorman (1981), as 'having smooth strictly quasi-concave preferences, and being greedy'.

Stone (1954b) was the first to attempt to use this theory directly to confront the data. He started from a (general) linear expenditure system of the form

$$p_i q_i = \sum_j a_{ij} p_j + b_i x \qquad (30)$$

where a_{ij} and b_i are unknown parameters. Stone showed that, in general, the system (30) does not satisfy the four requirements, but will do so if, and only if, the parameters are restricted so that the model can be written in the form

$$p_i q_i = p_i \gamma_i + \beta_i (x - p \cdot \gamma) \qquad (31)$$

with the β-parameters summing to unity. In this form the model is known as the linear expenditure system. As Samuelson (1947–8) and Geary (1949–50) had earlier shown, the utility function corresponding to (31) has the form

$$u = \sum \beta_i \ln (q_i - \gamma_i), \qquad (32)$$

sometimes referred to (somewhat inappropriately) as the Stone–Geary utility function. It can be thought of as a sum of Bernoulli utility functions of the quantity of each good above the minimal γ's.

Stone's achievement lay not in deriving the demand functions, but in thinking to estimate them. The demand functions (30), even if fitted to the data by least-squares, require non-linear optimization, and Stone invented a simple and not very efficient scheme, but one that allowed him to obtain parameter estimates and a good fit to interwar British data for a six commodity disaggregation of expenditures. This was a major breakthrough, not only in demand analysis, but also in applied econometrics in general. Indeed, much of demand analysis for a decade or so after Stone's paper consisted of applying better algorithms and faster computers to the fitting of Stone's model to different data sets.

The linear expenditure system offers a demand model for a system of, say n goods, and requires only $2n - 1$ parameters, a degree of parsimony that was very important in allowing the model to be estimated on very short time series data. However, such economy brings its own price, and the linear expenditure system is very restrictive in the sort of behaviour that it can allow. In particular, and pathological cases apart, the model cannot allow inferior goods (goods the demand for which falls as total outlay increases), nor can it allow goods to be complements rather than substitutes. (As defined by Hicks (1939) goods i and j are complements if the (i, j)th term in the Slutsky matrix is negative, so that the utility compensated cross-price response of i to an increase in the price of j is positive.) Normal (non-inferior) goods that are substitutes for one another may be the most important case, but they do not encompass everything that we might want to study. The linear expenditure system also implies that the marginal propensity to consume each good is the same no matter what is the total to be spent, and many cross-section studies of household budgets have suggested that this is not in fact the case.

Unfortunately, it is quite difficult to write down utility functions that will lead to more general demand functions than those of the linear expenditure system, nor is there any obvious way of generalizing Stone's procedure of writing down functions and making them consistent with the theory. Progress was only really made once applied demand analysis started using 'dual' formulations of preferences to specify demands. In the demand context, duality refers to a switch of variables, from quantities to prices, so that utility becomes a function, not directly of quantities consumed, but indirectly of prices and total expenditure. This indirect utility formulation is given by the function $\psi(x, p)$, already used above, and this is simply the maximum attainable utility from total outlay x at prices p. Since $\psi(x, p) = u$, and the function is monotone increasing in x, it can be inverted to give $x = c(u, p)$, known as the 'cost function', since it gives the minimum necessary cost that is required to reach the utility level u. By a theorem usually attributed to Shephard (1953) and to Uzawa (1964), these two functions contain a complete representation of preferences; provided preferences are convex, and provided the functions satisfy homogeneity and convexity (or concavity) conditions, preferences can be reconstructed from knowledge of either of the two functions. It is also very easy to move from either cost or indirect utility functions to the demand functions. For the indirect utility function, we have Roy's identity (Roy, 1943).

$$q = -\nabla_p \psi(x, p)/\psi_x(x, p) \equiv g(x, p) \qquad (33)$$

which immediately yields demand functions from preferences in a form that are suitable for estimation, while for the cost function, we have Shepard's Lemma (1953),

$$q = \nabla_p c(u, p) = \nabla_p c[\psi(x, p), p] \equiv g(x, p) \qquad (34)$$

where, as in (33), the operator ∇ denotes a vector of partial derivatives.

Demand analysis now had a high road to specification. Think of some quasi-convex decreasing function of the ratios of price to total outlay and call it an indirect utility function, or think of some function of utility and prices that is increasing in its arguments and linearly homogeneous and concave in prices and call it a cost function. Either way, and with only simple differentiation, new (and sometimes) interesting demand functions will be generated. Alternatively, and even more importantly, it is possible to use theory to aid and check out empirical knowledge. If it is known that the marginal propensity to spend on food is a declining function of total expenditure, or if it is thought likely that some goods do not depend very directly on the prices of other goods, it is relatively straightforward to find out what preferences (if any) will yield the result. It becomes possible, not just to generate demand functions serendipitously, but to generate good and useful ones deliberately.

There are many examples that could be cited from the literature. One of the most widely used in the *translog* model which was first proposed in 1970 by Jorgenson and Lau, see Christensen, Jorgenson and Lau (1973) for a convenient reference. To derive the translog, write the indirect utility function in terms of the ratios of prices to outlay, $r = p/x$, and approximate the indirect utility function as a second order polynomial in the logarithms of r. Application of Roy's identity yields demand functions in which the budget share of each good is the ratio of two functions, each of which is linear in the logarithms of the price to outlay ratios. Estimation of these rational functions, like estimation of the linear expenditure system, requires the use of non-linear maximization techniques. A related model, the 'almost ideal demand system' (AIDS) has been proposed by Deaton and Muellbauer (1980a), and I use this to illustrate some of the issues that arise with the current generation of demand models. The AIDS is specified by the logarithm of its cost function which takes the form

$$\ln c(u, p) = \alpha_0 + \sum \alpha_k \ln p_k + 0.5 \sum \sum \gamma_{km} \ln p_k \ln p_m$$
$$+ u \exp\{\sum \beta_k \ln p_k\}, \qquad (35)$$

so that, applying Shephard's lemma and rearranging, we have demand functions

$$p_i q_i / x \equiv w_i = \alpha_i + \beta_i \ln (x/P) + \sum \gamma_{ij} \ln p_j \qquad (36)$$

where P is a linearly homogeneous price index, the form of which can readily be inferred from (35). The parameters of the model must satisfy certain restrictions if (35) is to be a proper (log) cost function, and (36) a proper system of demand functions. The matrix of γ-parameters can be taken to be symmetric in (35), but must be so in (36), and its rows and columns must add to zero for the homogeneity and adding-up properties to be satisfied. The β-parameters can be positive or negative, with positive values indicating luxury goods, and negative values necessities. The main advantage of the AIDS model in time-series applications is that the price index P can typically be approximated by some known price index selected before estimation, so that the demand system is linear in its parameters. In consequence, it can be estimated by ordinary least squares on an equation by equation basis, at least if the symmetry of the γ-matrix is ignored. The homogeneity restrictions can be tested equation by equation using a t- or F-test, and while imposing or testing symmetry requires an iterative procedure, estimation can be done by straightforward iterated restricted generalized least-squares, see Barten (1979) or Deaton (1974a) for further discussion.

The results of estimating the AIDS model are sufficiently similar to those from other models and other studies, see e.g. Barten (1969), Deaton (1974a), Christensen, Jorgenson and Lau (1973), and many others, that perhaps they can be taken as representative. What typically seems to happen is that the homogeneity restrictions appear *not* to be satisfied, so that in the application of AIDS to British data, Deaton and Muellbauer found, for example, that the F-test for transport had a value of 172 compared with the 5 per cent critical value of 4.8. Results on symmetry from AIDS and other systems are more mixed, and it now seems clear that testing symmetry is not usually possible given the amount of data typically available in time series, or put more positively, that there is no convincing evidence against symmetry. The difficulty is that symmetry involves a set of restrictions *across* different equations, so that unlike homogeneity, which involves tests *within* each equation, exact, small sample tests are not available. Researchers have therefore fallen back on asymptotically valid tests, and it turns out that these work very badly for the usual sort of samples, especially when there are more than a very small number of goods in the demand system. The papers by Laitinen (1978) and Meisner (1979) first established the problem, see also Evans and Savin (1982) and Bera, Byron and Jarque (1981) for further evidence.

The AIDS model, like the translog and several others, e.g. Diewert's (1973) 'generalized Leontief' system, fall into the class of 'flexible functional forms'. This criterion of flexibility, first proposed by Diewert (1971), is an important guarantee that the model is sufficiently richly parametrized so as to allow estimation of what are thought to be the main parameters of interest, typically the total expenditure elasticities, and the matrix of own and cross-price elasticities. A 'second order' flexible functional form is one that has sufficient parameters, so configured, that it is possible to set the value of the function, and of its first and second partial derivatives to any arbitrary set of (theoretically permissible) values. By applying Roy's identity or Shephard's lemma, it is clear that a cost or indirect utility function that is a second order flexible functional form will yield demand functions that are first-order flexible, so that it is possible for estimation to yield any set of price and expenditure elasticities that are consistent with utility theory. For empirical work, such a guarantee is important, because it ensures that the elasticities are being measured, not assumed. Contrast, for example, the linear expenditure system (31) with the AIDS model (36). Both could be fitted to the same set of data, and the parameter estimates of each could be used to generate a complete set of expenditure and price elasticities. But the linear expenditure system is *not* a flexible functional form, and so its estimated elasticities are not independent of one another, as is apparent from the fact that there are $2n - 1$ parameters compared with the total number of potentially independent elasticities, which is $(n - 1)(1 + n/2)$. (There are $n - 1$ independent demand equations, each of which has an expenditure elasticity, and n price elasticities; however, one price elasticity per equation is lost to homogeneity, and symmetry imposes a further $(n - 1)(n - 2)/2$ constraints.) The linear expenditure system does not therefore *measure* all the price and income elasticities, but determines them by a mixture of measurement and assumption, the main assumption being that of additive preferences, see Deaton (1974b) for further details. The AIDS, by contrast, has exactly the right number of parameters to allow for intercepts and a full set of elasticities, so that when it (or the translog, or the generalized Leontief) is estimated, so is the full set of elasticities.

Being able to do this is a great step forward in methodology, but just as the linear expenditure system probably asks too little of modern data, (although not of the data available to Stone and the early pioneers of the systems approach), the second-order flexible functional forms probably ask too much, or equivalently, put too little structure on the problem. The consequences show up in large standard errors, a high frequency of apparently chance correlations, and a lack of robustness to functional form changes within the class of flexible functional forms, in other words, in all the standard symptoms of over-parametrization. These problems are particularly acute for the measurement of *price* elasticities, because in most time-series data, commodity prices tend to move together with relatively little variation in relative prices. And although the focus of most research on demand analysis over the last thirty years has been on the estimation and testing of price responses, there is certainly no consensus on what numbers, if any, are correct. Estimates obtained from the linear expenditure system are not credible because they are forced to satisfy an implausibly restrictive structure, while those from flexible functional forms are not credible because the data are not informative enough to supplement the lack of prior structure. Some intermediate forms are clearly required.

One of the attractions of flexible functional forms is their ability to approximate quite general forms for preferences. However, the models so far considered offer only approximations, and there is no guarantee that they have satisfactory *global* properties. Partly this is the standard problem that a fitted model will be forced to give a reasonable account of the data over the sample used for estimation, but may predict very badly elsewhere. But there are other deeper issues. Taking the AIDS as an example, estimation of (36) subject to symmetry and homogeneity will produce a system of estimated demand functions that will satisfy adding-up, homogeneity and symmetry for *all* values of x and p. However, there are two other important properties that are not assured. First, there is

no guarantee that the predicted budget shares will necessarily lie between zero and one, so that there may be regions of price space in which the estimated model yields nonsensical predictions. Second, there is no way that the AIDS can be guaranteed to have a negative semi-definite Slutsky matrix for all prices, at least not without restricting parameters to the point where the model ceases to be a flexible functional form. The parameters could be chosen so as to satisfy negativity for some particular combination of prices and outlay, but there will be no guarantee that the law of demand will be satisfied elsewhere. In the translog model, it is possible to impose a restriction that guarantees negativity everywhere, but the model with the restriction has the property that all estimated own price elasticities must be less than minus one, independently of whether this is in fact true, and it almost certainly is not, see Diewert and Wales (1986). A demand system is described as 'regular' if it has a negative definite Slutsky matrix and predicts positive demands, and several empirical studies, see e.g. Wales (1977) for one of the first, found that estimated flexible functional forms were not regular over disturbingly large regions of even the parameter space used to estimate them. Caves and Christensen (1980), and later Barnett and Lee (1985) and Barnett, Lee and Wolfe (1985), investigated the same problem theoretically by taking a known utility function, choosing the parameters of flexible functional forms to match its level and derivatives at a point, and then mapping out the regions of price space in which the systems remained regular. The results at least for the translog and the generalized Leontief model, were not good.

These regularity issues may seem of limited importance in practice, but this is far from being the case. One of the major reasons for being interested in complete empirical demand systems is to be able to examine the consequences of price changes, particularly of price changes that follow changes in government policy. The United States relies relatively little on indirect taxation as a source of public finance, but such is not the case in most of Europe, and the vast majority of developing countries maintain complex systems of price wedges, particularly for foods and for agricultural production. The effects of such systems cannot be predicted without good information on how demands respond to price changes, nor can reforms be intelligently discussed. However, estimated demand systems that are not regular are not a great deal of help. All of the theory of welfare economics, of consumer surplus, of optimal taxation and of tax reform, *assumes* that demand behaviour is generated by utility maximization at the individual level, and implementation without regularity risks internal contradiction. For example, if compensated demand functions slope *upwards*, the government can generate a dead-weight gain by imposing a distortionary tax. Of course, it may not be the empirical work that is wrong, but the theory that we used to try to model behaviour. If so, the estimated demand functions are still not useful, since we now have no idea what to do with them. But I doubt that the evidence goes so far; it is not that behaviour itself is irregular, but that we have not yet found a good modelling strategy that contains a reasonable amount of prior information to supplement the paucity of data, and at the same time can deliver global regularity if it is warranted by the evidence.

A number of interesting experiments are currently under way that involve new modelling techniques. One possibility is that the Taylor series expansions that motivate most flexible functional forms are themselves inadequate to the task. In particular, Taylor approximations lose their ability to approximate if they are also asked to possess other properties of the functions that they are approximating. For example, we might want to test whether or not preferences are additively separable, as in the linear expenditure system. One strategy would be to write down some second-order approximation to preferences, estimate the resulting demand model, and then test whether or not the conditions imposed on the demands by additivity are satisfied. But this will not work in general, because there may be no additive system of demand equations that has the precise functional form demanded by the approximation. The same phenomenon is well illustrated by Stone's derivation of the linear expenditure system itself. The original general linear expenditure equations (29) can clearly be justified as a Taylor approximation to any set of homogeneous demand functions, and yet the imposition of only *symmetry* generates the demand system (30) which comes from the *additive* utility function (31). Additivity is not imposed, but linear expenditure systems are only symmetric if they are additive. Similarly many flexible function forms are only globally regular if they are homothetic, see for example, Blackorby, Primont and Russell (1977). Several recent studies have proposed alternative ways of making functional approximations. Gallant (1982) has proposed using Fourier series approximations while Barnett (1983) has suggested that Laurent series can be used to generate demand models with good properties. Gallant's models are even more heavily parametrized than standard flexible functional forms, and there must be some question as to the suitability of trigonometrical functions for demand functions. Barnett's 'miniflex Laurent' model does not use the full flexibility of the Laurent series, but appears to have quite good approximation and regularity properties in practice, see Barnett and Lee (1985) and Barnett, Lee and Wolfe (1985); even so, its estimation is complex, and many of the parameters have to be estimated subject to inequality constraints.

A second line of current research has abandoned the standard approach of econometric analysis, taking instead a completely non-parametric approach. Since many of the difficulties discussed above arise from choice of functional form, it is useful to ask how far it is possible to go without assuming any functional form at all. We know from standard revealed preference theory that two observed vectors of prices and quantities can be inconsistent with utility maximization; if bundle one is chosen when bundle two is available, so that bundle one is revealed preferred to bundle two, then no subsequent choice should reveal bundle two to be preferred to bundle one. Before embarking on the exercise of fitting some specific utility function to any finite collection of price and quantity pairs, one might then ask whether the collection is conceivably consistent with any set of preferences. If it is, then contradictions between an estimated system and the theory must be a matter of inappropriate functional form. The conditions for utility consistency of a finite set of data were originally derived by Afriat (1967), who proposed a condition called cyclical consistency. Much later Varian (1982) not only provided an accessible and clear account of Afriat's results, but also recast the cyclical consistency condition into a 'generalized axiom of revealed preference (GARP)' that runs as follows. A bundle q^i is strictly directly revealed preferred to a bundle q if $p^i q^i > p^i q$, while q^i is revealed preferred to q, if there exists a sequence $j, k, \ldots, m$ such that $p^i q^i \geqslant p^i q^j, p^j q^j \geqslant p^j q^k, \ldots, p^m q^m \geqslant p^m q$, so that q^i is directly or indirectly (weakly) revealed preferred to q. GARP is satisfied if for all q^i revealed preferred to q^j, it is not true that q^j is strictly directly revealed preferred to q^i, and given GARP the data can be rationalized by a continuous, strictly concave, and non-satiated utility function. Differentiability can also be ensured by a slight strengthening of GARP, see Chiappori and Rochet (1987). GARP is readily tested for any given set of data

by checking the pairwise inequalities and using a simple algorithm provided by Varian to map out the patterns of indirect revealed preference. Repeated applications of the method to time series data have nearly always confirmed the consistency of the data with the theory. In retrospect, it is clear that violations of GARP cannot occur unless some budget lines intersect, so that if, over time, economic growth has resulted in the aggregate budget line moving steadily outward with little change in slopes, GARP is bound to be satisfied. (However, post-war United States data budget planes do occasionally intersect, and Bronars (1987) has recently shown that hypothetical demands generated by selecting random points on the actual budget lines would more often than not fail GARP.)

The contradictions between the parametric and non-parametric approaches can perhaps be resolved by thinking of the latter as a modelling technique that uses a very large number of parameters, so that the failure of the parametric models to fit theory to data can be thought of as failure to parametrize the models sufficiently richly. But I have already argued that these models already have too many parameters, and adding more would only exacerbate the already serious problems of measurement. For many purposes, the theory is only useful if it is capable of delivering a description of the data that is reasonably parsimonious. There is also something rather simple minded about non-parametric techniques that tends to be disguised by the sophisticated and elegant expositions that have been given them by Varian and others. Consider a very simple theory that says variable x should move directly with variable y as, for example, in the Euler equation (15) above which says that, under certainty consumption should grow from period t to $t + 1$ if and only if the real interest rate from t to $t + 1$ is greater than some fixed constant. A non-parametric test on a finite set of data would accept the theory if, in fact, x, and y always did move together, and reject it if x and y ever moved in opposite directions. That such testing procedures are widely employed in the press and by the uninformed public is no reason for treating them seriously in economics.

I have so far discussed the formulation and estimation of demand functions, meaning the relationships between quantities, outlay, and prices, and this has been the topic of most applied demand analysis over the last thirty years. However, there is an older tradition of demand analysis, in which the object of attention is household budget data, and this literature has recently been enjoying something of a revival. Since household budget data typically come from a cross-section of households over a short period of time, usually within a single year, prices are treated as common to all sample points, so that the focus of attention becomes the relationship between demand and outlay and the influence of household composition on the pattern of household expenditures. The oldest, and perhaps only law of economics, Engel's Law that the share of food in the budget declines as total outlay increases, comes from Engel's (1857, published 1895) study of Belgian working-class families, and early empirical studies of demand were almost inevitably based on household surveys (see Stigler (1954) for a masterly review). The modern study of Engel curves, the relationships between expenditure and total outlay, begins (and almost ended) with Prais and Houthakker (1955). Prais and Houthakker studied the shapes of Engel curves, the relationship between demand and household composition, and the variation in unit values across households, particularly in relation to the choice of quality, a topic that has subsequently been unjustly neglected. The functional forms for Engel curves that Prais and Houthakker examined became the staple menu for most subsequent studies, even though only one of their forms, the linear Engel curve, is capable of satisfying adding-up, and the linear form typically performs very badly on the data. Since 1955 a number of other Engel curves have been proposed, notably the lognormal Engel curve of Aitchison and Brown (1957), and Leser's (1963) revival of the form suggested much earlier by Holbrook Working (1943). Working's form, which apparently escaped the attention of Prais and Houthakker, makes the budget share of each commodity a linear function of the logarithm of total outlay. The formulation is particularly useful, for not only is it capable of accounting for most of the curvature that is discovered in empirical Engel curves, but it is also consistent with utility theory, and corresponds to the case where the welfare elasticity of the cost of living is independent of income. Gorman (1981) has provided a general character-ization theorem for Engel curves of the form

$$p_i q_i = \sum_k a_{ik}(p)\xi_k(x) \tag{37}$$

and has shown that the $\xi_k(\ )$ functions can be powers of x (polynomial Engel curves), or x multiplied by powers of $\log x$ (Engel curves relating budget shares to powers of the logarithm of outlay), or have trigonometric forms. This last form includes Fourier representations of Engel curves, while the first two allow Taylor or Laurent expansions for the expenditure/outlay and for the share/log-outlay forms. The Working–Engel curve is the first member of Gorman's 'share to log' class, and the theorem tells us that we may add quadratic or higher order terms to improve the fit. However, Gorman's paper contains a remarkable result; the matrix of the a-coefficients in (37) has rank at most equal to three. In consequence, the share to log and log-squared Engel curves are as general as any, as are the Engel curves of the quadratic expenditure system, see Howe, Pollak and Wales (1979). Given Gorman's results, and the empirical success of the Working form, it and its quadratic generalization deserve wide use in the analysis of budget studies. There is also accumulating evidence that such forms are indeed necessary. Thomas (1986), in a wide-ranging examination of household survey data from developing countries, has shown that Engel's Law itself does not appear to hold among the very poor, so that, in many cases, the share of the budget devoted to food at first rises with total outlay before falling in con-formity with the Law.

Prais and Houthakker also proposed a much-used formu-lation for the effects of household composition on behaviour. It can be written

$$p_i q_i / m_i(a) = f_i\{x/m_0(a)\} \tag{38}$$

where a is a vector of household demographic characteristics (perhaps a list of numbers of people in each age and sex category) and m_i and m_0 are scalar valued functions known as the 'specific' and 'general scales' respectively. In this literature, scales are devices that convert family structure into numbers of equivalent adults, so that a family of two adults and two children might be two equivalent adults for theatre entertain-ment, three equivalent adults for food, and six equivalent adults for milk. The general scale is supposed to reflect the overall number of equivalent adults, so that the Prais and Houthakker model is a simple generalization of the idea that *per capita* demand should be a function of *per capita* outlay. Barten (1964), in a very important paper, took up the Prais-Houthakker idea of specific scales, but assumed that the arguments of the household utility function were the household consumption levels each deflated by the corresponding specific scale. The consequences of Barten's formulation are similar to those of Prais and Houthakker, but embody the additional insight that changes in family composition affect the effective shadow prices of goods, so that demographic changes will

exercise, not only income, but also substitution effects on the pattern of demand. The story is often summarized by the phrase, 'if you have a wife and child, a penny bun costs three-pence', quoted in Gorman (1976), but the really far-reaching substitution effects of children are probably on time use and labour supply, particularly of women.

Since household surveys typically contain large samples of households, there is less need for theory to save degrees of freedom, and it is possible to estimate quite general functional forms that link expenditures to household composition patterns and then to interpret the results in terms of the various models. In addition, neither the Prais–Houthakker nor the Barten model seem to yield easily implemented functional forms, e.g. linear ones, nor is it clear that either model is even identified on a single cross-sectional household survey in which all prices are constant, see for example Muellbauer (1980) and Deaton (1986a). However, some empirical results for the two models can be found in Muellbauer (1977, 1980) and in Pollak and Wales (1980, 1981) who also examine Gorman's (1976) extension of Barten's model in which additional people are supposed to bring with them fixed needs for particular commodities. The fixed needs model is close to the formulation proposed by Rothbarth (1943) for measuring the costs of children. Rothbarth pointed out that there are certain commodities, adult goods, that are not consumed by children, so that when children are added to a household, the only effects on the household's consumption of adult goods will be the income effects that reflect the fact that, with unchanged total resources, the household is now poorer. Deaton, Ruiz-Castillo and Thomas (1985) have recently attempted to test Rothbarth's contention, and in their Spanish data it seems possible to identify a sensible group of adult goods, the expenditure on each of which changes with additional children in the same way as they change in response to changes in outlay.

Studies of the effects of family composition on household expenditure patterns have frequently been concerned, not only with estimating demands, but also with attempts to measure the 'cost' of children. It would take me too far afield to do justice to this topic here. Readers interested in this controversial area should perhaps start with Rothbarth (1943), who in a few pages makes a very simple and quite convincing case, and look also at Nicholson (1975). Pollak and Wales (1979) weigh in on the opposite side, and claim that it is impossible to measure child costs from expenditure data. My own position is argued in Deaton and Muellbauer (1986); there are certainly grave problems to be overcome in moving from the analysis of household survey data to the measurement of the costs of children, and it is clear that identifying assumptions must be made that are more severe and more controversial than those required, for example, to go from demand functions to consumer surplus. But that does not mean that it is not possible for such assumptions to be proposed and to be sensibly discussed.

ANGUS DEATON

See also CONSUMPTION FUNCTION; DEMAND THEORY; FRIEDMAN, MILTON; LIFE-CYCLE HYPOTHESIS.

BIBLIOGRAPHY

Abowd, J.M. and Card, D. 1985. The covariance structure of earnings and hours changes in three panel data sets. Princeton University, mimeo.

Afriat, S.N. 1967. The construction of a utility function from expenditure data. *International Economic Review* 8, 67–77.

Aitchison, J. and Brown, J.A.C. 1957. *The Lognormal Distribution*. Cambridge: Cambridge University Press.

Altonji, J. 1986. Intertemporal substitution in labor supply: evidence from micro data. *Journal of Political Economy* 94, S176–215.

Altonji, J. and Siow, A. 1985. Testing the response of consumption to income changes with (noisy) panel data. Industrial Relations Section Working Paper No. 186, Princeton University, mimeo.

Ando, A. and Modigliani, F. 1963. The life-cycle hypothesis of saving: aggregate implications and tests. *American Economic Review* 53, 55–84.

Ashenfelter, O. 1984. Macroeconomic analyses and microeconomic analyses of labor supply. Presented to Carnegie-Rochester Conference, Bal Harbor, Florida, November 1983.

Ashenfelter, O. and Ham, J. 1979. Education. unemployment, and earnings. *Journal of Political Economy* 87, S99–116.

Barnett, W.A. 1983. New indices of money supply and the flexible Laurent demand system. *Journal of Business and Economic Statistics* 1, 7–23.

Barnett, W.A. and Lee, Y.W. 1985. The global properties of the miniflex Laurent, generalized Leontief, and translog flexible functional forms. *Econometrica* 53, 1421–37.

Barnett, W.A., Lee, Y.W. and Wolfe, M. 1985. The three dimensional global properties of the miniflex Laurent, generalized Leontief, and translog flexible functional forms. *Journal of Econometrics, 3–31.*

Barten, A.P. 1964. Family composition, prices, and expenditure patterns. In *Econometric Analysis for National Economic Planning*, ed. P.E. Hart, G. Mills, and J.K. Whitaker, London: Butterworth.

Barten, A.P. 1969. Maximum likelihood estimation of a complete system of demand equations. *European Economic Review* 1, 7–23.

Bean, C.R. 1985. The estimation of surprise models and the surprise consumption function. Centre for Economic Policy Research (London), Discussion Paper No. 54, mimeo.

Bera, A.K., Byron, R. and Jarque, C.M. 1981. Further evidence on asymptotic tests for homogeneity in large demand systems. *Economics Letters* 8, 101–5.

Bernanke, B.S. 1984. Permanent income, liquidity, and expenditure on automobiles: evidence from panel data. *Quarterly Journal of Economics* 99, 587–614.

Bernheim, B.D., Schleiffer, A. and Summers, L.H. 1985. Bequests as a means of payment. *Journal of Political Economy*, 1045–76.

Blackorby, C., Primont, D. and Russell, R.R. 1977. On testing separability restrictions with flexible functional forms. *Journal of Econometrics* 5, 195–209.

Blinder, A.S. 1975. Distribution effects and the aggregate consumption function. *Journal of Political Economy* 83, 447–75.

Blinder, A.S. and Deaton, A.S. 1985. The time series consumption function revisited. *Brookings Papers on Economic Activity* 2, 465–511.

Breeden, D. 1974. An intertemporal asset pricing model with stochastic consumption and investment opportunities. *Journal of Financial Economics* 7, 265–96.

Bronars, S.G. 1987. The power of non-parametric tests of preference maximization. *Econometrica*.

Browning, M.J., Deaton, A.S. and Irish, M.J. 1985. A profitable approach to labor supply and commodity demands over the life cycle. *Econometrica* 53, 503–43.

Campbell, J.Y. 1986. Does saving anticipate declining labor income? An alternative test of the permanent income hypothesis. *Econometrica*.

Campbell, J.Y. and Mankiw, N.G. 1986. Are output fluctuations transitory? National Bureau of Economic Research Working Paper 1916, processed.

Caves, D.W. and Christensen, L.R. 1980. Global properties of flexible functional forms. *American Economic Review* 70, 422–32.

Chiappori, P.-A. and Rochet, J.-C. 1987. Revealed preferences and differentiable demand. *Econometrica*.

Christensen, L.R., Jorgenson, D.W. and Lau, L.J. 1973. Transcendental logarithmic production frontiers. *Review of Economics and Statistics* 55, 28–45.

Cochrane, J.H. 1986. How big is the random walk in GNP? Department of Economics, University of Chicago, processed.

Davenant, C. 1699. *Essay upon the Probable Methods of Making a People Gainers in the Balance of Trade.* London.

Davidson, J.E.H. et al. 1978. Econometric modelling of the aggregate time-series relationship between consumers expenditure and income in the United Kingdom. *Economic Journal* 88, 661–92.

Davies, J.B. 1980. Uncertain lifetime, consumption and dissaving in retirement. *Journal of Political Economy* 89, 561–77.

Deaton, A.S. 1974a. The analysis of consumer demand in the United Kingdom, 1900–1970. *Econometrica* 42, 341–67.

Deaton, A.S. 1974b. A reconsideration of the empirical implications of additive preferences. *Economic Journal* 84, 338–48.

Deaton, A.S. 1975. The structure of demand in Europe 1920–1970. In *The Fontana Economic History of Europe*, ed. C.M. Cippola, London: Collins-Fontana, Vol. 5.

Deaton, A.S. 1977. Involuntary saving through unanticipated inflation. *American Economic Review* 67, 899–910.

Deaton, A.S. 1986a. Demand analysis. In *Handbook of Econometrics*, ed. Z. Griliches and M. Intriligator, Amsterdam: North-Holland, Vol. 3.

Deaton, A.S. 1986b. Life-cycle models of consumption: is the evidence consistent with the theory? NBER Working Paper No. 1910, processed.

Deaton, A.S. and Muellbauer, J. 1980a. An almost ideal demand system. *American Economic Review* 70, 312–26.

Deaton, A.S. and Muellbauer, J. 1980b. *Economics and Consumer Behavior.* New York: Cambridge University Press.

Deaton, A.S. and Muellbauer, J. 1986. On measuring child costs, with applications to poor countries. *Journal of Political Economy* 94, 720–44.

Deaton, A.S., Ruiz-Castillo, J. and Thomas, D. 1985. The influence of household composition on household expenditure patterns: theory and Spanish evidence. Woodrow Wilson School, Princeton University, processed.

Dickey, D.A. and Fuller, W.A. 1981. Likelihood ratio statistics for autoregressive time series with a unit root. *Econometrica* 49, 1057–72.

Diewert, W.E. 1971. An application of the Shephard duality theorem: a generalized Leontief production function. *Journal of Political Economy* 79, 481–507.

Diewert, W.E. 1973. Functional forms for profit and transformation functions. *Journal of Economic Theory* 6, 284–316.

Diewert, W.E. 1974. Intertemporal consumer theory and the demand for durables. *Econometrica*, 42, 497-516.

Diewert, W.E. and Wales, T.J. 1986. Flexible functional forms and global curvature conditions. *Econometrica*.

Dixit, A.K. 1976. *Optimization in Economic Theory.* Oxford: Oxford University Press.

Dolde, W. and Tobin, J. 1971. *Monetary and Fiscal Effects on Consumption in Consumer Spending and Monetary Policy: The Linkages.* Boston: Federal Reserve Bank of Boston, Conference Series no. 5.

Duncan, G.J. and Hill, D.H. 1985. An investigation of the extent and consequences of measurement error in labor economic survey data. *Journal of Labor Economics, 508–32.*

Durlauf, S.N. and Phillips, P.C.B. 1986. Trends versus random walks in time-series analysis. Cowles Foundation Discussion Paper No. 788, Yale University, New Haven, processed.

Eichenbaum, M.S., Hansen, L.P. and Singleton, K. 1984. A time series analysis of representative agent models of consumption and leisure choice under uncertainty. Graduate School of Industrial Administration, Carnegie-Mellon University, Pittsburgh, mimeo.

Engel, E. 1895. Die lebenkosten Belgischer Arbeiter-Familien früher und jetzt. *International Statistical Institute Bulletin* 9, 1–74.

Epstein, L. 1975. A disaggregate analysis of consumer choice under uncertainty. *Econometrica* 43, 877–92.

Evans, G.B.A. and Savin, N.E. 1982. Conflict among the criteria revisited; the W, LR, and LM tests. *Econometrica* 50, 737–48.

Evans, M.K. 1967. The importance of wealth in the consumption function. *Journal of Political Economy* 75, 335–51.

Fisher, I. 1930. *The Theory of Interest.* New York: The Macmillan Company.

Flavin, M. 1981. The adjustment of consumption to changing expectations about future income. *Journal of Political Economy* 89, 974–1009.

Flemming, J.S. 1973. The consumption function when capital markets are imperfect: the permanent income hypothesis reconsidered. *Oxford Economic Papers* 25, 160–72.

Friedman, M. 1957. *A Theory of the Consumption Function.* Princeton: Princeton University Press.

Gallant, A.R. 1982. Unbiased determination of production technologies. *Journal of Econometrics* 20, 285–323.

Geary, R.C. 1949–50. A note on 'A constant utility index of the cost of living'. *Review of Economic Studies* 18, 65–6.

Ghez, G. and Becker, G.S. 1975. *The Allocation of Time and Goods over the Life-cycle.* New York: Columbia University Press.

Goldberger, A.S. 1967. Functional form and utility: a review of consumer demand theory. Social Systems Research Institute, University of Wisconsin, processed.

Gorman, W.M. 1959. Separable utility and aggregation. *Econometrica* 27, 469–81.

Gorman, W.M. 1976. Tricks with utility functions. In *Essays in economic analysis,* ed. M. Artis and A.R. Nobay, Cambridge: Cambridge University Press.

Gorman, W.M. 1981. Some Engel curves. In *Essays in the Theory and Measurement of Consumer Behaviour in honour of Sir Richard Stone,* ed. A.S. Deaton, Cambridge: Cambridge University Press.

Gorman, W.M. 1982. Facing an uncertain future. IMSS Technical Report No. 359, Stanford University, processed.

Grossman, S.J. and Shiller, R.J. 1981. The determinants of the variability of stock market prices. *American Economic Review, w Papers and Proceedings* 71, 222–7.

Hall, R.E. 1978. Stochastic implications of the life cycle-permanent income hypothesis: theory and evidence. *Journal of Political Economy* 86, 971–87.

Hall, R.E. and Mishkin, F.S. 1982. The sensitivity of consumption to transitory income: estimates from panel data on households. *Econometrica* 50, 461–81.

Hansen, L.P. and Singleton, K.J. 1982. Generalized instrumental variables estimation of non-linear rational expectations models. *Econometrica* 50, 1269–86.

Hayashi, F. 1982. The permanent income hypothesis: estimation and testing by instrumental variables. *Journal of Political Economy* 90, 895–916.

Hayashi, F. 1985a. Permanent income hypothesis and consumption durability: analysis based on Japanese panel data. *Quarterly Journal of Economics, 183–206.*

Hayashi, F. 1985b. Tests for liquidity constraints: a critical survey. Osaka University and NBER, processed. Presented at the Fifth World Congress of the Econometric Society, Cambridge, Mass., August 1985.

Heckman, J.J. 1971. Three essays on the supply of labor and the demand for goods. Unpublished PhD thesis, Princeton University.

Hicks, J.R. 1939. *Value and Capital.* Oxford: Oxford University Press.

Houthakker, H.S. 1961. An international comparison of personal saving. *Bulletin of the International Statistical Institute* 38, 55–70.

Houthakker, H.S. 1965. On some determinants of saving in developed and underdeveloped countries. In *Problems in Economic Development,* ed. A.G. Robinson, London: Macmillan.

Houthakker, H.S. and Taylor, L.D. 1970. *Consumer Demand in the United States: Analysis and Projections.* 2nd edn, Cambridge, Mass.: Harvard University Press.

Howe, H., Pollak, R.A. and Wales, T.J. 1979. Theory and time series estimation of the quadratic expenditure system. *Econometrica* 47, 1231-47.

Koskela, E. and Viven, M. 1982a. Saving and inflation: some international evidence. *Economics Letters* 9, 337–44.

Koskela, E. and Viren, M. 1982b. Inflation and savings: testing Deaton's hypothesis. *Applied Economics* 14, 579–90.

Kotlikoff, L.J. and Summers, L.H. 1981. The role of intergenerational transfers in aggregate capital accumulation. *Journal of Political Economy* 89, 706–32.

Kuznets, S. 1946. *National Income: A summary of findings.* National Bureau of Economic Research. New York: Arno Press.

Kuznets, S. 1962. Quantitative aspects of the economic growth of nations: VII: the share and structure of consumption. *Economic Development and Cultural Change* 10, 1–92.

Kydland, F.E. and Prescott, E.C. 1982. Time to build and aggregate fluctuations. *Econometrica* 50, 1345–70.

Laitinen, K. 1978. Why is demand homogeneity so often rejected? *Economics Letters* 1, 187–91.

Leff, N. 1969. Dependency rates and saving rates. *Economic Journal* 59, 886–96.

Leser, C.E.V. 1963. Forms of Engel functions. *Econometrica* 31, 694–703.

Lucas, R.E. 1976. Econometric policy evaluation: a critique. In *The Phillips Curve and Labor Markets,* ed. K. Brunner and A. Meltzer, Carnegie-Rochester Conference Series on Public Policy 1, Amsterdam: North-Holland.

Lucas, R.E. 1981. Introduction. In R.E. Lucas, *Studies in Business Cycle Theory.* Cambridge, Mass.: MIT Press.

Lucas, R.E. and Rapping, L. 1969. Real wages, employment, and inflation. *Journal of Political Economy* 77, 721–54.

MaCurdy, T.E. 1981. An empirical model of labor supply in a life-cycle setting. *Journal of Political Economy* 89, 1059–85.

Mankiw, N.G. and Shapiro, M. 1985. Trends, random walks, and tests of the permanent income hypothesis. *Journal of Monetary Economics* 16, 165–74.

Mankiw, N.G. and Shapiro, M. 1986. Do we reject too often? Small sample properties of tests of rational expectations models. *Economics Letters* 20, 139–45.

Mankiw, N.G., Rotemberg, J.J. and Summers, L.H. 1985. Intertemporal substitution in macroeconomics. *Quarterly Journal of Economics* 100, 225–51.

Meisner, J.F. 1979. The sad fate of the asymptotic Slutsky symmetry test. *Economics Letters* 2, 231–3.

Mirer, T.W. 1979. The wealth–age relationship among the aged. *American Economic Review* 69, 435–43.

Modigliani, F. 1970. The life-cycle hypothesis of saving and inter-country differences in the saving ratio. In *Induction, Growth and Trade: Essays in Honour of Sir Roy Harrod,* ed. W.A. Eltis et al., Oxford: Clarendon Press.

Modigliani, F. 1986. Life cycle, individual thrift, and the wealth of nations. *American Economic Review* 76, 297–313.

Modigliani, F. and Ando, A. 1957. Tests of the life-cycle hypothesis of savings. *Bulletin of the Oxford Institute of Economics and Statistics* 19, 99–124.

Modigliani, F. and Brumberg, R. 1954. Utility analysis and the consumption function: an interpretation of cross-section data. In *Post-Keynesian Economics,* ed. K.K. Kurihara, New Brunswick: Rutgers University Press.

Modigliani, F. and Brumberg, 1979. Utility analysis and aggregate consumption functions: an attempt at integration. In *The Collected Papers of Franco Modigliani,* ed. A. Abel, Vol. 2, Cambridge, Mass.: MIT Press.

Muellbauer, J. 1977. Testing the Barten model of household composition effects and the cost of children. *Economic Journal* 87, 460–87.

Muellbauer, J. 1980. The estimation of the Prais–Houthakker model of equivalence scales. *Econometrica* 48, 153–76.

Muellbauer, J. 1985. Habits, rationality and the life-cycle consumption function. Nuffield College, Oxford, mimeo.

Nicholson, J.L. 1976. Appraisal of different methods of estimating equivalence scales and their results. *Review of Income and Wealth* 22, 1–11.

Phillips, P.C.B. and Perron, P. 1986. Testing for a unit root in a time series regression. Cowles Foundation Discussion Paper No. 795, Yale University, New Haven, processed.

Pollak, R.A. and Wales, T.J. 1979. Welfare comparisons and equivalent scales. *American Economic Review* 69, 216–21.

Pollak, R.A. and Wales, T.J. 1980. Comparisons of the quadratic expenditure system and translog demand system with alternative specifications of demographic effects. *Econometrica* 48, 595–612.

Pollak, R.A. and Wales, T.J. 1981. Demographic variables in demand analysis. *Econometrica* 49, 1533–51.

Prais, S.J. and Houthakker, H.S. 1955. *The Analysis of Family Budgets.* Cambridge: Cambridge University Press.

Ramsey, F.P. 1928. A mathematical theory of saving. *Economic Journal* 38, 543–59.

Rothbarth, E. 1943. Note on a method of determining equivalent income for families of different composition. Appendix 4 in C. Madge (ed.), *War-time Patterns of Saving and Spending,* Occasional Paper 4, National Institute of Economic and Social Research, London.

Roy, R., 1943. *De l'utilité: contribution à la théorie des choix.* Paris: Herman.

Runkle, D.E. 1983. Liquidity constraints and the permanent income hypothesis: evidence from panel data. MIT, processed.

Samuelson, P.A. 1947–8. Some implications of linearity. *Review of Economic Studies* 15, 88–90.

Shephard, R. 1953. *Cost and Production Functions*. Princeton: Princeton University Press.

Shorrocks, A.F: 1975. The age–wealth relationship: a cross-section and cohort analysis. *Review of Economics and Statistics* 57, 155–63.

Slutsky, E. 1915. Sulla teoria del bilancio del consumatore. *Giornale degli Economisti* 15, 1–26. English translation in *Readings in Price Theory*, ed. G.J. Stigler and K. Boulding, Chicago: Chicago University Press, 1952.

Smith, J.P. 1977. Family labor supply over the life cycle. *Explorations in Economic Research* 4, 205–76.

Spinnewyn, F. 1979a. Rational habit formation. *European Economic Review* 15, 91–109.

Spinnewyn, F. 1979b. The cost of consumption and wealth in a model with habit formation. *Economics Letters* 2, 145–8.

Stigler, G.J. 1954. The early history of empirical studies of consumer behavior. *Journal of Political Economy* 62, 95–113.

Stone, J.R.N. 1954a. *The Measurement of Consumers' Expenditure and Behaviour in the United Kingdom, 1920–1938*, Volume 1. Cambridge: Cambridge University Press.

Stone, J.R.N. 1954b. Linear expenditure systems and demand analysis: an application to the pattern of British demand. *Economic Journal* 64, 511–27.

Stone, J.R.N. 1964. Private saving in Britain, past, present, and future. *The Manchester School* 32, 79–112.

Stone, J.R.N. 1966. Spending and saving in relation to income and wealth. *L'Industria*, 471–99.

Surrey, M.J.C. 1974. Saving, growth, and the consumption function. *Bulletin of the Oxford Institute of Statistics* 36, 125–42.

Thomas, D. 1986. Essays on the analysis of Engel curves in developing countries. PhD thesis, Princeton University.

Uzawa, H. 1964. Duality principles in the theory of cost and production. *International Economic Review* 5, 216–20.

Varian, H.R. 1978. *Microeconomic Analysis*. 2nd edn, New York: Norton, 1984.

Varian, H.R. 1982. The non-parametric approach to demand analysis. *Econometrica* 50, 945–73.

Wales, T.J. 1977. On the flexibility of flexible functional forms: an empirical approach. *Journal of Econometrics* 5, 183–93.

Watson, M.W. 1986. Univariate detrending method with stochastic trends. *Journal of Monetary Economics*.

Working, H. 1943. Statistical laws of family expenditure. *Journal of the American Statistical Association* 38, 43–56.

Yaari, M.E. 1965. Uncertain lifetime, life insurance, and the theory of the consumer. *Review of Economic Studies* 32, 137–50.

Zeldes, S. 1985. Consumption and liquidity constraints: an empirical investigation. The Wharton School, University of Pennsylvania, processed.

consumer surplus. Let P_i, $i = 1, 2, \ldots, n$, be the (nominal) price of commodity i that a consumer faces, and let Y be his (or her) nominal income. Assuming that the consumer is a price taker, his (or her) demand function can be written as,

$$x_i = x_i(P, Y), \qquad i = 1, 2, \ldots, n,$$

where $P = (P_1, P_2, \ldots, P_n)$.

Now consider two alternative situations. Let $Q^0 = (P^0, Y^0)$ and $Q^1 = (P^1, Y^1)$, respectively, signify the 'initial' and the 'terminal' situations. Confining himself to the case of a single price change, i.e., $P_i^0 = P_i^1$, $i \neq 1$, and $Y = Y^0$, Marshall (1920) argued that the welfare impact on the consumer can be measured by the trapezoid to the left of the demand curve $x_1(P_1, P_2^0, \ldots, P_n^0, Y^0)$ formed by the given price change. This is the famous concept of *consumer surplus* by Marshall. Although this concept did not originate with Marshall (he

apparently developed the notion after reading the works of A.A. Cournot around 1868, and was also aware of Dupuit's now well-known work, 1844), he was instrumental in popularizing this concept as an important tool for applied welfare economics, and also he duly recognized the importance of the 'approximate constancy' of the marginal utility of income. Hence, we may call such a welfare measure the *Marshall–Dupuit measure*, or the $(M–D)$*-measure*.

Assuming that consumers are alike and that their utilities can be added up, Marshall summed the individual consumer's surpluses in a market to obtain an aggregate welfare measure, and in his practical use of the concept he always placed the apostrophe in consumers' surplus after the s. With the advent of the new welfare economics and the rejection of interpersonal comparison of utilities, it has become more customary to discuss the concept in terms of a single consumer, i.e. *consumer's surplus*. To avoid the problem of social choice which bulks large in the literature, here we mainly confine ourselves to consumer's surplus. Yet, even confined to a single consumer, this concept has generated substantial debate. In fact, the debate has become more heated recently, producing various interesting claims as well as useful surveys (e.g. Chipman and Moore, 1976; Ng 1980, chap. 4; Just, Hueth and Schmitz, 1982; McKenzie, 1983; Boadway and Bruce, 1984; and Takayama, 1984). Suzumura (1985) cites 181 references on this topic.

In an early stage of these discussions, Hicks introduced the four concepts of consumer's surplus, which he attributes to Alexander Henderson. All of these are different from the Marshall–Dupuit measure. Among the four concepts, compensating variation and equivalent variation have attracted the most attention. As Hicks now puts it (1981, p. 115), the chief motive for his introduction of these four concepts is that he wished to 'extend the analysis to cover cases in which more than one price is changing'. However, under such circumstances, a new problem arises. This is the problem of whether or not the welfare measure, whatever its definition, is independent of the particular path over which prices change. That there can be (infinitely) many paths that prices can take can be illustrated in Figure 1. It is then natural to hope that consumer's surplus, however, it is defined, takes a unique value regardless of the paths of price change.

Silberberg (1972) followed the Marshall–Dupuit tradition and defined consumer's surplus for the multi-price changing

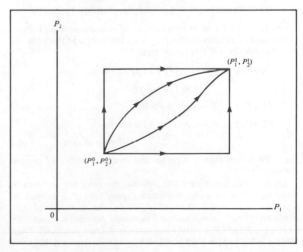

Figure 1   Paths of price changes

case by the following line integral (connecting P^0 to P^1),

$$T = -\int_{P^0}^{P^1} \sum_{i=1}^{n} x_i(P, Y^0)\, dP_i, \qquad (1)$$

which reduces to the usual (M–D)-measure when $P_i^0 = P_i^1$, $i \neq 1$ (with $P_1^1 > P_1^0$). He then found that the path independence condition requires the homotheticity of all demand functions x_i. In contrast to such a conclusion, it can be easily shown that compensating and equivalent variations automatically satisfy the path independence condition (e.g. Willig, 1979; Suzumura, 1985). Furthermore, the Hicksian measures (henceforth the *H-measures*) provide cardinal representation of the ordinal utility function. Thus they, good or bad, follow the 'ordinalist revolution' formally initiated by Hicks and Allen (1934), and yet they are 'simple, unambiguous, and allocatively operative within a Pareto context' (Mishan, 1977, p. 1).

NOTATIONS AND SOME BASICS

Here we introduce some basic materials necessary for the present topic. Consider a (usual price-taking) consumer who chooses a consumption bundle $x = (x_1, x_2, \ldots, x_n)$ so as to maximize a real-valued utility function $u(x)$ subject to the budget condition $P \cdot x (\equiv \Sigma P_i x_i) \leqslant Y$ and $x \geqslant 0$, where $Y > 0$. For simplicity, we assume that $P_i > 0$ for each i and $u_i (\equiv \partial u/\partial x_i) > 0$ for all i at the optimum, and that $u(x)$ is twice continuously differentiable. Then, assuming an interior solution, the first order conditions for an optimum are:

$$u_i(x) = \lambda P_i, \qquad i = 1, 2, \ldots, n, \qquad P \cdot x = Y, \qquad (2)$$

where λ is the Lagrangian multiplier. Clearly, $\lambda > 0$ at the optimum. Assuming that u is strictly quasi-concave, (2) furnishes a necessary and sufficient condition for a unique global maximum. From (2), we obtain the *demand functions*, $x_i = x_i(P, Y)$, $i = 1, 2, \ldots, n$, and $\lambda(P, Y)$, all of which are homogeneous of degree zero in P and Y. Assuming that $\lambda(P, Y)$ and the $x_i(P, Y)$'s are continuously differentiable, we have the *Hicks–Slutsky equation*,

$$\partial x_i/\partial P_j = S_{ij} - x_j \partial x_i/\partial Y, \qquad i, j = 1, 2, \ldots, n, \qquad (3)$$

where S_{ij} is the net substitution effect. The $n \times n$ matrix $S \equiv [S_{ij}]$ is known as the *Slutsky matrix*. Define function U by,

$$U(P, Y) = u[x(P, Y)]. \qquad \text{(indirect utility function)}$$

Clearly, $U(P, Y)$ is homogeneous of degree zero and twice continuously differentiable. Applying the envelope theorem, we at once obtain the following results.

$$\partial U(P, Y)/\partial P_i = -\lambda(P, Y)\, x_i(P, Y) < 0,$$
$$i = 1, 2, \ldots, n, \qquad (4a)$$

$$\partial U(P, Y)/\partial Y = \lambda(P, Y) > 0, \qquad (4b)$$

$$\partial U(P, Y)/\partial P_i + x_i \partial U(P, Y)/\partial Y = 0,$$
$$i = 1, 2, \ldots, n. \text{ (Roy's identity)} \qquad (4c)$$

Eq. (4b) states that λ signifies the *marginal utility of income* ('money').

Dual to the above problem, we may consider the problem of choosing an x so as to minimize expenditure $P \cdot x$ subject to $u(x) \geqslant u$ and $x \geqslant 0$. Let $x^*(P, u)$ be the solution of this problem (the *compensated demand function*), and let $e(P, u) \equiv P \cdot x^*(P, u)$ (the *minimum expenditure function*). Then letting $S^* \equiv [x_{ij}^*] \equiv [\partial x_i^*/\partial P_j]$, S^* is symmetric and negative semidefinite.

Major propositions of duality theory which are pertinent to the present topic are:

$$Y = e[P, U(P, Y)], \qquad x(P, Y) = x^*[P, U(P, Y)], \quad (5a)$$

$$x[P, e(P, u)] = x^*(P, u), \qquad (5b)$$

$$U[P, e(P, u)] = u. \qquad (5c)$$

Note that (5b), which follows from (5a), yields (3) upon differentiation in P_j where $S_{ij}(P, Y) = x_{ij}^*[P, U(P, Y)]$. Thus we may conclude that matrix S is also symmetric and negative semidefinite. Furthermore, we have: $\partial e/\partial P_j = x_j^*(P, u)$ (*Shephard (–L. McKenzie)'s lemma*).

COMPUTING THE HICKSIAN MEASURES

The results of the last section are well-known (e.g. Takayama, 1985, pp. 141–55), and are all obtainable from ordinal utility. Since the H-measures are based only on ordinal utility and are popular, we first take these up.

According to Hicks (e.g. 1956, p. 177; also Willig, 1976, p. 590), the *compensating variation* is the amount by which one would have to increase (or reduce) a person's income to make him just as well off after a change in prices as he had been in the initial situation. The compensating variation, which we shall denote by C, can be defined in symbols as:

$$U(P^0, Y^0) = U(P^1, Y^0 + C),$$
$$\{\text{or } C = e[P^1, U(P^0, Y^0)] - Y^0, \text{ by (5c)}\}. \qquad (6)$$

Given P^0 and P^1, the individual is better off compared with his initial situation if and only if $Y^1 - Y^0 > C$. On the other hand, the *equivalent variation* is defined as the amount of change in income which would have exactly the same effect upon a person's utility as a price change. Denoting the equivalent variation by E, it can be defined in symbols as:

$$U(P^1, Y^0) = U(P^0, Y^0 - E)$$
$$\{\text{or } E = Y^0 - e[P^0, U(P^1, Y^0)], \text{ by (5c)}\}. \qquad (7)$$

We may illustrate C and E diagrammatically in Figure 2, where we assume that $P_i = \text{constant}$ for all i except for 1.

An obvious difficulty of the H-measures is that they cannot be computed from empirical data since U is not observable. To overcome this, Willig (1976) argues that under certain assumptions, the (M–D)-measure can be used as an approximation to the H-measures. Seade (1978) obtains 'workable' formulas to compute the H-measures directly by assuming that all Engel curves are linear (which corresponds to Gorman's quasi-homotheticity). Hausman (1981) abandons such an assumption,

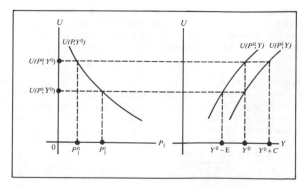

Figure 2 Compensating and equivalent variations

and attempts to obtain exact formulas to compute the H-measures by assuming that the observed demand functions are linear or log-linear. McKenzie and Pearce (1976, 1982) and McKenzie (1983) propose yet another approach to compute the H-measures, in which the Taylor expansion of the marginal utility of income plays an important role.

Vartia (1983) proposes an ingenious method to compute the H-measure. By recalling Shephard's lemma and (5b), we may obtain:

$$\frac{de}{dt} = \sum_{i=1}^{n} x_i[P(t), e] \frac{dP_i(t)}{dt}$$

where

$$\frac{de(P, u^0)}{dt} = \sum_{i=1}^{n} \frac{\partial e}{\partial P_i} \frac{dP_i}{dt}.$$

This can be viewed as an ordinary differential equation, in which $e(t)$ is the unknown function. Vartia proposed three algorithms to obtain the numerical solution of the above differential equation. His 'main algorithm' is then related to the Harberger (1971) welfare indicator. Nagatani (1984) pointed out that two of Vartia's methods are essentially the same as those used in Houthakker's well-known paper (1950) on revealed preference, and his 'main algorithm' is not particularly superior to the other two algorithms.

The recent popularity of the H-measures as indicated above seems to be based on the ordinalist revolution, for which Hicks (1946, p. 18) wrote, 'The quantitative concept of utility is not necessary to explain market phenomena. Therefore, on the principle of Occam's razor, it is better to do without it'. However, as Pareto was already well aware, this does not imply that utility cannot be cardinal (cf. Chipman, 1976). The ordinalist stance has also been shaken since the work of von Neumann and Morgenstern (1953) on the theory of behaviour under risk-taking circumstances. Following Georgescu-Roegen (1952), Chipman (1976, p. 76) also puts this metaphorically, saying 'Just because the equilibrium of a table is determined by three of its legs, we are not required by any scientific principle to assume that actual tables have only three legs, especially if direct observation suggests that they may have four'.

Regardless of which stance we adopt, we still see another important shortcoming in the H-measures. That is, we fail to see any convincing arguments in the literature as to why they should be the 'correct' welfare measures, nor do we see a clear discussion regarding which one of the H-measures we should choose when the discrepancy between them becomes great.

The discussion above refers to a single consumer. Suppose that more than one person is involved. We may, in concluding this section, ask the question whether we can use the sum of compensating variations (ΣC) as a measure of the gain or loss of the group as a whole. Putting this question in the following way, 'can we say if $\Sigma C > 0$, gainers can more than compensate losers, and the change in prices will at least lead to a potential Pareto improvement?' Boadway (1974) discovered that the answer to this question is negative. Since it is very tempting to give an affirmative answer to the above question, Ng (1980, p. 96) calls Boadway's discovery the *Boadway Paradox*.

THE CORRECT WELFARE MEASURE

To find the welfare impact of changes from Q^0 to Q^1, where $Q \equiv (P, Y)$, we first observe the following obvious relation:

$$dU = \sum_{i=1}^{n} U_i dP_i + U_Y dY,$$

where $U_i \equiv \partial U/\partial P_i$ and $U_Y \equiv \partial U/\partial Y$. It would then be natural

to *define* the welfare impact of changes in prices and income (denoted by ΔU) in terms of the following *line integral*:

$$\Delta U \equiv \int_{Q^0}^{Q^1} \left\{ \sum_{i=1}^{n} U_i dP_i + U_Y dY \right\}. \tag{8}$$

An important question here is: how do we know that the line integral on the r.h.s. of (8) is independent of the path connecting Q^0 to Q^1? However, this problem can easily be resolved by recalling the following well-known mathematical result (e.g. Apostol, 1957, pp. 280-81 and p. 292).

Lemma 1: Let $f(x)$ be continuously differentiable in an open convex subset D of the Euclidian space R^n. Then the line integral,

$$I = \int_A^B f_1(x) dx_1 + \cdots + f_n(x) dx_n, \qquad f_i \equiv \partial f/\partial x_i, \tag{9}$$

connecting every pair of end-points, A and B, in D by a piecewise smooth curve is independent of the path and I has a unique value, $I = f(A) - f(B)$.

Applying this to (8), we may at once conclude that ΔU is unique, i.e.,

$$\Delta U = U(Q^1) - U(Q^0), \tag{10}$$

and that the line integral in (8) connecting every end-point Q^0 and Q^1 by a piecewise smooth simple curve is independent of the path. Also, ΔU is homogeneous of degree zero in $Q \equiv (P, Y)$, so that ΔU is invariant with respect to changes in the unit of measurement of Q.

Furthermore, by a well-known mathematical result (e.g. Apostol, 1957, p. 293), the path independence of the line integral in (8) implies:

$$\frac{\partial}{\partial P_j} \frac{\partial U}{\partial P_i} = \frac{\partial}{\partial P_i} \frac{\partial U}{\partial P_j}$$

and

$$\frac{\partial}{\partial P_i} \frac{\partial U}{\partial Y} = \frac{\partial}{\partial Y} \frac{\partial U}{\partial P_i}, \qquad i, j = 1, 2, \ldots, n, \tag{11}$$

for all P and Y. This is satisfied since U is twice continuously differentiable (so that its Hessian matrix is symmetric). We may also assert that (11) is *sufficient* (as well as necessary) for the path independence of the line integral in (8).

To obtain the economic interpretation of (11), we obtain, by recalling (3) and (4):

$$\partial x_i/\partial P_j + x_j \partial x_i/\partial Y = \partial x_j/\partial P_i + x_i \partial x_j/\partial Y,$$

$$i, j = 1, 2, \ldots, n. \tag{12}$$

In view of (3), this condition is clearly equivalent to $S_{ij} = S_{ji}$, i.e. the symmetry condition of the Slutsky matrix. Note also that this condition provides the integrability condition of demand functions (e.g. Hurwicz, 1971). Thus, the existence of a utility function (whether ordinal or cardinal) almost trivially implies the path independence of our welfare measure, and conversely, the path independence condition requires the integrability condition, which in turn ensures the recoverability of a utility function. In summary, we have:

Theorem 1: The line integral in (8) is independent of the path, and $\Delta U = U(Q^1) - U(Q^0)$. The measure ΔU is unique depending only on Q^1 and Q^0, and is invariant with respect to changes in the unit of measurement of the P_i's and Y.

We are now ready to proceed further with our analysis. Substituting (4a) and (4b) into (8), we obtain the following fundamental formula:

$$\Delta U = \int_{Q^0}^{Q^1} \left\{ \sum_{i=1}^{n} (-\lambda x_i)\, \mathrm{d}P_i + \lambda\, \mathrm{d}Y \right\}. \tag{13}$$

From this it is clear that ΔU depends on λ, where $\lambda = \partial U / \partial Y$ signifies the *marginal utility of income* (MUI). Since λ in general depends on both P and Y, we need some assumptions, such as the 'constancy' of λ, to carry out the integration in (13) and obtain useful conclusions. In fact, Marshall (1920, p. 842), unlike Dupuit, was clearly aware of the importance of the assumption of the constant MUI. Marshall also realized that λ is not a strict constant, but it is only *approximately* constant. Unfortunately, however, the 'constancy' of MUI is subject to different interpretations.

One natural interpretation is that it is constant for all values of P and Y. However, this is impossible since U_Y is homogeneous of degree -1 in P and Y (cf. Samuelson, 1942). As Samuelson (1942) also pointed out, there are two other important interpretations of the constancy of MUI. One interpretation is that it is invariant with respect to changes in all prices, i.e.

$$U_Y(P, Y) = \gamma(Y), \qquad \text{for all } P \text{ and } Y. \tag{14}$$

According to Samuelson (1942), this assumption was made implicitly by Marshall. Since (14) implies that the demand functions are homothetic, we may, following Chipman and Moore (1976), call the interpretation in terms of (14), *the case of homothetic demands*. The second important interpretation is that MUI is independent of income and the prices of all goods except for one commodity (the 'numéraire' commodity, say, n). Namely,

$$U_Y(P, Y) = \gamma^*(P_n). \tag{15}$$

For reasons we shall explain later, we call this case *the case of vertical Engel curves*. Hicks (1941, 1946, 1956, etc.) interpreted Marshall's assumption of the constancy of MUI in the sense of (15), and such a specification is also widely used in the literature.

We now *illustrate* our approach via (13) by using these two alternative interpretations concerning the 'constancy' of MUI, where Roy's identity is useful in proving lemmas 2 and 3 below.

(A) THE CASE OF HOMOTHETIC DEMANDS: INTERPRETATION (14)
Lemma 2 (Samuelson, 1942): The constancy of MUI in the sense of (14) implies,

$$\gamma(Y) = a/Y, \qquad \text{where} \quad a \equiv \gamma(1), \tag{16}$$

and each demand function is homothetic, i.e. $x_i(P, Y) = \xi_i(P) Y$. Furthermore, (14) holds if and only if $u(x)$ can be written in the form of

$$u(x) = c_1 \log \phi(x) + c_2, \tag{17}$$

where $\phi(x)$ is homogeneous of degree one and c_1 and c_2 are some constant.

Note that $u(x)$ is (17) is *not* ordinal as it cannot be replaced by any strictly increasing transformation of itself. Using (13), (16) and $x_i = \xi_i(P) Y$, we may readily obtain:

$$\Delta U = a \log Y^1/Y^0 - a \int_{P^0}^{P^1} \sum_{i=1}^{n} \xi_i(P)\, \mathrm{d}P_i, \tag{18}$$

where $a \equiv \gamma(1)$ is a pure constant. Eq. (18) simplifies the formula obtained by Katzner (1970) and Chipman and Moore (1976). From (18), we may conclude that U is unique up to an increasing linear transformation of itself, and hence U is cardinal, and hence ΔU is also cardinal, where $\gamma(1)$ serves as the 'measuring stick' for cardinality.

When income and all prices except for P_1 are kept constant, (18') is reduced to,

$$\Delta U = - \int_{P_1^0}^{P_1^1} \xi_1(P_1, P_2^0, \ldots, P_n^0)\, \mathrm{d}P_1, \tag{18'}$$

where we set $\gamma(1) = 1$ by the proper choice of units. This corresponds to the (M–D)-measure except that x_1 is replaced by ξ_1.

We may now summarize some of the above results as follows:

Theorem 2: If the marginal utility of income is constant in the sense of (14), then ΔU is measured by (18), where we may set $a \equiv \gamma(1) = 1$. The utility measure ΔU is cardinal, where $\gamma(1)$ is the 'measuring stick', and ΔU is independent of the choice of the unit of measurement of the P_i's and Y.

Homothetic demands mean that Engel curves are all straight lines from the origin. There have been numerous budget studies which negate this assertion (at least globally), and this is often used to reject the constancy of MUI in the sense of (14). However, it may be possible to assume homothetic demands with (14) as a *local* approximation of true demand functions in the range of the price–income change from (P^0, Y^0) to (P^1, Y^1), and it is a testable hypothesis.

To forestall misunderstanding, we stress here that although (14) implies homothetic preferences (or demands), the converse does not necessarily hold. In other words, condition (14) specifies only a special class of homothetic preferences, as is clear from (17). To illustrate this, consider the utility function with two goods $u(x_1, x_2)$. If $u(x_1, x_2) = \log x_1 x_2$, then we may obtain $\lambda = 2/Y$ in which case (14) is satisfied. On the other hand, if $u(x_1, x_2) = x_1 x_2$, then we obtain $\lambda = Y/(2P_1 P_2)$, in which case (14) is *not* satisfied. Yet both utility functions $\log x_1 x_2$ and $x_1 x_2$ are homothetic and yield the *same* demand functions $x_i = Y/2P_i$, $i = 1, 2$. Note that $u = \log x_1 x_2 = 2 \log x_1^{1/2} x_2^{1/2}$ satisfies (17), while $u = x_1 x_2$ does not. This example would not be surprising, should we take the cardinalist stance. Also, this indicates that our Theorem 2 has a far-reaching implication: i.e. it can provide a basis for a scientifically legitimate theory of measurable utility. As Chipman argues, the assumption that the marginal utility of income is independent of prices is 'a proposition that carries strong empirical implications concerning consumer's preferences, which can be verified or refuted by observations on his market and demand behavior' (1982, p. 52).

(B) THE CASE OF VERTICAL ENGEL CURVES: INTERPRETATION (15)
Lemma 3 (Samuelson, 1942): Under condition (15), we have,

$$\gamma^*(P_n) = b/P_n, \qquad \text{where } b \equiv \gamma^*(1), \tag{19}$$

$$\partial x_i(P, Y)/\partial Y = 0, \qquad i = 1, 2, \ldots, n - 1. \tag{20}$$

Furthermore, (15) holds if and only if $u(x)$ can be written as,

$$u(x) = c_1 \Psi(x_1, x_2, \ldots, x_{n-1}) + (c_1 x_n + c_2), \tag{21}$$

where c_1 and c_2 are some constants.

Eq. (20) means that a change in income Y does not affect the demand for any commodities except for one commodity, commodity n. For $n = 2$, this means that the Engel curves are straight lines parallel to the axis of the numéraire commodity (commodity 2). The case of (15) was thus referred to as the case of vertical Engel curves, where commodity 2 is measured on the vertical axis. This case was popularized by Hicks (1946, pp. 38–41), in which all commodities except for commodity 1 are grouped together as a single 'composite commodity'. The assumption of vertical Engel curves is often justified for a commodity such as tea or salt, in which one person's expenditure on that commodity is a small part of his whole income. (However, see also Chipman and Moore, 1976.)

We now proceed with our analysis by setting $P_n = 1$. Letting p_i be the *normalized* price of commodity i and $p = (p_1, p_2, \ldots, p_{n-1})$, we obtain from (20),

$$x_i = h_i(p), \qquad i = 1, 2, \ldots, n-1,$$

$$x_n = h_n(p, y) \equiv y - \sum_{i=1}^{n-1} p_i h_i(p), \qquad (22)$$

where y is the income in terms of commodity n. Combining (13), (19), and (22), we obtain:

$$\Delta U = b(y^1 - y^0) - b \int_{p^0}^{p^1} \sum_{i=1}^{n-1} h_i(p) \, \mathrm{d}p_i. \qquad (23)$$

Clearly, ΔU in (23) is independent of choice of unit in measuring Q. As in (18), the utility measures U and ΔU are again cardinal, where $b \equiv \gamma^*(1)$, instead of $a \equiv \gamma(1)$, is the 'measuring stick' for cardinality.

If $n = 2$, (23) can be simplified as (by setting $b = 1$ by the choice of units):

$$\Delta U = (y^1 - y^0) - \int_{p_1^0}^{p_1^1} h_i(p) \, \mathrm{d}p_1. \qquad (23')$$

This corresponds to the formula obtained by Sono (1943, p. 95). If income is constant, this can further be reduced to,

$$\Delta U = - \int_{p_1^0}^{p_1^1} h_1(p) \, \mathrm{d}p_1. \qquad (23'')$$

This corresponds to the (M–D)-measure except that x_1 and P_1 are now replaced by h_1 and p_1, respectively.

In summary, we may conclude:

Theorem 3: Under the assumption of vertical Engel curves, (15), ΔU is measured by (23), and it is cardinal and is independent of the choice of the unit in measuring P and Y. The 'measuring stick' for cardinality is $\gamma^*(1)$.

THE HICKSIAN MEASURES UNDER THE CONSTANCY OF THE MARGINAL UTILITY OF INCOME

We now relate the two concepts of the Hicksian welfare measures, C and E, to the constancy of MUI. If λ is a constant in the sense of (14), we have formula (18). Then defining A and τ by,

$$A \equiv \int_{P^0}^{P^1} \sum_{i=1}^{n} x_i(P, Y^0) \, \mathrm{d}P_i$$

$$= Y^0 \int_{P^0}^{P^1} \sum_{i=1}^{n} \xi_i(P) \, \mathrm{d}P_i \quad \text{and} \quad \tau \equiv A/Y^0, \qquad (24)$$

we easily obtain:

$$C = Y^0(\mathrm{e}^\tau - 1). \qquad (25)$$

Note that if all the prices except for P_1 are kept constant, A measures the familiar area defined by the Marshallian triangle,

$$A = \int_{P_1^0}^{P_1^1} \xi_1(P_1, P_2^0, \ldots, P_n^0) Y^0 \, \mathrm{d}P_1. \qquad (24')$$

Likewise, the equivalent variation may be obtained from (18) and (27) as,

$$E = Y^0(1 - \mathrm{e}^{-\tau}). \qquad (26)$$

Then we may *unequivocally* conclude, for $P^0 \neq P^1$,

$$E < A < C. \qquad (27)$$

Example: Suppose the utility function is given by (17), and furthermore

$$\phi(x) \equiv x_1^{\alpha_1} x_2^{\alpha_2}, \ldots, x_n^{\alpha_n}, \quad \alpha_i > 0,$$

for all i, and

$$\sum_{i=1}^{n} \alpha_i = 1.$$

In this case, demand functions are homothetic and obtained as,

$$x_i = \alpha_i Y / P_i, \qquad i = 1, 2, \ldots, n,$$

so that $\xi_i(p) = \alpha_i / P_i$. Assume that income and the prices of all commodities except for P_1 are fixed. Then letting $z \equiv \Delta P_1 / P_1^0$, where $\Delta P_1 \equiv P_1^1 - P_1^0$, we may compute:

$$\bar{C} = (1 + z)^{\alpha_1} - 1, \qquad \tau = \alpha_1 \log(1 + z),$$

$$\bar{E} = 1 - (1 + z)^{-\alpha_1}, \qquad (28)$$

where $\bar{C} \equiv C/Y^0$, $\tau = A/Y^{0\circ}$ and $\bar{E} \equiv E/Y^0$.

The above example also shows that if z is sufficiently close to zero, we can see from (28) that C, A and E can all be approximated by $\alpha_1 z Y^0$. On the other hand, if z is not sufficiently close to zero, then the discrepancies of these three measures can be large. In particular, if $P_1^1 \to \infty$, as in the Marshallian triangle, then we may readily obtain from (28):

$$E \to Y^0, \qquad A \to \infty, \qquad C/A \to \infty.$$

Namely, the discrepancies among E, A and C can be very large as z gets large. Hence if we claim that C and E are the correct measures, then we would confront the difficulty that the discrepancies between the 'correct' measures can be infinitely large, *even* in a 'restrictive' situation in which (14) is imposed.

We may now summarize some of the above results as follows.

Theorem 4: If the marginal utility of income is constant in the sense of (14), then $-A/Y^0$ measures the true welfare change due to price changes with income constant, and we always have $E < A < C$. When $|A|$ is sufficiently small, the degree of over- and under-estimations of A by C and E are of a second order smallness. On the other hand, if $|A|$ is large, neither E nor C approximates A well; the discrepancies can be quite large.

To illustrate further the weakness of the Hicksian measures, consider a (single) price rise from P_1^0 to P_1^1, in which case the compensating variation can be illustrated by $P_1^0 AB' P_1^1$ as in Figure 3, where DD' is the ordinary demand curve and AB' is

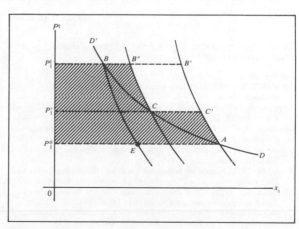

Figure 3   The Marshall–Dupuit measure and the compensating variation

the compensated one (passing through A). Note that DD' is flatter than AB' as long as the income effect is positive (as in the present case). Now suppose that the price rise takes place in two steps from P_1^0 to P_1' to P_1^1. Then the compensating variation would be the shaded area, $P_1^0 AC' P_1'$ plus $P_1' CB'' P_1^1$ in figure 3. Thus, it depends on the number of steps taken in a particular price rise. Similarly, the equivalent variation also depends on the number of steps for a particular price change. On the other hand, if we regard the price rise from P_1^0 to P_1^1 as consisting of a large number of steps, the compensating and the equivalent variations would both be close to the (M–D)-measure, $P_1^0 ABP_1^1$. Since we wish to require that the welfare measure be invariant with respect to the number of steps taken, this discussion also indicates the weakness of the H-measures.

Finally, if the constancy of MUI is interpreted in the sense of (15), then we may easily obtain the following well-known result:

$$E = A = C.$$

Namely, for the vertical Engel curve case, these three welfare measures all coincide. This result is hardly surprising, since the income effect is zero for this case, so that the compensated and the uncompensated demand curves coincide and we may recall figure 3.

CONCLUDING REMARKS

With the presence of income effects in the demand functions, H-measures cannot in general be the correct welfare measures, whereas the (M–D)-measure (with proper modifications) provides the correct welfare measure assuming the approximate constancy of MUI. Also, with the constancy of MUI, (indirect) utility can be cardinal, which conforms with the cardinalist stance of Marshall.

We may point out, however, that there can be other interesting cases in which we can carry out the computation of our welfare measure formula (13) *without* assuming the constancy of MUI (which may be too stringent an assumption for some readers). Here we only illustrated such a computation for historically important cases, i.e. (14) and (15).

Finally, we may observe that there is a close relation between the theory of consumer's surplus and that of index numbers (cf. e.g., Rader, 1976; Bruce, 1977; Vartia, 1983; Suzumura, 1985). The parallel study of both topics can be quite fruitful, though it appears that much work remains to be done in this context.

AKIRA TAKAYAMA

See also DUPUIT, ARSÈNE JULES ETIENNE JUVENAL; MARSHALL, ALFRED; PIGOU, ARTHUR CECIL.

BIBLIOGRAPHY

Apostol, T.M. 1957. *Mathematical Analysis*. Reading, Mass.: Addison-Wesley.
Bergson, A. 1975. A note on consumer's surplus. *Journal of Economic Literature* 13, March, 38–44.
Boadway, R.W. 1974. The welfare foundation of cost-benefit analysis. *Economic Journal* 84, December, 926–39.
Boadway, R.W. and Bruce, N. 1984. *Welfare Economics*. Oxford: Basil Blackwell.
Bruce, N. 1977. A note on consumer's surplus, the divisia index, and the measurement of welfare change. *Econometrica* 45, May, 1033–8.
Chipman, J.S. 1976. The Paretian heritage. *Cahiers Vilfredo Pareto, Revue européenne des sciences sociales* 14, 65–171.
Chipman, J.S. 1980. Compensating variation, consumer's surplus and welfare. *American Economic Review* 70, December, 933–49.
Chipman, J.S. 1982. Samuelson and consumption theory.

In *Samuelson and Neoclassical Economics*, ed. G.R. Feiwel, Boston: Kluwer Nijhof, 37–71.
Chipman, J.S. and Moore, J.C. 1976. The scope of consumer's surplus arguments. In *Evolution, Welfare and Time in Economics: Essays in Honor of Nicholas Georgescu-Roegen*, ed. A.M. Tang, F.M. Westfield and J.S. Worley, Lexington, Mass.: D.C. Heath, 69–123.
Dooley, P.C. 1983. Consumer's surplus: Marshall and his critics. *Canadian Journal of Economics* 16, February, 26–38.
Dupuit, J. 1844. On the measurement of the utility of public works. Trans. by R.H. Barback in *Readings in Welfare Economics*, ed. K.J. Arrow and T. Scitovsky, Homewood, Ill.: Richard D. Irwin, 1969, 255–83.
Georgescu-Roegen, N. 1952. A diagrammatic analysis of complementarity. *Southern Economic Journal* 19, July, 1–20.
Harberger, A.C. 1971. Three basic postulates for applied welfare economics: an interpretative essay. *Journal of Economic Literature* 9, September, 785–97.
Hausman, J.A. 1981. Exact consumer's surplus and deadweight loss. *American Economic Review* 71, September, 662–76.
Hicks, J.R. 1939. *Value and Capital*. 2nd edn, Oxford: Clarendon Press, 1946.
Hicks, J.R. 1941. The rehabilitation of consumer's surplus. *Review of Economic Studies* 8, February, 108–116.
Hicks, J.R. 1956. *A Revision of Demand Theory*. Oxford: Clarendon Press.
Hicks, J.R. 1981. The four consumer's surpluses. In J.R. Hicks, *Wealth and Welfare (Collected Essays on Economic Theory*, Vol. 1), Oxford: Basil Blackwell, 114–32.
Hicks, J.R. and Allen, R.G.D. 1934. A reconsideration of the theory of value. *Economica* 1, Part I, February, 52–76; Part II, May, 196–219.
Houthakker, H.S. 1950. Revealed preference and the utility function. *Economica* 17, May, 159–74.
Hurwicz, L. 1971. On the problem of integrability of demand functions. In *Preferences, Utility, and Demand*, ed. J.S. Chipman, L. Hurwicz, M.K. Richter and H.R. Sonnenschein, New York: Harcourt Brace Jovanovich, 194–214.
Just, R.E., Hueth, D.L. and Schmitz, A. 1982. *Applied Welfare Economics and Public Policy*. Englewood Cliffs, NJ: Prentice-Hall.
Katzner, D.W. 1970. *Static Demand Theory*. New York: Macmillan.
McKenzie, G.W. 1979. Consumer's surplus without apology: comment. *American Economic Review* 69, June, 465–74.
McKenzie, G.W. 1983. *Measuring Economic Welfare*. New York: Cambridge University Press.
McKenzie, G.W. and Pearce, I.F. 1976. A new operational procedure for evaluating economic policies. *Review of Economic Studies* 43, October, 465–8.
McKenzie, G.W. and Pearce, I.F. 1982. Welfare measurement – a synthesis. *American Economic Review* 72, September, 669–82.
Marshall, A. 1890. *Principles of Economics*. 8th edn, London, Macmillan, 1920.
Mishan, E.J. 1977. The plain truth about consumer surplus. *Zeitschrift für Nationalökonomie* 37, 1–24.
Nagatani, H. 1984. Algorithms for the Hicksian measures of consumer's surplus: Professor Houthakker revaluated. *Osaka University Economics (Osaka Daigaku Keizaigaku)* 34, 135–46 (in Japanese).
Neumann, J. von and Morgenstern, O. 1944. *Theory of Games and Economic Behavior*. 3rd edn, Princeton: Princeton University Press, 1953.
Ng, Y.K. 1980. *Welfare Economics*. New York: Wiley.
Rader, T. 1976. Equivalence of consumer surplus, the Divisia index of output, and Eisenberg's addilog social utility. *Journal of Economic Theory* 13, August, 58–66.
Samuelson, P.A. 1942. Constancy of the marginal utility of income. In *Studies in Mathematical Economics and Econometrics, In Memory of Henry Schultz*, ed. O. Lange, F. McIntyre and T.O. Yntema, Chicago: University of Chicago Press, 75–91.
Samuelson, P.A. 1947. *Foundations of Economic Analysis*. Cambridge, Mass.: Harvard University Press (enlarged edn, 1983).
Seade, J.K. 1978. Consumer's surplus and linearity of Engel curves. *Economic Journal* 88, September, 479–96.
Silberberg, E. 1972. Duality and the many consumer's surpluses. *American Economic Review* 62, December, 942–52.

Sono, M. 1943. On Dupuit's relative utility from the point of view of choice theory. *Economic Essays (Keizai Ronso)* 57, 88–97 (in Japanese).

Suzumura, K. 1985. Consumer's surplus and welfare evaluation. *Economic Review (Keizai Kenkyu)* 36, January, 53–66 (in Japanese).

Takayama, A. 1974. *Mathematical Economics.* Hinsdale, Ill.: Dryden Press; 2nd edn, New York: Cambridge University Press, 1985.

Takayama, A. 1984. Consumer's surplus, path independence, compensating and equivalent variations. *Zeitschrift für die gesamte Staatswissenschaft* 140, December, 594–625.

Vartia, Y.O. 1983. Efficient methods of measuring welfare change and compensated income in terms of ordinary demand functions. *Econometrica* 51, January, 79–98.

Willig, R.D. 1976. Consumers' surplus without apology. *American Economic Review* 66, September, 589–97.

Willig, R.D. 1979. Consumers' surplus without apology, reply. *American Economic Review* 69, June, 469–74.

consumption, conspicuous. *See* CONSPICUOUS CONSUMPTION.

consumption and production. Neoclassical economic analysis is carried out within a conceptual framework that views the economic process as a 'one way avenue' leading from 'factors of production' to 'consumption goods' (Sraffa, 1960, p. 93). This stands in striking contrast to the approach of classical political economy which views the system of consumption and production as a circular process. This perspective was first developed by Quesnay (1759) and elaborated by Marx (1859) in his analysis of the economy in general. Marx developed a distinction between 'production and productive consumption' and 'consumption and consumptive production' and related this to the concepts of exchange and distribution. This distinction fell into disuse with the rise of neoclassical economics but has been rehabilitated by Sraffa (1960) in his famous critique of modern economics. The concept 'production and productive consumption' provides the general conceptual framework within which his particular theory of commodities is elaborated (see Sraffa, 1960, p. 3). Sraffa's exposition not only advances our understanding of the theory of commodities, it also enables us to grasp the essence of Marx's important distinction between consumption and production. Marx expressed himself in rather obscure Hegelian terms and Sraffa's simple numerical examples clarify much of Marx's argument.

Following Sraffa, let us suppose that an extremely simple society is producing just enough wheat and iron to maintain itself. If 400 quarters of wheat (hereafter 400W) were produced using 280W and 12 tons of iron (12I) and 1/2 of the annual labour supply (1/2L) as inputs, while 20I were produced using 120W, 8I and 1/2L, then the methods of production and productive consumption can be tabulated as follows:

$$1/2L + 280W + 12I \rightarrow 400W$$

$$1/2L + 120W + 8I \rightarrow 20I$$

In order for the process to be repeated the wheat industry must exchange 120W for 12I. This restores the original distribution of products and enables the process to be repeated.

A three-product model takes us from barter to triangular trade: an n-product model to more complex forms of exchange and distribution.

The general formulation of the concept 'production and productive consumption' implicit in Sraffa's analysis is:

$$labour + things \rightarrow things.$$

In other words, the methods of production and productive consumption describe the process of the production of things by means of things and labour. The production by commodities by means of commodities is one historically specific form of these general relations. The emergence of things and labour as commodities presupposes private property and the emergence of a class of proletarians (Marx, 1867). This is only one of many social forms that things and labour can take. In tribal economies, for example, things and labour assume the social form of gifts. The social precondition for this to arise is a relatively egalitarian distribution of land between clans. Social data of this kind mean that the principles governing the exchange and distribution of products will vary greatly from economy to economy. In a 'pure' tribal economy, for example, profit maximization is not the central organizing principle of economic life and wages, prices and profits are not be found (Polanyi, 1944).

A corollary of this general formulation of production is that 'consumption and consumptive production' can be described as follows:

$$things + people \rightarrow people.$$

In other words 'consumption and consumptive production' describes the methods of production of people by means of people and things.

Neither Marx nor Sraffa analysed these relations which under capitalism would be called the 'household economy' or 'kinship'. However, anthropologists who have studied third world tribal and peasant societies have tended to focus almost exclusively on these relations, a fact, I would suggest, which tells something about the relative importance of production and consumption in capitalist and tribal/peasant societies respectively.

Some indication of what is involved in this concept of consumption can be gleaned by elaborating its meaning in the context of Sraffa's 'extremely simple economy'. Suppose that the iron and wheat were produced by two different households, each household consisting of a father (M), a mother (F), a boy (m) and girl (f). Reproduction of the households, and hence of labour, requires that the children set up new households and produce their own children. Incestuous relations aside, it is clear that the households must exchange children in a way that is analogous to the exchange of wheat for iron discussed above. This can be seen from the following formulation of the relations of consumption and consumptive production for this two-household economy:

$$M_1 + F_2 \rightarrow m_1 + f_1$$

$$M_2 + F_1 \rightarrow m_2 + f_2$$

where the subscripts represent the respective households. This particular example is an example of what anthropologists call 'cross cousin' marriage or 'sister exchange'. By tracing the relationships out it will be seen that a man marries his mother's brother's daughter who is also his father's sister's daughter. Take m_1 for example. His father is M_1, his father's sister is F_1, and the latter's daughter is f_2 with whom he will set up a household in the next generation. Tracing the relationships through m_1's mother (F_2) it is obvious that f_2 is also his mother's brother's daughter. Relations of this kind are very important in clan-based societies where a number of households, usually related either matrilineally or patrilineally, occupy a common piece of territory and forbid marriage within the households that make up the clan. In our own society, where the clan has no operational significance, and where marriage is a matter of personal choice rather than a formal arrangement between groups, the political and economic significance of kinship and marriage is relatively unimportant (Gregory, 1982).

Every economic analysis of a particular socio-economic form such as 'profits', 'prices' or 'wages' involves, either implicitly or explicitly, a general conceptual framework within which the analysis is carried out. The general model implicit in Quesnay's analysis of 18th-century French agriculture has been elaborated and developed to provide an extremely useful framework not only for the development of a 20th-century theory of the value and distribution of commodities but also for the analysis of comparative economic systems. By focusing on the circular process of production and reproduction, consumption becomes a dynamic process rather than the dead end of a one way avenue.

C. A. GREGORY

See also ECONOMIC ANTHROPOLOGY.

BIBLIOGRAPHY
Gregory, C.A. 1982. *Gifts and Commodities*. London: Academic Press.
Marx, K. 1859. *A Contribution to the Critique of Political Economy*. London: Lawrence & Wishart, 1971.
Marx, K. 1867. *Capital*, Vol. I. Moscow: Progress.
Polanyi, K. 1944. *The Great Transformation*. New York: Rinehart.
Quesnay, F. 1759. The 'Tableau Economique'. In *The Economics of Physiocracy*, ed. R. L. Meek, London: George Allen, 1962.
Sraffa, P. 1960. *Production of Commodities by Means of Commodities*. Cambridge: Cambridge University Press.

consumption function. Keynes (1936) introduced the consumption function as the relationship between consumption and income. Although Keynes (pp. 95–6) believed this relationship 'a fairly stable function', substantial shifts in the function were soon observed by empirical workers. Much work in the post-World War II era achieved functional forms by the 1970s which admirers and critics alike could agree were relatively shiftless. Most recent work has considered not functional form but whether or not observed changes in consumption are consistent with models of efficient markets.

THE KEYNESIAN CONCEPTION. Keynes conceived of the consumption function as relating consumption to disposable income as these are now conventionally measured in the national income accounts. These concepts were basic to the model of *The General Theory* and Keynes was doubtless pedagogically correct to posit a simple relationship which could be refined by future research.

The need for refinement became apparent shortly. In longer time series, consumption seemed to vary around a constant fraction of disposable income. In contrast, consumption functions fitted to depression-era or cross-section data seemed to indicate that this ratio (which Keynes called the average propensity to consume or APC) declined as disposable income rose. In other words, these studies estimated that the derivative of consumption with respect to disposable income (the marginal propensity to consume or MPC) was less than the APC.

Alvin Hansen (1939) among others predicted that a *secular stagnation* would result unless government spending filled this growing gap between output and consumption. When the gap failed to appear, the time was ripe for more sophisticated theories of the relationship between consumption and income. These theories were the earliest and perhaps still most successful resorts to microeconomic foundations for macroeconomics.

PERMANENT LIFE-CYCLES. In the early 1950s our two dominant models of consumption developed: the permanent-income and life-cycle hypotheses. While these models were once viewed as competing, they can now be seen as complementary with differences in emphasis which serve to illuminate different significant problems. Both models emphasized the distinction between consumer expenditures measured by the national income accounts and pure consumption which was to be explained by optimal allocation of present and future resources over time. The permanent income hypothesis (PIH) stressed stochastic variations in income (and consumption) over time and viewed saving in terms of a bequest motive. The life-cycle hypothesis (LCH) stressed predictable variations in income (and consumption) over the life cycle and viewed saving as resulting from the greater wealth and numbers of younger savers in comparison to older dissavers.

The original published references are to Friedman (1957) for the PIH and Modigliani and Brumberg (1954) for the LCH. Given the delays in NBER publication of Friedman's work which was widely circulated in manuscript form, the two hypotheses are generally regarded as distinct, contemporaneous responses to the described conflict between earlier studies and Simon Kuznets's data on the national income accounts for the 20th century. From the perspective of the monumental careers of the two principal proponents, priority does not seem an issue that need be resolved here.

The PIH relates (pure) consumption to the perpetuity stream that could be consumed forever. The agent is typically regarded as an infinitely lived individual. This represents the underlying notion of a family whose generations are linked by operative transfers from parent to child or vice-versa. Saving arises to equate the ratio of marginal utility of present and future consumption to the marginal rate of transformation implicit in market (real) interest rates. In this way the PIH is said to emphasize the bequest motive for saving.

In contrast, the strict LCH had individuals consuming their entire endowments over their lifetime. Saving was supposed to arise because young workers were more numerous and wealthy (due to technological progress) than the older generation who were dissaving to finance retirement. This provides an avenue by which faster growth can increase saving. Alternatively, as discussed below, factors such as social security which change the extent of mismatch between lifetime consumption and income patterns are predicted to have profound effects on aggregate saving.

These approaches – and their synthesis with intergenerationally linked utility functions – have led to a rich literature quite apart from the consumption function, but those developments are beyond the scope of this essay.

From the point of view of the consumption function per se, the PIH and LCH imply that pure consumption is a fraction (variable in principle but rarely in practice) of wealth or permanent income. Here wealth is inclusive of human as well as non-human capital and permanent income is a (conventionally constant) long-term *ex ante* real interest rate times this wealth. (Note that, contrary to Sargent (1978) and others this wealth is not the discounted present value of expected future income to the extent, as in the PIH, that future income is expected to rise through planned saving.) The empirical estimation of wealth or permanent income became a central issue in the specification of the consumption function.

Friedman proposed a computationally simple estimator of permanent income as a geometrically weighted average of past income. Since on this scheme, permanent income changes – besides normal growth – by a fraction, say β, of the difference between current income and permanent income, Friedman related this scheme to the adaptive-expectations approach recently introduced by his student Phillip Cagan (1956).

Modigliani and his associates proxied normal labour income by current income and the product of this variable and the unemployment rate and attempted to measure non-human wealth by collecting estimates of the national balance sheet at market values. In principle, this method seemed more clearly related to the underlying framework than Friedman's permanent-income proxy, but in practice it suffered several comparative disadvantages: (1) major components of non-human wealth had no market valuation; (2) the wealth estimates were not part of the national income accounts and competing variants were available with substantial delay and at irregular intervals; (3) for forecasting purposes, substantial additional equations were required to forecast (often poorly) future movements in wealth.

Darby (1974) reconciled these empirical measures of wealth by demonstrating that under the PIH, Friedman's geometrically weighted measure could be derived as the constant real interest rate β times a (backward-looking) perpetual inventory of wealth. This β value was estimated as about 0.10 per annum in contrast to higher values such as Friedman's 0.35 per annum. These higher values were explained by biases that arise as data deviate from pure consumption toward expenditures by consumers.

Empirical work on consumption functions has frequently floundered on the use of theories of pure consumption to explain data which are in whole or part consumer expenditures. Both the PIH and LCH were theories of pure consumption. Modigliani and Ando provided one link to consumer expenditures in their MPC model by modelling household investment in durable goods analogously to firm's investment behaviour. Operating in the PIH tradition, Darby (1972, 1974) argued that aggregate transitory income represented a change in wealth, part of which change would be invested in consumers' durable goods. (Darby (1972) in particular argued that because transitory income is received in non-human form, a disproportionate effect on durable-goods purchases may arise during the adjustment process, a result which explains the results of Hayashi, 1982.) Darby (1975, 1977–8) later combined pure consumption and durable investment equations to obtain a unified consumer expenditure function which avoided some of the inherent difficulties in dividing consumer expenditures into durable and nondurable portions.

The PIH and LCH thus evolved to explain aggregate consumer expenditures by wealth as a determinant of pure consumption and by *changes* in wealth and other variables which determine household investment in durable goods. The correlation of the determinants of this household investment with short-run (transitory) fluctuations in income explain a MPC which is substantial in magnitude even though substantially below the APC.

This brief development has omitted discussion of alternative views of the consumption function. Perhaps the most notable of these is the view that the substantial value of the MPC reflects liquidity constraints which prevent a substantial share of consumers (measured by wealth and consumption) from following their optimal intertemporal consumption plan. The author of this essay regards these alternative views as providing qualification of the dominant wealth-based view.

EFFICIENT-MARKET APPROACHES. Hall (1978) proposed to sidestep Friedman's backward-looking measure of wealth as well as the substantial empirical problems involved in measuring the market value of wealth. Instead, he posed the question of whether or not changes in consumption can be modelled empirically as determined by 'news'. Specifically, the assertion is that if wealth estimates and hence consumption are based on rational expectations, no past information including past changes in consumption or income should affect current changes in consumption.

Hall (1978) answered his question affirmatively, Flavin (1981) dissented, but Hayashi (1982) showed that excess sensitivity of spending to changes in wealth appeared to be confined to consumers' durable goods purchases. Taken as a whole, these studies seem to confirm the basic Friedman–Modigliani conceptions that aggregate consumption as determined by wealth but that it is important to distinguish between consumer expenditures and consumption.

BEQUEST VERSUS LIFE-CYCLE SAVING. Saying that consumers optimally allocate wealth leaves several important questions unanswered: Do consumers have operative linkages in utility functions across generations? Are consumers able to see through the veil of government to the ultimate production possibilities faced by society? If the first of these questions is answered affirmatively, transfer programmes such as social security which change the life-cycle pattern of income receipts will not affect aggregate consumption and saving. (The representative infinitely lived individual does not care whether he or she pays social security taxes which are refunded as equal benefits. Intergenerational transfers can be adjusted so that this representation is acceptable where utility functions are linked across generations.) If the second question is also answered affirmatively, then Ricardian equivalence holds (it is irrelevant whether government taxes or borrows) and the relevant income concept for the aggregate consumption function is net national product less government spending for goods and services.

Feldstein (1974) claimed that aggregate saving had been significantly reduced by the US social security programme. As pointed out by Barro (1978), this effect would not arise with intergenerationally linked utility functions. Using different methodology, White (1978) and Darby (1979) concluded that life-cycle motives accounted for an at most small fraction of aggregate saving and wealth. Kotlikoff and Summers (1981) relaxed Darby's assumptions on smooth growth of population and labour income without substantially changing the estimates on the range of assets attributable to life-cycle motives. These estimates seem to suggest that intergenerational linkages are indeed very important, as assumed by the PIH. The life-cycle effects highlighted in the LCH would appear more important for analysing cross-sectional data than as determinants of aggregate consumption.

The Ricardian equivalence idea was urged by Barro (1974) and Kochin (1974). It requires a certain suspension of disbelief to assume that bonds and taxes have equivalent effects on consumer behaviour, but the data are not very inconsistent with that notion. Indeed recent studies by Seater (1982) and Kormendi (1983) provide some evidence that Ricardian equivalence is a better working hypothesis than its denial.

CONCLUSIONS. The consumption function suggested by Keynes provided a useful challenge to theoretical and empirical economists. The relationship between changes in consumer expenditures and current income has been explained generally in a way which is consistent with microeconomic foundations and which is adequate in a multitude of specifications for most forecasting purposes. (Technical differences among empirical specifications are as large in number as they are uninteresting to the nonspecialist.) For policy analytic purposes, two key questions are outstanding: are life-cycle effects significant in the aggregate, and do individuals effectively see through government? This author's reading of the evidence suggests answers of no and maybe, but it is hard to put much certainty in any answer unless one starts with dogmatic priors.

The consumption function has faded as a topic of intense research largely because of the success of previous work in achieving a workable consensus. The unsettled issues, however, have crucial policy implications and there is much value yet to be added.

Michael R. Darby

See also CONSUMERS' EXPENDITURE; KEYNES'S GENERAL THEORY; LIFE-CYCLE HYPOTHESIS; REAL BALANCES; RELATIVE INCOME HYPOTHESIS; WEALTH EFFECT.

BIBLIOGRAPHY

Barro, R.J. 1974. Are government bonds net wealth? *Journal of Political Economy* 82(6), November–December, 1095–117.

Barro, R.J. 1978. *The Impact of Social Security on Private Saving: Evidence from the U.S. Time Series*. Washington, DC: American Enterprise Institute.

Cagan, P. 1956. The monetary dynamics of hyperinflation. In *Studies in the Quantity Theory of Money*, ed. M. Friedman, Chicago: University of Chicago Press.

Darby, M.R. 1972. The allocation of transitory income among consumers' assets. *American Economic Review* 62(5), December, 928–41.

Darby, M.R. 1974. The permanent income theory of consumption – a restatement. *Quarterly Journal of Economics* 88(2), May, 228–50.

Darby, M.R. 1975. Postwar U.S. consumption, consumer expenditures, and saving. *American Economic Review* 65(2), May, 217–22.

Darby, M.R. 1977–8. The consumer expenditure function. *Explorations in Economic Research* 4(5), Winter/Spring, 645-74.

Darby, M.R. 1979. *The Effects of Social Security on Income and the Capital Stock*. Washington, DC: American Enterprise Institute.

Feldstein, M. 1974. Social security, induced retirement, and aggregate capital accumulation. *Journal of Political Economy* 82(5), September/October, 905–26.

Flavin, M.A. 1981. The adjustment of consumption to changing expectations about future income. *Journal of Political Economy* 89(5), October, 974–1009.

Friedman, M. 1957. *A Theory of the Consumption Function*. NBER General Series, Vol. 63, Princeton: Princeton University Press.

Hall, R.E. 1978. Stochastic implications of the life cycle – permanent income hypotheses: theory and evidence. *Journal of Political Economy* 86(6), December, 971–87.

Hansen, A.H. 1939. Economic progress and declining population growth. *American Economic Review* 29, March, 1–15.

Hayashi, F. 1982. The permanent income hypothesis: estimation and testing by instrumental variables. *Journal of Political Economy* 90(5), October, 895–916.

Keynes, J.M. 1936. *The General Theory of Employment, Interest, and Money*. New York: Harcourt, Brace, and Co.

Kochin, L.A. 1974. Are future taxes anticipated by consumers? *Journal of Money, Credit, and Banking* 6(3), August, 385–94.

Kormendi, R.C. 1983. Government debt, government spending, and private sector behavior. *American Economic Review* 73(5), December, 994–1010.

Kotlikoff, L.J. and Summers, L.H. 1981. The role of intergenerational transfers in aggregate capital accumulation. *Journal of Political Economy* 89(4), August, 706–32.

Modigliani, F. and Brumberg, R. 1954. Utility analysis and the consumption function: an interpretation of cross-section data. In *Post Keynesian Economics*, ed. K.E. Kurihara, New Brunswick, NJ: Rutgers University Press.

Sargent, T.J. 1978. Rational expectations, econometric exogeneity, and consumption. *Journal of Political Economy* 86(4), August, 673–70.

Seater, J.J. 1982. Are future taxes discounted? *Journal of Money, Credit, and Banking* 14(3), August, 376–89.

White, B.B. 1978. Empirical tests of the life cycle hypothesis. *American Economic Review* 68(4), September, 647–60.

consumption-loan models. *See* INTERGENERATIONAL MODELS; OVERLAPPING GENERATIONS MODEL.

consumption sets. The idea of consumption sets was introduced into general equilibrium theory in July 1954 in Arrow and Debreu (1954, pp. 268–9) and Debreu (1954, p. 588), the name itself appearing only in the latter paper. Later expositions were given by Debreu (1959) and Arrow and Hahn (1971) and a more general discussion by Koopmans (1957, Essay 1). Although there have been several articles concerned with non-convex consumption sets (e.g. Yamazaki, 1978), in more recent years their role in general equilibrium theory has been muted, especially in approaches that use global analysis (see e.g. Mas-Colell, 1985, p. 69). Such sets play no role in partial equilibrium theories of consumer's demand, even in such modern treatments as Deaton and Muellbauer (1980). Since general equilibrium theory prides itself on precision and rigour (e.g. Debreu, 1959, p. x), it is odd that on close examination the meaning of consumption sets becomes unclear. Indeed, three quite different meanings can be distinguished within the various definitions presented in the literature. These are given below (in each case the containing set is the commodity space, usually R^n): M1 The consumption set C1 is that subset on which the individual's preferences are defined. M2 The consumption set C2 is that subset delimited by a natural bound on the individual's supply of labour services, i.e. 24 hours a day. M3 The consumption set C3 is the subset of all those bundles, the consumption of any one of which would permit the individual to survive. Each definition in the literature can (but here will not) be classified according to which of these meanings it includes. In probably the best known of them (Debreu, 1959, ch. 4), the consumption set appears to be the intersection of all three subsets C1–C3. M1 is plain. After all, preferences have to be defined on *some* proper subset of the commodity space, since the whole space includes bundles with some inadmissibly negative coordinates. M2 is also reasonable, although a full treatment of heterogeneous labour services does raise problems for what is meant by an Arrow–Debreu 'commodity' (see e.g. that of Arrow–Hahn, 1971, pp. 75–6). It is M3 that gives real difficulty, both in itself and in relation to the others.

First, there is little reason to expect either C1 or C3 to be a subset of the other, and so still less to expect M1 and M3 to define the same set. No individual would have any problem in preferring one bundle, the consumption of which would ensure her survival, to a second bundle, the consumption of which would result in her death by starvation. However, she might well prefer the second bundle to a third, whose consumption would cause her to die from thirst (the representation of such preferences by a real-valued utility function might pose problems, but that is another matter). On the other hand, the same individual might not be able to rank in order of preference two bundles each of which contains exotic food and drink, even though fully assured that the consumption of either bundle would allow her to survive.

More importantly, M3 implicitly introduces *consumption* activities, the actual eating and drinking and sheltering that are essential to survival. Such activities constitute what are sometimes called, by analogy with production, the consumption technology. Some partial equilibrium models, such as 'the new home economics' and the theory of characteristics, have treated aspects of such technologies but so far general equilibrium theory has not. In particular, Arrow–Debreu theory has not done so. As a consequence (and unlike some forms of the classical 'corn model') it does not give a coherent account of the birth and death of individual persons, any more than it does of the birth and death of individual firms (*see* GENERAL EQUILIBRIUM). Hence the third meaning M3, which in effect presumes that the model contains such an account when it does not, is hard to interpret. One major difficulty of interpretation arises with the Slater-like condition that each individual's endowment of goods and services, valued at the competitive prices $p*$, should be strictly greater than $\inf\{\langle x,p*\rangle: x\epsilon C\}$, where $\langle .,.\rangle$ denotes inner product and C is 'the' consumption set (see COST MINIMIZATION AND UTILITY MAXIMIZATION). This condition is important in proofs of existence of competitive equilibrium, to ensure for example that the budget correspondence is continuous, or that a compensated equilibrium is a competitive equilibrium. It is itself guaranteed by assumptions (discussed by McKenzie, 1981, pp. 821–5) on the relations between 'individual' consumption sets and the aggregate production set.

If C is taken to contain C3 then the assumptions just referred to imply that every consumer survives in every competitive equilibrium, not merely for one period but over the whole (finite) Arrow–Debreu span. This is a breathtaking assertion of fact which recalls irresistibly Hicks's wry observation: 'Pure economics has a remarkable way of producing rabbits out of a hat – apparently *a priori* propositions which apparently refer to reality. It is fascinating to try to discover how the rabbits got in' (1939, p. 23).

On the other hand if C is taken to be C1, then the assumptions take on a purely technical (and so less objectionable) aspect, whose role is essentially to ensure that the system stays within the (relative) interior of the sets concerned and so displays appropriate continuity. But then there is no presumption that individual agents survive in a competitive equilibrium, even for one period (cf. Robinson, 1962, p. 3). The multi-period versions of the Arrow–Debreu model are then at risk, since individuals disappear and take their labour service endowments with them. This should not come as a surprise – the problems of time in economics are really too complicated to be overcome simply by adding more dimensions to the one-period model.

Some models that include C3 in C attempt to justify Slater-like conditions directly, on the grounds that 'Not many economies in the present day are so extremely laissez faire as to permit people to starve' (Gale and Mas-Colell, 1975, p. 12). This justification clearly fails as long as the behaviour of the public agency whose actions allegedly prevent such starvation is not modelled *explicitly*, like that of the private agents.

It is usually assumed that consumption sets are bounded below, closed and convex. The first two assumptions are innocuous but the third poses issues of a conceptual kind, which spring from difficulties in interpreting the idea of a convex combination $x^1 = tx^1 + (1-t)x^2$ of two bundles x^1 and x^2, where $t\epsilon [0,1]$. Consider the example, sometimes used, in which x^1 is a house in London and x^2 a house in Paris. We cannot take seriously the claim that x^1 is a house in the Channel, so t cannot refer to distance. An alternative claim that t refers to the proportion of the period that is spent in London could arise from many different finite partitions of the time interval, not all of which need to be ranked equally by the individual. In effect, convexity of the consumption set comes down to the divisibility of consumer goods, an assumption which in the past has proved not such a bad approximation if one is interested mainly in general equilibrium aspects of market demand, and representative rather than actual consumers. Indivisibilities of producer goods are of course much more serious.

PETER NEWMAN

See also ARROW–DEBREU MODEL; COST MINIMIZATION AND UTILITY MAXIMIZATION; GENERAL EQUILIBRIUM; INDIVISIBILITIES.

BIBLIOGRAPHY
Arrow, K.J. and Debreu, G. 1954. Existence of an equilibrium for a competitive economy. *Econometrica* 22, 265–90.
Arrow, K.J. and Hahn, F.H. 1971. *General Competitive Analysis*. San Francisco: Holden-Day.
Deaton, A. and Muellbauer, J. 1980. *Economics and Consumer Behaviour*. Cambridge: Cambridge University Press.
Debreu, G. 1954. Valuation equilibrium and Pareto optimum. *Proceedings of the National Academy of Sciences* 40(7), 588–92.
Debreu, G. 1959. *Theory of Value*. Cowles Commission Monograph No. 17. New York: Wiley.
Gale, D. and Mas-Colell, A. 1975. An equilibrium existence theorem for a general model without ordered preferences. *Journal of Mathematical Economics* 2, 9–15.
Hicks, J.R. 1939. *Value and Capital*. Oxford: Clarendon Press.
Koopmans, T.C. 1957. *Three Essays on the State of Economic Science*. New York: McGraw-Hill.
McKenzie, L.W. 1981. The classical theorem on existence of competitive equilibrium. *Econometrica* 49, 819–41.
Mas-Colell, A. 1985. *The Theory of General Economic Equilibrium. A Differentiable Approach*. Cambridge: Cambridge University Press.
Robinson, J.V. 1962. The basic theory of normal prices. *Quarterly Journal of Economics* 76(1), 1–20.
Yamazaki, A. 1978. An equilibrium existence theorem without convexity assumptions. *Econometrica* 46, 541–55.

consumption taxation. Consumption taxes may be levied either as direct or indirect taxes. Indirect taxes on consumption include excise duties, wholesale or retail sales taxes, value added taxes, or other taxes on intermediate transactions, such as property taxes paid by business. The final incidence of these latter taxes may be calculated on the basis of assumptions about shifting and about the structure of production (see, e.g., Pechman and Okner, 1974; Nicholson and Britton, 1976).

Indirect consumption taxes may be varied according to commodity type. Sales taxes and value added taxes frequently have several rate bands, reflecting perceptions of the degree of luxuriousness of the commodity or of the incomes of those who purchase it. A direct consumption tax, by contrast, is based, not on the nature of the commodity, but on the aggregate consumption of the purchaser, and might be levied at progressive rates based on aggregate expenditure.

There is a long tradition of support for consumption rather than income as the principal tax base – a tradition inaugurated by Hobbes and strongly supported by John Stuart Mill and Irving Fisher. The seminal exposition of the argument for direct expenditure taxation is provided by Kaldor (1955) and this theme has more recently been developed by Meade (1978) and others. A direct tax on consumption would not be levied by compilation of aggregate household expenditure, but by indirect monitoring of net receipts from employment, investment and business activities. For this reason it is described by some writers (e.g., Andrew, 1974) as a 'cash-flow income tax'.

One argument favouring consumption taxes is that individuals should be assessed on what they take out of the common pool (their consumption) rather than in what they put in (their income). Thus Hobbes contrasted the burdens on a taxpayer who 'laboureth much, and, sparing the fruits of his labour' with that of another who 'liveth idley and splendeth all he gets', and Kaldor essayed a similar comparison between an Indian prince with a stock of gold and a beggar outside his palace gates, each of whom would pay no tax because they had no income.

But these arguments are less convincing on closer scrutiny. Over an individual's lifetime, what he takes out is necessarily equal to what he puts in, subject only to any gifts which he may receive or make. Thus the characters in Hobbes's or Kaldor's examples would enjoy different burdens at other times in their lifetime. Hobbes's taxpayer would pay when he chose to spend the fruits of his labour – Kaldor's prince when he saved to buy his stock of gold. Seen from this lifetime perspective, in fact, the consumption tax imposes the same burden on everyone with the same present value of lifetime consumption; an income tax discriminates in favour of those with accelerated consumption and against those who consume late in life.

Mill's principal concern was for the double taxation of savings implicit in an income tax, which taxes both savings and the return from savings, a form of double taxation which consumption taxation avoids. However the relevant economic issue is not how *often* something is taxed, but how heavily it is taxed. An income tax has the effect of taxing deferred consumption more heavily than current consumption. This is a distortion of consumer choice, but any feasible tax system necessarily involves some distortion of choice, and the issue to be considered is whether this particular one is more damaging, relative to the revenue it raises, than other effects of the tax system.

This issue has been a recent subject of both theoretical and empirical exploration. The theoretical issue concerns the appropriate relationship between the rates of taxation on present and future consumption. These will be identical if the utility function is separable as between consumption and leisure, and preferences are homothetic over consumption at different dates. Although these are not unreasonable assumptions, it is evident that only in special cases could one expect to find either that tax rates on consumption at all times should be identical or that they should be related in the complex and discriminatory way implied by an income tax. The importance of the distortions which result from the 'double taxation of savings' depends on the elasticity of supply or savings, a subject on which evidence is conflicting.

The incentive to work is generally of more concern to those who are disturbed by disincentive effects of taxation, and it is sometimes argued that consumption taxes are to be preferred to income taxes because they distort labour supply decisions less. Often this is the result of semantic confusion – if a tax is levied on income it does not necessarily mean that it discourages the earning of income more, for example, than a tax on the uses of income. In fact, if net saving is positive then a consumption tax will generally have a higher rate than an equivalent yield tax on income – which would be levied also on the return to life-cycle savings – and hence reduced distortions in the savings market may be bought at the price of greater distortions in the labour market.

The difficulties of determining income generates arguments for consumption taxes. Inflation aggravates these; the measurement of income requires that the real and nominal components in both investment income and capital gains should be distinguished, and moves to accomplish this have raised considerable political and practical difficulties everywhere. But this is only a symptom of more fundamental difficulties in maintaining an operational distinction between capital and income which does not give rise to administrative complexity and to opportunities for avoidance and evasion.

Reliance on traditional excises has tended to diminish in most countries, partly because these have often been levied as specific taxes whose nominal value has not been increased in line with inflation. No major country has yet adopted a direct expenditure tax, although there is a general tendency to provide increased relief for savings within the context of the income tax. The valued added tax has been very widely adopted as a primary broad based consumption tax. VAT is levied on all sales made by traders, but in computing liability tax paid on inputs may be deducted. Thus tax is collected on net value added at each stage of production, and by the final stage – at which tax is charged on a sale to a final consumer who is unable to recover any part of his liability – the whole of the value of the sale is subject to tax. VAT is frequently administered at multiple rates, differentiated by types of commodity. VAT can be applied to services as well as to the physical commodities which are subject of wholesale or retail sale taxes.

Primary areas of difficulty are housing – where there is no obvious measure of output – and financial services, where there is little or no marketed output of goods and services and income is normally earned from investments, or a difference between borrowing and lending rates, which does not fall within the scope of the value added tax. With these exceptions, VAT can be applied to more or less the whole of consumer expenditure and has now become the predominant consumption tax throughout the Western world.

JOHN KAY

See also EXPENDITURE TAX; HOBBES, THOMAS; VALUE-ADDED TAX.

BIBLIOGRAPHY

Andrew, W.D. 1974. A consumption type or cash flow personal income tax. *Harvard Law Review* 87, April, 1113–88.
Hobbes, T. 1651. *Leviathan*. London: Andrew Crooke.
Kaldor, N. 1955. *An Expenditure Tax*. London: Allen & Unwin.
Meade, J.E. 1978. *The Structure and Reform of Direct Taxation*. London: Allen & Unwin.
Nicholson, J.L. and Britton, A.J.C. 1976. The redistribution of income. In *The Personal Distribution of Income*, ed. A.B. Atkinson, London: Allen & Unwin.
Pechman, J.A. and Okner, B.A. 1974. *Who Bears the Tax Burden?* Washington, DC: Brookings.

contestable markets. Contestable markets are those in which competitive pressures from potential entrants exercise strong constraints on the behaviour of incumbent suppliers. For a market to be contestable, there must be no significant entry barriers. Then, in order to offer no profitable opportunities for additional entry, an equilibrium configuration of the industry must entail no significant excess profits, and must be efficient in its pricing and in its allocation of production among incumbent suppliers. This is so of a contestable market whether it is populated with only a monopolist or with a large number of actively competing firms, because it is potential competition from potential entrants rather than competition among active suppliers that effectively constrains the equilibrium behaviour of the incumbents.

Perfectly contestable markets (PCMs) are a benchmark for the analysis of industry structure – a benchmark based on an idealized limiting case. Perfectly contestable markets are open to entry by entrepreneurs who face no disadvantages *vis-à-vis* incumbent firms and who can exit without loss of any costs that entry required to be sunk. The potential entrants have available the same best-practice production technology, the same input markets and the same input prices as those available to the incumbents. There are no legal restrictions on market entry and exit, and there are no special costs that must be borne by an entrant that do not fall on incumbent firms as well. Consumers have no preferences among firms except those arising directly from price or quality differences in firms' offerings.

Potential entrants into perfectly contestable markets are profit-seekers who respond with production to profitable opportunities for entry. They assess the profitability of their marketing plans by making use of the current prices of incumbent firms. Thus, for example, an entrepreneur will enter a market if he anticipates positive profit from undercutting the incumbent's price and serving the entire market demand at the new lower price. Potential entrants are undeterred by prospects of retaliatory price cuts by incumbents and, instead, are deterred only when the existing market prices leave them no room for profitable entry.

These features of the behaviour of potential entrants are key to the workings of perfectly contestable markets, and they are fully rational only where entry faces no disadvantages and is costlessly reversible. Hence, the benchmark case of perfect contestability excludes the sunk costs, precommitments, asymmetric information, and strategic behaviour that characterize many real markets and that are the focus of much current research attention in the field of industrial organization. With irreversibilities and the inducements for strategic behaviour absent, industry structure in PCMs is determined by the fundamental forces of demand and production technology.

Of course, this is also true of perfectly competitive markets. However, this most familiar idealized limiting case is not a satisfactory benchmark for the study of industry structure in general, because it is intrinsically inapplicable to a variety of significant cases. In particular, where increasing returns to scale are present, perfectly competitive behaviour is logically inconsistent with the long-run financial viability of unsubsidized firms.

Perfectly contestable markets can serve in place of perfectly competitive markets as the general standard of comparison for the organization of industry whether or not scale economies are prevalent. Where they are not, perfectly competitive behaviour is necessary for equilibrium in PCMs, and where scale economies do prevail, equilibrium in PCMs entails behaviour different than that found in perfectly competitive markets but which none the less tends to exhibit desirable welfare properties. In other words, perfect contestability is a generalization of perfect competition that has strong implications in significant circumstances where the latter is inapplicable.

In order to clarify and expand on these ideas, subsequent sections offer analytic outlines of the theory of perfectly contestable markets and applications of the theory to single-product and multiproduct industries. Finally, observations are offered on the implications of this theory for the formulation of government policy towards industry.

PERFECTLY CONTESTABLE MARKETS: DEFINITIONS AND BASIC PROPERTIES. The theory presented here lies in the realm of partial equilibrium. It deals with the provision of the set of products $N = \{1, \ldots, n\}$, some of which may not actually be produced, and which is a proper subset of all the goods in the economy. The prices of these products are represented by vectors $p \in R^n_{++}$, and other prices are assumed to be exogenous and are suppressed in the notation. $Q(p) \in R^n_+$ is the vector-valued market demand function for the products in N, and it suppresses consumers' incomes which are assumed to be exogenous. For any output vector $y \in R^n_+$, $C(y)$ is the cost at exogenously fixed factor prices when production is efficient. The underlying technology is assumed to be freely available to all incumbent firms and all potential entrants. Where necessary, $C(y)$ and $Q(p)$ will be assumed to be differentiable.

Definition 1: A *feasible industry configuration* is composed of m firms producing output vectors $y^1, \ldots, y^m \in R^n_+$, at prices $p \in R^n_{++}$ such that the markets clear, $\Sigma^m_{i=1} y^i = Q(p)$,

and that each firm at least breaks even, $p \cdot y^i - C(y^i) \geqslant 0$, $i = 1, \ldots, m$.

Thus, the industry configuration is taken to be comprised of m firms, where m can be any positive integer, so that the industry structure is monopolistic if $m = 1$, competitive if m is sufficiently large, or oligopolistic for intermediate values of m. The term 'feasibility' refers to the requirements that each of the firms involved selects a non-negative output vector that permits its production costs, $C(y^i)$ to be covered at the market prices, p, and that the sum of the outputs of the m firms satisfies market demands at those prices.

Definition 2: A feasible industry configuration over N, with prices p and firms' outputs $y^1, \ldots, y^m$, is *sustainable* if $p^e \cdot y^e \leqslant C(y^e)$, for all $p^e \in R^n_{++}$, $y^e \in R^n_+$, $p^e \leqslant p$, and $y^e \leqslant Q(p^e)$.

The interpretation of this definition is that a sustainable configuration affords no profitable opportunities for entry by potential entrants who regard incumbents' prices as fixed (for a period sufficiently long to make $C(\cdot)$ the relevant flow cost function for an entrant). Here, a feasible marketing plan of a potential entrant is comprised of prices, p^e, that do not exceed the incumbents' quoted prices, p, and a quantity vector, y^e, that does not exceed market demand at the entrant's prices, $Q(p^e)$. The configuration is sustainable if no such marketing plan for an entrant offers a flow of profit, $p^e \cdot y^e - C(y^e)$, that is positive.

Definition 3: A *perfectly contestable market* (PCM) is one in which a necessary condition for an industry configuration to be in equilibrium is that it be sustainable.

A PCM so defined may be interpreted, heuristically, as a market subject to potential entry by firms that have no disadvantage relative to incumbents, and that assess the profitability of entry on the supposition that incumbents' prices are fixed for a sufficiently long period of time. Then, since one requirement for equilibrium is the absence of new entry, an equilibrium configuration in a PCM must offer no inducement for entry; i.e., it must be sustainable.

Definition 4: A feasible industry configuration over N, p; $y^1, \ldots, y^m$, is a *long-run competitive equilibrium* if $p \cdot y \leqslant C(y) \forall y \in R^n_+$.

So defined, a long-run competitive equilibrium has precisely the characteristics usually ascribed to it. Together, $p \cdot y^i \geqslant C(y^i)$ and $p \cdot y \leqslant C(y)$, $\forall y \in R^n_+$, imply that $p \cdot y^i = C(y^i)$ and that the $y^i \in \arg\max_y[p \cdot y - C(y)]$. Thus, each firm in the configuration takes prices as parametric, chooses output to maximize profits, earns zero profit, and equates marginal costs to prices of produced outputs. It is now easy to show

Proposition 1: A long-run competitive equilibrium is a sustainable configuration, so that a perfectly competitive market is a PCM.

Proposition 2: Sustainable configurations need not be long-run competitive equilibria, and a PCM need not be perfectly competitive.

The simplest example sufficient to prove this second proposition is an industry producing a single product with increasing returns to scale over the relevant range of output. Here, the only feasible configuration that is sustainable entails one firm producing the maximal output level y^* given by the intersection of the declining average cost curve with the industry demand curve, and selling at the price p^* given by the corresponding level of average cost. This configuration is sustainable because at a price equal to or less than p^*, sale of any quantity on or inside the demand curve yields revenue no greater than production cost; in this range, price does not exceed average cost. Yet, this configuration is not a long-run competitive equilibrium, as defined above, because sale of a quantity greater than y^* would earn positive profit if the price could remain at p^*, and because at y^* price exceeds marginal cost which is less than average cost. In fact, in this example there is no possible long-run competitive equilibrium since marginal cost lies below average cost throughout the relevant range of output levels given by demand. In contrast, there is a sustainable configuration.

Hence, Propositions 1 and 2 show that the sustainable industry configuration is a substantive generalization of the long-run competitive equilibrium, and that the PCM is a substantive generalization of the perfectly competitive market. The following propositions summarize some characteristics of equilibria in PCMs.

Proposition 3: Let $p; y^1, \ldots, y^m$ be a sustainable industry configuration. Then each firm must (i) earn zero profit by operating efficiently, $p \cdot y^i - C(y^i) = 0$; (ii) avoid cross-subsidization, $p_s \cdot y_s^i \geqslant C(y^i) - C(y_N^i - s)$, $\forall SCN$ (where the vector x_T agrees with the vector x in components $j \in T$ and has zeros for its other components); (iii) price at or above marginal cost, $p_j \geqslant \partial C(y^i)/\partial y_j$.

The interpretation of condition (ii) is that the revenues earned from the sales of any subset of the goods must not fall short of the incremental costs of producing that subset. Otherwise, in view of the equality of total revenues and costs, the revenues collected from the sales of the other goods must exceed their total stand-alone production cost. In PCMs, such pricing invites entry into the markets for the goods providing the subsidy.

Proposition 4: Let $p; y^1, \ldots, y^m$ be a sustainable configuration with $y_j^k < \Sigma_{h=1}^m y_j^h$. Then $p_j = \partial C(y^k)/\partial y_j$. That is, if two or more firms produce a given good in a PCM, they must select input–output vectors at which their marginal costs of producing it are equal to the good's market price.

The implications of this result are surprisingly strong. The discipline of sustainability in perfectly contestable markets forces firms to adopt prices just equal to marginal costs, provided only that they are not monopolists of the products in question. Conventional wisdom implies that, generally, only perfect competition involving a multitude of firms, each small in its output markets, can be relied upon to provide marginal-cost prices. Here we see that potential competition by prospective entrants, rather than rivalry among incumbent firms, suffices to make marginal-cost pricing a requirement of equilibrium in PCMs, even those containing as few as two active producers of each product. The conventional view holds that the enforcement mechanism of full competitive equilibrium requires the smallness of each active firm in its product market, in addition to freedom of entry. We see that the smallness requirement can be dispensed with, almost entirely, with exclusive reliance on the freedom of entry that characterizes PCMs.

Proposition 5: Let $p; y^1, \ldots, y^m$ be a sustainable configuration. Then, for any $\hat{y}^1, \ldots, \hat{y}^k$ with

$$\sum_{j=1}^k \hat{y}^j = \sum_{j=1}^m y^j, \qquad \sum_{j=1}^k C(\hat{y}^j) \geqslant \sum_{j=1}^m C(y^j).$$

That is, a sustainable configuration minimizes the total cost to the industry of producing the total industry output.

This proposition is a generalization to PCMs of a well-known result for perfect competition. It can be interpreted as a manifestation of the power of unimpeded potential entry to impose efficiency upon the industry. For example, the proposition implies that if a monopoly occupies a PCM it must be a *natural* monopoly – production by a single firm must minimize industry cost for the given output vector. Thus, Propositions 3, 4 and 5 are powerful tools for the analysis of industry structure in PCMs. Proposition 5 permits information on the properties of production costs to be used to assess the scale and scope of firms' activities in PCMs. Then, Propositions 3 and 4 permit inferences to be drawn about the corresponding equilibrium prices.

PCMS WITH A SINGLE PRODUCT. This analytic approach leads to very strong results in the single-product case. Propositions 3–5 show that there are only two possible types of sustainable configurations in single-product industries. The first type involves a single firm which charges the lowest price that is consistent with non-negative profit. The firm must be a natural monopoly when it produces the quantity that is demanded at this price. And, in this circumstance, the result maximizes welfare subject to the constraint that all firms in question be viable financially without subsidies. Such a second best maximum is referred to as a 'Ramsey optimum'.

The second type of sustainable configuration involves production by one or more firms of outputs at which both marginal cost and average cost are equal to price. Here, in the long run, all active firms exhibit the behaviour that characterizes perfectly competitive equilibrium. And, of course, the result involves both (first-best) welfare optimality and financial viability. Hence, in this case, Ramsey optimality and the first-best coincide. This establishes the result that in a single-product industry any sustainable configuration is Ramsey optimal.

However, in general, because of the 'integer problem', sustainable configurations may generally not exist. This problem arises, for example, where there is only one output at which a firm's marginal and average costs coincide, and where the quantity of output demanded by the market at the competitive price is greater than this, but is not an integer multiple of that amount. Then, no sustainable configurations exist.

There is, however, a plausible assumption, supported by empirical evidence, at least to some degree, that eliminates the integer problem. Suppose that a firm's average cost curve has a flat-bottom rather than being 'U'-shaped. In particular, suppose that the minimum level of average cost is attained not only at one output, but (at least) at all outputs between the minimum efficient scale, y_m, and twice the minimum efficient scale. Then any industry output, y^1, that is at least equal to y_m can be apportioned among an integer number of firms, each of which achieves minimum average cost. Specifically, y^1 can be divided evenly among $\lfloor y^1/y_m \rfloor$ firms (where $\lfloor x \rfloor$ is the largest integer not greater than x) and each firm's output, $y^1/\lfloor y^1/y_m \rfloor$, must lie in the (half-open) interval between y_m and $2y_m$. Hence, in this case, the Ramsey optimum can either be a sustainable configuration of two or more firms performing competitively, or a sustainable natural monopoly. Such a monopoly may either produce an output at which there are increasing returns to scale and it will then price at average cost, or it may produce an output between y_m and $2y_m$ with locally constant returns to scale and adopt a price equal both to average and marginal cost. This, together with the preceding argument, establishes the following result.

Proposition 6: In a single-product industry in which the firm's average cost curve has a flat-bottom between minimum efficient scale and twice minimum efficient scale, a configuration is sustainable if and only if it is Ramsey optimal.

This result shows that, under the conditions described, there is equivalence between welfare optimality and equilibrium in PCMs. This extends the corresponding result for perfectly competitive equilibria to cases of increasing returns to scale. Moreover, since the behavioural assumptions required for a PCM are weaker than those underlying perfectly competitive markets, the equivalence result is more sweeping. In particular, Proposition 6 implies that PCMs can be expected to perform well, whatever the number of firms participating in equilibrium. It is the potential competition of potential entrants, rather than the active competition of existing rivals, that drives equilibrium in PCMs with a single product to welfare optimality.

MULTIPRODUCT PERFECTLY CONTESTABLE MARKETS. In industries that produce two or more goods, a rich variety of industry structures become possible, even in PCMs. Here, while the constraints imposed upon incumbents by perfect contestability are not nearly as effective in limiting the range of possible outcomes as they are in single product industries, they nevertheless provide a helpful basis for analysis. In particular, Propositions 3–5 indicate connections among various qualitative properties of multiproduct cost functions and various elements of industry structure in PCMs. These connections constitute one theme of this section. The other theme is the normative evaluation of the industry structures that arise in multiproduct PCMs.

Before proceeding, it may be useful to provide definitions of some of the multiproduct cost properties that are used in the analysis.

Definition 5: Let $P = \{T_1, \ldots, T_k\}$ be a non-trivial partition of $S \subseteq N$. There are (weak) *economies of scope* at y_s with respect to the partition P if $\Sigma_{i=1}^{k} C(y_{Ti}) > (\geqslant) C(y_s)$. If no partition is mentioned explicitly, then it is presumed that $T_i = \{i\}$.

Definition 6: The *degree of scale economies* defined over the entire product set, $N = \{1 \ldots, n\}$, at y, is given by $S_N(y) = C(y)/y \cdot \nabla C(y)$.

Returns to scale are said to be increasing, constant, or decreasing as S_N is greater than, equal to, or less than unity. This occurs as the elasticity of ray average cost with respect to t is negative, positive, or zero; where *ray average cost* is $\mathrm{RAC}(ty^0) = C(ty^0)/t$.

Definition 7: The *incremental cost* of the product set $T \subseteq N$ at y is given by $\mathrm{IC}_T(y) \equiv C(y) - C(y_{N-T})$. The *average incremental cost* of T is $\mathrm{AIC}_T(y) \equiv \mathrm{IC}_T(y)/\Sigma_{j\in T} y_j$.

The average incremental cost of T is decreasing, increasing, or constant at y if $\mathrm{AIC}_T(ty_T + y_{N-T})$ is a decreasing, increasing, or locally constant function of t at $t = 1$. These cases are labelled respectively, increasing, decreasing, or constant *returns to the scale of the product line T*. The degree of scale economies specific to T is

$$\mathrm{IC}_T(y)/\sum_{i \in T} y_i \frac{\partial C(y)}{\partial y_i}.$$

Definition 8: A cost function $C(y)$ is *trans-ray convex* through some point $y^* = (y_1^*, \ldots, y_n^*)$ if there exists at least one vector of positive constants $w_1, \ldots, w_n$ such that for every two output vectors $y^a = (y_1^a, \ldots, y_n^a)$ and $y^b = (y_1^a, \ldots, y_n^b)$ that lie on the hyperplane $\Sigma w_i y_i = w_0$ through point y^*, $C[ky^a + (1 - k)y^b] \leqslant kC(y^a) + (1 - k)C(y^b)$ for $k \in (0, 1)$.

In view of the general result that sustainable configurations minimize industry-wide costs (Proposition 5), these cost properties permit inferences to be drawn about industry structure in multiproduct PCMs. The first issue that arises is when multi-

commodity production is characteristic of equilibrium in a PCM.

Proposition 7: A multiproduct firm in a PCM must enjoy (at least weak) economies of scope over the set of goods it produces. When strict economies of scope are present, there must be at least one multiproduct firm in any PCM that supplies more than one good.

The second basic question that arises is whether there can be two or more firms actively producing a particular good in a PCM. If there are, then, by Proposition 4, marginal cost pricing must result. The answer depends upon the availability of product-specific scale economies.

Proposition 8: Any product with average incremental costs that decline throughout the relevant range (i.e., that offers product-specific increasing returns to scale) must be produced by only a single firm (if it is produced at all) in a PCM. Further, such a product must be priced above marginal cost, unless the degree of product-specific scale economies is exactly one.

Thus, regardless of the presence or absence of economies of scope, globally declining average incremental costs imply that a product must be monopolized in a PCM. It is an immediate corollary that if all goods in the set N exhibit product-specific scale economies, and if there are economies of scope among them all, then the industry is a natural monopoly that must be monopolized in a PCM.

Another route to this result is provided by the 'weak invisible hand theorem of natural monopoly'.

Proposition 9: Trans-ray convexity of costs together with global economies of scale imply natural monopoly. If, in addition certain other technical conditions are met, a monopoly charging Ramsey-optimal prices is a sustainable configuration.

In general, there may exist natural monopoly situations in which no sustainable prices are possible for the Ramsey optimal product set. Further, even where sustainable prices exist, the Ramsey optimal prices may not be among them. However, under the conditions of the weak invisible hand theorem, the Ramsey optimal prices for the Ramsey optimal product set are guaranteed to be sustainable, so that PCMs are consistent with (second-best) welfare optimal performance by a natural monopoly.

PCMs will yield first-best welfare optimality if there exist sustainable configurations with at least two firms actively producing each good. For in this case Propositions 4 and 5 guarantee industry-wide cost efficiency and marginal-cost pricing of all products. Here, two issues must be resolved: Does industry-wide cost minimization require at least two producers of each good? And if so, do sustainable configurations exist?

The existence problem can be solved in a manner analogous to its solution in the case of single-product industries: by assuming that ray average costs remain at their minimum levels for output vectors that lie (on each ray) between minimum efficient scale and twice minimum efficient scale. And the presence of at least two producers (or one operating in the region where constant returns prevail) of each good is assured if the quantities demanded by the market at the relevant marginal-cost prices are no smaller than minimum efficient scale (along the relevant ray) and if the cost function exhibits trans-ray convexity.

POLICY IMPLICATIONS OF PCMS. One of the principal lessons of the analysis of PCMs is that monopoly does not necessarily entail welfare losses. Rather, the 'weak invisible hand theorem' shows that under certain conditions sustainability and Ramsey optimality are consistent, so that the total of consumers' and producers' surpluses may well be maximized (subject to the constraint that firms be self-supporting) in the equilibrium of a monopoly which operates in contestable markets.

Even stronger results follow from the discussed results that under certain conditions sustainability and a first-best solution are consistent in an oligopoly with a small number of firms. When minimization of industry cost requires that each good be produced by at least two firms, sustainability requires any equilibrium to satisfy the necessary conditions for a first-best allocation of resources. Thus, in these cases, the invisible hand has the same power over oligopoly in perfectly contestable markets that it exercises over a perfectly competitive industry.

This theory suggests that in a market that approximates perfect contestability, the general public interest is well-served by a policy of *laissez-faire* rather than active regulation by administrative or anti-trust means. Small numbers of large firms, vertical and even horizontal mergers and other arrangements which have traditionally been objects of suspicion of monopolistic power, are rendered harmless and perhaps even beneficient by the presence of contestability.

On the other hand, contestability theory does not lend support to the proposition that the unrestrained market automatically solves all economic problems and that virtually all regulation and anti-trust activity entails unwarranted and costly intervention. The economy of reality is composed of industries which vary widely in the degree to which they approximate the attributes of perfect contestability. Before the theory of contestability can be legitimately applied to reach a conclusion that intervention is unwarranted in a specific sector, it must first be shown that the sector lies unprotected by entry barriers and that the force of potential entry therefore actively constrains the behaviour of incumbent firms. This then becomes the appropriate first stage in an analysis of efficient government policy towards an industry. Only where the conditions of contestability are found to characterize the reality of an industry can there be validity in applying the normative conclusions of contestability theory concerning the power of potential competition actually to enforce efficient behaviour on incumbents.

Even where contestability is absent in reality, the formulation on efficient regulation can be usefully guided by the theory of contestable markets instead of the theory of perfectly competitive markets. The first-best lesson of the perfect competition model, calling for prices to be set equal to marginal costs, has no doubt contributed to the common regulatory ethos which *equates* price to *some* measure of cost. This doctrine has been used frequently where it is completely inappropriate and without logical foundation, that is, in cases where prices should be based on demand as well as cost considerations, because of the presence of economies of scale and scope. Such arbitrary measures as fully distributed costs cannot substitute for marginal cost measures as decision rules for proper pricing, and the search for a substitute is a remnant of inappropriate reliance on the model of perfect competition for guidance in regulation.

In contrast, contestability theory suggests cost measures that are appropriate guideposts for regulated pricing – incremental and stand-alone costs. The incremental cost of a given service is, of course, the increment in the total costs of the supplying firm when that service is added to its product line. In perfectly contestable markets, the price of a product will lie somewhere between its incremental and its stand-alone cost, just where it falls in that range depending on the state of demand. One cannot legitimately infer that monopoly power is exercised from data showing that prices do not exceed stand-alone costs, and

stand-alone costs constitute the proper cost-based ceilings upon prices, preventing both cross-subsidization and the exercise of monopoly power. A simple example will show why this is so.

First, suppose that a firm supplies two services, A and B, which *share no costs* and that each costs 10 units a year to supply. The availability of effective potential competition would force revenues from each service to equal 10 units a year. For higher earnings would attract (profitable) entry, and lower revenues would drive the supplier out of business. In this case, in which common costs are absent, incremental and stand-alone costs are equal to each other and to revenues, and the competitive and contestable benchmarks yield the same results.

Next, suppose instead that of the 20 unit total cost 4 are fixed and common to A and B, while 16 are variable, 8 of the 16 being attributable to A and 8 to B. If, because of demand conditions, at most only a bit more than 8 can be generated from consumers of A, then a firm operating and surviving in contestable markets will earn a bit less than 12 from B. These prices lie between incremental costs (8) and stand-alone costs (12), are mutually advantageous to consumers of both services, and will attract no entrants, even in the absence of any entry barriers. In contrast, should the firm attempt to raise the revenues obtained from B above the 12 unit stand-alone cost, it would lose its business to competitors willing to charge less. Similarly, the same fate would befall it in contestable markets if it priced B in a way that earned more than 8 plus the common cost of 4, less the contribution toward that common cost from service A.

Thus, the forces of idealized potential competition in perfectly contestable markets enforce cost constraints on prices, but prices remain sensitive to demands as well. Actual and potential competition are *effective* if they constrain rates in this way, and in such circumstances regulatory intervention is completely unwarranted. But if, in fact, market forces are not sufficiently strong, then there may be a proper role for regulation of natural monopoly, and the theoretical guidelines derived from the workings of contestable markets are the appropriate ones to apply. That is, prices must be constrained to lie between incremental and stand-alone costs. (This is the approach recently adopted by the Interstate Commerce Commission to determine maximum rates for US railroad services, and the method has already withstood appeals to the Federal courts.)

ROBERT D. WILLIG

See also ENTRY AND MARKET STRUCTURE; INCREASING RETURNS; NATURAL MONOPOLY.

BIBLIOGRAPHY
Baumol, W.J., Panzar, J.C. and Willig, R.D. 1982. *Contestable Markets and the Theory of Industry Structure.* New York: Harcourt Brace Jovanovich.
Baumol, W.J., Panzar, J.C. and Willig, R.D. 1985. On the theory of perfectly contestable markets. In *New Developments in the Analysis of Market Structure,* ed. J. Stiglitz and F. Mathewson, New York: Harcourt Brace.
Baumol, W.J. and Willig, R.D. 1987. New developments in contestability theory. *Oxford Economic Papers.*

contingent commodities. The theory of general competitive equilibrium was originally developed for environments where no uncertainty prevailed. Everything was certain and phrases like 'it might rain' or 'the weather might be hot' were outside the scope of the theory. The idea of *contingent commodity,* that was introduced by Arrow (1953) and further developed by Debreu (1953), was an ingenious device that enabled the theory to be interpreted to cover the case of uncertainty about the availability of resources and about consumption and production possibilities. Basically, the idea of contingent commodity is to add the environmental event in which the commodity is made available to the other specifications of the commodity. With no uncertainty every commodity is specified by its physical characteristics and by the location and date of its availability. It is fairly clear, however, that such a commodity can be considered to be quite different where two different environmental events have been realized. The following examples clarify this: an umbrella at a particular location and at a given date in case of rain is clearly different from the same umbrella at the same location and date when there is no rain; some ice cream when the weather is hot is clearly different from the same ice cream (and at the same location and date) when the weather is cold; finally, the economic role of wheat with specified physical characteristics available at some location and date clearly depends on the precipitation during its growing season. Thus, specifying commodities by both the standard characteristics and the environmental events seems very natural, whereas the role of the adjective in 'contingent commodities' is simply to make it clear that one is dealing with commodities the availability of which is contingent on the occurrence of some environmental event. With this specification the model with contingent commodities is very similar to the classical model of general competitive equilibrium and thus questions like the existence of equilibrium and its optimality (with the additional aspect of efficient allocation of risk bearing) are answered in a similar way. Note that although this model deals with uncertainty, no concept of probabilities is needed for its formal description.

To make things more explicit we look at a simple model with contingent commodities. Assume that, without referring to uncertain events, there are $k \geqslant 1$ commodities, indexed by i, and that there are $n > 1$ mutually exclusive and jointly exhaustive events (or states of nature), indexed by s, where k and n are finite. Thus a contingent commodity is denoted by x_{is} and the total number of these commodities is kn, which is greater than k but still finite. Consumption and production sets are thus defined as subsets of the kn-dimensional Euclidean space and the economic behaviour of firms and consumers naturally follow from profit maximization (by firms) and utility maximization (by consumers). The price p_{is} of the contingent commodity x_{is} is the number of units of account that have to be paid in order to have the ith commodity being delivered at the sth event. It is assumed that the market is organized before the realization of the possible events. Thus payment for the contingent commodity x_{is} is done at the beginning while delivery takes place after the realization of events and only in case event s has occurred. Note that the price of the (certain) ith commodity, i.e. the number of units of account that have to be paid in order to have the ith commodity *for sure*, is the sum over s of the prices p_{is}. For example, assume that the price of one quart of ice cream if the weather is hot is $2.00, the price of one quart of the same ice cream if the weather is cold is $1.00 and that $n = 2$ (either it is hot or it is cold). Thus the price of having one quart of that ice cream for sure is $2.00 + $1.00 = $3.00.

It should be noted that although the probabilities of the possible events do not explicitly enter the model, the attitude toward risk of both consumers and producers is of interest and do play a significant role in this framework. The preference relations of consumers defined on subsets of the kn-dimensional Euclidean space reflect not only their 'tastes' but also their subjective beliefs about the likelihoods of different events as well as their attitude toward risk. Convexity of consumers'

preferences, for example, is interpreted as risk aversion while, in the same spirit, profit maximization of firms is interpreted as risk-neutrality. It should be mentioned that both Arrow and Debreu basically assume expected utility maximizing behaviour, in the sense of the Savage (1954) framework. A more general approach to such preference relations can be found in Yaari (1969), where, again, convexity is taken to mean risk aversion.

A unified and more formal treatment of time and uncertainty using contingent commodities can be found in Debreu (1959, ch. 7). Radner (1968) presents an extension of the above model to the case in which different economic agents have different information.

ZVI SAFRA

See also ARROW-DEBREU MODEL; UNCERTAINTY; UNCERTAINTY AND GENERAL EQUILIBRIUM.

BIBLIOGRAPHY

Arrow, K.J. 1953. Le rôle de valeurs boursières pour la répartition la meilleure des risques. *Économétrie*, Paris: CNRS. English translation as 'The role of securities in the optimal allocation of risk-bearing' in *Review of Economic Studies* (1964); reprinted in K.J. Arrow, *Essays in the Theory of Risk-Bearing*, Chicago: Markham, 1971.

Debreu, G. 1953. Une économie de l'incertain. Mimeo, Paris: Electricité de France.

Debreu, G. 1959. *Theory of Value*. New York: Wiley.

Radner, R. 1968. Competitive equilibrium under uncertainty. *Econometrica* 36, January, 31–58.

Savage, L.J. 1954. *Foundations of Statistics*. New York: Wiley.

Yaari, M.E. 1969. Some remarks on measures of risk aversion and their uses. *Journal of Economic Theory* 1(3), October, 315–29.

continuity in economic history. Continuity and discontinuity are devices of story-telling, telling the story of monetary policy over the past few months or the story of modern economic growth. They raise certain questions in philosophy and lesser matters, such as precedence and politics.

It is well to have a case in mind. The most important is that of the British industrial revolution.

If it was a 'revolution', as it surely was, it happened sometime. There was a discontinuity, a before and after. When? Various dates have been proposed, down to the day and year: 9 March 1776, when the *Wealth of Nations* provided an ideology for the age; the five months in 1769 when Watt took out a patent on the high pressure steam engine and Arkwright on the cotton-spinning water frame; or 1 January 1760, when the furnaces at Carron Ironworks, Stirlingshire, were lit.

Such dating has of course an amateur air. A definite date looks handsome on a plaque or scroll but the precision does not fit well with sophisticated story-telling. The discontinuity is implausibly sharp, drawing attention to minor details. The Great Depression did not start on 24 October 1929; the deregulation of American banking was not completed with the fall of Regulation Q. Nicholas Crafts (1977) has pointed out that the detailed timing of the industrial revolution should not anyway be the thing to be studied, because small beginnings do not come labelled with their probabilities of developing into great revolutions. He is identifying a pitfall in story-telling. Joel Mokyr identifies another (1985, p. 44): rummaging among the possible acorns from which the great oak of the industrial revolution grew 'is a bit like studying the history of Jewish dissenters between 50 BC and 50 AD. What we are looking at is the inception of something which was at first insignificant and even bizarre', though 'destined to change the life of every man and woman in the West'.

What is destined or not destined to change our lives will look rather different to each of us. Each historian therefore has his or her own dating of the industrial revolution. Each sees another discontinuity. E.M. Carus-Wilson (1941, p. 41) spoke of 'an industrial revolution of the 13th century': she found that the fulling mill was 'due to scientific discoveries and changes in technique' and 'was destined to alter the face of medieval England'. A.C. Bridbury (1975, p. xix–xx) found in the late middle ages 'a country travelling slowly along the road ... that [it] travelled so very much more quickly in Adam Smith's day'. In the eyes of Marxist writers the 16th century was the century of discontinuity, when capitalism set off into the world to seek its fortune. John U. Nef, no Marxist, believed he saw an industrial revolution in the 16th century, centred on coal (1932), though admittedly slowed in the 17th century. A student of the 17th century itself, such as D.C. Coleman (1977), finds glimmerings of economic growth even in that disordered age. The most widely accepted period for the industrial revolution is the late 18th century, especially the 1760s and 1770s (Mantoux, 1928; Landes, 1969), but recent students of the matter (Harley, 1982; Crafts, 1984) have found much to admire in the accomplishments of the early 18th century. W.W. Rostow (1960) placed the 'takeoff into self-sustained growth' in the last two decades of the 18th century, but others have observed that even by 1850 the majority of British people remained in traditional sectors of the economy. And later still there was a second industrial revolution (of chemicals, electricity, and internal combustion) and a third (of electronics and biology).

Wider perspectives are possible, encouraging the observer to see continuity instead. Looking at the matter from 1907, the American historian Henry Adams could see a 'movement from unity into multiplicity, between 1200 and 1900, ... unbroken in sequence, and rapid in acceleration' (p. 498). The principal modern student of the industrial revolution, R.M. Hartwell, appealed for continuity against the jostling throng of dates (1965, p. 78): 'Do we need an *explanation* of the industrial revolution? Could it not be the culmination of a most unspectacular process, the consequence of a long period of economic growth?'

Such questions of continuity and discontinuity are asked widely in economics, though sometimes half consciously. They should not be left to historians. Economics is mainly contemporary history, and faces the problem of deciding when a piece of history has been continuous or not. For instance the crucial discontinuity in the growth of big government, as Robert Higgs (1987) points out, might be placed when the institutions of centralized intervention were conceived (1900–1918) or made (1930–45) or expanded (1960–70). Even recent history faces this narrative problem. When, if ever, did purchasing power parity break down in the 1970s? When did policy on antitrust alter to favour mergers? When did monetary policy last become expansionary? Where is the break?

The difficulty in answering the question has often been misconstrued as philosophical. The philosophical difficulty was first articulated in the 5th century BC by Parmenides and his student Zeno: that if everything is perfectly continuous, change is impossible (Korner, 1967). Everything is so to speak packed too tightly to move. The economist will recognize the point as analogous to an extreme form of economic equilibrium, or to the physicist's maximum entropy. If human nature doesn't 'really' change, then history will be a string of weary announcements that the more things change the more they

stay the same. If the economy is 'really' in equilibrium all the time, then nothing remains to be done.

Alexander Gerschenkron, the economic historian who has contributed most to the understanding of continuity and discontinuity in economics, noted that such a metaphysics would close the book of history (1962, p. 12). A history of economics that began with the Parmenidean continuum would never speak.

For purposes of social science Gerschenkron rejects the transition from the connectedness of all change to an absence of change. True, if you squint and fit a curve then no economic change looks discontinuous in the mathematical sense; but it is wrong then to deduce that 'really' there is no change at all, or that the industrial revolution is a mirage. 'Continuity' in the strict mathematical sense must be kept distinct from 'continuity' in the story-telling sense.

Economists have often been muddled about this philosophical distinction, drawing surprising ideological implications from it. Alfred Marshall enshrined on the title page of his *Principles* the motto 'natura non facit saltum' (nature does not make a jump; Leibnitz had invented it as 'la nature ne fait jamais des sauts'). Marshall himself perhaps believed that the ability to represent behaviour with differentiable functions implies that marginalism is a good description of human behaviour. It is less sure that he believed that the lack of jumps in nature (this on the eve of quantum physics) implies people should not jump either, and should change society only gradually. Anyway, both implications are non sequiturs. Though both have been attributed to neoclassical economics, neither is necessary for it. Much bitter controversy has assumed that neoclassical economics depends on smooth curves and in consequence must advocate smooth social policies. The peculiar alliance between discrete mathematics and Marxian economics has this origin, as does the enthusiasm of some conservative writers for continuities in economic history. Gerschenkron cursed both their houses; the social scientist should study change and continuity 'unbothered by the lovers and haters of revolutions who must find themselves playgrounds and battlegrounds outside the area of serious scholarship' (p. 39).

In one sense of 'continuity' it is trivial that economic history is continuous. History has causes (the fourth of five historically relevant definitions that Gerschenkron distinguishes). Continuity, then, can be viewed as being merely an impressively long causal chain. The exploitation of Scottish iron deposits in the 18th century was caused by bold investments, but these depended on a reliable law of property and commerce, which depended on certain legal developments in the 16th century, and on the growth of political stability in the early 18th century, which in turn depended on all manner of earlier events. Establishing continuities, as Gerschenkron remarks, is the historian's purpose – or, one might add, the economist's, who is doing historian's work when he is not doing philosopher's. The purpose might be to find a cause of, say, the Great Depression. It would be to find a chain of events the absence of which would have made a difference: the international irresponsibility of the United States, for instance, as Kindleberger argued; or the domestic irresponsibility of the Federal Reserve, as Friedman and Schwartz argued. Finding such chains has its own philosophical difficulties (see the article in this Dictionary on COUNTERFACTUALS).

The main problems of continuity and discontinuity, however, are not solvable in seminars on philosophy. They are practical problems in the uses of measurement, and must be solved in the economic or historical workshop. When shall we say that the industrial revolution happened? Gerschenkron gives an answer confined to industry, for in common with most economic historians he regards agriculture and services as laggards in economic growth.

In a number of major countries of Europe ... after a lengthy period of fairly low rates of growth came a moment of more or less sudden increase in the rates, which then remained at the accelerated level for a considerable period. That was the period of the great spurt in the respective countries' industrial development... . The rates and the margin between them in the 'pre-kink' and the 'post-kink' periods appear to vary depending on the degree of relative backwardness of the country at the time of the acceleration (pp. 33–4).

The level at which such discontinuity is to be observed is at choice. As Gerschenkron remarks,

If the seat of the great spurt lies in the area of manufacturing, it would be inept to try to locate the discontinuity by scrutinizing data on large aggregate magnitudes such as national income... . By the time industry has become bulky enough to affect the larger aggregate, the exciting period of the great spurt may well be over (pp. 34–5).

In a footnote to these sentences he remarks that 'Walt Rostow's failure to appreciate this point has detracted greatly from his concept of the take-off, which in principle is closely related to the concept of the great spurt as developed by this writer.'

The point is a good one, and applies to all questions of continuity in aggregate economics. Small (and exciting) beginnings will be hidden by the mass until well after they have become routine. Joel Mokyr has put it as a matter of arithmetic: if the traditional sector of an economy is growing at a slow one per cent per annum, and starts with 90 per cent of output, the modern sector growing at four per cent per annum will take three-quarters of a century to account for as much as half of output (1985, p. 5). We may call it the Weighting Theorem (or the Waiting Theorem, for the wait is long when the weight is small to begin with). There are parallel points to be made elsewhere in economics and in social science generally. In growth theory, for instance, as was noticed shortly after its birth, a century of theoretical time is needed in most models for a shift to yield growth as much as 90 per cent of its steady state. More generally, economists have long recognized the tension between microeconomic explanations and the macroeconomic things to be explained. And sociologists have been quarrelling along similar lines for a century, using even the same jargon of micro and macro.

In other words, the search for discontinuity in an aggregate time series raises the question of the level at which we should do our social thinking, the aggregation problem. Yet Gerschenkron himself did not answer the question well, and was hoist by his own petard. Calculating Italian industrial output he placed his 'big spurt' in 1896–1908, and wished to explain it with big banks founded in the 1890s. Stefano Fenoaltea, once his student, applied the Weighting Theorem to the case (Fenoaltea, 1987). Surely, Fenoaltea reasoned, the components of the industrial index – the steel output and the chemical output – are the 'real' units of economic analysis (note the similarity of this rhetoric to that advocating a micro foundation for macroeconomics). If the components started accelerating *before* the new banks appeared, becoming bulky only later, then the new banks could not have been the initiating force. Alas, the components did just this. They spoil Gerschenkron's bank-led story: the components accelerated not in the 1890s but in the 1880s, not after but before the

banks. To paraphrase Gerschenkron on Rostow, by the time the progressive components of industry had become bulky enough to affect the larger aggregate, the exciting period was well over.

Yet the moral is still Gerschenkron's: that continuity and discontinuity are tools 'forged by the historian rather than something inherently and invariantly contained in the historical matter... . [A]t all times it is the ordering hand of the historian that creates continuities or discontinuities' (p. 38). Gerschenkron nodded, but in nodding made the point. The multiple datings of the industrial revolution make it, too. So does any choice of smoothness or suddenness in economic story-telling.

The point is that history, like economics, is a story we tell. Continuity and discontinuity are narrative devices, to be chosen for their story-telling virtues. Niels Bohr said once that 'It is wrong to think that the task of physics is to find out how nature is. Physics concerns what we can say about nature.' It is *our* say. We can choose to emphasize the continuous: 'Abraham begat Isaac; ... begat ... begat ... and Jacob begat Joseph the husband of Mary, of whom was born Jesus.' Or the discontinuous: 'There was in the days of Herod, the king of Judea, a certain priest named Zacharias.' It is the same story, but its continuity or discontinuity is our creation, not God's. That it is out of God's hands does not make it arbitrary. Scholars speak of the industrial revolution as early or late, gradual or sudden. Other scholars believe or disbelieve their stories on the usual grounds.

DONALD N. McCLOSKEY

See also ECONOMIC HISTORY.

BIBLIOGRAPHY

Adams, H. 1906. *The Education of Henry Adams*. New York: Modern Library, 1931.

Bridbury, A.C. 1975. *Economic Growth: England in the later middle ages*. Brighton: Harvester.

Carus-Wilson, E.M. 1941. An industrial revolution of the thirteenth century. *Economic History Review* 11(1), 39–60. Reprinted in *Essays in Economic History*, Vol. 1, ed. E.M. Carus-Wilson, London: Edward Arnold, 1954.

Coleman, D.C. 1977. *The Economy of England 1450–1750*. Oxford: Oxford University Press.

Crafts, N.F.R. 1977. Industrial revolution in England and France: some thoughts on the question 'Why was England first?' *Economic History Review*, 2nd series 30(3), August, 429–41.

Crafts, N.F.R. 1984. *Economic Growth During the British Industrial Revolution*. Oxford: Oxford University Press.

Fenoaltea, S. 1987. *Italian Industrial Production, 1861–1913: a statistical reconstruction*. Cambridge: Cambridge University Press.

Gerschenkron, A. 1962. On the concept of continuity in history. *Proceedings of the American Philosophical Society*, June. Reprinted in A. Gerschenkron, *Continuity in History and Other Essays*, Cambridge, Mass.: Harvard University Press, 1968.

Harley, C.K. 1982. British industrialization before 1841: evidence of slower growth during the industrial revolution. *Journal of Economic History* 42(2), June, 267–90.

Hartwell, R.M. 1965. The causes of the industrial revolution: an essay in methodology. *Economic History Review*, 2nd series 18, August, 164–82. Reprinted in *The Causes of the Industrial Revolution in England*, ed. R.M. Hartwell, London: Methuen, 1967.

Higgs, R. 1987. *Crisis and Leviathan: critical episodes in the growth of American government*. New York: Oxford University Press.

Korner, S. 1967. Continuity. In *The Encyclopedia of Philosophy*, New York: Macmillan and Free Press.

Landes, D.S. 1969. *The Unbound Prometheus*. Cambridge: Cambridge University Press.

Mantoux, P. 1928. *The Industrial Revolution in the Eighteenth Century*. New York: Harper, 1961.

Mokyr, J. (ed.) 1985. *The Economics of the Industrial Revolution.* Totowa, NJ: Rowman and Allanheld.

Nef, J.U. 1932. *The Rise of the British Coal Industry.* 2 vols, London: Routledge.

Rostow, W.W. 1960. *The Stages of Economic Growth.* Cambridge: Cambridge University Press.

continuous and discrete time models. Most economists recognize that the use of discrete time is only an approximation, but assume (usually implicitly) that the error of approximation involved is trivially small relative to the other sorts of simplification and approximation inherent in economic theorizing. We consider below first the conditions under which this convenient assumption may be seriously misleading. We discuss briefly how to proceed when the assumption fails and the state of continuous time economic theory.

APPROXIMATION THEORY. Some economic behaviour does involve discrete delays, and most calculated adjustments in individual patterns of behaviour seem to occur following isolated periods of reflection, rather than continually. These notions are sometimes invoked to justify economic theories built on a discrete time scale. But to say there are elements of discrete delay or time-discontinuity in behaviour does not imply that discrete time models are appropriate. A model built in continuous time can include discrete delays and discontinuities. Only if all delays were discrete, multiples of a single underlying time unit, and synchronized across agents in the economy would modelling with a discrete time unit be appropriate.

None the less sometimes discrete models can avoid extraneous mathematical complexity at little cost in approximation error. It is easy enough to argue that time is in fact continuous and to show that there are in principle cases where use of discrete time models can lead to error. But it is also true in practice that more often than not discrete time models, translated intuitively and informally to give implications for the real continuous time world, are not seriously misleading. The analytical task, still not fully executed in the literature, is to understand why discrete modelling usually is adequate and thereby to understand the special circumstances under which it can be misleading.

The basis for the usual presumption is that, when the time unit is small relative to the rate at which variables in a model vary, discrete time models can ordinarily provide good approximations to continuous time models. Consider the case examined in detail in Geweke (1978), of a dynamic multivariate distributed lag regression model, in discrete time.

$$Y(t) = A * X(t) + U(t), \tag{1}$$

where $*$ stands for convolution, so that

$$A * X(t) = \sum_{s=-\infty}^{\infty} A(s)X(t-s). \tag{2}$$

We specify that the disturbances are uncorrelated with the independent variable vector X, i.e. $\mathrm{cov}[X(t), U(s)] = 0$, all t, s. The natural assumption is that, if approximation error from use of discrete time is to be small, $A(s)$ must be smooth as a function of s, and that in this case (1) is a good approximation to a model of the form

$$y(t) = a * x(t) + u(t) \tag{3}$$

where

$$a * x(t) = \int_{-\infty}^{\infty} a(s)x(t-s)\,\mathrm{d}s. \tag{4}$$

and y, a and x are functions of a continuous time parameter and satisfy $y(t) = Y(t)$, $x(t) = X(t)$ and $a(t) = A(t)$ at integer t. In this continuous time model we specify, paralleling the stochastic identifying assumption in discrete time, $\mathrm{cov}[x(t), u(s)] = 0$, all t, s. If the discrete model (1) corresponds in this way to a continuous time model, the distributed lag coefficient matrices $A(s)$ are uniquely determined by a and the serial correlation properties of x.

(We should note here that, though this framework seems to apply only to the case where X is a simple discrete sampling of x, not to the time-averaged case where $X(t)$ is the integral of $x(s)$ from $t-1$ to t, in fact both cases are covered. We can simply redefine the x process to be the continuously unit-averaged version of the original x process. This redefinition does have some effect on the nature of limiting results as the time unit goes to zero (since the unit-averaging transformation is different at each time unit) but turns out to be qualitatively of minor importance. Roughly speaking, sampling a unit-averaged process is like sampling a process whose paths have derivatives of one higher order than the unaveraged process.)

Geweke shows that under rather general conditions

$$\sum_{s=-\infty}^{\infty} \| A(s) - \tau a(s\tau) \|^2 \to 0 \tag{5}$$

as the time unit τ goes to zero, where '$\| \ \|$' is the usual root-sum-of-squared-elements norm. In this result, the continuous time process x and lag distribution a are held fixed while the time interval corresponding to the unit in the discrete time model shrinks.

This is the precise sense in which the intuition that discrete approximation does not matter much is correct. But there are important limitations on the result. Most obviously, the result depends on a in (3) being an ordinary function. In continuous time, well-behaved distributed lag relations like (3) are not the only possible dynamic relation between two series. For example, if one replaces (3) by

$$y(t) = \alpha(\mathrm{d}/\mathrm{d}t)x(t) + u(t) \tag{6}$$

then the limit of A in (1) is different for different continuous x processes. In a univariate model with second-order Markov x (i.e. with $\mathrm{cov}[x(t), x(t-s)] = 1 + \theta|s|)\,\mathrm{e}^{-\theta|s|}\mathrm{var}[x(t)])$, the limiting discrete time model, as τ goes to zero, is

$$Y(t) = a\{-0.02X(t+4) + 0.06X(t+3) - 0.22X(t+2)$$
$$+ 0.80X(t+1) - 0.80X(t-1) + 0.22X(t-2)$$
$$- 0.06X(t-3) + 0.02X(t-4)\} + U(t) \tag{7}$$

(see Sims, 1970).

This result is not as strange as it may look. The coefficients on X sum to zero and are anti-symmetric about zero. None the less (7) is far from the naive approximation which simply replaces the derivative operator with the first difference operator. In fact, if the estimation equation were constrained to involve only positive lags of X, the limiting form would be

$$Y(t) = \alpha\{1.27X(t) - 1.61X(t-1) + 0.43X(t-2)$$
$$- 0.12X(t-3) + 0.03X(t-4) - 0.01X(t-5)\} + U(t). \tag{8}$$

The naive approximation of (6) by $Y(t) = \alpha[X(t) - X(t) - 1] + U(t)$ is valid only in the sense that if this form is imposed on the discrete model a priori, the least squares estimate of α will converge to its true value. If the resulting estimated model is tested for fit against (7) or (8), it will be rejected.

Despite the fact that the underlying model involves only the contemporaneous derivative of x, (7) and (8) both involve fairly long lags in X. If x paths have higher than first order derivatives (e.g. if they are generated by a third order stochastic differential equation) the lag distributions in (7) and (8) are replaced by still higher order limiting forms. Thus different continuous time processes for x which all imply differentiable time paths produce different limiting discrete A. Here the fact that the time unit becomes small relative to the rate of variation in x does not justify the assumption that approximation of continuous by discrete models is innocuous. In particular, the notion that discrete differencing can approximate derivatives is potentially misleading.

It should not be surprising that the discrete time models may not do well in approximating a continuous time model in which derivatives appear. None the less empirical and theoretical work which ignores this point is surprisingly common.

If a is an ordinary function, there is still chance for error despite Geweke's result. His result implies only that the mean square deviation of a from A is small. This does not require that individual $A(t/\tau)$'s converge to the corresponding $a(t)$ values. For example, in a model where x is univariate and $a(t) = 0$, $t < 0$, $a(0) = 1$, $a(s)$ continuous on $[0, \infty)$, the limiting value for $A(0)$ is 0.5, not 1.0. Thus if $a(t) = e^{-\theta t}$ on $[0, \infty)$, making a monotone decreasing over that range, $A(t)$ will not be monotone decreasing. It will instead rise between $t = 0$ and $t = 1$. This is not unreasonable on reflection: the discrete lag distribution gives a value at $t = 0$ which averages the continuous time distribution's behaviour on either side of $t = 0$. It should therefore not be surprising that monotonicity of a does not necessarily imply monotonicity of A, but the point is ignored in some economic research.

Another example of possible confusion arises from the fact that if the x process has differentiable paths, $a(t) = 0$ for $t < 0$ does not imply $A(t) = 0$ for $t < 0$. The mean-square approximation result implies that when the time unit is small the sum of squares of coefficients on $X(t - s)$ for negative s must be small relative to the sum of squares on $X(t - s)$ for positive s, but the first few lead coefficients will generally be nonzero and will not go to zero as the time interval goes to zero. This would lead to mistaken conclusions about Granger causal priority in large samples, if significance tests were applied naively.

Geweke's exploration of multivariate models shows that the possibilities for confusing results are more numerous and subtle in that case. In particular, there are ways by which poor approximation of $\alpha_j(s)$ by $A_j(s/\tau)$ in some s interval (e.g. around $s = 0$) can lead to contamination of the estimates of other elements of the A matrix, even though they correspond to x_j's and a_j's which in a univariate model would not raise difficulties.

Since Geweke and I wrote on this subject, the amount of dynamic modelling involving least squares projection of one stochastic process (or vector of processes) y on another x has declined relative to the amount of work structured as estimation of a dynamic prediction model for a single vector y. Here the question becomes whether the continuous time dynamics for y, summarized in a Wold moving average representation

$$y(t) = a * u(t) \qquad (9)$$

has an intuitively transparented connection to the corresponding discrete time Wold representation

$$Y(t) = A * U(t). \qquad (10)$$

In discrete time the $U(t)$ of the Wold representation is the one-step-ahead prediction error, and in continuous time $u(t)$ also represents new information about y arriving at t. There are two related subquestions: Is the A function the same shape as the a function; and is the U vector related in a natural way to the u vector? The u vector is a continuous time white noise, so that U cannot possibly be a simple discrete sampling of u. None the less one might hope that U would be related to u by

$$U(t) = c * u(t), \qquad (11)$$

with $c(t)$ damping rapidly as t increases beyond 1.

Results analogous to those of Geweke for the distributed lag regressive model, displaying the limiting behaviour of the approximation as the time unit shrinks, are not yet available for this model. Some comforting results are clearly obtainable. For example, it is clear that if $a(0)$ is diagonal with all diagonal elements positive and a is continuous on $[0, \infty)$, then as the time interval shrinks to zero, $A(0)$ converges to a diagonal matrix and (11) makes

$$U_i(t) = \int_0^1 u_i(t - s) \, ds. \qquad (12)$$

This result is intuitively natural and appealing. However, the requirement that $a(0)$ be diagonal and full rank is restrictive. It implies that none of the elements of the y vector have differentiable paths. If $a(0) = 0$, but the kth right derivative of a at 0 is diagonal and full rank, then $A(0)$ will tend to diagonal form, but (12) will be replaced by a more complicated relation in which values of u_i lagged by more than 1 appear. If $a(0)$ is diagonal and less than full rank, $A(0)$ will not generally converge to diagonal form. It should be clear that the implications for dynamic multiple equation models which obtain identification by asserting serial and cross-serial correlation properties of disturbances could be far-reaching.

ESTIMATION AND CONTINUOUS TIME MODELLING. How can one proceed if one has a model like, say, (6), to which a discrete time model is clearly not a good approximation? The only possibility is to introduce explicitly a model for how x behaves between discrete time intervals, estimating this jointly with (6) from the available data. Doing so converts (6) from a single-equation to a multiple-equation model. That is, the device of treating x as 'given' and non-stochastic cannot work because an important part of the error term in the discrete model arises from the error in approximating $a * x$ by $A * X$. Furthermore, because separating the approximation error component of U from the component due to u is essential, one would have to model serial correlation in u explicitly. The model could take the form

$$\begin{bmatrix} y(t) \\ x(t) \end{bmatrix} = \begin{bmatrix} c(s) & a * b(s) \\ 0 & b(s) \end{bmatrix} * \begin{bmatrix} w(t) \\ v(t) \end{bmatrix}, \qquad (13)$$

where w and v are white noise processes fundamental (in the terminology of Rosanov, 1967) for y and x. To give b and c a convenient parametric form, one might suppose them rational, so that (13) can be written as a differential equation, i.e.

$$P(D)y(t) = P^{-1}(D)a * x(t) + w(t)$$
$$Q(D)x(t) = v(t), \qquad (14)$$

where P and Q are finite-order polynomials in the derivative operator, $Q^{-1}(D)v = b * v$, and $P^{-1}(D)w = c * w$.

A discrete time model derived explicitly from a continuous time model is likely to be nonlinear at least in parameters and therefore to be more difficult to handle than a more naive discrete model. None the less with modern computing power, such models are usable. Bergstrom (1983) provides a discussion of estimating continuous time constant coefficient linear stochastic differential equation systems from discrete data, the papers in the book (1976) he edited provide related discussions, and Hansen and Sargent (1981) discuss estimation of continuous time rational expectations models from discrete data.

CONTINUOUS TIME THEORY. Modelling in continuous time does not avoid the complexities of connecting discrete time data to continuous time reality – it only allows us to confront them directly. One reason this is so seldom done despite its technical feasibility is that it forces us to confront the weakness of economic theory in continuous time. A model like (14) makes an assertion about how many times y and x are differentiable, and a mistake in that assertion can result in error as bad as the mistake of ignoring the time aggregation problem. Economic theory does not have much to say about the degree of differentiability of most economic time series.

When, as in the case of most macroeconometric models for example, the theory underlying the model has no believable restrictions to place on fine-grained dynamics, it may be better to begin the modelling effort in discrete time. As is often true when models are in some respect under-identified, it is likely to be easier to begin from a normalized reduced form (in this case the discrete time model) in exploring the range of possible interpretations generated by different potential identifying assumptions.

Recent developments in financial economics have produced one area where there are continuous time economic theories with a solid foundation. No theory even in this area delivers continuous time white noise residuals from first principles.

Nevertheless, it is at least clear that stochastic differential equations provide a convenient and practically useful framework for modelling asset prices. For example, Harrison et al. (1984) show that differentiable paths for asset prices imply arbitrage opportunities. However, a process can have nondifferentiable paths without producing white noise residuals at any integer order of differentiation: e.g. a model satisfying (3) with $a(s) = s^{0.5} e^{-s}$. Such a process has continuous paths with unbounded variation and is not a semimartingale. That is, it is not the sum of a martingale and a process with bounded variation. Much of the theoretical literature in financial economics assumes such processes away at the start. As economists begin to connect financial sectors to the rest of the economy (see e.g. Grossman et al., 1985), more attention to time aggregation and continuous time modelling is likely to develop.

CHRISTOPHER A. SIMS

See also MULTIVARIATE TIME SERIES MODELS; TIME SERIES ANALYSIS.

BIBLIOGRAPHY

Bergstrom, A.R. (ed.) 1976. *Statistical Inference in Continuous Time Economic Models.* Amsterdam: North-Holland.

Bergstrom, A.R. 1983. Gaussian estimation of structural parameters in higher order continuous time dynamic models. *Econometrica* 51, 117–52.

Geweke, J. 1978. Temporal Aggregation in the Multiple Regression Model. *Econometrica* 46, 643–62.

Grossman, S., Melino, A. and Shiller, R. 1985. Estimating the continuous time consumption based capital asset pricing model. National Bureau of Economic Research Working Paper No. 1643.

Hansen, L.P. and Sargent, T.J. 1981. Formulating and estimating continuous time rational expectations models. Federal Reserve Bank of Minneapolis Staff Report No. 75.

Harrison, J.M., Pitbladdo, R. and Schaefer, S.M. 1984. Continuous price processes in frictionless markets have infinite variation. *Journal of Business* 57, 353–65.

Rosanov, Y.A. 1967. *Stationary Random Processes.* San Francisco: Holden-Day.

Sims, C.A. 1971. Approximate specifications in distributed lag models. In Proceedings of the 38th Session, *Bulletin of the International Statistical Institute* 44, Book I, 285–94.

continuous-time stochastic models. Models in which agents can revise their decisions continuously in time have proved fruitful in the analysis of economic problems involving intertemporal choice under uncertainty (cf. Malliaris and Brock, 1982). These models frequently produce significantly sharper results than can be derived from their discrete-time counterparts. In the majority of such cases, the dynamics of the underlying system are described by diffusion processes, whose continuous sample paths can be represented by Ito integrals. However, in selected applications, this assumption can be relaxed to include both non-Markov path-dependent processes and Poisson-directed jump processes.

An early application of this mode of analysis was the lifetime consumption-portfolio selection problem (Merton, 1969, 1971). Under the assumptions of continuous trading and asset returns generated by diffusion processes, the derived structure of optimal portfolio demands produce portfolio-separation or mutual fund theorems like those derived in the static Markowitz–Tobin mean-variance model, but without the objectionable assumption of either quadratic preferences or Gaussian-distributed asset prices. Indeed, in the special, but prototypical, case of lognormally-distributed asset prices, the intertemporal optimal rules are identical to those of the mean-variance model. The continuous-time analysis thus provides a reconciliation of this classic model, with models of general expected utility maximization in an environment where asset ownership has limited liability.

Using these same assumptions of continuous trading and lognormality of security prices, Black and Scholes (1973) derived a formula for pricing options that provided the foundation for subsequent development of a unified theory of corporation liability evaluation and general contingent-claim pricing. Cox, Ingersoll, and Ross (1985a) use the continuous-trading methodology with diffusion processes to derive a general theory for the term structure of interest rates.

Building on the continuous-time model of individual choice, Merton (1973), Breeden (1979), and Cox, Ingersoll and Ross (1985b) develop intertemporal models of equilibrium asset prices. Huang (1985) provides a stronger foundation for these models by showing that if information in an economy with continuous-trading opportunities evolves according to diffusion processes, then equilibrium security prices will also evolve according to diffusion processes.

In the intertemporal version of the Arrow–Debreu general equilibrium model with complete markets, the markets need only to be open 'once' because agents will have no need for further trade. The continuous-trading model is in this respect at the opposite extreme. Economies in which the dynamics of the system are described by diffusion processes will have a continuum of possible states over any finite interval of time. Thus, in the strict sense, to have complete markets in the continuous-time diffusion model requires an uncountable number of pure Arrow–Debreu securities. The continuous-trading model with diffusions, nevertheless, appears to have many of the important properties of the Arrow–Debreu model, but without nearly so many securities.

As is well known, in the absence of complete Arrow–Debreu markets, a competitive equilibrium does not in general produce Pareto optimal allocations. However, Radner (1972) has shown that an Arrow–Debreu equilibrium allocation can be achieved without a full set of pure time-state contingent securities if agents can use the available securities to implement dynamic trading strategies which replicate the payoff structure of the missing pure securities. There is much analysis to suggest that continuous-trading opportunities together with diffusion representations for the evolution of the economy provide a particularly fertile environment for fulfilling the Radner conditions.

Under reasonably general assumptions about agents' preferences and endowments Breeden (1979) among others has shown that the intertemporal equilibrium allocations generated in economies with continuous trading in a finite number of securities can be Pareto efficient. In the analysis of the individual portfolio selection problem underlying these equilibrium models, the derived portfolio-separation theorems show that the set of individually-optimal portfolios can be generated by combinations of relatively few composite securities or mutual funds.

The extensive literature on options and contingent-claims pricing provides further evidence that continuous-trading opportunities make possible a large reduction in the number of securities markets without loss of efficiency. Although typically partial equilibrium in nature, these analyses show that continuous-trading dynamic portfolio strategies using as few as two securities can replicate a wide range of state and time-dependent payoff structures.

In perhaps the most general analysis to date, Duffie and Huang (1985) study the role continuous trading plays in successfully implementing Arrow–Debreu equilibria with infinite-dimensional commodity spaces, using only a finite number of securities. In particular, they derive necessary and sufficient conditions for continuous-trading portfolio strategies with a finite number of securities to effectively complete markets in a Radner economy. By working with martingale representation theorems, Duffie and Huang show that the class of dynamics for which these results obtain extends beyond vector diffusion processes to include some non-Markov path-dependent processes. They also show that having heterogeneous probability assessments among agents provides no important difficulties with the results, provided all agents' subjective probability measures are uniformly absolutely continuous. Although there remain further technical issues to be resolved, it is evident that the continuous-trading models provide a strong foundation for the belief that a good substitute for having many markets and securities is to have fewer markets which are open for trade more frequently.

A sketch of the derivation of the portfolio separation theorem along the lines of Merton (1971, 1973, 1982a) and Breeden (1979) is a follows:

At each time t, each consumer-investor acts so as to

$$\text{Max } E_t \left\{ \int_t^T U[c(\tau), S(\tau), \tau] \, d\tau + B[W(T), S(T), T] \right\} \quad (1)$$

where E_t is the conditional expectation operator, conditional on information available at time t. $S(t) = [S_1(t), \ldots, S_m(t)]$ is a finite-m vector set of state variables which together with the consumer's current wealth $W(t)$ is sufficient to describe the state of the economy at time t. $c(t)$ denotes the instantaneous consumption flow selected at time t. U is a strictly concave, state-dependent utility function for consumption and B represents utility from bequests at date T.

The evolution of the state variables S is described by a Markov system of Itô stochastic differential equations

$$dS_i(t) = G_i(S, t) \, dt + H_i(S, t) \, dq_i, \quad i = 1, 2, \ldots, m \quad (2)$$

where $G_i(S, t)$ is the instantaneous expected change in $S_i(t)$ per unit time at time t; H_i^2 is the instantaneous variance of the change in $S_i(t)$, where it is understood that these statistics are conditional on $S(t) = S$. The dq_i are Wiener processes with the instantaneous correlation coefficient per unit time between dq_i and dq_j given by the function $\eta_{ij}(S, t)$, $i, j = 1, \ldots, m$.

At each point in time, the consumer chooses a consumption

flow and allocates his wealth among n risky securities and a riskless security whose instantaneous rate of return per unit time is the interest rate $r(t)$. The rate of return dynamics on risky security j can be written as

$$dP_j/P_j = \alpha_j(S, t) \, dt + \sigma_j(S, t) \, dz_j, \quad j = 1, 2, \ldots, n \quad (3)$$

where α_j is the instantaneous conditional expected rate of return per unit time; σ_j^2 is the conditional variance per unit time; and dz_j is a Wiener process. Denote by $\rho_{jk}(S, t)$ the instantaneous correlation coefficient per unit time between dz_j and dz_k, $j, k = 1, 2, \ldots, n$, and denote by $\mu_{ij}(S, t)$ the instantaneous correlation coefficient between dq_i and dz_j, $i = 1, 2, \ldots, m$ and $j = 1, 2, \ldots, n$.

The accumulation equation for the consumer's wealth can be written as

$$dW = [rW + y - c] \, dt + \sum_{j=1}^{n} w_j W[dP_j/P_j - r \, dt] \quad (4)$$

where $y = y(S, t)$ is the consumer's wage income; w_j is the fraction of his wealth allocated to risky security j at time t, and $[1 - \Sigma_j^n w_j]$ is the fraction allocated to the riskless asset.

The optimal consumption and portfolio rules, $c^*(W, S, t)$ and $w^*(W, S, t)$, are derived by the technique of stochastic dynamic programming. Among the first-order conditions to be satisfied by these optimal rules are the n conditions for the optimal portfolio holdings at time t, which can be expressed as $j = 1, 2, \ldots, n$

$$0 = \left\{ \alpha_j - r - \left(\sum_1^n w_i^* \sigma_i \sigma_j \rho_{ij} W + \sum_1^m A_i v_j H_i \mu_{ij} \right) \Big/ K \right\} \frac{\partial U}{\partial c} \frac{\partial c^*}{\partial W} W \quad (5)$$

where

$$K \equiv -\partial U/\partial c/[\partial^2 U/\partial c^2 \cdot \partial c^*/\partial W]$$

and

$$A_i \equiv -[\partial c^*/\partial S_i + (\partial^2 U/\partial c \partial S_i)/(\partial^2 U/\partial c^2)]/(\partial c^*/\partial W),$$
$$i = 1, 2, \ldots, m.$$

By inspection, the manifest characteristic of the system of equations (5) is that it is linear in the optimal demands for risky assets. Therefore, if none of the risky assets is redundant, then standard matrix inversion can be used to solve (5) explicitly for these demands. That is,

$$w_j^*(t) W(t) = K \sum_1^n v_{kj}(\alpha_k - r) + \sum_1^m A_i \zeta_{ij}, \quad j = 1, 2, \ldots, n \quad (6)$$

where v_{kj} is the $k - j$th element of the inverse of the variance–covariance matrix of returns

$$[\sigma_i \sigma_j \rho_{ij}] \quad \text{and} \quad \zeta_{ij} \equiv \sum_1^n v_{kj} \sigma_k H_i \mu_{ik}.$$

By inspection, $K, A_1, \ldots, A_m$ are the only elements in (6) that depend on the individual investor's preferences or endowment. As an immediate consequence, it follows that there exist $(m + 2)$ portfolios ('mutual funds') constructed from linear combinations of the available securities such that, independent of preferences, wealth distribution, or planning horizon, all investors will be indifferent between choosing their portfolios from combinations of just these $(m + 2)$ funds or combinations of all n risky securities and the riskless security. This portfolio-separation theorem is, of course, vacuous if $m \geq n + 1$. If, however, $m \ll n$, then it implies a nontrivial reduction in the number of securites required to generate the set of optimal portfolios.

Although not unique, a set of funds which meets the criterion of the theorem is: fund no. 1 holds the riskless asset; fund no. 2 holds fraction $\Sigma_1^n v_{kj}(\alpha_k - r)$ in security $j, j = 1, \ldots, n$ and the balance in the riskless asset; for $i = 1, 2, \ldots, m$, fund no. $(2 + i)$ holds fraction ζ_{ij} in security $j, j = 1, 2, \ldots, n$ and the balance in the riskless asset. Funds nos. 1 and 2, together generate the set of portfolios with maximum expected return for a given variance of the return (i.e. the mean-variance efficient set). Fund no. $(2 + i)$ provides the maximum feasible correlation between its return and the stochastic component of the instantaneous change in state variable $S_i(t)$, $i = 1, \ldots, m$. As discussed in detail in the cited Breeden and Merton papers, these latter portfolios serve the function of providing the best feasible hedges against utility losses caused by unanticipated changes in the state variables of the economy.

In the important case where the set of available securities is such that the return on fund no. $(2 + i)$ is perfectly correlated with the change in state variable $S_i(t)$ for each i, $i = 1, \ldots, m$, Breeden (1979) shows that the resulting intertemporal equilibrium allocations are Pareto-efficient. This is also the condition under which it is possible to replicate the payoff structure for the complete set of pure Arrow–Debreu securities using continuous-trading dynamic portfolio strategies with a finite number of securities.

The dynamic strategies for replicating the payoffs to pure Arrow–Debreu securities can be derived in a similar fashion to the derivation of contingent-claim prices in Merton (1977). Suppose that among the available traded securities, portfolios can be constructed whose returns are instantaneously perfectly correlated with changes in each of the state variables, $[S_1(t), \ldots, S_m(t)]$. Without loss of generality, assume that these portfolios are the first m risky securites (i.e. $dz_i = dq_i, i = 1, 2, \ldots, m$).

Let $F(S, t)$ satisfy the linear partial differential equation

$$0 = \frac{1}{2} \sum_1^m \sum_1^m H_i H_j \eta_{ij} \frac{\partial^2 F}{\partial S_i \partial S_j}$$

$$+ \sum_1^m [G_j - H_j(\alpha_j - r)/\sigma_j] \frac{\partial F}{\partial S_j} + \frac{\partial F}{\partial t} - rF \quad (7)$$

subject to the boundary conditions: $0 \leqslant F(S, t) \leqslant 1$ for all S and $t < \tau$; $F(S, \tau) = 1$ if $\bar{S}_k - \epsilon \leqslant S_k(\tau) \leqslant \bar{S}_k + \epsilon$ for each $k = 1, 2, \ldots, m$ and $F(S, \tau) = 0$, otherwise. Under mild regularity conditions on the functions H, η, G, α, σ and r, a solution to (7) exists and is unique.

Consider the continuous-trading portfolio strategy which allocates fraction $x_j(t) = (\partial F/\partial S_j) H_j/[\sigma_j V(t)]$ to security j, $j = 1, \ldots, m$ and $[1 - \Sigma_1^m x_j(t)]$ to the riskless security at time t, where $V(t)$ denotes the value of the portfolio. It follows from (3) and the prescribed allocation that the dynamics of the portfolio value can be written as

$$dV = V \left\{ \left[\sum_1^m x_j(\alpha_j - r) + r \right] dt + \sum_1^m x_j \sigma_j \, dz_j \right\}$$

$$= \left[\sum_1^m \frac{\partial F}{\partial S_j} H_j(\alpha_j - r)/\sigma_j + rV \right] dt + \sum_1^m \frac{\partial F}{\partial S_j} H_j \, dq_j \quad (8)$$

because $dz_j = dq_j$; $j = 1, 2, \ldots, m$.

As a solution to (7), F is twice-continuously differentiable. Thus, Itô's Lemma can be used to describe the stochastic process for F as

$$dF = \left(\frac{1}{2} \sum_1^m \sum_1^m H_i H_j \eta_{ij} \frac{\partial^2 F}{\partial S_i \partial S_j} + \sum_1^m \left[G_j \frac{\partial F}{\partial S_j} \right] + \frac{\partial F}{\partial t} \right) dt$$

$$+ \sum_1^m \frac{\partial F}{\partial S_j} H_j \, dq_j \quad (9)$$

where F is evaluated at $S = S(t)$ at each time t. Because F satisfies (7), (9) can be rewritten as

$$dF = \left[\sum_1^m \frac{\partial F}{\partial S_j} H_j(\alpha_j - r)/\sigma_j + rF \right] dt + \sum_1^m \frac{\partial F}{\partial S_j} H_j \, dq_j. \quad (10)$$

From (8) and (10), $dF - dV = r(F - V) \, dt$, which is an ordinary differential equation with solution $F[S(t), t] - V(t) = [F(S(0), 0) - V(0)] \exp[\int_0^t r(u) du]$. If, therefore, the initial investment in the portfolio is chosen so that $V(0) = F[S(0), 0]$, then $V(t) = F[S(t), t]$ for $0 \leqslant t \leqslant \tau$.

Thus, a dynamic portfolio strategy using $(m + 1)$ available securities is constructed that has a payoff at $t = \tau$ of 1 if $S_k - \epsilon \leqslant \bar{S}_k \leqslant \bar{S}_k + \epsilon, k = 1, 2, \ldots, m$ and 0, otherwise. By taking the appropriate limit as $\epsilon \to 0$, this portfolio exactly replicates the payoff to a pure Arrow-Debreu security which pays 1 if $\bar{S}_k(\tau) = S_k, k = 1, 2, \ldots, m$, and 0, otherwise. By changing the time and state parameters τ and $\bar{S}_k$, one can generate all of the uncountable number of pure securities. Moreover, F, the solution to (7) used to implement each strategy, will also be the equilibrium price for the corresponding pure Arrow-Debreu security.

Continuous trading, like any other continuous-revision process, is of course an abstraction from physical reality. If, however, the length of time between revisions is very short, then the continuous-trading optimal solutions will be a reasonable approximation to their discrete-time counterparts (see Samuelson, 1970 and Merton, 1975b; 1982b). From the work of Magill and Constantinides (1976), this conclusion appears to be robust even in the presence of transactions costs, which cause trading to be discrete almost certainly.

Whether the length of time between revisions is short enough for the continuous solution to provide a good approximation must be decided on a case-by-case basis by making a relative comparison with other time scales in the problem. The continuous-trading assumption appears to be especially appropriate for the analysis of security markets where the aggregate trading volume is large; the minimum unit-size for a transaction is relatively small, and the length of calendar time between successive transactions is quite short.

The continuous analysis may also provide a valid approximation in problems where the calendar length of time between revisions is not short. For example, Bourguignon (1974), Bismut (1975), and Merton (1975a) use this mode of analysis to extend the Solow model of economic growth to an uncertain environment and to analyse the stochastic Ramsey problem. It is the practice in such models to neglect 'short-run' business cycle fluctuations and to assume full employment. Moreover, the exogenous factors usually assumed to affect the time path of the economy in these models are either demographic or technological changes. Since major changes in either factor typically take rather long periods of time, the length of time between revisions in the capital stock, although hardly instantaneous, may well be quite short, relative to the time scale of the exogenous processes.

ROBERT C. MERTON

See also CONTINUOUS TIME STOCHASTIC PROCESSES: FINANCE; OPTIONS.

BIBLIOGRAPHY

Bismut, J.M. 1975. Growth and optimal intertemporal allocation of risks. *Journal of Economic Theory* 10, 239–57.

Black, F. and Scholes, M. 1973. The pricing of options and corporate liabilities. *Journal of Political Economy* 81, 637–54.

Bourguignon, F. 1974. A particular class of continuous-time stochastic growth models. *Journal of Economic Theory* 9, 141–58.

Breeden, D.T. 1979. An intertemporal asset pricing model with stochastic consumption and investment opportunities. *Journal of Financial Economics* 7, 265–96.

Cox, J.C., Ingersoll, J.E. Jr., and Ross, S.A. 1985a. A theory of the term structure of interest rates. *Econometrica* 53, 385–408.

Cox, J.C., Ingersoll, J.E. Jr., and Ross, S.A. 1985b. An intertemporal general equilibrium model of asset prices. *Econometrica* 53, 363–84.

Duffie, D. and Huang, C. 1985. Implementing Arrow–Debreu equilibria by continuous trading of a few long-lived securities. *Econometrica* 35, 1337–56.

Huang, C. 1985. Information structure and equilibrium asset prices. *Journal of Economic Theory* 35, 33–71.

Magill, M.J.P. and Constantinides, G.M. 1976. Portfolio selection with transactions costs. *Journal of Economic Theory* 13, 245–63.

Malliaris, A.G. and Brock, W.A. 1982. *Stochastic Methods in Economics and Finance.* Amsterdam: North-Holland.

Merton, R.C. 1969. Lifetime portfolio selection under uncertainty: the continuous-time case. *Review of Economics and Statistics* 51, 247–57.

Merton, R.C. 1971. Optimum consumption and portfolio rules in a continuous-time model. *Journal of Economic Theory* 3, 373–413.

Merton, R.C. 1973. An intertemporal capital asset pricing model. *Econometrica* 41, 867–87.

Merton, R.C. 1975a. An asymptotic theory of growth under uncertainty. *Review of Economic Studies* 42, 375–93.

Merton, R.C. 1975b. Theory of finance from the perspective of continuous time. *Journal of Financial and Quantitative Analysis* 10, 659–74.

Merton, R.C. 1977. On the pricing of contingent claims and the Modigliani-Miller theorem. *Journal of Financial Economics* 5, 241–9.

Merton, R.C. 1982a. On the microeconomic theory of investment under uncertainty. In *Handbook of Mathematical Economics*, ed. K.J. Arrow and M.D. Intriligator, Vol. 2, Amsterdam: North-Holland.

Merton, R.C. 1982b. On the mathematics and economics assumptions of continuous-time models. In *Financial Economics: Essays in Honor of Paul Cootner*, ed. W.F. Sharpe and C.M. Cootner, Englewood Cliffs, New Jersey: Prentice Hall.

Radner, R. 1972. Existence of plans, prices, and price expectations in a sequence of markets. *Econometrica* 40, 289–303.

Samuelson, P.A. 1970. The fundamental approximation theorem of portfolio analysis in terms of means, variances, and higher moments. *Review of Economic Studies* 37, 537–42.

continuous-time stochastic processes. Applications of continuous-time stochastic processes to economic modelling are largely focused on the areas of capital theory and financial markets. In these applications as in mathematics generally, the most widely studied continuous time process is a Brownian motion – so named for its early application as a model of the seemingly random movements of particles which were first observed by the English botanist Robert Brown in the 19th century. Einstein (1905), in the context of statistical mechanics, is generally given credit for the first mathematical formulation of a Brownian motion process. However, an earlier development of an equivalent continuous-time process is provided by Louis Bachelier (1900) in his theory of stock option pricing. Framed as an abstract mathematical process, a Brownian motion $\{B(t); t \in \mathscr{R}_+\}$ is described by the following properties: (1) for $0 \leqslant s < t < \infty$, $B(t) - B(s)$ is a normally distributed random variable with mean zero and variance $t - s$; (2) for $0 \leqslant t_0 < t_1 < \cdots < t_l < \infty$,

$$\{B(t_0); B(t_k) - B(t_{k-1}), k = 1, \ldots, l\}$$

is a set of independent random variables.

From this construction, Doob, Feller, Itô, Wiener, among others went on to develop the general theory of continuous-time stochastic processes.

During the half century of this development of the theory, its application in economics was confined primarily to the formulation and testing of hypotheses concerning time series properties of economic variables. It was not until the 1950s and early 1960s that the theory of continuous-time stochastic processes found its way into economic theory. Motivated by the rediscovery of Bachelier's work on options by L.J. Savage, Samuelson (1965) presents a theory of rational warrant pricing. Unlike Bachelier's assumption of a Brownian motion for a stock price process, Samuelson posits that the *logarithm* of a stock price follows a Brownian motion, and thereby, ensures that model stock prices exhibit non-negativity as required by limited liability. This process, called a *geometric Brownian motion* by Samuelson, remains to this day the prototypical process used by economists to describe stock price behaviour. Working with Samuelson, McKean (1965) uses the theory of optimal stopping to provide a rigorous derivation of the warrant price in Samuelson's theory.

Although it is the standard mode of analysis for warrant and option pricing theory today, the celebrated work on the stochastic integration by K. Itô (1944, 1951) was not introduced into economic analysis until the late 1960s. Merton (1969, 1971) was the first to use Itô's stochastic calculus in economics. He analysed an agent's optimal consumption and portfolio policies in a continuous time economy where asset prices are Itô processes.

Itô's contribution to the theory of stochastic processes lies in a definition of an integral with desired properties when the integrator is a Brownian motion. A pathwise definition in the Stieltjes sense may fail since a Brownian motion has sample paths that are nowhere differentiable with probability one. For a classical treatment of the Itô integral, see also Itô and McKean (1965) and McKean (1969). A good reference for modern treatments can be found in Chung and Williams (1983).

Itô's definition of a stochastic integral, in contrast to that of Stratonovich (1966), is much better suited for analysing intertemporal economic decision making. The *non-anticipating* integrand in Itô's definition captures the economic constraint that agents cannot anticipate future speculative price movements.

The most useful result of Itô's stochastic calculus is the so-called Itô's lemma: any twice continuously-differentiable function of an Itô process is itself an Itô process. This implies that the agent's wealth process is an Itô process and therefore the Bellman equation in the stochastic dynamic programming problem becomes a second-order partial differential equation. The latter allows one to analyse the portfolio problem by looking at just the first two moments of price processes and to achieve sharp characterizations. Merton (1973a) applied this technique further to study equilibrium relations among risky asset prices and arrived at the *Intertemporal Capital Asset Pricing Model*.

The introduction of Itô's stochastic calculus opened a whole new world for economists. With it, most of the static utility maximization models are readily extended to a dynamic setting with uncertainty. The continuous time set-up allows one to work with differential equations rather than with difference equations. For applications to capital theory and economic growth, see Bismut (1975), Brock and Magill (1979), and Merton (1975); to asset pricing models, see Cox, Ingersoll, and Ross (1985a, 1985b).

Itô's work was later extended by Kunita and Watanabe (1967) to the case where integrators are square-integrable martingales. They also proved a *martingale representation theorem* for a Brownian motion: any square-integrable martingale adapted to a Brownian motion filtration (see below) is representable as an Itô integral.

The most general notions of a stochastic process and a stochastic integral to date are in the terrain of the so-called *French School Probability Theory*, or the *General Theory of Processes*. Very abstract, and surely developed for intrinsic intellectual reasons, it nevertheless seems to have been invented for the study of financial markets; for references, see Dellacherie and Meyer (1978, 1982), Jacod (1979), and Meyer (1966, 1976).

Although making no explicit use of French probability theory, the seminal paper of Black and Scholes (1973) in the pricing of stock options nevertheless opens up the possibility of its application in financial economics. This work was subsequently generalized and formalized by Merton (1973b, 1977). The idea is that the payoff of a stock option can be *replicated* by continuous trading in its underlying stock and a riskless asset. The replicating strategy is *self-financing* in that after the beginning of this strategy there are neither additional funds invested into it nor funds withdrawn out of it. Thus, to rule out arbitrage opportunities, the stock option must sell for the exact value of the replicating portfolio at any point in time.

Black and Scholes's theory provided a strong incentive for financial economists to study continuous time stochastic processes. The key observation in this literature was made by Cox and Ross (1976). They noted that since the expected rate of return of the stock does not enter the Black and Scholes pricing formula for a stock option, the price of an option must be determined as if investors were risk neutral and had probability beliefs such that the stock earns an expected rate of return equal to the riskless rate. Harrison and Kreps (1979) formalized this observation in showing that *any* arbitrage-free price system can be converted into a martingale through a change of an equivalent probability after a suitable normalization. Note that this martingale connection of an arbitrage-free price system was vaguely foreshadowed in Samuelson and Merton (1969).

Harrison and Kreps (1979) and Harrison and Pliska (1981) make clear that the answer to whether a contingent claim can be replicated by dynamic trading is intimately related to the martingale representation theorem. A sketch of their arguments will be given.

Taken as primitive is a complete separable probability space $(\Omega, \mathcal{F}, P)$ and a *filtration* $\mathbf{F} = \{\mathcal{F}_t; t \in [0, 1]\}$. A filtration is an increasing family of sub-sigma-algebras of $\mathcal{F}$ representing information revelation over time. For simplicity, we take the time span of the economy to be $[0, 1]$. We assume that agents are endowed with the same information structure $\mathbf{F}$. Readers can think of a filtration to be like an event tree in a discrete time finite state setting. We also assume that agents at time zero know that the true state of the nature is an element $\omega \in \Omega$, which they will learn at time one.

Agents can only consume at time one. For simplicity again, we take the commodity space to be the space of square-integrable random variables defined on $(\Omega, \mathcal{F}, P)$, denoted by $L^2(P)$.

There are $N + 1$ long-lived securities traded indexed by $n = 0, 1, \ldots, N$. A long-lived security is a security available for trading all the time in $[0, 1]$ and is represented by a price process $\{S_n(t)\}$. It pays a dividend only at time one and is equal to $S_n(1)$ almost surely. Price processes are semimartingales (adapted to $\mathbf{F}$) and $S_n(1) \in L^2(P)$. In modelling a dynamic asset trading economy, before anything interesting can be said, one has to formulate a budget constraint. That naturally involves stochastic integrals. Jacod (1979) has shown that for stochastic integrals to have desired properties, it is necessary that integra-

tors be semimartingales. Thus, semimartingale price processes can be assumed without loss of generality.

In a Walrasian economy, only relative prices are determined. Thus we can assume that the price system has been normalized such that $S_0(t) = 1 \; \forall t \in [0, 1]$. We will call the 0th security the riskless security and the rest risky securities.

A trading strategy is an $(N + 1)$-dimensional predictable process $\theta = \{\theta_n(t); n = 0, 1, \ldots, N\}$, where we interpret $\theta_n(t)$ to be the number of shares of security n held from $t-$ to t before trading at time t. A process is predictable if its values at time t depend only upon the information available strictly before time t. Given the interpretation of θ, predictability is a natural information constraint.

A trading strategy is said to be *simple* if it is bounded and changes its value at most at a finite number of time points in $[0, 1]$.

A trading strategy θ is said to be *self-financing* if the stochastic integral

$$\int_0^t \theta(s)^{\mathrm{T}} \, dS(s)$$

is well-defined and if

$$\theta(t)^{\mathrm{T}} S(t) = \theta(0)^{\mathrm{T}} S(0) + \int_0^t \theta(s)^{\mathrm{T}} \, dS(s) \qquad \forall t \in [0, 1] \quad a.s., \quad (1)$$

where ^{T} denotes transpose. That is, the value of the portfolio θ at time t is equal to its initial value plus accumulated capital gains or losses from time zero to time t. There are neither new investments into nor withdrawals of funds out of the portfolio. This is just a natural budget constraint.

Harrison and Kreps (1979) and Kreps (1981) show that if all the simple self-financing trading strategies are allowed and if arbitrage opportunities are absent, then there exists a probability measure Q equivalent to P such that the Radon-Nikodym derivative $\xi \equiv dQ/dP$ is an element of $L^2(P)$ and that S is a martingale under Q, or a Q-martingale. Fix Q and note that since P and Q are equivalent, all the a.s. statements to follow apply to both.

Now we can specify the space of admissible strategies $\Theta[S]$. A self-financing trading strategy θ is admissible if

$$\int_0^t \theta(s)^{\mathrm{T}} \, dS(s) \qquad t \in [0, 1]$$

is a Q-martingale and $\theta(1)^{\mathrm{T}} S(1) \in L^2(P)$. [See Jacod (1979) for sufficient conditions for this to be true.] Then one can show that given $\Theta[S]$ indeed there are no arbitrage opportunities.

A contingent claim is an element of $L^2(P)$. A contingent claim x is said to be *marketed* if it can be dynamically manufactured by an admissible trading strategy. Formally, x is marketed if there exists $\theta \in \Theta[S]$ such that

$$x = \theta(0)^{\mathrm{T}} S(0) + \int_0^1 \theta(t)^{\mathrm{T}} \, dS(t) \qquad a.s.$$

The value of x at time t is $\theta(t)^{\mathrm{T}} S(t)$. By the definition of admissibility, we have

$$\theta(t)^{\mathrm{T}} S(t) = \theta(0)^{\mathrm{T}} S(0) + \int_0^t \theta(s)^{\mathrm{T}} \, dS(s) \qquad a.s.$$
$$= E^*[x \mid \mathcal{F}_t] \qquad a.s., \quad (2)$$

where $E^*[\cdot]$ is the expectation under Q. That is, the value of a marketed contingent claim is also a Q-martingale.

Before proceeding, we shall make one remark. Since $S_0(t) = 1$, the stochastic integral on the right-hand side of the first line of (2) is determined by S_n, $n = 1, 2, \ldots, N$. That is,

$$\int_0^t \theta(s)^\mathrm{T} \, \mathrm{d}S(s) = \sum_{n=1}^N \int_0^t \theta_n(s) \, \mathrm{d}S_n(s).$$

Now here is the key observation. Let x be a contingent claim. We know from relation (2) that if it is marketed, its value over time is equal to its initial value at time zero plus a stochastic integral with respect to N Q-martingales. Conversely, a contingent claim x marketed if the conditional expectation $E^*[x \,|\, \mathscr{F}_t]$, which is a Q-martingale, can be represented by a stochastic integral with respect to the N Q-martingales $\{S_n(t); n = 1, 2, \ldots, N\}$. [Here we should remark that any $x \in L^2(P)$ has a finite expectation under Q by the Cauchy–Schwarz inequality.] This observation turns on the machinery of the martingale representation theorem in the study of market completeness.

The security markets are said to be *dynamically complete* if all contingent claims are marketed. From the above discussion, it follows that markets are dynamically complete if all Q-martingales are representable as stochastic integrals with respect to the N risky Q-martingale prices. In such event, the N Q-martingales are said to have the *martingale representation property*. Readers might be curious by now that the riskless asset seems to disappear from the story. Indeed, whether a contingent claim is generated by a (not necessarily self-financing) trading strategy does not depend upon the riskless asset after time zero. The riskless asset, however, is a vehicle through which the budget is balanced over time.

The contribution made by Harrison, Kreps, and Pliska is methodological. They make available a powerful machinery for the study of financial/capital markets: the theory of martingales. Now we shall present some consequences of their work.

Since Merton's (1969, 1971, 1973a) analyses of optimal intertemporal consumption-portfolio policies and their implications on equilibrium asset prices, the conditions under which a price system is representable as an Itô process had been an open question for more than a decade. A short answer found in Huang (1985a) is as follows: Take the set-up of the economy as above and assume henceforth that there are no arbitrage opportunities. Moreover, assume that the information structure **F** is a Brownian motion filtration. We know S is a Q-martingale, so we can write

$$S_n(t) = E^*[S_n(1) \,|\, \mathscr{F}_t] \qquad a.s.$$
$$= \frac{E[S_n(1)\xi \,|\, \mathscr{F}_t]}{E[\xi \,|\, \mathscr{F}_t]} \qquad a.s.,$$

where the second equality follows from the Bayes' rule, and where we recall that $\xi = \mathrm{d}Q/\mathrm{d}P$, which is strictly positive by the fact that Q and P are equivalent. The numerator and the denominator of the above relation are both P-square integrable martingales. By the martingale representation theorem of Kunita and Watanabe (1967), we know that any P-square integrable martingale is representable as an Itô integral. Then S_n is an Itô process by Itô's lemma. Hence any arbitrage-free price system is an Itô process when the information structure is a Brownian filtration.

We can also study the sample path properties of a price system, which relates to examining empirically the so-called *efficient market hypothesis*. Much of the empirical work in financial economics and accounting concerns the response of capital/financial asset prices to information. The null hypothesis in this work is typically that the capital/financial markets are *efficient* in the sense that prices rapidly adjust to *new* information. But is it true that prices only make large adjustments

at surprises and what exactly is a *surprise*, mathematically? Here we turn to the classification of stopping times in the general theory of processes. In this context, a surprise is a non-predictable stopping time. We also know that a martingale must be continuous at predictable stopping times (provided that a minor technical condition is satisfied). Thus, S can make discrete changes only at nonpredictable stopping times or at surprises. This and other related issues can be found in Huang (1985a, b). A reference for the classification of stopping times is Dellacherie and Meyer (1978).

So we discover that a price system must be Itô process when the information is a Brownian motion filtration and when there are no arbitrage opportunities. There still remain further questions: does there exist an equilibrium where equilibrium price processes are Itô processes? More importantly, does there exist an equilibrium where although there are only a finite number of long-lived securites traded, the markets are dynamically complete and thus the equilibrium allocation is Pareto optimal? Note that in the Arrow–Debreu equilibrium theory, markets for all contingent claims are available at time zero. Agents trade to a Pareto optimal allocation. There is no need and no incentive for the markets to reopen after time zero. Of course, this does not conform with actual market structures. We do not have a complete set of contingent markets. What we do have are constantly-open financial markets where a finite number of long-lived assets are traded. Thus it is important to know whether there exists an equilibrium in such a world and to know the efficiency of the resulting allocation.

It follows from the earlier discussion on the martingale representation property of risky price processes that what is needed for an affirmative answer to the above questions: is that there be a riskless security with unit price throughout and a finite number of risky long-lived securities that have the martingale representation property. What complicates the story, however, is that the demand and supply of the long-lived securities must be equal in equilibrium. Thus these securities must be picked carefully. Moreover, it is not true that a finite number of martingales having the martingale representation property can always be found. Duffie and Huang (1985, 1986b) and Duffie (1986a), in exchange as well as in production economies, demonstrated a procedure to select long-lived securities having the desired properties and conditions under which the number is finite.

The martingale connection of an arbitrage-free system has been generalized to economies where securities can pay dividends and agents can consume at any time in [0, 1]. After a suitable normalization, a price system plus the accumulated dividends form a martingale under an equivalent probability measure. This is done in Huang (1985b). Similar theory is also valid in economies where agents have differential information. Interested readers are referred to Duffie and Huang (1986b) for details.

Although the focus of research has been on capital theory and financial markets, applications of the theory of continuous time stochastic processes to economic problems outside these areas can be found. For example, Duffie (1986b) applies classical potential theory as in the context of Markov processes to valuation of securities, and Li (1984) examines the stochastic theory of the firm in continuous time. He uses point processes to model stochastic demands for commodities and endogenizes a firm's demand for inventories, among other things. For applications of the theory of optimal stopping to game theory, see Hugues (1974) for zero-sum stopping games, and Huang and Li (1986) for nonzero-sum stopping games.

CHI-FU HUANG

See also CAPITAL ASSET PRICING MODEL; CONTINUOUS-TIME STOCHASTIC MODELS; OPTIONS.

BIBLIOGRAPHY

Bachelier, L. 1900. *Théorie de la speculation*. Paris: Gauthier-Villars.

Bismut, J. 1975. Growth and optimal intertemporal allocation of risks. *Journal of Economic Theory* 10, 239–7.

Black, F. and Scholes, M. 1973. The pricing of options and corporate liabilities. *Journal of Political Economy* 81, 637–54.

Brock, W. and Magill, M. 1979. Dynamics under uncertainty. *Econometrica* 47, 843–68.

Chung, K. and Williams, R. 1983. *An Introduction to Stochastic Integration*. Boston: Birkhauser.

Cox, J. and Ross, S. 1976. The valuation of options for alternative stochastic processes. *Journal of Financial Economics* 3, 145–66.

Cox, J., Ingersoll, J. and Ross, S. 1985a. An intertemporal general equilibrium model of asset prices. *Econometrica* 53, 363–84.

Cox, J., Ingersoll, J. and Ross, S. 1985b. A theory of the term structure of interest rates. *Econometrica* 53, 385–408.

Dellacherie, C. and Meyer, P. 1978. *Probabilities and Potential A: General Theory of Process*. New York: North-Holland Publishing Company.

Dellacherie, C. and Meyer, P. 1982. *Probabilities and Potential B: Theory of Martingales*. New York: North-Holland Publishing Company.

Duffie, D. 1986a. Stochastic equilibria: existence, spanning number, and the 'no expected gains for trade' hypothesis. *Econometrica*.

Duffie, D. 1986b. Price operators: extensions, potentials, and the Markov valuation of securities. Research Paper No. 813. Graduate School of Business, Stanford University.

Duffie, D. and Huang, C. 1985. Implementing Arrow–Debreu equilibria by continuous trading of few long-lived securities. *Econometrica* 53, 1337–56.

Duffie, D. and Huang, C. 1986a. Multiperiod securities markets with differential information: martingales and resolution times. *Journal of Mathematical Economics*.

Duffie, D. and Huang, C. 1986b. Stochastic production-exchange equilibria. Graduate School of Business, Stanford University.

Einstein, A. 1905. On the movement of small particles suspended in a stationary liquid demanded by the molecular kinetic theory of heat. *Annals of Physics* 17.

Harrison, M. and Kreps, D. 1979. Martingales and arbitrage in multiperiod securities markets. *Journal of Economic Theory* 20, 381–408.

Harrison, M. and Pliska, S. 1981. Martingales and stochastic integrals in the theory of continuous trading. *Stochastic Processes and their Applications* 11, 215–60.

Huang, C. 1985a. Information structure and equilibrium asset prices. *Journal of Economic Theory* 35, 33–71.

Huang, C. 1985b. Information structure and viable price systems. *Journal of Mathematical Economics* 14, 215–40.

Huang, C. and Li, L. 1986. Continuous time stopping games, Working Paper No. 1796–86, Sloan School of Management, MIT.

Hugues, C. 1974. Markov games. Technical Report No. 33, Department of Operations Research, Stanford University.

Itô, K. 1944. Stochastic integrals. *Proceedings of the Imperial Academy* 22, 519–24, Tokyo.

Itô, K. 1951. On stochastic differential equations. *Memoirs of the American Mathematical Society*. Rhode Island: The American Mathematical Society.

Itô, K. and McKean, H. 1965. *Diffusion Processes and Their Sample Paths*. New York: Springer-Verlag.

Jacod, J. 1979. *Calcul stochastique et problemes de martingales*. Lecture Notes in Mathematics 714, New York: Springer-Verlag.

Kreps, D. 1981. Arbitrage and equilibrium in economies with infinitely many commodities. *Journal of Mathematical Economics* 8, 15–35.

Kunita, H. and Watanabe, S. 1967. On square-integrable martingales. *Nagoya Mathematics Journal* 30, 209–245.

Li, L. 1984. A stochastic theory of the firm. Unpublished PhD thesis, Northwestern University.

McKean, H. 1965. Appendix: A free boundary problem for the heat equation arising from a problem in mathematical economics. *Industrial Management Review* 6, 32–39.

McKean, H. 1969. *Stochastic Integrals*. New York: Academic Press.

Merton, R. 1969. Lifetime portfolio selection under uncertainty: the continuous case. *Review of Economics and Statistics* 51, 247–57.

Merton, R. 1971. Optimum consumption and portfolio rules in a continuous time model. *Journal of Economic Theory* 3, 373–413.

Merton, R. 1973a. An intertemporal capital asset pricing model. *Econometrica* 41, 867–88.

Merton, R. 1973b. Theory of rational option pricing. *Bell Journal of Economics and Management Science* 4, 141–83.

Merton, R. 1975. An asymptotic theory of growth under uncertainty. *Review of Economic Studies* 42, 375–93.

Merton, R. 1977. On the pricing of contingent claims and the Modigliani–Miller theorem. *Journal of Financial Economics* 5, 241–9.

Meyer, P. 1966. *Probability and Potentials*. Blaisdell Publishing Company.

Meyer, P. 1976. Un cours sur les integrales stochastiques. In *Seminaires de Probabilité X*, Lecture Notes in Mathematics 511, New York: Springer-Verlag.

Samuelson, P. 1965. Rational theory of warrant pricing. *Industrial Management Review* 6, 13–32.

Samuelson, P. and Merton, R. 1969. A complete model of warrant pricing that maximizes utility. *Industrial Management Review* 10, 17–46.

Stratonovich, R. 1966. A new representation for stochastic integrals and equations. *SIAM Journal of Control* 4, 362–71.

continuum economies. *See* LARGE ECONOMIES; PERFECT COMPETITION.

contract curve. *See* CORES; EDGEWORTH, FRANCIS YSIDRO.

contract theory. *See* IMPLICIT CONTRACTS; INCENTIVE CONTRACTS; INCOMPLETE CONTRACTS; QUASI-CONTRACT.

contradiction.   The fundamental form of a contradiction is a pair of propositions, 'A' and 'Not A', one the negation of the other. If such an explicit contradiction is part of a body of propositions asserted by some individual or group at a given time, it follows that not all those propositions can be true: by thus impairing the reliability of the proponent, the occurrence of the contradiction throws doubt upon the truth of all the other propositions asserted.

Far more frequent than an overt or explicit contradiction is a hidden contradiction. A hidden contradiction is contained in a body of propositions when, by logically valid deductive reasoning, an explicit contradiction can be derived from them. Two quite different cases arise, according to the status of the original propositions from which the contradiction was derived. The first is that in which, as before, those propositions were all asserted by an individual or body of people. In this case, the hidden contradiction is as fatal to the joint correctness of those assertions as is the explicit one, although, of course, considerable work may have had to be expended in bringing it to light.

The second case is that in which at least some of the original propositions were not asserted, but merely advanced as suppositions to be considered. The formal conclusion now remains exactly the same: given that the contradiction was validly derived, not all the original propositions can be true. The effect, of course, is very different. Suppose that the original propositions – the premises from which the contradictory pair 'A' and 'Not A' have been derived – were four in number: 'B$_1$', 'B$_2$', 'C$_1$', and 'C$_2$'; and suppose that 'B$_1$' and 'B$_2$' were asserted outright, but that 'C$_1$' and 'C$_2$' were merely advanced for consideration. The contradiction shows that not all four can be true: without having to withdraw anything that he asserted, the proponent, still maintaining 'B$_1$' and 'B$_2$', is now in a position to assert 'If C$_1$, then not C$_2$' (or its equivalent, 'If C$_2$, then not C$_1$').

For this reason, derivation of a contradiction can be employed, not merely as a means of refuting the assertions of another, but as a method of demonstrating negative propositions: this is the celebrated mode of argument *reductio ad absurdum*. In conjunction with premisses, 'B$_1$' and 'B$_2$', say asserted outright, a proposition 'C' is presented as a hypothesis: not as a conjecture or supposition to be seriously entertained, but with an eye to proving its negation 'Not C'. From the premisses 'B$_1$' and 'B$_2$' and the hypothesis 'C', two contradictory propositions 'A' and 'Not A' are then derived: on the basis of the two premisses, the hypothesis now being dropped, its negation 'Not C' can now be definitely asserted. Two special cases fall under this general description. One is that under which 'A' is actually one of the two premisses, say 'B$_1$'. If from premisses 'B$_1$' and 'B$_2$' and the hypothesis 'C', the conclusion 'Not B', can be derived, one may assert 'Not C' on the strength of the two premisses. The other special case is that in which 'A' is the hypothesis 'C' itself. If from premisses 'B$_1$' and 'B$_2$' and the hypothesis 'C', the negation 'Not C' of the hypothesis can be derived, 'Not C' may be asserted outright on the strength of the two premisses.

As is well known, *reductio ad absurdum* arguments are frequent in mathematics. One of the simplest, as well as historically most important, is the proof that 2 has no rational square root. We may take as the premisses: (B$_1$) any rational number may be represented as a fraction whose numerator and denominator have no common factor; and (B$_2$) the square of an odd number is odd. As the hypothesis we may take: (C) 2 has a rational square root. From (B$_1$) and (C) it follows that, for some integers m and n, m and n have no common factor and $(m/n)_2 = 2$; hence $m^2 = 2n^2$. Hence, by the definition of 'even', m_2 is even, and from (B$_2$) it can be inferred that m is not odd, and hence is even. Thus $m = 2k$ for some k, and we have: $m_2 = 4k^2 = 2n^2$, and so $2k^2 = n^2$. Applying (B$_2$) once more, we infer that n is also even. Since m and n are both even, they have 2 as a common factor, which contradicts the earlier stipulation that they have no common factor. By arriving at this contradiction, we have achieved a demonstration that 2 has no rational square root, that is, a proof of the negation of our hypothesis (C).

The derivation of a hidden contradiction from premisses all definitely asserted may also be illustrated from mathematics. The most celebrated examples are the set-theoretic paradoxes which provoked the first 'crisis in the foundations' of mathematics in the early years of this century. Some of these, such as Burali-Forti's paradox and Cantor's paradox, demand some technical background; but Russell's paradox has the advantage of being statable in very simple terms. The propositions leading to this contradiction appear at first sight entirely harmless. They are: (1) to every property there corresponds a class, the class of things having that property; (2) the class of things having a given property F contains as members all and only those things that have the property F. Russell's contradiction arises from considering the property G of being a class that does not contain itself as a member. By assumption (1), there exists a class, which we may call W, of things having the property G. We now ask whether W contains itself as a member. It may then be argued by *reductio*

ad absurdum that it does not: we have first to suppose, as a hypothesis, that it does. By assumption (2), it therefore has property G. But property G is the property of being a class that does not contain itself: it follows, contrary to the hypothesis, that W does not contain itself. We may thus discard the hypothesis, and assert outright that W does not contain itself. Applying assumption (2) once more, we may then conclude that W lacks property G. It therefore is either not a class or does contain itself as a member; since it is by definition a class, it contains itself as a member. This now contradicts our earlier conclusion that it does not contain itself as a member: the two intuitively reasonable assumptions (1) and (2) have led to a contradiction.

Russell's contradiction is so simple to state and so easy to derive that those who are unaware of the importance in mathematics of the notion of a class or set are liable to think it no more than a trivial verbal puzzle. It is very far from trivial. It overthrew the life's work of the great logician Gottlob Frege, namely to provide unquestionably firm foundations for the theories of natural numbers and of real and complex numbers, just when he believed that he had accomplished it; and it cast the foundations of mathematics into confusion for some years. By showing that assumptions (1) and (2) cannot both be consistently made, it challenged mathematicians and logicians to find weaker assumptions that would be consistent: for which properties F do assumptions (1) and (2) hold good? This question proved exceedingly difficult to answer: hence the 'crisis in the foundations'.

Why is the discovery of a hidden contradiction so devastating? One answer is that, if a pair of contradictory propositions are both consequences of a given set of assumptions, then *every* proposition is a consequence of them. This holds good in virtue of the logical law, known to the medievals as *ex falso quodlibet*, that, from a pair of premisses 'A' and 'Not A', any proposition 'B' may be inferred. This law appears at first glance both useless and implausible; a natural first reaction is therefore to suggest repudiating it. That, however, is not easily done, since it is a consequence of two other, seemingly inescapable, laws concerning the logical constant 'or'. The first is the law now usually known as 'or'-introduction or disjunction-introduction, that, for any propositions 'A' and 'B', 'A or B' follows from 'A'. The second is that known in the traditional logic as *modus tollendo ponens*, that 'B' follows from the premisses 'A or B' and 'Not A'. It is quite obvious that, from the premisses 'A' and 'Not A' of the *ex falso quodlibet*, its conclusion 'B' can be reached by first applying 'or'-introduction and then *modus tollendo ponens*: but it is very hard to see how we could possibly reject either of the two latter laws, for they appear absolutely constitutive of the meaning of the connective 'or'. The best possible way to establish the truth of a disjunction – a statement of the form 'A or B' – is to establish the truth of one or other of the disjuncts 'A' and 'B': if the truth of 'A' does not guarantee the truth of 'A or B', what does 'or' mean? Conversely, the truth of a disjunction appears to *demand* that at least one of the disjuncts be true: so, if 'A or B' is true and 'A' is not true, 'B' must be true. If 'Not A' is true, 'A' cannot be true: so the validity of *modus tollendo ponens* appears likewise unquestionable.

Faced with the difficulty of rendering contradictions harmless by modifying our logic, some have proposed extruding the sign of negation altogether from the language. What use are merely negative propositions, they enquire: when we are tempted to assert one, we usually have to hand a more informative affirmative statement to take its place, and, when we do not, it will be a good thing to search for one. But the proposed remedy, drastic as it sounds, does not work: for, in place of the derivation of a contradiction, it is usually possible to exhibit a more direct method of deriving any proposition whatever. This may be illustrated by converting the Russell paradox into this form. Take any random proposition, say 'The Earth is flat': and consider the property H of being a class such that, if it contains itself as a member, the Earth is flat. By assumption (1), there exists a class, say Y, of things having the property H: let us ask, as before, whether Y contains itself as a member. Suppose, as a hypothesis, that it does. Then, by assumption (2), it possesses property H: that is, it is a class such that, if it contains itself as a member, the Earth is flat. Now, by hypothesis, it *does* contain itself as a member; hence, on this hypothesis, the Earth must be flat. We have now shown, on the hypothesis that Y contains itself as a member, that the Earth is flat: we may therefore assert outright, independently of the hypothesis, that, *if* Y contains itself as a member, the Earth is flat. From this we see that, since Y is by definition a class, it has property H. Hence, by assumption (2), Y contains it as a member: that is, Y really does contain itself as a member (and not just by hypothesis). We have now shown two things: first, that if Y contains itself as a member, the Earth is flat; and, secondly, that Y *does* contain itself as a member. It follows inescapably that the Earth is flat.

This version of the paradox lies in wait for any who would seek to escape it by tampering with the logical operation of negation. The idea, that some have had, that escape lies in rejecting the principle of bivalence (that every proposition is either true or false) or the closely related law of excluded middle (that, for any proposition 'A', 'A or not A' is a logical truth), does not even avoid the original paradox. It is tempting to open the argument by which the contradiction is derived with the declaration, 'Either W contains itself as a member or it does not': but it is quite unnecessary, and the foregoing statement of the argument neither began in this way, nor invoked the law of excluded middle at any other point. It turned principally on an application of *reductio ad absurdum*, in order to infer 'W does not contain itself as a member' from the fact that a contradiction followed from the hypothesis 'W contains itself as a member'. There are, indeed, logical systems in which the law of excluded middle does not hold. But, in the principal logical system of this kind, that known as intuitionistic logic, *reductio ad absurdum*, in the above form, is perfectly valid: indeed, all arguments and forms of argument hitherto considered are intuitionistically valid. It is true, indeed, that there is another, frequently used, version of *reductio ad absurdum* that is *not* intuitionistically valid. As *reductio ad absurdum* was characterized above, it always leads to a *negative* conclusion: the derivation of a contradiction from a hypothesis shows that hypothesis is *not* true. In the intuitionistically invalid version, a proposition is deduced to be true from the fact that the hypothesis that its negation is true leads to a contradiction. Certain propositions, say 'B₁' and 'B₂', are asserted as premises, and 'Not C' is assumed as hypothesis. A contradiction 'A' and 'Not A' is derived, and, on the strength of this, 'C' is asserted as following from the premises 'B₁' and 'B₂' alone. *This* form of argument does depend, for its validity, on the principle of bivalence. If we equate the falsity of 'C' with the truth of 'Not C', then the contradiction shows that 'C' cannot be false: to infer that it is actually true requires the presupposition that it is either true or false. Intuitionistic logic sanctions our treating large classes of propositions as satisfying bivalence, so that many applications of this extended form a *reductio ad absurdum* will be legitimate: but it objects to considering it generally valid, since

not all propositions can be regarded as necessarily being either true or false.

The devastating effect of the appearance of a hidden contradiction in a set of propositions asserted as true, or hitherto accepted as true, is not, of course, due to the fear that anyone will use the *ex falso quodlibet* law to deduce arbitrary conclusions: the utility of the *ex falso quodlibet* turns on its use in subordinate deductions (deductions under a hypothesis subsequently to be abandoned). The point is, rather, that we no longer have *any* reason to believe a proposition on the strength of its being a logical consequence of the given set, since every proposition is such a consequence: until we have discovered what gave rise to the contradiction, and have corrected it, no conclusion we derived from that set has any claim to be believed. The great philosopher Ludwig Wittgenstein scoffed at mathematicians for their 'superstitious awe and dread in face of a contradiction', and asked why they did not simply go round it: but, until it has been resolved, no one can be sure that the path he has taken does go round it. Analysis may show that the use of one particular notion is responsible for the contradiction, and we may then trust those conclusions, previously drawn, the argument to which in no way involved that notion: but, once the contradiction has appeared, only strong measures will supply us with any rational ground for believing any proposition that does involve it, directly or in the argument it is based on. It is not enough merely to find a way to weaken those of our former assumptions that involved the suspect notion so as to block the derivation of the contradiction. That was precisely what Frege did when Russell showed that his contradiction could be derived in Frege's logical theory: but it proved that another contradiction, similar though more complex, was lurking in the modified theory. We have, therefore, in such a case, not merely to weaken our assumptions, but to supply some argument that at least makes it plausible that the weakened assumptions are now consistent. When no hidden contradiction has been revealed, intuitive acceptability may be sufficient basis on which to treat our assumptions as true, even though it does not amount to proof. Once a contradiction has appeared, however, intuition is no longer to be trusted. The contradiction is evidence that the theory is diseased. It is no more enough to root out that particular contradiction than it is to eliminate a particular patch of dry rot: a thorough decontamination of the whole is called for.

The reason why the appearance of a contradiction is so dire a symptom lies not so much in any laws of inference as in the semantic notions of truth and falsity. A proposition and its negation cannot both be true, whereas it is inherent in the definition of 'follows (logically) from' that what follows from a set of true propositions must itself be true: hence, if 'A' and 'Not A' both follow from a set of assumptions, not every assumption in that set can be true. Appeal to semantic notions is in fact needed to explain the concept of the negation of a proposition. Logicians are accustomed to employ a negation operator, with the sense 'It is not the case that ...', which acts on whole propositions (sentences) to form their negations; and that has hitherto been tacitly done in this article. But natural language hardly possesses such an operator. Apart from the clumsy expedient of sticking the phrase 'It is not the case that ... in front of a sentence, natural language has no uniform way of forming negations. Admittedly, the negations of many sentences can be found by negating the main verb (in English, replacing 'is' by 'is not', 'resembles' by 'does not resemble', etc.), but this does not work for all. The negation of 'Someone is snoring' is not 'Someone is not snoring', but 'No-one is snoring'; the negation of 'You must attend' is not 'You must not attend', but 'You need not attend'; the negation of 'Whenever I look up, I see you yawning' is not 'Whenever I look up, I do not see you yawning', but 'I do not see you yawning whenever I look up'; and the negation of 'If taxes are cut, the government will be re-elected' is not 'If taxes are cut, the government will not be re-elected', but 'The government will not necessarily be re-elected if taxes are cut'. There is no uniform syntactic rule for determining the negation of any given proposition: to identify the negation of a proposition 'A', we have to advert to its characterization as that proposition which (in any given context) is true just in case 'A' is false.

This means that the notion of falsity is essential for an explanation of 'not' as used to qualify whole sentences: it does not mean that the notion is more fundamental than the uses of 'not' that occur in natural language. On the contrary, to identify the negations of most propositions, it is necessary to understand the word 'not' as it occurs in a variety of positions in a sentence, as illustrated in the above examples. It is therefore in no way inconsistent with the general characterization of the negation of a proposition in terms of truth and falsity to explain a proposition as being false just in case it is not true. It is, in fact, a mistake to think of truth and falsity as equally fundamental notions: the application to a proposition of only one of them is sufficient to determine its content. If this were not so, there could be one pair of propositions 'A' and 'B' differing only in that 'B' was neither true nor false in certain of the cases in which 'A' was false, and another pair 'C' and 'D' differing only in that 'D' was neither true nor false in certain of the cases in which 'C' was true, and these differences would entail that the two propositions in each pair diverged in content. But that is impossible, if 'content' is understood as here intended, namely as what is conveyed by the assertion of the proposition on its own. What was not laid down, in the foregoing stipulation, was whether, in asserting a proposition, a speaker is to be understood as excluding or as allowing for the case in which that proposition is neither true nor false. If he is to be understood as excluding it, what he conveys by his assertion is that the case in which the proposition is true obtains: the content of 'A' and of 'B' will therefore coincide. If, on the other hand, the speaker is to be understood as allowing for the case in which the proposition is neither true nor false, what he conveys by asserting it is that one of the cases in which it is not false obtains: if so, the content of 'C' and 'D' will coincide. To fix the content of a proposition, in the sense explained, we need to know, of any state of affairs specified in sufficient detail, whether an assertion of the proposition would rule it out or allow for it: and this does not provide for the introduction of two notions, those of truth and falsity, whose application is partially independent of one another.

The principle of bivalence rests on the conception that, to grasp the content of a proposition, one must know just what circumstances must obtain for it to be true, independently of whether or not these are circumstances which we are capable of recognizing as obtaining when they do. Given this conception, we may understand 'Not A' as being true in all circumstances save those in which 'A' is true: and so 'A' will be determinately either true or false. Likewise, the connective 'or' is so understood that 'A or B' is true in those circumstances in which 'A' is true, and in those in which 'B' is true, but in no others. Intuitionistic logic, on the other hand, is founded on the idea that the content of a proposition must be determined by our capacity to recognize it as true or as false. To grasp its content, we must know which recognizable circumstances render it demonstrably true: to assert it is to claim that such circumstances obtain. The meaning of 'or' must be explained by a rule determining the content of 'A or B', as given in this way, from the content of 'A' and of 'B', also so given: namely that those recognizable circumstances which render 'A' demonstrably true, and those which render 'B' demonstrably true, also count as rendering 'A or B' demonstrably true, but that no other recognizable circumstances do so. Since there is plainly no general guarantee, for any proposition 'A', that any recognizable circumstances will obtain that either render 'A' or render 'Not A' demonstrably true, the law of excluded middle 'A or not A' is not, in this logic, a valid law. (Some have seen in the requirement that a proof of 'A or B' constitute a proof either of 'A' or of 'B' an analogy with the legal conception of proof.)

How, then, is the operator 'not' to be understood in this logic? The usual explanation is to pick some patently absurd proposition, say 'Black is white', and explain 'Not A' as equivalent to 'If A, then black is white'. This throws us back on the intuitionistic explanation of 'if', which is that 'If A, then B' is demonstrably true in recognizable circumstances which would render 'B' demonstrably true, given that 'A' were demonstrably true. On the assumption that the absurd proposition 'Black is white' can never be demonstrably true, this amounts to counting 'Not A' as demonstrably true in circumstances which can be recognized as excluding the possibility that 'A' can become recognizably true. The assumption is not built into the logic, however. The fundamental laws governing negation are *reductio ad absurdum*, in the restricted form leading to a negative conclusion, and *ex falso quodlibet*. On the explanation of 'not' in terms of 'if', *reductio ad absurdum* is derivable from the laws governing 'if'. If from the hypothesis 'C' we can infer both 'A' and 'If A, then black is white', only one more step is needed to infer 'Black is white' from 'C': hence, dropping the hypothesis 'C', we may assert, 'If C, then black is white', which is 'Not C'. The *ex falso quodlibet*, however, is not derivable without a further assumption. We need to show that, from the premisses 'A' and 'Not A', we can infer any proposition. Since 'Not A' is 'If A, then black is white', the ordinary laws governing 'if' allow us to infer 'Black is white': so we need to assume that, from the absurd proposition 'Black is white', we can infer any proposition. The stronger assumption, that we shall never be able to assert 'Black is white', here plays no role. If we had a very restricted language, for which there was no absurdity in supposing that every proposition expressible in it might prove to be demonstrably true, it would be sufficient to understand what we have been calling the 'absurd' proposition as the conjunction of all other propositions expressible in the language: all the laws of intuitionistic logic would then hold good. In this sense, then, the intuitionistic meaning of negation – unlike those of the other propositional operators such as 'and' and 'or' – is relative to the language: the weaker the expressive power of the language, the weaker the meaning which logic requires us to impose on the word 'not'.

The word 'contradiction' is often used in a looser sense than the strict one so far discussed. When it is said that there is a contradiction in capitalist economies, it is not meant that the very notion of a capitalist economy involves a contradiction in the strict sense, or otherwise no such thing as a capitalist economy could exist. One of several things may be meant instead. (1) There is a formal contradiction, not in a *description* of a capitalist economy, but in the *justification* normally offered for it, or, perhaps, in any that could be offered. (2) A capitalist economy has a necessary tendency to evolve in each of two incompatible ways, and the resulting social and economic tensions will inevitably destroy it. (3) The term 'capitalist' applies to an economic system as the term 'smooth' applies to a surface, in virtue of its approximation to an unattainable limit: there really is a formal contradiction in the notion of a *pure* capitalist system – one that occupies the limiting position – but not in that of one that approximates to that limit and is hence ordinarily called 'capitalist'. It is in one of these senses, or a similar one, that the word 'contradiction', as customarily employed by Marxists and Hegelians, must be understood; but such a stretched use of it is best avoided. An explicit contradiction, in argument or testimony, is comparatively rare, although of course it does occur: but nothing deserves to be called a contradiction unless it genuinely implies an explicit one.

MICHAEL DUMMETT

See also AXIOMATIC THEORIES; EXISTENCE OF GENERAL EQUILIBRIUM.

contradictions of capitalism. Writers in the Marxist tradition frequently make use of the term 'contradiction of capitalism'. It is sometimes used, in a very loose sense, to describe virtually any malfunction or indeed objectionable feature of the capitalist system. But in Marx's theory of historical materialism the notion of contradiction played a more fundamental role. One of the central tenets of the theory is that there can be a contradiction between a society's system of economic organization and its capacity to develop its productive potential. Indeed it is precisely such a contradiction between the relations of production (relations of ownership, control etc.) and the forces of production (productive potential), which necessitates through some mechanism or other, a transformation of the economic system. Thus, argued Marx, at a certain stage the rigidities of the feudal system hampered economic growth, which required for its promotion the full and unfettered development of production for the market. The development of productive potential under capitalism formed the basis on which socialism *could* be constructed. The contradictions of capitalism, its inability in turn to take society forward beyond a certain stage, ensured that it *would* be superseded by socialism (see Elster, 1985, especially chapter 5).

LABOUR POWER AND THE LABOUR PROCESS. For Marx the defining feature of capitalism is that *labour power*, workers' capacity to work, becomes a commodity, which has to be sold by workers who do not have the means of production necessary to work on their own account. The capitalist class pays for this labour power at its value, that is, at a wage determined by social and historical circumstances. But labour power has the capacity to create more value than is contained in it – more precisely, the working class is forced to work longer than is required to produce the goods required to sustain it, leaving a surplus value to be appropriated by the capitalist.

This analysis of the source and nature of profit focuses attention on the factory floor as the locus of the exploitative relation between capital and labour. Labour power is a special commodity in that it cannot be detached from the worker. They do not literally leave their labour power at the factory gate each morning and pick it up in the evening in order to reconstitute it with food and sleep. While this is obvious, it has to be emphasized, since the conventional treatment of production as a matter of technically combining 'labour services' and 'capital services' pays no attention to the active participation of workers in the process of production (see

Rowthorn, 1980). In fact discipline, supervision, *control* over work are integral to the capitalist system. In turn this means that conflict between workers and employers over all aspects of the labour process is endemic.

Control over labour, and the conflict involved, is clearly a problem for the functioning of capitalism ignored by theories which describe it in terms of the harmonious cooperation between the classes (or owners of factors of production). But does it constitute a contradiction in the sense that it is unresolvable on the basis of private ownership of the means of production, and will lead to increasing malfunctioning of the system as a whole?

It is quite possible to conceive of situations in which inability to control labour in the labour process would become chronic. If it were the case that the development of capitalist production necessarily crowded workers into larger and larger factories, with deteriorating working conditions, but increasing opportunities for organization and resistance, then the question of control over labour could become critical. In fact trends have been more complex. In the advanced capitalist countries, firms have grown enormously in terms of numbers employed, but average plant size has grown much less. Whilst Ford-type production lines may have represented the ultimate in the imposition of capitalist control over the labour process by mechanical means, the continued requirement for skilled work, demanding judgement, has prevented such systems of work organization being instituted in all industries. Indeed in some industries, worker opposition, or a trend towards more sophisticated products, has led to a reversion to smaller-scale, more integrated methods of production where work is more varied, skilled and responsible.

What is striking, however, is that such trends have in part derived precisely from the resistance engendered by large-scale production. To take the case only of the motor industry, the development of worker resistance in US car plants in the 1960s led to widespread attempts to 'humanize' work by introducing team methods of production and payment. In Italy, conflict in Fiat car factories led to a deliberate policy of decentralizing the less skilled processes of production in order to overcome the problem of controlling 'mass work' in the factories. The production system of Japanese car companies is widely admired, whereby the most important and technically sophisticated stages of production are carried out in large factories, by trained workers, with high wages, paternalistic welfare provisions, tight labour discipline and a modicum of consultation, leaving many components to be produced in much smaller plants by subcontractors, paying lower wages and with less security of employment.

The most important point is a more general one. The shape of development of the capitalist system is determined by the problems and difficulties it encounters. It does not evolve out of some inexorable pattern of technical development; indeed, technology is consciously shaped to overcome social problems (like control over workers) as well as technical ones. A contradiction does not have to spell increasing malfunctioning, let alone capitalism's destruction, to heavily influence the way the system develops.

LABOUR SHORTAGE. If the first special characteristic of the commodity labour power is that its 'consumption' in the labour process involves the seller (the worker), the second is that its 'production' does not involve the capitalists. For workers are of course 'reproduced' in the home, not produced in factories. The supply of labour power, therefore, cannot like other commodities be increased by a simple redistribution of resources to the sector producing it. The supply of labour, while by no means independent of economic conditions, is not regulated by them as simply as other commodities. Availability of consumer goods does not spell availability of workers. This feature of labour power, together with the issue of control of work already discussed, explains why in analysing production workers cannot be represented by the consumer goods they live on.

The supply of labour is not entirely fixed, of course. Higher wages may increase population growth (as child mortality declines for example), but the social development which accompanies increased living standards may lead to smaller families. This in turn may permit greater participation by women in the labour force. But increased educational standards may delay entry into the labour force, welfare provisions may enable earlier retirement, and part of increased living standards may be taken in reduced hours of work. As pre-capitalist forms of production decline, the possibility for recruiting wage labour from their ranks is diminished; immigration from countries with a labour surplus may meet social and political barriers.

While the supply of labour depends on a host of these factors, not very amenable to short-term manipulation, the demand for labour depends on the rate at which capital is accumulated and its form. Rapid capital accumulation leads to increased demand for labour as workers are required for the new factories. But the new investment may be of a labour-saving variety, requiring fewer workers per machine as compared to earlier vintages. The rise in labour demand depends on the balance between these two forces. If accumulation is sufficiently rapid (as in the advanced capitalist countries in the 1950s and 1960s for example), so that demand for labour rises faster than the supply, then the reserve army of labour (the unemployed and underemployed) shrinks. This improves workers' bargaining position, with consequent difficulties for the employers in controlling work and wages. A crisis of 'overaccumulation' results.

Increased wages and difficulties in keeping up productivity levels both tend to reduce profits. This leads to reduced investment, insufficient demand for commodities and labour, and stagnation. The 'law of value' does not apply to labour power, so that shortage of supply does not lead to increased profitability in its production and thus increased supply. This can be seen as a fundamental 'contradiction' of capitalism, in the sense that the functioning of capitalism requires labour power to be fully a commodity, and yet this is impossible (see Itoh, 1980). Of course this does not establish that the contradiction is irresolvable. If the unemployment which results has the expected effect of reducing workers' bargaining power, then wages can be forced down and productivity up, profits and investment recover and a cyclical upturn results.

INDIVIDUAL AND CLASS INTERESTS. The development of such a crisis of 'overaccumulation' is an example of a more general category of problems. Each individual capitalist is attempting to maximize his profits through securing more labour; yet this leads to lower profits for the capitalist class as a whole as they bid up wages and find increasing problems in work organization. So the rationality of the individual economic agents conflicts with what is rational for the system as a whole. It seems very reasonable to describe this as a 'contradiction' in the functioning of capitalism (Elster, 1985). It would require a degree of coordination, which is actually impossible under normal circumstances in a competitive decentralized economy, for the individual employers to hold back from accumulating at a rate which in aggregate is unsustainable. There is no mechanism to tailor the rate of accumulation to what, given

the pattern of technical progress, is compatible with the growth of the labour supply, or adjust the pattern of technical progress to what is compatible with the other two variables. What has to 'give' is the rate of profit, and there is no guarantee that the response to a profit squeeze will be a smooth reduction in accumulation to the appropriate level.

There are other examples of 'contradictions' between the interests of individual capitalists and their class interest. Suppose an economic crisis has developed with unused capacity and unemployed labour. Each capitalist may try to improve his competitive position by cutting his employees' wages. But in aggregate the effect of such a strategy would be to reduce consumer demand, which could make the crisis worse. Exactly the same argument applies to the policies of individual capitalist countries trying to solve their problems by increasing their competitiveness. For the context may be a 'negative sum game', whereby cutting wages actually worsens the overall situation. Attempting to cut workers wages, whilst exhorting other capitalists' workers through advertisements to consume more, is a profoundly contradictory situation.

The famous example of this type of contradiction described by Marx was his Law of the Tendency of the Rate of Profit to Fall (LTRPF). He argued that the individual attempts of capitalists to maximize their profits led them to introduce techniques of production which reduced the profit rate for the class as a whole. As described elsewhere (see MARXIST ECONOMICS), Marx's argument is not satisfactory. But this weakness may not seem of great importance, since we have seen in the discussion of overaccumulation that it is perfectly possible to describe a situation where capitalists do act in such a way as to lead to lower profits for them all. The LTRPF leads to a prediction of a continuous decline in the profit rate, and a declining rate of accumulation, leading, if the process developed that far, to absolute stagnation. The actions of capitalists would, in the long run, destroy the very motor of the system, capital accumulation. Crises of overaccumulation, however, are less fundamental in the sense that they are contingent on a particular pattern of accumulation, technical progress and labour supply. Moreover, while they might be repeated there is no basis for asserting an inevitable tendency that they should become deeper and deeper. They can hardly be said therefore to amount to an absolute contradiction in the capitalist process of accumulation, which is the way Marx himself interpreted the LTRPF.

COMPETITION AND CONCENTRATION. The driving force of capitalism, according to Marx, is competition. This forces the individual capitalist to accumulate capital in the form of new factories, embodying the latest technology. If he fails to do this he will be defeated by his rivals in the battle for markets since his costs will be greater. In modern conditions, where investment is so necessary to generate new products, and where economies of scale in marketing are important alongside those in production, this pressure is stronger than ever. According to Marx the advantages of large-scale production lead to its concentration (he uses the term centralization) in the hands of fewer and fewer firms. As the most dynamic firms knock out, or take over, those that invest less effectively the degree of competition is reduced. At a certain stage this could weaken the pressure to accumulate and generate stagnation in the economy.

Such a contradiction was particularly emphasized by writers basing their ideas on the postwar dominance of giant US firms (see Baran and Sweezy, 1966). The development of Japanese and European industry, however, challenged this dominance and, during the 1960s, ushered in a great increase in competition on world markets. While monopolization has increased within each country, there has been a tremendous rise in competition through trade and foreign investment. Some of the Newly Industrialized Countries of South East Asia have begun to break into world markets as well.

The process of competition is, therefore, a complex one. The notion that increased concentration would both reduce the pressure to invest and increase the resources for investment (through higher prices and profits) does not stand as a convincing general trend. That is not to say however that, should a new era of protectionism develop, the high degree of industrial concentration within countries would not exacerbate a tendency to stagnation.

WASTED RESOURCES AND UNUSED POTENTIAL. Capitalist production is guided by profit, not social need, or to put it more abstractly, by exchange value rather than use value. The existence of unemployment is the most obvious example of such a contradiction. Unemployed workers could produce the very commodities which they, and the rest of society, need. But since production is for profit, they will only be taken on if the employers foresee a profit. In a situation of unemployment and unused capacity, capital accumulation and thus the introduction of new technology will be held back. The development of technology itself will be reduced if lower profits lead to cuts in research and development spending. For these reasons, society's capacity to produce will be reduced below what is feasible, as well as actual production being reduced below capacity.

These then are some of the senses in which capitalism has been deemed by Marxists to be a 'contradictory' system. The idea, prevalent in the 1950s and 1960s, that these contradictions had been overcome by the expansion of state activities or the advent of the managerial corporation, has disappeared with the collapse of the great postwar boom. Whether capitalism will find a way out of its problems, and lay the basis for rapid growth and full employment, depends of course on how fundamental these contradictions actually are. Even if less binding than some in the Marxist tradition have tended to assert, the idea that such contradictions generate powerful pressures for changes in the economic system remains a powerful and important one.

ANDREW GLYN

See also ECONOMIC INTERPRETATION OF HISTORY; MARXIST ECONOMICS.

BIBLIOGRAPHY

Baran, P. and Sweezy, P. 1966. *Monopoly Capital*. New York: Monthly Review Press; London: Penguin.
Elster, J. 1985. *Making Sense of Marx*. Cambridge: Cambridge University Press.
Itoh, M. 1980. *Value and Crisis*. London: Pluto.
Rowthorn, R.E. 1980. *Capitalism, Conflict and Inflation*. London: Lawrence & Wishart.

control and coordination of economic activity. The particular point of view of the present paper is that it looks upon the economy as a *control system*. This approach was pioneered in the 1950s by Simon (1952), Tustin (1953), Phillips (1954) and Geyer and Oppelt (1957). Lange (1965) attempted an early synthesis. In the 1970s the idea became widespread and developed in two directions. The first and more popular one applied control theoretical models to *economic policy-making*. In this case the structure of the controller is considered to be given and

the problem is to find values (time-paths) of the control variables such that the functioning of the economic system be acceptable (most often, stable and/or optimal) according to certain criteria. The second direction is related to the theory of economic systems, and this is where the present paper also belongs. A descriptive and explanatory *theory of economic mechanisms* is aimed at, which might be useful in the choice, change or construction of controllers. Although this research was certainly motivated by, and the findings often applied to, problems emerging in centrally planned economies, with particular reference to mechanism reform in East European countries, the theoretical framework is conceived in a more general setting. This research was initiated by Kornai (1971) and pursued further in Kornai (1980), and Kornai and Martos (1981).

In the first section I present the basic concepts and classifications, followed in the second section by the characterization of the elementary control processes, with the generation and transmission of information and decisions. The final section illustrates the usefulness of this framework by a microeconomic analysis of a non-Walrasian control model.

1. THE ECONOMIC CONTROL SYSTEM

At any point of time (t) an abstract economic system consists of the following ingredients:

A set $\mathcal{A}$ of *agents* (e.g. households, productive firms, banks, government agencies); they are the subjects of the economic activities.

A set $\mathcal{O}$ of *objects* upon which the economic agents act.

The natural, historical, social and economic environment $\mathcal{E}$, which is not a part of, but interacts with, the system.

A set $\mathcal{Y}$ of processes which connect elements of sets $\mathcal{A}$, $\mathcal{O}$ and $\mathcal{E}$ and changes their state.

When speaking about an economic system the first thing we have in mind is a national economy. However, most of the qualifications and methods we use can be applied to systems which are smaller or larger than that (e.g. an industry, a corporation, a region.)

For a consistent control-theory approach two kinds of economic processes (elements of $\mathcal{Y}$) must be distinguished:

Real processes ($\mathcal{Y}_r \subset \mathcal{Y}$), which change the state of physical objects. The most important real processes are production, storage, transfer of physical objects among agents, consumption (whether for productive or for final use). The objects of real processes form the set of *commodities* ($\mathcal{O}_r \subset \mathcal{O}$). The set of real processes consists of the real activities of the agents and the external effects of the environment. The former ones depend also on the control processes; the external effects cannot be controlled. The rules which connect the real processes are mostly the laws of nature (or more to the point, technology).

Control processes ($\mathcal{Y}_c \subset \mathcal{Y}$), which change the state of knowledge of the agents and regulate their behaviour. The objects of these processes ($\mathcal{O}_c \subset \mathcal{O}$) are called *signals*. The most important control processes are observation of real processes, signal generation and transmission among agents, and decision-making (the final signal generation) on real activities. A part of the signals may come directly from the environment as far as it is observable.

Since each agent $a \in \mathcal{A}$ performs both real and control activities, it is convenient not only to split the set of activities and objects into two (real vs control) subsets but also to consider each agent as consisting of two units: the *real unit* and the *control unit*, which perform real activities and control, respectively. Needless to say, this splitting of an agent into two units is only a conceptual separation, to which an actual separation of the functions may correspond with some kind of agents (e.g. large firms), but need not in any organized form exist with other kinds (e.g. households).

Finally, to make the dichotomy of the economic system complete, we can divide even the set $\mathscr{A}$ of agents into two subsets: that of *real agents* (or real organizations), $\mathscr{A}_r \subset \mathscr{A}$, whose *main* activities belong to the real processes (like households or productive firms) and that of *control agents* (or control organizations), $\mathscr{A}_c \subset \mathscr{A}$, whose *main* activity lies in information-processing and decision-making (like legislative bodies, local authorities, government agencies).

This classification of the agents requires some further comments. Firstly, there might be borderline agents (e.g. schools) whose classification is ambiguous and will be dependent on the role which they play in a given context. Secondly, the real units (real activities) of the control organizations are often negligible in theoretical considerations (just as the energy input of an electric control device might be negligible compared to the energy input of the physical process it controls). We also will make use of this simplification in the sequel and disregard the real activities of the control agents.

Finally, a few words are in order about the place of *fiduciary goods* (banknotes, accounting money, stocks and bonds), *monetary processes* (emission, exchange, income generation, credit) and *financial organizations* (banks, stockbrokers, tax offices) in the above dichotomy. Since it is not the physical transformation of fiduciary goods which is of economic interest (and hence they cannot belong to the real commodities), they belong to the control sphere by exclusion (in contrast with many other theoretical approaches where money is simply taken as one of the commodities). However, it must be kept in mind that the monetary sphere plays not only a particularly important part in the control of economic activities, but is in many aspects different from the rest of the control processes and obeys laws which are partly similar to the ones valid in the real sphere. A thorough discussion of the consequences of this reasoning would require a separate entry.

The economic control system can also be interpreted in the language of mathematical control theory. In a standard state-space representation of a continuously operating, multivariate, deterministic, externally commanded system, it consists of three equations:

Controlled subsystem:

$$\dot{x} = \Phi(t, x, u, z) \tag{1}$$

Measurement:

$$y = \Psi(x) \tag{2}$$

Controller:

$$u = \Theta(t, y - y^*), \tag{3}$$

where $t \geq 0$ denotes time and the dot above a variable differentiation with respect to time, $x(t)$ is the state vector, $u(t)$ is the control vector, $y(t)$ is the output vector, $y^*(t)$ is the command vector (the normal value of y), $z(t)$ is the vector of external effects on the state and Φ, Ψ and Θ are functions of their arguments as indicated.

The above system is said to be (globally) *viable* with respect to a closed convex subset $\mathscr{K}$ (the viability set) of the state space (the space of xs) if $x \in \mathscr{K}$ for all $t \geq 0$ and any given initial state $x(0) = x_0 \in \mathscr{K}$. If there is a state $\bar{x} \in \text{Int } \mathscr{K}$ and a number $\delta > 0$ such that $x \in \mathscr{K}$ for all $t \geq 0$ and any given initial state $x_0 \in \mathscr{K} \cap \{x \mid \|x - \bar{x}\| < \delta\}$, that is in the neighbourhood of $\bar{x}$, then the system is said to be *locally viable* at $\bar{x}$ with respect to $\mathscr{K}$.

It was proved by Aubin and Cellina (1983, theorem 5.4.1) that under some continuity, convexity and compactness assumptions there is a feedback rule Θ such that the system (1) to (3) is globally viable. It is to be noted, however, that this is an existence theorem from which no conclusion can be drawn, in this generality, as to how the appropriate feedback rule Θ can be constructed.

The form (1) to (3) is, of course, not the only mathematical form in which a control system can be represented, but it is general enough to cover many important cases and special forms, which are too numerous to list here even partially. I would rather mention systems which are not explicitly represented by the above formulation.

(a) *Intermittently operating systems.* It is frequently the case that, especially in economic applications, the measurement of the state is not done continuously but only at discrete points of time. In this case the value of the control variable remains constant in between. If the observation times are equidistant, the above formulation can easily be transformed to cover this case simply by replacing the differential operator of the left-hand side by a time shift operator $Ex(t) = x(t + 1)$.

(b) *Stochastic systems* arise if x and/or y and/or u represent stochastic processes, and consequently some of the operators, Φ, Ψ, Θ have stochastic values. In the case of a stochastic Φ, the controlled system works erratically; a stochastic Ψ indicates measurement errors; and a stochastic Θ indicates uncertain control behaviour. These are frequent cases in economic systems. (It is to be noted that any random disturbance on z and y^*, i.e. on variables representing the environment, does not make the system stochastic, that are the realizations which enter the functions.)

(c) *Optimum control*, in which case the control rule is not given in the form (3) but is rather a solution to the problem of maximizing a given functional

$$I = \int_0^T \mu(t, x, u) \, dt$$

subject to (1) and some other constraints which require the control variable u to belong to a given set $\mathscr{U}$, and where μ is a scalar function of the arguments.

(d) *Higher-order systems* (as contrasted to externally commanded systems) take different forms:

Self-command (or target modifying) systems produce the command signals y^* themselves.

Learning systems modify the form or parameter values characterizing the operator Θ; a learning mechanism improves the controller.

Self-organizing systems are capable of changing the control structures, the organizations and the interrelations among them both in the controlled subsystem and the controller.

Although it is clear that most economic systems perform such higher-order functioning, their mathematical analysis is difficult and mostly reduced to narrowly specified cases.

2. THE STRUCTURE OF THE CONTROLLER

The controller was typified in equation (3) in a very rough-and-ready way. In actual economic systems the controller has a rather complicated structure, consisting of many different elements which interact in various ways. Some of the elements make simple observations, routine calculations, bookkeeping, and so on; others collect, generate and disseminate important information or make crucial decisions and plans relying on a vast amount of preprocessed information. Some of them work

641

in parallel on different sets of data, and some form interactive or hierarchically ordered groups.

The study of such a structure must begin with the functioning of its constituent elements which are called *transfer elements*. A transfer element is an elementary part of a complex controller which cannot be divided further or has not been in a particular analysis.

There are three subsequent actions in the functioning of a transfer element:

Signal reception. The transfer element receives signals (information) from the observation of real processes, from the environment or from another transfer element. These are the *input signals* of the element.

Signal transformation or signal generation. The transfer element transforms, stores and combines the received signals and hereby generates new ones. The rules by which signals are generated form the *transfer function* of the element.

Signal emission. The transfer element transmits the generated signal (*output signal*) to one or more other transfer elements or to an agent which acts directly on real processes.

In the classification of the elementary control process we apply two criteria both with respect to the kinds of agents who participate in the process: – What kind of agent generates the signal? – Among what kind of agents is the signal transmitted?

With respect to *signal generation* we distinguish three kinds of processes:

Uncoordinated. The signal is generated by the control unit of a single real organization.

Interactive. The signal is generated jointly by the the control units of several real organizations.

Centralized. The signal is generated by a control organization or jointly by several control and perhaps real organizations.

With respect to *signal transmission* we also distinguish three kinds of process:

Non-communicative. The signal does not leave the organization where it was generated.

Transactional. The sender and the addressee are two different real organizations, and the signal refers to an (actual or potential) real transaction (usually transfer of a commodity) between the two real organizations (e.g. dispatch of an order, a price quotation, a bill).

Communicative (non-transactional). Any other signal transmission; for example, among more than two real organizations, or whenever a control organization is the sender or the addressee or both.

This dual classification of the transfer elements can be summarized as shown in Table 1. The two empty boxes represent signal generation–transmission combinations which cannot occur. (An interactive signal generation implies some kind of communication, since to generate signals jointly by several real organizations, they must communicate somehow. In the centralized signal generation a control organization takes part, hence it cannot be transactional.)

This simple classification scheme can be applied to elementary transfer units of the controller only. In a complex control process several transfer units are combined which differ with respect to their signal generation and transmission patterns.

Most of the actually existing economic control systems may be called *partially coordinated systems*, in which a considerable part of the decisions are taken by the real organizations in isolation, another part by their interaction (e.g. on the market) and yet another part by different control agents (e.g. legislative bodies, government agencies, banks, trade unions etc.). The problem of analysing (synthesizing) an economic control system

Table 1

Signal transmission	Signal generation		
	Uncoordinated	Coordinated	
		Interactive	Centralized
Non-communicative	+	∅	+
Transactional	+	+	∅
Communicative (non-transactional)	+	+	+

consists of the decision about whether one or the other function of the system is (should be) served by this or that kind of transfer unit and how these units are (can be) integrated into a viable or even efficient entity.

An essential feature of the above conceptualization of the structure of the economic control system is that it does not restrict the issue to 'control and coordination of economic activity' from the outside (done exclusively by specialized control organizations) but includes the control functions which work within the real organizations and interact among them. It is also to be noted that the classical distinction between centralized and decentralized control turned out to be insufficient and has been replaced by a more elaborate classification pattern.

3. A NON-WALRASIAN CONTROL STRUCTURE

The first economic theory which offered a mathematically rigorous representation of the control mechanism of a national economy is known under the term *General Equilibrium Theory*. Since neither Keynesian macroeconomics in capitalistic systems nor shortage phenomena in socialist economies could have been appropriately studied within the framework of this theory, a new approach emerged under various names: *disequilibrium theory, temporary equilibrium theory, theory of equilibria with rationing, non-Walrasian equilibrium theory*. Without discussing here merits and demerits of these approaches, it is to be noted that – as a rule – they were not based on mathematical control theory.

In what follows I present a non-Walrasian control model differing from the aforementioned approaches in many aspects:

(a) It is not only the (essentially static) equilibrium, its existence and efficiency which is studied, but rather the dynamics of the trajectories leading to an equilibrium state. Real and control processes run in parallel (out of equilibrium); there is no timeless *tâtonnement* process.

(b) No optimizing behaviour of the agents is assumed; adjustment to exogenous normal values of some output variables is the behavioural rule. When applying this 'control by norm' principle I assume that norms are formed by individual experience or social consent in a long-run process (which is not modelled here), and the norms remain constant along the short- and medium-run adjustment process.

(c) Information and decisions are not centralized as in the hands of an auctioning or rationing agent, but the whole control process is carried out by the control units of real organizations among themselves in an uncoordinated but transactionally communicative way. (This refers only to the particular model variant which follows. In other variants control organizations and coordination also appear.)

(d) Only observable variables are used (no fictitious 'effective demand') and hence the underlying assumptions can be, but generally have not been, empirically tested. (For an exception, see Kawasaki, McMillan and Zimmermann, 1982.)

Still it is to be admitted that this approach has not yet reached the generality and mathematical refinement of general equilibrium and disequilibrium theory.

The model. The economy consists of n producers (real organizations), each producing a single commodity. The technology is of the Leontief-type, with constant input coefficients. The environment acts upon the real processes by the final use (private and public consumption, investment) and on the control processes by past experiences, which determine the normal level of inventories (output stocks, input stocks) and backlog orders.

Notation: lower case – n-vector; upper case – $n \times n$ matrix; Greek lower case – scalar.

State variables:

q – vector of output stocks
V – matrix of input stocks
K – matrix of backlog orders
An asterisk * as a superscript refers to the exogenous normal values of the state variables.

Control variables:

r – vector of production ($\langle r \rangle$: the diagonal matrix formed from r)
Y – matrix of commodity transfers among producers
W – matrix of the transmission of new orders

Other notations:

$e = [1, 1, \ldots, 1]'$ – the summation vector
A – the input coefficient matrix
c – the vector of final uses
β, γ – control parameters
$\Gamma(\cdot) = -2\beta\gamma[d(\cdot)/dt] - \gamma^2 \cdot (\cdot)$ – differential operator.

Assumptions:

1. The final use is constant and semipositive, $c \geqslant 0$.
2. The input coefficient matrix A is constant and
   (a) non-negative
   (b) irreducible
   (c) productive, i.e. its spectral radius $\rho(A) < 1$.
3. $\gamma > 0$ (without loss of generality).

The real processes:

$$\dot{q} = r - Ye - c \tag{1}$$

$$\dot{V} = Y - A\langle r \rangle. \tag{2}$$

Equation (1) expresses the change of output stocks as the difference between the amounts produced and that transferred for productive and final use. Equation (2) tells that the change of input stocks equals the material purchases minus the materials used up in production.

The control processes:

$$\dot{K} = W - Y \tag{3}$$

$$\dot{r} = \Gamma(q - q^*) \tag{4}$$

$$\dot{W} = \Gamma(V - V^*) \tag{5}$$

$$\dot{Y} = -\Gamma(K - K^*). \tag{6}$$

Equation (3) describes the bookkeeping (at the supplier) of the backlog of orders; its change equals the difference between the incoming new orders and the deliveries. Equations (4) to (6) are the control equations proper, all of the same (linear) form, describing the assumed behaviour of the agents. The decisions on production level is dependent on the output stocks, the dispatch of orders (by the buyer) on the input stocks, and the deliveries (decided by the supplier) on the backlog of orders, in each case taking the deviation of the actual value from the normal value into account. None of these behavioural rules is at variance with common sense.

It is to be observed, that the transfer elements corresponding to equations (3) to (6) generate all the signals without any coordination; equations (3), (4) and (6) represent non-communicative elements, while there is transactional communication according to equation (5); namely, the orders are transmitted from the buyers to the suppliers.

The viability domain $\mathcal{K}$ for system (1) to (6) may be defined in the following way:

(a) All the variables are uniformly bounded, but the bounds are unspecified.

(b) The variables in q, V, K, r and Y are non-negative, but negative elements of W (withdrawal of orders) are permitted.

Although the theorem of Aubin and Cellina referred to above does not apply here, where we specified the form of the control equations (3) to (6), we can still guarantee local viability in the neighbourhood of the equilibrium state by an appropriate choice of the parameter β.

Theorem. Suppose that the following conditions are met:
(a) Assumptions (1) to (3) hold.
(b) The norms are positive: $q^* > 0$, $V^* > 0$, $K^* > 0$.
(c) $\beta > \max\{|\operatorname{Im}\sigma|/(2|\sigma|\sqrt{\operatorname{Re}\sigma})| -\sigma^3 + 2\sigma^2 - 2\sigma + 1 \in$ spectrum of $A\}$ and $\beta > \sqrt{6}/4$.
(d) The initial values at $t = 0$: $(q^0, V^0, K^0, r^0, Y^0, W^0)$ are close enough to the equilibrium state:

$$\bar{q} = q^*, \quad \bar{V} = V^*, \quad \bar{K} = K^*,$$

$$\bar{r} = (E - A)^{-1}c, \quad \bar{Y} = \bar{W} = A\langle(E - A)^{-1}c\rangle.$$

Then the system (1) to (6) is viable for $t \geqslant 0$ (local viability).

Remark: under (a) the relation (c) is both a necessary and sufficient condition of asymptotic stability.

A detailed analysis of the model and proof of the theorem (extended to varying c) is to be found in a forthcoming book by Martos. Models in a similar vein are analysed in Kornai and Martos (1981).

BÉLA MARTOS

See also DECENTRALIZATION; PLANNED ECONOMY; PLANNING; PONTRYAGIN'S PRINCIPLE OF OPTIMALITY.

BIBLIOGRAPHY

Aubin, J.P. and Cellina, A. 1983. *Differential Inclusions.* Berlin: Springer.
Geyer, W. and Oppelt, W. (eds) 1957. *Volkswirtschaftliche Regelungsvorgänge im Vergleich zu Regelungsvorgängen in der Technik.* Munich.
Kawasaki, S., McMillan, J. and Zimmermann, K.F. 1982. Disequilibrium dynamics: an empirical study. *American Economic Review* 72, 992–1003.
Kornai, J. 1971. *Anti-Equilibrium.* Amsterdam: North-Holland.
Kornai, J. 1980. *Economics of Shortage.* Amsterdam: North-Holland.
Kornai, J. and Martos, B. (eds) 1981. *Non-Price Control.* Amsterdam: North-Holland.
Lange, O. 1965. *Wstep do cybernetyki ekonomicznej* (Introduction to economic cybernetics). Warsaw: Państwowe Wydawnictwo Naukowe.
Phillips, A.W. 1954. Stabilization policy in a closed economy. *Economic Journal* 64, 290–323.
Simon, H.A. 1952. On the application of servomechanism theory in the study of production control. *Econometrica* 20, 247–68.
Tustin, A. 1953. *The Mechanism of Economic Systems.* London: Heinemann.

convergence hypothesis. This is the doctrine that the Soviet Union and 'similar countries' are becoming and will further become socially and economically similar to the United States and other advanced capitalist countries; or the other way round – so that eventually in either case political differences, and thus foreign policy tensions, will also disappear.

The doctrine takes many detailed forms, but is most often very unspecific. For instance does it mean: that Texan agriculture will be collectivized (each family farm is larger in area than a Soviet *Kolkhoz*); that there will be a stock exchange again in Moscow, where equity shares in Soviet businesses are freely traded; that the *zloty* will be made convertible; that Switzerland will introduce controls over all retail and wholesale prices; that British trade unions will be reduced to the status of Bulgarian trade unions, or vice versa; that Albania will allow a good deal of minor private enterprise; or even that both sides will converge upon self management in a market, *à la Yougoslave*?

The proponents of the doctrine seldom do it the courtesy of bringing it so close to brass tacks. Above all they fail to recognize just how numerous and diverse those brass tacks are. But the core of the doctrine is clear: advanced capitalism is (said to be) moving, through the large corporation (often public) and its intimacy with certain government departments, irreparably away from share-holder dominance, free enterprise and free markets, in respect of all sectors where small enterprise does not dominate; and a new socio-political type is coming to power, nearly indistinguishable in government and business, and very liable to swap jobs (corruptly, let us add). Meanwhile the advanced Communist states are admitting more and more the role of enterprise independence and markets for everyday small decisions; even the quasi-independence of associations of enterprises in larger decisions – the association would correspond to the corporation and the Communist enterprises to its separate, decentralized 'establishments'.

Hungary and France are of course very much further forward in convergence. A major problem, too for Convergence theorists and for sceptics alike, is China. Here, right at the bottom of the Communist income scale and without even having first introduced any central planning worthy of the name, 20 per cent of the human race is 'converging' very rapidly indeed. As partly too in Hungary, even private property in the means of production is making a comeback. It is not easy to fit this fact into the ordinary framework of debate.

As to a new socio-political type in power in government and 'business', in the USSR ideology is dying and the typical Party apparatchik is more and more obliged to have had some serious professional training and responsibility within the State machine. Meanwhile the obligatory Party membership of the senior technocrat continues to lie lightly on his shoulders. What then is this type, on both sides? It is above all a professional type: technically educated, pragmatic but accepting the particular value system of the given profession, believing in the rule of reason but unphilosophically confusing it with what was judged reasonable at professional school, striving for a higher 'earned' income as the right of competence in his chosen profession, and naive as to what constitutes the rule of reason in unprofessional matters (which are of course the very great majority of matters). One may think in 1986, as the fathers of Convergence certainly did not think, of the American term Yuppie (Young Upwardly Mobile Professionals). However, in the USSR Yuppies are much more idealistic and critical.

It is clear that every prophecy made about Communism in the previous paragraphs is coming true, and the Convergence theorists deserve praise for this – although it took much longer than they expected. The rule of reason is taking over, and the notion that the Soviet system is a frozen monolith, condemned to remain for ever its unpleasant and highly suboptimal (but rapidly growing!) self, is unfounded. But capitalism by no means shows the predicted unilinear change. Japan in one way ('industrial policy', unnaturally accommodating unions) and France in another (mild planning) used to be the showpieces of convergence from the other side. But recent Japanese financial reforms have tended to open up the country to free trade in money, and French planning is at present being down-graded. Monetarist and supply-sider attacks on the public sector and on taxes in the USA and the UK constitute divergence. So does the new tolerance for very heavy unemployment; even if Communist economic experts talk about the necessity for a little unemployment to discipline labour and create flexibility, the 'target' of Western levels is rapidly receding.

It is, then, capitalism that has 'misbehaved'. And if the rule of reason is eventually restored to economic affairs in the Western world, exactly how far, in so unreasonable a universe, will present divergent trends be reversed? We can at least be sure that protectionism – if that is reason – having flourished even under monetarism, will bloom yet taller under what succeeds it. Indeed under this or that institutional guise, protectionism is common to all systems except capitalist faire in the 19th century. Then too why should not the rule of reason be 'relaxed' again in the East? Besides, 'reason is and ought to be the slave of the passions': if the value systems of Communism and democratic Capitalism continue to diverge only half as much as now, this is cause enough for the reasonable choice of radically divergent policies and substantially divergent institutions.

These considerations alone give us pause before we can accept the basic optimism of Convergence theory. We pause to note that the seven questions of our second paragraph have not been answered at all. But there is worse – though outside of economics – to follow. Since when did resemblance make for peace? Since when was dissimilarity a cause of war? Especially in this ideological age, is not *minor* dissimilarity, or heresy, a major cause of war? For that matter, do not Third World capitalist countries make war on each other, quite unabashedly, over mere boundary disputes and ethnic irredentas in quite the old style? It is a very long way from convergence in respect of planning and the market, to international peace.

The alleged *aetiology* of convergence could, as set out above, be the existence of an optimal system somewhere in the middle, to which all existing systems gravitate simply because it is better. If, as is often reasonably claimed, the Yugoslav industrial system represents a third pole of equal theoretical importance, then moderate elements of self-management must be added to that optimal goal. But this is all mere wishful thinking: the judgements of politicians and (where they are counted) voters do not coincide all over the world with each other, let alone with the opinions of centre-left economists. An economic system good for some purposes (e.g. full employment, equality) is bad for others (e.g. rational resource allocation, stable prices, labour discipline). As we have seen, people *value* different sets of outcomes differently, and are also confused as to how in practice to obtain them.

But convergence through contact and competition is another matter. Since nearly all people are unthinking materialists, contact (say as an importer and an exporter) will sway them to imitate the at present more prosperous system: capitalism, to which may or may not be attached, in the perception of observers, parliamentary democracy. And this is truer of people living under Communism than of people in the Third World: for the latter are apt to attribute capitalist prosperity to the exploitation of themselves. Sheer economic contact undoubtedly influences Communist leaders in a capitalist direction, if only because of the overwhelmingly unfavourable balance of technological exchange.

Competition is the almost inevitable result of contact: both commercial and military. It goes without saying that competitors in an export market imitate each other, and not only in quality and technology embodied; but even the administrative systems of the enterprises producing the exports will converge on the one that is seen to be superior. Exporting is a sure and genuine source of convergence, that the most hard-nosed Sovietologist must accept. Military rivalry has much the same effects; for a country's forces also 'export' – a threat. But if the convergence of military technology and its maintenance and auxiliary equipment is of obvious relevance to economic systems, that of military doctrine and organization is not our subject. Still less is the convergence of para-military 'exports': training for guerrillas and terrorists, security systems for underdeveloped countries, espionage.

It can be seen that while high convergence theory is largely (but not altogether) hot air and wishful thinking, there exists a great deal of low-level convergence in fact, all of it easily explicable and much of it very regrettable.

P.J.D. WILES

See also BUREAUCRACY; COMMAND ECONOMY; MARKET SOCIALISM.

convexity. The importance of convexity of preferences and technology to many of the fundamental propositions of neo-classical economics, both positive and normative, is evidenced by scores if not hundreds of essays in this Dictionary. Two such propositions will suffice here. In general equilibrium theory the existence of competitive equilibrium is obtained by applying Brouwer's fixed point theorem or one of its extensions, each of which depends upon a suitable convex-valued mapping of a convex set to itself. In welfare economics, the one-to-one nature of Edgeworth–Pareto optimality and competitive equilibrium is assured by the Theorem of the Supporting Hyperplane applied to an appropriate convex set.

It is not always realised that many of the chief results of classical economics also depend, at least implicitly, on assumptions of convexity. This is obvious enough with the corn model and its accompanying Law of Diminishing Returns, but it is also implicit in the supposition that any divergence between market and natural prices, or in rates of profit, will be erased by some suitably convergent adjustment process of output and prices. One has only to think of the difficulties for such convergence imposed by that great classical nonconvexity, the Law of Increasing Return, to realize that buried deep down in their literary discussions the classical economists must have had some presumption, however crude, that a convex technology prevails.

It should be remarked (although a full discussion would be out of place here) that modern works which claim to inherit the classical tradition, such as that of Sraffa (1960), also depend upon assumptions of linearity, hence convexity, for most of their interesting results.

DEFINITIONS. A quotation from Young (1969, p. 95) will set the scene: 'Modern analysis works , . . . , much less with equality than with the relation of inequality $\geqslant$. The importance of convexity lies in the fact that it constitutes the higher dimensional generalization of this relation.'

The fundamental idea is that of a convex set, a concept which applies just as well to the whole genus of real vector spaces X

as it does to the leading species, Euclidean n-space R^n. When the statements below are quite generally applicable *without change*, the symbol X will be employed. Otherwise, however slight the change required, the discussion will be confined to the case $X = R^n$.

Any $C \subset X$ is *convex* if, given any two points x^1 and x^2 in C and any number t in the closed unit interval [0, 1], the point $x^t = tx^1 + (1-t)x^2$ also lies in C. More geometrically, C is convex if it contains the line segment joining any two of its points, so that pyramids are convex sets but frisbees are not. More algebraically, if two points are in C, then so is any of their internal weighted averages.

Economically, the implications of the requirement that a set be convex vary according to the context with the meaning of the word 'weighted'. For example, in its early days there was some confusion over the expected utility theory of von Neumann–Morgenstern (1947), when some economists thought that the 'mixture' $\alpha x + (1-\alpha)y$ in its Independence Axiom referred to the purchase (and consumption) of a bundle with actual components $(\alpha x_i + (1-\alpha)y_i, i = 1, 2, \ldots, n)$ rather than to its true meaning, which is simply that of a lottery ticket with chances α and $(1-\alpha)$, respectively, for the prizes x and y. This is by no means the only example of confusion about the economic meaning of such 'convex combinations' of bundles.

Given *any* convex set $C \subset R^{n+1}$, say, it is a simple matter to manufacture a convex function by taking the 'lower boundary' of C, as in the construction reported by Rockafellar (1970, p. 33). More formally, define $f: R^n \to [-\infty, \infty]$ by the formula

$$f(x) = \inf \{\xi : (x, \xi) \in C\} \tag{1}$$

where if there is no ξ such that (x, ξ) is in C, $f(x)$ is by convention put equal to $+\infty$ (the analogous procedure of taking the 'upper boundary' of C, thus replacing 'inf' in (1) by 'sup', and $+\infty$ by $-\infty$, manufactures a concave function g on R^n).

In a sense, the most general definition of a convex function reverses this construction. For any $f: X \to [-\infty, \infty]$ define its *epigraph* as that subset of $X \times R$ given by

$$\text{epi } f = \{x, \mu : x \in X, \mu \in R, \mu \geqslant f(x)\} \tag{2}$$

Then f is a *convex* function if epi f is a convex subset of $X \times R$; a function g is *concave* if $-f$ is convex. If it is known *a priori* that f is a real-valued function, defined say on some set $S \subset X$, then the previous definition specializes to the proposition that f satisfies *Jensen's Inequality*: for any x^1, x^2 in S and any t in [0, 1],

$$f[tx^1 + (1-t)x^2] \leqslant tf(x^1) + (1-t)f(x^2) \tag{3}$$

A real-valued function g is concave if the inequality is reversed. Notice that (3) makes no sense unless the set S is convex, for otherwise $tx^1 + (1-t)x^2$ does not lie in the domain of f.

DIFFERENTIAL CONVEXITY. Historically, explicit recognition of the importance of convexity and concavity in economics arose from the problem of finding stationary points by techniques of the ordinary calculus or of the calculus of variations. If f is a suitably differentiable function $f: S \to R$, for some $S \subset R$, then necessary conditions for it to have a local minimum at some point x^* are (i) that $f'(x^*) = 0$, and (ii) that $f''(x^*) \geqslant 0$. It is *sufficient* for x^* to be a local minimum that (ii) be restricted to the case of strict inequality. If x^* is to be a global minimum on S, then (ii) must be replaced by the condition (iii) that $f''(x) \geqslant 0$ for all x in S, which is equivalent to requiring that f be (differentiably) convex. (For the case of a local or global *maximum*, replace $\geqslant$ by $\leqslant$ and 'convex' by 'concave', wherever they occur.)

The earliest explicit example of a basic economic difficulty caused by non-convexity is perhaps the most famous of all. It is truly remarkable (not to say salutary) to realise how often it was forgotten and rediscovered over the course of almost 100 years. In spite of Marshall's allegation to the contrary (1891, p. 485n, which is an elaboration of 1890, p. 485n2), in fact Cournot was at great pains to point out that, for a producer maximizing profit under conditions of pure competition, if the cost function $C(x)$ is such that $C''(x) < 0$ for all x, then 'nothing would limit the production of the article'. Hence, if the producer is observed to be making a profit and $C''(\cdot)$ is observed to be negative, then that 'proves that the effect of monopoly is not wholly extinct ... [and] ... the variation of the amount produced by each individual producer affects the total production of the article, and its price, to a perceptible extent'. (1838, pp. 102–3; translation (1960 edition), pp. 91–92).

Suppose now that f is a suitably differentiable function of several variables. Then for x^* to be a local minimum of f, (iv) the value $\nabla f(x^*)$ of the gradient function must be zero, and (v) the Hessian matrix $H_f(x^*)$ must be positive semi-definite, i.e. f must be locally convex at x^*. A sufficient condition for x^* to be a local minimum is a modification of (v) to the effect that the Hessian is required to be positive definite at x^* (contrary to much economists' folklore, it is *not* sufficient for this latter condition that f be (locally) strictly convex (see Bernstein and Toupin, 1962)). If x^* is to be a global minimum of f on S, then $H_f(x)$ must be positive semi-definite for all x, which is equivalent to f being convex (Rockafellar, 1970, p. 27).

The first economist to consider convexity problems for nonseparable functions of several variables was Edgeworth (1881, pp. 34–6). Having written the utility function in the general form $u(x, y)$ for the first time ever, he needed his new-fangled indifference curves to be convex in order to show that the contract curve decreased as the number of agents increased. Jevons's assumptions that the utility function is additively separable and has diminishing marginal utility in each good ensure concavity of u, and hence convexity of indifference curves, via the property that finite sums of concave functions are concave (cf. Rockafellar, 1970, p. 33). But Edgeworth realized that in his case of a nonseparable u they do not. He could of course have assumed that each Hessian $H_u(.,.)$ was negative semi-definite, since that is equivalent to concavity; but that would have required the additional strong assumption that $u_{xx} u_{yy} \geqslant u_{xy}^2$.

Perhaps for this reason, or perhaps because the very idea of convex and concave functions was not developed systematically until early in the twentieth century (Hardy, Littlewood and Polya, 1934, p. 71), Edgeworth took a quite different route; certainly he would not have been deterred by the cardinality of utility that full concavity implies! Going beyond the Jevonian assumptions only in assuming that $u_{xy} < 0$, he proved the validity of a condition equivalent to a standard formula (as given for example in Allen, 1938, p. 375) that is sufficient for a function to be quasi-concave. A real-valued function f defined on a nonempty convex subset C of R^n is *quasi-concave* if for each real number α, the set $\{x: f(x) \geqslant \alpha\}$ is convex, or equivalently, if for any x^1, x^2 in C and $t \in [0, 1]$, $f[tx^1 + (1 - t)x^2] \geqslant \min[f(x^1), f(x^2)]$; this concept was first formally defined by de Finetti (1949) and Fenchel (1953, ch. III, p. 7). Exploration of the precise relations between its variants and the second order conditions for a *constrained* maximum (a problem which Edgeworth did not explore directly in this part of *Mathematical Psychics*) constitutes a small industry that was begun by Arrow and Enthoven (1961) and of which a recent report may be found in Ferland (1981).

CHARACTERIZATION OF CONVEX SETS. It seems fair to say that until World War II considerations of convexity made only an implicit appearance, in such systematic treatments of constrained optimization as those of Hicks (1939). The major exception is the great paper by von Neumann (1937), which, however, did not appear in English until the end of the war (von Neumann, 1945–6). During the War there appeared both game theory (von Neumann and Morgenstern, 1944) and the earliest rudiments of linear programming, due independently to Dantzig, Kantorovich and Koopmans (see the history of these developments in Koopmans, 1951). Both these new disciplines required the theory of convex polyhedra, and so the way was cleared for a more abstract approach to convexity in economic theory. Progress was quite rapid, sped along by such classic papers as those of Arrow (1951) and Debreu (1951) and the masterly expository essay by Koopmans (1957, Essay 1). So complete was this take-over that among its enthusiasts the use of calculus to explore problems of optimization soon came to be looked upon as an unnatural act. But that was a temporary aberration, which in the 1970s was superseded by an equal enthusiasm for the richness of result made possible by global analysis, in which functions are assumed to be as differentiable as desired (see e.g. Mas-Colell, 1985, Introduction).

An important mathematical result that characterizes convex sets in R^n was instrumental in making it clear just how intrinsic convexity is to optimization in economics. However, to explain this result requires some standard concepts from linear algebra and topology. Taking the latter concepts first (on which see e.g. Bushaw, 1963, ch. 2), for any set $S \subset R^n$ a point $x \in S$ is *interior* to S if there is a neighbourhood of x entirely contained in S, and a *boundary* (or frontier) point of S if it is neither interior to S nor interior to the complement S' of S in R^n. If all points of S are interior points, then it is *open* in R^n; if S' is open, then S is *closed*. The *closure* clS of S is the intersection of all the closed sets that contain S.

The set of all points x in R^n which satisfy the equation

$$\alpha_1 x_1 + \alpha_2 x_2 + \cdots + \alpha_n x_n = \beta \qquad (4)$$

for some α_i not all zero, is called a *hyperplane H* in R^n. Clearly, H divides R^n into the two 'open half-spaces' $\{x: \Sigma \alpha_i x_i > \beta\}$ and $\{x: \Sigma \alpha_i x_i < \beta\}$, one on each side of H. If H intersects a set $S \subset R^n$ in such a way that there are points of S in each of the two open half-spaces determined by H, then it is said to *cut S*. Finally, if H intersects clS and does not cut S, it is a *supporting hyperplane* of S.

We now have a two-part theorem (see, for example, Eggleston, 1958, pp. 20–21) which helps us to understand the structure of convex sets in R^n.

Theorem. (a) Through *every* boundary point of a convex set $C \subset R^n$ there passes at least one supporting hyperplane.

(b) If a set $S \subset R^n$:
   (i) is closed in R^n;
   (ii) has an interior point; and
   (iii) is such that through each of its boundary points passes a supporting hyperplane;
then it is convex.

If H is a supporting hyperplane to S at x^*, say, then it follows from (4) that $\Sigma \alpha_i x_i^* = \beta$ and that for all x in S, either $\Sigma \alpha_i x_i \leqslant \beta$ or $\Sigma \alpha_i x_i \geqslant \beta$, depending on which side of H the set S lies. Hence x^* maximizes (or minimizes) the linear functional represented by the vector of the α_i. If, for example, S were a production set and the α_i were input and output prices, then x^* would maximize profit over S at those prices. Again, if S were a 'better set' in the theory of consumer preferences, i.e.

$S = \{x \in R^n : x \succsim x^0\}$ where x^0 is some 'target' bundle, and the α_i were commodity prices, then x^* would minimize the expenditure needed at those prices in order to secure the level of satisfaction represented by x^0.

The economic force of the Theorem is then that, given the mild conditions (i) and (ii), (though the latter can be very severe in infinite-dimensional spaces), the set S is convex if and *only* if every one of its boundary points can be an optimizing point for *some* system of prices.

CONVEXITY AND NUMBERS. The relevance of the Theorem above depends upon optimizing with respect to a *linear* functional. In economics, why should the relevant functional be linear? The standard answer is that it represents the competitive prices which are taken as parameters by each agent, unaffected by that agent's behaviour. This is obviously a silly assumption if there are only a few agents, so such price-taking behaviour must presume a large enough number of agents. How many are large enough? That is a surprisingly subtle question which has provoked some remarkable research, beginning with Edgeworth (1881) and after almost 80 years' gap continuing right to the present (see the entries on CORES, LARGE ECONOMIES and PERFECT COMPETITION).

One unexpected set of results emerging from these enquiries is derived in the finite case from the Shapley–Folkman Theorem, and in the limiting case from Lyapunov's Theorem on the convexity of the range of a vector measure (see the entries on those Theorems). Although *individual* 'better sets', production sets, demand multifunctions etc. may be nonconvex, if the numbers of agents are large enough, then the *aggregate* set in each case, summed over all agents, will be approximately convex, and, in the limiting case, actually convex. In this way, proofs of existence of equilibrium may dispense with the assumption that individual preferences be convex.

But there is a snag, at least for production economies. If the number of producers is large, then we can appeal, Lyapunov-like, to the convexifying effect of large numbers on the aggregate production set even if the individual firms' production sets are not convex. But if individual production sets are nonconvex, then it is quite likely that we are in a world where increasing returns are significant, in which case the number of producers is likely to be relatively small. It is a classic Catch-22; large numbers of producers guarantee approximate convexity, but convexity is needed to ensure large numbers of producers.

CONCLUSION. With his awful example before us, it would be folly to claim in the manner of J. S. Mill (1864, Vol. 1, pp. 536–7) that 'Happily, there is nothing in the laws of Convexity which remains for the present or any future writer to clear up.' However, it is not so rash to argue that the role of convexity in economics is rather well understood, that as a result its use has reached a certain level of maturity, and that diminishing returns (convexity again!) have probably set in. Almost certainly, major improvements in this area of economic theory must wait on the creation of a satisfactory theory of increasing returns, of which there are as yet faint but unmistakable signs.

PETER NEWMAN

See also DUALITY; GAUGE FUNCTIONS; LAGRANGE MULTIPLIERS; LINEAR PROGRAMMING; NONLINEAR PROGRAMMING; OPTIMAL CONTROL AND ECONOMIC DYNAMICS.

BIBLIOGRAPHY

Allen, R.G.D. 1938. *Mathematical Analysis for Economists*. London: Macmillan.

Arrow, K.J. 1951. An extension of the basic theorems of classical welfare economics. In *Proceedings of the Second Berkeley Symposium on Mathematical Statistics and Probability*, ed. J.Neyman, Berkeley: University of California Press, 507–32.

Arrow, K.J. and Enthoven, A.C. 1961. Quasi-concave programming. *Econometrica* 29, 779–800.

Bernstein, B. and Toupin, R.A. 1962. Some properties of the Hessian matrix of a strictly convex function. *Journal für die reine und angewandte Mathematik* 210(1/2), 65–72.

Bushaw, D. 1963. *Elements of General Topology*. New York: John Wiley & Sons.

Cournot, A.A. 1838. *Recherches sur les principes mathématiques de la théorie des richesses*. Paris: Rivière. New edition, ed. G. Lutalla, Paris: Hachette, 1938. English translation by N.T. Bacon, 1897; repr. New York: Augustus M. Kelley, 1960.

Debreu, G. 1951. The coefficient of resource utilization. *Econometrica* 19, 273–92.

de Finetti, B. 1949. Sulle stratificazioni convesse. *Annali di Matematica Pura ed Applicata* 30, 173–183.

Edgeworth, F.Y. 1881. *Mathematical Psychics*. London: C. Kegan Paul & Co.

Eggleston, H.G. 1958. *Convexity*. Cambridge: Cambridge University Press.

Fenchel, W. 1953. Convex cones, sets and functions. Dept. of Mathematics, Princeton University, mimeo.

Ferland, J.A. 1981. Quasiconvexity and Pseudoconvexity of functions on the nonnegative orthant. In *Generalized Concavity in Optimization and Economics*, ed. S. Schaible and W.T. Ziemba, New York: Academic Press, 169–81.

Hardy, G.H., Littlewood, J.E. and Polya, G. 1934. *Inequalities*. Cambridge: Cambridge University Press. 2nd edn., 1951.

Hicks, J.R. 1939. *Value and Capital*. Oxford: Clarendon Press.

Koopmans, T.C. (ed.) 1951. *Activity Analysis of Production and Allocation*. Cowles Commission Monograph No. 13, New York: John Wiley & Sons.

Koopmans, T.C. 1957. *Three Essays on the State of Economic Science*. New York: McGraw-Hill.

Marshall, A. 1890. *Principles of Economics*, Vol. 1. London: Macmillan. 2nd edn, 1891.

Mas-Colell, A. 1985. *The Theory of General Economic Equilibrium: a differentiable approach*. Cambridge: Cambridge University Press.

Mill, J.S. 1864. *Principles of Political Economy*, Vol. I. 5th edn, New York: D. Appleton & Co.

Neumann, J. von. 1937. Über ein ökonomisches Gleichungssystem und eine Verallgemeinerung des Brouwerschen Fixpunktsatzes, *Ergebnisse eines mathematischen Kolloquiums* 8, 73–83. English translation as 'A model of general economic equilibrium', *Review of Economic Studies* 13, (1945 6), 1–9.

Neumann, J. von and Morgenstern, O. 1944. *Theory of Games and Economic Behavior*. Princeton: Princeton University Press. 2nd edn, 1947.

Rockafellar, R.T. 1970. *Convex Analysis*. Princeton: Princeton University Press.

Sraffa, P. 1960. *Production of Commodities by Means of Commodities: Prelude to a Critique of Economic Theory*. Cambridge: Cambridge University Press.

Young, L.C. 1969. *Lectures on the Calculus of Variations and Optimal Control Theory*. Philadelphia: W.B. Saunders Co.

convex programming. This essay covers the basic theory of convex optimization, together with enough introductory material on convex sets and functions so that the reader can follow the development. Its purpose is not only to introduce the reader to the fundamental theory of convexity, but also to prepare the way for other essays building on that theory.

The organization follows the sequence in which one enters the subject: first we cover convex and affine sets, then some of their topological properties, and next the basic theory of separation. After these elementary results, we examine several properties of convex cones that turn out to be helpful in dealing with general convex sets. We then introduce convex functions and their conjugates, examine their most important properties, and finally apply them to establish the fundamental structure and properties of perturbational duality.

The essay is entirely self-contained, in that it can be read by someone with no previous knowledge of convexity. However, two warnings are in order here: first, our arguments are often terse, and some work will be needed to fill in the blanks. Second, because of space limitations we have presented only the skeleton of the theory, and in particular we have given almost no examples. Real facility with the methods of convex optimization and duality comes only through actually using these tools on problems, and the reader should therefore work problems to bring out the significance of the mathematical results given here.

In our basic approach to the subject, we have followed the style and framework of Rockafellar (1970) and (1974), though in many places our particular methods or perspectives differ. In particular, in dealing with separation we have preferred to work with the form of the Hahn-Banach Theorem that is normally found in dealing with infinite-dimensional problems, and for that theorem we have followed the approach of Hermes and LaSalle (1969).

In order to make the work more accessible, and to conform to the limitations of space, we have cast the entire discussion in terms of finite-dimensional spaces. As just indicated, infinite-dimensional problems form an important application field for convex optimization; however, the technique required to deal with them is complicated by two unfortunate difficulties.

First, throughout this essay we use relative interiors of convex sets: that is, interiors relative to the smallest closed affine set containing the set in question. In finite-dimensional spaces, the relative interior is always nonempty if the set itself is nonempty. However, in infinite-dimensional spaces a nonempty convex set may not have such a relative interior. This means that, in general, one has to impose interiority conditions rather than relative interiority conditions in order to obtain many results, and the sharpness of the results is thereby reduced.

Second, many of our arguments here rest on the fact that in finite-dimensional spaces, closed bounded sets are compact. In the cases of infinite-dimensional spaces, this compactness property generally can be salvaged for closed bounded *convex* sets, but only with respect to a topology weaker than the norm topology. Therefore the compactness arguments have to be handled with much greater care when they can be done at all; in many cases the results just cannot be translated from the finite-dimensional to the infinite-dimensional case.

In the interest of simplicity, we have therefore limited the discussion here to the finite-dimensional case. However, for good discussions of convexity in infinite-dimensional spaces and some of its applications, one can refer to Ekeland and Temam (1974), Ekeland and Turnbull (1983), or (for special emphasis on economic applications) Aubin (1984). For an account of techniques in nonconvex analysis based on the methods of convexity, see Clarke (1983).

1. CONVEX SETS

1.1. *Basic definitions.* Here we introduce the most basic properties of convex sets, beginning with the even simpler class of *affine* sets in $\mathbb{R}^n$. These are defined by the property that for such a set, say A, if x and y belong to A then A contains the entire line $\{(1-t)x + ty \mid t \in \mathbb{R}\}$. Thus the affine sets are those that are 'flat'; in fact, they are just translates of subspaces. The dimension of such a subspace becomes the *dimension* of the corresponding affine set. Given any set S in $\mathbb{R}^n$, we define its *affine hull*, written aff S, to be the smallest affine set that contains S. An equivalent definition is that aff S is the set of all *affine*

combinations of the form $\Sigma_{i=1}^k t_i s_i$, where all s_i belong to S and the t_i sum to 1.

By analogy with affine combinations, we define *convex combinations* of the form $\Sigma_{i=1}^k t_i x_i$, where the x_i lie in $\mathbb{R}^n$ and the t_i are non-negative real numbers summing to 1. It is the non-negativity that distinguishes these t_i from those appearing in affine combinations, and this apparently minor change leads to a much richer structure.

We say a set C is *convex* if it contains all convex combinations of each pair of points of C, and it then follows that C contains any finite convex combination of its points. It is immediate that if C is convex, then so is its closure cl C. The *convex hull* of a subset S of $\mathbb{R}^n$ is the smallest convex set containing S; we write it conv S, and it is equally well described as the set of all finite convex combinations of points of S.

Certain simple convex sets play a special role in proofs; to introduce them we begin by saying that a collection of $k+1$ points in $\mathbb{R}^n$ is in *general position* if its affine hull has dimension k (for example, three points of $\mathbb{R}^n$ are in general position exactly when they are not collinear). We say that a *k-simplex* is the convex hull of $k+1$ points in general position. Examples of simplices are points, line segments, and (solid) triangles: these have dimension 0, 1 and 2 respectively, where we define the *dimension* of any convex set to be that of its affine hull.

1.2. *Relative interiors and closures of convex sets.* Although obviously convex sets do not always have interiors, they do always have a sort of interior that makes them much easier to handle than are general sets. The *relative interior* of a convex set C, written ri C, is just the interior of C relative to its affine hull: thus points of ri C are characterized by the property that all nearby points either belong to C itself, or lie outside aff C. If C coincides with its relative interior, we say it is *relatively open*, while we designate as the *relative boundary* of C those points of its closure that do not belong to the relative interior: that is, the set cl $C \setminus$ ri C.

A straightforward inductive construction establishes that if a convex set has dimension $k \geqslant 0$ then it contains a k-simplex. This has the very important consequence that *if a convex set is nonempty, then so is its relative interior.* Of course, this is a much stronger property than one has for general sets and their interiors, but one must keep in mind that the relative interior is in some important ways weaker than the interior: for example, it is *not* generally true that if $C \subset D$ then ri $C \subset$ ri D (think of C as one of the sides of a (solid) triangle D: then ri C and ri D are disjoint). This formula does hold, however, if C and D have the same affine hull.

An extremely important geometric property of the relative interior concerns line segments in a convex set C: if $x \in$ ri C and $y \in$ cl C, then the segment $[x, y)$ (defined to be $\{(1-t)x + ty \mid 0 \leqslant t < 1\}$) lies entirely in ri C. From this it follows at once that ri C is convex (take $y \in$ ri C too). The same property also yields an important characterization of ri C: x belongs to ri C if and only if for each $y \in C$ one can extend the line segment $[x, y]$ slightly beyond x without leaving C. This is equivalent to saying that for each such y there is $t > 1$ so that $(1-t)y + tx \in C$. These two simple properties of line segments underlie many proofs in convex analysis.

Using the definitions and the geometric properties we have just cited, one can prove the following fundamental result:

Theorem 1.1. Let C be a convex set in $\mathbb{R}^n$. Then the sets ri C, C, *and* cl C all have the same affine hull, the same closure, and the same relative interior.

It is a simple consequence of Theorem 1.1 that for convex C, one has $\operatorname{ri} \operatorname{cl} C = \operatorname{ri} C$ and $\operatorname{cl} \operatorname{ri} C = \operatorname{cl} C$. We shall use these formulas frequently.

Since linear operators commute with the operations of affine or convex combinations, it is easy to show that for a linear transformation $L: \mathbb{R}^n \to \mathbb{R}^m$ and a convex set $C \subset \mathbb{R}^n$, one has $L(\operatorname{aff} C) = \operatorname{aff} L(C)$ and $L(\operatorname{ri} C) = \operatorname{ri} L(C)$. The latter equation implies in particular that for two convex sets C and D in $\mathbb{R}^n$, $\operatorname{ri}(C + D) = \operatorname{ri} C + \operatorname{ri} D$. However, without additional conditions it is not generally true that $L(\operatorname{cl} C) = \operatorname{cl} L(C)$. We develop these conditions in Section 1.7.

Other formulations involving closures and relative interiors can be established if we assume a certain kind of regularity condition. To see why such a condition is needed, consider the solid triangle D in $\mathbb{R}^2$ with vertices $(1, 0)$, $(0, 1)$, and $(0, 0)$, and the linear transformation $L: \mathbb{R} \to \mathbb{R}^2$ defined by $Lx = (x, 0)$. Then the inverse image $L^{-1}(D)$ (defined to be $\{x \in \mathbb{R} \mid Lx \in D\}$) is $[0, 1]$, so $\operatorname{ri} L^{-1}(D) = (0, 1)$. But this does not equal $L^{-1}(\operatorname{ri} D)$, which is empty. To establish equality we need the hypothesis that the image of L actually meets $\operatorname{ri} D$. We use the notation $\operatorname{im} L = \{y \mid \text{for some } x, Lx = y\}$ for the image and, later, $\ker L = \{x \mid Lx = 0\}$ for the kernel.

Proposition 1.2. Let D be a convex set in $\mathbb{R}^m$ and L a linear transformation from $\mathbb{R}^n$ to $\mathbb{R}^m$. If $\operatorname{im} L$ meets $\operatorname{ri} D$, then

$$\operatorname{ri} L^{-1}(D) = L^{-1}(\operatorname{ri} D)$$

and

$$\operatorname{cl} L^{-1}(D) = L^{-1}(\operatorname{cl} D)$$

Under a similar assumption we can develop formulas for closures and relative interiors of intersections of sets:

Proposition 1.3. Let $\{C_\alpha \mid \alpha \subset A\}$ be a collection of non-empty convex sets in $\mathbb{R}^n$. Assume that $\bigcap_{\alpha \in A} \operatorname{ri} C_\alpha$ is nonempty. Then

$$\operatorname{cl} \bigcap_{\alpha \in A} C_\alpha = \bigcap_{\alpha \in A} \operatorname{cl} C_\alpha,$$

and

$$\operatorname{ri} \bigcap_{\alpha \in A} C_\alpha \subset \bigcap_{\alpha \in A} \operatorname{ri} C_\alpha,$$

with equality whenever A is a finite set.

To see the need for the finiteness assumption in the last assertion, let $A = \{1, 2, \ldots\}$ and take $C_n = [-1, 1 + n^{-1})$. Then $\operatorname{ri} \bigcap_n C_n = (-1, 1)$, whereas $\bigcap_n \operatorname{ri} C_n = (-1, 1]$.

1.3. Separation. All of the duality results that underlie convex programming come from the separation theory that we shall develop in this section. We are going to show how to separate pairs of convex sets by *hyperplanes*: that is, by affine sets of dimension one less than that of the space in which we are working. Such hyperplanes can be represented in the form $H = \{x \mid a(x) = \alpha\}$, where a is a nontrivial linear functional on $\mathbb{R}^n$ and α is a real number. Of course, we can always represent $a(x)$ by $\langle a^*, x \rangle$, where a^* is an element of $\mathbb{R}^n$ and $\langle \, , \, \rangle$ represents the standard inner product. The choice of H then determines the pair (a^*, α), but only up to multiplication by a nonzero scalar.

Given the above representation for H, we define its *upper closed (open) halfspace* to be the set $\{x \mid a(x) \geqslant (>)\alpha\}$, with a similar definition for the *lower closed (open) halfspace*. Then we say that H *separates* two convex sets C and D if each set belongs to a different closed halfspace. The separation is *proper* if $C \cup D \not\subset H$, and it is *strict* if C and D each belong to a different open halfspace. Finally, the separation is *strong* if, for some positive ϵ, H actually separates $C + \epsilon B$ and $D + \epsilon B$, where B is

the Euclidean unit ball: $B = \{x \mid \|x\| \leqslant 1\}$. These definitions are listed in increasing order of strength; as we shall see, the most useful is proper separation, and the next most useful is strong separation. We shall characterize each of these two.

Our fundamental tool for establishing separation will be a version of the Hahn–Banach extension theorem. This theorem holds in much more general settings than the present one; it deals with a real-valued function f on $\mathbb{R}^n$, assumed *positively homogeneous* (that is, for each $x \in \mathbb{R}^n$ and each $t > 0$, $f(tx) = tf(x)$) and *sublinear* (for each $x, y \in \mathbb{R}^n$, $f(x + y) \leqslant f(x) + f(y)$). The extension theorem asserts that if some linear functional minorizes f on a subspace of $\mathbb{R}^n$ then it can be extended so as to minorize f everywhere.

Lemma 1.4. (Hahn–Banach Theorem for $\mathbb{R}^n$). Let f be a positively homogeneous, sublinear functional on $\mathbb{R}^n$. Let M be a subspace of $\mathbb{R}^n$ and let a_M be a linear functional on M, with $a_M(m) \leqslant f(m)$ for each $m \in M$.

Then a_M can be extended to a linear functional a on $\mathbb{R}^n$, so that a agrees with a_M on M and $a \leqslant f$ everywhere on $\mathbb{R}^n$.

Proof. If there is some y not belonging to M, we will extend a_M from M to $M + \operatorname{span}(y)$. This construction then yields the required a in no more than n steps.

Note that for any p and q in M we have $a_M(p) - a_M(q) = a_M(p - q) \leqslant f(p - q) \leqslant f(p + y) + f(-q - y)$. Thus

$$\sup\{-f(-q - y) - a_M(q) \mid q \in M\}$$
$$\leqslant \inf\{f(p + y) - a_M(p) \mid p \in M\}, \quad (1)$$

so there is some real number s between the two sides of (1). It then follows that for any scalar t and any $m \in M$,

$$a_M(m) + ts \leqslant f(m + ty) \quad (2)$$

Now if $z \in M + \operatorname{span}(y)$ then we can write $z = m + ty$ for unique $m \in M$ and $t \in \mathbb{R}$. If we define a' on $M + \operatorname{span}(y)$ by $a'(z) = a_M(m) + ts$, then by (2) a' has the required properties. $\square$

With the extension lemma we can now prove the basic theorem about separation of a point from a convex set. The result about separation of two sets will follow easily from this.

Theorem 1.5. Let C be a nonempty convex subset of $\mathbb{R}^n$. Then C can be properly separated from $\{0\}$ if and only if $0 \notin \operatorname{ri} C$.

Proof (if): Let $D = \operatorname{conv}(\{0\} \cup C)$ and $M = \operatorname{aff} D$ (a subspace). Let $E = D + M^\perp$. We first prove that E has a nonempty interior that does not contain the origin. We have $\operatorname{aff} E = M + M^\perp = \mathbb{R}^n$, so $\operatorname{int} E = \operatorname{ri} E = \operatorname{ri} D + M^\perp$. If $0 \in \operatorname{int} E$ then $0 = d' + m'$ with $m' \in M^\perp$ and $d' \in \operatorname{ri} D \subset M$; thus $d' = 0$ so $0 \in \operatorname{ri} D$. Let $c \in \operatorname{ri} C$; then as $0 \in \operatorname{ri} D$ there is some $t > 0$ with $-tc \in C$. As C is convex we can find $s \in [0, 1]$ and $c' \in D$ with $-tc = (1 - s)0 + sc'$. Then $0 = ct/(t + s) + c's/(t + s)$, a convex combination of a point of $\operatorname{ri} C$ and a point of C. As $t > 0$ we have $0 \in \operatorname{ri} C$, contradicting the hypothesis. Hence $0 \notin \operatorname{int} E$.

Now let $-e \in \operatorname{int} E$ and set $E' = E + e$. Then $\operatorname{int} E'$ contains 0 but not e. Define the *gauge* of E' by

$$g(x) = \inf\{s \geqslant 0 \mid x \in sE'\}.$$

It is easy to show that g is a finite, positively homogeneous, sublinear function on $\mathbb{R}^n$; further, $\operatorname{int} E' = \{x \mid g(x) < 1\}$ and $\operatorname{cl} E' = \{x \mid g(x) \leqslant 1\}$. Now for $s \in \mathbb{R}$ let $a_e(se) = s$. If $s > 0$ then $a_e(se) = s \leqslant sg(e) = g(se)$, since we know $g(e) \geqslant 1$. On the other hand, if $s \leqslant 0$ then $a_e(se) = s \leqslant 0 \leqslant g(se)$. Hence a_e

minorizes g on span(e). Extend a_e to a linear functional a minorizing g on $\mathbb{R}^n$.

Now for any $w \in E$, we have $w + e \in E'$. Then

$$1 + a(w) = a(e + w) \leqq g(e + w) \leqq 1,$$

so that $E \subset \{x \mid a(x) \leqq 0\}$, and thus we have separated E from $\{0\}$ (and hence also C from $\{0\}$) by the hyperplane $H = \ker a$ (H is a hyperplane because $a(e) = 1$, so that a is nontrivial]). As $E = D + M^\perp$ we have $M^\perp \subset H$; if the separation were improper then we would have $H \supset \{0\} \cup C$ and hence $H \supset D$. Then $H \supset E$, contradicting $a(-e) = -1$ and $-e \in E$. Therefore H properly separates C from $\{0\}$.

(only if): Suppose a hyperplane H properly separates $\{0\}$ from C. If $0 \notin H$ then 0 certainly cannot belong to ri C. If $0 \in H$ then there is some $c \in C \backslash H$. If a is a linear functional with $H = \ker a$, then without loss of generality we can suppose $a(c)$ is positive. If $0 \in$ ri C then for some positive t, $-tc$ belongs to C. But $a(-tc)$ is negative, contradicting the separation assumption. Hence $0 \notin$ ri C. $\qquad \square$

With Theorem 1.5 established, it is now very easy to characterize proper and strong separation.

Theorem 1.6. Let C and D be nonempty convex subsets of $\mathbb{R}^n$. Then:

(a) C and D can be properly separated if and only if ri C and ri D are disjoint (equivalently, if and only if $0 \notin$ ri $(C - D)$).

(b) C and D can be strongly separated if and only if $0 \notin$ cl $(C - D)$.

Proof. For (a), let $E = C - D$. Then ri $E =$ ri $(C - D) =$ ri $C -$ ri D, and this set fails to contain the origin precisely when ri C and ri D are disjoint. By Theorem 1.5, this property is equivalent to proper separability of E from $\{0\}$. This, in turn, means that for some nontrivial linear functional a one has for each $c \in C$ and $d \in D$ the inequality $0 \leqq a(c - d) = a(c) - a(d)$, with strict inequality for some choice of c and d. But this can be rewritten as

$$\sup\{a(d) \mid d \in D\} \leqq \inf\{a(c) \mid c \in C\},$$

and any real number s between these values yields a hyperplane $H = \{x \mid a(x) = s\}$ properly separating C and D. This proves (a).

To prove (b), note that if $0 \notin$ cl $(C - D)$ then for some positive t, $2tB$ does not meet $C - D$. This is equivalent to saying that $C + tB$ and $D + tB$ are disjoint (and hence can be separated by (a)). This is strong separation of C and D.

On the other hand, if C and D can be strongly separated, then there exist a nontrivial linear functional a, a real number s, and a positive t, such that for each $c \in C$ and $d \in D$, and each v and w in B, we have

$$a(d + tv) \leqq s \leqq a(c + tw).$$

Taking the supremum in v on the left and the infimum in w on the right, we find that

$$a(d) + t \|a\| \leqq s \leqq a(c) - t \|a\|.$$

Rewriting this and employing the Schwarz inequality we finally obtain

$$2t \|a\| \leqq a(c - d) \leqq \|a\| \|c - d\|,$$

which implies that each element of $C - D$ has norm at least $2t$. Thus 0 does not belong to cl $(C - D)$. $\qquad \square$

Warning. To say $0 \notin$ cl $(C - D)$ is stronger than to say

that cl C and cl D are disjoint; hence we have a difference from the situation with relative interiors. To see this, consider $C = \{(x, y) \mid x > 0, xy \geqq 1\}$ and its reflection $D = \{(x, y) \mid (x, -y) \in C\}$. Here C and D are closed and disjoint, but strong separation is not possible.

However, we can still recover strong separation from disjointness if we require one of the sets to be compact. This is explained in the following corollary.

Corollary 1.7. Let C and D be nonempty disjoint convex sets in $\mathbb{R}^n$. If C is closed and D is compact then C and D can be strongly separated.

Proof. According to Theorem 1.6 we need only show that cl $(C - D)$ does not contain the origin. As C and D are disjoint, it is enough to show that $C - D$ is closed. If some sequence in $C - D$ converges to a point x, then by extracting a convergent subsequence of points of D we can show that actually $x \in C - D$, and so $C - D$ is closed. $\qquad \square$

1.4. Convex cones: basic facts. A subset S of $\mathbb{R}^n$ is a *cone* if for each $x \in S$, all positive scalar multiples of x lie in S. If S is a cone that is also a convex set, it is a *convex cone*. If a cone S is nonempty, its *polar* is $S^0 = \{y \mid$ for each $x \in S, \langle y, x \rangle \leqq 0\}$; this is a nonempty closed convex cone (since it is an intersection of closed convex cones, one for each x). The *lineality space* of a closed convex cone S is lin $S = S \cap (-S)$; this is the largest subspace contained in S.

We can introduce an operation to make any set into a cone by defining cone S to be $\{tx \mid x \in S, t > 0\}$ whenever $S \subset \mathbb{R}^n$. It is then possible to show that this operation commutes with the relative interior: that is, ri cone $S =$ cone ri S, when S is convex.

The hyperplane separation technique permits us to prove a basic duality theorem for cones. To establish our result it will be convenient first to note some special properties of separating hyperplanes when one of the sets being separated is a cone. We omit the proof since it is straightforward.

Proposition 1.8. Let C and D be nonempty convex sets in $\mathbb{R}^n$. Suppose that C is a cone and that C and D are separated by the hyperplane $H(s) = \{x \mid \langle y, x \rangle = s\}$, so that for each c in C and each d in D one has

$$\langle y, c \rangle \leqq s \leqq \langle y, d \rangle.$$

Then $y \in C^0$ and $s \geqq 0$; further, the hyperplane $H(0) = \{x \mid \langle y, x \rangle = 0\}$ also separates C and D. The separation by $H(0)$ is proper if and only if the separation by $H(s)$ was proper.

The following theorem is the basic duality result for cones.

Theorem 1.9. Let S be a nonempty cone in $\mathbb{R}^n$. Then

$$S^{00} = \text{cl conv } S.$$

Proof. If $q \in S^0$, then for each $x \in$ conv S it is obvious that $\langle q, x \rangle \leqq 0$. This means that $x \in S^{00}$, so $S^{00} \supset$ conv S. But S^{00} is closed, so $S^{00} \supset$ cl conv S.

Now suppose $x \notin$ cl conv S; we show $x \notin S^{00}$. Since cl conv S is closed and convex, Corollary 1.7 tells us that we can separate $\{x\}$ strongly from cl conv S. Thus for some $y \in \mathbb{R}^n$ and some real s, and for each $z \in$ cl conv S, $\langle y, z \rangle < s < \langle y, x \rangle$. By Proposition 1.8 we have $y \in S^0$ and $s \geqq 0$; thus $\langle y, x \rangle > 0$. But then $x \notin S^{00}$; hence we have shown that $S^{00} \subset$ cl conv S. $\qquad \square$

1.5. Recession cones of convex sets. In this section we introduce a tool for dealing with unbounded convex sets. If C is a nonempty convex set in $\mathbb{R}^n$, the *recession cone* of C, written rc C, is the set of points $z \in \mathbb{R}^n$ such that $C + z \subset C$: that is, for each $c \in C$ the point $c + z$ also belongs to C (sometimes the phrase *asymptotic cone* is used, see e.g. Debreu, 1959, p. 22). Evidently the origin belongs to rc C but other points may belong as well. It is easy to show from the definition that rc C is a convex cone. When C is also closed, then we have three other equivalent characterizations of rc C:

(i) rc C is the set of z such that for *some* $c \in C$ and all non-negative t, $c + tz \in C$.

(ii) rc C is the set of all limits of sequences of the form $t_k c_k$ where $c_k \in C$ and the t_k are positive numbers converging to zero. (As $C = \text{cl ri } C$, we can if we wish restrict the c_k to lie in ri C, and this is sometimes convenient).

(iii) rc C is the intersection over all non-negative s of the sets cl cone$[\{0\} \cup \{x \in C \mid \|x\| \geqslant s\}]$.

These three equivalent characterizations have several very useful consequences. For example, it is immediate from (iii) that rc C is closed, and that it is $\{0\}$ if and only if C is bounded. One can also prove the following properties of the recession cone with respect to various set operations.

Proposition 1.10. The recession cone has the following properties:

(i) If $\{C(\alpha) \mid \alpha \in A\}$ is a collection of closed convex subsets of $\mathbb{R}^n$ having a nonempty intersection, then the recession cone of their intersection is the intersection of their recession cones.

(ii) For a finite collection of nonempty closed convex sets, the recession cone of the Cartesian product is the Cartesian product of the recession cones.

(iii) If c is a closed convex subset of $\mathbb{R}^n$ and L is a linear transformation from $\mathbb{R}^m$ to $\mathbb{R}^n$ with $L^{-1}(C)$ nonempty, then rc $L^{-1}(C) = L^{-1}(\text{rc } C)$.

1.6. *The fundamental cone construction.* One of the reasons for paying so much attention to cones is that many important properties of convex sets can be illuminated by a certain construction that forms from a set in $\mathbb{R}^n$ a cone in $\mathbb{R}^{n+1}$. This construction is particularly useful in establishing and visualizing properties of the conjugate of a convex function. In this section we carry through the construction and establish its most important properties.

We have already seen how, from a set C in $\mathbb{R}^n$, we can construct a cone in $\mathbb{R}^n$ by taking positive scalar multiples to obtain cone C. However, this method has the disadvantage that if two points of C belong to the same half-line beginning at the origin, the cone operation causes them to lose their individual identities. In particular, given cone C we cannot recover the original set C.

To remedy this, we shall add a dimension by identifying C in $\mathbb{R}^n$ with the set $C \times \{-1\}$ in $\mathbb{R}^{n+1}$. We then form the set cl cone $(C \times \{-1\})$ and ask whether it displays any interesting information about C. It turns out that it does, and that we can recover from this cone not only cl C, but also ri C and rc cl C. This is explained in the following theorem, in which $\mathbb{R}_-$ denotes the set of non-positive reals.

Theorem 1.11. Suppose Q is a convex cone contained in $\mathbb{R}^n \times \mathbb{R}_-$ but not in $\mathbb{R}^n \times \{0\}$. Let $E = \{x \in \mathbb{R}^n \mid (x, -1) \in Q\}$. Then E is nonempty and we have

$$\text{cl } Q = \text{cone}[(\text{cl } E) \times \{-1\}] \cup [(\text{rc cl } E) \times \{0\}]$$

and

$$\text{ri } Q = \text{cone}[(\text{ri } E) \times \{-1\}].$$

Proof. By hypothesis there is some $(x, -s)$ in Q with $s > 0$. As Q is a cone, $(x/s, -1)$ belongs to E. This implies that ri $Q \subset \mathbb{R}^n \times (-\infty, 0)$. We have $Q = \text{cone } Q$, so ri $Q = \text{ri cone } Q = \text{cone ri } Q$. Hence ri Q is a cone each of whose elements is of the form $(x, -s)$ with $s > 0$, and it therefore consists of all positive scalar multiples of $(\text{ri } Q) \cap V(1)$, where we write $V(s) = \mathbb{R}^n \times \{-s\}$. But $(\text{ri } Q) \cap V(1) = \text{ri } [Q \cap V(1)] = \text{ri } (E \times \{-1\}) = (\text{ri } E) \times \{-1\}$, and so ri $Q = \text{cone}[(\text{ri } E) \times \{-1\}]$.

If $s > 0$ then $V(s)$ meets ri Q, and so we have

$$(\text{cl } Q) \cap V(s) = \text{cl}(Q \cap V(s))$$
$$= \text{cl } s[Q \cap V(1)] = s[(\text{cl } E) \times \{-1\}].$$

On the other hand, $(\text{cl } Q) \cap V(0)$ consists of those points $(x, 0)$ that are limits of sequences $(x_k, -s_k)$ in ri Q. Now x_k can be written as $s_k(x_k/s_k)$, where $x_k/s_k \in \text{ri } E$. As s_k converges to 0, the set of such limits x is exactly rc cl E. Putting together the results for $V(s)$ and for $V(0)$, we have the formula for cl Q. $\qquad \square$

Instead of starting with Q, we could begin with a nonempty convex set $E \subset \mathbb{R}^n$, and by defining Q to be cone $(E \times \{-1\})$ we could apply Theorem 1.11 to conclude that

$$\text{cl cone}(E \times \{-1\}) = \text{cone}[(\text{cl } E) \times \{-1\}] \cup [(\text{rc cl } E) \times \{0\}],$$

and

$$\text{ri cone}(E \times \{-1\}) = \text{cone}[(\text{ri } E) \times \{-1\}].$$

These formulas will be useful, for example, in dealing with conjugate functions in Section 2.3.

1.7. *Closure of linear images of convex sets.* Although it may seem appealing to conjecture that the image of a closed convex set C in $\mathbb{R}^n$ under a linear operator $L: \mathbb{R}^n \to \mathbb{R}^m$ should be closed, it is easy to see that this is false. For example, the image of the set $\{(x, y) \mid x > 0, xy \geqslant 1\}$ in $\mathbb{R}^2$, under the linear projector L defined by $L(x, y) = x$, is not closed. Since such images frequently occur in applications, we need to be able to predict when they will be closed. We can use the theory of Sections 1.5 and 1.6 for this purpose, and this section shows how to do so.

If we look carefully at the above example, we can see that for $k = 1, 2, 3, \ldots L$ carries the pairs $(1/k, k)$ into a sequence in $L(C)$ that converges to 0 (not in $L(C)$). The directions defined by the members of this sequence converge to the direction of $(0, 1)$, which belongs to the kernel of L and also to rc C. Thus, we might think it suitable to require that ker L have only the origin in common with rc C. This turns out to be slightly too strong: it suffices that the intersection of ker L and rc C (which is always a cone) actually be a subspace. Further, an appropriate version of this criterion works even when C itself is not closed.

To show this, we first notice that it is easy to prove when C is a convex cone. For suppose that Q is any nonempty convex cone (closed or not), and that $(\text{ker } L) \cap \text{cl } Q$ is a subspace M. We have $L(\text{cl } Q) \subset \text{cl } L(Q)$ by continuity of L; for the opposite inclusion it is enough to show that $L(\text{cl } Q)$ is closed. If we let $K = (\text{cl } Q) \cap M^\perp$, then cl $Q = M + K$ and $L(\text{cl } Q) = L(K)$; thus we need only prove that $L(K)$ is closed. If $K = \{0\}$ we are finished; if $K \neq \{0\}$ then since $(\text{ker } L) \cap K = M \cap M^\perp = \{0\}$, the minimum of $\|Lx\|$ on the compact set of points x in K with length 1 is a positive number, say $1/s$. This means that if $x \in K$, then $\|x\| \leqslant s \|Lx\|$. If $y \in \text{cl } L(K)$ then for each positive t the set $K(t) = \{x \in K \mid Lx \in y + tB\}$ is nonempty, closed, and (by what we have just shown) bounded, hence compact. The intersection of this nest of compact sets over all $t > 0$ is therefore nonempty, so $y \in L(K)$ and hence $L(K)$ is closed.

To prove the result for general C, we just combine the observation in the last paragraph with the cone construction of Section 1.6 to obtain the following theorem.

Theorem 1.12. Let C be a nonempty set in $\mathbb{R}^n$ and L a linear transformation from $\mathbb{R}^n$ to $\mathbb{R}^m$. If $(\ker L) \cap (\text{rc cl } C)$ is a subspace, then

$$L(\text{cl } C) = \text{cl } L(C)$$

and

$$L(\text{rc cl } C) = \text{rc cl } L(C).$$

Proof. Let $Q = \text{cone}(C \times \{-1\})$ and define a linear transformation L' from $\mathbb{R}^{n+1}$ to $\mathbb{R}^{m+1}$ by $L'(x, s) = (Lx, s)$. By Theorem 1.11,

$$\text{cl } Q = \text{cone}([\text{cl } C] \times \{-1\}) \cup ([\text{rc cl } C] \times \{0\}),$$

so $(\ker L') \cap Q = ([\ker L] \cap \text{rc cl } C) \times \{0\}$, and this is a subspace by hypothesis. Therefore $L'(\text{cl } Q) = \text{cl } L'(Q)$ by what we have already proved. But

$$L'(\text{cl } Q) = \text{cone}[L(\text{cl } C) \times \{-1\}] \cup [L(\text{rc cl } C) \times \{0\}],$$

and by Theorem 1.11,

$$\text{cl } L'(Q) = \text{cone}[\text{cl } L(C) \times \{-1\}] \cup [\text{rc cl } L(C) \times \{0\}].$$

Considering the sections of this cone whose $(n+1)$st components are -1 and 0 respectively, we find the formulas asserted in the theorem. □

2. CONVEX FUNCTIONS

2.1. Elementary facts. In this section we introduce extended real-valued functions on $\mathbb{R}^n$: that is, functions from $\mathbb{R}^n$ into the set $\overline{\mathbb{R}} = [-\infty, +\infty]$. The addition of $-\infty$ and $+\infty$ to $\mathbb{R}$ causes no real difficulty as long as we agree not to form the sum $(-\infty) + (+\infty)$. We postulate that either $+\infty$ or $-\infty$, when multiplied by zero, yields zero; otherwise we use the normal rules of addition and multiplication. In all of what follows, a function f on $\mathbb{R}^n$ will be assumed to be into $\overline{\mathbb{R}}$ (i.e. extended real-valued) unless some other range set is specified.

In dealing with extended real-valued functions it is very convenient to use the *epigraph* as a fundamental geometric device. The epigraph of f is the set

$$\text{epi } f = \{(x, s) \in \mathbb{R}^{n+1} \mid f(x) \leqslant s\};$$

note that s must be a real number (not $+\infty$ or $-\infty$).

The epigraph provides a convenient way to define convex functions: we say f is *convex* if and only if epi f is a convex set. As an example, we can define the *indicator* of a set $S \subset \mathbb{R}^n$ by setting $I_S(x) = 0$ if $x \in S$, and $+\infty$ otherwise. Evidently the function I_S will be convex precisely when S is a convex set. We say a function g is *concave* if $-g$ is convex. This is evidently equivalent to convexity of the *hypograph* of g, which is the set $\{(x, s) \mid g(x) \geqslant s\}$.

It is often convenient to have tests for convexity that use function values directly, and two such tests can be extracted directly from the definition. First, a function f is convex if and only if for each x and y in $\mathbb{R}^n$, each pair of real numbers r and s with $f(x) < r$ and $f(y) < s$, and each $t \in (0, 1)$, $f[(1-t)x + ty] < (1-t)r + ts$. Second, if the range of the function is confined to $(-\infty, +\infty]$, then f is convex if and only if for each x and y and for each t in $(0, 1)$,

$f[(1-t)x + ty] \leqslant (1-t)f(x) + tf(y)$. Using these tests one easily shows that if f is a convex function and s is a non-negative real number then sf is convex, whereas if f and g are convex functions from $\mathbb{R}^n$ to $(-\infty, +\infty]$ then $f + g$ is convex. Note that we did not allow the value $-\infty$, in order to avoid the possibility of forming the sum $(-\infty) + (+\infty)$.

Frequently in convex programming one uses the function value $+\infty$ to designate points that are *infeasible*: that is, they are not to be considered when minimizing the function. Therefore, for a function f the set $\{x \mid f(x) < +\infty\}$ is of particular interest. It is called the *effective domain* of f, abbreviated dom f. As dom f is the projection of epi f into $\mathbb{R}^n$, it is clearly convex if f is.

In most of the results we shall discuss here, differentiability plays no role. However, there is a differential test for convexity of a C'' function that is frequently useful in applications. It concerns a function f that is C'' on an open convex set in $\mathbb{R}^n$. We say that a function defined on a subset S of $\mathbb{R}^n$ is convex there if and only if its $+\infty$ *extension* (the function that agrees with f on S and is $+\infty$ elsewhere) is convex in the sense already defined.

Proposition 2.1. Let f be a real-valued C'' function on an open convex subset C of $\mathbb{R}^n$. Then f is convex on C if and only if for each $x \in C$, $f''(x)$ is positive semidefinite.

Instead of proving this proposition, we just outline the argument. First, convexity on C is equivalent to convexity of the functions from $\mathbb{R}$ to $\mathbb{R}$ that result from restricting f to the intersection of any line with C. The second derivative of such a function is of the form $\langle v, f''(x)v \rangle$, where the line containing x is $\{x + tv \mid t \in \mathbb{R}\}$. Positive semidefiniteness of $f''(x)$ is equivalent to non-negativity of all such inner products, and one then uses the fundamental theorem of calculus to obtain the convexity inequality.

2.2. Closure and lower semicontinuity. Convex functions need not, of course, be continuous. Instead, the basic condition for good behaviour of a convex function – at least, with respect to minimization – is closure, which we shall study here. To begin with, we say f is *lower semicontinuous* (lsc) at $x \in \mathbb{R}^n$ if $f(x) = \lim \inf_{y \to x} f(y)$, where

$$\lim \inf_{y \to x} f(y) = \sup_{V \in \mathscr{V}(x)} \inf_{y \in V} f(y),$$

and where $\mathscr{V}(x)$ denotes the neighbourhood system of x. This definition of limit inferior is slightly different from the classical one, which accounts for the equality in place of the inequality usually seen in the definition of lower semicontinuity. For an extended real-valued function f, one can show that f is lsc everywhere if and only if epi f is closed, and that these properties are further equivalent to the closedness of the level set $\{x \mid f(x) \leqslant s\}$ for each real s.

The closed convex functions are almost those that are lsc, but there is a slight twist: we say f is *closed* if it equals its *closure*, cl f, where cl f is (a) the *lower semicontinuous hull* of f (i.e., the function whose epigraph is cl epi f) if f never takes $-\infty$, or (b) the constant function $-\infty$, if f ever takes $-\infty$. This definition is devised so as to fit conveniently with the conjugate transforms that we shall introduce in the next section.

In addition to closure, another regularity classification is often useful: we say f is *proper* if it never takes $-\infty$ and is not identically $+\infty$, and *improper* otherwise. Using the elementary test for convexity discussed in the last section, one can show easily that an improper convex function f in fact takes $-\infty$ at each point of ri dom f.

One of the basic facts about convex functions is that if such a function does not take $-\infty$, then it is very nearly equal to its closure. We shall see how to state this precisely, but first we need a technical lemma.

Lemma 2.2. Let f be a convex function on $\mathbb{R}^n$. Then ri epi $f = \{(x, s) \in \mathbb{R}^{n+1} | x \in \text{ri dom} f, s > f(x)\}$.

Proof. If f is identically $+\infty$ this is clearly true, so we can assume dom f is nonempty. Define a linear transformation $P\colon \mathbb{R}^{n+1} \to \mathbb{R}^n$ by $P(x, s) = x$. Then $P(\text{ri epi} f) = \text{ri} P(\text{epi} f) = \text{ri dom} f$. We shall look at each point x in ri dom f, and show that the set (say S) on the right in the assertion of the lemma has the same intersection with a vertical line through x as does ri epi f.

Represent the line through x as $L = P^{-1}x$. Then $L = \text{ri} L$, and so ri L meets ri epi f since $x \in P(\text{ri epi} f)$. Therefore

$$L \cap \text{ri epi} f = \text{ri}(L \cap \text{epi} f) = \{(x, s)|s > f(x)\} = L \cap S. \quad \square$$

The next theorem develops the basic properties of the closure operation for convex functions.

Theorem 2.3. Let f be a convex function from $\mathbb{R}^n$ to $(-\infty, +\infty]$. Then cl f is closed and convex; it is proper if and only if f is proper. One has cl $f(x) = f(x)$ everywhere except perhaps on the relative boundary of dom f. Finally, cl dom $f \supset \text{dom cl} f \supset \text{dom} f$.

Proof. If f is improper then $f \equiv +\infty \equiv \text{cl} f$, so there is nothing to prove. Thus, we assume f is proper, so epi cl $f = \text{cl epi} f$ (and hence cl f is convex). If P is the linear transformation introduced in the proof of Lemma 2.2, then by continuity we have

$$\text{cl} P(\text{epi} f) \supset P(\text{cl epi} f) \supset P(\text{epi} f);$$

i.e.,

$$\text{cl dom} f \supset \text{dom cl} f \supset \text{dom} f,$$

which also implies ri dom cl $f = \text{ri dom} f$. Let x be an element of ri dom f and let $L = P^{-1}x$. As ri L meets ri epi f (Lemma 2.2), we have

$$L \cap \text{epi cl} f = L \cap \text{cl epi} f = \text{cl}(L \cap \text{epi} f) = L \cap \text{epi} f,$$

and therefore cl $f(x) = f(x)$. The equality also holds outside cl dom f since there both f and cl f take $+\infty$. As cl f agrees with f on ri dom $f (= \text{ri dom cl} f)$, we see cl f must be proper, since otherwise it would take $-\infty$ there. This in turn tells us that cl f *nowhere* takes $-\infty$; thus since epi cl f is closed, we see that cl f is closed. $\quad \square$

Theorem 2.3 tells us that cl f and f agree except perhaps at relative boundary points of dom f. In fact, if f is proper then the values of cl f can be obtained directly from f by taking limits along certain line segments, as we see next.

Proposition 2.4. Let f be a proper convex function on $\mathbb{R}^n$. If $x \in \mathbb{R}^n$ and $z \in \text{ri dom} f$, then cl $f(x) = \lim_{t \downarrow 0} f[(1 - t) \times x + tz]$.

Proof. Let $s > f(z)$; then $(z, s) \in \text{ri epi} f$. Assume for the moment that $x \in \text{dom cl} f$, and let $r \geqslant \text{cl} f(x)$. Then $(x, r) \in \text{cl epi} f$, so the relatively open line segment between (z, s) and (x, r) lies entirely in ri epi f, and thus for each small positive t, $f[(1 - t)x + tz] < (1 - t)r + ts$. But $\lim_{t \downarrow 0}(1 - t) \times r + ts = r \geqslant \text{cl} f(x)$, and since this is true for any $r \geqslant \text{cl} f(x)$, we have

$$\text{cl} f(x) \geqslant \lim \sup_{t \downarrow 0} f[(1 - t)x + tz].$$

On the other hand, since cl $f \leqslant f$ and cl f is lsc at x, we also have

$$\text{cl} f(x) = \lim \inf_{t \downarrow 0} \text{cl} f[(1 - t)x + tz]$$

$$\leqslant \lim \inf_{t \downarrow 0} f[(1 - t)x + tz].$$

This establishes the theorem if $x \in \text{dom cl} f$. But if $x \notin \text{dom cl} f$, the last inequality shows that

$$+\infty = \text{cl} f(x) \leqslant \lim \inf_{t \downarrow 0} f[(1 - t)x + tz],$$

so that in this case too the limit exists and agrees with cl f. $\quad \square$

2.3. *The conjugate transform.* Conjugacy is a device for associating with any convex function another such function in a correspondence that is essentially $1 - 1$. The paired functions display intricate mutual relationships that underlie all of the duality theory of convex optimization. In this section we introduce the conjugate function and derive its basic properties. Then in Section 2.4 we exhibit a useful application by establishing the duality correspondence between closed convex sets and their support functions.

The convex conjugate of a function is derived by considering affine minorants of the function. Of course, not every function has such a minorant, but every proper convex function does, as we now show.

Lemma 2.5. Let f be a convex function on $\mathbb{R}^n$. If $x \in \text{ri dom} f$, then there is some $x^* \in \mathbb{R}^n$ such that for each $z \in \mathbb{R}^n$.

$$f(z) \geqslant f(x) + \langle x^*, z - x \rangle.$$

Proof. If f is improper then $f(x)$ must be $-\infty$, so any x^* will do; thus assume f is proper. As $x \in \text{ri dom} f$ the point $[x, f(x)]$ does not belong to ri epi f (Lemma 2.2). Therefore we can properly separate $[x, f(x)]$ from epi f: this means that there is a pair (x^*, s^*) such that whenever $(z, s) \in \text{epi} f$ we have

$$\langle x^*, z \rangle + s^* s \leqslant \langle x^*, x \rangle + s^* f(x);$$

further, for some (z, s) the inequality is strict. Because of the form of epi f we obviously cannot have $s^* > 0$, whereas if $s^* = 0$ then x^* is the normal to a hyperplane properly separating x from dom f, which is impossible since we assumed $x \in \text{ri dom} f$. Therefore $s^* < 0$, and we can assume that (x^*, s^*) has been scaled so that $s^* = -1$. Then we have for each $(z, s) \in \text{epi} f$,

$$s \geqslant f(x) + \langle x^*, z - x \rangle,$$

which is enough to prove the assertion. $\quad \square$

Even if $x \notin \text{ri dom} f$, any point x^* having the property asserted by Lemma 2.5 is called a *subgradient* of f at x. We shall study subgradients further in Section 2.5.

Now for a given extended real-valued function f we can ask: among all affine functions of x having the form $\langle x^*, x \rangle - s^*$, with x^* fixed but s^* variable, which is the greatest that minorizes f (if any does)? This is equivalent to asking how small we could make s^* while still preserving the property that for each $x, f(x) \geqslant \langle x^*, x \rangle - s^*$. Obviously the answer to this question is that s^* should be the supremum over all $x \in \mathbb{R}^n$ of the quantity $\langle x^*, x \rangle - f(x)$ (where a value of $+\infty$ for s^* indicates that there is no minorant at all having the prescribed form). This value is defined to be that of the *convex conjugate function* f^* at the point x^*:

$$f^*(x^*) = \sup\{\langle x^*, x \rangle - f(x)\}.$$

We can also define the *concave conjugate* of f by replacing the 'sup' by 'inf' in the above expression. Since

$$\inf\{\langle x^*, x\rangle - f(x)\} = -\sup\{\langle -x^*, x\rangle - (-f)(x)\},$$

the concave conjugate of f has at x^* the value $-(-f)^*(-x^*)$, where the asterisk denotes the convex conjugate of $-f$. In this essay we will use the same notation (asterisk) for the convex and the concave conjugates of a function. Concave conjugates will be used only in Part 3, and it will generally be clear from the context when a conjugate is to be interpreted in the concave sense.

Certain properties of f^* follow directly from the definition and from our previous work.

Proposition 2.6. Let f be an extended real-valued function on $\mathbb{R}^n$. Then f^* is a closed convex function; if f is convex then f^* is proper if and only if f is proper.

Proof. The set $\operatorname{epi} f^*$ is the intersection of the closed convex sets $\{(x^*, s^*) | s^* \geqq \langle x^*, x\rangle - f(x)\}$ for $x \in \mathbb{R}^n$; hence it is closed and convex. If f is identically $+\infty$, then f^* is identically $-\infty$; otherwise f^* never takes $-\infty$. Thus f^* is a closed convex function. If f is improper then f^* will be either identically $-\infty$ or identically $+\infty$, and in either case it is improper too. If f is convex and proper then there is at least one affine function minorizing f (Lemma 2.5), so f^* is not identically $+\infty$. But as f is finite somewhere, f^* never takes $-\infty$, and therefore f^* is proper. □

The following theorem is the fundamental duality result of the theory of convex functions.

Theorem 2.7. If f is a convex function on $\mathbb{R}^n$, then $f^{**} = \operatorname{cl} f$.

Proof. If f ever takes $-\infty$ then $f^{**} \equiv -\infty \equiv \operatorname{cl} f$, while if $f \equiv +\infty$ then $f^{**} = f = \operatorname{cl} f$. So we can assume that f is proper. We shall use the cone construction of Section 1.6 to prove the theorem and at the same time gain some geometric insight into the nature of f^*.

Let $Q = \operatorname{cone}[(\operatorname{epi} f) \times \{-1\}]$; note that Q is not empty since f is proper. We know that (x^*, s^*) belongs to $\operatorname{epi} f^*$ if and only if for each $(x, s) \in \operatorname{epi} f, s^* \geqq \langle x^*, x\rangle - s$. This is equivalent to saying that

$$\langle (x^*, -1, s^*), (x, s, -1)\rangle \leqq 0,$$

where we have defined the inner product on $\mathbb{R}^{n+2}$ in the obvious way. That is, it is equivalent to saying that $(x^*, -1, s^*) \in Q^0$. Thus the sets $\{(x^*, -1, s^*) | (x^*, s^*) \in \operatorname{epi} f^*\}$ and $Q^0 \cap (\mathbb{R}^n \times \{-1\} \times \mathbb{R})$ are the same set, say E^*. E^* is nonempty because f^* is proper (Proposition 2.6). Further, since Q contains points $(x, s, -1)$ with arbitrarily large positive s, we see that $Q^0 \subset \mathbb{R}^n \times \mathbb{R}_- \times \mathbb{R}$, but $Q^0 \not\subset \mathbb{R}^n \times \{0\} \times \mathbb{R}$ since $\operatorname{epi} f^*$ is not empty.

We now apply Theorem 1.11 to conclude that $\operatorname{ri} Q^0 = \operatorname{ri} \operatorname{cone} E^*$. From the definition of conjugacy, we see that $(x, s) \in \operatorname{epi} f^{**}$ if and only if for each $(x^*, s^*) \in \operatorname{epi} f^*, s \geqq \langle x^*, x\rangle - s^*$. Just as we did above, we conclude that this is equivalent to saying that $(x, s, -1) \in [\operatorname{cone} E^*]^0$. But

$$[\operatorname{cone} E^*]^0 = [\operatorname{ri} \operatorname{cone} E^*]^0 = [\operatorname{ri} Q^0]^0 = Q^{00} = \operatorname{cl} Q,$$

by Theorem 1.9. Applying Theorem 1.11 once more, we see that $(x, s, -1) \in \operatorname{cl} Q$ if and only if (x, s) belongs to $\operatorname{cl} \operatorname{epi} f = \operatorname{epi} \operatorname{cl} f$. Hence $f^{**} = \operatorname{cl} f$. □

Using Theorem 2.7 one can show without difficulty that for any function f (convex or not), the operation f^{**} yields the greatest closed convex minorant of f. Indeed, f^{**} is closed and convex (Proposition 2.6), and the definition of conjugacy shows that f^{**} minorizes f. If g is a closed convex minorant of f, then $f \geqq g$ implies that $f^* \leqq g^*$, and hence that $f^{**} \geqq g^{**}$. So f^{**} is the greatest such minorant.

The construction used in the proof of Theorem 2.7 also yields valuable geometric insight into the conjugate transform: given f, one can often visualize $\operatorname{epi} f$, and therefore also Q and Q^0. By taking the intersection of Q with the hyperplane $\mathbb{R}^n \times \{-1\} \times \mathbb{R}$ we can then visualize the epigraph of f^*. This technique is often helpful in identifying geometric properties of f^* from those of f.

Another conjugate-like transform will be useful in our study of duality in Part 3. If F is a function from $\mathbb{R}^n \times \mathbb{R}^m$ to $\mathbb{R}$, we define the *adjoint of F in the convex sense* ('convex adjoint' for short) to be the function on $\mathbb{R}^m \times \mathbb{R}^n$ given by

$$F^A(y^*, x^*) = \inf_{x,y}\{-\langle x^*, x\rangle + \langle y^*, y\rangle + F(x, y)\}.$$

Note that $F^A(y^*, x^*)$ is $-F^*(x^*, -y^*)$ (convex conjugate); therefore F is a closed *concave* function. Similarly, the *adjoint of F in the concave sense* ('concave adjoint'), also written $F^A(y^*, x^*)$, is defined by replacing 'inf' in the above by 'sup'. It is therefore the same as $-F^*(x^*, -y^*)$ (concave conjugate), so it is a closed *convex* function.

If we begin by taking the convex adjoint of F, then the concave adjoint of the result, we obtain

$$F^{AA}(x, y) = \sup_{y^*, x^*}\{-\langle y^*, y\rangle + \langle x^*, x\rangle + F^A(y^*, x^*)\}$$
$$= \sup_{-y^*, x^*}\{\langle x^*, x\rangle + \langle -y^*, y\rangle - F^*(x^*, -y^*)\}$$
$$= F^{**}(x, y).$$

Hence if F is closed convex we have $F^{AA} = F$, and similarly $G^{AA} = G$ for closed concave G if we take first the concave adjoint, then the convex adjoint of the result.

The name 'adjoint' for this transformation comes from the fact that if L is a linear transformation from $\mathbb{R}^n$ to $\mathbb{R}^m$ and F is the convex indicator of its graph ($F(x, y) = 0$ if $y = Lx$ and $+\infty$ otherwise), then the convex adjoint of F is $F^A(y^*, x^*) = \inf_{x,y}\{-\langle x^*, x\rangle + \langle y^*, y\rangle | y = Lx\}$, and this is 0 if $L^*y^* = x^*$ and is $-\infty$ otherwise; hence F^A is the concave indicator of the graph of the adjoint linear transformation L^*. If we had begun with the concave indicator of graph L and had taken its concave adjoint, then we would have obtained the convex indicator of graph L^*.

2.4. *Application: the support function.* A good illustration of the power of the conjugacy correspondence comes from the theory of support functions of convex sets. Given any convex set C in $\mathbb{R}^n$, we define the support function of C by $I_C^*(x^*) = \sup\{\langle x^*, x\rangle | x \in C\}$. It is immediate that this is the same as $\sup\{\langle x^*, x\rangle - I_C(x)\}$, which explains the notation I_C^*.

We can see more of the nature of I_C^* if we examine its epigraph:

$$\operatorname{epi} I_C^* = \{(x^*, s^*) | \text{ for each } x \in C, \quad s^* \geqq \langle x^*, x\rangle\}$$
$$= \cap_{x \in C}\{(x^*, s^*) | \langle (x^*, s^*), (x, -1)\rangle \leqq 0\}.$$

Thus if C is nonempty then $\operatorname{epi} I_C^* = [\operatorname{cone}(C \times \{-1\})]^0$, a closed convex cone; if C is empty then $I_C^* \equiv -\infty$ and $\operatorname{epi} I_C^* = \mathbb{R}^{n+1}$. Since I_C is proper if and only if C is nonempty, if follows that I_C^* is a positively homogeneous closed convex function that is proper if and only if C is nonempty, in which case $I_C^*(0) = 0$.

Theorem 2.7 shows how to establish a very important correspondence between *closed* convex sets and their support functions. Specifically, given any closed convex set C we consider the set

$$\{x \mid \text{for each } x^*, \quad \langle x^*, x \rangle \leqslant I_C^*(x^*)\}$$
$$= \{x \mid \sup_{x^*} \{\langle x^*, x \rangle - I_C^*(x^*)\} \leqslant 0\}$$
$$= \{x \mid I_C^{**}(x) \leqslant 0\} = C,$$

where we have used Theorem 2.7 to conclude that $I_C^{**} = I_C$. Thus we can recover C from I_C^*. Similarly, given a positively homogeneous closed convex function p with $p(0) \leqslant 0$, define

$$P = \{x \mid \text{for each } x^*, \quad \langle x^*, x \rangle \leqslant p(x^*)\}.$$

If $x \in \mathbb{R}^n$ then $p^*(x) = \sup\{\langle x^*, x \rangle - p(x^*)\}$; if $x \in P$ then the supremum is 0 while if $x \notin P$ then there is some x^* with $\langle x^*, x \rangle > p(x^*)$, so the supremum is $+\infty$ by positive homogeneity. Thus $p^* = I_P$ and, since p is closed, Theorem 2.7 tells us that $p = p^{**} = I_P^*$. So we can recover p from P.

What we have just shown is that there is a $1-1$ correspondence between the class of closed convex sets C in $\mathbb{R}^n$ and the class of positively homogeneous closed convex functions p on $\mathbb{R}^n$ with $p(0) \leqslant 0$: namely, that which associates with each C the function $p = I_C^*$, and with each p the set $P = \{x \mid \text{for each } x^*, \langle x^*, x \rangle \leqslant p(x^*)\}$. This correspondence has many remarkable properties: for example, $C \subset D$ if and only if $I_C^* \leqslant I_D^*$, and $I_{C+D}^* = I_C^* + I_D^*$. Further, the support function enables us to establish various properties of a set C. As an example, we show that the origin belongs to the interior of a convex set C if and only if I_C^* is positive everywhere except at 0. The 'only if' direction is easy; for the 'if' direction note that I_C^* is closed, hence lsc, so if it is positive everywhere except at 0 then it attains a positive minimum, say m, on the set $\{x^* \mid \|x^*\| = 1\}$. Then for each x^* we have $I_C^*(x^*) \geqslant m \|x^*\|$, so by the above construction we find

$$C = \{x \mid \text{for each } x^*, \quad \langle x^*, x \rangle \leqslant I_C^*(x^*)\} \supset mB,$$

and hence $0 \in \text{int } C$. (Note that the above proof works whether or not m is finite!)

2.5. The subdifferential mapping.

Although a convex function will very often not be differentiable, every proper convex function f has at least one subgradient (Lemma 2.5). The multivalued function ∂f that associates with each $x \in \mathbb{R}^n$ the set $\partial f(x)$ of subgradients of f at x is called the *subdifferential* of f. The *domain* of ∂f, written $\text{dom } \partial f$, is the set of x for which $\partial f(x)$ is not empty. Note that from Lemma 2.5 and the definition of ∂f, we have $\text{ri dom } f \subset \text{dom } \partial f$ and, when f is not identically $+\infty$, also $\text{dom } \partial f \subset \text{dom } f$.

For a concave function g, subgradients at x are defined to be vectors x^* such that for each z, $g(z) \leqslant g(x) + \langle x^*, z - x \rangle$, and the set of all such subgradients is written $\partial g(x)$. One can check easily that with this definition $\partial(-f)(x) = -\partial f(x)$. In general, when dealing with convex functions we shall understand the subgradients to be defined in the convex sense, and similarly for concave functions. Thus, even though the notation is the same no confusion should arise.

If f is convex, then to say $x^* \in \partial f(x)$ is equivalent to saying that for each $x \in \mathbb{R}^n$, $\langle x^*, z \rangle - f(z) \leqslant \langle x^*, x \rangle - f(x)$. Thus in turn the function $\langle x^*, \cdot \rangle - f(\cdot)$ attains its maximum at x. In turn, this statement is equivalent to saying that $f^*(x^*) = \langle x^*, x \rangle - f(x)$. These equivalent forms yield different ways of describing the subdifferential. If f is closed, then by Theorem 2.7 we have $f^{**} = f$, so by applying the above reasoning to f^* we can see that in this case the statements that $x \in \partial f^*(x^*)$ and that $\langle \cdot, x \rangle - f^*(\cdot)$ attains its maximum at x^* are both equivalent to the above three properties. This tells us in particular that for closed convex functions f, ∂f and ∂f^* are

inverses in the sense of multivalued functions: that is, $x^* \in \partial f(x)$ if and only if $x \in \partial f^*(x^*)$. This is a very useful property.

Another useful fact following from this equivalence is that if f is proper convex, then for each $x \in \text{dom } \partial f$, $\partial f(x) = \partial(\text{cl} f)(x)$, and further that f agrees with $\text{cl} f$ on $\text{dom } \partial f$. To see this, suppose that $x \in \text{dom } \partial f$ and let $x^* \in \partial f(x)$. Then

$$f(x) \geqslant \text{cl} f(x) = f^{**}(x) \geqslant \langle x^*, x \rangle - f^*(x^*) = f(x)$$

Hence $f(x) = \text{cl} f(x)$. If $v^* \in \partial(\text{cl} f)(x)$, then for each $z \in \mathbb{R}^n$,

$$f(z) \geqslant \text{cl} f(z) \geqslant \text{cl} f(x) + \langle v^*, z - x \rangle = f(x) + \langle v^*, z - x \rangle,$$

implying that $\partial(\text{cl} f)(x) \subset \partial f(x)$. On the other hand, if $y \in \text{ri dom } f$ then by Proposition 2.4 we have, for each $z \in \mathbb{R}^n$, $\text{cl} f(z) = \lim_{t \downarrow 0} f[(1-t)z + ty]$. But for $t \in (0, 1)$,

$$f[(1-t)z + ty] \geqslant f(x) + \langle x^*, (1-t)z + ty - x \rangle.$$

Taking the limit, we find that

$$\text{cl} f(z) \geqslant f(x) + \langle x^*, z - x \rangle \geqslant \text{cl} f(x) + \langle x^*, z - x \rangle,$$

and hence $\partial f(x) \subset \partial(\text{cl} f)(x)$, so the two are actually equal.

We have described here only the most elementary properties of the subdifferential ∂f. There are many more aspects of ∂f that we have no space to discuss. Among these is the fact that if f is closed and proper, then ∂f is a maximal monotone operator; this provides a link with the large body of results established in recent years about maximal monotonicity. A good reference for this work is the monograph of Brézis (1973). There are also very important connections with directional differentiability and with other differentiability properties. For an introduction to these, see Rockafellar (1970).

2.6. Recession functions.

We can use the theory of recession cones (Section 1.5) to gain valuable information about the growth properties of proper convex functions. We do this by defining the *recession function* of a proper convex function f to be the function $\text{rec} f$, whose epigraph is the recession cone of $\text{epi} f$. Note that since f is proper, $\text{epi} f$ is nonempty, and therefore the origin belongs to $\text{rc epi} f = \text{epi rec} f$. Further, since this set is a convex cone we see that $\text{rec} f$ is a positively homogeneous convex function. If this function ever took $-\infty$, we would have for some y and *each* real s, $(y, s) \subset \text{rc epi} f$. This would imply that f took $-\infty$, contradicting the assumption that f is proper. Thus $\text{rec} f$ is proper and $\text{rec} f(0) = 0$. We can calculate values of $\text{rec} f$ by observing that (y, s) belongs to $\text{epi rec} f$ if and only if, for each $(x, r) \in \text{epi} f$, $(x + y, r + s) \in \text{epi} f$. Therefore, for a fixed y we must have $\text{rec} f(y) = \sup\{f(x + y) - f(x) \mid x \in \text{dom } f\}$.

If we assume f is closed, then we can prove more, as we now see.

Proposition 2.8. *If f is a closed proper convex function on $\mathbb{R}^n$ then $\text{rec} f$ is also closed proper convex and, for each $x \in \text{dom } f$ and each $y \in \mathbb{R}^n$,*

$$\text{rec} f(y) = \sup_{t > 0} t^{-1}[f(x + ty) - f(x)]$$
$$= \lim_{t \to +\infty} t^{-1}[f(x + ty) - f(x)]. \quad (1)$$

Proof. Since $\text{epi} f$ is closed, so is $\text{rc epi} f = \text{epi rec} f$, and since $\text{rec} f$ is proper convex, it must be closed. For any fixed $x \in \text{dom } f$, the pair (y, s) belongs to $\text{rc epi} f$ if and only if the half-line $\{[x, f(x)] + t(y, s) \mid t \geqslant 0\}$ belongs to $\text{epi} f$. Thus for each t, $f(x + ty) \leqslant f(x) + ts$, and since $\text{rec} f(y)$ is the infimum of the s that satisfy this requirement, we have the first equality in (1). We get the second just by noting that the difference quotient in question is nondecreasing in t. $\square$

The next theorem says in effect that in any given direction either f grows to $+\infty$ or it does not grow at all.

Theorem 2.9. Let f be a proper convex function on $\mathbb{R}^n$ and let $y \in \mathbb{R}^n$. If for some x we have $\liminf_{t \to +\infty} f(x + ty) < +\infty$, then

$$f(x + ty) \text{ is a nonincreasing function of } t. \qquad (2)$$

Further, (2) holds for each x in $\mathbb{R}^n$ if and only if $\mathrm{rec}\, f(y) \leqslant 0$, whereas if f is closed then (2) holds for each x if and only if it holds for one x in $\mathrm{dom}\, f$.

Proof. To say $\mathrm{rec}\, f(y) \leqslant 0$ is to say that $(y, 0) \in \mathrm{rc}\, \mathrm{epi}\, f$, which means for each x and each $t \geqslant 0$, $f(x + ty) \leqslant f(x)$. This is true if and only if (2) holds for each x in $\mathbb{R}^n$. If f is closed and there is some x in $\mathrm{dom}\, f$ satisfying (2), then by Proposition 2.8 $\mathrm{rec}\, f(y) \leqslant 0$, so (2) holds for all x.

Now let $x \in \mathbb{R}^n$ and suppose r is a real number greater than $\liminf_{t \to +\infty} f(x + ty)$. Let $g(t) = f(x + ty)$: this g is a proper convex function. Further, by assumption there is a sequence (t_k, r) in $\mathrm{epi}\, g$ with $t_k \to +\infty$. As $\mathrm{epi}\, g$ is convex, it must then contain a half-line of the form $\{(t', r) + s(1, 0) | s \geqslant 0\}$, and therefore $(1, 0) \in \mathrm{rc}\, \mathrm{epi}\, \mathrm{cl}\, g$ (note 'cl' is needed because we found the half-line at only one point in $\mathrm{epi}\, g$). But then $\mathrm{rec}\, \mathrm{cl}\, g(1) \leqslant 0$ and then, by what we have already proved, $\mathrm{cl}\, g$ is nonincreasing on $\mathbb{R}$. It follows that $\mathrm{dom}\, \mathrm{cl}\, g$ is an interval unbounded to the right. Thus the relative boundary of $\mathrm{dom}\, \mathrm{cl}\, g$ consists of at most one point, and this is the only place where g can differ from $\mathrm{cl}\, g$ (Theorem 2.3). So g is nonincreasing too, and so (2) holds. $\square$

Theorem 2.9 shows that the set of y for which $\mathrm{rec}\, f(y) \leqslant 0$ is important for studying the properties of f. This set is evidently a convex cone, closed if f is closed: we call it the *recession cone* of f (written $\mathrm{rc}\, f$ to distinguish it from the recession function $\mathrm{rec}\, f$). The lineality space of $\mathrm{rc}\, f$ is called the *constancy space* of f, since by Theorem 2.9 it is the set of directions along which f is constant.

The following result about level sets is of fundamental importance in convex programming.

Theorem 2.10. Let f be a closed proper convex function on $\mathbb{R}^n$, and for each real s define $L(s) = \{x | f(x) \leqslant s\} \Sigma$. Then for each s, either $L(s)$ is empty or $\mathrm{rc}\, L(s) = \mathrm{rc}\, f$.

Proof. If $L(s)$ is nonempty then it is closed, and a point y belongs to $\mathrm{rc}\, L(s)$ if and only if there is some x with $x + ty \in L(s)$ for each $t \geqslant 0$. But then by Theorem 2.9 $\mathrm{rec}\, f(y) \leqslant 0$, so $y \in \mathrm{rc}\, f$. Conversely, if $y \in \mathrm{rc}\, f$ then $\mathrm{rec}\, f(y) \leqslant 0$, so by Theorem 2.9 $f(x + ty)$ is nonincreasing in t for each x in $\mathbb{R}^n$. Choosing $x \in L(s)$ we find that $y \in \mathrm{rc}\, L(s)$. $\square$

Finally, the recession function enables us to develop a very important relationship between f and its conjugate.

Theorem 2.11. Let f be a proper convex function. The support function of $\mathrm{dom}\, f$ is $\mathrm{rec}\, f^*$; if f is closed then the support function of $\mathrm{dom}\, f^*$ is $\mathrm{rec}\, f$.

Proof. The second statement follows from the first since $f^{**} = \mathrm{cl}\, f$. To prove the first statement, note that the epigraph of f^* is the nonempty closed convex set $\bigcap_{(x,s) \in \mathrm{epi}\, f} \{(x^*, s^*) | s^* \geqslant \langle x^*, x \rangle - s\}$. Applying (i) and (iii)

of Proposition 1.10 we find that

$$\mathrm{epi}\, \mathrm{rec}\, f^* = \mathrm{rc}\, \mathrm{epi}\, f^* = \bigcap_{(x,s) \in \mathrm{epi}\, f} \mathrm{rc}\{(x^*, s^*) | s^* \geqslant \langle x^*, x \rangle - s\}$$

$$= \bigcap_{(x,s) \in \mathrm{epi}\, f} \{(x^*, s^*) | s^* \geqslant \langle x^*, x \rangle\} = \mathrm{epi}\, I^*_{\mathrm{dom}\, f}. \qquad \square$$

This theorem has a consequence that will be important in our study of duality in Part 3.

Corollary 2.12. Let f be a closed proper convex function. Then the origin belongs to $\mathrm{int}\, \mathrm{dom}\, f^*$ if and only if the level sets $L(s)$, defined in Theorem 2.10, are all compact.

Proof. The $L(s)$ are all closed and, for those that are not empty, $\mathrm{rc}\, L(s) = \mathrm{rc}\, f$ (Theorem 2.10). To say the $L(s)$ are all compact is to say that $\mathrm{rc}\, f = \{0\}$: equivalently, that $\mathrm{rec}\, f$ is positive everywhere except at the origin. But $\mathrm{rec}\, f = I^*_{\mathrm{dom}\, f^*}$ (Theorem 2.11), so this equivalent to $0 \in \mathrm{int}\, \mathrm{dom}\, f^*$ by the properties of support functions. $\square$

3. DUALITY THEORY OF CONVEX OPTIMIZATION

3.1. *Dual programming problems: general theory.* The term 'duality' in optimization refers to a certain parametrization problem: namely, given an optimization problem (which we shall take to be one of minimization) called the *primal*:

$$\inf_x f(x), \qquad (P)$$

where $f: \mathbb{R}^n \to \overline{\mathbb{R}}$, one wants to find a suitable parameter space and a function $K: \mathbb{R}^n \times \mathbb{R}^m \to \overline{\mathbb{R}}$, with $f = \sup_y K(\cdot, y)$. Then the problem (P) becomes $\inf_x \sup_y K(x, y)$, while the permuted problem $\sup_y \inf_x K(x, y)$ can be written as the so-called *dual* problem:

$$\sup_y g(y), \qquad (D)$$

just by defining g to be $\inf_x K(x, \cdot)$.

Of course, there are obviously many ways to select a K satisfying the stated requirements. Some are trivial (e.g. $K(x, y) = f(x)!$), but some yield important insights into the nature of the primal problem (P). The trick in establishing a duality scheme is to come up with the second kind of K rather than the first. This is easier to do when (P) has some special structure, and in particular when f is convex. Nevertheless, some important general properties of dual pairs of programming problems do not depend on the structure of (P). We state some of these in the following theorem. In it, we refer to a *saddle point* of K: this is a point $(x', y') \in \mathbb{R}^n \times \mathbb{R}^m$ such that for each $x \in \mathbb{R}^n$ and $y \in \mathbb{R}^m$, $K(x', y) \leqslant K(x', y') \leqslant K(x, y')$.

Theorem 3.1. Let K be a function from $\mathbb{R}^n \times \mathbb{R}^m$ to $\overline{\mathbb{R}}$. For any $x \in \mathbb{R}^n$ and $y \in \mathbb{R}^m$ define

$$f(x) = \sup_y K(x, y), \qquad g(y) = \inf_x K(x, y).$$

Then the following properties hold:

a. (Weak Duality): For each x' and y', $f(x') \geqslant g(y')$. Equivalently, $\inf_x \sup_y K(x, y) \geqslant \sup_y \inf_x K(x, y)$.

b. (Solvability/No Duality Gap): The dual optimization problems (P) and (D) are both solvable with equal extrema if and only if K has a saddle point. In that case, the set of saddle points of K is exactly the Cartesian product of the solution sets of (P) and (D), and for each pair (x, y) in this product the value of $K(x, y)$ is the common extremum of (P) and (D).

Proof. Choose any x' and y'. Then

$$f(x') = \sup_y K(x', y) \geqslant K(x', y') \geqslant \inf_x K(x, y') = g(y'), \quad (*)$$

so that $f(x') \geqslant g(y')$. The second assertion in (a) is proved from this by taking the infimum in x' and the supremum in y'.

For (b), suppose first that K has a saddle point, say (x', y'). For each x we have

$$f(x) = \sup_y K(x, y) \geqslant K(x, y') \geqslant K(x', y')$$
$$= \sup_y K(x', y) = f(x'),$$

and for each y,

$$g(y) = \inf_x K(x, y) \leqslant K(x', y) \leqslant K(x', y')$$
$$= \inf_x K(x, y') = g(y'),$$

so x' solves (P) and y' solves (D), and their common extremal value is $K(x', y')$. So, if the sets of primal and dual optimizers are X and Y respectively, and the set of saddle points of K is S, we have shown that $S \subset X \times Y$.

Now suppose that (P) and (D) are solvable with equal extrema. Let $x' \in X$ and $y' \in Y$. Then as $f(x') = g(y')$ we have a chain of equalities in (*), so the extremal value is $K(x', y')$ and the pair (x', y') is a saddle point. Thus $X \times Y \subset S$. Joining the two chains of reasoning we find that if the two equivalent conditions hold, then $S = X \times Y$ and the common extremal value is the same as the value of K at each saddle point. $\qquad\square$

Theorem 3.1 shows the equivalence between optimizing a pair of dual programming problems and finding a saddle point of the function K, which is commonly called the *Lagrangian* associated with (P) and (D). However, it does not yield a recipe for building nontrivial duality structures. One way to develop such a recipe is to introduce convexity into the problem, and this we do in the following section.

3.2. *Perturbational duality: the Rockafellar construction.* This section presents a general method, due to Rockafellar (1970) for obtaining a duality structure from any given primal objective function. The method can be applied even when the primal objective is not convex; an example of this is the so-called 'Lagrangian relaxation' method in integer programming. However, the method always produces a closed concave dual objective function, and the strongest results can be obtained when the primal objective is also closed and convex.

We proceed by taking a given extended real-valued function f on $\mathbb{R}^n$ and embedding it in another extended real-valued function F on $\mathbb{R}^n \times \mathbb{R}^m$ in such a way that $f = F(\cdot, 0)$. We call F the *perturbation function* associated with the duality structure (although that term is used differently by Rockafellar to denote what we prefer to call the value function).

In this setup, elements $p \in \mathbb{R}^m$ can be interpreted as *perturbations* of the original minimization problem: they perturb the objective function from its original form of $f = F(\cdot, 0)$ to $F(\cdot, p)$. The *value function* assigns to each such perturbation the resulting infimum:

$$v(p) = \inf_x F(x, p).$$

A good way to think about this construction is to imagine that we are trying to optimize an activity whose cost is given by $F(x, p)$. The variables x represent controls that are at our disposal, while the variables p represent external elements that we do not control (for example, very commonly they represent available resources). For each set of external elements p, the value function yields the least cost $v(p)$ that we can achieve by manipulating the control parameters x.

In order to set up the desired duality structure, we need to find a function to play the role of K in Section 3.1. Recall that the concave conjugate of a function h is defined by

$h^*(z^*) = \inf\{\langle z^*, z \rangle - h(z)\}$, so that $-h^*(0) = \sup_z h(z)$. We want to find an extended real-valued function L on $\mathbb{R}^n \times \mathbb{R}^m$ such that for each x, $f(x) = \sup_{p^*} L(x, p^*)$. This means that we want

$$F(x, 0) = f(x) = \sup_{p^*} L(x, p^*)$$
$$= -\inf_{p^*}\{\langle p^*, 0 \rangle - L(x, p^*)\} = -L(x, \cdot)^*(0), \quad (1)$$

where the conjugate is taken in the concave sense. This suggests starting with an F such that for each x the function $F(x, \cdot)$ is closed convex. If we define $L(x, \cdot)$ to be the conjugate in the concave sense of $(-F)(x, \cdot)$: i.e.,

$$L(x, p^*) = \inf_p\{\langle p^*, p \rangle + F(x, p)\}, \quad (2)$$

then $L(x, \cdot)$ is closed concave and we have

$$-L(x, \cdot)^*(0) = -(-F)(x, \cdot)^{**}(0)$$
$$= -(-F)(x, 0) = F(x, 0), \quad (3)$$

just as desired. This guarantees that $f(x)$ will be $\sup_{p^*} L(x, p^*)$ for each x.

The dual objective function $g(p^*)$ can now be found from L, according to the theory of Section 3.1, by setting

$$g(p^*) = \inf_x L(x, p^*) = -\sup_x\{\langle 0, x \rangle - L(x, p^*)\}$$
$$= -L(\cdot, p^*)^*(0), \quad (4)$$

where this time the conjugate is taken in the convex sense. An equivalent expression for g can be found by writing

$$g(p^*) = \inf_x L(x, p^*) = \inf_{x, p}\{\langle p^*, p \rangle + F(x, p)\}$$
$$= \inf_p\{\langle p^*, p \rangle + \inf_x F(x, p)\} = (-v)^*(p^*), \quad (5)$$

so that the dual objective function is the concave conjugate of the negative of the primal value function v.

We can now use the adjoint introduced in Section 2.3 to complete the picture of duality that we have developed. Referring to (5), we see that

$$g(p^*) = \inf_{x, p}\{-\langle 0, x \rangle + \langle p^*, p \rangle + F(x, p)\} = F^A(p^*, 0).$$

This suggests defining $G = F^A$ (convex sense) to be the perturbation function associated with (D), just as F was associated with (P), for then we have $g = G(\cdot, 0)$ just as $f = F(\cdot, 0)$. We can also define a dual value function by

$$w(x^*) = \sup_{p^*} G(p^*, x^*).$$

Concavity of G and elementary arguments then establish that w is concave.

Let us now assume that F is convex as a function of two variables. It then follows from the definition of v and the elementary tests for convexity that v is convex. If we assume also that F is closed, we have $G^A = F^{AA} = F$: that is, if we were to regard (D) as a primal problem and dualize it via the perturbation function G, we would obtain F as the dual perturbation function and hence f as the dual objective. This is the precise sense in which, in convex programming, 'the dual of the dual is the primal'.

Among the elementary properties of the subdifferential developed in Section 2.5 was the fact that for a convex function f, $\partial f(x)$ was exactly the set of points x^* at which $f^*(x^*) = \langle x^*, x \rangle - f(x)$. Of course, an analogous result holds for the concave subdifferential. Now we know that our dual objective function g is $(-v)^*$, so

$$-\partial v(0) = \partial(-v)(0) = \{p^* | (-v)^*(p^*)$$
$$= \langle p^*, 0 \rangle - (-v)(0)\} = \{p^* | g(p^*) = \inf f\}.$$

657

Similarly, if F is closed convex then $f = (-w)^*$, so

$$-\partial w(0) = \{x \mid f(x) = \sup g\}.$$

Now recalling Theorem 3.1, we see that *both* $\partial v(0)$ and $\partial w(0)$ will be nonempty precisely when the primal and dual problems are both solvable with equal extrema, and therefore that the set of saddle points of L is $[-\partial w(0)] \times [-\partial v(0)]$. If this set is nonempty then it consists of the pairs (x, p^*) such that $f(x) = \min(P) = \max(D) = g(p^*)$.

We now summarize the major properties we have discussed. Each has already been proved, so we only list them here.

Theorem 3.2. Let F be an extended real-valued function on $\mathbb{R}^n \times \mathbb{R}^m$, and let f be the function on $\mathbb{R}^n$ defined by $f = F(\cdot, 0)$. Define $L(x, p^*) = \inf_p \{\langle p^*, p \rangle + F(x, p)\}$ and $v(p) = \inf_x F(x, p)$.

If $F(x, \cdot)$ is closed convex for each x, then $L(x, \cdot)$ is closed concave and:

(1) For each x, $f(x) = -L(x, \cdot)^*(0) = \sup_{p^*} L(x, p^*)$.
(2) The dual objective function g defined by $g(p^*) = -L(\cdot, p^*)^*(0) = \inf_x L(x, p^*)$ is closed and concave, and $g = (-v)^*$, so that $\sup g = v^{**}(0) \leqslant v(0) = \inf f$.
(3) The dual perturbation function defined by $G = F^A$ is closed and concave, and the dual value function $w = \sup p^* G(p^*, \cdot)$ is concave, with $\sup g = w(0)$.

If F is convex, then:

(4) The primal value function v is convex, and $-\partial v(0) = \{p^* \mid g(p^*) = \inf f\}$. Any such p^* is a maximizer of g.

If F is also closed convex then:

(5) $F = G^A$, and $f = (-w)^*$, so that $\inf f = w^{**}(0)$.
(6) $-\partial w(0) = \{x \mid f(x) = \sup g\}$. Any such x is a minimizer of f.

Finally, the Lagrangian L has a saddle point if and only if the primal and dual problems are both solvable with equal extrema. The set of saddle points of L is $[-\partial w(0)] \times [-\partial v(0)]$.

At this point, it might be helpful to give an example showing one way in which the Lagrangian arises naturally in an economic context. Consider an economic agent operating some type of production process controlled by a vector of parameters $x \in \mathbb{R}^n$. We suppose that the agent has the freedom to buy certain inputs to the process; the quantities of these inputs bought will be denoted by $p \in \mathbb{R}^m$. The agent then operates the process at a cost $F(x, p)$ (which could, if negative, represent a net return to the agent). In this situation, if the control policy x and the market prices y^* of the inputs were fixed, the agent would clearly want to purchase quantities p so as to achieve the least overall cost: that is, the value

$$L(x, y^*) = \inf_p \{\langle y^*, p \rangle + F(x, p)\}.$$

For any fixed market prices y^*, the best policy for the agent to choose would be an x that achieves the value $\inf_x L(x, y^*)$. If the market attempts to maximize the amount extracted from the agent, it should therefore set prices to make this infimum as large as possible: that is, it should attempt to price the resources so as to attain the value

$$\sup_{y^*} \inf_x L(x, y^*).$$

Conversely, the agent (knowing that the market will value its resources in this way) should try to choose a control policy to attain

$$\inf_x \sup_{y^*} L(x, y^*).$$

Therefore in this example the primal minimization problem appears as the economic problem facing the agent, and the dual maximization problem represents that of setting appropriate market prices for the resources used. If L in fact has a saddle point, then this will provide values of x and y^* that simultaneously solve the problems confronting the two adversaries.

A very common form of the constrained minimization problem generating $F(x, p)$ is that in which the cost is given by a function $h(x)$, subject to the constraints $c_i(x) \leqslant p_i$, for $i = 1, \ldots, m$. In this case we just let $F(x, p)$ be $h(x)$ if the constraints $c_i(x) \leqslant p_i$ are all satisfied, and $+\infty$ otherwise. It is easy to verify that for fixed x, $F(x, p)$ is a closed convex function of p; further, if h and all of the c_i are closed convex in x, then F itself will be closed convex. Further, in this case the Lagrangian L will be given by

$$L(x, y^*) = \begin{cases} h(x) + \sum_{i=1}^m (y^*)_i c_i(x), & \text{if } y^* \geqslant 0, \\ -\infty, & \text{if } y^* \not\geqslant 0. \end{cases}$$

This form is so common that it is sometimes called the 'standard Lagrangian' in the literature. The elements of y^* are sometimes called 'Kuhn–Tucker coefficients' instead of the more standard term 'Lagrange multipliers', in recognition of the work of Kuhn and Tucker (1950) relating extrema and multipliers to saddle points of the Lagrangian in the case of inequality constraints. However, numerous earlier workers also dealt with the problem of inequality- constrained optimization, and much of this work has been overlooked until recently. An excellent historical survey has been given by Prékopa (1980).

Returning to the analysis of the primal and dual problems, we recall that Theorems 3.1 and 3.2 related solvability of the primal and dual problems to the existence of saddle points. However, it is convenient to have conditions on the problems themselves to ensure such solvability. The next theorem develops such conditions. In the general theory outlined here, these conditions play the same role as do 'constraint qualifications' in the optimization literature, as we shall see below.

In stating the theorem, we use the words 'maximum' and 'minimum' to indicate that the respective extrema are actually attained.

Theorem 3.3. Suppose the function F of Theorem 3.2 is convex. If $0 \in \mathrm{ri}\,\mathrm{dom}\,v$, then the infimum of f equals the maximum of g. If F is closed convex and if $0 \in \mathrm{ri}\,\mathrm{dom}\,w$, then the minimum of f equals the supremum of g. If both of these conditions hold, then the minimum of f and the maximum of g are the same finite real number.

Proof. Suppose $0 \in \mathrm{ri}\,\mathrm{dom}\,v$. Then by Lemma 2.5 $\partial v(0)$ is not empty. By (4) of Theorem 3.2 there is some p^* with $g(p^*) = \inf f$. Evidently p^* maximizes g, and the common extremal value is not $+\infty$ because we know $0 \in \mathrm{ri}\,\mathrm{dom}\,v$.

If F is closed convex then a similar argument using (6) of Theorem 3.2 establishes the second conclusion, along with the fact that the common extremal value is not $-\infty$. If both conditions hold, the value must therefore be finite. $\square$

To see how the conditions of Theorem 3.3 generalize the usual constraint qualifications, consider again the example in which F was defined in terms of the functions h and c_i. Assume first that for some x in $\mathrm{dom}\,h$, we have $c_i(x) < 0$ for each i. Then for some small positive t, and for each p belonging to the ball

tB about the origin, one has $c_i(x) < p_i$ for each i. Hence for such p, $v(p) \leqslant F(x, p) < +\infty$, and therefore $0 \in \text{int dom } v$.

The condition $c(x) < 0$ is usually called the 'Slater condition' in the optimization literature; see Slater (1950) and, for general discussion of constraint qualifications, Arrow, Hurwicz and Uzawa (1961) and Mangasarian (1969). Thus, the condition $0 \in \text{int dom } v$ can be thought of as a generalized Slater condition. It is clearly stronger than the condition $0 \in \text{ri dom } v$ of Theorem 3.3.

This stronger condition turns out to have an important geometric meaning. To see what it is, suppose for simplicity that F is closed convex and that the primal value function v does not take $-\infty$. Then Theorem 2.3 tells us that cl dom $v \supset$ dom cl $v \supset$ dom cl v, so that $0 \in \text{int dom } v$ if and only if $0 \in \text{int dom cl}(-v) = \text{int dom } g^*$. Applying Corollary 2.12, we see that the generalized Slater condition on the primal problem is equivalent to the requirement that the level sets of the dual objective function g be compact. Similarly, the generalized Slater condition on the dual problem ($0 \in \text{int dom } w$) is equivalent to the requirement that the essential objective function f of the primal problem have compact level sets.

The duality structure that we have outlined in this essay provides a powerful tool for attacking a great variety of problems, in fields ranging from mathematical economics to mechanics and physics. Although we have been able to present only the skeleton of this theory, the reader who has thoroughly understood the principles set out here should have at least a solid foundation on which to build the skills needed for applications.

STEPHEN M. ROBINSON

See also CORES; FUNCTIONAL ANALYSIS; LARGE ECONOMIES; LYAPUNOV THEOREM; PERFECT COMPETITION; QUASI-CONCAVITY; SHAPLEY–FOLKMAN THEOREM.

BIBLIOGRAPHY

Arrow, K.J., Hurwicz, L. and Uzawa, H. 1961. Constraint qualifications in maximization problems. *Naval Research Logistics Quarterly* 8, 175–91.

Aubin, J.-P. 1984. *L'analyse non linéaire et ses motivations économiques.* Paris: Masson.

Brézis, H. 1973. *Opérateurs maximaux monotones et semi-groupes de contractions dans les espaces de Hilbert.* North-Holland Mathematics Studies No. 5, Amsterdam: North-Holland.

Clarke, F.H. 1983. *Optimization and Nonsmooth Analysis.* New York: Wiley–Interscience.

Debreu, G. 1959. *Theory of Value,* New Haven: Yale University Press (6th Printing, 1975).

Ekeland, I. and Temam, R. 1974. *Analyse convexe et problèmes variationnels.* Paris: Dunod.

Ekeland, I. and Turnbull, T. 1983. *Infinite-Dimensional Optimization and Convexity.* Chicago Lectures in Mathematics, Chicago: University of Chicago Press.

Hermes, H. and LaSalle, J.P. 1969. *Functional Analysis and Time Optimal Control.* New York: Academic Press.

Kuhn, H.W. and Tucker, A.W. 1950. Nonlinear programming. In *Proceedings of the Second Berkeley Symposium on Mathematical Statistics and Probability,* ed. J. Neyman, University of California Press, Berkeley, 481–92.

Mangasarian, O.L. 1969. *Nonlinear Programming.* New York: McGraw-Hill.

Prékopa, A. 1980. On the development of optimization theory. *American Mathematical Monthly* 87, 527–42.

Rockafellar, R.T. 1970. *Convex Analysis.* Princeton: Princeton University Press.

Rockafellar, R.T. 1974. *Conjugate Duality and Optimization.* CBMS Regional Conference Series No. 16, Society for Industrial and Applied Mathematics, Philadelphia.

Slater, M. 1950. Lagrange multipliers revisited: a contribution to nonlinear programming. Cowles Commission Discussion Paper Math. 403, University of Chicago.

cooperative equilibrium. I. INTRODUCTION; II. THE DOMINANCE APPROACH; III. CONSISTENCY QUALIFICATIONS; IV. THE VALUATION APPROACH.

I. INTRODUCTION

The term 'cooperative equilibria' has been imported into economics from game theory. It refers to the equilibria of economic situations modelled by means of cooperative games and solved by appealing to an appropriate cooperative solution concept. The influence is not entirely one way, however. Many game theoretic notions (e.g. Cournot–Nash equilibrium, the Core) are formalizations of pre-existing ideas in economics.

The distinguishing feature of the cooperative approach in game theory and economics is that it does not attempt to model how a group of economic agents (say a buyer and a seller) may communicate among themselves. The typical starting point is the hypothesis that, in principle, any subgroup of economic agents (or perhaps some distinguished subgroups) has a clear picture of the possibilities of joint action and that its members can communicate freely before the formal play starts. Obviously, what is left out of cooperative theory is very substantial. The justification, or so one hopes, is that the drastic simplification brings to centre stage the implications of actual or potential coalition formation. In their classic book, von Neumann and Morgenstern (1944) already emphasized that the possibility of strategic coalition formation was the key aspect setting apart two from three or more players' games.

The previous remarks emphasize free preplay communication as the essential distinguishing characteristic of cooperative theory. There is a second feature common to most of the literature but which nonetheless may not be intrinsic to the theory (this the future will determine). We refer to the assumed extensive ability of coalitions' players to commit to a course of action once an agreement has been reached.

The remaining exposition is divided in three sections. Sections II and IV discuss the two main approaches to cooperative theory (domination and valuation, respectively). Section III contains qualifications to the domination approach.

An excellent reference for the topic of this entry is Shubik (1983).

II. THE DOMINANCE APPROACH

Suppose we have N economic agents. Every agent has a strategy set S_i. Denote $S = S_1 \times \cdots \times S_N$ with generic element $s = (s_1, \ldots, s_N)$. Given s and a coalition $C \subset N$, the expression s_C denotes the strategies corresponding to members of C. Letting C' complement of C, the expression $(s_C, s_{C'})$ defines s in the obvious way. For every i there is a utility function $u_i(s)$. If $u = (u_1, \ldots, u_N)$ is an N-list of utilities, expressions such as u_C or $(u_C, u_{C'})$ have the obvious meaning.

Example 1 (Exchange economies): There are N consumers and l desirable goods. Each consumer has a utility function $u_i(x_i)$ and initial endowments ω_i. A strategy of consumer i is an N non-negative vector $s_i = (s_{i1}, \ldots, s_{iN})$ such that $\sum_{j=1}^N s_{ij} \leqslant \omega_i$, i.e. s_i is an allocation of the initial endowments of i among the N consumers. Of course, $u_j(s) = u_j(\sum_i s_{ij})$.

Example 2 (Public goods): Suppose that to the model of Example 1 we add a public good y with production function $y = F(v)$. Utility functions have the form $u_j(x_j, y)$. A strategy for i is now an $(N+1)l$ vector $s_i = (s_{i1}, \ldots, s_{i, N+1})$ where $s_{i, N+1}$ is allocated as input to production. We have $u_j(s) = u_j[\sum_i s_{ij}, F(\sum_i s_{i, N+1})]$.

Example 3 (Exchange with private bads): This is as the first example, except that there is no free disposal, i.e. $\sum_{j=1}^N s_{ij} = \omega_i$

for every i. Some of the goods may actually be bads. To be concrete, suppose that $l = 2$, one of the goods is a desirable numéraire and the other is garbage. All consumers are identical and each owns one unit of numéraire and one of garbage (see Shapley and Shubik, 1969).

For a strategy profile s to be called a *cooperative equilibrium* we require that there is no coalition C that *dominates* the utility vector $u(s) = (u_1(s), \ldots, u_N(s))$, i.e. that can 'make effective' for its members utility levels u_i, $i \in C$, such that $u_i > u_i(s)$ for all $i \in C$. Denote by $V(C)$ the utility levels that C can 'make effective' for its members. The precise content of the equilibrium concept depends, of course, on the definition of $V(C)$. I proceed to discuss several possibilities (Aumann, 1959, is a key reference for all this).

(A) In line with the idea of Cournot–Nash equilibrium, we could define $V_s(C) = \{u_C : u_C \leqslant u_C(s'_C, s_C) \text{ for some } s'_C \in S_C\}$, that is, the agents in C take the strategies of C' as fixed. They do not anticipate, so to speak, any retaliatory move. The cooperative solution concept that uses $V_s(C)$ is called *strong Cournot–Nash equilibrium*. It is very strong indeed. So strong, that it rarely exists. Obviously, this limits the usefulness of the concept. It is immediate that it does not exist for any of the three examples above.

Note that $V_s(C)$ depends on the reference point s. We now go to the other extreme and consider definitions where when a coalition contemplates deviating, it readies itself for a retaliatory behaviour on the part of the complementary coalition; that is, the deviation erases the initial position and is carried out if and only if better levels of utility can be reached, no matter what the agents outside the coalition do. On defining $V(C)$, however, there is an important subtlety. The set $V(C)$ can be defined as either what the members of C cannot be prevented from getting (i.e. the members of C move second) or, more strictly, as what the members of C can guarantee themselves (i.e. they move first). More precisely:

(B) For every C, define:

$$V_\beta(C) = [u_C: \text{ for any } s_{C'} \text{ there is an } s_C$$

$$\text{such that } u_C \leqslant u(s_C, s_{C'})]$$

This is what C cannot be prevented from getting. The set of corresponding cooperative equilibria is called the β-core of the game or economy. For any s we have $V_\beta(C) \subset V_s(C)$, and so there is more of a chance for a β-core equilibrium to exist than for a strong Cournot–Nash equilibrium. But there is no general existence theorem. As we shall see, the β-core is non-empty in examples 1 and 2. It is instructive to verify that it is empty in example 3. By symmetry, it is enough to check that the strategies where each agent consumes its own endowment is not an equilibrium. Take the coalition formed by two of the three (identical) agents. At a retaliatory move, the third agent would, at worst, be dumping its unit of garbage on one of the members of the coalition (or perhaps splitting it among them), but the coalition can still be better off than at the initial endowment point by dumping its two units on the third member *and* transferring some money from the nonreceptor to the receptor of outside garbage.

(C) For every C define:

$$V_\alpha(C) = [u_C: \text{ there is } s_C \text{ such that}$$

$$u_C \leqslant u_C(s_C, s_{C'}) \text{ for any } s_{C'}].$$

This is what C can guarantee itself of getting. It represents the most pessimistic appraisal of the possibilities of C. The set of corresponding equilibria is called the α-core of the game or economy. For any s we have $V_\alpha(C) \subset V_\beta(C)$ and so there is more of a chance for an α-core equilibrium to exist than for a

β-core equilibrium. For the α-core there is a general existence theorem:

Theorem (Scarf, 1971): If S is convex, compact and every $u_i(s)$ is continuous and quasiconcave, then the α-core is non-empty.

The conditions of the above theorem are restrictive. Note that the quasiconcavity of u_i is required for the entire s and not only (as for Cournot–Nash equilibrium) for the vector s_i of own strategies. Nonetheless, it is a useful result. It tells us, for instance, that under the standard quasiconcavity hypothesis on utility functions, the α-core is non-empty in each of the three examples above. It will be instructive to verify why the initial endowment allocation is an equilibrium in example 3. In contrast to the β-core situation, a coalition of two members cannot now improve over the initial endowments because they have to move first and therefore cannot know who of the two will receive the outside member's garbage and will need, as a consequence, some extra amount of money.

If, as in examples 1 and 2, there are no bads, the distinction between V_α and V_β disappears. There is a unique way for the members of C' to hurt C, namely withholding its own resources. So in both the α and β senses the set $V(C)$ represents the utility combinations that can be attained by the members of C using only its own resources. This, incidentally, shows that the β-core is non-empty in examples 1 and 2 (since it is equal to the α-core!). There is another approach to existence in the no-bads case. Indeed, a Walrasian equilibrium (in the case of example 2 this takes the guise of a Lindahl equilibrium) is always in this core with no need of α or β qualification. In the context of example 1, the Core was first defined and exploited by Edgeworth (1881) (*see* CORES). Underlying both the α- and the β-core there is a quite pessimistic appraisal on what C' may do if C deviates. The next two remarks discuss, very informally, other, less extreme, possibilities.

(D) In the context of exchange economies (such as example 1) it seems sensible to suppose that a coalition of buyers and sellers in one market may neglect retaliation possibilities in unrelated markets. As it stands in subsections (B) and (C), it is very difficult for a group of traders to improve, since, so to speak, they have to set up a separate economy covering all markets. See Mas-Colell (1982) for further discussion of this point.

(E) For transferable utility situations (and for purposes more related to the valuation theory to be discussed in section IV), Harsanyi (1959), taking inspiration in Nash (1953), proposed that the total utility of the coalition C be defined as $\Sigma_{i \in C} u_i(\bar{s}_C, \bar{s}_{C'})$ where $(\bar{s}_C, \bar{s}_{C'})$ are the minimax strategies of the zero sum game between C and C' obtained by letting the payoff of C be $\Sigma_{i \in C} u_i(s_C, s_{C'}) - \Sigma_{i \in C'} u_i(s_C, s_{C'})$. Note: if the minimax strategies are not unique, a further qualification is required.

III. CONSISTENCY QUALIFICATIONS

In this section, several solution concepts are reviewed. Loosely, their common theme is that coalitions look beyond the one-step deviation possibilities.

A. The von Neumann–Morgenstern stable set solutions. Suppose that the game is described to us by the sets $V(C)$ that the members of coalitions of C can make effective for themselves. These sets do not depend on any reference combination of stratigies. They are constructed from the underlying situation in some of the ways described in section II. One says that the N-tuple of utilities $u \in V(N)$ dominates the N-tuple $v \in V(N)$ via coalition C, denoted $u \succ_C v$, if $u_C \in V(C)$. We write $u \succ v$ if

$\bar{u}$ dominates $\bar{v}$ via some coalition. A *core utility computation* is then any maximal element of $\succ$, i.e. any $u \in V(N)$ which is not dominated by any other imputation.

The following paradoxical situation may easily arise. An imputation u is not in the core. Nonetheless, all the members of any coalition that dominates u are treated, at any core imputation, worse than at u (consider for example, the predicament of a Bertrand duopolist at the joint monopoly outcome). If $\succ$ was transitive, then this could not happen, since (continuity complications aside) for any u there would be a core imputation directly dominating u. But $\succ$ is very far from transitive. The approach of von Neumann and Morgenstern consists in focusing on *sets* of imputations K, called *stable sets*, having the properties: (i) if $u \in K$ then there is no $v \in K$ that dominates u (internal stability) and (ii) if $u \notin K$ then $v \succ u$ for some $v \in K$ (external stability). Note that these are the properties that the set of maximal elements of $\succ$ would have if $\succ$ was transitive. The interpretation of K is as a standard of behaviour. If for any reason the imputations in K are regarded as acceptable, then there is an inner consistency to this: drop all the imputations dominated by an acceptable imputation and what you have left is precisely the set of acceptable imputations.

Important as the von Neumann–Morgenstern solution is, its impact in economics has been limited. There is an existence problem, but the main difficulty is that the sets are very hard to analyse.

B. The bargaining set.

This solution was proposed by Aumann and Maschler (1964) and is available in several versions. Describing one of them will give the flavour of what is involved. For an imputation u to be disqualified, it will be necessary, but not sufficient, that it be dominated (in the terminology of bargaining set theory: objected to) via some coalition C^*. The objection will not 'stick', i.e. throw u out of the negotiation table as a tentative equilibrium, unless it is found justified. The justifiability criterion is the following: there is no other coalition C^* having a $v_C^* \in V(C^*)$ with the property that $v_i \geq u_i$ for every i and which gives to every common member of C and C^* at least as much as they get at the objection. In other words, an objection can be countered if one of the members left out of the objecting coalition can protect themselves in a credible manner (credible in the sense that they can give to any member of C they need, as much as C gives them).

The bargaining set contains the core and, while it is conceptually quite different from a von Neumann–Morgenstern stable set solution, it still does avoid the most myopic features of the core. It is also much easier to analyse than the stable sets, although it is by no means a straightforward tool. But, again, its impact in economics has so far been limited.

A common aspect of stable set and bargaining set theory is that, implicitly or explicitly, a deviating coalition takes into consideration a subsequent, induced move by other coalitions. This is still true for the next two concepts, with one crucial qualification: a deviating coalition only takes into account subsequent moves of its own subcoalitions.

C. Coalition-proof Cournot–Nash equilibrium.

This solution concept has been proposed recently by Bernheim, Peleg and Whinston (1987). It can be viewed as a self-consistent enlargement of the set of strong Cournot–Nash equilibria. Consider the simplest case, a three-player game. Given a strategy profile $\bar{s}$, which deviations are possible for two players coalitions? If anything, then we are led to strong Cournot–Nash equilibria. But, there is something inconsistent about this. If the strategy profile $\bar{s}$ is not immune to deviations (i.e. there is no commit-

ment at $\bar{s}$), why should the deviation be so? That is, why should it be possible to commit to a deviation? This suggests that the deviation should be required to be immune to further deviations, that is, they should be Cournot–Nash equilibria of the induced two person game (the third player remains put at $\bar{s}$). Obviously, deviating becomes more difficult and the equilibrium set has more of a chance of being non-empty. Unfortunately, there is no general existence theorem. For three-person games, this is precisely the Coalition-Proof Cournot–Nash equilibrium. By recursion, one obtains a definition for any number of players.

D. The core.

It may be surprising to list the core in a section on concepts that attempts to be less myopic than the core. But, in fact, the core as a set can be made consistent against further deviations by *subcoalitions* of the deviating coalition. Simply make sure always to deviate via coalitions of smallest possible cardinality.

IV. THE VALUATION APPROACH

The aim of the valuation approach to games and conflict situations (of which the Shapley value is the central concept) is to associate to every game a reasonable outcome taking into account and compromising among all the conflicting claims. In games, those are expressed by sets $V(C)$ of utility vectors for which C is effective. The criteria of reasonableness are expressed axiomatically. Thus the valuation approach has to be thought of more as input for an arbitrator than as a descriptive theory of equilibrium. Except perhaps for the bargaining set, this point of view is strikingly different to anything discussed so far.

Sometimes the term 'fair' is used in connection with the valuation approach. There are at least two reasons to avoid this usage. The first is that the initial position [embodied in the sets $V(C)$] is taken as given. The second is that the fairness of a solution to a game can hardly be judged in isolation, i.e. independently of the position of the players in the overall socioeconomic game.

The valuation of a game will depend on the claims, i.e. on how the sets $V(C)$ are constructed. We saw in Section II that there was nothing straightforward about this. We will not repeat it here. It may be worthwhile to observe informally, however, that the valuation approach is altogether less strategic than the dominance one and that a useful way to think of $V(C)$ is as the utility levels the members of C could get if the members of C' did not exist, rather than as what the members of C could get if they go it alone [in defining $V(C)$ this point of view can make a difference].

Consider first games with transferable utilities (N, v) where N is a set of players and $v : 2^N \to R$ is a real valued function satisfying $v(\phi) = 0$. The restriction of v to a $C \in N$ is denoted (C, v). The *Shapley value* is a certain rule that associates to every game (N, v) an imputation $Sh(N, v)$, i.e. $\Sigma_{i \in N} Sh^i(N, v) = v(N)$.

The *Shapley value* was characterized by Shapley (1953) by four axioms that can be informally described as: (i) efficiency, i.e. $Sh(N, v)$ is an imputation, (ii) symmetry, i.e. the particular names of the players do not matter, (iii) linearity over games and (iv) dummy, i.e. a player that contributes nothing to any coalition receives nothing.

There is a simple way to compute the Shapley value. Put $P(\phi, v) = 0$ and, recursively, associate to every game (N, v) a number $P(N, v)$ such that

$$\sum_{i \in N} [P(N, v) - P(N/(i), v)] = v(N) \tag{1}$$

That is, the sum of marginal increments of P equals $v(N)$. This function is called the *potential* and it turns out that the marginal increments of P constitute precisely the Shapley valuations, i.e. $Sh^i(N, v) = P(N, v) - P[N/(i), v]$ for all (N, v) and $i \in N$. This is discussed in Hart and Mas-Colell (1985).

The Shapley value for transferable utility games admits several generalizations to the nontransferable utility case [with convex sets $V(C)$]. See Harsanyi (1959), Shapley (1969), Aumann (1985). Perhaps the most natural, although not necessarily the simpler to work with, was proposed by Harsanyi (1959) and has recently been axiomatized by Hart (1985). For a given game, an Harsanyi value imputation is obtained by rescaling individual utilities so as to guarantee the existence of an N-tuple $u \in V(N)$ satisfying, simultaneously, (i) the convex set $V(N)$ is supported at u by a hyperplane with normal $q = (1, \ldots, 1)$, (ii) if a potential P on the set of all games is defined by formula (1) (but replacing '$= v(N)$' by '$\in Bdry. V(N)$') then, as before, $u_i = P(N, V) - P(N/(i), V)$ for all $i \in N$.

One of the most striking features of the applications of Shapley value theory to economics is that, in economies with many traders, it has turned out to be intimately related to the notion of Walrasian equilibrium. Interestingly, this is in common with the dominance approach. Aumann (1975) is a representative paper of the very extensive literature on the topic.

A. MAS-COLELL

See also COLLUSION; CORES.

BIBLIOGRAPHY

Aumann, R. 1959. Acceptable points in general cooperative n-person games. *Annals of Mathematics Studies Series* 40, 287–324.

Aumann, R. 1975. Values of markets with a continuum of traders. *Econometrica* 43, 611–46.

Aumann, R. 1985. An axiomatization of the non-transferable utility value. *Econometrica* 53, 599–612.

Aumann, R. and Maschler, M. 1964. The bargaining set for cooperative games. In *Advances in Game Theory*, ed. M. Dresher, L. Shapley, and A.W. Tucker, Princeton: Princeton University Press, 443–7.

Bernheim, B.D., Peleg, B. and Whinston, M. 1987. Coalition-proof Nash equilibria I. Concepts. *Journal of Economic Theory*.

Edgeworth, F. 1881. *Mathematical Psychics*. London: Kegan Paul.

Harsanyi, J. 1959. A bargaining model for the cooperative n-person game. In *Contributions to the Theory of Games*, Vol. 4, ed. A.W. Tucker and R.D. Luce, Princeton: Princeton University Press, 324–56.

Hart, S. 1985. An axiomatization of Harsanyi nontransferable utility solution. *Econometrica* 53, 1295–314.

Hart, S. and Mas-Colell, A. 1985. The potential: a new approach to the value in multiperson allocation problems. Harvard Discussion Paper 1157.

Mas-Colell, A. 1982. Perfect competition and the core. *Review of Economic Studies* 49, 15–30.

Nash, J. 1953. Two-person cooperative games. *Econometrica* 21, 128–40.

Neumann, J. von and Morgenstern, O. 1944. *Theory of Games and Economic Behavior*. Princeton: Princeton University Press.

Scarf, H. 1971. On the existence of a cooperative solution for a general class of n-person games. *Journal of Economic Theory* 3, 169–81.

Shapley, L. 1953. A value for n-person games. In *Contributions to the Theory of Games*, Vol. 2, ed. H. Kuhn and A.W. Tucker, Princeton: Princeton University Press, 307–17.

Shapley, L. 1969. Utility comparison and the theory of games. In *La Décision*, Paris: Editions du CNRS, 251–63.

Shapley, L. and Shubik, M. 1969. On the core of an economic system with externalities. *American Economic Review* 59, 678–84.

Shubik, M. 1983. *Game Theory in the Social Sciences*. Cambridge Mass: MIT Press.

cooperative games. The title 'cooperative games' would be better termed games in coalitional form. The theory of games originally developed different conceptual forms, together with their associated solution concepts, namely, games in extensive form, in strategic form, and in coalitional form (von Neumann and Morgenstern, 1944). The game in strategic form is sometimes referred to as the game in normal form, while that in coalitional form is also referred to as the game in characteristic form.

The game in extensive form provides a process account of the detail of individual moves and information structure; the tree structure often employed in its description enables the researcher to keep track of the full history of any play of the game. This is useful for the analysis of reasonably well-structured formal process models where the beginning, end and sequencing of moves is well-defined, but is generally not so useful to describe complex, loosely structured social interaction.

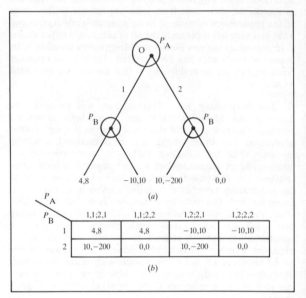

Figure 1

A simple example shows the connections among the three representations of a game. Consider a game with two players where the rules prescribe that Player A moves first. He must decide between two moves. After he has selected a move, Player B is informed and in turn selects between two moves. After B has selected a move the game ends and depending upon the history of the game each player obtains a payoff. Figure 1(a) shows this game in extensive form. The vertex labelled 0 indicates the starting point of the game. It is also circled to indicate the information structure. Figure 2(a) shows a game whose only difference from the game in Figure 1(a) is that in the latter Player B when called upon to select a move does not know to which of the choice points in his information set the game has progressed. In the game in Figure 1(a), when Player B makes his choice he knows precisely if Player A has selected move 1 or 2. Each vertex of the game is a choice point except the terminal vertices. Several vertices may be enclosed in the same information set. The player who 'owns' a particular information set is unable to distinguish among the choice points in a set. An arc (or branch of a tree) connecting a choice point with another choice point or a terminal point is a move. The moves emanating from any choice point are indexed so that they can be identified.

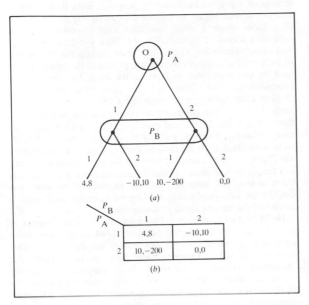

Figure 2

The final nodes at the bottom of the tree are not choice points but points of termination of the game and the numbers displayed indicate the value of the outcome to each player. The first number is the payoff to Player A and the second to Player B.

The extensive form may be reduced to the strategic form by means of strategies. A strategy is a plan covering all contingencies. Figure 1(b) shows that the moves and strategies for P_A are the same, choose 1 or 2. But P_B has four strategies as he can plan for the contingency that P_B selects 1 or 2. A sample strategy 1, 1; 2, 1 may be read as: 'If P_A selects 1, select 1; if P_A selects 2, select 1'.

The progression from extensive form to strategic form entails loss of fine structure. Details of information are no longer available. There are many extensive forms other than Figure 1(a) which are consistent with Figure 1(b).

A further compression of the game representation beyond the strategic form may be called for. At the level of bargaining or diplomacy details of strategy may be of little importance. Instead emphasis is laid upon the value of cooperation. The cooperative or coalitional form represents the game in terms of the jointly optimal outcomes obtainable by every set of players. If payoffs are comparable and side-payments are possible the gain from cooperation can be represented by a single number. If not then the optimal outcomes attainable by a set S of players will be a Pareto optimal surface in $s = |S|$ dimensions (where $|S|$ is the number of elements in S).

A game in cooperative form with side-payments can be represented by a characteristic function which is a superadditive set function. We use the symbol $\Gamma(N, v)$ to stand for a game in coalitional form with a set N of players and a characteristic function v defined on all of the 2^n subsets of N (where $n = |N|$).

The condition of superadditivity is a reasonable economic assumption in a transactions cost-free world. $v(S) + v(T) \leqslant v(S \cup T)$ where $S \cap T = \theta$ states that the amounts obtained by two independent coalitions S and T will be less than or at most equal to the amount that they could obtain by cooperating and acting together.

Returning to Figures 1(b) and 2(b) we can reduce them to coalitional form by specifying how to calculate $v(\theta)$, $v(\overline{1})$, $v(\overline{2})$ and $v(\overline{1, 2})$. The notation '$\overline{1, 2}$' reads as the set consisting of the players whose names are 1 and 2.

Let $\bar{S} = N - S$ be the complement to S. The worst that could happen to S is that $\bar{S}$ acts as a unit to minimize the joint payoff to S. Applying this highly pessimistic view to the games in Figures 1(b) and 2(b) letting $P_A = 1$ and $P_B = 2$ we obtain the following:

$$v(\theta) = 0, \text{ the coalition of no one obtains nothing, by convention.}$$

$$v(\overline{1}) = 0, \ v(\overline{2}) = 0$$

$$v(\overline{1, 2}) = 12$$

Although the extensive and strategic forms of these games differ, they coincide in this coalitional form. More detail has been lost. The coalitional form is symmetric but the underlying games do not appear to be symmetric. The pessimistic way of calculating $v(S)$ may easily overlook the possibility that it is highly costly for $\bar{S}$ to minimize the payoff to S. Thus it is possible that $v(S)$ does not reflect the threat structure in the underlying game. Prior to carrying out further game theoretic analysis on a game in characteristic function form the modeller must decide if the characteristic function is an adequate representation of the game. Harsanyi and Selten have suggested a way to evaluate threats (see Shubik, 1982).

APPLICATIONS. Depending upon the application, the extensive, strategic or coalitional forms may be the starting point for analysis. Thus in economic applications involving oligopoly theory one might go from economic data to the strategic form in order to study Cournot-type duopoly. Yet to study the relationship of the Edgeworth contract curve to the price system one can model the coalitional form directly from the economic data without being able even to describe an extensive or strategic form.

In any application, the description of the game in coalitional form is a major step in the specification of the problem. After the coalitional form has been specified a solution is applied to it. There are many solution concepts which have been suggested for games in coalitional form. Among the better known are the core, the value, the nucleolus, the kernel, the bargaining set and the stable set solutions. Only the core and value are noted here (for an exposition of the others see Shubik, 1982).

The core of an n-person game in characteristic function form was originally investigated by Gillies and adopted by Shapley as a solution. The value was developed by Shapley (1951) and has been considered in several modifications to account for the presence or absence of threats and sidepayments.

We define $\alpha = (\alpha_1, \alpha_2, \ldots, \alpha_n)$ where $\alpha_i \geqslant 0$ for all $i \in N$ and $\Sigma_{i \in N} \alpha_i = v(N)$ to be an imputation for the game $\Gamma(N, v)$. It is an individually rational division of the proceeds from total cooperation. The core is the set of imputations such that $\Sigma_{i \in S} \alpha_i \geqslant v(S)$ for all $S \subset N$. It is, in some sense, the set of imputations impervious to countervailing power. No subset of players can effectively claim that they could obtain more by acting by themselves. The core may be empty. An exchange economy with the usual Arrow–Debreu assumptions modelled as a game in coalitional form always has a core, and the imputation (or imputations) selected by the competitive equilibria of an exchange economy are always in the core of the associated market game.

The Shapley value is intuitively the average of all marginal contributions that an individual i can make to all coalitions. He developed the explicit formula to calculate the value imputation for any game in coalitional form with sidepayments. It is

$$\phi_i = \sum_{i \in S} \sum_{S \subset N} \frac{(n-s)!(s-l)!}{n!} [v(S) - v(S/i)].$$

The term $v(S) - v(S/i)$ measures the marginal contribution of i to the coalition S. The remaining terms provide the count of all of the ways the various coalitions involving i can be built up. For exchange economies with many traders a relationship between the competitive equilibria and the value can be established (for further discussion, see Shubik, 1984).

Many situations involving voting can be modelled as a game in coalitional form where the characteristic function takes only two values, 0 and 1. Such games are called simple games (Shapley, 1962). Shapley and Shubik (1954) suggested the use of the value to provide a power index for committee voting. The basic observation is that the power of a player increases in a nonlinear manner as the number of votes he controls increases. The value applied to a simple game provides an index of this power.

Cooperative games provide a way to carry out an analysis of many problems of interest to the social sciences without concern for the detail of the structure of process. Von Neumann and Morgenstern aptly noted that the difficulties to be encountered in the development of theories of dynamics in the social sciences were so large that the development of a primarily static theory of games in cooperative form was called for as a first step, bearing in mind that the eventual form of a theory of dynamics might have little resemblance to the statics. Some forty years after their seminal work much still remains to be done in the development of games in coalitional form.

MARTIN SHUBIK

See also COOPERATIVE EQUILIBRIUM; GAME THEORY; NASH EQUILIBRIUM; NON–COOPERATIVE GAMES.

BIBLIOGRAPHY
Shapley, L.S. 1951. The value of an n-person game. Rand Publication RM-670.
Shapley, L.S. 1962. Simple games: an outline of the descriptive theory. *Behavioral Science* 7, 59–66.
Shapley, L.S. and Shubik, M. 1954. A method for evaluating the distribution of power in a committee system. *The American Political Science Review* 48(3), 787–92.
Shubik, M. 1982. *Game Theory in the Social Sciences*, Vol. I. Cambridge, Mass.: Harvard University Press.
Shubik, M. 1984. *Game Theory in the Social Sciences*, Vol. II. Cambridge, Mass.: MIT Press.
Von Neumann, J. and Morgenstern, O. 1944. *The Theory of Games and Economic Behavior*. Princeton: Princeton University Press.

co-operatives. It is a very good question to ask why the factory system substituted capitalist for workers' control over the production process. As Andrew Ure remarked,

> To devise and administer a successful code of factory discipline, suited to the necessities of factory diligence, was the Herculean enterprise, the notable achievement of Arkwright ... it required, in fact, a man of a Napoleon nerve and ambition to subdue the refractory tempers of work-people, accustomed to irregular paroxysms of diligence ... such was Arkwright (*The Philosophy of Manufactures*, 1835).

Obviously factory discipline was learned reluctantly, and with understandable resentment. Co-operative association did not emerge as a coherent alternative, however, until Robert Owen and his school began to advocate them in the 1820s. Before that date, some friendly societies experimented with co-operative forms of distribution, by bulk purchases of grain and other necessities. Otherwise, those disaffected by the rise of industrial production were more prone, at the beginning, to look to the ownership of land as the basis for communistic experiments. True, there was the pioneering work of the Quaker John Bellers, who proposed a 'college of industry' as early as 1695. But producer co-operatives did not begin to flourish until the 1830s, and even then they had a high failure rate. Industrial disputes, notably the Derby turnouts of 1834, were associated with an insurrectionary idea of co-operation: the Derby workers appealed for help from surrounding towns, not simply to feed those locked out for supporting the Owenite trade union, but also to purchase machinery, so that they could enter into production on their own accord, and begin to construct the co-operative commonwealth.

The defeat of Owenism led to a more gradualist concept of co-operation, although the birth in 1844 of the consumer co-operative movement was far from a devaluation of older communistic ideas. Opening their shop in Toad Lane, the 'Rochdale pioneers' reaffirmed their intentions of raising money in order to embark upon co-operative production. As their initiative spread, it became possible to create a wholesale department servicing several societies, and to open a cornmill and a tobacco factory. Consumer co-operation established the principle of democratic control by its membership, with every member having only one vote, irrespective of the size of his or her capital investment. Profits were distributed in a dividend on purchases, after collective charges and interest payments had been met.

Because each co-operator votes only once, co-operation establishes a completely different principle of economic administration from that involved in the limited liability company. Retail co-operative societies in Britain frequently grew from the scale at which they could administer one local store to extended chains of shops covering an entire region. Each retail society would be governed by a management committee regularly elected by the membership. Consumer co-operation grew steadily, involving a million people by 1891, five million by 1926, and ten million by 1948. By the 1960s, consumer co-operatives reached a membership of over thirteen million.

With growth, however, there arose problems of involvement. In the original small ventures, all members would be directly involved not only in decision making but in a host of voluntary practical activities. As the movement grew, and recruited professional staff, so its internal democracy became greatly more attenuated. Rates of participation in management meetings declined, reaching very low levels by the middle of the 20th century. A commission under the chairmanship of Hugh Gaitskell and the secretaryship of Anthony Crosland, investigated the decline in co-operative membership involvement. They reported that 'only the few will ever wish to devote their evenings to voluntary public work. In the early days of the co-operative movement, when its total membership was numbered in thousands, almost the entire membership was drawn from among these few ... . Today, when the movement, has twelve million members, the few have become a small minority ... the figures of participation have fallen correspondingly.' The assumption of a fixed quota of activists only makes sense, however, on the basis of an assumption of fixed activities in which they might engage. Early co-operation involved a division of tasks among all members, and necessarily engendered high participation ratios. It was professionalization, not simply increase of scale, which changed this situation. As early as 1851, the Rochdale Society had resolved that 'No paid officer be a member of the Board, or a member of the Board a paid servant.' In other words, consumer co-operation in Britain had then established a professional civil service, which was constitutionally excluded from policy control, but increasingly expected to undertake executive management. This is an unreal separation of functions which inevitably eroded the effective powers of individual members. Indeed, when decline set in, apathy, if anything, increased. By 1984 members of co-operatives had declined to 8.5 million, but the 'fixed quota' of activists weighed, if anything, less than before, not more.

Things were quite different in the area of producer co-operation. This grew in labour-intensive industries, after the middle of the 19th century, following a successful lobby by Christian Socialists for legislation which could enable them to function. Between 1862 and 1880, 163 producer associations were registered under the Industrial and Provident Societies Acts, of 1852 and subsequently, which had been brought in as a result of careful lobbying by Ludlow, Neale and others. The First International welcomed these new co-operatives, saying of the movement that 'Its great merit is to practically show that ... the despotic system of the subordination of labour to capital can be superseded by the republican and beneficent system of the association of free and equal producers.' A new upsurge in experiments in co-operative workshops followed later, with the labour unrest out of which grew the 'New Unionism' and the 1889 dock strike.

By 1890 Beatrice Webb (Potter) distinguished four classes of producer co-operatives: those modelled on Christian Socialist doctrine, which elected their management committees, and only employed full members; those consisting only of full members who had accepted management by a person (or group) that was (or were) irremovable; those self-governing co-ops which employed outside labour; and those in which outside shareholders supplied most of the capital, but in which workers were encouraged or obliged to take shares, even though they were excluded from the management committee.

While Beatrice Webb documented some exploitative practices in the last three of these categories, she also pronounced strong judgement on those co-operatives which administered themselves according to strict principles. These, she thought, had a high failure rate, due to their propensity to eat their seed corn and thus fail to make adequate provision for investment. The Webbs' assumption became part of the conventional wisdom about workers' producer co-operatives until the 1970s, when Derek Jones undertook a careful study of the failure rate of producer co-operatives from 1875 onwards and showed that it was not greater than that of small businesses in general. By 1900 there were more than 100 producer co-operatives in Britain, the majority of which had joined forces in a body known as the Co-operative Productive Federation. This organization underwent slow decline, until it listed only 23 societies in the late 1960s. The largest of these, the Leicester Equity Boot and Shoe Manufacturers, employed 1600 people at its peak. Most societies were very much smaller, employing a few dozen.

Producer co-operation underwent a serious revival in the 1970s. Various organizations came into being to argue the case for industrial democracy. A growing discussion on workers'

control resulted in the formation of the Institute for Workers' Control (IWC) in 1968, and the extension of debate throughout the organizations of the Labour movement. A specialist body, the Industrial Common Ownership Movement (ICOM) began to organize new co-operatives outside the framework of the Co-operative Productive Federation. This was originally based on initiatives by the Scott Bader Commonwealth, a self-managed chemical company. The industrial policy of the 1974 Labour Government was influenced by the arguments of these new pressure groups, and producer co-operation received major publicity when attempts were made to rescue three failed enterprises from closure by converting them to co-operative management with funding from the Department of Trade and Industry, of which the Secretary of State was then Tony Benn. The 'Benn' co-operatives, as these became known, at Kirkby Manufacturing and Engineering near Liverpool, Triumph–Meriden and the Scottish Daily News, stimulated widespread debate and attracted a number of would-be imitators. A series of 'work ins' and sit-ins, beginning with that at the Upper Clyde shipyards in 1971 had encouraged workers not to accept plant closure when their employers' businesses failed, and some experiments in co-operative production resulted from these struggles. A women's co-operative manufacturing leather goods arose at Fakenham after a factory occupation, and Leadgate Engineering, in the North, followed the same pattern. By 1975, when Imperial typewriters closed their two factories in Hull and Leicester, it had become 'normal' to accept factory occupations as a reflex response to such decisions. The workers in Hull sat in, emblazoning a banner outside the factory, announcing 'We stay in till Benn says when.' But before the typewriter co-operative could be established, Mr Benn was relegated from the Department of Industry to that of Energy, and under his successor no more co-operatives of this kind were to be formed. Soon afterwards, KME and the Scottish Daily News failed for lack of adequate capital. The KME project had been particularly difficult, because it inherited a bizarre product mix, which had itself contributed to the collapse of the original enterprise. The Scottish Daily News came to an end after a series of agreements and disagreements with Robert Maxwell, the publishing entrepreneur, who had been brought in by the workers to assist in the rescue.

But as a result of such colourful events and the persistent lobbying of the industrial democrats, the Labour Party had committed itself to support new co-operatives, and a Co-operative Development agency was established in 1978, with limited funds to promote new organizations. The new agency was not without some opponents in the established co-operative movement, but it was soon to receive a remarkable fillip from the work of Local Government Enterprise Boards, which were established with the onset of slump in the late 1970s in an effort to create employment in local communities. The result was a rapid and spectacular increase in the number of producer organizations. By 1985 there were 750 organizations with an average turnover of £199,000. New co-operatives were being formed all the time, so that the number of new firms was growing at a rate of 20 per cent per annum.

The recovery of impetus by industrial co-operation already raises important questions for the consumer co-operative movement, and could generate pressures for its reform. It also begins to make possible closer involvement with producer co-operatives in Europe, where they have maintained, in many countries, a consistent strength and vitality. There can be little doubt that, if the upsurge of new co-operative continues, this will bring about-important changes in the political field, as the Labour Movement digests their implications.

KEN COATES

BIBLIOGRAPHY

Bailey, J. 1955. *The British Co-operative Movement.* London: Hutchinson.

Bradley, K. and Gelb, A. 1983. *Co-operation at Work: the Mondragon Experience.* London: Heinemann.

Carr-Saunders, A.M. et al. 1938. *Consumers' Co-operation in Great Britain.* London: Allen & Unwin.

Coates, K. (ed.) 1976. *The New Worker Co-operatives.* Nottingham: Spokesman.

Coates, K. 1981. *Work-ins, Sit-ins and Industrial Democracy.* Nottingham: Spokesman.

Cole, G.D.H. 1944. *A Century of Co-operation.* London: Allen & Unwin.

The Co-operative Directory (yearly). Manchester: Co-operative Union.

Derrick, P. and Phipps, J.F. 1969. *Co-ownership, Co-operation and Control.* London: Longmans.

Eccles, T. 1981. *Under New Management.* London: Pan.

Garnett, R.G. 1972. *Co-operation and the Owenite Socialist Communities in Britain.* Manchester: Manchester University Press.

Greater London Enterprise Board. 1984. *A Strategy for Co-operation: Worker Co-ops in London.* London: GLEB.

ICOM. *The Co-operative Way: Worker Co-ops in France, Spain and Eastern Europe.* London: ICOM Co-op Publications.

Jones, D. 1976. British producer co-operatives. In Coates (1976).

Labour Party Finance and Industry Group. 1983. *Towards Common Ownership.* London: Labour Party.

Marglin, S.A. 1976. What do bosses do? In *The Division of Labour,* ed. A. Gorz, Brighton: Harvester Press.

Ostergaard, G.N. and Halsey, A.H. 1965. *Power in Co-operatives.* Oxford: Blackwell.

Potter, B. 1907. *The Co-operative Movement in Great Britain.* London: Swan Sonnenschein.

Thomas, H.B. and Logan, C. 1982. *Mondragon: an Economic Analysis.* London: Allen & Unwin.

Thornley, J. 1981. *Workers' Co-operatives: Jobs and Dreams.* London: Heinemann.

Ure, A. 1835. *The Philosophy of Manufactures.* Edinburgh: Charles Knight.

Copland, Douglas Berry (1894–1971). Copland was born at St Andrews, New Zealand, in 1894 and died at Kilmore, Australia, in 1971. Australia's most public applied economist from the 1920s to 1960, he pioneered opportunities for professional economists. He was the first occupant of positions such as Professor of Economics at the University of Tasmania (1920–24), Professor of Commerce at the University of Melbourne (1924–44), President of the Economic Society of Australia and New Zealand (1925), chief editor of the *Economic Record* (1924–45), Australian/New Zealand representative for the Social Sciences Division of the Rockefeller Foundation (1925–54), Vice-Chancellor of the Australian National University (1948–53), Principal, Australian Administrative Staff College (1956–60), and Chairman, Committee for the Economic Development of Australia (1960–66).

Copland was particularly interested in monetary and capital flows and their relation to prices, business cycles and economic development. Stressing Australia's world position as a small, dependent, primary-producing country, his policy advice was often controversial. In 1929 he contributed to the Australian case for tariff protection. During the 1930s depression, he advocated the 'middle way' towards recovery – a policy-mix of deflationary cost, wage and fiscal measures, with reflationary exchange depreciation, expansionary monetary policy and tariff protection. In the 1950s he recommended that Australia avoid restrictions of the sterling area by pursuing a policy of rapid development based on dollar borrowings.

Copland's experiences as economic adviser to governments, Commonwealth Prices Commissioner (1939–45), Australian Minister to China (1946–8) and President of the Economic and Social Council of the United Nations (1955) while High Commissioner to Canada, led to publications on the parameters and mechanisms of economic control, especially within group frameworks – the Australian Commonwealth, the British Commonwealth and international organizations.

M. HARPER

SELECTED WORKS

1920. *Wheat Production in New Zealand: A Study in the Economics of New Zealand Agriculture.* Auckland: Whitcombe & Tombs.

1929. (With J.B. Brigden, E.C. Dyason, L.F. Giblin and C.H. Wickens.) *The Australian Tariff: An Economic Enquiry.* Melbourne: Melbourne University Press (Economic Series No. 6).

1930. *Credit and Currency Control: with special reference to Australia.* Melbourne: Melbourne University Press (Economic Series No. 9).

1934. *Australia in the World Crisis 1929–33.* Cambridge: Cambridge University Press.

1945. *The Road to High Employment: Administrative Controls in a Free Economy.* Sydney: Angus and Robertson.

1953. *Problems of the Sterling Area with special reference to Australia.* Essays in International Finance No. 17, September 1953. Princeton: Princeton University International Finance Section.

For a bibliography of academic works, see *Economic Record*, March 1960, 173–8.

cores. The *core* of an economy consists of those states of the economy which no group of agents can 'improve upon'. A group of agents can improve upon a state of the economy if, by using the means available to that group, each member can be made better off. Nothing is said in this definition of how a state in the core actually is reached. The actual process of economic transactions is not considered explicitly.

To keep the presentation as simple as possible, we shall consider only the core for exchange economies with an arbitrary number l of commodities, even though the core concept applies to more general situations.

Consider a finite set A of economic agents; each agent a in A is described by his *preference relation* $\precsim_a$ (defined on the positive orthant R^l_+) and his *initial endowments* e_a (a vector in R^l_+). The outcome of any exchange, that is to say, a state (x_a) of the exchange economy $\mathscr{E} = \{\precsim_a, e_a\}_{a \in A}$, is a *redistribution* of the total endowments, i.e.

$$\sum_{a \in A} x_a = \sum_{a \in A} e_a.$$

A *coalition* of agents, say $S \subset A$, can *improve upon* a redistribution (x_a), if that coalition S, by using the endowments available to it, can make each member of that coalition better off, that is to say, there is a redistribution, say $(y_a)_{a \in S}$, such that

$$y_a \succ_a x_a \text{ for every } a \in S \quad \text{and} \quad \sum_{a \in S} y_a = \sum_{a \in S} e_a.$$

The set of redistributions for the exchange economy $\mathscr{E}$ that no coalition can improve upon is called the *core* of the economy $\mathscr{E}$, and is denoted by $C(\mathscr{E})$.

The core is a rather theoretical, however, fundamental equilibrium concept. Indeed, the core provides a theoretical foundation of a more operational equilibrium concept, the *competitive equilibrium* which, in fact, is a very different notion of equilibrium. The allocation process is organized through markets; there is a price for every commodity. All economic agents take the price system as given and make their decisions independently of each other. The equilibrium price system coordinates these independent decisions in such a way that all markets are simultaneously balanced.

More formally, an allocation (x_a^*) for the exchange economy $\mathscr{E} = \{\precsim_a, e_a\}_{a \in A}$ is a *competitive equilibrium* (or a *Walras allocation*) if there exists a price vector $p^* \in R^l_+$ such that for every $a \in A$, $x_a^* \in \phi_a(p^*)$ and

$$\sum_{a \in A} x_a^* = \sum_{a \in A} e_a.$$

Here $\phi_a(p^*)$, or more explicitly, $\phi(p^*, e_a, \precsim_a)$ denotes the demand of agent a with preferences $\precsim_a$ and endowment e_a, i.e. the set of most desired commodity vectors (with respect to $\precsim_a$) in the budget-set $\{x \in R^l_+ \mid p^* \cdot x \le p^* \cdot e_a\}$.

The set of all competitive equilibria for the economy $\mathscr{E}$ is denoted by $W(\mathscr{E})$.

The core and the set of competitive equilibria for an economy with two agents and two commodities can be represented geometrically by the well-known Edgeworth–Box (see figure 1). The size of the box is determined by the total endowments $e_1 + e_2$. Every point P in the box represents a redistribution; the first agent receives $x_1 = P$ and the second receives $x_2 = (e_1 + e_2) - P$.

It is easy to show that for every exchange economy $\mathscr{E}$ a competitive equilibrium belongs to the core,

$$W(\mathscr{E}) \subset C(\mathscr{E}).$$

Thus, a state of the economy $\mathscr{E}$ which is decentralized by a price system cannot be improved upon by cooperation. This proposition strengthens a well-known result of Welfare Economics— every competitive equilibrium is Pareto-efficient.

The inclusion $W(\mathscr{E}) \subset C(\mathscr{E})$ is typically strict. Indeed, if the initial allocation of endowments is not Pareto-efficient, which is the typical case, then, if there are any allocations in the core at all, there are core-allocations which are not competitive equilibria.

This leads us to the *basic problem* in the theory of the core:

For which kind of economies is the 'difference' between the core and the set of competitive equilibria small? Or in other words, under which circumstances do cooperative barter and competition through decentralized markets lead essentially to the same result?

Naturally, the answer depends on the way one measures the 'difference' between the two equilibrium concepts. However this is done one expects that the economy must have a large number of participants.

In answering the basic question we try to be comprehensible (for example by avoiding the use of measure-theoretic concepts) but not comprehensive. Therefore, if we refer in the remainder

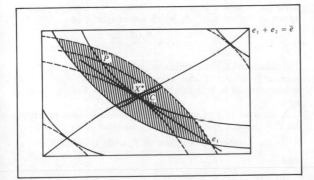

Figure 1

of this entry to an economy $\mathscr{E} = \{\precsim_a, e_a\}_{a \in A}$ we shall always assume that preference relations are continuous, complete, transitive, monotone and strictly convex. The total endowments $\sum_{a \in A} e_a$ of an economy are always assumed to be strictly positive. We shall not repeat these assumptions. Furthermore, if we call an economy smooth, then we assume in addition that preferences are smooth (hence representable by sufficiently differentiable utility functions) and individual endowments are strictly positive.

These assumptions simplify the presentation tremendously. For generalizations we refer to the extensive literature.

We remark that under the above assumptions there always exists a competitive equilibrium, and hence, the core is not empty.

LARGE ECONOMIES

The simplest and most stringent measure of difference between the two equilibrium sets, $C(\mathscr{E})$ and $W(\mathscr{E})$, which we shall denote by $\delta(\mathscr{E})$, can be defined as follows.

Let $\delta(\mathscr{E})$ be the smallest number δ with the property: for every allocation $(x_a) \in C(\mathscr{E})$ there exists an allocation $(x_a^*) \in W(\mathscr{E})$ such that

$$|x_a - x_a^*| \le \delta$$

for every agent a in the economy $\mathscr{E}$.

Thus, if $\delta(\mathscr{E})$ is small, then from every agent's view a core allocation is like a competitive equilibrium.

Unfortunately for this measure of difference, it is not true that $\delta(\mathscr{E})$ can be made arbitrarily small provided the number of agents in the economy $\mathscr{E}$ is sufficiently large (even if one restricts the agents' characteristics $(\precsim_a, e_a)$ to an *a priori* given finite set).

Consequently one considers also weaker measures for the 'difference' between the two equilibrium concepts $C(\mathscr{E})$ and $W(\mathscr{E})$. For example, define $\delta_1(\mathscr{E})$ and $\delta_2(\mathscr{E})$, respectively, as the smallest number δ with the property: for every $(x_a) \in C(\mathscr{E})$ there exists a price vector $p \in R^l_+$ such that

(δ_1) $\qquad |x_a - \phi_a(p)| \le \delta$ for every agent a in $\mathscr{E}$

or

(δ_2) $\qquad \dfrac{1}{\# A} \sum_{a \in A} |x_a - \phi_a(p)| \le \delta.$

Clearly, the measures δ_1 and δ_2 are weaker than δ since the price vector p is not required to be an equilibrium price vector for the economy $\mathscr{E}$. The number $\delta_1(\mathscr{E})$ (and, *a fortiori*, $\delta_2(\mathscr{E})$) does not measure the distance between the sets $C(\mathscr{E})$ and $W(\mathscr{E})$ but the degree by which an allocation in the core can be decentralized via a price system. Obviously one has $\delta_2(\mathscr{E}) \le \delta_1(\mathscr{E}) \le \delta(\mathscr{E})$.

One can show that $\delta_2(\mathscr{E})$ becomes arbitrarily small for sufficiently large economies. More precisely,

THEOREM 1. Let T be a finite set of agents' characteristics $(\precsim, e)$ and let b be a strictly positive vector in R^l. Then for every $\epsilon > 0$ there exists an integer N such that for every economy $\mathscr{E} = \{\precsim_a, e_a\}_{a \in A}$ with $\# A \ge N$,

$$\frac{1}{\# A} \sum_{a \in A} e_a \gtrless b$$

and $(\precsim_a, e_a) \in T$ one has

$$\delta_2(\mathscr{E}) \le \epsilon.$$

(The finite set T in Theorem 1 can be replaced by a compact set with respect to a suitably chosen topology: see Hildenbrand,

1974.) We emphasize that this result does not imply that in large economies core-allocations are near to competitive equilibria. In fact, Theorem 1 does not hold if δ_2 is replaced by the measure of difference δ or even δ_1. Theorem 1 does imply, however, that for sufficiently large economies one can associate to every core-allocation a price vector which 'approximately decentralizes' the core-allocation. Some readers might consider this conclusion as a perfectly satisfactory answer to our basic problem. If one holds this view, then the rest of the paper is a superfluous intellectual pastime. We would like to emphasize, however, that the meaning of 'approximate decentralization' is not very strong. First, the demand $\phi_a(p)$ is not necessarily near to x_a for every agent a in the economy; only the mean deviation

$$\frac{1}{\# A} \sum_{a \in A} |x_a - \phi_a(p)|$$

becomes small. Second, total demand is not equal to total supply; only the mean excess demand

$$\frac{1}{\# A} \sum_{a \in A} [\phi_a(p) - e_a]$$

becomes small.

There are alternative proofs in the literature, e.g. Bewley (1973), Hildenbrand (1974), Anderson (1981) or Hildenbrand (1982). These proofs are based either on a result by Vind (1965) or Anderson (1978).

Sharper conclusions than the one in Theorem 1 will be stated in the following sections. There we consider a sequence $(\mathscr{E}_n)_{n=1,\ldots}$ of economies and then study the asymptotic behaviour of $\delta(\mathscr{E}_n)$.

Before we present these limit theorems we should mention another approach of analysing the inclusion $W(\mathscr{E}) \subset C(\mathscr{E})$. Instead of analysing the asymptotic behaviour of the difference $\delta(\mathscr{E}_n)$ for a sequence of finite economies one can define a large economy where every agent has strictly no influence on collective actions. This leads to a *measure space without atoms* of economic agents (also called a *continuum of agents*). For such economies the two equilibrium concepts coincide. See Aumann (1964).

REPLICA ECONOMIES

Let $\mathscr{E} = \{\precsim_i, e_i\}$ be an exchange economy with m agents. For every integer n we define the n-fold *replica economy* $\mathscr{E}_n$ of $\mathscr{E}$ as an economy with $n \cdot m$ agents; there are exactly n agents with characteristics $(\precsim_i, e_i)$ for every $i = 1, \ldots, m$.

More formally,

$$\mathscr{E}_n = \{\precsim_{(i,j)}, e_{(i,j)}\}_{\substack{1 \leqslant i \leqslant m \\ 1 \leqslant j \leqslant n}}$$

where $\precsim_{(i,j)} = \precsim_i$ and $e_{(i,j)} = e_i$, $1 \leqslant i \leqslant m$ and $1 \leqslant j \leqslant n$. Thus, an agent a in the economy $\mathscr{E}_n$ is denoted by a double index $a = (i, j)$. We shall refer to agent (i, j) sometimes as the jth agent of type i.

Replica economies were first analysed by F. Edgeworth (1881) who proved a limit theorem for such sequences in the case of two commodities and two types of agents. A precise formulation of Edgeworth's analysis and the generalization to an arbitrary finite number of commodities and types of agents is due to Debreu and Scarf (1963).

Here is the basic result for replica economies.

THEOREM 2. For every sequence $(\mathscr{E}_n)$ of replica economies the difference between the core and the set of competitive equilibria tends to zero, i.e.,

$$\lim_{n \to \infty} \delta(\mathscr{E}_n) = 0.$$

Furthermore, if $\mathscr{E}$ is a smooth and regular economy then $\delta(\mathscr{E}_n)$ converges to zero at least as fast as the inverse of the number of participants, i.e., there is a constant K such that

$$\delta(\mathscr{E}_n) \leqslant \frac{K}{n}.$$

The proof of this remarkably neat result is based on the fact that a core–allocation (x_{ij}) assigns to every agent of the same type the same commodity bundle, i.e., $x_{ij} = x_{ik}$, This 'equal treatment' property simplifies the analysis of $\delta(\mathscr{E}_n)$ tremendously. Indeed, an allocation (x_{ij}) in $C(\mathscr{E}_n)$, which can be considered as a vector in $R^{l \cdot m \cdot n}$, is completely described by the commodity bundle of one agent in each type, thus by a vector $(x_{11}, x_{21}, \ldots, x_{m1})$ in $R^{l \cdot m}$, a space whose dimension is independent of n.

Thus, let

$$C_n = \{(x_{11}, x_{21}, \ldots, x_{m1}) \in R^{l \cdot m} | (x_{ij}) \in C(\mathscr{E}_n)\}.$$

One easily shows that $C_{n+1} \subset C_n$. It is not hard to see that Theorem 1 follows if

$$\cap_{n=1}^{\infty} C_n = W(\mathscr{E}_1).$$

But this is the well-known theorem of Debreu and Scarf (1963). The essential arguments in the proof go as follows. Let $(x_1, \ldots, x_m) \in \cap_{n=1}^{\infty} C_n$. One has to show that there is a price vector p^* such that $x \succ_i x_i$ implies $p^* \cdot x > p^* \cdot e_i$. For this it suffices to show that there is a p^* such that

$$p^* \cdot z \geqslant 0 \text{ for every } z \in \cup_{i=1}^m (\{x \in R_+^l | x \succ_i x_i\} - e_i) = Z,$$

i.e., there is a hyperplane (whose normal is p^*) which supports the set z. One shows that the assumption $(x_1, \ldots, x_m) \in \cap_{n=1}^{\infty} C_n$ implies that 0 does not belong to the convex hull of z. Minkowski's Separation Theorem for convex sets then implies the existence of the desired vector p^*.

The second part of the conclusion of Theorem 2 is due to Debreu (1975).

TYPE ECONOMIES

The limit theorem on the core for replica economies is not fully satisfactory since replication is a very rigid way of enlarging an economy. The conclusion '$\delta(\mathscr{E}_n) \to 0$' in Theorem 2, to be of general relevance, should be robust to small deviations from the strict replication procedure.

Consider a sequence $(\mathscr{E}_n)$ of economies where the characteristics of every agent belong to a given finite set of types $T = \{(\precsim_1, e_1), \ldots, (\precsim_m, e_m)\}$. We do not consider this as a restrictive assumption (considered as an approximation, one can always group agents' characteristics into a finite set of types). Let the economy $\mathscr{E}_n$ have N_n agents; $N_n(1)$ agents of the first type, $N_n(i)$ agents of type i. Of course the idea is that N_n tends to ∞ with increasing n. Consider the fraction $v_n(i)$ of agents in the economy $\mathscr{E}_n$ which are of type i, i.e.,

$$v_n(i) = \frac{N_n(i)}{N_n}.$$

The sequence $(\mathscr{E}_n)$ is a replica sequence of an economy $\mathscr{E}$ (not necessarily of $\mathscr{E}_1$) if and only if the fractions $v_n(i)$ are all independent of n. It is this rigidity which we want to weaken now.

A sequence $(\mathscr{E}_n)$ of economies with characteristics in a finite set T is called a *sequence of type economies* (over T) if

(i) the number N_n of agents in $\mathscr{E}_n$ tends to infinity

and

(ii) $v_n(i) = \dfrac{N_n(i)}{N_n} \xrightarrow[(n \to \infty)]{} v(i) > 0.$

EXAMPLE (random sampling of agents' characteristics):

Let π be a probability distribution over the finite set T. Define the economy $\mathscr{E}_n$ as a random sample of size n from this distribution $\pi(\cdot)$. The law of large numbers them implies property (ii): $v_n(i) \to \pi(i)$.

The step from replica economies to type economies – as small as it might appear to the reader – is conceptually very important. Yet with this 'small' generalization the analysis of the limit behaviour of $\delta(\mathscr{E}_n)$ or $\delta_1(\mathscr{E}_n)$ is made more difficult. Even worse, it is no longer true that for *every* sequence $(\mathscr{E}_n)$ of type economies one obtains $\delta(\mathscr{E}_n) \to 0$—even if the preferences of all types are assumed to be very nice, say smooth. There are some 'exceptional cases' where the conclusion $\delta(\mathscr{E}_n) \to 0$ does not hold. But these are 'exceptional' cases and the whole difficulty in the remainder of this section is to explain in which precise sense these cases are 'exceptional' and can therefore be ignored. We shall first exhibit the 'cases' where the conclusion fails to hold. Then we shall show that these cases are exceptional.

We denote by $\Pi(\mathscr{E})$ the set of normalized *equilibrium price vectors* for the economy $\mathscr{E} = \{(\precsim_a, e_a)\}_{a \in A}$. Thus, for $p^* \in \Pi(\mathscr{E})$ the excess demand is zero, i.e.,

$$\sum_{a \in A} [\phi_a(p^*) - e_a] = 0.$$

To every sequence $(\mathscr{E}_n)$ of type economies we associate a '*limit economy*' $\mathscr{E}_\infty$. This economy has an 'indefinitely large' number of agents of every type; the fraction of agents of type i is given by $v(i)$. The mean (per capita) excess demand of that limit economy $\mathscr{E}_\infty$ is defined by

$$z_v(p) = \sum_{i=1}^{m} v(i)[\phi(p, e_i, \precsim_i) - e_i].$$

An equilibrium price vector p^* of the limit economy $\mathscr{E}_\infty$ is defined by $z_v(p^*) = 0$. Let $\Pi(v)$ denote the set of normalized equilibrium price vectors for $\mathscr{E}_\infty$. Obviously for a replica sequence $(\mathscr{E}_n)$ we have $\Pi(\mathscr{E}_n) = \Pi(v)$ for all n. However, for a sequence of type economies the set $\Pi(\mathscr{E}_n)$ of equilibrium prices of the economy $\mathscr{E}_n$ depends on n, and it might happen that the set $\Pi(v)$ is not similar to $\Pi(\mathscr{E}_n)$ even for arbitrarily large n. To fix ideas, it might happen that $\Pi(\mathscr{E}_n) = \{p_n\}$ and $\Pi(v)$ contains not only $p = \lim p_n$ but also another equilibrium price vector. Such a situation has to be excluded.

We call a sequence of type economies *sleek* if $\Pi(\mathscr{E}_n)$ converges (in the Hausdorff-distance) to $\Pi(v)$.

It is known (Hildenbrand, 1974) that the sequence $(\Pi(\mathscr{E}_n))$ converges to $\Pi(v)$ if $\Pi(v)$ is a singleton (i.e., the limit economy has a unique equilibrium) or, in general, if (and only if) for every open set O in R^l with $O \cap \Pi(v) \neq \emptyset$ it follows that $O \cap \Pi(\mathscr{E}_n) \neq \emptyset$ for all n sufficiently large.

We now have exhibited the cases where a limit theorem on the core holds true.

THEOREM 3: For every sleek sequence $(\mathscr{E}_n)$ of type economies

$$\lim_{n \to \infty} \delta(\mathscr{E}_n) = 0.$$

Unfortunately there seems to be no short and easy proof. The main difficulty arises from the fact that for allocations in the core of a type economy the 'equal treatment' property, which made the replica case so manageable is no longer true. For a proof see Hildenbrand and Kirman (1976) or Hildenbrand (1982) and the references given there. The main step in the proof is based on a result of Bewley (1973).

It remains to show that non-sleek sequences of type economies are 'exceptional cases'.

The strongest form of 'exceptional' is, of course, 'never'. We mentioned already that a sequence $(\mathscr{E}_n)$ is sleek if its limit

economy has a unique equilibrium. Unfortunately, however, only under very restrictive assumptions on the set T of agents' characteristics does uniqueness prevail; for example,

(1)   if every preference relation leads to a demand function which satisfies gross-substitution (Cobb–Douglas utility functions are typical examples),

(2)   if every preference relation is homothetic and the endowment vectors $e_i (i = 1, \ldots, m)$ are collinear.

Since there is no reasonable justification for restricting the set T to such special types of agents we have to formulate a model in which we allow non-sleek sequences to occur provided, of course, this can be shown to be 'exceptional cases'. Let S^{m-1} denote the open simplex in R^m, i.e.

$$S^{m-1} = \left\{ x \in R^m \,|\, x_i > 0, \sum_{i=1}^{m} x_i = 1 \right\}.$$

The limit distribution $v(i)$ of a sequence of type economies with m types is a point in S^{m-1}.

A closed subset C in S^{m-1} which has $(m-1$ dimensional Lebesgue) measure zero is called *negligible*. Thus, if a distribution v is not in C then a sufficiently small change will not lead to C. Furthermore, given any arbitrary small positive number $\mathscr{E}$ one can find a countable collection of balls in S^{m-1} such that their union covers C, and that the sum of the diameters of these balls is smaller than $\mathscr{E}$. Thus, in particular, if $v \in C$ then one can approximate v by points which do not belong to C. Clearly, a negligible set is a small set in S^{m-1}.

THEOREM 4:   Given a finite set T of m smooth types of agents, there exists a negligible subset C in S^{m-1} and a constant K such that for every sequence $(\mathscr{E}_n)$ of type economies over T whose limit distribution v does not belong to C one has $\delta(\mathscr{E}_n) \leqslant K / \# A_n$, thus in particular, $\lim_{n \to \infty} \delta(\mathscr{E}_n) = 0$.

The convergence of $\delta(\mathscr{E}_n)$ follows from Theorem 3 and Theorems 5.4.3 and 5.8.15 in Mas–Colell (1985). For the rate of convergence see Grodal (1975).

WERNER HILDENBRAND

See also COOPERATIVE EQUILIBRIUM; EDGEWORTH, FRANCIS YSIDRO; EXISTENCE OF GENERAL EQUILIBRIUM; UNIQUENESS OF EQUILIBRIUM.

BIBLIOGRAPHY
There is an extensive literature on limit theorems on the core which contains important generalizations of the results given here. For a general reference we refer to Hildenbrand (1974) or (1982), Mas-Colell (1985), Anderson (1985) and the references given there.

Anderson, R.M. 1978. An elementary core equivalence theorem. *Econometrica* 46, 1483–7.
Anderson, R.M. 1981. Core theory with strongly convex preferences. *Econometrica* 49, 1457–68.
Aumann, R.J. 1964. Markets with a continuum of traders. *Econometrica* 32, 39–50.
Bewley, T.F. 1973. Edgeworth's conjecture. *Econometrica* 41, 425–54.
Debreu, G. 1975. The rate of convergence of the core of an economy. *Journal of Mathematical Economics* 2, 1–8.
Debreu, G. and Scarf, H. 1963. A limit theorem on the core of an economy. *International Economic Review* 4, 235–46.
Edgeworth, F.Y. 1881. *Mathematical Psychics*. London: Kegan Paul.
Grodal, B. 1975. The rate of convergence of the core for a purely competitive sequence of economies. *Journal of Mathematical Economics* 2, 171–86.
Hildenbrand, W. 1974. *Core and Equilibria of a Large Economy*. Princeton: Princeton University Press.
Hildenbrand, W. 1982. Core of an economy. In *Handbook of Mathematical Economics*, ed. K.J. Arrow and M.D. Intriligator, Vol. II, Amsterdam: North-Holland.

Hildenbrand, W. and Kirman, A.P. 1976. *Introduction to Equilibrium Analysis*. Amsterdam: North-Holland.

Mas-Colell, A. 1985. *The Theory of General Economic Equilibrium, A Differentiable Approach*. Cambridge: Cambridge University Press.

Vind, K. 1965. A theorem on the core of an economy. *Review of Economic Studies* 32, 47–8.

Corn Laws. The British Corn Laws were parliamentary statutes which attempted to regulate the trade in corn (mainly wheat, barley, rye, and oats) for the benefit of producers during periods of plenty and low prices. Legislation to prohibit or discourage importation can be traced back to the 15th century, though it only became effective with an Act of 1663, while bounties to encourage export date from the 14th century and became more systematic after an Act of 1689. However, no economic tracts or pamphlets seem to have been devoted exclusively to this subject before 1750 (Barnes, 1930, p. 16) and it was only in the 19th century that such legislation became controversial, mainly because the growth of population and especially of towns fuelled the concern about food supply that had been provoked by the scarcity of 1795 and by Malthus's *Essay* of 1798. In particular the 1815 Corn Law, which aimed to encourage domestic production by prohibiting importation until home prices had reached a certain level (80 shillings per quarter in the case of wheat), was the object of violent abuse both from radicals representing the interests of the consumer and also from middle-class manufacturers and exporters. In practice the 1815 Law satisfied no one. The sudden switch from total prohibition to total freedom of import at a particular price was destabilizing and failed to safeguard supply, since by the time (usually October or November) that prices reached the specified level, signalling a scarcity, the Baltic Sea was likely to have frozen over making cheap foreign imports unavailable for the remainder of the season. To meet these problems a sliding scale of duties was introduced in 1828, modified downwards in 1842, and finally abandoned seven years later after a major political crisis in 1846 had brought down Sir Robert Peel's second government and fundamentally divided the Conservative Party. The repeal of the Corn Laws was considered to mark the final triumph of free trade theories in Britain and quickly acquired symbolic importance, though with the drying up of European wheat supplies from the mid-1830s the Corn Laws had ceased to make very much practical difference to the trade in grain (Fairlie, 1965). Repeal did not (as was widely expected) lead to reductions in the price of wheat, though it did reduce fluctuations in the amounts annually imported.

An assessment of the place of the Corn Laws in political economy must depend on what is understood by 'political economy'. In the first half of the 19th century the term was often used in a vulgar sense, and often abusively, to denote the prescriptions of those members of the middle classes who were leading the attack on 'old corruption', as the monopoly of power and privilege by the landed elite was commonly termed. At this level the assault on protection generally, and on agricultural protection in particular, was the sharpest weapon in the political economist's armoury, and for many the work of the Anti-Corn Law League under Cobden and Bright, and the promptings of the *Economist* newspaper, marked 'the high tide of *laissez-faire*'. If, on the other hand, political economy is taken to denote a body of formal economic thought, the Corn Laws must be accorded considerably less significance. Smith had exempted food supply and defence from the areas of public life to which the maxim of free trade should be made to apply, and most of his 19th-century successors were similarly

well disposed to the Laws. Malthus consistently defended them while protesting that in all other matters he was a friend to free trade; Senior, who of all economists was the one most engaged in advising on public policy, and whose political views inclined him against the agricultural lobby, in fact had little to say on the subject. Even J.S. Mill, while welcoming Corn Law repeal, consistently played down the beneficial effects which were likely to flow from it (Blaug, 1968, pp. 192, 215). Probably only Ricardo placed hostility to the Corn Laws at the centre of his system. His corn model postulated that without access to cheap supplies of foreign grain, population pressure would either force domestic farmers onto more marginal land or else would compel them to cultivate the old land more intensively. In either case prices would rise, money wages would rise, profits would decline, and the economy would move towards a stationary state. Similar arguments were made by Torrens in his early work, though later he significantly qualified his opposition to the Corn Laws, and also by McCulloch, though he was always more concerned that the Laws caused excessive price fluctuations, and he eventually came to reject most aspects of the Ricardian corn model (O'Brien, 1970, pp. 378–95). Indeed it has been argued that even for Ricardo the corn model was essentially an abstraction, and that his real animus against the Laws was based on their contribution to price instability and the shelter which they afforded to inefficient producers (Hollander, 1979, pp. 605, 629–37, 647).

Moreover, the reduction and then finally the repeal of the Corn Laws seems to have owed little to economic doctrine. As early as 1821 Lord Liverpool's government envisaged the gradual dismantling of a system which it had always regarded as designed largely to ease the transition from a prolonged state of warfare and *de facto* protection (1793–1815) to a state of peace. Its main concern was with the supply situation, especially the unreliability of Ireland as a granary and increasing dependence on farmers in northern Europe in lean seasons. A subsidiary but significant factor was the return to the gold standard in 1821. It was now thought desirable to render the corn trade as regular (i.e. as little weather-related) as possible, in order to minimize fluctuations in bullion outflows (Hilton, 1977, pp. 98–126). Both these factors operated on Peel in the prelude to repeal in 1846. The Irish Famine of 1845–9 emphasized the precariousness of the situation with regard to domestic supply (though it served to confirm and excuse the policy of repeal rather than initiating it), while the Bank Charter Act of 1844 rendered the money supply more than ever sensitive to movements of bullion. Political factors also obtruded in the decision to repeal: especially, the Anti-Corn Law League's activities threatened a whig victory in the next general election unless something was done to undermine its existence (Prest, 1977, pp. 72–102). Undoubtedly there was also a mythical element in the campaign, the Corn Laws having become a symbol rather than a real guarantee of landed monopoly (Kemp, 1961–2). There was, however, one theoretical argument which may have counted in the decision. This was the adoption of a market theory of wages in preference to the subsistence theory derived from Ricardo and the labour theory of value. The market theory was hardly novel in the 1840s, having been espoused by Malthus, but it was not given public prominence until Cobden bruited it emphatically in his campaign for repeal. Thus Peel ascribed his change of heart on agricultural protection in part at least to a discovery that 'the wages of labour do not vary with the price of grain'. He seems also to have been moved by Cobden's claims that in free trade conditions agriculturists would find it easier to capitalize and to engage in the 'high farming' that would be their competitive salvation. Such confidence seemed to be justified by the 'Golden Age of English Farming' which succeeded repeal, the real challenge to agriculture not occurring until the appearance of imports from the New World in the last quarter of the 19th century. By then, however, the Corn Laws had taken their place with King Richard III and the Inquisition among the 'bad things' of history, so much so that the cry of 'cheap loaf' was to prove politically irresistible, and to impair all early 20th-century attempts at tariff reform and imperial preference.

B. HILTON

See also COBDEN, RICHARD; COMPENSATION PRINCIPLE; MANCHESTER SCHOOL.

BIBLIOGRAPHY

Barnes, D.G. 1938. *A History of the English Corn Laws from 1660–1846.* London: Routledge.

Blaug, M. 1968. *Economic Theory in Retrospect.* 2nd edn, London: Heinemann.

Fairlie, S. 1965. The nineteenth-century corn law reconsidered. *Economic History Review* 18, December, 562–75.

Hilton, B. 1977. *Corn, Cash, Commerce. The Economic Policies of the Tory Governments 1815–1830.* Oxford: Oxford University Press.

Hollander, S. 1970. *The Economics of David Ricardo.* London: Heinemann.

Kemp, B. 1961–2. Reflections on the repeal of the corn laws. *Victorian Studies* 5(3), March, 189–204.

O'Brien, D.P. 1978. *J.R. McCulloch. A Study in Classical Economics.* London: George Allen & Unwin.

Prest, J. 1977. *Politics in the Age of Cobden.* London: Macmillan.

corn model. This expression is commonly used to denote Sraffa's interpretation of the theory of profits formulated by Ricardo in his 1815 *Essay on Profits.* The characteristic feature of this theory is that in the production of corn there is a physical homogeneity between capital and product, because capital (which Ricardo tends to identify with the wages paid in the year) is conceived as entirely consisting of corn. Consequently the rate of profits in agriculture (production of corn) only depends upon the conditions of production of corn, and the amount of corn constituting the wage rate, and is determined independently of prices. The rate of profits of the other sectors will have to adjust to that of agriculture, by means of variations of the price of their product relative to corn. If r is the rate of profits established in agriculture, w the (corn) rate of wages, and L_i the number of workers employed in the production of commodity i, the price of i in terms of corn will be:

$$p_i = WL_i(1 + r)$$

where p_i is the only unknown.

In this conception, the production of corn plays virtually the same role as the Standard system in Sraffa's *Production of Commodities* (as Sraffa himself remarks: 1960, p. 93): corn, being the only basic commodity in the system, is also the Standard commodity (only, it is not a *composite* commodity).

The expression 'corn model' is slightly misleading, in that it may easily suggest that in Ricardo's *Essay* we have a one-sector model, whereas there are in it as many sectors as in his *Principles.* (The expression might perhaps more appropriately be employed for those stylized formulations of Ricardo's theory which, though assuming the existence of another sector beside agriculture, have much in common with one-sector models: e.g. Kaldor, 1955-6, pp. 211–15 and Pasinetti, 1960, pp. 6–10.) A more appropriate expression would be that employed by Sraffa: 'corn-ratio theory' of profits (Sraffa, 1951–73, I, p. xxxiii).

As Sraffa has written, the argument of the physical homogeneity of capital and product in agriculture 'is never stated by Ricardo in any of his extant letters and papers' (ibid., p. xxxi). Sraffa's reconstruction of Ricardo's argument has been questioned, in particular by S. Hollander, in his attempt to revive Marshall's interpretation of Ricardo's theory as an 'incomplete' version of marginalist theory (see Hollander, 1973 and 1979). It should be said, however, that Hollander does not deny the existence in Ricardo of a 'corn model'; he only denies its relevance in Ricardo's theoretical construction (Hollander, 1979, p. 146; for a discussion of Hollander's arguments, see Eatwell, 1975 and Garegnani, 1982).

A 'corn-ratio' theory of profits can be found in quite a few of Ricardo's comtemporaries (Hollander himself notices its existence in Malthus's *Measure of Value*: Hollander, 1979, p. 722). The most interesting case is that of Torrens, in whose 1820 *External Corn Trade* a 'corn-ratio' theory is formulated much more clearly than in Ricardo. The fact that Torrens explicitly avows the Ricardian parentage of this conception, appears as a strong confirmation of Sraffa's reconstruction of Ricardo's argument (see Langer, 1982 and de Vivo, 1985).

G. DE VIVO

See also CLASSICAL ECONOMICS; RICARDO, DAVID; SRAFFA, PIERO.

BIBLIOGRAPHY

De Vivo, G. 1985. Robert Torrens and Ricardo's 'corn-ratio' theory of profits. *Cambridge Journal of Economics* 9(1), March, 89–92.

Eatwell, J. 1975. The interpretation of Ricardo's *Essay on Profits. Economica* 42(166), May, 182 7.

Garegnani, P. 1982. On Hollander's interpretation of Ricardo's early theory of profits. *Cambridge Journal of Economics* 6(1), March, 65–77.

Hollander, S. 1973. Ricardo's analysis of the profit rate, 1813–15. *Economica* 40(159), August, 260–82.

Hollander, S. 1979. *The Economics of David Ricardo.* London: Heinemann.

Kaldor, N. 1955–6. Alternative theories of distribution. *Review of Economic Studies.* As reprinted in N. Kaldor, *Essays on Value and Distribution,* 2nd edn, London: Duckworth, 1980.

Langer, G.F. 1982. Further evidence for Sraffa's interpretation of Ricardo. *Cambridge Journal of Economics* 6(4), December, 397-400.

Pasinetti, L.L. 1960. A mathematical formulation of the Ricardian system. *Review of Economic Studies.* As reprinted in L.L. Pasinetti, *Growth and Income Distribution: Essays in Economic Theory,* Cambridge: Cambridge University Press, 1974.

Sraffa, P. (ed.) 1951–73. *The Works and Correspondence of David Ricardo,* Vols I–XI. Cambridge: Cambridge University Press.

Sraffa, P. 1960. *Production of Commodities by Means of Commodities. Prelude to a Critique of Economic Theory.* Cambridge: Cambridge University Press.

corporate economy. 'The Corporate Economy' is a term of art used loosely to refer to the way the economic system of rich industrialized societies evolved after 1900: a system in which a major part of the production side of the economy is organized by large limited-liability corporations whose shares are traded on organized stock markets. The phrase itself was first used openly in this sense in the title of a book edited by R. Marris and A. Wood published in 1971 (Marris and Wood, 1971). Associated with it are other terms such as 'The Organizational Revolution' (Boulding, 1953), 'The Managerial Revolution' (James Burnham, 1941) and more recently 'The Managerial Paradigm'. The last expression is intended to convey a body of ideas amounting to a picture of the world that is both internally consistent and an agenda of questions and answers. As such, the 'managerial' paradigm is clearly distinguished both from the neo-classical paradigm and from a more loosely conceived 'neo' Marxian paradigm. It particularly depends on the proposition that in the large corporation, owing to inherent difficulties for shareholders in monitoring the performance of managers, there is considerable separation between the vicarious role of stockholders, on the one hand, and the control, operating and policy-making roles of management, on the other. This state of affairs was first identified in a classic work published in 1932 by A.A. Berle and Gardner Means (Berle and Means, 1932).

In reality, the entities involved are diverse in character, and by no means confined to 'independent' or 'private' corporations or companies. They include nationalized industries producing for the market (such representing major elements, for example, in the second half of the 20th Century in the mixed economies of Western Europe), regulated public utilities (e.g. gas or electricity supply) or even, as in Yugoslavia, fairly large 'labour-managed' entities.

Although limited-liability laws were widely promulgated in most of the countries which we now called 'western' from around 1840, by 1910 the largest hundred industrial corporations typically controlled no more than 15 per cent of total industrial value-added (see Prais, 1976). Fifty years later, the figure had trebled. In 1890, Alfred Marshall had written 'there are few exceptions to the rule that large firms ... are, in proportion to their size, inferior to businesses of moderate size, in energy, resources ... and inventive power' (Marshall, 1980). Marshall automatically assumed that all business was family business, ignoring the potentiality of continuing organization. (See e.g. the famous passage comparing firms to 'trees of the forest' in his *Principles*, 1st edition.) Nevertheless, Marshall's characterization of industrial organization remained at the heart of neoclassical economics for the next hundred years. It assumes, almost axiomatically, that the basic economic agents on the production side of the economy, namely firms, must have decreasing returns to scale. By contrast, modern corporations attain gigantic scales with little evidence of increasing internal inefficiency. If returns to scale should be typically *increasing* or even merely constant, however, competitive equilibrium does not exist.

Institutionalist writers such as Thorsten Veblen or John Kenneth Galbraith have ascribed this internal contradiction of the neoclassical system to conspiracy, to defects of the method of economic science or to both. There is some force in either accusation.

It is not the case, however, that the problem has been studied by heterodox economists only. Since the late 1950s, an increasing number of mainstream writers have addressed the problem. The works of Masahiko Aoki, Robin Marris, Dennis Mueller, Hiroyuki Odagiri, Edith Penrose, Herbert Simon, Hirofumi Uzawa, Oliver Williamson and George Yarrow (alphabetical, not historical, order) may all be cited. Starting from the seminal book of Edith Penrose published in 1959, continuing through the later work of Williamson, Marris and Aoki, a sub-group of these writers have emphasized the significance of *organization* in the emergence of the corporate economy.

In the economic progress of the 20th century, in contrast to that of the 19th century, organization, and especially large-scale organization, has played a major role. The key factor has been the human race's ability to devise means to restrain administrative inefficiency. The proposition that provided it is properly led and organized, a large army will usually beat a smaller army, is as true in the economic as in the military sphere. The typical solution – the organizational hierarchy – is also similar in both spheres. Oliver Williamson (1970) was the first economist to emphasize the significance of the bureaucratic hierarchy in

business organization, but the seed of the idea is found in an earlier contribution of Williamson's teacher, Herbert Simon (1957). (The classic conceptualizations of bureaucracy and hierarchy in modern society are, of course, due to the sociologist Max Weber.) More generally, Williamson, in a massive life-work culminating in the publication, in 1985, of his *Economic Institutions of Capitalism*, has contributed to a reconstruction of the theory of the firm to accommodate modern realities. His approach is based on transactions-analysis: the business organization, large or small, is conceived as a hidden structure of implicit contracts, existing on account of the impracticality of competitive economic organization based mainly on explicit contracts. In Williamson's conception the problem of separation of ownership from control is thus an aspect of the general 'agency problem' (control of delegatee by delegator) which then inevitably arises.

IMPLICATIONS OF THE PARADIGM. From the nature of the case, the full implications of a paradigm cannot easily be summarized; if they are not diverse or unanticipated, the paradigm is not a paradigm. Questions especially addressed by the managerial paradigm are the theory of the growth of the firm; the cooperative-game theory of the firm; role of producer organizations in the stimulation of innovation and technical progress; mergers and business concentration; the micro foundations of macro economics; the theory of economic growth.

THE THEORY OF THE GROWTH OF THE FIRM. In the competitive paradigm, firms are neurons of the 'invisible hand'. Like actual neurons, they are not supposed to grow, nor indeed to have any motivation of their own. But in the corporate economy, if producer organizations can and do grow indefinitely, why has not the most successful among them swallowed the whole economy? More generally, *why* and *how* do firms grow? What forces stimulate, or, alternatively, constrain, the process? Is it possible that the standard model of neoclassical micro-theory, where the absolute sizes of firms are endogenous elements in the general solution for prices and quantities in industries and in the economy, can be replaced by a theory in which a similar role is played by the rate of change of size, i.e. by the firm's rate of growth?

Penrose postulated that both stimuli and constraints for growth arose out of the firm's inherent character as an administrative organization. Marris and Uzawa postulated closed models in which the stimuli arose from the internal motives of management, the constraints from external markets for goods, money and shares. The firm could grow faster by devoting more cash-flow to growth-creating activities – such as research and development – but in so doing reduced cash-flow available for dividends. If, thus created, growth was excessive, actual or potential owners of the shares would tend to become sellers, rather than buyers, tend to depress the market price of the stock, these results tending in turn to invite unwelcome attentions from take-over raiders. This type of model can be, and (especially in the hands of Odagiri, 1981) has been, developed to determine all other variables in the theory of the firm: product prices, production technology, research effort, diversification rate and profits.

From Marris onwards, all contributors have awarded the threat of merger a major role, as indicated, in *constraining* management. Mueller (1969), however, suggested that the other side of this coin could be equally significant. Who were the typical raiders? Mueller's answer was that they would be other managerially motivated corporations seeking mergers as a means to satisfy their own ambitions. Mueller (1972) also convincingly demonstrated a 'life-cycle' version of the managerial theory, in which the greatest potentiality for divergence of interest between management and stockholders came at a late stage of the life cycle, when special opportunities were exhausted and stockholders would do better with their money released to invest elsewhere.

COOPERATIVE THEORY OF THE FIRM. The 'managerialist' theories, such as those of Marris, Uzawa, Yarrow and Odagiri (historical order), assume that management-controlled firms are governed by managers for the benefit of managers, subject only to *constraints* from shareholders, workers or society. In sharp contrast, Aoki (1984) conceives of high management as arbitrator between the interests of existing employees and existing shareholders. This means that the high management will aim for a solution, which Aoki calls 'organizational equilibrium', that is equivalent to the solution that would be obtained if both sides were perfectly represented by agents who would behave according to the axioms of rational bargaining in game theory (see literature cited by Aoki, 1984, pp. 69 et seq.). In general such processes mostly conclude by equalizing each side's proportionate utility gain as compared with the respective expected outcomes if negotiation broke down. The result represents a distribution of *organizational rent*, the latter being the surplus derived by the organization, from society, through possessing specific synergistic human resources. The employees will usually have sufficient bargaining strength to obtain some share in this rent: so the wage will exceed the 'competitive' wage. Thus in the corporate economy, as conceived by Aoki, every business organization is engaged in a general game of monopolistic competition with every other, and each will divide the resulting proceeds in some way between rewarding existing workers, rewarding existing stockholders, and growth. At the micro level, the theory, like Odagiri's, can therefore uniquely determine price, output, wages, dividends, and growth.

FORMAL 'NEW' THEORIES OF THE FIRM. In the managerialist models, the firm is assumed to earn profit in a traditional way from existing activities, but to devote a part of the result to various activities intended to expand its own environment and permit long-term growth without falling profitability. The faster a firm attempts thus to grow, however, the more it is liable to become subject to what has become known as the 'Penrose effect', that is, increased costs and inefficiency caused by internal organizational problems associated with the speed of expansion. The latter costs, together with other developmental costs, are now called generically 'the costs of growth'. Normalized by reference to the size of the firm, they can be represented as an increasing function of the growth rate itself (see equation (1) below). For simplicity the resulting models were then formulated as steady-state growth models.

Unlike tangible investment expenditure, in business statistics costs of growth are usually treated as current expenses, deducted from cash flow before reporting profits. Reported profits are therefore operating profits less costs of growth; dividends are reported profits less cash retained for tangible investment in plant and inventory also associated with expansion. Assuming for simplicity that expansion is 100 per cent internally financed (it can be shown that the assumption is not important), the result (equation (2)) is a unique relationship between the level of the dividend and the growth rate. However, in steady state, with no new external finance, if the costs of growth are satisfied, growth occurs at a constant operating profit rate, hence, with a constant number of shareholders, the growth rates of assets and of dividends per share are equal. Thus the model generates a relationship, susceptible to *managerial* choice, between level of dividends and growth of dividends. It is then assumed that

current dividends and expected growth of dividends (the latter being the equivalent of anticipated capital gains), together determine stock market valuation: equation (3) is the standard formula for the present value of a stream of dividends growing to infinity at the rate g, discounted at the rate i, subject to the restriction $g < i$. Hence the end result is a managerial choice between growth rate and stock market value (equation (4)), now generally known as 'the v-g frontier'.

Management is then envisaged as possessing a utility function (equation (5)) whose arguments are, in fact, the dimensions of the frontier, the one (growth rate) representing the aspirations for future salary and psychic satisfaction, the other (valuation ratio) the aversion to risk of take-over. If management was motivated to maximize the interests of the stockholders only, caring nothing for growth per se, they would simply use equation (4) to maximize valuation; the resulting growth rate would be smaller but not necessarily zero.

The algebra is as follows:

$$p = a - p(g) \tag{1}$$

$$d = \{1 - r\}p = p - g \tag{2}$$

$$v = d/\{i - g\} = \{p - g\}/\{i - g\} \tag{3}$$

$$v = \{a - p(g) - g\}/\{i - g\} \tag{4}$$

$$U = U(g, v) \tag{5}$$

where p = profits per unit of assets; g = steady-state proportional growth rate of assets = proxy for growth rate of organization; a = 'operating profit rate' (p under zero growth); $p(g)$ = costs of growth ($p' > 0$); d = dividend per unit of assets; r = profit retention ratio (model assumes 100% internal financing hence $r = g/p$); v = stock market value of equity shares, per unit of assets ('valuation ratio'); i = rate at which stock market discounts expected future earnings; U = managerial utility ($g', v' \geqq 0$).

The above model was tested, with somewhat negative results, by Cubbin (1986). It has also been criticized on two major theoretical grounds, namely firstly (see Solow, 1971) that it can only determine the rate of change, and not the absolute level, of the size of the organization, a weakness which is most marked in applications of micro-economic general equilibrium; secondly that the utility function, and the v-g frontier are not independent (John Williamson, 1966; Yarrow, 1976; Odagiri, 1981). The first weakness is self-evident from the equations. The second arises from the fact that the strength of the fear of take-over (which must affect the 'shape' of the managerial U-function) partly depends on the attractiveness of the firm to outsiders, and the latter in turn depends on the maximum value that could be extracted under valuation-maximizing policies – i.e. on the location of the peak of the v-g frontier. In their different contexts, both flaws are serious.

Odagiri (1981) escapes both weaknesses first by marrying the model to a conventional static theory of the firm, with fully specified conventional elements (production function, factor prices etc.) and then by reconstructing the managerial utility-maximizing procedure. For the second stage, he assumes that (a) there is an exogenous 'cost of take over', i.e. premium over current market share price which, owing to capital-market imperfection, must be paid by any raider and (b) that management maximizes discounted expected future salary subject to the hazard of being taken over, i.e. subject to the hazard of employment and salary terminating entirely. As described below, Odagiri's further, major, achievement consisted of aggregating from the micro level, thus modified, to a macro-growth theory.

Similar algebra can also be used to illustrate Aoki's theory. In reviewing Aoki (1984) in a Japanese journal in 1986/7,

Marris suggested that the real wage in the Aoki theory would become,

$$w = 1/z + s(z - 1) \qquad (6)$$

where $z = 1 - 1/e$, and e = monopolistic competition elasticity of demand. From which it follows (assuming constant returns and no non-labour non-capital inputs) that the operating profit rate is given by (7),

$$a = \{k - w\}/c, \qquad (7)$$

where k = output per worker and c = capital output ratio. Hence

$$a = f(k, c, z, s). \qquad (8)$$

If (8) is substituted into (4) and U re-maximized subject to the reconstituted constraint it seems intuitively likely that the optimum growth rate, and the workers' bargaining share (s) will be negatively related. Aoki confirms rigorously that this is so (1984, pp. 78 et seq). Thus intuitive 'marriage' of Odagiri (see below) and Aoki suggests that other things being equal a corporate economy will grow faster (i) the less the workers' bargaining power; (ii) the less the shareholders' bargaining power (as reflected in take-over conditions); (iii) and the less the competitiveness of the economy as reflected in elasticity of demand! These are classic examples of conclusions from the managerial paradigm that cannot be obtained from the neo-classical paradigm.

GENERAL MICRO-ECONOMICS. At the end of the day, the concept of the 'industry' becomes blurred, and the production side of the economic stage becomes inhabited by agile dinosaurs, 'competing' for growth and profits but not necessarily engaging in strong price competition in individual markets. If the domestic economy becomes too small for them, they become multinational. Following a scheme suggested by Marris (1971), we may see an individual economy in this universe as a two-way table in which rows represent named organizations, columns, products or 'markets'. (In the Marshallian terminology, the rows would be 'firms', the columns 'industries'.) Elements in this matrix represent the contribution of a given organization to a given market. In the neoclassical paradigm, there is only one entry in each row (one firm, one industry) and many entries per column (perfect competition). In the corporate economy, there may be a number of entries in a row (any organization may be diversified); but, on account of economies of scale and the instability of competitive equilibrium, there will usually be only a moderate number of entries in columns, i.e. the typical situation is oligopoly.

It follows that the micro-economics of the corporate economy are essentially based on theories of imperfect competition and oligopoly; on this analysis the competitive economy is impossible.

But the matrix is not static. A major part of managerial effort is devoted to efforts to changing it. As a result of R&D, the list of columns (products) changes. As a result of mergers, the list of rows (organizations) changes. The general process needs analyzing by the micro theory of the growth of the firm, and, in turn, contributes to the micro foundations of macro growth economics.

ECONOMIC CONCENTRATION. In industrial economics it is usual to assess the potential competitiveness of a market by two factors, the proportion of sales controlled by the largest n firms (where n is a number like 4 or 5), and other elements in barriers to entry. In our matrix, 'industrial concentration' is therefore a characteristic of the columns. Entry occurs in the rows; its most likely cause is a previously zero element becoming positive; an existing organization enters a new field. Since existing organizations may well be large, the corporate economy does not reduce, and may increase, this type of competition. Nor does this system necessarily imply any long term tendency for increased average 'column-wise' (i.e. 'within-industry') concentration.

But another form of economic concentration occurs in the row-totals. Sometimes known as 'business concentration' or 'macro concentration', this type can be measured by the proportion of industrial output controlled by the m largest organizations, where m is a number like 100 or 200. That statistic increased sharply in all countries between 1910 and 1960, and is still apparently increasing in Europe. In the US, in the past twenty years, it has apparently been stabilized by new entry into the total organizational population (see Spillberg, 1985).

Macro concentration will be the product of two forces: (i) the internal growth of firms (organizations); (ii) mergers. Building on the earlier work of Gibrat (1931), Prais (1976) developed an elegant application of the theory of Markov chains to show how stochastic disturbance of internal growth rates could produce an automatic tendency to concentration without invoking any other systematic forces. Marris (1979) married this theory with the theory of the growth of the firm, and also with a managerialist/stochastic model of the merger process, to produce a general theory of concentration. If there are constant returns to scale, in the absence of macro new entry, business concentration will increase at a constant rate through time. With increasing returns, the process is exploding. With decreasing returns, concentration increases at a diminishing rate converging to an asymptote. (Although decreasing returns in respect of absolute size is supposedly ruled out in the managerial paradigm, the same results are also obtained if there are corresponding associations between absolute size and rate of change of size.)

MICRO FOUNDATIONS OF MACRO GROWTH ECONOMICS. One of the weaknesses of macro-economic growth theory, as it emerged in the aftermath of the Keynesian revolution, lay in depending on a general rate of technological progress which was not only exogenous but unexplained. An advantage of corporate-economy theory lies in being able to explain the growth rate, at least in part, from within the model. The proposition was hinted at in the last chapter of Marris (1964) but was not further developed before the appearance of an extremely comprehensive theory published by H. Odagiri in 1981. After refining and synthesizing the micro theory of the growth of the firm, Odagiri elegantly succeeds in aggregating to the economy-wide level, producing a model in which a number of interpretable behavioural or technical variables, together with government-policy variables, such as monetary and fiscal variables, actually determine the growth rate of the economy. The crucial factor is that, in striving for growth of itself, an organization creates (via induced technical progress) growth for the economy. Two micro factors are keys to Odagiri's macro growth rate; the strength of management's risk aversion when trading fear of take-over with desire for growth-led salary increase; and the institutional ease or difficulty of take-overs. In the second half of the 20th century, in Japan, on the one hand, under the system of 'life time employment' (informal security of tenure) managers, effectively locked into their firms, were in consequence likely to have comparatively strong growth preference, while on the other hand the organization of the Japanese capital market was not conducive to ease of take-overs. From such facts the managerial theory would predict fast growth of firms and the economy. The neoclassical theory, by contrast, would either have nothing to say, or give the opposite predictions. The actual result was that during this period, the growth rate of Japanese economy was by any standard exceptional; the 'Japanese miracle' may thus be seen as an outstanding achievement of the Corporate Economy.

R. L. MARRIS

See also ECONOMIC THEORY OF THE STATE; INDUSTRIAL ORGANIZATION.

BIBLIOGRAPHY

Alchian, A.A. (With H. Demsetz.) 1972. Production, information costs and economic organization. *American Economic Review* 62, December, 777–95.

Aoki, M. 1984. *The Co-operative Game Theory of the Firm.* Oxford: Oxford University Press.

Boulding, K.J. 1953. *The Organizational Revolution.* New York: Harper.

Burnham, J. 1941. *The Managerial Revolution.* New York: The John Day Co.

Cubbin, J. 1986. Testing the Marris model. *Managerial Economics,* June.

Galbraith, J.K. 1952. *American Capitalism.* Boston: Houghton Mifflin.

Galbraith, J.K. 1967. *The New Industrial State.* Boston: Houghton Mifflin.

Gibrat, F. 1931. *Les inégalités économiques.* Paris: Recueil Sirey.

Kuehn, D. 1975. *Takeovers and the Theory of the Firm.* London: Macmillan.

Marris, R.L. 1964. *The Economic Theory of 'Managerial' Capitalism.* London and New York: Macmillan.

Marris, R.L. (ed., with Adrian Wood.) 1971. *The Corporate Economy.* London and Cambridge, Mass.: Harvard University Press.

Marris, R.L. 1979. *The Theory and Future of the Corporate Economy.* Amsterdam: North-Holland Press.

Marris, R.L. 1986/7. Review of Aoki (1984) in *Keizai Kenko.*

Marshall, A. 1890. *Address to the British Association.*

Marshall, A. 1890. *Principles of Economics.* Successive editions, 1891–1920. London: Macmillan.

Means, G.C. (With A.A. Berle.) 1932. *The Modern Corporation and Private Property.* New York: Macmillan.

Mueller, D. 1969. A theory of conglomerate merger. *Quarterly Journal of Economics* 83(4), November, 643–59.

Mueller, D. 1972. A life cycle theory of the firm. *Journal of Industrial Economics* 20(3), July, 199–219.

Mueller, D. 1984. Further reflections on the invisible-hand theorem. In *Economics in Disarray,* ed. P. Wiles, Oxford: Oxford University Press.

Mueller, D. and Marris, R.L. 1980. The corporation, competition and the invisible hand. *Journal of Economic Literature.*

Odagiri, H. 1981. *The Theory of Growth in a Corporate Economy.* Cambridge: Cambridge University Press.

Odagiri, H. 1982. Anti-neoclassical management motivation in a neoclassical economy: a model of economic growth and Japan's experience. *Kyklos* 35(2), 223–43.

Penrose, E. 1959. *The Theory of the Growth of the Firm.* Oxford: Oxford University Press.

Penrose, E. 1985. The theory of the growth of the firm 25 years after. *Acta Universitatis Upsalienis,* Uppsala.

Prais, S. 1976. *The Evolution of Giant Firms in Britain.* Cambridge: Cambridge University Press.

Simon, H. 1957a. *Models of Man.* New York: Wiley.

Simon, H. 1957b. The compensation of executives. *Sociometry* 20(1), March, 32–5.

Simon, H. (With C. Bonini.) 1958. The size distribution of business firms. *American Economic Review* 48, September, 607–17.

Simon, H. 1972. Theories of bounded rationality. In *Decision and Organization,* ed. C. Maguire and R. Radner, Amsterdam: North-Holland.

Solow, R. 1971. Some implications of alternative criteria for the firm. In Marris and Wood (1971).

Uzawa, H. 1969. Time preference and the Penrose effect in economic growth. *Journal of Political Economy* 77, 628–52.

Veblen, T. 1923. *Absentee Ownership and Business Enterprise in Recent Times.* New York: B.W. Huebsch.

Weber, M. 1921. *Economy and Society.* Ed. G. Roth, New York: Bedminster Press, 1968.

Williamson, J. 1966. Profit, growth and sales maximization. *Economica* 33, 1–16.

Williamson, O. 1964. *The Economics of Discretionary Behavior.* Englewood Cliffs: Prentice Hall.

Williamson, O. 1970. *Corporate Control and Business Behavior.* Englewood Cliffs: Prentice Hall.

Williamson, O. 1975. *Markets and Hierarchies.* Englewood Cliffs: Prentice Hall.

Williamson, O. 1985. *The Economic Institutions of Capitalism.* New York: Free Press.

Yarrow, G. 1976. On the predictions of managerial theories of the firm. *Journal of Industrial Economics* 24(4), June, 267–79.

corporate taxation. *See* TAXATION OF CORPORATE PROFITS.

corporations. The concept 'corporation' has two distinct usages that cannot be subsumed under a single definition. The original meaning, dating back to medieval England, was a group that received a franchise (a special privilege or immunity) evidenced by a royal charter conveying a grant to them and their successors in perpetuity. The modern meaning, dating from the 17th century, is a legal and contractual mechanism for owning a business, using capital from investors that will be managed on their behalf by directors and officers.

MEDIEVAL CORPORATIONS. The earliest 'corporations' in medieval England were boroughs, guilds, churches and charities. Beginning in the 12th century, boroughs petitioned for the privilege of taxing themselves, thereby cutting out the king's rapacious middlemen, the tax-farmers. Guilds sought royal permission to enforce standardized prices and to regulate hours and wages for their journeymen and apprentices. Churches wanted their bishops and abbots to be classified as perpetual offices, so title to church lands would not escheat to the Crown whenever a bishop or abbot died. The creator of a charitable trust – a hospital or university, for example – needed the king's approval to transfer property to a board of trustees who, by choosing their own successors, could exist forever.

The church office was known as a 'corporation sole', the others were 'corporations aggregate', but none of them created any patterns or established any precedents relevant to voluntary business activity or to investment for profit. Therefore, they cannot be called the ancestors or forerunners of modern-day business corporations (Hessen, 1979).

DEFECTIVE DEFINITIONS. Those who hold the contrary view try to link medieval and modern corporations under a sweeping definition: a group of individuals who unite for a common purpose and act in a common name. This attempt fails because the definition equally well fits a partnership, or a labour union, and even a nation. Another definition – a group with continuity of existence despite changes in its membership – tries to encompass medieval and modern corporations, but it does so only by falsely implying that nearly every group is a corporation, even a family, an army, or the human race.

JOINT-STOCK COMPANIES. The apparent ancestors of today's corporations were the joint-stock companies that flourished in England during the 16th and 17th centuries. They were created to explore and trade overseas, raising capital by selling shares. Decision making was concentrated in the hands of the directors, so the shares were freely transferable from one investor to another. These companies had to secure a royal charter of incorporation because freedom of commerce – the right to travel and trade overseas – was not recognized by the Tudors and Stuarts. But they were not free market ventures as long as they asked for and accepted monopoly grants from the Crown to explore or colonize in a particular overseas area and to sell their imports in the British home market.

Joint-stock companies did not become the forerunners of today's corporations until they became fully private. At the end of the 17th century, British businessmen discovered they could create a corporate venture without bothering to acquire a charter. They simply copied the structure of the companies that held royal or parliamentary charters. This enabled them to create joint-stock associations that offered investors the attraction of freely transferable shares. However, in 1720, at the urging of a chartered corporation, the South Sea Company, which resented the newcomers' competition for investors' capital, Parliament passed the Bubble Act. It forbade companies without charters from issuing transferable shares or otherwise imitating corporate features.

CORPORATIONS DE FACTO. The Bubble Act backfired; businessmen and barristers soon devised a second way of acquiring corporate features without obtaining a charter. They combined two long-established common law forms, the partnership and the trust. By designating a few of the potentially numerous partners as trustees for all the others and by giving them exclusive authority to make contracts with outside parties, they concentrated managerial power in a few hands. Consequently, all other investors could be offered freely transferable partnership interests (virtually identical to corporate shares). The success of these unincorporated associations forced Parliament to relent: the Companies Act of 1844 set up a simple procedure for creating a corporation.

Although Parliament had extended the Bubble Act to the American colonies in 1741, the Act did not inhibit the formation of joint-stock companies. Like their British counterparts, American business promoters were able to create corporate features without incorporating. They attracted millions of dollars of capital from investors for large-scale, long-term enterprises, including textile factories and land development companies (Livermore, 1939).

THE ERA OF SPECIAL CHARTERS. Nonetheless, despite the easy availability of the unincorporated business association, some American firms continued to incur the expense of becoming corporations de jure. They did so because corporations and charters took on a new meaning in the late 18th century, after the American Revolution. The state legislatures were eager to encourage the investment of private funds to supply quasi-governmental services, so they began to create corporate franchises authorizing firms to build and operate a canal, bridge, wharf or harbour, a bank, or a water, fire-fighting or street-improvement company. Businessmen, who otherwise would have formed a partnership or an unincorporated business association, spent the money needed to secure a special charter from the state legislature because they thereby acquired privileges that were not otherwise available. These included a legally enforced monopoly, tax exemption, release of employees from militia and jury duty, power to exercise eminent domain, and authorization to hold lotteries as a means of raising capital.

THE ERA OF GENERAL INCORPORATION LAWS. These special charters, often expedited by bribery, were denounced by the Jacksonian reformers (William Leggett, John Vethake, Theodore Sedgwick and William Gouge). They called for the abolition of all legally protected monopolies and special privileges. Their viewpoint quickly triumphed. A new era

began in 1837 when Connecticut enacted the first all-purpose, general incorporation statute: it established a standardized, simplified procedure for creating a corporation.

Under Connecticut's law, which other states began to copy, the promoters of a corporation no longer had to obtain a special charter from the state legislature. Instead, they only had to file certain factual information with a state official. Therefore, in a literal sense, no governmental permission is needed to create a corporation. It is created by private contract. The state's role is simply to serve as a registry, just as it does for recording the birth of babies or transferring title to cars or land.

STATE RESTRICTIONS ON CORPORATIONS. The traditional explanation of why state incorporation laws are enabling or permissive, rather than restrictive, is that the various state legislatures engaged in a 'competition of laxity'. In 1935 Justice Louis D. Brandeis called it 'a race to the bottom' to see which state would impose the fewest restraints on corporations. For example, before the enactment of the general incorporation statutes, state legislatures had imposed limits on the amount of capital a corporation could raise and placed a strict time limit on its existence. Every charter had to specify the corporation's authorized purpose, and if any venture seemed to exceed the permissible scope, it was subject to challenge for being *ultra vires* (acts beyond a corporation's express and implied powers).

Corporations quickly found ways to thwart such restraints. In Massachusetts, for example, corporations were prohibited by law from owning any real estate, except the land required for their own factories and offices. They circumvented this barrier by acquiring real estate through a business trust. A trust – a common law device – can be a corporation *de facto*, featuring limited liability, freely transferable shares, centralized management, and continuity of existence. The availability of the Massachusetts trust as an alternative to incorporation forced legislatures to ease their efforts to restrict corporations.

CORPORATE ADVANTAGES WITHOUT INCORPORATION. In fact, the chief force that propelled the enactment of the general incorporation statutes was not a nefarious 'competition of laxity' between the states, but rather the easy availability of *three* organizational forms that would yield corporate advantages without incorporation. The first alternative was to create a limited partnership, a statutory form that concentrates managerial authority in the general partners, thus enabling the investors, the limited partners, to receive freely transferable interests. The second option was to create a joint-stock company, an unincorporated form in which investors receive no voice in management. Shares in a joint-stock company are freely transferable because unlike the situation in a partnership, the investors are not authorized to make valid contracts for the company, instead, managerial control resides only in the trustees or directors and their designated agents. The third possibility was to raise capital and sell freely transferable shares by creating a business trust. The investors, known as the beneficiaries of the trust, are entitled to the profits, but legal title and exclusive power of control over the assets is vested in the trustees.

ORGANIZATIONAL ALTERNATIVES. Those who criticize the permissiveness of the state incorporation laws overlook the fact that every organizational form is actually a contract, each with a particular mix of features that distinguishes it from other forms. They are like ready-to-wear clothes: if they fit well, they can be worn without alterations, or they can be modified until they fit better. With the right legal craftsmanship or tailoring, any form can be modified to suit the needs of any business. The choice of form is optional, not mandatory, and firms of all sizes can be operated under any organizational form (even a general partnership). Moreover, state incorporation laws are not intended to be prescriptive, that is, to set forth rules and procedures that must be obeyed. Instead, they are *suppletory*: they set forth a norm which applies only if no agreement to modify the norm has been made. (The laws of partnership and of intestacy – dying without a will – serve exactly the same purpose).

ARE CORPORATIONS 'CREATURES OF THE STATE'? Corporations usually are viewed as 'creatures of the state' because three features – entity status, perpetual duration and limited liability – allegedly can exist only by state creation.

Entity status means that a corporation can sue and be sued in its own name, whereas a partnership can only sue in the name of its individual owners. But entity status is an optional feature for all firms. The owners of an unincorporated business can designate trustees to represent them in lawsuits and to accept and convey title to property on their behalf.

Unlike a partnership, which automatically dissolves whenever one of the general partners dies, goes bankrupt, is expelled, or wishes to withdraw, a corporation is considered 'immortal' or 'eternal' because it continues to exist despite changes in the ranks of its owners, and because the promoters of a corporation may indicate 'perpetual duration' in the articles of incorporation. But the 'privilege' of perpetuity is no guarantee that a corporation will continue forever – more than half of all new corporate ventures fail and go out of existence within five years. Conversely, while partnerships are not automatically perpetual, firms of attorneys, accountants, architects and stockbrokers operated as partnerships for a century or more. Partners can easily make their enterprise perpetual by agreeing that the firm will not be liquidated if a general partner dies or withdraws.

At first glance, limited liability does seem to be a state-created benefit conferred exclusively upon corporations. According to legal theorists, a corporation is an entity distinct from the shareholders, so it contracts debts in its own name, not theirs. Hence 'they' (the owners) are not responsible for 'its' (the corporation's) debts. But there is no need to hypothesize 'artificial legal entities' or 'fictitious legal persons'. Limited liability derives from an implied contract between corporate shareholders and their creditors. Use of the symbols 'Inc.' or 'Corp.' constitutes a warning – constructive notice – to potential creditors that the shareholders do not accept unlimited personal liability. Creditors can, and often do, require that one or several of the shareholders become personal guarantors or sureties for the debt, but if they fail to insist on this safeguard, they are accepting limited liability by implied contract.

MUTUAL AGENCY VS. FREE TRANSFERABILITY. The crucial difference between a partnership and a corporation relates to agency authority. Partners are mutual agents, each able to sign contracts binding on all the partners, so restrictions are placed on the transferability of partnership interests. But since shareholders are *not* mutual agents, shares are freely transferable; they can be sold or given to anyone without placing the other investors at the mercy of a new owner's lack of wisdom, experience, or integrity. This means that a corporation's capital can be supplied by hundreds, thousands, or even millions of investors, each a stranger to all the others. By selling shares of stock, a corporation can raise sums of money that far exceed the assets of any one person or small group of investors. And it means that a corporation's

long-term capital needs can be supplied by a steady succession of short-term investors. Free transferability facilitates instant liquidity. There is no need to obtain the other owners' approval of a prospective new investor, no waiting period before one can sell one's shares, and no penalty for early withdrawal.

The special genius of the corporate form is its capacity to serve as a *financial intermediary* – a matchmaker between savers (investors) and borrowers (workers and managers). The success of corporations gives the lie to claims that industrialization and a rising standard of living require central planning, forced labour, or confiscating private savings to raise capital.

ROBERT HESSEN

See also INDUSTRIAL ORGANIZATION.

BIBLIOGRAPHY
Berle, A.A., Jr. and Means, G.C. 1932. *The Modern Corporation and Private Property*. New York: Macmillan.
Bromberg, A.R. 1968. *Crane and Bromberg on Partnership*. St Paul, Minnesota: West.
DuBois, A.B. 1938. *The English Business Company After the Bubble Act, 1720–1800*. New York: Commonwealth Fund.
Hessen, R. 1979. *In Defense of the Corporation*. Stanford: Hoover Institution Press.
Hessen, R. 1983. The modern corporation and private property: a reappraisal. *Journal of Law and Economics* 26(2), June, 273-89.
Livermore, S. 1939. *Early American Land Companies: Their Influence on Corporate Development*. New York: Commonwealth Fund.

corporatism. Corporatism is a set of political doctrines aimed at organizing civil society on the basis of professional and occupational representation in chambers called Estates or Corporations. It maintains that class conflict is not inherent in the capitalist system of production and ownership relations. Corporatism has its ideological roots mainly in 19th-century French and Italian Catholic social thought, as well as in German romanticism and idealism. Corporative ideas can be found in eminent European thinkers. Hegel, in his *Philosophy of Right*, thought of a corporate structure in which the Estates constituted the link between civil society and the State (Hegel, 1821). In France, Durkheim put forward a view of corporatism specifically related to the division of labour engendered by modern industry. According to Durkheim, the Corporations' task is to diversify at the level of each industry the general principles of industrial legislation formulated by the political assemblies (Durkheim, 1893).

The Catholic strand appeared first as a response to the social cleavages stemming from the industrialization of Europe. It advocated a return to the corporate form of guild associations of the Middle Ages, which it romantically viewed as based on social harmony. In 1891 the papal encyclical Rerum Novarum took a more reformist approach. It rejected the notion that 'class is naturally hostile to class, and that the wealthy and the working men are intended by nature to live in mutual conflict' (Rerum Novarum, 1891; in Camp, 1969, p. 81). At the same time it recognized the legitimacy of independent worker's unions, although preference was given to the creation of a single organization embracing employers and employees. In practice the Catholic movement opted for the first variant, partly because the industrialists rejected the idea of a single organization and partly because of the strength of the Socialist-led unions.

Where politics were concerned, in countries like Italy and Germany, the Catholics gradually reconciled their corporative social views with parliamentarism. In other instances, the

Catholic movement aimed at supplanting parliamentary institutions altogether. In Austria, for example, the alliance between the Social Christians and the fascist Heimwehr was the basis of the corporative Constitution passed before the assassination of Chancellor Dolfuss, in 1934.

Germany produced an important theoretician of corporatism: Karl Marlo. He wrote a comprehensive critique of liberalism in favour of Estate organizations (Marlo, 1885). His views are a reaction to the radicalization of the working class, which led to the 1848 Revolution. In that year, Marlo proposed to the Frankfurt Parliament that it form a social chamber composed by the representatives of all occupations whose task would be to formulate the social legislation to be approved by the political chamber.

Modern corporatism begins with the idealist jurist and Italian nationalist Alfredo Rocco. In his conception corporatism was an instrument for fostering the productive power of the nation. He considered the Estates to be merely organs of the State.

Italian fascism absorbed Rocco's views from its inception, although it combined them with elements of Catholic corporatism as well as with aspects of the doctrine of revolutionary syndicalism held by Georges Sorel (Togliatti, 1970). The syndicalist component was eliminated in 1926 when Rocco, who had become Mussolini's Minister of Justice, legally recognized the fascist unions only, banning all the others in existence. Under the pressure of the employers' association, Italian Confederation of Industry, shop floor committees, which the syndicalists wanted to retain, were also outlawed. The Italian corporative state was institutionalized when in 1927 a labour charter (Carta del Lavoro) was promulgated and, in 1934, a law was issued establishing 22 Estates. In 1939 their 500 delegates formed the Camera dei Fasci e delle Corporazioni, which replaced the Chamber of Deputies.

Italy's corporative state did not coordinate economic activity. Instead, it enabled the Government to control labour relations by making tutelage over the newly created labour unions legal. It enforced arbitration tribunals formed by a judge and two experts, thereby excluding any kind of worker representation even from the fascist unions (Salvemini, 1936; Rossi, 1955).

The rescue operations to save the Banca Commerciale which led to the formation in 1933 of the state-holding IRI (Institute for Industrial Reconstruction) are to be linked to the impact of the Depression on the endemic banking crisis in Italy rather than to any corporative economic programme. Already in 1922, Piero Sraffa pointed out that the frequent crises of Italy's banking system were caused by the fact that bank's activities were based on lending short while borrowing long. Sraffa showed that this was a structural characteristic of the Italian economy (Sraffa, 1922). The Depression magnified the above tendencies and the Government found itself compelled to intervene on an unprecedented scale.

The corporative juridical structure only played an indirect economic role. It legalized, as part of the Estates, a very subordinate form of unionism, while allowing the employers to struggle – within the Estates – for the creation of Consortia which, once approved, become compulsory (Rossi, 1955). Here there is both a similarity and a difference vis-à-vis the German case. The National Socialist regime pursued a policy of forced cartelization – an objective shared by many industrial groups well before 1933 – but not through a legal system of a syndicalist, corporative character. Workers were organized in a completely separate body called the Labour Front (Neumann, 1944; Kuczynski, 1945).

The juridically more complete nature of Italian corporatism became a reference for populist movements in South America. One important example is the Estado Novo established in Brazil under President Getulio Vargas in the years 1937–46. Following the Italian pattern a Labour Charter was issued. The decree-laws of 1939 legalized government prerogatives over labour unions, which were exercised by the Ministry of Labour.

Unlike Italy, Brazilian corporatism allowed the emergence of strong reformist demands. Although labour relations were governed by norms which prevented the formation of alliances between different groups of workers, the process leading to the corporative state marked also the appearance of formal unionism. Hence in Brazil during the liberal phase (1946–64) populist forces were capable of using institutions designed to control the working class for the purpose of giving political power to labour leaders (Erickson, 1977). Yet the strengthening of corporatism came from the conservative forces themselves, which after the coup d'état of 1964 tightened the controls over labour organizations.

The main element of modern corporatism consists in a detailed network of technical and juridical norms, enforced by ministerial bodies, aimed at controlling the labour movement. A formal system of Estates had either an incidental character (Italy) or was never implemented.

The economic views of the main advocates of corporatism have never reached an analytical dimension. During the 1930s in Italy some discussion took place around the issue of homo corporativus versus *homo oeconomicus* (Mancini, Parillo and Zagari, 1982).

JOSEPH HALEVI

See also ECONOMIC THEORY OF THE STATE; FASCISM.

BIBLIOGRAPHY

Camp, R. 1969. *The Papal Ideology of Social Reform. A Study in Historical Development, 1878–1967.* Leiden: E.J. Brill.

Durkheim, E. 1893. *The Division of Labour in Society.* London: Macmillan, 1933.

Erickson, K. 1977. *The Brazilian Corporate State and Working Class Politics.* Berkeley: University of California Press.

Hegel, G. 1821. *Hegel's Philosophy of Right.* London: Oxford University Press, 1967.

Kuczynski, J. 1945. *Germany: Economic and Labour Conditions under Fascism.* New York: International Publishers.

Mancini, O., Parillo, F. and Zagari, E. 1982. *La teoria economica del corporativismo.* Naples: Edizioni Scientifiche Italiane.

Marlo, K. 1885. *Untersuchungen über die Organisation der Arbeit.* Tübingen.

Neumann, F. 1944. *Behemoth; the Structure and Practice of National Socialism, 1933–1944.* New York: Octagon Books.

Rossi, E. 1955. *Padroni del vapore e fascismo.* Bari: Laterza.

Salvemini, G. 1936. *Under the Axe of Fascism.* New York: Viking Press.

Sraffa, P. 1922. The bank crisis in Italy. *Economic Journal* 32, June, 178–97.

Togliatti, P. 1970. *Lectures on Fascism.* New York: International Publishers, 1976.

correlation analysis. *See* REGRESSION AND CORRELATION ANALYSIS.

correspondence principle. In a pair of wartime papers, Paul Samuelson (1941, 1942) asserted the mutually supportive relationship of economic dynamics (the study of economies out of equilibrium) and comparative statics (the comparative study of economies in equilibrium). By formally modelling the dynamic processes by which economies respond to disequilibrium and then imposing the requirement that the processes be stable (converge to an equilibrium), one can derive fruitful theorems in comparative statics, that is, theorems concerning the effect of parametric changes (in tastes, techniques of production or taxes, for example) on equilibrium values of the variables; and, looking in the other direction, assumed properties of an equilibrium can yield information about the stability–instability properties of a parent disequilibrium system. That this mutually supportive or dualistic relationship exists was dubbed by Samuelson the correspondence principle. Initially, the principle was formulated in terms of local stability and local comparative statics, and it is still best known in that form. Later, however, Samuelson provided a one-variable global version of the principle; see Samuelson (1971 and 1975).

More recently, with the re-emergence of macro-growth and capital theory in the 1950s and 1960s, economists have sought to derive properties of steady states from conditions for the convergence of the growth process; and, conversely, they have sought to learn about the stability of the process from assumed properties of the steady states (for a striking example, see Burmeister and Long, 1977). Often, appeal is made to the correspondence principle. However, in modern growth and capital theory the economy is always in equilibrium. The new dualism therefore bears only a superficial similarity to Samuelson's Correspondence Principle.

So far, the principle has had only a modest impact on economic theory. Thus, even for quite small disequilibrium systems, stability conditions have been found to imply only very weak restrictions on the comparative-statical properties of the equilibrium; and knowledge of the latter properties rarely suffices to determine whether a parent disequilibrium system is stable. It is not surprising, then, that the principle has found its main fields of application in partial analysis, in the simple Keynesian macro-models of the immediate post-World War II period and in the small (two-by-two) general-equilibrium models characteristic of the theory of international trade.

Moreover, any particular system of equilibrium relationships can be imbedded in many more or less plausible parent disequilibrium systems; and each parent system has its own peculiar set of stability conditions. Thus even if it were the case that stability conditions always substantially restrict the parameters of equilibrium relationships there would remain the problem of choosing from alternative parent systems. In making that choice some guidance can be obtained from (the second branch of) the principle itself; that is, purely equilibrium information can be brought to bear on the problem of discriminating between competing disequilibrium formulations. However, such information will rarely be decisive.

A final source of scepticism is the fundamental postulate of dynamic stability. The typical comparative-statical exercise is conducted in the context of a model which is merely one part of a larger model. For the purpose of that exercise, it is quite proper to abstract from the rest of the system of artificially freezing some variables. For example, in exercises of the Stolper–Samuelson type one freezes commodity prices, thus sealing off the production or supply side of the system from the demand side. But then, in seeking to apply the correspondence principle, does one look at a disequilibrium extension of the larger equilibrium system or of its sub-system? The question has been extensively debated in recent years; see Mayer (1974), Neary (1978; 1980) and Herberg and Kemp (1980; 1982, Appendix). So far, no consensus has emerged. All

that can be said without controversy is that the smaller the equilibrium subsystem the weaker the justification for imposing stability on the parent disequilibrium subsystem. As a corollary, the smaller the equilibrium subsystem the more unconvincing is any attempt to reinforce (or diminish) comparative-statical results on the basis of the stability analysis of parent subsystems alone.

MURRAY C. KEMP

See also ADJUSTMENT PROCESSES AND STABILITY.

BIBLIOGRAPHY
Burmeister, E. and Long, N.V. 1977. On some unresolved questions in capital theory: an application of Samuelson's correspondence principle. *Quarterly Journal of Economics* 91(2), May, 289–314.
Herberg, H. and Kemp, M.C. 1980. In defence of some 'paradoxes' of trade theory. *American Economic Review* 70(4), September, 812–14.
Herberg, H. and Kemp, M.C. 1982. Some implications of variable returns to scale. In *Production Sets*, ed. M.C. Kemp, New York: Academic Press.
Mayer, W. 1974. Variable returns to scale in general equilibrium theory: a comment. *International Economic Review* 15(1), February, 225–35.
Neary, J.P. 1978. Dynamic stability and the theory of factor-market distortions. *American Economic Review* 68(4), September, 671–82.
Neary, J.P. 1980. This side of paradox, or, in defence of the correspondence principle: a reply to Herberg and Kemp. *American Economic Review* 70(4), September, 815–18.
Samuelson, P.A. 1941. The stability of equilibrium: comparative statics and dynamics. *Econometrica* 9, April, 97–120.
Samuelson, P.A. 1942. The stability of equilibrium: linear and non-linear systems. *Econometrica* 10, January, 1–25.
Samuelson, P.A. 1971. On the trail of conventional beliefs on the transfer problem. In *Trade, Balance of Payments, and Growth*, ed. J.N. Bhagwati et al., Amsterdam: North-Holland, 327–51.
Samuelson, P.A. 1975. Trade pattern reversals in time-phased Ricardian systems and intertemporal efficiency. *Journal of International Economics* 5(4), November, 309–63.

correspondences. *A correspondence Q from a domain set X to a range set Y associates with each element x in X a non-empty subset of Y, $Q(x)$. A function is a correspondence such that $Q(x)$ is a singleton for each x in X.* It is for this reason that a correspondence is also termed a *multi-valued function* or, more simply, a *multi-function*. Another name for a correspondence is a *set-valued mapping*.

Correspondences arise naturally in economic theory. One may think of an individual consumer's demand correspondence which associates with each price system the set of utility maximizing consumption plans; see, for example, Hildenbrand (1974, p. 92). An equally pervasive example is an individual producer's supply correspondence which associates with each price system the set of profit maximizing production plans, see for example, Arrow and Hahn (1971, pp. 54–5). The fact that these individual responses are correspondences rather than functions is simply a consequence of 'flats' in the underlying indifference surfaces and isoquants or, more precisely, of the constancy of marginal rates of substitution in consumption and in production over a range of commodity bundles. Indeed, the association of these marginal rates with the point at which they are evaluated is another example of a correspondence that arises naturally in economic theory, particularly in the study of marginal cost pricing equilibria in economies with increasing returns to scale; for example, Brown et al. (1986). The fact that there is no unique rate of substitution is simply a consequence of 'kinks' in the underlying function. In the case of a convex function, such a correspondence is termed the *subdifferential* correspondence, and for more general functions, it is *Clarke's generalized derivative*.

If the domain and range of a correspondence are *topological spaces*, one can formulate various notions of continuity of a correspondence. Recall that (X, τ_X) is a topological space if X is a set and τ_X is a collection of subsets of X that contains X and the empty set $\varnothing$ and is closed under finite intersection and arbitrary union. We can now present one formalization of the intuitive idea of continuity of a correspondence. A correspondence $Q: X \to Y$, X, Y both topological spaces, is said to be upper *semicontinuous* (u.s.c.) if for any V in τ_Y, the set $\{x \in X: Q(x) \subset V\}$ is in τ_X. Q is said to be lower *semicontinuous* (l.s.c.) if for any V in τ_Y, the set $\{x \in X: Q(x) \cap V \neq \varnothing\}$ is in τ_X. It is easy to convince onself that a correspondence may be u.s.c. without being l.s.c. and vice versa. It is also easy to show that if Y is a compact space, a correspondence Q is u.s.c. if and only if its graph, $\mathrm{Gr}Q$, $\mathrm{Gr}Q = \{(x, y) \in X \times Y: y \in Q(x)\}$ is such that its complement belongs to $\tau_X \times \tau_Y$. A correspondence is said to be *continuous* if it is both u.s.c. and l.s.c.

A very useful result for establishing u.s.c. of correspondences arising from maximization is Berge's *maximum theorem*. This states, in particular, that for any continuous correspondence Q from a topological space X to a topological space Y and any continuous function f from $X \times Y$ into the reals, the associated correspondence $\mu: X \to Y$ given by $\mu(x) = \{y \in Q(x): f(y, x) \geq f(y', x) \text{ for all } y' \in Q(x)\}$ is u.s.c. This theorem is used to show u.s.c. of the demand and supply correspondences in the theory of the consumer and of the producer.

A result which plays a significant role in the proof of the existence of a competitive equilibrium is Kakutani's *fixed point theorem* for convex valued, u.s.c. correspondences which take a non-empty convex compact subset of an Euclidean space to itself. The theorem states that such correspondences Q have a fixed point, i.e. an element x such that $x \in Q(x)$. Kakutani's theorem yields as an immediate corollary Brouwer's fixed point theorem and generalizes, word for word, to locally convex spaces as has been shown by Glicksberg and Ky Fan; see, for example, Berge (1963, p. 251).

It is of interest to know of conditions under which a correspondence $Q: X \to Y$ yields a *continuous selection*, i.e. a continuous function $f: X \to Y$ such that $f(x) \in Q(x)$ for all x in X. The celebrated selection theorems of Michael (see, for example, Bessaga and Pelczynski (1975, ch. II.7)) give a variety of sufficient conditions for this. One of these requires X to be a paracompact topological space, Y to be a separable Banach space and Q to be convex valued and l.s.c. This theorem has been used by Gale and Mas-Colell (1974) to show the existence of competitive equilibrium for economies in which consumer preferences need neither be complete nor transitive. If Q is u.s.c. rather than l.s.c., recent work of Cellina gives sufficient conditions under which one may obtain an *approximate continuous selection*.

So far in this exposition we have been considering results on correspondences whose domain and range are both topological spaces. An alternative setting is one where the range is a topological space but the domain is a *measurable space*. (T, Σ) is a measurable space if T is a set and Σ is a family of subsets that includes T and is closed under complementation and countable unions, i.e. Σ is a σ-*algebra*. Such correspondences arise naturally in the study of economies in which the set of agents is modelled as a measurable space. An obvious example of such a correspondence is one which associates with every agent his/her set of utility maximizing consumption plans under a given price system.

One can develop concepts analogous to continuity for correspondences from a measurable space to a topological space.

A correspondence $Q: T \to Y$ is said to be *measurable* if for any set V in τ_Y, the set $\{t \in T: Q(t) \cap V \neq \varnothing\}$ is an element of Σ. Variants of this definition have been presented in the literature along with conditions under which these variants are all equivalent. One particularly fruitful variant requires the measure space to be *complete* and the correspondence to have a *measurable graph*, i.e., $\mathrm{Gr}Q$ is a subset of $\Sigma \otimes \mathcal{B}(Y)$, the smallest σ-algebra generated by the sets in $\Sigma \times \mathcal{B}(Y)$ and where $\mathcal{B}(Y)$ is the smallest σ-algebra generated by sets in τ_Y.

We can now state a measure-theoretic analogue of Berge's theorem. Let Q be a correspondence with a measurable graph and f a $\Sigma \otimes \mathcal{B}(Y)$ measurable function from $T \times Y$ into the reals. Then a result due to the collective efforts of Debreu and Castaing–Valadier states that under a mild restriction on Y, namely Souslin, the correspondence $\mu: T \to X$, $\mu(t) = \{x \in Q(t): f(t, x) \geq f(t, x') \text{ for all } x' \text{ in } Q(t)\}$, has a measurable graph.

We have developed enough terminology to state a fundamental theorem due to the collective efforts of von Neumann, Aumann and St. Beuve. This states that under a restriction on the range space Y, namely Souslin, every correspondence Q with a measurable graph yields a *measurable selection*, i.e. a measurable function $f: T \to Y$ such that $f(t) \in Q(t)$ for all t in T.

Once we have a measurable selection theorem, we are in a position to formulate a satisfactory notion of an integral of a correspondence, a notion which may also be seen as a formalization of a sum of an infinite number of sets. However, one preliminary notion that still needs to be stated is that of a *measure* μ on (T, Σ). A measure μ is a set-valued function from Σ into (say) Euclidean space R^n such that

$$\mu(A) \geq 0, \mu\left(\bigcup_{i=1}^{\infty} A_i\right) = \sum_{i=1}^{\infty} \mu(A_i)$$

for all A, A_i in Σ and such that A_i are mutually disjoint. Now let us assume we know how to integrate a function with respect to μ and can therefore specify a function $f: T \to R^n$ to be an *integrable function* if its integral (Lebesgue integral) is finite. Following Aumann, we can define the integral of a correspondence Q, $\int_T Q(t) \, \mathrm{d}\mu$, to be the set $\{\int_T f(t) \, \mathrm{d}t: f \text{ an integrable function which is a measurable selection from } Q\}$. It is now clear that $\int_T Q(t) \, \mathrm{d}\mu$ is non-empty if Q has a measurable graph and if there exists an integrable function g with non-negative values and such that $|x| \leq g(t)$ for all $x \in Q(t)$ and for all $t \in T$.

Finally, we can state a consequence of Lyapunov's theorem on the range of an *atomless measure* that has played a fundamental role in the development of the theory of economies with a continuum of agents. A measure μ on a measurable space (T, Σ) is atomless if (T, Σ, μ) has no *atoms*, i.e. $A \in \Sigma$ such that $\mu(A) > 0$ and $B \in \Sigma$, $B \subset A$ implies $\mu(B) = \mu(A)$ or $\mu(B) = 0$. The Lyapunov–Richter theorem states that the integral of a correspondence $Q: T \to R^n$ is convex if μ is an atomless measure on (T, Σ).

In summary, a correspondence is a versatile mathematical object for which a deep and rich theory can be developed and which arises naturally in many diverse areas of applied mathematics, including economic theory. For an introduction to this theory and to its applications, the reader is referred to the following references which also contain all the concepts and results not referenced in this entry.

M. Ali Khan

See also FIXED POINT THEOREMS; LYAPUNOV THEOREM.

BIBLIOGRAPHY

Arrow, K.J. and Hahn, F.H. 1971. *General Competitive Analysis*. San Francisco: Holden-Day.

Aubin, J.P. and Cellina, A. 1984. *Differential Inclusions*. New York: Springer-Verlag.

Berge, C. 1963. *Topological Spaces*. New York: Macmillan.

Bessaga, C. and Pelczynski, A. 1975. *Selected Topics in Infinite-Dimensional Topology*. Warsaw: Polish Scientific Publishers.

Brown, D., Heal, G., Ali Khan, M. and Vohra, R. 1986. On a general existence theorem for marginal cost pricing equilibria. *Journal of Economic Theory* 38, 111–19.

Castaing, C. and Valadier, M. 1977. *Convex Analysis and Measurable Multifunctions*. Lecture Notes in Mathematics No. 580, New York: Springer-Verlag.

Clarke, F.H. 1983. *Optimization and Nonsmooth Analysis*. New York: John Wiley.

Gale, D. and Mas-Colell, A. 1974. An equilibrium existence theorem for a general model without ordered preferences. *Journal of Mathematical Economics* 2, 9–15. Erratum in ibid. 6, 297–8.

Hildenbrand, W. 1974. *Core and Equilibria of a Large Economy*. Princeton, NJ: Princeton University Press.

Klein, E. and Thompson, E.A. 1985. *Introduction to the Theory of Correspondences*. New York: John Wiley.

Rockafellar, R.T. 1970. *Convex Analysis*. Princeton, NJ: Princeton University Press.

Cossa, Luigi (1831–1896). Born in Milan, Cossa was Professor of Political Economy at the University of Pavia from 1858 to his death. He was influential both through his works and, perhaps even more, through his many pupils: Pantaleoni (who was not one of them) wrote in 1909 (p. 755) that Cossa was one of the 'three men [who] have been the direct teachers of all Italian economists' (the others being F. Ferrara and A. Messedaglia). Cossa is generally regarded as one of the Italian 'Socialists of the Chair', and as such he was attacked by Ferrara, who accused the 'Germanists' of being 'socialists, and corrupters of the Italian youth' (thus Cossa himself summarized Ferrara's onslaught: Cossa, 1876, p. 226).

Cossa had studied in Germany with Roscher and had been strongly influenced by him. The German influence is mainly revealed in his acceptance of the idea of the historical relativity of economic laws. He also maintained that a system of protection 'at certain times and under certain conditions ... has given notable advantages to industrial organisation and progress' (Cossa, 1876, p. 124). (All this, of course, sounded like blasphemy to Ferrara, a great admirer of Bastiat.) He was far from regarding the German economists as faultless, and never denied the importance, for some parts of political economy, of the deductive method. A good account of Cossa's position is that given by Edgeworth, who described him as 'hold[ing] the balance between the claims of historical observation and deductive reasoning with great fairness' (Edgeworth, 1892, p. 685).

Cossa did not go deeply into economic theory, keeping to a rather superficial eclecticism. But Pantaleoni wrote of him that he had the capacity of perfectly understanding books that he would have never been able to write (Pantaleoni, 1898, p. 250).

Cossa's fame is mostly due to the bibliographical essays he published, especially his 1876 *Guida allo Studio dell'Economia Politica*, the second edition of which was translated into English, and published by Macmillan, with a preface by Jevons, in 1880 (a new, greatly enlarged, edition issued in 1892, under the title *Introduzione allo Studio dell'Economia Politica* and translated into English, was also very successful). The *Guida*, like most of Cossa's works, mainly consisted of a 'Historical Part', containing an annotated bibliography of political economy. Another book which also attained some fame, and was translated into many languages (including even

Japanese, if we can trust Loria: 1896, p. 488) was *Primi Elementi di Economia Politica* (1875).

Cossa's bibliographies can still be instructive for a modern reader, especially the parts on Italian, and on French and German, economics. More interesting than those in his books are however those published in many instalments in the *Giornale degli Economisti*, from 1891 to 1900. These have only recently been reprinted in a single volume (L. Cossa, *Saggi bibliografici di economia politica*, con Prefazione di L. Dal Pane, 1963), but have not been translated into English. Cossa's scholarship could be exaggerated (Einaudi spoke of him as 'onnisciente'). For instance, he attributed to Edward Gibbon Wakefield the 1804 *Essay upon Political Economy* (see p. 245 of the volume just quoted) which had been written by his uncle Daniel (in 1804, E.G. Wakefield was only nine years old). It must however be said that his standards (especially when compared with those of many of his contemporaries) were generally of a fairly high level.

G. DE VIVO

SELECTED WORKS

1875. *Primi elementi di economia politica*. Milan: Hoepli.

1876. *Guide to the Study of Political Economy*. Translated from the second Italian edition [1877], with a Preface by W.S. Jevons, F.R.S. London: Macmillan, 1880.

1893. *An Introduction to the Study of Political Economy*. Translated by Louis Dyer, London: Macmillan.

1963. *Saggi bibliografici di economia politica*. Bologna: Forni.

BIBLIOGRAPHY

Edgeworth, F.Y. 1892. Review of L. Cossa, *Introduzione allo Studio dell'Economia Politica* (1892). *Economic Journal* 2, December, 685–7.

Loria, A. 1896. Obituary: L. Cossa. *Economic Journal* 6, September, 488–90.

Pantaleoni, M. 1898. Dei criteri che devono informare la storia delle dottrine economiche. As reprinted in *Erotemi di Economia*, Vol. I, Bari: G. Laterza, 1925.

Pantaleoni, M. 1909. Messedaglia, Angelo. In *Dictionary of Political Economy*, ed. R.H.I. Palgrave (Appendix), London: Macmillan.

cost and supply curves. In microeconomic theory we usually suppose that an individual firm has a production technology which can be characterized by a production function $\phi: \mathscr{R}^n_+ \to \mathscr{R}_+$; where the quantity $\phi(v)$, for $v \in \mathscr{R}^n_+$, is interpreted as the maximum quantity of output which can be produced, given the vector of quantities of inputs, v. Using the generic notation 'x' to denote the quantity of output, we also suppose that the firm's revenue and cost are described by functions $R: \mathscr{R}_+ \times P \to \mathscr{R}_+$ and $K: \mathscr{R}^n_+ \times \Omega \to \mathscr{R}_+$, where:

$R(x, \rho)$ is the revenue obtained by selling output $x \in \mathscr{R}_+$, given the market conditions for its output represented by $\rho \in P$; where ρ is assumed to be outside the firm's control, and

P is the space of possible output market conditions,

$K(v, \omega)$ is the cost incurred by the firm in employing the vector of input quantities $v \in \mathscr{R}^n_+$, given the input market conditions $\omega \in \Omega$; where ω is assumed to be outside the firm's control, and

Ω is the space of possible input market conditions.

The usual behavioural assumption made is that the firm chooses v in such a way as to maximise profits; that is, given $(\bar\rho, \bar\omega) \in P \times \Omega$, the firm chooses $v^* \in \mathscr{R}^n_+$ so as to satisfy:

for all $v \in \mathscr{R}^n_+$, $R[\phi(v), \bar\rho] - K(v, \bar\omega)$

$$\leqslant R[\phi(v^*), \bar\rho] - K(v^*, \bar\omega). \quad (1)$$

In what follows, we shall say that v^* *maximizes profits for* ϕ, given $(\bar{\rho}, \bar{\omega})$, iff v^* satisfies (1).

Define

$$\mathscr{R}_{++} = \{x \in \mathscr{R} \,|\, x > 0\}$$

and

$$\mathscr{R}^n_{++} = \{w \in \mathscr{R}^n \,|\, w_i > 0 \qquad \text{for } i = 1, \ldots, n\}.$$

In this essay we shall assume that P and Ω are non-empty subsets of

$$P^* = \{\rho \,|\, \rho\colon \mathscr{R}_+ \to \mathscr{R}_{++}\} \quad \text{and} \quad \Omega^* = \{\omega \,|\, \omega\colon \mathscr{R}^n_+ \to \mathscr{R}^n_{++}\},$$

respectively; and that R and K take the form

$$R(x, \rho) = \rho(x) \cdot x \qquad \text{for } (x, \rho) \in \mathscr{R}_+ \times P, \tag{2}$$

and

$$K(v, \omega) = \omega(v) \cdot v + C_0 \qquad \text{for } (v, \omega) \in \mathscr{R}^n_+ \times \Omega, \tag{3}$$

where $C_0 \geqq 0$ is the firm's fixed cost. Thus ρ and ω are, essentially, inverse demand (for output) and supply price functions for inputs, respectively. The basic idea of this representation, as it applies to demand functions, is as follows. Under the usual assumptions of microeconomic theory, the demand function for x can be written as:

$$x = d(p_x, p, m, \alpha),$$

where

$p_x =$ the price of good x,
$p = (p_1, \ldots, p_l)$ is the vector of prices of other commodities in the economy,
$m = (m_1, \ldots, m_k)$ is the vector of consumer incomes,
α is a parameter representing 'taste',

If, for each (p, m, α), $d(\cdot, p, m, \alpha)$ is strictly decreasing in p_x, we can invert the function to write

$$p_x = D(x, p, m, \alpha).$$

Each specification of (p, m, α) then determines a function $\rho\colon \mathscr{R}_+ \to \mathscr{R}_+$ defined by:

$$\rho(x) = D(x, p, m, \alpha) \qquad \text{for } x \in \mathscr{R}_+.$$

It is this sort of interpretation we have in mind by representing output market conditions by $\rho \in P^*$ and similar considerations apply to $\omega \in \Omega^*$. In accordance with this interpretation, we shall refer to elements of P^* and Ω^* as *output price* and *input supply price functions*, respectively.

Of particular importance to the analysis, however, is the case wherein the firm does not, by its own actions, change the market prices of the inputs which it uses; or the manager of the firm behaves as if this were the case (and thus is a 'price-taker' in input markets). In our formulation, this amounts to the assumption that

$$\Omega = \Omega^c, \tag{4}$$

where Ω^c is that subset of Ω^* consisting of all constant functions (*constant supply price functions*) on $\mathscr{R}^n_+$. In this situation $\omega \in \Omega^c$ corresponds to a unique value of $w \in \mathscr{R}^n_{++}$ (and conversely); and thus by a slight abuse of our notation, we can write the cost function (3) in the form:

$$K(v, w) = w \cdot v + C_0 \qquad \text{for } (v, w) \in \mathscr{R}^n_+ \times \mathscr{R}^n_{++}. \tag{5}$$

Since our principal concern will be with the theory of pure competition, we shall assume throughout our discussion of the behaviour of the individual firm that (4) and (5) hold. However, the more general specification of K will be useful when we turn to the discussion of competitive equilibrium for an industry.

When (4) and (5) hold, it is useful to break the firm's profit-maximization problem down into two parts, as follows.

1. Defining $X \subseteq \mathscr{R}_+$, the firm's *producible set*, by:

$$X = \{x \in \mathscr{R}_+ \,|\, (\exists v \in \mathscr{R}^n_+)\colon \phi(v) \geqq x\}, \tag{6}$$

we find, for each $(x, w) \in X \times \mathscr{R}^n_{++}$, $c(x, w)$, the minimum (variable) cost of producing x, given w. That is, given $(x^*, w^*) \in X \times \mathscr{R}^n_{++}$, we find $v^* \in \mathscr{R}^n_+$ satisfying:

$$\phi(v^*) \geqq x^* \quad \text{and} \quad w^* \cdot v^* \leqq w^* \cdot v \qquad \text{for all } v \in \mathscr{R}^n_+$$

such that $\phi(v) \geqq x^*$. (7)

Variable cost and total cost at (x^*, w^*), $c(x^*, w^*)$ and $C(x^*, w^*)$, respectively, are then given by:

$$c(x^*, w^*) = w^* \cdot v^*,$$

and

$$C(x^*, w^*) = c(x^*, w^*) + C_0.$$

2. Given the function C, and $\rho \in P$, we then find $x^* \in X$ satisfying

$$\text{for all } x \in X, \ R(x, \rho) - C(x, w) \leqq R(x^*, \rho) - C(x^*, w); \tag{8}$$

or equivalently,

$$\text{for all } x \in X, \ R(x, \rho) - c(x, w) \leqq R(x^*, \rho) - c(x^*, w); \tag{8'}$$

Because of the equivalance of (8) and (8'), we shall hereafter concern ourselves only with the variable cost function, c, and we shall refer to it as simply the 'cost function.' Similarly we define the firm's (gross) *profit function*, $\pi\colon X \times P \times \mathscr{R}^n_{++} \to R$ by

$$\pi(x, \rho, w) = R(x, \rho) - c(x, w); \tag{9}$$

and we shall say that $x^* \in X$ maximizes the profit function $\pi(\cdot, \rho, w)$ if, and only if, it satisfies (8').

It can be shown that if $R(\cdot, \rho)$ is non-decreasing in x on X, and v^* maximizes profits for ϕ, given (ρ, w), then

$$w \cdot v^* = c[\phi(v^*), w], \tag{10}$$

and $x^* \equiv (v^*)$ satisfies (8'). Conversely, if $x^* \in X$ satisfies (8'), and v^* satisfies (7), then v^* maximizes profits for ϕ, given (ρ, w). Thus, if $R(\cdot, \rho)$ is non-decreasing on X; the two procedures are logically equivalent. If $R(\cdot, \rho)$ is decreasing on a portion of X (the case of inelastic demand), the two-step procedure is not necessarily equivalent to maximizing profits for ϕ, given (ρ, w). However, in the situation we will be examining in detail, $R(\cdot, \rho)$ will always be non-decreasing on X.

One advantage of the two-step analysis of profit maximization is that the problem of maximizing the profit function, π, is much simpler, both conceptually and operationally, than the problem of finding a $v^* \in \mathscr{R}^n_+$ which maximizes profits for ϕ. However, a much more significant advantage of the two-step analysis is that the analysis of the cost function itself is applicable whatever the form of the revenue function, R. In particular, the relationship between a firm's production and cost functions, the examination of which will be our next order of business, is of interest whatever the (output) market structure under investigation.

In order to formally analyse the relationship between production and cost, let us say that a function $\phi\colon \mathscr{R}^n_+ \to \mathscr{R}_+$ is a *production function* if, and only if, $\phi(\cdot)$ satisfies the following three properties:

P.1 $\phi(0) = 0$ and for some $v^\tau \in \mathscr{R}^n_+$, $\phi(v^\tau) > 0$.
P.2 ϕ is non-decreasing on $\mathscr{R}^n_+$, i.e.,

for each $v, v' \in \mathscr{R}^n_+$, if $v \geqq v'$, then $\phi(v) \geqq \phi(v')$.

P.3 ϕ is upper semi-continuous on $\mathscr{R}^n_+$.

In the following treatment, we shall also define:

$$X_+ = \{x \in X \mid x > 0\} = \{x \in \mathscr{R}_+ \mid (\exists v \in \mathscr{R}_+^n): 0 < x \leqslant \phi(v)\}$$

and

$$\mathscr{R}_{++}^n = \{w \in \mathscr{R}_+^n \mid w_i > 0 \qquad \text{for } i = 1, \ldots, n\}.$$

The above conditions are generally fairly standard, and probably require no discussion, except perhaps the assumption that ϕ is upper semi-continuous. Generally speaking, continuity is *not* an empirically meaningful condition; that is, in investigating an actual production process we can do no better than to observe a finite collection of input vectors $[v^1, \ldots, v^\tau]$, together with the associated values of output $\{x^1, \ldots, x^\tau\}$. If these observations are consistent with the hypothesis that there exists a function $\phi: \mathscr{R}_+^n \to \mathscr{R}_+$ such that

$$x^t = \phi(x^t) \qquad \text{for } t = 1, \ldots, \tau; \tag{11}$$

then they are also consistent with the additional assumption that ϕ is continuous. Consequently, one might very legitimately ask why I have not simply made the more familiar assumption that ϕ is continuous. My reason for not doing so is that there are situations in which we may want to interpret the quantity of output as a stock, rather than a flow. In some situations where this is the case (e.g., 'finite production runs'), it is likely to be appropriate to assume that ϕ is discrete-valued; and while it is possible for a function $\phi: \mathscr{R}_+^n \to \mathscr{R}_+$ to be both upper semi-continuous and discrete-valued (an example is presented later in the text), it is not possible for such a function to be both discrete-valued and continuous. As it turns out, most of the analysis to follow requires only that ϕ be upper semi-continuous, and thus is applicable with either a stock or a flow interpretation of output quantities.

Turning now to the derivation of the cost function, let $(x^*, w^*) \in X \times \mathscr{R}_{++}^n$. Since ϕ is upper semi-continuous, it can be shown that there exists $v^* \in \mathscr{R}_+^n$ such that v^* satisfies (7) for $x = x^*$ and $w = w^*$. Thus it follows that if ϕ is a production function, by our definition, then the (variable) cost function $c: X \times \mathscr{R}_{++}^n \to \mathscr{R}_+$ is well-defined. In fact, it is fairly easy to show that the cost function $c(\cdot)$, corresponding to a given production function, $\phi(\cdot)$, will satisfy the following conditions. (Most of these properties are established in McFadden, 1978, and those which are not are proved in Moore, 1986.)

C.1. X, the producible set for ϕ, is a sub-interval of $\mathscr{R}_+$, and either

    a. there exists $\bar{x} > 0$ such that $X = [0, \bar{x}]$, or
    b. for each $w \in \mathscr{R}_{++}^n$, $c(\cdot, w)$ is unbounded on X.

C.2. for each $w \in \mathscr{R}_{++}^n$:

    a. $c(\cdot, w)$ is non-decreasing in x,
    b. $c(0, w) = 0$,
    c. $c(x, w) > 0$ for each $x \in X_+$,
    d. $c(\cdot, w)$ is lower semi-continuous on X.

C.3. for each $x \in X_+$, $c(x, \cdot)$ is:

    a. increasing in w.
    b. positively homogeneous of degree one in w.
    c. concave in w.
    d. continuous in w.

Since $C(\cdot)$, the *total cost function for* ϕ. is defined by

$$C(x, w) = c(x, w) + K_0 \qquad \text{for } (x, w) \in \mathscr{R}_{++}^n, \tag{12}$$

it follows at once that C also satisfies all of the above properties *except* C.2.b and C.3.b. We can also define the *average variable cost*, and *average cost* functions on $X_+ \times \mathscr{R}_{++}^n$ by:

$$a(x, w) = c(x, w)/x \qquad \text{for } (x, w) \in X_+ \times \mathscr{R}_{++}^n, \tag{13}$$

and

$$A(x, w) = C(x, w)/w \qquad \text{for } (x, w) \in X_+ \times \mathscr{R}_{++}^n, \tag{14}$$

respectively. However, under the assumptions we have been employing to this point, the marginal cost function, $c_x(\cdot, w)$, will not necessarily be well-defined. ['$c_x(x, w)$' denotes the partial derivative of c with respect to x, evaluated at (x, w)]. In fact, under the assumptions which we have been employing, a cost function may look rather unlike those used in traditional intermediate theory diagrams, as will be seen from the following example.

For each $x \in \mathscr{R}$, define $\lfloor x \rfloor$ and $\lceil x \rceil$ by:

$\lfloor x \rfloor$ = that unique integer, n, satisfying $n \leqslant x < n + 1$,

and

$\lceil x \rceil$ = that unique integer, n', satisfying:

$$n' - 1 < x \leqslant n'.$$

If we let $\alpha > 0$ be a positive real number, and define $\phi: \mathscr{R}_+ \to \mathscr{R}_+$ by

$$\phi(x) = \alpha \sqrt{\lfloor v \rfloor}, \qquad \text{for } v \in \mathscr{R}_+,$$

it can be shown that ϕ is a production function. Moreover, it is easy to see that the producible set for ϕ is given by:

$$X = \mathscr{R}_+,$$

and that the cost function for ϕ is given by:

$$c(x, w) = w \lceil (x/\alpha)^2 \rceil \qquad \text{for } x \in X \text{ and } w \in \mathscr{R}_{++}.$$

The graph of $c(\cdot)$ for $\alpha = w = 1$ is shown in Figure 1, below.

Obviously, the marginal cost function is not defined in this example.

Suppose now that the firm sells its output in a competitive market; that is, that the firm is a 'price-taker' in its output market. In terms of our formulation, this means that P is the set of all constant functions (*constant output price functions*); and by considerations similar to those used in our development of the cost function, we can write the firm's revenue function as:

$$R(x, p) = p \cdot x \qquad \text{for } (x, p) \in X \times \mathscr{R}_{++}. \tag{15}$$

Thus we are interested in whether or when, given $(p, w) \in \mathscr{R}_{++} \times \mathscr{R}_{++}^n$, there exists $x^* \in X$ satisfying

$$\text{for all } x \in X, \qquad p \cdot x - c(x, w) \leqslant p \cdot x^* - c(x^*, w). \tag{16}$$

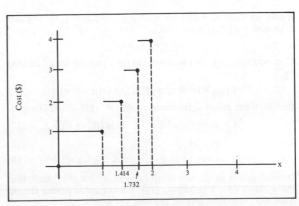

Figure 1

683

If, for each $(p, w) \in \mathcal{R}_{++} \times \mathcal{R}^n_{++}$, there exists a unique $x^* \in X$ satisfying (16), then there exists a function $s: \mathcal{R}_+ \times \mathcal{R}^n_{++} \to X$ such that for each (p, w), $s(p, w)$ is that unique value of x, x^*, satisfying (16). This function is called the firm's *supply function*; its value at each (p, w) is the firm's competitive (profit-maximizing) output, given the output price, p, and the vector of input prices, w. We shall briefly examine the conditions under which this function will exist, and its relationship to the firm's cost curve.

Suppose for the moment that the cost function is differentiable in x, and let '$c_x(x, w)$' denote the partial derivative of c with respect to x, evaluated at $(x, w) \in X \times \mathcal{R}^n_{++}$. The function $c_x(\cdot)$ is called the firm's *marginal cost function*, and it is customary in intermediate microtheory texts to state that the firm's supply curve is 'that portion of the marginal cost curve lying above the average variable cost curve'. Clearly the situation is a bit more complicated than this; and these complications, while perhaps not critical in the analysis of the individual competitive firm, become troublesome when we turn to the analysis of supply in a competitive industry.

In examining this problem, we shall restrict our attention to the case in which the text book treatment mentioned above is most nearly correct (or at least the most favorable case I can come up with); namely, that in which the firm's cost function satisfies the following condition.

C.4. Defining $\chi = \operatorname{Sup} X$ (χ may, of course, be equal to $+\infty$), c is continuously differentiable in x on $[0, \chi[\times \mathcal{R}^n_{++}$; and, for each $w \in \mathcal{R}^n_{++}$, $c_x(\cdot)$ is strictly increasing on $[0, \chi[$. [By '$c_x(0, w)$' we mean the right hand partial derivative.]

We shall not attempt to develop conditions on the firm's production function sufficient to ensure that c satisfies C.4. However, it is easy to show that if ϕ is strictly concave, then $c(\cdot, w)$ will be strictly convex in x, for each $w \in \mathcal{R}^n_{++}$. If in this case c is differentiable as well, then $c_x(\cdot, w)$ will be strictly increasing in x on $[0, \chi[$, for each $w \in \mathcal{R}^n_{++}$. Moreover, it follows from recent results on duality relationships between production and cost-functions that, given any cost function, c, satisfying (C.1–C.3 and) C.4, there exists a unique concave production function for which c is the corresponding cost function. (For an excellent survey of duality, see Diewert, 1982.)

Suppose, then, that c satisfies C.4. It is easy to see that, for each $w \in \mathcal{R}^n_{++}$,

$$\lim_{x \to \chi} c_x(x, w)$$

exists, although it may be equal to $+\infty$. Furthermore, if for each $w \in \mathcal{R}^n_{++}$, we define $a(w)$ and $b(w)$ by

$$a(w) = c_x(0, w) \quad b(w) = \lim_{x \to \chi} c_x(x, w);$$

it follows from C.4 that for each $p \in [a(w), b(w)[$, there exists a unique $x \in [0, \chi[$ such that

$$p = c_x(x, w).$$

Consequently, $c_x(\cdot, w)$ is invertible (in x) on the set π^0 defined by

$$\pi^0 = \{(p, w) \in \mathcal{R}_{++} \times \mathcal{R}^n_{++} \mid p \in [a(w), b(w)[\};$$

that is, there exists a function $\sigma: \pi^0 \to [0, \chi[\subseteq X$ satisfying:

$$\text{for each } (p, w) \in \pi^0, \quad c_x[\sigma(p, w), w] = p, \quad (17)$$

and

$$\text{for each } (x, w) \in [0, \chi[\times \mathcal{R}^n_{++}, \quad \sigma[c_x(x, w), w] = x. \quad (18)$$

If we define π as the set of all $(p, w) \in \mathcal{R}_{++} \times \mathcal{R}^n_{++}$ such that there exists $x^* \in X$ satisfying (16), the interested reader should have no great difficulty in proving the following.

S.1. $\pi^0 \subseteq \pi$

S.2. For each $(p, w) \in \pi$, the profit-maximizing output is unique; thus the firm's supply function has domain π, and is given by:

$$s(p, w) = \begin{cases} 0 & \text{if } 0 < p \leqslant a(w) \\ \sigma(p, w) & \text{if } p \in]a(w), b(w)[\\ \chi & \text{if } p \geqslant b(w) \end{cases} \quad \text{for } (p, w) \in \pi \quad (19)$$

S.3. For each $w \in \mathcal{R}^n_{++}$, $s(\cdot, w)$ is continuous and non-decreasing in p; and is strictly increasing in p on $[a(w), b(w)[$.

While, as already indicated, I shall leave the proof of the above result to the 'interested reader'; one or two explanatory comments seem to be in order. First, if c satisfies C.4, then marginal cost is always at least as large as average variable cost, i.e.,

$$\text{for each } (x, w) \in X_+ \times \mathcal{R}^n_{++}, \quad c_x(x, w) > c(x, w)/x \quad (20)$$

(this is easily established by the use of the mean value theorem). Secondly, the condition $p \geqslant b(w)$ and $(p, w) \in \pi$ is a bit misleading. The fact of the matter is, these two conditions can hold simultaneously only if X is of the form $X = [0, \chi]$, with χ finite (and positive. In this case also $\pi = \mathcal{R}_{++} \times \mathcal{R}^n_{++}$.) If this is not the case, then by C.1 we see that two other cases are possible.

Case 1: $X = [0, \chi[$ with χ finite. Here we have by C.1 that $c(\cdot, w)$ is unbounded in X, and this fact can be used to show that $b(w) = +\infty$, for each $w \in \mathcal{R}^n_{++}$. Thus in this case, $\pi = \mathcal{R}_{++} \times \mathcal{R}^n_{++}$, but we cannot have $p \geqslant b(w)$.

Case 2. $X = \mathcal{R}_+$. Here it is possible that $b(w)$ is finite. However, if this is the case, and (p, w) is such that $p \geqslant b(w)$, then no profit-maximizing solution exists. For example, consider the homothetic cost function

$$c(x, w) = f(x)\gamma(w), \quad (21)$$

where γ can be any function satisfying C.3, and f is given by:

$$f(x) = \alpha x + (x^2 + \beta^2)^{1/2} - \beta, \quad \text{with } \alpha, \beta > 0. \quad (22)$$

Here it is easily shown that c satisfies C.1–C.4, and that

$$a(w) \equiv c_x(0, w) = f'(x)\gamma(w) = \alpha\gamma(w), \quad (23)$$

while

$$b(w) \equiv \lim_{x \to +\infty} c_x(x, w) = \gamma(w) \lim_{x \to +\infty} f'(x) = (\alpha + 1)\gamma(w). \quad (24)$$

Here $b(w)$ is finite, but if $p \geqslant b(w)$, then no profit-maximizing output exists.

Turning our attention to suppy conditions for a competitive industry, suppose there are m firms producing a single (homogeneous) commodity, and let the ith firm's production function, cost function, and producible set be denoted by ϕ^i, c^i, and X_i, respectively. We shall use the generic notation x_i and v^i to denote the ith firm's output and vector of inputs employed, respectively; and we define the *producible set for the industry*, X, by

$$X = \sum_{i=1}^{m} X_i.$$

We assume that the market is competitive, so that each firm is a price-taker in both output and input markets; and we shall be interested in the competitive equilibria of the market (or industry), defined as follows.

We shall say that $(\bar{v}^1, \ldots, \bar{v}^m; \bar{\rho}, \bar{\omega})$ is a *competitive equilibrium for the industry* iff.

1. $\bar{v}^i \in \mathcal{R}^n_+$ for $i = 1, \ldots, m$,
2. $\bar{\rho} \in P^*$, $\bar{\omega} \in \Omega^*$, and
3. defining $\bar{p} = \bar{\rho} \left[\sum_{i=1}^{m} \phi^i(\bar{v}^i) \right]$ and $\bar{w} = \bar{\omega} \left(\sum_{i=1}^{m} \bar{v}^i \right)$,

the following condition holds: for each i $(i = 1, \ldots, m)$, $\bar{v}^i$ satisfies

$$\text{for all } v^i \in \mathscr{R}^n_+, \quad \bar{p} \cdot \phi^i(v^i) - \bar{w} \cdot v^i \leqq \bar{p} \cdot \phi^i(\bar{v}^i) - \bar{w} \cdot \bar{v}^i. \quad (25)$$

We shall also be interested in aggregate competitive equilibria for the industry, defined as follows.

We shall say that $(\bar{x}, \bar{v}, \bar{p}, \bar{\omega}) \in X \times \mathscr{R}^n_+ \times P^* \times \Omega^*$ is an *aggregate competitive equilibrium for the industry* iff there exist $\bar{v}^i \in \mathscr{R}^n_+$ for $i = i, \ldots, m$ such that

$$\bar{v} = \sum_{i=1}^{m} \bar{v}^i, \qquad \bar{x} = \sum_{i=1}^{m} \phi^i(\bar{v}^i),$$

and $(\bar{v}^1, \ldots, \bar{v}^m; \bar{p}, \bar{\omega})$ is a competitive equilibrium for the industry. We shall say that $(\bar{x}, \bar{p}, \bar{\omega}) \in X \times P^* \times \Omega^*$ is an aggregate output equilibrium for the industry iff there exists $\bar{v} \in \mathscr{R}^n_+$ such that $(\bar{x}, \bar{v}, \bar{p}, \bar{\omega})$ is an aggregate competitive equilibrium for the industry.

The first question I would like to consider is whether we can characterize the aggregate output equilibria as the set of points where supply equals demand, if by 'supply' we mean the summation of the supply functions of the individual firms. I don't believe that it will be necessary to go into a lot of detail to convince the reader of the truth of the following two assertions.

1. We cannot obtain the set of output equilibria for the industry by summing the individual supply curves and then finding the set of points at which this summation function equals demand unless we restrict our attention to cases in which $\omega \in \Omega^c$. This is a fairly serious difficulty, since this assumes that all m firms in the industry can simultaneously expand or contract input usage without appreciably affecting input prices, an assumption which is much more restrictive than assuming that each firm behaves as if its individual actions have no appreciable effect on input prices.

2. Even if we restrict our attention to the case where $\Omega = \Omega^c$, the analysis of the form of the summation supply function will be a very messy business. Suppose, for example, that each cost function c^i satisfies C.4, and denote the ith firm's supply function by s^i and its domain by π^i. Then the summation (industry) supply function will be defined on

$$\pi = \bigcap_{i=1}^{m} \pi_i,$$

and will be given by

$$s(p, w) = \sum_{i=1}^{m} s^i(p, w) \qquad \text{for } (p, w) \in \pi.$$

Given $\bar{w} \in \mathscr{R}^n_{++}$ and $\rho \in P^*$, $(\bar{x}, \bar{\rho}, \bar{\omega})$ will be an aggregate output equilibrium for the industry in this case if, and only if,

$$[\bar{p}(\bar{x}), \bar{w}] \in \pi \quad \text{and} \quad x = s[\bar{p}(\bar{x}), \bar{w}]. \quad (26)$$

In this case, therefore one can obtain the industry supply function by summing the supply functions of the individual firms, and this industry supply function can be conveniently utilized to obtain the aggregate output equilibria for the industry. However, if the reader will re-examine condition S.2, above [and particularly equation (19)], I am sure you will have no difficulty convincing yourself that the characterization of the form of π and $s(\cdot)$ will be a very messy business; even under the somewhat restrictive assumption that each c^i satisfies C.4. In fact, this is a fairly substantive problem, for suppose one wishes to estimate the supply function for a purely competitive industry. Given our present estimation techniques, this means that one needs to specify a functional form for $s(\cdot)$ (actually, a parametric family, the individual elements of which are determined by a finite set of parameters), whose parameters can

be estimated from data on aggregate output equilibria for the market. The question is, what sort of functional form is appropriate? Once again, a glance back at condition S.2 and equation (19) will suffice to convince the reader that the only practical means of deriving the form $s(\cdot)$ from assumptions about the functional form of the individual cost functions, c^i, is to assume that all of the individual firms have the same cost function; an assumption with which it is difficult to be comfortable.

Fortunately, there is a way of circumventing both of these difficulties, at least to a great extent. The relationships we shall develop to facilitate this alternative analysis are in some sense 'well known', but for some reason they do not seem to have found their way into microeconomic theory textbooks. We begin by considering the following problem, for an arbitrary $v \in \mathscr{R}^n_+$:

$$\text{Maximize } \sum_{i=1}^{m} \phi^i(v^i), \quad \text{subject to } \sum_{i=1}^{m} v^i \leqq v$$
$$\text{and} \quad v^i \in \mathscr{R}^n_+ \quad \text{for } i = 1, \ldots, m. \quad (27)$$

Since each ϕ^i is upper semi-continuous, the function

$$F(v^1, \ldots, v^m) \equiv \sum_{i=1}^{m} \phi^i(v^i)$$

is also upper semi-continuous; and, for each $v \in \mathscr{R}^n_+$, the set

$$V(v) = \left\{ (v^1, \ldots, v^m) \in \mathscr{R}^{mn} \,\middle|\, \sum_{i=1}^{m} v^i \leqq v \right\}$$

is compact. Therefore, for each $v \in \mathscr{R}^n_+$, the problem (27) has a solution, the value of which we shall denote by '$\phi(v)$', that is,

$$\phi(v) = \max \left\{ \sum_{i=1}^{m} \phi^i(v^i) \,\middle|\, (v^1, \ldots, v^m) \in V(v) \right\}. \quad (28)$$

We shall refer to the function ϕ as the *industry production function*; and for each $v \in \mathscr{R}^n_+$ we shall denote the solution set of (27) by '$V^*(v)$', that is,

$$V^*(v) = \left\{ (v^1, \ldots, v^m) \in V(v) \,\middle|\, \sum_{i=1}^{m} \phi^i(v^i) = \phi(v) \right\}. \quad (29)$$

It can be shown that ϕ is a production function; that is, it satisfies P.1–P.3. The industry production function does not necessarily retain other properties of the individual production functions, ϕ^i; for example, it may be the case that all the ϕ^i are quasi-concave but that ϕ is not quasi-concave. On the other hand, if all the ϕ^i are concave, or are all positively homogeneous of degree $r > 0$, then ϕ will be, respectively, concave or positively homogeneous of degree r. In any case, for our present purposes it suffices that ϕ is a production function, and thus has a cost function satisfying C.1–C.3. We can show that the set of aggregate competitive equilibria for the industry are the solutions of the following problem.

Given a production function, ϕ, and $(\bar{\rho}, \bar{\omega}) \in P^* \times \Omega^*$, we shall say that $\bar{v} \in \mathscr{R}^n_+$ *myopically maximizes profits for ϕ, given* $(\bar{\rho}, \bar{\omega})$ if $\bar{v}$ satisfies:

$$\text{for all } v \in \mathscr{R}^n_+, \quad \bar{p} \cdot \phi(v) - \bar{w} \cdot v \leqq \bar{p} \cdot \phi(\bar{v}) - \bar{w} \cdot \bar{v}, \quad (30)$$

where $\bar{p} = \bar{\rho}[\phi(\bar{v})]$ and $\bar{w} = \bar{\omega}(\bar{v})$.

One can then prove the following result; although, in the interest of brevity, I shall not do so here (a proof is included in Moore, 1986).

Proposition 1. If $\bar{v} \in \mathscr{R}^n_+$, myopically maximizes profits for ϕ (the industry production function), given $(\bar{\rho}, \bar{\omega}) \in P^* \times \Omega^*$, then $[\phi(\bar{v}), \bar{v}, \bar{\rho}, \bar{\omega}]$ is an aggregate competitive equilibrium for the industry [in fact, in this situation $(\bar{v}^1, \ldots, \bar{v}^m; \bar{\rho}, \bar{\omega})$ is a competitive equilibrium for the industry, for any

685

$(\bar{v}^1, \ldots, \bar{v}^m) \in V^*(\bar{v})]$. Conversely, if $(\hat{v}^1, \ldots, \hat{v}^m; \hat{\rho}, \hat{\omega})$ is a competitive equilibrium for the industry, and we define

$$\hat{v} = \sum_{i=1}^{m} , \hat{v}^i,$$

then

$$\phi(\hat{v}) = \sum_{i=1}^{m} \phi^i(\hat{v}^i),$$

and $\hat{v}$ myopically maximizes profits for ϕ, given $(\hat{\rho}, \hat{\omega})$.

There are a number of points which appear to be worth making with regard to the implications of the above result.

1. Given $(\bar{\rho}, \bar{\omega}) \in P^* \times \Omega^*$, one can find all aggregate competitive output and input equilibria corresponding to $(\bar{\rho}, \bar{\omega})$ by finding the set of v which myopically maximize ϕ, given $(\bar{\rho}, \bar{\omega})$. If there is a unique maximizing value of v, then there is correspondingly a unique aggregate competitive equilibrium for the industry. (This uniqueness question is explored in Moore, 1986).

2. One can estimate the industry production function, ϕ, from observations on aggregate output and input usage associated with competitive equilibria for the industry; since if $(\bar{v}^1, \ldots, \bar{v}^m; \bar{\rho}, \bar{\omega})$ is a competitive equilibrium for the industry, then

$$\sum_{i=1}^{m} \phi^i(\bar{v}^i) = \phi\left(\sum_{i=1}^{m} \bar{v}^i\right).$$

Similarly if one also has data on the values of w associated with each such competitive equilibrium, one can also estimate $\bar{\omega}$.

There is a complication connected with this last point, however. The situation I have been describing is one in which we have a series of competitive equilibria for the industry;

$$(x^t, v^t, \rho^t, \omega^t) \quad \text{for } t = 1, \ldots, T; \quad (31)$$

and we have observed

$$(x^t, v^t, w^t) \quad \text{for } t = 1, \ldots, T, \quad (32)$$

where

$$w^t = \omega^t(v^t) \quad \text{for } t = 1, \ldots, T. \quad (33)$$

Under the assumption that the individual production functions, ϕ^i, are unchanged over the period, then we can clearly estimate the industry production function from the relation

$$x^t = \phi(v^t) \quad \text{for } t = 1, \ldots, T, \quad (34)$$

where (34) holds by virtue of the fact that

$$x^t = \sum_{i=1}^{m} \phi^i(v^{it}), \qquad v^t = \sum_{i=1}^{m} v^{it},$$

and

$$\sum_{i=1}^{m} \phi^i(v^{it}) = \phi\left(\sum_{i=1}^{m} v^{it}\right).$$

Assuming that there exists $\bar{\omega} \in \Omega^*$ such that

$$\omega^t = \bar{\omega} \quad \text{for } t = 1, \ldots, T; \quad (35)$$

we can equally well estimate $\bar{\omega}$ from the relationship

$$w^t = \omega^t(v^t) = \bar{\omega}(v^t) \quad \text{for } t = 1, \ldots, T. \quad (36)$$

However, here it is well to keep in mind a point raised by Joan Robinson in her famous article 'Rising Supply Price' (1941): if the industry output price function changes from, say, ρ^1 to ρ^2, there will generally be a corresponding change in the input supply price function as well (in our framework, a change from some ω^1 to $\omega^2 \in \Omega^*$). In the situation under consideration here,

and under the assumption that the ϕ^i's are unchanged, we must have $\rho^t \neq \rho^{t'}$ if $(x^t, v^t) \neq (x^{t'}, v^{t'})$. Thus we have to allow for the possibility that $\omega^t \neq \omega^{t'}$ as well (unless, of course, $w^t = w^{t'}$ for all $t, t' = 1, \ldots, T$). This is essentially, an identification problem, and can be handled by methods similar to those used in conventional demand and supply estimation [on this, see, e.g., Fisher (1966)].

Robinson's point is also pertinent to the predictive use of the methods we have discussed here, however. Suppose we know, or have estimated, both the industry production function, ϕ, and the prevailing input supply price function $\bar{\omega}$; and we wish to predict the aggregate competitive equilibrium associated with $\hat{\rho} \in P^*$. It follows from Proposition 1 that we can find $(\bar{x}, \bar{v}, \hat{\rho}, \bar{\omega})$ by finding $\bar{v} \in \mathscr{R}^n_+$ such that $\bar{v}$ myopically maximizes profits for ϕ, given $(\hat{\rho}, \bar{\omega})$. The problem here, of course, is that if demand conditions change to $\hat{\rho}$, there may be a corresponding change to a new input supply price function, $\hat{\omega}$. While I have no suggestions regarding a way of circumventing this difficulty, one suspects that there are many more situations in which it is safe to assume that industry supply conditions remain unchanged for 'small' changes in ρ, than there are in which input prices themselves remain fixed for such changes in ρ.

3. Let us call the cost function, c, corresponding to the industry production function, ϕ, the *industry cost function*. It can be shown that if $(\bar{v}', \ldots, \bar{v}^m; \bar{\rho}, \bar{\omega})$ is a competitive equilibrium for the industry, and we define

$$\bar{w} = \bar{\omega}\left(\sum_{i=1}^{m} \bar{v}^i\right), \quad \text{and} \quad \bar{x}_i = \phi^i(\bar{v}^i) \quad \text{for } i = 1, \ldots, m,$$

then

$$\sum_{i=1}^{m} \bar{w} \cdot \bar{v}^i = c(\bar{x}, \bar{w}), \qquad \text{where } \bar{x} = \sum_{i=1}^{m} \bar{x}_i.$$

Thus one can estimate the industry cost function by observations on aggregate industry output, total industry factor cost, and $\bar{w}$. This fact is of particular interest in connection with our next point.

4. In the constant input supply price case ($\Omega = \Omega^c$), our analysis yields a simplified approach to obtaining (and analyzing the properties of) the industry supply function. From Proposition 1 and our discussion of profit maximization by the individual firm, we can see that if we derive the function $s: \pi \to X$ from the industry cost function in the same way that we derive the firm's supply function from its cost function (see the derivation of S.1–S.3 above), we can find the aggregate output equilibrium for the industry, given $(\bar{p}, \bar{w})$, by finding $\bar{x} \in X$ satisfying

$$\bar{x} = s[\bar{\rho}(\bar{x}), \bar{w}].$$

In other words, it is legitimate to approach the problem of estimating a supply curve for an industry by specifying a production function (or cost function) for the industry as an aggregate, and proceeding as if the industry were a single profit-maximizing entity.

The perceptive reader may, however, have detected a problem with the above procedure. We have shown that if each firm in a competitive industry has an individual production function (by the definition used here), then there is an associated total product function for the industry which is also a production function. The question remains, however, whether *any* production function could serve to describe industry output relationships in this manner. Insofar as I am aware, the answer to this general question is unknown, and deserves investigation. However, any *concave* production function can play such a role, as is shown by the following.

Proposition 2. Let $\phi: \mathscr{R}_+^n \to \mathscr{R}_+$ be a concave production function, and let m be a positive integer. Then there exist concave production functions
$\phi^i: \mathscr{R}_+^n \to \mathscr{R}_+$ for $i = 1, \ldots, m$, such that ϕ is the industry production function associated with the ϕ^i.

While I shall not provide a complete proof of Proposition 2 here, it can be established by showing that if ϕ is a concave production function, and one defines ϕ^i $(i = 1, \ldots, m)$ by

$$\phi^i(v^i) = (1/m)\phi(mv^i) \qquad \text{for } v^i \in \mathscr{R}_+^n;$$

then ϕ^i is a concave production function, and ϕ is the industry production function associated with $(\phi^1, \ldots, \phi^m)$. (Cf. Stigum, 1968).

JAMES C. MOORE

See also COST FUNCTIONS.

BIBLIOGRAPHY

Diewert, W.E. 1982. Duality approaches to microeconomic theory. In *Handbook of Mathematical Economics*, ed. K.J. Arrow and M.D. Intriligator, Vol. II, Amsterdam: North-Holland, 535–99.

Fisher, F.M. 1966. *The Identification Problem in Econometrics*. New York: McGraw-Hill.

Jacobsen, S.E. 1970. Production correspondences. *Econometrica* 38(5) 754–70.

Jacobsen, S.E. 1972. On Shephard's duality theorem. *Journal of Economic Theory* 4(3), 458–64.

McFadden, D. 1978. Cost, revenue, and profit functions. In *Production Economics: A Dual Approach to Theory and Applications*, ed. M. Fuss and D. McFadden, Amsterdam: North-Holland, 3–109.

Moore, J.C. 1986. A reconsideration of market supply and demand analysis. Purdue University, Mimeo.

Robinson, J. 1941. Rising supply price. *Economica*, N.S. 8, 1–8.

Shephard, R.W. 1970. *Theory of Cost and Production Functions*. Princeton: Princeton University Press.

Stigum, B.P. 1986. On a property of concave functions. *Review of Economic Studies* 35(4), 413–16.

Varian, H.R. *Microeconomic Analysis*. 2nd edn, New York: Norton.

cost–benefit analysis. Cost–benefit analysis is a widely used technique of applied welfare economics, which is used to throw light on the *social* desirability of undertaking an economic project. A project can be defined as an act of investment, introduction of a new commodity or a change in policy. Its analytical foundations go back to Dupuit (1844) who in his classic paper on 'consumers' surplus' can be said to have laid the foundations which in modified forms still inform a great deal of contemporary work. In an operational sense, there may be some justification for dating it back to the US Flood Control Act of 1936, as mentioned by Eckstein (1959). In postwar years, considerable impetus was imparted by the growth of a considerable literature on development programming where choice of investment projects figured very prominently. Tinbergen (1956, 1967) was amongst the first set of influential economists who strongly recommended the use of 'accounting prices', subsequently often referred to as 'shadow prices' for the appraisal of social worthwhileness of investment projects. Influential contributions were made in the 1960s by Little and Mirrlees (1969, 1974) which can be directly related to the work done by Tinbergen (1967). Marglin (1963) and Sen (1968) have provided major inputs into the discussion at different stages and were responsible along with P. Dasgupta in propounding a system of guidelines for project appraisal. The Little–Mirrlees work which was sponsored by the OECD has often been compared with the work done by Dasgupta, Marglin and Sen under the auspices of the United Nations through its specialized office at Vienna (UNIDO).

The leading idea behind cost–benefit analysis is that prevailing market prices involve significant distortions. These prices include the interest rate, the wage rate as well as the rate of foreign exchange. These distortions can arise from market imperfections of one sort or another. In addition, because of the presence of external effects, there may be an insufficiency of markets which make usual private profitability calculations misleading/inadequate as indicators for judging the desirability of introducing a specific *change* in the economic situation. Cost–benefit analysis does not question the fundamental theorems of welfare economics, rigorously worked by Barone (1935), Lange (1942) and Arrow (1951). It is believed that if *suitable corrections* are made to the prices of goods and factors, including the adoption of an appropriate rate of time discount, a 'proper measure of the benefit–cost ratio for a project can be obtained for purposes of ranking investment projects. For analytical reasons, the criterion generally adopted involves maximization of discounted present value of net benefits at an appropriately chosen rate of social discount rather than maximization of the 'internal rate of return', even though practising project planners often compute internal rates of return as the appropriate social rate of discount is often a matter of dispute.

1. In the literature on cost–benefit analysis, there are broadly speaking two major approaches which have been deployed by recent writers. One line goes back to the Marshallian surplus analysis as revived by Hotelling (1938) and by Hicks (1941). Despite the highly negative comments by Samuelson (1947), the appeal of the 'surplus' approach has proved very strong for certain economists for estimating the net loss to an economy because of the pressure of various distortions. Harberger (1971) has, in particular, argued the case for using the 'surplus approach' probably more forcefully than any other economist. Very recently, Willig (1976) has argued that the Marshallian measure which is strictly valid only on the assumption of the 'constancy of the marginal utility of money' can serve as a good enough approximation even when this assumption is not strictly valid. Willig has obtained bounds on the 'error' likely to be committed in the general case, the bounds being dependent on the parameters of the demand function. There is probably enough justification to describe the approach as a 'partial equilibrium' approach even though Harberger (1971) has questioned it and a formal extension to the n-commodity case had been worked out by Hotelling as early as 1938. Hotelling's extension depends on a mathematical theorem which need not be valid *in the large* for a market demand function.

A different approach which may be called the 'programming approach' views the cost–benefit analysis as a part of the decentralized planning procedure, intimately connected with the maximization of an overall social welfare function subject to various side conditions. Social welfare functions can be defined as functionals which include, inter alia, intertemporal extensions as well as distributive judgements. 'Shadow prices' associated with the constrained optimization exercises are treated as the 'correct estimates' of costs and benefits which can be utilized for evaluating a given project. According to this view, the 'plan' itself consists of an ensemble of interlinked projects. Apart from anything else, the validity of this approach rests on the assumption that 'shadow prices' are in some reasonable sense 'stable' which may involve, in particular, the assumption that the project in question is a 'marginal one', although not necessarily.

A variant of cost–benefit analysis is 'cost-effectiveness' analysis which is simpler to carry out. Here benefits are exogenously specified and the problem is to minimize the costs associated with a given profile of 'benefits'. This type of analysis is often applied where some precise, usually, non-pecuniary objective is exogenously stipulated.

2. Following Tinbergen (1967), the planning problem can be broken into three phases. The first and the main phase consists of derivation of an optimum savings path which is characterized by certain associated prices such as the 'wage rate' or the rate of interest or the price of foreign exchange.

At the second stage, the sectoral problems are solved including decisions about how much to produce at home, how much to export, or how much and what to import. This is the sector phase of the planning problem. Tinbergen introduced a distinction between 'tradeables' and 'non-tradeables', a distinction subsequently used by Little and Mirrlees as well. Tinbergen uses for the solution of the 'sector phase' a method of analysis known as the 'semi-input–output' analysis, which differs from the traditional input–output analysis pioneered by W. Leontief in so far as the inter-industry linkages are confined only to the subset consisting of non-tradeable commodities only. This can lead not merely to reduction of computations but also to savings in 'real resources' as well, especially if the economy is a small open economy where there are no upper bounds on exports.

While the sector phase of the planning problem is connected with problems of export substitution, the third phase which deals with 'project analysis' proper deals with evaluation of issues arising out of a specific act of investment pertaining to a given sector.

The 'three step procedure' is doubtless a convenient one but its validity depends on the assumption that 'feedback effects' are relatively insignificant from one phase to the other. Furthermore, the usefulness of introducing the middle phase depends on the distinction introduced between 'tradeables' and 'non-tradeables'. 'Non-tradeables' are generally defined to include construction, various services, electricity and local transportation activities. The distinction is not entirely independent of policy decisions. Hence, it is possible for two project evaluators to arrive at two independent benefit–cost estimates of a project, depending on which decisions of the government are to be regarded as part of 'data' of the problem.

While the three-step decomposition procedure is strongly emphasized by Tinbergen, Little and Mirrlees in their influential manual of industrial project appraisal have chosen to operate basically on a two-stage process treating phases two and three together. They treat foreign exchange as the *numéraire*, compute shadow wage rate and the accounting rate of interest from a macroeconomic optimizing model based on intertemporal utility maximization. Once these basic parameters are obtained, by valuing commodities at their 'border prices', they compute 'benefit–cost' ratios for projects, involving decisions as to which commodities to produce at home or which to import. If non-linearities are present on the export–import side, marginal export revenue and marginal import costs are used instead of fixed 'border' prices. Values of 'non-tradeables' are obtained by a suitable matrix operation which reduces them to an appropriately weighted sum of prices for 'tradeables' and 'labour'. Little and Mirrlees accept that in developing countries there exist an urban–rural wage gap as well as a state of sub-optimality of savings. The corrections to market prices are chiefly designed to correct these 'distortions'. In their analysis, various indirect taxes and subsidies as well as quotas and licences constitute distortion which the project evaluator ought to ignore in arriving at an estimate of 'true' social profitability.

In contrast with the Little–Mirrlees procedure, the UNIDO approach associated with Dasgupta, Marglin and Sen treats consumption as the *numéraire*, and accordingly estimates a shadow price for foreign exchange along with a shadow price for investment and a shadow wage rate. The authors of the approach show considerable cognizance of various government policy decisions which affect the project choice but are not being evaluated at a given time. Many national governments which take their planning seriously including desired levels of production of certain specified sectors and related policy decisions on matters of licensing and quotas based on considerations which are socially important even though not entirely price theoretic in character feel more at home with the UNIDO approach. This is particularly true of large size developing countries.

As Sen (1972) has pertinently observed, the question of defining the 'areas of control' is pertinent to cost–benefit computations as one is obliged to deal with a world where various departures from the optimum are the rule. In fact, the whole *raison d'être* of 'cost–benefit analysis' is the very fact that the world is imperfect and suitable corrections are called for in arriving at a proper estimate of how much net benefit accrues to society as a result of committing resources in a specified direction.

3. Important questions arise as to how to value external effects associated with a project. External economies and diseconomies are apt to be very significant in connection with certain types of projects, in the area of irrigation, power, heavy chemicals, steel, etc. The projects in these areas have significant effects on the environment or on the formation of skills in the labour force, etc. It is well known that in these cases a typical price system defined on the space of traditionally 'marketed' commodities cannot capture them. Ad hoc corrections to observed market prices will not do. If external effects are positive and the overall convexity of the feasible set is retained, it may be possible to augment the dimensionality of the commodity space to define magnitudes analogous to prices although their implementation will require complicated tax-subsidy schemes which may be information-intensive, besides being otherwise difficult to implement. With external diseconomies, the assumption of convexity of the production possibility set may cease to hold, making it impossible to implement a plan through price-based decentralized procedures.

4. Large-scale indivisibilities pose well known problems from the point of view of decentralized decision making. Mathematically, the corresponding programming models have mixed integer–linear character, assuming that the objective function is linear. While algorithms exist for solving these problems in the *primal* space, *duality* results in the usual sense do not hold even though Baumol and Gomory (1960) succeeded in defining a suitable 'dual' programme for these problems which 'permit the construction of a decentralized decision making arrangement which in principle, will achieve some of the possible efficient allocation of resources'. They also noted some special features which marked these dual prices. Problems posed by indivisibilities for cost–benefit analysis are thus non-trivial. However, when attempting choice of appropriate sites and designs of river valley development schemes, or of a large airport or for that matter setting up a large metal-fuel complex, one cannot avoid having to deal with problems where at least some variables can assume only integer values. While Harberger (1971) will not hesitate to use surplus based arguments even for these large changes, many

analysts cannot help having qualms about the ad hoc nature of the estimation of net benefits associated with his procedure. Sectoral programming models based on explicit articulation of inter-industrial linkages, as well as of the spatial distribution of activities along with exogenously given profiles of multiple specified benefits may be the more relevant theoretical approach enabling at least the mapping of relevant trade-offs.

5. An issue on which considerable discussion has taken place is the choice of a social discount rate. Basically, three approaches have been recommended and/or utilized. One is to use as the social discount rate the post-tax real rate of return on risk-free government bonds. This particular choice has been criticized by many economists for ignoring consumption externalities and for giving undue weighting to individual myopia, among others. Marglin (1963a) and Sen (1961) have given persuasive arguments as to why such a procedure may not be appropriate for discounting future benefits associated with public investment decisions. A second approach is to derive from the desired growth rate of the planner the underlying intertemporal substitution rate in consumption. The idea here is that properly specified intertemporal utility maximization exercised subject to production constraints will throw up as a solution the growth path of consumption along which the social rate of discount will equal the marginal rate of transformation through production (Ramsey, 1928). However, this equality will hold only if the government has the capacity to attain the desired rate of savings. Furthermore, such an exercise naturally has to assume that the relevant optimum exists, not an innocuous assumption as the literature on 'optimum savings' had demonstrated.

If, in a mixed economy, there are constraints which do not permit the government to achieve the desired level of investment, one has to take into account the social opportunity cost of capital which measures in terms of consumption, the loss inflicted by preemption of funds from private investment to public investment. Under suitable assumptions, Marglin (1963b) obtained a measure of the social opportunity cost of capital which depends on the social rate of discount (r), the rate of return from private investment in perpetuity (p) and a parameter θ_1 representing the amount of public investment displaced by each dollar of public investment ($0 \leqslant \theta_1 \leqslant 1$). Under these assumptions, the social opportunity cost of capital is measured by the expression $[\theta_1 p + (1 - \theta_1) r]/r$ (formula 4 in Marglin, 1963b).

Most developing economies are characterized by substantial amounts of 'structural unemployment'. Furthermore, they suffer from sub-optimality of savings as well. Under these circumstances, even if the opportunity cost of labour employed on industrial or infrastructure projects in terms of output foregone in the rest of the economy is zero, there is likely to be a cost associated with additional consumption that is connected with wage employment. If savings were at an optimal level, such consumption cannot be treated as a social cost. In the presence of government's inability to reach the appropriate level of savings, the 'market wage' will need to be corrected so as to reflect the social cost of employing additional labour, even though such labour would have remained unemployed otherwise. The 'shadow wage' rate which figures in social cost–benefit analysis is then, seen to depend upon three sets of considerations: (a) labour's opportunity cost, which may be zero, if extreme assumptions are made; (b) the industrial wage rate; and (c) the social opportunity cost of capital. Marglin (1976) and Sen (1968) have dealt with this problem in considerable detail.

Opinions are divided amongst economists as to whether cost–benefit analysts should pay explicit attention to considerations posed by income redistribution which are likely to arise in practice whenever an economy policy or an investment project is going to be implemented. Some argue that cost–benefit analysts should concentrate on the 'efficiency related' issues alone and thus ignore distributional considerations. Musgrave (1969) has talked about the pragmatic need for separating 'allocative' objectives from 'distributional' objectives. He has been supported in this case very forcefully by Harberger (1971). On the other side, Eckstein (1959), Marglin (1965) and others have strongly advocated the case for including distributional considerations alongside efficiency considerations. The question of how best to take into account the distributional considerations has also figured in the literature, should it be agreed that cost–benefit analysis cannot ignore these issues.

On the basic question of including distributional judgements explicitly, it would appear that the crucial point is that of identifying the major operative constraints. If the government has available to itself an armoury of non-distortionary taxes and subsidies, there could be pragmatic reason for ignoring distributional considerations. However, this is rarely the case. It would, then be quite appropriate to accord explicit distributional weights depending on the accrual of benefit streams to different classes or sections of society. The relevant issue, then, becomes, how best to express these weights. On this point, it is less easy to recommend any specific procedure although Benthamite and modified Benthamite weighting patterns have been recommended by several economists (Eckstein, 1964).

How do we evaluate the usefulness of cost–benefit analysis as a decision theoretic tool? Kornai (1979) has described cost–benefit analysis as 'enlightened orthodoxy', orthodox because of its adherence to the basic paradigm provided by neoclassical economic theory and 'enlightened' because it does recognize that reality differs in significant respects from the 'weltbild' of the neoclassical economist.

Kornai identifies three major axioms underlying cost–benefit analysis. These are the *existence* of a social welfare function, identification of the objective of decentralized decision makers with the maximization of the *social profit* function and finally the assumptions of *convexity* of production possibility sets along with the concavity of social welfare functions. With good reason, he raises significant doubts about the plausibility of all these three axioms. The important question, however, is whether these doubts invalidate the use of cost–benefit analysis as a practical tool.

Practical planning experience would appear to suggest that cost–benefit analysis has a useful role to play in conjunction with other instruments of economic policy which help to determine aggregative features of an economy along with the choice of appropriate production and foreign trade structures. If the cost–benefit analysis is viewed as a part of the broader argument for 'planning in stages', some of the criticisms levelled by Kornai would appear as less damaging than otherwise.

This is because such an approach avoids the necessity of viewing the entire planning problem as *one* grand optimization exercise, at one extreme (Frisch, 1976) and the reduction of the national plan to a mere ensemble of projects, on the other (Little and Mirrlees, 1974).

Planning in stages observes the need for devising a coherent macroeconomic policy and planning framework which ensures non-inflationary growth at a desired rate along with balance of payments equilibrium. In the process of implementing this, it also takes into account the indispensable inter-industry links as well. As a part of this procedure, the use of cost–benefit analysis can prove very useful as it avoids wasteful use of resources at the micro level along with preventing the emergence of additional distortions in the process of income generation if suitable distributional weights are allowed for.

Most importantly, it forces the collection of relevant data on the project level in a coherent framework. Along with the use of sensitivity analysis with respect to relevant national parameters, it can distinguish between projects which are more 'robust' from the social angle as distinguished from those which are just marginal or highly questionable. Finally, it helps significantly in enhancing the quality of the dialogue between the central planners on the one hand and planners who operate much lower down in the hierarchy of the decision making process.

SUKHAMOY CHAKRAVARTY

See also DEVELOPMENT ECONOMICS; PROJECT EVALUATION; SHADOW PRICING; WATER RESOURCES.

BIBLIOGRAPHY

Arrow, K.J. 1951. An extension of the basic theorems of classical welfare economics. In *Proceedings of the Second Berkeley Symposium*, Berkeley: University of California.

Arrow, K.J. and Hurwicz, L. 1960. Decentralization and computation in resource allocation. In *Essays in Honor of Harold Hotelling*, ed. R.W. Pfouts, Chapel Hill: University of North Carolina Press.

Barone, E. 1908. The Ministry of Production in the collectivist state. Trans. in *Collectivist Economic Planning*, ed. F.A. Hayek, London: G. Routledge & Sons, 1935.

Baumol, W.J. and Gomory, R.E. 1960. Integer programming and pricing. *Econometrica* 28, July, 521–50.

Dasgupta, P. 1972. A comparative analysis of the UNIDO guidelines and the OECD Manual. *Bulletin of the Oxford University Institute of Economics and Statistics* 34(1), February, 33–51.

Dupuit, J. 1844. *On the Measurement of the Utility of Public Works.* Trans. in *International Economic Papers* No. 2, London: Macmillan, 1952.

Eckstein, O. 1958.*Water Resource Development: The Economics of Project Evaluation.* Cambridge, Mass.: Harvard University Press.

Eckstein, O. 1959. A survey of the theory of public expenditure criteria. In *Conference on Public Finances: Needs, Sources and Utilization*, New York: NBER.

Eckstein, O. 1964. *Public Finance.* Englewood Cliffs: Prentice Hall.

Frisch, R. 1976. *Economic Planning Studies.* Ed. F.V. Long, Dordrecht: Reidel.

Harberger, A.C. 1971. Three basic postulates for applied welfare economics: an interpretative essay. *Journal of Economic Literature* 9(3), September, 785–97.

Harberger, A.C. 1972. Project evaluation. In A.C. Harberger, *Collected Papers*, London: Macmillan.

Layard, R. (ed.) 1976. *Cost-benefit Analysis, Selected Readings.* Harmondsworth: Penguin.

Little, I.M.D. and Mirrlees, J.A. 1968. *Manual of Industrial Project Analysis in Developing Countries.* Vol. II, *Social Cost Benefit Analysis.* Paris: OECD.

Little, I.M.D. and Mirrlees, J.A. 1974. *Project Appraisal and Planning for Developing Countries.* London: Heinemann Educational Books.

Hicks, J.R. 1941. The rehabilitation of consumers' surplus. *Review of Economic Studies* 8, February, 108–16.

Hotelling, H. 1938. The general welfare in relation to problems of taxation and of railway and utility rates. *Econometrica* 6, July, 242–69.

Kornai, J. 1979. Appraisal of project appraisal. In *Economics and Human Welfare*, ed. Michael J. Boskin, New York: Academic Press.

Marglin, S.A. 1963a. The social rate of discount and the optimal rate of investment. *Quarterly Journal of Economics* 77, February, 95–111.

Marglin, S.A. 1963b. The opportunity cost of public investment. *Quarterly Journal of Economics* 77, May, 274–89.

Marglin, S.A. 1967. *Public Investment Criteria.* London: Allen & Unwin.

Marglin, S.A. 1976. *Value and Price in a Labour Surplus Economy.* Oxford: Oxford University Press.

Musgrave, R.A. 1969. Cost-benefit analysis and the theory of public finance. *Journal of Economic Literature* 7(3), September, 797–806.

Pigou, A.C. 1932. *The Economics of Welfare.* 4th edn, London: Macmillan.

Prest, A.R. and Turvey, R. 1965. Cost-benefit analysis: a survey. *Economic Journal* 75, December, 683–735.

Ramsey, F.P. 1928. A mathematical theory of saving. *Economic Journal* 38, December, 543–59.

Sen, A.K. 1961. On optimising the rate of saving. *Economic Journal* 71, September, 479–96.

Sen, A.K. 1968. *Choice of Techniques.* 3rd edn, Oxford: Basil Blackwell.

Sen, A.K. 1972. Control areas and accounting prices: an approach to economic evaluation. *Economic Journal* 82, Supplement, March, 486–501.

Samuelson, P.A. 1947. *Foundations of Economic Analysis.* Cambridge, Mass.: Harvard University Press.

Tinbergen, J. 1958. *The Design of Development.* Baltimore: Johns Hopkins Press.

Tinbergen, J. 1967. *Development Planning.* London: Weidenfeld & Nicolson.

UNIDO (United Nations Industrial Development Organisation). 1972. *Guidelines for Project Evaluation.* Authors: P. Dasgupta, S.A. Marglin and A.K. Sen. New York: United Nations

Willig, R.D. 1976. Consumers' surplus without apology. *American Economic Review* 66(4), September, 589–97.

cost functions.

1. INTRODUCTION. Cost and expenditure functions are widely used in both theoretical and applied economics. Cost functions are often used in econometric studies which describe the technology of firms or industries while their consumer theory counterparts, expenditure functions, are frequently used to describe the preferences of consumers.

Cost and expenditure functions also play an important role in many theoretical investigations. This is due to the fact that a cost function embodies the consequences of cost minimizing behaviour on the part of a consumer or producer and so it is not necessary to spell out the details of the primal minimization problem that defined the cost function. This may seem like a very minor advantage, but when one is dealing with, say, the comparative statics of a general equilibrium problem, the use of cost functions leads to the analysis of a much smaller system of equations and hence the structure of the problem can be more easily understood.

Sections 2–5 below develop the theoretical properties of cost functions while Sections 6–8 are devoted to empirical applications of cost functions in the producer and consumer contexts.

2. PROPERTIES OF COST FUNCTIONS. One of the fundamental paradigms in economics is the one which has a producer competitively minimizing costs subject to his technological constraints. Competitive means that the producer takes input prices as fixed during the given period of time irrespective of the producer's demand for those inputs.

We assume that only one output can be produced using N inputs and that the producer's technology can be summarized by a *production function* $F: y = F(x)$ where $y \geqslant 0$ is the maximal amount of output that can be produced during a period, given the non-negative vector of inputs $x \equiv (x_1, \ldots, x_N) \geqslant 0_N$. We further assume that the cost of purchasing one unit of input i is $p_i > 0$, $i = 1, \ldots, N$ and that the positive vector of input prices that the producer faces is $p \equiv (p_1, \ldots, p_N) \gg 0_N$.

For $y \geq 0$, $p \gg 0_N$, the producer's *cost function* C is defined as the solution to the following constrained minimization problem:

$$C(y, p) \equiv \min_x \{p \cdot x : F(x) \geq y, x \geq 0_N\} \quad (1)$$

where $p \cdot x \equiv \Sigma_{n=1}^N p_n x_n$. Thus $C(y, p)$ is the minimum input cost of producing at least the output level y, given that the producer faces the input price vector p.

The minimization problem (1) can also be given a consumer theory interpretation: let F be a consumer's preference or *utility function*, let y be a utility or welfare level, let x be a vector of commodity purchases (rentals in the case of consumer durables), and let p be a vector of commodity (rental) prices. In this case, the consumer attempts to minimize the cost of achieving at least the target welfare level indexed by y, and the solution to (1) defines the consumer's *expenditure function*.

Unfortunately, the minimum in (1) may not exist in general. However, if we impose the following very weak regularity condition on F, it can be shown that C will be well defined as a minimum: *Assumption 1 on F*: F is continuous from above.

Assumption 1 means that for every y in the range of F, the *upper level set* $L(y) \equiv \{x : F(x) \geq y, x \geq 0_N\}$ is a closed set. The assumption is a technical one of minimal economic interest. It is also a very weak condition from an empirical point of view, since it cannot be contradicted by a finite set of data on the inputs and output of a producer.

Assuming that the production function F satisfies Assumption 1, it turns out that the cost function C has the following properties: *Property 1*: C is a non-negative function; i.e., $C(y, p) \geq 0$; *Property 2*: C is *linearly homogeneous* in input prices p for each fixed output level y; i.e., $C(y, \lambda p) = \lambda C(y, p)$ for $y \geq 0, \lambda > 0$ and $p \gg 0_N$, *Property 3*: C is *nondecreasing* in p for fixed y; i.e., $C(y, p^1) \geq C(y, p^2)$ for $y \geq 0$, $p^1 \geq p^2 \gg 0_N$; *Property 4*: C is *concave* in p for fixed y; i.e., $C(y, \lambda p^1 + (1 - \lambda)p^2) \geq \lambda C(y, p^1) + (1 - \lambda) C(y, p^2)$ for $y \geq 0$, $0 \leq \lambda \leq 1$, $p^1 \gg 0_N$ and $p^2 \gg 0_N$; *Property 5*: C is *nondecreasing* in y for fixed p; i.e., $C(y^1, p) \geq C(y^2, p)$ for $y^1 \geq y^2 \geq 0$ and $p \gg 0_N$; *Property 6*: C is *continuous from below* in y for fixed p, i.e., $\{y : C(y, p) \leq \alpha\}$ is a closed set for every α and $p \gg 0_N$.

Properties 1–4 for C were derived by Shephard (1953) under stronger regularity conditions on F and Properties 4, 5, and 6 were obtained by McKenzie (1957), Uzawa (1964), and Shephard (1970) respectively.

From the viewpoint of economics, all of the properties of C are intuitively obvious except Properties 4 and 6. Property 6 on C is the technical counterpart to Assumption 1 on F and is of minimal economic interest. However, Property 4 has some significant economic implications as we shall see in Section 5 below.

We can already draw some useful empirical implications from the fact that a cost function must satisfy Properties 1–6 above. For example, in industrial organization and applied econometrics, it is quite common to assume that the true functional form for a firm's or industry's cost function has the following functional form:

$$C(y, p) \equiv \alpha + \beta \cdot p + \gamma y \quad (2)$$

where $\alpha, \beta \equiv (\beta_1, \ldots, \beta_N)$ and γ are unknown parameters. However, Property 2 implies that α and γ must be zero in order for the cost function to be linearly homogeneous in input prices. But then $C(y, p) = \beta \cdot p$ does not depend on the output level y, which is very implausible.

3. DUALITY BETWEEN COST AND PRODUCTION FUNCTIONS. It is easy to see that the family of upper level sets, $L(y) \equiv \{x : F(x) \geq y, x \geq 0_N\}$, completely determines the production function F. Furthermore, the cost function C may be defined in terms of the production function by (1) or equivalently, in terms of the family of upper level sets as follows:

$$C(y, p) = \min_x \{p \cdot x : x \text{ belongs to } L(y)\}. \quad (3)$$

Thus given the production function F or the family of level sets $L(y)$, the cost function C is determined.

We now ask the following question: given a cost function C which has Properties 1 to 6, can we use C to define the underlying production function F?

For a given output level y and input price vector $p \gg 0_N$, define the corresponding isocost plane by $\{x : p \cdot x = C(y, p)\}$. From the definitions of $C(y, p)$ and $L(y)$, it is obvious that the set $L(y)$ must lie above this isocost plane and be tangent to it; i.e., $L(y)$ must be a subset of the set $\{x : p \cdot x \geq C(y, p)\}$ and this conclusion must be true for every positive input price vector p. Thus $L(y)$ must be a subset of the intersection of all of these sets which we denote by $M(y)$:

$$M(y) \equiv \bigcap_{p \gg 0}^N \{x : p \cdot x \geq C(y, p)\}. \quad (4)$$

The set $M(y)$ is called the free *disposal, convex hull of* $L(y)$; see McFadden (1966).

Each set $\{x : p \cdot x \geq C(y, p)\}$ is a halfspace and is a convex set. A set S *is convex* if and only if x^1 and x^2 belong to S and $0 \leq \lambda \leq 1$ implies $\lambda x^1 + (1 - \lambda)x^2$ also belongs to S. Since $M(y)$ is the intersection of a family of convex sets, $M(y)$ is also a convex set. $M(y)$ also has the following *free disposal* property:

x^1 belongs to $M(y)$, $x^1 \leq x^2$, then x^2 belongs to $M(y)$. (5)

We know $L(y)$ must be a subset of $M(y)$. If we want $L(y)$ to coincide with $M(y)$, then $L(y)$ must also be a convex set with the free disposal property. It can be shown that $L(y)$ will have these last two properties for every output level y if and only if the production function F has the following two properties: *Assumption 2 on F*: F is a *quasiconcave* function; i.e., for every y belonging to the range of F, $L(y) \equiv \{x : F(x) \geq y\}$ is a convex set. *Assumption 3 on F*: F is *nondecreasing*; i.e., if $x^2 \geq x^1 \geq 0_N$, then $F(x^2) \geq F(x^1)$.

We may now answer our earlier question about whether a cost function C can completely determine the production function F: the answer is yes if the production satisfies Assumptions 1–3.

More precisely, we have the following result: given a cost function C which satisfies Properties 1–6, then the production function F defined by

$$F(x) \equiv \max_y \{y : C(y, p) \leq p \cdot x \text{ for every } p \gg 0_N\}, \quad x \geq 0_N \quad (6)$$

satisfies Assumptions 1–3. Moreover, if we define the cost function C^* which corresponds to the F defined by (6) in the usual way [recall (1)], then $C^* = C$; i.e., this derived cost function C^* coincides with the original cost function C. Thus there is a *duality* between production functions F satisfying Assumptions 1–3 and cost functions C having Properties 1–6: each function completely determines the other under these regularity conditions.

Duality theorems similar to the above results have been established under various regularity conditions by Shephard (1953; 1970), Uzawa (1964), McFadden (1966; 1978a), and Diewert (1971; 1982).

4. THE DERIVATIVE PROPERTY OF THE COST FUNCTION. The following result is the basis for most of the theoretical and empirical applications of cost functions.

Suppose the cost function C satisfies Properties 1–6 listed in Section 2 and in addition, C is differentiable with respect to the components of p at the point (y^*, p^*). Then the solution $x^* \equiv (x_1^*, \ldots, x_N^*)$ to the cost minimization problem $\min_y \{p^* \cdot x : F(x) \geqslant y^*, x \geqslant 0_N\}$ is unique and

$$x_i^* = \partial C(y^*, p^*)/\partial p_i, \qquad i = 1, \ldots, N; \qquad (7)$$

i.e., the cost minimizing demand for the ith input is equal to the partial derivative of the cost function with respect to the ith input price.

The result (7) is known as the derivative property of the cost function (see McFadden, 1978a) or Shephard's Lemma, since Shephard (1953) was the first to obtain the result. It should be noted that Hicks (1946) and Samuelson (1947) obtained the result (7) earlier, but under different hypotheses: they assumed the existence of a utility or production function F and deduced (7) by analysing the comparative statics properties of the cost minimization problem (1). On the other hand, Shephard (1953) (1970) assumed only the existence of a cost function satisfying the appropriate regularity conditions.

A very elegant proof of (7) using the hypotheses of Hicks and Samuelson is due to Karlin (1959) and Gorman (1976). Their proof proceeds as follows.

Let x^* be a solution to $\min_x \{p^* \cdot x : F(x) \geqslant y^*, x \geqslant 0_N\} = C(y^*, p^*)$. Then for every $p \gg 0_N$, x^* is feasible for the cost minimization problem defined by $C(y^*, p) = \min_x \{p \cdot x : F(x) \geqslant y^*, x \geqslant 0_N\}$ but it is not necessarily optimal. Thus for every $p \gg 0_N$, we have the following inequality:

$$p \cdot x^* \geqslant C(y^*, p). \qquad (8)$$

We also have

$$p^* \cdot x^* = C(y^*, p^*). \qquad (9)$$

For $p \gg 0_N$, define the function $g(p) \equiv p \cdot x^* - C(y^*, p)$. From (8), $g(p) \geqslant 0$ for all $p \gg 0_N$ and from (9), $g(p^*) = 0$. Thus $g(p)$ attains a global minimum at $p = p^*$. Since g is differentiable, the first order necessary conditions for a minimum must be satisfied at p^*:

$$\nabla_p g(p^*) = x^* - \nabla_p C(y^*, p^*) = 0_N \qquad (10)$$

where $\nabla_p g(p^*) \equiv [\partial g(p^*)/\partial p_1, \ldots, \partial g(p^*)/\partial p_N]$ denotes the vector of first order partial derivatives of g with respect to the components of p evaluated at p^* and $\nabla_p C(y^*, p^*)$ denotes the vector of first order partial derivatives of C with respect to the components of p evaluated at (y^*, p^*). The second set of equalities in (10) can be rearranged to yield (7).

From an econometric point of view, Shephard's Lemma is a very useful result. In order to obtain a valid system of cost minimizing input demand functions, $x(y, p) \equiv [x_1(y, p), \ldots, x_N(y, p)]$ all we have to do is postulate a functional form for C which satisfies Properties 1–6 and then differentiate C with respect to the components of the input price vector p; i.e., $x(y, p) = \nabla_p C(y, p)$. It is not necessary to compute the production function F that corresponds to C via the Shephard Duality Theorem nor is it necessary to undertake the often complex algebra involved in deriving the input demand functions using the production function and Lagrangian techniques. In Section 6 below, we shall consider several functional forms for C that have been suggested for their econometric convenience.

5. THE COMPARATIVE STATICS PROPERTIES OF COST FUNCTIONS. Suppose that we are given a cost function C satisfying Properties 1–6 that is also twice continuously differentiable at (y^*, p^*) where $y^* > 0$ and $p^* \gg 0_N$. Applying Shephard's Lemma (7), the above differentiability assumption ensures that the cost minimizing input demand functions $x_i(y, p)$ exist and are once continuously differentiable at (y^*, p^*).

Define $[\partial x_i/\partial p_j] \equiv [\partial x_i(y^*, p^*)/\partial p_j]$ to be the N by N matrix of partial derivatives of the N demand functions $x_i(y^*, p^*)$ with respect to the N prices p_j, $i, j = 1, \ldots, N$. From (7), it follows that

$$[\partial x_i/\partial p_j] = [\partial^2 C(y^*, p^*)/\partial p_i \partial p_j] \equiv \nabla_{pp}^2 C(y^*, p^*) \qquad (11)$$

where $\nabla_{pp}^2 C(y^*, p^*)$ is the matrix of second order partial derivatives of the cost function with respect to the components of the input price vector evaluated at (y^*, p^*). The twice continuous differentiability property of C implies by Young's Theorem in calculus that $\nabla_{pp}^2 C(y^*, p^*)$ is a symmetric N by N matrix. Thus using (11), we have

$$[\partial x_i/\partial p_j] = [\partial x_i/\partial p_j]^{\mathrm{T}} = [\partial x_j/\partial p_i] \qquad (12)$$

where A^{T} denotes the transpose of the matrix A. Thus we have established the Hicks (1946) and Samuelson (1947) *symmetry restrictions* on input demand functions, $\partial x_i(y^*, p^*)/\partial p_j = \partial x_j(y^*, p^*)/\partial p_i$ for all i and j.

Since C is concave in p and is twice continuously differentiable with respect to the components of p at the point (y^*, p^*), it follows from a characterization of concave functions that $\nabla_{pp}^2 C(y^*, p^*)$ is a negative semidefinite matrix. Thus by (11),

$$z^{\mathrm{T}}[\partial x_i/\partial p_j] z \leqslant 0 \qquad \text{for all vectors } z. \qquad (13)$$

In particular, letting $z = e_i$, the ith unit vector, (13) implies

$$\partial x_i(y^*, p^*)/\partial p_i \leqslant 0 \qquad \text{for } i = 1, \ldots, N; \qquad (14)$$

i.e., the ith cost minimizing input demand function cannot slope upwards with respect to the ith input price for $i = 1, \ldots, N$.

Since C is linearly homogeneous in p, we have $C(y^*, \lambda p^*) = \lambda C(y^*, p^*)$ for all $\lambda > 0$. Partially differentiating this equation with respect to p_i for λ close to 1 yields the equation $C_i(y^*, \lambda p^*) \lambda = \lambda C_i(y^*, p^*)$ where $C_i(y^*, p^*) \equiv \partial C(y^*, p^*)/\partial p_i$. Thus $C_i(y^*, \lambda p^*) = C_i(y^*, p^*)$ and differentiation of this last equation with respect to λ yields when $\lambda = 1$:

$$\sum_{j=1}^{N} p_j^* \partial^2 C(y^*, p^*)/\partial p_i \partial p_j = 0 \qquad \text{for } i = 1, \ldots, N. \qquad (15)$$

Equations (11) and (15) imply that the input demand functions $x_i(y^*, p^*)$ satisfy the following N restrictions:

$$\sum_{j=1}^{N} p_j^* \partial x_i(y^*, p^*)/\partial p_j = 0 \qquad \text{for } i = 1, \ldots, N. \qquad (16)$$

A final general restriction on the derivatives of the input demand functions may be obtained as follows: for λ near 1 differentiate both sides of $C(y^*, \lambda p^*) = \lambda C(y^*, p^*)$ with respect to y and then differentiate the resulting equation with respect to λ. When $\lambda = 1$, the last equation becomes:

$$\sum_{j=1}^{N} p_j^* \partial^2 C(y^*, p^*)/\partial y \partial p_j = \partial C(y^*, p^*)/\partial y. \qquad (17)$$

The twice continuous differentiability of C at (y^*, p^*) and (7) imply:

$$\partial^2 C(y^*, p^*)/\partial y \partial p_j = \partial^2 C(y^*, p^*)/\partial p_j \partial y = \partial x_j(y^*, p^*)/\partial y \qquad (18)$$

Property 5 for cost functions implies that

$$\partial C(y^*, p^*)/\partial y^* \geqslant 0. \qquad (19)$$

Using (18) and (19), (17) is equivalent to:

$$\sum_{j=1}^{N} p_j^* \partial x_j(y^*, p^*)/\partial y \geqslant 0. \qquad (20)$$

Thus for at least one j, we must have $\partial x_j(y^*, p^*)/\partial y \geqslant 0$; i.e., as output increases, not every input demand can decrease.

We have shown that the assumption of cost minimizing

behaviour implies a number of restrictions on input demand functions that are potentially testable. Hicks (1946) and Samuelson (1947) obtained the restrictions (12), (13), and (16) using the first order conditions for the primal cost minimization problem (1) and the properties of determinants of bordered Hessian matrices; Samuelson also obtained (20). Our derivation of the restrictions on input demand functions using the dual approach is due to McKenzie (1957), Karlin (1959) and McFadden (1978a).

Hicks (1946) also showed that when $N = 2$, so that there are only two inputs, then (12), (13), and (16) imply that

$$\partial x_1(y^*, p_1^*, p_2^*)/\partial p_2 = \partial x_2(y^*, p_1^*, p_2^*)/\partial p_1 \geqslant 0. \quad (21)$$

Hicks (1946) called two distinct goods i and j *substitutes* if and only if $\partial x_i(y, p)/\partial p_j \geqslant 0$ and *complements* if and only if $\partial x_i(y, p)/\partial p_j < 0$. Thus in the two input case, the two goods must be substitutes. Hicks also showed that in the three input case, at least two of the three pairs of goods must be substitutes.

We turn now to empirical applications of cost functions.

6. FUNCTIONAL FORMS FOR COST FUNCTIONS. Shephard's Lemma (7) provides a convenient method for generating systems of cost minimizing input demand functions: simply postulate a functional form for $C(y, p)$ and then partially differentiate C with respect to each input price. Below, we present three examples to illustrate the technique.

Our first example is the *translog cost function* due to Christensen, Jorgenson and Lau (1971; 1973). The logarithm of the cost function is defined as follows:

$$\ln C(y, p) \equiv \alpha_0 + \sum_{i=1}^{N} a_i \ln p_i = (1/2) \sum_{i=1}^{N} \sum_{j=1}^{N} a_{ij} \ln p_i \ln p_j$$
$$+ \sum_{i=1}^{N} a_{iy} \ln p_i \ln y + a_y \ln y + (1/2)a_{yy} \ln y \ln y \quad (22)$$

where the a_i, $a_{ij}, = a_{ji}$, a_i, a_y and a_{yy} are $1 + N + (1/2)N(N + 1) + N + 2 = 3 + 2N + (1/2)N(N + 1)$ parameters determined by the technology of the firm or industry. Differentiating both sides of (22) with respect to the logarithm of the ith input price, $\ln p_i$, for $i = 1, \ldots, N$ yields the following system of equations:

$$s_i = a_i + \sum_{j=1}^{N} a_{ij} \ln p_j + a_{iy} \ln y, \qquad i = 1, \ldots, N \quad (23)$$

where the ith input cost share is defined as $s_i \equiv [p_i \partial C(y, p)/\partial p_i]/C(y, p) = p_i x_i(y, p)/C(y, p)$ where the last equality follows using (7).

By Property 2 for cost functions, $C(y, p)$ must be linearly homogeneous in input prices. This property will be satisfied by the translog cost function cost function if and only if the following $N + 2$ linear restrictions on the parameters hold:

$$\sum_{i=1}^{N} a_i = 1, \sum_{i=1}^{N} a_{iy} = 0 \text{ and } \sum_{j=1}^{N} a_{ij} = 0 \text{ for } i = 1, \ldots, N. \quad (24)$$

It is possible to append errors to equations (22) and $N - 1$ of the equations (23) and econometrically estimate the unknown parameters, given data on inputs, input prices and output. The symmetry restrictions $a_{ij} = a_{ji}$ and the restrictions (24) may be imposed or one can test for their validity. If these restrictions are imposed, then the resulting translog cost function will have $1 + N + (1/2)N(N + 1)$ free parameters.

What considerations are relevant in choosing a functional form for a cost function? The following four properties are desirable: (i) *flexibility*; i.e., the functional form for C should have a sufficient number of free parameters to be able to provide a second order approximation to an arbitrary twice continuously differentiable function with the appropriate the-

oretical properties, (ii) *parsimony*; i.e., the functional form for C should have the minimal number of free parameters required to have the flexibility property, (iii) *linearity*; i.e., the unknown parameters of C should appear in the system of estimating equations in a linear fashion in order to facilitate econometric estimation, and (iv) *consistency*; i.e., the functional form for C should be consistent with Properties 1–6 for cost functions. These considerations were first suggested by Diewert (1971) in an informal manner; the term parsimony is due to Fuss, McFadden and Mundlak (1978) and the term flexible is due to Diewert (1974). The equivalence of various definitions of the flexibility property is discussed by Barnett (1983).

How satisfactory is the translog cost function in the light of the above considerations? We consider the flexibility property first. In order to be able to approximate a function of $1 + N$ variables to the second order, we require $1 + (1 + N) + (1 + N)^2$ free parameters. However, if we assume that the cost functions are twice continuously differentiable, then we can reduce the number by $N(N + 1)/2$ due to the symmetry property of the second order partial derivatives. The linear homogeneity property of the cost function, Property 2, yields an additional $N + 1$ restriction on the first and second derivatives of C, (15) and (17), plus the following restriction (which follows using Euler's Theorem on homogeneous functions):

$$C(y, p) = \sum_{i=1}^{N} p_i \partial C(y, p)/\partial p_i, \quad (25)$$

Thus a flexible functional form for a cost function should have $1 + (1 + N) + (1 + N)^2 - [(1/2)N(N + 1) + N + 1 + 1] = 1 + N + (1/2)N(N + 1)$ free parameters, which is precisely the number the translog cost function has when the restrictions (24) are imposed. It can be shown that the translog cost function is indeed flexible and we have just shown that it is also parsimonious.

As can be seen by inspecting (22) and (23), the estimating equations are linear in the unknown parameters, so the linearity property is also satisfied.

If the restrictions (24) are imposed, Property 2 will be satisfied. In practice, the other properties that a cost function must have will be satisfied with the exception of Property 4, the concavity in prices property. If all of the a_{ij} and a_{iy} parameters are zero, then the translog cost function reduces to a Cobb–Douglas cost function which satisfies the concavity property globally. However, in the general case, the best we can hope for is that the concavity property is satisfied locally for a range of input prices.

If a production function is linearly homogeneous (i.e., $F(\lambda x) = \lambda F(x)$ for $\lambda \geqslant 0$ and $x \geqslant 0_N$) so that the technology is subject to constant returns to scale, then the corresponding cost function has the following property:

$$C(y, p) = yC(1, p); \quad (26)$$

i.e., total cost is equal to the output level y times the cost of producing one unit of output, $C(1, p) \equiv c(p)$, the *unit cost function*.

If C is twice continuously differentiable and satisfies (26), then one can show that the following $2 + N$ restrictions on the first and second derivatives of C must hold:

$$C(y, p) = y\partial C(y, p)\partial y; \quad (27)$$

$$\partial^2 C(y, p)/\partial y^2 = 0; \quad (28)$$

$$\partial C(y, p)/\partial p_i = y\partial^2 C(y, p)/\partial y\partial p_i, \qquad i = 1, \ldots, N. \quad (29)$$

However, in view of (25), it can be seen that only $N - 1$ of the restrictions (29) are new. Thus the assumption of a constant returns to scale technology imposes new restrictions on the derivatives of the cost function C.

It can be shown that necessary and sufficient conditions for the translog cost function defined by (22) and (24) to satisfy (26) are the following $N + 1$ restrictions:

$$a_y = 1, a_{yy} = 0 \quad \text{and} \quad a_{iy} = 0 \quad \text{for} \quad i = 1, \ldots, N - 1 \quad (30)$$

Of course (30) and (24) imply that $a_{Ny} = 0$ as well.

It can be shown that if the restrictions (24) and (30) are imposed on the parameters of the translog cost function defined by (22), then the resulting functional form is flexible in the class of cost functions that satisfy the constant returns to scale property (26). Note that we can test for the validity of the constant returns to scale property by testing whether the $N + 1$ linear restrictions (30) hold.

For our second example, consider the following functional form for a cost function:

$$C(y, p) \equiv c(p)y + \sum_{i=1}^{N} b_i p_i + b_{yy} \left(\sum_{i=1}^{N} \beta_i p_i \right) y^2; \quad (31)$$

$$c(p) \equiv \sum_{i=1}^{N} \sum_{j=1}^{N} b_{ij} p_i^{1/2} p_j^{1/2} \quad (32)$$

where the b_{yy}, b_i, $b_{ij} = b_{ji}$ and β_i are parameters which characterize the technology. If $b_i = 0$ for $i = 1, \ldots, N$ and $b_{yy} = 0$, then (31) reduces to the *Generalized Leontief cost function* defined by Diewert (1971). If in addition, $b_{ij} = 0$ for all $i \neq j$, then (31) reduces to the cost function $\sum_{i=1}^{N} b_{ii} p_i y$ which is dual to the Leontief (no substitution) production function, $F(x_1, \ldots, x_N) \equiv \min\{x_i / b_{ii} : i = 1, \ldots, N\}$.

In order for the cost function defined by (31) and (32) to satisfy the parsimony property, it is necessary for the empirical investigator to prespecify the β_i parameters; e.g., one could set β_i equal to 1 or to the average input quantity x_i observed in the sample of data. Under these conditions, the Generalized Leontief cost function has $(1/2)N(N + 1) + N + 1$ free parameters, which is just the required number for the flexibility property. In fact, Diewert and Wales (1986a) show that this cost function is flexible and parsimonious when the β_i are predetermined.

Applying (7), the input demand functions that correspond to (31) and (32) are:

$$x_i(y, p) = \sum_{j=1}^{N} b_{ij} p_i^{-1/2} p_j^{1/2} y + b_i + b_{yy} \beta_i y^2. \quad i = 1, \ldots, N \quad (33)$$

For the purpose of econometric estimation, errors can be appended to the N equations (33). If the β_i are predetermined, it can be seen that the system of estimating equations is linear in the unknown parameters.

If we wish to test for a constant returns to scale technology, then the following $1 + N$ linear restrictions on the parameters are necessary and sufficient for this property:

$$b_{yy} = 0 \quad \text{and} \quad b_i = 0 \quad \text{for} \quad i = 1, \ldots, N. \quad (34)$$

Note that the linear homogeneity in prices property is satisfied by the Generalized Leontief cost function. The other properties for cost functions will also be satisfied in practice with the exception of Property 4, the concavity in prices property. If all $b_{ij} \geq 0$ for $i \neq j$, then the concavity property will be globally satisfied, but this assumption rules out complementary pairs of inputs (recall the discussion about substitutes and complements at the end of the previous section). Thus in general, one can only hope that the concavity property will be satisfied locally, as was the case with the translog cost function.

For our third and final example, consider the following *normalized quadratic cost function* defined by (31) but now $c(p)$ is defined as follows:

$$c(p) \equiv \sum_{i=1}^{N} b_{ii} p_i + (1/2) \sum_{i=1}^{N} \sum_{j=1}^{N} a_{ij} p_i p_j \Big/ \left(\sum_{n=1}^{N} \alpha_n p_n \right) \quad (35)$$

where the N by N matrix $A \equiv [a_{ij}]$ is symmetric and satisfies the following restriction for some input price vector $p^* \gg 0_N$;

$$A p^* = 0_N. \quad (36)$$

This functional form is due to Diewert and Wales (1986a); it generalizes some functional forms due to Fuss (1977) and McFadden (1978b). The functional form has N b_{ii} parameters, $(1/2)N(N - 1)$ free a_{ij} parameters taking into consideration (36), N b_i parameters, 1 b_{yy}, N β_i and N α_n parameters or $1 + 3N + (1/2)N(N + 1)$ free parameters in all. In order for this functional form to have the parsimony property, it is necessary for the empirical investigator to prespecify the β_i and α_n parameters; we assume that this has been done and these parameters are non-negative and not identically equal to zero. Under these conditions, Diewert and Wales (1986a) show that this cost function is parsimonious and flexible at the point (y^*, p^*) where p^* is the price vector which appears in (36).

Applying (7), the system of input demand functions divided by the output, y is:

$$x_i(y, p)/y = b_{ii} + \sum_{j=1}^{N} a_{ij} p_j \left(\sum_{n=1}^{N} \alpha_n p_n \right)^{-1} - \left(\sum_{j=1}^{N} \sum_{k=1}^{N} a_{jk} p_j p_k \right)$$

$$\times \left(\sum_{n=1}^{N} \alpha_n p_n \right)^{-2} \alpha_i + b_i y^{-1} + b_{yy} \beta_i y, \quad i = 1, \ldots, N. \quad (37)$$

Errors can be appended to (37) and we obtain a system of estimating equations which is linear in the unknown parameters, provided that the α_n and β_i are prespecified.

If we wish to test for a constant returns to scale technology, then again the $1 + N$ linear restrictions (34) are necessary and sufficient for this property.

The normalized quadratic cost function with prespecified α_n and β_i is flexible, parsimonious and has linear estimating equations. As was the case with our first two examples, our third example has no problem in satisfying Properties 1, 2, 3, 5 and 6 for cost functions. It also turns out that our third example has no problem in satisfying Property 4: Diewert and Wales (1986a) using some results due to Lau (1978), show that the normalized quadratic cost function is globally concave if and only if the A matrix is negative semidefinite. They also indicate how this negative semidefiniteness property can be imposed if necessary without destroying the flexibility of the functional form; simply set $A = -SS^T$ where S is a lower triangular N by N matrix and S^T is its transpose. However, in this latter case, nonlinear regression techniques must be used in order to estimate the unknown parameters.

The extensive empirical literature on estimating cost functions is nicely reviewed by Jorgenson (1984).

7. APPLICATIONS TO THE ESTIMATION OF CONSUMER PREFERENCES. The cost function techniques described in the previous section can be used to obtain empirical descriptions of technologies. Those techniques can also be adapted to obtain empirical descriptions of consumer preferences.

As was noted in Section 2, y may be interpreted as a household's welfare level, F as a utility or preference function, p as a vector of commodity prices and $C(y, p)$ as the minimum cost of achieving at least the welfare level y.

However, the econometric techniques described in the previous section cannot be utilized immediately in the consumer context because utility cannot be observed whereas output can. We acknowledge this difference by using u, the consumer's utility or welfare level, in place of y in what follows.

The theory outlined in the previous sections is still valid: given a differentiable functional form for the cost function $C(u, p)$ that satisfies Properties 1 to 6, we may form the consumer's system of *constant real income* or *Hicksian demand functions* $x(u, p) \equiv [x_1(u, p), \ldots, x_N(u, p)]$ by differentiating the cost function with respect to each commodity price p_i [recall (7)]:

$$x_i(u, p) = \partial C(u, p)/\partial p_i, \qquad i = 1, \ldots, N. \tag{38}$$

We determine u as a function of the prices p and the consumer's observed expenditure on commodities during the period Y, say, by equating the minimum cost of achieving the welfare level u to the observed expenditure; i.e., we solve the following equation for u:

$$C(u, p) = Y. \tag{39}$$

The solution function g where $u = g(Y, p)$ is known as the consumer's *indirect utility function*. Now replace u in the right-hand side of (38) by $g(Y, p)$ and obtain the consumer's system of *market demand functions*:

$$x_i = \partial C(g(Y, p), p) \partial p_i, \qquad i = 1, \ldots, N. \tag{40}$$

If we multiply equation i in (40) by p_i, sum the resulting equations and use (7), (25) and (39), then we obtain the identity $\sum_{i=1}^{N} p_i x_i = Y$, so only $N - 1$ of the N equations in (40) are independent. Thus for econometric estimation purposes, we may add errors to $N - 1$ of the equations in (40), and given a functional form for C, we may use these equations to estimate the unknown parameters in C. We shall discuss this technique in more detail shortly, but first, we must discuss the problems involved in cardinalizing utility.

The scaling of utility is irrelevant in describing a consumer's preferences. However, when we postulate a functional form for a cost function, we are implicitly imposing a cardinalization of the consumer's utility. Hence, we might as well impose a convenient cardinalization: *money metric scaling of utility* (the term is due to Samuelson, 1974). This involves setting utility u equal to 'income' Y, holding prices constant at some specified price vector p^*, i.e., we have

$$Y = g(Y, p^*) \qquad \text{for all} \quad Y > 0. \tag{41}$$

In terms of the cost function, (41) may be rewritten as

$$u = C(u, p^*) \qquad \text{for all} \quad u > 0. \tag{42}$$

In examples 2 and 3 in the previous section, the cost function had the following form:

$$C(u, p) = c(p)u + \sum_{i=1}^{N} b_i p_i + b_{yy}\left(\sum_{i=1}^{N} \beta_i p_i\right)u^2. \tag{43}$$

In order to make (43) consistent with money metric scaling, (42), the following three restrictions on the parameters of C must be satisfied:

$$c(p^*) = 1, \quad \sum_{i=1}^{N} b_i p_i^* = 0 \quad \text{and} \quad b_{yy} = 0. \tag{44}$$

Using $b_{yy} = 0$, we find that the indirect utility function that corresponds to the C defined by (43) is

$$g(Y, p) = \left(Y - \sum_{i=1}^{N} b_i p_i\right)\bigg/ c(p). \tag{45}$$

Substitution of (45) into (40) yields the following system of consumer demand functions:

$$x_i = b_i + [\partial c(p)/\partial p_i]\left(Y - \sum_{i=1}^{N} b_i p_i\right)\bigg/ c(p). \qquad i = 1, \ldots, N. \tag{46}$$

Now add errors to $N - 1$ of the equations (46), calculate the partial derivatives of the $c(p)$ defined by (32) or (35), impose the normalizations (44) and we have a system of nonlinear estimating equations. An empirical example of this technique for estimating consumer preferences may be found in Diewert and Wales (1986b).

Finally, we note that cost functions of the type defined by (43) with $b_{yy} = 0$ have very convenient aggregation over consumers' properties; see Gorman (1953) and Deaton and Muellbauer (1980).

8. COST FUNCTIONS AND MEASURES OF WELFARE GAIN. Consider a consumer whose preferences can be represented by the differentiable cost function, $C(u, p)$. Suppose we can observe the consumer's choices x^1 and x^2 during periods 1 and 2 when prices p^1 and p^2 prevail. Let u^1 and u^2 be the welfare levels attained during those two periods. Then by (7),

$$x^i = \nabla_p C(u^i, p^i), \qquad i = 1, 2. \tag{47}$$

For many purposes in applied welfare economics, it is useful to evaluate the ex post welfare change of the consumer. Two natural measures, suggested originally by Hicks (1942), are his *equivalent* and *compensating variations* which we denote by $V(p^1)$ and $V(p^2)$:

$$V(p^1) \equiv C(u^2, p^1) - C(u^1, p^1);$$
$$V(p^2) \equiv C(u^2, p^2) - C(u^1, p^2). \tag{48}$$

From (47) and (25), $C(u^1, p^1) = p^1 \cdot x^1$ and $C(u^2, p^2) = p^2 \cdot x^2$. However, the costs $C(u^2, p^1)$ and $C(u^1, p^2)$ are not observable. Hence the following questions arises: can we form approximations to $V(p^i)$ that use only observable data?

Linear approximations to $C(u^i, p^j)$ may be obtained using Taylor's Theorem. Thus we have:

$$V(p^1) \cong [C(u^2, p^2) + \nabla_p C(u^2, p^2) \cdot (p^1 - p^2)] - C(u^1, p^1)$$
$$= [p^2 \cdot x^2 + x^2 \cdot (p^1 - p^2)] - p^1 \cdot x^1 \quad \text{using (47)}$$
$$= p^1 \cdot (x^2 - x^1) \tag{49}$$

and

$$V(p^2) \cong C(u^2, p^2) - [C(u^1, p^1) + \nabla_p C(u^1, p^1) \cdot (p^2 - p^1)]$$
$$= p^2 \cdot x^2 - [p^1 \cdot x^1 + x^1 \cdot (p^2 - p^1)] \quad \text{using (47)}$$
$$= p^2 \cdot (x^2 - x^1). \tag{50}$$

The first order approximations (49) and (50) are essentially due to Hicks (1942; 1946).

To obtain a second order approximation result, we proceed indirectly. Suppose the consumer's cost function is defined by

$$C(u, p) \equiv c(p) + \sum_{i=1}^{N} b_i p_i u \tag{51}$$

where $c(p)$ is the normalized quadrative unit cost function defined by (35) for some prespecified $\alpha \equiv (\alpha_1, \ldots, \alpha_N) > 0_N$.

It can be shown that the cost function defined by (51) can provide a second order approximation to an arbitrary twice continuously differentiable cost function that satisfies the money metric scaling of utility property (42).

Now use the parameters vector α which occurred in the definition of $c(p)$ in order to define the *normalized prices* v^i:

$$v^i \equiv p^i/p^i \cdot \alpha, \qquad i = 1, 2. \tag{52}$$

Straightforward calculations show that if C is defined by (51), then the following identity holds *exactly*:

$$(1/2) V(v^i) + (1/2) V(v^2) = (1/2)(v^1 + v^2) \cdot (x^2 - x^1) \quad (53)$$

where $V(v^1)$ and $V(v^2)$ are equivalent and compensating variations evaluated using the normalized prices v^i in place of the commodity price vectors p^i. Thus (53) says that an average of the Hicksian variations using normalized prices is exactly equal to the average of the normalized prices inner producted with the vector of quantity differences, $x^2 - x^1$, provided that preferences are defined by the cost function (51). Note that the right-hand side of (53) can be evaluated using observable price and quantity data. Since the formula on the right-hand side is exact for preferences which have a second order approximation property, we could call it a *superlative welfare gain measure* in analogy to the terminology used in index number theory. The term gain measure is due to King (1983).

W. E. Diewert

See also DUALITY; GAUGE FUNCTIONS; NEOCLASSICAL THEORY OF PRODUCTION; PRODUCTION AND COST FUNCTIONS; SUPPLY FUNCTIONS.

BIBLIOGRAPHY

Barnett, W.A. 1983. New indices of money supply and the flexible Laurent demand system. *Journal of Business and Economic Statistics* 1, 7–23.

Christensen, L.R., Jorgenson, D.W. and Lau, L.J. 1971. Conjugate duality and the transcendental logarithmic production function. *Econometrica* 39, 255–6.

Christensen, L.R., Jorgenson, D.W. and Lau, L.J. 1973. Transcendental logarithmic production frontiers. *Review of Economics and Statistics* 55, 28–45.

Deaton, A. and Muellbauer, J. 1980. *Economics and Consumer Behaviour.* Cambridge: Cambridge University Press.

Diewert, W.E. 1971. An application of the Shephard duality theorem: a generalized Leontief production function. *Journal of Political Economy* 79, 481–507.

Diewert, W.E. 1974. Applications of duality theory. In *Frontiers of Quantitative Economics,* Vol. II, ed. M.D. Intriligator and D.A. Kendrick. Amsterdam: North-Holland, 106–171.

Diewert, W.E. 1982. Duality approaches to microeconomic theory. In *Handbook of Mathematical Economics,* ed. K.J. Arrow and M.D. Intriligator, Vol. 2, Amsterdam: North-Holland, 535–99.

Diewert, W.E. and Wales, T.J. 1986a. Flexible functional forms and global curvature conditions. *Econometrica.*

Diewert, W.E. and Wales, T.J. 1986b. Normalized quadratic systems of consumer demand functions. Discussion Paper No. 86–16, Department of Economics, University of British Columbia, Vancouver, Canada, May.

Fuss, M.A. 1977. Dynamic factor demand systems with explicit costs of adjustment. Chapter 4 in E.R. Berndt, M. Fuss and L. Waverman, *Dynamic Models of the Industrial Demand for Energy,* Palo Alto, California: Electric Power Research Institute.

Fuss, M., McFadden, D. and Mundlak, Y. 1978. A survey of functional forms in the economic analysis of production. In *Production Economics: A Dual Approach to Theory and Applications,* Vol. 1, ed. M. Fuss and D. McFadden, Amsterdam: North-Holland, 219–68.

Gorman, W.M. 1953. Community preference fields. *Econometrica* 21, 63–80.

Gorman, W.M. 1976. Tricks with utility functions. In *Essays in Economic Analysis,* ed. M. Artis and R. Nobay, Cambridge: Cambridge University Press.

Hicks, J.R. 1942. Consumers' surplus and index-numbers. *Review of Economic Studies* 9, 126–37.

Hicks, J.R. 1946. *Value and Capital.* 2nd edn, Oxford: Clarendon Press.

Jorgenson, D.W. 1984. Econometric methods for modeling producer behavior. Discussion Paper 1086, Harvard Institute for Economic Research, Harvard University, Cambridge, Massachusetts. In *Handbook of Econometrics,* Vol. 3, ed. Z. Griliches and M.D. Intriligator, Amsterdam: North-Holland.

Karlin, S. 1959. *Mathematical Methods and Theory in Games, Programming and Economics,* Vol. 1. Palo Alto, California: Addison-Wesley.

King, M.A. 1983. Welfare analysis of tax returns using household data. *Journal of Public Economics* 21, 183–214.

Lau, L.J. 1978. Testing and imposing monotonicity, convexity and quasi-convexity constraints. In *Production Economics: A Dual Approach to theory and Applications,* Vol. 1, ed. M. Fuss and D. McFadden, Amsterdam: North-Holland, 409–53.

McFadden, D. 1966. Cost, revenue and profit functions: a cursory review. Working Paper No. 86, IBER, University of California at Berkeley, March.

McFadden, D. 1978a. Cost, revenue and profit functions. In *Production Economics: A Dual Approach to Theory and Applications,* Vol. 1, ed. M. Fuss and D. McFadden, Amsterdam: North-Holland, 3–109.

McFadden, D. 1978b. The general linear profit function. In *Production Economics: A Dual Approach to Theory and Applications,* Vol. 1, ed. M. Fuss and D. McFadden, Amsterdam: North-Holland, 269–86.

McKenzie, L. 1957. Demand theory without a utility index. *Review of Economic Studies* 24, 185–9.

Samuelson, P.A. 1947. *Foundations of Economic Analysis.* Cambridge, Mass.: Harvard University Press.

Samuelson, P.A. 1974. Complementarity – an essay on the 40th anniversary of the Hicks–Allen revolution in demand theory. *Journal of Economic Literature* 12, 1255–89.

Shephard, R.W. 1953. *Cost and Production Functions.* Princeton: Princeton University Press.

Shephard, R.W. 1970. *Theory of Cost and Production Functions.* Princeton: Princeton University Press.

Uzawa, H. 1964. Duality principles in the theory of cost and production. *International Economic Review* 5, 216–20.

cost minimization and utility maximization. Consider the following standard problem in the theory of demand: Find $x^* \geqslant 0$ so as to max $u(x)$ subject to $\langle x, p \rangle \leqslant \omega$ where $\langle x, p \rangle$ is the inner product of the n-dimensional commodity and price vectors, and $\omega > 0$ and u are the consumer's income and utility function respectively; this problem is here labelled max(p, ω).

The functional dependence of the *value* $v^*[\equiv u(x^*)]$ of this nonlinear programming problem on its parameters (p, ω) is denoted by $v(p, \omega)$, where v is the *indirect* utility function. The similar dependence of the *solution* x^* of max(p, ω) is written $f(p, \omega)$, where f is the *ordinary* (or *Marshallian*) demand function (or correspondence). If v^* does not exist then neither do v, x^* or f. Important though they are such non-existence problems are irrelevant here, so without further ado assume that every optimization problem has a solution.

Consider next a problem whose form is similar to that of max(p, ω) but whose objective is different, i.e. cost minimization rather than utility maximization. Specifically, find $x^{**} \geqslant 0$ so as to min$\langle x, p \rangle$ subject to $u(x) \geqslant \tau$ where x, p and u are as before and τ is a *target* level of utility; this new problem is labelled min(p, τ). The functional dependence of the value $\mu^{**}(\equiv \langle x^{**}, p \rangle)$ of min(p, τ) on its parameters (p, τ) is denoted $c(p, \tau)$, where c is the *cost* (or *expenditure*) function. The similar dependence of x^{**} on (p, τ) is written $h(p, \tau)$, where h is the *compensated* (or *Hicksian*) demand function (or correspondence).

Suppose now that max(p, ω) is solved and its value v^* is inserted into the second optimization problem, thus creating the problem min(p, v^*). Is each solution x^* of max(p, ω) necessarily also a solution of min(p, v^*)? Call this Question I. A similar question can be asked of the reverse situation, which is: For arbitrary (p, τ) solve min(p, τ), obtain it value μ^{**} and then solve the resulting max problem, max(p, μ^{**}). Question II is then: Is each solution x^{**} of $\min(p, \tau)$ necessarily also a solution of $\max(p, \mu^{**})$?

Problem $\min(p, v^*)$ has often been called the *dual* of $\max(\rho, \omega)$, from as far back as Arrow and Debreu (1954, pp. 285–6) to Deaton and Muellbauer (1980, pp 37ff) and beyond. Indeed, this usage is now so common that for most economists $\min(p, v^*)$ seems to be *the* leading species of the genus *dual problem*.

One can see why. It appears to be quite analogous to dual problems in linear programming (lp), with max becoming min, and objective and constraint functions becoming constraint and objective functions, respectively. However, the analogy with duals in lp is misleading, for each solution x^{**} of the alleged 'dual' $\min(p, v^*)$ is located in the *same* space as each solution x^* of its 'primal' $\max(p, \omega)$, whereas in lp the solutions to the dual all lie in the *dual* space. As Deaton and Muellbauer justly remark: 'The essential feature of the duality approach is a *change of variables*' (1980, p. 47, their italics). So a new term for the relation that $\min(p, v^*)$ bears to $\max(p, \omega)$ is needed in order to distinguish it from genuine duality; 'mirrored' (or 'reflected') problem is suggested in Newman (1982).

In demand theory it is sometimes recognized explicitly that Question I needs an answer (e.g. Samuelson, 1947, p. 103; McKenzie, 1957, p. 186) but more often not, probably because the usual assumptions on preferences are quite sufficient for coincidence of x^{**} with x^*. An explicit treatment appears unnecessary: '... clearly, the vector of commodities must in both cases be the same' (Deaton and Muellbauer, 1980, p. 37). In welfare economics, however, it has long been recognized that a suitably generalized form of Question I, simple as it is, has importance for the first fundamental theorem of welfare economics, namely that every competitive allocation is (strongly) Pareto-optimal.

Question II has always been considered more delicate than Question I. Indeed, it was not even put until Arrow (1950, pp. 527–8) exhibited his famous 'exceptional case' (now often known as the Arrow Corner) in which it receives a negative answer. Its relevance for proofs of existence of competitive equilibrium was fully grasped by Arrow and Debreu (1954, Sections 4 and 5), and later Debreu (1959, pp. 67–71), for essentially this reason, devoted four pages of his terse classic to a detailed examination of both Questions.

It is interesting that although the second Question is economically more subtle than the first, from a sufficiently abstract point of view the two are logically isomorphic (see Newman (1982), where in both Theorem (c) and Theorem (c') the assertion 'iff' is wrong and should be replaced by 'if'). While such extreme abstraction is irrelevant here, both $\max(p, \omega)$ and $\min(p, \tau)$ do need to be put into a form suitable for general equilibrium theory.

THE SETTING. The consumer is now endowed, not with an exogenous positive income, but with a nonzero bundle x^0, whose worth $\langle x^0, p \rangle$ may be zero. For simplicity (and only that), free disposal is assumed.

ASSUMPTIONS ABOUT PREFERENCES. The consumer has two disjoint binary relations $\succ$ ('preference') and $\sim$ ('indifference') each defined on some non-empty $S \subset R^n$; the union of $\succ$ and $\sim$ is denoted $\succsim$. Indifference is reflexive and symmetric (so that preference is irreflexive) and the statements $x^1 \succ x^2$ and $x^2 \sim x^3$ together imply $x^1 \succ x^3$. Neither completeness nor transitivity of preference is assumed, so a utility function need not exist.

The generalized version of $\max(p, \omega)$ is then: Find $x^* \in S$ for which $\langle x^*, p \rangle \leqslant \langle x^0, p \rangle$ and such that $x \succ x^*$ implies $\langle x, p \rangle > \langle x^0, p \rangle$. In words, '$x^*$ is feasible and anything preferred to it is unaffordable'. This problem is labelled $\max(p, x^0)$.

The generalized version of $\min(p, \tau)$ is: Find $x^{**} \in S$ for which $x^{**} \succsim t$ and such that $x \succsim t$ implies $\langle x, p \rangle \geqslant \langle x^{**}, p \rangle$. In words, 'anything at least as good as the target bundle $t \in S$ costs at least as much as x^{**}'. This problem is labelled $\min(p, t)$.

Note that in the absence of a utility function $\max(p, x^0)$ can have a solution but not a value, while $\min(p, t)$ can have both value and solution, just as before.

SOME DEFINITIONS. Any bundle $x^\#$ to which no $x \in S$ is preferred is called *bliss*, while a bundle $x_\#$ for which at prices p there is no cheaper $x \in S$ is called *p-minimal*. Preferences are *locally nonsatiated* at x^1 if *any* neighbourhood $N(x^1)$ contains $x \succ x^1$, while $x^2 \in S$ has *locally cheaper points* at p (a term apparently due to McKenzie, 1957) if *any* neighbourhood $N(x^2)$ contains a bundle $x \in S$ which at prices p is cheaper than x^2. If $x^\#$ is bliss it cannot be locally nonsatiated, and if $x_\#$ is p-minimal it has no locally cheaper points at p.

Following Bergstrom et al. (1976), preferences are said to have *open upper sections* if $x' \succ x^2$ implies the existence of a neighbourhood $N(x^1) \subset S$ for which $x \succ x^2$ for every x in it.

The following simple result answers both Questions satisfactorily and generalizes easily to a wide class of infinite-dimensional commodity spaces.

Theorem. (i) Assume (a) that if $x \in S$ is not bliss it is locally nonsatiated, and (b) that the solution x^* of $\max(p, x^0)$ is not bliss. Then x^* also solves $\min(p, x^*)$. Moreover, the value μ^{**} of $\min(p, x^*)$ equals $\langle x^0, p \rangle$.

(ii) Assume (c) that preferences have open upper sections, (d) that if $x \in S$ is not p-minimal it has locally cheaper points at p, and (e) that the solution x^{**} of $\min(p, t)$ is not p-minimal. Then x^{**} also solves $\max(p, \mu^{**})$, where $\mu^{**} = \langle x^{**}, p \rangle$.

Proof: (i) Suppose the result false, so there exists $x^1 \succsim x^*$ such that $\langle x^1, p \rangle < \langle x^*, p \rangle$. Now $x^1 \succ x^*$ cannot occur because if it did $\langle x^1, p \rangle < \langle x^*, p \rangle \leqslant \langle x^0, p \rangle$ would imply that x^* does not solve $\max(p, x^0)$, contrary to hypothesis. So $x^1 \sim x^*$.

Since the vector p represents a continuous linear function(al) there is a neighbourhood $N(x^1)$ all of whose points are cheaper at prices p than x^*. From (b) there exists $x \succ x^*$, and this and the symmetry of $\sim$ imply that $x \succ x^1$ as well, so that x^1 is not bliss either. Hence from (a) at least one member of $N(x^1)$, say x^2, is such that $x^2 \succ x^1$. Because $x^1 \sim x^*$ this leads to $x^2 \succ x^*$, which again contradicts the hypothesis. Thus x^* solves $\min(p, x^*)$, which implies $\mu^{**} = \langle x^*, p \rangle$.

Suppose $\langle x^*, p \rangle < \langle x^0, p \rangle$. By the continuity of p there exists $N(x^*)$ all of whose points are cheaper at prices p than is x^0, while from (b) and (a) at least one of them, say x^3, is such that $x^3 \succ x^*$. Yet again, this contradicts the hypothesis. So $\langle x^*, p \rangle = \langle x^0, p \rangle$.

(ii) By assumption $x^{**} \succsim t$. Suppose $x^{**} \succ t$. From (c) there exists $N(x^{**})$ such that $x \succ t$ for every x in it. From (e) and (d) x^{**} has locally cheaper points at p, so at least one x in $N(x^{**})$, say x^1, is cheaper than x^{**} at p. Since $x^1 \succ t$, this contradicts the hypothesis that x^{**} solves $\min(p, t)$. Hence $x^{**} \sim t$.

Suppose now that x^{**} does not solve $\max(p, \mu^{**})$, so there is an x^2 such that $x^2 \succ x^{**}$ and $\langle x^2, p \rangle \leqslant \langle x^{**}, p \rangle$. Hence $x^2 \succ t$. If x^2 were cheaper at p than x^{**} that would again contradict the hypothesis. So $\langle x^2, p \rangle = \langle x^{**}, p \rangle$.

From (e) there is an $x \in S$ cheaper at p than x^{**}, hence cheaper than x^2, so x^2 is not p-minimal either. Since $x^2 \succ t$, from (c) there exists $N(x^2)$ such that $x \succ t$ for every x in it and from (d) at least one of these must be cheaper than x^2 at p, and so cheaper than x^{**}, which again contradicts the hypothesis. Q.E.D.

One sees just how few and how weak are the assumptions on preferences that enable Questions I and II to be answered, as distinct (for example) from those needed to guarantee the *existence* of solutions x^* and x^{**}. Note that two assumptions are used for Question I and three for II, an inequality which occurs because the constraint in $\max(p, x^0)$ is linear and hence continuous, whereas in the problem $\min(p, t)$ some continuity in the (nonlinear) constraint has to be *imposed* by means of the 'extra' assumption (c). This asymmetry disappears in a more abstract treatment, with more general constraints.

The intuitions behind the proof help to see why Question II is a serious problem for general equilibrium theory. In the proof of (i) the bundle x^1 that is cheaper than x^* is made a little bigger, in effect increasing satisfaction by increasing expenditure, until a bundle is reached that is still affordable at income $\langle x^0, p \rangle$ but which is better than x^*; that expenditure can always be thus 'traded' for satisfaction is assured by local nonsatiation. In the proof of (ii) the bundle x^1 that is better than x^{**} is made a little smaller, lessening satisfaction in return for less cost, until a bundle is reached that is still as good as t but which costs less than x^{**}; such 'trading' of satisfaction for expenditure is guaranteed by the existence of locally cheaper points. However, if the expenditure on x^{**} at prices p is already least possible (i.e. if x^{**} is p-minimal) then 'trading' in *that* direction cannot occur – one cannot go below least cost.

Of the five assumptions of the Theorem the only one whose meaning is not transparent and whose restriction is not 'reasonable' is (e), so that it comes as no surprise that the main thing wrong at the Arrow Corner is that (e) does not hold there. For further discussion of this Slater-like assumption and its role in general equilibrium theory, see the entry on CONSUMPTION SETS.

PETER NEWMAN

See also DUALITY; GAUGE FUNCTIONS

BIBLIOGRAPHY

Arrow, K.J. 1951. An extension of the basic theorems of classical welfare economics. In *Proceedings of the Second Berkeley Symposium on Mathematical Statistics and Probability*, ed. J. Neyman, Berkeley, California: University of California Press, 507–32.

Arrow, K.J. and Debreu, G. 1954. Existence of an equilibrium for a competitive economy. *Econometrica* 22, 265–90.

Bergstrom, T.C., Parks, R.P. and Rader, T. 1976. Preferences which have open graphs. *Journal of Mathematical Economics* 3, 265–8.

Deaton, A. and Muellbauer, J. 1980. *Economics and Consumer Behaviour*. Cambridge: Cambridge University Press.

Debreu, G. 1959. *Theory of Value*. Cowles Commission Monograph No. 17, New York: John Wiley.

McKenzie, L. 1957. Demand theory without a utility index. *Review of Economic Studies* 24, 185–9.

Newman, P. 1982. Mirrored pairs of optimization problems. *Economica* 49, 109–19.

Samuelson, P.A. 1947. *Foundations of Economic Analysis*. Cambridge, Mass.: Harvard University Press.

cost of living. *See* HEDONIC FUNCTIONS AND HEDONIC INDICES.

cost of production. Adam Smith argued that competition would tend to establish the 'natural prices' of commodities produced, i.e. the prices at which 'the price of any commodity is neither more nor less than what is sufficient to pay the rent of land, the wages of labour, and the profit of stock employed . . . according to their natural rates' (Smith, 1776, p. 65). In other words, the price of any produced commodity will, under the pressure of competition, be equal to its cost of production.

Ricardo was later to use the term 'cost of production' as a synonym for the 'value' of a commodity, where by value is meant, in the *Essay on Profits*, the difficulty or facility of production of the commodity, and in the *Principles*, the relative quantity of labour necessary for the production of the commodity. The expression is used to represent the value of the commodity as manifest in terms of the standard of values used in the market. Ricardo dismissed the attempt by Malthus to draw a distinction between value and cost:

> Mr. Malthus appears to think that it is part of my doctrine, that the cost and value of a thing should be the same; – it is, if he means by cost, 'cost of production', including profits (1817, p. 47n).

Ricardo's identification of cost and value has led some authors to the belief that the classical theory of value is a 'cost of production' theory, which may be contrasted with the 'supply and demand' theory of neoclassical economics – an idea that was perhaps reinforced by Marshall's claim that classical theory was 'one-sided', was only one blade of the scissors:

> we might as reasonably dispute whether it is the upper or the under blade of a pair of scissors that cuts a piece of paper, as whether value is governed by utility or cost of production (1890, p. 548).

Walras, too, seems to suggest that 'cost of production' and demand are independent forces in the mutual determination of price.

In fact the condition that the cost of production of produced commodities is equal to their price is simply a definition of competitive equilibrium. The proposition that price is equal to cost is thus common to all theories of competitive value. The fact is not trivial, but is the outcome of competitive mobility. The meaningful question for any theory of value is what determines that cost and price.

The classical theory of value and distribution takes as data the size and composition of social output, the conditions of reproduction, and the real wage (Sraffa, 1960; Garegnani, 1984). In a model which contains only circulating capital these data may be formed into the following price equations:

$$Ap(1 + r) = p \qquad (1)$$

where A is the $n \times n$ input–output matrix, p the price vector and r the rate of profit. Wage goods are incorporated in the input coefficients. There is no presumption that A is invariant to changes in output.

Given that A is connected (all commodities are basic) then the equations may be solved for unique positive values of r and p. Although in (1) price is equal to cost of production, cost of production is not independent of price. Since A is connected the price of every commodity depends as much on its *own price* as on the price of other commodities (Sraffa, 1960, ch. 2).

The neoclassical theory of value takes as its data the preferences of individuals, the technology, and the endowment of factor services. In equilibrium the price of each produced commodity will equal the sum of the rentals of the factor services used in its production, i.e. its cost of production:

$$Bw = p \qquad (2)$$

where B is the $n \times m$ matrix of input coefficients of factor services, w is the vector of factor rentals, and p the vector of prices of commodities produced. In this case it might appear at first glance that cost of production is independent of price since prices on the left hand side of (2) do not appear on the right hand side. But the appearance is deceptive. The rentals which clear the markets for factor services are determined by the endowments of factor services and the demands for them, which are in turn functions of the prices of final products. Hence the prices of produced commodities are not 'determined' by their costs of production, but are determined simultaneously with their costs of production.

JOHN EATWELL

See also DIFFICULTY AND FACILITY OF PRODUCTION.

BIBLIOGRAPHY

Garegnani, P. 1984. Value and distribution in the classical economists and Marx. *Oxford Economic Papers* 36 (2), 291–325.

Marshall, A. 1890. *Principles of Economics*. London: Macmillan.

Ricardo, D. 1817. *Principles of Political Economy and Taxation*. Ed. P. Sraffa, Cambridge: Cambridge University Press, 1951.

Smith, A. 1776. *An Inquiry into the Nature and Causes of the Wealth of Nations*. London: Methuen, 1961.

Sraffa, P. 1960. *Production of Commodities by Means of Commodities*. Cambridge: Cambridge University Press.

cost-plus pricing. *See* AVERAGE COST PRICING.

cost-push inflation. The idea of cost-push inflation emerged in the post-World War II period as a description of inflation that resulted from labour unions pushing up wages despite the existence of excessive unemployment. It will be convenient to refer to this as wage-push to distinguish it from supply shock inflation, another form of cost-push that dominated world price developments in the 1970s when oil prices rose many-fold in two abrupt steps. The idea of both wage-push and supply shock inflation is that prices are pushed up by a shift up in supply schedules rather than by an increase in demand along an unchanged supply curve.

In the immediate postwar years, when the idea of wage-push was initially put forth, the Keynesian theory that dominated economic thinking provided no serious model of inflation. Keynesian theory emphasized that the economy could operate with inefficiently low utilization of its capital and labour resources and that expanding demand would employ those resources. Once full employment was achieved, further expansion of demand would only pull up nominal wages and prices. In contrast to this demand-pull inflation, wage-push implies supply behaviour that raises costs before resources are fully employed.

As clear as this initial distinction appears to be, the actual wage-price dynamics of a modern economy make it difficult either to provide a sharp analytical definition of wage-push or to identify instances of pure wage-push in the actual performance of economies.

By the 1960s, the short-run Phillips curve had emerged as an empirical description of the relation between inflation and unemployment over the business cycle. It described an empirical regularity according to which inflation got gradually, but continually, faster as unemployment declined. It appeared that the relation became steeper the lower the unemployment rate so that inflation speeded up only a little between, say, 8 per cent and 7 per cent unemployment but much more between 4 per cent and 3 per cent unemployment.

The empirical short-run Phillips curve blurs the simple distinction between cost-push and demand-pull inflation. There is a clear correspondence between the steep portion of the Phillips curve and the full employment region in the simple Keynesian model where demand-pull inflation exists. It is less clear whether to regard as a distinctive cost-push phenomenon the more modest inflation that appears systematically along the flatter, high-unemployment portion of the empirical Phillips curve. These systematic cyclical tendencies can instead represent the normal operation of heterogeneous labour markets in response to cyclical variations in demand. On this last interpretation, only departures from the normal response of wages over the business cycle, representing special instances of shifts in labour supply schedules, would qualify as distinctive wage-push phenomena.

The interrelations between prices and wages is another source of ambiguity about what constitutes wage-push. If labour supply schedules are defined in terms of real wages – that is wages relative to the average price level – then labour is on its supply schedule when nominal wages change proportionally in response to disturbances to the cost of living. The narrowest concept of wage-push would, therefore, include only shifts up in labour supply schedules that raise wages relative both to their normal response to cyclical demand conditions and to their normal response to consumer prices. Thus, in principle, wage-push could be identified by wage increases in excess of those predicted from these normal relations.

Empirically, instances of wage-push are hard to identify from historical data because of the normal interrelations among wages and prices in an economy. The great majority of product prices can be expected to respond fully to cost changes. Therefore, an exogenous wage-push will produce an almost corresponding rise in prices and nominal expenditures. And demand inflation will be kept going by induced wage increases. As a result of this two-way relation between wages and prices, wage and price variations will track each other closely, regardless of whether the variations originated in wage-push or from any other source, including excess demand.

Thus, a shift up in the empirical Phillips curve is not itself evidence of wage-push. In particular, sustained operation of the economy in the upper portion of the Phillips curve, where demand-pull inflation clearly exists, will push up the short-run Phillips curve. Wages will adjust to the higher ongoing and expected rate of inflation, and wage increases will be larger at every level of unemployment than they were before. Moreover, in a demand-pull inflation it may be wages that first respond to the excess demand. Hence, the timing of changes in wages and prices cannot be used to distinguish the two forms of inflation. Finally, if normal market forces within the labour market tend to keep relative wages in line, it is difficult to identify wage-push originating in the unionized sector because it will spread quickly to other wages.

Despite all these complications, a close examination of events suggests that important episodes of wage-push have occurred during the postwar period. In the late 1960s and early 1970s, abrupt accelerations in hourly compensation occurred in manufacturing industries in most European economies. For example, in Germany annual increases in hourly compensation jumped from $7\frac{1}{2}$ per cent in 1968 to $17\frac{1}{2}$ per cent in 1970, and in the United Kingdom the acceleration over the same period was from 7 per cent to $15\frac{1}{2}$ per cent. Unemployment was very low in this period, so strong demand was clearly part of the explanation. But the abruptness with which wages exploded qualifies these episodes as wage-push to most analysts.

During the 1970s, supply shocks to important raw materials prices dominated world price developments in the decade, producing the second main type of cost-push inflation. These supply shocks included the historic increases in oil prices in 1973–4 and again in 1979 and the food price explosion of 1973. Although world aggregate demand was relatively strong in both 1973 and 1979, the magnitude of the price increases that resulted cannot be explained by these demand conditions and instead has to be understood as a consequence of major shifts in world supplies. A succession of poor crops provoked the food price rise, while the successful organization of the OPEC oil cartel, aided by a levelling off in United States oil production, caused the oil price explosion.

Coincident with the 1973–5 supply shocks, further wage explosions occurred in several countries when the rise in world food and oil prices raised consumer price indexes sharply. In both the United Kingdom and Japan, annual increases in hourly compensation rose to over 30 per cent from less than half that rate in 1972. Most other major industrial countries experienced similar, though less dramatic, accelerations in wages. Although these wage developments were no doubt induced, in part, by the effects of the supply shocks on consumer prices, the differences across countries suggest that the wage changes were not merely a normal response to price changes in all countries. Thus, the period appears to offer further examples of wage-push. The rapid wage increases in turn boosted consumer prices significantly. The eventual changes in real wages, as well as the eventual increase in price levels, varied significantly among the industrial countries over this mid-1970s period. In the United States, both the speed-ups and slow-downs in wage increases and in price developments were far less dramatic than in Europe and Japan throughout this period. But over the decade of the 1970s as a whole, wages in the highly unionized sectors outpaced economy-wide wages substantially, indicating a modest but persistent wage-push from important major industries in this period.

Although the postwar record thus shows that both wage-push and supply shocks have been important in pushing up average price levels at times in the postwar period, several difficulties remain with the idea of cost-push as a distinct type of inflation, and these difficulties have led some analysts to reject the idea altogether. First of all, inflation refers to an ongoing rate of increase in prices. A one-term rise in the average price level will translate into some rate of increase in prices over a period spanning the rise. Without quibbling over how long a time period is needed before a measurement qualifies as an 'inflation rate', the distinction between a one-time rise in the price level and an ongoing inflation rate is important. Secondly, inflation refers to the general price level, not to a subset of prices. A rise in oil prices is, first of all, a rise in the relative price of oil. It is in principle conceivable that a rise in oil prices could be accompanied by a sufficient decline in other prices to keep the average price level unchanged.

Those who see monetary policy as able to control the overall price level would see a cost-push from some sectors as a relative price change that only becomes a change in the overall price level if it is accommodated by monetary policy. On this view, the accommodation rather than the cost-push causes the inflation. If most wages and prices were highly flexible and responded promptly to changes in the balance between demand and supply, then in the presence of non-accommodating macroeconomic policies cost-push shocks would indeed create only relative price changes; inflation, in the aggregate, would be impossible.

But monetarist reasoning ignores the actual nature of price and wage dynamics in modern economies and thus loses the important role that cost-push shocks have played in shaping the inflation performance of modern economies. There are strong positive correlations among most prices and wages in the economy. A cost-push supply shock will not only add directly to the average price level, but it will set in motion increases, not decreases, in other prices and wages. And those

tendencies are strong enough to persist for some time, even in the face of slowing demand and increasing underutilization of resources. Consequently, an attempt by monetary policy to hold the overall price level unchanged in the face of such a cost-push shock will result mainly in reducing output and employment. Only gradually will the upward movement of prices originating from a supply shock yield to restrictive monetary policies. On the other hand, because the initial shock induces positively correlated responses in wages and other prices, an accommodative policy that aims to maintain output and employment in the face of the shock will result in a rise in the overall price level that is substantially greater than the direct effect of the shock itself.

In light of these characteristics of modern economies, cost-push shocks as we have narrowly defined them can originate increases in the average price level even if, by themselves, they do not generate a faster ongoing inflation rate. Thus they can be an important part of the inflation problem that confronts stabilization policies. The extent to which the initial increase continues as an ongoing inflation depends on other characteristics of the wage-price system as well as on the extent to which aggregate demand policy accommodates. A cost-push shock will spread and be perpetuated more the greater the degree to which wages are indexed to prices, either formally or otherwise, and the greater the extent to which wages in some parts of the economy respond to wages elsewhere.

If an original wage-push shock represents a sustained attempt to enlarge real wages, then it will be repeated as prices and other wages rise in response. Such behaviour can thus result in a sustained or even in an accelerating wage–price–wage spiral. Most actual economies do not appear to be that fully indexed in their price-wage behaviour. Eventually, the initial forces of the cost-push peter out. But even so, a substantial bulge in the inflation rate can have occurred.

Because high-employment and price stability have both been goals of policy-makers, cost-push inflation has represented a stumbling block to good economic performance. Confronted by supply shocks or wage-push, governments with no policy tools at their disposal other than aggregate demand management have to choose between allowing higher inflation or raising unemployment in order to minimize the inflation.

The idea of cost-push inflation originating in excessive wage demands before full employment is achieved has prompted attempts in several countries to combine policies of aggregate demand management with specific wage-price policies or incomes policies as they came to be known in Europe. The idea initially was that demand management should aim at keeping the economy around full employment, while avoiding excess demand; at the same time, wage-price policies should aim at heading off cost-push inflation that might otherwise arise if unions with market power shifted up their labour supply schedule before full employment was achieved. That is, such policies should contain the inflation that would otherwise emerge along the flatter, high-unemployment portion of the Phillips curve. Similar policies could, in principle, also be useful in containing the effects of supply shocks by heading off the wage increases that such supply shocks might otherwise induce. The inevitable real wage adjustments associated with supply shocks might thus be made without inducing a price–wage–price spiral and without requiring higher unemployment to limit such a spiral. Where they have been tried in practice, incomes policies have relied on informal understandings among government, labour, and business.

There is some evidence that the original wage-price

guideposts that were implemented in the United States during the early 1960s did contribute to maintaining price stability through the middle of that decade. The guideposts had no legal authority or even real agreement with business and labour, and rested on Presidential persuasion for their effectiveness. They were abandoned once the Vietnam War buildup pushed the economy to full employment and then into the region where demand-pull inflationary forces were strong. In the United Kingdom, wage-price policies have been attempted with little evidence of sustained success. One obvious reason for their failure has been that such policies have generally been attempted in periods of low unemployment when demand-pull inflationary forces were strong. They were attempted as substitutes for demand management rather than as complements to it. In some other countries, such as Austria, informal incomes policies have apparently prevented outbursts of inflation originating in wage-push. And one interpretation of how Japan very quickly slowed wage increases after the wage explosions of the mid-1970s rests on an incomes-policy-like influence of the government on private-sector wage setting.

Because the enforceability of any guidelines to wage behaviour has rested on subtle political relations among government, labour, and business rather than on formulas with legal sanctions, the general applicability of such guidelines as a potential tool against cost-push inflation remains unproven.

There have been proposals to legislate tax incentives and penalties as a way of formalizing and strengthening an incomes policy. Such plans, known as tax-based incomes policies, had originated in proposals by Henry Wallich and Sidney Weintraub in the early 1960s. They received renewed attention and refinements in the 1970s, but were never made into law.

A more recent line of thought, also unproven, would rely on the credible commitment of policy-makers to stabilize prices through their conduct of fiscal and monetary policies. The idea here is that the decisions of market participants to raise wages or prices would be influenced by the knowledge that authorities would not tolerate any inflation in the aggregate. The decade-long rise in unemployment in Europe that started in the mid-1970s suggests either that such credibility can only be bought at very high cost in terms of high unemployment and extended stagnation, or that the power of credibility in this regard is greatly exaggerated because events or individual decisions that would lead to cost-push are uninfluenced by policy commitments, however credible, to stabilize the aggregate price level.

GEORGE L. PERRY

See also DEMAND-PULL INFLATION; INFLATION; INFLATIONARY EXPECTATIONS; SUPPLY SHOCKS IN MACROECONOMICS.

BIBLIOGRAPHY
Gordon, R.J. 1981. Output fluctuations and gradual price adjustment. *Journal of Economic Literature* 19, June, 493–530.
Gordon, R.J. 1985. Understanding inflation in the 1980s. *Brookings Papers on Economic Activity* 1, 263–99.
Gramlich, E.M. 1979. Macro policy responses to price shocks. *Brookings Papers on Economic Activity* 1, 126–66.
Okun, A.M. 1981. *Prices and Quantities: A Macroeconomic Analysis.* Washington, DC: Brookings.
Okun, A.M. and Perry, G.L. 1978. *Curing Chronic Inflation.* Washington, DC: Brookings.
Perry, G.L. 1980. Inflation in theory and practice. *Brookings Papers on Economic Activity* 1, 207–41.
Schultze, C.L. 1981. Some macro foundations for micro theory. *Brookings Papers on Economic Activity* 2, 521–76.
Schultze, C.L. 1985. Microeconomic efficiency and nominal wage stickiness. *American Economic Review* 75, March, 1–15.
Seidman, L.S. 1978. Tax-based incomes policies. *Brookings Papers on Economic Activity* No.2, 301–48.
Tobin, J. 1972. Inflation and unemployment. *American Economic Review* 62, March, 1–18.

costs of adjustment. *See* ADJUSTMENT COSTS.

counterfactuals. Counterfactuals are what ifs, thought experiments, *Gedankenexperimenten*, alternatives to actual history; they imagine what would have happened to an economy if, contrary to fact, some present condition were changed; in the philosophical literature therefore they are known also as 'contrary-to-fact conditionals'.

The notion has been used most self-consciously in historical economics. For example: 'If railroads had not been invented the national income of the United States in 1890 would have been at most 5 per cent lower.' Counterfactuals are implied, however, in many other parts of economics, such as macroeconomics: 'If a monetary rule with a small growth rate of M_1 were adopted then the rate of inflation would fall.' Or industrial organization: 'If the instant camera industry had 100 suppliers it would be competitive.'

The philosophical problem that counterfactuals raise, and part of the reason they have attracted the attention of modern philosophers, can be seen in the last example. We wish to contrast the present monopoly of instant cameras with (nearly) perfect competition. Perhaps we wish to do so in order to measure the welfare cost of the monopoly and to advise a judge. Now of course if somehow the instant camera industry were to have 100 sellers then each seller would be small relative to the whole demand or supply. Speaking mechanically, the usual formulas for elasticities imply that the elasticity of individual demand facing any one of them would be large, roughly 100 times the elasticity of total supply plus 100 times the elasticity of total demand. Such calculations are the heart of applied economics: If the cigarette tax were lowered what would be the new relative price of cigarettes? If the money supply were increased what would happen to the price level? If foreign doctors could practise freely in the United States what would happen to the cost of American medical care?

Such questions involve looking into a world having, say, an instant camera industry with 100 sellers rather than one. It would not be our world, which saw the miraculous birth of Polaroid, the struggle with Kodak, and the final triumph of patent over antitrust law. So much is clear. But how then is the counterfactual world to be imagined? A world in which the conditions of technology, personality, and law resulted in 100 Edwin Lands and 100 miniature Polaroid companies would be a different one — there's the condition contrary to fact.

The problems which can afflict counterfactuals are two: vagueness and absurdity. The vagueness arises when the model has not been fully specified. The world could arrive at 100 companies in many different ways, each with different implications for the original question about welfare. One can imagine getting 100 Polaroid companies, for example, by fragmenting edict now, well after the invention, in the style of the American Telephone and Telegraph case. Whatever the advantages, there might be inefficiencies in this. It would certainly change the future patent law. The change in law would in turn change things for good or ill elsewhere in the economy. A world in which patents are granted and then prematurely abrogated differs from the present world. Alternatively one might imagine subsidies in the 1940s that would have resulted originally in 100 alternative technologies of instant cameras (though actually only two were invented). This counterfactual likewise would have its costs, though different ones, changing for example the expectations of inventors about subsidies. A counterfactual requires a model broad enough to do the job.

Vagueness is solved by explicitness. The conditions required for various counterfactuals are made explicit, and being explicit can be tested for plausibility. Historical economists have been making counterfactuals explicit since the 1960s, using them to explore the causes of the American revolution and the consequences of American slavery (the counterfactual work is well surveyed by McClelland, 1975) .

In the most famous use of counterfactuals Robert W. Fogel (1964) calculated what the transport system of the United States in 1890 would have looked like without railroads. He argued that evaluating the 'indispensability' of the railroads entailed calculating what American life would have been like without them. Some historians were reluctant to talk about such a counterfactual, saying that it was ' "as if" history, quasi-history, fictitious history – that is not really history at all …, a figment' (Redlich, 1968, in Andreano (ed.), pp. 95f). But economists find the notion natural, and philosophers accept it as routine. Indeed, the philosophers point out that the following are nearly equivalent (Goodman, 1965, p. 44):

Scientific Law: All inflations arise from money growth.

Causal Assertion: Money growth alone causes inflation.

Factual Conditional: Since inflation has changed, money growth has changed.

Dispositional Statement: Inflation is controllable with money growth.

Parallel Worlds: In a world identical (or sufficiently similar) to ours except that money growth differed, inflation would be different.

Counterfactual: If money growth were to be held at zero, inflation would be zero.

The philosophy of counterfactuals revolves around the translation of one of these into another. Historians, not realizing that one is translatable into the other, flee the counterfactual in terror and cling to the causal statement. Yet economists have on this score no cause for smugness, since they have parallel philosophical fears. Economists flee the causal statement as historians flee the counterfactual, and believe as historians do that the thing itself can be avoided by suppressing its name.

Fogel's calculations stirred great controversy, but were robust (Fogel, 1979). Since he was interested in long-term economic growth he did not imagine a sudden closure of the railroads in 1890: that clearly would have resulted in a very large drop in national income. Mental experiments like this commonly lie behind claims that railroads (or airlines or postal services or garbage collection) are 'essential'. Fogel imagined instead what the American economy would have looked like without access to railroads from the beginning, forced from the 1830s onward to rely on substitutes.

Such an economy would have invested more in canals and roads (Fogel introduced some of these into his counterfactual world, using contemporary engineering studies proposing them). It would have been an economy closer to waterways, with a bigger St. Louis and a smaller Denver. It would doubtless have invented more improvements in road transport,

arriving at internal combustion a little earlier than the world we know.

Fogel could not specify every feature of the 'true' counterfactual world. But he suspected anyway that the true counterfactual would give a national income only a little below the actual. To test the suspicion, therefore, he biased the case against himself, choosing a 'practical' counterfactual world in which income would be if anything lower than in the true counterfactual: he did not introduce the internal combustion engine before its time; and he did not shift the location of the population to accommodate the non-railroad transportation. He forced his practical counterfactual to carry supplies by river, canal and horse cart (not by the motor trucks that might have been) to a Denver no smaller than it actually became at the height of the railroad age. The result was a calculable upper bound on the true impact on national income: since the 'true' counterfactual would have economized relative to the clumsy 'practical' counterfactual, a use of the practical counterfactual biases the case against a large impact. Fogel reckoned that the impact was at most five per cent of 1890 income, a couple of years of economic growth.

He was merely applying in a bold way the usual methods of economics. The usual method is to imagine an explicit economic model, M, with parameters, P, and initial conditions (or exogenous variables), I, and results by way of endogenous variables, R. The counterfactual varies some element of the setup, the simplest being a variation in I – where I might be a tax rate in a model of cigarette consumption or the number of firms in a naive model of instant camera pricing – and examines the results. Fogel removed from the initial conditions one of the technologies of transportation. In similar fashion a 500-equation model of the American economy permits experimentation in counterfactual worlds: What would happen if the price of oil fell? What would be the effect of a tax change? (The main empirical attack on Fogel's finding, indeed, was an highly explicit general equilibrium model of the Midwest and East (Williamson, 1974).)

Counterfactuals are one of the two main ways that economists at present explore the world (the third, controlled experiment, is still not common). The first is regression, or the comparative method, asking how *in fact* results have varied with initial or exogenous conditions. The second is the counterfactual, or simulation, asking how the results *would* vary. The regression infers parameters P from data on initial conditions I and results R and from arguments about the model, M; the counterfactual simulation infers R from data on P and from arguments about M and I.

But in solving the vagueness of counterfactuals by positing explicit models the economist runs against the other philosophical problem of counterfactuals: absurdity. Consider again the counterfactual of a 100-firm industry selling instant cameras. The problem is that the initial conditions that would lead to such an industry may themselves be absurd. Indeed, they may violate the very model used. The counterfactual assertion 'If the instant camera industry were perfectly competitive then price would be lower than it is now' takes on the character of the proverbial line 'If my grandmother had wheels she'd be a tram.' The model may be true (wheeled grandmothers may indeed be trams) but the counterfactual may be impossible – that is, a contradiction of the model itself or of some other, wider model felt to be persuasive.

It is possible to argue on these grounds that *all* counterfactuals are absurd. One might argue, as did Leibniz, that a world that did not invent the railroad would strictly speaking have to be a world different from ours right back to the big bang. Such a world might be one in which the seas were boiling hot or pigs had wings, with different transportation problems. The theory being violated by the counterfactual is the theory that the world hangs tightly together. As J.S. Mill remarked in attacking counterfactual comparison of free trade and protection, 'Two nations which agreed in everything except their commercial policy would agree also in that' (1872, p. 575).

A less intense scepticism on the matter has figured widely in economics. The theory of games, for example, can be viewed as an inquiry into counterfactuals, which sometimes violate wider theories (Selten and Leopold, 1982); the usual criticisms of the Cournot solution made by students of industrial organization involve the same point. Most notably, the Lucas Critique of econometric policy evaluation (Lucas, 1976) can be restated as a criticism of the usual counterfactual. The usual counterfactual imagines the effects of a change in the initial conditions I on a model M with given parameters P, fitted under the old regime. A new monetary policy would change the regime under which people believed they operated, changing P and M as much as I. Some broader model of how people adjust to regime changes is necessary to decide which would change: a new policy believed to be temporary would have very different effects from one believed to signal a revolution in government. The usual counterfactual violates the broader model, by supposing that people do not anticipate changes of regime or understand them when they occur. A broader model of rational expectations shows the counterfactual to be absurd.

John Elster, in a penetrating discussion of the role of counterfactuals in the economic sciences, posed the Basic Paradox of Counterfactuals: the less vague the theory, the more likely is a counterfactual using the theory to encounter absurdity. If Fogel had developed a theory of invention to draw a less vague picture of road transport without railroads he would have faced the problem that the very theory would predict the existence of railroads. After all, railroads were actually invented and therefore should be predicted by a sound theory of innovation. Elster wrote, 'If he attempted to strengthen his conclusion ... he would be sawing off the branch he is sitting on. In this kind of exercise it is often the case that more is less and that ignorance is strength' (1978, p. 206). The counterfactual must be 'capable of insertion into the real past'.

The Basic Paradox illuminates the discussion in economics about simplicity of models. A simpler model is harder to believe in its simulation because it is not so rich; but because of its lack of richness it is more likely to be insertable into the real past. A 500-equation model of the economy will more tightly constrain the past from which it comes than will a 10-equation model. Model selection has its own type I and type II errors.

Many of the meta-criticisms of economics, then, reduce to remarks about a counterfactual. This is scarcely odd, since counterfactuals are equivalent to causal statements and the point of economics is to make causal statements. The philosophical literature on counterfactuals is illuminating, though large, technical, and mainly inconclusive (Lewis, 1973; Goodman, 1965). It comes to a position more sophisticated than mere scepticism. Counterfactuals are a way economists speak, and philosophers wish usually to assist the speaking, not end it. Self-aware or not, economists will go on speaking counterfactually about non-cooperative games, macroeconomic policy, and the retrospective welfare calculations of historical economics. The task of a philosophy of the economic counterfactual would be to understand the practice, not to change it.

DONALD N. MCCLOSKEY

See also CLIOMETRICS; MODELS AND THEORY; PHILOSOPHY AND ECONOMICS.

BIBLIOGRAPHY

Elster, J. 1978. *Logic and Society: contradictions and possible worlds.* New York: Wiley.

Fogel, R.W. 1964. *Railroads and American Economic Growth: essays in econometric history.* Baltimore: Johns Hopkins Press.

Fogel, R.W. 1979. Notes on the social saving controversy. *Journal of Economic History* 39(1), March, 1–54.

Goodman, N. 1965. *Fact, Fiction and Forecast.* 2nd edn, Indianapolis: Bobbs-Merril.

Lewis, D.K. 1973. *Counterfactuals.* Cambridge, Mass.: Harvard University Press.

Lucas, R.E. 1976. Econometric policy evaluation: a critique. *Journal of Monetary Economics,* Supplementary Series 1, 19–46.

McClelland, P.D. 1975. *Causal Explanation and Model Building in History, Economics, and the New Economic History.* Ithaca, NY: Cornell University Press.

Mill, J.S. 1872. *A System of Logic.* 8th edn, London: Longmans; reprinted, 1956.

Redlich, F. 1968. Potentialities and pitfalls in economic history. *Explorations in Entrepreneurial History* II, 6(1), 93–108. Reprinted in *The New Economic History: recent papers on methodology,* ed. R.L. Andreano, New York: Wiley, 1970.

Selten, R. and Leopold, U. 1982. Subjective conditionals in decision and game theory. In*Studies in Contemporary Economics,* Berlin: Springer-Verlag.

Williamson, J.G. 1974. *Late Nineteenth-Century American Development: a general equilibrium history.* Cambridge: Cambridge University Press.

countertrade. Countertrade is an international commercial transaction in which the seller agrees to receive goods or services as partial or total settlement for goods or services delivered. In its simplest form, countertrade is a barter or a one-time swap of goods or services without cash payment.

Countertrade has been expanding rapidly since the beginning of the 1980s. But this is not a new phenomenon. Forms of countertrade in Europe can be traced back to before World War II and in the immediate postwar period bilateral trade and payments agreements were widespread among European countries pursuing trade despite non-convertibility of their currencies and/or lack of international liquidity. In Latin America barter-like deals were also common in the immediate postwar period, due to decreasing dollar and gold reserves. Later they receded, when international arrangements favoured a more open multilateral trading system (Outters-Jaeger, 1979, pp. 11–14). Centrally planned economies always favoured countertrade as part of their planning system. Therefore, for some decades, countertrade was typical in East–West trade.

The most common form of countertrade is the *counterpurchase,* in which importation by a firm or country is conditional on its trading partner accepting its exports. Often one side of the deal involves some homogeneous bulk product, agricultural or mineral. Crude oil became the single most important commodity in countertrade in the first half of the 1980s. By mid-decade some 25 per cent of OPEC oil production might have been involved in countertrade, from the settling of outstanding debt for construction work to the purchase of military equipment.

Another form, in which countertrade is in fact used to finance direct investment, is the *buy-back.* In buy-back arrangements, typically, a developed country supplies equipment or a turnkey plant and is paid in the future output of the project. Buy-back is often broader than the exchange of capital goods for resultant products, and might include loans, technology transfer, initial operation of the plant, the establishment of joint ventures and, sometimes, tripartite countertrade arrangements. For example, the Peruvian Government, in the early 1980s, contracted with a French engineering firm to build a petroleum refinery paid partly in refinery products. The French engineering firm, which had built petrochemical plants in Bulgaria, disposed of some of its countertrade obligations from Bulgaria by commissioning a Bulgarian engineering firm to supply and erect the storage tanks for the refinery in Peru.

A common form of countertrade among industrialized countries is the *offset*. Offset is the traditional title of compensatory transactions involving aircraft and military equipment. Offset can be directly related to the equipment sold, as the coproduction or subcontracting of some of the components in the buyer's country, the funding of operations of a joint company or the transfer of technology. But offset might take the form of a commitment to purchase goods and services unrelated to the military equipment sold (indirect offset). Thus, when a United States company sold F-5 fighter aircraft to Switzerland in 1975, the compensatory arrangements included finding export markets for various Swiss products, facilitating Swiss participation in foreign capital projects and assisting with tourist promotion. According to a survey of the US International Trade Commission, military offset represented 80 per cent of United States countertrade sales in 1984 (Group of Thirty, 1985, p. 6).

While at the beginning of the 1970s not much more than a dozen countries, mostly East European, were involved in countertrade, by the middle of the 1980s it had spread to nearly every country in the world. Most of the larger banks and corporations had established specialized countertrade divisions and a whole array of trading companies and law firms were in the business of matching potential countertrade partners (Jones, 1984). Countertrade might have surpassed 10 per cent of world trade in 1985.

Several reasons explain the latest surge in countertrade. The more recent requests came mostly from developing countries and they have been rising parallel to the worsening of the international economic environment for these countries and their mounting balance of payments difficulties (United Nations, 1986). Economic slack through much of the world and a weakening of the relationship between international trade and world output had among its manifestations depressed primary commodities markets and a persistent and fairly generalized decline in commodity prices in the first half of the 1980s. Terms of trade worsened for developing countries, which continued to accumulate debt. Subsequent debt servicing difficulties were followed by a dramatic decline in the flow of finance to developing countries. Demand for countertrade became more evident in developing countries particularly after the drying-up of voluntary bank lending and export credit cover that followed the Mexican debt crisis of 1982 (United Nations, 1986). With export earnings of developing countries falling or growing at a rate below the interest rate of their debt and with a high proportion of their export earnings tied up in debt repayment, countertrade became a way of assuring specific imports. In this sense, countertrade is a form of import finance for developing countries lacking alternative. Many developing countries are resorting to it owing to reciprocal impossibility of cash payments or credit. Thus, South–South trade, which suffered more than proportionately when developing countries had to produce a trade surplus and cut imports to pay their debt service, is gaining new impulse through countertrade.

When access to markets becomes more limited and uncertain, it can be expected that firms or countries will use their import potential as tool to open markets for their exports. In fact, firms from industrialized countries are increasingly offering countertrade as one more competitive peg in the battle for outlets. Countertrade may also be used to circumvent foreign exchange controls. When the import of a product has low priority in the foreign exchange allocations of a developing country, foreign suppliers have discovered that the obtaining of the contract might be quicker if they are willing to accept countertrade. In general, reciprocity demands – and countertrade can be seen as one of them – are tried as means of cutting through trade barriers and they grow with them. Countertrade tended to increase along with the erosion of the international trading system.

Critics of countertrade have argued that it necessarily imposes extra costs. The theoretical argument rests on the inefficiency implicit in arranging the 'double coincidence of wants' which is the prerequisite of any barter deal. The introduction of money reduced the cost of commercial transactions, because the efforts once wasted in trying to match sellers and buyers could be devoted instead to production. Therefore, if money exists as a means of exchange, barter (or countertrade) is irrational. However, the traditional case against barter was presented in the context of a closed economy. The implication of extending the argument to international trade is that all trading partners have equal access to the same monetary instruments. If access to hard currency is not present or is even partial, the theoretical case against barter does not hold, and we are back to the basic tenet that some trade (even barter) is better than no trade at all.

It is no coincidence that countertrade expanded in a period of sluggish world economic growth, of relatively slow growth in international trade and of proliferation of various forms of protectionism. Under these conditions, the observed increase in countertrade arrangements should not be seen in comparison with an ideal trade situation but rather as a pragmatic response to the peculiar conditions now prevailing in the international trading and financial system.

HELGA HOFFMANN

BIBLIOGRAPHY
Group of Thirty. 1985. *Countertrade in the World Economy*. New York.
Jones, S.F. 1984. *North–South Countertrade*. Special report No. 174, London: The Economist Intelligence Unit.
Organization for Economic Co-operation and Development. 1985. *Countertrade: developing country practices*. Paris: OECD.
Outters-Jaeger, I. 1979. *The Development Impact of Barter in Developing Countries*. Paris: Development Centre of the Organization for Economic Co-operation and Development.
UNCTAD. 1986. *Countertrade. Background note by the UNCTAD Secretariat*. New York: UNCTAD.
United Nations. 1986. Countertrade in developing countries: an inflicted option. *Supplement to the World Economic Survey 1985–1986*, New York: United Nations (Sales No. ST/ESA/188).

countervailing power. The concept of 'countervailing power' was perhaps most comprehensively adumbrated in John Kenneth Galbraith's classic, *American Capitalism* (1952). Galbraith argued that concentrations of economic power are not the social evil that orthodox economists – particularly antitrust proponents – had traditionally believed them to be. Countervailing power, not classical competition, he said, is the mechanism which effectively keeps concentrated power in check. Countervailing power, not antitrust, should therefore be the preferred weapon in the policy-maker's arsenal.

The actual or real restraints on a firm's market power are, according to Galbraith, vested not in its competitors but in its customers and suppliers; they are imposed not from the same side, but from the opposite side of the market. Thus, 'private economic power is held in check by the countervailing power of those who are subject to it. The first begets the second.' A monopoly on one side of the market offers an inducement to both suppliers and customers to develop the power with which they can defend themselves against exploitation. Thesis gives rise to antithesis, and there emerges a system of checks and balances which makes the economy as a whole workable, a *modus operandi* which lends stability to American capitalism. Most importantly, this system of checks and balances relieves the government of its obligation – imposed by the now antiquated antitrust laws – to launch any frontal attack on concentrated economic power. No longer need the government be concerned about the decline of competition or the sparsity of sellers in a particular market. Countervailing power can be relied on to eliminate the danger of any long-run exploitation by a private economic power bloc.

Put differently, countervailing power operates primarily through the creation of bilateral monopoly and/or oligopoly situations. A monopoly on one side of the market finds its power neutralized by the appearance of a monopoly on the other side of the market. Thus, a system of checks and balances is built on the foundation of bilateral power concentrations.

Galbraith cites the labour market as an area where the operation of countervailing power can be observed with the greatest clarity, for it is in the labour market that giant unions bargain on a national, industry-wide scale against groups of employers acting jointly either through a trade association or an informal ad hoc bargaining committee. Galbraith sees countervailing power at work in highly concentrated industries like the steel, rubber, and automobile manufacturing industries, and points out that not only has the strength of the corporations in these industries made it necessary for workers to develop the protection of countervailing power, it has provided unions with the opportunity for getting something more as well. If successful they could share in the fruits of the corporation's market power. Thus, Galbraith approves of bilateral monopoly in the labour market because it prevents unilateral exploitation, while simultaneously allowing one monopolist to share in whatever exorbitant gains may accrue to the other.

But bilateral monopoly in the labour market has further consequences. According to pure economic theory, this type of market structure is characterized by what Heinrich von Stackelberg aptly called *Gleichgewichtslosigkeit* – an incapacity to achieve a stable equilibrium (Stackelberg, 1934, p. 100). The inherent and irreconcilable conflict between bilateral monopolists can be rationally resolved (in the best interest of each party) only if they agree to enter into a vertical combination or conspiracy. Such coalition, of course, represents a compromise – a case of mutual forbearance – in order to achieve joint profit maximization. And, says Stackelberg, profits will be maximized for the bilateral monopolists if, for example, in labour-management confrontations, the employer (a monopsonist in the labour market) enjoys a monopoly in the sale of his products. In other words, market control or market dominance in the product market serves not only the best interests of management but also the best interests of labour. Hence, a bilateral monopoly situation naturally militates toward coalescence of power between management and labour, not antagonism or countervailance of power.

Understandably, this insight (which is neither profound nor esoteric) was used by the exponents of industrial cartels as a prime argument to persuade workers that cartels were in labour's best interests. Robert Liefmann (1927), for example, pointed out that cartels were in a better position than competitive firms to grant wage increases because they could pass the resulting cost increases on to consumers in the form of higher prices:

> Where the firms are in a cartel, they are more inclined to concede the workers higher wages than in a state of free competition, because they find it easier to pass the increased costs on to their customers by charging higher prices. The workers will therefore, generally speaking, find it easier to impose higher wages upon organized firms, and it is in their power, at least if they can form strong trade unions, to demand wages increasing with the cartel's prices, i.e., a *'sliding wage-scale'* (Liefmann, 1927, p. 80).

Thus, said Liefmann, market dominance and market control (i.e., cartels and monopolies) were in the best interests of labour as well as management, because the greater the market control the more ample the fruits to be shared through a system of vertical cooperation.

The consequence of such co-operation from the viewpoint of the public interest is, of course, another matter. In a prescient article written in 1890, Alfred Marshall observed that traditionally the public was protected by labour-management antagonism. Employers and employed 'have seldom worked together systematically to sacrifice the interests of the public to their own, by lessening the supply of their services or goods, and thus raising their price artificially'. However, Marshall, added,

> there are signs of a desire to arrange firm compacts between combinations of employers on the one side and of employees on the other to restrict production. Such compacts may become a grievous danger to the public in those trades in which there is little effective competition from foreign producers; a danger so great that if these compacts cannot be bent by public opinion they may have to be broken up by public force (Marshall, 1925, pp. 288–9).

In short, the absence of effective competition in product markets, when combined with vertical collusion between management and labour – whether tacit or overt – poses a central problem for public policy. Countervailing power is not a worthy substitute for antitrust policy, because countervailing power tends to be subverted by coalescing power and thus makes the problem of controlling market power more intractable than ever.

In a recent article (1983), Walter Adams and James W. Brock attempted an empirical test of the countervailing power hypothesis in four major American industries – airlines and trucking in the 'regulated' sector, and automobiles and steel in the 'private' sector of the economy. They found little evidence to support the Galbraith theory.

In airlines and trucking, inherently competitive industries, government regulation protected established firms from competitive entry and competitive rate cutting. It converted these erstwhile competitive industries into government-created and government-protected cartels. This, in turn, permitted management to maintain artificially high prices and to grant labour artificially high wage increases. (In trucking, for example, in a typical year, an estimated 74–97 per cent of the industry's excess revenues constituted monopoly rents accruing to capital and labour.) Not surprisingly, management and labour joined in support of this beneficent system of government regulation (protection), and lobbied ferociously against deregulation proposals which were eventually enacted by Congress (albeit in modified form).

In automobiles and steel, prices and wages since World War II tended to move in an almost perfectly synchronized upward spiral, securely protected by the industry's oligopoly structure and natural barriers to entry. With respect to automobiles, the phenomenon was graphically described by Charles L. Schultze, the former chairman of the US Council of Economic Advisers:

> In the mid-1960s hourly employment costs (wage and fringe benefits) in the major auto companies were about 20% above the average for manufacturing industries. Every three years since, the labour contract negotiated between industry and the union has widened the gap. By 1978 wages and fringes at the major auto companies had risen to almost 50% above the all-manufacturing average. Those extra costs were passed on in higher prices.
>
> Finally, in 1979 – faced with mounting interest rates, an incipient recession, sharply higher gasoline prices, growing resistance to large American cars and increased imports from Japan – what did the industry do? It negotiated a contract that by 1980 put auto wages and fringes about 60% above the manufacturing average (Schultze, 1981).

Predictably, when this price–wage–price spiral was threatened by foreign competition, management and labour joined forces to seek government protection in the form of tariffs, mandatory or voluntary quotas, orderly marketing agreements, and similar cartel devices. The objective was clear, that is, to persuade the government to stop import penetration of the US domestic market, and thus validate the industry's profits and labour's gains by making possible the price increases necessary to pay for them. In both automobiles and steel, coalescing (not countervailing) power seemed to operate with remarkable effectiveness.

Unless these case studies are egregiously unrepresentative, the following assessment of countervailing power – in the United States and, perhaps, other Western democracies – seems à propos:

(1) In industries where producers possess monopoly (or oligopoly) power in the product market, and where powerful trade unions dominate the relevant labour markets, there is an almost irresistible tendency toward tacit (if not, overt) vertical collusion. Countervailing power – ostensibly a structural safeguard of the public interest – is transmuted into coalescing power, a ready instrument for subverting the public interest.

(2) Tacit vertical collusion and coalescing power are sustainable only where product markets are immune from effective competition. Hence, a paramount objective of the labour-industrial complex is to obtain and/or preserve government protection from competition in the form of entry controls, minimum rate regulation, immunity from the antitrust laws, import restraints etc.

(3) The exercise of tacit vertical collusion and coalescing power has both micro-economic and macro-economic consequences. On the micro-economic level, it militates toward non-competitive structure in the affected industries which, in turn, leads to non-competitive conduct, which, ultimately, produces deficient industrial performance.

(4) On the macro economic level, the most serious consequence of tacit vertical collusion is a seemingly uncontrollable process of cumulative price–wage–price escalation – an engine of cost-push inflation that undermines the effectiveness of macro-stabilization policies. As Professor

Henry C. Simons of the University of Chicago recognized over three decades ago (Simons, 1948), the efficacy of such macro economic tools as monetary and fiscal policy vitally hinges upon an economy's underlying micro economic market structure. 'No amount of monetary or fiscal stimulation,' he wrote,

> will give us adequate employment or investment, if strategically situated unions and enterpriser monopolists insist upon utilizing improved demand conditions to increase their wages and prices rather than to increase employment, investment, and output – or to hold up prices where improved technology is markedly reducing costs. And there is no reason why organized producer groups, holding adequate organizational and political power, should, acting in their separate interest, forego the opportunity to improve their relative position in such circumstances. They may, to be sure, injure themselves along with the community, all or most of them being worse off by virtue of their restrictive measures than if none had practiced them. But each group may be better off than if it alone had behaved less monopolistically; and, short of dictatorship at one extreme and real competition at the other, there would appear to be no means for getting co-ordinated or co-operative action from such groups as a whole (Simons, 1948, p. 115).

Simons concluded that 'the inherent conflict of interest between each producer group and the community ... must be reconciled or avoided, either by the discipline of effective intragroup competition or by the dictation of absolute authority from above' (ibid. p. 120).

In sum, countervailing power is not a *deus ex machina* which solves the monopoly/oligopoly/cartel problem in advanced industrial societies. It does not provide a reliable mechanism for putting a lid on product prices. Nor does it preclude tacit or overt vertical collusion between organized power groups from dominating output and input markets.

WALTER ADAMS

See also ANTI-TRUST POLICY; COMPETITION POLICY; GALBRAITH, JOHN KENNETH.

BIBLIOGRAPHY
Adams, W. and Brock, J.W. 1983–4. Countervailing or coalescing power? The problem of labour management coalitions. *Journal of Post Keynesian Economics*, Winter, 180–97.
Galbraith, J.K. 1952. *American Capitalism: A Theory of Countervailing Power*. Boston: Houghton Mifflin.
Liefmann, R. 1927. *Cartels, Concerns, and Trusts*. New York: E.P. Dutton.
Marshall, A. 1925. *Memorials of Alfred Marshall*. Ed. A.C. Pigou, New York: Kelley and Millman, 1956.
Schultze, C.L. 1981. Against auto import protection. *The Wall Street Journal*, 20 March.
Simons, H. 1948. *Economic Policy for a Free Society*. Chicago: University of Chicago Press.
Stackelberg, H. von. 1934. *Marktform und Gleichgewicht*. Vienna: Julius Springer.

Courcelle-Seneuil, Jean Gustave (1813–1892). French economist and economic adviser. Born in the Dordogne, he studied law in Paris, then returned to his native region to manage an industrial firm. At the same time, during the July monarchy, he wrote for Republican newspapers and economic periodicals. After the 1848 Revolution, he held briefly a high position in the Ministry of Finance. In the following years, he became a frequent contributor to the *Journal des économistes*, and published a successful textbook on banking in 1852. In 1853, the Chilean government contracted him to teach economics at the University of Chile in Santiago, and to be available as official economic adviser; he stayed for ten years, until 1863, when he returned to France. While in Chile, he published his most ambitious work in economics, the *Traité théorique et pratique d'économie politique* (1858), which the Chilean Government arranged to bring out in a Spanish translation. After his return to France, he resumed his activity as prolific writer of books and articles on economic affairs. He also published several works on political and historical topics and translated into French John Stuart Mill's *Principles of Political Economy*, Sumner Maine's *Ancient Law* and William Graham Sumner's *What Social Classes Owe to Each Other*. He was appointed councillor of state in 1879, and three years later was elected member of the Académie des Sciences Morales et Politiques.

Throughout his life, Courcelle-Seneuil was a stalwart defender of free trade and *laissez faire*. Charles Gide, the co-author (with Charles Rist) of a well-known history of economic doctrines, wrote about him in rather sarcastic terms:

> He was virtually the *pontifex maximus* of the classical school; the holy doctrines were entrusted to him and it was his vocation to denounce and exterminate the heretics. During many years he fulfilled this mission through book reviews in the *Journal des économistes* with priestly dignity. Argus-eyed, he knew how to detect the slightest deviations from the liberal school (Gide, 1895, p. 710).

Courcelle-Seneuil's special interest, starting with the publication of a small book on bank reform in 1840, was the introduction of more freedom into banking or, to use a modern term, the 'deregulation' of this industry. Above all, he advocated the abolition of the Bank of France's exclusive right of issue. According to Gide, Courcelle-Seneuil was more esteemed in England and the United States than in France. In any event, adoption of his monetary and banking proposals was never seriously considered in his own country.

Once in Chile, Courcelle-Seneuil became a powerful policy maker and influential teacher. He arrived at a time when the international prestige of the *laissez faire* doctrine was at its height and when gold booms and subsequent busts in California and Australia caused considerable fluctuations in Chile's agricultural exports to these areas, creating a need for flexible short- and long-term credit facilities. This combination of events, joined with the prestige emanating from the foreign savant, permitted him to obtain in Chile what he had failed to achieve in his own country: under his guidance, the administration of Manuel Montt (1851–61) promulgated a banking law that established total freedom for any solvent person to found a bank and permitted all banks to issue currency subject only to one limitation: the banknotes in circulation were not to exceed 150 per cent of the issuing bank's capital.

Courcelle-Seneuil's advice was also sought in connection with a new customs tariff and here again he achieved substantial change: the level of protection was severely cut back, although some tariffs were retained for revenue purposes.

But the principal influence exercised by Courcelle-Seneuil resided in his forceful teaching: as the University of Chile's first professor of economics, he was apparently successful in instilling doctrinaire zeal in his students, some of whom later became influential policy makers. Thus, Chilean historians have not only traced the abandonment of convertibility in 1878 to the permissiveness of the 1860 Banking Law and the

lack of industrial development to the 1864 tariff; they also see Courcelle-Seneuil's indirect influence in the acquisition of the nitrate mines of Tarapacá by private foreign interests after Chile's victory over Peru in the War of the Pacific (1882) had given it title to the mines. Alienation of the mines was indeed recommended by a government committee dominated by Courcelle-Seneuil's disciples, who felt, like their teacher, that state ownership and management of business enterprises was to be strictly shunned. Secular inflation, industrial backwardness, domination of the country's principal natural resources by foreigners – all of these protracted ills of the Chilean economy have been attributed to the French expert.

Since the economically advanced countries were also those where economic science first flourished, they soon produced a peculiar export product: the foreign economic expert or adviser. Courcelle-Seneuil is probably the earliest prototype of the genre and his ironic career in Chile exhibits characteristics that were to remain typical of numerous later representatives. First, the adviser is deeply convinced that, thanks to the advances of economic science, he knows the correct solutions to economic problems no matter where they may arise. Secondly, the country which invites the expert looks forward to his advice as to some magic medicine which will work even when (perhaps especially In Chile foreign or foreign-trained experts have played key roles at crisis junctures, from Courcelle-Seneuil in the mid-19th century to Edwin Kemmerer in the 1920s, the Klein-Saks Mission in the 1950s, and finally to the 'Chicago boys' in the 1970s. Thirdly, the influence of the adviser derives not only from the intrinsic value and persuasiveness of his message, but from the fact that he usually has good connections in his home country and can therefore facilitate access to its capital market. Courcelle-Seneuil, for example, suspended his university courses in 1858–9 to accompany a Chilean financial mission that travelled to France in search of a railroad construction loan. Fourthly, the foreign adviser is often criticized for wishing to transplant the institutions of his own country to the country he advises, but his real ambition is more extravagant: it is to endow the country with those ideal institutions which exist in his mind only, for he has been unable to persuade his own countrymen to adopt them. Fifthly, history in general, and nationalist historiography in particular, is likely to be unkind to the foreign adviser. In retrospect he can easily become a universal scapegoat: whatever went wrong is attributed to his nefarious influence. This demonization is more damaging than the adviser himself could possible have been: It forestalls authentic learning from past experience.

ALBERT O. HIRSCHMAN

See also ADVISERS.

SELECTED WORKS

1840. *Le crédit et la Banque*. Paris.
1858. *Traité théorique et pratique d'économie politique*, 2 vols, Paris: Amyot.
1867. *La Banque libre*. Paris: Guillaumin.

BIBLIOGRAPHY

Encina, F. 1951. *Historia de Chile*. Santiago: Nascimiento, Vol. 18, ch. 58.
Fuentealba H., L. 1946. *Courcelle-Seneuil en Chile: errores del liberalismo económico*. Santiago: Prensas de la Universidad de Chile.
Gide, C. 1895. Die neuere volkswirtschaftliche Litteratur Frankreichs. *Schmollers Jahrbuch*.
Hirschman, A.O. 1963. *Journeys toward Progress*. New York: Twentieth Century Fund, 163–8.
Journal des économistes. July 1892. Obituary [of M. J.G. Courcelle-Seneuil].

Juglar, C. 1895. Notice sur la vie et les travaux de
  M. J.G. Courcelle- Seneuil. Académie des Sciences Morales et
  Politiques, *Compte Rendu*, 850–82.
Pinto S.C. 1959. *Chile, un caso de desarrollo frustrado*. Santiago: Edit.
  Universitaria.
Will, R.M. 1964. The introduction of classical economics into Chile.
  Hispanic-American Historical Review 44(1), February, 1–21.

Cournot, Antoine Augustin (1801–1877). Cournot was born at
Gray (Haute-Saône) on 28 August 1801 and died in Paris on
30 March 1877. Until the age of fifteen his education was at
Gray. After studying at Besançon he was admitted to the
Ecole Normale Supérieure in Paris in 1821. In 1823 he
obtained his licentiate in sciences and in October of that year
was employed by Marshal Gouvion-Saint-Cyr as literary
adviser to the Marshal and tutor to his son. In 1829 he
obtained his doctorate in science with a main thesis in
mechanics and a secondary one in astronomy. Through the
sponsorship of Poisson in 1834 he obtained the professorship
in analysis and mechanics at Lyon.

After a year of teaching he became primarily involved in
university administration. In 1835 he became rector of the
Académie de Grenoble and subsequently became inspector
general of education and from 1854 to 1862 was rector of the
Académie de Dijon. He became a Knight of the Legion of
Honour in 1838 and an Officer in 1845. He was afflicted with
failing eyesight and in the last part of his life was nearly blind.
In 1862 he retired from public life but continued his own
researches in Paris until his death.

Cournot was a prolific writer. His writings can be broadly
divided into three categories: (1) mathematics; (2) economics
and (3) the philosophy of science and philosophy of history.

In considering Cournot as an economist it is necessary to
place his major economic work, *Recherches sur les principes
mathématiques de la théorie des richesses* (1838) in the context
not only of *Principes de la théorie des richesses* (1863), which
can be regarded as a literary version of his work of a quarter
of a century earlier; and his *Revue sommaire des doctrines
économiques* (1877) which appeared in the last year of his life;
but also of his writings on probability and the philosophy of
science, in particular *Exposition de la théorie des chances et des
probabilités* (1843) and *Matérialisme, vitalisme, rationalisme:
Etudes des données de la science en philosophie* (1875).

It is possible to weave a broad cloth of interpretation taking
into account not merely Cournot's other works, but what
appears to be known of his personality and the considerable
social and political flux in France during the times in which he
lived. Guitton (1968) has suggested that Cournot had a rather
melancholic and solitary temperament and 'did nothing to
make his books attractive'. He notes that: 'Cournot was a
pioneer. He did nothing to court his contemporaries, and they,
in turn, not only failed to appreciate him but ignored him'.
Palomba ([1981] 1984) provides a sketch of the historical
background of his time, noting the growth of socialist ideas in
Europe, the political actions and reactions to the French
Revolution and the challenges to the concept of ownership.
Rather than challenge or repeat the broad contextual
interpretation of Cournot provided by Palomba, this essay is
confined primarily to the direct interpretation of his works in
economics and supporting texts in the light of many of the
developments in economics which are consistent with and may
be indebted to his original ideas.

The texts followed here include the French given in the
complete works of Cournot (1973) and the Nathaniel
T. Bacon translation (1899) entitled 'Researches into the

Mathematical Principles of the Theory of Wealth' which also
contains an essay by Irving Fisher on Cournot and
Mathematical Economics as well as a bibliography on
Mathematical Economics from 1711 to 1897. The 1929 reprint
of the 1897 edition was used.

The preface sets forth with great clarity Cournot's
fundamental approach to Political Economy. He states:

> But the title of this work sets forth not only theoretical
> researches; it shows also that I intend to apply to them the
> forms and symbols of mathematical analysis. Most authors
> who have devoted themselves to political economy seem
> also to have had a wrong idea of the nature of the
> applications of mathematical analysis to the theory of
> wealth.

> But those skilled in mathematical analysis know that its
> object is not simply to calculate numbers, but that it is also
> employed to find the relations between magnitudes which
> cannot be expressed in numbers and between *functions*
> whose law is not capable of algebraic expression. Thus the
> theory of probabilities furnishes a demonstration of very
> important propositions, although without the help of
> experience it is impossible to give numerical values for
> contingent events, except in questions of mere curiosity,
> such as arise from certain games of chance (p. 3).

Cournot continues in the preface to note that only the first
principles of differential and integral calculus are required for
his treatise. Professional mathematicians could be interested in
it for the questions raised rather than the level of mathematics
presented. He ends the preface with the caveat:

> I am far from having thought of writing in support of any
> system, and from joining the banners of any party; I
> believe that there is an immense step in passing from
> theory to governmental applications; I believe that theory
> loses none of its value in thus remaining preserved from
> contact with impassioned polemics; and I believe, if this
> essay is of any practical value, it will be chiefly in making
> clear how far we are from being able to solve, with full
> knowledge of the case, a multitude of questions which are
> boldly decided every day (p. 5).

The first chapter, 'of value in exchange or of wealth in
general', provides insight into the breadth of Cournot's
concern for the social and historical context of wealth.

> Property, power, the distinctions between masters, servants
> and slaves, abundance, and poverty, rights and privileges,
> all these are found among the most savage tribes, and seem
> to flow necessarily from the natural laws which preside
> over aggregations of individuals and of families; but such
> an idea of wealth as we draw from our advanced state of
> civilization, and such as is necessary to give rise to a
> theory, can only be slowly developed as a consequence of
> the progress of commercial relations, and of the gradual
> reaction of those relations on civil institutions (pp. 7–8).

He notes that: 'it is a long step to the abstract idea of *value in
exchange* which supposes that the objects to which such value
is attributed *are in commercial circulation*.'

In order to illustrate the distinction between the word *wealth*
in ordinary speech and value in exchange, he presents an
example of a publisher who destroys two thirds of his stock
expecting to derive more profit from the remainder than the
entire edition. The economics of elasticity is developed more
formally in chapter 4 on demand, but the concept is clear.

Chapter 2, 'on changes in value, absolute and relative',
begins by noting that 'we can only assign value to a
commodity by reference to other commodities'. This leads to a

discussion of the use of a corrected money which would serve as 'the equivalent of the mean sun of the astronomers'.

Chapter 3, 'of the exchanges', is the first in which formal mathematical manipulation is employed. He considers a silver standard in which all currencies are fixed in ratio to a gram of fine silver. He observes that the ratios of exchange for the same weight of fine silver cannot differ by more than transportation and smuggling costs. Given the volume of trade measured in silver he considers the arbitrage conditions for the $m(m-1)/2$ ratios among m centres. Fisher (1897) notes however that Cournot did not appear to be acquainted with determinants as he did not attempt a general solution of the exchange equations he proposed, but limited his calculations to three centres of exchange.

It is in chapter 4, 'on the law of demand', that the modernity of his approach stands out. He is interested in demand as it is revealed in sales at a given price. He represents the relationship between sales and price by the continuous function $D = F(p)$ and observes that this function generally increases in size with a fall in price and that the empirical problem is to determine the form of $F(p)$. He indicates an appreciation of the concept of elasticity of demand although he did not develop the formal measure.

Chapters 5 and 6 deal with monopoly without and with taxation; chapter 7, on the competition of producers and chapter 8 on unlimited competition. The ninth chapter is on the mutual relations of producers and the tenth on the communication of markets. The final two chapters are somewhat macroeconomic in scope. Chapter 11 is entitled 'of the social income' and 12 'of variations in the social income, resulting from the communication of markets'.

As our commentary is primarily on chapters 5–8, the order is reversed and 11 and 12 are dealt with first. Cournot explicitly avoids setting up the whole closed microeconomic system.

It seems, therefore, as if, for a complete and rigorous solution of the problems relative to some parts of the economic system, it were indispensable to take the entire system into consideration. But this would surpass the powers of mathematical analysis and of our practical methods of calulation, even if the values of all the constants could be assigned to them numerically. The object of this chapter and of the following one is to show how far it is possible to avoid this difficulty, while maintaining a certain kind of approximation, and to carry on, by the aid of mathematical symbols, a useful analysis of the most general questions which this subject brings up.

We will denote by *social income* the sum, not only of incomes properly so called, which belong to members of society in their quality of real estate owners or capitalists, but also the wages and annual profits which come to them in their capacity of workers and industrial agents. We will also include in it the annual amount of the stipends by means of which individuals or the state sustain those classes of men which economic writers have characterized as unproductive, because the product of their labour is not anything material or saleable (pp. 127–8).

But using a first order approximation he studies the effect of a change in price and consumption of a good on social income as a whole under competition, monopoly and when a new product is introduced.

Finally, although we make continuous and almost exclusive use of the word *commodity*, it must not be lost sight of (Article 8) that in this work we will assimilate to commodities the rendering of services which have for their object the satisfaction of wants or the procuring of

enjoyment. Thus when we say that funds are diverted from the demand for commodity A to be applied to the demand for commodity B, it may be meant by this expression that the funds diverted from the demand for a commodity properly so called, are employed to pay for services or vice versa. When the population of a great city loses its taste for taverns and takes up that for theatrical representations, the funds which were used in the demand for alcoholic beverages to to pay actors, authors, and musicians, whose annual income, according to our definition, appears on the balance sheet of the social income, as well as the rent of the vineyard owner, the vine-dresser's wages, and the tavern-keeper's profits (p. 149).

The last chapter considers international trade and national income and uses a first order approximation rather than a closed equilibrium system to study the benefits of opening up trade.

Moreover (and this is the favourite argument of writers of the school of Adam Smith), it should be inferred from the asserted advantage assigned to the exporting market, and the asserted disadvantage suffered by the importing market, that a nation should so arrange as always to export and never to import, which is evidently absurd, as it can only export on condition of importing, and even the sum of the values exported, calculated at the moment of leaving the national market, must necessarily be equal to the sum of the values imported, calculated at the moment of arrival on the national market (p. 161).

Cournot also notes the problem of analysing a tariff war.

The question would no longer be the same if establishment of a barrier for the benefit of A producers might provoke, by way of retaliation, the establishment of another barrier for the benefit of B producers, against whom the first barrier was raised. The government of A would then have to weigh the advantage resulting from the first measure to the citizens of A against the drawbacks caused by the retaliation. The two markets A and B would thus again be placed in symmetrical conditions, and each should be considered as acting the double part of an exporting and importing market (p. 164).

He closes his comments with:

We have just laid a finger on the question which is at the bottom of all discussions on measures which prohibit or restrict freedom of trade. It is not enough to accurately analyze the influence of such measures on the national income; their tendency as to the distribution of the wealth of society should also be looked into. We have no intention of taking up here this delicate question, which would carry us too far away from the purely abstract discussions with which this essay has to do. If we have tried to overthrow the doctrine of Smith's school as to barriers, it was only from theoretical considerations, and not in the least to make ourselves the advocates of prohibitory and restrictive laws. Moreover, it must be recognized that such questions as that of commercial liberty are not settled either by the arguments of scientific men or even by the wisdom of statesmen (p. 171).

He closes his work with the observation about theory that:

By giving more light on a debated point, it soothes the passions which are aroused. Systems have their fanatics, but the science which succeeds to systems never has them. Finally, even if theories relating to social organization do not guide the doings of the day, they at least throw light on the history of accomplished facts (p. 171).

Although the contribution of these last chapters is not as great as those to which we now turn, the spirit and style is that of a major theorist concerned deeply and objectively with application to practical affairs.

In chapters 5–9 Cournot develops his theory of monopoly, oligopoly and unlimited competition. This can be contrasted with Ricardo (1817) before and Walras (1874) after, who concentrated on unlimited competition with no aim at producing a unified theory involving numbers.

In chapter 5 Cournot deals with monopoly considering increasing, decreasing and constant returns and in chapter 6 the influence of taxation on a monopoly is considered. He notes direct taxes and indirect taxes as well as bounties and their influences on both producers and consumers; and closes with an examination of two variations of taxation in kind.

Chapter 7 provides a smooth transformation from single person maximization to noncooperative optimization where agents who mutually influence each other act without explicit cooperation.

We say *each independently*, and this restriction is very essential, as will soon appear; for if they should come to an agreement so as to obtain for each the greatest possible income, the results would be entirely different, and would not differ, so far as consumers are concerned, from those obtained in treating of a monopoly.

Instead of adopting $D = F(p)$ as before, in this case it will be convenient to adopt the inverse notation $p = f(D)$; and then the profits of proprietors (1) and (2) will be respectively expressed by

$$D_1 f(D_1 + D_2), \quad \text{and} \quad D_2 f(D_1 + D_2),$$

i.e. by functions into each of which enter two variables, D_1 and D_2 (p. 80).

It is at this point that Cournot switches from price to quantity of a homogeneous product as the strategic variable used by the competitors. His words and the mathematics do not quite match. He says, 'This he will be able to accomplish by properly adjusting his price.' The first order condition for the existence of a noncooperative equilibrium with quantity as the strategic variable are given. A diagram showing a stable equilibrium and another with a nonstable equilibrium are presented. The analysis is generalized to n producers including the possibility of an extra group of producers beyond n, all of whom produce at capacity. He obtains n symmetric equations for the firms with interior production levels and sets the others at capacity.

When he introduces n different general cost functions for the n firms he handles the situation with all having an equilibrium defined by the simultaneous satisfaction of the equations arising from the first order conditions. But he does not deal with the possibility that costs could be such that different subsets of firms could be active in different equilibria.

The criticism levelled by Bertrand (1883) in his review written well after Cournot's death concerns the modelling rather than the mathematics. As Cournot considered competition without entry among firms selling an identical product is was fairly natural to avoid the discontinuity in the payoff function caused by selecting price as an independent variable. But the observation of Bertrand matters for markets with a finite number of firms. The choice of strategic variable causes not only mathematical difficulties but raises questions concerning economic realism and relevance. Quantity, price, quality, product differentiation and scope can all be considered as playing dominant roles in different markets. But the general explanation of price and quantity as strategic variables was

and is critical to the development of economic theory. Cournot provided the foundations for the understanding of quantity. Bertrand, whose review of the books of Cournot and Walras was somewhat tangential to his professional interests offered only an example rather than a developed theory of price competition. It remained for Edgeworth (1925, pp. 111–42) to explore the underlying difficulties with the payoff functions for duopoly with increasing marginal costs; and it has only been in the last thirty years with the advent of the theory of games that there has been an adequate study of the properties of noncooperative equilibria in games with price and quantity as strategic variables, without or with product differentiation.

The thesis of Nash (1951) on the existence of non-cooperative equilibria for a class of games in strategic form provided a broad general underpinning for the concept of non-cooperative equilibrium. It was then immediately observable that although Cournot's work with equilibria of games with a continuum of strategies was not strictly covered by Nash's work, conceptually Cournot's solution could be viewed as an application of noncooperative equilibrium theory to oligopoly (see Mayberry, Nash and Shubik, 1953). The broader investigation of the price model and the interpretation of the instability of the Edgeworth cycle in terms of mixed strategy equilibria has only taken place recently. This also includes a growing literature on how to embed both the Cournot and Bertrand–Edgeworth models into a closed economic system or Walrasian framework. A summary of much of this work is presented by Shubik (1984).

It is important to appreciate that the developments in the theory of monopolistic competition such as those of Hotelling (1929) and Chamberlin (1933) and J. Robinson (1933) were based upon the Cournot–non-cooperative game model. Although it may be argued that Chamberlin's and Mrs Robinson's works possibly contained broader and richer models of competition among the few than that of Cournot, they represented a step backwards in their lack of mathematical sophistication and analysis. The Chamberlin discussion of large group equilibrium does have price as the strategic variable along with product differentiation and entry, but the solution concept is the non-cooperative equilibrium à la Cournot with the *caveat* that an attempt to produce a strict formal mathematical model of Chamberlin's large group equilibrium leads one to conclude that the game having price as a strategic variable is closer to Edgeworth's analysis than that of Cournot and a price strategy noncooperative equilibrium may not exist.

In chapter 8 Cournot shows his basic grasp of the important strategic difference between pure competition and oligopolistic competition. Using his own words, he states:

The effects of competition have reached their limit, when each of the partial productions D_2 is *inappreciable*, not only with reference to the total production $D = F(p)$, but also with reference to the derivative $F'(p)$, so that the partial production D_k could be subtracted from D without any appreciable variation resulting in the price of the commodity. This hypothesis is the one which is realized, in social economy, for a multitude of products, and, among them, for the most important products. It introduces a great simplification into the calculations, and this chapter is meant to develop the consequences of it (p. 90).

In modern mathematical economics, in the linking of competition among the few and the Walrasian system into a logically consistent whole, two approaches to the study of large numbers have been adopted. The first is replication and has its roots in Cournot and more formally, Edgeworth (1881) and following Edgeworth this method was used in cooperative core theory by Shubik (1959). The second involves considering a continuum of economic agents where each agent can be regarded as a set of measure zero. Cournot clearly saw the need to consider a market in which each individual firm is too small to influence price. But it remained for Aumann (1964) to fully formalize the concept of an economic game with a continuum of agents.

After twenty-five years during which his seminal work in mathematical economics was essentially ignored, Cournot demonstrated his concern for his ideas by publishing *Principes de la théorie des richesses* (1863), where he offered a nonmathematical rendition of his early work. This book is of considerably greater length than its predecessor and is divided into four books: Book 1, Les Richesses (eight chapters); Book 2, Les Monnaies (seven chapters); Book 3, Le Systeme économique (ten chapters) and Book 4, L'Optimisme économique (seven chapters).

This book met with no more immediate success than his original work and is not as deep. For example the chapters on money, although they contain discursive and historical material of interest, have little material of analytic depth.

In spite of the indifference of the environment to his writings in economics, Cournot regarded his contribution as sufficiently important that some fourteen years later, in the year of his death, he published his *Revue sommaire des doctrines économiques* (1877). This book was also longer, nonmathematical and of less significance than the work of almost forty years earlier. But Cournot's own sense of having been at least partially vindicated after forty-odd years is indicated in his *avant-propos*:

I was at that point in 1863, when I had the desire to find out whether I had sinned in the substance of ideas or only in their form. To that end, I went back to my work of 1838, expanding it where needed, and, most of all, removing entirely the algebraic apparatus which intimidates so much in these subjects. Whence the book entitled: 'Principes de la théorie des richesses.' Since it took me, I said in the preface, twenty-five years to lodge an appeal of the first sentence, it goes without saying that I do not intend, whatever happens, to resort to any other means. If I lose my case a second time, I will be left only with the consolation which never abandons disgraced authors: that of thinking that the sentence that condemns them will one day be quashed in the interest of the law, that is of the truth.'

When I took this engagement in 1863, I did not think that I would live long enough to see my 1838 case reviewed as a matter of course. Nevertheless, more than thirty years later, another generation of economists, to put it like Mr. the commander Boccardo, discovered that I opened up back then, though too timidly and too partially, a good path to be followed, on which I was even somewhat preceded by a man of merit, the doctor Whewell. While another Englishman, Mr. Jevons, was undertaking to enlarge this path, a young Frenchman, Mr. Leon Walras, professor of Political Economy at Lausanne, dared to maintain right in the Institute that it was wrong to pay so little attention to my method and my algorithm, which he used rightfully to expose a new theory, more amply developed.

Now, look at my bad luck. If I won a little late, without any involvement, my 1838 case, I lost my 1863 case. If one wanted in retrospective to make a case for my algebra, my prose (I am ashamed of saying it) did not get better success

from the publisher. The *Journal des Economistes* (August 1864) criticized me mainly 'for not having moved on from Ricardo,' for not having taken into account the discoveries that so many men of merit have made in twenty-five years in the field of political economy; thus the poor author that no one or the official world of French economists wanted to quote incurred the reproach of not having quoted others enough.

Cournot was central to the founding of modern mathematical economics. The average reader tends not to be aware that the textbook presentations of the 'marginal cost equals marginal revenue' optimizing condition for monopoly and 'marginal cost equals price' for the firm in pure competition come directly from the work of Cournot (including an investigation of the second order conditions).

He had to wait many years, for recognition, but when it came in the works of Jevons, Marshall, Edgeworth, Walras and others, it moved the course of economic theory. Marshall notes (*Memorials of Alfred Marshall*, pp. 412–13, letter 2, July 1900) 'I fancy I read Cournot in 1868', this was when Marshall was twenty-six, some thirty years after the book appeared. He acknowledges him both as a great master and as his source 'as regards the form of thought' for Marshall's theory of distribution. Jevons, in his preface to the second edition of *The Theory of Political Economy* records 'I procured a copy of the work as far back as 1872' and that it 'contains a wonderful analysis of the laws of supply and demand, and of the relations of prices, production, consumption, expenses and profits'. He excuses himself for his lateness in coming to Cournot observing: 'English economists can hardly be blamed for their ignorance of Cournot's economic works when we find French writers equally bad.' Walras in the preface to the fourth edition of *Elements of Pure Economics* (Jaffé translation, p. 37) acknowledges his 'father Auguste Walras, for the fundamental principles of my economic doctrine'; and 'Augustin Cournot for the idea of using the calculus of functions in the elaboration of this doctrine.' His liberal references to Cournot include his discussion of monopoly and the description of supply and demand.

The art of formal modelling is different from but related to the use of mathematical analysis in economics. The clarity and parsimony of Cournot's modelling stand out and have served as beacons guiding the development of mathematical economics.

An important feature missing from Cournot's seminal work is the discussion of the role of chance and uncertainty in the economy. He stressed the importance of chance in both his book *Exposition de la théorie des chances et des probabilités* (1843) and in *Matérialisme, vitalisme, rationalisme* (1875).

Although economics was the only social science he attempted to mathematize, he was well aware of the simplifications being made in cutting economic analysis from the context of history and society.

The economist considers the body social in a state of division and so to say of extreme pulverization, where all the particularities of organization and of individual life offset each other and vanish. The laws that he discovers or believes to discover are those of a mechanism, not those of a living organism. For him, it is no longer a question of social physiology, but of what is rightfully called social physics (p. 56). We mention that these cases of regression which imply that abstractions of the same kind, if not of the same type and of the same value, reappear in various stages of scientific construction.

Cournot's work on chance and probability does not appear to have provided any new mathematical analysis, but he made three distinctions concerning the nature of probability. His book of 1843 was a text with the dual purpose of teaching the non-mathematician the rules of the calculus of probability and of dissipating the obscurities on the delicate subject of probability. He stressed the distinction between objective and subjective probability. His opening chapters provide a discussion of the appropriate combinatorics and frequency of occurrence interpretation of probability.

Cournot stressed the distinction between objective probability where frequencies are known and subjective probability. He noted:

> We could, since then, relying on the theorems of Jacques Bernoulli, who was already aware of their meaning and scope, pass immediately to the applications those theorems had in the sciences of facts and observations. However, a principle, first stated by the Englishman Bayes, and on which Condorcet, Laplace and their successors wanted to build the doctrine of 'a posteriori' probabilities, became the source of much ambiguity which must first be clarified, of serious mistakes which must be corrected and which are corrected as soon as one has in mind the fundamental distinction between probabilities which have an objective existence, which give a measure of the possibility of things, and subjective probabilities, relating partly to one's knowledge, partly to one's ignorance, depending on one's intelligence level and on the available data (p. 155).

Subjective probability rests on the consideration of events which our ignorance calls for us to treat as equiprobable due to insufficient cause.

He added a third category which he entitled 'philosophical probability' (chapter 17) 'where probabilities are not reducible to an enumeration of chances' but 'which depend mainly on the idea that we have of the simplicity of the laws of nature' (p. 440).

Cournot's views on probability appear to be intimately related to his concern for social statistics and economic modelling. Although he did not establish formal links between his mathematical economics models and chance he regarded history and the development of institutions as dependent on chance and economics as set in the context of institutions.

Cournot was at best an indifferent mathematician. Bertrand clearly dominated him in that profession. But from his own writings it is clear that Cournot was well aware of both his purpose in applying mathematics to economics and his limitations as a mathematician. At the age of 58 he wrote his *Souvenirs* which he finished in Dijon in October 1859. They were published many years later with an introduction by Botinelli (1913). In these writings Cournot provides his self assessment as a mathematician.

> I was starting to be a little known in the academic world through a fairly large number of scientific articles. This was the basis of my fortune. Some of these articles ended up with Mr. Poisson, who was then the leader in Mathematics at the Institute, and mainly at the University, and he liked them particularly. He found in them philosophical insight, which I think was not all that wrong. Furthermore, he foresaw that I would go a long way in the field of pure mathematical speculation, which was (I always thought it and never hesitated to say it) one of his mistakes.

The general tenor of his *Souvenirs* is of a moderately conservative, quietly humourous, self-effacing man with considerable understanding of his environment and a broad belief in science and its value to society.

Regarding his work as a whole, his dedication and power as the founder of mathematical economics and the promoter of empirical numerical investigations emerges. He strove for around forty years to have his ideas accepted. He did so with persistence and humour (referring to his major work as 'mon opuscule'). He understood the need to wait for a generation to die. And before his death with the work and words of Jevons and Walras he saw the vindication of his approach.

MARTIN SHUBIK

See also BERTRAND, JOSEPH LOUIS FRANÇOIS.

SELECTED WORKS

1838. *Researches Into the Mathematical Principles of the Theory of Wealth.* Trans. N.T. Bacon, New York: Macmillan, 1929.
1841. *Traité élémentaire de la théorie des fonctions et du calcul infinitésimal.* 2nd edn, Paris: Hachette, 1857.
1843. *Exposition de la théorie des chances et des probabilités.* Paris: Hachette.
1861. *Traité de l'enchaînement des idées fondamentales dans les sciences et dans l'histoire.* New edn, Paris: Hachette, 1911.
1863. *Principes de la théorie des richesses.* Paris: Hachette.
1872. *Considérations sur la marche des idées et des évènements dans les temps modernes.* 2 vols, Paris: Boivin, 1934.
1875. *Matérialisme, vitalisme, rationalisme: Études des données de la science en philosophie.* Paris: Hachette, 1923.
1877. *Revue sommaire des doctrines économiques.* Paris: Hachette.
1913. *Souvenirs* (1760–1860). With an introduction by E.P. Bottinelli. Paris: Hachette. Published posthumously.
1973. *A.A. Cournot Oeuvres Complètes.* 5 vols, ed. André Robinet, Paris: Librairie Philosophique J. Vrin.

BIBLIOGRAPHY

Aumann, R.J. 1964. Markets with a continuum of traders. *Econometrica* 32, 39–50.
Bertrand, J.L.F. 1883. (Book Reviews of) *Théories Mathematique de la richesse sociale* par Léon Walras; *Recherches sur les principes mathématiques de la théorie de la richesse* par Augustin Cournot. *Journal des Savants*, 499–508.
Chamberlin, E.H. 1933. *The Theory of Monopolistic Competition.* Cambridge, Mass.: Harvard University Press.
Edgeworth, F.Y. 1881. *Mathematical Psychics.* London: Kegan Paul.
Edgeworth, F.Y. 1925. *Papers Relating to Political Economy*, I . London: Macmillan.
Guillebaud, C.W. (ed.) 1961. *Marshall's Principles of Economics.* Vol. II, *Notes.* London: Macmillan.
Guitton, H. 1968. Antoine Augustin Cournot. In *The International Encyclopedia of the Social Sciences*, Vol. 3, New York: Macmillan and Free Press.
Hotelling, H. 1929. Stability in competition. *Economic Journal* 34, 41–57.
Jevons, W.S. 1911. *The Theory of Political Economy.* 4th edn, London: Macmillan, 1931.
Mayberry, J., Nash, J.F. and Shubik, M. 1953. A comparison of treatments of a duopoly situation. *Econometrica* 21, 141–55.
Nash, J.F., Jr. 1951. Noncooperative games. *Annals of Mathematics* 54, 289–95.
Palomba, G. 1984. Introduction à l'oeuvre de Cournot. *Economie Appliquée* 37, 7–97. Trans. from Italian, extracted from *Cournot Opere*, Turin: UTET (1981).
Ricardo, D. 1817. *The Principles of Political Economy and Taxation.* London: J.M. Dent, 1965.
Robinson, J. 1933. *The Economics of Imperfect Competition.* London: Macmillan.
Shubik, M. 1959. Edgeworth market games. In *Contributions to the Theory of Games IV*, ed. A.W. Tucker and R.D. Luce, Princeton, NJ: Princeton University Press.
Shubik, M. 1984. *A Game Theoretic Approach to Political Economy.* Cambridge, Mass: MIT Press.
Walras, L. 1874–7. *Elements of Pure Economics.* Trans. W. Jaffé, London: George Allen & Unwin, 1954.

Court, Louis Mehel (born 1910). Court obtained his PhD degree in economics from Columbia University in 1942. He was at Columbia from the Summer Term of 1936 through the Spring Term of 1938 and held the Granville W. Garth Fellowship. He was a 'student at large' at the University of Chicago during the Winter and Spring Quarters of 1941. It is also known that he was an Instructor of Mathematics at Rutgers University during the years 1946–8. This sparse and sketchy information allows some gleaning into the intellectual influences on Louis Court.

Court's first published paper appeared in the *Journal of Mathematics and Physics* and concerned what would now fall under the heading of duality in mathematical programming. In particular he showed that:

if $\phi(q_1, \ldots, q_n)$ is maximized subject to the single constraint $\Sigma_{i=1}^n p_i q_i = m$ and $q_i(p_1, \ldots, p_n)$ $(i = 1, \ldots, n)$ [satisfy] the first order conditions for this maximization, then the function $\psi(p_1, \ldots, p_n) \equiv \phi[q_1(p_1, \ldots, p_n), \ldots, q_n(p_1, \ldots, p_n)]$ is minimized subject to the same constraint except that the p's are now regarded as the active variables.

Court returned to this result in his 1951 paper which he presented at the International Congress of Mathematicians and in which he not only generalized his result but also noted its relevance to isoperimetric problems in the calculus of variations and to possible applications concerning integrability problems in the theory of differential equations. He had by then already applied his result to statistical decision, theory. One can only wonder why he did not pursue applications in economic theory.

Louis Court's place among the pioneers of mathematical economics thus rests on his 1941 *Econometrica* articles in which he extended the theories of consumer and producer behaviour to a setting with infinitely many commodities. He introduced his paper with the following rather modern statement:

Apart from its utility in treating commodity groups embracing large, though not necessarily infinite numbers of items, the extension is stamped with true intellectual concinnity. The finite theories are contained, as very special cases, in the infinite analyses. . . . Housing provides an instance in which it is profitable to use the commodity-spectrum concept.

Court worked in the space of square Lebesgue integrable functions over a compact interval; saw the relevance of the theory of Hilbert spaces, still in its infancy; formulated the price system as an element of the topological dual of his commodity space and emphasized the distinction between functions and their equivalence classes (see ibid., footnote 5, p. 248). However, he did not see the relevance of Ramsey's (1928) work or the importance of the weak, weak star and Mackey topologies, the latter omission being justified by the fact that the basic papers dealing with these concepts had yet to be written. Court's results were extended to reflexive Banach spaces by Berger (1971).

In summary, Court's *Econometrica* papers may be seen as a first serious application of functional analysis (see, for example, Dieudonné, 1981) to economic theory and as a precursor of Debreu (1954), Hurwicz (1958), Bewley (1972) and of the burgeoning literature inspired by these contributions; and in another context, of Dornbusch–Fischer–Samuelson (1977). The evaluation of the (then) editor of *Econometrica*, Ragnar Frisch, still stands:

Even though considerable portions of [the] mathematical technique are in essence the same as that developed by Volterra and others, a presentation of this technique *shaped especially with the econometric problems in view*, is highly useful. Economic theory is now growing into a stage where much of the work will consist of a combination of mathematical and economic analyses so intimate that it is difficult to say where one begins and the other ends. Mr. Court's paper is a valuable contribution towards this type of work.

M. Ali Khan

See also FUNCTIONAL ANALYSIS.

SELECTED WORKS

1941. A theorem on maxima and minima with an application to differential equations. *Journal of Mathematics and Physics* 20, 99–106. Reviewed by J. Reid in *Mathematical Reviews* 2, 287.
1941. Entrepreneurial and consumer demand theories for commodity spectra. *Econometrica* 9, 135–62 and 241–97.
1944. A reciprocity principle for the Neyman–Pearson theory of testing statistical hypotheses *Annals of Mathematical Statistics* 15, 326–7. Reviewed by J. Wolfowitz in *Mathematical Reviews* 6, 93.
1951. A theorem on conditional extremes with an application to total differentials. *Proceedings at the American Mathematical Society* 2, 423–8. Reviewed by J. Reid in *Mathematical Reviews* 13, 215.

BIBLIOGRAPHY

Berger, M.S. 1971. Generalized differentiation and utility functionals for commodity spaces of arbitrary dimension. New York: *Preferences, Utility, and Demand*, ed. J.S. Chipman et al., New York: Harcourt Brace Jovanovich.
Bewley, T.F. 1972. Existence of equilibria in economies with infinitely many commodities. *Journal of Economic Theory* 4, 514–40.
Dieudonné, J. 1981. *History of Functional Analysis*. Amsterdam: North-Holland.
Dornbusch, R., Fischer, S. and Samuelson, P. 1977. Comparative advantage, trade and payments in a Ricardian model with a continuum of goods. *American Economic Review* 67, 823–39.
Hurwicz, L. 1958. Programming on linear spaces. In *Studies in Linear and Non-Linear Programming*, ed. K.J. Arrow et al., Stanford: Stanford University Press.
Ramsey, F.P. 1928. A mathematical theory of saving. *Economic Journal* 38, 543–59.

crawling peg. A 'crawling peg' denotes an exchange rate system in which the value of a country's currency is fixed but moveable. The country would undertake to keep its currency at a fixed, or 'par' value. But that par value itself would be *gradually* changed, if this were necessary to correct a 'fundamental disequilibrium' in the country's balance of payments. As elaborated by Williamson (1965) the rate of gradual adjustment would be limited to a maximum rate of one twenty-sixth of one per cent per week. Such a proposal had earlier been put forward by Meade (1964), and the idea originally came from Harrod (see Harrod, 1969, p. 92).

The reason for giving this proposal the label of 'crawling peg' should be apparent. The 'adjustable peg' of the Bretton Woods system was one in which changes in par values of exchange rates were carried out infrequently, suddenly, and in a sizeable, discrete step.

The 'crawling peg' was proposed as a system under which such par changes as occur are implemented slowly, in such a large number of small steps to make the process of exchange rate adjustment continuous for all practical purposes; a system therefore under which the peg crawls from one level to another (Williamson, 1965, p. 2).

If a 'crawling peg' system were not to give rise to large, and possibly disorderly, international capital flows, it would need to be accompanied by an appropriate interest rate policy. For example, if a country's exchange rate were crawling downwards by two per cent per year, then its interest rate would need to be two per cent higher than in other countries whose exchange rates were not moving, in order to avoid stimulating capital outflow.

The 'crawling peg' offered, in the late 1960s, considerable attractions. The 'adjustable peg' regime of the Bretton Woods system was then beginning to disintegrate under the influence of speculative capital flows. The trouble with the adjustable-peg system was that it delayed exchange rate adjustment until the point at which it had become a near certainty, encouraging a speculative attack which then precipitated the inevitable crisis (and which handed speculators a one way bet on a substantial capital gain). Such speculative attacks in the end broke the Bretton Woods system, and ushered in the era of floating exchange rates, with all its difficulties. The 'crawling peg' would have allowed countries to defend par values for their currencies and yet change these par values themselves without disrupting the whole system. A number of countries have, in fact, used the 'crawling peg' at some time (including Argentina, Brazil, Chile, Columbia, Israel, Uruguay and Vietnam). And there is 'rather general agreement' that it has succeeded in allowing them to neutralize efficiently the effects on their balance of payments of high inflation rates (see Williamson, 1977). Although these countries are underdeveloped, their favourable experience with the crawling peg may be relevant to the major industrialized nations.

The great difficulty about a 'crawling peg' system is, however, that it makes it very difficult, or even impossible, to use interest rate policy in the pursuit of domestic economic management. Consider a country in balance of payments deficit which was also experiencing the threat of unemployment. The exchange rate would crawl downwards (because of the deficit) and this would require a relatively high level of domestic interest rates (in order to prevent capital outflow) which would be inconsistent with combatting unemployment. If, instead, interest rates were lowered to combat the unemployment, then capital would flow out. In that case either the rate of downward crawl would increase (and become a cumulative downward spiral) or the capital outflow would become a torrent (as speculators anticipated the defeat of the crawling peg system by means of a large instant currency collapse). An implied great disadvantage of the 'crawling peg' is the fact that where large changes in the exchange rate prove necessary it is impossible to effect them immediately: this in effect means that the interest rate in the country may have to be tied down to offsetting the anticipated exchange rate change during a *very* lengthy adjustment period.

Nevertheless, the 'crawling peg' idea is still of contemporary relevance. There have been a number of recent proposals to reform the international monetary system in the direction of greater management of exchange rates, so as to limit the misalignments which are intrinsic to the present non-system of floating exchange rates. Such a new system would require 'target zones', or 'central rates', for its implementation (see Williamson, 1983; Meade, 1984). These target zones, or central rates, should crawl, rather than being rigidly pegged and discretely adjusted, for exactly the reasons discussed above. But the implications that this would have for domestic interest rate policy, so as to avoid destabilizing capital flows, should be clearly noted.

DAVID VINES

See also FIXED EXCHANGE RATES; FLEXIBLE EXCHANGE RATES; INTERNATIONAL FINANCE.

BIBLIOGRAPHY

Harrod, R.F. 1969. *Money*. London: Macmillan.
Katz, S.I. 1970. The interest-rate constraint and the crawling peg. In T.D. Willet, S.I. Katz and W.H. Branson, *Exchange-Rate Systems, Interest Rates, and Capital Flows*. Essays in International Finance No. 70, Princeton University, Department of Economics, International Finance Section.
Meade, J.E. 1964. The international monetary mechanism. *Three Banks Review*, September.
Meade, J.E. 1984. A Neo-Keynesian Bretton Woods. *Three Banks Review*, June.
Williamson, J.H. 1965. *The Crawling Peg*. Essays in International Finance No. 50, Princeton University, Department of Economics, International Finance Section.
Williamson, J.H. 1977. *The Failure of World Monetary Reform, 1971–74*. Sudbury-upon-Thames: Nelson.
Williamson, J.H. 1983. *The Exchange Rate System*. Policy Analyses in International Economics No. 5, Institute for International Economics, Washington, DC.

creative destruction. Schumpeter invented the phrase 'creative destruction' in his famous book on the development of capitalism into socialism (Schumpeter, 1942). In his view the process of creative destruction is the essential fact about capitalism and refers to the incessant mutation of the economic structure from within, destroying the old and creating a new.

In the footsteps of Karl Marx, Schumpeter argues that in dealing with capitalism we are dealing with an evolutionary process. It is by nature a form or method of economic change and not only never is, but never can be, stationary. The fundamental impulse that sets and keeps the capitalist engine in motion comes from new goods and new methods of production and transportation, created by the Schumpeterian entrepreneur, who is always on the outlook for new combinations of the factors of production.

The process of creative destruction takes time. For that reason there is no point in appraising its performance within a static framework. A system may produce an optimal allocation of resources at every point of time and may yet in the long run be inferior to a system without such optimal allocation, because the non-optimality may be a condition for the level and speed of long-run performances; in other words, for dynamic efficiency. Furthermore, the process of creative destruction in Schumpeter's vision must be seen as the background for individual decisions and strategies. Economic theory has a tendency to concentrate on decisions about prices by firms, who are assumed to maximize profits, within a given structure. Schumpeter argues that the relevant problem is how capitalism creates and destroys these structures.

Schumpeter's conception of creative destruction overturns the idea that price competition is the only component of the market behaviour of entrepreneurs. In fact, it is not that kind of competition which counts, but the competition from the new commodity, the new technology, the new source of supply and the new type of organization. Instead of marginal changes, fundamental upheavals are brought about by process and product innovations of existing firms and potential competitors.

Restrictive practices of monopolists and large firms are to be judged against the background of the perennial gale of creative destruction, rather than in the context of stationary development. The potential threat of process and product innovation reduces the scope and importance of restrictive practices that aim to guarantee the monopolist or big firm a quiet life. If however the profits are used to counterattack, restrictive practices may help to deepen the process of creative destruction and, therefore, the dynamic effects of capitalism.

The process of creative destruction as described by Schumpeter has been experienced again in the 1980s in the

United States, Japan and Western Europe. On the basis of new technologies many old firms, structures and professions have been swept away and new industrial organizations and labour relations have emerged. In particular, the introduction of the 'office of the future' is leading to major changes of a quantitative and qualitative nature in both the private and public sector of the economy. On the one hand, 'external' growth of already large firms which take over others is a feature of modern capitalism; on the other hand, every day new small firms are established, often created by former executives of existing (and long-lived) companies.

This extensive discussion of the process of creative destruction, illustrates Schumpeter's strong emphasis on the supply side of the economy. It would be an interesting question to study the impact of the process of creative destruction on employment. My guess would be that, on balance, the process of creative destruction is more creative than destructive, not only with regard to employment but also concerning broader perspectives of growth and welfare. This may be one of the reasons why Schumpeter's work has had a lasting and ever-increasing influence on economic theory.

ARNOLD HEERTJE

See also INNOVATION; MARKET STRUCTURE AND INNOVATION; SCHUMPETER, JOSEPH ALOIS.

BIBLIOGRAPHY
Heertje, A. (ed.) 1981. *Schumpeter's Vision: Capitalism, Socialism and Democracy after 40 years.* New York: Praeger.
Schumpeter, J. 1942. *Capitalism, Socialism and Democracy.* New York: Harper.

credit. While the volume and complexity of credit transactions has grown immensely over the centuries, the act of credit extension and debt creation, or lending and borrowing, as such, is probably as old as human society. To extend credit means to transfer the property rights on a given object (e.g. a sum of money) in exchange for a claim on specified objects (e.g. certain sums of money) at specified points of time in the future. To take credit, or go into debt, is the other side of the coin. Credit and debt have always posed some special problems of understanding for economists, beyond those associated with the production, trade and consumption of 'ordinary' goods like wheat or cloth, or factors of production like labour services. There exists, of course, a wide array of different forms of credit contracts in today's economies. Classifications are customary; for example, according to types of debtors or creditors (domestic or foreign, public or private, etc.), length of contract duration, type of security put forward by the debtor, or the use of the loan by the borrower. However, this essay will attempt to concentrate on the essential features common to all or most groups of credit transactions, rather than enumerate and describe the differences between specific types and forms of credit.

THE ECONOMIC FUNCTION OF CREDIT. The credit market is essentially a market for intertemporal exchange. Something is given up in the present in exchange for something else in the future – or vice versa, if seen from the point of view of the borrower. The future 'repayment' typically includes a compensation in excess of the original 'payment'; that is, interest. The rate of interest represents the relative price in the market for intertemporal exchange.

The possibility of intertemporal exchanges allows market participants the realization of utility gains, just as voluntary exchange in general is mutually advantageous. The basic reason for this is that individuals are not normally indifferent about the distribution of their consumption over time but care about it. This notion of 'time preference' – used here in its most general and neutral sense, which does not necessarily imply a preference for present over future consumption – was first clearly formulated by Fisher (1930), who viewed *dated* consumption possibilities as the consumer's objects of choice; that is, as separate arguments of his utility function. This allowed the application of the standard tools of microeconomic analysis to problems of inter-temporal choice and proved to be the clue to a clear understanding and analytical treatment of credit and debt. Fisher's treatment still captures the essence of credit and the function it performs in the economy. The given time profile of income (endowments) faced by individuals will often not represent their most desired distribution of the given total consumption over time. The existence of a credit market (the possibility of intertemporal exchange) allows them to transfer a given stream into a preferred stream – either by anticipating future consumption via borrowing ('deficit units') or by transferring consumption into the future via saving and lending ('surplus units'). Transactions of this kind can be mutually advantageous, due to differences in endowments and/or differences in preferences between individuals.

Given real investment opportunities (capital accumulation), the existence of a credit market in general also allows the choice of superior investment decisions, ultimately leading to a higher level of utility. Thus the presence of a credit market, like any other market, permits a more efficient allocation of inputs and outputs, especially with respect to time.

This Fisherian view of the credit market makes clear that it constitutes part of the 'real' economy. That is, it performs a 'real' function by helping to determine the 'real' equilibrium of the economy and the levels of satisfaction reached by its members. It also makes clear that credit can play an important role even in a pure exchange economy with no production and capital formation, given sufficient divergence in individual tastes and/or endowments. On the other hand, production and capital formation can, in principle, take place without credit. Resources can be set aside and invested directly by their owners (the savers). If the owners have no taste or ability for administering these investments, they can, in principle, hire labour (managers) to perform this job (wage, or equity, contracts instead of credit, or debt, contracts). That is, alternative contractual arrangements allowing capital formation and production are available. Of course, credit (debt) contracts, on the one hand, and work (equity) contracts, on the other hand, differ with respect to the way in which risks are shared between the parties involved and with respect to their incentive effects, and a credit market will in general, as already pointed out, be helpful in achieving an efficient allocation of resources and, ultimately, consumption.

CREDIT AND BUDGET CONSTRAINTS. A basic question arising with any credit transaction concerns the mechanisms which ensure that the debtor will meet his future payment obligations. As soon as he has obtained his credit, the borrower has, in principle, a strong incentive to 'run off'. This is linked to the question of the appropriate formulation of budget constraints in the presence of credit. What limits credit demand and present consumption (and the incentive to cheat)? Obviously, a credit market can come into existence and survive only if there exist disciplining mechanisms which serve to prevent, or at least severely restrict, dishonest behaviour. Penalties of one sort or another must be in force, be it through legal provisions (bankruptcy laws), social stigmatization or simply the exclusion from, or discrimination in, future credit market participation.

The appropriate formulation of intertemporal budget constraints, in view of a credit market, is comparatively unproblematic (1) as long as the future payment capacity of a potential debtor (his future income stream) is known with perfect certainty, and (2) if, due to social institutions guaranteeing complete enforceability, there is complete confidence in his willingness to fulfil his future payment obligations, as long as he objectively can. Under these conditions, the relevant magnitude serving to constrain an individual's lifetime consumption obviously is the present value of his lifetime income stream.

Matters are more complicated if the future is not perfectly foreseeable and/or contract enforceability is less than perfect. Unless credit extension is limited to the most pessimistic estimate of the debtor's future income or willingness to repay, there is then a possibility of default. Normally, creditors are willing to accept a certain positive probability of default in exchange for compensation in the form of a higher contractual rate of interest (a risk premium). However, the willingness to extend credit is affected, of course, by the possibility of default and its dependence on the amount of credit extended. Given a finite repayment capacity (finite future income), an increasing level of indebtedness increases the probability of default in two ways. First, for 'external' reasons: the possibility that the future payment obligations exceed the (uncertain) future repayment ability increases with increasing debt. Second, for 'internal' reasons (moral hazard): the incentive to 'run off' after credit has been obtained increases with an increasing repayment obligation; similarly, the incentive to produce future income may be lowered, since in case of partial default the debtor does not benefit from his own efforts. Given a finite repayment capacity, in fact, a point will be reached, sooner or later, where no increase in the contractual interest rate (no risk premium) can compensate the lender for the extra risk of non-payment resulting from a further increase in the level of debt, thus creating an absolute limit to the supply of credit to individuals. This was pointed out by Hodgman (1960), and has led him to speak of credit rationing.

An adequate level of trust in the implicit and explicit promises associated with outstanding debt contracts is an important prerequisite of a smoothly and efficiently operating financial system. Due to the intangible nature of 'trust', the danger of financial crises occurring whenever it is somehow weakened has always been inherent in a credit system. Institutional arrangements, such as a lender of last resort (usually the central bank) or an insurance system of one sort or another (e.g. deposit insurance) are important elements affecting the probability of such occurrences. They are traditionally seen as devices serving to eliminate, or at least contain, the risk of adverse chain reactions. Of course, one danger of institutions of this sort is that they may easily create a moral hazard problem themselves, by lowering the private costs of illiquidity and payment difficulties and thus reducing the private incentives to avoid excessive risks.

IMPERFECT INFORMATION AND THE CREDIT MARKET. In recent years the fact has been stressed that asymmetric information between market participants, and the results problems of adverse incentives and adverse selection, can lead to the breakdown of certain markets (incomplete markets) and to unusual types of market equilibria. These include equilibria with non-price rationing; that is, situations where the interest rate on a loan category is set by the lender at a given level and maintained there, even if there exists an excess demand for loans at this rate (Stiglitz and Weiss, 1981). Starting from the notion that the lender, due to asymmetric information, must, to a certain degree, lump heterogeneous loan customers together, the basic idea is that an increase in the loan rate (applying equally to all customers) will induce 'good' (high quality) customers to leave and 'bad' (low quality) customers to stay (adverse selection), or that individual customers will be induced by the higher loan rate to choose riskier investment projects (moral hazard). In either case, the average quality of loan customers is reduced. Thus an increase in the loan rate here has, in addition to its usual positive effect on lender return, a negative effect which may possibly dominate the former. If this is the case, it is not in the interest of the lender to raise the loan rate, even in the face of an excess demand for loans. The loan rate has then lost its traditional allocative role of bringing in line supply and demand, and instead serves as a device to limit the damages resulting from adverse selection and adverse incentives. Funds then must be allocated to customers in some other way.

This problem disappears again if creditors are able to overcome the underlying information asymmetries and identify different quality customers. Then they can offer different types of contracts (combinations of credit volumes and interest rates, possibly also of collateral levels and equity requirements) to different types of customers. One possibility which has been discussed, in analogy to similar problems in insurance and labour markets, concerns the feasibility of self-selection mechanisms. Under certain conditions it may be possible, by exploring the differences in preferences between high and low quality customers, to offer different types of contracts, so that each potential debtor has an incentive to choose of his own will the appropriate offer designed for his quality class. Another possibility concerns the ability of lenders to overcome the information deficiencies underlying the problems of adverse selection and incentives directly through information acquisition technologies of various sorts (direct screening and policing). Since this kind of information is customer-specific, this can encourage the development of long-term customer relationships. The empirical importance of the information-asymmetry models of credit-market behaviour referred to above thus will ultimately have to be judged in view of the empirical weight of these alternative response possibilities.

CREDIT AND CREDIT INSTITUTIONS. The role of credit as such must be clearly separated from the economic role of credit institutions, such as banks, playing the role of specialized intermediaries in the credit market by buying and simultaneously selling credit instruments (of a different type and quality). Since the ultimate borrowers and lenders can, in principle, do business with each other directly, without the help of such an intermediary, the function of these middlemen must be viewed as separate from that of credit as such.

Two main functions of institutions of this kind can be distinguished. The first is the function of risk consolidation or transformation. By dealing with a large number of creditors and debtors acting, to a considerable extent, independently of each other, the bank can, by exploiting the law of large numbers, achieve a consolidation of risks. In a world of subjective risk aversion, or if risk implies 'objective' costs of one sort or another (costs of adjusting to certain unfavourable states of the world), such a risk consolidation represents a utility gain for the individuals concerned, and this is a marketable service offered by these institutions to the public. Thus existence of risk and uncertainty (imperfect information) is fundamental for this first function of credit institutions.

The second major function of these institutions is that of a broker in the credit markets. As such, they specialize in producing intertemporal exchange transactions and owe their existence to their ability to bring together creditors and debtors at lower costs than the latter can achieve in direct transactions themselves. Transactions and information costs ('market imperfections') in the credit market, including the cost of evaluating credit risks as an especially important example, are fundamental for the financial intermediary in this second function. To summarize: the existence and function of credit institutions is linked in an essential way to the presence of uncertainty, imperfect information, and transactions costs in the credit market. In the absence of these elements, financial intermediaries would have no raison d'être (while credit as such can still perform an important function). Government, when issuing government bonds, can be viewed as an intermediary in a similar sense.

Another, basically similar, 'institutional' question concerns the marketability, or negotiability, of credit contracts and the existence of 'secondary' markets where they can be traded on a regular basis. This requires certain characteristics. In particular, the market cannot be too small, it must be comparatively homogeneous, and it must be possible to assess the quality of the traded contracts at reasonably low costs. The advantage to the creditor of such a resale market is, of course, its contribution to the liquidity of these assets.

CREDIT IN MACROECONOMIC THEORY. In macroeconomic theory, the credit market has frequently played the role of the 'hidden' market eliminated from explicit consideration via application of Walras' Law. Although not explicitly appearing, a credit market (in the form of a bond market) is, however, present in most traditional macromodels. This was clearly brought out, in particular, by Patinkin (1956). Credit has traditionally played a prominent role in some specific issues of macroanalysis, nevertheless. In particular, this is the case with respect to the question of wealth effects. To what extent does credit creation represent creation of net wealth (and in turn affect aggregate demand)? This became one of the dominant issues in monetary theory and macroeconomics during the 1950s and 1960s. See, in particular, Patinkin (1956). Aggregate demand for goods (as well as for money and other assets) was seen as depending on aggregate net wealth of the private sector, in addition to income and relative prices, and all assets were examined with regard to the existence of an equivalent and offsetting liability within the private sector. For most financial assets, such an offsetting liability obviously exists. The exceptions, in the traditional view, were money and – with less confidence, because of the question of the capitalization of future tax liabilities required to finance interest payments – government bonds. As Niehans (1978, p. 91) has argued, this emphasis on net wealth was misplaced in the sense that it failed to appreciate that demand effects arising from individual components of wealth can be powerful even if net wealth effects are negligible or nonexistent. That is, it is not just net wealth which affects the demand for goods and assets; rather, the stocks of the various wealth components given at any point in time, and their difference from the corresponding long-run desired levels, determine the economy's attempts to build up or reduce these components over time.

Another macroeconomic area where the credit market has traditionally played an important role is money supply theory or, more generally, aggregate models of the financial sector of the economy (e.g. Brunner and Meltzer, 1968; Tobin, 1969). Credit markets and credit creation are seen in these models in the light of their relation to money markets and money creation and nominal (price level) control of the system. Financial markets here are typically disaggregated into markets for assets serving as media of exchange (government money and bank demand deposits) and other (non-money) assets, such as bonds and other similar credit instruments. Models of this type have helped considerably to clarify the role of central bank policies in controlling monetary aggregates and, ultimately, the price level. In particular, they have shown that, as long as the degree of substitutability between money and other assets is less than perfect, central bank control over a comparatively narrow monetary aggregate, such as base money, is sufficient for nominal control of the system (price level control), a large menu and volume of private credit notwithstanding.

ERNST BALTENSPERGER

See also FINANCIAL INTERMEDIARIES.

BIBLIOGRAPHY
Brunner, K. and Meltzer, A.H. 1968. Liquidity traps for money, bank credit, and interest rates. *Journal of Political Economy* 76, January/February, 1–37.
Fisher, I. 1930. *The Theory of Interest.* New York: Macmillan.
Hodgman, D.R. 1960. Credit risk and credit rationing. *Quarterly Journal of Economics* 74(2), May, 258–78.
Niehans, J. 1978. Metzler, wealth, and macroeconomics: a review. *Journal of Economic Literature* 16(1), March, 84–95.
Patinkin, D. 1956. *Money, Interest, and Prices.* Evanston: Row & Peterson; 2nd edn, New York: Harper & Row, 1965.
Stiglitz, J. and Weiss, A. 1981. Credit rationing in markets with imperfect information. *American Economic Review* 71(3), June, 393–410.
Tobin, J. 1969. A general equilibrium approach to monetary theory. *Journal of Money, Credit, and Banking* 1(1), February, 15–29.

credit cycle. Prior to Keynes's *General Theory*, the resolution of the question why, in capitalist economies, aggregate variables undergo repeated fluctuations about the trend was regarded by economists as a main challenge for the profession. What was then called business (or trade) cycle theory grew quite independently from the classical and subsequently neo-classical corpus of price theory. In fact, for all economists, a clear cut distinction existed between the long-run forces at work in an economy – the subject of a rigorous value and distribution theory – and the more or less ad-hoc explanations of the short-run oscillations around such an (equilibrium) centre of gravity. Of course, from Ricardo and Thornton down the 19th century to Overstone and Mill, money and credit played a substantial, but independent, part in the business cycle. Along the same line, the founding fathers of marginalism (in particular Walras, Marshall and Jevons) failed to coordinate, even in a remotely satisfactory way, money and trade cycle with their then novel price theory.

Following Wicksell's and Mises's lead, it is only with the post-World War I attempts to integrate marginalist value and monetary theory, that theorists started pondering the possible 'incorporation of cyclical phenomena into the system of economic equilibrium theory' (Hayek, 1929, p. 33n.). The rediscovery of Tooke's (1844) income approach to the quantity theory of money is probably one of the earliest stepping-stones in the development of credit-cycle theories. This line of thought suggests that the explanation of money prices should start not from the quantity of money but from nominal income. Though another way of writing a Marshallian cash balance equation, Wicksell's (1898, p. 44) or Hawtrey's (1913, p. 6) emphasis on the 'aggregate of money income', on how it varies, is expanded or held, is a crucial turning-point on the road towards an analysis in terms of income, saving and investment. This shift of emphasis, together with the simultaneous progress in monetary theory proper (notably the development of a comprehensive and integrated monetary theory of interest), the 1914–18 inflationary episode and the post-war cyclical upheavals, provided in the 1920s and 1930s the right intellectual stimulus for credit-cycle theories to grow and multiply.

Explicitly or implicitly, to tackle this issue, Continental economists (e.g. Mises, Cassel, Hayek, Schumpeter and Aftalion), members of the Cambridge School then dominating in England (Keynes, Robertson, Pigou, Hawtrey), Fisher and Mitchell in the United States all used the common analytical framework established jointly by Walras, Menger, Marshall and Jevons. This is made up of two basic (though familiar) propositions: on the one hand, there is an inverse relation between the volume of investment and the rate of interest (i.e. a downward-sloping investment demand curve) and, on the other, despite short-run 'frictions', the interest rate is assumed to be sensitive enough to divergences between investment decisions and full employment saving.

The central theme of this argument (first expressed with great clarity in Wicksell's cumulative process) is that the market rate of interest oscillates in the short run around a natural rate of interest determined in the long run by the supply of and the demand for capital as a stock, which, in turn, guarantees the equality between planned investment and full employment saving. Once this logic is understood, it then emerges that the entire development of inte-war trade-cycle theories took place within the second proposition outlined above; namely that, in the long run, the interest rate is assumed to be sensitive enough to divergences between investment decisions and full employment saving. Hence, since the twin-concepts of an interest-elastic demand curve for investment and natural rate of interest were never called into question, the orgy of debates that took place in the 1920s and 1930s was conducted in terms of an analysis of various short-run forces which temporarily keep at bay the long-run forces of saving and investment.

These forces are, of course, of multiple nature. Of particular interest to inter-war economists, and one of the essential features of business cycle, with its recurrence of upswings and downswings, is a *credit cycle*, an alternation of credit expansion and credit contraction. But it was neither assumed that an alternation of prosperity and depression would not exist in a barter economy (or in a purely specie system) nor that cycles could be viewed as functions of monetary factors only.

In fact, and thanks to their common capital theory, none of the leading inter-war credit cycle theorists fell into either of these traps. Even Hawtrey who, with remarkable consistency kept claiming that business cycles are a purely monetary phenomenon, had clearly in mind a Wicksell-like cumulative process derived from Marshall's oral tradition in monetary theory. This common theoretical background and a deep interest in a then fast developing monetary theory make similarities between credit cycle theorists

> sufficiently pronounced to entitle us to speak of a single monetary theory [of the cycle], the votaries of which disagree on one issue only: whether bank-loan rates act primarily on 'durable capital' [Keynes, Robertson, Hayek] or via the stocks of wholesalers [Hawtrey] (Schumpeter, 1954, p. 1121).

In 1913, Hawtrey was amongst the first to provide a detailed analysis of the financial working of the cumulative process in an Anglo-Saxon environment. However, even if his theory usefully describes the ways in which money and credit behave in the cycle, the main weakness of his contribution is, of course, its almost exclusive emphasis on dealers' stocks in the course of a credit cycle. If Hawtrey does not deny altogether that a credit expansion/contraction has an influence on the volume of investment, he holds it however to be unimportant when compared with the direct influence on the wholesalers' stocks. He then logically disputes the existence of forced saving on the very ground of this availability of stocks and fails completely to link his credit cycle theory with the dominant Marshallian capital theory. Such a model led Hawtrey to give Bank Rate not only the crucial part to play in any counter-cyclical policy but also to consider its fluctuations as the only explanation of cyclical fluctuations. To sketch British inter-war depressions as almost exclusively functions of Bank Rate (itself a function of Britain's absorption of gold) is a rather bold simplification Hawtrey was never quite ready to abandon.

If the theoretical apparatus underlying the *Treatise on Money* proceeds from the same logic, Keynes's fundamental equations introduce, however, a number of very sophisticated and new variations on the basic credit-cycle theme. In particular, causes of credit cycles are of non-monetary nature (they result from fluctuations in the rate of investment relative to the rate of saving), the influence of Bank Rate on investment is not limited 'to one particular kind of investments, namely, investments by dealers in liquid goods [stocks]' (Keynes, 1930, I, p. 173), the cumulative process includes a theory of the demand for money beyond the traditional income motive (i.e. an early version of liquidity preference), and, in the short run, there is no longer a direct relation between the quantity of money/credit and the price level: monetary or credit changes do not foster *ipso facto* a forced/abortive saving process. Despite the higher degree of sophistication shown in the *Treatise*, in a classic chapter on the *modus operandi* of the Bank Rate, Keynes displays bold confidence in this mechanism to smooth any credit cycle, to fill the gap between saving and investment and to correct all temporary monetary divergences from the long-run full employment equilibrium. However, Keynes's disaffection with the forced saving doctrine and the purely static nature of his fundamental equations drew sharp criticisms from Robertson and Hayek. Though from different standpoints, they both considered Keynes's credit cycle analysis as no more than an attempt to spell out the appropriate banking policy which could maintain a monetary equilibrium. In particular, Keynes's version of credit cycle lacked, for the former, a proper sequential stability analysis and, for the latter, an explicit integration with capital theory.

Along lines very similar to Keynes's and, up to the late 1920s, in close cooperation with him, Robertson worked out a detailed sequential analysis of the interdependence of real and monetary magnitudes during the cycle. But clearly, for him, the cycle results from over-investment, this tendency to over-invest being a typical feature of decentralized economies stemming from the repercussions on the volume of investment of its gestation period. However, the largest part of Robertson's professional output was devoted to studying the monetary or credit symptoms of such economic fluctuations, i.e. how banks may respond to an increased demand for credit during expansion.

This led Robertson to a redefinition of the concept of saving in a monetary economy and to the rôle of this new concept in the cycle. This approach was linked with a sequential analysis of the lagged adjustments of output to monetary flows. In the 'forced saving' debate, central to all credit cycle theories, and contrary to Hayek who considered it as the villain of the piece, Robertson only saw that phenomenon as a relatively minor component of his theory, the factors at the root to his 'credit inflation' being the *real* cause of this expansion. Dragged among others by Keynes into endless discussions in the realm of monetary and interest theory, Robertson never managed however to offer an articulate and full-blown version of his theory of industrial fluctuations. In particular, the problem of the alteration in the structure of production, a question forming the core of Hayek's cycle theory, never received more than passing comment.

Grounded of course in the Austrian tradition and Wicksell's cumulative process (first extended by Mises, 1912 and Cassel, 1918), the distortion of the production time structure is absolutely central to Hayek's monetary cycle theory. The divergence between 'natural' and market rates of interest is linked by Hayek to the variability in forced saving and considered as the cause of cyclical fluctuations. Hayek's 'additional credit' theory places the cause of this gap between these two rates upon newly created money. The increase in loan capital resulting from a 'trailing market rate' makes investment surpass voluntary saving: a cumulative expansion results. Such an increase in investment alters the relative prices of capital and consumer goods in favour of the former. The increased output of capital goods distorts the production time structure. At a later stage, higher factor incomes drive up the demand for consumption goods, which through increased withdrawals from bank accounts will rise the market rate of interest and, finally, make some investment unprofitable. Then, the turnabout that takes place in the cycle brings a change in the other direction in the production structure, this time in favour of consumer goods. Clearly, crises are caused by over-investment, i.e. by a decline in the desire to purchase the flow of capital goods coming on the market. The reversal of the process initiated by credit inflation does take place (as in most credit cycle theories) whenever the market rate catches up with prices; and since, sooner or later, banks run up against the limits set to their lending by their reserves, this process cannot be explosive (Fisher also noticed, at least in his earliest writings, this stabilizing influence of the banking system [1911]).

Hayek's credit cycle theory thus marks a real break with what had come before. The theory of money is no longer a theory of the value of money 'in general' because relative prices may be changed by monetary influences and the Wicksellian full-employment assumption is dropped. The specific task of the trade cycle theorist is, for Hayek, to analyse short-period positions of the economy 'in successive moments of time' (1941, p. 23). The adoption of such an 'intertemporal equilibrium' approach to cycles (conceptually not different from modern temporary equilibrium) marks not only a crucial methodological turning point, but also the swan song of credit cycle theories.

On the one hand, this new method of 'intertemporal equilibrium' heralds the abandonment of the traditional framework in which cycles (defined as short-run disequilibria) are seen as temporary deviations from long-period equilibrium conditions determined by systematic and persistent forces at work in decentralized economies. In the present case, the 'natural' rate of interest determined in the long run by the supply of and the demand for capital is no longer the norm towards which the system is tending. It is in fact a property of such an 'intertemporal equilibrium' that not only will the price

of the same commodity be different at different points in time but also that the stock of capital will not yield a uniform 'natural' rate of interest on its supply-price.

On the other, the publication of Keynes's *General Theory* redirected research efforts away from this question into the problem of the determination of output at a point in time. It is only since the late 1960s, with the search for 'microfoundations for macroeconomics', and the subsequent advent of rational expectations and non-Walrasian equilibria, that this line of thought has been back on the theoretical agenda. However, given the extreme complexity of the problem and the relative crudeness of models still in their infancy, progress has so far been very modest.

P. BRIDEL

See also HAWTREY, RALPH GEORGE.

BIBLIOGRAPHY
Fisher, I. 1911. *The Purchasing Power of Money*. New York: the Macmillan Co.
Hawtrey, R.G. 1913. *Good and Bad Trade*. London: Constable.
Hayek, F.A. von. 1929. *Monetary Theory and the Trade Cycle*. Trans. by N. Kaldor and H.M. Crome, London: Jonathan Cape, 1933.
Hayek, F.A. von. 1941. *The Pure Theory of Capital*. London: Routledge.
Keynes, J.M. 1930. *A Treatise on Money*. Vol. I, *The Pure Theory of Money*. As in *Collected Writings*, vol. V, London: Macmillan, 1971.
Mises, L. von. 1912. *The Theory of Money and Credit*. Trans. by H.E. Batson, London: Jonathan Cape, 1934.
Schumpeter, J.A. 1954. *History of Economic Analysis*. London: Oxford University Press.
Tooke, T. 1844. *An Inquiry into the Currency Principle*. 2nd edn, London: Longman, Brown, Green & Longmans.
Wicksell, K. 1898. *Interest and Prices*. Trans. by R.F. Kahn, London: Macmillan, 1936.

credit markets. *See* CAPITAL, CREDIT AND MONEY MARKETS.

credit rationing Credit rationing is a condition of loan markets in which the lender supply of funds is less than borrower demand at the quoted contract terms. Credit rationing was briefly discussed in the context of usury ceilings by Adam Smith (1776) and was an issue in the bullion and currency controversies of 19th-century England (see Viner, 1937, pp. 256–7). Later, in his *Treatise on Money*, Keynes (1930, I, pp. 212–13; II, pp. 364–7) stressed the 'fringe of unsatisfied borrowers' as a factor influencing the volume of investment. Credit rationing came to prominence in the United States after World War II as part of the 'availability doctrine', first developed by Roosa (1951) and others in the Federal Reserve System. The focus of the availability doctrine, like Keynes's, is that credit rationing influences investment independently of variations in interest rates or in other factors that shift the demand schedules of borrowers.

MICROECONOMIC CREDIT RATIONING THEORY. The equivalent of credit rationing does not occur in well-functioning markets for goods and services because both suppliers and rationed demanders have incentive to raise the price. The price of a loan consists of the interest rate and possibly the non-rate terms such as collateral requirements. For rationing to exist on a continuing basis in loan markets, therefore, the interest rate must be maintained below the market-clearing level by special factors. Usury and other interest–rate ceilings represent an obvious case where exogenously imposed restrictions are the source of credit rationing. Such imposed restrictions aside, however, the goal of the theoretical credit-rationing literature is to identify as sufficient conditions those intrinsic factors that cause rational and unconstrained lenders to maintain loan rates below the market-clearing level on a continuing basis.

Hodgman (1960) was among the first to focus on the risk of default as a source of credit rationing, but he recognized that default risk *alone* is not a sufficient condition for credit rationing to occur. The basic reason is that, if the lender and borrower share and dependably act on the same information concerning default, then the interest rate can accurately reflect any expected default behaviour. Default risk thus does not remove the incentive ro raise the loan rate if there is excess demand. Nevertheless, Freimer and Gordon (1965) developed a credit-rationing model with rational lenders in the special case where the loan repayment is set equal to the *best* possible outcome of the investment project. If there exists borrower excess demand in this circumstance, then credit rationing occurs, because a higher interest rate cannot provide the lender with additional loan revenue. It was later recognized, however, that this rationing result depends on a peculiar form of asymmetrical information, in that the borrower must maintain an optimistic appraisal of the anticipated outcomes, while the lender considers default a certainty; otherwise there would be no basis for the excess demand.

Modern theory identifies the market failures of moral hazard and adverse selection as much more general features of loan markets that can be the source of credit rationing when there is asymmetrical information. Moral hazard and adverse selection occur when the interest rate or the loan size chosen by the lender affects borrower behaviour (moral hazard) or the riskiness of the applicant pool (adverse selection). There is also a class of customer-relationship models, based on the premise that long-standing customers receive priority access to credit, but it appears that these models also require a basis in asymmetrical information to generate credit rationing (Kane and Malkiel, 1965, and Fried and Howitt, 1980).

Jaffee and Russell (1976) developed a model of credit rationing based on moral hazard in the context of a consumer loan model with competitive lenders. The key feature of the model is that the propensity for default by certain borrowers rises as they are offered larger loans. The zero-profit, loan-contract, locus is therefore rising, with higher rates necessary to compensate lenders for the higher default experience on contracts with larger loans. The market-clearing contract is one point on this locus, but there also exists an alternative rationing contract with a lower interest rate, a lower loan size, and thereby a lower average default rate. Borrowers with low default propensities prefer and are able to enforce this rationing contract as the market equilibrium.

Stiglitz and Weiss (1981) developed an investment loan model of credit rationing that includes both moral hazard and adverse selection. The moral hazard feature of the model arises because individual borrowers choose to operate riskier projects at higher loan rates. The adverse selection feature arises because the relatively safe investments of some borrowers become unprofitable at higher loan rates, causing the remaining pool of loan applicants to become riskier. Thus, while higher loan rates increase the lender's expected revenue on any given project, higher rates may create moral hazard and adverse selection effects that reduce the lender's expected revenue for all borrowers. Given that the risk character of individual borrowers and projects cannot be identified *a priori*, it may be optimal policy for the lender to set the loan rate below the market-clearing level and to ration credit.

Lenders also have incentive to screen applicants, to set non-price terms such as collateral requirements, and to offer loan contracts that cause borrowers to identify their risk attributes as a function of their contract selection. The rationing propositions based on asymmetrical information have been criticized for ignoring lender use of such devices (Barro, 1976; Bester, 1985). In fact, however, while such devices may reduce the magnitude of credit rationing, they generally will not eliminate it. The key point is that the lender must control an additional independent instrument for each dimension of loan risk in order to eliminate the moral hazard and adverse selection that are the source of credit rationing. In practice, loan default is a complex, multi-dimensional process, and lenders have access to only relatively crude or costly devices for gaining information. It is thus unrealistic to assume that cost-effective use of these devices will reveal the precise risk attributes of individual borrowers.

EMPIRICAL AND MACROECONOMIC ASPECTS OF CREDIT RATIONING. Empirical tests of the existence and effects of credit rationing generally use indirect methods based on proxies and other measures with an assumed relationship to actual rationing. Direct measures of credit rationing are uncommon because they require data on applications and rejections, as well as loans made, and these are rarely available. The indirect methods used include survey data, proxy measures, and cross-section and time-series analysis. Jaffee (1971) provides a discussion of the various techniques and the evidence up to 1970.

Borrower surveys are made occasionally on an *ad hoc* basis, usually to study the determinants of investment demand. Interest rates are consistently rated the most important financial variable, but credit rationing is noted by about one-quarter of the firms, with a higher incidence among smaller firms. Lender surveys of loan rates and non-rate terms on business and mortgage loans are made on a continuing basis by the Federal Reserve and Federal Home Loan Bank systems, and some data are available for consumer loan markets as well. Studies of these data show that loan demand and corresponding real expenditures are negatively related to higher levels of the non-rate terms, such as higher collateral requirements, as well as to higher loan-rate levels.

These results confirm that non-rate terms can be treated symmetrically with loan rates as components of the vector that determine the price of a loan (Baltensperger, 1974 and 1978; Harris, 1974). There are alternative interpretations, however, with regard to the implications of this for credit rationing. In one view, the variability of non-price terms provides on *offset to credit rationing*, in that an excess demand for loans and thereby the need for credit rationing can be reduced by higher levels of non-price terms. In another view, the variability of non-price terms is considered a *form of credit rationing*, in that higher values of non-rate terms are used to ration the available supply of funds. This difference in view is a matter of definition, but it is important for monetary policy that the variability of non-price terms and the related 'credit rationing' provide a channel of impact on the real sectors of the economy that does not require variations in interest-rate levels.

Credit rationing proxy measures provide another empirical technique based on the theoretically expected effects of credit rationing. Most credit rationing theories imply that identifiably risk-free borrowers will not be rationed, and therefore that a higher proportion of total loans made to risk-free borrowers can be associated with greater rationing of risky borrowers, given that the ratio of demand between risk-free and risky borrowers has no corresponding variation. Jaffee and Modigliani (1969) implemented this technique, and tests of the proxy variable confirmed the existence of *dynamic* credit rationing, which occurs in the short-run as the loan rate adjusts to the market-clearing or equilibrium level, but did not consider *equilibrium* credit rationing, which occurs in a continuing equilibrium with the loan rate maintained below the market-clearing level.

A variety of time-series studies using special econometric methods for markets in disequilibrium have been carried out to test for the effects of credit rationing in mortgage and business loan markets (Fair and Jaffee, 1972; Sealey, 1979). Most studies have found some statistical evidence of credit rationing, but the quantitative magnitudes are generally inconsequential. Thus, while credit rationing may be a consistent feature of lender behaviour, an important impact on real investment expenditures has not been confirmed.

A basic explanation is that rationed firms may have access to alternative forms of credit. Trade credit, provided between non-financial firms, is particularly important in this respect because the amount outstanding in the US is of the same order of magnitude as business loans. There is the question, however, of why the problems of asymmetrical information do not cause lending firms, just as they cause lending banks, to ration credit. Theory on this point has been slow to develop, but it is plausible that the degree of asymmetrical information may be less between two firms acting as buying and seller of the same commodity than between one firm and a lending institution.

Credit rationing activity in mortgage and consumer loan markets in the US has been dominated by interest-rate ceilings. *Usury law ceilings* (Goudzwaard, 1968) become restrictive if the ceilings are not adjusted in line with rapidly rising market rates of interest, and lending activity is reduced in areas with the lowest ceilings. *Deposit rate ceilings* indirectly affect loan markets by restricting the flow of funds to depository institutions during high rate periods; the effect of these ceilings on mortgage lending and housing activity is especially clear (see Jaffee and Rosen, 1979). Most usury and deposit rate ceilings in the US were removed during the early 1980s, and it is anticipated that credit rationing in these markets will decline.

Recent discussions regarding credit rationing and monetary policy are taking place in the context of the major financial market innovations and deregulation of the early 1980s. The competitive and innovative forces in financial markets are expanding rapidly, with the result that loan markets, which specialize in originating risky instruments, and capital markets, which traditionally trade low-risk securities, are becoming integrated. This process includes the entry of capital market firms directly into loan markets, and the development of new capital market securities that consist of individual loans and that carry insurance of other guarantees against default. A possible result is that credit rationing and the availability channel of monetary policy will become less important features of the financial markets.

At the same time, the unique role played by loan markets and lending institutions in allocating capital to risky borrowers has received renewed attention (Bernanke, 1983; Blinder and Stiglitz, 1983: Stiglitz, 1985). Also, it has been argued that credit flows may provide a better indicator for monetary policy than traditional money supply measures (Friedman, 1983). Consequently, while the recent innovations and deregulation may change the location and reduce the magnitude of credit rationing, they do not change the fundamental problems of market failure under asymmetrical information, and credit rationing in one form or another is likely to continue.

DWIGHT M. JAFFEE

See also FINANCE; MONEY, CREDIT AND CAPITAL MARKETS.

BIBLIOGRAPHY
Baltensperger, E. 1976. The borrower-lender relationship, competitive equilibrium, and the theory of hedonic prices. *American Economic Review* 66, June, 401–5.
Baltensperger, E. 1978. Credit rationing: issues and questions. *Journal of Money, Credit, and Banking* 10(2), May, 170–83.
Barro, R. 1976. The loan market, collateral, and the rate of interest. *Journal of Money, Credit and Banking* 8(4), November, 439–56.
Bernanke, B. 1983. Nonmonetary effects of the financial collapse in the propagation of the Great Depression. *American Economic Review* 73(3), June, 257–76.
Bester, H. 1985. Screening versus rationing in credit markets with imperfect information. *American Economic Review* 75(4), September, 850–55.
Blinder, A. and Stiglitz, J. 1983. Money, credit constraints, and economic activity. *American Economic Review* 73(2), May, 297–302.
Fair, R. and Jaffee, D. 1972. Methods of estimation for markets in disequilibrium. *Econometrica* 40(3), May, 497–514.
Freimer, M. and Gordon, M. 1965. Why bankers ration credit. *Quarterly Journal of Economics* 79(3), August, 397–416.
Fried, J. and Howitt, P. 1980. Credit rationing and implicit contract theory. *Journal of Money, Credit, and Banking*, August, 305–14.
Friedman, B. 1983. The roles of money and credit in macroeconomic analysis. In *Macroeconomics, Prices and Quantities: Essays in Memory of Arthur Okun*, ed. J. Tobin, Washington, DC: Brookings Institution.
Goudzwaard, M. 1968. Price ceilings and credit rationing. *Journal of Finance* 23, March, 177–85.
Harris, D. 1974. Credit rationing at commercial banks: some empirical evidence. *Journal of Money, Credit, and Banking* 6(2), May, 227–40.
Hodgman, D. 1960. Credit risk and credit rationing. *Quarterly Journal of Economics* 74, May, 258–78.
Jaffee, D. 1971. *Credit rationing and the Commercial Loan Market*. New York: John Wiley.
Jaffee, D. and Modigliani, F. 1969. A theory and test of credit rationing. *American Economic Review* 59(5), December, 850–72.
Jaffee, D. and Rosen, K. 1979. Mortgage credit availability and residential construction activity. *Brookings Papers on Economic Activity* No. 2, 333–76.
Jaffee, D. and Russell, T. 1976. Imperfect information, uncertainty, and credit rationing. *Quarterly Journal of Economics* 90(4), November, 651–66.
Kane, E. and Malkiel, B. 1965. Bank portfolio allocation, deposit variability, and the availability doctrine. *Quarterly Journal of Economics* 79(2), February, 113–34.
Keynes, J.M. 1930. *A Treatise on Money*. London: Macmillan.
Rosa, R.V. 1951. Interest rates and the central bank. In *Money, Trade, and Economic Growth: Essays in Honor of John H. Williams*, ed. H.L. Waitzman, New York: Macmillan.
Sealey, C. 1979. Credit rationing in the commercial loan market: estimates of a structural model under conditions of disequilibrium. *Journal of Finance* 34(3), June, 689–702.
Smith, A. 1776. *An Inquiry into the Nature and Causes of the Wealth of Nations*. Ed. E. Cannan, London: Methuen, 1961.
Stiglitz, J. 1985. Credit markets and the control of capital. *Journal of Money, Credit, and Banking* 17(2), May, 133–52.
Stiglitz, J. and Weiss, A. 1981. Credit rationing in markets with imperfect information. *American Economic Review* 71(3), June, 393–410.
Viner, J. 1937. *Studies in the Theory of International Trade*. New York: Harper & Brothers.

crime and punishment. 'Economics of Crime' revives an old tradition in economic thought in its reliance on the unifying power of economic analysis to explain human behaviour and resource allocation choices both within and outside the conventional market place. Classical economists such as Beccaria, Paley, and Bentham devoted considerable attention

721

to the explanation of crime in rational economic terms, and to the formulation of optimal rules for punishing offenders, based on utilitarian principles. Motivated, in part, by the rapid growth of reported offences in recent decades, economists have regained interest in the issue. Several studies in the 1960s, notably the seminal work by Becker (1968), have inspired the development of the 'economic approach to crime'.

The essence of the approach lies in the assumption that offenders respond to incentives, both positive and negative, and that the volume of actual offences in the population is therefore influenced by the allocation of private and public resources to law enforcement and other means of crime prevention. For this approach to provide a useful approximation of the complicated reality of crime, it is not necessary that all those who commit specific offences respond to incentives, (nor is the degree of individual responsiveness prejudged); it is sufficient that a significant number of potential offenders so behave on the margin. By the same token, the theory does not preclude a priori any category of crime, or any class of incentives. Indeed, economists have applied this approach to a myriad of illegitimate activities, from tax evasion and violations of minimum wage laws to auto-theft, skyjacking, and murder.

THEORY

In Becker's analysis the equilibrium volume of crime was produced through the interaction between offenders and the law enforcement authority, and the focus was on propositions concerning the socially optimal probability, severity, and type of criminal sanction. Later work centred on a more complete formulation of the components of the system, especially the supply of offences, the production of law enforcement activities, and the criteria for optimal law enforcement. Attempts have also been made to expand the notion and scope of the 'market' for illegitimate activities by expounding the roles played by offenders (supply), consumers and potential victims (private demand), and enforcement and prevention (government intervention), and by augmenting the relevant market equilibrium analysis.

Supply. The offender's choice is generally modelled to involve an optimal allocation of time among competing legitimate and illegitimate activities which differ in the mix of their uncertain pecuniary and non-pecuniary consequences, and offenders are presumed to act as expected-utility maximizers. The basic opportunities affecting choice are identified as the (perceived) probabilities of apprehension, conviction, and punishment, and the marginal penalties imposed ('deterrence variables'); the deterrence variables associated with related crimes; the marginal returns on competing illegal and legal activities and the risk of unemployment; and initial wealth. Entry into a specific criminal activity is shown to be related inversely to its own deterrence variables, and directly to the differential return it provides. Moreover, a one per cent increase in the probability of apprehension is shown to generate a larger deterrent effect than corresponding increases in the conditional probabilities of conviction given apprehension, and specific punishments given conviction (see Ehrlich, 1975). Essentially due to conflicting income and substitution effects, some results for active offenders are more ambiguous: a strong preference for risk may reverse the deterrent effect of sanctions (Ehrlich, 1973) and the results are even less conclusive if one assumes (as do Block and Heineke, 1975) that the length of time spent in crime, not just the moral obstacle to entering it, generates disutility. The results become less ambiguous at the aggregate level, however, as one allows for non-homogeneity of offenders

due to differences in personal opportunities or preferences for crime: a more severe sanction can reduce the crime rate by deterring the entry of potential offenders even if it has little effect on actual ones.

Demand. The incentives operating on offenders often originate with, and are partially controlled by, consumers and potential victims. Transactions in illicit drugs and stolen goods, for example, are patronized by consumers who generate a direct or derived demand for the underlying offences (cf. Vandaele, 1978). But even for crimes that inflict pure harm on victims there exists an indirect (negative) demand, which is derived from a positive demand for safety. By their choice of optimal self-protective efforts through use of locks, safes, and alarms, or selective avoidance of travel, potential victims influence the marginal returns to offenders, and thus the implicit 'demand' for crime. And since optimal self-protection generally increases with the perceived risk of victimization (the crime rate), private protection and public enforcement will be interdependent.

Public intervention. Whereas crime is an external diseconomy and crime control measures are largely a public good, collective action is needed to augment individual self-protection. Public intervention typically aims to 'tax' illegal returns through the threat of punishment, or to 'regulate' offenders via incapacitation and rehabilitation programme. All control measures are costly. Therefore, the 'optimum' volume of offences cannot be nil, but must be set at a level where the marginal cost of each measure of enforcement or prevention equals its marginal benefit.

To assess the relevant net benefits, however, one must adopt a criterion for public choice. Becker (1968) and Stigler (1970) each chose maximization of a concept of 'social income' as the relevant criterion, requiring the minimization of the sum of social damages from offences and the cost of law enforcement activities. This approach can lead to powerful propositions regarding the optimal magnitudes of probability and severity of punishments for different crimes and different offenders, or, alternatively, the optimal level and mix of expenditures on police, courts, and corrections. It reaffirms the proposition that, in equilibrium, the deterrent effect of the optimal probability of apprehension will exceed that of the conditional probabilities of conviction and of specific punishments, and it makes a strong case for the superiority of monetary fines as a deterring sanction. Different criteria for public choice, however, yield different implications regarding the optimal mix of probability and severity of punishment, as is the case when the social welfare function is expanded to include concern for the distributional consequences of law enforcement and other concepts of justice in addition to aggregate income (see Polinsky and Shavell, 1979; and Ehrlich, 1982). Furthermore, a positive analysis of enforcement must address the behaviour of the separate agencies constituting the enforcement system and the constraints of the political market. Studies which focus on the production of and demand for specific agencies, such as police and courts (see, e.g., Landes, 1971), have often adopted decision rules which deviate from the social welfare maximizing criterion.

Market equilibrium. A general equilibrium analysis of the market for offences involving the joint determination of the volume of offences and the net returns from crime in a system of interrelated markets is still at an embryonic stage. One important implication of the market model already developed is that the efficacy of deterring sanctions cannot be assessed merely by reference to the elasticity of the aggregate supply of offences, but depends on the elasticity of the private demand schedule as well. Likewise, the efficacy of rehabilitation and incapacitation programme cannot be inferred solely from knowledge of their impact on individual offenders. It depends crucially on the elasticities of the market supply and demand schedules, as these determine the extent to which successfully rehabilitated offenders will be replaced by others responding to the prospect of higher net returns (see Ehrlich, 1981; van den Haag, 1975). A market setting has also been applied by economists to analyse various aspects of organized crime.

EMPIRICAL ANALYSES

Largely due to the paucity of theoretically relevant data, little has been done thus far to implement a comprehensive market model of illegitimate activity (but see Vandaele, 1978). In particular, few studies have sought to estimate the private demand for self-protection as part of a complete market system (see Bartel, 1975; Clotfelter, 1977). Many researchers have attempted, however, to implement a simultaneous equation model of crime and law enforcement activity consisting, typically, of three sets of basic structural equations (see Ehrlich, 1973): supply-of-offences functions linking the rate of offences with deterrence variables and other measurable incentives; production functions of law enforcement activity linking conditional probabilities of arrest, conviction, and punishment with resource inputs and other determinants of productivity; and demand-for-enforcement functions linking resource spending with determinants of public intervention. The bulk of the econometric work concerns the first two structural relationships. (For surveys see Palmer, 1977; Andreano and Siegfried, 1980; and Pyle, 1983.)

The econometric applications have been hampered by a number of methodological problems. For example, FBI crime reports are known to understate true crime rates, and related errors of measurement in estimated punishment risks may expose parameter estimation to biases and spurious correlations. The inherent simultaneity in the data requires systematic use of identification restrictions to assure consistent estimation of structural parameters. In testing offenders' responsiveness to incentives, estimates of the deterrent effect of imprisonment must be distinguished from those of its incapacitative effect. Efficient functional forms of structural equations must be selected systematically. And then there is the ubiquitous possibility that results would be biased by 'missing variables' (including links to markets for illicit drugs or handguns). While these problems have been recognized from the outset, not all studies have attempted to resolve them by applying relevant statistical remedies.

Most studies of specific offences report similar findings: probability and length of punishment are generally found to be inversely related to crime rates, and the estimated elasticities of the latter with respect to the conditional risk of apprehension are often found to exceed those with respect to the conditional risk of apprehension are often found to exceed those with respect to the conditional risks of conviction and punishment. Crime rates are often found to be directly related to measures of income inequality and community wealth (presumably due to the link between affluence and criminal opportunities). Estimates of unemployment effects are somewhat ambiguous, however, depending, in part, on whether they are derived from time-series or cross-section data (see the survey by Freeman, 1983), and such is the case also with demographic variables. This pattern of results is derived from studies using aggregate data from different countries and locations, FBI as well as Victimization Survey statistics, and

even individual crime data. There also is some evidence that police output measures are weakly responsive to additional resource inputs, although studies differ in their definitions of output and in their specification of the relevant production functions.

Not all research, however, is consistent with the deterrence hypothesis (e.g. Forst, 1976; but see its critique by Wadycki and Balkin, 1979). Also, criticism has been raised as to the validity of the estimated deterrent effects on grounds of potential biases due to errors of measurement and the identification restrictions used (see Blumstein et al., 1978). Critics have argued that the apparent deterrent effects may mask a deterrent effect of crime on punishment variables. These issues are clearly debatable (see Ehrlich and Mark, 1977).

The applicability of the economic approach to the crime of murder, and whether the death penalty constitutes a specific deterrent have raised greater controversy. The centre of debate has been the study by Ehrlich (1975) in which the approach was found to be not inconsistent with time-series evidence (see Blumstein et al., 1978; and Ehrlich and Mark, 1977). The controversy has generated additional empirical research, some inconsistent with the deterrence hypothesis (e.g., Passell, 1975; Forst, 1977; Avio, 1979; Hoenack and Weiler, 1980) and some quite corroborative (e.g. Ehrlich, 1977; Wolpin, 1978; Phillips and Ray, 1982; Layson, 1983 and 1985).

It is early to assess the degree to which the various econometric studies on crime have produced accurate estimates of critical behavioural relationships. Some studies attempting to test the theory have not, in fact, taken sufficient account of it. Both theory and econometric design, however, must be further developed to account for missing elements of the general market model, thereby facilitating the substantive identification of structural equations and, indeed, the explanation of observed crime variations. While a consensus seems to emerge among researchers regarding the potential power of the economic approach in studying both the illegal sector of the economy and its interaction with the legal economy, future progress will greatly depend on better data.

ISAAC EHRLICH

See also FAMILY; LAW AND ECONOMICS.

BIBLIOGRAPHY

Andreano, R. and Siegfried, J.J. 1980. *The Economics of Crime.* Cambridge, Mass.: Schenkman.

Avio, K.L. 1979. Capital punishment in Canada: a time-series analysis of the deterrent hypothesis. *Canadian Journal of Economics,* November, 647–76.

Bartel, A.P. 1975. An analysis of firm demand for protection against crime. *Journal of Legal Studies* 4(2), June, 433–78.

Becker, G.S. 1966. Crime and punishment: an economic approach. *Journal of Political Economy* 76(2), March/April, 169–217.

Becker, G.S. and Landes, W.M. (eds) 1974. *Essays in the Economics of Crime and Punishment.* New York: Columbia University Press.

Block, M.K. and Heineke, J.M. 1975. A labor theoretic analysis of the criminal choice. *American Economic Review* 65(3), June, 314–25.

Blumstein, A., Cohen, J. and Nagin, D. (eds) 1978. *Deterrence and Incapacitation: Estimating the Effects of Criminal Sanctions on Crime Rates.* Washington, DC: National Academy of Science.

Carr-Hill, R.A. and Stern, N.H. 1979. *Crime. The Police and Criminal Statistics.* London: Academic Press.

Clotfelter, C.T. 1977. Public services, private substitutes, and the demand for protection against crime. *American Economic Review* 67(5), December, 867–77.

Ehrlich, I. 1973. Participation in illegitimate activities: theoretical and empirical investigation. *Journal of Political Economy* 81(3), May–June, 521–65. Reprinted with supplements in Becker and Landes (1974).

Ehrlich, I. 1975. The deterrent effect of capital punishment: a question of life and death. *American Economic Review* 65(3), June, 397–417.

Ehrlich, I. 1977. Capital punishment and deterrence: some further thoughts and additional evidence. *Journal of Political Economy* 85(4), August, 741–88.

Ehrlich, I. and Mark, R. 1977. Fear of deterrence. *Journal of Legal Studies* 6, June, 293–316.

Ehrlich, I. 1981. On the usefulness of controlling individuals: an economic analysis of rehabilitation, incapacitation and deterrence. *American Economic Review* 71(3), June, 307–22.

Ehrlich, I. 1982. The optimum enforcement of laws and the concept of justice: a positive analysis. *International Review of Law and Economics* 2(1), June, 3–27.

Fleisher, B.M. 1966. *The Economics of Delinquency.* Chicago: Quadrangle.

Forst, B.E. 1976. Participation in illegitimate activities: further empirical findings. *Policy Analysis* 2(3), Summer, 477–92.

Forst, B.E. 1977. The deterrent effect of capital punishment: a cross-state analysis of the 1960s. *Minnesota Law Review* 61(5), May, 743–67.

Freeman, R.B. 1983. Crime and unemployment. In *Crime and Public Policy,* ed. J.Q. Wilson, San Francisco: ICS.

Heineke, J.M. (ed.) 1978. *Economic Models of Criminal Behavior.* Amsterdam: North-Holland.

Hoenack, S.A. and Weiler, W.C. 1980. A structural model of murder behavior. *American Economic Review* 70(3), June, 327–41.

Landes, W.M. 1971. An economic analysis of the courts. *Journal of Law and Economics* 14(1), April, 61–107.

Layson, S. 1983. Homicide and deterrence: another view of the Canadian time-series evidence. *Canadian Journal of Economics* 16(1), February, 52–73.

Layson, S. 1985. Homicide and deterrence: a reexamination of the United States time-series evidence. *Southern Journal of Economics* 52(1), July, 68–89.

Palmer, J. 1977. Economic analyses of the deterrent effect of punishment: a review. *Journal of Research in Crime and Delinquency* 14(1), January, 4–21.

Passell, P. 1975. The deterrent effect of the death penalty: statistical test. *Stanford Law Review* 28(1), November, 61–80.

Phillips, L. 1981. The criminal justice system: its technology and inefficiencies. *Journal of Legal Studies* 10(2), June, 363–80.

Phillips, L. and Ray, S.C. 1982. Evidence on the identification and causality dispute about the death penalty. In *Applied Time Series Analysis,* ed. O.D Anderson and M.R. Perryman, Amsterdam: North-Holland.

Polinsky, A.M. and Shavell, S. 1979. The optimal trade-off between the probability and magnitude of fines. *American Economic Review* 69(5), December, 880–91.

Pyle, D.J. 1983. *The Economics of Crime and Law Enforcement.* London: Macmillan.

Stigler, G.J. 1970. The optimum enforcement of laws. *Journal of Political Economy* 78(3), March–April, 526–35.

Tullock, G. 1967. The welfare costs of tariffs, monopolies, and theft. *Western Economic Review* 5(3), June, 224–32.

Vandaele, W. 1978. An econometric model of auto theft in the United States. In Heineke (1978).

Van den Haag, E. 1975. *Punishing Criminals.* New York: Basic Books.

Wadycki, W.J. and Balkin, S. 1979. Participation in illegitimate activities: Forst's model revisited. *Journal of Behavioral Economics* 8(2), Winter, 151–63.

Witte, A.D. 1980. Estimating the economic model of crime with individual data. *Quarterly Journal of Economics* 94(1), February, 57–84.

Wolpin, K. 1978. Capital punishment and homicide in England: a summary of results. *American Economic Review, Papers and Proceedings* 68(2), May, 422–7.

crises. The term 'crisis' as used in economics is principally associated with Marx. While other writers use the term, Marx attempted rigorously to theorize crises as they occur in capitalism. It is therefore his work which will be discussed here.

In one sense, what Marx meant by an economic crisis accords perfectly well with the common use of the term: for example, it would be quite appropriate to use it to describe the liquidation of a company due to bankruptcy or a major financial disruption, involving the collapse of a number of banks. Marx however used the term 'crisis' rather more precisely, applying it to any situation where the process of renewal and expansion of capital was interrupted. Thus, for example, overproduction by one sector of the economy would cause a crisis, whether restricted to that one sector alone, or not. The term also includes the most general crises, affecting all branches of the economy and many national economies simultaneously.

For Marx, long periods of economic decline or stagnation were not 'crises'. Neither should it be thought that by *the* crisis is meant solely the final demise of capitalism. For crises were (and are) a normal and frequent feature of capitalism, and they represent not only a breakdown in the process of capital accumulation, but also the means through which capital reorganizes itself for a fresh burst of accumulation.

Two important points must be made about Marx's theory of crises. The first is that Marx identified the forces which give rise to the possibility of crisis within the process of capitalist production itself. While not disputing that economic crises could also arise as a result of disturbances from outside the economic sphere (such as natural disasters), these were not Marx's concern. Marx attempted to show that crises could be generated 'internally' by capitalism. The second point is to emphasize that there is a distinction within the theory between the analysis of the features of capitalism which give rise to the possibility of crisis, and the analysis of those conditions which turn this latent possibility into reality. Although the 'theory of the possibility of crisis' grows over into the consideration of crises proper, it inevitably precedes it and lays the foundation for this analysis.

Most analyses of the actual content of crises begin with the circuit of capital, M–C–M. The purpose of theory of the possibility of crisis is to show why that form, M–C–M, contains the *potential* for crisis. It is that theory which will be discussed here.

Capitalist production is the production of commodities. To show that crises were intrinsic to capitalism, Marx had therefore to develop the theory of the possibility of crisis from his analysis of the commodity.

A commodity, Marx observed, is a product produced for exchange. It is not produced to meet the needs of the person who produces it. The commodity has two sides to it, its use-value (or usefulness) which is entirely dependent on its physical properties, and its value, the magnitude of which is measured by the amount of socially necessary labour time required for its production. As it is produced for exchange, it has to pass through a series of distinct forms: firstly as 'commodity' then as money and then again as 'commodity'. This commodity circuit is usually depicted as C–M–C.

It is worth explaining this in a little more detail to avoid any ambiguity. Suppose that I manufacture an item for sale. At this stage, my commodity is in its natural or 'commodity' form. Suppose now that I succeed in selling it. My commodity now takes the form of money. It is still a commodity (money is a commodity) but it now takes the form of money where previously it took a physical form. If I now use this money to make a purchase, my commodity has now once more reverted to a natural, 'commodity' form. C–M–C refers to the phases through which the one commodity has to pass, though its circuit is of course intertwined with the circuits of other commodities. In accordance with common sense, the first phase (C–M) is the sale and the second (M–C), the purchase.

A number of observations may now be made. Since the commodity is produced for sale, it must undergo the metamorphosis from 'commodity' to money. Whether it succeeds in this depends on conditions which are external to the commodity, conditions which may or may not prevail. The fact that it must attempt this transformation, the success of which depends upon conditions external to the commodity, is what creates 'the germ of the possibility of crisis' (Marx, 1861, p. 507). The possibility of crisis arises from the fact that the commodity may fail to complete this metamorphosis: it may fail to be sold.

It may seem that Marx was doing no more than state the obvious: a commodity must be sold. Such an assessment would be wrong for two reasons. It should be remembered that it is a result derived from his analysis of the commodity, not merely an assertion. Secondly, it is significant that those who deny that crises are an inevitable feature of capitalist production, do so essentially by ignoring or assuming away the very characteristics which Marx's analysis uncovered.

To illustrate this, it is worth looking at how Marx challenged Ricardo's denial of the possibility of general overproduction. Ricardo's position was that: 'Productions are always bought by productions, or by services; money is only the medium by which the exchange is effected' (Ricardo, 1821, pp. 291–2). To this, Marx replied:

> Here ... the exchange of commodities is transformed into mere barter of products, of simple use-values. This is a return not only to the time before capitalist production, but even to the time before there was simple commodity production: and the most complicated phenomenon of capitalist production – the world market crisis – is flatly denied by denying the first condition of capitalist production, namely that the product must be a commodity and therefore express itself as money and undergo the process of metamorphosis (Marx, 1861, p. 501).

But if the possibility of crisis lies firstly in the simple metamorphosis of the commodity, in the commodity circuit C–M–C, it is far from fully developed. 'For the development of this possibility into reality', Marx observed, 'a whole series of conditions is required which do not yet even exist from the standpoint of the simple circulation of commodities' (Marx, 1867, p. 209). Thus the theory of the possibility of crisis must be extended to take account of the implications of the circuit of capital.

Although the circulation of commodities is the starting point of capital, the circuit of capital is a dramatic transformation of that followed by the commodity. Instead of C–M–C, the capital circuit is M–C–M (Money–'Commodity'–Money). In the capital circuit, capital, as money, is firstly used to buy commodities (means of production, raw materials and labour-power). These are then put to use to produce items for sale which are then sold, if possible, at a profit. With this sale, capital has once more returned to the money form.

It is worth noting that money plays a quite different role in C–M–C, compared with M–C–M. In the circulation of the commodity, money acts merely as money, as medium of circulation, whereas 'money which describes the latter course in its movement is transformed into capital, becomes capital, and from the point of view of its function, is capital' (Marx, 1867, p. 248).

Two more points of contrast between M–C–M and C–M–C should be mentioned. Firstly, the goal of the simple circulation of the commodity is the acquisition of further commodities for their use-value: the goal is consumption. In contrast, the driving force of the circulation of capital, its determining purpose, is exchange value (Marx, 1867, p. 250). Secondly, although both C–M–C and M–C–M contain a sale phase and a purchase phase, the order of the two phases is inverted. In C–M–C, it is selling in order to buy. In M–C–M, it is buying in order to sell.

This inversion has a direct bearing on the development of the possibility of crisis. For obviously, if the circuit is broken, it will be during the sale phase. This creates a problem even under the simple circulation of commodities but its impact is likely to be limited. Once the circuit becomes a capital circuit, a failure to sell has more far-reaching consequences, because it means that the very purpose of production has been thwarted.

Marx illustrated this in his discussion on money as a means of payment. Essentially, a chain of mutual financial obligations develops: should the cloth fail to be sold, then many capitalists will be affected, not just the cloth merchant. The weaver will not be paid; he in turn will be unable to pay the spinner; neither will be able to pay the machine manufacturer and he in turn will be unable to pay the suppliers of iron, timber and coal. 'This is nothing other than the possibility of crisis described when dealing with money as a means of payment; but here – in capitalist production – we can already see the connection between the mutual claims and obligations, the sales and purchases, through which the possibility can develop into actuality' (Marx, 1861, p. 512).

Ricardo's denial of the possibility of general overproduction is now worth another look. His main argument was this:

> No man produces, but with a view to consume or sell, and he never sells but with an intention to purchase some other commodity, which may be immediately useful to him, or which may contribute to future production. By producing, then, he necessarily becomes either the consumer of his own goods, or the purchaser and consumer of the goods of some other person. It is not to be supposed that he should, for any length of time be ill informed of the commodities which he can most advantageously produce, to attain the object which he has in view, namely, the possession of other goods; and therefore, it is not probable that he will continuously produce a commodity for which there is no demand (Ricardo, 1821, p. 290).

Marx found fault with this on three counts. Firstly, in saying that a man may produce in order to consume, Ricardo was again overlooking the fact that commodities are produced to be sold, and not to meet the needs of the producer. It is true that where production is for the direct satisfaction of the producer, there are no crises. But such a situation is not even simple commodity production, let alone capitalist production (Marx, 1861, p. 502).

Marx's second criticism goes to the very heart of the matter:

> A man who has produced does not have the choice of selling or not selling. He must sell. In the crisis there arises the very situation in which he cannot sell or can only sell below the cost price or must even sell at a positive loss. What difference does it make to him or us that he has produced in order to sell? The very question we want to solve is what has thwarted that good intention of his? (Marx, 1861, p. 503).

Finally, 'no man sells but with an intention to purchase'? Not so, said Marx, who added that a capitalist may sell in order to pay, especially during a crisis. And:

During the crisis, a man may be very pleased if he has sold his commodities without immediately thinking of a purchase ... The immediate purpose of capitalist production is not 'possession of other goods' but the appropriation of value, of money, of abstract wealth (Marx, 1981, p. 503).

In the circulation of capital, M–C–M, the possibility of crisis is developed to its fullest extent. Firstly, it is a development of the 'simple' circulation of commodities, C–M–C, and therefore contains the 'simple' possibility of crisis, namely that commodities must (yet may not be able to) undergo a sequence of transformations. Secondly, under capitalist production, money as means of payment introduces a far-reaching set of connections between capitals. Thirdly, the fact that the goal of capitalist production is the acquisition of abstract wealth, rather than other use-values, means that the presence of use-values for sale is no longer sufficient to ensure that sales will take place, let alone at prices which will give the desired return.

Marx's criticism of Ricardo has a wider significance. Ricardo was criticized here not for erring in his deductions, but rather because the starting point for those deductions, his 'model', was inappropriate. Leaving aside those unfortunate moments when he was using arguments relevant only to a barter economy, Ricardo's model was one of simple commoditiy production, characterized by the circuit C–M–C. This was inappropriate, said Marx, because the circulation of capital, M–C–M, contains new possibilities for crises, not contained in the simple circulation C–M–C.

If Marx was right about this, then any model of production and exchange where the objective is consumption (that is, the acquisition of use-values rather than value in general) by its very nature excludes those specifically *capitalist* causes of the possibility of crisis.

The converse of this is that a proper consideration of capitalist crisis must consider not only use-values but value too: 'value, abstract wealth, money'. In this respect, Keynes's introduction of effective demand into the orthodox theory of his time can be seen as an attempt to remedy the same one-sidedness of that theory which Marx criticized in Ricardo. Indeed, the theory of the possibility of crisis can help show why 'effective demand' – a monetary quantity – is important in its own right and why Keynes was justified in elevating it to a place of considerable importance (Kenway, 1980).

Ricardo denied that crises could arise out of the production process itself. In his defence, Marx commented that Ricardo himself did not actually experience any such crises (Marx, 1861, p. 497). All the crises between 1800 and 1815 could be attributed to external conditions: poor harvest; interference with the currency by the authorities; the wars. After 1815, the crises could be explained quite readily by reference to the strains of the change from war to peace. Yet as Marx observed, these interpretations were not available to Ricardo's followers. And neither, of course, are they available today.

P. KENWAY

See also BUSINESS CYCLES; MARXIST ECONOMICS; TRADE CYCLES.

BIBLIOGRAPHY
Kenway, P.M. 1980. Marx, Keynes and the possibility of crisis. *Cambridge Journal of Economics* 4(1) March, 23–36.
Marx, K. 1861. *Theories of Surplus Value*, Part 2. London: Lawrence & Wishart, 1969.
Marx, K. 1867. *Capital*, Vol. I. Harmondsworth: Penguin, 1976.
Ricardo, D. 1821. *Collected Works and Correspondence*, Vol. I. Ed. P. Sraffa, Cambridge: Cambridge University Press, 1951.

critical path analysis. When consumers plan vacations, manufacturers schedule production, and governments tackle budget deficits, each must deal with a myriad of interrelated activities. In large projects, managing these interrelationships is very difficult due to three major factors: the precedence ordering of activities, the uncertainty about activity durations, and the possibility of reallocating resources.

Even if there were only one way to perform an activity and if the time it took to complete it were known for sure, there would still be the problem of determining when an activity can begin. A book cannot be bound until it is printed, cannot be printed until it is edited, and cannot be edited until it is written. When one realizes that there are hundreds of activities in book publishing, it is clear that effective management requires some way of keeping track of the precedence order of activities.

A further complexity is the uncertain duration of activities. People get sick, buildings burn down, funds are scarce and so activities often take longer than expected. Although delays in some activities will be relatively unimportant, delays in others will delay the whole project. Effective project management must focus attention on such critical activities.

The third major complication is due to the multiplicity of ways in which things can be done. By allocating more resources, an activity can be speeded up. By allocating fewer resources, costs can be held down, although delays will probably occur. Project managers need a way of determining how resources can be effectively allocated.

Critical path analysis (CPA) is the generic name for a set of techniques to help people deal with the problems of managing projects. The basic elements in CPA are: (i) the specification of activities necessary to complete a project; (ii) their precedence order represented by a directed, acyclic network diagram; (iii) the identification of the critical activities, especially those activities on the longest path through the network (i.e., the critical path); and (iv) the determination of cost-time tradeoffs for the whole project.

Critical path analysis can be viewed as the consolidation and extension of the ideas of Henry Gantt and Vilfredo Pareto. In the early 1900s, Gantt proposed a graphical method for scheduling and controlling production activities. A Gantt chart represents each production activity as a row with a bar drawn to scale representing how long the activity takes. The bar is positioned in calendar time by taking into account the precedence relationships among activities, although these relationships are not shown directly.

Pareto suggested that a small proportion of components had an undue effect on the performance of a system. For example, 10 per cent of a company's sales force often account for 90 per cent of the sales. This concept, sometimes under the label of the 'Pareto principle', became adopted as a regular management control technique. Both John Commons and Chester Barnard incorporated this concept of the 'critical factor' or 'strategic factor' in their economic theories of organization.

In the late 1960s two independent techniques, PERT (Program Evaluation and Review Technique) and CPM (Critical Path Method), were created to help manage very large projects. PERT was used in handling the tens of thousands of activities in developing weapon systems for Polaris submarines for the US Navy (Malcolm et al., 1959). CPM was developed for controlling large construction projects in industry (Kelley and Walker, 1959). Both methods can be viewed as a Gantt chart embedded in a network that shows the interdependencies among activities. This representation shows how the expected start and completion times of any activity depend on the progress of the activities that precede it. By identifying which activities can delay the whole project and which can expedite the project, the concept of critical factors is developed into a concept of a 'critical path'. By associating time-cost trade-offs with each activity, it becomes clear that one speeds up a project by allocating resources to critical activities and one saves money by withdrawing resources from non-critical activities.

Even though both PERT and CPM used very similar ideas in network representation and the identification of critical paths, each technique had its own unique features. In PERT, the arcs in a network represented the activities and the nodes represented starting and ending points, while in CPM the nodes represented the activities and the arcs indicated the precedence relationships. A more significant difference was that PERT allowed for uncertainty in the duration of an activity while CPM exhibited time-resource trade-offs. Since both uncertainty and resource trade-offs are key elements of any large project, both PERT and CPM made distinctive contributions.

PERT assumed that the uncertainty in the duration of an activity could be represented by a Beta distribution, the parameters of which are derived from three time estimates, a most likely time, an optimistic time, and a pessimistic time provided by project managers. Using the Central Limit Theorem, the overall project time is normally distributed with a mean (variance) equal to the sum of the means (variances) of activity distributions along the critical path. The possible errors in the PERT assumptions, at both the level of individual activities and at the level of the whole project have been analysed (MacCrimmon and Ryavec, 1959). The assumption of independence among activities (allowing means and variances to be summed) is particularly weak. Environmental events that delay one activity are likely to delay other activities and so the estimated completion time will tend to be optimistic. Methods have been proposed for grouping network elements to reduce bias and for using simulation techniques to overcome some of the analytical difficulties.

While PERT focuses on time management, CPM focuses on the cost of performing activities. Piecewise linear time cost tradeoffs are developed from information provided by project managers. For any desired project completion time, linear programming can be used to ascertain the minimum project variable cost subject to resource availabilities. By varying the project completion time parameter, a frontier of tradeoffs of total variable cost and completion times is obtained. By focusing only on the cost of the resources, the allocation of specific resources remains to be determined separately. The resources for speeding up one activity may be committed elsewhere.

Clearly, both PERT and CPM can help to plan and control large projects. By combining the best features of each, there is promise for developing more powerful methods. One of the first modifications was the development of PERT–COST which took into account project costs, although in more of a monitoring role than in CPM. Over time the original distinctions between PERT and CPM have become blurred and it is reasonable to focus on a generic CPA. Advances have taken place in two main areas, handling uncertainty and managing resources.

Handling project uncertainty has been improved by de-emphasizing the single most critical path. When delays occur, other paths may become the critical path, thus activities that are common to several of these paths should be monitored carefully. Methods allowing for a more flexible treatment of uncertainty in the activity durations have also been developed (Elmaghraby, 1977).

There is also uncertainty in how a project can be carried out. As the project goes along, the results of early activities influence the way later activities are performed. For example, the outcome of research and development on a new kind of memory may have major implications for the construction of a computer. More advanced network models, then, allow for uncertainty in network structure such as disjunctive activities whereby one activity is performed in lieu of another (Pritsker and Sigal, 1983).

A second major area of improvement has been in handling resources (Dean and Chaudhuri, 1980). Procedures for resource smoothing were used to avoid costly fluctuations such as continual hiring and firing in the labour force. Methods have been proposed for splitting jobs, allowing for halting the performance of one activity and transferring resources to where they are most needed. More sophisticated techniques have been developed for handling multiple categories of resource types and for handling uncertainty about the availability of resources. Other advances have incorporated information about the quality of performance of the activity.

Critical path analysis is now widely used in one form or another. Many actual applications, however, involve only the most basic elements such as the network representation. Why aren't some of the more advanced methods used? As one manager is reported to have said about the time estimates required in PERT, 'activity durations are too uncertain to try to use more than one time estimate'! With better analytical training, with microcomputers, and with sophisticated computer programs, perhaps the uses of critical path analysis will begin to catch up with the developments in the methods.

KENNETH R. MACCRIMMON

See also COMBINATORICS; OPERATIONS RESEARCH.

BIBLIOGRAPHY
Dean, B.V. and Chaudhuri, A.K. 1980. Project scheduling: a critical review. *TIMS Studies in the Management Sciences* 15, 215–33.
Elmaghraby, S.E. 1977. *Activity Networks: Project Planning and Control by Network Models.* New York: Wiley.
Kelley, J.E. and Walker, M.R. 1959. Critical path planning and scheduling. *Proceedings of the Eastern Joint Computer Conference.*
MacCrimmon, K.R. and Ryavec, C.A. 1959. An analytical study of the PERT assumptions. *Operations Research* 7(5), 16–37.
Malcolm, D.G., Rosenboom, J.H., Clark, C.E. and Fazar, W. 1959. Applications of a technique for research and development program evaluation. *Operations Research* 7(5), 646–69.
Pritsker, A.A.B. and Sigal, C.E. 1983. *Management Decision Making: A Network Simulation Approach.* Englewood Cliffs, NJ: Prentice-Hall.

Croce, Bendetto (1866–1952).   Croce was a southern Italian idealist philosopher and historian. His *Philosophy of Spirit* was intended as a secular religion capable of encompassing all aspects of human life. He regarded as his greatest innovation the addition of the category of the Useful to the classical triad of the Beautiful, the True and the Good. He elaborated this theory in the course of his early writings on Marx (1900b) and a debate with Pareto 'On the Economic Principle' (1900a). He argued that human practical activity was orientated to solving the immediate problems of everyday life, and hence highly contingent. We only discover the moral worth of an act *post facto*, when the consequences can be evaluated. Our action is therefore directed at the Useful and only indirectly at the Good. Whilst all moral acts are economic, the reverse is not the case. He rejects hedonism and egoism as ethical theories, since happiness and self-interest may be good guides to the utility of an act to an agent at a given time, but not necessarily to its ultimate moral worth. He therefore disputed Pareto's contention that you could develop a science of economics based on certain constant features of human behaviour. All human activity is conditioned by chance and the diversity of beliefs different individuals hold. This fact similarly vitiated Marx's historical materialism. These ideas were later expanded into his *Philosophy of the Practical* (1908). However, in a later debate he denied Luigi Einaudi's conclusion that his theory implied classical liberal *laissez-faire* policies (1928). He asserted that certain conditions could warrant welfare socialism. A moderate conservative rather than a liberal, he belatedly opposed fascism, partly because his philosophy provided few action guiding principles in the present beyond the endorsement of whatever succeeds. The judgement of events is left to history.

R. BELLAMY

See also PARETO, VILFREDO.

SELECTED WORKS

1900a. On the economic principle: a letter to Professor V. Pareto. In *International Economic Papers*, ed. A.T. Peacock et al., London: Macmillan, 1953.

1900b. *Historical Materialism and the Economics of Karl Marx.* Trans. C.M. Meredith, London: Howard Latimer Ltd, 1931.

1908. *Philosophy of the Practical.* Trans. D. Ainslee, London: Macmillan, 1913.

1928. Free enterprise and liberalism. In B. Croce, *Politics and Morals*, trans. S.J. Castiglione, London: George Allen & Unwin, 1946.

BIBLIOGRAPHY

Bellamy, R.P. 1986. *Modern Italian Social Theory.* Cambridge: Polity Press, ch. 5.

Crosland, Anthony (1918–1977). Born in 1918, Crosland read classics at Trinity College, Oxford (1937–40). Always a socialist, he led the undergraduate faction that opposed the Communist creed embraced by many left-wing intellectuals of that period. War service, as a paratrooper, claimed him for the next five years. Returning to Oxford, he became President of the Union, took a first class degree in politics and economics, and was appointed to a Fellowship at Trinity College. He taught economics for three years, then in 1950 began a political career as a Labour Member of Parliament.

His most important book, *The Future of Socialism* (1956), sought to define the role of a Socialist government in a modern industrial state. Essentially anti-utopian and revisionist, it was as opposed to latter-day Marxism as to Toryism. Crosland insisted that Socialism was about equality, not the ownership of the means of production. Greater equality was facilitated by economic growth, and high levels of government expenditure and intervention were also required.

For 20 years his views strongly influenced the Labour Party. Between 1964 and his sudden death in 1977 when he had been Foreign Secretary only 10 months, he held four senior Cabinet posts in which he initiated measures born of his political philosophy, particularly in education and housing. But government failure to achieve sufficient growth frustrated many of his aspirations. And after his death his blueprint for the future of socialism became less realizable. Always an optimist, he underestimated the economic and social forces that would obstruct his programmes.

I.M.D. LITTLE

See also FABIAN SOCIALISM; SOCIAL DEMOCRACY.

SELECTED WORKS

1956. *The Future of Socialism.* London: Jonathan Cape.

cross-elasticity. *See* ELASTICITY.

cross-section analysis. *See* CENSORED DATA MODELS; DISCRETE CHOICE MODELS; SELECTION BIAS AND SELF-SELECTION.

crowding out. 'Crowding out' refers to all the things which can go wrong when debt-financed fiscal policy is used to affect output. While the initial focus was on the slope of the LM curve, 'crowding out' now refers to a multiplicity of channels through which expansionary fiscal policy may in the end have little, no or even negative effects on output.

DIRECT CROWDING OUT AND RICARDIAN EQUIVALENCE. A first line of argument questions whether fiscal policy will have any effect at all on spending.

Changes in the pattern of taxation which keep the pattern of spending unaffected do not affect the intertemporal budget constraint of the private economy and thus may have little effect on private spending. This argument, known as the 'Ricardian equivalence' of debt and taxation, holds only if taxes are lump sum. Some taxes which induce strong intertemporal substitution, such as an investment tax credit on firms, will have stronger effects if they are temporary; for most others, such as income taxes, changes in the intertemporal pattern may only have a small effect on the pattern of spending. The Ricardian equivalence argument is not settled empirically and its validity surely depends on the circumstances: a change in the intertemporal taxation of assets such as housing or firms, leaving the present value of taxes the same will have little effect on their market value, thus on private spending; an explicitly temporary income tax increase may have little effect on spending while the anticipation of long prolonged deficits may lead taxpayers to ignore the eventual increase in tax liabilities. Evidence from specific episodes, such as the 1968 temporary tax surcharge in the US, suggests partial offset at best.

Changes in the pattern of government spending obviously have real effects. But here again, various forms of direct crowding out may be at work. Public spending may substitute perfectly or imperfectly for private spending, so that changes in public spending may be directly fully or partially offset by consumers or firms. Even if public spending is on public goods, the effect will depend on whether the change in spending is thought to be permanent or transitory. Permanent changes, financed by a permanent increase in taxes, will, as a first approximation, lead to a proportional decrease in private spending, with no effect on total spending. Temporary changes in spending, associated with a temporary increase in taxes, lead to a smaller reduction in private spending and thus to an increase in total spending.

Thus one should not expect any change in taxation or government spending to have a one for one effect on aggregate demand. An eclectic reading of the discussion above may be that only sustained decreases in income taxation, or the use of taxes which induce strong intertemporal substitution, or temporary increases in spending can reliably be used to boost aggregate demand. The focus will be on these forms of fiscal expansion in what follows.

CROWDING OUT AT FULL EMPLOYMENT. Not every increase in aggregate demand translates into an increase in output. This is clearly the case if the economy is already at full employment. While tracing the effects of fiscal expansion at full employment is of limited empirical interest, except perhaps as a description of war efforts, it is useful for what follows.

If labour supply is inelastic, output is fixed and any increase in aggregate demand must be offset by an increase in interest rates, leaving output unchanged. In the case of an increase in public spending, private spending will decrease; in the case of a decrease in income taxation, private spending will in the end be the same, but its composition will change as the share of interest sensitive components decreases. To the extent that labour supply is elastic, intertemporal substitution of labour in response to a temporary change in interest rates may lead to temporarily more output and employment.

But this is just the beginning of the story. Over time, changes in capital and debt lead to further effects on output. The decrease in investment in response to higher interest rates leads to a decline in capital accumulation and output, reducing the supply of goods. If fiscal expansion is associated with sustained deficits, the increase in debt further increases private wealth and private spending at given interest rates, further increasing interest rates and accelerating the decline in capital accumulation. How strong is this negative effect of debt on capital accumulation likely to be? One of the crucial links in this mechanism is the effect of government debt on interest rates; empirical evidence, both across countries and from the last two centuries shows surprisingly little relation between the two.

Allowing for uncertainty, and recognizing that debt and capital have different return characteristics, complicates the story in a potentially interesting way. Depending on the relation between human wealth and debt on the one hand, and human wealth and capital on the other, an increase in the share of debt in portfolios may increase or decrease the rate of return on capital. It is therefore conceivable that while the increase in the level of debt increases the overall level of interest rates, the increase in the share of debt in portfolios decreases the required rate of return on capital relative to that on debt; if this is the case, the steady increase in debt may have a small net effect on the required rate of return on capital, and on capital accumulation. Theoretical and empirical evidence suggest however that this portfolio effect is small and can probably be ignored.

Worse can happen: it may be that the fiscal programme becomes unsustainable. There is no reason to worry about a fiscal programme in which debt grows temporarily faster than the interest rate. But there is reason to worry when there is a positive probability that, even under the most optimistic assumptions, debt will have to grow forever faster than the interest rate. When this is the case, this implies that the government can only meet its interest payments on existing debt by borrowing more and more. What happens then may depend on the circumstances. Bond holders may start anticipating repudiation of government debt and require a risk premium on the debt, further accelerating deficits and the growth of the debt. If they instead anticipate repudiation through inflation, they will require a higher nominal rate and compensation for inflation risk in the form of a premium on all nominal debt, private and public. What is sure is that there will be increased uncertainty on financial markets and that this will further contribute to decreases in output and in welfare. The historical record suggests that it takes very large deficits and debt levels before the market perceives them as potentially unsustainable. England was able in the 19th century to build debt to GNP ratios close to 200 per cent without apparent trouble. Some European countries are currently running high deficits while already having debt to GNP ratios in excess of 100 per cent, without any evidence of a risk premium on

government debt. Sustainability seems in fact rarely to be an issue.

But even if one excludes this worst case scenario, fiscal expansion can clearly have adverse effects on output at full employment. The relevant issue is however whether the same dangers are present when fiscal expansion is implemented to reduce unemployment, which is presumably when it is most likely to be used.

CROWDING OUT AT LESS THAN FULL EMPLOYMENT. The historical starting point of the crowding out discussion is the fixed price IS–LM model. In that model, a fiscal expansion raises aggregate demand and output. The pressure on interest rates does not come from the full employment constraint as before but from the increased demand for money from increased output. Thus the fiscal multiplier is smaller the lower the elasticity of money demand to interest rates, or the larger the elasticity of private spending to interest rates. Fiscal expansion crowds out the interest sensitive components of private spending, but the multiplier effect on output is positive. As output and interest rates increase, it is quite possible for both investment and consumption to increase.

What happens however when the model is extended to take into account dynamics, expectations and so on? Can one overturn the initial result and get full crowding out or even negative multipliers?

Even within the static IS–LM, one can in fact get zero or negative multipliers. This is the case for example if money demand by agents is higher than by the government and the change in policy redistributes income from the government to agents. While this case is rather exotic, a much stronger case can be made if the economy is small, open, with capital mobility and flexible exchange rates, as in the 'Mundell–Fleming' model. In this case, with the interest rate given from outside, and fixed money supply, money demand determines output; fiscal policy only leads to exchange rate appreciation. Exchange rate sensitive components are now crowded out by fiscal expansion. The multiplier is equal to zero.

When dynamic effects are taken into account, other channels arise for crowding out. The analysis of these dynamic effects, taking into account the dynamics of debt accumulation, was initially conducted under the maintained assumption of fixed prices and demand determination of output. Then, as debt was accumulating, private wealth and spending increased, leading to even larger effects of fiscal policy on output in the long run than in the short run. But the assumption of fixed prices, while debt and capital accumulation are allowed to proceed, is surely misleading; when prices are also allowed to adjust, the effects of fiscal policy become more complex and crowding out more likely; this is because some of the full employment effects come back into prominence:

If fiscal expansion is maintained even after the economy has reached full employment, then the perverse effects of higher interest rates on capital accumulation and full employment output come again into play. This is true even if deficits disappear before the economy returns to full employment; the economy inherits a larger level of debt, and thus must have higher interest rates and lower capital accumulation than it would otherwise have had. The fiscal expansion trades off a faster return to full employment for lower full employment output.

Anticipations of these full employment effects are likely to feed back and modify the effects of fiscal policy at the start, when the economy is still at less than full employment. Faced with an increase in deficits, agents now anticipate not only faster return to full employment, but also higher interest rates for the foreseeable future. Depending on the strength of the two effects, the multiplier associated with fiscal policy may be larger or smaller than in the simple IS–LM. If the interest rate effect dominates, the effect of fiscal policy on output may be small.

The recent US experience has also brought into focus another but related perverse anticipation effect, that of anticipated future deficits on output. Anticipated deficits lead to expectations of higher interest rates, higher output and, if the economy is open, exchange rate appreciation. This in turn leads to high long rates and exchange rate appreciation today. If the interest rate and exchange rate effects dominate, the anticipation of deficits will decrease aggregate demand and lead to a recession. This negative multiplier is however transitory and disappears when fiscal expansion actually takes place.

Finally, confidence effects may again come into play. Fiscal programmes which eventually imply government bankruptcy, debt repudiation or monetization may well introduce sufficient additional uncertainty to decrease or change the sign of the fiscal multiplier. But such a scenario requires a fiscal expansion of very large magnitude, much in excess of what is likely to be needed to get the economy back to full employment.

CROWDING OUT: AN ASSESSMENT. Should one conclude from this that fiscal policy is an unreliable macroeconomic tool, with small and sometimes negative effects on output? The answer is clearly negative. Fiscal policy is likely to partly crowd out some components of private spending, even in the best circumstances but there is little reason to doubt that it can help the economy return to full employment.

Ricardian equivalence and direct crowding out warn us that not any tax cut or spending increase will increase aggregate demand. But there is little question that temporary spending or sustained income tax cuts will do so.

Results of full crowding out at less than full employment, such as the Mundell–Fleming result are simply a reminder that the monetary fiscal policy mix is important. In all cases, monetary accommodation of the increased demand for money removes the negative or the zero multipliers.

That fiscal expansion affects capital accumulation and output adversely at full employment, and that unsustainable fiscal programmes may lead to crises of confidence is a reminder that fiscal expansion should not be synonymous with steady increases in the debt to GNP ratio even after the economy has returned to full employment. This shows one of the difficulties associated with fiscal expansion: if done through tax cuts, it has to be expected to last long enough to affect private spending, but not lead to expectations of runaway deficits in the long run. The room for manoeuvre is however substantial. Some taxes, such as the investment tax credit work best when temporary. The historical record shows how large the margin of safety is before a fiscal programme becomes truly unsustainable.

OLIVIER JEAN BLANCHARD

See also DEFICIT FINANCING; DEFICIT SPENDING; INVESTMENT; NEOCLASSICAL SYNTHESIS.

Crowther, Geoffrey (1907–1972). Crowther was educated at Leeds Grammar School, Oundle and Clare College, Cambridge, where after studying modern languages he proceeded to win a high first in Part II of the Economics Tripos. Lionel Robbins remembered one of his examination answers as being only a few sentences: 'the way he put it left nothing more to be said' (Robbins, 1972, p. 23). This ability to go to the heart of the matter Crowther carried into his work at *The Economist*.

Prior to this however he went to Yale and Columbia Universities as a Commonwealth Fund Fellow (he married an American, Margaret Worth, in 1932) and then worked for two years in a London merchant bank. This led to his appointment as economic adviser on banking to the Irish government. Crowther gave up the Irish appointment to join *The Economist* in 1932, becoming assistant editor in 1935 and editor in 1938. Crowther was the longest major editor of the newspaper, holding the post from 1938 to 1956 – Robbins compared him to the paper's previous great editor, Walter Bagehot. After 1956 he maintained his contact with the journal, first as Managing Director and later as Chairman.

Under Crowther *The Economist* changed radically in its format so as to widen its appeal to a broader readership both in the UK and overseas, expanding its circulation from 10,000 to 55,000 and becoming one of the most influential weekly papers in the world. Crowther was also responsible for the establishment of the Economist Intelligence Unit just after World War II and for the newspaper's successful development of its St James's property. He was also one of the first newspaper editors to appoint women, such as Barbara Ward, to the staff in significant positions.

His major theoretical work on economics was *An Outline of Money* (1940), which, like his journalistic writings, had 'a clarity and expository power which few academics could muster' (Robbins, 1972, p. 23) as well as a lively style and was quickly popular with both students and the general public. His other works on economics, such as *Ways and Means* (1936) stemmed from broadcasts or lectures.

Crowther's magnetic personality and prodigious capacity for work made him an outstanding public servant (Goode, 1974). His principal public interest was in education. He was Chairman of the Central Advisory Council for Education (England) from 1956 to 1960, whose report '15 to 18' was a landmark in the expansion of further education. As the first Chancellor of the Open University (1968) he played a major part in its early development. He then took on the joint responsibilities of chairing both the Royal Commission on the Constitution and the Committee on Consumer Credit, whose report (1971) recommended the complete reform of consumer credit law (embodied in the Consumer Credit Act of 1974) and of personal property security law. Crowther was knighted in 1957 for his services to journalism and in 1968 he became a life peer, taking his title from Headingley, the place of his birth.

R.J. BIGG

SELECTED WORKS
1936. *Ways and Means: a study of the economic structure of Great Britain today*. London: Macmillan.
1940. *An Outline of Money*. London: Thomas Nelson & Sons.
BIBLIOGRAPHY
Goode, R.M. 1974. A Credit Law for Europe? *International and Comparative Law Quarterly* 23(1), April, 227–91.
Robbins, L.S. 1972. Lord Crowther: Memorial address. *The Economist*, 25 March.

culture. *See* ECONOMIC ANTHROPOLOGY.

cumulative causation. The notion of 'cumulative causation' constitutes a basic hypothesis on the workings of the market mechanism. The operation of markets is conceived as a continuous process in which economic forces interact upon one another in a cumulative way, thus making for changes in one direction to induce supporting changes which push the system further away from its initial position. In essence, this is the notion which Myrdal refers to as the 'principle of circular and cumulative causation' and which plays an organizing role in his analysis of 'uneven development' (Myrdal, 1957).

Although the term 'cumulative causation' is due to Myrdal, the basic hypothesis appears in Young's analysis of 'economic progress' (Young, 1928). It is on this basis that Kaldor puts forward a definite 'cumulative causation' approach to the 'economic process' (Kaldor, 1966, 1967, 1970, 1972, 1974, 1975, 1978, 1978b, 1981, 1981b, 1985); a similar approach, even if less developed, is found in Svennilson's analysis of economic growth (Svennilson, 1954).

YOUNG'S INCREASING RETURNS. Young's increasing returns constitute the dynamic counterpart of Adam Smith's dictum 'the division of labour – cause of the increased productive powers of labour – is limited by the extent of the market' (Smith, 1776). In Young's interpretation, the expansion of markets leads to an 'increasing use of roundabout methods of production' and to a 'progressive division and specialization of industries' which result in a rising 'efficiency of production' (Young, 1928).

The 'progressive division and specialization of industries' refers to the tendency (implied by the expansion of markets) for industries to be broken up into more specialized concerns which concentrate on a narrower range of output.

The growth of markets makes possible a progressive 'horizontal diversification' of consumer goods industries that relates to the introduction of new products and the increasing differentiation of basically the same type of goods. As for intermediate and capital goods industries, the process of specialization is both 'horizontal' and 'vertical' ('vertical disintegration', Stigler, 1951). To a large extent, this process depends on the occurrence of 'technological convergence' which itself depends on the expansion of markets. (Hirschman, 1957; Rosenberg, 1976; Kaldor, 1985). This notion refers to the accumulated backward linkages of industries at a given stage in the network of interindustry relations which come to share basically the same process of production, thus allowing and inducing the progressive specialization of industries at successive lower stages.

In this view, 'efficiency' appears as a *dynamic, macroeconomic-structural* phenomenon; for it relates to the processes of mechanization and structural transformation which, in turn, refer to the expansion of manufacturing as a whole. This, however, does not imply that efficiency is uniform across industries. On account mainly of the differential incidence of the process of mechanization and of technical progress, the *'opportunity for efficiency'* varies widely across industries which, indeed, gets reflected both in the level and in the rate of change of efficiency. Notionally, for each industry, 'opportunity' defines a 'standard' both for the level and for the rate of change of efficiency. The actual performance of the different industries can then be measured relative to the respective standards.

Relative efficiency gains in a given industry depend on mechanization and specialization which depend on the growth of markets. On account of manufacturing's internal linkages and of 'technological convergence', the growth of markets depends on the growth and specialization of other industries which, in turn, depend on the growth and specialization of yet other industries, and so on; thus, the relative rise in efficiency in an industry depends on the overall expansion of

manufacturing. At the same time, the specialization of an individual industry is but the result of the general process of 'division and specialization of industries'; to a large extent, an industry gets specialized, comes to concentrate on a narrower range of output insofar as other industries do. (complementary and subsidiary industries).

On this account, therefore, an industry's (relative) rise in efficiency depends on the expansion and internal development of manufacturing as a whole as much as it depends on the internal development of the industry itself. Moreover, due to the interindustry linkages internal to manufacturing, the rise in efficiency that notionally refers to a particular industry gets spread to other industries and, eventually, to the whole sector. In this sense, the development of particular 'key' industries characterized by a high 'opportunity' for efficiency and/or by rapidly growing markets benefits the development and efficiency of other industries across the sector; in this way, 'mature' industries may benefit and receive a new 'lease of life' from developments initiated elsewhere within the sector.

Efficiency, as macroeconomic phenomenon, reflects the process of growth in terms of capital accumulation and structural transformation; in the process, as different 'tensions, disproportions and bottlenecks' are continuously being solved, the efficiency of production rises all across manufacturing. At any one time, the level of efficiency is the reflection of the structure of manufacturing in terms of the degree of mechanization and of specialization and diversification of industries as well as in terms of the strength of the network of interindustry relations. In this sense, the level of efficiency is an index of the level of development and the rate of change is an index of the growth and development performance over a period.

On this basis, a given industry located in different countries will tend to show in each country a level and a rate of change of efficiency in correspondence with the overall development (and efficiency) and the rate of output growth (and efficiency gains) of the respective national manufacturing sectors. Thus, countries experiencing (relative to their competitors) higher rates of growth and transformation and, therefore, higher rates of efficiency as regards manufacturing as a whole will tend to experience higher corresponding rates as regards individual industries as well (see Eatwell, 1982). Yet, a proviso must be made here; for 'opportunity for efficiency' varies across countries as well. The degree of 'opportunity' is related to the dependence of efficiency on learning, on the accumulation of experience and mastery and on technical progress. As regards individual industries, a high degree of opportunity results from the industries' efficiency being dependent on (intensive in) learning, mastery and technical progress. As regards countries, the opportunity for efficiency, as it depends on learning and technical progress, is related to the growth and development of manufacturing. Thus, the intercountry differential in 'opportunity' is related to the interindustry differential; the lower the opportunity of the industry is, the lower the intercountry differential and, vice versa, the higher the opportunity of the industry, the higher the intercountry differential. Thus, the correspondence between the rate of change of efficiency in manufacturing and that in individual industries will tend to be more accurate for high opportunity industries.

SAY'S LAW AS 'CLOSURE' OF THE SYSTEM. In Young's analysis, based on the 'classical version' of Say's Law, the growth of markets is defined by the rise in the volume of production, which, in turn, is determined by the rise in efficiency; on account of increasing returns, the latter is determined by the growth of markets itself. Hence, 'the growth of markets is determined by the growth of markets'. This, as Young points out, 'is more than mere tautology'; the expansion of markets leads to the rise in efficiency through mechanization and structural transformation which open up *new opportunities for further change which would have not existed otherwise*'. In the normal operation of markets any given 'impulse' is amplified cumulatively, the growth of demand results in an endless 'chain reaction' of sectoral supplies and demands all through the network of interindustry relations. In the process, 'each sector receives impulses' for change and, in turn, 'sends impulses' for further change. Thus, *change becomes progressive and propagates itself in a cumulative way*' (Young, 1928; Kaldor, 1972, 1973).

Young's analysis embodies the essence of the principle of cumulative causation; however, what is essentially a matter of impulses and inducements what is a 'potentiality' is transformed into 'actuality'; for, by definition, demand always responds to the inducement to further growth provided by structural change and the all-round improvement in efficiency; the actuality of an endless chain of circular and cumulative causation is thus ensured. Due to Say's Law, there is no 'degree of freedom', no independent leading element in the system. In this sense, the analysis remains as it were 'hanging in the air'.

LEARNING AND TECHNICAL PROGRESS. (a) To a large extent, economic growth is to be seen as a *learning process* (Rosenberg, 1976). Economic growth involves a series of ongoing activities, decisions and events, ranging from the operation of plant and equipment and decisions taken about production and investment to the occurrence of structural change and the introduction and development of technology. As those activities, decisions and events materialize, different problems, 'tensions, disproportions and bottlenecks', are encountered. Successful growth requires that solutions be found to those problems; and learning results from discovering and facing problems and from searching for and finding solutions to them. Moreover, the faster growth takes place, the more will problems assert themselves, the more will the need to solve them be felt and, therefore, the stronger will the inducement to learn be (see Arrow, 1962). To the extent that learning is effective, experience and knowledge are accumulated and skills and capabilities developed. On this basis, each successive step in the normal process of growth and transformation becomes (potentially) easier. As a result, the efficiency of production and that of the growth and learning processes themselves are raised. Thus, learning depends on the growth of output, results in efficiency gains and induces further growth and transformation.

(b) Within the cumulative causation framework, normal technical progress is conceived of as a *non-random, evolutionary* process; it is *non-random* in that the direction of change is defined by the 'state of the art of the technologies already in use' and it is *evolutionary* in that it normally involves the 'rejection of parts of the old technology' rather than its total rejection. Moreover the process tends to be *cumulative*; for the likelihood of success in the completion of a new technology depends on past developments and on the accretion of experience, knowledge and technological mastery that results from the 'learning process' that the development of technology implies (see Dosi, 1984; Rosenberg, 1976; Nelson and Winter, 1982).

A new technological concept (product, equipment, technique) does not come about as a 'perfectly known', 'fully grown' output of R&D activities. At this stage, there is a fundamental lack of understanding and a great deal of uncertainty as to the actual performance of the new concept. Most commonly the resolution of that uncertainty and the acquisition of knowledge require experience in the production and operation of the new concept as well as further research and development.

At the same time, the introduction of a new technological concept faces fundamental uncertainties as to the nature of demand. Consumers are both uncertain about their preferences and unaware of the characteristics of new products and of how they compare with possible substitutes. Users of capital equipment are, in turn, uncertain as to the exact nature of their requirements and lack basic knowledge and face fundamental uncertainty as to the characteristics of new technological alternatives and as to how they fit in the process of production. It is only through actual experience in consumption (Pasinetti, 1982; 'product-cycle'model: Vernon, 1966) and in the effective use of equipment in production that uncertainty can be resolved and knowledge increased. ('learning by using': Rosenberg, 1982).

Technical progress manifests itself in a *sequence of problem-solving activities* along the chain '*demand–production–R&D*'. In this sequence, faults, weak spots and technical problems of a new technological concept will be discovered. To the extent that solutions are found and that, through operating experience, consumers/users are able to improve the specification of their preferences/requirements, there will be frequent modifications and improvements of the new concept. At the same time the discovery of problems, the search for and the actual finding of solutions will result in a better understanding of the new technology and in the accumulation of skills, experience and knowledge; in this sense, technical progress is in itself a *learning process*.

So technical progress depends on the dynamics of demand in a fundamental manner. On the one hand, technical progress is, to a large extent, *induced* by the expectation of demand. As regards capital goods industries there is an 'external impulse', signalled by the rate of investment, to accommodate specific requirements of different industries, particularly, of fast growing, highly innovative ones (see Schmookler, 1966; Rosenberg, 1976). As for consumer goods, technical change is induced by the expected evolution of consumer's 'wants' and by the expectation of extending given patterns of consumption to lower brackets of the income distribution structure. At the same time, the success (and further development) of technological advances depends on the actual dynamics of demand; the effective development of technology requires that the expectations of demand be fulfilled, i.e. it requires *validation* of the effective growth of markets.

On the other hand, the *efficiency* and *effectiveness* of the process of technical change depend largely on the growth of markets. A faster growth of markets makes it easier to ascertain the 'new ways of expansion' as well as to switch from one path of expansion to another; in this sense, it provides the innovative process with a '*higher degree of flexibility*' which lowers the risks and costs involved, thus leading to a higher rate of innovative effort. In addition, a faster growth of markets leads to a faster and more effective learning process; it leads to a higher rate of accumulation of skills, knowledge and mastery and, therefore, to a more efficient and effective handling of the sequence of problem-solving activities that the process of technical change entails.

The process of technical progress appears intrinsically connected to Young's increasing returns; for, both through the introduction and differentiation of goods and through the development of new technologies of production, it induces and, at the same time, is induced by the processes of mechanization and of division and specialization of industries.

EFFECTIVE DEMAND. By combining the dynamics of 'efficiency' as it results from Young's increasing returns and from learning and technical progress with the principle of effective demand in a dynamic setting, Kaldor provides the definitive development of the principle of cumulative causation. On this account, the growth of demand constitutes the 'leading factor' of the 'self-reinforcing dynamics' internal to manufacturing. The growth of demand determines the growth of output and leads to a rising efficiency of production; whether the process keeps its momentum and becomes cumulative or gets stopped (and probably reversed) depends on the 'next round' of demand, on the response of demand to the *inducement* to further growth provided by the rise in efficiency. In this sense, the growth of demand (as 'leading factor') is the 'weak-link' of the internal dynamics of manufacturing. Thus, effective demand provides the circular process of cumulative causation with a 'degree of openness' that contrasts with the 'continuity' that, owing to Say's Law, Young's analysis implied.

In the last analysis, the key role of demand rests on the 'independence' of capital accumulation as the driving force of the process of economic growth; capital accumulation is central to technical progress and adds both to demand and to capacity, i.e. it 'provides the incentives and the means of further expansion' (Kaldor, 1966). On this basis, the *potential* for a continuous self-expansion of the system finds no limit; as Joan Robinson puts it, 'carrying itself by its own bootstraps is just what a capitalist economy *can* do' (Joan Robinson, 1962).

The fact that investment is the fundamental independent variable of the system does not mean that the rate of accumulation is fixed, invariant with respect to economic conditions; actually, the assumed degrees of freedom in investment behaviour are to a large extent the reflection of the many factors, economic and non-economic, that influence investment decisions. In the context of the 'self-reinforcing dynamics' of manufacturing it is the response of investment to the growth of markets and to the resulting rise in efficiency along with the more direct dependence of consumption on industrial expansion that accounts for the 'reverse link' and, thus, for the circular and cumulative nature of the dynamics itself.

The rise in (quantitative) efficiency that results from industrial expansion, leads to the growth of consumer demand through the rise in real income and through the expansion of consumption to lower brackets of the income distribution structure. Owing to the different growth elasticities of demand for different goods and for different income levels, the overall growth of consumption and, therefore, the overall growth effect of the interaction 'industrial expansion–consumption' depend largely on the composition of consumption in terms both of goods and of income groups. In this regard, at high income levels there is a tendency for the growth of demand to slow down and, even, to stagnate; this tendency, however, is continuously being overcome by the 'innovation' and 'quality-differentiation' effects of efficiency (technical change, structure diversification); these effects are, thus, crucial to keep the 'drive' for expansion alive (Pasinetti, 1982). As regards capital goods, the 'price' and 'quality-obsolescence' effects of technical change constitute fundamental determinants of investment activity. In addition, investment is induced by industrial growth itself both through the interindustry expansion of markets and through the growth of consumption it entails.

In the sequence 'industrial growth – consumption –

investment – industrial growth', the growth of real wages is of special significance; for wages are both income and cost of production. (Kalecki, 1939). As income, the growth of real wages leads to demand and output growth which lead to productivity growth; as a result, it may lead to higher rates of investment. As cost, the growth of wages has two contradictory effects. On the on hand, it may induce a process of dynamic substitution *à la* Marx, thus, leading to a higher rate of investment and productivity. On the other hand, to the extent that the growth of real wages 'eats up' in profits, it may result in a lower rate of investment. On the basis of the 'substitution' and 'demand' effects, the growth of real wages can be seen to imply a 'cumulative causation' pattern of growth. The growth of real wages leads to demand growth and to dynamic substitution, therefore to investment and to productivity growth which, in turn, lead to higher growth of wages and so on and so forth.

MANUFACTURING AS THE ENGINE OF GROWTH. If capital and labour, as resources used in production, were exogeneously given in fixed quantities, the circular and cumulative dynamics of manufacturing would not materialize; economic growth would be effectively 'resource-constrained'. Yet the quantity and quality as well as the sectoral distribution of labour and capital cannot be taken as 'given' independently of the growth progress itself.

Insofar as the effective labour force (participation) varies in direct relation with demand and, most significantly, insofar as there is *surplus labour* in other sectors such as agriculture and services, at no time can the labour force be considered fully and optimally employed. As manufacturing expands, labour is drawn from those 'reserves' and gets allocated to other uses where its contribution to the economy's output is greater than before; moreover, in the process, 'efficiency' in the surplus labour sectors is enhanced. As for capital, in no significant sense can it be regarded as a 'scarce' resource; capital, as produced means of production, is output and, as such, is the result of economic activity. The quantity, quality and sectoral distribution of capital and labour, as determined by investment, learning and technical progress, are the 'effect' of the process of development as much as the 'cause' of it (see Kaldor, 1978).

In the course of its expansion, manufacturing *generates* its own resources, it mobilizes labour and produces capital; thus, the expansion of manufacturing represents a net addition to the effective use of resources and, therefore, to the overall growth of the system. The growth of manufacturing and, thus, overall economic growth, are not constrained by resources; rather, they are led by the expansion of markets, by the growth of demand for manufactures. Moreover, as other sectors depend largely on manufacturing for the provision of their inputs, the overall efficiency of the economy is mainly determined by that of manufacturing.

Economic growth, centred on the 'self-reinforcing dynamics' internal to manufacturing, is a circular process of cumulative causation governed by the growth of demand. The growth of demand for manufactures leads to the growth of output and to efficiency gains both in manufacturing and in the economy as a whole (capital accumulation-mechanization, structural transformation, reallocation of resources, learning and technical change) which *induce* further growth of demand and so on. In this view, a 'pause' in the expansion of the system may well lead to (structural) stagnation; for, on account of dynamic economies of scale, a shortage of effective demand tends to get amplified throughout the economy. Such a cumulative downturn is but the manifestation of the free workings of the market as mechanism that *transmits impulses and inducements*; in the same way as change calls forth supporting change, the absence of change leads to stagnation; for it is in the nature of the manner of operation of markets and competition that 'growth requires growth', 'success requires success'; the market system is prone to cumulative movements, once in a growth path it tends to cumulative self-expansion; yet should growth lose its momentum and slow down, a tendency towards a cumulative downturn ensues; 'a capitalist economy cannot afford to stay still because, it it stops expanding, it falls back' (Pasinetti, 1982). This is circular and cumulative causation. (Compare Marx's account of the process of capitalist development and of competition as a dynamic process.)

FOREIGN TRADE. At a more concrete level of analysis, as regards the 'open economy', foreign trade in manufactures asserts itself as a 'built-in' element making for the continuity of the circular process of cumulative causation. The growth and composition of net exports (exports minus imports) are fundamental elements in shaping the process of growth and structural change of the economy and, in turn, as determined by competitiveness which results from efficiency, they are mostly determined by economic growth itself. The growth and the change in the composition of demand, including those of net exports, lead to 'efficiency gains' which, via price and non-price factors, give competitiveness which leads to growth and changes in the composition of net exports and, thus, of demand and output and so on and so forth.

On the other hand, foreign trade, through the balance of payments position, may impose an 'effective constraint' on growth. But for the possibility of attracting a continuous net inflow of capital, in the long run an economy's growth rate cannot be higher than the rate of growth consistent with balance of payments equilibrium on current account. This growth rate Thirlwall (1980) refers to as 'balance of payments equilibrium growth rate'. This rate depends fundamentally on the trade balance in manufactures and, therefore, on the growth rate and on the 'normal' competitiveness of manufacturing (given the 'normal' time paths of the other components of the current account). The significance of the equilibrium rate as ceiling to the actual rate is to be understood in relation to the growth rate that can be considered as 'socially necessary' in terms of economic development (output and employment growth, structural transformation learning and technical progress) (cf.Singh's notion of an 'efficient manufacturing sector': Singh, 1977). In this regard, a situation in which, due to a 'weak' competitive position, the 'equilibrium' rate is lower than the 'socially necessary' rate tends to be 'self-perpetuating', as it will result in a lower rate of efficiency gains, lower growth of net exports, and, eventually, in a lower equilibrium rate.

The dynamics of foreign trade and, thus, economic growth in a given economy depend also on economic growth and efficiency abroad. Foreign growth 'complements' domestic growth insofar as it widens the opportunities for the expansion of domestic net exports. At the same time foreign growth enlarges the supply of commodities which can 'compete' with domestic production, and, by raising foreign efficiency, lowers domestic competitiveness, thus making for a lower growth of domestic net exports (Sayers, 1965; Singh, 1977). In addition, the competitive process in world markets entails a fundamental 'composition effect'; fast growing countries tend to gain market shares particularly in those trades with the highest 'opportunity for efficiency' and with the highest potential for market expansion while 'weak' countries tend to be pushed out of those trades. (cf. above, 'bias' in the correspondence across countries between efficiency in manufacturing and in individual industries). In this regard, if, in the course of growth, the 'competitive' aspects of growth elsewhere come to dominate, the ensuing disequilibrium may develop into a cumulative downturn in which a lower growth of net exports leads to lower growth of output, lower rates of investment, lower rates of transformation and technical change, thus leading to a still lower growth of net exports and so on; eventually, the country will find itself 'balance of payments constrained' as the equilibrium rate falls below the 'socially necessary' rate. This is a *'vicious circle of cumulative causation'*. The cumulative fall in competitiveness and the resulting 'vicious circle' are worsened as other countries will be experiencing a *'virtuous circle'* in which high rates of growth of demand result in high rates of investment, transformation and technical progress, high growth of net exports (increasing market shares) and so on. A fundamental feature of this process rests in the fact that the 'vicious circle' results from developments initiated elsewhere, i.e. by the rise in growth rates and in efficiency elsewhere in the world system; thus, the need to expand, the need to keep the pace in the process of structural transformation and technical change appears more stringent in the presence of foreign trade. On the foregoing account, the dynamics of the world economy, as regulated by the free operation of markets, appears characterized by an inherent tendency towards *unequal growth* across countries; for, in a dynamic world where the expansion of manufacturing is characterized by the operation of 'dynamic economies of scale', where technology is 'developed' and not universally accessible, where technical progress unfolds as an evolutionary and cumulative learning process and where the dynamics of effective demand determine the dynamics of the system, any given 'competitive advantage' in terms of growth, transformation and technical change tends to be compounded through the interdependence that exists among countries via foreign trade.

The tendency towards 'unequal growth' entails a *'deflationary bias'* and an intrinsic and progressive instability in the dynamics of the world economy. As the growth of 'weak' countries is held back, the overall expansion of the world economy tends to slow down. This is normally offset by the faster growth of 'strong' countries which actually enables weak countries to grow faster than would otherwise be the case. In this sense, the long-rung deflationary tendency embodied in the dynamics of the system remains as it were 'disguised' in the very process of expansion. Yet, the pattern of uneven growth makes for the cross-country 'differential' in competitiveness to grow wider over time; in this respect, the dynamics of the world economy appears inherently and progressively unstable. Over time, a tendency develops for weak countries to experience a 'fundamental disequilibrium' (constraint) in the balance of payments. In these circumstances, an exogenous 'deflationary shock' or, simply, a slowdown in the expansion of the 'leaders', would make the constraint binding. But, even in the absence of any such shock, as long as the weak countries' loss of competitiveness is left 'to look after itself' and actually becomes cumulative, the tendency towards 'fundamental disequilibrium' will eventually materialize. In the event, a general slowdown in the expansion of markets could only be avoided by enabling weak, 'structural' deficit countries to grow at rates higher than the respective balance of payments equilibrium rate, thus effectively allowing them to run continuous current account deficits. If, on the contrary, the burden of adjustment were brought to bear upon weak countries by forcing them 'to live within their means', a generalized contraction of effective demand would ensue; the lower growth and weak countries and, thus, the lower growth of effective demand, would be spread from country to country through the operation of the dynamic foreign trade multiplier. In this way, a generalized deflationary process would set in. The fundamental point to stress here is that the occurrence of such a process constitutes the long-run consequence of the progressively increasing differential of competitiveness implied by the pattern of unequal growth, transformation and technical progress inherent in the normal dynamics of the world economy as regulated by the free operation of markets.

At the same time, the normal dynamics of the world economy are characterized by a pattern of uneven development. In this regard, the sectoral structure of the economy is of the utmost significance. The dynamics of the different countries' net exports, as determined by relative efficiencies, reflects the process of development. At any one time, the structure of net exports reflects the past process of development in terms of Young's increasing returns, learning, technical change and both the potential for market expansion and the opportunity for efficiency characterizing the existing economic structure. In turn, the process of development and, thus, the economic structure reflect the dynamics of foreign trade.

As regards a 'representative' underdeveloped country, the economy is characterized by a low degree of mechanization, by a lack of inter- and intra-industry diversification and specialization and by a low degree of sectoral interdependence; in this sense, underdevelopment can be described in terms of the market-induced structural inability to realize Young's increasing returns. In addition, production processes are characterized by a very low intensity in skills, knowledge and technical progress which result in the absence of induced learning. On this basis, the export composition appears basically centred on primary commodities and a few 'mature' manufactured products for which the growth of demand tends to be rather low and unstable while the 'opportunity for efficiency' is practically nil.

As for a 'representative' advanced country, its economic structure, centred on the manufacturing sector, is highly diversified and interdependent; in turn, the different industries are highly specialized in terms of products and methods of production; the latter are further characterized by a high average degree of mechanization and by a high average intensity in accumulated experience, knowledge and technological mastery.

In the normal (free) operation of markets the pattern of 'specialization' as between advanced and 'poor' countries tends to be perpetuated and the corresponding differential and efficiency tends to be grow wider over time; due to the operation of dynamic economies of scale, industrial activities tend to concentrate in a few 'established centres' which benefit from the 'freeing' and 'widening' of markets at the expense of the industrial development of 'backward' countries; 'the free play of market forces works towards inequality' (Myrdal, 1957).

CARLOS J. RICOY

See also INCREASING RETURNS; KALDOR, NICHOLAS.

BIBLIOGRAPHY

Arrow, K.J. 1962. The economic implications of learning by doing. *Review of Economic Studies* 28(3), 155–73.

Cornwall, J. 1977. *Modern Capitalism: its Growth and Transformation.* Oxford: Martin Robertson.

Cripps, F. and Tarling, R. 1973. *Growth in Advanced Capitalist Economies, 1950–1970.* Cambridge: Cambridge University Press.

Dosi, G. 1984. *Technical Change and Industrial Transformation.* London: Macmillan.

Eatwell, J. 1982. *Whatever Happened to Britain?* London: Duckworth.

Hirschman, A. 1958. *The Strategy of Economic Development.* New Haven: Yale University Press.

Kaldor, N. 1966. *Causes of the Slow Rate of Economic Growth of the United Kingdom.* Cambridge: Cambridge University Press.

Kaldor, N. 1967. *Strategic Factors in Economic Development.* Ithaca: Cornell University Press.

Kaldor, N. 1970. The case for regional policies. *Scottish Journal of Political Economy* 17(3), November, 337–48.

Kaldor, 1972. The irrelevance of equilibrium economics. *Economic Journal* 82, 1237–55.

Kaldor, N. 1974. Teoria del equilibrio y teoria del crecimiento. *Cuadernos de Economia.* Reprinted in translation in *Economics and Human Welfare: Essays in Honour of T. Scitovsky,* ed. M.J. Boskin, London: Academic Press, 1979.

Kaldor, N. 1975. Economic growth and the Verdoorn Law: comment on Mr. Rowthorn's article. *Economic Journal* 85, December, 891–6.

Kaldor, N. 1978a. *Further Essays on Economic Theory.* London: Duckworth.

Kaldor, N. 1978b. *Further Essays on Applied Economics.* London: Duckworth.

Kaldor, N. 1981a. Discussion. In *Macroeconomic Analysis,* ed. D. Currie, R. Nobay and D. Peel, London: Croom Helm.

Kaldor, N. 1981b. The role of increasing returns, technical progress and cumulative causation in the theory of international trade and economic growth. *Economie Appliquée* 34(4), 593–617.

Kaldor, N. 1985. *Economics without Equilibrium.* Cardiff: University College Cardiff Press.

Kalecki, M. 1966. *Studies in the Theory of Business Cycles 1933–1939.* Oxford: Basil Blackwell.

Myrdal, G. 1957. *Economic Theory and Underdeveloped Regions.* London: Duckworth.

Nelson, R. and Winter, S. 1982. *An Evolutionary Theory of Economic Change.* Cambridge, Mass.: Harvard University Press.

Nurkse, R. 1953. *Problems of Capital Formation in Underdeveloped Countries.* Oxford: Oxford University Press.

Pasinetti, L. 1981. *Structural Change and Economic Growth.* Cambridge: Cambridge University Press.

Prebisch, R. 1950. *The Economic Development of Latin America and its Principal Problems.* New York: United Nations.

Prebisch, R. 1959. Commercial policy in underdeveloped countries. *American Economic Review, Papers and Proceedings* 49, May, 251–73.

Robinson, J. 1962. *Essays in the Theory of Economic Growth.* London: Macmillan.

Robinson, J. 1965. The new mercantilism. In *Collected Economic Papers of Joan Robinson,* Oxford: Basil Blackwell.

Rosenberg, N. 1976. *Perspectives on Technology.* Cambridge: Cambridge University Press.

Rosenberg, N. 1982. *Inside the Black Box: Technology and Economics.* Cambridge: Cambridge University Press.

Sayers, R.S. 1965. *The Vicissitudes of an Export Economy: Britain since 1880.* University of Sidney.

Schmookler, J. 1966. *Invention and Economic Growth.* Cambridge. Mass.: Harvard, University Press.

Singh, A. 1977. U.K. industry and the world economy: a case of de-industrialisation? *Cambridge Journal of Economics* 1(2), June, 113–36.

Singh, A. 1978. North Sea oil and the reconstruction of the UK industry. In *De-Industrialisation,* ed. F. Blackaby, London: Heinemann.

Smith, A. 1776. *An Inquiry into the Nature and Causes of the Wealth of Nations.* Ed. E. Cannan, London: Methuen, 1904.

Stigler, G. 1951. The division of labour is limited by the extent of the market. *Journal of Political Economy* 59, June, 185–93.

Svennilson, I. 1954. *Growth and Stagnation in the European Economy.* Geneva: UN Economic Commission for Europe.

Symposium. 1983. Kaldor's Laws. *Journal of Post-Keynesian Economics* 5(3), Spring, 341–429.

Thirlwall, A.P. 1980. *Balance of Payments Theory and the United Kingdom Experience.* London: Macmillan.

Vernon, R. 1966. International investment and international trade in the product cycle. *Quarterly Journal of Economics* 80, May, 190–207.

Young, A. 1928. Increasing returns and economic progress. *Economic Journal* 38, 527–42.

cumulative processes The first well-known analysis of cumulative processes was developed by Knut Wicksell in his book *Interest and Prices*, which was published in 1898. It grew out of an attempt to reformulate the quantity theory of money. In this context the cumulative process is intimately connected with the development of the saving–investment approach, which is one mechanism through which a change in the quantity of money can influence prices and quantities.

Wicksell considered the main proposition of the quantity theory, namely, that the value of the purchasing power of money varies in inverse proportion to its quantity, to be basically correct. At the same time the quantity theory was in its original formulation too restrictive and in conflict with reality, since it was based on the assumption that everybody uses their own cash, which is both legal tender and the monetary base, for buying and selling and all have to maintain a cash balance. Therefore the followers of the quantity theory sometimes argued 'as though the quantity of money, or of that part that at any moment finds itself in the hands of the public, must act as a *direct* and *proximate* price-determining force' (Wicksell, 1898, p. 43). This is the so-called direct mechanism, which works via a real-balance effect and it is still stressed by Friedman in his development of modern monetarism. However, in a developed credit economy the keeping of individual cash-balances has almost faded away and it has been replaced by current and deposit accounts and the use of claims of various kinds in monetary transactions. The banks, in their turn, only hold a smaller part of the deposited sums as cash, which shows that Wicksell developed the quantity theory for a banking system based on fractional reserves.

THE BACKGROUND TO THE CUMULATIVE PROCESS. The following quotation gives the analytical basis for the cumulative process:

> Every rise or fall in the price of a particular commodity presupposes a disturbance of the equilibrium between the supply and the demand for that commodity, whether the disturbance has actually taken place or is merely prospective. What is true *in this respect* of each commodity separately must doubtless be true of all commodities collectively. A general rise in prices is therefore only conceivable on the supposition that the general demand has for some reason become, or is expected to become, greater that the supply. This may sound paradoxical because we have accustomed ourselves, with J.B. Say, to regard goods themselves as reciprocally constituting and limiting the demand for each other. And indeed *ultimately* they do so; here, however, we are concerned with precisely what occurs, *in the first place*, with the middle link in the final exchange of one good against another, which is formed by the demand of money for goods and the supply of goods for money (Wicksell, 1935, pp. 159–60).

Wicksell proceeded from an approach based on Marshallian partial equilibrium to an aggregate approach for analysing secular changes in the general price level. Furthermore, the central problem is the analysis of a system out of equilibrium (i.e. a disequilibrium analysis), which implies criticism of the quantity theory for analysing and comparing equilibrium situations only and leaving out the dynamic process itself.

The cumulative process takes its point of departure in an analysis of the relation between the actual rate of interest on loans, the money rate, and the natural rate or the normal rate. The *natural rate* is defined as the anticipated profit to be made by the use of a bank loan. The *normal rate* is defined as that particular level of the money rate which guarantees the equality of the demand for loan capital from investors and the supply of savings or loan capital from lenders; this rate corresponds to the natural rate.

The level of the *money rate* of interest is ultimately determined by the normal rate. But in the first instance, the money rate of interest is a separate variable which is set autonomously by the banks in the market for borrowing and lending of money. In this institutional setting, where bankers fix the money rate, the money supply is assumed to be endogenous and determined by demand. Therefore disturbances emanate from variations in the demand for money due to changes in the natural rate, which is then passively supported by an expansion of the money supply from the private banks, and it is not active changes in the monetary base initiated by the Central Bank which are the source of the disturbance. The equality of the money rate with the normal rate, which, according to Wicksell's analysis, implies stability of the price level and that saving equals investment, is thus a separate equilibrium condition, which was later called monetary equilibrium.

THE MECHANISM OF THE CUMULATIVE PROCESS. In the following example it is supposed that the natural rate increases, which may be due to an increase in productivity, while the money rate as fixed by the banks stays the same. It implies that the value of the total product at the end of the production period – the duration of the period is the same in all lines of production – has increased, but the entrepreneurs have to pay back less to the bank. They now have a surplus profit, which eventually will lead to an attempt to expand production. An expansion in real quantities is ruled out since full employment is assumed (Wicksell's analysis was concerned with changes in the price level and not with changes in quantities.) In any case, even if capital accumulates, it would still take some time before the results accrue, so there would be no immediate counteracting effects. However, the entrepreneurs will try to increase their demands for inputs and these prices will rise, and it is assumed that the increase is equal to the value of the expected surplus profit. The owners of inputs, in their turn, will increase their demand for consumer goods and the price level will rise proportionately. At the end of the year, the entrepreneurs have in their hands, at the new price level, consumer goods of a higher value than at the end of the previous period, while their debts to the banks are the same. Hence, they will still have a surplus profit, and the tendency to expand output will persist despite the change of the price level. The whole process will repeat itself. This is the minimum requirement for denoting a process as cumulative: it should have an endogenous mechanism which keeps the process going.

If it is assumed that the entrepreneurs always anticipate that the price level for consumer goods will be the same at the beginning as well as the end of the period, then we can imagine that a steady and more or less uniform rise in the price level will ensue. In the case of entrepreneurs expecting future rises in prices, then the actual rise will be higher and the cumulative process will be more and more rapid.

In the reverse case, where the money rate is larger than the natural rate, the process will be similar since Wicksell assumed that prices and wages have the same flexibility in both directions. It is likely that full employment could be preserved during the downward process; the fall in entrepreneurial demand for labour and land will induce workers and landlords to reduce their claims for wages and rents and the activity will be maintained at its former level. Wicksell did not rule out the existence of unemployment during a downward cumulative process, but it would not be a cumulative change.

The cumulative process may come to an end through internal causes. The changes in the price level will act as an equilibrating mechanism via its effect on the level of bank reserves. The increase in prices will lead to a higher requirement of means of exchange, which implies that to maintain a rate of interest permanently below the natural rate it is necessary to increase continually the amount of reserves. The Central Bank can therefore play a role by changing the monetary base.

In the new equilibrium the current price level will not change since the entrepreneurs can pay the increased wages etc. and still earn the normal profit. This is the basis for Wicksell's discussion of the difference between a stable equilibrium of relative prices and a *neutral/indifferent equilibrium* for the general price level, which implies that there is no tendency to resume the old equilibrium position of the price level. In fact, in an equilibrium situation value theory will determine relative prices while the quantity theory of money gives the absolute height of the price level. Wicksell did not challenge the classical dichotomy as long as it is a comparison of equilibrium situations. However, during a cumulative process, which is a disequilibrium phenomenon, the connection between value theory and monetary theory proceeds via the difference between the money rate and the normal rate. This difference determines changes in the price level and not the level itself. Thus the cumulative process is in the first instance an analysis of changes in the general price level and its main concern is not with changes in output and employment. This is explicit in the formal analysis of *Interest and Prices*, where it is assumed that the real system is in a stationary equilibrium even during the cumulative process.

THE CUMULATIVE PROCESS AND MONETARY POLICY. Wicksell applied his reconstruction of the quantity theory to Tooke's criticism of the quantity theory; rising prices mainly coincide with rising or high interest rates, which Keynes called Gibson's paradox. The object of this debate is the secular increase in the price level, which may be exemplified by the period 1850–1873. Wicksell explained this fact by the tardiness of the banks to change the loan rate in relation to changes in the natural rate. It is thus changes in the natural rate which often trigger off the cumulative process. It has already been seen that Wicksell did not put the blame on the Central Bank and the private banks are now exempted from initiating disturbances, which are mainly due to changes in real factors affecting the private demand for money. This analysis obviously has a place for an active monetary policy where the Central Bank tries to influence the money rate so as to dampen the cumulative process.

FURTHER DEVELOPMENT OF CUMULATIVE PROCESSES. It is of fundamental importance for later developments that Wicksell analysed movements in the general price level via the effects of changes in the rate of interest (both money and normal) on savings and investment, that is, the indirect mechanism.

The Wicksellian influence on Keynes's *Treatise on Money* came probably not through Wicksell's works but via Cassel's *The Theory of Social Economy*, which was translated in 1923. Keynes used the idea of a difference between the natural and the market rate or between savings and investment, and its

influence on profit, which is defined as windfall gains, as the basis for his attempt to find the dynamical laws of the disequilibrium process. Like Wicksell, he criticized the long run equilibrium character of the propositions of the quantity theory, since it did not distinguish the factors which operated during the transition process between two equilibrium positions. Keynes's theoretical constructions, the Fundamental Equations, were not supposed to be a complete substitute for the quantity theory, but to add an analysis of short period situations which was most important, from a practical point of view, for studying monetary phenomena. Keynes extensively studied, in particular in the Fundamental Equations, the dynamics of the price level, but he went beyond Wicksell by analysing credit cycles, which involve the mechanics of the wage-price-employment structure. However, the incorporation of quantity changes in the disequilibrium process does not imply that Keynes had determined an equilibrium level of output and employment which is different from full employment.

Mises stressed that the difference between the two interest rates had differential impacts on the prices of consumption goods and the prices of capital goods, that is, an analysis of relative prices was incorporated in the dynamic process. Hayek started from Mises's contribution. He was not interested in the dynamics of the price level as such, because this magnitude, which is a statistical artifact, has no influence on the decisions of individuals. It is the direct influence on relative prices from changes in the money supply and the money rate which is important. These changes determine the level and the direction of production. This is a clear rejection of the proposition that changes in the money supply can only lead to disturbances via the general price level. Hayek's position is linked to the substitution of the old notion of a long run equilibrium by intertemporal equilibrium. The central problem is therefore not changes in the price level but disturbances of the equilibrium relation between the rates of intertemporal exchange. This spills over into the problem of neutral money: to define the conditions under which changes in the money supply might leave intertemporal price relationships unchanged, which is one development of the notion of monetary equilibrium.

Wicksell's Swedish followers, Lindahl and Myrdal in particular, used the notions of ex ante and ex post to determine the factors which constitute the ex post equality between saving and investment during a cumulative process. This analysis puts the difference between ex ante saving and ex ante investment as the main condition for monetary equilibrium, where the latter is a criterion of a cumulative process. They also made a thorough analysis of the definition of the normal rate which would guarantee monetary equilibrium, in an attempt to make this rate practically useful in a monetary analysis. In this analysis they used new equilibrium concepts like temporary equilibrium and sequence analysis, which became one of the hallmarks of the Stockholm School.

During the 1930s two different strands of thought superseded the cumulative process as an approach to the relation between savings and investments. On the one hand there is the macrodynamic analysis developed by Frisch and Tinbergen, which is centred on cyclical behaviour in prices and quantities and on the existence and stability of equilibrium in a dynamic system. On the other hand Keynes's *General Theory* focused on the determination of a short run equilibrium of output and employment. Comparative statics was used to study the effects of changes in exogenous factors and Keynes showed very little interest in the accommodation process outside equilibrium.

In the wake of the neo-Walrasian interpretations of Keynes (e.g. Clower and Leijonhufvud), which imply a disequilibrium approach, there have been attempts to reinterpret and develop Wicksell's cumulative process from this point of view (e.g. Laidler, 1972). The neo-Walrasians stress income-constrained aggregate demand functions and a dynamic process with trading at disequilibrium prices, which is opposed to the traditional tâtonnement process with an auctioneer and recontracting. From this angle, Wicksell's modern element lies in the explicit analysis of the behaviour of an economy in disequilibrium and with no recontracting, which generates an income constrained process. However, the assumption of flexible wages and prices, in particular downwards, leads only to a cumulative process in the price level while output is constant. According to Laidler (1972), it is enough to introduce the Keynesian assumption of rigid wages and sticky prices into Wicksell's cumulative process and a Keynesian income constrained process would follow immediately. In this process changes in quantities do all the adjusting necessary in disequilibrium, which may produce cumulative forces that tend to move employment away from full employment equilibrium.

BJÖRN HANSSON

See also WICKSELL, JOHAN GUSTAF KNUT; WICKSELL'S THEORY OF CAPITAL.

BIBLIOGRAPHY

Haberler, G. 1937. *Prosperity and Depression*. 5th edn, London: George Allen & Unwin, 1964.

Hayek, F. von. 1931. *Prices and Production*. London: George Routledge & Sons.

Keynes, J.M. 1930. *A Treatise on Money*. Vols I-II. Reprinted in Vols V-VI of *The Collected Writings of John Maynard Keynes*, London: Macmillan, 1971.

Laidler, D. 1972. On Wicksell's theory of price level dynamics. *Manchester School of Economics and Social Studies* 40(2), June, 125-44.

Lindahl, E. 1930. *Penningpolitikens medel*. Lund: C.W.K. Gleerup. Trans. as 'The rate of interest and the price level' in Lindahl, *Studies in the Theory of Money and Capital*, London: George Allen & Unwin, 1939.

Milgate, M. 1979. On the origin of the notion of 'intertemporal equilibrium'. *Economica* 46, February, 1-10.

Mises, L. von. 1912. *Theorie des Geldes und der Umlaufsmittel*. Munich: Duncker & Humblot; 2nd edn, 1924. Trans. as *The Theory of Money and Credit*, London: Jonathan Cape, 1934.

Myrdal, G. 1931. Om penningteoretisk jämvikt. En studie över den 'normala räntan' i Wicksells penninglära. *Ekonomisk Tidskrift* 33. Trans. as *Monetary Equilibrium*, London: Hodge, 1939.

Patinkin, D. 1952. Wicksell's 'cumulative process'. *Economic Journal* 62, December, 835-47.

Patinkin, D. 1956. *Money, Interest, and Prices*. 2nd edn, New York: Harper & Row, 1965.

Uhr, C.G. 1960. *Economic Doctrines of Knut Wicksell*. Berkeley and Los Angeles: University of California Press.

Wicksell, K. 1898. Penningeräntans inflytande på varuprisen. *Nationalekonomiska föreningens förhandlingar*, vol. I. Trans. as 'The influence of the rate of interest on commodity prices', in Wicksell, *Selected Papers on Economic Theory*, London: George Allen & Unwin, 1958.

Wicksell, K. 1898b. *Geldzins und Güterpreise*. Jena: Gustav Fischer. Trans. as *Interest and Prices*, London: Macmillan, 1936.

Wicksell, K. 1919. Professor Cassels nationalekonomiska system. *Ekonomisk Tidskrift* 21. Trans. as 'Professor Cassel's System of Economics', in Wicksell (1934-5).

Wicksell, K. 1934-5. *Lectures on Political Economy*. Vols I-II. Trans. from the third Swedish edition of *Föreläsningar i nationalekonomi*, vols I-II, 1928-9, London: George Routledge & Sons.

Cunningham, William (1849–1919).   A member of the English Historical School, Cunningham was educated at the Universities of Edinburgh and Cambridge. He held various posts as lecturer at Cambridge and was elected Fellow of Trinity College in 1891. From 1891 to 1897 he was Tooke Professor of Statistics of King's College London. In addition, he pursued a religious career. He was ordained in 1874 and rose to be Archdeacon of Ely (1907–19).

Cunningham was one of the most important pioneers in economic history. His *Growth of English Industry and Commerce* (1882) was the first textbook in the field, widely used for several decades and an important foundation on which English economic history was to be constructed, and he relentlessly fought for the recognition and establishment of economic history as an independent discipline.

Cunningham became increasingly hostile towards economic theory. He felt that its assumptions about human behaviour and the institutional framework were leading to insufficiently complete analyses and were blatantly unrealistic for most periods in history. In 1892 he started the English Methodenstreit by attacking Marshall for constructing economic history from general principles instead of empirical data. The debate was partly the result of his personal and professional antagonism towards Marshall and his wish to apply economics to politics.

Cunningham shifted from an internationalist and free-trader to a nationalist and protectionist, making the preservation and strengthening of the nation-state his most weighty political and economic objective. By the time of the fiscal controversy in 1903 he fully endorsed the tariff reform movement and subscribed to imperialism, with the great empire securing peace and order.

O. KURER

SELECTED WORKS

1882. *The Growth of English Industry and Commerce*. Cambridge: Cambridge University Press.

1892a. The perversion of economic history. *Economic Journal* 2, 491–506.

1892b. The perversion of economic history. A reply to Professor Marshall. *Pall Mall Gazette*, 29 September 1892 and *Academy*, 1 October 1892, 288.

1904. *The Rise and Decline of the Free Trade Movement*. Cambridge: Cambridge University Press.

1911. *The Case Against Free Trade*. Preface by Joseph Chamberlain. London: John Murray.

BIBLIOGRAPHY

Cunningham, A. 1950. *Wiliam Cunningham: Teacher and Priest*. Preface by F.R. Salter. London: Society for Promoting Christian Knowledge.

Foxwell, H.S. 1919. Archdeacon Cunningham (obituary). *Economic Journal* 29, 382–90.

Maloney, J. 1976. Marshall, Cunningham, and the emerging economics profession. *Economic History Review* 29, 440–51.

Maloney, J. 1985. *Marshall, Orthodoxy and the Professionalisation of Economics*. Cambridge: Cambridge University Press.

Scott, W.R. 1920. William Cunningham, 1849–1919. *British Academy, Proceedings* 9, 465–74.

Semmel, B. 1960. *Imperialism and Social Reform: English Imperial Thought 1895–1914*. London: George Allen & Unwin.

Wood, J.C. 1983. *British Economists and the Empire, 1860–1914*. 1860–1914. Beckenham, Kent: Croom Helm.

Cunynghame, Henry Hardinge (1848–1935).   Soldier, lawyer, civil servant, polymath and amateur economist, Sir Henry Cunynghame was born of distinguished forebears on 8 July 1848 at Penshurst. He died at Eastbourne on 3 May 1935, having been knighted in 1908. In 1870 he entered St John's College, Cambridge, to study law, throwing over a promising military career. There he became a favourite of Alfred Marshall and was infected by an enthusiasm for 'geometrical political economy', a topic on which he was eventually to publish one of his many books (Cunynghame, 1904). There too he invented for Marshall a machine (now lost) for drawing a grid of rectangular hyperbolae (Guillebaud, 1961, Vol. II, pp. 37–8). Called to the Bar in 1875, Cunynghame had a varied career in law and government, but always retained his interest in economics. He occasionally lectured on the subject (his *Notes on Exchange Value* (1880) were printed for one such course) and in the later 1880s belonged to the economic discussion group which met at the Hampstead home of Henry Ramée Beeton. (P.H. Wicksteed, G.B. Shaw, H.S. Foxwell and F.Y. Edgeworth were among the regulars.) There he presented a paper (Cunynghame, 1888) defending Marshall's supply curve against Wicksteed's criticisms. The analysis of external effects in production and consumption, his most significant theoretical contribution, first appeared here, the arguments being amplified, but not much clarified, in Cunynghame (1892). His other notable contribution, the use of back-to-back demand-supply diagrams to analyse markets linked by trade, appeared in Cunynghame (1903). The 1904 book, although lively and praised by J.M. Keynes, added little and, indeed, rather compounded earlier ambiguities by a certain flabbiness of thought. Cunynghame's last economic publication (1912), was a valedictory address on methodology. For further biographical detail see Keynes (1935) and Ward and Spencer (1938). Consult also letters by Marshall reproduced in (Pigou, 1925, pp. 447–52; Guillebaud, 1961, Vol. II, pp. 809–13) and Edgeworth's review (1905) of Cunynghame (1904).

J.K. WHITAKER

SELECTED WORKS

1880. *Notes on Exchange Value*. London, privately printed.
1888. *Some Remarks on Demand and Supply curves, and their interpretation*. London, privately printed.
1892. Some improvements in simple geometrical methods of treating exchange value, monopoly, and rent. *Economic Journal* 2, March, 35–52.
1903. The effect of export and import duties on price and production examined by the graphic method. *Economic Journal* 13, September, 313–23.
1904. *Geometrical Political Economy*. Oxford: Clarendon Press.
1912. Address to the Economic Science and Statistical Section of the British Association for the Advancement of Science. *Journal of the Royal Statistical Society* 76, December, 88–98.

BIBLIOGRAPHY

Edgeworth, F.Y. 1905. Review of Cunynghame (1904). *Economic Journal* 15, March, 62–71. Reprinted in F.Y. Edgeworth, *Papers Relating to Political Economy*, Vol. 3, London, Macmillan, 1925.
Guillebaud, C.W. (ed.) 1961. Alfred Marshall, *Principles of Economics*. Ninth (Variorum) Edition, London: Macmillan.
Keynes, J.M. 1935. Obituary: Sir Henry Cunynghame. *Economic Journal* 45(178), June, 398–406. Reproduced in J.M. Keynes, *Collected Writings*, Vol. X (*Essays in Biography*), London: Macmillan, 1972.
Pigou, A.C. (ed.) 1925. *Memorials of Alfred Marshall*. London: Macmillan.
Ward, C.H.D. and Spencer, C.B. 1938. *The Unconventional Civil Servant: Sir Henry Cunynghame*. London: Michael Joseph.

currencies. Any commodity is capable of being used as a medium of exchange and history furnishes us with an almost endless list of commodities that have been used in this way: cattle, cacao, beans, salt, silk, furs, tobacco, dried fish, wheat, rice, olive oil, cloth, cowry shells, iron, copper, silver and gold. However, not all of these commodities are efficient means of exchange and the natural properties of cowry shells, gold, silver and copper led to their emergence as the most popular form of currency. The relative scarcity of gold and its indestructibility made this form of money highly desirable as a store of value; the relative abundance of cowry shells, combined with their uniformity and divisibility, made them an ideal medium of exchange for low valued transactions; silver and copper have natural properties that made them useful for transactions intermediate between these two extremes.

The rise of nation states and the emergence of paper money and metallic tokens led to a decline in the use of commodity monies as currency. The principal problem with gold, silver, copper and cowries was that even though their relative values remained remarkably stable for centuries these ratios were incapable of being fixed. For example, the exchange ratio of silver to gold in Europe deviated little from its average of 13 to 1 in the eight hundred years prior to the emergence of the gold standard towards the end of the 19th century (Shaw, 1895); in West Africa the cowry/gold ratio varied between 15,000 and 20,000 to 1 over the period 1700 to 1850 (Johnson, 1970, p. 334). The ratios were determined by the conditions of production, unlike the relation of the English penny to the pound which was fixed by government fiat at 240 to 1.

Fixed ratios of the various units of a currency are essential if it is to perform its function as a standard of price efficiently. Thus 'bad' state money, which has no intrinsic value but fixed ratios between its subordinate parts, forced out the 'good' commodity monies according to the principles of Gresham's Law. Cowry shells were first to go and they disappeared from Africa and Asia in the mid to late 19th century following the colonization of the regions by the British empire and the establishment of the Sterling currency area. Silver followed next but only after much resistance from the European countries whose currencies were based on the silver or bimetal standard. Gold, too, disappeared from circulation but only to take up residence underground where central banks clung to it as a store of value. It too seemed to be on the way out in the post World War II period as the US dollar emerged as world currency. However, the rapid rise in the US dollar price of gold following the deregulation of the gold market in 1971 has effectively remonetized gold. In 1982, for example, gold accounted for only 9% of total foreign reserves held by all countries. However, this estimate values gold at the official rate of 35 SDR. If market price values are used (375 SDR) the percentage of gold to total reserves jumps to 51 per cent. Gold will no doubt continue to fulfil this function until a world government establishes a world paper currency. As there is no prospect for this happening for some time yet, gold is likely to be around for some time as a symbol of the anarchy and mistrust that characterizes the world economy.

The rise to dominance of paper money and coin tokens at the expense of metallic currencies is not difficult to understand. It was a technological advance in the sphere of exchange that was brought about by the technological changes in the sphere of production: the upsurge in the production of commodities required the development of an efficient medium for their exchange and distribution. What is difficult to explain, however, is why some 'archaic' currencies have not only continued to exist but have flourished under the impact of colonization. For example, the establishment of one of the world's largest copper mines on Bougainville Island, Papua New Guinea, has generated an enormous upsurge in demand for traditional shell currency. This has to be imported from Malaita Islands in the neighbouring Solomon Islands, some

550 kms away (Connell, 1977). This is not an isolated case as similar evidence comes from other parts of the country (e.g. Chowning, 1978).

At one level this can be seen as a minor problem of trying to understand the process by which a very small country of some three million people has been integrated into the world economy. At another level, however, it challenges us to reflect on the nature of our own money and society and to examine it within a comparative context. Early attempts to come to terms with the problem did so within the framework of a 'primitive money/modern money' dichotomy (Einzig, 1948; Quiggin, 1949). This formulation, which still has its adherents today (e.g. Melitz, 1974), confuses the issue by labelling as 'primitive' what is obviously very much a 'modern' phenomenon. What is needed is a theoretical framework that gets beyond the terminological and conceptual inadequacies of the 'primitive/modern' dichotomy. Karl Polanyi and his followers have made important contributions in this regard (see Polanyi, 1977). The 'gift/commodity' distinction (Gregory, 1982), which has its origins in the theories of Mauss (1925) and Marx (1867) respectively, is a recent attempt to come to terms with the problem from a somewhat different theoretical perspective. The issues here are complex and controversial and the debates surrounding this issue will no doubt continue for some time to come.

C.A. GREGORY

See also COMMODITY MONEY; FIAT MONEY; FIDUCIARY ISSUE; MONEY SUPPLY.

BIBLIOGRAPHY

Chowning, A. 1978. Changes in West New Britain trading systems. *Mankind* 11, 296–307.
Connell, J. 1977. The Bougainville connection: changes in the economic context of shell money production in Malaita. *Oceania* 48(2), 81–101.
Einzig, P. 1948. *Primitive Money*. London: Eyre & Spottiswoode.
Gregory, C.A. 1982. *Gifts and Commodities*. London: Academic Press.
Johnson, M. 1970. The cowrie currencies of West Africa. *Journal of African History* 11, 17–49; 331–53.
Marx, K. 1867. *Capital*. Moscow: Progress.
Mauss, M. 1925. *The Gift*. London: Routledge.
Melitz, J. 1974. *Primitive and Modern Money*. Reading, Mass.: Addison-Wesley.
Polanyi, K. 1977. *The Livelihood of Man*. London: Academic Press.
Quiggin, A.H. 1949. *A Survey of Primitive Money*. London: Methuen.
Shaw, W.A. 1895. *The History of Currency. 1252–1894*. London: Wilson & Milne.

currency boards. Once ubiquitous in the colonial regimes of Africa, Asia and the Caribbean, currency boards now survive only in such small countries as Singapore, Brunei and Hongkong. The main characteristic of the currency board system is that the board stands ready to exchange domestic *currency* for the foreign reserve currency at a specified and fixed rate. To perform this function the board is required to hold realizable financial assets in the reserve currency at least equal to the value of the domestic currency outstanding. Hence in the currency board system there can be no fiduciary issue. The backing to the currency must be at least 100 per cent. Although in principle it is the currency board that is required to convert on demand all offers of domestic or reserve currency, in practice, where there is a banking system, however elementary, it is the banks that have carried out most of the exchange business. The buying and selling rates for both currencies have a sufficient spread so that the costs of exchanged are covered. This convertibility of currencies in the currency board system does not extend to bank deposits or any other financial assets. If a person has a bank deposit and wishes to use the currency board to convert it to foreign currency then the deposit must be first converted into domestic currency and then presented to the currency board.

These disciplines of convertibility and the avoidance of deficit financing were characteristic of much of 19th-century Britain and France. The principle of the currency board was enshrined in the provisions of the (British) Bank Charter Act of 1844. The Issue Department of the Bank of England was to act like a currency board. It is not surprising that this principle was considered proper for the newly acquired colonies. At first, settlers and officials used the notes and coin of the imperial power as a normal extension of imperial trade. The metropolitan currency and coin, since it was widely accepted and considered 'as good as gold', served as a stable means of exchange and as a store of value in those largely inflation-free days of colonial occupation.

There were disadvantages of circulating the metropolitan currency, for example sterling notes and gold sovereigns, in the colonies. First, there was a high risk of destruction or loss. Second, real resources were locked into the circulating media and produced no return. Any loss of currency notes would be to the benefit of the issuer (e.g. the Bank of England) and the colony would correspondingly lose the real value of the notes. The institution of a currency board enabled the colony to avoid such loss. The Bank of England note could be stored in the currency board's vaults and local currency issued to the same value. Thus the accidental loss of a domestic note would not diminish the net assets of the colony. In addition, the currency board would find it efficient to replace worn notes from its stock without having its assets tied up in sending battered Bank of England notes back to London for reissue.

In practice the currency board did not need to hold all its reserves in Bank of England notes. It could buy interest-bearing financial assets of suitable liquidity. Provided these assets could be converted at sufficiently short notice without significant loss into bank notes (or provided the currency board could borrow notes on such security), the principles of convertibility, 100 per cent reserves and no fiduciary issue were satisfied. This more sophisticated currency board system could be used to earn at least some of the profits of seignorage for the benefit of the colony.

Most colonies developed a currency board system, although a few continued to circulate some foreign notes and coins as parallel currencies. The non-colonial countries of Liberia and Panama, however, have used the United States dollar as a circulating medium. In the case of Liberia it was argued that there were doubts whether the people would have confidence in a currency board supervised by the government of Liberia. In particular, there were fears – alas not groundless – that the monetary system would be used improperly to finance government spending.

As colonies became independent states in the 1950s and 1960s they generally eschewed the currency board system and formed Central Banks to manage their currencies, ostensibly for 'development' purposes. The central banks, as distinct from the currency boards that they replaced, required the commercial banks to hold reserves as deposits at the Central Bank. And the government could create money and finance government deficits by borrowing from the newly created Central Bank. Some countries, such as Singapore, continued to operate a sophisticated currency board system. And Hong Kong, after experimenting with an unpegged currency from 1972, returned to a currency board system based on the United States dollar in October 1983.

The financial experience of countries which departed from currency board systems has not been auspicious. Increasing inflation, generated largely by deficit financing through Central Bank credit and note issue, has been characteristic of most of the two or three decades since independence. The objective of promoting growth and development has not been generally achieved; indeed, in Africa the experience and the forecast is one of degeneration. It is difficult to avoid the conclusion that the financial instability brought in train by the abrogation of the currency board system has played a considerable role in this process. Nevertheless, it is unlikely that, whatever the arguments in favour of the currency board system, there will ever be a resuscitation of what is wrongly regarded as a manipulative monetary mechanism of colonialism or neo-imperialism.

The claims for a currency board system are many, some clearly dubious. One main claim is that the currency board system provides an annual increment of the money supply which is simply the mirror image of the surplus on the current balance of payments. If there were no banks, or if the banks acted only as depositories or 'cloakrooms' for currency, and if there were no imports or exports of capital in the form of foreign currency, then this assertion would be correct. The only way in which the residents could acquire foreign currency, and so swap for domestic currency, would be through net earnings from trade. When there is a surplus on the current account the money supply grows by that amount, and when a deficit appears the money stock contracts by the value of the deficit. This one-to-one relationship was thought to provide an automatic system which ensured that monetary behaviour always moved to eliminate a deficit or a surplus.

With notes and coin as the sole form of money and with no capital imports of foreign currency this one-to-one model was clearly valid. However, with the additional elements of bank deposits and credit the issue becomes much less clear cut. A proportional relation still holds even with a fully developed system of bank deposits acting as money and bank credit, provided first that there were no foreign capital movements, second that the banks maintain domestic currency in their reserves as a constant fraction of their deposit liabilities, and third that the public hold a constant ratio of domestic currency to bank deposits. All these fixed ratios would ensure that the M_1 definition of the money supply (currency plus checking accounts) would expand proportionally, but not one-to-one with the current balance.

If there are capital flows other than those required to settle the net bills of the trade account, then the proportionality disappears. A flow of capital, such as a colonial branch bank borrowing from its parent, will entail the acquisition of a foreign financial asset (as well as the corresponding liability). The branch bank, if required to hold reserves in domestic currency, will exchange its foreign financial asset (or strictly currency) at the currency board and acquire domestic currency reserves. So, keeping the reserve fraction constant, it will extend loans and expand deposits, thus increasing the deposit component of the money supply. The limit to such borrowing and domestic credit creation is set by the demand for credit in the colony, which in turn depends on the marginal profitability of credit in the colony relative to the interest rate. (This rate will normally be at a slight premium over the metropolitan interest rate.) In practice, the limit to such borrowings will be set by judgements of bankers and businessmen of the capacity and willingness of domestic borrowers to pay the servicing charges.

There is one set of circumstances which would insulate the monetary system from external capital flows. This would be the case where the importation of capital is effected only to supply the foreign exchange component of a domestic investment which would otherwise not occur. The insulation is complete if the investment generates profits in foreign exchange which just offset the servicing charges. These conditions of foreign capital flows were probably a fair approximation to reality for the period covered by the currency board era. But with the dominance of Western commercial bank lending to Third World governments, they are hardly characteristic of modern capital flows. Capital flows normally do affect monetary conditions.

The proportionality proposition is also upset by changes in the reserve–deposit ratios and by any changes in the fraction of the money stock which the public desires to hold in the form of currency. Prudential control of banks, often the responsibility of the Central Bank in the parent bank's country, usually takes the form of specifying *minimum* reserves which may be less than the prudential reserves held normally by banks. The branch banks may thus decide to extend credit and deposits, when conditions of confidence and credibility change, by running down their reserve to deposit ratio to somewhere near the specified minimum. The ability of branch banks generally to borrow from the head office in London gives considerable latitude to their liquidity requirements and virtually guarantees the solvency of the branch in the colony.

In the long run, much more important than the reserve–deposit ratio are changes in the currency-deposit ratio of the public. The modern process of financial innovation economizes on cash. The use of the cheque rather than cash is the predominant financial trend in all countries. For any given quantity of currency and other bank reserves the choice of the public for a larger ratio of deposits to currency has provided the main impetus for an expansion of the money supply (M_1) in currency board systems. The stability and confidence generated by the currency board system undoubtedly much encouraged the use of deposits.

This phenomenon nullifies one of the main criticisms of the currency board system, namely that it provides a stultifying monetary constraint on development and inhibits growth in the colony. It is perhaps ironic that the countries that have retained their currency board arrangements, Singapore and Hongkong, have been the highest growth economies in the oil-importing Third World. Their money supply has expanded partly through current balance surpluses and capital imports, but mainly through the increased use of deposits associated with the financial stability of the currency board system. Both Singapore and Hong Kong inflated during the late 1960s and 1970s at roughly the same relatively low rates as the currencies on which they were based. Thus they avoided the excessive inflation which affected many Third World countries which had adopted more 'advanced' systems of central bank finance.

Another important criticism was thought to be not only the preclusion of counter-cyclical monetary and budgetary policy, but also the promotion of an actually pro-cyclical policy. Many currency board colonies produced export crops which were sold in markets with widely fluctuating prices. The collapse of commodity prices in a world recession generally gave rise to a large deficit on the current balance and so induced the currency board to contract the money supply. The isomorphic case of a boom in export prices was thought to be less onerous. Under a liberal trade regime the increase in foreign exchange receipts from exports could be offset in part by an expansion of imports which would damp down the inflationary pressure generated by the rise in export prices. Although no monetary manipulation can turn a one-commodity export economy into a nicely diversified recession-proof system, there was no reason, apart from extraneous regulations, why the authorities as well as firms and persons could not hold or transfer foreign assets as a precaution against such oscillations. In the case of the Hong Kong currency board, the freedom to hold assets in any form and any currency is the *sine qua non* of the financial system. And, for many decades, the government of Hong Kong has held a large portfolio of foreign financial assets which can be used to expand or contract the money supply and hence influence the currency board issue.

It has been thought that the currency board system is likely to exacerbate liquidity shortages and even the solvency of the domestic banking system, and so make it difficult to contain runs on banks and all the fear and instability that inevitably follows. Again, this criticism has proven largely invalid. Since most banking business was carried out by the branches of metropolitan banks, there was little fear of a run on a particular branch causing solvency problems, and liquidity shortages could be covered quickly by transfer. Moreover the knowledge that the resources of the parent banks lay behind the branch gave rise to a singular confidence and so nipped any incipient run in the bud. For the local banks, which has no such recourse, the ebb and flow of confidence were much more serious (as in the United States in 1931-3 and Hong Kong in 1983 and 1985). Insofar as the currency board system promotes international branch banking, so it promotes stability.

Although the currency board system did not have all the virtues or faults which were attributed to it, it did have some singular advantages. To some extent it depoliticized the monetary system and insulated the public purse from plundering politicians. There was no resort to the printing press to reward political allies or ruin one's opponents. It gave a real credibility to the fixed exchange rate so that people willingly held both currency and deposits knowing that they would maintain their value. Similarly it precluded the possibility that the exchange rate would be used to attempt to solve political and social problems. These constraints, once thought to be vices, are now widely regarded as virtues. The evident failure of trying to promote growth or equality by inflationary finance may create a new respect for currency boards. The return of Hong Kong in 1983 to a full currency board system based on the US dollar was in response to political uncertainties as well as the realization that such financial stability was sorely needed.

It would be rash, however, to imagine that currency boards are the wave of the future. One suspects that they may be used rather more frequently in small economies that are heavily dependent on large trading partners. Similarly they are likely to remain the basic system for the great trading centres such as Singapore and Hong Kong where they have worked so well. The most demanding requirement of a currency board system is that, even under the most trying conditions, the financial community have faith that the board will honour its exchange obligations at the specified parity. Few Third World governments command such credibility. Thus, the currency board is unlikely to be the main vehicle for monetary and fiscal rectitude in the Third World.

ALAN WALTERS

See also CENTRAL BANKING; FINANCIAL INTERMEDIARIES.

BIBLIOGRAPHY

Drake, P.J. (ed.) 1966. *Money and Banking in Malaya and Singapore*. Singapore: Malayan Publications.

Greaves, I.C. 1953. *Colonial Monetary Conditions*. London: HMSO.

Greenwood, J.G. 1984. Why the HK\$/US\$ linked rate system should not be changed. *Asian Monetary Monitor* 8(6), November–December.

Newlyn, W.T. and Rowan, D.C. 1954. *Money and Banking in British Colonial Africa*. London: Oxford University Press.

currency school. *See* BANKING SCHOOL, CURRENCY SCHOOL AND FREE BANKING SCHOOL.

Currie, Lauchlin Bernard (born 1902). Currie was born in Nova Scotia on 8 October 1902 and was educated at St Francis Xavier College in Antigonish, the London School of Economics (BSc, 1925), and Harvard University (PhD, 1931). During a long, varied, influential and productive career as a macroeconomic policy adviser he developed and applied theoretical insights and new data sources to improve national well-being. From 1934 to 1945, Currie advised the New Deal on monetary and fiscal policies for recovery, full employment, maximum production for war and price stability. After 1949 he focused on development, primarily in Colombia, where he became a citizen in 1958. Well-trained in economics and an inveterate reformer, Currie sought public policies that would allow competitive markets to yield high saving and investment required for productivity and stable growth.

By 1933 Currie had coherently described banking powers and institutional forces affecting supplies of money, defined as cash and demand deposits (less interbank accounts). An active policy, he noted, could have expanded money supplies during the depression. Currie (1934a, p. 177) criticized the Federal Reserve for accommodating commercial credit needs while ignoring 'the best monetary theory, which holds that its task is rather the control of the volume of means of payment for the purpose of controlling in turn monetary incomes and the rate and character of their expenditure in relation to the rate and character of the output of goods'. In 1934, he proposed a 100 per cent reserve banking system and later drafted bills to strengthen central bank powers.

Working for the Federal Reserve until 1939, Currie directed studies of federal income-increasing expenditures in relation to other components of national income accounts. By 1935, he had demonstrated how deficits would stimulate depression-weakened incentives for investment, compared the government's actual net contribution to increased national income with a deficit necessary for full recovery, and related fiscal policies to effective monetary controls that would maintain full employment and stable prices. His policy advice for Marriner Eccles and other liberals in government anticipated Keynesian insights and led to the acceptance of countercyclical deficit spending as Roosevelt's recovery programme.

Currie applied these insights to the recession in 1937–8; in 1939 he became the first professional economist appointed as Administrative Assistant to the President. During World War II, he supported public policies to maximize output, administered Lend Lease for China, and fostered macroeconomic studies to assess curbs on inflation. He hoped progressive taxes and comprehensive income-maintenance programmes would assure high consumption and full employment after the war.

In 1949, after trying private enterprise, Currie undertook a World Bank-supported national study of economic development for Colombia. He urged improved health, education and public administration, as well as expanded transportation systems, exports and international borrowing. Since 1960 he has advocated a Leading Sector Strategy based on efficiently combining inputs through new techniques and more specialization possible with larger markets. He emphasized housing through planned communities, owner construction, and savings banks indexed to inflation along with a more equal distribution of income and social welfare.

B.L. JONES

SELECTED WORKS

1934a. The failure of monetary policy to prevent the depression of 1929–32. Journal of Political Economy 42, April, 145–77.

1934b. The Supply and Control of Money in the United States. Cambridge, Mass.: Harvard University Press. 2nd edn revised, 1935. 1st edn reprinted, New York: Russell & Russell, 1968.

[1935] 1978. Comments on pump priming and federal income-increasing expenditures, 1932–1935. History of Political Economy 10(4), Winter, 525–33, 534–40.

[1938] 1980. Causes of the recession. History of Political Economy 12(3), Fall, 316–35.

1939. Testimony. US Congress, 76th Congress, 1st Sess., Temporary National Economic Committee. Hearings Part 9, Washington, DC: Government Printing Office, 3520–38.

1950. The Basis of a Development Program for Colombia. Baltimore: Johns Hopkins Press.

1966. Accelerating Development: The Necessity and the Means. New York: McGraw-Hill.

1974. The 'leading sector' model of growth in developing countries. Journal of Economic Studies 1, May, 1–16.

1976. Taming the Megalopolis: A Design for Urban Growth. New York: Pergamon Press.

1981. The Role of Economic Advisers in Developing Countries. Westport, Conn.: Greenwood Press.

custom. *See* ECONOMIC ANTROPOLOGY.

customs unions. A customs union consists of two or more countries which have no tariff barriers between themselves and a common tariff against the rest of the world. There are variants which involve a greater or lesser degree of economic integration. A free trade area has no common external tariff; a union with free movement of production factors, particularly of labour, is often called a common market.

Theorizing about customs unions goes back to the classical economists, but contemporary theory, which has been mainly concerned with the welfare effects of union, is founded on the work of Jacob Viner (1950). He introduced the concepts of trade creation and trade diversion. Trade creation occurs when the removal of the tariff on intra-union trade shifts members' demand from domestic production to lower-cost output from a union partner, diversion when the tariff preference for union members shifts demand from a non-union source to a higher-cost union supplier. The establishment of the union, according to the theory, improves welfare if trade creation predominates and worsens it if trade diversion predominates.

The removal of tariffs between union members might appear to be a move towards free trade, and presumed to be beneficial. The possibility that trade diversion will predominate shows the inadequacy of that presumption. Viner's analysis exemplifies the 'theory of the second best', showing that an incomplete move towards the optimum – the removal of some, but not all tariffs – may, in fact, make matters either better or worse.

The definition of trade creation and diversion was usefully widened by Johnson (1962) to include consumption effects. Changes in the pattern of consumption following union may either increase or decrease consumers' surplus, depending on whether there is a shift to a lower or a higher cost source of satisfying demand. The distinction between this consumption effect and the production effect of the tariff-induced price changes can be expressed as that between inter-commodity and inter-country substitutions.

Discussion stimulated by Viner's analysis was particularly concerned with establishing general conditions determining whether a union was trade creating or diverting, and the consequent welfare effects. Various assumptions were relaxed – such as that of constant costs or of fixed proportions in consumption – and various results obtained. However, no universal law of customs unions, and few conclusions of practical importance, emerged (Krauss, 1972).

Meade (1955) and Johnson (1962), consistent with Viner's view that confident judgements cannot be made for customs unions in general and in the abstract, produced tentative and practically-oriented analyses of the conditions which favour a union's being on balance trade-creating, and there would be wide agreement on the following list:

1. Many union members.

2. Trade a small proportion of members' production, a high proportion giving more opportunity for a trade-diverting switch from non-union to union supply.

3. A high proportion of what trade there is being with members, and a low proportion with the outside world, again reducing trade diversion possibilities.

4. A low common external tariff as compared with the members' pre-union average tariff, further reducing the likelihood of diversion.

5. A wide overlap in the activities protected by the tariff in the different member countries, since with no overlap, there can be no trade-creating production effect through a shift in demand from a domestic to a union supplier, and a trade-diverting switch from a non-union supplier is probable.

6. Wide differences between union members in the cost of producing particular commodities.

These last two conditions provide for the countries forming the union to be actually competitive but potentially complementary.

In the light of these conditions, less-developed countries appear as most unlikely candidates for membership of a beneficial customs union. The theory deals with production and consumption shifts towards a more or a less efficient use of resources and satisfaction of consumer preferences. In developed, diversified economies such shifts can take place in response to price changes. The theory is much less adequate as an explanatory device for export-oriented, less-developed economies which produce a narrow range of commodities, and in which increased welfare requires primarily the growth and diversification of output. Yet there has been much activity in the formation of unions of such countries. Extension of the theory was required to explain this paradox, and to determine whether or not the formation of a union was economically rational: Johnson (1965); Cooper and Massell (1965). There has, however, been little development of a theory of customs unions in the context of economic growth (see Robson, 1983, ch. 2).

The basic theory acknowledges the existence of economies of scale. These may have cost-reduction effects with increased sales to union partners bringing domestic producers to a lower point on their supply curves. They may also have 'trade suppression' effects, with a switch to domestic products (in contrast with the standard trade diversion switch to products of union partners) from lower-cost (ex-tariff) non-union imports. These two effects may be thought of as parts of trade creation and trade diversion, respectively.

In a union of less-developed countries, economies of scale may have a much more central role. They may allow the development of competition between enterprises which would have monopolistic powers within the small domestic markets. Within the domestic markets many goods can be produced, if at all, only with extremely high protection. Access to the larger market allows a more efficient level of production. It also provides, above all, a stimulus to investment and economic growth. Many industries, operating with economies of scale, will be established only if they have access to the protected union market. These new industries, established to supply a demand previously satisfied entirely by imports, are by definition import-substituting and trade diverting. From this viewpoint, trade diversion becomes beneficial. In fact, it has become a major purpose of the union.

Other aspects of a customs union must be embraced by an extended theory if it is to be of particular relevance to less-developed economies. There is the existence of non-tariff barriers, which are often more serious restraints on trade than tariffs. There is the role of transport, because in many less-developed countries transport routes do not satisfactorily link potential union members, so that the removal of tariffs between them would be largely a formality, without any great effect on their trade. And there is the question of the distribution of the effects of union. For example, the location of new industries may be very unequal between members, so that some control of location or other equalizing procedures may be required. The basic theory says little or nothing about these matters, but in practice measures to deal with them are of fundamental importance to the viability of any customs union.

There is a further difficulty with the basic theory. It shows the circumstances in which the establishment of a customs union brings an improvement over protection on a national basis. However, precisely the same arguments about the efficient distribution of resources also show that free trade is better than a customs union. So why should customs unions be formed when, at their trade-creating best, they are inferior to the non-discriminatory removal of tariffs? Are customs unions simply irrational?

An explanation of why countries form customs unions, and why it can be rational for them to do so, requires the theory to be extended beyond the confines of the conventional assumption that welfare depends on private consumption alone. The inclusion of public goods, or public preferences, in the welfare function allows for policies to be counted as beneficial that would otherwise be irrational.

This approach provides a rationale for the policy commonly found in less-developed countries of attempting to secure a level of industrialization higher than would result from the operation of a free market. The preference for industry may have a non-economic basis, but it may also have economic rationality. It may be based on a belief in the importance of external economies created by industry and their beneficial effects on economic growth. In other words, the preference may have a long-run, growth-oriented basis, rather than a short-run allocation-oriented basis. The preference results in a policy of industrial protection as against free trade. Given economies of scale, this public preference for industry can be satisfied more efficiently within a customs union than within the smaller markets provided by protection on a national basis.

The device of counting as beneficial what would otherwise be seen as the opposite may be applied to a range of policies. The difficulty is that it can too easily be misinterpreted to justify any policy; a preference that cannot be questioned may be what the governments of less-developed countries want, but not what the people need.

Customs unions were sometimes a feature of colonial arrangements, as in East Africa and Southern Africa. Many schemes have been formulated and some put into effect in the era of independence. They have not been across-the-board preferential systems, relying on the response of the market to the resulting price signals, as in the theoretical model. They have recognized the need for complex regulations if an acceptable distribution of the gains is to be achieved. There has been planned industrial specialization and location, partial protection for particular industries within the union, and fiscal redistribution. Despite these arrangements, success has been less than assured. The East African union was dissolved. In Central America the customs union, though not formally dissolved, is effectively moribund. In general, schemes failed to progress once the force of the original initiative faded.

ARTHUR HAZLEWOOD

See also ECONOMIC INTEGRATION; INTERNATIONAL TRADE; MEADE, JAMES EDWARD; VINER, JACOB.

BIBLIOGRAPHY

Cooper, C.A. and Massell, B.F. 1965. A new look at customs union theory. *Economic Journal* 75(300), December, 742–47.
Corden, W.M. 1972. Economies of scale and customs union theory. *Journal of Political Economy* 80(3), May–June, 465–75.
Johnson, H.G. 1962. *Money, Trade and Economic Growth.* London: George Allen & Unwin.
Johnson, H.G. 1965. An economic theory of protectionism, tariff bargaining, and the formation of customs unions. *Journal of Political Economy* 73(3), June, 256–83.
Krauss, M.B. 1972. Recent developments in customs union theory: an interpretive survey. *Journal of Economic Literature* 10(2), June, 413–36.
Lipsey, R.G. 1960. The theory of customs unions: a general survey. *Economic Journal* 70(279), September, 496–513.
Meade, J.E. 1955. *The Theory of Customs Unions.* Amsterdam: North-Holland.
Robson, P. 1980. *The Economics of International Integration.* London: George Allen & Unwin.
Robson, P. 1983. *Integration, Development and Equity.* London: George Allen & Unwin.
Viner, J. 1950. *The Customs Union Issue.* New York: Carnegie Endowment for International Peace.

cycles in socialist economies. In the Marxist–Leninist project of socialist economy the elimination of cycles in economic activity is the expected result of central planning replacing the 'anarchy' of capitalist markets. *Ex-ante* coordination of the activities of government, households and firms according to a consistent, feasible and efficient plan should, in principle, ensure the continued full employment of labour and other resources along smooth growth paths instead of the recurring bouts of booms and recessions and persistent unemployment characteristic of capitalism.

The experience of those capitalist countries which, especially since World War II, have tried to implement a social-democratic version of this project while maintaining free enterprise does not differ significantly, at least qualitatively, from that of more conventional capitalist economies. Built-in stabilizers and anticyclical management of demand may have reduced the amplitude of fluctuations and the depth of unemployment (though some government intervention has been deemed cyclical because of leads and lags); the individual cost of fluctuations and unemployment has been partly collectivized by the welfare state; but the undesired phenomena have persisted. The same is true for Yugoslavia, a country which has implemented an associationist form of socialism introducing self-management on a large scale but has retained enterprise initiative and markets.

Other countries attempted to implement the marxist-leninist project – state ownership, central planning, equalitarianism, 'democratic centralism' under the leadership (and practical monopoly of power) of the communist party, as the Soviet Union, the East European Six, Mongolia, China, Cuba and the other countries loosely classed as centrally planned economies or CPEs. These countries have been successful in eliminating fluctuations in the degree of labour employment. Full employment of labour was reached in the Soviet Union at the inception of the First Five-Year Plan (1928) as a result of full-scale mobilization of labour and in the other countries in the course of reconstruction after the wars that brought about the new system. Ambitious accumulation policies maintained full employment; the wage pressure generated by labour shortage itself, combined with government commitment to price stability, added sustained excess demand for consumption which contributed further to full employment stability, without any need for specific policies to support it. Full employment has been the by-product of growthmanship. In view of the persistent microeconomic inefficiency of central planning and the underfulfilment of labour productivity targets it can also be said, in a sense, that full employment of labour has been achieved 'by default'. If, however, the decentralization process currently undertaken in most centrally planned economies were to reproduce unemployment tendencies no doubt specific policies would be adopted to restore and stabilize full employment.

Outside labour employment the performance of socialist planning has been less satisfactory than originally expected. In the Soviet Union, since the completion of reconstruction and the launching of accelerated industrialization in 1928, and in the other socialist countries since the corresponding dates in their economic history, fast growth of all performance indicators in peacetime until *circa* 1960 has smoothed small-scale cyclical phenomena, reducing them to fluctuations of positive growth rates rather than of levels of income and consumption. Since then, partly because of the gradual exhaustion of labour reserves and of easily accessible natural resources, partly because of the systemic microeconomic inefficiency exacerbated by the lack of such reserves, a discernible slowdown of growth trends has been accompanied by the appearance of negative rates, i.e. fluctuations of levels as in capitalist countries. Instances range from the early minor case of Czechoslovakia in 1963 to the large-scale income drop of one third in three years in Poland 1980–82.

These phenomena are only partly attributable to exogenous shocks and their echoes, whose persistence in the socialist economy was recognized by Oskar Lange (1969), or to adjustment processes such as accelerator-type movements, whose persistence in the socialist economy had been anticipated by Aftalion already in 1909 and recognized by Notkin (1961) and Coblijc–Stojanovic (1968). Partly – indeed mostly – these phenomena are caused by systemic factors which could be classed under three groups: (i) the lack, or at any rate the slowness, of automatic adjustment feedbacks in the economic life of centrally planned economies; (ii) the acceleration of economic activity towards the end of the planning period – be it a month, a year or five years – to avoid the formal and informal penalties of underfulfilment of targets and to obtain the rewards associated with fulfilment and overfulfilment, followed by slackening at the beginning of the next period; (iii) the presence of political feedbacks, such as popular discontent and unrest resulting from deteriorating economic performance, the changes in political centralization induced by manifestations of unrest, the economic management changes associated with political changes; these phenomena adding up to a systemic mechanism of economic/political cycles.

Markets, like all servomechanisms or homeostatic (self-regulating) devices, are neither costless nor instantaneous but are automatic in their operation; at the cost of unemployment and possibly with a considerable lag, for example, an unexpected contraction in world trade can be gradually accommodated through lower wages and prices than would otherwise have prevailed, lower exchange rate and higher interest rates regardless of government intervention, capital flows etc. Central planning, like manual control, may or may not be faster and cheaper, or more accurate, than automatic servomechanisms, depending on the relative quality of alternative controls and the actual circumstances, but is never automatic. The experience of centrally planned economies has shown repeated and sometimes glaring instances of inertia and sluggish response to exogenous change, such as persistent accelerated accumulation in the face of rising labour shortages, wage and price stability administratively enforced in spite of rising excess demand for labour and goods, systematic underpricing of imported materials and of exportables in spite of sharpening external imbalance. Reliance on monetary budget constraints and the continued presence of consumers' discretion (if not sovereignty) and some managerial room for manoeuvre make these forms of inertia and delayed response an important handicap for central planners trying to outperform market adjustments. It is precisely inadequate central response to a changing environment (including inadequate ability to innovate institutions and technology) that has given impetus to repeated attempts at reform in the last two decades.

The incentive system typical of central planning, strongly and discontinuously geared to the degree of fulfilment of physical targets, leads to frantic speeding-up of activity (*shturmovshchina* in Russian, literally 'storming') towards the end of the planning period. For monthly plans this haste leads to frequent quality deterioration; for yearly plans 'storming' leads to output being overestimated, or 'borrowed' from the subsequent period (i.e., made up through subsequent unrecorded additional output); so much so that the ratio of December output to that of the following January can be regarded as an index of economic centralization (Rostowski and Auerbach, 1984). For five years plans' 'storming' implies a concentration of investment project completions towards the end of the period and a spate of new starts at the beginning, with corresponding fluctuations. Moreover, the generalized growthmanship and emphasis on capital accumulation typical of the centrally planned economy leads usually to the inclusion in investment plans of more projects than can be completed on schedule, through 'investors' (local authorities, ministries, enterprises) underestimating true requirements in order to get a place in the plan and later escalating their demands, and through central planners systematically overestimating capacity and especially labour productivity prospects. Sometimes investment ambition leads to additional investment projects being added after or outside the plan balance (as in Gierek's Poland). As they say in East European literature, 'the investment front widens'. Sooner or later specific or generalized bottlenecks of productive or import capacity slow down implementation and reduce or block new starts. Efficiency falls due to investment resources being frozen for periods longer than economically and technically justified, and possibly because of disruption elsewhere in the economy due to resources being sucked in by investment projects given priority over current operations (a 'supply-multiplier' effect). Capital – i.e. in Marxian terminology 'dead labour' – is made unemployed instead of live labour. The cyclical pattern of starts and completions of projects, mostly within the plan period but sometimes overstepping it, leads to cyclical patterns of capacity and output endogenously generated by the system and not justified by exogenous factors. These processes have been investigated theoretically and empirically by Olivera (1960), Goldman (1964 and 1965), Baijt (1971), Bauer (1978), Dahlstedt (1981), Dallago (1982) and above all by Bauer (1982, in Hungarian, forthcoming in English).

Political factors induce cycles in socialist economy directly, through successive leaders trying to reinforce the legitimacy of their rule by appeasing their subjects with short-lived but significant spurts of consumption before the standard growth and accumulation oriented policy typical of socialist governments is resumed and comes up against the constraints discussed in the previous paragraph (Mieczkowski, 1978; Hanson, 1978; Bunce, 1980; Lafay, 1981). The association of economic and socio-political factors is investigated by Eysmontt and Maciejewski (1984), who apply discriminant analysis to a large number of indicators of such factors over time in order to identify – and anticipate – periods of crisis; they do not, however, have a model of the actual interaction of political and economic factors. An attempt at constructing such a model is made by Nuti (1979, 1985): a critical relationship is assumed between political centralization and popular unrest, inverse up to a threshold level and direct beyond it; economic centralization is directly related to political centralization and affects – through its impact on investment policy – the level of shortages and inefficiency which in turn fuel political unrest. A recursive model with lagged variables is shown to simulate the kind of recurring rounds of reform attempts and accumulation drives observable in actual socialist economies. Screpanti (1985) has modified such a model applying catastrophe theory and obtaining a political/economic accumulation cycle similar to that of capitalist economies.

The further progress of economic reform in centrally planned economies towards market socialism is bound to attenuate and ultimately eliminate the systemic types of economic cycles discussed above. However, as Maurice Dobb had already anticipated in 1939, the diffusion of markets instead of solving the instability problems of the centrally planned economy transforms them into those typical of capitalist economies.

D.M. NUTI

See also BUSINESS CYCLES; MARKET SOCIALISM; POLITICAL BUSINESS CYCLE; SOCIALISM; TRADE CYCLES.

BIBLIOGRAPHY

Aftalion, A. 1909. La réalité des superproductions générales. *Revue d'économie politique* 23(3), 201–29.

Baijt, A. 1971. Investment cycles in European socialist economies: a review article. *Journal of Economic Literature* 9(1), March, 56–63.

Bauer, T. 1978. Investment cycles in planned economies. *Acta Oeconomica* 21(3), 243–60.

Bauer, T. 1982. *Tervezès, beruchàzàs, ciklusok.* Budapest: KJK.

Bunce, V. 1980. The political consumption cycle: a comparative analysis. *Soviet Studies* 32(2), April 280–90.

Coblijc, N. and Stojanovic, L. 1969. *The Theory of Economic Cycles in a Socialist Economy.* New York: IASP.

Dallago, B. 1982. *Sviluppo e Cicli nelle Economie Est-Europee.* Milan: Angeli.

Dobb, M.H. 1939. A note on saving and investment in a socialist economy. *Economic Journal* 43, December, 713–28.

Eysmontt, J. and Maciejewski, W. 1984. Kryzysy spoleczno-gospodarcze w Polsce – ujecie modelowe (Social-economic crisis in Poland–a model approach). *Ekonomista.*

Goldmann, J. 1964. Fluctuations and trends in the rate of economic growth in some socialist countries. *Economics of Planning* 4(2), 88–98.

Goldmann, J. 1965. Short and long term variations in the growth rate and the model of functioning of a socialist economy. *Czechoslovak Economic Papers* 5, 35–46.

Hanson, P. 1978. Mieczkowski on consumption and politics: a comment. *Soviet Studies* 30(4) October, 553–6.

Lafay, J.-D. 1981. Empirical analysis of politico-economic interaction in East European countries. *Soviet Studies* 33(3), July, 386–400.

Lange, O. 1969. *Theory of Reproduction and Accumulation.* Oxford: Pergamon.

Mieczkowski, B. 1978. The relationship between changes in consumption and politics in Poland. *Soviet Studies* 30(2), April, 262–9.

Notkin, A. 1961. *Tempy i proportsii sotsialisticheskogo vosproizvodstva* (The rate and proportions of socialist reproduction). Moscow: IEL.

Nuti, D.M. 1979. The contradictions of socialist economies: a Marxian interpretation. *Socialist Register*, London: The Merlin Press.

Nuti, D.M. 1985. Political and economic fluctuations in the socialist system. European University Institute Working Paper No.85/156, Florence.

Olivera, J. 1960. Cyclical growth under collectivism. *Kyklos* 13(2), 229–52.

Rostowski, J. and Auerbach, P. 1984. Storming cycles and central planning. Discussion Paper in Political Economy No.52, Kingston Polytechnic.

Screpanti, E. 1985. A model of the political economic cycle in centrally planned economies. European University Institute Working Paper No.85/201, Florence.

cyclical fluctuations. *See* BUSINESS CYCLES; CREDIT CYCLES; GROWTH AND CYCLES; TRADE CYCLE.

D

Dalton, Edward Hugh John Neale (1887–1962). British fiscal economist and prominent Labour politician, Hugh Dalton was a student of A.C. Pigou and J.M. Keynes. His main professional interest was in the use of taxation as an instrument for the redistribution of income and wealth, an interest inspired by Pigou's teaching and by his revulsion at the contrast between the sufferings inflicted on younger generations by World War I and the material gains of those who financed or profited from the war itself. (Dalton spent four years on military service in France and Italy and lost several close friends, including the poet Rupert Brooke.) His main contribution was to investigate the properties of a modification of Bernoulli's formula $dw = dw/x$ where $w =$ economic welfare and $x =$ income but in which equal increases in welfare should correspond to more than proportionate increases in income, a condition satisfied by Dalton's formula $dw = dx/x^2$ so that $w = c - 1/x$ where c is a constant. Using this formula he concluded that economic welfare would be improved by transfers from rich to poor (Dalton, 1935), a proposition that has excited the interest of 'modern' public finance theorists of the neo-utilitarian school (see Fishburn and Willig, 1984). He elaborated his ideas in several works including his highly successful standard text *Principles of Public Finance* and in his lectures as Reader in Economics at the London School of Economics (1923–36). There he was responsible for teaching and for recommending Lionel Robbins to be Professor of Economics, a typical example of his desire not only to 'corrupt the young' (as he termed it) but also to promote the interests even of those with whom he disagreed.

Dalton combined teaching with a political career throughout the 1920s and 1930s, rising to political eminence as a member of Churchill's coalition government during World War II. As Minister of Economic Warfare he was responsible for setting up the famous sabotage team, the Special Operations Executive (SOE). Later as President of the Board of Trade he formulated plans for post-war distribution of industry designed to prevent mass unemployment. In the Attlee Labour Government of 1945 he reached the pinnacle of his political career as Chancellor of the Exchequer, one of his first acts being to nationalize the Bank of England. His famous attempt to drive down interest rates through a cheap money policy in order to float off an issue of Treasury stock at 2.5 per cent is a classic example of the failure of even an experienced and able economist to understand that, other than in the short run, governments can control either the price or the supply of bonds but not both.

ALAN PEACOCK

BIBLIOGRAPHY

Davenport, N. 1961–70. Hugh Dalton. In *Dictionary of National Biography*, Oxford: Oxford University Press, 266–9.

Dalton, H. 1935. *The Inequality of Incomes*. 4th Impression, London: George Routledge & Sons, especially the Appendix.

Fishburn, P.C. and Willig, R.D. 1984. Transfer principles in income redistribution. *Journal of Public Economics* 25(3), December, 323–8.

Pimlott, B. 1985. *Hugh Dalton*. London: Jonathan Cape.

Darwinism. *See* NATURAL SELECTION AND EVOLUTION.

Davanzati, Bernardo (1529–1606). Merchant, classical scholar, translator and economist, Davanzati was born in Florence where, apart from a period of residence in Lyon as a merchant, he worked until his death. His contributions to economics are contained in *Notizia dei cambi* (1582) which explains the operation of the foreign exchanges, and *Lezione delle Monete* (1588), translated into English in 1696 as *A Discourse Upon Coin* presumably because of its relevance to the recoinage controversies. Besides these economic writings, Davanzati produced a history of the English Reformation (1602) and a translation of Tacitus (1637) frequently described as a masterpiece of Italian literature.

Davanzati's observations on the foreign exchanges present a detailed discussion of the origins and practice of this art classified by him as the third type of mercantile transaction, the others being barter (goods for goods) and trade (goods for money). The analysis demonstrates how exchange rates fluctuate between gold points according to the supply and demand of bills, the gold points being determined by a risk premium, transport costs and interest lost while the funds are in transit. His illustration of a foreign exchange transaction by bills of exchange involving six parties residing in Lyon and Florence (1582, pp. 62–8) has been argued by De Roover (1963, p. 113) to be so instructive that had it been more thoroughly studied by historians and economists, 'fewer blunders in the history of banking' would have been made.

Davanzati's lecture on coin is one of the earliest presentations of the metallist view of the origin and nature of money. He stresses the advantages of money over barter in facilitating both the division of labour and trade of 'superfluities' between cities and nations. In the metallist tradition, money is defined as 'Gold, Silver, or Copper, coin'd by Publick Authority at pleasure, and by the consent of Nations, made the Price and Measure of Things' (Davanzati, 1588, p. 12). Non-metallic and non-convertible money can only be made acceptable to the public through coercion. Money is therefore a human convention and its intrinsic value is small relative to its value as means of exchange. To explain this value, Davanzati presents an early quantity theory which relates the value of stocks of commodities to the world's money stock. Although he is aware of the importance of monetary circulation (he compares it to the importance of the circulation of blood in the animal body), he does not develop a concept of its velocity. The lecture on money concludes with a forceful critique of the practice of debasing the coinage, based on analysing its consequences and illustrated with many examples of the practice. Davanzati argues that this 'evil' can only be avoided by making 'Money pass according to its Intrinsick Value' (1588, p. 24). Davanzati's lecture has also been noted because of its hints at the so-called 'paradox of value' and its references to elements of scarcity and usefulness in the determination of commodity prices. This and other aspects of his work were noted by Galiani (1750). Earlier his views appear to have been well received by Locke who owned, annotated and may even have inspired the Toland translation (Harrison and Laslett, 1965, p. 120).

PETER GROENEWEGEN

SELECTED WORKS

1582. *Notizia de'Cambi a M. Giulio del Caccia*. In *Scrittori classici Italiani di economia politica*. Parte Antica vol. 2, ed. Pietro Custodi, Milan: G.G. Destefanis, 1804.
1588. *Lezione delle Monete*. Translated by John Toland as *A Discourse Upon Coin*, London: Awnsham and Churchill, 1969.
1602. *Scisma d'Inghilterra sino alla morta della reina Maria ristretto in lingua propria Fiorentina*. Milan.
1637. *Gli Annali di C. Cornelio Tacito ... con la traduzione in volgar Fiorentino*. Florence: Landini.

BIBLIOGRAPHY

De Roover, R. 1963. *The Rise and Decline of the Medici Bank*. Cambridge: Mass.: Harvard University Press.
Galiani, F. (ed.) 1750. *Della Moneta*. In *Della Moneta e scritti inedite*, ed. Alberto Merola, Milan: Feltrinelli, 1963.
Harrison, J. and Laslett, P. 1965. *The Library of John Locke*. Oxford: Clarendon Press, 1971.

Davenant, Charles (1656–1714). Economist and administrator. Born in London, eldest son of William Davenant, the playwright and Poet Laureate, he was educated at Cheam School, Surrey, and entered Balliol College, Oxford, in 1671, going down in 1673 without a degree to take over the management of his father's theatre. In 1675 he wrote a tragedy, *Circe* (Davenant, 1677), but the theatre gained him little financial success. He also obtained an LL.D from Cambridge in 1675 and practised law for a short period. From 1678 to 1689 he was Commissioner of Excise. He sat as MP for St Ives from 1685 to 1688 and represented Great Bedwin in the Tory interest following the elections of 1698 and 1700. The financial consequences of his loss of office as Excise Commissioner in 1689 and unsuccessful attempts in 1692 and 1694 to obtain other positions in the revenue service appear to have inspired a career as pamphleteer, starting in 1695. Until 1702, when he again obtained preferment by being appointed Secretary to the Commission for negotiating the union between England and Scotland, he produced a steady flow of political and economic writings dealing with aspects of taxation, public debt, monetary and trade questions, foreign policy and criticisms of Whig policy in general. In June 1703 he obtained the post of Inspector-General of Exports and Imports in the Customs Office, a position he retained till his death in 1714. Most of his political and commercial writings were collected by C.E. Whitworth (1771) but two manuscript works on money and credit (Davenant, 1695b and 1696) were not published till 1942 (Evans, 1942).

Davenant's position in the history of economics rests on a variety of contributions. Initially, his work was largely depicted as typically that of an 'adherent of the mercantile theory' (Hughes, 1894, p. 483), but 'Tory free trader' (Ashley, 1900, p. 269) better describes his pronouncements on foreign trade policy as he particularly advocated the removal of trade restrictions, such as those affecting woollen exports, which benefited the landed interest by raising land values (Davenant, 1695a, pp. 16–17; 1697, pp. 98–104). His free trade position is not unambiguous. Although Davenant's remark that 'Trade is by its nature free, finds its own channel, and best directeth its own course ...' (1697, p. 98) is often quoted, the contradictory view that 'it is the prudence of a state to see that [its] industry, and stock, be not diverted from things profitable to the whole,

and turned upon objects unprofitable, and perhaps dangerous to the public' (1697, p. 107) is less frequently noticed. Schumpeter's (1954, p. 196, n.4, and p. 242) depiction of Davenant's work as 'comprehensive quasi-system' emphasizing the interdependence of economic activity is also rather difficult to sustain though it is possible to quote isolated remarks from Davenant's works in support. For example, Davenant's statement that 'all trades have a mutual dependence one upon the other, and one begets another, and the loss of one frequently loses half the rest' (1697, p.97) cannot really by described as the general theoretical proposition it appears to be. Its only use is to provide a basis for some special pleading on behalf of the East India trade. Waddell's conclusion (1958, p. 288) that Davenant was a person neither of 'exceptional ability, nor of any great strength of character' and 'a competent publicist' rather than 'an original thinker' or 'practical man of affairs' seems a more appropriate assessment from an examination of his economic writings.

Davenant's plea for the importance of 'political arithmetic' or 'the art of reasoning by figures, upon things relating to government' (1698, p. 128) provides a further claim to fame, partly because it made more readily available the fairly sophisticated national income and expenditure estimates of his friend Gregory King (1696). Most of Davenant's political arithmetic application relates to taxation and estimating the gains from trade in terms of bullion but he himself also made a useful contribution to the collection of international trade data as part of his duties as Inspector-General of Exports and Imports.

The precise details of Davenant's association with Gregory King are not fully known, but their names are also linked in another famous 'statistical' exercise, the so-called King–Davenant law of demand, first noted by Thornton (1802) and Lauderdale (1804), and later extensively discussed by Jevons (1871, pp. 154–8), who on the evidence available to him cautiously attributed to Davenant the data on which the law is based (but see Barnett, 1936, pp. 6–7). However, apart from providing these data, Davenant himself characteristically drew no such analytical conclusions from this information (1698, Part II, pp. 224–5; see Creedy, 1985, for a detailed discussion).

Davenant's contributions to the recoinage debates (1695b, 1696) are less well known because they were not included in Whitworth (1771). Full recoinage was not necessary in Davenant's view when the inferior (because clipped or worn) coins were still usefully employed in small retail transactions. In addition, the detrimental effects on the exchange rate and commodity prices of the deteriorating currency were greatly exaggerated. The rise in prices, Davenant argues, could be attributed to a great many other causes; the depreciated exchange rate was more easily explained by the substantial overseas remittances induced by the European war and was therefore better remedied by floating a public loan in Holland. Although in these essays, Davenant's exposition is not always complete, Evans (1942, p. vi) regards them as containing 'all the essential elements of the analysis of money and credit' and integrating 'the entire problem of currency and public finance'. Finally, Davenant's contributions to tax administration need to be recognized. They have been described as 'translating into principles, and trying to provide a reasonable justification for the practices that the more methodical and innovating officials (such as Pepys at the Navy Office and Admiralty, and Downing and Lowndes at the Treasury ...) were adopting and enforcing' and that in these matters of administrative thinking, unlike his economics, 'Davenant's viewpoint steadily became [dominant] in the course of the next century or so' (Hume,

1974, p.477). His writings also remain a useful source for much information on trade and finance over the final decades of the Stuart monarchy.

PETER GROENEWEGEN

See also KING, GREGORY.

SELECTED WORKS

1677. *Circe, A Tragedy. As it is acted at His Royal Highness the Duke of York's Theatre*. London: Richard Tonson.
1695a. *An Essay on Ways and Means of Supplying the War*. In Whitworth (1771), vol. I.
1695b. *A Memorial Concerning the Coyn of England*. Reprinted in Evans (1942).
1696. *A Memoriall Concerning Creditt*. Reprinted in Evans (1942).
1697. *An Essay on the East-India Trade*. Reprinted in Whitworth (1771), Vol. I, 85–123.
1698. *Discourses on the Public Revenues, and on the Trade of England in Two Parts*. Reprinted in Whitworth (1771), Part I in vol. I, 127–459, Part II in vol. II. 1–382.

BIBLIOGRAPHY

Ashley, W.J. 1900. The Tory origin of free trade policy. In W.J. Ashley, *Surveys Historic and Economic*, London: Longmans.
Barnett, G.E. 1936. *Two Tracts by Gregory King*. Baltimore: Johns Hopkins Press.
Creedy, J. 1985. On the King–Davenant 'Law' of Demand. University of Durham, Working Paper No. 74, Department of Economics.
Evans, G. Heberton. 1942. *Two Manuscripts by Charles Davenant*. Baltimore: Johns Hopkins Reprints of Economic Tracts.
Hughes, D. 1894. Charles D'Avenant (1686–1714). In *Dictionary of Political Economy*, ed. R.H.I. Palgrave, London: Macmillan, Vol. I.
Hume, L.J. 1974. Charles Davenant on financial administration. *History of Political Economy* 6, 463–77.
Jevons, W.S. 1871. *Theory of Political Economy*. 4th edn, London: Macmillan, 1911.
King, G. 1696. *Natural and Political Observations and Conclusions upon the State and Condition of England*. Reprinted in Barnett (1936).
Lauderdale, James Maitland, Eighth Earl of. 1804. *An Inquiry into the Nature and Origin or Public Wealth*. Edinburgh. Reprinted with an introduction and revisions from the second edition, New York: Kelley, 1966.
Schumpeter, J.A. 1954. *History of Economic Analysis*. London: Allen & Unwin, 1959.
Thornton, H. 1802. *An Inquiry into the Nature and Effects of the Paper Credit of Great Britain*. London.
Waddell, D. 1958. Charles Davenant (1656–1714), a biographical sketch. *Economic History Review* 11, 279–88.
Whitworth, Sir Charles E. 1771. *The Political and Commercial Works of that Celebrated Writer Charles D'Avenant LL.D*. London.

Davenport, Herbert Joseph (1861–1931). Davenport was born on 10 August 1861, in Wilmington, Vermont, and died on 16 June 1931, in New York City. He commenced a professorial career at the age of 41 after having been a land speculator (initially successful, but wiped out in the Panic of 1893) and high school teacher and principal. His academic work was at the University of South Dakota, Harvard Law School, Leipzig, Paris and Chicago (PhD, 1898). He taught at Chicago (1902–8), Missouri (1908–16) and Cornell (1916–29). He was president of the American Economic Association in 1920.

A leading, albeit somewhat iconoclastic, economic theorist of his day, he contributed to the reformulation of microeconomics from absolutist value theory to relativistic price theory. He stressed that while there were real forces at work in the economy, identifying them as human desires and productive capacities, price itself reflected nothing more fundamental than a temporary equation of demand and supply. Prices are not determined *by* the margins but *at* the margins. Recognizing the limits imposed by a resultant superficiality and simultaneity of determination, he felt that economists *qua* economists need not inquire into the formation of desires or institutions but should study the pecuniary logic of phenomena from the standpoint of price in a society dominated by the private and acquisitive point of view. His economics focused on entrepreneurial opportunity-cost adjustments and encompassed a non-normative distribution theory based directly on price theory.

While differing from his close friend Thorstein Veblen on certain substantive issues, Davenport's work nonetheless reflected the impact of Veblen's critiques of traditional theory and of the actual market economy. Emphasizing positive economics and rejecting apologetics (economic theory was not to be the monopoly of reactionaries), Davenport was willing to recognize that the search for private gain did not always conduce to social welfare, but this conclusion was not to be considered a part of economic science *per se*.

WARREN J. SAMUELS

SELECTED WORKS

1896. *Outlines of Economic Theory*. New York: Macmillan.
1897. *Outlines of Elementary Economics*. New York: Macmillan.
1908. *Value and Distribution*. Chicago: University of Chicago Press.
1913. *Economics of Enterprise*. New York: Macmillan.
1935. *The Economics of Alfred Marshall*. Ithaca: Cornell University Press.

Davidson, David (1854–1942). Born into a Jewish merchant family in Stockholm, Davidson studied law and economics at Uppsala University from 1871, became a docent in 1878, professor extraordinarius from 1880 to 1889, and then professor ordinarius for 30 years until he retired in 1919. Frequently called on to serve on parliamentary committees from 1891 to 1931, Davidson's influence was strongly felt on Sweden's monetary and tax policies, for instance the 'gold exclusion policy' of 1916–24.

In 1899 Davidson launched Sweden's first economic journal, *Ekonomisk Tidskrift*, to which he contributed almost all his work over 40 years as its owner and editor (in 1965 it was renamed *The Swedish Journal of Economics* and issued in English). This journal greatly stimulated economic research in Sweden with numerous contributions from, among others, Wicksell, Cassel, Lindahl, Myrdal and Ohlin.

Unlike Wicksell and Cassel, who published their works in German (later translated into English), all of Davidson's writings are in Swedish, none of them translated. This, and the fact that his work – five tracts 1878–89, over two hundred articles in his journal on a variety of subjects, plus chapters in several government reports – was never systematized in treatise form, accounts for his contributions to economics having been known, until recently, only to Scandinavian academics.

In his dissertation, *Bidrag till läran om de ekonomiska lagarna för kapitalbildningen* (A contribution to the theory of capital formation), Davidson anticipated Böhm-Bawerk's *Positive Theory of Capital*. To Davidson, capital was generated in the main by the unequal distribution of income. To the wealthy, increases in present goods have small and declining utility relative to that of future goods. The latter are obtained in greater quantity, variety and value by investing savings for a return – interest – in production of capital goods which, indirectly, increase productivity. This perspective inverts the first of Böhm-Bawerk's famous 'three grounds' for interest, and transforms the third to a marginal productivity theory of waiting. In his later work Davidson adopted the substance of Wicksell's amendments and reconstruction of Böhm-Bawerk's capital theory.

Davidson's monetary theory is best understood from his response in articles of 1908–25 to his friend Wicksell's pathbreaking work in this area. *Inter alia*, Davidson criticized Wicksell's monetary norm of price level stability as inappropriate in conditions of 'commodity shortage'. Eventually, by 1925, Wicksell was moved to amend his norm to accommodate Davidson's critique (Uhr, 1960, chs X and XI).

In his early tract *Om beskattningsnormen vid inkomstskatten* (A taxation norm for the income tax, 1889), Davidson urged the replacement of Sweden's several property taxes and most of its excises by a progressive income tax with a uniquely broad base. Its base was to include 'the citizen's potential consumption power' by levying the tax (i) on any increment in his net worth accrued (*whether realized or not*) between the end and the beginning of the tax year; and (ii) also on his actual consumption spending during the year. Net worth increments accrue to a person as the value of his assets increases over that of his liabilities, due to savings, capital gains, bequests etc. Such gains confer potential consumption power, which should be taxed along with actual consumption spending out of income.

Over the years, aware of difficulties his proposed tax base would encounter as it called for annual balance sheet and income–consumption statements, Davidson conceded some simplifications on the tax declarations, and to taxing capital gains only when realized by the sale of value-appreciated assets. He also agreed that the tax rates levied on net worth increments would have to be lower than the rates levied on consumption expenditures.

These concessions notwithstanding, Sweden's parliament in its first comprehensive income tax of 1910 adopted only one part of Davidson's proposal. It passed a progressive tax on income as usually defined (rather than on consumption spending as such), and added to it a second title, a tax on net worth increments at rates substantially lower than on income. Largely due to Davidson, this combination of an income and a net worth increments tax has remained a standard feature in Sweden's tax system since 1910.

CARL G. UHR

SELECTED WORKS

1878. *Bidrag till läran om de ekonomiska lagarna för kapitalbildningen* (A contribution to the theory of capital formation). Uppsala.
1889. *Om beskattningsnormen vid inkomstskatten* (A taxation norm for the income tax). Uppsala.

BIBLIOGRAPHY

Böhm-Bawerk, E. von. 1884. *The Positive Theory of Capital.* Trans. W. Smart, New York: G.E. Stechert & Co., 1930.
Heckscher, E.F. 1952. David Davidson. *International Economic Papers* 2, 111 ff.
Uhr, C.G. 1960. *Economic Doctrines of Knut Wicksell.* Berkeley: University of California Press.
Uhr, C.G. 1975. *Economic Doctrines of David Davidson.* Studia Oeconomica Upsaliensis, Uppsala.

dear money. The obverse of cheap money, 'dear money' is also used to denote episodes in which central banks have raised (short-term) interest rates deliberately to bring about a contraction of money or credit, often in order to preserve a fixed exchange rate. The historical episodes are memorable for their effects on economic activity and on subsequent monetary theory and policy.

The major financial crises of the 19th century were accompanied by the Bank of England's raising of its discount rate (Bank rate) to at least 5% (the maximum permitted under the usury laws until 1833) in order to protect the gold reserve from an internal or external drain. The tradition as it developed after the Bank Charter Act of 1844 was for the Bank to act as a lender of last resort even when that involved an expansion of the fixed fiduciary note issue imposed by the Act, but at a penal rate. Hence Bank rate went to 8% in 1847, 10% in 1857 and again in 1866, 9% in 1873, but only 6% in the Baring crisis of 1890, the smooth handling of which was seen as a success for the Bank's methods (Hawtrey, 1938, chs 1 and 3; Morgan, 1943, chs 7–9; Clapham, 1944, Vol. 2, ch. 6; Sayers, 1976, pp. 1–3). In the early 20th century the events of the crisis of 1907 seemed to confirm the utility of central banks in general and the efficacy of Bank rate in particular. When the American stock exchange boom broke, Bank rate was quickly raised to 7% in response to gold outflows from London. The outflows were swiftly reversed while a banking panic in the US turned into a severe though short-lived slump. The outcome in the US was the establishment of the National Monetary Commission in 1908 and the Federal Reserve System which it recommended, in 1914. In Britain, belief in the power of interest rates to influence economic activity was reinforced, and lasted for a generation (Hawtrey, 1938, pp. 115–18; Friedman and Schwartz, 1963, pp. 156–74; Sayers, 1957, pp. 62–4; Sayers, 1976, pp. 54–60; Keynes, 1930, Vol. I, ch. 13).

After World War I dear money was applied again, vigorously but after some hesitation, in both Britain and America to curb the postwar boom: Bank rate went to 6% in November 1919, 7% in April 1920, the Federal Reserve Bank of New York rediscount rate to 6% in January 1920. In both countries the rises came too late and were too strong: the restocking boom was already breaking and the subsequent slump was severe and (in the UK) prolonged (Friedman and Schwartz, 1963), pp. 221–39; Howson, 1974, and 1975, ch. 2). The Federal System continued to experiment in the 1920s with the use of interest rates to control the domestic economy (Chandler, 1958; Friedman and Schwartz, 1963, ch. 6), but elsewhere, with many countries struggling to return to or maintain the international gold standard, dear money, in the sense of high (short-term) interest rates was frequently and widely used for balance of payments reasons (Clarke, 1967; Moggridge, 1972). It was with considerable relief that countries falling off the gold standard in the 1930s took advantage of their new-found monetary independence to promote cheap money. The revival of monetary policy on both sides of the Atlantic after 1951 did not involve the use of dear money in traditional ways: concern with price stability was initially tempered by the objective of 'full employment' and in Britain at least interest rate rises for the sake of external balance were usually employed only as one element in 'packages' of deflationary measures; by the time the reduction of inflation became an important objective dear money as a target or as an indicator of monetary policy had been replaced by the rate of growth of the money supply (Dow, 1964, ch. 3; OECD, 1974; Blackaby, 1978, chs 5 and 6).

SUSAN HOWSON

See also BANK RATE; CHEAP MONEY.

BIBLIOGRAPHY

Blackaby, F.T. (ed.) 1978. *British Economic Policy 1960–74.* Cambridge: Cambridge University Press.

Chandler, L.V. 1958. *Benjamin Strong: Central Banker.* Washington, DC: Brookings Institution.

Clapham, Sir John. 1944. *The Bank of England.* Cambridge: Cambridge University Press.

Clarke, S.V.O. 1967. *Central Bank Cooperation 1924–31.* New York: Federal Reserve Bank of New York.

Dow, J.C.R. 1964. *The Management of the British Economy 1945–60.* Cambridge: Cambridge University Press.

Friedman, M. and Schwartz, A.J. 1963. *A Monetary History of the United States 1867–1960.* Princeton: Princeton University Press.

Hawtrey, R.G. 1938. *A Century of Bank Rate.* London: Longmans Green & Co.

Howson, S. 1974. The origins of dear money, 1919–20. *Economic History Review* 27(1), February, 88–107.

Howson, S. 1975. *Domestic Monetary Management in Britain 1919–38.* Cambridge: Cambridge University Press.

Keynes, J.M. 1930. *A Treatise on Money.* London: Macmillan for the Royal Economic Society, 1971.

Moggridge, D.E. 1972. *British Monetary Policy 1924–1931.* Cambridge: Cambridge University Press.

Morgan, E.V. 1943. *The Theory and Practice of Central Banking 1797–1913.* Cambridge: Cambridge University Press.

OECD. 1974. *Monetary Policy in the United States.* Paris: OECD.

Sayers, R.S. 1957. *Central Banking After Bagehot.* Oxford: Clarendon Press.

Sayers, R.S. 1976. *The Bank of England 1891–1944.* Cambridge: Cambridge University Press.

death duties. *See* INHERITANCE TAXES.

death processes. *See* BIRTH AND DEATH PROCESSES.

death rate. *See* MORTALITY.

débouchés, théorie des. Generally regarded as the main original contribution of J.B. Say to economic science, this *theory of outlets* or *of vent* affirms that a general glut or general over-production is impossible. If all products could be had for nothing, men would everywhere spring into existence to consume them. Products are bought with other products. Therefore each product is more in demand as other products increase and bid against it. In other words, as the same product constitutes the producer's demand and the consumer's supply, a general excess of supply over the general demand is absurd. Moreover, human desires expand indefinitely. So long as these are unsatisfied there can be no over-production except from lack of purchasing power arising from under-production on the part of the would-be purchasers.

Hence it is concluded that to maximize production is the interest of all; that industry is *solidaire*; and that cosmopolitanism in commerce is true wisdom, imports stimulating the sale of indigenous products. This theory, Say predicted, 'will change the politics of the world' (*Traité*, 5th edn, 1826, I. ciii).

The theory was resisted by Malthus and Sismondi, but was supported by James Mill and Ricardo, whose friendship grew out of this agreement, as we learn from J.S. Mill (*Principles*, 1875 edn, III. xiv). The last-mentioned writer's examination of the theory, though enforcing the strength of the main position, leaves still something to be desired. Arguments are used which take no account of the relativity of demand to price, the imperfection of the world market, or the element of time necessary to create new habits of production or consumption

or to raise up a new generation of consumers. The case is, however, conclusive against those whose view involves the fallacy of a general fall of values, or who mistake the phenomenon of a commercial crisis, in times of contracting credit, for over-production. The remedy, says J.S. Mill, for 'what may be indiscriminately called a glut of commodities or a dearth of money, is not a diminution of supply, but the restoration of confidence'.

[HENRY HIGGS]
Reprinted from *Palgrave's Dictionary of Political Economy.*

See also SAY'S LAW.

debt. *See* INTERNATIONAL INDEBTEDNESS; NATIONAL DEBT; PUBLIC DEBT; RICARDIAN EQUIVALENCE THEOREM.

decentralization. The main question to be answered by the theory of resource allocation, or by the theory of economic organization, concerns the performances of alternative systems characterized by different degrees of centralization of decision taking. A fully centralized system runs the risk of being inefficient because it does not create proper economic incentives and the centre is poorly informed. A pure market system with its high degree of decentralization runs the risk of bringing inequitable results and being inefficient because markets can never be complete, externalities exist and public wants tend to be neglected. Can these risks be avoided within the two opposite extremes of pure centralization or full decentralization? Can intermediate systems better resolve the difficulties? And if so, how?

Basic to the discussion are two features: the nature of the *information* held by various agents, and the *incentives* that should lead them to behave in conformity with collective requirements. These features and the issue of decentralization do not only appear for full economic systems, which this entry will consider, but also for the internal organization of firms or communities. They are stylized in the principal–agent problem: which rules should determine how to share the proceeds of an activity between the principal owner and his better-informed agent? (Ross, 1973; Grossman and Hart, 1983).

For the clarification of the complex issues involved, theory starts from a model of the conditions of economic activity. It makes assumptions such that, independently of economic organization, there exists a best outcome, or at least a set of 'optimal' outcomes. It then asks how well alternative forms of organization succeed in finding, implementing or at least approaching this best outcome or set of optimal outcomes.

By so doing, the theory discussed here neglects two related questions: how to determine what should be considered as 'the best' outcome in a society with many individuals, and which non-economic considerations interfere with the issue of decentralization? The theory of social choice shows the fundamental difficulty of the first question (Arrow, 1951), which is avoided when optimality is identified with Pareto efficiency. As for the second, philosophers may find in human nature or in the aims pursued by human societies reasons that favour some organization, beyond its economic performance; in particular, the right of individuals to autonomy appears fundamental in Western culture and is an important justification of decentralization, and even of the market system for such economists as Hayek (1944).

FORMAL CONCEPTS AND PRELIMINARIES. The following conceptual apparatus, although not yet common, is well suited to the purpose (see Hurwicz, 1960; Mount and Reiter, 1974).

An *economic environment* is defined by a set of commodities and their possible uses, by a list of agents and their characteristics (technology, endowments, preferences etc), and by an initial information structure (what each agent knows). The feasible set of economic environments defines 'the economy'.

An important property of an economy is its higher or lower degree of *decomposability*, which concerns agents' characteristics and the information structure. The highest decomposability is assumed in competitive equilibrium theory, where all consumption is private, no external effect exists and a *private information structure* prevails (each agent perfectly knows its own characteristics and the situation on all markets, but nothing else). But models with public goods, for instance, usually admit some decomposability, which matters for the validity of the results.

An *optimality correspondence* $P : E \to A$ defines which vectors of actions simultaneously taken by the various agents are optimal when the economic environment is e, i.e. optimal vectors belong to $P(e)$ (clearly, E is the set of feasible e, i.e. 'the economy', while A is the set of feasible vectors a, each one of them defining the actions taken by all the agents). For instance $P(e)$ may be the set of Pareto efficient vectors. But in the theory discussed here, it is often more narrowly defined so as to take equity considerations into account: a social utility function may have to be maximized or a rule on the consumers 'income distribution' satisfied.

A *resource allocation mechanism* $f : E \to A$ should select one $a = f(e)$ for each environment e (in some cases f may be multivalued, i.e. become a correspondence). The best formalized mechanism is the competitive equilibrium of a 'private ownership economy'. A study of decentralization requires a careful specification of the mechanism, which is typically viewed as operating in two stages: first, an iterative exchange of messages, usually between the agents and a centre, resulting in a message correspondence $g : E \to M$ (the message $0\ m = g(e)$ specifies what information about e have been collected at the centre), second an outcome function $h : M \to A$. For instance, the competitive mechanism is often specified as resulting from the tâtonnement process in which an auctioneer learns which demands and supplies are announced at various proposed vectors of prices and searches for the equilibrium prices; once these prices are found, the outcome function gives the equilibrium exchanges, hence productions and consumptions.

The performances of alternative mechanisms of course concern the final result: one must know whether the outcome $f(e)$ belongs to the optimal set $P(e)$ for all environments in E, or at least for a precise subset of E, and how close it is to $P(e)$ otherwise. But interesting performances also concern intermediate features of the mechanism, which usually is iterative. At step t the previously collected message m_{t-1} is enriched according to $m_t = g_t(m_{t-1}, e)$ and, if necessary, the process could end by $a = h_t(m_t)$. In a *finite* procedure it does end at T with $m = m_T$ and $h(m) = h_T(m_T)$; but most mechanisms assume an infinite sequence of m_t for $t = 1, 2 \ldots$ ad infinitum. One must then know whether and how $h_t(m_t)$ approaches $P(e)$, monotonically or otherwise. Since the transmission of information is costly, the nature and size of the message space M_t to which m_t belongs are also important characteristics (Mount and Reiter, 1974).

THE PLANNING PROBLEM. Early in this century many economists objected to socialist planning programmes that could not be implemented, because they unrealistically assumed that a central administration could have the knowledge and computing power required for an efficient control of economic activity. The leading figure was L. von Mises (1920 in particular); but Hayek (1935) was first to emphasize the problems raised by the decentralization of information. Socialist economists answered that decentralized mechanisms could operate, either mimicking the market system while being free of its deficiencies (Lange, 1936) or using different well conceived modes of information gathering (Taylor, 1929). The debate was, in the interwar years, the subject of the '*economic theory of socialism*'. (For a well-documented survey, see Bergson, 1948.)

The problem was again taken up during the 1960s, in particular because the logic of efficient planning was discussed in Eastern and Western Europe (Arrow and Hurwicz, 1960; Kornai, 1967; Malinvaud, 1967; Heal, 1973). Many planning procedures were rigorously studied as resource allocation mechanisms. Their definition implied an iterative exchange of information between a Central Planning Board and firms, sometimes also representative consumers. The additional messages provided by the function g_t at step t then consisted of *prospective indices* announced by the Board, for instance prices for the various commodities, and replies called *proposals* sent to the Board by firms and other agents, for instance preferred techniques of production and their input requirements, or supplies and demands.

In this discussion it is common to distinguish between price-guided procedures, in which the Board announces price vectors, and other procedures, in which quantity indices or targets worked out at the centre play a more or less important role. The nature and properties of the environment are then found to be crucial for the determination of the relative performances of alternative procedures, in particular of price-guided against quantity-guided procedures (Weitzman, 1974).

The analytical study of various procedures usually assumes that decentralized agents exactly follow specified rules for the determination of their proposals and so faithfully reveal part of their private information. Some procedures are then found to be efficient and to permit achievement of distributive objectives. But efficiency is typically easier precisely in those environments that are also favourable to the efficiency of free competition. Besides the possibility of incorrect reporting, the main difficulty concerning the relevance of this literature is to know whether its models provide an approximate representation of procedures that are actually used, or at least administratively feasible. Manove (1976) has made this claim for his representation of Soviet planning.

THE PUBLIC GOOD PROBLEM. The most relevant field of application may very well be the theory of public goods. Decisions concerning the provision of public services and their financing cannot be fully decentralized; but the knowledge required is dispersed and must be gathered in a proper way. Hence even the positive theory of public goods was often formulated along lines that look like those of planning procedures (Malinvaud, 1971). The same remark applies to decisions concerning public projects with large fixed costs, even if their output is privately consumed.

Considered as a planning procedure, the search for the best decision is often viewed as involving 'prospective indices' that define amounts of service to be provided, ask for corresponding individual marginal utilities and look whether the sum of the latter would cover the cost of additional service. This is compatible with the dual arrangement for private goods, prices being announced, supplies and demands being the replies. The procedure is then quantity-guided for public goods and price-guided for private goods (Drèze and Vallée Poussin, 1971).

The collective consumption of many types of public goods is not really national but limited to local communities (primary education, city transports etc.). Administrative science sees the decentralization issue as being to know at which level should decisions be taken: at the national level, so as to distribute fairly these services among communities, or at the local level, so as to permit better adaptation to local needs and wishes. Economists do not seem to have contributed to this issue; their discussion of local public goods assumes full administrative decentralization (Tiebout, 1956).

INCENTIVE COMPATIBILITY. The study of a decentralized system has to consider whether the actual reports and behaviour of individual agents do not deviate from what they are supposed to report and do; in case of deviations, how are the performances of the system affected? The problem is serious: once the rules of organization and decisions are known, individual agents may benefit from misreporting their private information or from behaving in a way that, although deviant, does not clearly appear to be so. In other words, they may act as players in a game, rather than as members of a team, and this may be more or less detrimental for the optimality of the final result.

The problem has long been known for organizations in which some agents do not individually benefit from what is achieved and therefore lack the incentive to do their best. Monopolistic or other non-competitive behaviour is often interpreted as a breach of the normal rules of resource allocation. In the theory of public good the 'free rider problem' occurs as soon as some individuals, having a high marginal utility for the public good, would benefit from hiding this fact so as to contribute little to the financing of the good.

Study of the problem has been active during the past two decades (Green and Laffont, 1979). The fundamental difficulty has been exhibited by such results as the following one: in the classical model of an exchange economy with a finite number of consumers, no procedure can be found that would necessarily lead to a Pareto efficient result in which individuals, acting as players in a non-cooperative game, would faithfully report (Hurwicz, 1972). However, misreporting may not prevent a procedure from eventually leading to an optimum, as was proved in a number of cases.

Experiments moreover show that the game-theoretic approach to the incentive problem may be misleading because it neglects non-economic motivations that individuals may find for accepting a team-like behaviour and therefore for faithfully reporting (Smith, 1980).

E. MALINVAUD

See also MARKET SOCIALISM; PLANNED ECONOMY; PLANNING.

BIBLIOGRAPHY

Arrow, K. 1951. *Social Choice and Individual Values.* New York: Wiley.
Arrow, K. and Hurwicz, L. 1960. Decentralization and computation in resource allocation. In *Essays in Economics and Econometrics in Honour of Harold Hotelling,* ed. R. Pfouts, Chapel Hill: University of North Carolina Press.
Bergson, A. 1948. Socialist economics. In *A Survey of Contemporary Economics,* ed. H. Ellis, Philadelphia: Blakiston.
Drèze, J. and Vallée Poussin, D. de la. 1971. A tâtonnement process for public goods. *Review of Economic Studies* 38, 133–50.
Green, J. and Laffont, J.-J. 1979. *Incentives in Public Decision-Making.* Amsterdam: North-Holland.
Grossman, S. and Hart, O. 1983. An analysis of the principal-agent problem. *Econometrica* 51(1), January, 7–45.
Hayek, F. 1935. Socialist calculation: the state of the debate. In *Collectivist Economic Planning,* ed. F. Hayek, London: G. Routledge & Sons.
Hayek, F. 1944. *The Road to Serfdom.* Chicago: University of Chicago Press.
Heal, G. 1973. *The Theory of Economic Planning.* Amsterdam: North-Holland.
Hurwicz, L. 1960. Optimality and information efficiency in resource allocation processes. In *Mathematical Methods in the Social Sciences,* ed. K.J. Arrow, S. Karlin and P. Suppes, Stanford: Stanford University Press.
Hurwicz, L. 1972. On informationally decentralized systems. In *Decision and Organization,* ed. R. Radner and C. McGuire, Amsterdam: North-Holland.
Kornai, J. 1967. *Mathematical Planning of Structural Decisions.* Amsterdam: North-Holland.
Lange, O. 1936. On the economic theory of socialism. *Review of Economic Studies* 4, 53–71, 123–42.
Malinvaud, E. 1967. Decentralized procedures for planning. In Malinvaud, E. and Bacharach, M., *Activity Analysis in the Theory of Growth and Planning,* Macmillan: London.
Malinvaud, E. 1971. A planning approach to the public good problem. *Swedish Journal of Economics,* 11, 96–112.
Manove, M. 1976. Soviet pricing, profit and technological choice. *Review of Economic Studies* 43(3), October, 413–21.
Mises, L. von. 1920. Economic calculation in the socialist commonwealth. First published in German in *Archiv für Sozialwissenshaft,* April; English translation in *Collectivist Economic Planning,* ed. F. Hayek, London: G. Routledge & Sons, 1935.
Mount, K. and Reiter, S. 1974. The informational size of message spaces. *Journal of Economic Theory* 8(2), June, 161–92.
Ross, S. 1973. The economic theory of agency: the principal's problem. *American Economic Review* 63(2), May, 134–9.
Smith, V. 1980. Experiments with a decentralized mechanism for public good decisions. *American Economic Review* 70(4), September, 584–99.
Taylor, F.M. 1929. The guidance of production in a socialist state. *American Economic Review* 19, March, 1–8.
Tiebout, C.M. 1956. A pure theory of local expenditures. *Journal of Political Economy* 64, October, 416–24.
Weitzman, M. 1974. Prices versus quantities. *Review of Economic Studies* 41(4), October, 477–91.

decision theory. To decide is to choose from sets of alternatives. Decision theory is concerned with *rationality* in choice.

1. An individual faces a set of alternatives, C. Over the set of alternatives, the individual has preferences described by a binary relation R: c is preferred or indifferent to (at least as good as) c' if and only if cRc'. The following postulate then characterizes rationality.

Postulate: The preference relation R is complete and transitive.

If cRc' and $c''Rc'$, $c''Rc$; for any c' and c, either $c'Rc$ or cRc'. Rationality in this simple framework is thus a consistency requirement.

From $A \subseteq C$ the individual chooses $d(A) \subseteq A$, not necessarily a singleton, the set of elements of A which are maximal for R: $d(A) = \{c \in A : cRc'$ for all $c' \in A\}$; the definition of the choice correspondence d is sometimes considered an additional aspect of rationality.

Note as an example that, if C is the consumption set, R is the individual's preference relation over commodity bundles, prices and income generate budget sets A, and d is the demand correspondence.

We are often interested in the following aspects:

Representability: A function u defined on the set of alternatives C represents the preference relations on R, if $u(c) \geqslant u(c')$ if and only if cRc'. When such a function exists, it is the objective function of the individual; in the special case of the consumer, it is referred to as the utility function. Note that if a function u represents the relation R, so does any monotonically increasing transformation of u; the representation is thus ordinal. The classical theorem on representability is due to Debreu (1954): A transitive and complete preference relation R on a set C is representable by a (continuous) objective function as long as the set of alternatives C is a connected, separable topological space, and the relation R is continuous: for all $c \in C$, the sets $\{c' \in C: c'Rc\}$ and $\{c' \in C: cRc'\}$ are closed. Debreu also gave an example of a relation which fails to be representable: Let C be the non-negative orthant of two-dimensional Euclidean space, and let the relation R be defined as follows: $c = (c_1, c_2)$ $Rc' = (c_1', c_2')$ if $c_1 > c_1'$ or $(c_1 = c_1'$ and $c_2 > c_2')$; this is known as the lexicographic relation. A straight-forward argument shows that the representability of R (not necessarily by a continuous function) would imply that the set of real numbers is countable, a contradiction. Representability is thus a strictly stronger requirement than rationality. Beyond representability and rationality, one may investigate the correspondence between qualitive properties of the relation R and the functional form of some representation u. Additive separability turns out to be of interest, as we shall see when we impose more structure; and the main result is due again to Debreu (1959): Let $N = \{1, \ldots, n\}$, $n > 2$, and let $C = \Pi_{j \in N} C_j$ be a connected and separable topological space. A transitive, complete and continuous relation R on C has an additively separable representation $u(c) = \Sigma_{j \in N} u_j(c_j)$ if and only if for every $J \subseteq N$ and $c_J = (c_j)_{j \in J}$ the induced relation R_{c_J} on $C_{N/J} = \Pi_{j \in N/J} C_j$ is independent of c_J, and at least three factors $j \in N$ are essential: a factor $j \in N$ is essential if not all elements of $C_{N/j}$ are mutually (preferred or) indifferent under the induced relation R_j. The case of only two essential factors can be treated separately.

Observability and recoverability: The preference relation R is an unobservable characteristic of the individual. What is, in principle at least, observable is the choice correspondence d on a class A of subsets of C. Samuelson (1938) first, in the context of consumer theory, gave a definition of rationality in terms of the observable characteristics of the consumer. Elaborating on Samuelson, Richter (1966) defined a consumption bundle, c, to be directly revealed preferred to another bundle, c', cVc', if, for some budget set A, $c \in d(A)$ while $c' \in A$. A bundle c is indirectly revealed preferred to another, c', cWc', if there exists a finite sequence of bundles, $c^1, \ldots, c^n$, such that $c = c^1 Vc^2, \ldots, Vc^{n-1} Vc^n = c'$, The consumer is congruous if, for all $c, c' \in C$ and all budget sets A, whenever $c \in d(A)$, $c' \in A$ and $c'Wc$, $c' \in d(A)$. Richter proceeded to show that congruence, which characterizes the observable choice correspondence, is equivalent to the earlier definition of rationality: A consumer satisfies the congruence axiom if and only if he is rational. Sen (1971) extended the argument beyond consumer theory, to general choice situations. Closely related to observability is the issue of recoverability. Even when the choice correspondence is known to be generated from the maximization of some underlying complete and transitive preference relation, knowledge of d need not suffice to identify unambiguously and recover R; the generating binary relation need not be unique. Mas-Colell (1977), in the context of consumer theory, showed that recoverability is indeed possible under mild regularity assumptions. Questions of prediction require recoverability based on the observation of the choice correspondence on a restricted domain, for which further qualitative assumptions on the underlying binary relation are necessary.

Existence and computability: For an arbitrary $A \subseteq C$ no maximal element for the relation R needs to exist. The choice correspondence is then defined on a restricted class A of subsets of the set of alternatives. Even if maximal elements can be shown to exist for $A \subseteq C$, there remains the issue of computability.

2. Under uncertainty, the objects of choice are not what ultimately determines the welfare of the individual. We follow the formalization of Savage (1954). States of the world are $s \in S$; a state of the world is an exhaustive and exclusive description of the environment. Consequences are $c \in C$; a consequence is what ultimately determines the welfare of the individual. Acts are $f \in F$, an act is a function $f: S \to C$, which associates consequences to states. The set F is the set of all possible acts; elements of the set F are the objects of choice of the individual. An event is a subset $B \subseteq S$: an event is said to occur if it contains the true or actual state of the world; for an event B, its complement is $\bar{B} = S/B$. Certainty is the limiting case in which S is a singleton and the sets of acts, F, and of consequences, C, coincide.

A series of postulates which characterize rationality under uncertainty imply that the individual's preferences over acts, described by the preference relation R, have an expected utility representation $E_p u$, where E is the expectation operator, p is a probability measure on the set of states of the world S, and u is a cardinal utility index on the set of consequences C, unique up to monotonically increasing, linear transformations. Note that the existence of such a probability measure is not taken for granted.

Postulate (i): The preference relation R over acts is transitive and complete.

This is the exact analogue of the postulate of rationality under certainty. Thus, under the additional technical assumptions of the representation theorem of Debreu (1954), the preference relation R is representable by an objective function $v: v(f) \geqslant v(f')$ if and only if fRf'.

The set of consequences C can be identified with the subset of constant acts, the acts which yield the same consequence at all states. It follows that implicit in the preference relation over acts is a preference relation over consequences.

Postulate (ii): For facts f, f', g and g' and an event B, of $f = f'$ and $g = g'$ on B, while $f = g$ and $f' = g'$ on $\bar{B}$, fRg if and only if $f'Rg'$.

Preferences over acts do not depend on the consequences they yield on states at which their consequences coincide; this is known as the sure thing principle and it corresponds, when probabilistic beliefs are taken as given, to the strong independence axiom. The sure thing principle guarantees the additive separability of the objective function across states; up to technical conditions, additive separability follows from the theorem of Debreu (1959) on additively separable representations. The sure thing principle is tenable as an aspect of rationality as long as states are exhaustive and exclusive descriptions of the environment. It has been challenged, however, on the ground that it is frequently violated in experimental set ups. The most famous such refutation is due to Allais (1953): Let $S = \{s^1, s^2, s^3\}$ and $C = [0, \infty)$, and consider the following acts:

$$f = \begin{bmatrix} s^1 \to 1 \\ s^2 \to 1 \\ s^3 \to 1 \end{bmatrix}; \quad g = \begin{bmatrix} s^1 \to 0 \\ s^2 \to 5 \\ s^3 \to 1 \end{bmatrix}; \quad f' = \begin{bmatrix} s^1 \to 0 \\ s^2 \to 1 \\ s^3 \to 0 \end{bmatrix}; \quad g' = \begin{bmatrix} s^1 \to 0 \\ s^2 \to 5 \\ s^3 \to 0 \end{bmatrix}.$$

According to the sure thing principle $(B = \{s_1, s_2\}, \sim B = \{s_3\})$ fRg if and only if $f'Rg'$. It is most often the case, however, that with payoffs (consequences) dominated in units of $1,000,000$ and the probability of occurrence of the states known to be $(0.01, 0.1, 0.89)$, individuals state their preferences as fRg and $g'Rf'$. Machina (1982) has argued that the sure thing principle can be understood as characteristic of an approximation to a general preference relation.

With postulate (ii), conditional preferences are well defined: For an event B, fR_Bg if and only if there exist acts f' and g' such that $f'Rg'$ and f coincides with g on B while, on B, f' coincides with g'. Knowledge of the restriction of f and g on B determines unambiguously the individual's preferences between f and g conditional on B; it suffices to complete f_B and g_B so that they coincide on B.

An event B is null if and only if fR_Bg for any acts f, $g \in F$.

Postulate (iii): For any constant acts f and g and any non-null event B, fR_Bg if and only if fRg.

This excludes state-dependent preferences. For any s, $s' \in S$ the representations v_s and $v_{s'}$ of the conditional preferences R_s and $R_{s'}$ must be ordinally equivalent. It may seem that one can introduce state dependence by replacing the set of consequences C by the product $C^* = C \times S$; this allows for state dependence since states of the world are now part of the specification of the consequences of an act. This may, however, be just empty formalism; the construction would oblige the individual to contemplate acts assigning to, say, states s the consequence (c, s'), while s and s' are mutually exclusive states of the world. For postulate (iii) to be tenable it is necessary to keep clear the distinction between acts and consequences.

Postulate (iv): For consequences c, c', d and $d' \in C$, acts f, f', g and $g' \in$, and events A and B

$$c'Rc, f = \begin{bmatrix} c \text{ on } A \\ c' \text{ on } \sim A \end{bmatrix}, \quad g = \begin{bmatrix} c \text{ on } B \\ c' \text{ on } \sim B \end{bmatrix}$$

and

$$d'Rd, f' = \begin{bmatrix} d \text{ on } A \\ d' \text{ on } \sim A \end{bmatrix}, \quad g' = \begin{bmatrix} d \text{ on } B \\ d' \text{ on } \sim B \end{bmatrix}$$

then fRg if and only if $f'Rg'$.

The individual has consistent probability beliefs. In addition to yielding a probability measure on the set of states, S, postulate (iv) will imply that the conditional objective functions v_s, $s \in S$, are not simply ordinally equivalent, but differ only by a monotonically increasing linear transformation; $v_s = p_s u$.

With postulate (iv), it makes sense to speak of one event B being at least as probable as another event $B': BR^*B'$ if there exist acts f and g and consequences c and c' such that

$$cRc', f = \begin{bmatrix} c \text{ on } B \\ c' \text{ on } \sim B \end{bmatrix}, \quad g = \begin{bmatrix} c \text{ on } B' \\ c' \text{ on } \sim B' \end{bmatrix}$$

and gRf.

Postulate (v): There exists at least a pair of consequences c and c' such that cRc' but not $c'Rc$.

This is simply to avoid the case of a preference relation which leaves the individual indifferent between any two acts. Such a preference relation could not be used to elicit the individual's probability beliefs which, by definition, must assign higher probability to some events than others.

We now proceed to outline the argument first for the derivation of a probability measure and then for the expected utility representation.

It is straightforward to check that the binary relation R^* over events is indeed a qualitative probability; that is, a complete and transitive relation which in addition satisfies the conditions that BR^*B' if and only if $(B \cup B'')R^*(B' \cup B'')$ whenever $(B \cap B'') = \phi$, $BR^*\phi$, and $SR^*\phi$ but not ϕR^*S. A probability measure p on S is a positive function such that $p(B \cup B') = p(B) + p(B)$ whenever $B \cap B' = \phi$ and $p(S) = 1$. If S carries a probability measure p and a qualitative probability R^* such that $p(B) \geqslant p(B')$ if and only if BR^*B, p agrees with (represents) R^*. Even for finite S, however, there exist qualitative probabilities for which no agreeing probability measure can be found. A probability measure p which agrees with R^* exists as long as an additional continuity condition is satisfied. We shall assume that this condition holds; thus p exists and is unique. Note that the definition of probability requires finite and not countable additivity; thus we avoid the need to specify the σ-field on which the measure is defined. The continuity assumption which we employ to guarantee that a probability measure exists implies that this probability measure satisfies a certain non-atomicity property; it excludes finite and even countable state spaces; to relax the condition is, however, cumbersome. Finally, observe that the representation of qualitative probability by a probability measure extends to conditional probability; indeed, we obtain Bayes' rule for every non-null event $B': p(B') = p(B \cap B')$.

With the probability measure p on S, every action $f \in F$ induces a probability measure μ_f on the set of consequences C: for $A \subseteq C$, $\mu_f(A) = p\{s \in S: f(s) \in A\}$. A probability measure is simple if it has finite support: acts which induce simple measures are gambles. Let M^* be the subset of the set M of all probability measures on C of simple measures. Observe that M^* is a mixture set: to each $\alpha \in [0, 1]$ and each pair of elements μ, $\mu' \in M^*$ there corresponds unambiguously an element $\alpha\mu + (1 - \alpha)\mu'$ such that $1\mu + 0\mu' = \mu$, $\alpha\mu + (1 - \alpha)\mu' = (1 - \alpha)\mu' + \alpha\mu$ and $\alpha[\alpha'\mu + (1 - \alpha')\mu'] + (1 - \alpha)\mu' = \alpha\alpha'\mu + (1 - \alpha\alpha')\mu'$. It follows from the postulates, and this is the key step in the construction, that acts are evaluated by the individual only with respect to the measures which they induce on the set of preferences. Equivalently, the preference relation R on F induces unambiguously a complete and transitive binary relation on M^*, which we also denote by $R: \mu R\mu'$ if $\mu = \mu_f$, $\mu' = \mu_f$, and fRf'. Furthermore, for μ, μ', $\mu'' \in M^*$ and $\alpha \in [0, 1]$, $\mu R\mu'$ if and only if $[\alpha\mu + (1 - \alpha)\mu'']R[\alpha\mu' + (1 - \alpha)\mu'']$, while for μ, μ', $\mu'' \in M^*$ with $\mu R\mu' R\mu''$, there exists a unique $\alpha(\mu'; \mu, \mu'') \in [0, 1]$ such that $[\alpha\mu + (1 - \alpha)\mu'']R\mu'$ and $\mu' R[\alpha\mu + (1 - \alpha)\mu'']$. The cardinal utility index u on C such that, restricted to the subset $F^* \subseteq F$ of gambles, $v = E_p u$ is constructed as follows: For a given pair of consequences $\bar{c}$ and $\underline{c}$ with $\bar{c}R\underline{c}$, let $u(\bar{c}) = 1$, $u(\underline{c}) = 0$; for c such that $cRcR\underline{c}$, let $u(c) = \alpha(\mu_c; u_{\bar{c}}, u_{\underline{c}})$; the extension of u to all of C is straightforward. Evidently, the cardinal utility index is unique up to monotonically increasing linear transformations. Under additional technical restrictions which involve the boundedness of the cardinal utility index (or, equivalently, the continuity of the preference relation with respect to the appropriate topology on the set of probability measures over consequences) the expected utility representation can be extended to acts which are not necessarily gambles. The Savage postulates do not allow for state dependence of the cardinal utility index u. Additional structure is required, as in Dreze (1984), for state dependence to be introduced and for probability beliefs to be distinguished from state dependence.

3. Choice may occur *sequentially*. We revert to a framework of certainty. The set of alternatives over which the individual has preferences and among which he chooses is C: for simplicity, we take it to be finite. The individual is characterized by his preference relation R and C, which is transitive and complete. Let $\mathcal{C}$ be the power set of all subsets, A, of C. The preference relation R on C induces unambiguously a preference relation $\bar{R}$ on $\mathcal{C}$, which inherits its transitivity and completeness: $A\bar{R}A'$ if and only if cRc' for some $c \in A$ and all $c' \in A'$. Note that the definition of $\bar{R}$ embodies the principle of backward induction: Faced with the choice between sets of alternatives A and A', the individual prefers A if a subsequent choice among the elements of A is at least as good as any possible choice among the elements of A'.

The problem of (time) *consistency* arises, as Strotz (1955–56) has noticed, when the individual's preferences over C change between the point at which he chooses among sets of alternatives and the subsequent point at which he chooses among alternatives in the set he chose earlier: Let R^2 be the final preference relation over C and let R^1 be the preference relation over C when he chooses over C. Two preference relations on C can be induced by the pair (R^1, R^2). The naive preference: $AR^N A'$ if and only if cRc' for some $c \in A$ and all $c' \in A'$; in this case the individual ignores the subsequent change of preferences which he may be able to foresee. The sophisticated preference: $AR^S A'$ if and only if cR^1c' for some $c \in A$ and some $c' \in A'$ such that cR^2c'' and $c'R^2c''$ for all $c''' \in A$ and all $c''' \in A'$, respectively; in this case, the individual foresees his subsequent change of preferences and attempts to commit himself to the extent that the choice out of A which will be made according to R^2 is as good as possible according to the current ranking, R^1. Again, the use of backward induction is evident. The individual is consistent if R^1 and R^2 and hence R^N and R^S coincide.

The resolution of uncertainty may occur sequentially. States of the world, acts, and consequences are as before. The individual's preferences over acts are represented by the objective function v. Let S be a partition of S. For $S^0 \in S$, let F^0 be the set of all acts $f^0 : S^0 \to C$. The question follows whether there exists an objective function on F^0 which is naturally induced by v. When the objective function v has an expected utility representation, the answer is straightforward: it suffices to replace the probability measure p by the conditional probability measure $p^0 = p | S^0$, thus obtaining $v^0 = E_{p^0}u$. Formally, the domain of v^0 is F, not F^0; yet no ambiguity arises, since, for any act $f \in Fv^0(f)$ depends only on the restriction of f to S^0. Suppose C and hence F are well as linear spaces (addition and scalar multiplication are well defined). If the individual has taken act $\bar{f} \in F$ before S^0 is realized, he ranks elements $f^0 \in F^0$ according to $v^0(\bar{f} + f_0)$, where f_0 is the unambiguous extension of f^0 to F which takes the value zero on S/S^0. When the objective function v does not have an expected utility representation, the argument breaks down. It is formally possible to ignore the resolution of uncertainty and rank acts $f^0 \in F^0$ according to $v^0(\bar{f} + f_0) = v(\bar{f} + f_0)$. But this is contrived: it amounts to considering as 'occurring' states of the world $s \in S/S^0$ when they are known not to have occurred.

4. We have concentrated on individual behaviour. Alternatively, it may be only aggregate behaviour which is observable or of interest. Suppose that the set of alternatives is a linear space: Let $h = 1, \ldots, H$ be a collection of individuals, and let $Q = (\ldots, Q^h, \ldots)$ be a distribution scheme: to any subset $A \subseteq C$ in a class **A**, it assigns a vector of subsets $(\ldots, A^h \subseteq C, \ldots)$ such that $A^1 + \cdots + A^h + \cdots \, A^H = A$. Let d be the aggregate choice correspondence restricted to **A**. Two questions follow: Under what conditions do there exist individual preference relations $R^1, \ldots, R^h, \ldots, R^H$ such that the aggregate correspondence coincide with d? Note that the question is well posed only with reference to a distribution scheme Q. Alternatively, under what conditions on the individual preference relations $R^1, \ldots, R^h, \ldots, R^H$ and the distribution scheme Q can the aggregate choice correspondence be derived from the optimization of a representative preference relation? In the context of consumer theory both questions have been studied extensively. Sonnenschein (1972) first suggested that as long as the number of individuals is large relative to the number of commodities, the income distribution scheme is derived from an arbitrary but fixed distribution of initial endowments, and only the excess demand of individuals is observed as prices vary, homogeneity with respect to prices and the budget constraint (Walras' Law) are the only constraints which aggregate behaviour must display; individual rationality fails to have observable implications in the aggregate. Alternatively, as Gorman (1953) has shown, if individual preferences are identical and homothetic (cRc' if and only if $(\lambda c)R(\lambda c' M)$, $\lambda > 0$) as well, the aggregate behaves like a single, rational individual. Note that a qualitative restriction on the preference relation is employed for individual rationality to have observable implications in the aggregate.

5. Throughout, the alternative which obtained was determined unambiguously by the decision of the individual and the resolution of exogenous uncertainty. We have ignored issues of feasibility, equilibrium and strategy.

H.M. Polemarchakis

See also ARROW-DEBREU MODEL; EXCHANGE; ORGANIZATION THEORY; STATISTICAL DECISION THEORY; UNCERTAINTY.

BIBLIOGRAPHY

Allais, M. 1953. Le comportement de l'homme rationel devant le risque; critique des postulats et axiomes de l'école Americaine. *Econometrica* 21, 503–46.

Debreu, G. 1954. Representation of a preference ordering by a numerical function. In *Decision Processes*, ed. R.M. Thrall, C.H. Coombs and R.L. Davis, New York: Wiley, 159–65.

Debreu, G. 1959. Topological methods in cardinal utility. In *Mathematical Methods in the Social Sciences*, ed. K.J. Arrow, S. Karlin and P. Suppes, Stanford: Stanford University Press, 16–26.

Gorman, W.M. 1953. Community preference fields. *Econometrica* 21(1), 63–80.

Green, J.R., Lau, L.J. and Polemarchakis, H.M. 1979. Identifiability of the von Neumann–Morgenstern utility function from asset demands. In *General Equilibrium, Growth and Trade*, ed. J.R. Green and J. Scheinkman, New York: Academic Press.

Machina, M. 1982. 'Expected utility' analysis without the independence axiom. *Econometrica* 50(2), 277–323.

Mas-Colell, A. 1977. The recoverability of consumers' preferences from market demand functions. *Econometrica* 45(6), 1409–30.

Richter, M.K. 1966. Revealed preference theory. *Econometrica* 34(3), 635–45.

Samuelson, P.A. 1938. A note on the pure theory of consumers' behaviour. *Economica* 5(1), 61–71.

Savage, L.J. 1954. *The Foundations of Statistics*. New York: John Wiley & Sons.

Sen, A.K. 1971. Choice functions and revealed preference. *Review of Economic Studies* 38(2), 307–17.

Sonnenschein, H. 1972. Market excess demand functions. *Econometrica* 40(3), 549–63.

Strotz, R.H. 1955–56. Myopia and inconsistency in dynamic utility maximization. *Review of Economic Studies* 23(3), 165–80.

declining industries. Logically, there are two meanings to the term declining industries. Industries can decline because their products have been replaced by new and better products, or industries can decline because what used to be most cheaply produced in country A is now most cheaply produced in country B and exported to country A. In the first case, the word processor replaces the typewriter. In the second case, steel production moves from the United States to Brazil and American needs are met with imports from Brazil.

In economic discussions the term declining industries is almost always used in conjunction with the shift of industries from one country to another. This occurs because there is little public controversy about the first type of decline and much public controversy about the second.

With a shift from one product to another it is immediately obvious to everyone that to prevent such declines is to hold one's standard of living below where it otherwise would be.

New products and the better jobs that go with them have to be held back to maintain a market for old products and old jobs. To do so is to retard progress and no one seriously proposes such actions.

It is equally true that to prevent the second type of decline is to hold one's standard of living below where it might otherwise be, but this conclusion is not as immediately obvious. Everyone can see in the first type of decline that additional new jobs serve as a counterbalance to the loss of old jobs and that the consumer get a better product. In the second type of decline the lost jobs are politically visible at home and the new jobs are politically invisible abroad. The home gain in real income comes via lower costs for consumers who replace expensive domestic products with cheap foreign products.

Most often the producers who lose their jobs suffer large immediate reductions in their incomes but are small in number, while the consumers are large in number but reap only small gains in their real incomes. The aggregate gains exceed the aggregate loss but the losses are highly visible while the gains are so small on a per capita basis as to be almost invisible politically. Combine this with a world where producer interests almost always have more political clout than consumer interests, and you have the political ingredients for policies to protect declining industries despite the fact that a country lowers its rate of growth by so doing.

Almost all countries protect their declining industries to some extent. Steel, for example, benefits from various forms of protection in Europe, the United States and Japan since none of them is today the low cost producer for basic steel products. The more extensive the protection, however, the more harm a country does to its economic future.

The pattern of events is well known. Given protection in the home market, cheap foreign producers first drive the home industry out of its unprotected export markets. After World War II, the American steel industry first lost its export markets. Without those export markets home production falls. The home producers of unsophisticated metal products then find that they cannot compete against foreign producers who can buy cheap foreign steel while they have to buy expensive domestic steel. Products such as nails and wire start to be produced abroad and imported into the United States. Home production again falls. Eventually, foreign producers of sophisticated metal-using products such as cars find that their lower cost of materials is one of their advantages in competing against the American auto industry with its high material costs. The steel that is not exported as steel is exported as cars. As the case of steel indicates, protection can serve to slow down the rate of decline, but it is almost never possible to stop it.

To protect a declining industry is to weaken related industries and set in motion spreading waves of decline and protection. As a result, protecting declining industries is much like poking a balloon: for every successful indentation there is an equal expansion somewhere else.

While it is clear that a country should not seek to delay declines in industries where comparative advantage has shifted abroad, it is often not clear as to whether comparative advantage really has shifted. This occurs since currency values have not moved smoothly to maintain national balances between exports and imports as they should have done if they had operated as expected from textbook models. They have often in the past 15 years given very misleading signals – and very rapidly changing signals – as to where a country's real comparative advantage lies.

Thus in February 1985 the value of the dollar was so high that foreign wheat could be sold for less in the United States than American wheat; yet it is clear that the United States still has a comparative advantage in the production of wheat. It just does not seem to be so because of the temporarily high value of the dollar and the markets, such as the Common Market, that have rules and regulations essentially closing them to American exports.

Since the transition costs of closing an industry when the value of the dollar is high and reopening the industry when the dollar falls are very large, it may not make sense to allow the market to operate as it would without government interference. The question then becomes one of whether the right solution is protection or subsidies for the affected domestic industries, or international actions to moderate the movements between major currencies and to open closed foreign markets. Given that protection once in place is difficult to remove politically, international actions to moderate currency movements and open markets would seem to be the preferable solution.

When one analyses a declining industry, one seldom finds an industry in total decline without competitively viable parts. In the steel industry, for example, there are parts – mini-steel mills using electric furnaces and low cost scrap iron, speciality high-tech alloy steels – that could be competitively operated in the United States given a value of the dollar that would balance exports and imports. To say that an industry is a declining industry is not to say that it will disappear.

A declining industry also need not lead to declining firms. While it is certainly true that modern industrial economies need less steel per unit of GNP produced, it is also true that there is a new growing high-tech industry in new materials – powdered metals, composites, pressed graphite – that is the new steel industry of tomorrow. Today's declining steel firms could be tomorrow's expanding new material firms. But most often they are not.

If one asks why not, it is clear that firms find it very difficult to develop new products that will destroy large old markets that they dominate. The firm has a large vested interest in the old markets and entrenched forces within the firm make it very difficult for it to move into these new areas quickly. Thus IBM, the dominant force in the office typewriter business, was slow to develop a word processor despite the fact that it was the world's leader in computers. At General Electric, the dominant vacuum tube division sat on the transistor and prevented General Electric from becoming a leader in transistors. The classic example is of course the railroads, which saw themselves as railroads rather than as transportation companies.

While decline is the flip side of progress, real costs are involved. Most of these costs come in the form of human resources that are not easily transferred to new areas. An unemployed 55-year-old Pennsylvania steel worker is not apt to be retrained to be a California computer assembler. Such an individual faces a large cut in expected income over the remainder of his working life and society may well find itself burdened with higher social welfare costs.

Economic theory has little to say about these transition problems and costs since it assumes that mobility is easy and that transition costs either do not exist or are very marginal. With its concept of equilibrium, wage workers forced out of work in old industries quickly find jobs in new industries with closely comparable wages. In contrast, those who have actually followed workers forced out of work in declining industries in the United States find that most of them find work only with a long time lag and then only with much lower wages. The losses in real incomes are not the marginal ones assumed by economic theory.

As a result there is a real issue in how a nation manages decline. A nation cannot and should not prevent declining industries from shrinking, but it still has to fact the issue of how it manages the transition of human resources from old sunset industries to new sunrise industries and what it does about those human resources that are essentially junked in the transition.

LESTER C. THUROW

See also MANUFACTURING AND DEINDUSTRIALIZATION; VERDOORN'S LAW.

BIBLIOGRAPHY

Borrus, M., Millstein, J. and Zysman, J. 1982. U.S. Japanese competition in the semiconductor industry. *Policy Papers in International Affairs*, No. 17, Berkeley: Institute of International Studies, University of California.

Eckstein, O., Caton, C., Brinner, R. and Duprey, P. 1984. *The DRI Report on U.S. Manufacturing Industries*. New York: McGraw-Hill.

Hatsopoulos, G.N. 1983. *High Cost of Capital: Handicap of American Industry*. Waltham, Mass.: American Business Conference, Thermo Electron Corp.

Konaga, K. 1983. Industrial policy: the Japanese version of a universal trend. *Journal of Japanese Trade and Industry* 4, 21f.

Krist, W.K. 1984. The U.S. response to foreign industrial policies. In *High Technology Public Policies for the 1980s*, Washington, DC: a National Journal Issues Book.

Krugman, P. 1984. The United States response to foreign industrial targeting. *Brookings Papers on Economic Activity* (1), 77–121.

Labor-Industry Coalition for International Trade. 1983. *International Trade, Industrial Policies, and the Future of American Industry*. Washington, DC: Labor-Industry Coalition for International Trade, 40f.

Lawrence, R.A. 1984. *Can America Compete?* Washington, DC: Brookings.

Magaziner, I. 1983. New policies for wealth creation in the United States. In *Growth with Fairness*, Institute on Taxation and Economic Policy.

McKenna, R., Borrus, M. and Cohen, S. 1984. Industrial policy and international competition in high technology – Part I: Blocking capital formation. *California Management Review* 26(6), Winter, 15–32.

Melman, S. 1984. The high-tech dream won't come true. *INC Magazine*, August.

Office of Technology Assessment. 1981. *US Industrial Competitiveness: A Comparison of Steel, Electronics and Automobiles*. Washington, DC: Congress of the US, Office of Technology Assessment.

Phillips, K. 1984. *Staying on Top: The Business Case for a National Industrial Strategy*. New York: Random House.

Piore, M.J. 1982. American labor and the industrial crisis. *Challenge* 25, March–April, 5–11.

Reich, R.B. 1982. Why the United States needs an industrial policy. *Harvard Business Review* 60(1), January, 74–80.

Schultze, C. 1983. Industrial policy: a dissent. *The Brookings Review* 2, Fall, 3–12.

Zysman, J. 1983. *Governments, Markets, and Growth*. Ithaca: Cornell University Press.

declining population. Population decline is much less common than population growth. Looking at the geographical areas occupied by present-day nations, or by their administrative subdivisions, one sees that over the last millenium the number of years when the human population declined is almost always much exceeded by the number when it grew. Reflecting this fact, economics has devoted much more attention to the growth of population than to its decline. The preoccupation with growth, however, may be ending as more countries experience lengthy periods of reduced fertility.

Many of the economists writing on the growth of population, from Malthus to the Club of Rome, are notorious for their bleak view of the future. If population growth is a bad thing, one might be excused for thinking that its decline might be beneficial. But much of the writing on decline is equally alarmist. Does this indicate a general tendency towards pessimism in demographic commentary? Or is the model used for analysing the consequences of population change genuinely asymmetrical, in the sense that increases and decreases of population do not produce opposite effects? Or are different models being used for growth and decline?

Before considering the consequences of population decline, it is desirable first to consider the causes, because in many respects the consequences are conditioned by the causes. The population of a given geographical area can decrease because of a reduction in fertility, an increase in mortality or an increase in net emigration. Of these three factors, fertility reduction has had the least importance as a historical cause of depopulation. Most areas in the world have indeed experienced prolonged periods of fertility decline, particularly within the past 200 years, but these declines have normally been accompanied by significant reductions in mortality, and indeed many would argue that the fall in fertility has been partly a consequence of the fall in mortality, particularly infant mortality. The result has been that populations have continued to grow even when the total fertility rate (the number of live childbirths per woman during the childbearing period, assuming age-specific birth rates to stay at their current levels) has been reduced by as much as 75 per cent, from a 'traditional' level of about eight to a 'modern' level of about two.

Of course, when the total fertility rate falls below the long-run replacement level, which in modern conditions of mortality is about 2.1 children per woman, the population must eventually diminish, in the absence of net immigration. However, some decades may elapse between the decline of the total fertility rate below this critical level and the subsequent decline of the population, because a pyramidal age-structure inherited from earlier regimes of high fertility can sustain the absolute number of births at a high level for several years even while age-specific birth rates are falling. In the United States, for example, the total fertility rate has been below 2.1 since 1972, but in 1984 the annual number of births was still 80 per cent greater than the number of deaths.

Increases in death rates, on the other hand, have often been so extreme and abrupt as to produce an immediate decline in population. Historically there have been three main causes of sudden increases in mortality: famine, disease and war. The three causes are not unrelated to each other. War has often caused famine, for example, and famine has caused disease. Famine, besides sometimes resulting from war and other political disorder, has been the product of natural disasters like drought and floods. Cases when disease has caused sudden increases in mortality include epidemics, like the bubonic plague in medieval Europe, and the importing of new infections into populations without immunity. A classic example of the latter is the decline of American Indian populations after their encounter with the measles, influenza, tuberculosis and other diseases brought by Europeans.

Regarding the future likelihood of these catastrophic causes of population decline, it is not easy to be optimistic, because our own 20th century provides numerous examples of such catastrophe. There have been large-scale famines leading to extensive depopulation. Probably the worst was the Chinese famine of 1959–61, caused by natural disasters and the dislocations of the Great Leap Forward. It is thought that in those years, 30 million deaths took place because of starvation (Banister and Kincannon, 1984). In the 1980s certain regions in Ethiopia and the African Sahel have been depopulated for similar reasons. As for disease, some 20th-century epidemics have reached vast proportions, in particular the influenza epidemic of 1918–19, which took 20 million lives worldwide. War and armed conflict have had even more serious depopulating effects in this century than earlier, as warring states and factions have increasingly resorted to the mass extermination of civilians. Large areas of Russia and Poland suffered population declines for this reason between 1941 and 1945, and similar declines are alleged to have occurred elsewhere during the century (Cambodia, Armenia, Uganda, Punjab).

The third cause of population decline, net emigration, is frequently encountered, but unlike mortality increases, it can often be regarded as benign. Emigration occurs in response to 'push' factors or 'pull' factors. In any individual case it is often difficult to tell whether 'push' or 'pull' is stronger, but it is certainly safe to say that in many instances, the decision to emigrate should be seen as a hopeful determination to explore new opportunities rather than as an escape from distress. Indeed, in a dynamic, expanding economy, it is to be expected that changes in demand and technology will shift the comparative advantages and disadvantages of particular regions, and that some regions will lose population to others as labour markets respond to these shifts.

At the regional or sub-national level, net emigration is often substantial enough to produce an actual decline in population. For example, in the United States between 1980 and 1983, four of the 50 states lost population, even though in all states the number of deaths during that period was less than the number of births. At the national level, net emigration is less commonly a cause of depopulation, largely because of the legal and other obstacles to international migration.

We turn now to the consequences of population decline, which, as noted above, will be found to vary according to the cause of the decline. The consequences of decline have been investigated with particular thoroughness in France, where the subject has been a matter of active political and academic discussion since the defeat of France by a more populous Germany in the war of 1870–71. In general, the tendency of the French population to stagnate has been deplored. A typical statement is found in the preamble to the Family Code of 1939, a set of pro-natalist measures adopted by the Daladier government on the eve of World War II (cited by Tomlinson et al., 1985):

> Our military and economic forces are in danger of wasting away; the country is ruining itself little by little; by contrast, the individual tax burden is increasing the whole time; each citizen is having to pay more to support the social welfare system; industry is gradually deprived of its market; land remains untilled; overseas expansion loses its momentum; and beyond our frontiers, our intellectual and artistic prestige is extinguished.

There are three themes in this bleak picture which have remained important in demographic analysis and which deserve further comment here: the increased burden of dependency said to result from a declining population, the weakening of military forces and the fall in aggregate demand.

The burden-of-dependency argument contends that in a declining population there is an increase in the ratio of dependants to workers. This causes heavier burdens on workers, both because of the increased taxes they must pay to finance public services provided to the dependent part of the population, and because of the increased levels of private consumption they must support. A fall in the rate of saving is the probable result. But there are some qualifications which should be made to this argument. First, if the population decline is due to the emigration of young adult males – a not untypical situation – there may well be an increase in the ratio of dependants to non-emigrant workers, but no corresponding additional burden on non-emigrants, since the dependants of emigrants will be supported in part by remittances.

Second, if the population decline is caused by a reduction in fertility, the rising fraction of elderly in the population will be at least partly offset by a diminishing fraction of children, with little change occurring in the ratio between all dependants and all workers (except in the very long run). The American case is illustrative. Between 1960, near the start of the current fertility decline in the United States, and 1983, the fraction of the population aged 65 or over rose from 9 per cent to 12 per cent, but the fraction aged under 18 fell from 36 per cent to 27 per cent, so that the fraction aged 18–64 actually rose from 55 per cent to 61 per cent. These numbers may even understate the real reduction in dependency burdens occurring during this period, since the fertility decline facilitated an increase in labour-force participation rates among females, reducing still further the number of dependants per worker.

While fertility declines like those occurring in the United States may not lead to much change in the ratio between all dependants and all workers, they certainly produce changes in the structure of dependency. Whether these structural changes lead to an additional fiscal burden on workers depends on the relative costs of public services for the elderly (pensions, health care) and those for children (education).

A third qualification which should be made to the burden-of-dependency argument is as follows: to the extent that the elderly finance their own consumption out of earlier saving, undertaken through a funded pension scheme or otherwise, their presence does not constitute an economic burden. For this reason and others, there is much complexity in the 'economics of aging populations', which has become an area of active enquiry in Europe and elsewhere as anxieties have developed on such issues as the future financing of social security.

The military implications of population decline do not seem very clear, despite what French strategists have argued. A country can gain the upper hand over a more populous adversary by conscripting a larger fraction of its population, by possessing more advanced weaponry, by receiving assistance from allies, or by any of several other methods. In the 20th century there is no shortage of examples of smaller countries defeating larger (Japan against Russia in 1904, Germany against Russia in 1917, Japan against China in 1937, Israel against Egypt in 1967, Vietnam against the United States in 1975).

The aggregate-demand argument is Keynesian in nature, and suggests that in a declining population, there will be large reductions in demand for certain kinds of investment goods and consumption goods (e.g. housing and children's clothing). Weak demand in these markets could lead to a deficiency of aggregate demand and to an equilibrium with considerable unemployment. However, if there is a Keynesian problem of this nature, a Keynesian solution could also exist. Expansionary fiscal and monetary measures could in principle restore aggregate demand to its full-employment level.

There are other elements in the case against a declining population, a case developed in recent years with particular vigour by Alfred Sauvy and Julian Simon (see, for example, Dumont and Sauvy, 1984; Simon, 1981). Many of these elements are difficult to evaluate, since they concern the allegedly deleterious effects of depopulation on certain intangible characteristics of a society that are not easily measured – such as the dynamism of its artists, or its spirit of adventure, or its readiness to innovate. Also difficult to evaluate is the 'Beethoven–Einstein' argument, which says that a smaller population has a smaller probability of producing a great genius. (If that is true, perhaps such a population is also less likely to produce an evil genius on the scale of Hitler.)

Generally absent from the alarmist views on population decline is the admission that decline does have some beneficial tendencies. These may indeed be swamped by the undoubted negative tendencies, but not necessarily so. Perhaps the most powerful benefit of population decline is its immediately favourable effect on the ratio between physical resources and the labour force. In the short run, the stock of natural resources and capital is fixed, and so any reduction in labour inputs will raise the ratio of natural resources to labour, the ratio of capital to labour, the marginal product of labour, and most probably the wage rate. In the longer run, what happens to the capital–labour ratio when the labour force is diminishing is more difficult to say: the outcome depends among other things on what is happening to dependency burdens and the rate of saving. But even in the longer run, the stock of many types of utilized natural resources will be practically independent of the size of the labour force, and to that extent a smaller labour force is likely to mean a higher income per capita. To make this point, it suffices to look at the economies of Kuwait and Nigeria, which in recent years have produced roughly the same substantial volume of crude oil. But Kuwait's population is only two per cent of Nigeria's, and largely in consequence, its per capita income is about 20 times higher.

The reasoning here is the same as that employed in standard neoclassical models of migration. It is assumed that higher wages in one area will attract migrants; this movement will lower the marginal product of labour in the area of destination and raise it in the area of origin, thus narrowing wage differentials and leading to an equilibrium rate of migration. The point of interest in the present context is that declines in the labour force tend to raise output per worker, certainly in the short run and perhaps in the long run as well.

Closely related to these economic benefits from depopulation are some environmental benefits. The increase in natural resources per capita which tends to raise income per capita also tends to alleviate problems like air and water pollution, the rapid depletion of mineral resources, urban congestion and excessive use of recreational space. The environmental advantages of smaller populations have been one of the main themes of contemporary anti-natalist movements like Zero Population Growth.

In sum, it is not difficult to think of benefits as well as costs of population decline. In many of the countries now facing population decline as a result of their recent fertility history, the benefits and costs are regarded as fairly evenly balanced, or at least, 'the sense of urgency over population decline is still far from acute' (McIntosh, 1981). According to the World Bank (1984), there were 22 countries which in 1982 had a total fertility rate less than 2.1. Seventeen of these were high-income OECD countries, three were East European (East Germany, Hungary and Yugoslavia), and the others were Cuba and Singapore. In some of these countries, like France and Hungary, there is considerable anxiety about depopulation. But in others, many people seem to feel that 'smaller is better'.

ROBIN BARLOW

See also AGEING POPULATIONS; DEMOGRAPHIC TRANSITION; SOCIAL SECURITY; STAGNATION.

BIBLIOGRAPHY

Banister, J. and Kincannon, L. 1984. Perspectives on China's 1982 census. Paper presented at the International Seminar on China's 1982 Population Census, Beijing.
Dumont, G.F. and Sauvy, A. 1984. La montée des déséquilibres démographiques: quel avenir pour une France vieillie dans un monde jeune? Paris: Economica.
McIntosh, C.A. 1981. Low fertility and liberal democracy in Western Europe. Population and Development Review 7(2), 181–207.
Simon, J. 1981. The Ultimate Resource. Princeton: Princeton University Press.
Tomlinson, R., Huss, M.M. and Ogden, P.E. 1985. France in peril: the French fear of dénatalité. History Today 35, April, 24–31.
World Bank. 1984. World Development Report 1984. New York: Oxford University Press.

defence economics. As armed conflicts among nations have evolved into total war, economic power has become a key factor in the modern nation's ability to defend or extend its sovereignty. Beginning in World War II, economics and economists have been employed increasingly both to understand the structure of and to manage the resource base underpinning national security. As new, more complex problems associated with total warfare emerged, and as a need arose for quantitative analytic methods to resolve them, the capability to provide analysis developed rapidly during and immediately after the War. Such fields as operations research and logistics management were conceived in response to wartime need (e.g. ship convoy techniques, submarine search methods, inventory and supply analysis, transport network analysis), and specific tools for management developed apace (such as inventory theory, input–output analysis, linear programming, activity analysis, and the theory of games).

World War II not only provided a powerful impetus for focusing economic technique on problems of conflict and security but the United States' predominant economic position at its end and at the beginning of the Cold War presented a special opportunity to apply national economic strength to foreign policy objectives. In response, aid, initiated as the Marshall Plan, provided the foundation for military build-up around the globe and for a vast network of alliances including NATO. Moreover it was the economic strength of the Soviet Union, as reflected in its foreign and strategic agenda, which furnished the West with the incentive to marshall its economic strength for an enduring competition. From this context was born a national security need to understand the structure of the Soviet and other Eastern economies, and how they conditioned our adversary's options and choices.

The need for economic analysis became crucial from the early days of the strategic nuclear era. That time mark the beginning of a still continuing technological explosion in war preparation. Thus, rapidly on the heels of economic analyses of mobilization and production, logistics management etc. came a new brand of economic study centred on the risks and dilemmas created by the bilateral accumulation of nuclear inventories and delivery systems. Such milestones as Herman Kahn's On Thermonuclear War (1961), Bernard Brodie's Strategy In The Missile Age (1959) and Thomas Schelling's Strategy of Conflict (1960) record the fascination with problems of national defence which captured many of the best minds in America and in the economics profession in particular. The period 1950–60 was also a time of rapid development of applications of economics throughout the public sector. Benefit cost analysis, conflict theory, systems analysis, and the theory of public expenditure generally have their foundations in this period.

DEFENCE ECONOMICS IN THE 1960s

As the economic approach to defence management crystallized, a summary of concept and technique for application to security was published in Hitch and McKean's *Economics of Defense in The Nuclear Age* (1961). With this statement and the simultaneous installation of Charles Hitch as financial manager of the Pentagon, economics acquired new recognition as a tool for national security decision makers. As such 'economics of national defence' then came to denote a family of adaptations of micro-economics and operations research to the development and management of military force.

More than programme management, however, defence economics came to denote an application of the discipline imposed by resource limits at the highest level of national security issues. Included in the scope of this management are decisions on what security actions a nation should prepare to undertake and which options to preserve. Specifically, how many wars must be prepared for, of what extent, duration, intensity, locations, weapons employment, and under what constraints; what methods to employ to pursue national security interests, whether diplomatic, economic, psychological, or ultimately military. Economics has pervaded these questions of national security because of the awareness that resource restriction limits the set of commitments a nation can effectively and credibly adopt. Moreover, which commitments a country should undertake must depend on a comparison of their associated costs and benefits. And while economists had no special expertise for comparing the political benefits of securing one area of the world or another, their dismal science did strike a warning against casual accumulation of national security obligations.

The actual application of economic notions to components of national security required an ambitious extension of economic methods into decisions as to the size, equipment, deployment and support of military forces, all of which has injected defence economics into military planning. This has required: (1) new, comprehensive, system-wide definitions of costs and benefits; (2) quantification of benefits and costs and reduction thereof into dollar values; (3) a search for – and comparison between – alternative programmes/systems to achieve measurable goals; (4) calculation of cost minimizing force compositions, based upon trade-offs among components with, (5) multi-year decisions based on present values calculations; and (6) a growing appreciation of adversarial reaction as an active component in defence analysis.

The practical ability of governments to make effective use of this awareness of the strategic, interactive nature of their international relationships is still severely limited. Nevertheless, the academic study of such interdependence was elaborately developed during the 1950s and 1960s – with economics providing the central paradigm. Direct, straightforward applications of duopoly theory and game theory to arms competition and arms race models demonstrated how economics as a theory of human choice could be used to deepen the insights of mechanical analogues previously drawn from biological and ecological systems. Such models were productively extended to analysis of competing doctrines of deterrence, including the spectrum from assured destruction to assured survival. Similarly, economic models of price war and predatory selling behaviour were usefully extended to the Cold War and East–West competition. The uses of risk as a threat and, more generally, the nature of deterrent threats, promises,

and commitments were extensively explored. As a result, the manner in which states might be led into war – by mistake, misperception, misunderstanding, or even deliberate calculation – have been better understood.

ECONOMICS OF DEFENCE IN THE 1980s

The economics of national security in the 1960–1970 period drew mainly on the conceptual framework of microeconomics, in sharp contrast with the older schools of a macro-orientation that had emphasized natural resource and national mobilization bases of defence. Nevertheless, these more contemporary, analytic, approaches did not spare the United States from mistaken national security decisions nor from the growing constraints imposed by gradual dilution of its hegemony and geopolitical predominance. Partly for this reason, the centre of defence economics has shifted in the past decade in a direction perhaps more congenial to earlier geopolitical strategists. Micro-economic applications have been relegated to a less decisive role than during the 1960s; defence management and its techniques should now be regarded as merely one of several components of national security economics. The field has evolved to include a still broader range of topics than when it first emerged. Economics of defence began on a premise of the utility of analyses of how the United States might most effectively conduct the East–West struggle. But concern now turns increasingly on the needs for and methods of collaboration among allies, for example on how to promote the viability of the alliance networks so arduously built up over the Cold War era, how to share resource allocation burdens and strategic decisions in an era of increased interdependence, how to wage a very long run multidimensional competition with the Warsaw Pact, and how to harmonize security interests with the rising interdependencies which derive from trade growth, resource scarcities, and shifts in the technological basis of national power.

Originating in this history, the contributions of economics to problems of war and peace can now usefully be organized into four categories as outlined in the following summary description. Of course economics and economists are by no means the only contributors to the study of national defence. But economics has made crucial contributions in each category. Moreover, the number of fields in economics that include national security applications has increased. For example, the economic analysis of cartel formation, stability, and behaviour, once a topic of industrial development, now has a weighty national security component. The growing quantitative importance of international trade no longer seems to be essentially of welfare or distribution significance; it now is recognized that nations become thereby increasingly interdependent and therefore increasingly vulnerable to transmission of disturbance from abroad. All of these factors continue to enlarge the scope of 'defence economics', that is, to increase the number and type of questions which bear on national security.

i. POLITICAL ECONOMY OF NATIONAL AND INTERNATIONAL SECURITY

(a) Foundations of national security. Included in this category is the study of how resources, geography, and international trade contribute to a nation's power and survival. Resources include minerals, fuels, land, and climate, tangible capital of various types, population, skilled and unskilled labour, technological expertise, and resource mobility. Geography includes strategic location, accessibility to friends or enemies,

value of territory to others, as well as size shape and terrain. Trade is both a source of strength (because it indicates a country's ability to supply others needs) and vulnerability (because trade creates a dependence on the demands of others especially by causing a country to specialize in meeting the demands by others).

(b) National security in the international system of allies and rivals. Under this heading we include both normative and positive study of the relationships among trade and security in systems of alliances (for example, how economic and security interests lead to the formation of blocs of nations).

II. NATIONAL DEFENCE AND THE NATIONAL ECONOMY

How a country's defence efforts affect its economic health, stability, and growth has been a topic of recurring interest since World War II. Both peacetime defence levels and wartime maximum efforts are of interest for developed and developing nations across the political spectrum. This area includes the following topics.

(a) Effects of defence on the macro-economy, including technological advance, investment, growth, prices, and unemployment.

(b) Economic capacities to support defence efforts, population structure, social and economic opportunity costs of defence.

(c) East–West–Soviet comparative defence economics.

(d) Economic effects of arms control.

III. NATIONAL DEFENCE STRATEGY AND STRUCTURE

Economists bring the discipline of a resource constraint to bear on the problem of how to formulate ultimate and intermediate security objectives in a world with purposeful adversaries. Concepts and techniques developed from game and duopoly theory are of importance here. (The value of having the last move or of imposing the last move on the opponent, is one example; the value and utilization of information is another.) In addition to technical issues, rather profound questions of value may be involved when very long-run competition with an adversary entails imposing costs on the adversary and its population.

Possibly more fundamental still, consideration must be given to framing precisely the objective and meaning of national security. How does economic security count as a national security objective. Moreover how can a country exploit its own economic strengths for the goal of 'security'?

VI. BENEFIT COST ANALYSIS, PROGRAMME DECISIONS, AND DEFENCE MANAGEMENT

This category conventionally came to be called 'defence economics' in the 1960s. Essentially it is an application of micro-economics to a multi-billion command economy. Systems engineering and economic analyses are central to the beginnings of even passably acceptable decision-making over staggeringly costly defence systems. Once technically inferior options are identified and discarded, wide scope remains for traditional economic analyses based on models of consumer and producer behaviour, labour market supply, retirement, retention and investment decisions. The range of options opened up extends from pricing and other incentive mechanisms in production, procurement, and usage of facilities, to game theoretic allocation problems in such diverse applications as anti-submarine warfare, missile-anti-missile assignment analyses, and tactical engagements in general.

Micro-economics contributes to numerous other highly important security topics; value of intelligence, effectiveness of military aid, or rational incentive mechanisms in a risky nuclear world are only a few examples. While this essay affords only a limited description of the applications of economics to national security, it attempts to convey three main ideas relevant to the subject. First, economic analysis may contribute to security through an understanding of the international system and the national economy as foundations of a country's security and assets to be protected. Second, the formulation of a nation's security strategy is in principle a constrained maximization problem strongly coloured by oligopoly elements in execution. Last, implementations of a strategy requires effective utilization of resources through various available instruments. In this last arena, technical expertise in economics may be most readily appreciated, since the relevance of economic method is most undeniable in this realm. But although it is most readily accepted at the level of technique, economics is no less indispensable to intelligent treatment of the larger issues.

MARTIN C. McGUIRE

See also ARMS RACES; MILITARY EXPENDITURE; WAR ECONOMY.

BIBLIOGRAPHY

Boulding, K. 1962. *Conflict and Defense*. New York: Harper and Row.

Brodie, B. 1959. *Strategy In the Missile Age*. Princeton: Princeton University Press.

Hitch, C.J. and McKean, R.N. 1961. *Economics of Defense in the Nuclear Age*. Cambridge, Mass.: Harvard University Press.

Kahn, H. 1961. *On Thermonuclear War*. Princeton: Princeton University Press.

Kennedy, G. 1983. *Defense Economics*. New York: St Martins Press.

McKean, R.N. (ed.) 1967. *Issues in Defense Economics*. New York: National Bureau of Economic Research.

Olvey, L.D., Golden, J.R. and Kelly, R.C. 1984. *The Economics of National Security*. Wayne, NJ: Avery Publishing Group.

Schelling, T.C. 1960. *The Strategy of Conflict*. Cambridge, Mass.: Harvard University Press.

deficit financing. Government budget deficits directly affect both the level of aggregate demand and its composition. Less directly, by influencing the amount of national saving and investment, they also influence the growth rate of real income in the longer run. The expected size and predictability of each of these effects is the subject of continuing empirical investigation. Because revenues and some transfer payments automatically rise and fall with cyclical movements in the economy, it is important at the outset to distinguish between actual deficits and structural deficits. The latter are calculated as the deficits that would prevail at some trend level of GNP, while actual deficits grow as the economy falls below this trend and shrink as the economy rises above it. In the rest of this discussion, deficits will mean structural deficits defined in this way, so that changes in the deficit refer to shifts in the deficit that would exist at a given utilization rate of economic resources.

The effects of deficits on the level of aggregate demand, commonly referred to as fiscal policy, became an important focus of governments' budget planning after Keynesian stabilization analysis became absorbed into policy-making. We first consider the basic relationship developed in Keynesian analysis before considering complications that may diffuse it. In the basic case, effects of larger or smaller deficits are symmetric and come about through changes in either government expenditures or tax revenues at given levels of income. Higher levels of government purchases raise demand directly while higher transfers or lower taxes raise incomes, which lead to higher levels of private demand. Whether an expansion of demand results entirely in higher real output or shows up partly in the price level depends on other considerations, such as how much slack exists in the economy and need not concern us at this level of exposition. For now we assume at least part of any change in GNP is a change in real GNP.

Because higher aggregate demand leads to higher levels of employment and incomes, any initial effects of deficits on demand are amplified through subsequent induced increases in spending out of the induced higher levels of income. So long as these increments to spending are a fraction less than 1.0 of the increments to gross national product, this process converges to a higher equilibrium level of aggregate income and output. The ratio of the eventual higher level of GNP to the initial fiscal stimulus is known as the multiplier. Thus if the multiplier on government purchases is 2.0, an initial $1 billion increase in the deficit resulting from $1 billion more in government purchases leads to a level of GNP $2 billion higher than the initial level. An equivalent way of expressing these effects is to note that an initial expansion of the deficit is a reduction in government, and therefore national, saving. In response, GNP expands to the point where national saving again equals investment.

We may now consider the main qualifications to this basic fiscal policy model. They are all possible reasons why offsets may occur to the apparent increments to demand coming from a fiscal action.

The first issue has to do with monetary policy and is partly definitional. Pure fiscal policy effects, which we are discussing here, should mean the effects that occur when the budget deficit shifts but monetary policy is unchanged. Depending on the definition of unchanged monetary policy that is used, a portion of the fiscal effects on demand may be offset by higher interest rates. The most common notion of unchanged monetary policy is an unchanged money supply. If the GNP were determined simply as a proportion of the money supply, then on this definition of unchanged monetary policy, whatever added demands came from the budget deficit would necessarily be offset by reduced demands elsewhere. This 'crowding out' would occur as a result of a rise in interest rates that directly reduced domestic interest-sensitive demands such as housing or business investment or that reduced the foreign trade balance by appreciating the exchange rate.

However, both theory and empirical evidence reject this model of a fixed relation between money and GNP. The interest rate increase that would reduce some private demands will also lead to economizing on money balances, thus breaking the fixed link between GNP and money demand. Nonetheless, to the extent that a fixed money supply forces interest rates to change in response to a fiscal change, a fixed money supply will reduce the effect on GNP that we attribute to a pure fiscal impact. Some private demands will change in response to the change in interest rates, offsetting part of effect on total GNP of the fiscal change.

Under alternative definitions of an unchanged monetary policy, we arrive at different assessments of what is here called the pure fiscal impact. Other candidates for defining an unchanged monetary policy include unchanged levels of bank reserves or borrowed reserves. Because the supply of money is itself elastic with respect to interest rate changes, the rise in interest rates that accompanies a change in fiscal policy is somewhat smaller under this definition than if the money supply is assumed fixed. As a consequence, a greater impact on

demand is attributed to pure fiscal policy. Finally, if we define unchanged monetary policy as an unchanged real interest rate, fiscal policy would have the full impact on GNP described in the basic model above. Although such a policy would be unsustainable with over-full employment, it is not logically inferior to a constant money supply definition. Furthermore, targeting interest rates corresponds to the way monetary policy has been conducted.

The next set of qualifications to the basic fiscal policy model concerns the behavioural response of private sector agents. One issue concerns the possible difference in consumers' response to temporary and permanent fiscal changes. The permanent income hypothesis relates current consumption to consumers' expected permanent income. A fiscal change that is known to be temporary will therefore have a much smaller effect on current consumption than would the same size fiscal change if it were taken to be permanent. However, if many consumers are constrained in their spending by a lack of liquidity, because they cannot freely borrow at near market interest rates against their future incomes, consumption will not be governed by permanent income. In this case, by relieving the binding liquidity constraint, temporary fiscal changes could have nearly the same effect on current spending as permanent ones.

Although the issue is unsettled because it is difficult to model consumers' expectations of future income, the balance of the evidence suggests that personal tax reductions that are known to be temporary, such as one-time tax rebates, have a smaller effect on spending than do other types of fiscal changes. But this is not a general result for all types of temporary tax change, some of which may have exceptionally large effects. An enlargement of investment tax credits for a limited period of time may have such an exceptionally large effect by shifting investment projects forward in time to take advantage of the temporary tax incentive. The reverse effect could occur from a temporary suspension of a tax credit. Such temporary changes have been used for stabilization by various governments in the past. However such special inducements that shift demand through time only alter demand now at the expense of demand later.

A more extreme argument against fiscal changes affecting GNP is the so-called Ricardian equivalence hypothesis, which asserts that deficits directly bring forth an offsetting change in private saving. This idea, which has been associated in modern times with Robert Barro, presumes that consumption decisions are based on an optimizing strategy over an infinitely long time horizon so that people today adjust their own consumption and saving in response to the after-tax incomes they expect to flow to themselves and their heirs over the indefinite future. Because in this model added deficits today will require higher taxes in the future, consumers fully offset increased government deficits with increased personal saving, thereby eliminating any effect of deficits on GNP.

Although it has renewed interest in modelling fiscal effects more carefully, there is little empirical support for this extreme proposition. However whether deficits, which directly change total national saving, induce some partial offset in saving in other sectors remains an unsettled empirical question. Such direct offsets appear to be more likely in response to some sources of change in deficits than others. Quite apart from the Barro-like effects just discussed, conventional consumption functions predict that a minor fraction of changes in disposable income will be saved, so that a shift in the deficit coming from personal tax reductions would induce a small rise in personal saving. A shift in the deficit coming from reduced business taxation could produce a shift in net business saving depending on how much the tax change affects business investment. In part, how important such effects are will depend on the time horizon in question. For example, some tax changes may have significant effects on investment in the first instance as business adjusts to a different desired capital stock. But once the new desired stock is achieved, investment demand will be changed much less. Further time lags may be involved as firms adjusted dividend payouts and individuals adjust their consumption. But leaving aside such transitory complications, in a steady state the directly induced effects of deficits on private saving appear to be small. Therefore shifts in deficits do shift total saving, total demand and GNP.

We turn next to the effects of a shift in the deficit with the level of GNP held constant. This case is relevant for analysis of the medium run, when departures of real GNP from its trend are averaged out. It is also relevant whenever monetary policy or real limits on expansion are assumed to constrain total real GNP. As before, the shift in the deficit represents a shift in government saving; but since GNP cannot change, this shift must be offset by a corresponding shift in saving net of investment of one or more other sectors.

Much of the adjustment to deficits appears to take place through induced changes in interest rates rather than directly. Higher interest rates reduce business investment, residential construction and spending on consumer durables. They may also affect personal saving, and therefore consumption more generally, although there is little evidence that such effects are large enough to be important. In some circumstances, a major part of a shift in the deficit may be offset by a decline in net foreign investment or, equivalently, a decline in the current account balance. Such an effect was an important part of the adjustment to the historically large US budget deficits of the 1980s.

The offsets to a deficit will not generally remain unchanged through time. At first, a modest rise in interest rates may induce an appreciation of the currency and a decline in the current account balance. This minimizes the effect of the deficit on domestic investment. But as foreigners' holdings of the deficit country's assets continue to increase, it may take ever-higher interest rates to maintain the currency at its appreciated level; and this, in turn, will reduce domestic investment further, thus shifting more of the adjustment to the deficit onto domestic sectors.

Because, in general, larger deficits lead to higher interest rates at any level of GNP, they reduce the share of GNP devoted to investment and increase the share devoted to consumption and government spending. To the extent that investment is crowded out by higher interest rates, the future capital stock will be smaller, thus reducing future real incomes and consumption. Even if domestic investment is sustained by increased net investment by foreigners, the earnings on this investment will accrue to foreigners, so again real domestic incomes will be reduced. If the deficit is increased as a consequence of higher government investment or other growth-inducing expenditure such as research and education, growth might not suffer absolutely. It would still be reduced relative to a budget that financed such outlays with higher taxes that suppressed present consumption.

These outcomes do not imply that a zero deficit, or any particular level of surplus or deficit, is optimal at all times or even, on average, in the long run. Sustained deficits can be too large in the sense that they lead to an explosive growth in the ratio of debt to GNP. But apart from such a limiting case, the appropriate deficit to GNP ratio will depend on the prevailing ratio of private saving to GNP and on the desired ratio of foreign investment or disinvestment to GNP. These ratios

have varied substantially across countries for reasons that have to do with the generosity of public retirement programmes, established lending practices and policies for home-ownership and other factors that determine private saving propensities and foreign investment schedules. In part they reflect different states of maturity in economies that make the return to saving and investment higher in some than in others. But whatever these fundamental characteristics of economies may be, within a range, varying deficits can be used to alter the ratio of national saving and investment to GNP.

GEORGE L. PERRY

See also BURDEN OF THE DEBT; CROWDING OUT; DEMAND MANAGEMENT; FINE TUNING; FISCAL POLICY; PUBLIC DEBT; RICARDIAN EQUIVALENCE THEOREM.

deficit spending. Interest in the economics of deficit finance began to all intents and purposes with the absorption of the economics of the *General Theory*. Before that, though with a few exceptions, the economic discussion of the public finances was based on the assumption of a fully employed economy and the notion of using deficit finance to stimulate output was accordingly not at issue.

Despite the fact that the economics of deficit finance begin with the Keynesian Revolution, it has been conclusively established by Kregel (1985) that Keynes himself 'did *not* ever directly recommend government deficits as a tool of stabilization policy' (Kregel, p. 32). Keynes played a conservative political hand and viewed budget deficits with a 'clearly enunciated lack of enthusiasm'. Although Kregel's discovery is both true and startling, the founder of the Keynesian theory of public finance, Abba Lerner, described what he termed the concept of functional finance as 'first put forward in complete form by J.M. Keynes in England' (Lerner, 1943). This seems to be, therefore, another example of Keynes himself being unaware of the full implications of his own theory or, alternatively, of Keynes himself being aware of political reasons why it would be inappropriate to declare publicly the full implications of his theory for the public finances. (It remains unclear which of these propositions has the greater part of the truth.)

The doctrine of functional finance says that the balance of spending and taxation in the budget should be manipulated so as to produce the desired result for output and employment and not in the interests of realizing a balance or surplus (or deficit) *per se*. This is entirely in tune with the income–expenditure analysis of the determination of income which became the central interpretation of the *General Theory*; since output is driven by demand, output can be altered by government action to raise or lower its own expenditures and to raise or lower, via taxation, the spending of the private sector. It is in this (simple and straightforward) sense that deficit finance and Keynesian economics are closely and correctly linked together. Strictly speaking (and this was fully recognized by Lerner), the objective is not output *per se* but 'internal balance'; this is important, because in conditions of full employment, potential excess demand and inflation the doctrine may indicate that a budget surplus is more appropriate than a deficit. The suggestion that Keynesian economics leads to excessive budget deficits does not therefore seem at all correct, although it is one to be encountered in the writings of some critics.

The deficit in the budget *per se* is of course an endogenous item, in the sense that tax revenues and some components of expenditures depend directly upon the level of output and economic activity. In order to obtain measures of deficit finance which are free of this endogeneity, it has become customary to estimate the 'structural' deficit, or the deficit at a normalized level of activity. Measures of the structural budget deficit are standard fare as summary measures of the stance of fiscal policy.

In recent years, the dominance of the principles of functional finance has declined and arguments have been erected (or resurrected) to show that deficit finance may not have the properties ascribed to it in the principles of functional finance; in particular, it has been argued that deficit finance is no different from deferred taxation and deferred taxation no different from current taxation. Hence the case for deficit finance has to be made on some different ground. This argument, perversely referred to as the 'Ricardian equivalence' doctrine (perverse because Ricardo, having entertained it, rejected it) takes its point of departure in a perfect foresight, full information (and fully employed) economy. In such an economy, if individuals are infinitely lived (or care about the welfare of their heirs), a current deficit financed by the issue of bonds creates the expectation of corresponding tax liabilities in the future. The wealth embodied in the bonds (equal to the present discounted value of the flow of coupons and repayment of principal) is precisely offset by the present discounted value of the stream of extra taxes required to service the coupons and repayment of principal. The two are equivalent and cancel out. The bond issue might as well be cancelled in favour of an increase in taxes since private sector savings must rise to meet the obligation to pay future taxes in any case. This argument against deficit finance, put forward most forcefully by Barro (1974) must be regarded as unacceptably extreme. A number of objections may be made to it, as a doctrine of real world relevance; a break in the chain of inheritance, lack of information, imperfect capital markets, less than full employment states are all objections. It is right to qualify these objections by pointing out that it is not in every particular case that the validity of the objection restores the assumptions of the functional finance income–expenditure model as the alternative correct model. Although the Ricardian equivalence theorem appears to be unacceptably extreme it is of interest to note that if it is accepted, a case for loan finance may still exist if only taxes are not lump sum. For if they are not and as usually assumed, welfare losses rise there then proportionately with the tax rate, there is a presumption in favour of smoothing tax rates; hence if expenditures or the tax base are erratic, a case for deficit finance reappears.

In practice, however, it is other considerations which have reduced the dominance of functional finance priciples and resurrected arguments for being concerned about deficit finance. Two, in particular, may be mentioned: first, the connection, real or presumed, between fiscal deficits and monetary growth in periods when monetary targeting has become a central policy objective; second, the structural problem raised by the deceleration of economic growth. Overlying these considerations is the point that with better information flows and increased financial integration, asset markets dominated by forward looking expectations have considerable power to check a fiscal policy that seems adventurous. In particular, if deficit finance is conducted on so large a scale as to raise doubts about its substainability, the market may conclude that rather than change the policy, the result will be explosive growth in the money supply. As a result, bond prices fall currently, and the exchange rate plummets. Scenarios of this type are responsible for an increasing emphasis being placed on targets for the ratio of public sector debit to GNP, an integral control version of

deficit/GNP ratios. In contrast to the destabilizing character of the latter, however, targets for the ratio of debt to potential GDP allow the stabilizers to be 'turned on' as output deviated from potential and provide a compromise between the flexibility and complete discretion and the potentially destabilizing rigidity of deficit targeting. Whether the compromise is the best that can be achieved remains to be discovered. All that is really required is that the market should trust the government, in following the principles of functional finance, not abuse them. To suppose that this trust can be inspired by adopting a target which implies a large degree of sacrifice of these principles may be wrong.

M.J. ARTIS

See also DEFICIT FINANCING; DEMAND MANAGEMENT; FINANCE.

BIBLIOGRAPHY

Barro, R. 1974. Are government bonds net wealth? *Journal of Political Economy* 82(6), 1095–117.

Kregel, J. 1985. Budget deficits, stabilization policy and liquidity preference: Keynes' post-war proposals. In *Keynes's Relevance Today*, ed. F. Vicarelli, London: Macmillan.

Lerner, A.P. 1943. Functional finance and the federal debt. *Social Research* 10, February, 38–51.

De Finetti, Bruno (1906–1985). De Finetti was born in Innsbruck, Austria, and died in Rome. After a degree in mathematics at Milan University, he chose practical activities rather than an academic career, and worked at the Istituto Centrale di Statistica (1927–31) and then at the Assicurazioni Generali (1931–46). Only later did he turn to an academic career and win a chair in Financial Mathematics at Trieste University (1939); from 1954 to 1961 he held the chair in the same subject at the University of Rome and from 1961 to 1976 the chair of Calculus of Probabilities at the same university. He was a member of the Accademia Nazionale dei Lincei and Fellow of the International Institute of Mathematical Statistics.

De Finetti's fame rests on his contributions to probability and to decision theory, but he also worked in descriptive statistics, mathematics and economics.

Together with Ramsey and Savage, de Finetti is one of the founders of the subjectivist approach to probability theory. The first illustrations (in non-technical terms) of his conception are in (1930a) and (1931b). He considers probability as a purely subjective entity 'as it is conceived by all of us in everyday life'. The probability that a person attributes to the occurrence of an event is nothing more or less than the measure of the person's degree of confidence (hope, fear, ...) in this event actually taking place. This can be interpreted as the amount (say, 0.72) that the person deems it fair to pay (or receive) in order to receive (or pay) the amount 1 if the event in question occurs. The mathematical theory was presented in his 1935 lectures at the Institut Poincaré (1937); see also (1970) and (1972).

De Finetti also introduced the important concept of *exchangeability* in probability (1929, 1930b, 1937, 1938) and proved the theorem on exchangeable variables named after him. Exchangeability is a weaker concept than independence and has been receiving increasing attention in probability theory (in fact, the natural assumption for a Bayesian is not independence, but exchangeability). In his 1935 Poincaré lectures (1937) he also treated the relations between the subjectivist point of view and the concept of exchangeability, which in his vision are at the basis of sound inductive reasoning and behaviour and, hence, of (statistical) decision theory (1959, 1961). It goes without saying that his position on the subject of statistical inference is fundamentally Bayesian.

In descriptive statistics he adhered to the functional concept according to which a statistic is an index selected on the basis of the single case (the aspects that one wants to stress, the aim of the statistical investigation, etc.); in (1931a) he stressed the importance of means which have the property of being associative.

Among his mathematical contributions the (1949) paper is especially interesting for economists. Here de Finetti investigates the conditions under which a concave function can be associated with a given 'convex stratification' (i.e. a one-parameter family of convex sets, one interior to the other as the parameter varies). The author also discusses the conditions for a quasi-concave function to be transformed into a concave one by means of an increasing function. This paper started the literature on the 'concavification' of quasi-concave functions. As the author pointed out, these investigations also bear on consumer theory – where the convex stratification is the indifference map and the associated function is the utility function.

De Finetti also wrote on economic problems, where he stressed the importance of rigorous reasoning and verification, and emphasized the idea that the scope of economics, freed from the tangle of individual and corporative interests, should always and only be that of realizing a collective optimum (in Pareto's sense) inspired by criteria of equity (1969). An important initiative of his for the diffusion and correct application of mathematical and econometric methods in economics was the annual CIME (Centro Internazionale Matematico Estivo) seminar that he organized from 1965 to 1975; this enabled young Italian economists to benefit from courses given by Frisch, Koopmans, Malinvaud, Morishima, Zellner, to mention only a few of the lecturers.

GIANCARLO GANDOLFO

See also BAYESIAN INFERENCE; CONVEXITY; SAVAGE, LEONARD JIMMIE; SUBJECTIVE PROBABILITY.

SELECTED WORKS

A full bibliography of de Finetti's works up to 1980 is contained in B. de Finetti, *Scritti (1926–1930)*, ed. L. Daboni et al., Padua: Cedam, 1981, with an autobiographical note.

1929. Funzione caratteristica di un fenomeno aleatorio. In *Atti del Congresso Internazionale dei Matematici* (1928), Bologna: Zanichelli, 179–190.

1930a. Fondamenti logici del ragionamento probabilistico. *Bollettino dell'Unione Matematica Italiana* 9, December, 258–61.

1930b. Funzione caratteristica di un fenomeno aleatorio. *Memorie della Reale Accademia dei Lincei*, Classe di scienze fisiche, matematiche e naturali, Vol. IV, fasc. 5.

1931a. Sul concetto di media. *Giornale dell'Istituto Italiano degli Attuari* 2, 369–96.

1931b. *Probabilismo. Saggio critico sulla teoria delle probabilità e sul valore della scienza.* Naples: Perrella; also in *Logos*, 1931, 163–219.

1937. La prévision: ses lois logiques, ses sources subjectives. *Annales de l'Institut Henri Poincaré*, vol. VII, fasc. I. Trans. as 'Foresight: its logical laws, its subjective sources', in *Studies in Subjective Probability*, ed. H.E. Kyburg Jr. and H.E. Smokler, New York: Wiley, 1964.

1938. Sur la condition de 'équivalence partielle'. (Conférence au Colloque consacré à la théorie des probabilités, University of Geneva, 1937.) In *Actualités Scientifiques et Industrielles*, no. 739, Paris: Herman.

1949. Sulle stratificazioni convesse. *Annali di matematica pura e applicata*, Series IV, Vol. XXX, 173–183.

1959. La probabilità e la statistica nei rapporti con l'induzione, secondo i diversi punti di vista. In *Atti corso CIME su Induzione e Statistica* (Varenna), Rome: Cremonese, 1–115.

1961. Dans quel sens la théorie de la décision est-elle et doit-elle être 'normative'. In *Colloques internationaux du Centre National de la Récherche Scientifique*, Paris: CNRS, 159–169.

1969. *Un matematico e l'economia.* Milan: F. Angeli (anthology of previously published papers).

1970. *Teoria delle probabilità. Sintesi introduttiva con appendice critica.* Turin: Einaudi, 2 vols. Trans. as *Theory of Probability*, 2 vols, New York: Wiley, 1974–5.

1972. *Probability, Induction and Statistics.* New York: Wiley (anthology of writings).

Defoe, Daniel (1660–1731). Born Daniel Foe in 1660, son of a London tradesman and Nonconformist, Defoe's early life was that of a merchant with a diversity of interests and ambitions. After his support for the Monmouth rebellion of 1685 he welcomed the accession of the Prince of Orange in 1688, later being given employment by the government. A financially advantageous marriage followed, and then his fortunes reversed with the collapse of his ventures in 1692 owing £17,000. His efforts at clearing his debts first turned him towards journalism, and this was to be his major occupation for the remainder of his life. In the early years of the 17th century he met with some literary success, but in 1702 he was imprisoned for libel. His release in 1704 was conditional on his undertaking to establish an intelligence network for the Government, and in the succeeding years he travelled widely, gathering information and assessing popular opinion. In 1713 he was imprisoned once more, this time for anti-Jacobite writings; pardoned in 1715, he returned to literary work and in the period until his death in 1731 produced the majority of the works for which he is known today.

Defoe published a number of tracts upon directly economic issues, chief among them his *Plan of the English Commerce* which argued that the employment of labour on the working-up of domestic produce (in particular, wool) was the true path to prosperity. He is perhaps best known for his novel *Robinson Crusoe* and his two accounts of English society, *Journal of the Plague Year* and *Tour through the whole Island of Great Britain*. The first of these was published anonymously in 1719 and was, until Defoe admitted authorship, thought to be a true account of the life of a castaway. In his defence, Defoe suggested that he had included much of his own experience, and it is shown today that the work is based on the experience of Alexander Selkirk. This blending of 'fiction' and 'fact' is typical of the other two works; for while they are based upon Defoe's observations, the form in which they are cast is fictional. The *Journal* records events that occurred when Defoe was five and the *Tour*, published in 1724–6, is in fact a compilation drawing in part on the travels of Defoe some 20 years previously. For all this, they are no less valuable as accounts of contemporary society, and were regarded as models by later observers.

K. TRIBE

BIBLIOGRAPHY
Moore, J.R. 1960. *A Checklist of the Writings of Daniel Defoe.* Bloomington: Indiana University Press.

degree of monopoly. If the term 'monopoly' is taken in its literal meaning, then there is no room for such a thing as a 'degree of monopoly'. For 'monopoly' means – taking into account the Greek origins of the term – a single seller; and there cannot be any 'degrees' of singleness. In fact, all through the 19th and well into the 20th century, economic thinking tended to look at monopoly in this way. Monopoly referred to the market form with a single seller as opposed to Competition, where several firms appear on the market. When the two market forms and their consequences were analysed it was soon realized that the two types were not quite sufficient to cover all decisive elements, and some in-between forms were taken into account as, for instance, in Cournot's duopoly analysis or in Marshall's insights into imperfect competition. But all the time monopoly remained more or less unscathed as a clearly defined juxtaposition to competitive market forms.

This situation became undermined from two different sides: rather gradually from a practical–political angle, when at the turn of the century a growing concern with big-business practice led to demands for anti-monopolistic legislation, and – later on – more dramatically in the theoretical sphere when the almost simultaneous appearance of Joan Robinson's (1933) and Edward H. Chamberlin's (1933) treatises on monopolistic competition provided a new perspective for market form analysis. In practical affairs it had soon become obvious that *exclusive* control of supplies of a certain commodity by a single firm was rather an exception, but that all the suspected evils of monopoly – high prices, displacement of actual or potential competitors, curtailment of production etc. – could also be detected when big firms or cartels dominate a market, even if there are numerous smaller competitors. Monopolistic power thus became connected with the question of concentration, and varying degrees of concentration could be seen as expressions of varying degrees of monopoly. This led to various proposals of a *descriptive–statistical nature* to measure degrees of monopolistic domination.

On the theoretical plane the development originated from a growing sophistication in the analysis of 'pure' market forms. On the one hand it became clear that there cannot be such a thing as a completely isolated monopolist free from competitive pressures, because there always exist substitutes which limit his room for manoeuvring; and on the other hand the heterogeneity of goods, location, and availabilities so departmentalizes competitive markets that the individual firm can have a certain amount of monopoly-like freedom for price-setting which could not exist on perfectly competitive markets. The classical juxtaposition of monopoly and competition had lost its simplicity; the 'pure' cases turned out to be limiting concepts in a world characterized by an intermixture of monopolistic and competitive elements. Thus the 'monopolistic competition revolution' gave rise to a series of attempts to find a suitable *theoretical* tool for measuring the 'degree of monopoly' with the main stress being put on the conceptual and analytical basis while the question of quantitative expression was largely neglected or remained unsolved.

Before giving a short presentation of the more important indices used for measuring the 'degree of monopoly' it is necessary to enumerate some of the formidable difficulties that beset *any* attempt to find a suitable (single) expression which could provide a unique and comprehensive index. First of all there is the firm–industry problem. As long as a monopoly is conceived in its narrowest sense – a single supplier of a certain commodity – the problem does not arise: the monopolistic firm coincides with the entire industrial branch. But once we allow for *degrees* of monopoly in multi-firm industries and for heterogeneous goods, all indices which try to measure monopolistic power within an industry come up against the problem of where to draw the lines for a meaningful group. If we want to estimate the monopolistic position of firms in the motor-car industry, are we to take as the decisive industrial group all motor-cars, or motor-cars of a certain size, motor-cars of a certain type, or what? Obviously one wants to draw the line where products cease to be serious substitutes for the commodity in question. But this involves necessarily a somewhat arbitrary decision and the results will be affected by it. Some writers, following Triffin (1940), have argued that in a world of heterogeneous goods and inter-industrial competition the concept of industry should be dropped altogether and the degree of monopoly of a firm should be measured exclusively vis-à-vis *single* other firms with the aid of cross-elasticities of demand. These would be zero in the case of complete monopolistic independence. But this approach would lead to an enormous number of cross-elasticities for every firm, and it neglects the fact that we do deal with industrial groups and problems in practice.

A further problem arises from the fact that indices of relative size within an industrial group do not tell us sufficiently how far other factors – like regional dispersion, marketing activities etc. – influence the monopolistic status of big and small firms. Measures which rely on realized prices and profits can only tell us something about *actual*, but not about *potential* monopoly power. Finally, there is always – in view of business secrecy and incomplete statistics – a serious data and estimation problem when it comes to quantitative judgements.

But the most important reason for coexistence of various degree of monopoly indices is that the monopoly problem has different aspects which require different measuring rods. Thus, the problem of monopoly power may be seen as a problem of relative market power within an industry, that is the problem of big firms versus small firms. This aspect plays an important role in anti-trust and fair-competition legislation. From the point of view of traditional economic theory, the question of monopolistic price formation with its effects on optimal allocation and economic welfare is the dominant one. Others – as for instance Marx or Kalecki – have stressed the distributional aspects of monopoly power, particularly with regard to the wage–profit relation. Finally, a political–economic viewpoint looks at the problem of the influence of monopolies on the state in the age of 'Monopoly Capitalism'.

The search for suitable indices originated in connection with political concerns over the growing concentration in certain industries. This gave rise to a demand for descriptive–statistical measures to be used as diagnostic instruments. A widely used index of long standing is the so-called 'concentration ratio' which measures the weight of the biggest enterprises in an industry on the basis of the percentage share of the biggest firms in total output, or sales, or employment, or capital assets.

The advantages of this index are obvious: the required data are usually available and its meaning is easily appreciated. It can certainly act as a rough indicator of levels and changes in monopolistic positions in individual industries. If shares of the biggest firms in *total* manufacturing output (employment etc.) are measured, we obtain hints with regard to the Monopoly–State problem. The main disadvantage of the concentration ratio is that it completely disregards information about the number and size of firms beyond the few leading firms. But their structure can influence the monopolistic context. As an alternative (or complement) to the concentration ratio we, therefore, find suggestions to measure the degree of monopoly with the aid of distributional indices like the Lorenz curve or the Herfindahl index which measure overall inequalities of distribution – greater inequalities (in output etc.) to be taken as higher degrees of monopoly. This is, however, hardly satisfactory because it does not give sufficient weight to concentration at the upper end (biggest firms) which is decisive for the monopoly problem.

When we turn to the theoretically oriented indices of degree of monopoly we meet a greater variety. Most of the proposals were born in the two decades after the publication of Chamberlin's and Robinson's books; since then the interest in further developments has died down. The pioneering study appeared in 1934 when Lerner (1934) proposed an index based on the theoretical idea that pure competition should be taken as the benchmark. Taking into account that in pure competition equilibrium prices will equal marginal costs he took as his indicator of degree of monopoly the excess of price over marginal cost relative to price (i.e. (p-c)/p, with p=price and c=marginal cost). This index equals zero in case of pure competition and can rise to a maximum of one when marginal costs are zero. What it measures is the deviation of a firm's price from the competitive ideal, with consequences for allocation and welfare. But since the index is (in equilibrium, with marginal revenue equal to marginal costs) equivalent to the reciprocal value of the price elasticity of demand, it does not take into account cost and supply considerations. The main advantage of the Lerner index is that it does not require the definition of an industry group. The same is true for Weintraub's (1949) suggestion of an index which measures the ratio between the actual output of a firm and the output it would produce under pure competition. This index equals one in the fully competitive case and becomes smaller with growing monopolistic deviations. Difficulties arise with regard to suitable data.

Also based on the individual firm and avoiding the ambiguous industry concept is an index by Bain (1941) which starts from the commonly acknowledged idea that monopoly power is acquired in order to obtain higher profits. Bain, therefore, proposes to use the ratio between a firm's profit rate and a 'normal' competitive profit rate as a degree of monopoly indicator. Since actuarial profit data do not meet theoretical requirements this approach also runs into estimation problems. To lay stress on profits is an advantage, but the index cannot distinguish monopoly-caused profits from other types (demand shifts, windfalls, etc.).

Some other indices take into account the (intra-industrial) interdependence of firms. Rothschild (1942), referring back to Chamberlin's 'two demand curves' facing a firm – a special one, when it alone varies the price, and a general one, when all firms together change their price – takes as his index the ratio of the slopes of the special and the general demand curve. In full competition the slope of the special curve and the index are equal to zero, and the index rises to one in pure monopoly when both curves coincide. Estimation problems are as formidable as before. Morgan (1946) and Papandreou (1949) both build on Triffin's idea of making cross-elasticities of demand a decisive criterion, but expand his ideas. Morgan makes monopoly power vis-à-vis other firms a function of the firm's share in their combined output and of the heterogeneity of goods (measured by cross-elasticities). Both enter positively into the index. Papandreou, in a combination of two complex indices, takes into account not only the cross-elasticities of demand (which determine the degree of 'insulation' when other prices are changed) but also output capacities (which determine the power of 'penetration' into other markets when demand is increased).

A special word must be said about Kalecki's (1938) 'degree of monopoly' which has become the most important specimen in theoretical literature. *Formally* it is similar to Lerner's but the theoretical underpinnings and uses are quite different. In contrast to Lerner, Kalecki starts from a (manufacturing) world in which oligopoly and imperfect competition are the rule. Pure competition cannot be the standard. All firms work below capacity; their marginal production costs tend to be constant and equal to average production costs. Prices are 'administered' by a mark-up on average production costs. The higher the mark-up the greater the difference between price and average cost (=marginal cost) and the higher, therefore, the 'degree of monopoly' in the definition of Lerner. Since the mark-up determines gross profits one obtains a theoretical framework where the 'degree of monopoly' is a decisive factor in determining the income distribution between production workers' wages and gross profits. But it is important to realize that in this setting (general under-utilization of capacity) the 'degree of monopoly' has a very wide meaning: in addition to monopoly power in the narrower sense and the higher profits that go with it, it also covers other non-wage items such as salaries and depreciation.

In more recent years Cowling (1978) and others have taken up Lerner's and Kalecki's indices in modified form to study postwar developments in welfare losses and distributional effects of growing monopolization and oligopolization. The fact of growing management influence which can transform monopoly profits into 'costs' and managerial advantages is taken into account and the index of the degree of monopoly is supplemented by an index of the degree of managerial discretion. The greater the latter, the smaller will be the apparent degree of monopoly as measured by reported profits.

The various conceptual and statistical attempts to find a suitable index for the 'degree of monopoly' have contributed to a better understanding of the issues involved. While most of them can shed *some* light on the monopoly problem, this is far too complex and many-sided to be compressed into one single index or to be fully describable in purely quantitative terms.

KURT W. ROTHSCHILD

See also ELASTICITY; KALECKI, MICHAL; LERNER, ABBA PTACHYA; MONOPOLISTIC COMPETITION; MONOPOLY.

BIBLIOGRAPHY

Bain, J.S. 1941. The profit rate as a measure of monopoly power. *Quarterly Journal of Economics* 55, February, 271–93.

Chamberlin, E.H. 1933. *The Theory of Monopolistic Competition.* Cambridge, Mass.: Harvard University Press.

Cowling, K. 1978. Monopoly, welfare and distribution. In *Contemporary Economic Analysis,* ed. M.J. Artis and A.R. Nobay, London: Croom Helm.

Kalecki, M. 1938. The determinants of the distribution of the national income. *Econometrica* 6, April, 97-112.

Lerner, A.P. 1934. The concept of monopoly and the measurement of monopoly power. *Review of Economic Studies* 1, June, 157-75.

Morgan, T. 1946. A measure of monopoly in selling. *Quarterly Journal of Economics* 60(3), May, 461-3.

Papandreou, A.G. 1949. Market structure and monopoly power. *American Economic Review* 39, September, 883-97.

Robinson, J. 1933. *The Economics of Imperfect Competition.* London: Macmillan.

Rothschild, K.W. 1942. The degree of monopoly. *Economica* 9, February, 24-39.

Triffin, R. 1940. *Monopolistic Competition and General Equilibrium Theory.* Cambridge, Mass.: Harvard University Press.

Weintraub, S. 1949. *Price Theory.* New York: Pitman Publishing Corporation.

degree of utility. This phrase was first made current by Jevons in his *Theory of Political Economy,* 1871. Its precise significance will be best elucidated by an analogy. 'Degree of utility' stands in the same relation to 'total utility' as 'velocity' to 'space traversed'. Suppose we have a body projected vertically upwards from rest, at a given speed. We may inquire *first* at what height the body will be found at any moment after its projection, and *second* at what rate it will be moving at any point of its course, and clearly the rate of its movement is the rate at which its height is increasing (whether positively as it rises, or negatively as it falls). This rate may be measured in feet per second, or in miles per hour, or in any other suitable unit, but in any case it varies from point to point and does not continue the same during any period, however short.

We must now extend the idea of measurement to such economic conceptions as 'satisfaction' and 'utility'. Measurement consists essentially in determining the ratio of the magnitude investigated to some other magnitude adopted as a standard; and a 'satisfaction' would accordingly be measured if we could determine its ratio to some standard satisfaction, or, which amounts to the same thing, some standard dissatisfaction. Thus if I wish to measure the satisfaction derived by a hungry man from the consumption of a certain quantity of bread, I may inquire how much labour he would perform, under stated conditions, rather than go without it; or what he would pay for it sooner than go without if an unscrupulous monopolist exacted from him the extreme famine price. Thus if we take any standard we choose we can, ideally at least, conceive of any concrete 'utility' or 'satisfaction' being measured in it. But we must remember that such measurements are based on the relative magnitudes of different satisfactions, etc., to one and the same person, and do not profess to give us means of comparing a satisfaction experienced by one mind with a satisfaction experienced by another; for no one can say that the standard unit of satisfaction selected means the same thing to two different men. Nor shall we find that any such absolute measurement is needed for the purpose in hand.

Having premised so much, we may now work out the economic analogue of the projected body. Suppose we take such a commodity as bread supplied to a hungry man. *Firstly*, we may inquire what amount of satisfaction the man has derived from the consumption of any given quantity of bread; in which case we shall be investigating the 'total utility' or 'value in use' of that quantity of bread, to that man, under those conditions. *Secondly*, we may inquire at what *rate* (per ounce, per pound, etc.) the consumption of the bread is conferring satisfaction upon the man at any point in the course of his meal; and in that case we shall be investigating the 'degree of utility' of the bread. This 'degree of utility' will of course vary from point to point. When the man was at his hungriest he would be deriving relatively great satisfaction per ounce of bread consumed, and towards the end of his meal, when nearly satisfied, his satisfaction per ounce would be relatively small; and, theoretically, it will not remain constant during any period, however short. Now this 'degree of utility' is obviously the rate at which the 'total utility' is increasing; just as the velocity of a rising or falling body is the rate at which 'space traversed' or 'height' is increasing.

The precise relation of velocity to space traversed, and of degree of utility to total utility, is expressed mathematically by saying that the former are the 'differential coefficients', 'first-derived functions', or 'fluxions' of the latter; and, graphically, if the latter are expressed by areas the former will be expressed by lines. In the figure, if we imagine the line *cd* moving from O in the direction of the arrow-head, at a uniform rate, to represent the lapse of time, and if we imagine the area *aOcd*, to represent the space traversed by the projected body in the O*c*, then the intercept *cd* will be the differential coefficient of *aOcd* and will represent the velocity of the body, or the rate at which it is rising, at the point of time represented by *c*. Perhaps this will be sufficiently obvious to the non-mathematical reader if he reflects that velocity represents the rate at which height is increasing, as time lapses, and observes that the length of the intercept *cd* likewise determines the rate at which the area *aOcd* increases as the vertical line moves in the direction of the arrow-head.

Now let the movement of the vertical from O represent the consumption of the bread, so that O*c* represents the amount consumed up to any given point of the meal; and let *aOcd* represent the total satisfaction derived from the consumption up to the point reached, then *cd* will still be the differential coefficient of *aOcd*, and will represent the rate per unit (ounce, etc.) at which the consumption of the bread is now increasing the total satisfaction reaped by the consumer. That is to say *cd* represents the degree of utility of bread at the point *c*, the amount represented by O*c* having already been consumed.

It should be observed, however, that when we are dealing with economic quantities, the line *ad* will probably never be a straight line, but always a curve of more or less complexity; and it will seldom or never be possible to determine its actual form with any precision.

The main interest naturally attaches to the degree of utility of that increment of a commodity which the consumer expects to obtain next, or which he may have to relinquish, that is to say the last increment he has secured or the next he hopes to secure. This is called by Jevons the 'final degree of utility'. The analogy of the moving body insisted on above was developed by Professor Léon Walras of Lausanne, and was first suggested by his father, A.A. Walras.

[P.H. WICKSTEED]
Reprinted from *Palgrave's Dictionary of Political Economy*.

See also FINAL DEGREE OF UTILITY.

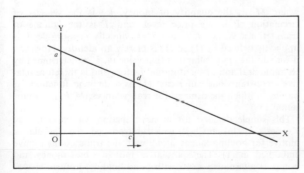

Figure 1

deindustrialization. *See* MANUFACTURING AND DEINDUSTRIALIZATION.

delivery lags. *See* INVENTORIES.

Del Mar, Alexander (1836–1926). Born in New York City and educated as a mining engineer at New York University, Del Mar formulated views on monetary economics on the basis of numerous empirical investigations which he undertook both on his own during the Civil War, and while serving as the first director of the US Bureau of Statistics.

Del Mar anticipated modern monetary analysis along a broad front. While an exponent of the long-run neutrality of money, he argued that in the short-run money is non-neutral. Specifically, he placed emphasis on evaluating the impact of monetary changes in the context of dynamic analysis and developed a broad monetary transmission mechanism (termed the 'precession of prices') which depended upon the marketability of assets (1864). Since he perceived that labour was the least marketable of assets, its price was the last to respond to a monetary change. The perceived tendency of wages to lag behind prices, the observed pro-cyclical nature of velocity, due to the effect of price expectations, and Del Mar's link-up between anticipations of price changes and variations in nominal interest rates, allowed him to formulate such concepts as self-generating expectations and money illusion (Tavlas and Aschheim, 1985).

From the 1860s to the 1880s, Del Mar undertook perhaps the first attempts in the US literature to estimate both the value of velocity and the annual rate of increase of national wealth. Based on his estimates, in *The Science of Money* (1885) he advocated as a policy-guide the first numerical monetary growth-rate rule in the professional literature. His work, however, was largely overlooked by the profession, except for Irving Fisher. Fisher cited Del Mar over the course of nearly 40 years.

JOSEPH ASCHHEIM AND GEORGE S. TAVLAS

SELECTED WORKS
1862. *Gold Money and Paper Money*. New York: A.D.F. Randolf.
1864. The dynamics of finance. *The New Nation* 1, 1–4.
1865. The growth of national wealth. *New York Social Science Review: Devoted to Political Economy and Statistics* 1, 193–218.
1880. *A History of the Precious Metals*. London: George Bell.
1885. *The Science of Money*. London: George Bell.
1886. *A History of Money in Ancient Countries*. London: George Bell.

BIBLIOGRAPHY
Tavlas, G.S. and Aschheim, J. 1985. Alexander Del Mar, Irving Fisher, and monetary economics. *The Canadian Journal of Economics* 18(2), May, 294–313.

Del Vecchio, Gustavo. *See* VECCHIO, GUSTAVO DEL.

De Malynes, Gerard. *See* MALYNES, GERARD DE.

demand, empirical studies of. *See* CONSUMERS' EXPENDITURE.

demand, integrability of. *See* INTEGRABILITY OF DEMAND.

demand for money: empirical studies. The relation between the demand for money balances and its determinants is a fundamental building block in most theories of macroeconomic behaviour and is a critical component in the formulation of monetary policy. Indeed, a stable demand function for money has long been perceived as a prerequisite for the use of monetary aggregates in the conduct of policy. Not surprisingly, then, the demand for money has been subjected to extensive empirical scrutiny.

Several broad factors have shaped the evolution of this research. First, there is the evolving nature of theories of the demand for money. The simple versions of the so-called quantity theory were followed by the Keynesian theory of liquidity preference and then by more modern variants. As theory evolved, so did empirical research. A second factor is the growing arsenal of econometric techniques that has permitted more sophisticated examinations of dynamics, functional forms, and expectations. These techniques have also provided researchers with a wide variety of diagnostic tests to evaluate the adequacy of particular specifications.

Finally, and perhaps most importantly, research has been spurred by the apparent breakdown of existing empirical models in the face of newly emerging data. These difficulties have been particularly evident since the mid-1970s. In many countries this period has been marked by unusual economic conditions including severe bouts of inflation, record-high interest rates, and deep recessions. This period also coincided with the widespread adoption of floating exchange rates and, in a number of major industrial countries, with substantial institutional changes brought about by financial innovation and financial deregulation. The period since 1974 thus provided a very severe test of empirical money demand relationships. As we shall see, this period succeeded in exposing a number of shortcomings in existing specifications of money demand functions. Where institutional change was particularly marked, it also led to a change in what we think of as 'money'.

It is perhaps ironic that the emergence of these shortcomings roughly coincided with the adoption by a number of central banks of policies aimed at targeting monetary aggregates. Some have argued that this association is more than mere coincidence. In any event, given the vested interest of policy-makers in the existence of a reliably stable money demand function, it is hardly surprising that employees of central banks were among the most active contributors to the most recent literature on money demand. The Federal Reserve System of the United States, with its dominant market share of monetary economists, was particularly active in this regard.

As noted, appreciation of empirical research on money demand requires a bit of background on monetary theory and it is with this that we begin our discussion. We next consider some measurement issues and then turn to the early empirical results. After briefly documenting the emerging difficulties with these results, we finally consider recent reformulations of the demand for money.

I. THEORETICAL OVERVIEW. One of the earliest approaches to the demand for money, the *quantity theory of money* starts with the *equation of exchange*. One version of the equation can be written

$$MV \equiv PT \qquad (1)$$

where M is the quantity of money, V is the velocity of circulation, P is the price level, and T is the volume of transactions. While M, P and T are directly measurable, V is implicitly defined by (1) so (1) is merely an identity. However, if we add the key assumption that velocity, V, is determined by technological and/or institutional factors and is therefore relatively constant, one can recast (1) as a demand function for money in which the demand for real balances, M/P, is proportional to T.

This simple demand for money function was modified by Keynes's (1936) analysis which introduced the speculative motive for holding money along with the transactions motive embodied in (1). The speculative motive views money and bonds as alternative assets with bond holding, in turn, viewed as depending on the rate of return on bonds. This introduction

770

of the interest rate into the demand for money, where it joined the transactions variable suggested by the quantity theory is the main empirical legacy of Keynes. Once the interest rate is introduced, there is no presumption that velocity will be constant from period to period.

Post-Keynesian developments moved in several different directions. One is represented by Friedman (1956), whose restatement of the quantity theory dispensed with the individual motives posited by Keynes and treated money like any other asset yielding a flow of services. This view emphasized the level of wealth as one of the major determinants of money demand. Friedman also suggested that a quite broad range of opportunity cost variables including the expected rate of inflation have theoretical relevance in a money demand function. (Given this emphasis, it is ironic that Friedman's early empirical results (Friedman, 1959) seemed to suggest that interest rates were unimportant in explaining velocity movements.)

While Friedman's approach sidestepped the explicit role of money in the transactions process, other influential post-Keynesian developments reconsidered and expanded on the transactions motive. William Baumol (1952) and James Tobin (1956) both applied inventory-theoretic considerations to the transactions demand for money. This led to the so-called *square-root law* with average money holdings given by

$$M = (2bT/r)^{1/2} \qquad (2)$$

where r is the interest rate on bonds and b is the brokerage charge or transactions cost for converting bonds into cash. Dividing both sides of equation (2) by the price level, makes the real transactions demand for money depend on 'the' interest rate, real brokerage charges and the level of real transactions. Miller and Orr (1966) extended this analysis to allow for uncertainty in cash flows, providing the insight that a firm's average money holdings depends on the variance of its cash flow viewed as a measure of the uncertainty of the flow of receipts and expenditures.

Keynes's speculative motive has also been reformulated – largely in terms of portfolio theory (Tobin, 1958). However, given the menu of assets available in most countries, this approach actually undermines the speculative demand for money. The reason is that if there is a riskless asset (e.g. a savings deposit) paying a higher rate of return than money (presumed to be zero in most models), then money is a dominated asset and will not be held. One can resurrect an asset demand for money by combining the portfolio approach with transaction costs but this has yet to be done in a fully general way. One partial attempt in this direction (Ando and Shell, 1975) demonstrates that in a world with a riskless and a risky asset the demand for money will not depend on the rate of return on the risky asset. This approach suggests using only a small number of interest rates, pertaining to riskless assets, in empirical work.

II. SOME MEASUREMENT ISSUES. Empirical estimation of a money demand function requires choosing explicit variables measuring both money and its determinants. Even if guided by a particular theory, such choices are often less than clear-cut. Given the diversity of theories, the range of possible variables is wider yet. This is immediately evident when one considers how to measure 'money'; the sharp distinction between money and other assets turns out to be a figment of the textbook. Moreover, what passes for money can be readily altered by changing financial institutions.

In general, theories based on the transactions motive provide the most guidance and lead to a so-called *narrow* definition of money that includes currency and deposits transferable by cheque (also called checkable deposits). In some institutional settings a plausible measure of checkable deposits is readily apparent. In the United States, for example, for many years only demand deposits at commercial banks were checkable. In other settings, there may well be a spectrum of checkable assets without any clear-cut dividing line. For example, a deposit account may limit the number of cheques per month or may have a minimum cheque size. Other accounts may permit third-party transfers only if regular periodic payments are involved or may permit cheque writing only with substantial service charges. When such deposit accounts should be included in a transactions-based definition of money is not obvious.

Furthermore, even in a world in which the definition of checkable deposits is relatively unambiguous, it is not clear that currency and checkable deposits should be regarded as perfect substitutes, a view that is implicit in simply adding them together to produce a measure of money. Currency and checkable deposits may differ in transactions costs, risk of loss, and ease of concealment of illegal or tax-evading activities. It may thus be preferable to estimate separate demand functions for currency and checkable deposits.

Once one moves away from a transactions view of the world, the appropriate empirical definition of money is even less clear. A theory that simply posits that money yields some unspecified flow of services must confront the fact that many assets may yield these services in varying degrees. Such theories have typically relied on a relatively broad definition of money but the definitions utilized are inevitably somewhat arbitrary. (This issue is taken up again in section IV.)

As with the definition of money, alternative theories have different implications for the relevant set of explanatory variables. As we have seen, the most prominent variables suggested by theory include the level of transactions, wealth, the opportunity cost of holding money, and transaction costs. Each of these involves measurement problems, even in a world of certainty. When uncertainty is allowed for, and expectational issues therefore arise, matters are even worse.

The level of transactions (T in equation (2)) is typically measured by the level of income or gross national product (GNP). While the term 'gross' in GNP makes it sound comprehensive, GNP is much less inclusive than a general measure of transactions. In particular, it excludes all sales of intermediate goods, purchases of existing goods, and financial transactions, all of which may contribute to a demand for money. The empirical use of GNP as a proxy for T therefore presumes that GNP and T move in a proportionate way. Unfortunately, this key assumption is extremely difficult to test because reliable data on T are nonexistent. (Moreover, it is not the case that all transactions are equally 'money intensive'. To cope with this empirically might require separately introducing the various components of T or, as an approximation, of GNP.)

As an alternative to GNP, some researchers have used permanent income, typically measured as an exponentially weighted average of current and past-values of GNP. This is generally done in the spirit of the modern quantity theory where permanent income is a proxy for wealth. As an empirical matter, given the high correlation of GNP and permanent income, a permanent income variable could easily 'work' even if money demand is dominated by transactions considerations. One can, of course, use a measure of wealth directly (only non-human wealth is readily available). This is certainly consistent with the quantity theory view and, given that financial transactions may generate a demand for money, can fit into a transactions view.

Before leaving measures of transactions, we should note one further problem that arises because of issues of aggregation. Most theories of the demand for money apply to an individual behavioural unit but are generally estimated with aggregate data without much attention to the details of aggregation. This failure may lead to the omission of potentially important variables. For example, in the context of a transactions variable, aggregation may suggest that the distribution of income, as well as the level of income, matters. However, with a few exceptions discussed below, we shall not focus on problems of aggregation.

Another set of measurement issues is presented by the opportunity cost of holding money. We consider in turn the two parts to this story: the rate of return on assets alternative to money; and the own rate of return on money. Under the transactions view, the relevant alternative is a 'bond' that is used as a temporary repository of funds soon to be disbursed. As a practical matter this has led to the use of one or more of the following rates: the yield on short-term government securities; the yield on short-term commercial paper; and the yield on time or savings deposits. As we have seen, the relevant set of alternatives under the modern quantity theory is much broader and empirical research in this spirit has also used long-term bond rates, either government or corporate. Indeed, a few studies have attempted to use proxies for the entire term structure of interest rates. In addition, some investigators use the rate of return on corporate equities and/or the expected rate of inflation.

The own rate of return on money obviously depends on the concept of money chosen for analysis. The seemingly simplest case occurs with a narrow definition of money that bears an explicit zero rate of return. In such cases, most investigators have treated the own rate of return as zero. This, however, is not precisely correct since holders of deposits may earn an implicit rate of return, either because they receive services or because service charges may be foregone as the level of deposits rises. Measuring this implicit return is no easy matter. Matters are considerably more complicated when broader definitions of money are used and some components of money bear explicit interest, especially when there are several components each carrying a different rate of return. The aggregate own rate of return would then be a complex function of the interest rates, shares, and elasticities of each of the components. For the most part, researchers have not faced this issue squarely. However, the advent of interest-bearing checkable deposits that exist alongside zero-return demand deposits means that even those using narrow definitions of money must address this issue.

A final variable that appears prominently in equation (2) is the transactions cost, b. This is sometimes interpreted as the brokerage charge for selling 'bonds' or as the 'shoe-leather' cost of going to the bank. Whatever the interpretation, however, such variables have generally been conspicuous by their absence from empirical work. Researchers have thus implicitly assumed that real transactions costs are constant. The validity of this assumption has grown increasingly questionable as innovation and technical change have spread through the financial sector. Unfortunately, there are only highly imperfect proxies available to measure b. The consequences of this are examined below.

III. EMPIRICAL FINDINGS: THE EARLY RESULTS. Before considering empirical results, a word needs to be said about the types of data that have been used. While there have been some cross-section studies using data at a variety of levels of aggregation, the vast majority of available studies employ highly aggregated time series data. Initially these were confined to annual observations, but increasingly the focus has been on shorter periods such as quarterly, monthly, or even weekly data. In part this shift stems from the availability of short-period data but, more importantly, from the related perception that the quarterly or monthly time frame is more useful for guiding monetary policy.

The earliest empirical work in monetary economics primarily involved producing estimates of velocity, characterizing its behaviour over time and identifying the institutional factors responsible for longer-run movements in velocity. (For a discussion of this literature, see Selden, 1956.) Modern empirical studies of money demand first appeared a few years after the publication of Keynes's *General Theory* in 1936. Not surprisingly, these studies focused on testing the prediction of the hypothesis of liquidity preference that there was an inverse relationship between the demand for money and the interest rate. One approach to this problem was to establish a positive correlation between interest rates and velocity.

A second approach involved distinguishing between 'active' and 'idle' balances and then relating idle balances to the interest rate. Conceptually this amounted to positing a demand function for money of the form

$$M/P = ky + f(r) \qquad (3)$$

where y is income or GNP. With k assumed known, idle balances, given by $(M/P - ky)$, can then be related to r. Tobin (1947), using data from 1922 to 1945, calculated k by assuming idle balances were zero in 1929 and found a relatively close relationship between idle balances and r of a roughly hyberbolic shape. Of course, as was recognized at the time, there is an element of arbitrariness in the definition of idle balances, and it is a short step to estimate equation (3) directly, obviating the necessity of distinguishing between active and idle balances. Indeed, this approach had already been suggested in 1939 by A. J. Brown who estimated a variant of (3). (Brown's paper, which is surprisingly modern, both conceptually and statistically, is also noteworthy for the inclusion of the rate of inflation in the demand for money.)

Initially at least, typical estimates of the demand-for-money function were based on annual data and used a log-linear specification, which has constant elasticities. Thus, a typical equation used in empirical work was of the form

$$\ln(M_t/P_t) = \beta_0 + \beta_1 \ln y_t + \beta_2 \ln r_t. \qquad (4)$$

As before, y is a scale variable such as income or wealth and r represents the interest rate. Sometimes several scale variables or interest rates were used; additional variables were also included on occasion. From the late 1950s on many studies estimated equations like (4) for a number of countries. These studies differed in terms of the sample period (sometimes going back as far as the late 1800s) and the specific choice of dependent and independent variables. While these studies hardly produced identical conclusions, at least through the early 1970s a number of common findings did emerge. For the United States (see Laidler, 1977): (1) Various interest rates – sometimes several at once – proved to be of statistical significance in (4) with elasticities of short-term and long-term rates generally ranging from -0.1 to -0.2 and -0.2 to -0.8, respectively. (2) Income, either measured or permanent, and non-human wealth all achieved statistical significance, although typically only when these variables were included one at a time. Some studies viewed the matter as a contest between these several variables, the winner often depending on the sample period, the definition of M, and econometric details. Estimated scale elasticities ranged from about $\frac{1}{2}$ to nearly 2, but most estimates were in the lower end of the range. (3) As judged by a variety of procedures, both formal and informal, the demand function for money exhibited a reasonable amount of stability over time.

While many of the early studies using annual data tended to ignore dynamic aspects of the specification, a number did address this issue, most frequently by the simple device of including a lagged dependent variable in the money demand equation. One rationale for this is the partial adjustment model, which posits the existence of a 'desired' level of real money balances M^*/P, and further assumes that the actual level of money balances adjusts in each period only part of the way toward its desired level. This idea is captured in the logarithmic adjustment equation

$$\ln(M_t/P_t) - \ln(M_{t-1}/P_{t-1})$$
$$= \gamma \ulcorner \eta(M_t^*P_t) - \ln(M_{t-1}/P_{t-1})] \quad (5)$$

where M_t/P_t denotes the actual value of real money balances. The parameter γ governs the speed of adjustment; $\gamma = 1$ corresponds to complete adjustment in one period (i.e. $M_t = M_t^*$). Implementation of (5) is achieved by expressing M_t^*/P_t as a function of y_t and r_t as in (4) and substituting into (5). The resulting equation gives M_t/P_t as a function of y_t, r_t, and M_{t-1}/P_{t-1}. As we shall see below, the partial adjustment model is not without its shortcomings.

Not surprisingly, allowance for dynamics proved of particular importance once investigators began using quarterly data. Dynamics aside, results obtained with quarterly data generally confirmed the findings with annual data. Quarterly data did suggest it was preferable to work with narrow definitions of the money stock. Indeed, some studies suggested there was a further payoff to disaggregating the narrow money stock, either into its components (i.e. currency and checkable deposits) or by type of holder (e.g. household vs. business). On the whole, however, these refinements were not necessary to yield a serviceable quarterly money demand function. A simple specification in which real narrow money balances depended on GNP, a short-term market interest rate, a savings deposit rate, and lagged money balances appeared to be adequate for most purposes (Goldfeld, 1973).

As the 1970s unfolded, however, this happy state of affairs unravelled. Difficulties were particularly pronounced with United States data, but instabilities appeared with equations for other countries as well (Boughton, 1981; Goldfeld, 1976). In the United States these difficulties first surfaced around 1974. Had past behaviour held up, the behaviour of real GNP and interest rates from the end of 1973 to the end of 1975 should have produced a mild decline in money demand in 1974 followed by a recovery in 1975. Instead, real money balances steadily declined, falling by about 7 per cent during this period. The economy seemed to be making do with less money. Or put another way, conventional money demand functions made sizeable and unprecedented overprediction errors. From 1974 to 1976 the cumulative drift was about 9 per cent. Another indication of the difficulty emerged when the post-1973 data were added to the estimation sample. Inclusion of the recent data tended to change the parameter estimates in the conventional money demand function, generally yielding quite unsatisfactory estimates. For example, the parameter γ tended to hover close to zero, implying implausibly long adjustment lags. These same difficulties were picked up by formal econometric tests that rejected the hypothesis that the structure of the money demand function had remained constant. Prior to 1974 these tests had given no indication of instability.

Stimulated by these difficulties, the last decade has witnessed a veritable outpouring of research on money demand. The primary emphasis has been on 'fixing' matters by improving the specification and/or using more appropriate econometric techniques. While progress has been made, even improved specifications have not proved immune from episodes of apparent instability.

IV. RECENT REFORMULATIONS. A substantial part of recent research has focused on the United States, but the issues are of general relevance for other countries. It should be noted that open-economy considerations, which have received only limited attention in the literature on the United States, would be more relevant for many other countries. On the other hand, the emphasis on financial innovation and deregulation in the case of the United States is probably of lesser importance for many countries.

The idea that financial innovation contributed to the instability of money demand in the United States stemmed from two observations: (1) the errant behaviour of money demand in the mid-1970s appeared to be concentrated in business holdings of checkable deposits; and (2) marked improvements were evident in business cash management techniques. These improvements, including such arcane-sounding devices as cash concentration accounts, lockboxes and zero balance accounts, altered the nature of the transactions process and permitted firms to economize on the need for transactions balances. These improvements stemmed both from exogenous technological innovations (e.g. in telecommunications) and from endogenous decisions whereby firms, stimulated by the high opportunity cost of holding cash, invested in new transactions technologies. In the context of the Baumol Tobin inventory-theoretic model of money demand, those changes can be modelled as a reduction in transactions costs, b, while in the Miller–Orr variant one can view these innovations as reducing the uncertainty of receipts and expenditures. While early innovations in the United States appeared concentrated in the business sector, more recent innovations – such as money market mutual funds – and financial deregulation have affected households as well. (As an aside, it should be noted that the constraints of regulation stimulated financial innovation that in turn forced deregulation. To the extent that innovation and deregulation contributed to instability in money demand, regulation, which was in part aimed at improving the workings of monetary policy, sowed the seeds of later difficulties for policy.)

Explicit consideration of financial innovation in an econometric specification has, however, proved extremely difficult. The basic problem is that there are no reliable direct data on transactions costs. What indirect evidence there is stems from the use of time trends to capture exogenous technical change or of some function of previous peak interest rates as a proxy for endogenous reductions in transactions costs. The idea behind the latter variable is that high interest rates create an incentive to incur the fixed costs necessary to introduce a new technology but that once interest rates decline the technology remains in place. The use of a previous peak variable is meant to capture this irreversibility and researchers using such a variable have found that it improves the fit of money demand functions. Unfortunately, however, the resulting estimates do not appear very robust, either to small changes in specification or to the use of additional data. Some economists have played down the potential importance of financial innovations, pointing to the fact that high interest rates did not appear to stimulate the same degree of innovation in other countries. Nevertheless, most empirical researchers remain quite uneasy with their inability to capture adequately relevant changes in transactions costs since it raises the possibility of a continuing source of specification error.

Of course, financial innovation is not the only conceivable source of specification error, and when money demand functions began misbehaving, other elements of the conventional specification were re-examined. In particular, researchers again considered the use of alternative measures of transactions, wealth, and interest rates. They also relaxed the assumption of a constant elasticity implicit in equation (4) and re-examined the benefits of disaggregating money holdings by type of holder (e.g. business vs. households). In contrast with earlier work, these efforts suggested a greater role for wealth and some evidence on the importance of allowing for a nonconstant interest elasticity and for introducing a measure of the own rate of return on money. They also reconfirmed that there are gains to disaggregation by types of holder. Nevertheless, these improvements still left unexplained much of the aberrant behaviour of money demand.

Another approach was to reconsider the definition of money. Since a substantial volume of monetary data is available, economists who are unhappy with the official definitions are free to construct their own. Research along these lines has been in two diametrically opposed directions. The first has regarded the official definitions of even 'narrow' money as too broad, at least from a purely transactions point of view. This concern has led some to suggest using a disaggregated approach in which separate empirical demand functions are estimated for each monetary asset. This sidesteps the definitional issue and at the same time permits the use of econometric techniques that take account of the interrelated nature of the demand functions. In practice, however, the application of this approach has been complicated by the appearance of new financial instruments brought about by deregulation, and such efforts have not been fully successful.

The second approach, noting that the line between transactions and other motives has become empirically murky, has considered whether relatively broad definitions of money could yield a stable demand function. However, conventional broad monetary aggregates obtained by simply adding together quantities of different assets are subject to the criticism that they combine components that offer differing degrees of monetary services. Consequently, most recent research along these lines has involved the weighting of the various components of a broad measure of money by the degree of 'moneyness' or 'liquidity' of each component. Although, the way in which this is done is inevitably somewhat arbitrary, in recent years some progress has been made in applying index-number theory to this issue (Barnett, 1982). Indeed, the Federal Reserve now regularly publishes a number of such weighted money measures, sometimes called Divisia indexes. Thus far, this research seems to suggest that only the broadest of such monetary measures appear to yield a stable demand function. Even this result, however, is not without its difficulties. For one, a complete understanding of this result requires an economic explanation of the behaviour of the weights used to construct the measures. (Especially where the weights are based on relative velocity or turnover data, there appears to be some circularity in the construction of the measures that will give the appearance of stability.) Second, it is important for the results to be useful in formulating policy that these weights be forecastable. On the whole, while promising, the verdict on the Divisia approach is still out, either as an explanation of instability or for use in the policy process.

Yet another feature of money demand that has received recent attention is the dynamics of the adjustment process. As

noted above, the so-called real partial adjustment model of equation (5) formed the basis of much early work. However, this model has come in for a wide variety of criticism. One aspect of this can be seen by rewriting (5) as follows:

$$\ln M_t - \ln M_{t-1} = \gamma [\ln(M_t^*/P_t) - \ln(M_{t-1}/P_{t-1})] + \Delta \ln P_t. \quad (6)$$

As (6) shows, since the coefficient of $\Delta \ln P_t$ is unity, the specification presumes as immediate adjustment to changes in the price level. As this assumption seems unwarranted, more recent research has used the so-called nominal adjustment model given by

$$\ln M_t - \ln M_{t-1} = \gamma (\ln M_t^* - \ln M_{t-1}). \quad (7)$$

Estimation of (7) is quite similar to (5) except that the variable M_{t-1}/P_t replaces the variable M_{t-1}/P_{t-1}. A variety of empirical tests suggest that the nominal model is to be preferred, but also indicate clearly that this change does not repair the money demand function.

Other re-examinations of dynamics have suggested that the simple partial adjustment model, either nominal or real, is more fundamentally flawed. Some writers point to the fact that the Miller–Orr transactions model predicts that money holders, facing a fixed cost of adjusting, will either make no adjustment or a complete adjustment. Partial adjustment would not be observed for an individual money holder. However, the applicability of this feature of the Miller–Orr model to aggregate data is not fully clear. Other attempts to derive an adjustment model from an optimizing framework have suggested models with a variable speed of adjustment with the speed parameter γ depending on income or interest rates. However, there has been only limited empirical work with such models.

Considerably more empirical work has been done with models where the speed of response of money holdings to some shock depends on which variable is producing the change in desired money holdings. This would accommodate the suggestion that changes in real income, especially when such changes are paid in the form of money, should yield quicker adjustments of money holdings than changes in interest rates. To allow for these effects, one must relax the rigid geometrically distributed lag implicit in (5) or (7) and use instead a more general distributed lag specification. Data for the United States do seem to provide some support for this more general adjustment model but, as with other suggested improvements, this change is not sufficient to yield a single acceptable function that fits the post-World War II data.

A final attack on the partial adjustment model involves a more general reconsideration of the adjustment process. The point can be seen most clearly if we assume that the monetary authorities exogenously fix the nominal money supply. In such a world the desired nominal stock of money must adjust to the given stock, presumably by adjustments to variables influencing desired holdings. A particularly simple version of this idea would dispense with the partial adjustment model of (7) and replace it with an adjustment equation for prices as in

$$\ln P_t - \ln P_{t-1} = \lambda (\ln M_t - \ln M_t^*) \quad (8)$$

While this obviates the need for a short-run money demand function, long-run money demand appears in (8) via M_t^*.

A variant of this approach would estimate the money demand function by imposing the assumption of rationality on price expectations. For example, one could begin with (4) or even (7) and use it to solve for the price level. Then, via the Fisher equation expressing the nominal rate of interest as the sum of the real rate and the expected rate of inflation, one can use the hypothesis of rational expectations to express the actual price level (or the rate of inflation) as a function of income, the money stock, and the real rate of interest. If we further posit the stochastic process for income, for the money stock (e.g. via a money supply rule) and for the real rate (e.g. the real rate is constant), we can use the resulting equation to estimate the parameters of the money demand function.

The estimation of money demand via (8) or its rational expectations variant is, however, not without its difficulties. One problem is that this approach implies that the inflation rate reacts quickly to changes in output or the money supply. Put another way, it assumes that the rate of inflation moves like an asset price determined in financial markets. This approach conflicts with the evidence of the stickiness of prices in response to shocks of various sorts. One way around this difficulty is to posit that the adjustments to 'disequilibrium' in the money market are effected in interest rates and/or output. (See Laidler and Bentley (1983), for a small model with these features.)

A second difficulty is the assumption that the money supply is exogenously set. For the United States, at least, the assumption seems most relevant for the period October 1979 to October 1982, the three years during which the Federal Reserve officially adopted monetary targeting. However, stated official policy notwithstanding, some have argued that the Federal Reserve never really pursued a policy of monetary targeting while others have suggested that such a policy began well before October 1979. This suggests that it is not always easy to identify changing monetary regimes. Nevertheless, it is clear that changes in the rules governing monetary policy can have implications for the proper specification and estimation of a money demand function. That is, conventional specifications may work in some circumstances but not others. Indeed, it has been suggested that failure to allow for this accounts for at least part of the apparent instability of conventional money demand functions (Gordon, 1984).

While it is undoubtedly important to view the money demand function as part of a more complete system, to date this has not been empirically done in a satisfactory way. Part of the problem stems from the need to specify the money supply process in some detail; a task made difficult by changing policy strategies and deregulation. Moreover, there is yet another complication, the question of the time unit of the analysis. Practitioners of monetary policy tend to have a relatively short decision-making horizon so that capturing the money supply process may require weekly or monthly data. In contrast, most money demand estimation has used quarterly or annual data. Put another way, proper attention to the dynamics of the monetary sector may require more care in the choice of the time unit of analysis. It may also require some sophisticated econometric techniques to perform estimation in the face of changing monetary regimes.

V. CONCLUSION. The current state of affairs finds the empirical money demand function to be in a bit of disarray, especially if one judges success by our ability to specify a single function that appears stable over the postwar period. To be sure, there are ample potential explanations – perhaps embarrassingly many – for the observed difficulties with conventional models. However, data inadequacies or econometric problems mean that it is not always easy to incorporate these explanations into an empirical demand function for money. Some have concluded from this that greater instability in money demand is a fact, not to be repaired in any simple way. It is the challenge of future research to overcome these difficulties. Given progress to date, it seems likely that further research will yield a more satisfactory statistical explanation of money demand. However, the flimsy nature of past apparent successes and the theoretical and empirical difficulties alluded to above alert us to the need for substantial scrutiny in evaluating new models. Ultimately, of course, such models need to stand the forward-looking test of time; that is, they need to continue to hold outside the period of estimation.

STEPHEN M. GOLDFELD

See also QUANTITY THEORY OF MONEY; RATIONAL EXPECTATIONS.

BIBLIOGRAPHY

Ando, A. and Shell, K. 1975. Demand for money in a general portfolio model. In *The Brookings Model: Perspectives and Recent Developments*, Amsterdam: North-Holland.

Barnett, W. 1982. The optimum level of monetary aggregation. *Journal of Money, Credit and Banking* 14(4), Part II, November, 687–710.

Baumol, W.J. 1952. The transactions demand for cash: an inventory theoretic approach. *Quarterly Journal of Economics* 66, November, 545–56.

Boughton, J.M. 1981. Recent instability of the demand for money: an international perspective. *Southern Economic Journal* 47(3), January, 579–97.

Brown, A.J. 1939. Interest, prices, and the demand schedule for idle money. *Oxford Economic Papers* 2, May, 46–69. Reprinted. in *Oxford Studies in the Price Mechanism*, ed. T. Wilson and P. Andrews, Oxford: Clarendon Press, 1951.

Friedman, M. 1956. The quantity theory of money – a restatement. In M. Friedman, (ed.) *Studies in the Quantity Theory of Money*, Chicago: University of Chicago Press.

Friedman, M. 1959. The demand for money: some theoretical and empirical results. *Journal of Political Economy* 67, August, 327–51.

Goldfeld, S.M. 1973. The demand for money revisited. *Brookings Papers on Economic Activity* No.3, 577–638.

Goldfeld, S.M. 1976. The case of the missing money. *Brookings Papers on Economic Activity* No.3, 683–730.

Gordon, R.J. 1984. The short-run demand for money: a reconsideration. *Journal of Money, Credit and Banking* 16(4), Part I, November, 403–34.

Keynes, J.M. 1936. *The General Theory of Employment, Interest, and Money*. London: Macmillan.

Laidler, D.E.W. 1977. *The Demand for Money: Theories and Evidence*. New York: Dun-Donnelley.

Laidler, D.E.W. and Bentley, B. 1983. A small macro-model of the post-war United States. *Manchester School of Economics and Social Studies* 51(4), December, 317–40.

Miller, M.H. and Orr, D. 1966. A model of the demand for money by firms. *Quarterly Journal of Economics* 80, August, 413–35.

Selden, R. 1956. Monetary velocity in the United States. In *Studies in the Quantity Theory of Money*, ed. M. Friedman, Chicago: University of Chicago Press.

Tobin, J. 1947. Liquidity preference and monetary policy. *Review of Economics and Statistics* 29, May, 124–31.

Tobin, J. 1956. The interest-elasticity of transactions demand for cash. *Review of Economics and Statistics* 38, August, 241–7.

Tobin, J. 1958. Liquidity preference as behavior towards risk. *Review of Economic Studies* 25, February, 65–86.

demand for money: theoretical studies. In any discussion of the demand for money it is important to be clear about the concept of money that is being utilized; otherwise, misunderstandings can arise because of the various possible meanings that readers could have in mind. Here the term will be taken to refer to an economy's *medium of exchange*: that is, to a tangible asset that is generally accepted in payment for any commodity. Money thus conceived will also serve as a store of value, of course, but may be of minor importance to the economy in that capacity. The monetary asset will usually also serve as the economy's medium of account – that is, prices will be quoted in terms of money – since additional accounting costs would be incurred if the unit of account were a quantity of some asset other than money. The medium-of-account role is, however, not logically tied to the medium of exchange (Wicksell, 1906; Niehans, 1978).

Throughout much of Western history, most economies have adopted as their principal medium of exchange a commodity that would be valuable even if it were not used as money. Recently, however, fiat money – intrinsically worthless tokens made of paper or some other cheap material – has come to predominate. Under a commodity money arrangement, the exchange value of money will depend upon the demand for the monetary commodity in its non-monetary as well as its monetary uses. But in a discussion of money demand, as distinct from a discussion of the price level, any possible non-monetary demand for the medium of exchange – which will be absent anyhow in fiat money system – can legitimately be ignored.

The quantity of money demanded in any economy – indeed, the set of assets that have monetary status – will be dependent upon prevailing institutions, regulations and technology. Technical progress in the payments industry will, for instance, tend to alter the quantity of money demanded for given values of determinants such as income. This dependence does not, however, imply that the demand for money is a nebulous or unusable concept, any more than the existence of technical progress and regulatory change in the transportation industry does so for the demand for automobiles. In practice, some lack of clarity pertains to the operational measurement of the money stock, as it does to the stock of automobiles or other commodities. But in an economy with a well-established national currency, the principle is relatively clear: assets are part of the money stock if and only if they constitute *claims* to currency, unrestricted legal claims that can be promptly and cheaply exercised (at par). This principle rationalizes the common practice of including demand deposits in the money stock of the United States, while excluding time deposits and various other assets.

The rapid development during the 1960s and 1970s of computer and telecommunications technologies has led some writers (e.g. Fama, 1980) to contemplate economies – anticipated by Wicksell (1906) – in which virtually all purchases are effected not by the transfer of a tangible medium of exchange, but by means of signals to an accounting network, signals that result in appropriate debits and credits to the wealth accounts of buyers and sellers. If there were literally *no* medium of exchange, the wealth accounts being claims to some specified bundle of commodities, the economy in question would be properly regarded and analysed as a non-monetary economy, albeit one that avoids the inefficiencies of crude barter. If, by contrast, the accounting network's credits were claims to quantities of a fiat or commodity medium of exchange, then individuals' credit balances would appropriately be included as part of the money stock (McCallum, 1985).

BASIC PRINCIPLES. An overview of the basic principles of money demand theory can be obtained by considering a hypothetical household that seeks at time t to maximize

$$u(c_t, l_t) + \beta u(c_{t+1}, l_{t+1}) + \beta^2 u(c_{t+2}, l_{t+2}) + \cdots \quad (1)$$

where c_t and l_t are the household's consumption and leisure during t and where $\beta = 1/(1 + \delta)$, with $\delta > 0$ the rate of time preference. The within-period utility function $u(\cdot, \cdot)$ is taken to be well behaved so that unique positive values will be chosen for c_t and l_t. The household has access to a productive technology described by a production function that is homogeneous of degree one in capital and labour inputs. But for simplicity we assume that labour is supplied inelastically, so this

function can be written as $y_t = f(k_{t-1})$, where y_t is production during t and k_{t-1} is the stock of capital held at the end of period $t-1$. The function $f(\cdot)$ is well behaved, so a unique positive value of k_t will be chosen for the upcoming period. Capital is unconsumed output, so its price is the same as that of the consumption good and its rate of return between t and $t + 1$ is $f'(k_t)$.

Although this set-up explicitly recognizes the existence of only one good, it is intended to serve a simplified representation – one formally justified by the analysis of Lucas (1980) – of an economy in which the household sells its specialized output and makes purchases (at constant relative prices) of a large number of distinct consumption goods. Carrying out these purchases requires *shopping time*, s_t, which subtracts from leisure: $l_t = 1 - s_t$, where units are chosen so that there is 1 unit of time per period available for shopping and leisure together. (If labour were elastically supplied, then labour time would have to be included in the expression.) In a monetary economy, however, the amount of shopping time required for a given amount of consumption will depend negatively upon the quantity of real money balances held by the household (up to some satiation level). For concreteness, we assume that

$$s_t = \psi(c_t, m_t) \quad (2)$$

where $\psi(\cdot, \cdot)$ has partial derivatives $\psi_1 > 0$ and $\psi_2 \leqslant 0$. In (2), $m_t = M_t/P_t$, where M_t is the nominal stock of money held at the end of t and P_t is the money price of a consumption bundle. (A variant with M_t denoting the start-of-period money stock will be mentioned below.) The transaction variable is here specified as c_t rather than $c_t + \Delta k_t$ to reflect the idea that only a few distinct capital goods will be utilized, so that the transaction cost to expenditure ratio will be much lower than for consumption goods.

Besides capital and money, there is a third asset available to the household. This asset is a nominal bond; i.e., a one-period security that may be purchased at the price $1/(1 + R_t)$ in period t and redeemed for one unit of money in $t + 1$. The symbol B_t will be used to denote the number (possibly negative) of these securities purchased by the household in period t, while $b_t = B_t/P_t$.

In the setting described, the household's budget constraint for period t may be written as follows:

$$f(k_{t-1}) + v_t \geqslant c_t + k_t - k_{t-1} + m_t - (1 + \pi_t)^{-1}m_{t-1}$$
$$+ (1 + R_t)^{-1}b_t - (1 + \pi_t)^{-1}b_{t-1} \quad (3)$$

Here v_t is the real value of lump-sum transfers (net of taxes) from the government, while π_t is the inflation rate, $\pi_t = (P_t - P_{t-1})/P_{t-1}$. Given the objective of maximizing (1), first-order conditions necessary for optimality of the household's choices include the following, in which ϕ_t and λ_t are Lagrangian multipliers associated with the constraints (2) and (3), respectively:

$$u_1(c_t, 1 - s_t) - \phi_t\psi_1(c_t, m_t) - \lambda_t = 0 \quad (4)$$

$$-u_2(c_t, 1 - s_t) + \phi_t = 0 \quad (5)$$

$$-\phi_t\psi_2(c_t, m_t) - \lambda_t + \beta\lambda_{t+1}(1 + \pi_{t+1})^{-1} = 0 \quad (6)$$

$$-\lambda_t + \beta\lambda_{t+1}[f'(k_t) + 1] = 0 \quad (7)$$

$$-\lambda_t(1 + R_t)^{-1} + \beta\lambda_{t+1}(1 + \pi_{t+1})^{-1} = 0. \quad (8)$$

These conditions, together with the constraints (2) and (3), determine current and planned values of $c_t, s_t, m_t, k_t, b_t, \phi_t$, and λ_t for given time paths of v_t, R_t, and π_t (which are exogenous to the household) and the predetermined values of k_{t-1}, m_{t-1}, and b_{t-1}. (There is also a relevant transversality condition, but it can be ignored for the issues at hand.) Also l_t values can be obtained from $l_t = 1 - s_t$ and, with P_{t-1} given, P_t, M_t, and B_t values are implied by the π_t, m_t, and b_t sequences.

The household's optimizing choice of m_t can be described in terms of two distinct concepts of a money-demand function. The first of these is a proper demand function; that is, a relationship giving the chosen quantity as a function of variables that are either predetermined or exogenous to the economic unit in question. In the present context, the money-demand function of that type will be of the form:

$$m_t = \mu(k_{t-1}, m_{t-1}, b_{t-1}, v_t, v_{t+1}, \ldots, R_t,$$
$$R_{t+1}, \ldots, \pi_t, \pi_{t+1}, \ldots) \quad (9)$$

where the variables dated $t + 1$, $t + 2, \ldots$ must be understood as anticipated values. Now, it will be obvious that this relationship does not closely resemble those normally described in the literature as 'money demand functions'. There is a second type of relationship implied by the model, however, that does have such a resemblance. To obtain this second expression, one can eliminate $\beta\lambda_{t+1}(1 + \pi_{t+1})^{-1}$ between equations (6) and (8), then eliminate λ_t and finally ϕ_t from the resultant by using (4) and (5). These steps yield the following:

$$-u_2(c_t, 1 - s_t)\psi_2(c_t, m_t) = [u_1(c_t, 1 - s_t)$$
$$- u_2(c_t, 1 - s_t)\psi_1(c_t, m_t)][1 - (1 + R_t)^{-1}]. \quad (10)$$

Then $\psi(c_t, m_t)$ can be used in place of s_t, and the result is a relationship that involves *only* m_t, c_t, and R_t. Consequently, (10) can be expressed in the form:

$$f(m_t, c_t, R_t) = 0 \quad (11)$$

and if the latter is solvable for m_t one can obtain:

$$M_t/P_t = L(c_t, R_t). \quad (12)$$

Thus the model at hand yields a *portfolio-balance* relationship between real money-balances demanded, a variable measuring the volume of transactions conducted, and the nominal interest rate (which reflects the cost of holding money rather than bonds). It can be shown, moreover, that for reasonable specifications of the utility and shopping-time functions, $L(\cdot, \cdot)$ will be increasing in its first argument and decreasing in the second.

There are, of course, two problems in moving from a demand function (of either type) for an individual household to one that pertains to the economy as a whole. The first of these involves the usual problem of aggregating over households that may have different tastes and/or levels of wealth. It is well known that the conditions permitting such aggregation are extremely stringent in the context of any sort of behavioural relation; but for many theoretical purposes it is sensible to pretend that they are satisfied. The second problem concerns the existence of economic units other than households – 'firms' being the most obvious example. To construct a model analogous to that above for a firm, one would presumably posit maximization of the present value of real net receipts rather than (1), and the constraints would be different. In particular, the shopping-time function (2) would need to be replaced with a more general relationship depicting resources used in conducting transactions as a function of their volume and the real quantity of money held. The transaction measure would not be c_t for firms or, therefore, for the economy as a whole. But the general aspects of the analysis would be similar, so we shall proceed under the presumption that the crucial issues are adequately represented in a setting that recognizes only economic units like the 'households' described above.

The distinction between the proper money-demand function (9) and the more standard portfolio-balance relation (12) is important in the context of certain issues. As an example, consider the issue of whether wealth or income should appear as a 'scale variable' (Meltzer, 1963). From the foregoing, it is clear that wealth is an important determinant of money demand in the sense that k_{t-1}, m_{t-1}, and b_{t-1} are arguments of the demand function (9). Nevertheless, formulation (12) indicates that there is no separate role for wealth in a portfolio-balance relation if appropriate transaction and opportunity-cost variables are included.

An issue that naturally arises concerns the foregoing discussion's neglect of randomness. How would the analysis be affected if it were recognized that future values of variables cannot possibly be known with certainty? In answer, let us suppose that the household knows current values of all relevant variables including P_t, R_t, and v_t when making decisions on m_t and c_t, but that its views concerning variables dated $t + 1, t + 2, \ldots$ are held in the form of non-degenerate probability distributions. Suppose also that there is uncertainty in production, so that the marginal product of capital in $t + 1$, $f'(k_t)$, is viewed as random. Then the household's problem becomes one of maximizing the expectation of (1), with $u(\cdot, \cdot)$ a von Neumann-Morgenstern utility function, given information available in period t. Consequently, the first-order conditions (4)–(8) must be replaced with ones that involve conditional expectations. For example, equation (7) would be replaced with:

$$- \lambda_t + \beta E_t\{\lambda_{t+1}[f'(k_t) + 1]\} = 0 \quad (7')$$

where $E_t(\cdot)$ denotes the expectation of the indicated variable conditional upon known values of P_t, R_t, v_t, and so on. With this modification, the nature of the proper demand function becomes much more complex – indeed, for most specifications no closed form solution analogous to (9) will exist. Nevertheless, the portfolio-balance relation (12) will continue to hold exactly as before, for the steps described in its derivation above remain the same except that it is $E_t[\beta\lambda_{t+1}(1 + \pi_{t+1})^{-1}]$ that is eliminated between equations corresponding to (6) and (8). From this result it follows that, according to our model, the relationship of M_t/P_t to the transaction and opportunity–cost variables is invariant to changes in the probability distribution of future variables.

Another specification variant that should be mentioned reflects the assumption that it is money held at the start of a period, not its end, that facilitates transactions conducted during the period. If that change in specification were made and the foregoing analysis repeated, it would be found that the household's concern in period t would be to have the appropriate level of real money balances at the start of period $t + 1$. The portfolio–balance relation analogous to (12) that would be obtained in the deterministic case would relate m_{t+1} to c_{t+1} and R_t, where $m_{t+1} = M_{t+1}/P_{t+1}$ with M_{t+1} reflecting money holdings at the end of period t. Consequently, M_{t+1}/P_t would be related to R_t, planned c_{t+1}, and P_t/P_{t+1}. Thus the theory does not work out as cleanly as in the case considered above even in the absence of randomness, and is complicated further by the recognition of the latter. The fundamental nature of the relationships are, however, the same as above.

Another point deserving of mention is that if labour is supplied elastically, the portfolio-balance relation analogous to (12) will include the real wage-rate as an additional argument. This has been noted by Karni (1973) and Dutton and Gramm (1973). More generally, the existence of other relevant margins of substitution can bring in other variables. If stocks of commodities held by households affect shopping-time requirements, for example, the inflation rate will appear separately in the counterpart of (12) (see Feige and Parkin, 1971).

Finally, it must be recognised that the simplicity of the portfolio-balance relation (12) would be lost if the intertemporal utility function (1) were not time-separable. If, for example, the function $u(c_t, l_t)$ in (1) were replaced with $u(c_t, l_t, l_{t-1})$ or $u(c_t, c_{t-1}, l_t)$, as has been suggested in the business cycle literature, then the dynamic aspect of the household's choices would be more complex and a relation like (12) – i.e. one that includes only contemporaneous variables – could not be derived.

HISTORICAL DEVELOPMENT. The approach to money-demand analysis outlined above, which features intertemporal optimization choices by individual economic agents whose transactions are facilitated by their holdings of money, has evolved gradually over time. In this section we briefly review that evolution.

While the earlier literature on the quantity theory of money contained many important insights, its emphasis was on the comparison of market equilibria rather than individual choice; that is, on 'market experiments' rather than 'individual experiments', in the language of Patinkin (1956). Consequently, there was little explicit consideration of money-demand behaviour in pre-1900 writings in the quantity theory tradition. Indeed, there was little emphasis on money demand *per se* even in the classic contributions of Mill (1848), Wicksell (1906) and Fisher (1911), despite the clear recognition by those analysts that some particular quantity of real money holdings would be desired by the inhabitants of an economy under any specified set of circumstances. Notable exceptions, discussed by Patinkin (1956, pp. 386–417), were provided by Walras and Schlesinger.

In the English language literature, the notion of money demand came forth more strongly in the 'cash balance' approach of Cambridge economists, an approach that featured analysis organized around the concepts of money demand and supply. This organizing principle was present in the early (c 1871) but unpublished writings of Marshall (see Whitaker, 1975, p. 165–8) and was laid out with great explicitness by Pigou (1917). The Cambridge approach presumed that the quantity of money demanded would depend primarily on the volume of transactions to be undertaken, but emphasized volition on the part of money-holders and recognized (sporadically) that the ratio of real balances to transaction volume would be affected by foregone 'investment income' (i.e., interest earnings). In this regard Cannan (1921), a non-Cambridge economist who was influenced by Marshall, noted that the quantity of money demanded should be negatively related to anticipated inflation – an insight previously expressed by Marshall in his testimony of 1886 for the Royal Commission on the Depression of Trade and Industry (Marshall, 1926). In addition, Cannan developed very clearly the point that the relevant concept is the demand for a *stock* of money.

Although the aforementioned theorists developed several important constituents of a satisfactory money-demand theory, none of them unambiguously cast his explanation in terms of marginal analysis. Thus a significant advance was provided by Lavington (1921, p. 30), in a chapter entitled 'The Demand for Money', who attempted a statement of the marginal conditions that must be satisfied for optimality by an individual who consumes, holds money, and holds interest-bearing securities. But despite the merits of his attempt, Lavington confused – as Patinkin (1956, p. 418) points out – the subjective sacrifice of permanently adding a dollar to cash balances with that of adding it for only one period. Thus it was left for Fisher (1930, p. 216) to provide a related but correct statement. The dis-

cussions of both Lavington and Fisher are notable for identifying the interest rate as a key determinant of the marginal opportunity cost of holding money.

In a justly famous article, Hicks (1935) argued persuasively that progress in the theory of money would require the treatment of money demand as a problem of individual choice at the margin. Building upon some insightful but unclear suggestions in Keynes's *Treatise on Money* (1930), Hicks investigated an agent's decision concerning the relative amounts of money and securities to be held at a point in time. He emphasized the need to explain why individuals willingly hold money when its return is exceeded by those available from other assets and – following Lavington and Fisher – concluded that money provides a service yield not offered by other assts. Hicks also noted that the positive transaction cost of investing in securities makes it unprofitable to undertake such investments for very short periods. Besides identifying the key aspects of marginal analysis of money demand. Hicks (1935) pointed out that an individual's total wealth will influence his demand for money. All of these points were developed further in chapters 13 and 19 of Hicks's *Value and Capital* (1939). The analysis in the latter is, some misleading statements about the nature of interest notwithstanding, substantively very close to that outlined in the previous section of this article. Hicks did not, however, provide formal conditions relating to money demand in his mathematical appendix.

The period between 1935 and 1939 witnessed, of course, the publication of Keynes's *General Theory* (1936). That work emphasized the importance for macroeconomic analysis of the interest-sensitivity of money demand – 'liquidity preference', in Keynes's terminology – and was in that respect, as in many others, enormously influential. Its treatment of money demand *per se* was not highly original, however, in terms of fundamentals. (This statement ignores some peculiarities resulting from a presumably inadvertent attribution of money illusion; on this topic, again see Patinkin, 1956, pp. 173–4.)

The importance of several items mentioned above – payments practices, foregone interest and transaction costs – was explicitly depicted in the formal optimization models developed several years later by Baumol (1952) and Tobin (1956). These models, which were suggested by mathematical inventory theory, assume the presence of two assets (money and an interest-bearing security), a fixed cost of making transfers between money and the security, and a lack of synchronization between (exogenously given) receipt and expenditure streams. In addition, they assume that all payments are made with money. Economic units are depicted as choosing the optimal frequency for money-security transfers so as to maximize interest earnings net of transaction costs.

In Baumol's treatment, which ignores integer constraints on the number of transactions per period, the income and interest-rate elasticities of real money demand are found to be $\frac{1}{2}$ and $-\frac{1}{2}$, respectively. Thus the model implies 'economies of scale' in making transactions. Tobin's (1956) analysis takes account of integer constraints, by contrast, and thus implies that individuals respond in a discontinuous fashion to alternative values of the interest rate. In his model it appears entirely possible for individual economic units to choose corner solutions in which none of the interest-bearing security is held. A number of extensions of the Baumol–Tobin approach have been made by various authors; for an insightful survey the reader is referred to Barro and Fischer (1976).

Miller and Orr (1966) pioneered the inventory approach to money demand theory in a stochastic context. Specifically, in their analysis a firm's net cash inflow is generated as a random walk, and the firm chooses a policy to minimize the sum of transaction and foregone-interest costs. The optimal decision rule is of the (S, s) type: when money balances reach zero or a ceiling, S, the firm makes transactions to return the balance to the level s. In this setting there are again predicted economies of scale, while the interest-rate elasticity is $-\frac{1}{3}$. For extensions the reader is again referred to Barro and Fisher (1976).

The various inventory models of money demand possess the desirable feature of providing an explicit depiction of the *source* of money's service yield to an individual holder. It has been noted (e.g. by Friedman and Schwartz, 1970) that the type of transaction demand described by these models is unable to account for more than a fraction of the transaction balances held in actual economies. Furthermore, their treatment of expenditure and receipt streams as exogenous is unfortunate and they do not generalize easily to fully dynamic settings. These points imply, however, only that the inventory models should not be interpreted too literally. In terms of fundamentals they are closely related to the basic model outlined in the previous section.

A quite different approach was put forth by Tobin (1958), in a paper that views the demand for money as arising from a portfolio allocation decision made under conditions of uncertainty. In the more influential of the paper's models, the individual wealth-holder must allocate his portfolio between a riskless asset, identified as money, and an asset with an uncertain return whose expected value exceeds that of money. Tobin shows how the optimal portfolio mix depends, under the assumption of expected utility maximization, on the individual's degree of risk aversion, his wealth, and the mean-variance characteristics of the risky asset's return distribution. The analysis implies a negative interest sensitivity of money demand, thereby satisfying Tobin's desire to provide an additional rationalization of Keynes's (1936) liquidity-preference hypothesis. The approach has, however, two shortcomings. First, in actuality money does not have a yield that is riskless in real terms, which is the relevant concept for rational individuals. Second, and more seriously, in many actual economies there exist assets 'that have precisely the same risk characteristics as money and yield higher returns' (Barro and Fischer, 1976, p. 139). Under such conditions, the model implies that no money will be held.

Another influential item from this period was provided by Friedman's well-known 'restatement' of the quantity theory (1956). In that paper, as in Tobin's, the principal role of money is as a form of wealth. Friedman's analysis emphasized margins of substitution between money and assets other than bonds (e.g. durable consumption goods and equities). The main contribution of the paper was to help rekindle interest in monetary analysis from a macroeconomic perspective, however, rather than to advance the formal theory of money demand.

A model that may be viewed as a formalization of Hicks's (1935, 1939) approach was outlined by Sidrauski (1967). The main purpose of Sidrauski's paper was to study the interaction of inflation and capital accumulation in a dynamic context, but his analysis gives rise to optimality conditions much like those of equations (4)–(8) of the present article and thus implies money-demand functions like (9) and (12). The main difference between Sidrauski's model and ours is merely due to our use of the 'shopping time' specification, which was suggested by Saving (1971). That feature makes real balances an argument of each individual's utility function only indirectly, rather than directly, and indicates the type of phenomenon that advocates of the direct approach presumably have in mind. Thus Sidrauski's implied money-demand model is the basis for the one presented above, while a stochastic version of the latter, being fundamentally similar to inventory or direct utility-yield specifications, is broadly representative of current mainstream views.

ONGOING CONTROVERSIES. Having outlined the current mainstream approach to money-demand analysis and its evolution, we now turn to matters that continue to be controversial. The first of these concerns the role of uncertainty. In that regard, one point has already been developed; i.e., that rate-of-return uncertainty on other assets cannot be used to explain why individuals hold money in economies – such as that of the US – in which there exist very short-term assets that yield positive interest and are essentially riskless in nominal terms. But this does not imply that uncertainty is unimportant for money demand in a more general sense, for there are various ways in which it can affect the analysis. In the basic model outlined above, uncertainty appears explicitly only by way of the assumption that households view asset returns as random. In that case, if money demand and consumption decisions for a period are made simultaneously then the portfolio-balance relation (12) will be – as shown above – invariant to changes in the return distributions. But the same is not true for the proper demand function (9). And the arguments c_t and R_t of (12) will themselves be affected by the extent of uncertainty, for it will affect households' saving, as well as portfolio, decisions. The former, of course, impact not only on c_t but also on the economy's capital stock and thus, via the equilibrium real return on capital, on R_t. In addition, because R_t is set in nominal terms, its level will include a risk differential for inflation uncertainty (Fama and Farber, 1979).

Furthermore, the invariance of (12) to uncertainty breaks down if money must be held at the start of a period to yield its transaction services during that period. In this case, the money demand decision temporally precedes the related consumption decision so the marginal service yield of money is random, with moments that depend on the covariance matrix of forecast errors for consumption and the price level. Thus the extent of uncertainty, as reflected in this covariance matrix, influences the quantity of real balances demanded in relation to R_t and plans for c_{t+1}.

There is, moreover, another type of uncertainty that is even more fundamental than rate-of-return randomness. In particular, the existence of uncertainty regarding exchange opportunities available at an extremely fine level of temporal and spatial disaggregation – uncertainties regarding the 'double coincidence of wants' in meetings with potential exchange partners – provides the basic *raison d'être* for a medium of exchange. In addition, the ready verifiability of money enhances the efficiency of the exchange process by permitting individuals to economize on the production of information when there is uncertainty about the reputation of potential trading partners. Thus uncertainty is crucial in explaining why it is that money holdings help to facilitate transactions – to save 'shopping time' in our formalization. In this way randomness is critically involved, even when it does not appear explicitly in the analysis. (Alternative treatments of uncertainty in the exchange process have been provided by Patinkin, 1956; Brunner and Meltzer, 1971; King and Plosser, 1986).

An important concern of macroeconomists in recent years has been to specify models in terms of genuinely structural relationships; that is, ones that are invariant to policy changes. This desire has led to increased emphasis on explicit analysis of individuals' dynamic optimization problems, with these expressed in terms of basic taste and technology parameters. Analysis of that type is especially problematical in the area of money demand, however, because of the difficulty of specifying rigorously the precise way – at a 'deeper' level than (2), for example – in which money facilitates the exchange process. One prominent attempt to surmount this difficulty has featured the application of a class of overlapping-generations models – i.e. dynamic equilibrium models that emphasize the differing perspectives on saving of young and old individuals – to a variety of problems in monetary economics. The particular class of overlapping-generations models in question is one in which, while there is an analytical entity termed 'fiat money', the specification deliberately excludes any shopping-time or related feature that would represent the transaction-facilitating aspect of money. Thus this approach, promoted most prominently in the work of Wallace (1980), tries to surmount the difficulty of modelling the medium-of-exchange function of money by simply ignoring it, emphasizing instead the asset's function as a store of value.

Models developed under this overlapping-generations approach typically possess highly distinctive implications, of which the particularly striking examples will be mentioned. First, if the monetary authority causes the stock of money to grow at a rate in excess of the economy's rate of output growth, no money will be demanded and the price level will be infinite. Second, steady-state equilibria in which money is valued will be Pareto optimal if and only if the growth rate of the money stock is non-positive. Third, open-market changes in the money stock will have no effect on the price level. It has been shown, however, that these implications result from the models' neglect of the medium-of-exchange function of money. Specifically. McCallum (1983) demonstrates that all three implications vanish if this neglect is remedied by recognition of shopping-time considerations as above. That conclusion suggests that the class of overlapping-generations models under discussion provides a seriously misleading framework for the analysis of monetary issues. This weakness, it should be added, results not from the generational structure of these models, but from the overly restrictive application of the principle that assets are valued solely on the basis of the returns that they yield; in particular, the models fail to reflect the non-pecuniary return provided by holdings of the medium of exchange. On these points see also Tobin (1980).

Recognizing this problem but desiring to avoid specifications like (2), some researchers have been attracted to the use of models incorporating a *cash-in-advance* constraint (e.g. Lucas, 1980; Svensson, 1985). In these models, it is assumed that an individual's purchases in any period cannot exceed the quantity of money brought into that period. Clearly, imposition of this type of constraint gives a medium-of-exchange role to the model's monetary asset and thereby avoids the problems of the Wallace-style overlapping-generations models. Whether it does so in a satisfactory manner is, however, more doubtful. In particular, the cash-in-advance formulation implies that start-of-period money holdings place a *strict* upper limit on purchase during the period. This is a considerably more stringent notion than that implied by (2), which is that such purchases are possible but increasingly expensive in terms of time and/or other resources. Thus the demand for money will tend to be less sensitive to interest-rate changes with the cash-in-advance specification than with one that ties consumption and money holding together less rigidly. More generally, the cash-in-advance specification can be viewed as an extreme special case of the shopping-time function described in (2), in much the same way as a fixed-coefficient production function is a special case of a more general neoclassical technology. For some issues, use of the special case specification will be convenient and not misleading, but care must be exerted to avoid inappropriate applications. It seems entirely unwarranted, moreover, to opt for the cash-in-advance specification in the hope that it will be

more nearly structural and less open to the Lucas critique (1976) than relations such as (2). Both of these specificational devices – and probably any that will be analytically tractable in a macroeconomic context – should be viewed not as literal depictions of technological or social constraints, but as potentially useful metaphors that permit the analyst to recognize in a rough way the benefits of monetary exchange. (On the general topic, see Fischer, 1974).

A final controversy that deserves brief mention pertains to an aspect of money demand theory that has not been formally discussed above, but which is of considerable importance in practical applications. Typically, econometric estimates of money-demand functions combine 'long run' specifications such as (12) with a *partial adjustment* process that relates actual money-holdings to the implied 'long run' values. Operationally, this approach often results in a regression equation that includes a lagged value of the money stock as an explanatory variable. (Distributed-lag formulations are analytically similar.) Adoption of the partial adjustments mechanism is justified by appeal to portfolio-adjustment costs. Specifically, some authors argue that money balances serve as a 'buffer stock' that temporarily accommodates unexpected variations in income, while others attribute sluggish adjustments to search costs.

From the theoretical perspective, however, the foregoing interpretation for the role of lagged-money balances (or distributed lags) appears weak. If is difficult to believe that tangible adjustment costs are significant, and in their absence there is no role for lagged money balances, in formulations as such as (12) when appropriate transaction and opportunity-cost variables are included. Furthermore, typical estimates suggest adjustment speeds that are too slow to be plausible.

These points have been stressed by Goodfriend (1985), who offers an alternative explanation for the relevant empirical findings. A model in which there is full contemporaneous adjustment of money-holding to transaction and opportunity-cost variables is shown to imply a positive coefficient on lagged money when these determinants are positively autocorrelated and contaminated with measurement error. Under this interpretation, the lagged variable is devoid of behavioural significance; it enters the regression only because it helps to explain the dependent variable in a mongrel equation that mixes together relations pertaining to money-demand and other aspects of behaviour. (This particular conclusion is shared with the 'buffer stock' approach described by Laidler (1984), which interprets the conventional regression as a confounding of money-demand with sluggish price-adjustment behaviour.) Furthermore, the measurement error hypothesis can account for positive autocorrelation of residuals in the conventional regression and, if measurement errors are serially correlated, the *magnitude* of the lagged-money coefficient typically found in practice.

BENNETT T. McCALLUM AND MARVIN S. GOODFRIEND

See also LIQUIDITY PREFERENCE; QUANTITY THEORY OF MONEY; VELOCITY OF CIRCULATION.

BIBLIOGRAPHY

Barro, R.J. and Fischer, S. 1976. Recent developments in monetary theory. *Journal of Monetary Economics* 2(2), April, 133–67.

Baumol, W.J. 1952. The transactions demand for cash: an inventory theoretic approach. *Quarterly Journal of Economics* 66, November, 545–56.

Brunner, K. and Meltzer, A. 1971. The uses of money: money in the theory of an exchange economy. *American Economic Review* 61(5), December, 784–805.

Cannan, E. 1921. The application of the theoretical apparatus of supply and demand to units of currency. *Economic Journal* 31, December, 453–61.

Dutton, D.S. and Gramm, W.P. 1973. Transactions costs, the wage rate, and the demand for money. *American Economic Review* 63(4), September, 652–65.

Fama, E.F. 1980. Banking in the theory of finance. *Journal of Monetary Economics* 6(1), January, 39–57.

Fama, E.F. and Farber, A. 1979. Money, bonds, and foreign exchange. *American Economic Review* 69(4), September, 639–49.

Feige, E. and Parkin, M. 1971. The optimal quantity of money, bonds, commodity inventories, and capital. *American Economic Review* 61(3), June, 335–49.

Fischer, S. 1974. Money and the production function. *Economic Inquiry* 12(4), December, 517–33.

Fisher, I. 1911. *The Purchasing Power of Money*. New York: Macmillan.

Fisher, I. 1930. *The Theory of Interest*. New York: Macmillan.

Friedman, M. 1956. The quantity theory of money: a restatement. In *Studies in the Quantity Theory of Money*, ed. M. Friedman, Chicago: University of Chicago Press.

Friedman, M. and Schwartz, A.J. 1970. *Monetary Statistics of the United States*. New York: Columbia Press for the National Bureau of Economic Research.

Goodfriend, M. 1985. Reinterpreting money demand regressions. *Carnegie-Rochester Conference Series on Public Policy* 22, Spring, 207–42.

Hicks, J.R. 1935. A suggestion for simplifying the theory of money. *Economica* 2, February, 1–19.

Hicks, J.R. 1939. *Value and Capital*. Oxford: Oxford University Press.

Karni, E. 1973. The transactions demand for cash: incorporation of the value of time into the inventory approach. *Journal of Political Economy* 81(5), September–October, 1216–25.

Keynes, J.M. 1930. *A Treatise on Money*. 2 vols, London: Macmillan.

Keynes, J.M. 1936. *The General Theory of Employment, Interest and Money*. London: Macmillan.

King, R.G. and Plosser, C.I. 1986. Money as the mechanism of exchange. *Journal of Monetary Economics* 17(1), January, 93–115.

Lavington, F. 1921. *The English Capital Market*. London: Methuen.

Lucas, R.E., Jr. 1976. Econometric policy evaluation: a critique. *Carnegie-Rochester Conference Series on Public Policy* 5, Autumn, 19–46.

Lucas, R.E., Jr. 1980. Equilibrium in a pure currency economy. In *Models of Monetary Economies*, ed. J.H. Kareken and N. Wallace, Minneapolis: Federal Reserve Bank of Minneapolis.

McCallum, B.T. 1983. The role of overlapping generations models in monetary economics. *Carnegie-Rochester Conference Series on Public Policy* 18, Spring, 9–44.

McCallum, B.T. 1985. Bank deregulation, accounting systems of exchange, and the unit of account: a critical review. *Carnegie-Rochester Conference Series on Public Policy* 23, Autumn, 13–45.

Marshall, A. 1926. *Official Papers by Alfred Marshall*. Ed. J.M. Keynes, London: Macmillan.

Meltzer, A.H. 1963. The demand for money: the evidence from the time series. *Journal of Political Economy* 71, June, 219–46.

Mill, J.S. 1848. *Principles of Political Economy*. 2 vols. London: John W. Parker.

Miller, M.H. and Orr, D. 1966. A model of the demand for money by firms. *Quarterly Journal of Economics* 80, August, 413–35.

Niehans, J. 1978. *The Theory of Money*. Baltimore: Johns Hopkins University Press.

Patinkin, D. 1956. *Money, Interest, and Prices*. New York: Harper and Row.

Pigou, A.C. 1917. The value of money. *Quarterly Journal of Economics* 32, November, 38–65.

Saving, T.R. 1971. Transactions costs and the demand for money. *American Economic Review* 61(3), June, 407–20.

Sidrauski, M. 1967. Rational choice and patterns of growth in a monetary economy. *American Economic Association Papers and Proceedings* 57, May, 534–44.

Svensson, L.E.O. 1985. Money and asset prices in a cash-in-advance economy. *Journal of Political Economy* 93(5), October, 919–44.

Tobin, J. 1956. The interest-elasticity of transactions demand for cash. *Review of Economics and Statistics* 38, August, 241–7.

Tobin, J. 1958. Liquidity preference as behavior toward risk. *Review of Economic Studies* 25, February, 65–86.

Tobin, J. 1980. Discussion. In *Models of Monetary Economies*, ed.

J.H. Kareken and N. Wallace, Minneapolis: Federal Reserve Bank of Minneapolis.

Wallace, N. 1980. The overlapping generations model of fiat money. In *Models of Monetary Economies*, ed. J.H. Kareken and N. Wallace, Minneapolis: Federal Reserve Bank of Minneapolis.

Whitaker, J.K. (ed.) 1975. *The Early Economic Writings of Alfred Marshall, 1867–1890*. 2 vols, New York: Free Press.

Wicksell, K. 1906. *Lectures on Political Economy*. Trans. E. Classen, London: Routledge & Kegan Paul, 1935, Vol. II.

demand management. The expression 'demand management' came into general use after World War II. The idea has its roots in the *General Theory of Employment, Interest and Money* (1936), in which Keynes had argued that in capitalist economies the aggregate demand for goods and services could fall short of the capacity of the economy to produce, with resultant unemployment. A deficiency of demand could be made good by governments increasing their expenditure or lowering taxes, or by the monetary authorities lowering interest rates to stimulate investment. Contrariwise, if there was excess demand, fiscal and monetary policy could be used in a restrictive manner. In the United States, 'demand management' never wholly displaced the term 'stabilization policy'.

Demand management presupposes that the working of the economy is sufficiently well understood for reasonable assessments to be made of the likely evolution of such variables as private and public consumption and investment, exports and imports and the level of prices. If the assessment indicated an 'inflationary gap' between total expenditure and available supplies, that would call for higher taxes or lower public expenditure. In the case of demand deficiency, the task was to estimate the additional demand needed to bring the economy to capacity output at full employment. Demand management was not intended to influence capacity output itself, which would be determined by such longer-term factors as the growth of the labour force, technical progress and the stock of capital equipment: it was aimed at correcting shorter-term deviations of output from its sustainable trend. The feasibility of policy intervention depends on the successive periods of time elapsing between the recognition of the need for action, taking the decision to act, the making of the policy change and the effect on the targeted variable. The effectiveness of demand management depends on the accuracy of forecasts: it also depends on the political constitution, which determines the speed and frequency with which policy interventions, such as tax changes, can be made. In Britain the annual Budget was initially the main pillar of demand management, tax changes rather than alterations in expenditure being the main instruments; later on, adjustments between Budgets became more frequent. When restraint was called for, fiscal policy was supplemented by the control of consumer credit and by regulating the investment programme of the public sector. Monetary policy was directed towards the balance of payments. During the 1950s and 1960s most European countries followed policies of active demand-management, though there were differences in the mix of fiscal and monetary policy; the United States did not embark on fiscal expansion until the 1960s.

In the quarter-century following World War II, the average annual growth of output was historically high, the rate of unemployment very low and the amplitude of fluctuations about the trend of output also historically low. Some would argue that the contribution of demand management to high activity and reduced instability can only be tested with the aid of macroeconometric models, and these, with the appropriate data series, are not available for most of the period in question. But a number of more limited studies have been made. Commenting on these, three members of the OECD Secretariat (Llewellyn et al., 1985) concluded that, in general, policy was stabilizing. They also endorsed the observation of Matthews (1968) that because economic agents and entrepreneurs believed that the authorities would use policy to control activity, the private sector invested on a scale and with a smoothness which contributed to the stability of the whole economy. Throughout the 1950s and 1960s there were in nearly all advanced countries regular annual rises in nominal wages and prices, but at rates which would be considered moderate by subsequent standards, price increases averaging less than 2 per cent a year in some countries and not more than 5 per cent a year in any. These increases were seen not so much as symptoms of excess demand as evidence of wage–price and wage–wage spirals, and a number of countries operated formal or informal 'incomes policies' designed to contain the rise in the general wage level. Despite occasional misgivings, the wage inflation was reckoned acceptable, and monetary policy was accommodatory.

The postwar 'golden age' came to an end in the early 1970s. After 1973 there was a sharp slowdown in productivity growth in all advanced countries, accompanied in most cases by rising unemployment and rising inflation. The 'stagflation' of the 1970s was followed by world recession in the early 1980s, when output in the OECD countries as a whole almost stopped rising altogether and unemployment reached levels not seen since the 1930s. On the face of it, this was a time when the thrust of demand management might have been expected to be expansionary. In fact, with some notable exceptions, both fiscal and monetary policy became increasingly restrictive. How can this paradox be explained?

Two factors may be singled out as contributing to the doubling of the average rate of inflation in OECD countries in the 1970s: a change into a higher gear of wage inflation in a number of countries at the end of the 1960s, and the fourfold increase in the price of oil of OPEC 1 in 1973–4. The latter was of particular significance since it boosted cost inflation while at the same time acting to reduce demand in oil-importing countries. While the typical inflation of the 1960s might have been acceptable, the higher rate was not, and notwithstanding the recession of output and employment in the mid-1970s, governments began to direct demand management towards reducing inflation. An element of the expansionist mode of demand management can still be seen in the outcome of the Bonn Summit meeting of the major powers in 1978, whereby those countries with low inflation and balance of payments surpluses, notably Germany and Japan, were to engineer a modest domestic expansion and act as 'locomotives' to pull up the rest of the world, but this initiative was swiftly overtaken by OPEC 2, re-igniting inflation and renewing the determination of major countries to pursue restrictive policies. This intensified the recession until the United States broke ranks in 1982.

So long as the response to cost inflation is restrictive fiscal and monetary policy, then clearly demand management is not available to combat unemployment. However, there has also been a theoretical reappraisal of the potential role of demand management. The theme of the 'monetarist' reaction launched by Friedman in 1968 was that there was no lasting trade-off between unemployment and inflation. In his view, if unemployment was pushed below a certain 'natural' rate, determined by the characteristics of the real economy, there would be not merely higher, but accelerating, inflation. In addition, the numerous and uncertain time-lags between the diagnosis of the need for action and the effects on the economy of the appropriate policy change rendered discretionary demand-management hazardous. Accordingly, Friedman recommended the adoption of a simple rule governing the growth of the money supply. Monetarism was influential in leading some countries to adopt monetary targets; in particular, the monetary aggregate 'Sterling M3' was the focal point of the Medium Term Financial Strategy adopted by the British government in 1980. Inflation did come down, though it brought monetarism down with it, for the chosen measure of money supply rose quite out of line with the price level, and the target was officially abandoned five years later. A more radical critique of demand management emerged from the 'rational expectations' analysis being developed at the end of the 1970s. This analysis raises important questions in economic theory and in econometric modelling, but it is the marriage of the rational expectations hypothesis with the 'natural rate' in the 'New Classical Economics' which has the most serious consequences for demand management, for it leads to the denial of any possible influence on the real economy of any systematic policies of this kind. This, however, is a result for a theoretical economy in which all markets clear all the time. It does not apply to a 'disequilibrium' economy in which important markets, such as the labour market, do not clear.

Though by no means conclusive, these critiques have raised important questions about the scope and limitations of demand management. Economists in the Keynesian tradition argue that its potential to influence real output and employment still remains; in their view what happened in the 1970s and 1980s was a change of the objective of demand management towards reducing inflation. If it is to be restored to its original role, an alternative means of restraining inflation is required, and that means a viable incomes policy. Others advocate switching the target of demand management from real output to the stabilization of the growth of the nominal value of GDP. By itself, this is not unlike what monetarism hoped to achieve, but New Keynesians, such as Meade, go a step further and also invoke incomes policy. But their idea is that wage settlements should be targeted on maximizing employment, whereas conventional incomes policy is conceived as restraining nominal incomes.

The risk of renewed inflation if demand management was given back its old role of reducing unemployment appears to be less in some countries than others, but in a number of countries this restoration is unlikely unless a viable incomes policy can be put in place. An equally powerful inhibition is the fear of exchange-rate depreciation. Those who advocated floating exchange rates had argued that the abandonment of fixed rates would allow countries to follow their own domestic policies of demand management without balance of payments crises cutting them short. But it seems to have been a case of jumping out of the frying pan into the fire. Countries attempting to expand out of recession unilaterally have quickly experienced a sharp fall in their exchange rate: only the dominant United States economy has so far been able to combine internal expansion with stability of the external value of its currency. Joint action among other countries seems to be required to counter the destabilizing effects of excessive currency fluctuations. Some tentative moves in this direction began to appear in the mid-1980s. In retrospect, the Bretton Woods arrangements are seen to have constituted a high peak of international economic cooperation, and some advocate the creation of a 'new Bretton Woods' on a world-wide basis. Others pin their faith on the strengthening of regional groupings, such as the European Community. In any case, the prospects for demand management resuming its role as an instrument for expansion and high employment are bound up with the extent to which major countries can contrive to coordinate their separate national policies.

G.D.N. WORSWICK

See also DEFICIT SPENDING; FISCAL POLICY.

BIBLIOGRAPHY
Friedman, M. 1968. The role of monetary policy. *American Economic Review* 58, March, 1–17.
Keynes, J.M. 1936. *The General Theory of Employment, Interest and Money.* In *Collected Writings of John Maynard Keynes,* London: Macmillan, 1973, Vol. VII.
Llewellyn, J., Potter, S. and Samuelson, L. 1985. *Economic Forecasting and Policy.* London: Routledge & Kegan Paul.
Matthews, R.C.O. 1968. Why has Britain had full employment since the war? *Economic Journal* 78, September, 555–69.
Vines, D., Maciejowski, J. and Meade, J.E. 1983. *Demand Management.* London: Allen & Unwin.

demand price. Earlier economic literature doubtless contains casual usages of the phrase 'demand price', but its appropriation as a technical term appears to date from Alfred Marshall's *Principles of Economics* (Marshall, 1890: see Marshall, 1920, pp. 95–101). Marshall applied the term in the contexts of both individual and market demand. Starting with a commodity (tea) purchasable in integral units of a pound's weight, an individual's demand price for the xth pound is the price he is just willing to pay for it given that he has already acquired $x - 1$ pounds. The basic assumption is that this demand price is lower the larger is x. A schedule of demand prices for all possible quantities (values of x) defines the consumer's demand schedule. Its graph is naturally drawn with quantity on the horizontal axis. In the case of a perfectly divisible commodity, the demand price of quantity x must be redefined as the price *per unit* which the consumer would be willing to pay for a tiny increment, given that he already possesses amount x. The demand schedule then graphs as a continuous negatively-sloped demand curve showing demand price in this sense as a function of x.

If the individual is free to buy any quantity at a fixed price, his 'marginal demand price' is the demand price for that quantity 'which lies at the margin or terminus or end of his purchases' (Marshall, 1920, p. 95). For a perfectly divisible commodity marginal demand price must equal market price. For a commodity purchasable in integral units only, market price may lie anywhere below marginal demand price, but not so low as to make the next unit marginal.

Marshall's discussion of consumer behaviour is based on two general assumptions, although these are informally relaxed at various points. The first is that the utility obtained from consuming a commodity depends only on the amount of that commodity. The second is that the marginal utility of 'money', or expenditure on all other goods, remains approximately constant with respect to variation in the expenditure on any particular commodity – the presumption being that the latter expenditure is only a small fraction of total expenditure. These assumptions have convenient consequences for the concept of demand price. If $u(x)$ denotes the utility a consumer obtains from consuming quantity x of a given good in a specified period, while λ is the constant marginal utility of money to him, then demand price for quantity x is $(du/dx)/\lambda$ in the case of divisible quantity and $[u(x) - u(x-1)]/\lambda$ in the case when only integral quantities are feasible. In either case, given the value of

λ, demand price depends on x alone and is proportional to marginal utility. The hypothesis of diminishing demand price is tantamount to that of diminishing marginal utility. A further advantage is that the demand price for quantity x is independent of the pecuniary terms on which the earlier units were, or are to be, acquired, as these terms will not change the marginal utility of money.

Although demand price is, on the above assumptions, proportional to marginal utility it has the great advantage of being measured in operational money units. This permits a monetary measure of the net benefit or consumer surplus obtained from the option of buying the commodity in question on specified monetary terms, rather than having to divert the expenditure to other goods. The distinction between demand price and market price is an operational version of the classical distinction between value in use and value in exchange.

The concept of demand price features prominently in Marshall's analysis of the market for a single commodity sold at a fixed price which is uniform to all buyers. Demand price is now interpreted as the maximum *uniform* price at which any specified aggregate quantity of the commodity can be sold on the market during a given period. The negatively-sloped market demand curve is simply a lateral addition of the individual demand curves and expresses the common demand price as a function of the aggregated quantity. Marshall recognized (1920, p. 457n) that it would be more natural when dealing with market demand to view quantity as a function of price, as Cournot (1838, pp. 44–55) had done, but chose the converse approach to maintain symmetry with his treatment of supply. Believing in the importance of scale economies in production, he deemed it generally impossible to treat quantity supplied per unit of time as a single-valued function of market price. Instead, adopting what he took to be the businessman's perspective, he introduced the concept of 'supply price'; the minimum uniform price at which any given quantity will be supplied to the market.

Market equilibrium occurs at any quantity whose demand price and supply price are equal, so that the market demand curve intersects the market supply curve – the latter the graph of supply price as a function of aggregate quantity supplied, a lateral sum of individual supply curves. Equilibrium is locally stable if the demand curve cuts the supply curve from above at the equilibrium quantity. This result is justified by the argument that the rate of supply will increase if the current market price (always determined by demand price) exceeds supply price at the current quantity, so that additional production offers excess profit, decreasing in the opposite case (Marshall, 1920, pp. 345–7). The resulting dynamic process is usually referred to as the Marshallian adjustment process.

It is probably due to Marshall's influence that English-speaking economists still graph demand and supply curves with quantity on the horizontal axis even though adopting a more Walrasian perspective which treats quantities demanded and supplied as functions of market price.

Marshall's conception of the demand price of a lone commodity, segregated from other commodities by an assumed constancy of the marginal utility of money, does not feature prominently in modern theoretical work. Instead, a multicommodity formulation of utility and demand is typically adopted. Consider a consumer maximizing the utility function $u(x_1, x_2, \ldots, x_n)$ subject to the budget constraint $\Sigma p_i x_i = M$. (Here the x_i are quantities and the p_i prices of the n commodities and M is a preset total expenditure level. The utility function, u, is assumed strictly increasing, strictly quasi-concave, and differentiable.) This maximization implies the consumer's direct demand functions $x_i = d_i(p_1/M, p_2/M, \ldots, p_n/M)$, $i = 1, 2, \ldots, n$, sometimes (but with dubious justification) referred to as Marshallian demand functions to distinguish them from Hicksian compensated or constant-utility demand functions. These demand functions can usually be inverted to yield the indirect or inverse demand functions $p_i/M = g_i(x_1, x_2, \ldots, x_n)$, $i = 1, 2, \ldots, n$. However, these can be obtained more immediately from the budget constraint and the first-order conditions $\partial u/\partial x_i = \lambda p_i$, $i = 1, 2, \ldots, n$ (where λ is the Lagrange multiplier associated with the budget constraint). We have, for $i = 1, 2, \ldots, n$,

$$\frac{p_i}{M} = \frac{\partial u/\partial x_i}{\lambda M} = \frac{\partial u/\partial x_i}{\Sigma \lambda p_j x_j} = \frac{\partial u/\partial x_i}{\Sigma x_j(\partial u/\partial x_j)} \equiv g_i(x_1, x_2, \ldots, x_n) \quad (1)$$

(The g_i are clearly unaffected by a monotone increasing transformation of u and reduce to $(\partial u/\partial x_i)/u$ if u is homogeneous of degree one.) The indirect demand functions (1) are the natural generalization of Marshall's demand-price concept at the individual level, defining an n-vector of normalized prices at which a given n-vector of commodities will be demanded.

Indirect demand functions may be useful in the contexts of central planning or rationing, where they can indicate the prices planners should choose to clear markets given the quantities available, or the notional prices at which ration allotments would just be freely purchased (see Pearce, 1964, pp. 57–64). But unfortunately, although indirect demand functions are readily obtained for the individual, they are not as easily aggregated to the market level as are direct demand functions. The asymmetry arises from the fact that individuals face identical prices but do not make identical quantity choices. Thus, market-level indirect demand functions must generally be obtained by first aggregating the individual direct demand functions and then inverting the resulting market functions.

The modern duality approach to consumer behaviour has revealed fundamental symmetries in the roles of prices and quantities. The alternatives of viewing quantity demanded as a function of price or demand price as a function of quantity can now be seen as only one of a variety of dual alternatives which considerably enrich theoretical and econometric analysis. (See Gorman, 1976, for a simple treatment.)

J.K. WHITAKER

See also MARSHALL, ALFRED.

BIBLIOGRAPHY

Cournot, A.A. 1838. *Mathematical Principles of the Theory of Wealth.* New York: Macmillan, 1897.

Gorman, W.M. 1976. Tricks with utility functions. In *Essays in Economic Analysis*, ed. J.J. Artis and A.R. Nobay, London: Cambridge University Press.

Marshall, A. 1890. *Principles of Economics*, Vol. I. London: Macmillan.

Marshall, A. 1920. *Principles of Economics: An Introductory Volume.* London: Macmillan. Eighth edition of Marshall (1890).

Pearce, I.F. 1964. *A Contribution to Demand Analysis.* Oxford: Clarendon Press.

demand-pull inflation. The basic idea of demand-pull inflation is that the price level rises when demand exceeds productive capacity on an economy-wide basis. Although it is not clear when the term 'demand-pull' was first coined, it has a clear representation in simple early Keynesian models. In such models, a full employment level of unemployment defines the productive capacity of the economy. At full employment, real resources are optimally utilized. If the economy is initially at a point of excess unemployment and spare capacity, an expansion of demand raises output and employment rather than producing inflation. But if total demand exceeds the

economy's productive capacity, it spills over into demand-pull price increases. The demand-pull region of unemployment rates is thus equivalent to the excess demand region.

An important reason for identifying demand-pull inflation is its implications for policy-making. In the model just described, the task of managing aggregate demand is well-defined. Policy-makers should aim to achieve the level of demand that just produces full employment because this optimally utilizes resources and avoids demand-pull inflation. Higher levels of demand generate inflation and lower levels waste productive resources.

Having defined demand-pull in this highly stylized model, we can now consider some difficulties with applying the idea more realistically. Full employment must be regarded as a region of unemployment rates rather than a precise point. The unemployment rates where demand-pull arises must be regarded as a region also, with demand-pull inflation becoming more severe as unemployment is reduced further within this region. But if the concept of demand-pull inflation is to have a useful, distinctive meaning, it must still be kept distinct from the more general proposition that prices are responsive to demand. And it must be distinguishable from other causes of inflation. No one generally agreed theory exists that explains the range of inflationary experience. But, the idea of demand-pull as outlined above does contribute to an overall understanding of that experience.

Episodes of inflation in which demand-pull was clearly the dominant factor can be identified. At times of major wars, maximizing output has been the paramount goal of governments even if it meant expanding demand well beyond the normal full-employment point. The demand-pull inflation generated by operating in this excess demand region has generally been moderated, but not completely suppressed, by rationing and price controls during major wars. Demand-pull was also a feature of the industrial economies in the late 1960s, when United States military spending was greatly enlarged and labour and product markets became extremely tight for an extended period throughout the industrial world.

Yet even this episode displays a mixture of causes of inflation. An abrupt explosion of wage increases at the end of the 1960s in most European countries suggests that wage-push also contributed to the inflation of that period. The abruptness with which wage demands jumped indicates a wage-push that was not caused entirely by a corresponding increase in demand; but the ongoing strength of total demand and tightness of labour markets in the period provided unions the opportunity to greatly enlarge their wage demands. We need not choose between demand-pull and cost-push explanation of that period when both were present.

The ambiguity in defining just what constitutes demand-pull inflation is apparent in considering the more general behaviour of prices and wages along the empirical relation known as the short-run Phillips curve. Inflation gets gradually, but continually, faster as unemployment is reduced cyclically. It is useful to characterize the higher inflation that arises at very low rates of unemployment as being of the demand-pull variety, with those unemployment rates constituting the demand-pull region. But the cause of the inflation that emerges when there is still ample slack in labour and product markets is harder to characterize. It is not demand-pull in the distinctive sense described above because labour and capital resources on the whole are not being optimally utilized.

Another complication in defining demand-pull inflation is the presence of an ongoing inflation rate. Whether it originated from supply shocks, as it did in the mid-1970s when energy prices exploded, or from demand-pull or wage-push, an ongoing inflation will persist long after the initiating shocks have disappeared and long after a reduction of demand has eliminated any excess demand-pull on the economy. Because of this inertia in an ongoing inflation rate, reduced demand results initially in excess capacity and high unemployment and only gradually in reduced inflation.

The inertia of inflation, the presence of cost-push as a source of inflation, and the variation of inflation along the short-run Phillips curve all discredit the idea that demand-pull is always the central source of inflation and that inflation can be eliminated efficiently simply by reducing demand to a point where labour and product markets are not excessively tight. Inflation is responsive to the strength of total demand, and avoiding levels of demand that would produce overly tight markets will avoid setting off a demand-pull inflation. However, in the face of either cost-push shocks or an ongoing inflation rate of whatever origin, reducing demand will mainly reduce output and employment in the short run, and only gradually reduce inflation, even if the economy is kept operating at rates well below the demand-pull region.

Because of these characteristics of economies, the demand management chore confronting policy-makers is not merely avoiding excess demand, as in the simplified Keynesian model, but rather choosing how much to accommodate inflation and how much to give up in output and employment in order to suppress inflation. As a related point, the identification of inflation with money in some models does not necessarily identify money as causing inflation in the sense of creating demand-pull, or 'too much money chasing too few goods'. Money may correlate with inflation whatever its cause unless policy-makers refuse to accommodate it at all and accept sharply lower output and employment levels instead.

Some models of inflation developed in the 1970s and 1980s maintain the essential features of the demand-pull inflation model but in a modified form that takes explicit account of the inertia in inflation. These models specify that there exists a natural rate of unemployment such that inflation accelerates when unemployment is below the natural rate and decelerates with unemployment above it. In their behavioural underpinnings, they assume wages are established in auction-like markets that would clear continuously except for uncertain expectations about inflation on the part of both firms and workers. They thus differ from models that are rooted in the original Keynesian insights about unemployment, which assume firms set wages in the context of more complicated long-run employment relations. In these models featuring long-term attachments between firms and workers, firms respond to reductions in demand primarily with layoffs rather than with market-clearing wage adjustments. Wasteful levels of unemployment can thus exist for extended periods.

The natural rate of unemployment is the analytical counterpart of full employment in Keynesian models, and unemployment rates below the natural rate correspond to the demand-pull region. These natural rate models can fit the historical data reasonably well if they make an important allowance for cost-push events and for inertia in inflation so that the response of inflation to economic slack is severely damped. Empirical testing thus far has been unable either to accept or reject some of the key features of the natural rate models. But there is little objective evidence that the natural unemployment rate that is empirically identified in these models corresponds to an optimal utilization of real resources in the same way that full employment represents an optimal operating level in the simpler Keynesian models. Avoiding excess demand, and thereby demand-pull inflation, is a clear prescription of both types of model; but because the presence

of inflation or even its worsening need not imply the existence of excess demand, avoiding inflation altogether while still fully utilizing labour and capital resources remains a difficult, and perhaps unattainable, goal for aggregate demand management.

GEORGE L. PERRY

See also COST-PUSH INFLATION; DEMAND MANAGEMENT; INFLATION.

BIBLIOGRAPHY

Friedman, M. 1968. The role of monetary policy. *American Economic Review* 58, March, 1–17.

Gordon, R.J. 1981. Output fluctuations and gradual price adjustment. *Journal of Economic Literature* 19, June, 493–530.

Gordon, R.J. 1985. Understanding inflation in the 1980s. *Brookings Papers on Economic Activity* No. 1, 263–99.

Hall, R.E. (ed.) 1982. *Inflation: Causes and Effects.* Chicago: University of Chicago Press for the National Bureau of Economic Research.

Nordhaus, W. 1981. Macroconfusion; the dilemma of economic policy. In *Macroeconomics, Prices, and Quantities,* ed. J. Tobin, Washington, DC: Brookings.

Okun, A.M. 1975. Inflation: its mechanics and welfare costs. *Brookings Papers on Economic Activity* No. 2, 351–90.

Okun, A.M. 1981. *Prices and Quantities: A Macroeconomic Analysis.* Washington, DC: Brookings.

Perry, G.L. 1980. Inflation in theory and practice. *Brookings Papers on Economic Activity* No. 1, 207–41.

Schultze, C.L. 1981. Some macro foundations for micro theory. *Brookings Papers on Economic Activity* No. 2, 521–76.

Schultze, C.L. 1985. Microeconomic efficiency and nominal wage stickiness. *American Economic Review* 75, March, 1–15.

Taylor, J.B. 1981. Rational expectations and the invisible handshake. In *Macroeconomics, Prices, and Quantities,* ed. J. Tobin, Washington, DC: Brookings.

Tobin, J. 1972. Inflation and unemployment. *American Economic Review* 62, March, 1–18.

demand theory. The main purpose of demand theory is to explain observed consumer choices of commodity bundles. Market parameters, typically prices and income, determine constraints on commodity bundles. Given a combination of market parameters, a commodity bundle or a non-empty set of commodity bundles, which satisfies the corresponding constraints, is called a demand vector or a demand set. The mapping which assigns to every admissible combination of market parameters a unique demand vector (or a non-empty demand set) is called a demand function (or a demand correspondence). Traditional demand theory considers the demand function (or correspondence) as the outcome of some optimizing behaviour of the consumer. Its primary goal is to determine the impact on observed demands for commodities of alternative assumptions on the objectives and behavioural rules of the consumer, and on the constraints which he faces. The traditional model of the consumer takes preferences over alternative commodity bundles to describe the objectives of the consumer. Its behavioural rule consists in maximizing these preferences on the set of corresponding commodity bundles which satisfy the budget constraint imposed by the market parameters. If there is a unique preference maximizer under each budget constraint, then preference maximization determines a demand function. If there is at least one preference maximizer under each budget constraint, then preference maximization determines a demand correspondence.

Once the traditional view is adopted the occurrence of demand correspondences cannot be avoided. Compatibility of observed demand, which is always unique, with some demand correspondence is a minor problem in general. However, the correspondence should be obtained through preference maximization. The last requirement leads to the main issues of modern demand theory: Which demand correspondences are compatible with preference maximization? Given any conditions necessary for demand correspondences to be compatible with preference maximization, are they sufficient? Which demand correspondences are compatible with a special class of preferences? What type of preferences yields a particular class of demand correspondences? When addressing these issues, modern demand theory attempts to link two concepts: preferences and demand.

Historically, the important concept was utility rather than preference. Before Fisher (1892) and Pareto (1896), utility was conceived as cardinal, that is it was assumed to be a measurable scale for the degree of satisfaction of the consumer. Fisher and Pareto were the first to observe that an arbitrary increasing transformation of the utility function has no effect on demand. Edgeworth (1881) had already written utility as a general function of quantities of all commodities and employed indifference curves. It is now widely accepted in demand theory that only ordinal utility matters. A utility function is merely a convenient device to represent a preference relation, and any increasing transformation of the utility function will serve this purpose as well.

The representability by utility functions imposes some restrictions on preferences. The problem of representability of a preference relation by a numerical function was solved by Debreu (1954, 1959, 1964) based on work by Eilenberg (1941), and by Rader (1963), and Bowen (1968).

While still assuming cardinal utility, Walras (1874) developed the first 'theory of demand': His demand was a function of all prices and endowment, obtained through utility maximization. Slutsky (1915) finally assumed an ordinal utility function with enough restrictions to yield a maximum under any budget constraint and testable properties of the resulting demand functions. In particular, he obtained negativity of diagonal elements and symmetry of the 'Slutsky matrix'.

Antonelli (1886) was the first to go the opposite way: construct indifference curves and a utility function from the so-called inverse demand function. Pareto (1980b) took the same route. Katzner (1970) reports on recent results in this direction. The construction of preference relations from demand functions was achieved in two ways: (1) Samuelson (1947) and Houthakker (1950) introduced the concept of revealed preference into demand theory. Considerable progress in relating utility and demand in terms of revealed preference was achieved by Uzawa (1960), further refinements being due to Richter (1966). (2) Hurwicz and Uzawa (1971) contributed to the following so-called integrability problem: construct a twice continuously differentiable utility representation from a continuously differentiable demand function which satisfies certain integrability conditions (including symmetry and negative semidefiniteness of the Slutsky matrix). Kihlstrom, Mas-Colell and Sonnenschein (1976) unified the two approaches under (1) and (2) in that they related the axioms of revealed preference to properties of the Slutsky matrix.

Since there exists a sizeable literature on demand theory, many of the concepts and results are well established and well known. These have become so much part of standard knowledge in economic theory that they are included in any microeconomic textbook today and other surveys. It would reduce the available space for a presentation of the new results of the last fifteen years substantially if an extended introductory account of demand theory were to be included here as well.

1. COMMODITIES AND PRICES

Consumers purchase or sell commodities, which can be divided into goods and services. Each commodity is specified by its physical quality, its location and the date of its availability. In the case of uncertainty, the state of the nature in which the commodity is available may be added to the specification of a commodity. This leads to the notion of a contingent commodity (see Arrow, 1953 and Debreu, 1959). We assume as in traditional theory that there exists a finite number l of such commodities. Quantities of each commodity are measured in real numbers. A *commodity bundle* is an l-dimensional vector $x = (x_1, \ldots, x_l)$. The set of all l-dimensional vectors $x = (x_1, \ldots, x_l)$ is the l-dimensional Euclidean space $\mathbb{R}^l$ which we interpret as the *commodity space*. $|x_h|$ indicates the quantity of commodity $h = 1, \ldots, l$. Commodities are assumed to be perfectly divisible, so that their quantity may be expressed as any (non-negative) real number. The standard sign convention for consumers assigns positive numbers for commodities made available to the consumer (inputs) and negative numbers for commodities made available by the consumer (outputs). Hence, any commodity bundle $x \in \mathbb{R}^l$ is conceivable.

The price p_h of a commodity $h, h = 1, \ldots, l$, is a real number which is the amount in units of account that has to be paid in exchange for one unit of the commodity. For the consumer, p_h is given and has to be paid now for the delivery of commodity h under the circumstances (location, date, state) specified for commodity h. A *price system* or *price vector* is a vector $p = (p_1, \ldots, p_l)$ in $\mathbb{R}^l$ and contains the prices for all commodities. The value of a commodity bundle x given the price vector p is $px = \Sigma_{h=1}^{l} p_h x_h$. This means that commodity bundles are *linearly priced*.

2. CONSUMPTION SETS AND BUDGET SETS

Typically, some commodity bundles cannot be consumed by a consumer for physical reasons. Those consumption bundles which can be consumed form the consumer's *consumption set*. This is a non-empty subset X of the commodity space $\mathbb{R}^l$. A consumer must choose a bundle x from his consumption set X in order to subsist. Traditionally, inputs in consumption are described by positive quantities and outputs by negative quantities. So in particular, the labour components of a consumption bundle x are all non-positive, unless labour is hired for a service. One usually assumes that the consumption set X is closed, convex, and bounded below. Vectors $x \in X$ are sometimes called *consumption plans*.

Given the sign convention on inputs and outputs and a price vector p, the value px of a consumption plan x defines the net outlay of x, that is the value of all purchases (inputs) minus the value of all sales (outputs) for the bundle x. Trading the bundle x in a market at prices p implies payments and receipts for that bundle. Therefore, the value of the consumption plan should not exceed the initial wealth (or income) of the consumer which is a given real number w. If the consumer owns a vector of initial resources $\omega \in \mathbb{R}^l$ and the price vector p is given, then w may be determined by $w = p\omega$. The consumer may have other sources of wealth: savings and pensions, bequests, profit shares, taxes or other liabilities. Given p and w, the set of possible consumption bundles whose value does not exceed the initial wealth of the consumer is called the *budget set* and is defined formally by

$$\beta(p, w) = \{x \in X \mid px \leqslant w\}.$$

The ultimate decision of a consumer is to choose a consumption plan from his budget set. Those vectors in $\beta(p, w)$ which the consumer eventually chooses form his *demand set* $\phi(p, w)$.

3. PREFERENCES AND DEMAND

The choice of the consumer depends on his tastes and desires. These are represented by his *preference relation* $\succsim$ which is a binary relation on X. For any two bundles $x, y \in X, x \succsim y$ means that x is at least as good as y. If the consumer always chooses a most preferred bundle in his budget set, then his demand set is defined by

$$\phi(p, w) = \{x \in \beta(p, w) | x' \in \beta(p, w)$$

$$\text{implies} \quad x \succsim x' \text{ or not } x' \succsim x\}.$$

Three basic axioms are usually imposed on the preference relation $\succsim$ which are taken as a definition of a rational consumer.

Axiom 1 (Reflexivity). If $x \in X$, then $x \succsim x$, i.e. any bundle is as good as itself.

Axiom 2 (Transitivity). If $x, y, z \in X$ such that $x \succsim y$ and $y \succsim z$, then $x \succsim z$.

Axiom 3 (Completeness). If $x, y \in X$, then $x \succsim y$ or $y \succsim x$.

A preference relation $\succsim$ which satisfies these three axioms is a complete preordering on X and will be called a *preference order*. Already Axioms 2 and 3 define a preference order, since Axiom 3 implies Axiom 1. A preference relation $\succsim$ on X induces two other relations on X, the relation of strict preference, $\succ$, and the relation of indifference, $\sim$.

Definition. Let $\succsim$ be a preference relation on the consumption set X. A bundle x is said to be *strictly preferred* to a bundle y, i.e. $x \succ y$, if and only if $x \succsim y$ and not $x \succsim x$. A bundle x is said to be *indifferent to* a bundle y, i.e. $x \sim y$, if and only if $x \succsim y$ and $y \succsim x$.

LEMMA. *Suppose $\succsim$ is reflexive and transitive. Then*

(i) $\succ$ *is irreflexive, i.e. not $x \succ x$, and transitive;*
(ii) $\sim$ *is an equivalence relation on X, that means $\sim$ is reflexive, transitive, and symmetric, i.e. $x \sim y$ if and only if $y \sim x$.*

For $Z \subset X, x \in Z, x$ is called *maximal in Z*, if for all $z \in Z$, not $z \succ x$. x is called a *best element of Z* or *most preferred in Z*, if for all $z \in Z, x \succsim z$. Best elements are maximal; maximal elements are not necessarily best elements. If $\succsim$ is complete, then best and maximal elements coincide. Obviously for any price vector p and initial wealth w,

$$\phi(p, w) = \{x \in \beta(p, w) | x \text{ is maximal in } \beta(p, w)\}.$$

Axioms 1–3 are not questioned in most consumer theory. However, transitivity and completeness may be violated by observed behaviour. Recent developments in the theory of consumer demand indicate that some weaker axioms suffice to describe and derive consistent demand behaviour (see, for example Sonnenschein, 1971; Katzner, 1971; Shafer, 1974; Kihlstrom et al., 1976; Kim and Richter, 1986).

In an alternative approach, one could start from a strict preference relation as the primitive concept. This may sometimes be convenient. However, the weak relation $\succsim$ seems to be the more natural concept. If the consumer chooses x, although y was a possible choice as well, then his choice can only be interpreted in the sense of $x \succsim y$, but not as $x \succ y$.

For the remainder of this section, let us fix a preference order $\succsim$ on X and a non-empty subset B of $\mathbb{R}^{l+1}$ such that for every $(p, w) \in B$, there is a unique $\succsim$-best element in $\beta(p, w)$; i.e. maximization of $\succsim$ defines a *demand function* $f : B \to X$, $\phi(p, w) = \{f(p, w)\}$ for all $(p, w) \in B$.

Let $x, x' \in X, x \neq x'$. We call x *revealed preferred to* x' and write xRx', if there is $(p, w) \in B$ such that $x = f(p, w)$ and $px' \leqslant px. xRx'$ implies that both x and x' are in the budget set $\beta(p, w)$ and x is chosen. Since f is derived from $\succsim$-maximization, xRx' implies $x \succ x'$. We call x *indirectly revealed preferred to* x' and write xR^*x', if there exists a finite sequence $x_0 = x, x_1, \ldots, x_n = x'$ in X such that $x_0 Rx_1, \ldots, x_{n-1} Rx'$. Obviously, R^* is transitive. Since $\succ$ is transitive, xR^*x' implies $x \succ x'$. Consequently, the following must hold. (Otherwise $x \succ x'!$)

(SARP) $xR^*x' \Rightarrow$ not $(x'R^*x)$.
(SARP) implies
(WARP) $xRx' \Rightarrow$ not $(x'Rx)$.

(SARP) is called the *strong axiom of revealed preference*; (WARP) is called the *weak axiom*. Hence $\succsim$-maximization implies the strong axiom. For the inverse implication, see Chapters 1, 2, 3, and 5 of Chipman et al. (1971).

4. CONTINUOUS PREFERENCE ORDERS AND UTILITY FUNCTIONS

The Axioms 1–3 have intuitive appeal. This is less so with the topological requirements of the following Axiom 4.

Axiom 4 (Continuity). For every $x \in X$, the sets $\{y \in X | y \succsim x\}$ and $\{y \in X | x \succsim y\}$ are closed relative to X.

Closedness of $\{y \in X | y \succsim x\}$ requires that for any sequence $y^n, n \in \mathbb{N}$, in X such that y^n converges to $y \in X$ and $y^n \succsim x$ for all n, the limit in y also satisfies $y \succsim x$. If $\succsim$ is a preference order, then Axiom 4 is equivalent to:

For every $x \in X$, the sets $\{y \in X | y \succ x\}$ and $\{y \in Y | x \succ y\}$ are open in X.

Openness of $\{y \in X | y \succ x\}$ means that if $y \succ x$, then $y' \succ x$ for any y' close enough to y.

The sets $\{y \in X | y \succsim x\}$ are called *upper contour sets* of the relation $\succsim$ and the sets $\{y \in X | x \succsim y\}$ are called *lower contour sets* of $\succsim$. For $x \in X$, the set $I(x) := \{y \in X | y \sim x\}$ is called the *indifference class* of x with respect to $\succsim$ or the $\succsim$-*indifference surface* through x or the $\succsim$-*indifference curve* through x. In case $\succsim$ is reflective and transitive, $I(x)$ is the equivalence class of x with respect to the equivalence relation $\sim$.

There is a preference order $\succsim$ on $\mathbb{R}^l, l \geqslant 2$, which does not satisfy Axiom 4, namely the *lexicographic order* defined by $(x_1, \ldots, x_l) \succsim (y_1, \ldots, y_l)$ if and only if there is $k, 1 \leqslant k \leqslant l$ such that $x_j = y_j$ for $j < k$ and $x_k > y_k$, or $x = y$. Few studies of the relationship between the order properties of Axioms 1–3 and the topological property of Axiom 4 have been made. We emphasize the following result:

THEOREM (Schmeidler, 1971). *Let $\succsim$ denote a transitive binary relation on a connected topological space X. Assume that there exists at least one pair $\bar{x}, \bar{y} \in X$ such that $\bar{x} \succ \bar{y}$. If for every $x \in X$,* (i) *$\{y \in X | y \succsim x\}$ and $\{y \in X | x \succsim y\}$ are closed and* (ii) *$\{y \in X | y \succ x\}$ and $\{y \in X | x \succ y\}$ are open, then $\succsim$ is complete.*

Definition. Let X be a set and $\succsim$ be a preference relation on X. Then a function u from X into the reals $\mathbb{R}$ is a (*utility*) *representation* or a *utility function* for $\succsim$, if for any $x, y \in X, u(x) \geqslant u(y)$ if and only if $x \succsim y$.

Clearly, if u is a utility representation for $\succsim$ and $f : \mathbb{R} \to \mathbb{R}$ is an increasing transformation, then $f \circ u$ is also a representation of $\succsim$. If $u : X \to \mathbb{R}$ is any function, then $\succsim$, defined by $x \succsim y$ if and only if $u(x) \geqslant u(y)$ for $x, y \in X$, is a preference order on X and u is a utility representation for $\succsim$.

Most utility functions used in consumer theory are continuous. If u is continuous and $\succsim$ is represented by u, then by necessity $\succsim$ is a continuous preference order. In our case where $X \subset \mathbb{R}^l$, the opposite implication also holds. If $\succsim$ is a continuous preference order, then it has a continuous utility representation.

THEOREM (Debreu, Eilenberg, Rader). *Let X be a topological space with a countable base of open sets (or a connected, separable topological space) and $\succsim$ be a continuous preference order on X. Then $\succsim$ has a continuous utility representation.*

A preference order $\succsim$ on X, which is not continuous, need not have a utility representation. For instance, the lexicographic order on $\mathbb{R}^l$ does not have a utility representation, not even a discontinuous one. As an immediate consequence of the representation theorem for preference relations, one obtains one of the standard results on the non-emptiness of the demand set $\phi(p, w)$ since any continuous function attains its maximum on a compact set (Weierstrass' Theorem).

COROLLARY. *Let $X \subset \mathbb{R}^l$ be bounded below and closed, $\succsim$ be a continuous preference order on X, $p \in \mathbb{R}^l_{++}$ (i.e. $p \gg 0$), and $w \in \mathbb{R}$. Then $\beta(p, w) \neq \varnothing$ implies $\phi(p, w) \neq \varnothing$.*

5. SOME PROPERTIES OF PREFERENCES AND UTILITY FUNCTIONS

Some of the frequent assumptions on preference relations correspond almost by definitions to analogous properties of utility functions, while other analogies need demonstration. We discuss the assumptions most commonly used.

MONOTONICITY

Definition. A preference order $\succsim$ on $X \subset \mathbb{R}^l$ is *monotonic*, if $x, y \in X$, $x \geqq y$, $x \neq y$ implies $x \succ y$.

This property means desirability of all commodities. If a monotonic preference order has a utility representation u, then u is an increasing function (in all arguments). Inversely, if $\succsim$ is represented by an increasing function, then $\succsim$ is monotonic.

NON-SATIATION

Definition. Let $\succsim$ be the preference relation of a consumer over consumption bundles in X and let $x \in X$.

(i) x is a *satiation point for* $\succsim$ if $x \succsim y$ for all $y \in X$, i.e. x is a best element in X.

(ii) The preference relation is *locally not satiated at x*, if for every neighbourhood V of x there exists $z \in V$ such that $z \succ x$.

Consider a utility representation u for $\succsim$. $x \in X$ is a satiation point if and only if u has a global maximum at x. $\succsim$ is locally not satiated at x if and only if u does not attain a local maximum at x. Local non-satiation excludes that u be constant in a neighbourhood of x. If $\succsim$ is locally not satiated at all x, then $\succsim$ cannot have thick indifference classes or satiation points.

CONVEXITY

Definition. A preference relation $\succsim$ on $X \subset \mathbb{R}^l$ is called

(i) *convex*, if the set $\{y \in X \mid y \succsim x\}$ is convex for all $x \in X$;

(ii) *strictly convex*, if X is convex and $\lambda x + (1 - \lambda)x' \succ x'$ for any two bundles $x, x' \in X$, such that $x \neq x'$, $x \succsim x'$, and for any λ, such that $0 < \lambda < 1$;

(iii) *strongly convex*, if X is convex and $\lambda x + (1 - \lambda)x' \succ x''$ for any three bundles $x, x', x'' \in X$ such that $x \neq x'$, $x \succsim x''$, $x' \succsim x''$, and for any λ such that $0 < \lambda < 1$.

Definition. $u : X \to \mathbb{R}$ is called

(i) *quasi-concave*, if $u(\lambda x + (1 - \lambda)y) \geqq \min\{u(x), u(y)\}$ for all $x, y \in X$ and any λ, $0 \leqslant \lambda \leqslant 1$;

(ii) *strictly quasi-concave*, if $u[\lambda x + (1 - \lambda)y] > \min\{u(x), u(y)\}$ for all $x, y \in X$, $x \neq y$, and any λ, $0 < \lambda < 1$.

Let u be a representation of the preference order $\succsim$. u is (strictly) quasi-concave if and only if $\succsim$ is (strictly) convex. Quasi-concavity is preserved under increasing transformations, i.e. it is an ordinal property. In contrast, concavity is a cardinal property which can be lost under increasing transformations. With respect to the difficult problem to characterize those preference orders which have a concave representation, we refer to Kannai (1977).

Clearly, if $\succsim$ is locally not satiated at all x, then $\succsim$ does not have a satiation point. In general, the inverse implication is false. If, however, $\succsim$ is strictly convex and does not have a satiation point, then $\succsim$ is locally not satiated at all x. Moreover, if $\succsim$ is strictly convex, then $\succsim$ has at most one satiation point. An immediate implication is the following lemma.

LEMMA. *Let $X \subset \mathbb{R}^l$ be bounded below, convex, and closed. Let $\succsim$ be a strictly convex, continuous preference order on X, $p \in \mathbb{R}^l_{++}$, and $w \in \mathbb{R}$. Then $\beta(p, w) \neq \varnothing$ implies that $\phi(p, w)$ is a singleton.*

SEPARABILITY. Separable utility functions were used in classical consumer theory long before associated properties of preferences had been defined. All early contributions to utility theory assumed without much discussion an additive form of the utility function over different commodities. It was not until Edgeworth (1881) that utility was written as a general function of a vector of commodities. The particular consequences of separability for demand theory were discussed well after the general nonseparable case in demand theory had been treated and generally accepted. Among the many contributors are Sono (1945), Leontief (1947), Samuelson (1947), Houthakker (1960), Debreu (1960), Koopmans (1972). We follow Katzner (1970) in our presentation.

Let $N = \{N_j\}_{j=1}^k$ be a partition of the set $\{1, \ldots, l\}$ and assume that $X = S_1 \times \cdots \times S_k$. Let $J = \{1, \ldots, k\}$ and for any $j \in J$, $y \in X$, $y = (y_1, \ldots, y_k) \in \Pi_{i \in J} S_i$ write $y_{-j} = (y_1, \ldots, y_{j-1}, y_{j+1}, \ldots, y_k)$ for the vector of components different from j. For any y_{-j}, a preference order $\succsim$ on X induces a preference order $\succsim_{y_{-j}}$ on S_j which is defined by $x_j \succsim_{y_{-j}} x'_j$ if and only if $(y_{-j}, x_j) \succsim (y_{-j}, x'_j)$ for $x_j, x'_j \in S_j$. In general, the induced ordering $\succsim_{y_{-j}}$ will depend on y_{-j}. The first notion of separability states that for any j, the preference orders $\succsim_{y_{-j}}$ are independent of $y_{-j} \in \Pi_{i \neq j} S_i$. The second notion of separability states that for any proper subset I of J, the induced preference orders $\succsim_{y_{\mathcal{N}}}$ on $\Pi_{i \in I} S_i$ are independent of $y_{\mathcal{N}} \in \Pi_{i \notin I} S_i$.

Definition. Let $\succsim$ be a preference order on $X = \Pi_{j \in J} S_j$.

(i) $\succsim$ is called *weakly separable* with respect to N if $\succsim_{y_{-j}} = \succsim_{z_{-j}}$ for each $j \in J$ and any $y_{-j}, z_{-j} \in \Pi_{i \neq j} S_i$.

(ii) $\succsim$ is called *strongly separable* with respect to N if $\succsim_{y_{\mathcal{N}}} = \succsim_{z_{\mathcal{N}}}$ for each $I \subset J$, $I \neq \varnothing$, $I \neq J$ and any $y_{\mathcal{N}}, z_{\mathcal{N}} \in \Pi_{i \notin I} S_i$.

Definition. Let $u : \Pi_{j \in J} S_j \to \mathbb{R}$. u is called

(i) *weakly separable* with respect to N, if there exist continuous functions $v_j : S_j \to \mathbb{R}$, $j \in J$, and $V : \mathbb{R}^k \to \mathbb{R}$ such that $u(x) = V[v_1(x_1), \ldots, v_k(x_k)]$.

(ii) u is called *strongly separable* with respect to N, if there exist continuous functions $v_j : S_j \to \mathbb{R}$, $j \in J$, and $V : \mathbb{R} \to \mathbb{R}$ such that $u(x) = V[\Sigma_{j \in J} v_j(x_j)]$.

The two important equivalence results on separability are due to Debreu and Katzner. The version of Debreu's Theorem given here is slightly weaker than his original result.

THEOREM (Katzner, 1970). *Let $\succsim$ be a continuous, monotonic preference order on $X = \Pi_{j \in J} S_j$ with $S_j = \mathbb{R}^N j$ for all $j \in J$. Then $\succsim$ is weakly separable if and only if every continuous representation of it is weakly separable.*

THEOREM (Debreu, 1960). *Let $\succsim$ be a continuous, monotonic preference order on $X = \Pi_{j \in J} S_j$ with $S_j = \mathbb{R}^N j$ for all $j \in J = \{1, \ldots, k\}$ and $k \geqslant 3$. Then $\succsim$ is strongly separable if and only if every continuous representation is strongly separable.*

Under the assumptions of this theorem, if $\succsim$ is strongly separable with representation $u(x) = V[\Sigma_{j \in J} v_j(x_j)]$, then V must be increasing or decreasing. Therefore,

$$v(x) = \begin{cases} \Sigma_{j \in J} v_j(x_j) & V \text{ increasing} \\ -\Sigma_{j \in J} v_j(x_j) & V \text{ decreasing} \end{cases}$$

is also a representation of $\succsim$. This is the form of separable utility used by early economists who thought that each commodity h had its own intrinsic utility representable by a scalar function u_h. The overall utility was then simply obtained as the sum of these functions, $u(x) = \Sigma_h u_h(x_h)$. Such a formulation is given by Jevons (1871) and Walras (1874) and implicitly contained in Gossen (1854).

For $k = 2$, weak and strong separability of preferences coincide. But there are separable preferences which do not admit a strongly separable utility representation, for instance $X = \mathbb{R}_+^2$, $N_j = \{j\}$ for $j = 1, 2$, $\succsim$ given by $u(x_1, x_2) = \sqrt{x_1} + \sqrt{x_1 + x_2}$.

Separability of preferences imposes restrictions on demand correspondences and on demand functions (for details see Barten and Böhm, 1982, sections 9, 14, and 15).

6. CONTINUOUS DEMAND

Given any price-wealth pair $(p, w) \in \mathbb{R}^{l+1}$, the budget set of the consumer was defined as $\beta(p, w) = \{x \in X \mid px \leqslant w\}$. Let $S \subset \mathbb{R}^{l+1}$ denote the set of price-wealth pairs for which the budget set is non-empty. Then β describes a correspondence from S into X, i.e. β associates to any $(p, w) \in S$ the non-empty subset $\beta(p, w)$ of X. There are two standard notions of continuity of correspondences, upper hemi-continuity and lower hemi-continuity (see Hildenbrand, 1974).

Definition. A compact-valued correspondence Ψ from S into an arbitrary subset T of $\mathbb{R}^l$ is *upper hemi-continuous* (u.h.c.) at a point $y \in S$, if for all sequences $(y^n, z^n) \in S \times T$ such that $y^n \to y$ and $z^n \in \Psi(y^n)$ for all n, there exist $z \in \Psi(y)$ and a subsequence z^{n_k} of z^n such that $z^{n_k} \to z$.

Definition. A correspondence Ψ from S into an arbitrary subset T of $\mathbb{R}^l$ is *lower hemi-continuous* (l.h.c.) at a point $y \in S$, if for any $z \in \Psi(y)$ and any sequence y^n in S with $y^n \to y$ there exists a sequence z^n in T such that $z^n \to z$ and $z^n \in \Psi(y^n)$ for all n.

Definition. A correspondence is *continuous* if it is both lower and upper hemi-continuous.

For single-valued correspondences, the notions of lower and upper hemi-continuity coincide with the usual notion of continuity for functions. For proofs of the following lemmas, see Debreu (1959) or Hildenbrand (1974).

LEMMA. *Let $X \subseteq \mathbb{R}^l$ be a convex set. Then the budget correspondence $\beta : S \to X$ has a closed graph and is lower hemi-continuous at every point (p, w) for which $w > \min\{px \mid x \in X\}$ holds.*

Combining a previous Corollary on the non-emptiness of the demand set and a fundamental theorem of Berge (1966) yields the next result.

LEMMA. *Let $X \subseteq \mathbb{R}^l$ be a convex set. If the preference relation has a continuous utility representation, then the demand correspondence is defined (i.e. non-empty valued), compact-valued, and upper hemi-continuous at each $(p, w) \in S$ such that $\beta(p, w)$ is compact and $w > \min\{px \mid x \in X\}$.*

It follows immediately from the definitions, that $\phi(\lambda p, \lambda w) = \phi(p, w)$ for any $\lambda > 0$ and any price-wealth pair (p, w), i.e. demand is homogeneous of degree zero in prices and wealth. For convex preference orders, the demand correspondence is convex-valued. For strictly convex preference orders, the demand correspondence is single-valued, that is one obtains a demand function. The results of this section and of section 4 are summarized in the following lemma which uses the weakest assumptions of traditional demand theory to generate a continuous demand function.

LEMMA. *Let $S' := \{(p, w) \in S \mid \beta(p, w)$ is compact and $w > \min\{px \mid x \in X\}\}$. If $\succsim$ denotes a strictly convex and continuous preference order, then $\phi(p, w)$ defines a continuous demand function $\phi : S' \to X$ which satisfies: (i) homogeneity of degree zero in prices and wealth and (ii) the strong axiom of revealed preference.*

7. CONTINUOUS DEMAND WITHOUT TRANSITIVITY

Transitivity is often violated in empirical studies. This excludes utility maximization, but not necessarily preference maximization. However, as the next theorem indicates, existence and continuity of demand do not depend on transitivity as crucially as one may expect. The theorem follows from a result by Sonnenschein (1971).

THEOREM. *Let $S^* = \{(p, w) \in S \mid \phi(p, w) \neq \varnothing\}$, X compact, and $\succsim$ complete and with closed graph.*

(i) *If $\{x' \subset X \mid x' \succ x\}$ is convex for all $x \in X$, then $\phi(p, w) \neq \varnothing$ whenever $\beta(p, w) \neq \varnothing$ (i.e. $S^* = S$).*

(ii) *If $S^* = S$ and $(p^\circ, w^\circ) \in S$ such that β is continuous at (p°, w°), then ϕ is u.h.c. at (p°, w°).*

The assumption that X is compact is not necessary. For case (i) it suffices that all budget sets $\beta(p, w)$ under consideration be compact. For case (ii) it is sufficient that there are a compact subset X° of X and a neighbourhood S° of (p°, w°) such that $\phi(S^\circ) \subset X^\circ$.

To complete this section we state a lemma on the properties of a demand function obtained under preference maximization without transitivity. This contrasts with the lemma at the end of the previous section. Nontransitivity essentially implies that the strong axiom of revealed preference need not hold. The lemma follows from the theorem by Sonnenschein and from the result by Shafer (1974).

LEMMA. *Let $X = \mathbb{R}_+^l$, $B = \mathbb{R}_{++}^{l+1}$. Suppose continuity and strong convexity of $\succsim$ (in addition to completeness). Then preference maximization yields a continuous demand function $f : B \to X$ which satisfies (i) homogeneity of degree zero in prices and wealth and (ii) the weak axiom of revealed preference.*

The converse statement of the lemma does not hold. For $l = 2$, $X = \mathbb{R}_+^2$, $B = \mathbb{R}_{++}^3$, there is a C^1-function $f : B \to X$ which fulfills (i), (ii), and (iii) $pf(p, w) = w$ for all $(p, w) \in B$, but which cannot be obtained as the demand function for a continuous, complete and strictly convex preference relation (John, 1984; Kim and Richter, 1986).

789

8. SMOOTH PREFERENCES AND DIFFERENTIABLE UTILITY FUNCTIONS

Due to the representation theorem of section 5, continuity of a utility function and continuity of the represented preference order are identical under the perspective of demand theory. When continuous differentiability of demand is required, continuity of the preference relation will not suffice in general. The first rigorous attempt to study 'differentiable preference orders' goes back to Antonelli (1886). We follow the more direct approach of Debreu (1972) to characterize 'smooth preference orders'. Smoothness of preferences is closely related to sufficient differentiability of utility representations and the solution of the integrability problem (see Debreu, 1972, also Debreu, 1976, Hurwicz, 1971, and section 12 below).

For the purpose of this and subsequent sections, let P denote the interior of $\mathbb{R}_+^l$ and assume that $X = P$. Let $\succsim$ be a continuous and monotonic preference order on P which we may consider as a subset of $P \times P$, i.e. $(x, y) \in \succsim \Leftrightarrow x \succsim y$ for $(x, y) \in P \times P$. Also, the associated indifference relation $\sim$ will be considered as a subset of $P \times P$. To describe a smooth preference order, differentiability assumptions will be made on the (graph of the) indifference relation in $P \times P$.

For $k \geq 1$, let C^k denote the class of functions which have continuous partial derivatives up to order k, and consider two open sets X and Y in $\mathbb{R}^n$. A bijection $h : X \to Y$ is a C^k-diffeomorphism if both h and h^{-1} are of class C^k. $M \subset \mathbb{R}^n$ is a C^k-hypersurface, if for every $z \in M$, there exist an open neighbourhood U of z, an open subset V of $\mathbb{R}^n$, a hyperplane $H \subset \mathbb{R}^n$ and a C^k-diffeomorphism $h : U \to V$ such that $h(M \cap U) = V \cap H$. A C^k-hypersurface has locally the structure of a hyperplane up to a C^k-diffeomorphism. Considering the indifference relation $\sim$ as a subset of $P \times P$, the set $\tilde{I} = \{(x, y) \in P \times P \mid x \sim y\}$ gives the 'indifference surface' of the preference relation. Then $\succsim$ is called a C^2-preference order (or smooth preference order), if $\tilde{I}$ is a C^2-hypersurface.

THEOREM (Debreu, 1972). *Let $\succsim$ be a continuous and monotonic preference order on P and $\tilde{I}$ be its indifference surface. Then $\succsim$ is a C^2-preference order if and only if it has a monotonic utility representation of class C^2 with no critical point.*

9. PROPERTIES OF DIFFERENTIABLE UTILITY FUNCTIONS

Utility functions of class C^2 provide the truly classical approach to demand theory (see, for example, Slutsky, 1915; Hicks, 1939; Samuelson, 1947).

Let $\succsim$ be a monotonic, strictly convex C^2-preference order on P and $u : P \to \mathbb{R}$ be a C^2-utility representation of $\succsim$ with no critical point. Then u is continuous, increasing in all arguments, and strictly quasi-concave. Moreover, all second-order partial derivatives $u_{ij}(x) = (\partial^2 u / \partial x_i \partial x_j)(x)$, $i, j = 1, \ldots, l$, $x \in P$, exist, all u_{ij} are continuous functions of x and $u_{ij} = u_{ji}$ for $i, j = 1, \ldots, l$. Let $D^2 u = (u_{ij})$ denote the Hessian matrix of u. Then $D^2 u$ is symmetric. The first-order derivatives $u_i(x) = (\partial u / \partial x_i)(x)$, $i = 1, \ldots, l$ are continuous functions of x. Assume that $u_i(x) > 0$ for $i = 1, \ldots, l$, $x \in P$ and define

$$Du(x) = \begin{bmatrix} u_1(x) \\ \vdots \\ u_l(x) \end{bmatrix}$$

as the gradient of u at x. For many $m \times n$-matrix M, let M' denote the transpose of M.

THEOREM. *If $u : P \to \mathbb{R}$ is a strictly quasi-concave utility function of class C^2, then*

$$z' D^2 u(x) z \leq 0 \quad \text{for all} \quad x \in P \quad \text{and} \quad z \in \{\tilde{z} \in \mathbb{R}^l \mid \tilde{z} Du(x) = 0\}.$$

(For a proof, see Barten and Böhm, 1982).

It will be shown in the next section that the conclusion of this theorem does not guarantee the existence of a differentiable demand function. The following definition strengthens the property of strict quasi-concavity.

Definition. u is called *strongly quasi-concave* if

$$z' D^2 u(x) z < 0 \quad \text{for all} \quad x \in P, \quad z \neq 0$$

$$\text{and} \quad z \in \{\tilde{z} \in \mathbb{R}^l \mid \tilde{z} Du(x) = 0\}.$$

Consider the bordered Hessian matrix

$$H(x) = \begin{bmatrix} D^2 u(x) & Du(x) \\ [Du(x)]' & 0 \end{bmatrix}.$$

Then u is strongly quasi-concave whenever u is strictly quasi-concave and $H(x)$ is non-singular. (For a proof see Barten and Böhm, 1982).

The properties of strict and strong quasi-concavity are invariant under increasing C^2-transformations. For other results and consequences of differentiable utility functions the reader may consult Barten and Böhm (1982) and the references listed there, or Debreu (1972), Mas-Colell (1974).

10. DIFFERENTIABLE DEMAND

Section 7 gave sufficient conditions on preferences for the existence of a continuous demand function which is homogeneous of degree zero in prices and wealth and satisfies the strong axiom of revealed preference. In this section, the implications of smooth preferences for differentiability of demand will be studied.

Consider an assumption (D), consisting of the following three parts:

(D1) $X = P$
(D2) $\succsim$ is a monotonic, strictly convex C^2-preference order on X and the closure relative to $\mathbb{R}_+^l \times \mathbb{R}_+^l$ of its indifference surface $\tilde{I}$ is contained in $P \times P$.
(D3) The price-wealth space is $B = \mathbb{R}_{++}^{l+1}$.

Given (D), there exists a demand function $f : B \to X$ with $p \cdot f(p, w) = w$ for all $(p, w) \in B$. Let u be an increasing strictly quasi-concave C^2-utility representation for $\succsim$. The following key result on the differentiability of demand was first given by Katzner (1968). For a detailed proof see Barten and Böhm (1982).

THEOREM. *Let $(\bar{p}, \bar{w}) \in B$ and $\bar{x} = f(\bar{p}, \bar{w})$. Then the following assertions are equivalent:*

(i) *f is C^1 in a neighbourhood of $(\bar{p}, \bar{w})$.*

(ii) $\begin{bmatrix} D^2 u(\bar{x}) & \bar{p}' \\ \bar{p} & 0 \end{bmatrix}$ *is non-singular.*

(iii) $H(\bar{x}) = \begin{bmatrix} D^2 u(\bar{x}) & Du(\bar{x}) \\ [Du(\bar{x})]' & 0 \end{bmatrix}$ *is non-singular.*

Once the demand function f is continuously differentiable, it is straightforward to derive all of the well-known comparative statics properties, for the proof of which we refer again to Barten and Böhm (1982). Let $f = (f^1, \ldots, f^l)$ be a demand function of class C^1 and define

$$f_w = (f_w^1, \ldots, f_w^l) = \left(\frac{\partial f^1}{\partial w}, \ldots, \frac{\partial f^l}{\partial w} \right),$$

$$f_j^i = \frac{\partial f^i}{\partial p_j}, \qquad i, j = 1, \ldots, l,$$

$$s_j^i = f_j^i + f_w^i f^j, \quad i, j = 1, \ldots, l.$$

We obtain the Jacobian matrix of f with respect to prices, $J = (f_j^i)$, and the *Slutsky matrix* $S = (s_j^i)$.

THEOREM.

(i) $p f_w = 1$, $pJ = -f$,
(ii) $Sp' = 0$,
(iii) S is symmetric,
(iv) $y S y' < 0$, if $y \in \mathbb{R}^l$, $y \neq \alpha p$ for all $\alpha \in \mathbb{R}$,
(v) $rank\ S = l - 1$.

Property (iv) implies that all diagonal elements of S are strictly negative, i.e. $s_i^i = f_i^i + f_w^i f^i < 0$. If $f_w^i \geqslant 0$, then $(\partial x_i / \partial p_i) < 0$, i.e. commodity i is a *normal good*. $f_w^i < 0$, i.e. commodity i is an *inferior good*, is a necessary, but not sufficient condition that $(\partial x_i / \partial p_i) > 0$, i.e. that commodity i is a *Giffen good*.

11. DUALITY APPROACH TO DEMAND THEORY

With the notion of an expenditure function, an alternative approach to demand analysis is possible which was suggested by Samuelson (1947). For the further development and details, we refer to Diewert (1974, 1982).

As a matter of convenience and for ease of presentation assumption (D) will be imposed on the preference relation $\succsim$. Let u denote a strictly quasi-concave increasing C^2-utility representation for $\succsim$ and let $f: B \to X$ be the demand function derived from preference maximization. Let us further assume that $u(X) = \mathbb{R}$. (This requirement can always be fulfilled by means of an increasing transformation.) Define the *indirect utility function* $v: B \to \mathbb{R}$ associated with u by $v(p, w) = u(f(p, w))$ for $(p, w) \in B$.

Given a price system $p \in \mathbb{R}_{++}^l$ and a utility level $c \in \mathbb{R}$, let $e(p, c) = \min \{ p \cdot x \mid x \in X, u(x) \geqslant c \}$. Since u is strictly quasi-concave and increasing, there exists a unique minimizer $h(p, c)$ of this problem such that $e(p, c) = ph(p, c)$. $h: \mathbb{R}_{++}^l \times \mathbb{R} \to \mathbb{R}_{++}^l$ is called the *Hicksian (income-compensated) demand function* and $e: \mathbb{R}_{++}^l \times \mathbb{R} \to \mathbb{R}_{++}$ is called the *expenditure function* for u.

Since assumption (D) holds, preference maximization and expenditure minimization imply the following properties and relationships:

(1) $c = v[p, e(p, c)]$ for all (p, c).
(2) $w = e[p, v(p, w)]$ for all (p, w).
(3) $v(p, \cdot)$ and $e(p, \cdot)$ are inverse functions for any p.
(4) $h(p, c) = f[p, e(p, c)]$ for all (p, c).
(5) $f(p, w) = h[p, v(p, w)]$ for all (p, w).
(6) e is strictly increasing and continuous in c.
(7) e is non-decreasing, positive linear homogeneous, and concave in prices.
(8) v is strictly increasing in w, and continuous.
(9) v is non-increasing in prices and homogeneous of degree zero in income and prices.

Moreover, some interesting and important consequences of these properties can be obtained if the functions are sufficiently differentiable.

THEOREM.

(i) e is C^k if and only if v is C^k. $\qquad (k = 1, 2)$.
(ii) If e is C^1, then $\partial e / \partial p = h$.

If f is C^1, then

(iii) v is C^2.
(iv) $f = -(\partial v / \partial p)/(\partial v / \partial w)$ (*Roy's identity*).
(v) 'e is C^1 if and only if h is C^1'.
(vi) h is C^1 and e is C^2, and $\partial h / \partial p = S$ (*Slutsky equation*) with $\partial h / \partial p$ evaluated at $[p, v(p, w)]$ and S at (p, w).

12. INTEGRABILITY

A review of the previous discussions and analytical results involving the concepts of:

$\succsim$ preference
u utility
h income-compensated demand
e expenditure function
v indirect utility
f (direct) demand

makes apparent their relationships which can be characterized schematically by the following diagram:

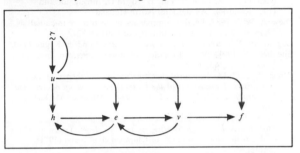

where $a \rightarrow b$ indicates that concept b can be derived from concept a under certain conditions.

The integrability problem is to establish $f \to u$, i.e. to recover the utility function from the demand function f. For details see the separate entry of Sonnenschein.

VOLKER BÖHM AND HANS HALLER

See also CHARACTERISTICS; COMPENSATED DEMAND; DUALITY; ELASTICITY; INCOME EFFECT; INTEGRABILITY OF DEMAND; REVEALED PREFERENCE; SEPARABILITY; SUBSTITUTES AND COMPLEMENTS.

BIBLIOGRAPHY

The present bibliography contains only those publications which are cited directly in the text. For more comprehensive bibliographies we refer to Barten and Böhm (1982), Chipman et al. (1971) and to Katzner (1970).

Antonelli, G.B. 1886. *Sulla Teoria Matematica della Economia Politica*. Pisa, Nella Tipografia del Folchetto. Translated as 'On the mathematical theory of political economy' in J.S. Chipman et al. (eds) (1971), chapter 16.

Arrow, K.J. 1953. Le rôle des valeurs boursières pour la répartition la meilleure des risques. *Économétrie, Colloques Internationaux du Centre National de la Recherche Scientifique*, Paris, Vol. 11, 41–7.

Arrow, K.J. and Enthoven, A.C. 1961. Quasi-concave programming. *Econometrica* 29, 779–800.

Arrow, K.J. and Intriligator, M.D. (eds) 1982. *Handbook of Mathematical Economics*, Vol. II. Amsterdam: North-Holland.

Arrow, K.J., Karlin, S. and Suppes, P. (eds) 1960. *Mathematical Methods in the Social Sciences*. Stanford: Stanford University Press.

Barten, A.P. and Böhm, V. 1982. Consumer theory. Chapter 9 in K.J. Arrow and M.D. Intriligator (eds) (1982).

Berge, C. 1966. *Espaces topologiques. Fonctions multivoques*. Paris: Dunod. Trans. as *Topological Spaces*, Edinburgh: Oliver and Boyd, 1973.

Bowen, R. 1968. A new proof of a theorem in utility theory. *International Economic Review* 9, 374.

Chipman, J.S., Hurwicz, L., Richter, M.K. and Sonnenschein, H.F. (eds) 1971. *Preferences, Utility, and Demand.* New York: Harcourt Brace Jovanovich.

Debreu, G. 1954. Representation of a preference ordering by a numerical function. In *Decision Processes*, ed. R.M. Thrall et al., New York: John Wiley.

Debreu, G. 1959. *Theory of Value.* New York: John Wiley. Press.

Debreu, G. 1960. Topological methods in cardinal utility theory. In K.J. Arrow et al. (1960), 12–26.

Debreu, G. 1964. Continuity properties of Paretian utility. *International Economic Review* 5, 285–93.

Debreu, G. 1972. Smooth preferences. *Econometrica* 40, 603–15.

Debreu, G. 1974. Excess demand functions. *Journal of Mathematical Economics* 1, 15–23.

Debreu, G. 1976. Smooth preferences. A corrigendum. *Econometrica* 44, 831–2.

Dierker, E., Dierker, H. and Trockel, W. 1984. Price-dispersed preferences and C^1 mean demand. *Journal of Mathematical Economics* 13, 11–42.

Diewert, W.E. 1974. Applications of duality theory. In *Frontiers of Quantitative Economics*, Vol. II, ed. M.D. Intriligator and D.A. Kendrick, Amsterdam: North-Holland.

Diewert, W.E. 1982. Duality approaches to microeconomic analysis. Chapter 12 in Arrow and Intriligator (eds) (1982).

Edgeworth, F.Y. 1881. *Mathematical Psychics.* London: Kegan Paul.

Eilenberg, S. 1941. Ordered topological spaces. *American Journal of Mathematics*, 63, 39–45.

Fisher, I. 1892. Mathematical investigations in the theory of value and prices. *Transactions of the Connecticut Academy of Arts and Sciences* 9, 1–124. Reprinted, New York: Augustus M. Kelley, 1965.

Frisch, R. 1926. Sur un problème d'économie pure. *Norsk Matematisk Forenings Skrifter, Serie 1*, 16, 1–40. Trans. as 'On a problem in pure economics' in Chipman et al. (eds) (1971), chapter 19.

Gossen, H.H. 1854. *Entwicklung der Gesetze des menschlichen Verkehrs und der daraus fließenden Regeln für menschliches Handeln.* Braunschweig. 2nd edn, Berlin: Prager, 1889.

Hicks, J.R. 1939. *Value and Capital.* Oxford: Clarenden Press.

Hildenbrand, W. 1974. *Core and Equilibria of a Large Economy.* Princeton: Princeton University Press.

Hildenbrand, W. 1980. On the uniqueness of mean demand for dispersed families of preferences. *Econometrica* 48, 1703–10.

Hildenbrand, W. 1983. On the 'Law of Demand'. *Econometrica* 51, 997–1019.

Houthakker, H.S. 1950. Revealed preference and the utility function. *Economica, N.S.* 17, 159–74.

Houthakker, H.S. 1960. Additive preferences. *Econometrica* 28, 244–57; Errata: *Econometrica* 30 (1962), 633.

Hurwicz, L. 1971. On the problem of integrability of demand functions. In J.S. Chipman et al. (eds) (1971), chapter 9.

Hurwicz, L. and Uzawa, H. 1971. On the integrability of demand functions. In J.S. Chipman et al. (eds) (1971), chapter 6.

Jevons, W. S. 1871. *Theory of Political Economy.* London: Macmillan.

John, R. 1984. A counterexample to a conjecture concerning the nontransitive consumer. University of Bonn, Sonderforschungsbereich 21, Discussion Paper No. 151.

Kannai, Y. 1977. Concavifiability and construction of concave utility functions. *Journal of Mathematical Economics* 4, 1–56.

Katzner, D.W. 1968. A note on the differentiability of consumer demand functions. *Econometrica* 36, 415–18.

Katzner, D.W. 1970. *Static Demand Theory.* New York: Macmillan.

Katzner, D.W. 1971. Demand and exchange analysis in the absence of integrability conditions. In J.S. Chipman et al. (eds) (1971), chapter 12.

Kihlstrom, R., Mas-Colell, A. and Sonnenschein, H. 1976. The demand theory of the weak axiom of revealed preference. *Econometrica* 44, 971–8.

Kim, T. and Richter, M.K. 1986. Nontransitive-nontotal consumer theory. *Journal of Economic Theory* 38, 324–63.

Koopmans, T. 1972. Representation of preference orderings with independent components of consumption. In *Decision and Organization*, ed. C.B. McGuire and R. Radner, Amsterdam: North-Holland.

Leontief, W. 1947. Introduction to a theory of the internal structure of functional relationships. *Econometrica* 15, 361–73. *Reprinted in Selected Readings in Economic Theory*, ed. K.J. Arrow, Cambridge, Mass.: MIT Press, 1971.

Mas-Colell, A. 1974. Continuous and smooth consumers: approximation theorems. *Journal of Economic Theory* 8, 305–36.

Mas-Colell, A. 1977. The recoverability of consumers' preferences from market demand behavior. *Econometrica* 45, 1409–30.

Mas-Colell, A. 1978. On revealed preference analysis. *Review of Economic Studies* 45, 121–31.

Pareto, V. 1896. *Cours d'économie politique.* Lausanne: Rouge.

Pareto, V. 1906a. *Manuale di Economia Politica, con una Introducione alla Scienza Soziale.* Milan: Società Editrice Libraria. Second edition: *Manuel d'Economie politique*, Paris: V. Giard et E. Brière, 1909.

Pareto, V. 1906b. L'ofelimità nel cicli non chiusi. *Giornale degli economisti* 33, 15–30. English translation: as 'Ophelimity in non-closed cycles' in: J.S. Chipman et al. (eds) (1971).

Rader, T. 1963. The existence of a utility function to represent preferences. *Review of Economic Studies* 30, 229–32.

Richter, M.K. 1966. Revealed preference theory. *Econometrica* 34, 635–45.

Samuelson, P.A. 1947. *Foundations of Economic Analysis.* Cambridge, Mass.: Harvard University Press.

Samuelson, P.A. 1950. The problem of integrability in utility theory. *Economica*, N.S., 17, 355–85.

Schmeidler, D. 1971. A condition for the completeness of partial preference relations. *Econometrica* 39, 403–4.

Schneider, E. 1970. *Einführung in die Wirtschaftstheorie.* 3rd edn, Vol.I, Pt IV Tübingen: J.C.B. Mohr (Paul Siebeck).

Shafer, W. 1974. The nontransitive consumer. *Econometrica* 42, 913–19.

Shafer, W. and Sonnenschein, H. 1982. Market demand and excess demand functions. Chapter 14 in Arrow and Intriligator (1982).

Slutsky, E. 1915. Sulla teoria del bilancio del consumatore. *Giornale degli Economisti e Rivista di Statistica 51*, 1–26. Trans. as 'On the theory of the budget of the consumer', chapter 2 in *Readings in Price Theory*, ed. G.J. Stigler and K.E. Boulding, Homewood, Ill.: R.D. Irwin, 1953.

Sondermann, D. 1975. Smoothing demand by aggregation. *Journal of Mathematical Economics* 2, 201–24.

Sonnenschein, H. 1971. Demand theory without transitive preferences, with applications to the theory of competitive equilibrium. In: J.S. Chipman et al. (eds) (1971), Chapter 10.

Sonnenschein, H. 1973. Do Walras identity and continuity characterize the class of community excess demand functions? *Journal of Economic Theory* 6, 345–54.

Sono, M. 1945. The effect of price changes on the demand and supply of separable goods. *Kokumni Keizai Zasski 74*, 1–51 (in Japanese). English translation: *International Economic Review* 2 (1960), 239–71.

Trockel, W. 1984. *Market Demand.* Lecture Notes in Economics and Mathematical Systems, Vol. 223, Berlin: Springer-Verlag.

Uzawa, H. 1960. Preference and rational choice in the theory of consumption. In K.J. Arrow et al. (eds) (1960). Reprinted in J.S. Chipman et al. (eds) (1971), chapter 1.

Volterra, V. 1906. L'economia matematica ed il nuovo manuale del prof. Pareto. *Giornale degli economisti 32* (1906), 296–331. Trans. as 'Mathematical Economics and Professor Pareto's New Manual' in J.S. Chipman et al. (eds) (1971), ch. 17.

Walras, L. 1874. Elements d'économie politique pure. Lausanne: Corbaz. Trans by W. Jaffé as *Elements of Pure Economics.* London: Allen & Unwin, 1954.

Wold, H.O.A. 1943. A synthesis of pure demand analysis. *Skandinavisk Aktuarietidskrift* 26, 85–118, 220–63.

Wold, H.O.A. 1944. A synthesis of pure demand analysis. *Skandinavisk Aktuarietidskrift* 27, 69–120.

demographic transition. The demographic transition is a specific change in the reproductive behaviour of a population that is said to occur during the transformation of a society from a traditional to a highly modernized state. The postulated change is from near equality of birth and death rates at high levels to near equality of birth and death rates at low levels. In the pre-modern state women who survive to age 50 have borne a large number of children; in the fully modernized society women bear only a small number. In a traditional society high mortality rates imply a low average duration of life; in highly modernized societies low mortality rates permit a long average duration of life.

A compilation of standard measures of current fertility and mortality in regions that the United Nations classifies as 'more developed' confirms the generalization that fertility and mortality are low in modernized populations. A measure of fertility often used by demographers is the total fertility rate (TFR), which is the average number of children that would be born (per woman) among women progressing from age 15 to age 50 subject to the birth rates at each age in the population in question. (The TFR of 1.8 in the United Kingdom in 1982 means that at 1982 rates, women would end childbearing having had an average of 1.8 births.) A measure of mortality that demographers often use is the expectation of life at birth (e(o)), or the average length of life of persons subject at each age to the death rates of the population in question. (The e(o) of 77 for females in the UK in 1982 means that women subject from birth on to 1982 death rates would survive to an average age of 77 years.) The United Nations category of 'more developed' countries includes Japan, the United States and Canada, Australia and New Zealand, the Soviet Union, and all of Europe. In 1975–80, the TFR in all of these countries except Ireland, Romania, Spain and Albania was between 1.4 and 2.5 children per woman; e(o) for females was between 74 and 80 years in all but Albania, Portugal and Romania.

Modernized countries have thus arrived at a remarkably homogeneous reproductive state. Moreover, the combination of the TFR and e(o) typical of these countries would produce in the long run nearly equal birth and death rates. The overall TFR in more developed countries in 1975–1980 was 2.05; female e(o) was 75.7 years. This combination would produce in the long run nearly equal birth and death rates of 12.8 and 13.6 per thousand respectively.

The demographic history as well as the current fertility and mortality levels of these modernized countries supports the generalization that their social and economic transformation has been accompanied by the postulated demographic transition. In each of the more developed countries in which TFR is low and e(o) is high, women bore at least twice as many children one or two centuries earlier; and experienced mortality leading to an average lifetime less than half the present average. In order words, much higher fertility and mortality (as implied by the transition) was characteristic of the pre-industrial era in countries now fully modernized. Because of the scarcity of valid early data on births and deaths, the evidence that birth and death rates were nearly equal in the pre-modern experience of these countries is mostly indirect. The near equality is inferred from the impossible numerical consequences that would follow the continuation for several centuries of a modest difference between the birth rate and the death rate – an average annual rate of increase of only one-half of one per cent causes a population to be multiplied by a factor of more than 12 in five centuries. Only under special circumstances such as those enjoyed by the early European settlers in North America could a pre-modern society experience any such multiplication. Populations inhabiting limited territory for hundreds of years and employing a gradually evolving technology, were limited to a low average rate of increase. Estimates of the growth of population in England show that before the Industrial Revolution, the population doubled in two centuries (from 1541 to 1741), yielding an average rate of increase of 0.35 per cent per year.

The term 'demographic transition' has wider connotations than the simple (and correct) statement that in the economically most advanced countries, fertility and morality are much lower than before modern development began. Another feature of the transition is that the decline in mortality normally preceded the decline in fertility. This sequence created a widened gap between the birth rate and death rate, a gap that was closed only after the delayed reduction in fertility again brought the two rates close together. Because of this gap, the transition includes a period of rapid growth in population.

The more important, complex, and uncertain connotation of the demographic transition is a set of hypotheses about the causal relation between industrialization (or economic development) and the reduction in fertility and mortality.

CAUSES OF THE DECLINE IN MORTALITY IN THE MORE DEVELOPED COUNTRIES. There is a disagreement among medical, social and economic historians concerning the relative role of various factors in lowering mortality in Europe beginning in the mid-18th century, a time that might be considered the first phase of the demographic transition. A number of innovations in preventive and curative medicine in the 18th and 19th centuries certainly contributed to lower mortality, including: vaccination for smallpox; the invention of anaesthesia; the discovery of the germ theory of disease and accompanying improvements in sterile conditions in surgery, and in hospitals; the pasteurization of milk; and the spread of an empirical approach to medical care so that doctors abandoned standard harmful treatments such as bleeding and purging. Specific reductions in mortality in specific areas (such as particular cities) can be identified as the result of the documented new provision of clean water or the construction of an adequate sewage system. A sustained reduction in mortality and the accompanying acceleration in population growth would not have been possible without an expanded and more regular food supply, resulting from the importation of food, from innovations in agriculture in Europe, including the introduction of new varieties of food plants from the Western Hemisphere, and from improvements in transport and extensions of markets, so that a local crop failure need no longer cause a rise in death rates. Improved diets may also have contributed to lower mortality. Also cited is a change in personal habits, such as more frequent bathing, and washing of hands and clothing.

Increases in e(o) since World War I, and especially after World War II, have been derived from the increasingly scientific basis of medical practice. Research has identified the causes of many diseases; medical technology has created the first really effective treatment (chemotherapy and antibiotics) for bacterial diseases and effective vaccines have been found for many viral diseases not susceptible to drug therapy.

In a broad sense, all of these factors contributing to reduced mortality are a natural part of modern industrialization, which both depended on and fostered the growth of modern science, and its application to agriculture, transportation, manufacturing, communications, and indeed almost every facet of life, naturally including medicine.

CAUSES OF THE TRANSITIONAL DECLINE OF FERTILITY. The first 'transitional' reductions in fertility large enough to affect national birth rates occurred in France and the United States – beginning within a decade or two of 1800. Since the United States was known for its rapid rate of increase and high birth rate (because it combined the moderately high marital fertility of European populations with much earlier marriage than in Western Europe), the early beginning of a decline in American fertility was not much noticed, especially since births were not registered, and the decline could only be inferred indirectly from changes in age composition. The decline in French fertility was well recognized; by 1900 the birth rate in France was only 22 per thousand, and the TFR only 2.8, low levels not attained until the 1920s or later in other European countries. Indeed, the generalization that the decline of mortality occurred before the decline in fertility applies very poorly to the French transition; throughout the 19th century, the fall the birth rate closely paralleled the fall in the depth rate. As a result the increase in the population of France was much less than in other major European countries. The slow growth of population was a matter of great concern in France, where it was blamed for the decline in the power of France relative to Germany, as exemplified in the outcome of the Franco-Prussian war.

French social scientists were the first to propose explanations of the modern decline in fertility. Arsène Dumont, writing before 1900, attributed the reduction in the birth rate to what he called 'social capillarity' (Dumont, 1890). He explained that in democratic societies where there are opportunities for social and economic advancement, a small family provides an opportunity for improvement in position. The small family rises in social and economic level, just as fluid rises in a small diameter tube, or capillary. In traditional societies, the opportunity for advancement is absent, and so is the incentive to have a small family. A French economist, Leroy-Beaulieu, expressed before World War I surprisingly modern-sounding views about why fertility was low in advanced societies (Leroy-Beaulieu, 1913). He said that in primitive societies expenditures of money and effort on children are limited, that children begin work at an early age and are soon contributing more to the family than they consume. In an advanced civilization child labour is outlawed, education is compulsory, and the emancipated young make many trying demands on their parents. Fertility is depressed by social ambition and the desire for comfort and luxury. Emancipated women find marriage less attractive, and may find a professional career competitive with maternity.

From the 1920s to the 1950s, Warren Thompson, C.P. Blacker, Frank Notestein and Kingsley Davis developed full and systematic statements of the typical changes in reproductive behaviour during industrialization, introduced the term demographic transition, and provided additional hypotheses to explain the fall in fertility (Thompson, 1930; Blacker, 1947; Notestein, 1953; Davis, 1945). Prominent among these is the decline in mortality itself. Lower death rates increase the size of family to be supported, and diminish the number of births needed to attain a given target number of children who survive to adulthood. Another factor suggested was the introduction of new forms of support for the aged (pensions, insurance policies and savings accounts), institutions that substituted for the traditional support of aged parents by their children, and thus reduced one of the incentives for childbearing.

The transition theorists disproved the conjectures of some biologists, who suggested that modern urban women had less reproductive capacity than their ancestors. (Clinical research showed that urban American women not practising contraception conceived at a rate as high as colonial Americans.) They also provided evidence that much of the restriction in fertility was attained by folk methods of contraception (especially *coitus interruptus*), with the implication that the transition in fertility had not been the result, primarily, of the invention of new contraceptives (although these inventions also contributed to the decline). In short, the decline in fertility had been to a large degree a change in the motivation to bear children, as suggested earlier by the pre-World War I French writers.

RECENT RESEARCH ON THE DEMOGRAPHIC TRANSITION. Since about 1960 both historical studies and theoretical analysis have broadened, but seldom simplified, our knowledge of transitional changes in fertility and mortality. An important contribution is Louis Henry's concept of *natural fertility* (Henry, 1961). In analysing fertility rates in different populations in which there is little or no practice of contraception, Henry found large variations in the level of fertility among married women. These variations are caused by differences in the duration and intensity of breastfeeding (which delays the resumption of ovulation and lengthens the interval between births); by taboos on intercourse while a mother is nursing; or by periodic separation of spouses. The distinctive characteristic of *natural fertility* is that behaviour of the sort described above that lengthens interbirth intervals is not parity specific; that is, the behaviour is practised after the first birth as well as after the fifth or sixth. Parity is the state of having born a certain number of children; a six parity woman is one who has had six births. On the other hand, *controlled fertility* occurs when married couples alter their behaviour to reduce their fertility after a certain number of children have been born.

Various evidence from contemporary less developed countries (and from historical research, including the analysis of parish registers and genealogies in the pre-modern stage of more developed countries) shows that under pre-modern conditions, marital fertility is and has been little affected by parity-related restriction. Modern evidence includes interview responses about the practice of contraception in less developed countries; historical evidence is mostly in the form of the age pattern of marital fertility, which has a characteristic structure of continued relatively high rates to higher ages when fertility is natural.

In pre-modern societies with long established traditions governing marriage and reproduction, the level of fertility has usually been surprisingly moderate. In Western Europe before 1800, marital fertility was rather high; if marriage had been early and universal, the total fertility rate would have been between eight and nine children. In fact, marriage was late (23 to 28 years average age at first marriage for women) and many remained single at age 50 (10–20 per cent). The actual TFR, therefore, was as low as four to five and a half children. In many non-European traditional societies marriage was early and universal; but marital fertility was moderate, being checked by various non-parity-related restrictions. Thus the TFR of rural China in about 1930 was only 5.5, and the TFR of India in 1901-1911 was only about 6.2, instead of the eight or higher that would have occurred with Asian marriage patterns and European marital fertility rates.

Moderate fertility rather than very high fertility has evident advantages for a long–enduring traditional society. The combination of fertility and mortality that such a society experiences determines the average rate of increase, which cannot be very different from zero over a long period. A TFR of eight would produce a rate of increase of two per cent annually if e(o) were 30 years; at this rate of increase, the population would be multiplied by 1,000 in 350 years! Thus a TFR of over eight would be sustainable only if e(o) were less than 20 years. The TFR of 5.5 in China produces a zero rate of increase in combination with an e(o) of 25 years, just about the mortality of the rural Chinese population. By maintaining customs that restricted fertility (late marriage, or prolonged nursing) traditional societies could achieve a more favourable mortality level, and have more resilience in the face of disaster, or more success in competing with rivals.

Fertility reduction as part of the demographic transition has consisted essentially of the replacement of moderate 'natural' fertility in the pre-modern era by very low controlled fertility achieved by contraception in the highly modernized state.

The circumstances under which the European decline in fertility began and under which it continued have been the subject of an extended research project centred since 1963 at the Office of Population Research at Princeton University. Its strategy is to construct indexes of fertility in all (or nearly all) of the 700 provinces of Europe from as early as data permit until a major decline in marital fertility (characteristically of fifty per cent or more) had occurred, and to collect and analyse information on the concurrent changing social and economic conditions in the different provinces (Coale and Watkins, 1986).

The project was undertaken to provide a firmer and more extensive foundation for generalizations concerning the demographic transition. It has undermined or strongly qualified previously accepted interpretations of the decline in fertility, in addition to suggesting a number of additional factors related to the decline.

The timing of the reduction in fertility is one of the surprises that this project provided. The decline began in France many decades before a sustained reduction in marital fertility was initiated in other European populations. Some of the French *départements* in which the reduction began no later than 1800 contain mostly peasant populations with low levels of literacy and high infant mortality. England, the acknowledged pioneer in the Industrial Revolution, having the highest proportion living in cities in Europe, did not begin to reduce fertility at an especially early date; later, for example, than Belgium or Switzerland, in each of which the proportion of the labour force in agriculture was twice as high, and the fraction living in cities only half as great as in England.

The research on fertility in Europe did not establish a checklist of characteristics (a threshold) that would serve as a sure indication that fertility reduction was about to begin. Reduction began under various conditions, in rural populations with little education, and high mortality, as well as in the expected context of highly literate populations with mostly non-agricultural occupations. It revealed a frequent geographic clustering of similar trends and levels of fertility. Adjacent provinces sharing the same language or ethnic origin were often alike in fertility even though different in educational levels, infant mortality and the proportions living in cities. At the same time, adjacent provinces that had a different cultural background (suggested, say, by a differing language or dialect) were not alike in fertility.

Low fertility or early decline is found in provinces in which voting patterns indicate secularized attitudes; for example, marital fidelity was already low in 1911 in Italy in provinces that 60 years later voted in favour of more liberal divorce laws. High fertility and late decline is found in provinces in which household industry (small-scale agriculture and handicrafts) was especially prevalent.

THE DEMOGRAPHIC TRANSITION IN LESS DEVELOPED COUNTRIES. In the 1940s, the authors of the demographic transition foresaw a postwar period of very rapid growth in the poorer parts of the world (those now labelled as less developed by the United Nations). They predicted what was later referred to as the 'population explosion' before it began. This foresight was derived from their interpretation of earlier demographic changes in Europe and other industrialized areas. Improvement in living conditions would reduce mortality in the poorer countries; fertility would at first remain high, as it had in most of the richer countries, because customs that maintain moderately high fertility are slow to change.

These forecasts underestimated the acceleration of growth in the less developed countries (ldc's), partly because unprecedented progress in low-cost curative and preventive medicine made possible unprecedented reductions in mortality, even in countries in which other forms of social and economic progress were slight. Until the 1960s, only a few areas had experienced a quantitatively important reduction in fertility, but in the 1970s a fall of a sufficient magnitude in fertility has occurred in a sufficient fraction of the less developed world to reduce the overall rate of increase, despite continuing reductions in mortality.

As in the demographic transition in Europe, the association in the less developed countries between changing fertility and specific features of social and economic progress is complex. Differences in traditional beliefs and customs appear to play a part in determining whether or not the rate of childbearing falls, in addition to such differences as education and per capita income. In several areas with a culture that derives from China – Singapore, Hong Kong, Taiwan, and South Korea – there have been reductions of 50 per cent or more in the total fertility rate. Social and economic development has been very rapid in these same areas. The TFR in Singapore is now lower than the average in more developed countries. In per capita income, life expectancy, energy consumption and educational attainment, Singapore has surpassed the poorer countries among those classified as more developed. It can thus be considered an instance of exceptionally rapid attainment of more developed status, including the current mortality and fertility levels typical of such status.

The sequence of fertility and mortality levels in other less developed countries is less consistent with the demographic transition. Kuwait has a per capita income ($20,000) nearly double that in the United States; 76 per cent of persons of appropriate age are enrolled in secondary school, the population is 91 per cent urban, and e(o) for females is 75 years; but the TGR is 5.7. In China per capita income is estimated as 310 dollars, 44 per cent of the appropriate age group is enrolled in secondary school, the population is 21 per cent urban, and e(o) for females is about 69 years; but the TFR is about 2.5. The Central Asian Republics of the Soviet Union constitute an instance of a population in which educational attainment at least through primary school is nearly universal among women under 40, and mortality is low, yet rural fertility remains very high.

In short, there are examples of populations that have reduced fertility while still low in income and rural in residence, and of others that have retained high fertility while making extraordinary gains in life expectancy, income, and education.

A high enough degree of modernization is accompanied by the full demographic transition; it is a sufficient condition for very low fertility and mortality, but not a necessary one. Religion and social tradition influence how resistant a population may be to reduced fertility as modernization occurs; information campaigns, expansion of family planning clinics, and incentives can speed the process.

ANSLEY J. COALE

See also AGEING POPULATIONS; DEMOGRAPHY; POPULATION; STABLE POPULATION THEORY.

BIBLIOGRAPHY

Blacker, C. 1947. Stages in population growth. *Eugenics Review* 39(3), October, 88–102.

Coale, A. 1979. The use of modern analytical demography by T.R. Malthus. *Population Studies* 33(2), July, 329–32.

Coale, A. and Watkins, S. (eds) 1986. *The Decline of Fertility in Europe.* Princeton: Princeton University Press.

Davis, K. 1945. The world demographic transition. *Annals of the American Academy of Political and Social Science* 237, January, 1–11.

Dumont, A. 1890. *Dépopulation et civilisation. Etude démographique.* Paris: Lecrosnier and Babe.

Henry, L. 1961. Some data on natural fertility. *Eugenics Quarterly* 8(2), June, 81–91.

Landry, A. 1934. *La révolution démographicque.* Paris: Sirey.

Leroy-Beaulieu, P. 1913. *La question de la population.* Paris: F. Alcan.

Notestein, F. 1953. Economic problems of population change. *Proceedings of the Eighth International Conference of Agricultural Economists.*

Thompson, W. 1930. *Population Problems.* New York: McGraw Hill.

demography. Demography is the analysis of population, including both techniques and substance. It is applied most often to human populations, and includes the gathering of data, the construction of models, interpretation of population changes, policy recommendations. The *data* used by demographers are partly cross-sectional in the form of censuses and sample surveys, partly flow data consisting of time series of births and deaths. *Models* that express the relation between the flow series of births, deaths and migration on the one side and the cross sections on the other are a main tradition of demography, running through the work of Lotka, Leslie and many others. *Interpretation* includes tracing causes of changes, and assessing their future consequences. *Policy* recommendations aim at lowering birth rates in countries of rapid growth, and raising it in countries below replacement.

Demography on the whole belongs to social science, though part of it (some of the analysis of mortality, was well as questions of fecundity) falls within the field of biology. It draws from and overlaps with other social sciences, especially sociology and economics. Reliability engineers deal with the life and demise of equipment and face problems analogous to those of human mortality; the mathematics they use is in many respects the same as that of demography, with superficial differences of notation. Epidemiology deals with some of the same problems as demography, though it too has developed a different tradition of exposition and notation. In so far as demographers collect and interpret data they necessarily borrow the techniques of statistics, including probability and stochastic processes. Ecology, a branch of biology, makes use of demographic techniques and results (Sauvy, 1954; Scudo, 1984).

For the more numerically minded demographer the subject begins with John Graunt (1662), who published his *Observations on the Bills of Mortality* more than three centuries ago. Yet Graunt's close study of the primitive death certificates of his day is not often referred to by working demographers now More often mentioned as a predecessor is Lotka, who applied the renewal equation, developed in mathematical physics about the beginning of the century, to the renewal of a human population. The part of his long career, with publications dating all the way from 1907 to 1948, that is most remembered was devoted to developing the consequences of that one equation. Those who see demography as emphasizing forecasting are likely to think of Cannan (1895), Bowley (1924), and Whelpton (1936), whose components method was put into convenient matrix form by Leslie (1945).

DATA. The most fundamental of all demographic data is the Census. Census taking is by no means novel. Ten cases of enumeration of the whole people (the earliest under Moses (Exodus xxxviii) and the last under Ezra (Ezra ii, 64)) are reported in the Old Testament, and one very famous occasion by the Romans is reported in the New Testament (Luke ii, 2). For a time the Romans took a census every five years. Classical Chinese literature contains innumerable references to counts in one part of the country or another. Premodern censuses were taken primarily to establish obligations on payment of taxes and military service, and they were correspondingly subject to evasion.

Modern censuses have been associated with the national state, as were other kinds of statistics: the word statistics itself itself reminds us of the association. Among the early acts of the revolutionary government of France was legislation providing for collection of data, including the taking of censuses. This was anticipated by Sweden, whose series of censuses goes back to the 18th century. Depending on the definition, the first census of modern times was taken in Sweden, Canada, or Virginia.

The association of the census with the national state has been seen in many of the new countries established after World War II. Countries seized on censuses to legitimate their nationhood, just as did France two centuries ago.

What characterizes modern censuses is (a) that they take place periodically, (b) that the enumeration is name-by-name, (c) that they seek to include all the persons belonging in a given area, (d) that they ask questions on age, sex, activity, etc., some of the questions often being on a sample, (e) that they recognize the problem of error and omission.

Geographic preparation is a major part of the effort to attain accuracy and completeness. The country is divided into enumeration areas on maps, with boundaries indentifiable on the ground, and each such area is assigned to an enumerator to be held responsible for its coverage. This principle of a division, first on maps and then on the ground, into an exhaustive set of non-overlapping areas is the essential principle of census-taking. It was apparently Morris H. Hansen who first applied the fact that every such area need not be covered for surveys (for example, population surveys taken between censuses). In area sampling the identification of individuals with a point on the map constitutes an implicit listing; the sample is specified in such a way that all individuals, including those unknown to the sample designers, have a prescribed chance of inclusion.

Equally valued with censuses for demographic calculations, though much less widely available, are accurate vital statistics. Partial records of births and deaths are to be found in many places and in many historical epochs, but effectively complete registration was largely a 19th-century innovation; the Swedish series going back to the 1700s is virtually unique.

Only under modern conditions do citizens need passports and other identification that depend on birth registration, and the citizen co-operation that is a condition for good vital statistics comes only with modernization. Censuses have now been taken in most countries of the world, but accurate vital statistics, covering current births and deaths, are to be had for countries including no more than about 30 per cent of the world's population. If we had to wait for the general awakening of public statistical consciousness that is required for a complete vital statistics system the population problem of the world would be solved before it could be measured.

COMPARISON. One of the oldest demographic problems is the simple comparison of mortality level as between two populations, or one population between two points of time. US advances in longevity were slow and uncertain in the 1950s and 1960s; it is a statistically delicate question whether mortality was lower in the United States in 1980 than it was in 1950 and by how much. A first attempt to answer it is comparison of crude rates, and we find that for white females the crude rate, deaths D divided by population P, was the same in both years. But this is not a pure comparison of mortality. If the populations number p_x^1 and p_x^2 at age x, and their death rates are μ_x^1 and μ_x^2, then the comparison of crude rates is D^1/P^1 versus D^2/P^2 or

$$\frac{\sum p_x^1 \mu_x^1}{\sum p_x^1} \quad \text{versus} \quad \frac{\sum p_x^2 \mu_x^2}{\sum p_x^2},$$

whose sole advantage as an index is that it may be calculated from the number of deaths and the number of exposed population at each of the two times, without any breakdown of the data by age. The p_x^1 and the p_x^2 confound the comparison, and if they are systematically different then the comparison of crude rates tells little about relative mortality. In particular one population having a larger proportion of old people than the other badly distorts the comparison.

To meet this difficulty, basic information was collected by age as far back as the 18th century in Sweden. To eliminate the different age weighting of the two populations from the comparison, it is common to use the directly standardized index with fixed p_x^1:

$$\frac{\sum p_x^1 \mu_x^2}{\sum p_x^1 \mu_x^1},$$

whose analogue in economics is the base-weighted aggregative price index. (The μs are similar to prices, and the ps to quantities used.) This formula gives for white females 6.5 in 1950 and 4.1 in 1980, a major difference from the crude rates, that were unchanged. Other formulas, for instance that obtained by replacing p_x^1 by p_x^2, give different answers, and the choice among them is difficult to make on logical grounds. Thus the famous price index number problem carries over to demographic comparison, though not the difficulty that rising or falling prices by themselves affect the amounts purchased. (Kitagawa and Hauser, 1973).

Demography has a resource not available to the study of price changes: the life table model. If the death rates of this year, including all ages at which anyone is living, can be seen as the successive ages in the life of an individual, then the individual subject to those rates would have a certain expectation of life. No real person will have such an expectation, but the model providesw what is the most common means of interpreting a current pattern of mortality.

If $\mu(x)$ is the age-specific death rate at age μ to $\mu + dx$ then the chance of a baby living to age α is $l(\alpha) = \exp[-\int_0^a \mu(x)\,dx]$, this being the solution of the differential equation defining the death rate,

$$\mu_x = \frac{1}{l(x)} \frac{dl(x)}{dx}.$$

The expectation of life at age x is then

$$e_x^0 = \frac{\int_x^\omega l(a)\,da}{l_x},$$

where ω is the highest age to which anyone lives. US white females showed e_0^0 equal to 72 years in 1950, 79 years in 1980. Elandt-Johnson, Regina and Johnson (1980) apply the expectations comparisons in clinical follow-up studies.

MORTALITY AND ITS CHANGES. To classify mortality according to the single parameter of life expectancy captures a good part of the variation in age incidence from one population to another, but not all. For instance a population may have high infant mortality and low mortality in later life while, in another, mortality may be low for infants and high in later life, with the two populations having the same overall expectations. Two dimensions differentiate among patterns much better than one. Coale and Demeny (1983) show four families of model tables. The United Nations (1985) show a Latin American, a Chilean, a South Asian, and a Far Eastern pattern. A particularly effective set of tables is due to William Brass (1971), who regresses the l_x column of a given table on that of a standard table, after both have been transformed by logits, and the regression of the one on the other turns out to be close to a straight line. Given the standard table, Brass's is a two constant system.

As mortality improves along the path that we have seen in advanced countries over the past generation the age specific rates at all ages go down, most being reduced by half in each generation. Because the span of life has changed little, a given per cent fall in age specific rates now has a much smaller effect on life expectancy than an equal percentage fall 50 years ago. In fact a drop of 1 per cent now in all age specific rates causes a rise of only about 0.10 to 0.15 per cent in life expectancy; 50 years ago it caused a rise of 0.30 per cent. This number, the derivative of the life expectancy with respect to the age specific rates, has been called H:

$$H = -\frac{\int_0^\omega l(x) \ln[l(x)]\,dx}{\int_0^\omega l(x)\,dx}.$$

On the present course it is becoming smaller and smaller, as we proceed to a time when everyone dies at about the same age. Demetrius (1974) has carried this analysis further.

Note that the progress against mortality need not go this route. We can imagine a slowing of the ageing process by which the l_x curve moves out to the right, rather than merely moving up to a horizontal line with a fixed boundary on the right. A slowing of the ageing process by 50 per cent would mean an extension of average life not of $50H$ per cent, or about 7 years, but a full doubling of life expectancy. One of the questions that physicians, pension officials and demographers ask one another is which of the two courses will be taken in the future by mortality improvements, especially at the oldest ages which count more and more for this as mortality under age 70 becomes small.

The life table with one exit – death – can be extended to several exits, representing the several causes of death, and on from these to several increments, taking place not only at age zero, but at arbitrary ages.

FERTILITY MEASURES. Children are born to women only at a restricted range of ages, so comparison for births are a somewhat different problem than for deaths. If we divide the number of births B by the whole population P to obtain a crude birth rate then we are subject to the irrelevant variation of the young and old people in the denominator; it is better to divide by the number of women in the childbearing ages. Some further small gain in precision of comparison is obtained by working with age-specific rates, the births $_5B_{15}$ to women 15–19 years at last birthday divided by the number of women $_5P_{15}$ in the population of that age at mid-period, and similarly for the six other ages under 50. With single years of age, if B_x is average girl births during a year to women aged x, then the rates are $f_x = B_x/P_x$, and these over the childbearing ages may be added to obtain the Gross Reproduction Rate (GRR):

$$GRR = \sum f_x = \sum (B_x/P_x).$$

including boy and girl births in the numerator B_x gives the total fertility rate (TFR), approximately double the GRR.

For measuring the natural increase of a population survivorship l_x is incorporated in the formula to give the net reproduction ratio (NRR), $R_0 = \Sigma\, l_x f_x$, where now f_x is again the girl birth rate. R_0 is the number of girl children expected to be born to a girl child on a particular set of rates of birth and death. By virtue of that definition it is the ratio of the number of persons in one generation to the number in the preceding, taken in abstraction from any irregularities in the age distribution, and disregarding the length of time over which one generation is replaced by another.

Estimating the effect of abortion and contraception raises some further issues. Since one abortion of a conception leading to a live birth reduces the number of live births in the population by 1, it might be thought that 1000 abortions would reduce the number of births by 1000, but this is not so. If the probability of a conception that leads to a live birth in a given month is p, and the sterile period following conception is s months, then there will be a birth on the average every $(1/p) + s$ months. If the sterile period following conception when abortion occurs is α, then there will be an abortion on the average every $(1/p) + \alpha$ months. Hence the number of abortions that avoid one birth is

$$\frac{\dfrac{1}{p} + s}{\dfrac{1}{p} + \alpha}.$$

This can come out above 2 if no contraception is used, but is only slightly over 1 if the abortion is a backstop to more or less efficient contraception (Potter, 1972).

MOMENTUM. With an NRR equal to unity a population will just replace itself over the long run; population in this condition of bare replacement will ultimately become stationary. If it drops to bare replacement after a history of rapid increase, then because of its young age distribution, with many women in the childbearing ages, it will continue to increase for one or two generations, until it attains a number that may be as much as 70 per cent higher than when its NRR dropped to unity, a phenomenon called population momentum. If the population has been increasing uniformly over a considerable period of time the ratio of the ultimate population to that at the onset of bare replacement is simply expressed as

$$\text{Ratio} = \left(\frac{b}{r}\right)\frac{e_0^0}{\mu}\left(\frac{R_0 - 1}{R_0}\right),$$

where b is the birth rate, r the rate of natural increase, μ the mean age in the stationary population (Keyfitz, 1985, p. 156).

This result is exact under the assumptions stated, and is one of numerous inferences from stable population theory.

PENSION COST AS A FUNCTION OF THE RATE OF INCREASE. Stable population theory also tells us the relation between certain

variables when other circumstances are held constant. A pension of unity to all members of the population over age 65 will cost those aged 20 to 64 at last birthday the annual premium

$$p(r) = \frac{\displaystyle\int_{65}^{\omega} e^{-rx}\, l(x)\, dx}{\displaystyle\int_{20}^{65} e^{-rx}\, l(x)\, dx},$$

and this cost can be approximated as

$$p(r) = p_0 \exp\left[r(m_1 - m_2) - \frac{r^2}{2}(\sigma_1^2 - \sigma_2^2)\right]$$

where m_1 and m_2 are the mean ages of the 20–64 and the 65 and over respectively, and σ_1^2 and σ_2^2 their variances. Since $m_1 < m_2$ and the term in r^2 is small, the premium is necessarily a decreasing function of the rate of increase of the population (Keyfitz, 1985, p. 106).

KINSHIP. If the population can be assumed to be stable and some assumptions of continuity are made then kin relations become determinate. Knowing the age specific rates of birth and death, and supposing the various demographic events are independent, we can find exact expressions for the probability that a person aged α has a living mother, living grandmother, as well as the expected aunts, cousins etc. (Goodman, Keyfitz and Pullum, 1974).

Lotka (1931) gives the probability that a girl aged α has a living mother. His answer is obtained in two steps: (1) with the condition that at the girls's birth the mother was x years old the probability is simple: $l_{x+\alpha}/l_x$; (2) removal of the condition by averaging over all ages of mothers at childbearing gives, on the stable assumption:

$$M_1(\alpha) = \int_\alpha^\beta \frac{l_{x+\alpha}}{l_x} e^{-rx}\, l(x)\, f(x)\, dx.$$

From this it follows that the probability of a living grandmother is

$$M_2(\alpha) = \int_\alpha^\beta M_1(x + \alpha)\, e^{-rx}\, l(x)\, f(x)\, dx,$$

and so on. Other expressions are obtainable for sisters, aunts, cousins (Le Bras, 1973). Noreen Goldman (1978) has applied the formulas for younger sisters and older sisters, equating the ratio as given in theory to the ratio observed in a sample of a population, and solving for the intrinsic rate. Her method for finding the rate of increase has the advantage of requiring no knowledge of age on the part of respondents.

Notice that the preceding formulas, like others based on stable theory, are essentially comparative statics, and give a result very different in meaning from one based on observed age data. They answer questions like 'What happens to the premium for old age pensions in the stable condition with the given parameters?' The formula for $M_1(\alpha)$ gives the fraction of girls aged α who have a living mother given the life table and birth rates, and disregarding all else. The observed fraction of girls aged α who have a living mother takes account of all other elements affecting the real population.

INFERRING VITAL RATES BY INDIRECT METHODS. In the absence of complete vital statistics much effort has had to be devoted to inferring vital rates from censuses, and one early method was based on the stable age distribution. In a fast growing population the preponderance of numbers is shifted to the younger ages, and this fact makes it possible to infer the rate of growth from examination of the age distribution. If birth rates and death rates are constant and the population closed, then as we saw the number of persons aged x per current birth is $e^{-rx}l_x$. If the l_x can be taken from a reference or model table, and a census gives c_x persons at age x and c_y persons at age $y > x$, then the equation

$$\frac{c_x}{c_y} = \frac{e^{-rx}\, l_x}{e^{-ry}\, l_y}$$

can be solved to find

$$r = \frac{1}{y-x} \ln\left(\frac{c_x/l_x}{c_y/l_y}\right)$$

(Bourgeois-Pichat, 1966).

The matter is not that simple in practice, since growth is irregular, censuses are subject to error, and one does not know what life table to apply. In general any pair of ages combined with a life table gives an estimate, and one can try to use ages that are less vulnerable to reporting error. The theory is readily extended to populations in which mortality is falling (Coale, 1963). More recently methods have been developed that do not depend on the assumption of stability (Brass, 1975; Preston and Coale, 1982; Coale, 1984; United Nations, 1985).

PERIODS AND COHORTS. Demography moves back and forth between consideration of a population existing at a given moment or period of time, and a cohort that is a group of individuals followed from birth or some other event. Comparison of mortality can be made between periods or between cohorts. The same formulas apply to both, for standardization as well as the life table. In fact, the usual life table is referred to as a synthetic cohort: it treats a set of age-specific rates referring to a particular moment as though they were applicable to individuals and extended over time. Cohorts are in a sense more real than periods, but being only calculations after the last individual member has died, they can never be up-to-date (Ryder, 1964).

The cohort – a number of individuals observed from a given starting point – is a demographic unit appropriate to fields other than mortality; one can assemble death and divorce statistics from individual data by following the marriages occurring in a particular year to the time where the couple divorces or one member of the couple dies (Henry, 1957a,b; Pressat, 1961).

MULTI-DIMENSIONAL DEMOGRAPHY. The above questions and techniques have been largely concerned with counts of people, and in disregard of characteristics other than age and sex. But for many purposes we need to examine marital status, or labour force status, or place of residence within a country. We need to take account of the transitions of individuals, for instance between the states of married and single, between school and labour force, etc. Combinations of sequences are numerous in any of these matters, and in order to bring the number down the Markov assumption is usually introduced, whereby the probability of a person moving into the several states in each period depends only on the last previous state the person was in, and not at all on the path by which he or she arrived at that state.

It fortunately happens that the ordinary life table can be extended to the multi-dimensional case, with matrix analogues for the most common formulas. If $\mu_{ij}(x)$ is the *rate* at which people aged x are moving from the jth state to the ith state, then the *probability* of going from the jth state at the beginning of a period to the ith state at the end of the period, is the ijth element of $\mathbf{P}_x$, where $\mathbf{M}_x$ is the matrix of the μs

$$\mathbf{P}_x = (1 + \mathbf{M}_x/2)^{-1}(1 - \mathbf{M}_x/2).$$

and so on through all the usual life table formulas (Rogers, 1975). This way of handling the arithmetic has the convenience of simple formulas, easily implemented on a computer. An equivalent method that dispenses with matrices is due to Robert Schoen (1975) and Leo A. Goodman (1961, 1969).

MIXTURES AND HETEROGENEITY. Everything said so far supposes that the several members of the population in any one category have the same probabilities – of dying, of giving birth, or of migrating – an assumption that cannot be correct. The usual demographic models recognize age, sex, and a few other sources of variation among individuals; they make no allowance for statistically unobserved heterogeneity.

Yet we know that some people are in vigorous condition, while others of the same age, sex, etc. are moribund. Among a group of individuals who are not all in the same condition the less vigorous die sooner, leaving the remainder with more favourable mortality than an unselected group would average. This process goes on through life, and the observed death rates, arising as they do from a population selected by differential mortality towards the more robust, are too low to represent an individual who at the start is of average frailty.

If we each had a mark on us indicating our degree of frailty then in estimating our own chances of survival we would use the experience of a group with the same mark as ourselves. We could avoid the unsatisfactory procedure of applying to ourselves the experience of a collection of people among whom average robustness was steadily increasing. Not knowing our condition, we must choose one of two ways of expressing our ignorance and deriving a probability. We can take ourselves as average at the start, and then we must accept that we will have an expectation lower than the published tables show; or else we can take ourselves as the average of the surviving population throughout the whole course, in which case we are supposing that we as individuals are steadily improving in robustness (Vaupel and Yashin, 1985).

The recognition of heterogeneity can explain some of the crossovers that are otherwise puzzling, for instance the fact that in the United States blacks show higher mortality than whites at ages up to 70, and beyond that they have lower mortality. Selection by the higher mortality at the younger ages is a way of explaining this; another explanation is defective data.

The curious paradoxes that arise through mixed distributions have been explored by reliability engineers (Mann, Schafer and Singpurwalla, 1974). In application to demography, the familiar rise in the proportion of divorces with duration of marriage, reaching a peak at five to ten years, could be due to married couples being of two kinds – one group that has a low and constant probability of divorce, not changing with duration of marriage, and another group that has a steadily rising probability with duration of marriage. First the overall rate, following this latter group, rises, but as these divorce and so drop out of the exposed population the rate falls towards that of the lower group. Neither of the component groups has a peak in rates at any time, yet the mix shows such a peak and subsequent fall because those more prone are eliminated from the exposed population.

The point is particularly important in respect of pregnancy. If we follow a group of fertile women through time, and note when they become pregnant we have the same problem of a changing mix, as those that are more fertile drop out, leaving less and less fertile ones behind. That may be a matter of fecundity, the biological ability to have a child, or it may be skill in using birth control, and both of these vary among women (Potter, 1972; Potter and Parker, 1964). It was Gini (1924) who showed that only in the first month can the rate refer to an unselected group. Goodman (1961) provides methods for the corresponding problem in migration, that had earlier been introduced by Blumen, Kogan and McCarthy (1955).

The order of magnitude of the effect can be very large in respect of susceptibility to pregnancy, or in respect of divorce; for mortality it cannot be so large because the event in question can only occur once to each member of the population. If a population were divided into three groups, one with an expectation of life of 65 years, one with 73 years, and one with 80 years, then the expected lifetime for the mixed population would be about one year greater than the expected lifetime of the middle group, that we take as the prospect for an individual who is initially of average frailty. About the only general statement that can be made is that expectation as given in published life tables is anything up to one year higher than the initially average person can expect to live.

FORECASTING. The activity of demographers that is most often noticed by the public is forecasting: estimating the future population of a country or other area (Brass, 1974). The forecasting problem is essentially unsolvable, just as is extrapolating from previous stops to estimate where the wheel will next stop in a casino. There is somewhat more continuity in the demographic than in the casino serials, but to know in advance the major turning points, especially in births, is at least for the present impossible.

While the public may think of demography as principally concerned with the forecasting of population, yet the literature of demography does not give a great deal of attention to this subject, and the best-known demographers have in recent years turned their attention to other problems; explaining the past is providing difficult enough, and until one can say why past events have occurred there is not much prospect of foretelling future ones.

Demographic forecasts are bound to be subject to especially large error for two reasons: they concern the long-term future, and they are self-contained within the narrow set of demographic variables. Forecasting a year ahead would be extremely useful in regard to the unemployment rate or housing construction, not to mention the stock market, while for a year ahead the population is so close to that of today that the forecast is of no interest. Demographic forecasts are typically for 10, 25, and more years into the future.

Since what the population will do depends on many variables outside of demography, it has often been suggested that demographers take into account these non-demographic variables. But that would require knowing future attitudes towards work and the family, and other matters more resistant to forecasting than population itself. Beyond that problem, even if we knew all of these independent variables for the next 25 years, the nature of the functional relation between them and population is beyond present knowledge.

During the present century death rates have been decreasing in most parts of the world, and extrapolations have been moderately successful. The increase in life expectancy has typically been almost three years per decade in developed countries, and has often reached five years per decade elsewhere.

What affects forecasts most is the birth rates assumed, and here is where the biggest failures have been. There was no way to forecast the postwar rise in births shown by developed countries, and equally little understood is the decline of births in the 1960s, and why birth rates continue to be so low. It was during the prosperity of the 1960s that the birth rates started to fall, and during the depressed late 1970s and 1980s that they fall even lower, so we do not know whether births depend directly or inversely on income. A theory that has strong logic on its side, that of Richard Easterlin (1980), by which the small cohort finds itself prosperous and produces a large cohort in its turn has not so far seemed precise enough either in timing or in quantity of the effect to be used by practising forecasters.

Migration is even more difficult for those few countries in which it is substantial. We do not know the amount of immigration into the United States now, let alone the amount that will occur during the 21st century.

Once the future mortality, fertility and migration are assumed, the forecast is easily made. In the usual projection by age and sex one starts with females, sets up a vertical vector P_0 consisting of the numbers at each age, premultiplies that vector by a matrix whose first row is the age-specific fertility rates for girl children, and whose subdiagonal is the survivorship rates. if M is the matrix with fertility rates m_{1j} in its first row, and survivorships $m_{j+1,j}$, $j = 1, \ldots, n-1$, in the sub-diagonal, then the age vector at time 1 is

$$P_1 = MP_0$$

and at time t is

$$P_t = M^t P_0,$$

if the rates are assumed constant over time (Leslie, 1945), If the rates change, the matrix being M_1 in the first period, M_2 in the second period. then

$$P_t = M_t, \ldots, M_2 M_1 P_0.$$

The assumed migrants would be added in each time period.

Experiments have shown that extrapolating birth and death rates does better, though not by much, than supposing that birth and death rates will continue unchanged at their level at the jumping-off point.

Even simpler than projecting with fixed birth rates is using fixed absolute numbers of births into the future. This method, that might be called instant stationarity, also gives results not much inferior to the usual assumption of changing future rates. A rationale for the fixed absolute numbers is provided by the Easterlin hypothesis, by which birth rates are higher for small parental cohorts.

FORECASTING ERROR. Badly needed are probability methods. Some have been proposed (e.g. Pollard, 1966) for *ex ante* computation of error, but so far these have had little influence on forecasting practice.

Ex post the problem is simpler. The assessment of earlier projections, leading to an estimate of the intrinsic error of the process, demands first of all a metric that will be comparable between different points of time for a given population, and between large and small populations, growing and declining populations, long- and short-range projections. Such a metric has been found to be the difference between the forecast rate of growth of the population in question and the (subsequently known) realized rate:

$$\text{Error} = \sqrt{\sum \left[\left(\frac{\hat{p}_t}{\hat{p}_0} \right)^{1/t} - \left(\frac{p_t}{p_0} \right)^{1/t} \right]^2}$$

where $\hat{p}_t$ is the forecast population at time t, p_t the realized population, t being the time interval between when the forecast was made and the date to which the projection applies. For some 300 forecasts applying to 15 developed countries, error as so measured turns out to be about 0.003, or 0.3 percentage points.

To interpret this result, consider an estimate for the United States of 268,000,000 for the year 2000, when we are now (1984) at 236,000,000. This is a projected annual rate of increase of 0.8 per cent, so odds are 2 to 1 of the true outcome falling within the range 0.8 ± 0.3 or $0.5 - 1.1$; one can bet 2 to 1 odds that the population in the year 2000 will be in the range $(236)(1.005)^{16}$ to $(236)(1.011)^{16}$, or 256 to 281 millions. This supposes that the present forecast is no better and no worse than the 300 similar forecasts on which this estimate of error has been based (Keyfitz, 1981).

EXPONENTIAL AND LOGISTIC GROWTH. There may have been situations in the past when populations were growing uniformly and it was possible to make some kind of credible prediction by supposing constant increase for the future. By definition of the rate of increase,

$$r = \frac{1}{P_t} \frac{dP_t}{dt},$$

so that the population at time t is

$$P_t = P_0 \, e^{rt}.$$

It is hard to think of cases where such exponential growth persists over more than a very short period.

The patent defect of the exponential that nothing can grow uniformly for very long suggested a further factor in the differential equation to produce the curve known as logistic:

$$r_t = \frac{1}{P_t}\left(1 - \frac{P_t}{A}\right)\frac{dP_t}{dt},$$

where A is the asymptotic population at which growth stops. The rate of increase r_t is no longer constant, and the solution of the equation is

$$P_t = \frac{A}{1 + be^{-ct}},$$

where b and c are constants.

The logistic seemed to have merit when births were slowing and total population growth tapering off. It reached the height of its popularity when the Americas could be seen as empty, and as they filled would move towards a population ceiling. Unfortunately the ceiling keeps changing with changing society and technology.

One might take a different line in support of the logistic: not the logic of the model but goodness of fit to the historical series. That does not work either; an inverse tangent, or a cumulative normal fit just as well as a logistic, and an impossible curve, a hyperbola moving off to infinity in a near future, is not much inferior to any of the three in fitting the past (Cohen, 1984).

For animal populations the story is different; real niches filling under constant conditions do appear, and in ecological studies the logistic has on occasion provided a useful representation of the process.

DIFFICULT MATTERS. Some demographic results are perfectly explicable: when Romania suddenly banned abortion, the birth rate, which presumably included a proportion of unwanted children, rose sharply; after the public adapted to the ban the birth rate settled back to where it was. Others remain puzzles even after much study: why does West Germany stay at the lowest recorded fertility of all time, much lower than neighbouring France? The effectiveness of determined population policy in East Germany is partly explained by the large expenditure on it, but not Hungary's extremely low fertility after the war, and the subsequent partial recovery.

Similarly, there is much to explain in poor countries; some countries have seen their fertility fall drastically, while others remain high. Cultural inheritance is apparently a factor. Islamic populations have higher fertility than non-Islamic that are otherwise similar; thus for 1980–85 the UN (1985) estimates Pakistan's TFR (Total Fertility Rate) at 5.84 and Bangladesh's at 6.15 against India's 4.41. What feature of Islam is the cause of the differential remains to be discovered.

A key question in contemporary demography is whether and how quickly the countries whose death rates have fallen can follow through with declines in birth rates that will bring them to zero growth. No one knows for sure whether the fall of deaths – for instance and especially of infant mortality – in and by itself brings about a decline of births; the literature contains proofs that it does and proofs that it does not. Even if we knew for sure that the demographic transition to a stationary condition will take place everywhere, forecasting for the years ahead is impeded by our ignorance of how quickly it will come. And professional opinion on the effectiveness of family planning programmes is by no means unanimous.

NATHAN KEYFITZ

See also DEMOGRAPHIC TRANSITION; HISTORICAL DEMOGRAPHY; LIFE TABLES; STABLE POPULATION THEORY.

BIBLIOGRAPHY

Arthur, W.B. and Vaupel, J.W. 1984. Some general relationships in population dynamics. *Population Index* 50(2), Summer, 214–26.

Blumen, I., Kogan, M. and McCarthy, P.J. 1955. *The Industrial Mobility of Labor as a Probability Process*. Vol. VI of Cornell Studies of Industrial and Labor Relations, Ithaca: Cornell University Press.

Bogue, D.J. 1985. *The Population of the United States: Historical Trends and Future Projections*. New York: Free Press.

Bourgeois-Pichat, J. 1966. *The Concept of a Stable Population: Application to the Study of Populations of Countries with Incomplete Population Statistics*. ST/SOA/Series A 139, New York: United Nations.

Bowley, A.L. 1924. Births and population of Great Britain. *Journal of the Royal Economic Society* 34, 188–92.

Brass, W. 1971. On the scale of mortality. In *Biological Aspects of Demography*, ed. W. Brass, London: Taylor and Francis, 69–110.

Brass, W. 1974. Perspectives in population prediction, illustrated by the statistics of England and Wales. *Journal of the Royal Statistical Society*, Series A 137, 532–83.

Brass, W. 1975. *Methods for Estimating Fertility and Mortality from Limited and Defective Data*. An Occasional Publication. Chapel Hill: University of North Carolina, International Program of Laboratories for Population Statistics.

Cannan, E. 1895. The probability of cessation of growth of population in England and Wales during the next century. *Economic Journal* 5, 505–15.

Coale, A.J. 1963. Estimates of various demographic measures through the quasi-stable age distribution. In *Emerging Techniques in Population Research* (39th Annual Conference of the Milbank Memorial Fund, 1962), New York: Milbank Memorial Fund, 175–93.

Coale, A.J. 1966. *Methods of Estimating Fertility and Mortality from Censuses of Population*. Princeton: Office of Population Research.

Coale, A.J. 1984. Life table construction on the basis of two enumerations of a closed population. *Population Index* 50(2), Summer, 193–213.

Coale, A.J. and Demeny, P. 1983. *Regional Model Life Tables and Stable Populations*. 2nd edn, New York: Academic Press.

Cohen, J.E. 1984. Demographic doomsday deferred. *Harvard Magazine* 86(3), January–February, 50–51.

Demetrius, L. 1974. Demographic parameters and natural selection. *Proceedings of the National Academy of Sciences* 71, 4645–7.

Easterlin, R.A. 1980. *Birth and Fortune: The Impact of Numbers on Personal Welfare*. New York: Basic Books.

Elandt-Johnson, R.C. and Johnson, N.L. 1980. *Survival Models and Data Analysis*. New York: John Wiley & Sons.

Gini, C. 1924. Premières recherches sur la fecondabilité de la femme. *Proceedings of the International Mathematics Congress*, Vol. 2, 889–92.

Goldman, N. 1978. Estimating the intrinsic rate of increase from the average numbers of younger and older sisters. *Demography* 15, 499–508.

Goodman, L.A. 1961. Statistical methods for the mover-stayer model. *Journal of the American Statistical Association* 56(296), 841–68.

Goodman, L.A. 1969. The analysis of population growth when the birth and death rates depend upon several factors. *Biometrics* 25, 659–81.

Goodman, L.A. Keyfitz, N. and Pullman, T.W. 1974. Family formation and the frequency of various kinship relationships. *Theoretical Population Biology* 5, 1–27.

Graunt, J. 1662. *Natural and Political Observations Made upon the Bills of Mortality*. London. Ed. Walter F. Willcox, Baltimore: Johns Hopkins University Press, 1939.

Henry, L. 1957a, Fécondité et famille. Modèles mathématiques I. *Population* 12, 413–444.

Henry, L. 1957b. Fécondité et famille. Modèles mathématiques II. *Population* 16, 27–48, 261–82.

Kaplan, E.L. and Meier, P. 1958. Nonparametric estimation from incomplete observations. *Journal of the American Statistical Association* 53, 457–81.

Keyfitz, N. 1981. The limits of population forecasting. *Population and Development Review* 7(4), 579–93.

Keyfitz, N. 1985. *Applied Mathematical Demography*. 2nd edn, New York: Springer-Verlag.

Kitagawa, E.M. and Hauser, P.M. 1973. *Mortality in the United States. A Study in Socioeconomic Epidemiology*. Cambridge, Mass.: Harvard University Press.

Le Bras, H. 1973. Parents, grandparents, diaeresis bisaieux. *Population* 28, 9–37. Trans. and ed. K. Wachter as *Statistical Studies of Historical Social Structure*, New York: Academic Press, 1978.

Lee, R.D. 1974. The formal dynamics of controlled populations and the echo, the boom and the bust. *Demography* 11, 563–85.

Leslie, P.H. 1945. On the use of matrices in certain population mathematics. *Biometrika* 33, 183–212.

Lotka, A.J. 1931. Orphanhood in relation to demographic factors. *Metron* 37–109.

Lotka, A.J. 1939. *Théorie analytique des associations biologiques*. Part II: *Analyse démographique avec application particulière à l'espèce humaine*. Actualités Scientifiques et Industrielles, No. 780, Paris: Hermann et Cie.

Mann, N.R., Schafer, R.D. and Singpurwalla, N.D. 1974. *Methods for Statistical Analysis of Reliability and Life Data*. New York: John Wiley and Sons.

Pollard, J.H. 1966. On the use of the direct matrix product in analysing certain stochastic population models. *Biometrika* 53, 397–415.

Potter, R.G. 1972. Births averted by induced abortion: an application of renewal theory. *Theoretical Population Biology* 3, 69–86.

Potter, R.G. and Parker, M.P. 1964. Predicting the time required to conceive. *Population Studies* 18, 99–116.

Pressat, R. 1961. *L'analyse démographique: méthodes, résultats, applications*. Paris: Presses Universitaires de France, for Institut National d'Etudes Démographiques.

Preston, S.H. and Coale, A.J. 1982. Age structure, growth, attrition, and accession: a new synthesis. *Population Index* 48(2), 217–59.

Rogers, A. 1975. *Introduction to Multiregional Mathematical Demography*. New York: John Wiley and Sons.

Ryder, N.B. 1964. The process of demographic transition. *Demography* 1(1), 74–82.

Sauvy, A. 1952–1954. *Théorie générale de la population*. Vol. 1: *Economie et population*. Vol. II: *Biologie sociale*. Paris: Presses Universitaires de France.

Schoen, R. 1975. Constructing increment-decrement life tables. *Demography* 12, 313–24.

Scudo, F.M. 1984. The 'golden age' of theoretical ecology; a conceptual appraisal. *Revue Européenne des sciences sociales* 22(67), 11–64.

United Nations. 1985. *World Population Prospects: Estimates and Projections as Assessed in 1982*. ST/ESA/SER.A/82, New York: United Nations.

Vaupel, J.W. and Yashin, I.Y. 1985. The deviant dynamics of death in heterogeneous populations. In *Sociological Methodology 1985*, ed. N.B. Tuma, San Francisco: Jossey-Bass.

Whelpton, P.K. 1936. An empirical method of calculating future population. *Journal of the American Statistical Association* 31, 457–73.

De Moivre, Abraham (1667–1754). De Moivre was born in Vitry-le-François on 26 May 1667, of French Protestant stock. Following the revocation of the Edict of Nantes in 1685 he fled to London, where he earned a precarious living as a mathematical author and tutor until his death there on 27 November 1754.

De Moivre was the most important writer on probability of his day, building on the work of Pascal, Fermat, Huygens and James Bernoulli. His *De mensura sortis* (On the measurement of lots) appeared in the *Philosophical Transactions* for 1711 and in ever-expanding form in English as the *Doctrine of Chances* (1718, 1738, 1756). It contained the first publication of the expression for the binomial distribution for general chances. The second edition (1738) included an English translation of the privately-circulated Latin pamphlet of 1733 in which De Moivre gave his celebrated Normal approximation to the binomial distribution '*A method of approximating the Sum of the Terms of the Binomial $(a+b)^n$ expanded into a Series from whence are deduced some practical Rules to estimate the Degree of Assent which is to be given to Experiments*.' De Moivre was fully seized of the importance of Bernoulli's limit theorem and its application to the problem of estimating a binomial parameter; this work replaced Bernoulli's 'very wide limits' by an approximation.

De Moivre also made important contributions to the 'Gambler's Ruin' problem, involving the question of the duration of play, to the use of generating functions, and to the study of annuities.

A.W.F. EDWARDS

dependency. The general field of study of dependency analysis is the development of peripheral capitalism. Its most important contribution is its attempt to analyse it from the point of view of the interplay between internal and external structures. Its most well-known feature is the internal debate about whether capitalism remains 'historically progressive' in the Third World (i.e. capable of developing the productive forces of these societies and thus able to lead them towards socialism).

With the necessary degree of simplification which every classification of intellectual tendencies entails one can distinguish four major approaches – not mutually exclusive from the point of view of intellectual history – in dependency analysis. The first two have in common the fact that they analyse the process of capitalist development in the periphery as historically progressive, but do so in a different way from the one predicted by Marx and Engels (for the classical marxist view on capitalist development in the periphery, see Palma, 1978). The main difference between these two first approaches to dependency lies in the fact that each has a different reason for their disagreement with classical marxist analysis. While one approach departs from it mainly arguing changes in 'circumstances' – the world capitalist system has been transformed in such a way that the industrialization of the periphery cannot take place in the way predicted by Marx and Engels – the other puts the emphasis on changes in 'diagnosis'; Marx's analysis is itself over-optimistic regarding the possibilities of industrialization in the backward areas of the world.

The other two approaches have in common their extreme scepticism regarding the possibilities of industrialization in the periphery – a postulate that goes against the spirit and the letter of Marx's writings. The main difference between these two second approaches is that while for one not only is there no possibility of capitalist development in the periphery at present, but there has never been one and there will never be one (i.e. there is no escape from the 'development of underdevelopment' within this system); for the other approach there are still certain alternatives to this supposed 'accumulation of backwardness'.

DEPENDENCY AS A THEORY OF 'INHIBITED' CAPITALIST DEVELOPMENT IN THE PERIPHERY. Ever since the end of the 19th century (the period of the 'Classics of Imperialism') Marxist analysis has put emphasis in the necessity of a 'bourgeois democratic revolution' as an essential requirement for any backward society to be able to embark in a process of capitalist development proper. In the words of Rosa Luxemburg '[bourgeois] revolution is an essential for the process of capitalist emancipation. The backward communities must shed their obsolete political organizations, and create a modern State machinery adapted to the purpose of capitalist production' (1913, p. 395). The main intellectual and political concern of this approach to dependency analysis is an attempt to explain why this 'bourgeois-democratic' revolution has not taken place as expected after the process of political independence in the Third World, and how this is inhibiting their process of capitalist development.

In the Marxist literature, the 'bourgeois democratic' revolution is defined as a revolt of the forces of production against the old outmoded relations of production. In this way the structure of the old political and legal system would be broken and a new economic expansion would be expected to take place. This revolution would be based on an alliance between the bourgeoisie and the proletariat, the principal battle line would be between the bourgeoisie and the traditional oligarchies, between industry and land, capitalism versus pre-capitalist forms of monopoly and privilege; because it is the result of the pressure of a rising class whose path is being blocked in economic and social terms, the revolution would bring not only political emancipation but economic progress as well (i.e. it could be seen as a 'supply side' explanation to the obstacles to economic development in the Third World).

Nevertheless, the political independence of the backward nations has not been followed by these developments, contrary to the expectations of the 'Classics of Imperialism'. Even more, in the case of most of the periphery it is precisely in the post-colonial period that the development of individual nations (with the due economic and political variations) has taken upon itself the articulation with the advanced capitalist countries which the classical writers on imperialism noted in the colonies – the growth of their productive sectors concentrated on primary products, whether mineral or agricultural; the limited degree of industrialization; and financial dependence. For this reason, this group of dependency writers attempt to explain why the 'bourgeois-democratic' revolution is being hindered and what the consequences of this are. Their main argument is that the process of industrialization in the backward countries is contradictory not only with some internally dominant groups, but also with imperialism. For this reason, the ability of the incipient national bourgeoisies to develop in the post-colonial phase would depend upon their political capacity to assert themselves over these two groups. This double contradiction in capitalist development in the periphery (particularly in the process of industrialization) would tend to be transformed into a single contradiction through the alliance of the groups in question (the so-called 'feudal-imperialist alliance'). This type of approach to dependency figures prominently in the political and economic analysis of large sectors of the Latin American left (including some Communist parties of the subcontinent). Furthermore, it seems to have had an important influence – albeit an unacknowledge one – upon the original ECLA analysis of the obstacles facing Latin American development (see STRUCTURALISM).

DEPENDENCY AS AN ANALYSIS OF CONCRETE PROCESSES OF DEVELOPMENT. The two main characteristics of this approach to dependency are, first, that it does not take classical marxist theory of development as a mechanical continuum of discrete stages through which each backward society must pass, not least because when this theory was formulated it was not based on any concrete experience of capitalist development in the periphery (although when it was formulated there were already several experiences of it, particularly in Latin America), but mainly on an extrapolation of the experience of Western Europe. Secondly, from a methodological point of view, it does not aspire to build an alternative mechanico-formal theory of development applicable to all the periphery and at all times, but to concentrate on the study of what have been called 'concrete situations of dependency'. In the words of F.H. Cardoso,

> The question which we should ask ourselves is why, it being obvious that the capitalist economy tends towards a growing internationalization, societies are divided into antagonistic classes, and that the particular is to a certain extent conditioned by the general, with these premises we have not gone beyond the partial – and therefore abstract in the Marxist sense – characterization of the Latin American situation and historical process (1974, pp. 326–7).

Briefly, this second approach to the analysis of dependency (which emerged with the publication of Cardoso and Faletto, 1967) can be expressed as follows:

(i) In common with the other approaches to dependency, this second approach sees the peripheral economies as an integral part of the world capitalist system, in a context of its increasing internationalization; it also argues that the central dynamic of that system lies outside the peripheral economies and that therefore the options which lie open to them are limited (but not determined) by the development of the system at the centre; in this way the particular is in some way conditioned by the general. Therefore, a basic element for the understanding of these societies is given by the 'general determinants' of the world capitalist system, which is itself changing through time; the analysis therefore requires primarily an understanding of the contemporary characteristics of the world capitalist system. One characteristic of this approach to dependency, and one which has been widely recognized, has been to incorporate more successfully into its analysis of Latin American development the transformations which are occurring and have occurred in the world capitalist system, and in particular the changes which became significant towards the end of the 1950s in the rhythm and the form of capitalist movement, and in the international division of labour, one of the most important being the emergence of the so-called multinational corporation which progressively transformed centre–periphery relationships, and relationships between countries of the centre. As foreign capital has increasingly been directed towards manufacturing industry in the periphery, the struggle for industrialization, which was previously seen as an anti-imperialist struggle, in a way has become increasingly the goal of foreign capital. Thus dependency and industrialization cease to be 'contradictory' and a path of 'dependent development' becomes possible.

(ii) Furthermore, this approach not only accepts as a starting point and improves upon the analysis of the location of the economies of the periphery in the world capitalist system, but also accepts and enriches their demonstration that these societies are structured through unequal and antagonistic patterns of social organization, showing the social asymmetries and the exploitative character of social organization which arise from its socio-economic base; it also gives considerable importance to the effect of the diversity of natural resources, geographical location, and so on, of each economy, thus extending significantly the analysis of the 'internal determinants' of the development of the peripheral economies.

(iii) But while these improvements are important, the most significant feature of this approach is that it goes beyond these points, and insists that from the premises so far outlined one necessarily arrives at a *partial*, *abstract* and *indeterminate* characterization of the peripheral historical process, which can only be overcome by understanding how the 'general' and 'specific' determinants interact in particular and concrete situations. It is only by understanding the specificity of the movement in these societies as a dialectical unity of both, and a synthesis of these 'internal' and 'external' factors, that one can explain the particularity of social, political and economic processes in the dependent societies.

DEPENDENCY AS A THEORY OF THE 'DEVELOPMENT OF UNDERDEVELOPMENT'. This approach to dependency analysis was first developed at the end of the 1950s, and took off with the publication of Paul Baran's *Political Economy of Growth* (1957). It is characterized by the acceptance, almost as an axiomatic truth, of the argument that no third world country can now expect to break out of a state of economic dependency and advance to an economic position closest to that of the major capitalist industrial powers. This is a very important proposition since it not only establishes the extent to which capitalism remains historically progressive in the modern world, but also thereby defines the economic background to political action. Yet, too often, the question is ill defined; it is not at all self-evident; its intellectual origins are obscure; and its actual foundations are in need of a fuller analysis.

Starting out with this 'stagnationist' analysis, André Gunder Frank (1967) attempted to develop the thesis that the only political solution is a revolution of an immediate socialist character, totally de-linked from the world capitalist system for within its context there could be no alternative to underdevelopment. Although Frank did not go very far in his analysis of the capitalist system as a whole, its origins and development – and why it could only offer destruction to the periphery – Immanuel Wallerstein tackled this tremendous challenge in his remarkable book (1974).

The central line of Frank's analysis regarding the complete lack of historical progressiveness of capitalism in the third world is continued (among many others) by Dos Santos (1970), Marini (1972), Caputo and Pizarro (1974), and Hinkelamert (1970). This type of approach to dependency analysis has been criticized from all sides, and on almost every point in their analysis: see Laclau (1971), Brenner (1977), Cardoso (1974), Warren (1980) and Palma (1978).

DEPENDENCY AS A REFORMULATION OF THE ECLA ANALYSIS OF LATIN AMERICAN DEVELOPMENT. Towards the middle of the 1960s the ECLA analyses were overtaken by gradual decline, in which many factors intervened. The statistics relating to Latin American development in the period after the Korean War presented a gloomy picture which was interpreted in different ways as indicating the failure of the policies ECLA had been proposing since its foundation. Furthermore, the first attempts to introduce into the traditional ECLA analysis a number of 'social aspects' (Prebisch, 1963) far from strengthening the analysis, revealed its fragility (see Cardoso, 1977). One of the results of the relative decline in the influence of ECLA's analysis was the emergence of an attempt to reformulate its thought.

This attempt took place just at the time when an important sector of the Latin American left was breaking with the first approach discussed above (capitalist development was both necessary and possible but hindered by the 'feudal-imperialist alliance') and moving towards the third one ('development of underdevelopment'). Not only did the different processes of reformulation take place at the same time, but they had an extremely important element in common: *pessimism* regarding the possibility and viability of capitalist development in the periphery.

The irony was that while both groups were busy writing and publishing different versions of stagnationist theories which did not take into account the cyclical pattern characterist of capitalist development (the most sophisticated perhaps being Furtado, 1966), international trade was picking up, the terms of trade were changing in favour of Latin America, and some countries were able to take advantage of the favourable situation and accelerated rapidly the rhythm of their economic development. Thus, as Cardoso (1977, p. 33) remarks, 'history has prepared a trap for pessimists'.

But if the attempt at reformulation which followed the crisis in ECLA school of thought did not succeed in grasping the transformations which were occurring at that moment in the world capitalist system, it did in time produce together with the abandonment of stagnationist theories, a movement towards a more structural-historical analysis of Latin America (of the type discussed in the second approach above). The first substantial critique of stagnationist theories came from Tavares and Serra (1970); see also Pinto (1965 and 1974), Sunkel and Paz (1970) and Cariola and Sunkel (1982) among others.

J.G. PALMA

See also COLONIALISM; DEVELOPMENT ECONOMICS; IMPERIALISM; NATIONALISM; PERIPHERY; TERMS OF TRADE AND ECONOMIC DEVELOPMENT.

BIBLIOGRAPHY
Amin, S. 1972. Underdevelopment and dependence in Black Africa: origins and contemporary forms. *Journal of Modern African Studies* 10, 503–25.
Amin, S. 1973. *Neocolonialism in West Africa*. Harmondsworth: Penguin.
Amin, S. 1976. *Unequal Exchange*. Brighton: Harvester.
Baran, P.A. 1957. *The Political Economy of Growth*. New York: Monthly Review Press.
Brenner, R. 1977. The origins of capitalist development: a critique of neo-Smithian Marxism. *New Left Review* 104, 25–93.
Caputo, O. and Pizarro, R. 1974. *Dependencia y relaciones internacionales*. San José, Costa Rica: Editorial Universitaria Centroamericana.
Cardoso, F.H. 1972. Dependency and development in Latin America. *New Left Review* 74, 83–95.

Cardoso, F.H. 1976. The consumption of dependency theory in the US. *Latin America Research Review* 12, 17–24.

Cardoso, F.H. and Faletto, E. 1979. *Dependency and Development in Latin America*. Trans. by Marjory Mattingly Urquidi, Berkeley: University of California Press. (A translation and revision of *Dependencia y desarrollo en América Latina*, Mexico: Siglo Veintiuno Editores, 1971; first version, 1967.)

Cariola, C. and Sunkel, O. 1982. *Un Siglo de Historia Económica de Chile, 1830–1930*. Madrid: Ediciones Cultura Hispanica. Also in *The Latin American Economies: growth and the export sector, 1880–1930*, ed. R. Cortez Conde and S.J. Hunt, New York: Holmes and Meier.

Dos Santos, T. 1969. The crisis of development theory and the problems of dependency in Latin America. In *Underdevelopment and Development*, ed. H. Bernstein, Harmondsworth: Penguin.

Dos Santos, T. 1970. The structure of dependency. *American Economic Review, Papers and Proceedings* 60, 231–6.

Frank, A.G. 1967. *Capitalism and Underdevelopment in Latin America. Historical Studies of Chile and Brazil*. New York, London: Monthly Review Press.

Frank, A.G. 1977. Dependency is dead, long live dependency and the class struggle: an answer to critics. *World Development* 5, 355–70.

Furtado, C. 1966. *Subdesarrollo y Estancamiento en América Latina*. Buenos Aires: Editorial Universitaria de Buenos Aires.

Hinkelamert, 1970. *El Subdesarrollo Latinoamericano: un caso de desarrollo capitalista*. Santiago: Ediciones Nueva Universidad, Universidad Catolica de Chile.

Laclau, E. 1971. Feudalism and imperialism in Latin America. *New Left Review* 67, 19–38.

Lenin, V.I. 1899. *The Development of Capitalism in Russia*. Moscow: Progress Publishers, 1964.

Luxemburg, R. 1913. *Die Akkumulation des Kapitals, ein Beitrag zur ökonomischen Erklärung des Imperialismus*. Berlin: P. Singer. Trans. by Agnes Schwarzschild as *The Accumulation of Capital*, London: Routledge and Kegan Paul, 1951.

Marini, R.M. 1972. Brazilian sub-imperialism. *Monthly Review* 9, 14–24.

O'Brien, P. 1975. A critique of Latin American theories of dependency. In O. Oxaal, T. Barnet and D. Booth, *Beyond the Sociology of Development*, London: Routledge & Kegan Paul.

Owen, R. and Sutcliffe, B. 1972. *Studies in the Theory of Imperialism*. London: Longman.

Palma, J.G. 1973. *La Via Chilena al Socialismo*. Mexico: Siglo XXI Editores.

Palma, J.G. 1978. Dependency: a formal theory of underdevelopment or a methodology for the analysis of concrete situations of underdevelopment? *World Development* 6, 881–924.

Pinto, A. and Knakel, J. 1972. The centre–periphery system 20 years later. In *International Economics and Development: Essays in Honour of Raul Prebisch*, ed. L.E. di Marco, New York and London: Academic Press.

Prebisch, R. 1963. *Hacia una dinámica del desarrollo latinoamericano*. Mexico: Fondo Cultura Económica. Trans. as *Towards a Dynamic Development Policy for Latin America*. New York: United Nations.

Rodriguez, O. 1980. *'La Teoria' del Subdesarrollo de la CEPAL* . Mexico: Siglo XXI Editores.

Serra, J. 1974. *Desarrollo Latinoamericano: Ensayos Criticos*. Mexico: Fondo de Cultura Economico.

Sunkel, O. 1973. Transnational capitalism and national disintegration in Latin America. *Social and Economic Studies* 22, 132–76.

Sunkel, O. and Paz, P. 1970. *El subdesarrollo latinoamericano y la teoria del desarrollo*. Mexico: Siglo XXI Editores.

Tavares, M.C. and Serra, J. 1970. Mas allá del estanciamento. In Serra (1974).

Walicki, A. 1969. *The Controversy Over Capitalism*. London: Oxford University Press.

Wallerstein, I. 1974a. *The Modern World-System: Capitalist Agriculture and the Origins of the European World-Economy in the Sixteenth Century*. New York: Academic Press.

Wallerstein, I. 1974b. Dependency in an interdependent world: the limited possibilities of a transformation within the capitalist world-economy. *African Studies Review* 17, 1–26.

Warren, B. 1973. Imperialism and capitalist industrialization. *New Left Review* 63, 3–44.

Warren, B. 1980. *Imperialism: Pioneer of Capitalism*. Ed. John Sender, London: Verso.

depletion. The concept of depletion is that counterpart of depreciation which is normally applied in extractive industries. The need for a different concept may fairly be questioned; as in many facets of economics, the explanation is more historical than analytical. Traditionally, land has been regarded as a non-depreciable asset, yet mineral rights have most often (though by no means always) been viewed as attached to the land. The special term *depletion* thus applies to the special circumstances where land loses value (actually or potentially) through a process of extraction of some non-reproducible element in the soil or subsoil.

The foregoing definition should make it clear that it is in principle not the land that is depleted, but the mineral deposits contained therein. It would accordingly not be appropriate in principle to allow that the full amount paid for a property should be deductible in concept of depletion. In practice, the full cost is frequently allowed, but typically only in circumstances where the mineral rights constitute the lion's share of the market value of the holding.

When the corporation income tax was introduced in the United States in 1909, the legislation embodied the concept of cost depletion. There was a transition provision (grandfather clause), however, which applied to mineral deposits that were already being exploited at the time of the law's enactment. Here, the allowable basis on which depletion could be claimed was the fair market value of the mineral holding when the law took effect. Ironically, this tiny and apparently innocuous clause contained the seeds of the half-century of political controversy and of the billions of dollars of economic waste that resulted from 'percentage depletion'.

The process began with the clamour for oil to fuel the World War I effort of Britain, France, and their allies, as the United States from 1916 onward abandoned any pretence of neutrality and moved step by step toward the status of a direct belligerent. Those involved in the oil industry were quick to point out that the wells discovered as a result of their own exploration activities were being taxed more heavily than 'old wells' that had already been functioning when the income tax law took effect. The oil interests succeeded by 1918 in obtaining parity of treatment: that is, newly discovered wells could now claim depletion allowances based not on their cost, but on their 'discovery value' – their market value at the time of their discovery.

Economists might well wonder how replacing cost depletion by discovery depletion could be so bad, since economic forces normally work to bring about a close relationship between the value produced by an economic activity and its cost. This normal tendency was slightly marred by the tax-paying entity being allowed to opt each year for the larger of discovery or cost depletion, but this was only a minor flaw in the legislation. The major flaw lay in the difficulty of reconciling legal and economic concepts of cost in face of the aleatory nature of petroleum exploration.

Petroleum exploration (and the search for most other minerals) has always been a rather risky business. Firms have typically drilled something like ten exploratory wells for each successful find. The economists' concept would say that the economic cost of each firm's successes was that of all the wells it drilled, and that the cost of all discoveries to a whole economy was the full cost of all exploration undertaken, whether successful or not. One way of reflecting the economists' concept would be to require that a firm capitalize all of its exploration costs (whether successful or not), and then write off the sum total of these costs over the economic life of the successful finds. This can prove difficult, for much exploration is undertaken by consortia, formed *ad hoc* for a particular series of attempts. The alternative actually followed under cost depletion was to permit the deduction of the specific costs of each successful well against the revenues therefrom, while the costs of dry holes simply became losses, to be written off against income from any source. As long as income was present against which to write off dry hole costs, they were in effect, under this treatment, allowed to be expensed. This gave oil exploration – even under cost depletion – a certain tax advantage over other types of investment, whose total costs were required to be capitalized initially, then written off gradually over the asset's useful life (yielding, of course, a present value of total write-off equal to only a fraction of the costs when incurred).

This relatively modest tax advantage of oil exploration was greatly magnified when discovery depletion was introduced. Assume that the value of the successful wells is precisely equal to the total economic costs incurred in finding them, and that the latter include 80 per cent of dry hole costs. Under discovery depletion the total write-off would turn out to be 180 per cent of exploration costs. The successful wells would obtain over their economic life a write-off equal to their discovery value (100 per cent of total exploration costs), while the 80 per cent of exploration costs incurred on what turned out to be dry holes would end up as losses written off against other income from any source.

The possibility of writing off more than 100 per cent of costs is the nub of the debate that raged for decades concerning percentage depletion. For percentage depletion, at least as it was first introduced and as it prevailed for many, many years was simply discovery depletion in another guise. It was introduced in 1926 precisely for the purpose of breaking a log-jam of litigation over the appropriate value to set on newly discovered wells. The precise percentage ($27\frac{1}{2}$ per cent of the gross value of oil or gas at the wellhead) was chosen so as to approximate the relationship between actual depletion allowances (based on legally sanctioned discovery values) and the production values to which they applied.

The tragedy of the depletion story did not really begin to unfold until much later. At the time discovery depletion was introduced, the US corporation income tax rate was 12 per cent; over the decade of the 1920s it oscillated between 10 and 13.5 per cent. At such tax rates even the double deduction of the cost of capital assets would have relatively little effect. If the tax consequence of the extra deduction is considered to be like a subsidy, its effects would be similar to those of a subsidy which caused the equilibrium rate of return to be about 9 per cent in investments in oil exploration if it would normally be 10 per cent in other activities – hardly a gross distortion.

The problems came later as tax rates first crept, then zoomed upward to finance a growing government and finally a major war effort. The corporation income tax rate was 52 per cent for many years following World War II; gradual reductions brought it to 46 per cent in 1981. Unfortunately, the same tax provisions have very different incentive effects at a 52 per cent rate than at one of 12 per cent or so.

A simple way of representing an equilibrium situation of a firm with respect to investment in a particular type of capital asset is to equate, at the after-tax rate of discount (r) the costs of the asset to the firm (net of tax offsets, if any) with the present value of the net-of-tax income stream produced by the asset. Let the present value (at the discount rate r) of the gross-of-tax income stream produced by the asset be Y. Let the asset's cost

be C_a; this is also the amount which will be written off over time in the form of depreciation allowances. The present value of those allowances will be dC_a; d is a positive fraction, which is smaller the larger is r, the longer is the period over which depreciation is spread, and the later within that period the allowances are concentrated. The equating of costs with benefits yields

$$C_a = Y - t(Y - dC_a), \tag{1}$$

or

$$C_a = Y(1 - t)/(1 - dt), \tag{2}$$

where t is the applicable tax rate.

The effect of discovery depletion was to permit the writing-off of the full value of the successful wells, while at the same time allowing the writing-off of dry-hole costs. If β is the fraction of total exploration costs represented by dry holes, the equilibrium investment under discovery depletion would be characterized by

$$C_d(1 - \beta t) = Y(1 - t)/(1 - dt). \tag{3}$$

Here C_d is the cost which would characterize an oil exploration investment producing a gross-of-tax income stream whose present value (discounted at the rate r) is Y, where the fruits of the investment are subject to discovery depletion, and the costs of dry holes are written-off against other income that is taxable at the normal rate, t.

It is easily seen, comparing (3) with (2) that

$$C_d/C_a = 1/(1 - \beta t). \tag{4}$$

This means that under discovery depletion, if (as was approximately the case) dry-hole costs amount to some 80 per cent of exploration costs, a marginal investment producing a given income stream would have costs equal to $1/(1 - 0.096)$ times those of an ordinary corporate investment producing a similar income stream when the tax rate was 12 per cent; this same equilibrium at the margin would with a 52 per cent tax rate be generated by an investment whose costs were $1/(1 - 0.416)$ times those corresponding to an ordinary investment producing the same income stream. The mere upward drift of tax rates, then, magnifies the distortion from a fraction of just a little over 10 per cent to a fraction of more than 2/3.

Percentage depletion differed from discovery depletion in specifying that the depletion allowance should be a specified fraction ($27\frac{1}{2}$ per cent for oil and gas) of the gross value of the product as it emerged from the wells (or mine). Gross value of product differs from the gross income attributable to capital by the amount of labour and materials costs involved in the extractive process. These costs are not great for oil and gas; for a typical well, the depletion allowances averaged about 35 per cent of the cash flow attributable to capital when the statutory depletion rate was $27\frac{1}{2}$ per cent of a broader income concept. Denoting this observed fraction (depletion allowance/cash flow attributable to capital) by p, and by C_p the costs which would yield the after-tax rate r under percentage depletion treatment, we have

$$C_p(1 - \beta t) = Y - t(Y - pY), \tag{5}$$

or

$$C_p = Y(1 - t + tp)/(1 - \beta t). \tag{6}$$

Investments under percentage depletion (with expensing of dry-hole costs) and under ordinary income taxation can be compared by looking at the relative amounts of cost that it would be barely worthwhile to incur in order to produce similar income streams under the two tax treatments. This is given by equation (7)

$$C_p/C_a = [(1 - t + tp)(1 - dt)/[(1 - \beta t)(1 - t)].\qquad (7)$$

For $p = 0.35$, $d = 0.65$ (an approximate figure for oil and gas wells under cost depletion when $r = 0.1$), and $\beta = 0.8$, this ratio comes to 1.07 for $t = 0.12$ and to 1.62 for $t = 0.52$. Ironically, the great bulk of the economic inefficiency produced by percentage depletion came long after it was enacted, as a result of tax rate changes that were debated, passed and signed into law without even the most cursory consideration being given to their consequences in magnifying the anti-economic incentive effects of percentage depletion.

Various factors have led to the progressive reduction of these anti-economic incentives. Beginning with the Tax Reform Act of 1969, the statutory rate of percentage depletion was reduced. Indeed, after the 1974 oil crisis, percentage depletion was eliminated for integrated firms, and after the crisis of 1979 an (ostensibly transitory) windfall profits tax was enacted. In addition, the percentage depletion rate for independent producers and royalty owners, and for secondary and tertiary production, was reduced in stages to 15 per cent as of 1984. Finally, the corporation income tax rate itself was reduced, reaching the level of 46 per cent in 1979, and accelerated depreciation was authorized for a wide range of assets of ordinary (non-extractive) businesses, consequently raising the value of d.

Some notion of the prospective level of the relative incentive to oil exploration, as of this writing, can be obtained by assuming $d = 0.8$ (compared with 0.65), $p = 0.2$ (compared with 0.35), and $t = 0.46$ (compared with 0.52). This calculation yields a value for C_p/C_a of 1.17 (without taking any account of the transitory windfall profits tax which, so long as it remains in effect, further reduces the incentive in question).

In a real sense, the saga of percentage depletion, so far as the oil and gas industry of the United States is concerned, may be said to have passed into history. Once a source a major economic distortion and of bitter political battles, it has become (for oil and gas) a comparatively innocuous piece of special-interest incentive legislation.

But that is not the whole story. Percentage depletion only began with oil and gas in 1928. Coal, metals, and sulphur were added in 1932; fluorspar, rock asphalt, and ball and sagger clay came into the list in 1945; other additions were made in 1944, 1947, and 1951 (when even sand, gravel, slate, and stone came to be included); and finally, in 1954, percentage depletion treatment was extended to 'all other minerals' (with a few stated exceptions).

The incentive works in a significantly different way for most other minerals than for oil and gas, because of the great importance of a continuing process of exploration and discovery in the latter case. The analysis presented above for oil and gas treats the exploration activity as the fundamental act of investment, and the production process as simply the reaping of its fruits. For minerals like coal, sulphur, clay, gypsum, and many of the metals, reserves are well known and exploration is an insignificant element in the economic picture. In these cases, assuming reserves to be large and the true loss of property value through depletion to be small, the effect of percentage depletion allowances is substantially equivalent to that of a subsidy at a rate equal to the depletion rate times the applicable rate of tax. Thus, for many of the products subject to it, percentage depletion works as a subsidy to extraction rather than exploration.

ARNOLD C. HARBERGER

See also EXHAUSTIBLE RESOURCES; NATURAL RESOURCES; NEUTRAL TAXATION; TAXATION OF CAPITAL; TAXATION OF CORPORATIONS.

BIBLIOGRAPHY

Agria, S.R. 1969. Special tax treatment of mineral industries. In *The Taxation of Income from Capital*, ed A.C. Harberger and M.J. Bailey, Washington DC: The Brookings Institution.

Gravelle, J.C. 1985. Effective federal tax rates on income from new investments in oil and gas extraction. *The Energy Journal* 6, Special Tax Issue, 145–53.

Harberger, A.C. 1955. The taxation of mineral industries. In U.S. Congress, Joint Economic Committee, *Federal Tax Policy for Economic Growth and Stability*, Washington, DC: GPO, November, 439–49.

Harberger, A.C. 1961. The tax treatment of oil exploration. *Proceedings of the Second Energy Institute*. Washington, DC: The American University, 256–69.

Robinson, M.S. 1983. Essays on the taxation of oil and natural gas. Doctoral Dissertation, Stanford University.

Steiner, P.O. 1959. Percentage depletion and resource allocation. US House of Representatives, Committee on Ways and Means, *Tax Revision Compendium*. Washington, DC: GPO, volume II, 949–66.

Wright, D. 1976. The taxation of petroleum production. Doctoral Dissertation, Havard University.

depopulation. *See* DECLINING POPULATION.

depreciation. Depreciation estimates the decline in the value of capital as a result of ageing, its maximum value being near its age of manufacture and its minimum value when it is dismantled and sold as scrap. It is of great importance to capital accounting, for the rate of dividend is calculated as the ratio of the surplus to the current value of assets. The reduction in value of equipment comes about from two causes – firstly that its productivity may fall with age; and secondly, that as time advances, the expected remaining earning life of the plant is shorter. Hence, the capitalized value of the present value of expected future stream of quasi-rents from an old piece of equipment is smaller for any given rate of interest than for a younger machine.

'ONE-HOSS SHAY' ASSUMPTION. The influence of declining productivity over time may be eliminated by assuming a 'one-hoss shay' type of equipment, which keeps its efficiency constant over its service life and falls to pieces at the end. However, the product of a process is not only its current output but the stock of equipment which remains at the end of the production period – as stressed by von Neumann (1933) and by Sraffa (who in 1960 referred to Robert Torrens as having insisted in the years 1818 and 1821 on its being considered as a part of output).

On account of the shorter remaining service life of equipment at the end of a period (and the consequent smaller number of expected items of quasi-rent in its stream of earnings), there is lesser value of capital remaining at the end of a production period – a so-called 'year'. This reduction in value of a stock output affects adversely the productivity in value terms (even with 'one-hoss shay' equipment) and it measures the depreciation. There is, therefore, an aggravated tendency of the value of capital embodied to fall as the plant is older.

SHAPE OF DECLINE IN VALUATION CURVE. In a straight line approximation, depreciation is taken as constant in absolute amount per year. In a formula using the exponential concept depreciation is at a constant rate; hence, the fall in value is more when machines are younger and higher priced, than when they are older – as in radioactive decay, i.e. it indicates a curve convex to the origin. But depreciation is at higher rates for older capital in service – not as would be given by an exponentially falling value of equipment at a constant rate with respect to time. When there is a rising rate of reduction of value, it makes the decline more than exponential as the machines are older, and yields a steeply falling value towards the end of the service life, i.e. it yields a curve with respect to time which is concave to the origin. The straight line approximation of value of capital (with respect to its age) which is used in some calculations is thus wide of the mark; and even the exponentially falling value according to a constant rate of reduction does not make the value of old machines decline sufficiently markedly.

In a Sraffa or von Neumann valuation of capital (of different ages taken as different commodities) this decline is well brought out automatically, for differences between value of the commodity called 'equipment t years old' and the one called '$t+1$ years old', increases as t becomes larger.

This aspect of the Sraffa system (1960) was not known to Joan Robinson or to Professor Richard Kahn and D.G. Champernowne in 1954 when the text of *Accumulation of Capital* (1956) was being finalized – especially its Mathematical Appendix (to a part of which the latter two had contributed as authors, their names appearing in the original printed text). It is all the more remarkable that it was discovered that in the measurement of value of ageing equipment, one could strike upon another useful device – of balanced age-composition of capital.

BALANCED AGE-COMPOSITION OF CAPITAL. In demographic studies as part of the subject of manpower, it is well known that for a population of human beings growing at g per cent, there are higher numbers of children of age t in comparison to those a year older (of age $t+1$) by the factor $(1+g)$. To a population of plants the same principle can be applied, and we can derive a universe of plants ordered according to their ages in this particular manner. One can try to ascertain what are the number of plants in a cohort of each age and the value of capital embodied in each cohort.

The value of plant at the centre of gravity of the age-composition pyramid, may then be used as the standard unit of measurement of the value of a plant of any particular age. The result would be in agreement with the well-known, but rather mystifying, Kahn–Champernowne formula of the reciprocal value of a new plant in terms of value of the plant of average age. This reciprocal will be called a K–C unit in honour of those two authors who worked out the said formula.

KAHN–CHAMPERNOWNE UNITS OF MEASUREMENT. In a generalized version of this concept, as the set of pieces of capital of constant physical productivity and of balanced age-composition growing exponentially at a steady rate, keep the composition in terms of relative sizes of cohorts constant; hence the value of the average plant does not change. This is the justification of the K–C units.

In terms of a balanced age-composition of equipment (with T years expected service life since its manufacture), a piece of equipment t 'years' old is replaced at the end of t years by a piece which is $t-1$ years old in the beginning of the year. Except for this replacement by equipment which is now of the same age as the piece it substitutes, there is no depreciation visible in the physical system or its statistical depiction.

REDUNDANCE OF GROSS AND NET CONCEPTS. It is to be remembered that Joan Robinson had correctly realized that depreciation was not a physical phenomenon but a notional or value one. The implication of depreciation not being a physical phenomenon in terms of effect upon the concepts of gross and net investment had to wait until the von Neumann model was integrated (in 1960) with the Robinsonian golden-age system. In traditional analysis the system is depicted as z machines (newly produced and added) in a factory, and at the same time another z machine rendered inoperative (by completion of their natural life). But the net investment is not an act of accretion–depreciation in physical terms; for the machines added through current investment are new ones and the depletion is of old machines – and it makes no sense if value measurement were not resorted to for calculating the excess of accretion over depreciation.

The balanced age-composition is a device by which one can realize that in a von Neumann system as a growing economy m machines of age t years exist and $m(1+g)$ of age t-1 years are automatically substituted a year later by $m(1+g)$ machines – also now of t years age. The stock as well as each age-cohort grows at rate g, and depreciation of value by ageing is exactly counter-balanced by that much capital of erstwhile younger age and erstwhile higher value (but now of the same age and the same value as the m plants at the beginning of the year) replacing it. In addition one has mg times more machine of age t. The total stock grows at a given rate of growth, and depreciation is also compensated for exactly, for $m(1+g)$ is equal to m for replacement, and mg for accumulation for each age-cohort.

In Sraffa–von Neumann analysis (as a simplified purposive model combining the two general constituents of those two models and integrating the resultant with the Robinsonian golden-age system), this fact was noticed in 1961, and it was discovered that in a state of steady growth and balanced age-composition depreciation of a stock of inputs in terms of writing down of value of equipment (due to ageing) is a dispensable concept (Mathur, 1965). Each age-cohort is replenished exactly by an age-cohort from within the system in physical numbers and value, and there is nothing to be written down of any piece of equipment by a chartered accountant at the end of the year. The pieces of equipment of each age are higher by the rate g, and valuation is required for finding out cumulative accumulation of equipment in each age-cohort. In a body of equipment of balanced age-composition as the value of capital of different ages differs by the amount of depreciation, the concept of depreciation is required for measuring aggregate accumulation due to ageing, not for decumulation due to ageing as was required in the traditional concept.

It is because of the total absence of writing down of value of stock of any age that it was realized that there is no concept of gross or net necessary in such a reckoning (Mathur, 1965), and depreciation is important not as the difference between gross and net investment, but as the difference of value of an older machine in relation to a younger one for purposes of measuring accumulation (of positive-age equipment from within the firm and of new equipment from the manufacturers). It is only when the age-composition is grossly unbalanced – as for newly established firms – that it may be necessary to use depreciation in the traditional sense of writing down value of stocks. But in that case measurement of depreciation or of amount to be written off is itself a procedure not entirely free from logical doubts.

DEPRECIATION AND MAINTENANCE. In manpower-employment

terms, total new employment is given by gross investment not by net investment, because the amount spent on activities of maintaining capital intact (repairing, renovating) also creates employment, and not only the building of new capital. Hence, in national income statistics, it is gross investment which creates manpower employment and not net investment by itself. The difference between gross and net is taken to be depreciation, but in manpower terms it does not so follow – for employment created for maintenance of a machine (like a sealed unit) might be very low, and yet the reduction of its value year by year very high due to ageing. When viewing manpower statistics, the activity of operatives of a particular type ought to be supplemented by statistics of valuation (Mathur, 1983). While figures in terms of counting heads are important for a physical count, greater economic significance would be acquired if the productivity of each type of human equipment were determined and its true value calculated in K-C units with respect to a balanced age-composition and age-structure (Mathur, 1964). But depreciation in value terms alone without the physical counterpart of replacement (of equipment or manpower) also tells us an incomplete story, and only valuation and quantification (in physical terms) together give the full picture.

GAUTAM MATHUR

See also AMORTIZATION; MAINTAINING CAPITAL INTACT; TAXATION OF CAPITAL.

BIBLIOGRAPHY

Champernowne, D.G. and Kahn, R.F. 1956. The value of invested capital. Mathematical Note appended at the end of Robinson (1956).
Mathur, G. 1964. The valuation of human capital for manpower planning. *Applied Economic Papers*, (Hyderabad), 4(2), September, 14–35.
Mathur, G. 1965. *Planning for Steady Growth*. Oxford. Basil Blackwell; New York: Augustus Kelly.
Mathur, G. 1983. Web of inequity. Presidential Address to the Silver Jubilee Session of the Indian Labour Economic Association, Lucknow, 1982. *Indian Journal of Labour Economics*, Sec. VIII
Neumann, J. von. 1933. A model of general economic equilibrium. *Review of Economic Studies* 13, (1945), 1–9.
Robinson, J. 1956. *The Accumulation of Capital*. London: Macmillan.
Sraffa, P. 1960. *Production of Commodities by Means of Commodities*. Cambridge: Cambridge University Press.

depressions. Modern economies have a tendency to grow, but their growth is irregular. The periodic variations of most indicators and even occasional reversals of direction inevitably prompt the question whether these changes are of a random nature, or indicate broader sweeps, swings or cycles. The trade cycle, or *Juglar* cycle (named after Clément Juglar) of an average duration of about seven years appeared frequently enough in the course of the nineteenth century to be generally recognized as a cyclical phenomenon. Other possible recurrent movements were the inventory *Kitchin* cycles (Joseph Kitchin) of 2–3 years, and the longer *Kuznets* (Simon Kuznets) swings of 20–25 years, indicating alternate phases of European and American long-term investment and of transatlantic migration.

By general consent, the trough phases of none of these are normally termed depressions. That term is reserved for longer periods of more serious adversity on an international scale, in particular the Great Depressions of c1873–96 and of the 1930s. By analogy, the distressed years following the Napoleonic wars and the years since the downturn of 1973 have also been included in that category. In view of the fact that these seem to have occurred at fairly regular intervals, attempts have not

been lacking to explain them as part of an alternating movement also.

The first major theory of long swings was that of N.D. Kondratieff, who published his findings in 1922–8 (Kondratieff, 1935), following some earlier Marxists, notably J. van Gelderen in 1913. Kondratieff's cycles are essentially price movements, including swings of other indicators expressed in money, such as wages and foreign trade. His depression periods of 1810/17–1844/51, and 1870/5–1890/6, were periods of falling prices. In addition to prices, Kondratieff also considered variations in some key industrial products such as coal and iron, and noted the particularly sharp deterioration of agriculture in the depressions. According to him, upswings were preceded by technological innovations and rises in gold production, while wars and revolutions also take place then; in the depressions their effects fade. Although essentially presented as a set of empirical findings, Kondratieff's swings may be interpreted as investment cycles of long duration.

Kondratieff's views were rejected in his own country, and found little echo in the west at first. They were introduced to a wider audience by being incorporated by J.A. Schumpeter (1939) in a grand concept of a cyclical development of modern capitalism. In this scheme, each Kondratieff consisted of six Juglars, the depression phase containing three Juglars in which the peaks tended to be weaker, the troughs more pronounced than in the upswing. Schumpeter's periodization was similar to Kondratieff's, except that the first turning point was set in 1842 3 rather than 1844 51. His depressions were periods which lacked the stimulus of what to him was the major driving force of industrial capitalistic society, the appearance of bunched major innovations, such as railways, steel or electricity. Each depression was introduced by a major crisis, including a high level of unemployment, following an exceptional investment boom or wartime expansion. Schumpeter also did not fail to notice the serious agricultural price fall and the pervasive agrarian distress that was part of each depression period.

The notion that bunched innovations are associated with recurrent depressions, that their introduction leads to loss of jobs, and that the depression can be reversed, in the end, only by a renewed massive introduction of a new technology, has also reappeared in the depression of the 1970s, in such theories as those propagated by Gerhard Mensch (1975), Ernest Mandel (1975) and Robert Boyer (1979). Mensch noted that the previous depressions were started by panics, in 1825, 1873 and 1929 respectively, among those who had the responsibility for economic policy, but he held that their basic cause was the diminishing returns on technical innovations, as major breakthroughs are completed, leaving room for only minor adjustments of ever lesser significance, while at the same time on the demand side there is a diminishing rate of growth of marginal utility, as markets become saturated with the new commodity or new productive technique. A renewed upward movement would therefore require a new set of major innovations.

Boyer's theory is a complex one. According to him, expansion periods are periods of 'extensive' accumulation (which may roughly be translated as investment), when capital of a known kind is spread into new areas. By contrast, depressions are periods in which opportunities for investment of the current type have become exhausted, and new techniques are being developed in what he terms 'intensive' accumulation. Since this has to be undertaken ahead of demand, it tends to be unprofitable and the general profit level therefore tends to fall until new structural parameters evolve, including new wage labour relations, competitive systems, capital relations, monetary and currency systems, and a redefined role of individual economies within the international division of labour. These then allow a renewed period of 'extensive' accumulation. Depressions are thus hinge periods of structural change between growth periods.

A Keynesian version of the Kondratieff was developed by W.W. Rostow in the 1940s (Rostow, 1978). His depression period extended over 1815–48, 1873–96 and 1920–36, and they were thus more in line with the reference cycles, made up of numerous indicators which have been developed since then by other scholars. The main characteristics of these depressions were falling prices, especially agricultural prices, falling interest rates and low profits, while incomes shifted in favour of wage earners, or at least in favour of those who remained in employment. Their cause lay in declining employment opportunities for capital, or, expressed in different terms, a failure of investment to mop up all available savings. The preceding prosperity periods had been marked, in each case, by investment in long gestation projects such as railways, as well as by major wars with their positive employment effects. In the depressions, the earlier investments were bearing fruit in lower costs which contributed to the fall in prices. The effects of the major gold discoveries at the onset of each upward phase, in c1850 and in the 1890s, were not forgotten, and the possible contribution of their diminishing yields to the deflationary tenor of the age, measured against the growing demand for gold owing to expanding world transactions and the extension of the gold standard, especially after 1873, was noted. However, in view of the growth of paper credit, the relationship between the amount of gold mined annually and the world price level was clearly a complex one, while the coincidence of the gold discoveries just at the point when gold was at its most valuable, i.e. when prices were lowest, could not be ignored.

Not surprisingly, the same descriptive emphases as well as the same building bricks of explanations tend to recur in most of these cyclical theories. None of them, however, entirely succeeds in clarifying the question whether the depressions were part of an immanent, endogenous rhythm of world capitalist development, or whether they were in each case the result of a fortuitous conjunction of circumstances. The bunching of innovations, for example, which occurs repeatedly as part of the explanatory model, sometimes in addition linked explicitly to a succeeding phase in which investment opportunities are exhausted, might derive either from a 'law' of the workings of market economies, or they might have a wholly exogenous explanation. Such a 'law' might be based on mass psychology, the successive waves of optimism or pessimism among entrepreneurs; it might be based on economic functions, according to which innovations gain by being accompanied by others; or it might conceivably have some other inherent mechanism as its source, according to which each phase necessarily bears the seeds of the next phase within itself. On the other hand, the bunching might have exogenous causes, such as development breakthroughs in science and technology which make several related processes possible at once, the opening up of overseas mineral supplies, overseas markets or the peopling of free land in empty continents. Most theories on offer balanced carefully between these two possibilities without coming down on either side. Similar ambiguities might be found in the other explanations offered, such as changes in relative costs and prices, the 'terms of trade', on an international scale. In any case, a mere three cycles at most were too few to provide certainty that endogenous swings or cycles were at work.

The alternative of looking at each of the depression periods as a unique historical event has therefore found many adherents. The first to be studied in any depth was the 'Great Depression' of 1873–96 (to use the terminal dates which today would command most support). It was particularly marked in Britain, where in consequence it has received the greatest amount of attention, and this, in turn, was associated with the fact that it coincided with a turning point, or 'climacteric', in British economic fortunes in international comparison. This was the period in which foreign manufacturing competition became a serious threat to Britain for the first time, and in which, therefore, a mood of general pessimism could spread more easily. Further, as modern research shows, the secular growth of the British economy did indeed experience a marked slow-down in those decades, showing that the instinct of contemporaries was sound. The continuation of the slow-down, bringing growth practically to a complete halt in the following upswing phase of 1896–1914 does, however, throw some doubt on the decline of the long-term growth rate as a characteristic of the 'depression' which allegedly came to an end in c1896. By contrast, both the USA and Germany, the other leading industrial nations, were then in a phase of rapid secular growth so that they were much better able to overcome the effects of a depression which by no means passed them by entirely.

The depression was ushered in by the collapse of what was perhaps the most expansive boom of the century (1871–3), particularly in the capital goods industries. It had been marked by much speculation and was followed by numerous bankruptcies. Overseas borrowing countries defaulted on their debts, home investments, made at a time when costs peaked, proved unprofitable, and the French indemnity to Germany, paid in part through London, further upset financial markets. In the period as a whole it was not only financiers who had a thin time but indeed all profit earners, though their plight may have been exaggerated, and interest rates were low. These low interest rates, part of the 'Gibson paradox', have frequently been used as a proof against the proposition that the depression was brought about by deflationary conditions which, in turn, derived from a shortage of gold, for in that case, interest rates should have been high.

In real terms, however, the 'depression' was far less clear-cut. Serious unemployment existed only in the late 1870s and in 1884–7, and even then it was mild by the standards of the 20th century. GNP failed to grow in three years only, and in each case the decline was marginal, never exceeding 0.5 per cent of the preceding year. It was, in fact, part of the persistent complaint of industrialists, before the Royal Commission on the Depression of Trade reporting in 1886 and elsewhere, that competition forced them to sell large quantities for which the unit profit margin had become exceedingly small. Real wages rose satisfactorily.

Even in agriculture, the sector which complained most loudly, the sharp decline in profits and in income was limited to the grain farmers. Here the combination of much reduced transport costs by rail and steamship, and much reduced production costs in the fertile lands above all of North America, but also of Russia, Australia and India, had led to a particularly rapid collapse in prices, to which home growers had not had time to adjust. This may be considered to be part of a long-term, and economically desirable process of an international division of labour in which Britain turned increasingly to producing manufactures and importing food. By contrast, producers of meat and dairy products, market gardeners and horse breeders did not fare too badly, benefiting rather than suffering from the cheap grain imports.

Thus it was essentially profit earners, and financiers for whom the period was one of depression. The standard of living of the rest of the population went up satisfactorily. But it is precisely profit earners and financiers who control the press and shape 'informed' economic opinion. Perhaps they have misled us. The 'Great Depression', in the view of some, was a myth (Saul, 1969).

The depression of the 1930s has possibly an even stronger claim to be considered a unique event, with its own particular explanation for which no parallels can be found in other periods. Marxists saw it as heralding the frequently predicted final end of capitalism, while other ascribed its severity to the direct and indirect consequences of the war. Its terminal dates are not entirely unquestioned. Most indices show a more drastic fall in 1920–21 than in 1929–30. Moreover, the inflation in Germany and some other countries in the early 1920s was, in some ways, more devastating than anything that happened in the 1930s. At the other extreme, the trade cycle boom of 1937 was extremely weak and carried many signs of turning into a further severe depression, which was avoided only by the preparations for war. In more normal circumstances, the whole of the three Juglars, 1920–39 or even 1920–45, might have been taken as the depression, in parallel with the dating of 1873–96. However, such was the extent of their economic adversity, that it is only the four to six years following the New York stock exchange crash of autumn 1929 which are commonly referred to as the 'Great Depression' (van der Wee, 1972).

The share collapse at the beginning was soon followed by other financial disasters. The failure of the Austrian Creditanstalt, by far the largest bank in the country, caused waves which also brought down some German banks. Britain, unable to stand the international drain on her gold reserve, went off the gold standard maintained precariously at high cost up to then, and was followed by many other countries. As the crisis deepened, American banks and finance houses went under in large numbers. Profits and interest rates fell. The British bank rate at two per cent ushered in an unprecedented period of 'cheap money'.

More significant for this depression than financial crashes was the collapse in the real world of production and trade, and above all the unprecedented unemployment. Unemployment of registered labour affected 15–30 per cent of the population at risk in many countries, while many more workers had removed themselves from the register, having lost all hope of finding work, and others worked short time only. Even after the onset of the recovery in 1933–4, a large hard core of intractable unemployment remained almost everywhere. Similarly unprecedented was the decline in output and in real national income over several years. The American GDP, for example, fell for four consecutive years, from an index of 163.0 in 1929 to 115.0 in 1933 (1913 = 100), or by almost 30 per cent; in Germany, the drop in the same years was from 121.6 to 102.0, or by 16 per cent; and even in the United Kingdom there was a six per cent drop over the two years 1929–31.

For several of the contributory causes of the depression and for its severity, the war could be held responsible. Thus it was in the war years, above all, that overseas countries had been encouraged to increase their food supplies to Europe where agricultural output suffered in the fighting, and when, afterwards, Europe returned to its previous output levels, growing world food surpluses began to burden world markets in the 1920s. Similar exceptional wartime demands had brought about an over-capacity in some industrial sectors also, such as shipbuilding, leading to exceptionally heavy unemployment there, but it was in primary products that the price fall was particularly severe in the depression, bankrupting overseas countries and their firms, though benefiting those Europeans who still had an income.

Among other consequences of the war were international war debts, the reparations imposed on Germany, and the creation of new, small, non-viable states in Europe. Debts and reparations bedevilled political relations, helped to radicalize the German electorate and inhibited the German chancellor Brüning from conducting a more vigorous reflationary policy in 1930. The hostility engendered then contributed to the protectionist and beggar-my-neighbour reactions of most governments to the depression so that trade was reduced, real costs rose, and the world became divided into several currency blocs, of the pound sterling, the dollar, the franc and the mark, severely restricting trade and payments between them. Britain, meanwhile, had become too weak to keep the world's exchanges in balance, as she had done in the 19th century, and the USA, which had emerged from the war as the leading economic power, was unwilling to accept that role, so that it went by default (Kindleberger, 1973).

Lastly, the war had strengthened the trade unions everywhere, and had led to greatly extended state welfare provisions, including more extensive unemployment benefits. This led to a rigidity of wages downwards, which, according to some, prevented an early adjustment to the depression and helped to account for its exceptional severity. Such views, widely held at the time, were strongly opposed by Keynes, whose comprehensive theory appeared in print only in 1936, well after the worst of the depression was over. According to him, cutting wages would have done little or nothing to improve employment; what was wanted was the creation of new purchasing power, which in the final analysis would have to come from the Government.

Keynes's view on the depression was dominant in the following decades, though by no means accepted by all. In the 1960s, an alternative theory, developed by Milton Friedman and others in the USA, began to gain wider support. In their view, the money supply, which to the Keynesians played only a subordinate role via the rate of interest, occupied the centre of the stage. As it happened, as far as the cure for a deep depression occurring in a deflationary phase was concerned this view did not differ too widely from Keynes's. According to Friedman and his associates, the depression had been greatly aggravated, at any rate in the USA, by repeated reductions in the quantity of money made available to the system, whereas the economy could have been revived by a controlled monetary expansion.

It is in their relative assessments of cause and cure of the depression of the 1970s, which is marked by a concurrent monetary inflation, that Keynesians and Monetarists are totally at loggerheads. The depression itself was triggered by the floating of the dollar in 1973 and the drastic oil price rises engineered by the OPEC countries in 1973–4 and again in 1979, but these themselves were symptoms and consequences of a creeping inflation which had accompanied the remarkable world boom of 1945–73. Depressed conditions at a time of inflation, 'stagflation', could not really occur according to the Keynesians, and the fact that it did, helped to discredit them, at least for a time. The underlying inflation after the war was, no doubt, at least to some extent due to Keynesian-type employment policies on the part of most governments. It is the monetarist view that only severe cuts in the expansion of the money supply, bringing with them at least temporarily drastic increases in unemployment, offer a way out.

Inflation apart, the current depression bears some marked similarities to the experience of earlier ones. Among them there is the technological explanation of unemployment, this time looked for in the electronics field; there is the rise of economic nationalism, fostered by subsidies, hidden tariffs, and industries maintained as status symbols, especially by weaker economies; there is the rigidity explanation, blaming trade unions and social insurance schemes for the unwillingness to change occupations or reduce wages; there is, despite international agreements to the contrary, the use of currency manipulation to gain trading advantages; there is also a huge international indebtedness, which the debtors are unwilling or unable to pay, and the creditors unwilling or unable to forego. In duration, if not in severity, the current depression is likely to match its predecessors.

SIDNEY POLLARD

See also KONDRATIEFF CYCLE; LONG SWINGS IN ECONOMIC GROWTH; TRADE CYCLE.

BIBLIOGRAPHY

Boyer, R. 1979. La crise actuelle: une mise au point en perspective historique. Critiques de l'économie politique, April–September, 5–113.

Brunner, K. (ed.) 1981. The Great Depression Revisited. Boston and The Hauge: Nijhoff.

Friedman, M. and Schwartz, A. 1963. A Monetary History of the United States. Princeton: Princeton University Press.

Kindleberger, C.P. 1973. The World in Depression, 1929–1939. Berkeley: University of California Press.

Kondratieff, N.D. 1935. The long waves in economic life. The Review of Economic Statistics 17(6), November, 105–15.

Mandel, E. 1975. Late Capitalism. London: New Left Books.

Mensch, G. 1975. Das technologische Patt. Innovationen überwinden die Depression . Frankfurt: Fisher.

Rostow, W.W. 1978. The World Economy: History and Prospect. Austin: Texas University Press; London: Macmillan.

Saul, S.B. 1969. The Myth of the Great Depression. London: Macmillan.

Schumpeter, J.A. 1939. Business Cycles. 2 vols. New York: McGraw-Hill.

Temin, P. 1976. Did Monetary Forces Cause the Great Depression? New York: Norton.

van der Wee, H. (ed.) 1972. The Great Depression Revisited. Essays on the Economics of the Thirties. The Hague: Nijhoff.

De Quincey, Thomas (1785–1859). The son of a prosperous merchant, De Quincey was born in 1785, and, after a brilliant literary career, died in 1859. That a genius of so high an order of imagination found the abstract reasoning of political economy 'Not harsh and crabbed as dull fools suppose' is instructive. The fascination which the severer aspect of the science had for De Quincey is expressed in that passage of the Confessions of an Opium Eater where the writer describes how he was aroused from lethargy by the study of Ricardo's Political Economy (1818). The fruit of that study appeared in the Dialogues of Three Templars (1824), a brilliant exposition and defence of the Ricardian theory of value. The paradox, for so De Quincey admits it to be in a good sense, that real value is measured by quantity of labour, that

> a million men may produce double or treble the amount of riches, of 'necessaries, conveniences, and amusements', in one state of society that they could in another, but will not on that account add anything to value (Ricardo, Political Economy; chapter on 'Value and Riches')

is expounded by the disciple even more fearlessly than by the master.

'My thesis,' says X, the Socrates of the dialogues, who represents the author's views, 'is that no such connection

subsists between the two [the quantity obtained and the value obtaining] as warrants any inference that the real value is great because the quantity it buys is great, or small because the quantity it buys is small.' 'I have a barouche,' says the objector, 'which is worth about 600 guineas at this moment. Now, if I should keep this barouche unused in my coach-house for five years, and at the end of this term it should happen from any cause that carriages had doubled in value, my understanding would lead me to expect double the quantity of any commodity for which I might then exchange it, whether that were money, sugar, besoms, or anything whatsoever. But you tell me no.' ... 'You are in the right,' replies X, 'I do tell you so ... If A double its value, it will not therefore command double the former quantity of B' [B representing any assignable thing] (Fourth Dialogue).

The intelligent Bailey might well be stirred by these startling deductions to attempt a reply (preface to Critical Dissertation). In the later dialogues Ricardo's theory of value is defended against Malthus. This controversy had been commenced in the 'Measure of Value', published in the London Magazine for December 1823. An article on 'Malthus' in an earlier number of the same journal contains a mild attack on the theory of population. Some of the points are elucidated in a letter to Hazlitt which appeared in the London Magazine, December 1823. To the same period belongs a sort of éloge of Ricardo, which De Quincey, shortly after the death of his revered master, contributed to the London Magazine, March 1824.

De Quincey's latest and greatest economical work is the Logic of Political Economy (1844). The more original portion of this book may be described as a vindication of the part played by utility in the determination of value. The cause is just and the reasoning ingenious; yet the censure with which J.S. Mill tempers his copious citation from this discourse seems deserved (Political Economy, bk. iii, ch. ii, §1, and §3 end). Certainly De Quincey's illustrations are perfect. The rhinoceros which in the reign of Charles II was sold for a figure far above the cost of importation; the Valdarfer copy of Boccaccio which Lord Blandford bought for £2240 and afterwards, when in pecuniary embarrassments, was sold by auction and purchased for £750 by Lord Spencer, whom he outbid at the first sale; Popish reliques which had a high value, but no cost of production (p. 60 et seq., 1844 edn); these and other 'shining instances' throw light upon an obscure subject. The 'dry light' of logic is intensified by a coruscation of wit. Sometimes, however, the doubt occurs whether the writer was as competent to point a moral as to adorn a tale. Thus, in the case of the pearl-market, and the vividly pictured slave-market (ibid. p. 77 et seq.) is it correctly stated that for 'the plebs amongst the slaves', and the 'ordinary pearls', value is determined by cost of production, while 'the natural aristocracy amongst the slaves, like the rarer pearls, will be valued on other principles'?

Even the famous parable of the musical snuff-box (cited by Mill, Political Economy, bk. iii, ch. ii, § 1) is not rightly interpreted by its author. It is not in general true of a bargain between two isolated individuals that the price will be 'racked up to U' (ibid. pp. 25 – 27)–the measure of the 'intrinsic worth of the article in your individual estimate for your individual purposes'; in other words its total utility to the purchaser (cp. Mill, §1 end). The following passage seems more correct.

> The purpose which any article answers and the cost which it imposes must eternally form the two limits within which the tennis-ball of price flies backwards and forwards. Five guineas being, upon the particular article X, the maximum

of teleologic price, the utmost sacrifice to which you would ever submit, under the fullest appreciation of the natural purposes which X can fulfil, and then only under the known alternative of losing it if you refuse the five guineas, this constitutes one pole, the aphelion, or remotest point to which the price for you could ever ascend.

The other limit is fixed by the cost of reproduction. These are 'the two limits between which the price must always be held potentially to oscillate' (ibid., pp. 105, 106). But even here it is not clearly stated that, in the absence of competition, the terms are indeterminate; the 'tennis-ball' may fall anywhere between the extreme limits. It is nowhere stated that in the presence of competition the upper limit is formed, not by *total*, but *final degree of utility*. De Quincey is far removed from the recent theorists to whom he bears a superficial resemblance by his not having attended to final utility and cognate conceptions. The connection between demand and value is denied by him on the strength of exceptional though striking instances (ibid., p. 331, quoted by Mill, bk. iii, ch. iii, § 2). 'A crazy maxim,' he says, 'has got possession of the whole world: viz. that price is, or can be, determined by the relation between supply and demand.' This imperfect conception of supply and demand is the special object of Mill's severe remarks on De Quincey. Mill's censure is endorsed by Sir Leslie Stephen in his article on De Quincey in the *Fortnightly Review* (1871). Mr. Shadworth Hodgson in one of his *Outcast Essays* has traversed this unfavourable verdict.

Whatever be the fate of De Quincey's cardinal tenets, it is certain that his occasional suggestions, the minor pearls of his discourse, enhanced as they are by a setting of consummate literary perfection, will preserve a lasting worth. Some important corrections of Ricardo's expressions deserve particular notice. De Quincey perceived, just as clearly as more recent critics, that 'the current rate of profits, as a thing settled and defined, must be a chimera'. He exposes

the puerility of that little receipt current among economists, viz. unlimited competition for keeping down profits to one uniform level... . Everybody must see that it is a very elaborate problem to ascertain even for one year, still more for a fair average of years, *what* has been the rate of profits upon the capital employed in any one trade (ibid., p. 237 *et seq.*).

What more could Cliffe Leslie say? De Quincey complains much that Ricardo, while insisting on the tendency towards the degradation of soils (the law of diminishing returns) has not sufficiently emphasized the counter-tendency towards improvement in the arts of cultivation. 'The land is travelling downwards, but always the productive management of land is travelling upwards' (ibid., p. 239). De Quincey discerns what a handle is afforded by Ricardo's partial statement to 'the systematic enemies of property' ... 'the policy of gloomy disorganising Jacobinism'. Rent is referred by De Quincey not to the 'indestructible', but the *differential* powers of the soil. Rent is defined as '*that portion of the produce from the soil (or from any agency of production) which is paid to the landlord for the use of its differential powers as measured by comparison with those of similar agencies operating on the same market*'.

The parenthesis exemplifies the pregnancy of De Quincey's occasional suggestions. In presenting the theory of rent, De Quincey employs an admirable geometrical construction. As in the construction which Prof. A. Marshall has made familiar (*Economics of Industry*, bk. ii, ch. iii), the *ordinate* in De Quincey's diagram represents produce. But the *abscissa* represents not doses of capital but qualities of soil. The two constructions have been combined by the present writer in an illustration of the *abstract theory of rent*, contributed to the British Association (Report, 1886). Referring to the use of diagrams, De Quincey well says:

A construction (i.e. a geometrical exhibition) of any elaborate truth is not often practicable; but, wherever it is so, prudence will not allow it to be neglected. What is called *evidentia*, that sort of demonstration which shows out ... is by a natural necessity more convincing to the learner. And, had Ricardo relied on this constructive mode of illustration his chapters upon rent and upon wages, they would not have tried the patience of his students in the way they have done.

Had De Quincey pursued his mathematical studies further, and applied the conceptions of the infinitesimal calculus to the theory of value, he would have escaped his capital error of having confused integral (or total), with differential (or final) utility. If he had worked with dU, instead of U, he might have anticipated Jevons.

[F.Y. EDGEWORTH]
Reprinted from *Palgrave's Dictionary of Political Economy*.

SELECTED WORKS
1844. *The Logic of Political Economy*. Edinburgh, London: William Blackwood & Sons.
1889–90. *The Collected Writings of Thomas De Quincey*. 14 vols, ed. David Masson, Edinburgh: Adam & Charles Black.
1890. *The Uncollected Writings of Thomas De Quincey*. 2 vols, ed. J. Hogg, London: Sonnenschein & Co.

deregulation. *See* REGULATION AND DEREGULATION.

derived demand. The idea that the demand for intermediate goods is *derived* from the demand for the final goods they help produce is obvious and appealing. It was implied by Cournot ([1838], 1897, pp. 99–116) and explicitly stated by Gossen ([1854], 1983, pp. 31, 113) and Menger ([1871], 1981, pp. 63–7). That the British classical school failed to make use of such a perspective – Mill's famous proposition that 'demand for commodities is not demand for labour' (1848, Bk. I, ch. V) came close to denying it – was doubtless due to the strong emphasis placed on prior accumulation of capital as a prerequisite for production. But it was Alfred Marshall in his *Principles of Economics* ([1890], 1920, pp. 381–93, 852–6) who introduced the term 'derived demand' and developed the concepts of the derived demand curve for an input and the elasticity of derived demand.

Marshall focused on a case in which a commodity is produced by the cooperation of several inputs, which are thus jointly demanded for the purpose, the demand for each being derived from the demand for the product. His formal analysis proceeded on the assumption that the inputs were all combined in fixed proportions (which might vary with the scale of output) although he suggested that the variable-proportions case would be similar.

A derived demand curve can be constructed for a selected input on the assumptions that production conditions, the demand curve for output, and the supply curves for all other inputs remain fixed, and that the competitive markets for output and all other inputs are always in equilibrium. The resulting derived demand curve can most easily be interpreted as the outcome of a hypothetical experiment. Make the selected input available, perfectly elastically, at an arbitrary price, y, per unit. Now ascertain, under the above conditions about the markets for output and other inputs, what quantity,

813

x, of the selected input would be demanded. All other markets must be in equilibrium, and each seller or buyer must be optimally adjusted to the assumed terms of availability of the selected input. Repeating this experiment for different values of y would generate the inverse of the relationship between *x* and *y*, $y = f(x)$, whose graphical representation is Marshall's derived demand curve for the selected input. Bringing this demand curve into conjunction with the actual supply curve of the selected input will determine the actual equilibrium price and quantity for this input and thereby implicitly determine the actual equilibrium prices and quantities of output and all other inputs. But the point of obtaining the derived demand curve is not to permit such a two-stage determination of the actual equilibrium. It is rather to permit a simplified analysis of the effect of *changes* in the supply conditions of the selected input when supply conditions of other inputs, as well as technology and the demand conditions for output, remain unaltered.

Marshall invoked a simple example in which the final product, a knife, is obtained by joining costlessly a unit each of the two inputs, blades and handles. The derived demand curve for handles is then given by the rule that *y*, the derived demand price for *x* handles, is the demand price for *x* knives less the supply price for *x* blades.

Marshall analysed the conditions producing a low elasticity of derived demand for an input, a condition which would encourage supply restriction. The first condition, the lack of a good substitute, is already implied by the fixity of production coefficients. The second is that the demand for the final output be inelastic. The third, aptly described by Henderson (1922, p. 59) as 'the importance of being unimportant', is that expenditure on the input in question be only a small fraction of total production cost. The final condition is that cooperating inputs be in inelastic supply. These last three conditions ensure that a large rise in the price of the input will not raise product price much, that a rise in the product price will not reduce sales much, and that a reduction in sales and production will lower the cost of cooperating inputs substantially.

The next major contribution was that of Hicks (1932, pp. 241–6) who formally relaxed the assumption of fixed production coefficients. He analysed the consequences of input substitutability for a two input case with constant returns to scale in production, making use of his newly invented concept of the elasticity of substitution. His principal finding was that, to get a low elasticity of derived demand, 'It is "important to be unimportant" only when the consumer can substitute more easily than the entrepreneur': i.e. only when the elasticity of demand for the product exceeds the elasticity of input substitution (1932, p. 246). This finding, which is not easily explained intuitively, has been the subject of intermittent controversy, aptly summarized and resolved in Maurice (1975). The extension of Hicks's analysis to the many-input case has been accomplished by Diewert (1971), using an elegant dual approach based on the cost function concept. However, modern theoretical work is more prone to work explicitly and symmetrically with complete systems of input demand equations for firm and industry.

More or less contemporaneously with Hicks, Joan Robinson (1933, chs 23, 24) was studying the derived demand curve for an input in cases where the final product is sold by a monopolist, who might also acquire cooperating inputs monopsonistically. The question of when areas under a derived demand curve can be given a welfare interpretation, analogous to consumer surplus for a final demand curve, has been broached by Wisecarver (1974).

The concept of derived demand finds its main application in discussions of labour-market questions and Marshall's tools still play a significant part in the teaching and writing in that area.

J.K. WHITAKER

See also ACCELERATION PRINCIPLE; MARSHALL, ALFRED; NEOCLASSICAL PRODUCTION THEORY.

BIBLIOGRAPHY

Cournot, A.A. 1838. *Mathematical Principles of the Theory of Wealth.* Trans., New York: Macmillan, 1897.
Diewert, W.E. 1971. A note on the elasticity of derived demand in the n-factor case. *Economica* 38, May, 192–8.
Gossen, H.H. 1854. *The Laws of Human Relations.* Trans., Cambridge, Mass.: MIT Press, 1983.
Henderson, D.H. 1922. *Supply and Demand.* London: Nisbet.
Hicks, J.R. 1932. *The Theory of Wages.* London: Macmillan.
Marshall, A. 1890. *Principles of Economics*, Vol. I. 8th edn, London: Macmillan, 1920.
Maurice, S.C. 1975. On the importance of being unimportant: an analysis of the paradox in Marshall's third rule of derived demand. *Economica* 42, November, 385–93.
Menger, C. 1871. *Principles of Economics.* Trans., New York: New York University Press, 1981.
Mill, J.S. 1848. *Principles of Political Economy.* London: Parker.
Robinson, J. 1933. *The Economics of Imperfect Competition.* London: Macmillan.
Wisecarver, D. 1974. The social costs of input-market distortions. *American Economic Review* 64(3), June, 359–72.

de-skilling. The proposition that there is a long run tendency for workers to become de-skilled as part of the basic operation of capitalist economies can be found in Marx (1867). The change in capitalist stages from Cooperation to Manufacture was distinguished by the division of labour under individual capitalists. The effect of this on workers is that they are ordered to specialize in a narrow range of tasks. The worker is transformed from an all-round craftsman into what Marx calls a detail worker. His detail dexterity becomes overexercised, and he is thereby turned into a 'crippled monstrosity'. The de-skilling process continues with the next stage of capitalism, Modern Industry. Under Manufacture, the traditional skills of workers are still required collectively even if individual workers may lose the ability to perform all the tasks required in a single trade. With Modern Industry the heart of the labour process becomes the machine. Workers become appendages of the machines. Their tasks concern feeding, minding and maintaining machines rather than parts of a skilled labour process.

This process of de-skilling is viewed by Marx as fundamental to the logic of capitalist development. Under competitive pressure capitalists must reduce costs. Labour costs can be reduced considerably if the skill required of workers is removed. This widens the supply of suitable workers, thereby swelling the reserve army of labour, and keeps wages down to subsistence levels. It means that expensive apprentice schemes do not have to be supported. It also means that workers, both individually and as a collectivity, do not possess the secrets that were the basis of the guilds' power to limit labour through long apprenticeships, even after most individual workers no longer used their acquired skills, This facilities the employment of women and children and reduces further the level of wages because now workers do not have to be paid a family wage.

That the division of labour could have a de-skilling effect on workers was well known before Marx. Smith (1776), the champion of the division of labour for its effects on productivity, noted that specialization could produce boredom and a loss of traditional skills. However, this was not emphasized by Smith, and he believed that the harmful effects could be effectively countered by public education.

One of the main benefits to employers of the division of labour was that tasks which were divided up into segments each requiring different skill levels, in principle could then be given out to workers with just those skills required to do the job. This would allow employers to pay for only those skills actually used in the labour process. This effect of the division of labour, known now as the Babbage Principle (Babbage, 1835), was reiterated by Marx.

There are two counter-arguments to the de-skilling hypothesis which have become very influential. The first is associated with Durkheim (1893). The effect of the division of labour is specialization. However, for Durkheim specialization means stimulating a diversity of skills rather than a loss of general skill. Diversity means that individuals are able to act in accordance with their own individualized preferences rather than preferences which are homogenized by social pressures. This allows an organic solidarity to be achieved in society as opposed to the mechanical solidarity of undifferentiated individuals which Durkheim primarily associates with primitive societies. A similar attitude towards the division of labour underpins the human capital view of skill (Becker, 1964). Specialization requires specialist skills. The opportunities are thereby created which allow individuals to choose to invest in acquiring those skills by foregoing immediate earnings.

The second argument against de-skilling is one which accepts Marx's judgement for the nineteenth century and early twentieth century, but which claims that he is now outdated. According to this view, skill requirements depend on overall types of technologies used in production (Woodward, 1958; Blauner, 1964). The shift from unit and small-batch production techniques to large-batch and mass-production techniques involved a loss of craft skills and a rise in worker alienation. However, it is argued that more recently technology has been changing once more, this time towards process production technologies. These require new skills associated with scientific and technical training and result in work which is also less alienating.

Both groups arguing against the de-skilling thesis have pointed to the universal rise in years of formal education and the relative growth in white-collar jobs as evidence against the de-skilling hypothesis.

The de-skilling hypothesis was revived by Braverman (1974). Braverman's argument was essentially that capitalism had not changed. At base the trend to de-skilling had continued. Although certain changes had occurred since Marx's time, they amounted to a change in the methods of de-skilling rather than in the fundamental direction of de-skilling. For Braverman the process of de-skilling involves four processes. First, the shop floor loses the right to design and plan work; that is, the separation of planning from doing or conception from execution, in an overall sense. Second, work is fragmented into meaningless segments. Third, tasks are redistributed among unskilled and semi-skilled labour according to the Babbage Principle, and conceptual activities are concentrated on as few workers as possible. Fourth, work is monitored closely.

According to Braverman, the essential problem for management is to control the variability and uncertainty associated with the transformation of worker's capacity to work (labour power) into actual work. Control over this transformation is the key to profitability. This has not changed since Marx's time. What has changed is the application of scientific principles to this task. The 20th century is distinguished by the application of Frederick Taylor's system of scientific management to this task.

Braverman accuses the Durkheimian school of concentrating only on what Marx would have called the social division of labour, the separation of trades or broad occupations, and ignoring what Marx called the manufacturing division of labour, the dividing up of work tasks within individual firms. He also argues against the straightforward determination of social processes by technology. Skill levels depend on the uses made of technology and on the social organization through which technology is used. This depends on the purposes of the agents in control of that social organization. That is, it is the fundamental needs of capitalists, not the technology itself, which should be the starting point of the analysis of skills. In particular, Braverman notes that the rise in white-collar work has not primarily occurred by a rise in the proportion of highly skilled technicians. Most white-collar occupational growth has been due to a rise in the proportion of low-level clerical staff. They have been de-skilled in precisely the same way as manual workers. Concerning rising levels of formal education, Braverman cites the considerable evidence that educational achievement required for recruitment exceeds the actual requirements for carrying out work in most job categories.

The de-skilling hypothesis has received considerable critical attention by theorists who have been inspired by Braverman. For Edwards (1979), what has grown during the 20th century is capitalist control over the labour process. This has occurred by substituting personal and direct ways of controlling labour with structural methods, such as by building controls into the overall pattern of machine design for whole factories or by bureaucratic procedures governing worker behaviour which apply to all workers. This change involves de-skilling some workers and re-skilling others at the same time.

Friedman (1977) associates de-skilling with one of two general types of management strategy: the Direct Control strategy. This strategy focuses on reducing the discretion individual workers can exercise. The alternative strategy, Responsible Autonomy, focuses on achieving high flexibility from workers by allowing them high discretion and by encouraging their loyalty to to the firm. According to Friedman, there is a perpetual tension between these strategies. During times of severe product market competition based on price (rather than quality), and times of excess labour supply, managers will be pushed toward Direct Control strategies and de-skilling. However, in the opposite environmental conditions, or when pushed by strong worker resistance, they will be encouraged to move towards Responsible Autonomy strategies.

Littler (1982) also notes that the problem of high-cost skilled workers can be avoided rather than confronted, by firms moving to new sites or when technological changes lead to new firms making products which had been made using skilled workers. The overall effect may be to change the composition of skills required, but individual skilled jobs are not directly redefined, they simply disappear.

Braverman has been widely criticized for ignoring the effects of worker resistance on managerial behaviour. According to Edwards, the Taylorist programme was a failure due to strong worker resistance. Friedman criticizes Braverman for presuming that the basic problem of management is to deal with worker variability and uncertainty. Managers often take actions to counter specific moves by workers, rather than merely to reduce the harmful effects that unanticipated worker resistance may cause. Also, by reducing the opportunities for workers to disrupt production, managers lose the advantages to be gained by harnessing worker initiative and loyalty. These circumstances allow the Responsible Autonomy strategy, and its attendant re-skilling possibilities, to be profitable.

Currently, while most of the post-Braverman theorists view de-skilling as an important symptom of capitalist development, it is viewed as a process which directly affects particular groups of workers in only limited episodes of capitalist development. Often the process occurs simply by capital moving around highly skilled groups. Also, the redivision of labour does not always run in the de-skilling direction. Sometimes capitalist development involves strategies which allow re-skilling.

A.L. FRIEDMAN

See also DIVISION OF LABOUR; DURKHEIM, EMILE.

BIBLIOGRAPHY

Babbage, C. 1835. On the economy of machinery and manufacture. Excerpted in Design of Jobs, ed. L.E. Davis and J.C. Taylor, Harmondsworth: Penguin, 1972.

Becker, G. 1964. Human Capital. New York: Columbia University Press.

Blauner, R. 1964. Alienation and Freedom: The Factory Worker and his Industry. Chicago: University of Chicago Press.

Braverman, H. 1974. Labor and Monopoly Capital. New York: Monthly Review Press.

Durkheim, E. 1893. The Division of Labour in Society. New York: Free Press, 1964.

Edwards, R. 1979. Contested Terrain. London: Heinemann.

Friedman, A.L. 1977. Industry and Labour. London: Macmillan.

Littler, C.R. 1982. The Development of the Labour Process in Capitalist Societies. London: Heinemann.

Marx, K. 1867. Capital, Vol. 1. London: Lawrence & Wishart, 1970.

Smith, A. 1776. An Inquiry into the Nature and Causes of the Wealth of Nations. Ed. E. Cannan, London: Methuen, 1961.

Woodward, J. 1958. Management and Technology. London: HMSO.

Destutt de Tracy, Antoine Louis Claude

Destutt de Tracy, Antoine Louis Claude (1754–1836). French philosopher and economist, Tracy was born into a noble family of the ancien régime at Paris on 20 July 1754 and died in the same city on 10 March 1836. His life spanned the most tumultuous period of French history, from the twilight of the Old Regime to the dawn of capitalism, romanticism and socialism. One of the last philosophes, Tracy began as an 18th-century classical metaphysician, preoccupied with the sensationalist doctrine of Locke and Condillac, and ended up, in the words of Auguste Comte, as the philosopher 'who had come closest to the positive state'. In the interim he knelt at the feet of Voltaire; served alongside Lafayette in the Royal Cavalry, and as deputy to the French Estates General and the Constituent Assembly; was imprisoned during the Reign of Terror; released after Thermidor (escaping the guillotine by a mere two days); subsequently helped to establish his country's first successful national programme of public education; led the opposition to Napoleon from his seat in the French Senate; regained his title under the Bourbon Restoration; counted among his associates the likes of Mirabeau, Condorcet, Cabanis, DuPont de Nemours, Jefferson, Franklin, Lavoisier, Ricardo and Mill; and retained his early sympathies for liberty throughout.

Long before it took on its pejorative sense at the hands of Marx, Tracy coined the term 'ideology' (by which he meant the science of ideas) to describe his philosophy, which embraced and intertwined psychological, moral, economic and social phenomena, but which gave primacy to economics because he thought that the purpose of society was to satisfy man's material needs and multiply his enjoyments. Tracy rejected the physiocratic notion of value, substituting a labour theory that Ricardo subsequently endorsed in his Principles. Like Say, he denied Smith's distinction between productive and unproductive labour. But unlike Smith or Say, he reduced all wealth, including land, to labour. On numerous other topics (i.e. wages, profits, rents, exchange, price variations, international trade) he was far less thorough and rigorous than either Smith or Say, but his exposition of the capitalization theory of taxation was superior to the rest. In the final analysis, his Traité was not properly a treatise on political economy so much as a part of a general study of the human will. Yet the resulting lack of depth did not impair his remarkable ability to allure great minds. Ricardo found him 'a very agreeable old gentleman', and Jefferson was influenced to the point of including 'ideology' among the ten projected departments in his plan for the University of Virginia.

Along with Say, Destutt de Tracy was one of the earliest members of the French liberal school. Patrician, philosopher and patriot, caught in the grips of major social and economic upheaval, he denounced the interests of his own class (the rentiérs) and became the spokesman of a nascent capitalism in which he had neither role nor vested interest.

R.F. HÉBERT

SELECTED WORKS

1804–18. Eléments d'idéologie. 5 vols, Paris: Courcier.

1811. A Commentary and Review of Montesquieu's Spirit of Laws. Trans. from the French, Philadelphia: William Duane.

1817. A Treatise on Political Economy. Ed. T. Jefferson, New York: Augustus M. Kelley, 1970.

BIBLIOGRAPHY

Allix, E. 1912. Destutt de Tracy, économiste. Revue d'Economie Politique 26, 424–51.

Kennedy, E. 1978. Destutt de Tracy and the Origins of 'Ideology'. Philadelphia: American Philosophical Society.

Picavet, F.J. 1918. Les Idéologues. Paris: F. Alcan, chs 5 and 6.

determinism

determinism. The proposition that every event has a cause sounds clear and simple. It is neither. On a very strong reading it asserts a grand inevitability about the workings of the universe, which leaves only one course of history possible. Many economists will associate determinism, taken in this sense, with Marx (1859):

> In the social production which men carry on they enter into definite relations that are indispensable and independent of their will; these relations of production correspond to a definite stage of development of their material powers of production. The sum total of these relations of production constitutes the economic structure of society – the real foundation, on which rise legal and political superstructures and to which correspond definite forms of social consciousness ... . It is not the consciousness of men that determines their existence, but, on the contrary, their social existence determines their consciousness (A Contribution to the Critique of Political Economy, Preface).

Since anyone who agrees is plainly a determinist, it is easy to presume that those who disagree with Marx are not. For, on this account, determinism seems opposed to freedom, because it excludes all individual voluntarism. Indeed, the passage contrasts so starkly with neoclassical analyses of choice, where the emphasis is on the role of individuals, that the opposition between determinism and individual freedom appears to capture a vital difference between marxian and neoclassical economists. But this would be too casual an appeal to a popular distinction between freedom and determinism, doing justice to neither school.

The first point to note is that determinism need not be as specific as in the economic variety pressed by Marx above. The proposition that every event has a cause, on a weaker reading, claims only that every event is predictable from its antecedents. The prediction need not be underpinned by Marx's relations and forces of production nor, more generally, by any set of natural laws, which involve real necessities. According to Hume (1748), prediction requires causal laws only in the sense of correlations or patterns which we have come to notice and expect. If he is right in his analysis of causation, then all economists, who seek empirical regularities in order to predict and explain effects from their antecedents, are determinists.

For example, neoclassical economists use causal laws to explain action. The neoclassicist conceives of economic man in such a way that his actions can in principle be predicted, given his environment, preferences and stock of information. The antecedent cause of an action is preference combined with environment and information. This is plain in the simple model of consumer choice or production, where the agent is no more than a mechanical throughput between environment and outcome. It also applies, however, in more complex models, where outcomes are not uniquely determined. Stochastic models are often referred to as non-deterministic, and mixing strategies can produce varying outcomes in the same game. Nevertheless, they are examples of determinism on a weaker, Humean, definition. The only difference is that what is being determined (or predicted) is not unique events but the probability distributions of events.

This may surprise those who take neoclassical economics to be wedded to ideas of free choice which are incompatible with determinism. After all, it is easy to assume that a caused action cannot be a chosen action. But many philosophers (compatibilists) deem this a mistake. Free actions are those which translate the agent's wants into effect; those where the agent is compelled to act against his wishes are unfree. Since *both* kinds of action are caused, however, the traditional dispute between free will and determinism has been misconceived (see e.g. Hume, 1748; Mill, 1843; Ayer, 1954). Indeed, the point carries over to the more striking claim that actions can be free only if they are also determined. Lack of freedom is a matter of interference between the agent's wants, his action and its intended outcome. Typical obstacles to freedom are coercion, ignorance and randomness. Free agents therefore need to be able to count on their actions being in conformity with their wants and on consequences being as foreseen. Where they cannot count on these causal sequences, they cannot be sure that they will satisfy their preferences by their actions. The advance of a deterministic science of economics is thus a positive help in making the outcome less clouded and opaque and hence in choosing the actions which satisfy preferences.

This compatibilist line reconciles freedom and determinism in a way which lends weight to the popular distinction between positive and normative economics. Normative economics is concerned with what is good or bad, right or wrong. It includes value judgements about which causes of action are morally justified and which outcomes morally desirable. It seeks to set the boundary between coerced and free actions. But these are normative distinctions within the realm of caused actions and outcomes. Positive economics, by contrast, views the same realm solely for purposes of explanation. It asks why economic agents behave as they do and not whether they

should. This kind of question is distinct from the others and will only be hampered by letting normative disputes obscure it. Indeed, by being left to get on with advancing deterministic explanations, and thus increasing knowledge of how to bring about desired ends, it offers an ever more powerful service to those individuals or policy-makers, whose normative judgements are to be respected.

Compatibilism is thus a tempting doctrine for any economist who shares Enlightenment hopes that a determinist, predictive science is an aid to progress in the pursuit of human happiness (or any other prescribed goal). It is also a useful doctrine for those who maintain the methodological unity of the sciences and the modelling of the social sciences on a positivist account of the natural sciences. But its reconciliation of freedom with determinism does not go unchallenged. There is bound to be a suspicion that, in assimilating human beings to other complex creatures or objects in nature and in embracing a scientific method designed for nature, a special quality of free human action has been lost. The suspicion is hard to focus precisely but Austin (1961) offers a sharp challenge. It is not enough, he holds, for an action to be free that, in other conditions or with other preferences, the agent *would have* acted differently. Free will requires that the agent *could have* chosen differently in the same conditions. 'Could have' does not reduce to 'would have, if ...'. This implies that an economic science, which treats economic decision as a throughput between environment and outcome, *via* preferences which are exogenously given, must somehow be denying free will.

Compatibilists retort that an alternative choice in the same conditions and with the same preferences would be a very puzzling phenomenon. In special cases a rational agent might deliberately adopt a randomizing strategy. But, in general, it looks as if free will is being supposed to require an unpredictable choice of action and hence an inexplicable one. If free actions cannot be explained in terms of what an agent in those circumstances, with those wants and beliefs, predictably did, then they are beyond the scope of scientific enquiry.

To dispose of the retort one needs a rival to causal explanation. An obvious candidate is rational or intentional explanation, although it may turn out not to be genuinely a rival. This kind of explanation focuses less on the situation and more on the agent's own understanding of it. The agent intends a certain result and has reason to believe that the chosen action is the likeliest way to achieve it. Explanation becomes the rational reconstruction of this process of decision. Provided that agents' judgements are reconstructed as not automatic but the work of their own understanding, perhaps the agent *could have done otherwise* in the same conditions, as Austin required. But a shift of emphasis from environment to psychology will not be philosophically significant, unless psychological explanations are non-causal. So the obvious counter-move is to point out that psychology too has often been regarded as a law-governed deterministic science.

Yet that may be to miss the point that the social world depends on agents' beliefs about it, whereas the natural world does not depend on what atoms believe. Granted a distinction between regularities in nature and rules or norms in human society, one might suggest that the social world is furnished and activated in ways which call for a different approach to psychology. At any rate, whether or not the workings of the mind are causal and law-like, the beliefs of agents affect the outcomes which economists observe. This peculiarity of social life is itself enough to open some interesting possibilities. For example, Keynes can be read as harnessing the point to show how different but plausible beliefs in the face of uncertainty would lead to different outcomes. The more recent literature finding rational expectations consistent with multiple equilibria takes it further. Choices become genuine, in Austin's sense, because what happens genuinely depends on what agents expect to happen.

Uncertainty and freedom become, so to speak, two sides of the same coin (cf. Shackle, 1969). The theme is developed in the post-Keynesian reminders that historical time differs from logical time. In logical time the series of events is complete and only human ignorance distinguishes the known past from the unknown future. Natural science theories commonly conceive the world in this timeless way (although perhaps adding direction through an idea of irreversible change). Economics, on the other hand, can or even should accommodate the thought that agents can make a future discontinuous with the past. They are not just discovering what a supreme intelligence could have predicted from the start, given the first state of the world and the forces acting in it. (This is a reference to Laplace, 1820.) If so, economic theories need to recognize the fact that economic events occur in historical time, in a way which natural science theories can abstract from.

One consequence is to undermine the positive/normative distinction. Economic agents are affected by beliefs, including beliefs about how the economy works. Economic theories (unless kept secret) thus affect outcomes. Economic science ceases to be an impartial description and, since rival theories involve differing normative commitments, the material for an allegedly positive science is hopelessly corrupted by normative elements in its data and by its own feedback through the beliefs of its subject matter. Whether an observed correlation amounts to a causal law threatens to depend on whether the positive economist can persuade people that it does! In place of the image of the economist as technician, we have an image of the economist as ideologue *malgré lui*, and the vision of economics as a moral science is restored.

This article has separated two ways of construing the relevance of determinism to economics. The more familiar starts from the popular contrast between determinism and freedom and with the tendency in economics to associate the former with Marx. This creates an impression that neoclassical economics rejects determinism, especially given the volume of neoclassical work on stochastic models. But if determinism claims only that outcomes are governed by causal laws and that events are accordingly predictable from their antecedents, the popular contrast disappears. Marxism and neoclassicism become alternative deterministic theories. There is still room for argument, however, about the success of compatibilism. To insist that choice implies 'could have acted otherwise' and not merely 'would have, if ...' is to reinstate the dispute. It then matters whether economic agents have an open future, whereas (random factors aside) atoms do not. If so, uncertainty in economics differs crucially from anything implied by an Uncertainty Principle in physics. In particular, economic theories may affect what people believe and hence what economic science tries to describe and explain. In that case economics cannot help being a normative science.

SHAUN HARGREAVES-HEAP AND MARTIN HOLLIS

See also DIALECTICAL MATERIALISM; DIALECTICAL REASONING; ECONOMIC INTERPRETATION OF HISTORY.

BIBLIOGRAPHY

Ayer, A.J. 1954. Freedom and necessity. In A.J. Ayer, *Philosophical Essays*, London: Macmillan.
Austin, J.L. 1961. Ifs and Cans. In J.L. Austin, *Philosophical Papers* Oxford: Clarendon Press.
Hume, D. 1748. *An Enquiry Concerning Human Understanding.* Sect. VII, pts I and II.
Laplace, P. 1820. *Théorie analytique des probabilités*. Paris.
Marx, K. 1858. *A Contribution to the Critique of Political Economy.* Moscow: Progress Publishers, 1970
Mill, J.S. 1843. *A System of Logic.* Book VI. London: J.W. Parker.
Shackle, G.L.S. 1969. *Decision, Order and Time.* Cambridge: Cambridge University Press.

De Tocqueville, A. *See* TOCQUEVILLE, ALEXIS DE.

devaluation. *See* EXCHANGE RATE POLICY.

developing countries, fiscal and monetary policies. *See* FISCAL AND MONETARY POLICIES IN DEVELOPING COUNTRIES.

development economics. As we are often reminded nowadays, economic development – in the sense of regular progress and rising prosperity – was a preoccupation of the classical economists. What has come to be called Development Economics, however, is of much more recent origin. Both during and immediately after World War II, the conditions of poverty, illiteracy, disease and mortality in backward agrarian countries aroused keen interest and concern in the West, inspired by humanitarian considerations and, no doubt, those ensuing from the Cold War. The search for ways whereby their people could escape such misery and enjoy rising prosperity engendered a body of diverse doctrines and strong controversy, which has by no means fully subsided.

Then, as now, the comparatively affluent living standards in industrialized societies provided a clear example of what was, in principle, possible. Of course, to reduce thus the problem of economic development to that of building an industrial society is to do it a good deal of violence. For those who place the realization of individual potential at the centre of things, dignity, liberty and satisfaction at the workplace count for quite as much as material affluence; see, for example, Seers (1969). And some writers in a more classical tradition emphasized the importance of expanding the range of choices open to individuals. Yet without claiming any causal connection, there appear to be quite strong associations between the share of industry in national income and at least some of the attributes of a decent life for the mass of the population, a set of regularities explored in considerable detail by Kuznets (1966) and Chenery and Syrquin (1975). There is also the point that industrialism is what most countries in the Third World aspire to. Together, these must do as a defence for the drastic reduction of the problem I have chosen in order to make the scope of this essay manageable.

Two themes are pursued. First, poor countries are starting out in a world in which there are already rich countries. As most of the latter are industrial economies and the former are still heavily agricultural, they will be referred to henceforth as pioneers and latecomers, respectively. In this context, pioneers are inventing new products and processes, even – where legal obstacles are not insuperable – new institutions, such as the joint stock company and the multinational corporation, or, in centrally plannned economies, Gosplan. This ferment in capitalist pioneers is the object of Schumpeter's (1926) celebrated work on economic development. Although modern development economics is concerned with the progress of latecomers, an important strand in much thinking on development is that the options and prospects facing latecomers are necessarily influenced by what is going on in pioneers. The very fact that pioneers and latecomers trade in goods, labour, capital and ideas itself suggests that latecomers are affected, though whether they gain or lose thereby is still controversial.

Secondly, much doctrine – and controversy – has been concerned with certain problems of economic coordination that arise in the course of industrialization. In this field, there has been no shortage of challenges to the proposition that economic coordination is best effected by the market mechanism, nor any lack of vigorous defence. It seems fair to say, however, that this is a field in which étatisme is a well-rooted doctrine, which finds ample reflection in the active role played by the state in many latecomers.

Finally, while the classical influence is still strong, development economics has come to absorb a good deal from other fields that are noticeably more 'modern'. Indeed, it might be argued that development economics has been absorbed back into the mainstream, and now enjoys no separate existence. That, too, will be assessed.

1. PIONEERS AND LATECOMERS: CATCHING UP. A summary record of the technological progress of pioneers can be thought of as a metaphorical 'book of blueprints'. Free access to this book is valuable to latecomers, inasmuch as they are then spared the expense of recreating what is already known. This seems to imply that latecomers have a potential advantage over pioneers, an advantage of backwardness, as Gerschenkron (1952) would call it.

While the above proposition looks virtually unassailable, some questions arise. First, is access to the book free? True, knowledge has some of the characteristics of a public good; so that the prices of goods produced by well established and widely diffused methods are unlikely to contain a significant element of rent corresponding to such knowledge. Where newer goods and processes are concerned, however, patent laws and the fact that key elements of know-how are often embodied in factors specific to the firm usually ensure some return to the knowledge possessed. In these cases, therefore, the question is whether the latecomer would be better off developing an alternative technique from whatever knowledge is freely available. Much proprietary knowledge is embodied in specific capital goods, which, with some exotic exceptions, are rarely produced by monopolies. Thus, unless the firm owning the knowledge and/or the producer(s) of the capital goods are able to pursue strategies that leave latecomers at their reservation levels, which may not always be possible, latecomers ought to enjoy a modest surplus over going it alone.

Secondly, many techniques in the 'book of blueprints' that have been discarded by pioneers are no longer available. The firms that produced the capital goods may have gone out of business or lost the intangible knowhow to make the process work; so that if the technique is to be revived, skills and resources will be needed. In many instances, current practice in pioneers will be the only techniques on offer, though it should be noted that this menu still contains many marginal methods, to pioneers at least. For this reason alone, there will be a tendency for latecomers to adopt 'advanced' techniques of production, relative to the pioneers at a comparable stage of their development.

Thirdly, is it socially desirable for latecomers to adopt 'advanced' techniques? To the extent that there is a real choice,

advanced techniques may not reflect real scarcities in the economy: loosely speaking, they may be too 'capital-intensive'. In that case, the remedy is to change the incentives favouring advanced techniques through policy reforms, or to licence investments based on their profitability at shadow prices which reflect social scarcities (see Section 5).

If, however, the spectrum of techniques itself is unsatisfactory, rather different considerations arise. If the output(s) in question can be imported, foreign trade provides an alternative to producing them at home. Yet the point at issue is the absence of so-called 'appropriate' techniques for production at home. Now there is always the option of devoting resources to the development of new, 'appropriate' techniques. If such inventive activity is lacking or very limited, it is important to establish why this activity is unattractive relative to, say, producing textiles. It is sometimes argued that latecomers lack the engineers and technicians to undertake such work; but pioneers do not seem to have been greatly handicapped by a lack of card-carrying graduates when they set out. Others argue that the people in question have the wrong sort of training and attitudes, and aspire to emulate inventive activity in pioneers, where many of them were trained. There is some truth in this, inasmuch as men seek prestige as well as profit; but it is not wholly persuasive. It seems more plausible that the limited inventive activity in latecomers directed at 'appropriate' techniques stems largely from its uncertain profitability. Market prices may favour advanced techniques, while the legal system may hold out little prospect that private agents will recover their outlays in royalties or monopoly profits afforded by patent protection. Similarly, it is not clear that the incentives facing public sector agencies, which often employ the majority of a latecomer's technical personnel, are conducive to the development of appropriate techniques.

More generally, if the trappings of modernity are a merit want for governments, entrepreneurs, engineers and final consumers, then 'advanced' is also, for them, 'appropriate'. It can be argued, therefore, that the existence of pioneers is damaging to latecomers, not through the exercise of monopoly power or conspiracy, but through the inevitable demonstration effects on the tastes of latecomers.

In any event, the fact that latecomers face a different spectrum of techniques at the outset leads naturally to the question: will they grow faster than pioneers did at comparable stages, and so eventually catch up? Gerschenkron (1952) argues that this was certainly the case in the 19th century. In the leading sectors, latecomers adopted the latest techniques, and the plants in question were usually larger in scale than representative plants in pioneers. The evidence, such as it is, suggests that some recent latecomers are growing faster still, again drawing heavily on current 'best practice' embodied in large scale plants, albeit not in all industries. While the performance of some other latecomers cautions against any strong claims, this part of Gerschenkron's thesis is given some support by contemporary experience.

Now, if there are constant returns to scale and some measure of choice, it will not usually be efficient for latecomers to adopt the 'best practice' technique – unless, of course, the latter dominates all others in the sense of requiring no more of any input per unit of output and less of at least one input. If, however, there are increasing returns to scale embodied in 'best practice' plant, then slavish imitation of the pioneers' path may be inferior to a leap straight to the most advanced methods. This is a slightly more formal way of stating Gerschenkron's contention that latecomers grow faster because there is a greater tension between current practice at the outset in latecomers and unexploited possibilities in the form of current best practice in pioneers. Certainly, it is easier to see how this might be when there are increasing returns.

In the course of adopting and adapting new techniques, increasing returns also appear in the guise of learning-by-doing (Arrow, 1962; Kaldor, 1957). While the process of learning is by no means automatic, firms can expect the efficiency with which they use new techniques to improve following their adoption. Hence, if firms in latecomers organize themselves so as to profit from their accumulated experience as fully as do firms in pioneers and such improvements have a ceiling that is reached in finite time or cumulative output, as seems plausible, then catching up in that particular line of production with the technique in question will be complete.

Thus far, no mention has been made of natural endowments. As a matter of history, industrialisation was launched in temperate climates, and most contemporary latecomers are in the tropics and sub-tropics, where pests harmful to man flourish the year round. Advances in medical science and public health, which originated in pioneers and were subsequently put to work in latecomers, have gone a long way towards eliminating this disadvantage, at fairly modest recurrent costs. That leaves the sapping effects of heat and humidity on human effort and efficiency, and poor soils as salient disadvantages of the tropics. Air conditioning deals with the former, just as heating takes care of winter's cold in temperate climes. As for poor soils, these are of no consequence for footloose industries, though a prosperous and productive agriculture may have a beneficial influence on the speed and sacrifice with which an industrial society is built. Besides, the examples of Switzerland, Denmark, Japan and, lately, Singapore and Taiwan indicate that ingenuity and flexibility may count for more than expanses of fertile land and/or an invigorating climate.

2. GROWTH: BALANCED AND UNBALANCED. It has just been argued that the transfer of knowledge and technique from pioneers to latecomers is an inescapable feature of growth in latecomers. Little was said, however, about the nature of the growth process itself, how it might be launched and sustained, or the forms of economic organization which would make the associated investments in plant and equipment. In particular, the role of the State went virtually unmentioned.

Although the doctrine of 'balanced' growth, as first set out by Rosenstein-Rodan (1943) and subsequently developed and elaborated by Nurkse (1953), certainly appeals to the notion that latecomers can draw on an existing stock of knowledge and techniques, the central problem, as its protagonists saw it, was to get growth started by inducing investment in industry. Now, why did investment have to be induced at all, as opposed to arising naturally and optimally as the result of profit seeking by entrepreneurs? First, it is argued, ruling market prices do not convey all relevant information to private investors. Not only are market structures imperfect, they are also incomplete, insurance markets being conspicuously thin and limited. Secondly, firms perceive their demand schedules to be rather inelastic where an expansion of output is concerned. This assumption of 'elasticity pessimism' was perhaps a natural legacy from the inter-war period. Nurkse, certainly, was pessimistic about the prospects for international trade; but the distinction between tradeable and non-tradeable goods, which is central to Section 5, was not made clearly. In any event, if firms perceive their respective demand schedules to be at all inelastic, they must have significant size, actually or potentially, in their respective markets. Thus, if one firm expands its output, the consequences for other firms are not, in general, completely summarized by market prices.

In Rosenstein-Rodan's example, the workers employed in a new shoe factory spend most of their income not on shoes, but on other wage goods, thereby making it profitable for the industries producing the latter to expand. In turn, an expansion of those industries will lead to a rise in the demand for shoes, but not necessarily such as to validate the initial investment in shoe-making capacity. What matters in establishing equilibrium, therefore, is firms' perceptions of the strategic responses of other firms, not only in competing lines of production, but potentially in all lines. Of course, this is immensely demanding of information for the individual firm, which may confine itself to conjectures about the responses of the firms in the more obvious complementary lines, while entirely ignoring wider ramifications. The more restricted the scope of these conjectures, the more limited is the expansion of output likely to be.

In the case of constant returns to scale – or, more precisely, constant average costs – some output will be produced, provided average cost is less than (perceived) marginal revenue at zero output. If, as seems plausible, initial perceptions are on the conservative side, firms will find demand conditions somewhat more favourable than expected, so that further rounds of expansion may occur. Nevertheless, with Nash conjectures, the resulting equilibrium will still be based on restricted assessments of the ramifications of an individual firm's actions.

The assumption of constant costs does not, however, sit very well with the notion that firms have significant size relative to their respective markets. It seems more fitting to assume that there are increasing returns to scale, at least in the form that the minimum efficient scale of production is large relative to perceived demand, so that average costs may well be falling over the relevant range. In this case, the indivisibility of investment requires the firm to make a substantial and irreversible commitment if any output is to be produced. This it will be reluctant to do, even if it makes extensive and possibly sanguine conjectures about the actions of other firms, unless it has strong assurances that the other firms will make their investments simultaneously. With obvious advantages to hanging back over moving first, it is quite possible that the outcome of this prisoners' dilemma game will be that no investments are made at all. This extreme outcome seems closer to the preoccupations of the balanced growth school than that of limited investment under constant costs, and better to characterize an agrarian economy in which modern industry has not yet been established. Indeed, Rosenstein-Rodan recognizes the importance of increasing returns in drawing upon Young's (1928) example of the tube line. In any event, the resulting failure of economic coordination under the conditions discussed here is greatly intensified in the presence of increasing returns.

Thus far, we have dealt with potentially beneficial effects of an expansion of one firm on the profits of others. But firms also use some of the same inputs, so that simultaneous expansion will raise costs more sharply, unless the inputs in question are in perfectly elastic supply. Thus, there are competitive as well as complementary effects to be considered (Fleming, 1955). The two resources used across the board are, of course, labour and investment.

Where raw, unskilled workers are concerned, no difficulties were anticipated, in view of what was presumed to be a great 'reserve army' of underemployed and unemployed labourers in peasant agriculture and petty trade, which could meet any conceivable (initial) expansion of organized industry. The discipline and rhythms of industrial life, as well as many specific skills, could be acquired on the job through learning-by-doing. Certain special skills, especially those of a technical and managerial nature, might not be so readily created, however, so that they would command a scarcity premium, which would increase with the overall scale of expansion, until additional supplies of such skills were forthcoming. This rise in costs is potentially damaging to the case for simultaneous expansion of all lines of production. In the short run, it could be mitigated by importing foreign technicians. Over the longer run, the training and education of nationals abroad and/or at home would be possible; but the gestation period for workers of this sort is so long that reliance on this option is scarcely feasible if a large programme of industrialization is to start straightaway.

The other resource for which firms clearly compete is capital goods. In a closed economy, the capacity of the machine-building sector will impose a limit on how much investment can be undertaken in other industries even if there is a willingness to save more, a point that is central to the models of Feldman–Domar (1957) and Mahalanobis (1953). If world supplies of such goods are highly elastic, imports remove this bottleneck, so that domestic savings become the limiting factor, provided they can be transformed into foreign exchange through exports. Most proponents of balanced growth assumed that there was plenty of global capacity to supply the plant and equipment needed at home; but they were less sure that all potential domestic savings could be converted into foreign exchange. Besides, a strong push on many fronts with significant indivisibilities of investment would entail heavy sacrifices in current consumption, even if such conversion were possible at parametric terms of trade. Hence the strong accompanying plea for foreign aid to get the process going without undue pain.

A case for strong government intervention to coordinate individual investments is beginning to emerge from the balanced growth argument. Before addressing it, however, we must also consider the contrary thesis of Hirschman (1958), namely, that the right strategy is to pursue unbalanced growth. In such a strategy, the complementarities discussed above are not simply ignored; rather imbalances between supply and demand are deliberately induced after an examination of where the complementarities lie. The difficulty with Hirschman's thesis is that, unlike the doctrine of balanced growth, it has defied attempts to state it in a formal and rigorous way. This does not, of course, mean that it is wrong; but comparisons with balanced growth are rendered much more difficult thereby.

There are two features of Hirschman's argument that are particularly relevant here. First, he dismisses all so-called 'obstacles to development' save one, namely, the capacity to make rational economic decisions. If this capacity is adequate, so his argument runs, all the other 'obstacles', should they have an independent existence, will be easily surmountable. Now, the one thing that is needed above all else in pursuing a strategy of balanced growth is the ability to coordinate complementary investments without much help from the price system, so that balanced growth makes intensive demands on the very resource that Hirschman believes to be the scarcest.

How does unbalanced growth economize on this resource? In part, the answer goes, by giving up the attempt at detailed, centralized coordination implied by balanced growth. At first sight, this looks like no strategy at all – if it be granted that the price mechanism is defective – so we move on to the second feature of Hirschman's argument, which is at once poetic and slippery. When growth is unbalanced, capacity in some sectors will outrun others in such a way as to create an imbalance between supply and demand at 'normal' prices. The tension stemming from this excess demand is supposed to induce supplies of whatever is most lacking – savings, entrepreneurship, a decision to build a new road, or whatever. In effect, such tensions focus attention and resources on what should be done, and the stronger the tension, the sharper the focus. This, too, is a form of economic coordination; but if there is anything novel in Hirschman's thesis, it must exert its influence by something other than a change in relative prices under the pressure of excess demand. It is easier to coin descriptive phrases for the process – 'creative tension', for example – than to pin down what is at work and how it operates.

One possible interpretation is that unresolved excess demand induces additional supplies through changes in tastes, endowments or even both. Faced with a particularly lucrative and unusual opportunity a peasant may revise his ideas about how much current consumption and leisure he should sacrifice in order to finance it. Similarly, the need to solve a particularly pressing problem may jolt managers and technicians from their ordinary routines, causing them to summon up hitherto unknown reserves of ingenuity and energy. (The performance of British industry on a three-day work week during the miners' strike of 1974 is perhaps an example.) These changes, it should be emphasized, are not the consequences of changes in relative prices with given tastes and endowments. Rather, they are changes in tastes and endowments triggered by the gap between market and 'shadow' prices when there is unresolved excess demand. Interpreted thus, the theory appears overtly and heavily 'psychological' – and formidably difficult to state precisely, let alone test. Welfare comparisons are also rendered moot, for once a man has eyed a prospect under such conditions, he is no longer the man he was. The idea that individuals are thus transformed by experience is not wholly alien to economics; but many economists would be bemused, rendered giddy even, by this version of it.

As strategic doctrines, balanced and unbalanced growth appear to call for very different roles for the State as an agent in promoting industrialization. Given its assumptions, balanced growth really expresses the desirability of exploiting complementarities through central coordination when the price mechanism cannot do the job efficiently. Inspired perhaps by the Soviet example, the proponents of balanced growth drew the conclusion that an optimal level and pattern of industrial development requires that all investment decisions be made centrally. In the presence of increasing returns and lumpy investments, the problems of isolation and assurance would also arise in a particularly acute form, with a high prior probability of bankruptcy for the individual firm acting in isolation. Thus, if firms were privately owned, they would have to have a voice in the proceedings. The desire to reduce current sacrifices to manageable proportions through foreign aid and commercial capital also introduced lender's risk and lender's interest. These foreign agencies were therefore to have their seats on Rosenstein-Rodan's Investment Board as well. Thus, what starts out as an argument for the desirability of central coordination begins to look like a manifesto for the Corporate State. Even leaving aside this inherent element of political economy, one is still struck by the staggering demands for detailed information that such a central body would make in its attempts to realize a full optimum.

A government pursuing an unbalanced growth strategy will clearly eschew any scheme of the above kind, but it will not leave matters entirely to the market. To the extent that such things can be assessed, it will promote growth in sectors that generate the right measure of creative tension, and this will need occasional revision as the process unfolds. The promotion could take a number of forms, from taxation to investment by the state itself. Moreover, the decision concerning which sectors to promote is itself a central one, requiring much information, though not as much as balanced growth. Thus, unbalanced growth certainly implies an active role for the state, though its rationale favours intervention in a decentralized form.

In this connection, Hirschman makes an orthodox and telling argument against balanced growth – or rather, the centralized mechanism balanced growth demands. Although the Investment Board might succeed in exploiting complementarity and increasing returns in a given state of knowledge, the very detail and scope of its investment plan would maße it resistant to changes. If new information or more efficient techniques of production become available, the Board's tidy scheme of things may be upset by attempts to accommodate them. In an unbalanced growth strategy, however, such disturbances may be positively welcomed, since they offer the opportunity to shake up the system. Moreover, in a decentralised system, agents will have stronger incentives to keep an eye out for new developments. Although the context is rather different, this is tantamount to standing Schumpeter's conclusion about monopoly on its head: by practising static virtue, the Investment Board falls into dynamic vice.

Finally, it is not clear that a presumption of market failure warrants the conclusion that direct, central coordination of investments is necessary. For if isolation and assurance are the problem, then an alternative way to get firms to commit themselves is to offer subsidies, the schedules of which depend on whether other firms have made commitments. Those moving early would receive larger subsidies until other firms followed. As more firms made commitments, subsidies would fall, since profits (losses) would rise (fall) as complementarities in demand began to make themselves felt. Once all firms had moved, all subsidies would cease and profits would be taxed according to some schedule announced in advance. Indeed, with the information available to the Investment Board, it should be possible to devise a schedule of subsidies that would induce firms to commit themselves in an optimal sequence, the resulting final pattern of investment being identical to that chosen by the Board. In practice, however, such refined calculations seem a rather implausible ideal. Instead, crude calculations would underpin an initial announcement of the schedule of subsidies. If no firms moved, the subsidies to early movers could be increased until some found it worthwhile to make investments, and further revisions would almost certainly be needed as the process unfolded. A lurching sequence of this sort, prodded by occasional revisions to tax policy, looks uncommonly like a form of unbalanced growth, even though its ultimate object is a balanced growth allocation that exploits complementarities in demand and economies of scale. Of course, as new data and techniques become available, revisions to the schedule of subsidies will be in order; but in this decentralized setting, only the schedule will be of inherent interest to the individual firms considering new investments.

3. THE DUAL ECONOMY. As we have seen, the assumption that labour is in highly elastic supply is an important element in balanced growth doctrine; for if wages are bid up significantly by a big push on many fronts, the very profitability of that coordinated effort may be undermined. Yet above all else, elastic supplies of labour bring to mind the classical tradition, and hence Lewis's (1954) celebrated article. Lewis was not, however, so much concerned with the problem of coordinating

investment that exercised Rosenstein-Rodan and Nurkse. True to the classical tradition, what mattered to Lewis is that capital be continuously accumulated and hence that there be a high marginal propensity to save. This would come about, for example, if the proceeds of growth accrued largely to capitalists and capitalists were abstemious – though whether the capitalists were private entrepreneurs or state functionaries was all the same to Lewis. (One should add that Hirschman's thesis makes light of a possible shortage of savings: if the right inducements to invest are present, such shortages will simply vanish.)

Perfectly elastic supplies of labour play a crucial role in Lewis's model. At a constant real wage, capitalists will choose a particular technique of production and, if there are constant returns to scale, earn a constant rate of profit. With classical savings behaviour, the rate of growth of the capitalist sector will be equal to the rate of profit multiplied by capitalists' marginal propensity to save. In the face of a stagnant subsistence sector, therefore, the structure of the economy will become steadily more capitalistic and the overall growth rate will continue to accelerate until the capitalist sector has exhausted all reserves of labour in the subsistence sector. If, at length, the wage should rise, the rate of profit will fall (in both Solovian and neo-Ricardian worlds). Thus, progressive rises in wages induced by the expansion of the capitalist sector will cause growth to peter out.

A notable feature of this process is that the distribution of national income shifts steadily in favour of profits so long as the real wage remains constant. Once the real wage begins to rise, the share of profits may continue to increase for a while if the share of the capitalist sector is still rising rapidly enough; but eventually it seems to have a tendency to fall. In any event, an increasing share of profits is likely to go with a more unequal distribution of incomes. To that extent, the evolution of Lewis's dual economy is consistent with Kuznets's hypothesis (1955) that the distribution of income at first becomes less equal as development proceeds and does not improve until industry accounts for a rather large share of national income.

There has been some dispute as to whether the marginal product of labour in the subsistence sector must be zero for Lewis's argument to go through. As should now be clear, all that matters is that the capitalist sector be able to attract workers at a constant real wage as it expands. Whether this constancy comes about through population growth, changing attitudes towards the participation of women in the labour force, a constant marginal product of labour in the subsistence sector, or some combination thereof is immaterial. Once the real wage begins to rise, however, Lewis's story is at an end.

Lewis's economy is certainly 'dual', in the sense that reproducible capital is used only in the capitalist sector and output per worker is much higher in that sector. Yet nowhere in the above account has it been necessary to appeal to increasing returns. This prompts one to ask whether Lewis's account of the development of the dual economy needs to be modified for successive waves of latecomers. If, at the outset, latecomers adopt more 'advanced' techniques, as embodied in large scale plants, dualism will be sharper than it was in pioneers. A higher rate of profit will yield a higher rate of growth of the capitalist sector, but if the latest techniques are adopted for their own sake, that will scarcely improve profits. Moreover, if such techniques employ fewer workers for each unit of investment, employment in the capitalist sector will be lower in latecomers than in pioneers at a comparable stage of development. Hence, the onset of rising real wages as a result of a depleted reserve army in the subsistence sector will be delayed. Dualism, therefore, will be not only sharper, but also more protracted than was the case historically.

4. GROWTH AND TRADE. Section 1 dealt mainly with the transfer of knowledge, albeit some of it embodied in specific capital goods and skilled workers. The consequences of trade between pioneers and latecomers will now be addressed in greater detail.

In the early literature, the thesis that the net barter terms of trade have a secular tendency to move against latecomers, which are presumably exporters of primary products, was stated by Prebisch (1950) and Singer (1950). This adverse shift stems, so the argument runs, from a combination of low price and income elasticities of demand for such products and an alleged bias towards the saving of raw materials in technical progress in industrialized countries. Thus, economic forces in pioneers produce damaging effects on latecomers. If true, the thesis implies that the later the start, the greater the difficulties of getting started. It was also used to support the argument that industrialization in latecomers should not be shaped by the prevailing structure of world prices for traded goods.

In the orthodox view, the individual latecomer to industrialization is a small country facing parametric prices for traded goods, in a given state of knowledge and with given endowments and tastes. The latecomer has the potential advantage of access to a larger set of techniques through transfers of knowledge, though the modern theory of distortions warns us that the right economic policies are needed to realize this advantage (Bhagwati and Ramaswami, 1963). As for the opportunities presented by trade, these are completely summarized by world prices. The latter may be more or less favourable to today's latecomers than those of a century ago, but the only relevant thing is their structure. There is no room in this account for the explicit operation of the kind of 'system' embracing pioneers and latecomers that is central to the dependencia school. If there were such a mechanism, the movements of the barter terms of trade would be, for the orthodox, a sufficient statistic of its inner working.

Accepting this conclusion for the moment, what has actually happened to the barter terms of trade between pioneers and contemporary latecomers over the past century? Despite fierce controversy, the answer is: probably not much (Spraos, 1980). This agnostic conclusion is strengthened if allowance is made for improvements in the quality of manufactures, which are inadequately reflected in individual price series. If a recent and much shorter period is taken – the one favoured by proponents of the Prebisch–Singer thesis is from the peak of the Korean boom to the recession of the early 1980s – and petroleum is excluded, then things do look rather bleak for latecomers. The appeal to such a short period is, however, questionable. Thus, theory and the facts appear to combine to confer a distinct advantage on today's latecomers.

It is still interesting to examine the gloomy case. Suppose, therefore, that manufactures become more expensive relative to primary commodities, which are exported. The standard 2×2 model tells us that with given knowledge and endowments, the domestic output of manufactures will increase. If the objective is a larger share for industry, the shift in relative prices is welcome – though there is an attendant loss of real income.

The assumption of just two goods and perfectly malleable and mobile capital may, however, obscure rather than illuminate matters. Industrial capital, in the sense of plant and equipment, is made up of produced goods. In the shorter run, this stock is specific and fixed. Over the longer run, latecomers cannot augment it by drawing upon a stock of malleable stuff called capital that was previously employed in the sector producing primary commodities for export. The plant and equipment in question is produced only in pioneers: for latecomers, it is a non-competitive import, and must be paid for with primary exports.

To capture this aspect, three goods are needed: primary exportables; standard manufactures, including simple producer goods like cement and fertilizers, plants for which can be bought off the shelf; and sophisticated producer goods, including cement and fertilizer plants. Now, with three goods, the conditions for technology and tastes to be well-behaved do not always suffice to ensure uniqueness of equilibrium; so that the usual caveat applies to what follows. When the relative price of manufactures rises, a shift towards standard manufactures at the expense of primary exportables looks attractive; but the purchasing power of exports over producer goods falls even with unchanged domestic production, so that an important element in the cost of producing standard manufactures also rises in terms of primary commodities. If (i) the real wage declines and (ii) domestic labour is a good substitute for producer goods, a substantial shift towards standard manufactures may still be profitable. Even though condition (i) may be satisfied, (ii) looks distinctly dubious, so that only a modest shift may be warranted. More generally, if producer goods from pioneers form a large and indispensable component of capital formation in latecomers, adverse movements in the barter terms of trade will certainly slow accumulation in the latter. For domestic savings measured in units of exportables are likely to fall, too. This, therefore, is a fairly orthodox argument that the industrialization of latecomers may be set back by a secular decline in their terms of trade – if such a process is at work.

In a departure from orthodoxy, consider the effects of increasing returns in the form of learning-by-doing. Here, knowledge is not freely transferable, but must be acquired through independent effort and experience. The people who acquire such knowledge become specific factors by virtue of their experience, and so are produced factors. Thus, if latecomers and pioneers face nominally identical prices, pioneers will have lower costs: latecomers will catch up, but they cannot compete. This apparent paradox is resolved if pioneers encounter rising costs as the gains from learning are largely exhausted. Rising real wages in pioneers, for example, will then open the door to competition from latecomers. Industries which are mature in the sense of having little further scope for learning-by-doing will tend to shift from pioneers to latecomers, leading to product-cycle trade.

Some arguments for the (temporary) protection of infant industries also hinge on an appeal to learning-by-doing, but some care is needed. If all the effects thereof are internal to the individual firm, capital markets are perfect and there are no other distortions, there is no case for protection. If learning-by-doing does produce factors and inventive activity in the form of adaptation that are not wholly specific to the firm, then there is a prima facie case for protecting industry in latecomers at the expense of agriculture, given that such externalities are weak or non-existent in agricultural pursuits. It is not, however, an argument for uniform protection, since there are scant grounds for supposing that all industries produce equally strong externalities of this sort.

We must now consider what the existence of international trading opportunities at parametric prices does to the arguments for balanced growth. In the face of perfectly elastic demand schedules, the prisoner's dilemma problem vanishes for firms considering the production of tradeables. Moreover, there will be no reasons for (static) economies of scale to remain unexploited for want of demand. The only reservation here is that the 'natural' wedge between c.i.f. and f.o.b. prices be not so large as to make domestic prices appreciably sensitive to domestic demand and cost conditions. With this proviso, the problem of economic coordination that was the focus of Section 2 disappears.

Does this sound the knell for balanced growth and the Investment Board? Not quite; for there are still the non-tradeables to be considered, some of which – utilities, transportation and communications, for example – have precisely the characteristics of increasing returns and lumpiness in investment which sharpen the argument for some form of central coordination. Thus, there seems to be a sort of reprieve for balanced growth doctrine, the exact form of which is deferred until the next section.

5. PROTECTION AND COST–BENEFIT ANALYSIS. As it turned out, industry in the Third World has grown at a fast clip since 1950, though somewhat more slowly since 1974. Both the pace and pattern of industrial growth have been influenced by a plethora of protective tariffs, subsidies, rebates, quotas and licences, as well as direct investments by activist states. These interventions began to attract the attention of development economists in the sixties, many of whom were exercised by the effects of these interventions on incentives and resource allocation. The patterns of nominal protection revealed, on further investigation, quite higgledy-piggledy structures of effective protection, the only discernible regularity being the taxation of agriculture and the subsidization of industries as a group, and especially those producing consumer goods (Balassa, 1971; Little, Scitovsky and Scott, 1970).

In such a setting, market prices are a poor, if not quite misleading, guide to relative scarcities. To get at the latter, however, something more precise and firmly grounded in theory is needed than the concept of effective protection, particularly in the face of imperfections in factor markets. Rigorous foundations were supplied by the theory of optimal taxation (Diamond and Mirrlees, 1971), which yielded an important and fairly robust result: that, in the small country case, the relative scarcities of tradeable goods are the same as their relative world prices. Thus, the point of departure is the same as that for a calculation of effective protection. Next, suppose that non-tradeables are produced under constant returns to scale with no joint production. Then, if the shadow price of a non-tradeable is equal to its social marginal cost of production, we have

$$p'_N = p'_T A_{TN} + p'_N A_{NN} + \omega l_N \tag{1}$$

where p'_N and p'_T are the vectors of shadow prices of non-tradeables and tradeables, respectively, A_{NN} and A_{TN} are their respective submatrices of input-output coefficients for producing non-tradeables, ω is the shadow wage rate and l_N is the vector of labour input coefficients for non-tradeables. The shadow wage rate, in turn, comprises the value of the worker's marginal product (at shadow prices) in alternative employment (m) plus the social cost of the worker's additional consumption, if any, arising out of his transfer from such alternative employment.

$$\omega = m + \lambda(p'_T, p'_N)b \cdot \Delta y \tag{2}$$

where b is the vector of the amounts of goods consumed by the worker out of an extra unit of income, Δy is the increase in income arising from a shift from alternative employment and λ is the social value of an extra unit of private income relative to the *numéraire*, which in this case is uncommitted government income. Given p_T, λ, b, Δy and the technology for producing

non-tradeables (A_{TN}, A_{NN}, l_N), the shadow prices of non-tradeables and labour follow at once from (1) and (2).

This, in essence, is the scheme advocated by Little and Mirrlees (1969), a work that has been deeply influential since its appearance. Non-tradeables are produced by means of tradeables, non-tradeables and labour; labour, in turn, produces tradeables or non-tradeables in alternative employment and spends any extra income on tradeables and non-tradeables. Thus, non-tradeables and labour can be decomposed ultimately into tradeables valued at world prices, a process of decomposition which corresponds to the matrix inversion needed to solve (1) and (2) for p_N and ω.

What does all this have to do with balanced growth? In the balanced growth schema, all goods are non-tradeables at the margin. Specializing (1) and (2) appropriately, it is immediately clear that, aside from commodity taxes, market prices will then diverge from shadow prices only if there is a distortion in the labour market or savings are deemed socially suboptimal ($\lambda < 1$). In most LDCs, one can safely assume one or the other, if not both, so that trade and other tax distortions aside, market prices are still not 'right'.

When tradeables are introduced at parametric world prices, all shadow prices get anchored to the latter. Yet the derived demands for non-tradeables arising from the extra output and final consumption of non-tradeables are very much at work in (1) and (2). Indeed, they are precisely expressed by the matrix inversion that yields p_N and ω. It should be added that labour is usually assumed to be drawn ultimately from a 'subsistence' sector, where its marginal product is constant (not necessarily zero) but income is lower than in organized employment. Thus, the 'dual' economy makes an appearance, too. Shorn of increasing returns and straitjacketed by international trading opportunities at parametric prices, this is the residue of balanced growth doctrine to have survived in the modern approach to assessing the social profitability of projects in distortion-ridden economies.

The focus on projects rather than plans is significant. True, good plans need good projects; but in the balanced growth scheme of things what is a good project cannot be determined independently of all the other projects making up the plan. The salient feature of the system of shadow prices derived above, however, is that it permits investment decisions to be decentralized. When the Ministry of Industry considers a proposal to build a textile factory, it need not worry about road-building proposals before the Ministry of Works. This arrangement is a far cry from Rosenstein-Rodan's Investment Board; but one thing they do have in common is the use of similar information. A glance at (1) and (2) reveals that there is not much difference in procedure between the derivation of shadow prices and the sort of calculations pursued by the 'traditional' sort of planners with input–output models. Dismissal of the latter as outmoded, if not positively harmful, therefore implies distrust of the former, a connection that some critics of 'planning' seem not to have recognized.

Be all that as it may, the widespread adoption of systems of project appraisal based on the use of the world prices carries another implication. For the individual country, world prices are the pivot on which all scarcities turn. True, the shadow prices of non-tradeables and labour will not bear exactly the same relation to the shadow prices of tradeables across all countries; but the latter exercise such a strong influence on the former that world prices will often exert a decisive influence over what is judged to be profitable, especially where industrial projects are concerned. In that case, these systems of shadow prices seem to impose the disciplines of free trade by stealth. Taken individually, each latecomer should benefit if the necessary conditions for the associated shadow prices to reflect real scarcities are satisfied. Taken as a group, however, the allocation of resources thus induced may worsen the terms of trade, which each latecomer has taken as parametric, so that problems of coordination may reappear at another level.

6. CONCLUDING REMARKS. The early writings in development economics are by no means doctrinally monolithic. Some can claim a classical lineage, while others are eclectic. If they share anything in common, it is a distrust of the proposition that matters can be left to the market. Even here there are exceptions, Bauer's being a notable (and sustained) voice of dissent; see, for example, Bauer and Yamey (1957). In fairness to Bauer, it should be said that while he has extolled the unalloyed virtues of individual enterprise and the importance of keeping markets free of intervention, he has never advocated pure laissez-faire. On the whole, however, the early writings have a decidedly étatiste flavour.

Thereafter, there has been a steady intrusion of what can be loosely termed 'neoclassical' influences. In pursuing the themes of this essay, these influences have appeared in the shape of the theories of international trade and optimal taxation. Together, they have quite transformed the discussion of how industrialization should be approached. Even institutions do not survive unscathed: the full blooded Ministry of Planning is replaced by the mild-mannered Central Office of Project Evaluation. Where the other theme is concerned – that today's numerous latecomers are setting out in a world in which there are many mature pioneers – it is natural that international economics should have a prominent place in the study of development problems. Indeed, the ubiquitous term 'Trade and Development' suggests that the latter is a sort of dependent companion of the former. What is troubling is that the 'Trade' partner in this pairing is usually unswervingly neoclassical. Thus, the implicit claim that economic relations are mutually beneficial makes 'Development' appear as a corollary to 'Trade'. Perhaps the proposition is correct; but it needs critical scrutiny.

This suggests that development economics is being drawn back into the fold, where it might lose its claim to an independent existence. In that case, students of the subject would require no special preparation: the usual drilling in micro- and macroeconomics, suitably buttressed by field courses in trade, public economics and labour economics, would suffice. No doubt some movement of this sort is occurring. Yet two closing remarks are in order.

First, the traffic in ideas is not wholly in one direction. For example, in struggling to understand the persistent macroeconomic problems that have plagued Latin American economies for several decades, writers in both the 'structuralist' and orthodox traditions have influenced writing on mature economies. Similarly, the diverse contractual arrangements found in the markets for labour, tenancies and credit in agrarian economies have inspired a good deal of work in some branches of microeconomic theory, especially risk-sharing, incentives and the economics of information. (The peasant, who is the leading player in this drama, is no longer a creature of habit and tradition, but rather a relentless maximizer within the scope of the control variables at his disposal.)

Secondly, although it is difficult to sustain all of the structuralist's assumptions of rigidity in the face of the accumulated evidence of the responsiveness of individuals and markets, it does not follow that reservations about the efficacy of the market mechanism can be set aside. LDCs, in which insurance and forward markets are conspicuously thin and incomplete, are very far removed from the Arrow–Debreu

ideal; and in the absence of a complete set of markets, market outcomes will not, in general, be (constrained) efficient. Thus, (neoclassical) theory lends no immediate support to the contention that intervention will invariably make matters worse. One cannot, however, rush to the opposite conclusion: that the case for direct interventions and control by the state is, once more, nicely sewn up. Indirect intervention through the market may be superior to direct allocations, and doing nothing may be better than either. Whether to intervene and if so, in what form, will depend on circumstances. This sort of pragmatic tinkering will not appeal to doctrinal purists; but if development economics is to make further progress towards becoming a mature branch of applied economics, these are among the important questions to be posed and answered.

CLIVE BELL

See also COST-BENEFIT ANALYSIS; DUAL ECONOMIES; LABOUR-SURPLUS ECONOMIES; LINKAGES; PROJECT EVALUATION.

BIBLIOGRAPHY
Arrow, K.J. 1962. The economic implications of learning by doing. *Review of Economic Studies* 28(3), June, 155–73.
Balassa, B. et al. 1971. *The Structure of Protection in Developing Countries*. Baltimore: Johns Hopkins University Press.
Bauer, P.T. and Yamey, B.S. 1957. *The Economics of Underdeveloped Countries*. Chicago: University of Chicago Press.
Bhagwati, J.N. and Ramaswami, V.K. 1963. Domestic distortions, tariffs and the theory of optimum subsidy. *Journal of Political Economy* 71, February, 44–5.
Chenery, H.B. and Syrquin, M. 1975. *Patterns of Development. 1950–1970*. London: Oxford University Press.
Diamond, P. and Mirrlees, J.A. 1971. Optimal taxation and public production I: Production efficiency and II: Tax rules. *American Economic Review* 61, January and June, 8–27 and 261–8.
Domar, E.D. 1957. *Essays in the Theory of Economic Growth*. New York: Oxford University Press.
Fleming, J.M. 1955. External economies and the doctrine of balanced growth. *Economic Journal* 65, June, 241–56.
Gerschenkron, A. 1952. Economic backwardness in historical perspective. In *The Progress of Underdeveloped Countries*, ed. B. Hoselitz, Chicago: Chicago University Press.
Hirschman, A.O. 1958. *The Strategy of Economic Development*. New Haven: Yale University Press.
Kaldor, N. 1957. A model of economic growth. *Economic Journal* 67, December 591–624.
Kuznets, S.S. 1955. Economic growth and income inequality. *American Economic Review* 45, March, 1–28.
Kuznets, S.S. 1966. *Modern Economic Growth: Rate, Structure and Spread*. New Haven: Yale University Press.
Lewis, W.A. 1954. Economic development with unlimited supplies of labour. *Manchester School* 22, May, 139–91.
Little, I.M.D., and Mirrlees, J.A. 1969. *Manual of Industrial Project Analysis in Developing Countries*, Vol. II, *Social Cost-Benefit Analysis*. Paris: OECD.
Little, I.M.D., Scitovsky, T. and Scott, M. 1970. *Industry and Trade in Some Developing Countries*. London: Oxford University Press.
Mahalanobis, P.C. 1953. Some observations on the process of growth of national income. *Sankhya* 12(4), September, 307–12.
Nurkse, R. 1953. *Problems of Capital Formation in Underdeveloped Countries*. Oxford: Blackwell.
Prebisch, R. 1950. *The Economic Development of Latin America and Its Principal Problems*. New York: United Nations.
Rosenstein-Rodan, P.N. 1943. Problems of industrialization of Eastern and South-Eastern Europe. *Economic Journal* 53, June–September, 202–11.
Schumpeter, J.A. 1926. *Theorie der Wirtschaftlichen Entwicklung*. 2nd edn, Leipzig: Duncker & Humblot. Trans. as *The Theory of Economic Development*, Cambridge, Mass.: Harvard University Press, 1934.
Seers, D. 1969. The meaning of development. *International Development Review* 11(4), 2–6.

Singer, H.W. 1950. The distribution of gains between investing and borrowing countries. *American Economic Review, Papers and Proceedings* 40, May, 473–85.

Spraos, J. 1980. The statistical debate on the net barter terms of trade between primary commodities and manufactures. *Economic Journal* 90, March, 107–28.

Young, A.A. 1928. Increasing returns and economic progress. *Economic Journal* 38, December, 527–42.

development planning. Conscious plans for development of the economy as a whole over an extended period (say, five or ten years) were drawn up for the first time in the Soviet Union in the 1920s. The socialist countries of Eastern Europe, and the People's Republic of China have since then been the most consistent practitioners of development planning. However, the practice of drawing up development plans soon spread from the Soviet Union to non-socialist countries and some of the plans promulgated by the respective governments were also implemented, with different degrees of success.

In socialist countries, the broad outlines of the development plan have to be approved by the highest authority which may be the praesidium of the supreme legislative and executive body or the Party Congress convened for the purpose. However, the political and administrative authorities at the lower levels of administration, such as the county or the province, transmit information upwards regarding both the availability of resources and the felt needs of development. The actual implementation of the plan and the detailing of the outputs to be produced and the inputs to be used for executing the plan are delegated to the lower level authorities. As we shall see later, in socialist countries an almost continuous debate has been conducted regarding the degree of devolution of administrative authority and decentralization of economic decision-making. By and large, the central leadership in socialist countries have taken the decisions regarding the strategic and long-term variables, such as the rate and sectoral composition of investment, the degree of openness of the economy, and the allocation of resources as between different regions, while leaving the tactical or short-run production decisions to the lower-level authorities.

Long-term development plans have to be based on a depiction of the structure of the economy and its probable evolution under the influence of different types of intervention by the government. In the Soviet Union in the 1920s, inspiration for the construction of models of a planned economy was drawn mainly from the works of Karl Marx. (For an anthology of translations of Soviet writings on the subject, see Spulber, 1964.) In particular, by drawing on the schemes of expanded reproduction constructed by Marx (1893 and 1894), G.A. Fel'dman constructed a two-sector model of development by assuming the economy to be closed and dividing it into two vertically-integrated sectors, one producing capital goods and the other consumer goods (Fel'dman, 1928 and Domar, 1957). Fel'dman assumed that capital goods were the only limiting factor of production. An analytically equivalent model was constructed by P.C. Mahalanobis (1953). One interesting result of the Fel'dman–Mahalanobis model is the demonstration that given a constant technology and a constant capital–output ratio, the long-term rate of growth of the economy is determined by the proportion of investment devoted to the expansion of the capital goods sector.

In Fel'dman's model, the capital goods sector included all the intermediate goods needed for producing the final goods, as did the consumer goods sector. But the actual calculation of the output of a particular intermediate good needed to sustain a desired level of a particular capital good or consumer good could be made only after all the direct and indirect uses of the corresponding intermediate good had been traced. In trying to solve this problem, the Soviet planners early evolved the method of the material balances, under which, once, let us say, a given volume of output of finished steel had been decided upon, all the inputs directly and indirectly needed to sustain that level of output in the way of iron ore, coal, limestone, blast furnace and steel-smelting facilities, transport services and power would be worked out. This would generally involve several iterations until the demands and supplies of the different inputs converged. These exercises would be carried out for all the major items entering planning – and these could run to several hundred items (Montias, 1959).

Wassily Leontief later worked out what has come to be known as the input–output method of analysis, which can be regarded as the logical completion of the method of material balances. (For a succinct summary of the available elaborations of the input–output models used in plan exercises, see Taylor, 1975.)

In the Soviet Union and other socialist countries, considerable attention was paid to the use of mathematical methods for solution of large-scale planning problems and for finding out least-cost methods of carrying out given projects or programmes. The Russian mathematician L.V. Kantorovich has been credited with the discovery of the method of linear programming though the first convenient algorithm for solving such a programme was invented by G.B. Dantzig (Kantorovich, 1965). However, the real problems of planning in the Soviet Union and other socialist economies have centred on questions of the use of prices or simulation of planning by markets, on the degree of decentralization of decision-making, and on the level and composition of maintainable investment, rather than on questions of which techniques to use to draw up plans.

Socialist economies such as the Soviet Union and China, soon after the beginning of planning, attained very high rates of investment: the rate of investment during the first five-year plan in Russia went up, for example, from 15 per cent to 44 per cent of national income between 1928 and 1932 (Ellman, 1975). In China the ratio of investment to national income went up to 25 per cent at the end of her first five-year plan (1953–7), and in the 1970s the investment–income ratio generally stayed above 30 per cent. One result of the drive to raise the rate of investment and construction was that the huge labour surpluses in these countries which had been prevalent in pre-revolution days were mopped up after the first few years of planning.

The problems that the socialist countries typically faced were well summed up by Mao Zedong in his famous talk on the ten major relationships (Mao, 1956). According to Mao, in the context of Chinese development, maintenance of a balance was crucial in the relationships (i) between heavy industry, light industry and agriculture; (ii) between industry in coastal regions and industry in the interior; (iii) between civil investment and defence construction; (iv) between the state, the units of production and the actual producers; (v) between the central and local authorities; (vi) between Han, that is, the majority nationality, and the minority nationalities; (vii) between Communist Party authorities and cadres and non-members of the Party; (viii) between different policies fostering revolution rather than counter-revolution; (ix) between rewarding the correct policy-executors and punishing the wrongdoers; and (x) between China and the foreign countries. The relations (vi), (vii), (viii) and (ix) are political questions of broad importance involving socialist legality, the correct treatment of counter-revolutionary elements, but also questions with a mainly Chinese orientation. But the other relations involve mainly questions of economic strategy and have appeared in many different contexts. It has been felt in many socialist countries that not enough attention was paid until recently to the aim of raising the standards of living of the people. Too many resources were devoted to the development of heavy industry and too few to the growth of light industries catering for mass consumption (cf. Kalecki, 1969).

It was also felt that because of the highly centralized character of management, the stress on investment and a general atmosphere of scarcity within which managers were to achieve certain quantitative goals, there is a tendency at the enterprise level in a socialist economy to hoard resources and to invest too much (Kornai, 1980). Moreover, it was thought that in the drive to raise the rate of industrialization, while keeping prices stable by ensuring the supply of an adequate quantity of agricultural goods at fixed prices to the non-agricultural sector, plans had tended to discriminate against the rural producers. The allegation that Soviet industrialization was mainly financed by Russian peasants has been called into question by recent research (Ellman, 1975; Vyas, 1979). However, in many socialist countries, including China, moves have been made in recent years to increase the incomes of agricultural producers significantly and prices of agricultural products have been raised drastically with the same end in view. In China, deliberate attempts have also been made to bring down the ratio of accumulation (investment) to national income, to increase the rate of growth of light industry, and to provide greater incentives to peasants and industrial enterprises to change their product mix in response to changing demand patterns, to economize on scarce resources and to bring about a greater degree of flexibility of management (Ma Hong, 1983, and Xue Muqiao, 1981). But the chief instruments of adjustment and reform have been changes in prices paid to producers of specified goods, especially agricultural commodities, and political and administrative decentralization, rather than allowing producers to change their prices or their investment patterns independently of political authorities. The main underpinnings for an egalitarian distribution of income in the shape of a comprehensive public distribution and social security system and of stability in consumer prices have so far been maintained in all socialist economies. One reason for this is that there is no simple way in which an economy-wide reform can be instituted so that prices either equal prices of production or equalize supplies and demands in all markets but do not bring about other undesirable side-effects in the form of an increase in inequality of income distribution or unemployment.

Socialist economies have been concerned in recent years with making a transition from a regime of extensive to one of intensive growth, that is, from one where economic growth is accelerated by raising the rate of investment or the application of labour to one where it can be raised by increasing the productivity of agents of production. Economic reforms are seen as one means of doing this. Increasing the rate of innovation and adaptation and absorption of imported technology are seen as other means of doing this. It is in the latter area that the relations between socialist countries and advanced capitalist economies become crucial. Socialist economies are striving to import improved technologies from the USA, the EEC countries and Japan without becoming dependent on them or becoming heavily indebted to them. On the other side, the advanced capitalist countries are trying to increase their markets in socialist countries without selling them technologies which could make them economically or militarily stronger than the capitalist countries in the future.

The problems that the non-socialist countries have faced in formulating credible development plans have been far more complex than those discussed above and their success in implementing them has been far more mixed.

While the Soviet theorists and Mao took a socialist system to be the environment in which a development plan was to be located, most other theorists were not explicit about the kind of system they had in mind when they proposed specific plans for development of the underdeveloped economies. Paul Rosenstein-Rodan's pioneering attempt to formulate appropriate plans for development of the Eastern European countries after World War II can be taken to be the genesis of what came to be known as the 'balanced growth' doctrine (Rosenstein-Rodan, 1943). Ragnar Nurkse (1953) developed some of these ideas further in his writings. According to these theorists, in a poor underdeveloped economy, a credible development plan would have to consist of a programme for a simultaneous and balanced development of all the important sectors in the economy, so that expanding demands are met by matching supplies, and vice versa. Moreover, this process of balanced growth would lead to the realization of internal economies of scale and external effects arising from learning processes, and a decline in uncertainty faced by buyers, sellers and investors (see, in this connection, Dobb, 1960, ch. 1). Maurice Dobb (1951), Nurkse and Lewis (1954) all stressed the necessity and possibility of mobilizing underemployed and unemployed labour for the purpose of capital formation in underdeveloped economies.

The balanced growth doctrine has the advantage that it can be embodied in specific development plans elaborated out of the Fel'dman–Mahalanobis models, and the input–output models devised by Leontief and his co-workers and later followers. But even before such models had been elaborated to take account of all the interconnections involved in a dynamic income generation process, it was clear that in a non-socialist economy, a development plan, however well-formulated, was likely to run into problems because of the lack of concordance between planners' goals and private sector goals and lead to political side-effects which could derail it before it had really had time to run its course.

It is useful to analyse some of these problems by using the four-sector model of development which Mahalanobis (1955) used as the scaffolding for drawing up the draft second five-year plan of India. In this model, the economy is divided into four vertically integrated sectors, the first producing capital goods by factory methods, the second producing consumer goods by factory methods, the third producing consumer goods by handicraft methods and the fourth producing services by labour-intensive methods. The idea behind this classification was that a designated proportion of the output of capital goods industries would be devoted to their own expansion in order to promote growth, while the handicraft and service sectors would meet much of the demand for consumer goods and services generated by increasing incomes and at the same time mobilize underemployed and unemployed labour thus minimizing the need to divert investible resources to the factory sector for production of more consumer goods.

However, one of the basic conditions for employment of more labour would be that the new workers can be fed and clothed (Nurkse, 1953; Lewis, 1954). It cannot be assumed that some automatic mechanism would spring up for diverting food from the farms to factories in urban or rural areas. Kalecki (1955) was one of the first to emphasize the importance of ensuring a smooth supply of wage goods and keeping the rate of saving high by curbing consumption for financing development in Third World countries.

Most Third World countries were, however, characterized by various kinds of landlordism or other semi-feudal constraints such as debt bondage, the use of non-market coercion, etc., limiting farm output. The failure to carry out thorough-going land reforms which would vest the ownership and management of the land in the hands of the actual cultivators also meant that traders and moneylenders could continue to prosper by exacting extortionate margins on goods sold or bought and charging usurious interest rates on loans to the poor in the countryside. These conditions also facilitate political coalitions between landlords, traders and moneylenders blocking the process of reforms to endow the peasants with the incentive and wherewithal to produce more and meet the needs of industrialization.

As Kalecki (1955) realized, if the marketed surplus fails to go up, an increase in the rate of investment as envisaged by all development plans would soon meet an inflation barrier (since the income elasticity of the demand for food is high and its price elasticity is low). A rising output of farm products does not in itself guarantee a rising volume of marketed surplus. If the consumption of the suppliers of farm products rises proportionately more than farm output, then the marketed surplus will fall. With a landlord-dominated farm sector, traders and landlords generally command enough credit and other assets to ensure that the rest of society pays a stiffly rising price for farm products whenever the output of agriculture falters (say, because of adverse weather conditions or floods or pests). If the government can be persuaded to run a procurement programme so that it is committed to buying up any agricultural supplies coming on the market at a minimum price, but cannot force the landlords or traders to deliver the grain (or cotton or oilseeds) at that price, then a ratchet is put under the prices of farm products. Thus the physical rate of growth of farm output puts only an outside limit on the rate of growth of non-agricultural output: the actual limit (which is lower) is set by the ownership pattern of agricultural assets and by the conditions of sales of agricultural commodities. When the farm sector is dominated by landlords, the rate of growth of agricultural output interacts with such factors as luxury consumption of the rich, the tendency to speculation whenever the harvest is poor, the extremely skewed distribution of credit, and public support for farm prices to produce a constricting limit on industrial growth. In a socialist economy, with fixed prices of food grains, a comprehensive public distribution system and the abolition of speculation, a similar rate of agricultural growth would be consistent with a much higher rate of industrial development. (A non-socialist economy with a relatively egalitarian distribution of landholdings would pose lesser problems for growth than a landlord-dominated society.) Thus, referring back to the four-sector Mahalanobis model, it can be seen that mobilization of labour to produce labour-intensive consumer (or capital) goods would require as a precondition a durable solution of the problem of supply of the needed foodgrains and other agricultural goods.

It can also be seen that stepping up the rate of investment in the economy would require stepping up the rate of savings to an equivalent amount. Such a stepping up of saving would not normally occur on a voluntary basis in an underdeveloped economy which had been stagnating before the onset of development planning. So the government would have to tax the rich in order to release the necessary resources for investment and keep the demand for foodgrains and other goods with inelastic supplies within reasonable bounds (compare Kalecki, 1955).

However, in a non-socialist economy the government generally fails to curb the increase in the purchasing power in the hands of the rich to an adequate extent. The rich then not only demand and commandeer more of the scarce resources which should go into investment, they also do not purchase sufficient amounts of the handicrafts or the labour-intensive consumer goods which, in the four-sector Mahalanobis model, are supposed to satisfy the increasing demands released in the economy. Thus excess capacity emerges (or continues) in many sectors of the economy (including capital goods turned out by government and private factories), with attendant unemployment, even while there is excess demand in other sectors (see Bagchi, 1970). In particular, the rich generally demand newer types of luxury goods produced in the advanced capitalist countries. If these cannot be produced at home, they will be imported from abroad. Since the failure to step up the rate of aggregate saving to an adequate extent or channel investment into the sectors which accelerate the growth of the economy in any case lead to balance of payments deficits, most Third World countries attempting to plan their development will also have foreign trade regimes characterized by exchange controls, high tariffs on permitted imports, and quantitative restrictions on imports and exports. Under these circumstances, restricted importables will normally fetch high premia in domestic currency and it will be profitable to smuggle them in or produce them behind the walls of the high tariffs and quantitative restrictions of various kinds, thus leading to further diversion of resources.

Some of the difficulties underdeveloped countries faced in obtaining enough foreign capital inflows for financing development were approached via the so-called 'two-gap' models of aid, trade and development (Chenery and Bruno, 1962; Manne, 1963; and McKinnon, 1964). In these models, on plausible assumptions about the desired rate and pattern of growth, a gap between *ex ante* exports and imports and a parallel gap between *ex ante* investment and savings are estimated. Since exports of most underdeveloped primary-commodity-producing countries are price and income-inelastic, and many of them also face non-price barriers in trade, whereas their planned investment is often relatively import-intensive, it was often found that the *ex ante* trade gap was larger than the *ex ante* investment-saving gap (Landau, 1971). It was argued then that the planning authorities of the country concerned should plan to borrow or canvas for aid to cover the larger of the two gaps, and then development could proceed as planned.

Few countries were, however, in the happy position of being able to borrow or receive as aid whatever foreign capital inflow the planning exercises indicate as the optimum amount, even in the days when official grants and loans were less niggardly than they have become in the last decade or more. Moreover, the two-gap models themselves did not indicate the desirable or the feasible method of adjustment of the two gaps to each other *ex post*, and to the amount of foreign capital actually received. Even if the foreign aid or loans equalled the larger of the two gaps, the planning authorities could not leave the adjustment process to autonomous market forces, but had to adopt specific policies to bring about an appropriate adjustment process (Vanek, 1967, ch. 6). When the foreign trade gap is dominant, for example, it is appropriate to allow savings to go down, in order to make the investment–savings gap rise to the export–import gap rather than stimulate (import-intensive) investment and increase the trade gap further. Under a wide variety of conditions, both policy-induced and market-induced adjustment processes would lead to a rise in consumption and a slowing down of investment (because of the uncertainty as regards the availability of imports and because of inventory accumulation as a result of excess capacity in import-constrained sectors). Thus where foreign capital inflows are a binding constraint, a negative relation may well be observed between inflows of aid and domestic savings effort (Rahman, 1968; Griffin, 1970).

Moreover, with overvalued foreign exchange and with a perceived disadvantage in investing in fields requiring new, foreign-controlled technology, there may also be hidden outflows of domestic capital to safe havens of hoarding or investment even while a substantial amount of foreign capital is coming in under official auspices.

Besides two-gap models, there were other advances in the understanding of development plans. It was realized that where the supply of foreign exchange was a constraint, planners might try to build up intersectoral linkages so as to provide for machines to produce machines or produce higher-order intermediate goods, and so attempt to accelerate economic development to the maximum possible extent (Raj and Sen, 1961). Optimizing exercises involving time-lags could be carried out with the same class of models. However, the implementation of the indicated development plans by non-socialist developed countries would flounder on their inability (a) to buy the technology, which was often patented or otherwise owned by transnational corporations, on reasonable terms, (b) to devise appropriate social and organizational mechanisms for absorbing and diffusing the technology, and for exacting the needed savings and allocation of investment out of the economy (see Bagchi, 1982, ch. 9).

In the field of application of input–output analysis and social accounting matrices to development plan models there have also been significant advances. Although it was sometimes suggested that different clusters of industries of the economy (such as heavy industry, light industry and agriculture) could grow at very different rates, because the current input–output flow system regularly displayed gaps between some sectors and close ties as between others (Manne and Rudra, 1965), it was realized that the flows of demands generated by the planning process would tie the growth patterns of different sectors tightly together, as we have seen already. Significant advances have been made in applying the social accounting matrices to plan models, and the implicit multipliers relating the growth of particular sectors or factor incomes to the rest of the economy have been utilized to predict the income generation and distributional implications of different patterns of plan expenditures (Pyatt and Round, 1979; Taylor, 1979).

However, it is one thing to devise models for development and another thing to implement them in underdeveloped countries with big landlords, propertied classes which are divided among themselves and which are continually attracted to the metropolitan centres by the lure of more modern life styles, safety of investments against threats of revolutions, and other considerations. Rosenstein-Rodan (1943) had conceived of the development plan as being carried out by a 'trust' which could internalize all external effects and all secondary effects of investment. In actual fact the limits of organization either through the market or in firms or governmental organizations, and the temptation to resort to opportunistic behaviour to the detriment of the collective good have been far more prevalent in non-socialist underdeveloped countries than in the socialist economies. The propertied, or more narrowly, capitalist groups have found it very difficult to evolve codes of cooperation without which confidence in the future and long-term investment become very fragile plants (see Axelrod, 1984).

Even while the balanced growth doctrine was being evolved, Albert Hirschman had proposed exploiting the profitability-signalling property of disequilibrium situations to recommend a path of development along which imbalances were deliberately engineered (Hirschman, 1958). In fact, as it turned out, capitalists more often reacted the 'wrong' way to disequilibria, by cornering scarce commodities, using political levers to raise barriers against entry into their favoured pastures, playing intertemporal arbitrage games to defeat the planners' intentions (see Bagchi, 1966; Hirschman, 1968). The obstacles to the execution of development plans in non-socialist countries had been foreseen in the 1950s by many Marxists, of whom Paul Baran was the most prominent, (Baran, 1952, 1957), and by other social scientists such as Gunnar Myrdal (1957). In the general atmosphere of crisis in the world economy, there is sometimes an agreement between proponents at both extremes of the political spectrum that development planning is impossible in Third World countries. What both experience and analysis indicate, however, is that the implementation of development plans is likely to be fraught with contradictions. There will be imbalances between regions, increasing differentiation of peasantry, tensions between development of the public and private sectors, conflicts between interests of local development and interests of transnational corporations and their local collaborators, and questions will be raised and often resolved through bloody confrontations regarding the appropriate political regimes. It is through the mobilization of ordinary people to tackle these manifold contradictions and to fight the vested interests blocking the progress of development programmes that further advances will be made. National planning, in that sense, has been and will always be, intimately tied up with politics. But for most Third World countries development planning remains an essential part of the programme for charting their own future.

AMIYA KUMAR BAGCHI

See also FEL'DMAN, GREGORII ALEXANDROVICH; MAHALANOBIS, PRASANTHA CHANDRA; PLANNED ECONOMY.

BIBLIOGRAPHY
Axelrod, R. 1984. *The Evolution of Cooperation.* New York: Basic Books.
Bagchi, A.K. 1966. Shadow prices, controls and tariff protection in India. *Indian Economic Review*, New Series, 1(1), April, 22–44.
Bagchi, A.K. 1970. Long-term constraints on India's industrial growth 1951–8. In *Economic Development in South Asia*, ed. E.A.G. Robinson and M. Kidron, London: Macmillan.
Bagchi, A.K. 1982. *The Political Economy of Underdevelopment.* Cambridge: Cambridge University Press.
Baran, P.A. 1952. The political economy of backwardness. *Manchester School of Economic and Social Studies* 20(1), January, 66–84.
Baran, P.A. 1957. *The Political Economy of Growth.* New York: Monthly Review Press.
Chenery, H.B. and Bruno, M. 1962. Development alternatives in an open economy: the case of Israel. *Economic Journal* 72, March, 79–103.
Dobb, M.H. 1951. *Some Aspects of Economic Development.* Delhi: Delhi School of Economics.
Dobb, M.H. 1960. *An Essay on Economic Growth and Planning.* London: Routledge & Kegan Paul.
Domar, E. 1957. A Soviet model of growth. In E. Domar, *Essays in the Theory of Economic Growth*, New York: Oxford University Press.

Eckstein, A. 1977. *China's Economic Revolution.* Cambridge: Cambridge University Press.

Ellman, M. 1975. Did the agricultural surplus provide the resources for the increase in investment in the USSR during the first five year plan? *Economic Journal* 85, December, 844–63.

Fel'dman, G.A. 1928. K teorii narodnogo dokhoda. *Planvoe khoziaistvo* 11, 12. Trans. as 'On the theory of growth rates of national income', I and II, in Spulber (1964).

Griffin, K. 1970. Foreign capital, domestic savings and economic development. *Bulletin of the Oxford University Institute of Economics and Statistics* 32(2), May, 99–112.

Hirschman, A. 1958. *The Strategy of Economic Development.* New Haven: Yale University Press.

Hirschman, A. 1968. The political economy of import-substituting industrialization in Latin America. *Quarterly Journal of Economics* 82(1), February, 1–32.

Kalecki, M. 1955. The problem of financing economic development. *Indian Economic Review* 2(3), February, 1–22.

Kalecki, M. 1969. *Introduction to the Theory of Growth in a Socialist Economy.* Oxford: Basil Blackwell.

Kantorovich, L.V. 1965. *The Best Use of Economic Resources.* Oxford: Pergamon.

Kornai, J. 1980. *Economics of Shortage.* 2 vols, Amsterdam: North-Holland.

Landau, L. 1971. Saving functions for Latin America. In *Studies in Development Planning*, ed. H.B. Chenery et al., Cambridge, Mass.: Harvard University Press.

Lewis, W.A. 1954. Economic development with unlimited supplies of labour. *Manchester School of Economic and Social Studies* 22, May, 139–91.

Lockett, M. and Littler, C.R. 1983. Trends in Chinese enterprise management 1978–1982. *World Development* 11(8), August, 683–704.

McKinnon, R.I. 1964. Foreign exchange constraints in economic development and efficient aid allocation. *Economic Journal* 74, June, 388–409.

Mahalanobis, P.C. 1953. Some observations on the process of growth of national income. *Sankhya* 12(4), September, 307–12.

Mahalanobis, P.C. 1955. The approach of operational research to planning in India. *Sankhya* 16(1 and 2), December, 3–130.

Ma Hong. 1983. *New Strategy for China's Economy.* Beijing: New World Press.

Manne, A. 1963. Key sectors of the Mexican economy. In *Studies in Process Analysis*, ed. A.Manne and H.M. Markowitz, New York: John Wiley.

Manne, A. and Rudra, A. 1965. A consistency model of India's Fourth Plan. *Sankhya*, Series B 27(1 and 2), September, 57–144.

Mao Zedong. 1956. On the ten major relationships. In *Selected Works of Mao Tse-tung*, Vol. V, Peking: Foreign Languages Press, 1977.

Marx, K. 1893. *Capital: A Critique of Political Economy*, Vol. II. Trans. from the 2nd German edn of 1893, ed. F. Engels, Moscow: Foreign Languages Publishing House, 1957.

Marx, K. 1894. *Capital: A Critique of Political Economy*, Vol. III. Trans. from original German edn of 1894, ed. F. Engels, Moscow: Foreign Languages Publishing House, 1966.

Montias, J.M. 1959. Planning with material balances in Soviet-type economies. *American Economic Review* 49, December, 963–85.

Myrdal, G. 1957. *Economic Theory and Underdeveloped Regions.* London: Duckworth.

Nurkse, R. 1953. *Problems of Capital Formation in Underdeveloped Countries.* Oxford: Basil Blackwell.

Nuti, D.M. 1981. Socialism on earth. *Cambridge Journal of Economics* 5(4), December, 391–403.

Pyatt, G. and Round, R.I. 1979. Accounting and fixed price multipliers in a social accounting matrix framework. *Economic Journal* 89(356), December, 850–73.

Rahman, M.A. 1968. Foreign capital and domestic savings: a test of Haavelmo's hypothesis with cross-country data. *Review of Economics and Statistics* 50, February, 137–8.

Raj, K.N. and Sen, A.K. 1961. Alternative patterns of growth under conditions of stagnant export earnings. *Oxford Economic Papers* 13(1), February, 43–52.

Rosenstein-Rodan, P.N. 1943. Problems of industrialisation of eastern and south-eastern Europe. *Economic Journal* 53, June–September, 202–11.

Spulber, N. (ed.) 1964. *Foundations of Soviet Strategy for Economic Growth: Selected Soviet Essays, 1924–1930.* Bloomington, Indiana: Indiana University Press.

Taylor, L. 1975. Theoretical foundations and technical implications. In *Economy-Wide Models and Development Planning*, ed. C.R. Blitzer, P.B. Clark and L. Taylor, London: Oxford University Press.

Taylor, L. 1979. *Macro Models for Developing Countries.* New York: McGraw-Hill.

Vanek, J. 1967. *Estimating Foreign Resource Needs for Economic Development: Theory, Method and a Case Study of Colombia.* New York: McGraw-Hill.

Vyas, A. 1979. Primary accumulation in the USSR revisited. *Cambridge Journal of Economics* 3(2), June, 119–30.

Xue Muqiao. 1981. *China's Socialist Economy.* Beijing: Foreign Languages Press.

De Viti de Marco, Antonio. *See* VITI DE MARCO, ANTONIO DE.

dialectical materialism. Dialectical materialism is what Engels in the Preface to the second edition of the *Anti–Dühring* calls 'the communist world outlook'. The term 'dialectical materialism' was probably first used by 'the father of Russian Marxism', Plekhanov, in 1891. It was unknown to Marx himself. Engels came close to coining it, and it was in fact Engels who was chiefly responsible for founding dialectical materialism: the relevant books are his *Anti-Dühring* (published 1877–8), *Dialectics of Nature* (written 1878–82, first published 1927) and *Ludwig Feuerbach and the End of Classical German Philosophy* (published 1886–8).

Marx's distinctive intellectual work was a theory of society, specifically of economics as the basis of society, and in particular, in his *Capital*, of the economics of capitalism. This social theory is known as 'historical materialism'. Dialectical materialism is distinguished from and related to historical materialism in various ways. For a start, it is a theory not simply about society but about reality as a whole, nature as well as society. The presupposition of dialectical materialism, in the words of the Preface to the second edition of the *Anti-Dühring*, is that 'in nature ... the same ... laws ... force their way through as those which in history govern ... events'. Thus the basic theories of dialectical materialism are formulated as laws of a completely universal application, governing 'nature, society, and thought' (*Anti-Dühring*, pt. I, ch. xiii). Second, in accordance with this claim of complete universality, dialectical materialism is generally regarded as philosophy, whereas historical materialism claims to be not philosophy but science, social science. Third, and further to its status as philosophy rather than science, it yields a very general account of the structural relations of the special sciences.

What we have here is a traditional rather than distinctively modern conception of philosophy and its relation to science. A philosophy is a 'world outlook', a synoptic view of the totality of things achieved in this case by revealing in the special sciences a common content, an underlying general conception of reality that they all share and express. This philosophy is therefore itself regarded as scientific, a kind of 'natural philosophy' exemplified in and supported by the findings of the special sciences as they investigate their own limited domains of reality.

Engels' case for dialectical materialism has a special political point for Marxism: namely to argue its scientificity. The case is that historical materialism shares with the natural sciences not, or not only, a method of inquiry but the same 'world outlook'. Historical materialism's claim to scientific status is of crucial importance to it. Marxism rejects as more or less unscientific both other (bourgeois) social theories and other forms of socialism such as ethical or utopian socialism. It seeks to recruit to its support the cognitive authority of science, distinguishing itself within the socialist movement as what Engels called 'scientific socialism'.

With the rise of the bourgeoisie, the Scientific Revolution and Enlightenment had seen the establishment of the natural sciences of astronomy, physics and chemistry. But it was not until the late 18th and early 19th centuries that the social sciences began to develop, in a process in which social theory sought to transform itself from philosophy into science. When in the 1840s Marx and Engels embarked on their construction of a unified and comprehensive social science they rejected as models not only the existing (bourgeois) forms of social theory, such as classical political economy, but also the earlier forms of the modern natural sciences. In their view each major social revolution, basically in the dominant mode of production, involves also an ideological revolution, a revolution in world outlook. Thus in the transition from feudalism to capitalism the religion-dominated ideology of the Middle Ages had given way to a general conception of reality shaped decisively by natural science. A central element in this 'natural philosophy' of the bourgeois era was the so-called 'mechanical philosophy'. According to this, the objective reality investigated by science is a mechanism of matter in motion, a kind of cosmic clockwork, and understanding this reality is knowing the laws governing the mechanism. Between this and the new world outlook of the rising working class there would be both continuities and breaks, but even the breaks would be prepared in bourgeois society. Thus for Marx and Engels the natural sciences in the later part of the 18th century had already begun to change in a significant way, developing one of the most basic and characteristic aspects of the new communist point of view.

Newton has said that in the beginning God threw the planets round the sun, creating processes ruled by the laws of motion and gravity, processes of repetitive or cyclical movement in a system that itself remained essentially unchanged and unchanging. But the Kant–Laplace nebular hypothesis rejected this static conception and replaced it with a theory representing the present solar system as the latest stage in a long and continuing evolution. For Marx and Engels, what this showed was that 'Nature has a history' and that the natural sciences were themselves evolving from a static conception of nature towards a recognition of its historicity. Lyle's geology and Darwin's biology seemed to confirm this tendency.

The key to understanding this mode of non-cyclical (progressive) change, according to Marx and Engels, had already been prepared within philosophy, by Hegel. This key was the dialectic. They believed, however, that in Hegel the dialectic suffers a deformation characteristic of philosophy, especially bourgeois philosophy. Its form is idealist, not materialist. For Hegel, in other words, reality is ideal, is the activity and product of spirit or mind, so that its dialectical nature is its nature as an essentially non-material process.

Dialectical materialism, then, results from the crossing of two bourgeois philosophies, Hegel's dialectical idealism and the mechanistic materialism of the Scientific Revolution and Enlightenment. Hegel's idealism is incompatible with materialism, and the mechanicism of traditional materialism is incompatible with dialectic. They are therefore rejected, leaving a conception of reality that is both dialectical and materialist.

In this unification of dialectic and materialism both doctrines are transformed. Traditional materialism, being non-dialectical, is reductive, a 'nothing-but' theory: it holds that reality is nothing but matter in motion, and thus that processes that appear to be otherwise are really not otherwise because they are 'reducible' to matter in motion. Ideas, for example, are reducible to and ultimately identical with material processes. On this view change itself, that is the development of difference and novelty, is really nothing but the continuation of the same basic processes and laws. The dialectical point of view, on the contrary, claims that concrete reality is a unity, but a differentiated unity in which the elements are all essentially interrelated and integrated but not reducible to one another. Indeed, differentiation means opposition and contradiction. Thus the material and ideal themselves are really different and opposed, but they exist and are related within a unity in which the material is basic: matter can exist without mind but not mind without matter. Epistemologically, then, physics yields, contrary to idealism, knowledge of an objective mind-independent reality, and forms the base of a unified system of the special sciences that, contrary to traditional materialism, are nevertheless not reducible to physics. Moreover, differentiation is not a static condition but an active process. Reality is a unity that is specifically contradictory, and it is the conflict of opposites within unity that drives reality onwards in a historical process of progressive change. This change is both evolutionary and revolutionary, both quantitative and qualitative: its revolutionary or discontinuous moments yield genuine novelty, change of a qualitative kind. Mind itself on this view is such an emergent novelty.

This dialectical world outlook is standardly summarized in the form of three fundamental laws: (1) the law of the unity of opposites, according to which concrete reality is a unity in conflict, a unity that is contradictory; (2) the law of the negation of the negation, which says that in the conflict of opposites one term negates the other, but preserves something of the negated term and is then itself negated in a historical process that in this way rises to ever higher levels; (3) the law of the transformation of quantity into quality, which says that in the evolutionary process of gradual quantitative change contradictions intensify to the point at which a revolutionary qualitative change occurs. The popularized version of these laws represents dialectic as a triadic process of thesis, antithesis and synthesis.

Dialectic claims to revolutionize our thinking at all levels, including – even most particularly – the intellectually fundamental level of logic. Among its most controversial elements is its use of the logical category of contradiction. Dialectic presupposes the doctrine that there are contradictions in reality, and is thought to imply that therefore traditional formal logic, with its central principle of non-contradiction, must be superseded by a logic that permits contradictory propositions as true of this contradictory reality. The orthodox rejoinder has argued that two *ideas* can be contradictory but that such ideas cannot both be true, i.e. that reality itself cannot be contradictory. Hegel rejects this distinction between ideas and reality, but may be seen as ultimately accepting, through his idealism, the orthodox view that contradiction is a relation between ideas. What is distinctive, even outrageous, about dialectical materialism is that it takes the logical category of contradiction to be applicable to material reality.

What are the implications of dialectical materialism for

economics? Economic theory, on this view, takes the form of laws in which major contradictions are identified within the processes of production, exchange, and distribution, and are used to explain historical change in society. In particular, these laws reveal how the gradual intensification of contradictions leads to crisis and ultimately to a revolution in which a qualitatively new economic system establishes itself.

But dialectical materialism has implications not only for the form of economic theory but also for the relation in which economics stands to the other social sciences, such as political science. First, the totalizing perspective of dialectic, according to which all things are so closely integrated that they can be understood only in their interrelation, rejects the conception of economics as a specialist social science capable of understanding its own domain of social phenomena independently of other domains and other social sciences. For the dialectic, economics is less a social science than an integral part or aspect of social science, of a comprehensive and unified theory about a unified, if contradictory, social totality. Second, however, materialism asserts that within the social totality economic processes have overriding importance. The general philosophical materialism associated with the rise of natural science contrasts matter with mind and ideas, and holds that matter is the most fundamental, or even the only ultimate, component of reality. In application to society in distinction from nature, materialism contrasts ideas and theory with practice and claims that the most fundamental aspect of any social system is its most material practice, its economic practice, and in particular its mode of (material) production. Thus for dialectical materialism, social structure and social change in general are explained ultimately in terms of economic structure and economic change. Economics is the most basic part of social science.

Indeed, under the sway of dialectical materialism Marxism has tended to exaggerate this doctrine to the point of vulgarization. In representing the scientificity of historical materialism as consisting in its sharing a world outlook with the natural sciences, dialectical materialism conceives historical materialism as a natural science of society. This attempt to combine dialectic and materialism within the general perspective of natural science has been a standing temptation to leave within 'the communist world outlook' unreconstructed residues from the bourgeois world outlook. The result has been a variety of intellectual pressures converging on an influential distortion, namely the vulgar version of Marxism that Lenin labelled 'economism'.

On the side of dialectic, the orthodox view that contradiction, as a logical relation, is a relation between ideas seems incompatible with its application to material reality. In consequence, the category of contradiction has tended to be identified with that of conflict (conflict of forces) and its specifically logical and critical content evacuated. What this has helped to undermine is the possibility of conceiving the social science of historical materialism as social *critique*.

On the side of materialism, classical scientific materialism is reductive and determinist, and conceives of 'matter' as an inert substance subject to 'iron laws' of nature. For a Marxism under the influence of this tendency, the political and theoretical superstructure are epiphenomena of society's material base. Only that material base, the economy, and perhaps only its most material aspect, technology, has real causal agency. The effect of this on socialist strategy is anti-Marxist: concentration on working-class action within the economic base rather than its extension to politics and the state. In fact, even this limited activity is threatened as either impossible or unnecessary by the conception of the science of

economics encouraged by a materialism of the natural science sort. Though it was Engels who was chiefly responsible for dialectical materialism, Marx himself sometimes lends support to this version of economics. In the Preface to the first German edition of *Capital* he refers to 'the natural laws of capitalist production' as 'tendencies working with iron necessity towards inevitable results'; and in the Afterword to the second German edition he speaks favourably of the reviewer who says that 'Marx treats the social movement as a process of natural history, governed by laws not only independent of human will, consciousness and intelligence, but rather, on the contrary, determining that will, consciousness and intelligence ...'. Whatever space this leaves for socialist action, if any, it seems inadequate for anything as large in scale and conscious in purpose as revolutionary class war. Lenin, though a committed believer in dialectical materialism, found it necessary to argue persistently against the anti-revolutionary tendencies of economism.

Marx once declared that he was not a Marxist. It was among the first generation of his followers after Marx's death that Marxism took shape, in the period that culminated in the Russian Revolution. Those followers learned their Marxism chiefly from the two most famous books of the founders, Marx's *Capital* and Engels' *Anti-Dühring*, the former regarded as constituting the basic economic science of historical materialism, the latter the philosophy of Marxism, specifically dialectical materialism. Dialectical materialism was an essential component of that first-generation Marxism, the generation of the Second International. It became, and remained, equally central to Soviet communism and to the Communist Party orthodoxy established under Soviet leadership. Between the two world wars, as Soviet communism slid into the tyranny of Stalinist dictatorship and party bureaucracy, this first Marxist philosophy of dialectical materialism came under attack from within that part of the Marxist movement outside the USSR and began to give way to a second form of Marxist philosophy. This was Marxist humanism, since then the characteristic form of 'Western Marxism'. Its chief theorists were Lukacs, Korsch and Gramsci, followed by the thinkers of the Frankfurt School and by Sartre's attempt to fuse Marxism and Existentialism. They attacked the materialism of the natural sciences, and in emphasizing Marx's debt to Hegel and dialectic insisted on the necessary roles in social change of politics and ideology. Their revisions of Marxism found some confirmation in the rediscovery, in the 1920s and 1930s, of Marx's early writings, especially his *Economic and Philosophical Manuscripts* of 1844. In their turn, since the 1960s these Hegelianizing tendencies have themselves come under attack, chiefly from Althusser and his followers. But 'diamat' (to use the abbreviated name of dialectical materialism common in the USSR) has remained characteristic mainly of Soviet communism and of the Communist Parties dominated by Russia.

ROY EDGLEY

See also DIALECTICAL REASONING; ECONOMIC INTERPRETATION OF HISTORY; MODES OF PRODUCTION.

BIBLIOGRAPHY

Colletti, L. 1969. *Marxism and Hegel*. London: NewLeft Books, 1973.
Colletti, L. 1975. Marxism and the dialectic. *New Left Review* 93.
Engels, F. 1877–8. *Anti-Dühring*. Moscow: Foreign Languages Publishing House, 1954.
Engels, F. 1886–8. *Ludwig Feuerbach and the End of Classical German Philosophy*. In K. Marx and F. Engels, *Selected Works*, Vol. 2, Moscow: Foreign Languages Publishing House, 1962.
Engels, F. 1927, written 1878–82. *Dialectics of Nature*. Moscow: Progress Publishers, 1974.

Graham, L.R. 1973. *Science and Philosophy in the Soviet Union*. London: Allen Lane.

Jordan, Z.A. 1967. *The Evolution of Dialectical Materialism*. London: Macmillan.

Lefebvre, H. 1939. *Dialectical Materialism*. London: Jonathan Cape, 1968.

Lenin, V.I. 1895–1916. *Philosophical Notebooks*. Vol. 38 of the *Collected Works*, Moscow: Foreign Languages Publishing House, 1963.

Lenin, V.I. 1902. *What is to be Done?* Moscow: Progress Publishers, 1969.

Lenin, V.I. 1908. *Materialism and Empirico-Criticism*. Moscow: Foreign Languages Publishing House, 1952.

Mao Tse-tung. 1937. On Contradiction. In *Selected Works*, Vol. 2, London: Lawrence and Wishart, 1954.

Marx, K. 1888, written 1845. *Theses on Feuerbach*. In K. Marx and and F. Engels, *The German Ideology* (written 1845–6), London: Lawrence & Wishart, 1970.

Norman, R. and Sayers, S. 1980. *Hegel, Marx and Dialectic*. Brighton: Harvester.

Plekhanov, G.V. 1908. *Fundamental Problems of Marxism*. London: Lawrence & Wishart, 1969.

Sartre, J.-P. 1960. *Critique of Dialectical Reason*. London: New Left Books, 1976.

Stalin, J.V. 1924. *Problems of Leninism*. Moscow: Foreign Languages Publishing House, 1945.

Wetter, G.A. 1952. *Dialectical Materialism*. London: Routledge and Kegan Paul, 1958.

dialectical reasoning. This notoriously elusive and multifaceted notion assumed importance in the history of political economy because Marx's 'critique of political economy', *Capital*, and particularly its first draft, the *Grundrisse* of 1857–8, were presented in a dialectical form. Part of the difficulty of encapsulating the dialectic within any concise definition derives from the fact that it may be conceived as a method of thought, a set of laws governing the world, the immanent movement of history or any combination of the three. The dialectic originated in ancient Greek philosophy. The original meaning of '*dialogos*' was to reason by splitting in two. In one form of its development, dialectic was associated with reason. Starting with Zeno's paradoxes, dialectical forms of reasoning were found in most of the philosophies of the ancient world and continued into medieval forms of disputation. It was this form of reasoning that Kant attacked in his distinction between the logic of understanding which, applied to the data of sensation, yielded knowledge of the phenomenal world, and dialectic or the logic of reasoning, which proceeded independently of experience and purported to give knowledge of the transcendant order of things in themselves. In another form of dialectic, the focus was primarily upon process: either an ascending dialectic in which the existence of a higher reality is demonstrated, or in a descending form in which this higher reality is shown to manifest itself in the phenomenal world. Such conceptions were particularly associated with Christian eschatology, neo-platonism and illuminism, and typically patterned themselves into conceptions of original unity, division or loss, and ultimate reunification.

For practical purposes, however, the form in which the dialectic was inherited and modified by Marx was that in which it had been elaborated by Hegel. 'Hegel's dialectics is the basic form of all dialectics, but only *after* it has been stripped of its mystified form, and it is precisely this which distinguishes my method' (Marx, letter to Kugelmann, 6 March 1868).

In Hegel, the dialectic is a self-generating and self-differentiating process of reason (reason being understood both to be the process of cognition and the process of the world). The Hegelian Absolute actualizes itself by alienating itself from itself and then by restoring its self-unity. This corresponds to the three basic divisions of the Hegelian system: the *Logic*, the *Philosophy of Nature* and the *Philosophy of Mind*. It is free because self-determined. Its freedom consists in recognizing that its alienation into its other (nature) is but a free expression of itself. The truth is the whole and it unfolds through a dialectical progression of categories, concepts and forms of consciousness from the most simple and empty to the most complex and concrete. Each category reveals itself to the observer to be incomplete, lacking and contradictory; it thus passes over into a more adequate category capable of resolving the one-sided and contradictory aspects of its predecessor, though throwing up new contradictions in its turn. Against Kant, this process of dialectical reason is not concerned with the transcendent, but is immanent in reality itself. Reflective understanding is not false, but partial. It abstracts from reality and decomposes objects into their elements. Analytic understanding represents a localized standpoint which sets up an unsurpassable barrier between subject and object and thus cannot grasp the systematic interconnection between things or the total process of which it is a part. The absolute subject contains both itself and its other (both being and thought) which is revealed to be identical with itself. Human history, human thought are vehicles through which the absolute achieves self-consciousness, but humanity as such is not the subject of the process. Thus the absolute spirit dwells in human activity without being reducible to it, just as the categories of the *Logic* precede their embodiment in nature and history.

The character of the marxian dialectic is yet harder to pin down than that of Hegel. In some well-known lines in the Post-Face to the Second Edition of *Capital* in 1873, Marx stated,

> I criticised the mystificatory side the Hegelian dialectic nearly thirty years ago ... [but] the mystification which the dialectic suffers in Hegel's hands by no means prevents him from being the first to present its general form of motion in a comprehensive and conscious manner. With him it is standing on its head. It must be inverted in order to discover the rational kernel within the mystical shell (Marx [1873], 1976, pp. 102–3).

This statement has satisfied practically no one. How can a dialectic be inverted? How can a rational kernel be extracted from a mystical shell? To critics from empiricist, positivist or structuralist traditions, anxious to free Marx from the clutches of Hegelianism, the dialectic is intrinsically unworkable and must either be dropped or stated in quite other terms (e.g. Bernstein, 1899; Della Volpe, 1950; Althusser, 1965; Cohen, 1978; Elster, 1985). To a second group, the dialectical understanding of capitalism is only a particular instance of more general dialectical laws which govern reality as a whole, both natural and social (Engels, dialectical materialism). To a third group, the Hegelian roots of Marx's thought are not sufficiently emphasized in this statement; Marxism is only Hegelianism taken to its logical revolutionary conclusions in the discovery of the proletariat as the subject–object of history and the 'totality' as the distinguishing feature of its world-outlook (Lukacs, 1923 and much of 20th-century Western Marxism). This *methodenstreit* cannot be discussed here. All that can be attempted is to give some sense to Marx's statement and in particular to indicate how it informed his critique of political economy.

Marx specifically criticized 'the mystificatory side of the Hegelian dialectic' in his 1843 *Critique of Hegel's Philosophy of Right* and in the concluding section of the *1844 Manuscripts* (both of which were only published in the 20th century). In these texts, Marx followed Feuerbach in considering Hegelian philosophy to be the conceptual equivalent of Christian theology; both were forms of alienation of man's species attributes; Christianity transposed human emotion into a religious Godhead, while Hegel projected human thinking into a fictive subject, the Absolute Idea, which in turn then supposedly generated the empirical world. Employing Feuerbach's 'transformative method' (the origin of the inversion metaphor) subject and predicate were reversed and hence the correct starting point of philosophy was the finite, man. Nature similarly was not the alienated expression of Absolute Spirit, it was irreducibly distinct. Thus there could be no speculative identity of being and thought. Man, however, as a natural being, could interract harmoniously with nature, his inorganic body. Once the absolute spirit had been dismantled and the identity of being and thought eliminated, it could be argued that the barrier against the harmonious interpenetration of man and nature and the free expression of human nature, was not 'objectification', the division between subject and object constitutive of the finite human condition, but rather the inhuman alienation of man's species life activity in property, religion and the state. True Communism, humanism, meant the reappropriation of man's essential powers, the generic use of his conscious life activity. In contrast to the predominant Young Hegelian position, therefore, which counterposed Hegel's revolutionary 'method' (the dialectic) to his 'conservative system', Marx argued that there was no incompatibility between the two. For while Hegel's dialectic ostensibly negated the empirical world, it covertly depended upon it. Not only was the moment of contradiction a prelude to the higher moment of reconciliation and the restoration of identity, but the ideas themselves were tacitly drawn from untheorized experience. The effect of the dialectical chain which embodied the world was not to subvert the existing state of affairs, but to sanctify it.

In the crucial period that followed, that of the *German Ideology* and the *Poverty of Philosophy*, in which the basic architecture of the 'materialist conception of history' was elaborated, the attack upon speculative idealism was made more radical. The generic notion of 'conscious life activity', 'praxis', was replaced by the more specific notion of production. Hegel and the Idealist tradition were given credit for emphasizing the active transformative side of human history, but castigated for recognizing this activity only in the form of thought. Thought itself was now made a wholly derivative activity. The fundamental activity was labour and what developed in history were the productive powers men employed in their interaction with nature, 'the productive forces'. Stages in the development of these productive forces were accompanied by successive 'forms of human intercourse', what became 'the relations of production'. Finally, 'man' as a generic being was dispersed into the struggle between different classes of men, between those who produced and those who owned and controlled the means of production.

In this new theorization of history, explicit references to Hegel were few and the dialectic scarcely mentioned. But Hegel re-entered the story as soon as Marx attempted to write up a systematic theory of the capitalist mode of production in 1857-8. To see why, we must briefly survey his economic writings up to that date.

Marx's 1843 critique of Hegel had led him to the conclusion that civil society was the foundation of the state and that the anatomy of of civil society was to be found in political economy. However, if his preoccupation with political economy dated from this point, it was not that of an economist. In the 1844 Manuscripts what is to be found is a humanist critique of both political economy and civil society: not an alternative theory of the economy, but rather a juxtaposition between the 'economic' and the 'human', the former being judged in terms of the latter. No distinction is made between political economy and the economic reality it purports to address, the one is simply seen as the mirror of the other.

The first attempt to define capitalism as an economic phenomenon occurred in the *Poverty of Philosophy* (1847). However, whatever the significance of that work in other respects, it did not outline any specifically marxian portrayal of the capitalist economy. As in 1844 there was no internal critique of classical political economy. The main difference was that whereas in 1844, Marx saw that economy through the eyes of Adam Smith, he now saw it through the eyes of Ricardo. In particular, he adopted what he took to be Ricardo's theory of value and belaboured Proudhon for positing as an ideal – the equivalence of value and price – what he considered to be the actual situation under capitalism. The only critique of Ricardo to be found there was a purely external historicist one: that Ricardo was the scientific expression of the epoch of capitalist triumph, but that that epoch had already passed away, that its gravediggers had already appeared and that its collapse was already at hand.

When Marx resumed his economic studies after the 1848 revolutions, Proudhonism was still the main object of attack. It occupied a major part of his unfinished economic manuscripts of 1850-51 and the attack on the Proudhonist banking schemes of Darimon took up the first part of the written-up notebooks of 1857-8, the *Grundrisse*. Proudhonism was the main object of attack because it could be taken for the predominant form of socialist or radical reasoning about the economy. Ricardo could again be utilized to attack such reasoning in order to argue that it represented a nostalgia for petty commodity production under conditions of equal exchange, a situation supposedly preceding modern capitalism rather than representing an emancipation from it. However, if the capitalist mode of production and its historical limits were to be grasped in theory, this would have to involve a critique of Ricardo himself.

The form this critique took, involved problematizing Ricardo's theory of value (or rather Marx's reading of it; Steedman (1979) has argued strongly that Marx misconstrued Ricardo's theory, though Ricardo's shifting of position between the three editions of the *Principles* and the fact that Marx only used the third edition, makes his mistake an understandable one). On the one hand, it raised a question never posed by Ricardo: the source of profit in a system of equal exchange. On the other hand, it involved juxtaposing wealth in the form of productive forces, i.e. as a collection of use values against the translation of all wealth into exchange values within capitalism. Ricardo, it was argued, possessed no criterion for distinguishing between the content – or the material elements – and the form of the economy, such as Marx possessed in the distinction between forces and relations of production. Ricardo never problematized the 'value form'; he linked the object of measurement with the measurement itself. For this reason, Ricardo was considered to possess no conception of the historicity of capitalism. Once the material could be distinguished from the social, the content from the form, the capitalist mode of production could be conceived as a dynamic system whose principle of movement could be located in the contradictory relationship between matter and form.

It is here that Hegel came in. We know that during the writing of the *Grundrisse* at the beginning of 1858, Marx re-read Hegel, in particular the *Science of Logic*. He wrote to Engels, 'I am getting some nice developments, e.g. I have overthrown the entire doctrine of profit as previously conceived. In the method of working, it was of great service to me that by mere accident I leafed through Hegel's *Logic* again' (Marx to Engels, 16 January 1858).

It is not really mysterious what Marx found so useful in his reading of Hegel's *Logic* at this time. It suggested a way of elaborating the contradictory elements that Marx had discerned in the value form into a theorization of the trajectory of the capitalist mode of production as a whole. The point is emphasised by Marx in his Post-face to Capital: the dialectic 'includes in its positive understanding of what exists a simultaneous recognition of its negation, its inevitable destruction; because it regards every historically developed form as being in a fluid state, in motion, and therefore grasps its transient aspect as well ([1879] 1976, p. 103). The dialectic offered a means of grasping a structure in movement, a process – the subtitle of *Capital*, Volume I was 'the process of capitalist production'. If capitalism could be represented as a process and not just a structure, then concomitantly its building blocks were not factors, but, as in Hegel, 'moments'. As Marx put it in the *Grundrisse*:

When we consider bourgeois society in the long view and as a whole, then the final result of the process of social production always appears as the society itself i.e. the human being itself in its social relations. Everything that has a fixed form, such as the product etc., appears as merely a moment, a vanishing moment in this movement. The conditions and objectifications of the process are themselves equally moments of it, and its only subjects are the individuals, but individuals in mutual relationships, which they equally reproduce and produce anew ... in which they renew themselves even as they renew the world of wealth they create (Marx [1857–8], 1973, p. 712).

Marx's attempt to utilize the *Logic* can be seen most clearly in the *Grundrisse*. There one can see the genesis of particular concepts which in *Capital* appear in more polished form. What is clear, is that the *Logic* is used as a first means of setting terms in relation to each other. The text is littered with Hegelian expressions and turns of phrase; indeed sometimes it appears as if lumps of Hegelian ratiocination have simply been transposed, undigested, to sketch the more intractable links in the chain. Here, for instance, is money striving to become capital: '... already for that reason, value which insists on itself as value preserves itself through increase; and it preserves itself precisely only by constantly driving beyond its quantitative barrier, which contradicts its character as form, its inner generality' (ibid., p. 270). But at the same time we can see Marx remind himself to correct the 'idealist manner of presentation, which makes it seem as if it were merely a matter of conceptual determination and of the dialectic of these concepts' (ibid., p. 151).

But the interest of dialectical logic for Marx was not simply that it offered him a way of outlining a structure in movement; more fundamentally it enabled him to depict contradiction as the motor of this movement. This was why the dialectic was 'in its very essence critical and revolutionary' (Marx [1873], 1976, p. 103), in that both in Hegel and in ancient Greek usage, movement was contradiction. This appears closely in the dramatic relationship that Marx sets up between the circulation system and the production system in *Capital*. The system of exchange, of the market is the public face of capitalism. It is 'in fact a very Eden of the innate rights of Man' (ibid., p. 280). Exchanges are equal. To look for the source of inequality in the exchange system, like the Proudhonists, is to look in the wrong place. Yet, if exchanges are equal how does capital accumulation take place? Equal exchange implies the principle of identity, of non-contradiction. It is, in Hegel's sense, the sphere of 'simple immediacy', the world as it first appears to the senses. It cannot move or develop, because it apparently contains no contradictory relations.

But this surface of things is not self-sufficient. It is 'the phenomenon of a process taking place behind it'. As a surface it is not nothing, but rather a boundary or limit. Contradiction and therefore movement is located in production. Here there is non-identity, the extraction of surplus labour disguised by the surface value form and its tendency to limitless expansion.

Thus, there are two processes, on the one hand that of the surface, that of immediate identity lacking the motive power of its own regeneration; on the other hand, that beneath the surface, a process of contradiction. Thus in Hegelian terms, the whole could then be defined as 'the identity of identity and non-identity'. In this whole, contradiction is the overriding moment, but the surface places increasingly formidable obstacles to its development, for the surface places increasingly formidable obstacles to its development, for instance, so-called 'realization' crises. Values can only be realized in an act of exchange and the medium of this exchange is money. But there is no guarantee that these exchanges must take place. The 'anarchy' of the market place is such that overproduction or disproportionality between sectors of production can only be seen after the event. Hence trade crises and slumps (see M. Nicolaus, Introduction to Marx, 1857–8).

This is only one example of how Marx employed dialectical principles in his attempt to conceptualize the process or movement of a contradictory whole. Another would be the six books Marx originally planned to write in 1857–8, the original blueprint of *Capital*. Their order would have been: Capital, Wage Labour, Landed Property, State, World Market, Crises. This plan is reminiscent of Hegel's *Encyclopaedia*. It describes a circle in a Hegelian sense. The point of departure is not capital *per se*, but commercial exchange as appearance, then proceeding through the contradictory world of production and eventually returning to commercial exchange again as the world market, but this time enriched by the whole of the preceding analysis.

There has been much controversy about the proximity or distance between the Hegelian and Marxian dialectics. Those who like Althusser (1965) argue for their radical dissimilarity, are on their strongest ground when arguing that in Marx the terms of the dialectic have been radically transformed. The contradiction between forces and relations of production cannot be reduced to the ultimate simplicity of that between Hegel's master and slave or of that between proletariat and bourgeoisie in the hegelianized marxist account of Lukacs. But it is far more difficult to establish as unambiguously the difference in the relationship between the terms in their respective dialectics. On the one hand, the relation between matter and form in Hegel is only one of apparent exteriority. Matter relates to form as other only because form is not yet posited within it. Once the terms are related, they are declared to be identical. Marx, on the other hand, insists upon the irreducible difference between matter and form, between the material and the social (even if he is not wholly successful in keeping them apart). Not only are matter and form different,

835

but the one determines the other: value is determined in relation to the material production of use value; the opposite is not true. Relations of determination would seem to exclude identity, and this is confirmed by Marx's avoidance of the Hegelian notion of 'sublation' (*Aufhebung*), the higher moment of synthesis. The dialectical clash between forces and relations of production in the capitalist mode of production does not of itself produce a higher unity (socialism); rather what crises do, is to make manifest the otherwise hidden determination of value by use value, of form by matter. Against this, however, must be set one or two passages, including a famous peroration in *Capital* Volume 1, where Marx does conceive the end of capitalism as a return to a higher but differentiated unity and does employ the notion of the negation of the negation (Marx [1873], 1976, p. 929), and, despite the best efforts of some modern commentators, it is difficult honestly to deny the strongly teleological imagination which underpins the whole enterprise of *Capital*.

Finally, in two important respects, Hegelian dialectic, however surreal, is less vulnerable than that of Marx. Firstly, Hegel's *Science of Logic* takes place outside spatio-temporal constraints. It is a purely logical progression of concepts, even if the principles on which one ontological category is derived from another 'have resisted analysis to this day' (Elster, 1985, p. 37). Marx's effort to avoid giving any impression of the 'self-determination' of the concept, took the form of attempting to demonstrate that 'the ideal is nothing but the material world reflected in the mind of man and translated into forms of thought' (Marx [1873], 1976, p. 102). In practical terms this implied that there was some systematic relationship between the logical sequence of concepts in the exposition of the argument and the chronological order of their appearance in historical time. But this turned out to impose insurmountable difficulties in terms of presentation (and it is significant that having begun with the product in the *Grundrisse*, he began with the commodity in *Capital*). Thus Marx both stated his position and violated it, bequeathing insoluble ambiguities surrounding his interpretation of value, of the meaning of 'reflection' and of the relationship between history and logic which have plagued even his closest followers ever since. Secondly, when it came to applying his dialectic to history, Hegel was categorical in refusing to project his theory into the future. The philosopher could explain the rationality of what had happened; it was only then that it could be grasped in thought. Marx, despite all his strictures against the voluntarism of other Young Hegelians and some of his fellow revolutionaries, was unable by the very nature of his project, fully to abide by the Hegelian restriction. Thus, while Hegel's owl of Minerva flew at dusk, the marxian owl, unfortunately, took flight at high noon.

GARETH STEDMAN JONES

See also DETERMINISM; DIALECTICAL MATERIALISM; ECONOMIC INTERPRETATION OF HISTORY; HEGELIANISM.

BIBLIOGRAPHY

Althusser, L. 1965. *For Marx*. London: Allen Lane, 1969.
Bernstein, E. 1899. *Evolutionary Socialism*. Stuttgart. English trans. by Edith C. Harvey, London: Independent Labour Party, 1909.
Bhaskar, R. 1983. *Dialectic, Materialism and Human Emancipation*. London: New Left Books.
Cohen, G. 1978. *Karl Marx's Theory of History: A Defence*. London: Oxford University Press.
Elster, J. 1985. *Making Sense of Marx*. Cambridge: Cambridge University Press
Hegel, G.W.F. 1812–16. *The Science of Logic*. London: Allen & Unwin, 1961.

Kolakowski, L. 1978. *Main Currents of Marxism*. Vol. I: *The Founders*, Oxford: Oxford University Press.
Lukács, G. 1923. *History and Class Consciousness*. London: Merlin, 1971.
Marx, K. 1844. *Economic and Philosophical Manuscripts of 1844*. In K. Marx and F. Engels, *Collected Works*, Vol. 3, London: Lawrence & Wishart, 1975.
Marx, K. 1847. *The Poverty of Philosophy*. In *Collected Works*, Vol. 6, London: Lawrence & Wishart, 1976.
Marx, K. [1857–8]. *Grundrisse*. Harmondsworth: Penguin 1973.
Marx, K. 1873. *Capital*, Vol. I. 2nd edn. Harmondsworth: Penguin, 1976.
Rosdolsky, R. 1968. *The Making of Marx's Capital*. Trans. by Peter Burgeis, London: Pluto Press, 1977.
Steedman, I. 1979. Marx on Ricardo. University of Manchester, Department of Economics, Discussion Paper 10.
Volpe, G. della. 1950. *Logica come scienza positiva*. Messina: G. d'Anna.

Dickinson, Henry Douglas (1899–1969). Dickinson went from the King's School, Wimbledon, to Emmanuel College, Cambridge, where he took the Part II Tripos in both Economics and History. He carried out research at the London School of Economics under Cannan, then went to teaching posts at Leeds and Bristol, where he held the Chair of Economics from 1951 to 1964. Although his *Institutional Revenue* (1932) is of interest for generalizing the concept of institutional rents, he is deservedly known for a series of writings which attempted to reconcile choice and individual freedom with socialist planning, in the tradition of market socialism. Together with Taylor, Lange and Lerner he provided a rebuttal (based on actual markets) of von Mises's view that rational allocation under socialism was impossible. He saw 'the beautiful systems of economic equilibrium' not as 'descriptions of society as it is but prophetic visions of a socialist economy of the future' (1933, p. 247). During the 1930s his writings were well known to intellectuals of the Left, including Cole, Dalton, Durbin and Laski. The best-known of his works is the *Economics of Socialism* (1939). His technical prowess was later exhibited in a *Review of Economic Studies* article of 1954–5 in which he formulated a constant elasticity of substitution production function (CES) for the first time and anticipated some of the neo-classical growth results of Solow and Swan. 'Dick', as he was universally known, was a much loved, unworldly, eccentric figure with a keen sense of fun and a most astute mind.

DAVID COLLARD

SELECTED WORKS

1932. *Institutional Revenue. A study of the influence of social institutions on the distribution of wealth*. London: Williams & Norgate.
1933. Price formation in a socialist community. *Economic Journal* 43, June, 237–50.
1939. *Economics of Socialism*. London: Oxford University Press.
1955. A note on dynamic economics. *Review of Economics Studies* 22(3), 169–79.

Diderot, Denis (1713–1784). Philosophe and editor of the *Encyclopédie raisonée* (1751–72). Born at Langres he was educated locally by the Jesuits and moved to Paris in 1728 to complete his education at the University of Paris and earn his living as a writer and translator. Diderot is ensured immortal fame for his role in commencing, editing and publishing the famous *Encyclopédie*, initially with D'Alembert but, after final government prohibition in May 1757, by himself. This task took close to half his lifetime; it was first mooted in 1746 and in 1772 the last volumes of engravings were published. The first volume of text appeared in 1751, the last in 1765; those containing the important economic contributions by Quesnay (1756, 1757) and Turgot (1757) appearing just before its official proscription by the censor. The completion of this task allowed Diderot time for a seven-month visit to Catherine the Great, whom he advised on various matters including economic policy.

In 1774 homesickness induced his departure from St Petersburg for his beloved Paris, where he died in 1784. His departure from St Petersburg has also been ascribed to a practical joke executed by Euler but inspired by the Czarina herself because of Diderot's boorish behaviour at Court. This involved an algebraic proof of the existence of God. Euler is said to have confronted Diderot with the following statement, spoken in a tone of perfect conviction.

$$\text{`Sir,}\quad \frac{a + b^n}{n} = x,\quad \text{hence God exists, reply!'}$$

Not at all skilled in mathematics Diderot had no answer, and humiliated by the unrestrained laughter which greeted his silence he asked, and received, Catherine's permission to return immediately to France (Bell, 1937, pp. 159–60).

As Bauer (1894, p. 577) noted, 'there is hardly a single branch of science which does not owe some debt of gratitude to the universal genius of this very able and characteristic French writer.' Because Bauer (1894) also gives a detailed summary of Diderot's economic contributions particularly for the *Encyclopédie*, other aspects of Diderot's importance for economics are mentioned here, particularly the role he played in disseminating French economics through its pages. This included work by Quesnay and Turgot and from lesser economic lights like Forbonnais, Leroy and Morellet. Beccaria and Verri learnt of Physiocracy from this source; likewise Sir James Steuart (1767, I p. 110) who cited Quesnay (1757a), while Adam Smith (1756, p. 246) in his second published article praised the *Encyclopédie* as a work promising 'to be the most compleat of this kind which has ever been published or attempted in any language'. The fact that Diderot enabled Quesnay to publish his first two economic essays in this work is particularly noteworthy, when it is realized these provide both the analytical foundations and the actual impetus for the creation of a Physiocratic school. Groenewegen (1983, pp. xii–xiii) has surmised that the reasons for this may have been Quesnay's considerable influence with Mme de Pompadour and its potential usefulness to Diderot for solving the continuing censorship crises the *Encyclopédie* was facing. Sadly, the censor ultimately prevented Quesnay from publishing two further contributions and consequently these remained virtually unknown for nearly 150 years after they were written. Likewise, official proscription made Turgot decline Diderot's invitation to write articles on topics including the rate of interest and taxation. Diderot appears also to have had an initial enthusiasm for Physiocratic thought, sufficiently strong to praise Mercier (1767) but in 1770 he actively supported Galiani's (1770) anti-Physiocratic grain trade position by first seeing the *Dialogues* through the press and then defending them against Morellet's criticisms (Mason, 1982, pp. 324–6).

Diderot's influence on some prominent nineteenth century thinkers may also be briefly noted. Diderot (1761) is distinguished by being the only modern work cited in Hegel's *Phenomenology of Spirit*. Marx singled it out as a 'masterpiece from beginning to end', describing Diderot as one of his favourite authors (Mason, 1982, pp. 184, 367). Marx's views were probably inspired by both Diderot's vigorous materialism and his wit, but may also derive from his views on the philosopher's role, so similar to Marx's own: 'What use is philosophy if it is silent? You must either speak out, or

renounce the title of instructor of the human race. You will be persecuted, that is your destiny...' (Diderot, 1778, p. 365). Only such sentiments could have sustained the 15 years lonely and arduous labour of completing his task of 'collecting the scattered knowledge of the world, revealing its overall structure and passing it to future generations' (Diderot, 1755, p. 174) as he himself defined his work on the *Encyclopédie*.

PETER GROENEWEGEN

SELECTED WORKS

1755. Encyclopédie. In *Encyclopédie ou dictionnaire raisonné des sciences, des arts et des métiers*, Paris, Vol. 5.
1761. *Rameau's Nephew*. Trans. L.W. Tencock. Harmondsworth: Penguin Books, 1966.
1778. *Essay on the Reigns of Claudius and Nero*. Extracts translated in Mason (1982).

BIBLIOGRAPHY

Bauer, S. 1894. Denis Diderot. In *Dictionary of Political Economy*, ed. R.H.I. Palgrave, London: Macmillan, Vol. I, 577–9.
Bell, E.T. 1937. *Men of Mathematics*. Harmondsworth: Pelican Books, 1953.
Galiani, F. 1770. *Dialogues sur le commerce des bléds*. Paris.
Groenewegen, P.D. 1983. Introduction to Quesnay, *Farmers*. Sydney: Department of Economics, Sydney University.
Mason, J.H. 1982. *The Irresistible Diderot*. London: Quartet.
Mercier de la Rivière, P.P. 1767. *L'ordre naturel et essential des sociétés politiques*. Paris.
Smith, A. 1756. A Letter to the Authors of the Edinburgh Review. In *Essays on Philosophical Subjects*, ed. W.P.D. Wightman, J.C. Bryce and I.S. Ross, Oxford: Clarendon, 1980, 242–54.
Steuart, Sir James. 1767. *Principles of Political Oeconomy*. London.

Dietzel, Carl August (1829–1884). German writer on public finance; Privatdozent of Heidelberg and later Professor of Public Finance, Marburg. Dietzel was struck by the contrast between British views on public debt such as those of Hume – 'if the Nation does not destroy Credit, Credit will destroy the Nation' – and the fact that the notable growth in British public debt during the 19th century had not been accompanied by the ruin of the British economy. Writing in 1855 he attacked the orthodox view that state borrowing required a Sinking Fund, arguing that government investment financed by renewable loans was a necessary condition for the growth in national production. His views were endorsed by several prominent German writers, notably Adolph Wagner, and were recalled during the post-1936 debate in support of Keynesian views on public debt policy.

ALAN PEACOCK

SELECTED WORKS

1855. *Das System der Staatsanleihen im Zusammenhang der Volkswirtschaft betrachtet*. Heidelberg.

BIBLIOGRAPHY

Stettner, W. 1948. Carl Dietzel, public expenditures and the public debt. In *Income, Employment and Public Policy: Essays in Honor of Alvin H. Hansen*, ed. L.A. Metzler, New York: Norton.

Dietzel, Heinrich (1857–1935). Born in Leipzig, Dietzel was appointed to a chair at the University of Dorpat in 1885 after studies in economics and law in Heidelberg, Göttingen and Berlin. In 1890 he accepted a chair in the philosophy faculty in Bonn. There he died in 1935.

Dietzel was a respected figure in circles of 19th–century German economists (such as Rau, von Thünen, von Hermann, von Mangoldt and Wagner) who were endeavoring to defend, pursue and modify classical methods and principles. He kept a sceptical distance from both the younger Historical School and the Austrian School, and was sharply opposed to popular Marxism. Nevertheless his excellent biography of Rodbertus and his writings on the early socialists are proof of his academic openness and liberal fairness. Enthusiastically though not successfully engaged in propagating free trade, Dietzel (in contrast to Manchester liberalism) was not dogmatic concerning the functions of the state in a concrete mixed economy.

His most important contribution to theory, the *Theoretische Sozialökonomie* (1895), unfortunately remained a torso. It is a pioneering analysis of the two main orders of an economy, namely the individualistic system of competitive markets and the collective system of compulsion of the state. This concept of the two (centralized and decentralized) elementary forms replaced the unscientific notions of capitalism and socialism, with their ideological bias. It opened the way to the foundation of an order theory that his disciple in Bonn, Walter Eucken, and the Freiburg School further developed and later on applied in Germany.

Though Dietzel dealt with self-interest, methodological theory (*Selbstinteresse*, 1911) and value theory, he and his followers (as Smithians) did not attempt to unify Smith's three systems of ethics, economics and politics to an integrated order theory via reconstructing and developing his 'obvious and simple system of natural liberty'. They also failed to produce an analysis of state and collective failures while they originally stressed the state's responsibility for ensuring sufficient market competition.

Nevertheless they made a number of contributions to the field and pointed to the right road to be taken in the future.

H.C. RECKTENWALD

SELECTED WORKS

1882. *Über das Verhältnis der Volkswirtschaftslehre zur Sozialwirtschaftslehre.* Berlin: Puttkammer und Mühlbrecht.

1886-8. *Karl Rodbertus: Darstellung seines Lebens und seiner Lehre.* 2 vols, Jena: G. Fischer.

1895. *Theoretische Sozialökonomie, I.* Leipzig: Winter.

1911. Selbstinteresse und Methodenstreit in der Wirtschaftstheorie. In *Handwörterbuch der Staatswissenschaften*, Vol. VII, Jena: G. Fischer.

1921. *Vom Lehrwert der Wertlehre und vom Grundfehler der Marxschen Verteilungslehre.* Leipzig-Erlangen: Scholl.

1922. *Technischer Fortschritt und Freiheit der Wissenschaft.* Bonn–Leipzig: Schroeder.

BIBLIOGRAPHY

Recktenwald, H.C. 1985. Über das Selbstverständnis der ökonomischen Wissenschaft. *Jahrbuch der Leibniz-Akademie der Wissenschaften und der Literatur.* Wiesbaden: Steiner.

Recktenwald, H.C. and Samuelson, P.A. 1986. Über Thünen's 'Der isolierte Staat'. *Wirtschaft und Finanzen*, Darmstadt–Düsseldorf.

differential games. A differential game studies system dynamics determined by the interactions of agents with divergent purposes. As a limit form of multi-stage games, its non-cooperative solution is subgame perfect; thus it may facilitate the study of credible threats and repeated play. Reducing each stage to a single point in continuous time, differential game applies control theoretic tools (including phase diagrams) to yield results more general and more detailed than other methods. Its applications range from common-property resource utilization to macro-economic stabilization.

MODEL. A differential game has four components: (a) a *state space*, X, where x in X embodies all relevant data at a particular stage, (b) a *time horizon*, T: a closed interval with a final instant equal to infinity or decided by some termination rule, (c) *a set of players*, $\bar{N} = \{1, \ldots, i, \ldots, N\}$, with each player distinguished by four aspects: (1) a *space for possible moves* (or 'controls'), K_i; (2) a *point-to-set correspondence for allowable moves*, $C_i: X \times T \rightrightarrows K_i$, $(x, t) \mapsto C_i(x, t)$, which vary with (x, t); (3) a *space for admissible 'strategies'* (or 'policies'), $R_i = \{r_i r_i: X \times T \to \cup_{X \times T} C_i(x, t)$ and r_i satisfies *additional conditions*\}, where each r_i assigns an allowable move at every (x, t); and (4) the *instantaneous payoff* $u_i: X \times T \times \Pi_j K_j \to R$, $((x, t), (c_j)) \mapsto u_i((x, t), (c_j))$. The additional conditions include (i) any restrictions on the information used for decisions, (ii) regularity conditions (e.g., being step-wise continuous) needed for a well defined model (d) a *state equation* for state transition, $F: X \times T \times \Pi_j K_j \to X$, $((x, t), (c_j)) \mapsto \dot{x}$, X and $K_1, \ldots, K_n$ are all subsets of Euclidean spaces.

Players select *strategies* at the outset, not piecemeal *moves*. Strategies are defined here as state-and-time dependent or 'feedback' strategies including the subclass which are 'open-loop' or time-dependent (only).

AN EXAMPLE WITH TWO VARIATIONS. Two users share a natural resource, which may be a petroleum reserve or fishery, under common-property tenure. The state space X is the set of all non-negative resource levels and the time horizon is $T = [0, t_f]$ where $t_f = +\infty$ or the instant when all the resource is used up. For all (x, t), $i = 1, 2$, the 'allowable moves' form a set $C_i(x, t) = K_i = R_+$, the set of all non-negative rates of use. Specimens of strategies include $r_i = kx$ for some $k \geq 0$, or $r_i = g(t)$ for some non-negative-valued function. The instantaneous payoffs of both players are assumed to be: $u_i = \exp(-at) \log c_i$ for some $a > 0$. The 'state equation' is: $dx/dt = f(x) - c_1 - c_2$ where: $f(x) = 0$ for the case of petroleum reserves, and $f(x) = x(b - \log x)$ for the fishery. The latter form agrees with the Gompertz recruitment function.

SOLUTION CONCEPTS. How players choose strategies under various scenarios is summarized as three *solution concepts*, e.g. (1) *The noncooperative equilibrium* (Cournot–Nash): each player's choice is his 'best reply' to the choices of all other players. This choice must be 'best' for all initial (x, t); (2) *The cooperative equilibrium* (Pareto): all players make choices such that no modification can benefit any player without harming another. This property holds for all initial (x, t); (3) *The hierarchical equilibrium* (Stackelberg): the 'leader' selects a committed choice to elicit the followers' 'best replies' so that the leader's payoff is maximized.

An equilibrium is a vector of strategies, one for each player, which is not liable to change. In differential games, players may change strategies in midgame, unless prevented by prior commitment (as in (3)), or by requiring the choices to be appropriate, once *and* forever (as in (1) and (2)). Significantly, the Cournot–Nash solution is thus subgame perfect à la Selten.

The Cournot–Nash solution is most frequently used. In particular, it depicts externalities under laissez-faire. For any problem it can be compared to Pareto solutions which assess any extra gains resulting from cooperation.

If an acknowledged leader (e.g. the *government* in a macro-economy) can offer credible commitments, he prefers to play Stackelberg (with a higher payoff for himself) rather than Cournot–Nash, since all followers' best replies are now under his influence rather than given independently.

The differential game sheds light on two additional features: (i) the *credibility* of the leader's professed strategy which is at issue, since he has both (a) the opportunity to renege on promises made and honoured at different times, and (b) the incentive to renege (his choice is subgame imperfect); (ii) 'Reputation' (rather than 'enforcement') is often the reason why commitments are kept, and may be modelled as a state variable suggested in Clemhout and Wan (1979). Hence credibility is established from a balance of the gains of reneging with the damage from reputation lost. This suggests a synergistic approach between Cournot–Nash and Stackelberg.

ALTERNATIVE FORMULATIONS OF COURNOT–NASH MODELS OVER TIME. To characterize the Cournot–Nash differential game in feedback strategy, one contrasts it with alternative versions of differing assumptions, 'what information players use' and 'the modelling of time'. Examples show that:

(a) To explain *reality* and provide *policy relevance*, 'feed-back' strategies are preferable to 'open-loop' strategies for two reasons; (1) in non-cooperative games, the subgame-perfect equilibrium is the image of reality, and (2) in models of common-property resources, policy relevance hinges on identifying the source of inefficiency. Our petroleum example (cf. Clemhout and Wan, 1985a) is a non-cooperative model of common-property utilization, and thus should have an *inefficient* but *subgame-perfect* equilibrium. This is the case when strategies are 'feedbacks'. The opposite is true if strategies are modelled as 'openloop' in which all equilibria are then *efficient* and *subgame-imperfect* and each is compatible only with one initial resource stock.

(b) For *reasonableness* and *convenience*, 'history-dependent state variables' are preferable to 'history-dependent strategies'. While history matters in contexts such as performance contracts, history-dependent strategies tend to require an infinite amount of information at every move. The use of history-dependent state variables (Smale, 1980, cf. Clemhout and Wan, 1979) is a reasonable alternative for players with bounded rationality. It also conforms to the finite-dimensional state space in differential games.

(c) For *game-theoretic* and *analytic* reasons 'continuous time' is preferable to 'discrete time'. Our fishery example (Clemhout and Wan, 1985a) illustrates two points. First only in continuous time is the model a game, according to Ichiishi (1983). To ensure non-negativity of the resource level, discrete-time models require the allowability of one player's move to depend upon the moves of all others at the same time, thus they become 'pseudo-games' by losing playability. The second point is that only in continuous time are the dual variables (which are analytically important) derivable from the conditions necessary for optimality whether the recruitment function is concave or not. This is because the adjoint system, in differential equation form, involves the slope of the recruitment function alone and not its curvature.

STRENGTHS OF DIFFERENTIAL GAMES. Differential games can obtain precise results either independently of particular functional forms, or by using empirically validated formulations. In our fishery example these include characterization of the resource level: (a) does it reach a sustained level? (b) does it approach extinction asymptotically, if so, how rapidly? (c) is it heading for extinction in finite time? (d) what difference do risks of random perturbation or extinction make? (e) what if several harvested species form pre-predator chains? and (f) do tax-incentives improve allocation efficiency? (Clemhout and Wan, 1985a,b,c).

In contrast with differential games, intuitive reasoning or simple examples (in two or three periods) can suggest certain outcomes, but cannot rule out the opposite outcome occurring

in plausible situations. Simulation models can start from any assumptions but cannot assure equilibrium.

In macro-economics, the linear-quadratic-Gaussian differential game can further analyse quantitatively real-life data. The estimation and interpretation of the parameters in such models is still subject to ongoing research. The same model also yields deep economic insights in their micro-economic applications.

CONCLUDING REMARKS. Pioneered by Isaacs and generalized by Case, the theory of differential games is now covered by excellent texts (e.g., Baser and Olsder, 1982), with reference to contributions by Blaquiere, Berkovitz, Cruz, Fleming, Friedman, Haurie, Ho and Leitmann, among others. Further progress in its economic applications now hinges on the development of 'techniques of analysis', akin to phase diagrams in control theory. Using these techniques one can deduce implications crucial to economists working with particular classes of models. This is often accomplished by utilizing structural properties common to entire families of models. The explicit solutions are neither required nor derived. Such feats are clearly attainable for differential games, as they have been for control models: the phase diagram itself has been recently applied to some models (Clemhout and Wan, 1985b) and contraction mappings in others (Stokey, 1985). Given the state of the art in this field, additional advances in theory (e.g., generalizing the model, proposing new solution concepts, etc.) are certainly most welcome, but no longer crucial for economic applications.

SIMONE CLEMHOUT and HENRY Y. WAN, JR.

See also GAME THEORY; NON-COOPERATIVE GAMES; OPTIMAL CONTROL AND ECONOMIC DYNAMICS; REPEATED GAMES.

BIBLIOGRAPHY
Basar, T. and Olsder, G.J. 1982. *Dynamic Noncooperative Game Theory.* New York: Academic Press.
Clemhout, S. and Wan, H., Jr. 1979. Interactive economic dynamics and differential games. *Journal of Optimization, Theory and Applications* 27(1), 7–30.
Clemhout, S. and Wan, H., Jr. 1985a. Resource exploitation and ecological degradations as differential games. *Journal of Optimization, Theory and Applications,* August.
Clemhout, S. and Wan, H., Jr. 1985b. Cartelization conserves endangered species? In *Optimal Control Theory and Economic Analysis 2,* ed. G. Feichtinger, Amsterdam: North-Holland.
Clemhout, S. and Wan, H., Jr. 1985c. Common-property exploitations under risks of resource extinctions. In *Dynamic Games and Applications in Economics,* ed. T. Basar. New York: Springer-Verlag.
Ichiishi, T. 1983. *Game Theory for Economic Analysis.* New York: Academic Press.
Smale, S. 1980. The Prisoner's Dilemma and dynamical systems associated to non-cooperative games. *Econometrica* 48(7), November, 1917–34.
Stokey, N. 1985. The dynamics of industry-wide learning. In *Essays in Honour of Kenneth J. Arrow,* ed. W.P. Heller, R.M. Starr and D.A. Starrett, Cambridge: Cambridge University Press.

difference principle. *See* JUSTICE.

differential rent. *See* EXTENSIVE AND INTENSIVE RENT.

differential topology. *See* GLOBAL ANALYSIS.

difficulty of attainment. A phrase used by De Quincey, Mill, and others, to denote a condition which must be superadded to utility in order that there should exist value in exchange.

> Any article whatever, to obtain that artificial sort of value which is meant by exchange value, must begin by offering itself as a means to some desirable purpose; and secondly, even though possessing incontestably this preliminary advantage, it will never ascend to an exchange value in cases where it can be obtained gratuitously and without effort (De Quincey, *Logic of Political Economy*, p. 13; quoted by Mill, *Political Economy*, book iii, ch. ii, § 1).

The difficulty of attainment here indicated is primarily that which is experienced by the purchaser. But it is usual to extend the term to the difficulty experienced by the producer. Thus De Quincey continues:

> Walk into almost any possible shop, buy the first article you see; what will determine its price? In the ninety-nine cases out of a hundred simply ... difficulty of attainment. ... If the difficulty of producing it be only worth one guinea, one guinea is the price which it will bear.

So Mill, of what he considers the general case, 'the obstacle to attainment consists only in the labour and expense necessary to produce the commodity' (ibid., § 2). And by others difficulty of attainment is used as equivalent to cost of production. Thus Walker (*First Lesson in Political Economy*, Art. 67), 'Cost of production is only another name for difficulty of attainment.' This transition from the sense in which the difficulty, like the other factor utility, is experienced by the individual purchaser is legitimate, where there exists such perfect 'industrial' competition that it is free to any one to enter any occupation. In that case the sacrifice made to attain a commodity by purchase tends to be equivalent to the efforts and sacrifices made in attaining it by production. If the value in exchange were higher, the commodity would not be purchased; if lower, it would not be produced.

The wider conception is particularly appropriate to the case which Mill, dividing the different kinds of difficulty, places second; where, 'without a certain labour and expense it [the commodity] cannot be had; but, when any one is willing to incur this, there needs be no limit to the multiplication of the product' ... up to a point which there is no need, for practical purposes, to contemplate (*Political Economy*, book iii, ch. ii, §1). In this case difficulty of production has a certain pre-eminence over the co-factor utility, both as (*a*) a cause, and (*b*) a measure of value. (*a*) The cause of a phenomenon being usually a somewhat arbitrarily selected portion of its total antecedent (Mill, *Logic*, book iii, ch. v, § 3; Venn, *Empirical Logic*, p. 57 *et seq.*), it is not paradoxical that sometimes utility, sometimes cost, should be regarded as the cause of value. Utility indeed is invariably an antecedent. But the scale of utility may, in the case supposed, be varied without any variation of value. 'If the demand for hats should be doubled, the price would immediately rise; but that rise would be only temporary, unless the cost of production of hats ... were raised' (Ricardo, *Political Economy*, ch. xxx). Whereas, if the cost of production of an article is varied, its value varies concomitantly. 'Diminish the cost of production of hats, and their price will ultimately fall to their new natural price, although the demand should be doubled, trebled, or quadrupled' (Ricardo, ibid.). Prediction, the prerogative of causation, is attached to cost rather than utility. (*b*) Accordingly, in the case supposed, the comparative difficulty of producing two commodities affords a simple measure of their relative value. It is true also that value is proportioned to

final utility. But this measure cannot be read until the measurement is already given. We cannot tell what the final utilities will be till we know the values. In some cases indeed (see below (4) and (5)) it is conceivable that, given the dispositions, the Demand-Curves of all the dealers in a market, we could deduce the rate of exchange which will be set up. The calculation is indicated by Professor Walras in his *Éléments d'économie politique pure*, Art. 50. Still difficulty of production, in the case most favourable to its operation, measures value directly, as a clock measures time; whereas utility at best is a measure like the shadow cast by the sun, which can only be interpreted by a difficult calculation.

This theory is subject to several reservations and exceptions. (1) The pre-eminence of difficulty of production as a regulator of value depends largely on the assumption that labour is perfectly homogeneous. If all labour consisted of raising weights in precisely similar circumstances, the theory might be literally true. 'If ... it usually cost twice the labour to kill a beaver which it does to kill a deer, one beaver should naturally exchange for or be worth two deer' (Adam Smith, quoted by Ricardo), there being only one mode of labour, work being as homogeneous as, say, gold. But suppose, besides effort of exertion, the sacrifice of waiting is required. Then, as between commodities involving these elements in different proportions (cf. Ricardo, ch. i, § 4), it would no longer be possible to assign the rate of exchange between the commodities without being given the comparative remuneration for the two kinds of sacrifice. But this datum could not in general be obtained *a priori*, but only as a result of the higgling of the market. (This reservation holds even upon the imaginary supposition that there existed a competition so perfect that it is free to any one to choose whether he will labour or abstain, *a fortiori*, when, as in reality the abstainers form a 'non-competing group'; and so fall under head (3).) Now, in fact, there are not only two, but many, kinds of sacrifice. The general principle is that the 'net advantages' (Marshall, *Principles of Economics*, vol. i, 2nd edn, p. 136) in occupations between which there is 'industrial competition' (Cairnes), tend to be equal. Accordingly the statement that the 'quantity of labour realised in commodities' (Ricardo) regulates their exchangeable value, can be true only on an average with wide deviations. Take the case put by De Quincey of a pearl-diver who sometimes obtains, along with 'ordinary', superior pearls. The true principle is that the net advantages of pearl-diving are the same as those of any other occupations between which there is industrial competition. How much truth is there in the proposition that the value of any pearl is proportioned to the 'quantity of labour realised' in it? The instance taken is a mild case of plural occupations, or joint production. The application of the general principle of net advantages here affords little light as to the value of particular articles (cf. Sidgwick, *Political Economy*, book ii, ch. ii, §10).

(2) The pre-eminence of difficulty over utility, as a regulator of value, disappears altogether when we pass from Mill's second case to a category comprising both Mill's third case (*Political Economy*, book iii, ch. ii, § 2), in which the cost of production increases with the quantity produced, according to the law of Diminishing Returns, and the converse case, in which the cost of production diminishes with the quantity produced according to the law of Increasing Returns. In this case the two factors, utility and value, become coordinate. As Professor Marshall says (*Economics of Industry*, 1st edn, p. 148),

> the amount produced and its normal value are to be regarded as determined simultaneously under the action of

economic laws. It is then incorrect to say as Ricardo did, that cost of production alone determines values; but it is no less incorrect to make utility alone, as others have done, the basis of value.

With reference to what Jevons calls the 'mechanics of industry' it seems trifling to inquire whether the force or the resistance contributes more to the determination of equilibrium. The *simultaneousness* of the two conditions is indicated by Jevons in his discussion of cost of production (*Theory*, ch. v). Jevons there entertains the unreal conception that it is free to the producer to apply his efforts in 'doses' to different kinds of production. This at most is true of the mere inventor as distinguished from the *entrepreneur* and operative. Still the conception may be usefully employed as symbolical of the actual working of competition in a regime of division of labour (Pantaleoni, *Principii. Theorema di Ricardo ed Marshall*). The simultaneousness of the two conditions may best be shown by imagining the disutility, as well as the utility, to be of the sort called 'final'.

(3) The coordinateness of difficulty of production with utility disappears when industrial competition is no longer supposed. In this case the assumed equation between the purchaser's and the producer's difficulty of attainment fails. The typical instance is international trade. There is no correspondence between the efforts of the Chinese producer of tea and the sacrifices which the English purchaser incurs to obtain it. It is pointed out by Cairnes that the principle of international trade governs domestic industry where 'non competing groups' exist. With reference to this case, as well as the preceding, Dr. Sidgwick justly says: 'It is not merely inconsistent with facts but with other parts of Mill's teaching, to say broadly that 'the value of things which can be increased at pleasure does not depend ... upon demand' (*Political Economy*, book ii, ch. ii, § 9). In this case the value of an article is proportioned to its final utility for the purchaser in the same sense as in the preceding cases. But it is not proportioned to the difficulty of attainment in the same sense.

(4) The coordinateness of difficulty of production with utility is not even supposable, when we pass to another category, Mill's first: 'things of which it is physically impossible to increase the quantity beyond certain narrow limits;' such as 'ancient sculptures' ... 'rare books or coins' ... 'houses and building-ground in a town of definite extent,' and 'potentially all land whatever' (*Political Economy*, book iii, ch. ii, § 2).

(5) With Mill's first class go those commodities which are temporarily 'unsusceptible of increase of supply' (ibid. § 5); in short all cases of Market as distinguished from Normal Value.

(6) Lastly, all cases of monopoly must be excepted from the sphere within which the difficulty of attainment experienced by the purchaser is equateable with the difficulty production. Outside this sphere the difficulty experienced by the purchaser is due to the niggardliness of his fellow-man, rather than the stubbornness of nature; and is measured only by his own reluctance to part with some useful commodity, and not also by his (potential) effort in producing the article purchased.

It is easier to refine upon these logical distinctions than to prove what is the relative extent and importance of the categories defined; which conception, if any, may be taken as typical of the facts. This is a matter of judgment rather than demonstration; about which there is much disagreement between economists of the last and the present generation. The case which one treats as the general rule, another treats as exceptional or non-existent. Mill speaks of his second category as 'embracing the majority of all things that are bought and sold' (*Political Economy*, book iii, ch. ii, § 2). To the same

effect Ricardo on the very first page of his *Principles*. The reservations which are here indicated under heading (1) are waived by Ricardo. Of the effect of the rate of profits on value he says, 'the reader however should remark that this cause of the variation of commodities is comparatively slight in its effects' (ibid., ch. i, § iv.) The difficulties caused by the difference in the qualities of labour he dismisses in a few sentences (ch. i). The extreme recoil from Ricardo's position is marked by the Austrian School, who emphasize utility as the determining principle of value, and assign quite a secondary place to Cost. See especially Professor Wieser, *Ueber den Ursprung ... des wirthschaftlichen Werths*; and Dr. Böhm-Bawerk, *Kapital und Kapitalzins*, interpreted by Mr James Bonar in the *Quarterly Journal of Economics*, October 1888, January 1889. In this attitude they had been anticipated by Jevons. But Jevons, as has been shown, admitted cost of production as a simultaneous factor. The simultaneousness of the two conditions in a regime of industrial competition has been defended by the present writer in the *Revue d'Économie Politique* for October 1890. In fine there are those who regard all abstract theory as futile. Cliffe Leslie, Adolf von Held, Brentano and others, harp on the unreality of the Ricardian assumptions. Neumann's article on prices in Schönberg's *Handbuch* teems with cases which it is difficult to reconcile with any theory of the relation between value and difficulty of attainment.

[F.Y. EDGEWORTH]
Reprinted from *Palgrave's Dictionary of Political Economy*.

BIBLIOGRAPHY
Böhm-Bawerk, E. von. 1884–9. *Kapital und Kapitalzins*. Innsbruck: Wagner.
Marshall, A. (With Mary Paley.) 1871. *The Economics of Industry*. London: Macmillan.
Marshall, A. 1891. *Principles of Economics*. 2nd edn, London: Macmillan.
Mill, J.S. 1843. *A System of Logic*. London: J.W. Parker.
Mill, J.S. 1848. *Principles of Political Economy*. London: J.W. Parker.
Ricardo, D. 1817. *Principles of Political Economy and Taxation*. London: J. Murray.
Sidgwick, H. 1883. *Principles of Political Economy*. London: Macmillan.
Venn, J. 1884. *The Principles of Empirical or Inductive Logic*. London and New York: Macmillan.
Walras, L. 1874–7. *Eléments d'économie politique pure*. Lausanne: Corbaz.
Wieser, F.F.B. 1884. *Ueber den Ursprung ... des Wirthschaftlichen Werthes*. Vienna: Holder.

difficulty or facility of production. The materialist view of the world characteristic of the writings of the classical economists was manifest not only in their concern with production and accumulation, but also in their theories of value. Petty and Cantillon, for example, both argued that the value of commodities is determined by the *amounts* of land and labour used in their production. Smith dropped land from the calculation, and argued that the value of commodities is determined by the quantity of labour used to bring them to market (at least in the early and rude state of society), though this material approach was somewhat blurred by reference to the 'toil and trouble' involved.

In the writings of Ricardo, however, the link between the material conditions of production and the value of commodities is both clear and prominent. In the *Essay on Profits*, prior to the formulation of his theory of value, Ricardo argued that

wherever competition can have its full effect, and the production of that commodity be not limited by nature, as in the case with some wines, the difficulty or facility of their production will ultimately regulate their exchangeable value (1815, p. 60).

To this proposition he appended a footnote:

Though the price of all commodities is ultimately regulated by, and is always tending to, the cost of their production, including the general profits of stock, they are all subject, and perhaps corn more than most others, to an accidental price, proceeding from temporary causes (1815, p. 60n).

The equation between 'difficulty or facility of production' and the 'cost of production', or value, of commodities remained a dominant theme in Ricardo's treatment of value in the three editions of the *Principles of Political Economy and Taxation* (1817, 1819, 1821) and in the papers on Absolute Value and Exchangeable Value, written in 1823 in the last few months of his life. In the draft version of these papers he declared, 'to me it appears a contradiction to say a thing has increased in natural value while it continues to be produced under precisely the same conditions as before' (1823, p. 375).

For Ricardo, difficulty of production referred only to the produced means of production and the labour required to produce a commodity. Non-produced means of production, such as the services of land, are not included. The limited availability of fertile land will be manifest in the extent to which more commodities and/or labour may be required to produce a further unit of output; i.e. the extent to which the difficulty of production will be increased.

But whilst the notion of difficulty of production is intuitively clear, it is not at all obvious how it may be represented as a single magnitude and so related to the exchangeable value of commodities. It was this latter relationship which was to be the source of the considerable difficulties which Ricardo encountered in the formalization of his theory of value and distribution, in particular once the influence of changes in distribution on exchange value was taken into account.

The representation of difficulty of production as a single magnitude is possible only if that magnitude is the quantity of labour embodied directly and indirectly in the production of the commodity. Changes in this quantity can derive only from changes in the technology – where by technology is meant the produced means of production and the labour used in total in the production of a commodity, i.e. the means of production and labour of the integrated sub-system which would (hypothetically) have as its net product one unit of the commodity in question (Sraffa, 1960, appendix A). So Ricardo's adoption of the labour theory of value was a natural outcome of his materialist view of economic relations, allowing him to move freely from material conditions of production to rates of exchange, and from material net product to the general rate of profit.

Yet it was exactly Ricardo's material conception of cost which exacerbated the contradictions which emerge once the influence of changes in distribution upon exchangeable value is considered. In 1823 he commented sadly that 'the increased or diminished facility of producing them' was 'by far the greatest cause' of variation in the exchangeable value of commodities, though 'it is not strictly the only one' (1823, p. 367). The focus on *variation* in the value of commodities, rather than the *difference* between labour values and natural prices, precipitated the fruitless search for an invariable standard of value as a means of tying variations in prices to variations in the difficulty or facility of production alone.

These difficulties notwithstanding (and the story of their resolution may be followed in Garegnani, 1984) Ricardo's persistent use of the idea of difficulty of production is indicative of his materialist conception of political economy. The variables from which his theory of value and distribution is constructed are objective (in the sense that they are all, in principle, directly observable and measurable), being the empirical description of the process of production and the real wage determined by the concrete institutional characteristics of economic society. And Ricardo's link between conditions of production and value is neither misplaced nor archaic – the dominant explanation of *changes* in relative values in modern economies is, surely, the differential rates of technological progress as between the production processes of different commodities, i.e. changes in the difficulty or facility of production.

JOHN EATWELL

See also CLASSICAL ECONOMICS; COST OF PRODUCTION.

BIBLIOGRAPHY

Garegnani, P. 1984. Value and distribution in the classical economists and in Marx. *Oxford Economic Papers* 36(2), May, 291–325.

Ricardo, D. 1815. An essay on the influence of a low price of corn on the profits of stock. Reprinted in *The Works and Correspondence of David Ricardo*, ed. P. Sraffa, Vol. IV, Cambridge: Cambridge University Press, 1951.

Ricardo, D. 1823. Notes on 'Absolute Value and Exchangeable Value'. Reprinted in *The Works and Correspondence of David Ricardo*, ed. P. Sraffa, Vol. IV, Cambridge: Cambridge University Press, 1951.

Sraffa, P. 1960. *Production of Commodities by Means of Commodities*. Cambridge: Cambridge University Press.

diffusion of technology. Technological change results in a change in the production function of an existing product or in an addition to the list of technically feasible products. An invention, when applied for the first time, is called an innovation. Many economists, ranging from Karl Marx to Joseph Schumpeter, have stressed that the diffusion of technological innovations is of great importance; for example, in the case of a process innovation, it determines how rapidly productivity increases in response to the new process. However, until the late 1950s and early 1960s, economists devoted little or no attention to the factors determining an innovation's rate of diffusion.

Studies carried out in the past 25 years have provided a considerable amount of data concerning the rate of diffusion of various innovations. According to these data, it takes about five or ten years, on the average, before one-half of the major firms in an industry begin using an important innovation. The rate of imitation varies widely: although it sometimes takes decades for firms to install a new technique, in other cases they follow the innovator very quickly. For example, it took about fifteen years for half of the major pig-iron producers to use the by-product coke oven, but only about three years for half of the major coal producers to use the continuous-mining machine.

Even when a firm begins using a new technique, this does not mean that the diffusion process is over for this firm. It generally takes a number of years before a firm completes the substitution of the new technique for the old. For example, it took about nine years, on the average, for an American railroad to increase its stock of diesel locomotives from 10 per cent to 90 per cent of the total. And there was wide variation among firms in the intrafirm rate of diffusion. For example, some firms took only a few years to go from 10 to 90 per cent, whereas others took fourteen years or more.

What determines how rapidly the use of a particular new process spreads from one firm to another? Given that one firm has begun using a new technique, what determines how rapidly other firms begin using it? Mansfield (1961) suggested that the following simple model might be of use: letting $\lambda_{ij}(t)$ be the proportion of firms in the ith industry not using the jth innovation at time t that introduce it by time $t + 1$, he proposed that

$$\lambda_{ij}(t) = f_i[P_{ij}(t), \pi_{ij}, S_{ij}, \ldots], \qquad (1)$$

where $P_{ij}(t)$ is the proportion of firms in this industry that have introduced it at time t, π_{ij} is the profitability of installing this innovation relative to that of alternative investments, and S_{ij} in the investment required to install this innovation as a percentage of the average total assets of the firms. In other words, the model assumes that the probability that a non-user will use the innovation between time t and $t + 1$ is dependent on the proportion of firms already using the innovation, the profitability of using the innovation, and the investment required to install the innovation.

Several reasons were given for expecting this probability to increase with increases in $P_{ij}(t)$, the proportion of firms already using the innovation. The larger the proportion of the firms already using the innovation, the less risky it is for a non-user to begin using it, and the more competitive pressure there may be on a non-user to begin using it. Also, there tends to be a 'bandwagon' effect. Turning to the effects of π_{ij}, it seems reasonable that more profitable innovations will tend to be accepted more rapidly. Also, one would expect that increases in S_{ij}, the investment required to introduce the innovation (as a percent of the average total assets of the firms), would result in a slower rate of diffusion.

Assuming that $\lambda_{ij}(t)$ can be approximated adequately by a Taylor's expansion that drops third and higher-order terms, and assuming that the coefficient of $P_{ij}^2(t)$ in this expansion is zero, it can be shown that the growth over time in the number of firms having introduced the innovation should conform to a logistic function. Specifically,

$$P_{ij}(t) = [1 + e^{-(l_{ij} + \Phi_{ij}t)}]^{-1}. \qquad (2)$$

It can also be shown that the rate of imitation depends only on Φ_{ij}, and on the basis of the model's assumptions,

$$\Phi_{ij} = b_i + a_1\pi_{ij} + a_2S_{ij} + z_{ij}, \qquad (3)$$

where the as and bs are parameters and z_{ij} is a random error term. (For discussion of the logistic stochastic process, see Mansfield and Hensley (1960). Parzen (1962) provides a basic treatment of stochastic processes.)

This model has been tested against data for dozens of innovations in a wide variety of industries, the results generally being quite favourable. Many studies have found that the growth in the number of users of an innovation can be approximated by a logistic curve. (For a well known agricultural study, see Griliches, 1957.) There is definite evidence that more profitable innovations and ones requiring smaller investments had higher rates of imitation, the relationship being similar to that predicted in equation (3). This model provides a good fit to data regarding the diffusion process in a variety of nations, such as Canada, Hong Kong, and the United States. Although this model is oversimplified in many respects, it has proved useful in forecasting the rate at which particular innovations, like numerically-controlled machine tools, have spread (see Mansfield et al., 1977).

In recent years, attempts have been made to construct models of the diffusion process based on Bayesian learning models. However, they have thus far proved to be intractable empirically. Also, models have been developed that regard firm size as the critical variable in determining whether or not a firm will begin using a new technique.

From both analytical and policy points of view, it is also important to know the characteristics of the firms that are relatively quick to begin using new techniques. Based on studies of over a dozen major industrial innovations in a number of quite different manufacturing industries, it is reasonably clear that firms where the expected returns from the innovation are greatest tend to be quickest to introduce the innovation and that firms where the expected returns from the innovation are lowest tend to be slowest to introduce the innovation. This, of course, is what we would expect. A firm's introduction of a new technique is delayed if the return is not deemed adequate to offset the risk involved.

Another factor that can influence how quickly a firm begins to use an innovation is its size. Holding constant the profitability of the innovation, big firms often tend to introduce an innovation before small firms. In some industries, this may be due to the fact that larger firms – although not necessarily the largest ones – tend to be more progressive than smaller firms. But even if the larger firms are not more progressive and do not introduce more than their share of the innovations, one might expect them to be quicker, on the average, to begin using a new technique than smaller firms, for the following reasons.

Suppose that a new type of equipment is put on the market and that the kth firm will eventually own α_k units of this equipment. Suppose that x_{ik}, the length of time that elapses (from the date when the innovation is first put on the market) before the kth firm's ith unit ($i = 1, \ldots, \alpha_k$) is installed, is a random variable with cumulative distribution function, $F(x)$, and that the time elapsing before one of its units is installed is independent of that for another unit. Under these highly simplified circumstances, the expected length of time a firm with an eventual complement of α units will wait before beginning to use the innovation is

$$\bar{X}_\alpha = \alpha \int_0^L x[1 - F(x)]^{\alpha-1}F'(x)\,dx$$

$$= \int_0^L [1 - F(x)]^\alpha\,dx,$$

where L is the maximum value of x_{ik}. Thus, if α_k is proportional to the kth firm's size, the expected length of time a firm waits should decrease at an increasing rate with increases in its size. (That is, $(\bar{X}_\alpha - \bar{X}_{\alpha+1}) > 0$, and $(\bar{X}_\alpha - \bar{X}_{\alpha+1}) - (\bar{X}_{\alpha+1} - \bar{X}_{\alpha+2}) > 0$.)

Other factors that often seem to be associated with how rapidly a firm begins using a new technique are the education and age of the relevant management personnel. Both in agriculture and in the tool and die industry, there is evidence that firms with better educated and younger managers tend to be quicker to begin using techniques than firms with less educated and older managers. In industries with bigger firms, no such tendency is found, but this may be because the data used pertain to the wrong managers – the presidents of the firms, who are quite far removed from the decision to introduce many innovations.

Firms that are relatively slow to begin using an innovation tend to substitute for older techniques more rapidly than those that are quick to begin using it. In other words, the late starters tend to 'catch up'. For example, railroads that began using diesel locomotives in the 1950s made the transition from 10 per cent to 90 per cent of full use of diesels much more quickly, on the average, than did railroads that began using diesel locomotives in the 1940s. The same sort of process occurs on the international scene: countries that are slow to begin using an innovation tend to substitute it for older techniques more rapidly than countries that are quick to begin using it.

843

Finally, the diffusion process may be slowed by bottlenecks in the production of the innovation, and by the policies adopted by relevant labour unions. The extent of advertising and other promotional activities used by producers of the new product or equipment will also have an effect. So too will the innovation's requirements with respect to knowledge and coordination: The diffusion process tends to be impeded if the innovation requires new kinds of knowledge on the part of the user, new types of behaviour, and the coordinated efforts of a number of organizations.

EDWIN MANSFIELD

See also GIBRAT'S LAW; INNOVATION; MARKET STRUCTURE AND INNOVATION.

BIBLIOGRAPHY

Griliches, Z. 1957. Hybrid corn: an exploration in the economics of technological change. *Econometrica* 25, October, 501–22.

Mansfield, E. 1961. Technical change and the rate of imitation. *Econometrica* 29, October, 741–66.

Mansfield, E. 1968. *Industrial Research and Technological Innovation.* New York: W.W. Norton.

Mansfield, E. et al. 1977. *The Production and Application of New Industrial Technology.* New York: W.W. Norton.

Mansfield, E. and Hensley, C. 1960. The logistic process. *Journal of the Royal Statistical Society,* Series B 22(2), 332–7.

Parzen, E. 1962. *Stochastic Processes.* San Francisco: Holden-Day.

dimensional invariance. *See* TRANSFORMATIONS AND INVARIANCE.

dimensions of economic quantities. A unit is a concrete magnitude selected as a standard by reference to which other magnitudes of the same kind may be compared. A derived unit is a unit determined with reference to some other unit. Thus the unit of area may be derived from the unit of length by being defined as the area of the square, erected on the unit of length. The unit of speed may be derived from the unit of length and the unit of time, by being defined as that speed at which the unit of length is traversed in the unit of time. In relation to the derived units of area and speed, the units of length and time would then be fundamental—'fundamental' being a term correlative to 'derived'.

The theory of dimensions is concerned with 'the laws according to which derived units vary when fundamental units are changed' (Everett). A fundamental unit, together with the magnitudes of like kind referred to it, is regarded as having one dimension. Thus a length had the dimension L. The unit of length enters twice into the unit of area, first determining the base and then the altitude of the unit rectangle, and therefore the dimensions of an area are LL, usually written L^2. If we alter the unit of length, say from a foot to an inch (1:12) the unit of area will be reduced in the same ratio twice successively (1:144 in all). The variations of the unit of area, therefore, are directly as the squares of the variations in the unit of length. The units of length and of time enter once each into the unit of speed, but they do not enter on the same footing. If the unit of time be the minute, and the unit of length the foot, the unit of speed will be a foot per minute. This unit will become smaller if we make the unit of *length* smaller, since an inch per minute is a smaller speed than a foot per minute; but it will become larger if we make the unit of *time* smaller, a foot a second being a greater speed than a foot a minute. This is expressed by saying that the dimensions of time T enters *negatively* into speed. The dimensions of speed, then, are expressed as LT^{-1}. A unit into which a dimension enters negatively is always a unit of rate, and measures amount of *x per unit* of *y*, *−y* being the quantity the dimension of which enters negatively.

We have now examined simple cases of the variations of derived *units*, but it is obvious that the *numerical values* of concrete magnitudes vary inversely as the units by reference to which they are estimated. The smaller the unit the greater the numerical value of any given magnitude. The numerical value of a magnitude, therefore, will vary inversely as the unit whose dimension enters into it positively, and directly as the unit whose dimensions enters into it negatively. Thus, let the unit of speed (dimensions LT^{-1}) be a foot per minute, and let the numerical value of a certain concrete speed be 10, *i.e.* let the speed be *ten* per minute. Then change the unit of length to an inch (1:12) and the unit of time to a second (1:60); the derived unit will now be an inch per second, and its relation to the former derived unit is obtained by altering directly in the ratio of 1:12 (dividing by 12) and inversely in the ratio of 1:60 (multiplying by 60), so that the new unit is five times as great as the old one, an inch per second being five times as great a speed as a foot per minute; but the numerical value of the concrete speed we had to express must be altered inversely as 1:12 and directly as 1:60, and is now only 2 − *i.e.* the speed is *two* inches per second – or one-fifth of what it was before.

If we are measuring such a magnitude as feet of vertical motion per foot of horizontal motion in the path of a projectile, the dimensions will be LL^{-1} and will cancel each other. No change in the unit of length, then, will in any way affect the numerical value of this magnitude, and as no other dimension enters into it at all, it may be said to have no dimensions. Angular magnitudes, defined as ratios between arcs and radii, trigonometrical functions, and ratios generally are of this nature. They have no selected units, and their numerical values are absolute.

When the elements of the theory of dimensions have been thoroughly grasped it will be easy to apply it to economic questions; and it will be found an invaluable check in the more intricate problems of co-ordination and analysis. Thus, if the unit of value-in-use or utility be taken as fundamental, and regarded as having the dimension U, and if the commodity we are considering be taken as having the dimension Q, then degree of utility of the commodity, being the rate at which satisfaction is secured per unit of *commodity* consumed, will have dimensions UQ^{-1}, and, will be readily distinguished from rate of enjoyment, accruing to the consumer, per unit of *time*, with dimensions UT^{-1}. *Price*, determined by *marginal*, or final, degree of utility, will have dimensions UQ^{-1} or P; and *hire*, being price per unit of time, will obviously have dimensions PT^{-1} or $UQ^{-1}T^{-1}$. When the thing hired is money and is used commercially, the utility derived from it is a commodity of like nature with itself. The dimension U then becomes Q, and the dimensions of interest (as a rate) are $QQ^{-1}T^{-1}$ or T^{-1}, which will be found on reflection and experiment to be correct.

The theory of dimensions should be applied to economics in close connection with the diagrammatic method. But of course the connection between dimensions, as now explained, and the geometrical dimensions of the diagrams is purely arbitrary. The physicist may, according to his convenience, represent the height of a projectile – a magnitude of one dimension – by a line, or by an area, and speed by a line of an inclination. So the economist may represent a magnitude measured by a complicated derived unit by a line, or a magnitude measured by a fundamental unit by an area or a solid; and if he keeps the theory of dimensions well before him he may vary his methods indefinitely without any danger of confusion. In all cases, however, the dimensions of those quantities represented by areas or solids will be compounded of the dimensions of those represented by the lines which determine them. Again, those who have any acquaintance with the elements of the calculus will see that if the equation of a curve be differentiated to x then the area of the derived curve will have the same dimensions as the ordinate of the fundamental curve; the ordinate of the derived curve will have the dimensions of the ordinates of the fundamental curve positively, and those of its abscissae negatively; and the abscissae of the two curves will have the same dimensions. In other words, differentiation introduces the dimensions of the variable to which we differentiate negatively, and integration introduces the dimensions of the variable to which we integrate positively.

BIBLIOGRAPHY

Everett, J.D. 1875. *Illustrations of the Centimetre-Gramme-Second System of Units, with tables of physical constants.* London.

Fourier, J. 1822. *Theorie analytique de chaleur.* Paris.

Jevons, W.S. 1871. *The Theory of Political Economy.* London: Macmillan.

Jevons, W.S. 1887. *Principles of Science.* London: Macmillan.

Wicksteed, P.H. 1889. On certain passages in Jevons's *Theory of Political Economy. Quarterly Journal of Economics* 3, 293–314.

Wicksteed, P.H. 1888. *The Alphabet of Economic Science.* London: Macmillan.

Wicksteed, P.H. 1895. *A Symposium on Value.* Ed. J.H. Levy, London: Macmillan.

Wicksteed, P.H. 1910. *The Common Sense of Political Economy.* London: Macmillan.

diminishing returns. *See* RETURNS TO SCALE.

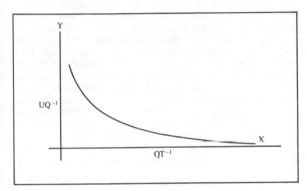

Figure 1

By way of illustration take a figure, on the ordinate of which intensity of desire, or degree of utility, is represented, while supply of commodity per unit of time is measured on the abscissae. Now imagine a third axis (of Z) perpendicular to the page, along which time is measured. Such a figure will enable us to represent all the quantities we have to deal with in an ordinary problem of consumption. Rate of supply is represented on axis of X, dimensions QT^{-1}; degree of utility on axis of Y, dimensions UQ^{-1}; time on axis of Z, dimension T; rate of enjoyment on areas parallel to plane of axes of X and Y, dimensions $UQ^{-1}QT^{-1}$ or UT^{-1}; total enjoyment on solid figure, dimensions $UQ^{-1}QT^{-1}T$, or U; total supply on areas parallel to plane of axes of X and Z, dimensions $QT^{-1}T$, or Q, and in like manner price, hire, total sum paid, etc., may be read, and their dimensional relations seen at a glance.

[The theory of dimensions was (according to Jevons, *Principles of Science*, 1887, p. 325) first clearly stated by Joseph Fourier. He expounded it with great lucidity in his *Théorie Analytique de la Chaleur*, 1882, §§ 159–62. An excellent popular statement of the theory, as it has since been elaborated, will be found in the beginning of J. D. Everett's *C.G.S. System of Units*, 1891. Jevons was the first to suggest the application of the theory to economics (*Theory of Political Economy*, 1888, pp. 232–52), but he unfortunately fell into some apparent errors and confusions which made the suggestion barren in his hands. A criticism of his treatment of the subject and an independent working-out of his suggestion, by the writer of the present article will be found in the American *Quarterly Journal of Economics* for April 1889, pp. 297–314.]

[P. H. WICKSTEED]

Reprinted from *Palgrave's Dictionary of Political Economy.*

directly unproductive profit-seeking (DUP) activities. Directly unproductive profit-seeking (DUP) activities are defined (Bhagwati, 1982) as ways of making a profit (i.e. income) by undertaking activities which are directly (i.e. immediately, in their primary impact) unproductive, in the sense that they produce pecuniary returns but do not produce goods or services that enter a conventional utility function or inputs into such goods and services.

Typical examples of such DUP (pronounced appropriately as 'dupe') activities are (i) tariff-seeking lobbying which is aimed at earning pecuniary income by changing the tariff and therefore factor incomes; (ii) revenue-seeking lobbying which seeks to divert government revenues towards oneself as recipient; (iii) monopoly-seeking lobbying whose objective is to create an artificial monopoly that generates rents; and (iv) tariff-evasion or smuggling which *de facto* reduces or eliminates the tariff (or quota) and generates returns by exploiting thereby the price differential between the tariff-inclusive legal and the tariff-free illegal imports.

While these are evidently profitable activities, their *output* is zero. Hence, they are wasteful in their primary impact, recalling Pareto's distinction between production and predation: they use real resources to produce profits but no output.

DUP activities of one kind or another have been analysed by several economic theorists, among them (i) the public-choice school's leading practitioners, their major work having been brought together in Buchanan, Tullock and Tollison (1980), (ii) Lindbeck (1976) who has worked on 'endogenous politicians', and (iii) the Chicago 'regulation' school, led by Stigler, Peltzman, Posner and recently Becker (1983).

However, a central theoretical breakthrough has come from the work of trade theorists who have systematically incorporated the analysis of DUP activities in the main corpus of general equilibrium theory.

The early papers that defined this general-equilibrium-theoretic approach, and which were set in the context of the theory of trade and welfare, were: Bhagwati and Hansen (1973) which analysed the question of illegal trade (i.e. tariff-evasion), Krueger (1974) which analysed the question of rent-seeking for rents associated with import quotas specifically and quotas more generally, and (iii) Bhagwati and Srinivasan (1980) who analysed the phenomenon of revenue-seeking, the 'price' counterpart of Krueger's rent-seeking, where a tariff resulted in revenues which were then sought by lobbies.

The synthesis and generalization of these and other apparently unrelated contributions, showing that they all related to diversion of resources to zero-output activities, was provided in Bhagwati (1982a) where they were called DUP activities. The following significant aspects of the theoretical analysis of DUP activities are noteworthy.

First, they are generally related to policy interventions (but they need not be: plunder, for instance, pre-dates the organization of governments). In so far as policy interventions induce DUP activities, they are analytically divided into two appropriate categories (Bhagwati and Srinivasan, 1982):

Category I: Policy-triggered DUP activities. One class consists of *lobbying* activities. Examples include: rent-seeking analysis of the cost of protection *via* import licences (Krueger, 1974); revenue-seeking analysis of the cost of tariffs (Bhagwati and Srinivasan, 1980), of shadow prices in cost-benefit analysis (Foster, 1981), of price *versus* quantity interventions (Bhagwati and Srinivasan, 1982), of non-economic objectives (Anam, 1982), of rank-ordering of alternative distorting policies such as tariffs, production and consumption taxes (Bhagwati, Brecher and Srinivasan, 1984), of the optimal tariff (Dinopoulos, 1984), of the transfer problem (Bhagwati, Brecher and Hatta, 1985), and of Voluntary Export Restrictions relative to import tariffs (Brecher and Bhagwati, 1987).

Another class consists of *policy-evading* activities. Examples include: analysis of smuggling (Bhagwati and Hansen, 1973), its implication for optimal tariffs (Johnson, 1974 and Bhagwati and Srinivasan, 1973), and alternative modelling by Kemp (1976), Sheikh (1974), Pitt (1981) and Martin and Panagariya (1984).

Category II: Policy-influencing DUP activities. The other generic class of DUP activities is not triggered by policies in place but is rather aimed at influencing the formulation of the policy itself. The most prominent DUP-theoretic contributions in this area relate to the analysis of tariff-seeking. Although Brock and Magee (1978) (1980) pioneered here, the general equilibrium analyses of endogeneous tariffs began with Findlay and Wellisz (1982) and Feenstra and Bhagwati (1982), the two sets of authors modelling the government and the lobbying activities in contrasting ways. Notable among the later contributions are Mayer (1984), who extends the analysis formally to include factor income-distribution and therewith voting behaviour, and Wellisz and Wilson (1984). Magee (1984) has an excellent review of many of these contributions. The implication of endogenizing the tariff for conventional measurement of the cost of protection has been analysed in Bhagwati (1980) and Tullock (1981).

The *choice* between alternative policy instruments when modelling the response of lobbies and governments to import competition, has also been extensively analysed. The issue was raised by Bhagwati (1982b) and analysed further by Dinopoulos (1983) and Sapir (1983) in terms of how different agents (e.g. 'capitalists' and 'labour') would profit from different policy responses such as increased immigration of cheap labour and tariffs when import competition intensified. It has subsequently been explored more fully by Rodrik (1986) who compares tariffs with production subsidies.

Second, Bhagwati (1982a) has noted, generalizing a result in Bhagwati and Srinivasan (1980), that DUP activities, while defined to be those that waste resources in their direct impact, cannot be taken as *ultimately* wasteful, i.e. immiserizing, since they may be triggered by a suboptimal policy intervention. For, in that event, throwing away or wasting resources may be beneficial. The shadow price of a productive factor in such

'highly distorted' economies may be negative. This is the obverse of the possibility of immiserizing growth (Bhagwati, 1980). Thus, Buchanan (1980), who has addressed the issue of DUP activities and *defined* them as activities that (ultimately) cause waste, has been corrected in Bhagwati (1983): the definition of DUP activities cannot properly exclude the possibility that DUP activities are ultimately beneficial rather than wasteful. This central distinction between the direct and the ultimate welfare impacts of DUP activities is now universally accepted. DUP activities are therefore defined now, as in Bhagwati (1982b) and subsequent contributions, as wasteful only in the direct sense.

Third, Bhagwati, Brecher and Srinivasan (1984) have raised yet another fundamental issue concerning DUP activities. Thus, where DUP activities belong to Category II distinguished above, full endogeneity of policy can follow. If so, the conventional rank-ordering of policies is no longer possible. We have the *Determinacy Paradox*: policy is chosen in the solution to the full 'political-economy', DUP-theoretic solution and cannot be varied at will. These authors have therefore suggested that, where full endogeneity obtains, the appropriate way to theorize about policy is to take variations around the observed DUP-theoretic equilibrium. Thus, traditional economic parameters such as factor supply could be varied; similarly now the DUP-activity parameters such as, say, the cost of lobbying could be varied. The impact on actual welfare resulting from such variations can then be a proper focus of analysis, implying a wholly different way of looking at policy questions from that which economists have employed to date.

Finally, DUP activities are related to Krueger's (1974) important category of rent-seeking activities. The latter are a subset of the former, in so far as they relate to lobbying for quota-determined scarcity rents and are therefore part of DUP activities of Category II distinguished above (Bhagwati, 1983).

JAGDISH N. BHAGWATI

See also BRIBERY; RENT-SEEKING.

BIBLIOGRAPHY

Anam, M. 1982. Distortion-triggered lobbying and welfare: a contribution to the theory of directly-unproductive profit-seeking activities. *Journal of International Economics* 13, August, 15–32.

Becker, G.S. 1983. A theory of competition among pressure groups for political influence. *Quarterly Journal of Economics* 93, August, 371–400.

Bhagwati, J. 1980. Lobbying and welfare. *Journal of Public Economics* 14, December, 355–63.

Bhagwati, J. 1982a. Directly-unproductive profit-seeking (DUP) activities. *Journal of Political Economy* 90, October, 988–1002.

Bhagwati, J. 1982b. Shifting comparative advantage, protectionist demands, and policy response. In *Import Competition and Response*, ed. Jagdish Bhagwati, Chicago: Chicago University Press.

Bhagwati, J. 1983. DUP activities and rent seeking. *Kyklos* 36, 634–7.

Bhagwati, J. and Hansen, B. 1973. Theoretical analysis of smuggling. *Quarterly Journal of Economics* 87, 172–87.

Bhagwati, J. and Srinivasan, T.N. 1973. Smuggling and trade policy. *Journal of Public Economics* 2, 377–89.

Bhagwati, J. and Srinivasan, T.N. 1980. Revenue-seeking: a generalization of the theory of tariffs. *Journal of Political Economy* 88, December, 1069–87.

Bhagwati, J. and Srinivasan, T.N. 1982. The welfare consequences of directly-unproductive profit-seeking (DUP) lobbying activities: price *versus* quantity distortions. *Journal of International Economics* 13, 33–44.

Bhagwati, J., Brecher, R. and Hatta, T. 1985. The generalized theory of transfers and welfare: exogenous (policy-imposed) and endogenous (transfer-induced) distortions. *Quarterly Journal of Economics* 100(3), 697–714.

Bhagwati, J., Brecher, R. and Srinivasan T.N. 1984. DUP activities and economic theory. In *Neoclassical Political Economy: The Analysis of Rent-seeking and DUP Activities*, ed. David Colander, Cambridge, Mass.: Ballinger & Co.

Brecher, R. and Bhagwati, J. 1987. Voluntary export restrictions and import restrictions: a welfare-theoretic comparison. In *Essays in Honour of W.M. Corden*, ed. Henryk Kierzkowski, Oxford: Basil Blackwell.

Brock, W. and Magee, S. 1978. The economics of special interest politics: the case of the tariff. *American Economic Review* 68, May, 246–50.

Brock, W. and Magee, S. 1980. Tariff formation in a democracy. In *Current Issues in International Commercial Policy and Diplomacy*, ed. John Black and Brian Hindley, New York: Macmillan.

Buchanan, J. 1980. Rent seeking and profit seeking. In *Towards a General Theory of the Rent-seeking Society*, ed. James Buchanan, Gordon Tullock and R. Tollison, College Station: Texas A&M University Press.

Buchanan, J., Tullock, G. and Tollison, R. (eds) 1980. *Towards a General Theory of the Rent-seeking Society*. College Station: Texas A&M University Press.

Dinopoulos, E. 1983. Import competition, international factor mobility and lobbying responses: the Schumpeterian industry cases. *Journal of International Economics* 14, May, 395–410.

Dinopolous, E. 1984. The optimal tariff with revenue-seeking: a contribution to the theory of DUP activities. In *The Neoclassical Political Economy: The Analysis of Rent-seeking and DUP Activities*, ed. David Colander, Cambridge, Mass.: Ballinger & Co.

Feenstra, R. and Bhagwati, J. 1982. Tariff seeking and the efficient tariff. In *Import Competition and Response*, ed. Jagdish Bhagwati, Chicago: Chicago University Press.

Findlay, R. and Wellisz, S. 1982. Endogenous tariffs, the political economy of trade restrictions, and welfare. In *Import Competition and Response*, ed. Jagdish Bhagwati, Chicago: Chicago University Press.

Foster, E. 1981. The treatment of rents in cost-benefit analysis. *American Economic Review* 71, March, 171–8.

Johnson, H.G. 1974. Notes on the economic theory of smuggling. In *Illegal Transactions in International Trade*, ed. Jagdish Bhagwati, Series in International Economics, Amsterdam: North-Holland.

Kemp, M. 1976. Smuggling and optimal commercial policy. *Journal of Public Economics* 5, 381–4.

Krueger, A. 1974. The political economy of the rent-seeking society. *American Economic Review* 64, June, 291–303.

Lindbeck, A. 1976. Stabilization policies in open economies with endogenous politicians. Richard Ely Lecture. *American Economic Review* 66, May, 1–19.

Magee, S. 1984. Endogenous tariff theory: a survey. In *Neoclassical Political Economy: The Analysis of Rent-seeking and DUP Activities*, ed. David Colander, Cambridge, Mass.: Ballinger & Co.

Martin, L. and Panagariya, A. 1984. Smuggling, trade, and price disparity: a crime-theoretic approach. *Journal of International Economics* 17, November, 201–18.

Mayer, W. 1984. Endogenous tariff formation. *American Economic Review* 74, December, 970–85.

Pitt, M. 1981. Smuggling and price disparity. *Journal of International Economics* 11, 447–58.

Rodrik, D. 1986. Tariffs, subsidies and welfare with endogenous policy. *Journal of International Economics*, November.

Sapir, A. 1983. Foreign competition, immigration and structural adjustment. *Journal of International Economics* 14, May, 381–94.

Sheikh, M. 1974. Smuggling, production and welfare. *Journal of International Economics* 4, 355–64.

Tullock, G. 1981. Lobbying and welfare: a comment. *Journal of Public Economics* 16, 391–4.

Wellisz, S. and Wilson, J.D. 1984. Public sector inefficiency, a general equilibrium analysis. Columbia University International Economics Research Center Discussion Paper Series No. 254.

direct taxes. The distinction between direct taxes and indirect taxes traditionally rests on a view of the incidence of the two kinds of tax. The incidence of a tax identifies who suffers loss of income or welfare as a result of the imposition of the tax. This may differ from the location of the legal liability for payment of the tax if the payer is able to shift part or all of this liability to some other agent. The capacity to shift the tax burden in this way depends on the elasticities of demand and supply of the taxed factor or commodity. Direct taxes are those for which the legal liability and the incidence are identical: indirect taxes are those where the tax is shifted, most usually to final consumers.

Thus income taxes are generally regarded as direct taxes and commodity taxes as indirect. This supposes that factor supplies are completely inelastic and commodity supplies perfectly elastic, an empirical observation which may hold in particular cases but which cannot be seen as a universal truth. In reality, all taxes are shifted to some extent and none completely. A more recent reformulation of the direct/indirect distinction (Atkinson and Stiglitz, 1980) describes indirect taxes as those differentiated by the nature of the transaction and direct taxes are those differentiated by the identity of the transactors; but this too breaks down on closer examination and the classification is one with no particular economic significance. The most important direct taxes are progressive wealth, income and expenditure taxes levied on individuals, and tax imposed on the income of corporations.

Before the emergence of modern systems of public finance, ad hoc wealth taxes were a primary source of revenue. But this was possible only when wealth mostly took the form of real property and revenue requirements were relatively minor. Many countries still have a tax on wealth, but there is none in which it makes an important contribution to revenue. Taxes are often levied on transfers of capital, on death or sometimes when substantial gifts are made. Such a tax may be donor or donee based. An inheritance tax levied on the donor is a progressive tax based on the total of gifts made by the tax payer. An accession tax on the donee is one in which the rate of tax is based on the cumulative total of gifts received.

Although there is extensive academic discussion of the potential of a direct tax on expenditure, no major country has adopted one. Direct taxes are primarily income taxes, on the incomes of individuals and of corporations. We begin by looking at the base of the tax and then consider the criteria which should determine the rates at which income – personal or corporate – should be taxed.

It seems trite to observe that in order to tax income it is necessary to define it, but in fact the taxing statutes of most states do not attempt to do so. Income is exemplified rather than defined. For economists, the classic definition of income is that of Hicks (1939) – 'income is the maximum value which a man can consume during a week and still be as well off at the end of the week as he was at the beginning'. By the same principle, corporate income might be defined as the maximum which a company can distribute, and still be as well off at the end of the accounting period as at the beginning. But these are not operational concepts for a tax inspector. How is he to determine what a man expects? And what is he to do if these expectations are unreasonable?

Thus attention has instead been devoted to the concept of 'comprehensive income', or Haig–Simons income, so-called after its principal advocates (Simons, 1938). As Hicksian income looks forward, so Haig–Simons looks back, and measures not what a man could have expected to consume but what he could in fact have consumed. If expectations are always fulfilled, then the two concepts are identical: but windfall gains, excluded from the Hicksian concept of income, fall within the Haig–Simons one. It follows that Haig–Simons income requires that all accruing capital gains should be included within the tax base and taxed as income. In fact no country has gone as far as this; some tax certain capital gains as income; almost all tax most kinds of capital gain more lightly, if at all.

The application of either a Hicksian or a Haig–Simons measure of real income implies indexation of the tax base. This means not only that capital gains should be adjusted for inflation, but that investment income – paid or received – should be adjusted also.

Such inflation adjustment should relate to individual income, to capital gains, and to the income of corporations. Inflation adjustment to the income of individuals is very rare, although several countries now provide for indexation in calculating capital gains. Most attention to the effects of inflation on the measurement of income has been given in the corporate sector inflation. Accounting profit becomes a misleading indicator of the returns earned by a company under inflation because depreciation is generally based on the historic cost rather than the current cost of equivalent assets; because the rise in the price of goods held in stock (stock depreciation) is included in profits; and because interest paid or received is expressed in nominal rather than real terms. All countries with recent experience of high rates of inflation have considered changes to accounting standards to remove these distortions but agreement on appropriate adjustments has proved elusive.

In the absence of accepted accounting principles, tax systems have responded to inflation in ad hoc ways. The inadequacy of historic cost depreciation allowances has been partly compensated for by acceleration of the rate at which such allowances may be taken. Relief for the effect of inflation on stock values has been given, either by accepting accounting practices such as LIFO (last in, first out) which automatically give relief at current prices, or by particular measures of stock relief. Tax authorities have been much more reluctant to make allowance for the effect of inflation in eroding the value both of the monetary assets of companies and of their debts.

A tax system which was fully indexed in this way would be neutral with respect to the rate of inflation, but it would not equalize pre- and post-tax rates of return because the real return earned by the company would continue to be subject to tax. Full neutrality could be achieved by means of a cash flow tax, which allows immediate deductibility of all capital expenditure – either in stocks or on fixed assets – but denies any relief for financing costs, whether interest or otherwise. Such a tax was proposed by the Meade Committee (1978) and it uses as its base the flow of funds from the real operations of the company to those who finance it.

Once income has been defined, at what rate should it be taxed? Differentiation between types of personal income was a principal issue when income tax was introduced in the 19th century. The argument rested on the precariousness of income from employment relative to property income, and this, is was suggested, provided a reason for taxing investment income more heavily. These arguments read rather oddly in a 20th-century context, in which inflation and economic fluctuations have generally made property income appear more precarious than earnings, and this argument has largely vanished from discussion and its consequences from tax schedules.

A tax schedule is progressive if the average rate of tax increases with income. This does not require that marginal tax rates are increasing and indeed a linear tax schedule is progressive if its intercept is positive. There is no unambiguous measure of progressivity, and the same term is sometimes used to cover both the extent to which the schedule deviates from

proportionality and the redistributive effect of tax structure. It will be apparent that a tax which departs substantially from proportionality but generates little revenue will have less redistributive effect than a more nearly proportional but heavier tax.

19th-century utilitarian arguments suggested alternative rate structures. The principle of equal sacrifice, for example, demanded a schedule which imposed equal utility losses on all the taxpayers. This implied payments from those with higher incomes, but not necessarily proportionately larger payments, the outcome depending on the elasticity of the marginal utility of income. Utility maximization subject to a revenue constraint requires equal *marginal* sacrifices, with similar implications.

However, these analyses take no account of the effects of tax schedules on labour supply. Like indirect taxes, income taxes impose a deadweight loss or excess burden in addition to the revenue which they raise. The magnitude of these losses depends on marginal tax rates and the wage elasticity of labour supply. It follows that there is a direct conflict between the progressivity of a tax schedule – which implies high marginal rates of tax – and its efficiency properties – which require low marginal rates.

Mirrlees (1971) was the first to examine this trade-off explicitly and although a substantial literature on optimal income tax structures has developed since, relatively few results of general application have emerged. There is some indication that marginal tax rates should be lower at the extremes of the distribution than in the middle of it. The disincentive effects of high marginal tax rates depend on the numbers of individuals in the relevant range, whereas their redistributive function depends on the number of individuals above that range. As we move up the income distribution, this redistributive effect steadily diminishes, while the disincentive effect remains; and thus the balance between the two factors changes in a direction which points to lower marginal rates of tax. Similar arguments can be applied at the lower end of the distribution.

While the welfare effects of income taxation are principally the product of marginal rates, the overall effect on labour supply is determined by both income and substitution effects, and is therefore influenced by the average as well as the marginal tax rate at any point in the distribution. For this reason, while the efficiency costs of increasing taxation are unambiguous the labour supply effect may be positive or negative in sign. Labour supply is presumably zero at tax rates of 100 per cent, however, and if an interior maximum exists (which is by no means certain) then there will be some rate below this which yields maximum revenue. This observation yields what has become known as the Laffer curve.

The structural issues which influence redistribution across the income distribution are concerned with vertical equity in taxation. Horizontal equity reflects its concern with the relative tax burdens at the same point in the income distribution. Horizontal equity implies that individuals in the same circumstances should be treated similarly and would exclude, for example, random taxation (even though this might, under certain circumstances, be efficient). However the principle of horizontal equity has limited application because of the difficulty of agreeing an objective definition of 'similar circumstances'. The most important issue of horizontal equity in practice concerns the tax treatment of the family, an area of taxation in which there is direct conflict between two conflicting principles – the desire to respect the right of individuals to individual treatment, which points to an individual basis for taxation, and the desire to relate liability to the whole of an individual's circumstances, which necessarily includes the circumstances of those with whom he or she lives. Most tax systems incorporate elements of both individual and unit bases.

In fixing the rate of corporate income tax, it is necessary to begin by asking why we tax corporate income at all. Although corporations have distinct legal personalities, they have no economic personality and ultimately generate no command over resources other than those of the individuals who work for them, manage them, buy their products, or own their shares. It is these individuals who pay corporation tax. The economic rationale for corporate income taxes therefore requires justification.

One such argument is that they are there: the phenomenon of tax capitalization implies that if particular assets, such as the equity of corporations, are subject to discriminatory taxation then these taxes will be reflected in the prices of the assets concerned. To remove such a tax would effect no current efficiency gain, and would confer windfall gains on current shareholders; this is the rationalization of the traditional maxim that 'an old tax is a good tax'. Corporation tax may also enable countries to derive revenue from the assets of non-residents; this is a powerful argument for such a tax in many countries.

An important point is that in the absence of corporate income tax, individuals would avoid the personal income tax through incorporation. This suggests that the income of corporations should be attributed to its owners and taxed as their income. Although the possibility of full *integration* of corporate and personal income taxation has been discussed, and was recommended for Canada by the Carter Commission (1966), no country has yet adopted it. The *classical* system of corporation tax is one in which the income of corporations is taxed at a flat rate entirely separate from the income of shareholders. This is the system used in the United States; most European countries, however, now employ an imputation system in which the shareholder receives some credit against his own income tax bill on dividends for corporation tax paid by the company from which he receives them. This relieves the element of double taxation implicit in the classical system, but still tends to tax income accruing through corporations more heavily than other kinds of income.

Corporation tax has usually been seen as a tax on capital employed in the corporate sector. It follows that this purpose is discriminated against relative to other uses of capital in the domestic economy, such as agriculture or property. This is the approach adopted in Harberger's classic (theoretical) analysis of the incidence of corporation tax (Harberger, 1962), which traced its effects on returns to capital in different sectors of the economy. It is also implicit in most empirical studies of the impact of corporation tax, such as those of Musgrave and Krzyzaniak (1964), which have considered the question of the extent to which a tax on the capital employed by corporations can be shifted forward into the prices of goods produced by the corporate sector. Their work suggested that the extent of such shifting might be substantial.

More recent analysis has challenged this approach to the incidence of company taxation (Stiglitz, 1976). The argument is that corporation tax cannot appropriately be represented as a tax on capital employed. Most corporate taxes allow extensive deductions for capital costs, such as interest and depreciation. If capital costs are fully deductible, then the corporate tax system is *neutral*. Such neutrality can be achieved either if all investment costs can be expensed, or if depreciation allowances correspond to true economic depreciation and financing costs are fully deductible, through tax

relief on interest paid and imputation for company dividends. If the tax regime provides – as is common in many countries – both for deductions for the costs of finance and for accelerated depreciation, then the corporation tax may actually act as a subsidy to corporate capital rather than a tax. The post-tax rate of return may exceed the pre-tax rate. Such a tax may still yield revenue, since it will still fall on pure profits, i.e. returns earned by the firm which are not directly attributable to its capital employed.

Pure profits are generated by entrepreneurship, a word which may describe the classic entrepreneurial function of bringing different factors of production together; the exploitation or establishment of monopoly rents; or the generation of new means of organization or invention. Thus the new view of corporation tax sees it as a levy on those items, combined with a rather arbitrary array of taxes and subsidies to different types of investment. The rates of these taxes and subsidies depend on the degree to which a given activity can be financed by debt rather than equity and the relationship between true economic depreciation and what is permitted for tax purposes.

Direct taxation can be adjusted sensitively to bold social and economic objectives, and as modern states have developed and their revenue requirements have grown so reliance on them has tended to increase. More recently, however, dependence on personal income tax has been seen to imply excessive rates. The result has been some moves back towards broadly based indirect taxes, particularly the value added tax, which has been introduced throughout the European community and in about thirty other states.

Similar pressures have been evident in the corporate sector. Taxing corporate income is therefore not the only means of taxing corporations and, given the difficulties involved in identifying the country within which income arises, measuring income in a period of inflation, and taxing declining real profitability, taxes on corporate income have tended to diminish in importance. The average share of total OECD tax receipts derived from corporation tax fell from 9.2 per cent to 7.4 per cent between 1965 and 1983. At the same time, however, other taxes on business, particularly payroll and social security taxes, have tended to increase: implying an overall shift in relative tax rates on capital and labour as factors of production.

JOHN KAY

See also CORPORATE TAXATION; TAXATION OF INCOME; TAXATION OF WEALTH.

BIBLIOGRAPHY

Atkinson, A.B. and Stiglitz, J.E. 1980. *Lectures on Public Economics.* New York: McGraw Hill.

Carter Commission. 1966. *Report of the Royal Commission on Taxation.* Ottawa.

Harberger, A.C. 1962. The incidence of the corporation income tax. *Journal of Political Economy* 70, 215–40.

Hicks, J.R. 1939. *Value and Capital.* Oxford: Clarendon Press.

Meade, J.E. (chairman) 1978. *The Structure and Reform of Direct Taxation.* London: Allen & Unwin.

Mirrlees, J.A. 1971. An exploration in the theory of optimal income taxation. *Review of Economic Studies* 38, 175–208.

Musgrave, R.A. and Krzyzaniak, M. 1964. *The Shifting of the Corporation Income Tax.* Baltimore: Johns Hopkins Press.

Simons, H.C. 1938. *Personal Income Taxation.* Chicago: Chicago University Press.

Stiglitz, J.E. 1976. The corporation tax. *Journal of Public Economics* 5(3–4), 303–11.

discommodities. *See* GOODS AND COMMODITIES.

discount. *See* PRESENT VALUE.

discrete choice models. These are those statistical models which specify the probability distribution of discrete dependent variables as a function of independent variables and unknown parameters. They are sometimes called *qualitative response models*, and are relevant in economics because the decision of an economic unit frequently involves discrete choice: for example, the decision regarding whether a person joins the labour force or not, the decision as to the number of cars to own, the choice of occupation, the choice of the mode of transportation, etc.

Despite their relevance, however, it is only recently (approximately in the last twenty years) that economists have started using them extensively. There seem to be three reasons for a recent surge of interest in such models: (1) Economists have realized that econometric models using only aggregate data cannot accurately explain economic phenomena nor predict the future values of economic variables well. (2) Large scale disaggregated data on consumers and producers have become available. (3) The rapid development of computer technology has made possible estimation of realistic models of this kind.

Note that when aggregated over many individuals, discrete variables behave almost like continuous variables and therefore can be subjected to standard regression analysis. A discrete choice model becomes necessary when we want to model the behaviour of an individual economic unit.

As econometric applications of these models have increased, we have also seen an increase of theoretical papers which address the problem of their specification and estimation. Biometricians have in fact used such models longer than have econometricians, using them, for example, to analyse the effect of an insecticide or the effect of a medical treatment. However, since the versions that econometricians use are generally more complex than those used by biometricians, it has been necessary for the former to develop new models and new methods of statistical inference.

There are cases where a discrete decision of an economic unit is closely interrelated with the determination of the value of a continuous variable. For example, a decision to join the labour force necessitates the decision of how many hours to work and at what wage rate. A decision to buy a car cannot be separated from the decision of how much to spend on a car. The joint determination of the values of discrete variables and continuous variables belongs to the topic of *limited dependent* variables.

Other closely related topics are *Markov chain models* and *duration* (or survival) *models*. These models introduce the time domain into discrete choice models thereby making the models dynamic. In Markov chain models time changes discretely, whereas in duration models time moves continuously.

Those who wish to study the subject in more detail than the present entry are referred to Amemiya (1981 and 1985), Maddala (1983), and McFadden (1984).

1 UNIVARIATE BINARY MODELS

1.1 *Model specification.* The simplest type of a discrete choice model is a univariate binary model which specifies the binary (1 or 0) outcome of a single dependent variable. Let y_i be the ith observation on the binary dependent variable and x_i the ith observation on the vector of independent variables. Then a general univariate binary model is defined by

$$P(y_i = 1) = F(x_i'\beta), \qquad i = 1, 2, \ldots, n, \qquad (\text{I})$$

where P stands for probability, F is a particular distribution

function, and β is a vector of unknown parameters. For example, the event $y_i = 1$ may signify that the ith individual buys a car and the elements of the vector x_i may include the income of the ith individual and the price of the car the individual must pay if he decides to buy a car.

Note that we have assumed the argument of F in (I) to be a linear function of the independent variables. As in the linear regression model, this linearity assumption is more general than appears at first, because x_i need not be the original economic variables like income and price, but instead could contain various transformations of the original variables. However, the model in which the function F depends on a nonlinear function of the independent variables and unknown parameters can be handled with only a slight modification of the subsequent analysis.

A variety of models arises as we choose different distribution functions for F. The most commonly used functions are the standard normal distribution function Φ and the logistic distribution function Λ. These functions are defined by

$$\Phi(x) = \int_{-\infty}^{x} (2\pi)^{-1/2} \exp(-2^{-1}t^2)\, dt$$

and

$$\Lambda(x) = (1 + e^{-x})^{-1}.$$

When $F = \Phi$, the model is called the *probit* model, and when $F = \Lambda$, it is called the *logit* model.

The decision regarding which function to use should be based both on theoretical considerations and on how well a model fits the data. However, as long as a researcher experiments with various independent variables and with various ways in which the independent variables appear in the argument of F, the particular choice of F is not crucial.

Let us consider by way of an example how this model arises as the result of an individual maximizing a utility function. Consider the decision of a person regarding whether he drives a car to work or travels by public transport. We suppose that a level of utility is associated with each alternative and the person is to choose the alternative for which the utility is greater. Let U_{i1} and U_{i0} be the ith person's utilities associated with driving a car and travelling by public transport respectively. We assume that they are linear functions of independent variables with additive error terms as follows:

$$U_{i1} = x_{i1}'\beta_1 + \epsilon_{i1},$$

and

$$U_{i0} = x_{i0}'\beta_0 + \epsilon_{i0}.$$

Here, the vector x_{i1} may be thought of as consisting of the time and the cost which would be incurred if the ith person were to drive a car, plus his socio-economic characteristics. The error term may be regarded as the sum of all the unobserved independent variables. Defining $y_i = 1$ if the ith person travels by car and $y_i = 0$ if he travels otherwise, we have

$$P(y_i = 1) = P(U_{i1} > U_{i0})$$
$$= F(x_{i1}'\beta_1 - x_{i0}'\beta_0),$$

where F is the distribution function of $\epsilon_{i0} - \epsilon_{i1}$. Thus, a probit model will result from the normality of $\epsilon_{i0} - \epsilon_{i1}$. The normality may be justified on the ground of a central limit theorem.

If a probit model fits the data well, so will a logit model because the logistic distribution function is similar to the standard normal distribution function.

1.2 *Estimation.* Let us consider the estimation of the parameter vector β in the model (I). We shall first discuss the maximum likelihood (ML) estimator and second, the minimum chi-square (MIN χ^2) estimator.

The likelihood function based on n independent binary observations $y_1, y_2, \ldots, y_n$ is given by

$$L = \prod_{i=1}^{n} F(x_i'\beta)^{y_i} [1 - F(x_i'\beta)]^{1-y_i}.$$

The ML estimator $\hat{\beta}$ is obtained by maximizing $\ln L$. Under general conditions $\hat{\beta}$ is consistent and asymptotically normal with the asymptotic variance–covariance matrix given by

$$V\hat{\beta} = \left\{ \sum_{i=1}^{n} \left[\frac{f^2(x_i'\beta)}{F(x_i'\beta)[1 - F(x_i'\beta)]} x_i x_i' \right] \right\}^{-1},$$

where f is the derivative of F.

Since an explicit formula for the ML estimator cannot be obtained for this model, the calculation of the estimator must be done by an iterative method. The log likelihood function can be shown to be globally concave in the probit and logit models. In these models, therefore, a standard iterative algorithm such as the Newton–Raphson method will generally converge to the global maximum.

The MIN χ^2 estimator, first proposed by Berkson (1944) for the logit model, works only if there are many observations on y for each of the values taken by the vector x. Let us suppose that x_i takes T vector values $x_1, x_2, \ldots, x_T$ and classify integers $1, 2, \ldots, n$ into T disjoint sets $I_1, I_2, \ldots, I_T$ by the rule: $i \in I_t$ if $x_i = x_t$. Define $n_t =$ number of integers contained in I_t and $\hat{P}_t = n_t^{-1} \Sigma_{i \in I_t} y_i$. Then, by a Taylor expansion, we have approximately

$$F^{-1}(\hat{P}_t) \simeq x_t'\beta + \{f[F^{-1}(P_t)]\}^{-1}(\hat{P}_t - P_t),$$

where F^{-1} denotes the inverse function of F. The MIN χ^2 estimator $\tilde{\beta}$ is the weighted least squares estimator applied to this last heteroscedastic regression equation; that is,

$$\tilde{\beta} = \left[\sum_{t=1}^{T} w_t x_t x_t' \right]^{-1} \sum_{t=1}^{T} w_t x_t F^{-1}(\hat{P}_t),$$

where

$$w_t = n_t f_t^2 [F^{-1}(\hat{P}_t)]/[\hat{P}_t (1 - \hat{P}_t)].$$

The MIN χ^2 estimator has the same asymptotic distribution as the ML estimator. Its advantage over the latter is computational simplicity, while its weakness is that it requires many observations for each value of the independent variables. The required number of observations increases with the number of the independent variables. If an independent variable takes many values it may be necessary to group the values into a small number of groups in order to define the MIN χ^2 estimator. But such a procedure will introduce a certain bias to the estimator.

2 MULTINOMIAL MODELS

A multinomial model is a statistical model for independent discrete variables, some of which take more than two values: Supposing that y_i takes $m_i + 1$ integer values $0, 1, \ldots, m_i$, the model is defined by specifying the $\Sigma_{i=1}^{n} m_i$ probabilities:

$$P(y_i = j) = F_{ij}(x, \beta), \qquad \begin{array}{l} i = 1, 2, \ldots, n \\ j = 1, 2, \ldots, m_i. \end{array} \qquad \text{(II)}$$

Note that $P(y_i = 0)$ need not be specified because the sum of the $m_i + 1$ probabilities is one for each i. It is important to let m depend on i because the number of alternatives available to different individuals may differ.

Defining $\Sigma_{i=1}^{n} (m_i + 1)$ binary variables

$$y_{ij} = 1 \quad \text{if} \quad y_i = j$$
$$= 0 \quad \text{if} \quad y_i \neq j, \qquad i = 1, 2, \ldots, n$$
$$j = 0, 1, \ldots, m_j,$$

the likelihood function of the model can be written as

$$L = \prod_{i=1}^{n} \prod_{j=0}^{m_i} F_{ij}(x, \beta)^{y_{ij}}.$$

Note that this reduces to the L equation of Section 1 if $m_i = 1$ for all i.

The ML estimator of β is consistent and asymptotically normal with its asymptotic variance–covariance matrix given by

$$V\hat{\beta} = -\left[E \frac{\partial^2 \log L}{\partial \beta \, \partial \beta'} \right]^{-1},$$

which will be equal to $V\hat{\beta}$ equation in Section 1 in the binary case. The MIN χ^2 estimator can be also defined for the multinomial model, although the definition will not be given here.

2.1 *Ordered models.* An ordered multinomial model arises when there is an unobserved continuous random variable y_i^* which determines the outcome of y_i by the rule

$$y_i = j \quad \text{if and only if} \quad \alpha_j < y_i^* < \alpha_{j+1},$$
$$j = 0, 1, \ldots, m, \quad \alpha_0 = -\infty, \quad \alpha_{m+1} = \infty.$$

Such a rule may be appropriate, for example, if $y_i = j$ signifies the event that the ith individual owns j cars and y_i^* refers to a measure of the intensity of the ith individual's desire to own cars. If the distribution function of $y_i^* - x_i'\beta$ is F, the last equation leads to an ordered model defined by

$$P(y_i = j) = F(\alpha_{j+1} - x_i'\beta) - F(\alpha_j - x_i'\beta).$$

As in the binary case, the choice of Φ and Λ for F is most frequently used.

An ordered model is attractive because of its simplicity. However, in many economic applications it may be an oversimplification to assume that the outcome of a multinomial variable can be completely determined by the outcome of a simple continuous variable. For example, for owning cars it is probably more realistic to assume that the ith person owns j cars if $U_{ij} > U_{ik}$ for all $k \neq j$, where U_{ij} is the utility that accrues to the ith person if he owns j cars. In this case m continuous variables $U_{ij} - U_{i,j+1}, j = 0, 1, \ldots, m$, determine the outcome of the discrete variable.

A multinomial model which is not an ordered model is called an unordered model. The models discussed in the next parts of this section are all unordered.

2.2 *Multinomial logit model.* A multinomial logit model is described below by defining the probabilities of the ith individual who faces three alternatives $j = 0, 1,$ and 2. A generalization to the case of more alternatives can be easily inferred. The three probabilities are given by

$$P(y_i = 2) = D^{-1} \exp(x_{i2}'\beta)$$
$$P(y_i = 1) = D^{-1} \exp(x_{i1}'\beta),$$
$$P(y_i = 0) = D^{-1},$$

where $D = 1 + \exp(x_{i1}'\beta) + \exp(x_{i2}'\beta)$.

McFadden (1974) showed how a multinomial logit model can be derived from the maximization of stochastic utilities. Suppose that the ith individual's utility U_{ij} associated with the jth alternative is the sum of the nonstochastic part μ_{ij} and the stochastic part ϵ_{ij} and that the individual chooses the alternative for which the utility is a maximum. Suppose further that ϵ_{i0}, ϵ_{i1} and ϵ_{i2} are independent and identically distributed according to the distribution function $\exp[-\exp(-\epsilon)]$ – called the *type I extreme value distribution*. Then we can show

$$P(y_i = 2) = P(U_{i2} > U_{i1}, U_{i2} > U_{i0})$$
$$= \exp(\mu_{i2})/[\exp(\mu_{i0}) + \exp(\mu_{i1}) + \exp(\mu_{i2})],$$

and similarly for $P(y_i = 1)$ and $P(y_i = 0)$. Thus, the model defined by the three equations above follows from putting $\mu_{i2} - \mu_{i0} = x'_{i2}\beta$ and $\mu_{i1} - \mu_{i0} = x'_{i1}\beta$.

The multinomial logit model has been extensively used in economic applications, such as the choice of modes of transportation, the choice of occupations, and the choice of types of appliances. The likelihood function of the model can be shown to be globally concave; consequently, the ML estimator can be computed with relative ease.

A major limitation of the multinomial logit model lies in its independence assumption. Consider the choice of transportation modes and suppose first that the alternatives consist of car, bus, and train. Then the assumption of independent utilities may be reasonable. Next, to use McFadden's famous example, suppose instead that the choice is among a car, a red bus, and a blue bus. Then it is clearly unreasonable to assume that the utilities associated with the red bus and the blue bus are independent. In the next subsection we shall consider a multinomial model which corrects this deficiency.

2.3 *Nested logit model.*

We continue the last example. Let $U_j = \mu_j + \epsilon_j$, $j = 0$, 1, and 2, be the utilities associated with car, red bus, and blue bus, respectively. (The subscript i is suppressed to simplify notation.) Following McFadden (1977), suppose ϵ_0 is distributed according to the type I extreme value distribution and independent of ϵ_1 and ϵ_2 and that the joint distribution of ϵ_1 and ϵ_2 is given by

$$F(\epsilon_1, \epsilon_2) = \exp\{-[\exp(-\rho^{-1}\epsilon_1) + [\exp(-\rho^{-1}\epsilon_2)]^\rho\},$$
$$0 \leqslant \rho \leqslant 1.$$

This distribution is called *Gumbel's type B bivariate extreme value distribution*. The correlation coefficient is $1 - \rho^2$, and if $\rho = 1$ (the case of independence), $F(\epsilon_1, \epsilon_2)$ becomes the product of two type I extreme value distributions.

Under these assumptions it can be shown that

$$P(y = 0) = \exp(\mu_0)/\{\exp(\mu_0) + [\exp(\rho^{-1}\mu_1) + \exp(\rho^{-1}\mu_2)]^\rho\}$$

and

$$P(y = 1 | y \neq 0) = \exp(\rho^{-1}\mu_1)/[\exp(\rho^{-1}\mu_1) + \exp(\rho^{-1}\mu_2)].$$

The other probabilities can be deduced from the above. Note that the last equation shows that the choice between red bus and blue bus is made according to a binary logit model, while the previous equation shows that the choice between car and noncar is also like a logit model expect that a certain weighted average of $\exp(\mu_1)$ and $\exp(\mu_2)$ is involved.

2.4 *Multinomial probit model.*

A multinomial probit model is derived from the assumption that the utilities $U_{i0}, U_{i1}, \ldots, U_{im_i}$ are multivariate normal for every i. Its advantage is that general assumptions about the correlations among the utilities are allowed. Its major disadvantage is that the calculation of the choice probability requires the evaluation of multiple integrals of joint normal densities, which is feasible only for a small number of alternatives.

3 MULTIVARIATE MODELS

A multivariate discrete choice model specifies the joint probability distribution of two or more discrete dependent variables. For example, the joint distribution of two binary variables y_1 and y_2 each of which takes values 1 or 0 is determined by the four probabilities $P_{jk} = P(y_1 = j, y_2 = k)$, $j, k = 0, 1$. (Of course, the sum of the probabilities must be equal to 1.)

A multivariate model is a special case of a multinomial model. For example, the model of two binary variables mentioned in the preceding paragraph may be regarded as a multinomial model for a single discrete variable which takes four values with probabilities P_{11}, P_{10}, P_{01}, and P_{00}. Therefore, all the results given in section 2 apply to multivariate models as well. In this section we shall discuss three types of models which specifically take into account the multivariate feature of the model.

3.1 *Log-linear model*

A log-linear model refers to a particular parameterization of a multivariate discrete choice model. In the previous bivariate binary model, the log-linear parameterization of the four probabilitites is given as follows:

$$P_{11} = D^{-1}\exp(\alpha_1 + \alpha_2 + \alpha_{12}),$$
$$P_{10} = D^{-1}\exp(\alpha_1),$$
$$P_{01} = D^{-1}\exp(\alpha_2),$$

and

$$P_{00} = D^{-1}, \tag{III}$$

where $D = 1 + \exp(\alpha_1) + \exp(\alpha_2) + \exp(\alpha_1 + \alpha_2 + \alpha_{12})$.

There is a one-to-one correspondence between any three probabilities and the three α parameters of the log-linear model; thus, the two parameterizations are equivalent. An advantage of the log-linear parameterization lies in its feature that $\alpha_{12} = 0$ if and only if y_1 and y_2 are independent.

Equations (III) may be represented by the following single equation:

$$P(y_1, y_2) \propto \exp(\alpha_1 y_1 + \alpha_2 y_2 + \alpha_1 \alpha_2 y_1 y_2).$$

Each equation of (III) is obtained by inserting values 1 or 0 into y_1 and y_2 in this equation. This formulation can be generalized to a log-linear model of more than two binary variables. The case of three variables is given below:

$$P(y_1, y_2, y_3) \propto \exp(\alpha_1 y_1 + \alpha_2 y_2 + \alpha_3 y_3 + \alpha_{12} y_1 y_2$$
$$+ \alpha_{13} y_1 y_3 + \alpha_{23} y_2 y_3 + \alpha_{123} y_1 y_2 y_3).$$

The first three terms in the exponential function are called the main effects. Terms involving the product of two variables are called second-order interaction terms, the product of three variables third-order interaction terms, and so on.

Note that the last equation has seven parameters, which can be put into one-to-one correspondence with the seven probabilities that completely determine the distribution of y_1, y_2, and y_3. Such a model, without any constraint among the parameters, is called a *saturated* model. Researchers often use a constrained log-linear model, called an *unsaturated* model, which is obtained by setting some of the higher-order interaction terms to zero; e.g. Goodman (1972). See also Nerlove and Press (1973) for an example of a log-linear model in which some of the α parameters are specified to be functions of independent variables and unknown parameters.

3.2 *Multivariate nested logit model*

The multivariate nested logit model is a special case of the nested logit model discussed in section 2.3, which is useful whenever a set of alternatives can be classified into classes each of which contains similar alternatives. It is useful in a multivariate situation because the alternatives can be naturally classified according to the outcome of one or more of the variables.

For example, in the bivariate binary case, the four alternatives can be classified according to whether $y_1 = 1$ or 0. Let U_{jk} be the utility associated with the choice $y_1 = j$ and $y_2 = k, j, k = 0, 1$ and assume as before that $U_{jk} = \mu_{jk} + \epsilon_{jk}$, where μ's are nonstochastic and ϵ's are random. As a slight generalization of the Gumbel distribution in section 2.3 assume that

$$F(\epsilon_{j1}, \epsilon_{j0}) = a_j \exp\{-[\exp(-\rho_j^{-1}\epsilon_{j1}) + \exp(-\rho_j^{-1}\epsilon_{j2})]^{\rho_j}\},$$

$$j = 1, 0.$$

and that $(\epsilon_{11}, \epsilon_{10})$ are independent of $(\epsilon_{01}, \epsilon_{00})$. Then the resulting multivariate nested logit model is characterized by the following probabilities:

$$P(y_1 = 1) = a_1[\exp(\rho_1^{-1}\mu_{11}) + \exp(\rho_1^{-1}\mu_{10})]^{\rho_1}$$
$$\div \{a_1[\exp(\rho_1^{-1}\mu_{11}) + \exp(\rho_1^{-1}\mu_{10})]^{\rho_1}$$
$$+ a_0[\exp(\rho_0^{-1}\mu_{01}) + \exp(\rho_0^{-1}\mu_{00})]^{\rho_0}\},$$

$$P(y_2 = 1 | y_1 = 1)$$
$$= \exp(\rho_1^{-1}\mu_{11})/[\exp(\rho_1^{-1}\mu_{11}) + \exp(\rho_1^{-1}\mu_{10})],$$

$$P(y_2 = 1 | y_1 = 0)$$
$$= \exp(\rho_0^{-1}\mu_{01})/[\exp(\rho_0^{-1}\mu_{01}) + \exp(\rho_0^{-1}\mu_{00})].$$

We may further specify $\mu_{jk} = x'_{jk}\beta$.

3.3 *Multivariate probit model.* This model is conceptually different from the models of the preceding two sections in that here the marginal probabilities are specified first and the joint probabilities are then defined in a certain natural way.

As an example of a bivariate binary probit model, let us suppose $y_j^* \sim N(\mu_j, 1)$, $j = 1$ and 2, and y_j^* is unobservable and its value determines the value of the observable binary variable y_j by the rule

$$y_j = 1 \quad \text{if } y_j^* > 0$$
$$= 0 \quad \text{otherwise.}$$

This rule determines the marginal probabilities

$$P(y_j = 1) = \Phi(\mu_j), j = 1 \text{ and } 2.$$

Thus, the model will be complete when we specify the joint probability $P(y_1 = 1, y_2 = 1)$. A natural way to specify it would be to assume that y_1^* and y_2^* are jointly normal with a correlation coefficient ρ and define

$$P(y_1 = 1, y_2 = 1) = P(y_1^* > \mu_1, y_2^* > \mu_2).$$

Usually, a researcher will further specify $\mu_1 = x'_1\beta$ and $\mu_2 = x'_2\beta$ and estimate the unknown parameters β and ρ; see Morimune (1979) for an econometric example of this model.

A bivariate logit model may be defined similarly. But, unlike the probit case, there is no natural choice among many bivariate logistic distributions with the same marginal univariate logistic distributions.

4 CHOICE-BASED SAMPLING

In models (I) or (II), the independent variables x_i were treated as known constants. This is equivalent to considering the conditional distribution of y_i given x_i. This practice was valid because it was implicitly assumed that y_i and x_i were generated according to either *random sampling* or *exogenous sampling*.

Under random sampling, y and x are sampled according to their true joint distribution $P(y|x)f(x)$. Thus the likelihood function denoted L_R, is given by

$$L_R = \prod_{i=1}^n P(y_i|x_i)f(x_i).$$

Under exogenous sampling, a researcher samples x according to a certain distribution $g(x)$, which may not be equal to the true distribution $f(x)$ of x in the total population, and then samples y according to its true conditional probability $P(y|x)$. Thus the likelihood function, denoted L_E, is given by

$$L_E = \prod_{i=1}^n P(y_i|x_i)g(x_i).$$

In either case, as long as the parameters that characterize $P(y|x)$ are not related to the parameters that characterize $f(x)$ or $g(x)$, the maximization of L_R or L_E is equivalent to the maximization of

$$L = \prod_{i=1}^n P(y_i|x_i),$$

which is equivalent to the L of Section 2.

Under choice-based sampling, a researcher samples y according to fixed proportions $H(y)$, and then, given y, samples x according to the conditional density $f(x|y)$. By the formula of conditional density,

$$f(x|y) = P(y|x)f(x)/Q(y),$$

where $Q(y) = E_x P(y|x)$, and E_x denotes the expectation taken with respect to the random vector x. Thus, the likelihood function under choice-based sampling, denoted L_c, is

$$L_c = \prod_{i=1}^n Q(y_i)^{-1}P(y_i|x_i)f(x_i)H(y_i).$$

Unlike random sampling or exogenous sampling, choice-based sampling requires new analysis because the maximization of L_c is not equivalent to the maximization of L on account of the fact that $Q(y)$ depends on the same parameters that characterize $P(y|x)$.

In particular, it means that the standard ML estimator which maximizes L is not even consistent under choice-based sampling. The reader should consult Amemiya (1985) or Manski and McFadden (1981) for the properties of the choice-based sampling ML estimator which maximizes L_c in various situations.

Choice-based sampling is useful when only a small number of people sampled according to random sampling are likely to choose a particular alternative. For example, in a transportation study, random sampling of individual households in a community with a small proportion of bus riders may produce an extremely small number of bus riders. In such a case a researcher may be able to attain a higher efficiency of estimation by sampling bus riders at a bus depot to augment the data gathered by random sampling.

An interesting problem in choice-based sampling is how to determine $H(y)$ to maximize the efficiency of estimation. Although there is no clear-cut solution to this problem in general, it is expected that if $Q(j)$ is small for some j then the value of $H(j)$ which is larger than $Q(j)$ will yield a more efficient estimator than the value of $H(j)$ which is equal to $Q(j)$. Note that if in the formula for L_c, $H(j) = Q(j)$ for every j, than L_c is reduced to L_R.

5 DISTRIBUTION-FREE METHODS

Consider the univariate binary model (I). There, we assumed that the function $F(\cdot)$ is completely specified and known.

Recently, Manski (1975) and Cosslett (1983) have shown how to estimate β consistently (subject to a certain normalization) without specifying $F(\cdot)$.

Manski's estimator is based on the idea that as long as F satisfies the condition $F(0) = 0.5$, one can predict y_i to be 1 or 0 depending on whether $x_i'\beta$ is positive or negative. His estimator of β is chosen so as to maximize the number of correct predictions. If we define the characteristic function χ of the event E by

$$\chi(E) = 1 \text{ if } E \text{ occurs}$$

$$= 0 \text{ otherwise,}$$

the number of correct predictions can be mathematically expressed as

$$S(\beta) = \sum_{i=1}^{n} [y_i \chi(x_i'\beta \geqq 0) + (1 - y_i)\chi(x_i'\beta < 0)].$$

Manski calls this the score function – and hence his estimator the maximum score estimator. The estimator has been shown to be consistent, but its asymptotic distribution is unknown.

Cosslett proposed maximizing the likelihood function L in Section 1.2 with respect to both β and F, and called his estimator the generalized ML estimator. For a given value of β, the value of F which maximizes that L is a step function, and Cosslett showed a simple method of determining it. Finding the optimal value of β, however, is the computationally difficult part. Like the maximum score estimator, the generalized ML estimator of β is consistent but its asymptotic distribution is unknown.

TAKESHI AMEMIYA

See also CENSORED DATA MODELS; LABOUR SUPPLY OF WOMEN; LIMITED DEPENDENT VARIABLES; LOGITS, PROBITS AND TOBITS; SELECTION BIAS AND SELF-SELECTION.

BIBLIOGRAPHY

Amemiya, T. 1981. Qualitative response models: a survey. *Journal of Economic Literature* 19, 1483–1536.

Amemiya, T. 1985. *Advanced Econometrics*. Cambridge, Mass.: Harvard University Press.

Berkson, J. 1944. Application of the logistic function to bioassay. *Journal of the American Statistical Association* 39, 357–65.

Cosslett, S.R. 1983. Distribution-free maximum likelihood estimator of the binary choice model. *Econometrica* 51, 765–82.

Goodman, L.A. 1972. A modified multiple regression approach to the analysis of dichotomous variables. *American Sociological Review* 37, 28–46.

McFadden, D. 1974. Conditional logit analysis of qualitative choice behavior. In *Frontiers in Econometrics*, ed. P. Zarembka, New York: Academic Press, 105–42.

McFadden, D. 1977. Qualitative methods for analyzing travel behavior of individuals: some recent developments. Cowles Foundation Discussion Paper No. 474.

McFadden, D. 1984. Econometric analysis of qualitative response models. In *Handbook of Econometrics*, ed. Z. Griliches and M.D. Intriligator, Vol. 2, Amsterdam: North-Holland, 1385–1457.

Maddala, G.S. 1983. *Limited-Dependent and Qualitative Variables in Econometrics*. Cambridge: Cambridge University Press.

Manski, C.F. 1975. The maximum score estimation of the stochastic utility model of choice. *Journal of Econometrics* 3, 205–28.

Manski, C.F. and McFadden, D. (eds) 1981. *Structural Analysis of Discrete Data with Econometric Applications*. Cambridge, Mass.: MIT Press.

Morimune, K. 1979. Comparisons of normal and logistic models in the bivariate dichotemous analysis. *Econometrica* 47, 957–76.

Nerlove, M. and Press, S.J. 1973. Univariate and multivariate log-linear and logistic models. R-1306-EDA/NIH, Santa Monica: Rand Corporation.

discrete time models. *See* CONTINUOUS AND DISCRETE TIME MODELS.

discriminating monopoly. In *The Wealth of Nations*, Adam Smith refers to two instances of price discrimination. In Book V, Chapter I, Part III, he ruminates on the problem of finding the best set of levies for toll roads and commends the practice of charging for luxurious carriages more than for working men's wagons even though the vehicles are of the same weight. He suggests that the rich can subsidize the poor by this tariff scheme. In Book IV, Chapter V, he notes that some groups of producers have sold their produce abroad at lower prices than at home. He views this as cross-subsidization and deplores the high prices which he sees as resulting in the domestic market. Smith's first problem, how to set tolls, has occupied economists to this day, although the solution was laid out in principle by Dupuit (1844) and with considerable precision by Edgeworth (1910): let each user's levy in excess of his or her marginal cost of usage (which may be zero on a toll bridge) be proportional to his or her intensity of preference as expressed by his or her elasticity of demand. Edgeworth in fact worked out details of two sorts of price discrimination – that practised by a private profit-maximizing monopolist and that practised by a 'state monopoly' interested in raising Z dollars of profit from the users of the monopoly while at the same time reducing welfare as little as possible. The solution to this state monopoly or public utility pricing problem we refer to today as Ramsey pricing (Ramsey, 1927, who attributes the idea for his paper to Pigou).

Smith's second instance of price discrimination can most usefully be viewed as the case of a monopolist selling at distinct prices in two separate markets, domestic and foreign, with distinct demand curves. Barone (1921, pp. 291–2) analysed it from this perspective diagrammatically and Yntema (1928) filled in the algebraic details.

Pigou (1920) presented his synthesis of results and introduced the terms first, second and third degree price discrimination – degrees referring to the fineness with which separate prices can be assigned to separate units demanded of the monopolist. He graphically worked out the two market case with linear demands in his Appendix III, pointing out that given two markets, only one might be served under uniform pricing whereas both might be served under price discrimination. In 1904 he had in fact independently of Dupuit analysed what we now call perfect price discrimination, or the situation in which each unit produced by a monopolist fetches a different price, each of which being bounded above by the buyer's willingness to pay. In her synthesis, J. Robinson (1933, p. 205) asked whether the monopolist would produce more under third degree price discrimination relative to his output under a uniform price.

The toll-setting problem turns on the fact that if users were charged commensurate with the wear and tear they cause (marginal cost pricing), insufficient revenue would generally be raised to cover the cost of building an obviously desirable road, bridge, railroad, telephone network etc. For example, the wear and tear caused by the marginal bridge user is approximately zero and thus no revenue would be raised by charging according to costs of usage. Dupuit realized that an individual's willingness to pay for a trip could far exceed his or her incremental cost of usage and suggested collecting revenue on the basis of each individual's maximum willingness to pay. The revenue so collected 'would not have the slightest relation to the costs of production' (p. 271) but would reflect the total utility in dollars per day's use of the project. This is price discrimination: each user pays generally a different price for the same service.

To sharpen his exposition Dupuit turned to shipping tons of ore across a bridge. At high prices obviously fewer tons will be shipped, since buyers of the ore will be obliged to absorb the charges and will demand less at high prices inclusive of delivery charges. Dupuit discussed the hypothetical case of each additional ton crossing the bridge 'paying' a slightly lower toll evaluated at the maximum willingness to pay for the ton in question. This is the case of perfect price discrimination and a variant is practised in the form of *block pricing*. Firms occasionally sell the first say 1000 bricks at $3 each, the second thousand at $2.50 each, the third thousand at $2.25 and so on. Robinson reflected on the issue of the monopolist brick seller selecting the break points (1000 bricks, 2000 bricks etc.) simultaneously with price per brick in order to maximize profits. One can see that perfect price discrimination is a procedure for transferring consumer surplus (the area under an individual's demand curve up to the quantity consumed less the amount actually paid) to the seller of the product.

Price discrimination is practised by a monopolist because it permits profits to rise above what they would be if a single or uniform price were charged. To see this suppose that in two separate markets the monopolist were practising price discrimination and maximizing aggregate profit. If he were now obliged to sell in both markets at a single uniform price his optimand can never rise since the single price represents a new constraint on his pursuit of maximum profit. Pursuing this case in more detail, let $Q_1(p)$ be the demand curve for gadgets by citizens abroad (or for return rail car trips for wheat shippers on a line) and $Q_2(p)$ the demand curve for gadgets from local people (or for return rail car trips for potash producers located in the wheat farming area). Then the monopolist's profit under price discrimination is $\pi = p_1 Q_1(p_1) + p_2 Q_2(p_2) - C(Q_1 + Q_2)$ where $C(\cdot)$ is total cost, increasing and convex in $Q = Q_1 + Q_2$, and p_i is the price in market i with quantity sold $Q_i(p_i)$. Profits attain a maximum when $C_Q = p_i[1 + (1/\epsilon_i)]$, where

$$C_Q \equiv dC/dQ \quad \text{and} \quad \epsilon_i = \frac{dQ_i}{dp_i} \cdot \frac{p_i}{Q_i} < -1$$

is the elasticity of demand in market i. This profit-maximizing condition is referred to as the Robinson–Yntema condition and was first set out by Edgeworth (1910). The left-hand side is marginal cost and the right-hand side is the marginal revenue in market i. For $|\epsilon_1| \gtreqless |\epsilon_2|$, $p_1 \lesseqgtr p_2$. For $n > 2$, the analysis is the same. (Edgeworth made C_Q a constant at c, defined his elasticity as

$$\frac{dQ}{d(p_i - c)} \cdot \frac{(p_i - c)}{Q}$$

and arrived at his 'equal elasticity condition' for profit-maximizing monopoly price discrimination.) A monopolist forced to sell at a single price (presumably because the product can be readily resold) will maximize profit when $C_Q = p\{1 + [1/(\omega_1\epsilon_1 + \omega_2\epsilon_2)]\}$, where $\omega_i = Q_i/Q$.

Edgeworth investigated when deviations in p_1 and p_2 from a uniform p would increase welfare (consumer surplus), while Robinson argued that price discrimination would raise Q from the level corresponding to a uniform profit-maximizing price if the more elastic demand curve is concave and the less elastic demand curve is convex.

The basic first order condition for monopoly price discrimination can be written as

$$\frac{\Delta Q_1}{Q_1} = \frac{\Delta Q_2}{Q_2} = 1,$$

where

$$\Delta Q_i = [p_i - C_Q] \frac{dQ_i}{dp_i}.$$

This illuminating formula indicates that each output would to a first approximation rise proportionately if there were no monopoly and no price discrimination, and it can orient one's intuition in viewing Robinson's result on concavity and convexity of demand schedules. Schmalensee (1981) and Varian (1985) have pointed out that a necessary condition for total net consumer surplus to rise as the monopolist switches from a uniform price to profit-maximizing price discrimination is that there be a rise in total output delivered.

The public utility or state monopoly problem in price discrimination is to raise Z dollars of profit by charging diverse prices to distinct customers while reducing welfare least. These profits might be assigned to cover the fixed costs of a public facility. Let $B_1(p)$ and $B_2(p)$ be the areas under each demand curve for price p. The state monopoly pricing problem is to maximize $W = B_1(p_1) + B_2(p_2) - C(Q_1 + Q_2)$ subject to $Z = p_1 Q_1 + p_2 Q_2 - C(Q_1 + Q_2)$. The first order condition can be expressed as

$$\frac{\Delta Q_1}{Q_1} = \frac{\Delta Q_2}{Q_2} = \lambda,$$

where λ is a function of the level Z of profit sought and the ΔQ_i's were defined above. This problem is an instance of Ramsey (1927) optimal excise tax analysis and has been put into a general equilibrium context in Hartwick (1978). Contemporary price discrimination schemes (e.g. Oi, 1971) have incorporated income elasticities of demand as well as price elasticities and arrived at two-part tariffs involving a 'membership' fee and a user's fee for service.

In closing, we note that high prices in peak times and low in off-peak times are not forms of monopoly price discrimination, since such peak-load prices vary with changes in the marginal costs of production. Under price discrimination, prices deviate from marginal costs of production only in accord with variations across buyers in their 'intensities' of demand. Marginal cost remains the same for each buyer.

JOHN M. HARTWICK

See also BASING-POINT SYSTEMS; CONSUMERS' SURPLUS; MONOPOLY; PRICE DISCRIMINATION; PUBLIC UTILITY PRICING.

BIBLIOGRAPHY

Barone, E. 1921. Les syndicats (cartels et trusts), *Révue de métaphysique et de morale* 28(2), April–June, 279–309.
Dupuit, J. 1844. On the measurement of the utility of public works. Reproduced in *Readings in Welfare Economics*, ed. K.J. Arrow and T. Scitovsky, American Economic Association, Homewood, Illinois: Irwin, 1969.
Edgeworth, F.Y. 1910. Applications of probabilities to economics. *Economic Journal* 20, 284–304, 441–65. Reprinted in F.Y. Edgeworth, *Papers Relating to Political Economy*, Vol. II, New York: Burt Franklin, 1925.
Hartwick, J.M. 1978. Optimal price discrimination. *Journal of Public Economics* 9(1), February, 83–9.
Oi, W.Y. 1971. A Disneyland dilemma: two-part tariffs for a Mickey Mouse monopoly. *Quarterly Journal of Economics* 85(1), February, 77–96.
Pigou, A.C. 1904. Monopoly and consumers' surplus. *Economic Journal* 14, September, 388–94.
Pigou, A.C. 1920. *The Economics of Welfare*. London: Macmillan.
Ramsey, F. 1927. A contribution to the theory of taxation. *Economic Journal* 37, March, 47–61.
Robinson, J. 1933. *The Economics of Imperfect Competition*. London: Macmillan.

Schmalensee, R. 1981. Output and welfare implications of monopolistic third-degree price discrimination. *American Economic Review* 71(1), March, 242–7.

Smith, A. 1776. *The Wealth of Nations*. Ed. E. Cannan, reprinted, New York: Modern Library, 1937.

Varian, H. 1985. Price discrimination and social welfare. *American Economic Review* 75(4), September, 870–75.

Yntema, T. 1928. The influence of dumping on monopoly price. *Journal of Political Economy* 36(6), December, 686–98.

discrimination. Discrimination may be said to occur in a market where individuals face terms of trade that are determined by personal characteristics which do not appear directly relevant to the transaction. Most concern has centred on differential treatment by race or ethnic group, and by sex. The primary focus has been on the labour market and housing market, with research motivated, in large part, by controversy over the role of government in maintaining or eliminating observed differentials.

The first extensive literature on the economics of discrimination dates to the equal pay controversy in Britain beginning before the turn of the century, focusing on the lower wages of women. Although interest in the economics of pay differentials by sex abated in the two decades following World War II, many aspects of the more recent theory appeared in this literature. The modern development of systematic models of economic discrimination began with the publication of Gary Becker's *The Economics of Discrimination* (1957). With the passage of laws prohibiting discrimination in the US, Britain and other countries in the 1960s and 1970s, research in the area has again grown.

MARKET DISCRIMINATION AND PERSONAL PREFERENCES. Becker's (1957) treatment took market discrimination to be the result of personal tastes of participants, providing a simple, closed model with a variety of testable implications. Earnings differentials, and discrimination in housing and other markets stem from the attempts of owners, workers and customers to avoid contact or interaction with certain groups.

Consider first the influence of employer preferences. Rather than maximizing profits, employers maximize a utility that incorporates the personal characteristics of employees. If employers prefer to hire workers from group A rather than group B and are willing to sacrifice profits to do so, they may be said to have discriminatory tastes. Where such employers dominate the market, the relative wages of group B workers must adjust downward if any are to be hired, and the resulting difference equals the pecuniary value of the employed preference. Where there are variations in taste among employers, relative wages are determined by the shape of the taste distribution, and the proportion of A and B workers to be hired.

Employees may also be taken to have discriminatory preferences over the group membership of their co-workers. If discriminating workers and members of the group they shun are perfect substitutes in production, employers have an incentive to provide separate facilities for groups, but no wage differential between groups will occur. In order for such preferences to cause wage differentials, the technology of production must preclude complete separation. For example, if it is necessary for supervisors to interact with assembly line workers, and supervisors prefer one group of workers to another, an employer who has no taste for discrimination and faces a competitive labour market will hire members of both groups only if their wages differ correspondingly.

Customers' tastes may also influence market wages in the absence of employer preferences. The extension of this approach to a variety of markets is clear. Housing discrimination would occur if owners required a premium in order to sell or rent to individuals in certain groups. However, in markets for goods, in contrast to services, no appreciable price differential could survive unless restrictions on resale were binding.

In any of these cases, some market participants may have a taste for discrimination without market differentials occurring if there are a sufficient number of non-discriminating participants to interact with the disliked group. One obvious source of non-discriminating participants is fellow group members. If groups are equally represented among employers, various kinds of workers, and customers, complete segregation can occur without economic loss to any group. Preferences against trading with those outside one's own group can only affect terms of trade where groups have different resources or skills. The formal model is, however, silent on the source of such differences.

COMPETITION AND DISCRIMINATORY PREFERENCES. It is widely argued that, in the long run, competition in markets for output and capital will drive out discriminating employers. Since discrimination by race and sex has long existed, this result has frequently been taken as grounds for rejecting the model (Arrow, 1972). In fact, this conclusion follows only from a particular version of the model, in which the taste for discrimination imposes a direct utility loss on the employer for each employee hired from the disliked group. Since non-discriminating employers suffer no such utility loss, under free competition, where they can expand production or buy out discriminators, they will take over the market. This need not be the case. A polar example has been termed nepotism, in which preferences for hiring one group act much like a net subsidy for the employer. In this case, those with the strongest discriminatory preferences ultimately dominate the market.

In general, discriminating employers earn lower money profits than those who do not discriminate, but this does not imply that under competition they will be driven from the market. Foregone profits must be recognized as consumption expenditures, and, so long as employer resources are sufficient to permit any consumption, there is no inconsistency between perfect competition and the existence of stable, long-run wage differentials stemming from employer preferences.

While market discrimination may survive competition, restrictions on competition will often result in more severe discrimination. In a competitive market, any market differential translates into a pecuniary cost that the discriminating employer must pay. But where prices do not equalize supply and demand, the employer's cost of discrimination may decline.

An effective minimum wage or, during times of economic decline, a wage that is downwardly rigid, allows the employer to hire both more productive workers and those most preferred without paying a higher wage. In contrast, if wages do not adjust immediately in an economic upturn, the cost of discrimination will increase.

Where a union successfully bargains for wages above the competitive level, discriminatory hiring, on the basis of either employers' or union members' preferences may take place at lower cost. In fact, discrimination against blacks by unions in the US was explicit and widespread until the 1930s, but by the 1960s union representation for blacks and whites was nearly identical. Black representation has been greatest in industrial unions, where unionization often hinges on the ability to organize both black and white workers, and proportionally lowest in craft unions, where unions frequently exercise power by limiting membership. Despite the historically high level of union discrimination, it appears to have contributed relatively little to observed black–white wage differentials in the US.

The cost of discrimination to firms may decline where there are restrictions on profit maximization. Those who manage non-profit organizations, regulated monopolies or government bureaucracies will devote more resources to improving their own working conditions; unless faced with direct constraints, they will be more likely to exercise personal preferences in the kinds of workers they hire (Alchian and Kessel, 1962).

Finally, in markets with search costs, discrimination may occur even if there are sufficient non-discriminating participants to trade with members of the disliked group, since the appropriate matching cannot occur.

DISCRIMINATION AS EXPLOITATION. It is frequently asserted that discrimination is engaged in because it is profitable. In general, there is some level of discrimination by members of any group that will improve the terms of trade so as to increase their money incomes. Discrimination by white employers, under some conditions, may increase the incomes of whites by increasing both employer profits and the earnings of white workers. Similarly, tastes that restrict blacks and women to certain kinds of jobs may increase money income both for employers and white male employees.

If discriminators' preferences are taken seriously, however, the impact of discriminatory preferences on money income is irrelevant. Although Becker's original treatment calculated such welfare effects, like any such comparison it required an arbitrary normalization to compare individuals with differing preferences. Changes in money income due to discrimination can be taken to represent group welfare if discriminatory behaviour does not reflect actual personal preference. However, individual incentives in a competitive market can no longer explain discrimination, since those who discriminate least receive the greatest gains. It is necessary that some process exist by which the group enforces its will on individual choices. Exploitation must have its roots in a social or political process.

Historically, there is no question that the enactment of discriminatory laws and provision of unequal public services has often represented the exploitation of groups with little political power. J.S. Mill (1869) argued that limitations on women's legal rights and the restrictions they faced in entering certain occupations, were part of a policy to provide men both with higher earnings in the labour market and greater authority over their wives at home. The history of governmental action regarding blacks in America since the Civil War is replete with examples of policies designed to benefit whites with political power at the expense of blacks.

Despite the government's often central role in furthering dominant group interests, there are clearly other channels by which groups exercise influence. An ethnic group is generally bound together by an ideology that dictates members' actions in a wide variety of contexts. Although some members may internalize such ideology, compliance is enforced by systems of social norms and sanctions within the group. The process by which such systems develop is not well understood, although it has been shown that discriminatory norms may be self-enforcing once established (Akerlof, 1976). Nonetheless, it is clear empirically that economic relations among groups, and their relations within the power structure, are critical in determining group ideology and, in turn, individual actions.

For example, it is a recurrent observation that severe ethnic or racial antagonism often can be traced to the point at which groups first find themselves competing in the labour market. Some writers have argued that all discrimination by race or ethnic group can be traced to such a dynamic, in which groups mobilize political and economic resources to further their material interests. The goal of such action is seen to be the exclusion of the competing group from the labour market or, failing this, the creation of a caste system providing the dominant group with preferential treatment (Bonacich, 1972).

As a rule, it is among lower income groups that racism appears most virulent and associated violence most common. In part, this reflects the fact that racism is a source of power to those groups whose alternatives are limited. In some measure, social norms, personal animosity and collective violence substitute for political power and state action.

In contrast to the assumption of the preference-based model, the treatment here implies that discriminatory preferences cannot be taken as exogenous. Tastes, or apparent tastes, may develop to further group interests. This is not to say that individual actions are ever completely determined by group interests, even where these are unambiguous. Within the most tightly structured groups, for example where ethnic identity is strong, discriminatory collusion against outsiders relies heavily on the availability of explicit policing mechanisms. Where individual behaviours are difficult to observe, and the benefits of violating collusive rules are great, discrimination will be less successful.

It must be stressed that many of the conclusions of the taste-based model may apply even where groups' interests play a critical role in shaping individuals' actions. For example, the model tells us that if white workers who compete with black workers merely refuse to work with them, white workers obtain no net gain in income. It is only through the adoption of discriminatory practices by employers that white workers realize gains.

STATISTICAL DISCRIMINATION. Participants in a market have an incentive to consider personal characteristics if these provide information that is relevant to the exchange but costly to obtain by other means. Statistical discrimination occurs where an ascribed characteristic serves this function. The widely accepted use of sex in markets for various kinds of insurance is an obvious example. Markets for credit and rental housing have similar structures, as does the market for labour. Initial screening is particularly critical in hiring for entry level positions in firms with internal labour markets, where a firm often undertakes extensive worker training, and implicit contracts limit the employer's ability to adjust wages in accord with realized productivity.

Some labour market analysts have attempted to limit the term statistical discrimination to contexts in which an employer distinguishes groups that do not differ in average productivity (Aigner and Cain, 1977). For example, where an employer favoured men over women because women were more likely to quit after receiving firm-specific training, this would not be labelled discrimination. In contrast, statistical discrimination would be said to occur if an employer screened by race in jobs where expected ability was critical because he was unable to judge the abilities of blacks. Such a distinction becomes muddied when it is recognized that matching the worker to the job is part of the productive process.

In certain respects, observed patterns of employment for women and blacks are consistent with statistical discrimination. Both are seriously under-represented in jobs offering extended promotion ladders, and, historically, firms often explicitly reserved for white males the training that prepared an employee for promotion.

Since such persistent statistical discrimination results from the efficient use of information, the basis of wage differentials would seem to rest on pre-market influences, not market dynamics. However, it is possible that group differences are themselves the result of employer expectations. Assume employers believe that members of a particular group have lower levels of the skills necessary for success in screened jobs. In so far as performance is ultimately rewarded for those placed in screened positions, members of this group, because they are less likely to be hired into such positions, will have reduced incentives to invest in relevant skills. Any one employer who hired members of that group into these positions would find workers to be less productive, so beliefs would be confirmed.

In addition to a number of technical conditions (Arrow, 1972), in order for such a 'self-fulfilling prophecy' to be stable, the actions of a single firm must not alter individual incentives. If it were possible for a firm to contract with individuals to fill positions prior to the point when they acquire such skills, individuals who entered contracts, whatever their group membership, would face the same incentives to obtain skills, and the vicious circle would be broken. The acquisition of such skills must therefore occur well in advance of the point that individual workers and firms can easily enter into agreements. Differences in socialization by sex, or cultural differences by race or ethnic group, if in response to disparate treatment in the labour market, could reflect this kind of vicious circle.

EXPLAINING MARKET DIFFERENTIALS. Earnings for women have been appreciably below those of men in almost all societies, past and present. Differences in levels of market participation and other observable personal attributes explain only a portion of the differential. Historically, some of the difference may be identified with governmental or institutional discrimination. Nevertheless, the enactment of laws in many countries prohibiting discrimination in the 1960s and 1970s have had little effect on the overall distribution of wages by sex. There is no obvious way to identify the impact of discrimination in explaining observed differences. Any unobserved direct market discrimination may induce differences in labour market participation and measurable pre-market factors, yet any unmeasured differences between men and women that are not due to discriminatory treatment, may also contribute to the wage differential.

Women have historically performed the bulk of household work and child care, participating in the labour market less continuously and less intensively than have men. Given this division of labour within the family, women who expect to marry have less incentive to develop skills requiring continuous labour market participation. Non-discriminating employers may simply pay women less because they have not invested in those skills that are most valuable in the market.

How the earnings gap is viewed must depend partly on the source of the family's division of labour. If it results from market discrimination, or social norms constructed to benefit dominant males, it may be analysed in terms of the models of discrimination. However, such a division is also consistent with joint optimization by husband and wife: if the bearing and rearing of children are even weakly complementary, it is efficient for the family to have the women specialize in both these non-market tasks. Sex-typed socialization would then merely reflect preparation for anticipated roles.

That perfect equality would occur in the absence of all labour market discrimination seems unlikely. Nonetheless, unless there are strong sanctions, employers have an incentive to practise statistical discrimination, magnifying whatever sex differences would occur in its absence.

The labour market disadvantages suffered by many ethnic and racial groups is similarly open to interpretation. Thomas Sowell (1981) has argued that cultural differences between arriving immigrant groups and blacks in the US are more important in explaining their economic progress than the levels of discrimination they faced. While it is clear that cultural factors are critically important, the degree to which these or other pre-market differences explain observed earnings differentials is unclear. The theory implies that discrimination will be most common and most damaging against groups with low levels of resources, those who would be disadvantaged in its absence.

For blacks in the US, slavery and subsequent governmental discrimination induced shortfalls in human resources that would have limited black achievement under the best of conditions. Nonetheless, up through the 1960s, measured pre-market differences explained only a modest portion of observed earnings differentials. Although unobserved pre-market differences may have played a role, given the pervasiveness of explicit market discrimination, it seems likely that discrimination further depressed the black position. To what degree labour market differences that persist despite the prohibition of discrimination since 1965 – most notably in rates of unemployment – are due to unmeasured pre-market differences, possibly associated with statistical discrimination, or to other market discrimination, is an open question.

PETER MUESER

See also EQUALITY; GENDER; HUMAN CAPITAL; INEQUALITY BETWEEN PERSONS; INEQUALITY BETWEEN RACES; INEQUALITY BETWEEN SEXES; LABOUR SUPPLY OF WOMEN; SIGNALLING; WOMEN'S WAGES.

BIBLIOGRAPHY

Akerlof, G. 1976. The economics of caste and of the rat race and other woeful tales. *Quarterly Journal of Economics* 90(4), November, 599–617.

Aigner, D. and Cain, G. 1977. Statistical theoies of discrimination in labor markets. *Industrial and Labor Relations Review* 30(2), January, 175–87.

Alchian, A. and Kessel, R. 1962. Competition, monopoly, and the pursuit of pecuniary gain. In *Aspects of Labor Economics*, NBER Special Conference Series, Princeton: Princeton University Press.

Arrow, K. 1972. Models of job discrimination. In *Racial Discrimination in Economic Life*, ed. A. Pascal, Lexington, Mass.: D.C. Heath.

Becker, G. 1957. *The Economics of Discrimination*. 2nd edn, Chicago: University of Chicago Press, 1971.

Bonacich, E. 1972. A theory of ethnic antagonism: the split labor market. *American Sociological Review* 37, October, 547–59.

Mill, J.S. 1869. *The Subjection of Women*. New York: Stokes, 1911.

Sowell, T. 1981. *Ethnic America: A History*. New York: Basic Books.

diseconomies of scale. *See* ECONOMIES AND DISECONOMIES OF SCALE.

disequilibrium analysis. A convenient way to define 'disequilibrium' is of course as the contrary of 'equilibrium'. Unfortunately this leaves us with no unique definition as the word equilibrium itself has been used in the economic literature with at least two principal meanings. The first one refers to market equilibrium, i.e. the equality of supply and demand on markets. This is the meaning we shall retain in this entry, and therefore the disequilibrium analysis we shall be concerned with here is the study of nonclearing markets, also called non-Walrasian analysis by reference to the most elaborate model of market clearing, the Walrasian model.

The second meaning of equilibrium is somewhat more general. A typical definition is given by Machlup (1958) as '... a constellation of selected interrelated variables, so adjusted to one another that no inherent tendency to change prevails in the model which they constitute'. Dealing with disequilibrium in this second meaning would be a quite formidable (and actually extremely imprecise) task, which is why we want to limit ourselves in this entry to disequilibrium analysis in the first sense.

We should note that the entry RATIONED EQUILIBRIA presents concepts of equilibria in the second, but not in the first sense of the word, i.e. more specifically equilibria without market clearing, or non-Walrasian equilibria.

THE ESSENCE OF THE THEORY. Disequilibrium analysis is best appraised by reference to the standard equilibrium market clearing paradigm, corresponding to the notions of Marshallian or Walrasian equilibrium. There all private agents receive a price signal and assume that they will be able to exchange whatever they want at that price. They express demands and supplies, sometimes called 'notional', which are functions of this price signal. An equilibrium price system is a set of prices for which demand and supply match on all markets. Transactions are equal to the demands and supplies at the equilibrium price system.

Two characteristics deserve to be stressed: all private agents receive price signals and make rational quantity decisions with respect to them. But no agent makes any use of the quantity signals sent to the market. Also no agent actually sets prices, the determination of which is left to the 'invisible hand' or to the implicit Walrasian auctioneer. This logical hole of the theory was pointed out by Arrow (1959) when he noted there was '... a logical gap in the usual formulations of the theory of the perfectly competitive economy, namely, that there is no place for a rational decision with respect to prices as there is with respect to quantities', and more specifically 'each individual participant in the economy is supposed to take prices as given and determine his choices as to purchases and sales accordingly; there is no one left over whose job is to make a decision on price'.

Disequilibrium analysis takes this strong logical objection quite seriously, and its purpose is to build a consistent theory of the functioning of decentralized economies when market clearing is not axiomatically assumed. The consequences of abandoning the market clearing assumption are actually quite far-reaching: (i) The transactions cannot be all equal to demands and supplies expressed on markets. Rationing will be experienced and quantity signals will be formed in addition to price signals (ii) Demand and supply theory must be substantially modified to take into account these quantity signals. One thus obtains a theory of effective demand, as opposed to notional demand which only takes price signals into account (iii) Price theory must also be amended in a way integrates the possibility of non-clearing markets, the presence of quantity signals, and makes agents themselves responsible for price making, (iv) Finally expectations, which in market clearing models are concerned with price signals only, must now include quantity signals expectations as well.

HISTORY. Though roots may be found earlier, an uncontestable grandfather of disequilibrium analysis in the sense we use here is of course Keynes (1936). He rightfully perceived that one of his main contributions in the *General Theory* was the introduction of quantity adjustments, and more specifically income adjustments, in the economic process, whereas the then dominant 'classical' economists focused on price adjustments only. As Keynes (1937) wrote 'As I have said above, the initial novelty lies in my maintaining that it is not the rate of interest, but the level of incomes which ensures equality between savings and investment'.

Unfortunately for many decades things did not go much further: macroeconomists added the level of income in their equations, thereby allowing for unemployment. But concentration on the 'equilibrium' of the goods and money markets, exemplified by the dominant IS–LM model, obscured the 'disequilibrium' nature of the model. As for microeconomics, it was basically unaffected by the Keynesian revolution, and correlatively a growing gap developed between microeconomics and macroeconomics.

A few isolated contributions in the post-war period made some steps toward modern disequilibrium theories. Samuelson (1947), Tobin and Houthakker (1950) studied the theory of demand under conditions of rationing. Bent Hansen (1951) introduced the ideas of active demand, close in spirit to that of effective demand, and of quasi-equilibrium where persistent disequilibrium created steady inflation. Patinkin (1956, ch. 13) considered the situation where the firms might not be able to sell all their 'notional' output. Hahn and Negishi (1962) studied non-tâtonnement processes where trade could take place before a general equilibrium price system was reached. Hicks (1965) discussed the 'fixprice' method as opposed to the flexprice method.

A main impetus came from the stimulating works of Clower (1965) and Leijonhufvud (1968). Both were concerned with the microeconomic foundations of Keynesian theory. Clower showed that the Keynesian consumption function made no sense unless reinterpreted as the response of a rational consumer to a disequilibrium on the labour markets. He introduced the 'dual-decision' hypothesis, a precursor of modern effective demand theory, showing how the consumption function could have two different functional forms, depending on whether the consumer was rationed on the labour market or not. Leijonhufvud (1968) insisted on the importance of short-run quantity adjustments to explain the establishment of an equilibrium with involuntary unemployment.

These contributions were followed by the macroeconomic model of Barro and Grossman (1971, 1976), integrating the 'Clower' consumption function and the 'Patinkin' employment function in the first 'disequilibrium' macroeconomic model.

Then the main development was that of microeconomic concepts of non-Walrasian equilibrium proposed notably by Benassy (1975, 1976, 1977, 1982), Drèze (1975) and Younès (1975). These, which generalize the notion of Walrasian general equilibrium to non-market clearing situations, gave solid microeconomic foundations to the field. The main concepts are reviewed in the entry RATIONED EQUILIBRIA.

From then on, the field has developed quite rapidly, notably in the direction of macroeconomic applications and econometrics, as we shall outline below. We shall review quickly the main elements of disequilibrium analysis. Longer developments can be found notably in Benassy (1982).

NON-CLEARING MARKETS AND QUANTITY SIGNALS. A most important element of the theory is obviously to show how transactions can occur in a market in disequilibrium, and how quantity signals are generated in the decentralized trading process. To make things clear and intuitive, we shall start with the simple case of two agents, one demander and one supplier in a market which does not necessarily clear. They meet and express, respectively, an effective demand $\tilde{d}$ and supply $\tilde{s}$ (note that we do not use notional demands and supplies which are fully irrelevant in this context). We shall now indicate how transactions and quantity signals are formed in this example. Transactions will be denoted d^* and s^* respectively and they must of course satisfy $d^* = s^*$.

The first principle we shall use is that of voluntary exchange, i.e. that no agent can be forced to trade more than he wants on a market. This condition is quite natural and actually verified on most markets, except maybe for some labour markets which are regulated by more complex contractual arrangements. It is written in this example:

$$d^* \leqslant \tilde{d} \qquad s^* \leqslant \tilde{s}$$

which implies that:

$$d^* = s^* \leqslant \min(\tilde{d}, \tilde{s})$$

Actually in this simple example, there is not reason why these two agents would exchange less than the minimum of demand and supply, as they would be both frustrated in their desires of exchange. This simple 'efficiency' assumption leads us to take the transaction as:

$$d^* = s^* = \min(\tilde{d}, \tilde{s})$$

the well-known 'rule of the minimum'.

Now at the same time as transactions take place, quantity signals are set across the market: faced with the supply $\tilde{s}$, and under voluntary exchange, the demander knows that he will not be able to purchase more than $\tilde{s}$. Symmetrically the supplier knows that he cannot sell more than $\tilde{d}$. Each agents thus receives from the other a quantity signal, respectively denoted as $\bar{d}$ and $\bar{s}$, which tells him the maximum quantity he can respectively buy and sell. In this example:

$$\bar{d} = \tilde{s} \qquad \bar{s} = \tilde{d}$$

and the transactions can thus be expressed as:

$$d^* = \min(\tilde{d}, \bar{d})$$

$$s^* = \min(\tilde{s}, \bar{s})$$

Let us move now to the general case (which is explored more formally in the entry on RATIONED EQUILIBRIA). Agents, indexed by i, exchange goods indexed by h. On each market h a rationing scheme transforms inconsistent demands and supplies, denoted $\tilde{d}_{ih}$ and $\tilde{s}_{ih}$, into consistent transactions, denoted d_{ih}^* and s_{ih}^*, which balance identically (i.e. total purchases always equal total sales). At the same time, and continuing to assume voluntary exchange, each agent receives a quantity signal, respectively $\bar{d}_{ih}$ or $\bar{s}_{ih}$ for demanders and suppliers, which tells him the maximum quantity he can buy or sell, and the rationing scheme is equivalently written:

$$d_{ih}^* = \min(\tilde{d}_{ih}, \bar{d}_{ih})$$

$$s_{ih}^* = \min(\tilde{s}_{ih}, \bar{s}_{ih})$$

where $\bar{d}_{ih}$ and $\bar{s}_{ih}$ are functions of the demands and supplies of the other agents on the market. These quantity signals may result from the signals set to each other by agent in decentralized pairwise meetings (as in the above two agents example) or result from a more centralized process (as in a uniform rationing scheme).

We thus see that on a market we may have unrationed demanders or suppliers, or rationed ones. The rationing scheme is called efficient if there are not both rationed demanders and rationed suppliers in the same market. An efficient rationing

scheme implies the well-known 'rule of the minimum', according to which aggregate transactions equal the minimum of supply and demand. Such an assumption, which was very natural for our example with two agents, may not be valid if one considers a macroeconomic market, as not all demanders and suppliers meet pairwise. In particular it is well known that the property of market efficiency may be lost in the process of aggregating submarkets, whereas voluntary exchange remains. Note, however, that the concepts that follow do not require that property of market efficiency.

Now it is clear that the quantity signals received by the agents hould have an effect on demand, supply and price formation. This is what we shall explore now.

EFFECTIVE DEMAND AND SUPPLY. Demands and supplies are signals that agents send to the 'market' (i.e. to the other agents) in order to obtain the best transactions according to their criterion. The traditional 'notional' or Walrasian demands and supplies are constructed under the assumption (which is actually verified ex-post in a Walrasian equilibrium) that each agent can buy and sell as much as he wants on each market. There is thus an equality between the signal the agent sends to the market (demand or supply) and the transaction he will obtained from it.

In disequilibrium analysis there is of course a difference between the signals sent (effective demands and supplies) and their consequences (the transactions actually realized). Effective demands and supplies expressed by an agent in the various markets are the signals which maximize his expected utility of the resulting transactions, knowing that these transactions are related to the demands and supplies by equalities of the type seen above, i.e.:

$$d_{ih}^* = \min(\tilde{d}_{ih}, \bar{d}_{ih})$$

$$s_{ih}^* = \min(\tilde{s}_{ih}, \bar{s}_{ih})$$

The results of such expected utility maximization programmes may be quite complex, depending for example on whether quantity constraints are expected deterministically or stochastically, or whether agents act or not as price markers, as we shall see in the next section. In the case of deterministic constraints, there exists a simple and workable definition of effective demand, which generalizes Clower's original 'dual decision' method: effective demand (or supply) on one particular market is the trade which maximizes the agent's criterion subject to the constraints encountered or expected on the other markets. This definition thus naturally integrates the well-known 'spillover effects', which show how disequilibrium in one market affects demands and supplies in the other markets.

We shall immediately give an illustrative example of this definition, due to Patinkin (1956) and Barro and Grossman (1971), that of the employment function of the firm. Consider a firm with a production function $y = F(l)$ exhibiting diminishing returns, and faced with a price p on the output market and a wage w on the labour market. The traditional 'notional' labour demand results from maximization of profit $py - wl$ subject to the production constraint $y = F(l)$, which yields immediately the usual Walrasian labour demand $F'^{-1}(w/p)$. Assume now that the firm faces a constraint $\bar{y}$ on its sales of output (i.e. a total demand $\bar{y}$). According to the above definition the effective demand for labour $\tilde{l}$ is the solution in l of the following programme:

$$\text{Maximize} \quad py - wl \quad \text{s.t.}$$

$$y = F(l)$$

$$y \leqslant \bar{y}$$

the solution of which is:

$$\tilde{l} = \min\{F'^{-1}(w/p), \quad F^{-1}(\bar{y})\}$$

We see that the effective demand for labour may have two forms: the Walrasian demand just seen above if the sales constraint is not binding, or, if this constraint is binding, a more 'Keynesian' form equal to the quantity of labour just necessary to produce the output demand. We see immediately on this example that effective demand may have various functional forms, which intuitively explains why disequilibrium models often have multiple regimes (see for example the three goods–three regimes model in the entry FIX-PRICE MODELS).

In the case of stochastic demand, the programme yielding the effective demand for labour becomes evidently more complex. One obtains some results quite reminiscent of the inventories literature as developed for example by Arrow, Karlin and Scarf (1958) or Bellman (1957). See Benassy (1982) for the link between these two lines of work.

PRICE MAKING. We shall now address the problem of price making by decentralized agents, and we shall see that there too quantity signals play a prominent role. It is actually quite intuitive that quantity signals must be a fundamental part of the competitive process in a truly decentralized economy. Indeed, it is the inability to sell as much as they want that leads suppliers to propose, or to accept from other agents, a lower price, and conversely it is the inability to buy as much as they want that leads demanders to propose, or accept, a higher price. Various modes of price making integrating these aspects can be envisioned. We shall deal here with a particular organization of the pricing process where agents on one side of the market (usually the suppliers) quote prices and agents on the other side act as price takers. Other modes of pricing (bargaining, contracting) are currently studied, but have not yet been integrated in this line of work. As we shall see this model of price making is quite reminiscent of the imperfect competition line: Chamberlain (1933), Robinson (1933), Triffin (1940), Bushaw and Clower (1957), Arrow (1959), Negishi (1961).

Consider thus, to fix ideas, the case where sellers set the prices (things would be quite symmetrical if demanders were setting the prices), and in order to have only one price per market, let us characterize a market by the nature of the good sold and its seller (we thus consider two goods sold by different sellers as different goods, a fairly usual assumption in microeconomic theory since these goods differ at least by location, quality, etc . . .). On each 'market' so defined we thus have one seller, the price maker, facing several buyers. As we saw above, for a given price this seller faces a quantity constraint $\bar{s}$, actually equal to the demand of the other agents on that market. But the price level is now a decision variable for the seller, and this quantity constraint (the others' total demand) can be modified by changing the price: for example in general the seller who wants to sell more knows that, others things being equal, he should lower the price. The relation between the maximum quantity he expects to sell and the price set by the price maker is called the expected demand curve. If demand is forecasted deterministically, this expected demand curve will be denoted as:

$$\bar{S}(p, \theta)$$

where θ is a vector of parameters depending on the exact functional form of that curve (for example elasticity and a position factor for isoelastic curves). If demand is forecast stochastically, the expected demand curve will have the form of a probability distribution on $\bar{s}$ (i.e. total demand) conditional on the price.

For a given expected demand curve, the price maker chooses the price which will maximize profits, given the relation between price and maximum sales. For example, continuing to consider a firm with production function $F(l)$, the programme yielding the optimum price is the following in the case of a deterministic expected demand curve:

$$\text{Maximize} \quad py - wl \quad \text{s.t.}$$
$$y = F(l)$$
$$y \leqslant \bar{S}(p, \theta)$$
$$l \leqslant \tilde{l}$$

where $\tilde{l}$ is the constraint the firm possibly faces on the labour market, where it is a 'wage taker'. Note that, according to our definition above, the effective demand for labour of this same firm would be given by the above programme, from which the last constraint would be deleted.

Both the price and quantity decisions of price makers depend on the parameters θ. Of course it would require quite heroic assumptions on the computational ability and information available to price setters to assume that they know the 'true' demand function (i.e. the 'true' functional form with the 'true' parameters). But the theory developed here gives a natural way of learning about the demand curve. Indeed, each realization $p, \bar{s}$ in a period is a point on the 'true' demand curve in that period (Bushaw and Clower, 1957). Using the sequence of these observations, plus any extra information available (including for example the price of its competitors), the price maker can use statistical techniques to yield an estimation of the demand curve. Whether this learning would lead to the 'true' demand curve is still an unresolved problem.

EXPECTATIONS. Of course, the modifications we outlined concerning the signal structure affect not only the current period, but the future periods as well, and as compared to traditional 'competitive' analysis, disequilibrium analysis introduces expected quantity signals in addition to expected price signals. Such an introduction allows for example to rationalize the traditional Keynesian accelerator (Grossman, 1972). The introduction of such quantity expectations into the microeconomic setting was made in Benassy (1975, 1977b, 1982). Macroeconomic applications of the corresponding concepts can be found in Hildenbrand and Hildenbrand (1978), Muellbauer and Portes (1978), Benassy (1982, 1986), Neary and Stiglitz (1983).

SCOPE AND USES OF DISEQUILIBRIUM ANALYSIS. We have briefly outlined the basic elements or building blocks of disequilibrium analysis. We saw that it generalizes the traditional theories of demand, supply and price formation to cases where, in the absence of an auctioneer, markets do not automatically clear. This theory is thus a quite general one, and the scope of its applications very broad. Up to now there have been in the literature three particularly active areas of development: (1) The construction of various concepts of equilibria with rationing, or non-Walrasian equilibria. These concepts, which generalize the traditional notion of Walrasian equilibrium to the cases where not all markets clear, show how mixed price-quantity adjustments can bring about a new type of equilibrium in the short run. (2) The development of numerous macroeconomic applications, which basically use the above concepts in the framework of aggregated macromodels, and derive policy implications, for example to fight involuntary unemployment. (3) Finally new econometric methods have been developed to deal with such models, as traditional methods were more suited to the study of equilibrium markets.

Microeconomic concepts of non-Walrasian equilibria are reviewed in the entry RATIONED EQUILIBRIA. We shall now very briefly outline the macroeconomic and econometric developments.

MACROECONOMIC APPLICATIONS. Many contributions in the field started from a reconsideration of Keynesian models, and it is therefore no surprise that many macroeconomic applications have been made. The early model of Barro and Grossman (1971) has been followed by a huge macroeconomic literature, notably aimed at policy analysis and the study of involuntary unemployment. A very valuable feature of disequilibrium macromodels in that, like the microeconomic models, they endogenously generate multiple regimes in which various policy tools may have quite different impacts. These models are thus a particularly useful tool for synthesizing hitherto disjoint macroeconomic theories. One finds a number of macroeconomic applications in books by Barro and Grossman (1976), Benassy (1982, 1986), Cuddington et al. (1984), Malinvaud (1977), Negishi (1979). We may note that the same methods can also be used to study the problems of centrally planned economies (Portes, 1981).

A few lessons can be drawn from these macrodisequilibrium models. The first is that, even though these models were at the very beginning aimed at bridging the gap with Keynesian analysis, they proved to be of quite more general relevance, and able to generate non-Keynesian results as well as the traditional Keynesian results. Secondly, and more generally, whether or not a policy tool is efficient may depend very much on the 'regime' the economy is in. A famous example is the Barro and Grossman fixprice macroeconomic model, with its 'Classical unemployment' and 'Keynesian unemployment' regimes. Finally, it appears that the results of these models are quite sensitive to both the price formation mechanism on each market, as well as on the expectations formation mechanisms on both price and quantities (cf. for example, Benassy (1986), which experiments with various hypotheses).

This quite naturally leads to the need of further theoretical work, and to the necessity of empirically testing these models, an issue to which we now turn.

DISEQUILIBRIUM ECONOMETRICS. In order to estimate microeconomic or macroeconomic disequilibrium models a whole new econometric technology has developed in recent years. Let us consider the very simplest case, that of a single market with a rigid price. The most basic system to estimate is then:

$$X^d = a_d Z_d + \epsilon_d$$
$$X^s = a_s Z_s + \epsilon_s$$
$$X = \min(X^d, X^s)$$

where X^d is quantity demanded, Z_d is the set of variables affecting demand, a_d is the vector of corresponding parameters and ϵ_d is a demand disturbance term (and symmetrically on the supply side). The market is assumed for the moment to function efficiently so that transaction X is the minimum of demand and supply X^d and X^s. The problem in estimating such a model, as compared with an equilibrium model, where by assumption

$$X = X^d = X^s$$

is that only X is observed, not X^d or X^s. Techniques for dealing with these problems are reviewed in Quandt (1982). Of course this is the simplest possible model, and numerous extensions are now considered: (1) The prices may be flexible, either within the period of estimation, or between successive periods. The price equation must then be estimated simultaneously with the demand-supply system. (2) Since some applications are made on macroeconomic markets, the 'minimum' condition may not be satisfied, and is replaced by an explicit procedure of aggregation of submarkets. (3) Finally models with several markets in disequilibrium have been estimated, notably at the macroeconomic level.

CONCLUDING REMARKS. The development of disequilibrium analysis has clearly led to an enlargement and synthesis of both traditional microeconomics and macroeconomics.

Usual microeconomic theory in the market clearing tradition has been generalized in a number of directions: the study of the functioning of non-clearing markets and the formation of quantity signals, a theory of demand and supply responding to these quantity signals as well as to price signals, the integration of quantity expectations into microeconomic theory. This line of analysis further includes a theory of price making by agents internal to the system which also bridges the gap with the traditional theories of imperfect competition.

As for the corresponding macroeconomic models, they turn out to be a very useful synthetical tool, as they cover all possible disequilibrium configurations. They are more general than either traditional Keynesian macromodels, which considered only excess supply states, or than 'new classical' macromodels which postulate market clearing at all times. They are of course the natural tool to study problems such as involuntary unemployment.

Still richer developments lie ahead with further developments in the theories of price and wage formation in markets without an auctioneer. The methodology outlined here will permit to derive the micro and macro consequences, as well as the consequences in terms of economic policy prescriptions. Much is also to be expected of the development of the associated econometric methods, which should allow to choose the most relevant hypotheses, and to characterize specific historical episodes.

JEAN-PASCAL BENASSY

See also EQUILIBRIUM: AN EXPECTATIONAL CONCEPT; RATIONED EQUILIBRIA; TEMPORARY EQUILIBRIUM; UNCERTAINTY AND GENERAL EQUILBRIUM.

BIBLIOGRAPHY

Arrow, K.J. 1959. Towards a theory of price adjustment. In *The Allocation of Economic Resources*, ed. M. Abramowitz, Stanford: Stanford University Press.

Arrow, K.J., Karlin, S. and Scarf, H. 1958. *Studies in the Mathematical Theory of Inventory and Production*. Stanford: Stanford University Press.

Barro, R.J., and Grossman, H.I. 1971. A general disequilibrium model of income and employment. *American Economic Review* 61, 82–93.

Barro, R.J., and Grossman, H.I. 1976. *Money, Employment and Inflation*. Cambridge: Cambridge University Press.

Bellman, R. 1957. *Dynamic Programming*. Princeton: Princeton University Press.

Benassy, J.P. 1975. Neo-Keynesian disequilibrium theory in a monetary economy. *Review of Economic Studies* 42, 502–23.

Benassy, J.P. 1976. The disequilibrium approach to monopolistic price setting and general monopolistic equilibrium. *Review of Economic Studies* 43, 69–81.

Benassy, J.P. 1977a. A Neo–Keynesian model of price and quantity determination in disequilibrium. In *Equilibrium and Disequilibrium in Economic Theory*, ed. G. Schwodiauer, Boston: D. Reidel Publishing Company.

Benassy, J.P. 1977b. On quantity signals and the foundations of effective demand theory. *Scandinavian Journal of Economics* 79, 147–68.

Benassy, J.P. 1982. *The Economics of Market Disequilibrium*. New York: Academic Press.

Benassy, J.P. 1986. *Macroeconomics: An Introduction to the Non-Walrasian Approach.* New York: Academic Press.

Bushaw, D.W., and Clower, R. 1957. *Introduction to Mathematical Economics.* Homewood, Ill.: Richard D. Irwin.

Chamberlin, E.H. 1933. *The Theory of Monopolistic Competition.* Cambridge, Mass.: Harvard University Press.

Clower, R.W. 1965. The Keynesian counterrevolution: a theoretical appraisal. In *The Theory of Interest Rates,* ed. F.H. Hahn and F.P.R. Brechling, London: Macmillan.

Cuddington, J.T., Johansson, P.O. and Lofgren, K.G. 1984. *Disequilibrium Macroeconomics in Open Economies.* Oxford: Basil Blackwell.

Drèze, J.H. 1975. Existence of an exchange equilibrium under price rigidities. *International Economic Review* 16, 301–20.

Grossman, H.I. 1972. A choice-theoretic model of an income investment accelerator. *American Economic Review* 62, 630–41.

Hahn, F.H., and Negishi, T. 1962. A theorem on non tatonnement stability. *Econometrica* 30, 463–9.

Hansen, B. 1951. *A Study in the Theory of Inflation.* London: Allen & Unwin.

Hicks, J.R. 1965. *Capital and Growth.* London: Oxford University Press.

Hildenbrand, K. and Hildenbrand, W. 1978. On Keynesian equilibria with unemployment and quantity rationing. *Journal of Economic Theory* 18, 255–77.

Keynes, J.M. 1936. *The General Theory of Money, Interest and Employment.* New York: Harcourt Brace.

Keynes, J.M. 1937. Alternative theories of the rate of interest. *Economic Journal* 47, 241–52.

Leijonhufvud, A. 1968. *On Keynesian Economics and the Economics of Keynes.* Oxford: Oxford University Press.

Machlup, F. 1958. Equilibrium and disequilibrium: misplaced concreteness and disguised politics. *Economic Journal* 68, 1–24.

Malinvaud, E. 1977. *The Theory of Unemployment Reconsidered.* Oxford: Basil Blackwell.

Muellbauer, J. and Portes, R. 1978. Macroeconomic models with quantity rationing. *Economic Journal* 88, 788–821.

Neary, J.P. and Stiglitz, J.E. 1983. Towards a reconstruction of Keynesian economics: expectations and constrained equilibria. *Quarterly Journal of Economics* 98, supplement, 199–228.

Negishi, T. 1961. Monopolistic competition and general equilibrium. *Review of Economic Studies* 28, 196–201.

Negishi, T. 1979. *Microeconomic Foundations of Keynesian Macroeconomics.* Amsterdam: North-Holland.

Patinkin, D. 1956. *Money, Interest and Prices.* New York: Row, Peterson & Co.; 2nd edn, New York: Harper & Row, 1965.

Portes, R. 1981. Macroeconomic equilibrium and disequilibrium in centrally planned economies. *Economic Inquiry* 19, 559–78.

Quandt, R.E. 1982. Econometric disequilibrium models. *Econometric Review* 1, 1–63.

Robinson, J. 1933. *The Economics of Imperfect Competition.* London: Macmillan.

Samuelson, P.A. 1947. *Foundations of Economic Analysis.* Cambridge, Mass.: Harvard University Press.

Tobin, J. and Houthakker, H.S. 1950. The effects of rationing on demand elasticities. *Review of Economic Studies* 18, 140–53.

Triffin, R. 1940. *Monopolistic Competition and General Equilibrium Theory.* Cambridge, Mass.: Harvard University Press.

Younès, Y. 1975. On the role of money in the process of exchange and the existence of a non-Walrasian equilibrium. *Review of Economic Studies* 42, 489–501.

disguised unemployment. Marx set out the notion that a 'reserve army' of unemployed labour is more or less continuously maintained in the course of capitalistic development. In the initial phases, this reserve army may be created through the destruction of the pre-capitalistic modes of production while, in later phases, a systematic bias in favour of labour-displacing innovations could serve the same purpose. This entails a broad vision of capitalistic development under extremely elastic supply conditions for labour where the actual level of wage employment is usually demand-determined. This means that the supply of labour tends to adjust to its demand through various routes such as, higher participation rate (e.g. as more married women join the labour force or the average schooling period is shortened), interregional and international migration of labour etc., all this taking place against the background of continuous induced innovations. Under these circumstances, it is not very useful to think of a 'natural' rate of growth, set by the growth of labour force and of labour productivity, as the maximum feasible growth rate of a capitalist economy (Marglin, 1984 pp. 103–8).

The elastic nature of the labour supply and its adjustability to the level of demand entail the existence of open or disguised unemployment as an untapped reservoir of labour in the normal course of capitalist development. However, such disguised unemployment although real is a somewhat amorphous phenomenon in an advanced capitalist economy for two distinct reasons. First, under normal circumstances, many potential entrants (e.g. married women, late school-leavers, young people on the farm) may not actually even try to enter the labour market unless demand is seen to be high with all sorts of job vacancies exceeding their corresponding numbers in registered unemployment. Second, the economic nationalism in the richer countries often takes the form of strictly regulating the migration of 'guest-workers' so that open unemployment in the (potentially) labour-exporting countries, rather than disguised unemployment in the advanced capitalist countries, becomes the normal pattern. And yet, prolonged stagnation in economic conditions in an advanced capitalist country may make this phenomenon of disguised unemployment more visible, as the redundant workers either seek various forms of self-employment with virtually no invested capital or try to sell their labour services directly as porters, odd-jobmen, domestic servants, farm-hands etc. (Robinson, 1956, pp. 157–8). Their earnings in these peripheral jobs would then become the 'reservation price' of this marginalized labour force. When unemployment dole and social security set a higher reservation price, some of this unemployment may come out in the open instead of being disguised. In this sense, it is probable that the growth of the welfare state may openly register as unemployed some who would have been otherwise unemployed in a disguised fashion earlier. And, the reverse could happen if the social security measures are cut by the government.

The existence of such disguised unemployment on a significant scale is usually accommodated by a secondary or informal labour market mostly in the service sector. This is much more easily visible in the phenomenon of massive migration to urban centres from rural areas in many developing countries. While all such migrants from rural areas aspire to limited job opportunities in organized industries located in urban areas, only a small fraction among them are actually able to find proper jobs at any given point of time. The rest spend their time, waiting in search of appropriate jobs. In the meantime, they somehow manage to disguise their unemployment either by self-employing themselves with tiny amounts of invested capital (e.g. polishing shoes, cleaning cars etc.) or by selling their labour services directly in odd jobs or even, simply taking recourse to the support of the elaborate kinship system in more traditional societies e.g. by living off better-placed relatives and migrant workers from their home areas. Thus, the phenomenon of disguised unemployment in the urban areas of many developing countries becomes closely linked with the massive migration from rural areas during the course of industrialization.

A distinguishing feature of disguised unemployment in such an informal sector is the irregular and often long hours of work per day. This is evident enough in the case of most self-employed persons in the informal sector; but even those who are employed on a wage-labour basis usually have highly flexible wage contracts in many respects (e.g. domestic servants, odd-jobmen etc.). Partly the explanation lies in the lower unionization of this sector. However, a deeper explanation lies in the fact that most self-employed persons as well as workers paid at the piece-rate have to work extended hours per day simply to make a livelihood. But this also could have a limited advantage for some of them insofar as the entire family can participate in the work (e.g. traditional carpet making, weaving and other types of artisan work are often done by many members of the family working together). In this context, we have to make a sharp distinction between labour-service and the labourer providing such service: the same amount of labour service (say, 18 hours per day) may be spread out over several family members working as labourers (say, three). In some cases, each family member (labourer) may on an average have a lighter work load (of only six hours) per day compared to an average worker in the organized industry. This brings us to a somewhat different analytical dimension of disguised unemployment: some persons may be unemployed in a disguised manner not only in the sense of having a very low earning rate i.e. *income-wise* unemployment but also in the sense of relatively light work-intensity per day, i.e. *time-disposition-wise* unemployment. And, unless one believes in the neoclassical proposition that income necessarily reflects the marginal product, one would have to devise, a third (and separate) criterion of disguised unemployment in terms of abnormally low *productivity* of labour. However, given the structure of reward in a capitalist economy, one needs to be careful in applying these concepts. Thus, an 'important person' belonging to the board of directors of several large corporations, may be making a well-above-average income by attending only a couple of board meetings per month. Such a person may very well be considered to be disguised unemployed by the time-disposition criterion and even perhaps by the labour-productivity criterion although, he cannot, by any means, be considered unemployed, disguised or not, by the income criterion! Also recall in this context that 'unproductive labour' was a common category used in the classical tradition of political economy and, all those engaged in unproductive labour (e.g. 'priests, prostitutes and professors' according to a picturesque phrase employed by Rosa Luxemburg) could be considered to be disguised unemployed by the productivity criterion.

In the normal organization of factory work under the capitalist system, the threefold distinction between income-wise, time-wise and productivity-wide disguised unemployment may not be particularly relevant. Thus, an unemployed industrial worker is both income– and time-wise unemployed and of course, he does not have much a chance to be productive either. However, such a distinction can be highly relevant in the context of traditional, family-based agriculture, especially for characterizing such phenomena as rural poverty or the existence of surplus labour. Consider for example a typical rural woman in the poorest strata: in addition to all her other work inside and outside the house, she may have to spend long hours collecting wood for fuel and carrying water home from a distance. Although she has exceptionally hard and long working hours every day and must be considered time – and disposition-wise fully employed and certainly productive in every normal sense of the term, in keeping her family going under most difficult circumstances, in all probability she would *not* be classified as 'gainfully employed' by the income criterion. Indeed her case is the opposite of that

our 'important person' who has a high income by attending a couple of board meetings every month. It is to be noted that the worst kind of rural poverty is often concentrated among people who are fully employed by the time-disposition criterion, but may be described as disguised unemployed by the income criterion, because of their miserably low earning rate per hour of work. After all, this is what the phrase 'eking out a living' usually means.

There can hardly be any serious doubt that in the backward agriculture of many populous countries (e.g. in South Asia), a high proportion of the population engaged in cultivation have extremely low income and, in this sense suffers from disguised unemployment by the income-criterion. Nevertheless, it is far more problematic to identify what such disguised unemployment by the income criterion implies in terms of either the time-disposal or the productivity criterion. If one were to believe in the ideologically potent neoclassical slogan that all 'factors of production' including labour always tend to get paid according to their marginal product even in pre-capitalist, backward agriculture, then that proportion of population with extremely low income could be said to be rather unproductively engaged in agriculture. Their low income would be the 'evidence' of their low productivity which in turn would imply a corresponding level of disguised unemployment in agriculture. But this would involve implicit theorizing based on the dubious assumption that income (earning) is always positively associated with productivity, even in traditional agriculture.

Such implicit theorizing apart (a sophisticated example of which is the so-called 'efficiency wage' hypothesis e.g. Bliss and Stern, 1978) the important question remains as to whether there is any meaningful sense in which one can argue about the existence of significant surplus labour and disguised unemployment in backward agriculture, judged by the productivity criterion. This would imply that some surplus labour can be withdrawn from agriculture without adversely affecting the level of agricultural output. Or, in more textbookish jargon, 'at the margin' labour contributes nothing to output so that, the marginal product of labour is zero in such agriculture.

Put in such general terms, the formulation is too fuzzy to be useful. For instance, if by 'margin', one means the *intensive* margin of higher labour input per unit of land, then considerable empirical evidence exists, at least in India, to suggest that the smaller-sized land holdings usually do use family labour more intensively, both in current agricultural operations *and* in direct investment of labour for improving land quality. As a result, the total output, taking all crops together over the year, tends to be higher per unit of land on smaller holdings (Bharadwaj, 1974, chs. 2, 3 and 7 provide an excellent account). This tendency towards an *inverse* relation between farm size and productivity per acre in traditional agriculture would tend to cast doubt on the simple-minded proposition that the 'marginal' product of labour is zero, especially if the notion of intensive margin is used.

Without going into such finer points of intensive and extensive margin, Schultz (1964, ch. 4) proposed the 'epidemic test': the 1918–19 influenza epidemic in India killed 6.2% of the 1918 population and 8.3% of the working population in agriculture (the latter according to Schultz's estimate). Schultz found that, although the weather conditions were roughly similar in 1916–17 and in 1919–20, in the latter year agricultural output was lower by about 3.8%, providing circumstantial evidence that withdrawal of labour from agriculture did affect output level. However, apart from many statistical and conceptual problems (e.g. the relation between acrage change in the sense of extensive margin and output change which is a resultant of both extensive and intensive margin in his macro-level statistical investigation), this 'epidemic test' must be deemed to be over-simplistic despite its apparent ingenuity. At best, it showed that a *random x%* withdrawal of labour from cultivation did affect the acrage and/or output level. But it does in no way establish the impossibility of *selectively* withdrawing *x%* labour through suitable reorganization of agricultural production at the family and regional level (e.g. Sen, 1967). And yet, most of the important initial proponents of the 'surplus labour' doctrine had in mind such selective (but not random) withdrawal of labour that may be induced by industrialization and expansion in urban employment opportunities (Nurkse, 1953; Lewis, 1954). And, once it is recognized that such withdrawal of labour from agriculture can be accompanied by reorganization of labour in the family farm through adjusting the hours of work of the family members staying back on the farm or through higher availability of land per cultivating family, it seems plausible to argue analytically (e.g. Takagi, 1978) as well as empirically that, labour can usually be released from agriculture without adversely affecting the level of agricultural output. Indeed, post-revolutionary experiences of agrarian reorganization in China and Vietnam demonstrated the possibility of using surplus labour to improve the quality of land through better drainage and irrigation without significant drop in short-run agricultural output, despite all the serious problems of lack of adequate incentive to private production in cooperative and collective agriculture.

AMIT BHADURI

See also HARRIS-TODARO MODEL; LABOUR SURPLUS ECONOMIES; ROBINSON, JOAN VIOLET.

BIBLIOGRAPHY

Bharadwaj, K. 1974. *Production Conditions in Indian Agriculture* (A study based on farm management surveys). Occasional Paper 33, Department of Applied Economics, Cambridge: Cambridge University Press.

Bliss, C. and Stern, N. 1978. Productivity, wages and nutrition, Parts I and II. *Journal of Development Economics* 5(4), 331–98.

Lewis, W.A. 1954. Economic development with unlimited supplies of labour. *Manchester School of Economic and Social Studies* 22, May, 139–91.

Marglin, S.A. 1984. *Growth, Distribution, and Prices.* Cambridge, Mass.: Harvard University Press.

Nurkse, R. 1953. *Problems of Capital Formation in Underdeveloped Economies.* Oxford, Clarendon Press.

Robinson, J. 1956. *The Accumulation of Capital.* London: Macmillan.

Schultz, T.W. 1964. *Transforming Traditional Agriculture.* New Haven: Yale University Press.

Sen, A.K. 1967. Surplus labour in India: a critique of Schultz's statistical test. *Economic Journal*, 154–60.

Takagi, Y. 1978. Surplus labour and disguised unemployment. *Oxford Economic Papers* 30(3), November, 447–57.

disintermediation. 'Intermediation' generally refers to the interposition of a financial institution in the process of transferring funds between ultimate savers and ultimate borrowers. The forms of services that such financial intermediaries provide, the characteristics of their liabilities and assets, and the rationale for their existence is described elsewhere. For this purpose, we only need to assume that a certain pattern of financial intermediation is given, say by actual historical development, or is theoretically optimal.

Disintermediation is then said to occur when some intervention, usually by government agencies for the purpose of controlling, or regulating, the growth of financial intermediaries, lessens their advantages in the provision of financial services, and drives financial transfers and business into other channels. In some cases the transfers of funds that otherwise would have gone through the books of financial intermediaries now pass directly from saver to borrower. An example of this is to be found when onerous reserve requirements on banks leads them to raise the margin (the spread) between deposit and lending rates, in order to maintain their profitability, so much that the more credit-worthy borrowers are induced to raise short-term funds directly from savers, for example, in the commercial paper market. Another, more recent, example arises when stringent capital adequacy requirements lead banks to provide funds to borrowers in a form that can be packaged into securities of a kind that can be on-sold to ultimate savers, rather than kept on the books of the banks involved, and thereby need larger capital backing.

Disintermediation not only refers to those instances where financial flows are constrained by intervention to pass more directly from saver to borrower (than in an unconstrained context), but also where such flows pass through different, and generally less efficient, channels than would otherwise be the case. This latter is just as common in practice. For example, where constraints and regulations are imposed on some sub-set of domestic financial institutions, substitute services of a similar kind will become provided by 'fringe' financial institutions that are not so constrained. More generally, in the absence of exchange control, constraints and burdens on the provision of domestic financial services will encourage financial institutions to provide these same services abroad, notably in the international Euro-markets. Indeed, the development of the Euro-markets provides a case study of the power of disintermediation out of more rigorously controlled domestic financial markets into an international milieu not subject to such controls.

The likelihood of such disintermediation imposes a limit on the authorities' ability to impose controls and regulations on financial intermediaries. If such controls are to be effective, they presumably force financial intermediaries to behave in a way that they would not voluntarily do, and hence represent a burden on them. There will then be an incentive for the controlled financial intermediary to seek to escape such a burden, for example through disintermediation. This represents a perennial problem for the monetary authorities. Logically, it might seem to lead to a tendency for the authorities to be forced to extremes, either to prevent disintermediation altogether by extending the ambit of controls to all forms and kinds of financial intermediation, or alternatively to allow complete laissez-faire within the financial system, despite the dangers of financial instability that might ensue. In practice, however, the authorities try to seek a compromise in the form of regulations sufficiently well-designed to maintain monetary control and financial stability, without being sufficiently burdensome to cause large-scale disintermediation. This is not, however, an easy exercise and requires continuous adjustment by the authorities as the financial system evolves.

CHARLES GOODHART

See also FINANCIAL INTERMEDIARIES; MONETARY POLICY.

distance functions. *See* GAUGE FUNCTIONS.

distortions. The voluminous literature on distortions, including a masterly survey by Jagdish Bhagwati (1971), contains no formal definition of the term distortion. The analysis often proceeds in terms of specific examples. Bhagwati analyses distortions in the context of foreign trade policies and the welfare of home consumers. He characterizes distortions as departures from the equality of the marginal rate of transformation of one commodity into some other through foreign trade (the so-called foreign rate of transformation) with transformation through domestic production (the domestic rate of transformation) and with the marginal rate of substitution in the consumption of the same pair of commodities by each consumer. Also, the failure to achieve aggregate production efficiency, in the sense of not producing on the boundary of the set of production possibilities given available resources and technology, is deemed a distortion.

Given non-interdependent consumer preferences the above equalities and production efficiency are indeed necessary conditions (leaving aside corner optima) for a feasible allocation to be Pareto Optimal. Any combination of production, consumption, and foreign trade vectors such that there is no positive excess demand for any commodity is feasible. Pareto Optimality ensures that no other feasible allocation can make at least one consumer better off without making some other consumer worse off. These conditions are also sufficient if it is assumed that the aggregate production set and individual preferences are convex. Further, if each consumer has a positive endowment of every commodity, any such Pareto Optimal allocation can be sustained as a competitive equilibrium provided redistribution of endowments among consumers or of their incomes through lump sum transfers in feasible. This is in essence the second fundamental theorem of neoclassical welfare economics.

Bhagwati, and others analysing distortionary taxation (Atkinson and Stiglitz, 1980), factor market distortions (Magee, 1976) etc., all seem to take (implicitly) the second fundamental theorem as the point of departure. This suggests the following definition: *a distortion exists in an economy in which lump sum transfers or their equivalents are feasible redistribution instruments, if some Pareto Optimal allocations from the point of view of consumers of that economy cannot be characterized as competitive equilibria*. This is consistent with the argument of Arrow (1964) that

> the best developed part of the theory (of externalities) related only to a single problem: the statement of a set of conditions, as weak as possible, which insure that a competitive equilibrium exists and is Pareto-efficient. Then the denial of any of these hypotheses is presumably a sufficient condition for considering resort to nonmarket channels of resource allocation – usually thought of as government expenditures, taxes, and subsidies.

A distortion can clearly arise in situations when some of the premises of the theorem are violated. Obviously, if lump sum income transfers are infeasible, even if all the other premises are satisfied some Pareto Optima cannot be characterized as competitive equilibria. Hence any redistribution achieved through other instruments may be Pareto dominated by an equilibrium achievable with lump sum transfers. Violations of other premises will in general call for the use of additional policy instruments besides lump sum transfers. If externalities or increasing returns in production lead to non-convexity of the aggregate production set, in general, a set of Pigouvian taxes and subsidies are the needed additional instruments. If price-taking producers and consumers do not perceive a country's market power in its foreign trade then taxes on foreign trade are needed.

The preceding discussion implicitly views the distortions as structural features of the economy or in Bhagwati's terminology, as endogenous and the policies as 'first best' responses that assure Pareto Optimality. However, if the same policy instruments are used in the absence of distortions or at levels that are not 'first best optimal' in their presence, the resulting equilibrium will be Pareto dominated by another achievable equilibrium by refraining from their use in the former case and by using them at first best optimal levels in the latter. Bhagwati characterizes such inappropriate use of policy as autonomous policy imposed distortion.

Policymakers may have other objectives besides consumer welfare. Johnson (1965) termed such social concerns non-economic objectives. The literature that followed (Bhagwati and Srinivasan, 1969) addressed two policy questions. The first derives the 'first best' policy that achieves a given non-economic objective, with the least cost in terms of consumer welfare. One feasible policy for achieving the non-economic objective has a higher cost than another, if the equilibrium associated with the former is Pareto dominated by an equilibrium achievable using the latter and making lump sum transfers between consumers as needed. The second question is the ranking of alternative feasible policies starting from the 'first best' to 'second best', 'third best' etc. in terms of their cost in achieving the non-economic objective.

Governments may wish to raise the output (for instance, for reasons of national defence) of some industry above its level in a laissez-faire competitive equilibrium through policy intervention. A production subsidy (or its equivalent) to that industry is the appropriate first best policy for achieving the production (non-economic) objective. Such a subsidy would be non-optimal, and hence a distortion, in the absence of the objective. Bhagwati characterizes such interventions as policy imposed instrumental distortions, the word instrumental signifying that the policy is an instrument for achieving non-economic objectives. Trade tariffs and quotas, consumption taxes and subsidies, wage subsidy and similar factor use taxes or subsidies turn out to be the first best policy instruments for achieving suitably specified non-economic objectives. Each such policy could also be a feasible policy for achieving non-economic objectives for which it is not the first best.

The impacts, measured in alternative ways, of particular policies or processes in the presence of a distortion rather than the optimal policy response to it have been analysed. An example is the impact of an import tariff in an economy with a distortion in the labour market in the form of a minimum wage above its market clearing level. The literature on immiserizing growth (Bhagwati, 1968) and its offshoots analyse the impact of the processes factor accumulation, technical change, external capital inflow, etc. on an economy with a tariff distortion. This diverse literature establishes two important common propositions. First, given an existing distortion, the impact of policies other than the first best or of processes could be in a direction opposite to that they would have taken had there been no distortion or had the distortion been addressed with a first best policy. For example, the accumulation of capital which would have increased consumer welfare had there been an optimal tariff could be welfare-worsening in its absence. The shadow price of a factor to be used in social cost benefit analysis is a small open economy with a distortionary tariff can be negative. Thus the withdrawal of that factor from its existing employment for use in a project instead of adding to the project's cost increases its social value! (Srinivasan and Bhagwati, 1978). An implication of this is that some of the production activities in an economy are subtracting rather than adding value at shadow prices, while obviously their value added at market prices is positive.

The second proposition shows that policies other than the first best, even if distortionary, can increase welfare. Thus given an existing distortion, introduction of another can improve welfare. In the so called Harris-Todaro (1970) economy a distortionary minimum wage is enforced in urban manufacturing activity. Rural workers migrate to urban areas as long as their expected wage (taking into account the probability of being unemployed) exceeds the rural wage. If the first best policy of a wage subsidy to both sectors is not feasible, an output subsidy to agriculture can improve welfare compared to the laissez-faire equilibrium. The second proposition is an illustration of the general theorem of the second best: 'if there is introduced into a general equilibrium system a constraint which prevents the attainment of one of the Paretian conditions, the other Paretian conditions, though still attainable, are in general, not desirable' (Lipsey and Lancaster, 1956). The constraint of this theorem is the equivalent of a distortion and violating other attainable Paretian conditions is equivalent to introducing other distortions. The theory of the second best is rigorously analysed by Guesnerie (1979, 1980).

The literature on rent seeking (Krueger, 1974) and directly unproductive profitseeking (DUP) activities (Bhagwati, 1982) has highlighted another aspect of distortions. A distortion by raising the demand price of a commodity above its relevant supply price creates a rent that may trigger a competition for acquiring it. For example, an import quota (tariff) by raising the domestic price above the import price could trigger a competition for quota rents (tariff revenues), thereby diverting resources from production. However, such a diversion takes place in the context of an existing distortion (an inappropriate quota or tariff) and as such, paradoxically, it can improve consumer welfare if it succeeds in reducing the welfare loss associated with the distortion more than the welfare loss it creates in reducing resources available for production. It has also been shown that the welfare ranking of policies that achieve a given non economic objective can be reversed once seeking activities triggered by such policies are taken into account.

To sum up, a distortion by definition creates a welfare loss; first best optimal policies could often be devised to offset this loss; if for some reason, first best policies are infeasible, other welfare-improving policies may exist and sometimes, they can be ranked as 'second best', 'third best' etc.; however, such policies, can have effects in directions opposite to those they would have had in the absence of a distortion; distortions have implications for social cost–benefit analysis; finally distortions can trigger rent-seeking activities.

T.N. SRINIVASAN

See also OPTIMAL TARIFFS; PARETO EFFICIENCY; PARETO OPTIMALITY; SECOND BEST; TAXES AND SUBSIDIES.

BIBLIOGRAPHY

Arrow, K.J. 1964. Political and economic evaluation of social effects and externalities. In *Analysis of Public Output*, ed. J. Margolis, New York: National Bureau for Economic Research, 1970.

Atkinson, A.B. and Stiglitz, J.E. 1980. *Lectures on Public Economics*. New York: McGraw Hill.

Bhagwati, J.N. 1968. Distortions and immiserizing growth: a generalization. *Review of Economic Studies* 35, 481–5.

Bhagwati, J.N. 1971. The generalized theory of distortions and welfare. Chapter 12 in *Trade, Balance of Payments and Growth: Papers in International Economics in Honor of Charles P. Kindleberger*, ed. J.N. Bhagwati, R.W. Jones, R. Mundell and J. Vanek, Amsterdam: North-Holland.

Bhagwati, J.N. 1982. Directly unproductive profit– seeking (DUP) activities. *Journal of Political Economy* 90, 988–1002.

Bhagwati, J.N. and Srinivasan, T.N. 1969. Optimal intervention to achieve non-economic objectives. *Review of Economic Studies* 36, 27–38.

Guesnerie, R. 1979. General statements on second best Pareto optimality. *Journal of Mathematical Economics* 6, 169–94.

Guesnerie, R. 1980. Second-best policy rules in Boiteux tradition. *Journal of Public Economics* 13, 51–8.

Harris, J.R. and Todaro, M.P. 1970. Migration, unemployment and development: a two sector analysis. *American Economic Review* 60, 126–42.

Johnson, H.G. 1965. Optimal trade intervention in the presence of domestic distortions. Chapter 11 in *Trade, Growth and the Balance of Payments*, ed. R.E. Caves, H.G. Johnson and P.B. Kenen, Amsterdam: North-Holland.

Krueger, A. 1974. The political economy of the rent-seeking society. *American Economic Review* 64, 291–303.

Lipsey, R.G. and Lancaster, K. 1956. The general theory of the second-best. *Review of Economic Studies* 24, 11–32.

Magee, S.P. 1976. *International Trade and Distortions in Factor Markets*. New York: Marcell Dekker.

Srinivasan, T.N. and Bhagwati, J.N. 1978. Shadow prices for project selection in the presence of distortions: effective rates of protection and domestic resource costs. *Journal of Political Economy* 86, 97–116.

distributed lags. *See* MULTIPLE TIME SERIES MODELS.

distribution, ethics of. The primary fact of economics is the production of wealth. The division of the product among those who create it is secondary in logical order and, in a sense, in importance. Yet the most important subject of thought connected with social economy is distribution. If the term be used broadly enough it designates all of the economic process that presents moral problems for solution. On the settlement of the ethical questions concerning the division of the social income depends not only the peace of society but the fruitfulness of industry. It is a striking fact that Ricardo, whose studies carried economic science forward in the direction of the truth concerning distribution, but stopped short of that goal, and so strengthened the hands of social agitators, realized the paramount importance of the subject on which his thought was chiefly concentrated: 'To determine the laws which regulate this distribution,' he says in his preface, 'is the principal problem in political economy.'

Scientific errors concerning the law of distribution react more harmfully on production than do errors of doctrine concerning production itself. Among self-asserting people, industry loses fruitfulness whenever the belief is widely diffused that products are shared according to an unjust principle. If it were a general conviction that social evolution is in the direction of iniquity – that distribution already robs the workers and will rob them more hereafter – no force could prevent a violent overturning of the social order.

Industry has its fruits and its sacrifices; it creates useful things at the cost of working and waiting. Where production is carried on in a collective way, both the products and the burdens of the process have to shared by different classes of men according to some principle. The apportionment that has to be made is not only of products, which represent positive values, but of sacrifices, which may be treated as negative values of a 'subjective' kind. While the term distribution, as currently used, designates only the apportionment of the positive values, or products, it is capable of being used in a more complete sense, and made to include the apportionment of the negative ones also. It would then include all of economic science that involves moral problems.

Both parts of this twofold distributive process must in any case be studied if the ethical questions connected with industry are to be solved. There is no independent standard of justice in the distribution of products only. What a man ought to get out of the collective income of mankind depends on how much he or some one who represents him has sacrificed in helping to create it. The apportionment of the positive values referred to is inseparably connected with that of the negative values. Political economy must tell us how both products and burdens are actually shared, and ethics must tell us how both of them ought to be shared, if the existing plan of social industry is to be morally tested.

Political economy has not as yet furnished a theory of the actual distribution of positive values, or products of industry, that has met with general acceptance. It has scarcely attempted to furnish a theory of the distribution of the negative values. Ethical science has not furnished a clear standard of justice in the double apportionment.

Every producer experiences in his own person the double effect of industry; he is first burdened and then rewarded. The net effect of the two influences on the man's well-being may be termed the subjective resultant of production. A complete science of distribution must study the economic resultants in the case of different classes of men. How is a labourer on the whole affected by industry? What is the measure of the net benefit that comes to him from this source? How is a capitalist affected? How do the net effects compare with each other? What tendencies are at work to change the two, both absolutely and relatively? These are economic questions; while the ethical question is what the resultants in the two cases ought to be.

The personal resultant of industry is always a positive quantity. Work yields a net gain; the fruits of it are worth more than they cost. For the most hardly-used classes an industrial life is, by economic tests, more than worth living. The hours of labour in a day are increasingly burdensome as the period of work is prolonged. A man might labour three hours a day with little weariness and no injury. The eighth hour is wearying, and the tenth is more so. There comes a time at which work naturally stops, if the man is free, because working longer would cost more in the way of pain than it would secure in the way of pleasure. Final or marginal labour is that which just pays for the weariness that it costs. The gain that comes through labour offsets the burden that it entails at the point in the working day at which the burden is greatest. The less onerous labour of the earlier hours affords a net personal gain. If the man is paid by the hour he earns a part of his wages very easily. Intramarginal labour, as we may term it, affords a net subjective gain, what some would call producers' rent.

Though the wages of all hours may be equal by money standards, they are of unequal utility to the man who gets them. His first earnings are spent on necessities, later ones on comforts, and final or marginal ones on things that figure in his estimate as luxuries. The last hour of his labour may ensure to him only the least important thing that he gets at all. It is the minimum benefit secured by an hour's labour that offsets the maximum sacrifice caused by it. There is therefore a second net gain coming to the worker in the spending of his money. As the sixpence or dime that is spent for a luxury benefits the man enough to offset the weariness of final or most fatiguing labour, those that are spent for food, clothing, etc., afford an additional benefit. The man enriches himself whenever he buys a loaf of bread. In general the sacrifices and the benefits of production just offset each other at the point at which the sacrifices are the greatest and the gains are the least.

Everywhere except at the margin the gains are greater and the sacrifices are less.

Again the positive resultant of industry is increased by social organization. Anarchy, even if it were peaceful, would increase sacrifices and diminish rewards. Whatever might be true of a sparsely settled world, a crowded world is dependent on the multiplying of productive power that combination brings. All classes are debtors to society. No serious case can be made against the existing social order on the ground that it lessens the gain that labour naturally brings.

The indictments brought against the social order are based on the comparative treatment that society accords to men of different classes. Are the benefits conferred on different ones what they ought to be relatively? Does society proceed capriciously in the allotment of rewards and sacrifices? Do some classes fail to get the proportionate benefit that is properly theirs? Are social tendencies in the direction of equity or away from it? These are the ethical questions to be solved by a comparision of the ideally just distribution with the actual one.

Of the ideals of distribution that have been advanced none has been crude enough to provide for the apportionment of the products of industry and take no account of the burdens. A rule of equal rewards for unequal sacrifices would have no moral support. Ethical studies in this field really have as their object the attainment of a rule for adjusting what we have termed the personal resultants of industry, or a rule that, if followed in practice, would make the net effect of industry on the welfare of different classes equitable. Communistic theories make equality nearly synonymous with equity; but the thing that is to be equalized is seldom mere property or income. If the principle of equality be carried into refinements, so as to bring to one level the net benefits that society confers on all its members, the rule approaches, though it is still far from reaching, the ultimate moral ideal of distribution.

The better socialistic ideals are refinements of the rule of equality. In applying the rule to individuals, inheritance is the first disturbing influence encountered. The law of inheritance is based on a certain solidarity of families. Where it is in force the sacrifices of a parent may accrue to the benefit of a child. What we have termed the resultant of industry in the case of the heir to an estate is not to be measured by adding together positive values, represented by the enjoyments that the property brings, with negative values, represented by the inheritor's own sacrifices. If he be considered apart from his family the values in the case are nearly all positive. A crude levelling of individuals' net gains accruing from industry demands the abolition not only of inheritance, but of gifts from parents to children. Where it is advocated it is in the interest of purely individualistic equality.

The handing over of all capital to the state sweeps away even more completely inequalities of wealth in permanent possession. In theory it might avoid the evil connected with the abolition of inheritance, that, namely of reducing the capital that is necessary if wages are to be sustained at a high rate; since it is conceivable that the state itself might accumulate capital with needed rapidity. This measure also would, in effect, disregard the solidarity of families and tend to put men on a footing of individualistic equality.

Economic difficulties do not need to be considered in the shaping of a moral ideal. The vesting of all capital in the state would save the student of applied ethics one serious difficulty, that, namely, of determining whether the sacrifice of abstinence is unduly rewarded as compared with that of labour, or, in other words, whether interest is too high as compared with wages. A socialistic state has its moral duty simplified, since it has only to reward different kinds of labour equitably.

A scheme that is too crude to have much support makes the wages and the working hours equal for all. Estimate the wages in money or its equivalent, gauge labour by time only, and bring both to an equality in the case of the whole adult population. Even the rewards are not thus in reality equalized, and the sacrifices are very unequal. In real rewards unmarried men would be favoured and large families would suffer. The real sacrifices incurred would vary according to the nature of the work performed.

An improvement on this scheme provides a stipend for each dependent member of a family, and tries to equalize sacrifices by so reducing the number of hours of labour per day in occupations that are disagreeable or hurtful, as to bring all employments to a certain uniformity of burdensomeness. In the case of very disagreeable work the hours would be reduced to a minimum, while in occupations that are less and less repellent they would be shortened proportionately less. Production would of course suffer by this arrangement, and the ideal that the plan of division presents is that of small but equal pay, with easy work, for all.

Another scheme does not content itself with equalizing what we have termed the personal resultants of industry, but aims to level inequalities of condition that lie at the back of industry itself. Society should do more for the lame and the blind than for those who have all faculties in possession, in order that the ultimate condition of all may be made as nearly equal as is possible. Here is the levelling policy in perhaps its most ambitious mood. It is not the treatment of men by society that is to be equalized, but the treatment of them both by nature and society. The industrial organism is to deal with its members unequally in order that it may somewhat neutralize the partiality of nature.

A rule of division that is often regarded as ethically lower than either of those above specified is that of compensation according to actual production. Give to a man the wealth that he creates, neither more nor less. Every one owns what he brings into existence; let not society wrest or filch from him any part of it. Let it keep itself clear from robbery and fraud.

If workers lived side by side in peaceful anarchy, with no division of labour and no exchanges, each man would get what he created. He would get little, but he would get all that would be his own. Introduce now a social union that multiplies products ten-fold but increases some men's returns only five-fold, and you seem to benefit these men and to rob them at the same time. If in organized industry some of the product that is distinctly attributable to labour itself finds its way into the hands of men who do not create it, the labourer suffers a wrong, even though the share that he still keeps may be larger by reason of the fact of his connection with the men who rob him. Such is the conception of industrial society that exists in many minds. The socialistic indictment against society is that it filches from workers a part of their share of the *extra* product of industry due to organization. Does society, under natural law, take from labour a product that is distinctly attributable to it? This is one of the most important questions in economics. A successful analysis of social production answers it. What needs to be known is what part of the composite result of industry is distinctly due to labour itself. In a land peopled by isolated producers and managing to live in peace, each man would get his own; does exchange vitiate this result? If so, organization proceeds here on an unusual principle; since the complications of society as a rule disguise essential facts of primitive industry, but do not annul them. The presumption is that the man who got his own when he

worked alone gets it when he trades with his neighbour on terms of genuine freedom, and that a true analysis of social relations will show the fact. If so, society tends actually to conform to the rule 'to every man the product that is distinctly attributable to the sacrifices that he or others in his interest have made'. There is common honesty in the distribution that takes place under natural law.

The literature of the subject of economic ethics is not as scanty as it is one-sided. The basis of the socialistic movement is ethical, and much of the literature is designed to prove that society is organized on a plan that systematically wrongs workers in the apportionment of the social income. A defence would naturally aim to show that the law of distribution is not itself iniquitous, however many particular cases of injustice might arise under it. A weak point in the defence is the lack of a clear demonstration of the complete nature of the actual law of distribution, a lack that, as is hoped, may soon be supplied. In the meanwhile statistics are appealed to on both sides to prove, on the one hand, that the actual apportionment of wealth is departing more and more from the ideal standard, and, on the other, that it is tending towards it.

[J.B. CLARK]
Reprinted from *Palgrave's Dictionary of Political Economy*.

distribution, law of. The most important share of the income of society is the one falling to labour. The so-called 'wage fund' theory accounted for the rate at which labourers are paid on the ground that wages come from a fund of capital devoted to this purpose, and that the rate per man depends on the size of the fund and the number of the claimants. The discovery of the fact that wages come from the product of industry, and not from capital, has made a new theory necessary, and has opened the way to the discovery of a general law of distribution.

The parties in the division of the general product of industry are – (1) those who contribute to production the element labour; (2) those who contribute instruments, or wealth in productive forms; and (3) those who bring labour and productive wealth into co-ordination by hiring both of these agents, and receiving and selling their products. The labour furnished includes the work of management, as well as other kinds of industrial effort; and the productive wealth, as the term is here used, includes land as well as other instruments. The co-ordinating function is, in this enumeration, kept distinct from the other two; the man who performs it is not to be treated in this connection as a labourer or as a capitalist, but as the employer of both labour and capital.

The shares to be accounted for are thus wages, interest, and pure profit, and these shares will include the rent of land and the wages of superintendence. The generic varieties of gain come from putting forth productive effort of some kind, from furnishing productive wealth in some form, and from bringing the effort and the wealth into coordination.

The scientific law of distribution determines what reward shall attach to the performing of one of these functions. It does not gauge the income of a particular man, since a man nearly always performs more than one function. A capitalist usually works, a labourer usually has capital, and an *entrepreneur*, or coordinator of labour and capital, almost invariably owns some productive wealth, and does some directive work. A scientific study aims to discover what determines the gain that attaches to the working, to the saving, and to the coordinating. As a man is a composite functionary, it tells us how much he naturally gets in each of his various capacities.

The nature of the distributive process. Social production is a synthesis of distinguishable elements. Distribution is an analysis; and it reverses the synthetic operation step by step. In organized production one worker does not complete a product from the beginning; if he applies his energy to crude nature and begins the making of something that the wants of society require, he passes the product in an incomplete state to a successor. This man in turn advances the article nearer to completion and hands it over to a third man. The product, when ready for final use, has passed through the hands of a series of workers each of whom has put his touch on it and passed it to his successor.

Subproduct	Resulting from:
1. Elementary utility: wool	Joint result of Capital and Labour.
2. Place utility: transporting	Joint result of C' and L'.
3. Form-utility: manufacturing	Joint result of C'' and L''.
4. Form-utility: tailoring	Joint result of C''' and L'''.

Table 1 Synthesis resulting in the completed product, clothing.

The process may be represented by Table 1. The garment, when completed, is an aggregate of distinct utilities, and we use the term sub-product to denote the quality imparted to it by each specific group of producers. The sharing of the value that a coat represents among the groups that have performed the specific operations of production is an analytical operation, that follows, in a reverse direction, the steps of the productive synthesis.

The first sub-product in the series is wool. It embodies an 'elementary utility', or one that results from calling a raw material into existence. The merchant's sub-product is only the special utility imparted to the wool by conveying it to his warehouse, assorting it, and dividing it into quantities convenient for purchasers. It is mainly a 'place utility', which is the service-rendering quality that a thing acquires by being taken to the place where it can be used; though in a complete statement it would be necessary to recognize a 'form-utility' due to assorting and dividing. The manufacturer's sub-product is not the cloth, but the 'form-utility' imparted to the wool by transmuting it into cloth. The tailor's sub-product is the further 'form-utility' imparted to the cloth by making a coat of it. Each specific utility is created by the joint action of labour and capital; and each of these agents must have its share of the value embodied in its sub-product.

In order that the action of labour and capital within the sub-groups may be a joint-action at all, it is necessary that a certain coordinating act be done. Some one must hire labour of the right kind, borrow capital and invest in the proper forms, and cause the two to cooperate. This is the work of the entrepreneur, in an unusually limited sense of the term. This functionary, in his capacity as entrepreneur, is not a capitalist and not a labourer, however frequently it may happen that the man who performs the coordinating function may perform others as well. The coordinator, as such, is not a business manager or superintendent. The performing of this function does not require salaried labour; indeed, after the process is begun, it scarcely requires effort at all.

Bargaining operations first divide the total product of industry among the general groups of which society as a whole is composed. How much wealth shall come to the entire group of workers, capitalists, and entrepreneurs who are engaged in the creating of the finished products, woollen garments? That depends on the price for which the garments sell. A myriad of

finished products from other groups in the world at large must come, by way of exchange, to minister to the wants of the men in this one group; and the quantity and quality of those products is fixed by the sale of the clothing. This sale, and others like it, perform the first and most generic dividing act that takes place in the process of distribution. It determines the total income of those who contribute to the production of clothing.

What fixes the part of the income of this general group that goes to each of the sub-groups that compose it? Bargains again. Each group must buy the utilities made by those that come earlier in the series, and sell them, with the addition of its own utility, to the group that succeeds it. The manufacturing group buys wool and sells cloth; and what it receives, less what it pays, constitutes the reward of the manufacturing operation. As the first division of the income of society resolves it into rewards of general producing groups, the first subdivision resolves the portion falling to one general group into shares for the sub-groups that constitute it.

A further division is to be effected: it is that of the shares falling to labourers, to capitalists, and to entrepreneurs in each sub-group. Here is the test operation of distribution; in this smallest of fields is created and divided the wealth that rewards each class in industrial society.

The productive operation from the fruit of which labour and capital get their pay is *intra-groupal*; it goes on within the specific industry in which a particular force of men and their quota of capital are engaged. The value that rewards woollen weavers and spinners and the men who furnish them capital is created wholly within the mill, and the sum that is divided between these classes is a sum on which no others have any claim. Yet the fact that labour and capital both migrate freely from group to group, so that workers from any group are able to share in the special gains that may come to the earners in any other, creates a certain solidarity of labour on the one hand, and capital on the other. Give to the wool spinners an advance of wages, and movements of labour will in the end distribute the gain among the whole working class. On the other hand, change the cardinal relations of labour and capital as a whole, and you change them in the end within every sub-group. Labour is in reality *trans-groupal*, and capital is the same. Each is a productive agent, the field of which extends directly across the sub-groups of the diagram. It is the relation of all capital to all labour that determines wages and interest. The law of wages is nothing if not general, and the same is true of the correlative law of interest.

It is a familiar fact that interest and wages tend toward uniformity in different occupations. Men of different productive powers may earn different rewards, even within a single trade; and the labour of management regularly receives more than work of the ordinary kinds. Men differ in the amount of working force that they possess, but men of like power tend to receive uniform wages throughout the series of industrial groups. If wages are high in the woollen mill the young men and women who are about to enter the field seek out this part of it, and by their competition reduce the wages there prevalent to the rate that prevails elsewhere. Interest tends to a similar uniformity; under free competition it tends to keep the same rate in all industries.

With interest has often been vaguely grouped what we have termed pure profit itself; the gross gains loosely attributed to capital tend toward equality. It is, however, in a special way that the element that we have distinguished as pure profit tends toward equality in different industries. Wherever it comes into existence it sets at work forces that tend to sweep it again out of existence. In a way this gain is self-annihilating.

The uniform rate toward which pure profit tends – though it never reaches it in all groups at once – is a zero rate. Here indeed, we reach controverted ground, and can claim only to present one theory, not a view that has universal support; but the evidence in favour of the correctness of the view is simple and conclusive. Competition tends to annihilate pure profit. The existence in one sub-group of a gain that is in excess both of interest on all the productive wealth that is there used, and of pay for all labour, is an inducement to the entrepreneurs of the group to hire in the market both capital and labour, and secure the pure profit that their joint industry creates. Let woollen mills pay wages, including salaries, and a double interest on the capital that they use, and the mills will speedily enlarge their capacity. The increase in the product will then reduce the price of it, and ultimately bring the enlargement to an end. Under natural law the sub-groups are in stable equilibrium when, aside from insurance and taxes, each earns wages on all labour, including the labour of management, interest on all capital employed, and nothing more. On this point the testimony of experience confirms the conclusions of theory.

The equilibrium is never in practice perfect. Causes that cannot here be analysed in any fulness cause the element pure profit to continually reappear. Inventions, as applied in particular industries, give to one and another of the sub-groups a gain that is in excess of that which perfectly stable conditions would afford. The occupation of new land creates, in a local way, a pure profit for the earlier comers. Continually appearing in particular parts of the field, and slowly disappearing by reason of competition – such is this element of the social income. If we watch a single sub-group we find the profit at intervals appearing and disappearing; if we watch the industrial field as a whole we find it everywhere present, though not long at the same points.

Pure profit depends on a relation between industrial groups. What the manufacturer pays to the earlier groups in the series above represented, and what he receives from the tailoring group, determine this part of his gain. The actual position of the entrepreneur himself, in the diagram that describes the sub-groups, is on the line that separates his own industry from the following one. He is a purchaser of everything that is produced on the left of that line. In the buying of materials he purchases the products of the earlier sub-groups, and in the paying of wages and interest he virtually buys the sub-product created in the group to which he himself belongs. The entrepreneur of the woollen mill buys wool, and so pays for the sub-products created by wool growers and merchants; and he buys the form-utility created in the woollen mill itself by making bargains with workmen and capitalists, giving them fixed sums, and inducing them to relinquish their claims on the cloth. As the place of a particular workman and of a particular amount of capital is, in the diagram, *intra-groupal*, so that of a particular entrepreneur is *inter-groupal*. Workers and capitalists get their pay from results secured wholly within their own industries, while entrepreneurs get theirs from the fruits of mercantile transactions between earlier groups and later ones. Pure profit does not depend on the relation between capital and labour. Moreover, where this profit exists it is local, it depends on the relations between adjacent groups.

We have shown that there is no law of wages that is merely local. There is no force that gauges the pay of wool-spinning independently of the wages paid in other employments. There is a level toward which all wages tend. There is likewise a level toward which interest in every group tends. What is the law that fixes these levels? What is the general law of wages and interest? Here again we are on ground that is actively

contested, and we therefore only indicate the nature of a certain theory without claiming for it a position of general acceptance, and without arguing any points in controversy.

In presenting it we may utilize a Ricardian formula for determining the rent of land. If we apply to a fixed area of land an increasing amount of labour, we get returns that diminish *per capita*. The first man set working on 100 acres creates a certain amount of wealth as the result of the tillage. Adding a second man does not double the crop. Adding a third does not increase by a half the product due to the former two. Each man, as he comes into the field, adds less to the total output of the industry than did any of his predecessors.

This hypothesis makes the men enter the field in a certain order of time, and the one who is the final man is so in a literal sense – he is the last to arrive. Actually putting the men into the field one at a time is not necessary in order to reveal the principle that governs the final productivity of labour. Let the full complement of men occupy the field at once, and there will still be what may be treated as the final increment of labour. Take any man away from the force that tills the field, and the remaining men will gain in *per capita* productivity by reason of his absence. The departure of one man out of a force numbering twenty does not reduce the crop by a twentieth, since the nineteen men remaining work at better advantage by reason of the withdrawal of one. The final productivity of labour is gauged by what would be lost if one man out of the force were to stop working. We may, by way of illustration, actually set the men working one at a time, and find what the last comer creates; or we may set them all working at once and see what would be lost by the departure of one. The conclusion is the same in either case: the final unit of labour is the least productive.

If, now, land were the only form of productive wealth that figured in the case, wages would equal the amount created by this final or twentieth man. That would gauge the amount that the employer would lose through the departure of any one man in the force. It would determine what he could afford to pay to any one. Each man tends to get what he is separately worth.

What would be true in the case of labour applied to land, and using no other capital worth considering, is actually true of labour applied to a fixed amount of general capital, or to a fixed quantum of wealth in all productive forms, including both land and other instruments. For the field of limited extent in the Ricardian illustration substitute a fixed value, expressible in pounds or dollars, and invested in such appliances of every kind as working the needs of the working community require. If there are a hundred men in the force, the departure of one of them will not reduce the product by 1 per cent. His departure will add somewhat to the productivity of the remaining workers. After he is gone the capital will adapt itself in form to the needs of the ninety-nine, and it will be in a slight degree more ample in quantity per man. Wages are gauged, as in the former case, by the final productivity of labour. What on the whole is lost by the departure of one man fixes the importance to employers of every man. If each man gets what employers would lose by his absence, he gets that he is effectively worth.

This principle in a reversed application fixes the rate of interest. It is the productivity of the final increment of capital, as employed by a fixed labour force, that gauges the pay of each increment. Let there be 100 men using 100 units of capital. Take, now, one unit of capital away, and you will not reduce the product by 1 per cent. The 99 units of capital will have gained in productivity per unit in consequence of the departure of the hundredth. The loss inflicted on the entrepreneur by the withdrawal of the one unit of capital gauges the importance of any single unit. Each unit of capital gets as its compensation what would be lost if one unit of capital were withdrawn. This diminution of the total product due to the departure of the final unit of capital gauges the importance to the entrepreneur of each separate unit. It determines what he will pay for the use of each one. Interest is therefore gauged by the final productivity of capital. Each pound or dollar tends, under natural law, to secure for its owner what, in production, it is separately worth.

[J.B. CLARK]
Reprinted from *Palgrave's Dictionary of Political Economy.*

BIBLIOGRAPHY

Böhm-Bawerk, E. von. 1884–9. *Kapital und Kapitalzins.* Innsbruck: Wagner.

Cairnes, J.E. 1874. *Some Leading Principles of Political Economy.* London: Macmillan.

Clark, J.B. 1886. *The Philosophy of Wealth.* Boston: Ginn & Co.

Clark, J.B. 1888. *Capital and its Earnings.* Baltimore: American Economic Association.

Clark, J.B. and Gidding, F.H. 1888. *The Modern Distributive Process.* Boston: Ginn & Co.

George, H. 1879. *Progress and Poverty.* New York: Appleton.

Longe, F.D. 1886. *A Refutation of the Wage-Fund Theory of Modern Political Economy.* London: Longmans, Green.

Thornton, W.T. 1869. *On Labour.* London: Macmillan.

Walker, F.A. 1876. *The Wages Question: A Treatise on Wages and the Wages Class.* New York: H. Holt & Co.

Walker, F.A. 1883. *Political Economy.* New York: H. Holt & Co.

Wieser, F.F.B. 1889. *Der Natürliche Werth.* Vienna: Hölder.

distribution-free estimation. *See* SEMI-PARAMETRIC ESTIMATION.

distribution-free methods. *See* NON-PARAMETRIC METHODS.

distribution theories: classical. The terms 'classical economists' and 'classical political economy' were first used by Marx, whose monumental survey of economic theory from the middle of the 17th century up to the early 1860s was contained in the manuscript written between January 1862 and July 1863 which the author called *Theorien über den Mehrwert.* Marx used the terms to describe 'the critical economists', 'the economic investigators ... like the Physiocrats, Adam Smith and Ricardo' whose 'urge' was 'to grasp the inner connection of the phenomena'; he also referred to Ricardo as 'the last great representative' of classical political economy (cf. Marx, 1862–3, Vol. III, pp. 453, 500 and 502; 1873, p. 24).

Marx's description implies that not only authors like Senior, Bastiat, Wilhelm Roscher and John Elliot Cairnes are extraneous to classical political economy, but also such faithful Ricardians as James Mill, McCulloch and John Stuart Mill do not properly fit into it. This can only be understood if one bears in mind that the ranking of the various authors in *Theorien über den Mehrwert* is centred upon the nature of their contributions to the related subjects of Distribution and Value: the explanation of profit and the formation of a normal or general rate of profit; the relation between wages and profits, the difficulties in the theory of value that arise in connection with the wage–profit relationship and the formation of a general rate of profit are the chief theoretical questions in the light of which the various authors are surveyed.

Thus a first discriminating factor in Marx's critical survey is provided by each author's attitude towards the main analytical difficulties: whether this or that author shows himself to be aware of their presence and tries to solve them, albeit at the cost of falling into further difficulties and contradictions, or

rather tends to present the theory as a fully satisfactory body of propositions by denying the difficulties and 'immediately adapting the concrete to the abstract' (Marx, 1862–3, Vol. III, p. 87). This factor explains why Marx is inclined to treat both Torrens (1815, 1821) and Malthus (in particular, 1827) as classical economists, while regarding James Mill as the beginner of the 'disintegration' of the Ricardian theory.

A second factor is the *weight* of the 'vulgar' element present in the contributions of the various authors – meaning by this the tendency to confine one's attention to the 'superficial appearance of the phenomena' *versus* 'the urge to grasp [their] inner connection'. As an important example of this factor one may refer to the increasing tendency, after Ricardo, to explain distribution by competition and 'the [changing] state of supply and demand' (J. Mill, 1844, p. 42; cf. also J.S. Mill, 1848, p. 337, and Cairnes, 1874, pp. 168–74) – thereby gradually abandoning the classical conception according to which demand and supply can only determine the oscillations of distribution and prices either above or below their 'natural' values. A third discriminating factor is the 'vulgar' element represented by the mere apology for the existing state of affairs (cf. Marx, 1962–63, Vol. III, p. 168), or, as Cannan was later to put it, by the 'desire to strengthen the position of the capitalist against the labourer' (Cannan, 1917, p. 206). Finally, a fourth factor may be indicated in the tendency to deny the existence of economic laws altogether, and to substitute shallow empiricism for theoretical analysis (think of the so-called historical school of German political economy).

The theoretical approach to distribution and value 'of the old classical economists from Adam Smith to Ricardo has been submerged and forgotten since the advent of the "marginal" method' (Sraffa, 1960, p. v). A contribution to this effect certainly came from the fact that *Theorien über den Mehrwert* remained largely unknown among economists. (It was only in the early 1950s that some sections of the 1905–10 Kautsky edition were translated into English, whilst the complete English translation from the edition based on the original manuscript was made in 1963–71.) In what follows, we shall take 'Classical Theory of Distribution' to mean the main elements which can be regarded as characterizing the approach to the problem of the division of the national product among classes followed by the English classical economists from Adam Smith to David Ricardo, later by Karl Marx, and, more recently, by Piero Sraffa – this century's greatest exponent of the 'classical' approach to distribution.

The classical method of approaching the problem of distribution is based upon a distinction between two parts in the annual product of society: that part which is necessary for its reproduction (which includes the necessary subsistence of the workers employed in the economy) and that part which can be 'freely' disposed of by the society and which constitutes its 'net product' or 'surplus' – what remains of the social product after deducting the necessary subsistence of the workers and the replacement of the means of production. It is the aim of the classical theory to explain the circumstances governing the size of the surplus and its distribution among classes: 'To determine the laws which regulate this distribution, is', according to Ricardo, 'the principal problem in Political Economy' (Ricardo, 1821, p. 5). In the course of his work he succeeded in 'getting rid of rent', so as to concentrate on the problem of the distribution between capitalists and workers; in what follows rent will be left entirely out of account – one may suppose that fertile lands abound – and the essential features of the surplus approach to distribution will be illustrated with reference to the determination of wages and profits.

Contrary to the supply-and-demand approach, which has been the dominant method over the last hundred years, in the theoretical approach to distribution of the classical economists and of Marx, the real wage rate and the rate of profit are not symmetrically and simultaneously determined on the basis of the relative scarcity of labour and capital. Within the classical approach, one of the two distributive variables is explained independently from both the social product and the other distributive variable, and the other one is determined as a residual.

Both the classical economists and Marx considered the real wage as constituting the independent or 'given magnitude' in the relation between the two distributive variables, maintaining that its normal level is determined by 'subsistence'. Normal profits, reckoned gross of interest, are determined as a residual, on the basis of the dominant techniques of production. Given the dominant techniques, the level of the wage rate is thus the only circumstance upon which the normal rate of profit depends and no increase in the latter can be conceived of but through a fall in the former.

WAGES AND PROFITS. It is in the context of this relation between wages and profits that the problem of value arises within the classical theory. All the surplus product of the annual labour of the economy, exceeding the portion absorbed by labour itself in the form of wages, must be divided among the individual capitalists according to the capitals they have employed in production. It is the very task of relative prices ('natural prices' or 'prices or production') to ensure such proportional division of the profit share of the surplus, and in order to perform their task relative prices are bound to change in the face of any increase or fall in the quantities of the various commodities accruing to the labourers as wages. This change in relative prices, and in the value of the social product, which must necessarily take place whenever nothing changes but distribution, makes it difficult to determine the effect on profits of a rise and fall in wages; it obscures the inverse relationship between wages and profits which would be apparent if output and its means of production were the same in kind, or if their values remained unaffected by changes in the division of the product. Hence Ricardo's search for a measure of value which would be invariant to changes in wages (Ricardo, 1821, ch. I, sections IV, V and VI; Sraffa, 1951, pp. xlviii–xlix); hence, also, Marx's determination of the general rate of profit *before and independently from* the 'prices of production', on the basis of magnitudes (the quantities of labour bestowed in the production of the relevant heterogeneous aggregates of commodities) invariant to changes in the division of the product (Marx, 1894, ch. 9).

Only recently was a solution provided (Sraffa, 1960) to the difficulties inherent in the theory of value that were left unresolved by Ricardo and Marx. The picture outlined above, however, points to a clear subordination of the problem of value to the determination of distribution. This contrasts sharply with the dominant supply-and-demand approach, where the theory of value – the conception of equilibrium prices as allocators of given factor endowments and their determination simultaneously with normal outputs and the equilibrium prices of factor services (distribution) – comes almost to coincide with economics itself.

As mentioned above, the real wage rate is explained by the classical authors in terms of 'subsistence'. They included in this notion 'not only the commodities which are indispensably necessary for the support of life, but whatever the custom of the country renders it indecent for creditable people, even of the lowest order, to be without', and 'the want of which would

be supposed to denote that disgraceful degree of poverty, which no body can well fall into without extreme bad conduct' (Smith, 1776, vol. II, p. 399). Their conception, in other words, was that the normal wage rate 'depends not merely upon the physical, but also upon the historically developed social needs, which become second nature. But in every country, at a given time, this regulating average wage is a given magnitude' (Marx, 1894, p. 859; cf. also Torrens, 1815, pp. 62–3).

The classical authors also ascribed to the conditions of competition on the labour market the possibility of influencing real wages for fairly long periods of time, and hence of causing shifts away from the normal distribution of income between capitalists and workers. Smith referred to the possibility that under certain circumstances, connected with the pace of accumulation and the growth in productivity of labour, 'the scarcity of hands' or a 'scarcity of employment' may move the wage above or below the normal average level (Smith, 1776, vol. I, pp. 77 and 80). Starting from Smith's analysis, Marx went on to consider the movements of wages in the periodic alternations of the industrial cycle as regulated 'by the varying proportions in which the working-class is divided into active and reserve army, ..., by the extent to which it is now absorbed, now set free' (Marx, 1883, p. 596).

Normal wages having been explained in terms of subsistence, the normal rate of profit must be determined as a residual on the basis of the dominant techniques of production. Those firms which, within each sphere of production, employ more backward or more advanced techniques than the dominant ones, earn profits that are respectively smaller or greater than normal.

In this conception, the conditions of competition amongst capitalists do not have any role to play as regulator of the normal distribution of income between wages and profits. It is easy to see on the basis of Sraffa's price equations (Sraffa, 1960, paras 1–4) that, given the wage in terms of specified necessaries and the methods of production, if there is a surplus product in the economy then the system necessarily determines, together with prices, also a positive general rate of profit which no competition whatsoever among capitalists can eliminate or change. If real wages, in other words, determined by historical and social conditions independently from prices and from the rate of profit, absorb only a part of the net product of the economy, it is simply impossible for competition, however intense it may be, to determine prices such as to render nil or 'as low as possible' what remains of the value of the product after the means of production have been reintegrated and the wages paid.

It is true that the competition amongst the owners of capital plays an important role in Smith's theory: he makes the level of the 'natural' rate of profit depend on it. But this is precisely where the basic contradiction in Smith's theory may be seen. On the one hand he considers the real wage to be determined by subsistence; on the other he maintains that the rate of profit is determined by competition amongst capitalists, which, by growing more intense as accumulation proceeds, would make 'the ordinary rate of profit as low as possible' (Smith, 1776, vol. I, p. 106). In short, his reasoning proceeds as if *both* distributive variables could be determined independently from each other.

Leaving aside Smith's contradiction, it can be affirmed that in classical and Marxian theory competition is envisaged essentially as the mechanism whereby, in each sphere of production, a single price tends to be established: the price that enables the means of production to be reintegrated on the basis of the dominant production techniques, and wages and profits to be paid at their normal rates. These latter must be explained independently from competition, and, as Marx puts it, it is they that regulate competition, rather than being regulated by it (cf. Marx, 1894, p. 865). The competition amongst firms within each sphere of production and the free transferability of capital from one sphere to another – hence the process whereby profit rates gravitate towards their respective normal levels – may be impeded by the presence of monopoly elements in this or that sphere of production. This however will affect the division of profits amongst the particular stocks making up social capital, but not the normal distribution of net output between wages and profits (Marx, 1894, p. 861).

INTEREST AND PROFITS. Profits on capital employed in production normally include, according to the classical economists, besides interest, also a remuneration for the 'risk and trouble' of productively employing it, or what may be termed a normal profit of enterprise. Production and accumulation would not continue, Ricardo argues, if the profits of the farmers and the manufacturers were 'so low as not to afford an adequate compensation for their trouble and the risk which they must necessarily encounter in employing their capital productively' (Ricardo, 1821, p. 122). Such 'adequate compensation' will be different in the various employments of capital, according to 'any real or fancied advantage which one employment may possess over another' (Ricardo, 1821, p. 90). On the basis of this conception, natural prices will have to be such as to ensure that, in each sphere of production, what remains of the value of the product after deducting wages and the replacement of the means of production, is sufficient to 'adequately' remunerate the 'risk and trouble' and pay interest at an uniform rate. It can thus be said that interest and profit of enterprise are conceived in the classical analysis as the two magnitudes into which normal profits – determined by real wages and production techniques – resolve themselves.

The money rate of interest emerges from this picture as a magnitude subordinate to the normal rate of profit, being ultimately determined by those real forces, the real wage rate and production techniques, which explain the course of the normal rate of profit. But what if actual experience did not validate the conception of the money rate of interest as a subordinate phenomenon? A few significant modifications would be called for within the classical-Marxian approach to distribution, if it had to be acknowledged that the level of the rate of interest in any one country is strongly influenced by circumstances which have nothing to do with the real forces regarded by the classical economists as governing the rate of profit. These modifications, as will be apparent from the determination of distribution outlined below, would lead to a view of the real wage as the residual rather than the independent or 'given' variable in the relation between profits and wages.

It is important to notice that the replacement of the wage by the rate of profit as the independent distributive variable is fully compatible with the surplus approach to distribution (cf. Garegnani, 1984, pp. 320–2). The concept of profits as surplus product is not under discussion when asking which of the two distributive variables should be regarded as 'given' in the present reality of the capitalist economy. The question is whether the relations that workers and capitalists establish with one another tend *primarily* to act upon the real wage or upon the rate of profit, once the view is abandoned that real wages consist of the necessary subsistence of the workers and

the possibility of variations in the division of the social surplus is admitted.

Actual experience seems in fact to validate the conception of an autonomous determination of the money rate of interest – autonomous in the sense that interest rates *do* experience lasting changes which are very reasonably explainable without any need to refer to a *primum movens* represented by changes in the normal profit rate. Interest rates in any one country depend directly on monetary policy; interest rate policy decisions, however, are taken under a wide range of constraints having different weights both amongst the various countries and for the same country at different times: external constraints, monetary and fiscal constraints, distributive constraints. The important point is that interest rate policies, both in the short and in the long run, do not appear to be constrained by a predetermined normal profitability of capital. Once this point is acknowledged, then, given the necessary (and generally admitted) long-run connection between the rate of interest and the rate of profit, it will also be acknowledged that it is the former which 'sets the pace' and that the latter will have to adapt itself. On this basis, one can proceed to discover the actual mechanism whereby the causation occurs and to study its implications (see Pivetti, 1985).

The actual mechanism whereby lasting changes in interest rates are susceptible of causing corresponding changes in normal profit rates, can be understood by following a three-stage line of reasoning. The first stage simply consists in regarding competition as the mechanism by which prices tend to be equated to normal costs. The second stage of the reasoning consists in looking at the rate of interest as a determinant of production costs, together with money wages and production techniques. Thus, lasting changes in interest rates *constitute* changes in normal costs, which, *ceteris paribus*, will result in corresponding changes of the price level. The third stage of the reasoning comes about as a consequence of the first two: by the competition amongst firms within each industry, a lasting change in interest rates causes a change in the same direction in the level of prices in relation to the level of money wages, thereby generating changes in income distribution.

The rate of interest thus emerges from our picture as the regulator of the ratio of prices to money wages. The reader will note the main difference between this view and the so-called post-Keynesian theory of distribution: whilst in that theory changes in the level of prices in relation to the level of money wages are determined by changes in aggregate demand, according to the present explanation of distribution they are determined by lasting changes in interest rates.

By taking into consideration also the excess of profit over interest, or profit of enterprise, our conception of the rate of interest as the regulator of the ratio of prices to money wages requires us to assume that lasting changes in the rate of interest do not tend, and are not likely, to be associated with opposite changes in the normal profit of enterprise. This assumption is largely consistent with classical conceptions as regards the normal excess of profit over interest: if profit *does* normally exceed interest (if competition, that is, does not tend to equalise profit and interest), then the excess of the former over the latter must cover objective elements of 'risk and trouble' or elements which are regarded as objective by the majority of the investing public. By taking into account all such elements, we can say that the normal rate of profit in each particular production sphere will be arrived at by adding up *two* autonomous components: the long-term rate of interest or 'pure' remuneration of capital, plus the normal profit of enterprise or the remuneration for the 'risk and trouble' of productively employing capital in that sphere of production. Provided this remuneration is a sufficiently stable magnitude, lasting changes in the rate of interest will cause corresponding changes in profit rates, and inverse changes in the real wage.

REAL WAGES AS A RESIDUE. As we saw above, interest and profit of enterprise are conceived by the classical economists as the two magnitudes into which normal profits resolve themselves, whereas, according to our view, the same two magnitudes should rather be regarded as the *determinants* of the rate of profit. Given the money wage, the real wage appears here as a residue on the basis of the price level reflecting the dominant techniques in the different spheres of production and the normal profit rate determined in each sphere in the way we have just indicated. From this determination of distribution, quite different views from the classical ones may be developed concerning the role of competition amongst capitalists.

Since in our view the real wage constitutes the residual variable, the presence of monopoly elements in this or that sphere of production may affect not only the division of profits amongst the different employments of capital, but also the distribution between profits and wages. Given in fact the money wage, the possibility for some commodities to obtain a monopoly price which rises above the 'price of production' will translate into a ratio price-level/money wage which will be higher than it would be if there were no monopoly elements, and hence into a lower real wage. Assuming the long-term rate of interest to be unaffected by the presence of monopoly elements, it follows that lasting effects of the conditions of competition on distribution may only be obtained in one direction: higher profits than normal. For the long-term interest rate and the normal remuneration of 'risk and trouble' establish, in each sphere of production, the minimum or necessary level below which the profit rate cannot go, over the long run, however intense one may suppose the forces of competition to be.

The possibility must also be admitted that the conditions of competition influence the normal profit rate via the long-term interest rate. At the root of this possible influence of competition there is the fact that the level of the real wage constitutes *in any case* an important constraint on the freedom of monetary policy to establish the level of interest rates. To acknowledge that lasting variations in the rate of interest determine variations in the normal distribution between profits and wages, is not to concede that the real wage may move to any level whatsoever. In each concrete situation, it would be hard to carry on the productive process in an orderly manner if the real wage were lower than certain levels reflecting institutional and historical as well as economic circumstances. Thus, if the conditions of competition have a negative effect on wages – via the levels of profits of enterprise or the methods of production adopted – then beyond certain limits, which will vary from one situation to another, a compensatory effect will have to be sought in the level of interest rates.

According to our view, then, the money rate of interest should be looked on as the magnitude on which the respective powers of capitalists and workers discharge themselves *in the first place*. Wage bargaining and monetary policy are regarded as the main channels through which class relations act in determining distribution, and those relations are seen as tending to primarily act upon the profit rate, via the monetary rate of interest, rather than upon the real wage rate as maintained by both the classical economists and Marx. The level of the real wage prevailing in any given situation is the *final* result of the whole process by which distribution of income between workers and capitalists is actually arrived at.

It seems to us that in the conditions of modern capitalism it is difficult to conceive of the real wage rate as the independent or given variable in the relationship between wages and profits – the difficulty, as we see it, arising from the fact that the direct outcome of wage bargaining is a certain level of the money wage, while the price level cannot be determined before and independently from money wages. Given distribution between profits and wages, and given the methods of production, the level of prices simply depends on the level of money wages. Thus, in our picture, the long-term rate of interest enters into the determination of the price level because it contributes to regulating the ratio of the latter to the money wage – that is, distribution between profits and wages.

If instead the real wage is taken as given, the ratio of prices to money wages will be determined by the condition that it must be such as to ensure the given level of the real wage; and on this basis wage bargaining, in determining money wages, can be thought of as determining also the price level. In such a picture monetary policy plays a purely passive role: the level of the rate of interest having to accommodate to lasting changes in the ratio of prices to money wages, rather than governing that ratio. Now what we are ultimately facing here is a conception of the ratio of prices to money wages as being determined by a magnitude, the real wage rate, which is not actually known before that ratio is known. This explains in our opinion why of the two alternative propositions – that the ratio of prices to money wages depends on the real wage rate, or that the real wage rate depends on the ratio of prices to the money wage – the latter is easier to digest: in actual fact, there are no circumstances determining real wages as distinct from those acting through money wages, the level of prices and the ratio of prices to money wages.

MASSIMO PIVETTI

See also INTEREST AND PROFIT; SURPLUS APPROACH TO VALUE AND DISTRIBUTION.

BIBLIOGRAPHY

Cairnes, J.E. 1874. *Some Leading Principles of Political Economy Newly Expounded.* New York: Harper & Brothers.

Cannan, E. 1917. *A History of the Theories of Production and Distribution in English Political Economy from 1776 to 1848.* 3rd edn, London: King.

Garegnani, P. 1984. Value and distribution in the classical economists and Marx. *Oxford Economic Papers* 36(2), June, 291–325.

Malthus, T.R. 1827. *Definitions in Political Economy, Preceded by an Inquiry into the Rules That Ought to Guide Political Economists in the Definition and Use of Their Terms; With Remarks on the Deviations from These Rules in Their Writings.* Reprinted, New York: Kelley, 1971.

Marx, K. 1862–63. *Theories of Surplus Value*, Vols I–III. Moscow: Progress Publishers, 1963–71.

Marx, K. 1873. Afterword to the 2nd German edition of *Capital*. In Marx (1883).

Marx, K. 1883. *Capital: A Critique of Political Economy*, Vol. I. 3rd edn, reprinted, London: Lawrence & Wishart, 1977.

Marx, K. 1894. *Capital: A Critique of Political Economy*, Vol. III. London: Lawrence & Wishart, 1977.

Mill, J. 1844. *Elements of Political Economy*. 3rd edn, New York: Kelley; 1965.

Mill, J.S. 1848. *Principles of Political Economy with Some of Their Applications to Social Philosophy.* Toronto: University of Toronto Press and London: Routledge & Kegan Paul, 1965.

Pivetti, M. 1985. On the monetary explanation of distribution. *Political Economy – Studies in the Surplus Approach* 1(2).

Ricardo, D. 1821. *Principles of Political Economy and Taxation.* 3rd edn, in *The Works and Correspondence of David Ricardo*, ed. P. Sraffa, Vol. 1, Cambridge: Cambridge University Press, 1951.

Smith, A. 1776. *An Inquiry into the Nature and Causes of the Wealth of Nations.* Ed. E. Cannan, London: Methuen, 1961.

Sraffa, P. 1951. Introduction to Ricardo's *Principles*. In *Collected Works of David Ricardo*, Vol. 1, Cambridge: Cambridge University Press.

Sraffa, P. 1960. *Production of Commodities by Means of Commodities*. Cambridge: Cambridge University Press.

Torrens, R. 1815. *An Essay on the External Corn Trade*. London: Hatchard.

Torrens, R. 1821. *An Essay on the Production of Wealth. With an Appendix in Which the Principles of Political Economy Are Applied to the Actual Circumstances of This Country*. Reprinted, New York: Kelley, 1965.

distribution theories: Keynesian. As Kaldor has pointed out, Keynes was never interested in the problem of distribution of income as such; the determination of its level was his main concern: 'One may nevertheless christen a particular theory of distribution as 'Keynesian' if it can be shown to be an application of the specifically Keynesian apparatus of thought' (Kaldor, 1956, p. 94). Since the middle Fifties a large number of neo- or post-Keynesian models of economic growth and income distribution have appeared, originating mainly in the University of Cambridge. Post-Keynesian distribution theory now occupies an undisputed place in most macro-economic textbooks. These models have been labelled as 'post-Keynesian' since savings passively adjust to the externally given full-employment investment, via redistribution of income between wages and profits and/or among social classes. This contrasts with the pre-Keynesian or neo-classical framework, where investment is governed by saving, and where the production function and marginal productivity theory play a crucial role in determining income distribution. The 'post-Keynesian' model also differs from the static Keynesian scheme, where changes in the level, rather than in the distribution, of income ensure equality between saving and investment.

THE ROLE OF SOCIAL CLASSES. In order to study income distribution in classical, post-Keynesian and neo-Ricardian theories it is relevant to define what kind of relationships exist between property and income earners. Property rights are fundamental determinants of distribution if the production process requires some form of cooperation from individuals having the power of 'withdrawing' certain essential inputs. As in most classical theories, social classes remain crucial for post-Keynesian theories, and their distinctive feature is given by their saving and consumption behaviour. In more sophisticated theories (Pasinetti) the assumption of 'separate appropriation' of each production factor is no longer in the foreground, and workers' income is made up by wages and profits on accumulated savings. In a general sense in post-Keynesian theories different rates of saving are associated with different economic or social classes. And the distribution of income among classes will be such as to yield an overall saving equal to the desired level of full-employment investment. We shall start by considering the origin of Keynesian income distribution theories.

THE HARROD–DOMAR DILEMMA. When in the late Thirties and in the Forties the first macro-economic models of economic growth were developed, the theory of income distribution was caught in an impasse, represented by the well-known Harrod–Domar equilibrium condition $s = g(K/Y)$, where s is the aggregate saving ratio, g the natural rate of growth (which can include 'labour saving' technical progress), and K/Y the capital/output ratio. If these three variables are all given, then it is unlikely that the Harrod–Domar condition can be satisfied. Hence, in order to have a model in which the possibility of steady growth is assured, it is necessary to relax one or another of the assumptions. The equality between s and $g(K/Y)$ can be obtained by: (a) flexibility in K/Y (also referred to as the technology assumption); (b) flexibility in s (saving assumption); (c) flexibility in g (labour-market and/or labour-supply assumption).

The above three cases can, of course, be combined in various ways as, for instance, in Samuelson and Modigliani's (1966) model, where (a) and (b) appply simultaneously.

TWO DIFFERENT WAYS OF ANSWERING THE HARROD–DOMAR DILEMMA. Solution (a) above was adopted by the neoclassical or marginalist school:

> Instead of there being fixed coefficients in production there may exist a production function offering a continuum of alternative techniques, each involving different capital–labour ratios; ... The consequence is that the capital–output ratio v is adjustable, instead of being fixed, and this provides a way in which s/v and n may be brought into equality (Hahn and Matthews, 1964, p. 785).

The second answer to the Harrod–Domar dilemma, that is, the assumption of a flexible aggregate saving ratio, was primarily adopted by the (neo-) Keynesian or Cambridge School. Of course there are many ways in which one can give flexibility to s; but the one which has played the major role is the hypothesis of a two-class society (namely workers and capitalists, or consumers and entrepreneurs), each with a different (constant) propensity to save. In this way there always exists a distribution of income between the two classes which produces precisely that saving ratio that will equal the value $g(K/Y)$, so satisfying the Harrod–Domar equilibrium condition. The validity of this approach is reinforced by the fact that the assumption of a uniform aggregate saving ratio ignores all possible differences in saving (and consumption) behaviour between, for instance, different classes of income receivers, or categories of income or even different sectors of the economy. Moreover the problem of aggregating savings might give rise to particular and unknown difficulties, so that it may be safer to consider it in a disaggregate way, as the neo-Keynesian model does. Thirdly, this assumption also receives empirical support from the observed high rates of saving out of corporate profits and lower rates out of labour income. Considering a full-employment long-run equilibrium growth model with a capitalists' class (whose income is derived entirely from capital) and a workers' class (whose income is derived from wages and accumulated savings), both with constant propensities to save, the Cambridge economists were in a position to (1) provide a solution to the Harrod–Domar dilemma (by specifying an aggregate saving ratio s which equals $g(K/Y)$, where g and K/Y are both exogenously given); (2) determine the long-run equilibrium value of the rate of profits, the distribution of income between profits and wages, and the distribution of disposable income between the two classes; (3) allow the existence of an income residual, namely the wages, consistent with the assumption of a relationship between the savings of that class of individuals (the capitalists) who are in the position to control the process of production and the patterns of capital accumulation; and (4) give some insights into the process of accumulation of capital by specifying the equilibrium capital shares of the two classes. This range of results is obtained within a fairly simple framework and on the basis of relatively few assumptions, much less 'hybrid, opposite and extreme' than those of the marginalist model.

KALDOR'S THEORY OF DISTRIBUTION. Kaldor's distribution theory plays a fundamental role in the Cambridge or post-

Keynesian theories of income distribution. His original analysis appeared first in the *Review of Economic Studies*, 1956 and, in a slightly different form in *Essays on Value and Distribution* in 1960. Kaldor considers a one-sector growing economy in which there are two classes: one whose income is derived entirely from capital (the capitalists, who are not wage-earners) and a second one which derives its income uniquely from wages (the workers). At each of these two groups he attaches a fixed propensity to save, s_c and s_w respectively, higher for the capitalists and lower for the workers. Kaldor's model, as well as all other neo- or post-Keynesian models, is based on the assumption of long-run, full-employment equilibrium.

Assuming that national income (Y) is divided into wages (W) and profits (P) and a situation of steady growth, where all variables grow at the same rate g and where all ratios among macro-economic variables remain constant, Kaldor derives explicit formulae for the overall rate of profits and share of profits in national income. Additionally, by making the 'classical' assumption that s_w (the propensity to save of the workers) is zero, he obtains the following two simple relationships: $P/K = g/s_c$ and $P/Y = g\bar{K}/s_c$. The first solution shows that the equilibrium rate of profits depends only on the exogenously given rate of growth (g) and on the constant propensity to save of the capitalists' class. The second solution shows that the long-run share of profits in national income is determined by the rate of growth, the capital/output ratio ($\bar{K}$) and the propensity to save of the capitalists (all exogenously given).

PASINETTI'S THEOREM. As we have seen, Kaldor's saving function considers, essentially, two types of income. What happens if we assume that the saving propensities differ, not according to classes of income, but according to classes of individuals (a more realistic assumption, referring to the weak definition of social class discussed above)? It is at this point that the basic contribution of Pasinetti may be brought in, where he assumes that saving propensities differ by class (assumed intergenerationally stable), rather than by type of income. His contribution, in his own words

> has come from the discovery of a fundamental relation (passed unnoticed in the whole of previous economic literature) which links profits to savings through the ownership of the capital stock. This relation simply follows from the institutional principle that profits are distributed in proportion to the ownership of capital and that the ownership of capital derives from accumulated savings (Pasinetti, 1974, p. 127)

In this way the workers' class is allowed to own a share of the total capital stock, from which it derives an interest income. By solving the model Pasinetti obtains an explicit value for the rate of profits and share of profits in national income; in particular the former turns out to be $P/K = g/s_c$, which has been defined as Pasinetti's Theorem, or 'Cambridge equation' (as a matter of fact it should be defined as the 'New Cambridge equation', since the original one had been found by Kaldor). Pasinetti's analytical results are similar to those obtained by Kaldor; there is, however, a fundamental difference, since Pasinetti's solutions have been obtained without making any assumption whatsoever on the propensity to save of the workers, which may assume positive values indeed. These results are undoubtedly of importance and establish a direct and simple relationship between the rate of profits and the rate of growth, through the interaction only of the capitalists' propensity to save. More precisely, the value of the rate of profits shows that on the long-run equilibrium growth path, the propensity to save of the workers, through influencing the distribution of income

between capitalists and workers, does not influence the distribution of income between profits and wages.

IMPLICATIONS OF THE 'NEW CAMBRIDGE EQUATION'. The first thing that can be stressed is that the rate of profits and the share of profits in national income both vary inversely with s_c. Hence, all other things being equal, the less the capitalists save and the greater is their return on capital (but with a smaller share of the capital stock). Exactly the opposite is true for the workers: the more they spend, the less they will receive for their future consumption (through a reduced share of the capital stock).

Secondly, as Pasinetti himself points out in the original exposition and more recently (Pasinetti, 1974, ch. VI) the irrelevance of workers' propensity to save gives the neo-Keynesian growth model much more generality than it appears at first sight. It is not necessary to make any hypothesis whatever on the aggregate saving behaviour of the workers for the simple reason that both the rate of profits and the distribution of income are determined independently of the propensity to save of the workers. Therefore the workers could be divided into any number of sub-categories we wanted. Again, the particular saving behaviour of any sub-category of workers would influence the distribution of income among the various sub-classes of workers and, of course, between the workers and capitalists, but the distribution of income between wages and profits would not be affected at all, given the constancy of the capitalists' propensity to save.

Third and finally, the 'New Cambridge equation' shows and uncovers, for the first time in modern economic theories, the 'absolute strategic importance' of the saving behaviour of just one group of individuals (the capitalists) for the determination of the most vital relationships of the model. On the other hand the saving behaviour of the other class (or sub-classes) has nearly no power at all: they can save as much as they want, and of course receive an interest on it, but they will not influence the distribution of income between profits and wages. Moreover the share of wages in national income is a residual, once the share of profits (a function of the capital/output ratio, the rate of growth and the propensity to save of the capitalists) has been determined. The concept of residual of the classical economists is to be found again: but while for Ricardo the residual was represented by profits, in post-Keynesian models wages are a residual, once profits have been determined.

THE MARGINALISTS' REPLY TO THE 'CAMBRIDGE EQUATION'. The results obtained by the neo-Keynesian economists did of course attract the attention of the neoclassical economists, who defined the Cambridge equation of income distribution as a 'paradox'. Their reaction was not surprising, since the Cambridge equation makes the whole 'well-behaved' production function framework irrelevant. With the aim of defending the theory of marginal productivity of capital, Meade (1963, 1966) and Samuelson and Modigliani (1966) set out to find a condition for which Kaldor–Pasinetti's Theorem would be prevented from operating, by arguing that when the propensity to save of the workers is exactly equal to the propensity to save of the capitalists times the profits share, then the capitalists cannot in equilibrium survive in the system and their propensity to save cannot determine the rate of profits. In such a situation all equilibrium savings of the system would be provided by the workers only, and the two-class system would become a single-class model where the marginalist scheme could be applied again to determine income distribution. But, as the ensuing debate has shown, such a situation is very unlikely to happen in the real world and, more importantly, it does represent a 'knife-edge' solution since in equilibrium it applies only when

$s_w = s$. To devise one 'knife-edge' in order to answer another one (the Harrod–Domar's) may not represent the best counter-argument.

OTHER CRITICISMS OF THE 'CAMBRIDGE EQUATION'. The most common criticisms of post-Keynesian income distribution models (cf., for instance, Bliss, 1975, ch. 6; Samuelson and Modigliani, 1966) seem to concentrate on: (a) the assumption of the equality, in the long-run, between the rate of profits earned by the capitalists and the rate of interest earned by the workers on their accumulated savings; (b) the constancy of the propensity to save of the two classes, exogenously given and hence independent of other variables as, for instance, the rate of interest or the rate of population growth; and (c) the assumption and identification of individuals who retain their class identity forever, that is, of classes which are inter-generationally stable.

Let us consider these points in some detail. In the late Sixties and early Seventies several authors have suggested that if one were to assume a differentiated rate of return for workers' and capitalists' savings, the Cambridge equation would no longer apply. As a matter of fact, as Pasinetti (1974, pp. 139–41) has formally proved, this may not be true: the hypothesis of a differentiated interest rate comes to reinforce his analysis, since 'A rate of interest lower than the rate of profit has the same effect of a higher propensity to save of the capitalists, as it redistributes income in favour of the class that owns the physical capital stock.' The second criticism was put forward by economists who thought that the introduction of the life-cycle hypothesis on savings into the two-class model (where individuals would make their saving plans on the basis of the level of the interest rate and of other life-cycle parameters) would make the equilibrium interest rate a function of all parameters of the model. The assumption of the life-cycle hypothesis is of course not strictly compatible with the neo-Keynesian framework, where investment is independent of savings; nonetheless it has been shown that even in the context of a two-class life-cycle model, as long as there exists a class of 'pure' capitalists, the equilibrium interest rate is a function of the behavioural parameters of the capitalists only. The third main criticism concerns the assumption of intergenerationally stable classes; one would expect that the relaxation of this assumption would invalidate the relevance of the Cambridge theorem. But it is not really so, as few authors seem to conclude.

Vaughan (1979), for instance, in his analysis obtains a third solution for the interest rate, which approaches Pasinetti's solution when the net transference of individuals between classes is low, as it may be the case over the very long run which constitutes the framework of these models.

CONCLUSIONS. Summing up we may say that post-Keynesian theories place themselves half-way between classical and marginalist theories of income distribution, since on the one hand they reject the strong version of the social-class theory of distribution postulated by classical economists, where each income share meets a strong 'claim' associated with the property of an essential input (labour, capital or land). Instead post-Keynesian theories put forward a much more flexible concept of social class, characterized by a given saving and consumption behaviour (for Pasinetti the workers may even be divided into sub-classes). But on the other hand post-Keynesian theories differentiate themselves from the models of competitive economics where individuals react only with respect to the markets on which they have little effect. Post-Keynesian theories do moreover allow for elements of monopoly power, and retain the concepts of residual income and circularity of the

production process contemplated by classical economists. It may well be that their extension to include certain elements of the life-cycle theory of saving and consumption behaviour will give them some micro-foundations.

MAURO BARANZINI

See also KALDOR, NICHOLAS; WIDOW'S CRUSE.

BIBLIOGRAPHY
Baranzini, M. 1975. The Pasinetti and the anti-Pasinetti theorems: a reconciliation. Oxford Economic Papers 27, 470–73.
Baranzini, M. and Scazzieri, R. 1986. Knowledge in economics: a framework. In Foundations of Economics: Structures of Inquiry and Economic Theory, ed. M. Baranzini and R. Scazzieri, Oxford and New York: Basil Blackwell.
Bliss, C.J. 1975. Capital Theory and the Distribution of Income. Amsterdam: North-Holland.
Hahn, F.H. and Matthews, R.C.O. 1964. The theory of economic growth: a survey. Economic Journal 74, 779–902.
Harcourt, G.C. 1972. Some Cambridge Controversies in the Theory of Capital. Cambridge: Cambridge University Press.
Kaldor, N. 1956. Alternative theories of distribution. Review of Economic Studies 23(2), 83–100.
Kaldor, N. 1960. Essays on Value and Distribution. London: Duckworth.
Meade, J.E. 1963. The rate of profit in a growing economy. Economic Journal 73, 665–74.
Meade, J.E. 1966. The outcome of the Pasinetti process: a note. Economic Journal 76, 161–5.
Pasinetti, L.L. 1962. The rate of profit and income distribution in relation to the rate of economic growth. Review of Economic Studies 29, 267–79.
Pasinetti, L.L. 1974. Growth and Income Distribution, Essays in Economic Theory. Cambridge: Cambridge University Press.
Pasinetti, L.L. 1981. Structural Change and Economic Growth. A Theoretical Essay on the Dynamics of the Wealth of Nations. Cambridge: Cambridge University Press.
Robinson, J. 1962. Essays in the Theory of Economic Growth. London: Macmillan.
Samuelson, P.A. and Modigliani, F. 1966. The Pasinetti paradox in neoclassical and more general models. Review of Economic Studies 33, 269–302.
Vaughan, R.N. 1979. Class behaviour and the distribution of wealth. Review of Economic Studies 46, 447–65.

distribution theories: Marxian. It is hard to imagine a more important topic within Marxian economics than the distribution of income and the means of production among the principal classes in capitalist economies. For example: (1) The share of profits (or, inversely, the share of wages) constitutes one important component of the rate of profit. (2) The rate of profit operates as a fundamental determinant of the pace of investment and, therefore, of accumulation. (3) The rate of accumulation serves as a kind of life-force invigorating capitalist economies over time – regulating their growth and development, and the wealth of their participants. (4) Distribution, production and accumulation are thus fundamentally interconnected, forming the foundation of lives and livelihoods in capitalist societies.

In this respect, indeed, Marx himself regarded 'distribution relations' as part of the core of the capitalist economy. Criticizing those who ventured an 'initial, but still handicapped, criticism of bourgeois economy' by seeking to distinguish between the level of priority of production and distribution, Marx affirmed that both production relations and distribution relations are part of the 'material foundations and social forms' of any given historical epoch. Distribution relations and production relations are 'essentially coincident', he argued, since 'both share the same historically transitory character'. (Marx, 1894, pp. 883, 878).

And yet, despite these reasonably self-evident theoretical connections, the analysis of distribution has remained substantially underdeveloped in the historical evolution of Marxian economics. While such classic issues as crisis theory, the transformation problem and the usefulness of the labour theory of value have been intensively and vigorously reviewed, the determination of distribution patterns over time and cross-sectionally has been elided in synthetic treatments of Marxian analytics and largely ignored in more focused scholarly investigations.

More recent developments in Marxian economics, fortunately, have finally begun to overcome this traditional reticence. This essay provides a brief review of traditional attention – or, more accurately, *in*attention – to the problem of distribution and then surveys some promising recent cultivations of this historically fallow terrain.

TERMS OF ANALYSIS

Before beginning that review, however, it will be useful to clarify the defining boundaries of this topic.

It is probably most useful to begin with the role of distribution in the determination of profitability, that central fulcrum of economic behaviour. A familiar accounting identity reminds us that the rate of profit of the individual firm, r, can be expressed as the product of the share of profits in firm value-added, s_r, the ratio of output to utilized capital stock, y_u, and the ratio of utilized to owned capital stock, k^*, or

$$r \equiv s_r \cdot y_u \cdot k^*, \qquad (1)$$

where

$$r \equiv \Pi/K_0; \quad s_r \equiv \Pi/Y; \quad y_u \equiv Y/K_u; \quad k^* \equiv K_u/K_0; \qquad (2)$$

and Π is firm profits, K_0 is the value of the firm's owned capital stock, Y is firm value-added, and K_u is the portion of the owned capital stock which is currently utilized. In the aggregate, abstracting from variation among firms for such purposes, the same accounting identity applies.

In this accounting identity, distribution relations primarily affect the level of and changes in s_r, the share of profits in firm revenue. Factors affecting the rate of capital accumulation and the productivity of the means of production primarily affect y_u. Secular trends in the robustness of aggregate demand and its fluctuations over the business cycle have their most direct impact on k^*.

At this first level of approximation, then, analysis of distribution relations among the principal classes of a capitalist economy can begin with a focus on the determinants of s_r. Such analyses would immediately concern themselves with the wage share, s_w, as well, since $s_w \equiv (1 - s_r)$.

This is, of course, only a first level of approximation. At a second level of investigation, we must deal with three further refinements of focus.

1. Accounting equation (1) is formulated in revenue terms, not in value terms, so it does not yet encompass the Marxian concern with the value-theoretic determinations of economic relations. But this additional consideration requires simply that we add an analysis of the *rate of exploitation* (or the rate of surplus value), ϵ, to the definition of our task, since conventional Marxian value analytics establish a straightforward transformation between the profit share and the rate of exploitation. In one simple formulation, for example, the rate of exploitation is equal to the ratio of profits (Π) to wages (W) weighted by the capital–labour ratio (k_L), or $\epsilon \equiv k_L \cdot (\Pi/W)$. (See Marglin, 1984, pp. 57–60 and 191–2, for a useful elaboration of these relations of equivalence.)

2. The first level of approximation, represented by equations (1) and (2), also allows for the existence of only two classes in capitalist economies, abstracting from all other relevant economic groupings or subsidiary classes. At a second level of approximation, therefore, we must also consider the existence of and determination of the shares of any other categories of economic agents, beyond our starting groups of capitalists and workers, which may seem relevant or necessary for our analyses.

3. A share of revenue need not necessarily translate into an exactly equivalent share of real income, since the prices confronting workers and capitalists may not exactly parallel each other over time. The relative purchasing power of their revenues received, and therefore the distribution of income, may consequently vary as a result of changes in the relative prices of capital goods and wage goods as well. It is conceivably useful, therefore, to decompose the profit share in equation (1) into two terms, one involving a ratio of 'real' profits to real income and the other a ratio of capital-goods prices to an index of (weighted) output prices. (See Weisskopf, 1979, for useful elaboration of this kind of decomposition.)

A final consideration seems critical for defining the scope of our analysis. It is taken for granted within the Marxian tradition that a given class's share of revenues is conditioned, at the most basic level, by the extent of its power over the means of production. And yet, over time, a given class's relative control of the means of production will be responsive to systematic changes in its share of revenues. It is not at all inappropriate, therefore, to treat the class distribution of revenues and the class distribution of control over the means of production as interdependent and mutually-determining over the long term. We may therefore define our task most broadly, in this respect, as *the analysis of the determination of class (and group) shares of revenue (and therefore of income) and of the class distribution of relative control over the means of production*.

Marx was himself clear on the importance of defining the analysis of distribution in both of these two senses. 'It may be said ...,' he wrote at the end of Volume III of *Capital* (1894, p. 879), 'that capital itself ... already presupposes a distribution: the expropriation of the labourer from the conditions of labour [and] the concentration of these conditions in the hands of a minority of individuals ... .' This underlying dimension of distribution 'differs altogether', he continued, 'from what is understood by distribution relations ... [as] the various titles to that portion of the product which goes into individual consumption'. This does not in any way suggest, he insisted, that distribution in this former sense does not involve 'distribution relations' or should somehow remain peripheral to our analysis:

> The aforementioned distribution relations, on the contrary, are the basis of special social functions performed within the production relations by certain of their agents ... . They imbue the conditions of production themselves and their representatives with a specific social quality. They determine the entire character and the entire movement of production.

TRADITIONAL ANALYSIS

Inherited approaches to the problem of distribution are most easily viewed through three somewhat separable lenses: the growth-theoretic perspective, crisis-theoretic hypotheses of a rising profit share, and antipodal crisis theories based on a falling profit share.

Long-term trajectories. Marxian economics has not always found it congenial to reflect upon the long-term growth paths of capitalist economies, since such perspectives are tainted in some minds by associations with concepts like 'stability' and 'equilibrium'. It is nonetheless possible to extract from traditional Marxian analyses a clear approach to the logic of determination of 'steady-state' tendencies – provided this exercise is understood, in Marglin's words (1984, p. 52), 'as a subset of Marxian theory and not as an attempt to represent the whole'.

It seems reasonably clear, in that context, that distribution relations are exogenously given to the traditional model, determined *outside* the set of basic interactions which jointly establish 'equilibrium' rates of growth and rates of profit. Historical conditions, not directly subject to internal economic analysis, establish a 'customary' wage. Existing levels of productiveness, also exogenous to the system, determine the level of output per hour and therefore, given the wage, the profit share as a residual. The behavioural hypothesis that capitalists save all profits combines with the determination of consumption by customary wage levels to create the conditions for a feasible and warranted steady-state combination of profit rates and growth rates. Marglin concludes (1984, p. 62): 'In contrast with the inherited neoclassical approach, in which resource allocation determines income distribution, causality here runs from [exogenously-determined] distribution to growth.'

There is, of course, nothing intrinsically wrong with these assumptions about directions of causality. Treating distribution as exogenous to the internal operations of the capitalist economy has simply meant that Marxian economists have tended to elide the factors determining distribution, setting them aside as consequences of 'historical and moral elements' and the 'technical' conditions of production.

Hypotheses of a rising profit share. Distribution has played a somewhat more explicit role in analyses of tendencies toward economic crisis. One group of theories has built upon hypotheses of a secular tendency toward an increasing profit share.

Perhaps the first systematic example of this hypothesis emerges in Lenin's account of imperialism and monopoly capitalism (1917). In its essence, Lenin's argument begins with the relatively simple hypothesis of increasing oligopoly and therefore, 'since monopoly prices are established' (p. 241), of relatively reduced competitive pressures. With the help of financial oligarchies, corporations are able to achieve a continuously rising profit share and therefore to amass 'an enormous "surplus of capital"' (p 212). With this surplus of capital, capitalists are prompted to export capital overseas and, eventually, to reduce efforts at technical improvements. Over time, 'the *tendency* to stagnation and decay, which is characteristic of monopoly, continues to operate ...' (p. 241; emphasis in the original).

The model begins, therefore, with a strong hypothesis about distribution – presuming a strong initial tendency under monopoly capitalism towards a rising profit share. And yet, the conditions which would be necessary to derive this as a prevailing long-term tendency are unexplored. There is no real analysis of wages, although prevailing assumptions about competitive labour markets are implicitly incorporated into the model. There is equal taciturnity about the initial

determination of real productivity, even though the rate of growth of real productivity must exceed the growth of real wages for the initial condition of a rising profit share and an ultimate 'surplus of capital' to hold. And, despite the international orientation of the analysis, there is no real incorporation of a model of international pricing and exchange which would support the hypothesis of rising profit shares in all the advanced countries.

These elisions are subsequently reproduced in most 20th-century analyses of underconsumption and monopoly capital. The models begin with a premise of growing capitalist power, most frequently from increasing monopoly control over product markets. This power leads to a rising 'surplus' and therefore to a rising profit share. From that set of initial premises, the problems of effective demand and urgent efforts to absorb the surplus follow naturally (Bleaney, 1976; Baran and Sweezy, 1966). As with Lenin, however, there is remarkably little attention to the conditions which permit this initial increase in the profit share. What about wages? Or labour productivity? Or conditions of international pricing? There is, in general, the simple presumption that conditions have evolved in a such a way as to permit consistent increases in the profit share, but little reflection on the relations which make those conditions possible. Baran and Sweezy admit some of this inattention, particularly to the social relations which would allow real productivity growth to outstrip real wage growth (1966, pp. 8–9):

> We do not claim that directing attention to the generation and absorption of surplus gives a complete picture of this or any other society. And we are particularly conscious of the fact that this approach, as we have used it, has resulted in almost total neglect of a subject which occupies a central place in Marx's study of capitalism: the labour process.

Hypotheses of a falling profit share. For completeness, it is useful to consider the alternative hypothesis of a falling profit share, although attention to this possibility has only emerged within Marxian analysis more recently, primarily in the post-World War II era.

This hypothesis has relatively simple analytic foundations. For whatever reasons, working-class power may increase sufficiently to allow wages to rise more rapidly than labour productivity and therefore to result in a persistent increase in the wage share of revenues.

The hypothesis follows most naturally in a cyclical context and bears close connections to Marx's own analysis of cyclical dynamics in Chapter XXV of Vol. I of *Capital* (1867). In the short run, rapid expansion may lead to tight labour markets, increasing workers' bargaining power and resulting in a rising wage share. (Boddy and Crotty (1975) provide a useful development of this cyclical model in relatively traditional terms.)

The hypothesis needs further grounding in order to serve as the basis for a theory of economic crisis, however. The forces which lead to tight labour markets in short-term expansions could plausibly result in comparably slack labour markets during short-term contractions and therefore to a recovery of the profit share. In order properly to ground a theory of secular crisis upon this hypothesis of a falling profit share – and therefore fully to develop a 'profit squeeze' theory of economic crisis – one must show why cyclical contractions do not restore the profit share and, other things equal, the rate of profit. This requires analyses of conditions which permit rising worker power – even in the age of oligopolistic competition – from one business cycle to the next. Until the mid-1970s, Glyn and Sutcliffe (1972) were the principal Marxian economists to have formally developed such an analysis, and in their case primarily for the sole case of England.

Even in their case, however, the analytic requirements for the secular version of the 'profit squeeze' theory of crisis are not fully developed. What are the explicit conditions of labour market competition which explain particular patterns of wage growth? Under what conditions in the organization of production and the promotion of technical change would real productivity growth fail to keep pace with real wage growth? What are the conditions of international economic linkages which would or would not support tendencies towards a falling profit share? A further problem involves the closeness of the relationship between profits and surplus value; Shaikh (1978) reviews some of the problems with casual assumptions about this connection.

Kalecki and Mandel as connecting writers. We can find in the work of Michal Kalecki and Ernest Mandel some early instances of the kinds of concerns which have fuelled more recent explorations.

Particularly in his later essays, Kalecki identifies but does not yet develop some of the lines of inquiry which would be necessary for a more advanced analysis of distribution. In 'Class Struggle and Distribution of National Income' (1971), Kalecki refines the analysis of the relationship between wages and the profit share, noting that analyses of the conditions of product market competition are necessary 'to arrive at any reasonable conclusion on the impact of bargaining for wages on the distribution of income' (p. 159); that trade union power is likely, *ceteris paribus*, to reduce the level of the mark-up; and that, in general,

> class struggle as reflected in trade-union bargaining may affect the distribution of national income but in a much more sophisticated fashion than expressed by the crude doctrine: when wages are raised, profits fall *pro tanto* (p. 163).

In 'Trend and Business Cycle' (1968), Kalecki develops what he regards as a more satisfactory analysis of the relationship between short- and longer-term determinants of investment and therefore, *a fortiori*, the conditions which are likely to affect movements in the profit share over time.

Both of these analyses are entirely preliminary, however, since they constitute more of a programme for further work than a report on completed analyses. In particular, Kalecki notes that most of his analysis hangs on a handful of coefficients which he takes as given for his purposes, including the level of labour productivity, the share of gross profits flowing into capitalist consumption, capitalists' propensities to invest, and the rate of embodied technical progress. 'To my mind', he concluded, 'future inquiry ... should be directed ... towards treating ... the coefficients used in our equations ... as slowly changing variables rooted in past development of the system' (p. 183). The real problem, in short, is not to assume the central parameters of the determination of profits and investment but rather to derive them from determinant structural and historical analysis.

Mandel serves as a transitional figure in a different way. Although much of Mandel's analysis is hard to pin down precisely, he has nonetheless helped highlight the importance of an integration between formal Marxian analytics and structural/historical analysis. In *Late Capitalism* (1972), in particular, he suggests the rich possibilities for analysis of the particular conditions which might or might not give rise to variations in the rate of surplus value. There is much to learn, he urged (p. 183):

Late capitalism is a great school for the proletariat, teaching it to concern itself not only with the immediate apportionment of newly created value between wages and profits, but with all questions of economic policy and development, and particularly with all questions revolving on the organization of labour, the process of production and the exercise of political power.

RECENT EXPLORATIONS

As this review is being written, a rich range of Marxian work on distribution in advanced capitalist societies has recently been completed or is currently under way. Since much of it is still in progress and unpublished, full references are difficult and probably inappropriate for an enduring encyclopedia. This final section will therefore concentrate on a synthetic review of the kinds of explorations which have recently been undertaken and the promising possibilities which have begun to emerge.

Changing power relations. One central problem in traditional Marxian analysis, which the examples of Kalecki and Mandel as connecting figures help to highlight, was the reluctance to forge determinate linkages between formal analytic categories, on one side, and the structure of and changes in power relations, on the other. Many appear to have felt either that these two loci of investigation operated at different levels of logical abstraction or that power relations, with all the social complexity of phenomena like the class struggle, could not be rendered analytically or studied empirically in any kind of formal or rigorous fashion. One is left with analyses, to quote Harris (1978, p. 166), which remain 'essentially ad hoc and tentative'.

Recent work has begun to overcome these hesitations. It has pursued careful and analytically determinate investigations of the relationship between power relations and, among other variables, the profit share. Attention has been focused primarily on three different dimensions of power relations: capital–labour relations, global linkages, and contests over state policy and practice.

Capital–labour relations. It has been recognized since Marx that class struggle over wages could conceivably affect distribution. But the formal linkage of conditions of class struggle to the determination of wage and profit shares has been hampered by the impression that levels and rates of change of productivity are determined orthogonally – by technical conditions and the pace of investment – and therefore that the two kinds of concerns could not somehow be combined into a single, inclusive, determinate analysis of changes in the profit share itself.

This problem appears to have been overcome. In recent work, particularly by Weisskopf, Bowles and Gordon (1983), a 'social model of productivity growth' has formally linked factors affecting capital–labour relations with the more traditional analyses. Several hypotheses about factors affecting the level of labour intensity in production have been both elaborated mathematically and tested empirically. This 'social model' appears to provide a robust explanation of variations in rates of productivity in the United States in the decades following World War II.

One crucial insight in that work is also beginning to invigorate Marxian wage analysis. Traditional perspectives on wage determination, building upon the 'reserve army' effect, focused on the relationship between wage bargaining and the threat of unemployment. As capitalist societies have developed, however, the threat of unemployment has been tempered by the availability of various components of what is typically called the 'social wage' – such as unemployment insurance and income maintenance expenditures. This has prompted the development of a more inclusive measure of the threat to workers of job dismissal: an index of 'the cost of job loss'. It calculates the expected income loss resulting from job termination, usually calculated as a percentage of the expected annual income if still employed, and incorporates estimates of the average wage in employment, expected unemployment duration, available income-replacing benefits, and available non-income-replacing benefits (which workers receive whether employed or not). (For provisional definition and measurement, see Weisskopf, Bowles and Gordon, 1983.) Building upon these insights, it is likely that we will soon see much more fully developed and sophisticated analyses both of the determinants of wage growth and of the relationship between wage growth and labour demand.

Taken together, these new hypotheses about wage change and productivity growth themselves combine to provide the possibility of much more advanced hypotheses about determinants of changes in the profit share. Given that it is formally true that the rate of change of the real profit share is equal to the rate of change of real productivity minus the rate of change of real wages, analytic determinations of changes in the class distribution of revenues can now properly reflect both 'social' and 'technical' determinations.

Global power. As noted above, another elision in traditional Marxian analyses of distribution has involved international connections. Traditional analyses have either assumed perfect competition, an awkward first approximation, or have tended, following models of monopoly capitalism, to assume a constant or rising price mark-up. But in an open economy, neither assumption seems useful, even as a first approximation, because of the likelihood of secular changes in a given economy's relations with other suppliers and buyers in global markets. And these changes are quite likely to affect the distribution of revenues, since they are bound to affect either relative input prices or the mark-up and through either path potentially to influence the real profit share.

Analyses of international linkages have lagged behind studies of capital–labour relations, but some promising initial explorations are under way. Two principal avenues of approach seem to be emerging. One seeks explicitly to model the effects of changes in the level and variability of the terms of trade on domestic productivity and profitability. The other aims at understanding and eventually modelling the effects of changing conditions of international power and, in particular, the effects of the internationalization of capital and growing multinational corporate leverage over domestic labour. (Bluestone and Harrison (1982) provide a useful early account of some of these latter effects for the US.) This kind of work is still in its early stages but seems increasingly essential in a more and more interdependent economy.

State policy and practice. The state can obviously have important effects on the private distribution of income among classes, both through tax policies and through the effects of expenditures on the costs of production and the relative bargaining power of the respective classes. Work on these connections has not yet moved beyond its early stages. Gough (1979) reviews the paths of likely effect on both the tax and expenditure side. Bowles and Gintis (1982) provide one provisional study of the effects of state policies on the profit share in the United States. And some of the studies of capital–labour relations discussed above are beginning to shed

important light on the effects of 'social wage' expenditures on private-sector wage and productivity determination.

Combined effects. These three dimensions of power relations need not be quarantined in separate cells of analytic isolation. It is possible to derive an inclusive model of their combined effects which retains a focus on the power relationships incumbent in each. Bowles, Gordon, and Weisskopf (1986) provide one such model of the determination of the profit rate; it includes factors affecting labour intensity, relative international power, and relationships with the state. Applied econometrically, the model appears to provide the most robust account available of variations in the rate of profit in the US in the postwar era. Although the study focuses on the rate of profit as a dependent variable, its approach could also permit more focused analysis of the profit share as a potentially separable component of profitability.

Comparative analysis. It seems equally important, finally, to advance our understanding of the factors which explain cross-sectional variations in the levels and time patterns of the class distribution of revenues and income. This task must inevitably come rather late in the game, since it largely presupposes the availability of existing models of distribution which work for at least one country or groups of countries on their own terms. At the time of writing, some promising initial studies of cross-national variations in the determination of profit rates and shares are just under way. The best existing review of the political economic history upon which such studies must build is the excellent comparative analysis provided by Armstrong, Glyn and Harrison (1984).

One, two … many classes? One final analytic task remains. Almost all recent studies of distribution have accepted the traditional preoccupation with a two-class model of capitalist economies – focusing almost exclusively on the single pair of opposing magnitudes, the profit share and the wage share. It is important at least to consider the possibility that a more variegated categorization of individuals would be fruitful, even for traditional Marxian problematics. What about managers? The petty bourgeoisie? Financiers? Different strata of the working class?

Empirical analyses aimed in this direction have lagged in large part because of continuing uncertainty and conflict over the appropriate definition of group boundaries and their inter-relationships. Two main approaches appear to have emerged as the principal lines of inquiry within the Marxian perspective.

One approach seeks to derive a more complex mapping of primary and 'intermediate' or 'subsumed' classes from the method and essential categories of traditional Marxian analysis. Sharp debates nearly overwhelmed these efforts in the mid- to late-1970s, but it is conceivable that a relatively widespread agreement on the terms of analysis may be emerging in the mid- to late-1980s. Almost all of these analyses presuppose the usefulness of a single category of 'productive workers' and seek to distinguish, as carefully as possible, among various groups of intermediate agents and non-productive workers whose incomes largely draw upon realized surplus value. Wright (1978) offers one useful early review of the possibilities and problems in this approach, while Resnick and Wolff (1985) present an interesting recent treatment.

A second approach, usually encompassed under the general heading of 'segmentation theory', has paid primary attention to the importance of various divisions within the working class. Different analyses of labour segmentation have emerged in studies of various countries, and it is not at all clear that a single uniform model of labour segmentation in advanced capitalist formations can or should emerge. These studies nonetheless suggest the promise and importance of studying (a) the effects of different structures of production and labour on the opportunities and realized incomes of individual members of the working class; and (b) the potential impact of systematically structured divisions within the working class on the wage share of the class as a whole. Gordon, Edwards and Reich (1982) provide one important analysis of segmentation for the United States; Wilkinson (1981) offers one useful early compilation of comparative studies; while Bowles and Gintis (1977) provide a formal analytic integration of segmentation analysis within the value-theoretic context of more traditional Marxian theory.

These two approaches are potentially complementary, not conflicting, since the former concentrates largely on the group distribution of realized surplus value while the latter primarily explores the group distribution of variable capital. They have not yet been properly vetted, compared, and integrated, however, so we still await a complete and satisfactory theoretical and empirical account of the distribution of revenues among all the relevant categories of individuals in capitalist economies.

DAVID M. GORDON

See also MARXIAN VALUE ANALYSIS; SURPLUS APPROACH TO VALUE AND DISTRIBUTION; SURPLUS VALUE.

BIBLIOGRAPHY

Armstrong, P., Glyn, A. and Harrison, J. 1984. *Capitalism since World War II*. London: Fontana.
Baran, P.A. and Sweezy, P.M. 1966. *Monopoly Capitalism*. New York: Monthly Review Press.
Bleaney, M. 1976. *Underconsumption Theories*. New York: International Publishers.
Bluestone, B. and Harrison, B. 1982. *The Deindustrialization of America*. New York: Basic Books.
Boddy, R. and Crotty, J. 1975. Class conflict and macro policy: the political business cycle. *Review of Radical Political Economics*, Spring.
Bowles, S. and Gintis, H. 1977. The Marxian theory of value and heterogeneous labour: a critique and reformulation. *Cambridge Journal of Economics*, 1(2), June 173—92.
Bowles, S. and Gintis, H. 1982. The crisis of liberal democratic capitalism: the case of the U.S. *Politics and Society*, Winter.
Bowles, S., Gordon, D.M. and Weisskopf, T.E. 1986. Power and profits: The social structure of accumulation and the profitability of the postwar U.S. economy. *Review of Radical Political Economics*, Spring-Summer.
Glyn, A. and Sutcliffe, B. 1972. *British Capitalism, Workers and the Profits Squeeze*. Harmondsworth: Penguin.
Gordon, D.M., Edwards, R. and Reich, M. 1982. *Segmented Work, Divided Workers*. New York: Cambridge University Press.
Gough, I. 1979. *The Political Economy of the Welfare State*. London: Macmillan.
Harris, D.J. 1978. *Capital Accumulation and Income Distribution*. Stanford: Stanford University Press.
Kalecki, M. 1968. Trend and business cycle. In M. Kalecki, *Selected Essays on the Dynamics of the Capitalist Economy, 1933–1970*, Cambridge: Cambridge University Press, 1971.
Kalecki, M. 1971. Class struggle and distribution of national income. In M. Kalecki, *Selected Essays*, op. cit.
Lenin, V.I. 1917. Imperialism, the highest stage of capitalism. In *Selected Works*, one-volume edition, New York: International Publishers, 1971.
Mandel, E. 1972. *Late Capitalism*. English edition, trans. Joris De Bres, London: New Left Books, 1975.
Marglin, S. 1984. *Growth, Distribution, and Prices*. Cambridge, Mass.: Harvard University Press.
Marx, K. 1867. *Capital*, Vol. I. New York: International Publishers, 1967.
Marx, K. 1894. *Capital*, Vol. III. New York: International Publishers, 1967.
Resnick, S.A. and Wolff, R.D. 1985. A Marxian reconceptualization of income and its distribution. In *Rethinking Marxism*, ed. S.A. Resnick and R.D. Wolff, Brooklyn, NY: Autonomedia.
Shaikh, A. 1978. An introduction to the history of crisis theories. In *U.S. Capitalism in Crisis*, New York: Union for Radical Political Economics.
Weisskopf, T.E. 1979. Marxian crisis theory and the rate of profit in the postwar U.S. economy. *Cambridge Journal of Economics* 3(4), December, 341–78.
Weisskopf, T.E., Bowles, S. and Gordon, D.M. 1983. Hearts and minds: a social model of U.S. productivity growth. *Brookings Papers on Economic Activity*, No. 2.
Wilkinson, F. (ed.) 1981. *The Dynamics of Labour Market Segmentation*. London: Academic Press.
Wright, E.O. 1978. *Class, Crisis, and the State*. London: New Left Books.

distribution theories: neoclassical. Whenever a theory becomes involved in controversy the question of what constitutes that theory itself becomes a contentious issue, and the neoclassical theory of distribution is no exception to that general rule. Some have seen marginal productivity as an essential feature of neoclassical theory. Others have regarded the aggregation of capital or an aggregate production function (even a function of the Cobb–Douglas form) as essential. Neoclassical distribution theory is viewed as general equilibrium theory by many but Friedman has defended the 'Marshallian' or partial equilibrium approach.

The truth is that any body of ideas widely maintained for a long time inevitably develops and transforms itself, absorbs some ideas, discards others, and fathers traditions and sub-traditions. As the neoclassical theory of distribution has been the predominant view in the leading countries for the development of economics for over 100 years, it is not surprising that it conformed to this pattern and expressed itself in diverse even contradictory voices. Many, whether or not they like neoclassical theory, hold that one voice represents the true message, but neoclassical theory, like christian doctrine, may stand on certain fundamentals but is not and could not be monolithic.

It is important to distinguish between 'neoclassical theory' on the one hand and the history of the development of that theory on the other. Both are valid subjects for study but a scientific assessment of the theory should address itself to the best modern statements. This principle has not always been respected, particularly in the heat of controversy, and some maintain that the theory went wrong from the start, and that if one could only go back to where the vital mistakes were made everything would become clearer. (For an extensive development and discussion of this line of argument, see Baranzini and Scazzieri, 1986.) However, the development of economic theory is not like a complicated calculation in which every step is supported by every earlier step. As with any other discipline, the logical standing of a theory and the history of the development of that theory are distinct entities.

By way of illustration of the last point, consider the way in which the theory developed in its early stages. The 'neoclassical' movement, whose leading members may be taken to include Böhm-Bawerk, Edgeworth, Gossen, Jevons, Marshall, Menger, Walras, Wieser and Wicksell, did not begin with a theory of distribution but quite neglected that side of the economic problem. By focusing on marginal utility and the demand for given resources in a barter economy, the neoclassical economists were able to develop a powerful and flexible method, the marginal principle, so impressive that it has often been taken to define their approach. The so-called 'psychic' notion of marginal utility represented the refinement, no more, of the old idea of 'value in use'. However with its help the neoclassicals eventually succeeded in clarifying, as Smith, Ricardo and Mill had all failed to clarify, how value in use, value in exchange and cost of production could coexist. Only the Austrians with their concept of 'imputation' hung on to the idea that utilities were in some sense primary and other values derived.

Put in unashamedly modern terms, the central neoclassical idea is that the pricing of goods and the pricing of factors of production are governed by common principles, mainly the forces of supply and demand generated by agents who maximize their objectives. From the perspective of the history of the development of the theory the definition is anachronistic. Economics did not develop and refine the notion of a factor of production or the concept of maximizing an objective and later arrive at the neoclassical theory of distribution. Rather the two processes took place in tandem. Despite the lip service to classical ideas paid by some members of the neoclassical school, notably Marshall, neoclassical is a misnomer. The neoclassicals were not revivalists of classical economic ideas, an Oxford Movement of classical political economy. They were revolutionaries.

THE DISTRIBUTION OF INCOME. The theories with which we are concerned are designed to explain the levels of payment to the various factors of production – rents, wage rates, and rates of profit – and by extension the shares of the various factors in the total product. That is to say that they are concerned with the *functional* distribution of income.

We shall not discuss the distribution of personal or household incomes, sometimes called the *size distribution*. The size distribution of household incomes takes the form of a function relating the level of income and the number of units receiving that income. It is true that given the distribution of the ownership of factors among units, strictly the quantities supplied to the various markets, and given also the rates at which those factors are remunerated, the size distribution may be derived. However, except in the short run, the interrelationship between the functional and size distributions is more complicated. This is mainly so because the quantities of factors which may be accumulated by individual units, land and capital, and even the quantity of labour, respond to rates of return to the various factors. Pasinetti (1962) presents a model which unusually takes this inter-relationship into account. For a discussion of the Pasinetti model and some of the criticisms which it has attracted, see Marglin (1984, pp. 324–8). On the distribution of personal income and wealth, see Atkinson (1975).

FACTORS OF PRODUCTION. It is not surprising that the concept of a factor of production plays a leading role in neoclassical theory because it lends itself to the view that the inputs used in production stand to each other in a relation of symmetry, governed by common principles. This is not to say that no differences between the conditions applying to factors are admitted. The symmetry is most marked in the treatment of the demand for factors, while on the supply side important differences are recognized.

The membership of the trinity of land, labour and capital, which have always been taken to be factors of production, goes back to the classical writers, and an additional factor called 'entrepreneurship' is widely recognized by neoclassical and classical writers alike. The development of the theory

along formal lines has tended until recently to suppress the role of the entrepreneur and to make the firm into a rather lifeless object. However lately the increasing employment of economic theory in industrial economics has given rise to some richer treatments of the firm.

The employment of the concept of a factor of production has been criticized. It has been argued that labour in particular does not submit itself to the laws of supply and demand like any other input. The introduction of distinctive features of the various factors and their markets tends to undermine the simple symmetry of pure theory. Some have detected apologetics in the designation of capital as a factor of production. On this see the discussion of ideology below.

MARGINAL PRODUCTIVITY AND THE DETERMINATION OF FACTOR PRICES. Do marginal productivities determine factor rewards? This apparently straightforward question conceals conceptual complications and, depending on the context to which the question is applied, either 'no' or 'yes' may be defended as reasonable answers. Robertson (1931) argued that the wage rate 'measures' the marginal productivity of labour. The reference is to the demand curve for labour, which is the schedule of the marginal productivities of various quantities of labour. Robertson was reminding his readers that the wage rate in a competitive market is determined by the intersection of the demand curve and the supply curve – both blades of the scissors cut the paper. If marginal productivities are values determined by the equilibrium solution as much as are wages and prices, talk of one determining the other is misplaced. The same point applies when the marginal product of capital and the return to capital are under consideration.

In certain contexts however it is reasonable to see marginal productivity as the determinant and the payment to the factor as determined. Consider the claim that managers of large enterprises are paid very large salaries because the marginal value productivity of a good manager amounts to a great deal of money. Supposing this argument correct, the high marginal productivity is a general feature which does not depend upon solving out the whole equilibrium. Contrast this with the case of a micro unit, say a farm, facing a given wage rate for labour and able to vary the quantity of labour employed. For that exercise the wage rate is given and the marginal product is determined by it.

A SIMPLE NEOCLASSICAL MODEL. In this section we examine a static model. Growth and capital will be considered below. The idea is to construct a model in which factor prices will drive everything else, including goods prices through cost functions. This requires special assumptions but makes for a model which can be easily presented and which suffices to illustrate some points about the neoclassical model of distribution. For a much more thorough review of neoclassical models, see Ferguson (1969).

We assume factors and goods to be distinct and that factors are not directly consumed. Let there be F factors available in given quantities, and G goods producible from those factors, F and G need not be equal and there may be more goods than factors, or less or the same number. The production function for the ith good is:

$$v^i = f^i(x^i) \qquad (i = 1, \ldots, G); \qquad (1)$$

where v^i is the output of the ith good and x^i is a vector of factor inputs to the production of the ith good. $f^i(\ )$ is a concave constant returns production function. The cost function shows the unit cost of producing good i given factor prices. Factor prices are a vector w and the unit cost of the ith good is $C^i(w)$, where $C^i(w)$ is the solution to the programme:

$$\min_{x^i} w \cdot x^i; \tag{2}$$

subject to:

$$f^i(w^i) \geqslant 1. \tag{3}$$

We denote the prices of goods by vector $c(w)$, where the ith element of $c(w)$ is $C^i(w)$. There are H households. Let the hth household own factors x^h, in which case its income will be $w \cdot x^h$. All the household's income is assumed spent on goods and the vector of goods demanded by household h is denoted z^h and is given by the hth household's demand function:

$$z^h = z^h[c(w), w \cdot x^h] \qquad (h = 1, \dots, H). \tag{4}$$

Now note that factor prices w imply demands for factors as may be seen by the following line of reasoning. Given w, we have household incomes $w \cdot x^h$ and goods prices $c(w)$. Hence we have total demands for goods:

$$\sum_h z^h[c(w), w \cdot x^h] = z. \tag{5}$$

The amount of factor j used in the production of good i is the partial derivative of $C^i(w)$ with respect to w^j, denoted c^i_j. The matrix of these coefficients, denoted C, depends on w only. Hence demand for factors is $C \cdot z$, supply is Σx^h, and we have shown that excess demands for factors are a function of factor prices.

To prove the existence of factor prices such that factor demands and supplies are equal (strictly such that there is excess demand for no factor), one has to establish the continuity of the relationship between factor prices and excess demands for factors, and then employ a fixed point theorem (see Arrow and Hahn, 1971, ch. 5).

We note some salient features of this model. First, prices of factors are determined by the supply and demand for those factors although demands for factors are derived demands depending on their employment to produce goods. Secondly, both the technology of production and tastes influence the solution for factor prices. Thirdly, factor prices measure the marginal products of factors, a property which is ensured by the process of cost minimization. However there is clearly no sense in which marginal products are prior to prices.

MORE AND LESS GENERAL MODELS. The model of the previous section is designed to illustrate the manner in which the determination of the distribution of income may be viewed as the outcome of a general equilibrium of supplies and demands for factors of production. The model is less general than the standard general equilibrium model. It exhibits, for example, constant returns to scale production functions, no joint production and no direct consumption of factor services. Also, goods are not used as inputs to the production of goods. The introduction of those features would undermine the model's neatness without introducing fundamentally new principles.

More striking results are produced when the model is made still more specialised. The factor input coefficients may be treated as constants independent of w. In this fixed coefficient case the marginal product of a factor in producing a good is undefined. In an extreme case there is only one factor, usually labour, with the result that relative goods prices are independent of demand. (For a discussion of this non-substitution result and its extension to an economy which uses fixed capital, see Bliss, 1975, ch. 11.) Models of this kind typically introduce the use of goods as intermediate inputs to the production of goods. However so long as there is no genuine joint production (the term genuine joint production is used to distinguish the production of final demands jointly from the notional joint production that arises when fixed capital goods are treated as one of the products of the productive process.), the inputs used to produce final output may all be reduced to the quantities of the factor incorporated in them.

The model of Sraffa (1960), sometimes known as the neo-Ricardian model, will be seen to be a version of the model, but including an elegant extension to fixed capital goods. Hahn (1982) has argued against the claim that the neo-Ricardian approach leads to new insights by pointing out that the model is a special case of the general equilibrium model.

THE PROBLEM WITH CAPITAL. The introduction of capital into the theory of distribution raises two issues which should be distinguished, even though they are not entirely unrelated. One is the aggregation of capital, the other is the nature of the supply of capital in the long run.

Although many expositions of the theory have been expressed in terms of an aggregate called capital, and there have even been attempts to formally underwrite this approach, it is now generally recognized that there is no rigorous method of aggregating a heterogeneous collection of capital goods. (The most famous attack on the use of aggregate capital is Robinson, 1953–4); see also Champernowne, 1953–4; Harcourt, 1972 and Marglin, 1984, ch. 12.) In this respect capital stands on a par with other types of input, labour for example. Highly aggregated models should therefore be seen as simple devices for illustrating how a type of model functions and not as descriptions of the world. Unfortunately, some writers who emphasize the problems of aggregating capital are quite cavalier when it comes to discussing the aggregation of labour or output. Formally however there is little difference between the cases.

With many distinct capital goods, demands for inputs are demands for the services of particular capital goods. However the supply of capital in the long run is the supply of saving, which may translate itself as required into particular capital services. Hence a long-run neoclassical theory of distribution depends on a model of long-run saving, a point which deserves emphasis.

We show how the solution for the quantities of capital goods and equilibrium prices may be obtained in a simple constant returns growth model. Let there be N goods, and let the quantities of them which make up the capital stock used by one unit of labour be represented by the elements of a vector x. Let consumption be proportional to a vector c_o, and γ the rate of growth of the labour force. Let y be the total stock of goods available next period for consumption and as inputs to next period's production. The production function corresponding to a unit labour input is:

$$F(y, x) = 0. \tag{6}$$

In steady state growth with a per capita consumption of αc_o, y will be $\alpha c_o + (1 + \gamma)x$. Hence:

$$F[\alpha c_o + (1 + \gamma)x, x] = 0. \tag{7}$$

Given a particular per capita consumption αc_o, (7) may be satisfied by various values of x, but only one of these will be the efficient and equilibrium value. To see this let $V(x^1)$ be the maximum value of β such that βc_o is a sustainable per capita consumption starting with a capital stock x^1. If x^1 is the steady state composition of the capital stock for consumption βc_o then $x^2 = x^1$ must solve:

$$\max_{x^2} \alpha \tag{8}$$

subject to:

$$F[(1 + \lambda)x^2 + \alpha c_o, x^1] \geqslant 0; \qquad (9)$$

and

$$V(x^2) \geqslant \beta c_o. \qquad (10)$$

Let the Lagrange multipliers attaching to the constraints (9) and (10) be respectively μ and η, and let F_i $(i = y, x)$ denote the vector of partial derivatives of F with respect to the output and input vectors. The necessary conditions for a solution to (8)–(10) are:

$$1 + \mu c_o \cdot F_y = 0; \qquad (11)$$

and

$$\mu F_y(1 + \lambda) + \eta V_x = 0. \qquad (12)$$

Equation (12) states that the marginal rates of substitution between outputs of the various goods shall be equal to the marginal rates of substitution between those same goods as inputs to the long-term provision of future consumption; compare Dorfman et al. (1958, ch. 12). This condition reduces the degrees of freedom enjoyed by the steady state capital stock to one. That last degree of freedom depends on the level of steady state consumption the determination of which requires a saving condition.

THEORY AND IDEOLOGY. According to its Marxist critics, neo-classical distribution theory is irredeemably apologetic in character, and it is indeed the case that some economists in the past saw the theory, and in particular the concept of marginal productivity, as throwing a relatively favourable light on capitalism. When the justification for the earnings of capital owning rentiers was being questioned, the notion that capital earns no more than its 'contribution' to production was not unwelcome in the salons. The idea that the rich are rewarded according to the marginal productivity of their 'waiting' sounded better still.

It can need a positive effort to see that all this is strictly irrelevant to the scientific standing of neoclassical theory. No one supposes that Newton's mechanics should be dismissed because its author saw in it the justification of a hierarchical organization of social life. A play on the overtones of words such as 'earning' or 'waiting' to justify the distribution of income should be similarly disregarded. Of course the neoclassical theory of distribution can be used to analyse the effects of policy, including policies to redistribute income. In a perfect world the conclusions which emerged from such investigations would be independent of the political stance of the investigator. We do not live in a perfect world, but the fact that the scientific ideal is never fully attainable should not lead us to conclude that economics can know nothing but self-serving apologetics.

CHRISTOPHER BLISS

See also ADDING-UP PROBLEM; CLARK, JOHN BATES; MARGINAL PRODUCTIVITY THEORY; WICKSTEED, PHILIP HENRY.

BIBLIOGRAPHY

Arrow, K.J. and Hahn, F.H. 1971. *General Competitive Analysis.* Amsterdam: North-Holland.

Atkinson, A.B. 1975. *The Economics of Inequality.* Oxford: Clarendon Press.

Baranzini, M. and Scazzieri, R. 1986. *The Foundations of Economic Knowledge.* Oxford: Basil Blackwell.

Bliss, C.J. 1975. *Capital Theory and the Distribution of Income.* Amsterdam: North-Holland.

Champernowne, D.G. 1953–4. The production function and the theory of capital: a comment. *Review of Economic Studies* 21(2), 112–35.

Dorfman, R., Samuelson, P.A. and Solow, R.M. 1958. *Linear Programming and Economic Analysis.* New York: McGraw-Hill.

Ferguson, C.E. 1969. *The Neoclassical Theory of Production and Distribution.* Cambridge: Cambridge University Press.

Hahn, F.H. 1982. The neo-Ricardians. *Cambridge Journal of Economics* 6(4), December, 353–74.

Harcourt, G.C. 1972. *Some Cambridge Controversies in the Theory of Capital.* Cambridge: Cambridge University Press.

Marglin, S.A. 1984. *Growth Distribution and Prices.* Cambridge, Mass.: Harvard University Press.

Pasinetti, L.L. 1962. Rate of profit and income distribution in relation to the rate of economic growth. *Review of Economic Studies* 29, October, 267–79.

Robertson, D.H. 1931. Wage grumbles. In D.H. Robertson, *Economic Fragments,* London: P.S. King & Son.

Robinson, J.V. 1953–4. The production function and the theory of capital. *Review of Economic Studies* 21(2), 81–106.

Sraffa, P. 1960. *The Production of Commodities by Means of Commodities.* Cambridge: Cambridge University Press.

distributive justice. Social justice is justice in all of the relationships occurring in society: the treatment of criminals, children and the elderly, domestic animals, rival countries, and so forth. Distributive justice is a narrower concept for which another name is economic justice. It is justice in the economic relationships within society: collaboration in production, trade in consumer goods, and the provision of collective goods. There is typically room for mutual gain from such exchange, especially voluntary exchange, and distributive justice is justice in the arrangements affecting the distribution (and thus generally the total production) of those individual gains among the participants in view of their respective efforts, opportunity costs, and contributions.

In earlier times the discussion of distributive justice tended to focus upon the obligations of the individual toward those with whom he or she had exchanges. So an employer was expected to be just or not to be unjust, and the problem was to demarcate employer injustice. With the rise of governments capable of redistribution and the spread of economic liberalism, the focus shifted to the distributional obligations of the central government. Let enterprises and households pursue their self interests while the government attends to distribution (within the limits of its just powers). Distributive justice is largely about redistributive taxation and subsidies. The latter may take many forms such as public expenditures for schooling and vocational training (beyond the point justified only by the Pareto principle from the status quo ante) as well as cash subsidies for the employment of labour or low-wage labour (whether paid to employer or employee).

Note that the so-called negative income tax, whatever the claims for or against it as a tool of social justice, does not appear to be an instrument for distributive justice unless restricted somehow to those participating (more than some threshold amount?) in the economy (and thus in the generation of the gains to be (re)distributed). In any case, it will not be discussed here, although some propositions about subsidies apply also to the negative tax.

The suggestion that distributive justice might (at least in principle) require subsidies, not merely tax concessions or tax forgiveness for the working poor, tends to raise the eyebrows of some and accounts for the fact that distributive justice raises the hackles of a few. As long as the Iroquois and the Sioux have no contact, there are no gains to be distributed and distributive justice does not apply; if they are let free to engage in bilateral inter-tribal exchanges, however, the payment of a subsidy to pull up the wage of the lowest earners, who are

Sioux, say, would come partly or wholly at the expense of the Iroquois. Now some commentators object to the notion that the Sioux, whose exchanges with the Iroquois are entirely voluntary and all of whom have benefited (or could have), we may suppose, might deserve an additional payment from the Iroquois, perhaps through some supra-tribal authority. Ayn Rand (1973), for example, argues that it is one thing to require of a poor person a fare for riding a bus with empty seats that the other riders can finance out of the benefits they receive from the bus – she has no qualms about such a free ride – and another thing for the poor person to tax the other riders. But she has got the economics wrong in the application of her (actually rather Rawlsian) ethical premise. Up to a point, a subsidy to the poorest-earning group (the Sioux in the above example) would leave the others (the Iroquois) still with a net gain – a gain after the tax needed to pay the subsidy. This is because of diminishing returns: When the group of Sioux workers is added to the fixed pool of Iroquois' labour and land, the extra product added by the first arrivals – and, more generally, the average of the extra products added by the succession of Sioux workers – is larger than the extra product resulting from the last of these workers, which is the 'marginal product' of Sioux labour; the Iroquois could afford a subsidy equal to the excess of the average extra product over the marginal product. Correctly applied, then, the Randian objection is to a gain-erasing or, at any rate, a gain-reversing subsidy, not to *any* subsidy whatsoever.

Another objection to the concept of distributive justice and to the admissibility of subsidies argues that if these notions were sound it would make sense, by analogy, to apply them to marriage allocation, to the matching of husbands and wives; since we never hear of such applications the ideas are presumably unsound. Of course, it would strike us as novel and foreign to see a proposal for a tax on marriage with Iroquois men and a subsidy to marriage to Sioux men on the ground that the former were apparently more attractive to women (from either tribe) and the resulting inequality of benefits unjust and demanding correction. But the reasons might be other than the supposed unacceptability of the ideas of distributive justice. Maybe the impracticality of deciding on the taxes and subsidies stands in the way. Perhaps a marriage subsidy would be demeaning while employment subsidies would not, being graduated or even a flat amount per hour. Yet the key observation may be that, although there is economic exchange here and although racial discrimination or racial prejudices could cause real injustices, the Sioux and Iroquois men in this example are not cooperating for mutual gain and so no problem about the just division of such gains can arise; they are competing, or contesting, for partners, not forming partnerships with one another. Thus distributive justice cannot apply here.

The terms offered to the working poor, as already implied, is the locus classicus to which notions of distributive justice have been applied. However, two other arenas in which issues of justice are being fought out should be mentioned. One of these is the problem of inter-generational justice. It was first addressed in a celebrated paper in 1928 by Frank Ramsey, who adopted as the criterion of optimality the standard associated with utilitarianism – the sum of utilities over time. This conception of intergenerational justice encountered difficulties when in the 1960s it was applied to optimum saving of a society in which the population is to grow without bound, although that odd demographic case may have put utilitarianism to an unfair (and absurd) test. In 1970 John Rawls struggled with the problem of intergenerational justice in a famously problematic section of his, only to conclude that '...

the difference principle [i.e., Rawls's maximin or, more accurately, leximin principle] does not apply to the savings problem. There is no way for later generations to improve the situation of the least fortunate first generation.' This seems to say that inter-generational justice, if there is such a thing, is not a problem of distributive justice, since there is no cooperation for mutual gain among generations, not even between adjacent ones in the chain. But the premise that the current generation cannot be helped by succeeding generations appears, on the face of it, to be a slip in Rawls's economics. In a closed economy, we can help future generations by providing them with more capital – even in an open economy enjoying perfect capital mobility, we can provide them with social overhead capital that the world capital market would not provide (or not so cheaply) – and, if overlapping with us, they can help us by meeting consumption claims we make through our issue of public debt and pension entitlements. Thus distributive justice does apply here, with a precision fit. What Rawls may be interpreted to mean is that if, being the least fortunate owing to heaven-sent technological discoveries over the future, the present generation were permitted to invest nothing (not even gross of depreciation!) – rather as we can imagine the poorest in the static problem to begin by sullenly asking for equality – the future generations could not bribe the present one to do something in their mutual interest – unlike the static problem in which the rich can explain the benefits of trickle-down. But in fact the next generation *can* bribe the present one with some old-age consumption in return for some investment. It may be conjectured that a maximin-optimal growth path would still exist in a model along the lines of the Phelps–Riley model notwithstanding the introduction of technological progress.

The other arena in which we find a debate over distributive justice is the international trade field. When a giant nation trades with a small number of pygmy countries, not large enough even in the aggregate to influence relative prices in the giant state, the latter receive all the gains from trade and the former gets nothing and loses nothing; this is exactly the Rawlsian maximin solution if perchance the pygmy countries are poorer (in some suitably defined way) than the giant. But if these tiny countries 'spoil the market', worsening their terms of trade in the course of exporting to and importing from the giant, because they are not of negligible size at least in the aggregate, then the Rawlsian solution is not obtained by the free market. The recent North–South problem of which the 'Southern' countries complain can be understood as the tendency of the 'Northern' countries that are already the richest countries, such as the North American and European countries, to retain the gain from trade resulting from the aforementioned change in the terms of trade caused by the 'Southern' countries through their trade with the 'Northern' ones. The 'Southern' countries believe justice to require that the 'Northern' countries arrange to give back that gain through some appropriate international transfer mechanism.

There are able and serious philosophers who would be happy to see distributive justice left to the economists. In fact, the history of philosophy has been seen as a process of divesting itself of a sub-field as soon as it could thrive independently. Likewise, there are economists who would leave the subject to philosophers. But, whichever group receives the lion's share of the contract to work on it, it seems that the economics (as well as philosophy) of the problems being studied is an essential element of the subject. In this sense and for this reason, the necessary cross listing notwithstanding, distributive justice is an important field under economics.

EDMUND S. PHELPS

887

See also ENTITLEMENTS; EQUALITY; EQUITY; EXPLOITATION; JUSTICE.

BIBLIOGRAPHY

Phelps, E.S. and Riley, J.G. 1978. Rawlsian growth: dynamic programming of capital and wealth for intergeneration 'maximin' justice. *Review of Economic Studies* 45(1), February, 103–20.

Ramsey, F.P. 1928. A mathematical theory of saving. *Economic Journal* 38, December, 543–59.

Rand, A. 1973. Government financing in a free society. In *Economic Justice*, ed. E.S. Phelps, Harmondsworth: Penguin.

Rawls, J. 1970. *A Theory of Justice*. Oxford: Oxford University Press; Cambridge, Mass.: Harvard University Press.

diversification of activities. Diversification is the process by which the modern corporation extends its activities beyond the products and markets in which it currently operates. It is a major determinant of the structure of modern industrial economies and has important implications for competition and efficiency. Robinson (1958, p. 114) defines diversification as 'the lateral expansion of firms neither in the direction of their existing main products, as with horizontal integration, nor in the direction of supplies and outlets, as with vertical integration, but in the direction of other different, but often broadly similar, activities'. The extent of diversification can be measured in a number of ways, but is hampered by the difficulty of precisely defining the boundaries between different products, markets and industries. It is not a simple task to assess the degree to which a firm spreads its operations over different activities. The more narrowly defined are these activities the greater will be the apparent degree of diversification. These problems are not unique to the measurement of diversification and similar difficulties arise in the measurement of concentration in industry. Indeed the process of diversification itself has played a major part in blurring the distinction between industries and in creating these measurement problems. However, it is clear that diversification must involve the firm in producing new products which are sufficiently different from its existing products to involve the firm in new production or distribution activities. Diversification may therefore involve only a small change of direction, or a dramatic switch into an entirely new line of business. In the literature the former is referred to as related, or narrow spectrum diversification and the latter as unrelated, or broad spectrum diversification.

One possible measurement of the extent of diversification involves identifying the number of industries, or products in which the firm is involved. The other main approach is to measure the proportion of the firm's activity in its core business in comparison with the proportions in its diversified activities. This measure has been refined in a number of ways to take account of the number and importance of these diversified activities (e.g. Berry, 1975; Jacquemin and Berry, 1979; Utton 1979).

The process of diversification is not a new phenomenon, but the principal empirical studies (Gort, 1962; Rumelt 1974; Berry, 1975; Utton, 1979) have demonstrated a marked increase in the degree of diversification over the past few decades. The studies suggest that diversification tends to be narrow spectrum diversification into similar industries. However, both Gort and Rumelt were able to discern some shift towards broad spectrum diversification. The intensity of narrow spectrum diversification was found to be industry related, but the extent of broad spectrum diversification was independent of the primary industry from which diversification was occurring. Rumelt was also able to identify a growth in importance of acquisitive conglomerates and there can be little

doubt that their importance has grown further since his study. There was general agreement that firms tended to diversify into industries characterized by high research and development intensity and rapid technological change. The industries also tended to be faster growing, but showed no significant differences in terms of profits variability, or the degree of concentration, than industries less popular with diversifying firms. The industries from which higher levels of diversification occurred were not slower growing than other industries, but did tend to be characterized by a higher degree of seller dominance. Such industries might give less scope for firm growth by capturing market share. The more rapid diversifiers tended to be larger firms with higher proportions of scientific and technical employees and this is consistent with the importance of technological industries as diversification choices which was noted above. Finally firms with above average rates of diversification tended to have above average rates in subsequent periods. This may be related to the organizational changes associated with diversification which have been identified by Chandler (1963) and others (e.g. Williamson, 1970; Channon, 1973). This issue is explored further below.

The growth of firms and the role of diversification in this growth process were elucidated in the pioneering work of Penrose (1959). Penrose identified three explanations for diversification: first, as a response to specific opportunities; second, as a response to specific threats; and third, as a general strategy for growth. The opportunity to diversify arises naturally as a byproduct of the existing activities of the firm. A key area is the research and development activities of the firm. Such activities develop the firm's knowledge of its technology which is unlikely to be product specific. Furthermore whether research is carried out only to improve the firm's existing products, or the develop new products, it is likely to provide new opportunities for diversification. The knowledge of the markets for its existing products and their channels of distribution provide the firm with other opportunities for diversification. Another opportunity for diversification arises from retained earnings from existing activities. The finding that these earnings are invested in diversification rather than, for example, paying dividends, is probably associated with the growth orientation of management and the tax position of shareholders. Thus the normal operations of the firm create both new opportunities for expansion and the availability of unused productive resources to meet these opportunities. The second explanation offered by Penrose concerns the exposure undiversified firms face due to permanent, or temporary, declines in demand for their products. Diversification is a means of spreading risk through reducing the firm's dependence on a few products. The reduction in perceived risk may also reduce the cost of capital to the firm. Diversification may also occur in response to diversification by a competitor. This type of competitive strategy raises the question of the implications of diversification for competition and this issue is examined below. Finally diversification may occur as part of a general policy for growth. This part of Penrose's work has been taken further by Marris (1964). Marris gives diversification a central role in his model of the growth of firms. The management of firms have a strong motivation to seek growth since it confers on them improved status, salary and security. But growth within their existing markets will eventually be limited by the growth of demand for these products and diversification is the means by which this demand constraint may be overcome. It has been argued above that a certain degree of diversification will be both natural and beneficial as opportunities are exploited. However, Marris argues that management will be prepared to press growth, and hence diversification, beyond the level which is optimal for shareholders. The drawback of too rapid a rate of diversification is a higher failure rate of new products due to a lack of managerial, financial, development and marketing resources. This may be a less reasonable proposition when the possibility of growth through merger is recognized. However before considering this it is worth looking at the changing structure of firms which has evolved with diversification.

The development of the M-form, divisionalized company was identified by Chandler (1963) to be a response to the growth and, more particularly, diversification of the modern corporation. Subsequent research (e.g. Channon, 1973; Rumelt, 1974; Williamson, 1970, 1975) has reinforced their inter-connection to such a degree that it is necessary to interpret the consequences of diversification within the context of the divisionalized company structure. In this structure responsibility for profitability is restored to divisional managers whose performance can be assessed. Top management is freed from day-to-day operational decisions and can concentrate on the allocation of funds between the divisions and other aspects of strategy. The divisional structure significantly reduces the organizational constraints of diversified growth, particularly growth by acquisition. The acquisition of new divisions, or sub-divisions, by takeover can be achieved quickly and with minimum disruption. Diversification through merger is often seen as less risky since it involves the acquisition of the physical assets, existing products and channels of distribution required and brings with it management and employees who are experienced in this area of activity. Furthermore, entry is achieved without initially having to compete for a market share. On the other hand if the motive for diversification is to utilize spare resources within the firm, or to exploit some technological development, then diversification by internal growth may be preferred. It appears that the importance of diversification mergers has increased in recent decades, partly as a response to the increase in strength of competition policy.

The US merger laws have evolved into a potent deterrent against sizeable horizontal and vertical mergers. It is doubtful, however, whether they have had much impact on the overall level of merger activity which has continued at high levels (Scherer, 1980, p. 588).

A substantial controversy surrounds the question of what impact diversification has on competition and efficiency. At first sight the creation of large, non-specialized firms would be expected to reduce both, but there are counter arguments. The evidence does not suggest that diversification raises market concentration. Indeed, broad spectrum diversification may be a force for reducing concentration in individual markets. Large firms diversifying are able to overcome many barriers to entry and may promote competition by their entry. Diversification may be the only means by which firms may grow large enough to reap pecuniary economies of scale, without becoming too dominant in a single market. It is also argued that the diversity of products, as well as large size, brings a greater potential benefit from research. Therefore large, diversified firms may be more likely to engage in intensive research and development, to the benefit of the whole economy. The associated introduction of the M-form organization is argued to lead to improved internal efficiency of the firm as divisions strive to meet profit targets and compete for funds. It is also argued that the internalizing of the capital market within the large, diversified firm can lead to improved allocative efficiency. This is created by top management, who hold better information than investors, allocating funds to their most profitable use. On the other hand there are several arguments which suggest that the growth of the diversified firm has the potential to create reduced competition and efficiency. It was noted earlier that there has been a high proportion of narrow spectrum diversification.

At least one possible interpretation of this finding is that the diversification that has led to relatively rapid rates of corporate growth (or has accompanied it) has not in general been to markets where the entering firm is a new and potentially competitive force. Rather, that 'diversification' has been to markets that are related to – and potentially if not actively competitive with – those in which the entering firm will frequently share what ever market power already exists. This kind of diversification is only one small step removed from the consolidation of market power through horizontal acquisition (Berry, 1975, pp. 74–5).

Furthermore, the internalizing of capital markets has led to the removal of information and decision-making from the investor and led to a concentration of economic power. 'This means that the diversified, divisionalized firm is increasingly becoming the arbiter of intersectional shifts in funds' (Rumelt, 1974, p. 155). Another focus of concern has been the potential for predatory pricing behaviour in which the diversified firm uses cross-subsidization between divisions to eliminate, or discipline, more specialized rivals and so achieve higher long-run profits. A further possibility is reciprocal purchasing agreements when a firm is significant both as a seller to and buyer from another firm. It is argued that such practices are more likely to be found amongst large, diversified firms, but there is little evidence for the widespread existence of either predatory pricing, or reciprocal purchasing behaviour. Finally there is the spheres of influence hypothesis which recognizes the pervasive influence of large, diversified firms in almost all markets. Conglomerates might recognize that aggressive behaviour against another conglomerate in one market would have adverse consequences in other markets. It is possible that a symmetry of market power might emerge which would blunt competition. The answers to many of the empirical issues concerning diversification are as yet unresolved. This is in part due to a lack of sufficient research, but also in part due to the fact that the process of diversification is continuing. When, and if, a more stable period emerges the uncompetitive consequences outlines above may become more apparent.

A. COSH

BIBLIOGRAPHY

Berry, C.H. 1975. *Corporate Growth and Diversification.* Princeton: Princeton University Press.

Chandler, A.D. 1963. *Strategy and Structure: Chapters in the History of the Industrial Enterprise.* Cambridge, Mass.: MIT Press.

Channon, D.F. 1973. *The Strategy and Structure of British Enterprise.* London: Macmillan.

Gort, M. 1962. *Diversification and Integration in American Industry.* Princeton: Princeton University Press.

Jacquemin, A. and Berry, C.H. 1979. Entropy measure of diversification and corporate growth. *Journal of Industrial Economics* 27(4), June, 359–69.

Marris, R.L. 1964. *The Economic Theory of Managerial Capitalism.* London: Macmillan.

Penrose, E.T. 1959. *The Theory of the Growth of the Firm.* Oxford: Basil Blackwell.

Robinson, E.A.G. 1958. *The Structure of Competitive Industry.* Rev. edn, Cambridge: Cambridge University Press.

Rumelt, R.P. 1974. *Strategy, Structure and Economic Performance.* Cambridge, Mass.: Harvard University Press.

Scherer, F.M. 1980. *Industrial Market Structure and Economic Performance.* Chicago: Rand McNally.

Utton, M.A. 1979. *Diversification and Competition.* The National Institute of Economic and Social Research Occasional Paper No. 31, London: Cambridge University Press.

Williamson, O.E. 1970. *Corporate Control and Business Behavior: An Enquiry into the Effects of Organisation Form on Enterprise Behavior.* Englewood Cliffs, NJ: Prentice-Hall.

Williamson, O.E. 1975. *Markets and Hierarchies: Analysis and Anti-trust Implications, a Study in the Economics of Internal Organization.* New York: Free Press.

divided populations and stochastic models.

1. INTRODUCTION. The title of this entry requires some explanation. I use the term 'stochastic models' to distinguish those theoretical models which include one or more stochastic variables from 'determinist models' which do not. I shall confine attention to some stochastic models which are obtained by introducing into a determinist model a single stochastic variable (which can be multivariate, but will in illustrative examples be univariate). I shall use the term 'generating system' to mean a determinist model in which from an initial state of the system an unending sequence of successive states of the system can be exactly predicted by means of a set of rules such as lagged equations. It is convenient to distinguish generating systems from stochastic models rather than extend the former class to include some or all of the latter. The important feature of stochastic models is that they can make allowance for wide margins of uncertainty and ignorance.

By a 'divided population' I shall generally mean a frequency distribution most of which is closely clustered around two or possibly more peaks, but fairly empty elsewhere: an extreme case would be that where the peaks were completely separated by an unoccupied stretch. However, the term 'divided population' can occasionally be extended to refer to a society which is divided into groups with contrasted living conditions, prospects and aims.

The term 'crisis' refers to an unstable situation where a small disturbance could tip the scales between the prospects of two widely different eventual outcomes. In a determinist model the representation of such a crisis would be a point of unstable equilibrium, and in a stochastic model based on that determinist model, one would still regard the point of instability as indicating crises facing that part of the population found close to it, by 'crises' meaning here the crises that chance might play a predominant part in determining their future prospects.

As a preliminary to the main discussion, it will be helpful to consider some standard tools for use with determinist models involving divided populations and crises.

2. SOME STANDARD METHODS FOR THE STUDY OF UNSTABLE SITUATIONS. A standard method of constructing a model of the response of an economic system to the passage of time, or to possible changes of policy or of outside influences, is to set up a generating system giving a set of initial conditions containing the present and recent values of a set of economic variables and policy parameters, together with a set of rules for calculating the set of the same variables one time-unit later and repeating this operation successively for any required number of time-units. Such rules would normally take the form of a number of equations giving the values of each variable as functions of the values of other variables, mainly at earlier dates, taking account of the present values assumed for any policy parameters. We may confine attention to very simple examples of such models.

It is quite usual to find in simple models that given the initial information, the application of the system of rules with fixed policy parameters will generate a sequence of sets of values of the variables which tend to a long-run equilibrium set, apart possibly from one or more constant common growth-rates. But it is also possible to frame fairly simple rules which lead to oscillations which persist at a constant amplitude. Often these will be smooth and sinusoidal, but there is another possibility which is the one relevant to crises, where there are periodic jumps from one smooth steady path (which we might call boom) to another smooth steady path (which we might call slump) alternately to and fro indefinitely.

A convenient tool for the representation of such systems when there are sufficiently few equations involved is the phase diagram. If we are dealing with difference equations of the kind just described, the axes of the diagram could measure the values of one important variable along the horizontal axis as independent variable and the change of that same variable over the next time-unit along the vertical axis as dependent variable. In such diagrams the curve relating the change of the variable as a function of the value itself will reveal points of equilibrium by its intersections with the horizontal axis: however, where the curve cuts the axis from below on the left, the equilibrium will evidently be unstable, and we shall call such equilibrium points crisis points. Figure 1 is a phase diagram applicable to the determinist model described below in section 3.

In Figure 1 the horizontal axis is cut by the graph *ITJKLSB* in three points *J*, *K* and *L* denoting equilibrium levels of the index of prosperity, but the point *K* is a '*crisis* point' indicating an *unstable* equilibrium value. The arrows following the paths starting from *A* and from near *K* illustrate how, given the level of the index in an initial period, the chart may be used to predict its values in later periods assuming the rules of the model to be obeyed. For example, to follow the changes from the initial value of 1000 at *A* on the horizontal axis, measure horizontally the same (negative) distance AA_1 as the vertical distance of the graph from *A*. Having marked A_1, for the value after one unit of time, repeat the operation from A_1 to mark in A_2 and so continue as illustrated in Figure 1. It is apparent that the series of such values must converge to the value marked by *S*, and similarly that starting from *C*, near *K* on the right, when the distances concerned will now be positive, (to the right or upwards), it should again be clear that the series obtained must converge to the same stable equilibrium value *S*. Finally, starting from any point to the left of *K*, the usual procedure must result in a series arriving at the other stable equilibrium point *T*: (this is so because the gradient of the line *ITJ* is -1 in this example, which entails that as soon as the path hits *ITJ* it leads directly to *T*). This illustrates why the equilibrium at points, such as *K*, where the axis is cut by the curve from below on the left are unstable, while the points such as *T* and *S* mark stable equilibrium values.

Figure 1 will be used again in section 3 to illustrate the numerical example there, which involves equations (3) to (6): Table 1 in that section provides the first few values of the sequences that would be obtained by applying the rules, starting from values 1000, 100 and 70 respectively.

An early example of a determinist economic model involving oscillation between two points of stable equilibrium across a gap containing a crisis point of unstable equilibrium, due to the interventions of a disturbing force moving the phase-curve, was the model of the trade cycle published by Kaldor in the March 1940 issue of the *Economic Journal*. This contained a diagram closely related to a phase diagram of the elementary type shown here in Figure 1, and which relied on the property that the curve itself moved upwards or downwards, depending on whether the currently relevant point representing equilibrium was on the right or left of the diagram.

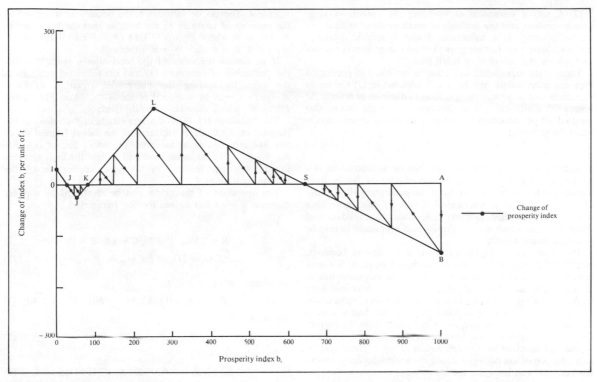

Figure 1 Phase diagram with crisis point K.

Figure 2 is a transposition of Kaldor's diagram into a phase diagram of the type outlined above. Three positions of the curve are shown marked 0, + and *. Initially the relevant point of intersection is *B* a stable prosperous stable equilibrium point: *K* and *S* mark the currently irrelevant *crisis* and slump equilibrium points on this curve. During the boom the curve moves down to the position + + + at which *B* and *K* meet at the point *K* + of tangency and the curve loses contact with the horizontal equilibrium axis so that the relevant equilibrium shifts rapidly to *D**, the slump stable equilibrium, and now the curve moves upwards past position 0 to position +, at which *S* and *K* coalesce at the new point *K** of tangency, and again the curve loses contact with the equilibrium line, so that now the relevant

stable equilibrium moves rapidly to the right to *B**, the boom stable equilibrium. Then the curve moves downwards again through the position 000 and the story is repeated again and again with alternative stable equilibria *D* and *S* in boom and in slump.

Since World War II a number of models have been based on such non-linear differential or difference equations to produce fairly regular switching between temporarily stable situations of slump and boom. An early and particularly neat example was provided by R. M. Goodwin in a paper delivered in June 1955 to a meeting of the International Economic Society in Oxford. An account of that and other such early models will be found in chapter 8 of *Mathematical Economics* by R. G. D. Allen (London: Macmillan; New York: St Martin's Press, 1956).

The model in section 3 with its crisis point has much in common with those of Kaldor and Goodwin and later writers, but in section 5 we shall develop it in a different direction by introducing stochastic disturbances so that it may be used for modelling the development of bimodal distributions. The point which that model is intended to illustrate is that a few simple ingredients which may underlie a number of complex situations in which bimodal frequency distributions may alone be sufficient to produce bimodality, without any of the many further influences which may also be possible explanations of it. It is quite plain that such a model is not in fact a complete explanation, but it may be helpful as illustrating a method of taking a first step in a variety of investigations of situations where divided populations are observed.

The simple ingredients alluded to above are as follows:

(1) A set of largely unidentifiable and unexpected disturbances to each member value of the population whose distribution is being generated. This may well increase the dispersion.

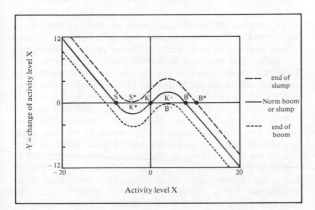

Figure 2 Phase diagram: three curve positions

(2) A set of influences encouraging the growth of large member values and the declines of small member values.

(3) Opposing these influences, 1 and 2: specific measures taken to discourage further growth of very large member values and reverse the fall of very small ones.

These three ingredients will often be sufficient to produce a bimodal distribution. We have not included in (3) the many influences that there may be operating to diminish or reverse the effects of ingredient (2) at intermediate levels: where this omitted set of influences is strong, a unimodal distribution is likely to be found.

3. RULES FOR A MODEL GENERATING LINES OF BEQUESTS. In this section we consider a population consisting of family lines within which bequests are passed down generation after generation according to a mechanical system of rules governing inheritance, earnings, consumption, taxation, subsidies and dividends, and which lead all family lines eventually to ruin or to considerable wealth.

The same rules apply to each and every line of bequests, which differ only in the level of the initial bequest. We may denote the level of the initial bequest in a representative line as B_0 and the level of the bequest in that line t generations later as B_t. We shall set out in the next paragraph a set of rules which entail that the following bequest, B_{t+1}, in the line is always obtainable from one or two linear equations from the current bequest B_t. For reference these equations (1), (2), are set out below and followed by an explanation of the notation and by a description of the rules governing the accumulation of wealth for bequests and implying these equations.

When $B_t < WEX$,

$$B_{t+1} = e^{RT} \cdot [B_t - (C - E)/R] + (C - E)/R$$

if B_t exceeds P but otherwise

$$B_{t+1} = e^{RT} \cdot [P - (C - E)/(R)] + (C - E)/R \qquad (1)$$
$$\text{or if this is } < 0, B_{t+1} = 0.$$

When $B_t > WEX$,

$$B_{t+1} = e^{RT} \cdot [B_t - TAX \cdot (B_t - WEX) - (C - E)/R]$$
$$+ (C - E)/R \qquad (2)$$

Both (1) and (2) operate if $B_t = WEX$.

The meanings of the symbols T, E, C, R, TAX and WEX are as follows: T = length of generation in years: we take $T = 25$ for examples, E = level of earnings per annum: we take $E = 10$ for examples, C = consumption expenditure per annum: $C = 12$ for examples, R = interest rate for dividends per annum: $R = 2.5\%$ for examples, P = level up to which bequests less than it are subsidized, $P = 50$ for examples, TAX = rate of tax of bequests starting at exemption level WEX for tax on bequests: $TAX = 2/3$ or $3/5$; $WEX = 250$ or 400, in examples.

The four rules which lead to the equations (1) and (2) are:

Rule 1. So long as any of a bequest remains it constitutes a fund attracting interest at the rate R per annum and provides a source from which the excess expenditure $(C - E)$ can be maintained.

Rule 2. If the whole of a bequest gets used up before the end of a generation, consumption is cut from C to E, (debt is ruled out) and in this case the bequest (before subsidy) must be zero.

Rule 3. Every bequest consists of the accumulated fund at retirement (before tax or subsidy), which fund may be zero.

Rule 4. The tax or subsidy on the bequest B_t is applied at the moment of payment to the heir, so that the heir receives W_t out of B_t where $W_t = B_t - TAX.(B_t - WEX)$ if $B_t > WEX$, $W_t = P$ if $B_t < P$ and $W_t = B_t$ otherwise.

If we denote the value of the fund after u years by $F(u)$, the derivation of equations (1) and (2) follows directly from the rules by solving the differential equation $dF/Fu = R \cdot F(u) - C + E$ by standard methods to obtain $F(T)$ given $F(0) = W_t$ which may be found by Rule 4.

The equations (1), (2) and a knowledge of the values of the parameters T, E, C, R etc. and of the initial bequest B_0 of any line now enable us to derive the whole line of bequests B_0, B_1, B_2, ... as far as we wish and to find the limiting value in long-run equilibrium, by repeated application of the relevant equations.

The operation of the model can be illustrated by a phase diagram if we select values for the parameters.

Putting

$$R = 2.5\%, \ T = 25, C = 12, \ E = 10,$$
$$TAX = 2/3, \ WEX = 250, \ P = 50 \qquad (3)$$

we obtain, when $B_t < 250$,

$$B_{t+1} - B_t = 0.868246 \, (B_t - 80), \quad \text{if} \quad B_t > 40 \qquad (4)$$

but if $B_t < 40$;

$$B_{t+1} - B_t = 23.95 - B_t. \qquad (5)$$

But when $B_t > 250$,

$$B_{t+1} - B_t = -0.377251 \, B_t + 241.91465 \qquad (6)$$

and can derive the phase diagram, Figure 1 in which the curve cuts the horizontal axis in the three equilibrium points at T, K and S at which $B_t = 23.95$, 80 and 641.26. The values of the turning points J and L are those of P and WEX, 50 and 250 (see section 2).

Table 1 covers ten generations and gives the values of the bequests in three lines starting at 70, 100 and 1000.

Table 1 Three lines of bequests over ten generations

Generation number	1	2	3	4	5	6	7	8	9	10
					Level of bequest					
Line 1	70.0	61.3	45.1	24.0	24.0	24.0	24.0	24.0	24.0	24.0
Line 2	100	117	150	210	324	443	518	565	593	611
Line 3	1000	865	780	728	695	675	662	654	649	646

4. STATISTICAL METHODS FOR STUDYING DISTRIBUTIONS WITH MANY PEAKS. Twin-peaked distributions often arise in situations where there are three equilibrium points of which two are stable, but the third is unstable, and lies between them. In such unstable situations the fact that an initial distribution contains individuals on both sides of the unstable crisis point will ensure that the population will eventually be divided into two groups at or close to the two stable equilibrium points.

The same mathematical device that underlies the crisis models generating alternative progressions to the two stable equilibrium points, or in some models regular switching from one to the other across an unstable one, may be adapted to represent situations which produce a frequency distribution consisting of two peaked distributions each centred on stable equilibrium points on either side of an unstable one. The adaptation may consist of the introduction of rules for moving the curve that indicates the equilibrium points, as in Kaldor's models, or by the introduction of rules disturbing the point indicating the current state of affairs off that curve: that is the line we shall investigate.

The whole frequency distribution may either continue strictly positive across the neighbourhood of the unstable point between the two peaks, or be split into two entirely separate distributions, with the unstable point left in the gap between. In the class of models which will be discussed in section 5 of the entry, the split version can only emerge if the rules governing the stochastic disturbances to the movements of the points (representing the individual values whose frequency distribution is being generated) do not enable individuals to arrive at or cross the unstable equilibrium point. This is a very stringent condition, but it represents an intermediate case between the stochastic model generating the unbroken two-peaked equilibrium distribution and the cruder determinist models generating a long-term equilibrium with all individual points concentrated at the two stable equilibrium points. More elaborate determinist models with lagged variables may lead to undamped regular oscillations about a single equilibrium point, but these will not be further discussed in this entry.

In the past, economists were largely concerned with the study of equilibrium positions towards which market competition and other social and economic forces would drive the economic individuals and conglomerations involved. The particular concerns of the statisticians and econometricians were more often with the movements of those equilibrium points and with the dispersion of the individuals or groups around these points. In the simple cases where there was just a single equilibrium they might for example study the shapes of the frequency distributions of the one or more coordinates of the point, and suggest and test various theories to explain how such shapes could arise, as well as what caused the movement of the equilibrium point itself. Thus there have been theories to account for and predict the age-distributions of the populations of various territories, the size-distributions of their cities and the distribution of the shares of votes cast for a particular party in the various constituencies, and again the distribution of income, wealth and other measures of prosperity, both between individuals and between various groups of persons.

However, if stochastic disturbances can interfere with the equilibrating forces or even shift the three equilibrium points, there may be preserved a considerable spread of distribution around each stable equilibrium point, and if the stochastic disturbances are strong, there may still be movement between the two groups across the unstable equilibrium point. In the former case we should expect two separated equilibrium distributions, whose relative sizes would depend on the nature of the initial distribution, but in the latter case a single continuous but probably bimodal equilibrium distribution whose shape could well be independent of the initial distribution.

In those cases where a considerable valley between the two peaks of the long-term equilibrium distribution is preserved, the stochastic mechanism is quite different from the simple determinist explanation for such a bimodal equilibrium distribution: this determinist explanation is simply that two quite distinct populations have been juxtaposed and counted together as one population. For example, if a wealthy island were to annex an impoverished island with roughly the same population and then compiled wealth- or income-distribution figures for the two combined, one might expect a fairly stable bimodal wealth- or income-distribution. However, with good transport between the two islands one might expect eventually that the later generations sprung from the impoverished island

would acquire gradually some of the cultural and other advantages of the descendants of the wealthy islanders and, vice versa, some of the descendants of the wealthy islanders would be impoverished as a result of the competition of the more gifted immigrants from the other island. Thus in the long run the stochastic intermingling of the two races might make the stochastic model more relevant than the determinist analysis of the equilibrium distribution to be expected.

In section 5 we shall explain how to introduce a stochastic variable into our determinist model of lines of bequests so as to change it into a stochastic model of the distribution of bequests in successive generations and in the following section will provide some numerical examples to suggest some questions which such models might be helpful in answering if they were suitably elaborated. These questions will be related to situations featuring an apparent contrast between two overlapping groups, 'poor' and 'rich', where the 'persons' to whom the distributions refer may be individuals or households or localities or larger groups such as whole economies.

5. EASY RULES FOR A STOCHASTIC MODEL OF A DIVIDED POPULATION. In our stochastic model we shall consider the distribution of bequests in each generation over a series of value-ranges of equal proportionate extent g. We shall suppose the top of range 0 to be P, and we shall number the ranges so that for each integer i, positive or negative, the top of range i is Pg^i. We assume that initially all bequests are at the centres of the ranges, and we impose rules to ensure that the same is true in every ensuing generation. This simplification makes rather narrow ranges desirable so as to avoid introducing considerable inaccuracy, but in illustrative examples we shall have to use wide intervals with $g = 10^{.2} = 1.585$ or $10^{.1} = 1.26$ so as to be able to set out the results in the space available.

The stochastic model differs from the deterministic one of Section 3, in modifying the value of B_{t+1}, there calculated from B_t. Denote that value by $B_{t+1}(i)$ when B_t is at the centre of range i, then in the stochastic model we multiply it by a stochastic multiplier m_i, which when $N = 2$ scatters the bequests of $B_{t+1}(i)$ to the centres of 4 (or more generally, of $N + 2$) consecutive ranges, in proportions that leave their arithmetic mean equal to $B_{t+1}(i)$.

In section 6 the rules for choosing the ranges and the proportions of bequests moved to each of them will be set out but nonspecialists may prefer to skip that section and be content with Figures 3 and 4 below, which illustrate typical effects of the multiplier with (i) $g = 1.585$, $N = 2$ and (ii) $g = 1.26$, $N = 7$.

We may then work out for each range i from 0 upwards, the following bequest $B_{t+1}(i)$ by the formulae (1) and (2) of the determinist model and apply the stochastic multiplier to the

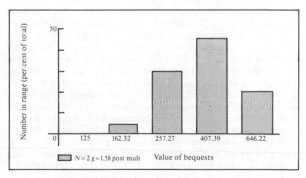

Figure 3 Stochastic disturbance about 400

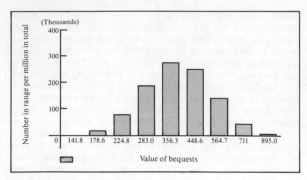

Figure 4 Disturbance about 400 (N = 7; g = 1.26)

bequests in lines from each range i, so as to split them into sets going, when $N = 2$ to the 4 (or more generally, $N + 2$) appropriate consecutive ranges. By using the information for every range containing at least one bequest where we round off to the nearest integer, assuming a total number of one million bequests in each generation, it is then a matter of arithmetic, to find the size-distribution of bequests in generation $t + 1$ from that of bequests in ranges with non-negative i in generation t.

We still have to explain how to handle bequests in the ranges with $i < 1$, namely the ranges below the level P. It is again assumed that all bequests in such ranges are subsidized up to the level P. Indeed, some such egalitarian measure as this is needed if we are to avoid all bequest lines eventually becoming permanently zero or in a range well below P, except possibly for a wealthy set all considerably above the crisis. level $(C - E)/R$. So in the calculations we merely have to lump all the bequests in ranges with i less than 1 into range 0. This need not prevent there being bequests *before subsidy* in each generation in other ranges below P, and it is the distribution of ranges before subsidy that we shall calculate in examples and which are relevant to the distributions of wealth and dividends which are all available towards the retiring age.

We shall give a very few numerical examples of such distributions in section 7 to which those uninterested in the details of the rules for the stochastic multiplier are advised to skip. Those rules will now be outlined in section 6.

6 RULES SETTING THE PROBABILITIES OF THE $N + 2$ VALUES OF m_i. These rules will be illustrated by the case $N = 2$, where normally m_i may take 4 values $g^j, g^{j+1}, g^{j+2}, g^{j+3}$, where j is an integer. There are, however, two simple special cases where only three consecutive integers are taken, the fourth value having no bequests dispersed to it. The rules ensure that these two cases give probabilities 0.25, 0.5, 0.25, 0 and 0, 0.25, 0.5, 0.25; the three non-zero terms are those of the binomial expansion $(0.5 + 0.5)^2$. Similarly, where N is any positive integer there are two special cases where $N + 1$ ranges only may be occupied with probabilities given by the $N + 1$ terms of the binomial expansion $(0.5 + 0.5)^N$. Returning to the special case $N = 2$, the rules further provide that the value of j and the proportions of the bequests should be so chosen that the four proportions are a weighted average with weights $1 - p$ and p $(0 < p < 1)$ of the two special cases with three terms each, and that the arithmetic mean of the bequests should equal the value $B_{t+1}(i)$ obtained in the determinist model. This entails that the four proportions should be the following: $(1 - p)/4$, $(2 - p)/4$, $(1 + p)/4$ and $p/4$. The arithmetic mean of the bequests must then be $(1 + pg) \cdot Pg^j(1 + g)^2/4$ so that our rules require

$$(1 + p(g - 1)) \cdot Pg^j(1 + g)^2 = 4B_{t+1}(i) \qquad (7)$$

where the right-hand side is known. This uniquely determines j and p and they may easily be derived.

In the general case where N is any positive integer the main modifications are that the binomial expansions in the special cases are now $(0.5 + 0.5)^N$ and that in equation (7) and the preceding line, 4 must be replaced by 2^N.

7. MODEL GENERATING 2-PEAKED-DISTRIBUTION: ILLUSTRATIVE CASES. In this section we shall illustrate the kinds of two-peaked distributions that are generated by such simplified stochastic models and the ways one might use them, by a few numerical exercises involving an imaginary set of a million lines of bequests. We shall mainly use arithmetic and diagrams for the exposition.

Let us start with the standard values for the parameters given in section 3 equation (3) as

$$R = 2.5\%, \quad T = 25, \quad C = 12, \quad E = 10,$$
$$TAX = 2/3 \quad \text{and} \quad WEX = 250$$

and in section 5 as

$$P = 50, \quad g = 10^{-2} \qquad (8)$$

The long-run equilibrium distribution obtained with this set-up will depend on how widely the stochastic multiplier disperses the bequests from each range in a single generation, and this is set by the parameter N. Figures 5 to 7 show that widening the dispersion in this example through the first four values, $N = 0, 1, 2$ and 3 already exhibits a wide variety of types of solution. Case $N = 0$. Two separated distributions: in ranges -2 and -1; and in ranges 10 and 11. The proportion of bequests in the two distributions will equal the initial

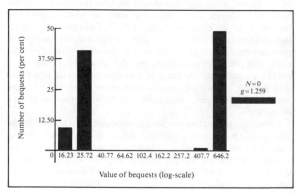

Figure 5 Equilibrium bequest–distributions

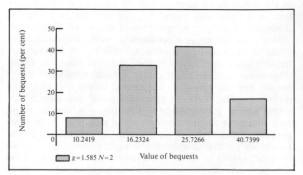

Figure 6 Equilibrium bequest distributions

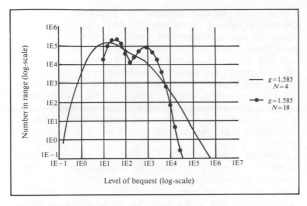

Figure 7 Equilibrium Pareto curve (non-cumulative)

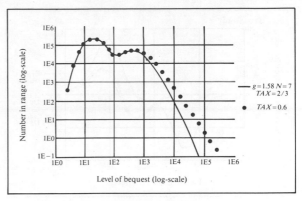

Figure 9 Effect of lower tax on bequests

proportions that were in ranges up to and including 1 and in ranges 2 and above. Cases $N = 2$ and $N = 3$. All bequests are in ranges immediately below P; 4 of them when $N = 2$ and 5 when $N = 3$. Cases $N = 4$ and over. All bequests are in a single distribution extending over many ranges from well below P up to well above WEX the tax exemption limit. These are the most interesting cases. Some have a pair of peaks separated by a valley, but those with N taking higher values have only a single peak.

Figure 5 illustrates the case $N = 0$ where we have assumed that half the bequests in the initial generation were in ranges 3, 4, 5 etc. . . . and half in the ranges 0, −1, −2 etc. The result, due to the minimum value of N, is a very divided distribution little different from the complete division that would be found in the determinist model: the case with $N − 1$, not shown, is less stark, allowing a spread over five ranges in the upper peak and over three in the lower peak. Figure 6 shows the unusual cases where in the long term there are no bequests in any range above P. With the particular values we took for the other parameters this unusual feature only occurs when $N = 2$ and $N = 3$. Figure 7 compares the typical bimodal form when $N = 4$ with the typical unimodal form when $N = 18$. The logarithmic scale used may given the deceptive impression that when $N = 4$ the valley between the peaks is not deep and therefore easily crossed, but a more careful inspection will reveal that it is very deep, since the valley floor indicates a range with roughly 10,000 bequests, whereas even the lower peak indicates one containing roughly 100,000 bequests.

Figures 8 and 9 are mainly concerned with a potentially instructive use of stochastic models for investigating the effects of altering one or more of the policy parameters. They do this for two examples of reflationary fiscal policies: raising WEX the tax-emption level from 250 to 400 (figure 8) and altering TAX from 3/5 and 2/3 to 50 per cent (figure 9). The effects of the higher exemption level are to deepen and widen the valley and shift the tail to the right along with the level of the exemption limit, without affecting its Pareto slope. The effect of the tax reduction is mainly to lessen the Pareto slope of the tail. Each measure greatly increases the total number of bequests above 5000; the tax reduction by four or fivefold and the higher exemption level by more than tenfold. This is perhaps the right moment to reiterate the warning that such examples are not meant to be more than indications of elementary methods for testing hunches of what are the probable logical effects of such changes given any set of artificial rules being mechanically obeyed.

All our discussion has been concerned with equilibrium distributions. However, as in so many branches of economic theory, knowledge of the eventual equilibrium corresponding to the present state of the economy and current policy decisions is virtually useless unless one knows how rapidly that equilibrium will be approached and particularly what will happen during the reasonably near future.

This also can be illustrated with our elementary example. It is to be expected that with low values of N, approach to equilibrium may be very slow and that is only too well confirmed by a wide variety of examples not further reported here. It is more interesting to give the stochastic disturbances considerable scattering influence by choosing quite a high value for N and then following the pace of approach towards equilibrium from an initial distribution of bequests chosen so as to differ considerably from that equilibrium distribution.

But in Figure 10 we have taken our standard example, with $N = 7$, and shown for each range the difference between the equilibrium number of ranges that would result from altering TAX from 3/5 to 2/3: we also show by the two intermediate curves how much of the approach to the new equilibrium would in each range be achieved after five and after ten generations of 25 years each. It will be seen how far from completed the transition is even after the 250 years.

Space forbids showing further examples of the short-run effect of altering policy or other parameters in such models, by methods similar to those used in studying long-run effects: naturally such short-term enquiry can be more important for obtaining conclusions remotely relevant to the real world, yet

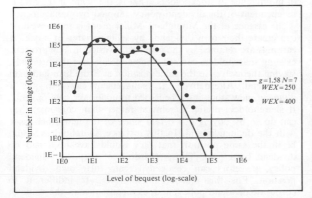

Figure 8 Effect of higher tax-exempt limit

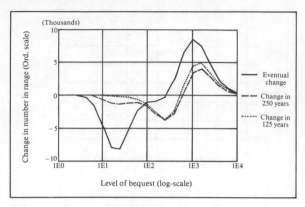

(Thousands)

Change in number in range (Ord. scale)

Level of bequest (log-scale)

Eventual change

Change in 250 years

Change in 125 years

Figure 10 Short-term moves to equilibrium

the theoretical approach to such investigations need differ little from that to the long-term ones discussed above.

8. CONCLUDING OBSERVATIONS. In the later sections of this entry we have provided an illustration of how, without introducing any of the more detailed causes of divided, i.e. of bimodal, frequency distributions, one can obtain a skeletal model of the development of such distributions by merely including the dispersive elements: (a) an ability and willingness on the part of the richer, to save a higher proportion of their income than on the part of the poorer, and (b) stochastic disturbances; both (a) and (b) tending to increase inequality; and the egalitarian elements: (c) to curtail (a) and (b) on the part of the very rich; and (d) subsidies to set a limit on the poverty of the very poor. We have hinted how models including at least these four basic elements, and thereby generating biomodal distributions, can provide some insight into possible long-run and short-run effects of altering policy parameters: in particular we have argued that considerations of long-run equilibrium can be very poor guides to short-run effects.

The next step is, naturally, to introduce into the model the more obvious and significant other causes acting to modify distributions of wealth, income, health, nourishment and other measures of well-being. That step is far too long for inclusion in an entry of this nature. Moreover, since although situations of the critical and divisive kinds, on which such research aims to throw some light become more frequent every year, statistics of these phenomena are patchy and unreliable. The development of stochastic methods to make allowance for the unreliability and incompleteness of information is by no means a minor step in such enquiries. It was this belief that prompted the submission of this methodological entry.

D. G. CHAMPERNOWNE

dividend policy. There are two major ways in which a firm can distribute cash to its common stockholders. The firm can either declare a cash dividend which it pays to call its common stockholders or it can repurchase stock. Stock repurchases may take the form of registered tender offers, open market purchases, or negotiated repurchases from a large shareholder. By far the most common method of distributing cash to shareholders is through the payment of cash dividends. For example, in 1985, US corporations paid over $83 billion in cash dividends.

Most firms pay cash dividends on a quarterly basis. The dividend is declared by the firm's board of directors on a date known as the 'announcement date'. The board's announcement states that a cash payment will be made to stockholders who are registered owners on a given 'record date'. The dividend checks are mailed to stockholders on the 'payment date' which is usually about two weeks after the record date. Stock exchange rules generally dictate that the stock is bought or sold with the dividend until the 'ex dividend date' which is a few business days before the record date. After the ex-dividend date, the stock is bought and sold without the dividend.

Dividends may be either labelled or unlabelled. Most dividends are not given labels by management. Unlabelled dividends are commonly referred to as 'regular dividends'. At times, managers will give a special label to the dividend. The most common label is the word, 'extra'. About 30 per cent of the *increases* in the dividend from the previous quarter are given some special label by management.

AN HISTORICAL PERSPECTIVE

Prior to 1961, academic treatments of dividends were primarily descriptive in nature, as, for example, in Dewing (1953). To the extent that economists considered corporate dividend policy, the commonly held view was that investors preferred high dividend payouts to low payouts (see, for example, Graham and Dodd, 1951). The only question was how much value was attached to dividends relative to capital gains in valuing a security (Gordon, 1959). This view was concisely summarized with the saying that a dividend in the hand is worth two (or some multiple) of those in the bush. The only question was – what is the multiple?

In 1961, scientific inquiry into the motives and consequences of corporate dividend policy shifted dramatically with the publication of a classic paper by Miller and Modigliani. Perhaps the most significant contribution of the Modigliani–Miller paper was to spell out in careful detail the assumptions under which their analysis was to be conducted. The most important of these include the assumption that the firm's investment policy is fixed and known by investors, that there are no taxes on dividends or capital gains, that individuals can costlessly buy and sell securities, that all investors have the same information and that investors have the same information as the managers of the firm, and, finally, that there are no contracting or agency costs associated with stock ownership. With this set of assumptions, Modigliani and Miller demonstrated that a firm's dividend policy is a matter of indifference to stockholders. That is, the value of the firm is independent of the dividend policy adopted by management.

The essence of the Modigliani–Miller proof is that investors can create their own dividends by selling shares of stock. If earnings are retained by the firm and invested in new projects, existing shareholders can sell stock and consume the proceeds, leaving themselves in the same position as if the firm had paid a dividend. Alternatively, if management elects to pay a dividend, new stock must be issued to undertake new projects. If shareholders prefer to reinvest rather than consume, they can do so by buying a pro rata share of the new stock issue with the dividends paid. In this instance, shareholders would be in the same position that they would have been had no dividend been paid. Thus, regardless of corporate dividend policy, investors can costlessly create their own dividend position. For this reason, stockholders are indifferent to corporate dividend policy, and, as a consequence, the value of the firm is independent of its dividend policy.

The conclusion that the market value of the firm is independent of its dividend policy means that corporate investment decisions can be made without regard to dividend policy. It is the case, though, that total cash inflows to and outflows from the firm do depend upon its investment decision. If the level of funds required for investment purposes exceeds internally generated funds, then new shares must be issued (or dividends retained) in order for firm value to be maximized. If internally generated funds exceed investment requirements, then shares must be repurchased or a cash dividend must be paid. Under the Modigliani–Miller assumptions though, the value of the firm is independent of the method used to distribute the cash.

After a brief flurry of debate, the Modigliani–Miller irrelevance proposition was essentially universally accepted as correct under their set of assumptions. There nevertheless remained an underlying notion that dividend policy must 'matter' given that managers and security analysis spend time worrying about it. If so, and if the Modigliani–Miller proposition is accepted, it must be due to violation of one or more of the Modigliani–Miller assumptions in the real world.

Since the early 1960s, the dividend debate has been lively and interesting as economists have analysed the effect on the value of the firm of relaxing the various Modigliani–Miller assumptions and have explored the data for evidence that dividend policy affects security prices and investor behaviour. Economists have focused on three related questions. First, does the *level* of dividends paid by the firm affect the value of the firm? That is, are high dividend-paying firms valued differently by the market than low dividend-paying firms, holding other factors constant? Second, do *changes* in an established dividend level affect the value of the firm? Third, does the method of cash payout affect the value of the firm? For example, are cash dividends valued differently than share repurchases and are labelled dividends valued differently than unlabelled dividends? We organize our discussion around these three questions.

FIRM VALUE AND THE LEVEL OF DIVIDEND PAYOUT

Taxes. Perhaps the obvious starting point for an investigation into the effect of relaxing the Modigliani–Miller assumptions is to introduce taxes. In the US, dividend payments by a corporation do not affect that firm's taxes. However, at least historically, dividends have been taxed at a higher rate than capital gains at the personal level. Thus, superficially, the US tax code appears to favour a low dividend payout policy.

Under the assumption that dividends and capital gains are taxed differentially, Brennan (1970) derived a model of stock valuation in which stocks with high payouts have higher required before-tax returns than stocks with low payouts. However, empirical tests of Brennan's model by Black and Scholes (1974), Litzenberger and Ramaswamy (1979) and Miller and Scholes (1982) have yielded ambiguous results, in which support for a dividend tax effect in stock returns appears to depend heavily upon the definition of dividend yield employed. In a provocative case study, Long (1978) has examined the prices of two classes of stock of Citizens Utility, which differ only in terms of dividends and tax treatments, and finds support for the notion that investors favour a high dividend payout.

As a counterpoint to Brennan, Miller and Scholes (1978) argue that the assumption that dividends are taxed disadvantagously relative to capital gains is inaccurate. They argue that, at least historically, under the US tax code there exist sufficient loopholes so that investors may shelter dividend income so as to drive the effective tax rate on dividends to zero. However, Feenberg (1981) and Peterson, Peterson and Ang (1985) examine data from actual tax returns which indicate the various methods of avoiding taxes described by Miller and Scholes are not used by investors who receive dividends.

Empirical investigation into the effects of taxes on the level of stock prices has not been limited to US data. For example, Poterba and Summers (1984) examine British stocks returns and Morgan (1980) examines Canadian stock returns with no more definitive conclusion than has been reached with US data.

Suffice it to say that, at this point, empirical studies on the relation among dividends, taxes, and firm value are inconclusive. Interestly, the most recent US tax legislation taxes dividends and capital gains at the same rate. The introduction of this legislation holds forth the prospect of providing an opportunity for a before-and-after examination of the data.

Agency costs. A second potentially important real world violation in the Modigliani–Miller assumptions is the existence of agency costs associated with stock ownership. In particular, managers of firms maximize their own utility, which is not necessarily the same as maximizing the market value of common stock. The costs associated with this potential conflict of interest include expenditures for structuring, monitoring and bonding contracts between shareholders and managers, and residual losses due to imperfectly constructed contracts (Jensen and Meckling, 1976).

Several authors have argued that dividends may be important in helping to resolve manager/shareholder conflicts. If dividend payments reduce agency costs, firms may pay dividends even though these payments are taxed disadvantageously.

Easterbrook (1984) and Rozeff (1982) argue that establishing a policy of paying dividends bonds managers to be evaluated periodically by the capital market. By paying dividends, the managers are required to tap the capital market more frequently to obtain funds for investment projects. Periodic review by the market is one way in which agency costs are reduced, which in turn, raises the value of the firm. If so, the value of the firm is no longer independent of dividend policy. It is still the case, however, that even in these models an 'optimal' dividend payout level is far from obvious.

At this point, no direct (or, even, indirect) tests of the agency cost explanations of corporate dividend policy have been reported. The dearth of empirical tests of these models is due, in part, to their recent development and, in part, to the relative lack of specificity of the theories.

FIRM VALUE AND CHANGES IN THE PAYOUT

While the evidence on whether the level of dividend payouts affects firm value is mixed, studies have consistently documented that stock returns around the announcement of a dividend change are positively correlated with the change in the dividend (Aharony and Swary, 1980; Asquith and Mullins, 1983; Brickley, 1983; Pettit, 1970). The leading explanation of this phenomenon is that dividend changes convey information about current or future earnings of the firm.

Contrary to the Modigliani–Miller assumption that investors have the same information as managers, the information content of dividends hypothesis is based on the assumption that managers possess more information about the prospects of the firm than individuals outside the firm. The hypothesis asserts that dividend changes convey manager's inside information to outsiders. This idea was suggested by Miller and Modigliani (1961) and has roots in Lintner's (1956) classic study on dividend policy. Lintner interviewed a sample of corporate managers. One of the primary findings of the interviews is that a high proportion of managers attempt to maintain a stable regular dividend. In Lintner's words, managers demonstrate a 'reluctance (common to all companies) to reduce regular rates once established and a consequent conservatism in raising regular rates' (p. 84). Lintner's argument is provided additional empirical support by Fama and Babiak (1968). If managers change regular dividends only when the earnings potential of the firm has changed, changes in regular dividend changes are likely to provide some information to the market about the firm's prospects.

More recently, formal models of dividends and information signalling have been developed. Models in which dividends convey information to outsiders include Bhattacharya (1979, 1980), John and Williams (1985), and Miller and Rock (1985). The assumptions under which these models are developed differ across the models. The major commonality is that managers are presumed to have information not available to outside investors. Typically, the information has to do with the current or future earnings of the firm.

The accumulated empirical evidence indicates that dividend announcements provide information to the market. As such, the evidence is consistent with the asymmetric information models of dividend changes. Whether these models actually capture the information to which the market is responding when dividend changes are announced is still an open question and which of the models best characterizes the process of information dissemination is still open to debate.

FIRM VALUE AND THE FORM OF THE PAYOUT

As with increases in regular cash dividends, specially labelled cash dividends and shares repurchases have been shown to be accompanied by permanent increases in stock prices (Brickley, 1983; Dann, 1981; Vermaelen, 1981). However, the factors that lead managers to choose one method over another are not well understood.

Given the Modigliani–Miller assumptions, the choice of the payout mechanism, like the choice of dividend policy itself, does not affect the value of the firm. Therefore, if the form of the payout is to matter, it must be due to violation of one or more of the Modigliani–Miller assumptions.

Economists have just begun to explore possible explanations as to why a particular form of payout is chosen. To develop a theory to explain the choice of payout mechanism, it must be that there are differential costs and/or benefits associated with the alternative payout methods. Given the preponderance of regular cash dividends relative to stock repurchases and specially-labelled dividends, a convincing explanation must credit regular cash dividends with substantial benefits or debit the alternatives with substantial costs. Furthermore, the relative benefits and/or costs must be especially significant because, at least historically, dividends have been tax-disfavoured (at the personal level) relative to share repurchases.

Two recently developed theories that attempt to explain the choice between cash dividends and share repurchases assume that managers have information not available to outside stockholders. Barclay and Smith (1986) and Offer and Thakor (1985) assume that managers can use this inside information to benefit themselves by means of share repurchases. In both cases, however, there are costs associated with the opportunis-tic use of the information. When the costs to the managers outweigh the benefits, dividends will be used to distribute cash instead of share repurchases.

As with various other hypotheses regarding corporate dividend policy, those explaining the choice between cash dividends and share repurchases have been developed only recently. As a consequence, they also have not yet undergone rigorous empirical testing. As regards the choice between regular cash dividends and specially labelled cash dividends reasonable explanations are even more scarce. However, Brickley (1983) does provide evidence that specially-labelled dividends convey a less positive message about firm value than do increases in regular cash dividends.

CONCLUSION

After twenty-five years of rigorous consideration, what is known about dividend policy is far outweighed by what is not known. We know that firms pay out to stockholders substantial amounts of cash annually and that the vast majority of this payout is in the form of regular cash dividends. Intermittently, firms also make specially labelled cash dividend payments and large-scale share repurchases. We also know that stock prices increase permanently when regular dividends are increased, when special dividends are declared, and when shares are repurchased and that stock prices decline when regular dividends are reduced. There is a growing consensus that the stock price changes come about because the dividend changes reflect information available to managers that is not otherwise available to outside investors. There is, however, little agreement as to what information management is providing to the market through the dividend payment and there is little agreement as to the linkage between the information released and the value of the firm. There also is little agreement as to whether the level of cash payout affects the value of the firm and there is little agreement as to whether the choice of the payout method matters and, if it matters, what factors favour one method relative to another.

It is tempting to conclude this essay on a disappointing note of frustration. But twenty-five years is a very short period of investigation for most economic phenomena. While what we do know about dividend policy is far less than we would like to know, we clearly know more about dividend policy now than we did twenty-five years ago. Undoubtedly, the next twenty-five years will witness further significant progress in understanding the determinants of corporate dividend policy.

JAMES A. BRICKLEY AND JOHN J. McCONNELL

See also CAPITAL BUDGETING; FINANCE; RETENTION RATIOS.

BIBLIOGRAPHY

Aharony, J. and Swary, I. 1980. Quarterly dividends, earnings announcements, and stockholder returns. *Journal of Finance* 35(1), March, 1–12.

Asquith, P. and Mullins, D. 1983. The impact of initiating dividend payments on shareholders' wealth. *Journal of Business* 56, January, 77–96.

Barclay, M. and Smith, C.W. 1986. Corporate payment policy. Cash dividends vs. share repurchases: Unpublished ms., August.

Bhattacharya, S. 1979. Imperfect information, dividend policy, and the 'Bird in the hand' fallacy. *Bell Journal of Economics* 10(1), Spring, 259–70.

Bhattacharya, S. 1980. Nondissipative signalling structures and dividend policy. *Quarterly Journal of Economics*, December 95, August, 1–24.

Black, F. and Scholes, M.S. 1974. The effects of dividend yield and dividend policy on common stock prices and returns. *Journal of Financial Economics* 1(1), May, 1–22.

Brennan, M.J. 1970. Taxes, market valuation, and corporate financial policy. *National Tax Journal* 23(4), December, 417–27.

Brickley, J.A. 1983. Shareholder wealth, information signalling, and the specially designated dividend: an empirical study. *Journal of Financial Economics* 12, August, 187–209.

Dann, L.Y. 1981. Common stock repurchases: an analysis of the returns to bondholders and stockholders. *Journal of Financial Economics* 9(2), June, 113–38.

Dewing, A.S. 1953. *The Financial Policy of Corporations.* 5th edn, New York: Ronald Press.

Easterbrook, F.H. 1984. Two agency-cost explanations of dividends. *American Economic Review* 74(4), September, 650–59.

Fama, E.F. and Babiak, H. 1968. Dividend policy: an empirical analysis. *American Statistical Association Journal* 63, December, 1132–61.

Feenberg, D. 1971. Does the investment interest limitation explain the existence of dividends? *Journal of Financial Economics* 9, September, 265–69.

Gordon, M.J. 1959. Dividends, earnings, and stock prices. *Review of Economics and Statistics* 41, May, 99–105.

Graham, B. and Dodd, D. 1951. *Security Analysis: Principles and Techniques.* New York: McGraw-Hill.

Jensen, M.C. and Meckling, W. 1976. Theory of the firm: managerial behavior, agency costs, and capital structure. *Journal of Financial Economics* 3(4), October, 305–60.

John, K. and Williams, J. 1985. Dividends, dilution and taxes: a signalling equilibrium. *Journal of Finance* 40(4), September, 1053–70.

Lintner, J. 1956. The distribution of incomes of corporations among dividends, retained earnings, and taxes. *American Economic Review, Paper and Proceedings* 46, May, 97–113.

Litzenberger, R.H. and Ramaswamy, K. 1979. The effect of personal taxes and dividends on capital asset prices: theory and empirical evidence. *Journal of Financial Economics* 7(2), June, 163–95.

Long, J.B. 1978. The market valuation of cash dividends: a case to consider. *Journal of Financial Economics* 6(2/3), June/September, 235–64.

Miller, M.H. and Modigliani, F. 1961. Dividend policy, growth, and the valuation of shares. *Journal of Business* 34, October, 235–64.

Miller, M.H. and Rock, K. 1985. Dividend policy under asymmetric information. *Journal of Finance* 40(4), September, 1031–51.

Miller, M.H. and Scholes, M.S. 1978. Dividends and taxes. *Journal of Financial Economics* 6(4), December, 333–64.

Miller, M.H. and Scholes, M.S. 1982. Dividends and taxes: some empirical evidence. *Journal of Political Economy* 90(6), December, 1118–41.

Morgan, I. 1980. Dividends and stock price behavior in Canada. *Journal of Business Administration*, Fall.

Offer, A. and Thakor, A. 1985. A theory of stock price response to alternative corporate cash disbursement methods: stock repurchases and dividends. Unpublished ms., December.

Peterson, P.P., Peterson, D.R. and Ang, J.S. 1985. Direct evidence on the marginal rate of taxation on dividend income. *Journal of Financial Economics* 14(2), June 267–82.

Pettit, R.R. 1972. Dividend announcements, security performance, and capital market efficiency. *Journal of Finance* 27(5), December, 993–1007.

Poterba, J.M. and Summers, L.H. 1984. New evidence that taxes affect the valuation of dividends. *Journal of Finance* 39(5), December, 1397–1415.

Rozeff, M.S. 1982. Growth, beta and agency costs as determinants of dividend payout ratios. *Journal of Financial Research* 2, Fall, 249–59.

Schleifer, A. and Vishny, R.W. 1986. Large stockholders and corporate control. *Journal of Political Economy* 94(3) pt1, June, 461–88.

Vermaelen, T. 1981. Common stock repurchases and market signalling: an empirical study. *Journal of Financial Economics* 9(2), June, 139–83.

Divisia, François Jean Marie (1889–1964). Divisia was born in Tizi-Ouzou, Algeria. He received baccalaureate degrees in mathematics and philosophy at Algiers. After two years in the Ecole Polytechnique he worked for the government as a civil engineer (Ponts et Chaussées). His graduate engineering work at the Ecole Nationale des Ponts et Chaussées was completed in 1919 after the interruption of World War I. After nearly ten years as a government engineer he joined the ministry of National Education to continue research and teaching economics. He became a professor of applied economics at the Ecole Nationale des Ponts et Chaussées (1932–50), the Conservatoire National des Arts et Métiers (1929–59), and the Ecole Polytechnic (1929–59). He was a founding member of the Econometric Society and its president in 1935. Subsequently he was also president of the Paris Statistics Society (1939) and of the International Econometric Society. He was a Fellow of the American Statistical Association and of the American Association for the Advancement of Science.

His major contributions to economics can be found centred in several books on economics and applied statistics. The Divisia Index, a variable-weight price index, was developed in *L'indice monétaire et la théorie de la monnaie* (1926). His *Economique rationnelle* (1928) was widely acclaimed in mathematical economics and was awarded prizes by the Academy of Sciences and by the Academy of Moral Sciences and Politics. Using a microeconomic perspective he cautioned against uncritical acceptance of macroeconomic research in *Traitement économétrique de la monnaie, l'intérêt, l'emploi* (1962).

DAVID E.R. GAY

SELECTED WORKS

1926. *L'indice monétaire et la théorie de la monnaie.* Paris.
1928. *Economique rationnelle.* Paris.
1931. *L'epargne et la richesse collective.* Paris.
1951–65. *Exposés d'économique.* Paris.
1962. *Traitement économétrique de la monnaie, l'intérêt, l'emploi.* Paris.

Divisia index. The Divisia index is a continuous time index number formula due to François Divisia (1925–26), which has been widely used in theoretical discussions of data aggregation and the measurement of technical change. It is defined with respect to the time paths of a set of prices $[P_1(t), \ldots, P_N(t)]$ and commodities $[X_1(t), \ldots, X_N(t)]$. Total expenditure on this group of commodities is given by:

$$Y(t) = P_1(t)X_1(t) + \cdots + P_N(t)X_N(t). \qquad (1)$$

Letting dots over variables indicate derivatives with respect to time, total differentiation of (1) yields:

$$\frac{\dot{Y}(t)}{Y(t)} = \sum_{i=1}^{i=N} \frac{P_i(t)X_i(t)}{Y(t)} \frac{\dot{P}_i(t)}{P_i(t)} + \sum_{i=1}^{i=N} \frac{P_i(t)X_i(t)}{Y(t)} \frac{\dot{X}_i(t)}{X_i(t)}. \qquad (2)$$

The first summation of the right-hand side of (2) defines the Divisia index of prices; the second summation defines the Divisia quantity index.

The Divisia price and quantity indexes are weighted averages of the growth rates of the individual $P_i(t)$ and $X_i(t)$, where the weights are the components' shares in total expenditure. The summations in (2) thus define the *rate of change* of the aggregate price and quantity indexes. The *levels* of these indexes are obtained by line integration over the trajectory followed by the individual prices and quantities over the time interval $[0, T]$.

For the quantity index, the line integral has the following form:

$$I_q(0, T) = \exp\left\{\int\int\left[\sum_{i=1}^{N} \frac{P_i(t)X_i(t)}{\Sigma P_j(t)X_j(t)} \frac{\dot{X}_i(t)}{X_i(t)}\right]\right\}$$

$$= \exp\left\{\int_\Gamma \phi(X)\,dX\right\}, \qquad (3)$$

where ϕ is a vector-valued function whose arguments are $P_i(t)/Y(t)$, prices are assumed to be a function of the X_i, and Γ is the curve described by X_i. A similar expression characterizes the Divisia price index (for a more extensive discussion of Divisia line integrals, see Richter, 1966 and Hulten, 1973).

The value of the index defined by (3) depends on the solution of the line integral. This can be obtained by identifying a 'potential function' Φ whose partial derivatives are the vector-valued function ϕ i.e. $\phi = \nabla\Phi$. Writing $\Phi = \log F$ function, the value of the index can be shown to equal $F[X(T)]/F[(X(0)]$, implying that the function F is unique only up to a scalar multiple.

In economic terms, the solution to (3) is associated with some underlying economic relationship among the variables being indexed. Assume, for example, there is a constant returns to scale production function $F(X)$ and $F_i = \lambda P_i$ (F_i denotes the partial derivative of F with respect to X_i and λ is a factor of proportionality). Then the function $\log F$ can serve as a potential function for (3), since $\nabla \log F$ equals the vector $[P_i/\Sigma_i X_i]$, which equals ϕ. In this case, the value of the Divisia index of inputs is the ratio of output at time T to output at time zero

If the form of the potential function is known a priori, the value of the index could be computed directly from the function F. However, the rationale for the Divisia index is that it provides a way of obtaining the ratio $F(X(T))/F(X(0))$ using data on prices and quantities alone, without direct knowledge of F. This is intuitively possible because, under sufficiently restrictive assumptions, information about the slope of the function F (as estimated by relative prices) over the path followed by the inputs is sufficient to characterize F up to a scalar multiple.

When the objective is to form an index of a subset of inputs – aggregate labour input, for example – the required potential function is a 'piece' of a production function. Specifically, if one wants to form a Divisia index of the first M inputs, the production function needs to be weakly separable into a function of these inputs: i.e. $F\{G[X_1(t), \ldots, X_M(t)], X_{M+1}(t), \ldots, X_N(t)\}$. The function $\log G$ serves as the potential function for the line integration.

These considerations apply to Divisia price indexes as well. The relevant potential function is now the factor price frontier $\Psi[P_1(t), \ldots, P_N(t)]$. A basic result of duality theory shows that the partial derivatives of Ψ are proportional to the corresponding $X_i(t)$.

The discussion suggests that the existence of the Divisia index is closely linked to the conditions for consistent aggregation. Furthermore, the required existence of potential function implies that aggregation cannot proceed with just any set of prices or quantities. There must be an *a priori* reason for supposing that the variables to be indexed are theoretically related.

Divisia indexes have the desirable property that they are invariant when the path of integration lies entirely in the same level set of the potential function. That is, if one input is substituted for another along a given isoquant, the value of the index will not change. However, there is no guarantee of invariance when the path of integration lies across several level sets. This reflects the mathematical property that line integrals are, in general, path dependent.

Path dependence means that the index (3) will generally have a different value for a path $\beta(t) \in \Gamma_1$ than path $\alpha(t) \in \Gamma$, even though the beginning and end points of Γ_1 and Γ are identical. This can lead to the following situation: the economy moves along Γ_1 from X from X' (which is on a different isoquant); the economy then returns along Γ to the original point X; because of path dependence, the vector of quantities represented by the vector X will have a different Divisia index value after the trip around the composite path, and subsequent circuits will produce still different values. The value of the Divisia index at any point X is thus arbitrary under path dependence.

The uniqueness of the Divisia index thus involves path independence. It turns out that the conditions discussed above lead to path independence: the existence of a potential function $\log F$ such that $\phi = \nabla \log F$, where ϕ is defined in (3). Given the existence of the potential function, the value of (3) is $F(X(T))/F(X(0))$, implying path independence since (3) depends only on the end points of the path, $X(0)$ and $X(T)$. Conversely, if (3) is path independent, there exists a potential function $\log F$ such that $\nabla \log F = \phi$.

This last condition requires that the vector $[F_i/F]$ equals $[P_i/\Sigma P_i X_i]$. In other words, path independence requires that F be linearly homogenous. This does not mean, however, that the Divisia index is restricted to situations where the underlying production or utility functions are linearly homogenous. Any homothetic transformation $F^*(X(t)) = H(F(X(t)))$, where $H' > 0$, can be indexed since F and F^* yield the same value of ϕ. In this case, $\log F$ still serves as the required potential function for (3) but the resulting value of the index will be $F(X(T))/F(X(0))$, not $F^*(X(T))/F^*(X(0))$.

We note, finally, that the Divisia index is defined using time as a continuous variable. This is appropriate for the theoretical analysis of many economic problems, but not for empirical analysis. Data on prices and quantieies typically refer to discrete points in time, and are therefore not suitable for use in the Divisia framework.

One approach to this problem is to approximate the continuous variables of (2) with their discrete time counterparts. Under the Törnqvist (1936) approach, the growth rates of prices and quantities are approximated by logarithmic differences, and the continuous weights by two period arithmetic averages. The Törnqvist approximation to the growth rate of the Divisia quantity index can then be written:

$$\sum_{i=1}^{i=T} \frac{1}{2}\left[\frac{P_{i,t}X_{i,t}}{Y_t} + \frac{P_{i,t-1}X_{i,t-1}}{Y_{t-1}}\right][\log X_{i,t} - \log X_{i,t-1}] \qquad (4)$$

A similar approximation applies to the growth rate of the Divisia index of prices.

While the Törnqvist index may be regarded as approximate, Diewert (1976) has shown that it is exact when the underlying potential function has the translog form.

The continuous Divisia index can also be approximated using chain indexing procedures. The Divisia index is sometimes regarded as a chain whose links are defined over infinitesimal time periods. Thus, an approximation can be obtained from a Paasche or Laspeyres (or other) index which is re-based in every time period.

CHARLES R. HULTEN

See also HEDONIC FUNCTIONS AND HEDONIC INDICES; INDEX NUMBERS.

BIBLIOGRAPHY

Diewert, W.E. 1976. Exact and superlative index numbers. *Journal of Econometrics* 4(2), May, 115–45.

Divisia, F. 1925–6. L'indice monétaire et la théorie de la monnaie. *Revue D'Economie Politique* 39(4), 842–64; (5), 980–1008;(6), 1121–51; 40(1), 49–81. Also separately at Paris, Société Anonyme du Recueil Sirey.

Hulten, C.R. 1973. Divisia index numbers. *Econometrica* 41(6), November, 1017–25.

Richter, M.K. 1966. Invariance axioms and economic indexes. *Econometrica* 34, October, 739–55.

Samuelson, P.A. and Swamy, S. 1974. Invariant economic index numbers and canonical duality: survey and synthesis. *American Economic Review* 64(4), September, 566–93.

Törnqvist, L. 1936. The Bank of Finland's consumption price index. *Bank of Finland Monthly Bulletin* 10, 1–8.

division of labour. The division of labour may be defined as the division of a process or employment into parts, each of which is carried out by a separate person. This includes the separation of employments or professions within society at large or *social division of labour* as well as the division of labour which takes place within the walls of a factory building or within the limits of a single industry, the *manufacturing division of labour*. Division of labour is associated with specialization and cooperation and their consequences for labour productivity and in its social form was analysed as early as the time of Greek philosophers such as Plato, Aristotle and Xenophon. Early analysis of a manufacturing division of labour had to await initial industrial developments of the 17th and 18th centuries and underwent further qualitative change in the 19th century. Hence manufacturing, or more detailed division of labour should not be seen as a simple continuum of the social division of labour. For example, under capitalism, social division of labour is largely a market influenced phenomenon, but manufacturing division is enforced by those who plan and control the manufacturing process. Furthermore, the one divides society; the other human activity in the workshop, and whereas social division of labour 'may enhance the individual and the species [in a manufacturing division], when carried on without regard to human capabilities and needs is a crime against the person and against humanity' (Braverman, 1974, p. 73). The notion of division of labour has also been applied to the household, hence *sexual division of labour*. When applied to locational specialization of industries both nationally and internationally, it has produced a variety of conceptions of the *territorial* or *international division of labour*.

Adam Smith (1776) placed the division of labour at the forefront of his discussion of economic growth and progress but neither in its social nor its manufacturing forms did the idea originate with him. It retained a varying, but often still very prominent place in 19th-century writings (particularly those of Senior, Babbage, John Stuart Mill, Marx and Marshall) but during the first half of the 20th century it disappeared as a major topic from economic texts. Reasons varied. Some felt such discussion to be more appropriate to technical handbooks of production engineering and factor management; others wished to confine analysis of its effects to sociological studies assessing the general impact of division of labour on society. The return of economic growth as an important part of the economist's research programme from the 1950s onwards, and earlier the work of Young (1928), carried renewed interest in the division of labour in its wake, as did growing dissatisfaction with the narrow view confining economics to studying 'the disposal of scarce commodities' (Robbins, 1932, p. 38). The different dimensions of division of labour raised in this preliminary overview suggest that a broad-brush treatment of these various aspects of the subject is warranted featuring highlights from its developments.

THE GREEKS. Many of the major Greek philosophers discussed aspects of the division of labour in their writings, particularly Plato and Xenophon. In Book 2 of the *Republic*, Plato states the necessity for a division of labour or specialization in occupations for social well-being and the adequate satisfaction of primary wants, linking the phenomenon with exchange, the requirement of 'a market, and a currency as a medium of exchange' (Plato, 380 BC, pp. 102–6). These and other aspects of Plato's work suggested to Foley (1974) that Smith's account may have substantially benefited from this early view on the subject. Aristotle, though also very conscious of the social need for a division of labour, did not depart much from Plato's earlier discussion (see Bonar, 1895, p. 34). More importantly, Xenophon linked division of labour and specialization to great cities, because they provided a substantial demand for individual articles while the subdivision of work raised the skill of individual workers. Xenophon's fresh insights appear also to have been known to Smith and possibly, Sir William Petty (see Gordon, 1975, p. 41).

PRE-SMITHIAN DEVELOPMENTS. Towards the end of the 17th century, English economic literature rediscovered the concept of the division of labour and began to analyse the more modern manufacturing form, linking it with productivity growth, cost reduction and increased international competitiveness, and associating its scope with the more extensive markets from increased urbanization. For example, Petty's *Political Arithmetick* written in 1671 compared the benefits of division of labour in textile production with specialization in ship building:

> for as Cloth must be cheaper made, when one Cards, another Spins, another Weaves, another Draws, another Dresses, another Presses and Packs; then when all the Operations above-mentioned, were clumsily performed by the same hand; so those who command the Trade of Shipping [need] to build ... a particular sort of Vessels for each particular Trade (Petty, 1671, pp. 260–61).

Ten years later, in *Another Essay on Political Arithmetic Concerning the Growth of the City of London*, Petty showed that a major gain from a vast city like London came from the improvement and growth of manufactures it encouraged.

> For in so vast a City *Manufactures* will beget one another, and each *Manufacture* will be divided into as many parts as possible, whereby the Work of each *Artisan* will be simple and easy; As for Example. In the making of a *Watch*, if one Man shall make the *Wheels*, another the *Spring*, another shall Engrave the *Dial-plate*, and another shall make the *Cases*, then the *Watch* will be better and cheaper, than if the whole Work be put upon any one man.

In continuing this argument Petty also suggested that specialization benefits could be achieved from concentrating certain manufactures on a particular location, partly because of the savings in transport and communication costs such concentration entailed (Petty, 1683, pp. 471–2). The anonymous author of *Considerations on the East India Trade* (1701, pp. 590–92) illustrated productivity gains from the division of labour by examples drawn from cloth making, watch making and ship building while he clearly indicated that sufficient demand and regular trade were a precondition for such improvements, which lowered manufacturing labour costs without the need to lower wages. During the 18th century, examples of authors aware of benefits and preconditions for a division of labour become more common. Practical writers like Patrick Lindsay (1733), Richard Campbell (1747) and Joseph Harris (1757) tended to concentrate on manufacturing division of labour using examples from linen and pin production as well as from the familiar watch making. Those writing from the position of moral or political philosophy, like Mandeville (1729), Hutcheson (1755) and Josiah Tucker (1755, 1774) concentrated more on aspects of the social division of labour.

Discussion of the division of labour was of course not confined to English economic literature. Among the Physiocrats, Quesnay dealt briefly with the social aspect of the subject in his article 'Natural Right' (1765, p. 51). Turgot developed the subject more thoroughly, making it the starting point of his *Reflections*, subsequently associating it with the introduction of money, the extension of commerce and the accumulation of capital (1766, pp. 44–6, 64, 70). Earlier, Turgot (1751, pp. 242–3) had linked the spread of social division of labour to inequality, arguing that this particular consequence of inequality improved living standards for even the humblest member of society and made possible cultivation of the arts and the sciences. Among the general principles with which Beccaria (1771, pp. 387–8) commenced the argument of this *Elementi*, the division of labour and its benefits in terms of increased skill and dexterity are clearly set out. Finally, it may be noted that the *Encyclopédie* of Diderot and d'Alembert in its article 'Art' discussed the essentials of the manufacturing division of labour, listing its consequences as improvements in skill, better quality product, saving of time and of materials, and 'of making the time or the labour go further, whether by the invention of a new machine or the discovery of a more suitable method'. In its article on pins ('Epingle') their manufacture is described as being generally subdivided into eighteen separate operations and therefore a prime example of the manufacturing division of labour (see Cannan, 1929, pp. 94–5).

ADAM SMITH'S TREATMENT OF THE DIVISION OF LABOUR. Adam Smith's discussion of the division of labour deserves separate treatment not because of its 'originality' or 'completeness of exposition' (Cannan, 1929, p. 96) but because 'nobody, either before or after [him], ever thought of putting such a burden upon division of labour. With A. Smith, it is practically the only factor in economic progress' (Schumpeter, 1954, p. 187). The first three chapters of the *Wealth of Nations* are devoted to its analysis because it provided one of two causes explaining increases in per capita output by which Smith defined the wealth of the nation. Although therefore only one of two causes, the other being 'the proportion between the number of those who are employed in useful labour, and that of those who are not so employed' (Smith, 1776, p. 10) it is the dominant one. Smith seems to have believed that scope for substantial increases in the proportion of the labour force devoted to productive activities was limited. Using the simple equation, $g = (k \cdot p/w) - 1$, developed by Hicks (1965, p. 38) to summarize the Smithian growth process, if change in k, the proportion of production and unproductive labour, is more or less ruled out, a substantial growth rate (g), given the real wage (w), depends exclusively on rising productivity (p) through extensions of the division of labour. Smith's *emphasis* on the division of labour as a factor in growth via its enormous influence on productivity makes his treatment on the subject so original. Surprisingly, this aspect of his contribution was taken up by few 19th-century writers and had to be largely rediscovered in the work of Young (1928)

and Kaldor (1972) who reiterated dynamic aspects of the phenomenon Smith was analysing.

Even though it was the most frequently revised part of his economics (see Meek and Skinner, 1973), Smith's basic account of the division of labour contains a number of weaknesses. First, Smith failed to develop aspects of the manufacturing division of labour with which he ought to have been familiar. Marglin (1974) points out that Smith ignored organizational features associated with a division of labour taking place within the one building of relevance to some well-established industries like textiles and the manufacture of metal implements. There arose from growing labour discipline problems, wasting time and materials, inherent in the putting-out system, then the dominant form of manufacturing organization. In fact it can be suggested that if this aspect of the division of labour is more fully taken into account, its important role in explaining economic growth so much emphasized by Smith is more easily integrated as a major factor explaining the industrial revolution (see Groenewegen, 1977). Marglin (1974) also questioned the force of 'the three different circumstances' by which Smith (1776, p. 17) explained the productivity gains from the division of labour: increased dexterity, saving of time, and invention of machinery. Although increased dexterity is clearly a product of a division of labour in a manufacturing process, this is rather limited when compared to that from the continual practice of surgeons, concert pianists and opera singers, to give a few examples. Time saved in eliminating time lost in passing from job to job is trivial and not the 'very considerable' benefit Smith (1776, pp. 18–19) had suggested. Savings in materials and time through transforming a putting-out to a factory system, an organizational feature of division of labour Smith had ignored, was more important. Rae (1834, pp. 164–5) saw savings in the use of tools as far more significant than time saved and for him (pp. 352–7) this provided the basic reason for extending a division of labour. Other 19th-century writers, particularly Babbage (1832), expanded further on this aspect of the matter. Smith's association of division of labour with inventions (1776, 19–22) covered both 'on the job improvements' and scientific invention by specialists originating from within a more sophisticated division of professions. It ignores, as Hegel (1821, p. 129) was one of the first to point out (cf. Stewart, 1858–75, vol. VIII, pp. 318–19), that as division of labour makes 'work more and more mechanical, ... man is able to step aside and install machines in his place', a feature of the process subsequently noted by Babbage (1832, pp. 173–4), Ure (1835, p. 21) and developed by Marx (1867). In short, the three circumstances Smith saw as explaining the productivity consequences from the division of labour derive their basic validity from reasons different to those Smith advanced. Further, Smith's remarks (1776, pp. 16–17) on the relatively smaller benefits from applying the division of labour to agriculture as compared with manufacturing have been contrasted with his quite different and controversial analysis of the primacy of agricultural investment in terms of its employment of productive labour and its more substantial contributions to gross revenue as subsequently argued (Smith, 1776, Book II, ch. 5), applied by him to define the 'natural' course of economic development (Book III, ch. 1) and recommended as superior practice for newly settled regions like the American colonies. Perelman (1984, p. 145) has solved this apparent contradiction in Smith by suggesting he is the 'first theorist of neo-imperialism' because Smith's strategy of development forces developing regions to specialize in raw material production whose terms of trade with manufactures are invariably poor. More likely, Smith's views on the productivity of agriculture relative to manufacturing are posed in terms of different yardsticks; agricultural activity by the very nature of its processes is less amenable to division of labour, even though its ability to employ productive labour is greater than that produced by equal investments in manufacture and trade. A final controversial issue from Smith's treatment of the division of labour concerns its social consequences, an argument he placed in the context of public education. The 'few simple operations' which under a division of labour most ordinary labouring people are asked to perform, renders them 'as stupid and ignorant as it is possible for a human creature to become' and increased 'dexterity at his own particular trade' is purchased with a reduction in 'intellectual, social and martial virtues ... unless government take some pains to prevent it' through providing general education (Smith, 1776, pp. 781–5). Smith was not alone in presenting this disadvantage of an extensive division of labour: similar views were put by Kames (1774) and Ferguson (1767, p. 280). The last described 'ignorance as the mother of industry' and argued that prosperous manufactures arise 'where the mind is least consulted, and where the workshop may ... be considered as an engine, the parts of which are men'. At the turn of the century and after, German philosophers (for example, Schiller, 1793; Hegel, 1821, and the young Marx, 1844) developed this into a humanist critique of industrial society, suggesting like Smith that such detrimental consequences were removable by education, especially aesthetic education. Such sentiments were resurrected in mid 19th-century England by Carlyle (1843) and Ruskin (1851–3, pp. 197–8). For others, Smith's remarks were an aberration, 'as unfounded [a statement] as can well be imagined' (McCulloch, 1850, p. 350) or even a contradiction with the division of labour's ability to inspire inventive faculties in labourers (West, 1964).

Despite such shortcomings, Smith's account of the division of labour proved particularly hardy and was invariably praised in most general terms by major textbook writers of the 19th century and after, though few followed the emphasis he gave it as a key factor explaining growth. Cannan (1929, p. 97) ascribed this success to 'the popularity of its form'. It can also be attributed to the striking productivity increase inherent in the pin example (cf. Mill, 1821, p. 215) and the unambiguous connection Smith drew between increased division of labour, extending the market and human proclivities 'to truck and barter' (McCulloch, 1825, pp. 54–5). The account of the division of labour is undoubtedly one of Smith's best remembered performances in economics.

19TH-CENTURY DEVELOPMENTS. With the growth of the factory system and more extensive use of increasingly sophisticated machinery, the manufacturing form of division of labour was considerably expanded. Consequently, some economic writers focused on a number of new aspects of the phenomenon, linking the division of labour with developments in the machine tool industry, large scale production and its advantages, and hence, on a more theoretical level, with increasing returns to scale and explicit recognition of a different pattern of productivity growth in manufacturing as compared with agriculture.

Charles Babbage was in many respects the pioneer in presenting the division of labour as 'the most important principle on which the economy of a manufacture depends' (1832, p. 169). He therefore carefully revised the advantages of a division of labour as first expounded by Smith. In this discussion, time (and cost) saving were also related to time saved in learning a skill and reduced waste of materials during the learning process (pp. 170–71), economy in tool using (p. 172), while the association between division of labour, dexterity and the introduction of new machines was developed more precisely and rigorously. Most important, Babbage pointed to a hitherto ignored additional advantage of the division of labour he had derived from observation but had earlier been discussed by Gioja (1815–17), whose interesting contribution to this subject is analysed by Scazzieri (1981, ch. 3).

By dividing the work to be executed into different processes of skill or of force, ... the master manufacturer ... can purchase exactly that precise quantity of both which is necessary for each process; whereas, if the whole work were executed by one workman, that person must possess sufficient skill to perform the most difficult, and sufficient strength to execute the most laborious, of the operations into which the art is divided (Babbage, 1832, pp. 175–6; original italics).

This economy of skill, Babbage demonstrated from a pin example, not only reinforced the cost advantages traditionally associated with division of labour, but was also a major cause of establishing large factories: 'When the number of processes in to which it is most advantageous to divide it, and the number of individuals to be employed in it, are ascertained then all factories which do not employ a direct multiple of this number, will produce the article at a greater cost' (Babbage, 1832, p. 213). Detailed division of labour, Babbage also argued, as in its manufacturing form, can also be applied to mental labour (p. 191) and an illustration of its application to mining highlights its control and information gathering features, two aspects of the division of labour to which Babbage paid particular attention. His analysis of the division of labour is even more important because the process as he described it is made interdependent with machine production, increased factory size, lower costs and prices from such concentration of industry and hence induces growth in demand and an extended market (see Corsi, 1984).

Ure's (1835) contribution must also be noted. It likewise linked development of the factor system to division of labour, summarizing 'the principle of the factory system ... as substituting mechanical science for hand skill, and the partition of a process into its essential constituents' (1835, p. 20). Ure commented on two other consequences of the division of labour in modern factories: de-skilling of the workforce when workers become 'mere overlookers of machines' and the development of mechanical engineering since the 'machine factory displayed the division of labour in manifold gradations' and facilitated the substitution of skilled hands by the planing, the key-groove cutting, and the drilling machines' (pp. 20–21).

Accounts of the division of labour by economists of the middle of the century were generally less innovative than those of Babbage and Ure, though they did occasionally provide some new point of departure. Senior (1836, pp. 74–5, 77) after classifying division of labour as one major advantage from the use of capital, concentrated on listing its benefits additional to those given by Smith. Illustrating from the post office, he argued that 'the same exertions which are necessary to produce a single given result are often sufficient to produce many hundred or many thousands similar results' was one aspect omitted by Smith. The development of retailing as a separate profession was likewise something inadequately dealt with by Smith. More importantly, for a number of reasons but particularly the division of labour, he suggested 'additional Labour when employed in Manufactures is MORE, when employed in Agriculture is LESS efficient in proportion', linking manufacturing activity implicitly to increasing returns to scale (1836, pp. 81–2). Mill (1848) treated division of labour as an important aspect of cooperation, arguing that irrespective of its well-recognized productivity advantages, without this complex cooperation in the modern division of labour 'few things would be produced at all' (p. 118). In discussing the productivity advantages, Mill cited the modification and additional advantages provided by Babbage (1832) and Rae (1834), adding little to their discussion. However, in the following chapter dealing with large and small scale production, he highlighted the point, so ably 'illustrated by Mr. Babbage ... [that] the larger the enterprise, the farther the division of labour may be carried ... as one of the principal causes of large manufactories' (1848, p. 131), thereby bringing this argument firmly into the corpus of economics. Mill's account was largely followed by Fawcett (1863) and in most of its essentials, by Nicholson (1893).

Marx's account (1867, chapters 13–15) combines much of this discussion, endowing it in the process with sharper analytical insights derived from his careful study of both the technical literature and his profound appreciation of the significance of the qualitative changes underlying the evolution of the division of labour. To Marx is owed the important distinction between manufacturing and social division of labour, as well as the precise assessment of the organizational features of its application to modern manufacture derived from his careful study of Babbage, Ure and many other sources. No wonder, that Nicholson (1893, p. 105) described Marx's treatment as 'both learned and exhaustive and ... well worth reading' while more recently, Rosenberg (1976) expressed regret that Marx's close study of 'both the history of technology and its newly emerging forms' has had so few imitators among contemporary economists.

Marshall is another economist from the second half of the 19th century who fully appreciated the importance of the division of labour and revealed it in its more modern form. He devoted no less than three chapters to division of labour in his *Principles* (1890, Book IV, chs 9–11) not only covering most of the points traditionally dealt with under this heading, but often introducing subtle modifications. For example, Marshall (1890, p. 263) discounted detrimental social consequences from monotonous work by pointing to the mental stimulus from the 'social surroundings of the factory' and the view that factory work was not inconsistent with 'considerable intelligence and mental resources'. Likewise, he extended Babbage's principle of 'economy of skill' to economy of machinery and materials (1890, p. 265), used it as a major explanatory factor for the localization of specialized industry (p. 271) and made it the chief advantage of large scale production in his famous discussion of economies of scale (p. 278). Later Marshall applied these aspects of his work to his detailed study of industry and trade to explain such things as America's leadership in standardized production (seen by Marshall, 1919, p. 149, as an 'unprecedented' application of 'Babbage's great principle of economical production'), the successful specialization of plant during World War I, and new issues concerning the growth of the firm. It is therefore paradoxical that Marshall's work in other respects induced the demise of the importance of division of labour in theoretical literature. This arose from the incompatibility of increasing returns to scale with stable supply and demand equilibrium, as he himself showed in Appendix H of the *Principles*. Apart from this, modern equilibrium analysis found it difficult to come to grips with the dynamic features of the division of labour process, and it is presumably at least partly for this

reason that division of labour was dropped as an important subject from the economic textbooks (see Kaldor, 1972).

INTERNATIONAL DIVISION OF LABOUR. Torrens (1808) appears to have been the first economist to distinguish the territorial division of labour from the mechanical division, suggesting that the former is inspired by 'different soils and climates [being] adapted to the growth of different production' thereby inducing regional specialization in those products which best suit 'the varieties of their soil' and climate. Taking advantage of territorial division of labour through regional and international trade enhances productivity and increases the wealth of the nations as much as a manufacturing division of labour. Senior (1836, p. 76) also drew attention to this aspect of the division of labour, attributing its discovery to Torrens. Marshall (1890, pp. 267–77) covered territorial division of labour under localization of industry while Taussig (1911, pp. 41–7) called it the 'geographical division of labour', with gains arising from 'the adaption of different regions to specific articles' for climatic and resources endowment reasons as well as from the general increase in proficiency which all specialization brings. During the 1970s a new dimension of the international division of labour was analysed, concentrating on its direct foreign investment aspects. Its novel features were a tendency to 'undermine the traditional bisection of the world into a few industrialized countries on the one hand, and a great majority of developing countries integrated into the world economy solely as raw material producers on the other, and [secondly, to compel] the increasing subdivision of manufacturing processes into a number of partial operations at different industrial sites throughout the world' to take advantage of advantageous labour market circumstances, relatively cheap transport opportunities, tax breaks and other government inducements for foreign investors (Fröbel et al., 1980, p. 45). This multi-national dimension to application of the division of labour is a direct descendent from the concept as understood by Smith, Babbage, Ure and Marx.

SEXUAL DIVISION OF LABOUR. The first explicit reference to a sexual division of labour in economic literature I could find is Hodgskin (1829, pp. 111–12). He argued that

there is no state of society, probably, in which division of labour between the sexes does not take place. It is and *must* be practised the instant a family exists. Among even the most barbarous tribes, *war* is the exclusive business of the males; they are in general the principal hunters and fishers ... the woman labours in and about the hut ... In modern as well as in ancient times, ... we find the men as the rule taking the out-door work to themselves, leaving the women most of the domestic occupations ... . The aptitude of the sexes for different employments, is only an example of the more general principle, that every human being ... is better adapted than another to some particular occupation.

Marx and Engels (1845–6, pp. 42–3) ascribed beginnings of division of labour 'originally [to] nothing but the division of labour in the sexual act' and only later to that 'spontaneously' or 'naturally' derived from predisposition, needs, accidents and so on. Subsequently, Engels (1884, esp. p. 311) elaborated further on the matter presenting the sexual division of labour in the family as a barrier to the 'emancipation of women'. Such an emancipation, he argued, was 'possible only as a result of modern large-scale industry [which] actually called for the participation of women in production and moreover, strives to convert private domestic work also into a public industry'. Both aspects of the sexual division of labour to which Engels referred in the context of women's emancipation have been taken up in more recent research. The role of domestic labour has been analysed by contemporary writers (see, for example, Himmelweit and Mohun, 1977; Gershuny, 1983) while attention has also been drawn to the shift in the provision of services from domestic production to production for the market (laundromats, take-away food) as a result of a gradual breakdown of the traditional sexual division of labour within the family (Gouverneur, 1978). Sexual division of labour issues have also been applied in segmented labour market analysis, thereby enriching this particular aspect of labour economics.

DECLINE AND REHABILITATION OF DIVISION OF LABOUR IN THE 20TH CENTURY. The association between division of labour and increasing returns, the consequent possibility of falling supply and cost curves created problems for marginalist equilibrium analysis already noted as a factor explaining decline emphasis on division of labour if not its complete elimination from the theoretical literature. Attempts to remove division of labour from economics were also based on other grounds. Robbins (1932, pp. 32–8) argued that study of the 'technical arts of production' belonged to engineering and not to economics, or in the case of 'motion study' to industrial psychology even if this meant removal of traditional topics like division of labour from economics. To some extent this followed Sidgwick's (1883, pp. 104–7) treatment which removed all technical aspects from the topic, leaving only its pure economic side. Others suggested it was better to leave its discussion to sociologists because Durkheim, and before him, Comte and Herbert Spencer, had absorbed division of labour within this then emerging discipline. However, several economists during the 20th century protested that removal of the division of labour constituted a major deficiency in economic understanding particularly that concerned with the dynamics of economic progress.

Allyn Young (1928) was the first of these economists. He made Adam Smith's theorem that the division of labour is limited by the extent of the market the central theme of his presidential address to section F of the British Association, arguing this was 'one of the most illuminating and fruitful generalisations which can be found in the whole literature of economics' (1928, p. 529). Rather than covering all aspects of the division of labour, Young concentrated on two interdependent matters: 'growth of indirect and roundabout methods of production and the division of labour [or increased specialisation] among industries' (ibid.), but the former, as Kaldor (1975, pp. 355–6) pointed out, was not to be confounded with the Austrian capital theoretic notion. From this he deduced division of labour as a cumulative, self-reinforcing process, because every reorganization of production, sometimes narrowly described as a new invention, involves fresh application of scientific progress to industry,

> alters the conditions of industrial activity and initiates responses elsewhere in the industrial structure which in turn have further unsettling effects ... The apparatus of supply and demand in their relation to prices does not seem to be particularly helpful for the purposes of an inquiry into these broader aspects of increasing returns (1928, p. 533).

However, apart from this damaging conclusion for competitive price theory, by ignoring these factors of greater specialization, better combinations of advantages of location, and a consequent increased number of specialized producers between basic raw materials and final producers, the 'possibility of economic progress' could not be fully understood (1928, pp. 538–40).

Kaldor was one of the few major economists who took up Young's challenge in both its critical (Kaldor, 1972, 1975) and more constructive aspects (Kaldor, 1966, 1967). The major thrust of Kaldor's positive argument suggests that faster growth is derived from faster growth in the manufacturing sector, partly because of the cumulative features which link the growth of manufacturing to growth of labour productivity via static and dynamic economies of scale, or the notion of increasing returns as developed by Young from the division of labour. This strong and powerful interaction of productivity growth and manufacturing growth is also included in Verdoorn's Law (1949) but its association with aspects of the discussion of division of labour is what is relevant here. Faster manufacturing growth draws labour from other sectors of the economy, inducing faster productivity growth but as the scope of transferring such labour from lower productivity sectors like agriculture dries up, the growth process slows down (see Thirlwall, 1983). A key feature of the process, as Rowthorn (1975, p. 899, n. 1) noted in one of his skirmishes with Kaldor on the subject, is that it is an interdependent, cumulative historical process where 'higher productivity means more exports which means greater industrial output which via its effects on investment, innovation and *scale of production* reacts back on productivity growth'. The importance of such a process was given detailed empirical examination in a discussion of the Taiwan machine tool industry in the 1970s as an application of a dynamic division of labour, envisaged as increases in output increasing productivity, with 'technological change, broadly defined, sandwiched in between' (Amsden, 1985, p. 271).

Viewed dynamically within the context of economic growth, as Smith (1776) and others had intended the division of labour to be viewed, it continues to be a powerful tool for understanding the process of economic growth, and on this ground alone can therefore not be jettisoned from economics as unwanted baggage as Robbins mistakenly had suggested. When its importance for understanding aspects of the labour process, the labour market and the theory of production contemplated at the plant and industry level is included, this argument is even stronger. The importance of the division of labour for economics is finally underlined by the fact that the greatest economic minds of the past invariably included it in their treatises on the subject.

PETER GROENEWEGEN

See also DURKHEIM, EMILE; INCREASING RETURNS; RANK; SMITH, ADAM; YOUNG, ALLYN ABBOT.

BIBLIOGRAPHY
Amsden, A.H. 1985. The division of labour is limited by the rate of growth of the market; the Taiwan machine tool industry in the 1970s. *Cambridge Journal of Economics* 9, 271–84.
Anonymous, 1701. *Considerations on the East-India trade.* In *A Select Collection of Early English Tracts on Commerce*, ed. J.R. McCulloch, London, 1856. Reissued Cambridge: Cambridge University Press, 1954.
Babbage, C. 1832. *On the Economy of Machinery and Manufactures.* London. Fourth enlarged edn of 1835, reissued New York: Augustus M. Kelley, 1963.
Beccaria, C. 1771. *Elementi di economia publica.* In *Opere*, ed. S. Romagnoli, Florence: Sansoni, 1958.
Bonar, J. 1893. *Philosophy and Political Economy.* 3rd edn, London: Allen & Unwin, 1967.
Braverman, H. 1974. *Labor and Monopoly Capital. The Degradation of Work in the Twentieth Century.* New York: Montly Review Press.

Campbell, R. 1747. *The London Tradesman.* London.

Cannan, E. 1929. *Review of Economic Theory.* London: P.S. King & Son.

Carlyle, T. 1843. *Past and Present.* London: Chapman & Hall. Another edn, London: G. Routledge & Sons, 1893.

Corsi, M. 1984. Il sistema di fabbrica e la divisione del lavore; il pensiero di Charles Babbage. *Quaderni di Storia dell' economia politica* 3, 111–23.

Engels, F. 1884. *Origin of the Family, Private Property and the State.* Reprinted in *Marx–Engels Selected Works* Vol. II, Moscow, 1958.

Fawcett, H. 1863. *Manual of Political Economy.* London and Cambridge: Macmillan & Co.

Ferguson, A. 1767. *An Essay on the History of Civil Society.* Edinburgh.

Foley, V. 1974. The division of labour in Plato and Smith. *History of Political Economy* 6(2), 220–42.

Fröbel, F., Heinrichs, J. and Kreye, O. 1980. *The New International Division of Labour.* Trans. Pete Burgess, Cambridge: Cambridge University Press.

Gershuny, J. 1983. *Social Innovation and Division of Labour.* Oxford: Oxford University Press.

Gioja, M. 1815–17. *Nuovo Prospetto delle scienze economiche.* Milan: G. Pirotta.

Gordon, B. 1975. *Economic Analysis Before Adam Smith.* London: Macmillan.

Gouverneur, J. 1978. *Contemporary Capitalism and Marxist Economics.* Trans. R. le Fanu, Oxford: Robertson, 1983.

Groenewegen, P. 1977. Adam Smith and the division of labour: a bi-centenary estimate. *Australian Economic Papers* 16, 161–74.

Harris, J. 1757. *An Essay Upon Money and Coins.* Part I. London: G. Hawkins.

Hegel, G.W.F. 1821. *Philosophy of Right.* Trans. T.M. Knox, Oxford: Clarendon Press, 1962.

Hicks, J.R. 1965. *Capital and Growth.* Oxford: Clarendon Press.

Himmelweit, S. and Mohun, S. 1977. Domestic labour and capital. *Cambridge Journal of Economics* 1, 15–31.

Hodgskin, T. 1827. *Popular Political Economy.* London: C. Tait. Reissued, New York: A.M. Kelley, 1966.

Hutcheson, F. 1755. *A System of Moral Philosophy.* Glasgow.

Kaldor, N. 1966. *Causes of the Slow Rate of Economic Growth of the United Kingdom.* Cambridge: Cambridge University Press.

Kaldor, N. 1967. *Strategic Factors in Economic Development.* Ithaca: State School of Industrial and Labor Relations, Cornell University.

Kaldor, N. 1972. The irrelevance of equilibrium economics. *Economic Journal* 82, 1237–55.

Kaldor, N. 1975. What is wrong with economic theory? *Quarterly Journal of Economics* 89, 347–57.

Kames, H.H. 1774. *Sketches of the History of Man.* Edinburgh: W. Creech; London: W. Strathan and T. Cadell.

Lindsay, P. 1733. *The Interest of Scotland Considered.* Edinburgh: R. Fleming & Co.

McCulloch, J.R. 1825. *Principles of Political Economy.* Reprinted London: Murray, 1870.

McCulloch, J.R. 1850. Introduction and notes to Adam Smith, *An Enquiry into the Nature and Causes of the Wealth of Nations.* 4th edn, Edinburgh: A. and C. Black; London: Longman.

Mandeville, B. 1729. *The Fable of the Bees.* Part 2. London: J. Roberts.

Marglin, S. 1974. What do bosses do: the origins and function of hierarchy in capitalist production. *Review of Radical Political Economics* 6, 60–112.

Marshall, A. 1890. *Principles of Economics.* 8th edn, London: Macmillan & Co., 1920.

Marshall, A. 1919. *Industry and Trade.* 3rd edn, London: Macmillan & Co.

Marx, K. 1844. *Economic and Philosophic Manuscripts.* Reprinted Moscow: Foreign Languages Publishing House, 1959.

Marx, K. 1867. *Capital,* Vol. 1. Moscow: Foreign Languages Publishing House, 1959.

Marx, K. and Engels, F. 1845–6. *The German Ideology.* Reprinted Moscow: Progress Publishers, 1964.

Meek, R.L. and Skinner, A.S. 1973. The development of Adam Smith's ideas on the division of labour. *Economic Journal* 83, 1094–116.

Mill, J. 1821. Elements of Political Economy. 3rd edn reprinted in *The Selected Economic Writings of James Mill,* ed. D.N. Winch, Edinburgh: Oliver & Boyd for the Scottish Economic Society, 1966.

Mill, J.S. 1848. *Principles of Political Economy.* Available in *Collected Works on John Stuart Mill,* Vols II and III, ed. J.M. Robson, Toronto: University of Toronto Press, 1965.

Nicholson, J.S. 1893. *Principles of Political Economy.* 2nd edn, London: A. & C. Black, 1902.

Perelman, M. 1984. *Classical Political Economy: Primitive Accumulation and the Social Division of Labour.* London: Rowman & Allenheld.

Petty, W. 1671. *Political Arithmetick.* In *Economic Writings of Sir William Petty,* ed. C.H. Hull, reissued New York: A.M. Kelley, 1963.

Petty, W. 1683. *Another essay on political arithmetick concerning the growth of the city of London.* In *Economic Writings of Sir William Petty,* ed. C.H. Hull, reissued New York: A.M. Kelley, 1963.

Plato, 380 BC. *The Republic.* Trans. H.D.P. Lee, Harmondsworth: Penguin Classics, 1955.

Quesnay, F. 1765. *Natural Right.* Extracts trans. in R.L. Meek, *The Economics of Physiocracy,* London: George Allen & Unwin, 1962.

Rae, J. 1834. *Statement of Some New Principles on the Subject of Political Economy.* Reissued New York: A.M. Kelley, 1964.

Robbins, L. 1932. *An Essay on the Nature and Significance of Economic Science.* 2nd edn, London: Macmillan & Co., 1935.

Rosenberg, N. 1976. Marx as a student of technology. *Monthly Review* 28, 56–77. Reprinted in N. Rosenberg, *Inside the Black Box; Technology and Economics,* Cambridge: Cambridge University Press, 1982.

Rowthorn, R.E. 1975. A reply to Lord Kaldor's comment. *Economic Journal* 85, 897–901.

Ruskin, J. 1851–3. *The Stones of Venice.* In *The Complete Works of John Ruskin,* ed. E.T. Cook and A. Wedderburn, London: George Allen, 1904.

Scazzieri, R. 1981. *Efficienza, produttiva e livelli di attivatà.* Bologna: Il Mulino.

Schiller, F. 1793. *On the Aesthetic Education of Man.* Translated by R. Snell, New York: Ungar, 1980.

Schumpeter, J.A. 1954. *History of Economic Analysis.* New York, London: Oxford University Press.

Senior, N. 1836. *An Outline of the Science of Political Economy.* Reprinted, London: G. Allen & Unwin, 1938, 1951.

Sidgwick, H. 1883. *Principles of Political Economy.* 2nd edn, London: Macmillan & Co., 1887.

Smith, A. 1776. *An Inquiry into the Nature and Causes of the Wealth of Nations.* Ed. R.H. Campbell and A.S. Skinner, Oxford: Clarendon Press, 1976.

Stewart, D. 1858–75. *Collected Works of Dugald Stewart.* Edited by Sir William Hamilton, Edinburgh.

Taussig, F.W. 1911. *Principles of Economics.* 3rd edn, New York: The Macmillan Co., 1936.

Thirlwall, A.P. 1983. A plain man's guide to Kaldor's growth laws. *Journal of Post-Keynesian Economics* 5, 345–58.

Torrens, R. 1808. *The Economists Refuted.* Reprinted, Sydney:Sydney University, Department of Economics, Reprints of Economic Classics, 1984.

Tucker, J. 1755. *The Elements of Commerce and Theory of Taxes.* London.

Tucker, J. 1774. *Four Tracts on Political and Commercial Subjects.* 2nd edn, Gloucester: R. Raikes.

Turgot, A.R.J. 1751. Lettre à Madame de Graffigny sur les lettres d'une Péruvienne. In *Oeuvres de Turgot et Documents le concernant,* Vol. I, ed. G. Schelle, Paris: F. Alcan, 1913.

Turgot, A.R.J. 1766. *Reflections on the Production and Distribution of Wealth.* In *The Economics of A.R.J. Turgot,* ed. P.D. Groenewegen, The Hague: Nijjhoff, 1977.

Ure, A. 1835. *The Philosophy of Manufactures.* London: C. Knight. Reissued London: Cass, 1967.

Verdoorn, P.J. 1949. Fattori che regolano lo sviluppo della produttività del lavoro. *L'Industria* 1, 45–53.

West, E.G. 1964. Adam Smith's two views of the division of labour. *Economica* 3, 23–32.

Young, A. 1928. Increasing returns and economic progress. *Economic Journal* 38, 327–42.

Dmitriev, Vladimir Karpovich (1868–1913). Vladimir Karpovich Dmitriev was the first Russian mathematical economist. His *Economic Essays on Value, Competition and Utility* (1898, 1902; English edition 1974) are a classic text in economic literature.

Vladimir Karpovich Dmitriev was born on 24 November 1868 on the Rai Estate in Smolensk Gubernia, Smolensk Uezd. On completing his classical education at the Tula Classical Gymnasium he went to Moscow University to study medicine but subsequently transferred to the Law Faculty where he began his studies in Political Economy. After graduation in 1896 he married T.A. Vatatsi and left to take the post of excise controller in the small town of Von'kovitsy in Podol'sk Gubernia. He served there for three years but contracted lung tuberculosis and had to leave the service. He was in great need all his life and his chronic illness eventually aggravated and caused his death on 30 November 1913.

Dmitriev's First Essay on *The theory of value of D. Ricardo* was published in 1898, followed in 1902 by a Second Essay on *The competition theory of A. Cournot* and a Third Essay on *The theory of marginal utility* (published together and with a Conclusion); the three essays were reprinted and issued together in 1904. He also published a large volume on the consumption of alcohol in Russia (with an introduction by P.V. Struve) in 1911 and half a dozen articles on the same topics as his books. He was planning at least three further Essays on rent, on industrial crises and on monetary circulation, which apparently were never written or at any rate published.

Dmitriev's contributions to economic theory include: (i) the development of an input–output method for the determination of the quantity of labour directly and indirectly embodied in commodities; (ii) a theory of production prices based on dated labour, similar to that of Piero Sraffa; (iii) a statement of 'wage–profit frontier' derived from technology and alternative level of real wage; (iv) a theory of non-productive costs in competition between firms. While these contributions do not amount quite to the 'organic synthesis of the labour theory of value and the theory of marginal utility' promised in the title page of the 1902 and 1904 editions of the *Essays*, they are highly original and remarkable in their anticipation of subsequent work. Dmitriev's propositions on labour values and production prices gained early recognition (Chuprov, 1905; Bortkiewicz 1907, who praised and used extensively 'this remarkable work'; Struve 1908, who hailed Dmitriev as a 'logically and mathematically thought-out Ricardo'; and Shaposhnikov's memorial lecture a year after his death, 1914). Until shortly after the October revolution Dmitriev was widely mentioned in Russian economic literature, then he was entirely forgotten until the Soviet school of mathematical economists brought him out of his official oblivion circa 1960 (Nemchinov, 1959; Belkin, Grobman, Lunts, in Aganbegyan–Belkin, 1961) attracting the attention of Western scholars (Nove–Zauberman, 1961; Zauberman, 1962).

In his first Essay Dmitriev considers the question 'how is it possible to calculate the amount of labour expended for the production of a given economic good from the very beginning of history, when man managed without capital, down to the present time' (p. 43 of the English edition, to which all page references are made here). He answers that there is no need for 'historical digressions' of this kind; the quantity of labour N_A which goes directly and indirectly into the production of commodity A is expressed by the equation

$$N_A = n_A + \frac{1}{m_1} N_1 + \frac{1}{m_2} N_2 + \cdots + \frac{1}{m_M} N_M \qquad (1)$$

where n_A is the *direct* labour input of a unit of commodity A: $1/m_i$ is the amount of the ith commodity *used up* in the production of commodity A, where $i = 1, 2, \ldots, M$; and N_i is the labour directly and indirectly embodied in the ith commodity (this is equation (6) in the First Essay, p. 44). The coefficient $1/m_i$ here is to be interpreted either as the inter-mediate inputs requirement for the production of the A commodity, or as the straight-line amortization of the ith fixed capital good (assuming uniform productiveness over its lifetime); some of these coefficients may be equal to zero, as in Dmitriev's system of equations (7) in the First Essay. For each of the M other commodities there is an equation of the same form, relating labour (directly and indirectly) embodied to input coefficients and the labour embodied in the inputs (p. 44). We obtain a system of $(M + 1)$ equations in $(M + 1)$ unknowns,

> which is always adequate for the determination of N, giving the required sum of the labour expended on the production of product A. Therefore, without any digressions into the prehistoric times of the first inception of technical capital, we can always find the total sum of the labour directly and indirectly expended on the production of any product *under present day production conditions*, both of this product itself and of those capital goods involved in its production (p. 44, emphasis in the text).

This is clearly a full-fledged input–output system, where N_i are the full coefficients of labour, the N_i are the direct labour inputs, and the $1/m$ are identical with Leontief's input–output coefficients. The analytical apparatus provided by Leontief four decades later adds two things: (i) a method for the actual computation of the solution, namely the inversion of the matrix $(I\text{-}A')$, where I is the identity matrix and A' is the transpose of the matrix of technical coefficients; and (ii) the generalization of notion of full input (i.e. direct and indirect input requrements) from labour to other production inputs. In Leontief's type of notation, if we call a_{ij} the amount of ith product required per unit of the jth product, A the $[a_{ij}]$ matrix: a_{oj} the direct labour input of product j, and a the column vector $[a_{oj}]$; and f_{ij} the full-input coefficient, i.e. the element of the $(I\text{-}A')^{-1}$ matrix, we obtain

$$f_{ik} = \sum_{j=1}^{n} a_{ij} f_{jk} + \delta_{ik} \qquad (2)$$

where $i, k, j = 1, 2, \ldots, n$; and f_{ik} is Kronecker's delta, i.e. is equal to zero except for $i = k$ when it is equal to unity. If we indicate full labour inputs (i.e. Dmitriev's Ns) by f_{ok}, Leontief's approach gives

$$f_{ok} = \sum_{j=1}^{n} a_{oi} f_{jk} \qquad (3)$$

or

$$\mathbf{f}_o = (\mathbf{I} - \mathbf{A}')^{-1} \mathbf{a} \qquad (4)$$

where $\mathbf{F}_o = [f_{ok}]$ Dmitriev's formulation of full labour inputs is

$$f_{ok} = a_{ok} + \sum_{j=1}^{n} f_{oj} a_{jk} \qquad (3')$$

or

$$\mathbf{f}_o = \mathbf{a} + \mathbf{A}' \mathbf{f}_o \qquad (4')$$

which is just another way of rewriting Leontief's equation (4).

The importance of Dmitriev's approach for socialist planning was already understood in the 1920s; A.V. Chayanov (1926) developed Dmitriev's scheme into an input–output table for agriculture. In the 1960s the ability to claim Russian priority in the discovery of input–output equations in the work of Dmitriev was an important step in the struggle for the use of mathematical methods in socialist planning. In 1962 the Central Statistical Administration produced an 83×83 intersectoral balance of labour outlays in the Soviet economy for 1959–60, using the first *ex-post* input-output tables for the Soviet economy, compiled for 1959. This balance shows, in terms of labour, the inter-industrial flows, the formation of the final bill of goods, the formation of national product and cost incurred in the non-productive sphere (see Eidel'man, 1962, Zauberman, 1963). This calculation corresponds exactly to the Dmitriev–Leontief full labour coefficients.

Dmitriev also had a theory of *prices of production* which is a reformulation and development of Ricardian price theory and corresponds to Marxian production prices. Dmitriev starts from the refutation of the criticism levied in his time (for instance by Walras) against the 'classical' theory of price determination based on production costs, 'that it defines price from prices, that it defines one unknown from other unknowns' (p. 41). This allegation, Dmitriev argues, can be levied against Adam Smith, who did not deal with the problem of the determination of the profit rate, except for a vague reference to the demand for and supply of capital, i.e. going outside the sphere of production. But Ricardo is not subject to this criticism; indeed 'The most important point in Ricardo's theory is undoubtedly his theory of the conditions defining the "average" profit rate...' and 'Ricardo's immortal contribution was his brilliant solution of this seemingly insoluble problem' (pp. 50 and 58, First Essay).

For the study of *prices* (or *values*, in his terminology) Dmitriev uses a framework slightly different from that employed for the study of *labour values* (or labour embodied in commodities). Instead of extending his *point input–point output* framework, whereby commodities are produced by means of labour and other commodities (equation (1)), he uses an Austrian-type model where commodities are produced by dated labour, i.e. a *flow input-point output* framework, whereby commodities are produced by dated labour. For each commodity Dmitriev formulates a price equation of the type:

$$X_A = n_A a X_a (1+r)'^A + n_1 a X_a (1+r)'^{A1} + \cdots$$
$$\cdots + n_m a X_a (1+r)'^{Am} \quad (5)$$

where X_A is the price of commodity A, a is the amount of wage good (say, corn) consumed by workers, X_a is the unit price of the wage good; $n_A, n_1, \ldots, n_m$ are the labour inputs required respectively $t_A, t_{A1}, \ldots, t_{Am}$ time units before the output of commodity A becomes available (this is equation (25), p. 54). If there are M commodities in addition to the wage good, we have $(M+1)$ equations; there are M relative prices to be determined, in terms of an arbitrary commodity whose price is taken as unit of account, plus the profit rate; the system is complete and can simultaneously determine relative price and the profit rate.

It is to Ricardo's credit that he was the first to note that there is one production equation by means of which we may determine the magnitude of r *directly* (i.e. without having recourse for assistance to the other equations). This equation gives us the production conditions of the product a to which in the final analysis the expenditure on all the products, $A, B, C, \ldots$, is reduced (p. 59).

For the wage good, with labour inputs N_i,

$$X_a = a X_a [N_a (1+r)^{t_a} + N_I (1+r)^{t_{a1}} + \cdots + N_1 (1+r)^{t_{aq}}]. \quad (6)$$

From this (equation (44), First Essay) we can obtain

$$a_i = \frac{1}{\sum_i N_i (1+r)^i} \quad (7)$$

which today is familiar as the 'wage-profit frontier': Dmitriev writes it instead in the implicit form

$$r = F(N_a, N_1, \ldots, N_q; t_a, t_{a1}, \ldots, t_{aq}; a). \quad (8)$$

Dmitriev then extends this analysis to the case where workers consume not a single commodity but a number of commodities in fixed proportions. The condition for a positive profit rate to arise is that 'we can obtain a *larger* quantity of the same product within some finite period of time as a result of the production process' (p. 62).

Dmitriev, in sum, considers 'production of commodities by means of dated labour', not 'production of commodities by means of commodities' (at least when discussing the determination of the profit rate), with wages being advanced, not 'posticipated' as in Sraffa (1960). Their similarity descends from the common Ricardian root. Although Dmitriev's approach is close to Marx, he goes out of his way to *deny* the Marxian theory of exploitation and to show, 'proceeding from Ricardo's analysis, that the origin of industrial profit does not stand in any "special" relationship to the human labour used in production' (p. 64), In order to do this, Dmitriev investigates the properties of an imaginary system where work is performed exclusively by animals and machines. The conditions for a positive profit rate are shown to be quite general; however, the fact that we do not usually talk of 'exploitation' of animals and machines does not in any conceivable sense rule out the proposition of *human* exploitation when *human* labour *is* actually used in production.

Having formulated and developed Ricardian propositions on prices of production Dmitriev proceeds to show that these propositions hold only under the most restrictive assumptions. Among these are constant returns to scale, i.e. zero rents, *and* perfect competition of a kind that brings prices down to the (constant) necessary costs of commodities (including profit at a rate determined by technology and the real wage). He decidedly parts company from Ricardo and shows that whenever at least one of these conditions is not satisfied prices depend on *demand conditions* as well, and not even 'long-run' equilibrium prices can be obtained purely from the knowledge of technology and the real wage.

Already at the end of the First Essay, Dmitriev shows that a demand price based exclusively on production conditions cannot handle the cases of monopoly prices and of positive rent. But the greatest blow to the Ricardian theory of price determination is given in the Second Essay, where Dmitriev most emphatically argues that demand conditions contribute to price determination also for 'goods which are infinitely reproducible by labour under conditions excluding the possibility of the occurrence of rent' (p. 92) even under competitive conditions. In order to do this, Dmitriev challenges the proposition that 'competition lowers prices' (p. 93) and starting from Cournot's analysis of competition he constructs a theory of unrestricted but not-so-perfect competition.

Dmitriev argues that the assumption that supply = production contradicts not only economic reality, but also the other basic hypothesis of competitive analysis, 'that every individual tends to pursue the greatest advantage' (p. 118). He relaxes the assumption to allow for stocks and unused capacity, representing *potential* supply. Dmitriev postulates that *for a given volume of production* rational behaviour of producers leads them to a tacit collusion on price, i.e. joint profit maximisation as in the monopoly case, but (i) such collusion is enforceable only because of the existence of a potential threat in the form of a potential supply greater than the collusion sales level, and (ii) competition between producers takes the form of expanding the level of potential supply, with sales lagging behind. For a given number *n* of producers there is an equilibrium potential supply such that the price corresponds to what would be charged by a monopolist. For *n* tending to infinity, the cost of the potential supply tends to equal the revenue from actual sales; profit (over and above the interest component of production costs) is zero, as in the customary competitive equilibrium, not because price is equal to the necessary production cost of the output sold, but because the additional cost of holding stocks or installing unused capacity brings the total cost of potential output up to the level of actual sales revenue and wipes out profits completely (p. 134).

A further instance of unproductive expenditure is mentioned by Dmitriev in his Conclusion, namely 'advertising' to expand sales of an individual entrepreneur *when the total sales level remains the same.* In a notable passage Dmitriev compares the role of commodity stocks with the strategy of 'intensified armament of the Powers in peace time' (pp. 148–9). It follows from this analysis that unrestricted competition has a cost for the economy, i.e. a *social cost of wasted output*, excess inventories, unused capacity or redundant advertising. This is only partly compensated by consumers' gain from prices lower than monopoly prices.

A most important implication of Dmitriev's analysis is his account of the economic consequences of technical progress (Section 7), which raises the level of potential supply at which the *temporary profit*, obtained by individual producers breaking their tacit price-collusion, disappears. 'Therefore an *expansion of output following a reduction of production costs will, in general, extend not only to an expansion of supply but also to an increase in excess commodity inventories* (p. 171). The building up of excess commodity inventories following technical progress gives rise to fluctuations in the levels of output capacity, capacity utilization, and inventory levels (pp. 173–8). When technical progress takes place, 'overproduction' periodically occurs, and this '*is in no sense a result of errors of economic judgement,* i.e. it is not a consequence of the inability of production to adapt to excessively variable demand...but is a direct result of the struggle of competing entrepreneurs, *each of whom is motivated in his own actions by quite correct economic judgement*' (p. 117).

The only way of eliminating wasted output, excess inventories and unused capacity, and the non-productive costs which these involve, is the establishment of forward markets (*Terminhandel*): 'forward contracts make non-productive "reserve stocks" unnecessary since they make it possible to sell goods which have still not been produced but merely can be produced...' (p. 178, footnote 1). Dmitriev relegates this qualification to a footnote, but this is really a central point in his argument, except that – we now know – forward markets would have to be not only complete but also exclusive (i.e. no future spot markets could reopen), which is neither practical nor advisable.

For Dmitriev the short-run equilibrium of an economic system is determined by the given levels of supply and the demand functions. He concludes that if prices of commodities happen to coincide with their necessary reproduction costs, actual prices will correspond to the solution of the Walrasian system. But if the supply level of a commodity is such that its price exceeds its necessary reproduction costs, the question of the distribution of the extra-normal profit lies, for Dmitriev, 'outside the sphere of economic research', because it is the result of a 'struggle' and is taken as a question of fact by economic theory. There may be 'a general sociological solution' (p. 207); 'Otherwise we should have to admit that the question cannot have any general solution at all' (*ibid*). Ultimately, price theory becomes the theory of the self-defeating attempts, by economic agents, to gain from a social struggle which is rational by the standards of individuals though not of society, and the theory of the ensuing waste and fluctuations.

D.M. NUTI

SELECTED WORKS

1898. *Ekonomicheskie Ocherki*, Vyp, I, 'Teoriya tsênnosti D. Ricardo (opyt' tochnago analyza)' [*Economic Essays*, Issue I, 'The theory of value of D. Ricardo, an attempt at a rigorous analysis']. Moscow.

1902. *Ekonomicheskie Ocherki*, 'Chast' l-aya (opyt' organicheskago sinteza trudovoi teorii tsênnosti i teorii predêl'noi poleznosti)', Vypuski 2-i i 3-i. Ocherk 2-i: 'Teoriya konkurrentsii Og. Kurno (Velikago "zabytago" ekonomista)'. Ocherk 3-i: 'Teoriya predêl'noi poleznosti' [*Economic Essays*, Part I, Attempt at an organic synthesis of the labour theory of value and the theory of marginal utility, Issues 2 and 3. Second Essay: The theory of competition of A. Cournot (the great 'forgotten' economist). Third Essay: The theory of marginal utility]. Moscow.

1904. *Ekonomicheskie Ocherki* (Seriya l-aya: 'opyt' organicheskago sinteza trudovoi toerii tsênnosti i teorii predêl'noi poleznosti') [*Economic Essays*, First Series: Attempt at an organic synthesis of the labour theory of value and the theory of marginal utility]. Moscow.

1911. *Kriticheskie izslêdovaniya o potreblenii alkogolya v Rossii*, s predisl. P.B. Struve, Issledovaniya i raboty po polit. ekonomii i obshchestv. znaniyam, izd. pod red. P.B. Struve, Vyp. I [*Critical Studies on the consumption of alcohol in Russia*, with an introduction by P.V. Struve: Studies and works in political economy and social sciences, edited by P.V. Struve, Issue I]. Moscow. (With an English translation of the table of contents.)

1974. *Economic Essays on Value, Competition and Utility*. Edited with an introduction by D.M. Nuti, Cambridge: Cambridge University Press.

BIBLIOGRAPHY

Belkin, V.D. 1961. Natsionalnyi dokhod i mezhotraslevoy balans [National income and intersectoral balance]. In *Primenenie matematiki i elektronnoy tekhniki v planirovanii* [The use of mathematics and electronic techniques in planning], ed. A.G. Aganbegyan and V.D. Belkin, Moscow.

Bortkiewicz von L. 1906. Wertrechnung und Preisrechnung im Marxschen Sistem, (in three parts). *Archiv für Sozialwissenschaft und Sozialpolitik* 23(1) 1907, 25(1); 1907, 25(2). The second and the third parts are translated into English, as 'Value and Price in the Marxian System', *International Economic Papers*, 1952, no. 2.

Eidel'man, M.R. 1962. Pervyi mezhotraslevoi balans zatrat truda v narodnom khoziaistve SSSR [The first intersectoral balance of labour expenditures in the national economy of the USSR]. *Vestnik Statistiki*, no. 10, 1962.

Leontief, W.W. 1941. *The Structure of the American Economy 1919–1939*. New York: Oxford University Press.

Leontief, W.W., et al. 1953. *Studies in the Structure of the American Economy: Theoretical and Empirical Explorations in Input Output Analysis*. White Plains, NY: International Arts and Science Press.

Nemchinov, V.S. 1959. The use of mathematical methods in economics. In *The Use of Mathematics in Economics*, ed. V.S. Nemchinov Moscow. English translation edited by A. Nove, London, 1964.

Nemchinov, V.S. 1961. *A model of an economic region*, Moscow. Translated in *Mathematical Studies in Economics and Statistics in the USSR and Eastern Europe*, Vol. 1, 1964, p. 14.

Nemchinov, V.S. 1963. Basic elements of a model of planned price formation. *Voprosy Ekonomiki*, no. 12. Translated in *Socialist Economics*, ed A. Nove and D.M. Nuti, Harmondsworth: Penguin, 1972.

Nove, A. and Zauberman, A. 1961. A resurrected Russian economist of 1900. *Soviet Studies* 13, July, 96–101.

Shaposhnikov, N.N. 1914. *Pervyi Russkii ekonomist-matematik Vladimir Karpovich Dmitriev, Doklad v posvyashchennom pamyati Dmitrieva zasêdanii O-va im. A.I. Chuprova* [The first Russian mathematical economist V.K. Dmitriev, a lecture as a meeting of the A.I. Chuprov Society, held in memory of Dmitriev]. Moscow.

Sraffa, P. 1960. *Production of Commodities by Means of Commodities.* Cambridge: Cambridge University Press.

Zauberman, A. 1962. A few remarks on a discovery in Soviet economics. *Bulletin of the Oxford Institute of Economics and Statistics* 24 November, 437–45.

Zauberman, A. 1963. A note on the Soviet inter-industry labour input balance. *Soviet Studies* 15, July, 53–7.

Dobb, Maurice Herbert (1900–1976). Maurice Dobb was undoubtedly one of the outstanding political economists of this century. He was a Marxist, and was one of the most creative contributors to Marxian economics. As Ronald Meek put it, in his obituary of Dobb for the British Academy, 'over a period of fifty years [Dobb] established and maintained his position as one of the most eminent Marxist economists in the world'. Dobb's *Political Economy and Capitalism* (1937) and *Studies in the Development of Capitalism* (1946) stand out as his two most outstanding contributions to Marxian economics. The former is primarily concerned with economic theory (including such subjects as value theory, economic crises, imperialism, socialist economies), and the latter with economic history (particularly the emergence of capitalism from feudalism). These two fields – economic theory and economic history – were intimately connected in Dobb's approach to economics. He also wrote an influential book on Soviet economic development. This was first published under the title *Russian Economic Development since the Revolution* (1928), and later in a revised edition as *Soviet Economic Development since 1917* (1948).

Maurice Dobb was born on 24 July 1900 in London. His father Walter Herbert Dobb had a draper's retail business and his mother Elsie Annie Moir came from a Scottish merchant's family. He was educated at Charterhouse, and then at Pembroke College, Cambridge, where he studied economics. This was followed by two postgraduate years at the London School of Economics, where he did his PhD on 'The Entrepreneur'. The thesis formed the basis of his book *Capitalist Enterprise and Social Progress* (1925). Dobb returned to Cambridge at the end of 1924 on being appointed as a Lecturer in Economics. He taught in Cambridge until his retirement in 1967. He was a Fellow of Trinity College, and was elected to a University Readership in 1959. He received honorary degrees from the Charles University of Prague, the University of Budapest, and Leicester University, and was elected a Fellow of the British Academy. After retirement he and his wife, Barbara, stayed on in the neighbouring village of Fulbourn. He died on 17 August 1976.

Dobb was a theorist of great originality and reach. He was also, throughout his life, deeply concerned with economic policy and planning. His foundational critique of 'market socialism' as developed by Oscar Lange and Abba Lerner, appeared in the *Economic Journal* of 1933, later reproduced along with a number of related contributions in his *On Economic Theory and Socialism* (1955). His relatively elementary book *Wages* (1928) presented not merely a simple

introduction to labour economics, but also an alternative outlook on these questions, including their policy implications, leading to interesting disputations with John Hicks, among others. In later years Dobb was much concerned with planning for economic development. In three lectures delivered at the Delhi School of Economics, later published as *Some Aspects of Economic Development* (1951), Dobb discussed some of the central issues of development planning for an economy with unemployed or underutilized labour, and his ideas were more extensively developed in his later book, *An Essay on Economic Growth and Planning* (1957).

Maurice Dobb also published a number of papers on more traditional fields in economic theory, including welfare economics, and some of these papers were collected together in his *Welfare Economics and the Economics of Socialism* (1969). In his *Theories of Value and Distribution since Adam Smith: Ideology and Economic Theory* (1973), he responded *inter alia* to the new developments in Cambridge political economy, including the influential 'Prelude to a Critique of Economic Theory' by Piero Sraffa (1960). Maurice Dobb's association with Piero Sraffa extended over a long period, both as a colleague at Trinity College, and also as a collaborator in editing *Works and Correspondence of David Ricardo*, published in eleven volumes between 1951 and 1973 (on the latter, see Pollitt, 1985).

In addition to academic writings, Maurice Dobb also did a good deal of popular writing, both for workers' education and for general public discussion. He wrote a number of pamphlets, including *The Development of Modern Capitalism* (1922), *Money and Prices* (1924), *An Outline of European History* (1926), *Modern Capitalism* (1927), *On Marxism Today* (1932), *Planning and Capitalism* (1937), *Soviet Planning and Labour in Peace and War* (1942), *Marx as an Economist, An Essay* (1943), *Capitalism Yesterday and Today* (1958), and *Economic Growth and Underdeveloped Countries* (1963), and many others. Dobb was a superb communicator, and the nature of his own research was much influenced by policy debates and public discussions. Dobb the economist was not only close to Dobb the historian, but also in constant company of Dobb the member of the public. It would be difficult to find another economist who could match Dobb in his extraordinary combination of genuinely 'high-brow' theory, on the one hand, and popular writing on the other. The author of *Political Economy and Capitalism* (from the appearance of which – as Ronald Meek (1978) rightly notes – 'that future historians of economic thought will probably date the emergence of Marxist economics as a really serious economic discipline', was also spending a good deal of effort writing pamphlets and material for labour education, and doing straightforward journalism. It is not possible to appreciate fully Maurice Dobb's contributions to economics without taking note of his views of the role of economics in public discussions and debates.

Another interesting issue in understanding Dobb's approach to economics concerns his adherence to the labour theory of value. The labour theory has been under attack not only from neoclassical economists, but also from such anti-neoclassical political economists as Joan Robinson and, indirectly, even Piero Sraffa. In his last major work, *Theories of Value and Distribution since Adam Smith* (1973), Maurice Dobb speaks much in support of the relevance of Sraffa's (1960) major contribution, which eschews the use of labour values (on this see Steedman, 1977), but without abandoning his insistence on the importance of the labour theory of value. It is easy to think that there is some inconsistency here, and it is tempting to trace the origin of this alleged inconsistency to Dobb's earlier writings, which made Abram Bergson remark that 'in Dobb's analysis the labour theory is not so much an analytic tool as excess baggage' (Bergson, 1949, p. 445).

The key to understanding Dobb's attitude to the labour theory of value is to recognize that he did not see it just as an intermediate product in explaining relative prices and distributions. He took 'the labour-principle' as 'making an important qualitative statement about the nature of the economic problem' (Dobb, 1937, p. 21). He rejected seeing the labour theory of value as simply a 'first approximation' containing 'nothing essential that cannot be expressed equally well and easily in other terms' (Dobb, 1973, pp. 148–9). The description of the production process in terms of labour involvement has an interest that extends far beyond the role of the labour value magnitudes in providing a 'first approxima- tion' for relative prices. As Dobb (1973) put it,

> there is something in the first approximation that is lacking in later approximations or cannot be expressed so easily in those terms (e.g., the first approximation may be a device for emphasising and throwing into relief something of greater generality and less particularity) (pp. 148–9).

Any description of reality involves some selection of facts to emphasize certain features and to underplay others, and the labour theory of value was seen by Dobb as emphasizing the role of those who are involved in 'personal participation in the process of production *per se*' in contrast with those who do not have such personal involvement.

> As such 'exploitation' is neither something 'metaphysical' nor simply an ethical judgement (still less 'just a noise') as has sometimes been depicted: it is a factual description of a socio-economic relationship, as much as is Marc Bloch's apt characterisation of Feudalism as a system where feudal Lords 'lived on the labour of other men' (Dobb, 1973, p. 145).

The possibility of calculating prices without going through value magnitudes, and the greater efficiency of doing that (on this see Steedman, 1977), does not affect this descriptive relevance of the labour theory of value in any way. Maurice Dobb also outlined the relationship of this primarily descriptive interpretation of labour theory of value with evaluative questions, e.g., assessing the 'right of ownership' (see especially Dobb, 1937).

The importance for Dobb of descriptive relevance is brought out also by his complex attitude to the utility theory of value. While he rejected the view that the utility picture is the best way of seeing relative values ('by taking as its foundation a fact of individual consciousness'), he lamented the descriptive impoverishment that is brought about by replacing the subjective utility theory by the 'revealed preference' approach.

> If all that is postulated is simply that men *choose*, without anything being stated even as to how they choose or what governs their choice, it would seem impossible for economics to provide us with any more than a sort of algebra of human choice (Dobb, 1937, p. 171).

Indeed as early as 1929, a long time before the 'revealed preference theory' was formally inaugurated by Paul Samuelson, Dobb had warned:

> Actually the whole tendency of modern theory is to abandon such psychological conceptions: to make utility and disutility coincident with observed offers in the market; to abandon a 'theory of value' in pursuit of a 'theory of price'. But this is to surrender, not to solve the problem (Dobb, 1929, p. 32).

Maurice Dobb's open-minded attitude to non-Marxian traditions in economics added strength and reach to his own Marxist theorizing. He could combine Marxist reasoning and methodology with other traditions, and he was eager to be able to communicate with economists belonging to other schools. Dobb's honesty and lack of dogmatism were important for the development of the Marxist economic tradition in the English-speaking world, because he occupied a unique position in Marxist thinking in Britain. As Eric Hobsbawm has noted,

> for several generations (as these are measured in the brief lives of students) he was not just the only Marxist economist in a British university of whom most people had heard, but virtually the only don known as a communist to the wider world (Hobsbawm, 1967, p. 1).

The Marxist economic tradition was well served by Maurice Dobb's willingness to engage in spirited but courteous debates with economists of other schools. Dobb achieved this without compromising the integrity of his position. The distinctly Marxist quality of his economic writings was as important as his willingness to listen and dispassionately analyse the claims of other schools of thought with which he engaged in systematic disputation. The gentleness of Dobb's style of disputation arose from strength rather than from weakness.

Dobb's willingness to appreciate positive elements in other economic traditions while retaining the distinctive qualities of his own approach is brought out very clearly also in his truly far-reaching critique of the theory of socialist pricing as presented by Lange, Lerner, Dickinson and others in the 1930s. Dobb noted the efficiency advantages of a price mechanism, especially in a static context. He was, however, one of the first economists to analyse clearly the conflict between the demands of efficiency expressed in the equilibrium conditions of the Langer–Lerner price mechanism (and also of course in a perfectly competitive market equilibrium), and the demands that would be imposed by the requirements of equality, given the initial conditions. In his paper called 'Economic Theory and the Problems of a Socialist Economy' published in 1933, Maurice Dobb argued thus:

> If carpenters are scarcer or more costly to train than scavengers, the market will place a higher value upon their services, and carpenters will derive a higher income and have greater 'voting power' as consumers. On the side of supply the extra 'costliness' of carpenters will receive expression, but only at the expense of giving carpenters a differential 'pull' as consumers, and hence vitiating the index of demand. On the other hand, if carpenters and scavengers are to be given equal weight as consumers by assuring them equal incomes, then the extra costliness of carpenters will find no expression in costs of production. Here is the central dilemma. Precisely because consumers are also producers, both costs and needs are precluded from receiving simultaneous expression in the same system of market valuations. Precisely to the extent that market valuations are rendered adequate in one direction they lose significance in the other (Dobb, 1933, p. 37).

The fact that given an initial distribution of resources the demands of efficiency and those of equity may — and typically will — conflict is, of course, one of the major issues in the theory of resource allocation, with implications for market socialism as well as for competitive markets in a private ownership economy. As a matter of fact, Marx had *inter alia* noted this conflict in his *Critique of Gotha Programme*, but in the discussion centring around Langer–Lerner systems, this deep conflict had attracted relatively little attention, except in the arguments presented by Maurice Dobb. The fact that even a socialist economy has to cope with inequalities of initial resource distribution (arising from, among other things, differences in inherited talents and acquired skills) makes it a relevant question for a socialist economy as well as for competitive market economies, and Dobb's was one of the first clear analyses of this central question of resource allocation.

The second respect in which Maurice Dobb found the literature on market socialism inadequate concerns allocation over time. In discussing the achievements and failures of the market mechanism, Maurice Dobb argued that the planning of investment decisions

> may contribute much more to human welfare than could the most perfect micro-economic adjustment, of which the market (if it worked like the textbooks, at least, and there were no income-inequalities) is admittedly more fitted in most cases to take care (Dobb, 1960, p. 76).

In his book *An Essay in Economic Growth and Planning* (1960), Dobb provided a major investigation of the basis of planned investment decisions, covering overall investment rates, sectoral divisions, choice of techniques, and pricing policies related to allocation (including that over time).

This contribution of Dobb relates closely to his analysis of the problems of economic development. In his earlier book *Some Aspects of Economic Development* (1951), Dobb had already presented a pioneering analysis of the problem of economic development in a surplus-labour economy, with shortage of capital and of many skills. While, on the one hand, he anticipated W.A. Lewis's more well-known investigation of economic growth with 'unlimited supplies of labour', he also went on to demonstrate the far-reaching implications of the over-all savings rates being socially sub-optimal and inadequate. Briefly, he showed that this requires not only policies directly aimed at raising the rates of saving and investment, but it also has implications for the choice of techniques, sectoral balances, and price fixation.

In such a brief note, it is not possible to do justice to the enormous range of Maurice Dobb's contributions to economic theory, applied economics and economic history. Different authors influenced by Maurice Dobb have emphasized different aspects of his many-sided works (see, for example, Feinstein (ed.), 1967, and Maurice Dobb Memorial Issue, 1978). He has also had influence even outside professional economics, particularly in history, especially through his analysis of the development of capitalism.

Dobb (1946) argued that the decline of feudalism was caused primarily by 'the inefficiency of Feudalism as a system of production, coupled with the growing needs of the ruling class for revenue' (p. 42). This view of feudal decline, with its emphasis on *internal* pressures, became the subject of a lively debate in the early 1950s. An alternative position, forcefully presented by Paul Sweezy in particular, emphasized some *external* developments, especially the growth of trade, operating through the relations between the feudal countryside and the towns that developed on its periphery. No matter what view is taken as to 'who won' the debates on the transition from feudalism to capitalism, Dobb's creative role in opening up a central question in economic history as well as a major issue in Marxist political economy can scarcely be disputed. Indeed, *Studies in the Development of Capitalism* (1946) has been a prime mover in the emergence of the powerful Marxian tradition of economic history in the English- speaking world, which has produced scholars of the eminence of Christopher Hill, Rodney Hilton, Eric Hobsbawm, Edward Thompson and others.

It is worth emphasizing that aside from the explicit contributions made by Maurice Dobb to economic history, he also did use a historical approach to economic analysis in general. Maurice Dobb's deep involvement in descriptive richness (as exemplified by his analysis of 'the requirements of a theory of value'), his insistence on not neglecting the long-run features of resource allocation (influencing his work on planning as well as development), his concern with observed phenomena in slumps and depressions in examining theories of 'crises', and so on, all relate to the historian's perspective. Dobb's works in the apparently divergent areas of economic theory, applied economics and economic history are, in fact, quite closely related to each other.

Maurice Dobb was not only a major bridge-builder between Marxist and non-Marxist economic traditions (aside from pioneering the development of Marxist economics in Britain and to some extent in the entire English-speaking world), he also built many bridges between the different pursuits of economic theorists, applied economists and economic historians. Dobb's political economy involved the rejection of the narrowly economic as well as the narrowly doctrinaire. He was a great economist in the best of the broad tradition of classical political economy.

AMARTYA SEN

SELECTED WORKS

1925. *Capitalist Enterprise and Social Progress*, London: Routledge.
1928. *Russian Economic Development since the Revolution*. London: Routledge.
1928. *Wages*. London: Nisbet; Cambridge: Cambridge University Press.
1929. A sceptical view of the theory of wages. *Economic Journal* 39, December, 506–19.
1933. Economic theory and the problems of a socialist economy. *Economic Journal* 43, December, 588–98.
1937. *Political Economy and Capitalism: Some Essays in Economic Tradition*. London: Routledge.
1946. *Studies in the Development of Capitalism*. London: Routledge.
1948. *Soviet Economic Development since 1917*. London: Routledge.
1950. Reply (to Paul Sweezy's article on the transition from feudalism to capitalism). *Science and Society* 14(2), Spring, 157–67.
1951. *Some Aspects of Economic Development: Three Lectures*. Delhi: Ranjit Publishers, for the Delhi School of Economics.
1955. *On Economic Theory and Socialism*. London: Routledge.
1960. *An Essay on Economic Growth and Planning*. London: Routledge.
1969. *Welfare Economics and the Economics of Socialism*. Cambridge: Cambridge University Press.
1973. *Theories of Value and Distribution since Adam Smith: Ideology and Economic Theory*. Cambridge: Cambridge University Press.

BIBLIOGRAPHY

Bergson, A. 1949. Socialist economics. In *A Survey of Contemporary Economics*, ed. H.S. Ellis, Philadelphia: Blakiston.
Hobsbawm, E.J. 1967. Maurice Dobb. *Socialism, Capitalism and Economic Growth: Essays Presented to Maurice Dobb*, ed. C. Feinstein, Cambridge: Cambridge University Press.
Maurice Dobb Memorial Issue. 1978. *Cambridge Journal of Economics* 2(2), June.
Meek, R. 1978. Obituary of Maurice Herbert Dobb. *Proceedings of the British Academy 1977* 53, 333–44.
Pollitt, B.H. 1985. Clearing the path for 'Production of Commodities by Means of Commodities': Notes on the Collaboration of Maurice Dobb in Piero Sraffa's edition of 'The Works and Correspondence of David Ricardo'. Mimeographed.
Sraffa, P. 1960. *Production of Commodities by Means of Commodities: Prelude to a Critique of Economic Theory*. Cambridge: Cambridge University Press.
Sraffa, P., with the collaboration of M.H. Dobb. 1951–73. *Works and Correspondence of David Ricardo*. 11 vols, Cambridge: Cambridge University Press.
Steedman, I. 1977. *Marx after Sraffa*. London: New Left Books.

Dodgson, Charles Lutwidge. *See* CARROLL, LEWIS.

Domar, Evsey David (born 1914). Domar (Domashevitsky) was born in 1914 in Lodz, Russia (now Poland), spent most of his early life in Harbin, Manchuria, and moved permanently to the United States in 1936. His undergraduate degree in economics (1939) was from the University of California (Los Angeles); his graduate work was at the Universities of Michigan (MA, Mathematical Statistics) and Harvard (PhD, 1947), where he studied with Alvin Hansen, the leading American Keynesian and most important single intellectual influence on Domar. Domar is best known for his leadership role, along with Roy Harrod, in the initiation of modern growth theory.

His first position was with the research staff of the Board of Governors of the Federal Reserve System, where he worked on fiscal problems from 1943 to 1946. His subsequent academic career took him briefly to the Carnegie Institute of Technology, the Cowles Foundation and the University of Chicago, the Johns Hopkins University in 1948 for ten years, and the Massachusetts Institute of Technology in 1958, from which he retired in 1984. An avid traveller, he has held more than a dozen visiting professorships in universities at home and abroad.

While the claim to the earliest statement of the famous Harrod–Domar growth model was clearly Harrod's (1939), Domar arrived independently at a structurally similar model but from a different point of view (1946, 1947). By incorporating into static Keynesian analysis the capacity changes associated with investment, he found that steady-state capacity growth required investment to grow at a rate equal to the savings rate multiplied by the capital–output ratio. From this simple beginning, growth theory took off to become a major focus, one might almost say obsession, of the profession in the 1950s and 1960s. He also made important contributions to some of its conceptual and measurement problems, such as the proper treatment of depreciation (1953) and the measurement of technological change (1961), and he coined the term 'residual' for the fraction of expanding output unexplained by the contribution of factors of production.

In fiscal theory, his early investigation, with Richard Musgrave (1944a), of the effect of a proportional income tax, with and without loss offsets, on portfolio choice was very similar in style and approach to portfolio theory of a decade later. Given individual preferences, the portfolio decision was modelled as a choice between alternative portfolios weighing their expected net returns against their risks (expected losses). The unconventional conclusion was reached that, given risk aversion, the imposition of a proportional income tax with symmetrical treatment of gains and losses would induce individuals to adjust their portfolios toward riskier assets. The reminder that expected risks and yields are both reduced by an income tax continues to be an important correction to a simplistic focus on yields alone.

As an applied theorist, Domar has had the knack of getting important results with simple theory. At a time when deficit finance was harshly criticized for increasing the debt burden and tax rate, Domar showed (1944b) that in a growing economy even continuous deficit finance resulted in only limited debt-income ratios and tax rates. Second, he made a fertile historical hypothesis (1970) – that the economic basis for the introduction of serfdom (or slavery) was a low land-to-labour cost – that is still being actively explored. Third, he ingeniously modified the administrative rules that guided the behaviour of collective farms (1966) or that determined the compensation of socialist managers (1974) to induce them toward more efficient price–output decisions.

Domar's work is informed by a rare combination of historical, empirical and theoretical breadth. His profound scholarship, in several languages, periods, and areas has often resurrected important findings of earlier writers previously overlooked.

E. CARY BROWN

See also HARROD-DOMAR MODEL.

SELECTED WORKS

1944a. (With Richard A. Musgrave.) Proportional income taxation and risk-taking. *Quarterly Journal of Economics* 58, May, 388–422.
1944b. The burden of the debt and the national income. *American Economic Review* 34, December, 798–827. Reprinted in Domar (1957).
1946. Capital expansion, rate of growth, and employment. *Econometrica* 14, April, 137–47. Reprinted in Domar (1957).
1947. Expansion and employment. *American Economic Review* 37, March, 34–55. Reprinted in Domar (1957).
1948. The problem of capital accumulation. *American Economic Review* 38, December, 777–94. Reprinted in Domar (1957).
1952. Economic growth: an econometric approach. *American Economic Review, Papers and Proceedings* 42, May, 479–95. Reprinted in Domar (1957).
1953. Depreciation, replacement and growth. *Economic Journal* 63, March, 1–32. Reprinted in Domar (1957).
1957. *Essays in the Theory of Economic Growth.* New York: Oxford University Press.
1961. On the measurement of technological change. *Economic Journal* 71, December, 709–29.
1966. The Soviet collective farm as a producer cooperative. *American Economic Review* 56, September, 734–57.
1970. The causes of slavery or serfdom: a hypothesis. *Journal of Economic History* 30(1), March, 18–32.
1974. On the optimal compensation of a socialist manager. *Quarterly Journal of Economics* 88(1), February, 1–18.

BIBLIOGRAPHY

Harrod, R.F. 1939. An essay in dynamic theory. *Economic Journal* 49, March, 14–33. Errata, June 1939, 377.
Harrod, R.F. 1948. *Towards a Dynamic Economics. Some recent developments of economic theory and their applications to policy.* London: Macmillan.

Domesday Book. Domesday Book is the name which, at least since the 12th century, has been borne by the record of the great survey of England made by order of William the Conqueror. Apparently the decree for the survey was issued at a moot held at Gloucester at the midwinter of 1085–86, and the work was completed in the course of the following year. Royal commissioners (*legati*) were sent into each shire with a list of interrogatories, to which they were to obtain sworn answers from local juries. Their procedure seems to have been this – they held a great shire moot, at which every hundred or wapentake of the shire was represented by a jury, while every vill was represented by a deputation of villagers. From each hundred-jury they obtained a verdict about all the land in the hundred, the villagers being at hand to correct or supplement verdicts, while 'the whole shire' was also present, and from time to time appeal could be made to its testimony. The statement thus supplied was reduced into writing and duly transmitted to the king. It was afterwards methodised and abstracted, and fairly transcribed in the great volume of Domesday and deposited in the royal treasury at Winchester, amongst the other muniments of the realm. It still exists, fresh and perfect as when the scribe put pen to parchment, the oldest cadastre, or survey of a kingdom, now existing in the world (Palgrave, *History of Normandy and England*, vol. iii, p. 575).

Our best information about the form of the original verdicts is contained, not in Domesday Book itself, but in a document known as the 'Inquisitio Comitatus Cantabrigiensis'. This seems to be a copy made in the 12th century of the verdicts delivered by the juries which represented some of the hundreds of Cambridgeshire. The verdicts having been obtained, they were sent to the king's treasury, and a digest was made of them by the royal officers. This digest is Domesday Book. If we may draw a general inference from Cambridgeshire, the materials supplied by the commissioners were subjected to a process of rearrangement. A scheme that was wholly geographical gave way to one which was partly geographical, partly proprietary. Domesday book deals with each shire separately, but within the shire it collects, under the name of each 'tenant in chief', all the estates that he holds, no matter in what hundred they may be. For example, the Cambridgeshire verdicts showed that Count Alan had lands in many hundreds. In the original verdicts the entries relating to his estates were therefore scattered about; in Domesday Book they are all collected together. Domesday Book consists of two volumes, sometimes called 'Great Domesday' and 'Little Domesday'. The latter deals with Essex, Norfolk, and Suffolk; the former with so much of the rest of England as was surveyed. A document in the keeping of the cathedral chapter of Exeter, and known as 'the Exon Domesday', contains an account of a large part of the south-western shires, which is very closely connected with that given by what, for distinction's sake, is sometimes called 'the Exchequer Domesday'. Seemingly this Exon Domesday is independent of the Exchequer Record, and goes back by a different route to the original verdicts. The same may perhaps be said of the 'Inquisitio Eliensis', an account of the estates held by the church of Ely. This Ely inquest must not be confused with the Cambridgeshire inquest.

Domesday Book was printed and published in 1783 in two folio volumes. A third volume containing indexes was published in 1811, and this was followed in 1816 by a fourth volume containing the Exon Domesday, the Ely Inquest, and some other matters. Of late years useful facsimiles have been published by the Ordnance Survey Office of various parts of the great Exchequer Record, and can be obtained at moderate prices. The important Cambridgeshire Inquisition was first published by N.E. Hamilton in 1876.

A large literature has gradually been collecting round Domesday Book. Among the older books Robert Kelham's *Domesday Book Illustrated* (1788) and the essays of Philip Carteret Webb deserve to be mentioned. Sir Henry Ellis, in his *General Introduction to Domesday Book* (1833), supplied valuable indexes, and summed up the older learning. In the fifth volume of E.A. Freeman's *Norman Conquest* good use has been made of all that bears on political history, on the history of great men, great churches, great events. James F. Morgan's *England under the Norman Occupation* (1858) is a good introduction to the study of Domesday, and the like may be said of W. de Gray Birch's *Domesday Book* (1887). A new epoch in the scientific exploration of the record is marked by the various works of R.W. Eyton dealing with Dorset, Somerset, Lincoln, and Stafford, especially by the key to Domesday Book. Two volumes of essays by various writers, called *Domesday Studies* (1888–91), contain two valuable

papers by J.H. Round, besides other matters. In some county histories Domesday has been well used, but here it is possible to name only the books of general importance. F. Seebohm's *English Village Community* has done much to awaken a new and an economic interest in our oldest statistics.

Much remains to be done. The student who approaches Domesday from the economic side will at once see that he has before him a vast mass of detailed statistics which ought to tell him much about agriculture, prices, rents, and the like. At the same time he will feel that he is debarred from making use of these precious materials by the difficulty of discovering the meaning of the crabbed formulas which are repeated on page after page. The difficulty is a very real one. Domesday Book stands alone. It is so far removed in time from the documents which most nearly resemble it, the extents of manors which are found in monastic cartularies, that we have to explain it out of itself or not at all, for we shall look in vain for help elsewhere. Then again the terms that it employs as technical terms are, we may say, derived from two different languages which have only of late come into contact with each other. About half of them have been introduced by the Norman conquerors, while the other half are words which were in use in England under Edward the Confessor. Hence many puzzles; for example, what word did English juries say when French clerks wrote down *villanus*? Then again, the more our record is studied, the more plainly do we see that one main purpose governs both its form and its matter. King William is not collecting miscellaneous information in the spirit of a scientific inquirer. He is in quest of geld. Domesday Book is a geld book, a tax book. Geldability, actual or potential, this is its main theme. If then we are to understand its statistics, the first thing necessary is a theory of geld, of the manner in which the great tax has been and is assessed and collected. Towards the construction of such a theory not a little has been done by modern writers, especially by Eyton and Round, but until the work has been completed, speculations about rents and values seem doomed to failure. Everywhere, for example, the question meets us whether we are reading of real areal units of land or of units which are the results of a rude system of taxation, and a great deal of labour must yet be spent on the book before this question will have been adequately answered.

[F.W. Maitland]
Reprinted from *Palgrave's Dictionary of Political Economy*.

BIBLIOGRAPHY

Brich, W. de G. 1887. *Domesday Book*. New York: E. & J.B. Young & Co.; London: Society for Promoting Christian Knowledge.
Dove, P.E. (ed.) 1888–91. *Domesday Studies*. London and New York: Longmans, Green & Co.
Ellis, H. 1833. *General Introduction to Domesday Book*. London.
Eyton, R.W. 1878. *A Key to Domesday*. London.
Freeman, E.A. 1869–79. *The History of the Norman Conquest*, Vol. 5. Oxford.
Kelham, R. 1788. *Domesday Book Illustrated*. London.
Maitland, F.W. 1897. *Domesday Book and Beyond*. Cambridge: Cambridge University Press.
Morgan, J.F. 1858. *England under the Norman Occupation*. London.
Palgrave, F. 1851–64. *The History of Normandy and of England*. Vols 1 and 2, London: J.W. Parker; vols 3 and 4, London: Macmillan.
Seebohm, F. 1883. *The English Village Community*. London: Longmans & Co.
Webb, P.C. 1756. *A Short Account of Some Particulars Concerning Domes-day*. London.

domestic labour. The term domestic labour entered economic vocabulary in the early 1970s as a result of feminist interest in criticizing and expanding economic categories to incorporate women's activities. Both mainstream and critical traditions in economics tried to grapple with the problem of how to account for the difference between men's and women's position on the labour market. One approach was to relate women's lesser training and skills in paid employment to competing demands made on a (married) woman's time by domestic commitments, with a tacit, though unexplained, acceptance that for women paid employment has to fit into time left over after the allocation of that needed for domestic labour, while for men it is the other way round. It is only by the addition of such an assumption that the analysis of domestic labour can be said to have had anything to say about *women*.

Neoclassical economists have seen domestic labour as one of three competing claims on people's time, the others being paid work and leisure. A household maximizes 'its' utility, which is a function of the consumption goods bought with income received from paid work by members of the household, the direct consumption of the products of time spent in domestic labour and a variety of ways of spending remaining leisure time (Becker, 1965). Women have a comparative advantage to men in domestic labour over paid work and so one or other partner should specialize; either a woman should not take paid employment or her husband should do no housework. Even if there is no intrinsic difference between men and women initially, specialized human capital can be acquired in each type of labour, so it makes sense for a division of labour to take place and for at most only one member of a household to work both in the home and outside. This is taken to explain both why the majority of domestic labour is performed by women and also why women work shorter hours in paid employment than men, accumulate less market-oriented training and skills, and have broken employment histories.

Two criticisms can be mounted of this approach. The first is that the comparative advantage itself needs explanation. At an individual level it can be accounted for by the lower relative earnings of women. But the outcome of individual household choices cannot, without circularity, then in turn be used to explain women's inferior earnings by the lesser time spent in the labour market acquiring appropriate human capital. At best such an approach can account for the division between houseworkers and paid workers, and if combined with an assumption that sex is used as a screening mechanism by employers, a form of rational statistical discrimination, why one sex as a whole will be more likely to constitute the houseworkers and the other the employees. But to explain why sex presents itself as a variable by which to screen, and why it is the *female* sex that constitutes the homeworkers, recourse must be made to biological differences in aptitude, an acceptable fall-back to some, but not to those who wish to show the power of the neoclassical economic approach to explain everything, nor to the feminist movement whose claims that a woman's place was socially rather than *naturally* in the home had led to the initial interest in the question.

The second criticism poses more fundamental problems for this type of analysis. The concept of a household's 'utility function' is a very shaky one. Individualism, upon which neoclassical economics is based, takes individuals as the only actors and decision makers, rejecting thereby, for example, the marxist notion of class interests and forces. The idea of a household utility function cannot therefore be entertained unless either all members of the household have identical preferences concerning the allocation of resources and leisure time among themselves or some rule for aggregating diverse preferences is adopted. Quite apart from the difficulty of devising such a rule which satisfies fairly minimal criteria to ensure that household preferences represent some meaningful aggregate of those of its members (Samuelson, 1956; Arrow, 1951), there is little evidence that households, rather than individuals, make decisions at all. Indeed, feminists would argue that such an approach obscures one of the key questions it was supposed to illuminate, differential power and thus an unequal division of labour within the household (Pahl, 1980).

This problem can be overcome by assuming one member of the household is sufficiently powerful, well-endowed and altruistic that all other members of the household are or aspire to be 'his' beneficiaries (Becker, 1974). Then the interest of all family members are serviced by the maximization of family income and the whole family can behave as one single decision-making unit. The assumptions of this model, which might seem appropriate only to an idealized picture of a Victorian patriarchal family, are necessary in order to avoid oligopolistic decision making, and even then care has to be taken to ensure that the paterfamilias is not driven into a corner solution, whereupon the unity of the family breaks down.

Marxist approaches criticize neoclassical analyses for failing to take account of the different social relations involved in wage and housework. The categories of marxist analysis are particularly appropriate to the analysis of unequal power relations, making marxism seem to some feminists more likely to offer a useful approach. The marxist notion of exploitation is based upon the characterization of *specific* forms of surplus extraction. The attempt to analyse domestic labour in these terms would therefore illuminate power relations within the household, without falling into the trap of conflating housework with paid labour, by recognizing its relations of production, not just its product, to be specific.

Accounts which characterized domestic labour as a separate mode of production came both from writers claiming to be orthodox marxists, extending rather than revising Marx's work, and from others who saw themselves more as using parts of Marx's mode of analysis to criticize and reformulate orthodox Marxism. Of the latter group Christine Delphy, for example, argued that there is a transhistorical family mode of production in which wives' labour power is exploited by their husbands which has coexisted with and outlasted the modes of production Marx described (Delphy, 1970). Harrison, on the other hand, sees the domestic mode of production as a specific subordinate counterpart to a capitalist mode of production unchanged from that of traditional marxist analysis.

Other accounts rejected the characterization of domestic labour as a separate mode of production on the grounds that a mode of production must be capable of independent self-perpetuation, since the term was used for the characterization of whole societies. The notion of a social formation encompassing two or more modes of production articulated with each other, while appropriate to the analysis of transition between modes, was not appropriate to the continued mutually dependent symbiotic relationship which exists between housework and wage work for capital. The alternative was to extend the notion of the capitalist mode of production to include housework (Gardiner, Himmelweit and Mackintosh, 1975). That extension was needed because the transformation of the wage into reproduced labour power is a process requiring labour and taking place under specific relations of production, and not the unproblematic natural process that Marx took it to be (O'Brien, 1981).

The effect within marxist theory of characterizing housework as a separate mode of production is to make housewives a class, exploited through performing surplus labour above the amount needed to reproduce their own labour power. This surplus was appropriated, according to different versions, either by their husband directly or transferred through lowering the value of his labour power to the capitalist who employed him. But if housework was seen as part of the capitalist mode of production, a housewife's class position, like that of anyone else, would be determined by her access to the means of production, and for most women that would put them in the working class along with their husbands.

Another area of dispute was whether domestic labour should be seen as value and/or surplus value producing. Some argued that it did produce value, because it produced the commodity labour power (Dalla Costa, 1973). In so far as the housewife worked longer hours than that needed to reproduce her own labour she also produced surplus value. Against this it could be argued that the housewife by producing use-values needed to reproduce labour power did not thereby make labour power her product, any more than the baker, butcher or obstetrician did (Seccombe, 1975). Labour power is an attribute of a living human being and is not, *pace* Marx, a commodity like any other in that it is not directly produced by labour at all. In that case the labour that a housewife expands is use-value but not value creating, and therefore *a fortiori* not surplus value creating.

The dispute as to whether domestic labour counted as productive labour turned upon the same issue, since within the capitalist mode of production labour is productive, according to the Marxist definition, if and only if it produces surplus value. Those who argued that domestic labour produced surplus value could therefore also claim that it was productive labour. But against this could be put Marx's own demonstration that productive labour must, to produce surplus value, take place between two exchanges: in the first labour power is bought for a wage, in the second the product is sold. Domestic labour requires neither exchange and therefore is technically outside the classification into productive and unproductive labour, which applies only to wage labour (Fee, 1976).

The 'domestic labour debate' as it became known failed to answer the question to which it was addressed: what is the material basis of women's oppression? To do so, it would have had to do more than classify domestic labour using the existing categories of Marxist analysis. By using those developed for the study of wage labour for capital it fell into a similar trap to the neoclassical approach.

The neoclassical approach failed to recognize that the different social relations under which domestic labour went on rendered the use of the theory of utility maximization developed to model market decision-making inappropriate. The assumptions needed in order that the division of labour within the home could be set up as a soluble decision-making problem had to turn the gender-divided household into a homogeneous single decision-making unit. Divisions within the household disappeared and its individual members became indistinguishable by anything that could be remotely related to gender except by recourse to some form of biological reductionism. Circularity is a common problem with utility analysis and in this case the only way to avoid it was by appeal to supposed biological differences, the very suppositions which feminists had rejected as insufficient to explain the social construction of gender-divided work patterns.

Marxism can escape the charge of circularity because its method is a historical one. Circularity thus becomes recast as the reproduction through time of the conditions which give rise to a gender-divided society. But ultimately marxism fell into the same trap. Although it did recognize that domestic labour and wage labour go on under different relations of production, it failed to give those different relations any constructive effect, seeing domestic labour as simply labour that did not have all the attributes of waged labour for capital. To have got further it would have been necessary to relate the analysis of domestic labour to the sex of those who performed it and to its fundamental characteristic of being labour involved in *reproduction* rather than just another form of production (Himmelweit, 1984).

S. HIMMELWEIT

See also FAMILY; HOME WORK; LABOUR SUPPLY OF WOMEN.

BIBLIOGRAPHY

Arrow, K.J. 1951. *Social Choice and Individual Values*. Cowles Commission Monograph No. 12, New York: John Wiley & Sons.

Becker, G. 1965. A theory of the allocation of time. *Economic Journal* 75, September, 493–517.

Becker, G. 1974. A theory of social interactions. *Journal of Political Economy* 82(6), November–December, 1063–93.

Dalla Costa, M. 1973. Women and the subversion of the community. In *The Power of Women and the Subversion of the Community*. 2nd edn, Bristol: Falling Wall Press.

Delphy, C. 1970. The main enemy. *Partisans* (Paris), Nos. 54–55.

Fee, T. 1976. Domestic labour: an analysis of housework and its relation to the production process. *Review of Radical Political Economy* 8(1), Spring, 1–8.

Gardiner, J., Himmelweit, S. and Macintosh, M. 1975. Women's domestic labour. *Bulletin of the Conference of Socialist Economists* 4(2). Reprinted in *On the Political Economy of Women*, CSE Pamphlet No. 2, London: Stage One, 1976.

Harrison, J. 1973. The political economy of housework. *Bulletin of the Conference of Socialist Economists* 3(1), Winter, 35–52.

Himmelweit, S. 1984. The real dualism of sex and class. *Review of Radical Political Economics* 16(1), 167–83.

O'Brien, M. 1981. *The Politics of Reproduction*. London: Routledge & Kegan Paul.

Pahl, J. 1980. Patterns of money management within marriage. *Journal of Social Policy* 9(3), July, 313–35.

Samuelson, P.A. 1956. Social indifference curves. *Quarterly Journal of Economics* 70(1), February, 1–22.

Seccombe, W. 1975. Domestic labour – reply to critics. *New Left Review* 94, November/December, 85–96.

Donisthorpe, Wordsworth (1847–?). Wordsworth Donisthorpe was born on 24 March 1847 in Harrogate, graduated from Trinity College, Cambridge in 1869 and was called to the Bar at the Inner Temple in 1879. Thereafter he lived and practised law in London. I have not been able to find his date of death, but what is apparently the last of his many books and pamphlets was published in 1913, his habitual enthusiasm as yet undimmed.

He is of interest to economists because of his first book, *Principles of Plutology* (reviewed in the *Saturday Review*, 9 September 1876, pp. 331–2). In it his vigorous and eccentric style, reminiscent of that of Fleeming Jenkin's last two papers in economics (Colvin and Ewing, 1887, Vol. II, pp. 122–54), is already there in full spate. While showing traces of Cairnes and Jevons, the book is for the most part subjectively original and objectively mediocre. Chapter IX on 'The Laws of Value' is an interesting exception. His clear understanding of the importance of the Law of One Price ('[This] proposition is the fundamental one', p. 133) is refreshing and unusual for its time, as is his Wicksteedian insistence on the reservation price of the seller, so that 'sellers and buyers are not two classes, but one class' (p. 132).

In the same chapter he discusses substitutes and complements ('co-elements'). Although attempting no rigorous definitions he does lay down various 'laws' concerning them, i.e. propositions of comparative statics. Thus, the Third Law reads: 'Other things equal, a rise in the value of a co-element is followed by a fall in the values of its co-elements, and a fall by a rise, but not necessarily at the same rate' (p. 153), while the Fourth Law is: 'Other things equal, a rise in the value of any commodity is followed by a rise in the value of its substitutes, and a fall by a fall, but not necessarily at the same rate' (ibid.). He points out that, depending on the circumstances, two commodities may stand in both relations to each other, e.g. wool and cotton as inputs to cloth are often co-elements while as individual consumer goods they are usually substitutes.

Perhaps disappointed at the book's reception (I know of no economist's reference to it) Donisthorpe soon left economics for political philosophy and became a leading pamphleteer for anarchic Individualism, a libertarian movement that perhaps owed as much to fear of Henry George as to admiration for Herbert Spencer. It took the complacent view that the state should interfere with individual activities only when deemed necessary to protect the rights of private property, a view which aroused such derisive epithets as 'tomtits of Anarchy' from its opponents (see *Westminster Gazette*, 3 and 11 August 1894).

However, a streak of Yorkshire shrewdness and wit kept Donisthorpe from becoming quite as doctrinaire and saintly an Individualist as, say, Auberon Herbert. For example, the last chapter of his *Law in a Free State* (1895) contains an uproarious but penetrating account of the problems posed to the Individualist polity, by what we would now call externalities of various kinds, economic, political, social and moral.

PETER NEWMAN

SELECTED WORKS
1876. *Principles of Plutology*. London: Williams & Norgate.
1880. *The Claims of Labour; or, serfdom, wagedom and freedom*. London: Tinsley.
1889. *Individualism: A System of Politics*. London: Macmillan.
1891. The limits of liberty. In *A Plea for Liberty*, ed. T. Mackay, New York: D. Appleton.
1893. *Love and Law: an essay on marriage*. London: W. Reeves.
1895a. *Law in a Free State*. London: Macmillan.
1895b. *A System of Measures of length, area, bulk, weight, value, force &c.* London: Spottiswoode.
1898. *Down the Stream of Civilization*. London: G. Newnes.
1913. *Uropa. A new philosophically-constructed language based on Latin roots*. Guildford: W. Stent & Sons.

BIBLIOGRAPHY
Colvin, S. and Ewing, J.A. (eds) 1887. *Papers, Literary, Scientific &c., by the late Fleeming Jenkin, F.R.S.,LL.D.* With a memoir by Robert Louis Stevenson. 2 vols, London: Longmans, Green.

Dorfman, Joseph (born 1904). Historian of American economic thought, Dorfman was born in Russia in 1904 and educated at Reed College and at Columbia University, where he earned a PhD degree in 1935 and taught from 1931 until his retirement forty years later. Dorfman was a student of Clarence Ayres at Reed, and of Wesley C. Mitchell and John Maurice Clark at Columbia. Mitchell in turn had been a student of Thorstein Veblen. These four economists, all with institutional leanings, stand out among the formative influences that affected Dorfman's early career. He made Veblen the subject of his doctoral dissertation, which was published under the title *Thorstein Veblen and his America* in 1934. This was at the time the only book-length appraisal of a modern economist that gave close attention not only to the

subject's writings but also to biographical detail, the contemporary climate of opinion, and the general social and cultural setting of the work.

This type of holistic approach is characteristic also of Dorfman's monumental *The Economic Mind in American Civilization*, a five-volume work that he published from 1946 to 1959. It is dedicated 'To the pioneering spirit of Thorstein Veblen and the first-born of his intellectual heirs, Wesley C. Mitchell'. The work is a detailed history of American economic thought from colonial times to 1933, the first of its kind and not likely to be replaced for many years. It is based on extensive research and in many instances provides the first comprehensive account of a writer's life and work. Dorfman sees a break of emphasis in the history of American economic thought at the time of the Civil War: it was commerce before, and industry later. He notes with respect the achievements of the past, and is a critical but tactful chronicler of past foibles. He was a pioneer in exploring not only the printed page but also archival material made up of 'papers', 'letters', and similarly elusive sources of information, the first writer to do so on a large and systematic scale in the history of economic thought.

HENRY W. SPIEGEL

SELECTED WORKS
1934. *Thornstein Veblen and His America*. New York: Viking Press.
1935. (With R.G. Tugwell.) *William Beach Lawrence: Apostle of Ricardo*. New York, reprinted from *Columbia University Quarterly*, September 1935.
1940. *The Economic Philosophy of Thomas Jefferson*. New York: Academy of Political Science.
1946–59. *The Economic Mind in American Civilization*. 5 vols, New York: Viking Press.
1954. Introduction to Adams, H.C., *Relation of the State to Industrial Action, and Economics and Jurisprudence. Two Essays*, ed. J. Dorfman, New York: Columbia University Press.
1960. (With R.G. Tugwell.) *Early American Policy: six Columbian contributors*. New York: Columbia University Press.
1967-9. Introduction to W.C. Mitchell, *Types of Economic Theory; from Mercantilism to Institutionalism*, ed. J. Dorfman, New York. A.M. Kelley.

double-entry bookkeeping. Firms of all kinds need, in different degrees, to maintain records of their transactions with other firms and persons, of the debts they owe or are owed, and of their assets. The records they keep for this purpose constitute their accounting records. Traditionally they have consisted of account-books of various kinds, but they can take the form also of magnetic tapes and so on. If the records are kept on a systematic basis, one can speak of an accounting system. From the accounting records one can prepare a variety of accounting statements in which the detailed accounting information is rearranged, regrouped and presented in summary form. The balance sheet and the profit-and-loss (or income) account or statement are important examples of such accounting statements.

Double-entry bookkeeping is a system or method for the arrangement and classification of accounting information. It developed in Italy, possibly in the second half of the 13th century. A description of the system was first published in Venice in 1494 as one part of a famous compendium of mathematical and commercial information: Luca Pacioli's *Summa de Arithmetica Geometria Proportioni et Proportionalità*. Knowledge of the double-entry system spread gradually from Italy to the rest of Europe by way of commercial contacts, schools and published treatises. It is not possible to establish how widely the system was used by merchants and others, say, in the 18th century. But by the 19th century it had become the standard system for accounting records. Today it is used by virtually all corporate enterprises and many other firms as well as non-profit-making organizations in the West and also elsewhere. It has also proved suitable to serve as a useful scaffolding for the construction of the national income and related accounts for countries or regions.

Double-entry bookkeeping is no more than a system for arranging and organizing accounting information. It does not itself define the scope and detail of that information. Thus, for example, the double-entry system does not require that all transactions with third parties should be recorded, although it is the convention now to record all of them. What is more important, it does not prescribe with occurrences or changes that do not involve external transactions should be recorded in the accounts. Thus it does not prescribe whether changes in the value of the firm's assets should be recorded, how they should be determined, or how they should be recorded. Double entry neither generates nor requires any particular set of valuation rules or profit concepts. Different valuation bases or conventions, and different treatments for changes in the value of money, are all compatible with the use of the double-entry system. The system itself is highly adaptable, since it is concerned with arrangement and organization rather than with scope and content. Its adaptability has made it possible for it to serve as the basis for arranging the records needed by the relatively small-scale merchants in the early modern period of economic expansion as well as for those of the largest corporate enterprises operating today. But this does not mean that asset values were recorded and profits calculated in the same way by 17th-century merchants as they are by today's largest corporate enterprises. In fact, 17th-century merchants used several alternative bases for recording changes in asset values. And some of these would not be used by companies today.

Moreover, although all the companies within the same jurisdiction are subject to the same laws and the same institutional constraints (e.g. those imposed by the stock-market authorities and those reflecting professional accounting standards), there is still scope for considerable variation in the determination and statement of accounting profits and asset values. However, because of developments in legislation and in the other constraining forces operating on corporate enterprises, it is no longer the case that a company chairman in the United Kingdom would be able to say (as Arthur Chamberlain, chairman of Tube Investments said in 1935) that he 'would almost undertake to draw up two balance-sheets for the same company, both coming within an auditor's statutory certificate, in which practically the only recognizable items would be the name and the capital authorised and issued'.

Double entry requires that each transaction (or other change) recorded in the accounting system must be recorded twice, and for the same money amount, once in debit form and once in credit form. In double entry, as Pacioli expressed it, 'all the entries placed in the ledger must be double, that is if you make a creditor (entry) you must make a debtor (entry)'. The debit and credit entries are made in the ledger, on the basis of the information entered in preliminary records. The ledger, which may for convenience be subdivided into a series of specialized ledgers, consists of a number of ledger accounts, pertaining, for example, to particular debtors or creditors, particular assets or particular categories of expenditure. It is the convention that the debit entry is made on the left-hand (debit) side of the appropriate ledger account, and the

corresponding off-setting credit entry on the right-hand (credit) side of the other appropriate ledger account.

The duality of entries for each transaction (or other recorded event) ties together the ledger accounts into an interlocking system of recorded information. Moreover, as each transaction gives rise to two equal but opposite entries, the system of accounts (if properly kept) is always in balance or equilibrium. The total of debit entries must be equal to the total of credit entries. Similarly, the total of the balances on all ledger accounts that have debit balances must be equal to the total of the balances on all the remaining ledger accounts that have credit balances. (If debit balances are taken as positive amounts and credit balances as negative amounts, the algebraic sum of the balances on all ledger accounts is zero.) The equality of debits and credits is the basis for the trial balance. This is a list of the balances on all open (i.e. unbalanced) accounts in the ledger, distinguishing between debit and credit balances. If the trial balance does not balance, there is some error in the ledger. Postlethwayt in his *Dictionary* (1751) wrote of the 'agreeable satisfaction' of getting a trial balance to balance, and said that the trial balance will 'shew you that this (double entry), of all methods, is the most excellent'. The fact that a trial balance does not balance is proof that the ledger does contain some error. The converse is, of course, not correct.

Roger North, son of the prominent Turkey merchant Sir Dudley North, wrote in 1714 as follows: 'The making true *Drs.* (debtors) and *Crs.* (creditors) is the greatest Difficulty of Accompting, and perpetually exerciseth the Judgment; being an Act of the Mind, intent upon the Nature and Truth of Things.' Writers of instructional books on bookkeeping and accounts through the centuries have devised various lists, rules or approaches to help the accountant decide which debit and credit entries he should make for the various categories of transaction.

An early rule, widely used, was as follows (taken from a verse, 'Rules to be Observed', in a book of 1553 by James Peele):

To make the thinges Receivyd, or the receiver,
Debter to the thinges delivered, or to the deliverer.

This rule is obviously readily applicable to many categories of transaction. If cash is received from a debtor, debit the cash account; and credit the debtor's account. If office furniture is bought on credit, debit the furniture account; and credit the supplier's account. If the owner withdraws cash from the business, debit the capital (i.e. owner's) account; and credit the cash account. But it is evidently a straining of the language to say, when an amount is written off the book value of, say, a ship, in order to reflect diminution of value due to wear and tear, that the profit-and-loss account, which is to be debited, 'receives' something that has been 'delivered' to it by the ship account. Teachers and textbook writers not surprisingly looked for a rule that is robust enough to cover comfortably all transactions and events to be recorded, and to indicate unambiguously in each case where the debit and where the credit are to be placed.

The most common rule or approach adopted today in transaction analysis in the double-entry system derives from the so-called balance-sheet equation. The earliest formulation of this approach can be traced to the work of a Dutchman, Willem van Gezel, published in 1681.

The basic balance-sheet equation is:

Owner's Equity
(or the firm's net worth) = Assets − Liabilities = Net Assets
or Owner's Equity + Liabilities = Assets.

The ledger contains accounts for the various assets and liabilities; and there are accounts in it for the capital contributed or withdrawn by the owner(s) and for any increases (decreases) in 'net worth' resulting from the activities of the firm. In the double-entry system, increases in assets are indicated by debits to an asset account – the extent to which assets are subdivided into separate ledger accounts is for each firm to decide. Conversely, decreases in assets are recorded as credits to asset accounts. The total of a firm's assets is represented by the same total of claims on those assets; namely, its liabilities (i.e. its debts to third parties) and its owner's equity. The total of these claims must be a credit amount that equals the debit amount representing the assets. An increase (decrease) in a claim is therefore represented by a credit (debit) in a liability account or an equity account. (Again, the extent to which claims are subdivided into various ledger accounts is a matter for each firm to decide. As regards the equity element, it is common for a ledger to contain separate accounts for each major category of business expenditure and income, a trading account, perhaps subdivided by type of activity, for showing the gross profit, and a profit-and-loss account to bring together the results from all the subordinate ledger accounts.)

Transaction analysis follows readily. The payment of salaries reduces the asset 'cash' and reduces the owner's equity, since the payment, taken by itself, represents a loss to the firm: hence, debit the salaries (eventually, profit-and-loss) account; and credit the cash account. The depreciation of an asset likewise reduces an asset and reduces the equity: debit the depreciation account (eventually profit-and-loss) account; and credit the ship account.

As has already been emphasized, the double-entry system does not itself dictate whether or in what circumstances increases or decreases in assets are to be recognized in the accounts. Neither does the system dictate the basis on which, or the circumstances in which, assets are to be revalued in the accounts. Decisions of these kinds are accounting decisions; and whenever such decisions are taken, the double-entry system of recording will accommodate them in accordance with its own logical structure. It follows from this that, although the value of the owner's equity in the ledger will always be equal to the value of the firm's net assets (i.e. assets minus liabilities to those outside the firm) as stated in the accounts, those two values depend on the bases on which the values of assets are stated in the accounts.

Subject to this crucial qualification, it follows from the equilibrium feature of the double-entry system that the change (increase or decrease) in the value of the net assets of a firm over a period will be reflected as entries in the various ledger accounts that represent the owner's equity. Those entries in the various equity accounts that relate to the firm's operations, when they are brought together in the profit-and-loss account, yield a balance that is equal to the change in the value of the net assets over the period. It is the profit (loss) for the period. This profit is equal to the change in the value of the net assets over the period (allowance being made for any contributions or withdrawals of assets by the owner). It may be noted that the same profit figure would be established if one took the difference between the totals of two inventories of the firm's net assets taken, respectively, at the beginning and at the end of the period, provided that the same valuations were used and the same allowance made for the owner's contributions and withdrawals. The method of profit calculation by means of successive inventories of assets and liabilities was widely used in the past. The surviving 16th-century records of the large-scale commercial, financial and mining enterprise of the Fugger family of Augsburg provide examples of this procedure.

The equality – Profit (Loss) = Change in Net Assets – evidently holds only if all the changes recorded in asset and liability accounts (other than the owner's contributions or withdrawals) are also recorded in equity accounts that, in turn, are closed into the profit-and-loss account. In contemporary corporate financial accounting it is permissible to allow the counter-entries representing certain changes in asset values, depending upon the circumstances, to bypass the profit-and-loss account (e.g. by recording these changes as debits or credits to one or other reserve account). This practice breaks the nexus between changes in net asset values and profits. It does, however, allow more 'realistic' values to be used in asset accounts where, otherwise, their use might produce 'distortions' in the profit figures that could mislead users such as investors and investment advisers. Both 'realistic' and 'distortions' are words that give rise to much debate in accounting circles. The double-entry recording system can accommodate the practice of bypassing the profit-and-loss account as comfortably as it can the alternative. The system itself imposes no discipline or constraint upon accountant or management – except the constraint that for each transaction or change recorded in the firm's accounting system, equal but offsetting debit and credit entries have to be made in accounts in the ledger.

The German economic historian, Werner Sombart, claimed that 'capitalism without double-entry bookkeeping is simply inconceivable', and that double-entry was one of the most significant inventions or creations of the human spirit. In similar vein, Oswald Spengler asserted that the creator of double-entry bookkeeping could take his place worthily beside his contemporaries Columbus and Copernicus. These scholars evidently attributed to the double entry system a role that goes well beyond what one might think appropriate to ascribe to a system of organizing and arranging accounting data. In a nutshell, Sombart argued that, historically, the double-entry system opened up possibilities and provided stimuli that enabled capitalism to develop fully. It clarified the acquisitive ends of commerce and provided the rational basis on which this acquisition could be carried on. It provided the basis for the continued rational pursuit of profits, and virtually compelled its users to pursue the acquisition of wealth. It also enabled the firm or enterprise to be separated from its owners, thus facilitating the development of corporate enterprises.

These views are in their details either untenable or grossly exaggerated. To note only a few points: the profits of an enterprise and its capital employed can be calculated without double-entry bookkeeping; joint-stock companies, such as the Dutch East India Company, have existed and flourished without double-entry bookkeeping; 16th- and 17th-century merchants, like the Fugger, who did not use the system do not seem to have been any less acquisitive, rational and successful than those who did use the system; and the adoption of the double-entry system could not have changed, or even have reinforced, the temperament, commercial acumen, motivation or goals of those who adopted it for organizing their accounting records.

To reject grandiose claims made for double-entry bookkeeping is not to deny the more workaday usefulness of the system. A method or system for recording and classifying accounting data that has been used increasingly over a period of six centuries must indeed have had substantial practical merit. Double entry is a useful and versatile method for organizing accounting data, its value increasing with the volume and complexity of the data to be organized. In turn, the efficient organization of data helps management at various levels in many ways, more notably in large organizations. But its contribution to efficiency does not proceed along the lines emphasized by Sombart.

BASIL S. YAMEY

See also ACCOUNTING AND ECONOMIC; ASSETS AND LIABILITIES.

BIBLIOGRAPHY
Edey, H.C. 1978. *Introduction to Accounting.* 4th edn, London: Hutchinson (for a concise introductory treatment of bookkeeping and accounts).
Yamey, B.S. 1964. Accounting and the rise of capitalism. *Journal of Accounting Research* 2, 117–36 (for a discussion of Sombart's views on double-entry bookkeeping and capitalism).

Douglas, Clifford Hugh (1879–1952).   Major Douglas, the founder of the Social Credit movement, was born in Stockport, Cheshire, in 1879. After a period at Pembroke College, Cambridge, he trained as an engineer and then served with the Royal Flying Corps. He died at Dundee, Scotland, in 1952.

Major Douglas is best known for his A+B theorem, which his followers used to impress laypersons and exasperate academic economists. It was based on the claim that all productive organizations make two kinds of payments: Group A payments, made up of wages, salaries and dividends; and Group B payments, made up of all other payments to banks and suppliers of materials. In his own words (Douglas, 1924):

> Since all payments go into prices, the rate of flow of prices cannot be less than A plus B. Since A will not purchase A plus B, a proportion of the product at least equivalent to B must be distributed by a form of purchasing power which is not comprised in the description grouped under A.

By first reducing prices below cost to the individual consumer and then making up this difference between price and cost by a Treasury issue to the producer, Douglas argued that such an issue of 'Social Credit' would enable underconsumption to be eliminated without inflation. The anti-socialist Douglas appeared oblivious to the fact that his scheme would have required an army of inspectors to fix and supervise the huge number of individual price reductions involved.

Social Credit ideas had the largest following in the Dominion economies of Canada, Australia and New Zealand. The province of Alberta had a Social Credit government between 1935 and 1971 and British Columbia one from 1952 to 1972. In other countries, his followers ranged from the 'Red Dean' (the Very Reverend Hewlett Johnson, Dean of Canterbury) through to the neo-fascist author Ezra Pound.

DAVID CLARK

See also GESELL, SILVIO; MONETARY CRANKS.

SELECTED WORKS
1920. *Economic Democracy.* London: Stanley Nott.
1921. *Credit Power and Democracy.* London: Cecil Palmer.
1924. *Social Credit.* London: Eyre & Spottiswoode.
1931. *Warning Democracy.* London: Stanley Nott.

BIBLIOGRAPHY
Dobb, M.H. 1936. *Social Credit Discredited: being an examination in terms of Political Economy of the much advertized nostrums of Major Douglas, which are subject to a devastating analysis and found wanting as a solution to the troubles of our time.* London, no publisher given.
Mairet, P. (ed.) 1934. *The Douglas Manual.* London: Stanley Nott.

McConnell, W.K. 1932. *The Douglas Credit Scheme: A Simple Explanation and Criticism.* Sydney: Angus & Robertson.

Douglas, Paul Howard (1892–1976).   Born in 1892 in Salem, Massachusetts, Paul Douglas attended Bowdoin College in Maine (BA, 1913) and Columbia University (PhD, 1921). After holding a number of teaching posts between 1916 and 1920, he joined the faculty of the University of Chicago where he remained (apart from service in World War II) until 1948, when he became a United States Senator from Illinois. After his retirement from the Senate in 1966, he taught at the New School for Social Research for two years (1967–9).

Paul Douglas first became well known for his massive theoretical and factual studies (e.g. 1930) of all the available information on wages in the United States from 1890. This work required laborious following up of old, obscure records, and repairing gaps in the available knowledge, such as domestic service wages. Douglas also collected information on prices so as to make an estimate of the movement of real wages.

In Britain there was almost complete cessation of the growth of real wages between 1896 and 1914. Understandably, it was a period of growing social tension. Sir Henry PhelpsBrown called it the 'climacteric'. We still do not really understand its cause; there was some sociological evidence about the deterioration of the quality of businessmen. D.H. Robertson found at least a partial explanation in economic causes, namely that of the two leading British export industries, cotton was produced under constant returns and coal under diminishing returns.

This problem remains of primary interest to economic historians, and naturally they enquire whether there is any evidence of a similar 'climacteric' in other countries. In Germany there was a slowing down of the rate of rise in real wages, but not very marked. Douglas's American data likewise do not show such a 'climacteric'. Recent research, however, has thrown some doubt not on Douglas' wage data, but on his price data; and perhaps there was some slowing down of the rate of growth of real wages.

Douglas became famous to the whole economic world through the 'Cobb–Douglas function' (e.g. 1934, 1950). Working in conjunction with Charles W. Cobb, a mathematician from Amherst College, and using Massachusetts State annual factory returns, Douglas in 1928 established the following relation: Let product be P, labour input L, capital input C, and k a constant. Then $P = kL^aC^b$. (The same formula, with land in place of capital, had already been used by Wicksell (e.g. 1900), but he gave it neither theoretical nor empirical development.)

We may, if we wish, constrain a and b to add up to one; but we get much the same results unconstrained. If a and b add up to more than one this is an indication of economies of scale (increasing returns) – a uniform increase in the quantities of inputs giving a more than proportionate increase in product.

Annual data, which many economists have been using, give results mainly dependent on fluctuations in the short-period business cycle – which is not what we want at all. It is only when we have data for such a long period as to make it possible to average out the business cycle that we can draw conclusions about productivity. This has been done by Solow in the United States, Aukrust in Norway, and Niitamo in Finland. In each case it was found, in the long run, that the product was rising much more rapidly than expected from inputs and their exponents. This difference is generally held to be due to technical advance, though some look for economies of scale. Some difficult but promising work by Denison further analyses the labour input by numerous categories, male and female, adult and juvenile, and various levels of education. These methods reduce the unknown factor – but it does not disappear.

Differentiating the Cobb–Douglas formula to obtain marginal productivities, then aggregate earnings of the factors should be proportional to a:b – assuming that each factor is remunerated according to its marginal productivity. When he first made this calculation (so he told me) Douglas fully expected the aggregate income of labour to be below that indicated by its marginal productivity. He was surprised, however, to find that it was almost exactly what was to be expected – about 75 per cent of the product.

The Cobb–Douglas formula has had abundant application in agricultural economics, especially for cross-section studies, where each farm may be considered an independent piece of evidence. Land is introduced as a factor, and also data for other inputs – fertilizers, insecticides, etc. – even (in one study in Sweden) the age of the farmer – a negative factor.

Douglas was very much a political economist. Organized labour in the United States did not attempt to form a political party of its own as in Britain, but instead played the two existing parties off against each other in demanding concessions. But in the 1920s this was not fully agreed. The other element in the population with a grievance against the current state of affairs were the farmers, and an attempt was made to form a Farmer–Labour political party. Douglas took an active part in these negotiations, and was national treasurer of the organization. But with the Roosevelt reforms of the 1930s the prospects of a Farmer–Labour party died away.

Chicago had acquired a worldwide reputation for corruption and crime; and the ruling Democratic Party considered that their 'image' would be improved by an upright professor of economics on the city council. Douglas assured me that some improvement had taken place, though less than was hoped for. Later, the despotic Mayor Daley achieved a real reduction in crime. But once I asked Douglas whether, if I wished to set up a milk distribution business in Chicago, he could guarantee my safety. He replied that, 'regrettably', he could not.

Douglas was a Quaker, and in World War I applied for exemption from military service on religious grounds. But in World War II he felt very differently. In spite of his age, he obtained a commission in the Marines through Roosevelt's personal intervention, and took part in the bloody landing on Iwojima. He sustained an injury to his hand which was with him for the rest of his life.

From city councillor he advanced to become Senator for Illinois. On the very day that he arrived in Washington he found a vanload of furniture which had been offered to him as a gift. He sent it back. This episode prompted him to write a little book, *Ethics in Government* (1952). He saw no harm in the small presents customarily exchanged among businessmen and politicians – calendars, cigars, etc., but instructed his staff to return any present valued at over $4.

COLIN G. CLARK

See also COBB-DOUGLAS FUNCTIONS.

SELECTED WORKS

1928. (With C.W. Cobb.) A theory of production. *American Economic Review*, Supplement, 18, March, 139–65.
1930. *Real Wages in the United States, 1890–1926.* Boston and New York: Houghton Mifflin Company.
1934. *The Theory of Wages.* New York: The Macmillan Company.
1936. *Social Security in the United Sates; an analysis and appraisal of the Federal social security act.* New York, London: Whittlesey House, McGraw-Hill.

1947. (With E.H. Schoenberg.) Studies in the supply curve of labour; the relation in 1929 between average earnings in American cities and the proportions seeking employment. *Journal of Political Economy* 45, February, 45–79.
1939a. The effect of wage increases upon employment. *American Economic Review* Supplement 29, March, 138–57.
1939b. (With H.G. Lewis.) Some problems in the measurement of income elasticities. *Econometrica* 7, July, 208–20.
1939c. (With M. Bronfenbrenner.) Cross-section studies in the Cobb–Douglas function. *Journal of Political Economy* 47, December, 761–85.
1948. Are there laws of production? *American Economic Review* 38, March, 1–41.
1952. *Ethics in Government.* (The Godkin Lectures at Harvard University, 1951.) Cambridge, Mass.: Harvard University Press.
1972. *In the Fullness of Time; the memoirs of Paul H. Douglas.* New York: Harcourt Brace Jovanovich.
1976. The Cobb–Douglas production function once again: its history, its testing and some new empirical values. *Journal of Political Economy* 84, October, 903–15.

BIBLIOGRAPHY
Wicksell, K. 1900. Marginal productivity as the basis of distribution in economics. *Ekonomisk Tidskrift*. English trans. In *K. Wicksell: Selected Papers in Economic Theory*, ed. E. Lindahl, London: Allen & Unwin, 1958.

dual economies. The concept of a 'dual economy' relates to various asymmetries of production and organization that exist in developing countries. The term was originally coined by Boeke (1953), in the context of his socioeconomic studies in Indonesia, to represent an economy and a society divided between the traditional sectors and the modern, capitalist sectors in which the Dutch colonialists operated. This organizational asymmetry also turns out to be a significant feature of the classic Lewis (1954) model of development. However, the notion of 'dualism' goes wider than asymmetry between a modern and traditional sector. A number of models have appeared in the literature, since Lewis' celebrated paper, which employ or emphasize asymmetries and rigidities of different types. Our object is to view these contributions as equally valid representations of dualism, and to compare and contrast their findings with those of earlier writers.

Dual economy models are a subclass of two-sector models of growth. They are intended to capture particular features of developing countries so as to enable a more accurate analysis of development paths and policies. The famous two-sector model of Uzawa (1961–3), for example, would *not* be regarded as a dual economy model. In that model product and factor markets clear instantaneously across sectors, and although the two sectors each produce a commodity which is different with respect to input requirements and consumption characteristics, this is where the 'asymmetry' between the two sectors stops. Both sectors use capital and labour (although with different production functions) and production decisions in both sectors are characterized by profit maximization.

The 'asymmetry' in the Uzawa model is, of course, the minimal necessary to make a two-sector model interesting – without asymmetry in production or consumption we would be back to a one-good world. However, the various dual economy models can be seen as departures from this minimal asymmetry; different models introduce different types of asymmetries, in different combinations, to highlight different points of interest.

In comparison with the Uzawa model, the Lewis model displays several types of asymmetries. In the former, there are two factors of production, capital and labour. Both factors are used in each sector, and factors are perfectly mobile between the two sectors. The Lewis model has three factors of production – land, labour and capital – and the two sectors are agriculture (or the traditional sector) and manufacturing (or the modern sector). But agriculture uses no capital and manufacturing uses no land while both sectors use labour. One way of viewing this asymmetry in production is as extreme factor immobility of two of the factors of production across the two sectors, and we will return to the factor mobility assumptions in dual economy models presently. However, attention has focused on yet another asymmetry in the Lewis model, and it is to this that we now turn.

In the Lewis model, manufacturing sector production decisions are made with the objective of maximizing profits, while in the agricultural sector the distribution of product is according to 'conventional norms' rather than marginal products. This is precisely what is meant by duality in the mainstream of development thought. As Little (1982) observes:

> Duality can be defined in many ways. But a useful analytic institutional definition would seem to be that an economy is dualistic when a significant part of it operates under such a paternalist or quasi-feudalist regime, while another significant part operates under a system of wage employment – which may be capitalist or socialist (if state capitalism is regarded as a variety of socialism). Surplus labour may exist in such a situation, but not necessarily so.

Little's final comment introduces the notion of 'surplus labour', and highlights the fact that this is in principle independent of the organizational asymmetry which lies at the heart of dualism. If by surplus labour is meant that the marginal product of labour is close to zero, then a competitive allocation of product is not possible in the agricultural sector – the wage so determined would be too low for survival. It is in such a situation that distribution of product according to norms may arise. However, the use of norms may be present even when the marginal product of labour is positive and sufficiently large.

What the conventional norms are matters for the Lewis story. If, for example, the traditional sector consists of family farms and distribution is according to average product, the consequences are different from the case where the traditional sector consists of landlords who maintain a work force at some income level above marginal product. In the latter case, when a worker leaves for the modern sector the landlords appropriate his income. In the former case, as one worker leaves, the average product rises and affects the supply price of the remaining workers.

From the point of view of static analysis, dual economies give rise to economic inefficiency. For maximization of national output what is required is that the marginal product of each factor be equalized across the two sectors. But the production asymmetry means that capital is not used at all in agriculture and land is not used at all in industry, while the organizational asymmetry means that even when returns to labour are equalized across the sectors by labour mobility, it is not the marginal products of labour in the two sectors which are so equalized.

In fact, in comparison with a neo-classical model it is clear that the agricultural sector is too large and the manufacturing sector is too small relative to the efficient outcome. In this sense accumulation of capital plays a double role – not only does it increase the level of national output, but it also moves the composition of national output in the direction of the efficient outcome. For Lewis, however, the role of accumulation and growth of the modern sector with unlimited supplies of labour at a fixed real wage was to demonstrate how the savings ratio could increase rapidly under such dualistic development, it being assumed that the only saving was undertaken by capitalists in the modern sector.

Jorgenson's (1961) model has many similarities with the Lewis model. The feature of the model emphasized by Jorgenson is production asymmetry between the two sectors:

> Productive activity in each sector may be characterized by a function relating output to each of the factors of production – land, labour and capital. The special character of the theory of development of a dual economy is a certain asymmetry in production relations. If the two production functions were essentially symmetric, that is, if each function included all three productive factors, the resulting model would be suited to the problems of industrial balance in an advanced economy or to dynamic problems in the theory of international trade. In the theory of a dual economy the output of the traditional or agricultural sector is a function of land and labour alone; there is no capital accumulation ... . Land does not appear as a factor of production in the manufacturing sector; the level of manufacturing output is a function of capital and labour alone.

Jorgenson also introduces organizational asymmetry:

> While it is not unreasonable to assume that profits are maximized in the advanced sector, there seems to be much less reason for making such an assumption for the agricultural sector ... It is assumed through the analysis that follows that the classical model applies.

Jorgenson's model is that of a closed economy, in which the terms of trade between agriculture and manufacturing determine accumulation and the rate of growth, and these terms of trade are themselves determined by the balance of supply and demand. Lewis (1954) considers both the closed and the open economy model, and discusses how accumulation may run into food-supply problems in the former case. Thus both models are distinguished by an inefficient sectoral allocation of labour owing to organizational asymmetry, by a focus on the rate of profit in manufacturing as the engine of growth given the production and savings assumptions, and by a recognition of the role of food supply in permitting growth to continue in the closed economy context. The model of Fei and Ranis (1964) also has similar characteristics (see Dixit, 1973, for a comparison of the behaviour of the Jorgenson and Fei–Ranis models).

The Lewis (1954) and Jorgenson (1961) models are not the only ones in the development literature that depart from the symmetry of two sector neo-classical models of growth. A number of more recent papers in the literature emphasize other asymmetries, and we wish to incorporate these into our overview of dual economy models. The celebrated model of Harris and Todaro (1970) is one such example. In fact, accumulation barely makes an appearance in this model. It is a standard, two-sector neo-classical model except for one particular asymmetry – the wage in manufacturing is above the market clearing level. Otherwise, and in contrast to the models of Lewis and Jorgenson, both sectors use capital and labour and the labour market in agriculture is competitive. In common with Lewis and Jorgenson, capital is immobile between the two sectors, and it is labour which is the equilibrating flow. The sectoral allocation of labour equilibrates at that value which equalizes the agricultural wage with the manufacturing wage times the employment rate in the manufacturing sector. The terms of trade can be taken as endogenous or, in the small open economy case, as exogenous.

The key feature is the inefficiency caused by the fact that the marginal products of labour in the sectors are no longer equal. The literature contains many papers which consider policy responses to this inefficiency, such as Bhagwati and Srinivasan (1974), and others which modify the capital mobility assumptions, such as Corden and Findlay (1975). But the family resemblance between the Harris–Todaro model and the Lewis and Jorgenson models should be clear. In all models, marginal products of the mobile factor are not equalized across the sectors because of an institutional asymmetry in the manner in which returns to the factor are determined in each sector. In the Harris–Todaro model it is manufacturing that departs from marginal product pricing of labour; in the Lewis–Jorgenson models this role is played by agriculture.

In all three models discussed so far, it is assumed that product markets are perfectly competitive – the focus of the asymmetry is the determination of the returns to factors. However, a class of models has recently been developed by Taylor (1983) and associates which introduces a non-clearing product market for the output of one of the sectors, manufacturing. Together with a non-clearing labour market, this introduces Keynesian features into the dual economy. Implicit in the models of Taylor is a 'sink' into which unsatisfied purchasing power goes, and out of which it can be attracted by means of government policy. In contrast to these Keynesian features of the manufacturing sector, with its output being demand constrained, the agricultural sector output is modelled as having a flexible price which adjusts to equate supply and demand. The asymmetry attempts to capture the stylized facts that agricultural commodity markets are largely competitive while manufacturing product markets are oligopolistic. Such dualism is a departure from the earlier models of Lewis, Jorgenson and Harris–Todaro, but it is an asymmetry that needs to be investigated more closely. In particular, the different models each highlight a particular asymmetry but do not bring this together in a way that can pinpoint the contribution of each – this we would consider to be an important area of research.

Asymmetries of factor and product markets are certainly a major distinguishing feature of various dual economy models. However, there is another strand running through these models and that is the different assumptions regarding *factor mobility*. In the Uzawa two-sector model, the two factors are perfectly mobile between the sectors. In effect, therefore, there is a unified market for each factor across the two sectors. The various dual economy models make different assumptions with regard to different factors. As already noted, in the Lewis model capital is used only in the manufacturing sector (and land is only used in the agricultural sector), which can be treated as a production asymmetry or as an extreme assumption of the mobility of the two factors – they are perfectly immobile. This is similarly true of the Jorgenson model. But in both the Lewis and Jorgenson models, it is assumed that there is a (constant) wage differential between the two sectors. Two interpretations are given for this differential. One is simply in terms of compensating differences – the urban wage is higher to compensate for the disadvantages of the urban lifestyle (for a model which incorporates this explicitly, see McIntosh, 1975). The other seems to be more akin to a statement that the differential is an equilibrium phenomenon, generated by less than perfect mobility of labour across the two sectors. While the two interpretations may be indistinguishable as equilibrium phenomena, whether or not labour (or any other factor) is instantaneously mobile affects the *dynamics* of the model significantly, as is shown in Kanbur and McIntosh (1985). The

long run stability and time path of a model can be altered radically depending on whether or not intersectoral factor movements are assumed to be fast relative to the rate of accumulation.

A similar situation arises in the Harris–Todaro model with respect to speeds of adjustment of the labour force across the two sectors. In the original paper the labour migration process and equilibrium is analysed *conditional* on a given capital stock. In other words, they assume this adjustment to be infinitely fast relative to the rate of accumulation. This seems an implausible specification, but it would not matter if the nature of the specification were irrelevant to the dynamics and the equilibrium of the model. However, as Bartlett (1983) has shown, allowing sectoral labour adjustment to occur at a speed commensurate with the rate of capital accumulation can introduce instability into the model with important consequences.

Thus the implications of alternative assumptions on the speed of intersectoral reallocation of factors in dual economy models, especially for the dynamic behaviour of these models, remains an extremely important area of analysis. The variety of time paths generated by different assumptions should alert us to their critical importance. However, there is another aspect of long run analysis that needs to be discussed. If dualism is to do with asymmetries and factor immobilities, is not the end of dualism to do with the end (or a severe diminishing) of these asymmetries and immobilities? Given their particular definition of dualism, and their particular specification of intersectoral factor movement speeds, the models discussed here all trace out the consequences of accumulation with unchanged assumptions. But none of the models surveyed here, and indeed none of the models we are aware of, incorporates the end of dualism itself as a long run outcome. Even in the Lewis model, the end of the surplus labour phase may or may not herald the end of organizational asymmetry between the two sectors. There is, thus, a gap in the literature; there are dual economy models of development, and there are non-dual economy models of growth but there are no models which treat the degree of factor immobility and asymmetry as endogenous and, hence, there are no models which analyse the path of dualism itself. This is clearly a major area for further research.

So far we have interpreted dualism to mean intersectoral asymmetries at the national level. However, in the wake of the policy debates on the new international economic order, there has developed a class of 'North–South' models which can essentially be viewed as models of dualism on the international scale. So far as asymmetries are concerned, these models share many of the features of standard dual economy models. As Findlay (1984) notes: 'I use the term "North–South" model to refer to any model in which there is some basic asymmetry related to the stage of development between the two regions.' Findlay (1980) has himself explored asymmetries in the operation of factor markets, with 'surplus labour' in the South and neo-classical conditions in the North. Taylor (1983) has modified this to make the North Keynesian by introducing non-clearing factor and product markets.

As in standard dual economy models, factor mobility assumptions are crucial to models of international dualism. All of the best known North–South models share the feature that labour is immobile between the regions (although international migration models tackle this aspect, they are not in an explicitly 'North–South', i.e. asymmetry based, framework). In this North–South models differ from single economy models because in many ways the essence of the latter is the shift of labour from the traditional to the modern sectors. However, recent models in the North–South genre focus on *capital mobility* (e.g. Burgstaller and Saavedra-Rivano, 1983), and in this way they differ again from standard models, which on the whole disregard capital mobility across sectors.

As with standard dual economy models, North–South models do not entertain to any great extent the end of dualism itself as the world economy progresses. However, an equally obvious problem is that at the level of global interaction a two-sector classification is perhaps too coarse to capture some basic questions of interest. In particular, the neglect of OPEC and COMECON as trading blocks in the world is difficult to justify empirically, and it is difficult to see how the special features of these blocks can be fitted into a two-region framework. Surplus labour is hardly a characteristic of OPEC, and they do not produce a manufactured product. Some attempts have been made a build Three Regions Model of Global Interaction incorporating North, South and OPEC (Gonzalez-Romero and Kanbur, 1986; Taylor, 1983; and van Wijnbergen, 1985), but much more work is needed here, and the incorporation of COMECON is still an open question.

The need for a finer level of disaggregation at the world level raises the question of whether the two-sector classification is adequate at the economy level. Of course, it depends on the questions being asked. As Sen (1975) observes, 'A million x million matrix is not a joy to handle.' Thus, there are costs to disaggregation and the optimal level of disaggregation depends on the purpose at hand. But it can be argued that for some purposes the dual structure may not be adequate, in particular where the nature of dualism is changing and the economy is characterized, for example, by an advanced capitalist sector which produces goods for export, an intermediate manufacturing sector which produces non-traded goods for domestic consumption, and a traditional agricultural/urban-informal sector. In these cases the insights of dual economy models need to be extended in order to shed light on the development process.

R. KANBUR AND J. MCINTOSH

See also HARRIS-TODARO MODEL; TWO-SECTOR MODELS.

BIBLIOGRAPHY

Bartlett, W. 1983. On the dynamic instability of induced-migration unemployment in a dual economy. *Journal of Development Economics* 12, 85–95.

Bhagwati, J. and Srinivasan, T.N. 1974. On reanalyzing the Harris–Todaro model: policy rankings in the case of sector-specific sticky wages. *American Economic Review* 64, 502–8.

Boeke, J.H. 1953. *Economics and Economic Policy of Dual Societies as Exemplified by Indonesia.* New York: Institute of Pacific Relations.

Burgstaller, A. and Saavedra-Rivano, N. 1983. Capital mobility and growth in a North–South model. *Columbia University Economics Department Discussion Paper No. 111.*

Corden, W.M. and Findlay, R. 1975. Urban unemployment, intersectoral capital mobility and development policy. *Economica.* 42, 59–78.

Dixit, A.K. 1973. Models of dual economies. *Models of Economic Growth,* ed. J.A. Mirrlees and N.H. Stern, New York: John Wiley and Sons, pp. 325–57.

Fei, J.C.H. and Ranis, G. 1964. *Development of the Labour Surplus Economy: Theory and Policy.* Homewood: Irwin.

Findlay, R. 1980. The terms of trade and equilibrium growth in the world economy. *American Economic Review* 70, 291–9.

Findlay R. 1984. Growth and Development in Trade Models. In *Handbook of International Economics,* Vol. 1, ed. R.W. Jones and P.B. Kenen. Amsterdam: North-Holland, 187–232.

Gonzalez-Romero, A. and Kanbur, S.M.R. 1986. Oil and the North–South terms of trade. University of Essex Discussion Paper.

Harris, J.R. and Todaro, M.P. 1970. Migration, unemployment and development: a two-sector analysis. *American Economic Review* 60(1), March, 126–42.

Kanbur, S.M.R. and McIntosh, J. 1986. Dual economy models: retrospect and prospect. University of Essex Discussion Paper.

Jorgenson, D.W. 1961. The development of a dual economy. *Economic Journal* 71, 309–34.

Lewis, W.A. 1954. Economic development with unlimited supplies of labour. *Manchester School of Economics and Social Studies* 22, 139–91.

Little, I.M.D. 1982. *Economic Development: Theory, Policy, and International Relations.* New York: Basic Books.

McIntosh, J. 1975. Growth and dualism in less developed countries. *Review of Economic Studies* 42, 421–43.

Sen, A.K. 1975. *Employment, Technology and Development.* Oxford: Oxford University Press.

Taylor, L. 1983. *Structuralist Macroeconomics.* New York: Basic Books.

Uzawa, H. 1961–3. On a two-sector model of economic growth. *Review of Economic Studies,* Pt. I, 29, October 1961, 40–47, Pt. II, 30, June 1963, 105–18.

van Wijnbergen, S. 1985. Interdependence revisited: a developing countries perspective on macroeconomic management and trade policy in the industrial world. *Economic Policy* 1, November, 81–317.

duality. Good and evil, knowing and being, subject and object even (quotes the *OED*) 'appls and pearz', all have been called dualities, testifying to the almost mystical power the word has had on the human mind. Such profusion testifies also to multiplicity of meaning. Sometimes it means just the sharp apparent contrast in pairs of ideas or objects, like mind and matter, 'meat and drinke'. Sometimes much more is implied, the alleged unity in seeming diversity or the two-sided nature of single beings. Put like that, duality appears as a special case, $n = 2$, of Marshall's famous Hegelian motto (1919, p. v): 'The many in the one, the one in the many'.

Ideas of duality have played important roles in academic disciplines as apparently widely separated as theology and physics. The word is in constant use in quite different branches of mathematics, in abstract set theory and functional analysis, to name only two. In economics it is also much bandied about, with correspondingly wide variation in meaning. For example, in such phrases as 'dual economies' and 'dual labour markets' it seems to mean just contrasting kinds of economy and of markets, whereas its main use in economics stems directly from the natural pairing of quantities and prices.

This pairing leads to the treatment of quantity space and price space as dual to one another, whether in the simple self-duality of finite-dimensional Euclidean space, or in the more subtle dualities of functional analysis that are appropriate to infinitely many goods (see e.g. Bewley (1972) and Peleg and Yaari (1970)). To treat all such dual aspects of quantity and price would widen the scope of this entry absurdly, making it as broad as general equilibrium theory itself. Instead, the focus will be on explicit 'duality schemes', the consistent use of which leads both to economy of proof and to sharper understanding of theoretical structure. Their advantages have been expressed well by Eggleston (1958, p. 25): [Duality] ... 'often suggests alternative proofs of known results; it suggests new results which are "dual" to known results; it helps to clarify existing knowledge and to coordinate diverse results'.

(a) Approaches to duality. Duality schemes occur in two major branches of economic theory, namely the analysis of linear economic models, and of 'convex' economies, by which is meant those neoclassical models that assume preferences and

technologies to be convex. (Of course, the latter models subsume the former but that will be ignored here.) Important examples of duality in linear models are: (i) the dual left and right eigenvectors of the production matrix in Sraffian economics, which give equilibrium relative prices and the weights of the standard commodity, respectively; (ii) the famous Duality Theorem of linear programming, due to von Neumann; (iii) the equally famous duality between growth rate and interest rate in von Neumann's canonical model of dynamic general equilibrium. These examples are discussed elsewhere in the Dictionary so are not considered here.

Four different meanings of 'duality' can be distinguished in the analysis of convex economies, one of which is not duality at all in the vector space sense of that term. It is important to sort these meanings out, since putting the same label on different things makes it harder to think straight. Indeed, a mixture of dualities and pseudo-dualities may be just what is needed to tackle a given problem, and then it will surely help to know which is which.

Consider a consumer facing competitively determined prices p and maximizing utility $u(.)$ subject to limited wealth. Let the value of any solution z^* of this 'primal' problem be written $\tau^* = u(z^*)$. The problem of finding a bundle z^{**} to minimize the cost of achieving at least τ^* at prices p is often called the dual to the maximization problem, a practice that goes back at least to Arrow and Debreu (1954, pp. 285–6). But for reasons spelled out in the entry on COST MINIMIZATION AND UTILITY MAXIMIZATION this usage seems inappropriate. The clue that something is amiss is that the solution z^{**} to the alleged 'dual' lies in the same space as (indeed, is often the same bundle as) the solution z^* to the primal, whereas if it solved a genuine dual problem it would, as in linear programming, lie in the space of dual variables. Hence such problems are not dual at all in the vector space sense.

Moving on to genuine duality schemes for convex economies, the label 'duality' is sometimes attached to any approach that uses only functions of dual variables, such as cost or profit functions. The formal duality scheme at work here is usually that of *support functions*, and it is best regarded as a special case of either one of the remaining two schemes (see e.g. CONVEX PROGRAMMING).

Most of the several original uses of duality in economics (e.g. Debreu (1951), Malmquist (1953) and Shephard (1953)), and much of the subsequent work, have been based on explicit or implicit use of the second genuine duality scheme, known as *gauge functions*. However, the formal mathematical treatment of this approach is currently incomplete, missing a large part that is of major importance for economists. It will be discussed, under that title, in a separate entry.

The third scheme has received scattered rather than systematic application in economics, even though it has been very thoroughly developed (and is of major importance) in that branch of mathematics known as *convex analysis*. It has many names, perhaps the most common usage in English being *conjugate convex functions*. The name used here, *Fenchel transforms*, is due to Rockafellar (1974). It is simple and commemorates the seminal work of Fenchel (1949). It also suggests the hope that in due course transforming a function à la Fenchel will be as routine as taking a Fourier or Laplace transform now is in everyday applied mathematics. (For economists, however, this hope is tempered by the thought that we have very few explicit functional forms to transform.)

(b) Scope of this entry. The rest of this entry is divided into four sections, the first two of which apply the tools of Fenchel transforms and superdifferentials, respectively, to the usual partial equilibrium theory of the individual consumer. The third part applies the same tools, plus that of infimal convolution, to prove a standard general equilibrium theorem in welfare economics, the so-called Second Fundamental Theorem. The final section applies all the previous tools, plus that of saddle functions, to an extension of the latter Theorem to an exchange economy with public goods.

The emphases on consumer's equilibrium and general equilibrium are quite deliberate, since such applications are rather scarce in the literature. Instead, the use of duality schemes in economics has tended to concentrate (though of course not exclusively) on partial equilibrium models of the firm and industry, and on concomitant econometric problems.

The discussion is limited to convex, finite-dimensional economies. The restriction to finite-dimensions is for exposition only, since all the techniques and many of the results apply in a wide class of infinite-dimensional spaces, that of locally convex topological vector spaces 'in duality'. A very few indications of such possible extensions are given along the way. The restriction to convex economies is more serious, but does reflect the state of the art. However, it is likely that progress in the theory of nonconvex economies will tend to come from building appropriately on techniques for convex economies, much as nonlinear functional analysis builds on its linear sibling; a good example is Clarke's brilliant extension of subdifferentials to nonconvex functions (see e.g. Clarke (1983) and Rockafellar (1981)).

Proofs and references will be notably rare. On Fenchel transforms and convex analysis, the entry on CONVEX PROGRAMMING should be consulted, while standard treatises are Moreau (1967), Rockafellar (1970), Ekeland and Temam (1976), Ioffe and Tihomirov (1979) and van Tiel (1984). On applications of duality schemes to cost functions, see the entry on that subject, while the whole field of applications to microeconomics is admirably surveyed in Diewert (1982), which contains a large bibliography.

I. FENCHEL TRANSFORMS AND INDIVIDUAL PREFERENCES

Each commodity bundle is a non-negative vector z in R^{n+1}. No subscripts are needed since there is only one agent, who is assumed to have two binary relations $\succ$ ('strict preference') and $\sim$ ('indifference'), each defined on some non-empty set $S \subset R^{n+1}$. The union of these relations is written $\succeq$ and referred to simply as *preferences*.

The assumptions that $\succ$ is asymmetric and $\sim$ symmetric and reflexive are obviously justified by the everyday meanings of 'strictly preferred' and 'indifferent' and will be maintained throughout, without labels. The following properties of preferences are less compelling and will be assumed only as needed:

A1 Transitivity
$\forall z^1, z^2, z^3 \in S \quad (z^1 \succeq z^2 \,\&\, z^2 \succeq z^3) \rightarrow (z^1 \succeq z^3)$

A2 Upper Closure
$\forall z^1 \in S \quad B^1 = \{z \in S: z \succeq z^1\}$ is closed

A3 Convexity
$\forall z^1 \in S$ The 'better set' B^1 is convex.

Two common assumptions not on this menu are *completeness* (for all $z^1, z^2 \in S$ either $z^1 \succeq z^2$ or $z^2 \succeq z^1$) and *strict monotonicity* (for all $z^1, z^2 \in S$, $z^1 > z^2$ implies $z^1 \succ z^2$, where $z^1 > z^2$ means $z^1 \geq z^2$ and $z^1 \neq z^2$). Lacking completeness, preferences will not be faithfully representable by a utility function in the usual way.

(a) Representations of preferences. A commodity is now singled out and a function defined, their properties and meaning to be

clarified in the sequel. Choose some commodity ξ and if necessary renumber to make it the last (or first, it makes no real difference). Each z can then be written (x, ξ), with $x \in R^n$ and $\xi \in R$. Define the function $f: R^n \times S \to [0, \infty]$ by the formula

$$f(x, z') = \inf\{\xi \geqslant 0: (x, \xi) \gtrsim z'\} \qquad (1)$$

where z' is mnemonic for a given *target* commodity bundle. In effect, (1) defines a family of functions $f(\,.\,, z')$ indexed by the parameter z'. Infimum (greatest lower bound) is used since a minimum may not exist, e.g. when the set in parentheses is empty.

Such a scheme is very flexible, and not just for demand theory. In production theory z' might be an output vector producible from any one of a set of input vectors y. In the theory of 'characteristics' z' might be a target vector of nutrients, contained in various diets z. Partitioning of z into (x, ξ) is often possible even when z (and so x) are infinite-dimensional. This is obvious when the space is of countable dimension but may hold also in more complicated spaces, like those of Dornbusch, Fischer and Samuelson (1977, 1978) and Wilson (1980) in international trade, which have one or two primary factors and a continuum of producible commodities.

Since it can take the value ∞, f is not real-valued but *extended* real-valued. Any function whose possible range is $[-\infty, \infty]$ is called *numerical* (see e.g. Choquet, 1966, p. 127). The *effective domain* dom F of any numerical $F: R^n \to [-\infty, \infty]$ is defined by

$$\text{dom } F = \{x \in R^n: F(x) < \infty\}$$

Putting $R^{n+} = \{x \in R^n: x \geqslant 0\}$, for each target z', $\text{dom} f(\,.\,, z') \subset R^{n+}$. Moreover, it is easy to show that

$$\forall z' \in S \quad \text{dom} f(\,.\,, z') = \{x \in R^n: \exists \xi \in R \ni (x, \xi) \gtrsim z'\}$$

A numerical function is *proper* if it is $-\infty$ nowhere and finite somewhere. By definition $f(\,.\,, z') > -\infty$ for all z', while since $z' \sim z', f(x', z') \leqslant \xi' < \infty$; hence each $f(\,.\,, z')$ is proper. (Observe that $f(x', z') < \xi'$ cannot be ruled out, even with A4 below.) Next, define the *epigraph* epi F of any numerical $F: R^n \to [-\infty, \infty]$ by

$$\text{epi } F = \{(x, \xi) \in R^{n+1}: \xi \geqslant F(x)\}$$

so that for functions $f(\,.\,, z')$,

$$\forall z' \in S \quad \text{epi} f(\,.\,, z') = \{(x, \xi) \in R^{n+1}: \xi \geqslant f(x, z')\} \qquad (2)$$

Next comes an assumption about ξ which would hold if that good were freely disposable, and is in any case quite reasonable. It obviously places some restriction on the choice of ξ.

A4 Weak Monotonicity of $\gtrsim$ in ξ.
$$\forall z' \in S, \quad \forall x \in \text{dom} f(\,.\,, z') \xi' \geqslant \xi'' \to (x, \xi') \gtrsim (x, \xi'')$$

The next two results show when epi $f(\,.\,, z')$ is the same as B', the better set of z'.

Lemma 1: Given A1 and A4, $\forall z' \in S$, cl epi $f(\,.\,, z') = \text{cl } B'$ where 'cl' denotes the closure of a set. An immediate consequence is

Theorem 1: Given A1, A2, and A4, $\forall z' \in S$, epi $f(\,.\,, z') = B'$.

Since a numerical function on R^n is *lower semicontinuous* (lsc) iff its epigraph is closed in R^{n+1}, there also follows

Corollary 1: Given A1, A2 and A4, $\forall z' \in S, f(\,.\,, z')$ is lsc.

What is the economic meaning of $f(\,.\,, z')$? If preferences were as in the textbooks, complete, continuous, convex, and strictly increasing in every commodity, then the graph of $f(\,.\,, z')$ would simply be the indifference surface through z'. As it is, for any z' its indifference surface may not exist and even

if it did may be 'thick', in which case $f(\,.\,, z')$ yields its lower boundary. More importantly, unlike the usual indifference surface $f(\,.\,, z')$ is defined on the whole of R^n. Indeed, since it is numerical and not real $f(x, z')$ remains defined (but infinite valued) even when x contains one or more inadmissibly negative elements, for then $\{\xi \geqslant 0: (x, \xi) \gtrsim z'\} = \varnothing$ and by convention inf $\varnothing = \infty$, just as sup $\varnothing = -\infty$.

To give an example, suppose that in the two-good case the agent must have at least 1 unit of the single commodity x per unit of time in order to live. Then for any $x < 0$ and $z' \geqslant (1, 0)$, $f(x, z') = \infty$ (drawing a diagram is helpful here). The flexibility that comes from representing preferences by numerical rather than real functions enables problems such as this one of 'survival' to be analysed naturally, without artifice.

It is not hard to show that given A1, $z^1 \gtrsim z^2$ iff $B^1 \subset B^2$, and second, that given A1, A2 and A4, $z^1 \gtrsim z^2$ iff $f(\,.\,, z^1) \geqslant f(\,.\,, z^2)$. The second result provides a sense in which the functions $f(\,.\,, z')$ do indeed represent preferences faithfully, since it is just a generalization of the obvious statement that $z^1 \gtrsim z^2$ iff the indifference surface through z^1 lies nowhere below that through z^2.

(b) *The cost function.* Assume now that ξ is a *numéraire* good, which requires that its (nominal) market price always be nonzero. Then each vector of prices in R^{n+1}, expressed in units of ξ, can be written $(p, 1)$. The value of a commodity bundle $z = (x, \xi)$ at those prices is then $\langle (x, \xi), (p, 1) \rangle$, where in this finite dimensional case $\langle \,.\,, .\, \rangle$ denotes inner product; in infinite dimensions the same notation, $\langle x, p \rangle$ say, stands for the value of the linear functional p at the point x.

The assumption that ξ is a numeraire does of course impose further restriction on its choice, beyond that already imposed by A4. In the partial equilibrium setting of this section however, the restriction involved is surely not great.

The next step is to derive the consumer's *cost* (or *expenditure*) *function*, using an optimization procedure that conceptually has two stages. In the first, $f(x, z')$ is computed for given $x \in R^n$ and given $z' \in S$. This yields the least amount of ξ (in the sense of infimum) that is needed, in conjunction with x, for the agent to be at least as well off as at z'. But that is for *given* x. Therefore, to find for prices $(p, 1)$ the least expenditure in units of ξ needed to obtain a bundle at least as good as z', in the second stage x is varied so as to find

$$\inf\{\langle x, p \rangle + f(x, z'): x \in R^n\} \qquad (3)$$

Notice that the value of (3) depends only on p and z' (the x's having been 'inf-ed' out as it were), so it can be written as a numerical function $\Phi(p, z')$. Allowing Φ to be numerical is tantamount to saying that (3) always has a value (which could be $\pm \infty$), although it may well not have a solution, i.e. even if the value is finite there may be no x which achieves it.

Before the powerful tool of Fenchel transforms can be applied, expression (3) needs some rearrangement. There are two equivalent ways of doing this, the choice between them a matter of personal taste. The first method has the advantage of using only ordinary (i.e. convex) Fenchel transforms, but involves also the awkwardness of writing price vectors as $-p$ rather than p, while the second (used here) involves the less usual *concave* Fenchel transforms but takes the p vectors as they come.

First, define $g: R^n \times S \to [-\infty, 0]$, the negative of f, by

$$g(x, z') = -f(x, z') \qquad (4)$$

See Figure 1. For $g(\,.\,, z')$, the terms dom, epigraph, and proper used previously for $f(\,.\,, z')$ have to be translated respectively to *n-dom* (i.e. the set of x's whose $g(\,.\,, z')$ value

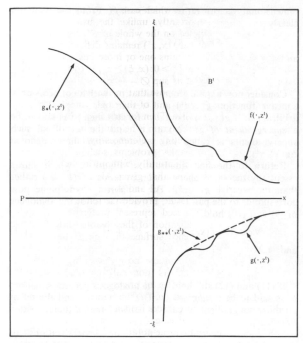

Figure 1

is greater than $-\infty$), *hypograph* [i.e. the set of (x, ξ) for which $\xi \leqslant g(x, z^t)$], and *n-proper* (i.e. $+\infty$ nowhere and finite somewhere). Define $g_*: R^n \times S \to [-\infty, \infty]$, the *concave Fenchel transform of* $g(\,.\,, z^t)$, by

$$g_*(p, z^t) = \inf\{\langle x, p \rangle - g(x, z^t) : x \in R^n\} \qquad (5)$$

Substituting (4) into (3) yields the right hand side (RHS) of (5), which proves

$$g_*(p, z^t) \equiv \Phi(p, z^t)$$

The concave Fenchel transform $g_*(\,.\,, z^t)$ is therefore the cost function, showing for relative prices p the least cost (in units of ξ) of being at least as well off as at z^t. The theory of such transforms demonstrates that it is concave and upper semicontinuous (usc) in p, whatever functional form $g(\,.\,, z^t)$ may have (see Figure 1). Its definition does not need preferences to be representable by a utility function. Indeed, $g_*(\,.\,, z^t)$ may itself represent those preferences, in the sense that given A1, $z^1 \gtrsim z^2$ implies $g_*(\,.\,, z^1) \geqslant g_*(\,.\,, z^2)$; the much more useful reverse implication does however require all of A1–A4, for reasons that will become clear.

(c) The second dual. Dizzy with success, let us go on to transform the transform, sending the dual function $g_*(\,.\,, z^t)$ defined on prices into a second dual function $g_{**}(\,.\,, z^t): R^n \to [-\infty, \infty]$ defined on quantities, by means of a formula completely analogous to (5), namely

$$g_{**}(x, z^t) = \inf\{\langle x, p \rangle - g_*(p, z^t) : p \in R^n\} \qquad (6)$$

The function thus created is called the *concave Fenchel transform of* $g_*(\,.\,, z^t)$, or the *second* concave Fenchel transform of $g(\,.\,, z^t)$. Since the operation on the RHS of (6) is the same as that in (5) it should (and does) give the same result, namely that $g_{**}(\,.\,, z^t)$ is concave and usc, this time in x rather than p. The meaning of the operation on the RHS of (5) followed easily from (3) but the RHS of (6) has no such

immediate economic interpretation, if only because the optimizing is done over the space of (relative) prices rather than quantities.

So change the question and ask not what the optimization problem in (6) means but what its result means. What is the economic meaning of $g_{**}(\,.\,, z^t)$? The answer is simple: It is the *concavification* of $g(\,.\,, z^t)$, i.e. the function whose hypograph is the *closed convex hull* of the hypograph of $g(\,.\,, z^t)$ (see Figure 1). Hence $g_{**}(\,.\,, z^t)$ represents preferences $\gtrsim^{**}$ that have been 'convexified' from the original $\gtrsim$, so that their better set B^{t**} is the closed convex hull of the original B^t (again see Figure 1). Moreover, one can see that *any* preferences that yield B^{t**} as the convexification of their better set for the target z^t will generate $g_{**}(\,.\,, z^t)$ as their second Fenchel transform.

When is $g(\,.\,, z^t)$ the 'onlie begetter' of $g_{**}(\,.\,, z^t)$? From the last remarks it is equivalent to ask: When are they the *same* function? Since $g_{**}(\,.\,, z^t)$ is concave and usc it is clearly necessary for such coincidence that $g(\,.\,, z^t)$ itself have both those properties. Because $g = -f$ this in turn means that $f(\,.\,, z^t)$ must be convex and lsc. For convexity a definition of convex function that is applicable to any numerical F is needed. This is quite simple: F is convex iff epi F is a convex set. Theorem 1 says that $B^t = $ epi $f(\,.\,, z^t)$, so it only needs the addition of A3 to make epi $f(\,.\,, z^t)$ a convex set, hence $f(\,.\,, z^t)$ convex and (by Corollary 1) lsc.

Necessity thus secured, sufficiency requires the use of the 'concave' version of the so-called Fenchel-Moreau Theorem. This fundamental result is formally equivalent to two better-known theorems in functional analysis (Hahn-Banach and 'the' Separating Hyperplane) and it applies in a much wider setting than R^n, namely, that of a pair of locally convex separated topological vector spaces that are 'in duality' (for which idea see e.g. Dieudonné, 1942).

Theorem 2: (Fenchel–Moreau, concave version). If $G : R^n \to [-\infty, \infty]$ is *n-proper*, then $G_{**} = G$ iff G is concave and usc.

Proof: See e.g. van Thiel, 1984, Chapter 6 for the convex version.

Theorem 3: Given A1–A4, $\forall z^t \in S$, $g(\,.\,, z^t) = g_{**}(\,.\,, z^t)$.

Proof: It has already been shown that $f(\,.\,, z^t)$ is proper, so $g(\,.\,, z^t)$ is *n-proper*. Similarly, it was demonstrated above that if A1–A4 hold then $g(\,.\,, z^t)$ is concave and usc. The result then follows from the Fenchel–Moreau Theorem. Q.E.D.

It turns out that $g_{***}(\,.\,, z^t)$, the transform applied thrice and so the concave Fenchel transform of $g_{**}(\,.\,, z^t)$, is the same function as the first transform $g_*(\,.\,, z^t)$, and so on for the fourth, fifth,... transforms. Hence the taking of Fenchel transforms stops with the second dual of $g(\,.\,, z^t)$, no matter what its functional form may be. Let us be thankful and pass on.

(d) Definition by optimization. For any $z^t \in S$ each $g_*(p, z^t)$ and $g_{**}(x, z^t)$ is defined, by (5) and (6) respectively, as the solution to an optimization problem. Perhaps the significance of this is best seen if $f(\,.\,, z^t)$, and so $g(\,.\,, z^t)$, are assumed to be differentiable. Then in (5) inf becomes min and in order for $g_*(p, z^t)$ to be defined it follows that the first-order conditions

$$\forall z^t \in S \quad p = \nabla g(x^1, z^t) \qquad (7)$$

must be satisfied at any minimizing x^1, where the RHS denotes the gradient ∇ of $g(\,.\,, z^t)$ at x^1, i.e. the vector of partial derivatives $g_i(x^1, z')$ of $g(., z')$ with respect to (wrt) x_i, for $i = 1, 2, \ldots, n$.

A moment's reflection (helped by reference again to Figure 1) shows that the partial derivative of $f(x^1, z')$ wrt x_i measures the marginal rate of substitution (mrs) of commodity ξ for i at x^1, in the sense of Hicks–Allen (1934, 1981), i.e. the rate at which the consumer must be compensated with ξ for losing i. Thus $f(., z')$ might be called *substitution-generating*. The convexity of $f(., z')$ assured by A3 makes each mrs an increasing function of x_i, and also implies that the first-order conditions (7) are sufficient as well as necessary for x^1 to yield a minimum in (3), thus dispensing with bordered Hessian determinants and all that.

So for differentiable preferences (7) says that for the cost function to be *defined* at any p the Hicks–Allen 'price ratio equals mrs' condition must be satisfied for every pair of commodities.

Turn now to (6) and assume that $g_*(., z')$ is differentiable; roughly speaking, this requires that $f(., z')$ be *strictly* convex (see Rockafellar, 1970, Theorem 26.3, pp. 253–4). Arguing as before it follows that the first-order conditions

$$\forall z' \in S \quad x = \nabla g_*(p, z') \tag{8}$$

must hold at any price vector p^2 that achieves the minimum in (6). Since $g_*(., z')$ is concave, $-g_*(., z')$ is convex, and so (8) is sufficient as well as necessary for p^2 actually to yield a minimum. But because $g_*(., z')$ is the cost function, (8) is quite simply the Hotelling–Shephard Lemma (Hotelling, 1932, p. 594; Shephard, 1953, p. 11) applied to consumer's demand, which must hold if the concavification $g_{**}(., z')$ is to be defined at any x.

The final step is simply to observe that if assumptions A1–A4 hold, then from Theorem 3 $g_{**}(., z') = g(., z')$. Therefore (8) must hold *unconditionally*, because $g_{**}(., z')$ is then defined not only by optimization as in (6) but also as $g(., z')$ itself. Indeed, the Fenchel–Moreau Theorem shows that every n-proper usc concave function lives a double life as it were – as Dr Jekyll its inoffensive self (e.g. $g(., z')$) and as Mr Hyde the functional solution (e.g. $g_{**}(., z')$) to an infinite family of optimization problems such as (6). It is this double perspective on concave (and convex) functions which lies at the heart of duality theory, and is mainly responsible for its beneficial Jekyll-like results.

Notice how the standard equilibrium conditions for the consumer, the Gossen equations (7) and the Hotelling equations (8), arise naturally from the two 'sides' of the duality, i.e. the first and second duals of $g(., z')$, respectively. Just how close is the connection between these two classic results will be seen below.

II. SUPERDIFFERENTIALS AND DEMAND ANALYSIS

Duality theory is not confined to differentiable functions. For concave and convex functions it is possible to generalize the usual differentials of multivariable calculus in a very natural way, and thereby gain further insight into the structure of the theory. It seems odd, therefore, that mathematics took so long to reach this generalization (cf. Minty, 1969).

(*a*) *Dual pairs of points.* In the fourth quadrant of Figure 2 $g(., z')$ has been assumed concave throughout, but not differentiable at x^1. However, as drawn it has infinitely many 'lines of support' there (more generally, 'supporting hyperplanes'). Of these, only that corresponding to the pair $(p^2, -\beta^2) \in R^{n+1}$ is shown, so that its graph is the straight line $-\xi = \langle x, p^2 \rangle - \beta^2$, where x and p are treated here as one-

dimensional vectors rather than scalars. From the diagram, clearly

$$\forall x \in R^n \quad g(x, z') \leqslant \langle x, p^2 \rangle - \beta^2 \tag{9}$$

and

$$g(x^1, z') = \langle x^1, p^2 \rangle - \beta^2 \tag{10}$$

Consider now a quite general situation, with a not necessarily concave function $g(., z')$ and a pair $(p^2, -\beta^2) \in R^{n+1}$, for arbitrary n. If $g(., z')$ obeys (9) and (10) then p^2 is said to be a *supergradient* of $g(., z')$ at x^1, and the set of all such supergradients is called its *superdifferential* there, denoted $\Delta g(x^1, z')$.

Return to the first quadrant of Figure 2, which shows essentially the same phenomenon in terms of $f(., z')$ rather than its negative $g(., z')$. The supporting hyperplane now corresponds to the pair $(-p^2, \alpha^2)$, and the following analogues of (9) and (10) hold.

$$\forall x \in R^n \quad f(x, z') \geqslant \langle x, -p^2 \rangle + \alpha^2 \tag{11}$$

and

$$f(x^1, z') = \langle x^1, -p^2 \rangle + \alpha^2 \tag{12}$$

If (11) and (12) still hold in the analogous general situation, p^2 is said to be a *subgradient* of $f(., z')$ at x^1, and the set of all those subgradients is called its *subdifferential* there, written $\partial f(x^1, z')$.

Sub- and superdifferentiability are generalizations of differentiability that have been tailored (by Minty and Moreau, independently of each other) to be applicable to convex and concave functions respectively. However, most work in convex analysis, dealing mainly with convex functions, normally uses the same terminology (subgradients and subdifferentials) and notation (∂f) for both sub- and supergradients, and sub- and superdifferentials.

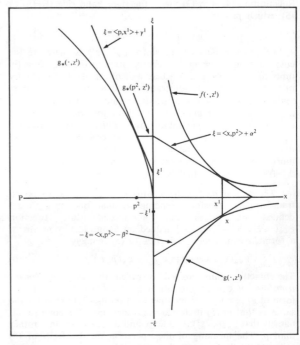

Figure 2

From (10) one sees that for $g(.,z^t)$ to be superdifferentiable at x^1 it must be finite there, while a further necessary condition is easily shown to be $g(x^1, z^t) = g_{**}(x^1, z^t)$. This in turn implies that $g(.,z^t)$ must be at least locally concave at x^1, since $g_{**}(.,z^t)$ is globally concave. It is also not hard to prove the important

Lemma 2: For any $g(.,z^t)$,

$$p^2 \in \Delta g(x^1, z^t) \equiv [g(x^1, z^t) + g_*(p^2, z^t) = \langle x^1, p^2 \rangle] \quad (13)$$

which implies at once that in (10) and (12) and Figure 2, $\beta^2 = g_*(p^2, z^t) = \alpha^2$. To see what Lemma 2 means in economic terms, observe that (13) can be written $g_*(p^2, z^t) = \langle x^1, p^2 \rangle + f(x^1, z^t)$, so that the bundle $(x^1, f(x^1, z^t))$ minimizes the cost of being in B^t at prices $(p^2, 1)$. Hence the Lemma says that this cost-minimization is *equivalent* to p^2 being a supergradient of $g(.,z^t)$ at x^1, which in turn is a natural generalization of the Gossen–Hicks–Allen conditions (7).

Turn next to the second quadrant in Figure 2, where p is measured positively from right to left. Theorem 4 will make it clear why $g_*(.,z^t)$ has (x^1, γ^1) as a supporting hyperplane precisely at p^2, i.e. $x^1 \in \Delta g_*(p^2, z^t)$. A result needed prior to that is simply the dual of Lemma 2.

Corollary 2: For any $g(.,z^t)$,

$$x^1 \in \Delta g_*(p^2, z^t) \equiv [g_*(p^2, z^t) + g_{**}(x^1, z^t) = \langle p^2, x^1 \rangle] \quad (14)$$

Equation (14) does not have so direct an economic meaning as (13), but the condition $x^1 \in \Delta g_*(p^2, z^t)$ is clearly a generalization of the Hotelling–Shephard Lemma (8).

Theorem 4: (a) For any $g(.,z^t)$,

$$p^2 \in \Delta g(x^1, z^t) \to x^1 \in \Delta g_*(p^2, z^t)$$

(b) Given A1–A4,

$$x^1 \in \Delta g_*(p^2, z^t) \to p^2 \in \Delta g(x^1, z^t)$$

Proof: (a) From Lemma 2 (13) holds, and since $\Delta g(x^1, z^t) \neq \emptyset, g(x^1, z^t) - g_{**}(x^1, z^t)$. Substituting for this in (13) yields (14), and the result then follows from Corollary 2. (b) From Corollary 2 (14) holds, while from Theorem 3 $g_{**}(.,z^t) = g(.,z^t)$. Substituting this into (14) yields (13), and the result then follows from Lemma 2. Q.E.D.

Part (a) of Theorem 4 shows that the generalized price-ratio-equals-mrs condition implies the Hotelling Lemma. Part (b), which is a consequence of the Fenchel–Moreau Theorem, shows in conjunction with part (a) that when each better set B^t is closed and convex, the generalized Hicks–Allen condition and the generalized Hotelling–Shephard Lemma are logically *equivalent*, each proposition implying the other.

For any $g(.,z^t)$ denote by μ the operation that takes each $x \in R^n$ into the set $\Delta g(x, z^t) \subset R^n$, so that μ is a *correspondence* (set-valued mapping, multifunction). Similarly, for $g_*(.,z^t)$ let h be the correspondence which takes each $p \in R^n$ into $\Delta g_*(p, z^t) \subset R^n$. Theorem 4 shows that under very general conditions μ and h are mappings inverse to each other, in the sense that $p \in \Delta g(x, z^t)$ iff $x \in \Delta g_*(p, z^t)$. Pairs (x, p) that stand in this relationship are called *conjugate*, or *dual pairs of points*.

(b) *Compensated demand correspondences.* The generalized Hotelling–Shephard Lemma $x^1 \in h(p^1, z^t)$ must hold when (x^1, p^1) are a dual pair, so that $h(.,z^t)$ is a *compensated* (or *Hicksian*) *demand correspondence*. Similarly, the generalized Hicks–Allen conditions $p^1 \in \mu(x^1, z^t)$ must also hold, p^1 being a vector of prices for which $(x^1, f(x^1, z^t))$ is a cost-minimizing response to target z^t. Hence, μ is an *inverse* compensated demand correspondence. Precisely because both h and μ are

superdifferential mappings, convex analysis has much to say about their properties. For simplicity only the inverse correspondence μ will be discussed here, but usually the same properties will hold also for h.

The simplest correspondence is an ordinary function, with one-element image sets. Since these singleton subsets are closed, convex, non-empty and bounded, the most tractable general correspondences are those whose image sets also have those four properties. For superdifferential mappings the first two properties are easily verified, because $\Delta g(x, z^t)$ is for any x the solution set to the infinite family of weak linear inequalities given by (9) and (10), and so is closed and convex.

Two useful results together help to establish when $\mu(x, z^t) \neq \emptyset$. First, any n-proper concave function that is continuous at a given point will have a non-empty superdifferential there; and second, any numerical concave function defined on R^n is continuous at every point of the relative interior (ri) of n-dom F (Rockafellar, 1970, pp. 82–3; on ri's see CONVEX PROGRAMMING). Hence if A1–A4 hold $\mu(x, z^t) \neq \emptyset$ for all $x \in $ ri n-dom $g(.,z^t)$, which at least for finite dimensions is quite satisfactory; in more general spaces the continuity of a concave function is a more delicate matter. (Observe that since $g_*(.,z^t)$ is n-proper iff the $g(.,z^t)$ is itself n-proper and concave, $h(.,z^t)$ like $\mu(.,z^t)$ needs A1–A4 before the first result can be applied.)

Because $\mu(x, z^t)$ is always a closed set, in finite dimensions its compactness is equivalent to its boundedness, though again the matter is much less simple in infinite-dimensional spaces. However, even in finite dimensions compactness does impose sharper restrictions: $\mu(x, z^t)$ will be bounded iff x belongs to the interior (int) of n-dom $g(.,z^t)$ (Rockafellar, 1970, p. 217). For infinite-dimensional spaces 'in duality', non-emptiness and (weak) compactness of $\mu(x, z^t)$ both follow if the concave n-proper function $g(.,z^t)$ is continuous throughout int n-dom $f(.,z^t)$, *and* the latter set is non-empty – often a strong restriction.

Collecting these results for finite-dimensional commodity spaces, the inverse demand correspondence will have non-empty convex compact image subsets $\mu(x, z^t)$ in R^n, for each $x \in $ int n-dom $g(.,z^t)$.

To apply fixed-point theorems it is essential that correspondences have suitable properties of continuity. Here again, the fact that $\mu(.,z^t)$ and $h(.,z^t)$ are superdifferential mappings yields quite useful results. If $g(.,z^t)$ is a usc numerical function at x^1, and there exists a neighbourhood $N(x^1)$ on which $g(.,z^t)$ is bounded from below, then $\mu(.,z^t)$ will be an upper semicontinuous correspondence (USC) at x^1 (Moreau, 1967, p. 79; for a definition of USC, see Correspondences). Another result on such USC mappings refers not to x but to the target z^t, and is useful for proofs of existence of equilibrium. Suppose that the set S to which the z^t belong is compact. Assume further that there is an open set G containing x^1 such that the mapping $z^t \to g(x, z^t)$ is continuous on S for every $x \in G$. Then the mapping $z^t \to \mu(x^1, z^t)$ is USC in z^t (Valadier, 1970a, Theorem 2.18).

Another useful property of superdifferentials has occasioned misunderstanding by economists. If $g(.,z^t)$ is superdifferentiable at x^1 and $p^1 \in \Delta g(x^1, z^t)$, then since $g(x^1, z^t)$ must be finite, (9) and (10) imply

$$\forall x \in R^n \quad g(x, z^t) \leqslant g(x^1, z^t) + \langle x - x^1, p^1 \rangle \quad (15)$$

This important relation is usually called the *supergradient inequality* (reversing $\leqslant$ gives the *sub* gradient inequality). Together with the stipulation that $g(x^1, z^t)$ be finite, it is actually equivalent to (9) and (10).

Let $x^1, x^2, x^3, \ldots, x^k$ be any finite chain of points at which

$g(\,.\,,z')$ is superdifferentiable, with $k \geqslant 2$ and corresponding supergradients $p^1, p^2, p^3, \ldots, p^k$. Then from (15), putting x successively equal to $x^2, x^3, \ldots, x^k, x^1$,

$$g(x^2, z') - g(x^1, z') \leqslant \langle x^2 - x^1, p^1 \rangle$$
$$g(x^3, z') - g(x^2, z') \leqslant \langle x^3 - x^2, p^2 \rangle$$
$$\ldots\ldots\ldots\ldots\ldots\ldots\ldots$$
$$g(x^1, z') - g(x^k, z') \leqslant \langle x^1 - x^k, p^k \rangle$$

On addition these inequalities yield

$$\Sigma \langle x^r - x^{r-1}, p^{r-1} \rangle + \langle x^1 - x^k, p^k \rangle \geqslant 0 \qquad (16)$$

where the summation is over $r = 2, 3, \ldots k$.

Any correspondence, such as $\mu(\,.\,,z')$, that satisfies (16) for every $k \geqslant 2$ is called a *cyclically monotone mapping*, a concept due to Rockafellar (see e.g. 1970, pp. 238–40). In particular, the case $k = 2$ yields the familiar relation

$$\langle x^2 - x^1, p^2 - p^1 \rangle \leqslant 0 \qquad (17)$$

for any pairs (x^1, p^1), (x^2, p^2) in the graph of $g(\,.\,,z')$. Relation (17) alone, without (16), implies that $\mu(\,.\,,z')$ is a *monotone mapping*. It has just been shown that (16) implies (17), but the reverse is not true unless R^n is actually R^2 (see Monotone Mappings). The apparent similarity of (17) to the situation envisaged by the Weak Axiom of revealed preference theory has misled some authors (e.g. Jorgenson and Lau, 1974, p. 190) into identifying it with that axiom. However, (17) applies only to quantity-price pairs in the graph of the inverse *compensated* demand correspondence, e.g. around an indifference curve, whereas Samuleson's Axiom applies to price-quantity pairs in the graph of the *ordinary* demand function and so allows also for income effects, which (17) does not do; a fortiori, cyclic monotonicity is not the same as the Strong Axiom of revealed preference.

Finally, although this section has concentrated on superdifferentials, there are many results to the effect that the sets of points at which a concave (or convex) numerical function on R^n fails to be differentiable in the ordinary sense is really quite small. Only two such results are quoted here. The first is an application of a classic result of Alexandroff (1939): Given A1–A4, $g(\,.\,,z')$ is twice differentiable almost everywhere on int n-dom $g(\,.\,,z')$, with equal second-order cross-partial derivatives. The second applies a result of Rockafellar (1981, p. 101): Under the same conditions, the set of x for which $\mu(x, z')$ has more than one point is of measure zero, and similarly for $h(\,.\,,z')$.

III. CONVOLUTION AND EFFICIENCY

The scene now changes from partial to general equilibrium. For brevity, only an exchange economy will be considered, having a finite number of agents indexed by $r = 1, 2, \ldots, s$ with preferences $\succsim_r$, and a finite number of commodities indexed by $i = 1, 2, \ldots, n$. The focus of attention is to prove the Second Fundamental Theorem of Welfare Economics, i.e. that any allocation that is Edgeworth–Pareto (EP) Optimal can be 'priced out' as a competitive equilibrium, with prices p^* and an allocation Z^* consisting of s bundles z_r^*, each of which is optimal for the agent concerned at those prices and with an appropriate distribution of the total endowments.

The method of attack uses both the mathematical operation of infimal convolution introduced by Moreau (1963), and an alternative approach to economic efficiency, introduced independently by Allais (1943, pp. 610–6, 637–44) and Scitovsky (1941–2). The use of convolution is the only novelty here, since Allais–Scitovsky efficiency is already present, explicitly or im-

plicitly, in standard treatments of this Welfare Theorem (e.g. in Debreu, 1959, especially pp. 96–7).

All summations are over the s agents. The notation ΣZ therefore means the n-vector of total usage of commodities in the allocation Z, so that $\Sigma Z^0 = z^0$, the total endowments.

An allocation Z^1 is *Edgeworth–Pareto (EP) Optimal for total endowments* z^0 if it is feasible (i.e. $\Sigma Z^1 = z^0$) and there exists no other feasible allocation Z such that $Z > Z^1$, where $>$ now means that $z_r \succsim_r z_r^1$ for each r and that strict preference occurs for at least one agent. If for some allocation Z^2 there is no Z such that $Z > Z^2$, then Z^2 is *bliss*.

Preferences are treated exactly as in Section I. The same commodity ξ is chosen for each agent r, so each z_r can be written (x_r, ξ_r). The rth agent's preferences are represented by the family of numerical functions $f_r(\,.\,,z_r')$, defined by

$$\forall x_r \in R^n, \forall z_r' \in S_r, \quad f_r(x_r, z_r') = \inf\{\xi \geqslant 0 : (x_r, \xi) \succsim_r z_r'\}$$

and their negatives $g_r(\,.\,,z_r')$ are defined analogously to (4). For simplicity, A1–A4 are always assumed. For $\xi < 0$, denote any vector of the form $(0, 0, \ldots, \xi)$ by s_ξ. Then the following addition to A4 will be needed.

A5 (Social usefulness of ξ). For any Z that is not bliss and any s_ξ there is an allocation Z^2 such that $\Sigma Z^2 = \Sigma Z + s_\xi$ and $Z^2 > Z$, i.e. ξ is always useful to somebody and rejected by nobody.

Under this assumption, ξ must have a positive nominal price and so can be used as *numéraire* for the exchange economy.

(a) Infimal convolution. Consider the programming problem: Choose vectors $(x_1, x_2, \ldots, x_m)$ so as to inf $\Sigma f_r(x_r, z_r')$ subject to $\Sigma x_r = x^0$. The value of this problem can be written as a numerical function of its parameters (x^0, Z'), where Z' is the m-fold array of the individual targets z_r'. More formally, letting $S = S_1 \times S_2 \times \ldots \times S_s$, the *infimal convolution* $f : R^n \times S \to [-\infty, \infty]$ of the s functions $f_r : R^n \times S_r$ is defined by

$$f(x, Z') = \inf\{\Sigma f_r(x_r, z_r') : \Sigma x_r = x\} \qquad (18)$$

Each f_r is bounded below by zero, so $f(x, Z')$ always exists but of course may be infinite. One can show that dom $f(\,.\,,Z') = \Sigma$ dom $f_r(\,.\,,z_r')$, while if each $f_r(\,.\,,z_r')$ is convex then the same property is inherited by $f(\,.\,,Z')$. Perhaps surprisingly, a similar inheritance is much harder to prove for lower semicontinuity. In this regard the next result is an application of a far from trivial theorem of Moreau (1963, pp. 21–3); our standard assumption that dom $f_r(\,.\,,z_r') \subset R^{n+}$ is important here.

Theorem 5: Given that A1–A4 hold for each r, (i) $f(\,.\,,Z')$ is proper, lsc and convex, and (ii) in (18) the inf is achieved as a minimum, i.e. for any $x^1 \in$ dom $f(\,.\,,Z')$ there is a division of x^1 into m vectors x_r^1 such that

$$f(x^1, Z') = \Sigma f_r(x_r^1, z_r^1)$$

Property (ii) is summarized here by saying that the allocation $\{x_r^1, f_r(x_r^1, z_r')\}$ *solves* $f(x^1, Z')$.

Theorem 6: Given A1–A4 for each r and A5, then if $Z^1 = \{x_r^1, \xi_r^1\}$ is EP Optimal for the endowments $z^0 = (x^0, \xi^0)$, it solves $f(x^0, Z^1)$. Hence, $\xi_r^1 = f_r(x_r^1, z_r^1)$ for each r.

Proof: Suppose the conclusion false, so $\Sigma \xi_r^1 - f(x^0, Z^1) = \xi^0 - f(x^0, Z^1) = \xi' > 0$. Put $s_\xi = (0, 0, \ldots, \xi')$. From Theorem 5 there exists an allocation Z^2 that solves $f(x^0, Z^1)$, and from A5 there exists Z^3 such that $\Sigma Z^3 = \Sigma Z^2 + s_\xi = \Sigma Z^1 = z^0$, and $Z^3 > Z^1$. But this contradicts the optimality of Z^1 for z^0. So $\Sigma \xi_r^1 = f(x^0, Z^1) = \Sigma f_r(x_r^1, z_r^1)$. Clearly, $\xi_r^1 \geqslant f_r(x_r^1, z_r^1)$ for all r, so from this and the last result equality must hold for each r. Q.E.D.

The most important aspect of the operation of infimal convolution is that it is dual to the operation of taking the *sum* of a family of convex Fenchel transforms. In the present case it is concave Fenchel transforms that are relevant, so the switch must be made from infimal convolution of the $f_r(\,.\,,z_r^t)$ to the *supremal convolution* $g(\,.\,,Z^t):R^n \to [-\infty,\infty]$ of the $g_r(\,.\,,z_r^t)$, defined by

$$g(x,Z^t) = \sup\{\Sigma g_r(x_r,z_r^t): \Sigma x_r = x\}$$

The next result is simple but very important,

$$\forall p \in R^n, \ \forall z_r \in S_r \qquad g_*(p,Z^t) = \Sigma g_{r*}(p,z_r^t) \qquad (19)$$

where the $g_{r*}(\,.\,,z_r^t)$ are the concave Fenchel transforms of the $g_r(\,.\,,z_r^t)$. In economic terms, the least total cost for the group as a whole is the sum of the individual least costs (a similar result applies when s has the power of the continuum, see e.g. Valadier, 1970b).

(b) *Compensated equilibrium.* An allocation Z^2 and a price vector p^2 constitutes a *compensated equilibrium* for the exchange economy consisting of s agents with preferences $\succsim_r$, and endowments z_r^t, if:

(A) Markets clear, i.e.

$$\Sigma x_r^2 = \Sigma x' \qquad (20)$$

(B) Each x_r^2 satisfies the individual budget constraint, i.e.

$$\forall r \quad \langle x_r^2,p^2\rangle + \zeta_r^2 = \langle x_z',p^2\rangle + \xi_r' \qquad (21)$$

(C) Each z_r^2 minimizes the cost at prices p^2 of achieving z_r^2, i.e.

$$\forall r \quad \langle x_r^2,p^2\rangle + \xi_r^2 = g_{r*}(p^2,z_r^2) \qquad (22)$$

This concept differs from competitive equilibrium in requiring the agents to minimize costs rather than maximize utility. There is no free disposal here, so the budget constraints must be satisfied as equalities. Note that from (20) and (21) $\Sigma\xi_r^2 = \Sigma\xi_r'$, so the ξ-market must be cleared as well (this is simply Walras' Law).

From Lemma 2 it is easy to prove

Lemma 3: Condition C is equivalent to the following conditions together:

$$\text{(i)} \quad \forall r \quad p^2 \in \Delta g_r(x_r^2,z_r^2) \qquad (23)$$

and

$$\text{(ii)} \quad \forall r \quad -\xi_r^2 = g_r(x_r^2,z_r^2) \qquad (24)$$

Since $f(\,.\,,Z^t)$ is proper, convex and lsc, then if $x^0 \in \text{ri dom} f(\,.\,,Z^t)$ the function will be continuous there and have a non-empty superdifferential; it follows also that there exists $p^1 \in \Delta g(x^0,Z^t)$. A decentralized 'pricing-out' theorem will therefore be proved if a link can be established between this fact and (23). To do this needs a simple but basic proposition of convex analysis that so far has not been required, at least explicitly. Adapted to the present situation, it reads

Young's Inequality. For any n-proper function $g_r(\,.\,,z_r^t)$,

$$\forall x_r, \ p \in R^n, \quad \forall z_r^t \in S_r \quad g_r(x_r,z_r^t)$$
$$+ g_{r*}(p,z_r^t) \leqslant \langle x_r,p\rangle \quad (25)$$

Notice that from Lemma 2, $p^2 \in \Delta g_r(x_r^1,z_r^t)$ is precisely the case of equality in (25).

The next result applies a lemma that is analogous to a result of Laurent (1972, pp. 366-8).

Lemma 4: The statement (iii) Z^1 solves $f(x^0,Z^1)$ and $p^1 \in \Delta g(x^0,Z^1)$ is equivalent to (iv) $p^1 \in \cap\{\Delta g_r(x_r^1,z_r^t): r = 1, 2, \ldots, m\}$

Proof: (for brevity, $g_r(x_r^1,z_r^t)$ will be written $g_r(x_r^1)$, etc.) (iv) $\to$ (iii). By the hypothesis and Lemma 2,

$$\forall r \quad g_r(x_r^1) + g_{r*}(p^1) = \langle x_r^1,p^1\rangle$$

which from (19) implies

$$\Sigma g_r(x_r^1) + g_*(p^1) = \langle \Sigma x_r^1,p^1\rangle \qquad (26)$$
$$= \langle x^0,p^1\rangle \qquad (27)$$

Since $f(x^0) \leqslant \Sigma f_r(x_r^1), g(x^0) \geqslant \Sigma g_r(x_r^1)$, so from this and (27),

$$g(x^0) + g_*(p^1) \geqslant \langle x^0,p^1\rangle$$

But from Young's Inequality (25),

$$g(x^0) + g_*(p^1) \leqslant \langle x^0,p^1\rangle$$

so actually

$$g(x^0) + g_*(p^1) = \langle x^0,p^1\rangle \qquad (28)$$

which from Lemma 2 implies $p^1 \in \Delta g(x^0)$. From (27) and (28), $g(x^0) = \Sigma g_r(x_r^1)$, which is the same as $f(x^0) = \Sigma f_r(x_r^1)$, so that Z^1 solves $f(x^0,Z^1)$.
(iii) $\to$ (iv). From the hypotheses, Lemma 2 and (19),

$$\Sigma g_r(x_r^1) + \Sigma g_{r*}((p^1)) = \langle \Sigma x_r^1,p^1\rangle \qquad (29)$$

By definition of each g_{r*},

$$\forall r \quad g_{r*}(p^1) \leqslant \langle x_r^1,p^1\rangle - g_r(x_r^1)$$

so

$$\forall r \quad g_r(x_r^1) + g_{r*}(p^1) \leqslant \langle x_r^1,p^1\rangle \qquad (30)$$

Then (29) and (30) together imply

$$\forall r \quad g_r(x_r^1) + g_{r*}(p^1) = \langle x_r^1,p^1\rangle$$

But Lemma 2 says that this is equivalent to

$$\forall r \quad p^1 \in \Delta g_r(x_r)$$

so

$$p^1 \in \cap\{\Delta g_r(x_r^1,z_r^t): r = 1, 2, \ldots, m\}$$

Q.E.D.

An immediate consequence is

Theorem 7: Assume A1–A4 for each r, A5, and $x^0 \in \text{ri dom} f(\,.\,,Z^1)$. Then if Z^1 is EP optimal for z^0, there exists a vector of relative prices p^1 such that (Z^1,p^1) form a compensated equilibrium for any individual endowments aggregating z^0 and satisfying the individual budget constraints (21).

Proof: Theorem 6 gives (20) and (24). Moreover, from the assumptions there exists $p^1 \in \Delta g(x^0,Z^1)$, which together with Theorem 6 again yields (iii) in Lemma 4. Then condition (iv) of that Lemma holds, which is in turn the same as (23). Lemma 3 implies that (20), (23) and (24) guarantee that Conditions A and C for a compensated equilibrium are satisfied. The left-hand-side (LHS) of (21), together with Theorem 6, yields $\langle x^0,p^1\rangle + \xi^0 = \langle \Sigma x',p^1\rangle + \xi'$, so any distribution of z^0 that satisfies (21) for each r will meet Condition B. Q.E.D.

The final step in the proof of the Second Welfare Theorem is to show that under certain conditions a compensated equilibrium is also a competitive equilibrium. This is not discussed here since it is a standard problem (see Arrow and Hahn, 1971, pp. 107–11; also COST MINIMIZATION AND UTILITY MAXIMIZATION). Essentially, it requires the existence of locally cheaper points at the compensated equilibrium.

Nowhere has it been assumed that individual preferences are either complete or representable by a utility function; nor was monotonicity assumed, except in ξ. Notice also that, taken in conjunction with Lemma 4, Theorem 7 gives interesting information about any price vector p^1 that 'supports' an EP optimum, since it must belong to the intersection of all the individual superdifferentials $\Delta g_r(x_r^1, z_r^1)$. This implies that the graph of the infimal convolution $f(., Z^1)$ – which is just a generalization of Scitovsky's community indifference curve — is likely to be smoother than the graphs of any of the individual $f_r(., z_r^1)$ whose convolution it is.

IV. SADDLE FUNCTIONS AND PUBLIC GOODS

A *saddle function* is defined here to be a numerical function with two vector arguments, in one of which it is concave and in the other convex. Considering the graph of such a function, the name appears apt. Quite apart from their standard uses in game theory and mathematical programming, saddle functions have many applications to problems both of partial and general equilibrium in economics, especially those involving *fixed* goods such as capital goods (industrial and domestic), rationed goods, and factor endowments (e.g. the 'National Product' and 'National Expense' functions of Samuelson, 1953–4). This section presents the example of a simple exchange economy with public goods, discusses the relevant dualities, and sketches a few of the results obtainable.

Saddle functions bring new and technically bothersome problems, of which only two are mentioned here. In Section I(b) it was pointed out that cost functions can be regarded either as concave Fenchel transforms, or as convex Fenchel transforms whose arguments (price vectors) have negative signs. With saddle functions, which are concave *and* convex, these problems of sign are unavoidably compounded, with the result that all price vectors appear here with non-intuitively negative signs attached. This is a nuisance but no more than that.

The second difficulty is more formidable. Suppose a real-valued saddle function F is defined on some subset $B \times C \subset R^n \times R^m$. It could be extended to a numerical function G defined on the whole of $R^n \times R^m$ by putting $G = F$ on $B \times C$, $G(x, y) = \infty$ for x in B and y not in C, and $G(x, y) = -\infty$ when x is not in B, no matter where y is. It could *also* be extended to another numerical function H by putting $H = F$ on $B \times C$, $= -\infty$ for x not in B and y in C, and $= \infty$ when y is not in C. If either $x \in B$ or $y \in C$ then $G = H$, but when $x \notin B$ and $y \notin C$ they differ as much as possible, one taking the value $-\infty$, the other $+\infty$. Yet it is easy to check that $\sup_x \inf_y G(x, y) = \sup_x \inf_y H(x, y)$!

Thus there is no unique way to extend a saddle function defined on a subset to a numerical saddle function defined on the whole space. The upshot is that one deals instead with *equivalence classes* of such functions. This involves a certain amount of mathematical busy-work that is passed over here.

(a) *A simple public exchange economy.* In this new exchange economy each agent has preferences over a subset S_r of R^{n+1+m}, choosing a bundle a_r consisting of $(n + 1)$ *private* goods (x_r, ξ_r) as before plus a bundle y (common to all) of m *public* goods. The economy's endowments z^0 consist only of private goods, the public goods being obtained by trading the *numéraire* ξ with foreigners at a given vector of exchange rates q^0, denominated in ξ. The data of this economy are therefore the $\succsim_r$, z^0, and q^0.

An alternative interpretation is that ξ is homogeneous labour, and the fixed q^0 are the constant marginal costs at which the society can extract public goods (armies, roads, pyramids) from Nature with the help of such labour. Since this interpretation involves production it is not pursued here.

In order to import public goods, the authorities require each agent to pay a vector of personalized subscription rates q_r, again denominated in ξ, some of which may be negative. Hence the rth agent's tax bill is $\langle y, q_r \rangle$. The social accounts consist of market clearing (equation (20)), government budget balance,

$$\Sigma q_r = q^0 \tag{31}$$

and the individual budget constraints,

$$\forall r \quad \langle x_r, p \rangle + \xi_r + \langle q_r, y \rangle = \langle x_r^0, p \rangle + \xi_r^0 \tag{32}$$

Summing (32) and using (20) and (31),

$$\Sigma \xi_r + \langle y, q^0 \rangle = \Sigma \xi_r^0 \tag{33}$$

Speaking loosely, the first term on the LHS of (33) is the domestic (or private) use of ξ, and the second term its foreign (or public) use. The job of the Guardians in this Lange–Lerner society is to pick private goods' prices $(p, 1)$ and public goods' quantities y in an efficient manner, subject to the constraints (z^0, q^0). The individual agents, on the other hand, treat $(p, 1)$ and y as parameters, responding with optimized choices of private goods' quantities z_r and public goods' subscription rates q_r. The criterion of social efficiency employed here is that of Allais–Scitovsky, and the decentralized solution sought will be an appropriately extended concept of compensated equilibrium, to include the subscriptions q_r. For reasons of brevity, no attempt is made to connect AS efficiency with EP optimality, nor this compensated Lindahl equilibrium with an ordinary ('competitive') Lindahl equilibrium.

Thus the main problem for consideration is a 'compensated' form of the Second Welfare Theorem, extended to public goods. Implementation of such equilibrium (especially problematic with free riders) will not be discussed.

(b) *Efficiency and costs, private and public.* For simplicity, all the assumptions of Section III are continued in force here, appropriately extended to the new commodity space that includes public goods. The f_r functions are easily extended to $f_r: R^n \times R^m \times S_r \to [-\infty, \infty]$ by the formula

$$f_r(x_r, y, a_r') = \inf\{\xi_r \geqslant 0: (x_r, \xi_r, y) \succsim_r a_r'\}$$

Their infimal convolution is now denoted $F: R^n \times R^m \times S \to [-\infty, \infty]$, given by

$$F(x, y, A') = \inf\{\Sigma f_r(x_r, y, a_r'): \Sigma x_r = x\} \tag{34}$$

Of course, given A1–A5 $F(., ., A')$ is (jointly) convex and lsc in (x, y), as in Section III. Unlike the case with a purely private economy, however, the infimal convolution given by (34) is not the appropriate function to depict social efficiency. For one thing it assumes the supply of public goods given at y, and there is no reason to expect this to be optimal, and for another it completely ignores the costs of public goods. Quantities not only of private goods but also of public goods must be varied so as to achieve the Allais–Scitovsky criterion of a minimal private and public use of ξ. This leads to a new function $W: R^n \times R^m \times S \to [-\infty, \infty]$ defined by

$$W(x, -q, A') = \inf\{F(x, y, A') - \langle y, -q \rangle: y \in R^m\} \tag{35}$$

Notice three things about W. First, unlike the relation between the f_r and F functions there are no individual W functions, the decisions concerning the supply of public goods being essentially social. Secondly, the operation on the RHS of (35) looks like a Fenchel transform but technically speaking it is not, being instead a *concave skew-conjugate* of $F(x, ., A')$; see Rockafellar (1968). Finally, given A1–A5 $W(., ., A')$ can be shown to be a convex–concave saddle function, convex in the first argument x and (closed) concave in the second, $-q$.

Turn now to cost functions. Given the provision y of public goods, the analysis of each agent's cost function for private goods is slightly different from that which led to (5). The relevant functions are the $V_r: R^n \times R^m \times S_r \to [-\infty, \infty)$, obtained from

$$V_r(-p, y, a_r^t) = \inf\{f_r(x_r, y, a_r^t) - \langle x_r, -p \rangle : x_r \in R^n\} \quad (36)$$

which is quite analogous to (3). The society's private cost function is obtained from the infimal convolution $F(.,.,A^t)$ by

$$V(-p, y, A^t) = \inf\{F(x, y, A^t) - \langle x, -p \rangle : x \in R^n\} \quad (37)$$

Again, notice three things about these V functions. First, as might have been predicted from (19),

$$V(-p, y, A^t) = \Sigma V_r(-p, y, a_r^t) \quad (38)$$

Secondly, like $W(.,.,A^t)$ the V functions are not Fenchel transforms but concave skew-conjugates of the functions $f_r(., y, a_r^t)$ and $F(., y, A^t)$, respectively. Finally, given A1–A5 it may be shown that each $V_r(.,.,a_r^t)$ is a concave–convex saddle function, (closed) concave in $-p$ and convex in y; and similarly for $V(.,.,A^t)$. This contrasts with the convex–concave W; in fact, the equivalence class containing W is skew-conjugate to that containing V.

The function $V(.,.,A^t)$ gives just private costs. In order to obtain the society's total cost function, public and private, one must both introduce the prices of public goods and allow their supply to vary. This leads to a new cost function $G: R^n \times R^m \times S \to [-\infty, \infty]$, defined by

$$G(-p, -q, A^t) = \inf\{\langle x, p \rangle + \langle y, q \rangle$$
$$+ F(x, y, A^t) : (x, y) \in R^{n+m}\} \quad (39)$$

$$= -\sup\{\langle x, -p \rangle + \langle y, -q \rangle$$
$$- F(x, y, A^t) : (x, y) \in R^{n+m}\} \quad (40)$$

The economic rationale of $G(.,.,A^t)$, again analogous to that for (3), is given by (39), while the fact that it is jointly concave and usc in $(-p, -q)$ is given by (40), since it is clearly the negative of the convex Fenchel transform of $F(.,.,A^t)$, regardless of the latter's functional form.

With this last function the quartet (F, W, V, G) of 'a canonical four-way one-to-one correspondence' (Rockafellar, 1968, Theorem 1) has been put in place, and forms the basis of the rich dualities present in this economy.

Before proceeding, however, it is worth a slight digression to give economic examples of the equivalent saddle functions mentioned earlier. Another approach to total private cost is to obtain it not directly, from $V(.,.,A^t)$ as before, but indirectly, subtracting public cost from total cost. This leads to a new function $v: R^n \times R^m \times S \to [-\infty, \infty]$ given by

$$v(-p, y, A^t) = \sup\{G(-p, -q, A^t)$$
$$+ \langle y, -q \rangle : -q \in R^m\} \quad (41)$$

A similar approach to social efficiency leads to another function $w: R^n \times R^m \times S \to [-\infty, \infty]$, defined by the formula

$$w(x, -q, A^t) = \sup\{G(-p, -q, A^t)$$
$$+ \langle x, -p \rangle : -p \in R^n\} \quad (42)$$

Both these functions are defined as *convex* skew-conjugates, the first of the concave $G(-p, ., A^t)$ and the second of $G(., -q, A^t)$. Given the usual assumptions, $v(.,.,Z^t)$ is a concave–convex saddle function that belongs to the same equivalence class as $V(.,.,A^t)$, and is actually equal to it

wherever the latter is subdifferentiable, while similar remarks apply, *mutatis mutandis*, to the relations between $w(.,.,A^t)$ and $W(.,.,A^t)$. Finally, the last two functions are respectively the least and greatest elements, under the natural ordering, of their equivalence class of saddle functions, and the same holds for the v, V pair.

(c) Subdifferentials and decentralization. Reasonably enough, a concave–convex saddle function H is *subdifferentiable* at (b^1, c^1) if the concave function $H(., c^1)$ is superdifferentiable at b^1 and the convex function $H(b^1, .)$ is subdifferentiable at c^1; and conversely for convex–concave saddle functions. The collection of the supergradients of $H(., c^1)$ at b^1 is written $\Delta_1 H(b^1, c^1)$, and the set of subgradients of $H(b^1, .)$ at c^1 denoted $\partial_2 H(b^1, c^1)$. The *subdifferential* of H at (b^1, c^1) is the Cartesian product $\Delta_1 H(b^1, c^1) \times \partial_2 H(b^1, c^1)$, denoted by $\partial H(b^1, c^1)$. The effective domain dom H of H is the Cartesian product of dom$_1 H = \{b : \exists c \ni H(b, c) > -\infty\}$, and dom$_2 H = \{c : \exists b \ni H(b, c) < +\infty\}$.

The next (and final) assumption is reasonable, saying essentially that for any agent r any small perturbation in the provision of public goods in the target bundle can be compensated for by an appropriate change in the quantities of private goods. For example, if the provision of national defence fell to zero this assumption could be violated, though even then sufficient self-protection might be possible.

A6. For any individual targets $a_r^t = (z_r^t, y^t)$,

$$y^t \in \text{ri dom}_2 V_r$$

The next result is an application of a major theorem of 'subdifferential calculus' known as the Moreau–Rockafellar Theorem (e.g. Ioffe and Tihomirov, 1979, pp. 47–50).

Lemma 5: Given A1–A6,

$$\forall \ p \subset R^n, \quad \forall y \in R^m, \quad \forall a_r^t \in S_r \quad \Sigma \partial V_r(-p, y, a_r^t)$$
$$= \partial V(-p, y, A^t) \quad (43)$$

The final major mathematical result needed is

Theorem 8: Given A1–A5, for any A^t the following statements are equivalent:

(a) $(x^0, -q^0) \in \partial V(-p^1, y^1, A^t)$;

(b) $(-p^1, y^1) \in \partial W(x^0, -q^0, A^t)$

(c) $(-p^1, -q^0) \in \partial F(x^0, y^1, A^t)$;

(d) $(x^0, y^1) \in \Delta G(-p^1, -q^0, A^t)$

(e) $F(x^0, y^1, A^t) + \langle x^0, p^1 \rangle$
    $+ \langle y^1, q^0 \rangle = G(-p^1, -q^0, A^t)$

The proof of this theorem is a rather lengthy extension of the kind of arguments that proved Theorem 4, and is not given here. Turn now to economic implications, which are only sketched because by now it will be apparent how they generalize those in Section III.

Provided $(x^0, q^0) \in \text{ri dom } W(.,.,A^t)$ that function is continuous there and has a non-empty subdifferential $\partial W(x^0, q^0)$. Any subgradient $(-p^1, y^1) \in \partial W(x^0, -q^0)$ assures the Guardians of control variables $(p^1, 1, y^1)$ that will, by (e), achieve Allais–Scitovsky efficiency for the targets A^t. In turn, provided $(-p^1, y^1) \in \cap \text{ri dom } V_r(.,.,A^t)$ these control variables announced à la Lerner–Lange and so inserted into the individual $V_r(.,.,a_r^t)$ will ensure cost-minimizing individual responses (x_r^1, q_r^t) for the targets a_r^t. Then Lemma 5 together with Theorem 8(a) guarantees that $\Sigma x_r^1 = x^0$ and $\Sigma q_r^t = q^0$, from which point the rest of the proof of the existence of a compensated Lindahl equilibrium is easy.

Finally, from Theorem 8(a) $x^0 \in \Delta_1 V(-p^1, y^1, A^t)$ and so from Lemma 5, $x^0 \in \Sigma \Delta_1 V_r(-p^1, y^1, A^t)$. In exactly the same way, $-q^0 \in \partial_2 V(-p^1, y^1, A^t) = \Sigma \partial_2 V_r(-p^1, y^1, A^t)$. Bearing in mind that if $V_r(., ., A^t)$ were differentiable, each $\partial V_r(-p^1, y^1, A^t)/\partial y_j$ would be the r's of ξ for the public good y_j, this last result is simply a generalization of the Samuelson (1954) rule for the pricing of public goods. It appears here as the second, public good, half of an optimality condition for the saddle function $V(., ., A^t)$, whose first half is a generalized aggregate Hotelling–Shephard Lemma for private goods. This illustrates well how the use of duality theory can reveal hidden symmetries in seemingly quite disparate ideas.

PETER NEWMAN

See also CONVEX PROGRAMMING; COST FUNCTIONS; FUNCTIONAL ANALYSIS; GAUGE FUNCTIONS; INTERNATIONAL TRADE.

BIBLIOGRAPHY

Alexandroff, A.D. 1939. Almost everywhere existence of the second differential of a convex function and some properties of convex surfaces connected with it (in Russian). *Annals of the Leningrad State University, Mathematical Series* 6, 3–35.

Allais, M. 1943. *A la récherche d'une discipline économique. Premiere partie, l'économie pure.* Paris: Ateliers Industria.

Arrow, K.J. and Debreu, G. 1954. Existence of an equilibrium for a competitive economy. *Econometrica* 22, July, 265–90.

Arrow, K.J. and Hahn, F.H. 1971. *General Competitive Analysis.* San Francisco, Holden-Day.

Bewley, T.F. 1972. Existence of equilibria in economies with infinitely many commodities. *Journal of Economic Theory* 4, 514–40.

Choquet, G. 1966. *Topology.* New York: Academic Press.

Clarke, F.H. 1983. *Optimization and Nonsmooth Analysis.* New York: Wiley.

Debreu, G. 1951. The coefficient of resource utilization. *Econometrica* 19, 273–92.

Debreu, G. 1959. *Theory of Value.* New York: Wiley.

Dieudonné, J. 1942. La dualité dans les éspaces vectoriels topologiques. *Annales Scientifiques de l'Ecole Normale Supérieure,* 3rd series, 59(2), 107–139.

Diewert, W.E. 1982. Duality approaches to microeconomic theory. In *Handbook of Mathematical Economics,* Volume II, ed. K.J. Arrow and M.D. Intriligator, Amsterdam: North-Holland, ch. 12, 535–99.

Dornbusch, R., Fischer, S. and Samuelson, P.A. 1977. Comparative advantage, trade and payments in a Ricardian model with a continuum of goods. *American Economic Review* 67, 823–39.

Dornbusch, R., Fischer, S. and Samuelson, P.A. 1980. Heckscher–Ohlin trade theory with a continuum of goods. *Quarterly Journal of Economics* 95, 203–24.

Eggleston, H.G. 1958. *Convexity.* Cambridge: Cambridge University Press.

Ekeland, I. and Temam, R. 1976. *Convex Analysis and Variational Problems.* Amsterdam: North-Holland.

Fenchel, W. 1949. On conjugate convex functions. *Canadian Journal of Mathematics* 1, 73–7.

Hicks, J.R. 1981. *Collected Essays on Economic Theory,* Volume I: *Wealth and Welfare.* Cambridge, Mass.; Harvard University Press.

Hicks, J.R. and Allen, R.G.D. 1934. A reconsideration of the theory of value. *Economica,* N.S.1, 52–76, 196–219. Reprinted in Hicks (1981).

Hotelling, H. 1932. Edgeworth's taxation paradox and the nature of demand and supply functions. *Journal of Political Economy* 40, 577–616.

Ioffe, A.D. and Tihomirov, V.M. 1979. *Theory of Extremal Problems.* Amsterdam: North-Holland.

Jorgenson, D.W. and Lau, L.J. 1974. The duality of technology and economic behaviour. *Review of Economic Studies* 41, 181–200.

Laurent, P.-J. 1972. *Approximation et optimisation.* Paris: Hermann.

Malmquist, S. 1953. Index numbers and indifference surfaces. *Trabajos de Estadistica.* 4, 209–241.

Marshall, A. 1919. *Industry and Trade.* London: Macmillan.

Minty, G.J. 1969. On some aspects of the theory of monotone operators. In *Theory and Applications of Monotone Operators,* ed. A.L. Ghizetti. Gubbio: Edizioni 'Oderisi'.

Moreau, J.-J. 1963. *Inf-convolution.* Montpellier: Seminaire de mathématiques, Faculté des Sciences. Mimeographed, 42 pp.

Moreau, J.J. 1967. *Fonctionelles convexes.* Seminaire sur les équations aux derivées partielles, II, Collège de France, mimeographed, 108 pp.

Peleg, B. and Yaari, M. 1970. Markets with countably many commodities. *International Economic Review* 11, 369–77.

Rockafellar, R.T. 1968. A general correspondence between dual minimax problems and convex programs. *Pacific Journal of Mathematics* 25, 597–611.

Rockafellar, R.T. 1970. *Convex analysis.* Princeton: Princeton University Press.

Rockafellar, R.T. 1974. *Conjugate Duality and Optimization.* Philadelphia: Society for Industrial and Applied Mathematics (SIAM).

Rockafellar, R.T. 1981. *The Theory of Subgradients and its Application to Problems of Optimization: Convex and Nonconvex Functions.* Berlin: Heldermann Verlag.

Samuelson, P.A. 1953. Prices of factors and goods in general equilibrium. *Review of Economic Studies* 21, 1–20.

Samuelson, P.A. 1954. The pure theory of public expenditure. *Review of Economics and Statistics* 36, 387–9.

Scitovsky, T. 1941–2. A reconsideration of the theory of tariffs. *Review of Economic Studies* 9, 89–110.

Shephard, R.W. 1953. *Cost and Production Functions.* Princeton: Princeton University Press.

Tiel, J. van 1984. *Convex Analysis.* New York: Wiley.

Valadier, M. 1970a. *Contribution a l'analyse convexe.* Thèse de Doctorat, University of Montpellier, Secretariat des Mathématiques, Publication No.92.

Valadier, M. 1970b. Integration de convexes fermés notamment d'epigraphes inf-convolution continué. *Revue Francaise d'Information et Recherche Operationelle* 4, 57–73.

Wilson, C.A. 1980. On the general structure of Ricardian models with a continuum of goods: applications to growth, tariff theory, and technical change. *Econometrica* 48, 1675–1702.

Dühring, Eugen Karl (1833–1921). Dühring was born on 12 January 1833 in Berlin and died on 21 September 1921 at Nowawes bei Potsdam. The son of a Prussian state official, Dühring studied law, philosophy and economics at the University of Berlin and practised law until blindness obliged him to abandon this career. He then became a *Privatdozent* at the University of Berlin where he taught philosophy and economics from 1863 to 1877, and began to write voluminously on a wide range of subjects, from the natural sciences to philosophy, social theory and socialism, his aim being to construct a system of social reform based upon positive science. His system was expounded in a series of books on capital and labour (1865), the principles of political economy (1866), a critical history of philosophy (1869), a critical history of political economy and socialism (1871), and courses in political economy and philosophy (1873, 1875). Dühring was an adherent of positivism, concerned in his philosophical works to expound a 'strictly scientific world outlook', in opposition particularly to the Hegelian dialectic. His economic writings emphasize the role of political factors in the development of capitalism, and he argued that social injustice is not caused primarily by the economic system, but by social and political circumstances, the remedy being to control the misuse of private property and capital (not to abolish them) through workers' organizations and state intervention.

Schumpeter, in his *History of Economic Analysis* (1954, pp. 509–10), praised Dühring's history of mechanics (1873), which was awarded an academic prize; suggested that he would retain a prominent place in the history of anti-metaphysical and positivist currents of thought; and noted that he made an important criticism of Marxist theory in his argument that political causes had played a major part in constituting the property relations of capitalist society. In other respects, however, Schumpeter considered that Dühring had made no significant contribution to economic theory.

Engels, in his well-known book (originally published as a series of articles), *Herr Eugen Dühring's Revolution in Science* [*Anti-Dühring*] (1877–8), which has done more than anything else to keep Dühring's name alive, took a much more critical view, deriding his work as a prime example of the 'higher nonsense' which infected German academic life. His philosophical views were dismissed by Engels as 'vulgar materialism' and compared unfavourably with the 'revolutionary side' of Hegel's dialectics; and in the chapter of *Anti-Dühring* devoted to the history of political economy (largely written by Marx, but not published in full until the third edition of the book in 1894), Dühring was castigated for his superficiality and theoretical misconceptions. It was, however, the concern with Dühring's programme of social reform, and its possible baleful effect on the developing labour movement (Bernstein, for example, was initially impressed by Dühring's *Cursus* of 1873, though soon repelled by his anti-Semitism) that originally provoked Engels's articles, and was countered in the final section of the book (frequently reprinted later as a separate text under the title *Socialism, Utopian and Scientific*) by an exposition of Marxist socialism which became enormously influential.

It seems doubtful that Dühring occupies more than a minor place in the history of economic and social thought, except for this encounter with Marx and Engels, though Schumpeter (1954, p. 509) called him a 'significant thinker' and the entry in the *Encyclopedia of the Social Sciences* (1931, vol. 5, p. 273) described his writings as 'among the important intellectual achievements of the nineteenth century'.

TOM BOTTOMORE

SELECTED WORKS

1871. *Kritische Geschichte der Nationalökomie und des Sozialismus.* Berlin: T. Grieben.
1873. *Cursus der National- und Sozialökonomie einschliesslich der Hauptpunkte der Finanzpolitik.* Berlin: T. Grieben.
1875. *Cursus der Philosophie als streng wissenschaftlicher Weltanschauung und Lebensgestaltung.* Leipzig: E. Koschny

BIBLIOGRAPHY

Albrecht, G. 1927. *Eugen Dühring: ein Beitrag zur Geschichte der Sozialwissenschaften.* Jena: G. Fischer.
Schumpeter, J.A. 1954. *A History of Economic Analysis.* London: Allen & Unwin.

dummy variables. In economics, as well as in other disciplines, qualitative factors often play an important role. For instance, the achievement of a student in school may be determined, among other factors, by his father's profession, which is a qualitative variable having as many attributes (characteristics) as there are professions. In medicine, to take another example, the response of a patient to a drug may be influenced by the patient's sex and the patient's smoking habits, which may be represented by two qualitative variables, each one having two attributes. The dummy-variable method is a simple and useful device for introducing, into a regression analysis, information contained in qualitative or categorical variables; that is, in variables that are not conventionally measured on a numerical scale. Such qualitative variables may include race, sex, marital status, occupation, level of education, region, seasonal effects, and so on. In some applications, the dummy-variable procedure may also be fruitfully applied to a quantitative variable such as age, the influence of which is frequently U-shaped. A system of dummy variables defined by age classes conforms to any curvature and consequently may lead to more significant results.

The working of the dummy-variable method is best illustrated by an example. Suppose we wish to fit an Engel curve for travel expenditure, based on a sample of n individuals. For each individual i, we have quantitative information on his travel expenditures (y_i) and on his disposable income (x_i), both variables being expressed in logarithms. A natural specification of the Engel curve is:

$$y_i = a + bx_i + u_i$$

where a and b are unknown regression parameters and u_i is a non-observable random term. Under the usual classical assumptions (which we shall adopt throughout this presentation), ordinary least-squares produce the best estimates for a and b.

Suppose now that we have additional information concerning the education level of each individual in the sample (presence or absence of college education). If we believe that the education level affects the travel habits of individuals, we should explicitly account for such an effect in the regression equation. Here, the education level is a qualitative variable with two attributes: college education; no college education. To each attribute, we can associate a dummy variable which takes the following form:

$$d_{1i} = \begin{cases} 1 \text{ if college education} \\ 0 \text{ if no college education} \end{cases}$$

$$d_{2i} = \begin{cases} 1 \text{ if no college education} \\ 0 \text{ if college education} \end{cases}$$

Inserting these two dummy variables in the Engel curve, we obtain the following expanded regression:

Specification I:

$$y_i = a_1 d_{1i} + a_2 d_{2i} + bx_i + u_i$$

which may be estimated by ordinary least-squares. Alternatively, noting that $d_{1i} + d_{2i} = 1$ for all i, we can write:

Specification II:

$$y_i = a_2 + (a_1 - a_2)d_{1i} + bx_i + u_i$$

which, again, may be estimated by ordinary least-squares.

It is easy to see how the procedure can be extended to take care of a finer classification of education levels. Suppose, for instance, that we actually have s education levels (s attributes). All we require is that the attributes be exhaustive and mutually exclusive. We then have the two following equivalent specifications:

Specification I:

$$y_i = a_1 d_{1i} + a_2 d_{2i} + \cdots + a_s d_{si} + bx_i + u_i$$

Specification II:

$$y_i = a_s + (a_1 - a_s)d_{1i} + \cdots + (a_{s-1} - a_s)d_{s-1,i} + bx_i + u_i.$$

Obviously, the two specifications produce the same results but give rise to different interpretations. Specification I includes all the s dummy variables but no constant term. In this case, the coefficient of d_{ji} gives the specific effect of attribute j. Specification II includes $s - 1$ dummy variables and an overall constant term. The constant term represents the specific effect of the omitted attribute, and the coefficients of the different d_{ji} represent the contrast (difference) of the effect of the jth attribute with respect to the effect of the omitted attribute. (Note that it is not possible to include all dummy variables plus an overall constant term, because of perfect collinearity.)

It is important to stress that by the introduction of additive dummy variables, it is implicitly assumed that the qualitative variable affects only the intercept but not the slope of the regression equation. In our example, the elasticity parameter, b, is the same for all individuals; only the intercepts differ from individual to individual depending on their education level. If we are interested in individual variation in slope, we can apply the same technique, as long as at least one explanatory variable has a constant coefficient over all individuals. Take the initial case of only two attributes. If the elasticity parameter varies according to the level of education, we have the following specification:

$$y_i = a_1 d_{1i} + a_2 d_{2i} + b_1 d_{1i} x_i + b_2 d_{2i} x_i + u_i.$$

Simple algebra shows that ordinary least-squares estimation of this model amounts to performing two separate regressions, one for each class of individuals. If, however, the model contained an additional explanatory variable, say z_i, with constant coefficient c, by simply adding the term cz_i to the above equation, we would simultaneously allow for variation in the intercept and variation in the slope (for x).

The dummy variable model also provides a conceptual framework for testing the significance of the qualitative variable in an easy way. Suppose we wish to test the hypothesis of no influence of the level of education on travel expenditures. The hypothesis is true if the s coefficients a_i are all equal; that is, if the $s-1$ differences $a_j - a_s$, $j = 1, \ldots, s-1$, are all zero. The test therefore boils down to a simple test of significance of the $s-1$ coefficients of the dummy variables in Specification II. If $s = 2$, the t-test applied to the single coefficient of d_{1i} is appropriate. If $s > 2$, we may conveniently compute the following quantity:

$$\frac{(SS_c - SS)/(s-1)}{SS/(n-s-1)}$$

which is distributed as an F-variable with $s-1$ and $n-s-1$ degrees of freedom. In the above expression, SS is the sum of squared residuals for the model with the dummy variables (either Specification I or II), and SS_c is the sum of squared residuals for the model with no dummy variables but with an overall constant term.

In some economic applications the main parameter of interest is the slope parameter, the coefficients of the dummy variables being nuisance parameters. When, as in the present context, only one qualitative variable (with s attributes) appears in the regression equation, an easy computational device is available which eliminates the problem of estimating the coefficients of the dummy variables. To this end, it suffices to estimate, by ordinary least-squares, the simple regression equation:

Specification III:

$$y_i^* = bx_i^* + u_i^*$$

where the quantitative variables (both explained and explanatory) for each individual are expressed as deviations from the mean over all individuals possessing the same attribute. For the dichotomous case presented in the beginning, for an individual with college education, we subtract the mean over all individuals with college education and likewise for an individual with no college education. Note, however, that the true number

of degrees of freedom is not $n-1$ but $n-1-s$. The same procedure also applies when the model contains other quantitative explanatory variables. The interested reader may consult Balestra (1982) for the conditions under which this simple transformation is valid in the context of generalized regression.

The case of multiple qualitative variables (of the explanatory type) can be handled in a similar fashion. However, some precaution must be taken to avoid perfect collinearity of the dummy variables. The easiest and most informative way to do this is to include, in the regression equation, an overall constant term and to add for each qualitative variable as many dummy variables as there are attributes minus one. Take the case of our Engel curve and suppose that, in addition to the education level (only two levels for simplicity), the place of residence also plays a role. Let us distinguish two types of place of residence: urban and rural. Again, we associate to these two attributes two dummy variables, say e_{1i} and e_{2i}. A correct specification of the model which allows for both qualitative effects is:

$$y_i = a_1 + a_2 d_{1i} + a_3 e_{1i} + bx_i + u_i.$$

Given the individual's characteristics, the measure of the qualitative effects is straightforward, as shown in the following table:

	Urban	Rural
College education	$a_1 + a_2 + a_3$	$a_1 + a_2$
No college education	$a_1 + a_3$	a_1

The specification given above for the multiple qualitative variable model corresponds to Specification II of the single qualitative variable model. Unfortunately, when there are two or more qualitative variables there is no easy transformation analogous to the one incorporated in Specification III, except under certain extraordinary circumstances (Balestra, 1982).

One such circumstance arises in connection with cross-section time-series models. Suppose that we have n individuals observed over t periods of time. If we believe in the presence of both an individual effect and a time effect, we may add to our model two sets of dummy variables, one corresponding to the individual effects and the other corresponding to the time effects. This is the so-called covariance model. The number of parameters to be estimated is possibly quite large when n or t or both are big. To avoid this, we may estimate a transformed model (with no dummies and no constant term) in which each quantitative variable (both explained and explanatory) for individual i and time period j is transformed by subtracting from it both the mean of the ith individual and the mean of the jth time period and by adding to it the overall mean. Note that, by this transformation, we lose $n + t - 1$ degrees of freedom.

To conclude, the purpose of the preceding expository presentation has been to show that the dummy-variable method is a powerful and, at the same time, simple tool for the introduction of qualitative effects in regression analysis. It has found and will undoubtedly find numerous applications in empirical economic research. Broadly speaking, it may be viewed as a means for considering a specific scheme of parameter variation, in which the variability of the coefficients is linked to the causal effect of some precisely identified qualitative variable. But it is not, by any means, the only scheme available. For instance, when the qualitative effects are generic, as in the cross-section time-series model, one may question the validity of representing such effects by fixed parameters. An interpretation in terms of random effects may seem more appealing. This type of consideration has led to the development of other schemes of parameter variation such as the error component model and the random coefficient model.

A final remark is in order. In the present discussion, qualitative variables of the explanatory type only have been considered. When the qualitative variable is the explained (or dependent) variable, the problem of these *limited* dependent variables is far more complex, both conceptually and computationally.

PIETRO BALESTRA

See also LIMITED DEPENDENT VARIABLES; RANDOM CO-EFFICIENTS.

BIBLIOGRAPHY

Balestra, P. 1982. Dummy variables in regression analysis. In *Advances in Economic Theory,* ed. Mauro Baranzini, Oxford: Blackwell, 273–92.

Goldberger, A.S. 1960. *Econometric Theory.* New York: John Wiley, 218–27.

Maddala, G.S. 1977. *Econometrics.* New York: McGraw-Hill, ch. 9.

Suits, D.B. 1957. Use of dummy variables in regression equations. *Journal of the American Statistical Association* 52, 548–51.

dumping. The term 'dumping' has been used for centuries in a general way to refer to export sales at a price low enough to cause significant harm to some interests in the importing country. Beginning early in this century, many countries instituted anti-dumping laws, and this has required a more precise definition of the term. The most common definition, both in the law and among professional economists, is export sales at a price below that at which similar goods are sold in the domestic market of the exporting country, taking into account differences in quality, attendant services and the like. However, an alternative definition, export sales at a price below the cost of production, is also incorporated into many of the laws, and this alternative has in recent years become of increasing practical importance.

Anti-dumping laws typically define the practice, prohibit it, provide for a penalty in cases where it nonetheless occurs, and establish an administrative procedure for determining in specific cases whether it has occurred and what penalty to impose. The penalty is usually in the form of an import levy related to the 'dumping margin', or difference between the export price and the source-country domestic price (or cost of production).

Such anti-dumping duties, though inherently at odds with most-favoured-nation treatment, are internationally accepted. The General Agreement on Tariffs and Trade (GATT) does not outlaw dumping, but it does countenance anti-dumping laws. The Tokyo Round of trade negotiations produced a code of conduct for antidumping legislation.

Numerous instances of alleged dumping have characterized recent tariff debates within and among the industrial countries. Recent changes in the administration of US anti-dumping and countervailing-duty statutes will likely further increase their use. More generally, the marked postwar reduction in tariffs on manufactured goods within the GATT framework on international responsibility, together with a secular convergence of cost structures in the industrial economies, prompt the conjecture that anti-dumping and anti-subsidy statutes will be a principal battle-ground for the 'new protectionism' concerning trade in manufactures among the developed economies. If so, the theory of dumping must become a major part of the positive theory of protection relevant to such trade.

The early literature generally defined dumping as price discrimination between national markets. This was the definition adhered to by Viner (1923) in his classic treatment and followed by most major authors (see Yntema, 1928;

Robinson, 1933; Haberler, 1937). Indeed, much of the early theory of price discrimination was developed in this context. Two problems arise when the phenomenon is viewed in this light. The first is why the firm is able to discriminate. This requires the firm to have some control over price; that is, imperfect competition is central. It also requires the firm to be able to segment markets on a national basis: tariffs or other trade barriers can serve this purpose. The second problem is why the export price should be lower than the domestic price rather than vice versa. One possible response is that such *reverse dumping* is indeed as common as dumping but is simply not a policy issue. For example, the sale of luxury German automobiles in the US at prices much higher than those in Germany brings forth not a whimper of an official threat from Washington, while the sales of low-priced European automobiles in the US was the occasion for a celebrated action some years ago. An alternative response is to hunt for circumstances that allow dumping to be more than a mere accident. One possibility is that the trade pattern is unidirectional and given by other considerations. Exporting firms thus compete only among themselves at home, but also with foreign firms in the export market. Thus, even if the *market* elasticity is the same in both countries, the elasticity facing each *firm* will be higher in the importing country, because more firms compete there. Thus, other things equal, exporters will charge lower prices abroad than at home (see Eichengreen and van der Ven, 1984).

A second possibility involves transport costs between markets. Other things equal, such costs result in a firm having a smaller share, in equilibrium, in its export market than in its domestic market. This again creates a presumption that the elasticity facing the firm is higher for foreign sales than for domestic sales. Furthermore, this reasoning does not require a unidirectional trade pattern; it is quite consistent with *reciprocal dumping*, or cross-hauling, with each country dumping in the other (see Brander and Krugman, 1983).

Most of the formal theory of dumping essentially consists only of the theory of monopolistic price discrimination between two markets. But by contrast the 'sales at a price below cost of production' criterion has gradually become relatively more important in recent years, both in practice and in revisions of anti-dumping laws. Economists have long recognized that the two criteria are not inconsistent. A price-discriminating firm might well price its exports below average cost in a slump as long as export revenues at least cover the variable cost of producing those exports (*sporadic* or *cyclical* dumping). Or the firm might permanently sell its exports below average cost if those exports allow it to realize sufficient economies of scale. *Predatory* dumping, to drive rivals from the market, has long received much public attention, but economists have typically minimized its importance (see Viner, 1923). How anti-dumping laws might in fact be applied in all these situations has, not surprisingly, concerned economists for years. More recently, attention has encompassed cases where export price does not cover even marginal cost. This might well occur *ex post* if the exporting firm must commit itself before demand conditions in the export market are fully known. Or the firm might do so deliberately if, instead of maximizing profit, it wishes to maximize sales subject to a profit constraint. More interesting, and closer to recent work in industrial organization, is the possibility that export sales, even at a low price, might make it easier for the firm to maintain excess capacity for the purpose of deterring entry by potential rivals (see Davies and McGuinness, 1982).

Even though economists no longer confine themselves to price discrimination, dumping has been treated (aside from sporadic instances) usually either as profit (or sales) maximization by a discriminating monopolist or as an oligopolistic tactic to eliminate competition, to deter entry, or to enforce a cartel. Industries with dumping (or allegations of dumping) are most often characterized by large fixed costs, factor-market rigidities, susceptibility to demand fluctuations and downward price rigidity. Though by no means inconsistent with oligopolistic rivalry in segmented markets, these characteristics involve much more. Thus our theory largely excludes those considerations fundamental to most contemporary problems: imperfectly adjusting factor markets in the presence of changing conditions of product demand. The earlier literature did consider the related problem of dumping to stabilize production over the business cycle. Viner (1923, p. 28), although conjecturing that 'it is probable that this is the most prevalent form of dumping', basically treated it as only a distinct motive. The interdependence between such dumping and factor-market equilibrium within the relevant industries of trading countries is critical. The ability to dump aboard during periods of slack demand allows a firm to offer its workers greater job security, and thereby allows that firm to pay lower wages over time than it would have to do if it did not offer that security. Thus the possibility of dumping influences the normal trading equilibrium. Furthermore, that equilibrium clearly must be sensitive to employment practices in different countries and to the relations between the business cycles of the various countries (see Ethier, 1982).

In addition to the deficient treatment of the fundamental issues involving factor markets, we have no theory of anti-dumping laws. The basic theory of tariffs applies of course to anti-dumping duties put in place and left there. But an anti-dumping *law* is a threat to impose (with considerably less than certainty) a duty in response to certain behaviour on the part of exporters and so will influence that behaviour even if not actually imposed. International trade theory has not yet addressed this issue. This is just one aspect, though an especially important one, of our prominent lack of a contemporary theory of protection. These two omissions (factor markets and anti-dumping laws) are serious, but the first is being addressed, and we have the technical equipment to deal adequately with both of them, so one would expect the deficiencies to be mended soon.

WILFRED J. ETHIER

See also DISCRIMINATING MONOPOLY; PRICE DISCRIMINATION; QUOTAS AND TARIFFS.

BIBLIOGRAPHY
Brander, J. and Krugman, P. 1983. A 'reciprocal dumping' model of international trade. *Journal of International Economics* 15(3/4), November, 313–21.
Davies, S.W. and McGuinness, A.J. 1982. Dumping at less than marginal cost. *Journal of International Economics* 12(1/2), February, 169–82.
Eichengreen, B. and van der Ven, H. 1984. US antidumping policies: the case of steel. In *The Structure and Evolution of Recent US Trade Policy.* ed. R.E. Baldwin and A.O. Kreuger, Chicago: University of Chicago Press, for the National Bureau of Economic Research.
Ethier, W.J. 1982. Dumping. *Journal of Political Economy* 90(3), June, 487–506.
Haberler, G. 1937. *The Theory of International Trade with its Applications to Commercial Policy.* New York: Macmillan.
Robinson, J. 1933. *The Economics of Imperfect Competition.* London: Macmillan.
Viner, J. 1923. *Dumping: A Problem in International Trade.* Chicago: University of Chicago Press.
Viner, J. 1931. Dumping. In *Encyclopedia of the Social Sciences,* New York: Macmillan.
Yntema, T.O. 1928. The influence of dumping on monopoly price. *Journal of Political Economy* 36, December, 686–98.

Dunbar, Charles Franklin (1830–1900). Dunbar's career illustrates the narrow gap between practical and academic economics in his lifetime, for he demonstrated that scholarly instincts, common sense and knowledge of current affairs could overcome deficiencies in formal academic training. Exactly 20 years after graduating from Harvard in 1851 he returned as Professor of Political Economy, having previously worked in a mercantile business, qualified and practised as a lawyer, and written articles on political questions for the *Boston Daily Advertiser*, of which he was sole proprietor and editor from 1865 to 1869. After President Eliot's invitation to Harvard, Dunbar spent two years travelling and studying in Europe, and subsequently served as Head of the Department of Political Economy for nearly 30 years, Dean of the College (1876–82) and the Faculty of Arts and Sciences (1890–95), and as editor from 1886 to 1896 of *The Quarterly Journal of Economics*, the first English-language scholarly periodical in the subject. His election as second President of the American Economic Association in 1892, following Francis A. Walker, testifies to his standing in the emerging economics profession. While he published comparatively little, his works on currency, finance and banking were widely respected, and his essays on the history, condition and methods of economics were wise and balanced at a time of intense controversy.

A.W. COATS

SELECTED WORKS
1891a. *Chapters on the Theory and History of Banking.* New York: G.P. Putnam's Sons. 2nd enlarged. edn, ed. O.M.W. Sprague, 1901; 3rd enlarged edn, 1917.
1891b. *Laws of the United States relating to currency, finance, and banking from 1789 to 1891.* Boston: Ginn & Co. Revised. edn, 1897.
1904. *Economic Essays.* Ed. O.M.W. Sprague, New York: Macmillan Co.

Dunlop, John Thomas (born 1914). Labour economists, practitioners and policy-makers have always paid closer attention to John T. Dunlop's thoughts on a subject than they have to those of most academic economists. They pay closer attention because Dunlop has combined academic research with unparalleled practical experience in solving problems and building institutions. His academic writings, which include several classic articles as well as major books, are the product of more than standard theorizing and empirical data analysis. They reflect incredible direct knowledge from participation and observation of social behaviour.

Dunlop first achieved academic attention with his 1938 *Economic Journal* article on the movement of real and money wages, which caused Keynes to admit that the *General Theory* was wrong on the relation between them over the cycle. Dunlop followed this with: the first theoretical model of unions as a maximizing institution; analyses of the cyclic variation of labour's share; development of the notion of 'wage contours' with accompanying stress on the role of product markets in influencing wages; development of the concept of 'industrial relations systems', and numerous analyses of wage determination, mediation and dispute resolution.

Dunlop's career spans a wide range of activities. Earning his AB (1935) and PhD (1939) from Berkeley, his first academic job was at Harvard, where he rose to Professor of Economics, Dean of the University (1970–73) and Lamont University Professor (1970–85). He worked for the National War Labor Board (1943–54), served as Secretary of Labor of the United States (1975–6), was participant or chairman on various stabilization agencies with dispute settlement responsibility. Director of the Cost of Living Council (1973–4), and member of labour-management committees, in areas ranging from missile sites to textiles to the public sector.

Underlying Dunlop's work has been the theme that, far from being a 'bourse', labour markets are pre-eminently a social institution for working out wage and other rules of the work place. His practical work has attempted to build institutions to resolve labour problems.

R.D. FREEMAN

SELECTED WORKS

1938. The movement of real and money wage rates. *Economic Journal* 48, September, 413–34.

1944. *Wage Determination under Trade Unions*. New York: Macmillan.

1948a. Productivity and the wage structure. In *Income, Employment and Public Policy: essays in honor of Alvin H. Hansen*, New York: W.W. Norton.

1948b. The development of labor organizations: a theoretical framework. In *Insights into Labor Issues*, ed. R.A. Lester and J. Shister, New York: Macmillan.

1957. The task of contemporary theory. In *New Concepts in Wage Determination*, ed. G.W. Taylor and F.C. Pierson, New York: McGraw-Hill.

1958. *Industrial Relations Systems*. New York: Henry Holt & Co.

1984. *Dispute Resolution*. Dover, Mass.: Auburn House Publishing Co.

BIBLIOGRAPHY

Segal, M. Post-institutionalism in labor economics: the forties and fifties revisited. *Industrial and Labor Relations Review* 39(3), April, 388–403.

Dunoyer, Barthélémy Charles Pierre Joseph (1786–1862). French economist and publicist, born at Carennac (southwest France) on 20 May 1786, died at Paris on 4 December 1862. Dunoyer studied law in Paris, where he befriended Charles Comte, who shared his liberalism and joined him in founding and editing *Le Censeur*, a journal of institutional and legal reform. The journal was discontinued in 1820 due to increasingly repressive press laws. Subsequently Comte went to Switzerland, whereas Dunoyer stayed in Paris and devoted himself exclusively to economics. He became professor of political economy at the Athénée, later publishing his lectures under the title *L'industrie et la morale considérées dans leurs rapports avec la liberté*. In 1832 he was elected to the French Institute, and in 1845 he became president of the Société d'Economie Politique. He spent two decades in public life, entering the government in 1830 under the bourgeois monarchy of Louis-Philippe, and withdrawing after the coup d'état of 1851. His articles appeared frequently in the *Journal d'Economie Politique* and in other French journals.

Dunoyer added nothing new to economic theory but he was part of a group of French radicals who helped create a powerful means of social analysis by fusing liberal historico-political thought with the economic orthodoxy of J.B. Say. Inspired by Turgot and Condorcet, Dunoyer and his cohorts advanced an evolutionary theory of history that identified progress with the gradual disintegration of authority and its replacement by the quiescent, voluntary relationships of the marketplace. These writers anticipated the flowering of *industriélisme*, of a kind apart from Saint-Simon's insofar as it

envisioned government as a mere subsidiary institution, charged mainly with the functions of preserving order and ministering to the needs of production. Having thus nested their basic anarchism in an evolutionary concept of social development, the group fit surprisingly well into the republican and constitutional framework of the July Monarchy.

The product of Dunoyer's mature thought was his three-volume work, *De la liberté du travail*. Despite its brilliance and good sense, it is more a history of civilization than a sustained economic treatise. Dunoyer anticipated Herbert Spencer by developing the idea that society is an organic composition of institutions and individuals with specific functions. Although he regarded government's role as minimal, the presence of government professionals finds justification in his conception of 'immaterial wealth' (i.e. services). Although he followed classical economics in most things, Dunoyer rejected Say's Law, holding that a general glut could arise due to the ignorance or error of entrepreneurs, or to the unequal distribution of wealth. Unlike Sismondi, however, whose ideas had a certain allure, he spurned government palliatives, trusting the growth of industry to gradually reduce entrepreneurial error and to smooth the distribution of income. Dunoyer also denied the classical theory of rent, because he admitted only one factor of production, labour. On population matters he was an unregenerate Malthusian, which tempered his basic faith in progress with a hint of pessimism.

R.F. HÉBERT

SELECTED WORKS

1825. *L'industrie et la morale considerée dans leurs rapports avec la liberté*. Paris: A. Sautelet. Revised, enlarged and reprinted as *Nouveau traité d'économie sociale*, 2 vols Paris: A. Sautelet, 1830.

1840. *Esprit et méthodes comparés de l'Angleterre et de la France dans les entreprises de travaux publics et en particulier des chemins de fer*. Paris: Carilian-Goeury et V. Dalmont.

1845. *De la liberté du travail*. 3 vols. Paris: Guillaumin.

BIBLIOGRAPHY

Allix, E. 1911. La déformation de l'économie politique libérale après J.B. Say: Charles Dunoyer. *Revue d'Histoire Economique et Sociale* 4, 115–47.

Villey-Desmeserts, E.L. 1899. *L'oeuvre économique de Charles Dunoyer*. Paris: L. Larose.

Weinburg, M. 1978. The social analysis of three early 19th-century French Liberals: Say, Comte and Dunoyer. *Journal of Libertarian Studies* 2, Winter, 45–63.

duopoly. A duopoly is a market in which two firms sell a product to a large number of consumers. Each consumer is too small to affect the market price for the product: that is, on the buyers' side, the market is competitive. Therefore, in its essence duopoly is a two player variable sum game. Each of the two duopolists is a rational decision-maker whose actions will affect both himself and his rival. Although the interests of the duopolists are intertwined, they are not wholly coincident nor wholly in conflict. In contrast to the agents in competitive markets, the duopolists must each concern themselves with what the other duopolist is likely to do.

The situation facing the duopolists is non-cooperative in the sense that they are barred from making binding agreements with one another. The relevance of this depends crucially on whether the model is a static market (i.e. a one-time-only, or one-shot market) or a market consisting of many time periods.

The first study of duopoly is the great contribution of Cournot (1838) in which the decision problem of the firms is posed for a homogeneous products market in a static setting.

The equilibrium concept proposed by Cournot, variously called the *Cournot equilibrium* or the *Cournot–Nash equilibrium*, has become a cornerstone of non-cooperative game theory. To sketch his model let x and y be the output levels of firms A and B, let $f(x + y)$ be the inverse demand function for the market, let $C(x)$ and $\Gamma(y)$ be the two firms' total cost functions, and let their respective profit functions be $\pi^A = xf(x + y) - C(x)$ and $\pi^B = yf(x + y) - \Gamma(y)$.

Cournot proposed as an equilibrium a pair of output levels (x, y) such that neither firm could have obtained higher profit by having chosen some other output. Thus π^A is maximized with respect to x (with y given), while, simultaneously, π^B is maximized with respect to y (with x given). If $x^c > 0$ and $y^c > 0$ the Cournot equilibrium is a solution to the simultaneous equations

$$\frac{\partial \pi^A}{\partial x} = f(x + y) + xf'(x + y) - C'(x) = 0$$

$$\frac{\partial \pi^B}{\partial y} = f(x + y) + yf'(x + y) - \Gamma'(x) = 0$$

The Cournot equilibrium defines consistency conditions. If firm A contemplates (x^c, y^c) as an outcome, and believes firm B is contemplating the same output pair, then firm A will see (a) that it cannot do better than to choose x^c (given the expectation that firm B will choose y^c) and (b) that, should firm B go through the same thought process, it will reach a parallel conclusion.

To translate this model into the language of game theory, player A chooses a *strategy* x from the set of all allowed output levels, say all $x \geq 0$. This set, $[0, \infty)$, is called the *strategy space* or *strategy set* of the player. Similarly for player B. The players' *payoff functions* are their respective profit functions. Thus the payoff function of a player gives his payoff as a function of the strategies of all players in the game. At a non-cooperative equilibrium (see Nash, 1951; Owen, 1968, or Friedman, 1986) no player could obtain a higher payoff through the use of a different strategy, given the strategies of the other players. Note, finally, that the actual behaviour of one duopolist cannot affect the actual behaviour of the other in this static setting, because they choose their output levels simultaneously. They do take one another into account in making decisions by analysing the game using *both* payoff functions.

Cournot's contribution went largely unnoticed for nearly half a century, after which it was scathingly reviewed by Bertrand (1883). Bertrand berates Cournot on two grounds. First he says that the firms will collude to achieve monopoly-like profits. This possibility is acknowledged by Cournot who made a conscious choice to explore behaviour in the absence of collusion. Bertrand's point was echoed later by Chamberlin (1933), although neither of them showed how the duopolists could be expected to maintain a collusive agreement nor did they solve the problem of the distribution of profits between the firms. These issues are addressed below in connection with recent developments.

Bertrand's second criticism is that price, not output, should be the firm's decision variable. Then, using Cournot's *mineral spring* example in which $C(x) = \Gamma(y) = 0$, he sketches the Bertrand equilibrium, arguing that consumers will buy from the firm charging the lower price, and showing that the only prices that can be in equilibrium are zero for both firms. Bertrand's equilibrium concept is precisely that of Cournot, transferred to the price choosing variant of Cournot's model. Bertrand's analysis was taken up, elaborated and extended by Edgeworth (1897). He supposed that the firms have production capacity limits, each of which is less than the market demand at zero price. Consequently no pair of prices is an equilibrium.

While the logic of Bertrand and Edgeworth is correct, the economic relevance is dubious. Real world firms choose both prices and output levels; however, the discontinuity of one firm's sales with respect to another firm's decision variable is *not* an obvious feature of economic life. Consequently, the Cournot formulation seems preferable. A way to reconcile price choosing firms with an absence of demand discontinuities is via differentiated products models.

Edgeworth and many of his contemporaries thought there was no worthwhile content in Cournot's duopoly theory. Edgeworth (1925, p. 111), writing forty years after Bertrand, said 'Now the demolition of Cournot's theory is generally accepted. Professor Amoroso is singular in his fidelity to Cournot'. Amoroso's good judgement was shared by Wicksell (1925). It is now generally accepted that Cournot was the first to perceive clearly and enunciate the game theoretic concept of *non-cooperative equilibrium*, which received a general statement from Nash (1951) and is the cornerstone of one of the main parts of game theory.

The next influential innovation is due to Bowley (1924) who invented the conjectural variation (which later received this name from Frisch, 1933). He wrote the two firms' first order conditions for equilibrium as $\partial \pi^A / \partial x + (\partial \pi^A / \partial y)(\partial y / \partial x) = 0$ for firm A and $\partial \pi^B / \partial y + (\partial \pi^B / \partial x)(\partial x / \partial y) = 0$ for firm B. The $\partial y / \partial x$ in firm A's condition indicates the way that A thinks B's output choice will vary according to the way that A varies his own output choice. A parallel meaning attaches to $\partial x / \partial y$ in B's first order condition. The presence of these conjectural variation terms is indefensible in a static model, but it shows the underlying concern that writers had with dynamic models, while, at the same time, limiting their formal analysis to static models. Given that the model is static with the two firms simultaneously selecting outputs, *and doing so only once*, there can be no conjectural variation. B's output choice will depend on what B expects A to do, but that expectation will not vary as A changes his mind about what output to select. B's expectation depends on B's thought processes and the information B has about the structure of the model, and does not depend on A's actual thought processes.

Dynamic elements of reaction of one firm to the choice of another go back to Cournot who performed a 'stability' analysis. He solved $\partial \pi^A / \partial x = 0$ to obtain $x = v(y)$ and $\partial \pi^B / \partial y = 0$ to obtain $y = w(x)$. He looked for conditions under which, starting from an arbitrary x^0, the sequence (x_n, y^{n+1}) for $n = 0, 2, 4, \ldots$ would converge to (x^c, y^c), the Cournot equilibrium. Bertrand and Edgeworth also wrote of actions and reactions, and Bowley introduces a new reactive element with his conjectural variation terms. Later Stackelberg (1934) posed the leader–follower duopoly in which one firm, say A, chooses x and, after that choice is communicated to B, y is chosen. B will always choose y according to $y = w(x)$ and this is known to A who maximizes $\pi^A = xf[x + w(x)] - C(x)$ with respect to x. Note that a conjectural variation term for A makes a legitimate appearance because B's decision is, in fact, a function of A's choice. Wicksell (1925) and Bowley (1928) anticipate Stackelberg's leader–follower equilibrium in their discussions of bilateral monopoly. All of these treatments strongly suggest an explicitly multiperiod formulation under which each firm maximizes a discounted profit stream and behaves according to a *reaction function* under which a firm's output choice in time t is selected as a function of the other firm's output choice in time $t - 1$. The last twenty years have seen such analysis, beginning with Friedman (1968).

The next major step in duopoly was the recognition that, in

many industries, the firms sell very similar, non-identical, products. In such a market, it is equally easy to represent the firms as price choosers or as quantity choosers. In either case, equilibrium can readily involve the firms selling at different prices. The pioneers here are Hotelling (1929) and Chamberlin (1933). To sketch a differentiated products duopoly, let the firm's prices be p and r, and let their demand functions be $x = \phi(p, r)$ and $y = \psi(p, r)$, respectively. The two firm's are assumed to produce gross (but imperfect) substitutes, so $\phi_r(p, r) > 0$ and $\psi_p(p, r) > 0$, but the own-price derivatives (ϕ_p and ψ_r) are negative and both firms' total revenues are bounded. Profit functions are $\pi^A = p\phi(p, r) - C[\phi(p, r)]$ and $\pi^B = r\psi(p, r) - \Gamma[\psi(p, r)]$. A non-cooperative (Cournot–Nash) equilibrium occurs at a price pair (p^c, r^c) for which π^A is maximized with respect to p (given $r = r^c$) and π^B is maximized with respect to r (given $p = p^c$).

Many writers have maintained that the Cournot equilibrium should not be expected to occur in practice because it does not lie on the firms' profit possibility frontier. In addition to Bertrand and Chamberlin there is a famous passage in Smith (1776) maintaining that people in the same line of business will attempt to collude whenever they get together. In response to such observations several points can be made. Smith's passage is a comment in passing that is not made within an analytical framework, so it cannot be closely judged. Bertrand and Chamberlin are discussing specific models within which their remarks do not hold up well, because the consistency condition embodied in the Cournot equilibrium is quite compelling and would be violated by collusive behaviour. Any agreement between the two firms – in a static setting where binding agreements cannot be made – will break down because at least one firm will note that, given the agreed decision for the rival, it can do better by violating its agreement. But both firms can perceive the incentives of either one of them, thus the only acceptable agreement in such circumstances is for a price pair (or output pair, if the firms are output choosers) such that, given the price of its rival, neither firm can gain by deviating from its agreement. Such a *self-enforcing agreement* is merely a non-cooperative equilibrium. We are back at Cournot.

However, this is far from the last word on collusion in the absence of legally binding agreements. Bertrand, Chamberlin, and others who have made, or agreed with, their assertion probably are motivated by a belief that voluntary collusion sometimes occurs in actual markets. They may be correct in their empirical observation; however, it remains true that voluntary collusion is not convincing in the traditional one-shot models. Therefore, the clear suggestion is that one-shot models are simply inadequate for analysing voluntary collusion. Suppose, then, that the model is changed to have an infinite horizon with each firm having a discount parameter of α. Then, letting t denote time, player A seeks to maximize

$$\sum_{t=0}^{\infty} \alpha^t \pi^A = \sum_{t=0}^{\infty} \alpha^t [p_t \phi(p_t, r_t) - C[\phi(p_t, r_t)]]$$

and the objective function of player B is

$$\sum_{t=0}^{\infty} \alpha^t \pi^B = \sum_{t=0}^{\infty} \alpha^t [r_t \psi(p_t, r_t) - \Gamma[\psi(p_t, r_t)]]$$

Strategy becomes much more complex than in the static model, because there will be an infinite succession of price choices by each firm and, prior to making a price choice any time after $t = 0$, the firm will know what past prices have been selected by its rival. For each t, a firm can choose its price according to a function (i.e. a rule) that depends on *all* past price choices of both of them. The rule for one period can be different from the

rule for another. A strategy for a firm is a collection of such rules, one for each period t.

In this model it may be possible to find a non-cooperative equilibrium that yields an outcome on the profit possibility frontier. Such an equilibrium is based on three critical prices for each firm. First there is (p^c, r^c), the Cournot price pair. Second there is (p^*, r^*), chosen so that profits at (p^*, r^*) are on the profit possibility frontier and are higher for each firm than at (p^c, r^c). Third define p' as the price for A that maximizes $\pi^A = p\phi(p, r^*) - C[\phi(p, r^*)]$, and define r' in a parallel way for B. Now consider the following strategy for firm A: $p_0 = p^*$, $p_t = p^*$ for $t > 0$ if $(p_k, r_k) = (p^*, r^*)$ for $k = 0, \ldots, t - 1$, and $p_t = p^c$ otherwise. Imagine a parallel strategy for B. These strategies amount to a firm saying 'I will begin by cooperating and will continue to cooperate as long as we both have cooperated in the past. If ever a lapse from cooperation occurs, I will revert to static Cournot behaviour'.

Whether this pair of strategies is a non-cooperative equilibrium depends on the sizes of α and the profits at (p^*, r^*), (p', r^*), (p^*, r'), and (p^c, r^c). A's choice boils down to comparing (i) receiving the profit associated with (p^*, r^*) in all periods or (ii) obtaining the larger profit associated with (p', r^*) for just one period and the reduced profit associated with (p^c, r^c) in all subsequent periods. If α is near enough to one, both firms will prefer alternative (i). Thus both firms can be better off following the 'cooperative' strategy. Note, however, that this cooperative outcome is the result of following non-cooperative equilibrium strategies. The strategy pair is chosen so that no single firm can increase its payoff by altering its strategy, given the strategy of the other firm. The strategies are designed so that deviating from cooperative behaviour is followed by punishment, and the punishment is carefully crafted so that it will be in the interests of all players to carry it out when the strategies call for it. This latter property, that the threats of punishment are credible because they are incentive compatible, is called *subgame perfection*. On the concept of subgame perfect non-cooperative equilibria, see Selten (1975) or Friedman (1986).

The work of Hotelling and Chamberlin raises an important issue that has received some recent attention: firms not only choose prices (or output levels), they decide on the design of their products. In deciding on how to design a product, the firm needs to know how design is related to cost of production and how it is related to consumers' tastes. The latter has been modelled by Lancaster (1979) in terms of inherent charactistics. The underlying notion is that consumers value certain attributes of goods that are analogous to the nutrients in foods. A particular product (e.g. a chair of a given design) is a specific bundle of characteristics. The product of a rival seller is a somewhat different bundle of characteristics. A difficulty with this approach in the most general form that Lancaster discusses is that it is difficult to define these characteristics. Less abstract versions are used in oligopoly models where, following Hotelling, physical location, is used as the only characteristic chosen by firms. Any single measurable attribute, such as sweetness of a bottled drink, can also be used.

Other topics treated in the duopoly theory literature include capital stock decisions, advertising, and entry. They can be found in Friedman (1983), along with a fuller account of the topics sketched above.

JAMES W. FRIEDMAN

See also BERTRAND, JOSEPH LOUIS FRANÇOIS; COURNOT, ANTOINE AUGUSTIN; NASH EQUILIBRIUM; OLIGOPOLY; STRATEGIC BEHAVIOUR AND MARKET STRUCTURE.

BIBLIOGRAPHY

Bertrand, J. 1883. Review of Cournot (1838). *Journal des Savants,* 499–508.

Bowley, A. 1924. *The Mathematical Groundwork of Economics.* New York: Kelley, 1965.

Bowley, A. 1928. Bilateral monopoly. *Economic Journal* 38, 651–9.

Chamberlin, E. 1933. *The Theory of Monopolistic Competition,* 7th edn, Cambridge: Harvard, 1956.

Cournot, A. 1838. *Recherches sur les principes mathématiques de la théorie des richesses.* Trans. N.T. Bacon, New York: Macmillan, 1927.

Edgeworth, F. 1897. The pure theory of monopoly. *Papers Relating to Political Economy,* vol. I, 111–42.

Edgeworth, F. 1925. *Papers Relating to Political Economy.* New York: Burt Franklin, 1970.

Friedman, J. 1968. Reaction functions and the theory of duopoly. *Review of Economic Studies* 35, 257–72.

Friedman, J. 1983. *Oligopoly Theory.* Cambridge: Cambridge University Press.

Friedman, J. 1986. *Game Theory with Applications to Economics.* New York: Oxford University Press.

Frisch, R. 1933. Monopole – polypole – la notion de force dans l'économie. *Festschrift til Harald Westergaard.* Supplement to *Nationalekonomisk Tidsskrift.*

Hotelling, H. 1929. Stability in competition. *Economic Journal* 39, 41–57.

Lancaster, K. 1979. *Variety, Equity, and Efficiency.* New York: Columbia University Press.

Nash, J. 1951. Noncooperative games. *Annals of Mathematics* 45, 286–95.

Owen, G. 1968. *Game Theory.* 2nd edn, New York: Academic Press, 1982.

Selten, R. 1975. Reexamination of the perfectness concept for equilibrium points in extensive games. *International Journal of Game Theory* 4, 25–55.

Smith, A. 1776. *An Inquiry into the Nature and Causes of the Wealth of Nations.* Ed. R.H. Campbell, A.S. Skinner, and W.M. Todd, Oxford: Clarendon Press, 1976.

Stackelberg, H. von. 1934. *Marktform und Gleichgewicht.* Vienna: Julius Springer.

Wicksell, K. 1925. Mathematical economics. In K. Wicksell, *Selected Papers on Economic Theory,* ed. Erik Lindahl, Cambridge, Mass.: Harvard University Press, 1958.

DUP activities. *See* DIRECTLY UNPRODUCTIVE PROFIT-SEEKING ACTIVITIES.

Du Pont de Nemours, Pierre Samuel (1739–1817). Economic writer and editor. Born in Paris, he trained for various occupations including medicine and watchmaking. A pamphlet on taxation (1763) brought him in contact with Mirabeau and Quesnay, under whose guidance he wrote a work on the grain trade (1764). He also befriended Turgot, with whom he diligently corresponded until Turgot's death. From 1766 to late 1768 he edited the *Journal de l'Agriculture* in the Physiocratic cause, then the *Éphémérides* until 1772. During this period he also published Quesnay's economics under the title *Physiocratie* (Du Pont, 1767) and summarized Mercier (1767), adding material on the history of the new science (Du Pont, 1768). From the early 1770s he developed a career as economic adviser through correspondence with the King of Sweden and the Margrave of Baden; the correspondence with the latter was subsequently published (Knies, 1892). In 1774 he was appointed tutor to the Polish royal family. On becoming *contrôleur-général,* Turgot required his friend's assistance and Du Pont was back in Paris by early 1775. Financial compensation for loss of his royal tutorship enabled him to purchase landed property near Nemours. Turgot's dismissal from office in 1776 did not end Du Pont's career in giving official economic advice; a highlight of which is his influence on the 1786 Anglo–French Commercial Treaty. Du Pont was politically active in the French revolution, serving from 1789 as Deputy for Nemours in the National Assembly and becoming its President during 1790; in 1794 to 1797 he was imprisoned for short periods. He migrated to the United States in 1799 but returned to Paris in 1802. From 1803 to 1810 he served in the Paris Chamber of Commerce, and in addition edited Turgot's works (Du Pont, 1808–11). In 1815 he returned to the United States and settled in Delaware, the town where his son Irenée had started the gunpowder factory from which the Du Pont chemical conglomerate developed, and where he died in 1817. Du Pont is now mainly remembered as a major propagator of Physiocracy, an early historian of economics, a pioneer in the use of diagrams in economic argument and, most importantly, as the editor of Quesnay and Turgot, whose works he helped to preserve. An assessment of his work as economist needs to take all facets of his career into account, as the one full-length attempt at this (McLain, 1977) has in fact done.

Virtually all Du Pont's economic work is characterized by dogmatic adherence to the Physiocracy developed by Quesnay and codified by Mercier de la Rivière. Turgot criticized this 'servitude to the ideas of the master' as totally inappropriate in matters of science (Schelle, 1913–23, II, p. 677). Despite such criticism Du Pont allowed his dogmatism to colour excursions into the history of economics (Du Pont, 1769) and more importantly, his preparation of Turgot's works for the press (see Groenewegen, 1977), particularly his editions of the *Reflections* (Turgot, 1766). Two examples of his more novel contributions to economics can be given. One is his use of diagrams in explaining economic policy, which Theocharis (1961, p. 60) described as the first use of a diagram by a professional economist for 'illustrating an economic argument set out in essentially dynamic time', thereby making Du Pont (1774) 'the earliest French contribution of importance in mathematical economics'. The problem analysed is the price effects of an excise reduction, the benefits of which are argued to accrue ultimately to the landowning class. The excise reduction's initial income effect on manufacturers and merchants allows them either to reduce their own prices or to pay higher prices for raw materials. By assuming this increased competition for raw materials to raise their price in each period by three-fourths of the increase in the preceding period, Du Pont shows how a new equilibrium price will be reached which transfers the benefits from excise reduction to the rural sector. His proof relies on the properties of diminishing geometrical progressions which also formed the basis for much of the analysis of the *Tableau économique.* Du Pont's analysis of the inflationary consequences from issuing assignats is a second example. Although much of this is similar to Turgot's (1749) analysis, some of it is of interest in explaining Smith's version of the specie mechanism to which Du Pont (1790, p. 28) explicitly refers. Issuing paper money by *assignats* makes silver superfluous as a circulating medium; this drives the metal out of the country because its only other use is to be sold abroad (Du Pont, 1790, p. 42), a specie mechanism like Smith's (1776, pp. 293–4) that is independent of relative price movements. Both examples of his more original economics relate to matters of economic policy and add force to the claim by McLain (1977, p. 255) that Du Pont represents 'the first important case of a professional economist turned government policy-maker, a tradition in which he would be followed by [many] others...'.

PETER GROENEWEGEN

SELECTED WORKS

1763. *Réflexions sur l'écrit intitulé: Richesses de l'état*. Paris.
1764. *De l'exportation et de l'importation des grains*. Soissons and Paris.
1767. *Physiocratie, ou Constitution Naturelle du Gouvernement le plus avantageux au genre humain*. Leyden and Paris.
1768. *De l'origine et des progrès d'une science nouvelle*. In *Physiocrates*, ed. E. Daire, Paris, 1846.
1769. *Notice abrégée des différents écrits modernes qui ont concours en France à former la science de l'économie politique*. In *Oeuvres Oeconomiques et Philosophiques de François Quesnay*, ed. A. Oncken, Frankfurt and Paris, 1888.
1774. *On Economic Curves*. Ed. H.W. Spiegel, Baltimore: Johns Hopkins Reprints of Economic Tracts, 1955.
1790. *The Dangers of Inflation*. Trans. Edmund E. Lincoln, Boston: Kress Library Publications, 1950.
1808-11. *Oeuvres de Turgot*. 9 vols, Paris.

BIBLIOGRAPHY

Groenewegen, P.D. 1977. *The Economics of A.R.J. Turgot*. The Hague: Nijhoff.
Knies, K. 1892. *Carl Friedrichs von Baden Brieflicher Verkehr mit Mirabeau und Du Pont*. Heidelberg.
McLain, J.J. 1977. *The Economic Writings of Du Pont de Nemours*. Newark and London: University of Delaware Press.
Mercier de la Rivière, P.P. 1767. *L'Ordre Naturel et Essentiel des Sociétiés politiques*. Paris.
Schelle, G. 1913-23. *Oeuvres de Turgot et documents le concernant*. 5 vols, Paris: F Alcan.
Smith, A. 1776. *An Inquiry into the Nature and Causes of the Wealth of Nations*. Ed. R H Campbell and A.S. Skinner, Oxford: Clarendon, 1976.
Theocharis, R.D. 1961. *Early Developments in Mathematical Economics*. London: Macmillan.
Turgot, A.R.J. 1749. *Letter on Paper Money*. In Groenewegen (1977).
Turgot, A.R.J. 1766. *Reflections on the Production and Distribution of Wealth*. In Groenewegen (1977).

Dupuit, Arsène-Jules-Emile Juvenal (1804–1866). French engineer and economic theorist, born at Fossano, Piedmont, Italy on 18 May 1804, when this region was part of the French empire; died 5 September 1866 in Paris. After his parents returned to Paris in 1814, Dupuit continued his education in the secondary schools at Versailles, at Louis-le-Grand and at Saint-Louis, where he finished brilliantly by winning a physics prize in a large group of competitors. Accepted to the Ecole des Ponts et Chaussées in 1824, Dupuit soon distinguished himself as an engineer and, in 1827, was put in charge of an engineering district in the department of Sarthe, where he concentrated on roadway and navigation work. Dupuit's numerous and trenchant engineering studies on such topics as friction and highway deterioration, floods and hydraulics, and municipal water systems made him one of the most creative civil engineers of his day. Decorated for such contributions by the Legion of Honour in 1843, Dupuit ultimately became director-chief engineer in Paris in 1850 and Inspector-General of the Corps of Civil Engineers in 1855.

No less profound were Dupuit's contributions to general economic analysis and to the economic evaluation of public works (cost-benefit analysis). In fact, Dupuit was the most illustrious contributor in the long French tradition of study, teaching and writing on economic topics at the Ecole des Ponts et Chaussées, whose professors and students included Isnard, Henri Navier, Charles Minard, Emile Cheysson and Charles Ellet.

Led by a desire to evaluate the economic or *net* benefits of public provision, Dupuit directed his considerable analytical

gifts to the utility foundation of demand and to its relevance to the welfare benefits of public works. In three substantial papers appearing in the *Annales des Ponts et Chaussées* (1844, 1849) and the *Journal des économistes* (1853), Dupuit became the first non-adventitious expositor of the theory of *marginal* utility, of (a variant of) marginal cost pricing, of simple and discriminating monopoly theory, and of pricing principles of the firm where location is a factor in expressing demand.

The font of Dupuit's contribution is the construction of a marginal utility curve and the identification of it with the demand curve or *courbe de consommation* (see Figure 1).

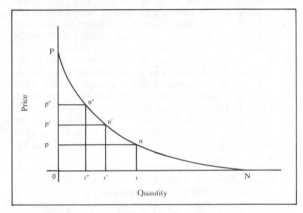

Figure 1

Arguing in the manner of Carl Menger, who later elaborated on the point, Dupuit showed that the marginal utility that an individual obtained from a homogeneous stock of goods is determined by the use to which the last units of the stock are put. In doing so, he clearly pointed out that the marginal utility of a stock or some particular good diminishes with increases in quantity and that each consumer attaches a different marginal utility to the same good according to the quantity consumed. The importance of Dupuit's invention rests in the fact that the psychological concept of diminishing marginal utility, and its ramifications, were carried over to the law of demand. With some, but not all, of the reservations and qualifications of Alfred Marshall, Dupuit *identified* the marginal utility curve with the demand curve, adding up the utility curves of individuals to obtain the market demand curve. Dupuit described his construction (see Figure 1), which applied to all goods, public and private, as follows:

> If ... along a line *Op* the lengths *Op*, *Op'*, *Op''* ... represent various prices for an article, and that ... *pn*, *p'n'*, *p''n''* ... represent the number of articles consumed corresponding to these prices, then it is possible to construct a curve *Nn'n''P* which we shall call the curve of consumption. *ON* represents the quantity consumed when the price is zero, and *OP* the price at which consumption falls to zero (1844, p. 106).

The identification of marginal utility and demand, of course, sets up the demand curve as a welfare tool and Dupuit made specific calculations. A measure of the welfare produced by the good (*utilité absolue*) at quantity *Or* is the definite integral of the demand curve between *O* and *r*. Given that *Op* is the (average) cost of producing quantity *Or*, consumers earn a surplus (*utilité relative*) equal to absolute utility (*OrnP*) less costs of production (*Ornp*). (Relative utility (*pnP*) is none other than Marshall's consumers' surplus without all the reservations that Marshall attached to the concept.) Importantly, Dupuit identified area *rNn* as lost utility (*utilité perdue*). Under competitive conditions this loss was inevitable due to the opportunity cost of resources. Under a monopoly structure, e.g. if, in Figure 1, *Op* were a monopoly price with zero production costs assumed, *utilité perdue* would be a loss to society – the 'deadweight' loss associated with excise taxes, tariffs or monopoly. Further, Dupuit advanced the theorem that the loss in utility was proportional to the *square* of the tax of price above marginal cost. This theorem, with attendant analysis, formed the base for large areas of neoclassical welfare economics, including the taxation studies of F.Y. Edgeworth and the marginal cost pricing argument of Harold Hotelling.

From this theoretical base, Dupuit investigated an impressive number of pricing systems and market models (1849). While Dupuit was an ardent and stubborn defender of laissez faire in most markets (1861), he was equally concerned that public works, provided or regulated by government as a *last* resort, should produce the maximum amount of utility possible. Thus tools such as marginal cost pricing find their theoretical foundations in the writings of Dupuit. Although Dupuit did not provide an explicit formulation of the principle, one of his bridge pricing examples and other statements strongly suggest the possibilities of such a technique to maximize welfare, but as a *long-run* proposition.

Dupuit analysed, independently of Cournot, who was apparently unknown to him, the profit-maximizing behaviour of the simple monopolist. He saw monopoly at the apex of a range of problems regarding the production of total welfare, being unconcerned about the 'distribution' of welfare between producers and consumers. His point was that the amount of 'absolute utility' (or what could be called net benefit) was lessened by monopoly profit maximization. This led him to defend the private practice of price discrimination and to produce an economic theory of discrimination. Price discrimination could exist, in Dupuit's view, with differences in 'buyer estimates', with the ability to segment markets either naturally or artificially, and with some degree of monopoly power. The motive was profit maximization, and although Dupuit discussed the effects of discrimination on price and revenue, he was primarily interested in the fact, as was Joan Robinson later, that discrimination could affect the size of the welfare benefit. This view was expanded to include the impact of price discrimination of welfare when buyers were spatially distributed (1849, 1854).

In the matter of policy, Dupuit recommended that tools be carefully fit to specific problems. If industries were to be collectivized or regulated by government, Dupuit proposed the maximization of net benefit under the constraint of covering total costs of production. The recovery of total cost might be achieved through regulated or constrained price discrimination or through a cost-based single price technique. However, Dupuit can hardly be credited with espousing an enlarged role for government or government intervention. A firm adherent of Smith's dictums concerning minimal government, Dupuit believed that free and open competition, along with vigorous antitrust or anticartel enforcement, would ensure optimal provisions in most cases, including transportation. Indeed, in the process of analysing the welfare principles of public works pricing, Dupuit discovered (in an uncommonly complete manner) some of the critical welfare-maximizing properties of a generalized competitive system.

ROBERT B. EKELUND, JR.

See also CONSUMERS' SURPLUS; PUBLIC UTILITY PRICING.

SELECTED WORKS

1844. On the measurement of the utility of public works. Translated by R.H. Barback from the *Annales des Ponts et Chaussées*, in *International Economic Papers*, No. 2, London: Macmillan, 1952.
1849. On tolls and transport charges. Translated by Elizabeth Henderson from the *Annales des Ponts et Chaussées*, in *International Economic Papers*, No. 11, London: Macmillan, 1962.
1853. On utility and its measure – on public utility. *Journal des économistes* 36, 1–27.
1854. Péages. In *Dictionnaire de l'Economie Politique*, Vol. II, Paris: Guillaumin.
1861. *La Liberté Commerciale*. Paris: Guillaumin.
1934. *De l'Utilité et sa Mésure: écrits choisis et republiés*. Ed. Mario de Bernardi, Turin: La Riforma Sociale.

BIBLIOGRAPHY

Ekelund, R.B., Jr. 1968. Jules Dupuit and the early theory of marginal cost pricing. *Journal of Political Economy* 76, May/June, 462–71.
Ekelund, R.B., Jr. 1970. Price discrimination and product differentiation in economic theory: an early analysis. *Quarterly Journal of Economics* 84(2), May, 268–78.
Ekelund, R.B., Jr. and Yeung-Nan Shieh. 1986. Dupuit, spatial economics, and optimal resource allocation: a French tradition. *Economica*.

Durand, David (born 1912). Durand was born in Ithaca, New York. He received his PhD at Columbia University in 1941. He was a member of the Research Staff of the National Bureau of Economic Research from 1946 to 1955 when he became a Professor at the Massachusetts Institute of Technology, where he remained throughout his career.

The early contributions of David Durand were in statistical methodology. His election as a Fellow of the American Statistical Association was based on his work in developing and applying statistical analysis in the field of finance, including the construction of historical series on the term structure of interest rates.

In a National Bureau Conference publication (1952), Durand authored a chapter which laid the foundation for later developments on cost of capital theory and measurement. Durand followed the premise that security appraisal is the key to measuring the cost of capital. He developed two alternative methods of appraisal, the Net Income (NI) method and the Net Operating Income (NOI) method. In the NI method, the cost of debt interest is deducted from net operating income and net income is capitalized at a constant rate; the value of the firm increases with higher debt leverage until both the cost of debt and of equity rise substantially. Under the NOI method a constant capitalization rate is applied to the net operating income so that the total value of all bonds and stocks is invariant so the degree of leverage employed. Durand leaned toward the NOI method, but recognized circumstances under which each model had applicability. Subsequent literature predominantly favoured the NOI approach until the 1980s, when Durand's views have essentially prevailed.

Durand also made contributions to the theory of capital budgeting. He emphasized an eclectic approach including the internal rate of return method and the net present value procedure. He also emphasized considering some measure of time to indicate how fast an investment project will liquidate itself. He argued that just as portfolio managers select bonds partly on the basis of term to maturity, financial managers responsible for capital budgeting should select investment projects partly on the basis of their weighted discounted payout period or duration.

J. FRED WESTON

SELECTED WORKS

1941. *Risk Elements in Consumer Installment Financing*. New York: National Bureau of Economic Research.

1942. *Basic Yields of Corporate Bonds: 1900–1942*. Technical Paper No. 3, New York: National Bureau of Economic Research.

1948. An appraisal of the errors involved in estimating the size distribution of a given aggregate income. *Review of Economics and Statistics* 30, 63–8.

1952. Costs of debt and equity funds for business: trends and problems of measurement. *Conference on Research in Business Finance*, New York: National Bureau of Economic Research, 215–47.

1954. Joint confidence regions for multiple regression coefficients. *Journal of the American Statistical Association* 49, 130–46.

1957. Growth stocks and the Petersburg Paradox. *Journal of Finance* 12, 348–63.

1971. *Stable chaos: an introduction to statistical control*. Morristown, NJ: D.H. Mark Publication of General Learning Press.

1974. Payout period, time spread and duration: aids to judgment in capital budgeting. *Journal of Bank Research* 5, 20–34.

1981. Comprehensiveness in capital budgeting. *Financial Management* 10(5), Winter, 7–13.

duration of life. *See* DEMOGRAPHIC TRANSITION; DEMOGRAPHY; MORTALITY.

Durbin, Evan Frank Mottram (1906–1948). Born in Devon, Durbin was a Scholar of New College, Oxford, won the Senior and Junior Webb Medley Scholarships, first class Honours in Politics, Philosophy and Economics and the Ricardo Fellowship to University College, London. Hired as an economics lecturer at the London School of Economics in 1930, he was later promoted to senior lecturer. During the war he was a personal assistant to Clement Attlee, the Deputy Prime Minister, and in 1945 he was elected Labour Member of Parliament for Edmonton. He served as Parliamentary Private Secretary to Hugh Dalton at the Treasury, and was appointed junior Minister of Works in March 1947. He was drowned in Cornwall in 1948. Durbin is best remembered for his book *The Politics of Democratic Socialism* (1940), an influential statement of the revisionist case in Britain, of which his close friend and professional colleague, Hugh Gaitskell, later commented: 'it marked the transition from the pioneering stage to that of responsibility and power.'

As a professional economist, Durbin published two books on macroeconomic theory and policy, and a number of articles on economic planning. In the intellectual turmoil of the early 1930s, he was searching for a theory to explain the trade cycle, because he believed that its control was essential to the socialist alternative to capitalism. He was strongly influenced by Hayek's cyclical theory of sectoral imbalance, although he argued that the crisis was precipitated by 'an excessive supply of money' in the consumers' sector, not capital scarcity in the producers' sector (Hayek's view). In further work, he introduced the role of the money market, an important advance on Hayek's model, which foreshadowed Keynes's use of uncertainty in *The General Theory*. Later scholars have also recognized his contributions to identifying the crucial growth problem of maintaining sufficient savings without causing sectoral imbalance. Together with Hugh Gaitskell, J.E. Meade and Douglas Jay, Durbin has also been credited with adapting the Keynesian revolution into practical policies for the British Labour Party. However, he always remained sceptical about some aspects of *The General Theory*; he did not believe it provided a solution of the cyclical problem, and he was

concerned about the inflationary potential of continued expansion.

Beginning in 1931 through the Fabian Society, Durbin and Gaitskell also organized systematic research into the theory and practice of socialist planning and the appropriate criteria for assessing efficiency in a socialist economy. Thus Durbin was in the forefront of the planning controversies of the Thirties, contributing articles to the development of the 'competitive' solution for market socialism and to the marginal cost-pricing debate. He was one of the first to argue that a mixed economy was fundamental to the notion of democratic socialism; the market provided individuals freedom to choose jobs and goods and incentives to innovate, and the government provided the programme and policies to sustain growth, to allocate resources in the public interest and to ensure social justice.

Durbin's main achievements were to present a practical forerunner of the postwar mainstream case for government intervention and to lay the intellectual foundations for the continuing debates about the nature of the socialist vision in Britain.

ELIZABETH DURBIN

See also FABIAN ECONOMICS; SOCIAL DEMOCRACY.

SELECTED WORKS

1933a. *Purchasing Power and Trade Depression*. London: Chapman & Hall.

1935a. *The Problem of Credit Policy*. London: Chapman & Hall.

1935b. The social significance of the theory of value. *Economic Journal* 45, December, 700–710.

1940. *The Politics of Democratic Socialism*. London: Routledge & Kegan Paul.

1949. *Problems of Economic Planning*. London: Routledge & Kegan Paul.

BIBLIOGRAPHY

Durbin, E. 1985. *New Jerusalems: The Labour Party and the Economics of Democratic Socialism*. London: Routledge & Kegan Paul.

Durkheim, Emile (1858–1917). Born in Epinal near Strasbourg, Durkheim attended the Ecole Normale Supérieure in Paris, taking his *agrégation* in 1882. His first important academic appointment was as Professor of Sociology and Education at Bordeaux in 1887. The Bordeaux appointment marked the first sociology professorship in France. In 1902 Durkheim was appointed as Professor of Sociology (and Education), at the Sorbonne where he remained until his death in 1917. Of Durkheim's four major works, *The Division of Labour* (1893), *The Rules of Sociological Method* (1895), *Suicide: A Study in Sociology* (1897) and *The Elementary Forms of Religious Life* (1912), the first three were written while he was at Bordeaux. At the Sorbonne, Durkheim devoted considerable effort towards the establishment of sociology as a professional discipline. He founded a journal, *L'année sociologique*, and was active in supervision of younger scholars, most notably Granet, Mauss, and Halbwachs.

The theoretical agenda of Durkheim's major works centred around understanding the collective bases for social order in modern societies characterized by increased individuation and autonomy. For Durkheim, a stable social order was possible only if the members of a group shared a common set of beliefs (*conscience collective*) governing individual behaviour. With the progression of the division of labour in society – which by definition leads to greater individuation and specialization of persons and roles – the values that increasingly heterogeneous individuals hold are seen to become more abstract, and are thus less able to shape and constrain individual social action. The social order, in this context, may become weak. Durkheim recognized that countervailing the weakness of the collective conscience in modern society was increased functional interdependence of persons. Yet, in *The Division of Labour*, Durkheim attacked the notion (attributed to Spencer as a representative utilitarian) that such interdependence (the need for individuals to exchange the products of their labour) was by itself robust enough to guarantee social stability. Rather, he asserted that exchange is possible only because of the existence of shared sentiments which govern the determination of 'individual interest' and behaviour. Contracts presume prior sentiments constraining self-interested social action.

Durkheim's fundamental methodological contribution to sociology is the recognition that macro-level outcomes cannot be accounted for from the analysis (or empirical observation) of micro-level (individual) action. Rather, he argued that social scientists must recognize that society is a 'reality sui generis', a 'thing' greater than, and not reducible to, its constituent parts. In this framework, sociology is the positive science of social facts, phenomena whose own structure can be used as an indicator of the social solidarity of a group which one cannot directly apprehend from observation alone.

Durkheim is considered a founder of modern sociology and anthropology. On both substantive and methodological grounds, his work can be considered a sustained attack on economic theory which typically elides the problem of social order and assumes that aggregate social outcomes are the products of individual social action and individual self-interest.

PETER BEARMAN

SELECTED WORKS

1893. *The Division of Labor in Society*. Trans. and ed. G. Simpson, New York: Free Press, 1947.

1895. *The Rules of Sociological Method*. Trans. S.A. Solovay and J.H. Mueller, ed. G. Catlin, New York: Free Press, 1958.

1897. *Suicide: A Study in Sociology*. Trans. J.A. Spaulding and G. Simpson, ed. G. Simpson, New York: Free Press, 1951.

1912. *The Elementary Forms of the Religious Life*. Trans. J.W. Swain, New York: Free Press, 1954.

BIBLIOGRAPHY

Lukes, S. 1973. *Emile Durkheim: His Life and Work: A Historical and Critical Study*. Harmondsworth: Penguin.

Parsons, T. 1968. Emile Durkheim. In *International Encyclopedia of the Social Sciences*, ed. D.L. Shils, New York: Macmillan.

dynamic programming and Markov decision processes. A great many problems in economics can be reduced to determining the maximum of a given function. Dynamic programming is one of a number of mathematical optimization techniques applicable in such problems. As will be illustrated, the dynamic programming technique or viewpoint is particularly useful in complex optimization problems with many variables in which time plays a crucial role. Unlike calculus-based techniques it does not require the function being optimized to be differentiable in the (decision) variables.

In a nutshell, dynamic programming is a mathematical approach designed for analysing decision processes in which the multi-stage or sequential character of the process is prominent. In particular, dynamic programming is likely to be applicable whenever an economic agent makes a sequence of decisions (such as how much to consume in year i) in a prespecified order (year i's decision is made prior to year $i + 1$'s decision). In contrast to the familiar first-order condition which, for

example, balances marginal revenues against marginal costs, the orientation of the typical dynamic programming approach entails balancing current profits against all future profits. In so doing, it transforms a complex n variable optimization problem into n simple one variable optimization problems.

While it is important to understand the conditions under which this approach induces a computationally attractive technique, economists' interest in dynamic programming emanates from its analytic rather than computational power. As empiricists we are interested in the numbers (for example, the optimal amount consumed in period 1), but wearing our theoretical or policy-making hats we are more interested in the intrinsic structure of the solution (for example, the optimal amount consumed in period 1 decreases in response to an increase in the riskiness associated with the income stream). With this in mind, we emphasize the use of dynamic programming as a conceptual framework enabling us to understand the nature of the solution to the decision-maker's problem.

The basic components describing a multi-stage decision process are states, stages, actions (decisions), rewards, state transitions or law of motion, and constraints. The relevant dynamic programming concepts are those of policy, return function, and functional equation. For pedagogical purposes we define and explain these objects in the context of consumption under uncertainty.

AN EXAMPLE. At the beginning of each of N periods (of equal length such as one year) our economic agent must decide how much of his current wealth to consume and how much to save. After making his consumption decision, his remaining wealth is invested and experiences a (possibly random) return of R per unit of capital. Assume $R \geqslant 0$ so that losing his entire investment is the worst that can happen. The agent is gainfully employed; accordingly, at the end of each period his wealth is augmented by his (possibly random) labour income L. To keep matters simple, assume that the $2N$ random variables are independent and that the distributions of both return on capital and on labour do not change with time. The agent's goal is to maximize the expected discounted utility of his consumption stream. The literature on this topic usually postulates that the agent's utility function is separable in time and that $u(c)$, the utility of consuming c units of capital in a given period, does not change with time and is strictly concave and strictly increasing. Denoting the one-period discount factor by $\beta > 0$, $\Sigma_{i=1}^{N} \beta^{i-1} u(c_i)$ is the utility associated with the consumption stream $c_1, c_2, \ldots, c_N$. Setting the agent's initial endowment at w_1, the problem specification is complete.

The *state* of the system or process is the agent's wealth, and the set of possible states, called the *state space*, is the nonnegative numbers. (Although typically the state is a real number or a vector of real numbers, occasionally the state is a more complicated object such as a probability measure.) The points in time when decisions must be made divide the process into *stages*. In this example, each period is a stage. The *action* or decision at each stage is how much to consume. Given a wealth of w, i.e., the agent finds himself in state w, the agent's consumption level c must satisfy the constraint $0 \leqslant c \leqslant w$. The agent's *action space* is $[0, w]$ and reflects the fact that his consumption cannot be negative and is not permitted to exceed his current wealth. (Thus, borrowing against future income is prohibited.)

In our consumption example the objective function or overall return (the functional being maximized, here $\Sigma_{i=1}^{N} \beta^{i-1} u(c_i)$) is additively separable in the consumption levels $c_1, c_2, \ldots, c_N$: the change in the overall return associated with a change in c_i to $\hat{c}_i$ is $\beta^{i-1}[u(\hat{c}_i) - u(c_i)]$ and does not depend upon any of the other consumption levels. (Of course, altering c_i has an impact upon the future wealth levels.) Consequently, we can speak of the *one-period reward function* u. Given the current state (wealth level) w, the system passes (the state is transformed) to a new state $T(w, c)$ in response to the action (consumption decision) c selected. The new state $T(w, c)$ is simply the state of the system at the beginning of the next stage or period. Thus $w_{j+1} = T(w_j, c)$ where w_j is the state of the system in period j. In our example, the *law of motion* or *transition function* is

$$T(w, c) = (w - c)R + L. \qquad (1)$$

It reflects the facts that labour income is unaffected by either consumption or the return on investment and that the investment has constant returns to scale.

It is often more convenient to label time backwards and to speak of the number of stages remaining. Accordingly, define $V_n(w)$ to be the maximum expected discounted utility obtainable when n stages remain and the current wealth is w, $n = 1, 2, \ldots$ and $w \geq 0$; V_n is called the n-period *return function*. Our immediate goal is to write a *functional equation* or recursive formula relating V_n to V_{n-1}.

In order to obtain our recursive relation, we shall employ implicitly Bellman's famous Principle of Optimality. Bellman stated it thus:

> An optimal policy has the property that whatever the initial state and initial decision are, the remaining decisions must constitute an optimal policy with regard to the state resulting from the first decision. (1, p. 83)

Our use of the Principle of Optimality will become clear as the development of the function equation (3) unfolds. To facilitate the connection between the functional equation and Bellman's Principle of Optimality one last piece of terminology requires introduction. A *policy* is a rule which specifies the decisions to be made as the system passes through the various states. Of course the decisions specified must be *feasible* in that they satisfy the system's constraints: each action selected must lie in the action space associated with the given state. While the action specified by the policy for state s at time n can be a (random) function of the history $(s_1, a_1, s_2, a_2, \ldots, s_{n-1}, a_{n-1}, s_n)$ of the system up to time n where s_i was the state at time i and a_i the action selected at time i, it is usually the case that attention can be restricted to policies under which the action specified for time n depends upon the history of the system only through the state of the system at time n; such a policy is referred to as a *Markov policy*. It may be helpful to think of a (Markov) policy as a contingency plan specifying the action to be selected if a given state is reached at a given stage rather than as a schedule of N actions that will occur. A policy is said to be an *optimal policy* if the return associated with using it equals the maximal return attainable.

DEVELOPING THE FUNCTIONAL EQUATION. To begin, recall that the agent's utility function u is nondecreasing, whence he consumes all his wealth in period N when one stage remains:

$$V_1(w) = u(w), \qquad \text{all} \quad w \geq 0. \qquad (2)$$

To obtain an expression for V_2 in terms of V_1, note that the total return when two stages remain consists of the immediate reward $u(c)$ from the first stage plus the discounted return from the second stage. At the second stage the agent will have an amount $(w - c)R + L$ of wealth to allocate between consumption and saving; clearly, it must be allocated in the best possible manner – in this instance all of it is consumed – in order to obtain an optimal two stage allocation. Thus, given an initial consumption of c, an additional return of $\beta V_1[(w - c)R + L]$ is

garnered if consumption in the final stage is chosen optimally. Therefore, the total expected return for the two stage process when c is the consumption in the first of the two stages is simply $u(c) + \beta E V_1[(w - c)R + L]$, where E denotes the expectation with respect to the random variables in the state description. Finally, by selecting the best consumption level in the first of the two stages we obtain the desired relationship between V_1 and V_2:

$$V_2(w) = \max_{0 \leq c \leq w} \{u(c) + \beta E V_1[(w - c)R + L]\},$$
$$\text{all} \quad w \geq 0. \qquad (3a)$$

Utilizing the same logic, the return function V_2 can be employed to compute V_3 and, more generally, V_{n-1} can be used to compute V_n as follows:

$$V_n(w) = \max_{0 \leq c \leq w} \{u(w) + \beta E V_{n-1}[(w - c)R + L]\},$$
$$n = 2, 3, \ldots, N, \quad \text{all} \quad w \geq 0. \qquad (3b)$$

For each n and w, define $c_n(w)$ to be the largest value of c for which the maximum in (3) is attained. Then the policy which consumes the amount $c_n(w)$ when in state w with n stages remaining is an optimal policy. When the optimal return exists, it is unique, but it is often the case that there is more than one optimal policy.

STRUCTURE OF THE OPTIMAL POLICY. As noted earlier, the problem is not solved until the structure of an optimal policy is exhibited. Our analysis of the consumption problem is typical and illustrative of many analyses of finite planning horizon ($N < \infty$) dynamic programming problems; in particular, mathematical induction is critical to the analysis.

To ensure a positive level of consumption each period, assume $u'(0) = \infty$ and $L \geq \epsilon > 0$ (so labour income is bounded away from zero whence $V_n(w) > -\infty$ for $w > 0$ as $Eu(L) \geq u(\epsilon) > -\infty$). The first condition provides the incentive to consume and the second provides the capital. If R and/or β is small, the agent's optimal policy may entail the corner solution of consuming all of his wealth in a given period. Assume R and β are sufficiently large – e.g., $u'(\epsilon) < \beta E(R) Eu'(L)$ – to ensure $c_n(w) < w$ for $n > 1$.

It is our intention to illustrate common analytical approaches as well as lay bare the structure of the optimal policy. In so doing the nature of the return function V_n is also characterized.

One technique often employed is that of computing the return of a suboptimal policy which mimics the actions of another (perhaps optimal) policy. Mimicking is the method of proof of the following minor result, which we facetiously interpret as 'life is worth living'.

Lemma 1. If $Eu(L) > 0$, then $V_{n+1} > V_n$.

Proof: Let the consumption $\pi_i(w)$ dictated by policy π when i stages remain and the current wealth is w be specified as follows: $\pi_1(w) = w$ and $\pi_{i+1}(w) = c_i(w)$ for $i \geq 1$. Thus, when $i + 1$ stages remain, π acts like an optimal policy if there were but i stages remaining. Consequently, π yields a return of $V_n(w) + \beta^n Eu(L) > V_n(w)$. The result now follows as the optimal return $V_{n+1}(w)$ is at least as large as the return from using π for $n + 1$ stages. Q.E.D.

The return function often inherits properties of the one-period reward function. For example, using induction it can be shown the return function is strictly concave and strictly increasing like u. Doing so in this instance is a bit more difficult than usual.

Lemma 2. The return function V_n is strictly increasing and strictly concave. Consequently, there is a unique optimal policy: $c_n(w)$ is the unique optimal level of consumption.

Proof: By (2) V_1 is trivially seen to be strictly increasing. Noting that $c_n(w + \delta)$ need not equal $c_n(w) + \delta$ for $\delta > 0$, we have

$$V_n(w + \delta) \geqslant u[c_n(w) + \delta] + \beta EV_{n-1}\{[w - c_n(w)]R + L\}$$
$$> u[c_n(w)] + \beta EV_{n-1}\{[w - c_n(w)]R + L\} = V_n(w)$$

so V_n is strictly increasing.

Strict concavity is proved by induction. Clearly V_1 is strictly concave. Assume V_{n-1} is strictly concave. It is easy to demonstrate (see Heyman and Sobel 1984, p. 535) that the function $J(w, c) = V_{n-1}[(w - c)r + l]$ is jointly concave in w and c on the convex set $C = \{(w, c): 0 \leqslant c \leqslant w, w > 0\}$. (The concavity is strict if $r > 0$.) As the sum of concave functions is itself concave, $EV_{n-1}[(w - c)R + L]$ is strictly concave on C as is $\bar{J}(w, c) = u(c) + \beta EV_{n-1}[(w - c)R + L]$. While the maximum of a set of concave functions need not be concave, a standard result (ibid. p. 525) reveals that V_n, the maximum of the jointly strictly concave function $\bar{J}$, is strictly concave on C. This completes the induction argument. Strict concavity of $\bar{J}(w, c)$ ensures uniqueness. Q.E.D.

The decreasing marginal utility of wealth readily implies that optimal consumption increases with, but not as quickly as, wealth.

Lemma 3. The optimal level of consumption $c_n(w)$ satisfies

$$0 < c_n(w + \Delta) - c_n(w) < \Delta \quad \text{for} \quad \Delta > 0. \tag{4}$$

Proof: For ease in presentation only, assume that u'' exists so that V''_{n-1} and $\mathrm{d}^2 EV_{n-1}[(w - c)R + L]/dc^2$ both exist. Differentiating the first order condition $u'[c_n(w)] - \beta E\{RV'_{n-1}[(w - c_n(w))R + L]\} = 0$ with respect to w yields

$$c'_n(w)u''[c_n(w)] - [1 - c'_n(w)]$$
$$\times E\langle R^2 V''_{n-1}\{[w - c_n(w)]R + L\}\rangle = 0, \tag{5}$$

As $u'' < 0$, $R^2 \geqslant 0$, and $V''_{n-1} < 0$, $c_n \leqslant 0$ would violate (5). Similarly, $c'_n \geqslant 1$ violates (5). Q.E.D.

In the context of a teenager's lament and the associated parental response, the two intuitive inequalities in (4) have the interpretations 'What is money for if not to spend?' and, 'Don't let it burn a hole in your pocket!'

The demonstration that the overall return increases with the time remaining offered in the proof of Lemma 1 was straightforward. Verifying that the marginal utility of wealth declines with the agent's age, whence consumption increases with age, entails the application of a frequently employed induction technique we call bootstrapping induction.

Lemma 4. The marginal utility of wealth decreases and the optimal level of consumption increases with age:

$$c_n(w) > c_{n+1}(w)$$

and

$$V'_n(w) < V'_{n+1}(w).$$

Proof: For ease in presentation assume only that u'' exists. Corner solutions have been eliminated: the assumption $u'(\epsilon) < \beta E(R)Eu'(L)$ ensures $c_n(w) < w$ for $n > 1$ whereas $u'(0) = \infty$ and $L \geqslant \epsilon$ ensures $c_n(w) > 0$ for $n \geqslant 1$. Therefore, the marginal benefit $u'[c_n(w)]$ of immediate consumption equals the marginal benefit $\beta E\langle RV'_{n-1}\{[w - c_n(w)]R + L\}\rangle$ of savings for $n > 1$. Consequently, regardless of the percentage of marginal increase in wealth the agent allocates to savings, we find

$$V'_n(w) = u'[c_n(w)], \quad n \geqslant 1. \tag{6}$$

From (2) and the guarantee of an interior solution for $n > 1$ we have $c_1(w) = w > c_2(w)$, whereas (6) and u' strictly decreasing yield $V'_1(w) = u'[c_1(w)] < u'[c_2(w)] = V'_2(w)$. Assume

$$c_n(w) > c_{n+1}(w), \quad \text{all} \quad w > 0 \tag{7a}$$
$$V'_n(w) < V'_{n+1}(w), \quad \text{all} \quad w > 0. \tag{7b}$$

Applying (7b) to the future return results in

$$\frac{\mathrm{d}}{\mathrm{d}_c} \beta EV_n[(w - c)R + L] = -\beta E\{RV'_n[(w - c)R + L]\}$$
$$> -\beta E\{RV'_{n+1}[(w - c)R + L]\} = \frac{\mathrm{d}}{\mathrm{d}_c} \beta EV_{n+1}[(w - c)R + L].$$

from which we obtain immediately

$$c_{n+1}(w) > c_{n+2}(w). \tag{8a}$$

Now (6), (8a), and u' strictly decreasing yield

$$V'_{n+1}(w) = u'[c_{n+1}(w)] < u'[c_{n+2}(w)] = V'_{n+2}(w). \tag{8b}$$

Having established (8), the induction argument is complete. Q.E.D.

The impact on consumption of increased uncertainty (in the sense of second order stochastic dominance) in capital income R or labour income L has been a focal point of the literature which models the agent's allocation between immediate consumption and saving. Will the prospect of either uncertainty vis-à-vis certainty or increased uncertainty induce the agent to increase his immediate consumption as a hedge against the (increasingly) uncertain future in which nature herself may, in effect, consume his wealth, or will the agent decrease his immediate consumption in an attempt to provide against an adverse future? The former strategy adopts a 'get while the getting's good' philosophy while the latter evokes one of 'save for a rainy day'.

The best response to an increase in uncertainty depends on the shape of the utility function as well as the source of the uncertainty. On this account, the family $\{u_\gamma\}$ of utility functions with constant relative risk aversion plays an important role:

$$u_0(c) = \ln c \quad \text{and} \quad u_\gamma(c) = c^\gamma/\gamma, \quad \text{for} \quad \gamma < 1, \quad \gamma \neq 0.$$

When the utility function has a positive third derivative and there is pure income risk (i.e. R is a constant), consumption decreases in the face of an increase in risk (see Miller, 1976). For $\gamma < 1$, $u'''_\gamma > 0$. When there is pure capital risk (i.e. L is a constant) and the utility function exhibits constant relative risk aversion, an increase in risk causes consumption to decrease if $\gamma < 0$ and increase if $\gamma > 0$ (see Phelps, 1962 or Mirman, 1971).

Of course the dynamic programming approach can be gainfully employed to address other interesting questions such as the conditions which imply capital will (on average) accumulate, whether V_n converges, and the impact of an uncertain lifetime. The second question is a recurring one in dynamic programming models; in this instance, V_N converges as $N \to \infty$ provided $\beta ER < 1$. If p_i is the probability the agent lives i or more years and $p_{N+1} = 0$, then the return function V_n satisfies (2) and (3) with $u(c)$ replaced by $p_{N-n+1}u(c)$ and an increase in consumption is the agent's response to an increase in the risk associated with his own longevity when there is neither income nor capital risk and $u = u_\gamma$ for $\gamma < 1$ (see Levhari and Mirman, 1977).

MARKOV DECISION PROCESSES. The consumption model was considered in unctuous detail for several reasons. It is intrinsically interesting to economists, it is relatively simple to describe, and its risk structure can be ascertained without undue effort. In addition, the analytical approach and the techniques employed as well as the formulation of the functional equation are standard fare in dynamic programming models. The most important reason, however, emanates from the fact that it is an example of the seemingly ubiquitous *Markov Decision Process* (MDP).

A discrete time MDP is a process that is observed at time points $0, 1, 2, \ldots$; the kth observation finds the process to be in some states $s_k \in S$. When in state s at time n, an action $a \in A_s$ is chosen. As a result of this action a reward $r(s, a)$ is received and the next state of the process is determined according to the transition probability of a stationary Markov process. The objective is to maximize the sum of the expected discounted rewards. Thus, if S is indexed by the non-negative integers, the optimal return function V for this infinite stage process can be shown (see Ross, 1983 for the standard proof when r is bounded and Lippman, 1975 for appropriate conditions on r and P when r is unbounded) to satisfy the functional equation

$$V(i) = \max_{a \in A_i} \{r(i, a) + \beta \sum_{j=0}^{\infty} P_{ij}(a)V(j)\}, \quad j = 0, 1, 2, \ldots \quad (9)$$

where $P_{ij}(a)$ is the conditional probability that the process will be in stage j at time $n + 1$ given that it was in state i at time n and action a was selected.

The theory of MDP, including the roles played by successive approximation and policy iteration, is rather extensive, though not by comparison with its host of applications. Excellent modern treatments emphasizing theory and computation, respectively, are given in Heyman and Sobel (1984) and Ross (1983) and in Denardo (1982). Bellman's original book (1957) on dynamic programming remains a very worthwhile read as does Howard's book (1960) on MDP.

STEVEN A. LIPPMAN

See also OPTIMAL CONTROL AND ECONOMIC DYNAMICS; STOCHASTIC OPTIMAL CONTROL.

BIBLIOGRAPHY

Bellman, R.1957.*Dynamic Programming*. Princeton: Princeton University Press.

Blackwell, D. 1962. Discrete dynamic programming. *Annals of Mathematics and Statistics* 33, 719–26.

Blackwell, D. 1965. Discounted dynamic programming. *Annals of Mathematics and Statistics* 36, 226–35.

Denardo, E. V. 1967. Contraction mappings in the theory underlying dynamic programming. *SIAM Review* 9, 165–77.

Denardo, E. V. 1982. *Dynamic Programming*. Englewood Cliffs, NJ: Prentice-Hall.

Hakansson, N. H. 1970. Optimal investment and consumption strategies under risk for a class of utility functions. *Econometrica* 38, 587–607.

Heyman, D. and Sobel, M. 1984. *Stochastic Models in Operations Research, Vol.II* New York: McGraw-Hill.

Howard, R. A. 1960. *Dynamic Programming and Markov Processes*. Cambridge, Mass: MIT Press.

Levhari, D. and Mirman, L. J. 1977. Savings and uncertainty with an uncertain horizon. *Journal of Political Economy* 85, 265–81.

Lippman, S. 1975. On dynamic programming with unbounded rewards. *Management Science* 21, 1225–33.

Miller, B. L. 1974. Optimal consumption with a stochastic income stream. *Econometrica* 42, 253–66.

Miller, B. L. 1976. The effect on optimal consumption of increased uncertainty in labor income in the multi period case. *Journal of Economic Theory* 13, 154–67.

Mirman, L. J. 1971. Uncertainty and optimal consumption decisions. *Econometrica* 39, 179–85.

Phelps, E. S. 1962. The accumulation of risky capital: a sequential utility analysis. *Econometrica* 30, 729–43.

Ross, S. 1983. *Introduction to Stochastic Dynamic Programming*. New York: Academic Press.